"The electronic version of the book is a great concept. I have no idea how successful the sales on this book have been, but I have put out constant advertisement for it, and my personal recommendation. I have been in some aspect of the IT business for 25 years and can spot a good product, which the *Encyclopedia of Networking* is. It's still the best I have come across, and a product I can be enthusiastic about."

—Thomas Taylor, lonebyte.com

"Tom Sheldon's electronic edition of the *Encyclopedia of Networking* is a tour-de-force. Buy it, and you will have almost unconditional knowledge about networking at your fingertips! If you want information about how to network two quantum computers, you'll have to go back to graduate school. But if you want the background on how to get your job done, while still having fun, this is the book for you."

—Daniel Gold,
   Director of Research and Development, Intropy Inc.

"I am thoroughly impressed with your book and I look forward to seeing your new edition. I often used your book in my studies for the MCSE and I continue to use it on the job as an NT Systems Administrator."

—Mike Pilkington, MCSE, NT Systems Administrator,
   Landmark Graphics Corporation

"I bought this book early in 1998, right after it was released, and I still think it is the number one reference book on networking. The author is very well-informed even about the latest novelties in networking. The book contains clear explanations combined with quality drawings and networking diagrams. Great work!"

—Peter van Herwaarden, Senior Partner,
   Atlas Consultancy & Networks
   (management consulting firm in the Netherlands)

"It's an excellent encyclopedia for almost any level of networking experience. Please publish more frequent editions of this electronic edition to keep readers abreast of this highly volatile field."

—Gautam Mukherjee,
   Dy. General Manager-R&D, HFCL,
   New Delhi, India

"Great book! Let me know when the next edition comes out. I want one!"

—Tim Hull, Director of Management Information
   Systems, EPIC, Yakima, WA

"Just a quick note to say thanks for the support. I am using your reference material daily and find that I can use many sections as training tools."

—Kevin Bowyer,
   Regional Manager for Technical Support,
   Qwest Communications International

"A very useful reference tool in the fast-changing global environment. In the rapidly-converging disciplines of voice and data networks, I haven't found any other source that provides the coverage that *EON* provides. I am not speaking about just topics, but also the explanations, related entries, and information on the Internet. I keep wondering how you were able to do it. Please notify me regarding future updates."

—Randy Johnson, Applications Engineer,
   Nokia IP Telephony Business Unit

"The *Encyclopedia of Networking* was the best reference I could find as a student learning about networks. It offered easy-to-locate information and provided necessary links to more. It did more to help me understand networks than any text I was assigned."

—Joe Huggins, Southwest Memorial Hospital,
   Director Education/Telemedicine

McGraw-Hill
Encyclopedia of Networking
& Telecommunications

About the Author. . .

Tom Sheldon is no stranger to the computer industry. Since the late 1970s, he has worked as a computer programmer, consultant, and network administrator. He has been designing and building networks since the invention of the Ethernet. He has been instrumental in many major network installations at Lockheed Space Operations and various government and educational institutions on the West Coast. Tom has written more than 30 books, and his articles have appeared in major computer and networking magazines. Tom is president of Big Sur Multimedia, a computer networking research and testing laboratory. The company tests products for major vendors, develops training material, and provides consulting services throughout the country. Tom is familiar to thousands of computer users who have learned about computers and Microsoft Windows by watching his best-selling LearnKey educational videotapes. He lives on the Big Sur coast of California and enjoys mountain biking, ocean kayak fishing, and golfing.

McGraw-Hill
Encyclopedia of Networking
& Telecommunications

Tom Sheldon

Osborne/**McGraw-Hill**
New York Chicago San Francisco
Lisbon London Madrid Mexico City
Milan New Delhi San Juan
Seoul Singapore Sydney Toronto

Osborne/**McGraw-Hill**
2600 Tenth Street
Berkeley, California 94710
U.S.A.

To arrange bulk purchase discounts for sales promotions, premiums, or fund-raisers, please contact Osborne/**McGraw-Hill** at the above address. For information on translations or book distributors outside the U.S.A., please see the International Contact Information page immediately following the index of this book.

McGraw-Hill Encyclopedia of Networking & Telecommunications

1234567890 DOC DOC 01987654321

Book p/n 0-07-212005-3 and CD p/n 0-07-212005-3
parts of
ISBN 0-07-212005-3

Publisher
    Brandon A. Nordin

Vice President & Associate Publisher
    Scott Rogers

Acquisitions Editors
    Wendy Rinaldi and Ann Sellers

Project Editor
    Lisa Wolters-Broder

Acquisitions Coordinator
    Timothy Madrid

Technical Editor
    Dan Logan

Copy Editor
    Dennis Weaver

Proofreaders
    Linda and Paul Medoff

Indexer
    Jack Lewis

Computer Designers
    Michelle Galicia
    Tara A. Davis

Illustrator
    Michael Mueller

Series Design
    Peter F. Hancik

Cover Design
    Amparo del Rio

This book was composed with Corel VENTURA™ Publisher.

To all the readers
of the previous edition
who sent me positive comments
or posted messages on the Web.
Your comments kept me going
and pushed me to make this edition
better than ever.

Contents

Foreword xxxv

Alphabetical Reference of Terms 1
10/100/1000Base-T 2
6Bone and IPv6 2
802 Standards, IEEE 2
Abilene 2
ABONE (Active Backbone) 3
Access Control 3
Access Method, Network 8
Access Provider 9
Access Rights 9
Account, User 9
Accounting on the Internet 12
Accounting Services 13
ACID (Atomicity, Consistency, Isolation, Durability) 14
Acknowledgments 14
ACL (Access Control List) 15
Acrobat 15
Active Directory 16
Active Documents 16
Active Networks 16
Active Server Page 17

ActiveX 18
Adapter 21
ADC (Analog-to-Digital Conversion) 21
ADCCP (Advanced Data Communications Control Procedure) 23
Address Resolution Protocol 23
Addresses, Electronic Mail 23
Addresses, Network 24
ADM (Add-Drop Multiplexors) 27
Administrator Account 27
Admission Control 30
ADPCM (Adaptive Differential Pulse Code Modulation) 31
ADSL (Asymmetrical Digital Subscriber Line) 31
ADTM (Asynchronous Time Division Multiplexing) 31
Advanced Intelligent Network 31
Advertising and Advertising Services 31
AFP (AppleTalk Filing Protocol) 32
AFS (Andrew File System) 33
Agent, Internet 35
Agent, Network Management 36
Aggregate Route-Based IP Switching 36
Aggregation, Routing 37
Aggregation of Links 37
AIN (Advanced Intelligent Network) 37
AIX (Advanced Interactive Executive) 37
ALB (Adaptive Load Balancing) 38
ALOHA 38
AMPS (Advanced Mobile Phone Service) 38
Analog Transmission Systems 38
Andrew File System 39
Anonymous (Guest) Access 39
ANSI (American National Standards Institute) 40
Antivirus Software 41
Anycasting 41
AnyNet 42
Apache 43
API (Application Programming Interface) 43
APPC (Advanced Program-to-Program Communications) 44
Apple Computer 45
Apple Open Transport Protocol 46
AppleShare 46
AppleTalk 47
Application Layer, OSI Model 48
Application-Level Gateway 49
Application Server 49

Applications, Networks 50
APPN (Advanced Peer-to-Peer Networking) 50
Archiving of Data 54
ARCNET 54
ARDIS (Advanced National Radio Data Service) 55
ARIN (American Registry for Internet Numbers) 56
ARIS (Aggregate Route-based IP Switching) 56
ARP (Address Resolution Protocol) 56
ARPANET (Advanced Research Projects Agency Network) 58
AS/400, IBM 59
ASIC (Application-Specific Integrated Circuit) 59
ASP (Application Service Provider) 60
Associations 62
Asymmetrical Multiprocessing 62
Asynchronous Communications 63
ATM (Asynchronous Transfer Mode) 65
AT&T 82
Attacks and Attackers 84
Attenuation 84
Attributes 85
Auditing 85
Authentication and Authorization 88
Authenticode, Microsoft 93
Autonomous System 93
Availability 95
AWG (American Wire Gauge) 95
Baby Bells 96
Backbone Networks 96
Back-End Systems 100
Backplane Architecture 100
Backup and Data Archiving 101
BACP (Bandwidth Allocation Control Protocol) 102
Bandwidth 102
Bandwidth Brokerage 108
Bandwidth Management 108
Bandwidth on Demand 110
Bandwidth Reservation 111
Banyan VINES 111
BAP and BACP 112
BAP (Bandwidth Allocation Protocol) and BACP
    (Bandwidth Allocation Control Protocol) 112
Baseband Network 113
Bastion Host 113
Baud 113

Beans 114
Bell Modem Standards 114
Bell Operating Companies 114
Bellman-Ford Distance-Vector Routing Algorithm 114
Benchmarking 115
BeOS 115
Best-Effort Delivery 115
BGP (Border Gateway Protocol) 117
Bindery 123
Biometric Access Devices 124
B-ISDN (Broadband ISDN) 126
BISYNC (Binary Synchronous Communications) 127
Bit-Oriented Protocol 128
Block Suballocation 129
Block Transmission 129
Bluetooth 129
Bonding 133
BOOTP (BOOTstrap Protocol) 134
Bootstrapping or Booting 134
Bots 135
Breakout Box 136
BRI (Basic Rate Interface) 136
Bridges and Bridging 136
Broadband Communications and Networking 144
Broadcast 147
Broadcast Address 148
Broadcast Domain 148
Broadcast Networking 149
Broadcast Storm 150
Broadcasting on the Internet 150
Brouter (Bridge/Router) 151
Browsers, Web 151
Burst and Bursty Traffic 152
Bus Architectures 153
Bus Topology 153
Byte-Oriented Protocol 154
C2 Security Rating 155
Cable and Wiring 155
Cable (CATV) Data Networks 172
Cache and Caching Techniques 174
Call Center Operations 176
Campus Network 178
Capacity 181
Capacity Planning 181

CAPs (Competitive Access Providers) 182
Capstone 183
CardBus 183
Carrier Signal 183
Carriers and Carrier Services 184
CCITT (Consultative Committee for International Telephony
  and Telegraphy) 184
CDDI (Copper Distributed Data Interface) 185
CDE (Common Desktop Environment) 185
CDMA (Code Division Multiple Access) 186
CDPD (Cellular Digital Packet Data) 188
CDSA (Common Data Security Architecture) 188
CEBus (Consumer Electronic Bus) 189
Cells and Cell Relay 189
Cellular Communication Systems 190
Central Office 190
Centrex (CENTRal Exchange) 190
CERN 191
CERN Proxy Services 191
CERT (Computer Emergency Response Team) 191
Certificates and Certification Systems 191
CGI (Common Gateway Interface) 195
Challenge/Response Protocol 196
Channel 196
Channel Banks 198
CHAP (Challenge Handshake Authentication Protocol) 198
Chat 201
CICS, IBM 202
CIDR (Classless Inter-Domain Routing) 203
CIFS (Common Internet File System Protocol) 208
CIM (Common Information Model) 210
CIP (Classical IP Over ATM) 210
CIP (Common Indexing Protocol) 212
CIR (Committed Information Rate) 213
Circuit 214
Circuit Relay Firewall 216
Circuit-Switching Services 216
CISC (Complex Instruction Set Computer) 218
CIX (Commercial Internet eXchange) Association 219
Class of Service 219
CLEC (Competitive Local Exchange Carriers) 219
Client 220
Client/Server Computing 220
CLNP (Connectionless Network Protocol) 224

Cluster Controllers 225
Clustering 225
CMIP (Common Management Information Protocol) 228
CNRP (Common Name Resolution Protocol) 228
CO (Central Office) 229
Coaxial Cable Media 230
Collaborative Computing 231
Co-Location Services 232
Collisions and Collision Domains 233
COM (Component Object Model) 234
Commercial Building Wiring Standard 237
Communication 237
Communication Controller 237
Communication Server 237
Communication Services and Providers 238
CompactPCI 240
Component Software Technology 241
Compound Documents 241
Compression Techniques 242
Computer-Telephony Integration 244
Concentrator Devices 244
Conferencing 244
Configuration Management 245
CBQ (Class-Based Queuing) 245
Congestion Control Mechanisms 245
Connection Establishment 254
Connection Technologies 258
Connection-Oriented and Connectionless Services 258
Constraint-Based Routing 260
Container 261
Container Objects, Directory Services 261
Content Distribution 261
Contention 263
Convergence 263
Convergence of Routing Tables 264
Cookies 264
Copper Distributed Data Interface 266
COPS (Common Open Policy Service) 266
CORBA (Common Object Request Broker Architecture) 266
Core Network 270
CoS (Class of Service) 270
CPCP (Coffee Pot Control Protocol) 272
CPE (Customer Premises Equipment) 272
CPI-C (Common Programming Interface for Communication), IBM 272

CPL (Call Processing Language) 273
Cryptography 273
CSMA/CD (Carrier Sense Multiple Access/Collision Detection) 280
CSR (Cell Switched Router), Toshiba 281
CSU/DSU (Channel Service Unit/Data Service Unit) 282
CTI (Computer-Telephony Integration) 283
Customer Premises Equipment 284
Cut-Through Architecture 284
Cut-Through Routing 285
Cyclic Redundancy Check 286
DAC (Discretionary Access Control) 287
Daemon 287
DAFS (Direct Access File System) 287
DARPA (Defense Advanced Research Projects Agency) 289
Data Broadcasting 290
Data Center Design 290
Data Communication Concepts 293
Data Compression 304
Data Encoding 304
Data Encryption 304
Data Link Layer, OSI Model 305
Data Link Protocols 305
Data Management 308
Data Mart 309
Data Migration 309
Data Mining 310
Data Protection 311
Data Striping 312
Data Switches 312
Data Transfer Rates 313
Data Transmissions 313
Data Warehousing 313
Database 318
Datagram and Datagram Services 319
DAV (Distributed Authoring and Versioning) 321
DAVIC (Digital Audio Visual Council) 322
DB2, IBM 323
DBMS (Database Management System) 323
DBS (Direct Broadcast Satellite) 331
DCE (Data Circuit–Terminating Equipment) 333
DCE (Distributed Computing Environment) 334
DCOM (Distributed Component Object Model) 335
DDE (Dynamic Data Exchange) 335
DDR (Dial-on-Demand Routing) 335

DECnet 336
Dedicated Circuits 336
Delay, Latency, and Jitter 337
DEN (Directory Enabled Networks) 341
Denial of Service Attack 344
DES (Data Encryption Standard) 344
Dfs (Distributed File System), Microsoft 344
DFS (Distributed File System), The Open Group 347
DHCP (Dynamic Host Configuration Protocol) 347
DHTML (Dynamic HTML) 347
Diagnostic Testing Equipment 348
Dial-Up Line 348
DIAMETER 348
Digest Algorithm 349
Differentiated Services (Diff-Serv) 350
Diffie-Hellman 357
Diff-Serv (Differentiated Services) 357
Digital Signal (DS) Standards 357
Digital Signatures 357
Digitize 360
Dijkstra Algorithm 361
Directory Attributes and Management 361
Directory Services 361
Disaster Planning and Recovery 368
Discovery Services 370
Discretionary Access Control 371
Disk Storage Systems 371
Diskless Workstations 371
Distance-Vector Routing 372
Distributed Applications 374
Distributed Computer Networks 376
Distributed Database 380
Distributed File Systems 380
Distributed Object Computing 380
DLC (Data Link Control) 385
DLC (Digital Loop Carrier) 385
DLSw (Data Link Switching) 385
DMI (Distributed Management Interface) 387
DMTF (Distributed Management Task Force) 388
DNA (Digital interNet Application) 388
DNS (Domain Name Service) and Internet Domains 389
DOCSIS (Data Over Cable Service Interface Specification) 395
Document Management 397
DOM (Document Object Model) 400

Domains, Internet 400
Domains, Windows NT 400
Downsizing 402
DPT (Dynamic Packet Transport) 403
DRDA (Distributed Relational Database Architecture) 403
DSA (Digital Signature Algorithm) 405
DSL (Digital Subscriber Line) 405
DSP (Digital Signal Processing) 408
DSS (Digital Satellite System) 408
DSS (Digital Signature Standard) 408
DSU/CSU (Data Service Unit/Channel Service Unit) 409
DSx (Digital Signal-x) 409
DTE (Data Terminal Equipment) 410
DTM (Dynamic Synchronous Transfer Mode) 410
Dublin Core Metadata for Resource Discovery 412
DUN (Dial Up Networking) 412
Duplexed Systems 412
DWDM (Dense Wavelength Division Multiplexing) 412
Dynamic Routing 412
E Carrier 413
EAP (Extensible Authentication Protocol) 414
E-Commerce 415
Edge Devices 415
EDI (Electronic Data Interchange) 416
EGPs (Exterior Gateway Protocols) 420
EIA (Electronic Industries Alliance) 420
EIA/TIA Structured Cabling Standards 421
EIP (Enterprise Information Portal) 421
ELAN (Emulated LAN), ATM 421
Electromagnetic Interference 421
Electromagnetic Spectrum 421
Electronic Commerce 425
Electronic Mail 436
Electronic Software Distribution and Licensing 444
E-mail 445
Embedded Systems 445
EMI (Electromagnetic Interference) 451
Emulated LAN 452
Encapsulation 452
Encryption 453
End Systems and End-to-End Connectivity 453
Enterprise Network 454
ENUM 456
ERP (Enterprise Resource Planning) 456

Error Detection and Correction 457
ESCON (Enterprise Systems Connection) 458
ES-IS (End System-to-Intermediate System) Routing 459
EtherLoop 459
Ethernet 460
EtherTalk 476
Explicit Routing 477
Express Forwarding 477
Exterior Routing 478
Extranet 478
Fabric, Switched 480
Failover 480
Fast EtherChannel 480
Fast Ethernet 480
Fast IP 485
Fault Management 486
Fault Tolerance and High Availability 486
FAX Servers and Network Faxing 492
FDDI (Fiber Distributed Data Interface) 494
FDM (Frequency Division Multiplexing) 497
Fiber-Optic Cable 497
Fiber to the Curb/Fiber to the Home 504
Fiberless Optical Networking 504
Fibre Channel 504
File and Directory Rights and Permissions 508
File Server 508
File Sharing 508
File Systems 512
File Transfer Protocols 518
Filtering 519
Find/Search 520
Finger 520
Firewall 520
FireWire 526
Flapping 527
Flow 527
Flow-Control Mechanisms 528
FORTEZZA 531
Forwarding 532
Fractional T1/Fractional T3 533
FRAD (Frame Relay Access Device) 533
Fragmentation and Reassembly 533
Frame 537
Frame Relay 537

Frame Switch 549

Framing in Data Transmissions 549

FreeSpace Optical Network 553

Front-End Processor 553

Front-End System 553

FTAM (File Transfer Access and Management) 553

FTP (File Transfer Protocol) 554

FTTH (Fiber to the Home) 555

Full-Duplex Transmissions 556

FutureShare, Apple 557

G Series ITU Recommendations 558

Gateway 558

Gateway-to-Gateway Protocol 560

GBE (10-Gigabit Ethernet) 560

Gigabit Ethernet 560

GigaPOP 568

GII (Global Information Infrastructure) 568

G.lite 569

Gopher 569

GPRS (General Packet Radio Service) 570

GPS (Global Positioning System) 570

Grid Environments 570

Grounding Problems 570

Groups 570

Groupware 570

GSM (Global System for Mobile Communications) 572

GSMP (General Switch Management Protocol) 572

GSN (Gigabyte System Networking) 572

Guided Media 572

H.100/H.110 Computer Telephony Bus Standard 573

H Series ITU Recommendations 573

H.323 Multimedia Conferencing Standard 573

Hacking and Hackers 575

HALO (High Altitude Long Operation) 576

Handle System 577

Handshake 579

Hash Functions 579

HDLC (High-Level Data Link Control) 581

HDML (Handheld Device Markup Language) 583

HDR (High Data Rate) 584

HDSL (High-Bit-Rate Digital Subscriber Line) 584

HFC (Hybrid Fiber/Coax) 584

High-Availability Systems 585

High-Speed/High-Performance Networking 585

HiperLAN (Higher-Performance Radio LAN) 587
HIPPI (High-Performance Parallel Interface) 587
HMAC (Hashed Message Authentication Code) 588
Home Networking 589
Hop 590
Host 591
Host Connectivity, IBM 591
HPR (High-Performance Routing), IBM 591
HSRP (Hot Standby Router Protocol) 592
HSSI (High-Speed Serial Interface) 592
HTCP (Hypertext Caching Protocol) 592
HTML (Hypertext Markup Language) 592
HTTP (Hypertext Transfer Protocol) 595
Hubs/Concentrators/MAUs 599
Hypermedia and Hypertext 599
I^{2}O (Intelligent I/O) 601
IAB (Internet Architectural Board) 601
IADs (Integrated Access Devices) 601
IAHC (International Ad Hoc Committee) 601
IANA (Internet Assigned Number Authority) 602
IBM (International Business Machines) 602
IBM Host Connectivity 602
ICANN (Internet Corporation for Assigned Names and Numbers) 603
ICMP (Internet Control Message Protocol) 603
ICP (Internet Cache Protocol) 604
ICQ (I-Seek-You) 604
ICSA (International Computer Security Association) 605
ICW (Internet Call Waiting) 605
IDPR (Interdomain Policy Routing Protocol) 605
IEC (International Electrotechnical Commission) 605
IEEE (Institute of Electrical and Electronic Engineers) 606
IEEE 802 Standards 606
IESG (Internet Engineering Steering Group) 608
IETF (Internet Engineering Task Force) 608
IGMP (Internet Group Message Protocol) 608
IGP (Interior Gateway Protocol) 609
IGRP (Interior Gateway Routing Protocol) 609
IIOP (Internet Inter-ORB Protocol) 610
IISP (Interim Inter-switch Signaling Protocol) 610
IKE (Internet Key Exchange) 610
ILEC (Incumbent Local Exchange Carriers) 610
IMA (Inverse Multiplexing over ATM) 611
Imaging 612
IMAP (Internet Message Access Protocol) 612

IMP (Interface Message Processor) 614
IMT-2000 (International Mobile Communications-2000) 614
IN (Intelligent Network) 614
Incident Response 616
InfiniBand 616
Information Appliance 618
Information Warehouse 618
Information Warfare 618
Infrared Technologies 619
Instant Messaging 622
Integrated Access Devices 626
Integrated Services (Int-Serv) 626
Intelligent Network 629
IntelliMirror 629
Internet 630
Internet2 636
Internet Appliances 637
Internet Architecture and Backbone 637
Internet Connections 645
Internet Entertainment 649
Internet Organizations and Committees 650
Internet Protocol Suite 654
Internet Radio 658
Internet Standards 659
Internet Telephony 661
Internetworking 661
InterNIC (Internet Network Information Center) 662
Interoperability 662
Intranets and Extranets 664
Intrusion Detection Systems 665
Int-Serv (Integrated Services) 665
Inverse Multiplexing 666
IOS (Internetwork Operating System) 667
IOTP (Internet Open Trading Protocol) 668
IP (Internet Protocol) 669
IPC (Interprocess Communication) 677
IPMI (Intelligent Platform Management Interface) 678
IP over ATM 678
IP over SONET 682
IPP (Internet Printing Protocol) 682
IPPM (IP Performance Metrics) 683
IPSec (IP Security) 683
IP Storage 685
IP Switching, Ipsilon (Nokia) 687

IP Telephony 688
IPX/SPX (Internetwork Packet Exchange/Sequenced Packet Exchange) 688
IRC (Internet Relay Chat) 690
IRR (Internet Routing Registry) 692
ISDN (Integrated Services Digital Network) 692
IS-IS (Intermediate System-to-Intermediate System) Routing ... 694
ISO (International Organization for Standardization) 694
ISOC (Internet Society) 695
Isochronous Services 695
isoEthernet 695
ISO/IEC-11801 Cabling Standards 695
ISPs (Internet Service Providers) 696
ITU (International Telecommunications Union) 699
IXC (Interexchange Carrier) 700
JAIN 701
Java 701
Jigsaw 706
Jitter 706
Jukebox Optical Storage Devices 707
Jumbo Frames 707
Kerberos Authentication Protocol 708
Kernel 711
Key Distribution and Management 711
Key Encryption Methods 715
KeyNote Trust Management System 715
Key Telephone Systems 716
L2TP (Layer 2 Tunneling Protocol) 717
Label Switching 719
Lambda Circuits 722
LAN (Local Area Network) 722
LAN Drivers 725
LANE (LAN Emulation) 726
LAN Emulation 727
LAN Management 727
LAN Manager, Microsoft 727
LAN Server, IBM 727
LAP (Link Access Procedure) 728
Last Mile Services 730
LATA (Local Access and Transport Area) 730
Latency 731
Layer 2/Layer 3/Layer 4 Switching 731
Layered Architecture 731
LDAP (Lightweight Directory Access Protocol) 731
LDP (Label Distribution Protocol) 734

Learning Bridges 735
Leased Line 735
LEC (LAN Emulation Client) 736
LEC (Local Exchange Carrier) 736
LECS (LAN Emulation Configuration Server) 736
Legacy Systems 736
LEO (Low Earth Orbit) Satellite 736
LES (LAN Emulation Server) 737
Licensing, Electronic 737
Line Conditioning 737
Link Aggregation 738
Link-State Routing 740
Linux 741
LISTSERV 743
LLC (Logical Link Control) 743
LMDS (Local Multipoint Distribution Service) 745
Load Balancing 748
Local Loop 753
Local Procedure Calls 754
LocalTalk 754
Login Scripts 755
Logons and Logon Accounts 755
Long-Distance Carriers 756
Lotus Domino 756
Lotus Notes 756
LU (Logical Unit) Entities 757
LVDS (Low-Voltage Differential Signaling) 757
MAC (Media Access Control) 758
Mac OS 759
MAE (Metropolitan Area Exchange) 760
Mailing List Programs 760
Mainframe 761
Majordomo 763
MAN (Metropolitan Area Network) 763
Managed Systems 765
Management 765
MAPI (Messaging Application Programming Interface) 765
Markup Language 766
Media Access Control Methods 766
Media Gateway 766
Megaco 766
MEMS (Micro-Electromechanical Systems) 768
Message Digest Protocols 768
Message-Oriented Middleware 768

Messaging Services, Mobile 768
Messaging Systems 769
Metadata 769
Metadirectories 772
Metro Access Network 772
MGCP (Media Gateway Control Protocol) 773
MIB (Management Information Base) 773
Microsoft 774
Microsoft.NET 774
Microsoft Active Directory 776
Microsoft BackOffice 777
Microsoft DNA (Digital interNet Application) 778
Microsoft Exchange 778
Microsoft Windows 779
Microsoft Windows File Systems 780
Microwave Communications 782
Middleware and Messaging 785
MIME (Multipurpose Internet Mail Extension) 788
Mirroring 790
MLPPP (Multilink PPP) 792
MMDS (Multichannel Multipoint Distribution Service) 793
Mobile Computing 794
Mobile IP 796
Modems 798
Modulation Techniques 803
MOM (Message-Oriented Middleware) 805
MOSPF (Multicast OSPF) 807
MOSS (MIME Object Security Services) 807
Motif 807
MP3 808
MPLS (Multiprotocol Label Switching) 808
MPλS (Multiprotocol Lambda Switching) 813
MPOA (Multiprotocol over ATM) 813
MPP (Massively Parallel Processor) Systems 813
MSP (Management Service Provider) 813
MTA (Message Transfer Agent) 814
MTU (Maximum Transmission Unit) 814
Multicasting 815
Multihoming 818
Multilayer Switching 819
Multilink Point-to-Point Protocol 823
Multimedia 823
Multiplexing and Multiplexers 828
Multiprocessing 834

Multitiered Architectures 838
NADH (North American Digital Hierarchy) 843
NAK (Negative Acknowledgment) 844
Name Services 844
Named Pipes 846
NAP (Network Access Point) 847
NAS (Network Access Server) 848
NAS (Network Attached Storage) 849
NAT (Network Address Translation) 852
NBMA (Nonbroadcast Multiple Access) 855
NC (Network Computer) 856
NCP (NetWare Core Protocol) 856
NDIS (Network Driver Interface Specification) 856
NDMP (Network Data Management Protocol) 857
NDS (Novell Directory Services) 858
NetBIOS/NetBEUI 859
Netcasting 862
NetPC 862
Netscape 862
NetWare, Novell 862
Network Access Methods 862
Network Access Services 862
Network Addressing Schemes 865
Network Analyzers 865
Network Appliances 868
Network Applications 869
Network Architecture 870
Network Computer Devices 874
Network Concepts 874
Network Connection Technologies 878
Network Core Technologies 879
Network Design and Construction 883
Network Interface Card 891
Network Layer Protocols 891
Network Management 892
Network Operating Systems 894
Network Operations Center 896
Network Processors 896
Network, Public 897
Network Service Providers 897
Newsfeed Services 897
Newsgroups 898
NFS (Network File System) 898
NGN (Next Generation Network) 900

NHRP (Next Hop Resolution Protocol) 900
NIC (Network Interface Card) 901
NII (National Information Infrastructure) 902
NIS (Network Information System) 903
NIST (National Institute of Standards and Technology) 904
NLSP (NetWare Link Services Protocol) 904
NNI (Network Node Interface), ATM 904
NNTP (Network News Transport Protocol) 904
NOC (Network Operations Center) 906
Node 906
NOS (Network Operating Systems) 906
Novell 906
Novell Directory Services 907
Novell NetWare 907
Novell NetWare File System 908
NPN (New Public Network) 910
NREN (National Research and Education Network) 912
NSA (National Security Agency) 912
NSF (National Science Foundation) and NSFnet 913
NSP (Network Service Provider) 914
NTFS (New Technology File System) 914
NTP (Network Time Protocol) 914
NUMA (Non-Uniform Memory Access) 914
OAG (Open Applications Group) 915
OBI (Open Buying on the Internet) 915
Object Management Architecture 916
Object Technologies 916
OC (Optical Carrier) 918
ODBC (Open Database Connectivity) 920
ODI (Open Data-Link Interface) 922
ODMA (Open Document Management API) 922
OFDM (Orthogonal Frequency Division Multiplexing) 922
OIM (Open Information Model) 924
OLAP (Online Analytical Processing) 924
OLE (Object Linking and Embedding) 925
OLE DB 925
OLTP (Online Transaction Processing) 926
OMA (Object Management Architecture) 926
OMG (Object Management Group) 927
One-Time Password Authentication 927
One-Way Hash Functions 928
OpenDoc 928
Open Group 928
Open Source Software 929

Open Systems 930
Open Transport Protocol 930
OpenView Management System 930
OpenVMS 931
Operating Systems 931
OPSEC (Open Platform for Security) 931
Optical Carrier Standards 932
Optical Libraries 932
Optical Networks 933
Optimization 940
Oracle 940
ORB (Object Request Broker) 940
Organizations 941
OS/2 Warp 941
OSI (Open Systems Interconnection) Model 941
OSP (Open Settlement Protocol) 945
OSPF (Open Shortest Path First) Routing 945
OSRP (Optical Signaling & Routing Protocol) 952
OTP (Open Trading Protocol) 952
Outsourcing 952
OXYGEN 953
P2P (Peer-to-Peer Communications) 954
P3P (Platform for Privacy Preferences) 954
PacketCable 954
Packet over SONET 955
Packet Radio Data Networks 955
Packet Rings 957
Packets and Packet-Switching Networks 957
PAN (Personal Area Network) 962
PAP (Password Authentication Protocol) 962
Parallel Interface 962
Parallel Processing 964
Partitions and Partition Management 964
Passwords 964
Path MTU Discovery 965
PBX (Private Branch Exchange) 965
PCI (Peripheral Component Interface) 968
PDH (Pleiochronous Digital Hierarchy) 968
Peer-to-Peer Communication 968
Peering 970
PEM (Privacy-Enhanced Mail) 972
Performance Measurement and Optimization 972
Perl 972
Permissions in Windows NT/Windows 2000 973

Personal Area Network 973
PGP (Pretty Good Privacy) 973
Physical Layer, OSI Model 974
PICS (Platform for Internet Content Selection) 975
PIM (Protocol Independent Multicast) 975
Ping (Packet Internet Groper) 975
PINT (PSTN and Internet Interworking) 976
Pipes 977
PKCS (Public-Key Cryptography Specification) 978
PKI (Public-Key Infrastructure) 978
PKIX (Public-Key Infrastructure X.509) 983
PNNI (Private Network-to-Network Interface) 983
Point-to-Point Communications 986
Policy-Based Management 986
Policy-Based Routing on the Internet 990
Polling 990
PON (Passive Optical Network) 990
PoP (Point of Presence) 993
POP (Post Office Protocol) 995
Portal 996
Ports, TCP/IP 998
PoS (Packet over SONET) 999
POTS (Plain Old Telephone Service) 1001
Power and Grounding Problems and Solutions 1002
Power Line Access Services 1005
PPP (Point-to-Point Protocol) 1005
PPP Multilink 1008
PPS (Packets per Second) 1008
PPTP (Point-to-Point Tunneling Protocol) 1008
Premises Distribution System 1008
Presence Monitoring 1008
Presentation Layer, OSI Model 1008
Printing 1009
Prioritization of Network Traffic 1009
Privacy 1011
Private-Key Cryptography 1011
Private Network 1012
Promiscuous Mode 1012
Propagation Delay 1012
Protocol Analyzers 1012
Protocols and Protocol Stacks 1012
Proxy Caching 1013
Proxy Servers 1013
PSTN (Public-Switched Telephone Network) 1014

Public-Key Cryptography 1014
Public-Key Infrastructure 1017
Public Networks 1017
Push and Pull 1017
PVC (Permanent Virtual Circuit) 1017
QAM (Quadrature Amplitude Modulation) 1018
Qbone 1018
QoS (Quality of Service) 1018
Quantum Cryptography 1027
Queuing 1028
Radio Communication and Networks 1033
Radio LANs 1034
Radio on the Internet 1034
RADIUS (Remote Authentication Dial-In User Service) 1034
RAID (Redundant Arrays of Inexpensive Disks) 1037
RAP (Resource Allocation Protocol) 1040
RARP (Reverse Address Resolution Protocol) 1040
RAS (Remote Access Server) 1041
Rate Control 1041
RBOCs (Regional Bell Operating Companies) 1041
RDF (Resource Description Framework) 1042
Real-Time Network Services 1042
Real-Time Operating System 1042
Redirector 1042
Redundancy 1042
Registries on the Internet 1043
Relational Database 1044
Reliable Data Delivery Services 1044
Remote Access 1047
Repeater 1049
Replication 1050
Repository 1055
Requester Software 1056
Reservation of Bandwidth 1056
Residential Broadband 1056
Resilient Packet Rings 1058
Resolver Services 1059
Resource Discovery Services 1059
Resource Management 1060
Retransmission 1061
RFC (Request for Comment) 1061
Ricochet 1061
Rights and Permissions 1061
Ring Network Topology 1062

RIP (Routing Information Protocol) 1063
RIPE (Réseaux IP Européens) 1065
RISC (Reduced Instruction Set Computer) 1065
Rlogin 1066
RMI (Remote Method Invocation) 1066
RMOA (Rcal Time Multimedia Over ATM) 1067
RMON (Remote Monitoring) 1067
Roaming 1068
Route Aggregation 1070
Routers 1071
Route Servers and Routing Arbiter 1075
Route Switching 1075
Routing 1075
Routing, Multilayer 1082
Routing on the Internet 1082
Routing Registries 1083
RPC (Remote Procedure Call) 1084
RPSL (Routing Policy Specification Language) 1086
RSA 1087
RSIP (Realm-Specific IP) 1087
RSVP (Resource Reservation Protocol) 1088
RTCP (Real-Time Control Protocol) 1091
RTFM (Real-Time Traffic Flow Measurement) 1091
RTOS (Real-Time Operating System) 1091
RTP (Real-time Transport Protocol) 1092
RTSP (Real-Time Streaming Protocol) 1092
SAA (Systems Application Architecture) 1094
Samba 1094
SANs (Storage Area Networks) 1094
SAN (System Area Network) 1099
SAP (Service Advertising Protocol) 1099
SAP (Session Announcement Protocol) 1099
SATAN (Security Administrator's Tool for Analyzing Networks) 1100
Satellite Communication Systems 1100
SBM (Subnet Bandwidth Manager) 1102
Schema 1103
SCSI (Small Computer System Interface) 1103
SCSP (Server Cache Synchronization Protocol) 1107
SCTP (Stream Control Transmission Protocol) 1107
SDH (Synchronous Digital Hierarchy) 1108
SDLC (Synchronous Data Link Control) 1108
SDP (Session Description Protocol) 1108
SDSL (Symmetric Digital Subscriber Line) 1109
Search and Discovery Services 1109

Secret-Key Cryptography 1114
Security 1115
Security Auditing 1120
Segment, Network 1123
Segment, TCP 1124
Sendmail 1124
Sequencing of Packets 1124
Serial Communication and Interfaces 1124
Servers 1126
Service Advertising and Discovery 1131
Service Providers and Carriers 1133
Session Layer, OSI Model 1136
SET (Secure Electronic Transaction) 1136
SFT (System Fault Tolerance) 1137
SGML (Standard Generalized Markup Language) 1137
S-HTTP (Secure Hypertext Transfer Protocol) 1138
Signaling for Call Control 1139
Signals 1140
SIP (Session Initiation Protocol) 1143
SKIP (Simple Key Management for Internet Protocols) 1145
SLA (Service-Level Agreement) 1146
Sliding-Window Flow Control 1147
SLIP (Serial Line Internet Protocol) 1147
Slow Start 1148
SLP (Service Location Protocol) 1148
Smart Cards 1150
SMB (Server Message Blocks) 1151
SMDS (Switched Multimegabit Data Service) 1152
SMIL (Synchronized Multimedia Integration Language) 1152
S/MIME (Secure Multipurpose Internet Mail Extension) 1152
SMP (Symmetric Multiprocessing) 1153
SMR (Specialized Mobile Radio) 1153
SMS (Short Messaging Service) 115
SMTP (Simple Mail Transfer Protocol) 158
SNA (Systems Network Architecture) 1159
Sniffer 1159
SNMP (Simple Network Management Protocol) 1160
SOAP (Simple Object Access Protocol) 1161
Socket 1162
Sockets API 1162
SOCKS 1163
Softswitch 1165
Software Distribution 1165
Solaris, SunSoft ....

Soliton 1165
SONET (Synchronous Optical Network) 1166
Source Routing 1172
Spanning Tree Algorithm 1172
SPIRITS (Service in the PSTN/IN Requesting InTernet Service) 1172
Spread Spectrum Signaling 1173
SPX (Sequenced Packet Exchange) 1174
SQL (Structured Query Language) 1174
SS7 (Signaling System 7) 1175
SSA (Serial Storage Architecture) 1177
SSH (Secure Shell) 1177
SSL (Secure Sockets Layer) 1178
SSO (Single Sign-On) 1183
SSP (Storage Service Provider) 1183
Standards Groups, Associations, and Organizations 1184
STAR TAP 1185
Stateful Inspection Technology 1186
Stateful and Stateless Connections 1186
Stateless and Call-Back Filing Systems 1187
Static Routing 1187
Storage Management Systems 1188
Storage over IP (SoIP) 1188
Storage Service Provider 1189
Storage Systems 1189
Store-and-Forward Networking 1189
Streaming Transmission 1189
Striping 1190
Structured Cabling Standards 1190
Subnetting 1190
Sun Microsystems 1190
Sun Microsystems Solaris 1191
Supercomputer 1191
Supernetting 1192
SVC (Switched Virtual Circuit) 1192
S/WAN (Secure WAN) 1193
Switch Fabrics and Bus Design 1193
Switching, Multilayer 1203
Switching and Switched Networks 1203
Symmetrical Multiprocessing 1206
Synchronous Communications 1206
SystemView, IBM 1208
ers 1209
(Terminal Access Controller Access Control System) 1211
ing 1212

TAPI (Telephony API) 1212
Tariff 1213
TCP (Transmission Control Protocol) 1213
TCP/IP (Transmission Control Protocol/Internet Protocol) 1220
TDD (Time Division Duplexing) 1220
TDM (Time Division Multiplexing) 1220
TDMA (Time Division Multiple Access) 1220
TDM Networks 1221
Telecommunications and Telephone Systems 1224
Telecommunications Regulation 1232
Telecommuting 1235
Teledesic 1235
Telematics 1236
Telephony 1236
Telnet 1236
Terabit Routers 1237
Terminal Servers 1237
Terminal Services 1237
Testing, Diagnostics, and Troubleshooting 1239
TFTP (Trivial File Transfer Protocol) 1240
Thin Clients 1241
Three-Tier Client-Server Model 1243
Throttling 1243
Throughput 1243
TIA (Telecommunications Industry Association) 1245
TIA/EIA Structured Cabling Standards 1245
Time Synchronization Services 1250
TLS (Transport Layer Security) 1251
TMN (Telecommunications Management Network) 1252
TN3270 1252
Token and Token-Passing Access Methods 1253
Token-Based Authentication 1254
Token Bus Network 1256
Token Ring Network 1256
Topology 1257
ToS (Type of Service) 1259
Traffic Management, Shaping, and Engineering 1259
Transaction Processing 1265
Transfer Rates 1270
Transport Layer, OSI Model 1270
Transport Layer Security (TLS) 1270
Transport Protocols and Services 1270
TRIP (Telephony Routing over IP) 1272
Troubleshooting 1272

Trunking 1272
Trust Relationships and Trust Management 1272
T Series ITU Recommendations 1276
Tunnels 1276
Two-Factor Authentication 1278
Two-Phase Commit 1278
Two-Tier Client/Server Model 1278
UDA (Universal Data Access) 1279
UDDI (Universal Description, Discovery, and Integration) 1279
UDP (User Datagram Protocol) 1279
ULSNET (Ultra Low-Speed Networking) 1283
UML (Unified Modeling Language) 1283
UMTS (Universal Mobile Telecommunication Services) 1283
UNI (User Network Interface) 1284
Unified Messaging 1284
Universal Service 1285
UNIX 1285
UNIX File System 1288
UPS (Uninterruptible Power Supply) 1290
URI (Uniform Resource Identifier) 1292
URL (Uniform Resource Locator) 1293
URL Parsing 1293
URN (Uniform Resource Name) 1294
USB (Universal Serial Bus) 1295
USENET 1295
Users and Groups 1296
UTP (Unshielded Twisted-Pair) Cable 1297
UUCP (UNIX to UNIX Copy Program) 1298
UWB (Ultra Wideband) 1298
VBI (Vertical Blanking Interval) 1299
vBNS (Very high speed Backbone Network Service) 1299
VI Architecture 1300
Videoconferencing 1301
VINES, Banyan 1305
Virtual Circuit 1305
Virtual Dial-Up Services 1306
Virtual Machine, Java 1306
Virtual Reality 1306
Virus and Antivirus Issues 1306
VLAN (Virtual LAN) 1308
VLSM (Variable Length Subnet Masking) 1313
VMS (Virtual Memory System) 1313
VoATM (Voice over ATM) 1313
VoFR (Voice over Frame Relay) 1313

Voice/Data Networks 1313
Voice Mail 1318
Voice over IP (VoIP) 1318
VoIP (Voice over IP) 1328
Volume and Partition Management 1328
VPN (Virtual Private Network) 1328
VRML (Virtual Reality Modeling Language) 1329
VRRP (Virtual Router Redundancy Protocol) 1329
VSAT (Very Small Aperture Terminal) 1330
VTAM (Virtual Telecommunications Access Method 1330
W3C (World Wide Web Consortium) 1331
WAN (Wide Area Network) 1331
WAP (Wireless Application Protocol) 1334
Wavelength Division Multiplexing 1334
Wavelength Routing 1334
WBEM (Web-Based Enterprise Management) 1335
WCCP (Web Cache Communication Protocol) 1336
WCS (Wireless Communications Service) 1337
WDM (Wavelength Division Multiplexing) 1337
Web 1340
Web3D 1340
Web Appliance 1340
Web-Based Network Management 1340
Web Caching 1341
Webcasting 1349
WebDAV 1351
Webmaster 1352
WebNFS (Network File System) 1353
Web Technologies and Concepts 1354
WebTV Networks 1356
Whiteboard Applications 1356
White Pages Directory Services 1357
WHOIS ("Who Is") 1357
Windows, Microsoft 1357
WINS (Windows Internet Naming Service) 1358
WinSock 1358
Wired for Management 1358
Wireless Broadband Access Technologies 1359
Wireless Communications 1369
Wireless IP 1372
Wireless LANs 1373
Wireless Local Loop 1377
Wireless Messaging 1378
Wireless Mobile Communications 1378

Wireless Optical Networking 1385
Wireless PANs (Personal Area Networks) 1385
Wiretapping 1386
Wiring and Wiring Standards 1386
WML (Wireless Markup Language) 1386
Workflow Management 1387
Workgroups 1390
World Wide Web 1390
World Wide Web Consortium 1390
WPAN (Wireless Personal Area Network) 1390
X12 Accredited Standards Committee 1391
X.25 1391
X.400 Message-Handling System 1392
X.500 Directory Services 1392
X.509 Certificates 1393
xDSL 1395
XHTML 1395
XML (Extensible Markup Language) 1395
X/Open 1397
XSL (Extensible Style Language) 1397
X Series ITU Recommendations 1398
X Window 1398
Z39.50 1399
Zero Administration for Windows Initiative 1399
Zones and Zone Servers 1400
Index 1401

Foreword

One of my favorite quotes about networking comes from RFC 1000 (The Request for Comments Reference Guide, August 1987). Stephen Crocker writes about the development of the early ARPANET. It is the late 1960s and Crocker and his cohorts are building the packet-switching system envisioned by Paul Baran, Larry Roberts, and Leonard Kleinrock that would eventually become the Internet. Apparently, they thought somebody else knew how to build the system, but it turned out that *they* were the designated experts:

> We had no official charter. Most of us were graduate students and we expected that a professional crew would show up eventually to take over the problems we were dealing with.

Back in the 1970s and 1980s, a lot of people wrapped up in LAN networking, IBM SNA systems, and other networking technologies were unfamiliar with what was developing in the Internet community. In fact, the early ARPANET (and eventually the Internet) served as the model for many of these other technologies, including the OSI model. RFC 871 (A Perspective On The Arpanet Reference Model, September 1982) says it best:

> It is an historical fact that many now widely-accepted, fundamental concepts of intercomputer networking were original to the ARPANET Network Working Group. The designers of the ARPANET protocol suite have had a reference model of their own all the long, but workers in the ARPA-sponsored research community were busy with their work or were perhaps somehow unsuited temperamentally to do learned papers on abstract topics.

It is incredibly ironic that the OSI protocols, which were extensively written and published never amounted to much in the way of actual implementation. In contrast, the Internet protocols were created to work with real systems. In many cases, they were written down after actual systems were fully developed.

An important design philosophy of the early Internet was an open approach to networking in a world that was dominated by proprietary, vendor-specific systems. The concept was to allow any system, regardless of vendor, to connect to an open-protocol network. This open approach has become pervasive throughout the computing and networking industry. Today, hardly anyone talks about "interoperability" problems because the Web and Web technologies have mostly solved those problems.

One of the best descriptions of the new world of open information comes from Simon Phipps, IBM's evangelist for Java and XML. He points out the following progression of events.

- TCP/IP has become the near-universal communications protocol for connecting information systems.

- Browsers have become the common space into which solutions can be loaded.

- Component technologies such as Java are now established as the standard for platform-neutral computing.

- Data was the last gap. An open data-formatting specification was needed. XML is that specification.

One last story. In the April 9, 2001 issue of *InformationWeek.com*, John Rendleman reported the following:

> The University of North Carolina has finally found a network server that, although missing for four years, had not missed a packet in all that time. Try as they might, university administrators couldn't find the server. Working with Novell, IT workers tracked it down by meticulously following cable until they literally ran into a wall. The server had been mistakenly sealed behind drywall by maintenance workers.

Now, that says something about networking! Information systems have become so big that entire servers get lost but still keep going. Maybe somebody sent a purchase order for a firewall to a construction firm.

See "Internet Entertainment" for more amusement.

Acknowledgments

Mom, Dad, Janie, John and Suzy, Jim and Peggy, Marty Mathews, Dario and Cindy, Becky and Alicia and Mikey and Christina, my golf pals, Gordon and Julia, and Jim and Andrea. Thanks also to the following people at Osborne: Wendy Rinaldi, Emily Rader, Ann Sellers, Lisa Wolters-Broder, Tim Madrid, Mark Karmendy, and everybody else who asked if I was done with "that book" yet.

Special thanks to Dan Logan for the technical edits.

Heartfelt thanks to Jim and Beth Sheldon for all technical, programming, cross-referencing, checking, and other assistance.

Introduction

This book is designed to provide quick references and executive summaries of the latest networking topics. You'll also find historical information that is meant to provide background information about technologies. Many of the historical documents mentioned are written by the original architects of the Internet or other technologies.

One of my objectives for this book was to create a reference that would help you continue your research into a particular topic. Read the topics to learn concepts and understand the underlying technologies, then refer to the Related Entries or Web sites for more information.

But this book doesn't end with the printed version. Obviously, there are only so many pages you can stuff in a book binding. At one point, the page count for this book was up to 2,000 pages. That extra information is posted at the Linktionary! Web site. There you will find an extended version of many of the topics discussed here, along with updated information, reader comments, fixes for broken Web links, and new Web links.

Visit http://www.linktionary.com.

So, what is the best way to read this book? Obviously, it is an alphabetical reference, so you can pick it up any time and look up a subject. Acronyms are favored over actual spell-outs. If you don't know how to find a particular topic, look in the index or search on the CD-ROM. You can also look up a topic that you think is related to the one you were originally looking for. At the bottom of each section in the book is a list of Related Entries that may lead you to an appropriate topic. On the CD-ROM, Related Entries appear as green hyperlinks. Additional topics, which usually follow such wording as "See—" or "See also—" are hyperlinked in orange on the CD-ROM.

If you want to read this book in an organized way, refer to the following topics. They provide a brief overview and links to related topics in this book.

Bandwidth Management
Cable and Wiring
Collaborative Computing
Communication Services and Providers
Data Communications Concepts
Distributed Computer Networks
Distributed Object Computing
Electronic Commerce
File Systems
Hypermedia and Hypertext
Internet
Internet Architecture and Backbone
LAN (Local Area Network)
Metadata
Mobile Computing
Multimedia
Multiprocessing
Multitiered Architecture
Network Access Services
Network Architecture

Network Concepts
Network Core Technologies
Network Design and Construction
Network Management
Network Operating Systems
Object Technologies
Optical Networks
Packets and Packet-Switching Networks
QoS (Quality of Service)
Routing
Search and Discovery Services
Security
Service Advertising and Discovery
Standards Groups, Associations, and Organizations
Telecommunications and Telephone Systems
Voice/Data Networks
Web Technologies and Concepts
Wireless Communications

About the CD-ROM

The CD-ROM contains the full text of this book in an electronic form. Instructions for loading the CD-ROM are in the back of the book. You'll also find a complete set of Internet RFCs on the CD-ROM, with a tab that provides a title index. Many of the topics provide hyperlinks to important RFCs. On the CD-ROM, links to the RFCs are displayed in red. When you click these links, the RFC is displayed. You don't need to be online.

The CD-ROM also contains a complete set of hyperlinks to Web sites on the Internet that provide more information about the topic under discussion. If you are online, click any of the blue links to go directly to the Web site.

I plan to develop updated CD-ROMs that will keep up with the latest changes in the industry, fix outdated hyperlinks, and provide information about new RFCs and other documents. Please check the Linktionary! Web site (http://www.linktionary.com) for more information. We can add your name to an Alert List to let you know when updates are available.

Encyclopedia

Millennium Edition

Alphabetical Reference of Terms

10/100/1000Base-T

See Ethernet; Fast Ethernet; *and* Gigabit Ethernet.

6Bone and IPv6

The 6Bone is an experimental test bed for IP version 6 that exists to help vendors and users participate in the actual evolution and transition to IPv6. Refer to RFC 2471 (IPv6 Testing Address Allocation, December 1998) and RFC 2546 (6Bone Routing Practice, March 1999) for additional information.

Related Entries   Abilene; GII (Global Information Infrastructure); Internet; Internet2; IP (Internet Protocol); Network Core Technologies; NII (National Information Infrastructure); NPN (New Public Network); *and* Routing on the Internet

Linktionary! – Tom Sheldon's Encyclopedia of   http://www.linktionary.com/6bone.html
Networking updates

6Bone home page (Links to everything you want to   http://www.6bone.net
know about 6Bone)

802 Standards, IEEE

See IEEE 802 Standards.

Abilene

In early 1999, Abilene, the newest addition to the Internet backbone, was brought online. Abilene was developed by University Corporation for Advanced Internet Development (UCAID), a consortium of 132 universities. The new backbone will eventually connect over 100 universities using the Qwest nationwide fiber-optic network and is the first part of UCAID's Internet2 project. Internet2 is a high-speed Internet backbone initiative outlined by Vice President Al Gore. Major contributions include the following:

- Fiber-optic network capacity provided by Qwest
- SONET transmission equipment provided by Northern Telecom
- Gigabit switch routers provided by Cisco

The current Internet backbone runs at 45 Mbits/sec. Another Internet backbone addition called vBNS was developed by MCI and operates at 62 Mbits/sec. The goal of Internet2 is to eventually boost this speed up to 9.6 Gbits/sec.

UCAID members will use the Abilene network for current research projects that require high bandwidths and as a platform for developing new applications that can take advantage of high bandwidth. Due to its high speed, the network supports real-time video for specialized applications such as, for example, remote monitoring of medical procedures. Abilene is also providing a test bed for implementing QoS (quality of service) and traffic prioritization techniques that are essential for real-time voice and video traffic on the Internet.

The actual fiber network provided by Qwest (called the Macro Capacity Fiber Network) is over 18,499 miles in length, making it the largest test network in the world. Qwest's physical network spans the United States and Mexico. It also extends via submarine cable across the Atlantic to Europe and across the Pacific to Pacific Rim countries. The network topology is a bidirectional ring architecture that is built for reliability. Its self-healing design provides instant rerouting of traffic in the event of a line failure.

Related Entries GII (Global Information Infrastructure); Internet; Internet2; Internet Architecture and Backbone; Internet Organizations and Committees; Network Core Technologies; NII (National Information Infrastructure); NIST (National Institute of Standards and Technology); NPN (New Public Network); Optical Networks; Routing on the Internet; *and* vBNS (Very high speed Backbone Network Service)

Linktionary! – Tom Sheldon's Encyclopedia of Networking updates	http://www.linktionary.com/abilene.html
UCAID (University Corporation for Advanced Internet Development)	http://www.ucaid.edu
Merit's High Performance Networking page, "The Internet2 Initiative" (includes Abilene links)	http://www.merit.edu/i2/
National Science Foundation (NSF) High Performance Networking, Next Generation Internet and Internet2 Web page	http://www.nsf.gov/od/lpa/news/media/fs325.htm
Qwest Macro Capacity Fiber Network information	http://www.qwest.com/network/network.html
Abilene Project links at Yahoo!	http://dir.yahoo.com/Computers_and_Internet/Internet/Internet_2__Abilene_Project/
Advanced Network & Services, Inc.	http://www.advanced.org/internet2.html

ABONE (Active Backbone)

ABONE is an experimental network that is being used to explore and test the concept of Active Networks, a new technology that adds intelligence to data packets so they can direct themselves through networks, rather than rely on routers. This is not to be confused with the Asia-wide Internet backbone that connects a number of Asian countries, including Japan and Thailand.

Related Entry Active Networks

Access Control

Access controls are the security features that block or control the ability of a user or system to communicate and interact with another system. Access controls manage access to computers systems, networks, Web servers, extranets, and a variety of other systems and devices. Access controls protect systems from unauthorized access and in most cases determine what levels of authorization are appropriate for a user or system that has been previously validated by an authentication system.

Access control starts with a logon procedure that attempts to identify and validate a user. The user provides some unique credentials such as a password, but fingerprint, voice, or eyeball scanning devices may also be used. A more common access control option is a smart card, which displays a unique access number that the user enters, along with some remembered logon information.

The easiest time for hackers to break into a system is during the logon process. Weak passwords, such as dog's names, are easily guessed by malicious users. Passwords should contain a combination of uppercase and lowercase characters such as "Qp&yTx." However, these are easy to forget, so "acronym passwords" are useful. For example, the complex password "Mbiot4oJ" is derived from "My birthday is on the 4th of July."

Network administrators can usually implement workstation and time restrictions (depending on the operating system) to prevent user access to specific systems at specific times of the day. For example, an administrator can restrict a user from logging on to all computers except the one in their office or from logging on to any computer after closing time. This prevents users from working on unsupervised systems or during off hours. The reason for this is to prevent users from performing illegal activities like downloading the customer database and carrying it out the door.

During logon, the system being accessed may do one of the following:

■ It may run its own authentication procedure, comparing the user-supplied information with information it has stored in its own security databases.

■ It may hand off the authentication to a *security server* that handles all network authentications.

The latter method is the most secure because user IDs and passwords are stored on a server that is presumably in a secure physical location where it is professionally managed. The first is less secure because the computer itself holds the security information, which could be hacked by someone who gains physical access to the system.

Once a user has been authenticated, access to system resources is controlled by the security system. A good example is the security system in Windows NT/Windows 2000:

■ All resources (folders, files, printers, etc.) are viewed as objects.

■ Each object has its own security descriptor, which simply holds security information about the object, such as which users are allowed to access it and what type of access they are allowed.

■ When a user wants to access an object, the Windows NT security system checks an ACL (access control list) defined by the security descriptor. If the ACL has an entry for the user, the system allows the user to access the object.

This process is covered further under "Discretionary Access Control," later in this section.

Most network-connected systems implement a single logon feature, in which the user logs on once to access resources anywhere on the network. Once the user is authenticated by the security system, he or she is given a special access token that verifies who the user is to other systems on the network. In Windows NT/Windows 2000, the access token contains the user's SID (security ID), the IDs of the groups the user belongs to, and other security information. When a user wants to access a resource on a server, the security system on that server evaluates the user's access token to determine the level of access for the user.

This scheme works well if all the servers on the network are using the same operating system and thus have compatible authentication schemes. However, most enterprise networks consist of a variety of systems that use different authentication schemes. To solve this problem, an enterprise can use directory services such as NDS (Novell Directory Services), Microsoft Active Directory, and NIS (Network Information Service). These systems provide a single storehouse for user information, including personal information, and are expanding to allow authentication and access control for all types of systems. See "Directory Services" for more information.

Auditing is a part of the access control process. An auditing system can track when specific users log on and what resources they access. A typical auditing system can be configured to track specific events, such as access to sensitive files or activities that are performed by administrators. See "Auditing" and "Security Auditing" for more information.

Discretionary Access Controls

Discretionary access control, or DAC, is a form of access control that allows more granular control over access to resources (directories and files). One user can be granted read access, while another can be granted read/write access. This is possible because each user has an individual user account that can be assigned different access controls. In some systems, a user can grant another user access to resources that they own. RFC 1825 (Security Architecture for the Internet Protocol, August 1995) discusses DACs.

In Windows NT/Windows 2000, all resources (called *objects* here) are assigned a *security descriptor* by the operating system. Figure A-1 shows a security descriptor for a folder. The security descriptor is a data structure that contains security information. The most important

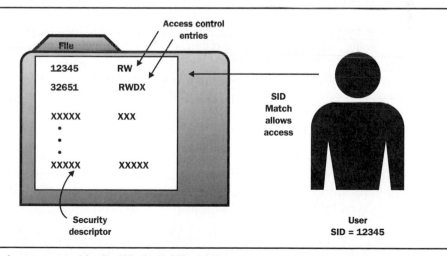

Figure A-1.   *Access control in the Windows NT environment*

structure in the security descriptor for this discussion is the DACL (discretionary ACL), which contains a list of who can access the object and how they can access it.

The owner of the object decides who can access the object and the type of access. When a user is granted access, an ACE (access control entry) is made into the DACL. A DACL may hold many such entries for users, groups, and even applications and system processes, all identified by SIDs (security IDs). The operating system identifies users, groups, and so on by SIDs—not by well-known names.

So far, we have an object for which a list of users (or system services) has been created that can access the object. Now let's look at what happens when one of those lucky users attempts to access the object. Assume JHendrix attempts to access a file called Music.doc. The owner of this file has already granted JHendrix read access rights. The security system compares JHendrix's SID with the SIDs in each entry (ACE) of the ACL. When the entry is found, the security system allows JHendrix to access the object according to the permissions defined in the ACE. The security system prevents JHendrix from changing the file because the ACE indicates that he may only read it.

Novell NetWare, UNIX systems, and Cisco routers offer other examples of how ACLs are implemented. They also use the concept of objects to define system resources such as folders, and access to these objects is defined by access control lists.

- **UNIX**   ACLs in UNIX systems have many similarities to the Windows NT access scheme just described. Objects have an ACL that consists of ACEs. The ACE entry starts with a keyword such as permit or deny, followed by the type of access (read, write, and so on), followed by the name of a user or group. You may use **chmod** to manage file permissions in most UNIX environments and commands such as **acledit** or **chacl** to modify access control lists (depending on the UNIX version).

- **Novell NetWare**   In this environment, system resources like files and folders are objects that are stored in the NDS (Novell Directory Services) directory tree. ACLs are associated with every object and define how trustees (users of those objects) are allowed to access the objects.

- **Cisco router access lists**   Cisco routers are involved with forwarding packets, so ACLs provide the filtering criteria that either *permits* or *denies* the forwarding of a packet. Each entry in the ACL has information that identifies specific packets or types of packets and how they should be handled. As a packet enters the router, information such as the source and destination address, protocol type, ports, sockets, and flags, is read from the packet and compared to entries in the list. If a match is found, the packet is either permitted or denied, depending on what is defined by the entry.

Other Access Control Systems

Proxy Servers and firewalls have the job of protecting internal network resources on networks that are connected to the Internet. A proxy server lets internal users access Web sites by acting as a proxy for those users. Internet Web sites then interact only with the proxy server and not the actual user. This has the advantage of hiding the internal addresses, which reduces the possibility of attacks on those addresses by outside hackers. A proxy server also gives network administrators control over the Internet sites that internal users can access. For example, an

A

administrator can restrict users from accessing Internet sites that are not related to the business of the company. Refer to "Proxy Servers" for more information.

A firewall has a much bigger job than a proxy server because it allows external users to access internal network resources. There are a variety of methods for controlling user access to internal resources. One method is to filter IP addresses, allowing only users who have a particular IP address to access internal systems. However, this method is susceptible to spoofing. Another method is to use a reverse proxy server, which intercepts incoming requests, evaluates those request for security and appropriateness, and then proxies those requests for internal systems. External users only interact with the proxy server and never the internal systems. Refer to "Firewalls" for more information.

Mobile users and work-at-home users who need to access corporate networks can do so by dialing into access servers located on those networks. Once again, local user databases and authentication methods may be used to allow access to those computers.

Another method is to use RADIUS (Remote Authentication Dial-In User Service) servers to control access. Many ISPs use RADIUS or TACACS (Terminal Access Controller Access Control System). See "Remote Access" and "NAS (Network Access Server)". Also see RFC 1492 (An Access Control Protocol, Sometimes Called TACACS) and RFC 2138 (Remote Authentication Dial In User Service, April 1997).

Organizations connected to the Web need specialized security devices to control who can access the company's Web site, receive broadcast information, or perform electronic commerce transactions.

While a company's internal servers are accessible by employees who have user accounts, a company's Web site will be accessed by new unknown users. One way to identify these users is with certificates. A certificate contains information about a person that can be used for authentication. The certificate is created and encrypted by a trusted certificate authority and can only be opened with that certificate authority's public key. Therefore, if the certificate authority is trusted, the contents of the certificate itself can be trusted. Refer to "Certificates and Certification Systems" for more information.

See "Security" for additional topics related to access control.

Related Entries   Authentication and Authorization; Biometric Access Devices; Certificates and Certificate Servers; CHAP (Challenge Handshake Authentication Protocol); Firewalls; Kerberos; Logons and Logon Accounts; One-Time Password Authentication; Proxy Servers; RADIUS (Remote Authentication Dial-In User Service); Rights and Permissions; Security; Smart Cards; TACACS (Terminal Access Controller Access Control System); Token-Based Authentication; *and* Trust Relationships and Trust Management

Linktionary!—Tom Sheldon's Encyclopedia of Networking updates	http://www.linktionary.com/a/access_control.html
Access control for the Web	http://www.isoc.org/HMP/PAPER/107/abst.html
Microsoft access control information	http://www.microsoft.com/WINDOWS2000/ library/planning/security/secdefs.asp

Acola access control technologies (including smart cards)	http://acola.com
PassGo access control products	http://www.passgo.com
RSA Data Security	http://www.rsa.com
Axent access control products	http://www.axent.com
Shiva's white paper on remote access security	http://www.shiva.com/remote/prodinfo/security/

Access Method, Network

Local area networks (LANs) are typically shared by a number of attached systems, and only one system at a time may use the network cable to transmit data. An access method defines how a system gains access to a shared network in a cooperative way so its transmissions do not interfere with the transmissions of other systems. Simultaneous access to the cable is either prevented by using a token-passing method or controlled with a carrier sensing and collision detection method.

The primary access methods listed below. The first is used by Ethernet. The last is used by Token ring networks.

- **CSMA/CD (Carrier Sense Multiple Access/Collision Detection)**   Carrier sensing implies that network nodes listen for a carrier tone on the cable and send information when other devices are not transmitting. Multiple access means that many devices share the same cable. If two or more devices sense that the network is idle, they will attempt to access it simultaneously (contention), causing collisions. Each station must then back off and wait a certain amount of time before attempting to retransmit. Contention may be reduced by dividing networks with bridges or using switches. See "CSMA/CD (Carrier Sense Multiple Access/Collision Detection)" and "Ethernet" for more information.

- **CSMA/CA (Carrier Sense Multiple Access/Collision Avoidance)**   This access method is a variation on the CSMA/CD method. Nodes estimate when a collision might occur and avoid transmission during that period. This method is cheaper to implement, since collision detection circuitry is not required; however, it imposes more delay and can slow network throughput.

- **Token Passing**   ARCNET and token ring networks use the token-passing access method. A workstation must have possession of a token before it can begin transmission. The token is passed around the network. Any station that needs to transmit must grab the token. See "Token and Token-Passing Access Methods."

Carrier sensing methods tend to be faster than token-passing methods, but collisions can bog down the network if it is heavily populated with devices. Token ring does not suffer from collision problems, but the current throughput rates on token ring networks are restrictive when compared to new high-speed Ethernet networks.

Related Entries   Collisions and Collision Domains; CSMA/CD (Carrier Sense Multiple Access/ Collision Detection); Ethernet; Fast Ethernet; Gigabit Ethernet; MAC (Medium Access Control); *and* Token Ring Network

 Linktionary! – Tom Sheldon's Encyclopedia of   http://www.linktionary.com/a/access_method.html Networking updates

Access Provider

An access provider is a service company that provides communication links into other networks. The most common example is an ISP (Internet service provider). Another example is a local or long-distance phone carrier.

An ASP (Application Service Provider) offers services that are the equivalent of renting software and provide a way for companies to outsource the management of the applications, especially groupware, collaboration, electronic commerce, and business-to-business applications.

An OSP (online service provider) is best characterized by AOL (America Online), which provides nationwide access to an enhanced set of information services and an "online community." These services are only available to subscribers, and as any AOL user will tell you, are quite popular with users. For example, AOL has an "instant messaging" service that can alert you when a friend logs on and let you exchange messages with that person in real time.

Related Entries   ASP (Application Service Provider); Communication Services and Providers; Internet Connections; ISP (Internet Service Provider); Network Access Services; POP (Point of Presence); *and* Service Providers and Carriers

 Linktionary! – Tom Sheldon's Encyclopedia of   http://www.linktionary.com/s/service_providers.html Networking updates

Access Rights

See Rights and Permissions.

Account, User

User accounts are fundamental to the security of information systems. Most network operating systems such as Windows NT, NetWare, and others require that users have an account. If a person is not assigned a specific account, access is often allowed through a guest account or with an anonymous user account. For example, your access to Web sites on the Internet is through anonymous user accounts at the site that do not require a logon name or password.

The user account holds information such as username, user information, logon restrictions to the network, and other information. Network administrators control user access by either changing values in individual user accounts or by setting global controls for all users or groups of users. For example, an administrator can disable an account while a user is on vacation or stop access to that account if illegal activities are taking place. Time limits can be assigned to accounts in the case of temporary employees. An account can also be configured so that user logons are restricted to certain hours of the day (say, 8:00 A.M. to 5:00 P.M.) or to a specific computer.

User accounts may also hold general information, such as the address of the user's workstation, phone number, or department name. In a directory services system like NDS (Novell Directory Services), user accounts appear as objects in the directory tree. Other users can scan through the directory tree, select a user, and view information about that user unless security restrictions prevent such access.

Information about users and user accounts can be seen in Figure A-2. This is the dialog box you see if you select a user in the NDS tree. Note that you can access other information about the account such as login restrictions, password restrictions, and login scripts.

Groups are collections of users that simplify system management. A user that is added to an administrative group or a special workgroup receives all the rights and permissions assigned to that group. Most network operating systems have default groups for various system management tasks and regular users groups for normal access. Special groups can be created at any time.

User Accounts in UNIX

In UNIX operating systems, an administrator assigns a UID (unique user identification number) to new user accounts. The system uses the UID to identify the user when he or she logs on, runs programs, accesses files, and so on. User account information on UNIX systems

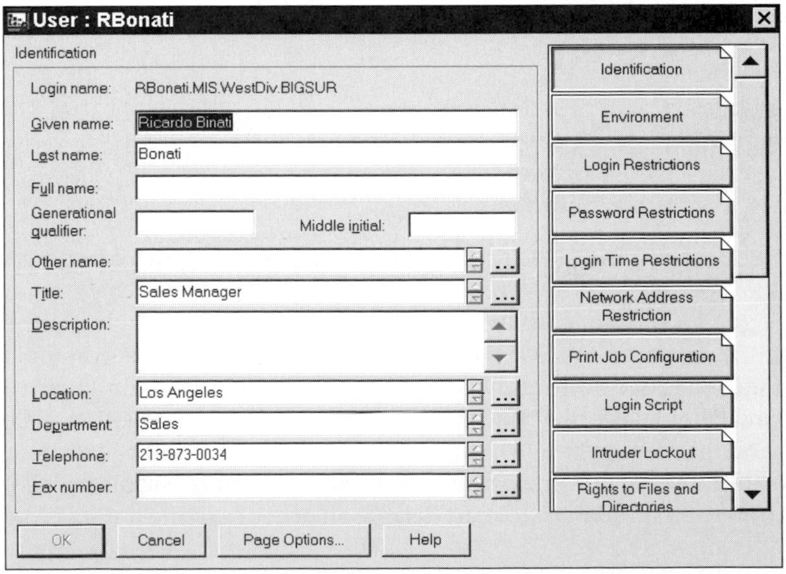

Figure A-2.   *User account information in NetWare*

is stored in a password file located in /etc/passwd. The password itself is coded for secrecy, but keep in mind that hackers can easily crack this file to obtain logon passwords, so you need to secure your systems physically. Each group has a unique GID (group ID). Group information is stored in /etc/group.

You add user accounts in UNIX by running commands such as **usercfg** or **adduser** (if they are available on your version of UNIX). The manual approach is to edit the /etc/passwd file. This should be covered in your UNIX manual, but the basic steps are to insert a line in the file that includes the username, password, UID, GID, real name, home directory, and login shell. You place an asterisk in place of the password, then run the **passwd** command, which adds an encrypted form of a password you specify into the password file.

User Accounts in Windows NT and Windows 2000

You manage user accounts and groups in Windows NT 4 by running User Manager or User Manager for Domains (on domain servers). The application provides a user interface that makes user account management a simple task. User accounts are assigned a unique number called a SID (security identifier) that is created by the operating system from a combination of the user information, time, date, and domain information. This ID is used internally by the system to manage access rights and other security features related to the account.

There are two built-in accounts on every system: administrator and guest. The administrator user account has full access to the system while the guest account has very restricted access. As for group, there is an Administrators group on each system for local use, a Domain Administrators group for users that administer the local domain, and a Domain Users group for users who can access systems in the domain (as opposed to accessing just the local system).

All user accounts are automatically added to the Everyone group, and no accounts may be excluded from this group. Another group, called Interactive, includes any user that is currently logged on to a server. There is also a Network group that includes all users that have performed a network logon.

Rights are assigned to user accounts with the User Manager program. Rights allow users to perform activities on a system or network, such as change the system time, load device drivers, manage auditing and security logs, and shut down the system. Any user or group may be assigned these rights. Users are granted permissions to access resources such as folders and files. Permission is granted at the resource, not to the user account. For example, to grant Joe and Bob access to the file Duck.doc, you right-click Duck.doc, choose Sharing, then choose Joe and Bob from a list of users.

Related Entries   Attributes; Authentication and Authorization; Directory Services; File Sharing; File Systems; Logons and Logon Accounts; Microsoft Windows; Network Operating Systems; Novell NetWare; Rights and Permissions; Security; UNIX; *and* Users and Groups

Linktionary! – Tom Sheldon's Encyclopedia of   http://www.linktionary.com/a/account.html
Networking updates

Accounting on the Internet

Some work has been done to support various forms of accounting on the Internet. An early paper describing the NREN (National Research and Education Network) had this to say:

> To encourage use of the Network by commercial information service providers, where technically feasible, the Network shall have accounting mechanisms that allow, where appropriate, users or groups of users to be charged for their usage of copyrighted materials over the Network. (RFC 1259, September 1991)

However, accounting has been difficult to implement, and not popular. In addition, many organizations post free information to attract visitors. Since RFC 1259 was written, most of the work related to accounting involves some method of metering traffic and charging the responsible party, or tracking "roaming users" who move among ISPs but maintain a formal relationship with only one ISP.

Metering

An early work was RFC 1272 (Internet Accounting: Background, November 1991), which described an "Internet Accounting Architecture." The focus of the paper was to define a meter service and a usage reporting service for measuring network utilization. The RFC specifies how accounting information is structured, collected, and used by accounting applications.

RFC 1672 (Accounting Requirements for IPng, August 1994), draws on the work in RFC 1272 by describing a model for policy-based routing and accounting in which packets carry accounting tags that can be used like vouchers to identify a party that is responsible for, and willing to pay for, a packet transmission. A tag initially identifies the party who sent it, but the tag could be changed along its routed path to reflect changes of the party responsible for the packets. Accounting meters would identify the parties responsible for traffic flows without having to deduce this using tables of rules, thus simplifying accounting for traffic that crosses network boundaries. The information could be used at higher layers of the protocol stack, for example, to allow an application server to inform a client about its usage of a resource.

RFC 2063 (Traffic Flow Measurement: Architecture, January 1997) references 1272 and discusses an architecture for the measurement and reporting of network traffic flows. It describes traffic meters that count attributes such as the number of packets and bytes and classify them as belonging to "accountable entities," identified by source/destination addresses. Accountable entities are the responsible parties "who pay for the traffic." A *traffic flow* is described as the logical equivalent to a call or connection that is generated by an accountable entity. The RFC also describes other entities required in the accounting system, including traffic measurement managers, meters, and meter readers.

oaming and Accounting

Roaming allows Internet users to connect at different points on the Internet while maintaining a billing relationship with only one ISP. ISPs participate in "roaming consortiums" in which they maintain authentication and accounting services that support roaming users. Roaming on the Internet is defined as "the ability to use any one of multiple Internet service providers (ISPs), while maintaining a formal, customer-vendor relationship with only one."

RFC 2477 (Criteria for Evaluating Roaming Protocols, January 1999) describes a roaming architecture that consists of a phone book subsystem (phone number presentation, exchange,

compilation, and updating), an authentication subsystem (connection management, authentication, authorization, routing, and security), and an accounting subsystem. The accounting subsystem enables all the participants in the roaming consortium to keep track of the resources clients use during a session, such as how long the user was connected, the connection speed, port type, and other information.

The roaming standard will also support RADIUS, due to its ubiquity as an authentication, authorization, and accounting solution. RADIUS accounting provides a way to generate packets that signal the start and end of services that require accounting. RADIUS accounting is described in RFC 2139 (RADIUS Accounting, April 1997).

Related Entries   Authentication and Authorization; Bandwidth Management; Policy-Based Network Management; RADIUS (Remote Authentication Dial-In User Service); *and* Roaming

Linktionary! – Tom Sheldon's Encyclopedia   http://www.linktionary.com/accounting_internet.html
of Networking updates

IETF Accounting, Authentication,   http://www.ietf.org/html.charters/aaa-charter.html
Authorization (aaa) Working Group

Accounting Services

Accounting services are provided by some network operating systems to track the usage of resources and the users who access those resources. Accounting systems also provide network asset tracking. Typical network resources tracked by accounting systems include

- Files accessed
- Disk space used
- User logons and logoffs
- Messages transferred by users
- Bytes transferred by users
- Applications started
- Access to resources such as printers and databases

In most cases, it is possible for the administrator or supervisor of a network or server to set limits on the amount of time a user can access the system, the amount of disk space a user can use, and the resources a user can access. Users can be granted a certain amount of time or access to resources, which gets used up as the user accesses the resources. The user can then request or purchase additional time or resources. The values are tracked in the user's account. The accounting system in NetWare can track and charge users for blocks read and written to disk, connect time, or service requests.

Related Entries   Auditing; Security Auditing

Linktionary! – Tom Sheldon's Encyclopedia of   http://www.linktionary.com/auditing.html
Networking updates

ACID (Atomicity, Consistency, Isolation, Durability)

The four states defined by the acronym ACID (atomicity, consistency, isolation, and durability) relate to a successful transaction, usually a database transaction. All of these characteristics must be present, or the transaction must be completely reversed (undone or rolled back).

Related Entries   Data Protection; DBMS (Database Management System); *and* Transaction Processing

Acknowledgments

An acknowledgment is a confirmation of receipt. When data is transmitted between two systems, the recipient can acknowledge that it received the data. Acknowledgments compensate for unreliable networks. However, acknowledgments can reduce performance on a network. If every packet sent requires an acknowledgment, then up to half of the data transmission is spent exchanging acknowledgments.

Modern networks such as LANs and WANs are considered highly reliable. There is little need to acknowledge every packet, so acknowledgments are used for groups of packets or not at all. Unreliable networks still exist, however, especially if you are building WANs in third-world countries or using wireless devices to transmit data. Acknowledgments may be handled in the data link layer for each frame. Doing this in the network is extremely wasteful of bandwidth, but often there is little choice. X.25 packet-switching networks use this technique. The alternative is to acknowledge higher up in the protocol stack and use the network to send data as fast as possible.

The TCP portion of the TCP/IP protocol suite implements an "expectational acknowledgment" system. The sender transmits packets and waits for an acknowledgment of receipt. The wait time is handled by a timer, which is set when the packets are sent. If the timer runs out before an acknowledgment is received, the sender retransmits the packets. In some cases, the actual data link may be broken, so to prevent endless retransmissions, the sender stops retransmitting after a set number of attempts.

TCP's acknowledgment scheme uses a sliding window technique in which the sender sends multiple packets at a time—say, packets 1, 2, and 3—then waits for the receipt. The receiver acknowledges receipt by requesting the next packets. The sender then sends segments 4, 5, and 6. The receiver requests a retransmission, if necessary (because packets are corrupted or lost), by failing to acknowledge a set of packets. RFC 813 (Window and Acknowledgement Strategy in TCP, July 1982) provides more information.

Three other RFCs of interest are RFC 1072 (TCP Extensions for Long-Delay Paths, October 1988), RFC 1323 (TCP Extensions for High Performance, May 1992), RFC 2001 (TCP Slow Start, Congestion Avoidance, Fast Retransmit, and Fast Recovery Algorithms, January 1997)

TCP SACK (selective acknowledgment is an enhancement to the TCP windowing and acknowledgment scheme that provides a way for the sender to retransmit only the packets that are missing in a window of data, rather than the entire window. FACK (forward acknowledgment) is an algorithm that can provide congestion control during the packet recovery process. RFC 2018 (TCP Selective Acknowledgment Options, October 1996) provides more information about SACK. See the Pittsburgh Supercomputing Center Web site (listed at the end of this topic) for more information.

A

Related Entries   Congestion and Congestion Control; Connection Establishment; Data Communications Concepts; Flow-Control Mechanisms; Fragmentation of Frames and Packets; Handshake Procedure; NAK (Negative Acknowledgment); Reliable Data Delivery Services; Sliding Window Mechanism; TCP (Transmission Control Protocol); *and* Transport Protocols and Services

Linktionary! – Tom Sheldon's Encyclopedia of Networking updates	http://www.linktionary.com/a/ack.html
Acknowledgments and related hyperlinks in a training course by Godred Fairhurst	http://www.erg.abdn.ac.uk/users/gorry/eg3561/dl-pages/ack.html
TCP papers links list (satellite, congestion, performance, acknowledgements, transactions, wireless)	http://tcpsat.lerc.nasa.gov/tcpsat/papers.html
Pittsburgh Supercomputing Center SACK and FACK information	http://www.psc.edu/networking/sack-fack.html

ACL (Access Control List)

See Access Control.

Acrobat

Acrobat is a product from Adobe Systems Incorporated that strives to be a universal document formatter and viewer. You can create document layouts and formats using any variety of typefaces, font sizes, layouts, and graphical information and then save those documents in Adobe Portable Document Format (PDF), which can be read by an Acrobat reader. Many documents available on the Internet and Web are available for download as Acrobat documents. Note the following:

- Acrobat is designed to assist companies in distributing their documents over the Internet, on disk and CD-ROM, or via electronic mail messages. Adobe also recommends Acrobat for long-term archiving of documents.

- You use the Acrobat toolset to create Acrobat documents. It costs about $250 and is available for Windows and Macintosh platforms. The toolset includes tools for converting files created in other applications into the Adobe PDF format. Converted files have the PDF filename extension.

- Acrobat readers are free and available at the Adobe site or at most sites that provide Acrobat files for downloading.

- Acrobat readers are available for Windows, Macintosh, Linux, and a variety of other UNIX systems.

- PDF files support security options and digital signatures to protect documents from unauthorized tampering, copying, or printing.

- Web site designers can create forms with PDF files.

The Adobe Web site is at http://www.adobe.com.

Related Entry   Document Standards and Document Management

Active Directory

Microsoft's Active Directory is the directory service included with Windows 2000 Server. Windows 2000 is the successor to Windows NT Server 4.0. Active Directory extends the feature set found in Windows NT domain services and adds new features. It is a secure directory database that can be partitioned and distributed via replication throughout the network. Active Directory is also scalable, and is designed to work in an environment with thousands of servers and millions of objects.

Related Entry   Directory Services; Microsoft Active Directory

Active Documents

An active document is a document that has links to programs or other information sources. The link may display information in the document that is either continually updated, updated only when the document is loaded, or updated when the user requests it. See "Compound Documents."

Active Networks

Active Networks (or Active Nets) is a DARPA (Defense Advanced Research Projects Agency) program to develop a next-generation Internet with a more dynamic routing model. Participating in the program are a number of universities, including MIT and the University of Pennsylvania, as well as Network Associates, Inc. and GTE-BBN Internetworking.

The Active Network concept is to move from static routers to active nodes that can handle "smart packets" (also called *capsules*) that have their own executable code. According to the paper "From Internet to ActiveNet" (see Web site below):

> Active Networks represent a new approach to network architecture that incorporates interposed computation. These networks are "active" in two ways: routers and switches within the network can act on (i.e., perform computations on) user data flowing through them; furthermore, users can "program" the network by supplying their own programs to perform these computations.

The Active Network concept goes beyond IPv6, which operates in static mode. In an Active Network, nodes that are dubbed active can look inside capsules and run the executable code in those capsules. Alternatively, the capsule may contain a pointer that references some code already located on the network. Network nodes may change their behavior based on the code or modify the capsule contents in order to affect network nodes down the line. A capsule may define its own path through the network.

In one case, routes are altered based on where information is cached on the network. This can eliminate the need for packets to move to and from the original source of the information and help reduce traffic. Packets are instead directed to the cached information, which may be closer to the user that requested it.

The Active Network concept is to make the network more flexible in terms of being able to change how it operates and to take advantage of new networking technologies.

Related Entries GII (Global Information Infrastructure); Internet; Internet2; Internet Architecture and Backbone; Internet Organizations and Committees; NII (National Information Infrastructure); NIST (National Institute of Standards and Technology); NREN (National Research and Education Network); Routing; Routing on the Internet; *and* vBNS (very high speed Backbone Network Service)

Linktionary! – Tom Sheldon's Encyclopedia of Networking updates	http://www.linktionary.com/a/active_network.html
DARPA Active Networks page	http://www.darpa.mil/ito/research/anets/index.html
"From Internet to ActiveNet," a paper by D. L. Tennenhouse, S. J. Garland, L. Shrira and M. F. Kaashoek	http://www.tns.lcs.mit.edu/publications/rfc96/
ActiveNets information page at MIT	http://www.sds.lcs.mit.edu/darpa-activenet/
ActiveNets home page at MIT	http://www.sds.lcs.mit.edu/activeware/
The SwitchWare Project at the University of Pennsylvania	http://www.cis.upenn.edu/~switchware/
Active Networks – A Survey	http://www.cis.ohio-state.edu/~jain/cis788-97/active_nets/
Active Networking research at Georgia Tech	http://www.cc.gatech.edu/projects/canes/
Smart Packets page at BBN	http://www.ir.bbn.com/documentation/techmemos/
A Survey of Active Network Research (IEEE Communications Magazine)	http://www.tns.lcs.mit.edu/publications/ieeecomms97.html
Active Network Archives	http://www.ittc.ukans.edu/Projects/ActiveNets/
Computer Science Laboratory Active Network Backbone Web page	http://www.csl.sri.com/activate/
Network Associates Inc.	http://www.nai.com
White Paper: "Implementation of a Prototype Active Network"	http://www.ittc.ukans.edu/~kulkarn/docs/OpenArch98/

Active Server Page

Active server pages (called ASP here to be concise) are part of Microsoft's Internet Information Server. ASP was originally released with version 3.0, and was enhanced in later versions of the software. ASP assists in the programming of dynamic content Web pages and Web-based applications.

Basically, an Active Server Page is an HTML page that has been created on the fly at the server before being sent to the user. The ASP itself contains a script that takes information that has been input by the client and uses it to build a database query. The results of the query returned by the database server are used to build a custom Web page that is created on the spot and forwarded to the client.

ASP scripts provide the same results as CGI (Common Gateway Interface) and ISAPI (Internet Server API) applications, but are much easier for programmers to create. ASP maintains the state of a session with the server, thus reducing the amount of information that must be sent back and forth between the client and the server. ASP can work with information entered in HTML forms as well as information embedded as parameters in the URL (Uniform Resource Locator). An ISAPI extension called Asp.dll compiles and caches ASP files in memory at runtime.

With ASP, programmers can create pages that provide interactivity no matter which browser the client might be using. In addition, scripts can be kept on the server for proprietary reasons, rather than being sent as part of a Web page to the client. In addition, programs can create scripts using a number of languages, including VBScript, JScript, PerlScript, REXX, or Python.

Related Entries   ActiveX; Client/Server Computing; COM (Component Object Model); Distributed Object Computing; Java; Multitiered Architectures; Object Technologies; SOAP (Simple Object Access Protocol); *and* Web Technologies and Concepts

Linktionary! – Tom Sheldon's Encyclopedia of Networking updates	http://www.linktionary.com/a/aspages.html
Microsoft (search for "ASP")	http://www.microsoft.com
Active Server reference site	http://www.15seconds.com/

ActiveX

ActiveX is Microsoft's component technology based on Microsoft's COM (Component Object Model), which itself is based on OLE (Object Linking and Embedding). OLE provides a linking technology in which an object inserted into documents (such as a pie chart created in Excel) is automatically updated when the parent object (in the Excel spreadsheet) is updated. Documents with objects created in multiple programs are called *compound documents* and are discussed elsewhere in this book.

COM is a development technology that advances OLE. It allows multiple objects and programs on the same computer to communicate, which promotes component application development. COM also promotes component reuse, meaning that components can be designed to work with multiple programs. DCOM (Distributed COM) extends COM onto networks, allowing two components on different computers to communicate and work together.

ActiveX is a natural extension of COM and DCOM that provides many advantages for building software components that can communicate over the Internet or intranet.

> **Note**   *ActiveX (and Java) are considered "mobile code." The code "travels" across networks and executes on client computers. Web users greatly benefit from this technology, but there are security implications in downloading executable programs, so security schemes are necessary.*

ActiveX programs are composed of *ActiveX controls,* which are modular components that perform tasks such as retrieving and displaying information or presenting a user interface feature such as a pull-down window on a Web page. Like Java applets, ActiveX controls are used primarily in the Web client and server environment, although that role has expanded. ActiveX controls run within a host process referred to as an ActiveX container. Web browsers and Microsoft Office applications such as Word are ActiveX containers that can host ActiveX controls. ActiveX controls can be developed with a variety of programming languages, including Visual C++, Visual Basic, and Java.

Microsoft promotes ActiveX technology as a tool for building dynamic and active Web pages and distributed object applications. When a user visits an ActiveX Web site, ActiveX controls are downloaded to the user's browser, where they remain in case the user visits the site again. ActiveX controls may display a moving object or banner, or they may provide a sophisticated program that calculates amortization schedules or financial information. Further, ActiveX controls may provide components that give clients direct access to data servers using protocols that are more sophisticated and efficient than the Web's HTTP (Hypertext Transfer Protocol). This is covered under "Distributed Object Computing."

Advantages for Web Sites

Companies that are involved in Internet commerce are especially interested in technologies like ActiveX (and Java) because they make the Web user's experience at their sites more dynamic and active with special multimedia effects, audio, video, virtual reality, and sophisticated applications. The whole idea is to make a site worth returning to. Executable component technology is also considered crucial to doing business on the Web. ActiveX can work in concert with the MTS (Microsoft Transaction Server) to ensure that transactions are either complete or are backed out to preserve database integrity. See "Transaction Processing."

For the Web site developer, ActiveX controls provide a way to manage and update Web content and client systems easily. Sophisticated applications in the form of many ActiveX components can be put up at the site for users to download. Initially, it may take some time for the user to download all the components, but updates and upgrades are easy because only specific components need to be copied to the user's computer.

ActiveX Server is a set of service technologies that speed deployment of component-based applications across the Internet and corporate intranets. These services include the following:

- **Transactions**   Traditional rollback and recovery for component-based applications in the event of system failure

- **Queuing**   The integration of component communication with reliable store-and-forward queues, which enables component applications to operate on networks that are occasionally unavailable

- **Server scripting**   The easy integration of component applications on the server with HTML-based Internet applications
- **Legacy access**   The integration of component applications with legacy production systems, including mainframe systems running CICS and IMS

Another advantage of ActiveX controls is that they can work closely with the user interface of the target operating system, especially Windows systems, since ActiveX is based on COM technology that has been a traditional part of Windows. With ActiveX Scripting, ActiveX controls and/or Java applets can be integrated and controlled from the server or browser.

Some of the other features available in ActiveX are as follows:

- An API called ADO (ActiveX Data Objects) allows programmers to allow programs access to back-end database systems easily. Web clients that visit a Web site where this technology has been implemented can make database requests directly from their Web browser. ADO uses the OLE DB interface to connect with databases. OLE DB is discussed elsewhere in this book.
- Web browsers can display ActiveX documents with non-HTML information, such as Microsoft Excel and Word files.
- With Active Scripting, ActiveX controls and/or Java applets can be integrated and controlled from the server or browser.
- ActiveX integrates software components in networked environments using any language, including Java.
- With ActiveX Server, Web servers can provide security and access back-end databases to provide information from the database to users.

ActiveX development is relatively easy, and there are already sites where developers can download prebuilt and reusable ActiveX controls. Other controls are available for sale.

Microsoft has developed ADO to support access to databases. ADO program statements are included on Active Server Web pages.

More Information

To promote ActiveX as a standard, in October 1996 Microsoft turned control of ActiveX over to the Open Group, which formed a subgroup called the Active Group specifically to manage the evolution of ActiveX technologies. It also provides development, branding, testing, and licensing services.

While Java and ActiveX compete in the market, there is a considerable amount of support for running both in the same environments, so you don't need to choose one over the other. Java applets can link to ActiveX controls, which in turn provide a link to higher-level operating system functions. Vendors that Support ActiveX, COM, and DCOM are listed here:

Metrowerks	http://www.metrowerks.com
Bristol Technologies	http://www.bristol.com
Mainsoft Corp	http://www.mainsoft.com

CMPnet WebTools site	http://www.webtools.com
Microsoft COM site	http://www.microsoft.com/activex
The Open Group Web site	http://www.opengroup.org/
Active Server Pages Web application development software	http://www.drumbeat.com
Active Server reference site	http://www.15seconds.com/default.htm
BrowserWatch ActiveX control information	http://browserwatch.internet.com
CNET's freeware and shareware ActiveX controls page	http://www.download.com/PC/Activex
TegoSoft ActiveX controls	http://www.tegosoft.com/OCXKit.htm
ActiveX links at Yahoo!	http://dir.yahoo.com/Computers_and_Internet/Internet/World_Wide_Web/

Related Entries   Active Server Pages; Client/Server Computing; COM (Component Object Model); Component Software Technology; Compound Documents; Distributed Applications; Distributed Computer Networks; Distributed Object Computing; Java; Microsoft Windows DNA (Digital interNetwork Application); Middleware and Messaging; Multitiered Architectures; Object Technologies; OLE (Object Linking and Embedding); SOAP (Simple Object Access Protocol; *and* Web Technologies and Concepts

Linktionary! – Tom Sheldon's Encyclopedia of Networking updates	http://www.linktionary.com/a/activex.html

Adapter

An adapter is an add-in board that expands the capabilities of a computer system. In the network environment, a NIC (network interface card) is the typical adapter that provides connections to Ethernet, token ring, or other types of networks.

Related Entry   NIC (Network Interface Card)

ADC (Analog-to-Digital Conversion)

ADC, or digitizing, converts analog waveforms to digital representations that can be processed and stored in computers. The analog wave is "sampled," or read, hundreds or thousands of times per second to map out the wave digitally. Digital music requires extremely high sampling rates (44,100 samples/sec), while it is usually acceptable to sample voice at 11,000 samples/sec or higher. There is also a factor that determines the precision of the captured signal—the more bits used to record the value of the sampled signal, the higher its resolution and the better its sound when played back. However, the more bits used, the more disk space is required for storage or bandwidth for transmission. For example, one minute of sampling at 44.1 kHz using 16 bits per sample (the compact disc specification) requires 5.292MB of disk space.

The telephone companies convert analog voice calls to digital at their central offices (there is one in your neighborhood) for transmission across trunk lines to other central offices or to long-distance systems. Voice converted to digital requires a 64-Kbit/sec channel, which happens to be a worldwide standard called DS0 (digital signal, level zero) for transmitting voice calls.

Analog-to-digital converters are used in a variety of information-processing applications. Information collected from analog phenomena such as sound, light, temperature, and pressure can be digitized and made available for digital processing. A codec (coder/decoder) is the device that transforms the analog signals to digital signals. The process involves sampling, quantizing, and digitizing. The amplitude of a signal is measured at various intervals. The tighter these intervals, the more accurate the recording. Figure A-3 illustrates how a wave is sampled 16 times per second, with a sampling rate of 16Hz. While sampling at this rate is impractical for voice or music, it illustrates how each sample records a different amplitude value for the sound. Generally, a rate of 8,000 samples per second or higher using 8 bits per sample is adequate for voice-quality signals. Quantizing is the process of replacing the sampled value with the nearest value within the range of the device and the sampling rate. Digitizing completes the process.

Scanners are devices that record the differences in dark and light areas in photographs and convert the differences to digital values. The picture becomes a matrix of dots, and each

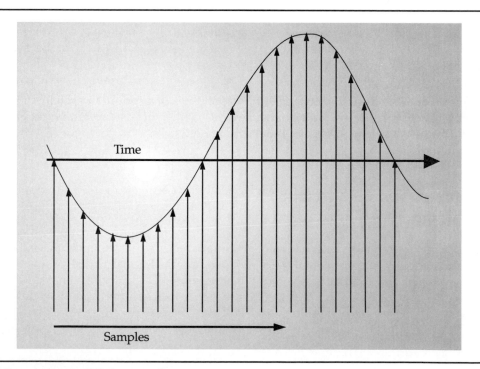

Figure A-3.   *Analog-to-digital conversion*

dot is represented in memory as a color or gray-scale value that can be displayed on a screen or transmitted to another device. Fax machines have built-in scanners.

Related Entries   ADPCM (Adaptive Differential Pulse Code Modulation); Compression; Multimedia; G Series ITU Recommendations; Telecommunications and Telephone Systems; Voice/Data Networking; *and* VoIP (Voice over IP)

Linktionary! – Tom Sheldon's Encyclopedia of   http://www.linktionary.com/adc.html
Networking updates

ADCCP (Advanced Data Communications Control Procedure)

ADCCP is a data link layer protocol that places data on a network and ensures proper delivery to a destination. ADCCP is basically an ANSI modification of IBM's SDLC (Synchronous Data Link Control) protocol. It is the ANSIX3.66 standard. The ISO then modified ADCCP into HDLC and the CCITT, now ITU, modified HDLC for its LAPB (Link Access Protocol-Balanced) protocol. The other protocols are described in this book under appropriate headings. See "HDLC (High-level Data Link Control)"

Address Resolution Protocol

See ARP (Address Resolution Protocol).

Addresses, Electronic Mail

Electronic mail systems have specific addressing schemes that identify users and resources on the network. These addressing schemes identify the area or domain and the specific node within the area or domain in which a user or resource exists .

The Internet, a global network of users, employs a hierarchical naming scheme as part of its DNS (Domain Name System). An address for a user attached to a local area network or a network attached to the organization's e-mail hub might be the following, which addresses John Doe (jdoe) at the library, University of California, Berkeley. The last portion, "edu," is the Internet top-level domain name indicating an educational institution.

jdoe@library.berkeley.edu

Two other standards should be mentioned. The X.400 specifications are a set of e-mail communications standards developed by the CCITT (Consultive Committee for International Telegraphy), now the ITU-T (International Telecommunication Union-Telecommunications Sector). Basically, X.400 set some precedents for e-mail, but never became as popular as Internet mail.

X.500 is a directory services standard that provides so-called *white pages* naming services for enterprise networks. While X.500 never became a popular standard for use in electronic mail addressing, a subset of X.500 standards has been implemented in LDAP (Lightweight Directory Access Protocol). White page services are important because they help users locate other users for a variety of activities, including addressing electronic mail to them. Note that with LDAP, the predominant addressing scheme is the Internet address.

Related Entries   Directory Services; DNS (Domain Name Service); Electronic Mail; Instant Messaging; Name Services; Search and Discovery Services; White Pages Directory Services; WHOIS ("Who Is"); X.400 Message Handling System; *and* X.500 Directory Services

Addresses, Network

There are two types of network addressing schemes. One is for identifying nodes on a shared Data Link layer LAN. The other is used to identify hosts in an internetwork environment.

- **LAN addressing**   A LAN is a shared media access system. Each node has a MAC (Media Access Control) address that is factory-programmed into its NIC (network interface card). One node transmits on the cable, and all the rest listen. Frames are addressed to either one of the nodes or, in the case of a broadcast, all of the nodes.

- **Internetwork addressing**   An internetwork is a collection of LANs and/or other networks that are connected with routers. Each network has a unique address and each node on the network has a unique address, so an address is network address/ node address combination. In the TCP/IP protocol suite, IP is responsible for network layer addressing.

While MAC addresses are hardwired, internetwork addressing is part of a logical addressing scheme that "overlays" the MAC layer addressing scheme. MAC addressing is part of the data link layer, while internetwork addressing is part of the network layer.

Network nodes can have multiple addresses. A server with two NICs will have two MAC layer addresses. Each of those NICs is attached to a separate LAN segment. Software in the server may either bridge the LAN segments into a single larger network or provide routing, in which case, each NIC will have network layer addresses.

The best way to think of these two addressing schemes is in terms of the postal system. MAC addressing is like local addressing, while internetwork addressing is like intercity mail, with ZIP codes providing an intercity message routing system.

Figure A-4 illustrates the hierarchy of MAC and network layer addressing schemes in a TCP/IP network. Data transmitted on a LAN is sent in frames. Each frame has a destination MAC address for a target node on the same LAN. If data is being transmitted to a node on another LAN, then frames are sent to the router that interconnects the LANs.

Note   *A multicast is a one-to-many transmission in which one station sends packets to a select group of systems. Refer to "Multicasting" in this book. An anycast address is an address assigned to one or more network interfaces that provide services as a group. A packet will go the one address that is best able to service it. See "Anycasting."*

MAC Addressing

The data link layer of the OSI protocol stack is divided into the MAC (Media Access Control) and LLC (Logical Link Control) sublayers, with MAC being below LLC. These sublayers are defined by the IEEE, and the addressing scheme used in the MAC layer is administered in such a way by the IEEE that no two network interface cards should ever have the same MAC address. This lets you install any NIC on a LAN without worrying about address conflicts.

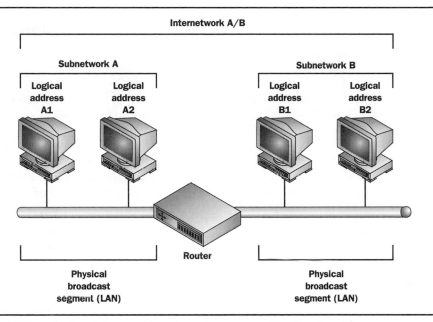

Figure A-4.   *MAC and network layer addressing schemes in a TCP/IP network*

The addressing layout is 48 bits in length. The first 24 bits hold the OUI (organization unique identifier), which is a number that identifies a manufacturer of NICs. The IEEE allocates OUIs. The second 24 bits contain a unique number assigned by the manufacturer or vendor to identify the NIC.

The following list shows some MAC addresses for Linksys and D-Link NICs. Note that the first six digits are the same for cards from the same vendor.

Linksys Ethernet card	00 40 05 1D 8E 7E
Linksys Ethernet card	00 40 05 2A 57 4B
D-Link Ethernet card	00 80 C8 C1 91 6D
D-Link Ethernet card	00 80 C8 C1 74 8B

Internetwork Addressing

An internetwork consists of interconnected LANs with attached nodes (called *hosts*) and routers. Each device has a physical connection to the network that has a MAC layer address, and each node has a logical internetwork address.

Figure A-5 illustrates the network with IP internetworking addresses applied. The left-hand network has the network address 192.168.1.0, and the right-hand network has the network address 192.168.2.0. The zero in the host field at the end of the address indicates the entire network.

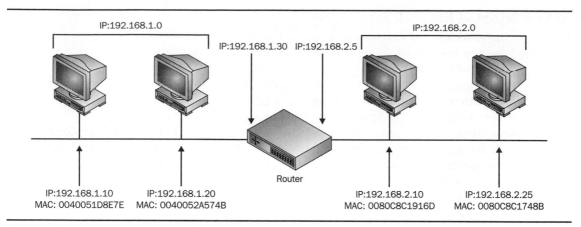

Figure A-5.   *Internetwork addressing*

Suppose host 192.168.1.10 wants to send a message to host 192.168.2.25 (at the far end of the network). A simplified description of this procedure follows.

1. Host 192.168.1.10 sends the message in a frame (or frames) addressed to the MAC address of the router.

2. The router reframes the data for the 192.168.2.0 network addressing the frames to the MAC address of 192.168.2.25.

3. Node 192.168.2.25 receives the frames.

Additional information about IP addressing may be found under the heading "IP (Internet Protocol).

Higher-Level Addressing

The application level is the level at which people interact with computers. Instead of using complex IP addresses to refer to other computers, names are used that are much easier to remember. For example, to access Microsoft's Web site, you type **www.microsoft.com** in the Address field of your Web browser. Your Web browser then goes to a specified DNS site and translates this name into an IP address. The IP address is used from then on to access the site.

Applications such as HTTP Web browsers or FTP use port addresses to connect with similar applications running on other computers. A combination of a port address and an IP address is known as a *socket*. For example, Web servers use port 80, so to contact a Web server at IP address 192.168.2.25, you could type **192.168.2.25:80**, However, the port numbers is assumed if you are running a Web browser, so people don't normally type them. There are well known ports for most applications. See "Ports, TCP/IP."

Connection-Oriented Network Addressing

The IP internetworking scheme is a connectionless networking scheme. Each packet is forwarded, hop by hop across routers to the destination. Routers read the address in each packet and forward the packet.

A connection-oriented network is one in which a path through the network is set up in advance. This path mimics a physical circuit and is called a *virtual circuit* in ATM networks, frame relay networks, and other connection-oriented networks.

On connection-oriented networks, the path through the network is assigned an identifier. This identifier is used in place of a destination address. It identifies the complete path to the destination, rather than the destination itself. As the packet traverses the network, switches read the identifier to determine which preassigned circuit to forward the packet on. This process reduces overhead and boosts performance. Refer to "ATM (Asynchronous Transfer Mode)," "Frame Relay," and "Virtual Circuit" for more information.

Related Entries   Data Link Layer; IP (Internet Protocol); Network Concepts; MAC (Medium Access Control); NAT (Network Address Translation); *and* NIC (Network Interface Card)

Linktionary! – Tom Sheldon's Encyclopedia of Networking updates	http://www.linktionary.com/addresses_network.html
Gorry Fairhurst's Data Communications course (see sections MAC and IP)	http://www.erg.abdn.ac.uk/users/gorry/eg3561/syllabus.html
Medium Access Control (MAC) course at University of Aberdeen	http://www.erg.abdn.ac.uk/users/gorry/course/lan-pages/mac.html
Understanding IP Addressing by Chuck Semeria (3COM)	http://www.3com.com/nsc/501302s.html
WRQ Guide Services, "IP Addressing Fundamentals"	http://support.wrq.com/tutorials/tcpip/tcpipfundamentals.html

ADM (Add-Drop Multiplexors)

See Multiplexing and Multiplexors; Optical Networks; *and* SONET (Synchronous Optical Network).

Administrator Account

Normally, an administrator is a person with a high level of control. The *administrator account* is a user account that exists on several popular network operating systems and has the highest level of control over a system and/or network. On a UNIX system, the *root* user account is the highest level account, with unrestricted access to the system. Root is often called the *superuser* account.

In older versions of NetWare, a person who installed a server became the *supervisor* for that server only, with unlimited rights to manage that server. In versions of NetWare that implement NDS (Novell Directory Services), the management structure for administrators has been expanded. The administrator account manages NDS and all the servers, users, and resources tracked by it. The administrative user can assign other people as subadministrators for part of the directory tree, if necessary, to enable distributed management.

Microsoft's new Active Directory for Windows 2000 implements a hierarchical administration scheme similar to NDS, in which one administrator has control over the entire network and can delegate subadministrators to manage other parts of the directory tree.

In the traditional Windows NT environments, a person becomes administrator by installing the first server in a domain. That server becomes the PDC (primary domain controller) for the domain, and other servers become BDCs (backup domain controllers). The administrator can manage all the servers in the domain. Of course, other domains can be created, but they can have their own administrators.

Administrator Activities

With most secure operating systems, the person who installs the operating system is the one who has first shot at becoming the administrator/root user. However, this is not always practical in a situation in which many systems are being set up at once by several people, but only one person should have administrator/root status. In this case, the real administrator should change the administrator/root password as soon as the system is installed to avoid security problems.

All administrative users should have a separate logon account that they use to access the network when performing nonadministrative tasks. Administrator-level access should not be taken lightly. Make sure no one watches you enter a password, and ensure that systems are in a safe location so that intruders can't install software that might act as a Trojan horse and steal your password. For security reasons, you can prevent the administrators of your systems from logging in over the network. This will reduce the chance of attacks from the network by allowing administrator logon only at the physical system.

The system administrator's password is the master key to the system. Try to use a complex password that is easy to recall by using the phrase system. For example, the password Mbiot4thoJ is derived from "My birthday is on the Fourth of July." Another suggestion is to create a two- or three-word password and then give a portion of the password to two or three people in the company. This "fail-safe" approach ensures that others can gain administrative access to the server should something happen to the administrator. To gain access, they must do so together.

In NetWare, a separate auditor account exists that can monitor the activities of the administrator. This is a good idea. When the system is first installed, an administrator enables auditing and creates the auditor account. Once the auditor is given control of the account, he or she can change the password to ensure that the administrator can no longer access it. The auditor can track the activities of the administrator but not perform any other tasks that the administrator can perform.

Generic Administrator Task List

Here's the generic list of administrator tasks. We pulled it out of the last edition to save space, but some readers requested it for use in job descriptions and service contracts:

- Install servers.
- Create the initial administrator password.
- Change the administrator password periodically for security reasons.
- In a directory services environment, administer the directory tree.
- Create directory structures for programs and data on servers.
- Install applications.
- Create, manage, and delete user accounts.
- Set logon and access restriction policies.
- Designate users as managers with special rights to manage systems and other users.
- Troubleshoot system problems and failures.
- Ensure that system security features such as authentication systems, access controls, and firewalls are properly installed and configured.
- Ensure that data is properly protected with backup procedures and system fault tolerance (SFT) features.
- Ensure that systems are physically secure. Malicious users have an easier time breaking into systems if they are at the system, rather than accessing it over the network.
- Monitor the system for malicious activity. This includes running monitoring tools and evaluating activity logs.
- Recommend new equipment or manage the expansion of the network when it becomes overloaded.
- Consider the repercussions of being the person of last resort to call during critical events such as system failures or disasters.
- Put training classes and conferences into your IT budget so you can keep up to date.
- Monitor the performance and integrity of the network.
- Purchase cable-testing equipment and protocol analyzers to troubleshoot your networks if they are large enough to justify it.
- Build a network-testing platform so you can try new software and hardware, and experiment with new network technologies.
- Handle whining users with diplomacy.
- Increase help desk budget so you can hire someone else to handle whining users.

Related Entries   Access Control; Auditing; Network Operating System; Network Management; Rights and Permissions; Security; Users and Groups; *and* Webmaster

Linktionary! – Tom Sheldon's Encyclopedia of   http://www.linktionary.com/a/administrator.html
Networking updates

Admission Control

In a bandwidth-managed network in which QoS (quality of service) is being provided, a mechanism is required that can estimate the level of QoS that a new user session will need and whether there is enough bandwidth available to service that session. If bandwidth is available, the session is *admitted*. Think about getting a seat on an airplane. The reservation agent provides admission by issuing a ticket if there are seats available.

There will be competition among sessions and flows for network bandwidth. An easy method for admission control is to service flows based on arrival time. This is often called *CAC (capacity-based admission control)*. With CAC, new flows are indiscriminately admitted until capacity is exhausted (First Come First Admitted). New flows are not admitted until capacity is available.

Another method is to allow some flows to preempt others based on *priority settings*. RFC 2751 (Signaled Preemption Priority Policy Element, January 2000) and RFC 2815 (Integrated Service Mappings on IEEE 802 Networks, May 2000) describe admission control in a priority-queued system. However, adding traffic to a higher priority queue can affect the performance of lower-priority classes, so priority queued systems must use sophisticated admission control algorithms.

One aspect of admission control is the ability to monitor, control, and enforce the use of network resources and services with *policy-based management*. The criteria for policy-based management includes identifying users and applications or identifying traffic based on how, when, and where it enters the network. RFC 2753 (A Framework for Policy-based Admission Control, January 2000) describes a policy-based control framework for admission control.

RFC 2814 (Subnet Bandwidth Manager: A Protocol for RSVP-based Admission Control over IEEE 802-style networks, May 2000) describes a signaling method and protocol for LAN-based admission control over RSVP flows.

RFC 2816 (A Framework for Integrated Services Over Shared and Switched IEEE 802 LAN Technologies, May 2000) discusses methods for supporting RSVP in LAN environments. It describes a BA (bandwidth allocator) that is responsible for performing admission control and maintaining state about the allocation of resources in the subnet. End stations request services such as bandwidth reservation that are processed by the BA.

Related Entries   Bandwidth Management; Congestion and Congestion Control; CoS (Class of Service); Differentiated Services (DiffServ); Policy-Based Network Management; Prioritization of Network Traffic; QoS (Quality of Service); RSVP (Resource Reservation Protocol); *and* Traffic Management, Shaping, and Engineering

Linktionary! – Tom Sheldon's Encyclopedia of   http://www.linktionary.com/a/admission.html
Networking updates

Newbridge Networks paper: "Connection Admission Control: A Key Service Differentiator in the ATM Infrastructure"	http://www.newbridge.com/doctypes/ technewbridgenote/pdf/cac_atm.pdf
Managing Admission Control Services	http://www.micronpc.com/programs/NT/ resources/pdf/techbriefs/tb5.pdf

ADPCM (Adaptive Differential Pulse Code Modulation)

ADPCM is a more efficient version of the digitizing method called PCM (pulse code modulation). It converts analog signals to digital data and is used to transmit analog voice over digital channels. Organizations that establish digital lines between remote sites can transmit both voice and data over these lines by digitizing the voice signals before transmitting. ADPCM uses a lower bit rate than normal PCM, which permits more voice channels to be transmitted over a typical digital line. The difference between samples is used and the coding scale can be dynamically changed to compensate for amplitude and frequency variations.

Related Entries   ADC (Analog-to-Digital Conversion); Multiplexing and Multiplexers; *and* T-Carriers

ADSL (Asymmetrical Digital Subscriber Line)

The telephone system in the United States is largely digital, even though most telephones are analog devices. The so-called "last mile" is the local loop of wire that stretches from most homes to the telephone company's central office (usually in the same neighborhood). This local loop is copper twisted-pair wire that has carried voice in a narrow band below 400 Hz. DSL technologies expand the bandwidth usage of this cable. DSL technologies use line encoding to provide very high data transmission rates over the local loop. ADSL is one form of DSL technology.

Refer to "DSL (Digital Subscriber Line)" for more information. You can also refer to the ADSL Forum home page at http://www.adsl.com.

ADTM (Asynchronous Time Division Multiplexing)

See Multiplexing and Multiplexers.

Advanced Intelligent Network

See AIN (Advanced Intelligent Network).

Advertising and Advertising Services

Advertising is a technique used by a server to announce the services it has available. Advertising was traditionally used in the NetWare environment, although that has changed recently. The NetWare operating system used SAP (Service Advertising Protocol) to broadcast information about available services on the network that other network devices can listen to. A server sends out SAP messages every 60 seconds. A server also sends out SAP messages to inform other devices that it is closing down. Workstations use SAP to find services they need on the network. For example, a workstation can send a SAP message to a local router to obtain the address of a node on another network.

SAP is a legacy protocol that has been used in almost all versions of NetWare. However, excessive SAP messages can sap network throughput. In NetWare 4, NDS (Novell Directory Services) helps reduce the need for SAP because the NDS database can be consulted for service locations. However, SAP is still used on NetWare 4.*x* networks because many network devices require it.

While SAP and similar protocols provide a way to advertise services on local networks, services on the Web are found using search services, word of mouth, or paid advertisements that catch the eye of readers and viewers. Recently, several methods have been proposed to help users locate services in domains on the Internet. The Service Location Protocol described in RFC 2165 eliminates the need for a user to know the DNS name of a host that provides a particular service. Instead, users can find services by specifying the type of service they need along with attributes of that service. Refer to "SLP (Service Location Protocol)" for more information.

Another scheme is the Dublin Core Metadata Initiative, which is working to develop conventions for resource discovery on the Web. Metadata refers to data structure that describes some other data, just like a library card describes a book. The Dublin Core is designed to provide a flexible way to represent resources and relationships among resources in both traditional and digital formats that simplify resource discovery. Refer to "Dublin Core" for more information.

Still another protocol, PIP (Presence Information Protocol), provides a way to alert users when another user logs on, thus allowing those users to exchange instant messages.

Emerging service advertising techniques are discussed under "Service Advertising and Discovery."

Related Entries   Directory Services; Instant Messaging; Metadata; Name Services; Service Advertising and Discovery; SAP (Session Announcement Protocol) *and* SLP (Service Location Protocol)

 Linktionary! – Tom Sheldon's Encyclopedia of   http://www.linktionary.com/a/advertising.html
Networking updates

AFP (AppleTalk Filing Protocol)

AFP is the file protocol in the Macintosh environment that lets users access files on other systems. AFP uses AppleTalk for communication between systems, although the latest incarnation—called AFP over TCP/IP—allows users to access AFP servers over TCP/IP networks.

AFP passes user commands down the protocol stack to lower-layer protocols that handle establishing connections and monitoring data flow between systems. AFP itself resides in the presentation and application layers of the AppleTalk protocol stack. It has the following features:

- AFP sets up an environment for a user that appears as if files on a remote file server are available locally.

■ Access to server files is handled using the same procedures as access to local files, except that a user must initially establish a connection to the remote file server.

■ AFP provides security features that can restrict user access to files.

AppleShare is Apple's client and server software that allows Mac OS (operating system) users to access shared files and printers. It is based on AFP. Macintosh users access AppleShare servers through AppleShare client software. Note that starting with the Macintosh System 7 OS, Macintosh users were able to share files on their own systems with other users.

In 1995, Apple introduced its Open Transport software, which allows the Macintosh system to support multiple protocols. This move was made primarily to add support for TCP/IP and the full suite of Internet protocols. In this scheme, AFP is tunneled across the TCP/IP network, allowing users to gain access to AppleShare servers, Web servers, FTP servers, and other services across intranets.

Related Entries   Apple Computer; AppleShare; AppleTalk; File Sharing; File Systems; *and* MacOS

 Linktionary! – Tom Sheldon's Encyclopedia of   http://www.linktionary.com/afp.html
Networking updates

AFS (Andrew File System)

AFS was developed by the ITC (Information Technology Center) at Carnegie Mellon University; its current development and marketing is in the hands of Transarc Corporation. A version of AFS called the DFS (Distributed File System) is a component in the OSF (Open Software Foundation) DCE (Distributed Computing Environment). AFS is architecturally similar to the NFS (Network File System). Basically, AFS/DFS provides a way to join dissimilar server and client machines into a global shared information system.

AFS is specifically designed to provide reliable file services in large distributed environments. It creates manageable distributed environments with a structure based on cells. A cell is a collection of file servers and client systems within an autonomous area that is managed by a specific authority. It typically represents the computing resources of an organization. Users can easily share information with other users within the cell. They can also share information with users in other cells, depending on access rights granted by the authorities in those cells.

A major objective of AFS/DFS is to make the way users retrieve information the same from any location, allowing users to collaborate and share information. It removes the barriers that separate the file systems of each different network operating system.

AFS/DFS provides the following features:

■ A file server process responds to client workstation requests for file services, maintains the directory structure, monitors file and directory status information, and verifies user access.

■ A BOS (basic overseer) server process runs in a "BOS-designated server." It monitors and manages processes running other servers and can restart server processes without human assistance.

- A volume server process handles file system operations related to volumes, such as volume create, move, replicate, backup, and restore.

- Replication automatically locates replicas of information across multiple locations. Replication can take place while users remain online.

- Optimized performance is provided by buffering commonly accessed files on local drives with the guarantee that the information in the files is up to date. This helps avoid network bottlenecks.

  Files can be moved around to different systems to adjust loads on servers. A VL (volume location) server process provides location transparency for volumes so that if volumes are moved, users can access them without the knowledge that they have moved.

- Security mechanisms are provided for controlling access to information according to users and groups. It uses encrypted login mechanisms and flexible access control lists for directories and files. The authentication system is based on Kerberos.

- Management of clients and server machines can be done from any point, allowing smaller numbers of administrators to manage more systems. A system-monitoring tool provides a view of system loads and alerts administrators of potential problems.

- It provides support for building scalable Web servers.

- Cluster computing in DFS allows administrators to run processor-intensive jobs across a network with portions of the processing task running on different computers.

- Clustering in DFS also allows files to be stored on a collection of smaller, lower-cost machines, as opposed to one big server.

DFS competes with Sun Microsystems' NFS in some environments. Transarc developed the following comparison between DFS and NFS:

- **File access**   In DFS, the filename is independent of the file's physical location. NFS filenames must be addressed by referencing physical file locations.

- **Performance**   DFS uses client data caching to reduce network load. NFS does not.

- **Replication**   DFS supports replication. NFS does not.

- **Availability**   With DFS, files are available during system maintenance. This is not true with NFS.

- **Security**   DFS supports encrypted login and data transmission. NFS does not.

- **Access control**   DFS supports access control lists for user and group accounts. NFS does not.

Related Entries   DCE (Distributed Computing Environment); DFS (Distributed File System), Microsoft; DFS (Distributed File System), Distributed Computer Networks; Open Group; File Sharing; File Systems; Network Operating Systems; *and* NFS (Network File System)

Linktionary! – Tom Sheldon's Encyclopedia of Networking updates	http://www.linktionary.com/a/afs.html
AFS and DFS information	http://www.transarc.com
AFS—Andrew File System; Fermilab Final Evaluation Report and Implementation Recommendations	http://www.hep.net/hepnrc/reports/afs-eval.html
Andrew II home page at Carnegie Mellon	http://andrew2.andrew.cmu.edu/ANDREWII/AndrewII.html
AFS resources and links	http://www.alw.nih.gov/WWW/AFS-resources.html
U.S. Navy AFS Q & A	http://amp.nrl.navy.mil/code5595/afs-support/
AFS paper at University of Alberta	http://gpu.srv.ualberta.ca/HELP/afs/afs2.html

Agent, Internet

Internet agents are software entities that are designed to seek out information intelligently on the Internet or on intranets. They are similar to Web search engines, except that they are designed to find information specific to a user's request and deliver it in a form that is similar to a newspaper. A typical agent is directed to find specific types of information. It then begins searching public and private networks (where authorized) and returns its results to the user. Agents may operate during off-hours to take advantage of low-traffic periods.

An agent product from Autonomy Systems called AgentWare automates the process of finding information and presenting it in a personal way to a user. Autonomy's pattern-matching technology enables AgentWare to identify and encode the unique "signature" of the key concepts within text documents. This signature of the concept then seeks out and uncovers the presence of similar concepts in volumes of content, such as a set of Web sites, a newsfeed, or an e-mail archive.

Search engines such as AltaVista can provide Internet searching through literally millions of Web documents that have already been indexed. One of the best sites about agents on the Internet is BotSpot.

Related Entries   Handle System; Metadata; Name Services; Search and Discovery Services; Service Advertising and Discovery; *and* URN (Universal Resource Naming)

Linktionary! – Tom Sheldon's Encyclopedia of Networking updates	http://www.linktionary.com/agent.html
Miningco.com. Bots and other interesting and related information	http://ai.miningco.com

"Robots in the Web: Threat or Treat?" by Martijn Koster of NEXOR	http://info.webcrawler.com/mak/projects/robots/threat-or-treat.html
Martijn Koster's "The Web Robots FAQ"	http://info.webcrawler.com/mak/projects/robots/faq.html
BotSpot at Internet.com	http://www.botspot.com
UMBC AgentWeb site	http://www.cs.umbc.edu/agents/
Autonomy Systems	http://www.autonomy.com/tech/index.html
AltaVista	http://www.altavista.com
Intelligent Agents page by Prof. Jeffrey MacKie-Mason	http://china.si.umich.edu/telecom/net-commerce-agents.html

Agent, Network Management

In general, an agent is a background process that performs an action at a specified time or when an event occurs. In the realm of networking, an agent is part of a network management system that resides in workstations or other network devices (called *managed elements*) and collects information to report back to a management system about those devices. The management system runs at a central location, but in a distributed management system, management subsystems may reside at various points in the network to collect local information that is periodically transferred to the main management system. Note that a client/server relationship exists between the agent and the management system, but the term "agent" is often used for management systems to avoid confusion.

In the SNMP (Simple Network Management Protocol) system, which provides a tool for tracking workstations and compiling information about them, agents are called *network agents*. As shown in Figure A-6, agents reside in devices on the network and monitor activities on those devices. For example, an agent in a router can monitor packet transmissions, error conditions, and connections. The agents then make this information available to NMSs (network management stations). The NMS is the controlling device that gathers information from network agents, stores it in an MIB (management information base) on disk, and presents it to network administrators or supervisors for evaluation. Statistical information can show how the network is reacting to its current load and provide a way to detect potential problems.

Related Entries   Network Management; SNMP (Simple Network Management Protocol)

Linktionary! – Tom Sheldon's Encyclopedia of Networking updates	http://www.linktionary.com/a/agent_net.html

Aggregate Route-Based IP Switching

See ARIS (Aggregate Route-Based IP Switching).

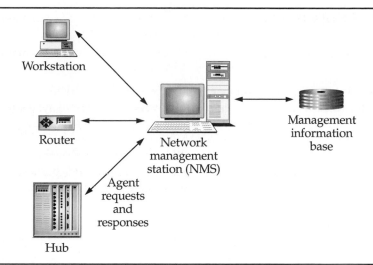

Figure A-6.   *Network agents*

Aggregation, Routing

Aggregation is the process of combining multiple contiguous network routes into a single route that can be advertised to other routers, thus reducing the amount of routing information that is advertised over the network. This is especially important on the Internet, where the number of networks has grown rapidly. Route aggregation is an important part of CIDR (Classless Inter-Domain Routing).

Related Entries   Anycasting; Autonomous System; CIDR (Classless Inter-Domain Routing); IP (Internet Protocol); ISP (Internet Service Provider); Link Aggregation; Load Balancing; NAT (Network Address Translation); OSPF (Open Shortest Path First) Protocol; Route Aggregation; *and* Routing

Aggregation of Links

See Link Aggregation; Load Balancing.

AIN (Advanced Intelligent Network)

See Telecommunications and Telephone Systems.

AIX (Advanced Interactive Executive)

See IBM AIX (Advanced Interactive Executive).

ALB (Adaptive Load Balancing)

See Link Aggregation.

ALOHA

ALOHA is a system for coordinating and arbitrating access to a shared communication channel. It was developed in the 1970s at the University of Hawaii. The original system used terrestrial radio broadcasting, but the system has been implemented in satellite communication systems.

A shared communication system like ALOHA requires a method of handling collisions that occur when two or more systems attempt to transmit on the channel at the same time. In the ALOHA system, a node transmits whenever data is available to send. If another node transmits at the same time, a collision occurs, and the frames that were transmitted are lost. However, a node can listen to broadcasts on the medium, even its own, and determine whether the frames were transmitted.

This technique is simple and elegant, but another method called *slotted* ALOHA was devised in 1972 to double the capacity. In the slotted scheme, distinct time slots are created in which systems can transmit a single frame. One node emits a signal at the start of each slot to let all other nodes know when the slot is available. By aligning frames on slots, overlaps in the transmissions are reduced. However, nodes must wait a fraction of a second for the beginning of a time slot before they can transmit. Also, data may be lost if nodes contend for the same slot. However, tests have shown that slotted ALOHA has a performance advantage.

One of the interesting things about ALOHA is that it inspired Robert Metcalfe in his design of Ethernet in 1972-1973 as discussed under "Ethernet."

Related Entries   Broadcast Networking; Collisions and Collision Domains; CSMA/CD (Carrier Sense Multiple Access/Collision Detection); Ethernet; Internet; *and* Satellite Communication Systems

Linktionary! – Tom Sheldon's Encyclopedia of Networking updates	http://www.linktionary.com/a/aloha.html
How the Internet Came to Be, By Vinton Cerf, as told by Bernard Aboba	http://www.bell-labs.com/user/zhwang/vcerf.html
Spread ALOHA Wireless Multiple Access: The Low-Cost Way for Ubiquitous, Tetherless Access to the Information Infrastructure	http://bob.nap.edu/html/wpni3/ch-21.html

AMPS (Advanced Mobile Phone Service)

See Wireless Mobile Communications.

Analog Transmission Systems

There are analog transmission systems and digital transmission systems. In an analog transmission system, signals propagate through the medium as continuously varying electromagnetic waves. In a digital system, signals propagate as discrete voltage pulses (that is, a positive voltage represents binary 1, and a negative voltage represents binary 0), which are measured in bits per second.

The medium for an analog transmission may be twisted-pair cable, coaxial cable, optical-fiber cable, the atmosphere, water, or space. A technique called "modulation" is used to combine an input signal (the data) onto a carrier signal. The carrier signal is a specific frequency. When tuning a radio, you select a particular carrier frequency in order to tune in that radio station. There are two primary modulation techniques: amplitude modulation, which varies the amplitude (height) of the carrier signal; and frequency modulation, which modulates the frequency of the carrier. Refer to "Modulation Techniques" for more information.

The frequency ranges of several analog transmission systems are listed here:

300–3,000 kHz	AM radio
3 to–30 MHz	Shortwave and CB radio
30–300 MHz	VHF television and FM radio
300–3,000 MHz	UHF television and cellular telephones, and microwave systems

In data communications, analog signals are used to transmit information over the telephone system or over radio transmission systems (such as satellite links). A modem converts digital data to analog signals. Alternatively, analog signals can be converted to digital information using a *codec (coder/decoder).* This process is called *digitizing.* Phones that connect to all-digital communication links use codecs to convert analog voice signals to digital signals. The phone company digitizes voice transmissions between its central offices and long-distance sites. In fact, the only remaining analog portion of the phone system is the twisted-pair wire that runs between homes and the telephone companies' central offices, which are usually less than a mile distance from the subscriber.

Related Entries   ADC (Analog-to-Digital Conversion); Bandwidth; Cable and Wiring; Data Communications Concepts; Electromagnetic Spectrum; Modulation Techniques; Signals, *and* Wireless Communication

Linktionary! – Tom Sheldon's Encyclopedia of   http://www.linktionary.com/a/analog.html
Networking updates

Andrew File System

See AFS (Andrew File System).

Anonymous (Guest) Access

Many computer systems and network servers provide what is called "anonymous" or "guest" access. An account is set up with the name anonymous or guest. Multiple users can log in to the account at the same time. Typically, an annonymous account does not require a password, although users are sometimes asked to type a username. The anonymous/guest account user usually has very restricted access to the system and is often only allowed to access special public files. Such accounts are used on FTP (called *Anonymous FTP*) and Web servers on the Internet (and intranets). The accounts are also used for kiosk information systems in public areas or in organizations that make computers available to employees that need to look up information such as pension fund data or archival data.

Two Internet RFCs of interest are RFC 1635 (How to Use Anonymous FTP, May 1994) and RFC 2245 (Anonymous SASL Mechanism, November 1997)

Internet RFC 2245 explains anonymous servers and provides some guidelines for managing them.

Anonymous accounts should only have read access rights to limit attacks on the system. Any user requiring write access should be required to log in under a specific user account with a secure password.

Anonymous or guest access accounts should be disabled by default in most operating systems unless the system administrator has specific reasons to use them.

Anonymous accounts may provide what is called a "drop-box" feature, in which a user is allowed to submit a file to a server but is not allowed read or execute access to the drop-box folder. This prevents users from submitting and running executable programs that could damage the server.

Many Web sites allow access to anonymous accounts only after users have supplied additional information, such as their e-mail address. This information can be used to track the user later. Cookies are also used to track users. Note that trace information is easily faked by the client, so the authenticity of this information should always be questioned. This is especially important when messages and other information received by clients are posted for others to read.

Anonymous servers are susceptible to attacks. An anonymous user could instigate a "denial-of-service" attack on a server that does not have an idle time-out and that limits the number of anonymous users. The user could simply tie up the server by logging on multiple times (up to the user limit) and keeping the connection open.

Related Entries   Access Control; Account, User; Administrator Account; Attributes; Authentication and Authorization; Cookies; FTP (File Transfer Protocol); Logons and Logon Accounts; Network Operating Systems; Password; Security; *and* Users and Groups

Linktionary! – Tom Sheldon's Encyclopedia of Networking updates

http://www.linktionary.com/a/anonymous.html

ANSI (American National Standards Institute)

ANSI is an organization that defines coding standards and signaling schemes in the United States and represents the United States in the ISO (International Organization for Standardization) and within the ITU (International Telecommunication Union). ANSI was a founding member of the ISO and plays an active role in its governing. It is one of five permanent members to the governing ISO Council. ANSI promotes the use of U.S. standards internationally, advocates U.S. policy and technical positions in international and regional standards organizations, and encourages the adoption of international standards as national standards where these meet the needs of the user community.

According to ANSI, "it does not itself develop ANSs (American National Standards); rather it facilitates development by establishing consensus among qualified groups. The Institute ensures that its guiding principles—consensus, due process and openness—are followed by the more than 175 distinct entities currently accredited by the Federation." The U.S. standards are presented to international standards organizations by ANSI, where they may be adopted in whole or in part as international standards. Volunteers from industry and government carry out much of the technical work, so the success of ANSI's work largely depends on the amount of participation by U.S. industry and U.S. government.

Here are some well-known ANSI standards:

- Programming and query languages, including SQL (ANSI X3H2), C++ (ANSI X3J16), and Smalltalk (ANSI X3J30)

- EDI (Electronic Data Interchange) specifications (ANSI X12)

- FDDI (Fiber Distributed Data Interface) specifications (ANSI X3T9.5)

- ADSL (Asymmetric Digital Subscriber Line) specifications (ANSI T1.413-1995)

- SONET (Synchronous Optical Network), the ANSI specification for fiber-optic transmissions over a common global infrastructure

- Security standards (ANSI X9)

Note that the IEEE (Institute of Electrical and Electronic Engineers) has conforming standards in some cases.

Related Entries   IEEE; ISO (International Organization for Standardization); *and* Standards Groups, Associations, and Organizations

 ANSI Web site   http://www.ansi.org

Antivirus Software

See Virus and Antivirus Issues.

Anycasting

An anycast address, according to RFC 2526 (Reserved IPv6 Subnet Anycast Addresses, March 1993), is a "reserved address in IPv6 that is assigned to one or more network interfaces that may belong to different physical nodes with the property that a packet sent to an anycast address is routed to the *nearest* interface having that address, according to the routing protocols' measure of distance." Another feature is that an anycast address looks the same as a normal unicast address. Nodes sending packets to an anycast address don't necessarily need to know that it is an anycast address.

An earlier document, RFC 1546 (Host Anycasting Service, November 1993), discusses the motivation for anycasting, but at this time, IPv6 addressing had not yet been developed. The reasoning is that clients will require some service that is available from two or more different servers. The client doesn't care which one of those servers provides the service. An important point is to make finding services easier for the client. For example, instead of choosing from a list of information servers, a client could type a request and be connected to the nearest server. Anycasting also provides fault tolerance since other servers in a group can provide service in other go down.

RFC 2373 (IP Version 6 Addressing Architecture, July 1998) provides a more recent description and motivation:

> One expected use of anycast addresses is to identify the set of routers belonging to an organization providing internet service. Such addresses could be used as intermediate addresses in an IPv6 Routing header, to cause a packet to be delivered via a particular aggregation or sequence of aggregations. Some other possible uses are to identify the set of routers attached to a particular subnet, or the set of routers providing entry into a particular routing domain.

An anycast address has a topological region in which all the members belonging to the anycast address reside. Within that region, each member must be advertised as a separate entry in the routing system, but outside the region, the members are known by the single aggregate anycast address.

RFC 1546 discusses some potential problems. For example, IP is stateless and does not keep track of where earlier datagrams were delivered. If a client sends two datagrams to an anycast address, one may go to one server and one may go to another. A mechanism is needed to make sure that once an anycast server is selected, all further packets go to that server. There is also the possibility that anycast datagrams may be sent to all of the hosts that serve the anycast address. Given these problems, the RFC provides a more correct definition of IP anycasting as "a service which provides a stateless best effort delivery of an anycast datagram to at least one host, and preferably only one host, which serves the anycast address."

The RFC states that the solution is to require applications to maintain state by learning the address of the client during the first datagram exchange and using that address for all future conversations. You can refer to RFC 1546 for additional information about anycast addressing, its architecture, use in applications, security considerations, and other details. RFC 2526 provides more up-to-date proposals on how anycasting should be implemented with IPv6.

Related Entries   Addresses, Network; IP (Internet Protocol); Link Aggregation; Load Balancing; *and* Multicasting

 Linktionary! – Tom Sheldon's Encyclopedia of Networking updates   http://www.linktionary.com/a/anycasting.html

AnyNet

AnyNet is a family of access node and gateway products that help you integrate IBM SNA, TCP/IP, IPX, and NetBIOS networks with products on IBM AIX/6000, MVX/ESA, OS/2, OS/400, and the Microsoft Windows platform. The AnyNet family is based on MPTN (Multiprotocol Transport Networking) architecture, an X/Open standard. AnyNet basically makes it easier to build multiprotocol networks in IBM environments and eliminates the need to build parallel networks that provide interconnections between computing devices. If you are transitioning from an SNA (Systems Network Architecture) network to a TCP/IP network, AnyNet can help reduce conversion costs by allowing SNA applications to be accessed via the TCP/IP network.

Related Entries   IBM (International Business Machines); MPTN (Multiprotocol Transport Network); *and* SNA (Systems Network Architecture)

Google Web Directory (search for "AnyNet")	http://directory.google.com/Top/Computers/
IBM Redbooks site (search for "AnyNet")	http://www.redbooks.ibm.com

Apache

Apache is an open source Web server that runs on UNIX platforms. It has grown in popularity with Linux, another open source product. Apache was originally based on code and ideas found in the NCSA HTTP server (circa 1995), but Apache has evolved into what the Apache Web calls "a far superior system which can rival (and probably surpass) almost any other UNIX based HTTP server in terms of functionality, efficiency and speed." The name is derived from "A PAtCHy server," which provides some clue to the patch code roots of the server.

Like Linux, the server is supported by a network of users, newsgroups, and chat communities, as well as numerous Web sites.

Related Entries   HTTP (Hypertext Transfer Protocol); Linux; Proxy Server; *and* Web Technologies and Concepts

Apache Web site	http://www.apache.org

API (Application Programming Interface)

APIs are the language and messaging formats that define how programs interact with an operating system, with functions in other programs, with communication systems, or with hardware drivers. For example, an operating system provides a set of standard APIs that programmers can use to access common functions such as accepting user input, writing information to the screen, or managing files. The APIs in Microsoft Windows are quite sophisticated because they allow programmers to build programs that easily access features such as pull-down menus, icons, scroll bars, and more. In the network environment, APIs are available that interface network services for delivering data across communication systems. A cross-platform API provides an interface for building applications or products that work across multiple operating systems or platforms.

Several types of network communication APIs are conversational, RPC (remote procedure call), and message APIs. IBM's APPC (Advanced Program-to-Program Communications) model is conversational. RPC models have been developed by Sun Microsystems, by the OSF (Open Software Foundation), and by Microsoft in its Windows environment. Messaging models include IBM MQSeries and MSMQ (Microsoft Message Queue Server).

For example, MSMQ is a store-and-forward service that enables applications running at different times to communicate across networks and systems that may be temporarily offline. Applications send messages to MSMQ, and MSMQ uses queues of messages to ensure that the messages eventually reach their destination. MSMQ provides guaranteed message delivery, efficient routing, security, and priority-based messaging.

Related Entries ActiveX; Client/Server Computing; COM (Component Object Model); DCE (Distributed Computing Environment); Distributed Applications; Distributed Computer Networks; Distributed Object Computing; Java; Middleware and Messaging; MOM (Message-Oriented Middleware); Multitiered Architectures; Object Technologies; RPCs (Remote Procedure Calls); SOAP (Simple Object Access Protocol); Sockets; WinSock; *and* XML (eXtensible Markup Language)

Linktionary! – Tom Sheldon's Encyclopedia of   http://www.linktionary.com/a/api.html
Networking updates

APPC (Advanced Program-to-Program Communications)

APPC, APPN (Advanced Peer-to-Peer Networking), and CPI-C (Common Programming Interface for Communications) are networking technologies that are available on many different IBM and non-IBM computing platforms. APPC, also known as LU 6.2, is software that enables high-speed communications between programs on different computers, from portables and workstations to midrange and host computers over SNA (Systems Network Architecture), Ethernet, X.25, token ring, and other network topologies. APPC software is available for many different systems, either as part of the operating system or as a separate software package. It is an open and published communications protocol.

APPC represented a major strategy change for IBM when it was introduced. It demonstrated a shift in network control away from the centralized host systems to the systems that were attached to the network. Systems running LU 6.2 sessions do not need the services of a host system when establishing sessions.

LU 6.2 was developed to allow computers on the network with their own processing power to set up their own sessions. In the older hierarchical approach, terminals attached to host computers relied completely on the host to set up and maintain sessions. LU 6.2 provides peer-to-peer communications between systems other than hosts and allows those systems to run distributed applications like file sharing and remote access. The entire range of IBM platforms is supported by LU 6.2, including LANs, desktop systems, and mainframes.

LU 6.2 relies on SNA Type 2.1 nodes. Type 2.1 nodes are different than other SNA nodes in that they run CP (Control Point) software that allows them to engage in peer-to-peer connections with other Type 2.1 nodes. This arrangement became increasingly important as LANs were installed in IBM SNA environments. While the LAN provided a connection from a network node to a connected host, those LAN nodes could also use LU 6.2 to communicate directly with other LAN nodes, rather than go through the host.

Applications using the LU 6.2 protocols are called TPs (transaction programs). Examples of TPs are IBM DDM (Distributed Data Management), which provides file sharing and database sharing among systems that implement DDM, and DIA (Document Interchange Architecture), which is a document exchange standard that defines searching, browsing, printing, and the distribution of documents.

A TP opens a session, performs data transfers, and closes. A TP performs a "unit of work" on a channel that interconnects IBM systems. The sessions are designed to be short-lived because some systems cannot perform other tasks until they complete the transactions. A transaction is like a conversation, and a TP can hold multiple conversations with multiple systems. Each conversation has a name and buffers for sending and receiving data, along with a code that is returned to indicate success or failure of the transaction. The parameters are simple, so code can be portable among systems.

Programs use LU 6.2 services through an interface called the LU 6.2 Protocol Boundary or through the CPI-C (Common Programming Interface for Communications). CPI-C is the currently preferred method. CPI provides a common environment for the execution of programs on different IBM platforms, and the C version provides the LU 6.2 communication interface. Recently, IBM has implemented CPI-C in its Open Blueprint, which supports TCP/IP (Transmission Control Protocol/Internet Protocol).

Related Entries   APPN (Advanced Peer-to-Peer Networking); IBM; SAA (Systems Application Architecture); *and* SNA (Systems Network Architecture)

Linktionary! – Tom Sheldon's Encyclopedia of Networking updates	http://www.linktionary.com/appc.html
IBM APPN information	http://www.networking.ibm.com/app/aiwinfo/aiwintro.htm
IBM APPC tutorial	http://pclt.cis.yale.edu/pclt/COMM/APPC.HTM
IBM SNA tutorial	http://pclt.cis.yale.edu/pclt/COMM/SNA.HTM
IBM Redbooks site (search for "APPC")	http://www.redbooks.ibm.com

Apple Computer

Apple Computer is the manufacturer of the Macintosh line of computers and developed the AppleTalk networking system that works over LocalTalk, EtherTalk, TokenTalk, and FDDITalk networks. Apple is involved extensively in networking and distributed management. Its products are widespread and can be used as nodes on almost every available network operating system and topology. Its Macintosh System 7 and Mac OS operating systems are in use on Macintosh systems everywhere. In addition, Macintosh users have relied on the AppleTalk networking protocols and AppleShare servers for all their networking needs.

Apple Macintosh experienced a surge of popularity in 1998 and 1999 with the introduction of Apple's iMac systems (in five dazzling colors), Apple PowerBook G3s, and Power Macintosh G3s.

An important change for the company was its full support of the Internet Protocol suite in all of its products, coupled with a move away from AppleTalk. Novell has gone through similar changes by fully supporting Internet protocols and shying away from its traditional SPX/IPX protocol suite.

Related Entries   AFP (AppleTalk Filing Protocol); AppleShare; AppleTalk; *and* Mac OS

General information	http://www.apple.com
Macintosh operating systems information	http://www.macos.apple.com
Apple products	http://www.apple.com/products/
Developer information	http://www.apple.com/developer/

Apple Open Transport Protocol

Apple Open Transport is Apple's solution for transport-independent networking for the Mac OS. Transport independence is designed to free network developers and users from any need to know about the underlying network. Open Transport brings together the technologies to support transport-independent applications. It provides a consistent set of network services across multiple protocols, including AppleTalk and TCP/IP. It also provides a name-to-network address mapping service so users can access resources using familiar names rather than cryptic network addresses. New implementations of Mac OS protocol stacks have been released that replace existing AppleTalk and TCP/IP implementations, including support for PPP (Point-to-Point Protocol), NetWare NCP and IPX, Windows 95 and Windows NT (SMB/TCP/NetBIOS), DECnet, and LAT.

In late 1998, Apple introduced an Open Transport Protocol update with its Mac OS 8.5. The update includes support for DHCP (Dynamic Host Configuration Protocol) and SNMP (Simple Network Management Protocol). It also replaced PPP (Point-to-Point Protocol) with ARA (Apple Remote Access).

With the release of Open Transport, Apple minimized development work on its traditional AppleTalk protocol stack in favor of Open Transport. Likewise, MacTCP (the TCP/IP protocol stack in early releases of Mac OS) was pushed aside in favor of Open Transport.

Related Entries   Apple Computer; AppleTalk; Mac OS; Internet Protocol Suite; *and* Transport Protocols and Services

AppleShare

AppleShare is a file-sharing solution that Apple built on the AppleTalk protocols. It has been around for a number of years. Every Macintosh computer has built-in client software for accessing AppleShare servers. The latest incarnation of AppleShare is AppleShare IP, which operates on the TCP/IP protocol suite rather than AppleTalk, although AppleTalk is still supported.

AppleShare IP was specifically designed to work with Mac OS 8.5. It improves file, print, mail, and Web services for Macintosh users and other clients. Here is a complete list of features as outlined by Apple:

- Cross-platform file, print, mail, and Web services
- Extremely fast file transfers

A

- Searching of server volumes using Sherlock technology
- Remote server administration from any Web browser
- Built-in firewall security
- Native support for Windows clients through the SMB file-sharing protocol
- Web site multihosting—supports up to 50 Web sites from a single server
- All services managed through one integrated interface
- Support for IMAP (Internet Mail Access Protocol), SMTP (Simple Mail Transfer Protocol), and POP(Post Office Protocol)
- Remote administration of the message database from any IMAP client

AppleShare IP supports the AFP (Apple Filing Protocol), FTP (File Transfer Protocol), and SMB (Server Message Block) file transfer protocols. It provides a file-sharing system that makes information accessible over intranets, the Internet, or AppleTalk networks.

The Sherlock search engine lets AppleShare IP clients conduct content searches of server volumes. Administrators can limit client searches by assigning clients access only to specific documents. Administrators can also manage AppleShare servers by using a Web browser. Tasks include adding users, changing passwords, and administering jobs in a print queue.

A built-in firewall allows strict control over which clients may access each network service. Access to services can be allowed or denied based on a range of IP addresses or at the individual client level. AppleShare IP 6.1 can also protect against unauthorized electronic mail through powerful antispam controls.

Windows 95, 98, and NT clients can share access to the server along with Mac clients to access standard Internet services, such as Web, mail, and FTP. AppleShare IP 6.1 also provides native file services for Windows clients using the SMB protocol, and Windows clients can print to the AppleShare print server over TCP/IP networks.

Related Entries   Apple Computer; AFP (AppleTalk Filing Protocol); AppleTalk; File Sharing; File Systems; LocalTalk; Mac OS; *and* Network Concepts

Linktionary! – Tom Sheldon's Encyclopedia of   http://www.linktionary.com/appleshare.html
Networking updates

AppleTalk

AppleTalk has been the networking protocol for the Macintosh nearly as long as the Macintosh has been around. It provides a way for individual users to share files via AppleShare servers. It also supports printer sharing and remote access. But AppleTalk is showing its age. It was designed in the early 1980s when LANs were primarily for file exchanges and printer sharing. Apple is even downplaying the protocols in favor of TCP/IP. Its Macintosh Operating System (Mac OS) includes the full TCP/IP suite and an enhanced AppleShare server called AppleShare IP that provides file sharing via AFP (Apple Filing Protocol) over TCP/IP. That means Macintosh users can access AppleShare file servers over a TCP/IP network.

Apple will continue to support AppleTalk networking in future operating systems through its transport-independent networking suite called Apple Open Transport, which supports not only AppleTalk but TCP/IP and, eventually, other protocols such as IPX.

For this edition of the book, AppleTalk information has been removed to conserve space. A full description and the latest updates are available at the Linktionary Web site listed here.

Related Entries   AFP (AppleTalk Filing Protocol); Apple Computer; Apple Open Transport Protocol; AppleShare; LocalTalk; Mac OS; *and* Network Concepts

Linktionary! – Tom Sheldon's Encyclopedia of Networking updates

http://www.linktionary.com/a/appletalk.html

General information

http://www.apple.com

Neon Software's Understanding AppleTalk page

http://www.neon.com/atalk_routing.html

AppleTalk 101

http://www.cs.mu.oz.au/appletalk/aboutatalk.html

Application Layer, OSI Model

The application layer is the top layer of the OSI (Open Systems Interconnection) model. The OSI model guides software developers and hardware vendors in the design of network communications products. When two systems need to communicate, they must use the same network protocols. The OSI models divide protocols in seven layers, with the lowest layer defining the physical connection of equipment and electrical signaling. The highest layer defines how an application running on one system can communicate with an application on another system. Middle layers define protocols that set up communication sessions, keep sessions alive, provide reliable delivery, and perform error checking to ensure that information is transmitted correctly. See "OSI (Open Systems Interconnection Model" for more information on the complete OSI stack.

The application layer is the top layer in the OSI protocol stack. Applications that provide network features reside at this layer and access underlying communication protocols. Examples include file access and transfer over the network, resource sharing, and print services. The OSI model specifies that applications must provide their own layer 7 protocols. The OSI FTAM (File Transfer Access and Management) utility and the X.400 electronic mail standard provide services at the OSI application layer.

In the Internet world, the application layer resides directly on top of the TCP/IP protocol stack. In this model, the presentation layer and session layer of the OSI protocol stack are used. The application layer talks directly with the transport layer (TCP and UDP). Common Internet applications in the application layer include Telnet, FTP (File Transfer Protocol), NFS (Network File System), SMTP (Simple Mail Transport Protocol), and DNS (Domain Name System).

Related Entries   Data Communication Concepts, Network Architecture; *and* OSI (Open Systems Interconnection) Model;

Linktionary! – Tom Sheldon's Encyclopedia of Networking updates

http://www.linktionary.com/o/osi.html

Application-Level Gateway

An application-level proxy server provides all the basic proxy features and also provides extensive packet analysis. When packets from the outside arrive at the gateway, they are examined and evaluated to determine whether the security policy allows the packet to enter into the internal network. Not only does the server evaluate IP addresses, it also looks at the data in the packets for corruption and alteration.

A typical application-level gateway can provide proxy services for applications and protocols like Telnet, FTP (File Transfer Protocol), HTTP (Hypertext Transfer Protocol), and SMTP (Simple Mail Transfer Protocol). Note that a separate proxy must be installed for each application-level service. (Some vendors achieve security simply by not providing proxies for some services, so be careful in your evaluation.) With proxies, security policies can be much more powerful and flexible because all the information in packets can be used by administrators to write the rules that determine how packets are handled by the gateway. It is easy to audit just about everything that happens on the gateway. You can also strip computer names to hide internal systems and evaluate the contents of packets for appropriateness and security.

Related Entry   Firewalls; NAT (Network Address Translation); Proxy Server; *and* Security

Linktionary! – Tom Sheldon's Encyclopedia of   http://www.linktionary.com/f/firewall.html
Networking updates

Application Server

An application server is a server that runs programs in a network environment. The applications may be network versions of commercial, off-the-shelf software that allow multiple users to access and run the program. This avoids loading the program on each user's computer and allows central updates to take place on the server. Custom-built or off-the-shelf client/server applications may run on application servers as well. A client/server application distributes processing between the client and the server, with the server handling file and data access and the client handling presentation and user input. A database server is also an application server, but is optimized for disk I/O (input/output) and may include attached servers that contain replicas of the data for fault tolerance.

Application servers have more recently become middleware servers. More specifically, they are "middle servers" in a three-tiered architecture (an evolution of the two-tiered client-server model). Application servers interface with databases and information systems on the back end. On the front end, application server interface with clients, usually Web server clients. The servers may perform relatively simple functions such as building Web pages on the fly with data obtained from back-end servers. The servers may also provide more sophisticated functions, such as transaction processing in electronic commerce applications.

Application servers provide a variety of functions. They serve as a central hub for running services such as message routing, object exchange, transaction processing, and data transformation. They also may support CORBA, Microsoft COM/DCOM, and Enterprise JavaBeans. Additional features include the ability to connect with a variety of back-end database services and to load balance the traffic between the servers and users. The servers are also a logical place to implement advanced sercurity services. The related entries here provide more information.

Related Entries ASP (Application Service Provider); Client-Server Computing; DBMS (Database Management System); Distributed Object Computing; Electronic Commerce; Middleware and Messaging; MOM (Message-Oriented Middleware); Multitiered Architectures; Object Technologies; Transaction Processing; *and* Web Technologies and Concepts

Linktionary! – Tom Sheldon's Encyclopedia of Networking updates	http://www.linktionary.com/a/application_server.html
Application server information at Serversatch.Internet.com	http://serverwatch.internet.com/appservers.html
Application server page at Webreview.com	http://www.webreview.com/pub/app_servers/
Application server zone	http://www.appserver-zone.com

Applications, Networks

See Network Applications.

APPN (Advanced Peer-to-Peer Networking)

IBM's APPN was introduced by IBM in 1985 and integrated into SNA (Systems Network Architecture). It provides peer-to-peer networking services similar to but not quite the same as TCP/IP. One of the main reasons IBM introduced APPN was to provide distributed client/server computing services to users who might have moved to TCP/IP or other services. APPN is basically link-layer independent. It can run over token ring, Ethernet, FDDI, frame relay, ISDN, X.25, SDLC, and ultra high-speed networks such as B-ISDN and ATM.

APPN is based on the concept that computers on the network have enough processing power of their own to handle session management and routing. APPN moves various services from central control (such as that provided by a host mainframe computer) to decentralized control points that operate in a peer-to-peer relationship. In the old SNA model, a mainframe was required to control sessions. In the APPN model, user stations set up and maintain their own sessions.

APPN is compared to OSI (Open Systems Interconnection) and TCP/IP in Figure A-7. APPN is part of IBM's revision to SNA and is often called the "new SNA." APPN is still tightly integrated with SNA, and it uses the SNA LU 6.2 protocol that is marketed as APPC (Advanced Program-to-Program Communications). APPC was introduced in the early 1980s as an application interface for APPN. By providing a way for applications on separate systems to communicate without involving a host system, APPC forged the way for APPN. It provided the shift away from centralized mainframe control and allowed programmable devices like computers to control their own sessions. In addition, APPN implements a newer application interface, the CPI-C (Common Programming Interface for Communications). CPI is a set of APIs (application program interfaces) that provide a common environment for the execution of programs on different IBM platforms.

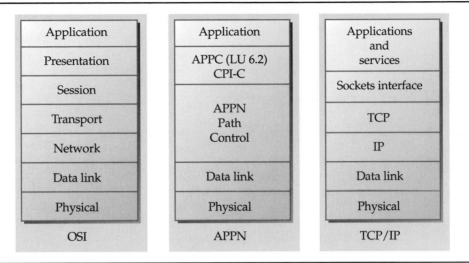

Figure A-7. *APPN architecture*

APPN provides routing services for APPC sessions. The routing environment consists of the following hierarchy, as pictured in Figure A-8:

■ **ENs (end nodes)**   An EN is a computer with its own operating system. It transmits information about itself and any locally attached resources to adjacent NNs (network nodes) when it logs in to the network. The NN then holds this information and provides it to other nodes on the APPN network. This reduces the need to search every EN when establishing sessions. IBM mainframe and midrange computers, as well as AIX or UNIX systems and desktop computers running OS/2 are end nodes. These larger systems can also be network nodes, as discussed next.

■ **NNs (network nodes)**   An NN is a routing node that moves traffic between end nodes. NNs exchange routing information with other NNs about the topology of the network as changes occur. To conserve network bandwidth, only information about recent changes is exchanged, rather than entire routing tables. NNs also locate resources and store the resource information for later use. Thus, NNs serve as distributed depositories for information about the network. This caching feature "improves with age" as more routes are added to the list, reducing the number of required route searches. IBM AS/ 400 minicomputers, IBM 6611 routers, and 3174 terminal controllers are devices that can serve as NNs.

■ **CNN (composite network node)**   A CNN provides seamless communications between an SNA subarea and APPN. The subarea network, which may contain a VTAM (Virtual Telecommunication Access Method) node and any number of NCP (Network Control

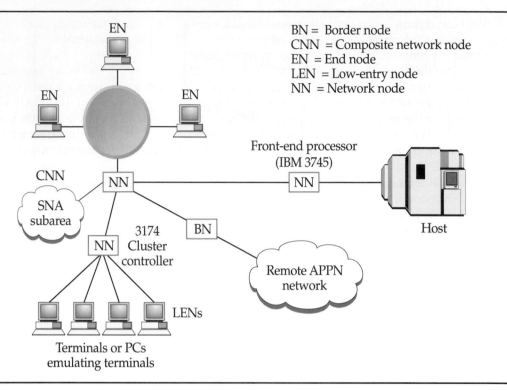

Figure A-8.   *APPN routing environment*

Program) nodes, emulates an NN. Note that VTAM provides users with access to network resources and information, and NCP is the control program that runs in an IBM FEP (front-end processor) such as an IBM 3745.

■ **LENs (low-entry nodes)**   A LEN can participate in a session with another LEN node on the network, but it requires the services of a network node to do so. This network node can be part of a local area network or directly connected to the LEN. PCs running DOS are examples of LEN nodes because they don't have the capability of operating as end nodes. OS/2, on the other hand, has full end-node capabilities.

■ **BN (border node) and EBN (extended border node)**   Subdivision of an APPN network is possible if a network broadcast becomes excessive. Division of the network isolates a broadcast to specific subnetworks. The BN or EBN routes information among subnetworks.

APPN NNs dynamically locate resources on the network and store the routing information locally. In older SNA networks, network elements were defined in a VTAM table stored in a mainframe. In contrast, APPN networks can configure themselves using route discovery methods. Network nodes work together to establish a path through a network so two end stations can set up a communication session. Each node contains a routing table used to establish the pathway for the link. One potential problem with APPN is that the selected path remains fixed for the duration of the session. If a node fails along the path, the session is not rerouted and fails as well. IBM fixed this with HPR (High Performance Routing), which was introduced in late 1994. You can refer to the HPR heading for more information. Also see RFC 2353 (APPN/HPR in IP Networks, May 1998).

Applications establish sessions with other destination nodes on the network by accessing logical unit software interfaces that correspond roughly to OSI session layer protocols. These high-level interfaces provide names for software entities that reside in ENs and NNs on the network. Note that applications go through LUs (logical units) to establish sessions, not directly to APPN. Basically, an LU in one station uses APPN services to locate a destination LU and set up a session. Think of LU sessions like pipes for transmitting data across the network from one application to another. Multiple applications can access a single LU, or applications can access multiple LUs.

APPN Developments

Some question the future of APPN. TCP/IP networks have proliferated in many organizations. However, SNA protocols are not routable, and APPN and TCP/IP do not mix. So, the network designers have a problem. They can build two networks or look for a solution that takes advantage of the internetworking features of TCP/IP to transport SNA traffic throughout the enterprise. A vendor consortium called the APPN Implementers Workshop is working to integrate TCP/IP and APPN. A protocol called DLSw (Data Link Switching) is based on its standards. It provides a way to move SNA traffic over TCP/IP networks by encapsulating the traffic into TCP/IP packets. The IETF (Internet Engineering Task Force) has also been working on DLSw.

Basically, DLSw provides a way for routers to route "unroutable" SNA traffic (and NetBIOS sessions) across an internetwork. The technique is to link the two SNA or NetBIOS systems with a pair of DLSw routers. The routers then take all traffic that is destined for the other SNA system, encapsulate it, and send it across the internetwork. RFC 2166 (APPN Implementer's Workshop DLSw v2.0 Enhancements, June 1997) discusses DLSw.

Web technology can provide a way to get at mainframe data as well. New methods for accessing SNA systems using Web browsers over TCP/IP networks are emerging, such as Cisco System's *IOS (Internetwork Operating System) for 390 TCP/IP* intranet software.

Browser-based access is especially attractive to remote and mobile users who make temporary connections into the corporate network. The best way for them to do that is through a single Web-based interface that gives them access to all the corporate information systems.

In general, SNA traffic on enterprise networks and on WANs will no doubt decrease significantly over the next few years as new methods for accessing traditional IBM systems are emerging.

Related Entries APPC (Advanced Program-to-Program Communications); DLSw (Data Link Switching), HPR (High-Performance Routing), IBM; SAA (Systems Application Architecture); and SNA (Systems Network Architecture)

Linktionary! – Tom Sheldon's Encyclopedia of Networking updates	http://www.linktionary.com/appn.html
APPN Implementers Workshop (AIW)	http://www.networking.ibm.com/app/aiwhome.htm
IBM Redbooks (search for APPN)	http://www.redbooks.ibm.com
APPN Links page at AIW	http://www.networking.ibm.com/app/aiwinfo/aiwsites.htm
IBM SNA tutorial	http://pclt.cis.yale.edu/pclt/COMM/SNA.HTM
IBM APPC tutorial	http://pclt.cis.yale.edu/pclt/COMM/APPC.HTM
Cisco Documentation: Designing APPN Internetworks	http://www.cisco.com/univercd/cc/td/doc/cisintwk/idg4/nd2006.htm
Cisco Documentation: IBM Systems Network Architecture (SNA) Protocols	http://www.cisco.com/univercd/cc/td/doc/cisintwk/ito_doc/ibmsna.htm
Cisco Documentation: IBM Systems Network Architecture (SNA) Routing	http://www.cisco.com/univercd/cc/td/doc/cisintwk/ito_doc/ibmsnaro.htm

Archiving of Data

See Backup and Data Archiving; Data Center Design; Data Migration; Data Protection; Disaster Planning and Recovery; Fault Tolerance and High Availability; Mirroring; Replication; Storage Management Systems; *and* Tape Backup Standards.

ARCNET

The ARCNET (Attached Resource Computing Network) is a baseband, token-passing network system that offers flexible star and bus topologies at a low price. Transmission speeds are 2.5 Mbits/sec. ARCNET uses a token-passing protocol on a token bus network topology. While ARCNET never became popular in the LAN environment, it is used extensively for embedded and real-time applications. Companies are using ARCNET for a number of tasks, including data acquisition, nuclear plant monitoring and control, closed-circuit cameras, building automation, process control, in-flight entertainment systems, phone switching systems, point-of-sale systems, stock exchange terminals, and machine control. The ARCNET Trade Association Web site provides a list of companies and their uses of ARCNET.

A typical ARCNET configuration is shown in Figure A-9. Although ARCNET is generally considered to have a slow throughput, it does support cable lengths of up to 600 meters when using active hubs. It is suitable for office environments that use text-based applications and where users don't often access the file server.

ARCNET connections are made to active and passive hubs. An active hub is a network relay that conditions and amplifies the signal strength. Most active hubs have eight ports to which workstations, passive hubs, or additional active hubs can be attached. A passive hub is a four-port connector with BNC jacks.

ARCNET uses 93-ohm RG-62 A/U coaxial cable, although twisted-pair and fiber-optic cable can also be used. Fiber-optic cable is used for backbones between active hubs and for outside runs.

Two Internet RFCs relate to ARCNET. These are RFC 1201 (Transmitting IP traffic over ARCNET networks, February 1991) and RFC 2497 (Transmission of IPv6 Packets over ARCNET Networks, January 1999)

Linktionary! – Tom Sheldon's Encyclopedia of Networking updates	http://www.linktionary.com/a/arcnet.html
ARCNET Trade Association	http://www.arcnet.com/home.html

ARDIS (Advanced National Radio Data Service)

See Packet Radio Data Networks.

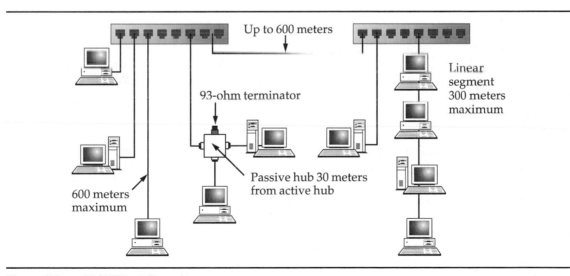

Figure A-9. *ARCNET configuration*

ARIN (American Registry for Internet Numbers)

On December 22, 1997, ARIN was officially made the authority of IP number administration in North America. This authority was transferred from Network Solutions, Inc. (InterNIC) by IANA (Internet Assigned Numbers Authority). ARIN is authorized by the National Science Foundation. Other registration agencies include RIPE NCC (Réseaux IP Européens Network Coordination Centre) and APNIC (Asia Pacific Network Information Centre). The topic CIDR (Classless Inter-Domain Routing) explains how these agencies are involved in Internet address allocation and registration.

Related Entries   CIDR (Classless Inter-Domain Routing); Internet Organizations and Committees; *and* Registries on the Internet

ARIS (Aggregate Route-based IP Switching)

A number of strategies have been defined to reduce the routing decision process that occurs at each router when a datagram travels the hop-by-hop route between source and destination. ARIS is one of those schemes. It is not as much a flow-driven scheme like IP Switching, but a tagging/labeling scheme like MPLS (Multiprotocol Label Switching) and Cisco's Tag Switching.

ARIS is IBM's scheme for switching IP datagrams. It is normally associated with ATM networks, but ARIS can be extended to work with other switching technologies. ARIS (and other IP switching technologies) takes advantage of integrated router switches. The idea is to map routing information to short fixed-length labels so that next-hop routers can be determined by direct indexing, rather than using the standard router packet evaluation and lookup process.

What ARIS does is set up a virtual circuit through a network based on the forwarding paths already established by routers that use routing protocols such as OSPF (Open Shortest Path First) and BGP (Border Gateway Protocol). IP datagrams are then switched through the network following these paths. No routing is done by any device along the VC. Instead, the datagrams are "tagged" with a label that is read by intermediate switches along the way, identified with a particular destination network, and sent along the appropriate circuit to that destination.

ARIS is very similar to MPLS. At the time of this writing, MPLS appears to be the major focus of the industry and is an emerging IETF standard. See "MPLS (Multiprotocol Label Switching)" and "Multilayer Switching" for more details.

Related Entries   IP Switching; MPLS (Multiprotocol Label Switching); Multilayer Switching; Routing; Switching and Switched Networks

    ARIS (IBM) (multilayer routing comparison)   http://www.watersprings.org/links/mlr

ARP (Address Resolution Protocol)

On TCP/IP networks, the ARP protocol is used to match up an IP (Internet Protocol) address with a MAC (Medium Access Control) address. An IP address is a high-level internetwork address that identifies a specific computer on a subnetwork of interconnected networks. A

MAC address is the hardwired address of a NIC (network interface card). MAC addresses are only used to forward frames between computers attached to the same network. They cannot be used to send frames to computers on other networks that are interconnected by routers. IP addressing must be used to forward frames across router boundaries (assuming TCP/IP networks).

Note   *RARP (Reverse Address Resolution Protocol) converts a MAC address into an IP address. The protocol was originally used to obtain an IP address for Ethernet-connected diskless workstations.*

ARP is used in all cases where one node on a TCP/IP network needs to know the MAC address of another node on the same network or on an internetwork. Basically, ARP lets a computer ask the question "will the computer with the IP address *w.x.y.z* send me its MAC address?" This ARP message is broadcast on the local network so all nodes hear it but only the node that has the IP address in question responds. The address resolution process is shown in Figure A-10.

Three subnetworks—A, B, and C—are connected by Router AB and Router BC. Hosts A1 and A2 are on network A, and Host C1 is on network C. Subnet B is an interconnecting LAN or a WAN. Assume Host A1 wants to transmit to Host A2. It knows the IP address of Host A2, but must have a hardware address to transmit on the network. To get the address, it creates an ARP request and "broadcasts" the frame on the network. All the other hosts on the network receive the broadcast, but only Host A2 (which owns the address in question) prepares an ARP response that contains its MAC address and sends it directly back to Host A1. The response is saved in a cache by Host A1 for future use.

If Host A1 wants to transmit to Host C1, Router AB must get involved. ARP is used to discover the MAC address of Router AB, and all frames for transmission to Host C1 are then sent to Router AB's MAC address. Router AB then forwards packets to Router BC, which we will presume has already used ARP to determine the MAC address of Host C1. It simply forwards the packets as frames addressed to Host C1 on the network that C1 is attached to.

To make ARP efficient, each computer caches IP-to-MAC address mappings to eliminate repetitive ARP broadcast requests. Most operating systems remove cached ARP entries if they are not used for some time. Entries are made to the ARP cache on a first-response basis.

Adding a permanent ARP entry can be useful to decrease the number of ARP broadcasts for frequently accessed hosts. Creating permanent ARP cache entries can speed performance

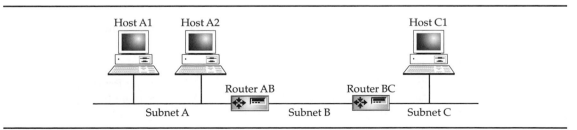

Figure A-10.   *Address resolution process*

to heavily used IP resources such as local servers and the default gateway. However, if the entries are invalid or the network interface card in the local server or default gateway changes, the permanent entry remains unless updated by an ARP from the server or default gateway. You can check for invalid ARP mappings with the ping command. It will display the message "Request timed out" if there is an invalid mapping.

The following RFCs are related to ARP:

- RFC 826 (An Ethernet Address Resolution Protocol, November 1982)
- RFC 903 (Reverse Address Resolution Protocol, June 1982)
- RFC 1027 (Using ARP to implement transparent subnet gateways, October 1987)
- RFC 1029 (More fault tolerant approach to address resolution for a Multi-LAN system of Ethernets, May 1988)
- RFC 1433 (Directed ARP, March 1993)
- RFC 1868 (ARP Extension, UNARP, November 1995)
- RFC 1931 (Dynamic RARP Extensions for Automatic Network Address Acquisition, April 1996)
- RFC 2320 (Classical IP and ARP Over ATM, April 1998)
- RFC 2390 (Inverse Address Resolution Protocol, August 1998)

Related Entries   Ethernet; Internet; IP (Internet Protocol); MAC (Medium Access Methods); RARP (Reverse Address Resolution Protocol); *and* Routing

Linktionary! – Tom Sheldon's Encyclopedia of Networking updates	http://www.linktionary.com/a/arp.html
ARP protocol overview	http://www.freesoft.org/CIE/Topics/61.htm
ARP page at Optimized Engineering Corporation	http://www.optimized.com/COMPENDI/ARP.htm
ARP page by Godred Fairhurst, University of Aberdeen	http://www.erg.abdn.ac.uk/users/gorry/course/ inet-pages/arp.html

ARPANET (Advanced Research Projects Agency Network)

ARPANET was a packet-switching network developed in the early 1970s. ARPANET was funded by ARPA (Advanced Research Projects Agency), which later became DARPA (Defense Advanced Research Projects Agency). The ARPANET network linked defense facilities, government research laboratories, and university sites. It evolved into the backbone of the Internet, and the term "ARPANET" was officially retired in 1990. However, MILNET (military network) was spun off from ARPANET in 1983. In addition, ARPANET spurred the development of one of the most important protocol suites available today, TCP/IP

(Transmission Control Protocol/Internet Protocol). TCP/IP is a set of communications procedures and standards that provide a basis for interconnecting dissimilar computers.

DARPA was interested in interlinking the many different computer systems that were spread out across the country as part of the nation's research and development effort. DARPA's goal was to create a set of nonproprietary communications protocols that would make it easy to connect many different computers together. Much of the original work was done at the Massachusetts Institute of Technology and with the help of companies such as BBN (Bolt, Beranek, and Newman, Inc.). In 1980, the first TCP/IP modules were installed.

One of the most important aspects of TCP/IP's development was the program of testing and certification carried out by the government to ensure that developers met published TCP/IP standards, which were (and still are) available to the public free of licensing arrangements. This ensured that developers did not alter the standard to fit their own needs and possibly cause confusion in the rest of the TCP/IP community. Today, the use of TCP/IP protocols virtually assures interconnection (and in some cases, interoperability) among systems that use it for communications.

Refer to RFC 2235 (Hobbes' Internet Timeline, November 1997). Also see "Routing on the Internet," which covers some of the historical aspects of routing.

Related Entries   DARPA (Defense Advanced Research Projects Agency); Internet; Internet Organizations and Committees; *and* Routing on the Internet

Linktionary! – Tom Sheldon's Encyclopedia of Networking updates	http://www.linktionary.com/a/arpanet.html
Internet History	http://www.linktionary.com/i/internet_history.html
Interview with Frank Heart, leader of the ARPANET design team	http://www.pretext.com/mar98/columns/intview.htm
Richard Martin's Dawn of the Internet paper	http://www.pretext.com/mar98/features/story1.htm
Yahoo! Birth of the Internet page	http://smithsonian.yahoo.com/internethistory.html

AS/400, IBM

See IBM (International Business Machines).

ASIC (Application-Specific Integrated Circuit)

An ASIC is a custom-designed processor that improves performance over a similar design with standard chips and lowers the cost of developing new systems. ASICs are commonly used in high-speed switches and routers. A typical device designed without ASICs will have many individual chips and components, and run many functions in software. An ASIC can consolidate the function of all of those chips, and even the software, onto a single chip. The resulting chip is often referred to as "customized silicon." The latest ASIC technology can put millions of logic gates on a single chip.

In the mid-1990s, ASICs provided layer 2 Ethernet switching functions. The chips read the MAC address and forwarded the frame. When layer 3 routing switches began to appear, ASICs took on the bigger task of evaluating the routing information within datagrams. Now switches that evaluate Layer 4 through Layer 7 information are common.

A customer who requires a custom ASIC goes to ASIC vendors, such as IBM, with their ASIC design. Special tools are used to lay out the logic of the chip, and connections are made on the layout to complete the design. This process has become more and more advanced, allowing for very complex functions to be added to ASICs, such as Layer 7 functionality.

The only problem with designing components and systems with ASICs is that the design is solidified once the chips are created. Applying updates is usually impractical. But many developers use a combination design that hardwires standard routines onto ASICs and puts less stable functions into programmable RISC (Reduced Instruction Set Computer) processors, at least until the design and/or standards are set.

ASICs are being targeted for tasks that require very intensive processing, such as VPN (virtual private network) data encryption, firewall packet processing, and policy-based management servers. Some ASICs have their own memory blocks so that special instructions and code changes can be added to the chip at a later time.

What might be considered the opposite of ASIC-based designs are RISC-based designs. RISC processors are off-the-shelf components that can be built into CPU-based systems (such as switches) for less than what might be spent to design and build custom ASICs. A RISC-based switch is more flexible in its ability to be reprogrammed and updated with software downloads. However, RISC designs are slower than ASIC designs.

Related Entries   Cut-Through Architecture; Network Processors; RISC (Reduced Instruction Set Computer); Routers; Switch Fabrics and Bus Design; *and* Switching and Switched Networks

Linktionary! – Tom Sheldon's Encyclopedia of Networking updates	http://www.linktionary.com/a/asic.html
An Anixter paper describing RISC and ASIC architectures	http://www.anixter.com/techlib/whiteppr/network/d0504p06.htm
Xaqti	http://www.xaqti.com
Vertex	http://www.vertex-networks.com
Altera Corp.	http://www.altera.com
LSI Logic Corp.	http://www.lsilogic.com
Vitesse	http://www.vitesse.com

ASP (Application Service Provider)

An ASP is a company that provides application hosting for customers in the same way that ISPs (Internet service providers) will host a company's Web site. The basic model is that mobile users or office users connect to the ASP to run their applications. The advantage is that the ASP has a fully managed data center run by professionals with all the facilities to provide fault tolerance, data backup, high availability, application maintenance, product support, and so on.

Users connect via Internet connections, or in some cases, private lines may connect companies with their ASPs.

> **Note** *ASPs figure into the network computing concept. Clients run applications at their ASP. The device they use does not need a hard drive. The ASP is the hard drive and stores the client's desktop. The device simply displays information and takes user input from the keyboard. All of this is done over the Internet. Refer to "NC (Network Computing)" for more information.*

Basically, ASPs provide outsourcing services. Many companies already outsource accounting functions such as payroll and employee benefits programs. The ASP can handle these applications, as well as many others, such as electronic mail, groupware, and collaboration software. Outsourcing these services can help companies reduce operating costs. For example, a company might wish to use Microsoft Exchange as its groupware application, but might not have the in-house expertise to manage the product. Outsourcing to an ASP takes advantage of the ASP's services and technical expertise. Costs may also be reduced in terms of software licensing and hardware.

ASPs may also host entire e-commerce and e-business (extranet) solutions. The ASP may provide essential add-on services such as credit card authorization, database management, and enhanced searching tools. They may use advanced Web hosting technologies including load balancing and caching of sites to multiple locations, possibly at other sites around the globe. ASPs may also provide high-speed direct links to the Internet to ensure adequate bandwidth for their customers and can provide additional services to take advantage of this bandwidth like QoS (quality of service) options.

Some ASPs provide specialized services to select groups. For example, an ASP might specialize in providing various accounting and specialty services for small contractors. Other ASPs may specialize in managing applications such as PeopleSoft or SAP products. The WebHarbor site listed later breaks out ASPs according to the following categories:

Human Resources	E-Commerce
Sales Force Automation	E-mail and Calendars
Remote Access	Customer Relationship Management (CRM)
Operations Management	Databases
Finance	Document Management
Project Management	Engineering/Scientific
Help Desk	Enterprise Resource Planning
Office Productivity	Marketing

Another critical service is security. Some organizations may wish to outsource applications that include customer, client, or patient records. This information must be kept private and secure. An ASP can provide professional security services, something that most companies have trouble doing on their own simply because there is a shortage of security experts.

The ASP Industry Consortium was formed in early 1999 with the goal of establishing guidelines and producing standards for application sharing. The consortium members include AT&T, Cisco Citrix, Compaq, Ernst & Young LLP, GTE, IBM, and Sun Microsystems, among others.

FirstSense and a number of other companies are developing software to help customers of ASP services monitor application service delivery and measure performance.

The ASP News Review site listed at the end of this topic has listings of ASPs and vendors that are in the ASP software and/or hardware business.

Related Entries   Application Server; Data Center Design; Electronic Commerce; Fault Tolerance and High-Availability Systems; ISP (Internet Service Provider); Outsourcing; Service Providers and Carriers; *and* Web Technologies and Concepts

Linktionary! – Tom Sheldon's Encyclopedia of Networking updates	http://www.linktionary.com/a/asp.html
ASP Industry Consortium	http://www.aspindustry.org
ASP Industry FAQ	http://www.aspindustry.org/ind.html
ASP News Review	http://www.aspnews.com
Web Host Guild	http://www.whg.org/index.htm
CNET Web Services "Ultimate Web Host List"	http://www.webhostlist.com
WebHarbor ASP Industry Portal	http://www.webharbor.com

Associations

See Standards Groups, Associations, and Organizations.

Asymmetrical Multiprocessing

Computer systems with multiple processors can utilize the processors in one of two ways. In asymmetrical multiprocessing, each CPU (central processing unit) is dedicated to a specific function, such as network interface card I/O (input/output) or file operations. In symmetrical multiprocessing, which is generally agreed to be superior to asymmetrical multiprocessing (but harder to implement), any CPU can handle any task if it is available to do so. Depending on the operating system and/or applications, tasks can be split up and simultaneously handled by multiple processors. Microsoft Windows NT/Windows 2000 and other new-generation operating systems perform symmetric multiprocessing.

Related Entries   Clustering; Distributed Computer Networks; Multiprocessing; SAN (Storage Attached Network); Servers; Switch Fabrics and Bus Designs

Linktionary! – Tom Sheldon's Encyclopedia of Networking updates	http://www.linktionary.com/m/multiprocessing.html

Asynchronous Communications

Asynchronous communication is the transmission of data between two devices that are not synchronized with one another via a clocking mechanism or other technique. Basically, the sender can transmit data at any time, and the receiver must be ready to accept information when it arrives. In contrast, synchronous transmission is a precisely timed stream of bits in which the start of a character is located by using a clocking mechanism.

In the mainframe/terminal environment, where asynchronous and synchronous transmissions were used abundantly, an asynchronous transmission is used to transmit characters from a terminal in which the user presses keys periodically. The receiving system knows to wait for the next keypress, even though that may take a relatively large amount of time. In contrast, synchronous transmissions are used as data links between large systems that transfer large amounts of information on a regular basis. The protocol is optimized to take advantage of slow links over public telephone systems, so extraneous bits are removed from the transmissions and clocks are used to separate characters.

In asynchronous communications, a character is coded as a string of bits and separated by a "start-of-character" bit and a "stop" bit. A parity bit is sometimes used for error detection and correction. The start-stop mode of transmission means that transmission starts over again for each new character, which eliminates any timing discrepancies that may have occurred during the last transmission. When discrepancies do occur, error detection and correction mechanisms can request a retransmission.

Asynchronous transmissions can take place between two nearby computers by connecting a null-modem cable between the asynchronous communications ports of each computer. If computers are at distant locations, a modem is required on each end to convert computer digital signals for transmission over analog phone lines. Asynchronous transmission can take place at speeds up to 56 Kbits/sec over normal switched (dial-up) or leased telephone lines.

A channel is a single communication path between two communicating devices that is created by physical connections or by multiplexing techniques. A circuit is an actual physical connection that provides a communication channel. The dial-up phone system provides circuits for channel communication between two systems. A simplex circuit is a unidirectional transmission path that transmits signals in one direction. A half-duplex circuit is a bidirectional transmission path that provides transmission in both directions, but only one direction at a time. A full-duplex link is a bidirectional transmission path that can transmit both ways at the same time over two circuits.

Error-Correction Methods

All transmission media are susceptible to interference and problems introduced by the medium itself, such as current resistance and signal attenuation. Outside interference may be introduced by background noise, atmospheric radiation, machinery, or even faulty equipment. As transmission rates increase, the number of bits affected by disturbances increases because there are more bits involved in the time frame of the disturbance. To correct these problems, error-detection and error-correction methods are used.

In parity checking, the numbers of 1s in groups must always be the same, either even or odd, to indicate that a group of bits was transmitted without error. Checking on a per-character basis is called VRC (vertical redundancy checking). Checking on a block-by-block basis is called LRC (longitudinal redundancy checking). Both systems must agree on the parity method before transmission begins. There is even parity (number of 1s must be even), odd parity (number of 1s must be odd), space parity (parity bit is always 0), and mark parity (parity bit is always 1).

Newer modems provide advanced error checking and correcting methods that are much more practical and efficient than those just discussed.

Interface Standards

The connections used for asynchronous communication are defined in the physical layer of the OSI (Open Systems Interconnections) reference model. This layer defines specifications related to connector types, pin-outs, and electrical signaling. Standards such as RS-232, RS-449, CCITT V.24, and others define these interfaces for various requirements.

Various standards are defined to ensure that connected devices can communicate with one another. The EIA (Electronic Industries Association) has set standards for transmitting asynchronous information across copper wires between computer devices. The EIA RS-232-C standard defines such things as the physical connections, signal voltages and timing, error checking, and other features. The standard defines serial transmissions of bit streams across a single wire. In contrast, a parallel transmission involves sending multiple bits simultaneously across multiple wires in the same cable, similar to a multilane freeway.

The EIA RS-232-C standard supports transmissions over short distances. For example, you use it to connect a computer to a modem. If the cable length becomes too long, the electrical current weakens, and the receiver may not be able to read it. The recommended maximum length of an RS-232 cable is 50 feet with a maximum signaling rate of 20 Kbits/sec (see "Serial Communication" for more details). To connect in-house systems over longer distances, set up a LAN. To connect with systems outside your own building, use a modem and the telephone system or other services provided by local and long-distance carriers (see "Communication Services").

Related Entries   Data Communication Concepts; Error Detection and Correction; Flow Control Mechanisms; Modems; Modulation Techniques; Serial Communication; *and* Synchronous Communication

Linktionary! – Tom Sheldon's Encyclopedia of Networking updates	http://www.linktionary.com/a/asynchronous.html
Sangoma.com (see TechDesk)	http://www.sangoma.com/
PC Communications over Modems and ISDN	http://pclt.cis.yale.edu/pclt/COMISDN/DEFAULT.HTM
Asynchronous-related topics at Optimized Engineering Corp.	http://www.optimized.com/COMPENDI/L1-R232.htm
Asynchronous communications by Godred Fairhurst	http://www.erg.abdn.ac.uk/users/gorry/course/ phy-pages/async.html

ATM (Asynchronous Transfer Mode)

ATM is a high-speed network technology that is designed for LANs, WANs, carrier and service provider networks, and Internet core networks. It is a connection-oriented switching technology, as opposed to a connectionless technology such as IP. ATM creates a virtual circuit (dedicated path) between source and destination across its switching fabric. These circuits can guarantee bandwidth and quality-of-service.

ATM's fixed cell size provides performance and predictable traffic flows. Picture a busy intersection. A semi tractor-trailer is attempting to negotiate a tight turn. All the rest of the traffic in the intersection is held up while this happens. Now picture the same intersection where all the vehicles are sports cars. In the latter case, traffic flows smoothly, and even predictably, because there are no traffic jams.

ATM cells negotiate ATM switches with the same efficiency, providing several benefits:

- Cell switching is efficient and fast for the reasons just described.
- Traffic flow is predictable due to the fixed cell size.
- Delivery of time-sensitive traffic (live voice and video) can be guaranteed.
- ATM includes QoS (quality of service) features that can be used to guarantee bandwidth for certain types of traffic.

There has been great debate over whether ATM is better than IP and vice versa. Many people find this debate odd, since the technologies are quite different and not even in the same protocol layer. The battle is really about whether networks should be *connection oriented* (ATM) or *best effort* (IP). ATM's fixed cell size and virtual circuit capability makes it the best choice for real time multimedia. Carriers and service providers use ATM in their core networks because it lets them provide service guarantees to their customers. However, IP's simple packet forwarding model has proved its usefulness in the Internet, where traffic is bursty and unpredictable. This model allows millions of people to share the bandwidth of the Internet without setting up virtual circuits in advance. However, the IP model starts to break down under traffic loads and congestion. In addition, the unpredictable delays of IP networks are a problem for real-time traffic.

ATM was originally defined by the telephone companies and has been heavily promoted by them as an end-to-end networking technology, as well as a voice technology. In this respect, ATM is both a LAN and WAN technology that can potentially allow customers to replace their separate voice and data networks with a single network to handle both voice and data, as well as other multimedia content such as video.

In the early 1990s, ATM was widely considered the next-generation networking technology that would extend all the way to the desktop. But broadcast LANs were already entrenched in most organizations and Internet technologies exploded on the scene. And while ATM was hyped for its speed, Gigabit Ethernet (1,000 Mbits/sec) and now 10 Gigabit Ethernet offer cheaper and more easily managed services.

Still, ATM is a viable technology for backbones, even in Gigabit Ethernet environments as discussed at the end of this topic. ATM is easily scalable and integrates with most existing technologies.

More recently, new technologies such as DWDM (Dense Wave-Division Multiplexing) and optical networking may undo ATM and even SONET. DWDM puts hundreds and potentially thousands of lambda circuits on a single fiber. That means core networks will support very high capacity switched optical circuits, reducing the need for packet switched core networks. Imagine having an entire beam (wavelength) of light allocated for your personal use, switched into place when you need it and taken down when you have finished. That is what the new optical networks could provide. See "Optical Networks" for more information.With those trends in mind, the following sections provide an overview of ATM technology.

ATM Network Design

ATM networks can be classed as private and public. Private ATM is the ATM network within an organization, while public ATM is a wide area networking service provided by carriers and service providers. As an organization implements ATM, the dividing line between public and private ATM shifts. For example, Figure A-11 illustrates the phases of ATM use. In the first phase, illustrated at the top, a customer uses a carrier's ATM network for wide area links. Notice that data frame and voice traffic from the customer site are delivered to the carrier's ATM switch over traditional leased lines. In this case, the carrier converts frames to ATM cells.

In phase 2, as illustrated at the bottom of Figure A-11, the customer installs an ATM edge device on the premises to handle frame-to-cell conversion and delivery. The carrier may provide this device. More likely, a customer installs ATM as a backbone or core networking technology and then uses an ATM-to-ATM connection between its sites and the carrier.

Organizations typically build private ATM networks in phases to accommodate their existing frame-based networks. Figure A-12 illustrates the initial phase and subsequent phases. On the left, an ATM switch is installed as a backbone, possibly replacing an existing FDDI (Fiber Distributed Data Interface) or Fast Ethernet backbone. Routers connect each of the existing networks into this backbone.

In the next phase, switching devices are added at various levels in the network hierarchy. Also, servers are moved to the backbone where they are more accessible to users. Note that cell switching is brought closer to the end user. A hybrid ATM/Gigabit Ethernet network design is presented at the end of this topic. This design takes advantage of high-speed Ethernet networking throughout the enterprise and uses ATM switching at the core. ATM switches can be configured into a mesh topology with multiple redundant load-sharing links. This scaleable mesh design is superior to Gigabit Ethernet backbones, which can become overwhelmed by traffic. In addition, the ATM core can provide QoS.

The ATM Model

ATM was originally defined as part of the B-ISDN (Broadband-Integrated Services Digital Network) standard. B-ISDN is public digital telecommunications network standard that is designed to offer high-end multimedia, television, CD-quality music, data networking, and other services to business and home users. ATM is the underlying network technology that makes B-ISDN possible.

The ITU-T is the international organization that sets ATM standards, but it implements recommendations made by the ATM Forum, a consortium of telephone companies and ATM equipment vendors that get together and hash out what they want ATM to do.

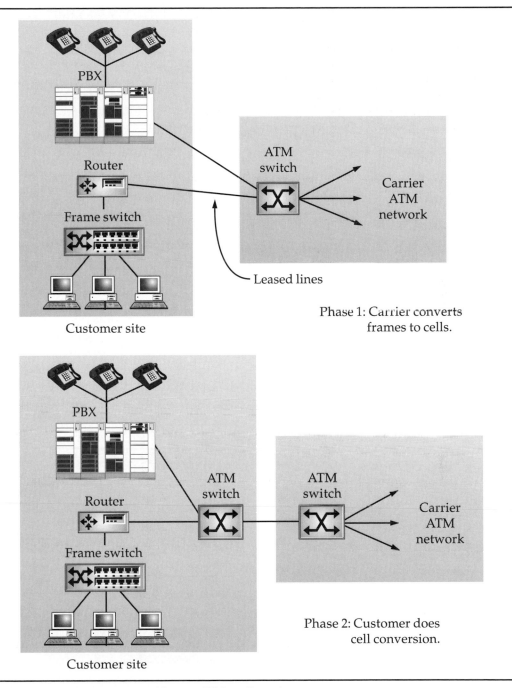

Figure A-11.   *Carrier/customer wide area ATM configuration*

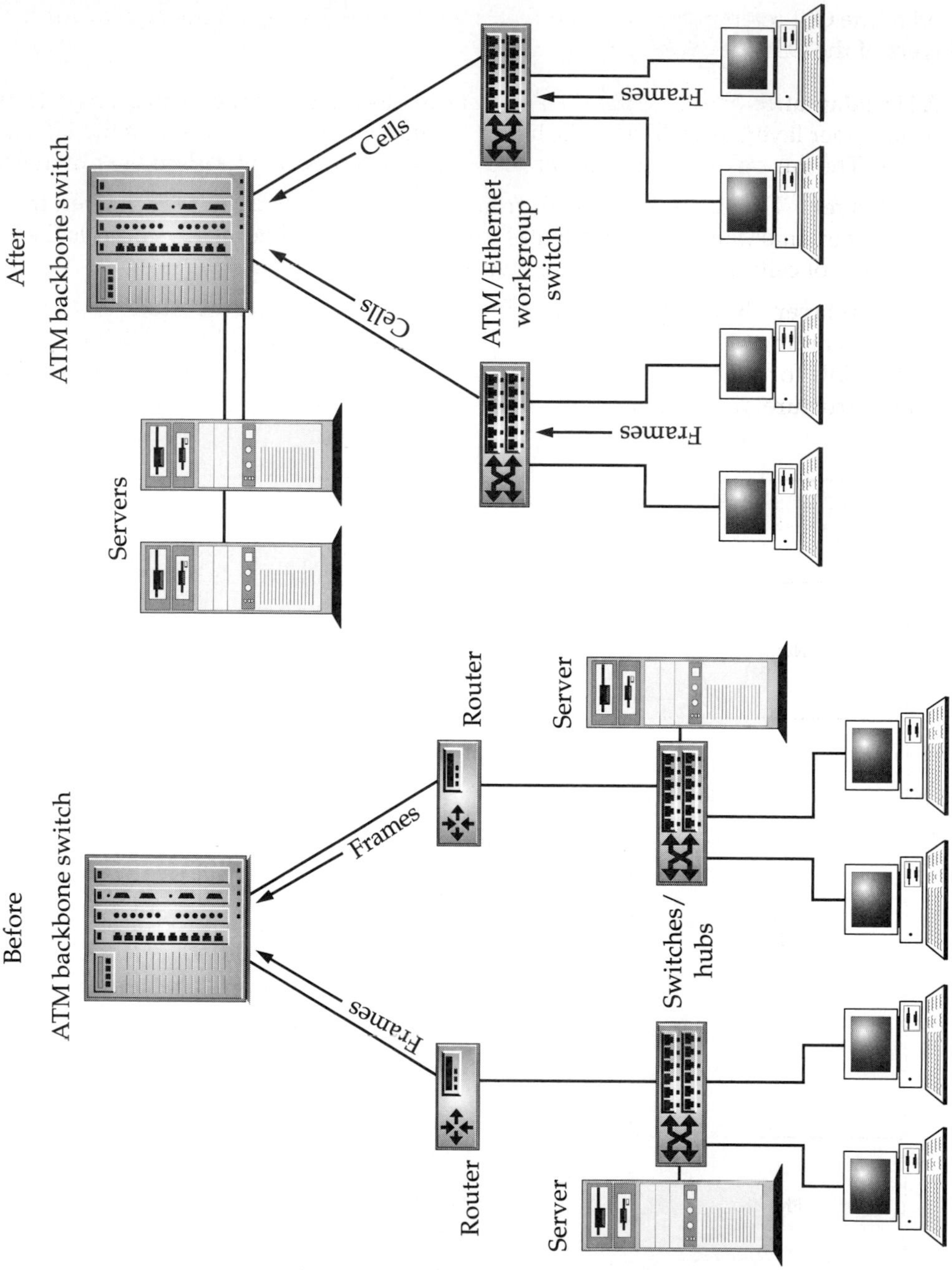

Figure A-12.   *Internal private ATM network construction*

The ATM reference model is shown in Figure A-13 and described below. Note that it is compared to the OSI reference model and that the two top ATM layers are equivalent to the lower layers of the OSI data link layer.

■ **ATM adaptation layer (AAL)**   This layer defines the process of converting information from upper layers into ATM cells, based on the type of delivery service the information needs. The various AAL services are discussed in a separate heading later in this topic.

■ **ATM layer**   This layer directs cells from the AAL layer to the physical layer. It establishes, maintains, and terminates virtual circuits and generally controls the transport of cells across the ATM network.

■ **Physical layer**   The physical layer connects with a physical medium that supports ATM, including SONET/SDH, DS-3/E3, Fibre Channel, and FDDI. The layer is responsible for converting outgoing cells to bits and for framing those bits into the frame structure of the network in use. Incoming bits are converted to cells.

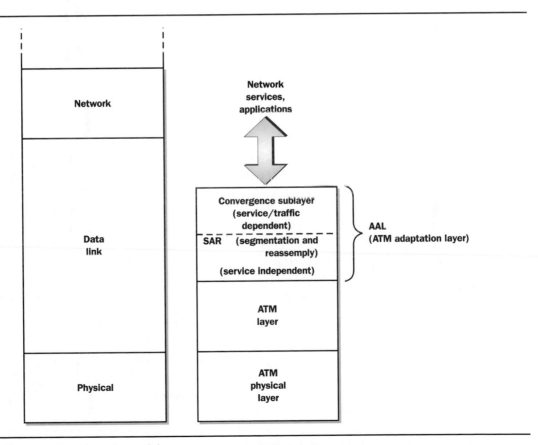

Figure A-13.   *ATM reference model*

The ATM physical layer does not define any one specific medium. SONET is usually associated with ATM, and many people believe that SONET is part of the ATM specification.

The ATM Cell

There are two types of ATM cells. One is the UNI (User-Network Interface), which is used in cells sent by users, and the other is the NNI (Network-to-Network Interface), which is sent by switches to other switches. The UNI and NNI cells are pictured in Figure A-14. The NNI cell does not have the GFC (Generic Flow Control) field. UNI and NNI are discussed later under "ATM Interfacing."

The ATM cell is 53 bytes in length: 48 bytes for payload and 5 bytes for header information. Note that header information is almost 10 percent of the cell, which adds up to extensive overhead on long transmissions. ATM cells are packets of information that contain "payload" (data) and header information that contains channel and path information to direct the cell to its destination. The information held by each field in the header is explained here:

- **GFC (Generic Flow Control)** This field is only in the UNI cell header and is used to control congestion on the user interface. This field uses 4 bits of what is the VPI field in the NNI cell.

- **VPI (Virtual Path Identifier)** Identifies virtual paths between users, or between users and networks. This field is 8 bits in UNI and 12 bits in NNI. VPIs are discussed later in this topic under "Virtual Circuits and Call Setup."

- **VCI (Virtual Channel Identifier)** Identifies virtual channels between users, or between users and networks. VCIs are discussed later in this topic under "Virtual Circuits and Call Setup."

- **PTI (Payload Type Indicator)** Indicates the type of information in the payload area, such as user, network, or management information.

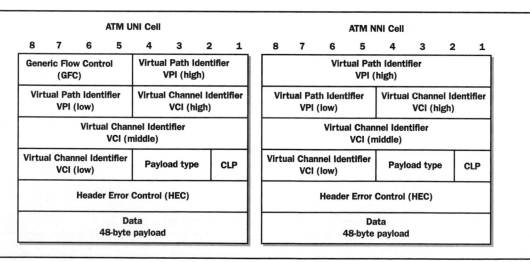

Figure A-14. *ATM cell layout (high, middle, and low refer to byte order)*

- ■ **CLP (Cell Loss Priority)**   Defines how to drop certain cells if network congestion occurs. The field holds priority values, with 0 indicating a cell of the highest value.
- ■ **HEC (Header Error Control)**   An 8-bit field that can provide FEC (forward error correction), a technique of sending information in the cell that can be used to fix errors, but only if a single bit is in error.

AAL (ATM Adaptation Layer)

AAL converges packets from upper layers into ATM cells. For example, in the case of a 1000-byte packet, AAL would segment it into about 21 fragments and place each fragment into a cell for transport.

Breaking packets up into many little cells and adding a header to each cell is one of the major drawbacks of ATM. All those additional header bits use up bandwidth!

Look again at Figure A-13. The AAL layer is divided into the convergence sublayer and the SAR (segmentation and reassembly) sublayer. The convergence sublayer prepares the message based on the class of ATM service required for transmission. These service classes are called AAL types and are described next. The SAR sublayer then chops the message up into fragments that will fit in the payload area of an ATM cell.

You can think of the ATM service classes in the same way you think of TCP and UDP services. TCP provides connection-oriented services, and UDP provides connectionless services. However, ATM's services classes are much more extensive. They take into consideration the need for timing and constant or variable bit rate as outlined in Table A-1. A description of these parameters is given later.

A service class is selected based on the type of application, (voice, video, high-priority data, low-priority data, and so on), the required quality of service, service contracts, and so on. The service classes are outlined here. Note that AAL-3/4 is a result of combining AAL-3 and AAL4. Originally, AAL-3 was defined for connection-oriented packet services such as X.25, while AAL4 was defined for connectionless services such as IP. However, differences were so small that they were combined. However, the engineers were still not happy, so they created AAL-5 to gain additional features not available in the other classes.

AAL Type	AAL-1 Class A	AAL-2 Class B	AAL-3/4 Class C	AAL-5 Class D
Connection mode	Connection-oriented	Connection-oriented	Connection-oriented and connectionless	Connection-oriented and connectionless
Timing requirements	Required	Required	Not required	Not required
Bit rate	Constant	Variable	Variable	Variable

Table A-1.   *Service Classes in the ATM Adaptation Layer*

- **AAL-1**   A connection-oriented service that emulates a TDM circuit (works like a T1 or T3 leased line). In other words, the bandwidth is allocated whether it is being used or not. This service is useful for live streaming audio and video applications. This service is expensive to use in terms of bandwidth and should only be used when necessary.

- **AAL-2**   This service is connection-oriented and meant for delivering audio and video, but it does not emulate a circuit like AAL-1, so is more efficient at using bandwidth (bandwidth is only used when there is something to send). This AAL is eliminated in UNI version 4.0 in favor of AAL-1 and AAL-5.

- **AAL-3/4**   A connection-oriented and a connectionless service for nonreal-time applications. AAL-3/4 has a fragmentation and reassembly service that is used to transport variable-length packets (such as IP packets) in fixed-length cells. AAL-3/4 inserts information in each cell that the destination uses to sequence and reassemble the packet. Multiplexing of packets from different sources is allowed. This AAL is eliminated in UNI version 4.0 in favor of AAL-1 and AAL-5.

- **AAL-5**   A connection-oriented and connectionless service that fragments frames for delivery in cells, but does so more efficiently than AAL-3/4. The trade-off is that this service does not allow multiplexing. The following discussion explains this further.

The distinction between AAL-3/4 and AAL-5 is important. When AAL-3/4 fragments a packet, it adds sequencing and reassembly information to each fragment *before* inserting it into a cell. Thus, the amount of actual data you can put in each cell is reduced by this information (the information does not go in the ATM cell header). Many ATM designers thought this was a waste of space in the data area.

AAL-5 was designed to use nearly the whole ATM cell payload for data. Multiplexing (interleaving) of transmissions from different sources is not allowed. AAL-5 advocates convinced the ATM Forum to allocate a single bit in the ATM cell header that could be used for a fragmentation and reassembly scheme. Basically, when the last fragment of a packet is sent, the bit is set to 1. When the recipient receives this last fragment, it knows that the next cell is the start of a new fragment.

A drawback to AAL-5 is the inability to multiplex transmissions from more than one source across a single circuit. While setting up circuits as needed may not be a problem on in-house networks, it can be expensive on carrier networks in which you must pay for circuits. Also, loss of any cell requires retransmitting the entire frame.

ATM Interfacing

There are a number of ways of connecting ATM, as illustrated in Figure A-15. Each of the interfaces shown in the figure is described here:

- **UNI (User-Network Interface)**   Defines the connection between user equipment and ATM equipment. When connected to an ATM WAN, the UNI is the link between the customer site and the carrier access point. It may be a T1 line or an ATM FUNI (Frame UNI). The latter transmits frames to the ATM network, where they are then converted to cells by the carrier. FUNI can reduce hardware costs.

- **NNI (Network-to-Network Interface)**   This is the interface between ATM devices within the same network or autonomous system. Note that the ATM Forum refers to the NNI connection between ATM devices in the same network as PNNI (Private Network-to-Network Interface).

- **ICI (Intercarrier Interface)**   This interface is designed for interconnecting different public networks, and for sending traffic across intermediate networks (transiting).

- **DXI (Data Exchange Interface)**   This provides an interface for legacy equipment such as routers into ATM using HDLC (High-level Data Link Control) framing. Packets, not cells, are transmitted to the ATM interface.

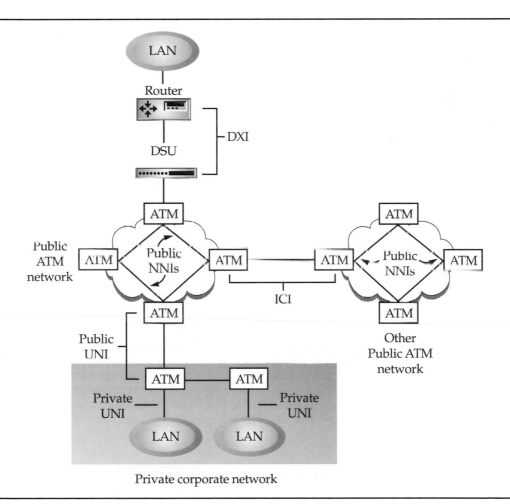

Figure A-15.   *ATM interfaces*

The important point is that the NNI components provide a way to construct full-mesh PVC-connected networks in the backbone of private and public networks automatically while the UNI component allows end systems to establish SVCs across switches in the ATM mesh network. Such mesh networks are described later.

UNI is a well-defined interface. UNI version 4.0 includes the call setup feature for SVCs. Earlier UNI versions supported only PVCs. The signaling specification for UNI is based on an ITU-T public signaling protocol called Q.2931, which is equivalent to the signaling used for narrowband ISDN. NNI signaling is based on SS7 (Signaling System 7).

PNNI (Private Network-to-Network Interface) is a routing protocol. ATM switches use it to map the topology of the network and determine the best path to use when establishing a connection. It maps the topology of the network so that connections can be made on the fly without human assistance. Its interconnection features allow for multiple links between switches, thus providing load sharing and redundancy. In addition, multiple connections allow for building mesh topologies among switches.

Refer to "PNNI (Private Network-to-Network Interface)" for more details.

Virtual Circuits and Call Setup

As mentioned, ATM is a connection-oriented technology, meaning that it sets up virtual circuits over which end systems communicate. Since ATM is a switching technology, little processing is required at each switch along a path to forward a cell to its destination. Each cell has an identifier that explicitly defines how the switch should forward the cell. Therefore, the network is very efficient at moving cells.

The terminology for virtual circuits is as follows and is pictured in Figure A-16.

- **VC (virtual circuit)**   Logical connections between end stations identified in a cell with a VCI (virtual circuit identifier

- **VP (virtual path)**   A bundle of VCs identified in a cell with a VPI (virtual path identifier)

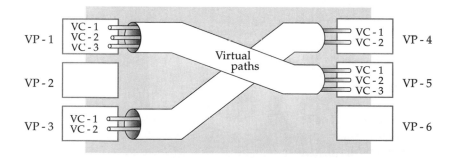

Figure A-16.   *ATM virtual circuits and virtual paths*

Think of a VP as a cable that contains a bundle of wires. The cable connects two points, and wires within the cable provide individual circuits between the two points. The advantage of this method is that connections sharing the same path through the network are grouped together and take advantage of the same management actions. If a VP is already set up, adding a new VC is easy, since the work of defining paths through the network is already done. Only the endpoints need to be established. In addition, if a VP changes to avoid congestion or a downed switch, all the VCs (potentially over 65,000) within the VP change with it.

There is another advantage. If the VP extends over a carrier network, the carrier does not need to keep track of every circuit within the path. This would require storing too much information in the carrier network. All the carrier has to do is maintain the VP between customer sites and let the customer equipment at each end handle the circuits (although carriers may manage the whole thing).

In an ATM cell header, a VPI (virtual path identifier) identifies a link formed by a virtual path, and a VCI (virtual channel identifier) identifies a channel within a virtual path. The VPI and VCI are identified and correspond to termination points at ATM switches. For example, in Figure A-16, a virtual path connects VP-1 and VP-5. Within this path are three virtual circuits. Note that VPIs identify the equivalent of a port specific to the network, while circuits are identified relative to a path.

ATM supports both PVCs (permanent virtual circuits) and SVCs (switched virtual circuits). PVCs are always set up. SVCs are set up on demand.

While PVCs are like a permanently connect telephone link, SVCs are like a dial-up telephone call. PVCs are usually set up manually by administrators to create a permanent link between two endpoints. Carriers have preferred to sell customers PVCs because it is easy to preconfigure them to provide a certain level of service.

While PVCs are usually created manually by the administrators of private and public ATM networks, the nature of SVCs requires that they be created quickly and automatically. Setting up VCs requires that each switch along the path ensure that it has capacity for the circuit. Switches contract with one another to build the VCs, and no data is transmitted until the VC is completely established across the network. Of course, setting up VCs is relatively time-consuming, so many switches are rated according to their call setup time.

Call setups are handled by UNI, which provides the signaling functions for setting up and taking down connections. PNNI is also involved in this process. It locates end systems and determines the best paths to reach them.

A connection setup starts with a connection request by an end device. The message contains the ATM address of the destination along with requests for specific levels of service (such as bandwidth). Signaling is done across a default virtual path.

The path selection is based on the destination address and the results of lookups in a network database (essentially a routing table). Each switch uses a procedure called CAC (connection admission control) to determine whether it can provide the services required by the connection. If not, the connection is rejected (think of getting a busy signal when making a phone call). Even though a switch may have available bandwidth at the moment, it may reject a connection to protect the bandwidth it has guaranteed to other connections.

Once a path is found, a VC number is assigned to it and returned to the end station requesting the connection. All transmissions are then addressed to the VC that leads to an end system, not the ATM address of the end system.

ATM Addressing

ATM is a connection-oriented networking scheme based on switching. Cells are transported to their destination based on the VCI. The VCI is an abbreviated address that identifies the circuit over which the cell needs to travel to its destination. But the VCI only identifies a path to a device, which is analogous to the way a highway number identifies a road to a particular city. Each device on the ATM network still needs a unique address to specifically identify it.

Unfortunately, ATM addressing is a somewhat bungled scheme. There are four addressing formats, and they are administered by different agencies:

- **DCC (Data Country Code)**   Designed for private ATM networks and administered by ANSI in the United States

- **ICD (International Code Designator)**   Originally designed for coding (bar codes, library codes) and not intended for network addressing; administered by the British Standards Institute

- **E.164**   A public networking scheme defined and administered by the ITU

- **E.164 NSAP (Network Service Access Point)**   Another version of E.164 defined by the ATM Forum, but not administered by it

The problem with all these schemes is which one to use. If you are building your own in-house network, DCC is usually recommended. It also doesn't matter much if you use PVCs over public networks. When it does matter is when you need SVCs across public networks, because then you will need to use addresses that conform to the rest of the world. Usually, E.164 is recommended because it follows an internationally recognized scheme. Refer to your switch vendor for the best advice.

The ATM address is a 20-byte string that includes fields for a country code, an administrative authority, a routing domain, an area identifier, an end-system identifier (a IEEE MAC address), an NSAP (Network Service Access Point), an international code, and an ISDN telephone number.

The end-system identifier holds a MAC address, making it easy to integrate ATM networks with LANs. The field is 6 bytes long, which holds 48-bit MAC addresses. Devices at the edge of ATM networks take this address, along with the packet and put them into ATM cells for delivery across an ATM backbone.

ATM Traffic Management, Quality of Service, and Service Contracts

Traffic management makes efficient use of network resources such as bandwidth and buffers. For customers of carrier ATM services, a traffic contract can guarantee (or attempt to guarantee) the level of service that the customer can expect. At the same time, contracts let carriers put constraints on how customers can use the network. The information in this section describes service contract parameters.

Note   *Refer to "Traffic Management, Shaping, and Engineering" for additional information on this topic.*

Contract negotiation is not limited to paper documents. Switches in ATM negotiate among themselves to establish connections across the network. An end system can make a request for a connection, and that request is propagated along the path to the destination. Each switch along the way determines whether it can meet the requested service levels (maximum data rates, average rates over time, and levels of acceptable cell loss and delay, and so on). If so, the switches set up the connection. When PNNI is used to set up SVCs on demand, switches advertise their QoS abilities so that the best path can be selected for building a connection that matches the QoS requested by the source.

ATM *service categories* are used to ensure that the service requirements of applications are met. They can provide higher priority for transmissions that need it. The service categories are described below. The traffic contract parameters mentioned in the following descriptions are described in Table A-2.

- **CBR (constant bit rate)**   Provides a fixed amount of bandwidth that is always available for streaming data such as voice and video, even if no data is being sent. CBR works like a TDM circuit. A PCR (peak cell rate) is specified, and if traffic exceeds this rate, cells may be dropped.

- **rt-VBR (real time-variable bit rate)**   This is similar to CBR in that a peak cell rate is specified, but network bandwidth is only used when data is sent. It is intended for voice and video which do not tolerate delay and variation. It supports bursty traffic (data flows are followed by idle periods). SCR (sustainable cell rate) is used to specify minimum levels of service, and burst rates are defined with PCR and MBS (maximum burst size).

- **nrt-VBR (non-real time-variable bit rate)**   This service is meant for bursty traffic of the type that is common on LANs. Like rt-VBR, SCR is used to specify minimum levels of service, and burst rates are defined with PCR and MBS.

- **UBR (unspecified bit rate)**   This parameter does not guarantee bandwidth or throughput. It allows cells to be dropped if there is not enough bandwidth. This is basically a best-effort service intended for non-real-time applications. Good for e-mail and other non-time-critical applications. Only PCR may be specified.

- **ABR (available bit rate)**   This parameter takes advantage of unused bandwidth. A customer gets a specific bandwidth, but can use more if it is available. An end system with an ABR connection can use flow-control mechanisms to adjust its rate of transmission dynamically, based on feedback from the network. ABR is relatively new and not yet fully utilized. ABR is designed to replace static VBR traffic constraints with a more dynamic approach. When the feedback rules are followed, there is generally low cell loss.

- **GFR (guaranteed frame rate)**   GFR is ATM's latest service class. It is designed to offer various quality of service commitments, specifically for IP traffic. Users may send at any rate up to PCR, but the network is only committed to sending MCR (minimum cell rate). GFR is an alternative to UBR services.

Traffic Contract Parameter	Description
PCR (peak cell rate)	The maximum amount of bandwidth allowed on a connection before packets are dropped (or carried at a more expensive rate). The carrier guarantees this rate. Customers might want to measure the line to ensure that they are receiving their guaranteed rate.
SCR (sustainable cell rate)	This parameter (used only by VBR services) specifies a guaranteed bandwidth during the variable transmissions.
MBS (maximum burst size)	This parameter (used only by VBR services) specifies the maximum number of cells that will be transmitted at PCR.
CDVT (cell delay variation tolerance)	This parameter specifies maximum allowable cell jitter (delay variance). This parameter is used to specify time-constraints for cell delivery.
MCR (minimum cell rate)	This parameter (used only by ABR services) specifies the rate in cells per second that the source may transmit.
ACR (allowed cell rate)	This parameter (used only by ABR services) is designed to work with ABR's feedback mechanism that determines cell rate.

Table A-2.   *Attributes of ATM Service Categories*

ATM is often used as an enterprise backbone networking technology. Ethernet and other LANs are connected to ATM switches. The switches put frames in cells and deliver them to another segment of the network. UBR is the most commonly used service in this scheme, but as traffic increases, ABR becomes more useful due to its traffic flow controls. As congestion increases, an ATM switch notifies downstream switches and end systems of the congestion by changing the Payload Type field in the ATM cell header. The destination then informs the sender to slow down its transmission. Another technique sends a management cell every 32 cells that informs the destination about congestion. The destination then in turn informs the sender.

GFR was designed from the start as a way to deliver IP traffic across ATM backbones, especially in service provider core networks. GFR can provide a certain type of throughput guarantees, something that is sorely missing in a traditional IP-routed internetwork. Keep in mind that ATM QoS is usually only available if you run ATM from end to end. In a situation where the core is ATM and Ethernet is used at the edges, QoS is difficult. GFR lets service providers offer guaranteed minimum bandwidth and extra bandwidth if necessary, minimizing lost frames.

The ATM Forum is also working to integrate the IETF's Diff-Serv (Differentiated Services) specification into ATM. Diff-Serv defines IP traffic classes, allowing them to be prioritized.

Refer to "QoS (Quality of Service)" for more information about how QoS is being implemented on carrier networks and the Internet.

ATM QoS Parameters

Table A-3 defines ATM QoS parameters that are used to *measure* the performance of a network. Note that QoS measurements only make sense when the traffic conforms to the contract's levels of service. If a customer is attempting to push too much traffic through a connection, the network will drop cells, so cell loss cannot be blamed on the carrier.

Conformance testing of CBR, VBR, UBR, and GFR can be done with the GCRA (Generic Cell Rate Algorithm), also referred to as the "leaky bucket" algorithm. For more information on GCRA, refer to the Web sites given later.

Traffic Management

Traffic management entails a number of techniques to control network traffic, including dropping cells and scaling back the transmissions of an end station. Here are some relevant features:

■ **CAC (connection admission control)**   CAC was mentioned earlier as the procedure that switches follow when setting up a virtual circuit to ensure that they can meet the requested QoS without affecting the QoS of existing connections.

■ **Policing, or UPC (usage parameter control)**   This is used to check for valid virtual circuits and virtual paths and determine the conformity of traffic-to-traffic descriptors. Invalid cells may be discarded completely or tagged with a CLP (Cell Loss Priority) of 1, indicating that they may be dropped if necessary to meet bandwidth requirements.

■ **Traffic shaping**   What traffic shaping does is change the spacing of cells on a connection, thus increasing the delay of those cells. Shaping is performed to better utilize network resources and meet traffic constraints (avoid dropping cells).

QoS Parameter	Description
CDV (cell delay variation) measurement	The difference between a cell's expected arrival time and its actual arrival time. Measures a circuit's ability to maintain bandwidth.
CTD (cell transfer delay) measurement	The time from exit at source to arrival at destination. This measure is important for real-time applications.
CLR (cell loss ratio) measurement	The ratio of cells lost to cells that reach their destination. Note that cells may be lost due to errors or dropped because contract parameters are exceeded.
CER (cell error ratio) measurement	The ratio of cells in error to cells that reach their destination.
CMR (cell misinsertion rate) measurement	The number of cells inserted on the wrong connection.
BER (bit error rate) measurement	A ratio of the total number of bit errors to the total number of bits transmitted.

Table A-3.   *QoS Parameters for Measuring the Performance of an ATM Network*

LAN Emulation and IP over ATM

The dream of ATM designers has always been an end-to-end ATM system in which all end systems have an ATM interface. Today, no one believes this will ever happen. ATM is perceived as a networking system that conforms to the old telephone network in a world that is dominated by IP packets.

Still, many enterprise network managers see ATM as a superior network backbone technology. ATM is also used at the core of many carrier and Internet service provider networks. This scheme is pictured on the right in Figure A-12. Note that frame-based networks such as Ethernet connect to ATM switches at the workgroup level. These workgroup-level switches are interconnected by core/backbone switches that handles all internetwork routing.

Both the ATM Forum and the IETF have developed different standards for implementing ATM in legacy network environments as shown in Table A-4. Note that all are IP overlay models except for LANE, which has the ATM network emulating a LAN like Ethernet. In other words, the ATM network operates as if it is a MAC layer network below the LLC sublayer of the data link layer. The IP overlay models treat the ATM networks as a data link bridging and/or routing network. Each of these specifications is discussed elsewhere in this book.

Some claim that IP will be able to offer ATM-like QoS as soon as Diff-Serv and MPLS come into widespread use. Diff-Serv lets routers set prioritization, and MPLS allows high-speed processing of IP packets across backbone. When that happens, ATM may become less important.

Refer to "IP over ATM" for a general overview of IP over ATM networking and a description of each of these topics. Also see "Label Switching."

Hybrid ATM *Networks*

An interesting exercise is to compare ATM to Ethernet. Not too many years ago, such a comparison would be laughable. Some considered Ethernet an outgoing technology, while ATM would be the new networking technology for the enterprise and carrier networks. Both ATM and Ethernet are layer 2 networking technologies, and IP will run over ATM or Ethernet.

The ATM people have advocated ATM's benefits for years: QoS, switching design, and speed, but while ATM technologies were subjects of endless debate and little standardization, Ethernet and IP technologies have moved forward together. Gigabit Ethernet (and now 10 Gigabit Ethernet) and IP prioritization and QoS technologies can provide many of the benefits of ATM, due in part to enhanced bandwidth availability.

Of course, while Gigabit Ethernet exceeds ATM's bandwidth, there is some doubt that the IETF's concept of QoS will actually work. ATM was designed from the ground up to provide

ATM Forum Specification	IETF Specification
LANE (LAN Emulation)	CIP (Classical Model IP over ATM), RFC 2225
MPOA (Multiprotocol Over ATM)	NHRP (Next Hop Resolution Protocol)
	MPLS (Multiprotocol Label Switching)

Table A-4. *ATM Forum and IETF Specification Comparison*

QoS, while much of the IETF's work is based on making a connectionless, best-effort networking scheme provide QoS!

The argument for ATM is that QoS is still needed at the core of the network. That is why many carriers and service providers use it. Building faster switches and bigger pipes is not always the solution. Ethernet networks are normally built with a hierarchical topology that can overwhelm the backbone. This is where ATM can save the day.

Look at the hybrid ATM/Gigabit Ethernet environment pictured in Figure A-17 and note the mesh topology that connects all the ATM switches. There are multiple, redundant links between each switch (thanks to PNNI). Not only do these redundant links provide fault tolerance, they also provide load sharing, which means that core bandwidth can scale up

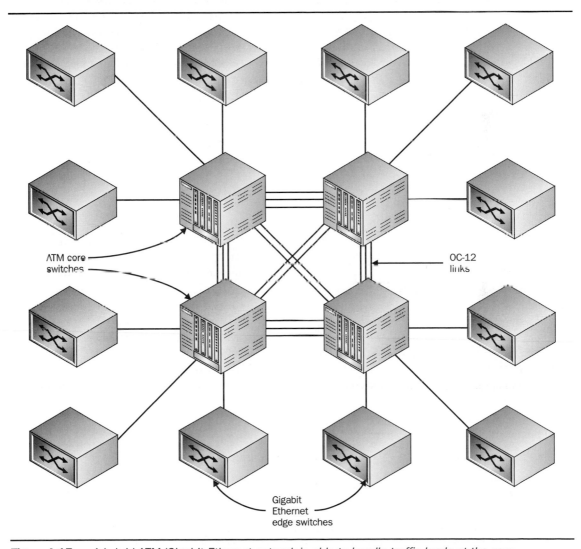

Figure A-17.   *A hybrid ATM/Gigabit Ethernet network is able to handle traffic loads at the core*

to a very high levels to avoid bottlenecks, no matter how many Gigabit Ethernet networks are connected to the ATM core.

While Ethernet has gained some QoS characteristics in the form of CoS (class of service), which prioritizes traffic, jitter and latency problems still exist. ATM was designed with full QoS capabilities in mind, so it can provide absolute QoS guarantees within the parameters of the network's capacity. In other words, ATM lets you set aside part of the bandwidth for a videoconference, and you will get that bandwidth. Of course, the more total bandwidth you have, the better—even with true QoS capabilities.

See "Bandwidth Management" and "QoS (Quality of Service)" for more information.

Related Entries   Bandwidth Management; Cell Relay; Gigabit Ethernet; IMA (Inverse Multiplexing over ATM); IP over ATM; IP Switching; Label Switching; LANE (LAN Emulation); MPLS (Multiprotocol Label Switching); MPOA (Multiprotocol over ATM); Multilayer Switching; Network Access Services; Network Concepts; Network Core Technologies; Network Design and Construction; NPN (New Public Network); Optical Networks; PoS (Packets over Sonet); PNNI (Private Network-to-Network Interface); QoS (Quality of Service); Switching and Switched Networks; *and* Virtual Circuits

Linktionary! – Tom Sheldon's Encyclopedia of Networking updates	http://www.linktionary.com/atm.html
The ATM Forum	http://www.atmforum.com
ATM Consortium at UNH InterOperability Lab (IOL)	http://www.iol.unh.edu/consortiums/atm/
Cell Relay Retreat (includes ATM FAQ and reference material)	http://cell-relay.indiana.edu/cell-relay/
ATM: Scan Technologies ATM tutorial (interesting and colorful illustrations!)	http://www.scan-technologies.com/tutorials/ATM%20Tutorial.htm
ATM resources links (extensive)	http://china.si.umich.edu/telecom/technical-atm.html
Links by Vasilios Apostolopoulos (very extensive)	http://www.webexpert.net/vasilios/telecom/telecom.htm
TechFest ATM links	http://www.techfest.com/networking/atm.htm
Cisco Documentation: Asynchronous Transfer Mode (ATM) Switching	http://www.cisco.com/univercd/cc/td/doc/cisintwk/ito_doc/atm.htm
Cisco Documentation: Designing ATM Internetworks	http://www.cisco.com/univercd/cc/td/doc/cisintwk/idg4/nd2008.htm
Cisco Documentation: Troubleshooting ATM Environments	http://www.cisco.com/univercd/cc/td/doc/cisintwk/itg_v1/tr1921.htm
Bitpipe (search for "ATM")	http://www.bitpipe.com/

AT&T

AT&T is the successor to Alexander Graham Bell's phone company. The company grew so large that the federal government had to regulate it. In 1913, the Department of Justice brought an antitrust suit against AT&T that resulted in the Kingsbury Commitment. It forced AT&T to divest itself of Western Union and allow independent carriers to use the long-distance network it had established. In 1956, the Justice Department limited AT&T to providing only regulated services to customers and, in 1968, ruled that customers could attach non-AT&T equipment to the public telephone network. The 1969 MCI Decision allowed MCI and other carriers to compete with AT&T for long-distance communications.

From 1982 to 1984, the Justice Department finalized its antitrust suit by forcing AT&T to break up and re-form into seven regional holding companies called RBOCs (regional Bell operating companies), or "Baby Bells." A manufacturing, research, and long-distance operation called AT&T Corporation was allowed to continue operation. Refer to "Telecommunications Regulation" for more information about the breakup.

More recently, AT&T has been getting back into local service markets. It now provides service in almost 100 major cities. AT&T acquired a number of companies, including TCG (Teleport Communications Group) and TCI (Tele-Communication, Inc.). AT&T is also in a joint venture with British Telecom and acquired IBM's global data network in December of 1998. The TCG acquisition gives AT&T access to a number of local service markets and the 38-GHz wireless spectrum that TCG owned. The wireless service gives subscribers access to AT&T's wireless local access service. The TCI acquisition gives AT&T access to broadband hybrid fiber-coax networks that reach almost one-third of U.S. households. TCI controlled @Home Network, which gives AT&T further access to services that support Internet users.

AT&T is also involved with the support of Internet traffic and voice/data networking. It is upgrading much of its network with Cisco gigabit routers and switches from Nortel and Lucent to handle packet-based voice traffic.

In January of 1999, AT&T announced INC (Integrated Network Connection), a multiservice access solution for small and large businesses that is similar to Sprint's ION (Integrated On-demand Network). In its initial offering, INC supports up to 40 voice calls simultaneously with 512 Kbits/sec of data and Internet Protocol (IP) traffic using an AT&T-owned ATM multiplexor located on the customer's premises. The multiplexor will automatically react to users' dynamic demands for different types of network traffic and allocate bandwidth accordingly, whether that be voice, frame relay, IP traffic, or video communications.

AT&T also provides extensive support for VPNs (virtual private networks). Its Enterprise Class Virtual Private Network (VPN) services combine frame relay, due to its reliability, and IP, due to its ubiquity and flexibility. The services implement some interesting features such as support for MPLS (Multiprotocol Label Switching), QoS (quality of service), and IPSec (IP Security) encryption techniques.

Related Entries   Carrier Services; RBOCs (Regional Bell Operating Companies); LATAs (local access and transport areas); LEC (local exchange carrier); Service Providers and Carriers; Telecommunications and Telephone Systems; *and* Telecommunications Regulation

AT&T Web site	http://www.att.com
Telecordia (formerly Bellcore)	http//www.bellcore.com

Attacks and Attackers

An attack is an attempt by an attacker (also commonly called a hacker) to access a system or take control of a system (a computer, network server, Web site, and so on) using a variety of methods. The intent of an attack is assumed to be malicious. The attacker may wish to view sensitive information, change information, shut down the system, or overload it to prevent other users from accessing it (a denial of service attack). Encrypted information may be attacked, meaning that the attacker is attempting to break the encryption and discover the secured information. Attackers are more commonly referred to as "hackers."

There are two primary types of attacks:

- **Passive attack**   Monitoring and collecting information about a system to be used in a later attack. An eavesdropper listens for information being transmitted that can be used in a later attack.

- **Active attack**   An active attack is one in which the attacker actually attempts to gain access to a system through unauthorized or illegal means.

An attacker may monitor the sessions of other users (a passive attack) and then take over the sessions (an active attack). In a *replay attack*, the attacker uses previously gathered information to gain access to a system by replaying it to the system, which thinks that it is dealing with a valid session.

Two important Internet RFCs provide information about attacks and attackers. RFC 2196 (Site Security Handbook, September 1997) provides extensive information on security policies, firewalls, authentication, and access. Most important, it described procedures for detecting and handling security incidents. RFC 2504 (User's Security Handbook, February 1999) decribes useful information for users that can help in preventing attacks.

Related Entries   Cryptography; Firewall; Hacking and Hackers; Security; *and* Security Auditing

Linktionary! – Tom Sheldon's Encyclopedia of Networking updates	http://www.linktionary.com/security/
Simulating Cyber Attacks, Defenses, and Consequences	http://all.net/journal/ntb/simulate/simulate.html

Attenuation

Attenuation is signal loss, measured in decibels, of a signal transmission over distance. The opposite of attenuation is signal amplification. On network cables, attenuation is the degradation of the digital signal or a loss of amplitude of an electric signal. Repeaters are used to regenerate signals by amplifying them but not changing their information content in any way. With a repeater, a network can be extended beyond its normal range.

Related Entries   Cable and Wiring; Data Communication Concepts; *and* Signals

Attributes

Attributes define user access to files and directories and the properties of files and directories. A common attribute is "Archive Needed," which indicates that a file has been modified and needs to be included in the next backup. This attribute is then turned off when the file is backed up, but is set on again if a user changes the file. Read-only attributes found on most network operating systems prevent users from changing the contents of files or deleting them.

NetWare 4.*x* has some interesting attributes. DI (Delete Inhibit) prevents a user from deleting a file or directory. IM (Immediate Compress) causes a file, or the files in a directory, to be compressed as soon as possible. DC (Don't Compress) prevents a file, or the files, in a directory from being automatically compressed.

Objects within object-oriented filing systems, databases, and programming languages have attributes called *properties*. If an object is compared to a record within a database, its properties are like the fields within a record that hold values.

Related Entries   File Sharing; File Systems; Network Operating Systems; *and* Rights and Permissions

Linktionary! – Tom Sheldon's Encyclopedia of   http://www.linktionary.com/attributes.html
Networking updates

Auditing

Auditing is the collection and monitoring of events on servers and networks for the purpose of tracking security violations and to keep track of how systems are used. A network auditing system logs details of what users are doing on the network so that malicious or unintended activities can be tracked. When auditing is in place, vast amounts of information may be recorded and even archived for future reference. Some audit systems provide event alarms to warn administrators when certain levels or conditions are met.

  Another form of auditing is security auditing, which uses scanners and other tools to detect security problems in servers and networks. Refer to "Security Auditing" for details.

Resource auditing is the most common form of auditing. You use it to track how users are using resources. Disk space usage is most often tracked, and many network operating systems allow administrators to set a disk usage limit. When a user reaches his or her limit, more disk space can be allocated. This may require that the user contact the administrator to request more space, at which time the user and administrator can evaluate disk space requirements and determine why the user has gone over their allocation (maybe they installed games or images from the Web).

In some environments, users are charged for the use of resources like disk space, printers, and so on. Auditing can provide the records need to charge for these resources. The charge may not be monetary, but only serve as a measure that indicates how users are using network resources.

Software metering and licensing is another area that requires auditing. Some operating systems and some software packages include metering functions that help companies track when the number of allowable licensed users for a software package has been exceeded so additional licenses can be purchased.

Network management systems provide centralized management features that help administrators and auditors keep track of systems throughout a network. Refer to "Network Management" for more details.

Auditing System Examples

NetWare 4.*x* provides a good example of an auditing system. It designates a network user known as the *auditor* to track events on the network. The events fall into two categories: volume tracking and container tracking. Each auditing category can have a distinct password, so, for example, the auditor who tracks volume events cannot track container events without the container password. However, one auditor can track all events if necessary.

One of the primary users to track with the auditing system is the network administrator, who basically has unlimited rights to the system. An auditor can keep administrators "honest" by passively tracking and monitoring all their activities. Initially, the network administrator creates a special auditor account, usually as directed by higher-level management. The auditor then logs in to the account and immediately changes the password, effectively blocking all access to the account, even by the network administrator.

The auditor can then set up auditing features, view audit logs, and work in designated audit directories. A record is kept for every activity that is designated for tracking. Events that can be tracked are listed here:

- Directory creation and deletion
- Creating, opening, closing, deleting, renaming, writing, and salvaging files
- Modifying directory entries
- Queue activities
- Server events, such as changing the date and time, downing the server, and mounting or dismounting volumes
- User events, such as logon, logoff, connection termination, space restrictions, granting of trustee rights, and disabling of accounts
- Directory services events, such as changes in passwords, security, and logon restrictions
- Activities of a specific user, such as a supervisor or network administrator

Auditing records can be viewed using special filters to produce reports that show specific activities. Filters can be applied to show specific date and time ranges, specified events, file and directory events, or user events.

The Windows NT auditing system lets you track events that occur on individual servers related to security policies, system events, and application events. Two types of auditing events can be tracked. The first is user account auditing, which tracks security events and logs them in the server's security log. The second is file system auditing, which tracks file system events. For example, to set up auditing in Windows NT, you open the dialog box shown in Figure A-18. Note that you can track the success and/or failure of an event. For example, you might want to always track logon failures.

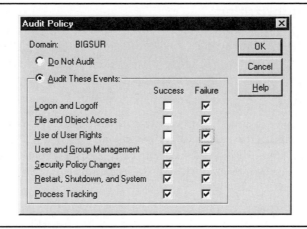

Figure A-18.   *Windows NT Audit Policy dialog box*

The syslog facility exists in the UNIX operating system to create audit trails. It is necessary to protect the audit records from alteration or destruction. They can, for example, be copied to another system that is accessible only by administrators or an auditor.

Administrators should be on the lookout for a large number of failed logon attempts or logins that take place at odd hours, which usually indicate that an intruder is attempting to access the system.

Section 4.6 in RFC 2196 (Site Security Handbook, September 1997) provides useful information about auditing such as collecting and handling auditing information, and preserving it for investigations and prosecutions. Also see RFC 2903 (Generic AAA Architecture, August 2000).

Related Entries   Licensing, Electronic; Network Management; Security; Security Auditing; *and* Software Metering

Linktionary! – Tom Sheldon's Encyclopedia of Networking updates	http://www.linktionary.com/a/auditing.html
Server Auditing article by Jay Milne at Network Computing Online	http://www.nwc.com/707/707work1.html

Authentication and Authorization

According to RFC 2828 (Internet Security Glossary, May 2000), authentication is "the process of verifying an identity claimed by or for a system entity." The key word here is *verify*, and the correct terminology is to say that "an authentication system verifies an identity."

Authentication can provide assurance that users (or systems) are who they say they are. Authorization refers to a user's ability to access resources on a network, usually based on user account rights and privileges. Refer to "Access Control" for details about how authenticated users are allowed to access system resources.

Authentication may be performed directly on the computer that the user is attempting to access, but in distributed environments, the user account and security information are usually stored and managed by a special security server. When a user logs on, the username and password are verified with the security server. Done properly, passwords are never sent across the wire. It is essential that the user's password be kept private and never cross the network, especially as readable text where eavesdroppers could easily capture the information and use it to access secure systems by masquerading as the user. Instead, unique handshake schemes are used to authenticate users in a secure way as discussed here.

While stand-alone security servers provide many benefits (centralized security and security management), authenticating users in distributed environments presents a number of interesting challenges.

For example, assume Sue wants to access a secure server called DOCS. When Sue logs in, her login information is used directly or indirectly to authenticate her. Now Sue attempts to access the DOCS server. Assume that DOCS "trusts" the security server and assumes that it can properly authorize Sue. Since the security server has already authenticated Sue, it does not make sense for DOCS to also attempt to authenticate her. What is needed is a "single sign-on" authentication scheme that lets Sue access any system within the trusted network environment without further logon requests, assuming she has one user account for the entire network. This may be accomplished as follows:

■ Sue's logon information may be cached. When she accesses another server, that server obtains the logon information and verifies it with the security server.

■ The security server may issue logon credentials to Sue when she first logs on. These credentials are used when accessing other systems for the duration of her logon session.

Paraphrasing RFC 1704 (On Internet Authentication, October 1994), a secure authentication scheme must provide "strong, mutual authentication" as described here:

■ **Mutual authentication**   The two parties involved in an exchange use a reliable means of learning the true identity of the other.

■ **Strong authentication**   Neither party obtains information that could be used to impersonate the other party in another session.

Passwords can be used for mutual authentication, but not for strong authentication. If one party gives its password directly to the other, it reveals something about itself that the other system can use to impersonate it. Basically, the first "speaker" gives out its passwords and becomes vulnerable. Eavesdroppers can also capture the password and use it later (except in the case of one-time passwords).

A strong authentication scheme allows both parties to reveal that they know a secret *without revealing the actual secret*. Using the previous example, Sue has a secret password. She must prove to the security server that she knows the password without transmitting it across the network. The following four-way handshake scheme is an example:

1. When Sue logs on, her computer generates a random number and encrypts it with the secret key. Note that this key is derived from the password or obtained from a local encrypted file that is only accessible when a correct password is entered.

2. The result is sent to the security server, which decrypts it with the shared secret key.

3. The security server now has the random number generated by Sue's computer. It increments the number by 1, then generates its own random number and encrypts both separately with the shared secret key.

4. Sue's computer receives the message and decrypts it. The first part of the message should be the random number it originally sent to the security server, incremented by 1, which verifies that it is in contact with a system that knows the shared secret key.

5. Next, Sue's computer increments the random number received from the security server by 1, encrypts it, and returns it to the server.

6. When the server receives this message, with its random number incremented by 1, it knows the client must be authentic.

After authentication, the client and server establish a new secret key to use for encryption during the remainder of the session. This minimizes the use of the logon secret key. Of course, the shared secret must be kept secret. If someone obtains it, that person can masquerade as either the client or server.

A number of authentication protocols and techniques have been developed over the years. CHAP (Challenge-Handshake Authentication Protocol) is discussed in RFC 1994 and under its own heading in this book. It is very similar to the procedure just described. Another protocol is EAP (Extensible Authentication Protocol), which is discussed in RFC 2284 and also discussed under its own heading in this book.

Several other more advanced schemes are outlined here:

■ **Two-factor authentication**   In this method, a token device such as a smart card is used that generates an additional logon code. This logon code is synchronized in time with a code that the server knows. Users enter the code, their username, and password when they log on. Thus two items are required to log on: something the user knows (his or her password) and something the user has (the token). This scheme requires that all users carry a smart card, and it is usually implemented for remote users. Refer to "Token-Based Authentication" for more information.

- ■ **Kerberos**   This is a well-established protocol that performs authentications based on tickets. A ticket is an encrypted packet of data that is issued by a special security server called the KDC (Key Distribution Center). A KDC is usually maintained in-house on the corporate intranet, which is the KDC's area of authority or realm. When a user logs on, authentication is handled by the KDC. If the user is properly authenticated, the KDC issues the user a ticket (called the Ticket Granting Ticket or TGT). When that user wants to access some network server, the KDC checks the TGT it previously gave to the user (to verify that they are still authentic) and then issues the user a service ticket that allows the user to access the target server. The target server has its own means of verifying that the ticket and thus the user are authentic and grants the user access based on predefined access controls. That is pretty much it in a nutshell. You can refer to the "Kerberos" topic in this book for more information.

- ■ **Certificates, public keys, and PKIs (public-key infrastructures)**   If you require secure logon to Internet servers or other public servers, the certificate scheme is appropriate. A certificate is basically a digital ID that is secured by a well-known certificate authority such as VeriSign. It can prove that the person on the other end of a connection is who they say they are. This scheme uses public-key encryption and provides a way for a user to provide you with his or her public key for authentication purposes and to encrypt a session between client and server. The difference between this scheme and Kerberos is that Kerberos requires an online security server to authenticate users. Certificates are self-contained packages that include everything needed to authenticate a user. However, it requires that some entity issue certificates. This may be done by a public service such as VeriSign, or by an internal certificate server in the case of a company that wants to issue its own certificates to employees. Refer to "Certificates and Certificate Servers" and "Public Key Cryptosystems" for more details.

RFC 1704 (On Internet Authentication) (October 1994), provides a comprehensive list of authentication protocols and a good description of the terminology of authentication, cryptography, and security. Three important RFCs related to AAA (authentication, authorization, and accounting) were released in 2000: RFC 2903 (Generic AAA Architecture, August 2000), RFC 2904 (AAA Authorization Framework, August 2000), and RFC 2905 (AAA Authorization Application Examples, August 2000).

Single Sign-On, The Holy Grail

The concept of SSO (single sign-on) is simple. A user only needs to type in their username and password one time (the first time they log on) in order to access any network resource. In some cases, SSO even allows access to extranet systems and Internet Web servers without further need for users to present their credentials.

Windows 2000 networks improve single sign-on features by using Kerberos and Secure Sockets Layer protocols. One advantage of these protocols is that they allow single sign-on in mixed network environments where some servers may be UNIX, Linux, or NetWare servers that also support the protocols. Microsoft SNA Server extends SSO capabilities to mainframe environments. Microsoft claims that Windows 2000 is the best choice to serve as an SSO *hub* in heterogeneous networks because SSO for Windows 2000 interoperates with so many other vendors' operating systems. In Windows 2000, every domain controller is a Kerberos Key Distribution Center that has a realm corresponding to the domain.

An important feature of any SSO is that it be attached to some directory service that serves as a single repository for network management information, including user accounts. Novell NetWare and Microsoft Active Directory are such directory services. A directory service provides a single authoritative listing of each user's rights and privileges on systems throughout the network, which simplifies management and control and allows administrators to change logon privileges and access rights at any time from a single location.

A number of SSO solutions are available and are listed here. You can refer to the Web sites of these vendors (listed at the end of this topic) for more information.

- **PassGo Authentication Server**   Provides single sign-on or one-click access to all resources on the corporate enterprise network and helps enforce corporate security standards and procedures.

- **Axent Technologies' Enterprise Security Manager**   Enterprise Security Manager gives you the ability to automate the planning, management, and control of your security policy from a single location.

- **CyberSafe TrustBroker Security Suite**   Features multiplatform, single sign-on authentication, including both public-key and Kerberos encryption. It secures your organization's intranet and extranet against inside and outside threats.

- **Platinum Technologies AutoSecure Single Sign On**   AutoSecure SSO is designed for heterogeneous environments including mainframes, distributed systems, and PCs. It is independent of platforms, applications, networks, and even other security mechanisms.

- **ZOOMIT VIA**   A metadirectory service that makes it easy to design, customize, and deploy unified enterprise directory services. Most important to this discussion, VIA provides single sign-on to multiple systems.

IETF Working Groups and RFCs

There are several IETF working groups related to authentication, authorization, and accounting. These are listed here. Refer to these groups for more information, including working documents and a list of related RFCs.

IETF Working Group: Authentication, Authorization, and Accounting (AAA). This group is working on base protocols related to a network access server, Mobile IP, and roaming.	http://www.ietf.org/html.charters/aaa-charter.html
IETF Working Group: One Time Password Authentication (OTP)	http://www.ietf.org/html.charters/otp-charter.html
IETF Working Group: Common Authentication Technology (CAT). This group has worked on Kerberos services and security APIs.	http://www.ietf.org/html.charters/cat-charter.html

A number of Internet RFC are worth investigating to further your knowledge of this topic. The most important are listed below.

- RFC 1507 (DASS - Distributed Authentication Security Service, September 1993)
- RFC 1510 (The Kerberos Network Authentication Service (V5, September 1993)
- RFC 1511 (Common Authentication Technology Overview, September 1993)
- RFC 1994 (Challenge Handshake Authentication Protocol, August 1996)
- RFC 2084 (Considerations for Web Transaction Security, January 1997)
- RFC 2222 (Simple Authentication and Security Layer, October 1997)
- RFC 2284 (PPP Extensible Authentication Protocol, March 1998)
- RFC 2289 (A One-Time-Password System, February 1998)
- RFC 2401 (Security Architecture for the Internet Protocol, November 1998)
- RFC 2444 (The One-Time-Password SASL Mechanism, October 1998)
- RFC 2716 (PPP EAP TLS Authentication Protocol, October 1999)
- RFC 2945 (The SRP Authentication and Key Exchange System, September 2000))

Related Entries   Access Control; Certificates and Certification Systems; CHAP (Challenge Handshake Authentication Protocol); Cryptography; Digital Signatures; EAP (Extensible Authentication Protocol); Hackers and Hacking; IPSec (IP Security); Kerberos; PAP (Password Authentication Protocol); Passwords; Public Key Cryptosystems; PKI (Public Key Infrastructure); Rights and Permissions; Security; Security Auditing; *and* Trust Relationships and Trust Management

Linktionary! – Tom Sheldon's Encyclopedia of Networking updates	http://www.linktionary.com/a/authenticate.html
Shiva's white paper on remote access security	http://www.shiva.com/remote/prodinfo/security/
"A Distributed Authorization Model for WWW" by Jose Kahan Oblatt	http://www.isoc.org/HMP/PAPER/107/abst.html
Microsoft Security page	http://www.microsoft.com/security/
Google Web Directory Authentication	http://directory.google.com/Top/Computers/Security/Authentication/
Bitpipe (search for "authentication")	http://www.bitpipe.com/
Cisco AAA Implementation Case Study	http://www.cisco.com/univercd/cc/td/doc/cisintwk/intsolns/aaaisg/
CyberSafe Corporation	http://www.cybersafe.com

Authenticode, Microsoft

Microsoft's Authenticode is part of its larger Internet Security Framework. It attempts to solve one of the larger questions facing the software industry today: How can users trust code that is published on the Internet? It provides a way to sign code so users know that programs obtained from the Internet are legitimate, just as shrink wrap and sealed boxes imply that off-the-shelf packaged software is authentic. Authenticode provides the following:

- Authenticity, so you know who published the code
- Integrity, so you know that code hasn't been tampered with since it was published
- A legitimate and safe way to exchange programs over the Internet

The basic procedure for signing code is for a publisher to get a certificate from a certification authority. The publisher then encrypts its digital signatures into the code with its private key to create a unique digital signature (note the signatures are inserted directly into the program file). The code can then be verified using functions that validate the digital signature, as discussed under "Certificates" in this book. The functions indicate whether the code is valid or whether it is possibly fake or has been tampered with.

While Authenticode is a Microsoft initiative, Netscape and JavaSoft have developed their own code-signing technology called JAR (Java Archive Format). Still other vendors are developing their own technologies. The W3C (World Wide Web Consortium) at http://www.w3.org is attempting to consolidate these digital signing and certificate technologies into a single framework called the Digital Signature Initiative.

Related Entries   Certificates; Digital Signatures; *and* Security

Microsoft Security and Cryptography page   http://www.microsoft.com/workshop/security/

Autonomous System

An AS (autonomous system) is a collection of networks, or more precisely, the routers joining those networks, that are under the same administrative authority and that share a common routing strategy. An AS has a single "interior" routing protocol and policy. Internal routing information is shared among routing within the AS, but not with systems outside the AS. However, an AS announces the network addresses of its internal networks to other ASes that it is linked to. On the Internet, an AS is an ISP (Internet service provider), but universities, research institutes, and private organizations also have their own ASes.

A group of autonomous systems that share routing information is called a "confederation of ASes" (an interesting phrase when pronounced incorrectly). Autonomous confederations are assumed to have a higher level of trust protection against routing loops among member systems.

Two Internet RFCs discuss autonomous systems: RFC 1930 (Guidelines for creation, selection, and registration of an Autonomous System, March 1996) and RFC 0975 (Autonomous confederations, February 1986)

According to RFC 1930, "Without exception, an AS must have only one *routing policy*. Here routing policy refers to how the rest of the Internet makes routing decisions based on information from your AS." Organizations with ASes are assigned 16-bit numbers by IANA (Internet Assigned Numbers Authority). Note: AS numbers are not related to IP addresses.

Figure A-19 illustrates two autonomous systems. IGPs (Interior Gateway Protocols) are used within the AS and EGPs (Exterior Gateway Protocols) are used between the ASes. IGPs provide basic routing within autonomous systems, while EGP is designed to provide *reachability information*, both about neighbor gateways and about routes to non-neighbor gateways. The IGPs collect the reachability information and the EGP advertises that information.

The following exterior gateway protocols operate within autonomous systems to gather internal routing information. These protocols are discussed elsewhere in this book.

- **RIP (Routing Information Protocol)**   A traditional and very common routing protocol included with most network operating systems and supported by all routers.

- **OSPF (Open Shortest Path First)**   OSPF is a more efficient routing protocol than RIP. It provides more control over the routing process and responds faster to changes.

- **IGRP (Interior Gateway Routing Protocol)**   A Cisco distance vector routing protocol.

The primary exterior gateway protocol used on the Internet is BGP (Border Gateway Protocol). Refer to the BGP topic in this book for more information about autonomous system design and structure.

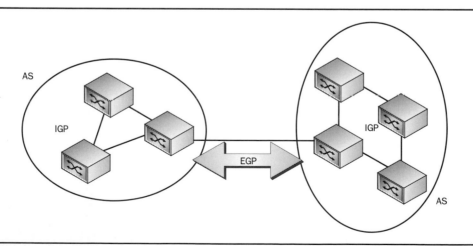

Figure A-19.   *Autonomous systems*

Refer to "Routing on the Internet" for a historical perspective on the development of autonomous systems and the protocols associated with them. The topic "Routing" provides additional information and links to associated sections.

Related Entries   BGP (Border Gateway Protocol); Internet; Internet Architecture and Backbone; Routers; Routing, *and* Routing on the Internet

 Linktionary! – Tom Sheldon's Encyclopedia of   http://www.linktionary.com/a/autonomous.html
Networking updates

Availability

See Data Center Design; Disaster Planning and Recovery; *and* Fault Tolerance and High-Availability Systems.

AWG (American Wire Gauge)

AWG is a measurement system for wire that specifies its thickness. As the thickness of the wire increases, the AWG number decreases. Some common cable conductor gauges are listed here:

Cable Type	Gauge
RS-232 serial cable	22 AWG and 24 AWG
Telephone cable	22 AWG, 24 AWG, and 28 AWG
Coaxial thick Ethernet cable	12 AWG
Coaxial thin Ethernet cable	20 AWG

Related Entry   Cable and Wiring

Baby Bells

The Baby Bells were the result of the restructuring agreement of AT&T in 1984. The agreement created 22 regional Bell operating companies (RBOCs).

Related Entries   AT&T; IXC (Inter-eXchange Carrier); LEC (Local Exchange Carrier); NPN (New Public Network); RBOC (Regional Bell Operating Companies); Service Providers and Carriers; Telecommunications and Telephone Systems; *and* Telecommunications Companies

Backbone Networks

The backbone network is an important architectural element for building enterprise networks. It provides a path for the exchange of information between different LANs or subnetworks. A backbone can tie together diverse networks in the same building, in different buildings in a campus environment, or over wide areas. Generally, the backbone's capacity is greater than the networks connected to it.

There are *distributed backbones* that snake throughout a building or campus to provide a connection point for LANs, and there are *collapsed backbones* that exist as wiring hubs and switches. The two topologies are illustrated in Figure B-1. A hybrid configuration ties together several collapsed backbone hubs or switches with a distributed backbone.

The distributed backbone on the left in Figure B-1 shows how the network (in this case, an FDDI ring) extends to each department or floor in a building. Each network is connected via a router to the backbone network. FDDI adds fault tolerance due to its ring topology. If one of the routers fails, the rest of the network stays connected.

In the collapsed backbone shown on the right, a cable runs from each department (or floor) network to a central hub or switch, usually located in a building wiring closet or management center. The backbone is reduced to a hub or switch and the network is configured with a star-wired topology. The hub or switch uses a variety of architectural designs, such as bus, shared memory, or matrix—as discussed under "Switch Fabric and Bus Design." A backbone is typically a network that interconnects other networks. In a switched network design, a backbone is not as clearly defined. It is usually just the high-speed switched that aggregates traffic from attached networks.

So far, our backbone has been limited to a single building. A backbone can link multiple networks in the campus environment or connect networks over wide area network links. These two approaches are pictured in Figure B-2. The fault tolerant ring topology of FDDI accommodates the campus backbone well. Another solution is Gigabit Ethernet fiber-optic links that connect to a central switch.

As for wide area networks, two approaches are possible. The private network approach is pictured on the right in Figure B-2. Dedicated leased lines are installed connecting all the sites—a costly proposition, especially if the sites are far from each other, because the cost of leased lines increases with distance.

B

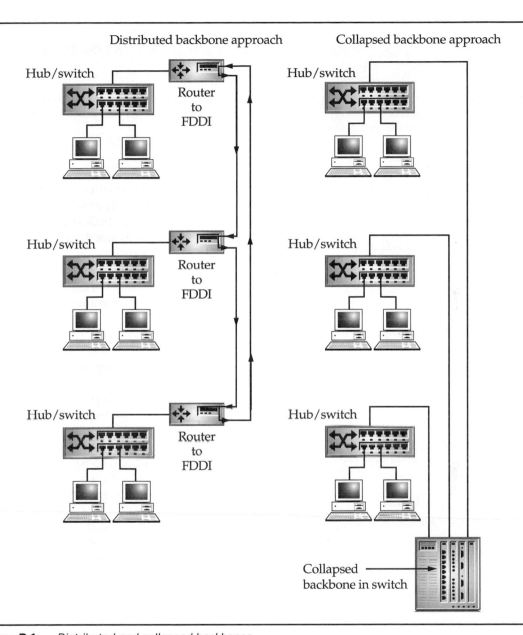

Distributed backbone approach   Collapsed backbone approach

Hub/switch

Router
to
FDDI

Hub/switch

Router
to
FDDI

Hub/switch

Router
to
FDDI

Hub/switch

Hub/switch

Hub/switch

Collapsed
backbone in switch

Figure B-1. *Distributed and collapsed backbones*

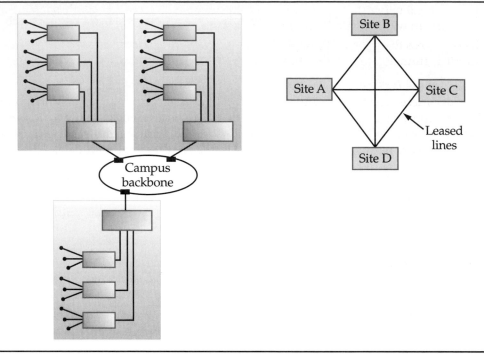

Figure B-2.   *Campus and wide area backbones*

A better approach to building wide area network backbones is to use carrier and service provider networks that provide frame relay, ATM, or other similar services, as discussed in "WAN (Wide Area Network)." Also see "Internet Architecture and Backbone."

The 80/20 and 20/80 Rules

An old rule for backbones was that 80 percent of the traffic stayed in the department, while 20 percent crossed the backbone. With this model, high data throughput rates on the backbone were not a priority. If your departmental networks used 10-Mbit/sec Ethernet, you could usually get by with a 100-Mbit/sec backbone.

However, the 80/20 rule no longer applies for most networks. In fact, it has reversed due to the following:

- Users that often communicate with one another are distributed throughout an organization rather than being in the same department.

- Servers may be physically located at a central site, so the majority of network traffic flows to the same place.

B

- Hierarchical networking schemes and centralized management naturally create a structure in which traffic flows to a central hub or switch.
- Users access the Internet through firewall gateways, which means that all Internet traffic is funneled to a central hub or switch and then out the Internet connection.

Because of these factors, there is a need to improve the performance of the backbone or come up with different network designs. Added to that is increased traffic load put on the network by multimedia applications, including live voice and videoconferencing applications.

ATM (Asynchronous Transfer Mode) has solved the traffic problems in many networks, including carrier core networks. Multiple ATM switches can be connected together in a mesh topology with redundant load-sharing links that handle high traffic loads at the core. An example is discussed in the ATM topic under the subheading "Hybrid ATM Networks."

Another choice is to build enterprise networks Gigabit Ethernet cores. It provides gigabit/sec (1,000-Mbit/sec) throughput on the backbone switch or between switches. It fits in well with existing Ethernet networks because the same frame format, medium access method, and other defining characteristics are retained. In most cases, a Gigabit Ethernet switch can replace older switches.

In general, switched-based building blocks are the components you need to build a high-speed hierarchical network that maintains high performance under big traffic loads. Refer to "Switching and Switched Networks" for more information on how to build the "new" networks. Also see "TIA/EIA Structured Cabling Standards."

In the wide area, many new approaches are available for connecting geographically dispersed networks. One method is to configure secure "tunnels" over the Internet in the form of VPNs (virtual private networks). Another approach is to connect with service providers that are taking advantage of optical networking technologies that significantly reduce WAN costs and improve performance and service options. Refer to "NGN (Next Generation Network)" and "WAN (Wide Area Network)" for more details.

Related Entries ATM (Asynchronous Transfer Mode); Cable and Wiring; FDDI (Fiber Distributed Data Interface); Frame Relay; Gigabit Ethernet; Internet Architecture and Backbone; Network Design and Construction; NGN (Next Generation Network); Switching and Switched Networks; VLAN (Virtual LAN); VPNs (Virtual Private Networks); *and* WAN (Wide Area Network)

Linktionary!—Tom Sheldon's Encyclopedia of Networking updates	http://www.linktionary.com/b/backbone.html
"Upgrading Your Network Backbone" article at Network Computing	http://networkcomputing.com/netdesign/bone1.html
"Strengthen Your Backbone" article at Information Week Online	http://www.informationweek.com/705/05olbck.htm
"Fortify Your Backbone" by Stephen Lawson	http://www.infoworld.com/cgi-bin/displayStory.pl?/features/980504backbone.htm
"Building High-speed Networks" by Tere Parnell (excerpt)	http://www.smartbooks.com/b911/bw902buildhispeednetchp.htm

Back-End Systems

"Back-end systems" loosely refers to servers, superservers, clustered systems, midrange systems, and mainframes that provide data services to users. The location of these services is often called the *server farm* or *data center*.

The server in client/server refers to the back-end systems. Client/server computing splits processing between a front-end application that runs on the client's workstation, and back-end services. Typical back-end services include database management systems (DBMSs), messaging systems (i.e., Lotus Notes and Microsoft Exchange), gateways to legacy systems such as IBM hosts, and network management systems.

Users interact with applications in front-end systems to make requests on back-end systems. The back-end systems then process the requests, searching and sorting data, serving up files, and providing other services. Back-end systems are *physically close* to data storage systems, so this arrangement uses the network efficiently.

Three-tier systems extend the client/server system by adding a middle system that performs some processing normally done by either the client or the server. Most important, the middle tier in mission-critical business environments holds the *business logic* (rules, procedures, and/or operational sequences) that is shared by all applications.

When Internet/intranet technologies are used, a Web server may exist at the middle tier. It accepts requests from clients, screens the requests, passes those requests to back-end systems, accepts the response, formats it into a Web page, and sends the Web page to the user. This system is scalable. If traffic increases, the Web server can distribute some of its workload to peer servers that are not as busy. See "Load Balancing."

For example, an online registration system built around Microsoft technology may employ Internet Explorer front-end interfaces and a Microsoft SQL Server back-end database. The middle tier consists of a Windows NT/Windows 2000 server running Microsoft Internet Information Server (IIS) that uses ActiveX technology and Active Server Pages (ASPs). When users access the Web server, the ActiveX components are downloaded to the client to provide client-side support for accessing the back-end database information.

Related Entries   Client/Server Computing; Clustering; Data Center Design; DBMS (Database Management System); Distributed Applications; Distributed Computer Networks; Distributed Object Computing; Load Balancing: Middleware and Messaging; Multitiered Architectures; *and* Web Technologies and Concepts

 Linktionary!—Tom Sheldon's Encyclopedia of   http://www.linktionary.com/b/back_end.html
Networking updates

Backplane Architecture

A backplane is a circuit board that includes peripheral connection slots into which I/O devices, processors, and other computer and networks components may be installed. The slots are connected to a high-speed communication bus or switching fabric that is controlled by an onboard processor and is also connected to onboard memory. A computer motherboard is the best example of a backplane, but other examples include backplanes in hubs, switches, and routers. There are various ways of implementing the bus architecture on a backplane in order to optimize performance. Several bus standards exist, as discussed in "Switch Fabrics and Bus Design."

B

Backup and Data Archiving

It is essential to back up the data on servers and other data systems throughout your network. That is obvious. This section describes a number of ways you can perform backups, including copying data to magnetic tape or optical disks, or by copying or replicating information to other systems. Before getting started, take note of the following terminology:

- A *backup* is a copy of online storage information that provides fault protection. An *archive* is a historical backup.

- An *online storage device* is a high-performance magnetic disk that stores information users access most often. *Nearline* and *offline storage devices* are slower, secondary storage devices that provide backup services or archiving services.

- *Hierarchical file systems* move little-used files or large image files from online storage to nearline storage systems such as optical disk, where they remain available to users. For more information, see "Storage Management Systems."

- *Tape backup systems* are the traditional backup medium while *optical disk systems* provide archiving and nearline storage requirements.

- *Real-time backups* take place at any time and must have a procedure for handling files that are open during backup. In most cases, the backup system tracks open files and returns to back them up later.

- *Disk mirroring* is a real-time strategy that writes data to two or more disks at the same time. If one disk fails, the other continues to operate and provide access for users. *Server mirroring* provides the same functionality, except that an entire server is duplicated. This strategy allows users to continue accessing data if one of the servers fails. See "Fault Tolerance and High Availability" for additional information on these strategies.

- *Replication* copies information to alternate servers on distributed networks to make that information more readily available to people in other locations. While replication is not necessarily a backup technique, replicated data on remote servers can be made available to local users should the server close to them go down.

- *Remote vaulting* is an automatic backup technique that transmits data to alternate sites. The alternate sites can be more than just warehouses for backups. They may be entire data centers that can be brought online when the primary data center goes offline in the event of a major disaster.

The traditional backup medium is magnetic tape. Tapes are relatively inexpensive, making it economical to devise an archiving scheme where you store tapes permanently at safe locations rather than reusing the tapes. You can refer to "Storage Systems and Management" for additional information.

This topic continues at Tom Sheldon's Linktionary! Web site. Refer to the Linktionary Web address listed at the end of this section. The link has an extensive list of backup and archiving vendors.

Related Entries   Clustering; Data Center Design; Data Migration; Data Protection; Disaster Recovery; Fault Management; Fault Tolerance and High Availability; Mirroring; Power and Grounding Problems and Solutions; Redundancy; Replication; Storage Management Systems; Storage Systems; *and* Technology

Linktionary!—Tom Sheldon's Encyclopedia of Networking updates	http://www.linktionary.com/b/backup.html
Availability.com	http://www.availability.com
Backup Strategies page at About.com (white papers and links)	http://compnetworking.miningco.com/compute/hardware/compnetworking/msubbackstrat.htm
Novell Research Network Services Topics (See Storage/Backup Services)	http://developer.novell.com/research/topical/network_services.htm

BACP (Bandwidth Allocation Control Protocol)

See BAP (Bandwidth Allocation Protocol) and BACP (Bandwidth Allocation Protocol).

Bandwidth

Bandwidth is the information-carrying capacity of a communication channel. The channel may be analog or digital. Analog transmissions such as telephone calls, AM and FM radio, and television are measured in cycles per second (hertz or Hz); and digital transmissions are measured in bits per second. For digital systems, the terms "bandwidth" and "capacity" are often used interchangeably, and the actual transmission capabilities are referred to as the data transfer rate (or just data rate).

It is helpful to think of a communication system like a water pipe or hose: the size of the pipe is analogous to bandwidth and the flow is analogous to data rate, as pictured in Figure B-3. Many people talk about the *speed* of a network system, but the term can be confusing. A bit propagates through a medium close to the speed of light. Now, how many bits can you transfer per second? That depends on the rate at which the transmitter can send data.

Communication systems have a stated bandwidth that defines the upper bounds of the system. For example, Fast Ethernet is rated at 100 Mbits/sec. But due to latency caused by congestion or other factors, a system may never operate at its optimal rate. *Throughput* is the "measured" performance of a system as opposed to its stated performance. It is a measure of an entire system, including transmitters, receivers, cable, and so on, and how much that system is affected by environmental factors like noise, data errors, attenuation due to cable distance, and so on. Because these conditions change, throughput varies over time and with each system. Refer to "Delay, Latency, and Jitter" and "Throughput" for additional information.

Copper cable, fiber-optic cable, and wireless communication systems all have different transmission characteristics and, thus, different bandwidths.

The telephone cable in the local loop has the potential of being a high-capacity link. However, the lines have traditionally been used for voice only, so the telephone company

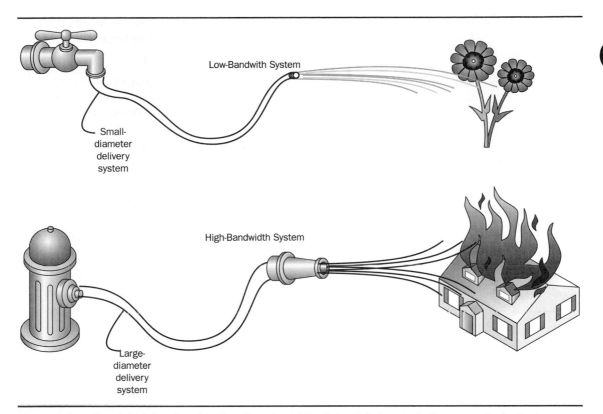

Figure B-3. *Bandwidth is related to the diameter of the "pipe." Data rate is the amount of actual information flowing through the "pipe."*

restricted the operating frequency of the cables to the voice range. Frequencies below 400 Hz and above 3,400 Hz are cut off, so the maximum bandwidth of the local loop is approximately 3,000 Hz. This is the passband, as pictured in Figure B-4. Modems convert digital information into analog signals that are transmitted in this range. Because the range is limited, data rates on telephone lines have been kept low. DSL removes this limitation.

Encoding and compression techniques have improved data rates. The higher the bandwidth of a data channel, the higher the transmission rate. For example, the fundamental frequency of Ethernet 1-BaseT (10 Mbit/sec) is 10 MHz, while Fast Ethernet (100 Mbits/sec) is 31.25 Mbits/sec. Still higher is fiber-optic cable, which uses the infrared light range (terahertz range) and has data rates in the multigigabit/sec range. Figure B-5 illustrates how higher frequencies transmit signal changes at a higher rate.

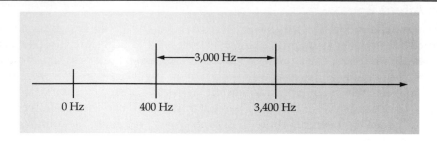

Figure B-4.   *Voice bandwidth on a telephone line*

There are some problems with increasing bandwidth. A large data file may be transferred to a system so quickly that the receiver does not have time to react. It may become overwhelmed with data before it can signal back to the sender to slow down. That causes dropped packets that must be resent. Networks that transfer bits in the gigabit-per-second range operate so fast that even a momentary delay within a single system along a transmission path may cause hundreds of packets to be dropped before the sender can be alerted to the problem.

Increasing bandwidth may not provide data rates that support real-time voice and video transfers. A single user transferring a large file can quickly consume all the bandwidth, holding up voice and video packets and causing delay distortions. The only real QoS solution is to reserve bandwidth in advance. Refer to "Bandwidth Management" and "QoS (Quality of Service)" for more details.

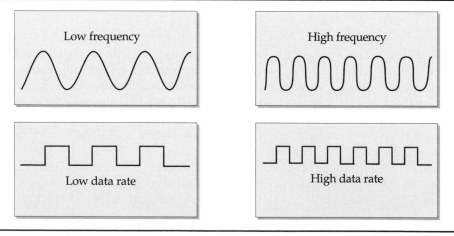

Figure B-5.   *Data rates for low and high frequencies*

How Protocols Affect Bandwidth

Packet overhead is a factor that reduces the actual data being sent. All packets contain some header information, so only a part of the packet is user data. In addition, some packets are used to send only control messages and no user data. As for Ethernet networks, the cable is shared by multiple users who must take turns using it. As more users access the network, contention increases and packets may require retransmission. In the end, a shared communication system like Ethernet may use only 20 percent to 40 percent of its stated capacity to deliver user data. Of course, switched Ethernet solves contention problems by reducing the number of users connected to a segment.

TCP has a set of mechanisms that are designed to find the most efficient way to transmit packets over network links. A sender will start transmitting at a slow rate and then build up its rate in order to avoid congesting the network. Congestion causes dropped packets. When the receiver fails to acknowledge receipt of packets, the sender starts to slow down. While the mechanism works, it relies on dropped packets as a signaling mechanism! So, alternative schemes have been proposed and developed.

An interesting measure of TCP performance is the "bandwidth x delay product," which measures the amount of data that can be pipelined (fill the data pipe). TCP uses *sliding window* mechanisms in which a large amount of buffer space at both the sender and receiver will allow the sender to maximize the throughput on the link (i.e., keep the pipeline full). Refer to "Sliding Windows Mechanisms," "Congestion Control Mechanisms," and "TCP (Transmission Control Protocol)" for more information.

Problems can arise on what are called "long, fat pipes" such as high-capacity packet satellite channels or cross-country fiber-optic paths running at 45 Mbits/sec and above. See the subheading "TCP Performance Issues" under the topic "TCP (Transmission Control Protocols)" for more information.

The following RFCs provide additional information about bandwidth utilization on TCP/IP Networks:

- RFC 1323 (TCP Extensions for High Performance, May 19920)

- RFC 2018 (TCP Selective Acknowledgemt Options, October 1996)

Bandwidth Requirements and Ratings

In the United States, the Federal Communications Commission (FCC) is in charge of allocating the electromagnetic spectrum and, thus, the bandwidth of various communication systems. In the electromagnetic spectrum, sound waves occupy low ranges, while microwaves, visible light, ultraviolet, and X-rays occupy upper ranges. The bandwidths occupied by various communication technologies are described in "Electromagnetic Spectrum."

The bandwidth requirements of various applications are listed in Table B-1. The rates are shown in bits/sec (bits per second), Kbits/sec (thousands of bits per second), Mbits/sec (millions of bits per second), and Gbits/sec (billions of bits per second). Compression and other techniques can reduce these requirements.

Application	Rate
Personal communications	300 to 9,600 bits/sec or higher
E-mail transmissions	2,400 to 9,600 bits/sec or higher
Remote control programs	9,600 bits/sec to 56 Kbits/sec
Digitized voice phone call	64,000 bits/sec
Database text query	Up to 1 Mbit/sec
Digital audio	1 to 2 Mbits/sec
Access images	1 to 8 Mbits/sec
Compressed video	2 to 10 Mbits/sec
Medical transmissions	Up to 50 Mbits/sec
Document imaging	10 to 100 Mbits/sec
Scientific imaging	Up to 1 Gbit/sec
Full-motion video	1 to 2 Gbits/sec

Table B-1.   *Bandwidth Requirements of Various Applications*

The transmission rates of various communication systems are listed in Table B-2. Compression techniques and signal encoding are used to boost data rates. For example, modems use the ITU V.42 bis data compression standard to compress data at a ratio of over 3 to 1. V.42 bis compresses and decompresses on the fly as data is sent and received by connected modems.

Type	Rate
Dial-up modem connection	1,200 bits/sec to 56 Kbits/sec
Serial port file transfers	2,000 bits/sec
ISDN (Integrated Services Digital Network)	64 Kbits/sec or 128 Kbits/sec
Fractional T1 digital WAN link	64 Kbits/sec
Parallel port	300 Kbits/sec
DirecPC (satellite) Internet downloads	400 Kbits/sec
DSL (Digital Subscriber Line)	512 Kbits/sec to 8 Mbits/sec

Table B-2.   *Transmission Rates of Various Communication Systems* (continues on next page)

Type	Rate
Cable (CATV) modems	512 Kbits/sec to 10 Mbits/sec (or higher)
T1 digital WAN link	1.544 Mbits/sec
ARCNET LANs	2.5 or 20 Mbits/sec
Token ring LANs	4 or 16 Mbits/sec
Ethernet LANs	10, 100, 1,000 Mbits/sec
T3 digital WAN link	44.184 Mbits/sec
HSSI (High-Speed Serial Interface)	52 Mbits/sec
FDDI (Fiber Distributed Data Interface)	100 Mbits/sec
Fibre Channel	1 Gbit/sec
Gigabit Ethernet	1 Gbit/sec
10GE (10 Gigabit Ethernet)	10 Gbits/sec
SONET (Synchronous Optical Network)	51.9 Mbits/sec to 2.5 Gbits/sec
Optical (lambda) networks implementing DWDM	Hundreds (or perhaps thousands) of lambdas per fiber, each running at 2.5 Gbits/sec

Table B-2.   *Transmission Rates of Various Communication Systems* (continued)

Related Entries   Bandwidth Brokerage; Bandwidth Management; Bandwidth on Demand; Broadband Communications; Cabling and Cable Installation; Channel; Circuit; Data Communication Concepts; Delay, Latency, and Jitter; Electromagnetic Spectrum; Modulation Techniques; Signals; *and* Throughput

Linktionary!—Tom Sheldon's Encyclopedia of Networking updates	http://www.linktionary.com/b/bandwidth.html
Jakob Nielsen's Law of Internet Bandwidth	http://www.useit.com/alertbox/980405.html
"Bandwidth and Latency: It's the Latency, Stupid" (Part 1) by Stuart Cheshire	http://www.tidbits.com/tb-issues/TidBITS-367.html#lnk4
"Bandwidth and Latency: It's the Latency, Stupid" (Part 2) by Stuart Cheshire	http://www.tidbits.com/tb-issues/TidBITS-368.html#lnk4
Tip Library "Bandwidth vs. Distance Latency"	http://www.pmg.com/tip_archive/July98.htm
"What is the speed of . . ." at Whatis.com (search for "bandwidth" and "speed")	http://www.whatis.com/thespeed.htm

Bandwidth Brokerage

A bandwidth brokerage treats bandwidth as a commodity that is easily resold. Bandwidth brokerages are essentially clearinghouses for bandwidth on public networks. The brokerages take advantage of the fact that bandwidth is no longer under the grip of traditional telecom pricing schemes. Telecom deregulation, competition, and the growing availability of bandwidth have affected these schemes.

 In another context, bandwidth brokers are "agents" that implement policy-based access control on intranets and the Internet as discussed in RFC 2768 (Network Policy and Services, February 2000). See "Policy-Based Management."

Clearinghouses make money by transacting bandwidth exchanges, usually between carriers and ISPs. Their goal is to make bandwidth trading easy. Clients can bid on the capacity they need or trade capacity they own but are not using. For example, a clearinghouse may post leased lines and telephone minutes for sale. Clients bid on the posting. The brokerage puts the bid winner together with a seller and charges a commission on the deal. Some brokerage services post the latest prices for leased lines and phone minutes, which network managers can use for comparison shopping.

Arbinet, in New York City, has developed what it calls the AGCN (Arbinet Global Clearing Network), which provides real-time authentication, authorization, least-cost routing, call placement, and settlement on a transaction-by-transaction basis. With AGCN, carriers gain access to information about the best rates and routing options without having to negotiate and contract separately with each supplier. According to Arbinet, AGCN members post for sale or purchase any capacity to any destination and attach specific parameters to define the conditions under which such trades will be authorized. The rest is performed automatically by the AGCN as it matches on a call-by-call basis any such available routes.

Related Entries Bandwidth; Bandwidth on Demand; Communication Services and Providers; *and* Telecommunications and Telephone Systems

Linktionary!—Tom Sheldon's Encyclopedia of Networking updates	http://www.linktionary.com/b/bandwidth_brokerage.html
Arbinet (New York)	http://www.arbinet.com
Band-X (London)	http://www.band-x.com
Cape Saffron (London)	http://www.capesaffron.com
Interxion (Amsterdam)	http://www.interxion.com
RateXchange Inc. (San Francisco)	http://www.ratexchange.com

Bandwidth Management

Bandwidth management is about making sure that enough bandwidth is available to meet traffic needs, and if not, managing the traffic in some way to ensure that critical traffic gets through. There are a number of topics in this book that deal with bandwidth management. Refer to the following topics for more information:

- **QoS (Quality of Service)**   This is the major topic in this book that covers the many ways that users and services are provided enough network bandwidth to ensure that data is delivered with minimal delay and packet loss.

- **CoS (Class of Service)**   CoS is a level of service that is promised to a client, not to be confused with QoS (quality of service). For example, you may choose next-day service from an express package service. That is a class of service. But the package may not arrive on time due to poor quality of service. You deserve a refund since the class of service you requested was not delivered.

- **Congestion Control Mechanisms**   This topic discusses why networks, especially packet-switched networks, cannot always deliver COS or QoS, even when adequate bandwidth appears to be available.

- **Differentiated Services (Diff-Serv)**   This topic covers work being done in the IETF Diff-Serv working group to define IP bandwidth management schemes using COS. In particular, the group is defining how to use the ToS (type of service) byte in the IP packet to identify prioritization of traffic.

- **Multimedia and Multimedia Networks**   This topic is not about bandwidth management, but it talks about why you are going to need it.

- **Policy-Based Management**   If bandwidth has to be allocated to specific users and applications in a fair (or unfair way), policies must be created to define who or what gets bandwidth and when. This topic describes how bandwidth is managed according to policies.

- **Traffic Management, Shaping, and Engineering**   The best example of traffic management and "shaping" is to use the analogy of how traffic management is done on crowded freeways. At on ramps, traffic lights may admit cars every few seconds in order to space them out and distribute the "load" on the freeway.

- **Load Balancing**   With load balancing, redundant network links and/or network services are provided to spread loads across redundant links or systems. At a Web site, traffic may come in over multiple aggregate links to a load-balancing system that will hand packets off to the least busy server or a server that is most appropriate for processing the packet.

- **VPN (Virtual Private Networks)**   A VPN is a tunneling technique that may provide QoS in some network environments. Protocols such as MPLS are meant to provide that over the Internet.

Finally, there are some topics that discuss how to build high-bandwidth networks, either in the enterprise or on the Internet. These topics include "Backbone Networks," "High-Speed/ High Perfomance Networking," "Link Aggregation," "MPLS (Multiprotocol Label Switching)," "Multilayer Switching," "Network Core Technologies," "Network Design and Construction," "NGN (Next Generation Network)," "Optical Networks," "Switch Fabrics and Bus Design," and "Switching and Switched Networks."

Linktionary!—Tom Sheldon's Encyclopedia of   http://www.linktionary.com/b/
Networking updates   bandwidth_management.html

Bandwidth on Demand

Bandwidth on demand is a data communication technique for providing additional capacity on a link as necessary to accommodate bursts in data traffic, a videoconference, or other special requirements. The technique is commonly used on dial-up lines and wide area networks (WANs) to temporarily boost the capacity of a link. Some call it "rubber bandwidth" because the capacity can be increased or decreased as needed. It is also called *dynamic bandwidth allocation* or *load balancing*. A similar technique is *bandwidth on time of day*, which refers to providing additional capacity at specific times of the day.

A network administrator who cannot be sure of traffic patterns between two sites can install routers that provide bandwidth-on-demand features. Such routers can automatically establish links on demand (dial-up, ISDN, or other switched services) to provide more capacity, and then bring the line down when traffic demands diminish. Home users with ISDN connections can aggregate two 64-Kbit/sec lines into a single 128-Kbit/sec line on demand.

Bandwidth on demand is both economical and practical. It makes sense to use a switched line and only pay for services as they are needed, rather than lease an expensive dedicated line that may go underused part of the time. Networks such as frame relay can automatically provide more capacity without the need to add additional lines, but the capacity is limited by the size of the trunk that connects a customer to the frame relay network.

Inverse multiplexing is typically used to combine individually dialed lines into a single, higher-speed channel. Data is divided over the lines at one end and recombined at the other end. Both ends of the connection must use the same inverse multiplexing and demultiplexing techniques. A typical dial-on-demand connection happens like this: A router on one end makes a normal connection, and then queries the router at the other end for additional connection information. When traffic loads are heavy, the additional connections are made to accommodate the traffic requirements.

The Lucent/Ascend Pipeline 75 remote access device determines when to add or subtract channels as follows. A specified time period is used as the basis for calculating average line utilization (ALU). The ALU is then compared to a target percentage threshold. When the ALU exceeds the threshold for a specified period of time, the Pipeline 75 attempts to add channels. When the ALU falls below the threshold for a specified period of time, it then removes the channels.

As an aside, a technique called *trunking* or *link aggregation* is like bandwidth on demand, but the bandwidth is usually made permanently available. Trunking is manually configured on internal network links to create additional bandwidth to high-volume servers and other devices. The usual configuration consists of two or more bonded Fast Ethernet channels between a switch and a server farm. See "Link Aggregation" and "Load Balancing" for more information.

Carrier Offerings

The telephone companies and other providers offer bandwidth on demand as part of their service offerings. Both ISDN and frame relay provide the services and have the potential to replace expensive dedicated leased lines such as T1 lines. As mentioned, basic rate ISDN has two 64-Kbit/sec B channels that can be combined into a single 128-Kbit/sec channel using bandwidth-on-demand techniques. For corporate users, AT&T provides worldwide switched digital services over an ISDN backbone that provides bandwidth on demand in increments of 64 Kbits/sec up to T1 rates (1.544 Mbits/sec).

A common telephone company offering called Multirate ISDN requires that you call the phone company in advance of needing the bandwidth and "demand" the extra bandwidth. This service is often used for videoconferencing where users need a specific bandwidth at a specific time.

An option for handling LAN traffic is MLPPP (Multilink PPP), an IETF recommendation. This protocol dynamically allocates bandwidth as needed and is supported in most vendors' routers. If you use MLPPP to get on the Internet, your ISP must have MLPPP equipment to support your dial-in connection. MLPPP is well suited for traffic bursts and overflows caused by backup sessions, conferences, large file transfers, or start-of-day traffic spikes. The protocol supports many different types of connections, including ISDN, frame relay, and analog lines; and it operates in software, making it more efficient for on-the-fly allocation of lines. BAP/BACP is an extension to the protocol that defines a way for devices from different vendors to negotiate bandwidth.

Related Entries   Bandwidth Management; BAP (Bandwidth Allocation Protocol) and BACP (Bandwidth Allocation Control Protocol); Bonding; Circuit-Switching Services; DDR (Dial-on-Demand Routing); Frame Relay; Inverse Multiplexing; ISDN (Integrated Services Digital Network); Link Aggregation; Load Balancing; MLPPP (Multilink PPP); *and* WAN (Wide Area Network)

Linktionary!—Tom Sheldon's Encyclopedia of Networking updates

http://www.linktionary.com/b/bandwidth_on_demand.html

Bandwidth Reservation

See Bandwidth Management.

Banyan VINES

Banyan VINES is a network operating system with a UNIX kernel that allows users of popular PC desktop operating systems such as DOS, OS/2, Windows, and those for Macintosh systems to share information and resources with each other and with host computing systems. VINES first appeared in the 1980s. It provides full UNIX NFS (Network File System) support in its core services and the Transmission Control Protocol/Internet Protocol (TCP/IP) for transport. It also includes Banyan's StreetTalk Directory Services, one of the first viable directory services to appear in a network operating system. In October of 1999, Banyan became ePresence, a provider of Internet services. At the same time, it announced the obsolescence of VINES and other Banyan products.

Banyan Product Support	http://products.banyan.com/
EPresence	http://www.epresence.com/
Cisco Internetworking Technology Overview (see Banyan Vines topic)	http://www.cisco.com/univercd/cc/td/doc/ cisintwk/ito_doc/
Cisco Troubleshooting Internetworking Systems (see "Troubleshooting Banyan VINES")	http://www.cisco.com/univercd/cc/td/doc/ cisintwk/tis_doc/index.htm

BAP (Bandwidth Allocation Protocol) and BACP (Bandwidth Allocation Control Protocol)

BACP is an Internet protocol that helps users manage a combination of dial-up links, usually over ISDN (Integrated Services Digital Network) connections. The protocol is defined in RFC 2125 (The PPP Bandwidth Allocation Protocol [BAP] and The PPP Bandwidth Allocation Control Protocol [BAPC], March 1997).

BACP provides what is called *dial on demand* (or *bandwidth on demand),* a technique for providing additional bandwidth as needed by combining two or more circuits into a single circuit with a higher data throughput rate. The technique is useful for accommodating bursts in traffic, videoconferencing, backup sessions, and other requirements.

Basic rate ISDN consists of two digital circuits for home or business use. The circuits can be used for two separate phone calls, a phone call and a computer connection, or two separate computer connections. Each circuit provides a data rate of 64 Kbits/sec. In addition, the circuits can be combined into a single 128-Kbit/sec channel. You use dial on demand to automatically combine channels when data traffic increases beyond the capacity of a single channel. One advantage of dialing on demand with ISDN is that calls are usually charged on a per-call basis. When the demand falls back, the second line is automatically disconnected to save phone charges.

BACP adds features to the IETF's MLPPP (Multilink PPP). BACP extends Multilink PPP by providing a way for different vendors' equipment to negotiate for additional bandwidth. Routers exchange BACP messages to negotiate link requirements for providing extra bandwidth or to take lines down when extra bandwidth is no longer needed.

Refer to RFC 2125 for more information, or the Network Computing article listed in the following, which put BAC/BACP into context with MLPPP.

Related Entries   Bandwidth Management; Bandwidth on Demand; Bonding; Circuit-Switching Services; DDR (Dial-on-Demand Routing); Inverse Multiplexing; ISDN (Integrated Services Digital Network); Link Aggregation; Load Balancing; *and* MLPPP (Multi-Link PPP)

Linktionary!—Tom Sheldon's Encyclopedia of Networking updates	http://www.linktionary.com/b/bap.html
"Getting the Most Out of Your Bandwidth" Network Computing article	http://networkcomputing.com/1023/ 1023ws1.html
BACP, PPP Bandwidth Allocation Control Protocol document at Network Sorcery	http://www.networksorcery.com/enp/protocol/ bacp.htm

B

Baseband Network

Baseband is a transmission method in which direct current pulses are applied directly to the cable to transmit digital signals. The discrete signal consists of either high- or low-voltage pulses that represent binary 1s and 0s or that hold binary information in encoded form. For more information, see "Signals." A baseband network is usually limited to a local area. Ethernet is a baseband network that transmits only one signal at a time.

The direct current signals placed on a baseband transmission system tend to degrade over distance due to attenuation and other factors. In addition, outside interference from electrical fields generated by motors, fluorescent lights, and other electrical devices can further corrupt the signal. The higher the data transmission rate, the more susceptible the signal is to degradation. For this reason, networking standards such as Ethernet specify cable types, cable shielding, cable distances, transmission rates, and other details that must be conformed to in order to guarantee quality service.

Compare baseband to broadband transmission. Most people refer to broadband as any date rate above what can be sent over a telephone circuit. That is 56 Kbits/sec for a standard line or 128 Kbits/sec for ISDN. A broadband system may have its bandwidth divided into channels—some for sending, some for receiving, and some for transmitting different types of information and data.

Related Entries   Bandwidth; Broadband Communications and Networking; Cable and Wiring; Ethernet; *and* Signals

Bastion Host

A bastion host is a security firewall that protects an internal network from attacks that come from external networks. A firewall may separate one department network from another, or an enterprise network from the Internet. The bastion host is the main point of contact to the outside and so is the most vulnerable system.

Related Entries   Firewall; Hacking and Hackers; Proxy Server; *and* Security

Baud

Baud is a measure of signal changes per second in a device such as a modem. It represents the number of times the state of a communication line changes per second. The name comes from the Frenchman Baudot, who developed an encoding scheme for the French telegraph system in 1877.

Baud is rarely used to refer to modem speeds because it does not have a relationship to the number of bits transferred per second on high-speed modems. If a modem transferred 1 bit for every signal change, then its bits-per-second rate and baud rate would be the same. However, encoding techniques are employed to make 1 baud, or signal change, represent 2 or more bits. Two bits per baud is known as dibit encoding and 3 bits per baud is known as tribit encoding.

Related Entries   Analog Signals; Broadcasts; Data Communication Concepts; Modems; Modulation Techniques; *and* Signals

Beans

Yes, there is a networking term called "beans." Well, JavaBeans, to be exact. Java Beans is an architecture that assists in the development of reusable software components and makes Java components interoperable in intranet and Internet environments.

See the "JavaBeans" subheading under "Java" for more information.

Bell Modem Standards

The Bell standards were the first modem communications protocols. The first of these standards was Bell 103, which paved the way for today's complex and efficient modem standards, such as V.32bis and V.42bis. While AT&T largely controlled the standardization of the original modem standards, the CCITT (Consultative Committee for International Telegraph and Telephone), established as part of the United Nations' ITU (International Telecommunications Union), controls most standardization today. The Bell standards are summarized here:

- **Bell 103**   Supports 300-baud full-duplex asynchronous modem transmissions.
- **Bell 113A and 113D**   A originates calls, and D answers calls.
- **Bell 201B**   Supports synchronous 2,400-bits/sec full-duplex transmissions.
- **Bell 202**   Supports asynchronous 1,800-bits/sec full-duplex transmissions.
- **Bell 208**   Supports synchronous 4,800-bit/sec transmissions.
- **Bell 209**   Supports synchronous 9,600-bit/sec full-duplex transmissions.
- **Bell 212A**   Supports 1,200-bit/sec full-duplex transmissions (equivalent CCITT V.22 standard).

Many other standards have been developed since these initial standards, such as the CCITT "V dot" series standards. Microcom, a modem and communications software vendor, developed several standards on its own that have also come into widespread use or been integrated into ITU standards.

Related Entries   Asynchronous Communications; Data Communication Concepts; MNP (Microcom Networking Protocol); Modems; Modulation Techniques; Serial Communications and Interfaces; *and* Synchronous Communication.

Bell Operating Companies

See AT&T; LEC (Local Exchange Carrier); RBOCs (Regional Bell Operating Companies); Service Providers and Carriers; *and* Telecordia Technologies.

Bellman-Ford Distance-Vector Routing Algorithm

The Bellman-Ford distance-vector routing algorithm is used by routers on internetworks to exchange routing information about the current status of the network and how to route packets to their destinations. The algorithm basically merges routing information provided by different routers into lookup tables. It is well defined and used on a number of popular networks. It also provides reasonable performance on small- to medium-sized networks, but on larger networks the algorithm is slow at calculating updates to the network topology. In some cases, looping occurs, in which a packet goes through the same node more than once. In general, most DVR (distance-vector routing) algorithms are not suitable for larger networks that have thousands of nodes, or if the network configuration changes often. In the latter case, the routing algorithm must be able to dynamically update the routing tables quickly to accommodate changes. A more efficient routing protocol is OSPF (Open Shortest Path First).

Related Entries   Distance Vector Routing; OSPF (Open Shortest Path First) Protocol; RIP (Routing Information Protocol; *and* Routing

Benchmarking

See Testing, Diagnostics, and Troubleshooting.

BeOS

BeOS is an operating system designed from the ground up to include all of the latest technologies available to desktop and network operating systems. Its designers hoped to avoid the problems that plague operating systems that evolve from, and must stay compatible with, older, legacy operating systems. In 1990, Jean-Louis Gassée, former president of Apple's product division, formed Be, Inc. to create BeOS.

BeOS is an operating system on the level of Windows 98 and Mac OS that runs on PowerPC and Intel processors. It supports preemptive multitasking and multithreading, symmetric multiprocessing, and an object-oriented application programming interface. In particular, the architecture is designed to support real-time, high bandwidth applications like audio and video. Some of the first applications available for BeOS were audio and video editing suites.

In terms of networking, BeOS fully supports the AppleTalk and TCP/IP protocol suites and can operate as a client to most popular network operating systems. It also provides file sharing through AppleTalk services; ftp; and, in the future, NFS (Network File System).

Related Entries   AppleTalk; Network Operating Systems; *and* NFS (Network File System)

Be, Inc., home page	http://www.be.com/
BEOSCENTRAL.COM	http://www.beoscentral.com/
A news site about BeOS	http://www.beforever.com/
OmicronSoft, a BeOS software developer	http://www.omicronsoft.com/

Best-Effort Delivery

Best-effort delivery describes a network service in which the network does not provide any special features that recover lost or corrupted packets. These services are instead provided by end systems. By removing the need to provide these services, the network operates more efficiently. The postal service delivers letters using a best-effort delivery approach. You don't know for sure whether a letter has been delivered. However, you can pay extra for a delivery confirmation receipt, which requires that the carrier get a signature from the recipient and return it to you.

In the TCP/IP protocol suite, TCP provides guaranteed services while IP provides best-effort delivery. TCP performs the equivalent of obtaining a delivery confirmation from the recipient and returning it to the sender. Because IP provided basic packet delivery services without guarantees, it is called a best-effort delivery service. It does its best to deliver packets to the destination, but takes no steps to recover packets that are lost or misdirected.

The early Internet protocol suite consisted only of TCP and IP (although IP was not differentiated as a separate service). During development, TCP protocol designers realized a need for timeliness rather than accuracy. In other words, speed was more important than packet recovery. In real-time voice or video transfers, a few lost packets are tolerable. Recovering them creates excessive overhead that reduces performance. To accommodate this type of traffic, TCP was reorganized into TCP, IP, and UDP. The basic addressing and packet-forwarding services in the network layer were called IP. TCP and UDP are in the transport layer on top of IP. Both use IP's services, but UDP is a stripped-down version of TCP that provides applications with access to IP's best-effort services. Applications go through UDP when they don't need TCP's services.

With best-effort services, packet discard is acceptable because recovery is handled by other services. Figure B-6 illustrates where discards may occur. In the lower physical and data link layers, frames may be corrupted and dropped. In the network layer, congested routers drop packets.

TCP is a reliable data delivery service that end systems use to recover packets that are dropped in the network due to congestion, or that are dropped at the end system itself due to overflowing buffers. In the network, packets may be dropped on purpose to "signal" congestion to the sender. When a packet is dropped in a TCP connection, the receiver fails to acknowledge it and the sender slows down its transmissions. These mechanisms are discussed further under "Congestion Control Mechanisms," "Flow Control Mechanisms," and "Reliable Data Delivery Services."

Related Entries   Anycasting; Acknowledgment; Congestion Control Mechanisms; Connection-Oriented and Connectionless Services; Data Communication Concepts; Data Link Protocols; Datagrams and Datagram Services; Flow-Control Mechanisms; Internet Protocol Suite; IP (Internet Protocol); Network Architecture; Network Concepts; Packet and Cell Switching; Packets; Reliable Data Delivery Services; Routing; TCP (Transmission Control Protocol); Throughput; *and* UDP (User Datagram Protocol)

Information on the Internet

Linktionary!—Tom Sheldon's Encyclopedia of Networking updates	http://www.linktionary.com/b/best_effort.html
Introduction to the Internet Protocols at Rutgers	http://oac3.hsc.uth.tmc.edu/staff/snewton/ tcp-tutorial/sec2.html

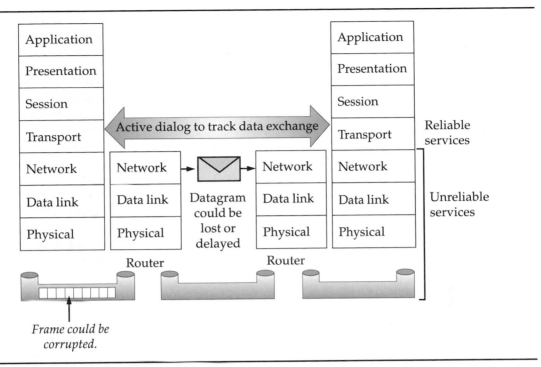

Figure B-6.   *Best-effort, connectionless services do not resolve transmission problems. That is done by the transport layer.*

BGP (Border Gateway Protocol)

BGP is a TCP/IP-based *exterior* routing protocol that is used between autonomous systems (ASs), primarily on the Internet. An AS is basically an Internet service provider in this context, although it defines any group of networks managed by a central authority. ASs are also referred to as *domains*.

In contrast, *Interior* routing protocols, such as OSPF (Open Shortest Path First), operate inside autonomous systems. Refer to RFC 1403 (BGP OSPF Interaction, January 1993) for information about interfacing between BGP and OSPF.

BGP runs in the routers that are connected to other autonomous systems. Those routers are called *boundary routers*. They are truly gateways because they provide connections to networks outside of the autonomous system. BGP exchanges routing and reachability information over these links.

Currently, BGP is in version 4, which supports CIDR (Classless Inter-domain Routing). Refer to "Routing on the Internet" for a historical perspective on the development of Internet routing, including information about the earlier EGP protocol.

| Note | RFC 1771 (Border Gateway Protocol 4, March 1995) describes the latest version of BGP. For a complete list of related RFCs, refer to the IETF Inter-Domain Routing (idr) Working Group Web site listed at the end of this topic. |

Generally, routing protocols discover the topology of an internetwork and create lookup tables that provide packet-forwarding information. A router looks in the table to determine the best way to forward a packet to its destination. On the Internet, packets are sent between domains and across domains. In the latter case, a packet transits across one or more domains to get to its destination. For example, a packet leaves your organization's domain, and transits your local ISP's domain and possibly other domains before arriving at its destination.

An analogy is useful here. A business owner makes a trip from her New York office to her LA office. She takes a cab to La Guardia, flies to LAX, and then takes a cab to the LA office. The cab drivers know about local topologies (intra-city routes). The airline knows about inter-city routes. There is no need for an airline to track the final destination of its passengers. It only needs to get the passenger to the destination city. All other "people routing" information is nonessential to the airline. In this analogy, the cities are domains. The airlines provide exterior routing and the taxis provide interior routing.

BGP is the routing protocol that service providers are now using across the Internet to exchange information about routes between and among ASs. Some large ISPs manage nearly 100,000 BGP routes in their Internet core backbone routers. In 1994, that number was only 15,000 routes.

Traffic exchange agreements and policies are put into place by connected autonomous systems. Your organization has a traffic exchange agreement with one or more ISPs. In the same way, ISPs have traffic exchange agreements with one another.

Autonomous Systems (Domains)

An autonomous system is a grouping of networks (in a much larger network) with one or more gateways that connect it with other autonomous systems. On the Internet, ISPs and national backbone service providers run their own autonomous systems. ASs have a unique identifying 16-bit number between 0 and 65,535. Some large organizations, such as universities, may have numerous internal autonomous systems and use BGP to route among those systems in the same way BGP is used on the Internet.

Gateways "announce" the networks that are reachable inside the AS. Since only network addresses are announced, the amount of routing information that is exchanged and stored in routing tables is minimized.

Figure B-7 shows three possible AS topologies. The single-homed stub AS on the left does not have any downstream ASs of its own. This could be your own organization's internal network. In this case, you don't really need BGP. Instead, you set up a default route to the ISP. This route then becomes a gateway to the outside world.

The middle configuration consists of a stub AS (no downstream AS) that is multihomed, meaning that it is connected to more than one upstream service provider. In this example, each upstream AS announces the routes of the stub AS. Finally, the right configuration is a multihomed transit AS. *Transit* implies that traffic from other ASs passed through it. For this to take place, the transit AS must obtain route information for other ASs that it can reach and provide it to the other ASs that it is attached to.

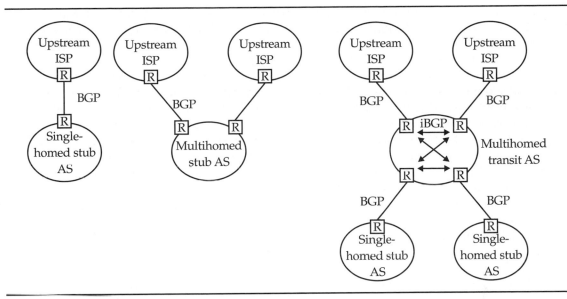

Figure B-7.   *Three possible AS topologies addressed by BGP*

As mentioned, an AS is defined by an AS number. However, private networks that are attached to a single ISP do not need an AS number. Those networks can become extensions of their ISP's AS number. But if an AS is multihomed (connected to multiple ISPs), it must have an AS number to identify it on each of the possible paths that are available.

iBGP

A version of BGP called iBGP is used to exchange BGP information internally within a transit AS to each of the AS's boundary routers. A default route is manually created across the internal network among the boundary routers for carrying the iBGP information. The internal network still uses an internal routing protocol.

When a packet arrives at a boundary router, a lookup may determine that its destination is not within the AS. The packet is then transmitted across the internal network to the appropriate border router and forwarded to the next AS.

BGP and CIDR

BGP version 4 supports CIDR (Classless Inter-domain Routing). Actually, the two are essential requirements for today's Internet. Both solved (at least temporarily) the Internet's scaling problem, which was becoming serious in the early 1990s.

CIDR provides topological addressing. The addressing scheme is hierarchical and, as the name implies, classless (the old class A, B, and C scheme is not used—see the "CIDR" heading and "IP" heading for more details). A major ISP is assigned a large block of contiguous addresses with a specific address prefix. This ISP then assigns network addresses to its customers from the contiguous block.

The important concept is that the address block is contiguous so that all the internal/ downstream networks can be reached by the major ISP's network prefix. Once an incoming packet reaches the ISP's network, internal routing directs it appropriately. All of this internal routing information is hidden to the larger Internet. Thus, routing information and routing table sizes are reduced at the top levels of the Internet.

The telephone system uses a similar scheme. An area code is assigned to a specific geographic area. People outside the area can connect with any phone within the area by first dialing the area code prefix, then the local phone number. Most important, the caller's telephone company does not need to keep a database of phone numbers available in other area codes. It just directs the call to that area where local switching equipment connects the call.

The whole BGP4/CIDR scheme provides *route aggregation*, which allows the Internet to scale. For example, less than 65,000 routes are exchanged across the Internet, which is a pretty small number when compared to the actual number of networks attached to the Internet. Refer to RFC 2519 (A Framework for Inter-Domain Route Aggregation, February 1999) for more information.

BGP Operation

BGP uses a combination of distance-vector and link-state routing algorithms. First, it constructs AS path information that defines how to get to a particular AS. Thus, BGP acts like a link-state protocol in the way that it obtains network topology information. Initially, an entire routing information table is exchanged between BGP routers, but after that, updates are transmitted on a periodic basis. This is a distance-vector protocol technique.

The BGP-4 routing tables contain information about paths to other networks. This information includes a network address and an *AS path* value. The network address identifies ASs and the AS path describes how to reach those ASs. A gateway with a packet to forward looks up the destination network number in the table and then forwards the packet along the AS path.

In the case of multiple paths, an administrator can use a metric to assign a preference for one path over another. This metric provides a form of policy routing in that values can be assigned based on criteria such as the bandwidth of a path or the autonomous systems that it passes through.

An example of the way BGP exchanges information is described next and pictured in Figure B-8. In this example, a multihomed AS (AS-1) announces its network number to the two upstream ASs (AS-2 and AS-3). Keep in mind that there are two paths between AS-1 and AS-5:

- ■ AS-1 sends path vector (20.10.0.0/16, AS-1) to AS-2 and AS-3.
- ■ AS-2 sends path vector (20.10.0.0/16, AS-2, AS-1) to AS-5.
- ■ AS-3 sends path vector (20.10.0.0/16, AS-3, AS-1) to AS-4
- ■ AS-4 sends path vector (20,10.0.0/16, AS-4, AS-3, AS-1) to AS-5

B

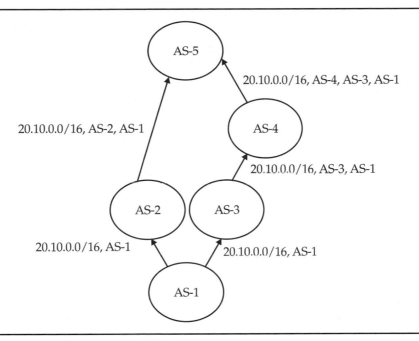

Figure B-8. *How BGP exchanges information*

RFC 1771 defines four types of BGP messages for transmitting information between BGP routers. These messages may be exchanged after the routers make a TCP connection. TCP is used because it provides reliable delivery. There four messages are

- **Open message** Opens a BGP communication session between peer BGP routers.
- **Keep-alive message** After a BGP session is opened, keep-alive messages are sent every 60 seconds to ensure that connections are still alive.
- **Update message** This message is used to exchange routing information such as updates to the routing table. Route withdrawals may also be sent to remove a route from a table.
- **Notification message** Used to report errors and close BGP communication sessions.

The contents of these fields are fully described in RFC 1771; however, a brief description of the update message is important since it describes the type of information that is exchanged between BGP routers. The message format is pictured in Figure B-9.

- **Unfeasible Route Length** The length of the next field (Withdrawn Routes). Value 0 indicates no withdrawn routes.
- **Withdrawn Routes** Address prefixes for the routes that are being withdrawn from service.

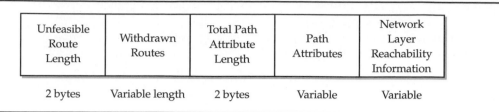

Unfeasible Route Length	Withdrawn Routes	Total Path Attribute Length	Path Attributes	Network Layer Reachability Information
2 bytes	Variable length	2 bytes	Variable	Variable

Figure B-9.   *BGP update message format*

- **Total Path Attribute Length**   The length of the next field (Path Attributes).
- **Path Attributes**   A variable-length sequence of path attributes that is present in every update message.

The Path Attributes field may contain the following information:

- **Origin**   Defines the origin of the path information (how learned), via interior routing protocol, exterior routing protocol, or other means.
- **AS Path**   Contains a sequence of AS path segments.
- **Next Hop**   Contains the IP address of the border router that should be used as the next hop to the destinations listed in the Network Layer Reachability field. This field changes as the messages pass through a border router, but not an interior router.
- **Multi Exit Disc**   An arbitrary metric that can be used to assign metrics to paths when more than one path exists to a destination.
- **Local Pref**   Used by a BGP speaker to inform other BGP speakers in its own autonomous system of the originating speaker's degree of preference for an advertised route.
- **Atomic Aggregate**   BGP speakers use this field to inform other BGP speakers that the local system selected a less specific route without selecting a more specific route that is included in it.
- **Aggregator**   Contains the last AS number that formed the aggregate route, followed by the IP address of the BGP speaker that formed the aggregate route.

As mentioned, RFC 1771 describes these fields and the functions in more detail. One of the most important features of BGP is its ability to avoid loops. This is achieved by routers refusing to accept route information that already contains the local AS as the AS path vector.

An aggregation scheme is also supported in which an upstream AS can aggregate routes from different downstream ASs if they have similar network prefixes (i.e., contiguous IP addresses). The route entries are combined into a single route entry that encompasses all the combined routes.

For more information, refer to the Web sites listed next, or contact specific router vendors to obtain details about the particular exterior routing protocol implementation in their systems.

Related Entries   Autonomous System; CIDR (Classless Interdomain Routing); IDPR (Inter-Domain Policy Routing Protocol); Internet; Internet Architecture and Backbone; IP (Internet Protocol); IS-IS (Intermediate System-to-Intermediate System) Routing; ISPF (Open Shortest Path First) Protocol; Routing; Routing Registies; *and* Routing on the Internet

Linktionary!—Tom Sheldon's Encyclopedia of Networking updates	http://www.linktionary.com/b/bgp.html
IETF Inter-Domain Routing (idr) Working Group (look here for relevant RFCs and drafts)	http://www.ietf.org/html.charters/idr-charter.html
IETF drafts about BGP (search for "BGP" at this site)	http://search.ietf.org/search/brokers/internet-drafts/query.html
Cisco Documentation: Border Gateway Protocol	http://www.cisco.com/univercd/cc/td/doc/cisintwk/ito_doc/bgp.htm
Cisco Documentation: Using the Border Gateway Protocol for Interdomain Routing (refer to this document for extensive coverage)	http://www.cisco.com/univercd/cc/td/doc/cisintwk/ics/icsbgp4.htm
Cisco documentation: "Designing Large-Scale IP Internetworks" (includes sections about IGRP, OSPF, and BGP)	http://www.cisco.com/univercd/cc/td/doc/cisintwk/idg4/nd2003.htm
Cisco BGP Technical Tips	http://cio.cisco.com/warp/public/459/18.html
"Internet Exterior Routing Protocol Development: Problems, Issues, and Misconceptions" by Tim Bass	http://www.silkroad.com/papers/html/pba/n1.html
Avi Freedman's BGP routing paper	http://www.netaxs.com/~freedman/bgp.html
Frequently Asked Questions on Multi-homing and BGP	http://info.connect.com.au/docs/routing/general/multi-faq.shtml#q1
NLANP BGP Statistics page	http://cabrienlanr.net/BGP/
Joe Lindsay's "The BGP Page" with a list of BGP RFCs	http://www.mindspring.com/~jlindsay/bgp.html

Bindery

The bindery is a database file in the NetWare network operating systems for versions previous to NetWare 3.*x*. It holds security, accounting, and name management information for the server on which NetWare is installed. Because NetWare servers that use binderies still exist in many environments, newer versions of NetWare provide bindery emulation to support them. NDS (Novell Directory Services) replaced the bindery in later versions of NetWare, although the bindery is still supported.

Every pre-NetWare 3.*x* server maintains its own bindery. The bindery contains *object* records. Objects are server entities, such as users, groups, and the server name. Objects have attributes, called *properties*, such as passwords, account restrictions, account balances, group membership, and so on. Properties have values, which are kept in a separate but related file.

For more information about the NetWare network operating system, see "Novell NetWare."

Novell list of paper about the Binder   http://developer.novell.com/research/topical/
                                                  netware_servers.htm

Biometric Access Devices

Biometrics adds another dimension to the logon/authentication process. Biometrics identifies some physical trait of the user logging on and uses that information, along with a username and password in most cases, to authenticate the user. Physical traits include fingerprints, voice, and facial and iris/retina features.

In many environments, username/password access is not strong enough to make network administrators feel comfortable that their systems are secure. To improve security, administrators may consider "smart card" token access devices (see "Token-Based Authentication") or biometric access devices, as covered here. Of course, other access methods are available, but they are somewhat esoteric and expensive. Others are just emerging or may only be applicable to certain situations. For example, the GPS (Global Positioning System) can be used to verify that a user is logging on from the location where his or her computer is located.

Biometrics identifies the actual person who has authorized access by his or her physical traits. In contrast, token-based systems are based on an external physical device that is carried by the person. Technically, both systems can be compromised with brute force—literally. For example, an attacker could force an authorized user to reveal his or her secret password, steal the token device, and then attempt to logon from any remote system that accepts the password and token code. In contrast, biometric logon usually only takes in specific locations in which the biometric devices are located. An attacker would need to force the authorized user to scan his or her fingers, eyes, face, and so on, at that location. If guards are posted or other people are around, this could be a little difficult.

Here are four types of biometric identification techniques:

■ **Face recognition**   A camera is used to capture a user's face and match facial features with a database of known users. Cheap video cameras, mounted on computer displays, may make this technology reasonable for every desktop. The cameras may also be used for videoconferencing. Face scanning is also non-intimidating to most users (as opposed to scanning eyes).

■ **Finger scanning**   A light scanner is used to read the unique whorls on fingertips. These devices are relatively inexpensive, but best suited for clean environments. Hand scanners may be more appropriate in dirty environments.

■ **Hand scanning**   This type of scanner scans an entire hand or the palm of a hand, which provides unique identification information without the higher resolutions required in finger scanners. The size and shape of the hand, as well as its unique lines, are used in the identification.

■ **Iris/retina scanning**   Eye scanners may provide the most accurate identification, but users may be apprehensive about using them. They are also the most expensive.

- **Signature recognition**   Devices that recognize signatures are categorized as behavioral devices because they recognize a nonphysical aspect of a person. Users write their signature on a small tablet-like device and features of the signatures are compared to a user database.

- **Voice recognition**   Like signature recognition devices, voice print devices are categorized as behavioral. The security system stores unique information about a person's voice that is compared to a phrase the user says when logging on. Voice recognition can be used over phone lines if necessary.

The Web sites listed in the following provide extensive information on biometric technologies. Many new products are emerging, and prices are sure to drop as development costs are recouped and the technologies take hold.

Related Entries   Access Control; Authentication and Authorization; Certificates and Certification Systems; CHAP (Challenge Handshake Authentication Protocol); Cryptography; Digital Signatures; EAP (Extensible Authentication Protocol); FORTEZZA; Hash Functions; Kerberos Authentication Protocol; Logons and Logon Accounts; One-Time Password Authentication; Passwords; Secret-Key Cryptography; Security; *and* Token-Based Authentication

Linktionary!—Tom Sheldon's Encyclopedia of Networking updates	http://www.linktionary.com/b/biometric.html
The Biometrics Consortium	http://www.biometrics.org/
The Biometric Digest	http://webusers.anet-stl.com/~wrogers/biometrics/
National Biometric Test Center (NBTC)	http://www-engr.sjsu.edu/biometrics/
Biometric Identification, Inc.	http://www.biometricid.com/
Identix Incorporated fingerprint security products	http://www.identix.com/
Miros face identification software	http://www.etrue.com
Mytec Technologies fingerprint security products	http://www.mytec.com/
SAC Technologies fingerprint, voice, and facial identification products	http://www.sacman.com/
American Biometrics Company	http://www.abio.com
SAFLINK Corporation fingerprint, voice, and facial identification products	http://www.saflink.com/home.html
Visionics	http://www.visionics.com
Who? Vision Systems, Inc., fingerprint identification	http://www.whovision.com/

B-ISDN (Broadband ISDN)

ISDN (Integrated Services Digital Network) development began in the 1980s as part of a plan by the carriers to develop a single integrated network transmitting voice, video, and data communications. B-ISDN development began in 1988 as developers saw a need for bandwidth above 155 Mbits/sec in anticipation of future video and multimedia services. ATM was developed from this work as the underlying transport, with B-ISDN being the overlying technology for controlling the network. Figure B-10 illustrates the B-ISDN architecture. ATM cells are delivered across a physical SONET network.

In general, ISDN is based on 64-Kbit/sec channels. These channels are just wide enough to handle a digitized voice call. All other ISDN implementations are some multiple of this basic service. A typical user signs up for basic rate ISDN, which consists of two 64-Kbit/sec channels (called the B channels) and one 16-Kbit/sec D channel used for signaling. The B channels can be used individually for separate voice calls or combined to create a 128-Kbit/sec data channel. Primary rate ISDN consists of 23 B channels and one 64-Kbit/sec signaling channel. ISDN is useful for networking because the customer can add bandwidth in increments of 64 Kbits/sec as needed.

ISDN is a switched service and is designed around intelligent switching components in the carrier network. It allows users to dial any other ISDN point on the network and create a high-speed digital link that can mimic point-to-point T1 lines. However, T1 lines are usually permanently established between two points, while ISDN allows the switching of the line between many different points by the customer. This is due to the intelligent network components. The intelligent network also supports a variety of other services, including call forwarding, caller ID, and channel bonding.

B-ISDN provides the intelligent telecommunications services above ATM. It manages the establishment of point-to-point and point-to-multipoint connections through the switched network. It supports on-demand, reserved, and permanent services, as well as connection-oriented and connectionless services. The carriers had big plans to use B-ISDN for services like videotelephony, videoconferencing, electronic newspapers, and TV distribution. Now, B-ISDN is rarely discussed. All you hear about is ATM.

SONET is the physical transport backbone of B-ISDN. It is a fiber-optic–based networking standard that defines a hierarchy of transmission rates and data-framing formats. It is used as a transmission medium to interconnect carrier-switching offices worldwide, and so forms the structure of the communications network. SONET is now used as the medium between

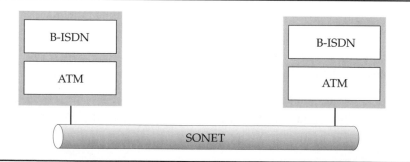

Figure B-10.   *B-ISDN network architecture*

carrier-switching offices and customers. SONET transmission rates start at 51.4 Mbits/sec and increase in 52-Mbit/sec building blocks.

ATM is the switching technology for B-ISDN and provides B-ISDN users access to the SONET fiber-optic network. Information received at the ATM layer is placed in fixed-length cells, addressed, and transmitted over the SONET network. ATM provides very high-speed switching of these packets between the links attached to the SONET network. ATM takes full advantage of the transmission speeds available on fiber-optic cable.

Note that neither ISDN nor B-ISDN has gained the popularity envisioned by the carriers. IP networking has gained in popularity and the latest trend is to build converged networks where voice travels in packets. See "NPN (New Public Network)," "Voice/Data Networking," and "VoIP (Voice over IP)."

Related Entries   ATM (Asynchronous Transfer Mode); ISDN (Integrated Services Digital Network); NADH (North American Digital Hierarchy); NPN (New Public Network); Optical Networks; SDH (Synchronous Digital Hierarchy); SONET (Synchronous Optical Network); Telecommunications and Telephone Systems; Voice/Data Networks; *and* WAN (Wide Area Network)

Linktionary!—Tom Sheldon's Encyclopedia of Networking updates	http://www.linktionary.com/b/bisdn.html
B-ISDN notes by Saleem Bhatti, University College London	http://www-dept.cs.ucl.ac.uk/staff/S.Bhatti/D51-notes/node35.html
Broadband ISDN Communications	http://www.geocities.com/SiliconValley/1047/bisdn.html
Dan Kegel's ISDN Page with extensive Web links	http://www.alumni.caltech.edu/~dank/isdn/index.html
B-ISDN and its relationship to ATM	http://ganges.cs.tcd.ie/4ba2/atm/index.html

BISYNC (Binary Synchronous Communications)

Binary synchronous communications, or BISYNC, is a character (byte)–oriented form of communication developed by IBM in the 1960s. It was originally designed for batch transmissions between the IBM S/360 mainframe family and IBM 2780 and 3780 terminals. It supports online and RJE (remote job entry) terminals in the CICS/VSE (Customer Information Control System/Virtual Storage Extended) environment.

BISYNC establishes rules for transmitting binary-coded data between a terminal and a host computer's BISYNC port. While BISYNC is a half-duplex protocol, it will synchronize in both directions on a full-duplex channel. BISYNC supports both point-to-point (over leased or dial-up lines) and multipoint transmissions. Each message must be acknowledged, adding to its overhead.

BISYNC is character oriented, meaning that groups of bits (bytes) are the main elements of transmission, rather than a stream of bits. The BISYNC frame is pictured next. It starts with two sync characters that the receiver and transmitter use for synchronizing. This is followed by a start of header (SOH) command, and then the header. Following this are the start of text (STX) command and the text. Finally, an end of text (EOT) command and a cyclic redundancy check (CRC) end the frame. The CRC provides error detection and correction.

SYNC	SOH	Header	STX	Text	EOT	CRC

Most of the bisynchronous protocols, of which there are many, provide only half-duplex transmission and require an acknowledgment for every block of transmitted data. Some do provide full-duplex transmission and bit-oriented operation. BISYNC has largely been replaced by the more powerful SDLC (Synchronous Data Link Protocol).

Related Entries   Asynchronous Communication; Bit-Oriented Protocol, Byte-Oriented Protocol; Data Communication Concepts; SDLC (Synchronous Data Link Protocol); *and* Synchronous Communication

Linktionary!—Tom Sheldon's Encyclopedia of Networking updates   http://www.linktionary.com/d/datacomm.html

Bit-Oriented Protocol

In any communication session between devices, control codes are used to control another device or provide information about the status of the session. Byte- or character-oriented protocols use full bytes (8 bits) to represent established control codes such as those defined by ASCII (American Standard Code for Information Interchange). Thus, a character-oriented protocol can only be used with its native character set because that character set has the specific control characters. In contrast, bit-oriented protocols rely on individual bits for control information and are the preferred method for transmitting data. Most data link protocols like those used for local area networks are bit oriented.

In a bit-oriented transmission, data is transmitted as a steady stream of bits. Before actual data transmission begins, special *sync* characters are transmitted by the sender so the receiver can synchronize itself with the bit stream. This bit pattern is usually in the form of a specially coded 8-bit string. IBM's SDLC (Synchronous Data Link Control) protocol is bit oriented. The sync character is the bit string 01111110, and this is followed by an 8-bit address, an 8-bit control field, and the data. Once the receiving system receives these start frames, it begins reading eight bits at a time (a byte) from the bit stream until an error check and an ending flag appear.

IBM's SDLC and HDLS (High-level Data Link Control) are bit-oriented protocols that control synchronous communication. HDLC is used in X.25 packet-switching networks; SDLC is a subset of HDLC.

Related Entries   Asynchronous Communication; Byte-Oriented Protocol; Data Communication Concepts; LLC (Logical Link Control); SDLC (Synchronous Data Link Control); *and* Synchronous Communication

Linktionary!—Tom Sheldon's Encyclopedia of Networking updates   http://www.linktionary.com/d/datacomm.html

Block Suballocation

This Novell NetWare operating system feature maximizes disk space. If there are any partially used disk blocks (usually a block is 8KB in size), NetWare divides them into 512-byte suballocation blocks for the storage of small files or fragments of files. For more information, see "Novell NetWare File System" and "Volume and Partition Management."

Block Transmission

When an application such as the FTP (File Transfer Protocol) needs to send a file from one computer to another, it can select from several transmission modes. A concern with any long data transmission is that the transmission might be interrupted or part of the transmission might be corrupted. A block transmission mode can assist in recovering an interrupted transmission.

Block-mode transmissions divide data into multiple blocks and treat each block as a record. Each record has a *count field*, *data*, and an *end of record* marker. The data is sent one block at a time. If the transmission fails, it can be resumed starting at the last record sent.

Related Entry   Data Link Protocols

Bluetooth

Bluetooth is the codename of a wireless personal area network specification that is being developed by the Bluetooth SIG (Special Interest Group). Bluetooth will enable electronic devices to spontaneously set up wireless networks within small areas. Bluetooth is designed for notebooks; telephones; and other devices, including wireless headsets, handheld and wearable devices (such as inventory scanners), and data/voice access devices. It also provides peripheral connections for printers, PDAs, desktops, fax machines, keyboards, joysticks, and virtually any other digital device.

The Bluetooth SIG (special interest group) includes hundreds of leading technology companies that are determined to make this specification pervasive. Bluetooth SIG members refer to Bluetooth as *third-generation mobile technology*. Unlike second-generation devices, such as GSM phones, which are optimized for voice communication, third-generation technology smart phones and communicators are designed for digital content such as speech, pictures, and video. A typical Bluetooth phone will have two radios for example, one for the metropolitan cellular system and one for the Bluetooth personal area network.

Other ventures that benefit Bluetooth are designed to promote the development of mobile devices and standardize access to the Internet:

- **Symbian**   A joint venture to develop and promote an operating system for wireless information devices called EPOC. The Symbian Web site is listed later.

- **WAP (Wireless Applications Protocol)**   A protocol to support wireless links between mobile devices and the Internet. The WAP Forum site listed later provides more information.

A typical mobile device can use Bluetooth to exchange information (such as electronic business cards, calendars, and phone book address information) with other Bluetooth devices. Bluetooth implementations are being developed for Windows and other popular operating systems.

A typical Bluetooth device will include software to discover other devices, establish links with those devices, and exchange information. In addition, the software should be able to discover higher-level applications running in other Bluetooth devices. For example, one device may discover that another device has an address book and automatically synchronize address information with it. The Bluetooth software framework uses existing software specifications, including OBEX, vCard/vCalendar, HID (Human Interface Device), and TCP/IP.

Automatic data exchange in mobile devices sounds a bit scary. Envision your personal notebook automatically exchanging address book information with unknown Bluetooth devices at the airport! However, connections can be tightly controlled. Bluetooth implements a challenge-response authentication scheme. Authentication allows a Bluetooth device to create a "domain of trust" with other Bluetooth devices, which is important for mobile users who carry their devices to untrusted areas.

In a typical connection scenario, one device may authenticate another, or both devices may authenticate one another. For example, a user can allow only his or her own devices to communicate with one another. The Bluetooth SIG considers these security mechanisms adequate in most cases, but recommends using stronger security mechanisms when appropriate.

Bluetooth also uses a data encryption scheme to obscure data being transmitted in the open. Bluetooth uses a stream cipher well suited for a silicon implementation with secret key lengths of 0, 40, or 64 bits.

Bluetooth Specifications

Bluetooth users connect their computing and telecommunications devices using short-range radio links rather than cables. Any peripheral devices can use the technology to gain connection to any computer device. It has built-in encryption and authentication to secure wireless signals. Vendors and manufacturers adopting the standard include software developers, network vendors, silicon vendors, peripheral and camera manufacturers, mobile PC and handheld device developers, consumer electronics manufacturers, car manufacturers, and test and measurement equipment manufacturers.

Bluetooth uses the ISM (industrial/scientific/medical) band in the 2.4-GHz range. This band is available globally without licensing requirements.

Bluetooth uses a fast acknowledgement and frequency-hopping scheme that combats fading and interference in a noisy radiofrequency environment. Devices avoid interference from other signals by hopping to a new frequency (up to 1,600 hops/sec) after transmitting or receiving a packet. Bluetooth's fast hops and small packet sizes make it more robust than competing systems. The specifications of the transmission system are outlined here:

- The Bluetooth air interface is based on a nominal antenna power of 0 dBm. Spread spectrum is used for optional operation at power levels up to 100 mW worldwide. The spreading is accomplished with 79 hops, displaced by 1 MHz, starting at 2.402 GHz and stopping at 2.480 GHz. This bandwidth is reduced in Japan, France, and Spain.

- The nominal link range is 10 centimeters to 10 meters, but can be extended to more than 100 meters by increasing the transmit power.

- Use of FEC (forward error correction) limits the impact of random noise on long-distance links.

■ Bluetooth can support an asynchronous data channel, up to three simultaneous synchronous voice channels, or a channel that simultaneously supports asynchronous data and synchronous voice.

■ Each voice channel supports a 64-Kbit/sec synchronous (voice) link.

■ The asynchronous channel can support an asymmetric link of 721 Kbits/sec in either direction while permitting 57.6 Kbits/sec in the return direction, or a 432.6-Kbit/sec symmetric link.

The Bluetooth Personal Area Network

The Bluetooth network consists of some interesting terminology and technology, as pictured in Figure B-11. First, the Bluetooth network supports both point-to-point and point-to-multipoint connections. The latter refers to the ability of one system to connect with and transmit to multiple other devices. A collection of two or more connected Bluetooth devices is called a *piconet*.

A *scatternet* is a collection of piconets that can potentially connect in any arrangement to form a larger piconet. Each piconet in a scatternet environment is linked together via a different frequency-hopping sequence and the devices within each piconet synchronize with the unique sequence of the piconet they want to communicate with. Data rates in scatternet environments that include as many as 10 fully loaded piconets can reach as high as 6 Mbits/sec, according to the Bluetooth SIG tests.

All devices have a peer relationship except that one device acts as a master device in order to coordinate the connection of other devices in the piconet. The master unit synchronizes with other piconet devices (called slaves) by going through various clocking and hopping sequences. Each device has a 3-bit MAC address to identify it in the piconet. Some units are *parked*, which means they are synchronized in the piconet but have given up their MAC addresses, while other units may go into *sniff and hold* mode, which means they have gone into power-saving mode but are ready to wake up if necessary. A temperature sensor is an example of a device that goes into low-power mode.

A Bluetooth device waits for a connection in standby mode, where it listens for messages every 1.28 seconds from other Bluetooth devices. A device listens on up to 32 hop frequencies defined for it. A Bluetooth device that wants to make a connection sends a message to a device indicating that it wants to establish a connection. This device becomes the master and the paged device becomes the slave. A master device may need to go into inquiry mode in order to locate a particular device with an unknown address.

There are two types of links:

■ **SCO (synchronous connection oriented)**   A symmetric link that supports real-time voice traffic. The packets in this link are transmitted at reserved intervals to ensure high voice quality. However, lost or corrupted packets are not retransmitted.

■ **ACL (asynchronous connectionless)**   Supports asymmetric packet-oriented traffic in which the master unit controls the bandwidth and how much is given to each slave. Slave devices are polled before they can transmit data. A broadcast message mode is also provided.

The topic "Service Advertising and Discovery" discusses methods in which network devices can advertise services they are offering or find out about services being offered on a

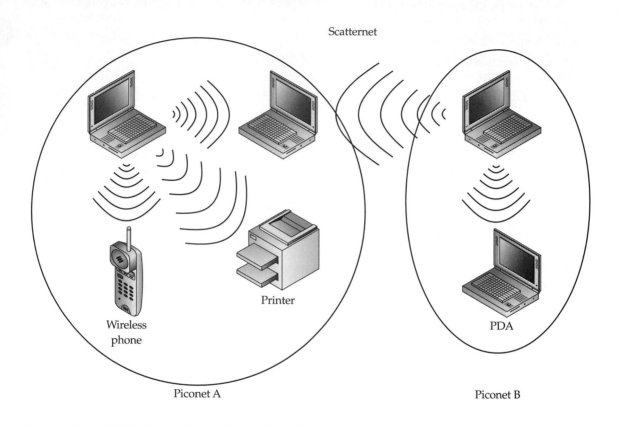

Scatternet

Printer

Wireless
phone

PDA

Piconet A

Piconet B

Figure B-11. *Bluetooth piconets within a Bluetooth scatternet*

network. This is important to Bluetooth devices that must dynamically discover the services that are available on networks that the user connects to. The topic discusses several service location models, including Salutation, JetSend (Hewlett-Packard), and Jini (Sun Microsystems).

Related Entries Cellular Communication Systems; Embedded Systems and Architectures; Home Networking; Java; Mobile Computing; Network Appliances; Peer-to-Peer Communication; Service Advertising and Discovery; SLP (Service Location Protocol); Thin Clients; Wireless Communications; Wireless Mobile Communications; *and* Wireless LANs

Linktionary!—Tom Sheldon's Encyclopedia of Networking updates	http://www.linktionary.com/b/bluetooth.html
Bluetooth Web site	http://www.bluetooth.com

B

Bluetooth Resource Centre at Palo Pacific Technology	http://www.palopt.com.au/bluetooth/
Motorola's Bluetooth Web site	http://www.motorola.com/bluetooth/
Nokia 3rd-Generation wireless technology information	http://www.nokia.com
Brainboxes Bluetooth Web page	http://www.brainboxes.com/bluetooth/
Brightcom (silicon and software solutions for Bluetooth)	http://www.brightcom.com/
Cerulic, The Bluetooth Portal Company	http://www.cerulic.com/
BlueTooth information at NIST	http://isdn.ncsl.nist.gov/misc/hsnt/projects.html
Symbian site (information about EPOC wireless operating system)	http://www.symbian.com
WAP Forum site (Wireless Applications Protocol)	http://www.wapforum.org

Bonding

Bonding is a technique of combining data channels to form a higher-capacity data channel. Bonding provides a way to obtain bandwidth on demand without contacting the phone company. You typically use it to obtain more capacity before a high-data-rate session such as a videoconference. A router that supports bonding will dial and/or connect one or more extra transmission lines and combine them into a single channel. After the videoconference, you terminate the bound channels. The purpose of bonding (and bandwidth on demand) is to obtain more capacity without obtaining an expensive dedicated line that might go underused most of the time.

Note that bonding takes place when the call is set up. The phone company can also perform bonding within its own system for customers. In addition, most new routers support MLPPP (Multilink Point-to-Point Protocol), which provides automatic bandwidth on demand at any time and is more appropriate for bursty and unpredictable local area network traffic.

In the ISDN (Integrated Services Digital Network) environment, bonding refers to combining the two 64-Kbit/sec B channels to create a higher-capacity 128-Kbit/sec channel. BACP (Bandwidth Allocation Control Protocol) provides a way to do this in conjunction with the carrier.

Trunking is a method for combining multiple LAN links into a single data channel with higher bandwidth. Refer to "Link Aggregation" for more information.

Related Entries   Bandwidth Management; Bandwidth-on-Demand; BAP (Bandwidth Allocation Protocol) and BACP (Bandwidth Allocation Control Protocol); Circuit-Switching Services; DDR (Dial-on-Demand Routing); Inverse Multiplexing; ISDN (Integrated Services Digital Network); Link Aggregation; Load Balancing; *and* MLPPP (Multilink PPP)

Linktionary!—Tom Sheldon's Encyclopedia of Networking updates	http://www.linktionary.com/b/bonding.html

BOOTP (BOOTstrap Protocol)

BOOTP is an Internet protocol that can provide network configuration information to diskless workstations, or other workstations if necessary, on a local network. Diskless workstations need to obtain a boot image from a disk on the network because they do not have their own disks from which to obtain this information. BOOTP is also used to initialize IP phones. The boot image provides all the files required to start the operating system on the computer.

BOOTP Enhanced what RARP (Reverse Address Resolution Protocol does. RARP obtains an IP address only. BOOTP obtains an IP address, a gateway address, and a name server address. BOOTP is designed for LANs and bridged networks. It can be used across routed internetworks if the routers support BOOTP forwarding.

When a workstation boots, it broadcasts a BOOTP message on the network. A BOOTP server receives this message, obtains the configuration information for the designated computer, and returns it to the computer. The booting system does not have an IP address when it sends out a BOOTP message. Instead, the hardware address of the NIC (network interface card) is placed in the message and the BOOTP server returns its reply to this address.

Information returned by the BOOTP server to the booting computer includes its IP address, the IP address of the server, the host name of the server, and the IP address of a default router. It also specifies the location of a boot image that the booting computer can obtain in order to complete its startup operation.

Note that administrators must manually configure the information on a BOOTP server. An IP address must be matched to the MAC (medium access control) addresses of computers on the network. To minimize this configuration requirement, DHCP (Dynamic Host Configuration Protocol) was developed to automatically allocate IP addresses to clients. Basically, BOOTP makes a request for IP Information while DHCP fulfills that request.

The following Internet RFCs discuss BOOTP and related protocols.

- RFC 951 (The Bootstrap Protocol, September 1985)
- RFC 1534 (Interoperation Between DHCP and BOOTP, October 1993)
- RFC 1542 (Clarifications and Extensions for the Bootstrap Protocol, October 1993)
- RFC 2132 (DHCP Options and BOOTP Vendor Extensions, March 1997)

Related Entries   ARP (Address Resolution Protocol); Bootstrapping or Booting; DHCP (Dynamic Host Configuration Protocol); Diskless Workstation; RARP (Reverse Address Resolution Protocol); *and* Thin Clients

Bootstrapping or Booting

When a computer is first started, a built-in routine (in ROM) provides it with enough logic to obtain startup programs from a permanent storage device. The built-in ROM routines are small—there is just enough code to direct the system to a disk where it can begin to load the much larger operating system files. But what if the computer is a diskless workstation (a computer with no local storage device)?

In the case of a diskless workstation, boot information is typically obtained from a network server. The diskless workstation has a special ROM inserted on its NIC (network interface card)

that directs it to contact a specific computer on the network. This computer then has a program that sends a startup disk image to the diskless workstation so it can boot. All subsequent disk access is performed on network servers.

Network computers need quite a bit of information to get started, including a network address and the location of important services. In the TCP/IP environment, a system needs an IP address, a default router address, a subnet mask, a DNS (Domain Name Service) server address, and some other parameters, depending on the environment. However, creating a startup configuration file for every diskless workstation on a network can be a daunting task, especially if the information changes often, as it might for mobile users. A number of protocols have been developed to dynamically assign IP addresses, as will be discussed in a moment.

The Internet protocol suite includes a protocol called RARP (Reverse Address Resolution Protocol) that allows a computer to obtain an IP address from a server. When a diskless TCP/IP workstation is booted on a network, it broadcasts a RARP request packet on the local network. This address packet is broadcast on the network for all to receive because the workstation does not know the IP address of the server that can supply it with an address. It includes its own physical network address (the MAC address) in the request so the server will know where to return a reply. The server that receives the request looks in a table, matches the MAC address with an IP address, and then returns the IP address to the diskless workstation.

Another protocol called BOOTP (BOOTstrap Protocol) provides a way for a server to supply even more configuration information to a workstation at boot time. For more information, see "BOOTP (BOOTstrap Protocol)" and "DHCP (Dynamic Host Configuration Protocol)." DHCP (Dynamic Host Configuration Protocol) can provide automatic and dynamic IP address allocation for some or all of the workstations on a network.

Related Entries   ARP (Address Resolution Protocol); BOOTP (BOOTstrap Protocol); DHCP (Dynamic Host Configuration Protocol); Diskless Workstation; RARP (Reverse Address Resolution Protocol); *and* Thin Clients

Bots

According to the BotSpot Web site, "a bot is a software tool for digging through data. You give a bot directions and it brings back answers. The word is short for *robot*, of course, which is derived from the Czech word *robota—meaning work*."

That pretty much says it all. In terms of the Internet, a typical bot visits Web sites and searches for information you request. But the bots don't visit all the sites on the Web every time you request a search! The wait would take forever! What most bots do is compile a list of Web sites and the information on them into a large database, and then index the database. When you request information, you're not using the bot yourself. You are only accessing the results of its work. Most Internet search sites use this technique.

Bots are also referred to as agents. In addition, bots are used for data mining, which refers to digging information out of databases using a series of refined searches.

The topic "Search and Discovery Services" provides a more detailed look at search services on the Internet.

Related Entries   Agent, Internet; Handle System; Metadata; Name Services; Search and Discovery Services; Service Advertising and Discovery; URN (Universal Resource Naming); *and* White Pages Directory Services

BotSpot at Internet.com	http://botspot.com
UMBC AgentWeb site	http://www.cs.umbc.edu/agents/
Robots in the Web: threat or treat? By Martijn Koster of NEXOR	http://info.webcrawler.com/mak/projects/ robots/threat-or-treat.html
Miningco.com information about bots, agents, data mining, and other related topics	http://ai.miningco.com/
The Web Robots FAQ	http://info.webcrawler.com/mak/projects/ robots/faq.html

Breakout Box

See Testing and Diagnostic Equipment and Techniques.

BRI (Basic Rate Interface)

The basic rate interface is the minimal service obtainable for ISDN (Integrated Services Digital Network). ISDN is a digital phone service that is meant to replace the traditional analog phone system.

BRI consists of two 64-Kbit/sec B channels and one 16-Kbit/sec D channel. Each B channel can carry a single digitized voice call or can be used as a data channel. The B channels can also be combined to form a single 128-Kbit/sec data channel. The D channel is used for call establishment and other signaling.

Related Entries   B-ISDN (Broadband ISDN); Bonding; *and* ISDN (Integrated Services Digital Network)

Bridges and Bridging

A *bridge* is a LAN connection device with two or more ports that forwards frames from one LAN (local area network) segment to another. In the past, the bridge was a small box with several LAN connectors or a server with several network interface cards. Today, bridges are more likely to appear in the form of switching devices, which are technically multiport bridges. Each port provides a separate LAN connection that is bridged to the other ports.

The bridge provides several important functions:

- ■ It allows a single LAN to be extended to greater distances.

- ■ You can join different types of network links with a bridge while retaining the same broadcast domain. For example, you can bridge two distant LANs with bridges joined by fiber-optic cable.

- ■ A bridge forwards frames, but a filtering mechanism can be used to prevent unnecessary frames from propagating across the network.

B

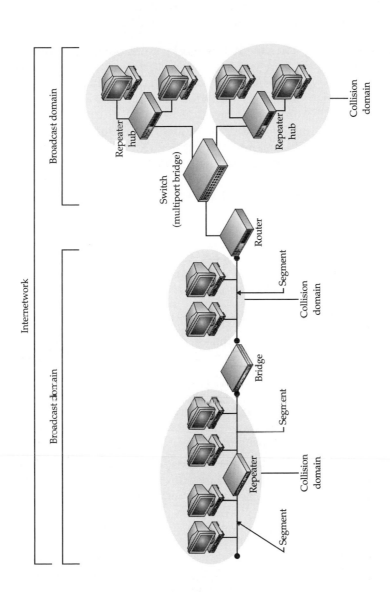

Figure B-12.   *A bridge subdivides a network into separate collision domains.*

- They provide a barrier that keeps electrical or other problems on one segment from propagating to the other segment.

- A bridge isolates each LAN from the collisions that occur on other LANs. Thus, it creates separate collision domains within the same broadcast domain.

The last point is important. On Ethernet networks, collisions occur when two nodes attempt to transmit at the same time. As more nodes are added to a network, collisions increase. A bridge can be used to divide a network into separate *collision domains* while retaining the broadcast domain. A broadcast domain is basically a LAN as compared to an internetwork, which is multiple LANs connected by routers. In a broadcast domain, any node can send a message to any other node using data link layer addressing, while a routed network requires internetwork addressing. See "Collisions and Collision Domains" for more information.

Figure B-12 illustrates the topology and the terminology for a typical bridged and routed network. Note that the router in the middle joins two separate networks into an internetwork. The network on the left has a flat topology (i.e., coaxial cable), while the network on the right has a hierarchical topology (i.e., twisted pair) in which workstations are connected to hub ports and hubs are connected to a switch.

Note the terminology used in the illustration:

- **Segment**   Each individual length of Ethernet coaxial cable in the network on the left is considered a segment. On the right-hand network, all the cables attached to a hub form what is best described as a "star configured multicable segment." Multiple hubs can be connected together to extend this topology.

- **Collision domain**   An Ethernet collision domain is defined as a single CSMA/CD network in which collisions may occur between any computers attached to the network. Repeaters and repeater hubs can be used to connect multiple segments to create larger collision domains.

- **Broadcast domain**   Bridges join network segments to create a much larger broadcast domain. Since they do not propagate collision signals, they effectively divide a network into separate collision domains.

- **Internetwork**   The router joins the two broadcast domains networks into an internetwork. No broadcast traffic propagates across the router, although the router will foward packets addressed to other networks.

The repeater on the left network propagates all traffic between the two networks it connects. Therefore, a repeater creates a larger collision domain. A bridge is a better choice for large networks because it can be used to split a network into separate collision domains, thus reducing collisions and boosting performance in each domain. A router is even better still if the network must be divided into workgroups, departments, and other divisions.

A modern LAN switch is essentially a *multiport bridge*. The switch can connect one port with any other port, and create a temporary network segment between those ports. You can connect as few as one computer to a switch port. In a configuration in which single computers are attached to each port and a switch connected between any two ports is a nonshared link in which collisions are essentially eliminated. Note that repeater hubs or other switches may be attached to switching port hubs, but the effect is the same: the number of collisions are reduced by reducing the number of nodes per segment.

Bridge Functionality

Bridges operate in "promiscuous" mode, which means they listen to all traffic on all connected segments. The bridge forwards frames to all attached segments, although it may be programmed to filter specific frames. Bridges can filter traffic based on MAC addresses.

There are generally three types of bridges: *local*, *remote link*, and *translation*. A local bridge, as shown on the bottom in Figure B-13, provides LAN connection ports for connecting two or more LANs within the same general area (a building). A remote bridge, as shown on the top in Figure B-13, has telecommunications ports for connecting over wide area networks. Bridges are also available to provide wireless connections in the campus environment, microwave links for metropolitan environments, or satellite links for global connections.

A translation bridge can be used to connect different types of LANs by resolving the differences between frame layout, transmission speed, and control codes. For example, token ring frame sizes are potentially much larger than Ethernet frames. In addition, token ring and Ethernet operating speeds are quite different. Also, Ethernet and token ring frames carry different protocol information. In most cases, routers are a better choice for joining different network types.

Bridging takes place in the data link layer relative to the OSI protocol model, as shown in Figure B-14. Ethernet, token ring, and FDDI are examples of networks that conform to IEEE 802 standards for MAC-level bridging. The data link layer is subdivided into the upper LLC (Logical Link Control) sublayer and the lower MAC sublayer. The modular MAC sublayer handles different types of medium access methods and the upper LLC layer acts as a sort of "switchboard" to move frames among the network modules in the MAC sublayer.

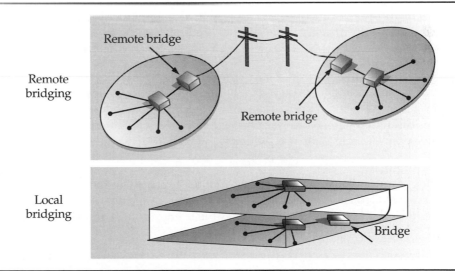

Figure B-13.   *Local and remote bridges*

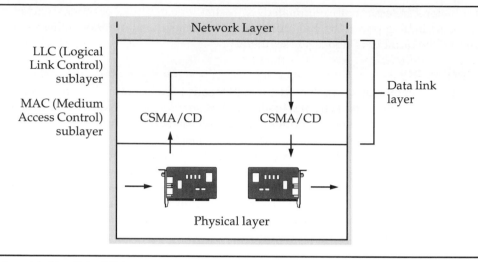

Figure B-14.   *A bridge links MAC layer devices.*

Bridges provide the following functions:

- **Frame forwarding**   As mentioned, a bridge will forward frames to another network if they are addressed for a device on that network.

- **Loop resolution**   Large-bridged LANs may have loops that could cause frames to travel continuously. Most bridges can detect such looping frames and intercept them.

- **Learning techniques**   Bridges build address tables that describe routes by either examining traffic flow (*transparent bridging*) or obtaining information from "explorer frames" that have learned about the network topology during their travels (*source routing*).

Early bridges required that network managers hand enter the address tables. This was a tedious task, and the tables had to be periodically updated if a workstation or user moved to another location. Today's advanced bridges can learn the address of other stations on the network using techniques discussed here. Note that transparent bridges are often called learning bridges and they use the spanning tree algorithm, which is the IEEE 802.1 standard.

Transparent Bridging
Transparent bridges automatically set about learning the topology of the network environment as soon as they are installed and powered up. When a frame from a new source arrives at a port, the bridge makes an entry in its table that associates the frame's source address with the port on

B

which it arrived. A typical table for two LANs is shown in Figure B-15. Note that the source address of a frame is associated with a port. Arriving packets are forwarded by the bridge based on the entries the bridge has in its table. The bridging table is constantly updated with new source addresses and updates as the network changes.

A discovery process is initiated if an address is not found in the table. A frame is sent to all segments except the one from which the frame originated. Eventually, the destination sends a response back to the bridge and the bridge makes an entry in its table that associates the address with the port on which it received the response. Given time, a bridge will learn the address of every node on the network.

If a bridge only connects two LANs, it is relatively easy to build a table that defines which nodes are on one side and which are on the other. How do you join multiple LANs? The network at the top in Figure B-16 must transmit packets from the left segment through the middle segment to reach the right segment. This can cause excess traffic and performance problems in the middle segment; however, only two bridges are required. An alternative method is to attach a bridge to each LAN and connect the bridges to a backbone network such as an FDDI ring, as shown at the bottom in Figure B-16. This eliminates the need to transmit frames through one segment to reach another segment—except for the backbone, which is installed specifically for shuttling frames between networks.

On large interconnected networks, multiple bridge paths are possible that can form a closed loop and cause packets to circle endlessly, reducing performance or crippling the network. In the worst case, *broadcast storms* occur when new packets are endlessly generated to correct the problem. But multiple paths are useful for providing fault tolerance, as shown in Figure B-17.

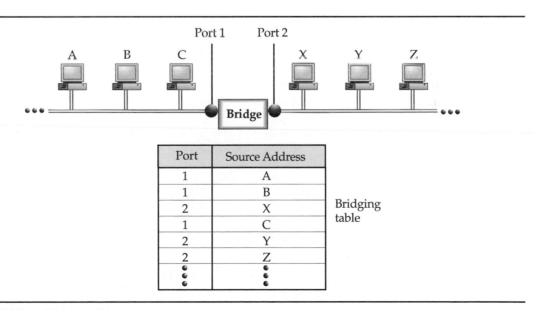

Figure B-15. *Bridging table*

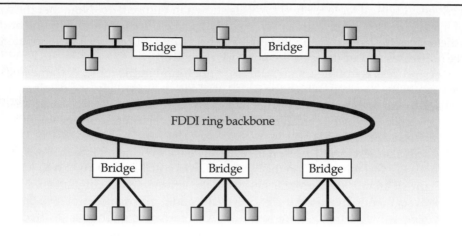

Figure B-16.   *Multisegment bridge networks and backbone networks*

If the link between LAN A and LAN B goes down, an alternative link is still available indirectly through LAN C. The STA (spanning tree algorithm) provides a way to create multiple paths while preventing loops. However, STA does this by blocking one path until it is needed. An alternative strategy, called *load sharing*, solves this problem somewhat, as discussed in a moment.

The Spanning Tree Algorithm

Spanning tree bridges detect and break circular traffic patterns by disabling certain links in Ethernet networks. The IEEE 801.2-D STP (Spanning Tree Protocol) inhibits loops in redundant

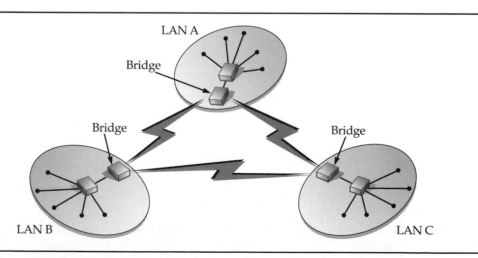

Figure B-17.   *Providing multiple bridge paths*

bridges by maintaining the secondary bridge as a backup. If the first bridge goes down, the secondary bridge takes over.

The algorithm assigns unique *identifiers* to each bridge. A *priority value* is also assigned to each bridge. Each port on every bridge is assigned a unique identifier. Each bridge port is then assigned a *path cost* that assigns a value to ports. The network administrator can change cost values manually to assign preferences for a particular port.

As the algorithm proceeds, a root bridge is selected from the set of bridges. The bridge with the lowest identifier is selected as the root. Once the root bridge is selected, other bridges determine which of their ports provides access to the root bridge at the least cost. This port becomes the *root port* of the bridge. If ports have the same costs, the one with the least number of bridge-to-bridge hops is used. The last step is to determine which bridges and bridge ports will provide a pathway through the network to the root based on the least path cost. This process enables some ports to ensure forwarding paths for some bridges and disables other ports to prevent loops.

Load-Sharing Bridges

When bridges use leased lines to span wide areas, it is not economically feasible in the minds of most network managers to block the line and use it only for a backup. Some bridges provide load-sharing features that are capable of using the backup link to share the network load without causing loops. The load-sharing bridge is the most efficient form of bridge. It uses a spanning tree–type algorithm, and it uses a dual link to transfer packets, thus improving internetwork performance.

Source Route Bridging

IBM Token Ring networks use source routing methods that tells the bridge not only where packets should go, but how to get to their destination. In source routing, the packets themselves hold the forwarding information. Path information is placed directly in packets so they can find their way through the network on their own.

Bridges that do source routing use a *discovery* method to first determine the route a packet should take to a destination. A source routing bridge is simply a forwarding device that knows the addresses of other bridges. Best-path routing information is contained within the packet. This has advantages for WANs (wide area networks). In transparent bridging, it is necessary to block some links to prevent loops. In source routing, loops are avoided, so it is much easier and safer to create parallel redundant paths over wide area links to remote locations.

Explorer packets are released by a source to discover a path through the network. If there are multiple bridges on the network, multiple explorer packets arrive at the destination from each intermediate bridge. The destination node forwards these responses to the original source node. The source node then picks the best path based on factors such as the number of bridge-to-bridge hops. This path is saved by the bridge and used for all subsequent deliveries.

Remote Bridging Techniques

There are a number of connection methods for remote bridges. The topic "Data Transfer Rates" defines rates for common network applications and activities that can help you determine transmission requirements. The most important consideration is that filtering is even more important on dial-up or leased lines because the lines usually have limited bandwidth.

The dial-up modem and asynchronous link are adequate for occasional low-volume internetwork traffic. For heavier traffic, dedicated analog lines or digital lines are necessary. A CSU/DSU (channel service unit/data service unit) links the bridge to the digital line, as shown in Figure B-18. If you plan to mix voice and data, you'll need a multiplexor.

Related Entries   Backbone Networks; Campus Network; Load Balancing; Network Concepts; Network Design and Construction; Repeaters; Routers; Switching and Switched Networks; *and* WAN (Wide Area Network)

Linktionary!—Tom Sheldon's Encyclopedia of Networking updates	http://www.linktionary.com/b/bridge.html
Bitpipe.com (search for "bridging")	http://www.bitpipe.com
Configuring Bridging Services at Bay Networks	http://support.baynetworks.com/library/tpubs/html/router/soft1000/bridge/2950A-1.html
Cisco Documentation: "Bridging and Switching Basics"	http://www.cisco.com
Cisco Documentation: Troubleshooting Transparent Bridging Environments	http://www.cisco.com/univercd/cc/td/doc/cisintwk/itg_v1/tr1920.htm
Cisco Documentation: Configuring Spanning Tree	http://www.cisco.com
Cisco Documentation: Configuring Source-Route Bridging	http://www.cisco.com/univercd/cc/td/doc/product/software/ios120/12cgcr/ibm_c/bcprt1/bcsrb.htm
Cisco paper: "Understanding and Designing Networks Using Spanning Tree and UplinkFast Groups"	http://www.cisco.com/univercd/ce/td/doc/product/lan/cat5000/rel_5.2/config/stp_enha.htm
IETF Bridge Working Group	http://www.ietf.org/html.charters/bridge-charter.html
RAD Data Networks Bridging paper	http://www.rad.com/networks/1994/bridges/bridges.htm
Novell's "Source Routing and the Spanning-Tree Protocol" application notes (very extensive)	http://developer.novell.com/research/appnotes/1991/august/01/index.htm
Scan Technologies bridging tutorial	http://www.scan-technologies.com/tutorials/Bridging%20Tutorial.htm
Bridge tutorial by Godred Fairhurst	http://www.erg.abdn.ac.uk/users/gorry/course/lan-pages/bridge.html
Bridge Functions Consortium at UNH InterOperability Lab (IOL)	http://www.iol.unh.edu/consortiums

Broadband Communications and Networking

Broadband communications is usually considered to be any technology with transmission rates above the fastest speed available over a telephone line. Broadband transmission systems typically provide channels for data transmissions in different directions and by many different

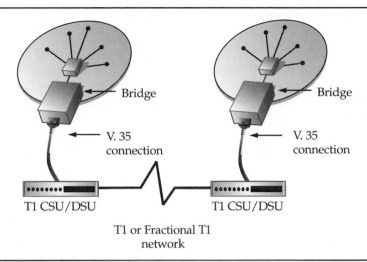

Figure B-18.   *Bridging across a T1 line*

users. For example, the coaxial CATV system is a broadband system that delivers multiple television channels over the same cable. In addition, it can handle data transmissions (primarily Internet access for home users) in an entirely different frequency spectrum.

    Refer to "Network Core Technologies" for information about transmission systems such as SONET and DWDM that are used at the core of carrier and service provider networks.

Typical broadband communication systems include the following:

- **ISDN (Integrated Services Digital Network)**   ISDN is implemented over existing copper telephone cables. The basic rate variety provides two channels of 64-Kbit/sec throughput that can be bonded to form a 128-Kbit/sec data channel. Primary rate ISDN provides additional bandwidth in increments of 64 Kbits/sec.

- **ATM (Asynchronous Transfer Mode)**   Another high-bandwidth service available from the carriers. The carriers use of ATM benefits everyone, but medium to large companies can install ATM equipment on-site to connect directly into carrier ATM networks and gain all the benefits of those systems. See the "ATM" heading for more information.

- **Frame relay**   A data networking and voice service offered by the carriers that is widely available. Like ATM, frame relay is primarily used for corporate rather than home connections.

- **Leased lines T1, T3**   Leased T1 lines provide dedicated throughput of 1.544 Mbits/sec over two-pair twisted wire. Existing telephone cable is usually adequate. T3 provides approximately 45-Mbit/sec throughput. Fractional T1 can be leased in increments of 64 Kbits/sec.

■ **DSL (Digital Subscriber Line)**   DSL is a whole family of high-bandwidth digital services that the telephone companies offer over copper telephone cable. Depending on the service, rates can reach into the multimegabit/sec rates.

■ **Cable (CATV)**   The cable TV system is a well-established broadband network that now makes its system available for data links and Internet access. Nearly 100 million homes in the U.S. have cable access, and it is estimated that 70 to 75 percent of those homes will be able to support Internet access in the year 2000.

■ **Broadband Wireless**   A variety of wireless broadband services are now available or under development, including satellite-based systems and terrestrial-based systems that are essentially fixed cellular systems. Broadband wireless uses microwave and millimeter wave technology to transmit signals from base stations to customers. See "Wireless Broadband Access Technologies."

DSL, cable, and broadband wireless will largely solve the problem of providing high bandwidth to home users. This is the so-called "last mile," although last mile has traditionally referred to the copper local loop that connects homes to local telephone central offices. In this respect, CATV and broadband wireless have never had a last-mile problem. DSL solves the last-mile problem in the local loop.

Another aspect of most of these broadband technologies (although not directly related to the definition of broadband) is that they provide direct access to the Internet. There is no need to dial up and hope you get a connection. You are always connected, in the same way that your TV is always connected to the CATV network.

As bandwidth increases, customers will gain access to higher qualities of service for voice, video, and data using packet-based Internet technologies. Global Internet-based telephone calls and videoconferences will become more commonplace, as will distance learning and high-resolution imaging as applied in areas like telemedicine.

An interesting technology that can provide broadband service is HALO (High Altitude Long Operation), which is a scheme to put high-flying planes or balloons above major metropolitan areas. Angel technologies is promoting HALO in the form of a 28-GHz LMDS system that typically uses three planes as aerial base stations. Data rates are in the 10-Mbit/sec range. Skystation International uses balloons that provide 1-Mbit/sec to 12-Mbit/sec transfer rates. The systems connect with ISP and carriers so that users can access the global telecommunications infrastructure.

Linktionary!—Tom Sheldon's Encyclopedia of Networking updates	http://www.linktionary.com/b/broadband.html
Broadband links	http://www.cs.ubc.ca/spider/mjmccut/broadband.html
Internet.com Cyber Atlas broadband page	http://cyberatlas.internet.com/markets/broadband
Bitpipe.com (search for "broadband")	http://www.bitpipe.com

Broadband Guide	http://www.broadband-guide.com/
Bandwidth on the Internet: "Nielsen's Law of Internet Bandwidth"	http://www.useit.com/alertbox/980405.html

Related Entries   ATM (Asynchronous Transfer Mode); B-ISDN (Broadband ISDN); Cable (CATV) Data Networks; Communication Services and Providers; DBS (Direct Broadcast Satellite); DSL (Digital Subscriber Line); Fiber to the Curb/Fiber to the Home; HALO (High Altitude Long Operation); High-Speed/High-Performance Networking; Home Networking; Internet Connections; ISDN (Integrated Services Digital Network); Last Mile Services; LMDS (Local Multipoint Distribution Service); Local Loop; Network Access Services; Residential Broadband; Satellite Communication Systems; Service Providers and Carriers; Telecommunications and Telephone Systems; WAN (Wide Area Network); Wireless Broadband Access Services; Wireless Communications; *and* Wireless Local Loop

Broadcast

In radio communication, a broadcast is a one-to-many signal transmission. *Transmitters* broadcast signals to *receivers*. In Ethernet networks, stations broadcast packet transmissions on a shared medium. Other stations listen to these broadcasts, but receive only packets addressed to them. This broadcast network metaphor is the opposite of a point-to-point network in which transmissions take place between two systems over a dedicated circuit or virtual circuit.

Applications that produce broadcast messages include ARP (used by hosts to locate IP addresses on a network), routing protocols like RIP, and network applications that "advertise" their services on the network. Some other variations include SLP (Service Locaton Protocol), a relatively new protocol used on the Internet to find services. PIP (Presence Information Protocol) alerts users when other users log on.

A discussion of broadcasting may be found in RFC 791 (Internet Protocol, September 1981) and RFC 919 (Broadcasting Internet Datagrams, October 1984).

A form of broadcasting is used on the Internet in which users choose to subscribe to information that is "published" by various services. These publishers are usually news services that deliver content to users at regular intervals. See "Broadcasting on the Internet" and "Webcasting."

Multicasting is a selective form of broadcasting that is supported on the Internet. It allows broadcasts to be directed to users who request to see the broadcast and limits broadcasts to only those parts of the network where users have requested it, thus controlling traffic where it is not needed.

Related Entries   Broadcast Address; Broadcast Networking; Broadcasting on the Internet; Data Communication Concepts, Multicasting; Service Advertising and Discovery; SLP (Service Location Protocol); *and* Webcasting

Linktionary!—Tom Sheldon's Encyclopedia of Networking updates	http://www.linktionary.com/b/broadcast.html

Broadcast Address

Broadcast address refers to the ability to address a message that is broadcast to all stations or hosts on a network. Ethernet networks are shared-media networks in which computers transmit signals on a cable that all other computers attached to the cable can receive. Thus, all the computers are part of the same "broadcast domain."

Normally, one computer transmits frames to only one other computer on the network by placing the MAC address of the destination computer in the frame. This frame is then transmitted on the shared media. Even though other computers see this frame on the network, only the target recieves it. A *broadcast message* is addressed to all stations on the network. The destination address in a broadcast message consists of all 1s (0xFFFFFFFF). All stations automatically receive frames with this address. Normally, broadcast messages are sent for network management and diagnostic purposes.

On IP networks, the IP address 255.255.255.255 (in binary, all 1s) is the general broadcast address. You can't use this address to broadcast a message to every user on the Internet because routers block it, so all you end up doing is broadcasting it to all hosts on your own network. The broadcast address for a specific network includes all 1s in the host portion of the IP address. For example, on the class C network 192.168.1.0, the last byte indicates the host address (a 0 in this position doesn't refer to any host, but provides a way to refer to the entire network). The value 255 in this position fills it with all 1s, which indicates the network broadcast address, so packets sent to 192.168.1.255 are sent to all hosts on the network.

Applications that produce broadcast messages include ARP (used by hosts to locate IP addresses on a network), routing protocols like RIP, and network applications that "advertise" their services on the network.

Related Entries   Addresses, Network; Broadcast; Broadcast Domain; IP (Internet Protocol); MAC (Media Access Control); *and* Multicasting

Broadcast Domain

A broadcast domain is a restricted area in which information can be transmitted for all devices in the domain to receive. More specifically, Ethernet LANs are broadcast domains. Any devices attached to the LAN can transmit frames to any other device because the medium is a shared transmission system. Frames are normally addressed to a specific destination device on the network. While all devices detect the frame transmission on the network, only the device to which the frame is addressed actually receives it. A special broadcast address consisting of all 1s is used to send frames to all devices on the network.

- A *repeater* is a device that joins two LANs to extend the distance of the LAN. All network traffic is sent across the repeater unaltered.

- A *bridge* is a device that joins two LANs into a single broadcast domain, but isolates them so that problems on one LAN do not propagate to the other LAN. In addition, bridges maintain separate collision domains, so that computers on each segment only contend with other computers on the same segment for access.

■ If multiple LANs are connected with *routers*, the router forms the boundary of the broadcast domain. Broadcast traffic and collision signals do not cross routers, although most routers can be configured to forward specific broadcast traffic.

Note that virtual LAN (VLAN) technology can create "virtual" broadcast domains. A network built with switching devices can treat each workstation as an independent entity and groups of these workstations can be joined into a virtual broadcast domain, no matter where they are attached to the physical network. For more information, see "Switched Networks" and "VLAN (Virtual LAN)."

Related Entries   Bridges and Bridging; Broadcast Address, Broadcast Networking; Collisions and Collision Domains; CSMA/CD (Carrier Sense Multiple Access/Collision Detection); Ethernet; MAC (Media Access Control); Switching and Switched Networks; *and* VLAN (Virtual LAN)

Linktionary!—Tom Sheldon's Encyclopedia of
Networking updates

http://www.linktionary.com/b/
broadcast_domain.html

Broadcast Networking

Broadcast networking refers to a type of networking that is done on shared-media networks such as Ethernet where multiple nodes are attached to the same LAN. It is a one-to-many method of transmitting information. All the devices attached to the network that receive the broadcast are part of the same broadcast domain.

In contrast, a *point-to point* link is an unshared connection between two systems. On a point-to-point link, there is no contention for the cable because it connects only the sender and receiver, not a number of shared devices. There are also NBMA (Nonbroadcast Multiple Access) networks such as ATM (Asynchronous Transfer Mode), frame relay, SMDS (Switched Multimegabit Data Service), and X.25. NBMA networks are the opposite of broadcast networks. They are constructed of a mesh of connections or a switching fabric, and virtual circuits are established to transmit information between two endpoints. There is no broadcasting. Data is sent directly across the circuit as if a physical wire connected the endpoints.

A transmission on a broadcast network consists of frames that include the MAC (Medium Access Control) address of the destination node. Network interface cards have built-in MAC addresses that are programmed at the factory. A sender puts the destination system MAC address in a frame and transmits it on the network. Each node listens to traffic on the network and reads the destination address in the frames. If a node receives a frame that has been addressed to it, it accepts the frame. Other nodes ignore the frame. There is also a *broadcast address* that is used to address frames to every node on the network.

Applications that produce broadcast messages include ARP (used by hosts to locate IP addresses on a network), routing protocols like RIP, and network applications that "advertise" their services on the network. *Multicasting* is a selective form of broadcasting that allows broadcasts to be directed to users who request to see the broadcast and limits broadcasts to only those parts of the network where users have requested it, thus controlling traffic where it is not needed.

A discussion of broadcasting may be found in RFC 791 (Internet Protocol, September 1981) and RFC 919 (Broadcasting Internet Datagrams, October 1984).

Related Entries   Bridges and Bridging; Broadcast Address; Broadcast Domain; Collisions and Collision Domains; CSMA/CD (Carrier Sense Multiple Access/Collision Detection); Data Communication Concepts; Ethernet; MAC (Medium Access Control); Multicasting; NBMA (Nonbroadcast Multiple Access); Network Concepts; *and* Point-to-Point Communications

Linktionary!—Tom Sheldon's Encyclopedia of   http://www.linktionary.com/b/
Networking updates   broadcast_network.html

Broadcast Storm

A broadcast storm occurs when a host system responds to a packet that is continuously circulating on the network or attempts to respond to a system that never replies. Typically, request or response packets are continuously generated to correct the situation, often making matters worse. As the number of packets on the network increases, congestion occurs that can reduce network performance or cripple it. See "Bridges and Bridging."

Broadcasting on the Internet

It is possible on the Internet to mimic the kind of wide-audience news broadcasting that radio and television can achieve. A Web site simply maintains a list of subscribers and then sends news to those subscribers via e-mail on a regular basis. Thus, the Web site "broadcasts" news (or just about any kind of information). *Webcasting* is a technique of delivering messages to a wide audience.

The concept of Webcasting is taken even further with *multicasting*, which is a method of broadcasting that does not require that the source maintain a subscriber address list. Instead, packets are transmitted using a special multicast IP address. People who want to receive the broadcast set their Web browsers (or multicast receivers) to receive packets with the specific multicast address.

Another form of Web broadcasting called *datacasting* has recently emerged that does not even use the Internet as its delivery platform. Instead, a server broadcasts data over the VBI (vertical blanking interval) portion of the television signal. The VBI is normally used for closed captioning. Note that data broadcasting is a transmit-only model. Users cannot interact with the Web server, but the technique is useful for delivering specific types of content such as stock quotes, sports news, and so on. A company called WavePhore transmits data over PBS stations nationwide. All you need is a TV card in your computer to receive the transmissions.

Related Entries   Multicasting; NNTP (Network News Transport Protocol); Push; *and* Webcasting

Linktionary!—Tom Sheldon's Encyclopedia of   http://www.linktionary.com/w/webcasting.html
Networking updates

Brouter (Bridge/Router)

A brouter is a hybrid device that merges bridging and routing technology. Basically, a brouter is a bridge that can bridge multiple protocols and provide routing for some of those protocols. In this sense, a brouter is a device that forwards packets between networks at the network layer and the data link layer in the OSI (Open Systems Interconnection) protocol stack. See "Bridges and Bridging" and "Routing."

Browsers, Web

It seems a little ridiculous to define a Web browser since they are as well known as television or radio, so this section contains mostly references to related topics and an extensive list of Web sites that have information on all the Web browsers available. Here are the basic facts about Web browsers:

■ Web browsers run on TCP/IP networks.

■ HTTP (Hypertext Transfer Protocol) is the protocol that a Web browser uses to access a Web server.

■ HTML is the traditional document formatting (markup) language used to display information inside Web browsers.

■ Hyperlinking is the most unique feature of Web browsers. Users click hyperlinks to move to related Web sites and documents. This is where the term "browser" comes from.

■ Web browsers are considered a "universal front end" for accessing information on almost any server, including Web servers, data base servers, and so on.

■ Web browsers are "containers" that are capable of displaying graphics and video content and running all sorts of applications

■ Component technologies such as ActiveX and Java were designed to take advantage of the container metaphor of the browser.

■ Plug-ins such as ShockWave give Web browsers additional capabilities (i.e., the ability to display multimedia files and presentations).

Microsoft Internet Explorer and Netscape Navigator are by far the most popular Web browsers on the market. They are available for free, and both Microsoft and Netscape have been locked in a feature battle for years. That's good for users and good for advancing Web technologies. But many other Web browsers are available for free. Check the Web sites listed later for more information.

In early 1999, Sun released a Java-based browser called the Personal Applications browser. The browser is designed to work in TV set-top boxes and small devices like cell phones. The browser's core requires only 280K of memory. One interesting feature is the ability to click on a hyperlink that dials an associated phone number. A zoom feature lets users zoom in on parts of a Web page that are difficult to see on a small LCD display.

Related Entries   Client-Server Computing; Multitiered Architectures; Thin Clients; *and* Web Technologies and Concepts

Linktionary!—Tom Sheldon's Encyclopedia of Networking updates	http://www.linktionary.com/b/browser.html
Bitpipe (search for "browser")	http://www.bitpipe.com
Navigating the World Wide Web (send your newbies here)	http://www.imaginarylandscape.com/helpweb/www/www.html
Web browser plug-ins with extensive links	http://www.stars.com/Software/Plugins/
Web browser plug-ins page at Netscape	http://home.netscape.com/plugins/index.html
BrowserWatch Web browser information	http://browserwatch.internet.com/
Browser Standards Project	http://www.webstandards.org/
Web Browser overview at RAD Data Communications	http://www.rad.com/networks/1997/browser/browser.htm
Mozilla.org (Mozilla is the original Netscape Navigator)	http://www.mozilla.org/
NCSA Mosaic	http://www.ncsa.uiuc.edu/SDG/Software/WinMosaic/HomePage.html
Web Monkey browser page	http://hotwired.lycos.com/webmonkey/browsers/?tw=browsers
Yahoo! Web links	http://dir.yahoo.com/Computers_and_Internet/Internet/World_Wide_Web/
Amaya Web browser	http://www.w3.org/Amaya/
Complete browser link list	http://www.stars.com/Vlib/Software/Browsers.html
Emacs/W3 Web browser	http://www.cs.indiana.edu/elisp/w3/docs.html
HotJava Web browser	http://java.sun.com/products/hotjava/index.html
Internet Explorer	http://www.microsoft.com/windows/ie/
Lynx	http://lynx.browser.org/
Netscape Navigator	http://www.netscape.com/navigator/
Opera Software	http://opera.nta.no/
Web-On-Call Voice Browser	http://www.netphonic.com/
Web technology links, Mark McCutcheon's Links	http://www.cs.ubc.ca/spider/mjmccut/technics.html

Burst and Bursty Traffic

A burst is a continuous transfer of data without interruption from one device to another. Microprocessors allow burst-mode block transfers of data to memory and onboard caches.

Disk and network adapters perform burst-mode transfers in which they control the system bus in order to send multiple blocks of data.

On a multiplexed data communication channel that normally merges and transfers data from several sources, burst mode provides a way to dedicate the entire channel for the transmission of data from one source. Normally, a timeslot is dedicated for each device that needs to transmit. Statistical multiplexing can handle bursts from one source.

Burst multiplexing is done on advanced "next generation" optical networks with a burst assembler at the edge. For example, IP traffic headed in the same general direction is assembled and routed as a burst through the network. The burst is carried on two wavelengths, one for data and another for header information that guides the burst through the network. The advantage of this scheme is realized in networks that are not fully optical. The header information, which requires optical to electrical translation, goes in a separate wavelength, while the data burst goes all the way through in the optical form.

Related Entries   Bandwidth on Demand; Bonding; Link Aggregation; Load Balancing; Multiplexing; *and* Optical Networks

Bus Architectures

See Switch Fabrics and Bus Design.

Bus Topology

The layout of a network's cable system and the methods that workstations use to access and transmit data on the cable are part of the topology of a network. A bus topology network consists of a single cable trunk that connects one workstation to the next in a daisy-chain configuration, as shown in Figure B-19. In an actual installation, the cable snakes its way through a building from office to office. All nodes share the same media, and only one node can broadcast messages at a time. While bus topologies are easy to install because they conform well to office layouts, a break in the trunk cable will disable the entire network.

The most common bus topology network is Ethernet. Coaxial cable has been its primary transmission media, although twisted-pair wire is now used in most new installations. Twisted-pair Ethernet (10Base-T) is a star-configured bus topology. The bus itself is collapsed into a small box called a *concentrator*. Wires branch out to workstations from the connection in a star configuration, as shown in Figure B-20.

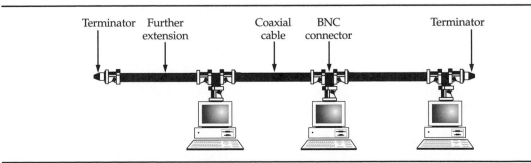

Figure B-19.   *Coaxial cable bus topology*

Related Entries   Ethernet; Network Design and Construction; *and* Topology

 Linktionary!—Tom Sheldon's Encyclopedia of   http://www.linktionary.com/t/topology.html
Networking updates

Byte-Oriented Protocol

In any communication session between devices, control codes are used to control another device or provide information about the status of the session. Byte- or character-oriented protocols use full bytes to represent established control codes such as those defined by the ASCII (American Standard Code for Information Interchange) scheme. In contrast, bit-oriented protocols rely on individual bits for control codes.

Byte-oriented protocols transmit data as strings of characters. The transmission method is asynchronous. Each character is separated by a start bit and a stop bit, and no timing mechanism is needed. Asynchronous protocols used with most modems and IBM's BISYNC (Binary Synchronous Communications) Protocol are byte-oriented protocols.

Related Entries   Asynchronous Communications; Bit-Oriented Protocol; *and* Modems

 Linktionary!—Tom Sheldon's Encyclopedia of   http://www.linktionary.com/d/datacomm.html
Networking updates

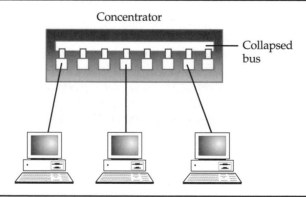

Figure B-20.   *Collapsed bus*

C2 Security Rating

The C2 security rating is a set of security specifications that define access-control methods for computer systems that computer vendors can follow to comply with Department of Defense security standards. A more comprehensive system is now defined by the ISO's Common Criteria; see "Security Auditing" later in this book.

Cable and Wiring

Current networking trends favor an integrated network that can support data, as well as multimedia, voice, and video. Fortunately, new structured wiring and networking standards have been defined to help network designers to plan, install, and test cable systems that support gigabit- and multigigabit-per-second data rates.

In the 1970s and 1980s, coaxial cable was the preferred LAN medium. But by the late 1980s, data-capable twisted-pair wiring emerged as the predominant network cabling scheme. While twisted-pair wire has cable distance limitations, a hierarchical wiring scheme, initially built around hubs (and more recently switches), overcomes those limitations. Workstations are attached to workgroup hubs/switches in nearby wiring closets and those hubs/switches are attached to wiring hubs/switches at centralized data centers via twisted-pair cable, or via fiber-optic cable over long distances.

Today, there are a variety of standards that define cable and component specifications, including the configuration, implementation, performance, conformance, and verification of cabling systems. The most prominent standards are listed here:

- **United States** TIA/EIA-568-A (Telecommunications Industry Association/Electronic Industries Association-568-A), defines how to design, build, and manage a structured wiring system. Note that the specification is also called the EIA/TIA-568 in some references. Refer to "TIA/EIA Structured Cabling Standards" for more information.

- **International** ISO/IEC IS 11801 (International Organization for Standardization/ International Engineering Consortium) defines generic cabling for customer premises. It is being used in Europe, Asia, and Africa. See ISO/IEC-11801 Cabling Standards.

- **Europe** Cenelec EN 50173 was derived from ISO 11801 and defines generic cabling and open-market cabling components.

- **Canada** CSA T529—Canadian Standards for Telecommunications Wiring Systems that closely follows the TIA/EIA-568 specifications.

- **Australia and New Zealand** SAA/SNZ HB27:1996. This standard is based on the TIA TSB67 standard. It specifies field testing of balanced copper cabling and the methodology of specifying field tester accuracy

You can learn more about international cabling standards by visiting the Agilent's wirescope.com Web page at http://www.wirescope.com/.

Transmission Media

This section outlines a variety of "guided" media for network communications. "Unguided" communication techniques are related to wireless networking.

Figure C-1 illustrates the primary types of cable used for data transmissions. These cable types are described here:

- **Straight cable** This is the simplest type of cable. It consists of copper wires surrounded by an insulator. The wire comes in bundles or as flat "ribbon" cables and is used to connect various peripheral devices over short distances. Cables for internal disk drives are typically flat cables with multiple transmission wires running in parallel.

- **Twisted-pair cable** This cable consists of copper-core wires surrounded by an insulator. Two wires are twisted together to form a pair, and the pair forms a balanced circuit (voltages in each pair have the same amplitude but are opposite in phase). The twisting protects against EMI (electromagnetic interference) and RFI (radio frequency interference). A typical cable has multiple twisted pairs, each color-coded to differentiate it from other pairs. *UTP (unshielded twisted-pair)* has been used in the telephone network and is commonly used for data networking in the United States. *STP (shielded twisted-pair)* cable has a foil shield around the wire pairs in a cable to provide superior immunity to RFI. Traditional twisted-pair LANs use two pairs, one for transmit and one for receive, but newer Gigabit Ethernet networks use four pairs to transmit and receive simultaneously. UTP and STP are constructed of 100-ohm, 24-AWG solid conductors.

- **Coaxial cable** This cable consists of a solid copper core surrounded by an insulator, a combination shield and ground wire, and an outer protective jacket. In the early days of LANs, coaxial cable was used for its high bit rates. An Ethernet Thinnet (10Base-2) network has a data rate of 10Mbits/sec and implements a bus topology in which each station is attached to a single strand of cable. Today, hierarchical wiring schemes are considered more practical, and even though more twisted pair wire is required to cable such a network, cost has dropped, making such networks very practical.

- **Fiber-optic cable** This cable consists of a center glass core through which light waves propagate. This core is surrounded by a glass cladding that basically reflects the inner light of the core back into the core. A thick plastic outer jacket surrounds this assembly, along with special fibers to add strength. Fiber-optic cable is available with a metal core for strength if the cable will be hung over distances.

Copper cable is a relatively inexpensive, well-understood technology. However, it has various electrical characteristics that impose restrictions on its use. For example, copper resists the flow of electrons, which limits the length of cables. It also radiates energy in the form of signals that can be monitored, and it is susceptible to external radiation that can distort transmissions. In contrast, fiber-optic cable transmits light (photons) through a core of pure silicon dioxide that is so clear, a three-mile-thick window of it would not distort the view. Thus, fiber cable has high transmission rates and is used for long distances. Photonic transmissions produce no emissions outside the cable and are not affected by external radiation. Thus, fiber cable is preferred where security is an issue.

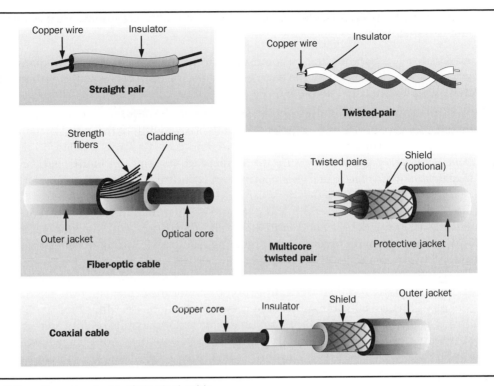

Figure C-1.   *Common types of physical cable*

A characteristic of cable that must not be overlooked is its fire rating. Cable installed in the plenum space, which is the airspace between the ceiling and the next floor or roof, must be installed in metal conduit, or must meet local fire codes. In the event of a fire, the cable must not produce noxious or hazardous gases that would be pumped to other parts of a structure through the plenum. *Nonplenum cables* have PVC (polyvinyl chloride) jackets while *plenum-rated cables* have jackets made with fluoropolymers such as Du Pont's Teflon.

The remainder of this section covers so-called *guided media* copper cabling, as opposed to *unguided media*. For a discussion of unguided media, see "Wireless Communications." Optical cabling is covered under "Fiber-Optic Cable." Also see "Optical Networks" and "WDM (Wave Division Multiplexing)."

Copper Cable Characteristics

Information is transmitted over copper cable by applying variable or discrete voltages at one end of the cable and reading those voltages at the other end. Data signals are discrete pulses of electricity (or light in the case of fiber cable). As mentioned, this discussion is oriented toward twisted-pair cable. Some of the characteristics discussed here only apply to wires that are twisted.

The following relationship exists between the frequency of the electrical signal and the rate at which data is transmitted:

- **Bandwidth**   The bandwidth of a communication system is the highest frequency range that it uses. This is defined by the engineering specification of the particular network. Some examples are listed in Table C-1.
- **Data rate**   The actual data throughput of a cable, after applying encoding and compression schemes to more efficiently use the bandwidth of the cable.

 Data rate is a more accurate measure of a transmission system's capabilities, but the term "bandwidth" is often used in a general way.

The relationship between bandwidth and data rate is illustrated in Figure C-2. You can think of the cable as a pipe, where bandwidth is the size of the pipe and the data rate is the amount of information you can push through the pipe. An encoding and compression scheme lets you use the pipe more efficiently. See "Signals."

For example, 100Base-TX uses an encoding scheme called 4B-5B, which first maps data to a table of efficient codes and then transmits the codes over the cable using the NRZ signal encoding scheme. Thus, an 80-MHz signal supports a data rate of 100 Mbits/sec.

In contrast, Gigabit Ethernet (IEEE 802.3ab or 1000Base-T) transmits on four wire pairs in *full-duplex* mode, meaning that signals are transmitted in both directions on each wire pair. With encoding applied, each wire pair supports a data rate of 250 Mbits/sec in each direction. See "Gigabit Ethernet" for additional information.

Data transmissions over copper cable are subject to attenuation, delay distortion, noise, and environmental problems. Qualified cable installers should test cable both before the cable is installed (to test for cable quality) and after it is installed (to test for proper installation). A table of test parameters is provided later. Also see "Testing, Diagnostic, and Troubleshooting."

Gigabit Ethernet can use existing high-performance Category 5 cable (described later) if the cable passes appropriate testing. It requires much better cable performance than was defined in the original Category 5 specification, so existing cable must be retested to ensure it supports higher frequencies. The minimum recommendations for Gigabit Ethernet cabling are outlined in TIA TSB-95 as described under "TIA/EIA Structured Cabling Standards." Test equipment

Network Type	Maximum Frequency Allowed	Actual Data Rate
10Base-T (Traditional Ethernet over twisted pair)	10 MHz	10 Mbits/sec
100Base-TX (Fast Ethernet)	80 MHz	100 Mbits/sec
ATM-155	100 MHz	155 Mbits/sec
1000Base-T (Gigabit Ethernet, four pairs)	100 MHz	1,000 Mbits/sec

Table C-1.   *Operating Frequency and Data Rate of Ethernet Networks*

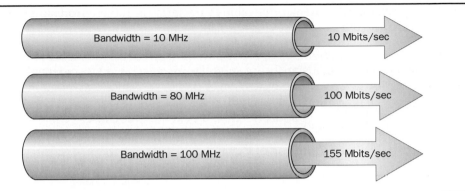

Figure C-2.   *Bandwidth is analogous to a pipe. Data rate is the amount of data that can be transmitted through the pipe.*

from Fluke (http://www.fluke.com), Agilent (http://www.wirescope.com), and other vendors can help you determine the performance of a cable installation.

High-performance cable requires special handling procedures. The physical shape of the cable cannot be drastically altered, meaning that it should not be stretched, twisted, or bent beyond a radius that is 10 times the outside diameter of the cable. Figure C-3 illustrates what can happen to wires that are excessively bent. The twisted pairs are pushed closer together, which causes signal interference between wire pairs and signal distortion.

Cable quality may be poor if a cable manufacturer has substituted some material because another material is in short supply, as happened several years ago during the worldwide shortage of FEP (Fluorinated Ethylene-Propylene Teflon). According to Anixter, there now exist more than 45 plenum and nonplenum cable designs that exhibit varying electrical performance characteristics but are still labeled Category 5 compliant. Moral: Have all existing cable installations tested and certified for use with the networking technology you plan to use. You may find that some existing cable runs will support high-speed networks, while others may need connector replacements, and still other require complete replacement.

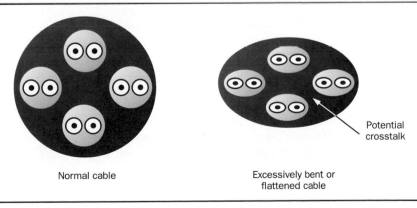

Figure C-3.   *Stressed cable becomes distorted, changing its electrical characteristics.*

The following sections discuss various cable characteristics and environmental conditions that affect performance and how those characteristics affect cable and network design.

Attenuation

Signal transmissions over long distances are subject to *attenuation,* a loss of signal strength or amplitude. Attenuation is also caused by broken or damaged cables. Attenuation is the main reason why networks have various cable-length restrictions. If a signal becomes too weak, the receiving equipment will interpret it incorrectly or not at all. This causes errors, which require retransmission, and loss of performance.

The following shows the weakening of signal due to attenuation:

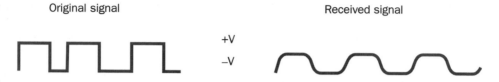

Original signal   Received signal

+V
−V

Attenuation is measured in dB (decibels) of signal loss. For every 3dB of signal loss, a signal loses 50 percent of its remaining strength. Attenuation can be measured by cable testers that inject signals with a known power level at one end of the line and measure the power level at the other end of the line. A typical readout from a Fluke tester is shown in the following illustration. Note that the cable is tested at increasing frequencies and the margin between the tested attenuation and the maximum allowable attenuation (based on Category 5 specifications) is listed.

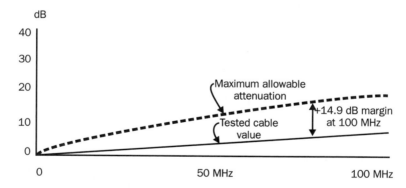

Attenuation is fairly easy to understand. The illustration is primarily meant to show how cable testers graphically display the test values of cable over the entire frequency range against the TIA-rated values.

Attenuation increases with frequency, so 100Base-TX at 80 MHz has higher attenuation than 10Base-T at 10 MHz. Attenuation also increases with temperature, so cable installers may need to plan shorter cable runs in hot environments. Metal conduit also increases attenuation and should be considered when planning cable length. Cable vendors should provide you with technical specifications for their cables.

Capacitance

Capacitance is the ability of a material to store a charge. Copper cables have capacitance that can distort signals by storing some of the energy of a previous signal bit. Capacitance is a measure of the energy that a cable and its insulator can store. Adjoining wires in wire bundles also contribute to the capacitance of a wire. Cable testers can check capacitance values to determine if a cable has kinks or has been stretched. All cable has known capacitance values that are measured in pF (picofarads). Twisted-pair wire used for network cabling is rated at 17–20 pF.

Test equipment from Fluke, Agilent, and other vendors can test for capacitance in order to identify cable link faults or installation problems. However, a TDR (time-domain reflectometer) is usually a better tool for finding such problems. Fluke testers use capacitance to determine if wiring problems like split pairs exist by testing at only one end of a cable (an adapter is not required at the other end of the cable).

Impedance and Delay Distortion (Jitter)

A signal is prone to delay distortion caused by *impedance*, which is resistance that changes at different frequencies. It can cause the different-frequency components within a signal to arrive out of step at the receiver. The effect is more problematic on high-data-rate networks that use high frequencies. Impedance may change abruptly due to kinks and excessive bends in the cable, which cause *signal reflections* that distort data. That leads to retransmissions and a loss in network performance. In the worst case, the network may not operate.

Different types of cable should not be mixed along the same signal path, since a change of impedance at the junction causes a signal reflection back to the source. On high-speed networks, a connector used to join two cables will almost certainly cause an impedance problem because of the untwisting of the wire pairs at the connector. Such connectors should never be used when high-performance networking is implemented over Category 5 cable.

Decreasing the cable length and/or lowering the transmission frequency may solve these problems. Note that the impedance value of a cable can be measured to detect breaks or faulty connections. Data-grade cable should have an impedance value of 100 ohms at the frequency used to transmit data. Category 5 cable meant to support Gigabit Ethernet must be tested for delay distortion.

Delay skew is a problem in networks that transmit on multiple pairs in the same direction at the same time, such as Gigabit Ethernet. It is caused when signals travel at different speeds in each of the wire pairs of a cable. A Gigabit Ethernet transmitter will send signals in parallel across all pairs, which must be reassembled by the receiver. Delay skew desynchronizes these signals, which may prevent reassembly. Category 5 cable meant to support Gigabit Ethernet must be tested for delay skew.

Noise

Transmission lines will have some amount of background noise that is generated by external sources. This noise combines with and distorts a transmitted signal. While noise may be minor, attenuation can enhance its effects. As shown here, the signal is higher than the noise level at the transmitter but is equal to the noise level at the receiver due to attenuation:

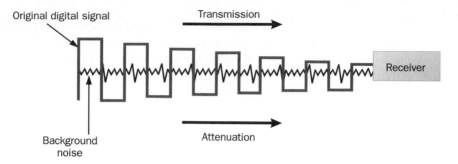

Ambient noise on digital circuits is caused by florescent lights, motors, microwave ovens, and office equipment such as computers, phones, and copiers. Technicians can certify wire by testing for noise levels. If noise is a persistent problem in some areas, it can be avoided by running wire away from sources of noise, by using shielded cable, or by using fiber-optic cable.

As mentioned, twisted-pair cable is supposed to form a balanced circuit where one wire in a pair is equal in amplitude but opposite in phase to the wire it is twisted with. If this characteristic changes due to cable distortion or other factors, the cable becomes unbalanced and starts acting like an antenna, picking up noise from all over, including machines, fluorescent lights, radio stations, and alien transmissions.

Inductance and NEXT (Near-End Crosstalk)

Inductance occurs when current flows on two adjacent metallic conductors. Electromagnetic fields created by the current flows can create signal distortions in adjoining wires. The biggest problem this creates is near-end cross talk (NEXT), which is basically the crossing over of a signal on one wire pair to another wire pair (electromagnetic disturbance). NEXT occurs near the transmitter and creates distortions that typically affect signals on adjacent receive pairs, as shown here:

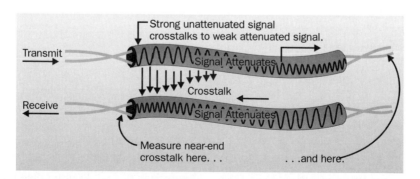

Note that strong fields from the transmit line may overwhelm the weak (attenuated) signal arriving on the receive line, which can lead to intermittent problems, lockups, or complete failure of the system. NEXT should be measured at both end of the cable.

A typical NEXT measurement is shown in the following illustration. This illustration is derived from a Fluke tester. NEXT is measured in dB, with higher values being better. Note that NEXT is measured for all frequencies between 0 and 100 MHz and that crosstalk varies across the spectrum. The lower line indicates the TIA minimum allowed value across the spectrum.

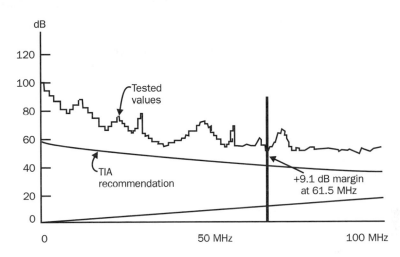

Twisting wire pairs is the primary method for reducing the effects of inductance, but the type of conductor and insulation also play a role. Twisting wire pairs cancels the positive and negative energy on the cable. Because of this, twists in cable must be preserved all the way up to the connection, especially on high-performance networks. In addition, wires cannot be untwisted more than one-half inch from their connection points.

NEXT is measured by injecting a signal on a wire pair and measuring its crosstalk on another wire pair. Every pair must be tested in this way. Fortunately, cable testers make this job easy and automatic. Keep in mind that NEXT refers to crosstalk at the near end, as the name implies. Crosstalk lessens down the cable as the signal strength weakens due to attenuation. However, this also implies that NEXT should be measured at both ends of a link.

FEXT (Far-End Crosstalk)

FEXT is a relatively new cable measurement requirement. It is a measure of the crosstalk noise that exists at the opposite end of a cable (at the receiver) and is only relevant on network technologies that transmit on multiple pairs in the same direction at the same time—that is, Gigabit Ethernet (1000Base-T). What happens is that crosstalk occurs between transmitters as signals are transmitted down the line.

FEXT can be tested by putting a test signal on one pair and measuring how much of that signal crosses over to the other pairs at the far end of the cable. You will often see FEXT discussed in terms of ELFEXT (equal-level far-end crosstalk). ELFEXT provides a standard way to measure far-end crosstalk no matter what the cable length, so that all cabling can be tested to the same certification levels. The ELFEXT test is required for Gigabit Ethernet cable certification.

ACR (Attenuation to Crosstalk Ratio)

ACR is the ratio at which crosstalk affects an attenuated signal. In other words, how much does the noise on the cable distort the signal I am receiving? If the noise is high, and the signal being received is attenuated, the bit error rate (BER) will be high and retransmissions will be necessary, which leads to a loss in network performance. ACR is important because it provides a useful indication of a cable's performance and is helpful when making purchasing decisions. High ACRs indicate high-capacity cables.

The ratio is calculated by dividing attenuation by NEXT. Most cable testers gather all the information about a cable and perform this calculation automatically. Figure C-4 illustrates the relationship between NEXT and attenuation. Note that at the point where NEXT and attenuation meet, the crosstalk and data signal are equal, and the crosstalk exceeds the signal strength at higher frequencies. A cable meter like that from Fluke will measure the ACR and compare it against a TIA limit for NEXT. The margins between the worst-case ACR and the TIA limit are outlined in Table C-2.

Categories of Twisted-Pair Cable

Twisted-pair cable has been used for decades to transmit both analog and digital information. The existing telephone system is mostly wired with voice-grade twisted-pair wires (the wire is not twisted in some cases). Twisted-pair wire is now the preferred wire for network cabling. The twisting of pairs, the quality of the conductive material, the type of insulator, and the shielding largely determine the rate at which data can be transmitted over twisted-pair cable.

The following categories of cable are recognized throughout the industry, and Category 3, Category 4, and Category 5 cable are specified in the TIA/EIA 568-A specification.

- **Category 1**   Traditional unshielded twisted-pair telephone cable that is suited for voice. Most telephone cable installed before 1983 is Category 1 cable. It is not recommended for network use, although modems do a good job of transmitting over it.

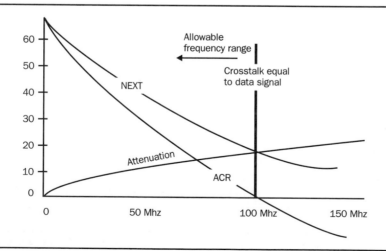

Figure C-4.   *ACR (attenuation to crosstalk ratio), source: Fluke*

- **Category 2**   Unshielded twisted-pair cable certified for data transmissions up to 4 Mbits/sec. This cable has four twisted pairs. It was commonly used for IBM mainframe and minicomputer terminal connections and was also recommended for low-speed ARCNET networks. This cable should not be used for high-speed networking.

- **Category 3**   This category is rated for signals up to 16 MHz and supports 10-Mbit/sec Ethernet, 4-Mbit/sec token ring, and 100VG-AnyLAN networks. The cable has four pairs and three twists per foot (although the number of twists is not specified). Costs are around 10 cents per foot. Plenum cable costs about 40 cents per foot. This cable is installed at many sites as telephone cabling.

- **Category 4**   This category is rated for signals up to 20 MHz and is certified to handle 16-Mbit/sec token ring networks. The cable has four pairs and costs under 20 cents per foot. Plenum cable costs under 50 cents per foot.

- **Category 5**   This category has four twisted pairs with eight twists per foot and is rated for signals up to 100 MHz at a maximum distance of 100 meters. Ethernet 100Base-TX, FDDI, and ATM at 155 Mbits/sec use this cabling. The cable has low capacitance and exhibits low crosstalk due to the high number of twists per foot. It costs under 30 cents per foot. Plenum cable costs under 60 cents per foot. This is the predominant cable installed in all new buildings since the early 1990s. Specifications for this cable are outlined in Table C-2.

Parameter	Category 5	Proposed Category 5E	Proposed Category 6, Class E (Performance at 250 MHz Shown In Parentheses)	Proposed Category 7, Class F (Performance at 600 MHz Shown in Parentheses)
Specified frequency range	1–100 MHz	1–100 MHz	1–250 MHz	1–600 MHz
Attenuation	24 dB	24 dB	21.7 dB (36 dB)	20.8 dB (54.1 dB)
NEXT	27.1 dB	30.1 dB	39.9 dB (33.1 dB)	62.1 dB (51 dB)
Power-sum NEXT	Pending	27.1 dB	37.1 dB (30.2 dB)	59.1 dB (48 dB)
ACR	3.1 dB	6.1 dB	18.2 dB (–2.9 dB)	41.3 dB (–3.1 dB)
Power-sum ACR	N/A	3.1 dB	15.4 dB (–5.8 dB)	38.3 dB (–6.1 dB)
ELFEXT	17 dB	17.4 dB	23.2 dB (15.3 dB	Pending
Power-sum ELFEXT	14.4 dB	14.4 dB	3.2 dB (12.3 dB)	Pending
Return loss	8 dB	10 dB	12 dB (8 dB)	14.1 dB (8.7 dB)
Propagation delay	548 ns	548 ns	548 ns (546 ns)	500 for ns (501 ns)
Skew	50 ns	50 ns	50 ns	20 ns

Table C-2.   *Channel Performance at 100 MHz/100 meters. Source:* Cabling Installation & Maintenance, *November 1998, p. 40, by Valerie Rybinski*

Even though Category 5 is widely used, there are many factors that can prevent a cabling system from delivering the intended data rate. Cable runs should not exceed 100 meters (300 feet). The TIA/EIA specification calls for 90-meter maximum runs from the wiring closet to the wall outlet. An extra 10 meters is allowed to connect computers to the wall outlet and to connect the cable runs to patch panels. Category 5 installations must use Category 5 connectors, patch panels, wall plates, and other components. In addition, proper twisting must be maintained all the way up to connectors.

Enhanced Cabling

Even though Category 5 was considered future-proof, new gigabit-per-second networking schemes have emerged that call for a better class of cable. As mentioned, you can have existing Category 5 cable tested to see if it supports Gigabit Ethernet, but if you are installing new cable for Gigabit Ethernet, choose Category 5E cable, or if you really want to future-proof your installation, consider Category 6 and Category 7 cable. The specifications for these cable types are outlined in Table C-2, earlier in this section.

- **Category 5E (Enhanced)**   This cable has all the characteristics of Category 5, but is manufactured with higher quality to minimize crosstalk. The cable has more twists than traditional Category 5. It is rated at frequencies up to 200 MHz, which is double the transmission capability of traditional Category 5. However, at these frequencies, crosstalk can be a problem, and the cable does not have shielding to reduce crosstalk. This cable is defined in TIA/EIA-568A-5 (Addendum 5).

- **TIA Category 6 and ISO Class E**   These cable types are designed to support frequencies over 200 MHz using specially designed components that reduce delay distortion and other problems. The TIA and ISO are cooperating on this category.

- **TIA Category 7 and ISO Class F**   These cable types are designed to support frequencies up to 600 MHz. Each pair is individually shielded and the entire cable is surrounded by a shielded jacket. Connectors are expected to be specially designed proprietary components. The TIA and ISO are cooperating on this category.

ACR (attenuation to crosstalk ratio) values for the above cable types are listed in the following table. Note that these values for Category 6 and Category 7 are still tentative. The table is meant to provide a comparison at this point in time. Always ensure that new cable is certified for the maximum bandwidth required. Category 5 and 5E cable should be tested at 100 MHz over a 100-meter cable. Category 6 should be tested at 250 MHz over a 100-meter cable.

Category 5 cable	6 to 10 dB ACR at 100 MHz
Category 6 cable	6 to 10 dB ACR at 130 MHz
Category 7 cable	6 to 10 dB ACR at up to 200 MHz

Category 6 and Category 7 specifications have been formulated by the ISO/IEC 11801 groups and the TIA TR42.1.2 committee. One of the best places to find information on these specifications is http://cabletesting.com.

Components of a Structured Cabling System

In the 1980s, vendors and standards organizations saw a need to standardize cabling schemes, and they eventually created the TIA/EIA 568 structured cabling standard. The typical components of a structured wiring scheme are illustrated in Figure C-5. The patch panel provides a place to terminate the horizontal wiring that fans out to work areas. The twisted pairs in the cable are directly attached to the back of the patch panel. The front of the patch panel then provides a place to attach patch cables that connect to network hubs and switches. This arrangement makes moves and changes easily. When someone must be moved to another workgroup or subnetwork, the patch cable on the port leading to his or her computer is moved to another port on a network hub or switch.

As network bandwidth has increased, high-quality cable and components are essential, and they must be installed to exact specifications. A Category 5 cabling system must test within the allowed specifications across the entire cable plant, including all connectors, outlets, patch panels, and cross-connects. This is especially important as networks move to gigabit-per-second speeds.

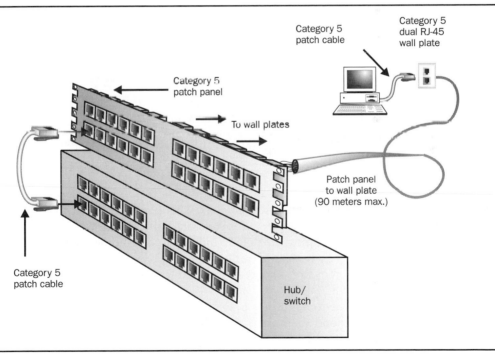

Figure C-5.   *Components of a structured cabling system*

As mentioned, it might be possible to use existing Category 5 cable for gigabit networks, but testing may indicate that some components need replacement.

For more information on cable installation, refer to "TIA/EIA Structured Cabling Standards." Also see "Network Design and Construction" and "Testing, Diagnostic, and Troubleshooting."

Also refer to the Linktionary! site for updates, additional information, and an extensive set of Web links.

Related Entries   Backbone Networks; Bandwidth; Campus Network; Capacity; Channel; Circuit; Data Communication Concepts; Delay, Latency, and Jitter; Electromagnetic Spectrum; Ethernet; Fast Ethernet; Fiber-Optic Cable; Gigabit Ethernet; ISO/IEC 11801 Cabling Standards; Modulation Techniques; Network Concepts; Network Connection Technologies; Network Design and Construction; Power and Grounding Problems and Solutions; Signals; TIA/EIA Structured Cabling Standards; Testing, Diagnostic, and Troubleshooting; Throughput; *and* Wireless Communications

Linktionary!—Tom Sheldon's Encyclopedia of Networking updates	http://www.linktionary.com/c/cabling.html
BICSI (Building Industry Consultants Services Int'l)	http://www.bicsi.org/
ACP (Association of Cabling Professionals) Wireville site	http://www.wireville.com/
Structured Cabling System paper at WebProForums	http://www.iec.org/tutorials/scs
Cabling links at TechFest	http://www.techfest.com/networking/cabling.htm
Anixter Technical Library	http://www.anixter.com/techlib/d0500p01.htm
Cabling Contractors Directory	http://www.cabling-contractors.com
Bitpipe (search for "cabling")	http://www.bitpipe.com
Yahoo!'s Wire and Cable links page	http://www.yahoo.com/Business_and_Economy/ Companies/Industrial_Supplies/Wire_and_Cable

CATV Architecture

The traditional CATV system consists of a shared coaxial cable network that transmits analog television signals to downstream subscribers. It is estimated that over 100 million homes are reachable by CATV cable, of which approximately 75 million of those homes are CATV subscribers.

The cable network mimics the over-the-air radio frequency broadcast signals that you would receive via a TV antennae, but they are carried on cable. Television signals are transmitted in 6-MHz channels.

CATV is a shared cable system that uses a tree-and-branch topology in which multiple households within a neighborhood share the same cable. The topology of the CATV system is pictured in Figure C-6.

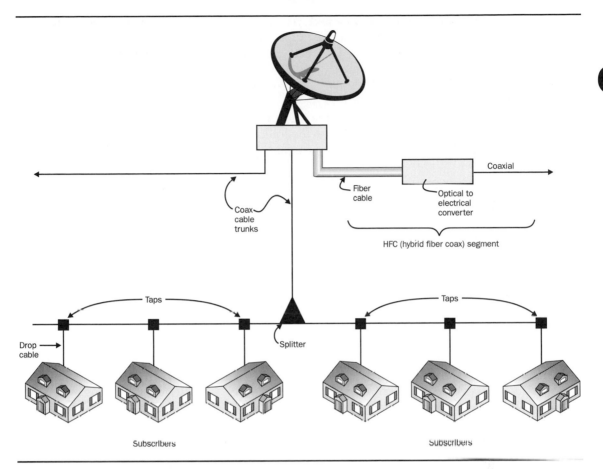

Figure C-6. *The traditional CATV system*

Note that early CATV systems were all coaxial cable. The figure shows a fiber cable trunk combined with a coaxial cable trunk. This dual system is called a hybrid fiber coax (HFC) system. The fiber-optic cable helps overcome attenuation of signals over long distances and problems related to aging components (aging coax cable is commonly replaced with fiber where appropriate). Fiber also provides more bandwidth for future expansion. In some areas, cable providers have been installing fiber cable all the way to the curb. These efforts are covered under "Fiber to the Curb/Fiber to the Home."

Since the CATV network was primarily designed for downstream transmission of television signals, most of the existing network is being refitted to support two-way data transmissions. For example, amplifiers are used at various points along the cable to boost signals, but these amplifiers only work in one direction. Upgrading those components, along with many other components has been a big and expensive task. A temporary solution to provide two-way communications is the dual-path approach, in which subscribers transmit data upstream via a separate telephone connection. This scheme is being phased out as full two-way systems are put into place, as described next.

Cable Data Network Operation

Cable data network subscribers connect to the system via a cable modem. Once connected, subscribers obtain a continuous connection to the Internet via the cable network. The modems are internal devices or connect to PC and home entertainment equipment via USB (Universal Serial Bus) and other interfaces.

The cable modem communicates with the CMTS (Cable Modem Termination System) in the head office. The CMTS provides connections for thousands of cable modems over a network that can stretch to over 100 km with potential data rates up to 50 Mbits/sec. The CMTS also connects to the Internet and other media sources, sending and receiving user packets.

The cable modem performs upstream and downstream conversions. In the downstream process, packet data from the Internet arrives at the cable network provider's head end as shown in Figure C-7. A processor module converts IP packets into MPEG packets and then error checks and modulates the packets onto a carrier wave using QAM/FEC (quadrature amplitude modulation/forward error correction). The output is then forwarded downstream to the subscriber. The subscriber's modem converts the radio frequency information back to IP packets and sends them to the end device. The head-end portion of the cable network can typically receive signals from a variety of sources, including terrestrial and satellite wireless transmissions.

The cable network uses FDM (frequency division multiplexing). As mentioned, TV channels are carried in 6 MHz bands, and one or more of these channels is dedicated to carrying data. The upstream channel typically occupies lower parts of the bandwidth not occupied by TV channels. Downstream rates are typically in the range of 30 Mbits/sec or less while upstream rates are in the range of 300 Kibts/sec to 10 Mbits/sec.

The actual downstream data rate available to users will fluctuate because the system is shared and not all users will be downloading information at the same time. There may be brief periods where all the bandwidth is available to just a few users, which would make for near instantaneous downloads for megabit-size files. The cable operator also has the flexibility to allocate more bandwidth by making additional channels available for data.

The upstream channel is a problem. When upstream channels are used on the cable network, they typically occupy lower frequencies that are subject to noise. In addition, the typical system uses TDMA, so users must contend for access to time slots. As more people access the network, performance drops. Some systems are so noisy that providers require users to use dial-up connections for upstream data.

Noise on the upstream connection is caused by electrical interference from home appliances, motors, and so on. The problem is only made worse by poor quality construction, old cable, loose connections, and improperly shielded cable. All combined, data is in for a rough ride on the way back to the head end. In fact, the noise problem puts a severe limit on the upstream bandwidth.

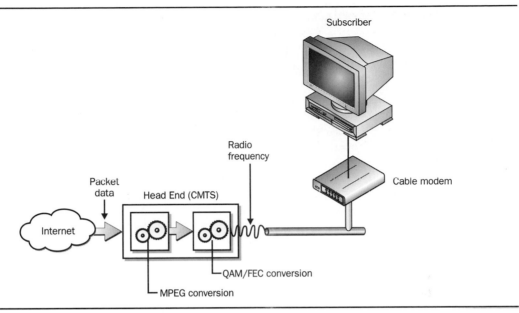

Figure C-7.   *Cable network downstream modulation process*

Many of the problems just discussed can be resolved with Terayon's S-CDMA (Synchronous Code Division Multiplexing). S-CDMA is a spread-spectrum modulation technique that uses available frequencies more efficiently and can operate more reliably than TDMA in noisy upstream channels. Because of the way that S-CDMA spreads its signals, it suffers less from external noise. In addition, S-CDMA synchronizes the upstream signals, which reduces mutual interference, thus opening up more bandwidth. See "CDMA (Synchronous Code Division Multiplexing)" for more information.

At first, one might think that downstream traffic naturally requires more bandwidth than upstream traffic. After all, a single mouse click by a user can unleash an avalanche of data from an Internet server. However, many people are using the Internet for voice calls and to exchange files, digital music, pictures, and video. In addition, many people are setting up Web sites that can potentially overuse the upstream channel. Cable operators have had to deal with this problem by preventing users from setting up Web sites at the far end of the network, where there is the most contention for the upstream channel. These Web sites are moved to data centers that are closer to the core of the Internet.

The shared nature of the cable network introduced security problems. Users armed with network snoopers can watch traffic and attempt to capture valuable information. The cable industry has worked out encryption techniques and other security measures that support privacy. Firewalls are now common in homes.

Cable (CATV) Data Networks

The television cable industry has become a major service provider by allowing data transport over upgraded CATV cable networks. The cable industry has had many plans for delivering unique services to its subscribers. High-resolution digital video has been part of the plan, as well as TV set-top boxes that provide interactive game interfaces, WebTV, and other features. Cable data networks make this possible.

This section describes how broadband services are delivered over the "cable network." It discusses the architecture of the cable network and several competing specifications that are attempting to define a universal cable network standard.

Cable data networks are one of several residential broadband schemes. Other schemes include DSL (Digital Subscriber Line), satellite systems such as Hughes Network System's DirecPC, and wireless data systems discussed under "Wireless Broadband Access Technologies." In fact, MMDS (Multichannel Multipoint Distribution Services) has been called a "wireless cable data network" solution because of its multipoint characteristics. See "Residential Broadband."

Cable Network Provider Services

Cable operators can add various types of Internet-related services to enhance their networks. For example, caching ensures that the benefits of high-speed Internet access available to cable network subscribers is not lost when accessing slower links and servers on the Internet. For example, a number of users in the system may frequently access a server that is connected to the Internet via a 56K modem link. The cable operator can cache this information on its local servers to make the information immediately available to subscribers. See "Content Distribution."

IP telephony support allows users to make voice telephone calls over the cable network. This requires a cable modem that provides integrated MTA (multimedia terminal adapter) support, which basically means it has a telephone jack and a computer connector. IP telephony over cable networks supports multiple phone and simultaneous calls, which are set up as virtual circuits. Additional virtual circuits can be created at any time, with available bandwidth and the number of handsets/headsets being the only restriction. Incoming calls are set up as another virtual circuit. At the cable operator end, an IP-to-PSTN (public-switched telephone network) gateway converts and routes IP-based telephone calls into the traditional telephone system. See "Voice/Data Networks."

Cable operators are working to provide a number of services to their customers, including audio and video servers that can serve up music and movies. A big player is @Home, a cable-specific ISP, meaning that it provides content to cable companies throughout the United States. Cable companies such as Cox Communications deploy @Home Network as part of interactive content for homes and workplaces. Cox is an equity partner in At Home Corporation, along with Comcast Corporation and Tele-Communications.

Corporate users should keep in mind that cable networks are primarily geared toward home users, not companies that want to build high-speed remote office connections, extranets, or other high-usage links. Many cable operators may discourage large organizations from connecting to their cable system. See "Network Access Servers" for alternatives.

Standards Development

Cable standards are designed to provide interoperability between cable modems and head-end gear. Subscribers should be able to buy off-the-shelf cable modems that are guaranteed to connect over the cable network with equipment installed at the cable operators site. Standards benefit both subscribers and operators by making connection easier and promoting new applications. The most important standards are outlined here:

- **DOCSIS (Data over Cable Interface Specification)**   DOCSIS is the result of work done by MCNS (Multimedia Cable Network System Partners Ltd.). This standard has become the most interesting and important, and is covered under the "DOCSIS" heading. Visit http://www.cablemodem.com/.

- **DAVIC (Digital Audio Visual Council)**   DAVIC was a non-profit group that promoted digital audio-visual applications and services based on specifications which maximized interoperability across countries and applications/services. DAVIC developed a digital video broadcast reference model that is popular in Europe and preferred by the European Cable Communications Association (ECCA), a European cable industry organization. DAVIC oriented toward delivering digital video to home users, while DOCSIS is better positioned for data delivery. DAVIC completed its work and closed in 2000. See the "DAVIC" topic and visit http://www.davic.org.

- **IEEE 802.14 Working Group**   This group is defining the physical layer and a MAC (Medium Access Control) layer protocol for HFC networks. The architecture specifies an HFC cable plant with a radius of 80 kilometers from the head end. The group's goal is to develop a specification for delivering Ethernet traffic over the network. ATM networking was also considered for the delivery of multimedia traffic. There has been some conflict between the work done by this IEEE group and the work done by MCNS, but MCNS is implementing part of the IEEE's physical layer work. Still, a paper about cable standards at the CATV Cyberlab claims that "the IEEE 802.14 effort was a failure." In fact, MCNS began work on DOCSIS because the IEEE was not working fast enough on its specification.

- **IETF IP over Cable Data Network (IPCDN) Working Group**   The IPCDN is defining how IP can be delivered over the cable network. Most of its work is centered on DOCSIS and addresses higher levels than the IEEE 802.14 Working Group, which is concentrating on physical and data link layer protocols. IPCDN is defining a specification to map both IPv4 and IPv6 into the HFC access networks. The group is interested in multicast, broadcast, address mapping and resolution (for IPv4), and neighbor discovery (for IPv6). IPCDN is also working on bandwidth management and guarantees using RSVP, security using IPSec, and management using SNMP. More information is at http://www.ietf.org/html.charters/ipcdn-charter.html. The Web site lists a number of Internet drafts that describe various aspects of delivering IP over cable networks.

Related Entries   Broadband; CDMA (Code Division Multiple Access); Communication Service Providers; DAVIC (Digital Audio Visual Council); DBS (Direct Broadcast Satellite), DOCSIS (Data Over Cable Interface Specification); DSL (Digital Subscriber Line); Fiber to the Curb/Fiber to the Home; HALO

(High Altitude Long Operation); Home Networking; Internet Connections; ISP (Internet Service Providers); Local Loop; Network Access Services; Residential Broadband; Satellite Communication Systems; Service Providers and Carriers; Telecommunications and Telephone Systems; Web Technologies and Concepts; Wireless Broadband Access Technologies; *and* Wireless Local Loop

Linktionary!—Tom Sheldon's Encyclopedia of Networking updates	http://www.linktionary.com/c/cabledata.html
Cable Labs	http://www.cablelabs.com/
Bitpipe (search for "cable modem" or "DOCSIS")	http://www.bitpipe.com
IETF Working Group: IP Over Cable Data Network (IPCDN)	http://www.ietf.org/html.charters/ipcdn-charter.html
CATV.org	http://www.catv.org
Cable Datacom News	http://www.cabledatacomnews.com
DOCSIS Consortium at UNH InterOperability Lab (IOL)	http://www.iol.unh.edu/consortiums/
Terayon (S-CDMA information)	http://www.terayon.com/
Links and information: CableModemInfo.com	http://www.cablemodeminfo.com/

Cache and Caching Techniques

A cache is a memory area that holds information so that it may be quickly accessed by the next person that needs it. A cache normally resides between a slow device and a fast device. It may be RAM memory, a disk storage area, or a combination of both. A cache may be a very small amount of memory used by a microprocessor for "shuffling" information during its processing operations, or a cache may be very large—that is, an entire server or cluster of servers that caches frequently accessed Web pages.

This topic covers caching in general. Web-related caching is a topic on its own. The topic "Content Distribution" discusses techniques like that used by Akamai in which content is copied from Web servers to special edge server at ISPs and automatically maintained and updated.

The primary purpose of caching is to keep information readily available for later access. When a process needs information, it first checks the cache to see if the information can be more quickly accessed there, rather than retrieving it from disk or in the case of a network, another server. Caches have *hit rates*, which is a measure of how often the cache information has been accessed. Information in a cache *ages*, meaning that at some point the information in the cache is no longer reliable or no longer needed, so caches are usually *flushed* on an ongoing basis by removing old information or updating it on a continuous basis.

The algorithms for discarding and updating cache information can get quite complex. An algorithm can evaluate all cache entries to decide which entries should be flushed based on how often those entries are used. For example, if a lot of people in your organization access the "Dilbert" Web site to view the latest cartoons, the caching server connected to the Internet may keep that information in the cache and constantly update it from the host site.

Different types of caches are described here.

- **Processor cache**   A processor cache is a block of memory that is part of the processor itself. Information in a processor's cache is much more accessible than information in RAM (random access memory) because it requires fewer cycles to access, is available on the internal bus, and is accessible at the clock rate of the processor rather than a slower external bus rate.

- **Cache RAM**   Many motherboards have slots for installing an intermediate type of memory that sits between the CPU cache and main memory. This memory is faster than main memory but not as fast as the processor cache.

- **Disk read buffer**   Most hard drives have built-in RAM caches that read information ahead of the next request (read-ahead). When an application requests a sector from disk, the disk will automatically read subsequent sectors into its cache in anticipation that the application will need those sectors as well. Without this type of caching, the next requested sector may rotate out of position enough to cause a relatively significant delay when factored over thousands of reads.

- **Disk write buffer**   In the case of hard drives, a write cache can be used to delay a write operation until the processor has a free moment to perform the write. This improves performance, but information in the write cache may be lost forever if the system loses power. The delay is usually only a fraction of a second, but in the case of a server, small amounts of information from many users may be in the cache, so a backup power supply is recommended.

- **Disk cache (in main memory)**   This disk cache should not be confused with the disk buffers discussed above. The disk cache is located in a computer's RAM memory, where it holds blocks of information (rather than whole files) that might be needed again. When information is requested, blocks are moved from disk to cache. In some cases, several blocks are moved into RAM in anticipation of future needs. Most disks also have their own built-in cache to improve performance.

- **Remote cache**   Remote users benefit from cached information since it reduces information exchanges across slow links. Users who access information on remote file servers over wide area networks may experience delays that can be resolved by caching information from remote servers on the local system. In this way, frequently accessed information only needs to cross the link once. Information that does not change often may be permanently cached on the remote user's hard drive.

- **Client/server cache**   In a client/server system, large chunks of data are "transferred" to a cache in the client workstation across the network in anticipation that the user will need that information. This helps the server satisfy the client needs and avoid future servicing, but the client and/or the server must ensure that data remains synchronized and consistent.

- **Intermediate server cache**   In a distributed client/server environment, information may be cached from a back-end server to an *intermediate workgroup server* to improve access for local users who access the same information. When clients in the workgroup request files, they are retrieved from the primary server and cached on the intermediate server in anticipation of future access. This arrangement is useful if the primary server is at a remote location.

- **Distributed directory caching**   Some distributed file systems cache directory information in users' workstations to improve access. This reduces network traffic and other overhead, since workstations can look in their own memory cache for file information.

- **Web server/proxy server cache**   Web servers cache often-accessed pages to improve access for Internet users. Refer to "Web Caching" for more information.

- **Content Delivery Service**   Content delivery has become popular on the Web as a way to improve information access to users around the globe. Typically, "origin" servers (as they are referred to by Digital Island), located at data centers around the globe, maintain and store real-time and dynamic information. Static information is stored at *distribution servers* located even closer to users—that is, at ISPs. Users' access is improved if the data they need is located at a local distribution center; otherwise, it is obtained from the origin servers.

In some distributed file systems (such as the Andrew File System), client workstations maintain a cache on a local hard disk (rather than in RAM memory) for information requested from servers. This cache can become quite large, which introduces consistency problems. There are two methods that help overcome this problem. One model has the client constantly checking with the server to see if information has changed, but this adds a great deal of overhead. Another model uses a call-back approach, in which the server informs clients when information they have in their cache is changed, but this technique requires that servers keep track of clients that have cached information. Refer to "Stateless and Call-Back Filing Systems" for more information.

Related Entries   Client-Server Computing; Content Distribution; Distributed File Systems; Firewall; Proxy Server; Stateless and Call-Back Filing Systems; Storage Systems; Web Caching; *and* Web Technologies and Concepts

Linktionary!—Tom Sheldon's Encyclopedia of Networking updates	http://www.linktionary.com/c/cache.html
Internet Caching Resource Center	http://www.caching.com/
Caching links at Yahoo!	http://dir.yahoo.com/Computers_and_Internet/Internet/World_Wide_Web/Caching/
Caching Links at Netfusion	http://www.nwfusion.com/netresources/caching.html
Merit's Internet Web Cache Project	http://www.merit.edu/michnet/cache/

Call Center Operations

A call center is a business or organizational facility where calls are taken and calls are made. Think of the pledge breaks on your local public television station. When people call to make pledges, an ACD (automatic call distribution) system routes those calls to an available representative. The caller may be put in a queue listening to music (and grumbling the whole time).

RFC 2458 (Toward the PSTN/Internet Inter-Networking—Pre-PINT Implementations, November 1998) provides an official description of a call center. See section 11.2, "Call Center Features."

Other call center examples include credit card authorization facilities, airline reservation systems, and customer service centers for large retail establishments. A common theme is *customer service*, usually 24 hours a day, 7 days a week. A call center may also be called a "customer contact center," a "customer care center," a "customer service center," or a "technical support center."

In the past, call centers were built with large premises telephone switches and mainframe computer systems. Today, the trend is to build call centers with CTI (computer-telephony integration) technologies that are integrated with customer account databases. This makes it possible to integrate call centers and Web site operations. It is now not uncommon to find "click-to-call" buttons on Web pages. In an online shopping scenario, a call center agent should be able to view historical information about a customer's activities while talking with the customer on the phone and dynamically interacting with the customer as they access a Web page.

Amazon.com and similar online stores have proven that users are willing to use a fully automated Web-based sales process, but there will always be cases where customers prefer to talk with a live operator, especially for customer support and help desk. New call center systems integrate Web technologies to help customers and operator/agents make a connection. For example:

1. A customer visits a Web site to view information about a product, event, or other item of interest.

2. A "click-to-call" button exists on the page that the customer clicks to be connected with a service representative.

3. An Internet call is made based on the link information in the button. Ideally the call is made to an agent that specializes in the topic of the Web page.

There are several ways to handle the call:

- In a simple system, the call button sends a message to the call center that a customer needs to be called back.

- Online live chat sessions may be initiated, in which customers and agents type and exchange messages in real time.

- In a computer-telephony integrated (CTI) system, a traditional voice call over the public telephone system is automatically established when the customer chooses the "click-to-call" button.

- In the fully integrated system that supports voice calls over IP networks, the call goes directly over the Internet using VoIP technology.

Enhancements to these models allow the agent and customer to navigate a Web site together. When a call comes in, the Web page the customer is working on pops up on the agent's screen so the agent knows the customer's exact context. In addition, systems linked to customer databases will identify a customer (via a cookie or by previous registration), and display information about the customer to the agent. This information may provide authentication (digital certificates), and help in order processing, the printing of shipping labels, and so on.

For additional information on call center operations, visit the Telephony World site listed at the end of this topic. There, you will find a complete list of vendors that offer call center products. Another good site is HelloDirect.com (The Phone Zone), which offers an incredible amount of information on call centers and Internet telephony. Go to the Network Information section for tutorials, white papers, analysis, and more.

Related Entries   Convergence; CTI (Computer Telephony Integration); PINT (PSTN-Internet Interworking); Telecommunications and Telephone System; Voice/Data Networking; *and* VoIP (Voice over IP)

Linktionary!—Tom Sheldon's Encyclopedia of Networking updates	http://www.linktionary.com/c/cti.html
Call Center Solutions at Telephony World.com	http://www.telephonyworld.com/callcntr/callcntr.htm
Computer Telephony.com, including CallCenter online magazine	http://www.telecomlibrary.com/
TMCnet, an online source from CTI, Internet telephony, and call center solutions	http://www.tmcnet.com/
Hello Direct.com (The Phone Zone)	http://www.hellodirect.net/
Call Centre Magazine	http://www.callcentre.co.uk/
3Com White paper: The Call Center Revolution	http://www.3com.com/news/ccrevolution_jp.html
CosmoCom call center solutions	http://www.cosmocom.com/

Campus Network

A campus network is an autonomous network under the management of a single entity that exists on a university campus or within a local geographic area such as a business park, a government center, a research center, or a medical center. While the network may be managed by a single entity, it may be used by different organizations. Often, a campus network provides and access path into a larger network, such as a metropolitan area network or the Internet.

A "campus network" is not necessarily a "backbone network." While a campus network may be designed with a backbone topology, the issues related to campus networks involve the type of media to be used between buildings, outside cable specifications, rights-of-way, avoidance of natural barriers, underground or aerial cabling requirements, line of site for interbuilding wireless transmissions, and security issues (for example, cables in the open can be tapped or cut). There are also access issues for the users and/or customers that connect to the network such as whether they are charged for usage.

A typical campus network and the various methods used to connect it are illustrated in Figure C-8.

Individual networks within buildings typically connect to the campus network via routers. Hierarchical topologies using high-performance switches may also be used as illustrated in Figure C-9. The Cisco Web site listed at the end of this topic hosts a number of papers on campus network design.

Related Entries   ATM (Asynchronous Transfer Mode); Backbone Networks; Cable and Wiring; MAN (Metropolitan Area Network); Network Access Services; Network Design and Construction; Switching and Switched Networks; TIA/EIA Structured Cabling Standards; *and* WAN (Wide Area Network)

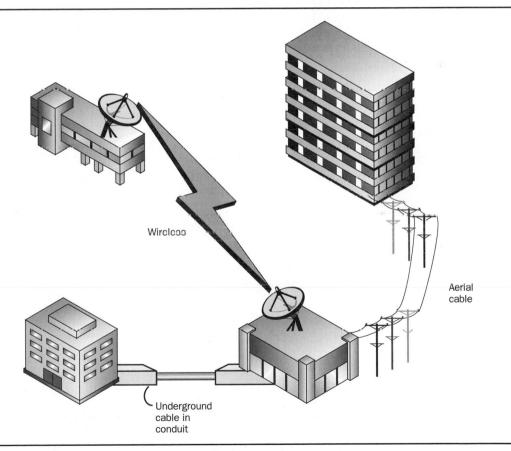

Wireless

Aerial cable

Underground cable in conduit

Figure C-8.   *Campus network connection methods*

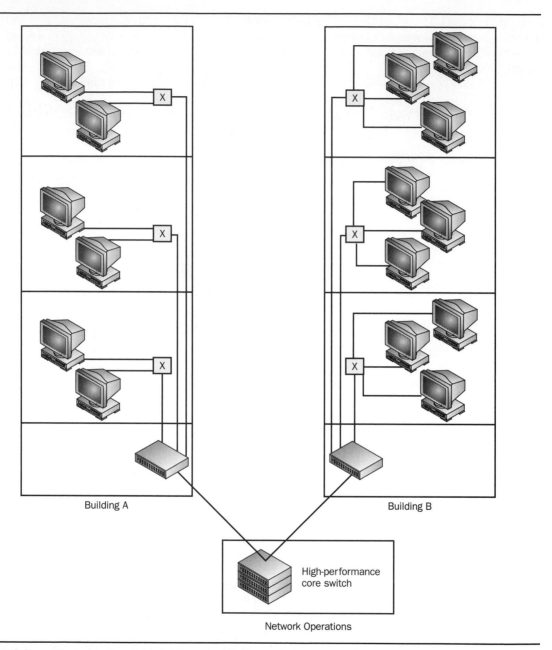

Figure C-9. *Hierarchical switched cabling topologies*

Linktionary!—Tom Sheldon's Encyclopedia of Networking updates	http://www.linktionary.com/c/campusnet.html
Cisco campus design papers (search for "campus network")	http://www.cisco.com/
Campus backbones paper, 3Com	http://www.3com.com/technology/ent_net/

C

Capacity

Capacity is another term for *bandwidth*. It is a measure of a communication system's data transmission capabilities. It is the "width" of the data pipe. For an analog system, it is also the frequency range of that system. A similar term is *throughput*, which refers to the actual measured capacity or bandwidth of a communication system after taking into account factors such as processor performance, media type, delay, transmission errors, and anything else that affects transmission.

A standard Ethernet network has a capacity of 10 Mbits/sec, while Fast Ethernet has a capacity of 100 Mbits/sec. After delay, contention, transmission problems, and other problems are factored in, the actual throughput of a system may be only half of its stated capacity.

Related Entries   Bandwidth; Broadband Communications; Cable and Wiring; Channel; Circuit; Data Communication Concepts; Delay, Latency, and Jitter; Electromagnetic Spectrum; Modulation Techniques; Signals; *and* Throughput

Linktionary!—Tom Sheldon's Encyclopedia of Networking updates	http://www.linktionary.com/b/capacity.html

Capacity Planning

Capacity planning is a technique that network administrators use to plan for network growth and ensure that they expand their network with equipment that will meet projected needs. Capacity planning involves most network systems, including servers, network components such as adapters and cable, switches, routers, and other equipment. It also involves network topologies—that is, planning the upgrade to switched networks over a period of time in anticipation of higher traffic rates and network-wide traffic patterns.

Capacity planning involves measuring current throughput rates. This may be done by analyzing reports and statistical information that is produced by servers and other equipment. Monitoring equipment may also be used to track network performance. Without capacity planning, administrators must deal with problems as they occur, typically by reacting to alarms that indicate that some threshold for a system has been exceeded. Capacity planning can help you deal with problems and disasters before they happen.

Third-party capacity planning tools can help. Such tools are specifically designed to help network administrators plan for the future and prevent impending disasters. They include network-mapping tools that document the network and keep track of problems. However, most important, these tools can simulate traffic on a network, which provides an administrator with a real view of how a network or parts of a network perform under pressure. You can even simulate a disaster to see where the worst problems will be in advance.

The capacityplanning.com Web site listed at the end of this section provides extensive coverage of this topic.

A number of capacity planning and simulation tools are in this section's Web list. These packages can be expensive ($10,000 plus), but are essential for large corporate networks.

- Concord's Network Health automates the collection, analysis, and reporting of network data. It discovers and collects data from existing devices in your network and then condenses it into a graphical presentation showing the most critical information.

- CACI Products Company COMNET Predictor can generate network traffic and vary changes in growth rate so you can examine traffic levels over time. You can perform WAN failures to monitor what happens when they fail. You can also set warnings, alarms, and overloads.

- NETClarity's Capacity Planner emulates network traffic and provides application simulation so you can uncover the impact of new application traffic or network changes before you implement them. It will predict when you will need to add LAN or WAN capacity and point out where bottlenecks are most likely to occur.

Related Entries   Network Management; Performance Measurement and Optimization, *and* Testing, Diagnostics, and Troubleshooting

Linktionary!—Tom Sheldon's Encyclopedia of Networking updates	http://www.linktionary.com/c/capacity_planning.html
CSS Interactive's capacityplanning.com Web site	http://www.capacityplanning.com/
Capacity Planning paper by Dr. Frederick Scholl	http://www.monarch-info.com/capplan.html
Concord Communications, Inc.	http://www.concord.com
CACI Products Co.	http://www.caciasl.com
LANQuest, Inc.	http://www.lanquest.com/
Bitpipe (search for "capacity planning")	http://www.bitpipe.com
ICCM (Institute for Computer Capacity Management)	http://www.iccmforum.com

CAPs (Competitive Access Providers)

A CAP is a service provider that provides LEC (local exchange carrier) services and other data services. An LEC is a telephone company that operates within a local area called the LATA (Local Access and Transport Area). The *ILECs (Incumbent LECs)* are the result of the breakup of AT&T in 1984, which created seven independent RBOCs (Regional Bell Operating Companies) in the U.S. These included Pacific Bell, NYNEX, GTE and others, but mergers and consolidations have changed the original gang of seven. Most ILECs operate across a number of LATAs.

The CAPs (Competitive Access Providers) and CLECs (Competitive LECs) compete with the ILECs in the same service areas. Any nonincumbent carrier is called an ITO (Independent Telephone Company), but some ITO operate area where they do not compete with ILECs.

The IXCs (Interexchange Carriers) provide inter-LATA service (basically long-distance service). Common IXCs are AT&T and MCI Worldcom. More recently, the CLECs are morphing into what are called *ICPs (Integrated Communications Providers)*, which provide a variety of "New Public Network" services including, including Web hosting, and Internet access.

Refer to "Service Providers and Carriers" for a more complete discussion of these service providers.

Capstone

Capstone is a U.S. Government's program to develop cryptography and security standards for protecting government communications as specified in FIPS (Federal Information Processing Standard). These standards must be used by government agencies and private companies that do business with the government. NIST (National Institute of Standards and Technology) and NSA (National Security Agency) are responsible for Capstone. Capstone's major components include an encryption algorithm called Skipjack (and a Skipjack encryption chip called Clipper), a hash function called SHA-1 (Secure Hash Standard-1), and DSA (Digital Signature Algorithm), which is the algorithm used in DSS (Digital Signature Standard). Capstone is also working on a key exchange protocol.

Related Entries   Authentication and Authorization; Cryptography; Digital Signatures; DSS (Digital Signature Standard); FORTEZZA; Hash Functions; Public-Key Cryptography; Secret Key Cryptography; *and* Security

CardBus

CardBus is the 32-bit high-performance bus mastering architecture enhancement to the PC Card. PC Cards are credit-card-size peripherals that plug into mobile computers to provide additional memory, mass storage, and I/O capabilities. PC Card and CardBus are developments of the PCMCIA (Personal Computer Memory Card International Association), a nonprofit trade association and standards body. The PCMCIA also promotes Miniature Card and SmartMedia cards. In the past, cards were known as "PCMCIA Cards," but the industry now refers to products based on the technology as "PC Cards," "PC Card Hosts," and "PC Card Software." CardBus adds high-bandwidth capabilities to the PC Card technology and helps it match the system performance achieved by today's PCI bus-based mobile computers. It is the preferred high-speed mobile interconnect bus. For more information, visit the PCMCIA Web site at http://www.pc-card.com/.

Carrier Signal

A *carrier* signal is a specific frequency in an analog communication channel that is modulated to carry information. Carrier signals are commonly used in AM, FM, and other radio transmissions to differentiate among channels. When you turn a radio dial, you are selecting a carrier frequency. The radio then amplifies the signal carried on the selected frequency. In AM (amplitude modulation), modulation changes the strength or amplitude of the carrier signal. In FM (frequency modulation), the frequency of the carrier signal is modulated.

Related Entries   Analog Transmission Systems; Bandwidth; Bandwidth Management; Cable and Wiring; Channel; Data Communication Concepts; Delay, Latency, and Jitter; Electromagnetic Spectrum; Modulation Techniques; Signals; *and* Throughput

Carriers and Carrier Services

Carrier refer to the local and/or long-distance telecommunication service providers that offer a range of data communication services. This topic is covered under "Service Providers and Carriers."

Related Entries   AT&T (American Telephone and Telegraph); Communication Services; ISP (Internet Service Provider); IXC (Interexchange Carrier); LATA (Local Access and Transport Area); LEC (Local Exchange Carrier); NPN (New Public Network); POP (Point of Presence); PSTN (Public Switched Telephone Network); RBOCs (Regional Bell Operating Companies); Service Providers and Carriers; *and* Telecommunications and Telephone Systems

CCITT (Consultative Committee for International Telephony and Telegraphy)

The CCITT is part of the ITU (International Telegraph Union), which has a history that stretches back to 1865. In that year, 20 countries agreed to standardize telegraph networks. The ITU was set up as part of the agreement to work on subsequent amendments. In subsequent years, the ITU got involved with telephony regulation, wireless radiocommunications, and sound broadcasting. In 1927, the union was involved in allocating frequency bands for radio services, including fixed radio, mobile radio (maritime and aeronautical), broadcasting, and amateur/experimental radio. In 1934, the union changed its name to the International Telecommunication Union to more properly define its role in all forms of communication, including wire, radio, optical, and electromagnetic systems.

After World War II, the ITU became a special agency of the United Nations and moved its headquarters to Geneva. Also at this time, it made mandatory the Table of Frequency Allocations, which allocates frequency bands for each radio service. This table is meant to avoid interference between aircraft and ground communications, car telephones, maritime communications, radio stations, and spacecraft communications.

Then, in 1956, two separate ITU committees, the CCIF (Consultive Committee for International Telephony) and the CCIT (Consultive Committee for International Telegraphy) were joined to create the CCITT to more effectively manage the telephone and telegraph communications.

In 1993, the ITU went through a reorganization. The ITU-T is the ITU's Telecommunications Standardization Sector. Two other main sectors formed at this time were the Radio communications Sector (ITU-R) and the Telecommunications Development Sector (ITU-D). The CCITT was integrated into this new structure.

Even though the ITU-T now creates recommendations and standards, the CCITT recommendations are still mentioned quite frequently, but they should be referenced as now being managed by the ITU.

Related Entries Electromagnetic Spectrum; ITU (International Telecommunication Union); Standards Groups, Associations, and Organizations; Telecommunications and Telephone Systems; *and* Telecommunications Regulation

 ITU Web site   http://www.itu.org

CDDI (Copper Distributed Data Interface)

CDDI is a version of FDDI (Fiber Distributed Data Interface) designed to run on shielded and unshielded twisted-pair cable. It is currently a standard that was developed separately by Cabletron and Crescendo, who combined their technology work and received ANSI standards approval in 1993. A typical CDDI network consists of concentrators with a number of ports for the connection of workstations. Because CDDI has limited cable distances, a CDDI concentrator can connect to an FDDI ring as a subnetwork.

Related Entry FDDI (Fiber Distributed Data Interface)

CDE (Common Desktop Environment)

The CDE is a graphical user interface for UNIX environments that was developed as a cooperative effort by members of The Open Group. CDE provides a user interface for UNIX systems that could be compared to the Microsoft Windows user interface. It also provides a common programming environment for developing off-the-shelf software that works across different vendors' versions of the operating system. Originally, CDE was jointly developed and licensed by Hewlett-Packard, IBM, Novell, and SunSoft. CDE is an important feature of Sun's Solaris operating system.

The Open Group was created in 1996 by the merger of X/Open and the Open Software Foundation. It provides a focal point for the development of international standard, advanced open systems research, and the management of an internationally recognized brand for open systems. For example, Microsoft turned its ActiveX specifications over to the group, and in 1996 the group took over custodianship for the X Window System technology. See "Open Group" for more information.

CDE supports end users, developers, and administrators with a consistent and customizable interface. The consistent interface simplifies software development and marketing. CDE also helps network administrators control desktops throughout the enterprise. It incorporates the Motif 2.1 application programming interface and additional interfaces for programming desktop services, as well as the X Window System. CDE also include a multimedia e-mail facility, Web browser, and an array of desktop tools.

The source code is available for evaluation, or you can purchase the full-distribution source code from The Open Group direct at 1-800-268-5245, or send e-mail to direct@opengroup.org.

Related Entries Network Operating Systems; Linux; Open Group; UNIX; *and* X Window

 The Open Group   http://www.opengroup.org/cde/

Sun Microsystems Solaris Web site   http://www.sun.com/solaris

CDMA (Code Division Multiple Access)

CDMA is an access technology and air interface for wireless digital cellular systems and other communication systems. CDMA was originally developed by Qualcomm, although the underlying technology has been around since the 1940. Qualcomm now holds the patents for CDMA and is greatly benefitting as it becomes the wireless access technology of choice around the world.

CDMA uses wideband spread spectrum techniques for signal transmission, as opposed to narrowband channel techniques used in conventional analog systems. CDMA's use in mobile communications systems is covered under the topic "Wireless Mobile Communications."

CDMA was approved as a digital multiple access technique for cellular telephony by the TIA (Telecommunications Industry Association) in 1993. It is also called "IS-95." The CDMA Development Group uses the trademarked named cdmaOne to describe a full IS-95 system with ANSI-41 switch interconnections and other standards. While CDMA has traditionally been a wireless technology, CableLabs recently adopted S-CDMA (Synchronous CDMA) as developed by Terayon for use in cable data network modems. S-CDMA synchronizes signals so that the signal do not create mutually generated interference. This reduces noise and allows more efficient use of the available spectrum.

In the traditional analog cellular system, the bandwidth is divided into channels using frequency division multiplexing. Each subscriber is allocated a channel for the duration of his or her call. AMPS (Advanced Mobile Phone Service) uses FDMA (Frequency Division Multiple Access). However, AMPS is wasteful of bandwidth because an entire channel is allocated during the call. Some AMPS systems were converted to use TDM (time division multiplexing), which divides each channel into time slots and then allocates time slots to users.

CDMA's spread spectrum technology spreads the information contained in calls over the available bandwidth. The technique has been used for years by the military because the signal is hard to detect and difficult to jam. Technically, CDMA calls are spread out to a rate of about 1.23 Mbits/sec. Spreading involves applying a code to data bits that specifically identifies the information belonging to a particular call (user) in the current cell. While this adds overhead, the bandwidth of the system is wide enough to handle it.

Note that the data bits for all users in the cell are simultaneously transmitted across the wide bandwidth of the system. When a user's device receives signals, it discards all the coded bits except those specifically targeted to it. It then strips off the code and restores the transmission to its original form.

Andrew S. Tanenbaum describes these access methods as follows in his book "*Computer Networks, Third Edition*" (Prentice-Hall PTR, 1996):

> In a large room, many pairs of people are conversing. TDM is when all the people are in the middle of the room, but they take turns speaking, first one then another. FDM is when the people group into widely separated clumps, each clump holding its own conversation at the same time as, but still independent of, the others. CDMA is when they are all in the middle of the room talking at once, but with each pair in a different language. The French-speaking couple just hones in on the French, rejecting everything

else as noise. Thus the key to CDMA is to be able to extract the desired signal while rejecting everything else as random noise.

CDMA advocates promote the security and privacy that spread spectrum can provide. Eavesdroppers have trouble picking up the signal because it is spread out and requires knowledge of a code to separate one call from another. In contrast, the AMPS system and TDMA systems concentrate channels into a narrow band that is easy to monitor with radio receivers.

An industry consortium called CDMA Development Group (CDG) develops products and services for CDMA and works to promote its adoption around the world. The CDG is composed of telecommunication service providers and manufacturers who are pushing for interoperability standards among related equipment vendors.

Qualcomm recently announced HDR (High Data Rate), a specialized data-only CDMA with asymmetric data rates up to 2.4 Mbits/sec when downloading to the mobile device. HDR works in the 1.25-MHz frequency range. HDR is designed to support Internet Protocols. Existing cellular operators can add HDR into their existing infrastructure. In addition, HDR can be installed by service providers to provide wireless Internet access.

CDMA cellular systems are going through transitions as they evolve to third-generation phone systems. In this migration, an interim standard called 1xRTT has been defined by Qualcomm and the CDMA Developers Group. 1xRTT adds packet data capabilities to cdmaOne at up to 144 Kbits/sec in mobile environments. Higher speeds are possible in stationary environments. 1xRTT also doubles the number of possible voice calls and can be easily integrated into existing systems.

The 1xRTT system is a step in the evolution to cdma2000, a full 3G technology. cdma2000 includes all the features of 1xRTT, but also supports both circuit switching and packet switching of voice or data. Data rates go as high as 2 Mbits/sec. cdma2000 is part of the ITU's IMT-2000 (International Mobile Communications-2000) global framework for third-generation wireless communications. Refer to "Wireless Mobile Communications" for more information.

Related Entries   Cable (CATV) Networks; Electromagnetic Spectrum; Mobile Computing; Satellite Communication Systems; Spread Spectrum Signaling; Wireless Communications; Wireless Broadband Access Technologies; *and* Wireless LAN

Linktionary!—Tom Sheldon's Encyclopedia of Networking updates	http://www.linktionary.com/c/cdma.html
CDMA Development Group	http://www.cdg.org
Qualcomm CDMA Web site	http://www.cdma.com/
Spread Spectrum Online (one of the best sites for tutorials, links, references, and more)	http://sss-mag.com/
Motorola CDMA information	http://www.mot.com/CNSS/CIG/Technology/cdma.html
Sierra Wireless Web site	http://www.sierrawireless.com/
Andrew Seybold's Wirelessroadmap.com	http://www.wirelessroadmap.com
Packet Radio Web site	http://www.tapr.org/tapr/html/pktf.html

CDPD (Cellular Digital Packet Data)

CDPD (Cellular Digital Packet Data) provides packet-switching data services on wireless analog cellular systems such as AMPS. CDPD is sometimes called wireless IP, although that term now means much more, as discussed under the "Wireless IP" section in this book. CDPD handles the types of bursty traffic that are common with network-connected users, such as short exchanges of information like electronic mail or database queries. Data is sent in packets across a wireless circuit that is shared by other users, or across any channel that is idle. Users are billed in subminute billing units to accommodate short data bursts. For more information, see "Wireless Mobile Communications."

CDSA (Common Data Security Architecture)

CDSA is essentially security *middleware*. It is a specification of The Open Group that provides a set of APIs that independent software developers can use to embed security into desktop and network applications. In particular, CDSA is designed for use in electronic commerce, communications, and content delivery applications.

An important feature of CDSA is its ability to provide the highest level of encryption allowable in the country where it is being used. International companies can use CDSA to comply with the government encryption regulations of the countries they operate in.

The architecture is designed around two themes:

- *Digital certificates* are used to identify users and to provide authorization information.

- *Portable digital tokens* are used to carry cryptographic keys and perform cryptographic operations.

These themes support data encryption, data integrity (the ability to detect tampering), authenticity (the ability to validate the sender), and nonrepudiation (the ability to prevent a sender from denying that they sent data). CDSA supports X.509 digital certificates, the Digital Signature Algorithm, and LDAP (Lightweight Directory Access Protocol).

The CDSA architecture is multilayered. The bottom *service provider modules* layer consists of cryptographic service providers, trust model libraries, certificate libraries, data storage libraries, and other yet to be defined services.

The next layer up is the CSSM (Common Security Services Manager) layer, which consists of published APIs that applications use to access security features such as cryptographic operations and certificate management operations. At the top of the system are security services and applications that are usually written in C, C++, and Java.

Related Entries   Authentication and Authorization; Certificates and Certification Systems; Cryptography; Digital Signatures; Middleware; *and* Security

Linktionary!—Tom Sheldon's Encyclopedia of Networking updates	http://www.linktionary.com/c/cdsa.html
The Open Group CDSA Web site	http://www.opengroup.org/public/tech/security/cdsa/
Intel Architecture Labs information on CDSA	http://www.intel.com/ial/security/
Open Information Interchange CDSA Web page	http://158.169.50.95:10080/oii/en/secure.html#CDSA

CEBus (Consumer Electronic Bus)

One of several network architectures designed for home and small business use. Other standards include X-100 and Lon Works. Refer to "Home Networks" for more information.

Cells and Cell Relay

Cells are the basic unit for packaging and transmitting data in ATM. Cell relay is the process of moving cells through switching elements. ATM cells are 53 bytes in length. The first 5 bytes contain header information such as source and destination address; the remaining 48 bytes are reserved for data. In contrast, frames are the basic unit of data transport in local area networks and frame relay networks. The main difference is that frames vary in size and may be up to 8,000 bytes in length. The difference between cells and frames is illustrated here:

Fixed-size cells can be switched at very high speed and add predictability to data transmissions. In contrast, variable-length frames produce unpredictable traffic patterns. Imagine a traffic intersection with a four-way stop sign. If all the vehicles entering the intersection are Porsche 911s, delays should be minimal. But if the vehicles are a mix of cars, buses, and trucks with trailers, only an average throughput can be determined.

ATM is ideal for deliverying real-time traffic like voice and video because its predictable traffic flows support QoS. It is a simple matter to reserve cells for specific types of traffic like voice to guarantee that traffic will get through. MPLS can be used in frame-based networks to add traffic engineering, which is step toward providing QoS in those networks.

On the downside, the 5-byte header tends to be excessive when transferring large amounts of data. The term "cell tax" is often used to describe the overhead imposed by ATM cells.

There has always been a rift between the telecommunication engineers who advocated cells and the data communication engineers who advocated packet switching. The outcome of this rift was summarized by Charles N. Judice writing in *IEEE Communications Magazine*, August 2000:

> I submit that the communication industry lost it when the computer guys could not get their 1000-byte packets into ATM standards. While those of us with the "Bell Shaped Heads" thought we won a great compromise in establishing 53 bytes as the ATM packet size, what we really did was demonstrate to the computer industry that we had little understanding of their requirements or the implications of their design. So rather than design the next-generation network with us, they just kept making their datagram network work harder and faster.

Related Entries   ATM (Asynchronous Transfer Mode); Datagram and Datagram Services; Framing in Data Transitions; MPLS (Multiprotocol Label Switching); Packet and Cell Switching Concepts; Switch Fabric and Bus Design; Switching and Switched Networks; *and* Virtual Circuits

Linktionary!—Tom Sheldon's   http://www.linktionary.com/c/cell_relay.html
Encyclopedia of Networking updates

Cell Relay Retreat   http://cell-relay.indiana.edu/cell-relay/index.html

Scan Technologies tutorials   http://www.scan_technologies.com/tutorials.htm/

Cellular Communication Systems

See Wireless Mobile Communication; Wireless Communications.

Central Office

See CO (Central Office).

Centrex (CENTRal Exchange)

A single telephone relies on the telephone company's switching equipment to set up call circuits. Organizations with many phones have a choice of relying on equipment at the telephone company to set up and control calls, or to set up their own switching equipment. A PBX is a telephone exchange device located at a customer premises site. All the company's phones are connected to this switch. The switch itself is then connected to the phone company via a single trunk line, usually a T1 or fractional T1 line.

Companies with PBXs typically have unique telephone numbers for each inside phone. The first few digits of these numbers are similar. In addition, people inside the company can call other insiders by dialing the last few unique digits of their "extension." Calls to the outside world go through the PBX over a trunk line connected to the local carrier.

Centrex is a PBX-like service offered by the RBOCs in which the switching equipment is located at the carrier site, not the customer premises. Basically, the carrier creates a PBX for a customer in their switching equipment. The main advantage of doing this is to get the PBX out of your building and locate it where qualified service technicians are available to service it. In addition, Centrex makes it easy to keep up with the latest telephone technologies. Carriers can easily offer you new Centrex phone services. In contrast, a PBX may require an expensive upgrade to support those same services. In a decision about whether to use Centrex or PBX, Centrex is usually the preferred solution for small to medium-size companies. Larger companies usually benefit from purchasing their own on-site PBX equipment.

The name "Centrex" is trademarked and was formerly owned by AT&T, but is now owned by the RBOCs.

As Internet telephony and voice/data networks take hold, managers should evaluate new VoIP (Voice over IP) equipment and standards as they emerge. An "IP PBX" installed on-site may be a viable solution. In contrast, many carriers are offering Centrex-like services that support voice/data networking. For example, AT&T's INC (Integrated Network Connection) services supports up to 40 voice calls simultaneously with 512 Kbits/sec of data and IP (Internet Protocol) traffic using an AT&T-owned ATM multiplexer located on the customer's premises.

Related Entries   PBX (Private Branch Exchange); Telecommunications and Telephone Systems; *and* Voice/Data Networking

CERN

CERN is the French acronym for the European Laboratory for Particle Physics, which is located in Geneva, Switzerland. CERN gained importance with regard to networking and the Internet because it is where Tim Berners-Lee and associates created the communication protocols that brought about the World Wide Web. The protocols allowed users with browsers to access information on Web servers. This work was extended in 1993 when the NCSA (National Center for Supercomputing Applications) released the graphically oriented Mosaic Web browser. Marc Andreessen, who headed up Netscape before it was purchased by AOL, was responsible for that work.

CERN Proxy Services

See Firewall; NAT (Network Address Translation); Proxy Server; RSIP (Realm Specific IP); *and* Security

CERT (Computer Emergency Response Team)

CERT is an Internet security advisory group that tracks security breaches and publishes advisory reports about them.

 CERT's Web site   http://www.cert.org

Certificates and Certification Systems

A certificate is a digital record that holds information about a person or organization, and usually the public key for that person or organization. In the words of Ron Rivest, one of the cofounders of RSA Data Security, "Digital certificates are your Internet calling card." They are personal digital IDs that can be used for a variety of security uses.

A certificate binds a public key to the owner of that key and provides a way to exchange keys in a reliable way. Once exchanged, keys are used to encrypt and decrypt messages. Briefly, the public-key scheme works like this:

1. Bob wants to send private messages to Alice. He generates a pair of keys using a special utility. These keys are unique and linked to one another. Data encrypted by one key may be decrypted by the other (and no other).

2. Bob keeps the private key and makes the public key available for public use.

3. When Bob is ready to send a private message to Alice, he encrypts it with his private key.

4. Upon receipt of the message, Alice decrypts it with Bob's public key.

A reverse path is also possible. Alice can encrypt a message with Bob's public key and send it to Bob. Upon receipt, Bob decrypts the message with his private key. Alternatively, Alice can encrypt a message with her private key and Bob can decrypt the message with Alice's public key.

The advantage of a CA is that it provides a way for Bob and Alice to exchange public keys in a secure and reliable way. If a key is in a CA-issued certificate, the key can be considered the authentic key of the person to which the certificate was issued.

Certificates are issued by certification authorities (CAs) such as Verisign or even the U.S. Post Office. Once issued, a certificate is usually made available to the public. Basically, by issuing a certificate, the CA is saying "We have verified that the information in this certificate about this person or organization is true and that the public key included in the certificate is a valid public key for the person or organization."

Not all certificates are designed for public key distribution. An *attribute certificate* binds descriptive data to someone or to a separate public key certificate. The data are digitally signed by an attribute authority, which guarantees the contents through its own signature. The certificates may include identifications, access control, security clearances, and so on. An interesting document is RFC 2693 (SPKI Certificate Theory, September 1999), which describes certificate usage for authorization, rather than authentication.

Certificates can be used in the authentication and secure message exchange procedures between clients and servers. Certificates can even be used in place of credit card numbers for online buying transactions. The SET (Secure Electronic Transaction) scheme developed by major credit card companies is designed to hide credit card numbers from merchants by substituting the card number with a digital certificate. See the "SET (Secure Electronic Transaction)" topic for more details.

The risk of message forgery is perhaps a more important reason to use public key infrastructures. As electronic commerce grows, the need to ensure that messages are authentic and have not been altered grows. Another problem is message repudiation—that is, the author of a message denies having sent a message. These problems can be averted by digitally signing messages. The message is combined with the user's key and hashed to create a unique message digest that can be used later to detect alteration and prove that a user signed the original message.

Creating Certificates

CAs provide a variety of services, including verifying the identities of people or organizations that apply for certificates, managing and renewing digital certificates, maintaining certificate revocation lists (certificates that have been revoked), and managing certificate servers and certificate information in a secure way.

Ideally, all certificates should have a standard format (layout, structure) so that they can be used anywhere around the world. The most accepted certificate standard is X.509 version 3 as defined by the ISO/IEC. The certificate layout consists of information fields such as the X.509 version number, serial number, issuing CA, expiration period, holder's name, holder's public key, and optional information that may be customized to fit the application. See "X.509 Certificates."

The following steps outline the basic certificate issuance procedure. Note that these steps also apply to enterprise certificate servers as well, although some verification steps may be skipped.

1. An individual needing a certificate generates a pair of keys, one public and one private.

2. The individual applies for the certificate by providing personal information and the keys to the CA.

3. The CA verifies that the information is accurate.

4. The CA creates a "digital document" from the information, including the public key, expiration date, user information, and so on.

5. The CA signs the digital document with its own private key. This "locks down" the contents of the document so that alterations can be detected and provides assurance that the document was issued by the CA.

A CA digitally signs the certificates it issues with its private key. The certificates can then be verified with the CA's public keys. The certificate contains a message digest that the CA created with its private key. If the client can create the same digest with the CA's public key, the certificate is considered valid and unaltered. Therefore, the public key in the certificate is considered valid for the owner of the certificate.

One must trust that the public key used to verify a certificate is itself authentic. The trust comes from the fact that a CA's public key is in a certificate that has been signed by a higher-level authority and this trust extends up a hierarchy of trust to authorities such as government agencies or international organizations. This hierarchy of trust is part of a public key infrastructure as discussed later.

Validating a Certificate

SSL (Secure Sockets Layer) is a common protocol used to secure communications between Web clients and Web servers. SSL provides one of the best examples of certificate usage. Typically, a Web client needs to authenticate a server to ensure that a site is not being spoofed. Servers may also require that clients have certificates for client authentication. Here are the steps for authenticating a server certificate:

1. Obtain the issuing CA's public key by getting a copy of its certificate. Software that uses certificates will often come with a collection of CA public keys. For example, you can view certificates in Internet Explorer 5 by choosing Internet Options on the Tools menu, then clicking Content and Certificates.

2. Validate the certificates signature with the CAs public key and check the certificate's validity period or the CAs revocation list to see if a certificate is outdated or has been revoked.

3. Verify the server's domain. The certificate lists the domain name of the server. The client compares this to the domain name of the server it is actually connected to. If they compare, the server must be real and not an imposter server.

4. Complete SSL connection. If all of the above checks out, the client and server continue with the steps in the SSL handshake and establish a connection.

See "SSL (Secure Sockets Layer)" for a complete discussion. A more elaborate scheme is IPSec (IPSecurity), which uses certificates to build secure VPNs (Virtual Private Networks). With the highest level of security in a secure VPN scheme, entire IP packets are hidden, including the headers, not just the packet payloads.

Certificate Authorities and Public-Key Infrastructure

A CA puts itself in the position of trust. It must implement certification policies and define the procedures for verifying certificate holders and revoking certificates, if necessary. It must also create and manage keys and ensure that certificate holder information and key information are kept confidential. The level of trust that a CA has depends on the thoroughness and accuracy of its certification policies.

> **Note** *Many organizations prefer to manage their own certificate issuance based on their own policies and certificate requirements. Most of the vendors listed at the end of this topic supply in-house systems.*

Verisign is a well-known certificate authority. You can visit its Web site for a complete description of the procedures the company uses to issue and manage certificates. VeriSign's class 1 certificate, which you can obtain for free, contains only a user's name and e-mail address. Higher-level certificates may contain more personal information. In fact, companies can work with Verisign to create custom containers with specific information fields.

The framework for managing keys (issuance, distribution, storage, revocation, etc.) is handled by a framework system that includes servers, server software, policies, and procedures. This combination is called PKI (public-key infrastructure). An important feature of a PKI system is to allow key distribution and a path of trust for users and organizations who do not know or necessarily trust each other, which is the case with electronic commerce on the Internet. Refer to "PKI (Public-Key Infrastructure)" for more information.

The IETF has two working groups that are working on PKI-related topics. The PKIX (Public-Key Infrastructure) Working Group is developing Internet standards needed to support an X.509-based PKI. The SPKI (Simple Public-Key Infrastructure) Working Group is committed to developing key certificate formats and associated protocols that are *simple* to understand, implement, and use. SPKI is designed to support security for Internet applications, including IPSEC protocols, encrypted electronic mail and Web documents, payment protocols, and other applications with support for a range of trust models. The following Internet RFCs are useful for continuing with this topic.

- RFC 2459 (Internet X.509 Public Key Infrastructure Certificate and CRL Profile, January 1999)

- RFC 2510 (Internet X.509 Public Key Infrastructure Certificate Management Protocols, March 1999)

- RFC 2511 (Internet X.509 Certificate Request Message Format, March 1999)

- RFC 2527 (Internet X.509 Public Key Infrastructure Certificate Policy and Certification Practices Framework, March 1999)

- RFC 2692 (SPKI Requirements, September 1999)

- RFC 2693 (SPKI Certificate Theory, September 1999)

Related Entries   Authentication and Authorization; Cryptography; Digital Signatures; Electronic Commerce; Hash Functions; Key Distribution and Management; PKI (Public-Key Infrastructure); Public-Key Cryptography; Security; SET (Secure Electronic Transactions); SSL (Secure Sockets Layer); TLS (Tranport Layer Security); *and* X.509 Certificates

Linktionary!—Tom Sheldon's Encyclopedia of Networking updates	http://www.linktionary.com/c/certificates.html
IETF Working Group: Public-Key Infrastructure (X.509) (PKIX)	http://www.ietf.org/html.charters/pkix-charter.html

IETF Working Group: Simple Public Key Infrastructure	http://www.ietf.org/html.charters/spki-charter.html
CommerceNet	http://www.commerce.net
VeriSign	http://www.verisign.com
Entrust	http://www.entrust.com/
Xcert	http://www.xcert.com/
OII Guide to Information Security	http://158.169.50.95:10080/oii/en/secguide.html

Note *For additional links, see "PKI (Public-Key Infrastructure)" and "Security."*

CGI (Common Gateway Interface)

CGI is a server extension that extends the capabilities of Web servers. You write server extensions to make your Web site more active and interesting. Instead of delivering a stale static page, CGI (and other server extensions) lets Web clients request information from Web servers. The user fills out a *form* that is submitted to the server. The server uses the submitted information to query a database or as input to a program. The results are then used to build a custom Web page and send it to the client. Note that there is no "back-and-forth" information between the server and client. A user must fill out a form and submit it. Blank fields or fields with incorrect information must be detected, and the client must be asked to resubmit the form.

CGI is nonconversational. It is not possible to stop in the middle of processing data from a Web browser and go back to the Web browser to ask for data to be corrected. CGI allows only for data to be input. The CGI processes the data, produces output, and then terminates. If a gateway needs to have data corrected, it can only run to completion and then start over when the data is re-presented by the Web server.

The *CGI interface* is the protocol that provides a two-way interface between Web clients and Web servers and the *CGI script* is the set of commands that determines what happens when they communicate. CGI was invented to extend the HTTP protocol. It consists of the following:

- The CGI *control tags* and *field specifiers* to be placed in HTML documents
- *Environment variables* in memory where the server places information used by scripts
- The flow of information between client, server, and script.

The steps that Web site developers follow to use CGI are to first create the HTML (Hypertext Markup Language) form and add the tags that define the input boxes, drop-down list boxes, and buttons that appear on forms to collect input from users. Next, a CGI script is written to accept the input that the end user types on the HTML form and do something with it, like make a query to a back-end database. Perl is a scripting and reporting tool that many programmers use to build CGI scripts. Refer to "Perl."

CGI is notoriously slow, so Open Market created a protocol called FastCGI to address the problem. FastCGI eliminates the need for servers to create address spaces every time it needs to run CGI by maintaining a pool of available CGI processes that are always available.

For more information on gateways, forms, and CGI, refer to the Web pages listed here, or refer to books on Web server design. Many books include disks that contain sample programs for collecting common information from Web clients.

Related Entries   Cookies; Distributed Object Computing; Java; PERL; Web Technologies and Concepts; *and* XML (Extensible Markup Language)

Linktionary!—Tom Sheldon's Encyclopedia of Networking updates	http://www.linktionary.com/c/cgi.html
W3C CGI Web page with links	http://www.w3.org/CGI/
NCSA CGI Web page with links	http://hoohoo.ncsa.uiuc.edu/cgi/
Alan Richmond's CGI page	http://www.stars.com/Authoring/CGI/
CGI Authoring Resources	http://www.stars.com/Authoring/CGI/Resources.html
Jonathan Roy's Unofficial FastCGI Page with plenty of links	http://www.fastcgi.com/
irt.org Home page (extensive information on CGI and Perl)	http://www.irt.org/
PC Lube and Tune CGI Tutorial	http://pclt.cis.yale.edu/pclt/WEBAPP/cgi.htm

Challenge/Response Protocol

See CHAP (Challenge Handshake Authentication Protocol).

Channel

A channel is essentially a communication circuit between two or more devices. You can think of a channel as a pipe for sending data between two systems. In a computer system, a channel provides an input/output interface between the processor and some peripheral device. In telecommunication, a channel may take one of the forms described below and pictured in Figure C-10. Keep in mind that a channel may be one of many channels that run over the same physical circuit. These channels are called *virtual channels* or *virtual circuits*.

- *One channel* carried on a physical wire or wireless medium between two systems. The twisted-pair copper wire in the local loop between your phone and the local central office is a dedicated channel that forms its own circuit.

- *Time-division multiplexed channels,* in which signals from several sources such as telephones and computers are merged into a single stream of data and separated by intervals of time.

- *Frequency-division multiplexed channels,* in which signals from many sources are transmitted over a single wire or wireless medium by modulating each signal on carriers at different frequencies.

- *Packet or cell switching,* in which packets from many sources are multiplexed and transmitted from endpoint to endpoint over a switched network.

C

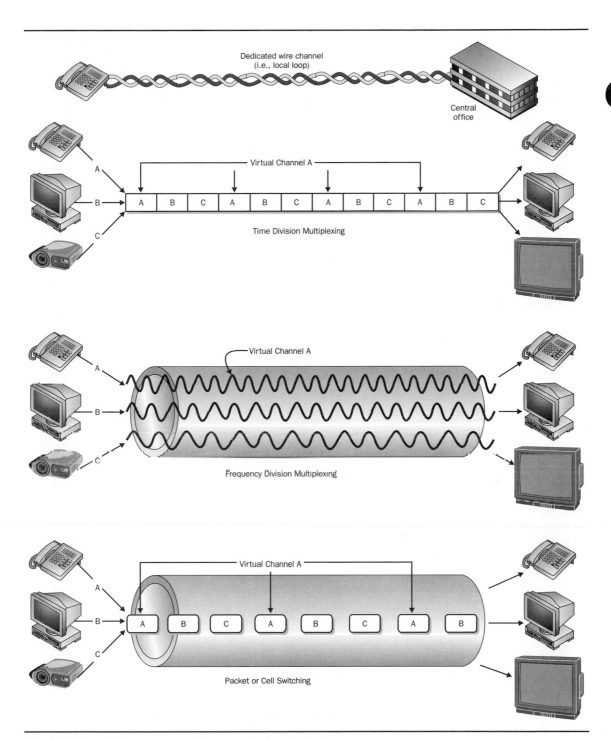

Figure C-10. *Different types of communication channels*

As for applications that use network communications, a channel is a logical link between applications and processes running on different systems. A system may have several logical channels operating at the same time, with many systems. When connected to the Internet, you can simultaneously obtain your mail and connect with a server to check stocks or news. Packets flow into your system over the same line, but those packets form connections that appear as channels between your system and the specific servers providing the services. Each connection is managed as a socket, which is essentially an IP address and a port number. See "Ports, TCP" and "Sockets API" for more information. Also see TCP (Transmission Control Protocol).

The topics "Bandwidth" and "Delay, Latency, and Jitter" discuss channel capacities and delay problems. A related topic is "Throughput." The topic "Cable and Cable Concepts" discusses cabling systems and things that affect transmissions, including interference, cable distance, and so on.

Related Entries   Bandwidth; Cable and Cable Concepts; Capacity; Circuit; Circuit-Switching Services; Data Communication Concepts; Modulation Techniques; Multiplexing; Switching and Switched Services; Throughput; *and* Virtual Circuits

Channel Banks

See PBX (Private Branch Exchange); Multiplexers.

CHAP (Challenge Handshake Authentication Protocol)

CHAP is an authentication protocol used for remote logon, usually between a client and server or Web browser and Web server. A challenge/response is a security mechanism for verifying the identity of a person or process without revealing a secret password that is shared by the two entities. It is also referred to as a three-way handshake. An important concept related to CHAP is that the client must prove to the server that it knows a shared secret without actually revealing the secret (sending the secret across the wire could reveal it to an eavesdropper). CHAP provides a mechanism for doing this.

When a client contacts a system that uses CHAP, the system (herein called the authenticator) responds by sending the client a "challenge." The challenge is some information that is unique for this authentication session. The client then takes this information and encrypts it using a previously issued password that is shared by both the client and authenticator. The result of this operation is then returned to the authenticator. The authenticator has the same password and uses it as a key to encrypt the information it previously sent to the client. It compares its results with the encrypted results sent by the client. If they are the same, the client is assumed to be authentic.

 These schemes are often called "proof of possession" protocols. The challenge requires that an entity prove possession of a shared key or one of the key pairs in a public key scheme.

This procedure is repeated throughout the session to verify that the correct client is still connected. Repeating these steps prevents someone from "stealing" the client's session by "replaying" information that was intercepted on the line.

The specifics of the routine are described next and pictured in Figure C-11. Note that this technique doesn't require that the client send a password in the open over the wire to the server (authenticator). The password is already shared by both the client and the authenticator, and each use it to execute their own separate hash functions.

1. The client connects with the authenticator.

2. The authenticator responds by sending a challenge to the client.

3. The client appends the shared secret to the challenge and runs the combination through one-way hash function, which creates a *message digest* that is impossible by current standards to revert to its original form (think of trying to reassemble a smashed pumpkin).

4. The client returns the results of this operation to the authenticator.

5. Separately, the authenticator performs this same operation. It combines and hashes the shared secret and the challenge it sent to the client. Then it compares its results with the results received from the client.

6. If they match, the client is considered authentic. If not, the connection is terminated.

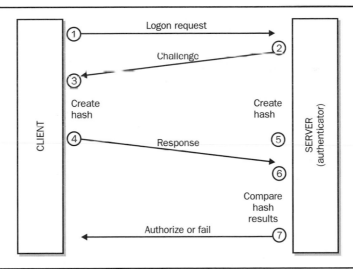

Figure C-11.   *The challenge/response mechanism*

Another important feature is that the authenticator issues a different challenge at every logon and periodically as the session progresses to detect session that have been taken over by a hacker. When each new challenge is sent, it must be hashed with the shared secret. If someone has taken over a session, it is presumed they don't have shared secret, which causes the authentication to fail, and the server will disconnect the session.,

In this scenario, the authenticator challenges the client—a one-way scheme. The client will also want to make sure it is connected to the right server, since a hacker could also break into a session and masquerade as a server. The solution is to run CHAP in both directions, but the shared secret for each CHAP session should be different

The CHAP packet format and method for exchanging packets during authentication reveal more detail about how CHAP works. The exchange is pictured in Figure C-12. Note that the CHAP packet size is variable depending on the type of packet being sent.

The fields in the CHAP packet are described here:

- **Code field**   The Code field contains a numeric value that identifies the type of CHAP packet as follows: 1 = Challenge packet (authenticator to client), 2 = Response packet (client to authenticator), 3 = Success packet (authenticator to client upon successful authentication), 4 = Failure (authenticator to client upon failed authentication). The authenticator terminates the link after sending a code 4 packet.

- **Identifier**   This field contains a value that identifies a particular authentication session. All the challenge and response packets have the same identifiers to distinguish the packets for other authentication sessions.

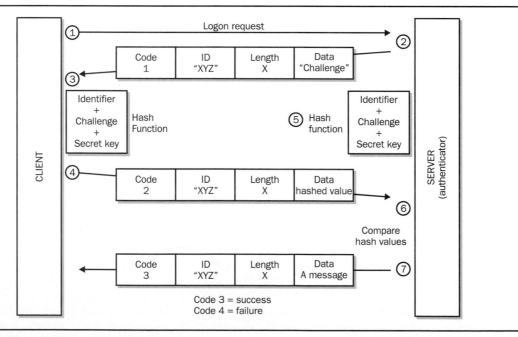

Figure C-12.   *CHAP packets exchange*

- **Length**   This field contains a value that indicates the length of the CHAP packet, including the Code, Identifier, Length, and Data fields.

- **Data (Value)**   This field has a variable size depending on the packet code type, and contains the following information:

    - **Challenge value (code 1)**   The value in the field is a unique and unpredictable value that is generated by the authenticator. This uniqueness prevents attackers from attempting to fool the authenticator with a previously intercepted value.

    - **Response value (code 2)**   The value field holds the one-way hash created by the client. The hash is created by encrypting a combination of the identifier, the secret key, and the challenge value. The hash is usually created by using MD5 encryption.

    - **Success or Failure value (code 3 and code 4)**   The value for these packets depend on the implementation, but is usually just a human-readable message that has no affect on the protocol operation.

In Figure C-12, note how the code values and the data values differ in the exchanged packets. Steps 3 and 5 occur at about the same time on the client and authenticator, and then the authenticator waits for the hash results from the client and compares them to its own. It then sends a success or fail packet, depending on the results of the comparison.

A challenge/authentication scheme can also be used with public keys to authenticate users. Assume Alice sends Bob a challenge. She encrypts the challenge with Bob's public key. Bob decrypts the challenge with his private key and returns the challenge to Alice, thus proving to Alice that he holds the private key associated with the public key Alice used to encrypt the challenge. Another technique is that Bob combines the challenge with some other information and signs it with his private key, returning the results to Alice. Alice performs the same operation with Bob's public key and compares the result of that operation with what she received from Bob. If they compare, the Alice knows Bob possesses the right key.

Several Internet RFCs cover CHAP in more detail. These are RFC 1994 (PPP Challenge Handshake Authentication Protocol, August 1996), RFC 2433 (Microsoft PPP CHAP Extensions, October 1998), and RFC 2759 (Microsoft PPP CHAP Extensions version 2, January 2000).

Related Entries   Access Control; Authentication and Authorization; Certificates and Certification Systems; Cryptography; EAP (Extended Authentication Protocol); Hash Functions; PAP (Password Authentication Protocol); Rights and Permissions; Security; *and* SSL (Secure Sockets Layer);

 Linktionary!—Tom Sheldon's Encyclopedia of   http://www.linktionary.com/c/chap.html
Networking updates

Chat

The Internet is famous for chat rooms—places where people meet and discuss topics of *any* nature. You join a chat room and start taking part in the conversation already underway, or start your own chat room. You might even take some of the participants of one chat room with you to a newly formed chat room. While chat rooms are an Internet phenomenon, they can also serve a useful purpose on company intranets, providing a place to hold virtual meetings, training sessions, and similar collaborative activities.

When you enter a chat room, you can use your name or, in the case of graphical chat rooms, take on an iconic representation (called an *avatar*) that represents your personality in cyberspace. Avatars may be famous people, monsters, or objects. If a chat room supports virtual reality, you can move around in 3-D space, bump into other avatars, and have a conversation with them. Of course, much of this technology is still developing. Voice- and video-based chat rooms will be supported more widely as bandwidth increases.

IRC (Internet Relay Chat) is one of the most popular chat systems. It has been around since the 1980 and has grown in features and popularity. IRC consists of a client that runs on users' computers and IRC servers, which exist all over the Internet but can also be installed on company intranets for internal use. The IRC tracks different discussions and makes sure that messages directed to discussions are broadcast to all the people participating in those discussions. Refer to "IRC (Internet Relay Chat)" for more information.

The popular Internet service AOL (America Online) has an instant messaging service that provides a service-wide chat scheme. As an AOL subscriber, you can create a buddy list of people you want to chat with when you sign on. When the people on your buddy list sign on, you are alerted and can send them instant messages. See "Instant Messaging."

An application from ICQ, Inc. called ICQ (pronounced "I seek you") provides a similar service for anyone on the Internet that runs the application. You create a list of people you want to communicate with and ICQ tracks when those people get on the Internet so you can exchange instant messages and join chat rooms. Note that ICQ Inc. was formerly known as Mirabilis, but AOL bought the company in 1998 and changed the name. PeopleLink (http://www.peoplelink.com) is another provider of these services.

Related Entries   Collaborative Computing; CU-SeeME; Electronic Mail; ICQ (I-Seek-You); IRC (Internet Relay Chat); Instant Messaging; Multicasting; Multimedia and Multimedia Network Services; Unified Messaging; Videoconferencing; VoIP (Voice over IP); *and* Webcasting

Linktionary!—Tom Sheldon's Encyclopedia of Networking updates	http://www.linktionary.com/c/chat.html
IRChelp.org	http://www.irchelp.org
Internet Chat Resources by Nerd World Media	http://www.tiac.net/users/dstein/nw681.html
Yahoo's Chat Links	http://dir.yahoo.com/Computers_and_Internet/Internet/Chat/
ICQ, Inc.	http://www.icq.com/

CICS, IBM

CICS (Customer Information Control System) is a family of client/server transaction-processing products that enables an organization to exploit applications and data on many different hardware and software platforms. It is an open platform for building an enterprise system. CICS client/server applications are portable across IBM and many non-IBM systems, interoperable across

LANs and WANs, scalable up to 1,000s of users, and manageable from a single point of control. CICS is normally found in large online networks and provides application compatibility with platforms like IBM's AIX, MVS, OS/2, OS/400 and VSE, as well non-IBM environments such as Windows NT, HP, Digital, and Sun.

Related Entries   DBMS (Database Management System); IBM; *and* Transaction Processing

CIDR (Classless Inter-Domain Routing)

In the early 1990s, Internet administrators began to address the potential problem of IP address space exhaustion. CIDR (pronounced "cider") is a solution that allows more scalability in the Internet under the current IP version 4 addressing scheme. It provides an interim solution until IP version 6 is put into place.

The key words here are "domain routing." The U.S. Postal Service ZIP code could be called a domain routing scheme. The first digit represents a large geographic area (domain). The second digit represents a region within that area (subdomain), and so on. Packages sent between domains are routed on the basis of the first digit. The remaining digits are only meaningful to the mail handlers within a domain.

To understand CIDR and why it is necessary, consider an analogy that greatly simplifies a network addressing scheme (since actual IP address manipulation can cause rapid head spinning). Assume an Internet is to be built that will have only 1,000 attached networks with the addresses 1000 to 1999. There are ten regional Internet service providers that will manage IP addresses and allocate addresses to organizations that connect to the Internet through their network services.

Using a *CIDR-like solution,* contiguous block of addresses are preassigned to each ISP. For example, ISP 0 would get addresses 1000 through 1099, ISP 2 would get 1100 through 1199, and so on. The first two digits indicate the ISP and the last two specify actual hosts. An advantage is that inter-ISP routing tables only require 10 entries.

ISP 0	10xx
ISP 1	11xx
ISP 2	12xx
ISP 3	13xx
ISP 4	14xx
ISP 5	15xx
ISP 6	16xx
ISP 7	17xx
ISP 8	18xx
ISP 9	19xx

To send a packet to network 1552, it is only necessary to consider the first two digits in the address (15) in a table lookup. The packet is sent to ISP 5, which handles all further routing within its own domain. *Each domain maintains its own internal routing tables.* The benefits of this scheme are as follows and aptly describe the benefits of CIDR in the actual Internet:

- Addresses are allocated in contiguous blocks (such as 1000 to 1099) so that all the routes behind an ISP are grouped together and can be represented with a single route. This is called *route aggregation.*

- The routing table for the Internet backbone has a small number of entries. It is easy to calculate and little bandwidth is used to transmit the table or table updates to other ISPs.

- All routing within an ISP is handled by the ISP's routers. Other ISPs only need to send packets to the ISP and don't need to know about its subnetworks.

- Changes to subnetworks within the ISP don't need to be propagated to other ISPs, which greatly reduces network traffic and table updates.

- ISPs can allocate their address spaces to fit the needs of their subscribers.

The last point is most important. For example, ISP 1 could assign a company block 111*x* (a block of 10 addresses), or it can assign a home user the single address 1121. This method of letting ISPs allocate their address block is efficient and practical.

The concept of aggregation can be explained by examining how the U.S. postal ZIP code system works. The scheme makes for efficient mail distribution by associating a hierarchical numbering scheme with geographic regions. For example, all mail with ZIP codes 9xxxx is directed to the West coast. A mail sorter on the east coast only need to know that all ZIP codes starting with 9 go west. On the West Coast, regional and local post offices sort the mail by looking further into the ZIP code. For example, 98xxx letters are sent to Washington, while 97xxx letters are sent to Oregon.

Now consider the real Internet and its very real addressing problems. While the Internet Protocol's 32-bit address space can in theory provide up to two billion addresses, a class system was implemented early on that makes inefficient use of the addresses. The class system was developed before it was conceived that the Internet would be as large as it is today.

Note   *In addition to this topic, you should also see "IP (Internet Protocol)" and "Routing Registries." For an historical perspective, refer to "Routing on the Internet." Also see "NAT (Network Address Translation," which solves IP address allocation problems by supporting private IP addressing schemes.*

One problem with the class system is a lack of a class that was appropriate for mid-sized organizations—that is, organizations that needed more host addresses than class C (254 hosts) but much fewer than class B (65,534 hosts). If you were allocated a class B network address block and needed only half of the host addresses within that block, the rest went unused, which exacerbated the address space problem.

Alternatively, you could obtain multiple class C addresses to fit your host-addressing needs, but you would then have multiple network addresses that required multiple router entries and an undesirable internal division of the network.

Another problem was the routing table size. Imagine the complexity of every major router on the Internet needing to keep track of tens of thousands of network addresses with changes occurring constantly. The task is unwieldy.

Route flapping is the frequent changing of routes. Some routers may continue to forward packets on routes that have changed until they receive an update. Thus, the packets are sent to what is called a *black hole*. With CIDR, routing changes are internalize within an ISP's domain. Since the ISP only advertises a single, *aggregated* network address on the Internet, route-flapping problems are significantly reduced.

One last problem was the impending exhaustion of the 32-bit IPv4 address space. At the time, it was estimated that only 10 to 20 percent of the actual addresses were being used. The unused addresses were "allocated" to organizations that did not need all the addresses in the block they were assigned. To make the problem worse, organizations that were assigned class A and class B addresses were supposed to return those addresses to the IP address pools, but so far, only one major organization has done so.

Today, organizations obtain IP addresses from an ISP, and those ISPs obtain addresses from regional registries, which in turn obtain addresses from top-level registries. This scheme is often referred to as "provider-based address allocation." Refer to Internet RFC 2050 (Internet Registry IP Allocation Guidelines, November 1996) for a more complete description of the Internet registries, and refer to "Registries on the Internet" and "Routing Registries."

BGP version 4 supports the CIDR *route aggregation* scheme. Together, they have allowed the Internet to scale. In 1995, there were close to 65,000 routes. As CIDR aggregation has been implemented, the number of routes in the global routing table has reduced to approximately 35,000 routes. Refer to RFC 2519 (A Framework for Inter-Domain Route Aggregation, February 1999) for more information.

How CIDR Works

The CIDR addressing scheme is hierarchical. Regional service providers such as Pacific Bell are allocated large blocks of contiguous Internet addresses. Pacific Bell then allocates parts of those blocks to other smaller ISPs or directly to organizations. The hierarchical scheme is illustrated in Figure C-13.

Because the ISP has a contiguous block of IP addresses, it need only advertise its single supernet address, which represents an aggregation of all the subnets within that supernet. The basic rule is to never distribute internal routing paths onto the Internet. *Supernetting* is the opposite of IP *subnetting*. Whereas subnetting subdivides a single IP network address into multiple subnets (but with fewer hosts per subnet), supernetting makes two or more smaller networks appear as a single network address.

For example, an ISP might be allocated the class C addresses 200.200.1.0 through 200.200.255.0. It can allocate these addresses in any way it likes. Note that blocks of addresses

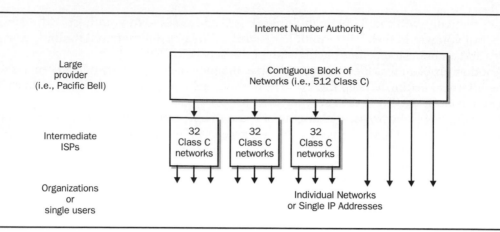

Figure C-13.   *CIDR address allocation example*

are identified by the first address in the block. Company X might get 200.200.2.0, while company Y might get 200.200.3.0. A company may even get a subnet of that, or the ISP can allocate single addresses to individual users. Thus, the ISP is able to allocate its block of IP addresses efficiently.

RFC 2008 (Implications of Various Address Allocation Policies for Internet Routing, October 1996) discusses how aggregation reduces the number of routes to advertise on the Internet. It also discusses address "ownership" and address "lending" concepts.

Note that the first two bytes of the address are the same and can be referred to as 200.200.0.0, where 0 in the last two bytes is a global value. The ISP only needs to advertise the address 200.200.0.0 on the Internet. Packets addressed to any host with the 200.200 network prefix are routed to the ISP. The ISP then routes the packets internally.

A CIDR address is a normal 32-bit IP address, but is classless. A special mask indicates how many bits in the address represent the network prefix. For example, the address 200.200.10.15/23 indicates that the first 23 bits of the binary form of this address represent the network. The remaining bits identify a specific host on that network.

Another way of describing this address is 200.200.10.15/255.255.254.0, where the numbers after the slash are the mask in dotted-decimal notation. The address mask relationship is shown below. Note that the mask has 23 binary 1s.

IP Address	200	200	10	15
Binary form	11001000	11001000	00001010	00001111
Mask (/23)	255	255	254	0
Binary form	11111111	11111111	11111110	00000000

Table C-3 lists the most commonly used prefixes, the mask represented by the prefix, and the number of host addresses available with a prefix of the type listed.

Mask as Prefix Value	Mask as Dotted Decimal Value	Number of Host Addresses
/27	255.255.255.224	32 hosts
/26	255.255.255.192	64 hosts
/25	255.255.255.128	128 hosts
/24	255.255.255.0 (class C)	256 hosts
/23	255.255.254.0	512 hosts
/22	255.255.252.0	1,024 hosts
/21	255.255.248.0	2,048 hosts
/20	255.255.240.0	4,096 hosts
/19	255.255.224.0	8,192 hosts
/18	255.255.192.0	16,384 hosts
/17	255.255.128.0	32,768 hosts
/16	255.255.0.0 (class B)	65,536 hosts
/15	255.254.0.0	131,072 hosts
/14	255.252.0.0	262,144 hosts
/13	255.248.0.0	524,288 hosts

Table C-3.   *CIDR masking scheme*

Routing protocols must support CIDR. Supporting protocols include the interior routing protocols RIP version 2 and OSPF version 2, EIGRP (Enhanced Interior Gateway Routing Protocol), and the exterior routing protocol BGP version 4. Earlier protocols like RIP, BGP-3, EGP, and IGRP do not support CIDR. Today, all ISPs and similar service providers are expected to support variable-length subnet masking and CIDR.

Despite the benefits of CIDR over the years, addressing problems still exist. This is addressed in RFC 2519, Inter-Domain Route Aggregation (February 1999). The RFC notes that "the ability of levels of the global routing to implement efficient aggregation schemes varies widely. As a result, the size and growth rate of the Internet routing table, as well as the associated route computation required, remain major issues today. To support Internet growth, it is important to maximize the efficiency of aggregation at all levels in the routing system." It then goes on to discuss some possible solutions.

See also the related topic "NAT (Network Address Translation)." NAT runs on a gateway between two networks, usually a private network and the Internet. NAT essentially hides internal network addresses by representing all of those addresses with a single IP address to the Internet. This scheme allows internal networks to use an addressing scheme that is not officially registered. It also provides security benefits since internal addresses are hidden. Private internal IP addressing is recommended, as discussed under "IP (Internet Protocol)."

  Note   *Refer to the Linktionary! site for a complete list of CIDR-related Internet RFCs.*

Related Entries   Addressing, Network; Autonomous Systems, BGP (Border Gateway Protocol); Internet Routing and Addressing; IP (Internet Protocol); NAT (Network Address Translation); OSPF (Open Shortest Path First) Routing; Registries on the Internet; Route Aggregation; Routing; Routing Registries; Routing on the Internet; RSIP (Realm-Specific IP); *and* TCP/IP (Transmission Control Protocol/Internet Protocol)

Linktionary!—Tom Sheldon's Encyclopedia of Networking updates	http://www.linktionary.com/c/cidr.html
IANA (Internet Assigned Numbers Authority)	http://www.iana.org/
Pacific Bell CIDR Overview	http://public.pacbell.net/dedicated/cidr.html
CIDR FAQ by Hank Nussbacher	http://support.digex.net/cst/ipcidr-faq.html
Subnetting and CIDR	http://www.freesoft.org/CIE/Course/Subnet
Internet Exterior Routing Protocol Development: Problems, Issues, and Misconceptions, by Tim Bass, SAIC, Center for Information Protection	http://www.silkroad.com/papers/html/pba/n1.html
Thomas Baumann's CIDR Web pages	http://www.heh.uni-hannover.de/books/os2-peer/peerfaq2/n019.html
IP Address Space (table showing allocation of address blocks to various registries).	http://www.isi.edu/in-notes/iana/assignments/ipv4-address-space

CIFS (Common Internet File System Protocol)

CIFS is an Internet file-sharing system developed by Microsoft in 1996 as a replacement for other Internet file protocols such as FTP (File Transfer Protocol). CIFS goes beyond FTP's simple file transfer facilities by providing a sophisticated and relatively secure file-sharing environment that can be used for collaborative applications over the Internet.

CIFS is an extension of Microsoft's existing SMB (Server Message Block), Microsoft's open, cross-platform file-sharing protocol is available in the Windows 95, Windows 98, Windows NT/Windows 2000, and OS/2 operating systems. SMB runs on other platforms as well, including Linux. CIFS allows users to share documents over the Internet in the same way they share documents when running peer networking services on their internal SMB networks. SMB is discussed elsewhere in this book.

Here are important features of CIFS:

■ CIFS uses the same multiuser open, close, read, and write operations, as well as file-sharing semantics that are used on most enterprise networks.

■ File and record locking prevents multiple users from overwriting the work that another person is doing on a file or record.

- CIFS runs over TCP/IP and uses the Internet's global DNS (Domain Naming Service).
- CIFS support fault tolerance and can automatically restore connections and reopen files that were open prior to interruption.
- CIFS is "tuned" to provide optimal performance over dial-up links.
- Users refer to remote file systems with an easy to use file naming scheme.
- CIFS is also widely available on UNIX, VMS, and other platforms.

CIFS complements standard Web protocols such as HTTP (Hypertext Transfer Protocol) by providing a more sophisticated file-sharing protocol. Users do not need to rely solely on their Web browsers to access Internet information because with CIFS, most existing applications can access that data directly by using the standard Open and Save dialog boxes that users are already familiar with.

The security features in CIFS include support both for anonymous transfers and for secure, authenticated access to named files. File and directory security policies are easy to administer and use the same paradigm as share-level and user-level security policies in Windows environments. Most major operating system and application developers support CIFS.

CIFS competes with Sun Microsystems' Web NFS, a distributed file system that Sun is integrating directly into Web browsers and other clients. Netscape Navigator includes embedded Web NFS. A paper at the Network Appliance Web site listed at the end of this topic compares NFS and CIFS.

CIFS is important to NAS (network attached storage). The Storage Networking Industry Association (SNIA) formed a working group in January 2000 to develop NAS concepts and how CIFS will work with NAS.

Related Entries   DAFS (Direct Access File System); DFS (Distributed File System), Microsoft; Distributed Applications; Distributed Computer Networks; File Sharing; File Systems; File Transfer Protocols; Internet; Microsoft Windows; Network Operating Systems; NAS (Network Attached Storage); NFS (Network File System); Rights and Permissions; Search and Discovery Services; Samba; SMB (Server Message Blocks); Stateful and Call-Back Filing Systems; SMB (Server Message Blocks); Storage Systems; Web NFS (Network File System); *and* Web Technologies and Concepts

Linktionary!—Tom Sheldon's Encyclopedia of Networking updates	http://www.linktionary.com/c/cifs.html
Microsoft's CIFS page	http://msdn.microsoft.com/workshop/c-frame.htm#/workshop/networking/cifs/
Microsoft CIFS document	http://www.microsoft.com/Mind/1196/CIFS.htm
Thursby's CIFS page	http://www.thursby.com/cifs/
Network Appliance Resource Library (see CIFS-related documents)	http://www.netapp.com/tech_library/
Storage Networking Industry Association (SNIA)	http://www.snia.org

CIM (Common Information Model)

CIM specifies how management information about logical and physical objects on a managed network is stored in management information databases. CIM attempts to provide a consistent and unified view of information so that it can be retrieved by any CIM-compliant network management systems. CIM is part of the WBEM (Web-based Enterprise Management) initiative, which is being defined by the majority of major network vendors and managed by the DMTF (Distributed Management Task Force). The DMTF also manages WBEM. Note that CIM was originally called HMMS (Hypermedia Management Schema).

According to the DMTF, CIM consists of the CIM specification and the CIM schema:

- The CIM specification describes the language, naming, Meta Schema, and mapping techniques to other management models such as SNMP MIBs, and DMTF MIFs.

- The Meta Schema is a formal definition of the model. It defines the terms used to express the model and their usage and semantics.

Related Entries   Metadata; Network Management; WBEM (Web-Based Enterprise Management); *and* XML (eXtensible Markup Language)

Linktionary!—Tom Sheldon's Encyclopedia of   http://www.linktionary.com/c/cim.html
Networking updates

CIP (Classical IP Over ATM)

Classical IP over ATM, or CIP as it is informally called, defines how to transmit IP datagrams over ATM networks. CIP was originally defined in RFC 1577 (Classical IP and ARP over ATM, January 1994). This RFC was made obsolete and replaced by RFC 2225 (Classical IP and ARP over ATM, April 1998).

CIP is an IETF standard. Alternative methods for integrating ATM into legacy networks have been developed by the ATM Forum and are outlined under the heading "IP over ATM." An ATM Forum standard called LANE (LAN Emulation) provides a way to integrate ATM with legacy LAN protocols such as Ethernet and Token Ring (and carry IP as if the ATM network were a LAN). Another ATM Forum standard is MPOA (Multiprotocol over ATM), which adds cut-through/shortcut routing to the LANE scheme. Both are discussed under separate headings.

CIP uses an ATM network as its underlying data link network. In this scheme, ATM is like any other data link network such as Ethernet and token ring. CIP implements the concept of a *LIS (logical IP subnet)*, which is a closed logical IP subnetwork (such as a department or workgroup) consisting of a group of hosts. Multiple LISs can exist on the same ATM network, but routers are still needed for inter-LIS communications.

There is some inefficiency in this configuration. If two LISs are on the same ATM network, a host on one LIS must go through a router to communicate with a host in the other LIS, even though the underlying ATM network is capable of setting up a virtual circuit that directly connects both hosts. This is by design, in order to retain the requirement that packets addressed to hosts in other subnets be sent to a default router. This is why it is called *classical* IP.

Later, the IETF defined NHRP (Next Hop Routing Protocol), which can set up direct ATM virtual circuit connections between end stations in different LISs. This is pictured in Figure C-14.

Each LIS includes a single ATMARP (ATM Address Resolution Protocol) server, which resolves IP to ATM addresses. When a host is turned on, it connects with the ATMARP server. The ATMARP server then requests the host's IP and ATM addresses, which are then stored in the ATMARP lookup table for future reference. Hosts and routers contact the ATMARP server when they need to resolve IP addresses into ATM addresses.

Alternative IP over ATM schemes are outlined under "IP over ATM." Also see "LANE (LAN Emulation)" and "MPOA (Multiprotocol over ATM)."

Besides RFC 2225, the following RFC provide useful information about IP over ATM:

- RFC 1755, (ATM Signaling Support for IP over ATM, February 1995)
- RFC 1754 (IP over ATM Working Group's Recommendations for the ATM Forum's Multiprotocol BOF, January 1995)
- RFC 1932 (IP over ATM: A Framework Document, April 1996)
- RFC 2226 (IP Broadcast over ATM Networks, October 1997)
- RFC 2382 (A Framework for Integrated Services and RSVP over ATM, August 1998)
- RFC 2336 (Classical IP and ARP over ATM to NHRP Transition, July 1998)
- RFC 2684 (Multiprotocol Encapsulation over ATM Adaptation Layer 5, September 1999)

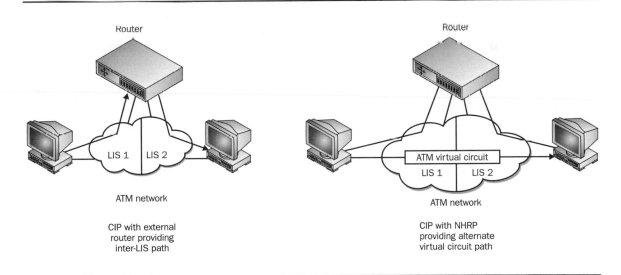

Figure C-14.   *CIP by itself requires inter-LIS routers. NHRP adds cut-through routing across the ATM fabric.*

Related Entries   ATM (Asynchronous Transfer Mode); ION (Internetworking over NBMA); IP over ATM; I-PNNI (Integrated-Private Network-to-Network Interface); IP Switching; MPOA (Multiprotocol over ATM); NHRP (Next Hop Resolution Protocol); *and* RSVP (Resource Reservation Protocol)

Linktionary!—Tom Sheldon's Encyclopedia of Networking updates	http://www.linktionary.com/c/cip_atm.html
Trillium papers about IP over ATM	http://www.trillium.com/whats-new/wp_ip.html
James Sterbenz's ATM page	http://www.ccrc.wustl.edu/~jpgs/research/atm/atm.html
Com21 (Communication for the 21st Century) on IP over ATM	http://www.com21.com/pages/ietf.html
Jun Xu's excellent page: "IP over ATM: Classical IP, NHRP, LANE, MPOA, PAR and I-PNNI"	http://www.cis.ohio-state.edu/~jain/cis788-97/ip_over_atm/
ATM Internetworking by Anthony Alles, Cisco Systems	http://cell.onecall.net/cell-relay/docs/cisco.html
Cell Relay Retreat	http://cell-relay.indiana.edu/

CIP (Common Indexing Protocol)

CIP is an evolution and refinement of Whois++, an Internet protocol for finding information about resources on networks. CIP provides a way for information servers to know the contents of other information servers by exchanging index information. Once indexes are exchanged, a server can look in its own index to answer a query, or look in the indexes received from other servers to see if the query can be answered elsewhere.

CIP is an indexing protocol that defines methods for creating and exchanging index information among indexing servers. It distributes searches across several instances of a single type of search engine to create a global directory. CIP can tie individual databases into distributed data warehouse.

CIP indexing servers can refer queries to other servers that might be able to answer the query. This process is called *query routing* and the network of servers is called a *referral mesh*. With query routing, a query is eventually directed to the server that can answer the query. The results are returned to the person making the query. The user is responsible for "collating, filtering, and chasing" the referrals.

RFC 2651 (The Architecture of the Common Indexing Protocol, August 1999) defines the CIP architecture. CIP is a protocol used by back-end servers, not people. It defines how queries and referrals are handled, how servers interface with one another, and search engine specifications. The servers holding the most likely data to satisfy a query are determined by referring to previously accumulated index information. RFC 2653 (CIP Transport Protocols, August 1999) describe how CIP requests, responses, and index objects may be carried over TCP, mail, and HTTP.

Whois++ used the concept of a *centroid*, which is a condensed block of index information (a form of metadata) that is exchanged between directory servers. Think of a library index card that describes a book. CIP uses a similar concept called *summary objects* (or an *index object*) to contain the information that is exchanged among indexing servers. This object is composed of three fundamental components:

- **Template**   A template defines how the information in the object is constructed. Many different templates can be defined, so this field indicates which template is being used.

- **URL**   The URL refers to the location of the document.

- **Attribute/value pairs**   These are named fields that can have some value. For example, the value of the "Name" field is the name of the document. For example, a generic template called "FILE" can be used to describe a variety of Web-based resources. Common attributes for the FILE template include Abstract (brief abstract about the object), Author (author of the object), Description (brief description about the object), and many more.

RFC 2655 (CIP Index Object Format for SOIF Objects, August 1999) describes SOIF (Summary Object Interchange Format), a machine-readable syntax for transmitting summary objects among servers. It provides a complete description of the FILE template type just mentioned. Templates may be registered or unregistered. Registered templates are well-known types that support interoperability. See RFC 2656 (Registration Procedures for SOIF Template Types, August 1999). RFC 2654 (A Tagged Index Object for use in the Common Indexing Protocol, August 1999) defines how index update information can be exchanged, rather than exchanging entire databases.

Related Entries   Handle System; Metadata; Name Services; Search and Discovery Services; Service Advertising and Discovery; SLP (Service Location Protocol); URN (Universal Resource Naming); *and* WebDAV

Recent developments in Indexing, Searching and Information Retrieval Technologies (REIS)	http://www.terena.nl/projects/reis/
Search Engine Watch	http://searchenginewatch.com/
OII (Open Information Interchange) Guides	http://158.169.50.95:10080/oii/en/guides.html
Searchtools.com	http://www.searchtools.com/info/
The American Society of Indexers	http://www.asindexing.org/

CIR (Committed Information Rate)

When you order a virtual circuit for a service such as frame relay or ATM, you can specify a guaranteed data rate that you want the carrier to provide. The data rate is negotiated with the carrier as the CIR (committed information rate).

When the data rate exceeds the CIR, the network starts dropping packets, so CIR should be a balance between the minimum and maximum bandwidth requirements. You can also negotiate a burst rate that lets you exceed the CIR rate to accommodate spikes in traffic. The ability to burst depends on whether bandwidth is available. CIR may also be negotiated as variable over time, so that during busy business hours more bandwidth is available.

Basically, CIR is the throughput rate that you negotiate with a service provider, and they will usually attempt to guarantee that rate. One way the carrier guarantees CIR is by dropping non-CIR traffic.

Carriers will often "overbook" the capacity of their networks, hoping that customers will not make excessive demands on the network at the same time. But if the carrier miscalculates, traffic will be dropped, even if it is guaranteed, although non-CIR traffic will be dropped first.

Related Entries   ATM (Asynchronous Transfer Mode); Circuit; Frame Relay; Leased Line; Packet and Cell Switching; SLA (Service Level Agreement); Virtual Circuits; *and* WAN

Circuit

In the world of computer networking, the term "circuit" is used in many different contexts. A circuit is a communication channel between two devices. Circuit types are shown in Figure C-15.

- **Physical circuit**   A wire that carries a single channel such as a telephone call, or multiplexed circuits as described here.

- **FDM (frequency division multiplexing)**   In this scheme, circuits are created by dividing available bandwidth into separate carrier frequencies and then modulating data onto the carriers.

- **WDM (wave division multiplexing)**   This is basically frequency division multiplexing with light, done on fiber-optic cables and open-air laser transmissions. Think of a "color" of light as being a circuit. See "WDM (Wave Division Multiplexing)" for more information.

- **TDM (time division multiplexing)**   In this scheme, circuits are created by dividing a signal stream into multiple time slots and allocating a regular repeating time slot to each user's transmission.

- **CDM (code division multiplexing)**   In this scheme, all transmissions are sent across one large channel, spread out across the bandwidth using spread spectrum technology. Each user's transmission is broken up into small segments that are coded, transmitted, and then reassembled at the receiving end. Refer to "CDMA (Code Division Multiple Access)" and "Spread Spectrum Signaling."

- **Virtual circuits**   This type of circuit exists in a mesh network in which cells, frames, or packets are transmitted among nodes in a network. A virtual circuit is a path between end systems through the mesh network.

The analog cellular telephone network is a circuit-switched FDM cellular system. When you make a call, you get a dedicated frequency for transmitting and another dedicated frequency for receiving. These basically act like hardwired dedicated circuits between caller and callee. Digital cellular systems extend the analog system with TDM or CDM technologies and digitizing voice.

Virtual circuits are common in WANs (wide area networks) and internal networks that use switches in the workgroup area and the backbone. Basically, a virtual circuit appears to the end systems as a dedicated wire for transmitting information across a communication system.

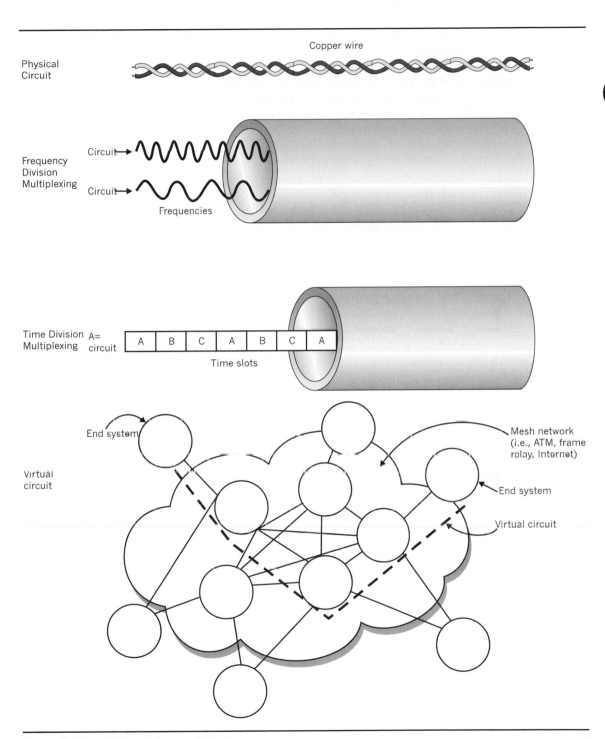

Figure C-15.   *Different types of circuits*

However, the underlying network consists of a path through one or more switches that is either permanent or switched, as described under "Virtual Circuit."

Circuits are also defined in higher layers of the protocol stack. The virtual circuit just described is a connection for transferring a variety of traffic between two points, usually over a layer 2 switched network. In contrast, a TCP connection-oriented circuit is established between software applications across a packet switched network. This connection allows both systems to manage the exchange of packets, recover lost packets, and actively control the packet exchange rate so that one system does not overwhelm the other or the network. See "Transport Protocols and Services" and "Reliable Data Delivery Services."

Higher up in the protocol stack, client/server applications may use RPC request/response mechanisms to exchange information as if there were a "communication circuit" between the systems. The opposite approach is to use a message passing, store-and-forward approach in which two systems exchange information by putting it in a message and forwarding the message to the other system. This is like two people exchanging e-mail.

Related Entries   Bandwidth; Cable and Cable Concepts; Capacity; Channel; Circuit-Switching Services; Connection Establishment; Connection-Oriented and Connectionless Services; Data Communication Concepts; Delay, Latency, and Jitter; Modulation Techniques; Multiplexing; Packet and Cell Switching; Point-to-Point Communications; Reliable Data Delivery Services; Switching and Switched Services; Throughput; Transport Protocols and Services; *and* Virtual Circuits

Linktionary!—Tom Sheldon's Encyclopedia   http://www.linktionary.com/c/circuit.html
of Networking updates

Circuit Relay Firewall

A circuit relay firewall is a type of security firewall (proxy server) that provides a controlled network connection between internal and external systems (that is, there is no "air gap"). A virtual "circuit" exists between the internal client and the proxy server. Internet requests go through this circuit to the proxy server, and the proxy server delivers those requests to the Internet after changing the IP (Internet Protocol) address. External users only see the IP address of the proxy server. Responses are then received by the proxy server and sent back through the circuit to the client. While traffic is allowed through, external systems never see the internal systems. This type of connection is often used to connect "trusted" internal users to the Internet. See "Firewall" and "NAT (Network Address Translation)" for more information.

Circuit-Switching Services

Circuit switching, as opposed to packet switching, sets up a dedicated communication channel between two end systems. Voice calls on the telephone networks are the best example. A phone connects to a local telephone switching center via twisted-pair cables. If the connection is between two phones in the same area, the local switch creates a connection between the circuits from each phone. This is pictured as connection A1-A2 in Figure C-16.

If the connection is between phones in two different areas, a circuit is set up through an intermediate exchange, as shown by circuit C1-C2. Long-distance circuits are made through

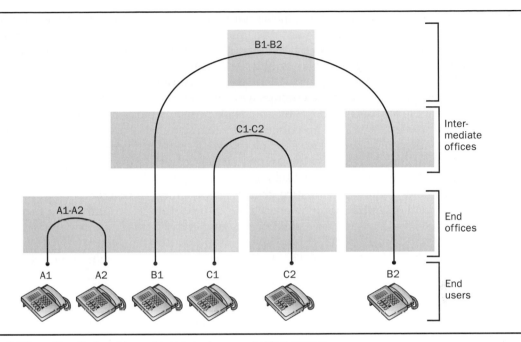

Figure C-16.   *Circuits in a hierarchical telephone switching system*

remote switching offices, as shown by circuit B1-B2. When telephone circuits are used for data, they provide private links with guaranteed bandwidth.

A *dedicated circuit* is a circuit that is switched on once and stays on. You lease the line from the local carrier or combination of local and long-distance carriers. Circuit services are often called TDM services because they use TDM (time division multiplexing). Data is transmitted in time slots that can guarantee bandwidth for time sensitive voice and video, assuming enough bandwidth is allocated in the circuit.

The advantage of switched circuit is that you can connect to a variety of preconfigured locations rather than a single location. This type of service is good for backing up and replicating data between remote systems, or for videoconferences. ISDN is an example of a circuit-switching service that is practical for home and small office users.

An alternative to circuit-switched services is packet-switching services. The main characteristic of packet-switching services is that you share a network with many other users and organization and connections can be made to a variety of endpoints. ATM (called *cell switching*), frame relay, and the Internet use this model. Packet switching is ideal for long-distance any-to-any connectivity. See "Packet and Cell Switching."

A *virtual circuit* is a dedicated end-to-end link over a packet- or cell-switched network. A dedicated path is selected through a mesh network for the transmission of a data. There are PVCs (permanent virtual circuits) and SVCs (switched virtual circuits). The former are preprogrammed and the latter are set up "on the fly."

While everyone has been advocating the advantages of packet-switched networks such as the Internet for metro and WAN connections, interesting developments are taking place in optical networking. As the bandwidth and capabilities of fiber-optic networks improve with DWDM (dense wavelength division multiplexing) and optical switching, the concept of "switched lambda circuits" has emerged. A lambda is an individual wavelength of light, and hundreds or thousands of lambdas can occupy a single fiber cable. DWDM makes so many wavelengths available that service providers can lease private lambda circuits to organizations on a switched or permanent basis. This circuit can stretch across the service provider's entire network and provide an economical way to link remote offices with very high bandwidth links. See "Optical Networking."

According to George Gilder (Gilder Technology Report, April 2000), "In a world of bandwidth abundance, bandwidth-wasting circuits become ideal once again. Rather than economizing on bandwidth by chopping everything into packets and multiplexing them into time slots, the mandate is to waste bandwidth. As in the old telephone system, the best approach is circuits."

DTM (Dynamic Synchronous Transfer Mode) is a form of circuit switching for fiber-optic networks that employs TDM (time division multiplexing) in a new way that dynamically reallocates available bandwidth to users that need it. DTM was designed to remove the bottleneck at fiber network access points. These bottlenecks are typically caused by the need to process and buffer data large amounts packet-based data. DTM seeks to limit complexity and use transmission capacity more efficiently. In particular, DTM can fully support high bit-rate real-time traffic and multicasting, and when used as a link layer for IP networks, can support strict QoS. See "DTM (Dynamic Synchronous Transfer Mode)."

Related Entries   Circuit; Communication Services and Providers; Connection-Oriented and Connectionless Services; Data Communication Concepts; DSL (Digital Subscriber Line); ISDN (Integrated Services Digital Network); Telecommunications and Telephone Systems; Virtual Circuits; VoIP (Voice over IP); *and* WANs (Wide Area Networks)

Linktionary!—Tom Sheldon's Encyclopedia of Networking updates	http://www.linktionary.com/c/circuit_switching.html
Godred Fairhurst's circuit switching course	http://www.erg.abdn.ac.uk/users/gorry/course/intro-pages/cs.html
Circuit-Switched Voice Carrier Services topics at Business Communication Review Magazine	http://www.bcr.com/widearea.htm#Voice

CISC (Complex Instruction Set Computer)

Computer processors contain instructions or microcode to carry out various functions. The richer the instruction set, the easier it is to write programs for the microprocessor, but a rich set of microcode can affect performance. This trade-off differentiates the two categories of microprocessors:

- *CISC (Complex Instruction Set Computer)* designs include a rich set of microcode that simplifies the creation of programs that run on the processor.

- *RISC (Reduced Instruction Set Computer)* designs, as the name implies, have a reduced set of instructions that improves the efficiency of the processor but requires more complex external programs.

RISC designs are based on work performed at IBM by John Cocke, who found that about 20 percent of a computer's instructions did about 80 percent of the work. Thus, RISC-designed systems are generally faster than CISC systems. His 80/20 rule spawned the development of RISC architecture.

Related Entries   ASIC (Application Specific Integrated Circuit); DSP (Digital Signal Processing); Network Processors; *and* RISC (Reduced Instruction Set Computer)

CIX (Commercial Internet eXchange) Association

The CIX Association is a nonprofit association of public service providers that promotes the public data internetworking services industry. It provides a forum for exchanging information about internetworking services. It also encourages technical research and development that benefits its members, suppliers, and customers of public data communication services. It also promotes and administers policies and standards among its members.

The CIX Web site is located at http://www.cix.org/.

Related Entries   Internet; Internet Architecture and Backbone; ISP (Internet Service Providers); NAP (Network Access Point); Peering; Routing; Routing on the Internet; Routing Registries; *and* Service Providers and Carriers

Class of Service

See CoS (Class of Service).

CLEC (Competitive Local Exchange Carriers)

An LEC is a telephone company that operates within a local area called the LATA (Local Access and Transport Area). The *ILECs (incumbent LECs)* are the result of the breakup of AT&T in 1984, which created seven independent RBOCs (Regional Bell Operating Companies) in the U.S. These included Pacific Bell, NYNEX, GTE and others, but mergers and consolidations have changed the original gang of seven. Most ILECs operate across a number of LATAs.

The CAPs (Competitive Access Providers) and CLECs (Competitive LECs) compete with the ILECs in the same service areas. Any non-incumbent carrier is called an ITC (Independent Telephone Company), but some ITCs operate in areas where they do not compete with ILECs (such as rural areas that are not covered by the RBOCs or any other phone companies). More recently, the CLECs are morphing into what are called *ICPs (Integrated Communications Providers)*, which provide a variety of "New Public Network" services, including Web hosting and Internet access.

Note   *An important feature of CLECs is that they can interconnect with the incumbent's SS7 network. See "SS7 (Signaling System 7)" for details.*

Refer to "Service Providers and Carriers" for a more complete discussion of these service providers.

CLECs provide bypass services. A bypass service provides a connection for organizations to IXCs that bypasses the ILECs. CLECs may also provide a variety of other services, such as wireless services, voice/data services, Internet access, and more. Originally, the CLECs tried to be like the incumbent carriers, but most found that deploying alternative services such as frame relay, ATM, and eventually Internet access, as well as DSL services, more profitable.

Related Entries   AT&T (American Telephone and Telegraph); Communication Services and Providers; ISP (Internet Service Provider); IXC (Interexchange Carrier); LATA (Local Access and Transport Area); LEC (Local Exchange Carrier); MAN (Metropolitan Area Network); Network Access Services; NPN (New Public Network); POP (Point of Presence; PSTN (Public Switched Telephone Network); RBOCs (Regional Bell Operating Companies); Service Providers and Carriers; *and* Telecommunications and Telephone Systems

Linktionary!—Tom Sheldon's Encyclopedia of Networking updates	http://www.linktionary.com/c/clec.html
CLEC News Magazine	http://www.clecnews.com/
CLEC.com	http://www.clec.com/

The topic "Service Providers and Carriers" provides a larger list of telecom Web sites.

Client

A client may be either a device or a user on a network that takes advantage of the services offered by a server. "Client" is often used in a loose way to refer to a computer on the network. It also refers to a user that is running the client side of a client/server application.

Related Entries   Client/Server Computing; Multitiered Architectures; *and* Web Browsers

Client/Server Computing

Client/server computing defines an architecture in which program logic is distributed between client systems and server systems. Client/server computing is a result of trends in the 1980s to populate desktops with powerful computers that were connected via LANs to back-end database servers or application servers. It was a model designed to replace the mainframe computing model in which all the processing was done by a centralized system.

   Interestingly, the old centralized model was resurrected in the form of the thin client, in which applications run on back-end megaservers, not on desktop computers. See "Thin Clients."

With the rise of the Internet, the client/server computing model has evolved from a two-way relationship (usually called a two-tiered model) to a three-tiered or multitiered model in which clients communicate with intermediate application servers or Web servers, which in turn communicate with back-end data servers and/or legacy systems. The intermediate servers then return the results of database queries back to clients. See "Multitiered Architectures" for a description and illustration.

C

There are several possible client/server configurations. In the most basic model, several clients access a single server; however, the distributed approach shown in Figure C-17 is more common. Servers in a distributed configuration can communicate with one another to provide coordinated services to clients.

In Figure C-18, a database is copied (replicated) to a remote system so that users at the remote site can access data at their local site rather than over a WAN (wide area network) link. The two servers periodically synchronize with each other to ensure that users are working with the latest information. On the right in Figure C-18, vast amounts of data for the enterprise are stored in a "data storage warehouse." Workgroups access a middle-tier "staging system" that caches commonly accessed data or makes queries to the back-end system for clients. For more on this topic, see "Data Warehousing."

These discussions have assumed that the client is software compatible with the server, but this is not always the case. An enterprise network may be a conglomeration of departmental LANs and applications and a variety of clients. Middleware helps meld these heterogeneous components together, as shown in Figure C-19, so that developers can hide the differences between applications and provide connections for a variety of clients. Middleware also provides a communication system in the form of a messaging system or a direct link between client and server. Refer to "Middleware and Messaging" for more information.

File servers, application servers, print servers, fax servers, communication servers, and so on, take advantage of the client/server model. The term *server* is used here to refer to both the system and system software. A server process running on a system waits for a request from a client. The request may be for a file or to initiate a complex transaction.

The back-end data servers run DBMS (database management systems) software, and clients query these systems via SQL (Structured Query Language) statements. SQL became popular as a form of client/server middleware on LANs because it was efficient at selecting and moving just the records that were needed. In addition, it could run stored procedures directly at the database server, rather than moving data to the client and then running procedures on the

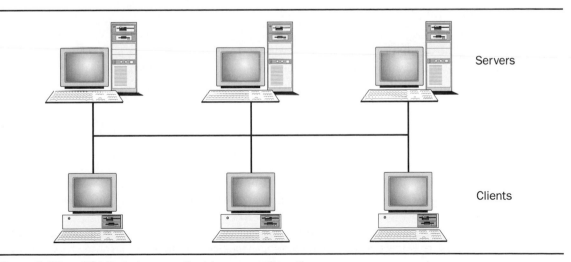

Figure C-17.   *Distributed server client/server configuration*

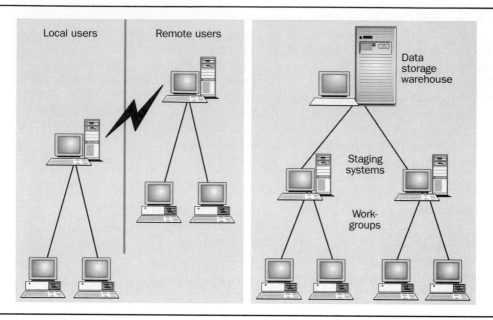

Figure C-18.   *Database replication and data warehousing in the client/server environment*

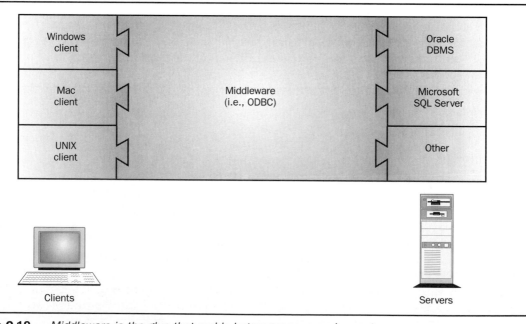

Figure C-19.   *Middleware is the glue that melds heterogeneous enviroments.*

client. Refer to "DBMS (Database Management System)" and "SQL (Structured Query Language)" for more information.

Servers provide services to many clients; so, for performance reasons, they must be powerful systems. In the so-called thin-client environment, the server does most of the work while the client basically displays information and takes input from users. Many thin clients do not even have hard drives. In a more balanced model, the client and server (or multiple servers) share the work. Most thin-client models are based on Java applets and applications. Refer to "Java" for a description of the Java distributed computing environment.

Here are some of the advantages in the client/server model:

- Client/server computing helps organizations "downsize" from mainframes and minicomputers to networks that provide an enterprise-wide data communication platform.

- The split between client and server allows programmers to take advantage of powerful client systems that run GUIs like Windows and Web browsers.

- Data is stored close to servers that work on that data, minimizing the amount of information sent over the network. Backups are easier.

- A large percentage of information is cached once into the server's memory rather than the memory of every workstation that needs it.

- Network traffic is reduced because the server only gives the client the information requested, not large blocks of information that the workstation must process.

- Large server systems can off-load applications that are better handled by personal workstations.

- Data is safe and secure in one location. Data warehousing provides a way to make specific data available at intermediate workgroup servers while maintaining control of the data.

- With centralized data, administrators can apply security controls to restrict data access and use tracking mechanisms to monitor data access.

- Multiple systems can get involved in parallel processing, in which they cooperate in the completion of a processing task.

Enhanced Client/Server Models

In the three-tier model, most of the data access and manipulation of that data is removed from the client and placed on a middle-tier system (data resides on the back-end tier). In a business environment, the middle-tier system may hold all the "business logic" for an organization. Business logic includes the rules, procedures, and operational sequences that provide services to data processing systems. By consolidating business logic on a shared system, all the rules are grouped onto a single server where they are easier to manage and where applications can more easily access them. See "Multitiered Architectures."

Distributed object computing involves the use of object-oriented components built with Java, ActiveX, and other languages. These components are created and distributed over intranets and the Internet, where they run inside Web browsers or other "containers" or are used to assemble full-fledges applications. Services such as application logic, information retrieval, transaction monitoring, data presentation, and management may each run on different computers on the network. The network provides a communication infrastructure on which these components communicate to provide the end user with an experience of working with a seamless application. Refer to "Distributed Object Computing" and "Middleware and Messaging" for more information.

Related Entries   COM (Component Object Model); CORBA (Common Object Request Broker Architecture); Data Warehousing; DBMS (Database Management System); Distributed Applications; Distributing Computer Networks; Distributed Object Computing; HTTP (HyperText Transfer Protocol); Java; Metadata; Middleware and Messaging; MOM (Message-Oriented Middleware); Multitiered Architectures; Object Technologies; ORB (Object Request Broker); RPCs (Remote Procedure Calls); SOAP (Simple Object Access Protocol); SQL (Structured Query Language); Transaction Processing; *and* XML (eXtensible Markup Language)

Linktionary!—Tom Sheldon's Encyclopedia of Networking updates	http://www.linktionary.com/c/clientserver.html
The Client-Server Factory	http://www.tcsf.com/
Client-Server Technology by Joseph O. Nattey	http://www.personal.kent.edu/~jnattey/natteypres.htm
Bitpipe (search for "client/server")	http://www.bitpipe.com/
An Approach for Constructing Web Enterprise Systems on Distributed Objects (IBM paper)	http://www.redbooks.ibm.com/REDP0025/redp0025.pdf
Links at CAIT	http://www.cait.wustl.edu/infosys/infosys.html
Client/Server Software Architectures—An Overview	http://www.sei.cmu.edu/str/descriptions/clientserver_body.html
3Com white paper on Client-Server Computing	http://www.3com.com/technology/tech_net/tech_briefs/500906.html
Client-Server in a Thin Client Environment	http://www.bcr.com/bcrmag/07/98p28.htm
Client-server FAQ (frequently asked questions)	http://www.faqs.org/faqs/client-server-faq/
Client-server FAQ by Lloyd Taylor	http://www.abs.net/~lloyd/csfaq.txt

CLNP (Connectionless Network Protocol)

CLNP is the equivalent of the IP (Internet Protocol) for OSI (Open Systems Interconnection) networks, with the primary difference being the size of the address. CLNP's address size is 20 bytes, as compared to IP's 4 bytes; so CLNP has an advantage over IP, which is experiencing an address shortage. However, the OSI protocols have not gained worldwide acceptance and do not appear to be viable for anything other than a reference model at this writing. CLNP exists in the network layer of the OSI protocol stack. As the name implies, it provides connectionless datagram services over OSI networks.

At one time, it was thought that OSI protocols would replace the Internet protocols on the government-funded Internet. The topic "Routing on the Internet" provides a historical perspective for this.

Related Entries   ES-IS (End System-to-Intermediate System) Routing; IDPR (Inter-Domain Policy Routing Protocol); IS-IS (Intermediate System-to-Intermediate System) Routing; OSI (Open Systems Interconnection) Model; OSPF (Open Shortest Path First); Routing; *and* Routing on the Internet

Cluster Controllers

A cluster controller is an IBM-manufactured or compatible device used to channel-attach 3270 terminals to a host system. This topic is covered in more detail at the Linktionary! site.

 Linktionary!—Tom Sheldon's Encyclopedia   http://www.linktionary.com/c/cluster_controller.html of Networking updates

Clustering

Clustering is a fault-tolerant server technology that provides availability and scalability. It groups servers and shared resources into a single system that can provide immunity from faults. Improved performance is a byproduct of such a system. Clients interact with clusters of servers as if they are a single system. Should one of the servers fail in the cluster, the other servers can take over its load.

An interesting aspect of clustering is that it can provide "four nines" of availability (99.99 percent uptime), which translates to 53 minutes of downtime per year. A complete description of availability is under "Fault Tolerance and High Availability."

Before discussing clustering, it is important to put the range of network server/storage devices and configurations into context. Here are the typical arrangements of servers and storage devices on enterprise networks and Web sites on the Internet:

- **SMP (symmetric multiprocessing) systems**   A single system with multiple processors, multiple power supplies, network interface cards, and multiple storage devices that provide "local" fault tolerance (if one processor, power supply, or interface fails, the others remain operational), but not disaster tolerance (flood or fire). These systems can provide scalable performance, but do not provide an ideal scalable storage environment.

- **LAN-based server configurations**   This is the traditional LAN or wide area network in which servers are attached to the LAN at various locations in a building or over a MAN or WAN. Replication can be used to copy data to different locations in the same building or the extended network. This provides protection against local disasters such as fires and equipment failures. However, the systems are loosely coupled and do not provide the performance and management benefits of the systems discussed next.

- **Clustering**   A clustered system is a set of servers and attached storage devices that are in the same location and in a configuration that provides fault tolerance against the failure of any one device. All of the servers appear as a single server to users. Requests are balanced between the servers, either by external load-balancing devices or by software provided in the operating systems. All servers have access to all the storage devices, so if one server goes down, access is still available to hard drives through other servers in the cluster.

■ **SAN (Storage Area Network)** SANs basically put storage devices on their own high-speed network, typically Fibre Channel. By having all the devices attached to the network, any storage device becomes easily accessible. The switching nature of the network allows servers to make direct connections to any device. See "SAN (Storage Area Network)" and "Fibre Channel." SANs are often created with multiple clustered systems.

■ **NAS (Network Attached Storage)** A NAS is now commonly referred to as a *network appliance*. The basic concept is to remove the server altogether and attach storage directly to the network, thus reducing cost and simplifying management. While a SAN is typically a system defined for enterprise use, a NAS is often installed at the department level. This concept relies on the fact that with standard document formats and XML, proprietary file formats used by servers are no longer needed and the server can be removed altogether. According to George Gilder, NASs are all about removing storage from the enslavement of server operating systems. See "NAS (Network Attached Storage)."

Note that clusters, SANs, and NASs all separate storage from servers, thus allowing any server to access any storage device. In addition, access to storage is not dependent on any one server since clients can get at storage through any server (or directly, in the case of NAS).

A simple clustering solution is pictured on the left in Figure C-20. In this case, two servers share the same hard disks. A cluster may also consist of more than two servers, as shown on the right in Figure C-20. The latter is often established to provide additional performance. In fact, a multicluster system is designed to allow scaling as well as fault tolerance. Additional servers are added to the cluster as processing requirements grow.

Clustering technology can provide better performance than large symmetric multi-processing servers because multiple systems provide better I/O (input/output) for a large number of network clients. Other important features and benefits are outlined here:

■ **Load balancing** Cluster software provides load balancing among the processors to ensure that processing is distributed in a way that optimizes the system.

■ **Failover** This is the term used to describe how other servers take over the load of a failed server.

■ **Fault-resilience** The ability to provide uninterrupted service. Obviously, this depends on the number of servers, disk arrays, backup power supplies, and quality of equipment.

■ **Multiport disk access** Each system in the cluster has access to the same RAID system. RAID systems have their own built-in fault tolerance.

■ **Scalability** The ability to scale the system up to handle more clients on an as-needed basis.

Both clients and network administrators view clusters of servers as a single server. A virtual IP (Internet Protocol) addressing scheme is implemented in which a single URL (Universal Resource Locator) points to the entire cluster of servers. A file system distributed over a cluster appears as a single file system even if one of the servers in the cluster fails. Network

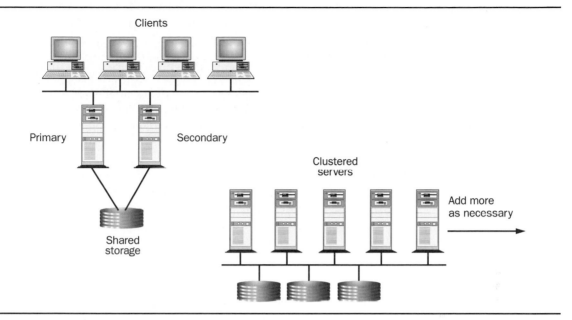

Figure C-20.   *Clustering configurations*

administrators can run a single management application to monitor the performance of
the cluster.

Some of the difficulties of clustering include handling failures of components, recovering
from failures, arbitration of access to disks in a shared environment, and cache coherency (a
disk is read by another user before update information in the cache is written).

Clustering is a typical configuration in multitiered network architectures where the cluster
represents the middle and back-end tiers. See "Multitiered Architectures" for more information.

Microsoft Windows 2000 DataCenter is designed for use at the core of enterprise networks.
It supports a four-node cluster with expanded support in the future. A related product is Microsoft
WLBS (Windows Load Balancing Service) for Windows NT. This is called NLB (Network Load
Balancing) in Windows 2000. In Windows 2000, a feature called CLB (Component Load Balancing)
balances the distribution of objects (software components) across a set of COM+ servers. Microsoft
developed the MSCS (Microsoft Cluster Service) API to support cluster development.

IBM's Netfinity servers support up to eight nodes in a cluster with software that was
designed using the Microsoft MSCS API. Novell's NWCS (NetWare Cluster Services) is
another clustering solution.

The Virtual Interface (VI) Architecture specification defines an industry-standard architecture
for communication within clusters of servers and workstations. The specification is designed
to boost I/O by reducing the time it takes to exchange messages between devices. ""The VI
architecture is promoted by Compaq, Intel, and Microsoft. More information is available at
the Web site listed at the end of this topic. Refer to "VI Architecture" for more information.

Load-balancing is a related technology for creating what are often called *virtual clusters*. Refer to "Load Balancing" for more information. Other interesting related technologies are described under "Infiniband" and "DAFS (Direct Access File System)."

Related Entries   DAFS (Direct Access File System); Data Center Design; Data Protection; Data Warehousing; DBMS (Database Management System); Disaster Planning and Recovery; Distributed Computer Networks; Fault Management; Fault Tolerance and High-Availability; Infiniband; Load Balancing; Multiprocessing; Multitiered Architectures; NAS (Network Attached Storage); Replication; SAN (Storage Area Network); SCSP (Server Cache Synchronization Protocol); Servers; Supercomputer; Switch Fabrics and Bus Design; UPS (Uninterruptible Power Supply); *and* VI Architecture

Linktionary!—Tom Sheldon's Encyclopedia of Networking updates	http://www.linktionary.com/c/clustering.html
The Beowulf Project	http://www.beowulf.org/
Network Appliance clustered systems paper	http://www.netapp.com/technology/level3/1004.html
Microsoft Clustering Technologies (search for "Clustering")	http://www.microsoft.com/windows2000
Compaq fault tolerance and high availability Web site	http://www5.compaq.com/enterprise/highavailability.html
3Com High-Availability papers	http://www.3com.com/technology/tech_net/white_papers/
VI (Virtual Interface) Architecture Web site	http://www.viarch.org/

CMIP (Common Management Information Protocol)

CMIP is an OSI (Open Systems Interconnection) model that defines how to create a common network management system. While both CMIP and the Internet SNMP (Simple Network Management Protocol) define network management standards, CMIP is more complex. In fact, CMIP is really only used by some telecommunications service providers for network management. In contrast, SNMP is an Internet protocol specifically designed for TCP/IP networks that is commonly used on corporate networks.

The Linktionary! Web page at http://www.linktionary.com/c/cmip.html has more information about CMIP.

CNRP (Common Name Resolution Protocol)

CNRP is an Internet protocol that relieves people from having to remember long and complicated Internet URLs (Universal Resource Locators). Instead, you type in "common names" to access resources. CNRP provides a "resolution service" that converts the common name into an Internet address. See RFC 2972 (Context and Goals for Common Name Resolution, October 2000).

Imagine your looking for a document on your company's Web server. You know it's the February meeting notes. In your Web browser's Address field, you type *Feb meeting notes* and the document appears. In the background, CNRP has taken your easy-to-remember document name and resolved it into an IP address (for example http://www.company.com/docserver/febmeeting.doc).

Common names and the CNRP protocol may be used in the following applications:

- **Business directories**   The common name is a company, and the resource referred to provides information about the company, its products, SEC filings, stock quotes, and so on.

- **White pages**   The common name is a last name, phone number, or e-mail address that provides information about a person.

- **E-commerce directories**   The common name is a brand name or description, and the resource referred to is a consumer item.

- **Publishing directories**   The title of a publication refers to a book, song title, or artist's name.

- **Entertainment directories**   Common names refer to movies, rock band, events, concerts, TV shows, and so on.

- **Yellow pages services**   A house for sale, a restaurant, a car dealership, or other type of establishment or service that can be found in the traditional yellow pages is referred to with a street address, the name of a business, or a description.

- **News feeds**   A headline refers to a press article.

Currently, RealNames uses the protocol at its Web site. Some of the authors of the CNRP protocol work for RealNames. Similar techniques have been implemented, including AOL's KeyWords, CompuServe's Go Words, NetScape Navigator's Smart Browsing, and others. CNRP is an attempt to standardize the concept.

Related topics include URN (Uniform Resource Names), which is a computer-to-computer naming scheme. A URN is a name with global scope that does not imply a location. It has the same meaning everywhere. It provides a persistent identifier for recognizing a resource and providing access to it via a URL (Uniform Resource Locator).

Related Entries   CIP (Common Indexing Protocol); Directory Services; Handle System; Metadata; Name Services; Search and Discovery Services; Service Advertising and Discovery; URI (Uniform Resource Identifier); URN (Universal Resource Naming); WebDAV; *and* White Pages Directory Services

Linktionary!—Tom Sheldon's Encyclopedia of Networking updates	http://www.linktionary.com/c/cnrp.html
IETF Common Name Resolution Protocol (cnrp) Working Group	http://www.ietf.org/html.charters/cnrp-charter.html
RealNames Web site	http://web.realnames.com/

CO (Central Office)

A CO is part of the telephone network in your area. It is a building in which the phone lines in your home or office terminate and connect to a much larger switching system. In large metropolitan areas, COs are more appropriately LOs (local offices), because they serve a local area. The term "CO" is from the early days of the telephone system when the local telephone company really did have only one central office in each area.

The telephone cable from the CO to your home or office is called the *local loop* and is, in most cases, the last remaining part of the telephone network that uses analog voice signaling over copper cables. The maximum distance of a CO-to-home/office cable is about 5 kilometers. A CO in a metropolitan area may provide service to over 100,000 local loops.

The CO is connected to a much broader switching system in which switching offices are interconnected with trunk lines that may be coax cable, fiber-optic cable, or microwave transmission systems. While the local loop is an analog circuit for voice calls, once a call gets to the CO, it is converted to a 64-Kbit/sec stream of digital data for routing through the switching system. A trunk line will carry hundreds of these digitized voice calls using multiplexing techniques. See "Multiplexing and Multiplexers" and "T-Carriers."

Telephone switching systems perform the task that was historically handled by telephone operators. They connect one phone line to another. There is a hierarchy of switches as pictured under the topic "Circuit-Switching Services." See "Telecommunications and Telephone System" for more details.

Related Entries   Circuit-Switching Services; Communication Services and Providers; DSL (Digital Subscriber Line); Line Conditioning; Local Loop; Modems; Network Access Services; NPN (New Public Network); PSTN (Public Switched Telephone Network); RBOCs (Regional Bell Operating Companies); Residential Broadband; Service Providers and Carriers; Telecommunications and Telephone Systems; *and* Wireless Local Loop

"Expecting 56k (V.90/X2/K56)?" (describes phone-line problems)

http://www.hal-pc.org/~wdg/56k.html

CO (Central Office) locator (to determine how far you are from your CO)

http://www.dslreports.com/coinfo

Coaxial Cable Media

Coaxial cable consists of a solid copper core surrounded by an insulator, a combination shield and ground wire, and an outer protective jacket, as pictured in Figure C-21. The primary types of coaxial cable used for networking are listed here:

- **RG-58A/U**   50-ohm cable used in Ethernet 10Base2 (Thinnet)
- **RG-59/U**   CATV cable (75 ohm)
- **RG-62/U**   93-ohm cable used in ARCNET and to connect IBM 3270 terminals

Coaxial cable can be cabled over longer distances (186 meters for 10Base2 Ethernet) than twisted-pair cable (about 100 meters); but because twisted-pair now offers higher data rates and is easier and cheaper to install, it is now favored over coaxial cable. The shielding on coaxial cable makes it less susceptible to interference from outside sources. Still, new categories of twisted-pair wire now allow data rates to surpass that available on coaxial cable. Coaxial cable requires termination at each end of the cable and a single ground connection. In long runs, there is a possibility that secondary grounds can form on the cable, causing noise problems and the potential for electric shock.

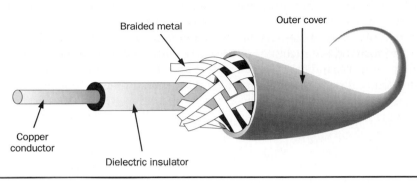

Braided metal

Outer cover

Copper
conductor

Dielectric insulator

Figure C-21.   *Coaxial cable*

While coaxial cable is the traditional media for Ethernet and ARCNET networks, twisted-pair and fiber-optic cable are more common today. New structured wiring system standards call for data-grade twisted-pair cable wire that transmits at 100 Mbits/sec, ten times the speed of Ethernet coaxial cable networks. Coaxial cable is most likely a dead-end cabling scheme for large office environments, although it may occasionally be used for long backbone connections.

Related Entries   Cable and Wiring; Fiber-Optic Cable; *and* TIA/EIA Structured Cabling Standards

Collaborative Computing

Collaborative computing allows users to work together on documents and projects, usually in real time, by taking advantage of underlying network communication systems. Whole new categories of software have been developed for collaborative computing, and many existing applications now include features that let people work together over networks. Here are some examples:

■ Application suites such as Microsoft Office and Exchange, Lotus Notes, and Novell Groupwise that provide messaging, scheduling, document coauthoring, rules-based message management, workflow routing, and discussion groups.

■ Videoconferencing applications that allow users to collaborate over local networks, private WANs (wide area networks), or over the Internet. See "Videoconferencing" for more information.

■ Internet collaboration tools that provide virtual meetings, group discussions, chat rooms, whiteboards, document exchange, workflow routing, and many other features. Multicasting is an enabling technology for groupware and collaborative work on the Internet that reduces bandwidth requirements. A single packet can be addressed to a group rather than having to send a packet to each member of the group. See "Multicasting" for more details.

■ Instant messaging is like electronic mail that happens in real time. When you log onto a company server or an Internet site that tracks your "presence," other people whom you designate are notified that you are online and available for instant messaging. They can send you a message that appears immediately on your screen. You can send an immediate reply. Instant message has huge potential in many applications. Companies can use it to form ad hoc meetings or organize meetings. It is even being used as a signaling protocol to indicate when a person changes their physical location so that Internet phone calls can be redirected to that location. Refer to "Instant Messaging" for more details.

■ Workflow management is about coordinating the flow of documents (invoices, reports, legal documents, etc.) within an organization from one person to another. Refer to "Workflow Management" for more details.

A good example of collaborative applications designed for Internet use are Microsoft's NetShow and NetMeeting. NetShow is a multimedia Web technology that enhances broadcasting with interactive content like audio, illustrated audio (images and sound), and video. This is delivered using multicast technology, which means that multiple users can receive the same broadcast at the same time. NetMeeting is a multimedia conferencing tool that works over the Internet or intranets. It provides what are essentially videophone services between users.

The topic "File Sharing" discusses some interesting services on the Web that support collaborative computing via personal shared file areas and chat rooms.

Related Entries   Chat; CU-SeeME; Document Management; Electronic Mail; Groupware; ICQ (I-Seek-You); Information Publishing; Instant Messaging; IRC (Internet Relay Chat); Lotus Notes; Microsoft Exchange; Multicasting; Multimedia and Multimedia Network Services; Unified Messaging; Videoconferencing; VoIP (Voice over IP); Webcasting; Whiteboard Applications; Workflow Management; *and* XML (eXtensible Markup Language)

Linktionary!—Tom Sheldon's Encyclopedia of Networking updates	http://www.linktionary.com/c/collaborate.html
Collaboration topics at TechGuide.com	http://www.techguide.com
Open Information Interchange (OII) guide to Workflow Management and Collaborative Authoring	http://158.169.50.95:10080/oii/en/workflow.html
Bitpipe (search for "collaborative computing")	http://www.bitpipe.com/
Collaborative Computing by Teemu Torvelainen	http://www.mli.hkkk.fi/classes/mis1997/collabor/
Mitre document: "Collaborative Virtual Workspace"	http://www.mitre.org/pubs/showcase/cvw/
Mitre Collaborative Technologies newsletter	http://www.mitre.org/pubs/edge/june_98/

Co-Location Services

Co-location, for the purposes of this discussion, is the outsourcing of Internet services (such as Web hosting). Outsourcing is when a company decides to let an outside service organization manage some aspect of its business. Outsourcing lets a company concentrate on what it does best and reduce the expenses associated with managing services that are better handled by outside experts.

The most common form of co-location is the outsourcing of Web services, commerce services, intranet servers, and extranet servers. A co-location provider such as AboveNet provides these services:

- Teleco-grade facilities with fire protection, clean power, and power backup
- High-bandwidth redundant Internet connections
- Peering arrangements with other service providers and Internet exchanges
- Management on a 24-hour, 7-day-per-week basis.
- Technical expertise in managing BGP4 routing, TCP/IP, and other Internet protocols

A co-location facility with high-bandwidth Internet connections is commonly called a gigaPOP (Point-of-Presence with gigabit connections).

The AboveNet Web site listed has additional information. You can also check with the Internet service providers in your area for additional information about co-location.

Related Entries   ASP (Application Service Provider); Data Center Design; Fault Tolerance and High-Availability; Internet Connections; ISP (Internet Service Provider); Outsourcing; POP (Point-of-Presence); Service Providers and Carriers; *and* Web Technologies and Concepts

Linktionary!—Tom Sheldon's Encyclopedia of Networking updates	http://www.linktionary.com/c/co-location.html
AboveNet co-location services	http://www.above.net/

Collisions and Collision Domains

Ethernet networks use a collision-sensing protocol called CSMA/CD (carrier sense multiple access/collision detection). The protocol allows multiple devices connected to a shared network cable to use that cable by taking turns accessing it. The basic strategy goes like this:

1. A computer listens on the cable to see if another computer is transmitting, which is indicated by a voltage change on the cable. If busy, the computer waits and listens.

2. When the cable is not busy, a computer attempts to transmit.

3. Another computer may attempt to transmit at the same time, which causes a *collision*.

4. Both computers that attempted to transmit must back off, wait, and then attempt to transmit again.

Computers on the network detect collisions by looking for abnormally changing voltages. Signals from multiple systems overlap and distort one another. Overlapping signals will push the voltage above the allowable limit. This is detected by attached computers, which reject the corrupted frames (called *runts*).

When a network becomes excessively busy, collisions increase dramatically, causing a need to retransmit frames, which compounds the problem. The last station to transmit usually gets to transmit first when the network recovers, which can cause delay problems that are unfavorable for multimedia traffic. 3Com's PACE solution attempts to prevent monopolization of a network by a single station due to this effect. PACE improves bandwidth utilization by managing traffic instead of letting the network manage itself. See "PACE (Priority Access Control Enabled)" for more information.

A late collision occurs when a cable is longer than allowed by the Ethernet specification. It may also be caused by cable or connector damage, too many repeaters, or interference problems. Assume the cable is too long. One station starts to transmit and its signals begin propagating down the cable. Because the cable is too long, a station at the other end of the cable does not detect that another node is transmitting and begins to transmit. In this case, a collision will occur, but the first transmitter may have completed its transmission and is no longer listening for collisions. The transmission becomes corrupted and other stations reject it. In addition, the transmitter will need to be told to retransmit the packet. Network performance is affected by the retransmission requirements.

An Ethernet LAN consists of *collision domains* and *broadcast domains*. Suppose you have a LAN with 100 computers. All 100 computers vie for access to the cable. The entire LAN of 100 computers is also a broadcast domain since any message sent by one computer can be heard by another. Now suppose you divide the LAN with a bridge into segment A and segment B, each with 50 computers. The bridge blocks collisions but allows broadcasts between the segments. Now there are only 50 computers in the collisions domain on segment A, which significantly reduces the possibility of collisions. But segments A and B are still in the same broadcast domain because the bridge will propagate frames between nodes on any segment.

 LAN switches, which are basically multiport bridges, are now considered the best way to build enterprise LANs. See "Switching and Switched Networks."

Related Entries   Addresses, Network; Bridges and Bridging; Broadcast Address, Broadcast Domain; Broadcast Networking; CSMA/CD (Carrier Sense Multiple Access/Collision Detection); Ethernet; MAC (Media Access Control); and Switching *and* Switched Networks

Linktionary!—Tom Sheldon's Encyclopedia of Networking updates	http://www.linktionary.com/c/collisions.html
Charles Spurgeon's "Collisions" page	http://www.host.ots.utexus.edu/ethernet/ enet-misc/collision/collision.html
Ethernet Collisions page at Optimized Engineering	http://www.optimized.com/COMPENDI/ EN-Colli.htm
Collisions by Godred Fairhurst	http://www.erg.abdn.ac.uk/users/gorry/course/ lan-pages/csma-cd.html
Collision Domains, by Transition Networks	http://www.transition.com/learning/ whitepapers/colldom_wp.htm

COM (Component Object Model)

COM (Component Object Model) is a Microsoft specification that defines the interaction between components in the Windows environment. A *component* is a self-contained coded module that provides some service to other components in an object-oriented environment. The topics "Object Technologies" and "Distributed Object Computing" describe this concept further.

COM was introduced in 1993, and its first major implementation was in Windows 95, although it is the basis of OLE (Object Linking and Embedding), which is an object-based service that allows applications running in the same computer to interact and share information. In 1996, Microsoft created ActiveX, which is basically OLE designed to work in Web-centric environments. ActiveX components are downloadable controls that enhance the Windows interface on a user's computer.

DCOM (Distributed Component Object Model) is the network version of COM that allows objects running in different computers attached to a network to interact. Microsoft describes DCOM as "COM with a long wire." DCOM works across a variety of network transports, but most important, it works across TCP/IP protocols and the Internet.

The latest version of COM, specifically designed to work in the Windows 2000 environment, is COM+. This new version has new services that enhance its ability to act as an ORB (object request broker). It supports messaging, directory services, and transaction services. In fact, MTS (Microsoft Transaction Server) was a separate product that Microsoft integrated with COM+. Other features include the ability to load balance traffic between servers in a clustered environment, enhanced security, and the ability of applications to operate in either a disconnected (asynchronous) or connected (synchronous) state (as described under the "Middleware and Messaging" topic).

One of the most important features of COM+ was added later. Microsoft replaced the interobject communication protocol with a message-passing approach that uses standard XML, thus advancing its component model into the realm of universal objects. Basically, it replaced RPC (remote procedure call) with a new protocol called SOAP (Simple Object Access Protocol), which is covered later in this book.

DCOM (Distributed Component Object Model)

The idea behind component technology is to break large and complex applications into smaller software modules that are easier to develop, modify, and upgrade. By breaking applications into parts, a modification or upgrade affects only specific components, not the entire program. Application logic, information retrieval, transaction monitoring, data presentation, and management may run on different computers that communicate with one another to provide end users with a seamless application interface.

Microsoft's DCOM takes all the qualities of COM and extends it over a network. It provides the underlying binding elements for extending components across networks. It is designed to run on Windows 9x, Windows NT, Windows 2000, Macintosh, UNIX, and legacy operating systems.

Microsoft openly licenses DCOM technology. In October of 1996, Microsoft turned control of ActiveX technology and DCOM over to The Open Group, an industry consortium that manages open software development. DCOM is also part of The Open Group's DCE (Distributed Computing Environment) technology. The Web sites are listed at the end of this topic.

Microsoft is also working with Internet standards bodies, including the IETF and the W3C (World Wide Web Consortium), to make DCOM viable on the Internet. Software AG has done extensive work with DCOM and has ported it to the Sun Solaris operating system.

To extend its component model to a model that supports sophisticated applications, Microsoft has integrated DCOM into its ActiveX Server, a series of technology services that speed deployment of component-based applications across the Internet and corporate intranets.

DCOM is also language neutral, meaning that components can be written in a variety of languages. The Web browser is the most common "container" for running components. Users download components at the sites they visit. The components may be stored permanently on the user's system for later use or may go into the cache, where they may be deleted after a period of nonuse. Most Windows applications also provide the container paradigm.

Communication techniques are required so that components can interact with one another across networks. As mentioned, the original DCOM used RPCs, but COM+ uses the message-passing approach of SOAP. SOAP messages are passed over networks via standard HTTP, and the format of the messages is defined in standard XML. With XML, the content of messages is standardized so that any application can read them. In addition, XML tags can be developed to define any kind of information, including how to handle security. Microsoft believes that the messaging paradigm, as opposed to the connection-oriented RPC method, is the best way to create scalable, decentralized intranets and Web application environments.

There is a need to register components and coordinate their activities when critical transactions are taking place. Microsoft Transaction Server (now integrated in COM+) coordinates the interaction of components and ensures that transactions are implemented safely. It provides transaction processing and monitoring, along with message queuing and other traditional features normally found on high-end transaction systems. Because it provides these features in an object-based environment, it is essentially a transaction-based *object request broker*. See "Transaction Processing."

DCOM competes with other object technologies, such as CORBA (Common Object Request Broker Architecture) and Sun's EJB (Enterprise JavaBeans). Refer to "Distributed Object Computing" for a comparison of these technologies.

Related Entries   ActiveX; Client/Server Computing; CORBA (Common Object Request Broker Architecture); Distributed Applications; Distributed Computer Networks; Distributed Object Computing; Java; Microsoft Windows DNA (Digital interNetwork Application); Middleware; MOM (Message-Oriented Middleware); Multitiered Architectures; Object Technologies; OLE (Object Linking and Embedding); ORB (Object Request Broker); RPCs (Remote Procedure Calls); SOAP (Simple Object Access Protocol); Transaction Processing; *and* Web Technologies and Concepts

Linktionary!—Tom Sheldon's Encyclopedia of Networking updates	http://www.linktionary.com/c/com.html
Microsoft COM and DCOM Web page	http://www.microsoft.com/com/
dev^x (development exchange)	http://www.devx.com/
COM/DCOM FAQ	http://www.vivid-creations.com/faq/comfaq.htm
COM/CORBA, Cetus Links—Object-Orientation	http://www.cetus-links.org/
White Paper: CORBA, COM, and other Object Standards and Their Relevance to Development of Interoperable Systems	http://www2.dcnicn.com/cals/cals_97f/task07/html/Non-CDRL/whitepaper.html

Commercial Building Wiring Standard

See ISO/IEC-11801 Cabling Standards; TIA/EIA Structured Cabling Standards.

Communication

See Data Communication Concepts.

Communication Controller

A communication controller manages data input and output to a host computer or computer network. The communication controller is often called a front-end processor because it is a separate device from the host system that handles all communication with external devices such as terminals. It also contains the adapter to connect with the host channel and interface units that connect with cluster controllers. This topic is covered in more detail at the Linktionary! site.

Related Entries   Cluster Controller; IBM; IBM Mainframe Environment; *and* SNA (Systems Network Architecture)

 Linktionary!—Tom Sheldon's Encyclopedia   http://www.linktionary.com/c/comm._controller.html of Networking updates

Communication Server

A communication server is a dedicated system that provides communication services for users on a network who need to transfer files or access information on systems or networks at remote locations over telecommunication links. The communication server provides communication channels for one or more users simultaneously, depending on the software and the hardware capabilities. Communication servers may provide one or more of the following functions:

- **Gateway functions**   These provide users with connections to host computers by translating between data formats, communication protocols, and cable signals.

- **Modems**   Communication servers provide banks of modems that internal users access for dial-out sessions or remote users access for dial-in sessions.

- **Access services**   These enable remote users to dial into the network from their home or other remote locations and obtain "remote node" or "remote control" access. With the remote node method, all processing takes place at the remote workstation. With the remote control method, the user connects to a dedicated workstation on the LAN (local area network) and all processing takes place at the LAN-attached dedicated workstation.

- **Bridge and router functions**   A communication server with these features maintains a dedicated or dial-up (intermittent) link with remote LANs and automatically transfers data packets between the LANs as necessary.

- **Electronic mail servers**   These automatically connect with other LANs or electronic "post offices" to pick up and deliver e-mail. The systems may call at timed intervals or whenever there is enough outgoing mail to make the call worthwhile.

Related Entries   DIAMETER; Internet Connections; Mobile Computing: Modems; NAS (Network Access Server); RADIUS (Remote Authentication Dial In User Service); Remote Access; Roaming; Servers; *and* VPN (Virtual Private Networks)

Communication Services and Providers

Communication services that support voice, video, and data are provided by a variety of carriers and service providers: "last-mile" local access services, metropolitan area services, or wide area services. The types of providers that sell these services include the following:

- **ILECs (incumbent local exchange carriers)**   The traditional telephone carriers that are usually the RBOCs (Regional Bell Operating Companies), although some areas have carriers that were never part of AT&T.

- **CLECs (competitive local exchange carriers)**   Carriers that compete with the ILECs within the same geographic area.

- **IXCs (interexchange carriers)**   These are the traditional long-distance carriers such as MCI Worldcom, Sprint, and AT&T, as well as new players.

- **ICPs (integrated communications providers)**   CLECs are morphing into ICPs, which provide a variety of "New Public Network" services, including Web hosting and Internet access.

- **Integrated voice-video-data service providers**   Service providers that have built infrastructure in local, metropolitan, or wide areas to provide a full range of voice, video, and data services.

- **CATV**   The traditional television cable networks, now providing voice, video, and high-speed data services over hybrid copper/fiber networks.

- **ISPs (Internet service providers)**   Traditional Internet service providers, some of which may offer local access in the form of fiber cables into buildings or wireless access systems.

- **WSPs (wireless service providers)**   A whole new breed of service providers that use radio or optical wireless systems to provide local access to homes and businesses. In addition, cellular phone system providers are boosting their data rates with new protocols and technologies.

- **HALO (High Altitude Long Operation)**   These are the newest local access providers that offer wireless services relayed from balloons or circling planes.

- **Satellite systems**   There are a number of satellite systems in place to deliver voice, video, and data services, including the LEO (low earth orbit) and geosynchronous systems.

Organizations build wide area enterprise networks to link remote users and create LAN-to-LAN links that allow users in one geographic area to use resources on LANs in other areas. A variety of carrier services are available to create these links:

- **Circuit switching (analog)**   Provides dial-up lines with relatively low throughput for point-to-point connections. This type of service is best for occasional traffic between two points, such as a single-user connection or file transfer.

- **Circuit switching (digital)**   Provides temporary connections between two points with rapid setup times. This type of service is preferred for periodic connections among a number of different points where speeds higher than dial-up lines is required. Circuits are usually virtual.

- **Dedicated line**   Provides a permanent connection between two points on a leased, month-to-month basis, usually with an initial setup charge. These lines are suitable for handling constant traffic between two sites.

- **Packet switching**   Provides the most flexible service for companies that need to connect with many different sites. A packet-switched network provides simultaneous connections to many points and bandwidth on demand in most cases. See "Packet and Cell Switching" for more information.

The following describes services available from the local and long-distance carriers. For additional information about the services provided by specific providers, refer to their Web sites. The Web pages listed at the end of this section provide links to carriers and service providers. Also see "Service Providers and Carriers." Many of these services can be defined as either access services for enterprise wide area networking and/or Internet access services for home and small business users. Refer to either "WAN (Wide Area Network)" or "Network Access Services."

- **Dial-up analog lines**   Connections are made only when needed for file transfers, e-mail connections, and remote users' sessions. See "Modems."

- **Permanent leased lines**   These analog lines provide the same data rates as dial-up lines, except that customers contract with the carrier to keep the lines available for immediate use when necessary. See "Leased Line," "T Carriers," and "TDM Networks."

- **Circuit switched ISDN (Integrated Services Digital Network)**   ISDN is a point-to point voice and data service with two switchable channels that provide a data rate of 64 Kbits/sec. See "ISDN (Integrated Services Digital Network)" for more details.

- **Dedicated digital TDM (time division multiplexing) services**   With TDM, data is transmitted across circuits that are divided into time slots, with individual users getting a regular repeating time slot. The traditional TDM digital line service is the *T1 channel*. See "T Carriers" and "TDM Networks."

- **DSL (Digital Subscriber Line) services**   These are emerging services that use the existing twisted-pair copper wire in the local loop to provide data rates up to the megabits-per-second range. DSL is an always-on circuit service for home and business use.

- **Cable (CATV)**   Existing CATV network providers are now offering Internet connection services over their networks, primarily to home users. See "Cable (CATV) Data Networks."

- **X.25 packet switching services**   This is a standard, well-tested, protocol that has been a workhorse packet-switching service since 1976. It is suitable for light loads and was commonly used to provide remote terminal connections to mainframe systems. However, frame relay and ATM services are more suitable for network traffic.

■ **Frame relay frame switching services**   This service provides many enhancements over X.25. It is an excellent choice for organizations that need any-to-any connections on an as-needed or permanent basis. See "Frame Relay" for more details.

■ **ATM (Asynchronous Transfer Mode)**   This service provides cell-switching services that can transmit data at megabit- and potentially gigabit-per-second rates. Most carriers already use ATM switching internally. Customers can take advantage of this service by installing ATM access devices on-site to route voice, video, and data across the carriers network. See "ATM (Asynchronous Transfer Mode)."

■ **Metro Ethernet and Ethernet WAN services**   Gigabit Ethernet and 10 Gigabit Ethernet are proving useful in the MAN (metropolitan area network) and WAN environments. A number of service providers are building mesh networks with these technologies and separating customer traffic with VLAN techniques. See "MAN (Metropolitan Area Network)," "Network Access Services," and "WAN (Wide Area Network)."

■ **Wireless mobile services**   The cellular phone service providers are extending their existing networks and frequency allocation rights with new protocols and technology that boost the data rates for which mobile users. Refer to "Wireless Mobile Communications" for more information.

■ **Wireless broadband**   A whole range of new high-speed wireless services is emerging that can provide access services in the gigabit-per-second range. See "Wireless Broadband Access Services" for more details.

Related Entries   ATM (Asynchronous Transfer Mode; Cable (CATV) Data Networks; Circuit; Circuit-Switching Services; DBS (Direct Broadcast Satellite); DSL (Digital Subscriber Line); Fiber to the Curb/Fiber to the Home; Frame Relay; Gigabit Ethernet; HALO (High Altitude Long Operation); High-Speed/High-Performance Networking; Internet Connections; ISDN (Integrated Services Digital Network); ISPs (Internet Service Providers); Local Loop; MAN (Metropolitan Area Network); Multiplexing and Multiplexers; Network Access Services; NPN (New Public Network); Packet and Cell Switching; Residential Broadband; Satellite Communication Systems; Service Providers and Carriers; SONET (Synchronous Optical Network); TDM Networks; Telecommunications and Telephone Systems; WAN (Wide Area Network); Wireless Broadband Access Services; Wireless Communications; Wireless Mobile Communications; *and* X.25

Linktionary!—Tom Sheldon's Encyclopedia of Networking updates	http://www.linktionary.com/c/commservices/html
Analysys Telecoms Virtual Library	http://www.analysys.co.uk/vlib/
Jeffrey K. MacKie-Mason's Telecom Information Resources on the Internet	http://china.si.umich.edu/telecom/telecom-info.html
Computer and Communication Hot Links	http://www.cmpcmm.com/cc/
FCC Consumer Information Bureau	http://www.fcc.gov/clib/

CompactPCI

See Switch Fabrics and Bus Design.

Component Software Technology

Component software technology breaks large and complex applications into smaller software modules called *components* or *objects* (in the Java environment, objects are called *applets*). By breaking applications into components, complex software is simplified. Each component is like a building block that performs a specific task and has an interface that lets developers combine it with other components to build applications. See "Distributed Object Computing" for more information.

Compound Documents

A compound document is like a container that holds text, graphics, and multimedia video and sound objects. Early on, Microsoft Windows and the Macintosh used this technology, which allows users to create documents with a word processor, spreadsheet program, or other program, and embed or link objects in the documents. An electronic mail message with an attachment such as a graphic is also a compound document.

Today, a Web page is the best example of a compound document. It holds text and individual objects like pictures, sounds, videos, Java applets, and ActiveX controls.

The original purpose of compound documents was to provide a single place where users could create a document that contained all the elements related to that document. When you save a compound document, you save all the text and objects under the same filename even though objects remain as separate files for editing or inclusion in other documents.

In the case of a Web server HTML document, a simple link or hyperlink to external objects is all that is needed to display those objects in documents. For example, an image of a company's logo can be stored on a Web server and then opened for display on any Web page. If the logo is called LOGO.GIF, a tag is placed in an HTML document to display the logo. The LOGO.GIF image file can be altered at any time. The next time a Web page is opened by a user, the new logo is displayed because the Web page simply searches for LOGO.GIF and displays it.

An active document contains objects or components that are manually or automatically updated from a source called the server. For example, if a compound document contains a link to a graphic image that has been updated by someone else, the graphic in the compound document is updated the next time the document is opened. This concept has been extended to the Internet and the Web. Java and ActiveX are now the primary tools for creating active documents that contain applets and components that perform a variety of actions or tasks.

One of the advantages of this technology is that the document signals the source when it needs to have its objects updated. This frees the server from having to continuously provide updates when it may be unnecessary. When an active document is opened, that is when updates can occur, but if necessary, an active document can be continuously updated. This is the case where information is updated in real time and the server broadcasts information on a continuous basis. See "Push" and "Webcasting" for more information on this technology.

On the World Wide Web, Web pages are active documents that are dynamically updated, often in real time. Note that Web pages may be either static or dynamic. A static page does not change except when the Webmaster makes changes to it. Everyone who accesses the page sees the same information. Dynamic Web pages, on the other hand, are created on-the-fly, based on information the user typed into a form or, based on other information such as the current time, date, and other information. For example, you may enter stock symbols into a form, and then get a personalized Web page back from the server that details the current value of your stock holdings.

Active documents are discussed in a document written by Sandy Ressler called "Perspectives on Electronic Publishing." The document is located at the U.S. government's NIST (National Institute of Standards) Web site. See the Web site listed at the end of this topic. It provides an example of a pie chart in a document that is automatically updated as data in a spreadsheet changes. In another case, a change to a document may initiate an electronic mail message that is sent to the author of the document or someone else responsible for its contents. The mechanisms that allow these updates are as follows:

- OLE (Object Linking and Embedding) in the Windows environment
- The Publish and Subscribe facility in the Macintosh environment
- RPC (remote procedure calls) on UNIX and Windows systems
- Component Software Technologies such as Java and ActiveX

Related Entries   Acrobat; ActiveX; Collaborative Computing; COM (Component Object Model); Distributed Applications; Distributed Object Computing; Document Management; HTML (Hypertext Markup Language); Hypermedia and Hypertext; Imaging; Java; Metadata; Object Technologies; OLE (Object Linking and Embedding); SGML (Standard Generalized Markup Language); Web Technologies and Concepts; Workflow Management; *and* XML (eXtensible Markup Language)

Linktionary!—Tom Sheldon's Encyclopedia of Networking updates	http://www.linktionary.com/c/compound_doc.html
Perspectives on Electronic Publishing by Sandy Ressler	http://www.nist.gov/itl/div894/ovrt/people/sressler/Persp/Views.html
W3C Compound Document Architecture page	http://www.w3.org/OOP/CompoundDoc.html

Compression Techniques

Data compression squeezes data so it requires less disk space for storage and less bandwidth on a data transmission channel. Communications equipment like modems, bridges, and routers use compression schemes to improve throughput over standard phone lines or leased lines. Compression is also used to compress voice telephone calls transmitted over leased lines so that more calls can be placed on those lines. In addition, compression is essential for videoconferencing applications that run over data networks.

Most compression schemes take advantage of the fact that data contains a lot of repetition. For example, alphanumeric characters are normally represented by a 7-bit ASCII code, but a compression scheme can use a 3-bit code to represent the eight most common letters.

In addition, long stretches of "nothing" can be replaced by a value that indicates how much "nothing" there is. For example, silence in a compressed audio recording can be replaced by a value that indicates how long that silence is. White space in a compressed graphic image can be replaced by a value that indicates the amount of white space.

Compression has become critical in the move to combine voice and data networks. Compression techniques have been developed that reduce the data requirements for a voice channel down to 8 Kbits/sec. This is a significant improvement over noncompressed voice (64 Kbits/sec) and older compression techniques yielding 32 Kbits/sec.

Two important compression concepts are lossy and lossless compression:

- **Lossy compression**   With lossy compression, it is assumed that some loss of information is acceptable. The best example is a videoconference where there is an acceptable amount of frame loss in order to deliver the image in real time. People may appear jerky in their movements, but you still have a grasp for what is happening on the other end of the conference. In the case of graphics files, some resolution may be lost in order to create a smaller file. The loss may be in the form of color depth or graphic detail. For example, high-resolution details can be lost if a picture is going to be displayed on a low-resolution device. Loss is also acceptable in voice and audio compression, depending on the desired quality.

- **Lossless compression**   With lossless compression, data is compressed without any loss of data. It assumes you want to get everything back that you put in. Critical financial data files are examples where lossless compression is required.

The removal of information in the lossy technique is acceptable for images, because the loss of information is usually imperceptible to the human eye. While this trick works on humans, you may not be able to use lossy images in some situations, such as when scanners are used to locate details in images.

Lossy compression can provide compression ratios of 100:1 to 200:1, depending on the type of information being compressed. Lossless compression ratios usually only achieve a 2:1 compression ratio. Lossy compression techniques are often "tunable" in that you can turn the compression up to improve throughput, but at a loss in quality. Compression can also be turned downed to the point at which there is little loss of image, but throughput will be affected.

This topic is continued at the Linktionary! Web site. See the hyperlink.

Related Entries   ADC (Analog to Digital Conversion); Encryption; IP (Internet Protocol); Videoconferencing; Voice/Data Networking; *and* VoIP (Voice over IP)

Linktionary!—Tom Sheldon's Encyclopedia of Networking updates	http://www.linktionary.com/c/compression.html
Iterated Systems' Web site	http://www.iterated.com
OII Guide to Image Compression	http://158.169.50.95:10080/oii/en/compress.html
Alien's Cyberhome Digial Audio Compression page	http://www.delysid.org/alien/sound/mpeg/mpeg.html
Compression FAQ	http://www.faqs.org/faqs/compression-faq/
LuraTech LuraWave information (be sure to browse this site and view the demos)	http://www.luratech.com
Ericsson Data Compression paper	http://www.ericsson.com/datacom/emedia/data_compression.pdf

Computer-Telephony Integration

See CTI (Computer-Telephony Integration).

Concentrator Devices

A concentrator is a device that provides a central connection point for the connection of terminal, computer, or communication devices. It can be a central point where cables converge. Technically, a concentrator merges a certain number of incoming lines with a number of outgoing lines, or provides a central communication link for a number of devices. Several types of concentrators are listed here:

- **Concentrators**   In the mainframe environment, a concentrator can merge the lines from a number of terminals and provides a link to another concentrator in a hierarchical arrangement, or links directly to the front-end processor of a host computer. Data from the low-speed terminal lines is transferred over a high-speed line using a multiplexing method or a contention method. In the multiplexing method, a terminal gets a fixed time slot in the multiplexed stream. In the contention method, each low-speed line gets full access to the high-speed line for a brief period. See "IBM Mainframe Environment" for more information.

- **Front-end processors**   A front-end processor is similar to the concentrator just described in function, but it is usually a dedicated computer in its own right that performs concentration functions at higher speeds and supports more attached devices. See "IBM Mainframe Environment" for more information.

- **LAN concentrators**   In the LAN (local area network) environment, concentrators have grown from simple wire management facilities to hub devices that provide "collapsed backbone," bridging, and routing functions. A collapsed backbone is equivalent to shrinking a bus cable system like Thinwire coaxial Ethernet down to the size of a small box. A separate wire of inexpensive twisted-pair wire then runs to each workstation. See "Hubs/Concentrators/MAUs" and "Ethernet."

- **Port-sharing and selector units**   Port-sharing units provide a way for multiple terminals at a remote site to share a modem connection to a computer or host system. The device fits in between the terminals and the modem.

- **Multiplexors**   The original design of a multiplexor was based on a need to reduce the cost of data transmissions for terminal devices that needed to communicate with a host device over a telecommunication link. A multiplexor is a device that merges the data from multiple terminals into one line and then ships the merged data over the link, where it is demultiplexed at the other end. Multiplexing cost-justifies the leasing of a high-speed digital line such as T1. See "Multiplexing and Multiplexers" for more details.

Conferencing

See Collaborative Computing; CU-SeeME; Groupware; ICQ (I-Seek-You); Instant Messaging; IRC (Internet Relay Chat); Multicasting; Multimedia and Multimedia Network Services; Unified Messaging; Videoconferencing; Webcasting; and Whiteboard Applications.

Configuration Management

Configuration management covers a wide range of network administration topics. It is often referred to as a practice for software development, but this topic is about network management.

In its simplest form, configuration management has to do with collecting and storing information about devices on the network (i.e., bridges, routers, workstations, servers, and other equipment). Administrators can refer to this information when changing configurations or to determine the cause of some failure. The database can hold important infrastructure information, such as physical connections and dependencies. In advanced systems, changes made to a central database automatically affect network devices. For example, changing a subnetwork number updates all the appropriate devices connected to that subnetwork.

Configuration management also deals with issues like password management, printing configurations, and user or group management. It also may provide software installation, updates, and reconfiguration from a single location. Version numbers and licensing can be tracked and updated.

On the hardware side, configuration management provides a way to configure systems once new hardware is installed and to report this information to dependent systems. Information such as serial numbers, settings, and version information are reported back to the management database. Once the management system knows where hardware is located, it can automatically update drivers and driver updates.

Related Entries   CIM (Common Information Model); DMI (Desktop Management Interface); DMTF (Desktop Management Task Force); Network Analyzers; Network Management; Performance Measurement and Optimization; RMON (Remote Monitoring); SNMP (Simple Network Management Protocol); Testing, Diagnostics, and Troubleshooting; WBEM (Wpb-Based Enterprise Management); Wired for Management; *and* Zero Administration for Windows Initiative

CBQ (Class-Based Queuing)

See "Traffic Management, Shaping, and Engineering."

Congestion Control Mechanisms

Congestion is a problem that occurs on shared networks when multiple users contend for access to the same resources (bandwidth, buffers, and queues). Think about freeway congestion. Many vehicles enter the freeway without regard for impending or existing congestion. As more vehicles enter the freeway, congestion gets worse. Eventually, the on-ramps may back up, preventing vehicles from getting on at all.

In packet-switched networks, packets move in and out of the buffers and queues of switching devices as they traverse the network. In fact, a packet-switched network is often referred to as a "network of queues." A characteristic of packet-switched networks is that packets may arrive in bursts from one or more sources. Buffers help routers absorb bursts until they can catch up. If traffic is excessive, buffers fill up and new incoming packets are dropped. Increasing the size of the buffers is not a solution, because excessive buffer size can lead to excessive delay.

Congestion typically occurs where multiple links feed into a single link, such as where internal LANs are connected to WAN links. Congestion also occurs at routers in core networks where nodes are subjected to more traffic than they are designed to handle. TCP/IP networks such as the Internet are especially susceptible to congestion because of their basic connection-less nature. There are no virtual circuits with guaranteed bandwidth. Packets are injected by any host at any time, and those packets are variable in size, which make predicting traffic patterns and providing guaranteed service impossible. While connectionless networks have advantages, quality of service is not one of them.

> **Note** *Shared LANs such as Ethernet have their own congestion control mechanisms in the form of access controls that prevent multiple nodes from transmitting at the same time. See "Access Control, Network" and "MAC (Media Access Control)."*

The following basic techniques may be used to manage congestion.

- **End-system flow control** This is not a congestion control scheme, but a way to prevent the sender from overrunning the buffers of the receiver. See "Flow Control Mechanisms."

- **Network congestion control** In this scheme, end systems throttle back in order to avoid congesting the network. The mechanism is similar to end-to-end flow controls, but the intention is to reduce congestion in the network, not the receiver.

- **Network-based congestion avoidance** In this scheme, a router detects that congestion *may* occur and attempts to slow down senders before queues become full.

- **Resource allocation** This technique involves scheduling the use of physical circuits or other resources, perhaps for a specific time period. A virtual circuit, built across a series a switches with a guaranteed bandwidth is a form of resource allocation. This technique is difficult, but can eliminate network congestion by blocking traffic that is in excess of the network capacity. A list of related topics is given at the end of this topic.

> **Note** *Caching is probably the ultimate congestion control scheme. By moving content closer to users, a majority of traffic is obtained locally rather than being obtained from distant servers along routed paths that may experience congestion. Caching has become a serious business on the Internet, as discussed under "Content Distribution."*

Queuing and Congestion

Any discussion of congestion naturally involves queuing. Buffers on network devices are managed with various queuing techniques. Properly managed queues can minimize dropped packets and network congestion, as well as improve network performance.

The most basic technique is FIFO (first-in, first-out), where packets are processed in the order in which they arrive in the queue. Going beyond this, a priority queuing scheme uses multiple queues with different priority levels so that the most important packets are sent first.

An important queuing technique is to assign flows to their own queues. This differentiates flows so that priorities can be assigned. Just as important, each flow is responsible for making sure that it does not overflow its own queue. Separating queues in this way ensures that each queue only contains packets from a single source.

See "Queuing" for more information.

Congestion Control in Frame Relay

While this topic is primarily about congestion problems in connectionless packet-switched networks, it is useful to examine the way congestion is handled in a connection-oriented network. Frame relay provides a good example.

Frame relay subscribers negotiate a CIR (committed information rate) with the service provider. The CIR is the guaranteed level of service, but providers usually allow subscribers to burst over this level if network capacity is available. However, frames in excess of the CIR are marked as *discard eligible*. If a switch on the network becomes congested, it will drop discard eligible frames. This ensures that the service providers can meet their negotiated CIR levels for subscribers.

Dropping frames is never a good idea, so two congestion avoidance mechanisms are available:

- **BECN (backward explicit congestion notification)** When a switch starts to experience congestion (i.e., the buffers/queues are getting full), it can send a frame in the backward direction to senders with the BECN bit set to inform senders to slow down.

- **FECN (forward explicit congestion notification)** When a switch starts congesting, it can send a frame in the forward direction to receiving nodes with the FECN bit set. This informs the forward nodes that they should inform the sender to slow down.

Note that sender or receiver do not need to respond to BECN or FECN, but eventually, network switches will drop frames as congestion continues to increase.

Congestion Control and Avoidance in TCP

Until the mid 1980s, the Internet was prone to a phenomenon called "congestion collapse." This would occur because there was little control over managing heavy network loads. Individual connections used flow controls between sender and receiver to prevent the sender from overwhelming the receiver. These are described in RFC 793 (Transmission Control Protocol, September 1981).

But these early flow controls were designed to prevent overflowing the receiver's buffers, not the buffers of network nodes. However, the early Internet consisted of a large number of relatively slow links, so congestion was not the problem it is today.

In the late 1980s, Van Jacobson developed the congestion control mechanisms that make TCP respond to congestion in the network. The basic "signal" is a dropped packet, which causes the host to stop or slow down.

Normally, when a host receives a packet (or set of packets), it sends an ACK (acknowledgement) to the sender. A window mechanism allows the host to send multiple packets with a single ACK as discussed under "Flow Control Mechanisms." Failure to receive an ACK indicates that the receiving host may be overflowing or that the network is congested. In either case, the sender slows down or stops.

A strategy called *additive increase/multiplicative decrease* regulates the number of packets that are sent at one time. If you graphed the flow, you would see a sawtooth pattern where the number of packets increases (additive increase) until congestion occurs and then drops off when packets start to drop (multiplicative decrease). The window size is typically halved when a congestion signal occurs.

What the host is doing is finding the optimal transmission rate by constantly testing the network with a higher rate. Sometimes, the higher rate is allowed, but if the network is busy, packets start to drop and the host scales back. This scheme sees the network as a "black box" that drops packets when it is congested. Therefore, congestion controls are run by the end systems that see dropped packets as the only indication of network congestion.

A sender that is transferring a large file will push for a higher rate until eventually it grabs all the bandwidth. Other hosts may have trouble getting packets through. Often, the host that has grabbed the bandwidth is transmitting the least important traffic. The effect is especially disruptive to real-time traffic such as voice. Even if a link has sufficient bandwidth to handle its load, ill-behaved hosts can saturate the link (although briefly) enough to disrupt voice traffic in a way that is perceptible to users.

Of course, the network can take an active role in managing congestion. That is where "active queue management" and congestion avoidance come into play, as discussed later. RFC 1254 (Gateway Congestion Control Survey, August 1991) describes congestion control and avoidance mechanisms that were reviewed by the IETF Performance and Congestion Control Working Group. The group divided congestion handling into the following:

- **Congestion recovery**   Restore the operating state of the network when demand exceeds capacity.

- **Congestion avoidance**   Anticipate congestion and avoid it so that congestion never occurs.

RFC 1254 states that the Internet would cease to operate without congestion recovery, but has operated a long time without congestion avoidance. Today, congestion avoidance is an important tool for improving the performance and QoS of the Internet.

RFC 2309 (Recommendations on Queue Management and Congestion Avoidance in the Internet, April 1998) states that router-based mechanisms for controlling congestion can be divided into "queue management" algorithms and "scheduling" algorithms. Refer to this RFC for useful information about congestion controls, congestion avoidance schemes, and queue scheduling techniques.

An important goal is to minimize the number of dropped packets. If a host is transmitting at a high rate and the network go into congestion, a large number of packets will be lost. Congestion avoidance attempts to prevent this without putting limits on network throughput. RFC 2309 points out that it is better to accept the fact that there will be bursts that overflow queues rather than try to maintain queues in a non-full state. That would essentially translate to favoring low end-to-end delay over high throughput. The RFC also notes the following:

> The point of buffering in the network is to absorb data bursts and to transmit them during the (hopefully) ensuing bursts of silence. This is essential to permit the transmission of bursty data. It should be clear why we would like to have normally-small queues in routers: we want to have queue capacity to absorb the bursts. The counter-intuitive result is that maintaining normally-small queues can result in higher throughput as well as lower end-to-end delay. In short, queue limits should not reflect the steady state queues we want maintained in the network; instead, they should reflect the size of bursts we need to absorb.

Keep in mind that bursts can disrupts multiple hosts. If a single hosts fills a queue being used by multiple hosts, all of the hosts will need to back off. This results in a period in which the network is underutilized because hosts are sending packets at a lower rate. But eventually, they start building back up with a need to retransmit dropped packets. What happens then is that all the hosts that previously backed off try to resend at about the same time, causing another congestion state. This is called the "global synchronization" problem.

Keep in mind is that TCP handles congestion control. UDP is typically used for real-time audio and video streams because there is no need to recover lost packets. UDP is an unreliable transport protocol that does not send ACK signals back to the source. Since there is no ACK, UDP streams cannot be controlled with traditional TCP congestion controls.

Lawrence G. Roberts, one of the early architects of the Internet, made some interesting comments about TCP and its congestion control schemes in a 1997 paper called "Explicit Rate Flow Control, A 100 Fold Improvement over TCP." His comments are paraphrased below.

> So long as TCP operates only in the end-stations its operation cannot be substantially improved . . . If TCP is not replaced, TCP will cause major overloads and outages on long haul networks like the Internet. Users are severely impacted by the slow start-up rate and high delay variance inherent with TCP. The IETF has not even considered revising TCP. In fact no study has been done by the IETF on flow control because everyone seems to believe, "if it worked in the past, it will continue to work". TCP must be replaced with a new flow control as good as explicit rate flow control as soon as possible.

RFC 2581 (TCP Congestion Control, April 1999) defines TCP's four intertwined congestion control algorithms: slow start, congestion avoidance, fast retransmit, and fast recovery. Each of these is discussed in the following sections.

Slow Start Congestion Control   Slow start reduces the burst affect when a host first transmits. It requires a host to start its transmissions slowly and then build up to the point where congestion starts to occur. The host does not initially know how many packets it can send, so it uses slow start as a way to gauge the network's capacity. A host starts a transmission by sending two packets to the receiver. When the receiver receives the segments, it returns ACKs (acknowledgements) as confirmation. The sender increments its window by two and sends four packets. This buildup continues with the sender doubling the number of packets it sends until an ACK is not received, indicating that the flow has reached the network's ability to handle traffic or the receivers ability to handle incoming traffic.

Slow start does not prevent congestion, it simply prevents a host from causing an immediate congestion state. If the host is sending a large file, it will eventually reach a state where it overloads the network and packets begin to drop. Slow start is critical in avoiding the congestion collapse problem. But new applications such as voice over IP cannot tolerate the delay caused by slow start and in some cases, slow start is disabled so the user can "grab" bandwidth. That trend will only lead to problems.

Fast Retransmit and Fast Recovery (Reno)   Fast retransmit and fast recovery are algorithms that are designed to minimize the effect that dropping packets has on network throughput. The *fast retransmit* mechanism infers information from another TCP mechanism that a receiver uses to signal to the sender that it has received packets out of sequence. The technique is to send several duplicate ACKs to the sender.

Fast retransmit takes advantage of this feature by assuming that duplicate ACKs indicates dropped packets. Instead of waiting for an ACK until the timer expires, the source resends packets if three such duplicate ACKs are received. This occurs before the timeout period and thus improves network throughput. For example, if a host receives packet 5 and 7, but not 6, it will send a duplicate ACK for packet 5 when it receives packet 7 (but not packet 6).

Fast recovery is a mechanism that replaces slow start when fast retransmit is used. Note that while duplicate ACKs indicate that a segment has been lost, it also indicates that packets are still flowing since the source received a packet with a sequence number higher than the missing packet. In this case, the assumption is that a single packet has been dropped and that the network is not fully congested. Therefore, the sender does not need to drop fully back to slow start mode but to half the previous rate.

Note that the preceding mechanisms are called Reno. RFC 2582 (The NewReno Modification to TCP's Fast Recovery Algorithm, April 1999) describes a modification to Reno to cover situations in which ACKs do not cover all of the outstanding data when loss was detected.

Active Queue Management and Congestion Avoidance

Dropping packets is inefficient. If a host is bursting and congestion occurs, a lot of packets will be lost. Therefore, it is useful to detect impending congestion conditions and actively manage congestion before it gets out of hand.

Active queue management is a technique in which routers actively drop packets from queues as a signal to senders that they should slow down. RFC 2309 lists the following advantages of active queue management:

- Burst are inevitable. Keeping queue size small and actively managing queues improves a router's ability to absorb bursts without dropping excessive packets.

- If a source overflows a shared queue, all the devices sharing that queue will slow down (the "global synchronization" problem).

- Recovering from many dropped packets is more difficult than recovering from a single dropped packet.

- Large queue can translate into delay. Active queue management allows queues to be smaller, which improves throughput.

- Lock-out occurs when a host fills a queue and prevents other hosts from using the queue. Active queue management can prevent this condition.

Several congestion avoidance schemes are described next. Keep in mind that the next step beyond these techniques involves traffic shaping, resource reservations, virtual circuits, and QoS techniques. More on this later.

RED (Random Early Discard)   RED is an active queue management scheme that provides a mechanism for congestion avoidance. RFC 2309, section 3 provides a description of RED. Sally Floyd and Van Jacobson wrote the basic paper describing RED gateways. That paper along with other papers and related resources may be found at Sally Floyd's Web site. The address is listed at the end of this section.

Unlike traditional congestion control schemes that drop packets at the end of full queues, RED uses statistical methods to drop packets in a "probabilistic" way before queues overflow. Dropping packets in this way slows a source down enough to keep the queue steady and reduces the number of packets that would be lost when a queue overflows and a host is transmitting at a high rate.

RED makes two important decisions. It decides when to drop packets and what packets to drop. RED keeps track of an average queue size and drops packets when the average queue size grows beyond a defined threshold. The average size is recalculated every time a new packet arrives at the queue. RED makes packet-drop decisions based on two parameters:

- **Minimum threshold (minth)**   Specifies the average queue size *below which* no packets will be dropped.

- **Maximum threshold (maxth)**   Specifies the average queue size *above which* all packets will be dropped

RED uses time-averaging, meaning that if the queue has recently been mostly empty, RED will not react to a sudden burst as if it were a major congestion event. However, if the queues remain near full, RED will assume congestion and start dropping packets at a higher rate.

RFC 2309 mentions that active queue management mechanisms in the Internet can have substantial performance benefits and that there appears to be no disadvantages to using the RED algorithm.

WRED (weighted RED) is a technique of dropping packets based on the type of traffic, where it is going, or other factors. WRED may also drop packets based on marking made to packets outside the network.

ECN (Explicit Congestion Notification)   The problem with RED is that it drops packets. A more efficient technique would be for a router to set a congestion notification bit in a packet, and then send the packet to the receiver. The receiver could then inform the sender to slow down via a message in the ACK. All the while, the receiver gets its packet and we avoid using packet drops to signal congestion.

ECN is an end-to-end congestion avoidance mechanism that adopts this technique. As the name implies, ECN provides direct notification of congestion rather than indirectly signaling congestion via dropped packets. ECN works when congestion is moderate. When congestion gets excessive, packet-drop techniques are used.

ECN-enabled routers set a CD (congestion experienced) bit in the packet header of packets from ECN-capable hosts when the length of a queue exceeds a certain threshold value. The packets are forwarded to the receiver, which then sends an ACK to the sender that contains the congestion indicator. This ACK is called an *ECN-Echo*. When the sender receives this explicit signal, it halves the rate at which it sends packets.

Note that ECN requires modifications to TCP. ECN is described in RFC 2481 (A Proposal to Add Explicit Congestion Notification to IP, January 1999). Refer to RFC 2884 (Performance Evaluation of Explicit Congestion Notification in IP Networks, July 2000) for further information. The IETF Endpoint Congestion Management (ecm) Working Group has additional information (Web site listed later).

TCP Rate Control   TCP rate control is a technique in which endpoints can adjust their transmissions based on feedback from network devices that perform rate control. Packeteer is an advocate of rate control and this section describes how the company implements it in its PacketShaper products. Packeteer's Web site has numerous papers on rate control and other congestion control topics.

TCP Rate Control is also known as ERC (explicit rate control). A form of ERC is implemented in ATM networks. The Lawrence G. Roberts paper mentioned earlier in this section describes ERC in both ATM and TCP networks.

Packeteer's PacketShaper maintains state information about individual TCP connections. This allows it to send feedback to the source that controls its behavior. The primary goal is to control bursts by smoothing out a source's rate of transmission. With bursts reduced, traffic management becomes easier.

The rate control process is performed within the network between the end systems. PacketShaper intercepts ACKs from receivers and holds them for an amount of time that is precisely calculated to make the sender transmit its next packet in a way that smoothes out the burst.

For example, a source sends a packet to the receiver. The receiver returns an ACK to the sender. PacketShaper intercepts the ACK and changes some internal settings such as the TCP window size. At the precise moment, PacketShaper sends the packet and the contents of the packet (ACK sequence number plus the window size) and tells the sender that it is time to transmit another packet.

This results in a steady flow of packets from sources and improved resource management. The downside is that routers must actively track each flow. In addition, changing the contents of in-transit packets may not be a good idea, depending on the network. Traffic management and QoS devices implement TCP rate control.

Other Schemes   Most of the schemes described in the preceding section are queue management schemes. If you wish to manage network traffic beyond what these schemes provide, you need to look at prioritization schemes, packet tagging schemes, virtual circuit schemes, and QoS schemes. Refer to the following topics for more information:

- Differentiated Services (DiffServ)
- Integrated Services (IntServ)
- Load Balancing
- MPLS (Multiprotocol Label Switching)
- Policy-Based Management
- QoS (Quality of Service)
- Traffic Management, Shaping, and Engineering

Congestion Management Resources

One of the best sources of information about congestion controls and especially congestion avoidance is Sally Floyd's Web site. The address is given later. The IETF Endpoint Congestion Management (ecm) Working Group has information on new congestion control schemes and documents that evaluates current congestion control schemes. Sally Floyd wrote RFC 2914 (Congestion Control Principles, September 2000). The IETF Transport Area Working Group (tsvwg) is working on new transport specifications.

RFC 2581 and RFC 2914 are two of the best sources for information on TCP's congestion control. Some earlier or related RFCs of interest are listed here:

- RFC 793 (Transmission Control Protocol, September 1981)
- RFC 813 (Window and Acknowledgement Strategy in TCP, July 1982)
- RFC 1122 (Requirements for Internet Hosts — Communication Layers, October 1989)
- RFC 2018 (TCP Selective Acknowledgment Options, October 1996)
- RFC 2414 (Increasing TCP's Initial Window, September 1998)
- RFC 2416 (When TCP Starts Up With Four Packets Into Only Three Buffers. September 1998)
- RFC 2488 (Enhancing TCP Over Satellite Channels Using Standard Mechanisms, January 1999)
- RFC 2525 (Known TCP Implementation Problems, March 1999)
- RFC 2757 (Long Thin Networks, January 2000)
- RFC 2861 (TCP Congestion Window Validation, June 2000)

Related Entries   Acknowledgment; Active Networks; Bandwidth Management; Connection Establishment; Constraint-Based Routing; Data Communication Concepts; Data Link Protocols; Differentiated Services (DiffServ); Flow Control Mechanisms; Handshake Procedures; Integrated Services (IntServ); Load Balancing; MPLS (Multiprotocol Label Switching); Policy-Based Management; Prioritization of Network Traffic; QoS (Quality of Service); RSVP (Resource Reservation Protocol); TCP (Transmission Control Protocol); Throughput; Traffic Management, Shaping, and Engineering; *and* Transport Protocols and Services

IETF Working Group: TCP Implementation (tcpimpl)	http://www.ietf.org/html.charters/tcpimpl-charter.html
IETF Transport Area Working Group (tsvwg)	http://www.ietf.org/html.charters/tsvwg-charter.html
The IETF Endpoint Congestion Management (ecm) Working Groups	http://www.ietf.org/html.charters/ecm-charter.html
"Congestion Control Principles" by Sally Floyd (in draft form at the time of this writing)	http://www.ietf.org/html.charters/ecm-charter.html
Papers by Sally Floyd and pointers to related information	http://www.aciri.org/floyd/

"The Causes of Network Delay" at The Digital Tools Group	http://www.dtool.com/delay.html
"Congestion Control Schemes for TCP/IP Networks" by Darius Buntinas	http://www.cis.ohio-state.edu/~jain/cis788-95/tcpip_cong/
LBNL's Network Research Group (members of this group did much of the work on TCP congestion control mechanisms)	http://ee.lbl.gov/
"A Taxonomy for Congestion Control Algorithms in Packet Switching Networks" by Cui-Qing Yang and Alapati V. S. Reddy	http://www.comsoc.org/pubs/surveys/yang/yang-orig.html
Comparison of ATM and TCP Congestion Control	http://www.halcyon.com/ast/tcpatmcc.htm
"Explicit Rate Flow Control, A 100 Fold Improvement Over TCP" by Lawrence G. Roberts	http://www.ziplink.net/%7Elroberts/Explicit-Rate/Explicit-Rate-Flow-Control.html
Links to various papers about congestion	http://www.cs.ubc.ca/spider/mjmccut/internet.html
Congestion-related documents at University of Massachusetts	http://www-net.cs.umass.edu/papers/papers.html
Packeteer research and articles related to congestion and TCP rate control	http://www.packeteer.com/technology/research.cfm
"Rate Control to Enhance Network Service Quality" by Eric Siegel, Net	http://www.netreference.com/Public/WhitePapers/RateCon.html
TCP papers links list (satellite, congestion, performance, acknowledgements, transactions, wireless)	http://tcpsat.lerc.nasa.gov/tcpsat/papers.html
Frank Kelly's links to congestion and rate control papers	http://www.statslab.cam.ac.uk/~frank/pf/
Hoov's Musings at Acuitive, Inc., on CoS (Class of Service) and TCP Rate Control	http://www.acuitive.com/musings/hmv1-3.htm

Connection Establishment

A connection is a link between two or more computer systems that need to exchange messages and data. On a shared network and internetwork, connections are usually virtual, meaning that a connection state is set up in software that tracks the exchange of data across what appears to be a dedicated circuit to the application that is using it. These connections take place in the transport layer and are handled by TCP in the Internet protocol suite. This topic discusses TCP connections. Refer to "Handshake Procedures" for information about other types of connections.

A connection is a requirement of a reliable data delivery service. It is set up before the actual data exchange takes place. The connection is used to acknowledge the receipt of packets and retransmit those that are lost. The opposite of this is a best-effort service. A file transfer is an example of a service that requires guaranteed delivery services. The delivered file must be an exact copy of the original. See "Reliable Data Delivery Services" and "Best-Effort Delivery Services."

To reliably exchange data, an application on one network system creates an *end-to-end connection* with an application on another network system. A single computer may establish and terminate multiple connections at any time. The packets from these connections are *multiplexed* over a single physical link, as shown in the following illustration. Thus, they are *virtual* connections. In addition, each connection is full duplex, allowing bidirectional packet exchange.

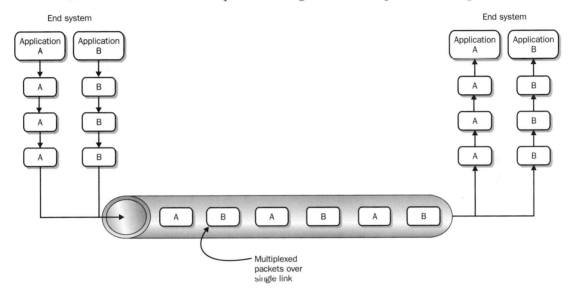

The first part of establishing a connection is to obtain a network address for the target host. If both the source and target are on the same LAN (or routed LANs), ARP (Address Resolution Protocol) can be used to obtain the hardware address of the target, assuming its IP address is already known. If the IP address is not known, a DNS server can be contacted to obtain this address. In Windows environments, NetBIOS naming provides a way to locate computer addresses. Once these addresses are known, the two computers set up a connection.

A connection must first be requested by the sender and granted by the receiver. This provides the first level of reliability by ensuring that the receiver is ready to receive data. It also points out how TCP manages data delivery. If an application were to pass data directly to IP for delivery, IP would simply start sending packets to the destination. But if the destination is offline or busy, those packets will be dropped and IP by itself has no way to inform the application that the packets were not delivered. TCP manages this by starting with a simple connection request, which IP delivers.

- The actual connection involves a three-way handshake process, in which three packets (called *segments* in the TCP layer) are exchanged across the network. Following is a description of this process between a client and server.

- The client uses a Sockets procedure called CONNECT, which creates a TCP segment that includes the server's IP address and the port number of the desired service. The SYN bit is set on and the ACK bit is set off to indicate that this is a *connection request*.

In addition, the client generates an initial sequence number and places it in the Sequence Number field of the header.

■ When the server receives this segment, it checks to make sure that the specified port is available and, if so, returns an *acknowledgment segment* back to the client. This segment has the SYN and ACK bit set on. To acknowledge that it has received the client initial sequence number, the server increments the sequence number by 1 and inserts it into the Acknowledgment field of the segment it returns to the client. In addition, it inserts its own sequence number into the Sequence Number field. This is the sequence number that the server will use to send segments to the client.

■ After the client receives the acknowledgement segment from the server, it returns an acknowledgement segment to the server with the ACK bit set. It also increments the sequence number received from the server by 1 and inserts it into the Acknowledgment field to indicate that it received the server's initial sequence number.

Note that SYN (synchronize) and ACK (acknowledgement) are flag bits in the TCP header that can be set either on or off. The sequence is pictured in the following flowchart in Figure C-22.

Following this exchange, data transmission can begin. After the transmission completes, both sides terminate the connection.

TCP may have to deal with a number of connection parameters during the connection setup phase. One of these is to establish transmission delay parameters. Suppose the client sends a segment to the server and the server returns an acknowledgment, but for some reason the acknowledgment does not arrive at the client in a reasonable time. The server must assume that the client did not receive its transmission, so it retransmits the segment. In the meantime, the "lost" acknowledgment may find its way to the client and the retransmission arrives at the server, which now has two of the same segment to deal with.

The amount of time that a sender should wait for an acknowledgment cannot be a fixed value because some links, such as satellites, have longer delays than others. TCP can negotiate

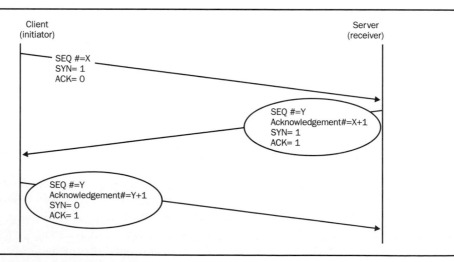

Figure C-22.   *A connection-oriented virtual circuit*

this value by measuring the time it takes to receive responses. It then estimates a round-trip delay value and uses this value to clock transmissions and acknowledgments for a connection.

The sender can attempt to find the best size for packets to avoid fragmentation as discussed under "Fragmentation and Reassembly." The sender starts its transmissions slowly to avoid congesting the network as discussed under "Congestion Control Mechanisms." It may then vary its transmission speed to avoid overflowing the receiver, as discussed under "Flow Control Mechanism." Refer to "Reliable Data Delivery Services" for more information about TCP's reliable services. Also refer to "TCP (Transmission Control Protocol)."

Refer to the following Internet RFCs for additional information:

- RFC 793 (Transmission Control Protocol, September 1981)
- RFC 1122 (Requirements for Internet Hosts—Communication Layers, October 1989) (see section 4.2)
- RFC 1180 (A TCP/IP Tutorial, January 1991)
- RFC 1379 (Extending TCP for Transactions, November 1992)

As an aside, this connection sequence is prone to sequence number guessing attacks, which allow an attacker to steal the session being established by a legitimate user and pretend to be that user to the target system. According to RFC 1948 (Defending Against Sequence Number Attacks, May 1996), it turns out that the initial sequence number is actually easy to predict. An attacker (Jack) makes a connection to the server and then waits for someone else (Joe) to make a connection. The server then sends Joe an acknowledgment segment. In the meantime, Jack has figured out what the next sequence number should be and sends an acknowledgement message back to the server with that sequence number and pretends to be Joe. The server accepts this connection and Jack can start executing commands on the server.

Related Entries   Acknowledgements; Best-Effort Delivery Services; Congestion Control Mechanisms; Connection-Oriented and Connectionless Services; Data Communication Concepts; Error Detection and Correction; Flow Control Mechanisms; Handshake Procedures; Reliable Data Delivery Services; Sliding Window Mechanism; TCP (Transmission Control Protocol); *and* Transport Protocols and Services

Linktionary!—Tom Sheldon's Encyclopedia of Networking updates	http://www.linktionary.com/c/ connection_setup.html
TCP Connection Open (course at Connected: An Internet Encyclopedia)	http://www.freesoft.org/CIE/Course/Section4/ 10.htm
Reliable Messages and Connection Establishment, by Butler W. Lampson	http://research.microsoft.com/lampson/ 47-ReliableMessages/WebPage.html
Connection Establishment and Termination topics by The Transport Group	http://ganges.cs.tcd.ie/4ba2/transport/5.pc.02.html
Godred Fairhurst's Data Communications Course: TCP page	http://www.erg.abdn.ac.uk/users/gorry/eg3561/ inet-pages/tcp.html
Albert P. Belle WinSock Tuning FAQ (information about tuning TCP/IP parameters)	http://www.cerberus-sys.com/~belleisl/ mtu_mss_rwin.html

Extension of Three-Way Handshake	http://www.isoc.org/HMP/PAPER/144/html/node5.html
Explanation of the Three-Way Handshake via TCP/IP (Microsoft document)	http://support.microsoft.com/support/kb/articles/q172/9/83.asp

Connection Technologies

See Network Connection Technologies.

Connection-Oriented and Connectionless Services

Two distinct techniques are used in data communications to transfer data. Each has its own advantages and disadvantages. They are the connection-oriented method and the connectionless method:

- **Connection-oriented**   Requires a session connection (analogous to a phone call) be established before any data can be sent. This method is often called a "reliable" network service. It can guarantee that data will arrive in the same order. Connection-oriented services set up virtual links between end systems through a network, as shown in Figure C-23. Note that the packet on the left is assigned the virtual circuit number 01. As it moves through the network, routers quickly send it through virtual circuit 01.

- **Connectionless**   Does not require a session connection between sender and receiver. The sender simply starts sending packets (called datagrams) to the destination. This

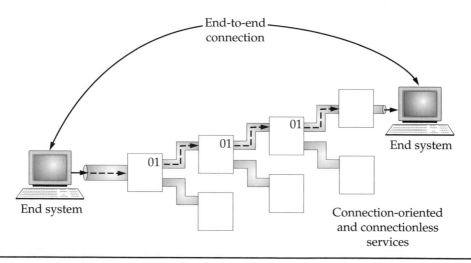

Figure C-23.   *Object Management Architecture*

service does not have the reliability of the connection-oriented method, but it is useful for periodic burst transfers. Neither system must maintain state information for the systems that they send transmission to or receive transmission from. A connectionless network provides minimal services, but connection.

These methods may be implemented in the data link layers of the protocol stack and/or in the transport layers of the protocol stack, depending on the physical connections in place and the services required by the systems that are communicating. TCP (Transmission Control Protocol) is a connection-oriented transport protocol, while UDP (User Datagram Protocol) is a connectionless network protocol. Both operate over IP.

The physical, data link, and network layer protocols have been used to implement guaranteed data delivery. For example, X.25 packet-switching networks perform extensive error checking and packet acknowledgment because the services were originally implemented on poor-quality telephone connections. Today, networks are more reliable. It is generally believed that the underlying network should do what it does best, which is deliver data bits as quickly as possible. Therefore, connection-oriented services are now primarily handled in the transport layer by end systems, not the network. This allows lower-layer networks to be optimized for speed.

LANs operate as connectionless systems. A computer attached to a network can start transmitting frames as soon as it has access to the network. It does not need to set up a connection with the destination system ahead of time. However, a transport-level protocol such as TCP may set up a connection-oriented session when necessary.

The Internet is one big connectionless packet network in which all packet deliveries are handled by IP. However, TCP adds connection-oriented services on top of IP. TCP provides all the upper-level connection-oriented session requirements to ensure that data is delivered properly. MPLS is a relatively new connection-oriented networking scheme for IP networks that sets up fast label-switched paths across routed or layer 2 networks.

A WAN service that uses the connection-oriented model is frame relay. The service provider sets up PVCs (permanent virtual circuits) through the network as required or requested by the customer. ATM is another networking technology that uses the connection-oriented virtual circuit approach.

Related Entries   Acknowledgments; Anycasting; Best-Effort Delivery Services; Circuit-Switching Services; Congestion Control Mechanisms; Connection Establishment; Data Communication Concepts; Flow Control Mechanisms; Handshake Procedures; IP (Internet Protocol); Network Concepts; Reliable Data Delivery Services; Session Communication and Management; TCP (Transmission Control Protocol); Transport Protocols and Services; UDP (User Datagram Protocol); *and* Virtual Circuits

Linktionary!—Tom Sheldon's Encyclopedia of Networking updates	http://www.linktionary.com/c/connections.html
Introduction to the Internet Protocols at Rutgers	http://oac3.hsc.uth.tmc.edu/staff/snewton/tcp-tutorial/sec2.html

Constraint-Based Routing

Constraint-based routing is a QoS (Quality of Service) routing technique that has become important with the development of MPLS (Multiprotocol Label Switching). However, RFC 2702, Requirements for Traffic Engineering Over MPLS (September 1999) notes that QoS routing is really a subset of a more broadly defined constraint-based routing approach.

MPLS is a protocol for carrier-based core networks that runs over MPLS-enabled IP routers and ATM switches. Such devices are called MPLS LSRs (label switch routers). An MPLS network permits the definition of *explicit paths,* which are predefined routes through networks as opposed to routes that are selected at each router on a hop-by-hop basis. Routing protocols such as OSPF and BGP determine these explicit routes in advance, and then build tables in each router that define the routes. Packets carry labels to indicate which explicit route they should be taking. Thus, labeled packets follow LSPs (label switched paths).

The preceding procedure of using standard routing protocols to define explicit paths is really the default procedure, and it can take place without operator intervention. In addition, MPLS is flexible enough to define paths based on various constraints such as available bandwidth, the priority setting of packets, the whims of an operator, or the directives of a policy-based server. Thus, MPLS also supports *CBR (constraint-based routing).*

For example, normal explicit routing methods using OSPF may find that a path through a set of routers is the shortest path to a particular destination. However, with CBR, a specific amount of bandwidth can be specified as the defining criteria for a route. In this case, another (possibly longer) route may be selected because it has enough bandwidth to meet the request. Similar methods can be used to distribute loads across multiple routes, ensuring that one route is not overloaded while another is underused.

With CBR, paths can be defined that ensure an adequate amount of bandwidth, allowing real-time voice traffic without the delays associated with IP networks. CBR gives MPLS-based networks traffic-engineering capabilities that were once only in ATM networks. CBR does require an enhanced link-state routing protocol, and that is provided by CR-LDP (Constraint-Based Routing Using Label Distribution Protocol). The Nortel paper mentioned at the end of this topic describes CR-LDP. Also see "MPLS (Multiprotocol Label Switching)." RFC 2702 (Requirements for Traffic Engineering Over MPLS, September 1999) provides additional information.

Related Entries   Congestion Control Mechanisms; MPLS (Multiprotocol Label Switching); QoS (Quality of Service); *and* Traffic Management, Shaping, and Engineering

Linktionary!—Tom Sheldon's Encyclopedia of Networking updates	http://www.linktionary.com/c/constraint_routing.html
IETF MPLS Working Group	http://www.ietf.org/html.charters/mpls-charter.html
Nortel MPLS white paper: "Using Constraint-Based Routing to Deliver New Services"	http://www.nortelnetworks.com/products/library/collateral/55046.25-10-99.pdf

Container

A container is a document or an application in which objects and components can be placed. A Web browser is an example of a container. It displays HTML (Hypertext Markup Language) pages that contain text and objects. Objects can be pictures, sounds, videos, Java applets, and ActiveX controls.

Related Entries   ActiveX; Browsers; COM (Component Object Model); Component Software Technology; Compound Documents; Java; Object Technologies; *and* Web Browsers

Container Objects, Directory Services

Container objects are part of a directory services structure such as NetWare Directory Services, a feature in Novell NetWare. Container objects hold other objects, including other containers, and so form branches in a hierarchical directory tree used to organize the user accounts and resources of an organization. Container objects usually represent the divisions or departments of a company, and contain the user accounts and resources belonging to the division or department. The managers or supervisors of the department have special management rights to the containers, which automatically give them rights to manage the objects within the container.

Related Entries   Directory Services Overview; X.500 Directory Services

Content Distribution

Content distribution, sometimes called *controlled content distribution* or *CCD*, provides a way to improve the performance of content delivery from Web sites for users. Content is typically moved to strategically placed servers around the globe where it is closer to users. Requests and responses may take only a few router hops rather than many hops.

The importance of moving content close to users can be seen in the amount of delay it takes to move Web objects from a distant server. A host on one side of the globe may wait up to 500 milliseconds to obtain a single object, such as a logo, from a server on the other side of the globe. Since Web pages have multiple objects, a page can take minutes to download. Obviously, moving this information to nearby servers reduces the delay.

By reducing delay, content distribution servers are often referred to as "Internet acceleration services." See the topic "Replication" for a general discussion of techniques that are used to duplicate information to multiple servers.

As an example, Digital Island's content delivery service, called Footprint, is aimed toward electronic commerce. Static content is pushed closer to users (forward-deployed) through Digital Island's Intelligent Network, which is essentially a collection of caching and mirroring servers around the globe:

■ **Caching**   Content that is typically requested multiple times is pulled from "origin" servers and placed on LCM (local content management) servers. Once information is cached locally, performance greatly improves for local users by minimizing the number of connection points or "hops" necessary to transmit critical data or rich media.

■ **Mirroring**   For customers with noncacheable content, mirroring (replication) can be used to place content closer to users. Noncacheable content includes authenticated FTP files, authenticated Web sites, and encrypted and compressed software packages. The content is first placed in a secure staging area, and then replicated to LCMs within Digital Island's Intelligent Network.

Real-time information is served from a core of servers with original content. There are thousands of distributed content servers located at Internet service provider facilities around the world. Digital Island's Footprint content delivery network is capable of distributing all major content types, including streaming media and dynamic content. Web site performance can improve up to ten times. As demand increases, Footprint is able to maintain this performance. The service is available on a subscription basis.

Akamai is also in the business. Its approach is based on its FreeFlow content delivery service. Web site owners that adopt FreeFlow tag the content to be served by Akamai's network. When users request content, the Akamai network delivers it from local servers to ensure high performance. The user's browser automatically points to an Akamai server rather than to the Web site. Based on Akamai's real-time network map, FreeFlow directs requests to the Akamai server best able to satisfy each request. Akamai has developed algorithms to disperse content to the servers from the central site in a way that guarantees that no server is ever overloaded by requests. As the number of requests for a document increases, so does the number of servers containing copies.

Inktomi's approach is its integrated Traffic Server and Content Delivery Suite. The architecture consists of a Content Distributor that detects changes in source content and propagates those changes to servers. Special agents receive content from the Content Distributor, monitor Web server performance in real time, and send statistics to a content management system. As content is updated at Web servers, Inktomi automatically informs the cache to retrieve the new pages, ensuring fresh and consistent content is served to the user.

Mirror Image, an Xcelera-owned company, uses a more storage-oriented approach, placing up to 75 percent of Web traffic in its CAP (content access point) servers around the world. In contrast, other services with less storage at the caching sites rely on fast routed paths back to the original content, which translates into delay.

Other vendors that provide content delivery systems and Web-caching technology include ArrowPoint (now Cisco), Compaq, Novell, and Network Appliance. The Web sites for all the companies described here are provided later.

A related form of content distribution is Internet distributed file sharing, sometimes called *p2p (peer-to-peer)*. Napster is the most common example. The concept is that information is massively distributed out to nodes, mostly end-user computers, where it is available for other users to access. A user-based search program or central database keeps track of where content is located. The concept took off with music sharing, but has spread to other forms of media. See "File Sharing" and "Peer-to-Peer Communication" for more information. Also see my Napster article at the Linktionary! Web site listed here.

Related Entries   Backup and Data Archiving; Caching; Data Center Design; Fault Tolerance and High Availability; File Sharing; Load Balancing; Network Appliance; Peer-to-Peer Communication; Proxy Caching; Proxy Server: Web Caching; *and* Web Technologies and Concepts

Linktionary!—Tom Sheldon's Encyclopedia of Networking updates	http://www.linktionary.com/c/content_distribution.html
Tom Sheldon's Napster article	http://www.linktionary.com/p/peer2peer.htm
Digital Island	http://www.digisle.net/
Akamai	http://www.akamai.com
Inktomi	http://www.inktomi.com/
ArrowPoint Communications (now Cisco)	http://www.arrowpoint.com/
Xcelera (Mirror Image)	http://www.xcelera.com/
Network Appliance	http://www.networkappliance.com/
Compaq Computer	http://www.compaq.com
Novell	http://www.novell.com

Contention

Contention occurs on shared-media networks in which multiple workstations vie to have access to the medium. Contention is part of CSMA (carrier sense multiple access) networks (i.e., Ethernet). Contention occurs when two or more devices attempt to use the channel at the same time. When contention does occur, the devices wait for a random amount of time, then attempt access again. If many devices are competing for the cable, the situation becomes worse because the wait time reduces performance—in addition to the need for workstations to continually attempt to access the cable.

Related Entries   Collision and Collision Domains; CSMA/CD; *and* Ethernet

Convergence

Convergence is a term usually applied to the merging of voice onto enterprise networks and across the Internet. Convergence of voice and data networks is seen as the first step to supporting even more multimedia types, such as streaming video and videoconferencing. For enterprise networks, the idea is to build one network instead of having two separate cabling systems, one for voice and one for data. There are many other advantages to bringing voice (and other multimedia) to IP networks and the Internet. The most important is that voice services can be combined with unique computer-related applications. In contrast, the traditional telephone system severely limits the number of add-on services. Call-waiting, caller-ID, call forwarding, and other telephone services pale in comparison to the types of voice-related applications that can be designed on data networks such as intranets and the Internet.

Related Entries   Multimedia; QoS (Quality of Service); *and* VoIP (Voice Over IP)

Linktionary!—Tom Sheldon's Encyclopedia of Networking updates	http://www.linktionary.com/c/convergence.html

Convergence of Routing Tables

In a packet-switched, mesh topology network (with the Internet being one of the biggest), networks are joined by routers, and routers keep track of routes to different parts of the network. Routers hold routing tables that indicate the best route to a particular location. These routing tables are created dynamically by obtaining neighbor and route information from other routers. Routers must be constantly updated to changes in the network topology. Routes may be added or removed, or routes may fail due to a break in the physical link.

Convergence is part of the routing table update process. When a link fails or changes, updates are sent across the network that describe changes in the network topology. Each router then runs a routing algorithm to recompute routes and build new routing tables based on this information. Once all the routers in the network have updated their routing tables, convergence is complete.

Convergence is a *dynamic* routing process as opposed to *static* routing. In static routing, an operator programs routes into routers. Static routing is appropriate for small networks or when dedicated links exist between networks.

Related Entry   Routing

Cookies

A cookie is a small file, stored on a client system by a server that contains data to be used during future sessions with the server. Cookies are primarily used on the Web, although they are useful in any Web-based client/server environment. The information in the cookie is read by the server the next time the client connects with the server. This allows the server to "remember" the client and information about that client. The cookie basically maintains "state" between client and server, either during connections within the same session or for future sessions.

For example, when you fill out a form at a Web site, some of the information may be stored in a cookie on your computer for future use. The next time you visit, the Web server reads the cookie to learn your name and other information about you to be used in the current session.

Cookies allow e-commerce sites to save information about clients, such as their logon information and customer ID. Thus, cookies provide a form of *single signon*—that is, the Web server gets logon information from the user's cookie rather than asking the user again. There are, of course, privacy and security issues involved with cookies (one bad cookie spoils the whole lot?). For example, cookies can track Web sites visited by users and pass that information on to a Web server, to be used for demographic purposes. The information might also be used to display an ad that fits the preferences of a user based on the type of Web sites visited. Some hacker attacks were also staged with cookies.

Almost all Web sites will attempt to place a cookie on a client's systems. A typical client may have hundreds or even thousands of cookies stored on their system at any one time. Most Web browsers have a feature to control cookies—the user can choose to reject all cookies or be asked before a cookie is stored, but setting these options is a nuisance because messages pop up constantly or Web sites refuse to cooperate with browsers. For example, as a test, I once set "Ask before saving cookies" on my Web browser, and then visited a popular Web site. In a very short time, over 40 "Ask" messages popped up on my screen.

To understand why cookies were created, you need to understand the concept of *state*. Originally, the Web was stateless (and still is, except for add-ons like cookies and some new protocols). Stateless means that a connection between two systems is done anonymously, and the server does not keep information about a client or the connection that could be used again. Stateless also means that a connection does not remain open to await further requests. Cookies provide a way to create state in the HTTP protocol. This is described further in RFC 2109 (HTTP State Management Mechanism, February 1997)."

Cookies are handled by CGI scripts on the server. When a user connects to a server that uses cookies, the server script asks the user's Web browser to accept and save cookie information. The Web browser puts the cookie in a special location (the cookie jar?) for future reference. The next time the Web site is visited, the cookie information is available for the Web server.

Netscape was the first to use cookies and develop a cookie proposal, but RFC 2109 eventually defined an interoperable standard. The RFC defines two new headers in the HTTP protocol: *Cookie* and *Set-Cookie*. A connection procedure using cookies goes like this:

1. The client contacts the server.

2. The server responds to the client with the Set-Cookie header option.

3. The client returns a Cookie request header (assuming it accepts cookies).

The Set-Cookie header contains the following information:

- **Name**   The name of the cookie as determined by the server.

- **Comment**   An optional value that may contain information about how the server intends to use the cookie. The user may inspect this information to decide whether it wants to accept the cookie.

- **Domain**   An optional value that includes the name of the server issuing the cookie.

- **Max-Age**   A value that defines the lifetime of a cookie in seconds. Cookies are discarded at the end of their lifetime. Cookies with a value of 0 are discarded immediately after being read.

- **Path**   Specifies the subset of URLs to which this cookie applies.

- **Secure**   Specifies that cookies should be used over secure connections to hide the contents of the cookie during transmission.

- **Version**   Specifies the version of the cookie where 1 is equal to RFC 2109.

RFC 2109 indicates that clients should have the ability to store at least 300 cookies with at least 4,096 bytes per cookie. It also recommends that each server or domain should be able to store at least 20 cookies. Denial-of-service attacks are possible in which a server could flood a client with numerous cookies, or large cookies, which would force out other cookies on the user's system, assuming there is a cookie limit and the oldest cookies are discarded first. Therefore, an upper limit should be set on the number of cookies acceptable from any one server.

Possible spoofing attacks are also discussed in the RFC, as well as privacy issues such as the ability of the user to track whether cookies are collecting information about the sites they visit.

A relatively new technique called *cookie cutting* is used to prioritize traffic at switches, especially Web switches. The technique lets Web sites designate some customers as premium users, forwarding their incoming packets to higher-performance servers. Cookie cutting is a technique discussed further under "Load Balancing" and "Switching and Switched Networks."

Related Entries   Browsers; Stateful and Stateless Connections; *and* Web Technologies and Concepts

Linktionary!—Tom Sheldon's Encyclopedia of Networking updates	http://www.linktionary.com/c/cookies.html
Cookie Central	http://www.cookiecentral.com/
URL and Cookie-Based Switching	http://www.arrowpoint.com/solutions/white_papers/WebNS.html
Wired Digital webmonkey page on cookies	http://www.hotwired.com/webmonkey/backend/backend_more.html#cookies

Copper Distributed Data Interface

See CDDI (Copper Distributed Data Interface).

COPS (Common Open Policy Service)

See Policy-Based Management.

CORBA (Common Object Request Broker Architecture)

CORBA is a distributed object technology defined by the OMG (Object Management Group) in its OMA (Object Management Architecture) specification. The architecture has also been adopted by The Open Group. Refer to "Object Technologies" and "Distributed Object Computing" for an introduction to object technologies in general.

CORBA is based on the OMG's Object Management Architecture as discussed in the next section. It was released in 1991 and defined how objects can interact over a special interface bus called an *object request broker*. CORBA version 2.0 defined how different ORBs from different vendors could work together. CORBA version 3.0, announced in 1999, includes an enhanced distributed component model, the ability to operate through firewalls, and other features.

OMA (Object Management Architecture)

The OMG developed the OMA architectural model as a vision of what a distributed environment should look like. CORBA follows this model. It consists of system-level and application-level components, as pictured in Figure C-23. The components are described here:

■ The *ORB (Object Request Broker)* manages communication among objects. It provides mechanisms for finding objects on a network that can satisfy a client request for services. It also prepares the target object to accept the request (there may be a difference in implementation).

■ *Object services* supplement the ORB by providing services to any objects, such as security services and transaction processing services.

■ The *Application interface* is on the end-user side of the model. OMA provides an interface for specific applications that are usually not shared by other objects, such as a word processing or spreadsheet program.

■ *Common facilities* are also end-user interfaces. OMA supports applications that many applications can access and share, such as a spelling checker, charting utility, or sorting routine.

Note that the ORB is often described as a "bus" that interconnects all objects. However, the ORB is really just a set of interfaces that interact with one another to provide object-to-object communications. The underlying network and the processes associated with object interfacing are hidden from the user, who sees only what appears to be a single application, even though the system may be interacting with objects on a remote multiplatform system.

CORBA Architecture

The initial task of the Object Management Group (OMG) was to create a standard architecture for developing object-oriented applications that would run across a diversity of multivendor products and operating environments. CORBA is the outcome of its work. So far, CORBA has been deployed within enterprises to provide connections to a variety of back-end databases and information systems.

Figure C-24 illustrates where CORBA fits relative to the OSI and TCP/IP protocol stacks. The top layers of CORBA provide the object interfaces into the GIOP (General Inter-ORB

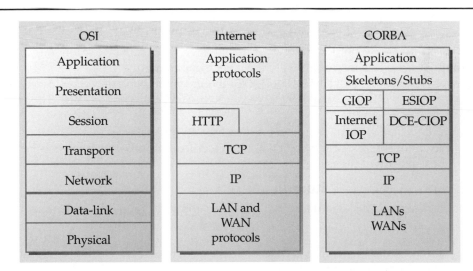

GIOP = General Inter-ORB Protocol

IOP = Inter-ORB Protocol

Figure C-24. *CORBA protocol model*

Protocol) or ESIOP (Environment Specific Inter-ORB Protocol) layer. GIOP defines the format and data representation of messages that are exchanged between ORBs.

Under GIOP is the IOP (Inter-ORB Protocol) layer, which provides an interface to network topologies. So far, CORBA has been mapped to TCP/IP, as shown, through IIOP (Internet Inter-ORB Protocol), but it could be mapped to other transport protocols, such as IPX, OSI, and SNA. Note that IIOP provides a way to map GIOP directly to TCP/IP.

IIOP was added in CORBA 2.0. It provides object interoperability among objects developed by different vendors. In particular, Java applets can use IIOP to communicate with objects on remote servers. IIOP improves connections over TCP/IP networks by removing the need to make multiple connections when downloading objects from Web pages. Basically, over a single connection, multiple objects may be accessed.

The OMG modified IIOP so that it supports the Java RMI (Remote Method Invocation). RMI allows objects in the Java environment to interact with one another. By modifying IIOP to support RMI, RMI can run on top of IIOP and use it as a transport protocol, allowing Java objects to conform to CORBA and operate over TCP/IP networks.

In Sun's J2EE (Java 2 Platform, Enterprise Edition), IIOP allows Java components to interact with non-Java programs written for CORBA in other languages, such as C++ and COBOL.

ESIOP accommodates interfaces that might have special requirements. Currently, DCE (Distributed Computing Environment) is supported with DCE-CIOP (DCE Common Inter-ORB Protocol), which binds DCE to TCP.

CORBA Object Interface and Operation

As mentioned, the ORB is often seen as a bus connecting client with objects that provide services. This can be seen in Figure C-25. The interface is "well defined" and is specified by the OMG's IDL (Interface Definition Language). IDL describes a consistent object interface.

Objects written to conform with IDL are essentially portable. IDL provides programming language independence and allows developers to create CORBA components using a language of choice. Objects created with IDL have a specific behavior that can be exploited by other CORBA-compatible objects, no matter how the object was created.

A client communicates with another object (called the *object implementation*) by passing requests through the ORB. The target object receives the request from the ORB. The object implementation is code and data.

To make a request, the client can access three different interfaces. Some system functions require that the client directly access the ORB interface. Two other interfaces are accessed, depending on the nature of the target object:

- The IDL Stubs interface is used when IDL is required to translate between different client and server implementations. In this case, the server-side IDL skeleton is involved in the connection.

- The DII (Dynamic Invocation Interface) interface allows inter-ORB interoperability. A client dynamically issues a request without requiring a specific IDL interface–specific stub. In this case, the server-side DSI (Dynamic Skeleton Interface) is involved in the connection.

C

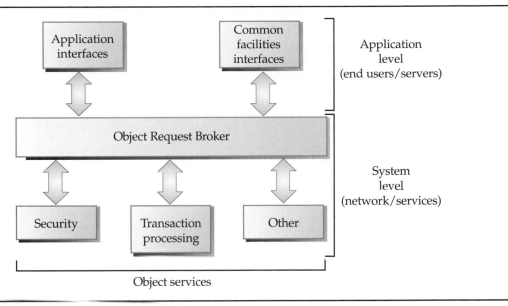

Figure C-25.   *CORBA interfaces and object interaction*

Finally, the OA (Object Adapter) helps the ORB to link object implementations with the ORB. The OA may provide support for special implementations such as an object-oriented database.

More detailed information for developers and programmers is available at the Web sites listed at the end of this section.

Related Entries   Client/Server Computing; DCE (Distributed Computing Environment); Distributed Applications; Distributed Computer Networks; Distributed Object Computing; Java, Middleware; MOM (Message-Oriented Middleware); Multitiered Architectures; Object Technologies; OMA (Object Management Architecture); OMG (Object Management Group); ORB (Object Request Broker); Transaction Processing; *and* Web Technologies and Concepts

Linktionary!—Tom Sheldon's Encyclopedia of Networking updates	http://www.linktionary.com/c/corba.html
OMG (Object Management Group)	http://www.omg.org
CORBA for Beginners (tutorial at OMG)	http://www.omg.org/gettingstarted/corbafaq.htm
Distributed Object Computing by Junichi Susuki	http://www.yy.cs.keio.ac.jp/nsuzuki/object/dist_comp.html
Vertel: CORBA info.	http://www.vertel.com/corba/
CORBA FAQ by Robert Appelbaum et al.	http://www.aurora-tech.com/corba-faq/

Manfred Schneider's Distributed Objects & Components: CORBA	http://www.cetus-links.org/oo_corba.html
Manfred Schneider's Distributed Objects & Components: CORBA ORBs and other software	http://www.cetus-links.org/oo_object_request_brokers.html
IONA Orbix	http://www.iona.com
Sun Microsystem's Solaris NEO	http://www.sun.com/solaris/neo/
Visigenic VisiBroker	http://www.inprise.com/visibroker/
White Paper: CORBA, COM, and Other Object Standards and Their Relevance to Development of Interoperable Systems	http://www2.dcnicn.com/cals/cals_97f/task07/html/Non-CDRL/whitepaper.html
Software Engineering Institute CORBA page	http://www.sei.cmu.edu/str/descriptions/corba.html
Software Engineering Institute ORB page	http://www.sei.cmu.edu/str/descriptions/orb.html
Object Technology page by Kang Sung-IL	http://rtlab.kaist.ac.kr/~sikang/oo/index.html

Core Network

A core network is a backbone network, usually with a mesh topology, that provides any-to-any connections among devices on the network. While the Internet could be considered a giant core network, it really consists of many service providers that run their own core networks, and those core networks are interconnected. A core network may consist of multiple ATM switches configured in a multilinked mesh topology, or it may consist of IP routers.

Significant to core networks is "the edge," where networks and users exist. The edge may perform intelligent functions that are not performed inside the core network. For example, if the core network is using MPLS (Multiprotocol Label Switching), an edge switch may examine packets and select a path through the network based on various properties of the packet. The core network then switches the packets (as opposed to doing hop-by-hop routing of the packets), which significantly improves performance. In this case, the core network is considered relatively "dumb" while the edge is considered "smart" because the path selection through the core is determined by the edge.

Related Entries   ATM (Asynchronous Transfer Mode); Edge Devices; End System and End-to-End Connectivity; MPLS (Multiprotocol Label Switching); Network Access Services; Network Core Technologies; NPN (New Public Network); Optical Networks; Routing; Routing on the Internet; Switching and Switched Networks; and WAN (Wide Area Network)

CoS (Class of Service)

CoS—not to be confused with QoS (Quality of Service)—is a form of priority queuing that has been used in a number of communication and networking protocols. It is a way of classifying and prioritizing packets based on application type (voice, video, file transfers, transaction processing), the type of user (CEO, secretary), or other settings.

CoS is a queuing discipline while QoS covers a wider range of techniques to manage bandwidth and network resources. CoS classifies packets by examining packet parameters or CoS markings and places packets in queues of different priorities based on predefined criteria. QoS has to do with guaranteeing certain levels of network performance to meet service contracts or to support real-time traffic. With QoS, some method is used to reserve bandwidth across a network in advance of sending packets.

> **Note**   *As an analogy, CoS is like classifying packages for delivery via regular mail, second-day delivery, or next-day delivery. QoS is what the delivery company does to ensure your packages are delivered on time (such as package tracking, air transport, door-to-door pickup and drop-off).*

While CoS techniques can give some traffic priority over other traffic, without QoS, there is no way to prevent even high-priority traffic from being delayed or losing packets. In fact, true QoS is only possible with ATM, which can provide predictable service due to its fixed cell size. With ATM, carriers and service providers know exactly how many 53-byte cells can be delivered within the capacity of their network. This predictability allows the carriers to write service-level agreements with guaranteed service levels.

Still, CoS techniques can reduce latency and ensure that important traffic gets through in a reasonable amount of time. CoS is practical on enterprise networks. It is possible to overprovision a network (provide more bandwidth than is needed on average) and then prioritize traffic to achieve acceptable service levels. By prioritizing traffic, network devices can drop the least important traffic before the highest priority traffic.

CoS techniques are listed next and described elsewhere in this book. For comparison, refer to "QoS (Quality of Service" and "Integrated Services (IntServ)" for a discussion of QoS techniques.

- **802.1p**   An IEEE standard for classifying traffic with up to eight levels of priority using three bits in the Ethernet frame header. Basically, it gives switches and other layer 2 networking equipment the ability to prioritize traffic. This is discussed under "Prioritization of Network Traffic" and "QoS (Quality of Service)."

- **Diff-Serv**   An IETF specification for prioritizing IP traffic. It specifies methods for setting the ToS (type of service) field in the IP header in ways that can prioritize traffic across IP networks. Diff-Serv is important because it can be used across internetworks and the Internet. See "Differentiated Services (DiffServ)" and "Prioritization of Network Traffic."

- **ATM service categories**   ATM has its own methods for categorizing traffic such as CBR (constant bit rate), VBR (variable bit rate), UBR (unspecified bit rate), ABR (available bit rate), and GFR (guaranteed frame rate). Refer to "ATM (Asynchronous Transfer Mode)" for more details.

A paper by Mark Hoover, president of Acuitive (see link at the end of this topic) provides an interesting perspective on CoS. Hoover claims that while CoS can reduce latency, CoS becomes less important as the speed of links increases. For example, delays under 200 milliseconds are barely noticeable. The latency of Fast Ethernet links is about 2.4 milliseconds. He notes that for a user to even notice a slight increase in latency, packets would need to "be going through almost 100 Fast Ethernet Switches, arriving behind 20 maximum-sized Ethernet frames at each." His assessment is that CoS most important is in the WAN, not Ethernet LANs.

Related Entries   ATM (Asynchronous Transfer Mode; Bandwidth Management; Cells and Cell Relay; Congestion and Congestion Control; Differentiated Services (DiffServ); Policy-Based Network Management; Prioritization of Network Traffic; QoS (Quality of Service); Queuing; SLA (Service-Level Agreement); *and* Traffic Management, Shaping, and Engineering

Linktionary!—Tom Sheldon's Encyclopedia of Networking updates	http://www.linktionary.com/c/cos.html
Intel paper that discusses QoS and CoS in particular	http://www.intel.com/network/white_papers/diff_serv/diffserv.htm
Hoov's Musings: "Class of Marketing" by Mark Hoover	http://www.acuitive.com/musings/hmv1-3.htm
Lucent white paper: QoS in the LAN	http://www.lucent.com/ins/library/pdf/white_papers/qos_in_lan.pdf

CPCP (Coffee Pot Control Protocol)

CPCP describes how to connect your coffee pot to the Internet. Hurry and get your network cable connected to the kitchen. No provisions are given for decaffeinated coffee, but who cares. The "tongue-in-cheek" protocol is described in RFC 2324 (Coffee Pot Protocol, April 1998). As the RFC mentions, future versions of this protocol may include extensions for espresso machines and similar devices. See "Internet Entertainment" for a list of similar humorous RFCs.

CPE (Customer Premises Equipment)

CPE is the telecommunications equipment owned by an organization and located on its premises. CPE equipment includes PBXs (private branch exchanges), telephones, key systems, facsimile products, modems, voice-processing equipment, and video communication equipment.

Previous to 1996, carriers were not allowed to be involved in the manufacturing, marketing, and sales of this equipment, but to promote competition, Congress opened up the telecommunications markets. Now companies like AT&T can provide one-source solutions for wide area networks by providing customers with on-site equipment and long-distance services.

Related Entries   PBX (Private Branch Exchange); Telecommunications and Telephone Systems; *and* Voice Networking

CPI-C (Common Programming Interface for Communication), IBM

CPI-C is a platform-independent API that interfaces to a common set of APPC (Advanced Program-to-Program Communication) verbs. It is simple and straightforward, and is portable across all platforms that support CPI-C. CPI-C is designed to provide a common environment for the execution of applications across IBM platforms, such as IBM MVS (Multiple Virtual Storage), VS (Virtual Storage), OS/400, and OS/2-based systems. This topic is continued at the Linktionary! Web site.

Related Entries   AIX (Advanced Interactive Executive); AnyNet, IBM; APPC (Advanced Program-to-Program Communications); APPN (Advanced Peer-to-Peer Networking); AS/400; DCE (Distributed Computing Environment); *and* IBM

Linktionary!—Tom Sheldon's Encyclopedia of Networking updates

http://www.linktionary.com/c/cpi-c.html

The Official CPI-C Home Page

http://www.networking.ibm.com/app/aiwconf/cpic.htm

C

CPL (Call Processing Language)

The CPL (Call Processing Language) is a language that can be used to describe and control Internet telephony services. It may be implemented on network servers or user agent servers. It is meant to be simple, extensible, easily edited by graphical clients, and independent of operating system or signaling protocol. It is suitable for running on a server where users may not be allowed to execute arbitrary programs, as it has no variables, loops, or ability to run external programs. See "VoIP (Voice over IP)" for more information.

Cryptography

Cryptography is a field of science and research in which *cryptographers* engage in the design and development of *cryptographic systems*, systems that can protect sensitive data from hackers, eavesdroppers, and industrial spies. Cryptographic methods are also used for *authentication* between users and between computer systems. Cryptographers actively attempt to break the very systems they create in order to understand their limitations. The concept of breaking something that you have created is common in manufacturing. It proves the reliability and safety of a product such as an automobile. Today, a common practice is to enlist the public help in breaking cryptographic schemes by offering prizes in the form of money and "prestige" for having broken a scheme.

Encryption transforms some input into an output that is impossible to read without the proper key. It is performed by running an *algorithm* that transforms some input called the *plaintext* into an encrypted form called the *ciphertext*. While the algorithm always operates the same way, the use of a key ensures that the output will always be different (given the same input). A different key used on the same plaintext will produce different ciphertext. The key is also used to unlock the encrypted data by using the same algorithm in reverse. Because algorithms are usually public and well known, good encryption relies on a solid algorithm and avoiding the use of *weak* keys.

There are three primary cryptographic techniques. Two are used to encrypt text, graphics, and other information in a form that can be recovered by someone who has an appropriate key. The third, used in authentication and integrity shemps, scrambles input without any intention to recover it.

■ **Secret-key cryptography** A single key is used to encrypt and decrypt information. This technique is called *symmetric key encryption*. Encrypted information may be stored on disk or transmitted over nonsecure channels. Since there is only one key, some form of secure key exchange is necessary (in-person, courier, and so on).

■ **Public-key cryptography** Two keys are used in this scheme—one to encrypt and one to decrypt. Thus, the scheme is *asymmetric*. Every person has a set of keys and one is held private while the other is made publicly available. To send a private message to someone, you encrypt it with the recipient's public key. The recipient then decrypts it with his or her private key. This eliminates the problems of exchanging keys in advance of using the encryption.

■ **Hash functions**   A hash function is an algorithm that produces a unique "fingerprint" of a message that can prove that it has not been altered since its creation. The output of the algorithm is called a *message digest*. A recipient that runs the same algorithm on the message should arrive at the same digest; otherwise, the message is suspect. The technique is used to digitally sign messages and documents. See "Hash Function" for more details.

Several other topics related to cryptography are covered elsewhere in this book. Refer to "PKI (Public Key Infrastructure)," "Public-Key Cryptography," and "Security."

The Encryption Process

One of the most well-known encryption algorithms is the U.S. Government–developed DES (Data Encryption Standard). It uses a 56-bit key and an algorithm that scrambles and obscures a message by running it through multiple iterations or rounds of an obfuscation algorithm. This process is pictured in Figure C-26, and is greatly simplified in the following description. To visualize the cryptographic process, imagine that the information being encrypted is split apart and then woven together like threads. The key value is used to "tint" the threads with different color during each twist (iteration) of the process.

1. The plaintext is divided into 64-bit blocks. Each block is worked independently through 16 iterations of the algorithm.

2. At the same time, the 56-bit key is divided in half. In each iteration, the bits in each half are shifted to the left to change the key values (like changing the color to be applied to the thread).

3. A 64-bit block is divided in half (now we have two threads) and the right half is combined with the two key halves created in step 2 (this is like coloring one of the threads).

4. The results of step 3 are converted again using some specific techniques (too complex to discuss here); then, the results are combined with the left half of the 64-bit block (like weaving in another thread).

5. The results of the preceding steps become the new right half. Now the next iteration for the same 64-bit block is ready to start. The right half from the previous iteration is brought down to become the new left half (the thread to be colored). Also, the left and right halves of the key are bit-shifted left and combined to create a new key (like changing the color).

6. The process repeats again using the new left half and new right half for 15 more iterations. This produces the first 64-bit block of ciphertext.

7. The next 64-bit block is processed using the same procedure.

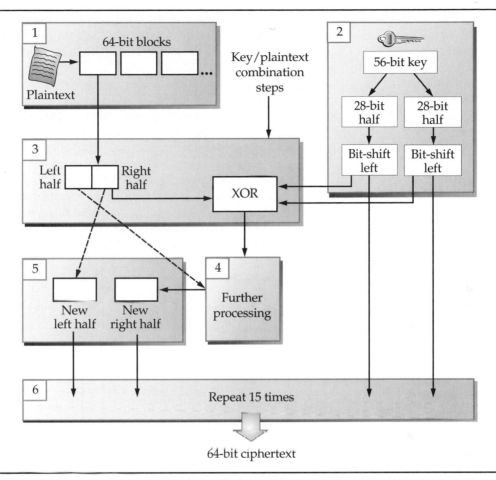

Figure C-26.   *DES encryption algorithm (simplified)*

Cryptanalysis

Cryptanalysis is the analysis of a cryptosystem to verify its integrity or find its weaknesses. An attacker may take the latter route to exploit a system or view sensitive information.

One of the interesting things about DES and other algorithms is that the algorithms are published and well known, so anyone that is trying to break your DES-encrypted ciphertext will presumably have the algorithm to work with. But in reality, the algorithm is not that useful to a "cracker." Instead, code breakers simply try to find the right key. But that is not a simple task. Crackers have employed arrays of hundreds or thousands of computers to try millions of keys until the right key is discovered.

The 56-bit key size of DES is no longer considered secure against attacks. The EFF (Electronic Frontiers Foundation) recently used a custom computer system costing $250,000 to crack

56-bit DES in three days! In another effort, the EFF organized 100,000 Internet-based personal computers to break DES in less than a day. Since then, the U.S. Department of Commerce has not recommended using 56-bit DES. It now recommends the use of Triple DES (discussed later in this topic).

Governments around the world have put controls on the use of encryption and limit the size of keys, but some governments have relaxed these controls due to the proliferation of hacking and code breaking. In 1999, the French government claimed that it was futile to control encryption technology in an attempt to keep it out of the hands of criminals.

One method is called the *brute force attack*. Every possible key is tried in an attempt to decrypt the ciphertext. Often, a dictionary of common passwords (freely available on the Internet) is used. This type of attack is often successful if weak passwords are used. A weak password is a common name, words out of the dictionary, and common abbreviations. Brute force attacks are difficult if long keys are used and if the keys consist of mixed numbers and characters in a nonsense pattern. It is estimated that a 100-bit key could take millions to billions of years to break. However, a weakness in a system might reduce the number of keys that need to be tried, thus making an attack feasible.

Another possibility is that the cryptanalyst knows something about what is inside an encrypted message and has the algorithm used to create the ciphertext. In this case, the cryptanalyst can analyze the original plaintext, the algorithm, and the resulting ciphertext to find some pattern or weakness in the system. Message content is often not hard to figure out. Documents created in popular word processors often have hidden formatting codes and header information. Invoices or other business documents have a company's name and address. The names of persons or systems may be repeated throughout a document.

The cryptanalyst might even find a way to get some text inserted into a sensitive document before it is encrypted, and then use the techniques just described to look for the message in the ciphertext. There are also some special techniques, called *differential* cryptanalysis, in which an interactive and iterative process works through many rounds and uses the results of previous rounds to break ciphertext.

Note *RFC 1984 IAB and IESG Statement on Cryptographic Technology and the Internet (August 1996) outlines the IAB (Internet Architecture Board) and the IESG (Internet Engineering Steering Group) concerns about security on the Internet and the policies of some governments that impose restrictions on cryptographic methods.*

One of the best sources of information on cryptography is the RSA Security System cryptography FAQ (Frequently Asked Questions). The Web site is given at the end of this topic.

Types of Ciphers

As mentioned, there are symmetric (single-key) and asymmetric (two-key) ciphers. Symmetric schemes are also called *secret-key* encryption schemes. A single key is used for both encrypting and decrypting messages. DES is a symmetric algorithm. If you send an encrypted message to someone, you must get them a copy of the key so he or she can decrypt the message. This is a problem in some environments, especially if you don't know the recipient and need to transport or transmit the key via people or methods you don't trust. How can you be sure the key has not been compromised? Asymmetric public-key schemes solve this problem.

With asymmetric *public-key cryptography* schemes, users get a pair of keys, one public and one private. The keys are linked so that messages encrypted with one key can only be decrypted with the other. The public key can be sent to other users or placed on public servers. The private key is kept by the owner and never revealed. To send a private message to someone, you encrypt the message with the recipient's public key. Upon receipt, the recipient decrypts the message with his or her private key. The public-key scheme has revolutionized computer security by providing ways to enable electronic commerce, authenticate users, validate and timestamp documents and programs, exchange secure electronic messages, and more. See "Public-Key Cryptography" for more details.

The rest of this section covers secret-key (symmetric) encryption.

A common secret-key system is Kerberos. It traditionally uses DES and relies on a third-party host system (typically a security server in an intranet environment) that holds the secret keys of all the users (and services) on a network. The Kerberos server handles things like creating credentials that users can present when they log on to network systems. See "Kerberos."

Symmetric algorithms have the following characteristics:

- **Block or stream cipher mode**   In block cipher mode, plaintext is divided up into blocks and each block is processed individually in multiple rounds (iterations). In stream cipher mode, streams of raw bits are processed. The stream mode is generally faster.

- **Key size**   The key size (number of bits) determines the strength of an algorithm, with larger keys providing better strength. Some algorithms have fixed key sizes, while others allow variable key sizes. The longer a key, the more time it takes to perform an encryption. When storing a will, a large key is desirable so that it will hold up a long time into the future. A short-lived transaction can get by with a smaller key size.

- **Block size**   For block ciphers, the size of the blocks that are processed.

- **Rounds**   The number of iterations that a block goes through during the encryption. The more rounds the better, but the more time the process will take.

The following sections describe the most common encryption algorithms. You can refer to the Linktionary! Web site for a list of Internet RFCs Web sites that provide additional information. Also see "Security" for additional links.

DES (Data Encryption Standard) and Triple DES

DES was developed by IBM in the 1970s. It was adopted by the National Bureau of Standards, which is now called the NIST (National Institute of Standards). DES became an official U.S. Government standard for data encryption in 1977. In 1997, NIST began looking for a DES replacement, as discussed later in this topic.

DES is a private-key cryptographic technique that uses an algorithm to encrypt data in 64-bit blocks using a 56-bit key. The 56-bit key provides quadrillions of possible key combinations. In addition, every block in the data stream is encoded using a different variation of the key, which reduces the chance that a coding scheme might be revealed over a lengthy transmission.

DES is fast compared to other methods, and it was originally designed to run in hardware. It is also simple to use, assuming key exchange can be handled safely. DES can also be used for personal use to encrypt stored information. A number of router vendors use DES to encrypt transmissions over public networks.

Because DES is faster than public-key methods, it is often used to encrypt the text of a message itself. The key for the DES encryption is then itself encrypted using a public-key encryption method and sent to the receiving party along with the message. This strategy works because the public-key method provides a secure way to distribute the key over a public network while DES provides fast encryption.

Due to the attacks discussed earlier in this section, DES now lacks public confidence.

Triple-DES is a secure form of DES (called 3DES) with a 156-bit key length that performs three DES operations (encrypt, decrypt, and encrypt) on each data block.

CAST-128, CAST-256

CAST-128 and CAST-256 are symmetric encryption algorithms. The name comes from the designers (Carlisle Adams and Stafford Tavares). CAST uses large key sizes that are designed to encrypt and protect data well into the 21st century, even as computer processing power improves. Symmetric encryption algorithms use a single key to encrypt and decrypt data. The key is kept by the person encrypting data and may be given to other people who might need to decrypt the data. In contrast, public-key cryptography is asymmetric in that there are two keys, a private key for encrypting and a public key for decrypting.

CAST-256 is the latest and most secure version of CAST. The original CAST was designed to deliver high software performance on general-purpose computers. CAST-256 was created in 1997. The Algorithms are now managed and distributed by Entrust Technologies (http://www.entrust.com).

CAST-256 can be used as a replacement for DES. It has a more flexible key size and a larger block size that provides higher levels of security. CAST-256 supports key sizes of 128, 160, 192, 224, and 256 bits and a block size of 128 bits. A primary advantage of CAST is its speed. It was designed to run at high-performance levels in either hardware or software, and can be tuned to provide even higher performance for special applications such as the encryption of bulk data transfers between systems.

Blowfish and Twofish

Blowfish is a freely available public domain data encryption cipher designed to protect data for many years into the future, despite advances in the ability to break or decipher (using cryptanalysis) such encryption. Blowfish was developed by Bruce Schneier in 1993 with design criteria developed with Niels Fergusen. The cipher is discussed at Bruce Schneier's Web site (http://www.counterpane.com).

The Blowfish Web site describes the cipher in more detail. Basically, Blowfish is a variable-length key (32 to 448 bits) block cipher that can be used to replace DES and IDEA. The algorithm goes through two phases of computation. In the first phase, the key supplied by the user of up to 448 bits is expanded in several subkey arrays totaling 4,168 bytes. In the second phase, data is divided into 64-bit blocks for encryption using the key array. Technically, "data encryption occurs via a 16-round Feistel network. Each round consists of a key-dependent permutation, and a key- and data-dependent substitution. All operations are XORs and additions on 32-bit words. The only additional operations are four indexed array data lookups per round."

More recently, Bruce created the *Twofish* algorithm, which he submitted as a replacement for the current DES (Data Encryption Standard) as described later in this topic under "NIST Advanced Encryption Standard (AES)." Twofish is based on Blowfish, but is more suited to 32-bit microprocessors, 8-bit smart card microprocessors, and dedicated hardware. Some trade-offs in design were used to allow an implementer to balance performance variables like encryption speed, key setup time, code size, RAM, ROM, and gate count. There is a $10,000 prize for the best attack against the Twofish algorithm. Check the Counterpane Systems Web site for more information.

CAST-128 is discussed further in RFC 2144 (The CAST-128 Encryption Algorithm May 1997). Cast 256 is discussed in RFC 2612 (The CAST-256 Encryption Algorithm June 1999).

Other Block Ciphers

You are likely to encounter a number of other block ciphers. The most important are listed below. Keep in mind that other encryption techniques exist, including public-key cryptosystems, discussed under "Public-Key Cryptography."

- **IDEA (International Data Encryption Algorithm)**   IDEA is a block-oriented secret-key (single-key) encryption algorithm developed by the Swiss Federal Institute of Technology. It uses a 128-bit key compared to DES's 56-bit key, and encrypts 64-bit blocks in eight rounds. IDEA is not fast in software, but it has been implemented on processor chips to improve performance. The algorithm is considered suitable for electronic commerce and is exportable around the world. As of this writing, there have been no known successful attacks on IDEA. However, over 250 weak keys were discovered that should not be used.

- **SAFER (Secure And Fast Encryption Routine)**   A byte-oriented block cipher that implements 64-bit blocks and a 64-bit key size. A version is also available that supports 128-bit keys. The number of rounds is user selectable. The cipher uses 1-byte operation, which makes it suitable for use in smart cards and other devices with limited processing power. The newest versions, SK-64 and SK-128, were strengthened against some weaknesses in the way keys are implemented. SAFER is nonproprietary.

- **Skipjack**   This encryption algorithm is used in the Clipper chip, a security device designed by the NSA for securing communications. The algorithm uses 80-bit keys and 64-bit blocks. Each chip also contains an 80-bit key that is split into two parts, with each part being stored at separate key escrow agencies. The key fragments can be obtained and combined (upon a court order) to recover information encrypted with a particular chip. Skipjack was originally classified, which meant that it could not be subjected to public cryptanalysis, so there was little trust in the system. Since then, the NSA has declassified the algorithm.

- **FEAL (Fast Data Encipherment Algorithm)**   This algorithm is not considered secure.

NIST Advanced Encryption Standard (AES)

In 1997, the U.S. National Institute of Standards announced that it wanted to replace DES with a new AES (Advanced Encryption Standard) that could provide strong encryption well into the first quarter of the 21st century. The key length was to be over 128 and variable in length. NIST evaluated algorithms developed by individuals and organizations. Fifteen submissions were received and NIST selected Rijndael in late 2000.

- **MARS**   Developed by IBM, which developed the original DES
- **RC6**   Developed by Ron Rivest, coinventor of RSA
- **Rijndael**   Co-developed in Belgium by Joan Daemen and Vincent Rijmen
- **Serpent**   Co-developed by Ross Anderson, Eli Biham, and Lars Knudsen of the United Kingdom, Israel, and Norway
- **Twofish**   Developed by Counterpane Systems, the developers of BlowFish

Information about the AES program may be found at the following Web sites:

NIST AES Home	http://csrc.nist.gov/encryption/aes/
Counterpane Systems	http://www.counterpane.com

Related Entries   Authentication and Authorization; Certificates and Certification Systems; Digital Signatures; FORTEZZA; Hacking and Hackers; Hash Functions; PKI (Public-Key Infrastructure); Public-Key Cryptography; Secret-Key Cryptography; *and* Security

Linktionary!—Tom Sheldon's Encyclopedia of   http://www.linktionary.com/c/cryptography.html
Networking updates

Also see the list of Web links under "Security."

CSMA/CD (Carrier Sense Multiple Access/Collision Detection)

CSMA is a network access method used on shared network topologies such as Ethernet to control access to the network. Devices attached to the network cable listen (carrier sense) before transmitting. If the channel is in use, devices wait before transmitting. MA (multiple access) indicates that many devices can connect to and share the same network. All devices have equal access to use the network when it is clear. Even though devices attempt to sense whether the network is in use, there is a good chance that two stations will attempt to access it at the same time. On large networks, the transmission time between one end of the cable and another is enough that one station may access the cable even though another has already just accessed it. There are two methods for avoiding these so-called collisions, listed here:

- **CSMA/CD (carrier sense multiple access/collision detection)**   CD (collision detection) defines what happens when two devices sense a clear channel, then attempt to transmit at the same time. A collision occurs, and both devices stop transmission, wait for a random amount of time, then retransmit. This is the technique used to access the 802.3 Ethernet network channel. This method handles collisions as they occur, but if the bus is constantly busy, collisions can occur so often that performance drops drastically. It is estimated that network traffic must be less than 40 percent of the bus capacity for the network to operate efficiently. If distances are long, time lags occur that may result in inappropriate carrier sensing, and hence collisions.

- **CSMA/CA (carrier sense multiple access/collision avoidance)**   In CA (collision avoidance), collisions are avoided because each node signals its intent to transmit before actually doing so. This method is not popular because it requires excessive overhead that reduces performance.

Linktionary!—Tom Sheldon's Encyclopedia of Networking updates	http://www.linktionary.com/c/csma/htm
CSMA/CD	http://www.erg.abdn.ac.uk/users/gorry/course/lan-pages/csma-cd.html
Charles Spurgeon's Ethernet Web Site	http://www.ots.utexas.edu/ethernet/

Related Entries   Access Methods; Collision and Collision Domains; Ethernet; IEEE 802 Standards; *and* Network Concepts

CSR (Cell Switched Router), Toshiba

CSR is a "route at the edge, switch in the core" technology designed for ATM networks. It is similar to other multilayer integration technologies, as discussed in the sections "Label Switching" and "Multilayer Switching." CSR was one of the first attempts at multilayer switching on ATM switches. Ipsilon's IP Switching was another. Both control an ATM device using IP protocols, making the ATM switch operate like a switch router.

CSR uses a data-driven model, in which individual traffic flows are detected and a binding is made to a virtual circuit if the flow is sufficient to warrant it. This is called *cut-through* or *shortcut routing*. Normal routing is used otherwise. This flow-driven approach limits the number of labels to the flows detected. However, switches must detect flows, which takes time. In some cases, by the time a flow is detected and a shortcut is set up, the flow may actually be ending. In this case, only the end of that flow may gain the benefit of being switched.

A CSR network is composed of CSR multilayer devices with ATM label-switching capabilities, and layer 3 packet routing and forwarding capabilities. The network is seen as a cloud with edge devices (ingress and egress nodes) that connect to legacy networks (standard IP networks running on top of LANs such as Ethernet).

A cut-through path is established from the ingress node to an egress node across intermediate CSR multilayer devices. The cut-through path is established by the ingress CSR and maintained by all the CSRs that make up the path.

Note that CSR solves many problems related to communicating between logical IP subnets (as is the case in overlay models like MPOA), since each device in the network has routing capabilities—not just the edge devices. At the same time, forwarding is handled with fast layer 2 switching.

Like IP switching, CSR was not considered scalable for service provider networks and was limited to use in enterprise LANs. For additional information, refer to the following RFCs:

- RFC 2098 (Toshiba's Router Architecture Extensions for ATM Overview, February 1997)
- RFC 2129 (Toshiba's Flow Attribute Notification Protocol (FANP) Specification, April 1997)

Related Entries   ATM (Asynchronous Transfer Mode); IP Navigator; IP Over ATM; IP Switching; Label Switching; Multilayer Switching; QoS (Quality of Service); Tag Switching; Traffic Management, Shaping, and Engineering; *and* VPN (Virtual Private Network)

MPLS Forum	http://www.mplsforum.com/
IETF MPLS Working Group	http://www.ietf.org/html.charters/mpls-charter.html
Noritoshi Demizu Multilayer Switching Page	http://www.waterspring.org/links/mlr/
Toshiba CSP page	http://www.toshiba.co.jp/about/press/1998_05/pr0401.htm
TechFest Multilayer Switching page	http://www.techfest.com/networking/mlayer.htm

CSU/DSU (Channel Service Unit/Data Service Unit)

Because digital signaling on the telephone network is different than the digital signaling used by computer equipment, special devices are required to connect the two types of transmission facilities together. The CSU/DSU is part of the hardware you need to connect digital computer equipment to telephone company digital transmission lines (T1 and T3 lines).

CSUs (channel service units) and DSUs (data service units) are actually two separate devices, as described next, but they are used in conjunction and often combined into the same box.

- **Channel service unit**   This inexpensive device connects with the digital communication line and provides a termination for the digital signal. The CSU provides various loop-back tests on the line and keeps the line connected if the other communication equipment attached to it fails. It also provides synchronization (clocking) with similar devices.

- **Data service unit**   This device, sometimes called a *digital service unit*, is the hardware component you need to transmit digital data over the hardware channel. The device converts signals from bridges, routers, and multiplexors into the bipolar digital signals used on the telephone company digital lines and ensures that voltage levels are correct.

The typical configuration is pictured in Figure C-27. CSU/DSUs are often included with multiplexors, which are devices that transmit voice signals and data over the same line.

ADC Kentrox is a major producer of telecommunications gear. Recently, it released a device called a SDU (service delivery unit) that it says obsoletes the CSU/DSU. The device has more sophisticated features that can monitor a line's performance to ensure that service-level agreements are being met. The device will even monitor who or what is using the line, and enforce usage policies. ATC Kentrox is at http://www.adc.com/.

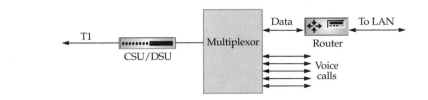

C

Figure C-27.   *CSU/DSU (channel service unit/data service unit)*

Related Entries   Network Connection Technologies; T Carriers; TDM Networks; *and* WAN (Wide Area Network)

CTI (Computer-Telephony Integration)

The term *convergence* is usually applied to the integration of voice and data services on the same network, either in the enterprise or over public networks such as the Internet. CTI is the integration of telephony services with computers, servers, PBX devices, and other computer-related equipment. These two areas, which are merging as organizations, install high-speed networks that can carry both voice and data.

Although the first implementations of CTI integrated computers with the circuit-switched voice phone network, new CTI products operate over IP data networks. A range of devices is possible, including:

- At the low end, a diskless device that integrates a Web browser and telephone functionality.

- At the high end, a desktop computer with telephone, videoconferencing, speech recognition, and just about anything else you might use in a telephony environment such as automatic answering, call forwarding, voice messaging, and so on.

IVR (Interactive Voice Response) is a CTI application. It is the front-end "computerized operator" that guides you through button-pushing options when you call a company (i.e., "press 1 for sales, press 2 for service"). Putting this on computers has simplified setup for administrators because an easy-to-use interface makes it easy to program selections and add or change a message. It is even possible to have messages change automatically based on programmed times or dates.

Universal in-box is another aspect of CTI. It can provide services such as voice mail, faxing, and e-mail on a company-wide basis. Information is stored on disk and accessible to users who dial into the server from their phone, or access it from their workstation. In the latter case, voice messages travel across the network to the recipient's computer where they are played back, so this is getting close to voice networking. However, stored messages are not real-time voice, so bandwidth requirements are not as strict. This is one of the biggest concerns with integrating voice over networks. The voice calls are live, and if enough bandwidth is not available, the conversation becomes garbled.

To provide a basis for CTI, Novell created TSAPI (Telephony Services API) and Microsoft created TAPI (Telephony API). TSAPI was enhanced in 1996 by a vendor consortium called Versit, which includes IBM, Siemens, and Apple Computer as its members.

Note, however, that these protocols do not combine voice and data networking. They allow a computer to manipulate telephone devices that are connected to telephone lines. In some cases, telephony devices might be connected over a network, but the signals that cross the network are for control. They are not voice signals.

Applications can use TSAPI or TAPI to interact with devices like phones, PBXs, and modems. Microsoft Windows uses TAPI in a number of built-in applications to interact with modems. For example, a phone dialer program lets you enter names and phone numbers in a notepad that can be selected and dialed at any time. Windows can do a number of other things as well using TAPI, like answer incoming phone calls and faxes, forward calls, and provide voice mail. A fax application is included that receives incoming faxes and displays them in a graphical interface where they can be manipulated as if working in a drawing program.

Related Entries   TAPI (Telephony API); Voice/Data Networking; *and* VoIP (Voice over IP)

Linktionary!—Tom Sheldon's Encyclopedia of Networking updates	http://www.linktionary.com/c/cti.html
Web ProForums (see various CTI topics)	http://www.iec.org/tutorials/
Computer Telephony.com	http://www.telecomlibrary.com/
Enterprise Computer Telephony Forum (ECTF)	http://www.ectf.org
Phonezone.com (a great resource for telephony information)	http://www.phonezone.com/
Internet & Telecoms Convergence Consortium	http://itel.mit.edu/
SCSA (Signal Computing System Architecture) Web site	http://www.scsa.org/

Customer Premises Equipment

See CPE (Customer Premises Equipment).

Cut-Through Architecture

Cut-through architecture is one method of design for packet-switching systems. When a packet arrives at a switch, the switch starts forwarding the packet almost immediately, reading only the first few bytes in the packet to learn the destination address. This technique improves performance.

The opposite approach is the *store-and-forward* technique that is commonly used in traditional bridges and routers. In this approach, the entire packet is received in a buffer before it is forwarded. The device performs error checking on the packet as well. The entire store-and-forward process takes time and adds latency, but reduces errors.

As network throughput has increased, the cut-through method became an essential part of switch design. It is no longer possible to hold packets up using the store-and-forward method. Some devices use both methods, switching to store-and-forward if network errors start to increase.

Related Entries   ASIC (Application Specific Integrated Circuit); Cut-Through Routing; Router Switch Fabrics and Bus Design; *and* Switching and Switched Networks

Cut-Through Routing

Routers receive packets from one or more inputs and make forwarding decisions about where to send the packets. Traditional software routers (as opposed to routing switches) read each packet header and examine the fields to determine how the packet should be forwarded. This takes time and affects performance. Add multiple router hops into the path between source and destination, and the requirement to also filter packets, perform accounting, and encrypt data, and you come up with a low-performance network link. Some routers use caching techniques that detect a flow of packets and store the routing information of the first packet in memory. Subsequent routing decisions are made from the information in memory, thus boosting performance somewhat.

Cut-through routing (sometimes called *shortcut routing*) is an approach in which devices on different subnets can directly communicate with one another without going through a router. The approach is used on switching fabrics such as ATM networks in which multiple LISs (logical IP subnets) overlay the ATM switching fabric. While routing is normally required between LISs, an end system in one LIS can connect directly with an end system in another LIS by using a cut-through route. The cut-through route is created between the end system as a virtual circuit across the ATM switching fabric.

Typically, the first few packets are initially routed, but if a long flow is detected, the ATM address of the destination is obtained by the source, which then sets up a virtual connection across the ATM fabric directly to the destination, switching all subsequent packets and bypassing the routers. This process is often referred to as "route once, switch many." The related entries, next, provide further information.

Related Entries   CSR (Cell-Switched Router); Cut-Through Architecture; Fast IP; IP Navigator; IP Over ATM; IP Switching; MPOA (Multiprotocol Over ATM); NHRP (Next Hop Resolution Protocol); *and* PNNI (Private Network-to-Network Interface)

Cyclic Redundancy Check

See Error Detection and Correction.

DAC (Discretionary Access Control)

See Access Control.

Daemon

Pronounced "demon," it is a background process or program on UNIX systems. Once started, daemons usually run on their own without any further need for input from an operator. A system administrator may need to set initial startup parameters and change those parameters occasionally.

DAFS (Direct Access File System)

DAFS is a new fast-and-simple way of accessing data from file servers. It is designed for use in SANs (Storage Area Networks) environments and NAS (Network Attached Storage) devices. DAFS is tied to the Virtual Interface architecture (VI architecture), which provides fast data transport in a local environment, such as data centers. VI architecture was originally designed for SANs. DAFS provides a performance gain that makes NAS (Network Attached Storage) devices suitable for high-volume transactions.

DAFS was developed by Network Appliance, Intel, Oracle and Seagate Technology. The DAFS Collaborative Web site (listed at the end of this topic) notes that application servers can benefit from using DAFS. An example is a set of diskless Web servers connected to one or more file servers that store Web information. Another example is a cluster of diskless servers running a highly available shared database that uses a file server to store database information. DAFS is primarily designed for clustered, shared-file network environments, in which a limited number of server-class clients connect to a set of file servers via a dedicated high-speed network.

To understand DAFS, you need to understand the VI architecture. To understand VI architecture, you need to understand how files are transferred on networks. That is best explained by reviewing traditional PC file access methods. When you request to open a file in Microsoft Word, the operating system talks to the disk interface (IDE, SCSI, and so on), which, in turn, reads blocks of data from disk and moves it into RAM where it is accessible by your application. A PC operating system adds a lot of overhead with its user-friendly interface, i.e., you get to request a file by name and the complexities of moving blocks from disk are handled in the background.

Accessing a file in the traditional way on a network server requires many more steps. The application request goes to the local operating system, which hands it to the network interface; the network interface, in turn, puts the request in a packet and sends it across the network. The server unpacks the request and sends it to the disk interface, which moves data blocks into output buffers on the network interface. In most cases, blocks of data must be split up and inserted into multiple packets for transport across the network. This whole process of moving data in and out of buffers and splitting it up is rather inefficient. A better approach is to move *whole* blocks directly from disk across the network into the memory of the requesting device. This is where DAFS, using VI architecture as its transport mechanism, comes into play.

VI architecture and DAFS help to eliminate the overhead and improve data access across network connections. VI architecture provides "consumers" (basically, clients such as other servers or thin clients) with a direct *virtual interface* into server hardware across the network connection. VI architecture supports transport-independent, memory-to-memory transfer methods across networks. In other words, data consumers have direct access to the disk and can transfer data from it directly into their own memory. There is no need to copy data to or from intermediate buffers, or to interrupt the operating system during file transfers. VI architecture supports bulk data transfers (block mode) and allows applications to directly access VI architecture hardware without operating system intervention.

VI architecture was designed for application interaction across SANs. SANs are usually constructed with highly available redundant interconnect fabrics, so SAN performance more closely resembles that of a memory subsystem than a traditional LAN. Traditional file access methods are inappropriate in these high-performance environments. That is why VI architecture was developed.

DAFS is a shared-file access protocol designed to work in SAN environments, where VI architecture is the underlying transport mechanism. DAFS offers these features:

- Provides high-speed, fault-tolerant, consistent views of files to a heterogeneous environment of servers that may be running different operating systems.

- Provides a consistent, cached locking mechanism that tolerates client or file server failures and failovers.

- Provides user authentication and cluster node access control for security.

- Negotiates optimal data packet sizes with the underlying VI architecture. This improves file sharing and file transfers.

- Allows clusters of application servers to efficiently share data while avoiding the overhead imposed by general-purpose operating systems.

- Accesses stored information by way of block addresses rather than filenames.

- Boosts file access by 40 percent by allowing direct memory-to-memory file access.

- DAFS and VI architecture in combination free up CPUs from excessive interrupts so servers have more time to process tasks other than disk I/O.

Not only do these feature reduce data transfer latency, but the CPU is freed from excessive interrupts and has more time to process other tasks. In addition, VIA-compliant adapters perform message fragmentation, message assembly, and other functions in their own hardware rather than relying on the CPU.

Note that the VI architecture is designed for high-speed interconnects, such as the Fibre Channel networks used in clusters and SANs (storage area networks). VI is also implemented in InfiniBand, the new high-speed fabric-switching architecture for servers and switches. See "Switch Fabrics and Bus Design" for more information about Infiniband.

One of the most important features of DAFS is its ability to do block-level storage access, which requires very few instructions to access a file, compared to higher-level file-system protocols. NAS vendors have implemented block-level storage protocols in their devices; but since NAS devices are connected to standard LANs (TCP/IP), the blocks are broken up and carried in IP datagrams, and this reduces performance. A VI architecture connection is preferred since it is more efficient at delivering blocks across network links and allowing memory-to-memory data exchange.

Giganet has developed VI/IP (Virtual Interface Over IP), which carries data blocks in VI architecture message over IP networks. Those networks can be Gigabit Ethernet networks, which provide a performance boost.

The IETF IP Storage (ips) Working Group is developing technologies that transport block storage traffic across IP-based networks. The idea is to transport protocols such as SCSI and Fibre Channel in IP packets. See "IP Storage."

Related Entries Client/Server Computing; Directory Services; Distributed Applications; Distributed Computer Networks; Embedded Systems and Architectures; File Sharing; File Systems; File Transfer Protocols; IP Storage; Network Operating Systems; Replication; Rights and Permissions; Search and Discovery Services; Stateless and Call-Back Filing Systems; Storage Management Systems; Storage Systems; VI Architecture; *and* Volume and Partition Management

Linktionary!—Tom Sheldon's Encyclopedia of Networking updates	http://www.linktionary.com/d/dafs.html
DAFS Collaborative Web site	http://www.dafscollaborative.org/
IETF	
Network Appliance Tech Library (Click "File Service" and choose a document.)	http://www.netapp.com/tech_library/
VI Architecture Specification	http://www.viarch.org
Intel's VI Architecture home page	http://developer.intel.com/design/servers/vi/
Giganet	http://www.giganet.com

DARPA (Defense Advanced Research Projects Agency)

In 1972, ARPA (Advanced Research Projects Agency) became DARPA (Defense Advanced Research Projects Agency). DARPA is an extension of the Department of Defense assigned to fund basic research. DARPA funded most of the basic research for the TCP/IP (Transmission Control Protocol/Internet Protocol) protocol suite and the Internet in the early 1970s. In fact, some of the original work took place at MIT (Massachusetts Institute of Technology) as far back as 1965 under a subcontract MIT had with ARPA.

Some early DARPA boards and committees became what are today known as the IETF (Internet Engineering Task Force) and the IRTF (Internet Research Task Force). Refer to "Internet Organizations and Committees" for more information. Also see "Internet." For a historical account of how routing technologies developed on the Internet, see "Routing on the Internet."

Related Entries ARPANET (Advanced Research Projects Agency Network); Internet; Internet Architecture and Backbone; Internet Organizations and Committees; Internet Protocol Suite; Routing on the Internet; *and* Standards Groups, Associations, and Organizations

Linktionary!—Tom Sheldon's Encyclopedia of Networking updates	http://www.linktionary.com/i/ Internet_Organizations.html

Data Broadcasting

See Broadcasting on the Internet; Content Distribution; Multicasting; Multimedia; Newsfeed Services; NNTP (Network News Transport Protocol); Peer-to-Peer Communications; Push; VBI (Vertical Blinking Interval); Videoconferencing; *and* Webcasting.

Data Center Design

A data center or NOC (network operations center) is a place to consolidate application servers, Web servers, communications equipment, security systems, system administrators, support personnel, and anything or anybody else that provides data services. A data center benefits from centralized management, support, backup control, power management, security, and so on. It may be housed in a single room or fill an entire building. Special equipment is usually installed to protect against power outages, natural disasters, and security breaches.

An organization may build its own data centers or outsource to companies that specialize in high-availability data services. Many small- to medium-size businesses cannot justify a large staff of network professionals. Outsourcing services to data centers and connecting to those data centers via high-speed connections provides a solution. These service providers include ISPs (Internet service providers), ASPs (application service providers), MSPs (management service providers), electronic commerce organizations, and electronic business support services.

Typical services provided by data centers include application management, Web server hosting, electronic mail services, backup services, security services (firewalls, VPNs, incident response, and so on), usage analysis, and monitoring/management services. As ASPs grow in popularity, so does the use of thin clients, which are stripped-down PCs that may not have any local storage. All client data is stored on the ASP servers and a thin client protocol, which transfers only screen and keyboard data, helping to reduce traffic loads on customer–to–data center connections. See "Thin Clients."

Some other characteristics of data centers include the following:

- Data centers are managed by people who specialize in *facilities management*.

- Data centers provide *managed services*, which are services provided to customers on equipment and software that is maintained and monitored by data center technicians.

- Data centers provide *co-location services*, which include providing rack space for customer equipment, power, and network connectivity (to other data center systems, the Internet, or other service providers).

A data center is usually designed to provide *high availability*, *reliability*, and *scalability* for mission-critical applications such as databases, groupware, electronic mail, and so on. These data centers are designed to provide service 24 hours a day, 7 days a week. Site mirroring is the creation of multiple data centers that provide a high level of availability. If any one data center is knocked out due to a local weather problem or other disaster, the other data centers pick up the load. See "Fault Tolerance and High Availability" for related information.

The design of a data center depends on its size and use. A data center designed to support full-time electronic commerce over the Internet or mission-critical applications has different requirements than a data center designed to support applications and databases for a small organization. In general, a data center should have the following characteristics:

- **Resiliency**   The ability of systems to avoid disasters, and even detect potential failures, with monitoring techniques, scheduled maintenance, or replacement of older components before they fail.

- **Redundancy**   Systems that are built with two or more of the most critical components are redundant. If some component should fail, the other can take over. Redundant components include power supplies, I/O cards, drives and drive arrays, buses, and switching fabrics, as well as entire servers, switches, routers, and so on. Refer to "Fault Tolerance and Availability" for more information on redundancy.

- **Manageability**   The ability to monitor systems to detect impending problems or to quickly react to problems as they occur. Thresholds are commonly used to warn against problems. A typical example is a "disk full" threshold that sounds an alarm when a disk is getting close to full capacity.

A data center with these characteristics can be designed with clustered servers, load-balancing equipment, storage area networks (SANs), aggregate links, firewalls, and backup power supplies and generators.

Figure D-1 illustrates a typical data center. The features of this design are covered in more detail in the Intel white paper "Planning and Building a Data Center." The Web site is listed at the end of this topic. The basic features are as follows:

- Raised floors to accommodate cables and trunks

- Power systems, generators, and battery backups

- High-speed data connections to carriers and the Internet

- Temperature control systems

- Fire detection and suppression system

- A physically secure building with secure access facilities and close-circuit television monitoring

- Private cages and secure vaults for customers who require additional security

- Racks that support hosting servers with convenient power and network connections

The system infrastructure includes network cabling and network devices that interconnect systems and provide access to external Telco and ISP services. Infrastructure equipment will also include load balancers, switches, backup systems, and so on. External connections should ideally connect to several service providers that can provide alternative and redundant services.

Servers and other equipment are located within racks in which they are supplied with power and network connectivity. The racks may also contain their own monitoring, management, and backup systems.

A relatively new and interesting technology for data centers is InfiniBand I/O interconnect technology, which implements a switched-fabric architecture with a packet-switching communication protocol. It can be used as a replacement for standard backplane buses, such as PCI, as an interconnect for system area networks (clusters) and storage area networks (disk access). It can also be used as a high-speed interconnection for parallel processing systems.

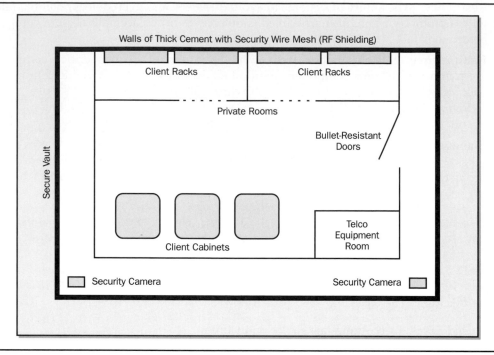

Figure D-1.   *Data Center design (courtesy: Intel)*

InfiniBand replaces familiar server bus architectures such as PCI with a switched fabric. In servers, InfiniBand allows system I/O to be removed from the motherboard and extended out via an InfiniBand link to external devices. I/O control is moved from the central processor to the switched fabric. This frees the CPU from I/O tasks and overcomes the bandwidth and slot restrictions of bus architectures. Servers become CPU modules in rack systems, along with disks and other components, all interconnected via InfiniBand. See "InfiniBand" for more information, or visit the InfiniBand Trade Association (IBTA) Web site listed at the end of this topic. The "Servers" topic provides additional information about rack mounting of servers.

The previously mentioned Intel white paper, "Planning and Building a Data Center," describes the service management center (SMC), which provides systems management for all services and monitoring for the network. A typical SMC requires the following:

- Dedicated management and monitoring tools, such as HP OpenView
- Automated backup facilities for all managed services
- An online call management system
- An integrated change management/asset management/configuration tool, such as Ultracomp Red Box (http://www.ultracomp.co.uk/)
- Help desk management system

You can learn more about data centers by visiting the Exodus Web site. Exodus pioneered the Internet Data Center market. It's Web site provides interesting illustrations of its "Internet Data Centers."

Related Entries   ASP (Application Service Provider); Backup and Data Archiving; Clustering; Co-Location Services; Data Protection; Data Warehousing; Disaster Planning and Recovery; Distributed Computer Networks; Embedded Systems; Fault Management; Fault Tolerance and High-Availability Systems; Fibre Channel; File Systems; Load Balancing; Multiprocessing; NAS (Network Attached Storage); Network Management; Outsourcing; PoP (Point of Presence); Power and Grounding Problems and Solutions; RAID (Redundant Arrays of Inexpensive Disks); Replication; SAN (Storage Attached Network); SAN (System Area Network); SCSI (Small Computer System Interface); Servers; Supercomputer; UPS (Uninterruptible Power Supply); *and* Web Caching

Linktionary!—Tom Sheldon's Encyclopedia of Networking updates	http://www.linktionary.com/d/data_center.html
Intel white paper: "Planning and Building a Data Center"	http://www.intel.com/network/white_papers/data_center/
Bitpipe (search for "data center")	http://www.bitpipe.com/
BRUNS-PAK Design/Build Solutions for Data Centers	http://www.datacenterconstruction.com/
Crossroads Systems (data center technologies)	http://www.crossroads.com/
Design for Nonstop E-Commerce, Cisco Advocates Three-Tiered Network Model for High-Availability Sites	http://www.cisco.com/warp/public/784/packet/july99/2.html
IBTA (InfinBand Trade Association)	http://www.infinibandta.org/
Exodus	http://www.exodus.com/
COLO.com	http://www.colo.com/
3Com paper: The Net Impact of Data Center Consolidation	http://www.3com.com/technology/tech_net/tech_briefs/500903.html
Availability.com Data Center Construction and Management	http://www.availability.com/layers/physical_environment/datacenter.cfm

Data Communication Concepts

Data communications is about transmitting information from one device to another. Protocols define the rules for communication so that sender and receiver can coordinate their activities. At the physical level, information is converted into signals that can be transmitted across a guided (copper or fiber-optic cable) or unguided (radio or infrared transmission) medium. Higher-level protocols define the packaging of information for transmission, flow controls, and techniques for recovering information that was lost or corrupted during transmission.

This section is an overview and referral section. It outlines data communication technologies and makes reference to other sections in this book.

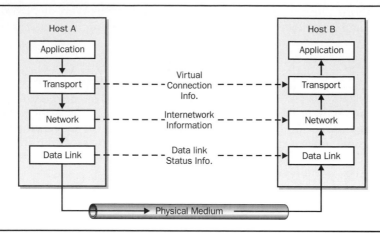

Figure D-2.   *Layered network architecture simplified for clarity*

Communication Protocols

Communication protocols can be compared to the diplomatic protocols used by foreign embassies. Diplomats of various rank handle different types of negotiations. They communicate with peer diplomats in other embassies. Likewise, communication protocols have a layered architecture. When two systems exchange data, the protocols in each layer communicate to handle various aspects of the communication. A simplified diagram is pictured in Figure D-2. These layers are discussed in the following sections. See "Network Architecture" for more information.

Long ago, the ISO (International Organization for Standardization) developed the seven-layer OSI (Open System Interconnection) model. While the OSI model never became a popular standard, it is still used to describe protocol layering. See "OSI (Open Systems Interconnection) Model" for more information.

Transmission Media and Signaling at the Physical Layer

A communication system consists of a transmission medium and the devices that connect to it. The medium may be guided or unguided, where guided media is a metal or optical cable, and unguided media refers to wireless transmissions. See "Cable and Cable Concepts."

Devices involved in data transmissions may be transmitters, or receivers, or both. If one system only transmits and the other only receives, the link is called *simplex*. If both devices can send and receive, but only one device at a time, the link is called *duplex*. A *full-duplex* link allows both systems to transmit and receive simultaneously.

Network communication may take the form of one-to-one transmissions, one-to-many, or many-to-many transmissions. A communication system that connects two devices is said to be a *point-to-point* system. In contrast, a *shared* system connects a number of devices that can transmit on the same medium, but only one at a time. Both systems are illustrated in Figure D-3.

In contrast to a point-to-point system, an *end-to-end link* refers to a link between two systems over multiple links. The link between system A and system Z in Figure D-3 is an end-to-end link.

D

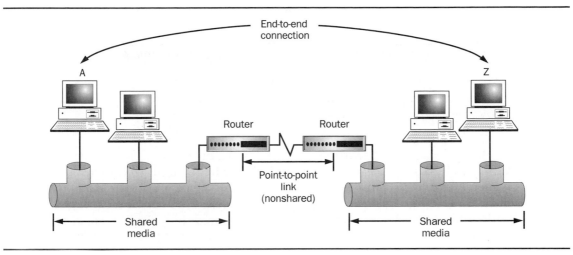

Figure D-3. *Shared and point-to-point communication systems*

Multiplexing is a technique of sending multiple transmissions across a single link. In a TDM (time division multiplexing) system, each channel is defined by periodic time slots in a stream of time slots. In an FDM (frequency division multiplexing) system, each channel occupies a specific frequency. In packet- and cell-switching systems, individual packets or cells traverse the network much like cars on a freeway. See "Multiplexing."

Analog and Digital Signaling

Devices are connected to a transmission medium with an adapter that generates signals for transmitting data over some medium. An *analog* communication system transmits continuous analog signals that vary in amplitude and frequency over time. The frequency of these sine wave signals is measured in cycles per second, or Hz (hertz). In contrast, a *digital* communication system uses discrete high- and low-voltage values to represent digital signals. See "Signals."

Bandwidth is the information-carrying capacity of a communication channel. The channel may be analog or digital. For digital systems, the term *capacity* refers to its information-carrying capability, which is usually expressed as the *data transfer rate* or *wire speed* of the channel. *Throughput* is the "measured" performance of a system as opposed to its stated performance. Throughput takes into account delay caused by congestion, hardware inefficiencies, and transmission distance. See "Bandwidth," "Throughput," and "Delay, Latency, and Jitter."

A modem (modulator/demodulator) is a device that can be used to transmit digital signals over analog transmission lines. A modem is required at both ends of a transmission to modulate, then demodulate, the signal. As shown in Figure D-4, the transmitting modem converts a digital signal into an analog signal and the receiving modem converts the signal back to discrete digital signals. See "Modems."

Figure D-4.   *Digital-to-analog-to-digital conversion*

When transmitting digital data over analog systems, the higher the frequency, the higher the data rate. Figure D-5 illustrates why this is so. In A, the frequency is low, so it is more difficult to transpose the discrete digital signal on the analog transmission. Note that the discrete signal is poorly represented, and this will result in distortion at the receiving end. In B, the bandwidth is much higher and more capable of representing the discrete digital signal without distortion.

Synchronous and Asynchronous Transmissions

Not all transmissions are a steady flow of characters. A transmission that consists of many starts and stops is an *asynchronous* transmission. Assume you are back in the 1960s, sitting at a dumb terminal connected to a mainframe computer. As you type, each character is transmitted to the computer over an asynchronous link. You pause and the transmission pauses. Because the systems operate in asynchronous mode, the receiver is not expecting a steady stream of bits. It waits for further transmission at any time and does not assume that the link has been disrupted when transmissions stop.

In contrast, a *synchronous* transmission is characterized by a long string of bits in which each character in the string is demarcated with a timing signal. Both types of transmissions are commonly used to connect computer systems over telephone lines or other channels.

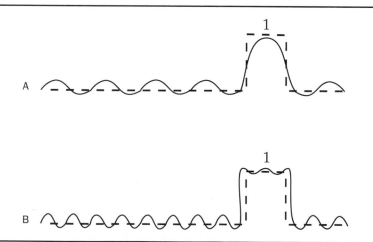

Figure D-5.   *Representing discrete digital signals on analog transmissions*

The choice of one over the other depends on the installation. In fact, modems that provide asynchronous operation for users may switch to synchronous mode for extended transmissions. See "Asynchronous Communications" and "Synchronous Communications."

Synchronous techniques are designed for continuous data transfers, while asynchronous techniques are better suited for individual user sessions.

Serial Interfaces

A standard interface is required to connect communication devices like modems to computers. The most common interface for modems is the EIA-232 standard, which was originally called RS-232. In this scheme, computers or other similar devices are called DTE (data terminal equipment) and devices like modems are called DCE (data circuit-terminating equipment). The interface connector has multiple wires that are wired through to the opposite connector. Each pin represents a channel on which data is transferred or a specific control signal is sent. For example, there is a *request to send* line that the DTE uses to signal that it wants to transmit. The DCE uses a *clear to send* line to indicate that it is ready to receive. See "Serial Communication and Interfaces" for more information about this subject.

Transmission Media

There are a variety of transmission media, including copper cable, fiber-optic cable, and wireless systems. Media is affected by attenuation (loss of signal over distance), distortion, background noise, and other factors. Designers of communication systems take all of these factors into consideration when designing network systems such as Ethernet, token ring, FDDI (Fiber Distributed Data Interface), and others. Therefore, networks must be built within their specifications to avoid problems.

Computer data can be transmitted over RFs (radio frequencies) or light (usually infrared) in cases in which wires are impractical. These transmissions take place between a transmitter and a receiver within a single room or across town. Wireless networks provide unique solutions for campus and business park environments when links are required across roads, rivers, and physical space (in general, where it is not practical to run a cable). Terrestrial microwave systems are visible on the top of buildings and towers.

Optical networks and satellite communication systems provide other solutions. See "Microwave Communication," "Satellite Communication Systems," "Optical Networks," and "Wireless Communications" for more details. Also see "Cable and Cable Concepts" and "Network Design and Construction."

Data Link Protocols

The data link layer is the layer just above the hardware (physical) layer in the OSI protocol stack. The protocols in this layer manage the flow of bits between connected systems. Packets from upper layers are framed and sent across the data link. Flow controls and error correction techniques are also used. The data link layer handles point-to-point or point-to-multipoint links. In the OSI protocol stack, the higher-level Network layer handles connections across multiple router-connect data links.

See "Data Link Protocols" for more information.

Framing

Framing provides a controlled method for transmitting bits across a physical medium. It provides error control and may provide data retransmission services, depending on the type of service. A block of bits is framed with a header and a checksum is appended so the frame can be checked for corruption. If a frame is corrupted or lost, only that frame needs to be resent rather than the entire set of data.

Frames have a specific structure, depending on the data link protocol in use. The frame structure for a popular data link protocol called HDLC (High-Level Data Link Control) is pictured in Figure D-6. Note that the Information field is where data is placed, and it is variable in length. An entire packet of information may be placed into the Information field. The Beginning Flag field indicates the start of the frame. The Address field holds the address of the destination, and the Control field describes whether the Information field holds data, commands, or responses. The FCS field contains error-detection coding.

See "Framing in Data Transmissions" for more information.

Error Detection and Control

The data link layer is also responsible for error detection and control. One error control method is to detect errors and then request a retransmission. Another method is for the receiver to detect an error and then rebuild the frame. This latter method requires that enough additional information be sent with the frame so the receiver can rebuild it if an error is detected. This method is used when retransmissions are impractical (i.e., transmitting information to a space probe comes to mind).

It is often inefficient to perform error recovery in the data link layer, so many network implementations rely on upper-level protocols for this task. In most cases, the data link layer is used to deliver data as fast and efficiently as possible without performing extensive data recovery. Upper-layer protocols provide recovery services.

These techniques are discussed further under "Error Detection and Correction."

Flow Control

A data transmission can be thought of as water flowing through a hose that fills up a bucket at the receiver. The receiver draws from the bucket, but some method is needed to cut back the

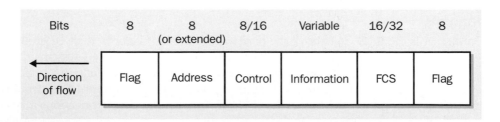

Figure D-6.   *HDLC frame format*

flow so the bucket doesn't overflow. In this analogy, the bucket represents data buffers that the receiver uses to hold incoming data that must be processed. The buffers on some NICs (network interface cards) are large enough to hold an entire incoming transmission. If the buffers overflow, frames are usually dropped, so it is useful for the receiver to have some way to tell the sender to slow down or stop sending frames. See "Acknowledgments," "Congestion Control Mechanisms," and "Flow-Control Mechanisms" for more information.

Network Access and Logical Link Control for Shared LANs

Access methods are necessary on networks that are shared by multiple devices. Only one device can transmit on the network at a time, so a medium access control method is needed to provide arbitration.

In the local area network environments defined by the IEEE, medium access protocols reside in a sublayer of the data link layer called the MAC (Medium Access Control) sublayer. The MAC sublayer sits below the LLC sublayer, which provides the data link control for any installed MAC drivers below it. The subdivision of the layers can be seen in Figure D-7.

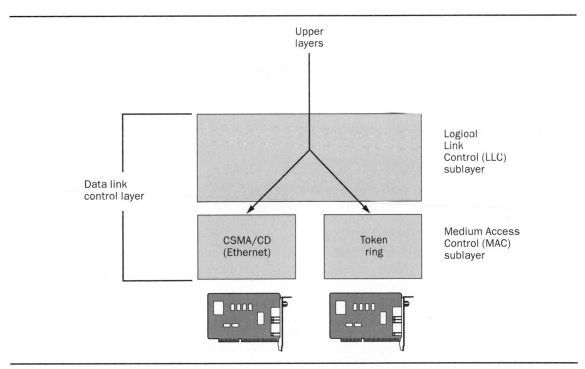

Figure D-7. *The data link layer consists of two sublayers: MAC (Medium Access Control) and LLC (Logical Link Control)*

The MAC sublayer supports a variety of different network types, each of which has a specific way of arbitrating access to the network. Three possible access methods are as follows:

■ **Carrier sense methods** With this technique, devices listen on the network for transmissions and wait until the line is free before transmitting their own data. If two stations attempt to transmit at the same time, both devices back off and wait a random amount of time before retransmitting.

■ **Token access methods** A token ring network forms a logical ring on which each transmission travels around the ring from station to station. Only a station that has possession of a special *token* can transmit.

■ **Reservation methods** In this scheme, every transmitting device has a specific slot of time or frequency allotted to it. TDM (time division multiplexing) is an example. A device can choose to place data in the slot for transmission. This technique can waste bandwidth if a device has nothing to transmit.

Refer to "Data Link Protocols," "MAC (Medium Access Control)," "Medium Access Control Methods," and "Multiplexing" for more information.

Bridging

A bridge is a device that connects two or more network segments into a single LAN. All the devices on the new joined LAN can communinicate with one another, but the bridge provides filtering features that prevent unwanted traffic from one segment from propagating to the other segment. A bridge is often used to divide a large LAN into two separate network segments. If the LAN is an Ethernet network, the bridge creates one broadcast domain and two collision domains. In Ethernet, a collision domain with fewer computers is better, so dividing a network with a bridge is advantageous. Note that switches (discussed next) are basically multiport bridges. See "Bridges and Bridging," "Broadcast Domain," and "Collisions and Collision Domains."

Switching

As mentioned, a bridge can be used to split a LAN into two segments, which effectively makes two smaller collision domains. A switch is a device that expands on this concept. Whereas a bridge typically has two ports to join two LAN segments, a switch has an array of ports for joining more than two segments. Figure D-8 illustrates how a switch provides bridging functions for multiple hubs. Each hub is a collision domain, but the entire network shown is a single broadcast domain. Each switch port is essentially a separate LAN segment that can be "bridged" to any other port on-the-fly by the internal circuitry in the switch. See "Switching and Switched Networks."

All of the benefits of bridging apply as mentioned in the preceding section.

Most switching devices provide a way to configure VLANs (virtual LANs). When building networks with switches, there is a tendency to build one large flat network instead of multiple distinct LANs (i.e., all nodes are part of the same broadcast network). VLAN techniques can be used to create virtual LANs in a flat switched environment. For example, if the hubs in Figure D-8 are replaced with VLAN-capable switches, workstations A and D could be configured into a VLAN; and workstations B, E, and H could be configured into another VLAN. Broadcasts from A are heard by D, and broadcasts from B are heard by E and H. A router is then needed to send packets between the VLANs. Refer to "VLAN (Virtual LAN)" for more details.

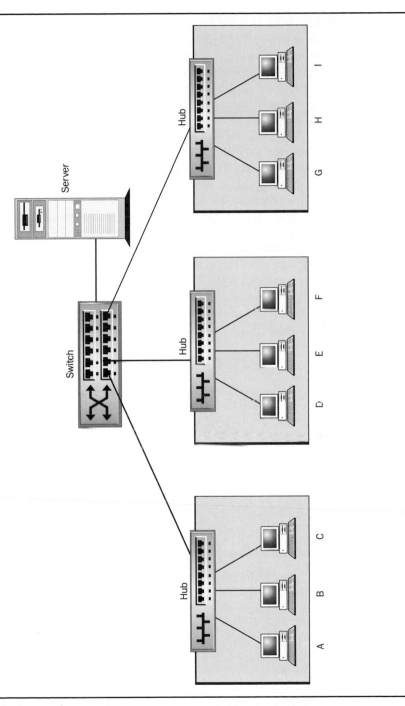

Figure D-8. *A switched network*

Routing, Internetworking, and the Network Layer

While a bridge joins two separate LAN segments into a single broadcast domain (or splits a large LAN into two or more distinct collision domains), a router provides internetworking capabilities. At the bridge level, information is transmitted to other systems in frames (frames are defined in the data link layer). At the router level, information must be packaged in packets that contain a target network address, and then forwarded across a router boundary. Routers join networks into internetworks.

At one time, you could mail a letter to someone in the same city by writing the address and the word "City" under the address. But if a letter has an "intercity" address, you'll need to write a city and ZIP code on the envelope. Likewise, an *internetwork* consists of many interconnected networks. The Internet is the largest internetwork. To send packets among different networks, a *hierarchical* naming scheme is required, one that identifies each of the networks with a name or number that can be used for routing purposes. The ZIP code scheme does this for the postal system. IP (Internet Protocol) is an internetwork addressing and routing protocol.

In Figure D-9, LANs are attached to routers and the routers form a mesh of interconnected paths over which packets may travel to get to their destinations. Note that any router and attached LAN in the network may be reached from any other point.

See the following topics for more information about internetworking: "Best-Effort Delivery Services," "Datagrams and Datagram Services Fragmentation and Reassembly," "Internetworking," "IP (Internet Protocol)," "Network Architecture," "Packets and Packet Switching," "Routers," "Routing," and "Routing on the Internet" (for historical information and trends).

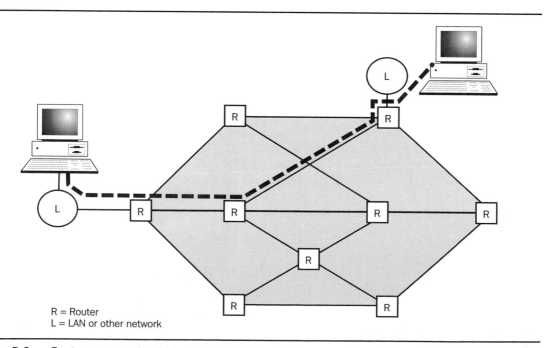

R = Router
L = LAN or other network

Figure D-9.   *Routers are used to build networks with multiple connection points and redundant paths.*

Transport Layer Services

The transport layer provides connection-oriented services, meaning that two systems can establish a session over which they engage in a "conversation" about the status of a data exchange. While a connection takes time to set up and adds some overhead to a data transmission, it provides services that guarantee to the sender that the receiver has received all of the data it has sent. The sender transmits a set of packets, and the receiver acknowledges that it has received the packets. If the receiver fails to acknowledgement receipt, the sender retransmits the packets. Session controls also provide flow control to prevent from overrunning the receiver or, in some cases, the network.

Figure D-10 illustrates how a transport layer session is a logical end-to-end connection that spans intermediate devices like routers. The two peer transport layers talk to one another across the connection-oriented virtual circuit.

The transport layer provides reliable *connection-oriented* services. For example, if a network link should temporarily fail, a connection-oriented session does not immediately give up the connection, but attempts to keep it alive until the underlying link is reestablished. Once the session is reestablished, data transmission continues from where it was interrupted. Refer to "Transport Protocols and Services" for more information.

The Application Layer

Applications that run at the highest level of the protocol stack are not really involved in communications, but they do use communication services and implement features in their user interfaces that take advantage of the underlying network. Network file-sharing services

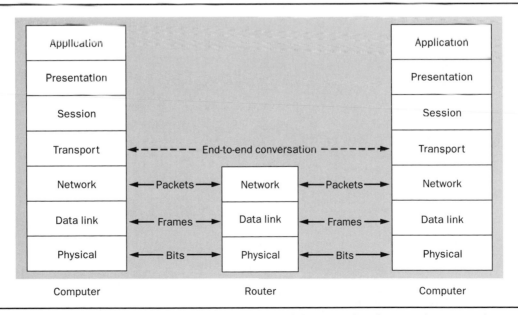

Figure D-10. *The transport layer can engage in end-to-end "conversations" across internetworks.*

like NCP (NetWare Core Protocol), NFS (Network File System) in the UNIX environment, or SMB (Server Message Blocks) in the Windows environment are specifically designed to use network services so that users can share files over networks.

In the TCP/IP environment, Sockets API provides a programming interface between applications and underlying network services. Also see "RPC (Remote Procedure Call)," "API (Application Programming Interface)," and "Distributed Applications."

Linktionary!—Tom Sheldon's Encyclopedia of Networking updates	http://www.linktionary.com/d/datacomm.html
Data communications course by Brian Brown	http://www.cit.ac.nz/smac/dc100www/dc_000.htm
Dwight Baker's tutorials links list (click Computers)	http://www.wizard.com/users/baker/public_html/
Data communication course at University of Aberdeen	http://www.erg.abdn.ac.uk/users/gorry/course/syllabus.html
Data communication topics at Optimized Engineering	http://www.optimized.com/COMPENDI/TabOfCon.htm
RAD data communication topics	http://www.rad.com/networks/tutorial.htm
3Com networking resources page	http://www.3com.com/technology/
IBM Redbooks	http://www.redbooks.ibm.com/
Network Magazine.com tutorials	http://www.networkmagazine.com/static/tutorial/index.html
Cisco documentation related to internetworking	http://www.cisco.com/univercd/cc/td/doc/cisintwk/
Web ProForum Data Communications and Telecommunication Tutorial	http://www.iec.org/tutorials/
Data communication links at ITPRC	http://www.itprc.com/
Introduction to serial communication	http://www.taltech.com/introserial.htm

Data Compression
See Compression Techniques.

Data Encoding
See Signals.

Data Encryption
See Cryptography; Security.

Data Link Layer, OSI Model

In the OSI (Open Systems Interconnection) model, the data link layer sits just above the physical layer. Therefore, it defines the protocols that directly interact with the physical components of the link, such as the network adapters and cable. It frames data and controls the flow of information across the link. Originally, data link protocols were designed for point-to-point links, and this is still the primary way that communication is handled, although shared LANs such as Ethernet require additional medium access control protocols to arbitrate access to the shared medium.

Related Entries   Data Link Protocols; Network Architecture; *and* OSI (Open Systems Interconnection) Model

Data Link Protocols

Often called layer 2 protocols, data link protocols exist in the protocol layer just above the physical layer relative to the OSI protocol model. Data link protocols provide communication between two devices. Because there are many different ways to connect devices, there are many different data link protocols. The defining factors are

- Dedicated point-to-point links between two devices, such as modem, bridges, or routers
- Shared media links in which multiple devices share the same cable (i.e., Ethernet LAN)

The PPP (Point-to-Point Protocol) that people use to connect to the Internet via a dial-up modem is an example of a data link protocol. Because the link between two systems is point to point, the bits are always delivered from sender to receiver in order. Also, unlike shared-media LANs in which multiple stations attempt to use the network, there is no contention.

Data link protocols may provide any of the following services:

- **Framing**   Data is broken up into frames that are transmitted as independent units. If errors are detected in a frame, it is only necessary to retransmit that frame.
- **Session setup and termination**   For reliable services, session control messages are used by end systems to exchange status information about the session.
- **Error detection**   Determines whether a frame has been delivered accurately. A checksum is calculated on a frame by the sender, and the receiver must perform the same calculation and come up with the same checksum. If not, the frame is considered corrupted. If reliable services are being used, the frame is retransmitted. For nonreliable services, the frame is dropped and upper-layer protocols are relied on to handle the problem.
- **Addressing on a multipoint medium such as a LAN**   A computer's address is usually the hardwired address of the NIC (network interface card).
- **Flow control**   A technique that prevents the sender from sending more, overflowing the receiver with more data than it can handle.

Reliable services were essential in the days of dumb terminals that did not have the capabilities to perform error or frame checking. Today, end systems have their own processing power, so reliability services are not essential in the network itself. Instead, reliable services are executed on end systems. TCP is a reliable transport layer protocols that can replace network-level reliability services.

Common Data Link Protocols

The most common data link level protocols are listed here with a short description. You will find more information about each protocol under appropriate headings in this book.

- **SDLC (Synchronous Data Link Protocol)**   This protocol was originally developed by IBM as part of IBM's SNA (Systems Network Architecture). It was used to connect remote devices to mainframe computers at central locations in either point-to-point (one-to-one) or point-to-multipoint (one-to-many) connections.

- **HDLC (High-Level Data Link Control)**   This protocol is based on SDLC and provides both a best-effort unreliable service and a reliable service. It is used with various serial interface protocols defined in the physical layer, such as EIA/TIA-232, V.24, V.35, and others.

- **SLIP (Serial Line Interface Protocol)**   SLIP is a data link control facility for transmitting IP packets, usually between an ISP (Internet service provider) and a home user over a dial-up link. SLIP has some limitations, including a lack of any error-detection and correction mechanisms. It is up to higher-layer protocols to perform these checks. Used over much of the same serial interfaces as HDLC.

- **PPP (Point-to-Point Protocol)**   PPP provides the same functionality as SLIP (i.e., it is commonly used for Internet connections over dial-up lines); but it is a more robust protocol that can transport not only IP, but also other types of packets. Frames contain a field that identifies the type of protocol being carried (IP, IPX, and so on). It is used over much of the same serial interfaces as HDLC.

- **LAP (Link Access Procedure)**   LAP has reliability service features and comes in three varieties. LAPB (LAP Balanced) is a protocol that provides point-to-point connections on X.25 packet-switched networks. LAPD (LAP D-Channel) provides the data link control over the D channel of an ISDN (Integrated Services Digital Network) connection. LAPF (LAP Frame-Mode Bearer Services) provides the data link for frame relay networks.

- **Frame Relay**   LAP used with X.25 is highly reliable, but it also has high overhead. Frame relay does away with the reliability services (i.e., error-correction mechanisms are removed) to improve throughput.

- **LLC (Logical Link Control)**   The IEEE (Institute of Electrical and Electronic Engineers) defines this protocol in its 802.x family of networks standards. The ANSI FDDI standard also uses this protocol. LLC is discussed further in the next section.

LAN Data Link Controls

The IEEE (Institute of Electrical and Electronics Engineers) has defined a number of LAN technologies in the data link layer, including Ethernet, Fast Ethernet, Gigabit Ethernet, and token ring. You can refer to related headings in this book for more information.

The actual data link layer is split into two sublayers, called the MAC (Medium Access Control) sublayer and the LLC (Logical Link Control) sublayer, as shown in Figure D-11. The lower MAC layer defines the media access method, which can be CSMA/CD (carrier sense multiple access/collision detection), token ring, or other IEEE physical interface. The LLC sublayer provides a way for the network layer to communicate with one of these protocols.

Data link layer devices include bridges and switches, which are discussed elsewhere in this book. Refer to "Bridges and Bridging" and "Switching and Switched Networks" for more information.

Frame relay is a high-speed data link protocol. It uses LAPF (Link Access Procedure for Frame-Mode Bearer Services). See "Frame Relay" for more information. ATM (Asynchronous Transfer Mode) is a cell-based data link–level service. See "ATM (Asynchronous Transfer Mode)" for more information.

Related Entries   Access Method, Network; Asynchronous Communications; Connection Establishment; Connection-Oriented and Connectionless Services; Data Communication Concepts; Data Link Layer, OSI (Open Systems Interconnection) Model; Encapsulation; Flow Control Mechanisms; Framing in Data Transmissions; HDLC (High-Level Data Link Control); LAN (Local Area Network); LAP (Link Access Procedure); LLC (Logical Link Control); Logical Links; MAC (Medium Access Control); Medium Access Control Methods; Network Concepts; Point-to-Point Communications; PPP (Point-to-Point Protocol); SDLC (Synchronous Data Link Control); Serial Communication and Interfaces; *and* Synchronous Communications

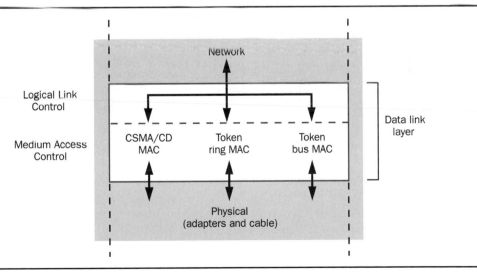

Figure D-11.   *The IEEE sublayers for LANs within the data link layer*

Linktionary!—Tom Sheldon's Encyclopedia
of Networking updates

http://www.linktionary.com/d/data_link.html

Data link protocols tutorial at University
of Aberdeen

http://www.erg.abdn.ac.uk/users/gorry/course/
syllabus.html

Data link layer protocols

http://www.protocols.com/protoc.htm

Data link protocol discussions at Optimized
Engineering

http://www.optimized.com/COMPENDI/
TabOfCon.htm

Cisco internetworking technology overviews

http://www.cisco.com/univercd/cc/td/doc/
cisintwk/ito_doc/

RAD Communications HDLC tutorial

http://www.rad.com/networks/1994/hdlc/
hdlc.htm

Synchronous Data Link Control and Derivatives

http://www.ics.muni.cz/cisco/data/doc/cintrnet/
ito/55172.htm

Data Management

Data management is concerned with the distribution of data to users and the protection of that data from loss such as fire, theft, or unauthorized access. Data management includes these areas:

- **Data protection**   Protecting data from catastrophic events, theft, or similar problems using archiving, backup, and other techniques. See "Backup and Data Archiving" and "Data Protection."

- **Data availability**   Making sure that data is available to users. See "Fault Tolerance and High Availability" and "Data Center Design."

- **Data migration**   Similar to archiving, but provides a way for users to quickly access files that have been archived. See "Data Migration" and "Storage Management Systems."

- **Data warehousing**   Data warehousing uses data summarization techniques to make large volumes of data available in a form that is easily accessible to data clients. See "Data Warehousing." A related topic is "SAN (Storage Area Network)."

- **DBMS (database management system)**   A database is a file that contains records with information in fields. A DBMS is a complete package that provides a query language and provides access to the data. See "DBMS (Database Management System)."

- **Distributed and replicated data**   Distributed data is stored on multiple servers across a network. The data is usually in the form of a database that is automatically replicated (copied) to other locations where it is easily accessible by users at those locations. See "DBMS (Database Management System," "Replication," and "Web Cabling."

- **Redundancy**   Redundancy methods are used to protect systems from failure, to protect data from loss and corruption, and to ensure that communication systems stay online and provide a required amount of performance. See "Redundancy."

- **Security**   User access rights, directory rights, and file rights all deal with restricting user access to specific files, directories, and servers. See "Security."

Linktionary!—Tom Sheldon's Encyclopedia   http://www.linktionary.com/d/data_management.html
of Networking updates

Data Mart

A data mart is a data warehouse for a single department or division of a company, as compared to a full-blown data warehouse, which attempts to store and make available all the data a company has available. Because full-blown data warehouses are difficult to implement, many companies start with data marts and then combine those data marts into data warehouses at a later date.

A data mart will have anywhere from 50 to 300 GB of data, while a data warehouse will house terabytes of data. A data mart is subject specific and usually departmental, while a data warehouse is a repository for an entire enterprise's data. Data marts are simpler to build (less than one year), while data warehouses are complex undertakings that take over a year to build. The cost of a data mart is in the thousands of dollars, while the cost of a data warehouse is in the millions of dollars.

A company called Appsco Software Ltd. claims its software makes data mart construction easy. AppsMart is a rapid application development tool that simplifies data mart construction using most popular SQL Server database applications.

Related Entries   Client/Server Computing; Clustering; Data Management; Data Migration; Data Mining; Data Protection; Data Warehousing; DBMS (Database Management System); IBM Host Connectivity; Multitiered Architectures; NAS (Network Attached Storage); OLAP (Online Analytical Processing); SAN (Storage Area Network); Servers; SQL (Structured Query Language); Storage Management Systems; Storage Systems; *and* Transaction Processing

 Linktionary!—Tom Sheldon's Encyclopedia of   http://www.linktionary.com/d/datamart.html
Networking updates

The Data Warehousing Institute	http://www.dw-institute.com
The International Data Warehousing Association	http://www.idwa.org
DM Review Magazine	http://www.data-warehouse.com/
Larry Greenfield's Data Warehousing Information Center (be sure to see the "White Papers" section)	http://pwp.starnetinc.com/larryg/index.html
Web ProForums (see data warehousing topics)	http://www.iec.org/tutorials/index.html
Washington University data warehousing links	http://www.cait.wustl.edu/infosys/infosys.html

Data Migration

Data migration is an archiving process that moves little-used or unused files to a secondary storage system, such as magnetic tape or optical disk. The files are typically imaged documents or historical information that needs to be readily accessible at any time in the future. Migration works in conjunction with backup strategies, and regular backups are still required.

Migration (and demigration) is a process that moves files off valuable high-speed magnetic disk space and onto secondary, high-volume media—primarily optical disk. Files remain available offline, but are accessible to users over the network.

This is accomplished by keeping a list of names for archived files in a directory on the primary media. When users need an archived file, they look in this directory, find the file, and open it as normal. The file is then *demigrated* from secondary storage (optical disk) to primary storage (magnetic disk). This process happens in the background, and users may not be aware that the file has been demigrated from optical disk. When users are done with the file, the file is migrated back to secondary storage. This migration can take place immediately, after a specific amount of time, or at the discretion of users or network administrators.

The Novell NetWare High Capacity Storage System (HCSS) is a data-archiving system that supports an offline optical jukebox storage device. A jukebox is an autochanger device that can select from a stack of rewritable optical disks. The HCSS system migrates files marked by users and network administrators and demigrates files as they are requested by users. Except for a slight delay in access, there is little indication that a file has been demigrated.

Related Entries   Backup and Data Archiving; Data Protection; Disaster Planning and Recovery; Fault Management; Fault Tolerance and High Availability; Imaging; Jukebox Optical Storage Devices; Mirroring; Optical Libraries; Replication; Storage Management Systems; *and* Storage Systems

 Linktionary!—Tom Sheldon's Encyclopedia   http://www.linktionary.com/d/data_management.html
of Networking updates

Data Mining

Data mining is about finding new information within existing data. Patterns, relationships, correlations, and dependencies are located by analyzing data using a variety of tools and techniques. Data mining has grown in popularity as computers and software have become available to handle the task.

Large amounts of data from a variety of sources are usually analyzed in this way. An organization might be able to extract new data out of its existing data by correlating it to a database obtained from some other source. For example, a customer database might provide new information if combined with a database from another source that contains additional information about those same customers. Mining may bring out unseen information beyond the basic relationships of the combined data. But data mining's potential goes beyond customer databases. Scientific databases are a prime candidate. For example, geological information can be "mined" to find potential mineral and oil sites!

 Linktionary!—Tom Sheldon's Encyclopedia   http://www.linktionary.com/d/data_mining.html
of Networking updates

A report on data mining   http://www.cs.usask.ca/homepages/grads/mgs310/
                                                 Cmpt826S3/node5.html

techguide.com white papers   http://www.techguide.com

Knowledge Discovery Nuggets Web site   http://www.kdnuggets.com/

IBM's Quest data mining project	http://www.almaden.ibm.com/cs/quest/
IBM's Business Intelligence	http://www4.ibm.com/software/data/busn-intel/
Information Discovery, Inc.	http://www.datamining.com/
Intellix data mining software	http://www.intellix.com/

Data Protection

Besides people, data is the most important asset to most organizations. Everything else can be replaced. If systems are destroyed, you can replace hardware in a day, but you can't bring your network back up and running if you don't have proper data backups. In addition, if your company is like most, even a day of downtime is intolerable, and thousands or millions of dollars could be lost while a system is not operating. The following list outlines some measures for protecting systems and data:

- **Data backup**   Data backup is essential, whether data is copied to other hard drives, tapes, optical disks, or even systems in other locations. See "Backup and Data Archiving."

- **Theft protection**   Theft of equipment can cause serious downtime, even if data has been backed up, considering replacement and reconfiguration costs. You can bolt equipment to desktops and floors, lock equipment in special rooms, and hire staff to look over equipment 24 hours a day. See "Security."

- **Protecting against fire and natural disasters**   Consider installing special fire-prevention equipment, such as halon gas systems, to reduce fire loss. To protect against natural disasters, consider what is necessary to protect the physical infrastructure. Alternative data centers may be necessary. Gasoline-powered generators can supply power to servers and workstations when electricity is cut off.

- **Recovery**   In the event of a physical security breach, hacker attack, fire, earthquake, or other disaster, you need to get systems back online as soon as possible. There are various resources available to help you do this. See "Disaster Planning and Recovery."

- **Management style**   There are advantages to both centralized management and distributed management. To centralize management, move network resources—servers, hubs, switches, routers, and other equipment—to central locations where trained staff can manage the systems in secure and protected areas. However, doing so puts you at greater risk of catastrophes such as earthquakes and fires. An alternative is to distribute network resources and automatically replicate data to remote sites on a regular basis. Use high-speed data links between the sites. See "Data Center Design" for more information.

- **Fault tolerance**   Network components should be protected against failure with techniques such as disk mirroring, disk duplexing, server duplexing, clustering, load balancing, replication, and a variety of other techniques, including the construction of multiple data centers. See "Fault Tolerance and High Availability" for more information.

- **Diskless devices**   Diskless workstations don't have disk drives, so users can't download valuable company data or upload information in an unsupervised environment. See "Diskless Workstations" and "Thin Clients."

- **Security**   Intruders may physically attack your system or gain access across unsecure networks. See "Security" for a discussion of this topic and links to other topics. Also see "Firewall" and "Virus and Antivirus Issues."

- **Administration**   Network administrators need to know all the ins and outs of network operating systems and their security features to protect against attacks, mismanagement, and data corruption or loss.

- **Network management**   Network management systems can spot problems before they occur and help improve performance so that users are better serviced. See "Network Management."

- **Training**   Properly trained users are your best resource against security breaches, attacks, mistakes, lost data, and so on.

- **Tracking and auditing**   Be sure logs and tracking utilities are enabled so you can track down problems after they occur. See "Auditing" and "Security Auditing."

Related Entries   Backup and Data Archiving; Clustering; Data Center Design; Data Migration; Data Warehousing; Disaster Planning and Recovery; Fault Tolerance and High Availability; Mirroring; Network Management; Power and Grounding Problems and Solutions; Redundancy; Replication; Security; SFT (System Fault Tolerance); Storage Management Systems; UPS (Uninterruptible Power Supply); *and* Virus and Antivirus Issues

Linktionary!—Tom Sheldon's Encyclopedia of Networking updates	http://www.linktionary.com/d/data_protection.html
Data Recovery, Inc. (recovery of hard drives and disaster planning)	http://www.datarecoveryinc.com/
Veritas	http://www.veritas.com/
Comdisco	http://www.comdisco.com/
Exabyte data recovery services	http://www.exabyte.com/suppserv/techsupp/recovery/in0230.html
Sun Microsystems document: Data Protection Solutions	http://www.sun.com/storage/white-papers/dataprotection.html
Network Appliance data protection strategies paper	http://www.netapp.com/tech_library/3066.html

Data Striping

See RAID (Redundant Arrays of Inexpensive Disks).

Data Switches

A device that links terminals, computers, and other computing devices to mainframe computers. They are basically concentrator devices that provide a way for a large number of devices to share a limited number of ports.

Related Entries   Cluster Controllers, IBM; Concentrator Devices; Ethernet; Network Connection Technologies; Switched Fabrics and Bus Design; *and* Switching and Switched Networks

Data Transfer Rates

Data transfer rates are a measure of the amount of digital information that can be transmitted through a channel per second. Data transfer rates are also referred to as *throughput* rates. A number of factors determine data transfer rates, including bandwidth of the line, transmission impairments, distance, media type, and so on.

Related Entries   Bandwidth; Cable and Wiring; Capacity; Channel; Delay, Latency, and Jitter; Electromagnetic Spectrum; Signals; *and* Throughput

Data Transmissions

There are an incredible number of ways to transmit data from one place to another. See "Data Communication Concepts" for a list of topics that provide a general overview of communications concepts. See "Network Connection Technologies" for a list of topics about the technologies available for communciations. These topics provide additional information:

- Cable and Wiring
- Data Communication Concepts
- Fiber-Optic Cable
- High-Speed/High-Performance Networking
- Internetworking
- LAN (Local Area Network)
- Microwave Communications
- Network Access Services
- Network Concepts
- Network Core Technologies
- Network Design and Construction
- Optical Networks
- Telecommunications and Telephone Systems
- WAN (Wide Area Network)
- Wireless Communications

Data Warehousing

Every day, organizations capture data that is essentially unavailable for use because there is no way to conveniently access, manipulate, and present it. Billions of bytes of data are essentially "locked up" on computer systems throughout an organization. *Data warehousing* defines strategies for making this data more accessible.

Industry analysts and system vendors long ago recognized that there are two types of information systems:

- **Operational systems**   These are the systems that handle day-to-day processes such as accounting, order entry, and inventory management. These are the systems that keep a business running.

- **Informational systems**   These are systems that people use to analyze data, make business management decisions, and plan for the future. These systems are often referred to as "executive management systems."

The important difference between the two systems for the purposes of this discussion is that operational systems deal with a specific set of data, such as the inventory, while information systems are concerned with extracting useful information from a variety of related information sources. Informational systems access and use data from the following information sources:

- **Legacy data systems**   The storehouse of data that an organization has collected over many years. Systems include older mainframe or minicomputer systems that run specific applications that are not easily accessible from more modern PC-based applications.

- **External data systems**   These are systems outside the organization, such as the Web servers or subscription data services, that provide a range of information (demographic data, economic trend data, product data, and so on).

- **Operational data systems**   As described earlier, operational data is the day-to-day data collected by and generated by accounting and other business systems.

A data warehouse can be thought of as a *three-tier system* in which a middle system provides usable data in a secure way to end users. On either side of this middle system are the end users and the back-end data stores. The data warehouse is typically made up of the following components, which are illustrated in Figure D-12:

- **Staging systems/data mart**   This is the place where selected data from back-end systems is stored for access by clients. The data is usually cleaned up and manipulated in a variety of ways before it is ready to be accessed, as discussed later. A data warehouse may consist of many data marts, one for each department in the company. While a data mart may store information extracted from a data warehouse, often data warehouses are built in stages by starting with departmental data marts and then combining the data marts.

- **Front-end client**   These are the end users who access data using PC-based applications that display data for analysis.

- **Middleware**   This is a layer of software that hides the differences between data management systems and allows clients to easily access those systems. See "DBMS (Database Management System)," "Middleware and Messaging," and "SQL (Structured Query Language)" for more information.

- **Messaging systems**   The data warehouse typically consists of multiple back-end systems and multiple clients. A message system is a delivery system that transports

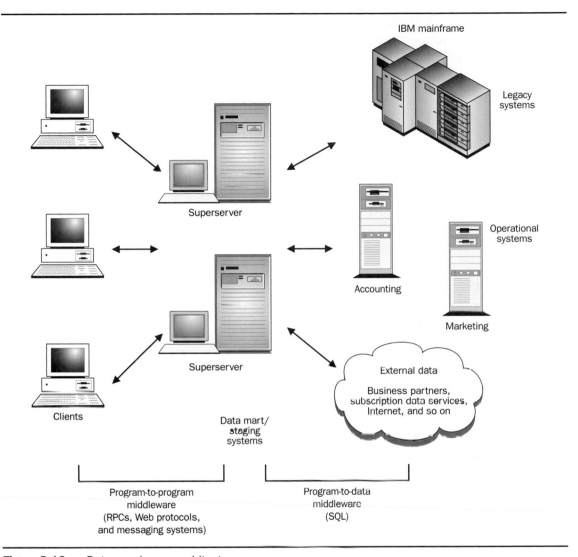

Figure D-12. *Data warehouse architecture*

requests and responses throughout the data warehouse. The messaging system uses the underlying network protocols and facilities to deliver information.

■ **Metadata**   This is information about the data in the data warehouse, much like the catalog cards in a library hold information about the books in the library. See "Metadata."

By looking at Figure D-12, you can see that clients have access to data stored on the data marts, although direct access to legacy, operational, or external systems is also possible. However, this staging approach provides a number of benefits, including security and client access to data that is tightly controlled by data analysts or data managers.

About Information in the Data Warehouse

The data warehouse can be thought of as a system that holds summary information from legacy, operational, or external data sources. Staging systems store only the latest information for read-only purposes. All data updates take place on operational systems, not on the staging system.

According to Prism Solutions (now Informix), there are different levels of summarization and detail in the data warehouse, as shown in Figure D-13 and explained here:

- Older detail data is historical or legacy data.

- Current detail data (typically operational data) is the most recent data. It is voluminous and requires extensive summarization to make it easily accessible.

- Lightly summarized data is data that has been distilled from the current detail data by a database analyst or some other process.

- Highly summarized data is compact and easily accessible by end users within specific departments.

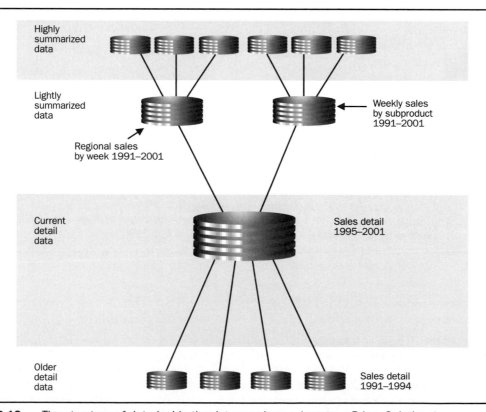

Figure D-13.   *The structure of data inside the data warehouse (courtesy Prism Solutions)*

It is assumed that data stored on legacy, operational, or external systems is encoded, structured, and stored in a number of different ways, and that over the years database designers have used their own conventions in building database structures. Therefore, the way that information is stored in one database is largely inconsistent with the way related information is stored in other databases.

When data is transferred to the staging systems, it must be "preprocessed" either by the database analysts or by applications specifically designed for the task. Processing involves extracting, cleaning, combining, altering, and manipulating data into new sets of data that are more relevant to end users. It may also include extensive integrity checking to ensure that end users access accurate and timely data.

A key feature of this process is to integrate data using common naming conventions and consistent attributes, coding, and structure. For example, date information from different databases may be in a variety of formats (Julian, *yymmdd*, *mmddyy*, and so on), but may be reformatted and stored in Julian format only on the staging system.

As mentioned, each department in a company may have its own staging system for lightly or highly summarized data. A database analyst usually handles the task of summarizing and extracting data from back-end systems and making it accessible to users. D2K, Inc. (http://www.d2k.com) calls these analysts "farmers," presumably because they work to extract data stored at the "server farm." The data farmers may use OLAP (online analytical processing) and "data mining" tools that help them correlate information, and discover interesting and meaningful relationships in the data. OLAP presents data as a multidimensional "cube" instead of the more traditional table format.

New and emerging software to support the data-warehousing concept can replace EIS (executive information systems) and DSS (decision support systems). These early systems did not benefit from the constant updating of data that can take place in a data warehouse and were limited in use to only a few decision makers.

The IDWA (International Data Warehousing Association) identifies a type of data warehouse it calls the "operational data warehouse." This warehouse offers dynamic access to back-end data that has been identified at the front-end system. The example it uses is a bank that has been called upon to identify all the assets of a particular company. The bank extracts relevant data from many different systems. The court then orders that all accounts be frozen. This is a problem if all the accounts are stored on many different legacy systems. Bank employees will need to close each account individually. With an operational data warehouse, all the accounts can be closed using the same software that was used to pull up the account information in the first place.

Planning and Building a Data Warehouse

An organization that decides to build a data warehouse faces the daunting task of making information available to users that is timely, accurate, and useful. There are many stories of misguided attempts to build data warehouses that end up providing inaccurate or inadequate information. Still, there is often no choice but to build a data warehouse. The alternative is to leave valuable data locked up on legacy systems.

There is a story about a company that built seven data warehouses. The first six were failed attempts that turned into learning experiences.

The process of building a data warehouse should start with a carefully planned strategy and a prototype. Before expensive hardware is purchased, developers should work closely with users to determine exactly what information is required on staging systems and how it will be used. This can often be done by building small systems that grow into full production systems.

Vendors have developed special systems for data warehousing. IBM has its Information Warehouse system. Parallel database systems are emerging that improve access to database systems. New data visualization tools (http://www.pyramid.com) has developed parallel processing systems specifically designed for this purpose.

The Web interface is perhaps the most important new aspect in data warehousing. A number of vendors, including D2K, Inc., are developing applications that deliver warehoused data to Web browsers. Push technologies are used to automatically provide subscribed users with the latest view of the data they are interested in. With Web technologies, it is only necessary to format data for display in a Web browser. Then users on any system, using any Web browser, can display the information.

Readers should check the Web sites listed at the end of this section for more information. There are many Web sites and white papers available on the topic from individuals and vendors. There are also many vendors' products that simplify the whole process.

Related Entries   Client/Server Computing; Clustering; Data Center Design; Data Management; Data Mart; Data Migration; Data Mining; Data Protection; DBMS (Database Management System); Distributed Object Computing; IBM Host Connectivity; Middleware and Messaging; Multitiered Architectures; NAS (Network Attached Storage); Object Technologies; OLAP (Online Analytical Processing); Redundancy; Replication; SAN (Storage Area Network); Servers; SQL (Structured Query Language); Storage Management Systems; Storage Systems; *and* Transaction Processing

Linktionary!—Tom Sheldon's Encyclopedia of Networking updates	http://www.linktionary.com/d/datawarehouse.html
The Data Warehousing Institute	http://www.dw-institute.com
The International Data Warehousing Association	http://www.idwa.org
DM Review Magazine	http://www.data-warehouse.com/
Larry Greenfield's Data Warehousing Information Center (be sure to see the "White Papers" section)	http://pwp.starnetinc.com/larryg/index.html
Data warehousing topics at WebProForums	http://www.webproforum.com/wpf_all.html
Washington University data warehousing links	http://www.cait.wustl.edu/infosys/infosys.html
Data warehousing links	http://juliet.stfx.ca/~rmackinn/dataware.htm

Database

An information storage system described under any one of the following topics, with "DBMS (Database Management System)" being the primary topic.

Related Entries   Client/Server Computing; Data Management; Data Mart; Data Mining; Data Warehousing; DBMS (Database Management System); Multitiered Architectures; OLAP (Online Analytical Processing); SQL (Structured Query Language); *and* Transaction Processing

Datagram and Datagram Services

A datagram is a unit of data in the network layers of the protocol stack. Like a message, it includes a destination network address so it can be forwarded across internetworks to a recipient. A datagram is a network layer protocol entity that encapsulates data from the upper transport layer, such as TCP segments. This is illustrated in Figure D-14 and described next.

- **Segment**   A unit of end-to-end transmission in the TCP protocol. It consists of a TCP header followed by application data. A segment goes inside an IP datagram.

- **IP datagram**   A unit of end-to-end transmission in the IP protocol. It consists of an IP header followed by the TCP segment.

- **Packet**   IP datagrams are subject to fragmentation. Packet is a generic way to refer to datagrams that are either whole or fragmented. Packets go inside frames.

- **Frame**   A unit of transmission in the data link layer, consisting of a frame header and a packet (IP datagram or IP datagram fragment).

A datagram is a package for carrying data across a packet-switched network. As mentioned, it is carried either whole or fragmented in data link layer frames (or cells,

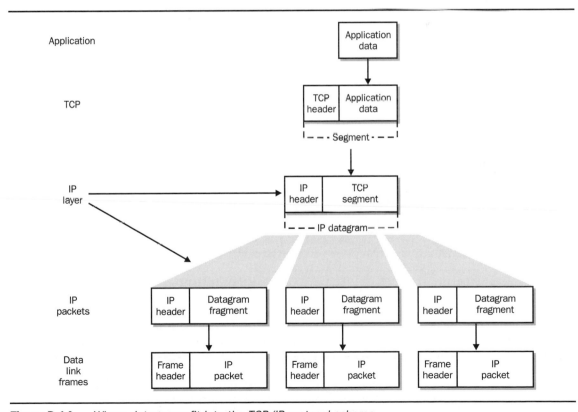

Figure D-14.   *Where datagrams fit into the TCP/IP protocol scheme*

as in ATM). It is transmitted using connectionless, best-effort delivery techniques. IPX (Internetwork Packet Exchange) and IP (Internet Protocol) are datagram services.

In contrast, SPX (Sequenced Packet Exchange) and TCP (Transmission Control Protocol) are connection-oriented services that provide additional reliability services on top of IPX and IP, respectively. Applications that don't need reliability services go through UDP rather than TCP, but both UDP and TCP use the underlying IP datagram services to move information across router-connected internetworks.

The concept that a reliable protocol such as TCP uses an unreliable protocol like IP is often confusing. One can think of a postal carrier as a datagram service provider. Her job is to delivery packets (letters). If you want a confirmation that a letter has been delivered, you need to fill out a receipt confirmation slip. That's an enhanced service provided by the post office. TCP is an enhanced service that applications can choose to use if they need delivery confirmations.

Figure D-15 illustrates the difference between the IP datagram and the TCP segment. Note that IP datagrams have fields for IP source and destination addresses, along with flags and a

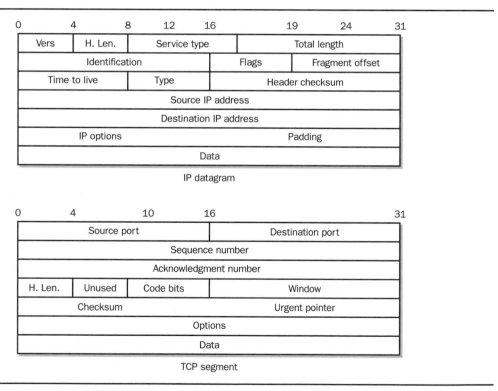

Figure D-15.   *Comparison of IP datagram to TCP segment*

Checksum field (to determine if a packet is corrupted). This information is all related to moving information across a network. A TCP segment, on the other hand, contains fields for information that is used to provide reliable delivery (sequence numbers and acknowledgement numbers), as well as port numbers, which identify the application processes that connect across the TCP virtual circuit.

There has always been a rift between the telecommunication engineers who advocated cells and the data communication engineers who advocated packet switching. The outcome of this rift was summarized by Charles N. Judice writing in *IEEE Communications Magazine*, August 2000:

> I submit that the communication industry lost it when the computer guys could not get their 1000-byte packets into ATM standards. While those of us with the "Bell Shaped Heads" thought we won a great compromise in establishing 53 bytes as the ATM packet size, what we really did was demonstrate to the computer industry that we had little understanding of their requirements or the implications of their design. So rather than design the next-generation network with us, they just kept making their datagram network work harder and faster.

Related Entries   Best-Effort Delivery Services; Connection-Oriented and Connectionless Services; Data Communication Concepts; Encapsulation, Fragmentation, and Reassembly; Framing in Data Transmissions; Internet Protocol Suite; Internetworking; IP (Internet Protocol); Network Architecture; Network Concepts; Network Layer Protocols; Packets and Packet Switching Networks; Reliable Data Delivery Services; Routing; TCP (Transmission Control Protocol); *and* UDP (User Datagram Protocol)

Linktionary!—Tom Sheldon's Encyclopedia   http://www.linktionary.com/d/datagram.html
of Networking updates

Datagrams versus virtual circuits information   http://www.erg.abdn.ac.uk/users/gorry/course/
at University of Aberdeen   intro-pages/datagrams.html

DAV (Distributed Authoring and Versioning)

The Web was originally designed as a read-only medium in which browsers are used to display prepublished content at Web sites. But from the beginning, many people saw a need for authors to be able to edit Web content from remote sites. For example, if you have an ISP host your Web site, you may need to edit Web pages on your own computer, and then copy the updated files to the ISP's host server using FTP. WebDAV is a set of extensions that defines how to perform distributed authoring and versioning directly on Web pages.

Related Entries   Collaborative Computing; Document Management; HTML (HyperText Markup Language); Hypermedia and Hypertext; Information Publishing; Metadata; RDF (Resource Description Language); Search and Discovery Services; Service Advertising and Discovery; URN (Universal Resource Naming); Web Technologies and Concepts; WebDAV; Workflow Management; *and* XML (eXtensible Markup Language)

Linktionary!—Tom Sheldon's Encyclopedia   http://www.linktionary.com/w/webdav.html
of Networking updates

DAVIC (Digital Audio Visual Council)

DAVIC is an audiovisual industry association composed of over 157 companies, government agencies, and research organizations around the world. DAVIC creates industry standards for end-to-end interoperability of broadcast and interactive digital audiovisual information, and of multimedia communication over satellite, fiber, radio, and cable distribution systems.

DAVIC's original goal was to promote interactive digital audiovisual applications and services by "promulgating specifications of open interface and protocols that maximize interoperability across geographic, industry, services, and application boundaries," according to DAVIC's Web site.

DAVIC is working to converge its specifications with the Internet to allow IP networking over cable TV systems. DAVIC is also developing initiatives for mobile and portable multimedia.

But while the DAVIC specification is popular in Europe, DOCSIS (Data Over Cable Interface Specification) has become more important in the United States. DOCSIS is the result of work done by MCNS (Multimedia Cable Network System Partners Ltd.). For more information about these standards, refer to "Cable (CATV) Data Networks."

DAVIC defines the following parts:

- Part 1   Description of Digital Audiovisual Functionalities
- Part 2   System Reference Models and Scenarios
- Part 3   Service Provider System Architecture
- Part 4   Delivery System Architecture and Interfaces
- Part 5   Service Consumer System Architecture
- Part 6   Management Architecture and Protocols
- Part 7   High and Midlayer Protocols
- Part 8   Lower-Layer Protocols and Physical Interfaces
- Part 9   Information Representation
- Part 10 Basic Security Tools
- Part 11 Usage Information Protocols
- Part 12 System Dynamics, Scenarios and Protocol Requirements
- Part 13 Conformance and Interoperability
- Part 14 Contours: Technology Domain

DAVIC is working to bring the benefits of high-quality and reliable, guaranteed multimedia services from a many-to-one toward a (mass) one-to-one topology. DAVIC's next initiative will be toward mobile and portable multimedia, adding this network platform to the existing list of satellite, fiber, radio, and cable distribution systems across which interoperability of interactive services is guaranteed.

More information about DAVIC may be found at the Web site listed at the end of this topic, including white papers and multimedia presentation.

Related Entries   Broadband Communications and Networking; Cable (CATV) Data Networks; Communication Services and Providers; DBS (Direct Broadcast Satellite); DOCSIS (Data Over Cable Service Interface Specification); DSL (Digital Subscriber Line); Fiber to the Curb/Fiber to the Home; HALO (High Altitude Long Operation); High-Speed/High-Performance Networking; Home Networking; Internet Connections; Last Mile Services; Local Loop, Multicasting; Network Access Services; Residential Broadband; Service Providers and Carriers; *and* Wireless Communications

 DAVIC, Digital Audio Video Council (DAVIC)   http://www.davic.org/

DB2, IBM

DB2 is a relational DBMS (database management system) from IBM. It first appeared on IBM mainframes and has had a long life of service. Today, DB2 is IBM's most important legacy database system and is available on all of its major platforms. SQL (Structured Query Language) has been the primary means of accessing data in DB2.

The latest incarnation of DB2 is DB2 Universal Database, a scalable, multimedia Web-enabled database that runs on Intel and UNIX platforms, as well as a variety of SMP (symmetrical multiprocessing) and MPP (massively parallel processing) environments. The product also supports Java and JDBC (Java Database Connectivity). It can also handle distributed multimedia data warehousing and includes database tools, World Wide Web connectivity, and multimedia object-relational support.

Related Entries   Client/Server Computing; Data Management; Data Mart; Data Mining; Data Warehousing; DBMS (Database Management System); DRDA (Distributed Relational Database Architecture); IBM Host Connectivity; OLAP (Online Analytical Processing); SQL (Structured Query Language); *and* Transaction Processing

 Linktionary!—Tom Sheldon's Encyclopedia   http://www.linktionary.com/d/dbms.html
of Networking updates

DB2 World Wide Web Connection   http://www.software.ibm.com/data/db2/www/

IBM DB2 Software Web site   http://www.software.ibm.com/data/db2/

International DB2 Users Group   http://www.idug.org/

DB2 Magazine Online   http://www.db2mag.com/

DBMS (Database Management System)

A DBMS is a software program that typically operates on a database server or mainframe system to manage structured data, accept queries from users, and respond to those queries. A typical DBMS has the following features:

- Provides a way to structure data as records, tables, or objects

- Accepts data input from operators and stores that data for later retrieval

- Provides query languages for searching, sorting, reporting, and other "decision support" activities that help users correlate and make sense of collected data

- Provides multiuser access to data, along with security features that prevent some users from viewing and/or changing certain types of information

- Provides data integrity features that prevent more than one user from accessing and changing the same information simultaneously

- Provides a data dictionary (metadata) that describes the structure of the database, related files, and record information

Most DBMS systems are client/server based and operate over networks. The DBMS is an engine that typically runs on a powerful server or cluster of servers, in a SAN (storage area network) environment or mainframe with a high-performance channel to a large data store. The DBMS accepts requests from clients that may require sorting and extracting data. Once the server has processed the request, it returns the information to the client.

There are a variety of back-end database systems, clients, and methods of access. Database middleware products are designed to provide a middle layer of software that hides the differences among databases. ODBC (Open Database Connectivity), originally designed by Microsoft, has been one of the most popular middleware products. The section "Database Connectivity" later in this topic discusses middleware. Also see the topic "Middleware and Messaging."

The common language for accessing most database systems is SQL (Structured Query Language), which is discussed under the main SQL heading, "SQL (Structured Query Language)." Z39.50 is an open ANSI standard that allows database searching and information retrieval among networked systems. See "Z39.50."

Metadata is information that describes data in a database. A raw data file would appear as a mass of letters, numbers, and symbols; but by knowing the format and structure of how that data is stored, you can display the data as records, fields, attributes, and elements with specific rules and properties (i.e., some fields are locked or the data is displayed a certain way). A metadata file provides this knowledge. Recall the Mars spacecraft that burned up in Mars orbit. The company that built the spacecraft was working with acceleration data in English units of pounds of force. NASA entered the data into a computer that assumed metric units called newtons. This was a tragic metadata error, in which the description of the data was misinterpreted. See "Metadata" for more information.

Most databases are operational databases, meaning that data going into the database is used in real time to support the ongoing activities of a business. A point-of-sale business accounting system is an example. As items are sold, the inventory database is updated and the inventory information is made available to the sales staff. The invoicing, order entry, and related systems are also updated.

Data analysts use OLAP (online analytical processing) systems to analyze database information in order to find trends or make business decisions. A *data warehouse* is a large-scale OLAP and/or data mining system that is specifically designed to extract, summarize, combine, clean up, and process information from a number of data sources—such as the operational databases, legacy (historical) databases, and online subscription databases—for the purpose of analysis. Metadata is especially important in this environment. See "Data Warehousing" for more information.

A *database server* is a computer attached to a network that runs a client/server DBMS (database management system). These systems may be superservers (multiprocessor systems), servers in a clustered arrangement, or even MPP (massively parallel processing) systems. Many systems are distributed, meaning that servers and databases are located in multiple physical locations on an enterprise network or the Internet. See "Clustering," "Distributed Computer Networks," "Servers," "Supercomputer," "SAN (Storage Area Network)," and "SAN (System Area Network)."

A recent trend is to put databases largely in memory on big servers, which eliminates disk latency. The acronym IMDS (in-memory database system) appears to be catching on. As memory drops in price, it becomes more feasible to put entire databases in memory. Busy Web servers benefit from this trend. Actually, the process can be quite complex. Data in memory that changes must be protected from loss, so it must be continually written to disk, and this should take place over two or more systems to provide fault tolerance. Check with vendors for more information.

Directory services are specialized types of databases that provide "lookup" services for people and resources on networks. The database contains objects and subobjects that are arranged hierarchically. Managers store information about people and resources in the directory and use it to manage resources. *Policies* may be stored in the database that define how and when users may access resources or, in the case of routers and switches, what their priority and/or bandwidth allocation will be. Network devices check with the database before allocating resources to users. See "Directory Services" and "Policy-Based Management" for more information.

Types of DBMS Systems

A simple database is a collection of records that contain fields of information. A simple name and address database is basically a *flat-file database*, since all the information can be stored in one file. Flat-file databases are usually inadequate for business applications. Instead, relational and/or object-oriented database systems are required, as described here.

With the Web, database vendors were forced to finally deal with a plethora of data types, not just structured data. When a Web user accesses a Web site, the server at the site must build dynamic pages based on the user's requests that include not only text, but images, sound, and even video. Most database vendors now provide hybrid RDBMS systems that provide storage for multimedia types. These systems are called object-relational databases or, more recently, *universal databases*. Microsoft's UDA (Universal Data Access) is a strategy for accessing information across any enterprise data source as discussed later in the section "Database Connectivity Tools."

RDBMS (Relational Database Management System)

An RDBMS is a system that stores data in multiple databases called *tables*. The tables can be related and combined in a number of ways to correlate and view data. A typical database for an accounting system might contain hundreds of tables that can potentially produce thousands of relationships. A common element, such as a customer number, may link information across the databases. A query for a particular customer may pull the customer's address from one database, an account balance from another, and some historical purchasing information from another.

The RDBMS is currently the most popular type of database. However, there is a growing need to store more than text and numbers—thus, the object-oriented DBMSs, as discussed next.

OODBMS (Object-Oriented Database Management System)

An object database is designed to handle a variety of different data types, including documents, images, audio, and video. The objects themselves store information that is used to access the object or define its properties. New object types can be created as necessary to define any type of information. This is in contrast to relational databases, in which procedures are designed into programs and data goes into the database. The program then works on the data in the database.

In an object-oriented database, procedures and data go together. An OODBMS consists of a model of all the data in the database. The database contains many different data types that can be defined in advance or at any time. Each data type can be assigned meaning that is relevant to the object it represents. There can be a class, such as "person," and subclasses of that class, such as "doctor," "lawyer," and "accountant." If a change is made to a class, the change is made to all objects in that class. Each class can have specific procedures associated with it, so programming and data manipulation are not separate. See "Object Technologies."

Distributed Database

A distributed computing system consists of data located at multiple sites. Users should be able to access that data without regard to its location. General guidelines for developing distributed database systems are listed here and were originally outlined by Chris J. Date, one of the designers of relational database systems:

- *Local autonomy* allows each site to maintain an independent nature so data and resources can be secured, protected, and managed by local authorities.

- *Noncentralization* eliminates central data sites that represent a single point of failure.

- *Continuous operation* provides services to users, even during backup.

- *Transparency* hides the location of the data from users so they don't need to be concerned where that data is or how to get to it.

- *Fragmentation* (partitioning) provides a way to split the database and store it at multiple sites.

- *Replication* provides a way to copy multiple fragments of the database to multiple sites.

- *Distributed query processing* provides a way for users to query remote sites using the best path to the site and the best resources to satisfy the query.

- *Distributed transaction processing* provides a way to ensure that writes to multiple databases are correctly written on all databases, or backed out if a failure occurs anywhere.

- *Hardware independence* implies support for multivendor computer systems and platforms.

- *Operating system independence* implies support for a number of operating systems.

- *Network independence* implies support for multiple network topologies and communication protocols.

■ *DBMS independence* allows users to access any database management system from their client application, as discussed in the next section.

Once data is distributed, transaction processing, fragmentation, and replication techniques are put in place to ensure the reliability, availability, and protection of data.

When data is distributed over many database servers, various protection mechanisms are required to ensure that data is properly written to all databases. For example, consider a customer account balance that is updated at three separate remote databases. If a connection to any database fails during the transaction write phase, the databases will be out of synchronization. Transaction processing solves this problem by monitoring the changes that must occur to all the databases involved. If any one of the writes fails, the transaction monitor backs them all out to ensure data integrity. See "Transaction Processing" for more details.

Partitioning is a method of splitting a database into related blocks of information, and *replication* is the process of copying those blocks to other locations. A master database is still maintained at one site, and a partition is a portion of that database that is replicated to another site. Partitioning and replication are used to provide fault tolerance and/or to make data physically available near users. See "Replication" for information about replicating entire databases or parts of databases to other locations in real time or by using a "publish and subscribe" model.

Object-oriented systems provide a unique solution for storing data and creating applications in enterprise environments. *Objects* are abstractions of real-world entities such as people in a customer database, invoices in an accounting system, or printers and servers in a network directory services database.

See "Object Technologies" and "Distributed Computer Networks" for more information.

Database Connectivity

In the early days of DBMSs, programmers spent a lot of time writing programs that allowed people to access data in a specific way on database systems. But users needed a better way to get at data, so query languages were developed that let users make requests directly to the database using commands (called *statements*) that were supposed to mimic spoken language. In the mid-1970s, IBM developed a query tool called SQL (Structured Query Language) that eventually became the recognized industry standard for database access. See "SQL (Structured Query Language)."

While SQL provided a standard for accessing databases, there were differences in the way each system was implemented. Database systems have traditionally been tied to a specific front-end interface that did not work with just any client-side application. One of the following programming interfaces is usually implemented:

■ **Embedded SQL**   In this approach, SQL statements are embedded into the source code of programs that are written in a host language, such as C. A typical embedded SQL program contains a number of SQL statements, but these statements cannot be directly compiled into C; so they are precompiled to make them compatible with the host language, and the program is then compiled for execution. The program can then operate directly with the database because the SQL statements are embedded in it.

■ **CLI (Call-Level Interface)**   With this approach, programs must call a set of external functions in an API library in order to work with the database. CLI is normally used when the client and server are on two different systems and the API is located on the client system. The client application makes a call to the API, and the API communicates with the DBMS.

It is usually the case that a client has a need to connect with many different back-end systems that may be from different vendors. In addition, clients need to access back-end data using common desktop applications such as Microsoft Access or Microsoft Excel. Given this, an interface is required that can transform client requests to match the target DBMS and that can provide a "universal" interface for any client application. This "middleware" layer must deal with a number of problems:

■ While SQL is a standard, each DBMS may implement SQL in a different way.

■ RDBMSs (relational DBMSs) often use different techniques for describing how information is stored in the database. This is often called "metadata" or the "data catalog."

■ Nearly every DBMS on the market uses different methods to transfer data and communicate information between the client and server, such as alerts, requests for data, and status information.

■ DBMSs typically use different IPC (interprocess communication) mechanisms to transport the messages just described. Some DBMSs use named pipes, some use TCP/IP sockets, and some use other methods.

Three-Tier Model

Database connectivity on the Web typically takes the form of the three-tier model shown in Figure D-16. The three-tier model consists of the presentation tier (Web browser), the business logic tier (Web server), and the data tier (back-end databases and mainframe systems). This model fully supports component software designs and a highly dynamic Web page construction. It is also scalable—additional servers can be added to the middle tier and the database tier to provide load balancing and handle increased Web user access.

The middle tier can provide a range of application services, such as transaction processing and monitoring functions, and it can host component software created with Java, ActiveX, and other technologies. A number of protocols for access to back-end data are discussed in an upcoming section. See "Middleware and Messaging" and "MOM (Message-Oriented Middleware)" for more information.

Middleware Application Servers

An application server is a "middle server" in a three-tiered architecture. Application servers interface with databases and information systems on the back end and clients on the front end. The servers may perform relatively simple functions, such as building Web pages on-the-fly with data obtained from back-end servers. The servers may also provide more sophisticated functions, such as transaction processing, shopping carts, and subscriber access functions for electronic commerce applications.

Application servers provide a variety of functions. They serve as a central hub where a variety of application services can take place, including message routing, object exchange,

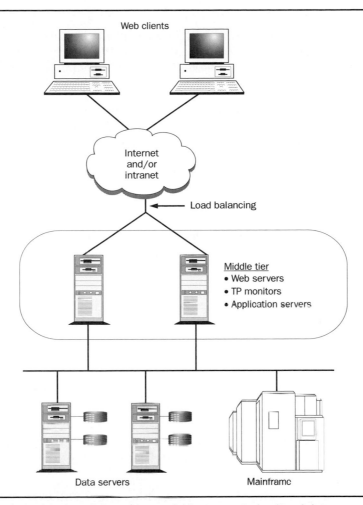

Figure D-16.   *The three-tiered model provides scalable access to back-end data*

transaction processing, data transformation, and so on. They also provide a development environment that may support CORBA, Microsoft COM/DCOM, and Enterprise JavaBeans. Additional features include the ability to connect with a variety of back-end database services and to load balance the traffic between the servers and users. The servers are also a logical place to implement advanced security services. The following Web sites provide useful information.

Application server information at Serverwatch.Internet.com	http://serverwatch.internet.com/appservers.html
Application server page at Webreview.com	http://www.webreview.com/pub/app_servers/
Application server zone	http://www.appserver-zone.com

Database Connectivity Tools

A number of tools are now available to access database information on legacy mainframe systems and networks servers. Most are designed to support Web servers' access to information on a back-end database based on client requests. The Web servers build dynamic Web pages based on information requested by users. The most common tools are listed here:

- **ODBC (Open Database Connectivity)**   This is an open standard architecture that defines how clients can access data on a variety of heterogeneous databases. It was originally defined by Microsoft, but is now used almost universally. See "ODBC (Open Database Connectivity)," for more information.

- **Microsoft OLE DB**   This is an extension of ODBC that defines access to universal data types (i.e., multimedia data, including pictures, sound, and video). See "OLE DB" for more information.

- **Microsoft ADO (ActiveX Data Objects)**   This is an ODBC-compliant set of interfaces that exposes all of the functionality in modern databases through accessible objects. ADO can be used with virtually any scripting language, such as JavaScript, VB Script, and Perl.

- **Microsoft UDA (Universal Data Access)**   This is Microsoft's strategy for providing access to information across the enterprise. UDA provides access to a variety of information sources, including relational and nonrelational, and an easy-to-use programming interface that is tool and language independent. Microsoft's UDA Web site is http://www.microsoft.com/data/.

- **JDBC (Java Database Connectivity)**   JDBC provides much of the same functionality as ODBC, but provides support for programs written in Java and JavaScript. See "Java" for more information.

- **J/SQL**   This is a thin-client JDBC standard developed by Oracle that provides an easy-to-use, high-level interface to relational databases. Oracle promotes J/SQL as an open standard. Refer to http://www.oracle.com.

- **DRDA (Distributed Relational Database Architecture)**   DRDA is an IBM standard for accessing database information across IBM platforms that follows SQL standards. See "DRDA (Distributed Relational Database Architecture)."

- **IBM DataJoiner**   This is an IBM information integration solution that allows access and/or joins to IMS, VSAM, DB2, Oracle, Microsoft SQL Server, Sybase, Informix, and other data seamlessly, within a single SQL statement through a single interface. Refer to http://www-4.ibm.com/software/data/datajoiner/ for more information.

- **XML (Extensible Markup Language)**   XML has become the standard way to access and share information across the Web. XML is a markup language that can define standard and customizable ways of describing data. Once data is extracted into an XML format, it can be shared with any XML system and easily transported across the Web. See "XML (Extensible Markup Language)."

Related Entries   Client/Server Computing; Clustering; Data Management; Data Mart; Data Migration; Data Mining; Data Protection; Data Warehousing; Distributed Applications; Distributed Computer Networks;

Distributed Object Computing; DRDA (Distributed Relational Database Architecture); IBM Host Connectivity; Middleware and Messaging; Multitiered Architectures; Object Technologies; ODBC (Open Database Connectivity); OLAP (Online Analytical Processing); OLE DB; Replication; SQL (Structured Query Language); Transaction Processing; *and* Z39.50

Linktionary!—Tom Sheldon's Encyclopedia of Networking updates	http://www.linktionary.com/d/dbms.html
CAIT Information Systems Meta-List (an extensive set of links)	http://www.cait.wustl.edu/infosys/infosys.html

An extensive set of links is available at the Linktionary! Web site.

DBS (Direct Broadcast Satellite)

DBS (direct broadcast satellite) and DSS (Digital Satellite System) are often used interchangeably; but DBS is a generic name for broadcast satellite systems that have been around since the early 1970s, while DSS is a trademark name owned by Hughes Corporation. Most DBS systems now provide digital TV broadcasting directly to users who are equipped with satellite dish equipment. Companies involved in DBS include EchoStar, Gilat Satellite Networks, DirecTV (Hughes), News Corporation, Primestar, and USSB (United States Satellite Broadcasting).

While DBS systems primarily offer television services, satellite Internet access is growing in popularity. The following companies are involved:

- The DirecPC system from DirecTV (Hughes) provides download speeds up to 400Kbits/sec. This system is discussed in the next paragraphs.

- Cyberstar from Loral Space and Communications Ltd. is a two-way satellite service targeted for business use. The data rate will be as high as 27 Mbits/sec. The service offers IP multicasting, which enables corporations to build extranets and perform large file distribution to company servers at remote locations. The service will also provide Internet access.

- StarBand is a two-way satellite system with download data rates in the 500 Kbits/sec range. The company is in partnership with Gilat Satellite Networks, Microsoft Corporation, and Echostar Communications.

- Teledesic Corporation is developing an "Internet-in-the-Sky" system using low-orbiting satellites that may be in place by 2003. The venture is being financed by Bill Gates, Craig McCaw, Motorola, and others.

The DirecPC system is based on the DirecTV system, in which users receive a digital broadcast TV signal on an 18-inch VSAT (very small aperture terminal) mounted to a rooftop or aerial. A modified 21-inch dish allows both TV and data access. PCs are connected to the dish via an internal adapter or an external device that connects to a PC's USB (Universal Serial Bus) port. Because the system is designed for download only, a separate modem connection is required to make Web requests, as shown in Figure D-17.

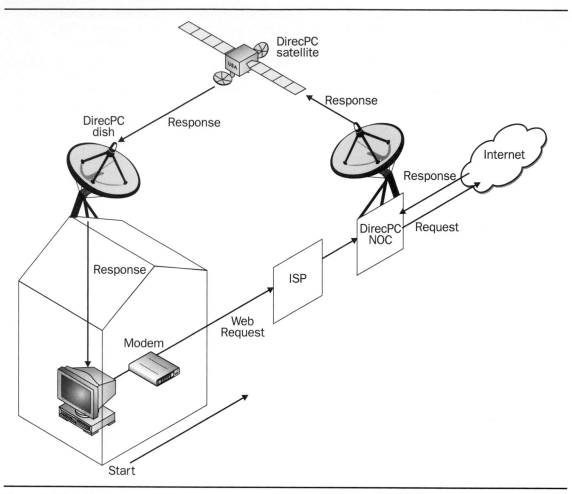

Figure D-17. *The DirecPC system*

Note that Web requests (called the upstream signal) are transmitted over the phone lines to an ISP and then to the DirecPC NOC (network operations center). The NOC sends the requests to the appropriate Web server on the Internet; receives the response; and then sends the response to its satellite, where they are beamed to the customer's dish at up to 400 Kbits/sec.

This whole scheme is a departure from the normal HTTP protocol. The DirecPC software in the user's computer directs requests to the DirecPC NOC and the NOC changes the IP packet header information so that it looks like the NOC is the source. The Web server then returns information to the NOC and the NOC sends this up to the satellite.

This scheme works well because the bulk of information travels to users in the download, which can be transmitted back to the user over the high-speed satellite link. The upstream requests are usually minimal in size, and so can travel over the modem links. The only real

D

problem is the inconvenience of having to connect to the Internet via two separate links and the need to pay two different service providers, although DirecPC now provides a single billing option.

However, there are limits to the number of users that can use a satellite. DirecPC users have been complaining about slow access as the system gains in popularity. DirecPC system managers implemented a "fair access policy" that reduced the bandwidth allocations of some users who were abusing the system. In some cases, users were providing ISP-like services for other users over their fast access links.

To accommodate more users, Hughes is launching new satellites and using special techniques such as spot beaming to target more users in smaller areas. In 2001, the company expects to launch Spaceway, a two-way satellite system that has a downstream data rate of 108 Mbits/sec and an upstream data rate of 6 Mbits/sec.

Related Entries Cable (CATV) Data Networks; HALO (High Altitude Long Operation); Internet Connections; Last Mile Services; LMDS (Local Multipoint Distribution Services); MMDS (Multichannel Multipoint Distribution Services; Network Access Services; Optical Networks; Residential Broadband; Satellite Communication Systems; Service Providers and Carriers; Wireless Communications; *and* Wireless Local Loop

Linktionary!—Tom Sheldon's Encyclopedia of Networking updates	http://www.linktionary.com/d/dbs.html
"Internet Via Satellite: The Hughes DirecPC Model" By Kristian Richards	http://oak.cats.ohiou.edu/~sl302186/direcpc.htm
DirecPC home page	http://www.direcpc.com/
StarBand	http://www.starband.com/
Telesat (Canada) DirecPC information	http://www.telesat.ca/direcpc/
Loral Cyberstar	http://www.cyberstar.com/
DBSDish.com DBS information site	http://www.dbsdish.com/
DBS Online	http://www.dbs-online.com/
MLSAT Web page (satellite information)	http://www.mlesat.com/

DCE (Data Circuit–Terminating Equipment)

DCE equipment is typically a modem or other type of communication device. The DCE sits between the DTE (data terminal equipment) and a transmission circuit such as a phone line. Originally, the DTE was a dumb terminal or printer, but today it is a computer, or a bridge or router that interconnects local area networks. In an IBM mainframe environment, a *communication controller* and a link-attached *cluster controller* are examples of DTEs.

A DCE provides a connection for the DTE into a communication network and back again. In addition, it terminates and provides clocking for a circuit. When analog telephone lines are the communication media, the DCE is a *modem.* When the lines are digital, the DCE is a CSU/DSU (*channel service unit/data service unit*).

DTE and DCE interfaces are defined by the physical layer in the OSI (Open Systems Interconnection) model. The most common standards for DTE/DCE devices are EIA (Electronic Industries Association) RS-232-C and RS-232-D. Outside the United States, these standards are the same as the V.24 standard of the CCITT (Consultative Committee for International Telegraphy and Telephony). Other DTE/DCE standards include the EIA RS-366-A, as well as the CCITT X.20, X.21, and V.35 standards. The later standards are used for high-speed communication over telephone lines.

DTE and DCE devices send and receive data on separate wires that terminate at a 25-pin connector. It is useful to know that DTE devices transmit on pin connector 2 and receive on pin 3. DCE devices are just the opposite—pin 3 transmits and pin 2 receives.

Related Entries   CSU/DSU (Channel Service Unit/Data Service Unit); Data Communication Concepts; *and* Modems

DCE (Distributed Computing Environment)

DCE is the product of the OSF (Open Software Foundation), which merged with X/Open Company Ltd. in February 1996 to form The Open Group. OSF was originally founded in 1988 to research and develop distributed computing environments. X/Open was founded in 1984 to provide compliance to open systems specifications. The newly formed Open Group's mission is to enable customer choice in the implementation of multivendor information systems. The Open Group's Web site is located at http://www.opengroup.org.

DCE is a suite of "enabling" software services that allow organizations to distribute processing and data across the enterprise. It hides the differences in multivendor products, technologies, and standards. Thus, DCE provides an independence from operating systems and networks. No specific network protocol is specified, so the underlying network can use IP, IPX, or SNA.

Much of the technology in DCE was acquired through a process called Request for Technology. Major hardware and software vendors submitted their technologies and OSF picked the best. A list is provided here:

- Hewlett-Packard and DEC's RPC (remote procedure call)
- DECdns directory naming services
- X.500 directory naming services from Siemens AG
- Kerberos security services from MIT with Hewlett-Packard extensions
- Andrew File System from Transarc
- LM/X PC integrated technology from Microsoft
- Concert Multi-Threads Architecture from DEC
- DECdts time services from DEC

The DCE architecture is a layered model that integrates the technologies just described. At the bottom are the most basic services (such as operating systems), and at the top are applications.

The services provided by DCE are designed to mask the complexity of multivendor network environments and let information easily flow to where it is needed. In this respect, DCE is middleware.

The DCE services are grouped into two categories: development tools and data-sharing services. The development tools help software developers create end-user services needed for distributed computing. They include RPCs (remote procedure calls), directory services, time services, security services, and threads services. Data-sharing services provide end users with capabilities built upon the development tools to easily access information. They include distributed file system and diskless workstation support.

Related Entries   AFS (Andrew File System); Directory Services; Distributed Computer Networks; Distributed Object Computing; *and* Network Operating Systems

 Open Group   http://www.opengroup.org

DCOM (Distributed Component Object Model)

COM (Component Object Model) is a Microsoft specification that defines the interaction between objects in the Windows environment. See "COM (Component Object Model)."

DDE (Dynamic Data Exchange)

DDE is an interprocess mechanism for exchanging messages between processes running in a computer. It is implemented in Microsoft Windows products. Successor technologies include OLE (Object Linking and Embedding), COM (Component Object Model), and DCOM (Distributed COM).

Related Entries   COM (Component Object Model); DCOM (Distributed Component Object Model); Distributed Object Computing; Object Technologies; *and* OLE (Object Linking and Embedding)

DDR (Dial-on-Demand Routing)

DDR provides a way to link two sites over a public network and provide needed bandwidth by setting up additional lines as required. DDR is a feature of routers from Cisco and other vendors. It allows a device to establish a circuit-switched asynchronous modem connection, an ISDN digital connection, or Switched 56 connections to a remote location. Switched connections can provide secondary links that back up primary communication lines when they become overloaded or when they fail. Switched lines are ideal for handling peaks in traffic, fax transmissions, backup sessions, bulk e-mail transfers, and temporary remote office connections.

A Cisco router running the DDR utility issues a dial-up command to the connected DCE (data circuit–terminating equipment) when it receives packets destined for remote networks. The network administrator can designate which packets can initiate a dial-on-demand sequence. Cisco routers use the CCITT V.25 bis protocol to initiate calls on automatic calling devices. DDR provides an alternative to leased lines that can help managers when making decisions about adding bandwidth for remote links.

Related Entries   BACP (Bandwidth Allocation Control Protocol); Bandwidth Management; Bandwidth on Demand; Bandwidth Reservation; Bonding; Circuit-Switching Services; Inverse Multiplexing; Load Balancing; MLPPP (Multi-Link PPP); Routers; *and* Trunking

 Cisco Paper: Designing DDR Internetworks   http://www.cisco.com/univercd/cc/td/doc/
                                                                  cisintwk/idg4/nd2010.htm

DECnet

DECnet is Digital Equipment Corporation's (now Compaq) name for the set of hardware and software products that implement DNA (Digital Network Architecture), a protocol suite that is very similar in structure to the OSI protocol model, except that an additional layer exists under the application layer for network management. DEC (Digital Equipment Corporation) was purchased in 1998 by Compaq Computer Corporation.

   DECnet information is available at the Linktionary! Web site, at http://www.linktionary.com/ d/decnet.html.

Dedicated Circuits

A dedicated circuit is a data-communication pathway between two communicating systems. The circuit may exist as a physical cable between two systems, or may exist logically within a multiplexed or switched communication network. Dedicated circuits are often called *leased lines* and are used to create private WANs (wide area networks). Leased lines are permanent point-to-point links through the public network that are usually billed based on the distance and capacity. A dedicated circuit is either a voice-grade analog line requiring modems at each end, or a digital line such as a T1-type service that provides transmission speeds up to 1.544 Mbits/sec or a T3 line at 45 Mbits/sec.

A dedicated circuit can also exist logically (as a virtual circuit) in switching networks such as X.25, frame relay, ATM networks, and the Internet. Depending on the network type, the carrier may predefine a path with a guaranteed bandwidth through the network.

Network administrators evaluating the use of these lines must weigh the cost of a leased line based on the amount of traffic that will traverse it and whether an uninterrupted connection must be maintained at all times. If traffic is light, or peaks during parts of the day, a dial-up line may be appropriate. A dial-up line may also supplement a dedicated circuit by providing occasional transmissions, such as bulk e-mail transfers or replication of server information to a remote office. Dedicated lines are best when traffic is constant and service requirements are immediate.

ISDN (Integrated Services Digital Network) provides temporary dedicated circuit capabilities and allows users to dial any other site. DSL (Digital Subscriber Line) services offer another possibility.

Related Entries   Capacity; Channel; Circuit-Switching Services; Communication Services and Providers; Leased Line; Multiplexing; Multiplexers; Point-to-Point Communications; T-Carriers; TDM Networks; Telecommunications and Telephone Systems; Throughput; Virtual Circuits; VPN (Virtual Private Network); *and* WAN (Wide Area Network)

Linktionary!—Tom Sheldon's Encyclopedia   http://www.linktionary.com/c/circuit.html
of Networking updates

D

Delay, Latency, and Jitter

Delay and *latency* are similar terms that refer to the amount of time it takes a bit to be transmitted from source to destination. *Jitter* is delay that varies over time. One way to view latency is how long a system holds on to a packet. That system may be a single device like a router, or a complete communication system including routers and links.

Closely related topics include *bandwidth* and *throughput*. These are illustrated in Figure D-18. Bandwidth is often used to refer to the data rate of a system, but it appropriately refers to the width of the frequency band that a system operates in. Data rate and wire speed are better terms when talking about transmitting digital information. The speed of a system is affected by congestion and delays. Throughput refers to the actual measured performance of a system when delay is considered.

Delays are caused by distance, errors and error recovery, congestion, the processing capabilities of systems involved in the transmission, and other factors. Even if you remove these hardware-type delays, you still have the speed-of-light delay. It takes nearly 30 ms to send a bit through a cross-country fiber-optic cable, a delay that can't be eliminated.

Delays of distance (called *propagation delays*) are especially critical when transmitting data to other countries (especially when you consider all the equipment along the way that adds delay). Delay is also significant with satellite transmissions; and don't forget that most communciations require a round-trip exchange of data, especially if the sender is waiting for an acknowledgement of receipt from the receiver. Increasing data rates allows you to send more bits in the same amount of time, but it doesn't help improve delay. Excessive delay may cause a receiving system to time out and request a retransmission. The delay factor has to be adjusted when excessive delay exists.

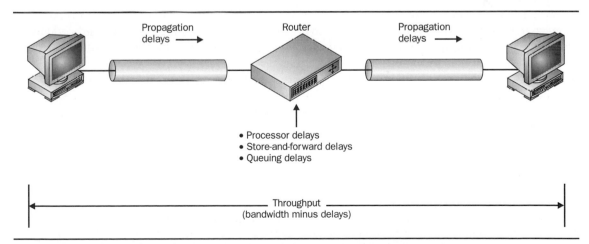

Figure D-18.   *The relationships among bandwidth, delay, and throughput*

Delay is problematic for real-time traffic like interactive voice calls and live video. Delay can also be a problem with time-sensitive transaction processing systems. Delay caused by congestion must be avoided; so bandwidth management, priority queuing, and QoS are important for live media to ensure that enough packets get through on time.

Variation in delay (jitter) is more disruptive to a voice call than delay itself. When delay is constant, you can get used to the slight pause in the conversation; but if the delay is variable, it's difficult to adapt. RTP (Real-Time Protocol) is a streaming protocol that has a packet resynchronization feature. The sender puts time stamps on packets, and the receiver uses these time stamps to play back the packets in a synchronized way so that jitter is smoothed out. RTP is discussed under "Multimedia."

Causes of Delay/Latency

Delay is caused by hardware and software inefficiencies, as well as network congestion and transmission problems that cause errors. Delay may be caused by the following:

- *Network congestion*, caused by excessive traffic.
- *Processing delays,* caused by inefficient hardware.
- *Queuing delays* occur when buffers in network devices become flooded.
- *Propagation delay* is related to how long it takes a signal to travel across a physical medium.

Congestion Delays

As traffic increases on the network, *congestion* increases. On freeways, congestion occurs at busy intersections. On networks, congestion occurs at routers and switches, causing delay that is variable (jitter).

Ethernet's shared medium is prone to congestion. A user must wait if the cable is being used, and collisions occur if two people try to transmit at the same time. Both wait and then try again, causing further delay for the end-user application.

When a TCP/IP host begins to transmit, it has no way to monitor the network for downstream congestion problems. The host cannot immediately detect that a router is becoming overburdened. Only when the sender is forced into retransmitting dropped packets does it get a sense that the network must be busy and then start to slow down its transmissions.

Several techniques have been developed to resolve congestion problems on TCP/IP networks, such as *slow start* and *congestion avoidance.* Congestion controls help hosts adapt to traffic conditions. A transmission starts slowly and builds up until congestion is detected (packets are being dropped). See "Flow-Control Mechanisms," "Congestion Control Mechanisms," and "Traffic Management, Shaping, and Engineering."

Hardware and Processing Delays

When networks become busy, routers and switches must be able to keep up with traffic demands and forward packets with as little delay and packet loss as possible. A typical router uses one of the following techniques to process packets:

- **Store and forward**   This technique is prone to delay. Packets must be fully received before they are processed.

■ **Cut-through forwarding** This technique helps reduce delay. The device will examine a packet header before it is fully received and forward it immediately.

Routers have to do a lot of work. They check for errors, and then perform a table lookup and make a routing decision for every packet. Processing power is critical, and a number of vendors have created gigabit and terabit routers to handle huge traffic loads. An alternative is to tag packets with information that eliminates the need to do a lookup for every packet. This is done by routing switches and label-switching devices. See "Label Switching."

Queuing Delays

After a router receives and examines a packet, it sends the packet to a buffer where it is queued up for transmission, usually on a first-in, first-out basis (FIFO). Routers receive packets from many different sources, so the devices can easily be overwhelmed.

Buffers start to fill up when the network gets busy. Traffic may move into a queue faster than it can be moved out. If packets are delayed long enough, the source systems may begin retransmitting packets under the assumption that packets have been lost. This adds to network congestion and delay.

As mentioned, queues are usually processed on a first-come, first-served basis. Priority queuing techniques give some packets precedence over others. Packets may be marked or tagged in advance so that they are directed into a queue that matches their priority. Alternatively, a device may examine packet contents to determine priority. Refer to "Queuing" and "Prioritization of Network Traffic." for additional information.

Link Delays

Once a packet has been queued up, it is ready to be forwarded onto the network link. The network link is subject to the maximum data rate of the networking technology in use (i.e., the number of bits per second the interface will pump onto the medium) and propagation delay.

Transmissions through a vacuum are near the speed of light, but cables are made of materials that cause propagation delay. For example, electrical signals travel through copper cable at approximately 2/3 the speed of light. A paper called "Propagation Delay" at the Optimized Engineering Corporation Web site (see the link at the end of this topic) describes the "length" of a bit as it crosses an Ethernet cable:

> Since we know that Ethernet operates at 10 Mbits/sec or 10,000,000 bits per second, we can determine that the length of wire that one bit occupies is approximately equal to 20 meters or 60 feet.

Propagation delay increases with distance. A 1,000-mile round trip for a bit on a fiber cable takes about 10 ms, which means that a cross-country round trip takes about 30 ms and a transmission to a geosynchronous satellite takes about 250 ms. To put this in perspective, consider that a round-trip delay of over 100 ms is considered unacceptable for a voice conversation.

Propagation delay and excessive cable length can cause problems in shared Ethernet networks. Assume a computer at one end of the cable puts a signal on the cable. At the same time, a computer at the other end of a cable begins its transmissions. Because of propagation delay and excessive cable length, neither station detects that the other station has begun transmitting. The signals collide and become corrupted. In some cases, the transmitter may never know this has occurred because it finishes transmitting before it can detect the collision. The receiver will discard the corrupted packets and require a retransmission.

The topic "TCP (Transmission Control Protocol)" has a subsection called "TCP Performance Issues" that discusses delay problems and solutions on TCP networks.

Monitoring and Controlling Delay

Increasing network bandwidth solves many performance problems, but some delay is inevitable. For example, in the case of a large file transfer, TCP/IP will first attempt to use all the bandwidth. This can put a stop to other transfers and seriously affect voice calls. Priority queueing and bandwidth reservation techniques can help. Another solution is to use traffic- shaping techniques that "smooth out" large file transfers over a longer period of time so that other traffic is not cut off. See "Traffic Management, Shaping, and Engineering."

"Chatty protocols" are communication protocols that send a lot of acknowledgment and control information back and forth. All that overhead cuts into the amount of actual data being sent. It takes longer to transfer a file with a chatty protocol (like the old X.25) as opposed to a nonchatty protocol (like frame relay). Some networks introduce a lot of overhead in the packet/cell, such as ATM. Stuart Cheshire's paper "Bandwidth and Latency: It's the Latency, Stupid" (see the upcoming Web link) does a good job of explaining why modem communications are subject to all sorts of latency problems.

Propagation delays over global networks are relatively small, but a lot of delay is added by all the devices that packets must go through when traversing these long-distance links. The more distant you are from a Web server on the Internet, the more networks, routers, and switches your packets must traverse—which adds up to delay. To solve this problem, many popular Web sites are mirrored (copied or cached) onto servers in specific geographic regions so the Web content is closer to the users in those regions. The topic "Content Distribution" covers this.

Many organizations run proxy servers that cache Internet information locally to make it quickly available to other users in the organization that might need it. The LowLat Project (Low Latency Project) has information on caching systems. The Web site is given at the end of this topic.

Some attempts were made to control delay, along with throughput and reliability, early in the development of the Internet Protocol. But these early attempts really never caught on. More recently, initiatives such as Differentiated Services are making progress in classifying and prioritizing traffic based on its class. Refer to "Differentiated Services (Diff-Serv)."

The IETF IPPM (IP Performance Metrics) Working Group is developing a set of standards for measuring the quality, performance, and reliability of Internet data delivery services. Network operators, end users, or independent testing groups can use the metrics to provide unbiased quantitative measures of performance. The Web address is listed at the end of this topic.

Related Entries   Bandwidth; Bandwidth Management; Channel; Circuit; Congestion Control Mechanisms; Data Communication Concepts; Differentiated Services (Diff-Serv); Electromagnetic Spectrum; Flow Control Mechanisms; QoS (Quality of Service); Queuing; Signals; Testing, Diagnostics, and Troubleshooting; Throughput; *and* Traffic Management, Shaping, and Engineering

Linktionary!—Tom Sheldon's Encyclopedia of Networking updates	http://www.linktionary.com/d/delay.html
IETF Working Group: IP Performance Metrics (ippm)	http://www.ietf.org/html.charters/ippm-charter.html
"Bandwidth and Latency: It's the Latency, Stupid" (Part 1) by Stuart Cheshire	http://www.tidbits.com/tb-issues/TidBITS-367.html#lnk4
"Bandwidth and Latency: It's the Latency, Stupid" (Part 2) by Stuart Cheshire	http://www.tidbits.com/tb-issues/TidBITS-368.html#lnk4
"The Causes of Network Delay" by Tom Porter	http://www.dtool.com/delay.html
"Propagation Delay in Ethernet Networks," a paper at Optimized Engineering Corporation	http://www.optimized.com/COMPENDI/TabOfCon.htm
Tip Library, "Bandwidth vs. Distance Latency"	http://www.pmg.com/tip_archive/July98.htm
The LowLat (Low Latency) Project	http://www.isi.edu/lowlat/
Satellite Data Networks by Rizwan Mustafa Mir (includes satellite delay information)	http://www.cis.ohio-state.edu/~jain/cis788-97/satellite_data/index.htm
Techniques for Web latency improvement	http://www.cs.virginia.edu/~ami4v/paper.html

DEN (Directory Enabled Networks)

DEN is a network management specification that integrates policy services and directory services in a way that provides configuration and policy-based access control to network resources—specifically, network bandwidth. According to the DEN specification, "directories must be transformed from a dumb warehouse to an authoritative, distributed, intelligent repository of information for services and applications." Some advocate that the directory service is now the heart of the network, the place where all network operations are defined and managed.

DEN defines a standard directory services architecture and schema that can be used to store network policy and configuration information. It is a blueprint that attempts to guarantee interoperability among vendors of network equipment, directory services, and applications. DEN's primary components include a distributed database (one that can be replicated to other locations); a consistent data model (structure of the data—that is, how real-world objects are defined in the directory); and LDAP (Lightweight Directory Access Protocol), a protocol that applications use to access the directory.

Microsoft first proposed the architecture and did early work with Cisco. Eventually, DEN was transferred to the DMTF (Desktop Management Task Force) to help promote its widespread standardization. The DMTF completed the initial specification in 1998, and has since expanded it. The IETF Policy Framework (policy) Working Group is working to define how policies and policy information is implemented in network environments. It is defining an extensible information model and schemata to represent policy. It is also addressing policy as it relates to QoS traffic management and Differentiated Services (Diff-Serv). Early directory services were more like the white pages telephone directory, mapping users with their e-mail information. Later, directory services became more like the yellow pages, storing information about objects on a network and their services. Users could search for a particular service and find the name of a device that provided that service. Administrators could organize and manage the devices through the directory. Directory services became a central place for managing the network. Users benefited from single sign-on—that is, the ability to log on once to the directory and access any other resources on the network.

DEN expands this concept by giving the directory an even more important role as *the place* to manage the configuration of network components such as routers, switches, remote access servers, printers, and other networking equipment. The directory also provides a central place to encode policy information, and a single place where people and applications can access it. Network devices check with the directory for configuration information and policies. The alternative is to manually program it into each device.

Bandwidth management is an important issue as networks take on real-time multimedia traffic, especially voice over IP. DEN provides the means for allocating bandwidth to users based on policies stored in the directory. Now, there are schemes to support prioritization and QoS, such as IEEE 802.1p and Diff-Serv. DEN works with these schemes. See "Policy-Based Management" and "Differentiated Services (Diff-Serv)."

If a central database is to be used, any network device must be able to access it. This requires a standard *schema*. A schema is a set of rules and syntax for storing data in a directory, much like the postal system defines a schema for addressing envelopes. The postal schema includes the elements name, address, city, state, and ZIP. The rules are that the name appear first, the ZIP code appear last, and so on. DEN provides a standard scheme that supports interoperability among different vendors' network devices.

DEN is an extension of the DMTF's CIM (Common Information Model), an enterprise management model that covers all aspects of network management. As an information model, CIM provides a schema that defines objects and the attributes, as well as how objects are managed and relate to one another. DEN extends CIM with new network elements and services. It maps information into an LDAP-compatible directory, and extends the information model so that the behavior of network elements can be described. The relationships among X.500, CIM, and DEN can be seen in Figure D-19.

DEN's schema draws on the existing objects and attributes already defined in CIM. User object information is drawn from X.500, as shown in Figure D-19. The lower part of the figure shows the DEN extensions.

Products using DEN include Microsoft Active Directory and Novell NDS. Microsoft worked closely with Cisco on the DEN standard. Novell's strategy includes ZENworks for Networks, a product that simplifies the task of establishing a quality-of-service infrastructure by using NDS to provide the user and group information necessary for successful policy-based management.

An interesting RFC that discusses developments in directories, policies, resource management, and QoS is RFC 2768, "A Report of a Workshop on Middleware," (February 2000).

Related Entries   Differentiated Services (Diff-Serv); Directory Services; LDAP (Lightweight Directory Access Protocol); Network Management; Policy-Based Management; QoS (Quality of Service); Traffic Management, Shaping, and Engineering; *and* VoIP (Voice Over IP)

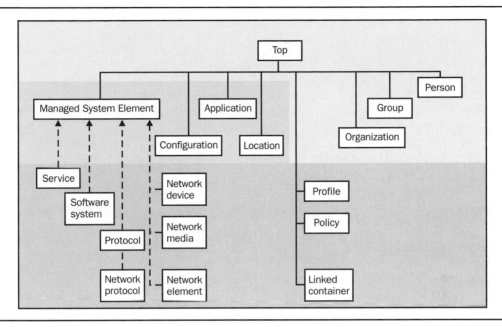

Figure D-19. *DEN directory scheme and information model (source: Cisco)*

Linktionary!—Tom Sheldon's Encyclopedia of Networking updates	http://www.linktionary.com/d/den.html
DMTF DEN home page	http://www.dmtf.org/spec/denh.html
DEN Ad Hoc Working Group	http://murchiso.com/den/#denspec/
The Directory Interoperability Forum	http://www.directoryforum.org/
IETF Policy Framework Working Group (policy)	http://www.ietf.org/html.charters/policy-charter.html
Directory Enabled Networks (DEN) links page	http://www.ee.umanitoba.ca/~blight/networks/DEN.html
3Com document: "Policy-Powered Networking and the Role of Directories"	http://www.3com.com/technology/tech_net/white_papers/500670.html
3Com paper: "Schema Standardization Efforts"	http://www.3com.com/technology/tech_net/white_papers/500665a.html
Cisco DEN paper	http://www.cisco.com/warp/public/784/packet/jan99/10.html
Network World information and articles about directory services	http://www.nwfusion.com/netresources/directories.html

DEN links at ITPRC	http://www.itprc.com/qos.htm
Complete list of directory services and LDAP RFCs	http://olymp.wu-wien.ac.at/manuals/rfc-ldap.html

Denial of Service Attack

See Security and RFC 2827, "Network Ingress Filtering: Defeating Denial of Service Attacks Which Employ IP Source Address Spoofing," (May 2000).

DES (Data Encryption Standard)

See Cryptography.

Dfs (Distributed File System), Microsoft

Microsoft Dfs is designed to make it easier to access files on networks. It provides a way to unite files on different computers under a single name space. To the user, files appear as if they are in one location, rather than on separate computers. A hierarchical tree provides a view of these files, and users can "drill down" through the tree to find just the information they are looking for.

 Microsoft's Dfs should not be confused with The Open Group's DFS (Distributed File System) discussed in the next topic. While they are both file systems, they have little in common.

The user does not need to know or care about the physical location of the file, only where it is located in the hierarchical view. That means that users no longer search for files by opening file servers and disk drives, and looking through a separate directory structure on each. Instead, users look through a logical directory that places shared information in a place that makes more sense to users and administrators alike. With Dfs, an administrator does up-front work to logically organize information, so users don't have trouble finding it later on.

As an analogy, think of a city library system in which the book catalog at each library lists all the books available at libraries throughout the city. You can order any book and it will be delivered from its current location. The important point is that there is one library catalog system that provides a list of all the books available, no matter what their physical location. Dfs provides a single "catalog" view of files on your network, no matter where those files are located.

Some of the benefits of Dfs are outlined here:

- In Windows 2000, Dfs takes advantage of the Active Directory. The Dfs tree topology is automatically published to the Active Directory, resulting in fault tolerance for the Dfs root.

- Users can access information with Dfs's hierarchical view of network resources. Administrators can create custom views to make file access easier for users.

- Volumes consist of individual shares, and those shares can be at many different locations. A share can be taken offline without affecting the rest of the volume. The volumes that you add to a Dfs root are the leaves or branch nodes that represent shared network directories.

- User access to Dfs volumes is controlled with standard Windows NT/Windows 2000 security, such as group access rights.

- To ensure that critical data is always available, administrators can set up alternate locations for accessing data by simply including the alternate locations under the same logical Dfs name. Client software automatically chooses to use data on a server that is closest to the user. If one of the locations goes down, another location is automatically selected.

- Response time can be improved by load balancing the system. Often-accessed files can be stored in multiple locations, and the system will automatically distribute requests across the drives to balance traffic during peak usage periods.

- Users don't need to know about the physical location of files. Administrators can physically move files to other drives; but to the user, the files still appear under the same location in the hierarchical tree.

- Client access to shares is cached to improve performance. The first time a user accesses a published directory, the information is cached and used for future references.

- Dfs simplifies enterprise backups. Since a Dfs tree can be built to cover an entire enterprise, the backup software can back up this single "tree," no matter how many servers/shares are part of the tree. The tree can include Windows 95 and Windows NT/Windows 2000 desktops as well.

- A graphical administration tool makes it easy to configure volumes, Dfs links, and remote Dfs roots.

Dfs fits into an organization's Internet and intranet strategy. The Web page of individual departments or even users can be included within the directory tree. Dfs can also hold HTML links; so, if linked pages are moved to a different physical location, all links pointing to the pages will not have to be reconfigured.

Dfs Volumes

A Dfs volume starts out by being hosted by a specific computer. There may be many individual Dfs volumes available on a network, and each will have its own distinct name. Windows NT/Windows 2000 servers are currently the only systems that can host Dfs volumes. An organization might have a master Dfs volume that contains *links* to other Dfs volumes at the department or division level. Another volume might tie together shares that are common in each department, such as public documents.

In the Dfs volume name shown here, the hosting computer name is *Server_Name*:

*Server_Name**Dfs_Share_Name**path**name*

Like a local file system, a Dfs volume has a root that is its starting point. This is represented by *Dfs_Share_Name*. The reference to *path**name* can be any valid pathname.

Figure D-20 illustrates how links work. Three departments—Marketing, Engineering, and Research—have set up their own name spaces to fit their own needs. The corporate Dfs volume links into specific parts of these shares as needed to provide corporate users with information from other locations in the organization. When a link is accessed, the junction between two

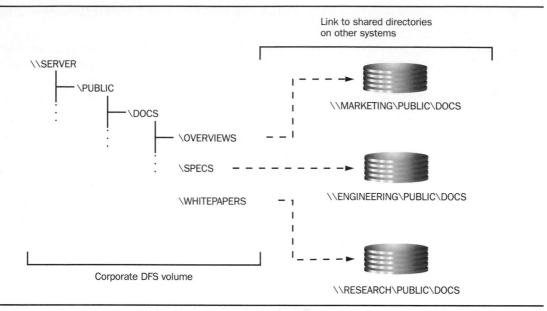

Figure D-20.   *Structure of a distributed file system*

different Dfs volumes is crossed and the server that provides the Dfs root changes. This is transparent to the user, however.

Related Entries   CIFS (Common Internet File System); Directory Services; File Systems; Microsoft Windows; Samba; *and* SMB (Server Message Blocks)

Linktionary!—Tom Sheldon's Encyclopedia of Networking updates	http://www.linktionary.com/d/dfs.html
Microsoft Dfs paper	http://www.microsoft.com/Windows/server/ Technical/fileprint/dfsnew.asp
Microsoft Dfs document: "Dfs Introduction: Building a Single, Hierarchical View of Multiple File Servers and File Server Shares on a Network"	http://www.microsoft.com/NTServer/fileprint/ exec/feature/dfsSummary.asp
Microsoft Dfs document: "Dfs In-Depth: A Logical View of Physical Hierarchy"	http://www.microsoft.com/NTServer/fileprint/ exec/feature/DFSWP.asp
Windows 2000 Magazine article: "Dfs: A Logical View of Physical Resources," by Sean Deuby and Tim Daniels	http://www.win2000mag.com/Articles/ Index.cfm?ArticleID=2871
Windows 2000 Magazine article: "Get a Head Start on Windows NT 5.0 with Dfs"	http://www.win2000mag.com/Articles/ Index.cfm?ArticleID=3105
John Savill's Windows 2000 FAQ Dfs page	http://www.ntfaq.com/Articles/ Index.cfm?DepartmentID=773

DFS (Distributed File System), The Open Group

DFS is a version of the AFS (Andrew File System) that is included with The Open Group's DCE (Distributed Computing Environment). Transarc is responsible for DFS. Its Web site is listed at the end of this section.

Related Entries   AFS (Andrews File System; DCE (Distributed Computing Environment); *and* File Systems

Linktionary!—Tom Sheldon's Encyclopedia of Networking updates	http://www.linktionary.com/f/file_systems.html
Transarc	http://www.transarc.com
The Open Group DCE information	http://www.opengroup.org/dce/

DHCP (Dynamic Host Configuration Protocol)

DHCP is designed to help reduce configuration time for TCP/IP networks by automatically assigning IP addresses to clients when they log on. DHCP centralizes IP address management on central computers that run the DHCP server program.

Although you can manually assign permanent IP addresses to any computer on your network, DHCP provides a way to automatically assign addresses. In order to have a client get its IP address from a DHCP server, you configure the client to obtain its address automatically from a host server. This option appears in the TCP/IP configuration area of most clients' operating systems. Once these options are set, the client "leases" an IP address from the DHCP server every time it boots. At least one DHCP server must exist on a network.

More information about DHCP is written up at the Linktionary! Web site given at the end of this topic. Also refer to the IETF Dynamic Host Configuration (dhc) site listed at the end of this topic for more information about these and other DHCP developments. All relevant Internet drafts and RFCs are located at the site.

Related Entries   Addresses, Network; BOOTP (BOOTstrap Protocol); Bootstrapping and Booting; Diskless Workstations; Internet Protocol Suite; IP (Internet Protocol); TCP (Transmission Control Protocol); Thin Clients; *and* WINS (Windows Internet Naming Service)

Linktionary!—Tom Sheldon's Encyclopedia of Networking updates	http://www.linktionary.com/d/dhcp.html
IETF Working Group: Dynamic Host Configuration (dhc) (This page has a list of relevant RFCs and drafts.)	http://www.ietf.cnri.reston.va.us/html.charters/dhc-charter.html
DHCP.org	http://www.dhcp.org/
DHCP reading room	http://www.ehsco.com/reading/dhcp.html

DHTML (Dynamic HTML)

See DOM (Document Object Model); HTML (Hypertext Markup Language).

Diagnostic Testing Equipment

See Testing, Diagnostics, and Troubleshooting.

Dial-Up Line

Dial-up networking is an important connection method for remote and mobile users. A dial-up line is a connection or circuit between two sites through a switched telephone network. In the data communication world, a dial-up line forms a link between two distant computers or local area networks. Dial-up lines provide any-to-any connections. The originating site can call any other site, unlike dedicated leased lines that provide a permanent connection between two sites. Modems are required on both ends of a dial-up line. The transmission rate can be as high as 56 Kbits/sec.

Dial-up lines can be aggregated, meaning that multiple dial-up lines can be combined to improve the capacity. The MLPPP (Multi-Link PPP) protocol allows users to dial a remote system (usually an ISP) and connect with a single line. Once authenticated, a second line is dialed automatically. The throughput increases from 56 Kbits/sec to 112 Kbits/sec.

Related Entries   Bandwidth on Demand; Bonding; Circuit-Switching Services; Communication Services; DDR (Dial-on-Demand Routing); Leased Line; Load Balancing; MLPPP (Multi-Link PPP); Mobile Computing; Modems; NAS (Network Access Server); Network Access Services; Point-to-Point Communications; PPP (Point-to-Point Protocol); RAS (Remote Access Server); Remote Computing; Telecommunications and Telephone Systems; *and* WAN (Wide Area Network)

DIAMETER

DIAMETER is a protocol that authenticates remote dial-up users. It evolved from the popular RADIUS protocol. Both protocols are AAA (authentication, authorization, and accounting) protocols, meaning that they are used to authenticate dial-up users and provide the authorizations users need to access systems. The accounting aspect handles back-end account tracking services. RADIUS has worked well, but it has some limitations—namely, that it is limited to working over the SLIP and PPP data link protocols used with modem connections. A number of new devices are being used to access the Internet, such as smart phones and hand-held devices that use different access protocols.

DIAMETER evolves the RADIUS scheme by adding new features, such as the ability to ask for additional logon information beyond the basic authentication. For example, DIAMETER uses the initial logon and authentication to identify a user, and then can continue to query the user for additional information that might be used to strengthen the authentication or to give the user access to additional systems.

DIAMETER supports user roaming. The IETF ROAMOPS (Roaming Operations) Working Group investigated whether RADIUS could be used to support roaming and concluded that it was ill suited to handle interdomain exchange of user and accounting information. DIAMETER is a new solution to this problem. See "Roaming" for more information.

Note that the base DIAMETER protocol is not used on its own but is always extended for a particular applications. DIAMETER is being worked into extensions under development by the following IETF working groups:

- ROAMOPS (Roaming Operations) is developing procedures, mechanisms, and protocols to support user roaming among groups of Internet service providers (ISPs).

- NASREQ (Network Access Server Requirements) is taking NAS design beyond simple dial-up into VPN support, smart authentication methods, and roaming.

- MobileIP (IP Routing for Wireless/Mobile Hosts) is developing routing support to permit IP nodes (hosts and routers) using either IPv4 or IPv6 to seamlessly "roam" among IP subnetworks and media types.

- AAA (Authentication, Authorization, and Accounting) is developing DIAMETER-related protocols with added accounting, transport, security, and proxy support.

DIAMETER was under development at the time of this writing. You can obtain a list of relevant documents by going to the IETF "Internet-Drafts" Web page mentioned at the end of this topic and searching for "DIAMETER." The previously mentioned Working Groups also list drafts and RFCs related to DIAMETER.

Related Entries   Access Control; Accounting on the Internet; Authentication and Authorization; Communication Server; EAP (Extensible Authentication Protocol); Mobile Computing; NAS (Network Access Server); RADIUS (Remote Authentication Dial-In User Service); Remote Access; Roaming; Security; TACACS (Terminal Access Controller Access Control System); Token-Based Authentication; *and* VPN (Virtual Private Networks)

Linktionary! —Tom Sheldon's Encyclopedia of Networking updates	http://www.linktionary.com/d/diameter.html
IETF Working Group: Authentication, Authorization, and Accounting (aaa)	http://www.ietf.org/html.charters/aaa-charter.html
IETF Working Group: Network Access Server Requirements (nasreq)	http://www.ietf.org/html.charters/nasreq-charter.html
IETF Working Group: IP Routing for Wireless/Mobile Hosts (mobileip)	http://www.ietf.org/html.charters/mobileip-charter.html

Digest Algorithm

There are cryptographic processes that can produce unique "fingerprints" of messages that prove to the receiving party that the messages have not been altered. Some part of the message, such as the header text, is run through a one-way hashing function, which produces an output that serves as a unique identification for the message. The output is called a *message digest*. When a person receives such a message, they can run a similar hash function to create a message digest that should exactly match the digest sent with the message. If the digests do not match, the message should be considered invalid since any alteration will change the results of the hash and produce a different message digest.

Related Entries   Digital Signatures; Hash Functions

Differentiated Services (Diff-Serv)

Diff-Serv is a CoS (class of service) model that enhances the best-effort services of the Internet. It differentiates traffic by user, service requirements, and other criteria; then, it marks packets so that network nodes can provide different levels of service via priority queuing or bandwidth allocation, or by choosing dedicated routes for specific traffic flows. A policy management system controls service allocation. Note that some of the concepts discussed here are covered in more detail under the topics listed in Related Entries at the end of this topic.

Various QoS (quality of service) techniques have been proposed or developed that attempt to provide predictable service on the Internet. One technique is Integrated Services (IntServ) and its associated RSVP protocol, as discussed in a moment. Some of the concepts in Diff-Serv grew out of the IntServ model. However, Diff-Serv is a CoS approach rather than a full QoS approach.

The traditional best-effort model of the Internet makes no attempt to differentiate between the traffic flows that are generated by different hosts. As traffic flow varies, the network provides the best service it can; but there are no controls to preserve higher levels of service for some flows and not others. What Diff-Serv does is attempt to provide better levels of service in a best-effort environment. RFC 2638, "Two-Bit Differentiated Services Architecture," (July 1999) uses the following analogy to describe differentiated services:

> We are motivated to provide services tiers in somewhat the same fashion as the airlines do with first class, business class and coach class. The latter also has tiering built in due to the various restrictions put on the purchase. A part of the analogy we want to stress is that best effort traffic, like coach class seats on an airplane, is still expected to make up the bulk of internet traffic. Business and first class carry a small number of passengers, but are quite important to the economics of the airline industry. The various economic forces and realities combine to dictate the relative allocation of the seats and to try to fill the airplane. We don't expect that differentiated services will comprise all the traffic on the internet, but we do expect that new services will lead to a healthy economic and service environment.

RFC 2990, "Next Steps for QoS Architecture," (November 2000) is one of the best documents to read with regard to QoS in the Internet. Geoff Huston of Telstra (Australia) did an excellent job documenting QoS problems and solutions. The next few paragraphs draw on his work.

IntServ is a bandwidth *reservation* technique that builds virtual circuits across the Internet. Bandwidth requests come from applications running in hosts. Once a bandwidth reservation is made, the bandwidth cannot be reassigned or preempted by another reservation or by other traffic. IntServ and RSVP are *stateful*, meaning that RSVP network nodes must coordinate with one another to set up an RSVP path, and then remember state information about the flow. This can be a daunting task on the Internet, where millions of flows may exist across a router. The RSVP approach is now considered too unwieldy for the Internet, but appropriate for smaller enterprise networks (or when used with Diff-Serv and other techniques, discussed shortly).

Diff-Serv takes a *stateless* approach that minimizes the need for nodes in the network to remember anything about flows. It is not as good at providing QoS as the stateful approach, but more practical to implement across the Internet. Diff-Serv devices at the edge of the network mark packets in a way that describes the service level they should receive. Network elements simply respond to these markings without the need to negotiate paths or remember extensive state information for every flow. In addition, applications don't need to request a particular service level or provide advance notice about where traffic is going.

In the IntServ/RSVP environment, applications negotiate with the network for service. IntServ is said to be application aware, which allows hosts to communicate useful information to the network about their requirements and the state of their flows. In contrast, Diff-Serv is not application aware (although work is underway to make it so). Since Diff-Serv does not listen to applications, it does not benefit from feedback that applications could provide. Since it doesn't know exactly what an application needs, it may fail to provide it with an appropriate service level. In addition, Diff-Serv is not in touch with the receiving host, so it doesn't know whether that host can handle the services it will allocate.

One could say that the Internet needs both RSVP (or some other full QoS model) and Diff-Serv. RFC 2990 mentions that both IntServ and Diff-Serv may need to be combined into an end-to-end model, with IntServ as the architecture that allows applications to interact with the network, and Diff-Serv as the architecture to manage admission and network resources. This is covered further in RFC 2998, "A Framework for Integrated Services Operation Over DiffServ Networks," (November 2000). One approach is to use Diff-Serv to carry RSVP application messages across the core to another RSVP network.

This discussion has so far compared Diff-Serv with IntServ and RSVP. Diff-Serv can be contrasted with MPLS, which implements connection-oriented virtual circuits on ATM, frame relay, or switched networks. MPLS adds labels (tags) to packets that indicate forwarding behavior, but packets travel across predefined circuits. MPLS is generally more sophisticated and complex than Diff-Serv, but provides better QoS capabilities.

Diff-Serv Architecture

RFC 2638 states that a differentiated services architecture should "keep the forwarding path simple, push complexity to the edges of the network to the extent possible, provide a service that avoids assumptions about the type of traffic using it, employ an allocation policy that will be compatible with both long-term and short-term provisioning, and make it possible for the dominant Internet traffic model to remain best-effort."

The IETF formed the Diff-Serv Working Group to develop a simple and coarse method for differentiating classes of service for Internet traffic. The primary Diff-Serv RFCs are RFC 2474, "Definition of the Differentiated Services Field in the IPv4 and IPv6 Headers," (December 1998), which defines the DS field and how it is used, and RFC 2475, "An Architecture for Differentiated Services," (December 1998), which describes techniques for implementing scalable differentiated services on the Internet.

Some important points about Diff-Serv are outlined here:

- Diff-Serv defines a new DS (Differentiated Services) field in the IP header that replaces the older ToS (Type of Service) field. Bit patterns in the field indicate the type of service and forwarding behavior at network nodes. The field is illustrated next. DSCP is the "differentiated services codepoint" (herein called DSCP, but also called the "DS codepoint," or simply "codepoint"), and CU indicates "currently unused."

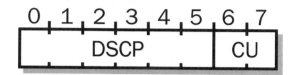

- The 6 bits in the DSCP field can define up to 64 discrete network service types.

- PHB (per-hop behavior) refers to a particular type of forwarding treatment for packets across the Diff-Serv network. The value of the DSCP field indicates the PHB to use.

- PHBs may satisfy a particular bandwidth requirement (i.e., to support real-time voice) or provide some priority service. Service characteristics may be designed to improve throughput or reduce delay, jitter, and packet loss.

- Differentiated services can accommodate different types of application requirements and allow service providers to price services according to their characteristics.

- Diff-Serv is designed to work within domains or end to end across the Internet (over different service provider domains).

- Rules that define service are set with policy-based management schemes (see "Policy-Based Management").

Per-Hop Behaviors

A PHB (per-hop behavior) is a basic hop-by-hop resource allocation mechanism. Think of PHB as a particular forwarding behavior that stretches across a network and that provides a particular class of service—being careful not to call it a path, because a path could imply state in the network.

RFC 2475 describes a PHB as a forwarding behavior applied to a particular DS behavior aggregate. A *DS behavior aggregate* is a collection of packets with the same DSCP value crossing a link in a particular direction. When a behavior aggregate arrives at a node, the node maps the DSCP to the appropriate PHB, and this mapping defines how the node will allocate resources to the behavior aggregate. Some example PHBs are described here:

- A PHB that guarantees a minimal bandwidth allocation across a link to a behavior aggregate.

- A PHB similar to the preceding with the added feature of being able to share any excess link capacity with other behavior aggregates.

- A PHB that has resource (buffers and bandwidth) priority over other PHBs.

- A PHB that has low delay and traffic loss characteristics

RFC 2474 and RFC 2475 include sections that describe guidelines for defining PHBs in order to promote consistency and standardization. The guidelines recommend that PHBs be designed to provide host-to-host, WAN edge–to–WAN edge, and/or domain edge–to–domain edge services.

A PHB is implemented with buffer management and packet -scheduling mechanisms. Routers examine the DSCP field, differentiate according to the markings, and then move packets into appropriate queues. An outgoing link typically has multiple queues with different priorities. A scheduling technique is used to move packets in the queues out to the next hop. See "Queuing" for additional information

Diff-Serv Network Elements

The Diff-Serv network consists of a variety of network elements and some specific terminology. Some of the elements are illustrated in Figure D-21 and explained next. All of these elements and their associated behaviors are designed to decouple traffic management and service provisioning functions from the forwarding functions, which are implemented within the core network nodes.

The most prominent features of Diff-Serv networks are the *DS domains* and the *DS boundary nodes*. The DS domains may be private intranets, but are typically autonomous service provider networks that have their own service-provisioning policies and PHB definitions. *DS Interior nodes* interpret the DSCP value and forward packets. They may perform some traffic conditioning functions and may remark packets. DS domains interconnect with other domains via boundary links. A *DS region* is a set of contiguous DS domains that offer inter-domain differentiated services.

The DS boundary nodes exist at the edge of the Diff-Serv network as either ingress or egress nodes. The ingress node is the most important because it classifies and injects traffic into the

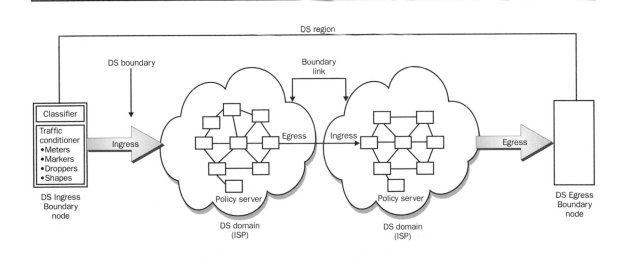

Figure D-21   *Diff-Serv Network elements*

network. It may also condition traffic to make sure it meets policy requirements. The boundary node contains the following elements.

- **Standard Classifier** Selects packets based on the DS codepoint value. Selected packets are then forwarded as appropriate or subjected to traffic conditioning if necessary.

- **Multi-Field Classifier** This classifier selects packets based on the content of some arbitrary number of header fields—typically, some combination of source address, destination address, DS field, protocol ID, source port, and destination port.

- **Marker** An entity that sets the value of the DSCP field.

- **Policy Systems/Bandwidth Brokers** Devices that are configured with organizational policies. They keep track of the current allocation of marked traffic and interpret new requests to mark traffic in light of the policies and current allocation. RFC 2638 provides a broad overview of these system requirements.

- **Traffic Conditioner** An entity that meters, marks, drops, and shapes traffic. A traffic conditioner may re-mark a traffic stream, or may discard or shape packets to alter the temporal characteristics of the stream and bring it into compliance with a traffic profile. The subcomponents of the traffic conditioner are listed here. See "Traffic Management, Shaping, and Engineering" for related details.

  - **Meter** Measures the rate of traffic streams selected by the classifier. The measurements are used by the following elements, or for accounting and measurement purposes.

  - **Policer** Evaluates the measurements made by the meter and uses them to enforce policy-based traffic profiles.

  - **Dropper** Droppers discard some or all of the packets in a traffic stream in order to bring the stream into compliance with a traffic profile. This process is known as "policing" the stream.

  - **Shaper** Delays packets within a traffic stream to cause it to conform to some defined traffic profile. A shaper may drop packets if there is not sufficient buffer space to hold the delayed packets.

Traffic conditioners are usually located within the DS ingress or egress boundary nodes, but may also be located in interior nodes within the DS domain. The ingress node of the source domain is the first to mark packets. An egress node that leads to another DS domain may re-mark packets if necessary.

Traffic conditioning rules are specified in a TCA (traffic conditioning agreement) and enforced by the traffic conditioner. TCA rules correspond to SLAs (service-level agreements) made between customers and service providers. These agreements specify the type of service a customer will receive. Note that DS domains within a region include ISPs that are peering with one another and have established peering SLAs.

Diff-Serv performs traffic conditioning to ensure that the traffic entering the DS domain conforms to the rules specified in the TCA, in accordance with the domain's service provisioning policy. The traffic classifier forwards packets to appropriate traffic conditioning elements.

Traffic conditioners use *traffic profiles* to determine how to condition traffic. A traffic profile defines the rules for determining whether packets are in-profile or out-of-profile. Out-of-profile packets may be queued until they are in-profile (shaped), discarded (policed), marked with a new codepoint (re-marked), or forwarded unchanged while triggering some accounting procedure. Out-of-profile packets may be mapped to an "inferior" behavior aggregate.

As mentioned in the preceding list, traffic conditioners contain meters, markers, shapers, and droppers. The meter measures traffic streams against the traffic profile, and the state of the meter affects whether a packet is marked, dropped, or shaped. The following illustration shows packets coming into the classifier. The meter measures the stream and passes information to other elements that trigger a particular action. The marker sets the DSCP value of a packet, effectively adding it to a particular behavior aggregate.

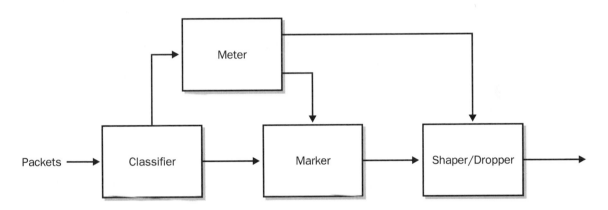

RFC 2597, "Assured Forwarding PHB Group," (June 1999) defines a method for defining drop precedence. IP packets are marked by customers or other ISPs with one of three possible drop precedence values. When congestion occurs, the congested DS node protects packets with a lower drop precedence value by discarding packets with a higher drop precedence value.

RFC 2598, "An Expedited Forwarding PHB," (June 1999) describes an expedited forwarding (EF) PHB that can be used to build a low-loss, low-latency, low-jitter, assured-bandwidth, end-to-end service through DS domains. Such a service appears to the endpoints like a point-to-point connection or a "virtual leased line." It is useful for voice over IP because it minimizes latency.

RFC 2697, "A Single Rate Three Color Marker [srTCM]," (September 1999) describes a way to mark packets according to three traffic parameters: Committed Information Rate, (CIR), Committed Burst Size (CBS), and Excess Burst Size (EBS). The srTCM is useful for ingress policing of a service, where only the length, not the peak rate, of the burst determines service eligibility.

RFC 2698, "A Two Rate Three Color Marker [trTCM]," (September 1999) describes a way to mark packets based on two rates, Peak Information Rate (PIR) and Committed Information Rate (CIR). The trTCM is useful for ingress policing of a service, where a peak rate needs to be enforced separately from a committed rate.

RFC 2859, "A Time Sliding Window Three Color Marker," (June 2000) describes a method of marking packets based on the measured throughput of the traffic stream, compared to the Committed Target Rate (CTR) and the Peak Target Rate (PTR). The marker is intended to mark packets that will be treated by the Assured Forwarding (AF) PHB in downstream routers.

Additional Diff-Serv Information

As previously mentioned, other sections cover functions that are performed in Diff-Serv networks and in many other types of networks. These topics include "Queuing," "Policy-Based Management," and "Traffic Management, Shaping, and Engineering."

The IETF Differentiated Services (diffserv) Working Group has a complete list of Diff-Serv–related RFCs and a list of drafts that describe the latest developments in Diff-Serv.

The IETF Internet Traffic Engineering (tewg) Working Group is defining traffic engineering techniques and mechanisms for intra-domain traffic engineering, including provisioning, measurement and control of intra-domain routing, and measurement and control aspects of intra-domain network resource allocation. It is developing traffic engineering models for ATM and frame relay overlay, MPLS, constraint-based routing, and Diff-Serv environments.

The IETF Policy Framework (policy) Working Group is defining policy frameworks, information models, and schemata to store, retrieve, distribute, and process policies. It is also defining intra-domain policies. The group is providing input to the Diff-Serv Working Group.

Finally, the Linktionary! Web site has additional information, including a more extensive set of links to Diff-Serv resources.

Related Entries   Admission Control; Bandwidth; Bandwidth Management; Capacity; Congestion Control Mechanisms; CoS (Class of Service); Data Communication Concepts; Delay, Latency, and Jitter; Flow Control Mechanisms; Integrated Services (IntServ); Label Switching; Load Balancing; MPLS (Multiprotocol Label Switching); Policy-Based Management; Prioritization of Network Traffic; QoS (Quality of Service); Queuing; RSVP (Resource Reservation Protocol); SLA (Service-Level Agreement); Throughput; ToS (Type of Service); Traffic Management, Shaping, and Engineering; Transport Protocols and Services; Voice Over IP; VLAN (Virtual LAN); *and* VPN (Virtual Private Networks)

Linktionary!—Tom Sheldon's Encyclopedia of Networking updates	http://www.linktionary.com/d/diffserv.html
IETF Working Group: Differentiated Services (diffserv)	http://www.ietf.org/html.charters/diffserv-charter.html
IETF Working Group: Internet Traffic Engineering (tewg)	http://www.ietf.org/html.charters/tewg-charter.html
IETF Working Group: Policy Framework (policy)	http://www.ietf.org/html.charters/policy-charter.html
"Differentiated Services for Internet2" by John Sikora and Ben Teitelbaum	http://www.internet2.edu/qos/may98Workshop/html/diffserv.html
Stardust.com quality of service channel	http://www.stardust.com/qos/
Intel document: "Differentiated Services"	http://www.intel.com/network/white_papers/diff_serv/

The QoS Alliance	http://www.qosalliance.org/
vBNS QBONE information	http://www.vbns.net/presentations/qbone-plan.html
Quality of service over IP references	http://www.cis.ohio-state.edu/~jain/refs/ipqs_ref.htm

Diffie-Hellman

Whitfield Diffie and Martin Hellman published the first public-key algorithm in 1976. However, Diffie and Hellman did not put their system to actual use. Ron Rivest, Adi Shamir, and Len Adleman developed the first practical system based on Diffie and Hellman's concepts in 1978. Their system became known as RSA (Rivest, Shamir, Adleman). Refer to "Public-Key Cryptography" for more information.

The Diffie-Hellman key exchange algorithm enables two parties to agree on a key that can be used to encrypt subsequent messages that are exchanged between the parties. Refer to "Key Exchange and Management" in this book. Also see RFC 2631, "Diffie-Hellman Key Agreement Method," (June 1999) and RFC 2875, "Diffie-Hellman Proof-of-Possession Algorithm," (July 2000).

Diff-Serv (Differentiated Services)

See Differentiated Services (Diff-Serv).

Digital Signal (DS) Standards

See DSx Standards.

Digital Signatures

Digital signatures are based on public-key cryptography. In the public-key scheme, each person has a pair of keys, one public and one private. The private key is never given out, while the public key is made freely available. To send a private message to someone, you encrypt the message with the recipient's public key. The recipient then decrypts the message with his or her private key. Thus, the message is kept private until the recipient receives it.

The public-key scheme associates a key with a person (or system). This association of user and key supports message signing, which can provide message authenticity, detect tampering and transmission errors, and provide nonrepudiation (someone denies being the sender of a message).

The signing process involves creating a unique digital fingerprint with the message itself using a hash function (discussed later in this topic). The fingerprint is then encrypted with the sender's private key. Since only the sender's public key will open the encrypted message, the message authenticity can be verified. The recipient can then check for tampering or errors by running the same hash function on the message as the sender. The unique fingerprint derived by both parties should be exactly the same, or the message is invalid.

As a side point, security expert Bruce Schneier wrote an interesting article about some of the problems with digital signatures and how they may not hold up in court. Refer to Schneier's November 15, 2000 Crypto-Gram at the address at the end of this topic for more information.

Digital signatures also prevent someone from denying that he or she sent a message. The signed message digest is proof that the message and its content are from the owner of the key that signed the message.

The public-key encryption and digital signature techniques are pictured in Figure D-22.

Suppose Bob wants to send a message to Alice, but Alice needs proof that the message is from Bob, that it has not been altered by someone else, and that there were no errors in communication. The steps are outlined here and pictured in Figure D-23.

1. Before sending the message, Bob runs the message through a *hash function* (see "Hash Functions"), which derives a unique block of information from the message, called a *message digest*.

2. Bob now encrypts the message digest with his private key and sends the message to Alice.

3. Alice decrypts the message digest with Bob's public key (which proves the message is from Bob, since only his public key can successfully decrypt the message digest).

4. Finally, Alice hashes the message using the same hash function as Bob. The resulting message digest should compare exactly with the one from Bob. Otherwise, the message is considered fake, altered, or in error.

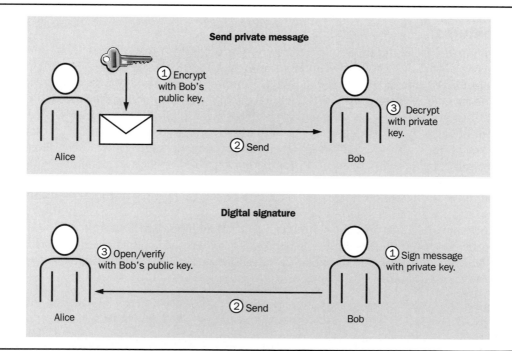

Figure D-22. *Two ways to perform public-key message authentication*

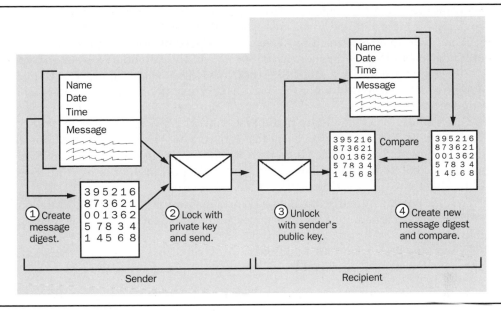

Figure D-23.   *Steps in the digital signature process*

The preceding process is relatively fast because only the small message digest must be encrypted. But this method does not hide the entire message, so eavesdroppers could view its contents. Still, the parties may only care about message integrity and not about privacy. To add privacy, Bob can encrypt the entire message with Alice's public key. Then, only Alice can open the message with her private key.

The W3C (World Wide Web Consortium) DSig (Digital Signature Initiative) is designed to develop trust on the Internet. DSig is a response to requests by vendors such as Microsoft, JavaSoft, and IBM to develop an interoperable infrastructure for digital signatures and code signing. DSig consists of digital signatures, identity certificates, packing lists, and content label technologies. There are two mechanisms at the core of DSig:

- Providing signature labels that allow a user or organization that signs an object to make statements about the object. These statements are called *assertions* and/or *endorsements*.

- Providing trust management systems that allow end users to verify the creator of downloadable code and what it does, by interpreting statements made by the signers of the objects.

For example, a digital signature may hold machine-readable code that makes assertions and endorsements. An example assertion might be "this Microsoft code was designed to run on Windows 2000." Another party can make assertions about the code as well, such as "Code x from Microsoft will run with our software." The mechanism for doing this is built into browsers.

DSS (Digital Signature Standard) and the DSA (Digital Signature Algorithm) are part of the U.S. government's Capstone program to develop cryptography and security standards for protecting government communications. DSS must be used by government agencies and private companies doing business with the government. NIST (National Institute of Standards and Technology) and NSA (National Security Agency) are responsible for Capstone. Capstone's major components include an encryption algorithm called *Skipjack* (and a Skipjack encryption chip called *Clipper*); a hash function called *SHA-1 (Secure Hash Standard)*; and DSA (Digital Signature Algorithm), which is the algorithm used in DSS. Capstone is also working on a key-exchange protocol.

The XML-Signature Working Group of the W3C is working with the IETF to develop an XML-compliant syntax that will represent the signature of Web resources, and portions of protocol messages and procedures for computing and verifying such signatures. Such signatures will be able to provide data integrity, authentication, and/or nonrepudiation. Refer to http://www.w3.org/Signature/ for more information.

The IETF XML Digital Signatures (xmldsig) Working Group is developing XML-compliant syntax to represent the signature of Web resources and portions of protocol messages (anything referencable by a URI).

The IETF working groups and the Linktionary! Web site listed at the end of this topic provide a list of relevant RFCs and Web sites.

Related Entries   Certificates and Certification Servers; Cryptography; Kerberos; PKI (Public-Key Infrastructure); Public-Key Cryptography; Security; *and* X.509 Certificates

In addition to the following links, others appear under "Security" in this book.

Linktionary!—Tom Sheldon's Encyclopedia of Networking updates	http://www.linktionary.com/security/
DSS (Digital Signature Standard), U.S. Department of Commerce/NIST	http://csrc.ncsl.nist.gov/fips/fips186.txt
W3C digital signature information	http://www.w3.org/DSig/
W3C general security information	http://www.w3.org/pub/WWW/Security
Digital signatures: Security standards list at OII	http://www2.echo.lu/oii/en/secure.html
RSA Data Systems	http://www.rsa.com
VeriSign	http://www.verisign.com
Bruce Schneier's November 15, 2000 Crypto-Gram (see "Why Digital Signatures are Not Signatures")	http://www.counterpane.com/crypto-gram-0011.html
IETF Working Group: XML Digital Signatures (xmldsig)	http://www.ietf.org/html.charters/xmldsig-charter.html

Digitize

Digitizing is the process of converting any kind of information to digital information (1s and 0s). An analog signal such as a voice telephone conversation is converted to digital for transmission across a digital link. Sound is digitized for storage in computers or on CD-ROMs. Pictures are digitized with scanners so they can be displayed on computer screens and stored on disk.

Related Entries   ADC (Analog-to-Digital Conversion); Imaging

Dijkstra Algorithm

The Dijkstra algorithm is used with link-state routing protocols to help find the shortest path through a mesh of network connections based on the path with the least cost. The algorithm runs through a series of calculations that eventually develop the cost of pathways to nodes, and the pathway that has the least cost.

Related Entries   Link State Routing; Routing Protocols and Algorithms

Directory Attributes and Management

See File Systems.

Directory Services

Directory services are to a network what white pages are to the telephone system. They store information about things in the real world, such as people, computers, printers, and so on, as objects with descriptive attributes. People can use the service to look up objects by name; or, like the yellow pages, they can be used to look up services.

Network managers use directories to manage user accounts and network resources. From a manager's viewpoint, a directory service is like an inventory of all the devices on the network. Any device can be located by using a graphic interface or by searching for its name or some properties (i.e., "color printer"). Once located, a manager can control the device (i.e., disable it or block certain users from accessing it). The directory is a central database where all objects and users are managed.

 DNS (Domain Name System) is a form of directory service. It holds information about domain names.

A directory service consists of a data store similar to a database, but it differs from the traditional database in a number of ways. The organization of a directory is hierarchical, with classes of objects and subclasses of objects. A directory is primarily used for lookup operations, rather than continuous reads and writes. The information does not change as often as a transactional database. Therefore, frequent updates to distributed copies of the database are less of a concern.

An early directory services standard was X.500, which is discussed elsewhere. Today, Microsoft Windows 2000 Active Directory and Novell Directory Services (NDS) build on that model. An important directory services protocol is LDAP (Lightweight Directory Access Protocol), an IETF-defined client/server protocol for accessing a directory.

Directories are now used to manage a wide range of information, including QoS, bandwidth management policies, profiles, electronic commerce information, and more. They also play an important security role related to authentication of users, firewall filtering, and VPN access. Most directory products now map certificates to user accounts in the directory, and a directory can provide single sign-on for users. DEN (Directory Enabled Network) is a directory services initiative that addresses the issues of policy-based networking and interoperable networks.

The role of directories in electronic commerce and business-to-business relationships is significant. Directories can hold important information about people outside the corporate network that can be used to identify them and define their access to network resources. Managers can apply policies across objects in the directory to quickly define access for groups of people, such as business partners.

Directory services provide a common location to store all types of information. At the same time, an organization may want to maintain multiple different directories for security or business-related reasons. *Meta-directories* are separate or integrated directory components that help link multiple different directories and synchronize the information in the directories. LDAP plays the role of connecting with other directories. XML can provide a standard way to represent information that needs to be communicated between directories.

Directory Structure and Operation

X.500 is a family of directory services standards ratified by the CCITT (now referred to as ITU-T) in 1988. It was originally designed to work with the X.400 messaging standard. Today, X.500 serves mainly as a model for commercial products. X.500 was designed to use the OSI protocol suite, but TCP/IP became the de facto network protocol. Consequently, most directory services today are modeled after X.500 and designed to run on TCP/IP. LDAP is a modification of an X.500 protocol made to run on TCP/IP networks.

The X.500 inverted hierarchical tree format is shown in Figure D-24. The directory consists of *entries* that are either *containers* or *leaf objects*. Containers are situated at branches in the tree and hold other containers and/or leaf objects. Leaf objects represent real-world objects like people, computers, printers, and storage volumes. Each of these objects has a CN (common name) and attributes, as discussed shortly. A DN (distinguished name) is a name that defines all the containers that form a path from the top of the tree to an object. In Figure D-24, Joe's DN is

    cn=Joe,ou=Eng,o=Bigcorp,c=US

Every entry in the database (the logical directory tree) has an object class. In Figure D-24, US and UK are of object class **Country**, while Microsoft and BigCorp are of object class **Organization**. Joe is of object class **Person**.

Each object class has a specific set of *attributes* (also called "properties" or "elements"). Attributes are basically fields in the database that can hold some value. An **Organization** entry will have attributes that describe a company, while a **Person** entry will have attributes that define people. The most common attributes are Common Name, Address, Mail, Department, Phone, Fax, and so on.

The concept of subclasses of objects is important. If you create an object and give it certain attributes, and then create a subclass under that object, the subclass will automatically "inherit" the attributes of the parent. If you change the parent, the subclass also inherits those changes. For example, an object **Printer** will have the basic attributes of all printers. Under this are subclasses of printers, such as color printer, collating printers, and so on. This scheme greatly benefits enterprise-wide management, especially as organizations grow and change.

RFC 1617, "Naming and Structuring Guidelines for X.500 Directory Pilots," (May 1994) provides useful information about directory services and guidelines for planning a directory structure.

D

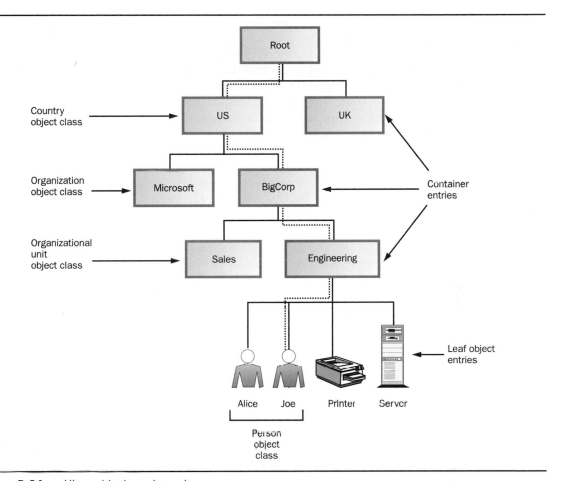

Figure D-24. *Hierarchical naming scheme*

LDAP (Lightweight Directory Access Protocol) is a common protocol for accessing a directory. It is a client/server protocol, in which a client operation may add and delete, or modify entry, or simply query the database about some entry. Clients can also search a database by specifying the attributes of an object they are looking for. Queries can be limited to specific branches of the tree. For example, in Figure D-24, you could execute a search for an object under the BigCorp entry in the database.

Directory Schema

Schema is a structural model that defines how objects in the real world such as people and computers are represented in the directory database. It defines the structure of the database, the names of the objects in it, and the attributes of those objects. RFC 2251, "LDAPv3," (December 1997) provides a good description of schema.

An analogy of a schema is the postal addressing scheme. An envelope is addressed with a name, address, city, state, and ZIP code. This same scheme is used throughout the country, which makes the mail system work well. Unfortunately, most directory services do not use the same schema, and so interoperability is difficult. Directory services like Novell NDS have a set of defined objects such as Person and Computer, but administrators can also make up their own objects. But once a directory is "customized" in this way, it is more difficult to merge the directory with another directory, as is necessary when two companies merge or when electronic business partners need to share directory information. Meta-directories and translation schemes, discussed next, are required to handle this.

The DEN (Directory Enabled Networks) Initiative defines a standard directory services architecture and schema that can be used to store network policy and configuration information for switches, routers, servers, and other devices. See "DEN (Directory Enabled Networks)" for more information.

Meta-Directories

A meta-directory adds interoperability to directory services by serving as a single point of access to other directory services. It is a form of middleware. A meta-directory provides a way for different directory services to exchange data. Think of a meta-directory as a sort of central hub to which directories connect to exchange information.

The following comes from "The Meta-Directory FAQ" by The Burton Group:

> In 1996, The Burton Group formalized the "meta-directory" concept, describing a functional specification of join, centralized registration, attribute flow, and other directory services.

The terminology is derived from metadata, which comes from the database world. Metadata describes data in a database in the same way that a card catalog describes books in a library. The Burton Group coined the term "meta-directory" to describe a class of products that were emerging to integrate and translate information among multiple directory services. According to the FAQ, "meta-directory services consolidate subsets of the information in multiple directories, including data on people, groups, roles, organizational units, locations, and other resources. This consolidation creates a join, or unified view, of the different directories in an organization. The meta-directory makes that unified view accessible via LDAP and Web-based access protocols."

The join aspect of meta-directories is best understood by considering that a single user has multiple identities on a network, such as his or her logon name and e-mail name. A meta-directory can also help resolve differences in naming schemes among the directories established within an organization or between business partners. All of this is done dynamically by a system that tracks changes and makes sure that information about those changes is updated appropriately.

There are two types of meta-directories:

■ **Consolidated meta-directory**   In this scheme, a separate directory is created that points to all the other directories. An administrator works with the meta-directory, and not necessarily each of the individual referenced directories. Isocor (http://www.isocor.com) uses this approach.

■ **Virtual meta-directory**   In this scheme, an additional directory is not created. Instead, a management application allows an administrator to work directly with the individual directories by providing a single view of the directory via an index-mapping scheme. Entevo (http://www.entevo.com) uses this approach.

Meta-directories resolve political problems related to which directory service should be used or, if multiple directories exist, which should be the top directory. Microsoft had originally designed its Active Directory to operate as the all-controlling directory, but realized that it needed to support heterogeneous directory environments. It bought a company called Zoomit for its Via meta-directory product and reworked it to create "Microsoft Meta-Directory Services."

Novell is using DirXML to obtain directory information from legacy directories. DirXML relies on LDAP to connect with other directories, and XML as a standard format for information exchange.

Eventually, interoperability services will no doubt be integrated into directory services.

DSML (Directory Services Markup Language)

DSML is a schema for describing directory services information in XML (Extensible Markup Language). DSML integrates XML and directories. It provides a way to access information in directories, package it, and ship it over an intranet or the Internet. Bowstreet is responsible for DSML, which is supported by major vendors including IBM, Microsoft, Novell, Oracle, Netscape, and Sun Microsystems.

DSML allows XML-based applications to take advantage of directories. Basically, a standard schema defines the content and structure of directory information. This information goes in a DCD (document content description), which can be transmitted to other applications that need to use the information. LDAP is used to access directory information as usual, but DSML provides a way for other applications to interpret directory information. With DSML as a standard, custom applications do not need to be written for every different directory. By expressing directory information in XML, any XML based application can use the information. The DSML and Bowstreet Web sites listed at the end of this topic provide more information on DSML.

Directory Enabled Networks and Policy Management

Policy-based networking and directories are joining up to provide a central place to manage and allocate network resources, including network bandwidth within network core and edge devices. By merging policy-based management and directories, administrators gain more control over the management of network equipment and the ability to manage QoS across multiple networks. Policy rules in a directory can define the type of QoS and traffic routing that will be assigned to a particular person, group, or service.

An important concept is that device configuration information moves to the directory where it benefits from the hierarchical management schemes that directories offer. Devices check with the centralized directory for update information or policy changes, rather than relying on an administrator to program that information into the devices themselves on a one-on-one basis.

Novell's ZENworks for Networks is a network services software product that automates policy management, using Novell's NDS as a repository for policy information. The product supports end-to-end QoS management and works with network equipment, such as switches and routers, from major network vendors. Administrators can use the software to assign bandwidth to applications and users.

DEN integrates policy services and directory services into an authoritative, distributed, intelligent repository of information.

See "Policy-Based Management," "QoS (Quality of Service)," and "DEN (Directory Enabled Networks)" for more information.

Replication and Partitioning

Most directory services support replication and partitioning. Replication is a way to copy the database to other locations and ensure that all copies are updated and synchronized. Partitioning splits a directory at branches in the tree so that the pieces (such as all the objects for a department) can be located on servers at other locations (such as a department). Partitioning and replication provide fault tolerance and allow users to access nearby information.

X.500 defines the master-slave database model of replication, in which all writes are made to a master copy and then written out to the slave copies from the master. The alternative is the multiple-master model in which changes must be made to multiple copies at the same time. The latter model is considered more difficult to implement and prone to a loss of data integrity.

Replicating and partitioning introduces the need for synchronization. Changes made in one database must be made as soon as possible in replicas. If a lot of administrators make frequent updates in different locations, the updates must occur more often. Reducing the number of people who can make changes helps solve the problem. Fortunately, directories are primarily "lookup" services that can tolerate longer update delays than traditional databases.

Novell uses a timestamp to indicate which updates are the most recent, while Microsoft's Active Directory uses a sequence numbering scheme to assign a number to the most current changes.

Available Services

The most important directory services are described next. At this writing, the two primary directory services are Microsoft Active Directory and Novell NDS. Active Directory runs only with Windows 2000, while NDS has been ported to a variety of platforms. One notable difference between the two is that with NDS, all access controls are managed from the directory. With Windows 2000, some access controls are in Active Directory, while others are at servers. NDS follows the more traditional X.500 model, while Active Directory still has elements of Microsoft Domain Model, a proprietary scheme.

■ **DCE Directory Services** (http://www.opengroup.org/)   The Open Group's DCE (Distributed Computing Environment) includes its own directory services that are integrated with other DCE components, as described under "DCE (Distributed Computing Environment)."

■ **IBM Network Directory** (http://www-4.ibm.com/software/network/directory/) IBM's entry into the directory services market is based on its DB2 database system. It is designed with e-commerce and business-to-business transactions in mind. IBM claims the service is more secure and scalable than Novell's NDS and Microsoft's Active Directory.

■ **Netscape Directory Server** (http://developer.netscape.com/tech/directory/) Netscape's Directory Server is designed to be a central place for adding, modifying, and removing user information. It can organize and distribute the information throughout a series of servers on an organization's intranet. The services can be integrated with Netscape's SuiteSpot to provide structured information and group information for the entire suite of applications. Directory Server implements advanced LDAP support and tools for writing directory enabled apps. It also includes enhancements for continuous operation and heterogeneous replication between LDAP servers.

■ **Novell Directory Services** (http://www.novell.com/products/nds/)   NDS (Novell Directory Services) is a feature in NetWare 4.*x* that implements a distributed directory service similar to the X.500 specification. Novell has adapted NDS for use on Windows NT and UNIX platforms. A special e-commerce version of NDS is also available. See "NDS (Novell Directory Services)" for more information.

■ **Microsoft Active Directory** (http://www.microsoft.com/windows2000/)   Active Directory combines features of the Internet's DNS locator service and X.500 naming. LDAP is the core access protocol for the service. LDAP will allow Microsoft's Active Directory to work across operating system boundaries and integrate multiple name spaces, thus allowing administrators to manage other vendors' directory services. See "Microsoft Active Directory" for more information.

The Directory Interoperability Forum was formed to advance open directories based on LDAP standards. The forum is a group of open directory providers who plan to work through standards bodies to accelerate the evolution and adoption of directory-based applications. Refer to http://www.directoryforum.org/ for more information.

IETF Working Groups

A number of IETF working groups have worked on or are working on directory services standards. A list of working groups is provided here.

IETF Working Group, Directory Services, LDAP Extensions (ldapext)	http://www.ietf.org/html.charters/ldapext-charter.html
IETF Working Group, Directory Services: LDAP Duplication/Replication/Update Protocols (ldup)	http://www.ietf.org/html.charters/ldup-charter.html
IETF Working Group: Policy Frameworks including directory services	http://www.ietf.org/html.charters/policy-charter.html

Related Entries   CIP (Common Indexing Protocol); CNRP (Common Name Resolution Protocol); DEN (Directory Enabled Networks); LDAP (Lightweight Directory Access Protocol); Metadata; Microsoft Active Directory; Name Services; NDS (Novell Directory Services); NIS (Network Information System); Search and Discovery Services; Service Advertising and Discovery; SLP (Service Location Protocol); URI (Uniform Resource Identifier); URN (Uniform Resource Name); WHOIS; *and* X.500 Directory Services

Linktionary!—Tom Sheldon's Encyclopedia of Networking updates	http://www.linktionary.com/d/dirserv.html
The X.500 Global Directory Service (Search the X.500 global directory for individuals.)	http://ganges.cs.tcd.ie/ntrg/x500.html
The Directory Interoperability Forum (DIF)	http://www.directoryforum.org/
DSML (Directory Services Markup Language) Web site.	http://www.dsml.org/
3Com papers (See directory topics and Policy-Powered Networking papers.)	http://www.3com.com/technology/tech_net/white_papers/index.html
Network World information and articles about directory services	http://www.nwfusion.com/netresources/directories.html
The Meta-Directory FAQ by The Burton Group	http://www.tbg.com/public/content/metafaq.asp
NETPRO Directory Resources (useful links)	http://www.netpro.com/directoryexperts/resources.asp
Complete list of directory services and LDAP RFCs	http://olymp.wu-wien.ac.at/manuals/rfc-ldap.html
X.500 and LDAP: Raw Bibliography of Relevant RFCs	http://www.stanford.edu/group/networking/directory/x500ldapfaq.biblio.html
Links to documents about directory services at Tumbleweed Communications	http://www.worldtalk.com/Standards%20and%20Tech/dirref.shtm
Bowstreet	http://www.bowstreet.com/
Novell	http://www.novell.com/edirectory/
Microsoft	http://www.microsoft.com/
FastLane Technologies, Inc.	http://www.fastlane.com/
Entevo (directory management products)	http://www.entevo.com/
Process Software Corp.	http://www.process.com/
ISOCOR (meta-directory solutions)	http://www.isocor.com/
Radiant Logic (directory design tools)	http://www.radiantlogic.com/

Disaster Planning and Recovery

Network managers must prepare for fires, earthquakes, storms, and theft. Disasters can disrupt user access to data and/or data communications. A downed server or failed communication link may be disastrous if those resources are needed for critical operations. A system may provide life-support or life-saving information, or may provide mission-critical business transaction services.

A disaster plan must define a recovery procedure that brings resources back online as fast as possible, or ensures that they are operational 24/7 (24 hours a day, 7 days a week). A downed business transaction server could mount up losses in the millions of dollars over only a few hours or days.

Disaster planning not only involves a plan to recover from the disaster, but also requires redundant components, systems, and even duplicate data centers that can continue operations. Systems must provide automatic failover if they are to provide high levels of service. The levels of service are gauged by metrics used throughout the industry. So-called "high-availability" systems have ratings in the "five-nines" (99.999%) availability. See "Fault Tolerance and High Availability."

The best disaster plan for large companies is to build an alternative data site or use public data centers. A public data center can host your Web operations and provide disaster protection, fault tolerance, and data replication to alternative sites. You can also use a public data center as a safe place to store your data, even if the site does not host your Web operations. Alternatively, you can build your own alternative data centers. This is common with many large companies. Another solution is to continuously replicate important information to servers at other corporate sites.

The best place to start is by evaluating the importance of your equipment and data for day-to-day operations. Consider how long your business can operate on backup systems. Consider what will happen if a disaster lasted for more than a few days. In the event of a fire in the lobby of an office building, officials may close down the entire building for weeks, not allowing anyone access to systems and data.

Evaluate the strategy you will use to replicate data to alternative sites. Keep in mind that replication may not take place immediately. The most current data at the main data center may not be replicated for a few minutes or even hours.

Consider that communication channels may fail during a local or regional disaster. You'll need to transfer information to an alternative site by physical means, and this requires a plan to move backups off-site and restore them on other systems. Back up data continuously to tapes, optical disk, or whatever means you use, and transfer this information regularly to the alternative site. Keep track of what has not been backed up in this way, and put a plan into place that will help people obtain that data at the last minute.

Your last-minute plans may fail if users can't even get into a building to implement your plan. Perhaps the best thing to do is to stop all operations well in advance if you know a disaster is pending (i.e., a hurricane is on the way). You may need a plan that continuously replicates a data center in real time to another site and provides fast automatic failover in the event of a disaster. Most Web hosting services have experience in this area, and the equipment and expertise is now readily available.

Test your plan using whatever means possible, including disaster simulations during off-hours. Document everything.

The January 11, 1999, issue of *Network Computing Magazine* includes an article by Brian Walsh called "Request for Proposal: Heading for Disaster?" It includes three proposals from Comdisco, Exodus, and IBM in response to a request for a "business-continuity plan of action to survive unforeseen calamities." You can find this article at the Web link provided at the end of this topic. Note that all of the companies mentioned in the article offer disaster services in the form of planning, system design, and maintenance. They also make their own data centers available for leasing by customers that prefer to outsource these services.

Related Entries   Backup and Data Archiving; Clustering; Data Center Design; Data Migration; Data Protection; Fault Management; Fault Tolerance and High-Availability; Mirroring; Power and Grounding Problems and Solutions; Redundancy; Replication; SAN (System Area Network); Security;

Storage Management Systems; UPS (Uninterruptible Power Supply); *and* VRRP (Virtual Router Redundancy Protocol)

Linktionary!—Tom Sheldon's Encyclopedia of Networking updates	http://www.linktionary.com/d/disaster.html
CERT (Computer Emergency Response Team) Coordination Center	http://www.cert.org
CIAC (Computer Incident Advisory Capability)	http://ciac.llnl.gov
Forum of Incident Response and Security Teams	http://www.first.org
Harris Disaster Recovery Associates	http://www.hdra.com/
IBM Emergency Response Service	http://www-1.ibm.com/services/continuity/recover1.nsf/ers/Home
Public Library Association digital disaster planning document	http://www.pla.org/ddp.html
Comdisco Continuity Services	http://www.comdisco.com/
The Disaster Center	http://www.disastercenter.com/
Disaster Survival Planning Network	http://www.disaster-survival.com/
Data Recovery, Inc. (recovery hard drives and disaster planning)	http://www.datarecoveryinc.com/
Exabyte data recovery services	http://www.exabyte.com/suppserv/techsupp/recovery/in0230.html
Binomial International Disaster Recovery Planning	http://www.disasterrecovery.com
3Com paper: Bulletproofing Networks for High-Availability Computing	http://www.3com.com/technology/tech_net/white_papers/500693.html
Sun Microsystems document: Data Protection Solutions	http://www.sun.com/storage/white-papers/dataprotection.html
Patrick H. Corrigan's disaster planning paper	http://www.sci.sdsu.edu/People/Diana/network/disaster.html
Network Computing Magazine article: "RFP: Heading for Disaster?" by Brian Walsh	http://www.networkcomputing.com/1001/1001f1.html
EnterEdge Technology (see "Disaster Planning" section)	http://www.enteredge.com/
Veritas	http://www.veritas.com/

Discovery Services

A variety of services are available or emerging that help users find and locate resources and services on intranet and the Internet. Refer to these topics for more information:

- CNRP (Common Name Resolution Protocol)
- Directory Services

- Handle System
- Metadata
- Name Services
- Search and Discovery Services
- Service Advertising and Discovery
- SLP (Service Location Protocol)
- URN (Uniform Resource Naming)

Discretionary Access Control

Discretionary access control, or DAC, is a form of access control to resources (directories and files) in which individual users can be assigned a unique type of access. For example, John can be allowed to both read and change a file, while Jim can be restricted to only reading the file. In contrast, nondiscretionary access control implies that all users accessing a resource receive the same rights—whatever share level you set for the resource.

Related Entry   Access Control

Disk Storage Systems

The following topics provide disk and storage information: Clustering; File Systems; NAS (Network Attached Storage); RAID (Redundant Arrays of Inexpensive Disks); SAN (Storage Area Networks); Servers; Storage Management Systems; Storage Systems; and Volume and Partition Management.

Diskless Workstations

Diskless workstations are inexpensive computers without floppy disk drives or hard disk drives. They provide users with network access at a reasonable price, and they offer data security because users can't download data to floppy disks and carry it off-site. Diskless workstations are a consideration for use by temporary employees or installation in unsupervised areas. See "Thin Clients" for the latest information about these types of systems.

When using diskless workstations, you'll need a network interface card that supports the use of a remote boot PROM (programmable read-only memory) chip. Most interface cards have this option, but it's a good idea to make sure. Remote boot PROMs cost are added to cards as an option. The PROM allows the workstation to boot from a boot file located on the network server.

Related Entries   ARP (Address Resolution Protocol); BOOTP; Bootstrapping or Booting; DHCP (Dynamic Host Configuration Protocol); NC (Network Computer) Devices; Network Appliance; RARP (Reverse Address Resolution Protocol); Terminal Servers; Thin Clients; *and* X Window

Distance-Vector Routing

The distance-vector routing is a type of algorithm used by routing protocols to discover routes on an interconnected network. The primary distance-vector routing algorithm is the Bellman-Ford algorithm. Another type of routing algorithm is the *link-state* approach, as covered elsewhere in this book. Routing protocols that use distance-vector routing include RIP (Routing Information Protocol), Cisco's IGRP (Internet Gateway Routing Protocol), and Apple's RTMP (Routing Table Maintenance Protocol). The most common link-state routing protocol is OSPF (Open Shortest Path First).

Dynamic routing, as opposed to static (manually entered) routing, requires routing algorithms. Dynamic routing protocols assist in the automatic creation of routing tables. Network topologies are subject to change at any time. A link may fail unexpectedly, or a new link may be added. A dynamic routing protocol must discover these changes, automatically adjust its routing tables, and inform other routers of the changes. The process of rebuilding the routing tables based on new information is called *convergence*.

Distance-vector routing refers to a method for exchanging route information. A router will advertise a route as a vector of *direction* and *distance*. Direction refers to a port that leads to the next router along the path to the destination, and distance is a metric that indicates the number of hops to the destination, although it may also be an arbitrary value that gives one route precedence over another. Internetwork routers exchange this vector information and build route lookup tables from it.

Router A receives a vector from its immediate neighbor, router B, that indicates that router C is its neighbor. Therefore, to router A, router C is one hop away in the direction of router B. This information is then used by routers to forward packets along the best possible path to their destination.

As an analogy, assume you are visiting a city and you want to see its museum. The city has conveniently posted directions at every intersection. The intersection right outside your hotel says "Museum, Go North, 5 blocks." So you head to the next intersection. There, a sign says "Museum, Go East, 4 blocks" and "Museum, Go North, 7 blocks." Two vectors. You can choose either, but one is farther than the other because it goes around a block. You might need to take that long route if the short route is blocked. You take the short route and proceed on to the museum by following the posted directions.

Now consider how those directions were obtained, pretending that you are a blind router with no concept of the topology. We'll also need some "agents" to write down route information and pass it around. At the museum, the agent posts directions at all the intersections that are one block away, something like "Museum, Go East, 1 block." Now an agent at each of those intersections takes the instructions to the next intersections outward from the museum and writes instructions such as "Museum, Go East, 2 blocks."

From this, you can see how the routing information is generated in steps outward from the museum. The operation in a network is pictured in Figure D-25 and described next. For clarity, note that only the last two bytes of the IP addresses are used.

- ■ **Time interval 1**   Each router builds its own table to describe its local interfaces. The hop count is 0 since they are locally connected.

- **Time interval 2**   Routers send their tables to neighbors (A sends to B, B sends to A and C, C sends to B). Each router calculates a new routing table based on the new entries it has received from neighbors, adjusting hop counts to reflect distance from the current location.

- **Time interval 3**   The routers once again exchange routing tables. Router B has information about network 1.0 and network 4.0, and it passes this on to the other routers. At this point, the network of three routers is converged.

A more interesting convergence takes place when multiple paths exist to a destination. For example, you could attach a router to Net 4 and then attach that router to Net 1. After convergence, routing tables would then reflect the hop count to any router going in either direction. Obviously, one direction will always have a higher hop count than the other direction; but if a link fails, that opposite direction becomes useful.

Routers will exchange routing tables on a periodic basis and then update their own tables with any new routes or routes that it determines are better, based on a smaller hop count.

Distance-vector routing is easy to manage and is a good choice for small corporate internetworks. However, it has some disadvantages. The entire routing table is transmitted periodically, reducing network bandwidth, even if no updates have taken place. In addition, it may take a while to complete table convergence; and while this is taking place, other problems may occur that are not included in the convergence.

Normally, if a network goes down, the router will inform other routers that a link has failed. But if a router goes down, other routers do not receive such a message. The solution

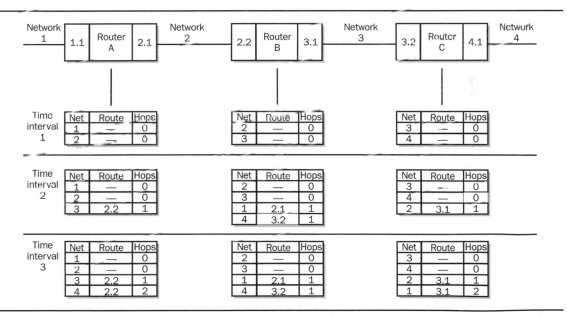

Figure D-25.   *Distance-vector routing table formation*

is for routers to set a time limit on the information they receive from other routers. If the router sending that information does not update it at the next interval, the information will be discarded after the time-out period (usually several update periods). This ensures that information is up to date.

Referring to Figure D-25, assume that network 4 goes down. Router C prepares to send an update to router B at the next update interval. In the meantime, router B sends its update to router C with an entry for network 4. This is obsolete information, but router C does not know that. It thinks, "Oh, I can get to network 4 through router B" and updates its table. When a packet arrives at router B, the router forwards the packet to router C. But router C thinks that router B is the path to network 4 and sends the packet back to router C. Router B returns it to router C, and the loop would continue indefinitely (called "count to infinity")—except that maximum hop counts are now implemented, in which a packet is dropped after being forwarded a set maximum number of times (usually 15).

To prevent this problem in the first place, a technique called *split horizon* prevents a router from sending route entries to a router that it has learned from that router. Another form of this technique, called *poisoned reverse*, actually returns the route entries to their source but marks them as unreachable.

RFC 1058, "Routing Information Protocol," (June 1988) is a good document to read for further information. Refer to "Distance Vector Routings."

Related Entries   IGRP (Interior Gateway Routing Protocol); IP (Internet Protocol); Link-State Routing; RIP (Routing Information Protocol) Router; Routing; Routing on the Internet; *and* VRRP (Virtual Router Redundancy Protocol)

Linktionary!—Tom Sheldon's Encyclopedia of Networking updates	http://www.linktionary.com/r/routing.html
IETF Working Group: Routing Information Protocol (rip)	http://www.ietf.org/html.charters/rip-charter.html
Cisco documentation: Routing Basics	http://www.cisco.com/univercd/cc/td/doc/cisintwk/ito_doc/routing.htm
Cisco Documentation: Routing Information Protocol (RIP)	http://www.cisco.com/univercd/cc/td/doc/cisintwk/ito_doc/rip.htm

Distributed Applications

Distributed applications allow users to interact with other systems on a network. A distributed application is traditionally divided into two parts—the front-end client and the back-end server. This is the *client/server* model, a model that balances processing loads between client and server. See "Client/Server Computing." *Distributed* means that clients may interact with many different servers all over the network.

Application/groupware suites like Microsoft Exchange, Novell GroupWise, Lotus Notes/Domino, and Netscape SuiteSpot are designed for distributed networks, while management applications that use SNMP can collect information from remote systems and report it back to management systems.

The Internet and the Web are "massively distributed networks." Web browsers provide a *universal client* for accessing applications and resources on local and remote systems, either within the organization or outside. The object/component approach breaks up complex programs into smaller components that make it easier to distribute and update applications, especially on the Internet.

Dan Nessett of 3Com points out some important and emerging concepts for object technologies in his excellent paper "Massively Distributed Systems" (see the link at the end of this section). He points out two ways of organizing computations on distributed systems:

- Move data to the processing, as is done with NFS (Network File System), World Wide Web, FTP, and Gopher.

- Move processing to the data, as is done with active networking and Java applets (i.e., objects move within the distributed system, and carry both code and data).

Nessett notes that "If the object consists primarily of data, it will closely approximate moving data to the processing. If it consists primarily of code, it will closely approximate moving processing to the data."

The three-tier model consists of clients on one end and servers on the other, and a middle tier that provides services, business rules, transaction management, and other business logic. The server side may consist of database servers, data marts, and data warehouses. See "Distributed Computer Networks," "Multitiered Architecture" "Distributed Object Computing," and "Object Technologies."

The middleware component is now commonly referred to as an *application server*. Application servers interface with databases and information systems on the back end and clients, usually Web server clients, on the front end. The servers may perform relatively simple functions, such as building Web pages on-the-fly with data obtained from back-end servers. The servers may also provide more sophisticated functions, such as transaction processing in electronic commerce applications

Application servers provide a variety of functions. They serve as a central hub for application services, including message routing, object exchange, transaction processing, data transformation, and so on. They also may support CORBA, Microsoft COM/DCOM, and Enterprise JavaBeans. Additional features include the ability to connect with a variety of back-end database services and to load balance the traffic between users and a cluster of servers.

Distributed Application Models

There are several models for creating distributed applications and providing a way for client, server, and components to communicate:

- **RPCs (remote procedure calls)**   A session-oriented communication protocol between computers connected across networks. RPCs are generally used for real-time, connection-oriented activities.

- **Messaging services**   Messaging services (usually called *MOM*, or *message-oriented middleware*) provide a way to exchange information between applications and components using queues and store-and-forward messaging. It is not appropriate for real-time communications. Newer techniques use XML. Microsoft's SOAP (Simple

Object Access Protocol) is a message-passing protocol that uses HTTP to carry XML-formatted messages.

■ **ORB (object-request brokering)** The best way to describe how ORBs fit into this picture is to describe their use in the Web client/server model. A user running a Web browser contacts a Web site and uses an ORB to locate a necessary component. Once he or she has the component, the client communicates through it to back-end services, and the original Web server is out of the picture.

For more information about middleware in general, see "Distributed Object Computing," and "Middleware and Messaging."

A transaction system protects data from damage that can occur if an in-process transaction fails due to hardware problems or communication problems. A business system may consist of data servers at far-flung locations that must contain the same information. If an inventory is stored over multiple servers to make data more available to local users, changes to the inventory in one location must be immediately posted to other locations. If a glitch occurs during the transaction, all the changes made so far must be backed out. No transaction is complete until it is fully written to all the data servers involved. This topic is covered further under "Transaction Processing."

Related Entries   ActiveX; Client/Server Computing; Collaborative Computing; COM (Component Object Model); DBMS (Database Management System); Distributed Computer Networks; Distributed Object Computing; Groupware; Instant Messaging; Java; Middleware and Messaging; MOM (Message-Oriented Middleware); Multitiered Architectures; Object Technologies; ORB (Object Request Broker); RPCs (Remote Procedure Calls); SOAP (Simple Object Access Protocol); Transaction Processing; *and* Unified Messaging

Linktionary!—Tom Sheldon's Encyclopedia of Networking updates	http://www.linktionary.com/d/dist_apps.html
Application server information at Serversatch.Internet.com	http://serverwatch.internet.com/appservers.html
Application server page at Webreview.com	http://www.webreview.com/pub/app_servers/
Application server zone	http://www.appserver-zone.com
CAIT Information Systems Meta-List	http://www.cait.wustl.edu/infosys/infosys.html
3Com paper: "Massively Distributed Systems"	http://www.3com.com/technology/tech_net/white_papers/503056.html
3Com paper: "The Net Impact of N-Tiered Applications"	http://www.3com.com/technology/tech_net/tech_briefs/500906.html

Distributed Computer Networks

Distributed computer networks consist of clients and servers connected in such a way that any system can potentially communicate with any other system. The platform for distributed systems has been the enterprise network linking workgroups, departments, branches, and divisions of an organization. Data is not located in one server, but in many servers; and these servers might be at geographically diverse areas, connected by WAN links.

Figure D-26 illustrates the trend from expensive centralized systems to low-cost distributed systems that can be installed in large numbers. In the late 1980s and early 1990s, distributed systems consisted of large numbers of desktop computers. Today, the Internet and Web technologies have greatly expanded the concept of distributed systems. The Web is a "massively distributed collection of systems," to paraphrase a 3Com paper mentioned in the next section. It consists of countless nodes ranging from servers, to portable computers, to wireless PDAs, not to mention embedded systems that largely talk to one another without human intervention.

A paper written by Simon Phipps of IBM (see the link at the end of this topic) discusses how distributed computing systems have been removing dependencies in the computing environment as follows:

- TCP/IP provides a network-independent transport layer.
- Web clients and servers remove platform and operating system dependencies.
- Component software (Java, ActiveX) eliminates the hassles associated with buying and installing software.
- XML makes data independent of software.

Networks built with Web technologies (i.e., intranets and the Internet) are truly advanced distributed computing networks. Web technologies add a new dimension to distributed computing. Web servers provide universal access to any client with a Web browser. The type of computing platform and operating system become less important, while communication and information exchange without limits takes hold.

A distributed environment has interesting characteristics. It takes advantage of client/server computing and multitiered architectures. It distributes processing to inexpensive systems and relieves servers of many tasks. Data may be accessed from a diversity of sites

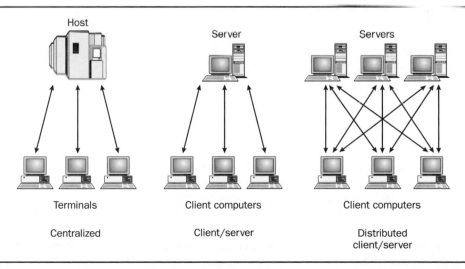

Figure D-26.   *Distributed computing has evolved from centralized and client/server computing.*

over wired or wireless networks. Data may be replicated to other systems to provide fault tolerance and place data close to users. Distributing data provides protection from local disasters. The distributed environment needs the following components:

- The network *platform* that supports multivendor products and communication protocols. TCP/IP has become the de facto standard protocol. See "Network Architecture."

- Application interfaces to exchange information between client and server, such as RPC (remote procedure call), message-passing systems, or Web protocols. See "Distributed Applications."

- A *directory naming service* that keeps track of resources and information, and where they are located. See "Directory Services."

- File systems and databases that support *partitioning* and *replication* to provide the distribution of data and ensure the availability, reliability, and protection of that data. See "Distributed File Systems."

- *Caching schemes* to place information closer to users and minimize the amount of time it must be transmitted across long-distance links. See "Caching" and "Content Distribution."

- Security features such as authentication and authorization, as well as trust relationships between systems at diverse locations. See "Security."

As mentioned, the Web is the ultimate distributed computer system. You can access Web servers all over the world that offer a nearly unlimited amount of content. Directory services help you locate sites. Search engines catalog information all over the Web and make it available for your queries. Caching techniques and "content distribution" are moving information closer to users.

Massively Distributed Systems

3Com has an interesting paper called "Massively Distributed Systems" by Dan Nessett (see the Web link at the end of this topic). The paper talks about the trend from high-cost centralized systems to distributed low-cost, high–unit-volume products, to massively distributed systems that are everywhere and that often "operate outside the normal cognizance of the people they serve." This paper is highly recommended for those who want to understand trends in distributed computing.

Nessett discusses two approaches to distributed processing. One method is to move data to the edge processors, as is done with the Web and Web-based file systems. The other approach is to move processing to the data, as is done with active networking and Java applets (i.e., objects move within the distributed system and carry both code and data). If the object consists primarily of data, it will closely approximate moving data to the processing. If it consists primarily of code, it will closely approximate moving processing to the data. Yet another approach is the thin-client approach, in which users work at graphical terminals connected to servers that perform all processing and store the user's data. See "Thin Client."

The World Wide Web is a massively distributed system full of objects. There are Web sites containing documents that contain both objects and referrals to other objects. Nessett talks about how the presentation of massively distributed objects to technically naïve users will require new interfaces. One example is to represent objects in virtual spaces that users navigate through as if walking through a 3D world.

Distributed and Parallel Processing

One aspect of distributed computing is the ability to run programs in parallel on multiple computers. There is distributed parallel processing, which is best described as multiprocessing that takes place across computers connected via LANs or the Internet; and there is dedicated parallel processing, which is best described as multiprocessing that takes place on systems that are locally attached via a high-speed interface. The former is discussed here because it represents a truly distributed processing environment. The latter is discussed under "Multiprocessing" and "Supercomputer."

Distributed parallel processing across multiple computer systems requires an authoritative scheduling program that can decide where and when to execute parts of a program. Distribution of tasks may take place in real time or on a more relaxed schedule. For example, distributed processing has been used to crack encrypted messages. Distributed.net is a project that employs thousands of users and their computers to crack codes. Users receive a small program that communicates with Distributed.net's main system, which distributes *pieces* of the challenge to users. The program runs when the user's computer is idle and returns its results to the main computer when done. The main computer eventually compiles all the results submitted by all the computers. Distributed.net claims its network of users has the "fastest computer on Earth."

HTC (high-throughput computing) environments are large collections of workstations, often called "grid environments." The Globus Project is an HTC project that helps scientists use idle cycles on pools of workstations and supercomputers. The system is based on Condor, a proven system that has been used to harness idle workstation time on LANs. The Web sites for Globus and Condor are listed at the end of this topic.

Related Entries   Client/Server Computing; Collaborative Computing; Data Management; Data Mart; Data Warehousing; Directory Services; Distributed Applications; Distributed Object Computing; Embedded Systems; Middleware and Messaging; MOM (Message-Oriented Middleware); Multiprocessing; Multitiered Architectures; Network Appliances; NPN (New Public Network); ORB (Object Request Broker); Peer-to-Peer Communication; Replication; RPCs (Remote Procedure Calls); Service Advertising and Discovery; SOAP (Simple Object Access Protocol); Supercomputer; Thin Clients; Transaction Processing; Web Technologies and Concepts; *and* Webcasting

Linktionary!—Tom Sheldon's Encyclopedia of Networking updates	http://www.linktionary.com/d/dist_computing.html
IETF Working Group: Distributed Management (disman)	http://www.ietf.org/html.charters/ disman-charter.html
Distributed applications and the Web	http://pclt.cis.yale.edu/pclt/WEBAPP/default.htm
Distributed Computing: An Overview	http://www.geocities.com/SiliconValley/Vista/4015/ pdcindex.html
Distributed computing links By Kang Sung-IL	http://rtlab.kaist.ac.kr/~sikang/middle.html

Distributed Computing, links at Washington University	http://www.cait.wustl.edu/infosys/infosys.html
Distributed Objects, Cetus Links— Object-Orientation	http://www.cetus-links.org/
Distributed.net (involved in code cracking distributed processing projects)	http:// www.distributed.net /
The Globus Project	http://www.globus.org/
Condor High Throughput Computing home page	http://www.cs.wisc.edu/condor/
XML: Completing the E-Business Picture, by Simon Phipps	http://www.ibm.com/developer/features/feature021599-javaxml.html
"AgentOS: The Agent-Based Distributed Operating System for Mobile Networks" by Larry T. Chen	http://info.acm.org/crossroads/xrds5-2/agentos.html
3Com paper: "Massively Distributed Systems"	http://www.3com.com/technology/tech_net/white_papers/503056.html
3Com paper: "The Net Impact of N-Tiered Applications"	http://www.3com.com/technology/tech_net/tech_briefs/500906.html
Distributed Science (peer-to-peer supercomputing technologies)	http://www.distributedscience.com/
Entropia (the computer the size of planet Earth)	http://entropia.com/
Parabon Computation (donate or sell idle computer time)	http://www.parabon.com/
Popular Power (donate or sell idle computer time)	http://www.popularpower.com/
Google Supercomputing Web Directory	http://directory.google.com/Top/Computers/Supercomputing/
"Internet Computing and the Emerging Grid," by Ian Foster at Nature.com (also see links at end)	http://www.nature.com/nature/webmatters/grid/grid.html

Distributed Database

See DBMS (Database Management System).

Distributed File Systems

See File Systems.

Distributed Object Computing

As discussed under the topic "Object Technologies," objects are encapsulated procedures and/or data, a building block of reusable code that can be combined with other objects to create programs or add functionality to existing programs. Programmers generally work with objects.

A *component* is a self-contained coded module that provides some service to other components in an object-oriented environment. You can think of a component as a mini-application. You've no doubt downloaded components such as sound and video players that enhanced the functionality of your Web browser. Think of Web browsers as containers that run components.

Distributed object computing is about building applications in a modular way with components. Components are typically designed for distribution across networks for use on multivendor, multiplatform computing systems. Because components are meant for distribution, standard interfaces and communication methods are important, as discussed shortly.

An interesting paper written by Simon Phipps of IBM (see the link at the end of this topic) provides insight into how the Web and component technology fit together:

- TCP/IP provide a network-independent transport layer.

- Web clients and servers remove platform and operating system dependencies.

- Component software (e.g., Java or ActiveX) eliminates the hassles associated with buying and installing software.

- XML makes data independent of software.

XML has become a critical part of component technologies because it allows for the exchange of structured information among any type of systems. XML creates a framework for documents in which data has meaning as defined by tags. Any system or application that understands XML tags can access data in XML documents. The distributed object/XML relationship is discussed further in the next section.

In an enterprise environment, components developed for in-house use may reside on multiple servers in multiple departments. Some objects are used throughout the organization and may be the core components of an application. Other components may add special functionality or exist temporarily on user systems. The component approach lets network administrators and develops quickly update components as needed, without changing the whole system.

If multiple companies are involved in business-to-business relationships over private networks (or the Internet), object technologies can be used to integrate business processes. All that is necessary is a standard object interface that lets each company access common data or objects.

Some of the advantages of component technology are listed next. While component technology may be used to build custom in-house applications, such as accounting systems, Web browsers and browser add-ins provide the most immediate example of component technology.

- If the application needs updating, only specific components need upgrading, not the entire application.

- New components can be added at any time to expand the functionality of the program.

- Users don't need to install every component that makes up an application, only the components they need.

- Individual components can be sold on the commercial market to provide functions that developers need to build applications or that users need to expand programs they already use.

■ Software development time is reduced because existing components can be reused to build new applications.

■ Using standard interfaces and programming languages like Java, components from different developers and vendors can be combined.

■ Maintenance costs are reduced because individual components can be upgraded without having to change the entire application.

Component models provide the basis for inter-service communications and component integration. Web sites can offer sophisticated services for users by performing interactive tasks that involve calls by one server to multiple other servers. These multitiered environments allow tasks to be broken up into different services that run on different computers. Services such as application logic, information retrieval, transaction monitoring, data presentation, and management may run on different computers that communicate with one another to provide end users with a seamless application interface.

Distributed Component Architectures

A standard component model and inter-component communication architecture are critical in furthering the use of component technology on the open Web. The most common component models are CORBA, EJB (Enterprise Java Beans), and Microsoft COM, as discussed shortly.

Distributing applications over networks leads to some interesting problems. In a stand-alone system, components run as a unit in the memory space of the same computer. If a problem occurs, the components can easily communicate that problem with one another. But if components are running on different computers, they need a way to communicate the results of their work or problems that have occurred.

An ORB (object request broker) handles the plumbing that allows objects to communicate over a network. You can think of the ORB as a sort of software bus, or backbone, that provides a common interface through which many different kinds of objects can communicate in a peer-to-peer scheme. One such ORB is CORBA (Common Object Request Broker Architecture). CORBA is cross-platform and allows components written for different operating systems and environments to work together.

An object makes a request and sends it to the ORB. The ORB then locates the requested object or an object that can provide services, and establishes communication between the client and server. The receiving object then responds to the request and returns a response to the ORB, which formats and forwards the response to the requester.

In this model, objects simply specify a task to perform. The location of the object that can satisfy the request is not important. The end user sees applications as being seamless, even though services and data may be coming from many places on the network.

The ORB process is similar to a remote procedure call with the added benefit that the ORB itself is capable of locating other objects that can service requests. Actually, an ORB is an alternative to RPCs (remote procedure calls) and message-oriented middleware.

To run sophisticated applications and transactions over networks, there is a need to register components and coordinate their activities so that critical transactions can take place. For example, if data is being written to multiple databases at different locations, a transaction monitor is needed to make sure that all those writes take place. Otherwise, they must all be rolled back. Microsoft Transaction Server is an example. It coordinates the interaction of components and ensures that transactions are implemented safely. Because it provides these features in an object-based environment, it is essentially a transaction-based *object request broker*. See "Transaction Processing" for more information.

The most important object models are described here:

- **CORBA (Common Object Request Broker Architecture)** The basic messaging technology specification defined by the OMG (Object Management Group) in its OMA (Object Management Architecture). CORBA has been implemented by a number of companies and is becoming an important standard for implementing distributed applications on the Internet. See "CORBA (Common Object Request Broker Architecture)."

- **COM/DCOM (Component Object Model/Distributed COM)** COM is Microsoft's basic object model. An early implementation was OLE (Object Linking and Embedding), which gave Windows applications their basic container and object-linking capabilities (within a single computer). DCOM is the network version of COM that allows objects running in different computers attached to a network to interact. The latest version of COM is COM+ for Windows 2000, which adds many new features and works by way of an XML-based message-passing approach. In 1999, Microsoft announced a DCOM replacement called SOAP (Simple Object Access Protocol) that uses XML as a universal data exchange mechanism. See "COM (Component Object Model)."

- **EJB (Enterprise Java Beans)** JavaBeans are software components that are based on the Java platform. EJB is contained within Sun's J2EE (Java2 Platform, Enterprise Edition). JavaBeans can be combined to build larger applications, in the same way that OLE objects can be combined into compound documents. Enterprise JavaBeans are components for enterprise networks. Recently, the best features of CORBA and EJB are merging into a model that can compete against the entrenched COM/DCOM model. See "Java."

DCOM is the most common of the technologies at this point, mainly because of existing support, developer knowledge, and the pervasiveness of Windows clients. CORBA has better multivendor, multiplatform support and is best for heterogeneous environments. CORBA was originally designed for tightly controlled enterprise network environments and well-managed inter-company connections. Both DCOM and CORBA are considered enterprise application development technologies, although both have been extended to work over the Internet. But they are considered too complex for most Web applications. EJB has gained the widespread support of Web developers. It is implemented in application servers from IBM, BEA Systems, and iPlanet (the Sun and Netscape Alliance). The CORBA 3.0 specification defines CORBA Beans, which combines features of CORBA and EJB with additional support for XML.

Microsoft's SOAP is important because it represents a move from the traditional remote procedure call method for exchanging information among objects to a message-passing scheme that uses XML. Microsoft now believes that messaging model best for the Web, as opposed to connection-oriented models such as RPC (remote procedure call) and Java's RMI (remote method invocation). By allowing objects to interact via XML, data interoperability is enhanced. SOAP carries XML messages across the Web via HTTP, which is pretty much a bottom line for interoperability.

The Object Management Group that managed CORBA standards has been working with OASIS (Organization for the Advancement of Structured Information Standards) to define how XML can be used to support CORBA services. EJB uses XML to provide information about Bean's interfaces, data types, and structure.

Related Entries ActiveX; Client/Server Computing; COM (Component Object Model); Compound Documents; CORBA (Common Object Request Broker Architecture); Distributed Applications; Distributed Computer Networks; Handle System; Java; Metadata; Middleware and Messaging; MOM (Message-Oriented Middleware); Multitiered Architectures; Object Technologies; OLE (Object Linking and Embedding); OMG (Object Management Group); ORB (Object Request Broker); RPCs (Remote Procedure Calls); SOAP (Simple Object Access Protocol); Transaction Processing; *and* XML (eXtensible Markup Language)

Linktionary!—Tom Sheldon's Encyclopedia of Networking updates	http://www.linktionary.com/d/distrib_objects.html
Open Applications Group (Best Practices and XML Content for eBusiness and Application Integration)	http://www.openapplications.org/
OASIS (Organization for Structured Information Standards), promoting SGML, HTML, and XML	http://www.oasis-open.org/
ComponentWare Consortium	http://www.componentware.com
Object Database Management Group	http://www.odmg.org
OMG (Object Management Group)	http://www.omg.org
Open Group	http://www.opengroup.org
W3C's Object page	http://www.w3.org/pub/WWW/OOP
Object-oriented links at Sysnetics (see links page)	http://www.sysnetics.com
Object computing links at Washington University	http://www.cait.wustl.edu/infosys/infosys.html
White Paper: CORBA, COM, and Other Object Standards and Their Relevance to Development of Interoperable Systems	http://www2.dcnicn.com/cals/cals_97f/task07/html/Non-CDRL/whitepaper.html
Object Technology page by Kang Sung-IL	http://rtlab.kaist.ac.kr/~sikang/oo/index.html
Cetus links for objects and components	http://www.cetus-links.org/
UserLand XML-RPC home page	http://www.xmlrpc.com
iPlanet (Sun/Netscape Alliance)	http://www.iplanet.com/
OII (Open Information Interchange) Guide to Objects and Components	http://158.169.50.95:10080/oii/en/objects.html
"XML: Completing the E-Business Picture," by Simon Phipps	http://www.ibm.com/developer/features/feature021599-javaxml.html
BoDO: The Best of Distributed Objects (some dated, but interesting articles)	http://www.bodo.org/

DLC (Data Link Control)

See Data Link Layer, OSI Model; Data Link Protocols.

DLC (Digital Loop Carrier)

A DLC system is a part of the copper-wire, local-loop telephone system. A DLC system aggregates the subscriber calls within a neighborhood, office building, or industrial park and multiplexes the calls over a single line (T1/E1 or fiber), back to the telephone company central office where all the switching equipment is located. DLC is an impediment to the expansion of DSL (Digital Subscriber Line) services. See "Telecommunications and Telephone Systems" and "DSL (Digital Subscriber Line)."

DLSw (Data Link Switching)

DLSw is a standard for encapsulating and tunneling IBM SNA (System Network Architecture) and NetBIOS traffic across IP (Internet Protocol) networks. The protocol is the result of a need to integrate SNA and non-SNA networks (i.e., Token Ring and Ethernet LANs), rather than deploy two separate networks or use a variety of proprietary schemes to tunnel SNA data over non-SNA networks.

As LANs became more popular throughout the enterprise, IBM and other vendors saw the benefits of using these networks for interconnecting SNA devices and as a way to allow network-connected PC users to access SNA mainframes. APPN (Advanced Peer-to-Peer Networking) was IBM's solution for building router-connected internetworks, but TCP/IP has since become more popular. DLSw was developed to meet the needs of sending SNA traffic over IP networks.

IBM originally submitted its definition of DLSw as RFC 1434, "Data Link Switching: Switch-to-Switch Protocol," (March 1993). This was replaced by RFC 1795, "Data Link Switching: Switch to Switch Protocol," (April 1995), which addressed some deficiencies in the earlier RFC. The AIW (APPN Implementers Workshop) did much of the development work. RFC 2166, "DLSw v2.0 Enhancements," (June 1997) defines what is called DLSw version 2. It provides enhancements for making networks more scalable, reduces the requirements of making some TCP connections (thus reducing overhead), and adds support for multicasting.

Running SNA traffic over TCP/IP networks via DLSw provides a number of benefits, such as the ability to build one network that services all enterprise communications. In the early days of LANs, some organizations had both LANs and host-to-mainframe communication systems installed on their premises. SNA benefits from the bandwidth improvements of running over LAN technologies.

DLSw works over DLSw-capable routers, which provide a link over an IP network, as shown in Figure D-27. Note that LANs carrying IBM LLC2 (Logical Link Control, Type 2) frames (a connection-oriented protocol) are connected to an IP network by way of the data link switch multiprotocol routers. The data link switches encapsulate the LLC2 frames in a TCP segment and transport them across the IP connection.

The DLSw device captures an SNA or NetBIOS session that must cross the IP link, and then terminates the session, encapsulates the frames, and transports the frames across the link.

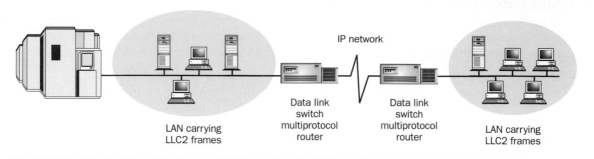

Figure D-27. *A DLSw-connected network*

At the other end of the link, the session resumes by making a connection to the appropriate end system. This scheme helps DLSw reduce the problem associated with source route bridging networks in which there can be no more than seven rings and bridges between devices.

Details about DLSw circuit establishment, flow control, network management, traffic management, and other features may be found in the Internet white papers listed at the end of this topic. Refer to TN3270 for information about software that allows clients to access IBM systems over TCP/IP networks.

Note that current trends favor extending TCP/IP all the way up to the SNA devices. Web technologies are providing a new way to get at corporate data, even data stored on mainframe systems. IBM and other vendors promote technology that provides SNA access via Web browsers. Cisco, for example, has its IOS/390 TCP/IP intranet software that provides access to mainframes. In 1999, Cisco bought IBM's networking operations and has since been pushing TCP/IP to the SNA community. Its SNASw (SNA Switching Services) carries SNA traffic directly across IP network without being encapsulated, as is done in DLSw.

Related Entries APPN (Advanced Peer-to-Peer Networking); IBM (International Business Machines); IBM Host Connectivity; SNA (Systems Network Architecture); *and* TN3270

Linktionary!—Tom Sheldon's Encyclopedia of Networking updates	http://www.linktionary.com/d/dlsw.html
AIW (APPN Implementers Workshop)	http://www.networking.ibm.com/app/aiwhome.htm
DLSw links list	http://www.networking.ibm.com/app/aiwinfo/aiwsites.htm
3Com's DLSw	http://www.3com.com/nsc/500605.html
Cisco paper: "Data-Link Switching Background"	http://www.cisco.com/univercd/cc/td/doc/cisintwk/ito_doc/dlsw.htm
Cisco paper: "Designing DLSw+ Internetworks"	http://www.cisco.com/univercd/cc/td/doc/cisintwk/idg4/nd2007.htm
Cisco SNA Switching Services (SNASw) Web page	http://www.cisco.com/warp/public/cc/cisco/mkt/iworks/wan/appn/prodlit/snasw_ov.htm

DMI (Distributed Management Interface)

The DMI is a programming and reporting standard for managing desktop workstations. It basically allows a managed device like a PC to "publish" information about itself in a standard way that allows any network management application to gather that information for reporting and management purposes. DMI was defined by the DMTF (Distributed Management Task Force). Note that the DMTF changed its name from "Desktop Management Task Force" to "Distributed Management Task Force" in May of 1999. DMI was changed from "Desktop Management Interface" to "Distributed Management Interface."

The DMI is an API that provides network managers with information about workstations on the network. The primary objective is to reduce network managers' workloads by providing them with vital workstation information, and assisting them with configuration and updating tasks. Managers can view information and carry out management tasks from their offices, saving time and even eliminating travel, in some cases.

The DMI defines how manufacturers of hardware products such as network interface cards or networking software can integrate "agents" into their products that collect information and report back to a management utility. Manufacturers don't need to worry about which protocols and operating systems end users will run with their management products. This is all handled by management software. The DMI is open to any management application or protocol, and all applications that adopt the DMI can call the same interface. DMI can be implemented in computers and peripheral components such as printers, modems, and storage devices.

Automation is the primary advantage of DMI. DMI-compatible agents perform tasks in the background and compile information that a normal network manager would never have time to gather using manual methods. This information can be vital to network managers for troubleshooting or to monitor changing conditions on the network. Potential problems may become evident through this process.

The DMI provides a common method for issuing requests and commands, called the *MI (management interface)*. Management systems that are DMI compliant use this interface to access management information. The CI (component interface) allows products to be managed by applications calling the DMI. The CI lets product manufacturers define the level of management needed for their products. One component defined in the DMI is the MIFF (management information format file). The MIFF is a text file that collects information about systems and makes it available to management programs. Vendors provide MIFFs with their DMI-compliant products.

Network administrators obtain information through a DMI interface, such as basic information about processor types, available memory, and disk space on desktop systems. Information about hardware and software components is also available, including how components are configured, whether they are working, and whether they may be due for an upgrade (based on versioning). This information can help managers quickly resolve problems and provide upgrades.

DMI version 2.0 was released in early 1998. In the meantime, the DMTF's CIM (Common Information Model) has gained the attention of network managers. CIM defines a hierarchical, object-oriented information model with a schema that can describe the full range of enterprise network management information. A core model is applicable to all areas of management; and a common model defines information in specific areas, including systems, applications, databases, networks, and devices. Extensions are also possible, such as the information model for DEN (Directory Enabled Networks). This goes well beyond DMI, but CIM also includes a specification that describes how CIM integrates with other management models, such as DMI and SNMP (Simple Network Management Protocol). Network management applications can use XML to display and exchange CIM information.

Related Entries   CIM (Common Information Model); DEN (Directory Enabled Networks); DMTF (Distributed Management Task Force); Network Management; SNMP (Simple Network Management Protocol); *and* WBEM (Web-Based Enterprise Management)

Linktionary!—Tom Sheldon's Encyclopedia of   http://www.linktionary.com/d/dmi.html
Networking updates

DMTF   http://www.dmtf.org

DMTF (Distributed Management Task Force)

The DMTF was founded in 1992 by a group of vendors, including Digital Equipment Corporation (now Compaq), Hewlett-Packard, IBM, Intel, Microsoft, and Novell. The DMTF changed its name from "Desktop Management Task Force" to "Distributed Management Task Force" in May of 1999.

The goal of the DMTF is to deliver management standards and initiatives for desktop, enterprise, and Internet environments. The DMTF manages the following initiatives and standards:

- **DMI (Distributed Management Interface)**   A common management framework for desktop systems. See "DMI (Distributed Management Interface)."

- **CIM (Common Information Model)**   An object-oriented specification for collecting and sharing enterprise-wide management information. CIM has rapidly become the leading management information model.

- **WBEM (Web-Based Enterprise Management)**   An initiative that uses Web technologies to manage systems. Web browsers are used as management interfaces, CIM is the inventory model, and XML is the data interchange format.

- **DEN (Directory Enabled Networks)**   An initiative to develop standard directory schema and interoperable directory services. Through DEN, managers use directory services to manage network services such as QoS, network addressing, and network policies.

Related Entries   CIM (Common Information Model); DEN (Directory Enabled Networks); DMI (Distributed Management Interface); Network Management; RMON (Remote Monitoring); SNMP (Simple Network Management Protocol); *and* WBEM (Web-Based Enterprise Management)

DMTF   http://www.dmtf.org

DNA (Digital interNet Application)

See Microsoft DNA (Digital interNet Application).

DNS (Domain Name Service) and Internet Domains

On the Internet, networks are connected to hierarchically organized routers, as shown in Figure D-28. A packet might only need to go through an intermediate router or be sent to

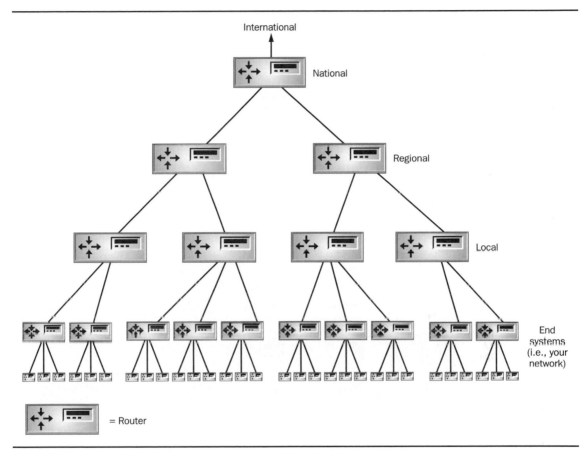

Figure D-28. *Hierarchical routing structure on the Internet*

a router at the very top of the hierarchy in order to find a path to its destination. Every router along the way knows about the networks that are connected to it. If a router does not know the path, it sends the packet up to the next highest router in the hierarchy.

Closely related to this routing hierarchy is the Domain Name Service (DNS), which links names to IP addresses. When you access Web sites on the Internet, you can type the IP address of the site if you know what it is and if you can remember it. But few people do this. Instead, we rely on DNS servers scattered throughout the Internet to translate the well-known names we can remember into IP addresses. The procedure for obtaining an IP address is mapped out in Figure D-29.

DNS servers are strategically located on the Internet. There is usually one either directly accessible to your system or accessible over as few as one router hop, although several servers may be queried as shown in Figure D-29. Most Internet service providers have DNS servers. When you type a domain name in a Web browser, a query is sent to the primary DNS server defined in your Web browser's configuration dialog box (or if no server is specified, a default DNS server).

If something goes wrong in the process, an error message appears, indicating that the site cannot be found. Usually, this is only a temporary problem due to busy networks and servers. Another attempt to access the site usually results in a DNS lookup and a successful connection.

The naming system is hierarchical, as Figure D-30 shows. The tree is inverted with the root level pictured at the top. The tree is divided into top-level domains (TLDs), and those domains

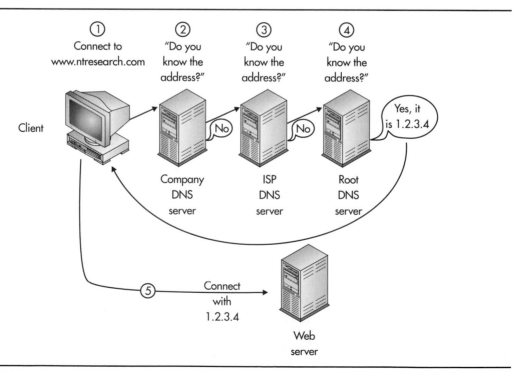

Figure D-29.   *Obtaining an IP address from a DNS server*

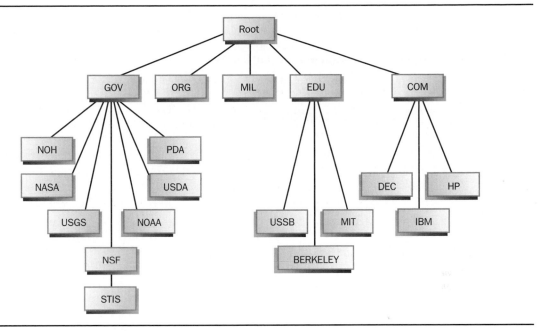

Figure D-30. *DNS naming hierarchy*

are divided into second-level domains (SLDs), and so on. Besides the TLDs shown (.com, .net, and .org), there are more than 200 national TLDs that are managed by their corresponding governments or private entities. The top-level nongovernment domains are listed here:

COM	Commercial
EDU	Education
GOV	Government
ORG	Organizational
NET	Networks
INT	International treaty organizations
MIL	U.S. military organizations

In February of 1997, the IAHC (International Ad Hoc Committee) announced seven new gTLDs (generic top-level domains), in addition to the existing ones (.com, .net, and .org), under which Internet names may be registered. The new fields are as follows:

.firm	Business or firms
.store	Businesses offering goods
.arts	Culture and entertainment

.rec	Recreational entertainment
.info	Information services
.web	Entities related to the Web
.nom	For individual or personal nomenclature

DNS Historical and Administrative Information

In 1998 and 1999, the entire management structure was revamped. A paper titled "Management of Internet Names and Addresses," published by the Unites States Department of Commerce, outlines the U.S. government's plan to "privatize the domain name system in a manner that increases competition and facilitates international participation in its management."

The Linktionary! Web site expands on this information, and provides links to papers that contain historical and administrative information.

In the early days of the Internet, when there were hundreds of users and not millions, Jon Postel maintained a list of host names and IP address mappings. The list was stored in an FTP server that others could access. It contained two columns of information: the IP address and the host name. A problem with this scheme was updating the file and making sure that everyone had the latest information. Changes and updates got to be a nightmare. A way was needed to automate the process and to make sure that no two hosts had the same name.

Paul Mockapetris eventually came up with what he called the "Domain Name Scheme." It was hierarchical and distributed. It also allowed one DNS server to query another if it did not know a name. The early DNS documents are RFC 1034, "Domain Names—Concepts and Facilities," (November 1987) and RFC 2035, "Domain Names—Implementation and Specification," (November 1987).

In 1991–92, the National Science Foundation (NSF) awarded Network Solutions, Inc. (NSI) with contracts to manage domain name registration and other services. Through most of the 1990s, NSI has handled name registration in the generic top-level domains (gTLDs) on a first-come, first-served basis. It also maintains a directory linking domain names with the IP numbers of domain name servers, and it maintains the authoritative database of Internet registrations. In this capacity, NSI played an important role as the Internet was commercially developed during the 1990s.

Up until 1999, the Domain Name System had the following structure:

- IANA coordinates the allocation of blocks of numeric IP addresses to regional IP registries (ARIN in North America, RIPE in Europe, and APNIC in the Asia/Pacific region). Large ISPs then apply to the registries for blocks of IP addresses. Those ISPs then allocate the blocks of addresses they have been assigned to smaller ISPs or to end users.

- IANA maintains technical parameters for the Internet protocol suite, including protocol numbers, port numbers, autonomous system numbers, management information base object identifiers, and others.

- DNS consists of a root server system that is physically contained in a set of 13 file servers. These servers contain the authoritative database that lists all top-level domains.

NSI operated the "A" root server, which maintains the authoritative root database and replicates changes to the other root servers on a daily basis. The U.S. government played a role in operating about half of these servers. The authoritative servers provide an important feature: universal name consistency on the Internet.

In 1999, The Internet Corporation for Assigned Names and Numbers (ICANN), a new nonprofit corporation, took over responsibility for the IP address space allocation, protocol parameter assignment, domain name system management, and root server system management functions that were formerly performed under U.S. government contract by IANA and other entities.

ICANN has adopted accreditation standards and applications procedures for prospective .com, .org, and .net registrars. By agreement with the U.S. government, Network Solutions, Inc., opened its Shared Registration System test bed for the .com, .org., and .net gTLDs to five registrars in April 1999, and to all accredited registrars in mid-1999. Since NSI lost its exclusive contract to assign Internet domain names, a number of other companies and organizations have taken up the job, including AOL (America Online, Inc.), AT&T, register.com, France Telecom, and several international consortiums. Eventually, many other firms will sell domains. NSI is still in the business and still maintains the "A" authoritative root database.

DNS Operations

An organization that is connecting its internal networks to the Internet can choose to install its own DNS server or use an external DNS server, such as the one located at its ISP. Some organizations may choose to use both internal and external DNS servers. Installing internal DNS servers involves properly maintaining the DNS server and its database so that the system interoperates with external DNS servers.

Since DNS consists of a distributed database, it exists on a number of servers that each hold part of the overall database. If DNS is used for private internal use, the entire database may be on one server, or can be split up into several servers, depending on the size of the network and the number of users that access it at one time.

On the Internet, distributing the database is an essential requirement. Servers in the DNS hierarchy hold a portion of the DNS database related to a *zone,* and the server is said to be authoritative for its zone. A zone may consist of one or more domains, and a zone server is authoritative for only those domains. With zones, the DNS database can be distributed and managed by separate DNS servers.

A DNS server contains zone files that include the name-to-IP address mappings. Zone files contain a *resource record* for each name-to-IP address mapping. These files are typically edited with a DNS management program that comes with the DNS software. They may also be manually edited.

DNS name servers on the Internet are required to have both a primary and secondary name server, with the primary name server containing the original name-to-IP address mapping and the secondary, containing a copy of those mappings. This provides redundancy and fault tolerance to ensure connectivity for Internet users.

A typical DNS server contains the following files:

- **Zone file**   Contains resource records that describe the name-to-IP address mapping for each host in the zone for which the DNS server is authoritative.

- **Cache file**   Contains name-to-IP address mappings for Internet root DNS servers and is used to resolve name queries for computers that are located outside the domain.

- **Reverse lookup file**   This file contains IP address-to-name mappings (called PTR records) that are used to provide a name when only the IP address is known.

Setting up a DNS server involves installing the DNS server software, creating the zone database file, specifying the primary domain, and adding the subdomains. You can then begin adding the host systems. Some operating systems automate this last process by using dynamic DNS techniques, in which hosts are located and their names/IP address information are entered into the database.

One final step is to ensure that network client's TCP/IP software is configured to indicate the IP address of the primary and secondary DNS servers. This allows the client system to go directly to the nearest DNS server first to resolve name-to-IP address mappings.

RFC 2901, "Guide to Administrative Procedures of the Internet Infrastructure," (August 2000) describes the administrative procedures for networks seeking to connect to the global Internet. This includes the steps and operations necessary for address space allocation and registration, routing database registration, and domain name registration.

Novell DNS/DHCP Services integrates DNS and DHCP (Dynamic Host Configuration Protocol) into Novell Directory Services (NDS). DHCP is a protocol that automatically assigns IP addresses to client systems. DNS/DHCP Services also support Dynamic DNS (DDNS), which dynamically updates the host name database with new IP addresses. With DNS/DHCP Services, administrators can centrally administer and manage IP addresses and host names through NDS.

In the Windows NT/Windows 2000 environment, DNS integrates with WINS (Windows Internet Naming Service) to provide a form of *dynamic* DNS. WINS is a system that tracks NetBIOS computer names on traditional Windows networks. With the release of Windows 2000, Microsoft is moving away from NetBIOS names and into DNS naming.

Security is a potential problem with DNS. Security breaches are possible due to server misconfigurations, firewall misconfigurations, and the failure to install the latest patches that fix known security breaches. The IETF Domain Name System Security (dnssec) Working Group is working on DNS security issues. See RFC 2541, "DNS Security Operational Considerations," (March 1999).

One last thing. The Berkeley Internet Name Domain (BIND) is the most common implementation of DNS and is available at the Internet Software Consortium (ISC), which is located at http://www.isc.org. Operating systems such as Novell NetWare and Windows NT/Windows 2000 are available with their own specific implementations of DNS, although you are free to run other implementations.

Related Entries   DHCP (Dynamic Host Configuration Protocol); Internet; Internet Architecture and Backbone; Internet Connections; Internet Organizations and Committees; Internet Protocol Suite; Peering; Registries on the Internet; Routing; *and* Routing on the Internet

Linktionary!—Tom Sheldon's Encyclopedia of Networking updates	http://www.linktionary.com/d/dns.html
IETF Working Group: Domain Name System Security (dnssec)	http://www.ietf.org/html.charters/dnssec-charter.html
DNS IXFR, Notification, and Dynamic Update (dnsind)	http://www.ietf.org/html.charters/dnsind-charter.html
DNS Resources Directory, a complete source of DNS information	http://www.dns.net/dnsrd/
DNS-related RFCs list at DNS Resources Directory	http://www.dns.net/dnsrd/rfc/
Active DNS–Related Internet Drafts at DNS Resources Directory	http://www.dns.net/dnsrd/docs/id.html
The Internet Corporation for Assigned Names and Numbers	http://www.icann.org/
World Intellectual Property Organization (WIPO)	http://www.wipo.org
Network Solutions, Inc.	http://www.networksolutions.com

DOCSIS (Data Over Cable Service Interface Specification)

DOCSIS is an ITU-approved international standard that specifies how data should be transmitted over cable networks. The original DOCSIS project was headed by a consortium of large cable operators called MCNS Holdings, L.P. (MCNS), which included as members Comcast Cable Communications, Cox Communications, Tele-Communications, and Time Warner Cable. The ITU approved DOCSIS as a standard in 1998, after it was reviewed and accepted by the SCTE (Society of Cable Telecommunications Engineers). The DOCSIS project is managed by Arthur D. Little, Inc.

DOCSIS is administered by CableLabs (Cable Television Laboratories, Inc.), a consortium of cable television system operators that plans and funds research and development projects for the cable industry. CableLabs has a certification program that performs interoperability testing for vendors that wish to label their cable modems as *DOCSIS compatible.*

DOCSIS is specifically designed to provide transparent bidirectional transmission of IP traffic (as opposed to using an awkward telephone modem connection for upstream data). The architecture is designed to take advantage of HFC (hybrid fiber/coaxial) networks. An important aspect of DOCSIS is its architecture for supporting real-time, integrated voice and video.

DOCSIS includes a set of interface specifications, illustrated in Figure D-31. All the components and interfaces inside the "distribution hub or head end" are located at a cable operator site. The components on the right are the fiber and coaxial cable trunks and the subscriber equipment. The left side is the Internet, telephone service connections, and connections to other services. The security services and the OSSI are significant parts of the system. OSSI provides management-layer interfaces that support basic business processes.

The physical-layer technology for DOCSIS has been refined to provide advanced, high-performance, two-way cable service. Two standards recently adopted are Terayon's SCDMA (Synchronous Code Division Multiple Access) technology and Broadcom's Advanced Frequency Agile (TDMA) technology.

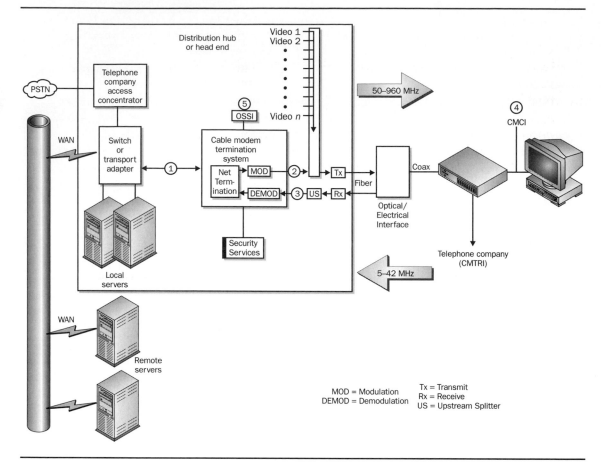

Figure D-31. *DOSCIS reference architecture*

Related Entry Cable (CATV) Data Networks

  Note *The Cable (CATV) Data Networks topic provides a major list of Web sites related to cable networks.*

  Linktionary!—Tom Sheldon's Encyclopedia http://www.linktionary.com/d/docsis.html
of Networking updates

CableLabs Web site http://www.cablemodem.com/

DOCSIS Consortium at UNH http://www.iol.unh.edu/consortiums/
InterOperability Lab (IOL)

Tutorial: Cable Modem Tutorial http://www.webproforum.com/nextlevel/index.html

Tutorial: Hybrid Fiber Coax	http://www.webproforum.com/sci-atlanta/index.html
Terayon Communication Systems	http://www.terayon.com/
Broadcom	http://www.broadcom.com/

Document Management

Document management systems are often called *electronic document management systems* or *EDMS* for short. According to AIIM (Association for Information and Image Management International), documents hold the "intellectual assets of organizations, the knowledge and expertise of its people, and the information and data they have compiled. These valuable assets must be managed and protected. Everything a company knows about itself, its products and services, its customers, and the business environment in which it exists are stored in documents."

Document management encompasses the storing, categorizing, exchange, and retrieval of documents, spreadsheets, graphs, and imaged (scanned) documents via electronic means (for the purposes of this book) across enterprise networks and the Internet. As an example, an EDMS for a law firm tracks all the activities occurring with a document, such as the number of keystrokes, revisions, and printings, so clients can be charged for the services. The exchange of computer information would be impossible without character formatting standards such as ASCII (American Standard Code for Information Interchange). Users on different computer platforms should be able to exchange documents and retain formats, even though the applications and operations are different. Newer document interchange standards such as Adobe Acrobat, HTML, and XML attempt to provide universal document formatting, and even data exchange.

A high-end EDMS system provides highly structured document management tracking and archiving features. Large enterprises and organizations use these systems to track documents for a variety of reasons, including the need to comply with local and federal government regulations. For example, airlines must document maintenance and repairs, pharmaceutical companies must document all research and testing, and nuclear power plants must document just about everything. EDMS systems are complex and management-intensive systems.

At the opposite end of the spectrum are unstructured document systems. The Web is an example of a massive document system with little document management—i.e., there is little indexing and cataloging of documents (although some standards have been proposed). Granted, some Web sites attempt to catalog Web pages and documents, but the amount of structure is nowhere near what is needed to find exactly the document you are looking for. Search engines such as Google.com do a good job of finding documents via keyword matches; but what the Web needs is a standard system for indexing, tagging, and locating documents. Be sure to check "Related Entries" listed at the end of this section for topics that discuss newer Web-based document standards.

Electronic commerce (e-commerce) has come to be associated with the buying and selling of goods on the Internet. If you think of e-commerce as an online retail sales and accounting system, its easy to see that electronic document management exchange is essential on the Internet. There are early EDI (Electronic Document Interchange) systems and newer systems that promote Web technologies. XML is perhaps the most important development on the Web in terms of document management. It provides a highly structured way of describing the contents of data in documents so that any system can read it.

According to AIIM, a document management system should do the following:

- Manage documents that are distributed and stored in repositories throughout an organization.

- Provide services such as storing, tracking, versioning, indexing, and searching for documents.

- Manage document revisions and "audit trails" to track where a document has been.

- Make information available both inside and outside the organization.

- Make it easier to access any kind of documents over computer networks.

- Perform document imaging and forms processing.

- Provide workflow and groupware technologies for transaction-oriented and collaborative document management.

Some popular applications, such as Microsoft Office, include document tracking and revision features. These features are useful in small offices and workgroups, but may not provide the sophisticated level of document management and tracking required by some organizations.

ODMA (Open Document Management API) is a document management integration standard developed in the mid-1990s by a coalition of document management companies. The standard is now managed by the AIIM. ODMA provides platform-independent APIs and platform-specific registration and binding specifications. It includes a set of interfaces that applications use to request services within a document management system. The API makes it easier for vendors to create products that use document management features. There is also an ODMA Extension for Workflow.

The following organizations support the document management industry. You'll find more information about document management and links to important document management sites.

AIIM (Association for Information & Image Management).	http://www.aiim.org/
ODMA (Open Document Management API) information	http://www.aiim.org/odma/odma.htm
Document Management Industries Association	http://www.dmia.org/
DISA (Data Interchange Standards Association)	http://www.disa.org/
OASIS, the Organization for the Advancement of Structured Information Standards	http://www.oasis-open.org/
Public Library Association	http://www.pla.org/
NISO (National Information Standards Organization)	http://www.niso.org/
D-Lib Forum (promotes global digital libraries)	http://www.dlib.org/

A number of topics in this book provide information about important related topics. The topic "Handle System" describes a global naming service that provides document persistence. If a document moves to a new location, people can still find it without knowing the new address.

The topic "Metadata" provides information about document description schemas and initiatives such as Dublin Core, RDF (Resource Description Framework), Digital Object Identifier (DOI) System, DDI (Data Document Initiative), and other technologies. The topic "Search and Discovery Services" provides an overview of search, labeling, and indexing services. The topic "Service Advertising and Discovery" describes new and existing technologies for describing and advertising documents and services on the Web. Finally, the topic "Storage Management Systems" describes online and near-line document archive systems.

Related Entries   Acrobat; Backup and Data Archiving; CIP (Common Indexing Protocol); CNRP (Common Name Resolution Protocol); Compound Documents; Directory Services; EDI (Electronic Data Interchange); Electronic Commerce; Groupware; Handle System; HTML (Hypertext Markup Language); Hypermedia and Hypertext; Imaging; Metadata; MIME (Multipurpose Internet Mail Extension); Name Services; Search and Discovery Services; Service Advertising and Discovery; SGML (Standard Generalized Markup Language); Storage Management Systems; URN (Universal Resource Naming); Workflow Management; *and* XML (eXtensible Markup Language)

Linktionary!—Tom Sheldon's Encyclopedia of Networking updates	http://www.linktionary.com/d/document_management.html
ODI (Open Information Interchange) document Interchange Standards (a very extensive list) Guide to Workflow Management and Collaborative Authoring	http://158.169.50.95:10080/oii/en/docstand.html
ODI (Open Information Interchange)	http://158.169.50.95:10080/oii/en/workflow.html
Form Magazine online	http://www.formmag.com
Document management links at *Form Magazine*	http://www.formmag.com/links.html
DocuWorld online	http://www.docuworld.com/
"Perspectives on Electronic Publishing" by Sandy Ressler	http://www.nist.gov/itl/div894/ovrt/people/sressler/Persp/Views.html
"Electronic Document Interchange and Distribution Based on the Portable Document Format, an Open Interchange Format"	http://bob.nap.edu/html/wpni3/ch-65.html
Good Documents document design advice	http://www.gooddocuments.com/
IBM E-Business Content Management Solutions	http://edms.solutions.ibm.com/
DocuCorp	http://www.docucorp.com/
Documentum	http://www.documentum.com/
e-Business Technologies	http://www.ebt.com/
Filenet	http://www.filenet.com
Hummingbird (PCDOCS)	http://www.hummingbird.com/
IntraNet Solutions	http://www.intranetsol.com/
OpenText	http://www.opentext.com/
SystemCorp	http://www.systemcorp.com/

DOM (Document Object Model)

DOM is an API (application programming interface) for HTML and XML documents. The W3C (World Wide Web Coalition) created DOM in 1998 with the intention of giving programmers a way to write programs that work the same way on all browsers. DOM provides a programming model that allows programmers to use whatever programming language they prefer.

DOM defines logical structure for documents, which are in most cases documents with data represented by XML. These XML documents contain elements and content that can be accessed, changed, deleted, or added using the Document Object Model. The term *DHTML (Dynamic HTML)* is often used to refer to HTML documents with scripts and programs that can make changes to the style, structure, and content of Web pages.

The name comes from the fact that DOM is an "object model" in which documents are modeled with objects. The model encompasses the structure and the behavior of documents.

Related Entries   Document Standards; HTML; Web Technologies and Concepts; *and* XML (eXtensible Markup Language)

DOM (Document Object Model) at W3C	http://www.w3.org/DOM/Activity
W3C DOM FAQ	http://www.w3.org/DOM/faq.html
The Legion of DOM	http://www.webreview.com/97/11/14/feature/index.html
BoDO: The Best of Distributed Objects	http://www.bodo.org/

Domains, Internet

See DNS (Domain Name Service).

Domains, Windows NT

Windows NT Server domains are collections of computers and computer users that are managed by a central authority. Domains may span departments, divisions, and/or workgroups, as well as other types of computer groups. You implement domains to make groups of computers more manageable and to apply a security policy to specific areas of your network. In addition, domains logically split up large networks into groups of resources that make it easy for users to find those resources.

A *distributed network* is one in which networks in different divisions, departments, or workgroups, all with different data sources, have been linked together to provide an enterprise-wide information system, as pictured in Figure D-32. Domains provide a way to maintain a single directory of users in large distributed-network environments. Because a domain is an administrative entity that encompasses a collection of computers, those computers might be next to each other or separated by some distance.

In a Windows NT domain environment, network users have user accounts that are maintained on a Windows NT Server *domain controller* in a *directory database*. Each domain has a PDC (primary domain controller) and may have one or more BDCs (backup domain controllers) as well. The directory database holds all the accounts and security information for a domain. It is replicated (copied) to other domain controllers in the domain for backup reasons and to

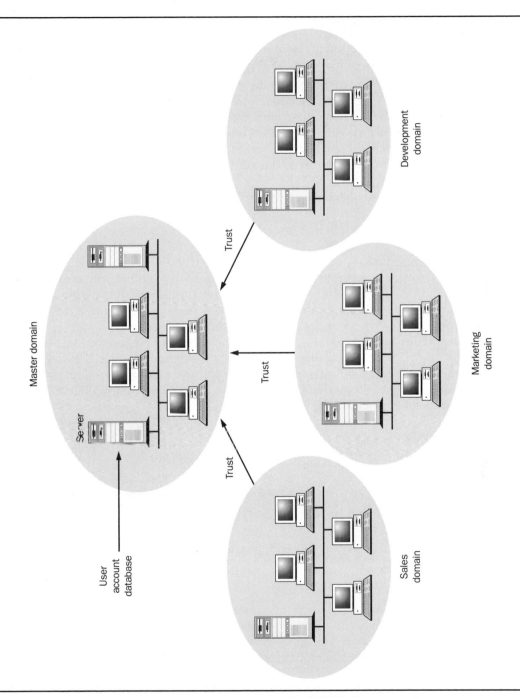

Figure D-32.   *Multiple domains can be centrally managed or individually managed*

make it more readily available to people in different geographic locations. Replication is automatic among domain controllers.

Of course, domains are an important part of security in the Windows NT environment. If a company has two separate divisions, each may implement its own domain, and the domains can provide an administrative barrier between the divisions that can be closely monitored and managed. Each domain may have its own administrator, and together those administrators determine how resources in one domain will be accessed by users in the other domain. Trust relationships make this work, as will be discussed next.

In the domain environment, there is usually a need for users in one domain to access resources in another domain. To allow cross-domain activities, domain administrators set up *trust relationships*.

If an organization has only one domain, trust relationships are not required; but in large organizations, many domains may exist, requiring trust relationships to allow information exchange. A single administrator can manage all the domains, or each domain can be managed separately with its own tight security.

There are one-way and two-way trust relationships. In a one-way relationship, one domain trusts the users in the other domain to use its resources, but not the other way around. In a two-way trust relationship, each domain trusts the other. Of course, after setting up trusts, the next step is to grant specific users and groups in one domain access to resources in another domain.

The best way to think of this is at the department level. For example, users in the accounting department often need a trust relationship with the sales department so that they can access daily sales information for accounting purposes. However, users in the sales department don't need a trust relationship with the accounting department, because the information on the servers in accounting is none of their business.

Related Entries   Microsoft Windows; Trust Relationships and Trust Management

Downsizing

Downsizing: An excuse to get rid of your highly paid senior employees and put in a workforce of "temps."

—*Upside Magazine*, Foster City, CA

Chainsaw Consultant: An outside expert brought in to reduce the employee headcount, leaving the top brass with clean hands.

—Source unknown

In the computer environment, downsizing has been associated with the process of replacing minicomputers and mainframes with LAN-based servers and workstations, typically associated with a move to UNIX boxes or powerful superservers, and a shift to client/server computing.

Many organizations have too much of an investment to completely move away from mainframe and minicomputer systems, or have special engineering and scientific applications that require their use, or find it is cost prohibitive to redesign for network systems.

DPT (Dynamic Packet Transport)

DPT is a SONET-like technology that transports packets across fiber-optic rings. Along with Gigabit Ethernet and DTM (Dynamic Synchronous Transfer Mode), Cisco's DPT is considered one of the technologies to use in new fiber-access metropolitan area networks. It provides the reliability and restorability associated with SONET and SDH networks, but is specifically designed for packet transport. Cisco labels the technology as "IP+Optical." Some of the features of DPT are listed here:

- Transports packets between Cisco DPT routers over two counter-rotating OC-12 fiber-optic rings.

- Both fibers are used concurrently to transport both data and control traffic, unlike SONET, which keeps one in standby mode until needed.

- DPT uses SRP (Spatial Reuse Protocol) as a media access protocol. SRP manages the add/drop process, controls bandwidth, and controls the propagation of messages on the packet ring.

- Cisco claims throughput is double what SONET can provide over the same ring.

The Cisco Web site at the end of this topic provides more information. You can also refer to "MAN (Metropolitan Area Network)" for information about metro access technologies in general.

Related Entries   DTM (Dynamic Synchronous Transfer Mode); MAN (Metropolitan Area Network); Multiplexing; Network Access Services; Network Core Technologies; NPN (New Public Network); Optical Networks; SONET (Synchronous Optical Network); *and* WDM (Wavelength Division Multiplexing)

Linktionary!—Tom Sheldon's Encyclopedia   http://www.linktionary.com/d/dpt.html
of Networking updates

Cisco's DPT Web page   http://www.cisco.com/warp/public/779/servpro/
                                              solutions/optical/dpt.html

DRDA (Distributed Relational Database Architecture)

DRDA is an IBM standard for accessing database information across IBM platforms that follows SQL standards. It is a key component in IBM's Information Warehouse framework, which defines large back-end servers that clients can access through smaller, workgroup-based intermediate servers. DRDA has the following capabilities:

- Defines protocols for providing interfaces between clients and back-end databases

- Provides a framework for interconnecting IBM's DB2, DBM, SQL/DS, and SQL/400 database systems

- Supports multivendor database systems

- Supports transaction (unit of work) processing over distributed databases

In DRDA, clients are called ARs (application requesters) and back-end servers are called ASs (application servers). A protocol called the ASP (Application Support Protocol) interfaces the ARs with the ASs. The whole process operates on SNA networks, but OSI and TCP/IP support is planned. An additional protocol, called the DSP (Database Support Protocol), lets an AS act as an AR to another server. In this way, servers can talk to servers and forward requests from client ARs, as shown in Figure D-33. The initial protocol supports one SQL statement to one database, but future versions will support multiple statements to one or more databases.

DRDA is one of the foundations for building client/server computing in IBM environments. The others are APPN (Advanced Peer-to-Peer Networking) and DDM (Distributed Data Management). Through the Information Warehouse and DRDN, IBM plans to keep its mainframes as central components in the enterprise as the storage platforms for all types of information, including multimedia.

DRDA was officially moved into the public domain in 1998, after it was adopted by The Open Group. More information about DRDA's current status may be found at The Open Group's Web site, given later. An alternative database connectivity standard is ODBC (Open Database Connectivity), which was originally developed by Microsoft. You can refer to "ODBC (Open Database Connectivity)" and "Database Connectivity" for more information.

Related Entries   APPN (Advanced Peer-to-Peer Networking); Data Warehouse; DBMS (Database Management System); IBM (International Business Machines); ODBC (Open Database Connectivity); *and* SQL (Structured Query Language)

Linktionary!—Tom Sheldon's Encyclopedia of Networking updates	http://www.linktionary.com/d/drda.html
IBM DRDA Web page	http://www-4.ibm.com/software/data/db2/os390/drda.html
The International DB2 Users Group	http://www.idug.org

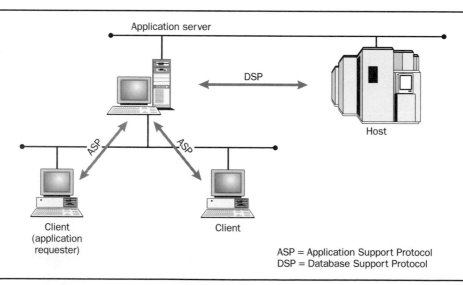

Figure D-33.   *The IBM Distributed Relational Database Architecture environment*

DSA (Digital Signature Algorithm)

See DSS (Digital Signature Standard).

DSL (Digital Subscriber Line)

DSL is a technology that provides high-speed data transmissions over the so-called "last-mile" of "local-loop" of the telephone network, i.e., the twisted copper wire that connects home and small office users to the telephone company central offices (COs). Demand for high-speed access methods is increasing with growing Internet access, electronic commerce, IP telephony, and videoconferencing. A number of methods for providing this bandwidth are available, including DSL technologies, cable (CATV) networks, and wireless and satellite technologies. All of these fit into the category of "residential broadband services."

This section provides a short briefing on DSL technologies. One of the best places to find DSL information is Telechoice's xDSL.com Web site at http://www.xdsl.com. There you will find the latest breaking DSL news, buyers guides, white papers, and company listings.

DSL technologies can enhance copper wire infrastructure to be the most effective way of delivering broadband services to the greatest number of people. In some cases, data rates up to 52 Mbits/sec can be achieved. DSL makes the local loop a multiservice access network that can support not only Internet access, but video and telephony services. No wiring upgrade is necessary for DSL. Only the equipment at the user end and at the telephone company end of the cable must be upgraded to new equipment.

While DSL transmission can share the same wire used to transmit traditional analog voice calls, it can also support multiple lines of digital telephony within the frequency range that it operates. Figure D-34 illustrates how ADSL modems use frequency division multiplexing to support three separate channels: a traditional analog voice channel, the low-speed upstream channel, and the high-speed downstream channel.

DSL connections are point-to-point dedicated circuits, meaning that they are always connected. There is no dial-up. There is also no switching, which means that the line is a

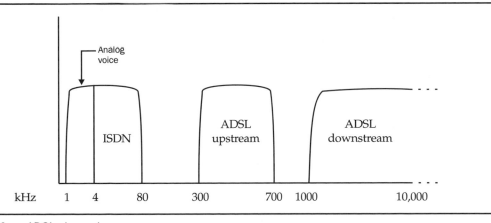

Figure D-34.   *ADSL channels*

direct connection into the carrier's system. DSL modems are required at the customer site and the carrier site. Because there are different modulation techniques, users must ensure compatibility between their equipment and the carrier's equipment. The carrier will usually recommend suitable equipment.

There are actually seven types of DSL service, ranging in speeds from 16 Kbits/sec to 52 Mbits/sec. The services are either symmetric (traffic flows at the same speed in both directions) or asymmetric (the downstream capacity is higher than the upstream capacity). Asymmetric services are good for Internet users because more information is usually downloaded than uploaded. For example, a simple button click to download a Web page may produce 1K of upstream traffic, and thousands or millions of bytes of downstream traffic.

With all DSL technologies, there is a trade-off between the data rate and cable distance. As distance between the home and CO increases, the data rate drops. For example, the highest speed DSL service requires that customers be within 1,000 feet of the central office. Not too many homes qualify for that service, but businesses, apartment buildings, and condominium structures in downtown areas might.

Following is a description of the different versions of DSL. Note that these versions are often collectively referred to as *xDSL*.

- **HDSL (High-Speed Digital Subscriber Line)**   HDSL is the most common and mature of the DSL services. It delivers data symmetrically at T1 data rates of 1.544 Mbits/sec over lines that are up to 3.6 kilometers (12,000 feet) in length. Generally, HDSL is a T1 service that requires no repeaters but does use two lines. Voice telephone services cannot operate on the same lines. It is not intended for home users, but instead is intended for the telephone company's own feeder lines, interexchange connections, Internet servers, and private data networks.

- **SDSL (Symmetric Digital Subscriber Line)**   SDSL is a symmetric bidirectional DSL service that is basically the same as HDSL, but operates on one twisted-pair wire. It can provide data rates up to the T1 rate of 1.544 Mbits/sec.

- **ADSL (Asymmetric Digital Subscriber Line)**   ADSL is an asymmetric technology, meaning that the downstream data rate is much higher than the upstream data rate. As mentioned, this works well for a typical Internet session in which more information is downloaded from Web servers than is uploaded. ADSL operates in a frequency range that is above the frequency range of voice services, so the same wire can carry both analog voice and digital data transmissions. The upstream rates range from 16 Kbits/sec to as high as 768 Kbits/sec. The downstream rates and distances are listed here.

Downstream Rate	Downstream Distance
1.544 Mbits/sec	5.5 km (18,000 ft.)
2.048 Mbits/sec	4.8 km (16,000 ft.)
6.312 Mbits/sec	3.6 km (12,000 ft.)
8.448 Mbits/sec	2.7 km (9,000 ft.)

- **VDSL (Very High–Data-Rate Digital Subscriber Line)**   VDSL is basically ADSL at much higher data rates. It is asymmetric and, thus, has a higher downstream rate than upstream rate. The upstream rates are from 1.5 Mbits/sec to 2.3 Mbits/sec. The downstream rates and distances are listed in the following table. VDSL is seen as a way to provide very high-speed access for streaming video, combined data and video, video-conferencing, data distribution in campus environments, and the support of multiple connections within apartment buildings.

Downstream Rate	Downstream Distance
12.96 Mbits/sec	1.4 km (4,500 ft.)
25.82 Mbits/sec	0.9 km (3,000 ft.)
51.84 Mbits/sec	0.3 km (1,000 ft.)

- **RADSL (Rate-Adaptive Digital Subscriber Line)**   This service is also similar to ADSL, but it has a rate-adaptive feature that will adjust the transmission speed to match the quality of the line and the length of the line. A line-polling technique is used to establish a connection speed when the line is first established.

- **DSL Lite (or G.Lite)**   DSL Lite is considered a "jump-start" technology that is meant to deliver DSL to the greatest number of users, as fast as possible. While it has a lower data rate than other DSLs, it does not require that the telephone company do anything to the lines. In addition, equipment to handle DSL Lite is becoming readily available at a low price.

A related technology is VoDSL (Voice Over DSL). This is discussed under the topic "Voice/Data Networking." This topic is expanded at the Linktionary! Web site listed at the end of this topic. There you will find additional information *and* Web links.

Related Entries   Broadband Communications and Networking; Cable (CATV) Data Networks; Carrier Services; Communication Services and Providers; Data Link Protocols; DBS (Direct Broadcast Satellite); Home Networking; Internet Connections; Last Mile Services; Local Loop; Network Access Services; Residential Broadband; Telecommunications and Telephone Systems; *and* Wireless Broadband Access Services

Linktionary!—Tom Sheldon's Encyclopedia of Networking updates	http://www.linktionary.com/d/dsl.html
ADSL Forum	http://www.adsl.com
Web ProForums (several DSL topics)	http://www.iec.org/tutorials/index.html
Telechoice xDSL.com Web site	http://www.xdsl.com/
Tut Systems	http://www.tutsys.com
CopperCom "voice of DSL" technology vendor	http://www.coppercom.com
DSL Sourcebook by Paradyne	http://www.paradyne.com/sourcebook_offer/

DSL Life Web site	http://www.dsllife.com/
InterOperability Lab Consortiums (see multiple DSL headings)	http://www.iol.unh.edu/consortiums/
Network World Fusion DSL Web page	http://www.nwfusion.com/netresources/dsl.html

DSP (Digital Signal Processing)

The technique of converting analog information such as sound, video, and still pictures into digital information. DSP is often used to refer to a chip or processor that performs these functions. They may also be used to manipulate this information and then output it as analog.

Related Entries   ASIC (Application-Specific Integrated Circuit); CISC (Complex Instruction Set Computer); Network Processors; RISC (Reduced Instruction Set Computer); *and* Switch Fabrics and Bus Design

FAQs (Frequently asked questions with answers) on Digital Signal Processing	http://www.bdti.com/faq/
Eg3 DSP page	http://www.eg3.com/navi/dsp.htm
Bitpipe (search for DSP)	http://www.bitpipe.com

DSS (Digital Satellite System)

See DBS (Digital Broadcast Satellite).

DSS (Digital Signature Standard)

DSS is part of the U.S. government's Capstone program to develop cryptography and security standards that must be used by government agencies and private companies doing business with the government as specified in FIPS (Federal Information Processing Standard). NIST (National Institute of Standards and Technology) and NSA (National Security Agency) are responsible for Capstone. Capstone's major components include an encryption algorithm called *Skipjack* (and a Skipjack encryption chip called *Clipper*); a hash function called *SHA-1 (Secure Hash Standard)*; and *DSA (Digital Signature Algorithm)*, which is the algorithm used in DSS. Capstone is also working on a key exchange protocol.

DSS, which was made a standard in 1994, provides authentication but not encryption. Therefore, it can only be used for digital signatures—as compared to the RSA system, which can be used for encryption and digital signatures. The DSA algorithm is based on the discrete logarithm system—as opposed to RSA, which is based on integer factorization. Another system growing in popularity and supposedly stronger than these is the ECC (elliptic curve cryptosystem). These methods are discussed further under "Public-Key Cryptography." The topic "Digital Signatures" provides additional information related to this topic.

RSA Laboratories makes some interesting points about DSS and the DSA in its "Frequently Asked Questions About Today's Cryptography":

D

■ DSA generates a signature faster than it can be verified, while RSA verifies faster than it can generate a signature. RSA notes that it is better to verify fast since generation only happens once and verification happens often.

■ DSA has been criticized for its lack of flexibility, compared to RSA's cryptosystem.

■ NIST chose DSA in a secret and arbitrary way with influence from the NSA, which led many people not to trust the system.

■ The original scheme had some security problems that were fixed, but still haunt it.

While these views obviously favor RSA, one should keep in mind that other companies such as Certicom are hot on the heels of RSA with advanced cryptosystems using systems such as elliptic curve cryptography.

Related Entries   Certificates and Certification Servers; Cryptography; Digital Signatures; PKI (Public-Key Infrastructure); Public-Key Cryptography; *and* Security

In addition to the following links, others appear under "Security" in this book.

Linktionary!—Tom Sheldon's Encyclopedia of Networking updates	http://www.linktionary.com/security/
DSS (Digital Signature Standard), U.S. Department of Commerce/NIST	http://csrc.ncsl.nist.gov/fips/fips186.txt
W3C DSS Signature Suite	http://www.w3.org/TR/1998/REC-DSig-label/DSS-1_0

DSU/CSU (Data Service Unit/Channel Service Unit)

A DSU (data service unit) is a communication device that connects a company's telephone premises equipment to digital communication lines, such as a T1. A CSU (channel service unit) provides line termination and signal regeneration. The DSU and the CSU are often combined in one device and connected to a channel bank, which provides analog-to-digital conversion and multiplexing of voice transmissions. See "CSU/DSU (Channel Service Unit/Data Service Unit)."

DSx (Digital Signal-x)

Digital signal refers to the rate and format of digital telecommunication circuits. DS is related to the T designations; but DS refers to multiplexing techniques while the T designations refer to the underlying equipment and signaling. There are various DS levels, as outlined here:

DS Level	T-Carrier Equivalent	Speed	Number of 64-Kbit/ sec Channels
DS0	Fractional T1	64 Kbits/sec	1
DS1	T1	1.544 Mbits/sec	24
DS3	T3	44.736 Mbits/sec	672

DS-0 represents a single voice telephone call, while DS-1 defines how to multiplex 24 phone calls onto a single circuit. This DS signal hierarchy is part of the NADH (North American Digital Hierarchy). Eventually, SONET (Synchronous Optical Network) will replace NADH. SDH (Synchronous Digital Hierarchy) is the European equivalent of SONET.

Related Entries   Circuit; E-Carriers; Leased Line; NADH (North American Digital Hierarchy); SONET (Synchronous Optical Network); T-Carriers; TDM Networks; Telecommunications and Telephone Systems; *and* WAN (Wide Area Network)

DTE (Data Terminal Equipment)

DTEs are the source or destination of data in a communication connection. DTEs are connected to DCE (data circuit–terminating equipment), which in turn is connected to the communication channel, as shown in Figure D-35. Dumb terminals were originally classified as DTEs, but computers also fall into this category. A DCE is a modem if the circuit is an analog voice line, or a DSU/CSU if the line is digital.

DTM (Dynamic Synchronous Transfer Mode)

DTM is a form of circuit switching for fiber-optic networks that employs TDM (time division multiplexing) in a new way that dynamically reallocates available bandwidth to users that need it. DTM was designed to remove the bottleneck at fiber network access points. These bottlenecks are typically caused by the need to process and buffer large amounts packet-based data. DTM seeks to limit complexity and use transmission capacity more efficiently. In particular, DTM can fully support high–bit-rate, real-time traffic and multicasting; and when used as a link layer for IP networks, it can support strict QoS.

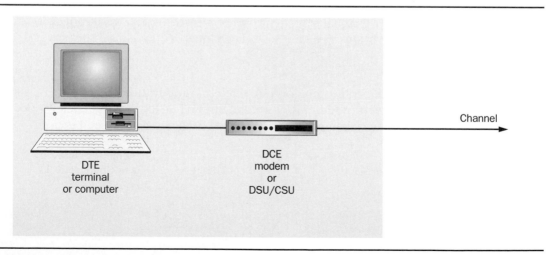

Figure D-35.   *A DTE/DCE connection*

Along with Gigabit Ethernet and Cisco DPT (Dynamic Packet Transport), DTM is considered one of the technologies to use in new fiber-access metropolitan area networks.

Circuit switching has always been more reliable than packet switching, and provides a nonblocking data transmission system (it's predictable because you get all the bandwidth you paid for). At the same time, packet switching has many benefits, including the ability to use bandwidth efficiently by multiplexing the transmissions of many users over mesh-topology links. The global Internet is testament to the advantages of packet switching. But as network capacity has improved due to fiber-optic cable, and as bandwidth requirements have increased for real-time traffic like voice and video, the need for circuits is real.

As mentioned, DTM is a circuit-switching scheme that uses TDM. Thus, DTM can guarantee bandwidth to users of the system. DTM uses SONET/SDH framing schemes, but extends the scheme with a dynamic reallocation mechanism that can redistribute bandwidth not being used by one user to another user who needs it. DTM basically allocates, on demand, any available bandwidth to other users. New channels can be set up at very high speed (less than a millisecond).

Users can be allocated bandwidth according to several schemes. The best scheme is *guaranteed bandwidth*, which allocates a certain number of time slots to a user that will guarantee the bandwidth the user needs. The *on-demand bandwidth* scheme gives users bandwidth when they ask for it, at an extra cost. Finally, the on-demand bandwidth with best effort is a scheme that gives users bandwidth when requested, but only when it is available.

While DTM is primarily circuit oriented, it differs in several ways. First, DTM channels are simplex to achieve high bandwidth. Interactive sessions between two hosts will require two channels. DTM supports multirate bandwidth allocation, from 512 Kbits/sec up to full link capacity. DTM also supports multicast so that any one channel can be connected to any number of receivers. DTM is fault tolerant. It supports identical nodes (master and slave) and redundant dual-fiber connections between adjacent dual nodes. The switching nodes are used in parallel, but provide immediate failover in case one fails.

More information about DTM is available at the upcoming Web sites. Dynarc and Net Insight are the two primary vendors advocating DTM. Net Insight developed an 8-port single-chip DTM switch that other vendors are using to build DTM equipment.

Related Entries   DPT (Dynamic Packet Transport); MAN (Metropolitan Area Network); Multiplexing; Network Access Services; Network Core Technologies; NPN (New Public Network); Optical Networks; SONET (Synchronous Optical Network); *and* WDM (Wavelength Division Multiplexing)

Linktionary!—Tom Sheldon's Encyclopedia of Networking updates	http://www.linktionary.com/d/dtm.html
Dynarc	http://www.dynarc.com/
Net Insight	http://www.netinsight.se/
Web ProForum Tutorial: "Dynamic Synchronous Transfer Mode (DTM) Fundamentals and Network Solutions"	http://www.iec.org/tutorials/dtm_fund/index.html
Light Reading (provides news and analysis on all optical networking topics)	http://www.lightreading.com/

Dublin Core Metadata for Resource Discovery

See Metadata.

DUN (Dial-Up Networking)

See Remote Access.

Duplexed Systems

A duplexed system provides data protection in the form of mirroring, in which data is simultaneously written in two places at once. Mirroring implies that two disks are present, but attached to one disk channel (adapter card). Duplexing implies that each disk is attached to its own adapter card, which adds another level of protection. The entire server can also be duplexed so users are never without a server should one server go down. Duplexed servers are attached with high-speed interfaces (fiber) and can be placed in separate locations to protect them from local disasters.

Related Entry   Mirroring

DWDM (Dense Wavelength Division Multiplexing)

See WDM (Wavelength Division Multiplexing).

Dynamic Routing

Dynamic routing is a process in which routers automatically adjust to changes in network topology or traffic. The opposite is static routing, in which the router manager enters the routes manually. Dynamic routing is used in all modern routers, but some amount of programming is still available for customizing routes if necessary. See "Routing" for more information.

E Carrier

The *E carriers* (E1, E3, and so on), like the North American *T carriers*, are communication systems and standards that provide multiplexed, multichannel, point-to-point communication links. It has been used by carriers to link remote telephone switching offices and is commonly used for customer-to-carrier access links.

The E carriers are defined by the European CEPT (Conference of Postal and Telecommunications Administrations) and are used in Europe, Mexico, and South America. The T carriers are part of the NADH (North American Digital Hierarchy). The CEPT format defines how digital information is formatted and multiplexed into the transmission system.

Conceptually, the two standards provide a similar type of service: transmission links that provide multiple time division multiplexed (TDM) channels. Traditionally, multiple voice calls are carried over the service, but data is also supported. The service is digital, meaning that analog phone calls piped into a TDM channel are first converted to digital signals. PCM (pulse code modulation) is used for analog-to-digital conversion.

The carriers originally used the services to connect outlying remote telephone switches with central office switches or to interconnect central offices. For example, if a new subdivision was built, a remote switch was installed near the subdivision to provide a connection point for new subscriber telephone lines (local loop copper wires). The subscriber lines then were multiplexed onto a single cable that connected the remote switch with the central office.

The basic channel in both systems is the 64-Kbit/sec channel that supports one voice call or data circuit, depending on how the customer wants to use it. But this is where to two systems diverge. The E carriers allocate the full 64-Kbits/sec channel to the user, while the T carriers rob some of the bits in the basic channel to use for signaling. The end results are the same, but the digital hierarchy is different. The E carrier hierarchy is listed here.

Circuit Name	Data Rate	Number of 64-Kbit/Sec Channels
E1	2.048-Mbit/sec circuit	Thirty voice channels plus two control and synchronization channels
E3	34.368-Mbit/sec circuit	Equivalent to 16 E1 circuits
E4	139.26-Mbit/sec circuit	Equivalent to 4 E3 circuits
E5	565.148-Mbit/sec	Equivalent to 4 E4 circuits

Note that an E1 carries 30 channels, while a T1 carries 24 channels. Since E1 circuits carry more channels than T1 circuits (24 channels), repeaters are required every 6,000 feet when copper wire is used. See "T Carriers" for information about the T carriers and "NADH (North American Digital Hierarchy)" for information about the signaling methods. See "TDM Networks" for information about building networks with E1/T1 links.

Related Entries   Circuit; Circuit-Switching Services; Communication Services and Providers; CSU/DSU (Channel Service Unit/Data Service Unit); Data Communication Concepts; Last Mile Services; Leased Line; Local Loop; MAN (Metropolitan Area Network); Multiplexing and Multiplexers; NADH (North American Digital Hierarchy); Network Access Services; Network Core Technologies; Optical

Networks; Point-to-Point Communications; Service Providers and Carriers; T-Carriers; TDM Networks; Telecommunications and Telephone Systems; *and* WAN (Wide Area Network)

 Linktionary!—Tom Sheldon's Encyclopedia of   http://www.linktionary.com/e/e-carrier.html
Networking updates

See "T-Carriers" and "TDM Networks" for more links.

EAP (Extensible Authentication Protocol)

EAP is a framework for extending authentication techniques in PPP (Point-to-Point Protocol). PPP is designed to transport datagrams over a point-to-point link. It is commonly used for dial-up connections. EAP is discussed in RFC 2284, "PPP Extensible Authentication Protocol" (March 1998).

Internet users use PPP when they dial into a remote access server. Built into PPP is a Link Control Protocol (LCP) that establishes a link between the systems. LCP can then optionally negotiate an authentication protocol that authenticates the user. The traditional authentication method has been either PAP or CHAP (PAP is not considered secure). RADIUS servers are typically used to authenticate users.

What EAP does is open up the possibilities to use a range of new authentication protocols, including token cards, one-time passwords, and biometric techniques. When EAP is configured, the selection of an authentication mechanism is bypassed during the LCP phase and handled during the authentication phase. The server being logged onto (authenticator) uses this opportunity to request additional information from the client before it decides which authentication technique to use. The authenticator can pass the authentication through to a back-end server if necessary.

When the authenticator requests additional information from the client, it makes that request via type fields in the request message. Request types include identity, MD5-challenge (similar to CHAP), one-time passwords, and generic token card, among others. The client sends a Response packet back to the authenticator that contains type field information related to the authentication method it supports.

RFC 2716, "PPP EAP TLS Authentication Protocol" (October 1999) describes how EAP works with TLS (Transport Layer Security), which defines high levels of mutual authentication, key exchange, and integrity-protected negotiations of security protocols.

EAPOE (Extensible Authentication Protocol Over Ethernet) is an IEEE development that extends the benefits of EAP to LANs, including the ability to authenticate users with a variety of protocols. Where EAPOE differs is that it couples EAP with Ethernet rather than PPP. In addition, it runs in Ethernet switches. When an Ethernet node attempts to access the Ethernet network, EAPOE initiates its authentication routine. A Request Identity message is sent to the Ethernet node. This serves as a challenge. The node puts its ID in a return message, and this is forwarded by the switch to a RADIUS server. The RADIUS server then challenges the node and an authentication ensues. CHAP may be used; but EAPOE, like EAP, is open to a variety of authentication techniques, as already mentioned.

Related Entries   Authentication and Authorization; Biometric Access Devices; Certificates and Certification Systems; CHAP (Challenge Handshake Authentication Protocol); Cryptography; DIAMETER; Digital Signatures; Hash Functions; IPSec (IP Security); Kerberos Authentication Protocol;

Mobile Computing; NAS (Network Access Server); PPP (Point-to-Point Protocol); RADIUS (Remote Authentication Dial-In User Service); RAS (Remote Access Server); Security; *and* Token-Based Authentication

Linktionary!—Tom Sheldon's Encyclopedia of Networking updates	http://www.linktionary.com/e/eap.html
IETF Point-to-Point Protocol Extensions (pppext) Working Group	http://www.ietf.org/html.charters/pppext-charter.html

E-Commerce

See Electronic Commerce.

Edge Devices

Edge devices are routers, switches, routing switches, IADs (integrated access devices), multiplexers, and a variety of MAN/WAN access devices that provide entry points into enterprise or carrier/service provider core networks. On an enterprise network, edge devices may connect Ethernet and token ring LANs to an ATM backbone, where the ATM network provides a bridge between the edge networks. This configuration is shown on the left in Figure E-1. Edge devices also provide connections into carrier and service provider networks, as shown on the right in Figure E-1. Note that the "end systems" are on the "outside" of the edge device.

In general, edge devices provide access to faster, more efficient backbone and core networks. The trend is to make the edge smart and the core "dumb and fast." Consequently, core networks are being designed with switches rather than routers. The topics "ATM" and "MPLS" provide examples of edge switches. Figure A-17 illustrates a core of ATM switches surrounded by Gigabit Ethernet edge switches. While a core of all routers may be easy to manage (routing protocols self-configure routes), they are not scalable and do not support traffic engineering and other techniques that support QoS. See "IPM over ATM."

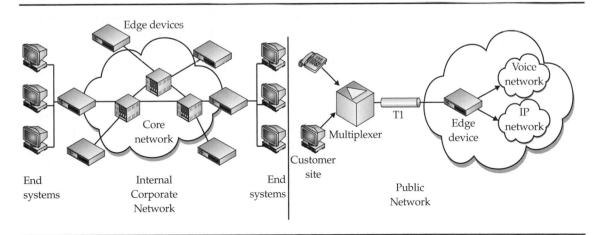

Figure E-1.   *Edge devices "at the edge" of ATM networks*

Edge devices may translate between one type of network protocol and another. For example, ATM networks send data in cells and use connection-oriented virtual circuits. An IP network is packet oriented; so if ATM is used as a core, packets must be encapsulated in cells and the destination address must be converted to a virtual circuit identifier. Edge devices are responsible for handling this conversion. There is an *ingress* (input) and *egress* (output) edge device for all connections. A number of techniques have been devised to move IP packets over switched network topologies. See "LANE (LAN Emulation)," "MPOA (Multiprotocol Over ATM)," "IP Over ATM," "Label Switching," "Multilayer Switching," and "MPLS (Multiprotocol Label Switching)."

An edge switch for a WAN may be a multiservice unit, meaning that it supports a wide variety of communication technologies, including voice and IP over dial-up connections, ISDN, T1 circuits, frame relay, and ATM. An edge device may provide enhanced services, such as VPN support, voice over IP, and QoS services. See "IADs (Integrated Access Devices)."

Related Entries   ATM (Asynchronous Transfer Mode); Connection-Oriented and Connectionless Services; Data Communication Concepts; Datagrams and Datagram Services; End Systems and End-to-End Connectivity; IADs (Integrated Access Devices); IP Over ATM; IP Switching; Label Switching; LANE (LAN Emulation); MPLS (Multiprotocol Label Switching); MPOA (Multiprotocol Over ATM); Multilayer Switching; Network Access Services; Network Concepts; Network Core Technologies; Network Design and Construction; Packets and Packet Switching Networks; Point-to-Point Communications; Reliable Data Delivery Services; Routing; Switching and Switched Networks; Transport Protocols and Services; Virtual Circuits; *and* VLAN (Virtual LAN)

Linktionary!—Tom Sheldon's Encyclopedia of Networking updates

http://www.linktionary.com/e/ edge_devices.html

EDI (Electronic Data Interchange)

EDI is a set of protocols for conducting electronic business over computer networks. Traditionally, these networks have been private WANS; but EDI is now done over the Internet. EDI defines the electronic exchange of structured business data, such as purchase orders, invoices, and shipping notices, typically between one organization and another. The relationship is usually between a vendor and customer. For example, EDI provides a way for a customer's computer to place orders for goods with a vendor's computers, based on reorder levels. The EDI system coordinates the transaction, initiates deliveries, and generates invoices.

It is important to differentiate between EDI and *electronic commerce*. Electronic commerce encompasses all aspects of electronic business exchanges, including person-to-person interaction (collaboration), money transfers, data sharing and exchange, Web site merchant systems, and so on. EDI is a subset of electronic commerce that encompasses the exchange of business information in a standardized electronic form. Standard form defines things like the layout of information for an invoice or purchase order.

EDI can reduce costs, workforce requirements, and errors associated with retyping orders, invoices, and other documents. With EDI, computer data already entered by one organization is made available to a business partner. EDI is typically handled using store-and-forward technologies similar to e-mail. A third party such as GEIS (General Electric Information Service) often serves as a "middleman" to help organizations establish business relationships and handle business transactions.

EDI can be thought of in terms of *messages* exchanged between businesses that are engaged in electronic commerce. Within a message is a basic unit of information called the *data element*. A message may consist of many data elements. For example, each line item on an invoice is a data element. All the data elements form a *compound document*, which is essentially a *business form*. An EDI message also includes a field definition table that provides information about the data elements in the message, such as whether an element is mandatory or optional, how many characters it has, and whether it is numeric or alphabetic. *String identifiers* define things like data element names and a data dictionary reference number. The *data element dictionary* defines the content and meaning of data elements.

EDI was first developed by the automobile/transportation industry in the 1970s. Today, it is widely used in a variety of industries, including distribution, finance and accounting, health care, manufacturing, purchasing, retail, tax form filing, and shipping. Early EDI packages used rather simple standard forms that forced companies to convert data to fit the forms. Newer EDI systems allow companies to create custom systems using simple programming or authoring tools. Even more recently, EDI has been adapted for the Internet and to work with XML, as discussed later.

There are two approaches to implementing EDI. Many large organizations acquire or build their own proprietary systems, often in association with their business partners. If a business partner is small, it may have little choice but to adopt the proprietary system of its much larger business associate. The other approach is to work with a VAN (value added network) provider, which provides EDI transaction services, security, document interchange assistance, standard message formats, communication protocols, and communication parameters for EDI. Most VANs also provide a network on which to transmit information. VAN providers include

- GE Information Systems   http://www.geis.com
- IBM Global Services   http://www.ibm.com/services/
- Sterling Commerce   http://www.stercomm.com

In many ways, the Internet is a better medium for implementing EDI than using value added network providers or installing private leased lines. The Internet is already in place as a business-to-business communication system. The startup costs are cheaper and, in most cases, the organization is already connected to the Internet. This makes it easier for more businesses to join the electronic commerce web, especially those who previously could not afford the expense of EDI.

The use of VPNs is growing for EDI and e-commerce–related traffic. A VPN can secure and give preferential treatment to EDI traffic. The term *extranet* is usually used to refer to a secure Internet connection between trading partners. The protocol for VPNs are L2TP (Layer 2

Tunneling Protocol), PPTP (Point-to-Point Tunneling Protocol), and the IETF's IPSec (IP Security). See "VPN (Virtual Private Network)."

EDI Standards and Initiatives

There are several EDI standards that have been around for many years. But as the Internet took hold, new techniques for implementing EDI developed in groups and consortiums such as the W3C (World Wide Web Consortium), Commerce-Net, Rosetta Net, and Open Buying on the Internet (OBI). The Web sites for these organizations are listed later.

New EDI standards are currently under development. Some examples are described here.

- **ANSI ASC X12 (American National Standards-X12)**   X12 is a standard that defines many different types of documents, including air shipments, student loan applications, injury and illness reports, and shipment and billing notices. The ANSI (American National Standards Institute) assigned responsibility for development of EDI standards to the ASC (Accredited Standards Committee) X12 organization in 1979. X12 has roots in work done in the shipping industry by the TDCC (Transportation Data Coordinating Committee) and work done in the food distribution industry by the UCC (Uniform Code Council).

- **UN/EDIFACT**   UN/EDIFACT (United Nations/Electronic Data Interchange for Administration Commerce and Transport) is an international set of EDI standards that are published by the United Nations Trade Data Interchange Directory (UNTDID). The standards include syntax rules and implementation guidelines; message design guidelines; and directory sets defining messages, data elements, and code sets, among other definitions. It is built upon X12 and TDI (Trade Data Interchange), the latter being a generic EDI standard used in Europe.

- **Open-EDI**   The ISO (International Standards Organization) and IEC (International Electrical Committee) are developing an EDI reference model under a joint committee called Open-EDI. The goal of Open-EDI is to allow electronic transactions among "multiple autonomous organizations" that may or may not have any prior business relationships. In other words, businesses should be able to establish trading partners over networks like the Internet upon first contact and without any pre-agreement, assuming trust systems are in place. See the Web site http://www.x12.org and http://enix.epa.gov.tw/enixnews/1999spring/FA_OOEDI.htm.

For additional information about standards, refer to the DISA (Data Interchange Standards Association) at the Web site given later. Another good Web site that lists common EDI and e-commerce standards is European Commission's Open Information Interchange (OII) Web site. The Web site addresses are given at the end of this topic.

EDI and XML

While EDI is still a widely used electronic commerce technology, smaller businesses often have a difficult time implementing it. XML is proving to be a good technology for business information exchange. In addition, existing EDI data formats can be translated into XML. At some point, EDI will blur into XML-based electronic commerce solutions. Many vendors have already developed transition products that help companies' integration of EDI and XML systems.

By combining EDI and XML, the previously designed message formats and element dictionaries of EDI carried into the XML realm, where file formats and schema exist to represent data and data structures. Data exchanged in XML is easy to search, decode, manipulate, and display in a consistent way. See "XML (Extensible Markup Language)" or visit the XML/EDI Group Web page listed later.

EDI and the IETF

A turning point for EDI on the Internet came in 1995, upon publication of RFC 1767, "MIME Encapsulation of EDI Objects" (March 1995). This RFC defines how electronic mail can be used as a delivery mechanism for electronic transactions. The specification defines how to encapsulate EDI exchanges into MIME messages. The RFC does not specify any changes to EDI itself. It simply defines another way to exchange EDI transactions beyond those already defined.

Internet RFC 1865, "EDI Meets the Internet Frequently Asked Questions About Electronic Data Interchange on the Internet" (January 1996) provides answers to many EDI-over-the-Internet questions. It points out the potential benefits of the Internet for EDI, including common standards and interoperability, traffic routing that makes any-to-any connections possible, and distributed directory services for identifying and contacting other organizations.

The IETF Working Group called "Electronic Data Interchange-Internet Integration (ediint)" was formed to expand the use of EDI on the Internet. The group is working on security issues such as EDI transaction integrity, privacy and nonrepudiation in various forms. It is also working on standards that are needed to ensure interoperability between EDI packages over Internet. In addition, it is also defining how current Internet standards can be used to achieve interoperable EDI for real-time transactions (a problem, since the Internet is based on best-effort IP services).

Related Entries   Collaborative Computing; Document Standards; Electronic Commerce; Electronic Mail; Extranet; Groupware; Instant Messaging; IPSec (IP Security); Security; VPN (Virtual Private Network); Web Technologies and Concepts; Workflow Management; *and* XML (Extensible Markup Language)

Linktionary!—Tom Sheldon's Encyclopedia of Networking updates	http://www.linktionary.com/e/edi.html
IETF Working Group: Electronic Data Interchange-Internet Integration (ediint)	http://www.ietf.org/html.charters/ediint-charter.html
DISA (Data Interchange Standards Association)	http://www.disa.org
DISA X.12	http://www.x12.org/
UN/EDIFACT	http://www.unece.org/trade/
CommerceNet	http://www.commerce.net/
Rosetta Net	http://www.rosettanet.org/
OBI Consortium Web site	http://www.openbuy.org/
XML/EDI Group	http://www.xmledi-group.org/
OII (Open Information Exchange) EDI Web site	http://158.169.50.95:10080/oii/en/edi.html
OII (Open Information Exchange) Electronic Commerce Web site	http://158.169.50.95:10080/oii/en/commerce.html

Harbinger EDI Software	http://www.harbinger.com
Sterling Commerce, Inc.	http://www.sterlingcommerce.com/
Prof. Jeff MacKie-Mason EDI Links page	http://china.si.umich.edu/telecom/ net-commerce-edi.html
GE Global Exchange Services	http://www.geis.com/
Google Web Directory (search for "EDI")	http://directory.google.com/Top/Computers/

EGPs (Exterior Gateway Protocols)

The Internet and TCP/IP networks are divided into autonomous systems, which are collections of hosts and routers that typically use the same routing protocol and are administered by the same authority. There are two categories of routing protocols to handle traffic for domains. While *interior routing protocols* are used within a domain, *exterior routing protocols* provide a way for two neighboring routers located at the edges of their respective domains to exchange routing information.

The primary interior routing protocols in use today are RIP (Routing Information Protocol) and OSPF (Open Shortest Path First). OSPF is now the most important on large networks and Internet service provider networks, but RIP is still popular for small private networks. The primary exterior routing protocol for exchanging routing information between autonomous systems is BGP (Border Gateway Protocol). An earlier protocol for doing this was EGP (Exterior Gateway Protocol), but it was replaced by BGP. The topic "Routing on the Internet" provides more information about these protocols.

Related Entries   Autonomous Systems; BGP (Border Gateway Protocol); IDPR (Inter-Domain Policy Routing Protocol); Internetworking; IP (Internet Protocol); RIP (Routing Information Protocol); Route Aggregation; Routing; *and* Routing on the Internet

Linktionary!—Tom Sheldon's Encyclopedia of Networking updates	http://www.linktionary.com/r/routing.html

EIA (Electronic Industries Alliance)

Founded in 1924, the EIA is a U.S. organization of electronics manufacturers. The EIA has published a number of standards related to telecommunication and computer communication, and works closely with other associates such as ANSI and the ITU.

The primary EIA standards for telecommunication define the serial interface between modems and computers. The most popular are the RS-232-C, RS-449, RS-422, and RS-423 serial interfaces. The physical layer specifications define 37-pin (DB-37), 25-pin (DB-25), and 9-pin (DB-9) connectors and associated cable, as well as electrical characteristics such as the type of signal used on each pin and the timing of those signals. See "Serial Communications and Interfaces."

Note that the EIA RS-232 standard is also the CCITT standard V.24. CCITT is part of the ITU. The CCITT V series protocols are more commonly used than the EIA standards, partly because they are used in Europe where government standards dictate the type of protocol to be used. For the most part, EIA standards have CCITT equivalents. For example, the Group 3 facsimile, which is the fax machine standard for transmissions rates up to 9.6 Kbits/sec, is the CCITT Recommendation T.4 and the EIA-465 standard.

In the area of structured cabling for networks, the EIA has recently joined with the TIA (Telecommunications Industry Association) to create the Commercial Building Telecommunications Wiring Standards (TIA/EIA 568 and 569), which define hierarchical wiring systems in campus environments using data-grade twisted-pair wire. These standards provide a wiring structure that building designers can use to facilitate high-speed data communication equipment without the need to know in advance what that equipment will be.

Related Entries   IEEE 802 Standards; Internet Organizations and Committees; Internet Standards; ISO (International Organization for Standardization); ITU (International Telecommunications Union); OSI (Open Systems Interconnection) Model; Serial Communications and Interfaces; Standards Groups, Associations, and Organizations; TIA (Telecommunications Industry Association); *and* TIA/EIA Structured Cabling Standards

 EIA (Electronic Industries Alliance)   http://www.eia.org

EIA/TIA Structured Cabling Standards

See TIA/EIA Structured Cabling Standards.

EIP (Enterprise Information Portal)

See Portal.

ELAN (Emulated LAN), ATM

See ATM (Asynchronous Transfer Mode); IP Over ATM; LANE (LAN Emulation); MPOA (Multiprotocol Over ATM); Switched Networks; *and* Virtual Circuits.

Electromagnetic Interference

See EMI (Electromagnetic Interference).

Electromagnetic Spectrum

Energy is transmitted in three ways: electromagnetic radiation, conduction, and convection (heat transfer). Because electromagnetic waves do not necessarily need a material medium for transmission, they are used for a wide range of communication, including communication over copper and fiber-optic cable, as well as through water, air, and the vacuum of space.

Electron movement causes electromagnetic radiation. The frequency is the number of oscillations per second of the resulting wave, also called Hz (hertz). The wavelength is the distance between crests in the wave. The higher the frequency, the shorter the wavelength. As outlined in Figure E-2, the length of a wave may be larger than the earth's diameter and smaller than an electron.

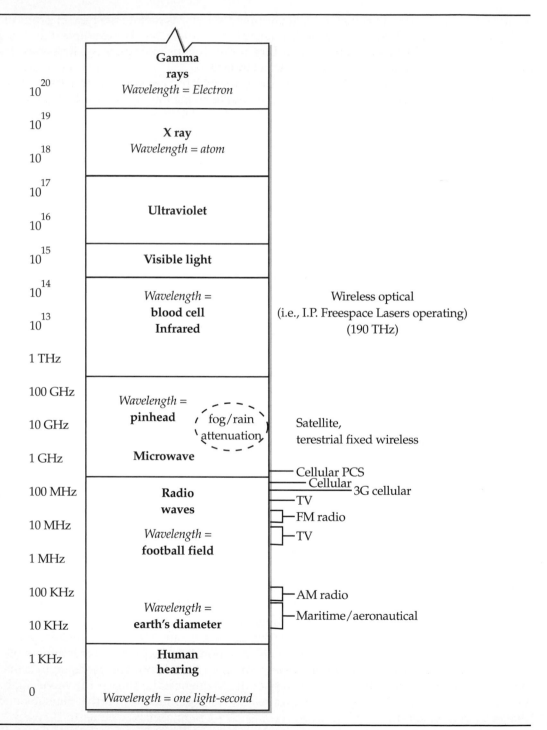

Figure E-2.   *The electromagnetic spectrum*

Wireless systems use specific bands in the radio, microwave, and infrared range, as shown in Figure E-2. The spectrum is allocated by governments and international organizations. In the United States, the FCC allocates the spectrum and sells it at auctions to companies that want to operate communication services in designated markets. Spectrum allocation is designed to prevent overlapping signals and interference. In fact, interference still occurs. Devices like microwave ovens, wireless LANs, and cellular phones operate in the same frequency. Some common frequency allocations are listed here.

Cordless telephones	46 to 49 MHz
Mobile radio (not telephone) services	30 to 300 MHz
Wireless local loop	420 to 450 MHz
Citizens band radio	462 to 467 MHz
UHF TV channels 60–69 (may be allocated to cellular)	747 to 762 MHz 777 to 792 MHz
Cellular services	824 to 849 MHz 869 to 894 MHz
Cellular services, GSM	890 to 914 MHz 935 to 959 MHz
Mobile satellite service and GPS (Global Positioning System)	1.2 to 1.3 GHz
3G bands (potential areas of use)	Other Cellular ranges 1.7 to 1.8 GHz Some MMDS 2-GHz ranges
Cellular PCS (personal communication system)	1.85 to 1.91 GHz (licensed) 1.93 to 1.99 GHz (licensed) 1.91 to 1.93 GHz (unlicensed)
High-speed unlicensed wireless LANs (IEEE 802.11b), home networking (e.g., Home RF), Bluetooth PAN (personal area network), cordless phones, and consumer electronics	2.4-GHz band
U-NII (Unlicensed National Information Infrastructure). IEEE 802.11a wireless LANs operate in this range.	5.15 to 5.35 GHz 5.725 to 5.825 GHz
MMDS (Multichannel Multipoint Distribution Service) fixed broadband wireless for local access (48 km/30 mi)	2.5 to 2.7 GHz 3.4 to 3.7 GHz
LMDS (Local Multipoint Distribution Services) fixed broadband wireless for local access (8 km/5 mi)	10 to 43 GHz (various bands)
Optical wireless, e.g., Terabeam's freespace laser system (no licensing required)	190 THz (infrared range)

In analog transmissions, information is transmitted by modulating either the wave's amplitude, frequency, or phase. A receiving device then "tunes" itself to the designated frequency and extracts the modulated signal. The higher the frequency, the higher the data rate, but the lower the signal range. Here are some examples:

- IEEE 802.11b wireless LANs operating in the 2.4-GHz band have a data rate of 11 Mbits/sec and a range of up to 100 meters. If OFDM (orthogonal frequency-division multiplexing) is used, data rates may go up to 30 Mbits/sec.

- IEEE 802.11a wireless LANs operating in the 5-GHz band have data rates up to 50 Mbits/sec.

- MMDS *wireless cable services* (2.5 to 3.7 GHz) covers a radius up to 48 km (30 mi) with a maximum data rate of 10 Mbits/sec.

- LMDS *wireless cable services* (10 to 43 GHz) covers a radius of only 8 km (5 mi) with a maximum data rate of 155 Mbits/sec.

Part of the microwave spectrum is especially susceptible to rain and fog. Basically, the water molecules absorb the radio energy. System designers must account for signal fading from fog and rain. High-frequency systems like LMDS also require line of sight (unlike FM radio) since the waves do not travel through buildings.

Because spectrum allocations have a finite bandwidth, carriers use whatever means possible to optimize the bandwidth. Cellular systems optimize their allocations by reusing frequencies in different, nonadjoining cells. LMDS is laid out in relatively small cells because their radio waves travel such short distances.

Lack of available frequencies has prompted the FCC to open up parts of the spectrum as unlicensed, meaning that anyone who wants to create a wireless device can use the frequency without regard for other devices that might be using it. Thus, the 2.4-GHz band hosts many different devices competing for the same frequencies. Some examples are cordless phones, wireless Ethernet LANs, Bluetooth personal area network devices, security systems, and video distribution services. Microwave ovens also operate in the band and, if leaking, can disrupt other devices in range. The FCC has created another unlicensed band in the 5-GHz range that will be used primarily for wireless LANs.

According to technologist George Gilder (*Gilder Technology Report*, January 2000), "there is a growing awareness that the information bearing power of the electromagnetic spectrum—its bandwidth or range of frequencies and wavelengths available to carry signals—is not severely limited, as previously believed, but essentially infinite. An infinitude of potential bandwidth implies the endless multiplication of spectrum use and reuse. Cellular technologies such as CDMA allow the reuse of all available bandwidth in every cell, the sharing of cellular bandwidth among many users, and the proliferation of local cells through the deployment of more antennas. The rise of Qualcomm (and its CDMA technology) is based on this potential of ubiquitous waves."

Related Entries   Analog Transmission Systems; Bluetooth; CDMA (Code Division Multiple Access); Fiber-Optic Cable; Home Networking; Infrared Technologies; Microwave Communication Systems; Mobile Computing; Multiplexing and Multiplexers; Network Concepts; Network Connection Technologies; Optical Networks; Packet Radio Data Networks; Radio Communications and Networks; Satellite Communication Systems; Signals; Spread Spectrum Signaling; TDMA (Time Division Multiple

Access); Throughput; UWB (Ultra Wideband); WDM (Wavelength Division Multiplexing); Wireless Communications; Wireless LAN, *and* Wireless Mobile Communications

Linktionary!—Tom Sheldon's Encyclopedia of Networking updates	http://www.linktionary.com/e/spectrum.html
Electromagnetic Spectrum: Data Communications, Radio	http://telecom.tbi.net/transmission.htm
Bennett Kobb's SpectrumGuide (independent sourcebook of U.S. radio frequency use)	http://www.newsignals.com/
NTIA (National Telecommunications and Information Administration) U.S. Frequency Allocation Chart (very detailed!)	http://www.ntia.doc.gov/osmhome/allochrt.html
FCC (Federal Communications Commission) home page	http://www.fcc.gov/
History of Wire and Broadcast Communications by FCC	http://www.fcc.gov/cib/evol.html
FCC Radio Spectrum Chart links	http://www.fcc.gov/oet/faqs/freqchart.html
U.S. Department of Defense joint spectrum chart	http://www.jsc.mil/images/speccht.jpg
Andrew Bateman radio design course: "Transmitter & Receiver Architectures"	http://www.avren.com/Courses/TX_RX_Architectures_plain.htm
WTB (Wireless Telecommunications Bureau) directory of wireless communication services	http://www.fcc.gov/wtb/services.html

Electronic Commerce

Electronic commerce (e-commerce) has come to be associated with the buying and selling of goods on the Internet or, more specifically, the Web because it takes advantage of Web protocols. It involves customer-oriented processes like those used at online shopping malls, including the presentation of online catalogs, shopping cart schemes, and payment authorization schemes. This customer-oriented e-commerce is often called B2C (business to consumer).

Electronic commerce also includes business-to-business (B2B) transactions, such as automatic inventory reordering and the exchange of electronic documents (purchase orders, invoices, and soon). B2B is usually built upon VPN-based extranets. A VPN is a private connection across the Internet or some other network, secured by an encrypting tunneling protocol such as IPSec (IP Security). B2B may integrate EDI (Electronic Data Interchange), an older technique of exchanging electronic business documents, in order to access legacy system and data. EDI has now been integrated into newer Web protocols. See "EDI (Electronic Data Interchange)" for more information.

Today, everyone is familiar with electronic commerce. Most computer users have purchased a book at Amazon.com. This topic is about the structural elements and protocols of electronic commerce. The Web sites given later provide more extensive information about planning, building, and securing electronic commerce sites.

E-Commerce Site Architecture

An electronic commerce site consists of one or more data centers, as pictured in Figure E-3. Note that this architecture is greatly simplified to illustrate the difference between B2C and B2B. An actual system may consist of several data centers and many firewalls, Internet connections, and extranet connections.

On the B2C client side, secure connections are established with protocols such as SSL (Secure Sockets Layer) and TLS (Transport Layer Security) to provide privacy and hide sensitive transaction information, such as credit card numbers. The use of certificates, public-key cryptography, and public-key infrastructure can enhance an e-commerce site by enabling authentication and access controls for a wide variety of users. See "PKI (Public-Key Infrastructure)" for more information.

On the B2B side, the e-commerce systems and applications are connected via secured private connections to trading partners and financial institutions. Inventory management may be handled automatically between the e-commerce site and its trading partners. The financial institutions provide credit card authorizations, banking transactions, and other financial services.

The most important physical component on the B2B side is the secure extranet connection. The current best protocol for implementing secure VPNs is IPSec. See "IPSec (IP Security)" and "VPN (Virtual Private Network)" for more information.

A busy e-commerce site should have multiple connections to an ISP to ensure adequate bandwidth and redundant connections. These connections should be physically diverse. Within the data center itself, there should be load-balancing devices and multiple servers to handle peak volume. Load balancers can examine a packet's contents and distribute the packets to appropriate servers. Fault tolerance and high availability are big issues for critical e-commerce sites, since lost connections translate to lost business. See "Load Balancing" and "Data Center Design" for more information on designs.

Security

To transact business, companies must have the means to conduct safe, private, and reliable transactions. To get to that level, the four cornerstones of secure electronic transactions must be present:

- The ability to prevent unauthorized monitoring of data transmissions
- A way to prevent the content of messages from being altered after they are sent and/or a way to prove that they have been altered
- The ability to determine whether a transmission is from an authentic source, or from someone or something masquerading as that source
- A way to prevent others from denying (repudiating) that they sent a message (such as a buy order) or that they received and read a message

Secure connections may be provided by SSL (Secure Sockets Layer) or TLS (Transport Layer Security). These secure channel services encrypt the data crossing the link between client and server. The protocols authenticate the client, and then exchange a master key that is used to

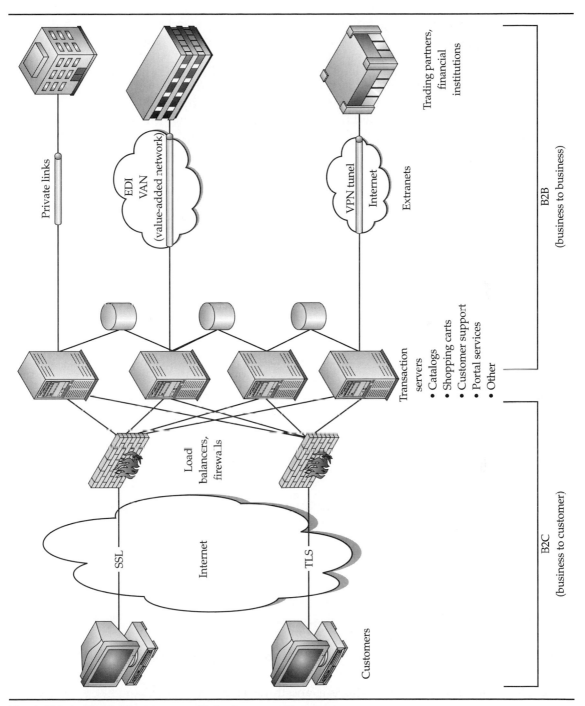

Figure E-3. *Electronic commerce Web site*

encrypt subsequent data exchanges. SSL is the current industry standard, but TLS is an IETF specification that may gain ground. See "SSL (Secure Sockets Layer)" and "TLS (Transport Layer Security)" for a description of how these security mechanisms work.

Public-key cryptography and public-key infrastructure (PKI) provide the basis for satisfying the other security requirements. With PKI, people and organizations that do not know each other can carry out secure transactions. For more information, refer to the following topics: "Certificates and Certification Systems"; "Digital Signatures"; "PKI (Public-Key Infrastructure)"; "Public-Key Cryptography"; and "X.509 Certificates."

Electronic Payment Schemes

Electronic payment/settlement systems on the Internet allow buyers to compensate sellers for goods or services. After a buyer selects an item to purchase, an electronic invoice is created and the method of payment is determined. The payment transaction is executed and the goods are delivered to the buyer.

Many Internet payment schemes have been developed. Some were developed by banks, some by credit card companies, and some by software vendors. Many of the schemes are not standards and may not exist by the time you read this. Some of the most important are described in this section. For more information, visit the following Web sites:

Electronic Payment Schemes by Dr. Phillip M. Hallam-Baker (W3C)	http://www.w3.org/ECommerce/roadmap.html
Internet Payment Systems page	http://www.geocities.com/CapeCanaveral/Lab/8967/Cash1.html
European Commission's Open Information Interchange (OII) Payment Standards Web page	http://158.169.50.95:10080/oii/en/payguide.html
European Commission's Open Information Interchange (OII) Electronic Payment Mechanisms Web page	http://158.169.50.95:10080/oii/en/payment.html

The following payment methods may be used. All are designed to work between unknown and untrusted parties.

- **Credit card**   This scheme uses the existing credit card infrastructure to compensate the seller. This scheme is transactional, meaning that a third party (bank or credit card company) must be involved. The most common transactional protocol is SET (Secure Electronic Transaction), which is discussed under its own heading in this book.

- **Electronic cash**   The user buys tokens from electronic cash vendors. These tokens represent cash at supporting Web sites. An analogy is the phone card, which can be purchased in various denominations and used to make phone calls until the "phone cash" is used up.

- **Electronic checks**   This scheme is a cross between the credit card and electronic cash schemes. A buyer uses a check, and the seller verifies with the check issuer that funds are available. The seller is compensated by the check issuer.

The electronic cash scheme revolves around cash values that are stored in some object held by the user. Sellers accept electronic cash as they would real cash. A typical place to store electronic cash is in a digital wallet (software based) or a smart card (a physical object). Wave Systems (http://www.wavesys.com) has developed a chip called EMBASSY that many vendors are integrating into their products. The chip stores secure information (public keys, electronic cash, and so on) and performs encryption and other security routines. It is basically a *security coprocessor* and *data vault*.

Important electronic payment schemes are outlined in the following list:

- **SET (Secure Electronic Transactions)**   The SET protocol was developed by Microsoft, IBM, Netscape, GTE, Visa, and MasterCard so merchants could automatically and safely collect and process payments from Internet clients. SET secures credit card transactions by authenticating cardholders, merchants, and banks, and by preserving the confidentiality of payment data. SSL and TLS are good at securing the link, while SET is designed to hide credit card details, including hiding the details from the merchant. SET requires digital signatures to verify that the customer, the merchant, and the bank are legitimate. It also uses multiparty messages that prevent credit card numbers from ending up in the wrong hands. See "SET (Secure Electronic Transaction)" for more information.

- **JEPI (Joint Electronic Payment Initiative)**   JEPI was a project managed by the W3C and CommerceNet that developed protocols for negotiating payment instrument (credit card, debit card, electronic check, electronic cash, and so on). It produced PEP (Protocol Extensions Protocol) and UPP (Universal Payment Preamble), both of which automate payment negotiations. Refer to http://www.w3.org/ECommerce/.

- **IOTP (Internet Open Trading Protocol)**   IOTP provides a framework for Internet electronic commerce. In particular, it allows purchasing software to operate independent of a particular payment mechanism, as described later. Also see the topic "IOTP (Internet Open Trading Protocol)."

Electronic Wallets

A wallet is an electronic cash component that resides on the user's computer or another hardware device such as a smart card. It stores personal security information such as private keys, credit card numbers, and certificates; can be moved from place to place so users can work at different computers; and has its access controlled by policies.

PFX (Personal Information Exchange) is a Microsoft protocol that enables users to transfer sensitive information from one environment or platform to another. For example, a user may have information such as certificates and keys stored on a PC in her office, but she also needs to securely transfer this information to her Macintosh at home. With this protocol, a user can securely export personal information from one computer system to another. Visit http://www.microsoft.com and search for information about PFX.

The Java Wallet is an extension to the core Java platform that allows developers to create electronic commerce applications with support for secure online transactional electronic commerce solutions. Java Wallet is part of the Java Commerce toolkit. Refer to http://java.sun.com/products/commerce/ for more information.

ECML (Electronic Commerce Modeling Language) is an open specification for the exchange of order and payment information between consumers and merchants. It helps streamline the purchase process. ECML was designed by the ECML Alliance (http://www.ecml.org/), which includes America Online, American Express, Brodia, Compaq, CyberCash, Discover, FSTC, IBM, MasterCard, Microsoft, Novell, SETCo, Sun Microsystems, Trintech, and Visa U.S.A. Online retailers supporting ECML include Beyond.com, Dell Computer Corp., fashionmall.com, healthshop.com, Nordstrom.com, and others.

ECML is documented in RFC 2706, "ECML v1: Field Names for E-Commerce" (October 1999) and at the ECML Alliance Web site. It defines a standard set of information fields (credit card number, billing address, and so on) that a customer fills out in order to complete a purchase or transaction at an online merchant site. ECML automates the process by automatically filling out these fields with information extracted from a "customer wallet." The data is input once into the wallet using the ECML standard format. Web sites can then read this information to fill out forms at the site for the customer.

Micropayments

A micropayment is a payment made with a very small amount of money, perhaps less than one cent. Publishers need to have an incentive for putting content up, and that incentive is profit; but if they charge too much, people won't access their systems. Micropayments produce a profit as long as enough people buy content. Messages like "access will require a charge of .25 cents" may become common on the Web.

The alternative is to just give things away and sell advertising space. In fact, micropayment systems will bridge the gap between things that are either free or cost hundreds of dollars.

The problem with micropayments is making it cost effective to collect money of that value. The W3C has worked on the problem and there is an information page at http://www.w3.org/ECommerce/Micropayments/.

E-Commerce and XML

XML has become a universally accepted method of describing information in a way that makes it easy to exchange data over the Web. XML is a markup language like HTML, but it goes well beyond HTML in functionality.

HTML provides a language that tells browsers how to display information, but it does not describe the information. If tables of data are sent to the browser and the user wants to extract that data for some other use, he or she must copy the data using tedious cut-and-paste techniques or custom programs. A list of stocks is an example. Web sites such as Yahoo allow users to create custom portfolios to track stocks and then display the most current stock data. If you want to collect the data for historical charting, you'll need to use difficult cut and paste. For example, here's how a single stock would appear in the HTML data:

```
<TR><TH ALIGN=LEFT><B>AMERICA ONLINE </B></TH><TD>$56.25</TD>
```

Most of the information has to do with table alignment and boldfacing the name. The power of XML is that it can be used to tag data with a name and specify attributes for the data. The equivalent XML page would describe the formatting and layout in one section, and put the data in another section, as follows:

```
<NAME>AMERICA ONLINE</NAME>
<PRICE>$56.25</PRICE>
```

Note that the fields are explicitly tagged ("NAME" and "PRICE"), making it easy to extract the data with an automated program or spreadsheets that recognize the tags. But people and programs must know the names and attributes of the tags. That information is defined by a *schema* and stored as *metadata* (data about XML data). Many industries, such as the automobile and medical industry, have defined standard schemas.

See "XML (Extensible Markup Language)" and "Metadata" for more information. Also refer to the following Web sites:

World Wide Web Consortium	http://www.w3c.org/
XML.org	http://www.xml.org/

E-Commerce Frameworks and Models

Electronic commerce frameworks and models simplify the task of building and integrating electronic commerce systems. They also ensure that clients can access such systems with ease. The only problem is that there are many frameworks and models available. Some examples are outlined here. Note that other frameworks exist, and some are described under the "Oasis ebXML" heading later.

EDI (Electronic Data Interchange)

Early techniques for exchanging electronic business information revolved around EDI. EDI defines ways to exchange structured business data, such as purchase orders, invoices, and shipping notices, typically between one organization and another. Store-and-forward technologies similar to e-mail have been used to exchange EDI information, or a third party such as GEIS (General Electric Information Service) may serve as a "middleman" to help organizations establish business relationships and handle business transactions.

EDI predates Internet electronic commerce, but there are still many legacy systems that use EDI. Today, it is considered a subset of electronic commerce and has been integrated with XML. It encompasses the exchange of business information in a standardized electronic form. Standard form defines things like the layout of information for an invoice or purchase order. While EDI had many advantages, it used a flat file structure and was too inflexible for the dynamic e-commerce environment of the Web. See "EDI (Electronic Data Interchange)."

OBI (Open Buying on the Internet)

OBI is a business-to-business Internet commerce framework developed by the OBI Consortium. The consortium was formed in 1997 with initial funding by SupplyWorks and American Express. Later, CommerceNet took over management of the OBI framework. A white paper at the OBI Web site describes the OBI framework as follows:

> A *requisitioner* at a *Buying Organization* uses a Web browser to interact with a specialized catalog at a *Selling Organization*. If the requisitioner places an order, the Selling Organization will transmit an *order request* to the Buying Organization's purchasing server for approval and/or additional information. The Buying

Organization may approve or reject the order, perhaps after passing it through a workflow process of some kind, and return an approved and completed order to the Selling Organization.

At one time, the OBI framework was considered one of the best solutions for B2B electronic commerce, but XML now provides a better solution. The OBI Web site is located at http://www.openbuy.org/.

IOTP (Internet Open Trading Protocol)

The Internet Open Trading Protocol is a framework that supports interoperable Internet commerce. The framework was originally conceived by the Open Trading Protocol Consortium, a large group of vendors involved in electronic payments and electronic commerce. The IETF has since taken responsibility for engineering aspects of IOTP and is developing it in its Internet Open Trading Protocol (trade) Working Group. See "IOTP (Internet Open Trading Protocol)."

BizTalk

BizTalk is a Microsoft initiative to promote the consistent adoption of XML for electronic commerce. Technology vendors such as SAP and CommerceOne are behind BizTalk. According to Microsoft, XML is so flexible that some guidelines are necessary to promote consistency and interoperability. The BizTalk Framework is a set of guidelines for how to publish schemas in XML and how to use XML messages to easily integrate software programs. Microsoft emphasizes that BizTalk itself is not a standard, but that XML is the standard. BizTalk is simply designed to accelerate XML's adoption.

BizTalk is essentially an XML schema repository. Schema are registered at the BizTalk.org Web site. The schemas are run through a verification test to ensure they are valid BizTalk Framework schemas. Anyone can then access the XML schemas within applications. Schemas may also be submitted to the BizTalk.org Web site for private use between trading partners. The site is organized and managed by Microsoft-independent companies and organizations. Note, however, that Microsoft's e-commerce platforms (BizTalk Server and Commerce Server) are wrapped around the BizTalk initiative. For more information, visit the BizTalk Web site at http://www.biztalk.org.

OASIS ebXML

OASIS (Organization for the Advancement of Structured Information Standards) is a nonprofit consortium dedicated to the adoption of product-independent formats such as SGML, XML, and HTML. It joined forces with UN/CEFACT (United Nations body for Trade Facilitation and Electronic Business) to establish the Electronic Business XML (ebXML) initiative. ebXML is a technical framework for exchanging business data in a consistent manner using XML. An objective is to make electronic data exchange easier and less expensive, opening it to smaller businesses and developing nations.

ebXML is an attempt to create a single global XML framework solution (interestingly, Oasis views Microsoft's BizTalk as an attempt to establish proprietary XML schemas). The goal is to provide an open technical specification that defines how XML will be used for the exchange of electronic business data in application-to-application, application-to-person, and person-to-application environments. ebXML is backed by companies such as IBM, Sun Microsystems, Commerce One, Dun & Bradstreet, Oracle, Visa International, General Motors, and many others around the globe.

More information is available at http://www.oasis-open.org and http://www.ebxml.org.

RosettaNet

RosettaNet is an XML-based framework that is designed to streamline the exchange of information and the alignment of business processes in the IT (information technology) supply chain. The framework is designed around XML-based business processes called PIPs (Partner Interface Processes) and dictionaries:

- **Dictionaries**   Common definitions for IT-related parts and business terms. Define properties for products, partners, and business transactions.

- **PIPs (Partner Interface Processes)**   PIPs provide common business/data models and documents. A PIP basically defines in an XML document how e-commerce transactions between trading partners take place. There are 12 PIPs at this writing, including PIPs for catalog information, technical specifications (software, memory, laptop, and so on), technical properties, partner properties, business properties, and others.

Companies involved in RosettaNet include Microsoft, Compaq, IBM, Hewlett-Packard, Cisco Systems, Arrow Electronics, Avnet, VEBA Electronics, and Toshiba. For more information about RosettaNet, refer to http://www.rosettanet.org/.

CBL (Common Business Library)

CBL is a Commerce One open specification designed to promote exchange of business documents across different industries. An important part of CBL is that it provides a transition path for businesses using EDI into XML-based electronic commerce, and a way to unify other standards such as OBI (Open Buying on the Internet) and IOTP (Internet Open Trading Protocol). For more information, refer to http://www.commerceone.com/.

Organizations Involved in E-Commerce

A number of organizations are involved in promoting electronic commerce on a global scale. Some of these organizations work with specific protocols, while others work to promote global electronic commerce in general.

W3C (World Wide Web Coalition)

The W3C is involved in many different aspects of Web development. It was organized to develop common protocols to promote interoperability on the Web and to help the Web evolve.

The W3C electronic commerce interest group is involved in a range of activities related to electronic commerce. These include micropayment schemes, metadata definitions, digital signatures, privacy and security, and electronic transaction protocols. For more details, refer to http://www.w3.org/ECommerce/.

FSTC (Financial Services Technology Consortium)

The Financial Services Technology Consortium (FSTC) is a nonprofit organization that sponsors project-oriented collaborative research and development on interbank technical projects affecting the entire financial services industry, with emphasis placed on payment systems and services. Members of the consortium include banks, financial services providers, research laboratories, universities, technology companies, and government agencies. Several FSTC projects are listed here. The FSTC Web site is http://www.fstc.org/.

- **FAST (Financial Agent Secure Transaction)**   Defines an Internet-based, technologically neutral framework that authenticates transactions between parties unknown to each other.

- **SDML (Signed Document Work Language)**   A message format structure that allows an entity such as a bill payer to provide an electronic document whose author and integrity can be authenticated. SDML documents may be digitally signed using public-key cryptographic signatures and hash algorithms.

- **PACES (Paperless Automated Check Exchange and Settlement)**   An FSTC initiative focused on moving the financial services industry toward image-based truncation.

- **EChecks**   An FSTC and CommerceNet initiative for electronic checks. It was selected as an electronic payment mechanism by the U.S. Treasury. Refer to http://www.echeck.org/.

- **BIPS (Bank Internet Payment System)**   A system for securely sending payments across the Internet. Transactions are secured with digital certificates and signatures.

- **Risk Management Project**   An FSTC project to research technological solutions for reducing fraudulent transactions. This includes investigating both ways of controlling fraud, such as the use of cryptographic, biometric, tamperproof, and tamper-evident technologies, as well as detecting fraud, including real-time anomaly detection.

VICS (Voluntary Interindustry Commerce Standards)

VICS is a volunteer organization that has the goal of establishing cross-industry standards to simplify the flow of products and information in the general merchandise retail industry, for retailers and suppliers alike. Some of its current projects are listed next. The VICS Web site is located at http://www.vics.org/.

- **Bill of Lading**   The VICS Bill of Lading is meant to simplify and standardize the key data elements for processing of goods through supply chains, to support the use of EDI documents between trading partners by standardizing the Bill of Lading number, and to support bar coding of the Bill of Lading number. Refer to http://www.vics.org/BOL.htm

- **CPFR (Collaborative Planning, Forecasting, and Replenishment)**   A VICS committee, made up of retailers, manufacturers, and solution providers, that has developed a set of business processes that entities in a supply chain can use for collaboration on a number of buyer/seller functions, toward overall efficiency in the supply chain. Refer to http://www.cpfr.org/.

■ **Internet Commerce Model**   The VICS Internet Commerce Model is a platform- and vendor-independent interoperable environment. The model is composed of existing standards and is outlined at http://www.vics.org/icm.doc.

■ **Direct to Consumer**   A committee that is addressing communication standards among customers, retailers, and manufacturers to facilitate direct-to-consumer commerce originating in self-service selling environments. Issues include interoperability, connumer interface, and the impact on enabling standards/technologies.

■ **VICS Logistics Model**   A model for documenting business processes and accompanying information flows commonly used throughout the industry.

Global Commerce Initiative

The GCI was formed in October of 1999 by some of the world's leading companies to define global electronic commerce for the consumer goods industry. The GCI is concentrating on five areas, including EDI (Electronic Data Interchange), product numbering and identification, standardized product tagging, global scorecard development, and extranet development. The goal of GCI is to make global supply chains more efficient by developing systems and standards for building supply chains across international boundaries.

Organization for Economic Cooperation and Development (OECD)

The OECD is a group of 29 member countries that provides governments a setting in which to discuss, develop, and perfect economic and social policy. The OECD has been involved in a number of international trade initiatives. It has a number of committees that are involved in economic policy, trade, finance, science and technology, education, food and agriculture, and many other areas. Most recently, it developed guidelines for electronic commerce consumer protection. Refer to http://www.oecd.org/ for more information.

Related Entries   ASP (Application Service Provider); Certificates and Certification Systems; Cryptography; Data Warehousing; DBMS (Database Management System); Digital Signatures; Document Standards; EDI (Electronic Data Interchange); ERP (Enterprise Resource Planning); Extranet; Groupware; Hash Functions; Intranets and Extranets; IOTP (Internet Open Trading Protocol); IPSec (IP Security); Metadata; Middleware and Messaging; Multitiered Architectures; OAG (Open Applications Group); OLAP (Online Analytical Processing); PKI (Public-Key Infrastructure); Public-Key Cryptography; Security; SET (Secure Electronic Transactions); S-HTTP (Secure Hypertext Transfer Protocol); SSL (Secure Sockets Layer); TLS (Transport Layer Security); Transaction Processing; VPN (Virtual Private Network); Web Technologies and Concepts; Workflow Management; X.509 Certificates; *and* XML (Extensible Markup Language)

Linktionary!—Tom Sheldon's Encyclopedia of Networking updates	http://www.linktionary.com/e/ecommerce.html
Electronic commerce: IETF Internet Open Trading Protocol (trade) WG	http://www.ietf.org/html.charters/ trade-charter.html
Advisory Commission on Electronic Commerce	http://www.ecommercecommission.org/
DISA (Data Interchange Standards Institute)	http://www.disa.org/

Google Web Directory E-Commerce page	http://directory.google.com/Top/Business/E-Commerce/
Bitpipe (see "Electronic Commerce" subject)	http://www.bitpipe.com/
Sterling Commerce (see electronic commerce resources list)	http://www.sterlingcommerce.com/
U.S. Government Electronic Commerce Policy	http://www.ecommerce.gov/
CommerceNet	http://www.commerce.net/
European Commission's Open Information Interchange (OII) guide to electronic commerce	http://158.169.50.95:10080/oii/en/commerce.html
CIO electronic business research center	http://www.cio.com/forums/ec/
Roger Clarke's Electronic Commerce Pages (an excellent site)	http://www.anu.edu.au/people/Roger.Clarke/EC/index.html
Planet IT E-Business site	http://www.planetit.com/techcenters/e-commerce
Cisco e-commerce information	http://www.cisco.com/warp/public/784/packet/july99/index.html
Ecommerce-Guide.com	http://ecommerce.internet.com/
Advisor.com (see E-Business sections on products and resources)	http://www.advisor.com/
ECompany.com (see "E-Commerce" option)	http://www.ecompany.com/
Web ProForums (see Electronic Commerce tutorial)	http://www.iec.org/tutorials/
Prof. Jeffrey MacKie-Mason's Electronic Commerce Directory	http://china.si.umich.edu/telecom/net-commerce-directories.html
Information Economy Commerce Links	http://www.sims.berkeley.edu/resources/infoecon/Commerce.html

Electronic Mail

Electronic mail (e-mail) is probably the most common application used on enterprise networks and the Internet. Some enterprise networks were built with e-mail in mind. Messaging has many obvious benefits. If a person isn't available to pick up a message immediately, the message is held in an e-mail box until it can be picked up. Files can be exchanged by attaching them to messages. Today, collaborative applications are built upon electronic messaging systems and messaging has become an important part of network applications.

Chat and instant messaging are forms of *synchronous communications*. Like a voice telephone call, a chat or instant messaging session is live and each user responds to the other in real time. In contrast, discussion forums and electronic mail are forms of *asynchronous communications*. Some amount of time may pass before a person responds to a message. In a discussion forum, a message sits in a message queue for other people to read and respond to at any time, or until the message falls out of the queue. These two forms of communication, which are accessible to any Internet user from just about any Internet-attached system, may be the most important aspect of the Internet. They promote a new form of instant global communication and collaboration. In the case of discussion forums and e-mail, the delay in communication is beneficial—it gives people time to think about and research their responses.

There are many different e-mail systems in use on networks, mainframe systems, and public networks. The Internet's message transport standard is SMTP (Simple Mail Transfer Protocol), which is supported by mail server protocols such as POP (Post Office Protocol) and IMAP (Internet Message Access Protocol). The growth of the Internet and intranets has promoted its acceptance almost everywhere. In addition, SMTP-compatible e-mail services are integrated into browsers. As a result, almost every Web user has an SMTP mail client available for their use.

Legacy mail systems include IBM PROFS (Professional Office System) and SNADS (SNA Distributed Services), which were used in the IBM mainframe environment, and VAXmail or All-In-1 in the DEC environment. A single organization might have numerous e-mail systems that were implemented in the days when departments or workgroups maintained their own LANs. As the organization was interconnected, e-mail gateway systems were often employed to translate messages among the different systems. The X.400 Message Handling System was supposed to provide a standard for exchanging messages among a wide variety of messaging platforms, but X.400 never caught on. Today, most network administrators prefer to use a single mail standard, and that has become the Internet messaging protocols. Vendors are also integrating the standard into their proprietary systems. Because of its pervasiveness, the Internet mail standard is covered in this section.

Still, three major messaging platforms are available that offer more than just electronic mail. Lotus Domino, Microsoft Exchange, and Novell GroupWise are enterprise collaboration and groupware platforms, as discussed later.

Electronic Mail Features

An electronic mail system for an enterprise network usually consists of the following components, which are illustrated in Figure E-4.

- A front-end application called a *UA (user agent)* or *client* that users use to create, address, send, receive, and forward messages. Other features include the ability to attach files and other information to messages, and the ability to manage a personal address book. One of the most popular Internet e-mail clients is Eudora, a Qualcomm product that is now free at http://www.eudora.com/. Pine (Program for Internet News & Email) is another free mail client available at http://www.washington.edu/pine/.

- A back-end *MTA (message transfer agent)* that transfers messages from the UA and delivers them to mail servers. A message might need to move among a number of mail servers before it reaches its destination. This is SMTP in the Internet environment.

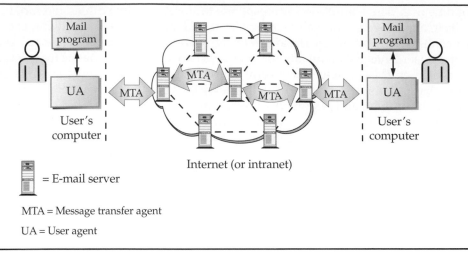

Figure E-4.   *Electronic messaging system components*

- Mails servers that run MTAs and provide temporary message stores. In the Internet environments, this would be servers running POP (Post Office Protocol) or IMAP (Internet Message Access Protocol).

- A directory service that maintains a database of users and services on the network. Users can access the service to locate a user and his or her e-mail address. LDAP (Lightweight Directory Access Protocol) is an example.

Additional features in some e-mail systems include the ability to secure messages with encryption, or add a digital signature to prove the authenticity of messages and prevent alterations. The ability to send and receive facsimiles is another feature included with many systems.

Here are the major protocols and standards that make up the Internet email system:

- **SMTP (Simple Mail Transfer Protocol)**   SMTP is the message-exchange standard for the Internet. It is familiar to most people by its addressing scheme— the *username@company*.com format. SMTP provides the very important function of moving messages from one e-mail server to another. SMTP is designed for TCP/IP networks. It works in conjunction with POP (Post Office Protocol) on many mail servers to receive and send mail. POP receives mail and holds it in a user's post office mailbox, while SMTP provides message transport services. See "SMTP (Simple Mail Transfer Protocol)" for more information.

- **POP (Post Office Protocol)**   POP is an Internet mail server protocol that provides an incoming and outgoing message server and storage system. It works in conjunction with the SMTP (Simple Mail Transfer Protocol). Many e-mail systems will be described as POP3 compatible. See "POP (Post Office Protocol)" for more information.

- **IMAP4 (Internet Mail Access Protocol 4)**   IMAP is considered the successor to POP. It is a store-and-forward mail server protocol that goes a step beyond POP. IMAP lets users access a mailbox on the mail server, as opposed to having mail delivered directly to the inbox in their SMTP-compatible client software. This is a useful feature for mobile users with portable diskless devices who want to save messages for later. IMAP4 is the latest version of IMAP and provides better mail server management capabilities. For example, administrators can manage folders from a remote location (i.e., over a WAN link). Mailboxes can also be replicated to benefit mobile users. See "IMAP (Internet Message Access Protocol)" for more information.

- **MIME (Multipurpose Internet Mail Extension) and S/MIME (Secure MIME)**   SMTP can only handle messages that contain 7-bit ASCII text. MIME provides a way to insert 8-bit binary data into messages. That includes multimedia objects like pictures and sound, and even voice-mail messages. The data is "attached" to the message in a format that is compatible with the SMTP message format. Lines are added to the header of the message to indicate the presence and structure of MIME information. S/MIME is a de facto standard for securing mail messages. See "MIME (Multipurpose Internet Mail Extension)" for more information.

- **LDAP (Lightweight Directory Access Protocol)**   LDAP is a directory services protocol that goes beyond simple e-mail address books by providing a way for e-mail clients to browse directories of users on any LDAP server. Almost every vendor of directory services products supports LDAP. See "LDAP (Lightweight Directory Access Protocol)" for more information.

- **MAPI (Messaging Application Programming Interface)**   MAPI is a set of interfaces that helps developers integrate support for a variety of e-mail systems into their applications. MAPI has become widely accepted in the industry. Today, most messaging systems provide support for MAPI. See "MAPI (Messaging Application Programming Interface)" for more information.

How Internet Mail Works

In the old days, e-mail was designed to run on mainframes; and since employees accessed the same system with their terminal, there was little need to transfer mail to different systems. As networks grew, it was necessary to interconnect e-mail servers and develop a protocol that would transfer mail between servers. SMTP was defined in 1982 for that purpose.

The Internet mail system must send and receive messages from potentially millions of different computers on thousands of different networks. The SMTP protocol is the protocol that defines the format of messages and how they are processed and delivered. A mail program running on a user's computer follows SMTP standards and presents an interface to the user for reading, creating, and deleting messages. When a user creates a message, the UA background process submits the messages for delivery to the MTA. The MTA then performs the task of moving the message to the destination. Mail servers must run continually in order to transfer messages at any time.

MTAs communicate with other MTAs on the Internet because the messaging infrastructure consists of many mail servers through which messages pass, as shown in Figure E-4. Messages are routed through the infrastructure from one mail server to the next, until the messages reach their destinations. The following describes the message transfer path:

1. Sender types message at mail interface connected to UA.

2. UA submits message to local MTA.

3. MTA to MTA to MTA (and so on, to destination MTA).

4. Destination MTA sends message to UA.

5. Recipient reads message.

The final message server in the chain provides a mailbox for the user and holds messages until the user asks for them.

To ensure reliable delivery, the UA on a sender's computer keeps a copy of a message until the receiving computer has stored the message. A server may also reject messages from some sources or prevent a particular system from receiving messages.

Messages can also be addressed to multiple users. If the users are all at the same location (i.e., have mailboxes at the same server), then a single message is sent to the server, which, in turn, sends copies to all the recipients listed in the message. This technique is especially useful in groupware and collaborative applications.

With regard to POP, messages are usually deleted on the server after the client retrieves them. This has been a source of frustration to many users, especially mobile users with small devices that don't have the memory or storage devices to keep messages for later viewing. IMAP4 solves this problem by providing a way to create a hierarchy of folders for message storage at the mail server.

Mailing list programs are programs that distribute messages to large numbers of recipients by taking advantage of the Internet mail protocols. A manager can create a mailing list and have all messages submitted to the listserver automatically forwarded to the names on the list. LISTSERV is the name of a mailing list product sold by L-Soft International, Inc., that has its roots in the original mailing listserver product created by Eric Thomas in 1986. A public package called Majordomo is also available. See "Mailing List Programs" for more information.

Secure E-mail

Like any data transmission, users may wish to protect e-mail from eavesdropping, alteration, and forgery. In addition, recipients need to know that a message is authentic, and that a message cannot be repudiated (disowned) by its sender.

Any security schemes must be shared by both sender and receiver. If a message is encrypted, the receiver must have the software to decrypt it, as well as the key that unlocks the encryption. Some examples are provided next, with more explanations under the topics of the same name:

■ **Public-Key Cryptography**   A way for different parties to exchange encryption keys.

E

- **Digital Signatures**   A way to "lock down" the contents of a message with your private key so the recipient knows it is authentic and has not been altered.
- **PGP (Pretty Good Privacy)**   An encryption and digital signature scheme that uses public-key cryptography.
- **S/MIME**   A security scheme developed by RSA Security that is an alternative to PGP. It has been standardized by the IETF. See "MIME (Multipurpose Internet Mail Extension)" for information about S/MIME.

Two early protocols for securing e-mail were PEM (Privacy-Enhanced Mail) and MOSS (MIME Object Security Services), which are discussed briefly under their own headings elsewhere. However, RFC 2316, "Report of the IAB Security Architecture Workshop" (April 1998) labeled PEM and MOSS as "not useful" because they have failed to catch on. PGP was labeled "useful but not core." According to RFC 2316, the designated core security mechanism for adding secured sections to MIME-encapsulated e-mail is Security/Multipart, as described in RFC 1847, "Security Multiparts for MIME: Multipart/Signed and Multipart/Encrypted" (October 1995).

While PGP is well known and well used, S/MIME has a solid industry backing. This is important for large organizations that need to standardize e-mail security for both intercompany and intracompany mail exchange. However, S/MIME requires a public-key infrastructure be in place, either in-house or by using any of the public certificate authorities. PGP users can manage their own keys. Two IETF working groups are developing these standards:

An Open Specification for Pretty Good Privacy (openpgp)	http://www.ietf.org/html.charters/ openpgp-charter.html
S/MIME Mail Security (smime)	http://www.ietf.org/html.charters/ smime-charter.html

E-mail Systems and Products

Internet e-mail systems can be set up using free software obtained on the Internet. Sendmail is a popular SMTP-compatible mail server package that has been around for over 20 years and is common in the UNIX environment. See "Sendmail." Many enterprises will prefer to use solutions from major vendors such as the following:

- **Lotus Domino**   This product is primarily a groupware application that also supports messaging. It is recommended where collaboration is a goal.
- **Microsoft Exchange**   This product is a good choice for enterprises that have standardized on Microsoft Office and BackOffice Products.
- **Novell GroupWise**   This product is tied with NDS (Novell Directory Services), which may provide a strong incentive for choosing it over other products.

All of these provide Internet messaging and a variety of other features, including the following:

- Mail server replication that protects the system and makes messages more readily available to users at other locations in the company
- Server-bound mailboxes that let users keep messages in a central location for later referral
- Directory services to make it easier for people to locate people and resources
- Public folders that serve as repositories for shared messages, forms, documents, applications, and other information
- Discussion databases and chat rooms that let people actively post and exchange messages on an ongoing basis, using the message thread approach
- Support for remote users that dial directly into the mail server
- The ability to build applications such as groupware and workflow products that take advantage of the services provided in the messaging server
- E-mail gateway services that provide relay and translation services between different types of e-mail systems

Here is a partial list of vendors that provide e-mail and messaging products:

Lotus Notes	http://www.lotus.com
Microsoft Exchange Server	http://www.microsoft.com
Novell GroupWise	http://www.novell.com
Syntegra messaging solutions	http://www.syntegra.com
Fujitsu TeamWare Messaging	http://www.teamware.com/
LAN-ACES Office-Logic	http://www.lan-aces.com
Software.com	http://www.software.com

Development Work

A number of working groups and organizations are involved in the development of electronic mail standards. The Internet Mail Consortium is an international organization that promotes electronic mail and electronic mail standards on the Internet. The IMC's Web site is a good place to find the latest information about electronic mail developments.

A complete list of IETF RFCs is available at the Linktionary! Web site given later.

Here is a list of IETF working groups that are developing standards associated with electronic messaging:

- **Detailed Revision/Update of Message Standards (drums)**   This working group is reviewing the original mail RFCs and determining the applicability of each of these to the future direction of the messaging on the Internet. See http://www.ietf.org/html.charters/drums-charter.html

- **Message Tracking Protocol (msgtrk)**   This working group is designing a diagnostic protocol for a message originator to request information about the submission, transport, and delivery of a message, regardless of its delivery status. See http://www.ietf.org/html.charters/msgtrk-charter.html.

- **S/MIME Mail Security (smime)**   This group is working on integrating S/MIME (Secure MIME) with Internet mail, including the encapsulation of encrypted and signed objects. S/MIME is a product of RSA Security. See http://www.ietf.org/html.charters/smime-charter.html.

- **An Open Specification for Pretty Good Privacy (openpgp)**   PGP is used for both protecting e-mail and file storage. It presents a way to digitally sign and encrypt information. This working group is integrating PGP with Internet mail. See http://www.ietf.org/html.charters/openpgp-charter.html.

- **MIME Encapsulation of Aggregate HTML Documents (mhtml)**   The MHTML Working Group has developed standards that permit the transport of compound structured HTML Web documents via Internet mail in MIME multipart/related body parts. The idea is to support interoperability between separate HTTP-based systems and Internet mail systems, as well as being suitable for combined mail/HTTP browser systems. See http://www.ietf.org/html.charters/mhtml-charter.html.

- **Internet Fax (fax)**   This working group will pursue a review and specification for enabling standardized messaging-based fax over the Internet. See http://www.ietf.org/html.charters/fax-charter.html.

- **Calendaring and Scheduling (calsch)**   This working group develops standards that help calendaring and group scheduling products interoperate and work across organizational boundaries. It develops MIME content types to represent common objects needed for calendaring and group scheduling transactions, and access protocols between systems and between clients and servers. See http://www.ietf.org/html.charters/calsch-charter.html.

Related Entries   Addresses, Electronic Mail; Directory Services; FAX Servers and Network Faxing; Groupware; IMAP (Internet Message Access Protocol); Instant Messaging; Mailing List Programs; Microsoft Exchange; MIME (Multipurpose Internet Mail Extension); MOM (Message Oriented Middleware); Name Services; POP (Post Office Protocol); Search and Discovery Services; SMTP (Simple Mail Transfer Protocol); Unified Messaging; *and* Workflow Management

Linktionary!—Tom Sheldon's Encyclopedia of Networking updates	http://www.linktionary.com/e/email.html
Internet Mail Consortium	http://www.imc.org/
Mail-related RFCs, complete list	http://www.imc.org/rfcs.html
Electronic Messaging Association	http://www.ema.org/
The IMAP Connection	http://www.imap.org
IMAP Information Center	http://www.washington.edu/imap

Emailman, electronic superhero (everything you ever wanted to know about e-mail)	http://www.emailman.com/
Email Guides	http://www.screen.com/start/guide/email.html
The Carnegie Mellon Enterprise Electronic Mail Project	http://asg.web.cmu.edu/cyrus/
Yahoo's e-mail links page	http://dir.yahoo.com/Computers_and_Internet/ Communications_and_Networking/Email/
Douglas W. Sauder's MIME Information Page	http://www.hunnysoft.com/mime/
Andrew Starr's Unofficial Eudora Site	http://www.emailman.com/eudora/

Electronic Software Distribution and Licensing

Electronic software distribution takes two forms. One form is downloading software from Internet sites. In this case, online software retailers have software packages that can be purchased online and downloaded, usually at a reduced charge because the packaging costs less. This topic is *not* about downloading retail software, although some sites that offer software download and licensing are listed at the end of this topic.

This topic is about the automatic installation and configuration of software on users' desktops. A "distribution server" transfers software code to a client machine, and then installs and configures the software based on preconfigured settings and policies. This form of electronic software distribution saves network administrators the time and expense of traveling to each client's computer and installing the software manually.

A typical organization may have thousands of workstations at diverse sites, some requiring more than one day's travel. It makes sense to rely on management software to handle the installation procedures. ESD provides automatic software updating, and ESL provides automatic tracking of software usage to ensure that an organization stays within its software licensing requirements.

Software distribution programs for in-house use ideally copy software to workstations, install the software, configure it, and provide periodic updates when necessary. The programs can look at system configurations and update the configurations if necessary.

Much of the work in software distribution and management programs is being handled by the DMTF (Distributed Management Task Force) and is defined in DMTF's DMI (Distributed Management Interface). Part of the DMI is an agent that collects information about network workstations and other nodes, and places the information in a file called the MIFF (management information format file). MIFFs provide information required to install and configure an application for a specific machine, such as its type of video, printer, and memory configuration.

Web "push" technologies are often employed to automatically distribute software to users, as opposed to "pull" technologies, in which users go get the software on their own.

Novell NAL (NetWare Application Launcher) is a software distribution utility included with NetWare and Novell's ZENworks product. NAL enables administrators to install and manage applications on Windows-based workstations across networks. It uses NDS (Novell Directory Services) as a central repository for all application information. Microsoft includes ESD functions in its SMS (System Management Server), which is part of the BackOffice suite. Administrators can time the installation events, set who can access shared software on servers, configure desktop settings, schedule commands on specific PCs, and perform a number of other tasks from the SMS console.

Other ESD packages include the following:

Computer Associates ShipIT	http://www.cai.com/
Tivoli Application Management Suite	http://www.tivoli.com/
Intel LANDesk Management Suite	http://www.intel.com/
Veritas Software WinInstall	http://www.veritas.com/
Symantec (formerly 20/20 Software) AutoInstall	http://www.symantec.com/
InstallShield NetInstall	http://www.installshield.com/

Licensing packages are used to ensure that a company is operating within its legal boundaries for software usage. A licensing package typically holds keys that allow users to access software applications. Each key is a license that has been purchased from the software vendor. The licensing program delivers keys to users who request the use of an application. When the keys are gone, other users can't access applications until a key frees up or more keys are added. Licensing programs usually include controls that prevent unauthorized users from accessing programs or prevent users from holding a key for too long.

The following sites handle online licensing and software downloads:

License Online	http://www.licenseonline.com/
Intraware	http://www.intraware.com/
CyberSource	http://www.cybersource.com/
Globetrotter Software	http://www.globes.com/

E-mail

See Electronic Mail.

Embedded Systems

An embedded system is a system within a larger system. It is often implemented on a single integrated circuit or as scaled-down software code. An embedded system typically has a specialized function with programs stored on ROM. Examples of embedded systems are chips that monitor automobile functions, including engine controls, antilock brakes, air bags, active suspension systems, environmental systems, security systems, and entertainment systems. Everything needed for those functions is custom designed into specific chips. No external operating system is required.

Another example is a chip for a microwave oven. It is specifically designed to run the front-panel controls and all the timing and electronics of the oven.

Network managers will need to manage more and more embedded systems devices, ranging from printers to scanners, to handheld computing devices, to cell phones. All of these have a need to connect with other devices, either directly or through a wireless or direct-connect network. Most will have custom operating systems or variations of existing operating systems (e.g., Microsoft Windows CE).

It's easy to picture nearly every electronic device as having an embedded system. For example, refrigerators, washing machines, and even coffee brewers will benefit in some way from embedded systems. A critical feature of an embedded system is its ability to communicate, so embedded systems support Ethernet, Bluetooth (wireless), infrared, or other technologies.

A weather station on top of a building can include an embedded system that gathers information from external sensors. This information can be pushed or pulled. In the push scenario, the data is automatically sent to devices that have requested it. In the pull scenario, users access the weather station to read the latest information.

If the weather station is connected to the Internet, it may have its own IP address and, ideally, will provide information to anyone that accesses the IP address. In this sense, the weather station is acting as a mini-Web server. In fact, many embedded systems are basically *Web servers on a chip*. The chips contain HTTP and HTML functions, and custom applications appropriate for the environment in which the chip will be used.

An interesting 3Com paper called "Massively Distributed Systems" by Dan Nessett discusses the growth of distributed computer networks with billions of new nodes, many of which will be embedded systems. While these embedded systems handle some computing and communication tasks on their own, many will need to off-load heavy computations to more capable systems. The paper discusses the potential architecture of distributed systems that include such embedded system devices. The paper is at the Web site listed later.

Another useful Web site is eg3.com, which is the oldest and largest Web resource devoted to electronic design, specifically embedded systems, real time, and DSP. The Web site is at http://www.eg3.com/.

Embedded Controllers and Systems

The number of devices using embedded controllers is increasing. A typical controller will combine RISC (Reduced Instruction Set Computer) with DSP (digital signal processing). RISC processors execute a limited number of instructions very quickly. DSPs convert analog information (voice, images, and so on) into digital, and then manipulate and compress it. The RISC processor runs an operating system, while the DSP handles the processing of signals. Some controllers also include Ethernet or wireless communication functions.

Combining these functions on a single chip reduces size and simplifies product development. Products using the controllers include advanced cell phones, DSL equipment, voice over IP equipment, Internet cameras, and just about anything that converts analog to digital and requires compression. In particular, cellular phones, DSL modems, and cable modems are using the controllers in record numbers, with some phones using multiple controllers.

Mercury Computer System's RACE architecture is a chip-level switch fabric for multiprocessing embedded systems. These systems are typically used for multichannel sensor-based I/O and processing in advanced real-time signal processing, simulation, and communications applications. The multicomputer interconnect consists of RACEway six-port crossbar switches. Ports on the chips may connect to other RACEway chips to form a fabric, or may provide a connection port for a processor. The architecture is discussed and illustrated further under "Switch Fabrics and

Bus Designs." Other embedded switching architectures are also discussed there, such a RapidIO, a chip-to-chip interconnection architecture for embedded systems.

Embedded system companies in this space are listed next. Additional companies involved in the embedded market are listed at the Embedded.com Web site listed later.

Analog Devices	http://www.analog.com
ARM Holdings	http://www.arm.com
Atmel Corporation	http://www.atmel.com
Hitachi Semiconductors	http://www.hitachi.com
Infineon Technologies	http://www.infineon.com/
Mercury Computer Systems	http://www.mc.com/
National Semiconductors	http://www.nsc.com
Texas Instruments	http://www.ti.com
Transmeta (Crusoe processor)	http://www.transmeta.com/

Embedded Operating Systems

The embedded operating system market is growing with the need for network appliances, thin client systems, and small handheld computers. A typical server running an embedded operating system may be managed remotely by an administrator using a Web browser. The embedded system does not need to support monitors, a mouse, a keyboard, and so on. There is no need for expansion capabilities, as the embedded OS is designed to deal with a very narrow set of tasks.

- **Microsoft Windows for Express Networks (WEN)**   This is basically Windows NT that has been stripped down to perform a specific task, such as managing network attached appliances. Intel uses WEN in its Small Office Network, which is a simplified server designed for easy setup in small businesses. The operating system is installed by the user, but the installation is simplified because of the reduced functionality of the operating system.

- **NeoLinux by Neoware Systems**   A version of the Linux operating system designed to be embedded within information appliances. The distribution is based on Red Hat Linux. It is typically installed on diskless devices. Refer to http://www.neoware.com/.

- **Inferno by Lucent Technologies**   A real-time network operating system that provides a software infrastructure for creating distributed network applications. Inferno is more like a file system that operates over a variety of transport protocols. It is designed to provide connectivity over the Internet, public telephone networks, cable television, and satellite broadcast networks. Inferno includes network and security protocols. It has a very small memory footprint and can be used as a stand-alone OS on information appliances.

- **Microsoft Windows CE**   Windows CE is an example of an embedded operating system. It is fairly complex compared to other embedded systems, but at the same time is a greatly stripped down version of the full-version Windows. Windows CE is an ideal

OS for handheld PCs, Web-enabled cell phones, video game consoles, TV set-top boxes, and network appliances such as smart printers and network attached storage. It is even used in vehicle navigation systems. Windows CE is also being used for more traditional embedded applications, such as data acquisition devices, point-of-sale terminals, and industrial controllers. Refer to http://www.microsoft.com/windows/embedded/.

■ **Wave Systems EMBASSY**   While not exactly an operating system, Wave System's EMBASSY provides unique related features. EMBASSY is a unique security processor and solid state data vault that enables secure transaction processing and distributed information metering in users' PCs and other end-user devices, such as set-top boxes. Refer to http://www.wavesys.com/.

Embedded Web Servers

The term "micro-Web servers" has been used by some vendors to describe network-connected devices that have embedded Web servers. The trend is to embed Web-based server protocols (HTTP and HTML) into embedded devices to provide a standardized access method for accessing and managing the devices. An embedded Web server may provide the basic HTTP server services, or go beyond that with additional features such as a CGI layer, authentication, and support for SNMP. Rapid Logic (http://www.rapidlogic.com/) is a company that has clearly defined the requirements of embedded Web servers. It defines an embedded server as a device with the following components:

■ **RTOS (real-time operating system)**   An operating system that supports a timely response to external events, and where errors occur if a response is not made in an appropriate time period. See "RTOS (Real-Time Operating System)" for more information and Web sites.

■ **SNMP (Simple Network Management Protocol) agent**   SNMP is an Internet management protocol. An SNMP agent resides in a device and collects information about that device to pass on to a management program.

■ **Application**   The program code that makes the device do what it is supposed to do.

■ **Glue code**   A layer of integration that makes parts of the applications available for management. The glue code takes into account the different ways that manufacturers represent their data internally.

■ **Backplane**   The backplane exposes the internal data elements to the external management system. The backplane maps presentation/control objects (VT-100 terminal, a Java-enabled Web browser, or an SNMP console) to data objects presented by the application through the glue code, or by the SNMP agent or RTOS.

Rapid Logic feels this architecture has several advantages. First, it has a tiny footprint with little overhead. Second, it is scalable and supports future protocols. Third, it uses existing standards such as SNMP. Finally, it supports Web browser–based management, a trend that the entire industry is following.

XML Strategies

The Rapid Logic system just described takes advantage of XML in its device management scheme. XML is a framework for defining markup languages that can be used for different types of applications, and this is especially useful in the embedded systems environment. Rapid Logic notes that XML is ideal for human-to-machine and machine-to-machine interfacing, primarily because it is text based.

A schema is defined for a particular application and stored in a DTD (Document Type Definition). The schema defines elements and the types of values those elements can have. Think of a schema as a dictionary that describes a common "grammar" for defining structured data. Applications that use the same dictionaries can exchange data.

In this scheme, XML doesn't do anything itself except to provide a way for developers to create unified methods of binding different network-enabled applications together. A developer creates the schema and then writes applications that use it. Java is currently the most popular programming language for building network applications.

Web browsers and server technologies are introduced into this scheme to provide management functions. For example, a device can implement an embedded Web server that provides information in XML form. Web browsers can then view this information, or collect and analyze it. An important aspect of XML is that data elements are tagged and are easily extracted and manipulated, unlike HTML, which simply presents data without describing what the data is. See "XML (Extensible Markup Language)."

Java Technologies

Java technologies are ideal for implementation into a range of consumer electronic devices and network peripheral devices. Sun has developed a number of technologies to support small devices and embedded technologies:

- **Java 2 Platform, Micro Edition**   A development environment for creating networked products, applications, and services for the consumer and embedded market.
- **K Virtual Machine (KVM)**   A "lean" Java runtime environment for devices with small memory footprints, such as cell phones, pagers, PDAs, and set-top boxes.
- **EmbeddedJava Application Environment**   An API and application environment for high-volume embedded systems.
- **Java Card**   Embedded Java for smart cards.

For more information, visit http://java.sun.com/ or http://www.sun.com/software/embeddedserver/.

Communication Protocols for Embedded Systems

Network-connected embedded systems need to communicate with one another, or administrators need to access the devices to gather management information. Consider the embedded systems in a smart building. Say the power goes out in part of the building. Other systems in the building may be queried to see if the power is out elsewhere. The security system may be queried to see if there is a breach. The fire protection system may be queried to see if part of the building is burning. A master system may assess all the information gathered to determine a course of action. Since the embedded systems may be from different manufacturers, a common communication method is needed.

Some products and strategies that target the embedded market are outlined here:

- **Universal Plug and Play** A Microsoft open standard technology for connecting appliances, PCs, and services by extending Plug and Play to support networks and peer-to-peer discovery and configuration. Refer to http://www.microsoft.com/homenet/upnp.htm.

- **Jini** A Sun network connectivity technology that supports distributed embedded applications. Jini allows devices to connect and communicate without going through external operating systems or without being configured first. Jini devices communicate immediately and form personal or community networks. Refer to the Web site http://www.sun.com/jini/.

- **Bluetooth** A wireless PAN (personal area network) technology that allows devices to instantly connect into small network groups. Bluetooth is designed for devices with small embedded operating systems, such as cell phones and peripherals. For example, a cell phone will have two radios, one for the cellular network and one for Bluetooth personal area networks. See "Bluetooth."

- **JetSend (Hewlett-Packard)** JetSend is implemented as embedded code in devices to allow them to directly exchange information. Devices become either senders or receivers. JetSend gives devices the intelligence to know their own capabilities and negotiate the best way to exchange information with other devices. No external operating systems need to get involved. No special drivers are needed to connect with other devices. All JetSend devices can immediately communicate. JetSend is a transport-independent protocol that works across any bidirectional transport, including TCP/IP, IR, IEEE 1394, and others. It is ideal for PDAs, digital cameras, copiers, network-attached printers and scanners, fax machines, and other devices. Refer to http://www.jetsend.com.

Along with billions of embedded devices is a need to find out where those devices are located and what they do. A number of network initiatives and protocols have been developed to provide service advertising and resource discovery. These are discussed under the topic "Service Advertising and Discovery."

Extend the Internet (ETI) Alliance

emWare, along with over 22 other technology companies, formed the ETI Alliance to develop solutions that allow any electronic device to be managed and controlled remotely over the Internet. emWare uses the term *device networking* to refer to connecting "intelligent" devices to networks, and controlling or gathering information from those devices via browsers, PDAs, telephones, or enterprise applications.

emWare sees the information coming from these networked devices as being more valuable than the individual devices themselves. However, the devices rarely need the full TCP/IP suite to communicate the information they have to offer. emWare's approach is to distribute networking functionality. Embedded products are given only the communication functionality they need in the form of a lightweight protocol called EMIT. These devices send packets to emWare's emGateway product, which bridges the lightweight devices to larger networks such as the Internet.

The ETI approach reduces the level of functionality required in embedded network devices and moves that functionality to the emGateways. ETI Alliance partners are delivering solutions like power meters that conserve energy; pay phones that can be diagnosed and repaired remotely; office equipment that can be upgraded from anywhere in the world, medical equipment that can be simultaneously viewed at the hospital, clinic, or home; and building environment controls data that can be viewed and configured over PDA, browser, or telephone interface.

Refer to http://www.emware.com/eti/ for more information on ETI.

Related Entries   Bluetooth; Directory Services; Home Networking; Java; Mobile Computing; Multiprocessing; Network Appliances; Network Operating Systems; Network Processors; Real-Time Network Services; RTOS (Real-Time Operating System); Servers; Service Advertising and Discovery; SLP (Service Location Protocol); Switch Fabrics and Bus Designs; *and* Thin Clients

Linktionary!—Tom Sheldon's Encyclopedia of Networking updates	http://www.linktionary.com/e/embedded.html
eg3.com (resources for embedded systems)	http://www.eg3.com/
Dedicated Systems Experts (real-time operating system information)	http://www.realtime-info.be/
Embedded.com	http://www.embedded.com/
Embedded Technology.com	http://www.embeddedtechnology.com/
Embedded Planet	http://www.embeddedplanet.com/
Embedded Systems at ChipCenter	http://www.chipcenter.com/embedsys/
Bitpipe (search for "embedded systems")	http://www.bitpipe.com/
3Com paper, "Massively Distributed Systems" by Dan Nessett	http://www.3com.com/technology/tech_net/white_papers/503056.html
Sun's Consumer and Embedded Solutions Web page	http://www.sun.com/consumer-embedded/
Distributed Communication "Architecture" by Hirschmann Network Systems	http://www.anixter.com/ind/pdf/2853.pdf

EMI (Electromagnetic Interference)

EMI is waves of energy that emanate from electrical devices and cables. The waves may interfere with the proper operation of nearby devices or the proper transmission of signals in nearby cabling systems. Electromechanical devices emit low-frequency waves, while computer chips and other integrated circuits emit high-frequency waves. If the emissions have sufficient energy and are close enough to another device, they will interfere with that device. United States and international regulatory agencies provide standards that ensure that devices do not exceed certain emission levels. The FCC (Federal Communication Commission) regulates emissions in the United States.

Emulated LAN

See ATM (Asynchronous Transfer Mode); IP Over ATM; LANE (LAN Emulation); MPOA (Multiprotocol Over ATM); Virtual Circuits; *and* VLAN (Virtual LAN).

Encapsulation

Encapsulation is the technique of putting information within a packet for delivery to some process or entity. In the networking world, encapsulation takes place in two primary ways:

- **Packetization**   When a network application or network process needs to communicate with an application or process on another system, data is sent down through the protocol stack. At each layer, the data from the upper layer is encapsulated within a new packet, and the protocol at that layer adds its own header information to the new packet. At the bottom layer (the physical layer), the packet is encapsulated into frames and transmitted across the network. Refer to "Network Architecture" for more information.

- **Tunneling**   A tunnel describes a way to transmit packets of one protocol across a network that uses a different protocol. Think of a ferry that carries cars across a river. Figure E-5 illustrates how an IPX packet is encapsulated in an IP packet and transported across a TCP/IP network. Another example is the use of tunnels to deliver nonroutable protocols like SNA and NetBEUI across a routed network (such as a TCP/IP intranets and the Internet). The SNA or NetBEUI packets are encapsulated within IP packets and delivered to an SNA or NetBEUI network on the other side of the IP network. DLSw (Data-Link Switching) is an IBM protocol designed to deliver SNA traffic across multiprotocol networks such as IP and IPX networks. See "Tunnels" for more information.

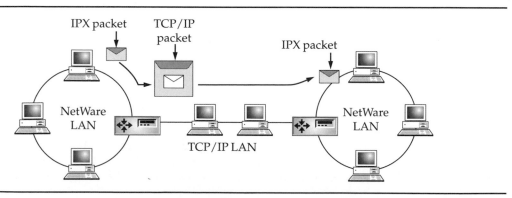

Figure E-5.   *Encapsulation of packets into other packets*

Actually, encapsulation takes place almost everywhere in the network environment. Data from host systems is encapsulated into the frames or cells of the underlying network. In the WAN, IP packets are encapsulated into ATM cells that are, in turn, encapsulated into SONET frames. In the campus environment, Ethernet frames may be encapsulated into the frames of an FDDI (Fiber Distributed Data Interface) backbone network for delivery to an Ethernet network in another building.

Most computers that are connected to the Internet with modems use the PPP (Point-to-Point Protocol), which is a serial point-to-point link protocol. The user's IP datagrams are encapsulated into the PPP frames and delivered across the modem link to the ISP access device. At that point, the datagrams are removed from the PPP frames and forwarded on to the Internet.

VPNs (virtual private networks) illustrate another form of encapsulation, in which many different types of network traffic are delivered across the Internet (or an internal TCP/IP network) in a private and secure way. Packet contents are encrypted to maintain security, but the packet headers remain readable so that packets may be routed as normal.

GRE (Generic Routing Encapsulation) is a protocol developed by Cisco for encapsulating just about any protocol inside IP. The result is a tunnel for delivering non-IP protocols across an IP network. Microsoft uses a modified version of GRE to encapsulate PPP frames in its PPTP (Point-to-Point Tunneling Protocol) solution.

Related Entries   Data Communication Concepts; Fragmentation and Assembly; Framing in Data Transmissions; Network Architectures; Network Concepts; Packets and Packet-Switching Networks; Tunnels; *and* VPN (Virtual Private Network)

Linktionary!—Tom Sheldon's Encyclopedia of Networking updates

http://www.linktionary.com/d/encapsulation.html

Encryption

See Cryptography.

End Systems and End-to-End Connectivity

End System (ES) is official terminology used in the OSI reference model and by the Internet community to describe a computer or user at the end of a communication link. End systems may be at either end of a straight through point-to-point link or at the edge of a multilink, multihop packet-switched network such as the Internet.

RFC 1136, "Administrative Domains and Routing Domains, A Model for Routing in the Internet" (December 1989) describes the terminology of Internet and TCP/IP-routed networks.

David P. Read, one of the people involved in the design of the TCP/IP protocols, discusses the importance of the end-to-end design for the Internet in his paper, "The End of the End-to-End Argument." By splitting the Internet protocols into two protocols (TCP and IP), the network was decentralized and turned into a basic datagram forwarding network. In this model, end systems implemented functions that were previously handled by networks, such as flow control, acknowledgements, and retransmissions. The decentralized model also allowed end-users to deploy applications on their own, so that instead of waiting for some central authority (like the phone company) to decide when a new application could be deployed, end users could run applications on their end xsystems that used IP's services. This was a radical departure from the network architectures of the time, and it has proved disruptive to the 100-year-old phone system. For example, you can run an Internet phone or videoconferencing application on your computer and communicate with any other Internet user running similar applications. There is no need to involve the telephone company, and the applications can have unique features that are not possible with the telephone system, such as whiteboarding. Read's paper is on the Web at http://www.reed.com/Papers/endofendtoend.html.

The most important feature of transport layer protocols like TCP is their ability to establish an end-to-end (host-to-host) communication session across a connectionless packet-switched network made up of many point-to-pint links. In connection-oriented networks like ATM and frame relay, virtual circuits are established from end to end across a network of switches.

RFC 2775, "Internet Transparency" (February 2000) is an interesting read. It describes the current state of the Internet from the architectural viewpoint and concentrates on issues of end-to-end connectivity and transparency.

Related Entries   Connection-Oriented and Connectionless Services; Data Communication Concepts; Datagrams and Datagram Services; Edge Devices; LAN (Local Area Network); Network Access Services; Network Concepts; Network Core Technologies; Network Design and Construction; Packets and Packet-Switching Networks; Point-to-Point Communications; Reliable Data Delivery Services; Routing; Switching and Switched Networks; TCP (Transmission Control Protocol); Transport Protocols and Services; Virtual Circuits; *and* VPN (Virtual Private Network)

Enterprise Network

During the 1980s, organizations began to install local area networks to connect computers in departments and workgroups. Department-level managers usually made decisions about what type of computers and networks they wanted to install.

Eventually, organizations saw benefits in building *enterprise networks* that would let people throughout the organization exchange e-mail and work together using collaborative software. An enterprise network would connect all the isolated departmental or workgroup networks into an intracompany network, with the potential for allowing all computer users in a company to access any data or computing resource. It would provide interoperability among autonomous and heterogeneous systems and have the eventual goal of reducing the number of communication protocols in use. Toward this goal, industry organizations were formed to create open standards, and vendors developed their own strategies.

An enterprise network is both local and wide area in scope. It integrates all the systems within an organization, whether they are Windows computers, Apple Macintoshes, UNIX workstations, minicomputers, or mainframes.

An enterprise network can be thought of as a "plug-and-play" platform for connecting many different computing devices. In this platform scenario, no user or group is an island. All systems can potentially communicate with all other systems while maintaining reasonable performance, security, and reliability.

This has largely been achieved with Internet protocols and Web technologies. TCP/IP is a unifying internetwork protocol that lets organizations tie together workgroup and division LANs, and connect with the Internet. Web protocols (HTTP, HTML, and XML) unify user interfaces, applications, and data, letting organizations build *intranets* (internal internets). A Web browser is like a universal client, and Web servers can provide data to any of those clients. Multitiered architectures are used, in which a Web client accesses a Web server and a Web server accesses back-end data sources, such as mainframes and server farms. See "Multitiered Architecture" for more detail.

Trends in Enterprise Networking

At one point, there was a trend toward building networks with stripped-down diskless clients and huge servers. This NC (Network Computer) strategy, championed by Oracle, never took off because full-function desktop and portable PCs became very cheap. But the number of handheld devices, smart phones, network appliances, and other devices that connect to networks, either directly or wirelessly, is increasing. See "Bluetooth," "Embedded Systems and Architectures," "Mobile Computing," "Network Appliances," and "Thin Clients."

An interesting 3Com paper called "Massively Distributed Systems," by Dan Nessett, discusses the growth of distributed computer networks to billions of nodes, many of which will be embedded systems. While these embedded systems will handle some computing and communication tasks on their own, many will need to off-load heavy computations to more capable systems. The paper discusses the potential architecture of distributed systems that include such embedded system devices. The paper is at the Web site listed later. Also see "Distributed Computer Networks."

New wireless Ethernet LAN protocols (IEEE 802.11a) support data rates over 50 Mbits/sec. See "Ethernet" and "Wireless LANs."

As interest in Voice Over IP (VOIP) increases, the need for higher-capacity networks, QoS, bandwidth management, and policy management will increase. See "QoS (Quality of Service)" and "VOIP (Voice Over IP)" for more details.

Another trend reduces the need for enterprise networks. If users can connect to the Internet with high-speed pipes (DSL, cable—or wireless), then the Internet—or at least a local service provider—can become the enterprise network. This becomes a reality when the bandwidth constraints of local access are lifted. An enterprise may provide connections to its application servers via the Internet, so that users go out on the Internet and then back in to the enterprise Web site. Alternatively, an enterprise may have an ASP (application service provider) host its applications. As more users become mobile and use wireless devices, a traditional enterprise network becomes a platform that ties them to the locations where they can connect to that network.

An excellent paper by Bill St. Arnaud discusses this trend. See "The End of the Enterprise Network" at the Web site listed later.

Related Entries   ASP (Application Service Provider); Backbone Networks; Campus Network; Client/ Server Computing; Data Center Design; Data Warehousing; DBMS (Database Management System); Directory Services; Distributed Computer Networks; Distributed Object Computing; Intranets and Extranets; LAN (Local Area Network); MAN (Metropolitan Area Network); Middleware and Messaging; Mobile Computing; Multitiered Architectures; Network Concepts; Network Design and Construction; Packets and Packet-Switching Networks; Peer-to-Peer Communication; Remote Computing; Switching and Switched Networks; Thin Clients; Voice/Data Networks; WAN (Wide Area Network); Wireless Communications; *and* Web Technologies and Concepts

Linktionary!—Tom Sheldon's Encyclopedia of Networking updates

http://www.linktionary.com/e/enterprise.html

3Com paper, "Massively Distributed Systems" by Dan Nessett

http://www.3com.com/technology/tech_net/ white_papers/503056.html

The End of the Enterprise Network by Bill St.   http://www.canarie.ca/~bstarn/enterprise.html
Arnaud, CANARIE

ENUM

The IETF Telephone Number Mapping (enum) Working Group is defining a DNS-based
architecture and protocols for mapping a telephone number to a set of attributes (e.g., URLs)
that can be used to contact a resource associated with that number. The efforts are designed
to integrate Internet telephony with the traditional PSTN (public-switched telephone network).

Related Entries   SIP (Session Initiation Protocol); Telecommunications and Telephone Systems;
Videoconferencing; Voice/Data Networking; *and* Voice Over IP (VOIP)

Linktionary!—Tom Sheldon's Encyclopedia of   http://www.linktionary.com/e/enum.html
Networking updates

IETF Working Group: Telephone Number   http://www.ietf.org/html.charters/
Mapping (enum)   enum-charter.html

ENUM World, a joint project of Telcordia   http://www.enumworld.com/
Technologies and VeriSign

ERP (Enterprise Resource Planning)

The goal of ERP software is to provide a platform for integrating dissimilar enterprise applications,
such as business-critical inventory, manufacturing, sales, marketing, and finance applications.
The idea is to provide a way to exchange information between systems and to help companies
plan ahead, usually in the development of products.

Deploying ERP is not easy. It involves a considerable amount of business analysis. Current
business processes must be evaluated, new workflow patterns must be established, and goals
must be established. There may also be a need to interoperate with other businesses and the
need to integrate with electronic commerce. Once installed, an ERP system helps companies
quickly respond to changing business markets.

SAP is one of the major ERP providers. The SAP Web site is at http://www.sap.com.

Related Entries   Client/Server Computing; Data Warehouse; DBMS (Database Management System);
Electronic Commerce; Extranet; Multitiered Architecture; *and* OLAP (Online Analytical Processing)

Linktionary!—Tom Sheldon's Encyclopedia of   http://www.linktionary.com/e/erp.html
Networking updates

ERP Supersite   http://www.erpsupersite.com/

ERP Links at Netfusion   http://www.nwfusion.com/netresources/
erp.html

ERP Systems—Using IT to Gain a Competitive Advantage, by S. Shankarnarayanan	http://www.expressindia.com/newads/bsl/advant.htm
System21 ERP Solutions	http://system21.geac.com/
CIO Enterprise Resource Planning Research Center	http://www.cio.com/forums/erp/

Error Detection and Correction

Data processing and transmission systems use a variety of techniques to detect and correct errors that occur, usually for any of the following reasons:

- Electrostatic interference from nearby machines or circuits
- Attenuation of the signal caused by a resistance to current in a cable
- Distortion due to inductance and capacitance
- Loss in transmission due to leakages
- Impulses from static in the atmosphere

It has been estimated that an error occurs for every 1 in 200,000 bits. While most LAN technologies and optical cable networks reduce errors considerably, wireless networks and WAN links can have high error rates.

Bit errors are errors that corrupt single bits of a transmission, turning a 1 into a 0, and vice versa. These errors are caused by power surges and other interference. *Packet errors* occur when packets are lost or corrupted. Packet loss can occur during times of network congestion when buffers become full and network devices start discarding packets. Errors and packet loss also occur during network link failures.

There are two solutions to this problem:

- **Error correction strategy**   Send enough additional information to correct problems at the destination. This is called *FEC (forward error correction)*.
- **Error detection strategy**   Send only enough extra information to detect an error; then request a retransmission from the source. This is called *ARQ (automatic repeat request)*.

ARQ is usually preferred because it requires that fewer bits be transmitted; but if many errors do occur, such as in wireless, retransmissions may occupy a large part of the bandwidth. FEC is used when retransmissions are not practical or possible. Sending program data to an interplanetary spacecraft comes to mind.

The "additional information" sent in either case is called *redundant bits*. These bits provide enough additional information to determine what a corrupted block of data should really be (as in FEC) or to determine if the block is corrupted (as in ARQ). FEC requires that more bits be sent with each transmission and does not use the transmission line efficiently (although you might consider it efficient if a lot of errors are occurring).

ARQ strategies allow a receiving device to detect errors in transmissions and request a retransmission from the sender. Different ARQ strategies are outlined here:

- **Parity check**   This is the simplest error-detection mechanism. A parity bit is appended to a block of data, normally at the end of a 7-bit ASCII (American Standard Code for Information Interchange) character. Two techniques—even parity or odd parity—are available, and which method is used is up to the user. In even parity, a parity bit is selected so that the character has an even number of 1s. In odd parity, the parity bit is selected so that the character has an odd number of 1s. So, for example, if even parity is selected and a computer receives a character with an odd number of 1s, it assumes an error and asks for a retransmission. This method easily breaks down. If two bits change, an error is undetectable by the receiver.

- **CRC (cyclic redundancy check)**   The CRC method operates on blocks of data called *frames*. Basically, the sender appends a bit sequence to every frame, called the *FCS (frame check sequence)*. The resulting frame is exactly divisible by a predetermined number. The receiving computer divides the frame by the predetermined number. If there is a remainder, the frame is considered corrupted and a retransmission is requested. This method is commonly used in many forms of communication. It provides a high level of error detection with speed and ease of use.

Related Entries   Acknowledgements; Asynchronous Communications; Data Communication Concepts; Data Link Protocols; Flow Control Mechanisms; NAK (Negative Acknowledgment); Redundancy; Reliable Data Delivery Services; Serial Communication and Interfaces; Signals; Testing, Diagnostics, and Troubleshooting; *and* Transport Protocols and Services.

Linktionary!—Tom Sheldon's Encyclopedia of Networking updates	http://www.linktionary.com/e/error.html
"A Painless Guide to CRC Error Detection Algorithms" by Ross Williams	http://www.riccibitti.com/crcguide.htm
Rad Data Communications Tutorials	http://www.rad.com/networks/tutorial.htm
Optimized Engineering Tutorials	http://www.optimized.com/COMPENDI/TabOfCon.htm

ESCON (Enterprise Systems Connection)

ESCON is an IBM fiber-optic channel connection technology that provides 17-MB/sec throughput. ESCON provides direct channel-to-channel connections between mainframe systems and peripherals over fiber-optic links at distances up to 60 kilometers (36 miles). It also provides a way for communication controllers and other devices to share a single channel to a mainframe.

Related Entries   Cluster Controllers; IBM (International Business Machines); Mainframe; *and* Storage Systems and Technology

ES-IS (End System-to-Intermediate System) Routing

ES-IS is an OSI (Open Systems Interconnection) protocol that allows communication between end systems (hosts on a network) and intermediate systems (routers that are attached to other networks). The protocol is a *discovery* protocol similar to the Internet's ARP (Address Resolution Protocol). It allows end systems to take part in internetwork routing.

During the discovery process, the ES and IS find each other. At regular intervals, ESs generate *ES Hello messages* and send them to every router on the network. Likewise, ISs generate *IS Hello messages* and send them to every host on their attached subnetworks. The messages transmit OSI network layer and OSI subnetwork addresses. While the process is similar to what happens on IP networks, the terminology is different and beyond the scope of this book, especially in light of the fact that there are very few networks running the OSI protocol suite. Refer to "OSI (Open Systems Interconnection) Model" for more information and Web site references.

At one time, it was thought that OSI protocols would replace the Internet protocols on the government-funded Internet. There are a number of Internet RFCs from the early 1990s that discuss a transition to OSI protocols.

Related Entries   CLNP (Connectionless Network Protocol); IDPR (Inter-Domain Policy Routing Protocol); Internetworking; IS-IS (Intermediate System-to-Intermediate System) Routing; Network Concepts; Network Layer Protocols; OSI (Open Systems Interconnection) Model; Packets and Packet-Switching Networks; *and* Routing

EtherLoop

EtherLoop is a communication technology for the local loop that uses the Ethernet protocol. It provides high-speed data access for home users over the twisted-pair wire loop that stretches from homes to the telephone company CO (central office) or remote offices. EtherLoop uses the basic concepts of DSL technologies, such as HDSL and ADSL, but overcomes many of the limitation of these technologies by using the Ethernet packet-delivery algorithms.

According to Elastic Networks, which developed the technology, EtherLoop provides a solution that is simple to install, robust over distances up to 21,000 feet, and efficient in power consumption. Current data rates are as high as 4 Mbits/sec up to 6,000 feet, and as low as 400 Kbits/sec at 18,000 feet.

EtherLoop was designed as a competitor for cable modems in the area of high-speed data access. It uses features of both DSL and Ethernet. Data is transmitted in bursts to get around the interference problems that are inherent in DSL. The Ethernet packet data model reduces cost by providing compatibility with existing standards. At the same time, the collision problems usually associated with Ethernet are nonexistent because the local loop is a point-to-point link between two devices. A device at one end becomes a server and the other becomes a client. The client only speaks when the server allows, thus eliminating collisions.

This client/server point-to-point arrangement has some performance benefits. If a file is being transferred, it is going in one direction, and most of the time and bandwidth is spent transmitting in that direction. A small amount of bandwidth is used to transmit occasional acknowledgements in the other direction.

EtherLoop monitors the signal during silent periods and measures crosstalk and interference to determine line quality. Crosstalk may occur between any of the 50 wires in the cable bundle that connects to the telephone company central or remote office. If necessary, EtherLoop will change internal frequencies to reduce crosstalk and avoid interference. This rate adaptation allows the EtherLoop modem to immediately adapt to any noise.

The user connection consists of a PC connected to an EtherLoop modem that, in turn, is connected to the phone line. This connects to the telephone company office where an EtherLoop multiplexer receives the signal and forwards packets to an Ethernet switch that, in turn, delivers the packets to one of several destinations: the Internet, a private intranet, or an ATM/frame relay network. Home users are assigned static or dynamic IP addresses.

Related Entries   DSL (Digital Subscriber Line); Ethernet; *and* Network Access Technologies

 Elastic Networks, Inc.   http://www.elastic.com/

Ethernet

Ethernet is a shared local area networking (LAN) technology that was developed in the early 1970s by some of the same pioneers who were working on the development of the Internet. The basic design consists of a shared transmission medium in the form of a coaxial cable or a multiport hub. If the medium is a cable, workstations (nodes) are tapped into the cable along its path through a room or building. If a hub is used, workstations connect to the hub via twisted-pair cables in a star-like configuration. Since the communication medium is shared, nodes must listen to make sure the cable is not in use before transmitting. This works well for small LANs, but the sharing scheme runs into problems as networks grow, as will be explained.

Historical Information

Dr. Robert Metcalfe was the chief designer of Ethernet, but several other people were involved in the project. The following historical information is paraphrased from "Where Wizards Stay Up Late, The Origins of the Internet," by Katie Hafner and Matthew Lyon (Touchstone, 1996).

In 1972, while on DARPA-related business for Xerox PARC (Palo Alto Research Center), Metcalfe stayed at the Washington, D.C., home of friend Steve Crocker. Steve Crocker and Vint Cerf were senior members of the UCLA group headed by Leonard Kleinrock that set up the first Internet router. See "Routing on the Internet" for more details.

At Crocker's home, Metcalfe found a paper written by Norm Abramson about the ALOHA network at the University of Hawaii. The ALOHA system was a radio and satellite network that used a time-slot system to prevent two stations from transmitting at the same time. Metcalfe immediately saw the deficiencies in the system and set out to improve it. His idea was to simply let packets collide, and then retransmit at a random time—which provided a vast improvement in the transmission rate when cable was used as the network medium. The cables would connect computers in a small area. Thus, Metcalfe defined the first *local area network*, or *LAN*.

Metcalfe also developed a *collision avoidance* scheme in which computers listen to the cable before transmitting to determine if another computer is transmitting. If the cable is busy, a computer waits for a few thousandths of a second and then tries again. Since it is possible that two computers might transmit at the same time, causing a "collision," a *collision detection* scheme was built into the system. When collisions occur, any packets being transmitted are corrupted, and thus collisions can be detected. When a collision occurs, both stations back off and try retransmitting later. As it turned out, this scheme scaled well even as transmission rates were increased and more computers were added to the network.

Metcalfe got the first Ethernet up and running at Xerox PARC in 1973 with the help of Butler Lampson, David Boggs, and Chuck Thacker. Metcalfe suggested the name Ethernet, recalling the hypothetical luminiferous medium that 19th century physicists used to explain how light traveled through empty space.

Commercial development of Ethernet took place in the 1980s. The system was jointly developed as a standard in 1980 by Digital Equipment Corporation, Intel, and Xerox. This standard became known as DIX Ethernet, in reference to the developers' names. The IEEE (Institute of Electrical and Electronics Engineers) 802.3 standard defines a similar scheme that uses a slightly different framing method. The IEEE 802.3 standard was adopted as an ISO (International Organization for Standardization) standard and is now used worldwide. The remainder of this discussion refers to IEEE 802.3 Ethernet.

General Ethernet Features

There are a number of adaptations to the IEEE 802.3 Ethernet standard, including adaptations with data rates of 10 Mbits/sec; 100 Mbits/sec (Fast Ethernet); 1,000 Mbits/sec (Gigabit Ethernet); and, most recently, 10 Gigabit/sec Ethernet. The original forms of Ethernet used coaxial cable, but today most Ethernet networks are connected with Category 5 twisted-pair cable.

- **Shared media**   All nodes attached to the network take turns using the media. If the network is not busy, a shared scheme is very efficient; but if the network gets busy, nodes must wait to transmit or, worse, collisions occur that reduce performance.

- **Broadcast domains**   Just like a TV broadcast, transmitted frames are "heard" by all, but nodes receive only the frames that are addressed to them. Special *broadcast* frames are addressed to all nodes. These are used for multicasting and network maintenance. See "Broadcast," "Broadcast Domain," and "Broadcast Networking."

- **CSMA/CD (carrier sense multiple access/collision detection) access method** On a shared media, some method is required to prevent two or more nodes from transmitting at the same time, and to detect "collisions" that occur if two stations begin transmitting at the same time. See "CSMA/CD (Carrier Sense Multiple Access/ Collision Detection)" for details.

- **Collision domains**   A collision domain consists of a set of networked nodes that share the same medium and that contend for access to the cable. In other words, their transmissions can collide. Suppose you have a busy 50-node network, and the number of collisions is reducing performance. You divide the network with a bridge to create two 25-node networks. Now you have two separate collision domains and one broadcast domain (the bridge will propagate broadcasts and appropriate traffic from one segment to the other). See "Collisions and Collision Domains."

- **Framing method**   Several framing methods were specified early on, but most systems now conform to IEEE 802.3 framing. More recently, the framing method was changed to support higher data rates (Gigabit Ethernet). The 802.3 frame is discussed later. Also see "Framing in Data Transmissions."

- **Full-duplex mode**   The twisted-pair Ethernet adaptations support full-duplex mode, in which signals are transmitted on one wire and received on another. Coaxial cable does not support full-duplex mode. Since both end stations are transmitting on separate wires, there is no contention (in a switched environment). This greatly improves transmission speeds.

- **Cable types**   The earliest Ethernet adaptations support coaxial cable in a bus topology configuration (the cable runs from one node to the next). Later versions supported twisted-pair cable in a star configuration (each node is individually wired to a hub). Combinations of cabling schemes are possible.

- **Cable length**   There are cable-length limitations, depending on the media type. Overextended networks are subject to signal propagation delays that can cause a failure in the collision detection mechanism. When a cable is too long, nodes at far ends may not detect that another has begun transmission. Collisions will go undetected, and there will be continuous network errors until the cable is shortened and the end stations are able to detect one another's transmissions.

- **MAC addresses**   All Ethernet NICs (network interface cards) come with a preassigned 48-bit network address. This address is made up of a 24-bit number that identifies the vendor of the card and a 24-bit number assigned by the vendor to identify the card. The address is globally unique and is called the MAC address because it defines a node on the network at the MAC (Media Access Control) layer.

Ethernet Adaptations

The common features of Ethernet are listed in the following sections. Note that Fast Ethernet and Gigabit Ethernet are discussed under their own headings. 10Base-2 and 10Base-T are discussed later in this topic.

See "IEEE 802 Standards" for a description of all IEEE 802 networking standards. The IEEE 802.11 committee defines wireless networking standards that are compatible with standard Ethernet. See "Wireless LANs."

Information about fiber-optic LANs is available at the FOLS (Fiber Optics LAN Section) of the TIA. The Web site is http://www.fols.org/.

Traditional Ethernet (10 Mbits/sec)

- **10Base-5**   This is a coaxial cable scheme, also called *Thicknet,* with maximum segment lengths of 500 meters; uses baseband transmission methods.

- **10Base-2**   This is another coaxial cable (RG-58 A/U), also called *Thinnet,* with maximum segment lengths of about 185 meters; uses baseband transmission methods.

- **10Base-T**   Twisted-pair cable with maximum segment lengths of 100 meters.
- **10Base-FL**   Supports fiber-optic cable backbones of up to 4 kilometers with transmission at 10 Mbits/sec. The TIA/EIA has approved this cable for cross-connects between campus buildings in its Commercial Building Wiring Standard.

Fast Ethernet, IEEE 802.3u (100 Mbits/sec)

- **100Base-TX**   Fast Ethernet (100 Mbits/sec) over two pairs of Category 5 UTP (unshielded twisted-pair) or Category 1 shielded twisted-pair cable.
- **100Base-T4**   Fast Ethernet (100 Mbits/sec) over four pairs of Category 3, 4, or 5 UTP wiring.
- **100Base-FX**   Fast Ethernet (100 Mbits/sec) over fiber-optic cable.

Gigabit Ethernet (1000 Mbits/Sec)

- **1000Base-LX** (IEEE 802.3z)   Implements long-wavelength laser transmissions with links up to 550 meters over multimode fiber-optic cable and 3,000 meters over single-mode fiber-optic cable.
- **1000Base-SX** (IEEE 802.3z)   Implements short-wavelength (850 nm) laser transmissions over multimode fiber-optic cable.
- **1000Base-CX** (IEEE 802.3z)   Designed for connecting devices over short distances (in the same wiring closet), this standard uses high-data-rate twisted-pair cable with a maximum distance of 25 meters.
- **1000Base-T** (IEEE 802.3ab)   Gigabit Ethernet transmissions over four-pair Category 5 cable, with a maximum distance of 100 meters per station to switch or 205 meters end to end.
- **10 Gigabit Ethernet (IEEE 802.3ae)**   As with 1 Gigabit Ethernet, 10 Gigabit Ethernet will preserve the 802.3 Ethernet frame format, as well as minimum and maximum frame sizes. It will support full-duplex operation only. The topology is star-wired LANs that use point-to-point links and structured cabling topologies. Also, 802.3ad link aggregation will be supported.

Ethernet-Related Specifications   The IEEE had developed or is developing the following additional Ethernet specifications. Note that this list is not complete. Refer to the IEEE Web site listed later for more details.

- **IEEE 802.1Q**   Defines a tag, inserted into Ethernet frames, that defines VLAN membership. See "VLAN (Virtual LAN)." Three of the bits in this tag are reserved for identifying priority as defined by IEEE 802.1p, as discussed next.
- **IEEE 802.1p**   Not really an Ethernet specification, but primarily targeted at improving prioritization on Ethernet networks. It prioritizes traffic by differentiating between classes of traffic. Frames are tagged with user priority levels ranging from 7 (highest

priority) to 0 (lowest priority). Routers and switches look at this tag and give high-priority traffic precedence over low-priority traffic. This is done by putting outgoing frames in up to seven different buffers. Thus, real-time traffic like voice can receive preferential treatment. See "QoS (Quality of Service)" and "Prioritization of Network Traffic." Note that 802.1p was merged into the IEEE 802.1D bridging standard.

- **IEEE 802.3ad (Link Aggregation)**   A trunking and link aggregation protocol that combines multiple Ethernet channels into a single logical channel. Multiple channels provide more throughput and fault tolerance. Fast Ethernet or Gigabit Ethernet may be aggregated. See "Load Balancing."

- **IEEE 802.3af (DTE Power via MDI Talk Force)**   This project is defining how to provide power to data terminal equipment with 802.3 interfaces over the Ethernet cable. The idea is to provide electrical power for a new class of small network devices, such as telephones so they have the same availability as traditional phone lines.

Ethernet Networking Devices

Ethernet and other LAN technologies are implemented in the data link layer of the OSI protocol model. Therefore, most Ethernet connection devices are referred to as layer 2 devices.

The data link layer is divided into two sublayers: the LLC (Logical Link Control) sublayer and the MAC (Media Access Control) sublayer. The LLC sits on top of the MAC, where it interfaces with higher-layer protocols. The MAC is where different networks are implemented, such as Ethernet and token ring. For example, an Ethernet network adapter is a MAC device that communicates with upper-layer protocols (IP or IPX) through the LLC. The LLC is important in devices that have more than one MAC interface (Ethernet and token ring, for example). It acts as a switch, forwarding packets to the appropriate interface.

In coaxial cable Ethernet implementations, workstations are connected in a daisy-chain fashion by attaching segments of cable to each station as shown in A in Figure E-6. The segments form a single, large cable system called the *trunk*. A signal is *broadcast* on the bus so that all nodes may listen. At the same time, all of the nodes participate in the same collision domain, so as more stations are attached, collisions increase and performance drops.

Coaxial cable networks will exhibit faults or fail if the cable is damaged or cut. A solution to this problem is the star-configured bus topology, as shown in B in Figure E-6. The bus is collapsed into a hub or switch, and nodes are connected to the hub via individual twisted-pair cable. A cut in any cable only disrupts the node attached to that cable.

Once again, all the nodes are part of the same broadcast and collision domain. All the nodes attached to the cable may transmit to any other node, and broadcast messages reach all the nodes. At the same time, all the nodes compete for access to the cable.

Repeaters and Repeater Hubs

Parts C and D of Figure E-6 show the use of a repeater, which is a physical layer device that extends the distance of a network by amplifying and retiming signals. A repeater corrects for attenuation problems that occur when a network extends over a long distance. A repeater does not segment a network. All the users are still sharing the same network media and are still part of the same broadcast and collision domain. In other words, frames transmitted by a node on one port are sent to every other node.

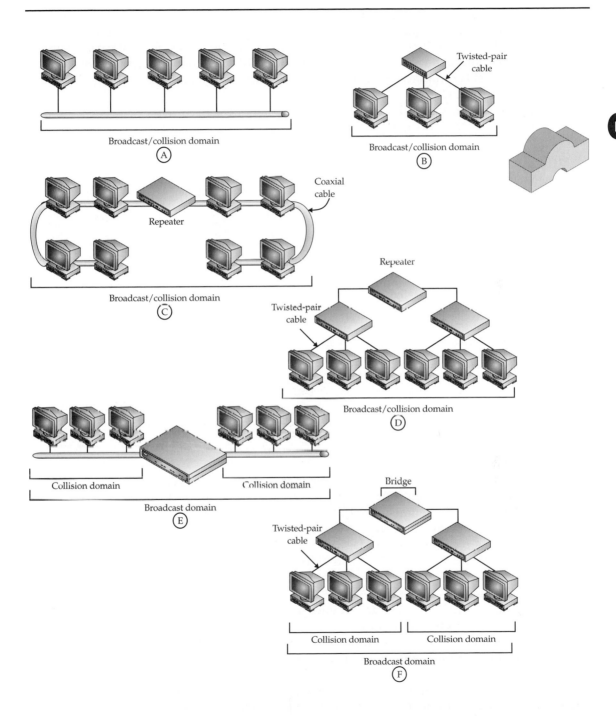

Figure E-6.   *Coaxial cable and twisted-pair Ethernet networks*

A hub is a 10Base-T device that is basically a repeater with multiple ports. Each port is an RJ-45 connector. Part D in Figure E-6 shows the nodes connected directly to the hub, but the usual configuration is as follows: a computer is connected to a wall jack, the wall jack is wired to a punchdown block in a wiring closet, the punchdown block is connected to a patch panel, and the patch panel is connected to the hub. This is outlined later under the heading "Ethernet 10Base-T (Twisted-Pair)."

Hubs may be interconnected via a stand-alone repeater or via connectors on the backs of hubs. Such connectors are often coaxial cable Ethernet, which allows a long run of cable between hub devices.

There are limitations to the number of repeaters that can be used, due to propagation delays. You cannot create a network that is so large that a station at one end cannot detect when a station at the other end has just begun to transmit. Both stations would end up using the cable at the same time.

Bridges

Parts E and F of Figure E-6 illustrate the use of a bridge. A bridge is a layer 2 device that divides a network into separate collision domains while retaining the broadcast domain. A bridge is a useful device for an Ethernet network because it can divide a network into segments with each segment having a reduced number of nodes that are competing for access to the transmission medium.

When a node transmits, only the nodes on its side of the bridge "hear" the transmission on the cable, and only those nodes contend for access to the medium.

But a bridge maintains the broadcast domain and allows nodes in either segment to communicate with one another. The bridge keeps a table of the nodes in each segment and forwards frames appropriately. The bridge also makes sure that broadcast/multicast frames are propagated to all attached segments. See "Switching and Switched Networks" for more information.

Switches

Figure E-7 illustrates a *multiport bridge,* or *switch.* A switch, like a bridge, is a layer 2 device that can temporarily bridge any port with any other port. This is possible because the switch has a switching matrix (sometimes called a "switching fabric") that can rapidly connect and disconnect ports, as shown on the right in Figure E-7.

Note that port A is bridged to port D, allowing the two computers attached to those ports to connect across a contentionless, full-bandwidth link. In other words, since only two devices are connected to the link, they are vying for the link with only one another, thus reducing contention dramatically.

Unlike a hub, a switch only forwards frames from one port to the required destination port—not to all other ports. This reduces traffic on the rest of the network and also improves security—since frames are only traveling between the end systems that are sending and receiving, rather than to all nodes in the broadcast domain.

Also note on the right in Figure E-7 that hubs may be attached to switch ports, thus allowing a group of nodes to share the same port. While not as efficient as the single-computer–per–port method, contention is still reduced in the same way that adding a bridge reduces contention in Figure E-6 E or F.

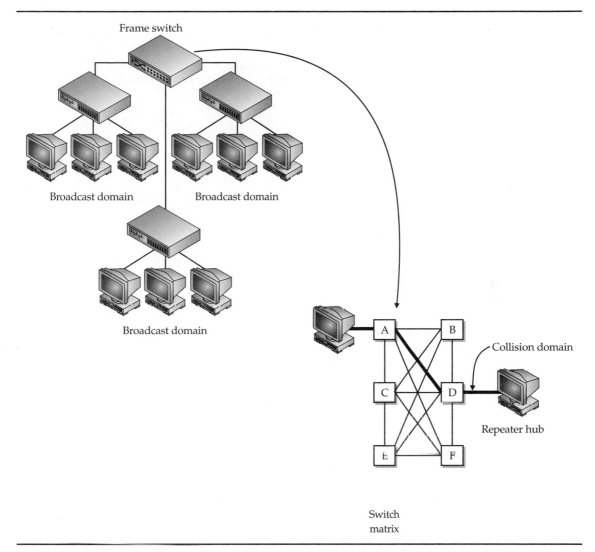

Figure E-7.   *A switch is a multiport bridge with a switching matrix*

Switches are ideal for building hierarchical networks, as shown in Figure E-8. Most multiport Ethernet devices sold today are switches rather than hubs, although hubs may still be used in small workgroup environments. Multilayer switches combine routing functions (discussed next) with switching to create an ideal network device. Many switches now provide full-duplex mode, which allows end systems to establish connections and then send and receive across separate twisted-pair, thus removing all contention and allowing both systems to transmit at full Ethernet speeds.

For more information about switching, see "Switching and Switched Networks."

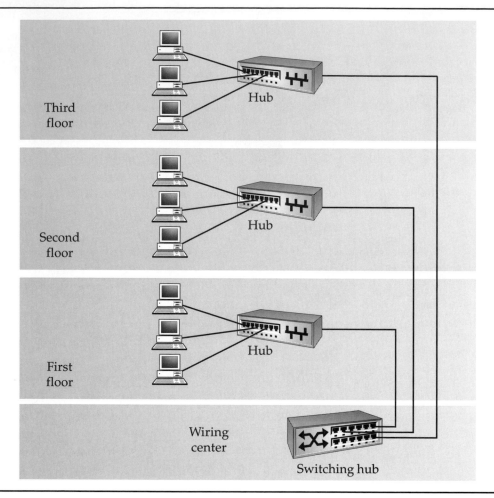

Figure E-8.   *Switches promote hierarchical network design.*

Routers

A router is a layer 3 device that separates networks into distinct broadcast areas. Networks on either side of a router maintain their own broadcast and collision domains. An internetworking scheme is required to send packets across the router to nodes on the other side. This requires a special addressing scheme. Figure E-9 illustrates a router-connected internetwork with IP as the internetwork address scheme. Ethernet LANs are on either side of the router. The Ethernet addressing scheme works in the MAC layer. It uses the address that is hardwired into network adapters, as discussed later. In order for a node on one network to address a node on another, an overlay addressing scheme is required. The router learns the addresses on either side and forwards packets appropriately.

Figure E-9 illustrates a router-connected internetwork. IP (Internet Protocol) is the internetwork addressing scheme. You can refer to the networks on either side of the router as *subnetworks*.

Every computer on a TCP/IP network has two addresses: a MAC address that is only used within the subnetwork, and an IP address that identifies the computer on the internetwork. In this configuration, two computers on the same subnetwork send each other messages by using the MAC address. If a message must be sent to another subnetwork, it is simply sent to the router. The router then forwards the message to the appropriate system on the other subnetwork.

Note *RFC 1042, "IP and ARP on IEEE 802 Networks" (February 1988) defines how IP is mapped into Ethernet frames.*

The usefulness of routers is well defined on the Internet. They separate all the private networks from one another while forwarding traffic that is destined for other networks. Routers also provide security by filtering packets.

In an enterprise environment, routers can separate all the departmental LANs while allowing packets to flow between networks as necessary. Often, a backbone network is installed and all the corporate LANs are connected to it via routers. See "Backbone Networks."

A better solution today is the multilayer switch, which is basically a switch with built-in routing capabilities. The important feature is that routing occurs at wire speed and is built into hardware. So, instead of having a bunch of expensive software-based slow routers, you have one multiport box with built-in routing capabilities that can provide the separation of networks that you need for departments and divisions. These layer 3 switches, as they are sometimes called, are essential for reducing network bottlenecks in areas like network aggregation points. See "Multilayer Switching."

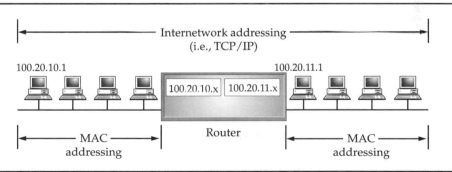

Figure E-9.   *Ethernet subnetworks in an internetwork configuration*

Frame Formats

An Ethernet frame format defines the layout for packaging data and control information into frames and transmitting it over a network. It defines the position of headers and control bits, and the position and size of the data. Figure E-10 shows the frame for IEEE 802.3 frames. Important fields in the frames are described here.

- **Preamble**   This field marks the start of a frame. It always contains the bit pattern 10101010. Interestingly, this pattern produces a clocking signal that appears as a 10-MHz square wave for 5.6 microseconds to the receiver.

- **SFD (start frame delimiter)**   This field indicates the actual start of the frame itself and always contains the bit pattern 10101011.

- **Destination and Source**   These fields hold the address of where the frame came from and where it is supposed to go.

- **Length (LEN) of Data field**   This field indicates the length of the data portion of the frame.

- **CRC (cyclic redundancy check)**   This field holds a value calculated on the packet by the sender. The receiver performs the same calculation to see if it comes up with the same CRC value. If not, the frame is considered corrupted and is retransmitted.

Ethernet 10Base-2

Ethernet 10Base-2 (also called Thinnet) is the most common and practical of the coaxial cable schemes. The other coaxial cable scheme, Ethernet 10Base-5 (Thicknet), provides longer trunk distances (500 meters compared to 185 meters); but its use of external transceivers and thicker cabling makes it harder to implement.

A Thinnet network is illustrated in Figure E-11. Figure E-12 illustrates the components of the wiring system.

The Web sites given later provide extensive technical details on 10 Mbit/sec Ethernet technologies.

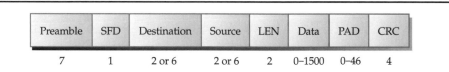

Preamble	SFD	Destination	Source	LEN	Data	PAD	CRC
7	1	2 or 6	2 or 6	2	0–1500	0–46	4

Figure E-10.   *Ethernet 802.3 frame*

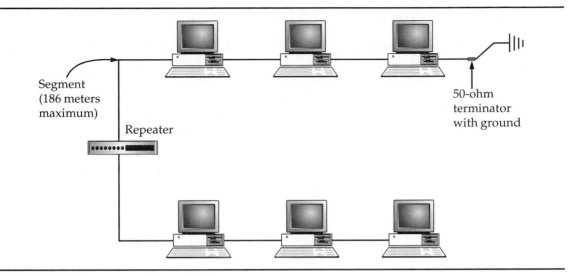

Segment
(186 meters
maximum)

Repeater

50-ohm
terminator
with ground

Figure E-11.   *Ethernet-6: Ethernet 10Base-2 coaxial cable network*

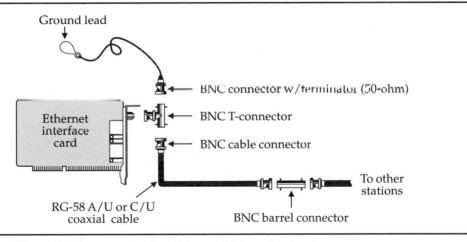

Ground lead

BNC connector w/terminator (50-ohm)

BNC T-connector

Ethernet
interface
card

BNC cable connector

To other
stations

RG-58 A/U or C/U
coaxial cable

BNC barrel connector

Figure E-12.   *Ethernet-7: Components of an Ethernet 10Base-2 network*

The components of a 10Base-2 network are described in the next sections.

- **Network interface card (NIC)** A card with a BNC adapter. Most boards today are dual function, supporting both 10- and 100-Mbits/sec Ethernet, and have both a BNC and an RF-45 connector (to support 10Base-T or 100Base-T). Boards with PROM (programmable read-only memory) slots support diskless workstations.

- **Thin Ethernet cable** The cabling used for Thin Ethernet is a 50-ohm 0.2-inch-diameter RG-58 A/U or RG-58 C/U coaxial cable. Cable is available as fire-safe plenum cable, nonplenum interior cable, underground-rated cable, and aerial-rated cable.

- **BNC cable connectors** BNC connectors must be attached to the ends of all cable segments. BNC cable-connector kits include a center pin, a housing, and a clampdown sleeve.

- **BNC T-connectors** A T-connector is attached to the BNC connector on the back of the Ethernet interface card. The T-connector provides two cable connections for signal-in and signal-out. You will need a T-connector for each workstation, even if it is the last station in the trunk, in which case the BNC *terminator* is attached to the open end of the T-connector.

- **BNC barrel connectors** BNC barrel connectors are used to join two cable segments together.

- **BNC terminators** Each cable segment must be terminated at both ends with a 50-ohm BNC terminator. For each cable segment, you need one terminator with a ground and one without.

10Base-2 Specifications

You must abide by the following rules and limitations when wiring Ethernet networks with RG-58 A/U or RG-58 C/U coaxial cable:

- A segment is a collection of up to 30 stations connected with cable in a daisy-chain fashion. The maximum segment length is 186 meters (607 feet).

- A trunk is a collection of up to five segments, connected together with repeaters. The maximum network trunk length is 910 meters (3,035 feet).

- When segments are joined to trunks with repeaters, the repeater counts as a station, allowing only 29 additional stations.

- On a trunk that consists of five segments, stations are allowed on only three of the segments. The others are used for distance.

- No piece of cable interconnecting two stations may be shorter than 0.5 meters (1.64 feet) in length.

■ A terminator must be placed at each end of a trunk, and one end (and only one end) must be grounded.

Note that once the cable and T-connectors are configured into a segment, the T-connector can be removed from and reattached to a station without bringing down the network. However, if the cable itself is disconnected from a T-connector, the network will stop working.

Ethernet 10Base-T (Twisted-Pair)

10Base-T's biggest advantage is a star, or distributed, topology, which allows for clusters of workstations in departments or other areas. It is easy to build hierarchical wiring systems. Even though cable segment distances are shorter, the hierarchical topology provides a cabling scheme that makes up for this deficiency.

A basic 10Base-T network is shown in Figure E-13. Workstations are attached to a central hub, or concentrator, that acts as a repeater. When a signal from a workstation arrives, the hub broadcasts it on all output lines. You can attach hubs to other hubs in a hierarchical configuration. Workstations are attached to the hub with a UTP (unshielded twisted-pair) cable that cannot exceed 100 meters (328 feet).

10Base-T connections use Category 3 cabling, as shown in Figure E-14. Two pairs of wires are used—one pair for receiving data and the other for transmitting data. The transmit wires connect to pins 1 and 2, and the receive wires connect to pins 3 and 6, as shown in Figure E-14. The twists in each pair must be maintained all the way up to the connection point. Higher grades of cable can be used, such as Category 5. This provides for future growth into faster transmission technologies such as 100Base-T or 1000Base-T.

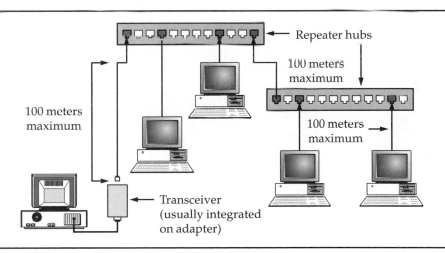

Figure E-13.   *Ethernet 10Base-T cabling example*

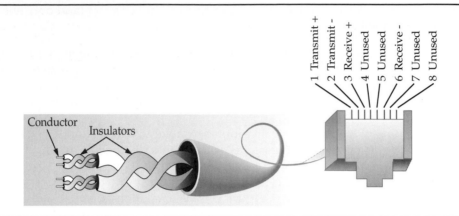

Figure E-14. *Category 3 cable configuration for 10Base-T*

Figure E-15 illustrates a small-office wiring configuration. Note that the hub in the wiring closet connects to a backbone that courses through the building, or connects to a central hub or switch. A 50-wire telephone jumper cable connects the concentrator to a punchdown block. Twisted-pair cable then runs from the punchdown block to wall faceplates near workstations. At the workstation, a cable is strung from the faceplate to a transceiver, which then connects to the workstation. Note that the Ethernet specification recommends a maximum of 90 meters

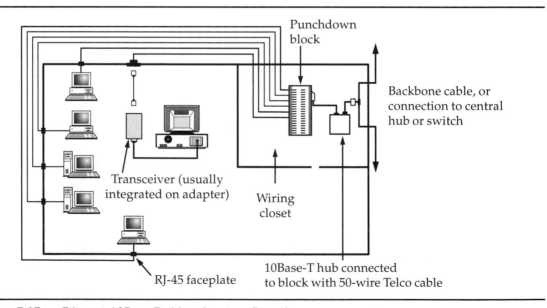

Figure E-15. *Ethernet 10Base-T wiring closet configuration*

from wiring closet to faceplate. The remaining 10 meters should be sufficient for the faceplate-to-station cable. This cable must be the same Category 3 or greater twisted-pair variety, and not the cables used to connect telephones.

The 10Base-T specifications are listed here. Note that some of these specifications are flexible, depending on the vendor. An entire connection from wall plate to hub is pictured in Figure E-16.

- The maximum number of nodes per segment is 1,024, not counting repeaters.

- Use Category 3, 4, or 5 unshielded twisted-pair cable.

- Use RJ-45 jacks at the end of cables. Pins 1 and 2 are "transmit" and pins 3 and 6 are "receive."

- The distance from a station to a hub cannot exceed 100 meters (328 feet).

- Up to 12 repeater hubs can be attached to a central hub to expand the number of network stations, but the number of repeaters cannot exceed 4 between any two end nodes.

- A bridge may be used to extend some of these limitations. Divide large networks with routers as discussed earlier.

Related Entries   ATM (Asynchronous Transfer Mode); Backbone Networks; Bridges and Bridging; Broadcast; Broadcast Domain; Broadcast Networking; Cabling and Cable Concepts; Collisions and Collision Domains; CSMA/CD (Carrier Sense Multiple Access/Collision Detection); Data Communication Concepts; Data Link Protocols; Fast Ethernet; Framing in Data Transmissions; Gigabit Ethernet; IEEE 802 Standards; LAN (Local Area Network); Load Balancing; Multilayer Switching; Network Concepts; Network Design and Construction; Switching and Switched Networks; TIA/EIA Structured Cabling Standards; VLAN (Virtual LAN); *and* Wireless LAN

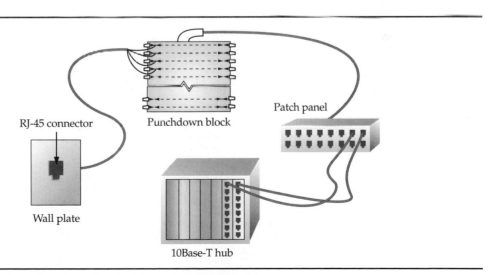

Figure E-16.   *Ethernet 10Base-T wall plate–to–hub configuration*

In addition to the following links, other links can be found under "Fast Ethernet" and "Gigabit Ethernet."

Linktionary!—Tom Sheldon's Encyclopedia of Networking updates	http://www.linktionary.com/e/ethernet.html
Ethernet, IEEE 802.3 Ethernet Working Group page	http://grouper.ieee.org/groups/802/3/
Optimized Engineering Corporation Ethernet information	http://www.optimized.com/COMPENDI/TabOfCon.htm
Enterasys Systems Technical Documentation (see Ethernet Technology guide)	http://www.enterasys.com/support/manuals/overview.html
Cisco's Ethernet Technology page	http://www.cisco.com/univercd/cc/td/doc/cisintwk/ito_doc/ethernet.htm
Cisco "Troubleshooting Ethernet" page	http://www.cisco.com/univercd/cc/td/doc/cisintwk/itg_v1/tr1904.htm
3Com's Networking Solutions Center	http://www.3com.com/technology/
Lantronix Networking Tutorials	http://www.lantronix.com/training/tutorials/
Gorry Fairhurst's communications and networking tutorial (see "Local Area Network" section)	http://www.erg.abdn.ac.uk/users/gorry/eg3561/syllabus.html
Charles Spurgeon's Ethernet Page	http://www.ots.utexas.edu/ethernet/
H. Gilbert's Ethernet document	http://pclt.cis.yale.edu/pclt/COMM/ETHER.HTM
Black Box Corporation (412) 746-5500	http://www.blackbox.com
Allied Electronics (800) 433-5700	http://www.allied.avnet.com
Extreme Networks white papers and technology guides	http://www.extremenetworks.com/technology/
TechFest Ethernet links	http://www.techfest.com/networking/lan.htm
Ethernet links at ITPRC	http://www.itprc.com/data.htm
Anixter Technical Library (very informative)	http://www.anixter.com/techlib/

EtherTalk

EtherTalk is an implementation of the IEEE (Institute of Electrical and Electronics Engineers) 802.3 Ethernet standard for Apple Macintosh computers. EtherTalk adapters provided by Apple include media adapters for thin coaxial cable, twisted-pair cable, and fiber-optic cable. The cards are called the Ethernet NuBus (NB) card for Macintosh IIs or the Ethernet LC card for Macintosh LCs. An external adapter is also available for non-NuBus systems. It attaches to the SCSI (Small Computer System Interface) port.

Related Entries   AppleTalk; Ethernet

Explicit Routing

Packet-switched networks are built on mesh topologies in which multiple paths to a destination exist. The links in the mesh are point-to-point links joined by routers. A path to a destination may go through any number of routers, and the path may change at any time due to traffic problems or failed links. In this environment, there are two possible packet-routing methods:

- **Hop-by-hop, destination-based routing**   This scheme is like getting directions along the way. A packet has a destination address. Each router looks at the address and makes a routing decision about how to forward the packet. Thus, decisions are made on a hop-by-hop basis *in the network* until the packet reaches its destination.

- **Explicit routing**   This scheme relies on a network made of switch routers or ATM switches. A predefined path is specified in advance for a packet. This is a virtual circuit in the ATM world. Since the path is predefined, the packet is switched at each node, thus eliminating the need to make routing decisions at every node along the path. Explicit routing is useful for traffic engineering, QoS (Quality of Service), and the prevention of routing loops. It requires path setup in advance, something that can be done in IP networks with MPLS (Multiprotocol Label Switching). *Source routing* is a form of explicit routing in which end systems discover a path through the network in advance of sending packets.

Setting up paths implies that the network will keep state information, something that was frowned on in the past due to its potential to reduce performance. But with the need for QoS and bandwidth management rising, explicit routing is now important and can be done much more efficiently due to higher-performance devices.

Explicit routing is usually done on service provider and carrier networks due to the traffic loads. Most enterprise networks can be provisioned to provide enough bandwidth for users. This is not always the case on the Internet or other wide area networks.

MPLS (Multiprotocol Label Switching) is the most important protocol that provides explicit routing. With MPLS, a simple designator for a path through a network is inserted in a label that gets attached to packets. An important feature of MPLS is that it provides a means to support traffic engineering, which means that certain routes through IP networks can be managed in a way that ensures certain traffic has the bandwidth it needs. Latency-sensitive traffic can be routed along a path that has been engineered for low latency.

Related Entries   Congestion and Control Mechanisms; Constraint-Based Routing; Cut-Through Routing: Differentiated Services (DiffServ); Label Switching; MPLS (Multiprotocol Label Switching); Multilayer Switching; QoS (Quality of Service); Routing; *and* Traffic Management, Shaping and Engineering

Express Forwarding

Cisco's Express Forwarding (CEF) technology is a layer 2 switching technology designed for enterprise IP networks. CEF includes Cisco NetFlow Switching technology and was part of Cisco's Tag Switching architecture, which were merged with the IETF's MPLS (Multiprotocol Label Switching) efforts. See "MPLS (Multiprotocol Label Switching)."

Exterior Routing

Exterior routing is a feature of very large networks such as the Internet. Consider the structure of the Internet. Your organization's internal network is connected to a local ISP. This local ISP is itself connected to a regional ISP. Finally, the regional ISP is connected to a national backbone network.

Each of these networks is an *autonomous system (AS)*, with its own *internal routing* scheme. The connections between these autonomous systems are referred to as *external routing*. Internal routing protocols are meant to exchange routing information with routers only within the autonomous system. Exterior routing protocols exchange routing information with other autonomous systems.

Early in the days of the Internet (the ARPANET at that time), there was a protocol called EGP (Exterior Gateway Protocol). This protocol evolved into BGP (Border Gateway Protocol). However, you will see the acronym "EGP" used in a generic way to refer to "exterior gateway protocols." These days, the actual EGP protocol is no longer used and the only exterior routing protocol of significance is BGP (BGP version 4, to be precise).

Note the significance of "gateway" in the phrase "exterior gateway protocol." While a gateway is a router, the term specifically implies a path or "doorway" to another AS.

The primary reason for having interior and exterior routing protocols is that the Internet is so large. It is not possible to maintain routing tables for all the networks on the Internet and pass that information around among different routers. The benefit of autonomous systems is that we can represent a large group of networks with a single piece of routing information and exchange just that entry with other exterior routers. This scheme allows the Internet to grow very large.

Refer to "Routing on the Internet" for historical information about the development of routing protocols and conception information about why they developed the way they did.

Related Entries   Autonomous Systems; BGP (Border Gateway Protocol); EGPs (Exterior Gateway Protocols); IDPR (Inter-Domain Policy Routing Protocol); Internet Architecture and Backbone; Internetworking; IP (Internet Protocol); OSPF (Open Shortest Path First); Peering; RIP (Routing Information Protocol); Route Aggregation; Routing; *and* Routing on the Internet

Extranet

The term "extranet" is an outgrowth of "intranet," a term that describes internal networks that are built with Internet technologies such as TCP/IP, and Web protocols such as HTTP, HTML, and XML. Independent organizations that need to connect their networks together to securely exchange documents or engage in business transactions can do so by using the same Internet and Web technologies—thus the term "extranet." Extranets are cross-business connections built with private leased lines or encrypted Internet links that allow people and businesses to engage in secure business relationships.

A typical extranet involves firewalls to protect internal resources, certificates to exchange security keys, metadirectories to integrate the directory services of the companies being connected, software distribution standards, and data exchange formats such as EDI (Electronic Data Interchange) and XML.

E

Setting up an extranet requires coordination between the partners involved. Both partners must set up firewalls to protect their own internal systems while letting appropriate traffic flow through. The firewalls essentially "dual" with one another. Secure encrypted tunnels are established using a VPN (virtual private network) protocol such as PPTP (Point-to-Point Tunneling Protocol), L2TP (Layer 2 Tunneling Protocol), or IPSec (IP Security). Another protocol is SSL (Secure Socket Layer), a client/server protocol typically used between Web browsers and Web servers. These protocols are discussed under their own headings.

However, extranets usually involve allowing a whole company or workgroups at that company to access databases and proprietary information like engineering drawings or customer lists. Beyond access to databases, partners may need to be involved interactively using collaborative applications like bulletin boards, chat groups, messaging, and workflow applications.

An extranet may be defined by simply granting users in the partner company access privileges to programs or data on your own systems. This is not much different than allowing your own mobile users to access corporate data and has many of the same security implications.

Related Entries   Collaborative Computing; EDI (Electronic Data Interchange); Electronic Commerce; Firewall; Groupware; Internet; Intranets and Extranets; IPSec (IP Security); Network Concepts; Network Design and Construction; Security; SSL (Secure Socket Layer); S/WAN (Secure WAN); VPN (Virtual Private Network); *and* Web Technologies and Concepts

Linktionary!—Tom Sheldon's Encyclopedia of Networking updates	http://www.linktionary.com/e/extranet.html
Aventail Corporation managed services	http://www.aventail.com/
Citrix Extranet	http://www.citrix.com/products/extranet/
Marimba extranet solutions	http://www.marimba.com/solutions/extranet_solutions.html
Bitpipe (search for "intranet" or "extranet")	http://www.bitpipe.com/
Smart Computing (search for "intranet" or "extranet")	http://www.smartcomputing.com/
CIO Intranet/Extranet Research Center	http://www.cio.com/forums/intranet/
CIR (Complete Internet Resources), also has extranet information	http://www.intrack.com/intranet/extra.shtml
Netscape Overview of Extranet Standards	http://sitesearch.netscape.com/products/whitepaper/extranetstds.html
ExtraNet Strategist	http://www.extranet-strategist.com/
Kerstin Forsberg's Extranet page	http://www.viktoria.informatik.gu.se/~kerstinf/extranet.htm
Extranet security paper at CSI	http://www.gocsi.com/extranet.htm

Fabric, Switched

Think of a multiconnection device in which a mesh of interconnections connects inputs on one side with outputs on the other side. Any input can be switched to any output almost instantaneously. This is a switching fabric. Now reduce it down to fit on a thumbnail-size (or smaller) chip. Switching fabrics allow fast internetwork connections between devices in LAN environments, on network backbones, or in Internet core networks.

Related Entry   Switch Fabrics and Bus Design

Failover

Failover occurs when a failing component is automatically removed from operation and a standby component is placed into service. The process of switching is called a *handover*. An important part of this process is *fault isolation*, where the failing component is isolated so it can't do any harm to the rest of the system. Some other terms related to this process include *hot spare* (a component, such as a disk drive, that is constantly updated with the latest information so that it can be switched into service) and *hot swap* (the process of handing over a hot spare).

In software systems, databases, and transaction processing systems, rollback is an important feature that ensures data integrity in the event that a transaction is not completed properly (for example, because of insufficient funds, lack of credit, a power loss, or a failed link). A *transaction monitor* is the program that monitors this process. As a user steps through a transaction, changes are made to a database. If the user needs to abort the transaction, the transaction monitor makes sure that all affected databases revert to their pretransaction states. See "Transaction Processing."

Related Entries   Clustering; Data Center Design; Disaster Planning and Recovery; Fault Tolerance and High Availability; Load Balancing; Mirrroring; RAID (Redundant Arrays of Inexpensive Disks); Replication; Storage Management Systems; Storage Systems; *and* Transaction Processing

Fast EtherChannel

See Ethernet; Link Aggregation.

Fast Ethernet

Fast Ethernet is traditional CSMA/CD (carrier sense multiple access/collision detection) access control at 100 Mbits/sec over twisted-pair wire. The original Ethernet data rate was 10 Mbits/sec.

During the early development of Fast Ethernet, two different groups worked out standards proposals—and both were finally approved, but under different IEEE committees. One standard became IEEE 802.3u Fast Ethernet and the other became 100VG-AnyLAN, which is now governed by the IEEE 802.12 committee. The latter uses the "demand priority" medium access method instead of CSMA/CD.

100VG-AnyLAN has not caught on, while Fast Ethernet enjoyed great success in enterprise LAN environments. At about the same time, switching technologies came on the scene to further improve network performance. More recently, Gigabit Ethernet has come on the scene to provide a high-speed upgrade path for Fast Ethernet users. It provides high-speed backbones that interconnect Fast Ethernet LANs. See "Gigabit Ethernet."

Fast Ethernet takes advantage of the scalability of CSMA/CD hierarchical networking. It is designed after the 10Base-T standard and can be built into hierarchical networking topologies like that shown in Figure F-1. This type of configuration is compatible with structured wiring strategies, as discussed under "TIA/EIA Structured Cabling Standards."

The primary concern of Fast Ethernet developers was to preserve the CSMA/CD medium access method of 802.3 Ethernet while boosting the data rate. In addition, the developers kept the frame format. Because of this, Fast Ethernet fits in well with traditional Ethernet installations. One version of the Fast Ethernet standard will run on older Category 3 cable installations. Multiple Ethernet types (10 and 100 Mbits/sec) may coexist. A Fast Ethernet-compatible hub simply needs to perform speed matching when exchanging frames. An autonegotiate feature allows devices to detect the speed of incoming transmissions and adjust appropriately.

There are four Fast Ethernet schemes:

- **100Base-TX**   Runs on two pairs of Category 5 data-grade twisted-pair wire with a maximum distance of 100 meters between hub and workstation.

- **100Base-T4**   Runs on four pairs of cable, including Category 3 cable, with a maximum distance of 100 meters between hub and workstation.

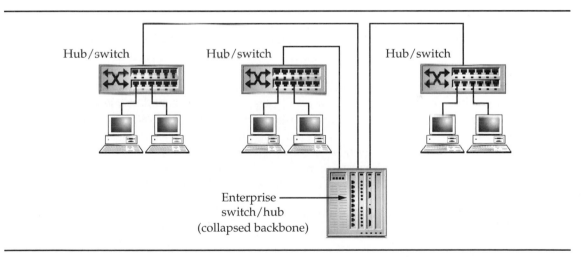

Figure F-1.   *Fast Ethernet supports hierarchical topologies.*

- **100Base-FX**   Runs on optical cable at distances up to 2 kilometers, and is used to connect hubs over long distances in a backbone configuration (e.g., a building in a campus environment).

- **100Base-SX**   Called Short Wavelength Fast Ethernet, this is a proposed standard (as of this writing) for a Fast Ethernet over fiber-optic cable using 850 nm wavelength optics. Refer to FOLS (Fiber Optics LAN Section) of the TIA at http://www.fols.org/.

The higher frequency used in the Fast Ethernet standard is prone to attenuation, so cable distance is more limited than in the Ethernet 10Base-T specification. If the encoding scheme of traditional Ethernet were used with Fast Ethernet, the high-end frequency would be above 200 Mhz. That is double the maximum frequency rating of Category 5 cable. To get around this, new encoding schemes were implemented to allow higher-frequency transmissions. Refer to the paper called "Specifications for Data Encoding in Fast Ethernet" at the Optimized Engineering Web site given later.

Note that the collision domain is $1/10^{th}$ the size of the collision domain in 10-Mbit/sec Ethernet. This is because of the 10-times increase in speed of the network. It also means that Fast Ethernet networks can only be one-tenth the physical size of a 10Base-T network.

Fast Ethernet can support full-duplex switched networking modes to provide even better performance. A full-duplex nonshared link (i.e., workstations are attached to switches, not hubs) doesn't even need CSMA/CD, because no other stations are trying to use the link, and each end system has its own channel to transmit on. Collision detection and loopback functions can be disabled. This arrangement is especially useful for backbone connections. If both end systems are transmitting at the same time, the combined data rate is 200 Mbits/sec.

100Base-TX

100Base-TX works with two pairs of UTP (unshielded twisted pair) or STP (shielded twisted pair). Transmission takes place on one pair of wires and collision detection takes place on the other pair of wires. Two types of cable can be used with this specification: Category 5 UTP and IBM's Type 1 STP. Category 5 cable has four pairs of wire. Since only two of the pairs are used, the other two are available for other uses or future expansion. However, it is not recommended that another *high-speed* network be used on the pairs.

Category 5 cable is designed to cancel out the effects of EMI and, therefore, has very stringent installation requirements. All the components in the cabling system must be Category 5 compliant, including connectors, patch panels, punchdown blocks, and hubs/switches. The twists in the cable must be maintained all the way up to within ½ inch of a connector. The twists in the cable help maintain proper signaling, especially at high data rates. Other 100Base-TX requirements are

- **Cable distance**   A link segment is the connection between a workstation and a hub or switch. The maximum link segment distance is 100 meters; but if faceplates are used, the specification recommends not exceeding 90 meters from hub to faceplate. This allows 10 meters for the faceplate-to-station connection.

- **Maximum collision domain size**   First, understand that a collision domain is a segment of a network in which all the stations on that segment hear the same broadcast. The maximum end-to-end distance between two systems within a 100Base-TX twisted-pair broadcast/collision domain segment is approximately 205 meters. This is illustrated in Figure F-2. These distances are flexible as long as the maximum is not exceeded. For example, the inter-repeater distance could be increased if the workstation-to-repeater distance is decreased.

- **Repeater hubs** Fast Ethernet repeaters are relatively sophisticated devices compared to standard Ethernet repeaters. They detect improper signals, perform data translations between different types of Fast Ethernet, monitor the network for faults, disconnect faulty ports, and partition off part of a network that is having problems so that the network can continue running. There are two types of repeater hubs in the 100Base-TX scheme:

  - *Class I repeaters* should be used if the network has mixed Fast Ethernet types (100Base-TX, 100Base-FX, and 100Base-T4) because they will change the data encoding between network types on different ports. One class I repeater is allowed per collisions domain (see "Collisions and Collision Domains" for an explanation).

  - *Class II repeaters* are strictly devices that send all incoming signals to all other ports without translation. They should be used when all the ports are supporting the same network type. Two class II repeaters are allowed per collision domain, but the link between the repeaters cannot exceed 5 meters.

F

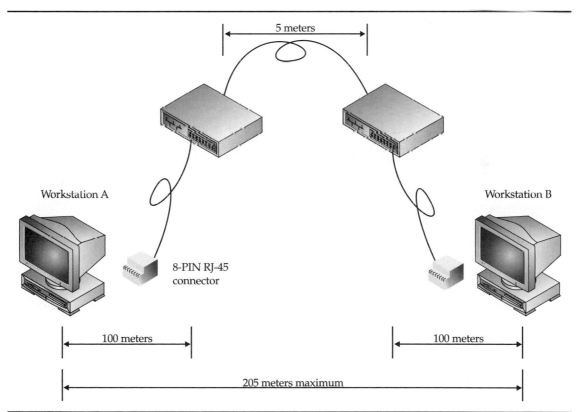

Figure F-2. *100Base-TX twisted-pair cabling configuration*

■ **Switching hubs**   To get around the hub count limitation just described, you can install switching hubs, which basically segment the network as a bridge would segment a network. Refer to "Ethernet" and "Switching and Switched Networks" for a discussion of switches and network design. Beyond plain switching is multilayer routing, which builds high-speed inexpensive routing right into the switches and allows network managers great flexibility in designing their networks. See "Multilayer Switching."

■ **Full-Duplex mode**   Full-duplex mode allows simultaneous data transmission between two end nodes without collisions. A 100Base-TX link operating in full-duplex mode has an effective bandwidth of 100 Mbits/sec. All components, including the hubs, must be full-duplex capable.

100Base-T4

The 100Base-T4 standard has the same cabling specifications as 100Base-TX in terms of distances and hub configuration. The difference is that 100Base-T4 uses all four wires in a half-duplex signaling scheme. Three pairs are used to either transmit or receive data, and the other pair is used for collision detection. 100Base-T4 also uses a special three-level encoding scheme (as opposed to two levels in other media) to reduce the clock rate. Spreading the 100-Mbit/sec signal over three pairs reduces the signal frequency and allows it to run on older Category 3 cable. Basically, 33.33 Mbits/sec is transmitted over each of the three pairs.

Higher-grade cable such as Category 5 is recommended for future expansion. Like 100Base-TX, the 100Base-T4 specification has a maximum hub-to-station cable length of 100 meters and an end-to-end maximum of 250 meters. 100Base-T4 also uses the same repeater classing scheme as 100Base-TX. Class I hubs allow a mix of different Fast Ethernet network types, and class II hubs allow only one scheme (refer to the description in the previous section).

100Base-FX

100Base-FX is the fiber-optic cable implementation of the Fast Ethernet standard. It is ideal for building backbone connections. Cable distance is limited to 412 meters; but if full-duplex mode is used, cable runs may be as long as 2 km. While fiber-optic cable can span longer distances, the limit is imposed to account for packet round-trip timing.

Fiber-optic cable is not prone to interference; and it does not emanate a signal, so it is more secure (especially for wiring across public areas). In addition, fiber-optic cable can scale up to higher transmission rates for future expansion.

100Base-FX requires a cable with two strands of 62.5/125-micron fiber. One strand is used for signal transmission while the other is used to receive and detect collisions. 100Base-FX also uses the same repeater classing scheme as 100Base-TX. Class I hubs allow mixed Fast Ethernet networks, and class II hubs allow only one scheme (refer to the description in the previous section).

Related Entries   Backbone Networks; Bridges and Bridging; Broadcast; Broadcast Domain; Broadcast Networking; Cable and Wiring; Collisions and Collision Domains; CSMA/CD (Carrier Sense Multiple Access/Collision Detection); Data Communication Concepts; Enterprise Network; Ethernet; Fast

EtherChannel; Gigabit Ethernet; IEEE 802 Standards; LAN (Local Area Network); Load Balancing; Multilayer Switching; Network Concepts; Network Design and Construction; Switching and Switched Networks; TIA/EIA Structured Cabling Standards; VLAN (Virtual LAN); *and* Wireless LANs

Linktionary!—Tom Sheldon's Encyclopedia of Networking updates	http://www.linktionary.com/f/fast_ethernet.html
Fast Ethernet Consortium	http://www.iol.unh.edu/consortiums/fe/
FOLS (Fiber Optics LAN Section) of the TIA	http://www.fols.org/
Anixter Technical Library (very informative)	http://www.anixter.com/techlib/
Charles Spurgeon's Ethernet Page	http://www.ots.utexas.edu/ethernet/100mbps.html
Optimized Engineering Corporation (see Fast Ethernet section)	http://www.optimized.com/COMPENDI/TabOfCon.htm
"Specifications for Data Encoding in Fast Ethernet" by Optimized Engineering	http://www.optimized.com/COMPENDI/FE-Encod.htm
Lantronix Networking Tutorials (see Fast Ethernet section)	http://www.lantronix.com/training/tutorials/
Cisco's Ethernet Technology page	http://www.cisco.com/univercd/cc/td/doc/cisintwk/ito_doc/ethernet.htm
Dan Kegel's Fast Ethernet Page	http://alumni.caltech.edu/~dank/fe
Network Design Guidelines by Extreme (an excellent paper describing routing, switching, and QoS considerations)	http://www.extremenetworks.com/extreme/solutions/whitepapers/pbqos.htm
Fast Ethernet Switching paper by Intel	http://www.intel.com/network/white_papers/fast_switching.htm
SMC Fast Ethernet Technology: Evaluation and Integration	http://www.ece.ac.ae/techstuff/networking/fetech.html

Refer to "Ethernet" for additional links related to this topic.

Fast IP

3Com's FastIP is a 3Com proprietary flow-driven, cut-through routing technique designed as an overlay for layer 2 switched networks. It is one of many schemes that attempt to take advantage of fast switching in layer 2 and avoid the overhead of routing every packet on a hop-by-hop basis. This topic is covered at the following Linktionary! site. Also see "Multilayer Switching" and "IP over ATM."

Linktionary!—Tom Sheldon's Encyclopedia of Networking updates	http://www.linktionary.com/f/fastip.html

Fault Management

Fault management is the ability to locate faults, determine the cause, and make corrections. It also includes implementing fault-tolerant hardware systems and fault-tolerant procedures, as discussed under "Fault Tolerance and High Availability." Fault management involves the following:

- Continuous monitoring and the collection of statistics on workstations, traffic conditions, and usage so potential faults can be forecast and avoided

- Setting threshold conditions that can warn you with alarms of conditions on the network that may cause failures

- Setting alarms that warn of performance degradation on servers, routers, and wide area network links

- Setting alarms that warn of resource usage problems, such as a server that is almost out of disk space

- The ability to remotely control workstations and other devices

- The ability to perform some or all of the preceding tasks from a single management location, which may be extremely remote from some sites

Fault management requires certain procedures, personnel, and equipment to handle alarm conditions, as listed here:

- Using pager devices to warn staff members who are not at the office

- Testing equipment such as protocol analyzers

- Preparing an inventory of spare parts

- Writing procedures that unskilled users can follow, if necessary

- Ensuring proper documentation of all systems

Management software and management protocols are available to handle some of these tasks. Some companies outsource these tasks. See "Network Management" for more information.

Related Entries   Backup and Data Archiving; Clustering; Data Migration; Data Protection; Disaster Planning and Recovery; Fault Management; Fault Tolerance and High Availability; Mirroring; Outsourcing; Power and Grounding Problems and Solutions; Redundancy; Replication; SAN (Storage Area Network); Security; Storage Management Systems; *and* Virus and Antivirus Issues

Fault Tolerance and High Availability

Fault tolerance and high availability is about keeping systems up and running 24 hours a day, 7 days a week, or at least keeping systems up and running with a reasonable amount of performance. Downed systems can cost an organization thousands of dollars per hour, as outlined in the following table:

The Cost of Internet Commerce Downtime

Web Site	Daily Internet Commerce Revenue as of 1/15/99 (U.S. $)	Lost Revenue per Hour of Downtime as of 1/15/99 (U.S. $)*
www.techdata.com	$1,000,000	$18,280
www.amazon.com	$2,700,000	$22,500
www.dell.com	$10,000,000	$91,320
www.cisco.com	$20,000,000	$182,640
www.intel.com	$33,000,000	$274,980

Lost revenue assumes a U.S. $1-million-per-day site where 20 percent of transactions are lost during downtime.
Source: Forrester Research

A fault-tolerant system is designed to keep running even after a fault has occurred. Fault-tolerant features in early network operating systems included mirrored disks, with both disks reading and writing the same information. If one disk failed, the other kept running in what is called "failover" mode. This fault tolerance was expanded to disk duplexing, in which the disks and disk controllers were duplicated. These redundant components not only provided fault tolerance, but also improved performance since disk reads could come from either disk (writes still had to be performed by both disks). Of course, fault-tolerant systems must provide more than just disk failover. Some other examples of redundant systems include the following:

- RAID disk systems combine multiple hard drives into fault-protected arrays.
- Redundant components (power supplies, I/O boards, and so on).
- Multiple servers are *clustered* to minimize problems if any of the servers should fail.
- Alternate pathing and load balancing improve throughput and provide redundant links.
- Multiple data centers to protect against local disasters.

An obvious benefit of providing these fault-tolerant features is improved performance through load balancing. In a clustered system, load balancing ensures that no single server is overworked while others are underused. At busy Web server sites, load-balancing devices can be used to balance traffic among multiple servers and to detect problems with servers or links as they occur, balancing traffic around those problems.

A failover is not a simple operation. A component may carry state information related to its activities before it failed. To maintain the highest levels of availability, this information must be tracked and carried over to another component. A sophisticated management system is necessary.

The architecture of such systems includes multiple node designs in which either both nodes are always active and providing services, or one node exactly mimics the activity of the other node in standby mode, waiting to take over should the primary fail.

High Availability

High availability (or resiliency) is a metric that indicates how well systems can function under various conditions and for a specific period of time. The goal is to provide no downtime by keeping systems up and available 24/7 (24 hour per day, 7 days a week). High-availability metrics give vendors and customers a way to gauge the level of performance they will get from a particular system. High availability is often referred to as *RAS (reliability, availability, serviceability),* referring to fault tolerance, continuous service, and the ability to service failed components without bringing a system down.

Two common ways of looking at availability are as follows:

- **MTTF (mean time to failure)**   The longer something runs, the more frequently it will fail. Therefore, it may be possible to predict the failure and replace or upgrade the units before they fail. A burn-in period is usually followed by a long running period, which then follows with failure periods.

- **MTTR (mean time to recover)**   This is a measure of downtime for a system and how long it takes to get it back up to normal operation. By installing failover components and systems, MTTR can be reduced to zero.

The reliability of different components will vary. Cables and connectors may last for hundreds of years, while circuit boards and disk drives may last only a few years. Researchers who study MTTF and MTTR have defined the following availability classes:

Availability Class	Availability Measurement	Annual Downtime
Two nines	99 percent	3.7 days
Three nines	99.9 percent	8.8 hours
Four nines	99.99 percent	53 minutes
Five nines	99.999 percent	5.3 minutes
Six nines	99.9999 percent	32 seconds

Vendors, carriers, and service providers use these values when making claims about the availability of their services or reliability of their products. The telephone switching system is a five nines system, and many people use it as a benchmark for comparing other systems. The Web sites listed at the end of this topic provide more details about these availability categories. In particular, the "High Availability" paper by Larisa Chistyakov evaluates the stages of a failure and failure response strategies.

High availability has become critical for Web e-commerce sites and mission-critical applications. But it is also a complicated endeavor. Many organizations simply choose to outsource their data centers to service providers that already have the facilities and experience to provide high availability. Examples of large data centers that are designed to provide high availability include Exodus Data Networks and GlobalCenter, a Global Crossing company. See "Data Center Design" and "NOC (Network Operations Center)."

Ways to Achieve Fault Tolerance and High Availability

Fault-tolerance techniques can be implemented by using redundant hardware and by using software techniques. There are a variety of fault-tolerant techniques, as described next:

- **Disk-level protection**   Network operating systems employ techniques to protect data being written to disk, including redundant file tables (stored in different disk locations), and hot-fix features that automatically detect bad disk blocks and move data elsewhere.

- **Transaction-monitoring systems**   A *transaction monitor* can ensure that incomplete disk writes are backed off the disk. This occurs if a system or communication link fails while information is being written to the disk. In distributed environments, a transaction can involve more than one system and database. If these databases are at different remote locations, any of the communication links or systems may fail during the write. It is the job of the transaction monitor to track the write events, and either commit or back them off. See "Transaction Processing."

- **Redundant components**   Communication devices, switches, servers, and other network devices should contain redundant components such as power supplies, multiple processors, buses, switching fabrics, fans, and I/O components ensure that no single components can bring down a system. A *hot swap* component can be replaced without downing a system.

- **Uninterruptible power**   Continuous power is an essential component. The level of power backup varies, however. Battery backups can be used for temporary outages on individual systems, but long-term outages for data centers will typically require gas- or diesel-powered generators.

- **Disk mirroring and duplexing**   Mirroring and duplexing provide protection against disk failure in servers. With mirroring, data is written to two disks at once. If one disk goes down, the other takes over until the disk is replaced. With duplexing, the disk drive adapter (channel) is duplicated as well to further protect against hardware failure. Since both disks are operational, they can provide a form of load balancing in which both disks can satisfy different read requests (writes must occur simultaneously). See "Mirroring."

- **RAIDs (redundant arrays of inexpensive disks)**   RAID systems are clusters of disks that appear as one disk to the operating system. If one disk in the array fails, the rest can still operate because a separate disk provides parity information that can supply the missing data. See "RAID (Redundant Arrays of Inexpensive Disks)."

- **Mirrored servers**   In this strategy, an entire server is duplicated to protect against the failure of any component. Data is written to both systems simultaneously, and they are interconnected with fast data links to ensure synchronization. The servers can be placed in different locations to protect against local disasters, but the links between systems must be very high speed, so the distance may be limited to the extent that a private fiber-optic link can be installed. NetWare SFT Level III for NetWare version 3 and 4 is an example. See "Mirroring" and "Servers."

- **Clustering**   A cluster is a set of servers that are connected together to provide greater availability, scalability, and performance. They can provide 99.99% availability when implemented properly. The systems often share the same storage devices. Connections among servers and storage devices are made with a gigabit/sec high-speed bus. The systems provide load balancing by sending user requests to an available server. The more systems that are added to the cluster, the better the performance and reliability. Should one server go down, the others can take over its load. See "Clustering" and "SAN (System Area Network)" for more information.

■ **Load balancing**   Load balancing refers to internal network solutions that provide multiple links among servers, switches, and routers. Loads are automatically distributed across the links. This not only improves the bandwidth, but also provides failover—if one link fails, the others can maintain communications. See "Load Balancing" for more information.

■ **Redundant communication links**   Redundant communication links between remote sites can ensure that communication stays active should one link fail. The links can be aggregated to improve throughput. Ideally, links should follow different paths to avoid local problems (storms, backhoes, or earthquakes). Note that many carriers can guarantee high levels of service, eliminating the need to establish multiple links with different carriers. See "Bonding," "Inverse Multiplexing," "Load Balancing," and "Trunking."

■ **Distributed computing**   In a distributed computing environment, data resources such as user databases or directory services are stored on multiple servers in different locations. Information is replicated from a master server and kept synchronized. Users can access data from local servers rather than servers that are at some remote site. Should a server fail, users can still access data on replicated servers. See "Distributed Computer Networks" and "Replication."

■ **Duplicate data centers**   This takes the distributed computing concept further by duplicating entire data centers to other geographic locations. One data center may run in standby mode only, continuously backing up the data at the primary data center; or a data center may run in active mode, providing services to users that are geographically in the same area. Some organizations running mission-critical applications and Web sites have no choice but to create multiple data centers or outsource some or all of their data services to service providers. See "Data Center Design" for more information.

Reliable server pools can be used to provide highly available services by using a set of servers in a pool. The IETF Reliable Server Pooling (rserpool) Working Group is developing an architecture and protocols for the management and operation of server pools supporting highly reliable applications, and for client access mechanisms to a server pool. The group is specifically addressing network fault tolerance, highly available services, resistance against malicious attacks, and scalability. The Working Group is located at http://www.ietf.org/html.charters/rserpool-charter.html.

Related Entries   ASP (Application Service Provider); Backup and Data Archiving; Clustering; Content Distribution; Data Center Design; Data Migration; Data Protection; Disaster Recovery; Distributed Computer Networks; Load Balancing; Mirroring; MPP (Massively Parallel Processor)

Systems; Multiprocessing; NUMA (Nonuniform Memory Access); Parallel Processing; Power and Grounding Problems and Solutions; RAID (Redundant Arrays of Inexpensive Disks); Redundancy; Replication; SAN (Storage Area Network); Storage Management System; Storage Systems; Symmetrical Multiprocessing; Transaction Processing; UPS (Uninterruptible Power Supply); *and* VRRP (Virtual Router Redundancy Protocol)

Linktionary!—Tom Sheldon's Encyclopedia of Networking updates	http://www.linktionary.com/f/fault_tolerance.html
Network Appliance paper: "Using NUMA Interconnects to Implement Highly Available File Server Appliances"	http://www.netapp.com/tech_library/1004.html
Compaq's fault tolerance and high availability Web site	http://www5.compaq.com/enterprise/highavailability.html
Microsoft's Reliability Web page	http://www.microsoft.com/technet/reliable/
High availability white paper by John Mehaffey	http://www.mvista.com/white/highavailability.html
Trillium links related to fault-tolerance/high availability	http://www.trillium.com/whats-new/rn_020.html
"High Availability" by Larisa Chistyokov	http://www.csdmag.com/tech/tech9803.htm
"Make It Run Forever" by Jeff Lawrence	http://www.tmcnet.com/articles/ctimag/0899/0899compass.htm
High Availability Center.com	http://www.highavailabilitycenter.com/
Novell Fault Tolerance papers	http://developer.novell.com/research/topical/netware_servers.htm
IP Metrics Software (Resiliency with NIC Arrays)	http://www.ipmetrics.com/ipms/Solutions.html
A Conceptual Framework for Systems Fault Tolerance	http://hissa.ncsl.nist.gov/chissa/SEI_Framework/framework_8.html
The Center for Reliable and High-Performance Computing	http://www.crhc.uiuc.edu/
3Com White papers (see High Availability Networks section)	http://www.3com.com/technology/tech_net/white_papers/index.html
Stratus	http://www.stratus.com/
Data Connection High Availability Framework	http://www.dataconnection.com/mpls/highavfr.htm
"Highly Available Embedded Computer Platforms Become Reality," a Web ProForums tutorial	http://www.iec.org/tutorials/ha_embed/
"Carrier-Grade, High-Availability Computing Platforms for Voice and Data Networks," a Web ProForums tutorial	http://www.iec.org/tutorials/car_grade/index.html

FAX Servers and Network Faxing

Fax servers are computers with fax devices that manage incoming and outgoing faxes. Users at workstations can avoid lines at the office fax machine by simply sending faxes from their desktop to the fax server. Because the fax server is shared by many users, it reduces the need to install many individual fax devices throughout a company. Most fax servers also provide inbound services, which route incoming faxes to users on a network. Fax servers can keep log files of faxing activities for later scrutiny and manage the fax address books for a company.

Faxing out is relatively easy compared to handling incoming faxes. There are a number of ways to handle inbound faxes. The easiest method is to print the faxes directly at the fax server, and then have someone distribute the faxes to recipients. But this method is inefficient and lacks privacy. Another method is to have someone at the fax computer route received faxes from the fax server across the network to recipients. Automated delivery systems that perform this task are the best. Many deliver faxes to the internal user's electronic mail box.

Some systems require that senders enter touchtone codes to direct faxes to specific recipients, but this puts too much reliance on the sender. Another method is called *DID (direct inward dialing)*, and it relies on the phone company to create a virtual fax phone number for each recipient in your organization but routes all incoming faxes to your fax server. The fax server then routes the faxes to the recipient's fax phone number. DID requires compatible fax boards, which can be more costly, but the price for the service from the phone company is relatively cheap.

A fax server will usually require quite a few telephone lines to handle the incoming and outgoing faxing requirements of an organization. Some of the companies mentioned in Related Entries provide boards that can handle multiple lines. In fact, some boards support the use of T1 lines, which provide 24 voice/fax channels. Check with the vendors listed in the next section for more information.

Companies can also set up fax information services. Users on the network or users dialing in can select from lists of documents by pressing buttons on their phones or choosing from menus on their computers. The information is then faxed to them by the fax server.

Internet Fax

Internet fax (sometimes called FoIP or Fax over IP) falls into the realm of IP telephony. The usual technique is to install an IP telephony gateway that provides an interface to the Internet. IP telephony gateways have become popular as companies take advantage of the Internet to handle some (if not all) voice calls.

One technique helps reduce the cost of long-distance charges. A fax is sent to a local fax gateway. This gateway may be part of an organization or a service provided within the local calling area. The fax is converted to electronic mail and forwarded over the Internet to a fax gateway in the calling area of the destination fax machine. This fax gateway sends the fax to the destination fax machine.

There are two primary methods for faxing over the Internet:

- **Store-and-forward fax** This is similar to e-mail in that it takes advantage of store-and-forward concepts. The fax is sent to an Internet fax server and then forwarded. This technique does not have the real-time aspect of standard fax transmission; but that is not always important, and it is often more efficient to send some faxes after hours to reduce traffic. The store-and-forward fax via e-mail technique is defined in the ITU T.37 fax protocol.

- ■ **Realtime fax over IP**   This is defined in the ITU T.38 standard. It defines the ability to send a fax in real time and receive confirmation of delivery. Basically, T.38 fax devices can communicate directly to Internet-capable communication devices, including T.38 gateways.

When a fax is sent as e-mail (T.37), the fax image is attached to the e-mail in the compressed TIFF (Tag Image File Format) format. This format represents the data content and structure generated by the current suite of ITU-T Recommendations for Group 3 facsimile. There are a number of ITU profiles as outlined in RFC 2301, "File Format for Internet Fax," (March 1998). RFC 2304, "Minimal FAX Address Format in Internet Mail," (March 1998) describes a simple method of encoding PSTN addresses of facsimile devices in the local part of Internet e-mail addresses. Also see RFC 2879, "Content Feature Schema for Internet Fax," (August 2000) and RFC 2880, "Internet Fax T.30 Feature Mapping," (August 2000).

The IETF Internet Fax Working Group did a lot of the work of standardizing message-based fax over the Internet. It completed its work, but you can still go to the group's Web page and access drafts and RFCs. The Web site is given below.

Related Entries   Access Server; Communication Services and Providers; Electronic Mail; Instant Messaging; Modems; PBX (Private Branch Exchange); Servers; Unified Messaging; *and* VoIP (Voice over IP)

Linktionary!—Tom Sheldon's Encyclopedia of Networking updates	http://www.linktionary.com/f/fax.html
IETF Working Group. Internet Fax (fax)	http://www.ietf.org/html.charters/fax-charter.html
Electronic Messaging Association (search for "fax")	http://www.ema.org/
Davidson Consulting (see Fax and Unified Messaging sections)	http://www.davidsonconsulting.com/
Voice and Fax over Internet Protocol (V/FoIP) Tutorial	http://www.webproforum.com/vfoip/
Hello Direct.com (search for fax in tutorials)	http://www.hellodirect.com/
Faximum "FAQ about Fax"	http://www.faximum.com/faqs/fax
The World Wide Web Virtual Library Facsimile section	http://www.faximum.com/w3vlib/fax
FAQ: "How can I send a fax from the Internet?"	http://www.savetz.com/fax/
MessageClick Unified Messaging Services	http://www.messageclick.com/
Bristol Group	http://www.bg.com
Brooktrout	http://www.brooktrout.com
Castelle	http://www.castelle.com
Dialogic	http://www.dialogic.com

Genoa Technology	http://www.gentech.com
Interstar Technologies	http://www.faxserver.com
Natural MicroSystems	http://www.nmss.com
NetCentric	http://www.netcentric.com
Optus Sofware	http://www.facsys.com
Softlinx	http://www.softlinx.com

FDDI (Fiber Distributed Data Interface)

FDDI is a 100-Mbit/sec networking technology developed by the ANSI (American National Standards Institute) X3T9.5 committee. It was originally designed for fiber-optic cable, but was later modified to support copper cable over shorter distances. Before Fast Ethernet and Gigabit Ethernet came along, FDDI was commonly used in the LAN and campus environment, as well as a backbone to tie together devices on service provider networks and at exchange points on the Internet. FDDI uses a redundant dual-ring topology that supports 500 nodes over a maximum distance of 100 kilometers (60 miles). Such distances also qualify FDDI for use as a MAN (metropolitan area network). The dual counter-rotating rings offer redundancy (fault tolerance). If a link fails or the cable is cut, the network continues operating as shown on the right in Figure F-3. Each station contains relays that join the rings in case of a break or bypass the station in case it is having problems.

FDDI has been used extensively as a network backbone topology. LAN segments, server farms, and mainframe systems are typically connected to the backbone. The usual configuration was to connect up to ten Ethernet LANs (10 Mbits/sec) to the FDDI network

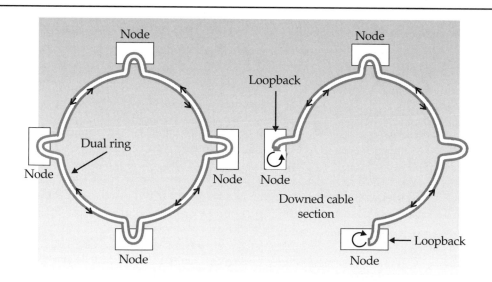

Figure F-3. *FDDI counter-rotating rings*

(100 Mbits/sec), and then attach servers to the FDDI ring itself. See "Backbone Networks" for more information.

FDDI operates over single-mode and multimode fiber-optic cable, as well as STP (shielded twisted-pair) and UTP (unshielded twisted-pair) copper cable, as discussed next.

CDDI (Copper Distributed Data Interface) is an alternative cabling technology that follows the FDDI standard. It uses UTP copper wire. It was originally proposed by IBM, DEC, Cabletron Systems, Crescendo Communications, and others. The ANSI TP-PMD (Twisted-Pair-Physical Medium Dependent) standard defines an FDDI network that runs over Category 5 data-grade cable and IBM Type 1 STP cable. It provides the features of normal FDDI, except for a difference in the distance of the cable. UTP supports 100 meters (330 feet) between nodes while fiber supports 2 kilometers between nodes.

At one point, there were attempts to extend FDDI. One attempt was FDDI-II, which was an attempt to support real-time traffic by dividing the bandwidth into 16 dedicated channels. FDDI-II failed as Fast Ethernet and other superior solutions appeared.

FDDI Configuration

As mentioned, the maximum ring length is 100 km. In addition, the maximum distance between adjacent stations is 2 km. The topology is what is called a physical ring of trees; but logically, the entire network forms a ring. The two FDDI rings are known as the primary ring and the secondary ring. Both may be used as a transmission path or one may be set aside for use as a backup in the event of a break in the primary ring.

Note in Figure F-4 that you can trace the route of the primary ring through each device. In this illustration, the secondary ring is basically in standby mode and is capable of re-forming the ring should any link in the network be broken.

There are three types of devices that can attach to the ring:

- **DAS (dual attached station)**   Connected to both rings, such as a critical server and other pieces of equipment
- **DAC (dual attached concentrator)**   Connected to both rings and provides a connection point for stations
- **SAS (single attached station)**   Attached to the primary ring via a concentrator

A dual-attached device can bridge the ring if it is cut at some point. Single attached devices cannot do this bridging, but they are cheaper. If a computer attached to an FDDI concentrator fails, the concentrator ensures the ring is maintained, not the FDDI adapter in the computer.

Because FDDI implements a logical ring in a physical star, you can build hierarchical networks. This can be done using an actual *cable ring* or a *concentrator-based ring*. To build a cable ring, you connect stations to one another in a ring configuration. A disadvantage of this technique is that if two stations fail or the cable is cut in two locations, the network will fail. The alternative is to build a concentrator-based ring. A concentrator is a multiport hub. Devices are attached to the hub. If any devices fail, the ring is maintained. This technique requires a cable from the concentrator to each device, but it is considered superior to the cable ring method.

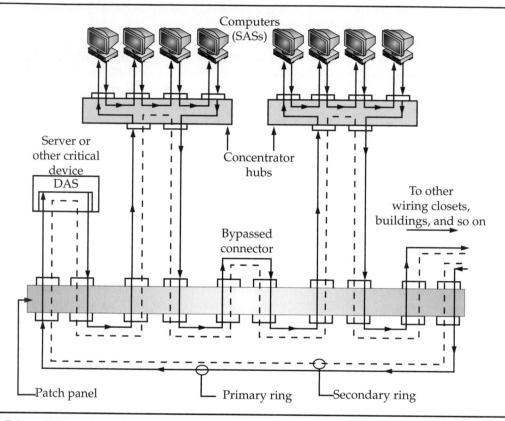

Figure F-4. *FDDI configuration*

FDDI Operation and Access Method

FDDI uses a token-passing access method. A token frame is passed around the network from station to station; if a station needs to transmit, it acquires the token. The station then transmits a frame and removes it from the network after it makes a full loop. A regulation mechanism is used to prevent one station from holding the token for too long. The FDDI frame size is 1,500 bytes.

To accommodate high-volume stations, the network administrator can prioritize the station, basically giving it a longer period of time to transmit before releasing the token. Note the features listed here:

- Directly attached FDDI stations act like repeaters. They receive packets from their upstream neighbor and send them to their downstream neighbor. When a node sees its own address in a packet, it copies the packet into its own memory.

- Multiple frames can exist on the network. If a station relinquishes the token while its frames are still in transit, other stations can begin transmitting.

- A management mechanism called *station management* enables system administrators to manage and monitor FDDI networks, isolate faulty nodes, and route traffic.

FDDI has two transmission modes. *Asynchronous ring mode* is token based. Any station can access the network by acquiring the token. In this mode, traffic is not prioritized. *Synchronous token-passing ring mode* allows prioritization. FDDI cards with synchronous capabilities give network managers the ability to set aside part of the bandwidth for time-sensitive traffic. Asynchronous workstations then contend for the rest. Synchronous capabilities are added via software upgrades.

Related Entries   Backbone Networks; Cable and Wiring; Data Communication Concepts; Fiber-Optic Cable; Network Concepts; Network Design and Construction; *and* Optical Networks

Linktionary!—Tom Sheldon's Encyclopedia of Networking updates	http://www.linktionary.com/f/fddi.html
FDDI Consortium (see FDDI sections)	http://www.iol.unh.edu/consortiums/
FDDI Frequently Asked Questions (FAQ)	http://www.cicese.mx/~aarmenta/frames/redes/fddi/FDDIFAQ.html
Optimized Engineering Corporation FDDI tutorial	http://www.optimized.com/COMPENDI/L1-FDDI.htm
Cisco FDDI documentation	http://www.cisco.com/univercd/cc/td/doc/cisintwk/ito_doc/fddi.htm
Cisco documentation: Troubleshooting FDDI	http://www.cisco.com/univercd/cc/td/doc/cisintwk/itg_v1/tr1905.htm
Cisco CDDI/FDDI Adapters and Concentrators	http://www.cisco.com/univercd/cc/td/doc/product/cddi/index.htm
ANSI X3T12 (FDDI) Home Page	http://www.nswc.navy.mil/ITT/x3t12/
FDDI Links at Netfusion	http://www.nwfusion.com/netresources/fddi.html

FDM (Frequency Division Multiplexing)

Multiplexing is a technique used to combine multiple channels of information onto a single circuit or within a specific bandwidth range of a wireless system. At the other end of the circuit, the information is demultiplexed so that the individual channels can be extracted. Frequency division multiplexing allocates bands at specific frequencies for each multiplexed channel. See "Multiplexing" for the complete discussion.

Related Entries   Channel; Circuit; Modulation Techniques; Multiplexing and Multiplexers; VOFDM (Vector Orthogonal Frequency Division Multiplexing); *and* Wireless Communications

Fiber-Optic Cable

Fiber-optic cable employs photons for the transmission of digital signals across a strand of ultrapure silica (or plastic in some cases). Photons pass through the cable with negligible resistance. The silica is so pure that, according to Michael Coden of Codenoll Technologies Corporation, a 3-mile-thick window made of the purified silica would give you the same view as a 1/8-inch-thick glass window. As optical system requirements increase, the purity of the cable becomes even more important. The best cable from Corning and Lucent is free of all but the smallest trace elements of iron and other metals, as well as hydroxyl ions, which are present due to water molecules in the cable.

Note that optical systems operate in the infrared range, but the term "light" is typically used for clarity.

A fiber-optic cable guides light from end to end. A signal is injected in one end by an LED (light-emitting diode) or by semiconductor lasers. LEDs can generate signals up to about 300 Mbits/ sec. Lasers can generate signals in the multi-gigabit/sec range. LEDs are used for short-distance optical links such as enterprise backbones while lasers are used for longer distance networks. Lasers are also capable of the higher power levels needed for long-haul backbone links.

Lasers produce light in "windows" of the near infrared range as listed in the following table. A window is an infrared range that is optimized for optical transmissions. The ITU recently defined the following spectral bands in order to clarify the terminology that is used for fiber-optic systems. These definitions are meant for classification purposes only.

Band	Descriptor	Range (nm)
O band	Original	1260 to 1360
E band	Extended	1360 to 1460
S band	Short wavelength	1460 to 1530
C band	Conventional	1530 to 1565
L band	Long wavelength	1565 to 1625
U band	Ultralong wavelength	1625 to 1675

Figure F-5 illustrates the structure of fiber-optic cable. The *core* is the transparent silica (or plastic) through which the light travels. The *cladding* is a glass sheath that surrounds the core. The cladding acts like a mirror, reflecting light back into the core. The cladding itself is covered with a plastic coating and strength material when appropriate.

Figure F-6 illustrates the different paths that light will take through a fiber cable, depending on the type of cable. If the core is wide and there is a sharp transition between the core and the

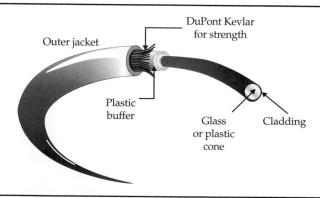

Figure F-5.   *Fiber-optic cable structure*

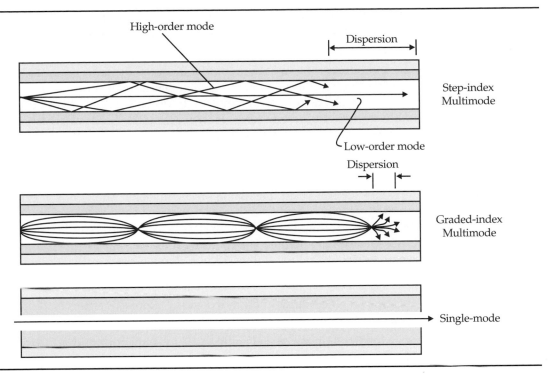

Figure F-6. *Light dispersion in fiber-optic cable*

cladding, high-order rays will follow reflected paths while low order modes will follow straighter paths. This causes some of the rays to arrive at the source at a different time— a phenomenon called *modal dispersion*, as discussed later. Dispersion limits cable distance. Graded-index cable can help resolve the problem, or a small core can be used as in the single-mode cable. An animation that demonstrates the way that light travels through fiber cable is at the Bell Labs Web site given later.

Plastic core cable is used for short-distance applications, such as airplane wiring and wiring for some buildings. The remainder of this topic covers silica-based fiber-optic cable.

Silica cable is categorized as either *multimode cable*, which is used for short-distance connections (LANs, campus networks, and short-distance metro networks), or *single-mode cable* that is used for long-distance (cross-country networks and intercontinental submarine links). The light source for the former is typically an LED, while the light source for the latter is a laser. Long-haul fiber-optic cable is often bundled with anywhere from 100 to 800 fibers per cable.

■ **Multimode cable** This cable has a relatively large diameter core (50 to 80 microns) and a total diameter of 125 microns. *Step-index multimode cable* has an abrupt change between core and cladding while *graded-index multimode cables* has a gradual change between core and cladding. The former is limited to about 50 Mbits/sec, while the latter is limited to 1 Gbit/sec. With graded cable, the amount of refraction gradually drops outward from the core. Light travels faster in a material in which refraction is lower. This causes the light traveling through the outer material to travel faster than light at the core. The end result is that all the light tends to arrive at the same time. But this fix still has distance limitations.

- **Single mode (monomode) cable**   The single-mode cables are the most important cables for long-haul use (carrier and Internet core). The cable has a small core (7 to 10 microns) that forces the light to follow a more linear single path down the cable, as opposed to the multipath reflections of multimode cable. However, another form of dispersion, called *chromatic dispersion*, is a problem (as discussed later). Lasers are the usual light source. This cable is the most expensive and hardest to handle, but it has the highest bandwidths and distance ratings.

Cable specifications list the core and cladding diameters as fractional numbers. For example, the minimum recommended cable type for FDDI (Fiber Distributed Data Interface) is 62.5/ 125-micron multimode fiber-optic cable. That means the core is 62.5 microns and the core with surrounding cladding is a total of 125 microns. The cladding diameter must be the same when joining cables because connectors typically use the cladding diameter as a guide for aligning the core.

- The core specifications for step-index and graded-index *multimode* cables is typically 50, 62.5, or 100 microns. The cladding diameter for step-mode cable is 125 microns.
- The core diameter for single-mode cable is typically 7 to 10 microns with a cladding diameter of 125 microns.

The ITU has defined a series of recommendations that describe the geometrical properties and transmissive properties of multimode and single-mode fiber-optic cables. The four most important recommendations are listed here:

- **ITU G.651**   Covers *multimode* graded-index fiber-optic cable having a 50-micron nominal core diameter and a 125-micron nominal cladding diameter.
- **ITU G.652**   Covers *single-mode* NDSF (non-dispersion-shifted fiber). This cable constitutes most of the cable that was installed in the 1980s. Transmissions take place in the 1,310-nm range where there is minimal signal dispersion. Dispersion causes signal problems over long distances, as described later. G.652 cable supports the following distances and data rates: 1000 km at 2.5 Gbits/sec, 60 km at 10 Gbits/sec, and 3 km at 40 Gbits/sec.
- **ITU G.653**   Covers *single-mode* dispersion-shifted optical fiber cable. The cable is designed in a way to "shift" the region where dispersion is minimized to the 1,550-nm wavelength range. At this range attenuation is also minimized, so longer distance cables are possible.
- **ITU G.655**   Covers *single-mode* NZ-DSF (nonzero dispersion-shifted fiber) cable, which takes advantage of dispersion characteristics that suppress the growth of four-wave mixing, an effect that is harmful to WDM (wavelength division multiplexing) systems. NZ-DSF supports high-power signals and longer distances, as well as closely spaced DWDM (dense WDM) channels at rates of 10 Gbits/sec or higher. Lucent True Wave

is an example of this cable. It supports the following distances and data rates: 6000 km at 2.5 Gbits/sec, 400 km at 10 Gbits/sec, and 25 km at 40 Gbits/sec.

G.655 is the latest development in fiber-optic cable. In particular, G.655 is optimized for WDM and long-distance cable runs such as submarine cables. It uses dispersion to advantage. Dispersion can help reduce an effect called *four-wave mixing (FWM)*, which occurs in DWDM systems when three wavelengths mix in such a way to produce a fourth wavelength that overlays and interferes with the original signals.

With DWDM, a single fiber can potentially carry thousands of lambda circuits. A lambda is a specific subwavelength of light within one of the windows of light. It provides all the capabilities of an individual circuit. Lambdas are set up using frequency division multiplexing. Think of each lambda as a specific color of infrared light transmitting at 10 Gbits/sec or more. An optical multiplexer divides the available spectrum on the cable up into many individual lambdas. For example, the Avanex PowerMux can put over 800 channels on a single fiber with spacing between channels of 12.5 gigahertz. With the potential of thousands of lambdas per fiber, it is practical for carriers to lease entire optical wavelengths to businesses. See "Optical Networks."

An alternative to DWDM are new optical modulation techniques that boost the capacity of existing cables. Kestrel Solution's Optical FDM combines FDM (frequency division multiplexing), DSP (digital signal processing), and optical modulation to improve performance on existing fiber cables, especially in metropolitan areas where low-quality fiber has been installed (due to short distances) and in SONET systems. Optical FDM gives full access to the total bandwidth of the cable.

Cable Performance Characteristics

Fiber cable has certain characteristics that limit its performance. Cable from different manufacturers may exhibit variations in these characteristics. The primary performance limiters are attenuation and dispersion.

Attenuation, EDFAs, and Raman Amplifiers

Attenuation is signal loss over distance. Think of the light pulses as loosing their energy and flattening out as they travel down the cable. High attenuation will result in errors at the receiver. Attenuation is not a problem for metro-area networks, but it puts distance limitations on long-haul backbone networks. Three types of devices may be used to overcome attenuation:

- **Electronic regenerator**   This device *regenerates* signals by first converting optical signals to electrical signals. The electrical signal is regenerated, converted back to optical, and injected back into the fiber. Regenerators are too inefficient for modern high-speed optical networks due to electrical regeneration requirements. On WDM systems, each wavelength requires its own opto-electric amplifier, an expensive proposition if there are many wavelengths.

- **EDFA (erbium-doped fiber amplifier)**   This device is an *amplifier* rather than a signal regenerator. It directly amplifies optical signals without a need to do the optical-to-electrical conversion. An EDFA contains a short strand of erbium-doped fiber and two signal inputs. One input is the optical signal that needs to be amplified. The other is light from a pump laser that excites the erbium atoms so that they give up photons that amplify incoming optical signal photons as described later. Thank Albert Einstein for this "trick" of light magic.

- **EDFA/Raman amplifier combination**   Raman amplification is an add-on component that enhances EDFA optical amplifiers. At each EDFA amplifier, a Raman pump injects high-power laser light into the fiber *in the opposite direction* of the source signal. The injected photons boost the optical signal where it is needed most—at the far end of the laser signal where it is experiencing the most attenuation. Raman amplification can create signal gain of up to 10 dB, which allows longer distance cable runs. It also allows optical networks to obtain transmission rates as high as 40 Gbits/sec.

EDFAs are crucial to WDMA systems because a single amplifier boosts all the wavelengths simultaneously. With older electrical regenerators, one regenerator is required for each wavelength, meaning that an entire stack of regenerators is needed at each regeneration point.

The 1,550 range (C band) is often called "erbium window" because the energy level of erbium ions is close to the energy level of photons in the C band. Through the process of stimulated emission, erbium can be coaxed into releasing energy that amplifies light in the C-band. The process is as follows. The EDFA amplifier pumps photons into the erbium-doped cable. Erbium atoms absorb photons, which cause electrons to jump to a temporary excited state. When an electron decays, it releases a photon that is absorbed by the signal photons. Thus, the optical signal passing through the cable is amplified without any electrical conversion.

Dispersion

Another characteristic is *dispersion,* which is the broadening of a light pulse as it travels down the cable. Excessive dispersion will make a signal difficult to read by the receiver. When an LED or laser sends light into a multimode fiber, a range of wavelengths of light is present. Some of those wavelengths travel at different speeds than others. The effect is to distort waveforms, which can cause errors in reading the signal at the other end of the cable. Graded-index cable is designed to minimize the delay of the slower wavelengths.

There are four types of dispersion:

- **Material dispersion**   Variations in the refractive properties of the cable cause signal dispersion.

- **Modal dispersion**   Occurs in multimode cable. Light takes different paths through the cable with light on some paths having a longer travel time than others. Graded cable balances this effect.

- **Chromatic dispersion**   This occurs because some wavelengths travel through a medium faster than others. The longer the cable, the worse the effect, and the harder it is to read the signal.

- **Waveguide dispersion**   This dispersion occurs in single-mode fiber due to the difference in the speed of the signal between the core and the cladding. It causes chromatic dispersion.

G.652 cable, used in most commercial systems, takes advantage of the 1,310-nm window where chromatic dispersion is minimized. This window is often called the *zero-dispersion point*—it is the range where chromatic dispersion is minimized because the waveguide dispersion cancels out material dispersion.

Long-haul carriers, on the other hand, have higher bandwidth and distance requirements, so G.653 and G.655 "dispersion-shifted" fiber operating in the C band is preferred. The C band is used for DWDM systems, which support many closely spaced channels at data rates of 10 Gbits/sec and higher. Two other bands are now being used to boost capacity and distance: the 1,460 nm to 1,530 nm S band and the 1565 to 1625 L band. A newer approach employs soliton technology, which can be used to create a cable system that stretches nearly halfway around the world. See "Soliton."

Note that it is possible to support DWDM on many older fiber cables. Standard single-mode fiber will support DWDM at lower data rates. Some older dispersion-shifted fibers were not able to handle DWDM, but these cables may be made to act like nonzero dispersion cable by using wavelength above and below the 1,550-nm window.

Corning and Lucent are the major providers of long-haul cable. Lucent's TrueWave and AllWave cables are made of single-mode nonzero dispersion fibers that support all the wavelength windows. TrueWave is specifically designed for optically amplified, high-powered long-distance DWDM networks operating in both the C band and the L band. Both cable types are manufactured with a patented purification process to remove water molecules in the core, thus allowing wider spectrum usage.

Corning's LEAF is a single-mode NZ-DSF fiber designed for DWDM systems. It combines low attenuation and low dispersion with an effective area that is 32 percent larger than non-NZ-DSF fiber. This allows more power to be pumped into the network over more channels without nonlinear effects that create noise, distort signals, and degrade performance. It can operate at 10 Gbits/sec or higher using high-output-power EDFAs.

Corning's MetroCor fiber is a single-mode NZ-DSF cable optimized for short-distance metropolitan usage. It does not require the powerful lasers that are required in the long-haul environment and so helps reduce the cost of implementing metropolitan fiber networks.

For more information about metropolitan optical networks, see "FTTH (Fiber to the Home)," "MAN (Metropolitan Area Network)," and "PON (Passive Optical Network)."

Related Entries   Backbone Networks; Cable and Wiring; Data Communication Concepts; DPT (Dynamic Packet Transport); DTM (Dynamic Synchronous Transfer Mode); Lambda Circuits; Network Concepts; Network Core Technologies; Network Design and Construction; OC (Optical Carrier); Optical Networks; OSRP (Optical Signaling & Routing Protocol); OXYGEN; PON (Passive Optical Network); Soliton; SONET (Synchronous Optical Network); Testing, Diagnostics, and Troubleshooting; TIA/EIA Structured Cabling Standards; *and* WDM (Wavelength Division Multiplexing)

Linktionary!—Tom Sheldon's Encyclopedia of Networking updates	http://www.linktionary.com/f/ fiber-optic.html
Bell Labs "Understanding Lightwave Transmissions" Web page	http://www.bell-labs.com/technology/ lightwave/
National Academy of Sciences laser and fiber-optic presentation	http://www4.nas.edu/beyond/ beyonddiscovery.nsf/web/laser

Web ProForum papers: "Fiber-Optic Technology" and "Raman Amplification Design in WDM Systems." (There are numerous other optical networking papers here.)	http://www.iec.org/tutorials/
Photonic Resources on the Web, sponsored by Avanex	http://www.photonicresources.com/
Corning Fiber	http://www.corningfiber.com
Lucent Optical Fiber Solutions page	http://www.lucent.com/ofs/
Lucent's Optical Networking Resources page	http://www.lucent-optical.com/resources/
Lightwave On-Line Magazine devoted to optical networking	http://lw.pennwellnet.com/home/home.cfm
Light Reading (Optical Networking information)	http://www.lightreading.com
Optimized Engineering Corporation Fiber Optics information	http://www.optimized.com/COMPENDI/L1-fiber.htm
Laser Glossary by Alessandro Nordio	http://docenti.ing.unipi.it/~d7384/com_ottiche/LaserGlossario.html

Fiber to the Curb/Fiber to the Home

See FTTH (Fiber to the Home); PON (Passive Optical Network).

Fiberless Optical Networking

See Optical Networks.

Fibre Channel

Fibre Channel is a gigabit interconnect technology for data center and SANs (Storage Area Networks). It is designed primarily to interconnect peripherals, mass storage systems, imaging and archiving systems, mainframes, supercomputers, engineering workstations, and other high-speed devices. Fibre Channel has features of a network, but it is not a network in the traditional sense. Instead, it is a high-speed switching system that uses fiber-optic cable to interconnect computing devices in a relatively local environment, such as a laboratory or a campus environment, as shown in Figure F-7.

Fibre Channel supports point-to-point links, scalable-bandwidth switched circuits, and arbitrated loops (shared-bandwidth loop circuits). It is an important connection technology in the SAN (Storage Area Network) environment. The speed of Fibre Channel is its most distinguishing feature: it provides bandwidth in the range of 266 megabits/second to over 4 gigabits/second over a variety of cable types, including multimode fiber, coaxial cable, and shielded twisted-pair wire. Fibre Channel also supports distances up to 10 km. Additional features are listed here.

- Delivery confirmation, used for reliability or disabled to improve performance
- Supports ARP, RARP, and other self-discovery protocols
- Connection-oriented virtual circuits to guarantee quality of service for critical backups or other operations

■ Supports real-time applications like video using fractional bandwidth virtual circuits

■ Variable frame sizes, allowing bulk data transfers to be done with the largest frame size possible.

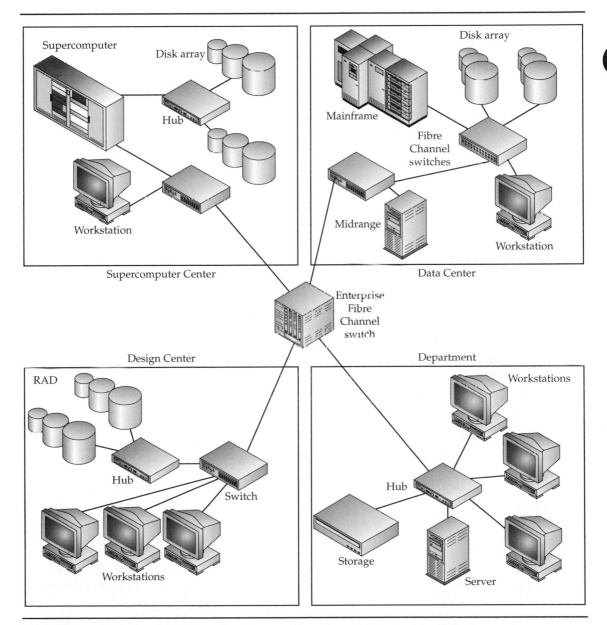

Figure F-7. *Fibre Channel configuration (source: Fibre Channel Industry Association)*

The ANSI (American National Standards Institute) X3T9 committee developed the Fibre Channel Interconnect standard. The NCITS (National Committee for Information Technology Standards) Technical Committee T11 is responsible for device-level interfaces and has been working on the Fibre Channel standard, as well as HIPPI (High Performance Parallel Interface). HIPPI is T11.1 and Fibre Channel is T11.2.

Where Fibre Channel Fits In

Existing network technologies such as Ethernet use data-framing techniques to transport data over a shared medium. This strategy is not ideal for communication between high-speed workstations and peripheral devices. LAN technologies such as Ethernet were not meant to handle the high-speed data processing in computer center environments.

The Fibre Channel interface dedicates circuits for transferring data, while allowing other devices to access the channel when it is free. If multiple sessions must run simultaneously, that is possible, too. There are three possible connection types with Fibre Channel:

- *Point-to-point device connections* for high transfer rates over greater distances. An example would be a direct connection between a RAID disk system and a superserver. Notice that this point-to-point connection can occur over a network that other users share, but the cable is unavailable until the communication session is complete.

- *Cluster (workgroup) connections* for high-speed workstations.

- *Switched connections* for supporting Ethernet, FDDI, and token ring networks that allow multiple, simultaneous point-to-point connections between workstations.

Fibre Channel transports data coming from devices by simply reading the buffer information, packaging it, and sending it across the switch fabric. Underlying data formats, packet structures, or frame types are not important in the switching scheme. Fibre Channel overcomes device restrictions, as well. Consider the SCSI interface. You can normally connect up to 8 or 16 devices to a SCSI adapter. With Fibre Channel switching, you could connect millions of devices.

As mentioned, Fibre Channel can establish dedicated, point-to-point connections between devices. These connections are like circuits, and multiple high-bandwidth circuits can exist simultaneously. The circuits are bidirectional and can provide gigabits/second throughput in both directions. When a device wishes to transmit over a switching device or network, it simply attempts to get a dedicated circuit to that device. See "SANs (Storage Area Networks)."

Fibre Channel can be compared to ATM. But Fibre Channel makes a better peripheral connection technology, while ATM is better for network backbones in the WAN environment, or for teleconferencing applications, due to its built-in QoS (Quality of Service). Latency (delay) is another thing to consider. Fibre Channel uses frame sizes that are 2KB in size. Only about 1.5 percent of this frame is used for header information. On the other hand, ATM cells are 53 bytes long, and 10 percent is used for header information. What this means is that Fibre Channel will transfer more data than ATM under comparable conditions. However, ATM's fixed cell size is better at multiplexing for large volumes of traffic from many different sources.

Fibre Channel can also be compared to Gigabit Ethernet. But Gigabit Ethernet is designed to be backward compatible with previous versions of Ethernet and it retains the same frame structure. Fibre Channel's frame structure is designed to move large amounts of data very quickly.

Network administrators should consider using Fibre Channel in storage environments and as network connections for high-bandwidth devices and users. The Web sites listed at the end of this section provide additional information on Fibre Channel usage.

Fibre Channel Arbitrated Loop (FC-AL) is a recent enhancement to the standard that supports copper media and loops containing up to 126 devices, or nodes. It was developed with storage connectivity in mind. Devices can be hot-swapped without disrupting the network, and the system is fault tolerant.

SCSI-FCP (Small Computer System Interface-Fibre Channel Protocol) is an implementation of Fibre Channel that transports SCSI protocols. SCSI is a disk interface technology that normally runs over a parallel connection. SCSI-FCP is a serial SCSI that allows SCSI-based applications to use an underlying Fibre Channel connection. SCSI-FCP is widely used to connect high-performance servers to storage subsystems, especially in the SAN environment. It provides higher performance (100 Mbits/sec), supports cable lengths up to 10km, and can address up to 16 million devices. Data is transferred in frames rather than blocks.

FICON (Fibre Connection) is a mainframe connectivity product for storage devices that IBM is using as a replacement to its ESCON (Enterprise Systems Connection) channels. While ESCON's throughput is 17 MB/sec, FICON operates at 100 MB/sec. FICON supports full-duplex operation.

FC-IP is a method of encapsulating Fibre Channel frames within TCP/IP packets. This allows different Fibre Channel networks to interconnect across a TCP/IP network. For example, an organization could connect two data centers running Fibre Channel SANs via FC-IP.

FSPF (Fabric Shortest Path First) is an inter-switch routing protocol that routes data among Fibre Channel switches. With FSPF, different vendors can build Fibre Channel switches that can work together.

RFC 2625, "IP and ARP over Fibre Channel," (June 1999) specifies how IP and ARP are encapsulated over Fibre Channel and describes a mechanism for IP address resolution.

The IETF IP Storage (ips) Working Group is developing protocols for encapsulating SCSI and Fibre Channel in an IP-based transport or transports. The Working Group's Web site is at http://www.ietf.org/html.charters/ips-charter.html

Emerging technologies that compete with Fibre Channel are covered in "Switch Fabrics and Bus Design."

Related Entries   ATM (Asynchronous Transfer Mode); Clustering; DAFS (Direct Access File System); Data Center Design; Data Communication Concepts; Firewire; Gigabit Ethernet; HPPI (High-Performance Parallel Interface); HSSI (High-Speed Serial Interface); IP Storage; LVDS (Low-Voltage Differential Signaling); Multiprocessing; Network Concepts; Network Connection Technologies; Network Design and Construction; Parallel Interface; SAN (Storage Area Network); SCSI (Small Computer System Interface); Serial Communication and Interfaces; Servers; SSA (Serial Storage Architecture); Storage Management Systems; Storage Systems; Switch Fabrics and Bus Design; Switching and Switched Networks; *and* VIA (Virtual Interface Architecture)

Linktionary!—Tom Sheldon's Encyclopedia of Networking updates	http://www.linktionary.com/f/fibre_channel
FCIA (Fibre Channel Industry Association)	http://www.fibrechannel.com/

CERN Fibre Channel home page	http://www.cern.ch/HSI/fcs/fcs.html
Fibre Channel Consortium	http://www.iol.unh.edu/consortiums/fc/
DataDirect Networks Fibre Channel SAN Technology page	http://www.datadirectnet.com/SAN/fibrechannel.htm
The T11 Home Page	http://www.t11.org/
Schelto's T11 Web page	http://www.schelto.com/
Brian A. Berg's Storage Cornucopia (great links!)	http://www.bswd.com/cornucop.htm
IETF Working Group: IP over Fibre Channel (ipfc)	http://www.ietf.org/html.charters/ipfc-charter.html

File and Directory Rights and Permissions

See Microsoft Windows File System; Novell NetWare File System; Rights and Permissions; *and* UNIX File System.

File Server

A computer that attaches to a network to provide file services for network users. In a traditional small office LAN, the file server was usually the place where all network management took place. It ran a network operating system that managed users accounts, access rights, permissions, disk management, and so on. Today, a file server may be a network-attached storage device that provides high-performance storage services, but none of the traditional network services. These are off-loaded to management servers that control file servers remotely.

Related Entries Client/Server Computing; Data Warehousing; Distributed Applications; File Sharing; File Systems; File Transfer Protocols; Microsoft Windows File Systems; NAS (Network-Attached Storage); Network Operating Systems; NFS (Network File System); Novell NetWare; Novell NetWare File System; Rights and Permissions; SAN (Storage Area Network); Servers; Storage Management Systems; Storage Systems; UNIX; *and* UNIX File System

File Sharing

File sharing has several meanings. When you put a file on a disk and give the disk to a friend, you are "file sharing." When you transfer a file via electronic mail, you are "file sharing." This topic is about "peer-to-peer file sharing," which refers to the ability of users to make files on their computers accessible to other users. It discusses Web-based file storage and community-based peer-to-peer information exchange over the Web. A related topic called "File Transfers" discusses the protocols used to transfer files.

Enterprise Network File Sharing

File sharing is a feature that allows users of network-connected computers to make files on their own systems available to other users or to access shared files on other systems. File sharing in this way is considered peer-to-peer networking since any system on the network can act as a server, not just dedicated file servers. For example, in Microsoft Windows 98, you can share a folder so that other network users can access that folder from their computers. The folder can be shared as read-only or read-write. In the read-only mode, users on the network can access files, but not write new files or changed files back to the shared drive. In the read-write mode, other users can write files to the shared drive or edit files that are already there.

An important difference between Windows 98 and more advanced operating systems like Microsoft Windows 2000 is the granularity of the sharing. In Windows 98, users can share an entire folder, but can't control the sharing of individual files within the folder. In Windows 2000, different levels of access for individual files may be specified for specific users.

Windows 2000 is a full-featured network operating system. It keeps track of users via user accounts and has strict logon procedures and security checks to ensure that users are authentic. Because Windows 2000 supports user account management, sharing can be done on an individual basis. For example, Joe can be granted read-only rights to a specific file in some directory, while Loretta can be granted read-write capabilities for the same file. Of course, this requires more management; but if the files contain critical information, the time and effort put into managing advanced security are worth it.

The only drawback to file sharing is that users are allowing other users to access their systems. This can be a problem if users are not properly trained on how to set file-sharing features. In Windows 98, a common mistake is to share an entire drive. This allows some unscrupulous person on the network (or from the Internet) to access critical directories such as the root of the boot drive, or the Windows and System directories. Viruses could be installed.

A new problem with file sharing occurs when users are connected to "always-on" Internet services such as DSL and cable. If a user is sharing a folder (or worse, a whole drive), it is possible for some hacker on the Internet to find the "always-on" system and access files on the drive or install damaging programs. The problem with "always-on" is that users get an IP address that is more permanent than the per-connect IP address that is obtained with most dial-up accounts. Hackers quickly discover these addresses and start attacking the system. Personal firewalls are needed. See "Firewall."

Internet File-Sharing Services

A number of services have popped up on the Internet that give people a place to store files other than their own hard drives. Users can then retrieve the files from another location (home, remote office, or hotel) or allow other people to retrieve the files.

The services discussed here are new only in that they sport Web interfaces and support collaborative applications now common on the Web. An early file-sharing protocol is FTP (File Transfer Protocol), which is discussed under its own heading.

Services such as click2send offer basic "deposit a file" and "pick up a file" services. Users can easily transfer any type of file, including graphics, audio, video, photos, and more, by using a Web browser interface that is easy to use and understand. Some services bill themselves as "virtual collaboration workspaces." Most services offer free limited disk space. Additional disk space is available at a charge.

The services provide security, logging, safe deposit boxes and other features that go beyond simple file transfer via e-mail or via anonymous servers. For example, at click2send, users must register with their full names (not handles), and accounts include the IP address from which the login session originated. The idea is to ensure security and privacy, and also record access to files for accounting, copyright, or other purposes. Note that these services represent what can be called "virtual networking," in which users run programs and access data at remote computers (enterprise or Internet data centers), not on their own computers. A user's computer may be a thin client, a PDA, or even a cell phone. The main point is that the user can go anywhere, hook up, and access data. In addition, the user can run most programs because the programs run on the servers at data center.

Following is a partial list of Internet file-sharing services, some of which offer 50MB or more of free disk space. For additional information about online storage sites, visit Brian A. Berg's Storage Cornucopia Web site at http://www.bswd.com/cornucop.htm.

Middlewire	http://www.middlewire.com/
DiskOnNet.com	http://www.diskonnet.com/
Critical Path Secure file services	http://www.docspace.com/
Driveway	http://www.driveway.com/
Filegenie.com	http://www.filegenie.com/
FreeDrive	http://www.freedrive.com/
i-drive	http://www.idrive.com/
Punch WebGroups File Collaboration Service	http://www.punchnetworks.com/
Skydesk (a Qualcomm-funded site)	http://www.skydesk.com/
vVault (caters to PDAs, WAP phones, and other wireless devices)	http://www.vvault.com/
X:drive (100MB free)	http://www.xdrive.com/

Internet Distributed File Sharing

While the Internet file-sharing services just described offer centralized file storage, distributed file-sharing services provide peer-to-peer file sharing across the entire Internet. Members belong to "sharing communities" where information is shared in an ad-free, censorship-free environment. This is reminiscent of the "ring-of-links" concept in which users share links to one another's Web pages so that visitors can quickly jump from one related site to another.

The peering phenomenon exploded with Napster, a music-sharing software model. The general concept with this type of software is that users install software on their computers and join a sharing community. Users then share the files with other community users. Users can search for a song on other user's computers. A list of available locations appears, some providing better bandwidth than others. The user can then immediately download the song. Napster caused a ruckus because it allowed users to infringe on copyrights and easily pirate music. In fact, Napster no longer exists in its original form because it was bought by a recording company!

Note that distributed file sharing and peer-to-peer software is not a new technology. It has been around in some form for a long time. Collaboration software and the ability to share folders in Windows clients are examples. What Napster did was introduce software that simplified peer-to-peer content distribution among users without any controls imposed by network administrators (or the owners of copyrighted material). Software features quickly expanded to support instant messaging, advanced searching, and mailing list support. In the enterprise (and on the Internet), peer-to-peer networking bypasses the central control that administrators have over information that is stored on file servers. The issue for network administrators is whether to maintain central control or suppress peer-to-peer networking.

At the time of this writing, Gnutella was the leading Internet file-sharing product. Several other services are available, listed next. All can be used to share audio and video media in a community-based exchange arrangement.

Napster	http://www.napster.com/
Gnutella Web page	http://gnutella.wego.com/
Flycode.com	http://www.flycode.com/
Another Gnutella Web page	http://welcome.to/gnutella
Gnutella downloads, links, and articles	http://daugava.com/gnutella.htm
Napster and OpenNap (open source Napster server)	http://opennap.sourceforge.net/
The Free Network Project, home of Freenet	http://freenet.sourceforge.net/
Yo!NK File Download Community	http://www.downloadcommunity.com/
NetBrilliant	http://www.netbrilliant.com/
FileSwap.com	http://www.fileswap.com/
Hotline	http://www.bigredh.com
Jungle Monkey (University of Michigan)	http://www.junglemonkey.net/

According to the Yo!NK community Web site, "Each member of the community shares a folder that receives new downloads and stores media that you would like others to download from you. You help define the community by the amount and type of files you have available. Your searches are broadcasted to the entire community, each Yo!NK member that matches your request will show you the files you want to download."

Related Entries   Access Rights; Account, User; Authentication and Authorization; Client/Server Computing; Collaborative Computing; Content Distribution; Directory Services; Distributed Computer Networks; File Systems; File Transfer Protocols; FTP (File Transfer Protocol); Groupware; Instant Messaging; Microsoft File System; Microsoft Windows NT ; Multimedia; Network Operating Systems; Novell NetWare File System; Peer-to-Peer Communication; Replication; Search and Discovery Services; *and* UNIX File System

Linktionary!—Tom Sheldon's Encyclopedia of Networking updates	http://www.linktionary.com/f/file_sharing.html
Linktionary! — Tom Sheldon's Encyclopedia of Networking updates	http://www.linktionary.com/p/peer2peer.html
Tom Sheldon's peer-to-peer article	http://www.linktionary.com/napster.html

| Google Web Directory: File Sharing | http://directory.google.com/Top/Computers/
Software/Internet/Clients/File_Sharing/ |
| Peer-to-Peer (P2P) page at About.com | http://compnetworking.about.com/compute/
compnetworking/cs/peertopeer/ |

File Systems

A file system provides persistent storage of information. It is the part of an operating system that interfaces with storage systems and provides a way to organize how information is stored. Users access files through command-line or graphical user interfaces.

Local file systems allow users to access storage on their own computers. However, most operating systems include peer-to-peer file-sharing functions that let users access files on other network computers or share (publish) files on their own computers. See "File Sharing" for a description and list of Web services that offer Web-based collaborative information exchange, file storage, and distributed file-sharing services.

File systems are organized into tree-structured directories. The metaphor is usually file cabinets (drives) and folders (directories). Folders are like containers that can hold other folders or files. Directories have rights or permissions such as read-only, read-write, and so on. These are assigned by the owner or network administrator. The right and permissions of top-level folders are passed down to sub-folders. This is called inheritance. Files also have their own set of attributes, depending on the operating system.

Common file systems are briefly described here. Some of these file systems are discussed elsewhere in this book, as noted.

- **FAT (file allocation table)**   The IBM/Microsoft DOS-based file system that is also used by Windows 9x versions. Windows NT also supports FAT, as well as NTFS (New Technology File System). FAT divides hard disks into one or more partitions that become drive letters, such as C:, D:, and so on. Disks are formatted into sectors, and sectors are grouped into clusters of from 4 to 32 sectors at the user's discretion. A FAT entry describes the location of files or parts of those files on the disk.

- **FAT32**   Windows 95 (release 2) and later versions of Windows 9x provide this update to FAT that allows for a default cluster size as small as 4K, as well as support for hard disk sizes in excess of 2GB.

- **HPFS (High-Performance File System)**   This file system was first introduced with OS/2 when Microsoft was working on the project with IBM. It supports large hard drives, supports extended names, and has more file security features. HPFS organizes directories like FAT, but adds features that improve performance. A design goal was to have HPFS allocate as much of a file in contiguous sectors as possible to increase speed.

- **NTFS (New Technology File System)**   NTFS is the file system for Windows NT. It builds on the features of FAT and HPFS, and adds new features or changes. NTFS provides advanced security features and better performance, especially for server operations. NTFS is a *recoverable file system*, meaning that it keeps track of transactions against the file system. See "Microsoft Windows File System" for more information.

- **NTFS 5**   NTFS 5 is the file system for Windows 2000. It has most of the features of NTFS, including support for FAT and FAT32 file systems. It also provides complete content indexing and built-in hierarchical storage management. A major new feature is dynamic volume management, which allows for live configuration changes without rebooting. There are also advanced backup, restore, and disaster recovery tools. NTFS 5 also supports I$_2$O, IEEE 1394, and Fibre Channel. NTFS 5 may also participate in Windows 2000 Dfs (Distributed file system), which provides load balancing, fault tolerance, and replication services. See "Microsoft Windows File System" for more information.

- **NetWare UFS (Universal File System)**   UFS is the file system for NetWare 3.*x*, a server-based operating system. All of its features are enhanced to provide high performance to multiple users. It includes such features as elevator seeking, background writes, overlapped seeks, Turbo FAT, file compression, and block suballocation. See "Novell NetWare File System" for details.

- **NWFS (NetWare File System)**   This Novell file system appeared in NetWare 4.1 and NetWare 4.11. It provides backward compatibility with previous file systems and supports loadable modules that support other file systems such as Windows 9*x*, OS/2, Windows NT, UNIX NFS (Network File System), and Apple Macintosh file systems. The maximum number of files supported is 16 million, with a maximum file size of 4 gigabytes. It also supports over 100 levels of directories. Other features include file compression, block suballocation, file salvage features, hot fix (data is redirected out of corrupted sectors), the ability to span volumes across 32 disks, a transaction tracking system to recover from failed transactions, mirroring, duplexing, and data migration (hierarchical storage management). File system security and quota information is stored in NDS (Novell Directory Services).

- **NSS (Novell Storage Services)**   This is the follow-up to NWFS that appeared with NetWare 5.0. It stores billions of files, and the maximum file size is 8 terabytes. Name space support for other operating systems is built in. Some features in NWFS were removed to improve performance, or because they were deemed unnecessary or considered add-ons. These include compression, block suballocation, transaction tracking, disk mirroring, and data migration.

- **UNIX file system**   The UNIX file system is based on the hierarchical directory tree structure like the file systems previously mentioned. The original file system was not specifically designed for remote file sharing, but these features were added later with NFS (Network File System), RFS (Remote File System), and AFS (Andrews File System). These network file systems are covered under their own headers. The UNIX file system maintains a set of attributes for each of its files. The attributes are stored in a structure called an *inode* (index node), which is stored on disk. The attributes include information about the type of file, its size, the device where it is located, and an inode number that uniquely identifies the file on disk. Other information included is the ID of the owner, timestamps, and permissions (read, write, and execute). See "UNIX File System."

- **WAFL (Write Anywhere File Layout)**   Network Appliance Corp. designs NAS (network-attached storage) devices. It created WAFL to provide a way to store files in a multiprotocol format. Files in this format can be shared via NFS, CIFS, or HTTP. WAFL essentially frees files from the restrictions imposed by specific operating systems and the file systems they use. With WAFL, users can access files no matter which operating system they use or how the files are stored. WAFL implements Snapshots, which are read-only clones of the active file system. WAFL uses a copy-on-write technique to minimize the disk space that Snapshots consume. WAFL also uses Snapshots to eliminate the need for file system consistency checking after an unclean shutdown. WAFL provides very high performance, and supports RAID and quick restart, even after an unclean shutdown. See "NAS (Network Attached Storage)" and "Network Appliance."

 The Network Appliance Web site has an extensive set of documents about all types of file systems. The Web site is given later.

As already mentioned, file sharing is an important aspect of network-connected systems. File-sharing systems take advantage of the underlying file systems just mentioned. For example, NFS is a file-sharing system that runs with existing UNIX file systems. Likewise, Microsoft's SMB (Server Message Blocks) takes advantage of FAT and NTFS, as does the newer CIFS (Common Internet File System). There are peer-to-peer and dedicated file-sharing systems:

- **Peer-to-peer sharing**   Users share files on their own workstations with other peer network users. The users are in control of the file and directory management, or it may be controlled by administrators.

- **Dedicated server sharing**   In this scheme, a dedicated and secure server running a network operating system such as Novell NetWare or Windows NT/Windows 2000 provides file services that are controlled by a network administrator. This scheme provides a high level of granular control over file access.

Distributed File Systems

Distributed file systems store files on multiple servers, replicate files among those servers, and present users with a single view of all the servers. Files are accessible to users by filename without regard to the physical location of the file. As an analogy, think of a city library system in which the book catalog at each library lists all the books available at libraries throughout the city. You can order any book and it will be delivered from its current location. There is one library catalog system that provides a list of all the books available, no matter what their physical location. A distributed file system provides a single "catalog" view of files on your network, no matter where those files are located. Distributed file systems automatically replicate files to mirror servers so users can access files on servers that are close to them.

Some of the most common distributed files systems are described here.

- **AFS (Andrew File System)**   AFS was developed by the Information Technology Center at Carnegie Mellon University, but is currently managed by Transarc Corporation. AFS has some enhancements that NFS does not. See "AFS (Andrew File System)."

■ **DFS (Distributed File System), DCE**   DFS is a version of AFS. It serves as the file system component in the Open Software Foundation's DCE (Distributed Computing Environment). See "DCE (Distributed Computing Environment), The Open Group."

■ **Microsoft Dfs (Distributed file system)**   Windows NT/Windows 2000 includes Microsoft's new hierarchical distributed file system. Dfs is a true distributed file system that lets administrators create custom hierarchical trees that group file resources from anywhere in the organization. See "Dfs (Distributed File System), Microsoft."

■ **NCP (NetWare Core Protocol)**   NCP is NetWare's proprietary set of service protocols that the operating system follows to accept and respond to service requests from clients and other servers. It includes services for file access, file locking, security, resource tracking, and other network-related features. See "NCP (NetWare Core Protocol)."

■ **NFS (Network File System)**   NFS was originally created by Sun Microsystems, Inc., as a file-sharing system for TCP/IP networks. NFS is running on millions of systems, ranging from mainframes to personal computers. See "NFS (Network File System)."

■ **SMB (Server Message Blocks)**   SMB is Microsoft's traditional shared-file system that runs on Windows 3.*x*, Windows 95, and Windows NT platforms. An independently developed version of SMB called Samba is also available for non-Windows systems. See "SMB (Server Message Blocks)" and "Samba."

■ **DAFS (Direct Access File System)**   DAFS is a shared-file access protocol designed to work in SAN (Storage Area Network) environments, in which VI architecture is the underlying transport mechanism. DAFS is primarily designed for clustered, shared-file network environments, in which a limited number of server-class clients connect to a set of file servers via a dedicated high-speed network. With DAFS and VI, data consumers have direct access to disks across the network and can transfer data from remote disks directly into their own memory. There is no need to copy data to or from intermediate buffers, or to interrupt an operating system during file transfers.

Several additional distributed file-sharing protocols have been developed for the Web. Traditionally, when a Web client connects with a Web server, a Web page is downloaded to the user's computer. This may require a series of connections and reconnections until the document is completely downloaded. The first connection downloads text, and subsequent connections download graphics and other page elements. New Web-based distributed file systems are designed to download all the related files with a single connection, thus improving performance. The two competing Web file systems are briefly described here:

■ **SunSoft's WebNFS**   Implements all the features of NFS and is optimized to run over the Internet or intranets. Also provides a way to implement file security mechanisms over the Web. See "NFS (Network File System)."

■ **Microsoft's CIFS (Common Internet File System)**   CIFS is an extension of Microsoft's SMB (Server Message Blocks) file protocol. Like WebNFS, it is optimized to run over the Internet or intranets and implements file-level security mechanisms. See "CIFS (Common Internet File System)."

Two interesting schemes for finding and locating files on the Internet are discussed under "Handle System" and "URN (Universal Resource Naming)." Also see "Search and Discovery Services."

Distributed File System Features

A distributed file system should provide clients with access to files no matter where they are located. Traditionally, file servers have been located throughout an organization (in departments and workgroups), and users have had to locate servers that held files of interest by searching, by referrals in applications or files, or by word of mouth.

Directory services change that. Administrators can use directory services to group files and file storage systems in a hierarchical tree under branches that make sense to people. For example, an administrator could create a branch of the tree called "White Papers," and then create links to all the directories on all the servers in the organization that contain white papers. Users only need to open the White Papers section in the directory tree to access files, rather than accessing a particular server. Novell's NDS (Novell Directory Services) and Microsoft's Dfs provide these features.

A distributed file system should also provide *replication*. If users throughout the organization require access to files on a particular server, it makes sense to replicate those files to a server that is closer to the user, especially if they are at remote offices. Replication can also minimize traffic on servers by distributing the load to other servers. A distributed file system should be able to retrieve a file from a server in a replicated set that is most available to handle the request or closest to the user making the request.

A distributed file system should also implement single sign-on so users do not need to enter a password every time they access a file on a connected or replicated system. One additional feature is encryption. If a user is going to access a sensitive file from a secure server, the transmission of the file should be encrypted, especially if the file is being transmitted over the Internet.

A common problem with any shared file system is that multiple users will need to access the same file at the same time. Concurrency controls are required to arbitrate multiuser access to files. These controls take the following forms:

- **Read-only sharing** Any client can access a file, but not change it. This is simple to implement. Web servers do this.

- **Controlled writes** In this method, multiple users can open a file, but only one user can write changes. The changes written by that user may not appear on the screens of other users who had the file open.

- **Concurrent writes** This method allows multiple users to both read and write a file simultaneously. The operating system must continuously monitor file access to prevent overwrites and ensure that users receive the latest updates.

Shared file systems differ in the way they handle concurrent writes. When a client requests a file (or database records) from a server, the file is placed in a cache at the client's workstation. If another client requests the same file, it is also placed in a cache at that client's workstation. As both clients make changes to the file, technically, three versions of the file exist (one at each client and one at the server). There are two methods for maintaining synchronization among the versions:

- **Stateless systems**   In stateless systems, the server does not keep information about what files its clients are caching. Therefore, clients must periodically check with the server to see if other clients have changed the file they are caching. NFS is a stateless system.

- **Call-back systems**   In this method, the server retains information about what its clients are doing and the files they are caching. The server uses a *call-back promise* technique to inform clients when another client has changed a file. This method produces less network traffic than the stateless approach. AFS is a call-back system. As clients change files, other clients holding copies of the files are called back and notified of changes.

There are performance advantages to stateless operations, but AFS retains some of these advantages by making sure that it does not become flooded with call-back promises. It does this by discarding callbacks after a certain amount of time. Clients check the expiration time in call-back promises to ensure that they are current. Another interesting feature of the call-back promise is that it provides a guarantee to a client that a file is current. In other words, if a cached file has a call-back promise, the client knows the file must be current unless the server has called to indicate the file changed at the server.

Related Entries, File Systems   AFP (AppleTalk Filing Protocol); AFS (Andrew File System); AppleShare; CIFS (Common Internet File System); DAFS (Direct Access File System); Dfs (Distributed file system), Microsoft; DFS (Distributed File System), Open Group; Linux; Microsoft Windows File Systems; NFS (Network File System); Novell NetWare; Novell NetWare File System; Samba; SMB (Server Message Blocks); UNIX; *and* UNIX File System

Related Entries, General   Access Control; Account, User; ACL (Access Control List); Attributes; Authentication and Authorization; Client/Server Computing; Compression Techniques; Content Distribution; Data Center Design; Data Management; Data Protection; Data Warehousing; Directory Services; Distributed Applications; Distributed Computer Networks; Distributed Database; Embedded Systems and Architectures; File Sharing; File Transfer Protocols; Logons and Logon Accounts; NAS (Network Attached Storage); Network Operating Systems; Replication; Rights and Permissions; SAN (Storage Area Network); Search and Discovery Services; Servers; Stateless and Call-Back Filing Systems; Storage Management Systems; Storage Systems; Transaction Processing; *and* Volume and Partition Management

Linktionary!—Tom Sheldon's Encyclopedia of Networking updates	http://www.linktionary.com/f/ file_systems.html
Network Appliance Tech Library (Click "File Service" and choose a document)	http://www.netapp.com/tech_library/
Microsoft File and Print Services Page	http://www.microsoft.com/ntserver/fileprint/
Novell Directory and File Information (see File Services under appropriate operating system heading)	http://www.novell.com/documentation/
Novell Research Network Services Topics (see File Services)	http://developer.novell.com/research/topical/ network_services.htm

AFS Directory and File Permissions paper at Pittsburgh Supercomputing Center	http://www.psc.edu/general/filesys/afs/setpermissions.html
AFS information at Transarc	http://www.transarc.com/Library/
AFS and NFS tutorials	http://www.cs.unc.edu/~pescator/dfs/implement.html
NFS Working Group at IETF	http://www.ietf.org/html.charters/nfsv4-charter.html
UNIX file system information	http://www.sao.nrc.ca/imsb/rcsg/documents/basic/node22.html
UNIX file permissions page	http://www.cs.umass.edu/rcfbbl/bbl_security_050395_files.html
UNIX directory information	http://www.mcsr.olemiss.edu/unixhelp/tasks/index.html
Distributed File Systems (IBM/Transarc DFSTM, Microsoft Distributed File System, Novell NetWare, Sun NFS), by Mitchell I. Kramer (December 1996)	http://www.tks.buffalo.edu/committees/ppc/Infra/dfs/seybold.html
Distributed file system info at NIST	http://snad.ncsl.nist.gov/snad-staff/olsen/pubs/titlehce/node6.html
DCE DFS Specifications at The Open Group	http://www.opengroup.org/public/pubs/catalog/p409.htm
IBM DCE DFS Administration Guide and Reference	http://www.univie.ac.at/dcedoc/A3U2M/A3U2MM02.HTM
JetFile Distributed File System paper by Björn Grönvall, Assar Westerlund, and Stephen Pink	http://www.sics.se/I/osdi99.html
Distributed File Systems paper by Jason Packer, March 1997	http://www.ccp.uchicago.edu/~jpack/dfs.html
IBM OS/390 Distributed File Service papers	http://www1.s390.ibm.com/os390/bkserv/dfs.html

File Transfer Protocols

File transfer protocols arbitrate the transfer of files from one system to another over local or remote networks. The previous sections, "File Sharing" and "File Systems," describe network operating systems that include file transfer capabilities. There are several specific protocols for transferring files:

- **FTP (File Transfer Protocol)**   This is perhaps the most well-known file transfer protocol. Before the Web and its graphical hyperlinked interface, people transferred files using text-based FTP. Files are stored on FTP servers on the Internet or corporate servers. Users running FTP clients access a particular FTP server and use a set of commands (such as list, get, put, and so on) to access files on the server. See "FTP (File Transfer Protocol)."

- **TFTP (Trivial File Transfer Protocol)**   A scaled-down version of FTP that uses UDP instead of TCP. TCP provides guaranteed delivery, but adds overhead. Some transfers do not require this and so can take advantage of TFTP.

- **UUCP (UNIX to UNIX Copy Program)**   A UNIX file transfer command for copying files between computers or for executing commands between computers. See the UUCP topic.

- **HTTP (Hypertext Transfer Protocol)**   HTTP has essentially replaced FTP for many users as an Internet file transfer protocol. It replaces FTP's command-oriented interface with a point-and-click interface that support hyperlinks. Files can also be saved directly to the user's disk (in Internet Explorer, right-click on a hyperlink and choose Save Target As). See "HTTP (Hypertext Transfer Protocol)."

- **FTAM (File Transfer Access and Management)**   This is an OSI file management and transfer service. It is similar in concept to FTP. See "FTAM (File Transfer Access and Management)."

See "File Sharing" for a description and list of Web services that offer Web-based collaborative information exchange, file storage, and distributed file-sharing services. Also see "File Systems" and "Peer-to-Peer Communication."

Filtering

In the context of networks, filtering is a firewall-like process performed by *screening routers*. Most routers today have filtering functions. These routers evaluate information in a packet, such as the source and/or destination address, or application type (based on port number).

The basic filtering rule is "all that is not expressly permitted is denied." In other words, drop all packets except those that have been previously specified as being acceptable. Routers look inside packets and evaluate any of the following:

- *Source addresses*, to determine whether the source is allowed to access systems on the other side of the router. For example, you could block a competitor from accessing your Web site.

- *Destination addresses*, to restrict packets from reaching a particular system. For example, you could block all packets from the Internet that are addressed to systems that should only be accessed by internal users.

- *Service ports*, to prevent someone from using an application such as Telnet, FTP, SMTP, or other utilities that might pose a security threat to internal systems.

- *SYN filtering*, to prevent an external system from establishing internal connections. A TCP packet with SYN set is trying to establish a connection. If such a packet is received from the outside, it is dropped. Note that internal systems can still establish external connections. A SYN packet is allowed to go out, and the target system returns an SYN+ACK packet, which is allowed through the router. See "Connection Establishment" for additional details.

One reason for blocking IP addresses is to prevent spoofing attacks. A spoofed packet originates from an unknown/unauthorized source and contains a fake source address. The fake address makes the packet appear to be from a system on your own internal network or a trusted system. A screening router will drop such packets. How does it know a packet is spoofed? Simple: if the packet arrives on the external port with an internal source address, it is fake.

See "Firewall" for more information about filtering and advanced network security techniques.

Linktionary!—Tom Sheldon's Encyclopedia of   http://www.linktionary.com/f/filtering.html
Networking updates

Find/Search

See Search and Discovery Services.

Finger

Finger is a UNIX and Internet utility that can be used to find out if a user is logged on. The command may display information about the user, depending on the operating system and security policies in place. The command requires the user ID or name of a user. For example, you could type **finger tsheldon@ntresearch.com** to see if I am working at my Web site.

RFC 1288, "The Finger User Information Protocol," (December 1991) describes the protocol. Some Finger sites are listed here.

DaveCentral Finger/Whois page   http://www.davecentral.com/finger.html

eMailman Finger page   http://www.emailman.com/finger/

The WWW to Finger Gateway with support for faces   http://www.cs.indiana.edu:800/finger/
                                                    gateway

Firewall

A *firewall* is a gateway that restricts and controls the flow of traffic between networks, typically between an internal corporate network and the Internet. Firewalls may also provide secure gateway services between internal networks. For example, a military installation may have two networks, one for non-classified general communications and another network that is connected to strategic defense systems. A very secure firewall must be in place to ensure that only authorized users access the defense network. In some cases, no connection may be the most secure policy.

This topic provides basic descriptions of firewalls and firewall terminology. A more complete description is available at the Linktionary! Web site.

Castles and castle defenses are often used as an analogy in describing firewalls. A castle is designed to protect the people on the inside from the storming hoards on the outside. There is a perimeter defense system that keeps attackers as far away as possible (outer walls, moats, and so on). The castle gate is the "choke point" through which people and supplies must pass to enter or exit the castle. It is the most heavily defended part of the castle.

A firewall is a "choke point" for internal networks that actively inspects and controls the flow of traffic between networks. In the case of a proxy firewall, traffic never flows directly between the networks. Instead, the proxy "repackages" request and responses. No internal host is directly accessible from the external network and no external host is directly accessible by an internal host. Think about the people in the castle. During times of tension, they may prefer to stay inside the castle and use proxy agents to take care of their business on the outside.

Part of the design of a secure Internet-connected network is to create what is called a "demilitarized zone" or DMZ, which is a network that exists between the protected and the unprotected network. The DMZ is protected by a perimeter defense system, much like the outer walls and moats of a castle. Picture the market yard of a castle. In medieval times, local townspeople and traders were usually allowed to enter the yard with relative ease so they could deliver or pick up goods. At night, the gates were closed and goods were brought into the castle—usually after close inspection. Guards were posted at the gates during the day to scrutinize all the people coming into the market yard. If known hooligans tried to enter, they were immediately pointed in the other direction and given the boot.

The DMZ between the protected and unprotected network follows this analogy. Internet users can freely enter the DMZ to access public Web servers, but screening routers exist at the access point to filter out unwanted traffic, such as floods of packets from hackers who are trying to disrupt operations. At the same time, the internal private network is protected by highly secure firewalls. Within the castle walls was the *keep*, a heavily fortified structure that provided the last defense against attackers.

Interestingly, the castle proved quite capable of withstanding attacks until the cannon came along. In the 16th century, Essex and Cromwell overran many castles in Ireland with little force. They simply blew the parapets off the top of castle walls to make them indefensible, and then scaled the walls. What similar weapons will our network defenses face?

Firewalls have become quite sophisticated over the years, but they are not an all-in-one security solution. Firewalls are just one tool in the arsenal of security tools available to security administrators. Note the following:

- A firewall may consists of several pieces of equipment, including a router, a gateway server, and an authentication server.

- Firewalls monitor incoming and outgoing traffic and filter, redirect, repackage, and/or discard packets. Packets may be filtered based on their source and destination IP address, source and destination TCP port numbers, setting of bits in the TCP header, and so on.

- In the case of a proxy firewall, the firewall is the endpoint of the incoming and outgoing connection. It can perform extensive security and validation scans on the packets it processes. The proxy runs safe, uncorrupted, and bug-free versions of protocols and software.

- Firewalls can enforce an organization's security policies by filtering the outgoing traffic of internal users to ensure that it complies with usage policies.

- Sophisticated logging, auditing, and intrusion detection tools are now part of most commercial firewalls.

RFC 2979, "Behavior of and Requirements for Internet Firewalls," (October 2000) describes other firewall characteristics.

Hackers and attackers just keep getting smarter, more aggressive, and more numerous. In 2000, China announced that it could not keep up with the United States militarily, and threatened to wage an information war on the United States. Computer systems at U.S. military installations are under constant attack by both sophisticated and unsophisticated attackers. How many undetected intruders are in those systems?

The castle analogy falls apart in the face of modern security threats, because the weapons available to attackers defy physical boundaries. For example, an attacker may set up an attack well in advance by using e-mail virus techniques to plant so-called "zombie" programs on hundreds or thousands of computers owned by innocent Internet users, many within your own network. The programs are set to wake up at specific times and begin launching attacks against other systems. The real attacker cannot be identified because the attacks are coming from innocent users all over the Internet. The entire Internet can become a weapon aimed at your private network.

Because of these threats, firewall-like software is now needed in nearly every Internet-connected computer, especially those that are connected to "always-on" services, such as DSL and cable (CATV) connections. A typical home setup is to network the parent's and the kid's computers together, and share a single DSL or cable connection to the Internet. Since the connection is always on, it has a continuous IP address that is posted like a flag on the Internet. Hackers will eventually find the IP address and keep coming back to examine and disrupt systems. Personal firewalls are designed to protect these systems while minimizing complex setup procedures.

Firewall Terminology

A standard firewall terminology helps remove the confusion surrounding firewall technology. RFC 2647, "Benchmarking Terminology for Firewall Performance," (August 1999) is one document that attempts to establish such terminology. The most important terms it describes are outlined next. Refer to the RFC for a more complete description. The following list has been reordered for clarity and reworded for conciseness.

- **Firewall**   A device or group of devices that enforces an access control policy among networks. Firewalls connect protected and unprotected networks, or support tri-homing, which allows a DMZ network.

- **Protected network**   A network segment or segments to which access is controlled. Protected networks are sometimes called "internal networks," but RFC 2647 states that the term is inappropriate because firewalls increasingly are deployed within an organization, where all segments are by definition internal.

- **Unprotected network**   A network segment or segments to which access is not controlled by the firewall.

- **Demilitarized zone (DMZ)**   A network segment or segments located between protected and unprotected networks. The DMZ may not be connected to the protected network in any way. The DMZ may also include *perimeter defense* systems. For example, The DMZ can be made to look like it is part of the protected network, luring hackers into traps that log their activities and attempt to track the source of the activity.

- **Dual-homed firewall**   A firewall with two interfaces, one attached to the protected network and one attached to the unprotected network.

- **Tri-homed firewall**   A tri-homed firewalls connect three network segments with different network addresses. Typically, these would be protected, DMZ, and unprotected segments.

- **Proxy**   A request for a connection made on behalf of a host. A proxy stands between the protected and unprotected network. Think of a quarantined area where people on the inside use a telephone to talk to people on the outside. All external connections leading into the proxy terminate at the proxy. This effectively eliminates IP routing between the networks. The proxy repackages the messages into new packets that are allowed into the internal network. The proxy also terminates internal traffic that is headed out to the Internet and repackages it in a new packet with the source IP address of the proxy, not the internal host. Most important, the proxy inspects and filters traffic. A predefined "rule set" is used to determine which traffic should be forwarded and which should be rejected. There are two types of proxies: application proxies and circuit proxies, as described shortly.

- **Network address translation**   A method of mapping one or more private, reserved IP addresses to one or more public IP addresses. NAT was defined to conserve IPv4 address space and refer to a specific block of IP addresses that are never recognized or routed on the Internet. It allows organizations to use their own internal IP addressing scheme. A NAT device translates between internal and external addresses, and is usually combined with proxy services. NAT devices are implemented in firewalls to support the private addressing scheme as defined in RFC 1918.

- **Application proxy**   A proxy service that is set up and torn down in response to a client request, rather than existing on a static basis (as is the case with circuit proxies). The application proxy performs all of the services of a proxy, but for specific applications. In contrast, a basic proxy performs generic packet filtering. The application proxy only processes packets related to the applications that it supports. If code is not installed for an application, those incoming packets are dropped. Packets are only forwarded after a connection has been made, which is subject to authentication and authorization.

- **Circuit proxy**   A proxy service that statically defines which traffic will be forwarded. The circuit proxy is a special function performed by application proxies, usually to support proxy connection between internal users and outside hosts. The packets are relayed without performing any extensive processing or filtering because the packets are from trusted internal users, and they are going outside. However, packets that return in response to these packets are fully examined by the application proxy services.

- **Policy**   A document defining acceptable access to protected, DMZ, and unprotected networks. Security policies set general guidelines for what is and is not acceptable network access.

- **Rule set**   The collection of access control rules that determines which packets are forwarded or dropped.

- **Allowed traffic**   Packets forwarded as a result of the rule set.

- **Illegal traffic**   Packets specified for rejection in the rule set.

- **Rejected traffic**   Packets dropped as a result of the rule set.

- **Authentication**   The process of verifying that a user requesting a network resource is who he, she, or it claims to be, and vice versa. The entity being authenticated might be the client machine or a user, so authentication may take the form of verifying IP addresses; TCP or UDP port numbers; passwords; and other advanced forms of identification, such as token cards and biometrics.

- **Security association**   The set of security information related to a given network connection or set of connections. This definition covers the relationship between policy and connections. Associations may be set up during connection establishment, and they may be reiterated or revoked during a connection.

- **Packet filtering**   The process of controlling access by examining packets based on the content of packet headers. Header information, such as IP address or TCP port number, is examined to determine whether a packet should be forwarded or rejected, based on a rule set.

- **Stateful packet filtering**   The process of forwarding or rejecting traffic based on the contents of a state table maintained by a firewall. When stateful filtering is used, packets are only forwarded if they belong to a connection that has already been established and that is being tracked in a state table.

- **Logging**   The recording of user requests made to the firewall. All requests are typically logged, including allowed, illegal, and rejected traffic.

A related topic in the book is "Security Auditing," which discusses auditing and intrusion detection systems. An intrusion detection system actively monitors network access points to detect hackers and track attacks as they progress.

SOCKS is a circuit-level proxy firewall service that attempts to provide a secure channel between two TCP/IP hosts, typically a Web client on an internal corporate network that wants to access an outside Web server (on the Internet, on another company's network, or on another part of an intranet). SOCKS provides firewall services, as well as auditing, management, fault tolerance, and other features. See "SOCKS."

Most firewalls also perform authentication to verify the identity of the users or processes. RADIUS is often used as the authentication service. It is the same authentication service used for dial-up network access by both enterprise networks and Internet service providers. By authenticating users, the firewall has additional information it can work with to filter packets. For example, it can allow a specific user to access some services but not others. Modern firewalls also support VPNs, which provide secure tunnels between a firewall and a remote user across the Internet. The firewall authenticates the user, encrypts all data, and ensures data integrity by using digital signature technology.

As the role of the firewall becomes more complex, one feature that should not be overlooked is speed. Firewalls must now operate at "gigabit" speeds to keep up with network traffic. Netscreen (http://www.netscreen.com) builds a "gigabit firewall" that is designed for Internet data center usage. The system is designed to support the firewall needs of up to 100 separate customers who have outsourced and collocated their Web servers and other equipment at the data center.

Refer to the following RFCs for more information about firewalls. Also refer to the Linktionary! Web site for the full text of this topic.

- RFC 1928, "SOCKS Protocol Version 5," (March 1996)
- RFC 2196, "Site Security Handbook," (September 1997), see section 3
- RFC 2647, "Benchmarking Terminology for Firewall Performance," (August 1999)
- RFC 2775, "Internet Transparency," (February 2000)
- RFC 2827, "Network Ingress Filtering: Defeating Denial of Service Attacks Which employ IP Source Address Spoofing," (May 2000)
- RFC 2828, "Internet Security Glossary," (May 2000)
- RFC 2979, "Behavior of and Requirements for Internet Firewalls," (October 2000)

Three firewall-related books I recommend are listed here:

- *Windows 2000 Security Handbook* by Tom Sheldon and Philip Cox (Osborne McGraw-Hill, 2001).
- *Firewalls and Internet Security: Repelling the Wily Hacker*, second edition by William R. Cheswick and Steven M. Bellovin (Addison-Wesley, 2001)
- *Building Internet Firewalls* by Brent Chapman, Elizabeth D. Zwicky, and others (O'Reilly & Associates, June 2000).

Related Entries   Access Control; Attacks and Attackers; Authentication and Authorization; Cryptography; Data Protection; DIAMETER; Extranet; Filtering; Gateway; Hacking and Hackers; IPSec (IP Security); NAT (Network Address Translation); OPSEC (Open Platform for Security); Policy-Based Networking; Proxy Server; RADIUS (Remote Authentication Dial-In User Service); RSIP (Realm-Specific IP); S/WAN (Secure WAN); Security; Security Auditing; SOCKS; Trust Relationships and Trust Management; Tunneling; VPN (Virtual Private Network); *and* Web Caching

Linktionary!—Tom Sheldon's Encyclopedia of Networking updates	http://www.linktionary.com/f/firewall.html
Security Portal has extensive coverage and testing of enterprise and personal firewalls	http://www.securityportal.com/
Zeuros Network Solutions firewall resources page	http://www.zeuros.co.uk/generic/resource/firewall/
Trusted Information Systems firewall toolkit	http://www.tis.com/research/software/

Great Circle Associates (home of the original firewall experts)	http://www.greatcircle.com/
Mark Grenman's "Firewall and Proxy Server HOWTO" page	http://www.grennan.com/Firewall-HOWTO.html
About.com firewalls, proxies, and caching page	http://compnetworking.about.com/compute/compnetworking/cs/proxyservers/index.htm
Bitpipe (search for "firewall")	http://www.bitpipe.com/
Google Web Directory firewall page	http://directory.google.com/Top/Computers/Security/Firewalls/
Chuck Semeria's "Internet Firewalls and Security" paper	http://www.3com.com/nsc/500619s.html
"Securing Your Network Against Source IP Spoofing Attacks" by Chuck Semeria	http://www.indy.net/~sabronet/secure/795inet.html
IETF Security Working Groups	http://www.ietf.org/html.charters/wg-dir.html#Security_Area

FireWire

FireWire is a peripheral connection technology developed by Apple Computer and Texas Instruments. The high-speed interface is suitable for real-time, full-motion video applications. Its high-speed bus supports data transfer rates of 100 Mbits/sec to 400 Mbits/sec, and the designers are working toward a 1-Gbit/sec data transfer rate. Officially, FireWire is IEEE 1394.

FireWire is an asynchronous technology that also supports real-time isochronous (time-dependent) data traffic such as full-motion video transfers. FireWire peripherals are daisy-chained from a controller port on a device such as a Macintosh. This daisy-chaining allows all the devices to be connected to a single port. Up to 63 devices can be connected without shutting down the rest of the system. FireWire provides its own bus power for peripherals.

FireWire devices include consumer electronic equipment like digital cameras, scanners, audio recorders, and video recorders, as well as computer peripherals like optical disks and high-performance disk drives.

FireWire has gained in popularity as more and more people buy digital cameras with the idea of editing video on their desktop computers. FireWire can handle the transfer of massive amounts of data from videotape to computer disk. It is also common on video editing equipment.

FireWire has many similarities to the SCSI (Small Computer System Interface) peripheral interface commonly used to connect hard drives to computers. However, FireWire has a much higher data rate and uses different cabling technology. Up to 63 devices can be connected to a single bus using twisted-pair cabling. Unlike SCSI, FireWire devices do not need to be connected in a line and terminated at the end. There is also no need to assign addresses to devices.

FireWire protocols include commands for controlling devices on the bus, including commands for starting and stopping devices like video recorders and players. FireWire will be a boon in the video production field because it provides a fast interface for not only controlling video devices, but also for streaming audio/video data to hard disks with little, if any, loss in quality.

A product that is often compared with FireWire is USB (Universal Serial Bus), discussed under its own topic. Apple Computer includes both USB and FireWire on its computers.

RFC 2734, "IPv4 over IEEE 1394," (December 1999) discusses how to transport IP datagrams over IEEE 1394.

Related Entries   Fibre Channel; Network Connection Technologies; Parallel Interface; SCSI (Small Computer System Interface); Serial Communication and Interfaces; SSA (Serial Storage Architecture); Throughput; *and* USB (Universal Serial Bus)

Linktionary!—Tom Sheldon's Encyclopedia of Networking updates	http://www.linktionary.com/f/firewire.html
Interoperability Lab IEEE 1394 information	http://www.iol.unh.edu/training/index.html
Apple Computer's FireWire page	http://www.apple.com/firewire/
1394 Trade Association	http://www.1394ta.org/
IEEE 1394 Related Links	http://rtlab.kaist.ac.kr/~sikang/soho/soho.html
Texas Instruments' IEEE 1394 page	http://www.ti.com/sc/docs/msp/1394/1394.htm
Skipstone (Adaptec) IEEE 1394 papers	http://www.skipstone.com/informat.html

Flapping

When a route in an IP network goes down, the router that knows about the change advertises it to neighboring routers. Those routers then recalculate their routes. Route flapping is when this occurs rapidly and possibly on a large scale. Route flapping can get out of control and affect network performance.

The Internet is protected from route flapping on private networks because private networks advertise only a summary of their internal routes. This is one reason for using both interior and exterior routing protocols—that is, OSPF (Open Shortest Path First) and BGP (Border Gateway Protocol).

Related Entries   BGP (Border Gateway Protocol); OSPF (Open Shortest Path First); *and* Routing

Flow

A flow is a stream of packets that is transmitted between a source and a destination. Flows generally follow the same route through a network, although that route may change at any time to bypass downed links and other problems. A voice or video session consists of long flows that usually require a certain amount of guaranteed bandwidth. An IP over ATM technique that provides QoS is to detect flows and set up switched paths across the ATM network that can satisfy the QoS requirements of the flows.

Flows may be implicit or explicit. An implicit flow is one in which the router detects a flow by inspecting header information in packets and then manages the flow as necessary. An explicit flow is a flow that is predefined, in other words, an end device tells the network that a flow is about to begin and the network sets itself up to handle the flow. In both cases, the network manages the flow in order to allocate resources (e.g., bandwidth and buffers) for the flow. When flows are recognized, congestion problems can be avoided.

Cut-through routing is a technique of detecting flows and switching the flows at high speed, using switching techniques rather than routing techniques. This case points out that flows are not related to routing because the routing functions are removed.

Flows are allocated some bandwidth, which means that some flows may have more bandwidth than others. This gets into issues of priority and/or fair sharing of bandwidth. See "Bandwidth Management" and "QoS (Quality of Service)."

Related Entries   Bandwidth; Bandwidth Management; Capacity; Channel; Congestion Control Mechanisms; Connection-Oriented and Connectionless Services; Cut-Through Routing; Data Communication Concepts; Delay, Latency, and Jitter; IP Switching; Multilayer Switching; QoS (Quality of Service); Reliable Data Delivery Services; TCP (Transmission Control Protocol); Throughput; *and* Transport Protocols and Services

Flow-Control Mechanisms

Network services can be categorized as *best-effort*, *connectionless* services or *reliable connection-oriented* services. In the Internet protocol suite, IP is a best-effort service and TCP is a reliable service. IP provides basic packet forwarding while TCP implements flow controls, acknowledgements, and retransmissions of lost or corrupted packets. This split in services "decentralizes" the network and moves the responsibility for reliable delivery to end systems. TCP is an end-to-end transport protocol, meaning that it runs in end systems, not the network. IP is a network protocol. This topic discusses flow control in terms of TCP, but flow controls are used by many other communication protocols, as mentioned later. The services offered by TCP include the following:

- *Flow-control mechanisms* control packet flow so that a sender does not transmit more packets than a receiver can process.

- *Reliable delivery mechanisms* provide a way for a receiving system to acknowledge that it has received a packet, and a way for the sender to know that it must retransmit a lost or corrupted packet. Refer to "Reliable Data Delivery Services."

- *Congestion control mechanisms* allow network systems to detect network congestion (a condition in which there is more traffic on the network than can be handled by the network or network devices) and throttle back their transmission to alleviate the congestion. Refer to "Congestion Control Mechanisms."

Congestion occurs on busy networks. When it occurs, end systems and the network must work together to minimize the congestion. In contrast, *flow controls* are used between end systems. A receiver uses flow controls to signal to the sender that it is overloaded. The sender then throttles back or stops its transmission.

Flow controls are necessary because senders and receivers are often unmatched in capacity and processing power. A receiver might not be able to process packets at the same speed as the sender. If buffers fill, packets are dropped. The goal of flow-control mechanisms is to prevent dropped packets that must be retransmitted.

Keep in mind that flow controls are used in the data link layer to control flow between devices that are directly connected. In contrast, TCP controls flow between devices that may be connected across a multihop routed network. Data link layer protocols include SDLC (Synchronous Data Link Control), HDLC (High-level Data Link Control), LAP-B (Link Access Procedure-Balanced), SLIP (Serial Line Internet Protocol), and PPP (Point-to-Point Protocol). Transport layer protocols include TCP (Transmission Control Protocol) and Novell SPX (Sequenced Packet Exchange).

When discussing data link layer protocols, the unit of transmission is the *frame*. In the transport layer, the unit of transmission for TCP is the *segment*. A segment is encapsulated in an IP datagram, which in turn is encapsulated in frames at the data link layer.

There are a few Internet RFCs related to flow control, including the original TCP RFCs:

- RFC 793, "Transmission Control Protocol," (September 1981)

- RFC 813, "Window and Acknowledgement Strategy in TCP," (July 1982)

- RFC 1016, "Something a Host Could Do with Source Quench: The Source Quench Introduced Delay," (July 1987)

- RFC 1180, "A TCP/IP Tutorial," (January 1991)

Types of Flow Control

Several flow-control schemes are discussed next. Each mechanism helps the sender and receiver synchronize their transmission and receive rates to prevent dropped packets. Dropped packets must be retransmitted, wasting network bandwidth.

Physical Layer Flow Controls

Physical layer connections include serial interfaces such as V.24 (RS-232) that are used to connect peripheral devices to computers or to connect two communication devices together, such as a computer serial port to a modem or a terminal connection. Flow controls are used to signal that the receiver is ready for a transmission and to signal that the transmission must stop because the receiver is overloaded.

There are two types of physical layer flow controls:

- **Hardware (out-of-band) flow controls**   In this scheme, specific leads (wires) on the physical interface are used to signal that transmission may begin or end. The RTS (Request To Send) is activated by the sending station when it is ready to transmit data. The CTS (Clear To Send) lead is activated by the receiving station when it is ready to receive data. If the receiver becomes overloaded, it deactivates CTS.

- **Software (in-band) flow controls**   In this scheme, special control characters called XON and XOFF are used to control flow. When the receiver is ready to accept data, it sends an XON character. When it becomes overloaded, it sends an XOFF character. When it is ready to receive more data, it sends another XON.

Stop-and-Wait Flow Control

The simplest flow control above the physical layer is the *stop-and-wait* mechanism. First, the sender transmits a packet to the destination. Upon receipt, the destination returns an *acknowledgment* packet to the receiver to indicate that it is ready to receive another packet. The source always waits for the acknowledgment packet before transmitting another packet. This technique naturally avoids overflowing the destination. If the destination needs time to process a packet, it holds up sending the acknowledgment.

This technique is useful if information can be sent in just a few packets. However, it is inefficient for long transmissions that require many packets. There is too much overhead in sending acknowledgments for each packet. In addition, some networks use small packets, which means there are more packets, and thus more acknowledgments.

Source-Quench Messaging

In this scheme, the sender starts sending packets to the receiver and continues sending until it receives a source-quench message from the receiver. The source-quench message instructs the sender to reduce its data transmission rate.

Source-quench does not take place until at least one packet has been dropped. Packets are dropped when the receiver's buffers are full. The receiver will send the source-quench to the sender, but other packets may be dropped before the sender starts slowing down. One source-quench message is sent for each message that is dropped. The sender starts slowing down and continues to slow down until the sender stops sending source-quench messages. Then it starts to pick up its transmission rate, buts slows down if more source-quench messages are received. The only problem with this scheme is that packets are dropped before the sender starts getting messages to slow down.

Sliding-Window Flow Control

Sliding-window flow controls are designed to provide reliable services in a more efficient way, using less network bandwidth for acknowledgments. The sliding-window technique basically lets the sender transmit multiple packets at a time and use the transmission channel as efficiently as possible. At the same time, its flow-control technique allows the receiver to indicate to the sender the status of its buffers. In the following discussion, the term "packet" refers to blocks of data, either frames or TCP segments.

You can understand the sliding-window technique as a conversation between sender and receiver. The sender starts out by saying, "I will send you x number of packets before you need to send me an acknowledgment." If the receiver starts to overflow, it says, "Scale back the number of packets being transmitted because my buffers are overflowing." The process is dynamic and automatically adjusts the number of packets that can be sent at one time. An adaptive sliding window will try to determine the best window size so that it sends as many packets as possible without overflowing the receiver. When the window gets too large, packets are dropped at the receiver and the sender scales the window size back.

TCP's window mechanism is an adaptive flow control that increases the data rate until it receives a signal to slow down. This signal is a dropped packet. When a receiver drops a packet (or doesn't receive one because the network is congested), it fails to acknowledge that packet. That is the signal that the sender uses to slow down or stop transmissions. The downside of this approach is that it relies on dropped packets and is not predictable. The flow may rapidly increase and decrease as traffic patterns change on the network. If an end system has plenty of buffers, a sender can increase its flow up to the point at which it saturates the network. On a fast network, the sender may complete its transmission before the sender receives a message to scale back. See "Congestion Control Mechanisms" and "TCP (Transmission Control Protocol)" for a continuation of this discussion.

Network Flow Controls

The preceding discussions describe flow controls as they are implemented in end systems. These flow controls were not originally implemented in the network because the network was meant to provide only basic packet forwarding. This improved performance and kept the network simple. More recently, network designers have become interested in traffic and flow controls in the network. One technique is to estimate the rate at which a particular traffic stream is arriving with a "rate estimator," and then mark packets according to how their rate compares to a CTR (committed target rate) and PTR (peak target rate). Packets are marked with a so-called color that indicates a drop precedence that is compatible with DiffServ (Differentiated Services). Packets below or equal to the CTR are marked "green," packets between CTR and PTR are marked "yellow," and packets above PTR are marked "red."

This particular method is outlined in RFC 2859, "A Time Sliding Window Three Colour Marker," (June 2000). This topic continues under "Traffic Management, Shaping, and Engineering." Also see "Differentiated Services" and "Congestion Control Mechanisms,"

Related Entries   Acknowledgments; Asynchronous Communications; Best-Effort Delivery Services; Connection Establishment; Congestion Control Mechanisms; Connection-Oriented and Connectionless Services; Data Communication Concepts; Data Link Protocols; Delay, Latency, and Jitter; Error Detection and Correction; Fragmentation and Reassembly; Network Architecture; Network Concepts; Packets and Packet-Switching Networks; Prioritization of Network Traffic; QoS (Quality of Service); Queuing; Reliable Data Delivery Services; TCP (Transmission Control Protocol); Traffic Management, Shaping, and Engineering; *and* Transport Protocols and Services

Linktionary!—Tom Sheldon's Encyclopedia of Networking updates	http://www.linktionary.com/f/flow_control.html
Flow Control in the Transport Area, by Michael Pierce	http://ganges.cs.tcd.ie/4ba2/transport/5.mp.1.html
Sliding window protocol analysis	http://paradise.caltech.edu/slide/
Sliding window flow control tutorial	http://www.ce.chalmers.se/~fcela/javis/tcp_slidwin.html

FORTEZZA

FORTEZZA is derived from the Italian word for fortress or fort. It is a registered trademark of the U.S. National Security Agency (NSA), and it describes a family of security products that were developed to create user-friendly, low-cost security devices for the Defense Message System. The Defense Department also uses FORTEZZA to encrypt voice communications over its secure telephones.

FORTEZZA cards (and other devices) are general-purposes cryptographic "co-processors" that can be used to provide authentication, data integrity, and confidentiality. Authentication (and nonrepudiation) is provided via DSA (Digital Signature Algorithm), which is part of DSS (Digital Signature Standard). Data integrity is provided via SHA (Secure Hash Algorithm).

Confidentiality is provided via KEA (Key Exchange Algorithm) and the SKIPJACK encryption algorithm. KEA and SKIPJACK were formerly classified. For more information about these individual algorithms and standards, refer to the related entries given later.

FORTEZZA-enabled devices include PCMCIA-based cards, serial port devices, Ethernet cards, and modems. FORTEZZA is being integrated into cellular telephones, pagers, PDAs, routers, and other devices. FORTEZZA crypto cards are tamper-resistant PCMCIA token authentication smart cards that support all of the preceding security schemes. Enhanced cards with more powerful processors are available to protect classified information.

Microsoft supports FORTEZZA in Windows 2000. There is also a Defense Message System–compliant version of Exchange, and an Outlook messaging and collaboration client. Microsoft Internet Explorer and Internet Information Server also support FORTEZZA.

Related Entries   Authentication and Authorization; Biometric Access Devices; Cryptography; Digital Signatures; DSS (Digital Signature Standard); Hash Functions; Key Distribution and Management; One-Time Password Authentication; Security; Smart Cards; *and* Token-Based Authentication

Linktionary!—Tom Sheldon's Encyclopedia of Networking updates

http://www.linktionary.com/f/fortezza.html

PC-Card Support Group (see FORTEZZA section)   http://fortezza-support.com/

Forwarding

Forwarding is the process used by a bridge, switch, or router to move a frame or packet from an input to an appropriate output port. Bridges and switches operate at layer 2 and handle frames. Routers operate at layer 3 and handle datagrams (packets).

The usual process is to *store-and-forward* packets, meaning that a packet must be fully received in memory before it is forwarded. But *cut-through* forwarding improves performance. Basically, the forwarding device looks at the forwarding address even before the packet is fully received and immediately begins to forward the packet.

The forwarding process in routers involves a table lookup to determine how a packet should be forwarded. Removing this step by using new label-switching techniques can improve performance. A label is a piece of information added to a packet at the edge of the network that identifies a specific network path through the network. By reading the label, devices in the network can immediately forward a packet without making routing decisions. Refer to "Label Switching" for more information.

Network nodes that implement the differentiated services enhancements to IP use a special field in the IP header to select a per-hop behavior (PHB) as the specific forwarding treatment for packets. Refer to "Differentiated Services (Diff-Serv)" for more information.

Related Entries   Bridges and Bridging; Data Communication Concepts; Differentiated Services (Diff-Serv); Framing in Data Transmissions; Label Switching; Multilayer Switching; Network Concepts; Packets and Packet Switching Networks; Routers; Routing; *and* Switching and Switched Networks

Linktionary!—Tom Sheldon's Encyclopedia of Networking updates

http://www.linktionary.com/f/forwarding.html

Fractional T1/Fractional T3

A fractional T1 line is a subchannel of a full T1 line. There are 24 fractional T1 lines in a full T1 line and each has a bandwidth of 64 Kbits/sec, which is just enough bandwidth to handle one digitized voice call. There are 28 T1 channels in a T3 line. Users can purchase one or more fractional lines without the need to purchase the full line and can add additional fractional lines at any time.

Related Entries   Multiplexing; NADH (North American Digital Hierarchy); T Carriers; *and* TDM Networks.

FRAD (Frame Relay Access Device)

See Frame Relay.

Fragmentation and Reassembly

Fragmentation is the process of breaking a packet into smaller pieces so that they will fit into the frames of the underlying network. The receiving system reassembles the pieces into the original packets. The term MTU (maximum transmission unit) refers to the maximum amount of data that can travel in a frame. Different networks have different MTU sizes, so packets may need to be fragmented in order to fit within the frames of the network that they transit. The process is illustrated in Figure F-8.

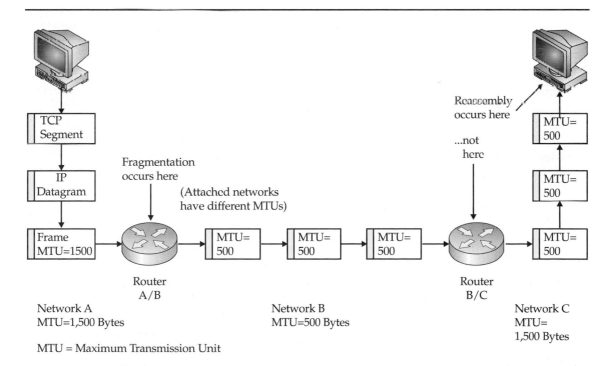

Figure F-8.   *Packets are fragmented to fit the frame size of the networks they must cross.*

RFC 791, "Internet Protocol" (September 1981) describes fragmentation and reassembly. RFC 815, "IP Datagram Reassembly Algorithms" (July 1982) also describes reassembly. RFC 1122, "Requirements for Internet Hosts—Communication Layers" (November 1990) also describes the process (see sections "3.3.2 Reassembly" and "3.3.3 Fragmentation"). A must-read document to understand fragmentation is RFC 879, "The TCP Maximum Segment Size and Related Topics" (November 1983). Also useful is RFC 1180, "A TCP/IP Tutorial" (January 1991).

Internetworking protocols such as IP use fragmentation because each of the networks that a packet may travel over could have a different frame size. Fragmentation occurs at routers that connect two networks with different MTUs. While it is possible to design an internal network with the same MTU size, this is not an option on the Internet, which includes thousands of independently managed interconnected networks.

Fragmentation is always undesirable because it reduces performance. In fact, fragmentation is not allowed in IPv6. Large packets are always preferable, especially if large files are being transferred on high-performance networks. But in some cases, trying to eliminate or reduce fragmentation may create additional problems. IP version 6 attempts to remove the need for fragmentation altogether by relying on end systems to discover the MTU across the entire delivery path. This is called *path MTU discovery* and it is already used in IP version 4, as discussed later. IPv6 will enforce it.

An important concept is that each fragment becomes a new, smaller IP datagram. That is because a new IP header is attached to the datagram that contains much of the information in the original datagram's IP header, plus information related to the fragmentation process. This new IP datagram is placed in a frame of the underlying network. The process is discussed and pictured later. The total size of the new datagram (IP header plus data) cannot exceed the MTU of that network.

Only the destination reassembles fragmented packets. Routers along a transmission path never perform reassembly. Consider that once a packet has been fragmented, its fragments may end up taking different paths to the destination. The only place where all of the fragments should appear again is at the destination. The receiver starts a timer and begins putting the fragments into a buffer, where they can be held until all the fragments arrive. If just one of the packet fragments fails to appear at the destination, the entire packet must be retransmitted since there is no mechanism for requesting and retransmitting individual fragments.

Since TCP segments go into IP datagrams and IP datagrams go into the frames of underlying networks, there are some interesting relationships to look at. First, TCP segments can be no bigger than IP datagrams minus the IP header. The maximum size of an IP datagram is 65,535 bytes minus the IP header, which may be 20 to 60 bytes in size. The size varies in increments of 4 bytes, depending on the header option settings. Few data link connections have MTUs that will accommodate 65K datagrams. Ethernet's MTU is 1,500 bytes and FDDI's MTU is 4,500 bytes.

Here are some other considerations that affect fragment size, as you'll see:

- Each IP datagram fragment must be a multiple of 8 bytes.
- An IP header is added to IP datagram fragments, so the total fragment size is (data fragment + IP header).
- The MTU specifies the maximum allowable fragment size (fragment + IP header)

Since the fragment must be a multiple of 8, the total size of a fragment may not always equal the MTU. Assume the MTU is 512 bytes and the header size is 20 (the header size is 20 if no options are used). Since IP datagrams can only be fragmented in multiples of 8 bytes, the largest fragment for this example network (before adding the header) is 488 bytes. After adding the header, the total fragment size is 508 bytes, which is under the 512-byte MTU limit. Note that the next multiple of 8 is 496 bytes. Adding a header would give a total fragment size of 516 bytes, which is over the MTU.

The following fields are used in the IP header to provide fragmentation information and control:

- **Packet Identifier**   A 16-bit field that identifies all the fragmented packets with a unique number. This number cannot be reused again until all the fragments have been processed by the receiver.

- **Fragment Offset**   Provides information to the receiver for reassembling the fragments into the original packet. The value indicates where the data in the fragment belongs in relation to the start of the data.

- **Don't Fragment flag**   When set to 1, the datagram should be transmitted without fragmentation. If that is not possible, the datagram should be dropped and an error message should be returned to the sender (using ICMP). This flag can be used in "scout" packets that are sent out to determine the largest MTU that can be sent across a network. See the upcoming section "Path MTU Discovery."

- **More Fragments flag**   When set to 1, this flag indicates that more fragments are coming. A 0 indicates that a packet is the last fragment.

Figure F-9 illustrates how a 1,300-byte datagram is fragmented into three datagrams on a network where the MTU is 500 bytes (values are rounded for clarity).

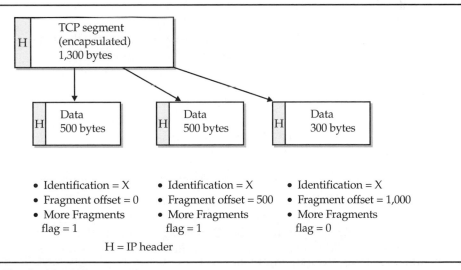

Figure F-9.   *The fragmentation process*

Note that routers must accept datagrams from attached networks that are the size of the specified MTU on those networks. In addition, they must accept a minimum datagram size of 576 bytes, a value that was defined in RFC 879 back in 1983 to help vendors create interoperable routers. The rule put forth in RFC 879 specifies that "hosts must not send datagrams larger than 576 bytes unless they have specific knowledge that the destination host is prepared to accept larger datagrams." Today, most routers support MTUs of 1,500 bytes, but the minimum value is still used when transmitting across nonlocal networks with unknown MTU sizes. Generally, networks on the Internet now support a minimum MTU of 576 bytes.

The other part of the long-established rule in RFC 879 is that the maximum TCP segment size (the data that goes into the IP datagram that, in turn, gets fragmented) is the maximum IP datagram size minus 40 bytes for header. Thus, the maximum TCP segment size is 536 bytes (576 bytes minus 40 bytes).

Most operating systems provide a way to change the MTU size. For example, in Windows 98, you can view and change dial-up network settings as follows. Open the Network utility in the Control Panel, click the Configuration tab, choose the Dial-Up Adapter, and then click Properties. On the Advanced tab, click IP Packet Size. The following values are available:

■ Automatic   The default setting

■ Large   1,500 bytes

■ Medium   1,000 bytes

■ Small   576 bytes

In Automatic mode, all PPP connections below 128 Kbps use an MTU of 576, while connections above 128 Kbps use an MTU of 1,500.

Path MTU Discovery

Path MTU is the smallest-size MTU over all the links in a path between a source and a destination node. Path MTU discovery is a process by which a packet is sent out like a "scout" on the network to discover the smallest path MTU. When the smallest MTU is found, the sender uses this value as the maximum IP datagram size so that packets are not fragmented during transmission. As mentioned earlier, fragmentation adds overhead and reduces performance. The large packet size should be used whenever possible.

Path MTU discovery is described in RFC 1191, "Path MTU Discovery" (November 1990), RFC 1981, "Path MTU Discovery for IP Version 6" (August 1996), and RFC 2923, "TCP Problems with Path MTU Discovery" (September 2000).

Path MTU discovery goes like this:

1. The sender transmits a packet (usually the default size for its local network) and sets the "Don't Fragment" flag to 1.

2. If the packet is larger than any network's MTU, the router connected to that network will drop the packet and return an ICMP message to the sender. This message indicates that the packet could not be forwarded without fragmentation and contains the MTU of the network that caused the problem.

3. The sender tries again with the new packet size and the process starts over as in step 1. A router further on in the network that is connected to a network with an even smaller MTU may drop the packet and return an error message.

By using Path MTU discovery, a system can send packets over multiple networks using the largest packet size possible without the overhead of fragmentation and reassembly.

However, Path MTU Discovery has its own costs. Actual data is not transmitted until the best MTU is discovered, which causes delays. Several routers may return error messages with new MTU sizes. In addition, discovery packets use network bandwidth and require additional processing by routers on the network. Still, this bandwidth use and processing is considered better than fragmenting datagrams.

Related Entries   Acknowledgments; Best-Effort Delivery Services; Connection Establishment; Data Communication Concepts; Datagrams and Datagram Services; Encapsulation; Flow-Control Mechanisms; Framing in Data Transmissions; Network Architecture; Network Concepts Packets and Packet-Switching Networks; Routers; Routing; TCP (Transmission Control Protocol); *and* Transport Protocols and Services

Linktionary!—Tom Sheldon's Encyclopedia of Networking updates	http://www.linktionary.com/f/ fragmentation.html
Godred Fairhurst's Data Communications Course: Maximum Transfer Unit (MTU)	http://www.erg.abdn.aoryusers/gorry/ eg3561/inet-pages/mtu.html
Albert P. Belle WinSock Tuning FAQ (see "Tuning MTU/MSS/RWIN")	http://www.cerberus-sys.com/~belleisl/ mtu_mss_rwin.html
"Fragmentation Considered Harmful" by Christopher A. Kent and Jeffrey C. Mogul (December 1987)	http://www.research.compaq.com/wrl/ techreports/abstracts/87.3.html
Path MTU Discovery and Filtering ICMP by Marc Slemko	http://www.worldgate.com/~marcs/mtu/
Lynn Larrow's Place (MTU/MSS page)	http://www.webcom.com/llarrow/ mtumss.html

Frame

See Data Link Protocols; Encapsulation; Framing in Data Transmissions; Network Architecture; *and* Packets and Packet-Switching Networks.

Frame Relay

Frame relay is a metropolitan and wide area networking solution that implements data link switching techniques. Data frames are sent across permanent or switched virtual circuits that are defined within a network of frame relay switches. Frame relay networks are operated by local and long-distance carriers such as Sprint, MCI, AT&T, and most of the RBOCs (Regional Bell Operating Companies).

Frame relay is an outgrowth of work done on ISDN (Integrated Services Digital Network). Basically, frame relay is the frame-switching component of ISDN, and it is now sold as a separate service. While ISDN is primarily a circuit-based service that mimics a telephone call, frame relay was designed into the service to provide reliable any-to-any connections across a switched network.

Subscribers contract for a virtual circuit between two points. The circuit has some guaranteed level of service. What the subscriber sees is a private data pipe with that level of service from one point to the other. Inside the network itself, the path of the pipe may vary, depending on traffic conditions, downed lines, and so on. However, because the service is switched, the network will quickly establish new circuit paths and maintain the levels of service guaranteed to subscribers. If the carrier cannot maintain the contracted service levels, the subscriber will obtain some form of credit.

Frame relay is an any-to-any service that is shared by many users. Virtual circuits can be established between any two devices attached to the nework. In contrast, leased TDM circuits such as T1 are set up between two points with a specific bandwidth. The advantage of frame relay is that many users share the network, which means that carriers can offer lower monthly rates. If one subscriber is not using its share of the bandwidth, that share is available for another subscriber to use. The data rate is more flexible. Instead of one fixed rate, bursts are allowed if the network has available capacity.

The downside of a shared network is that when traffic increases, service levels may drop. Carriers will write this into their contracts. For example, a carrier will add together the bandwidth requirements of all of its subscribers and then ensure that the network has enough capacity to deliver that bandwidth. This is the *committed rate* that it guarantees to subscribers. Figure F-10 illustrates the advantage of frame relay when compared to a network of private dedicated circuits such as T1 lines. There are four sites in different cities. The customer wants to inter-connect all sites. To do so with T1 circuits would require six long-distance links. With frame relay, subscribers simply connect each site via a short-distance circuit into a carrier's local frame relay cloud. The frame relay network then provides the long-distance component.

Once again, frame relay is a subscriber-shared network, so costs are lower per subscriber, but heavy traffic may affect performance.

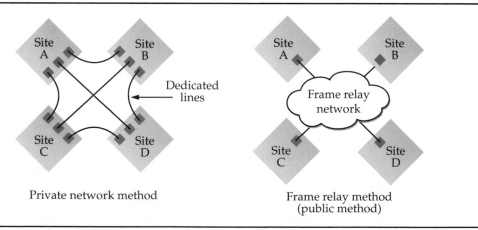

Figure F-10.   *A private leased line network compared to a frame relay virtual private network*

Frame relay has become one of the most widely deployed WAN technologies. It allows organizations to consolidate physical access circuits. Frame relay is well suited for moving SNA (Systems Network Architecture) traffic, and it has become a conduit for carrying voice calls between company sites. Frame relay is also used to carry Internet traffic in the access provider portion of the Internet.

Historical and Standards Information

Frame relay was one of the most quickly developed and adopted standards in the history of telecommunications. Users groups, industry consortiums, and international standards bodies worked on frame relay.

As mentioned, frame relay started out as part of the ISDN specification. The LAPD (Link Access Protocol-D channel) had been defined to carry signaling information on the ISDN D channel. LAPD had been designed with a provision for multiplexing virtual circuits in the data link layer. From this, developers created a set of standards for frame relay.

Both ANSI and the ITU defined the standards in cooperation. The standards are outlined here:

Frame relay service description	ANSI T1.606	ITU I.233
Core Aspects	ANSI T1.618	ITU Q.922 Annex A
Access Signaling	ANSI T1.617	ITU Q.933

The Frame Relay Forum is a nonprofit organization that promotes frame relay through implementation agreements. The agreements are meant to ensure interoperability and facilitate conformance testing. The Frame Relay Forum has done extensive work on extending frame relay with the implementation agreements listed next. Refer to the Frame Relay Forum Web site, given later, for more information.

FRF.1.1	User-to-Network (UNI) Implementation Agreement, January 1996
FRF.1.2	Frame Relay Network-to-Network (NNI) Implementation Agreement, July 1995
FRF.3.1	Multiprotocol Encapsulation Implementation Agreement (MEI), June 1995
FRF.4.1	SVC User-to-Network Interface (UNI) Implementation Agreement, January 2000
FRF.5	Frame Relay/ATM Network Interworking Implementation, December 1994
FRF.6	Frame Relay Service Customer Network Management Implementation Agreement (MIB), March 1994
FRF.7	Frame Relay PVC Multicast Service and Protocol Description, October 1994
FRF.8.1	Frame Relay / ATM PVC Service Interworking Implementation Agreement, February 2000
FRF.9	Data Compression over Frame Relay Implementation Agreement, January 1996
FRF.10	Frame Relay Network-to-Network SVC Implementation Agreement, September 1996
FRF.11	Voice over Frame Relay Implementation Agreement, May 1997, Annex J, added March 1999
FRF.12	Frame Relay Fragmentation Implementation Agreement, December 1997

FRF.13   Service Level Definitions Implementation Agreement, August 1998

FRF.14   Physical Layer Interface Implementation Agreement, December 1998

FRF.15   End-to-End Multilink Frame Relay Implementation Agreement, August 1999

FRF.16   Multilink Frame Relay UNI/NNI Implementation Agreement, August 1999

FRF.17   Frame Relay Privacy Implementation Agreement, January 2000

Note that FRF 15 and FRF 16 provide a way to split frame relay traffic over multiple lines that are aggregated to provide higher bandwidth.

Frame Relay Features and Operation

Frame relay is superior in many way to other networking protocols. Even as the Internet has grown, many organizations still prefer frame relay for building private WANs. Some of frame relays most important features are outlined here:

- **Dynamic bandwidth allocation**   The dynamic allocation of bandwidth is one of frame relay's strongest features. Bandwidth is cooperatively shared by customers. When one customer is not using bandwidth, it is available for others to use.

- **Frames versus time slots**   Frame relay is based on frames, which are individually addressable, as opposed to the fixed time slots in a TDM (time division multiplexing) circuit such as T1. This allows quick reconfiguration of the path, quick recovery from errors, and other useful features.

- **Frames versus packets**   IP relies on routers in the network to make hop-by-hop forwarding decisions for packets. In contrast, frame relay forwards frames across virtual circuits. When a frame arrives at a switch, the switch quickly forwards it based on the virtual circuit setting in the frame. No table lookup is required, as is the case with IP routing.

- **Speed due to simplicity**   Early WAN technologies such as X.25 were built to provide reliability in the network. This was in part due to the fact that end devices were dumb terminals. Early communication networks were also unreliable. As end devices became more intelligent and networks became more reliable, it no longer made sense to have the network provide reliability functions, so the excessive acknowledgment scheme of X.25 was removed to make the network fast and efficient.

- **Simple rule: "If there is a problem, discard the data"**   This simple rule is a result of making the network simple and relying on intelligent end nodes. If frames have errors, they are discarded. If devices are overloaded or the network is congested, frames are discarded (not randomly, but based on discard eligibility, as discussed later).

- **Protocol encapsulation and framing**   Frame relay will accept any type of protocol data and encapsulate it inside a frame relay frame. The frame size is variable to support different types of networks. The most common size is 1,600 bytes, but frame sizes up to 8,000 bytes are supported. Frame relay adds a 2-byte header to the frame. One of the fields in the frame is the DLCI (Data Link Connection Identifier), a 10-bit field that identifies the virtual circuit between two points (not a destination address, but a path that leads to the destination).

F

Figure F-11 illustrates the details of a typical frame relay network and end-to-end connection. Note that frame relay "routers" are pictured. Routers are necessary to make the decisions about whether to forward LAN packets across the frame relay network. These routers have built-in FRADs (frame relay access devices), which provide frame relay assembly/disassembly functions that encapsulate LAN frames into frame relay frames. Stand-alone FRADs also exist. These provide basic assembly/disassembly functions for LAN bridging

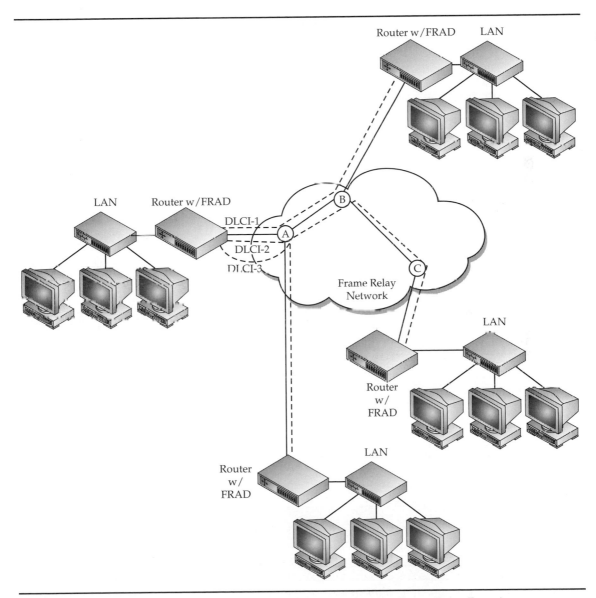

Figure F-11.   *Frame relay network and end-to-end connection (source: Frame Relay Forum)*

or connections of mainframe front-end processors to frame relay networks. This discussion will refer to all frame relay access devices as FRADs.

Note the DLCIs in Figure F-11. Each DLCI value identifies a destination across the frame relay network. The switches in the network (A, B, and C) perform a very fast and efficient frame-forwarding operation.

Frame Format

The frame format for frame relay contains special fields that hold control information for establishing and releasing connections. The frame is pictured in Figure F-12, and the fields are described here.

FLAG   The Flag field holds the "Start of frame" marker.

LINK INFO   This field holds the logical connection address and control fields described here:

- **DLCI (data link connection identifier)**   An address that identifies logical connections
- **C/R**   Command/Response bit (not used in frame relay)
- **EA (extended address)**   Used to extend the Header field to support DLCI addresses of more than 10 bits
- **FECN (forward explicit congestion notification)**   Warns receivers about network congestion
- **BECN (backward explicit congestion notification)**   Warns senders about network congestion
- **DE (discard eligibility)**   Indicates whether frames can be discarded if the network is congested

DATA   Control information or encapsulated data goes in this field.

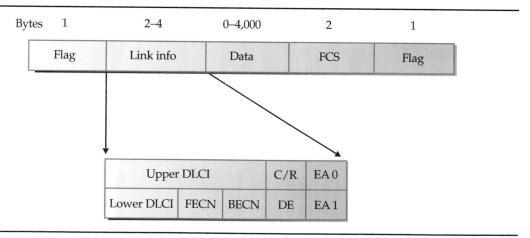

Figure F-12.   *The frame format for frame relay*

FCS (FRAME CHECK SEQUENCE)   FCS is a checksum used for error detection.

FLAG   This flag field holds the "End of frame" marker.

> **Note**   *RFC 2427, "Multiprotocol Interconnect over Frame Relay," (September 1998) describes an encapsulation method for carrying network interconnect traffic over a frame relay backbone. It covers aspects of both bridging and routing.*

PVCs (Permanent Virtual Circuits)

All frames are transmitted across virtual circuits, either permanent or switched. Carriers prefer PVCs (permanent virtual circuits) because they can be programmed in advance and customer billing is simplified. SVCs (switched virtual circuits) are just beginning to appear. They are useful for one-time events like videoconferences when the circuit is set up on demand and taken down immediately afterward. However, SVCs are relatively difficult to implement. Carriers like to manage bandwidth, and that is difficult if customers are setting up SVCs on the fly.

Once a PVC is established, it provides private line service with an agreed-upon bandwidth. Carriers and customers negotiate the features of PVCs as part of a service-level agreement (SLA). The agreed-upon capacity is called the CIR (committed information rate). The endpoints of the PVC are constant, but a carrier can usually reprogram a PVC in a short time. When evaluating frame relay services, a good thing to know is how responsive the carrier is to setting up PVCs and changing the endpoints if you move your office.

A customer with multiple sites will usually have multiple PVCs through the frame relay network, as shown in Figure F-13. These PVCs are statistically multiplexed across the access line from the customer site to the frame relay network. Once the circuits hit the frame relay network, they follow different paths to their destinations.

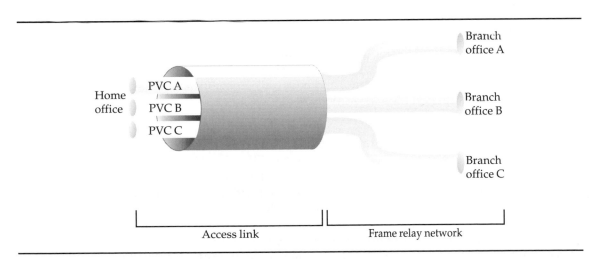

Figure F-13.   *Multiple PVCs on the same access line*

Connection Setup and Release

The following discussion concentrates on PVCs rather than SVCs. A PVC is set up at the time of registration by a carrier and exists until the subscriber and carrier agree to take it down. It provides an always-on connection that does not require dialing or any sort of connection establishment phase. A single FRAD can be programmed to support multiple PVCs, each of which provides a link to any location in the frame relay network.

The carrier assigns a specific DLCI number to each PVC. Once the FRADs on either end of the connection are set up, they can communicate immediately across the network. Note that frames carry the DLCI number, which is a path number, rather than the address of the destination. However, the DLCI value leads to that destination.

A management protocol called LMI (Local Management Interface) provides information about the status of PVC-to-network access devices. It defines management frames for monitoring the integrity of a link, and whether a link is active or inactive.

SVCs (Switched Virtual Circuits)

SVCs were added to the frame relay standard after the initial design work, although there was always the potential of using switched circuits. Only recently have carriers begun to offer SVCs for customer use. Customer premises equipment is now available to support SVCs as well. SVCs offer several benefits over PVCs, the most important being switched any-to-any connectivity. An organization can use frame relay SVCs to set up temporary connections to remote sites, business partners, or data center backup/replication servers. An SVC is also useful for applications such as teleconferencing and, of course, voice calls. They can also be used to handle overflow traffic or provide an alternate line if a primary link fails.

SVCs require call setup and call disconnect signaling. During the call setup, information about the call must be passed across the network. This includes required bandwidth parameters and endpoint addresses. Setting up an SVC is like setting up a phone call in the public telephone network. The requested destination must be contacted and it must accept the call. The network then builds an SVC between the source and destination. A path is determined and the forwarding information is programmed into each switch node along the way. When the SVC is no longer needed, one of the end systems notifies the network to take it down.

PVCs have not provided the kind of convenience that customers would like for some of the applications mentioned here. For example, to set up a teleconference over frame relay, the customer must call the carrier in advance and have a PVC established. This process may take hours or days, depending on the carrier. With SVCs, setting up such links can be as simple as making a phone call.

CIR (Committed Information Rate) and Bursts

The capacity of a PVC is negotiated in advance as the CIR (committed information rate). The network provides bandwidth to a PVC up to the CIR and then may allocate additional bandwidth for bursts in traffic, depending on what was negotiated with the customer. Unlike a leased line that has a fixed capacity that can never be exceeded, frame relay PVCs can be stretched if bandwidth is available and if a prior arrangement was made. This is like borrowing bandwidth from elsewhere in the network to fill a temporary need.

The bandwidth that is available for "borrowing" is bandwidth that is not in use on the network. Usually, there is no charge up to a certain rate. There is a maximum burst rate, called

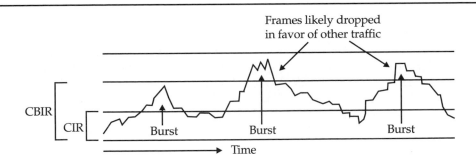

CBIR = Committed burst information rate
CIR = Committed information rate

Figure F-14. *Frame relay bursts*

the CBIR (committed burst information rate). Data can burst up to this rate and still get through the network, but bursts higher than the CBIR are likely to be dropped by the carrier in preference to other traffic if the network gets busy. This relationship is pictured in Figure F-14.

Ultimately, the access line between the customer and the network does determine the high-end data rate, but customers may choose to lease a line that has a data rate higher than the highest burst rate.

Error Detection and Recovery

Frame relay is usually compared to X.25, which was specifically designed for error-prone communication systems. X.25 performs extensive error checking and acknowledgments at the data link level to guarantee packet delivery. X.25 is still used in many countries where the telecommunication system is inadequate. As mentioned previously, it became apparent that the core network could run more efficiently if error checking and acknowledgment were pushed out to the end systems, which today are more powerful and capable of handling the tasks.

Figure F-15 illustrates how the X.25 network on the left requires acknowledgments at every hop along the transmission path. Transmitting a single frame through this network is a 12-step process! Frame relay, on the other hand, eliminates excessive traffic by requiring only the destination node to return an acknowledgment of successful delivery.

The only real error checking handled by the frame relay network is to determine whether a frame has become corrupted in transit. If so, the frame is immediately dropped. The end system must handle recovery.

Congestion Control

The frame relay network manages congestion by setting bits in frames that warn end devices that there is congestion on the network. The three congestion control devices, described next, correspond to the control fields in the frame relay frame shown earlier in Figure F-12.

■ **FECN (forward explicit congestion notification)** When a node in the network starts to become congested, it can warn downstream nodes (toward the destination) and the

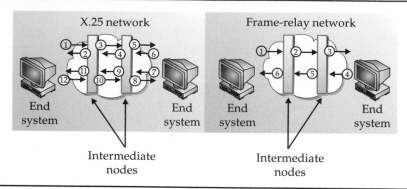

Figure F-15.   *Acknowledgments in X.25 and frame relay*

destination itself that congestion is occurring by setting the FECN bit in frames to 1. This information is not really useful to downstream nodes, except that they might use it as an indicator to slow down transmission in the reverse direction since traffic is congested. A high occurrence of the bits can also be used as an indicator to the carrier that some part of the network is underprovisioned for the amount of traffic going through it.

■ **BECN (backward explicit congestion notification)**   BECN is the most useful traffic control mechanism. If a node is experiencing congestion, it can set the BECN bit to 1 to indicate to the source that it needs to slow down its transmissions. Note that the BECN bit is set in frames that are already headed toward the source; the node does not create a frame to send to the source.

■ **DE (discard eligibility)**   As mentioned earlier, frame relay follows the simple rule of discarding frames in the event of congestion. However, it does not discard randomly. Doing so would cause all endpoints to initiate retransmission. Through the use of CIR, it is possible to predefine which frames should be dropped. When a circuit exceeds its CIR, its frames are eligible for discard. The DE bit is set to 1 at the customer site to indicate a preference for which frames may be dropped should congestion occur. However, DE provides no guarantees. If congestion continues to increase, even nonflagged frames may be dropped.

Voice over Frame Relay

Frame relay can help you fully consolidate voice, data, and fax into a single network. In the past, voice quality was poor because of delay problems and the quality of compression equipment. The current standard for voice compression is the ITU (International Telecommunications Union) G.729 algorithm, which can provide toll-quality voice and uses only 8 Kbits/sec of bandwidth per voice channel. Compare this to the traditional voice compression standard G.724, which compresses to 32 Kbits/sec.

The added benefit of voice over frame relay is that all calls are included in the price of the link and might be considered free to some manager's way of thinking. If numerous calls are made by employees to remote sites, there may be considerable savings in moving those calls from the carrier's voice network to the frame relay network. Most products can now carry voice, data, and other traffic (such as SNA traffic) over a single PVC, rather than setting up a different PVC for every traffic type.

The Frame Relay Forum implementation agreement FRF.11 defines VoFR (Voice over Frame Relay). FRF.11 established a standard that vendors can use to design interoperable VoFR equipment. FRF.11 specifies two classes of voice encoding/decoding. The first is G.727, a high-bit-rate class to preserve high-quality voice. The second is G.728, a low-bit-rate class for lower-quality voice. See "G Series ITU Recommendations."

Frame Relay/ATM Internetworking

Both the Frame Relay Forum and the ATM Forum have defined a method for internetworking between frame relay and ATM. The reason for internetworking with ATM is to support wide area networking with ATM cores. ATM has built-in QoS and can better support real-time traffic such as broadcast video. The following standards support frame relay to ATM internetworking:

- **FRF.5 (Frame Relay/ATM Network Interworking for PVCs)**   Allows frame relay devices (routers and FRADs) and end-user equipment to communicate across an ATM network or networking devices such as FRADs. The ATM network is in the middle and frame relay equipment is on either side of the cross-ATM link.

- **FRF.8 (Frame Relay/ATM Service Interworking for PVCs)**   This standard allows frame relay users to communicate with users who are connected to an ATM-based network. In other words, the users or devices on one side of the link are connected via ATM, not frame relay.

- **FUNI (Frame-based User-to-Network Interface)**   This is an alternative to Frame Relay/ATM Service Interworking. It primary function is to allow frame relay users and devices connected to ATM to maintain the QoS levels of the ATM network. With FUNI, the variable-length frames characteristic of frame relay may be transmitted over an access link to the ATM network. The idea is to move the frame-to-cell conversion to a switch that is directly attached to the ATM network where many users can share the equipment.

Developments

The Frame Relay Forum develops new capabilities for frame relay. The Multilink features described in FRF.15 and FRF.16 are examples of new developments that help frame relay compete with emerging IP services. With multilink services, frame relay bandwidth can be increased via inverse multiplexing.

MPLS (Multiprotocol Label Switching) has been developed as a way to provide virtual-circuit–like capabilities for IP. MPLS works over ATM and frame relay–based networks. MPLS provide VPN capabilities for IP.

Ordering Frame Relay Services

Most carriers now offer frame relay services. Each carrier has a specific number of places where customers can link into the network, called *points of presence*. Access to these points is through the LEC (local exchange carrier) or other service provider. Here are some things to consider when evaluating frame relay services or putting together requests for proposals:

- Are switched service offerings available for any-to-any connections? Are Internet virtual circuits available? Are voice services available?

- What kind of service guarantees are available and how are they available (in the form of credits)? What are the fees for additional offerings such as disaster recovery services and equipment management?

- What kind of access is available into the frame relay network? This access will depend on distance from your site to the frame relay access point, but it often involves a major portion of the cost to implement frame relay.

- What are the paths of the PVCs through the network? Ask to see a map so you can determine whether they pass through potentially congested areas.

- Establish a CIR (committed information rate) for your needs, and obtain a level of commitment from the carrier for providing services over that rate.

- Is usage-based billing available in which you are charged for the amount of traffic sent, usually above a low monthly fee? A maximum charge rate is usually set as well.

- Can you obtain usage and performance information from the carrier that will help you optimize your use of the network?

- What type of management facilities are available for monitoring and managing connections from your own site? Is SNMP (Simple Network Management Protocol) supported?

Related Entries   ATM (Asynchronous Transfer Mode); Communication Services and Providers; Data Communication Concepts; Internet Connections; ISDN (Integrated Services Digital Network); Network Access Services; Network Concepts; Network Design and Construction; Packets and Packet Switching Networks; Service Providers and Carriers; Switching and Switched Networks; Telecommunications and Telephone Systems; Virtual Circuits; WAN (Wide Area Network); *and* X.25

Linktionary!—Tom Sheldon's Encyclopedia of Networking updates	http://www.linktionary.com/f/frame_relay.html
Frame Relay Forum	http://www.frforum.com
Frame Relay paper by Norm Al Dude and Professor N. Erd (interesting and colorful illustrations!)	http://www.scan-technologies.com/tutorials/Frame%20Relay%20Tutorial.htm
IBM frame relay papers (with information pertinent to SNA; (search for frame relay)	http://www.redbooks.ibm.com/
Cisco paper: SNA Internetworking over Frame Relay Design and Implementation	http://www.cisco.com/univercd/cc/td/doc/cisintwk/dsgngde/snafr/index.htm
Cisco Frame Relay Troubleshooting Guide	http://www.cisco.com/univercd/cc/td/doc/cisintwk/itg_v1/index.htm

Cisco Frame Relay Background paper	http://www.cisco.com/univercd/cc/td/doc/cisintwk/ito_doc/frame.htm
Motorola Frame Relay Resources page (very extensive)	http://www.mot.com/networking/frame-relay/
Network World Fusion frame relay information, articles, and links	http://www.nwfusion.com/netresources/framerelay.html
Frame Relay	http://www.rad.com/networks/tutorial.htm
Protocols.com Frame Relay page with good information about standards	http://www.protocols.com/pbook/frame.htm
Frame Relay Resource Center, Alliance Datacom (extensive links and white papers)	http://www.alliancedatacom.com/framerelay.asp

F

Frame Switch

See Switch Fabrics and Bus Design; Switching and Switched Networks.

Framing in Data Transmissions

A point-to-point connection between two computers or devices consists of a wire in which data is transmitted as a stream of bits. However, these bits must be *framed* into discernible blocks of information. Framing is a function of the data link layer. It provides a way for a sender to transmit a set of bits that are meaningful to the receiver. Ethernet, token ring, frame relay, and other data link layer technologies have their own frame structures. Frames have headers that contain information such as error-checking codes.

There are three different types of framing, each of which provides a way for the sender to tell the receiver where the block of data begins and ends:

- **Byte-oriented framing**   Computer data is normally stored as alphanumeric characters that are encoded with a combination of 8 bits (1 byte). This type of framing differentiates one byte from another. It is an older style of framing that was used in the terminal/mainframe environment. Examples of byte-oriented framing include IBM's BISYNC protocol.

- **Bit-oriented framing**   This type of framing allows the sender to transmit a long string of bits at one time. IBM's SDLC (Synchronous Data Link Control) and HDLC (High-level Data Link Control) are examples of bit-oriented protocols. Most LANs use bit-oriented framing. There is usually a maximum frame size. For example, Ethernet has a maximum frame size of 1,526 bytes. The beginning and end of a frame is signaled with a special bit sequence (01111110 for HDLC). If no data is being transmitted, this same sequence is continuously transmitted so the end systems remain synchronized.

- **Clock-based framing**   In a clock-based system, a series of repetitive pulses are used to maintain a constant bit rate and keep the digital bits aligned in the data stream. SONET (Synchronous Optical Network) is a synchronous system in which all the clocks in the network are synchronized back to a master clock reference. SONET frames are then positioned within the clocked stream.

The advantage of using frames is that data is broken up into recoverable chunks that can easily be checked for corruption. A glitch in the line during the transmission will corrupt some frames. Only the lost frames and not the entire set of data needs to be retransmitted. Detecting and correcting errors is discussed under "Error Detection and Correction."

The general format for frames is a header followed by a data payload area. The frame size is usually fixed, while the data area is variable. Most data link networks use variable-size framing, which has advantages (more efficient use of the network) and disadvantages (unpredictable traffic flows and the inability to provide quality of service).

An Ethernet frame (IEEE 802.3), as pictured in Figure F-16, can hold up to 1,500 bytes of data. Note that the frame includes header and trailer bytes along with the encapsulated data. The information in the header adds overhead in the form of additional data that must be transmitted.

The preamble contains a set of bits that help the sender and receiver synchronize their transmissions. The Ethernet bit pattern is 10101010, which produces a 10-MHz square wave clocking signal for 5.6 microseconds. The SFD (start frame delimiter) indicates the actual start of the frame. The destination and source addresses are self-explanatory. The LEN (length) field indicates the length of the data portion of the frame. PAD (padding) is used for fill-in bits. CRC (cyclic redundancy checksum) is used for error checking.

Framing is specific to the data link layer. Upper-layer protocols also divide data into discernible "packets" of information, but the terminology used to define packets at each layer is different, as outlined next. Note that these descriptions assume the Internet protocol suite.

- **Message**   The actual application data, command, or instruction specified by the user or application. A message is encapsulated within a TCP segment assuming TCP is used.

- **Segment**   The packet of information exchanged between two connected systems (peers) that contains transport layer protocol information. TCP exchanges segments. Segments encapsulate upper-layer messages.

- **Datagram**   The packet of information that is exchanged between two connected systems that contains network layer protocol information. IP exchanges datagrams. Datagrams encapsulate segments.

- **Frame**   The packet of information at the data link layer with a layout that is specific to the protocol in use. Frames encapsulate datagrams.

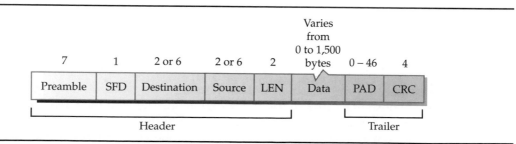

Figure F-16.   *An 802.3 (Ethernet) frame*

Figure F-17 illustrates how data is passed down the protocol stack and encapsulated by the protocols at each layer. The TCP/IP protocol is illustrated in this example. At the transport layer, TCP encapsulates upper-layer data and adds its own header to create a segment. At the network layer, IP encapsulates the segment and its own header into a datagram. Finally, the data link layer encapsulates the datagram into a frame or frames. Note that datagrams may be fragmented and placed into multiple frames. Refer to "Network Architecture" and "Fragmentation and Reassembly" for more information.

Framing is handled by the underlying network protocols and equipment. Ethernet, token ring, frame relay, ATM, and other data link technologies use their own framing standards (ATM frames are actually called "cells" and are a fixed size). Upper-layer protocols are generally designed to interface with any of these protocols and framing methods. When building a network application, you generally don't need to care about which underlying LAN will be used, as long as you ensure the application is compatible with a network protocol suite like TCP/IP.

Note that frames are confined to specific network segments. An internetwork consists of multiple data link segments, as pictured in Figure F-18. One segment may be Ethernet while another is token ring. The connecting bridge or router must remove the encapsulated data from

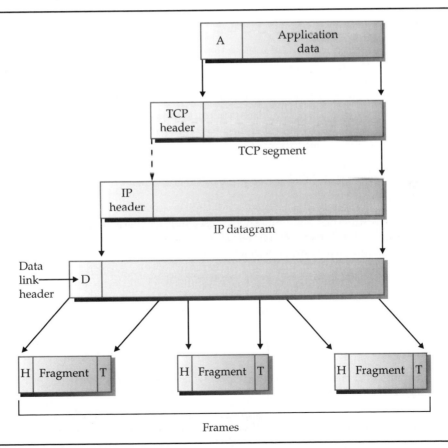

Figure F-17.   *Packets and frames in TCP/IP*

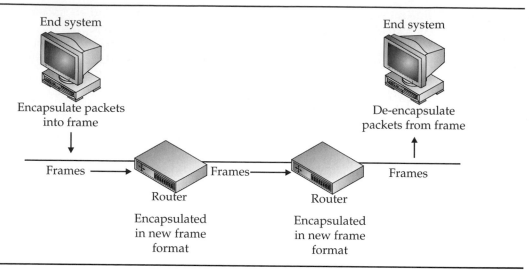

Figure F-18.   *Framing across internetworks*

the frames it receives and reencapsulate the data into the frame type of the next network. In some cases, the next network might require a smaller frame size, so the device might need to fragment the data before encapsulating it into frames. Note that once data is fragmented, it travels that way all the way to the final destination.

Alteon has proposed expanding the Ethernet frame size from its 1,500-byte size to a "jumbo frames" size of 9,000 bytes. The company claims that jumbo frames can provide a 300-percent increase in throughput for Gigabit Ethernet networks by reducing the number of frames that must be processed. Alteon believes that the 9,000-byte size (and not a larger size) is a good balance between efficiency and the processing requirements of error checking and handling large blocks of data.

Related Entries   Asynchronous Communications; Best-Effort Delivery; Bridges and Bridging; Data Communication Concepts; Data Link Protocols; Datagrams and Datagram Services; Encapsulation; Error Detection and Correction; Ethernet; Flow-Control Mechanisms; Fragmentation and Reassembly; Handshake; HDLC (High-Level Data Link Control); LAP (Link Access Procedure); Network Architecture; Network Concepts; Packets and Packet-Switching Networks; PPP (Point-to-Point Protocol); SDLC (Synchronous Data Link Control); Serial Communication and Interfaces; SONET (Synchronous Optical Network); Switching and Switched Networks; Synchronous Communications; *and* Token Ring

Linktionary!—Tom Sheldon's Encyclopedia of Networking updates	http://www.linktionary.com/f/framing.html
Ethernet frame format information at Optimized Engineering Corporation	http://www.optimized.com/COMPENDI/EN-FrFmt.htm
HDLC framing information	http://www.erg.abdn.a`oryusers/gorry/course/dl-pages/hdlc-framing.html

FreeSpace Optical Network

See Infrared Technologies; MAN (Metropolitan Area Network); Network Access Services; *and* Optical Networks.

Front-End Processor

A *front-end processor*, or *FEP*, is a dedicated computer that controls communication between an IBM host computer and the terminals that communicate with it. The IBM 3725 and 3745 are front-end processors that run the NCP (Network Control Program), which communicates with programs running in PUs (physical units). FEPs connect to IBM 3270 hosts.

The primary function of the front-end processor, or communication controllers as they are commonly called, is to free up the host computer to run applications. In this way, the host is not continually interrupted by the external devices.

Communication controllers establish sessions, manage communication links, detect and correct errors, and provide concentration points for cluster controllers. The older model 3705 provides up to 352 communication lines at line speeds up to 230.4 Kbits/sec and can attach to eight hosts. Newer models, such as the IBM 3745, provide full-duplex communication lines and dual processors for standby service and backup, as well as IBM Token Ring Network support. IBM 3745 also supports IBM SNA (Systems Network Architecture) networks and public packet-switched networks (with appropriate software).

Related Entries   Communication Controller; Mainframe; *and* SNA (Systems Network Architecture)

Front-End System

In a client/server environment, the front-end system is typically a computer on the network that a person uses to access data stored on a back-end server system.

Related Entries   Client/Server Computing; Distributed Computer Networks

FTAM (File Transfer Access and Management)

FTAM is an OSI standard that provides file transfer services between client (initiator) and server (responder) systems in an open environment. It also provides access to files and management of files on diverse systems. In these respects, it strives to be a universal file system. FTAM has worked well as a way to bring mainframe information systems into distributed environments, but FTAM has not caught on otherwise. A more complete description of FTAM is at the Linktionary! Web site listed shortly.

Related Entries   Client/Server Computing; Distributed File Systems; File Systems; File Transfer Protocols; Network Operating Systems; *and* OSI (Open Systems Interconnection) Model

| Linktionary!—Tom Sheldon's Encyclopedia of Networking updates | http://www.linktionary.com/f/ftam.html |
| FTAM standards listing at OII | http://158.169.50.95:10080/oii/en/ files.html#FTAM |

FTP (File Transfer Protocol)

FTP is an Internet file transfer service that operates on the Internet and over TCP/IP networks. FTP is basically a client/server protocol in which a system running the FTP server accepts commands from a system running an FTP client. The service allows users to send commands to the server for uploading and downloading files. FTP operates among heterogeneous systems and allows users on one system to interact with another type of system without regard for the operating systems in place, as long as the network protocol is TCP/IP.

FTP clients run an interactive, command-driven, text-based interface. The basic steps a client goes through to interact with an FTP server are described here:

1. Start the FTP command interface.

2. Type **?** to get command help.

3. Use the **open** command to specify the IP address or domain name of the FTP server to access.

4. Log on (at public sites, type **anonymous** as your logon name).

5. Use the **dir** or **ls** command to list files on the FTP server.

6. Use the **cd** command to switch directories.

7. Use the **get** command to download files or the **put** command to upload files.

8. Type **close** to close the current session (and **open** to access a different server).

9. Type **quit** to end the program.

In most cases, these steps represent most of what you will do when interacting with an FTP server. As mentioned, you can type **?** to see a complete list of commands, and there are many. Many FTP sites use minimal file access security because they provide files to the public. These sites are called *anonymous FTP* sites. As mentioned in step 4, you simply type **anonymous** as your logon name, and then type your e-mail address (or anything really) as your password.

FTP works across many different files systems, so users must be aware that file types on FTP servers may not be compatible with their systems. Text (txt) files are generally viewable by all, and new universal files types like Adobe's PDF (Page Description Language) make this less of a problem. One other thing: type **binary** before downloading graphics files or executables; type **ascii** before downloading text files.

The FTP client actually handles much of the command processing. It first interprets the user's commands and then sends a request to the FTP server using the FTP protocol.

Commands and data are sent across two different connections. When you start FTP and connect with an FTP server, a connection is opened to that server that remains open (is persistent) until you type the **close** command. When you request a file transfer, the file's data is transferred across a different connection, and that connection is taken down when the file transfer completes. Thus, a typical FTP session may have several open connections at the same time if multiple files are being transferred. Using this scheme to separate control and data means that the control connection can be used while data is transferred.

FTP has been defined over the years in numerous RFCs. The original specification goes back to 1971. The most current FTP-specific document is RFC 959, "File Transfer Protocol,"

(October 1985). A useful document is RFC 1635, "How to Use Anonymous FTP," (May 1994). Quite a few related RFCs exist, including RFC 783, "The TFTP Protocol," (June 1981). It describes the Trivial File Transfer Protocol, which is a scaled-down version of FTP that runs over UDP, not TCP. A complete list of RFCs is available at the Linktionary! Web site.

The IETF Working Group, called "Extensions to FTP (ftpext)," developed recent extensions for FTP. A list of relevant documents is at the Web site.

Related Entries   File Sharing; File Systems; File Transfer Protocols; Internet; Internet Protocol Suite; *and* Internet Standards

Linktionary!—Tom Sheldon's Encyclopedia of Networking updates	http://www.linktionary.com/f/ftp.html
FTP Extensions WP: Extensions to FTP (ftpext)	http://www.ietf.org/html.charters/ftpext-charter.html
The FTP Protocol Resource Center, by Jarle (jgaa) Aase	http://war.jgaa.com:8080/ftp/
"Using FTP for File Transfer" by CIRCA Network Services	http://www.circa.ufl.edu/handouts/networks/ftp.html
Globalscape.com (browser-based FTP software)	http://www.globalscape.com/

FTTH (Fiber to the Home)

The majority of the Internet and the carrier networks are constructed with optical fiber cable, which provides gigabit-level speeds within the core. In contrast, the "local loop" and the "last mile" are still largely copper cable in the form of the twisted-pair telephone line and coaxial cable (CATV). DSL and cable modems have boosted access rates for home and small business users, but promoters of fiber to the home have a bigger goal. They want to deliver voice (up to six lines), data, and television services over a single cable. Extending fiber all the way to the home is now getting more attention because of reduced equipment costs and a bigger demand for service.

Note that fiber to the home is similar to HFC (hybrid fiber/coaxial) networks, which are built with a combination of fiber and copper cabling. A similar hybrid system extends fiber cable to carrier remote terminals and then takes advantage of DSL services over the copper wire into homes.

A typical FTTH fiber installation consists of multiple splitters. A trunk cable extends from the central office to a remote terminal, where it is split into 8 separate cables that extend to clusters of homes. Near the homes, the cable is split again to service 4 homes. This allows a single trunk from the central office to service 32 homes. The first split can be up to 30,000 feet from the central office. The cable can then extend another 3,000 feet from this splitter. Note that some systems support many hundreds or thousands of users.

Inside the home, the cable terminates at an ONT (optical network termination) box that typically contains an Ethernet 10/100Base-TX network interface. This services an Ethernet network within the home. The ONT performs an optical-to-electrical conversion on the signal arriving from the central office. Multiple services may be extracted from the signal, including voice telephone signals, high-speed data, and television signals.

One method of transporting signals over the cable is ATM PON (Asynchronous Transfer Mode passive optical network), which is an ITU specification. ATM PON is a "passive" optical system that does not require power or active electronic components between the service provider and customer. It consists only of the optical fiber, splitters, splice points, and connectors. A single fiber services multiple customers, as compared to older systems that required a separate fiber to each customer. PONs can be used over great distances and are ideal for rural areas. See "PON (Passive Optical Network)."

While ATM PON is promoted by the telecommunication carriers, Ethernet PON is being promoted by new network providers that intend to build competitive broadband service networks in metropolitan areas. Another alternative is SONET PON.

Related Entries   Cable (CATV) Networks; Communication Services and Providers; Fiber-Optic Cable; HFC (Hybrid Fiber/Coax); Home Networking; Internet Connections; Last Mile Services; Local Loop; Network Access Services; Optical Networks; PON (Passive Optical Network); Residential Broadband; *and* Service Providers and Carriers

Linktionary!—Tom Sheldon's Encyclopedia of Networking updates	http://www.linktionary.com/f/fiber_home.html
Web ProForum (see "Fiber to the Home" tutorial)	http://www.iec.org/tutorials/index.html
FSAN (Full Service Access Network) consortium	http://www.fsanet.net/
Terawave Communications	http://www.terawave.com/
Optical Solutions	http://www.opticalsolutions.com/
IEEE Ethernet Web page (see "Ethernet in the First Mile Study Group")	http://grouper.ieee.org/groups/802/3/
Lightwave Magazine Online	http://www.light-wave.com
Light Reading ("the global site for optical networking")	http://www.lightreading.com/

Full-Duplex Transmissions

The simple explanation of full-duplex mode is that it is like the telephone, where both parties can talk at the same time. In contrast, a pair of walkie-talkies operates in half-duplex mode because only one party can talk at a time.

A full-duplex data transmission is one in which data flows in both directions at the same time. Two separate channels are required for full duplex—either two separate wire pairs or two multiplexed channels. In contrast, a half-duplex connection allows data to flow in only one direction at a time.

A typical serial connection (RS-232) between a computer and some other device like a modem or printer is pictured in Figure F-19. Note that this is the minimal wire configuration,

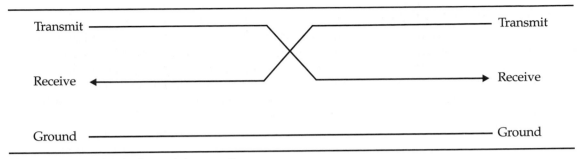

Figure F-19.   *A full-duplex serial connection*

and that the transmit and receive lines share the ground wire. An RS-232 cable will typically consist of additional wire for transmitting control signals.

FutureShare, Apple

See AppleShare.

G Series ITU Recommendations

The G Series of ITU recommendations are referred to as "Transmission systems and media, digital systems and networks." Most of the recommendations below G.600 are related to analog telephone equipment and circuits. The G.600 series is related to transmission media (twisted-pair, coaxial, and fiber-optic cable) for the telephone system. The G.700 series recommendations are related to digital transmission systems, in particular, coding of analog signals into digital signals. A list of these standards is at the Linktionary! Web site.

In particular, the G.711, G.723, G.726, G.728, and G.729 voice-coding techniques are the most important for multimedia networking. These techniques improve bandwidth, voice quality and other factors. G.723.1 defines a technique for compressing speech or audio at very low rates (5.3 and 6.3 Kbits/sec). The techniques are components of the IMTC (International Multimedia Teleconferencing Consortium) standard for Internet telephony. See "Compression Techniques" for more information, as well as "VoIP (Voice over IP)" and "Multimedia."

Related Entries   ADC (Analog-to-Digital Conversion); Cable and Wiring; Coaxial Cable; Compression; Fiber-Optic Cable; Frame Relay; H Series ITU Recommendations; H.323 ITU Recommendation; ISDN (Integrated Services Digital Network); ITU (International Telecommunications Union; Multimedia; T Series ITU Recommendations; Videoconferencing; Voice/Data Networking; VoIP (Voice over IP); *and* X Series ITU Recommendations

Linktionary!—Tom Sheldon's Encyclopedia of   http://www.linktionary.com/g/g_series.html
Networking updates

ITU G series recommendations   http://www.itu.int//itudoc/itu-t/rec/g/

Gateway

There are many types of gateways. One definition of a gateway is a computer system or other device that acts as a translator between two systems that do not use the same communication protocols, data-formatting structures, languages, and/or architecture. Unlike a bridge, which simply passes information between two systems without conversion, a gateway repackages information or changes its syntax to match the destination system. A gateway may also provide filtering and security functions, as in the case of a proxy server and/or firewalls. Note that most gateways operate at the application layer relative to the OSI protocol model, which is the topmost layer. Some examples of gateways are described in the following sections.

Another definition of a gateway is a router, which is a network layer gateway. In the early days of the Internet, routers were called "gateways." These devices provided links, initially between mainframe computers, and then later between LANs and other networks. The term "router" is more common now, but gateway is still used when configuring the IP protocol for host devices. Some networks have multiple routers that lead to other networks. A host can be configured so that one of the routers is selected over any of the others. It is usually called the "default gateway," meaning that it is the primary path to other networks. See "Routing." Other types of gateways are listed here.

■ **IBM Host Gateways**   An IBM host gateway allows workstations attached to LANs to connect with IBM mainframe systems. See "IBM Host Connectivity" for more information.

■ **LAN Gateways**   LAN gateways are used when joining networks that use different protocols, such as when a backbone network provides an interconnection for all the networks attached to it. For example, FDDI was a popular backbone networking technology used to interconnect many department and workgroup LANs. See "Backbone Networks" and "FDDI (Fiber Distributed Data Interface)."

■ **Electronic Mail Gateways**   Electronic mail gateways translate messages from one vendor's messaging application to another's so that users with different e-mail applications can share messages over a network. A typical e-mail gateway converts messages to the X.400 format for electronic mail messaging or uses Internet mail. See "Electronic Mail."

■ **Firewall**   A firewall is a device that allows internal network users to access the Internet while blocking Internet users from accessing the internal network. A full-featured firewall provides advanced screening, authentication, and proxy services to keep hackers and attackers from reaching vulnerable internal systems. See "Firewall."

■ **Proxy service**   With a proxy service, the packet generated by an internal user never goes out over the Internet. Instead, the proxy service reads the packet and creates its own to send out over the network. Incoming packets are handled in the same way. They are never allowed through the proxy server as is. See "Proxy Server."

■ **NAT (Network Address Translation)**   An internal network may have its own internal IP addressing scheme that does not comply with the Internet addressing scheme or is hidden for security reasons. An NAT translates between internal and external IP addresses. See "NAT (Network Address Translation)."

■ **Caching services**   A caching server may be part of a firewall and proxy server or a stand-alone device. It caches information that users have obtained from the Internet or external networks and keeps it available in case other users need that same information. See "Cache and Caching Techniques" and "Web Caching."

■ **Voice/Media Gateways**   The term "convergence" is often used to describe the integration of voice networks (i.e., the telephone system) and data networks. The idea is to build one network that carries both voice and data. But voice is a streaming technology, while data is typically packetized. Media gateways, which are part of the softswitch architecture, provide an interface between the circuit-based PSTN and the packet-based Internet. See "Softswitch" and "Voice over IP (VoIP)" for more information.

G

■ **NAS (network access servers)**   An NAS is a gateway into a larger network for dial-in users or ISDN users. It may also be classified as a RAS (remote access server). See "NAS (Network Access Server)" and "Remote Access."

Linktionary!—Tom Sheldon's Encyclopedia of Networking updates	http://www.linktionary.com/g/gateway.html
Yahoo! Gateways section	http://dir.yahoo.com/Computers_and_Internet/ Internet/World_Wide_Web/
IETF Working Group: Media Gateway Control (megaco)	http://www.ietf.org/html.charters/megaco-charter.html

Gateway-to-Gateway Protocol

This protocol is one of the first routing protocols developed for use on the Internet. It is similar to the Xerox Network System's RIP (Routing Information Protocol), but was found to be inadequate because it could not keep up with dynamic changes in the network. Eventually, the concept of autonomous systems (domains) was developed and IGPs (Interior Gateway Protocols), and EGPs (Exterior Gateway Protocols) were developed. See "Routing" and "Routing on the Internet."

GBE (10-Gigabit Ethernet)

Another name for IEEE 802.3ae, a 10-Gbit/sec version of Gigabit Ethernet. See "Gigabit Ethernet."

Gigabit Ethernet

Gigabit Ethernet is a 1-gigabit/sec (1,000-Mbit/sec) extension of the IEEE 802.3 Ethernet networking standard. Its primary niches are corporate LANs, campus networks, and service provider networks where it can be used to tie together existing 10-Mbit/sec and 100-Mbit/sec Ethernet networks. Gigabit Ethernet can replace 100-Mbit/sec FDDI (Fiber Distributed Data Interface) and Fast Ethernet backbones, and it competes with ATM (Asynchronous Transfer Mode) as a core networking technology. Many ISPs use Gigabit Ethernet in their data centers.

Gigabit Ethernet provides an ideal upgrade path for existing Ethernet-based networks. It can be installed as a backbone network while retaining the existing investment in Ethernet hubs, switches, and wiring plants. In addition, management tools can be retained, although network analyzers will require updates to handle the higher speed.

Gigabit Ethernet provides an alternative to ATM as a high-speed networking technology. While ATM has built-in QoS (quality of service) to support real-time network traffic, Gigabit Ethernet may be able to provide a high level of service quality by providing more bandwidth than is needed. The Gigabit Ethernet/ATM debate is discussed later in this topic.

Gigabit Ethernet Features and Specifications

Gigabit Ethernet was developed by the IEEE 802.3z Gigabit Task Force and was ratified as a standard in June of 1998. To speed up standardization, it was decided early in the process to leverage the ANSI Fibre Channel standard, which implements high-speed data transmissions over fiber-optic cable.

Some of the more important features of Gigabit Ethernet are outlined here:

- Supports the existing frame size and frame format of IEEE 802.3 Ethernet, which means it easily integrates with existing networks.

- Allows an easy upgrade path to high-performance networking while taking advantage of existing technologies and product knowledge.

- Supports *full-duplex mode* for switch-to-switch and switch-to-end-station connections. Most Gigabit Ethernet products being shipped are full duplex. In this mode, there are no shared-media contention problems.

- Supports *half-duplex mode* on shared network connections. In this mode, Gigabit Ethernet uses the same fundamental CSMA/CD medium access method as traditional Ethernet to resolve contention for the shared media.

- A packet bursting feature was added to CDMA/CD that allows servers, switches, and other devices to send bursts of small packets in order to fully utilize available bandwidth.

- Uses fiber-optic cable or Category 5 (preferably Category 5e) cable. See "Cable and Wiring" for a description.

As shown in Figure G-1, Gigabit Ethernet implements a hierarchical star topology. The core Gigabit Ethernet hub is a multilayer switch, meaning it includes wire-speed routing functions. Note that Gigabit Ethernet switches should be able to support a switching capacity that is an aggregate of all of its ports. For example, a 10-port Gigabit Ethernet switch should have a switching capacity of 10 Gbits/sec. See "Multilayer Switching" for details.

Figure G-2 illustrates the functional elements of Gigabit Ethernet. Note that the physical layer media includes fiber-optic cable and copper twisted-pair cable, as described shortly.

There are two primary Gigabit Ethernet committees. IEEE 802.3z pursued two fiber optic media specifications and one short-distance copper-based link. The IEEE 802.3ab committee pursued a long-distance twisted pair (Category 5 or better cable). The latter's work is now referred to as 1000BaseT. The different specifications are listed here:

- **1000Base-LX (IEEE 802.3z)**   Implements long-wavelength laser transmissions with links up to 550 meters over multimode fiber-optic cable and 3,000 meters over single-mode fiber-optic cable:

    - 50-micron multimode fiber-optic cable (550 meters)

    - 62.5-micron multimode fiber-optic cable (550 meters)

    - 9-micron single-mode fiber-optic cable (5 km)

- **1000Base-SX (IEEE 802.3z)**   Implements short-wavelength (850 nm) laser transmissions over the following links:

    - 50-micron multimode fiber-optic cable (500 to 550 meters)

    - 62.5-micron multimode fiber-optic cable (220 to 275 meters)

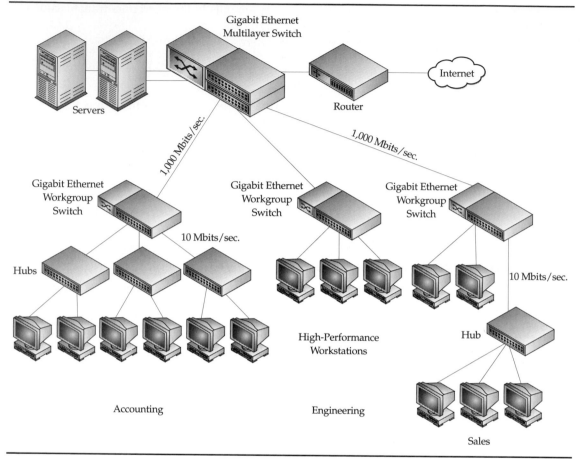

Figure G-1. *Typical Gigabit Ethernet hierarchical topology*

- **1000Base-CX (IEEE 802.3z)** Designed for connecting devices over short distances (in the same wiring closet), this standard uses high-data-rate shielded twisted-pair cable with a maximum distance of 25 meters.

- **1000Base-T (IEEE 802.3ab)** This standard allows Gigabit Ethernet transmissions over four-pair Category 5 cable with a maximum distance of 100 meters. This version is a good choice for server and high-performance desktop connections when the cost of fiber is a consideration.

- **10-Gigabit Ethernet (IEEE 802.3ae)** A 10-Gbit/sec version of Ethernet currently in the works. This version is being used in service provider metro-Ethernet networks to provide data services in metropolitan areas as an alternative to SONET. See "MAN (Metropolitan Area Network)."

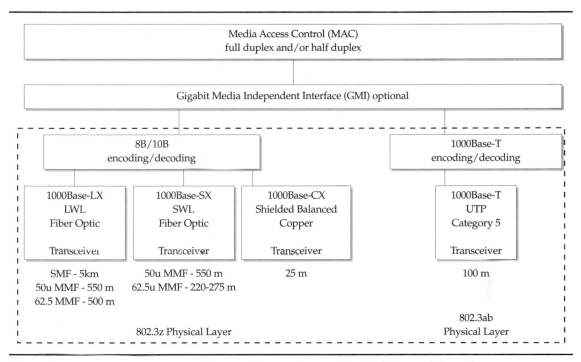

Figure G-2.   *Functional elements of Gigabit Ethernet (source: Gigabit Ethernet Alliance)*

A related IEEE standard of importance to Gigabit Ethernet networks is IEEE 802.1ad, which provides link aggregation. Link aggregation allows trunking of links between switches to improve bandwidth and provide redundancy. See "Link Aggregation" and "Load Balancing."

3Com's MPLA (MultiPoint Link Aggregation) is a link aggregation solution in which Gigabit Ethernet switches are a fundamental building block. It allows the bonding of multiple physical gigabit switch ports to form one logical channel expandable in gigabit increments.

Gigabit Ethernet over Copper (1000Base-T)

The 1000Base-T (IEEE 802.3ab) specification is actually a great piece of engineering work. But it also took a few years for developers to lock down a standard. Signals are sent simultaneously on all four pairs of a Category 5 cable, which requires special encoding and error monitoring. The specification is limited in distance to 100 meters. But that should not be a problem when a network's design is based on a hierarchical model where 1000Base-T is used to connect high-performance end systems to wiring closets and where fiber is used to connect the wiring closets to backbone switches. 1000Base-T is also ideal for data centers and server farm configuration when the distance is not a problem.

While Fast Ethernet uses two twisted pairs in a Category 5 cable, Gigabit Ethernet uses all four wires in a Category 5 cable. Basically, Gigabit Ethernet transmits 250 Mbits/sec per pair and aggregates the four pairs into a 1,000-Mbit/sec channel. You can think of the cable as a four-channel trunk with aggregate bandwidth of 1,000 Mbits/sec.

While Fast Ethernet uses a three-level encoding scheme, Gigabit Ethernet uses a five-level encoding scheme. That translates to a higher operating frequency that makes Gigabit Ethernet more susceptible to some copper-wire line conditions. The most common is FEXT (far-end crosstalk), which is a measure of the crosstalk noise that exists at the opposite end of a cable (at the receiver). What happens is that crosstalk occurs between transmitters as signals are transmitted down the line. See "Cable and Wiring" for more information about cabling tests and measurements.

While Gigabit Ethernet is supposed to run over properly installed Category 5 cable, a better bet for companies installing new cable is to use Enhanced Category 5 cable (Cat-5E).

All existing Category 5 cable must be tested to ensure that it will work with Gigabit Ethernet. Fluke, Scope, and other test equipment vendors sell equipment and train technicians that can certify cable as Gigabit Ethernet compliant. Note that failed segments can usually be fixed by redoing connections to tighter specifications or by replacing connectors. In some cases, the cable itself may have problems such as excessive bending or flattening that can be traced with an appropriate cable analyzer.

Gigabit Ethernet Switches

Typical Gigabit Ethernet switches may have a variety of port types, including 10-Mbit/sec Ethernet, Fast Ethernet, and Gigabit Ethernet. For example, Foundry Network's FastIron II Plus GC has 16 1000Base-T ports and 24 10/100Base-TX ports. Extreme Networks has an enterprise Gigabit Ethernet switch that supports a variety of port configurations and has built-in policy-based QoS (Quality of Service). Nortel Network's Accelar 8000 core switch has up to 64 1000Base-T ports.

Remember that a large number of gigabit ports is only impressive if the switch has enough switching capacity to handle all the traffic that might come into those ports simultaneously. Most Gigabit Ethernet switches use ASICs and/or network processors to ensure wire-speed throughput.

Most Gigabit Ethernet switches today are multilayer switches that provide layer 3 routing, as well as layer 2 switching. That means that each port can be separated from other ports via the packet-filtering and firewall-like functionality provided at layer 3. See "Multilayer Switching" for a more complete description of enterprise network switches.

Network Configurations

As mentioned, Gigabit Ethernet is designed for the campus or building environment as a high-bandwidth backbone and a way to connect routers, switches, hubs, repeaters, and servers. The designers do not expect the technology to be deployed directly to desktop systems, although that is possible in the future. Some configuration options are outlined next. See "Network Design and Construction" for more examples of how networks can be constructed with Gigabit Ethernet.

■ **Flat network or subnets**   A Gigabit Ethernet network for a small- to medium-size company can be built as one flat network without subnet boundaries. A flat network is one in which the entire network is built without routers. In other words, all network segments are bridged and there are no routers. This has some management advantages, but network broadcasts can be problem. See "VLAN (Virtual LAN)" for a description of some solutions. Multilayer switches provide an economical way to introduce routing back into a flat network. See "Multilayer Switching."

■ **Gigabit Ethernet backbones**   Gigabit Ethernet is a good replacement for older backbones such as Fast Ethernet or FDDI. This improves overall throughput among networks attached to the switch, which may run 100-Mbit/sec or 10-Mbit/sec Ethernet. As shown previously in Figure G-1, Gigabit Ethernet workgroup switches can provide a flat network topology within departments, while multilayer backbone switches can provide the necessary routing to interconnect different workgroup/department networks. Gigabit Ethernet supports the fiber-optic cable used in FDDI networks. In an FDDI upgrade, the organization can retain existing fiber-optic cabling but improve the aggregate bandwidth tenfold.

■ **Switch-to-server links**   In the scenario, the bandwidth to the server farm is increased by replacing the NICs (network interface cards) in the servers with Gigabit Ethernet NICs. This upgrade provides 1,000-Mbit/sec throughput to the servers. In Figure G-1, note that high-performance superservers are connected directly to the Gigabit Ethernet switch. Severs equipped with Gigabit Ethernet NICs must potentially handle over a million packets (and thus interrupts) per second. This is beyond the means of many servers, but a company called Alteon has developed a special NIC that off-loads interrupt handling to help in this task. Basically, if the server is busy and cannot handle interrupts, the card buffers incoming packets and then hands them to the server using a single interrupt.

■ **Gigabit Ethernet to the desktop**   In this scenario, a Gigabit Ethernet NIC is installed in a high-performance engineering or scientific workstation and connected directly to the Gigabit Ethernet network. Note the workstation attachment at the top in Figure G-2.

■ **Switch-to-switch links**   In this scenario, Gigabit Ethernet switches are linked together using fiber-optic cable. The links between the switches provide a high-performance backbone and promote a hierarchical network infrastructure.

Gigabit Ethernet Versus ATM

Gigabit Ethernet is often compared to ATM. A typical ATM corporate network operates at 622 Mbits/sec compared to Gigabit Ethernet at 1,000 Mbits/sec. However, ATM has built-in bandwidth management and QoS capabilities that can support real-time multimedia traffic such as voice and video. As this traffic increases, network managers will need to choose between bandwidth management and overprovisioning, or use some combination of the two:

■ **Bandwidth management**   This involves dividing the available bandwidth up and allocating a guaranteed amount of that bandwidth to applications that need it such as voice telephone calls. The remainder of the bandwidth is allocated for best-effort use.

■ **Overprovisioning**   The alternative is to provide more bandwidth than all the applications on the network ever need. If that bandwidth is relatively cheap (as it is with Gigabit Ethernet), then overprovisioning is a good solution.

Both solutions have merit. TCP/IP hosts have a habit of bursting traffic onto a network. The burst appears as a spike that hogs all bandwidth, and these spikes can disrupt real-time traffic. With ATM, virtual circuits can be set up to guarantee bandwidth to voice traffic. Traffic-management techniques are just emerging for TCP/IP networks. However, bandwidth management requires special software, policies, and management. Even with bandwidth management, overprovisioning may be required to keep up with growing traffic loads.

Gigabit Ethernet, combined with some bandwidth management, is a logical choice as multimedia traffic increases on your network. Some interesting QoS capabilities are being developed for both Ethernet and for TCP/IP that can provide QoS even in a packet-switched environment. And if you do run short on bandwidth, you can aggregate two or more Gigabit Ethernet channels to form a single larger-bandwidth trunk, as mentioned earlier. See "Link Aggregation" and "QoS (Quality of Service)" for more information."

Hybrid Gigabit Ethernet/ATM Core Network

The argument for ATM is that QoS is still needed at the core of the network. That is why many carriers and service providers use it. Building faster switches and bigger pipes is not always the solution. Ethernet networks are normally built with a hierarchical topology that can overwhelm the backbone. This is where ATM backbones are useful.

Look at the hybrid network pictured in Figure G-3. This design is meant for very large enterprises. A similar network is used in service provider networks, except that routers exist at the edge of the ATM network to connect different subscriber networks.

The core of the network is a mesh of multiple redundant links among the switches with Gigabit Ethernet switches at the edge. The ATM multilink mesh topology is possible thanks to PNNI (Private Network-to-Network Interface). Not only do these redundant links provide fault tolerance, they also provide load sharing, which means that core bandwidth can scale up to very high levels to avoid bottlenecks—no matter how many Gigabit Ethernet networks are connected to the edge of the ATM core. Each Gigabit Ethernet edge switch may service traffic within a department or division of the company, but send interdepartment or interdivision traffic across the ATM core.

10-Gigabit Ethernet

As if 1 Gbits/sec wasn't enough, the IEEE is working to define 10-Gigabit Ethernet (sometimes called "10 GE"). The new standard is being developed by the IEEE 802.3ae Working Group. Service providers will be the first to take advantage of this standard. It is being deployed in emerging metro-Ethernet networks. See "MAN (Metropolitan Area Network)" and "Network Access Services."

As with 1-Gigabit Ethernet, 10-Gigabit Ethernet will preserve the 802.3 Ethernet frame format, as well as minimum and maximum frame sizes. It will support full-duplex operation only. The topology is star-wired LANs that use point-to-point links, and structured cabling topologies. 802.3ad link aggregation will also be supported.

The new standard will support new multimedia applications, distributed processing, imaging, medical, CAD/CAM, and a variety of other applications—many that cannot even be

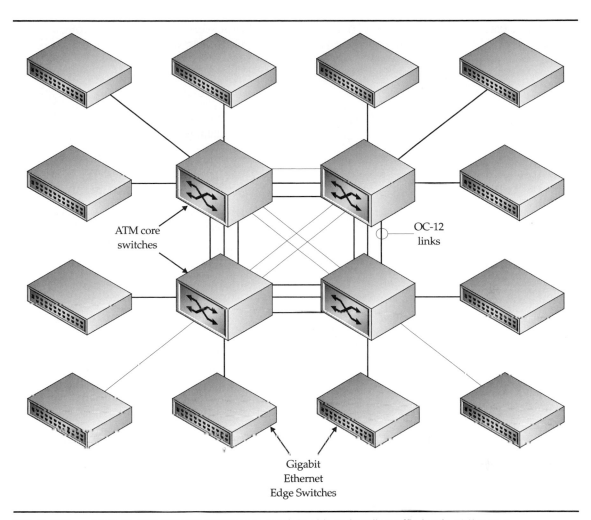

Figure G-3.   *A hybrid ATM/Gigabit Ethernet network is able to handle traffic loads at the core*

perceived today. Most certainly it will be used in service provider data centers and as part of metropolitan area networks. The technology will also be useful in the SAN (Storage Area Network) environment. Refer to the following Web sites for more information.

| 10 GEA (10 Gigabit Ethernet Alliance) | http://www.10gea.org/Tech-whitepapers.htm |
| Telecommunications article on 10 Gigabit Ethernet "Lighting Internet in the WAN" | http://www.telecoms-mag.com/issues/200009/tcs/lighting_internet.html |

Related Entries   ATM (Asynchronous Transfer Mode); Backbone Networks; Cable and Wiring; Data Link Protocols; Ethernet; Fast Ethernet; Fibre Channel; IEEE 802 Standards; Load Balancing; MAN (Metropolitan Area Network); Multilayer Switching; Network Access Services; Network Concepts; Network Design and Construction; Switching and Switched Networks; Throughput; TIA/EIA Structured Cabling Standards; *and* VLAN (Virtual LAN)

Linktionary!—Tom Sheldon's Encyclopedia of Networking updates	http://www.linktionary.com/g/ gigabit_ethernet.html
IEEE 802.3 Working Group home page	http://grouper.ieee.org/groups/802/3/
3Com Network Solution Center (see white papers or choose Gigabit Ethernet)	http://www.3com.com/nsc/
3Com paper: "Gigabit Ethernet Comes of Age"	http://www.3com.com/technology/tech_net/ white_papers/503003.html
Cisco's Gigabit Ethernet page	http://www.cisco.com/univercd/cc/td/doc/ cisintwk/ito_doc/ethernet.htm
Cisco technology brief: "Introduction to Gigabit Ethernet"	http://www.cisco.com/warp/public/cc/techno/ media/lan/gig/tech/gigbt_tc.htm
Extreme Networks technology page	http://www.extremenetworks.com/technology/ technology.asp
Google Web Directory for Gigabit Ethernet	http://directory.google.com/Top/Computers/ Data_Communications/Ethernet/Gigabit/
Bitpipe (search for "Gigabit Ethernet")	http://www.bitpipe.com

GigaPOP

See POP (Point-of-Presence); Internet2; Internet Architecture *and* Backbone; *and* ISP (Internet Service Provider).

GII (Global Information Infrastructure)

The GII was proposed by Vice President Al Gore in a 1994 speech to the ITU World Telecommunication Development Conference in Buenos Aires, Argentina. It is a vehicle for ensuring that all citizens of the world benefit from information and telecommunications technologies. The GII recognizes that these technologies are engines for development, economic growth, and infrastructure improvements around the world. It believes that a worldwide "network of networks" will create a global information marketplace that will encourage broad-based social discourse within and among all countries.

The GII is based on five principles: encouragement of private investment, competition, flexible regulatory frameworks, open network access, and universal service. A key goal is to open up overseas markets and eliminate barriers caused by incompatible standards. The U.S. contribution to the GII is the NII (National Information Infrastructure), which will link to the GII and provide Americans with access to the global community.

The *Global Information Infrastructure Commission (GIIC)* is an independent, non-governmental initiative involving communications-related industry leaders from developing as well as industrialized countries. GIIC was established to create dialog that will lead to a more rational set of public policies, trade agreements, and private-sector–coordinated self-regulatory initiatives.

Related Entries   6Bone and IPv6; Abilene; Active Networks; Internet; Internet2; Internet Architecture and Backbone; NII (National Information Infrastructure); NIST (National Institute of Standards and Technology); NREN (National Research and Education Network); Peering; Qbone; Routing on the Internet; STAR TAP; *and* vBNS (Very High Speed Backbone Network Service)

United States National Information Infrastructure Virtual Library	http://nii.nist.gov/
Global Information Infrastructure Commission	http://www.gii.org
NII White Papers	http://bob.nap.edu/html/wpni3/
Prof. Jeffrey MacKie-Mason's global information infrastructure links page	http://china.si.umich.edu/telecom/gii.html

G

G.lite

G.lite (sometimes called DSL.lite or ADSL.lite) is a DSL (Digital Subscriber Line) technology that is meant to help users quickly and cheaply obtain high bandwidth to the home. DSL allows high-bandwidth connections over existing copper telephone lines while retaining the traditional voice telephone circuit on the same line. G.Lite has the lowest data rate of any of the DSL technologies, but it can be installed quickly and without the need for the telephone company to send out a technician. Aware, Inc., pioneered the G.lite technology. See "DSL (Digital Subscriber Line)" or visit http://www.linktionary.com/g/glite.html.

Gopher

According to RFC 1436, "The Internet Gopher Protocol" (March 1993), a gopher is a burrowing mammal or an office worker that fetches or delivers documents for office staff. All of these describe the Gopher protocol, which is a system that assists users in searching and retrieving documents on distributed systems. Gopher became necessary in the early days of the hypertext Internet because of the number of documents that were being published in campus and research environments. These documents were stored not in one place, but in many computers—even desktop computers connected to the Internet.

Gopher allows users to search for keywords across multiple documents on multiple systems (it is distributed). The results are displayed as a series of nested menus that looks similar to the organization of a directory with subdirectories and files. Users can browse this list and explore, meaning that they can select a document to immediately see its contents.

Gopher supports gateways to other information systems such as the Web, WAIS, Archie, and WHOIS. Gopher is often the preferred method for navigating through files in an FTP server.

While RFC 1436 describes the Gopher system in detail, RFC 1580, "Guide to Network Resource Tools" (March 1994) provides a more concise description of how users can use Gopher and take advantage of its capabilities. This RFC also lists sites where the Gopher software can be obtained for free.

Related Entries   Directory Services; Handle System; Metadata; Name Services; NIS (Network Information System); Search and Discovery Services; URN (Universal Resource Naming); WebDAV; *and* WHOIS

Linktionary!—Tom Sheldon's Encyclopedia of   http://www.linktionary.com/g/gopher.html
Networking updates

GPRS (General Packet Radio Service)

GPRS is a technology for transmitting data over a GSM (Global System for Mobile communications) wireless network. It uses packet switching and supports IP. GPRS is a 3G (third-generation) cellular technology and was implemented in 1999 and 2000. Data rates are at least twice that of the fastest telephone modem.

Refer to "Mobile Computing" and "Wireless Mobile Communications" for more information.

GPS (Global Positioning System)

GPS is the now well-known network of satellites that offers global positioning and timing data for land and sea navigation. The system consists of 24 Navstar satellites that orbit at an altitude of 11,000 miles. It was originally put in place by the U.S. Department of Defense, but its services are now available free to anyone. GPS location devices are now sold in stores and included in automobiles as a way to track their position for driver navigation and servicing. The system has some interesting and unique uses for networking. Refer to the Linktionary! site for more information.

Related Entries   Mobile Computing; Network Appliances; Service Advertising and Discovery; *and* Wireless Communications

Linktionary!—Tom Sheldon's Encyclopedia of   http://www.linktionary.com/g/gps.html
Networking updates

Mitre GPS technology page   http://www.mitre.org/pubs/showcase/gps/

Grid Environments

See Distributed Computer Networks.

Grounding Problems

See Power and Grounding Problems and Solutions.

Groups

See "Users and Groups."

Groupware

Groupware is software that groups of people use together over computer networks and the Internet. It is based on the assumption that computer networks can help people increase their productivity by collaborating and sharing information. Electronic mail is a form of groupware. It lets users communicate with one another, coordinate activities, and easily share information. Electronic mail is the foundation and data transport system of many groupware applications.

Note   *This topic is covered in more detail at the Linktionary! Web site.*

Some example groupware applications are outlined here:

- A scheduling program that schedules a group of people into meetings after evaluating their current personal schedules.

- Instant messaging, which lets people contact one another in real time via pop-up messages. Initially, these messages are typed; but as network bandwidth and multimedia capabilities improve, instant messaging will use voice and video. See "Instant Messaging."

- A network meeting application that allows users to hold meetings over the network. Attendees sit at their workstations and collaborate on a joint project by opening documents on the screen and working on those documents together.

- A videoconferencing application that works in conjunction with the network meeting applications just described so attendees can see one another and collaborate on computers at the same time.

Groupware also comes in the form of *bulletin board, interactive conferencing, threaded discussions, and chat room* applications. These applications provide a place to post messages that other users see and can respond to, either in real time or over a period of time. All dialogs can be archived for future reference, and users can respond to them at any time. The archive provides a record of events, activities, problems, and solutions that can be referred to at any time.

Chat and instant messaging are forms of *synchronous communications*. Like a voice telephone call, a chat or instant messaging session is live and each user responds to the other in real time. In contrast, discussion forums and electronic mail are *asynchronous communications*. Some amount of time may pass before a person responds to a message. In a discussion forum, a message sits in a message queue for other people to read and respond to at any time, or until the message falls out of the queue. These two forms of communication, which are accessible to any Internet user from just about any Web-attached system, may be the most profound aspect of the Internet. They promote a new form of instant global communication and collaboration. In the case of discussion forums and e-mail, they provide delayed communication in which respondents have time to think about their response and gather information from other sources before responding.

One aspect of groupware is called *workflow,* which combines electronic messaging with document management and imaging. The messaging system is used as a transport that helps documents flow sequentially through different processes. Accounting and procurement systems can use workflow management, for example. A document moves through various stages of processing by being sent to appropriate people who work on the documents, authorize the documents, and validate them. Part of this automated process is the use of digital certificates so that a person receiving a document knows that it has come from an authorized person. See "Workflow Management" for more information.

Related Entries   Collaborative Computing; Compound Documents; Document Management; Electronic Mail; Extranet; Imaging; Instant Messaging; Intranets and Extranets; IRC (Internet Relay Chat); Lotus Notes; Microsoft Exchange; Multicasting; Multimedia; Unified Messaging; Videoconferencing; Webcasting; Workflow Management; *and* XML (Extensible Markup Language)

Linktionary!—Tom Sheldon's Encyclopedia of Networking updates	http://www.linktionary.com/g/groupware.html
Workflow Management Coalition	http://www.aiim.org/wfmc/
Perspectives on Electronic Publishing by Sandy Ressler	http://www.nist.gov/itl/div894/ovrt/people/sressler/Persp/Views.html
Groupware, Links at Washington University	http://www.cait.wustl.edu/infosys/infosys.html

GSM (Global System for Mobile Communications)

See Wireless Mobile Communications.

GSMP (General Switch Management Protocol)

GSMP (General Switch Management Protocol) is an Ipsilon protocol specification that is designed to control an ATM (Asynchronous Transfer Mode) switch. With GSMP, a controller can establish and release connections across the ATM switch, add and delete nodes on a point-to-multipoint connection, manage switch ports, request configuration information, and request statistics.

Related Entries   IP Switching; Label Switching

General Switch Management Protocol (gsmp)	http://www.ietf.org/html.charters/gsmp-charter.html
Multilayer Routing page by Noritoshi Demizu	http://www.watersprings.org/links/mlr/

GSN (Gigabyte System Networking)

GSN is a switched local networking technology that uses copper cable or fiber. GSN is nicknamed SuperHIPPI and is related to the HIPPI (High Performance Parallel Interface) standard. See "HIPPI (High Performance Parallel Interface)."

Guided Media

These include twisted-pair wire and coaxial cable, with copper being the preferred core transmission material for networks. Fiber-optic cable is available with either single or multiple strands of plastic or glass fiber.

Related Entry   Transmission Media, Methods, and Equipment

H.100/H.110 Computer Telephony Bus Standard

H.100 and H.110 are nonproprietary switching fabric implementations developed by the ECTF (Enterprise Computer Telephony Forum). The standards are implemented in CT (computer telephony) systems. CT systems integrate voice, fax, and data networking. See the related entries listed next, and refer to the Linktionary! Web site for a more complete description of this topic.

Related Entries   CTI (Computer-Telephony Integration); Switch Fabrics and Bus Design; Voice/Data Networks; *and* VoIP (Voice over IP)

Linktionary!—Tom Sheldon's Encyclopedia of Networking updates	http://www.linktionary.com/h/h100.html
ECTF (Enterprise Computer Telephony Forum)	http://www.ectf.org
SCSA (Signal Computing System Architecture)	http://www.scsa.org/
Dialogic	http://www.dialogic.com

H Series ITU Recommendations

The H series recommendations are ITU standards that define audiovisual and multimedia systems. Refer to the ITU Web site listed for a complete list and description of each recommendation. A list of important H series recommendations is at the Linktionary! Web site. H.323 is perhaps the most important H series recommendation. It describes voice and video (multimedia) over packet switched networks (the Internet). See "H.323 ITU Recommendation" and "Voice over IP (VoIP)" for more information.

Related Entries   G Series ITU Recommendations; H.323 Multimedia Conferencing Standard; ITU (International Telecommunications Union); Multimedia; T Series ITU Recommendations; Videoconferencing; Voice/Data Networks; Voice over IP (VoIP); *and* X Series ITU Recommendations

Linktionary!—Tom Sheldon's Encyclopedia of Networking updates	http://www.linktionary.com/h/h_series.html
ITU H series recommendations	http://www.itu.int//itudoc/itu-t/rec/h/

H.323 Multimedia Conferencing Standard

H.323 is part of a family of ITU-T recommendations that specify multimedia communications services such as real-time audio, video, and data over a variety of communication services, including videoconference. H.323 defines multimedia communications over packet-switched networks using desktop computers or audiovisual devices. Audio is a required component, while video and data are optional. Since packet-switched networks are not good at supporting real-time audio and video, H.323 addresses problems related to packet delay and packet loss on LANs, corporate intranets, and the Internet.

Note *This is a summary of the complete topic, which is located at the Linktionary! Web site given later in this topic. Also see "Voice over IP (VoIP)" for more information.*

The IETF's SIP (Session Initiation Protocol) competes with H.323. While H.323 is considered a traditional telecom standard oriented toward the old phone system, SIP and its family of protocol (RTP, RTCP, and SDP) are oriented toward the packet-oriented Internet. See "Multimedia."

An H.323 environment consists of H.323 terminals (PCs and other user devices), gateways, gatekeepers, and multipoint control units. An H.323 gateway connects IP-based H.323 terminals with the switched telephone network, for example. Gateways perform the appropriate mapping of call signals and control protocols between systems. Gatekeepers are systems that manage a group of H.323 terminals and gateways within a "zone," which is a management area. The gatekeeper translates between H.323 addresses and IP addresses, allows or rejects calls, manages bandwidth, and provides call signaling functions. The MCU supports multipoint conferences between three or more terminals.

The H.323 protocols include RTCP (Real-time Transport Control Protocol, and IETF-defined protocol that RTP (Real Time Protocol) uses to control and synchronize streaming audio and video. There is also a RAS (registration, admission, status) protocol that terminals and gateways use to exchange call registrations, admission, and termination information. The full protocol suite is discussed at the Linktionary! Web site.

Calls may be initiated directly between terminals or through the gatekeeper. The procedure is that the terminal asks the gatekeeper for permission to make a call. The gatekeeper either admits or rejects the call. If the call is allowed, the calling terminal sends a "setup" message to a target terminal, which responds with a "call proceeding" message. The called terminal gets approval from its gatekeeper to accept the call. If approved, the called terminal alerts its user of an incoming call. If the user picks up the call, the called terminal sends a "contact" message to the calling terminal.

Related Entries Collaborative Computing; Compression Techniques; Convergence; CTI (Computer-Telephony Integration); G Series ITU Recommendations; Groupware; H Series ITU Recommendations; ISDN (Integrated Services Digital Network); ITU (International Telecommunications Union); Megaco; MGCP (Media Gateway Control Protocol); Multicasting; Multimedia; NPN (New Public Network); PBX (Private Branch Exchange); PINT (PSTN-Internet Interworking); Prioritization of Network Traffic; QoS (Quality of Service); Signaling for Call Control; SIP (Session Initiation Protocol); SPIRITS (Service in the PSTN/IN Requesting InTernet Service); SS7 (Signaling System 7); T Series ITU Recommendations; Telecommunications and Telephone Systems; Videoconferencing; Voice/Data Networks; Voice over IP (VoIP); *and* X Series ITU Recommendations

Linktionary!—Tom Sheldon's Encyclopedia of Networking updates	http://www.linktionary.com/h/h323.html
H.323 tutorial at Web ProForums	http://www.iec.org/tutorials/h323/
GateKeeper Tutorial at Web ProForum	http://www.iec.org/tutorials/gatekeep/
"Packet Based Multimedia Communications Systems," at Queensland University of Technology	http://www.fit.qut.edu.au/~rolf/itn540/gallery/a199/hilton/s-hilton.htm

OII (Open Information Interchange) Electronic Conferencing Standards	http://158.169.50.95:10080/oii/en/confer.html
OpenH323 Project (creating open source H.323 implementation)	http://www3.openh323.org/

Hacking and Hackers

A hacker is a person who is knowledgeable enough about some computer system to be able to exploit that system in some way. This has both good and bad connotations. A hacker might work long hours to learn about a system, and then come up with some way to make that system do something it wasn't designed to do. Unfortunately, the more modern definition of a hacker is someone who illegally breaks into a system. Based on that description, the opposite of a hacker is a "good citizen."

 Note   *Refer to the Linktionary! Web site for a continuation of this topic.*

Related to hacking is *cracking* (breaking encryption schemes), *spoofing* (masquerading as another user to gain access to a system), *sniffing* (listening to traffic on a network to gain useful information), and *phreaking* (illegally gaining access to phone lines). These activities are performed by internal malicious users and the underground community of pranksters, hardened criminals, industrial spies, and international terrorists who want to break into your systems for profit and pleasure. John O'Leary of the Computer Security Institute says that "the biggest problem with the hacker threat is that hacking is fun!"

The following RFCs provide important information about protecting sites and systems against hacker attacks. Also see "Firewall" and "Security" for additional RFCs and Web links.

- RFC 1704, "(On Internet Authentication," (October 1994) describes authentication technologies that can protect systems.

- RFC 2196, "(Site Security Handbook," (September 1997) provides extensive information on security incident handling. See Section 5 in the RFC.

- RFC 2350, "(Expectations for Computer Security Incident Response," (June 1998) describes techniques for handling and reporting security intrusions.

- RFC 2504, "(Users' Security Handbook," (February 1999) provides user with information to help keep networks and systems secure.

- RFC 2827, "(Network Ingress Filtering: Defeating Denial of Service Attacks Which employ IP Source Address Spoofing," (May 2000) discusses filtering techniques to prohibit attacks.

- RFC 3013, "(Recommended Internet Service Provider Security Services and Procedures," (November 2000) discusses security requirements that the Internet community expects of Internet service providers.

Related Entries   Access Control; Attacks and Attackers; Authentication and Authorization; Cryptography; Data Protection; DIAMETER; Filtering; Firewall; NAT (Network Address

Translation); Ports, TCP/IP; Proxy Servers; RADIUS (Remote Authentication Dial-In User Service); Security; Security Auditing; SOCKS; *and* Trust Relationships and Trust Management

Linktionary!—Tom Sheldon's Encyclopedia of Networking updates	http://www.linktionary.com/h/hacking.html
Simulating Cyber Attacks, Defenses, and Consequences	http://all.net/journal/ntb/simulate/simulate.html
L0pht Heavy Industries	http://www.l0pht.com/
HNC Network	http://www.hack-net.com/
Google Web Directory—Hacking	http://directory.google.com/Top/Computers/Hacking/

HALO (High Altitude Long Operation)

In the late 1990s, a scramble to provide high-speed Internet access resulted in a number of strategies and technologies. These included the now well-established DSL and cable modem access methods, as well as some sideshow technologies such as access over electric power lines (which mostly failed). Satellite constellations were also deployed, but perhaps the most interesting were the flying/floating platforms called HALOs (High Altitude Long Operations).

HALOs offer network access services by providing communication platforms flying in the stratosphere above cities. The platforms provide uplink and downlink transmissions much like satellites, except that they are closer to Earth. The signal propagation times are shorter and the platforms stay over a particular area. HALOs are a good choice for enterprise Internet access. They provide data rates as high as 10 Mbits/sec. Two companies are involved in this business, both offering a different platform:

- **Angel Technologies**   This company flies airplanes above metropolitan areas and provides symmetrical service and Internet access up to 10 Mbits/sec. In the U.S., Angel's services operate in the LMDS (Local Multipoint Distribution Service) microwave ranges of 24 GHz, 28 GHz, and 38 GHz. In other countries, the 3- to 20-GHz range may be used. The airplane is similar to a corporate jet. It flies 10 miles above the target area in a 2.5-mile-diameter circle. The ground coverage area is up to 75 miles in diameter. Planes fly three shifts of 8 hours each. The 40-kilowatt signal is powered by the jet engines and can penetrate weather conditions normally adverse to microwaves. Angel is working with Raytheon for the communication link and with several companies that have pioneered high-flying, long-duration aircraft.

- **Skystation International**   Skystation has designed unmanned helium-filled blimps (the company prefers to call them "vehicles" or "aerostats") that can be used for a variety of applications, one of which is telecommunications/Internet access. The platform was also designed to be used for earth sciences applications. For communications, the platforms can maintain geostationary positions. The platforms may be moved around for earth sciences applications. It provides data rates of 2 Mbit/sec on the uplink and as high as 10 Mbits/sec on the downlink. Skystation uses spectrum in the 47-GHz band, which has been designated by the ITU and the FCC for use by high-altitude stratospheric platforms. The life expectancy is estimated to be up to 10 years.

You are not alone if you are somewhat skeptical at these proposals, but the ITU and FCC have already designated a frequency band for such platforms. Also, if you read the white papers at the company Web sites presented later, you will see that these schemes are well thought out and practical. The HALO network supports hundreds of thousands of broadband end users on a metropolitan distance scale. Since HALOs are situated high in the sky, they have access to nearly all rooftops within a city.

Proponents of these systems see the emergence of a "stratospheric communication layer" that may trigger a decline in the use of communication satellites. Skystation sees its platforms as being used to provide telephony for developing countries.

Related Entries   Communication Services and Providers; DBS (Direct Broadcast Satellite); Electromagnetic Spectrum; Last Mile Services; LMDS (Local Multipoint Distribution Service); MAN (Metropolitan Area Network); Microwave Communications; Network Access Services; Radio Communication and Networks; Satellite Communication Systems; Service Providers and Carriers; Wireless Broadband Access Technologies; Wireless Communications; *and* Wireless LANs

Linktionary!—Tom Sheldon's Encyclopedia of Networking updates	http://www.linktionary.com/h/halo.html
Angel Technologies	http://www.angeltechnologies.com
Skystation	http://www.skystation.com

Handle System

The Handle System is a global naming service for documents. It provides persistence for documents that might move to different locations so that users can always locate those documents, even after they have been moved. The strategy relies on uniquely identifying each document. This identity is stored in a name server along with the current location of the document. If the document is moved, the location information in the name server must be updated. When users need a document, they find it by referring to the name server.

The Handle System is a resolver service in that it resolves document names into URLs (Uniform Resource Locators), which are the actual Web site addresses where documents are stored. The Handle System provides a resolver service similar to DNS (Domain Name System), and like DNS, the Handle Service is distributed. There is a Global Handle Registry that will pass requests for documents over to local Handle services.

Assume you are writing an online report that requires a bibliographic reference. You want to hyperlink each reference so readers can quickly find them on the Web. The Handle System provides a solution. Following is an example of the kind of link you would include in your reference. This example is borrowed from Springer-Verlag, a developer of the DOI (Digital Object Identifier) system. DOI is an identification system for managing intellectual property in the digital environment. It helps link customers with publishers, facilitates electronic commerce, and enables automated copyright management:

http://dx.doi.org/10.1007/s00214990m180.

The first part of the link is a standard Web URL that refers to the location of the DOI name server where names are resolved to actual locations. The remaining part of the link is called a "handle." The handle prefix 10.1007 identifies the publisher (Springer-Verlag, in this case), and it was assigned by the DOI agency. The handle suffix s00214990m180 identifies an actual document and is analogous to the ISBN numbers that are assigned to books.

This link can be included in any document without worry that it might fail, assuming that the administrator of the site where the actual document is located keeps the DOI name server updated about the current location of the actual document.

A unique feature of the Handle System is that handles can refer to copies of the same document at different locations. This can help balance loads when documents are in high demand or a server is too busy to handle a user request for the document.

Web sites join the global handle namespace and are assigned a unique identifier. Springer-Verlag's ID is 10.1007 in the DOI system. All documents at the site retain their current local naming scheme. The Handle System simply provides a link into that naming scheme. The administrator of the site is responsible for making sure that the Handle System links match the current document locations.

The Handle System is hierarchical. At the top is the Global Handle Registry. Below this are all "local handle services," which are usually run by organizations that have documents to publish or act on behalf of document publishers. A Web site that wishes to publish documents can join the Handle System. In doing so, it obtains a handle prefix value and becomes known as a *naming authority* (since it has authority over its own local namespace).

The Global Handle Registry tracks the namespace for these naming authorities so that it can divert requests to the appropriate naming authority. When a user requests a document, a query may be sent to the Global Handle Registry to find the local service that knows how to process the handle. When the Global Handle Registry finds the local service, it communicates this information to the client who then accesses the home service directly.

The Public Library Association paper called "DOI: The Persistence of Memory" provides useful information about persistent documents, including links to other relevant sites. The Web address for this document is given at the end of this topic.

A document called "Handle System Overview" was submitted to the IETF in early 2000. This document is available at the Handle System Web site given later.

The IETF Uniform Resource Names (URN) Working Group is defining universal resource names, which are names that remain persistent over time, even if the documents move. The URN and the Handle System may sound similar, but, in fact, the Handle System is one case of what the URN Working Group is defining. See "URN (Universal Resource Names)" for more information.

A related technology is CIP (Common Indexing Protocol). CIP provides a way for information servers to exchange index information about the documents they hold. A server can then answer queries from its own index or look in the indexes received from other servers and make referrals to those servers. See "CIP (Common Indexing Protocol)."

Related Entries   CIP (Common Indexing Protocol); CNRP (Common Name Resolution Protocol); Directory Services; Document Management; LDAP (Lightweight Directory Access Protocol); Metadata; Name Services; Search and Discovery Services; Service Advertising and Discovery; SLP (Service Location Protocol); URI (Uniform Resource Identifier); URL (Uniform Resource Locator); URN (Universal Resource Name); Web Technologies and Concepts; WebDAV; *and* XML (Extensible Markup Language)

Linktionary!—Tom Sheldon's Encyclopedia of Networking updates	http://www.linktionary.com/h/handle_system.html
Handle System	http://www.handle.net
DOI (Digital Object Identifier) Web site	http://www.doi.org/
Public Library Association paper: "DOI: The Persistence of Memory"	http://www.pla.org/technotes/doi.html
Recent developments in Indexing, Searching and Information Retrieval Technologies (REIS)	http://www.terena.nl/projects/reis/isir/ reisnews9908sendex.html
IETF Uniform Resource Names (URN) Working Group	http://www.ietf.org/html.charters/urn-charter.html

Handshake

See Connection Establishment.

Hash Functions

A hash function is a form of encryption that takes some plaintext input and transforms it into a fixed-length encrypted output called the *message digest*. The digest is a fixed-size set of bits that serves as a unique "digital fingerprint" for the original message. If the original message is altered and hashed again, it will produce a different signature. Thus, hash functions can be used to detect altered and forged documents. They provide message integrity, assuring recipients that the contents of a message have not been altered or corrupted.

Hash functions are *one-way*, meaning that it is easy to compute the message digest but very difficult to revert the message digest back to the original plaintext (e.g., imagine trying to put a smashed pumpkin back to exactly the way it was). Hash function features are listed here:

- A hash function should be impossible for two different messages to ever produce the same message digest. Changing a single digit in one message will produce an entirely different message digest.

- It should be impossible to produce a message that has some desired or predefined output (target message digest).

- It should be impossible to reverse the results of a hash function. This is possible because a message digest could have been produced by an almost infinite number of messages.

- The hash algorithm itself does not need to be kept secret. It is made available to the public. Its security comes from its ability to produce one-way hashes.

- The resulting message digest is a fixed size. A hash of a short message will produce the same size digest as a hash of a full set of encyclopedias.

Hash functions may be used with or without a key; and if a key is used, both symmetric (single secret key) and asymmetric keys (public/private key pairs) may be used. The two primary algorithms are listed next and the RFCs listed later provide more information on the protocols. You may also refer to the Web site given later for links.

- **MD-5**   A hash function designed by Ron Rivest, one of the inventors of the RSA public-key encryption scheme. The MD-5 algorithm produces a 128-bit output. Note that MD-5 is now known to have some weaknesses and should be avoided if possible. SHA-1 is generally recommended. This is discussed later.

- **SHA-1 (Secure Hash Algorithm-1)**   SHA-1 is an MD-5–like algorithm that was designed to be used with the Digital Signature Standard (DSS). The United States agencies NIST (National Institute of Standards and Technology) and NSA (National Security Agency) are responsible for SHA-1. The SHA-1 algorithm produces a 160-bit MAC. This longer output is considered to be more secure than MD-5.

Keyed MD5 is a technique for using MD-5. Basically, a sender appends a randomly generated key to the end of a message, and then hashes the message and key combination to create a message digest. Next, the key is removed from the message and encrypted with the sender's private key. The message, message digest, and encrypted key are sent to the recipient, who opens the key with the sender's public key (thus validating that the message is actually from the sender). The recipient then appends the key to the message and runs the same hash as the sender. The message digest should match the message digest sent with the message.

The result of a hash function that combines a message with a key is called *a message authentication code*, or MAC. A MAC is a "fingerprint" or "message digest" of the input in combination with a key available to parties in the message exchange.

 This topic continues at the Linktionary! Web site, which lists relevant RFCs and other Web links.

Related Entries   Authentication and Authorization; Certificates and Certification Systems; CHAP (Challenge Handshake Authentication Protocol); Cryptography; Digital Signatures; DSS (Digital Signature Standard); EAP (Extensible Authentication Protocol); FORTEZZA; IPSec (IP Security); Kerberos Authentication Protocol; One-Time Password Authentication; Public-Key Cryptography; Secret-Key Cryptography; Security; *and* Security Auditing

Linktionary!—Tom Sheldon's Encyclopedia of Networking updates	http://www.linktionary.com/h/hash_function.html
RSA Data Systems	http://www.rsa.com
Security Links at Telecom Information Resources on the Internet	http://china.si.umich.edu/telecom/net-security.html

See also the list under "Security."

HDLC (High-Level Data Link Control)

HDLC is a bit-oriented, link layer protocol for the transmission of data over synchronous networks. It is an ISO standard, but is a superset of IBM's SDLC (Synchronous Data Link Control) protocol. SDLC was the successful follow-up to the BISYNC communication protocol and was originally introduced with IBM SNA (Systems Network Architecture) products. Another name for HDLC is ADCCP (Advanced Data Communications Control Procedure), an ANSI standard, but HDLC is the widely accepted name for the protocol. There are some incompatibilities between SDLC and HDLC, depending on the vendor.

HDLC is bit oriented, meaning that the data is monitored bit by bit. Transmissions consist of binary data without any special control codes. Information in the frame contains control and response commands, however. HDLC supports full-duplex transmission in which data is transmitted in two directions at the same time, resulting in higher throughput. HDLC is suitable for point-to-point and multipoint (multidrop or one-to-many) connections. Subsets of HDLC are used to provide signaling and control data links for X.25, ISDN, and frame relay networks.

When an HDLC session is established, one station, called the *primary station*, is designated to manage the flow of data. The other station (or stations) is designated as the *secondary station*. The primary station issues commands, and the secondary stations issue responses. There are three possible connection methods, as shown in Figure H-1. The top two support either

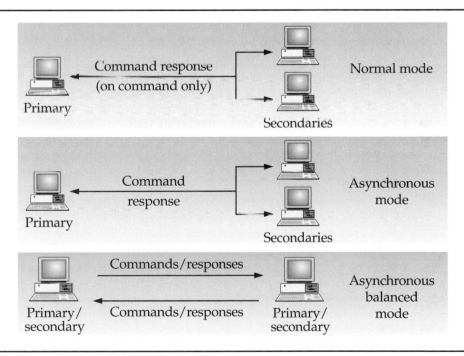

Figure H-1.   *HDLC connection methods*

point-to-point connections between two systems, or *multipoint* connections between a primary station and two or more secondary stations:

- The normal mode is unbalanced because the secondary station can only transmit when permitted to do so by the primary station.

- The asynchronous mode is also unbalanced, but the secondary station may initiate a transmission on its own.

- The asynchronous balanced mode is designed for point-to-point connections between two computers over a duplex line. Each station can send commands and responses over its own line and receive commands and responses on the duplexed line. This is the mode used to connect stations to X.25 packet-switched networks.

The HDLC frame defines the structure for delivering data and command/response messages between communicating systems. The frame is pictured in Figure H-2 and described here:

- The Flag fields contain the bit sequence 01111110, which indicates the beginning and end of the HDLC frame. If any portion of the data in the frame contains more than five 1 bits, a *zero-bit insertion* technique inserts a 0 bit to ensure that data is not mistaken for a flag.

- The Address field generally contains the address of a secondary station. This field is normally 8 bits, but extended addressing is possible for multipoint connections that contain many different addresses. A broadcast address can also be inserted in the field to send messages to all stations in a multipoint connection.

- The Control field identifies the information contained in the frame as data, commands, or responses. Commands are sent by the primary station, and responses are sent by the secondary station. The control information can acknowledge frames, request retransmission of frames, or request a suspension of transmission, as well as other commands and responses.

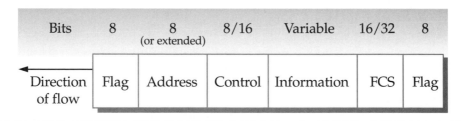

Figure H-2.   *HDLC frame definition*

A communication session starts by establishing connections between primary and secondary stations. The primary station transmits a special frame to either a single station or to multiple stations to initiate a setup procedure. The secondary stations respond with information that is used for error and flow control during the session. When everything is set up, data transmission begins; and when data transmission ends, the primary station sends a frame to initiate a disconnection of the session.

As mentioned, HDLC forms the basis for data link layer control in X.25 packet-switching networks. A subset of HDLC is LAP-B (Link Access Procedure-Balanced), which is designed for point-to-point connections, so the Address field is not necessary to identify the secondary stations. It provides the frame structure, error, and flow-control mechanisms for an asynchronous balanced-mode session. Another subset of HDLC is the LAP-D (Link Access Procedure D-channel) protocol associated with ISDN (Integrated Services Digital Network). The D channel is the signaling channel that controls the data flowing through the two B (bearer) channels. Think of the B channels as two separate phone lines and the D channel as the line that sets up the call.

Two Internet RFCs are related to HDLC. These are RFC 2687, "PPP in a Real-Time Oriented HDLC-like Framing," (September 1999) and RFC 1662, "PPP in HDLC-like Framing," (July 1994).

Related Entries   Data Communication Concepts; Data Link Protocols; Framing in Data Transmissions; ISDN (Integrated Services Digital Network); LAP (Link Access Procedure); LLC (Logical Link Control); Point-to-Point Communications; PPP (Point-to-Point Protocol); SDLC (Synchronous Data Link Control); Serial Communication and Interfaces; Synchronous Communications; *and* X.25

Linktionary!—Tom Sheldon's Encyclopedia of Networking updates	http://www.linktionary.com/h/hdlc.html
HDLC Tutorial at RAD Data Communications	http://www.rad.com/networks/1994/hdlc/hdlc.htm
Gory Fairhurst's HDLC protocol tutorial	http://www.erg.abdn.ac.uk/users/gorry/course/dl-pages/hdlc.html
Asynchronous HDLC FAQ	http://ftp.uni-erlangen.de/pub/other/Documents/ISO/async-HDLC

HDML (Handheld Device Markup Language)

HDML was developed by Unwired Planet (now Phone.com) as a markup language for pocket-sized devices such as cellular phones and two-way pagers that conform to Internet standards and protocols, and that are constrained to a few lines of display, a limited keypad, and little memory. It is a markup language similar to HTML (Hypertext Markup Language) in concept but designed for developing applications and services for cellular devices. It is compatible with all Web servers, uses little memory, makes efficient use of wireless network transmissions, and supports integrated phone features like voice. More information is at the Linktionary! Web site.

Related Entries   Bluetooth; Mobile Computing; Mobile IP; Packet-Radio Data Networks; Remote Access; SMR (Specialized Mobile Radio); WAP (Wireless Application Protocol); Wireless Broadband Access Technologies; Wireless Communications; Wireless IP; *and* Wireless Mobile Communications

Linktionary!—Tom Sheldon's Encyclopedia of   http://www.linktionary.com/h/hdml.html
Networking updates

HDR (High Data Rate)

HDR is a Qualcomm wireless technology that provides high-speed, high-capacity IP packet data services that carriers can deploy in metropolitan areas. It can provide up to a 2.4-Mbit/sec data transfer rate in a 1.25-MHz channel for use by stationary users, portable devices, and mobile services. Data rates for mobile users will be lower than data rates for stationary users. Basically, a user of a wireless device can be located anywhere within a cell site, including inside buildings, and get Internet access without wires.

HDR's high capacity is the result of maximizing the utilization of the available spectrum. It uses Qualcomm's CDMA air link technology. HDR is designed for data and it is "always on." Thus, it offers rapid connect time for users. By designing HDR for data and not for voice, Qualcomm engineers were able to avoid making compromises that would have reduced the performance of the system. HDR may be deployed alongside existing cellular/PCS networks, sharing the same cell sites, towers, and antennas. Basically, the carrier plugs an HDR card into their existing equipment and starts up the service. It will also need Internet connections to connect the base station to an Internet point of presence.

Related Entries   CDMA (Code Division Multiple Access); Wireless Broadband Access Technologies; Wireless Communications; *and* Wireless Mobile Communications

Linktionary!—Tom Sheldon's Encyclopedia of   http://www.linktionary.com/h/hdr.html
Networking updates

Qualcomm HDR Web site   http://www.qualcomm.com/hdr/

HDSL (High-Bit-Rate Digital Subscriber Line)

HDSL is one of the DSL (Digital Subscriber Line) options that permits high-speed data transmissions over the existing copper-based lines that provide telephone service between most homes and the telephone companies' central offices. See "DSL (Digital Subscriber Line)."

HFC (Hybrid Fiber/Coax)

An HFC network is a cable (CATV) network that includes a combination of fiber-optic and coaxial cable, with fiber-optic cable running from the cable company's facility to a location near a home and coaxial cable running from there into the home. The fiber cable provides high bandwidth to multiple users in a single neighborhood. It forms what is called the "trunk line" that stretches from cable office to neighborhoods. The coaxial cable is called the "feeder circuit." An upgrade to an HFC system usually requires replacement of existing coaxial trunk lines with fiber trunk lines. In addition, equipment is needed at the neighborhood junction to join the coaxial and fiber cables.

The original CATV systems were designed to support only downstream broadcasts to subscriber television sets. To provide full Internet access, service providers must also support upstream traffic (or else upstream traffic can travel across a separate phone line, which is inconvenient). Bidirectional traffic requires that all amplifiers and related equipment be upgraded. Subscribers install cable modems to access the data signals on the cable.

The data signals for Internet access are transmitted on the cable using frequency division multiplexing. The downstream signal from the providers occupies 450 MHz to 750 MHz, while the upstream signal occupies 5 MHz to 50 MHz. Normal television signals fall between these bands. The bandwidth is allocated to subscribers by using time division multiplexing. More recently, Terayon has pioneered a form of CDMA (Code Division Multiple Access) called S-CDMA (Synchronous CDMA) to support spread spectrum signaling. S-CDMA can support upstream data rates of up to 30 Mbits/sec.

Related Entries   Cable (CATV) Data Networks; CDMA (Code Division Multiple Access); Communication Services and Providers; Fiber-Optic Cable; FTTH (Fiber To The Home); Home Networking; Internet Connections; Last Mile Services; Local Loop; Network Access Services; Optical Networks; PON (Passive Optical Network); Residential Broadband; Service Providers and Carriers; *and* Spread Spectrum Signaling

Linktionary!—Tom Sheldon's Encyclopedia of Networking updates	http://www.linktionary.com/h/hdr.html
Web ProForums "Hybrid/Fiber Coax (HFC) and Dense Wavelength Division Multiplexing (DWDM) Networks Tutorial"	http://www.webproforum.com/sci-atlanta/
Web Pro Forums "Hybrid Fiber Coaxial (HFC) Telephony Tutorial"	http://www.webproforum.com/hfc_tele/
Terayon S-CDMA cable modems	http://www.terayon.com

High-Availability Systems

See Fault Tolerance and High Availability; Data Center Design; *and* Disaster Planning and Recovery.

High-Speed/High-Performance Networking

"High-speed networking" is a misnomer. Speed seems to imply that bits are moving faster. People use the term when they are really talking about high-performance networks with high *data rates*. A network medium that operates at gigabit/sec rates is perceived as *fast* because a typical file transfer occurs in a very short period of time compared to transferring the same file over a modem link, for example. "Fast" is based on user perception. *Data transfer rates* are measurable events. Similar terms are "wire speed," which is used to refer to the data transfer rate of a particular networking technology, and "throughput," which is the actual data rate, including delays caused by traffic conditions and system components.

However, "fast networks" and "speedy networks" have become synonymous with high-performance networking, and it is difficult to write about such networks without calling them fast. In many cases, it just sounds better to say "high-speed networking" or "fast networks" instead of "high-data-rate networking."

Several Internet RFCs cover high-performance networking. RFC 1077, "Critical Issues in High Bandwidth Networking," (November 1988) is an early paper that discusses gigabit networking. RFC 1323, "TCP Extensions for High Performance," (May 1992) discusses improvements to TCP that allow scaling for high-data-rate networks.

The following topics provide more information on high-performance networking.

High-Performance Networking Technologies   ATM (Asynchronous Transfer Mode); Cable (CATV) Data Networks; DBS (Direct Broadcast Satellite); DSL (Digital Subscriber Line); Fibre Channel; Frame Relay; FTTH (Fiber To The Home); Gigabit Ethernet; HALO (High Altitude Long Operation); HIPPI (High-Performance Parallel Interface); Infrared Technologies; ISDN (Integrated Services Digital Network); LMDS (Local Multipoint Distribution Services); Microwave Communications; MMDS (Multichannel Multipoint Distribution Services); Optical Networking; PON (Passive Optical Network); Residential Broadband; Satellite Communication Systems; SONET (Synchronous Optical Network); T Carriers; TDM Networks; WDM (Wavelength Division Multiplexing); Wireless Broadband Access Technologies; *and* Wireless Local Loop

Advanced Internet Networks   Abilene; Active Networks; GII (Global Information Infrastructure); Internet2; NPN (New Public Network); STAR TAP; *and* vBNS (Very High Speed Backbone Network Service)

Bandwidth Management Techniques   Bandwidth Management; Congestion Control Mechanisms; Link Aggregation; Load Balancing; MPLS (Multiprotocol Label Switching); Policy-Based Management; Prioritization of Network Traffic; QoS (Quality of Service); *and* Traffic Management, Shaping, and Engineering

Related Entries   Clustering; Data Communication Concepts; Distributed Computer Networks; Internet Connections; Internetworking; IP over AM; LAN (Local Area Network); Last Mile Services; Local Loop; Multilayer Switching; Multiplexing and Multiplexers; Multiprocessing; Network Access Services; Network Concepts; Network Connection Technologies; Network Core Technologies;Optical Networks; Residential Broadband; Switch Fabrics and Bus Design; Switching and Switched Networks; TDM Networks; Telecommunications and Telephone Systems; WAN (Wide Area Network); *and* Wireless Communications

Linktionary!—Tom Sheldon's Encyclopedia of Networking updates	http://www.linktionary.com/h/high_performance.html
Internet2 home page	http://www.internet2.org/
NGI (Next Generation Internet) Initiative home page	http://www.ngi.gov/
vBNS/vBNS+ home page	http://www.vbns.net/
High-performance networking info at NLANR site	http://www.nlanr.net/

High-performance networking proving ground: STAR TAP	http://www.startap.net/
High-performance Networking Forum	http://www.hnf.org/
IEEE 802.3 Higher Speed Study Group	http://grouper.ieee.org/groups/802/3/ 10G_study/public/
Networking at the Pittsburgh Supercomputing Center	http://www.psc.edu/networking/
Mitre High Performance Computing	http://www.mitre.org/technology/hpc/
High-speed networking links at About.com	http://compnetworking.miningco.com/compute/ hardware/compnetworking/msubtech.htm
Noritoshi Demizu's High Performance Networking page (links)	http://www.watersprings.org/links/inet/hpn.html
Noritoshi Demizu's Gigabit Networking page (links)	http://www.watersprings.org/links/inet/giga.html
Suzanne Woolf's Gigabits Networking Research (GIGA) Project page	http://www.isi.edu/div7/giga/

H

HiperLAN (Higher-Performance Radio LAN)

See Wireless LANs.

HIPPI (High-Performance Parallel Interface)

HIPPI is a high-performance interface originally designed to interconnect high-end workstations, supercomputers, and peripheral devices in a local network configuration. As the name implies, it is a parallel interface, as compared to the serial interfaces such as those described under "Serial Communication and Interfaces." It grew out of work done at the LANL (Los Alamos National Laboratory). HIPPI is ANSI standard X3T9.3 and it is also known as ANSI T11.1.

HIPPI has data transfer rates of 800 Mbits/sec in simplex mode (data transfers in one direction at a time), and 1,600 Mbits/sec total when set up as a duplex channel. A serial version is available that runs over fiber-optic cable.

The parallel interface specification calls for a cable that has 50 copper twisted-pair wires. Data is transferred on 32 of the wires at 25 Mbits/sec each, providing a total throughput of 800 Mbits/sec. This supports 32-bit bus operations; a 64-bit bus operating at 1,600 Mbits/sec is possible using dual cables. The actual distance of transmission on copper cables is limited to 25 meters (82.5 feet); but if fiber-optic connections are used, distances can range from 300 meters to 10 kilometers.

HIPPI-6400 is the newest version of HIPPI that operates at 6,400 Mbits/sec. It is sometimes called "SuperHIPPI" or "GSN (Gigabyte System Networking)." GSN is being developed by a group of vendors and research institutes known as the High-Performance Networking Forum (HNF). Members include Compaq, Silicon Graphics, Sun Microsystems, Los Alamos National Laboratories, and the European Center for Nuclear Research. GSN's copper cable uses 20 coaxial wires and has a maximum length of 40 meters. Fiber connections use parallel fiber cable with 10 multimode fibers for connections up to 300 meters. Transfer rates of 6.4 Gbits/sec are possible.

The transfer channel uses four multiplexed virtual channels (VC-0 through VC-1). Data is transferred in small micropackets of 32 bytes. Small packets make switching more efficient. Link control and look-ahead flow control is done with administrative micropackets that cross the network to learn about traffic conditions and manage services. GSN is technology independent, which means it may be combined with other network technologies such as Fibre Channel, ATM, and Gigabit Ethernet.

While HIPPI can be used for point-to-point connections, a more common setup is to use a switch with, typically, 8 to 32 ports. Each port has a specific address using a 24-bit addressing scheme. The switch sets up a point-to-point circuit between two different end systems. Essential Communications is the primary HIPPI switch manufacturer. The Web site is listed later.

There are request lines and connect lines used to establish connections, and parity-checking lines to ensure that data is transmitted correctly. A transmission sequence consists of bursts of data that form variable-length datagrams of 64KB to 4.3GB of data. The data dumps into frame buffers, and these buffers can continue filling while information in the buffers is processed.

Fibre Channel is an alternative to HIPPI that provides longer cable distances and data transfer rates. Translation is possible between HIPPI and Fibre Channel, so they can be used in the same environment.

Internet RFC 2067, "IP over HIPPI," (January 1997) describes the encapsulation of IP datagrams on HIPPI. Also see RFC 2834, "ARP and IP Broadcast over HIPPI 800," (May 2000) and RFC 2835, "IP and ARP over HIPPI-6400".

Related Entries   Fibre Channel; Network Connection Technologies; SAN (Storage Area Network); SCSI (Small Computer System Interface); Supercomputer; *and* Switching and Switched Networks

Linktionary!—Tom Sheldon's Encyclopedia of Networking updates	http://www.linktionary.com/h/hippi.html
The T11 Home Page	http://www.t11.org/
High Performance Networking Forum (complete HIPPI specifications)	http://www.hnf.org/
GSN Home page	http://hsi.web.cern.ch/HSI/gsn/gsnhome.htm
Essential Communications	http://www.esscom.com/highperf.shtml
CERN HIPPI home page	http://hsi.web.cern.ch/HSI/hippi/
MAGIC Gigabit Testbed HIPPI documents	http://www.msci.magic.net/docs/hippi/hippi.html
Los Alamos National Laboratory HIPPI document by Stephen C. Tenbrink and Donald E. Tolmie (1994)	http://lib-www.lanl.gov/la-pubs/00326726.pdf

HMAC (Hashed Message Authentication Code)

See Hash Functions.

Home Networking

As computer prices drop and more homes obtain multiple computers and/or Web appliances, there is a need to network those computers. A home network can give all users access to the same Internet access line, which is practical if the line is high-speed DSL or cable. A home network also lets family members share peripherals such as printers and quickly transfer files between computers. For example, family members may want to exchange photos. Since these files are usually large, it makes sense to do it over a network rather than copying to a disk. Disk devices can also be shared. If one system has a CD writer, other family members can access it as if it is a local drive and create their own CDs. Finally, computer gaming over networks allows multiple members to join in the same game.

There are a number of home networking technologies, including traditional Ethernet, phone line networks, power line networks, and wireless, but many people may prefer to use standard Ethernet. It's cheap, easy to install, and well supported. Some companies give older Ethernet adapters and cable to employees for home use. Chances are a family friend knows how to get things going in a jiffy. If you choose to do it yourself, go out and buy a cheap Ethernet switch and some preconfigured cables (the connectors are already installed), and then run the cables through the ceiling or walls by placing a few drill holes. If you want a "cleaner" installation, you'll need to buy faceplates, connectors, and a roll of cable, and then run the cable and install the connectors. Some people might prefer to call a professional, or maybe extend a dinner invitation to the cabling guy at work. Install Category 5 or better cable just to make sure you can support future standards. See "Cable and Wiring" for more information.

Some alternative home networking technologies are listed next. All of these technologies require network adapters in each PC, so the choice of which to use is often related to the cost of hardware rather than the wiring options. Another thing is that all computers share the line, so an access method, such as CSMA/CD or token passing, is necessary. See "MAC (Media Access Control)."

- **Telephone line networks**   Many homes have phone jacks in nearly every room, so it makes sense to use the cable to network home computers. Products that use phone lines transmit signals in frequency ranges that are above the range used by voice. DSL works over the phone lines using the same technique. There is no interference between voice calls and data transmissions because the transmission ranges are widely separated. The Home Phoneline Networking Alliance has specified standards for transmission over home telephone lines. Depending on the version and hardware, transfer rates can go as high as 10 Mbits/sec.

- **Power line networks**   Copper cable power lines are usually available in every part of the house, so using those power lines to build home networks is a flexible option. However, power lines are usually noisy, so transfer rates are lower to compensate. The top rate is usually less than 1 Mbits/sec. Encryption techniques are required to provide privacy because signals on the power line propagate out of the home to other homes in the vicinity.

- **Wireless home networking**   Wireless technologies are perhaps the best choice for many home users, especially because it is well understood since cordless phones, which use similar technology, are common in the home. Wireless networks also support mobility, so the home portable computer can be used in front of the TV for entertainment or taken to a study area. The range is usually about 250 feet. Wireless home networking uses either infrared (IR) or radio frequency (RF) technology. IR requires a line of sight with a transmitter/receiver, which limits its flexibility. RF is the preferred choice because users can roam anywhere in the home and remain connected. Like AM or FM radio, RF penetrates walls. Frequency ranges are in the 900 MHz, 2.4 GHz, and 5.8 GHz ranges. The last two ranges are part of the unlicensed band, which means that many types of devices transmit in these frequencies, including cordless phones. The 2.4 GHz range is the busiest. Choose products in the 5.8 GHz range. See "Wireless LANs" for more information about these technologies. Also see "Bluetooth" and "Wireless PANs (Personal Area Networks)" for related technology.

Several home networking standards have been developed, including those developed by the Home Phoneline Networking Alliance, mentioned in the preceding list. Another is CEBus, an open standard for home automation, which was officially released as EIA IS-60. The HomeRF Working Group is promoted by Motorola, Proxim, Compaq, Intel, National Semiconductor, Siemens, and others.

Related Entries   Bluetooth; Cable (CATV) Data Networks; DSL (Digital Subscriber Line); Electromagnetic Spectrum; FTTH (Fiber To The Home); Infrared Technologies; MAC (Media Access Control); Mobile Computing; Radio Communication and Networks; Remote Access; Residential Broadband; Wireless Communications; Wireless LANs; Wireless Local Loop; Wireless Mobile Communications; *and* Wireless PANs (Personal Area Networks)

Linktionary!—Tom Sheldon's Encyclopedia of Networking updates	http://www.linktionary.com/h/home_networks.html
Home Phoneline Networking Alliance	http://www.homepna.org/
HomeRF Working Group	http://www.homerf.org/
CDBus Products	http://www.acscontrol.com/cebus.htm
Microsoft home networking page	http://www.microsoft.com/HOMENET/
3Com home networking page	http://www.3com.com/homeoffice/products/networking.html
3Com paper: Introduction to Home Networking	http://www.3com.com/technology/tech_net/white_papers/503061.html
About.com home networking page (see Subjects list)	http://compnetworking.about.com/
Palowireless.com homeRF resource center	http://www.palowireless.com/homerf/
Intellon power line networking	http://www.intellon.com/

Hop

In a packet-switched internetwork that is connected by routers, such as TCP/IP networks and the Internet, a hop is a jump that a packet takes from one router to the next.

Related Entries Data Communication Concepts, Internetworking; IP (Internet Protocol); Network Concepts; *and* Routing

Host

In the TCP/IP networking environment, a host is basically a node on the network that has an IP address. In contrast, a router is a device that interconnects networks.

In a network environment in which multiple LANs are connected together with a series of routers, a host is often referred to as the *end system* or *ES*. For example, if the accounting department is connected to the sales department with a router, then workstations in each department are referred to as "hosts" (or "end systems"), and the router is referred to as an *intermediate system*. There may be a number of intermediate systems that a communication message has to cross between one end system and another.

In the IBM environment, "host" is the term normally applied to mainframe computer systems. More appropriately, they are called the "host processors." These hosts include the IBM model 3090, IBM model 4381, or IBM model 9370. These mainframes usually run the MVS (Multiple Virtual Storage) operating system, running as either XA (Extended Architecture) or ESA (Enterprise Systems Architecture). MVS is part of IBM's SAA (Systems Application Architecture). Refer to "Mainframe" for more details.

Host Connectivity, IBM

See IBM Host Connectivity.

HPR (High-Performance Routing), IBM

HPR is an internetworking protocol designed by IBM as an upgrade to its APPN (Advanced Peer-to-Peer Networking) protocol. It was originally referred to as APPN+, but is now officially referred to as APPN-HPR, or simply HPR. IBM designed the protocol to provide the same internetworking functionality as TCP/IP. HPR was designed as a transport for legacy data over frame- and cell-based networks. In fact, IBM designed it to fully exploit frame relay and ATM. In 1999, Cisco bought IBM's networking operations and has since been pushing TCP/IP to the SNA community.

This topic is covered in more detail at the Linktionary! Web site and the other Web sites listed here.

Related Entries APPN (Advanced Peer-to-Peer Networking); DLSw (Data Link Switching); BM Host Connectivity; IBM (International Business Machines); IMainframe; Routing; *and* SNA (Systems Network Architecture)

Linktionary!—Tom Sheldon's Encyclopedia of Networking updates	http://www.linktionary.com/h/hpr.html
IBM HPR Web page	http://www-4.ibm.com/software/network/technology/appnhpr/hpr.html

HSRP (Hot Standby Router Protocol)

HSRP is a Cisco protocol that switches to a backup router if a main router fails. The protocol provides automatic router backup (fault tolerance). HSRP is compatible with IP, Novell's Internetwork Packet Exchange (IPX), AppleTalk, and Banyan VINES, and it is compatible with DECnet and Xerox Network Systems (XNS) in certain configurations.

In a WAN configuration, HSRP can provide a way to forward packets on an alternate link should a primary link fail. HSRP is defined in RFC 2281, "Cisco Hot Standby Router Protocol," (March 1998) and at the Cisco Web site (see address following).

Related Entries   Fault Management; Fault Tolerance and High Availability; Redundancy; Routers; Routing; *and* Routing on the Internet

Linktionary!—Tom Sheldon's Encyclopedia of Networking updates	http://www.linktionary.com/h/hsrp.html
Cisco documentation: Using HSRP for Fault-Tolerant IP Routing	http://www.cisco.com/univercd/cc/td/doc/cisintwk/ics/cs009.htm
Cisco HSRP Web page	http://www.cisco.com/warp/public/619/

HSSI (High-Speed Serial Interface)

The HSSI (High-Speed Serial Interface) is a high-speed interface for connecting routers and multiplexers to high-speed communication services, such as frame relay and ATM. Cisco and T3plus Networking developed the protocol, but it is freely available for use.

HSSI has a synchronous data rate of up to 52 Mbits/sec, which allows support of T3 WAN connections. Maximum cable length is 50 feet over shielded twisted-pair wire. Many vendors now integrate this interface onto their router and multiplexer devices in place of serial interfaces such as V.35 and EIA-530 (EIA-422). Not only does it operate at much higher data rates, it also has superior flow control and additional loopback capability. The EIA-530 interface has a maximum data rate of about 10 Mbits/sec over short distances, and V.35 is even slower.

Related Entries   Data Center Design; Multiplexing and Multiplexers; Network Connection Technologies; Routers; Serial Communication and Interfaces; *and* Synchronous Communications

Linktionary!—Tom Sheldon's Encyclopedia of Networking updates	http://www.linktionary.com/h/hsrp.html
Cisco Documentation: High-Speed Serial Interface	http://www.cisco.com/univercd/cc/td/doc/cisintwk/ito_doc/hssi.htm

HTCP (Hypertext Caching Protocol)

See Web Caching.

HTML (Hypertext Markup Language)

HTML is a markup language that is used to create Web pages. Files are created using simple text with embedded tags. These files are stored on Web servers. When Web clients access a

Web site, a default or "home" Web page in the HTML format is sent to clients. The client's Web browser automatically interprets the HTML tags and formats the page to display in the browsers. This page may contain links to other pages at the same site or at other Web sites.

| **Note** | *This topic is covered in more detail at the Linktionary! Web site given at the end of this topic.* |

HTML documents have the filename extension "HTML" or "HTM." They can display images, sounds, and other multimedia objects. The objects are not actually stored in the document. Instead, an external reference to a picture or multimedia object is inserted in the text of the HTML document. When a user displays the HTML document in his or her Web browser, the external reference pulls the referenced object into the document. Thus, an HTML page actually consists of the HTML file itself along with any additional references, graphics, and multimedia files. All of these objects must be online and available to a user when the file is opened.

Hypertext is nonlinear text. It allows you to quickly switch to a reference or another source of information with the click of a button, and then jump back and continue reading where you left off. A historical perspective on hypertext is given under "Hypermedia and Hypertext."

As mentioned, HTML documents are plaintext documents that you can create in any word processor, although a number of development tools are available. An application like Microsoft FrontPage lets developers create Web sites without coding HTML. Text and objects are placed on the page and formatted using text formatting and graphics manipulation tools. All the coding is done in the background, and the end result is an HTML document that can be posted on a Web site.

You can view the HTML code for any Web page. Open your Web browser and go to your favorite Web page on the Internet. After the page opens, choose Source (or Document Source) from the View menu of your browser. With the source code open, you can see the HTML tags, which appear as items enclosed in angle brackets (< and >). There is an opening tag and a closing tag. For example, to boldface some text, you insert the tag <B> at the beginning of the text and insert the tag </B> at the end of the text. The Linktionary! Web site has more information about building Web pages.

The World Wide Web Consortium, or W3C, is the primary organization responsible for advancing HTML. Although Microsoft, Netscape, and others have improved the standard on their own, the W3C has attempted to corral these improvements and describe them as standards. Here is a brief history of HTML versions:

- **HTML 2**   Defined by the IETF in 1996, based on core work done in 1994. RFC 1866, "Hypertext Markup Language—2.0," (November 1995) describes this version.

- **HTML 3.2**   The W3C released this in 1996. It includes tables, applets, text flow, superscripts, and subscripts.

- **HTML 4.0**   The W3C released this in 1997 with a revision in 1998.

- **HTML 4.01**   The W3C released this in late 1999 to fix bugs in HTML 4.0.

- **XHTML**   HTML recast as XML (Extensible Markup Language).

The W3C's Metadata Activity Group is developing ways to model and encode metadata. The group has developed RDF (Resource Description Framework) and PICS (Platform for Internet Content Selection). A broad goal of RDF is to define a way to describe resources without being tied to any platform or application. RDF relies on XML to do this, a universal format for structuring and formatting documents. See "Metadata" for more information.

The Linktionary! Web site chronicles the improvements in HTML over the years and provides a list of HTML features.

XHTML

The HTML developments described in the preceding topic were done by extending existing versions of HTML. HTML has been great for presentation, but the Web is becoming more than just a presentation medium. It is becoming an electronic commerce medium, and the pages that people exchange must become more than just large blocks of unclassified information. XML can explicitly describe and tag a piece of information, such as an address or an invoice total, so other programs can extract that information automatically.

In 1999, the W3C recast HTML in XML, resulting in XHTML. XHTML is similar enough to HTML that developers will be able to make an easy transition to the world of XML. But while HTML is a specific markup language for displaying information in Web browsers (e.g., the tags are predefined for displaying information), XHTML follows a modular approach that supports the creation of documents that can be used in a variety of environments. For example, a document may have several associated templates, and each template describes how the document is displayed (or what it does) when opened by a particular device (PC with Web browser, PDA, or cell phone).

To understand XHTML, one must understand XML. HTML defines how to display information in a Web browser. Now suppose you want to display the same HTML document in the small display of a PDA. It's possible, but the display will not do justice to most Web pages. What is needed is another set of tags that describes how to display the same information with formatting that is appropriate for a PDA.

With XML, information about documents and their contents is defined in external documents called DTDs (Document Type Descriptions). DTDs define the rules, syntax, and grammar for marking up documents. For example, the medical and legal professions have defined their own document descriptions. Anyone working with the medical or legal industry can use the predefined DTD to display and work with medical or legal documents. With XML, the parts of a document are defined for what they are. For example, the elements of a table are named so you can pull the table directly into a spreadsheet program, rather than using tedious cut-and-paste-and-reformat techniques.

XHTML modules are separate documents that extend XHTML into a variety of existing and new platforms. The modules provide a framework for defining markup languages that fit particular applications and devices. Content providers will find it easier to produce content for a wide range of platforms, with better assurances about how the content is rendered. The concept takes into account that many different devices will be connected to the Web, including cell phones, PDAs, and other devices with varying display characteristics.

See "XML (Extensible Markup Language)" for more information. Also refer to the Web sites listed at the end of this topic.

Related Entries   Document Management; DOM (Document Object Model); Electronic Commerce; Handle System; HTTP (Hypertext Transfer Protocol); Hypermedia and Hypertext; Java; Metadata; Microsoft.NET; RDF (Resource Description Framework); Search and Discovery Services; Service Advertising and Discovery; SGML (Standard Generalized Markup Language); SOAP (Simple Object Access Protocol); URN (Universal Resource Name); WebDAV; Web Technologies and Concepts; *and* XML (Extensible Markup Language)

Linktionary!—Tom Sheldon's Encyclopedia of Networking updates	http://www.linktionary.com/h/html.html
World Wide Web Consortium home page for HTML	http://www.w3.org/MarkUp
W3C HTML activity statement	http://www.w3.org/MarkUp/Activity
OASIS (Organization for Structured Information Standards) promotes SGML, HTML, and XML	http://www.oasis-open.org/
OII (Open Information Interchange) document interchange standards	http://158.169.50.95:10080/oii/en/docstand.html
National Center for Supercomputing Application's "Beginners Guide to HTML"	http://www.ncsa.uiuc.edu/General/Internet/WWW/HTMLPrimer.html
Introduction to XHTML, with examples, by Alan Richmond	http://www.wdvl.com/Authoring/Languages/XML/XHTML/
HTML information at internet.com	http://www.stars.com/Authoring/HTML/
HTTP, Mark McCutcheon's HTTP and HTML links	http://www.cs.ubc.ca/spider/mjmccut/technics.html
Google Web Directory: Internet programming page	http://directory.google.com/Top/Computers/Programming/Internet/

HTTP (Hypertext Transfer Protocol)

The World Wide Web is built on top of the Internet and uses the Internet protocol suite. HTTP is the client/server application-level protocol specifically designed to support hypermedia information systems. Web browsers use HTTP to connect with Web servers and access information on those servers. The protocol sets up a connection between Web browser and Web server, and then manages the exchange of information.

HTTP first appeared in 1990 as HTTP version 0.9. Later, HTTP version 1.0 appeared, and is described in RFC 1945, "Hypertext Transfer Protocol—HTTP/1.0," (May 1996). The basic protocol is stateless, meaning that the client and server do not store information about one another during the session. The client connects with a server, the server transfers the requested information, and the connection is closed. The server doesn't need to know anything about the client. It simply gives the requested information.

In HTTP version 1.0, every object on a Web page (graphics images, for example) required that a new connection be established to transfer it. HTTP 1.1, described in RFC 2616, "HTTP/1.1," (June 1999), adds *persistence*, which makes client/server connections more efficient. Persistence allows the client and server to maintain a connection (not to be confused with state) until all objects on a page are transferred. The connection is then closed.

HTTP version 1.1 also supports cache management in the browser. Basically, a server page is compared with a page that a browser has in its cache. Only items that need updating are sent. Tests have shown that HTTP 1.1 provides approximately a 50-percent improvement in download times and reduces the number of packets by more than 50 percent. See "Web Caching."

HTTP 1.1 includes a feature that alleviates some of the problems with IP address depletion on the Internet. A field in the HTTP header allows multiple domain names to be assigned to a single IP address. On the lighter side, an amusing document is RFC 2324, "HyperText Coffee Pot Control Protocol," (April 1998).

HTTP Connections

HTTP is the request/response protocol that sets up communication between a client and a server, and passes messages between the two systems. HTML (and now XML) is the document formatting language. When a client types the URL for a server (or an IP address) in the Address field of a browser, the HTTP protocol locates the address and establishes a connection to port 80 (typically) on the designated Web server. The Web server automatically returns its default page (usually an HTML file called HOME.HTML or INDEX.HTML). This process is pictured in Figure H-3.

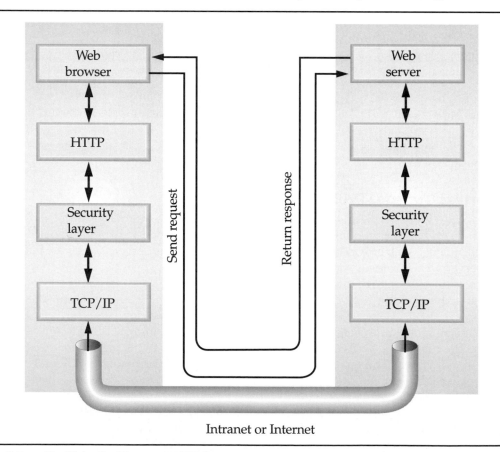

Figure H-3.   *The Web client/server architecture*

The connection process starts when you type the address of a Web site in your Web browser (or click a button). Here is an example of a URL that retrieves a document called info.html from the White House Web site:

www.whitehouse.gov/public/info.html

First, the IP address for this Web site is looked up in a DNS (Domain Name System) server. The name is converted to an IP address, and the IP address is returned to the Web browser. The Web browser then makes a direct connection to the Web server located at the IP address.

At That Point, The Server Will Respond To The Tail End Of The Url (Public/Info.Html). It Retrieves the file info.html in the public directory and transfers it via IP to the Web browser. The Web browser then interprets the HTML information in the file and displays it. As part of this process, Web servers may provide additional information to Web clients, such as the version of HTTP in use, status information about the request (was item found?), and the MIME (Multipurpose Internet Mail Extension) type that defines the media format (text, sound, pictures, video, and so on).

HTTP Secure Connections

HTTP connections can be secured using the S-HTTP (Secure HTTP) protocol or SSL (Secure Sockets Layer). Secure sessions encrypt information to prevent eavesdropping. Securing a session usually requires that the user or the Web site have a certificate that is issued by a certification authority (CA) such as VeriSign (www.verisign.com). See "Certificates and Certification Systems" for more information on CAs.

S-HTTP is a secure version of HTTP that is designed to coexist with HTTP and provide a variety of security mechanisms that can secure transactions between Web clients and servers. The existing HTTP transaction model is retained. Refer to "S-HTTP (Secure Hypertext Transfer Protocol)" for more information.

However, S-HTTP was never fully accepted by Web browser vendors such as Microsoft and Netscape. Instead, a similar protocol called SSL (Secure Sockets Layer) became more popular. SSL provides the same authentication and encryption functionality, but SSL has the added feature of being able to encrypt all data being passed between client and server at the IP socket level. See "SSL (Secure Sockets Layer)" for a detailed description of the procedure for setting up a secure session.

The IETF's TLS (Transport Layer Security) protocol is an SSL-like protocol being developed by the IETF Transport Layer Security (tls) Working Group.

RFC 2617, "HTTP Authentication," (June 1999) provides a specification for HTTP's authentication framework. RFC 2818, "HTTP over TLS," (May 2000) describes how to use TLS (Transport Layer Security) to secure HTTP connections over the Internet. RFC 2817, "Upgrading to TLS Within HTTP/1.1," (May 2000) describes how to use the upgrade mechanism in HTTP/1.1 to initiate TLS over an existing TCP connection. See "TLS (Transport Layer Security)."

HTTP Developments

The deficiencies in the HTTP protocol make it difficult to run sophisticated business applications over the Internet. Java and ActiveX have provided quite a lot of program functionality; but for critical business transactions, there is a need to maintain high levels of data integrity, reliability, and security. On intranets and extranets, these are processes that can be handled by transaction monitors, but getting such monitors to work over the Internet is a problem. See "Distributed Object Computing" and "Transaction Processing," for more details.

RFC 2774, "An HTTP Extension Framework," (February 2000) describes how HTTP can be dynamically extended with software components. Two other interesting RFCs include RFC 2964, "Use of HTTP State Management," (October 2000) and RFC 2965, "HTTP State Management Mechanism" (October 2000). See "Stateful and Stateless Connections."

Some vendors have come up with middleware solutions that basically bypass HTTP. Initially, a user accesses a Web server via HTTP. Some initial components downloaded to the user's system provide the middleware functionality between the client and an application server over the Internet. Basically, after the Web server does its job of setting up the user, it gets out of the way. All further interaction is directly between the client and the application server through the middleware components. See "Middleware and Messaging" for more information.

RFC 2756, "Hyper Text Caching Protocol," (January 2000) describes HTCP, a protocol for discovering HTTP caches and cached data, managing sets of HTTP caches, and monitoring cache activity. See "Web Caching."

The topics "URN (Universal Resource Names)" and "Handle System" describe "document persistence" (not to be confused with the connection persistence described earlier). Document persistence ensures that documents can be found independent of their URL address. In other words, the target documents specified by a hyperlink can be found even if the document is moved to a new location with a different URL.

RFC 2518, "HTTP Extensions for Distributed Authoring—WEBDAV," (February 1999) describes an extension to the HTTP 1.1 protocol that allows clients to perform remote Web content authoring operations. See "WebDAV" for more information.

Related Entries   Client/Server Computing; Distributed Object Computing; Handle System; HTML (Hypertext Markup Language); Hypermedia and Hypertext; Internet; Middleware and Messaging; Multitiered Architectures; Name Services; Service Advertising and Discovery; Stateful and Stateless Connections; TCP/IP (Transmission Control Protocol/Internet Protocol); Transaction Processing; URI (Uniform Resource Identifier); URL (Uniform Resource Locator); URN (Universal Resource Name); Web Caching; Webcasting; *and* Web Technologies and Concepts

Linktionary!—Tom Sheldon's Encyclopedia of Networking updates	http://www.linktionary.com/h/http.html
IETF Working Group: Transport Layer Security (tls)	http://www.ietf.org/html.charters/tls-charter.html
W3C HTTP Activity Statement	http://www.w3.org/Protocols/Activity.html
HTTP Made Really Easy by James Marshall	http://www.jmarshall.com/easy/http/
Optimizing Web Performance paper by James Rubarth-Lay	http://eunuch.ddg.com/LIS/CyberHornsS96/j.rubarth-lay/PAPER.html
HTTP, Mark McCutcheon's HTTP and HTML links	http://www.cs.ubc.ca/spider/mjmccut/technics.html

Google Web Directory: HTTP	http://directory.google.com/Top/ Computers/Internet/Protocols/HTTP/

Hubs/Concentrators/MAUs

See Network Connection Technologies; Network Design and Construction; Switch Fabrics and Bus Design; *and* Switching and Switched Networks.

Hypermedia and Hypertext

Hypermedia and hypertext are nonlinear information, presented to users in a way that lets them jump from one reference to another with the click of a button. On the Internet and the World Wide Web, people use hypermedia to access all sorts of information. The technology made using computers as easy as driving cars. Hypertext is linked text information, while hypermedia is both linked text and multimedia (graphics, sound, video, animation, and so on) information. The difference is trivial and most Web documents are now hypermedia documents. Hypermedia is well understood. This topic provides historical information, defines the terminology, and identifies related technologies.

Hypermedia is all about *hyperlinking*: while browsing through a hypermedia document, you can select a link and quickly jump to a reference or another source of information, and then jump back and continue reading where you left off. Vannevar Bush first suggested using electronic technology to access cross-links and references in an article that appeared in the August 1945 issue of *Atlantic Monthly!*

Ted Nelson actually coined the term *hypertext* back in 1965 and created a vision for a project called "Xanadu" that would implement hypertext on a Sun workstation. I heard Nelson speak about Xanadu in the early 1980s—how it would handle copyright laws and payments to authors for referenced works. I'm not sure if Ted Nelson was thinking about the Web when he came up with ideas, but he was certainly on the right track.

The most important feature is hyperlinking. With it, Web site authors can include the following kinds of links:

- **Links to other sections on the same document**   A common practice is to build a table of contents at the beginning of a Web document. When you click an item in the table, you will jump to a lower section in the document.

- **Links to other documents at the same Web site**   A hyperlink that opens another document at the same Web site, sometimes in a different directory.

- **Links to documents at other Web sites**   These require that the full URL to other Web sites be embedded in the HTML document.

One of the unifying concepts of the Internet is that all the documents stored on Web servers are created with HTML (and now XML). The HTML language is based on some early work done by IBM, and takes into account the fact that most documents have similar features. For example, the title is usually a large bold font, and the text is a smaller font with occasional underlined or italicized elements. In the late 1980s, IBM developed GML (Generalized Markup Language) as a way to tag or mark these elements so that documents could be moved from one place to another and retain their formatting.

GML is designed to be a universal document language. It was even standardized by the International Standards Organization, which called it SGML (Standard Generalized Markup Language). Tim Berners-Lee derived HTML from SGML in 1990 when he put together the first proposals for the World Wide Web.

The other component that makes hypermedia work on the Web is HTTP (Hypertext Transfer Protocol). HTTP is the protocol that Web browsers and Web servers use to set up a connection and exchange information. When a Web browser accesses a Web server, it requests a specific HTML page on that server. The server then responds by sending the page to the client using HTTP protocols.

XML is the latest Web development, and potentially the most significant. It goes beyond HTML by allowing developers to tag information in documents. With XML, if a document contains an address, it will be tagged as "Address." Other programs can then search the document for "Address" and extract the value stored there. XML documents are true information documents with the same benefits as database files or spreadsheets. With standard HTML documents, if you wanted to extract some information, you had to resort to cut-and-paste techniques. With XML, your database program can automatically extract information. What XML does is allow Web documents to participate directly in business applications, electronic commerce, and workflow applications. See "XML (Extensible Markup Language)."

Another interesting development is DAV (Distributed Authoring and Version), which is a set of extensions to HTTP that allows distributed Web authoring tools to perform, in an interoperable manner, versioning and configuration management of Web resources. See "WebDAV."

Yet another interesting development is Webcasting, which allows users to receive Web pages, updates, and broadcasts by subscribing to a service. Broadcasts can include multimedia audio and video. See "Webcasting."

Related Entries   ActiveX; Document Management; Handle System; HTML (Hypertext Markup Language); HTTP (Hypertext Transfer Protocol); Internet; Java; Metadata; Microsoft.NET; Search and Discovery Services; Service Advertising and Discovery; URI (Uniform Resource Identifier); URL (Uniform Resource Locator); URN (Universal Resource Name); Webcasting; WebDAV; Web Technologies and Concepts; *and* XML (Extensible Markup Language)

Linktionary!—Tom Sheldon's Encyclopedia of Networking updates	http://www.linktionary.com/h/hypermedia.html
W3C Markup Language page (see the section "Some early ideas for HTML")	http://www.w3.org/MarkUp/
History of the World Wide Web	http://www.webhistory.org/
History of the World Wide Web by Shahrooz Feizabadi	http://ei.cs.vt.edu/~wwwbtb/book/chap1/

I²O (Intelligent I/O)

See Servers; Switch Fabrics and Bus Design.

IAB (Internet Architectural Board)

See Internet Organizations and Committees *and* Standards Groups, Associations, and Organizations or visit the IAB Web site at http://www.iab.org/.

IADs (Integrated Access Devices)

An IAD is a customer premises device that provides access to wide area networks and the Internet. Specifically, it aggregates multiple channels of information including voice and data across a single shared access link to a carrier or service provider PoP (Point of Presence). The access link may be a T1 line, a DSL connection, a cable (CATV) network, a broadband wireless link, or a metro-Ethernet connection.

At the PoP, the customer's aggregated information is typically directed into a MSPP (multiservice provisioning platform), which is a complex and expensive device that sits between customers and the core network. It manages traffic streams coming from customers and forwards those streams to the PSTN (voice) or appropriate wide area networks (ATM, frame relay, or the Internet).

An IAD is sometimes installed by the service provider that a customer wishes to connect with. This allows the service provider to control the features of the access link and manage its operation during use. Competitive service providers are now offering access services over a variety of access technologies, including wireless optical (i.e., Terabeam) and metro-Ethernet networks. Old telco protocols and transport methods (T1 lines and time division multiplexing) are replaced with access methods that are appropriate for the underlying transport. Because of this, the provider will usually specify an appropriate IAD, or install an IAD.

See "Network Access Services" for a continuation of this topic.

Related Entries   DSL (Digital Subscriber Line); Gigabit Ethernet; HALO (High Altitude Long Operation); HDR (High Data Rate); Infrared Technologies; Internet Connections; Last Mile Services; LMDS (Local Multipoint Distribution Service); Local Loop; MAN (Metropolitan Area Network); Microwave Communications; MMDS (Multichannel Multipoint Distribution Services); Network Access Services; Packet-Radio Data Networks; Routers; Routing; Service Providers and Carriers; SONET (Synchronous Optical Network); Switching and Switched Networks; TDM Networks; Telecommunications and Telephone Systems; UWB (Ultra Wideband); WAN (Wide Area Network); Wireless Broadband Access Technologies; Wireless Communications; *and* Wireless Local Loop

 Linktionary!—Tom Sheldon's Encyclopedia of   http://www.linktionary.com/i/iad.html
Networking updates

IAHC (International Ad Hoc Committee)

The IAHC was dissolved on May 1, 1997, but the Web site is still available (although not being updated) and contains considerable background materials related to the work of the IAHC and other resources on the Internet DNS. *See* "Internet Organizations and Committees *and* Standards Groups, Associations, and Organizations" or visit the IAHC Web site at http://www.iahc.org/.

IANA (Internet Assigned Number Authority)

See Internet Organizations and Committees *and* Standards Groups, Associations, and Organizations or visit the IANA Web site at http://www.iana.org/.

IBM (International Business Machines)

IBM began operations in 1911 as the Computing-Tabulating-Recording Co. (CTR). In 1914, under the direction of Thomas J. Watson, CTR became IBM (International Business Machines). In 1953, IBM announced its first computer, the model 701, and shortly after, the model 650, which became its most popular model during the 1950s. The standard-setting computer for all modern IBM systems, the System/360, was introduced in 1964. An alternative line of computers, starting with the System/3, was introduced in 1970. The AS/400 is the current model in this series.

Mainframes are not going away any time soon. They still house up to 70 percent of the world data. This *legacy data* and the systems that store it will no doubt keep old IBM engineers and programmers busy with consulting work for years. In fact, IBM mainframes have been reborn in much smaller server-size packages that run older software and provide connections to legacy data.

 A discussion of IBM and IBM systems continues at the Linktionary! Web site. Also see the Related Entries listed here.

Starting in the mid-1990s, many IBM sites using SNA systems and APPN began moving to TCP/IP rather than using IBM networking schemes. In fact, IBM and other vendors like Cisco are developing hardware and software for integrating legacy systems into TCP/IP networks, not the other way around. These are discussed under "IBM Host Connectivity."

Related Entries   APPC (Advanced Program-to-Program Communication); APPN (Advanced Peer-to-Peer Networking); AnyNet; CPI-C (Common Programming Interface for Communication); Data Warehousing; DB2, IBM; DLSw (Data Link Switching); DRDA (Distributed Relational Database Architecture); HPR (High-Performance Routing); IBM Host Connectivity; Mainframe; SAA (Systems Application Architecture); and SNA (Systems Network Architecture)

Linktionary!—Tom Sheldon's Encyclopedia of Networking updates	http://www.linktionary.com/i/ibm.html
IBM Web site	http://www.ibm.com/
Yahoo! IBM resources page	http://dir.yahoo.com/Computers_and_Internet/Hardware/Systems/IBM/

IBM Host Connectivity

Nearly 70 percent of the world's data is stored in mainframe-based relational databases. Organizations that implement IBM mainframe and IBM AS/400 hosts need a way to let intranets, extranets, and Web users access data on those systems. A number of methods have been developed to provide host connectivity, including LAN-based access to mainframes, gateways that provide translation services, and Web technologies that provide a variety of middleware services.

Note   *The Linktionary! Web site listed below discusses some of these connectivity options. Also see the Related Entries and other Web sites listed at the end of this topic.*

More information about database connectivity in general may be found under the topics "DBMS (Database Management System)," "Middleware and Messaging," "MOM (Message-Oriented Middleware)," and "Multitiered Architectures."

Related Entries   APPN (Advanced Peer-to-Peer Networking); Client/Server Computing; Data Warehousing; DB2, IBM; DBMS (Database Management System); Distributed Applications; Distributed Computer Networks; Distributed Object Computing; DRDA (Distributed Relational Database Architecture); IBM (International Business Machines); Java; Mainframe; Middleware and Messaging; Multitiered Architectures; Object Technologies; ODBC (Open Database Connectivity); OLAP (Online Analytical Processing); SNA (Systems Network Architecture); SQL (Structured Query Language); Transaction Processing; XML (Extensible Markup Language); *and* Z39.50

Linktionary!—Tom Sheldon's Encyclopedia of Networking updates	http://www.linktionary.com/i/ibm_connectivity.html
APPN Implementer's Workshop	http://www.networking.ibm.com/app/aiwinfo/aiwsites.htm
Open Connect TCP/IP to SNA connectivity products	http://www.openconnect.com
Attachmate	http://www.attachmate.com
Cisco document: Enterprise 2000 Solutions for IBM Networks: Building an Infrastructure for the Future	http://www.cisco.com/warp/public/cc/so/neso/ibso/e2000_pl.htm
Microsoft's Technology Solutions Web page (see mainframe section)	http://www.microsoft.com/technet/techsol/

ICANN (Internet Corporation for Assigned Names and Numbers)

See Internet Organizations and Committees *and* Standards Groups, Associations, and Organizations or visit the ICANN Web site at http://www.icann.org/.

ICMP (Internet Control Message Protocol)

ICMP is an error-reporting protocol that works in concert with IP. If an error on the network occurs, such as a failure in one of the paths, IP sends an ICMP error message within an IP datagram. ICMP, therefore, requires IP as its transport mechanism.

Routers send ICMP messages in response to datagrams that cannot be delivered or had other problems. The router puts an ICMP message in an IP datagram and sends it back to the source of the datagram that could not be delivered.

The **ping** command uses ICMP as a probe to test whether a station is reachable. Ping packages an ICMP *echo request* message in a datagram and sends it to a selected destination. The user chooses the destination by specifying its IP address or name on the command line in a form such as:

ping 100.50.25.1

When the destination receives the echo request message, it responds by sending an ICMP echo reply message. If a reply is not returned within a set time, ping resends the echo request several more times. If no reply arrives, ping indicates that the destination is unreachable.

There are five ICMP error messages that may be returned to a sender in response to problems on the network or with datagrams. These messages can indicate information such as depleted buffers at the destination, lost packets, unreachable hosts, alternate network paths, and the need to fragment datagrams.

ICMP is discussed in the following RFCs:

- RFC 792, "Internet Control Message Protocol" (September 1981)
- RFC 1256 "ICMP Router Discovery Messages" (September 1991)
- RFC 1788 "ICMP Domain Name Messages" (April 1995)
- RFC 2463 "Internet Control Message Protocol (ICMPv6) for the Internet Protocol Version 6" (December 1998)
- RFC 2521 "ICMP Security Failures Messages" (March 1999)

Another utility that uses ICMP is *traceroute*, which provides a list of all the routers along the path to a specified destination.

Related Entries   Internet Protocol Suite; IP (Internet Protocol); Network Analyzers; Network Management; Performance Measurement and Optimization; Ping (Packet Internet Groper); RMON (Remote Monitoring); SNMP (Simple Network Management Protocol); *and* Testing, Diagnostics, and Troubleshooting

Linktionary!—Tom Sheldon's Encyclopedia of Networking updates	http://www.linktionary.com/i/icmp.html
Daryl's TCP/IP Primer (see Troubleshooting section)	http://ipprimer.2ndlevel.net/section.cfm
Gorry Fairhurst ICMP Web page	http://www.erg.abdn.ac.uk/users/gorry/course/ inet-pages/icmp.html
Ralph Walden's ICMP Message Web page	http://www.ee.siue.edu/~rwalden/networking/ icmpmess.html
Optimized Engineering Corporation ICMP Web page	http://www.optimized.com/COMPENDI/ICMP_1.htm

ICP (Internet Cache Protocol)

See Web Caching.

ICQ (I-Seek-You)

ICQ is an instant messaging system that informs users when someone they know is online and lets them instantly chat with one another. To participate in ICQ, you register with an ICQ server, which is connected to a broad network of servers spanning the Internet. At the time of registration, you receive a unique ICQ number and you can optionally provide personal information that allows other ICQ users to recognize you when you log on. Once you've registered, you can compile a selected list of friends and associates. ICQ uses this list to find your friends for you. When you log on, ICQ automatically detects the Internet connection, announces your presence to the Internet community, and alerts you when friends sign on or off. When someone you know logs on, you can instantly initiate a chat session; send messages; exchange files; or launch peer-to-peer applications such as games, Internet telephone calls, and videoconferences. ICQ has known security risks.

See "Instant Messaging" for more details, or refer to the ICQ Web site at http://www.icq.com.

ICSA (International Computer Security Association)

Formerly called NCSA (National Computer Security Association), this organization is devoted to computer security issues in corporations, associations, and government agencies worldwide. It is dedicated to continuously improving commercial computer security through certification, sharing of knowledge, and dissemination of information. The organization was founded in 1989 and is located in Carlisle, Pennsylvania.

ICSA delivers information through publications, conferences, forums, and seminars—in both traditional and electronic formats. You can obtain information at the Web site http://www.trusecure.net.

ICW (Internet Call Waiting)

The IETF PSTN/IN Requesting InTernet Services (SPIRITS) Working Group is developing specifications and protocols that describe how telephony services in IP networks can be started from the PSTN (public-switched telephone network) and IN (Intelligent Network) requests. ICW is being addressed by this working group and was a work in progress at the time of this writing.

RFC 2995, "Pre-SPIRITS Implementations" (November 2000) is dedicated to a discussion of Internet call waiting. See "Voice over IP (VoIP)" and refer to the SPIRITS Working Group Web page at http://www.ietf.org/html.charters/spirits-charter.html.

IDPR (Interdomain Policy Routing Protocol)

IDRP (Interdomain Routing Protocol) is an OSI *exterior* (interdomain) routing protocol that is used to exchange routing information between autonomous systems (ASs) of routers. The corresponding OSI *interior* (intradomain) routing protocol is IS-IS, which is designed to work within an autonomous system. IDRP was considered as a routing protocol for the Internet in the early 1990s when it was thought that OSI protocols would be used on the Internet. It has since fallen out of favor. Historical information is at the following Linktionary! Web site.

Linktionary!—Tom Sheldon's Encyclopedia of   http://www.linktionary.com/i/idpr.html
Networking updates

IEC (International Electrotechnical Commission)

See Standards Groups, Associations, and Organizations.

IEEE (Institute of Electrical and Electronic Engineers)

The IEEE is a nonprofit, technical professional association based in the United States that develops, among other things, data communication standards. It consists of committees that are responsible for developing drafts that are passed on to the ANSI (American National Standards Institute) for approval and standardization within the United States. The IEEE also forwards the drafts to the ISO.

The IEEE is composed of working groups that are involved in standards development in a number of areas, including aerospace electronics, circuits, communications, instrumentation, electrical code, nuclear engineering, power electronics, telecommunications, and vehicular technology, among many others. An information technology section includes working groups for bus architectures, local and metropolitan area networks, software engineering, storage systems, and testing technologies, among others. The LAN/MAN standards are known as the IEEE 802 standards and are covered in the next topic. A complete hyperlinked list of working groups is available at the Web site, listed here.

Related Entries   IEEE 802 Standards; Internet Organizations and Committees; and Standards Groups, Associations, and Organizations

IEEE Institute Web site	http://www.ieee.org/
IEEE Standards Association	http://standards.ieee.org/
Hyperlinked list of working group areas	http://standards.ieee.org/catalog/contents.html
IEEE Working Group Areas	http://grouper.ieee.org/
IEEE Communications Society	http://www.comsoc.org/
IEEE Communications Society Computer.org site	http://www.computer.org/

IEEE 802 Standards

The IEEE (Institute of Electrical and Electronic Engineers) is a technical association of industry professionals with a common interest in advancing all communications technologies. The previous topic discusses the IEEE organization. This topic describes the standards developed by the LAN/MAN Standards Committee (LMSC), which develops LAN (local area network) and MAN (metropolitan area network) standards, mainly for the lowest two layers in the OSI reference model. LMSC is also called the IEEE Project 802, so the standards it develops are referenced as IEEE 802 standards, described next. In general, IEEE 802 standards define physical network interfaces such as network interface cards, bridges, routers, connectors, cables, and all the signaling and access methods associated with physical network connections.

802.1 Higher Layer LAN Protocols Working Group   This working group defines the relationship between the IEEE 802 standards and other reference models. It focuses on LAN optimization of bridging/switching and cooperates with the IETF and ATM Forum. It is also working on VLAN (virtual LAN) standards. See "Bridges and Bridging" and "VLAN (Virtual LAN)."

802.2 Logical Link Control Working Group (Inactive)   This working group defines the IEEE LLC (Logical Link Control) protocol, which provides a connection to lower-layer MAC

(Medium Access Control) networks such as the IEEE 802 standards described here. See "Data Link Protocols," "LLC (Logical Link Control)," and "MAC (Media Access Control)."

802.3 Ethernet Working Group   This working group defines how the CSMA/CD (carrier sense multiple access/collision detection) method operates over various media, such as coaxial cable, twisted-pair cable, and fiber-optic medium. See "Ethernet" and "Gigabit Ethernet."

802.4 Token Bus Working Group (Inactive)   The token bus working group defines a broadband networking scheme that is used in the manufacturing industry. It is derived from the MAP (Manufacturing Automation Protocol). The network implements the token-passing method on a broadcast bus network. The standard is not widely implemented in the LAN environment.

802.5 Token Ring Working Group   The token ring working group defines the access protocols, cabling, and interface for token ring LANs made popular by IBM. See "Token Ring Network."

802.6 Metropolitan Area Network Working Group (Inactive)   The IEEE 802.6 MAN working group defines a high-speed protocol in which attached stations share a dual fiber-optic bus using an access method called DQDB (Distributed Queue Dual Bus). DQDB is the underlying access protocol for SMDS (Switched Multimegabit Data Service).

802.7 Broadband TAG (Inactive)   This working group provides technical advice to other subcommittees on broadband networking techniques. It is inactive at this writing.

802.8 Fiber Optic TAG   This working group provides advice to other subcommittees on fiber-optic networks as alternatives to existing copper-cable–based networks. Proposed standards are still under development at this writing.

802.9 Isochronous LAN Working Group   The IEEE 802.9 working group is working on the integration of voice, data, and video traffic to 802 LANs (basically, ISDN and Ethernet on the same wire). The specification has been called IVD (integrated voice and data), but is now commonly referred to as *isochronous Ethernet* or *isoEthernet*. See "isoEthernet" and "ISDN (Integrated Services Digital Network)."

802.10 Security Working Group   This working group is working on the definition of a standard security model that interoperates over a variety of networks and incorporates authentication and encryption methods. The group is also developing a mechanism that allows LAN traffic (frames) to carry an identifier that indicates which VLAN a frame belongs to. This would allow quick switching of information. Proposed standards are still under development.

802.11 Wireless LAN Working Group   This working group is defining standards for wireless networks. It is working on the standardization of mediums such as spread spectrum radio, narrowband radio, infrared, and transmission over power lines. See "Wireless Communications" and "Wireless LANs."

802.12 Demand Priority Working Group   This working group defined the 100-Mbit/sec Ethernet standard with the demand priority access method developed by Hewlett-Packard and other vendors. The access method uses a central hub to control access to the cable and support real-time delivery of multimedia information.

802.14 Cable Modem Working Group   This working group is chartered to create standards for data transport over traditional cable TV networks. The reference architecture specifies a hybrid fiber/coax plant with an 80-kilometer radius from the head end. The group is working on carrying Ethernet and ATM traffic. See "Cable (CATV) Data Networks."

802.15 Wireless Personal Area Network (WPAN) Working Group   This working group is developing standards for personal area networks, which are short-distance wireless networks such as Bluetooth. See "Bluetooth" and "Wireless PANs (Personal Area Networks)."

802.16 Broadband Wireless Access Working Group   This working group is developing standards and recommended practices to support the development and deployment of fixed broadband wireless access systems. See "Wireless Broadband Access Technologies."

802.17 Resilient Packet Ring Working Group   This working group is creating a standard for MAC-layer resilient packet rings. The group will define a resilient packet ring access protocol for use in local, metropolitan, and wide area fiber-optic networks. The goal is to optimize the current fiber-optic ring infrastructure for the demands of packet networks, including resiliency to faults. See "MAN (Metropolitan Area Network," "Optical Networks," and "Resilient Packet Rings."

Related Entries   ANSI (American National Standards Institute); IEEE (Institute of Electrical and Electronic Engineers); Internet Organizations and Committees; Internet Protocol Suite; Internet Standards; ISO (International Organization for Standardization); ITU (International Telecommunications Union); OSI (Open Systems Interconnection) Model; Standards Groups, Associations, and Organizations; Telecommunications and Telephone Systems; *and* TIA (Telecommunications Industry Association)

Linktionary!—Tom Sheldon's Encyclopedia of Networking updates	http://www.linktionary.com/i/ieee_standards.html
IEEE Institute Web site	http://www.ieee.org/
IEEE Standards Association	http://standards.ieee.org/
IEEE Working Group Area, LAN/MAN Standards Committee	http://grouper.ieee.org/groups/802/index.html
Networking Standards list at TechFest	http://www.techfest.com/networking/standard.htm

IESG (Internet Engineering Steering Group)

See Internet Organizations and Committees *and* Standards Groups, Associations, and Organizations or visit the IESG Web site at http://www.ietf.org/iesg.html.

IETF (Internet Engineering Task Force)

See Internet Organizations and Committees *and* Standards Groups, Associations, and Organizations or visit the IESG Web site at http://www.ietf.org/.

IGMP (Internet Group Message Protocol)

Multicast receivers must indicate their desire to be included in a multicast session. This is done with IGMP, a protocol that runs between hosts and their immediately neighboring multicast routers. Hosts use the protocol to inform the local multicast router that they want to receive transmissions from a particular multicast group, or that they no longer want to receive messages from a group. See "Multicasting."

IGP (Interior Gateway Protocol)

The Internet is divided into domains, or autonomous systems. A *domain* is a collection of hosts and routers that use the same routing protocol and are administered by a single authority. IGPs route within a domain. The EGP (Exterior Gateway Protocol) provides a way for two neighboring routers located at edges of their respective domains to exchange messages and information. On the Internet, IGP is used inside regions and EGP ties the regions together. Common IGPs include RIP (Routing Information Protocol), Cisco's IGRP (Interior Gateway Routing Protocol), the OSI's IS-IS (Intermediate System-to-Intermediate System), and the IETF's OSPF (Open Shortest Path First).

RFC 1371, "Choosing a Common IGP for the IP Internet" (October 1992) provides some insight into interior gateway protocols.

Related Entries   Autonomous System; IGRP (Interior Gateway Routing Protocol); Internetworking; IP (Internet Protocol); IS-IS (Intermediate System-to-Intermediate System) Routing; Network Concepts; OSPF (Open Shortest Path First) Routing; Packets and Packet-Switching Networks; RIP (Routing Information Protocol); Routing; *and* Routing on the Internet

IGRP (Interior Gateway Routing Protocol)

IGRP is a Cisco interior routing protocol based on distance-vector routing. An interior routing protocol is meant to be used inside an autonomous system (an organization's private network) while an exterior routing protocol operated between autonomous systems. IGRP is a distance-vector protocol, as opposed to a link-state protocol. While link-state protocols are superior, distance-vector protocols are appropriate for small internetworks, and require much less configuration and management. See "Distance-Vector Routing" for more information.

Cisco developed IGRP in the 1980s to provide an alternative to RIP (Routing Information Protocol). At the time, IGRP was a significant improvement over RIP, which had a hop count restriction that limited the size of an internetwork. IGRP supports internetworks with up to 255 hops.

Alternatives to IGRP are EIGRP (Enhanced Interior Gateway Routing Protocol) and OSPF (Open Shortest Path First). EIGRP is a distance-vector routing protocol similar to IGRP, but with many enhancements. OSPF is an IETF-developed link-state routing protocol that is suitable for large internetworks and the Internet. OSPF is now the preferred interior routing protocol.

This topic continues at the Linktionary Web site, with a discussion of IGRP and EIGRP.

Related Entries   Autonomous System; BGP (Border Gateway Protocol); Datagram and Datagram Services; Distance-Vector Routing; DNS (Domain Name Service) and Internet Domains; Fragmentation and Reassembly; Internet Architecture and Backbone; Internetworking; IP (Internet Protocol); Network Architecture; Network Concepts; Network Layer Protocols; OSPF (Open Shortest Path First) Routing; Packets and Packet-Switching Networks; RIP (Routing Information Protocol); Routing; *and* Routing on the Internet

    Linktionary!—Tom Sheldon's Encyclopedia of   http://www.linktionary.com/i/igrp.html
Networking updates

IIOP (Internet Inter-ORB Protocol)

IIOP is part of the CORBA (Common Object Request Broker Architecture). It provides a way to allow CORBA-based object interaction over TCP/IP protocol networks, including the Internet. IIOP basically works in conjunction with or replaces HTTP (Hypertext Transfer Protocol), the primary protocol for Web browser/server interaction.

See "CORBA (Common Object Request Broker Architecture)" and "Distributed Object Computing."

IISP (Interim Inter-switch Signaling Protocol)

IISP provides static routing in ATM networks. It is a subset of the NNI (Network-to-Network Interface) specification in ATM in which administrators manually configure routes. Signaling is also very limited. PNNI (Private Network-to-Network Interface) provides dynamic routing and advanced signaling. See "ATM (Asynchronous Transfer Mode)" and "PNNI (Private Network-to-Network Interface)."

IKE (Internet Key Exchange)

See Key Distribution and Management.

ILEC (Incumbent Local Exchange Carriers)

A local exchange carrier is a telephone service provider within a specific geographic area. In the Unites States, the ILECs are the service providers that are part of the old AT&T telephone system. When the government split AT&T up into separate entities, the separate operating units were called the RBOCs (regional Bell operating companies). The Telecommunications Reform Act of 1996 allowed the RBOCs to merge, so today it is more appropriate to refer to the incumbent carriers as "ILECs." The following mergers or acquisitions recently occurred:

- SBC Communications merged with PacBell (Pacific Telesis) in April 1996
- Bell Atlantic merged with Nynex in April 1996
- Qwest Communications bought US West in July 1999
- SBC Communications merged with Ameritech in October 1999
- Bell Atlantic merged with GTE in June 2000 and renamed itself Verizon

So, the current ILECs are SBC Communications, Bell Atlantic (now called Verizon), Qwest Communications, and BellSouth. The Act also attempted to increase competition by opening local markets. RBOCs were required to open their facilities to competitive providers called CLECs (competitive local exchange carriers). If the ILECs complied with the new rules of competition, they are allowed to expand into long-distance markets. This is discussed further under "Telecommunications Regulation." Also see "Service Providers and Carriers."

Related Entries   AT&T; Communication Services and Providers; ISPs (Internet Service Providers); NPN (New Public Network); PSTN (Public-Switched Telephone Network); Service Providers and Carriers; Telecommunications and Telephone Systems; Telecommunications Regulation; *and* WAN (Wide Area Network)

 Linktionary!—Tom Sheldon's Encyclopedia   http://www.linktionary.com/s/service_providers.html
of Networking updates

IMA (Inverse Multiplexing over ATM)

IMA is a specification defined by the ATM Forum that provides a way to combine an ATM cell stream over two or more circuits (i.e., T1 lines), thus allowing an organization to lease just the bandwidth it needs. When more than T1 and less than T3 is required, IMA provides a solution. It lets an organization purchase just the bandwidth it needs to transmit ATM cells across a carrier's network to its remote sites.

As shown in Figure I-1, IMA distributes traffic across multiple T1 circuits. The T1 lines act as a single circuit rather than multiple separate circuits. This optimizes bandwidth. For example, if separate ATM virtual connections were carried over separate T1 lines, some of the bandwidth on those lines might go unused. If each of the circuits only required 1 Mbits/sec of bandwidth rather than 1.544, the .544 Mbits/sec of bandwidth would go unused. IMA also allows bigger virtual connections. For example, if three T1 lines are aggregated, a virtual circuit can be as big as the three T1 lines combined.

A round-robin approach is used to distribute cells across the lines. Note in the figure that cell 1 is placed on line 1, cell 2 is placed on line 2, and so on. At the receiving end, the cells are recombined in their proper order to maintain ATM's quality-of-service characteristics.

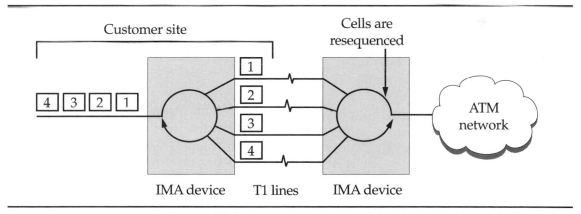

Figure I-1.   *Inverse multiplexing over ATM*

Related Entries   ATM (Asynchronous Transfer Mode); Bandwidth Management; Bandwidth on Demand; Bandwidth Reservation; BAP (Bandwidth Allocation Protocol); Bonding; DDR (Dial-on-Dem and Routing); Inverse Multiplexing; Link Aggregation; Load Balancing; Multiplexing and Multiplexers; Network Access Services; Network Design and Construction; TDM Networks; *and* WAN (Wide Area Network)

Linktionary!—Tom Sheldon's Encyclopedia of Networking updates	http://www.linktionary.com/i/ima.html
Larscom papers on inverse multiplexing	http://www.larscom.com/lib/lc_wp.htm
3Com paper: Inverse Multiplexing over ATM by Randy Brumfield	http://www.3com.com/technology/tech_net/white_papers/500642.html

Imaging

Imaging is the process of capturing, storing, displaying, and printing graphical information. This process includes the capturing of paper documents for archival purposes. Imaging procedures involve the use of scanners to capture the image and optical disks to store the many megabytes of information the captured images contain.

Imaging systems allow users on a network to store and call up imaged documents from centralized image storage systems. The network provides easy access to these files so users don't need to make a trip to the back-office storage area or request the files from an off-site location. Imaging is part of document processing and workflow applications that manage the way documents move through an organization.

This topic continues at the Linktionary! Web site. Also refer to the Related Entries and Web links here.

Related Entries   ADC (Analog-to-Digital Conversion); Collaborative Computing; Compound Documents; Compression Techniques; Document Management; EDI (Electronic Document Interchange); FAX Servers and Network Faxing; Groupware; Multimedia; Storage Management Systems; Videoconferencing; Webcasting; Whiteboard Applications; *and* Workflow Management

Linktionary!—Tom Sheldon's Encyclopedia of Networking updates	http://www.linktionary.com/i/imaging.html
Bitpipe (search for "imaging")	http://www.bitpipe.com/
Google Web Directory image processing page	http://directory.google.com/Top/Science/Technology/Electrical_Engineering/Image_Processing/
Techguide.com (see Document Management section)	http://www.techguide.com/

IMAP (Internet Message Access Protocol)

IMAP is an Internet protocol that allows a client to manipulate electronic mail messages that are stored on a mail server. IMAP is similar to POP (Post Office Protocol), but has new features.

It allows clients to manipulate a remote message folder (called a mailbox) in the same way they would manipulate local mailboxes. It supports mail operations that let users create, delete, and rename mailboxes; check for new messages; permanently remove messages; set and clear flags; and search.

IMAP (like POP) uses SMTP (Simple Mail Transport Protocol) as its transport mechanism. As an analogy, IMAP servers are like post offices while SMTP is like the postal carriers. An IMAP Internet mail server must run SMTP in order to receive incoming messages. At the same time, any outgoing messages are uploaded and forwarded as necessary. IMAP uses TCP to take advantage of its reliable data delivery services. The port that IMAP listens on is TCP port 143.

The latest version of IMAP is IMAP version 4, revision 1 (IMAP 4rev1), but the term "IMAP" is used here for simplicity. It is defined in RFC 2060, "Internet Message Access Protocol, Version 4rev1" (December 1996).

IMAP provides all the features of POP and can replace POP without disrupting current mail systems. Instead of requiring that users download all messages when they connect with a mail server, IMAP lets users store mail on the mail server for later retrieval. This is especially useful for mobile users who access mail at different computers, or with a palm device that doesn't have enough memory to hold mail that users might want to save for later reading or permanently archive in their desktop mail program.

Some important features available with IMAP that are not available in POP are described here:

- Clients can selectively download only the mail they want to read from the server by reviewing message headers.

- Clients may choose to download only part of a message. This is useful if a message has a large attachment and the user is working on a slow link. The attachment can be downloaded later.

- Shared mailboxes are available for workgroup use. All members of the workgroup are allowed to post and receive mail from the shared mailbox. The minutes of a meeting could be posted in the mailbox, for example.

- Allows the client to build a hierarchical message store on the server for storing messages.

- IMAP includes support for address books, and links to documents and USENET newsgroups.

- IMAP has strong authentication features. It supports Kerberos and other security protocols.

- Search commands are available that let users find messages based on their header, subject, or content information.

General electronic mail procedures are covered in more detail under the heading "Electronic Mail." A list of e-mail vendors that support Internet protocols and provide cross-platform support can also be found there. Refer to the Linktionary! Web site for a list of Internet RFCs related to IMAP and additional information.

Related Entries   Addresses, Electronic Mail; Collaborative Computing; Directory Services; Electronic Mail; FAX Servers and Network Faxing; Groupware; Instant Messaging; Mailing List Programs; Microsoft Exchange; MIME (Multipurpose Internet Mail Extension); Name Services; POP (Post Office Protocol); Search and Discovery Services; SMTP (Simple Mail Transfer Protocol); Unified Messaging; *and* Workflow Management

Linktionary!—Tom Sheldon's Encyclopedia of Networking updates	http://www.linktionary.com/i/imap.html
Internet Mail Consortium	http://www.imc.org/
Mail-related RFCs, complete list	http://www.imc.org/rfcs.html
Electronic Messaging Association	http://www.ema.org/
The IMAP Connection	http://www.imap.org/
IMAP Information Center	http://www.washington.edu/imap
Emailman, electronic superhero (everything you ever wanted to know about email)	http://www.emailman.com/
Email Guides	http://www.screen.com/start/guide/email.html
"IMAP: A New Internet Message Access Protocol" by Gordon Bennett	http://idm.internet.com/foundation/imap4.shtml

IMP (Interface Message Processor)

An IMP was a device used to connect the original Internet (then called the ARPANET). It was the precursor to today's routers. The IMP shielded the host computer (back in those days, the ARPANET was a network of mainframes). The IMP handled all the communications (message routing) between the hosts and, therefore, formed the network.

Related Entries   ARPANET; Internet; Internet Architecture and Backbone; Router; Routing; *and* Routing on the Internet

IMT-2000 (International Mobile Communications-2000)

See Wireless Mobile Communications.

IN (Intelligent Network)

IN is the intelligent portion of the public telephone network that contains the logic for routing calls, establishing connections, and providing advanced features such as unique customer services and custom programming of the network. You will also hear about the AIN (Advanced Intelligent Network). It was supposed to provide a way for customers to deploy services, but was never fully developed.

The IN consists of a signaling path that is separate from the actual voice call circuit. Call setup information is handled by SS7 (Signaling System 7), and the information is transferred via packets across an overlay packet-switching network. The primary advantage of a separate signaling system is that the phone network becomes more flexible and allows for the introduction of new services. For example, the IN allows for three-digit services such as the 800 and 900 services. It also supports caller ID, in which the caller's telephone number is transferred across the SS7 signaling path. Another service, called SRF (special resource function), plays recorded messages and prompts users to respond with inputs from the telephone keypad. See "Telecommunications and Telephone Systems" for more details.

The problem with the Intelligent Network is that services are created in the network and that end-devices (i.e., telephones) are relatively dumb terminals that use these services. In contrast, the Internet model assumes that end devices have processors and memory, and can run applications, while the network provides basic transport services. New services in the IN are difficult to create and deploy. New services in the Internet are a simple matter of users installing new programs on their computers.

Note *The user interface for the Internet is the Web browser, a graphical interface with powerful application capabilities. The user interface for the telephone system is the 12-key pad! How much longer must we put up with this relic from the 20th century?*

The NPN (new public network) is the convergence of the PSTN and the Internet. It allows Internet phone users to connect with PSTN telephone users and vice versa. It provides the reliability of the PSTN (five nines or 99.999% availability) with the flexibility of the Internet. Internet engineers have developed their own set of protocols that provide telephony services over the Internet and interconnection with the PSTN. See "Voice over IP (VoIP)."

With voice running over packets and telephony applications running in computers, many new and unique services are possible. For example, instant messaging can be used to "ring" someone's computer-attached telephone. A message might pop up like "Do you have time to talk right now?" Intelligent call forwarding can forward calls to you or alert you of incoming calls based on preset parameters in your address book. See the Related Entries for further discussion of the IN, the NPN, and Internet telephony services.

Related Entries   AIN (Advanced Intelligent Network); AT&T; NPN (New Public Network); Service Providers and Carriers; SS7 (Signaling System 7); T Carriers; Telecommunications and Telephone Systems; Telecommunications Regulation; Voice/Data Networks; Voice over IP (VoIP); *and* WAN (Wide Area Network)

Linktionary!—Tom Sheldon's Encyclopedia of Networking updates	http://www.linktionary.com/i/in.html
Intelligent Network Forum	http://www.inf.org/
Telecordia Technologies (formerly Bellcore)	http://www.telecordia.com/
Web ProForum Tutorial: "Fundamentals of Telecommunications"	http://www.iec.org/tutorials/fund_telecom/
Web ProForum Tutorial: "Signaling System 7 (SS7)"	http://www.iec.org/tutorials/ss7/
Web ProForum Tutorial: "Intelligent Network (IN)"	http://www. iec.org/tutorials/in/

Incident Response

A security incident is a breach of security, an attack by a hacker, a Trojan horse, a virus, and so on. Incident response deals with how these are handled. Administrators should be prepared in advance for such events and have a planned response. Appropriate mechanisms must be in place to detect security breaches and then do something about them. See "Security Auditing."

InfiniBand

InfiniBand is a new communication interconnect technology that was developed by the IBTA (InfiniBand Trade Association) in association with Compaq, Dell, Hewlett-Packard, IBM, Intel, Microsoft, Sun Microsystems, and other industry leaders. The architecture is a switched fabric with a packet-switching communication protocol. It also specifies links, host channel adapters, and adapter form factors.

InfiniBand evolved from previous work with I/O architectures called Future I/O and NGIO (Next-Generation I/O). These two were combined into System I/O and then redefined again into InfiniBand. The architecture was designed with multivendor interoperability in mind. It draws on the success of previous switched fabric architectures such as Fibre Channel.

A server is an example of a system that uses InfiniBand. An InfiniBand HCA (host channel adapter) replaces the PCI shared bus and provides a connection to an external InfiniBand switch. I/O devices also connect to the switch. Basically, the I/O controllers are moved off the server backplane to a separate switching device. The server then becomes just another device connected to the switch (via the HCA). With the I/O offloaded, the CPU is relieved of I/O interrupts and processing. In addition, slot restrictions of PCI are eliminated. Thus, servers can be reduced to rack-mount modules. In fact, InfiniBand can be thought of as a high-speed interconnect for rack-mount systems. A single rack could hold 30 or more servers in a clustered or parallel-processing configuration.

The InfiniBand topology is illustrated in Figure I-2. It consists of the four components listed here:

- **HCAs (host channel adapters)**   This is the InfiniBand interface for computer chassis. A link extends from it to InfiniBand switches. Compared to TCAs (see the next entry), HCAs can access memory directly in their hosts. This reduces CPU overhead.

- **TCAs (target channel adapters)**   This is the interface for noncomputer devices (i.e., peripherals such as network controllers and storage device controllers).

- **Switches**   While TCAs may connect directly to HCAs, a switch is best because it allows multiple devices to be connected. When a switch receives an incoming packet, it reads the destination address and forwards it to an appropriate output port.

- **Routers**   Interconnects multiple InfiniBand subnets.

Interdevice communication is handled via packet switching. Messages are routed around the system in data packets that have an address much like IP packets have addresses. Packets can be up to 4,096 bytes. Globally shared memory is supported, which, along with message passing, is crucial for multiprocessing environments.

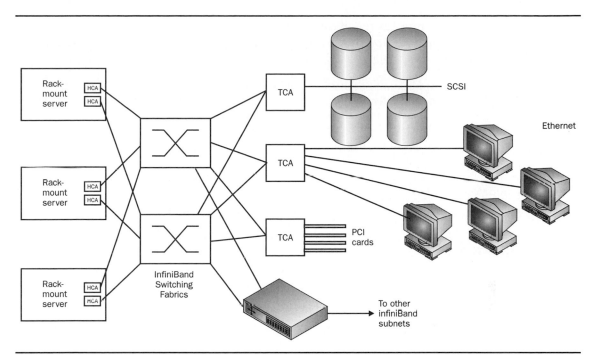

Figure I-2.   *InfiniBand network (topology of rack-mount system)*

A fabric manager controls the switching fabric. It determines the current topology and the nodes attached to the system, and establishes routing between the nodes. A channel communications model is used, in which devices directly connect with one another across the fabric. Since CPUs are decoupled from I/O, channel-connected devices can directly access host memory.

The basic interconnect is a four-wire LVDS link (two wires receive, two wires send). LVDS uses opposing signals on two wires, which helps the receiver discard induced noise. With noise reduced, voltages can be reduced, which leads to lower power requirements. See "LVDS (Low-Voltage Differential Signaling)."

InfiniBand connectors are high-speed serial I/O links, whereas PCI implements a parallel architecture. Serial links reduce the number of wires and the pin count, which improves cabling distance. Board design is simplified and boards can be reduced in size. In fact, the pin count on the actual processors can be reduced with InfiniBand. Since peripherals and peripheral connects are off-loaded, servicing and availability improve. Components are easily swapped out without bringing down the rest of the system.

Multiple links and multiple switches can be implemented to scale the system and provide redundancy. InfiniBand has several link bandwidth options. In the 1x mode, links consist of one differential transmit pair and one differential receive pair to provide full-duplex bandwidth of 500 MB/sec. This minimum configuration is the same bandwidth as PCI, but PCI is a single bus that all the devices attached to it must share, while InfiniBand uses multiple channels to create dedicated nonshared connections between devices.

A 4x (2 GB/sec) mode and 12x (6 GB full-duplex) mode are also available. Equipment can be upgraded at any time to support the higher rates. For example, a critical link could be upgraded to a higher capacity while less critical links remain the same.

Related Entries   ASIC (Application-Specific Integrated Circuit); Data Center Design; Distributed Computer Networks; Embedded Systems; LVDS (Low-Voltage Differential Signaling); Multiprocessing; Network Concepts; Network Connection Technologies; Network Processors; SAN (Storage Area Network); SAN (System Area Network); SCSI (Small Computer System Interface); Servers; Switch Fabrics and Bus Design; *and* Switching and Switched Networks

Linktionary!—Tom Sheldon's Encyclopedia of Networking updates	http://www.linktionary.com/i/infiniband.html
IBTA (InfiniBand Trade Association)	http://www.infinibandta.org/

Information Appliance

An information appliance is a device that attaches to a network to provide services to users, or it is a user access device usually called a "network appliance" or "Web terminal." These devices are usually preconfigured to operate out-of-the box. See the Related Entries listed next.

Related Entries   Embedded Systems; NAS (Network Attached Storage); Network Appliances; *and* Thin Client

Information Warehouse

An *information warehouse* is an entity that allows end users to quickly and easily access an organization's data in a consistent way. In the view of large system vendors like IBM, the information warehouse recasts mainframe and midrange computer systems as the central repository for current and historical data, as well as predefined data sets, reports, and catalogs of data. This strategy protects high-end system technology and customers' investments. The information warehouse provides a central point where all data is collected and made available, repackaged, or redistributed to end users. This topic is covered further under "Data Warehousing."

Related Entries   Client/Server Computing; Clustering; Data Center Design; Data Management; Data Mart; Data Mining; Data Protection; Data Warehousing; DBMS (Database Management System); IBM Host Connectivity; Multitiered Architectures; NAS (Network Attached Storage); OLAP (Online Analytical Processing); SAN (Storage Area Network); Servers; SQL (Structured Query Language); Storage Management Systems; *and* Storage Systems

Information Warfare

Information warfare is war waged in cyberspace against a competitor, a group, or another nation. The attacker targets the information resources of its opponent, eavesdrops on vital communications, and uses other techniques such as spying and social engineering to gain advantage.

Many people consider information warfare one of the most serious concerns of the information age, because it can be waged by anyone with minimal resources across the global

Internet. A group or nation may hire known hackers, out-of-work programmers, and experts in the field to wage wars over the global communications network.

An information war may involve attacks against banking systems, media and information Web sites, communication systems, the power companies, transportation and distribution systems, agricultural systems, and so on. In a well-planned attack, all of these attacks and more may take place simultaneously. In fact, many of the individual attacks that have been taking place over the years may only be "tests" designed to "sniff out" vulnerabilities in preparation for much larger attacks.

The InfoSysSec Web site listed here is the place to start your research into information warfare and security issues in general.

Related Entries   Attacks and Attackers; Firewall; Hacking and Hackers; Security; *and* Security Auditing

Linktionary!—Tom Sheldon's Encyclopedia of Networking updates	http://www.linktionary.com/i/infowar.html
Linktionary!—Tom Sheldon's Security Web page	http://www.linktionary.com/security/
InfoWar.com	http://www.infowar.com/
InfoSysSec (the most thorough and complete security site on the Web)	http://www.infosyssec.net/infosyssec/infowar1.htm
Dorothy Denning's "Cybercrime, Infowar, and Infosecurity" Web page	http://www.cs.georgetown.edu/~denning/infosec/

See "Security" for more hyperlinks.

Infrared Technologies

Infrared is the region in the electromagnetic spectrum that falls between radio waves and visible light. Infrared can't be seen, but it can be felt as heat given a strong energy source. A camera equipped with infrared-sensitive film can take pictures of "warm" objects in low-light environments. Most people are familiar with infrared as implemented in remote control devices.

Infrared signals for computer networks and computing devices may be either direct (point to point) or diffused (many to many). The *direct mode* systems implement point-to-point laser beams that require a clear line of sight between transmitter and receiver. The *diffused mode* spreads the light out and bounces it off walls, ceilings, and buildings so that it reaches a group of end systems (i.e., workstations in the same room). In contrast, radiofrequency signals penetrate walls, are subject to interference, and are regulated in most cases.

Diffused infrared signals are relatively secure from eavesdroppers. The signals do not travel far. Equipment vendors also employ encryption to secure signals, especially for equipment designed to operate across metropolitan areas. While infrared signals are immune to electromagnetic interference, they are susceptible to interference from some types of lighting. Direct mode systems may be necessary in some environments.

Infrared optical systems operate in a wavelength range that is specified in nanometers. Red blood corpuscles are about the same size as the wavelengths in the infrared range. A typical fiber-optic system operates in the 1,550-nm range, which has a frequency of 194,000 GHz

(194,000 billion cycles/sec). Shorter wavelengths yield higher operating frequencies. A decrease of only 1 nm increases the frequency by 133 GHz.

Infrared light is used in a number of communications systems, including the following:

- **Fiber-optic transmission systems**   Signals are transmitted by "lighting" the cable with LEDs (light-emitting diodes) or semiconductor lasers The infrared range for fiber-optic cable occupies specific frequency ranges called "windows." These are in the near-infrared range (850 nm, 1,320 nm, 1,400 nm, 1,550 nm, and 1,620 nm). See "Fiber-Optic Cable," "Optical Networks," and "WDM (Wavelength Division Multiplexing)."

- **Point-to-point metropolitan laser systems**   These systems are designed to bridge corporate networks across metropolitan areas, or provide "instant" data links for special events such as videoconferences or news service data uplinks. For example, Lucent provided point-to-point laser links between event locations at the Olympics in Atlanta.

- **Free space optical systems**   Systems in this category imitate fiber-optic cable, but don't use cable. Data signals are transmitted through open space via infrared light. The systems are narrowly focused and designed to provide subscribers with high-speed access to the Internet or other network connections without the need to lay cable. Terabeam's Fiberless Optical systems are installed at hub sites in metropolitan areas. Multiple subscribers place a transceiver in a window of their building to connect with Terabeam's switching hub. Switches at the hub use MPLS to provide virtual circuits for individual subscriber traffic, which may be routed to the Internet or directed to other networks. No licensing is required. Terabeam's system is based on IP over Ethernet over Infrared.

- **Infrared LANs and home networks**   Infrared LANs may operate in direct or diffused mode, or a combination of the two. Direct mode is used to bridge LANs, while diffused mode is used to connect multiple workstations to a base unit. Line-of-sight systems provide better distance and performance. Diffused systems allow multiple stations to participate in LAN connections, but there are distance and data rate limitations because diffusion causes a loss of energy. A typical infrared LAN operates in the wavelength range between 780 nm and 950 nm. Performance is typically in the range of 10 Mbits/sec to 20 Mbits/sec, although 100-Mbit/sec systems are possible. Some systems designed for metropolitan area links operate in the gigabits/sec range. Infrared LANs typically implement Ethernet or token ring access methods.

- **Infrared data interconnects**   The infrared technologies in this category are considered replacement technologies for serial and parallel data connectors. The technology has been standardized by IrDA (Infrared Data Association). IrDA cordless data connections are best known as the small dark red window on the sides of IrDA-compatible devices. The window covers the infrared transmitter and receiver. IrDA provides digital exchange at 9,600–115,200 bits/sec, with data rates up to 4 Mbits/sec in some units. Future products will achieve data rates of 50 Mbits/sec.

Infrared interconnect technologies began appearing in the early 1990s shortly after the formation of the IrDA. IrDA is an international nonprofit organization that creates standards for infrared communications and promotes interoperability among vendor products. The standards support a broad range of computing devices, including laptops, palm devices, communications equipment, printers, copiers, fax machines, overhead projectors, telephones, game controllers, headsets, and credit cards (yes, credit cards will have infrared links).

There are two IrDA infrared standards. *IrDA DATA* is designed for peer-to-peer data transmissions between compatible devices. *IrDA CONTROL* allows host devices to control peripherals such as keyboards, mice, game pads, joysticks, and pointing devices. Host devices include PCs, home appliances, game machines, and television/Web set-top boxes.

The IrDA DATA standard consists of the following protocols, which are required for interoperability with other devices. An optional set of protocols is also available, as discussed later.

- **PHY (Physical Signaling Layer)** The physical layer provides the infrared data signaling between devices. A high-power version is available that can achieve distances of about 2 meters. A low-power version is designed to conserve power and is limited to distances of under 30 cm.

- **IrLAP (Link Access Protocol)** This protocol provides a device-to-device connection for the reliable, ordered transfer of data, and defines procedures for discovering nodes.

- **IrLMP (Link Management Protocol)** Provides multiplexing of the IrLAP layer and supports multiple channels above an IrLAP connection. The Information Access Service protocol provides a service discovery procedure.

Optional protocols include Tiny TP (provides flow control), IrCOMM (provides serial and parallel port emulation), IrOBEX (provides object exchange services similar to HTTP, IrDA Lite (provides a "lite" reduced code set), IrTran-P (provides image exchange protocol used in digital image capture devices/cameras), IrMC (a specifications for exchanging data with telephony devices), and IrLAN (supports wireless LAN access).

Related Entries Bluetooth; Data Link Protocols; Electromagnetic Spectrum; Fiber-Optic Cable; Home Networking; IEEE 802 Standards; LAP (Link Access Procedure); LLC (Logical Link Control); Mobile Computing; Network Access Services; Network Connection Technologies; Optical Networks; Parallel Interface; Point-to-Point Communications; Serial Communication and Interfaces; Spread Spectrum Signaling; USB (Universal Serial Bus); WDM (Wavelength Division Multiplexing); Wireless Broadband Access Technologies; Wireless Communications; Wireless LANs; Wireless Local Loop; Wireless Mobile Communications; *and* Wireless PANs (Personal Area Networks)

Linktionary!—Tom Sheldon's Encyclopedia of Networking updates	http://www.linktionary.com/i/infrared.html
IrDA (Infrared Data Association)	http://www.irda.org/
Extended Systems	http://www.extendedsystems.com/
Terabeam "Fiberless Optical" technology	http://www.terabeam.com/
Microsoft's Infrared Technology page	http://www.microsoft.com/hwdev/infrared/
Clarinet Systems infrared LAN products	http://www.clarinetsystems.com/

Instant Messaging

Instant messaging, or IM, provides a way to send short messages to other people on the Internet, usually in real time, although delayed delivery is supported. Instant messaging could be compared to a combination of e-mail and Internet chat. Like e-mail, instant messaging supports message exchange between people; but, unlike e-mail, instant messaging is designed for two-way live chats. IM bridges the gap between voice calls and e-mail. What IM does not normally do is archive messages like e-mail programs. Business users may need to look for products that log conversations for later referral or for legal purposes.

Chat and instant messaging are forms of *synchronous communications*. Like a voice telephone call, a chat or instant messaging session is live and each user responds to the other in real time. But while voice calls require the immediate attention of the parties involved, IM gives people a chance (if only momentary) to think out responses. In contrast, discussion forums and electronic mail are *asynchronous communications*. Some amount of time may pass before a person responds to a message. A discussion forum is a non-real-time chat room where groups of people exchange messages in an asynchronous style. A message sits in a message queue for other people to read and respond to at any time, or until the message falls out of the queue.

Important aspects of IM are *presence monitoring (PM)* and what AOL calls "buddy lists" or just *lists*. A list is a group of people that you want to exchange instant messages with. A presence monitoring server keeps track of when people log on and notifies you. Likewise, the presence server keeps track of when you log on and notifies other people. You can specify exactly who in your list should know you are currently online. For example, you can specify that fellow employees only know you are online from 8:00 to 5:00.

A typical IM/PM system works as follows:

1. A central server logs users on and stores the user's current IP address.

2. The user's computer sends the server its current buddy list, or at least a sublist of who the user is willing to message with.

3. The server tells the user who in the list is currently online.

4. The user can send a message to an online user. It goes through the messaging server and displays on the recipient's screen.

5. The recipient receives the message immediately and can reply immediately.

One thing to consider is that even though your system may be listed as "online" to other users, you may not be physically present to receive instant messages. People who send you instant messages may think you are ignoring them. Consequently, instant messaging allows people to specify that they are online but temporarily unavailable. You can also designate your availability depending on the device you are using or the network you are attached to. For example, when you are on the road and using your palm computer, you may not want to receive messages from most of the people in your list. Alternatively, when you connect to the company network from your home computer, you may want to let everyone in your department or workgroup know you are available.

IM and PM have been getting a lot of attention in the last few years, but they are nothing new. Instant messaging has been available on centralized computing systems (mainframes and minicomputers) and LANs for years. On those systems, all users log on to a common system, so it is easy to track who is online. In the UNIX environment, the **who** and **finger** commands can be used to find out who is online, and the **write** and **talk** commands can be used to initiate a message exchange session. Instant messaging is also available to cellular phone users in the form of SMS (short messaging service), which lets users exchange short text messages with other cell phone users.

Extending PM to the Internet is more difficult. So far, IM and PM have worked well within the domains of service providers. If you belong to AOL, MSN (Microsoft Network), or Yahoo!, you can be alerted when other users of those services log on; but IM and PM don't work well between service provider networks due to differences in systems and protocols, and an unwillingness of the providers to share such information. AOL has been particularly protective of its popular Instant Messenger system. In early 2001, the FCC recommended to AOL as part of its merger with Time Warner that it demonstrate interoperability with other systems or give subscribers the ability to access other IM systems.

Presence information will grow more critical in all realms of communication. Presence databases are to the Internet what phone number directories are to the telephone system. IM/PM-oriented user databases must be shared among service providers in order to build a globally viable instant messaging and presence system.

The latest trend in instant messaging is to turn it into a global Internet service, but that is only the beginning. Presence monitoring and instant messaging are bridging the barrier between the Internet and the telephone network, and becoming service-enabling features for a whole new set of applications and services, including "instant" Internet telephony and "instant" conferencing. Some examples are described here:

- Instant messaging can serve as the "ringer" for Internet telephone calls. You send a message to some to find out if they are available to talk. If so, you initiate an Internet phone call.

- Instant messaging can be used to set up an ad hoc videoconference.

- IM users can send messages to cellular telephone users who already take advantage of SMS.

Instant messaging and presence protocols can also provide middleware functionality between applications, and between applications and people. For example, a news server could use instant messaging to deliver breaking news to your browser about stocks you own. Applications running on different servers could use instant messaging to instantly update one another as information changes.

Eventually, instant messaging and presence systems will provide a single point of contact that helps people get in touch no matter where they are or what type of device they are using. Presence monitoring provides reachability information that enhances business communications. It can even be tied in with calendars. As presence technologies expand, they will become the basis for a single communication system with *personal location services* that can locate people on whatever device they are currently using, whether that is a desktop computer, a PDA, or a cellular phone. The idea is to provide one-click access to people, rather than having to look in different lists (phone book, e-mail, pager, and so on).

Some people worry that privacy will be lost as messages follow them wherever they go, but messaging systems give users a high degree of control over when and where they can be contacted, as defined by rules and priority settings. In fact, presence protocols are becoming the most important tool that people use to control how they can be reached and how they reach other people.

Instant Messaging and Presence Protocols

As mentioned, detecting when other users are online is relatively easy on enterprise networks or within the same service provider network. Internetwork presence monitoring requires service agreements and the delivery of presence information across domains. That requires standard protocols so services providers can easily share information. Unfortunately, at the time of this writing, a number of groups have proposals that do not work well together.

The IETF working group called Instant Messaging and Presence Protocol (IMPP) was working on a model for IM and PM, but the group's work is currently on hold because its members and the industry were unable to agree on details. According to Jeff Pulver (http://www.pulver.com), "the IMPP working group's dual focus on IM and Presence has led to the dumbing down of presence management capabilities to keep IM protocols simple." In the meantime, the group asked for proposals from other parties with the intention of consolidating them into a single recommendation. The proposals may be found at the IMPP Information home page listed at the end of this topic.

Two RFCs developed by the IMPP working group provide general information about the requirements of an Internet-based IM/PM system. RFC 2778 (A Model for Presence and Instant Messaging, February 2000) defines an abstract IM/PM model, the various entities involved, the terminology, and the services it should provide. RFC 2779 (Instant Messaging / Presence Protocol Requirements, February 2000) defines a minimal set of protocols that are required so that independently developed IM/PM applications can interoperate across the Internet.

An instant messaging system consists of clients and servers, and protocols that transport messages between clients and servers. Clients may be users or user applications. The RFCs define messaging and presence as two separate client/server models, as described next. Both services may run side by side in an instant messaging and presence service, or be distributed in different servers. The relationships are pictured in Figure I-3.

- **Instant messaging**   This model includes *senders* and *instant inboxes*. A sender is a user or application that creates messages and forwards them to the IM service for delivery. Messages are sent to an instant inbox based on the instant inbox address attached to the message.

- **Presence**   This model includes *presentities* and *watchers*. Presentities store and distribute presence information. Watchers receive presence information from the service, and consist of *fetchers* and *subscribers*. A fetcher requests presence information from a presentity (either on command or at regular intervals), while a subscriber requests notification of changes in some presentitie's presence information.

The IM/PM protocol defines the interaction between the IM and PM entities (presentities and watchers in the presence service, and senders and instant inboxes in the instant messaging service). The protocols carry information such as requests for presence information, notification

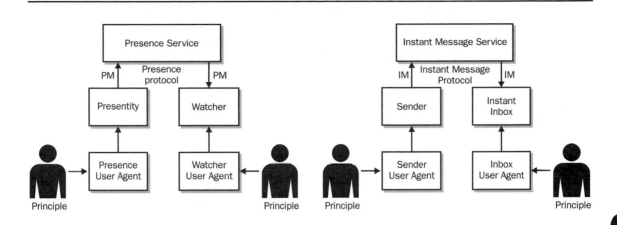

Figure I-3. *IM and PM protocols and service entities*

of presence, and text-based messages (or messages using other types of media). Presence information includes a user's current address and information about the IM/PM mechanisms in use. URLs are used for addressing and MIME is used for message transport. Data formatting and presentation is handled by XML.

Many of the proposed IMPP protocols define extensions to support SIP (Session Initiation Protocol). SIP is an IETF-defined application-layer signaling protocol used for setting up, maintaining, and terminating multimedia sessions such as voice calls, videoconferences, and instant messaging sessions. SIP and other protocols are being used in schemes to invoke PSTN telephone services from an IP network. These services include placing basic calls, sending and receiving faxes, and receiving content over the telephone. Since SIP defines how to register and keep track of users on a network, as well as redirect messages to other locations, it already provides services that are useful instant messaging. A related protocol is SDP (Session Description Protocol), which is used to describe multimedia sessions for the purposes of session announcement, session invitation, and other forms of multimedia session initiation. Microsoft and other major vendors are supporting SIP in their IM plans. See "SIP (Session Initiation Protocol)."

Interoperability is a major requirement. IMUnified is a coalition of AT&T, Excite@home, MSN, Odigo, Phone.com, Prodigy, and Yahoo! that is pushing for interoperable instant messaging standards that will allow Internet users to communicate freely with each other. The PAM (Presence and Availability Management) Forum was formed by Lucent and Novell to create a single API (called the PAM API) that all developers can use to build IM and PM products that are interoperable across networks and services. The APIs are designed to allow communication systems to share authorized information about a subscriber's identity, presence, and availability securely across telephony and IP technologies. In particular, the APIs are designed to work across both telephone and Internet networks and to have a strong emphasis on security and privacy mechanisms. The PAM Forum Web site has more information.

Related Entries   Chat; Collaborative Computing; Electronic Mail; Groupware; ICQ (I-Seek-You); IRC (Internet Relay Chat); Mailing List Programs; Search and Discovery Services; Service Advertising and Discovery; SIP (Session Initiation Protocol); Unified Messaging; Videoconferencing; Voice/Data Networks; VoIP (Voice over IP); Webcasting; *and* XML (Extensible Markup Language)

Linktionary!—Tom Sheldon's Encyclopedia of Networking updates	http://www.linktionary.com/i/instant_messaging.html
IETF Working Group: Instant Messaging and Presence Protocol (impp)	http://www.ietf.org/html.charters/impp-charter.html
IETF Working Group: SIP for Instant Messaging and Presence Leveraging (simple)	http://www.ietf.org/html.charters/simple-charter.html
IETF Working Group: Session Initiation Protocol (sip)	http://www.ietf.org/html.charters/sip-charter.html
IETF Working Group: Application Exchange (apex)	http://www.ietf.org/html.charters/apex-charter.html
IMPP Information home page	http://www.imppwg.org/
IMUnified home page	http://www.imunified.org/
PAM Forum	http://www.pamforum.org/
The Presence & Instant Messaging Web site (in association with Pulver.com)	http://www.instantmessaging.org/
Pulver.com (a great site for IP telephony)	http://www.pulver.com/
The SIP Center	http://www.sipcenter.com/
Google Messaging Services page	http://directory.google.com/Top/Computers/Software/Internet/Clients/Chat/Messaging_Services/
Microsoft Exchange Conferencing Server Web site	http://www.microsoft.com/exchange/
Jabber.com	http://www.jabber.com
dynamicsoft, Inc.	http://www.dynamicsoft.com/
MSN Messenger Service page	http://messenger.msn.com/
AOL Instant Messenger	http://www.aol.com/aim/
Web ProForums (see "Instant Messaging" paper by Ericsson)	http://www.iec.org/tutorials/

Integrated Access Devices

See IAD (Integrated Access Devices).

Integrated Services (Int-Serv)

Integrated Services, or Int-Serv, is a model for providing QoS on the Internet and intranets by using bandwidth *reservation* techniques. As originally designed, the Internet supports only best-effort delivery of data packets across multiaccess (shared) network links. There is little support for QoS (quality of service) due to the packet-oriented nature of the Internet and factors such as variable queuing delays and congestion losses.

The Int-Serv model defines methods for identifying traffic *flows*, which are streams of packets going to the same destination. An Internet voice call is an example. The Int-Serv concept reserves just the right amount of bandwidth to support the flow's requirements and protect it from disruptions caused by network congestion. Reservations are negotiated with each network device along a route to a destination. If each device has resources to support the flow, a reserved path is set up. RSVP (Resource Reservation Protocol) is the signaling protocol that sends messages in the forward direction to *request* reservations, and then sends messages in the reverse direction to *set up* the reservations if all devices in a route agree to reserve resources.

Many feel that Int-Serv concepts were too ambitious and too difficult to implement on the Internet (although it is appropriate for enterprise networks). In contrast, the IETF Diff-Serv model is a classification and packet-tagging system that is more concerned with CoS (class of service) than QoS. Packets are classified and tagged, either at the source or at the edge of a Diff-Serv network, and then given appropriate priority service as they cross the network. Diff-Serv is more practical to implement across the Internet. See "Differentiated Services (Diff-Serv)."

One of the earliest documents to discuss Int-Serv was RFC 1363 (A Proposed Flow Specification, September 1992). It proposed a *flow specification* that hosts could use to request special services of an internetwork (i.e., guarantees about how the internetwork will provide quality of communication between applications). The RFC describes a message structure with fields that a host could use to describe its flow requirements. The message was sent across the network and used to negotiate with devices for the required service levels.

The RFC also provides insight into traffic and delay characteristics, queuing problems and buffer space, delay variations, rate controls, and the need for networks to provide a range of guarantees. At the time, there was speculation about whether hosts should negotiate for network resources or whether the internetwork should infer the QoS requirements of a host from information embedded in the data traffic.

One of the main requirements of the reservation approach is to find a route that supports the QoS requirements. The information to be supplied to the routing systems includes *throughput requirements, delay sensitivity* (i.e., avoid satellite links if the flow is delay sensitive), *error tolerance* (is the application sensitive to dropped packets?), and *tolerance of delay variation* (voice cannot tolerate jitter). The expectation is that the network will either allow the flow (admittance) or reject it. Early designers considered a scheme in which a host "haggled" with the network until a suitable reservation could be agreed upon!

RFC 1363 makes one final note that there must be some mechanism to perform a short exchange of messaging in preparation for setting up a flow. This is where RFC 1633 (Integrated Services in the Internet Architecture: An Overview, June 1994) comes into the picture. It spells out a workable reservation system. In particular, the need for a resource reservation protocol is mentioned as a requirement for reserving QoS across a network. RSVP version 1 is covered in RFC 2205 (Resource ReSerVation Protocol—Version 1 Functional Specification, September 1997).

Integrated Services Architecture

The original Int-Serv specification called for two types of services targeted toward real-time traffic: guaranteed and predictive service. The goal was to go beyond the best-effort nature of the original Internet architecture to a model that could support real-time QoS by controlling end-to-end packet delays. The model specifies these features:

- **Controlled-link sharing** By controlling links, it was possible to monitor new flows into links and reject them if they would degrade the service already assigned to existing flows. This was a radical departure from the original best-effort shared model in which packets were sent into the network at will, even if the link was congested.

- **Resource reservation** Reserving bandwidth is a key feature of the Int-Serv model. RFC 1633 argues that guarantees can only be achieved through reservations. "Guarantees" in this case refers to a quality of service that allows a real-time application to operate in an acceptable way over the duration of its use.

- **Admission control** The ability to reject new flows that might degrade the quality of existing flows is also an important feature of the Int-Serv model.

To accommodate these requirements, the Int-Serv framework includes a *packet scheduler* to manage the forwarding of packet streams, a *classifier* that maps incoming packets into some class so that packets in the same class can get the same treatment, an *admission control* component that decides whether a new flow gets the QoS requested, and a *reservation setup protocol* (i.e., RSVP) that creates and maintains flow in the hosts and in routers along the path of a flow. The admission control component also handles the authentication functions, as well as accounting and administrative reporting. This implies a policy system that keeps track of user privileges and a system that charges users for bandwidth. See "RSVP (Resource Reservation Protocol)" and "Policy-Based Management."

The problem with RSVP is that it attempts to provide QoS by reserving bandwidth across multiple networks. This requires that each router reserve resources for the flows, and maintain state on potentially hundreds or thousands of flows at any one time. That goes against the basic architecture of the Internet, which is based on the concept that only end systems keep state information about flows and that routers remain relatively simple.

Upgrading the Internet protocols and routers to support flows and state information has been a daunting task. While RSVP now exists and routers support it, there are few implementations, especially on the Internet. Many have rejected the Int-Serv model, claiming that it has scalability problems and that with enough bandwidth, CoS techniques would be sufficient. That is the approach of the newer Diff-Serv model, which classifies and marks packets so that they receive specific per-hop forwarding at network nodes without the usual table lookup requirements. The important part is that Diff-Serv does the work at the edge so that network devices only need to get involved in properly queuing and forwarding packets.

Many alternative approaches also exist, including techniques to deliver multimedia streams more efficiently. See "QoS (Quality of Service)," "Multicasting," and "Multimedia."

RFC 2990 (Next Steps for the IP QoS Architecture, November 2000) describes the progress in defining QoS for the Internet, but also discusses problems that require further work. RFC 2998 (A Framework for Integrated Services Operation over Diff-Serv Networks, November 2000) describes how Int-Serv can take advantage of a Diff-Serv network to provide QoS.

RFC 2815 (Integrated Service Mappings on IEEE 802 Networks, May 2000) describes mappings of Int-Serv over switched IEEE 802 networks. RFC 2816 (A Framework for Integrated

Services over Shared and Switched IEEE 802 LAN Technologies, May 2000) includes background material on the capabilities of IEEE 802–like networks with regard to parameters that affect integrated services such as access latency, delay variation, and queuing support in LAN switches.

Additional RFCs are listed at the Linktionary! Web site, or you can refer to the IETF Working Group Web pages listed, which provide a complete list of drafts and RFCs related to integrated services, RSVP, and QoS-related issues.

Related Entries   Bandwidth; Bandwidth Management; Capacity; Congestion Control Mechanisms; CoS (Class of Service); Data Communication Concepts; Delay, Latency, and Jitter; Differentiated Services (Diff-Serv); Flow-Control Mechanisms; MPLS (Multiprotocol Label Switching); Multimedia; Policy-Based Management; Prioritization of Network Traffic; QoS (Quality of Service); Queuing; Routers; RSVP (Resource Reservation Protocol); RTP (Real-time Transport Protocol); RTSP (Real-Time Streaming Protocol); SLA (Service-Level Agreement); TCP (Transmission Control Protocol); Throughput; Traffic Management, Shaping, and Engineering; Transport Protocols and Services; VLAN (Virtual LAN); Voice over IP (VoIP); *and* VPN (Virtual Private Network)

Linktionary!—Tom Sheldon's Encyclopedia of Networking updates	http://www.linktionary.com/i/intserv.html
IETF Working Group. Integrated Services (Int-Serv)	http://www.ietf.org/html.charters/Intserv-charter.html
IETF Working Group: Resource Reservation Setup Protocol (rsvp)	http://www.ietf.org/html.charters/rsvp-charter.html
IETF Working Group: RSVP Admission Policy (rap)	http://www.ietf.org/html.charters/rap-charter.html
IETF Working Group: Integrated Services over Specific Link Layers (issll)	http://www.ietf.org/html.charters/issll-charter.html

Intelligent Network

See IN (Intelligent Network); Telecommunications and Telephone Systems.

IntelliMirror

IntelliMirror is a set of management technologies built into Microsoft Windows 2000 that provide desktop change and configuration management. With IntelliMirror, users' data, personal computer settings, and computing environment follow them to other locations. Based on policy definitions, IntelliMirror is able to deploy, recover, restore, or replace users' data, software, and personal settings in a Windows 2000–based environment.

Essentially, IntelliMirror provides users with follow-me functionality for their personal computing environment. Users have constant access to all of their information and software, whether or not they are connected to the network, with the assurance that their data is safely maintained and available.

IntelliMirror is an addition to the Zero Administration initiative for Windows (ZAWs). IntelliMirror allows an administrator to set policy definitions once and be confident that the policy will be applied without further administrative intervention. The core of IntelliMirror is user data management, software installation and maintenance, and user settings management.

Related Entries   Configuration Management; DMI (Distributed Management Interface); DMTF (Distributed Management Task Force); Microsoft Windows; Mobile Computing; Mobile IP; Network Management; Policy-Based Management; *and* Zero Administration for Windows Initiative

   Microsoft IntelliMirror information (search for "IntelliMirror")   http://www.microsoft.com

Internet

The Internet is a global web of interconnected computer networks—a "network of networks." Over the last 35 years, it has evolved into a global communication system that is analogous in many ways to the circuitry of the brain. In fact, the original concept of an interconnected mesh topology network with redundant links was conceived by Paul Baran of Rand Corporation in the early 1960s as he was thinking about the brain's neural network of redundant pathways.

Today, the Internet is huge and consists of millions of network connections. While the Internet was originally conceived as a communication network for researchers, today it is used by millions of people in business, in education, or for just everyday communication via e-mail, chat rooms, news services, webcasting, and so on.

No person, government, or entity owns or controls the Internet. One way to understand the Internet is to see it as a set of protocols (TCP/IP), standards, and acceptable use policies that are defined by open committees and organizations. Systems connected to the Internet must abide by these standards. The process of setting standards on the Internet is handled by organizations based on input from users, vendors, government agencies, and so on.

A volunteer organization called ISOC (Internet Society) controls the future of the Internet. ISOC manages the various organizations and standard-setting procedures. Other committees and organizations of the Internet include ICANN (Internet Corporation for Assigned Names and Numbers), which coordinates the assignment of Internet "identifiers" such as domain names, autonomous system numbers, IP address numbers, protocol numbers, and port numbers. Other organizations such as W3C (World Wide Web Consortium), NGI (Next Generation Internet), NSF (National Science Foundation), and GIIC (Global Information Infrastructure Commission) promote the development of interoperable technologies, advanced networking technologies, and global Internet infrastructures. These organizations are discussed under "Internet Organizations and Committees."

Internet technical specifications evolve through various levels of maturity called the "standards track." See "Internet Standards" for more information about the standards track process.

Funding for the Internet comes from many sources. The United States government has funded research into advanced networks, including the NSFNET of the later 1980s and early 1990s. At the time, this network was a platform for a high-speed Internet backbones and new routing structures. Today, commercial Internet service providers in conjunction with local and long-haul communication service providers have built a pay-for-service infrastructure that has greatly expanded the reach of the Internet.

There is a saying that the network is the computer. Emerging Internet and Web technologies are making this a reality. More and more people rely on the Internet for their computing needs.

For example, many organization are outsourcing application, storage, and management to Internet service providers that operate facilities that are staffed full time by professionals and that provide fault tolerance and high-availability. See "Data Center Design," "ASP (Application Service Provider)," "MSP (Management Service Provider," and "SSP (Storage Service Provider)."

Internet data centers have become huge facilities where ASPs, MSP, and SSPs can host their equipment and gain direct access to core networks. These regional facilities also support the exchange of information among service providers and core backbone networks. In addition, they host Internet caching and content distribution services. In fact, Internet data centers come close to caching almost the entire contents of the Internet. This means that end users access information at a relatively local site, rather than at servers that are thousands of miles and many router hops away. See "Content Distribution" and "Web Caching."

More users are accessing the Web via "thin clients" such as handheld devices, palm computers, and so on. These thin clients are often called "Internet appliances" or "Web terminals." Many are kitchen counter-top devices that provide Web browser services, electronic mail, and so on. The important point is that they have minimal storage and processing power and rely on Web servers for these needs. See "Network Appliance" and "Thin Client."

An example is a Web camera. It does two things really well. It takes pictures and it provides a Web browser–like interface. After taking pictures, you connect to the Web and upload pictures to a photo-processing Web site. Using the camera's Web browser interface, you can manipulate the pictures (crop, adjust colors, and so on), and then send them to other people or have pictures printed and sent to your home. The important point is that Web servers are doing all the processing and storage. The camera is just a Web interface. Other examples are presented under the topics "Distributed Computer Networks" and "Embedded Systems."

Internet History and Concepts

From the beginning, the thing that set the early Internet apart from other communication systems was its use of packet switching. Information was delivered in packets rather than as a single continuous transmission. If a glitch occurred during transmission, it was only necessary to resend the packets affected by the glitch.

 An expanded version of this historical information is available at the Linktionary! Web site. Also refer to the Computer Museum History Center Web site listed later.

Leonard Kleinrock developed the packet concept at MIT in the late 1950s and published a theory paper in 1961. Kleinrock later became a key figure in the construction of the early Internet. About the same time, Paul Baran of Rand Corporation developed a model of a distributed mesh topology network. He also developed the concept of multiplexing, in which packet transmissions from multiple sources may be traversing the network at the same time.

Baran was working on a U.S. Department of Defense project to build a communications network that could survive a variety of disruptions, including nuclear war. In thinking about the brain's neural network of redundant connections, he came up with the distributed mesh design shown on the right in the following illustration.

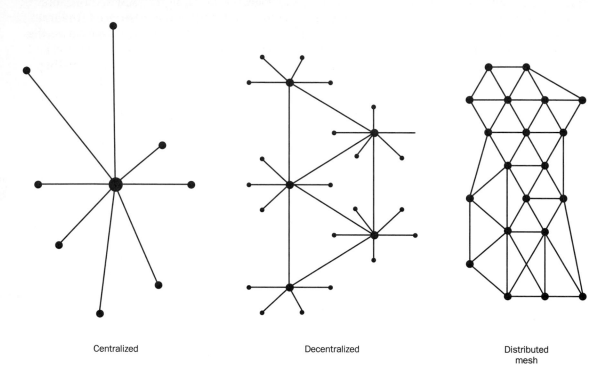

Centralized   Decentralized   Distributed mesh

The centralized model was common with mainframe systems of the time. Dumb terminals connected to central computers that controlled everything. The decentralized model was basically a group of mainframes that could exchange information. The distributed mesh model supports any-to-any connectivity, meaning that any node can directly connect with any other node. This requires a universal logical addressing scheme and a mechanism that allows packets to flow from source to destination essentially unaltered.

The network designers realized that there were a variety of different hosts to connect, so a separate message-handling device was created to handle the communication process in a standard way and provide a custom interface to the local time-sharing host system. The device was called an *interface message processor* or *IMP*, which was the forerunner of today's router. The first IMP went online in 1969, providing communication services between computers at UCLA and Stanford. At this point, the early Internet was really just a remote computing network, not an internetwork. But it would soon grow and be referred to as the ARPANET.

The early designers of the Internet were particularly interested in the concept of "open architecture networking." People working on the project wanted to connect with many different types of computer systems over many different types of transmission schemes, including low-speed, high-speed, and wireless connections. The IMP separated communication services from the actual computer. This allowed any type of device to connect to the network. The result of this open approach can be seen in the near universal connectivity provided by the Internet.

Bob Kahn of DARPA and Vinton Cerf at Stanford University began developing TCP (Transmission Control Protocol) in the early 1970s. The original protocol was called TCP (IP wasn't defined until later) and it provided a range of reliable connection-oriented services (flow control, acknowledgment, retransmission, and so on). But the designers soon realized that TCP's reliability features added overhead that disrupted the ability to deliver live voice across the network. So, in 1978, TCP was reorganized into TCP and IP, with TCP providing reliability, and IP handling basic networking functions such as addressing, routing, and packet forwarding. With this, applications that didn't need TCP's reliability functions could bypass it and go directly to IP through a new protocol called UDP (User Datagram Protocol). UDP is a scaled-down version of TCP. It provides port connections for applications but foregoes all the extra services in the interest of speed.

The official "birth" of the Internet and the transition from the ARPANET occurred on January 1, 1983. This was the day that all connected networks were required to run the new TCP/IP protocol suite. While the Internet has a history stretching back over 20 years, from that day on, it was called the "Internet."

ARPANET grew during the 1970s, partly because its open architecture made it easy to connect just about any system to the network. In fact, the more computers that were added, the better—in the same way that fax machines are more beneficial if everybody owns one. E-mail was probably one of the most significant contributors to Internet growth. Eventually, networks (and not just large computers) were attached to the network. Robert Metcalfe had created Ethernet, which immediately became a popular LAN technology. Also, the TCP/IP protocols were adopted by the UNIX community, which led to a rapid explosion in the number of users that could connect to the Internet.

In the early 1980s, the NSF (National Science Foundation) realized the benefits the ARPANET had on research and decided to build a successor to ARPANET that would be open to university research groups. Its project resulted in the creation of a high-speed backbone called the NSFNET, which changed the topology of the Internet from a distributed mesh to a hierarchical scheme in which regional networks connected to the backbone and local networks connected to the regional networks.

This model proved very successful and it is still with us today, except that the hierarchical model has reverted to a fully meshed model as new backbones were built and interconnected with one another. In addition, regional backbone operators built cross-links directly between their networks rather than going through the backbone. By 1995, the NSF had defunded NSFNET and implemented full commercialization of the Internet. See "Internet Architecture and Backbone" and "ISP (Internet Service Provider)" for more information.

In 1996, the Next Generation Internet (NGI) Initiative was announced to develop advanced networking technologies and applications on testbed networks that were 100 to 1,000 times faster than the networks of the day. This research is still continuing, and you can learn more at the NGI Web site at http://www.ngi.gov.

Internet2 is the latest testbed for the Internet. It is a collaborative project sponsored by UCAID (University Corporation for Advanced Internet Development), a consortium of over 180 U.S. universities that are developing advanced Internet technologies and applications to support research and higher education. See "Internet2."

The core of the Internet is now based on optical networking technologies and *light circuits* or *lambdas*. A lambda is a single wavelength of light that can carry huge amounts of data. Multiple lambdas may exist in a single fiber strand thanks to DWDM (dense wave division multiplexing). These circuits provide high-speed point-to-point links that cross entire continents, thus eliminating router hops and avoiding congestion. High-speed optical access networks are also being developed in metropolitan areas, displacing the need to lease voice lines in order to carry data. See "WDM (Wavelength Division Multiplexing), "MAN (Metropolitan Area Network)," "Network Core Technologies," "Network Access Services," "NPN (New Public Network)," and "Optical Networks."

RFCs Related to Internet History and Development

The following RFCs provide historical and developmental information about the Internet and the Internet protocols. Be sure to see "Internet Entertainment" for a list of RFCs that reflect the "lighter" side of the Internet.

- RFC 871 (Perspective on the ARPANET Reference Model, September 1982)
- RFC 920 (Domain Requirements, October 1984)
- RFC 1118 (Hitchhiker's Guide to the Internet, September 1989)
- RFC 1167 (Thoughts on the National Research and Education Network, July 1990)
- RFC 1180 (A TCP/IP Tutorial, January 1991)
- RFC 1207 (FYI on Questions and Answers—Answers to Commonly Asked "Experienced Internet User" Questions, February 1991)
- RFC 1208 (A Glossary of Networking Terms, March 1991)
- RFC 1296 (Internet Growth from 1981–1991, January 1992)
- RFC 1462 (FYI on 'What is the Internet?' May 1993)
- RFC 1463 (FYI on Introducing the Internet—A Short Bibliography of Introductory Internetworking Readings, May 1993)
- RFC 1480 (The US Domain, June 1993)
- RFC 1607 (A view from the 21st Century by V. Cerf, April 1994)
- RFC 1775 (To Be 'On' the Internet, March 1995)
- RFC 1935 (What Is the Internet, Anyway? April 1996)
- RFC 1958 (Architectural Principles of the Internet, June 1996)
- RFC 1983 (Internet Users' Glossary, August 1996)
- RFC 2151 (A Primer on Internet and TCP/IP Tools and Utilities. June 1997)
- RFC 2235 (Hobbes' Internet Timeline, November 1997)
- RFC 2664 (FYI on Questions and Answers—Answers to Commonly Asked 'New Internet User' Questions, August 1999)
- RFC 2990 (Next Steps for the IP QoS Architecture, November 2000)

Related Entries   Best-Effort Delivery; Connection-Oriented and Connectionless Services; Data Communication Concepts; Datagrams and Datagram Services; End Systems and End-to-End Connectivity; Internet Architecture and Backbone; Internet Connections; Internet Entertainment; Internet Organizations and Committees; Internet Protocol Suite; Internet Standards; Internetworking; Intranets and Extranets; IP (Internet Protocol); ISPs (Internet Service Providers); Multicasting; Multimedia; Network Architecture; Network Concepts; Network Layer Protocols; NII (National Information Infrastructure); OSI (Open Systems Interconnection) Model; Packets and Packet-Switching Networks; Reliable Data Delivery Services; Routers; Routing; Routing on the Internet; Standards Groups, Associations, and Organizations; TCP (Transmission Control Protocol); Transport Protocols and Services; UDP (User Datagram Protocol); *and* Web Technologies and Concepts

Linktionary!—Tom Sheldon's Encyclopedia of Networking updates	http://www.linktionary.com/i/internet.html
Tom Sheldon's Internet history timeline	http://www.linktionary.com/internet_history.html
Computer Museum History Center	http://www.computerhistory.org/exhibits/internet_history/
Library of Congress "Explore the Internet" page	http://www.loc.gov/global/
Google Web Directory Internet page	http://directory.google.com/Top/Computers/Internet/
IETF home page	http://www.ietf.org
Internet Society home page	http://www.isoc.org
Internet Society "All About the Internet" page	http://www.isoc.org/internet/
W3C (World Wide Web Consortium)	http://www.w3.org/pub/WWW
US National Information Infrastructure Virtual Library	http://nii.nist.gov
Internet and WWW history resource list	http://www.vissing.dk/Internet.History/ihistlist.html
Web ProForums communications technology tutorials	http://www.iec.org/tutorials/
History of the Internet by Gregory R. Gromov	http://www.internetvalley.com/intval.html
"Short History of the Internet" by Bruce Sterling	http://www.forthnet.gr/forthnet/isoc/short.history.of.internet
"The History of the Net" by Henry Edward Hardy	http://www.ocean.ic.net/ftp/doc/nethist.html
Microsoft's "The Complete Internet Guide and Web Tutorial"	http://www.microsoft.com/insider/internet/
About.com "Internet for Beginners" page	http://www.learnthenet.com/english/
About.com History and Future of Networking	http://compnetworking.about.com/compute/compnetworking/cs/networkfuture/

PreText Magazine special issue on the history of the   http://www.pretext.com/mar98/
Internet

Internet Overview (links to facts, figures,   http://www.srv.net/~gpilley/An_Overview.html
background, guides, and so on)

Russ Haynal's "Information Navigators"   http://navigators.com/
page (Internet courses, ISP info, Internet
architecture, and so on)

Internet.com, the Internet industry portal   http://internet.com/

Internet FAQs   http://www.faqs.org/faqs/internet/

IRT (Internet Related Technologies) Web page   http://www.irt.org/

Internet2

Internet2 is a testbed for developing advanced Internet technologies and services. It is a collaborative project sponsored by UCAID (University Corporation for Advanced Internet Development), a consortium of over 180 U.S. universities that are developing advanced Internet technologies and applications to support research and education.

The primary goal of Internet2 is to create a leading-edge research network that supports the deployment of new and revolutionary applications, and then deploy the knowledge and the technologies to the broader Internet community. Internet2 members are working in these five areas:

- **Advanced applications**   This area includes development of advanced collaborative applications including *tele-immersion* (collaborate at remote sites in real time using shared simulations—like being in the same room), *virtual laboratories* (an environment that enables people to work together on a common set of projects), *digital multimedia libraries*, and *learningware* (distributed instructions).

- **Middleware**   The layer of software between applications and networks is often called middleware. Internet2 members are working to deploy core middleware services such as identification, authentication, authorization, directories, and security as interoperable standards, rather than relying on individual applications to provide these services. RFC 2768 (Network Policy and Services: A Report of a Workshop on Middleware, February 2000) identifies the types of middleware of concern to Internet2.

- **New networking capabilities**   This area covers the deployment of testbeds for new IP network services that support QoS, network traffic engineering, and high performance.

- **Advanced network infrastructure**   This area covers advanced backbone networks, including Abilene, an advanced backbone that connects regional network aggregation points, called gigaPoPs, that support Internet2. Other advanced networks, including the Canadian CA*net3, are described at the Web site.

- **Partnerships and alliances**   This area promotes partnerships among corporations, government, and international organizations.

Related Entries   Abilene; Active Networks; GII (Global Information Infrastructure); Internet; Internet Architecture and Backbone; Internet Organizations and Committees; NAP (Network Access Point); NII (National Information Infrastructure); NIST (National Institute of Standards and Technology); NPN (New Public Network); NREN (National Research and Education Network); PoP (Point of Presence); STAR TAP; *and* vBNS (Very High Speed Backbone Network Service)

Linktionary!—Tom Sheldon's *Encyclopedia of Networking* updates	http://www.linktionary.com/i/internet2.html
Internet2 Web site	http://www.internet2.edu/
Internet2 and NGI links and resources	http://www.uazone.org/znews/internet2/internet2.html
Cisco's Web site describing Internet2-technologies	http://www.cisco.com/warp/public/784/packet/apr00/netizens.html
Merit Internet2 site	http://www.merit.edu/i2/
STAR TAP	http://www.startap.net/
vBNS	http://www.vbns.net/
Google Web Directory (search for "Internet2")	http://directory.google.com/Top/Computers/

Internet Appliances

See Embedded Systems; Internet; NAS (Network Attached Storage); Network Appliances; Servers; *and* Thin Clients.

Internet Architecture and Backbone

The Internet is a packet-switching network with a distributed mesh topology. Information travels in packets across a network that consists of multiple paths to a destination. Networks are interconnected with routers, which forward packets along paths to their destinations. The mesh topology provides redundant links. If a link fails, packets are routed around the link along different paths.

The Internet is sometimes called a backbone network, but this is misleading since the Internet is actually many backbones that are interconnected to form a mesh. The term "backbone" comes from an early research network called the NSFNET, which was funded by the U.S. National Science Foundation. This network created the hierarchical model that is still used today, in which local service providers connect to regional services, which, in turn, connect to national or global service providers. Today, many backbones exist and they are interconnected so that traffic can flow from any host to any other host. In addition, many regional networks directly connect with one another, bypassing the backbone networks.

The networks of the Internet are managed by large independent service providers such as MCI Worldcom, Sprint, Earthlink, Cable and Wireless, and others. There are NSPs (network service providers), ISPs (Internet service providers), and exchange points. NSPs build national or global networks and sell bandwidth to regional NSPs. Regional NSPs then resell bandwidth to local ISPs. Local ISPs sell and manage services to end users.

Internet Topologies

The history of the early Internet is outlined under the topic "Internet." This topic takes up the story in the mid-1980s with the creation of the NSFNET. As mentioned, the NSFNET redefined the Internet's early architecture and operation, and defined the hierarchy of networks and service providers that still applies today.

The NSFNET-connected sites included supercomputer centers, research centers, and universities, all of which connected on a no-fee basis. At the time, the network was considered a high-speed backbone. It was initially deployed as a series of 56 Kbits/sec links; but by 1991, it was running over T3 links with T1 on ramps. Organizations were connected with 28.8 or 56K connections.

As mentioned, the network was hierarchical. There was the top-level backbone to which regional networks connected. Local networks then connected to the regional networks via a relatively short link. The backbone network and the regional networks were managed by different authorities and provided bandwidth and transport services for local networks. Bandwidth was resold.

The ISP business model was developed by the early network providers and service providers. Entrepreneurs could set up facilities in their local area and purchase bandwidth, routing, and transport services from higher-level NSPs. The local ISP would then resell those services to end users. Many ISPs were started by one person who had extra bandwidth to sell. A typical ISP installs dial-up facilities (modems, modem banks, concentrators, access and authentication servers, and so on) and then metered and billed users for service.

Internet Exchanges

The NSFNET backbone concept worked well. Similar backbones had been created by other U.S. federal agencies, including MILNET (the military network), NSI (NASA Science Internet), and Esnet (Energy Sciences Network). Obviously, there was a need to exchange traffic among these networks, so two interconnection points called FIXes (Federal Internet Exchanges) were built. FIX-West was located in the Bay Area and FIX-East was located near Washington, D.C.

The FIXes are *Internet exchanges.* The participating agencies used the exchanges to peer with one another. *Peering* is a relationship in which different network authorities agree to exchange route advertisements and traffic. Each agency had a router at the FIX locations that exchanged routing information and traffic with the other agency's routers. The traffic flowing among these routers was constrained by policies of the individual agencies, as well as a federal AUP (acceptable use policy) that limited non-federal agency traffic.

By interconnecting different backbones, the Internet became a mesh network rather than a single backbone network. At this point, any reference to backbone refers to just one of the major trunks that provides transit services between mid-level networks. The hierarchical structure of the NSFNET with its top-level, mid-level, and feeder networks still remains, but there are multiple overlapping backbones, as shown in Figure I-4. Note the following:

- Major backbone interconnects and exchanges traffic at Internet exchange sites.
- Regional networks feed into the backbone via Internet exchange sites or direct connects.
- Some networks exchange traffic directly via private peering links that bypass the backbone networks.

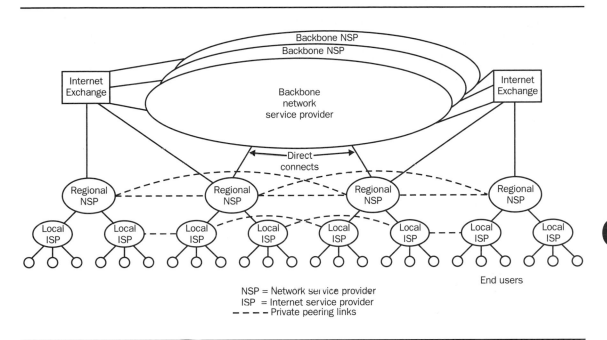

Figure I-4.   *The Internet in the early 1990s*

Internet Exchanges and NAPs (Network Access Points)

By 1993, the NSFNET decided to defund the NSFNET and do away with the AUP in order to promote commercialization of the Internet. Many commercial Internet networks came online during this time. In fact, the regional networks that were originally supported by the NSF turned into commercial service providers, including UUNet, PSINet, BBN, Intermedia; Netcom; and others.

The NSF's plan for privatization included the creation of NAPs (network access points), which are Internet exchanges with open access policies that support commercial and international traffic. One can think of the NAPs as being like airports that serve many different airlines. The airlines lease airport space and use its facilities. Likewise, NSPs lease space at NAPs and use their switching facilities to exchange traffic with other parts of the Internet.

Part of NSF's strategy was that all NSPs that received government funding must connect to all the NAPs. In 1993, the NFS awarded NAP contracts to MFS (Metropolitan Fiber Systems) Communications for a NAP in Washington, D.C., Ameritech for a NAP in Chicago, Pacific Bell for a NAP in San Francisco, and Sprint for a NAP in New York. MFS already operated MAEs (metropolitan area exchanges) in Washington, D.C. (MAE East) and in California's Silicon Valley (MAE West). A MAE is a fiber-optic loop covering a metropolitan area that provides a connection point for local service providers and businesses.

A NAP is a physical facility with equipment racks, power supplies, cable trays, and facilities for connecting to outside communication systems. The NAP operator installs switching equipment. Originally, NAPs used FDDI and switched Ethernet, but ATM switches or Gigabit Ethernet switches are common today. NSPs install their own routers at the NAP and connect them to the switching facilities, as shown in Figure I-5. Thus, traffic originating from an ISP crosses the NSP's router into the NAP's switching facility to routers owned by other NSPs that are located at the NAP. Refer to Geoff Huston's paper called "Interconnection, Peering, and Settlements" at the Web address listed later for a complete discussion of NAPs and peering.

Most NAPs now consist of core ATM switches surrounded by routers. Traffic is exchanged across ATM PVCs (permanent virtual circuits). Usually, a NAP provides a default fully meshed set of PVCs that provide circuits to every other NSP router located at the NAP. However, an NSP can remove a PVC to block traffic from a particular NSP. However, larger NSPs may not want to peer with smaller NSPs because there is no equal exchange of traffic. A rule of thumb is that NSPs with a presence at every NAP peer with one another on an equal basis.

NAP operators do not establish peering agreements between NSPs, but only provide the facilities where peering can take place. Peering agreements are bilateral agreements negotiated between NSPs that define how they will exchange traffic at the NAPs. In addition, all IP datagram routing is handled by the NSP's equipment. However, the NAP provides the switching equipment over which the packets traverse after being routed.

The NSF also funded the creation of the Routing Arbiter service, which provided routing coordination in the form of a route server and a routing arbiter database (RADB). Route servers

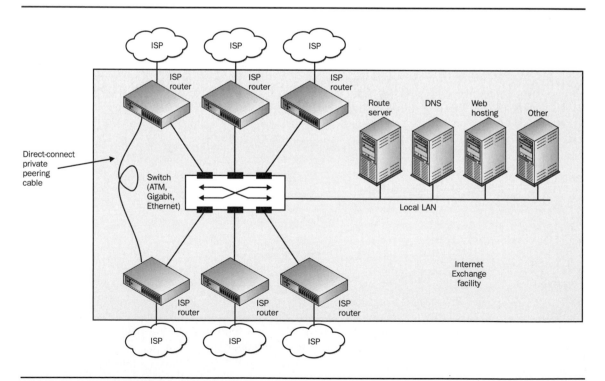

Figure I-5.   *NAP switching facilities*

would handle routing tasks at NAPs while the RADB generated the route server configuration files. RADB was part of a distributed set of databases known as the Internet Routing Registry, a public repository of announced routes and routing policy in a common format. NSPs use information in the registry to configure their backbone routers. See "Routing Registries."

You can learn more about the NAPs by referring to the following Web sites.

Worldcom MAE information site	http://www.mae.net/
MFS Communications MAE information	http://www.mfst.com/MAE/doc/mae-info.html
The Ameritech Chicago NAP home page	http://nap.aads.net/main.html
PAIX.net, a neutral Internet exchange	http://www.paix.net/
Equinix IBX (Internet business exchange)	http://www.equinix.com/
Above.net ISX (Internet service exchange)	http://www.above.net/

Today, Internet exchanges are only one part of the Internet architecture. Many NSPs establish *private peering arrangements*, as previously mentioned. A private connection is a direct physical link that avoids forwarding traffic through the NAPs switching facility, which is often overburdened. NSPs create private connections in two ways. One method is to run a cable between their respective routers at the NAP facility. Another more costly approach is to lay cable or lease lines between their own facilities.

Internap Network Services Corporation provides an Internet exchange service designed to maximize performance. Its Assimilator proprietary technology provides intelligent routing and route management to extend and enhance BGP4 routing. Assimilator allows the P-NAP to make intelligent routing decisions, such as choosing the faster of multiple backbones to route data if the destination is multihomed. Internap customer packets are sent immediately to the correct Internet backbone, rather than to a randomly chosen public or private peering point.

Networks and Autonomous Systems

The many individually managed networks that make up the Internet are called autonomous systems or ASs. An AS is both a management domain and a routing domain. A typical AS is operated by an NSP or ISP. Each AS on the Internet is identified by a number assigned to it by the Internet authorities (now ICANN).

An AS may use one or more *interior routing protocols* to maintain internal routing tables. The usual interior routing protocol is OSPF (Open Shortest Path First) or IS-IS (Intermediate System-to-Intermediate System).

An *exterior routing protocol* handles the exchange of routing information among ASs. An AS must present a coherent interior routing plan and a consistent picture of the destinations reachable through the AS. The exterior routing protocol for the Internet is BGP (Border Gateway Protocol). BGP runs in "border routers" that connect ASs with other ASs. A border router at the edge of one AS tells a border router at the edge of another AS about the routes on its internal networks. These routes are advertised as an aggregation of addresses. An analogy is the way that the ZIP code 934*xx* represents a group of postal areas on the central coast of California. Route aggregation is a way of using the IP address space more efficiently. ISPs can aggregate blocks of addresses and advertise those addresses on the Internet with a single network address. At the same time, ISPs can allocate those addresses any way they like, as single address, just a few addresses, or large blocks to distribute to lower-level ISPs.

See "Autonomous Systems," "BGP (Border Gateway Protocol)," "CIDR (Classless Inter-Domain Routing)," "Route Aggregation," "Registries on the Internet," "Routing," and "Routing Registries" for more information.

PoPs and Internet Data Centers

A PoP is any facility where customers can connect into a service provider's facilities and gain access to much larger networks. Some PoPs are designed for end-user access, while others are designed to allow ISPs to connect into NSP networks. A PoP is not an Internet-specific entity. The ILECs and CLECs have their own PoPs that house voice and data equipment.

An ISP may be large enough to build its own PoP facility or lease space in an existing PoP where it collocates its equipment. Collocation makes sense, since PoP facilities provide security, backup power, disaster protection, fast Internet connections, Internet exchange switches, Internet Web services, and so on. In some cases, the ISP does not own any equipment, but leases everything from an NSP. Such an ISP is basically in the business of reselling services to end users and supporting those end users.

Over the years, end-user dial-up connection methods have changed, especially with the introduction of 56K modem technology. Up until the mid-1990s, ISPs would install a bank of modems and access servers at their own facilities. End-users would then dial and connect with the ISP's modems. When 56K modem technology came along, full modem speed could only be achieved by trunking calls from the carrier's PoP to the ISP's facility over a digital connection (T1 or T3 lines). See "Modems" for more information. In many cases, ISPs simply collocate their modem pools and access servers to the carrier's facilities in order to avoid expensive leased lines, or lease a bank of modems that are installed at a carrier or service provider facility.

Figure I-6 illustrates the facilities for ISP and NSP. The lower part shows subscribers dialing into the ISP facility across the PSTN. The local ISP trunks its traffic into the regional NSP, which in turn forwards traffic onto Internet backbones or other connections. Note that the lower part of the illustration assumes subscribers access is through the PSTN. ISPs may support other access methods, such as metro-Ethernet and wireless access services.

Internet data centers have become huge facilities that provide collocation and outsourcing facilities. They provide security, disaster protection, professional services, high-bandwidth connections, and so on. As mentioned, many ISPs are really *virtual ISPs* that resell services provided by larger carriers instead of investing in their own ISP infrastructure. In this role, the virtual ISP becomes a pure Internet service retailer that basically acquires new Internet customers, provides help-desk services, and handles billing and customer management. See "ISP (Internet Service Provider)."

Private companies also use the facilities to host their Web sites and provide Internet access for their remote users via VPNs. See "VPN (Virtual Private Network)."

For a continuation of the topics discussed here, see "Network Access Services," "Network Core Technologies," "Internet Connections," and "Optical Networks."

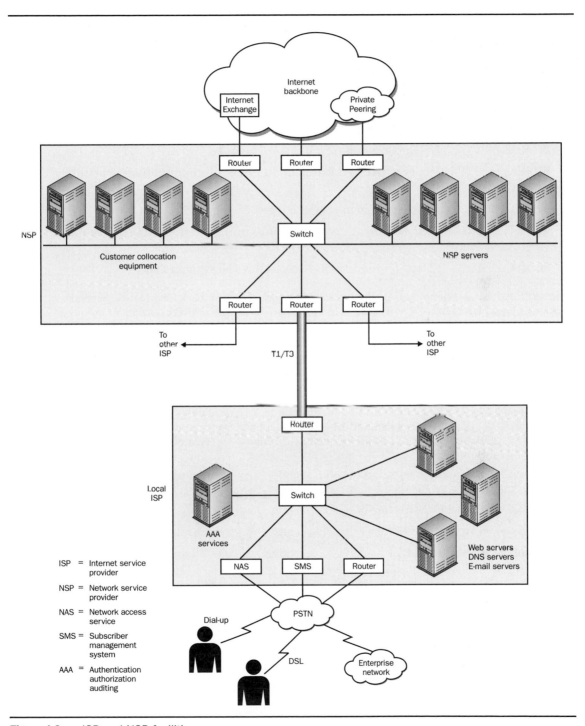

Figure I-6. *ISP and NSP facilities*

As mentioned, the Linktionary! Web site provides an extended version of this topic. It also lists a large set of related Internet RFCs. Some of the more important RFCs are listed here:

- RFC 1093 (The NSFNET Routing Architecture, February 1989)
- RFC 1136 (Administrative Domains and Routing Domains, a Model for Routing in the Internet, December 1989)
- RFC 1287 (Towards the Future Internet Architecture, December 1991)
- RFC 1480 (The US Domain, June 1993)
- RFC 1862 (Report of the IAB Workshop on Internet Information Infrastructure, November 1995)
- RFC 1958 (Architectural Principles of the Internet, June 1996)
- RFC 2901 (Guide to Administrative Procedures of the Internet Infrastructure, August 2000)
- RFC 2990 (Next Steps for the IP QoS Architecture, November 2000)

Related Entries   Abilene; Active Networks; Autonomous System; Backbone Networks; BGP (Border Gateway Protocol); CIDR (Classless Inter-Domain Routing); DARPA (Defense Advanced Research Projects Agency); DNS (Domain Name Service) and Internet Domains; GII (Global Information Infrastructure); Internet; Internet2; Internet Connections; Internet Organizations and Committees; Internet Standards; Internetworking; Intranets and Extranets; ISP (Internet Service Providers); NAS (Network Access Server); Network Access Services; Network Core Technologies; NII (National Information Infrastructure); NPN (New Public Network); OSPF (Open Shortest Path First); Peering; PoP (Point of Presence); RAS (Remote Access Server); Registries on the Internet; Route Aggregation; Routing; Routing on the Internet; Routing Registries; Service Providers and Carriers; Standards Groups, Associations, and Organizations; STAR TAP; Telecommunications and Telephone Systems; vBNS (Very high speed Backbone Network Service); WAN (Wide Area Network); *and* Web Technologies and Concepts

Linktionary!—Tom Sheldon's Encyclopedia of Networking updates	http://www.linktionary.com/i/internet.html
Internet Society internet Infrastructure page	http://www.isoc.org/internet/infrastructure/
Survey of Internet architecture by Network Manias	http://www.netmanias.com/internet/internet.htm
Internet architectures and topology links by Henning Schulzrinne	http://www.cs.columbia.edu/~hgs/internet/
Computer Museum History Center Internet historical outline	http://www.computerhistory.org/exhibits/internet_history/
Exodus Internet data center (take the visual tour)	http://www.exodus.net/idc/
ITPRC Internet architecture and ISP links	http://www.itprc.com/internet.htm
Web ProForums communications technology tutorials	http://www.iec.org/tutorials/

Russ Haynal's "Information Navigators" page (Internet courses, ISP info, Internet architecture, and so on)	http://navigators.com/
"Interconnection, Peering, and Settlements" by Geoff Huston	http://www.isoc.org/inet99/1e/1e_1.htm
"Internet Service Provider Peering" by Geoff Huston	http://www.users.on.net/tomk/docs/settleme.htm
Network Startup Resource Center	http://www.nsrc.org/
NLANR Engineering Services (Internet performance measurement, TCP tuning)	http://www.nlanr.net/NA/
NCNE GigaPoP (see architecture map)	http://www.ncne.net/
Cyber Geography Research (atlas of cyberspace)	http://www.cybergeography.org/
Internet Traffic Report	http://www.internettrafficreport.com/
CAIDA (Cooperative Association for Internet Data Analysis)	http://www.caida.org/
David Papp's Net.Presence page (ISPs, NSPs, MAEs, NAPs, and so on)	http://david.remote.net/connectivity/

Internet Connections

"Connecting to the Internet" means different things to different people. There are users (i.e., subscribers and consumers of information) of Internet services and providers of Internet services (Web sites, ecommerce sites, and so on). If you are a "user" of Internet services, then connecting to the Internet is relatively simple. You contact an ISP in your area and discuss the type of connections that are available. Connection types include dial-up modem access, cable modem access, wireless, and other services. See "MAN (Metropolitan Area Network)," "Network Access Services," and "WAN (Wide Area Network)."

According to RFC 1775 (To Be 'On' the Internet, March 1995), there are four types of Internet users. Full access users have permanent Internet connections with IP addresses that are visible to other Internet users. Client access is an indirect access method through a firewall, proxy server, or protocol translation device. Mediated access is a terminal-like service in which applications are run on Web-based servers and files are stored on Internet systems. Finally, messaging access is a noninteractive service level in which users access is limited to electronic mail and network news services.

Connections for enterprise networks and ISPs are more complex. The remainder of this topic describes the administrative procedures for networks seeking to connect to the global Internet, including the steps and operations necessary for address space allocation and registration, routing database registration, and domain name registration. These networks include ISPs (with many subscribers) and large organizations (with many internal users).

Note *This topic is a synopsis of the procedures outlined in RFC 2901 (Guide to Administrative Procedures of the Internet Infrastructure, August 2000). Refer to the RFC for complete details.*

The preliminary activities for setting up an Internet connection include

- Apply for a domain name. This can be done by contacting Network Solutions, Inc. (http://www.nsi.com) or by choosing an alternative registrar in the "Accredited Registrar Directory" at http://www.internic.net/.

- Designate an administrative contact person and a technical contact. The contact information will go in the Internet registry databases.

- Determine the type of connection to use (e.g., dial-up, dedicated T1, metro-Ethernet, wireless, and so on). See "Network Access Services" and "MAN (Metropolitan Area Network)" for more information.

- Determine where you will connect (a local ISP, a regional ISP, a telecommunications carrier, and so on)

- Evaluate your IP address requirements (either a single address or a block of addresses). Block allocations require address space evaluation and planning, and you may need to justify your need for the allocation you request.

- Determine whether an Autonomous System Number (ASN) will be necessary.

- Register domain names and configure reverse address resolution (IP address to domain name mapping).

Most organizations will contact local or regional ISPs for IP address space allocation. If an ISP cannot supply an appropriate block of addresses, you may need to contact a *regional registry*, which is an official organization that allocates IP addresses. The IP address space is managed at the highest level by ICANN, which delegates responsibility for address allocation to three RIRs (regional Internet registries): ARIN, RIPE, and APNIC. The RIRs, in turn, allocate address space to large service providers in regional areas. For example, ARIN is responsible for allocations in North and South America, the Caribbean, and sub-Saharan Africa. See "Registries on the Internet" and "Internet Standards and Organizations."

IP address requirements are determined by mapping out the network and its users. RFC 2901 and RFC 2050 (Internet Registry IP Allocation Guidelines, November 1996) provide some help in this area. Familiarize yourself with IP address aggregation as discussed under "Route Aggregation" and "CIDR (Classless Inter-Domain Routing)." RFC 2901 notes the following with regard to address space:

- RIRs usually assign address blocks based on immediate need and projected need (one year for end users and three years for ISPs).

- Address space allocation is based on CIDR bit boundaries.

- Registries will need the details of your network engineering and deployment plans in order to allocate address space.

If you obtain address space from a local ISP and then switch to another ISP, you may need to change your IP addressing scheme. To avoid this, you can petition an RIR for what is called a *routable block of IP addresses*. This requires paying a fee to the regional IR, but the block is not part of another upstream provider's address allocation. More details are in Section II-B and II-C of RFC 2901.

Obtaining address spaces from regional registries typically involves becoming a member of the registry, and then requesting the address space by sending a *database object* to the registry. The object is based on a template that includes fields with a tag and a value. An example template and the procedures for becoming a registry member are outlined in Section II-D of RFC 2901.

When an organization's routing policies are different from its providers, an ASN (autonomous system number) is necessary. Sites that are multihomed will require an ASN. *Multihomed* means that the site is connected to more than one upstream provider. This is often the case when a site wants to connect with an alternative provider to balance traffic into its site or provide a path for traffic from another region. Instructions for obtaining an ASN are in Section III of RFC 2901. Organizations that use the same routing policy as their service providers should use the service provider's ASN.

The next step in the Internet connection process is to register with a routing registry. A routing registry is a repository of routing policy information and provides a place where network operators can submit, maintain, and retrieve router configuration information. A registry maintains *route servers* (not to be confused with routers) that coordinate routes among service provider networks. Note that organizations that get their address space from an upstream ISP do not need to register with a routing registry since this is done by the ISP. Organizations that are multihomed should register with a routing database in order to describe the route configurations that have been established with the multiple connections. See "Routing Registries" and refer to Section IV of RFC 2901 for more information.

The last step is to manage domain name configurations. It is assumed you have already obtained a domain name. Section VI of RFC 2901 outlines how to register an IN-ADDR.ARPA domain, which is a mapping of IP addresses into domain names. The mapping is the opposite of the domain name to IP address resolution provided by DNS and so is often called "inverse addressing."

Of course, there will be other things to do, depending on where you are connecting and the equipment and link requirements. Contact your upstream service provider or exchange point for more information. For example, the MAE Internet exchange points owned and operated by WorldCom have connection guidelines that are outlined at http://208.234.102.97/MAE/doc/maecheck.html.

As mentioned, RFC 2901 describes the administrative procedures for networks seeking to connect to the global Internet. The following RFC provide additional information:

- RFC 1207 (FYI on Questions and Answers—Answers to Commonly Asked 'Experienced Internet User' Questions, February 1991)
- RFC 1291 (Mid-Level Networks Potential Technical Services, December 1991)
- RFC 1302 (Building a Network Information Services Infrastructure, February 1992)
- RFC 1359 (Connecting to the Internet, What Connecting Institutions Should Anticipate, August 1992)
- RFC 1480 (The US Domain, June 1993)

- RFC 1580 (Guide to Network Resource Tools, March 1994)

- RFC 1787 (Routing in a Multi-provider Internet, April 1995)

- RFC 1930 (Guidelines for the Creation, Selection, and Registration of an Autonomous System, March 1996)

- RFC 1958 (Architectural Principles of the Internet, June 1996)

- RFC 2050 (Internet Registry IP Allocation Guidelines, November 1996)

- RFC 2260 (Scalable Support for Multi-homed Multi-provider Connectivity, January 1998)

- RFC 2270 (Using a Dedicated AS for Sites Homed to a Single Provider, January 1998)

- RFC 2901 (Guide to Administrative Procedures of the Internet Infrastructure, August 2000)

- RFC 3013 (Recommended Internet Service Provider Security Services and Procedures, November 2000)

Related Entries   Autonomous System; BGP (Border Gateway Protocol); CIDR (Classless Inter-Domain Routing); Co-Location Services; DNS (Domain Name Service) and Internet Domains; DSL (Digital Subscriber Line); Internet; Internet Architecture and Backbone; Internet Organizations and Committees; Internet Protocol Suite; Internet Standards; Internetworking; Intranets and Extranets; IP (Internet Protocol); ISP (Internet Service Providers); NAS (Network Access Server); Network Access Services; Peering; PON (Passive Optical Network); PoP (Point of Presence); RAS (Remote Access Server); Registries on the Internet; Route Aggregation; Routing; Routing on the Internet; Routing Registries; Service Providers and Carriers; Standards Groups, Associations, and Organizations; Telecommunications and Telephone Systems; WAN (Wide Area Network); Web Technologies and Concepts; *and* Wireless Broadband Access Technologies

Linktionary!—Tom Sheldon's Encyclopedia of Networking updates	http://www.linktionary.com/i/ internet_connections.html
NSRC (Network Startup Resource Center)	http://www.nsrc.org/
ICANN (Internet Corporation for Assigned Names and Numbers)	http://www.icann.org/
ARIN (American Registry for Internet Numbers)	http://www.arin.net
RIPE NCC (Réseaux IP Européens Network Coordination Centre)	http://www.ripe.net/
APNIC (Asia Pacific Network Information Centre)	http://www.apnic.net/
CAIDA (Cooperative Association for Internet Data Analysis) provides tools to promote the engineering and maintenance of a robust, scalable global Internet infrastructure	http://www.caida.org/
InterNIC Accredited Registrar Directory	http://www.internic.net/regist.html
Network Solutions, a domain registrar	http://www.nsi.com
Top-level domain configuration	http://www.iana.com/ domain-names.htm

Google Web Directory Internet resources (see "Acess Providers," "Domain Names," and so on) — http://directory.google.com/Top/Computers/Internet/

Avi Freedman's Home Page (numerous articles related to multihoming and routing) — http://www.netaxs.com/~freedman/

Also see links under "ISP (Internet Service Provider)."

Internet Entertainment

The Internet RFCs provide valuable information about the Internet. But some authors, including well-known architects of the Internet, couldn't help but have a little fun with the technical jargon and documentation procedures. Here is a list of amusing RFCs:

- RFC 527 (ARPAWOCKY, R. Merryman, June 1973)
- RFC 602 ('The Stockings Were Hung by the Chimney with Care,' Bob Metcalfe, December 1973)
- RFC 748 (TELNET RANDOMLY-LOSE Option, M. Crispin, April 1978)
- RFC 968 ('Twas the Night Before Start-Up,' V. Cerf, December 1985)
- RFC 1097 (TELNET SUBLIMINAL-MESSAGE Option, B. Miller, April 1989)
- RFC 1121 (Act One—The Poems, Postel/Kleinrock/Cerf/Boehm, September 1989)
- RFC 1149 (A Standard for the Transmission of IP Datagrams on Avian Carriers, D. Waitzman, April 1990)
- RFC 1178 (Choosing a Name for Your Computer, D. Libes, August 1990)
- RFC 1216 (Gigabit Network Economics and Paradigm Shifts, Richard & Kynikos, April 1991)
- RFC 1217 (Memo from the Consortium for Slow Commotion Research (CSCR), V. Cerf, April 1991)
- RFC 1300 (Remembrances of Things Past, S. Greenfield, February 1992)
- RFC 1437 (The Extension of MIME Content-Types to a New Medium, Borenstein & Linimon, April 1993)
- RFC 1438 (Internet Engineering Task Force Statements of Boredom [SOBs], Chapin & Huitema, April 1993)
- RFC 1605 (SONET to Sonnet Translation, Shakespeare et al., April 1994)
- RFC 1606 (A Historical Perspective on The Usage of IP Version 9, J. Onions, April 1994)
- RFC 1607 (A View from the 21st Century, V. Cerf, April 1994)
- RFC 1882 (The 12 Days of Technology Before Christmas, B. Hancock, December 1995)
- RFC 1925 (The Twelve Networking Truths, R. Callon, April 1996)
- RFC 2100 (The Naming of Hosts, J. Ashworth, April 1997)

- RFC 2321 (RITA—The Reliable Internetwork Troubleshooting Agent, A. Bressen, April 1998)
- RFC 2322 (Management of IP Numbers by peg-dhcp, K. van den Hout et al., April 1998)
- RFC 2323 (IETF Identification and Security Guidelines, A. Ramos, April 1998)
- RFC 2324 (Hyper Text Coffee Pot Control Protocol, L. Masinter, April 1998)
- RFC 2325 (Definitions of Managed Objects for Drip-Type Heated Beverage Hardware Devices Using SMIv2, M. Slavitch, April 1998)
- RFC 2468 (I Remember IANA, V. Cerf, October 1998)
- RFC 2549 (IP over Avian Carriers with Quality of Service, D. Waitzman, April 1999)
- RFC 2550 (Y10K and Beyond, Glassman et al., April 1999)
- RFC 2551 (The Roman Standards Process—Revision III, S. Bradner, April MCMXCIX)
- RFC 2555 (30 Years of RFCs, April 1999)—A serious document, but also entertaining
- RFC 2795 (The Infinite Monkey Protocol Suite (IMPS), S. Christey, April 2000)

Internet Organizations and Committees

The Internet is a collection of autonomous and interconnected networks that implement open protocols and standards. No person, government, or entity owns or controls the Internet. Instead, a volunteer organization called ISOC (Internet Society) controls the future of the Internet. It appoints a technical advisory group called the IAB (Internet Architecture Board) to evaluate and set standards.

Input on protocols and standards can come from anybody—individuals, research groups, companies, and universities. A specification is submitted as an Internet draft and made available for review and comments. The Internet organizations evaluate whether these specifications should be advanced through a process that elevates the specification to different levels of maturity until it potentially reaches a standards status. The process is described under "Internet Standards."

The organizations and committees that oversee the Internet are charted in Figure I-7. These organizations are described next. In general, the IETF forms working groups to develop specifications, which are evaluated by the IESG in conjunction with the IAB (Internet Architecture Board). The Internet Society then publicizes the new standards. Web standards are promulgated by the W3C (World Wide Web Consortium) and other groups.

- **ISOC (Internet Society)**   The ISOC is a nongovernmental international organization to promote global cooperation and coordination for the Internet, and its internetworking technologies and applications. The ISOC approves appointments to the IAB from nominees submitted by the IETF Nominating Committee. The ISOC Web site is at http://www.isoc.org.
- **IAB (Internet Architecture Board)**   The IAB is a technical advisory group of the ISOC (Internet Society). Its responsibilities are to appoint a new IETF chair and IESG candidates, serve as an appeal board, manage editorial content and publication (RFCs),

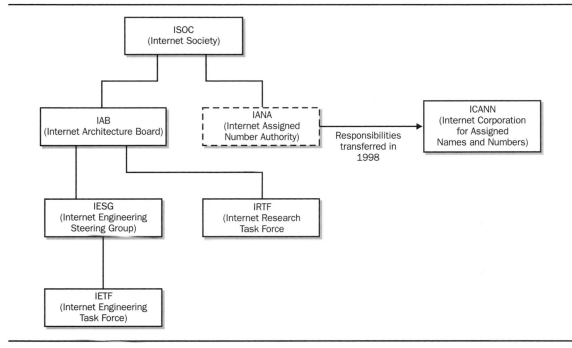

Figure I-7. *The organizations of the Internet*

and provide services to the Internet Society. The IAB Web site is at http://www.iab.org/iab.

■ **IESG (Internet Engineering Steering Group)**   The IESG is chartered by ISOC to provide technical management of IETF activities and the Internet standards process. The IESG manages the IETF working groups and is directly responsible for the actions associated with entry into and movement along the Internet "standards track," including final approval of specifications as Internet standards. The IESG Web site is at http://www.ietf.org/iesg.htm.

■ **IRTF (Internet Research Task Force)**   The purpose of the IRTF is to create research groups that focus on Internet protocols, applications, architecture, and technology. The groups are small and long term, and are put together to promote the development of research collaboration and teamwork in exploring research issues. Participation is by individual contributors rather than by representatives of organizations. The IRSG manages the research groups and holds workshops that focus on the evolution of the Internet and discuss research priorities from an Internet perspective. The IRTF Web site is at http://www.irtf.org.

■ **IETF (Internet Engineering Task Force)**   The IETF is a large open international community of network designers, operators, vendors, and researchers concerned with the evolution of the Internet architecture and the smooth operation of the Internet. The actual technical work of the IETF is done in its working groups, which include Applications, Internet, Network Management, Operational Requirements, Routing, Security, Transport, and User Services. Working groups are managed by members of the IESG. The IAB provides architectural oversight. The IETF also facilitates technology transfers from the IRTF to the wider Internet community. The IETF Web site is at http://www.ietf.org.

IP Address Allocation and Domain Registration Services

Historically, an Internet organization called IANA (Internet Assigned Numbers Authority) was chartered by ISOC to coordinate the assignment of Internet "identifiers" such as domain names, autonomous system numbers, IP address numbers, protocol numbers, and port numbers.

In the early 1990s, IANA coordinated the establishment of the InterNIC (Internet Network Information Center) with funding from the NSF (National Science Foundation). The InterNIC took responsibility for managing the top-level Internet domain names (.com, .org, .net, and so on) and the other Internet identifiers. InterNIC was a collaborative project of AT&T, General Atomics, and NSI (Network Solutions, Inc.). RFC 1400 (Transition and Modernization of the Internet Registration Service, March 1993) describes the services offered by the InterNIC. AT&T managed the InterNIC Directory and Database Services project, NSI managed the Registration Services project (domain registration and IP address allocation), and General Atomics managed the Information Services project, which was dropped from funding in 1995.

By the late 1990s, IANA and the U.S. government felt that the registration services, address allocations, and other functions should be handled by private-sector authorities. In October of 1998, a broad coalition of the Internet's business, technical, academic, and user communities created a nonprofit corporation called ICANN (Internet Corporation for Assigned Names and Numbers) and gave it responsibility for the functions previously managed by IANA. ICANN also coordinates the Internet's root server system and is dedicated to preserving the operational stability of the Internet. The IANA and ICANN Web addresses are as follows:

IANA (Internet Assigned Numbers Authority)	http://www.iana.org/
ICANN (Internet Corporation for Assigned Names and Numbers)	http://www.icann.org/

With the formation of ICANN, NSI lost the registration services monopoly it had with InterNIC. The for-profit company is now one of many organizations that register domain names. The InterNIC as it was established in 1993 is no longer in service. However, the site still has valuable information, such as a list of registrars. Since the word "InterNIC" is a registered service mark of the U.S. Department of Commerce, NSI no longer uses the name.

Domain name registration may be accomplished through a number of organizations, including NSI. The following Web site provides a directory of accredited registrars:

InterNIC Accredited Registrar Directory	http://www.internic.net/regist.html

While ICANN is responsible for IP address allocation *policies*, the actual management of IP address space is handled by registries. IP addresses are distributed in a hierarchical manner. At the top of the hierarchy is IANA, which allocates blocks of IP addresses to regional Internet registries (RIRs). The regional registries then further allocate blocks of IP addresses to local Internet registries within their geographic regions. Finally, the local registries assign addresses to end users. There are currently three RIRs:

ARIN (American Registry for Internet Numbers)	http://www.arin.net
RIPE NCC (Réseaux IP Européens Network Coordination Centre)	http://www.ripe.net/
APNIC (Asia Pacific Network Information Centre)	http://www.apnic.net/

Other Information

Many organizations are involved in the development of telecommunications and information technology standards. In many cases, these organizations share work with the Internet organizations mentioned earlier. In particular, organizations such as the IEEE (Institute of Electrical and Electronics Engineers), the ATM Forum, the ISO (International Organization for Standardization), and the ITU (International Telecommunication Union) create standards that are closely linked to Internet standards. See "Standards Groups, Associations, and Organizations" for a complete list of related organizations and their Web addresses.

Note *The Linktionary! Web site provides a list of related organizations. It also has a list of RFCs that provide current or historical information about the organization of the Internet and its committees.*

Related Entries   DNS (Domain Name Service) and Internet Domains; IEEE 802 Standards; Internet; Internet Architecture and Backbone; Internet Protocol Suite; Internet Standards; IP (Internet Protocol); ISO (International Organization for Standardization); ISPs (Internet Service Providers); ITU (International Telecommunications Union); OSI (Open Systems Interconnection) Model; Registries on the Internet; Routing on the Internet; *and* Standards Groups, Associations, and Organizations

Linktionary!—Tom Sheldon's Encyclopedia of Networking updates	http://www.linktionary.com/i/internet_organizations.html
Google Web Directory Internet organizations page	http://directory.google.com/Top/Computers/Internet/Organizations/
Internet organizations list at Yahoo!	http://dir.yahoo.com/Computers_and_Internet/Internet/Organizations/
Internet Theory Task Force, an independent information resource	http://ittf.vlsm.org/
David's Net.Presence Web site	http://david.remote.net/connectivity/
ITPRC (Information Technology Professional's Resource Center) Internet Operations page	http://www.itprc.com/internet.htm
Networking Standards list at TechFest	http://www.techfest.com/networking/standard.htm

Internet Protocol Suite

The Internet Protocol suite, usually referred to as "TCP/IP," is a full set of internetworking protocols that operate in the network layer, the transport layer, and the application layer. While TCP/IP refers to two separate protocols called TCP and IP, Internet Protocol suite refers to the entire set of protocols developed by the Internet community. Still, most people just say "TCP/IP" when they are referring to the Internet Protocol suite. Figure I-8 illustrates how the protocols compare to the OSI model.

Note that no Internet protocols exist at the data link and physical layer. This is because the Internet protocols were designed to accommodate any underlying network technology.

The global Internet is a success because of TCP/IP. It is hard to believe that there ever was a "protocol war," but during the 1980s and early 1990s, many organizations were indecisive about which protocols to use. TCP/IP was popular in academic, military, and scientific communities, but many businesses had installed LANs using Novell SPX/IPX and Microsoft's NetBEUI/NetBIOS, or were tied to legacy protocols such as IBM SNA. The Internet protocols

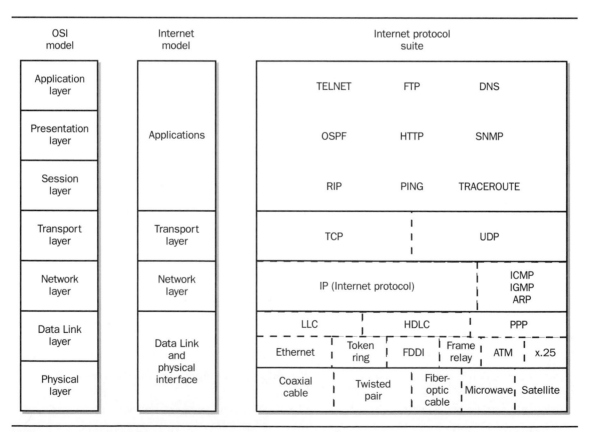

Figure I-8.   *The Internet protocol suite (data link and physical interfaces are non-Internet protocols)*

have been universally accepted because they support scalable internetworking, for which the global Internet is the best example.

In the late 1960s and early 1970s, the Internet began to take shape in the form of a wide area network (primarily continental United States) called ARPANET. ARPANET was funded by the DARPA (Defense Advanced Research Projects Agency). It consisted of computers that had been set up and connected using an experimental packet-switching system. At first, the systems used a client/server relationship, but it was decided that a host-to-host protocol was preferred. This protocol was called the NCP (Network Control Protocol).

By 1972, developers were connecting terminals to a variety of hosts. An early goal was to develop methods for supporting many different types of computers over many different types of transmission schemes, including low-speed, high-speed, and wireless connections. This open interoperable strategy accounts for the Internet protocol's enormous success.

Bob Kahn of DARPA and Vinton Cerf at Stanford University began developing TCP (Transmission Control Protocol) in 1973 with the objective of gaining knowledge about how the protocol would interface with existing operating systems. Originally, TCP connected large computers, not LANs and PCs. It was meant to support a nationwide system of approximately 256 networks, but this turned out to be too small in scale when LANs started appearing in the late 1970s.

Note that the original protocol was called TCP. It attempted to provide as many reliability services as possible, including connection-oriented sessions in which the sender and receiver exchange flow-control information and acknowledge the receipt of data. These reliable services help guarantee that data is received exactly as it was sent. But these services add overhead that disrupts real-time transmissions like voice, so TCP was reorganized into TCP, IP, and UDP (User Datagram Protocol), with UDP providing a way to bypass TCP for applications that don't need TCP's reliable services. Each of these protocols is discussed under its own heading.

 The Linktionary! Web site expands on this topic by describing the basic protocol operation.

The following RFCs provide additional information:

- RFC 768 (User Datagram Protocol, April 1980)
- RFC 791 (Internet Protocol, September 1981)
- RFC 793 (Transmission Control Protocol, September 1981)
- RFC 1122 (Requirements for Internet Hosts—Communication Layers, October 1989)
- RFC 1123 (Requirements for Internet Hosts—Application and Support, October 1989)
- RFC 1180 (A TCP/IP Tutorial, January 1991)
- RFC 1580 (Guide to Network Resource Tools, March 1994)
- RFC 1958 (Architectural Principles of the Internet, June 1996)
- RFC 2151 (A Primer on Internet and TCP/IP Tools and Utilities, June 1997)
- RFC 2700 (Internet Official Protocol Standards, August 2000)

Other Protocols and Services

While TCP, IP, and UDP provide transport and network services, many other protocols were added by the Internet community over the years, mostly at the applications level. These are listed next. Of course, hundreds of nonstandard services are also available. The protocols listed here are described in various Internet RFCs and many are described under their own heading in this book.

- **Archie**   A utility for gathering and indexing files on the Internet.

- **ARP (Address Resolution Protocol)**   Dynamically maps Internet addresses to physical (hardware) addresses on local area networks.

- **BGP (Border Gateway Protocol)**   A routing protocol that is used to exchange route information between autonomous systems (i.e., service provider networks on the Internet).

- **DHCP (Dynamic Host Configuration Protocol)**   A protocol that dynamically assigns IP addresses to host devices when they connect to a network.

- **DNS (Domain Name System**)   A service that resolves easy-to-remember host names into IP addresses.

- **DNS (Domain Name System)**   A hierarchical name service that matches up Internet host names with IP addresses.

- **FTP (File Transfer Protocol)**   A utility for transferring files between hosts on the Internet or any TCP/IP network.

- **Gopher**   A tool for searching for and retrieving documents stored hierarchically on Internet hosts.

- **HTML (Hypertext Markup Language)**   The markup and tagging language used to create Web pages.

- **HTTP (HyperText Transfer Protocol)**   The file transfer protocol that is the basis of the World Wide Web.

- **ICMP (Internet Control Message Protocol)**   A diagnostics and error-reporting protocol used to handle errors and control messages at the IP layer.

- **IGMP (Internet Group Management Protocol)**   A protocol for managing multicast groups.

- **IMAP (Internet Message Access Protocol)**   An Internet e-mail post office protocol that expands on the features of POP.

- **IPSec (IP Security)**   A set of protocols that support secure and encrypted data exchange at the network layer. IPSec supports VPNs.

- **IRC (Internet Relay Chat)**   A multiuser chat system.

- **LDAP (Lightweight Directory Access Protocol)**   A set of protocols for accessing directory services and directory service databases.

- **Listserv**   An automated mailing list system that users can subscribe to. Mailing lists are available on a variety of topics.

- **MIME (Multipurpose Internet Mail Extensions)**   Provides a way to use different file formats in e-mail and other documents.

- **NFS (Network File System)**   A shared file system developed by Sun Microsystems.

- **NNTP (Network News Transfer Protocol)**   A protocol for managing and distributing news articles.

- **OSPF (Open Shortest Path First)**   Another routing protocol. OSPF is now used on the Internet while RIP is still used for many internal networks.

- **PING (Packet Internet Gopher)**   A tool for determining the reachability of a host. It sends a request to a specified host and waits for a response.

- **POP (Post Office Protocol)**   A protocol that stores mail for users on a server and forwards that mail to them when they log on.

- **PPP (Point-to-Point Protocol)**   A protocol for transmitting IP datagrams and other protocols over telephone links or serial lines.

- **RARP (Reverse Address Resolution Protocol)**   A diskless host uses this protocol to find its Internet address at startup.

- **RIP (Routing Information Protocol)**   A protocol that routers use to exchange routing information.

- **RSVP (Resource Reservation Protocol)**   A protocol that allocates and reserves bandwidth across Internet links to support QoS.

- **RTP (Real-Time Protocol)**   A protocol that optimizes the delivery of real-time data such as live and/or interactive audio and video.

- **SIP (Session Initiation Protocol)**   A signaling protocol used for setting up, maintaining, and terminating multimedia sessions.

- **S-HTTP (Secure HTTP)**   A secure version of HTTP that encrypts HTTP transmissions.

- **SLIP   (Serial Line Internet Protocol)**   A protocol for transmitting IP datagrams and other protocols over telephone links or serial lines.

- **SMTP   (Simple Mail Transfer Protocol)**   The primary protocol for exchanging e-mail messages across TCP/IP networks. Works with POP and IMAP.

- **SNMP   (Simple Network Management Protocol)**   A network management protocol used to gather information about devices on a network.

- **Sockets**   An API (application programming interface) that applications use to access TCP/IP networking services.

- **SSL (Secure Socket Layer)**   A protocol that secures transmissions across IP networks by encrypting data.

- **Telnet**   A terminal protocol for logging on to remote hosts.

- **TFTP (Trivial File Transfer Protocol)**   A simplified version of FTP that provides no security and does not use TCP's reliability features.

- **Usenet**   A protocol that allows users to participate in newsgroups, where articles can be posted and viewed.

- **Veronica**   A search engine similar to Archie and built with Gopher.

- **WAIS (Wide Area Information Service)**   A distributed information service and search system.

- **WHOIS**   A protocol that displays information about an entity or person.

Related Entries   Acknowledgments; Best-Effort Delivery; Congestion Control Mechanisms; Connection Establishment; Connection-Oriented and Connectionless Services; Data Communication Concepts; Datagram and Datagram Services; Encapsulation; End Systems and End-to-End Connectivity; Error Detection and Correction; Flow-Control Mechanisms; Fragmentation and Reassembly; Framing in Data Transmissions; IEEE 802 Standards; Internet; Internet Architecture and Backbone; Internet Entertainment; Internet Organizations and Committees; Internet Standards; Internetworking; IP (Internet Protocol); MPLS (Multiprotocol Label Switching); Multicasting; Multimedia; Network Architecture; Network Concepts; Network Layer Protocols; OSI (Open Systems Interconnection) Model; Packets and Packet-Switching Networks; Point-to-Point Communications; Ports, TCP/IP; QoS (Quality of Service); Queuing; Reliable Data Delivery Services; Routers; Routing; Routing on the Internet; Security; TCP (Transmission Control Protocol); Transport Protocols and Services; UDP (User Datagram Protocol); *and* Web Technologies and Concepts

Linktionary!—Tom Sheldon's *Encyclopedia of Networking* updates	http://www.linktionary.com/i/internet_protocols.html
IETF (Internet Engineering Task Force) home page (Internet Working Groups, RFCs, Drafts)	http://www.ietf.org
Google Web Directory Internet page	http://directory.google.com/Top/Computers/Internet/
Uri Raz's "TCP/IP Resources List"	http://www.private.org.il/tcpip_rl.html
Daryl's TCP/IP Primer	http://ipprimer.2ndlevel.net/

Additional Web sites are at the Linktionary! Web site, and under "IP (Internet Protocol)" and "TCP (Transmission Control Protocol)."

Internet Radio

Internet radio brings radio stations from all over the world to your computer or "Internet radio device." Instead of receiving over-the-air radio broadcasts from relatively few local radio stations, you receive the radio programs of over 10,000 radio stations that have put their content on the Internet. The Web sites listed later provide links to important Internet radio sites and resources. At some sites, you can create your own radio format by specifying your likes and dislikes. The station then assembles play lists for your listening pleasure.

The requirements to receive Internet radio are a media player such as Windows Media Player or Real Player, a Web browser, a sound card and speakers, and a relatively fast and stable Internet connection. The Kerbango tuning service even sells an Internet radio that is dedicated to receiving radio programs from the Internet.

Internet radio uses streaming media, a method of delivering real-time or stored information such as audio and video across networks and the Internet. When you select a radio station, the live broadcast starts to stream to your computer from the Web site and continues to stream in the background as you listen. More information about streaming media is under the topic "Multimedia."

Anyone interested in Internet radio will also be interested in digital music technologies such as MP3 and peer-to-peer technologies. These technologies are focused on music files that can be exchanged among users, while Internet radio is streaming live media that is not stored locally. See "Peer-to-Peer Communication" and "MP3."

Related Entries   Compression Techniques; MP3; Multicasting; Multimedia; Peer-to-Peer Communications; QoS (Quality of Service); Webcasting; *and* Web Technologies and Concepts

 Linktionary!—Tom Sheldon's Encyclopedia of Networking updates — http://www.linktionary.com/i/internet_radio.html

Real.com Real Player applications — http://www.realaudio.com

Microsoft Media Player — http://www.microsoft.com/windows/windowsmedia/

Yahoo! Radio — http://radio.yahoo.com/

Kerbango Tuning Service — http://www.kerbango.com/

Netradio.com — http://www.netradio.com/

Radio sonicnet (lets you create your own format) — http://radio.sonicnet.com/

Internet Radio List — http://www.internetradiolist.com/

Radio-locator.com (formerly the MIT "List of Radio Stations on the Internet") — http://www.radio-locator.com/

Internetradioindex.com — http://www.internetradioindex.com/i

Internet Standards

The Internet, according to RFC 2026 (The Internet Standards Process—Revision 3, October 1996), is a "loosely-organized international collaboration of autonomous, interconnected networks that supports host-to-host communication through voluntary adherence to open protocols and procedures defined by Internet Standards." The Internet is not controlled by one government or entity, but by its users and the organizations that have formed to "watch over" and manage the Internet. These organizations include the IETF (Internet Engineering Task Force), ISOC (Internet Society), and other groups described under "Internet Organizations and Committees."

The IETF is a large open international community of network designers, operators, vendors, researchers, and just about anyone else who wants to get involved in the development of the Internet. The actual technical work of the IETF is done in its working groups, which are organized by topic into several areas (e.g., routing, transport, and security). These working groups are managed by AD (area directors) who are members of the IESG (Internet Engineering Steering Group). The IAB (Internet Architectural Board) provides architectural oversight. Finally, the IAB and IESG are chartered by the ISOC. These working groups are accessible by visiting the IETF Web site at http://www.ietf.org/.

Internet technical specifications evolve through various levels of maturity called the "standards track." A specification is first submitted as a draft specification and this draft is put up for review. The IESG may then choose to place it on the standards track. The standards track maturity levels are "proposed standard," "draft standard," and "standard." There are also "experimental" specifications, which do not follow the standards track, and "historical" specifications, which can be thought of as "retired." The complete process is outlined in RFC 2026.

At the time of this writing, there were only 61 specification elevated to "standard" status. You can see a list of these standards by visiting the Internet protocol standards index at http://www.faqs.org/rfcs/std/std-index.html. Also see http://www.faqs.org/rfcs/std/std1.html, which lists documents that are in various stages of review, including "proposed standard," "draft standard," and "standard."

RFCs provide a wealth of information about the Internet. They are numbered, starting with RFC 1, which is dated April 1969. There are currently over 3,000 RFCs. RFC 2555 (30 Years of RFCs, April 1999) describes the early history of the standards process and the role that Jon Postel played in creating the documentation format and standards process. Jon was the original keeper of the "big red three ring notebook" that contained notes and information about the RFC publication process. Other RFCs related to the standards process are listed here:

- RFC 1311 (Introduction to the STD Notes, March 1992)
- RFC 1796 (Not All RFCs Are Standards, April 1995)
- RFC 1818 (Best Current Practices, August 1995)
- RFC 2119 (Key Words for Use in RFCs to Indicate Requirement Levels, March 1997)
- RFC 2223 (Instructions to RFC Authors, October 1997)

The CD-ROM included with this book includes a very complete set of RFCs. Those not included on the disk may be obtained from the Internet.

One of the best sites for obtaining RFCs and information about RFCs and the Internet standards is FAQs.org. You can display RFCs by number, search through the archives for keywords, display a complete title-only index, or obtain other information. If you know an RFC number, you can also go to the following address, replacing *xxxx* with the RFC number (leading 0s required):

http://www.ietf.org/rfc/rfc*xxxx*.txt

Related Entries   IEEE 802 Standards; Internet Organizations and Committees; Internet Protocol Suite; ISO (International Organization for Standardization); ITU (International Telecommunications Union); OSI (Open Systems Interconnection) Model; Standards Groups, Associations, and Organizations; Telecommunications and Telephone Systems; *and* TIA (Telecommunications Industry Association)

Linktionary!—Tom Sheldon's Encyclopedia of Networking updates	http://www.linktionary.com/i/ internet_standards.html
IETF Working Group: Process for Organization of Internet Standards ONg (poisson)	http://www.ietf.org/html.charters/ poisson-charter.html
Internet RFC/STD/FYI/BCP Archives	http://www.faqs.org/rfcs/
Internet Protocol standards index	http://www.faqs.org/rfcs/std/std-index.html
Normos Internet Engineering Standards Repository (also includes ATM Forum, IEEE, ISO, and other standards)	http://www.normos.org/
Networking Standards list at TechFest	http://www.techfest.com/networking/standard.htm

Internet Telephony

Internet telephony (also called IP telephony) is about converting real-time voice conversations for delivery across packet-switched networks such as the Internet. Telephony also covers telephone-related services such as voice mail, and the integration of telephones and computers. Refer to the following topics for more information about Internet telephony:

■ **CTI (Computer-Telephony Integration)**   Covers the integration of telephones and computers into the same box and over the same networks.

■ **Multimedia**   Discusses how voice, video, and other multimedia are carried over data networks.

■ **Softswitch** Describes devices that support Internet telephony and convergence with the PSTN.

■ **Telecommunications and the Telephone System**   General overview of the PSTN (public-switched telephone network).

■ **Videoconferencing**   Covers videoconferencing over intranets and the Internet.

■ **Voice/Data Networks**   Describes how data networks can carry voice.

■ **Voice over IP (VoIP)**   Discusses products, standards, and techniques for carrying voice calls over IP networks and the Internet.

Internetworking

An internetwork is a set of interconnected networks that form a single communication system, allowing any node on any network to connect with any other node. The Internet Protocol suite (TCP/IP) and Novell's IPX/SPX protocol suite are the most common internetworking protocols. An internetwork has the following characteristics and features:

■ **End-to-end transparency**   Information may flow from source to destination essentially unaltered.

■ **Addressing**   Each interconnected network has its own unique network address, and each node has a unique address on the network to which it is attached.

- **Packets**   Information is delivered in packets, which contain parts of a complete transmission. If a packet is lost or corrupted, only that packet needs to be resent, not the entire transmission. Packets have a destination address, but not a defined path and, therefore, can be routed around failed links on the internetwork.

- **Routers and routing**   Routers are devices that interconnect the networks and forward packets to their destinations.

An internetwork protocol like IP provides an addressing scheme that overlays the connected networks. The postal ZIP code system provides an analogy. It is an overlay addressing scheme that uniquely identifies regions, cities, and individual post offices so that mail may be routed on a national scale. At the same time, each city retains its traditional addressing scheme (street addresses) for local mail delivery. Likewise, individual networks use their own MAC-based addressing schemes to forward frames of information to other nodes on the same LAN.

An internetwork may have a mesh topology, meaning that many routers are interconnected in a way that provides multiple paths through the network. Routers forward packets along the best path based on information that has been discovered about the topology of the network. Routing protocols provide the mechanism for finding these paths. Routers gather information about the networks they are connected to and then forward this information to other routers. Each router then builds forwarding tables based on this information. See "Routing."

The Internet is the biggest internetwork. It consists of thousands of interconnected public and private networks. Each network is called an autonomous system because it is managed by a distinct authority.

Related Entries   Autonomous System; Best-Effort Delivery; Connection-Oriented and Connectionless Services; Data Communication Concepts; Datagram and Datagram Service; Distributed Computer Networks; Enterprise Network; Internet; Internet Architecture and Backbone; IP (Internet Protocol); Network Architecture; Network Concepts; Network Layer Protocols; OSI (Open Systems Interconnection) Model; Packets and Packet-Switching Networks; Reliable Data Delivery Services; Routers; Routing; Routing on the Internet; TCP (Transmission Control Protocol); Transport Protocols and Services; UDP (User Datagram Protocol); Virtual Circuit; *and* WAN (Wide Area Network)

Linktionary!—Tom Sheldon's *Encyclopedia of Networking* updates	http://www.linktionary.com/i/internetworking.html
Noritoshi Demizu's Internetworking technical resources page	http://www.watersprings.org/links/inet/
Lucent's internetworking systems resource library (also see white papers section)	http://www.lucent.com/ins/library/

InterNIC (Internet Network Information Center)

See Internet Organizations and Committees.

Interoperability

Interoperability describes how different computer systems, networks, operating systems, and applications work together and share information. This is usually achieved by following published or de facto standards. Interoperability is the opposite of vendor proprietary solutions, which were pervasive in the days of IBM mainframe and minicomputer systems. When desktop computers appeared in the early 1980s, users were empowered but interoperability with other systems was a major problem.

Interoperability is a networking issue. In the days of centralized mainframe systems, all the components attached to the system were specifically designed to work together. With networks, it is possible to attach different computer platforms running different operating systems and different applications. Actually, the network itself provides the first level of interoperability. For example, all the workstations attached to an Ethernet network can potentially communicate with one another.

Until recently, it was difficult for PC, UNIX, and Macintosh users to simply exchange files, even when connected to the same network. The file storage techniques, formats, and file transfer programs on these systems were different. Users often converted files to simple ASCII text and transmitted them to one another using modems, losing formatting and control codes in the process.

Network servers solved the problem to some extent by providing a single place to store files. Most servers expanded to support a variety of clients, allowing them to store files in a single location for other clients to access. Standard file formats such as RTF (Rich Text Format) were developed to save formatting information and make them available to a variety of readers. Standard markup languages such as SGML provides another solution. Application interoperability was achieved across platforms with client/server computing and Web technologies. Middleware products and component software were developed to enable applications that work across platforms.

Simon Phipps, IBM's evangelist for Java and XML, likes to describe the transition to XML (Extensible Markup Language) as the "last gap" in defining a new world of information sharing. This has been achieved through the following progression of events:

- TCP/IP has become the near-universal communications protocol for connecting information systems.

- Browsers have become the common space into which solutions can be loaded.

- Component technologies such as Java are now established as the standard for platform-neutral computing.

- Data was the last gap. An open data-formatting specification was needed. XML is that specification.

Related Entries DBMS (Database Management System); Distributed Object Computing; ISO (International Organization for Standardization); Java; Middleware and Messaging; Object Technologies; Open Group; Open Systems; OSI (Open Systems Interconnection) Model; SGML (Standard Generalized Markup Language); Web Technologies and Concepts; *and* XML (Extensible Markup Language)

Linktionary!—Tom Sheldon's Encyclopedia of Networking updates	http://www.linktionary.com/i/interoperability.html
Simon Phipps' comments	http://www.ibm.com/developer/features/feature021599-javaxml.html
Microsoft's Interoperability Web site	http://www.microsoft.com/technet/interop/

Intranets and Extranets

An *intranet* is an internal network that implements Internet and Web technologies such as Web servers and Web browsers that use HTTP and HTML. An *extranet* is an intranet that has been extended outside the company to a business partner, with transmissions going over the Internet or across private lines. An intranet has the following characteristics:

- Intranets run the TCP/IP protocol and other Internet-related protocols.
- Web servers are used to publish information and provide access to back-end systems.
- Web browsers provide a universal client interface.
- Internet mail generally becomes the pervasive mail system.

Another significant characteristic of intranets is that they typically use private IP addressing rather than IP addresses that are assigned by Internet authorities. RFC 1918 (Address Allocation for Private Internets, February 1996) describes private IP network addressing schemes. In this scheme, the private network, called the "internal realm," uses unregistered IP addresses. The RFC recommends three address blocks, listed next. These address blocks are "safe" for security reasons because they are never routed on the global Internet, which helps keep hackers at bay. A NAT (network address translation) server is required to allow internal users to access the Internet. See "NAT (Network Address Translation)."

10	A single class A network
172.16 through 172.31	16 contiguous class B networks
192.168.0 through 192.168.255	256 contiguous class C networks

Internet and Web technologies are cross-platform. Web browsers running on UNIX, Macintosh, and Windows clients can access the same internal Web servers with no modifications. The technology is well known, and easy to learn and use. Interoperability is a plus because intranet products are based on the open architecture of the Internet. Other advantages include lowered user costs and quick development and deployment of systems or products.

The information publishing aspect of intranets is well understood. You can put any kind of information on a Web browser with the assurance that everyone in the company can access it, no matter what computer platform they use. Text and graphic information can be presented with hyperlinks to other Web sites, either on the intranet or on the Internet. Many products are available that allow users to access data on back-end systems with their Web browsers. The advantage is that one interface, the Web browser, can be used to access all types of information.

Some examples of applications that are easily deployed on intranet platforms are described next. See "Collaborative Computing" and "Groupware" for more information.

- Employee directory (phone number, personal interest, and so on) or personal Web pages for employees
- Collaborative applications such as calendaring/scheduling tools, group editing, and workflow software

■ Electronic meeting tools such as chat rooms, voice and videoconferencing, and whiteboard applications

■ Libraries for marketing, technical, or other types of information

An extranet is basically an intranet linked up with some other organization's intranet. The link may cross the Internet or use private network links. In either case, two organizations have decided to share information and allow users to interact between the organizations. Trading partners often do this using traditional EDI (Electronic Data Interchange). With EDI, the format and structure of electronic documents, such as invoices and purchase orders, follow published standards so that document flows can occur among organizations. EDI has been extended to Web technologies as well, either as traditional EDI or completely new business-to-business technologies.

This topic is covered further under "Extranet." Also see "EDI (Electronic Data Interchange)," "Electronic Commerce," "Firewall," and "Proxy Servers."

Related Entries   Collaborative Computing; EDI (Electronic Data Interchange); Electronic Commerce; Extranet; Firewall; Groupware; Internet; Internet Protocol Suite; IP (Internet Protocol); Network Concepts; Network Design and Construction; TCP (Transmission Control Protocol); Videoconferencing; Voice over IP (VoIP); VPN (Virtual Private Network); *and* Web Technologies and Concepts

Linktionary!—Tom Sheldon's Encyclopedia of Networking updates	http://www.linktionary.com/i/intranet.html
Bitpipe (search for "intranet" or "extranet")	http://www.bitpipe.com/
Smart Computing (search for "intranet"or "extranet")	http://www.smartcomputing.com/
About.com intranets and extranets page	http://compnetworking.about.com/compute/compnetworking/cs/intranets/index.htm
CIO Intranet/Extranet Research Center	http://www.cio.com/forums/intranet/
CIR (Complete Intranet Resources)	http://www.intrack.com/intranet/
Microsoft's Intranet Web site	http://www.microsoft.com/intranet/
Earthweb Intranet Journal	http://www.intranetjournal.com
Intranet Design Magazine	http://www.innergy.com/
Intranet News	http://www.internetnews.com/intra-news/
@Brint.com BizTech Network intranet resources page	http://www.brint.com/Intranets.htm
Intranets.com (Intranet hosting site)	http://www.intranets.com/
Intranet Roadmap	http://www.intranetroadmap.com/

Intrusion Detection Systems

See Security Auditing.

Int-Serv (Integrated Services)

See Integrated Services (Int-Serv).

Inverse Multiplexing

Inverse multiplexing is the process of splitting a data stream for transmission over multiple channels, as shown in Figure I-9. At the receiving end, the data is recombined into a single stream. The links may be dial-up or permanent leased lines. Inverse multiplexing provides more bandwidth and can provide bandwidth on demand by establishing additional links when loads increase beyond the capacity of existing links. Inverse multiplexing is the opposite of multiplexing, which combines data streams from multiple sources into a single line. See "Multiplexing and Multiplexers."

Inverse multiplexing solves the problem of trying to figure out how much bandwidth to allocate for MAN or WAN links. For example, a company may need more than the bandwidth of a T1 line but less than a full T3. Inverse multiplexing lets the company lease just the number of T1 lines that, when combined, provide just the bandwidth needed. An alternative scenario is to lease one line on a permanent basis and then lease additional lines on a switched basis. Then when extra bandwidth is needed, additional T1 lines are switched into place only for the time they are needed, thus reducing service charges. This feature is often called *channel aggregation, dial on demand, bandwidth on demand, rubber bandwidth,* or *bonding.* Inverse multiplexing also provides link fault tolerance. Should one link fail, the others still provide service.

Larscom Incorporated developed a bit-based inverse multiplexing scheme that uses a round-robin approach to transmit one bit at a time over as many as eight links. The receiving device recombines the bits in the proper order and uses buffering to compensate for differences in delivery time among the links. The advantage of bit-based methods is transparency—that is, any protocol can be transported over the aggregated links.

IMA (Inverse Multiplexing over ATM) is a method for distributing ATM cells across multiple links. The technique is often used by service providers to provide customers with higher bandwidth or bandwidth on demand. See "IMA (Inverse Multiplexing over ATM)."

MFR (Multilink Frame Relay) provides physical interface emulation for frame relay devices. It aggregates multiple T1 or E1 links into what are called "bundle links" that appear as a single "bundle" of bandwidth. The Frame Relay Forum has defined this standard in its FRF.16 standard (see Web site at the end of this topic). MFR is a frame-based inverse multiplexing scheme. Frame relay network operators create bundles for customers to provide more bandwidth than is available from single physical interfaces. It defines methods for dynamically adding and dropping links and support for fault tolerance.

MLPPP is a method for splitting, recombining and sequencing IP datagrams across multiple logical data links. The protocol was originally designed with ISDN in mind, but can also be

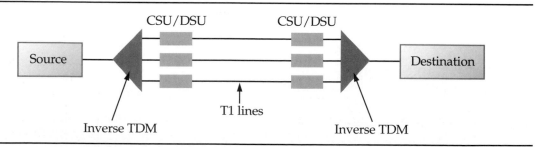

Figure I-9.   *Inverse Multiplexing combines multiple links into what appears to be a single link with high bandwith.*

used to bond multiple modem and dial-up lines. Microsoft Windows, Linux, and other operating systems support multilink. Many routers also support multilink PPP and the ability to connect remote LANs with multiple dial-up or ISDN lines. See "MLPPP (MultiLink PPP)" for more information.

The topic "BAP (Bandwidth Allocation Protocol) and BACP (Bandwidth Allocation Control Protocol)" discusses the IETF protocols that help users manage a combination of dial-up or ISDN links. BACP supports additional features such as the ability to dial multiple lines when the need for additional bandwidth is detected, or drop those lines when necessary. The protocol is defined in RFC 2125 (The PPP Bandwidth Allocation Protocol [BAP] and the PPP Bandwidth Allocation Control Protocol [BAPC], March 1997).

The topic "Link Aggregation" expands on the topic of aggregating links and sharing loads across multiple links. It discusses trunking techniques as defined by the IEEE 802.3 Link Aggregation Standard. A related topic is "Load Balancing," which discusses aggregation in terms of balancing traffic loads to servers and other networking devices.

Related Entries   Bandwidth on Demand; Bandwidth Reservation; Bonding; Circuit-Switching Services; DDR (Dial-on-Demand Routing); IMA (Inverse Multiplexing over ATM); Link Aggregation; Load Balancing; MLPPP (Multilink PPP); *and* Multiplexing and Multiplexers

Linktionary!—Tom Sheldon's Encyclopedia of Networking updates	http://www.linktionary.com/i/ inverse_multiplexing.html
"Getting the Most Out of Your Bandwidth," *Network Computing* article	http://networkcomputing.com/1023/1023ws1.html
Larscom papers on inverse multiplexing	http://www.larscom.com/lib/lc_wp.htm
3Com paper: Inverse Multiplexing over ATM by Randy Brumfield	http://www.3com.com/technology/tech_net/ white_papers/500642.html
Techguide.com (see inverse multiplexing paper under Communications category)	http://www.techguide.com/
Frame Relay Forum FRF.16: MFM (Multilink Frame Relay)	http://www.frforum.com/5000/Approved/ FRF.16/frf16.pdf

IOS (Internetwork Operating System)

IOS is Cisco's internetwork operating system. Just as PCs have operating systems and LANs have network operating systems, it is Cisco's belief that internetworks need their own operating systems. Cisco's goal was to create an operating system that could evolve as the network evolved. IOS supports change and migration through its ability to integrate all evolving classes of network platforms, including routers, ATM switches, LAN and WAN switches, file servers, intelligent hubs, personal computers, and other devices.

IOS spans the core network, workgroups, remote access, and IBM internetworking. It supports formal and de facto standard interfaces, including major network protocols such as IP, IPX NetBIOS, SNA, and AppleTalk. IOS provides four internetwork services:

- **Routing services**   Locates optimal paths using adaptive routing techniques that reduce cost by using network bandwidth efficiently. Also supports multilayer switching and virtual LANs.

- **WAN Optimization services**   Supports all WAN services, including circuit-switched and packet-switched services.

- **Management and security services**   IOS provides an array of network management and security features, including configuration services, monitoring and diagnostics, encryption, authentication, accounting, and logging.

- **Scalability services**   IOS addresses key areas for avoiding congestion, overcoming protocol limitations, and bypassing obstacles that cause bottlenecks.

On many systems, IOS is accessed by connecting a terminal or PC to a console port on a networking device. A terminal emulation package or Telnet is used to access the IOS software. IOS has a user command interface with several command modes, including a user EXEC mode for viewing basic information, a privileged EXEC mode for advanced management, a global configuration mode for configuring system options, and several other modes of operation.

IOS has an extensive command set that requires some time and skill to master. Fortunately, a built-in help facility is available by typing a question mark on the command line. A complete set of documentation for Cisco IOS is available at the Web site listed here.

Related Entries   Network Operating Systems; Routers; *and* Routing

 Cisco IOS Software Configuration

http://www.cisco.com/univercd/cc/td/doc/product/software/index.htm

IOTP (Internet Open Trading Protocol)

IOTP is a framework that supports commerce on the Internet by providing a familiar trading model and global interoperability. IOTP attempts to virtualize real-world buying, selling, and trading. IOTP is designed to promote business-to-business commerce on the Internet and make online shopping easier for consumers. It supports electronic commerce across sites, as in the case of different Internet sites that handle parts of the same transactions, such as catalogs and shopping carts, payment handlers, product delivery, and customer support.

    This topic is covered at the Linktionary! Web site.

Related Entries   Certificates and Certification Systems; Digital Signatures; EDI (Electronic Data Interchange); Electronic Commerce; OBI (Open Buying on the Internet); SET (Secure Electronic Transaction); *and* XML (Extensible Markup Language)

 Linktionary!—Tom Sheldon's Encyclopedia of Networking updates

http://www.linktionary.com/i/iotp.html

IETF Working Group: Internet Open Trading Protocol (trade)

http://www.ietf.org/html.charters/trade-charter.html

Robin Cover's IOTP Web page

http://www.oasis-open.org/cover/otp.html

Open Trading Protocol Consortium

http://www.otp.org

IP (Internet Protocol)

The Internet Protocol (IP) is the network layer protocol for the Internet. It is part of the suite of protocols referred to as the Internet protocol suite. Most people just refer to the Internet protocols as TCP/IP. See "Internet Protocol Suite" for a general overview of the entire set of Internet protocols and historical information about the development of those protocols.

 This is a synopsis of the full topic, which is located at the Linktionary! Web site given later.

As a network layer protocol, IP provides datagram routing services. Datagrams are the packets that carry user and application data end to end across router-connected networks. IP is defined in RFC 791 (Internet Protocol, September 1981). This RFC was later amended by many additional proposals and updates. A list of relevant RFCs is available at the Linktionary! Web site.

IP's primary task is to support internetwork addressing and packet forwarding. An internetwork consists of individual networks joined by routers, as pictured in Figure I-10. Networks A and B are connected to create internetwork A/B (I'm using this terminology to simplify the discussion up front).

Every computer on the Internet must have a unique address that IP can provide by way of a *hierarchical addressing scheme.* An IP address is a unique number that contains two parts: a *network address* and *host address.* The network address is used to forward packets across interconnected networks. Routers look at this address and forward a packet along a path toward the destination. When the packet arrives at the destination network, the host portion of the IP address identifies the destination host.

Routers interconnect different networks. Each network has its own IP network address. When a packet arrives at a router, it determines the best way to forward that packet (i.e., which output port to use). However, routers only need to determine the next best hop toward a destination, not the complete path to the destination. This is like getting directions—a person

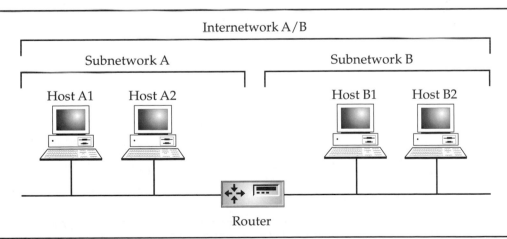

Figure I-10.   *IP is a communication protocol that supports interconnected networks with a global addressing scheme.*

may point you in the right direction at an intersection. At the next intersection, another person points you in the right direction. Eventually, you get to where you want to go—not by knowing the exact path from the start, but by being pointed along the way as you go. This is discussed further under "Routing."

Think of IP as an "overlay" addressing scheme for interconnected networks. The U.S. ZIP code is also an overlay scheme that identifies postal areas. Local addressing (street addresses, rural routes, P.O. boxes, and so on) identifies the final destination for mail.

As shown in Figure I-11, TCP and UDP are layered on top of IP and take advantage of IP's datagram delivery services. TCP is a transport layer end-to-end protocol that provides a set of reliable data delivery services not provided by IP. If an application does not need TCP's services, it goes through UDP.

Applications make calls to TCP or UDP to obtain network services. Application data or messages are encapsulated in TCP segments or UDP datagrams, and then passed down to IP. IP passes datagrams down to the underlying network, which frames the data into "blocks" for

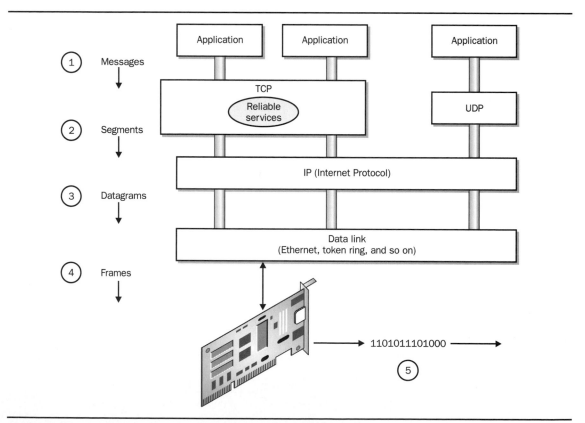

Figure I-11. *The TCP/IP protocol stack in relation to applications and the network*

transmission across the local network medium. The interaction between protocol layers is discussed further under "Network Architecture." Also see "TCP (Transmission Control Protocol)" and "Transport Protocols and Services" for a description of the services provided by TCP and the transport layer.

IP Datagrams

IP datagrams are the "envelopes" that carry data across IP networks. Datagrams are assembled by the source computer and sent out on the network. Routers transfer the datagram from one network to another. To traverse a particular network, datagrams are encapsulated within the frames of that network. However, not all networks have the same frame size, so a datagram that fits nicely in a single frame on one network may need to be fragmented and carried in multiple frames on another network. Routers handle this job. Each network has its own MTU (maximum transmission unit), which is the maximum size for an IP datagram. See "Fragmentation and Reassembly" for more on this.

The IP datagram header is pictured in Figure I-12. Data of variable length is attached directly after the header. The maximum length of the datagram including header and data cannot exceed 65,535 bytes. Also note that the datagram aligns on 32-bit boundaries.

The datagram fields are described in the following list:

- **Version**   The version number of the protocol.
- **IHL (Internet header length)**   Length of the header.
- **Type of service**   Specifies various levels of speed and/or reliability. This field is finally being put to use by new enhancements such as Diff-Serv. See "Differentiated Services (Diff-Serv)" for more details.
- **Total length**   The total length of the datagram, including the header.
- **Identification**   If a datagram is fragmented, this field contains a value that identifies a fragment as belonging to a particular datagram.
- **Flags**   DF (Don't Fragment) or MF (More Fragments). DF indicates that the datagram should not be fragmented and is used when attempting to discover the maximum packet size for networks. MF indicates that this is not the last fragment.
- **Fragment offset**   Where the datagram fragment belongs in the set of fragments.
- **Time to live**   A counter that is decremented with every pass through a router. When 0, the datagram is assumed to be in a loop and is discarded.
- **Protocol**   Identifies the transport layer process to receive the datagram.
- **Header checksum**   An error detection feature that indicates to the receiver whether a packet has been corrupted.
- **Source address**   The IP address of the host sending the datagram.
- **Destination address**   The IP address of the host to receive the datagram.
- **Options/padding**   Optional information and filler to ensure the header is a multiple of 32 bits.

Bit   0   16   31

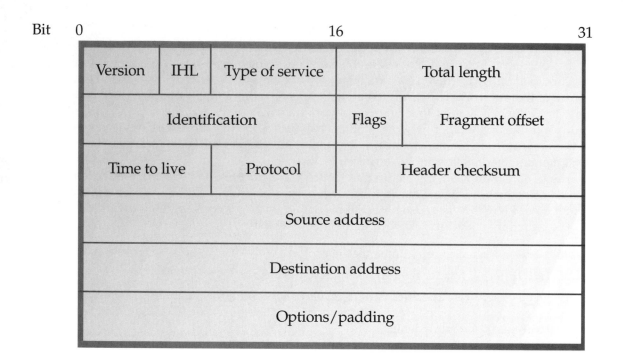

Figure I-12.   *IP datagram header*

IP Addressing and Host Names

An IP address is a 32-bit binary number that contains two separate pieces of information. The network portion identifies the network (a group of computers). The host portion identifies a specific computer on the network. While computers work with IP addresses as 32-bit binary values, humans normally use the dotted-decimal notation. A binary address and its dotted-decimal equivalent are shown here:

11000000.10101000.00001010.00000101 = 192.168.10.5

Note that the 32-bit address is divided into four 8-bit fields called *octets*. You can refer to these fields with the following abbreviated notation:

w.x.y.z

In the early days of the Internet, the 32-bit IP address space was allocated into three address classes: class A, class B, and class C. These are shown in the following table. A class D scheme also exists for multicasting. The first 4 bits (1110) identify the class, and the remaining 28 bits refer to a group of hosts, all of which receive the same IP packet. See "Multicasting."

Class	Network Address	Host Address	Number of Networks	Number of Hosts per Network
Class A	w	x.y.z	126	16,777,214
Class B	w.x	y.z	16,382	65,534
Class C	w.x.y	z	2,097,150	254

Keep in mind that the address is split, with the left part indicating the network and the right part indicating a host. The question is, where does the network part end and the host part begin? It varies, depending on which class of network address you are referring to. The IP address classes are pictured in Figure I-13.

Many of the Class A network addresses were allocated early to large service providers and organizations. The Class Bs were assigned to large companies or other organizations. Many of the Class Cs were still being allocated in the 1990s. For the record, the class scheme is no longer used on the Internet, except that many organizations still own large class-based address blocks. The classless scheme, called CIDR (Classless Inter-Domain Routing), was implemented in the early 1990s to help overcome an impending address shortage. Organizations were supposed to return their class-based addresses to the address pool and receive a contiguous set of classless addresses in return. This wasn't entirely successful since many organizations were not willing to give up their address assignments, especially since it meant renumbering internal networks. See "CIDR (Classless Inter-Domain Routing)" for more information.

To help with renumbering, a private addressing scheme was developed that allows users to implement an unregistered set of IP addresses for their internal networks. This requires NAT (network address translation) at the gateway between the Internet and the external network, which translates internal IP addresses to external addresses and vice versa. See "Proxy Server" and "NAT (Network Address Translation)" for more information.

The Linktionary! Web site discusses subnet masks, subnetting, supernetting, and other IP-related topics in detail.

A proposed Internet protocol called RSIP (Realm-Specific Internet Protocol) solves some of the address problems of IPv4, and provides better support for multimedia. The IETF has stated that RSIP is a replacement for NAT (network address translation) and a potential alternative to

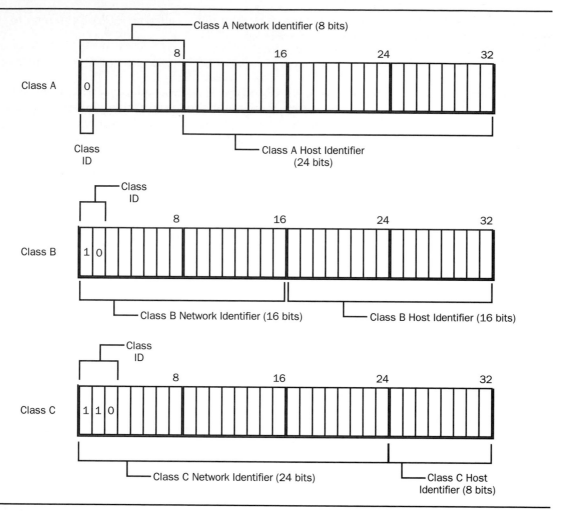

Figure I-13. *IP address classes*

IPv6. At the same time, RSIP provides a transition path to IPv6 for organizations that implement it. See "RSIP (Realm-Specific IP)."

IPv6 (Internet Protocol version 6)

IPv4 has served the Internet community well, but its limited address space has caused problems. The use of private network addressing and NATs, as well as the development of CIDR, has helped to resolve some of these address limitations and security problems, but they are considered temporary fixes. The next generation of the IP protocol is IPv6. IPv6 was officially deployed in 1999, but the Internet community has failed to make the complex transition, even though IPv6 features are sorely needed.

The IETF began working on a next-generation IP protocol in 1990. One of the original formulations of the proposals for a next-generation IP protocol was outlined in RFC 1752 (The Recommendation for the IP Next Generation Protocol, January 1995) and RFC 1753 (IPng Technical Requirements, December 1994). The current best document is RFC 2460 (Internet Protocol, Version 6 Specification, December 1998).

The two IETF working groups mentioned next have more information on IPv6 and list all the relevant drafts and RFCs. The 6Bone is a testbed for IPv6 that helps vendors and users participate in the actual evolution and transition to IPv6. The other Web sites listed here provide additional information.

IETF Working Group: IPNG (ipngwg)	http://www.ietf.org/html.charters/ipngwg-charter.html
IETF Working Group: Next Generation Transition (ngtrans)	http://www.ietf.org/html.charters/ngtrans-charter.html
6Bone (links to other important IPv6 sites)	http://www.6bone.net/
IPv6 Forum	http://www.ipv6forum.com/
Stardust.com IPv6 Channel (papers, mailing lists, news, and so on)	http://www.stardust.com/ipv6/
Cisco's IPv6 Web page	http://www.cisco.com/ipv6/
Microsoft's IP Version 6 papers (search for IPv6)	http://www.microsoft.com/windows2000/
Compaq's IPv6 InfoCenter	http://www.compaq.com/ipv6/
3GPP (Third-Generation Partnership Project)	http://www.3gpp.org

The most important feature of IPv6 is its longer 128-bit address space, compared to 16 bits for IPv4! While IPv4 is limited to four billion addresses (many of which are wasted due to class-based addressing), IPv6 supports 3.4×10^{38} addresses, which reportedly allows for 50,000 addresses for every square meter of land on Earth. While this number may seem high, many billions of addresses will be needed in the future to provide unique addresses for every person and device on the planet. IP addresses will be needed for the explosion in mobile wireless devices and embedded systems contained within everything from home entertainment systems to automobiles to alarm clocks. Most people will own multiple devices that each require a unique IP address. In addition, mobile users can have a temporary second address, called the "care-of" address, where messages are automatically forwarded if the user is not at the primary address.

IPv6 contains many *built-in* features, as opposed to *added-on* features, as was the case with IPv4. These include the following:

■ Support for class of service features that are compliant with the IETF Differentiated Services model. A 20-bit traffic-flow identifier can be used to provide bandwidth reservations, flow identification, and various levels of service that prioritize traffic across routers.

■ Security is supported through IPSec, which supports authentication, encryption of data, and data integrity. Header authentication can guarantee that a packet is from the real source address.

- IPv6 supports mobile users, unlike IPv4, which assumes that users always attach to networks at the same place.

- Autoconfiguration reduces system configuration and management. A node can create its own IP addresses by combining its MAC address with an IP address prefix obtained from a local router.

- IPv6 supports expanded multicasting and anycasting. An anycast address may be assigned to multiple devices that provide the same service. Packets sent to the address will go to the device that is closest or most available. See "Multicasting" and "Anycasting."

- An extension scheme is also included so that senders can add custom information into a datagram. This will allow flexible expansion of the design as new requirements appear.

Related Entries Active Networks; Address, Network; Anycasting; ARP (Address Resolution Protocol); Best-Effort Delivery Services; Broadcast Address; CIDR (Classless Inter-Domain Routing); Connection-Oriented and Connectionless Services; Data Communication Concepts; Datagram and Datagram Services; Differentiated Services (Diff-Serv); Encapsulation; Forwarding; Fragmentation and Reassembly; Framing in Data Transmissions; ICMP (Internet Control Message Protocol); Internet; IPSec (IP Security); Mobile IP; MPLS (Multiprotocol Label Switching); Multicasting; NAT (Network Address Translation); Network Architecture; Network Concepts; Packets and Packet-Switching Networks; Reliable Data Delivery Protocols; Route Aggregation; Routers; Routing; RSIP (Realm-Specific IP); TCP (Transmission Control Protocol); Transport Protocols and Services; *and* UDP (User Datagram Protocol)

Linktionary!—Tom Sheldon's Encyclopedia of Networking updates	http://www.linktionary.com/i/ip.html
Google Web Directory Internet protocols page	http://directory.google.com/Top/Computers/Internet/Protocols/
About.com (search for "IP")	http://compnetworking.about.com/
Network Magazine tutorials	http://www.networkmagazine.com/static/tutorial/index.html
Noritoshi Demizu's Internetworking technical resources page	http://www.watersprings.org/links/inet/
IBM Redbook: TCP/IP Tutorial and Technical Overview	http://www.redbooks.ibm.com/abstracts/gg243376.html/
IBM Redbook: IP Network Design Guide	http://www.redbooks.ibm.com/abstracts/sg242580.html
Information Technology Professional's Resource Center	http://www.itprc.com/tcp_ip.htm
Cisco document: Internet Protocols	http://www.cisco.com/univercd/cc/td/doc/cisintwk/ito_doc/ip.htm
"Understanding IP Addressing: Everything You Ever Wanted To Know" by Chuck Semeria	http://www.3com.com/nsc/501302.html
Uri Raz's "TCP/IP Resources List"	http://www.private.org.il/tcpip_rl.html
Daryl's TCP/IP Primer	http://ipprimer.2ndlevel.net/

IPC (Interprocess Communication)

IPC is a communication process used between programs and processes running in multitasking operating systems or between networked computers. There are two types of IPCs:

- **LPC (local procedure call)**   LPCs are used in multitasking operating systems to allow concurrently running tasks to talk to one another. They can share memory spaces, synchronize tasks, and send messages to one another.

- **RPC (remote procedure call)**   RPCs are similar to the LPC but work over networks. RPCs provide mechanisms that clients use to communicate requests for services to another network-attached system such as a server. If you think of a client/server application as a program that has been split between front-end and back-end systems, the RPC can be viewed as the component that reintegrates them over the network. RPCs are sometimes called *coupling* mechanisms.

One of the advantages of using IPCs is that programs can take advantage of processes handled by other programs or computers. The client/server model takes advantage of RPCs, as do distributed object architectures such as Microsoft's DCOM (Distributed Component Object Model) and CORBA (Common Object Request Broker Architecture).

The normal interprocess communication mechanism in UNIX is the *pipe*, and the *socket* is the interprocess communication mechanism that works across networks. It became a part of UNIX when the TCP/IP protocol stack was integrated into Berkeley UNIX in the early 1980s. This was a project funded by DARPA.

The IPC features described here are used if programs need to communicate with one another or share memory areas:

- **Shared memory**   Processes can exchange values in shared memory. The memory becomes a sort of bulletin board where processes can post status information and data that needs to be shared.

- **Queues**   A queue IPC is a structured and ordered list of memory segments where processes store or retrieve data.

- **Semaphores**   A semaphore provides a synchronizing mechanism for processes that are accessing the same resource. No data is passed with a semaphore—it simply coordinates access to shared resources.

- **Pipes**   A pipe provides a way for processes to communicate with one another by exchanging messages. Named pipes provide a way for processes running on different computer systems to communicate over the network. Mail slots is a store-and-forward messaging system that doesn't require stations to synchronize with one another.

Related Entries   API (Application Programming Interface); Client/Server Computing; COM (Component Object Model); Distributed Applications; Distributed Computer Networks; Distributed Object Computing; Java; Microsoft.NET; Middleware and Messaging; MOM (Message-Oriented Middleware); Multitiered Architectures; Named Pipes; Object Technologies; Pipes; RPCs (Remote Procedure Calls); Sockets API; Transaction Processing; *and* WinSock

| Linktionary!—Tom Sheldon's Encyclopedia of Networking updates | http://www.linktionary.com/i/ipc.html |
| Tom Christiansen's interprocess communications page | http://www.perl.com/CPAN-local/doc/ FMTEYEWTK/IPC/perlipc.html |

IPMI (Intelligent Platform Management Interface)

IPMI is a common management interface specification defined by Intel Corporation, Hewlett-Packard Company, NEC Corporation, and Dell Computer Corporation. IPMI monitors the physical characteristics of equipment such as servers, switches, PBXs, and other network equipment. Monitored characteristics include temperature, voltage, fans, power supplies, and chassis. IPMI interfaces with management software running on the host processor or in other management systems. With IPMI, administrators can proactively manage equipment, monitoring for potential problems and correcting them before they turn into major problems. IPMI is designed to work on its own, even when a host processor is down.

IPMI is designed into management controllers that are embedded in computer boards and other devices. The specification is the recommended interface for CompactPCI systems.

Related Entries Embedded Systems and Architectures; Network Management

| Linktionary!—Tom Sheldon's Encyclopedia of Networking updates | http://www.linktionary.com/i/ipmi.html |
| Intel's IPMI Web page | http://developer.intel.com/design/servers/ipmi/ |

IP over ATM

This topic discusses several approaches to integrating IP and ATM networks, including using ATM networks as the underlying data link for IP networks. If you are looking for Classical IP over ATM as defined by IETF RFC 1577, refer to "CIP (Classical IP over ATM)."

ATM has been a major influence in networking since the late 1980s. Many have claimed it to be a superior networking technology due to its speed and ability to provide QoS (quality of service). Today, other network technologies such as Gigabit Ethernet and multilayer switching provide performance benefits and ease of use over ATM. Still, ATM has been installed in many environments and its QoS capabilities support traffic engineering. Many organizations have a need to integrate ATM with their other networking technologies.

The IP over ATM technologies discussed here are generally "overlay models" that use ATM for layer 2 forwarding. In this context, ATM acts like a data link layer network that encapsulates packets and delivers them from one edge of the ATM network to the other. Therefore, the techniques described here are typically implemented in edge devices, although, in some cases, the ATM device is modified as well.

Keep in mind that ATM is connection oriented, while IP is connectionless. Before any data can be sent across an ATM network, *virtual circuits* must be set up across the switching fabric. Virtual circuits are either PVCs (permanent virtual circuits), which are manually configured for permanent use, or SVCs (switched virtual circuits), which are configured dynamically on demand. In contrast, IP is a network layer connectionless protocol. When a packet is sent across a multihop network, each router makes a decision about how to forward the packet based on the latest topology information it has obtained about the network. There is no predefined path. As a result, routing can induce processing delays and the paths chosen by routers may not be optimal, even when administrators carefully configure route metrics.

In contrast, ATM virtual circuits can provide fast forwarding of packets from one side of a network to another. Figure I-14 illustrates how a core ATM network can provide virtual circuits between any two edge devices, thus allowing any-to-any connections. The edge devices may be routers, Ethernet switches, or other devices. ATM-equipped Internet exchange points may use this method to provide any-to-any connections among all the NSP (network service provider) routers that have been collocated at the facility.

Another difference between ATM and IP is that ATM transports data in fixed-size 53-byte cells while IP uses packets that are variable in size. To transport IP packets in ATM cells, the packets must be broken into pieces and then reassembled at the destination (a process called

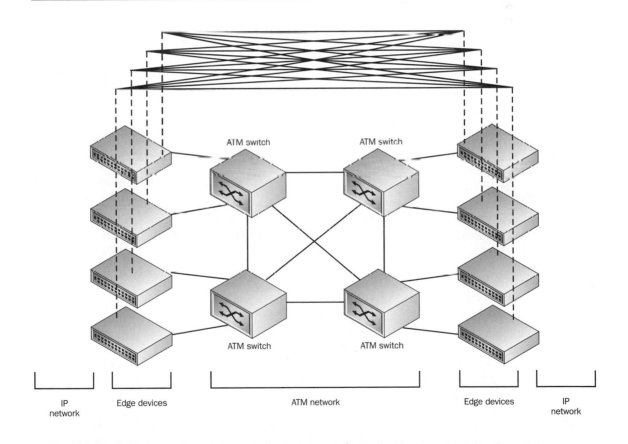

Figure I-14.   *ATM provides virtual circuits between any two edge devices.*

"segmentation and reassembly" or SAR). Since each cell has a header of its own, this leads to a lot of overhead (called the "cell tax"). In addition, ATM and IP use different addressing schemes, so address resolution must take place in order to set up connections between end systems.

When ATM is used instead of a LAN technology, such as Ethernet, you are replacing a broadcast networking technology with a circuit-oriented technology. Broadcasts and multicasts are important network technologies and they must be replaced in an IP over ATM scheme. This is usually done by installing a server that keeps track of all the end stations that belong to a particular virtual LAN (VLAN) and by sending broadcast messages to each of those stations on individual circuits. The servers also provide routing services, address translation, and broadcast emulation services.

The techniques in the following sections have been designed for carrying IP over ATM. Both the ATM Forum and the IETF defined different schemes, in some cases using protocols developed by the other organization. The basic schemes are *encapsulation*, *overlay models with flow-driven cut-through routing*, and *multilayer label switching*.

Encapsulation

In this scheme, non-ATM networks are connected to the periphery of ATM networks via ATM/LAN interfaces. Virtual circuits are created across the ATM backbone that provide direct connections to other peripheral networks. These circuits are usually created manually, although dynamic creation methods are supported. Upper-layer protocol packets are "encapsulated" into ATM cells and delivered across the ATM virtual circuits to a specific destination.

RFC 1483 (Multiprotocol Encapsulation over ATM Adaptation Layer 5, July 1993) is the document to refer to. Specifically, it defines two encapsulation methods:

- **VC-based multiplexing** This is a multicircuit method in which different protocols are carried over a separate ATM virtual circuit. It does higher-layer protocol multiplexing implicitly on ATM virtual circuits (VCs). This method is best within an enterprise, where there are usually no restrictions (such as cost) on the number of circuits that can be created.

- **LLC encapsulation** This is a single-circuit multiplexing method in which multiple protocols are carried over a single ATM virtual circuit. This method is best if a carrier ATM network is used where there are costs and circuit management limitations to consider.

Overlay Models with Flow-Driven Cut-Through Routing

Overlay models provide a way to create virtual layer 3 topologies on top of a physical network topology. The models described here can be used to create multiple IP subnetworks on top of the ATM network. These are virtual networks that exist on top of the layer 2 switching fabric. Routing is required between subnetworks, but cut-through connections can be created directly across the ATM fabric between any end system in any subnet, bypassing the need for hop-by-hop routing. Each of these is discussed under its own heading.

- **CIP (Classical IP over ATM)** This scheme is an IETF standard that defines how to transmit IP datagrams over ATM networks. It consists of creating one or more logical IP subnets (LISs) on top of the ATM switching fabric.

■ **LANE (LAN Emulation)**   LANE is an ATM Forum specification that defines how to use ATM networks like a LAN. LANE automates SVC (switched virtual circuit) setup across an ATM network for LAN clients. Previously, administrators had to manually configure PVC (permanent virtual circuits). See "LANE (LAN Emulation)."

■ **MPOA (Multiprotocol over ATM)**   MPOA provides a way to route multiple network layer protocols over ATM switching networks. It was originally designed for large networks and service providers. MPOA uses an overlay model that maps IP addresses (and other network layer addresses such as IPX) to ATM addresses. MPOA is not a routing protocol, but it does provide a way for ATM clients to query routers or route servers. The IETF's NHRP or the ATM Forum's I-PNNI routing protocols can be used, along with legacy protocols. See "MPOA (Multiprotocol over ATM)" and "NHRP (Next Hop Resolution Protocol)" for more details. Note that MPOA is based on LANE (LAN Emulation).

Multilayer Switching

Multilayer switching solutions were developed in the mid-1990s to provide an alternative to the overlay models just described. The goal was to eliminate the complex mapping of IP to ATM and provide better levels of QoS. ATM signaling and routing techniques are thrown out and replaced by signaling and label distribution protocols based on IP standards, These protocols are integrated with ATM switches to create a *hybrid multilayer switch* that has a layer 3 control plane and a layer 2 packet-forwarding plane. The control plane runs routing protocols and exchanges routing information with other switches. Layer 2 forwarding tables are constructed with the information gathered by the control plane.

Labels are added to packets to identify how the packets should be forwarded across networks. Two approaches to multilayer label switching are the *traffic-driven model* and the *control-driven model.*

Traffic-Driven Approaches

In this approach, individual traffic flows are detected and a binding is made to a virtual circuit if the flow is sufficient to warrant it. Normal routing is used otherwise. Switches must go through the process of detecting flows, which may introduce delays. Also, by the time a flow is detected, it may be nearly over and only the end of that flow may gain the benefit of being switched.

Toshiba's CSR (Cell Switch Router) and Ipsilon's IP Switching (Ipsilon is now part of Nokia) were the first two attempts at multilayer switching on ATM switches. Both control an ATM device using IP protocols, making the ATM switch operate like a switch router. These models were not suitable for large service provider networks due to the large number of flows that are possible. Ipsilon's IP Switching, introduced in 1996, generated a lot of interest and demonstrated that controlling ATM networks with something other than ATM Forum–defined controls was a viable solution. But the traffic-driven approaches never caught on.

Control-Driven Approaches

In this approach, label assignments already exist for routes in the network. These may be operator defined or established by mapping labels to routes that are discovered with standard IP routing protocols. Packets are classified, labeled, and mapped to specifically defined paths across the network. This is a form of *explicit routing* that allows path selection to accommodate

QoS, bandwidth requirements, minimum delay requirements, VPN membership, and so on. This approach is considered the most appropriate for large service providers.

Every packet is label switched, not just those that are part of a detected flow. Label assignments are based on control information from external sources or static configurations. Several different approaches were defined, including IP Navigator (developed by Cascade, which was bought by Ascend, which, in turn, was acquired by Lucent), IBM's ARIS (Aggregate Routed-based IP Switching), and Cisco's Tag Switching. Features from ARIS and Tag Switching were rolled into the latest approach, which is MPLS (Multiprotocol Label Switching), an IETF-developed label-switching standard. See "MPLS (Multiprotocol Label Switching)" and "Label Switching" for more information.

Related Entries   ATM (Asynchronous Transfer Mode); CIP (Classical IP over ATM); LANE (LAN Emulation); MPLS (Multiprotocol Label Switching); MPOA (Multiprotocol over ATM); Multilayer Switching; NHRP (Next Hop Resolution Protocol); PNNI (Private Network-to-Network Interface); Traffic Management, Shaping, and Engineering; *and* VPN (Virtual Private Network)

Linktionary!—Tom Sheldon's Encyclopedia of Networking updates	http://www.linktionary.com/i/ip_atm.html
The ATM Forum	http://www.atmforum.com
IETF MPLS Working Group	http://www.ietf.org/html.charters/mpls-charter.html
MPLS Forum	http://www.mplsforum.com/
Jun Xu's excellent page: "IP over ATM: Classical IP, NHRP, LANE, MPOA, PAR and I-PNNI"	http://www.cis.ohio-state.edu/~jain/cis788-97/ip_over_atm/
Noritoshi Demizu's Multi Layer Routing Web page	http://www.watersprings.org/links/mlr/
TechFest Multilayer Switching page with links	http://www.techfest.com/networking/mlayer.htm

IP over SONET

See PoS (Packets over SONET).

IPP (Internet Printing Protocol)

IPP is a protocol that supports remote printing in distributed environments. For example, IPP allows a user to print a document on a printer at another geographic location by choosing print options from a Web browser or by specifying an Internet URL. The idea is to provide users with the same printing controls and concepts that they use to print locally or to LAN-attached printers. IPP printing services can show the location of available printers, or allow users to inquire about printer capabilities and printer status. You can also choose printers interactively. The protocol supports installation, configuration, print job submission, and other management features, with appropriate security.

IPP may be embedded in a single physical output device, in which case clients talk directly to the printer. In addition, a printer server may support multiple IPP printer objects, where each printer object is associated with exactly one physical output device supported by the server. Finally, a printer server may support multiple physical output devices. All of these printers are similar and the server distributes print jobs to any available printer. Users see the array of printers as a single device.

In designing IPP, the needs of end users, operators, and administrators were considered, as outlined here:

- End users need to find or locate printers by name, location, or capability, create an instance (object) of the printer in their local operating system, view the status and capabilities of a printer, submit print jobs, view the status of print jobs, and cancel print jobs.

- Operators manage printers that accept print jobs through the Internet. They are responsible for making sure the printer has paper and toner and is working properly. IPP must alert operators of a need for service.

- Administrators are responsible for creating the printer instances and controlling which end users and operators are authorized to use and manage the printer. Administrators need tools, programs, and utilities to manage users and operators, manage print job features, manage security, and so on.

The IETF Internet Printing Protocol (ipp) Working Group is developing the IPP protocol. For more information, refer to http://www.ietf.org/html.charters/ipp-charter.html.

Related Entries   FAX Servers and Network Faxing; Imaging; Internet; *and* Internet Protocol Suite

 Linktionary!—Tom Sheldon's Encyclopedia of   http://www.linktionary.com/i/ipp.html
Networking updates

IPPM (IP Performance Metrics)

The IETF IP Performance Metrics (ippm) Working Group is developing a set of standard metrics that can be applied to the quality, performance, and reliability of Internet data delivery services. The metrics are designed to be used by network operators, end users, or independent testing groups. The information they produce is meant to be unbiased quantitative measures of performance.

RFC 2330 (Framework for IP Performance Metrics, May 1998) is the primary document that defines the objectives of the IPPM Working Group and the metrics it is developing. The RFC defines the criteria for IP performance metrics and fundamental concepts, such as metrics, measurement methodologies, and other issues. RFC 2498 (IPPM Metrics for Measuring Connectivity, September 1999) describes how basic Internet connectivity is measured.

See "Performance Measurement and Optimization" or refer to the IPPM Web site at http://www.ietf.org/html.charters/ippm-charter.html.

IPSec (IP Security)

IPSec has the goal of providing security services at the IP layer in the Internet protocol stack. Network communication is open to a variety of attacks as discussed under "Security" and

"Hacking and Hackers." IPSec is designed to provide end systems with a method of authenticating one another and to protect data in transit from eavesdropping and attacks.

 This topic is covered in more detail at the Linktionary! Web site. Refer to http:// www.linktionary.com/i/ipsec.html for the complete discussion.

IPSec relies on cryptography to protect communications in a variety of environments, including communication links between computers on private networks, links between corporate sites, and links between dial-up users and corporate LANs. IPSec is also used between trading partners (extranet connections) and for electronic commerce applications.

IPSec is a tunneling protocol designed for both IPv4 and IPv6. Tunnels are "paths" between a pair of hosts, between a pair of *security gateways* (typically firewalls), or between a security gateway and a host. One tunnel can be created to carry all traffic, or multiple tunnels can be created between the same endpoints to support a variety of TCP services.

An important feature of IPSec is that it provides end-to-end security across IP networks. Lower-layer security protocols only provide protection across a single link. But IPSec should be differentiated from upper-layer session protocols such as SSL (Secure Sockets Layer). SSL has been a mainstay of secure communication, primarily between Web servers and clients. SSL is still the preferred method for short client transactions such as buying a book from Amazon.com. But SSL only secures sessions, not the IP connections between hosts, as IPSec does. See "SSL (Secure Sockets Layer)" for more information.

IPSec has multiple modes and services, as outlined here:

- **Data origin authentication**   Parts of the header of a packet are signed (run through a hash algorithm) so the receiver can trust that the packets are authentic.

- **Connectionless integrity**   The signing process can assure the receiver that the packets have not been altered in transit.

- **Confidentiality**   Entire packets or parts of packets can be encrypted to hide their contents. Encryption hides the IP header of the original packet during transit, so an outer packet is required with a header that is readable by intermediate forwarding systems.

- **Replay protection**   By protecting/hiding vital packet information, IPSec protects against someone capturing packets and replaying them at a later time to gain access to a system.

- **Key management**   IPSec uses IKE (Internet Key Exchange) to manage the exchange of security keys between parties.

IPSec has been slow in coming. Part of the reason is that it was originally designed for IPv6 and IPv6's release date has been moved many times. There are problems with interoperability between vendor products. Encryption is processor intensive and may not be supportable in some environments. But vendors such as Intel have developed security adapters that speed up IPSec processing by offloading encryption.

RFC 2401 (Security Architecture for the Internet Protocol, November 1998) specifies the base architecture for IPsec-compliant systems. RFC 2411 (IP Security Document Roadmap,

November 1998) describes the interrelationship of IPSec documents. The following IETF working groups are developing IPSec and related protocols and extensions:

IETF IP Security (ipsec) Working Group	http://www.ietf.org/html.charters/ipsec-charter.html
IETF IP Security Remote Access (ipsra) Working Group	http://www.ietf.org/html.charters/ipsra-charter.html
IETF IP Security Policy (ipsp) Working Group	http://www.ietf.org/html.charters/ipsp-charter.html
IETF Layer Two Tunneling Protocol Extensions (l2tpext) Working Group	http://www.ietf.org/html.charters/l2tpext-charter.html

Related Entries   Authentication and Authorization; Certificates and Certification Systems; Cryptography; Digital Signatures; EAP (Extensible Authentication Protocol); Firewall; FORTEZZA; Hacking and Hackers; Hash Functions; Kerberos Authentication Protocol; Key Distribution and Management; OPSEC (Open Platform for Security); PKI (Public-Key Infrastructure); Private-Key Cryptography; Public-Key Cryptography; S/WAN (Secure WAN); Secret-Key Cryptography; Security; SSL (Secure Sockets Layer); TLS (Transport Layer Security); Trust Relationships and Trust Management; Tunnels; VPN (Virtual Private Network); *and* X.509 Certificates

Linktionary!—Tom Sheldon's Encyclopedia of Networking updates	http://www.linktionary.com/i/ipsec.html
Bitpipe (search for "ipsec")	http://www.bitpipe.com/
VPNC (Virtual Private Network Consortium)	http://www.vpnc.org/
ICSA (International Computer Security Association) certifies IPSec products	http://www.icsalabs.com/
CyLAN IPSec White Paper	http://www.cylan.com/files/whpaper.htm
Cisco IPSec white paper	http://www.cisco.com/warp/public/cc/techno/protocol/ipsecur/ipsec/tech/ipsec_wp.htm
IBM Redbooks (search for "ipsec")	http://www.redbooks.ibm.com/
IPSec Developers Forum	http://www.ip-sec.com/
IPSec discussion and comparisons at *Intranet Design* Magazine	http://idm.internet.com/foundation/tunneling.shtml
Virtual Private Networks: End-to-End Privacy or Open-Ended Problems? by Rik Farrow	http://www.gocsi.com/Virtual.htm

IP Storage

IP storage refers to technology for transporting *block-mode data* across IP/Ethernet networks. Block-mode is the raw mechanism used by SCSI and other disk drivers to directly access data on disks. Most applications go through higher-level *file access* protocols such as NFS, CIFS, and FTP to access disk information. However, file-mode access is slow and requires many operations compared to block-mode access. Block mode is usually performed between a computer and its directly attached storage devices and is the preferred access method for database applications.

The goal of IP storage is to run block-mode data calls over networks. Doing so can reduce complex file-mode data access, improve disk performance over existing networks, and reduce the need for secondary storage networks such as SANs (storage area networks). Many NAS (network attached storage) devices also work at the file level using protocols such as NFS and CIFS. The performance of these devices improves with support for block-mode data calls over existing networks.

The IETF IP Storage (ips) Working Group is developing standards that will enable block data calls over existing IP networks. The technology encompasses disk, tape, and optical storage devices. The logical terminology for IP storage is "storage over IP," but this terminology and its acronym "SoIP" are a trademark of Nishan Systems. CNT Corporation refers to its IP storage technology as "SAN over IP." Consequently, the IETF refers to the technology as "IP storage."

Currently, SANs implement Fibre Channel to interconnect storage devices in a separate LAN that is accessible to users, typically in an enterprise environment. However, Fibre Channel SAN solutions are difficult to install and manage, and organizations with high-speed networks see no reason to build a secondary network for storage if the existing network has the bandwidth to support high-performance network-attached storage. IP storage outlines how to build inexpensive IP-based SANs over existing infrastructure, preferably Gigabit Ethernet networks.

Gigabit Ethernet and 10-Gigabit Ethernet are now being used in metropolitan area access networks, which means that IP storage even becomes practical in the MAN and WAN in some cases. This allows remote disk access, synchronous and asynchronous remote mirroring, and remote backup and restore (tape vaulting). The protocols will ensure data reliability, cope with network congestion, automatically adapt retransmission strategies to WAN delays, and attempt to avoid the need for protocol conversion.

Proposals submitted to the IETF IP Storage Working Group fall into two categories:

- **Fibre Channel Tunneling**   Provides a way to interconnect two Fibre Channel SANs across an IP network by tunneling Fibre Channel controls and data across the IP network.

- **iSCSI**   This approach encapsulated SCSI controls and data inside IP packets, enabling the construction of inexpensive network-based SANs.

Adaptec has developed SCSI over IP solutions called EtherStorage. The company notes that IP storage technologies work well over high-bandwidth, low-latency switched Ethernet networks in computer room, LAN, and campus environments, but not over WANs, where latency is unpredictable. The company notes that "some applications will not be able to work efficiently with the unpredictable performance and latency of WAN storage configurations, but other applications (such as remote backups) will be able to use IP networks across WANs to provide valuable storage services."

A related technology is DAFS (Direct Access File System), which supports block-level data transfers between a client and a storage device over VI Architecture networks. With DAFS, a client can gain direct access to a disk and transfer data from it directly into local memory without the need to copy data to or from intermediate buffers or to interrupt the operating system during file transfers. See "DAFS (Direct Access File System)" and "VI Architecture."

Related Entries   Clustering; DAFS (Direct Access File System); Data Center Design; Distributed Computer Networks; Embedded Systems; Fibre Channel; File Sharing; File Systems; File Transfer Protocols; InfiniBand; Mirroring; NAS (Network Attached Storage); Replication; SAN (Storage Area Network); SAN (System Area Network); Search and Discovery Services; Servers; Stateless and Call-Back Filing Systems; Storage Management Systems; Storage Systems; Switch Fabrics and Bus Design; Switching and Switched Networks; *and* VI Architecture

Linktionary!—Tom Sheldon's Encyclopedia of Networking updates	http://www.linktionary.com/i/ipstorage.html
IETF Working Group: IP Storage (ips)	http://www.ietf.org/html.charters/ips-charter.html
IETF Working Group: IP over Fibre Channel (ipfc)	http://www.ietf.org/html.charters/ipfc-charter.html
The IP Storage page (document archives and links)	http://www.ece.cmu.cdu/~ips/index.html
Julian Satran's IP Storage archive (documents related to iSCSI)	http://www.haifa.il.ibm.com/satran/ips/
Brian A. Berg's Storage Cornucopia (see iSCSI (Internet SCSI)/IP Storage/SCSI over TCP/ Storage over IP) section	http://www.bswd.com/cornucop.htm
CNT (Computer Network Technology) storage over IP solutions	http://www.cnt.com/
Gadzoox Networks Fibre Channel over IP Solutions (see the SAN Library)	http://www.gadzoox.com/
Adaptec EtherStorage solutions	http://www.adaptec.com/products/solutions/ etherstorage.html
Crossroads Systems	http://www.crossroads.com/
Nishan Systems SoIP solutions	http://www.nishansystems.com/

IP Switching, Ipsilon (Nokia)

Ipsilon (now Nokia) pioneered IP Switching, a technique that combines layer 2 switching with layer 3 routing. An IP Switching device identifies a long flow of packets and switches the flow in layer 2 if possible, thus bypassing routers and improving throughput. IP Switching integrates fast ATM hardware directly with IP, thus preserving the connectionless nature of IP. Note that the term "IP switching" is often used to describe a variety of switch routing techniques. These other techniques are discussed under "IP over ATM."

IP Switching gained notoriety in the mid-1990s because its multilayer switching scheme bypassed traditional ATM signaling and addressing schemes, and replaced them with a scheme that integrated layer 2 and layer 3. Ipsilon's switch controller was basically a high-speed IP router that controlled an ATM switch.

IP switching is no longer an important technology. Label switching techniques are now considered more viable. See "Label Switching." More information is available at the Linktionary! Web page listed later. You can also refer to RFC 1953 (Ipsilon Flow Management

Protocol Specification for IPv4, May 1996). Noritoshi Demizu's multilayer routing Web page provides information about all the switching and routing techniques available today.

Related Entries   ATM (Asynchronous Transfer Mode); CIP (Classical IP over ATM); IP over ATM; Label Switching; MPLS (Multiprotocol Label Switching); MPOA (Multiprotocol over ATM); *and* NHRP (Next Hop Resolution Protocol)

Linktionary!—Tom Sheldon's Encyclopedia of Networking updates	http://www.linktionary.com/i/ip_switching.html
Noritoshi Demizu's multilayer routing Web page	http://www.watersprings.org/links/mlr/
Nokia Web site	http://www.nokia.com

IP Telephony

IP telephony is about the convergence of voice and telephony technologies with the packet-switched Internet technologies. See "Voice/Data Networking" and "Voice over IP (VoIP)" for details.

IPX/SPX (Internetwork Packet Exchange/Sequenced Packet Exchange)

IPX/SPX is the legacy internetworking protocol for Novell NetWare. It was derived from the XNS (Xerox Network System) protocol, which was developed in the 1970s. It is usually just called "IPX," although some sources refer to it as "IPX/SPX," "SPX/IPX," or "Novell protocol." Note that TCP/IP is now the primary Novell NetWare internetwork protocol.

Currently, a number of other network operating systems, including Windows NT, include IPX protocol stacks. The protocol is an easy-to-configure internetworking protocol, suitable for small networks, and it provides compatibility with legacy Novell NetWare networks. A number of network clients also support the protocol, including Microsoft Windows.

IPX provides datagram services over packet-switched internetworks. Its basic operation is similar to IP (Internet Protocol), but its addressing scheme, packet structure, and general scope are different. Internetworking protocols operate in the network layer and include routing services, as shown in Figure I-15.

The other member of the Novell NetWare protocol suite is SPX (Sequenced Packet Exchange), which resides in the transport layer. When compared to the TCP/IP protocol suite, IPX provides routing and internetwork services similar to IP, and SPX provides transport layer services similar to TCP. IPX and IP are connectionless datagram protocols, while SPX and TCP are connection-oriented protocols. See "Connection-Oriented and Connectionless Services" for additional information.

IPX addresses include a network address and a node address. Network addresses are assigned when setting up the primary server on a NetWare LAN. The node address is the hardwired address on a network interface card. A complete IPX address is a 12-byte hexadecimal number that may look similar to the following, where the first part is the network address and the second part is the hardwired node address:

4A87B321 14594EA221AE 0119

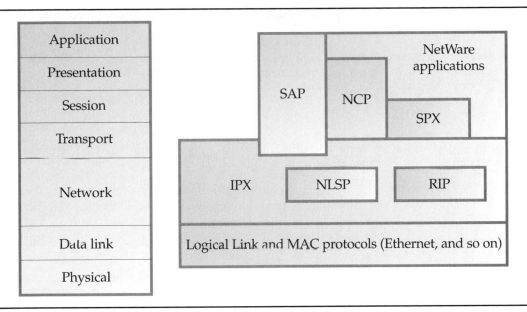

Figure I-15. *NetWare internetworking protocols in relation to the OSI reference model*

Two routing protocols are available in traditional NetWare environments: RIP (Routing Information Protocol) and NLSP (NetWare Link Services Protocol). RIP is the traditional routing protocol for NetWare. The preferred protocol is NLSP, which uses more efficient link-state routing algorithms. Link-state routing protocols track the status of other routers and links, and can adapt more quickly to changes in network topology. These protocols are discussed elsewhere.

Servers and routers on NetWare networks use *SAP (Service Advertising Protocol)* to broadcast a message that indicates the types of services they provide. These messages are broadcast every 60 seconds. SAP is similar to RIP in that it enables network devices to exchange information about their availability on the network. However, SAP broadcasting can add unnecessary traffic to networks. To reduce SAP broadcasts, you can increase the interval at which they occur or use Novell-provided filters that reduce SAP traffic over wide area links.

NCP (NetWare Core Protocol) is the principal protocol for handling service requests between NetWare servers and clients. NCP handles logon requests, and many other types of requests to the file system and the printing system. IPX is the underlying protocol that carries the transmission. NCP is a LAN protocol that was originally designed with the assumption that servers and workstations would be relatively close. When a router gets involved and connections are made over wide area network links, NCP causes traffic congestion. It uses a request/response scheme to manage server/workstation communication. If a workstation makes a request, it must first wait for a response from the server before making another request. This required acknowledgment adds excess traffic.

Additional information on IPX/SPX is posted at the Linktionary! Web site address listed here.

Related Entries   Best-Effort Delivery; Connection-Oriented and Connectionless Services; Data Communication Concepts; Datagram and Datagram Services; LAN (Local Area Network); NDS (Novell Directory Services); Network Architecture; Network Concepts; Network Layer Protocols; NLSP (NetWare Link Services Protocol); Novell; Packets and Packet-Switching Networks; Reliable Data Delivery Services; RIP (Routing Information Protocol); Router; Routing; *and* Transport Protocols and Services

Linktionary!—Tom Sheldon's Encyclopedia of Networking updates	http://www.linktionary.com/i/ipx.html
Novell	http://www.novell.com
Cisco documentation: NetWare Protocols	http://www.cisco.com/univercd/cc/td/doc/cisintwk/ito_doc/netwarep.htm
Cisco documentation: Troubleshooting Novell IPX	http://www.cisco.com/univercd/cc/td/doc/cisintwk/itg_v1/tr1908.htm
Linux IPX-HOWTO	http://www.linuxdoc.org/HOWTO/IPX-HOWTO.html
J Helmig's IPX/SPX configuration page	http://www.helmig.com/j_helmig/ipxspx.htm

IRC (Internet Relay Chat)

IRC is a real-time group messaging system that allows two or more people at remote locations to hold an ongoing conversation over the Internet. The conversation takes place via typed messages, although newer multimedia systems are emerging (i.e., Internet voice and videoconferencing). IRC was originally defined in RFC 1459 (Internet Relay Chat Protocol, May 1993), which describes IRC as a teleconferencing system. In this respect, it is analogous to a telephone party line except that users type messages rather than talk. Another analogy is CB radio, where users converse in an ongoing conversation. Thousands of IRC chats may be taking place at any one time, and these conversations are hosted inside so-called "chat rooms." Some people prefer to say that IRC conversations are held on "channels."

IRC, chat, and instant messaging are forms of *synchronous communications*. Like a voice telephone call, a chat or instant messaging session is live and each user responds to the other in real time. In contrast, *discussion forums* and electronic mail are *asynchronous communications*. Some amount of time may pass before a person responds to a message. In a discussion forum, a message sits in a message queue for other people to read and respond to at any time, or until the message falls out of the queue.

IRC servers are located all over the Internet. The Web sites listed later provide directories to various IRC hosting sites. Chats are listed according to topic. To participate in a chat, you connect to a particular IRC server and join a chat room. When a user posts a message, all the other participants in that chat room see the message. Anyone can start a new chat line at any time, even taking users in one chat room to a new chat room. Typical conversation may range from friendly ramblings to heated political debates. As important events take place in the world, chat room participation typically increases. The identity of participants is usually hidden. Users have "handles," which are short names that identify them within the conversation, but which may give no clue as to the real identity of the person. The ability to stay anonymous is one of the draws of chat, but there is also no way to enforce "adults only" conversations.

IRC servers provide a central control point for chat. The IRC server manages the chat rooms by receiving and posting messages as they arrive. People join and drop out of conversations spontaneously, so the server manages a list of current participants. Conversations are live and rarely archived due to the volume of messages, although participant's can often scroll backward in their chat software to see messages posted within the last few minutes. A history buffer can be adjusted to increase the size of the "scroll back" windows.

Several vendors have enhanced the IRC concept. For example, Microsoft NetMeeting is a collaborative application suite that provides multiuser applications and data sharing over intranets or the Internet. Two or more users can work together and collaborate in real time using application sharing, whiteboards, and an IRC-compatible chat feature called Microsoft Chat. NetMeeting is included in Microsoft's Internet Explorer.

Microsoft Chat has advanced features such as searching, which lets users easily locate chats of interest. A user can search chats by multiple attributes, including user alias, keyword, chat channel size, or channel type. Multiple chat channels are supported, including public, invite-only, persistent, authenticated, and auditorium chat channels. Chat also supports Unicode and ANSI characters for international language support.

The following RFCs provide updates to the existing IRC protocol. The updates were designed to support better scalability and allow the existing IRC networks to grow to sizes that were not anticipated when RFC 1459 was written.

- RFC 2057 (Source Directed Access Control on the Internet, November 1996)
- RFC 2150 (Humanities and Arts: Sharing Center Stage on the Internet, October 1997)
- RFC 2810 (Internet Relay Chat: Architecture, April 2000)
- RFC 2811 (Internet Relay Chat: Channel Management, April 2000)
- RFC 2812 (Internet Relay Chat: Client Protocol, April 2000)
- RFC 2813 (Internet Relay Chat: Server Protocol, April 2000)

RFC 2057 is interesting. It was created from a deposition that Scott Bradnet (Harvard University) submitted as a challenge to the Communications Decency Act of 1996, which was Part Of The Telecommunications Reform Act Of 1996. The Rfc Addresses The Issue Of Minors anonymously participating in chat rooms with adult content. RFC 2150 discusses IRC in terms of its usefulness to the Internet community.

Related Entries   Chat; Collaborative Computing; Electronic Mail; ICQ (I-Seek-You); Instant Messaging; Mailing List Programs; Multicasting; Multimedia; NNTP (Network News Transport Protocol); Unified Messaging; USENET; Videoconferencing; VoIP (Voice over IP); *and* Webcasting

Linktionary!—Tom Sheldon's Encyclopedia of Networking updates   http://www.linktionary.com/i/irc.html

Talk City, another one of the largest chat networks   http://www.talkcity.com/

Undernet, one of the largest real-time chat networks in the world	http://www.undernet.org/
IRChelp.org	http://www.irchelp.org/
MIRC, a shareware IRC (this site also has extensive IRC resources)	http://www.mirc.com/
Internet Chat Resources by Nerd World Media	http://www.tiac.net/users/dstein/nw681.html
Bitpipe (search for "chat")	http://www.bitpipe.com/
Google Web Directory IRC protocol page	http://directory.google.com/Top/Computers/Internet/Protocols/IRC/
Google Web Directory IRC chat page	http://directory.google.com/Top/Computers/Internet/Chat/IRC/
Chat links at Yahoo!	http://dir.yahoo.com/Computers_and_Internet/Internet/Chat/
About.com (search for "IRC")	http://compnetworking.about.com/compute/compnetworking/cs/intranets/index.htm

IRR (Internet Routing Registry)

The IRR is a repository of routing policies on the Internet. Currently, the IRR consists of five independent repositories that contain interdomain routing information and policies. See "Routing Registries"

ISDN (Integrated Services Digital Network)

ISDN is an all-digital telephone system that was originally designed by the world's telephone companies and service providers as a replacement for the aging analog telephone system. What ISDN does is extend the telephone company's digital network into the local loop all the way to the subscriber. Traditionally, the local loop is an analog voice circuit.

ISDN is based on 64-Kbit/sec channels. These channels are just wide enough to handle a non-compressed digitized voice call. The three ISDN implementations listed here are based on rate.

- **BRI (Basic Rate ISDN)**   The version of ISDN that is of most interest to consumers because it operates over the existing copper wire local loop to provide digital voice and data channels.

- **PRI (Primary Rate ISDN)**   Organizations with a need for ISDN at higher data rates (for network connections) get involved with PRI. It basically provides additional channels as required up to a total of 23 B channels and one 64-Kbit/sec D channel for a total bandwidth that is equivalent to T1 (1.544 Mbits/sec).

- **B-ISDN (Broadband-ISDN)**   The broadband version of ISDN designed to handle multimedia services in the carrier backbones. The B-ISDN architecture defines ATM (Asynchronous Transfer Mode) at the data link layer and so implements cell-based virtual circuits across the ATM network. SONET (Synchronous Optical Network) is the underlying physical network. See "B-ISDN (Broadband ISDN)."

The remainder of this section covers the consumer-oriented Basic Rate ISDN and Primary Rate ISDN. ISDN was one of the most well-funded projects in the history of the telecommunication industry, but it was slow to catch on. Obtaining ISDN service is still problematic in most areas, and the service is sometimes more expensive than competing services that offer better bandwidth. Competing services include DSL (Digital Subscriber Line) and cable modems.

ISDN Services and Connections

For businesses, ISDN can provide switched-circuit connections that are more practical than analog modems and more cost effective than leased lines if the bandwidth requirements vary. ISDN supports bandwidth on demand, as discussed later. The services take advantage of existing local loop cables, but give consumers direct access to the ISDN digital network created by the carriers. The ISDN circuit supports multiple devices at the same time via TDM (time division multiplexing).

In North America, the carrier installs an NT (network termination) device at the customer site. An NT1 device connects the customer with the telephone company's local loop. For home or small office connections (BRI), ISDN connects directly to the NT1. An NT2 supports the attachment of other devices, such as network switches, multiplexers, and PBXs.

The NT device provides a connection for TE (terminal equipment) and TA (terminal adapter) equipment to the local loop. TE devices are ISDN compatible, while TAs are devices that provide a connection point for non-ISDN equipment such as analog phones. A TA looks like an external modem, and usually has a jack for a telephone and a jack for a PC.

ISDN supports *bandwidth on demand*, an inverse multiplexing technique that combines multiple lines into a higher-bandwidth link when more bandwidth is required. For example, two 64K channels can be combined to provide a 128-Kbit/sec channel. With PRI, up to 23 channels can be combined as needed to provide a throughput rate up to 1,536 Mbits/sec (in the U.S.). This process can be automatic or programmed for specific times of the day. By switching circuits in and out, you only pay for the bandwidth you need. See "Inverse Multiplexing."

The ISDN D channel provides the signaling to set up calls. This signaling operates in the physical, data link, and network layers relative to the OSI protocol model. The protocols define message types that are exchanged between the customer equipment and the local exchange for setting up and maintaining calls. Refer to the Linktionary! Web site for more information.

Related Entries   ATM (Asynchronous Transfer Mode); Bandwidth on Demand; B-ISDN (Broadband ISDN); Circuit-Switching Services; Data Link Protocols; DSL (Digital Subscriber Line); G Series ITU Recommendations; Inverse Multiplexing; LAP (Link Access Procedure); Last Mile Services; Local Loop; Network Access Services; Residential Broadband; Service Providers and Carriers; Telecommunications and Telephone Systems; *and* WAN (Wide Area Network)

Linktionary!—Tom Sheldon's Encyclopedia of Networking updates	http://www.linktionary.com/i/isdn.html
NIUF (North American ISDN Users' Forum)	http://www.niuf.nist.gov/
NIC (National ISDN Council)	http://www.nationalisdncouncil.com/
Dan Kegel's ISDN page	http://www.alumni.caltech.edu/~dank/isdn/

ISDN Zone	http://www.isdnzone.com/
ISDN FAQs	http://www.cs.ruu.nl/wais/html/na-dir/isdn-faq/.html
Norm Al Dude and Professor N. Erd on the subject of ISDN	http://www.scan-technologies.com/tutorials/ISDN%20Tutorial.htm

IS-IS (Intermediate System-to-Intermediate System) Routing

IS-IS is an OSI (Open Systems Interconnection) *link-state* routing protocol that dynamically routes packets between routers or intermediate systems. OSPF (Open Shortest Path First) is an Internet link-state protocol based on IS-IS.

IS-IS (and OSPF) is an interior (intradomain) routing protocol designed to work within an autonomous system (AS). The corresponding OSI exterior (interdomain) routing protocol is IDRP (Interdomain Routing Protocol), which is designed to exchange routing information between autonomous systems. IDRP is based on the Internet BGP (Border Gateway Protocol) exterior routing protocol.

IS-IS routers flood an internetwork with link-state information. Other routers receive this information and build a database that describes all the routes on the network. A routing table is then calculated from this information.

IS-IS supports a two-level hierarchy in which groups of routers can be delegated to an area (domain). Routing information is then contained within the domain and summary information for those routes is exchanged with other areas. Some Internet documents that provide information about IS-IS are listed here:

- RFC 1074 (The NSFNET Backbone SPF Based Interior Gateway Protocol, October 1988)
- RFC 1195 (Use of OSI IS-IS for Routing in TCP/IP and Dual Environments, December 1990)
- RFC 2763 (Dynamic Hostname Exchange Mechanism for IS-IS, February 2000)

Related Entries   CLNP (Connectionless Network Protocol); IDPR (Interdomain Policy Routing Protocol); ES-IS (End System-to-Intermediate System) Routing; OSI (Open Systems Interconnection) Model; OSPF (Open Shortest Path First) Routing; *and* Routing

ISO (International Organization for Standardization)

The ISO is a worldwide federation of national standards bodies with representatives from over 100 countries. It is a nongovernmental organization established in 1947 with a mission to promote the development of worldwide standards that promote the international exchange of goods and services, and to develop cooperation in the spheres of intellectual, scientific, technological, and economic activity.

Of interest to readers of this book is the *OSI reference model*, which the ISO maintains. The OSI model is described under "OSI (Open Systems Interconnection) Model." It promotes open networking environments that let multivendor computer systems communicate with one another using protocols that have been accepted internationally by ISO members.

Related Entries   ANSI (American National Standards Institute); IEEE 802 Standards; Internet Organizations and Committees; Internet Protocol Suite; Internet Standards; ITU (International Telecommunications Union); OSI (Open Systems Interconnection) Model; Standards Groups, Associations, and Organizations; Telecommunications and Telephone Systems; *and* TIA (Telecommunications Industry Association)

Linktionary!—Tom Sheldon's Encyclopedia of Networking updates	http://www.linktionary.com/i/iso.html
ISO Online	http://www.iso.ch/

ISOC (Internet Society)

See Internet; Internet Organizations and Committees.

Isochronous Services

Isochronous (iso = same, chronous = time) network technologies are designed to deliver real-time voice and video over data networks. Isochronous is the opposite of asynchronous, in which data transmissions are broken up and not sent in a constant stream. Isochronous is similar to synchronous, but does not have the perfectly timed stream of bits or bytes that a synchronous stream adheres to. ATM is an isochronous technology. It provides predictable behavior by delivering data in fixed-sized cells across predefined virtual circuits. iso-Ethernet is another network technology that provides isochronous services.

Related Entries   ATM (Asynchronous Transfer Mode); IsoEthernet; Multimedia; QoS (Quality of Service); Videoconferencing; *and* Voice/Data Networking

isoEthernet

The isoEthernet standard (IEEE 802.9a) is a combination of Ethernet and ISDN (Integrated Services Digital Network) on the same cable. It provides 16.144-Mbit/sec throughput. Through the use of multiple dedicated circuits, it provides a 10-Mbit/sec Ethernet channel and 96 ISDN B-channels of 64 Kbits/sec. At the time of its development, IsoEthernet seemed like a good idea for providing voice and data over the same wire, but Fast Ethernet and Gigabit Ethernet, along with CoS (Class of Service) and QoS (Quality of Service) developments, have lessened interest in isoEthernet.

Linktionary!—Tom Sheldon's Encyclopedia of Networking updates	http://www.linktionary.com/i/isoethernet.html
Dave Hawley's isoEthernet Page	http://members.aol.com/dhawley/isoenet.html

ISO/IEC-11801 Cabling Standards

Cabling standards are developed to provide specifications and design criteria for cabling manufacturers, suppliers, building designers, network architects, service technicians, and others. Cabling standards for data transmissions are meant to define cabling specifications for many years into the future and to support future requirements for high-speed transmissions and network design.

One of the first cabling standards was TIA/EIA-568-A, which was developed by the TIA (Telecommunications Industry Association) and the EIA (Electronic Industries Association). TIA/EIA-568-A is a uniform wiring system, designed for voice and data networks, that supports multivendor products and environments. It defines how to design, build, and manage a structured cabling system. The standard defines a structured, hierarchical star-topology network in which high-speed cables (usually fiber optic) feed slower periphery networks.

ISO/IEC-11801 is an international cabling standard (also referred to as Generic Customer Premises Cabling). The standard was published in 1995. It is based on the ANSI/TIA/EIA-568 cabling standard. Note that the initial document is now considered obsolete. It was updated by ISO/IEC IS11801 AM2—1999, and later with ISO/IEC 11801 2nd Edition – 2000. These updates are outlined at the Cabletesting.com Web site given here.

See "TIA/EIA Structured Cabling Standards" for a more complete discussion of structured cabling. Cabling in general is discussed under the heading "Cable and Wiring."

Related Entries   Backbone Networks; Bandwidth; Cable and Wiring; Campus Network; Capacity; Channel; Circuit; Data Communication Concepts; Delay, Latency, and Jitter; Electromagnetic Spectrum; Ethernet; Fast Ethernet; Fiber-Optic Cable; Gigabit Ethernet; Modulation Techniques; Network Concepts; Network Connection Technologies; Network Design and Construction; Power and Grounding Problems and Solutions; Signals; Testing, Diagnostic, and Troubleshooting; Throughput; *and* TIA/EIA Structured Cabling Standards

ISO (International Standards Organization)	http://www.iso.ch/
Siemon Cabling Systems standards overview (excellent illustrations!)	http://www.siemon.com/standards/overview_ind.asp
Cabletesting.com Cabling standards documents (describes latest updates!)	http://www.cabletesting.com/Cabling_Standards_Documents_Overview.html
Structured Cabling article at *Voice & Data Magazine*	http://www.voicendata.com/aug99/s-cabling.html
BICSI Paper: "The Future of International Cabling Standards," by Alan Flatman	http://www.bicsi.org/prsump11.htm

ISPs (Internet Service Providers)

ISPs provide connections into the Internet for home users and businesses. There are local, regional, national, and global ISPs. However, the regional and national providers that provide bandwidth, transit, and routing services are more appropriately called NSPs (network service providers). The interconnection scheme is hierarchical in most cases, with local ISPs connecting into regional NSPs that, in turn, connect into national or global NSPs. These connections are discussed under "Internet Architecture and Backbone."

An ISP is usually a local service provider that is in the business of providing customers with Internet access and customer support. In contrast, the NSPs are more interested in network infrastructure and reselling bandwidth. Many ISPs are small offices with very little equipment. The ISP outsources all its equipment needs with an NSP or collocates equipment at a carrier or NSP POP (point of presence).

ISPs first appeared at the end of the 1980s. The National Science Foundation (NSF) had created the NSFNET, which defined a hierarchical network scheme in which local networks connected to regional networks that, in turn, connected to the NSFNET national backbone. Local networks included universities, government facilities, and research centers. The regional networks were started with funding from NSF, but the intention was that they would eventually become self-supporting entities by reselling services to lower-level service providers and customers.

The regional networks had an extraordinary opportunity. They were connected to a national backbone, and many organizations wanted access to that backbone. At the same time, the regional networks had incentive to resell bandwidth, since they bought it in large quantity at wholesale prices from carriers. Everything was in place for an explosion of commercial ISPs. Money was to be made. But the NSF had a policy that restricted commercial use of the NSFNET.

By 1993, the pressure to commercialize the Internet was too great. The NSF decided to privatize the Internet and announced its intention to defund the NSFNET and turn over operation of its existing network assets for commercial use. The commercialization of the Internet had begun. The regional networks that started with funding from NSF became commercial entities that began reselling bandwidth and transit services (allowing packets to cross a network to get to another network) to smaller ISPs. Today's major backbone carriers include Sprint, MCI Worldcom, Cable & Wireless, and others.

Internet service providers began appearing everywhere. The entry cost was low and potential profits were high. Local ISPs would buy wholesale services from higher-level ISPs and resell those services to end users. All they had to do was find customers, but there were plenty. The ISP installed dial-up facilities (modems, modem banks, concentrators, and so on) and then metered and billed users for service. Typically, an ISP existed within the area of a single telephone area code. Users dialed into the ISP and established TCP/IP sessions. The ISPs then forwarded user packets across high-speed trunks to higher-level service providers.

A typical ISP facility (PoP) is a secure location that houses routers, servers, storage devices, and other communications and networking equipment. Generally, a PoP has two main features: an access side and an Internet connection side. Between the access side and the Internet side is a core network or a switch that interconnects the two sides and provides connections for other equipment, such as RADIUS AAA (authentication, authorization, accouting) servers, DNS servers, electronic mail servers, Web servers, hosting systems, and so on. The POP also houses support equipment such as racks, power, cable trays, cages, security systems, and fire protection, as well as management services.

The POP funnels connections from many small networks and hundreds or thousands of individual users across its core to one or more high-speed trunks that lead to the Internet. Multiple Internet connections may exist, some going to other POPs owned by the service provider, some going to the Internet backbone, and some going directly to other regional networks. An ISP may offer collocation services, allowing business to house their equipment at the POP and take advantage of fast Internet connections.

The core of the earliest ISPs was often a simple LAN such as Ethernet. As network traffic increased and more subscribers signed up, the POP network equipment was usually upgraded to FDDI. In the late 1980s, FDDI at 100 Mbits/sec provided the best networking technology. Later, Fast Ethernet and switched Ethernet were used. Today, many ISPs use advanced core routers made by Cisco and other providers, or ATM switches. More recently, Gigabit Ethernet is being used in the ISP core networks.

The topic "Internet Architecture and Backbone" contains a subsection called "PoPs and Internet Data Centers" that describes and illustrates various service provider facilities. In particular, refer to Figure I-6.

Also see "Internet Connections," which describes the procedures that businesses and service providers follow to establish an Internet presence.

Several related topics discuss specialized service providers such as those that provide applications, management, and storage support. See "ASP (Application Service Provider)," "MSP (Management Service Provider)," and "SSP (Storage Service Provider)."

Related Entries   Autonomous System; Data Center Design; Fault Tolerance and High-Availability Systems; Internet; Internet Architecture and Backbone; Internet Connections; Internet Organizations and Committees; Internet Protocol Suite; Internet Standards; Internetworking; Intranets and Extranets; IP (Internet Protocol); NAS (Network Access Server); Network Access Services; Outsourcing; Peering; RAS (Remote Access Server); Registries on the Internet; Route Aggregation; Routing; Routing on the Internet; Routing Registries; Service Providers and Carriers; Standards Groups, Associations, and Organizations; Telecommunications and Telephone Systems; WAN (Wide Area Network); *and* Web Technologies and Concepts

Linktionary!—Tom Sheldon's Encyclopedia of Networking updates	http://www.linktionary.com/i/isp.html
Network Startup Resource Center (documents, tools, and links for configuring network services)	http://www.nsrc.org/
NANOG (North American Network Operators' Group)	http://nic.merit.edu/~nanog/
Internet Operators.org	http://www.iops.org/
ISPC (Internet Service Provider Consortium)	http://www.ispc.org/
CIX (Commercial Internet Exchange)	http://www.cix.org/
InterNAP (bypasses congested public NAPs and peering points)	http://www.internap.com/
Google Web Directory resources for ISPs	http://directory.google.com/Top/Computers/Internet/Access_Providers/Resources_for_ISPs/
ISPworld, the definitive ISP business tool (includes *Boardwatch*, the trade journal for ISPs).	http://www.ispworld.com/
Exodus Internet data center (take the visual tour)	http://www.exodus.net/idc/
Internet Service Provider Information Pages (extensive information and links)	http://www.spitbrook.destek.com/isp/

ISP Planet	http://www.isp-planet.com/
Resources for network operators and ISPs at Merit Networks (tools, statistics, performance management, and so on)	http://www.merit.edu/ipma/docs/isp.html
Randall S. Benn's ISP information page	http://www.clark.net/pub/rbenn/isp.html
ISP-Resource.com	http://www.isp-resource.com/
ITPRC (Information Technology Professional's Resource Center) Internet Operations page	http://www.itprc.com/internet.htm

Refer to "Internet Architecture and Backbone" for links specifically related to Internet architectures. See "Internet Connections" for other related links.

ITU (International Telecommunications Union)

The ITU is an agency of the United Nations that coordinates the establishment and operation of global telecommunication networks and services. It includes governments and the private sector organizations from around the world as its members. ITU activities include coordination, development, regulation, and standardization of international telecommunications, as well as the coordination of national policies. According to the ITU, its goals are "to foster and facilitate the global development of telecommunications for the universal benefit of mankind, through the rule of law, mutual consent and cooperative action."

See "CCITT (Consultative Committee for International Telephony and Telegraphy)" for historical information on the ITU.

The ITU makes the recommendations about various technologies and publishes those recommendations for use by the telecommunications industry. The recommendations are published in a series, labeled A through Z, that cover topics such as network operations, telephone services, telecommunications services (other than telephone), transmission systems, cabling plant construction and management, ISDN, switching, signaling, and data communications. A complete list of ITU recommendations may be found at http://www.itu.ch/itudoc/itu-t/rec.html.

The ITU also has specific study groups that gather information about technologies and make them available to anyone. There are groups that study telecom service operations, tariffs and accounting, network management and maintenance, cabling, audio and video transmissions, telephone signaling, and multimedia systems. For more information, refer to http://www.itu.ch/itudoc/itu-t.

Related Entries   ANSI (American National Standards Institute); CCITT (Consultative Committee for International Telephony and Telegraphy); G Series ITU Recommendations; H.323 Multimedia Conferencing Standard; H Series ITU Recommendations. IEEE 802 Standards; Internet Organizations and Committees; Internet Protocol Suite; Internet Standards; ISO (International Organization for Standardization); OSI (Open Systems Interconnection) Model; Standards Groups, Associations, and Organizations; Telecommunications and Telephone Systems; *and* TIA (Telecommunications Industry Association)

Linktionary!—Tom Sheldon's Encyclopedia of Networking updates

http://www.linktionary.com/i/itu.html

The ITU Web site

http://www.itu.int/

IXC (Interexchange Carrier)

An IXC is a telecommunications carrier that provides service between LECs (local exchange carriers). LECs may be the incumbent carriers that were formed by the breakup of AT&T (previously called the RBOCs or "regional Bell operating companies"), or they may be CLECs (competitive local exchange carriers), which operate as competitive carriers in the same area as the incumbent LECs.

LECs operate within one or more local areas called the LATA (local access and transport area). The IXCs (interexchange carriers) provide inter-LATA service (basically, long-distance service). They are allowed to co-locate equipment at LEC facilities and tap into the LEC's switching equipment so that LEC customers can make long-distance calls across the IXC's network. All LECs must provide interexchange carriers with an access point, called the PoP (point of presence). Common IXCs are AT&T, MCI Worldcom, and Sprint. This topic is covered in more detail under "Service Providers and Carriers" and "Telecommunication Regulation."

Related Entries   AT&T; Communication Services and Providers; ISPs (Internet Service Providers); NPN (New Public Network); PoP (Point-of-Presence); Service Providers and Carriers; Telecommunications and Telephone Systems; Telecommunications Regulation; *and* WAN (Wide Area Network)

Linktionary!—Tom Sheldon's Encyclopedia of Networking updates

http://www.linktionary.com/i/ixc.html

JAIN

JAIN is a set of Java technology-based APIs that enable the rapid development of new telecom products and services on the Java platform. JAIN is Sun Microsystem's initiative that can be used to define and build integrated networks. Information is available at http://java.sun.com/products/jain/. The Parlay Group is also involved in this area. Its Web site is http://www.parlay.org/. Also see http://www.linktionary.com/j/jain.html.

Java

Java is a programming language and development environment created by Sun Microsystems and launched in 1995. It took the computer industry by storm as a new platform and programming language for building object-oriented component-based applications.

Java programmers use the Java language to create Java applets (components that run inside browsers) and Java applications. Java applets and applications run inside what is called a *Java VM (Virtual Machine)*. Only the VM must be designed to be compatible with any specific platform. Once a VM is installed on a computing device, any Java applet will run inside the VM. Think of the VM as a software box where Java applications run.

Java's architectural model is pictured in Figure J-1. At the top are applets and applications, which connect to the Java base platform (black area) via Java Core API and Java Standard Extension API. The Java Virtual Machine is at the core of the platform. The Porting Interface lies between the Java Virtual Machine and the OS (operating system) or browser. This Porting Interface is platform independent. Connected to it are platform-dependent Adapters. The OS and JavaOS provide the user interface, filing system, and network functionality. Different machines can be connected by a network, as shown in the figure. The "Java on a desktop OS" represents a PC or Macintosh computer, while "Java on JavaOS" represents a thin client computer.

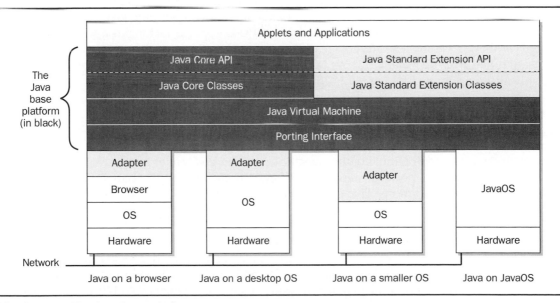

Figure J-1. *The Java base platform*

Java has grown into a sophisticated and widely supported development environment. Hundreds of companies are developing Java tools, libraries of code, and other enhancements to speed application development. Since Java is supported on multiple platforms, migration issues are simplified. Rapid application development and deployment are possible with Java's component model, and components can be reused to build or enhance other applications.

JavaOS is a relatively small operating system that executes Java applications directly on hardware platforms. The operating system can be stored in flash ROM or may be booted from the network. It is the smallest and fastest operating system for running Java on a broad range of devices, including computers, "smart" telephones, personal digital assistants, kiosks, and entertainment systems. The JavaOS architecture consists of a microkernel and memory manager, device drivers, the Java Virtual Machine, the JavaOS graphics and JavaOS windowing systems, networking classes, and support for the full Java applications programming interface.

Jini is a Sun technology that provides a way to connect digital devices into impromptu, expandable Java-oriented networks that let users immediately access network resources and services. The technology is designed to support any device that "passes digital information in or out" according to Sun. Devices register with the network when they connect, which makes them available to other devices. For example, when a printer is attached and gets registered, it makes its driver available on the network and this driver gets downloaded to clients when they need to use the printer. See "Service Advertising and Discovery" for related information.

Java is supported industrywide. The Java Fund is an industry consortium of vendors including IBM, Netscape, Oracle, and others that are working together on Java development. The Java Fund Web site is at http://www.kpcb.com/keiretsu/JavaFund.html.

The Java Virtual Machine

The VM is like a CPU that runs on software—a software CPU. With Java running on top of the hardware CPU as a software process, applications written to run with the Java VM can run on any computer platform, no matter what hardware CPU is in place, as long as a VM has been written for that processor. The advantage of this approach is that programmers can write one application that works on many different computer platforms rather than different versions of an application to run on different computing platforms.

The Java VM is so much modeled after a CPU that it even converts Java code into a language that is very similar to CPU-level machine language. The machine-like language it creates is specific to the hardware CPU that the VM was designed to work with. The VM has an upper layer and a lower layer. The upper layer is compatible with all Java applications, and the lower layer is compatible with a specific CPU. The VM makes hardware calls to the processor and these calls perform standard CPU operations. But the VM hides the platform specifics from Java applications. These applications only need to make calls to the Java VM.

JavaBeans

JavaBeans are components, written with the Java programming language, that run on any Java-enabled platform. Component technologies provide a building-block approach to application development. Components are reusable and can be combined in a variety of ways to create full applications or applets that run inside "containers" such as Web browsers. Like any object technology, components provide services to other components through their external interfaces.

The JavaBeans model consists of the *components* themselves; *containers*, which are the shells where objects are assembled; and *scripting*, which allows developers to write the directives that make components interact. A container is a place where components can register themselves and publish their interfaces so that other components know how to interact with them.

Enterprise JavaBeans are specialized "beans" that are designed to run on a server rather than as applications on a user system or applets within a browser. The Java 2 Platform, Enterprise Edition (J2EE), is a platform that defines how JavaBeans interact in a network and Internet environment. J2EE is discussed in the next section.

JavaBeans is a complete component model that supports common component architecture features such as properties, events, methods, and persistence, as described here.

- **Interface publishing and discovery**   When a component is placed in a JavaBean container, the object is registered so it can be identified by other objects. Its interfaces are also published so other objects can use those interfaces.

- **Event handling**   Allows objects to communicate via messaging.

- **Persistence**   Provides a way to store information about an event or object for later use.

- **Layout control**   Provides controls for visual appearance and the layout of components inside a container.

- **Application builder controls**   Allows components to expose their properties and behaviors to development tools so developers can quickly build applications.

The *InfoBus* is a compact Java programming interface that allows cooperating applets or Beans on a Web page or in a Java application to communicate data to one another. The InfoBus is a communication mechanism designed to run in a single client or a single server. It is not a network communication mechanism. Networking techniques are discussed next.

The InfoBus categorizes JavaBeans as "data providers" and "data consumers." Data providers access data from native stores such as a DBMS, spreadsheet, and flat files. The data is put on the InfoBus, where it is retrieved by data consumers. This technique allows data consumers to operate independent of the data they use. For example, a JavaBean does not need to know SQL (Structured Query Language) to access data from a SQL database.

For security reasons, developers can control the behavior of components to a fine degree using rules that determine what resources a component can access. This allows untrusted applets to be combined with trusted applications.

Java 2 Platform, Enterprise Edition (J2EE)

J2EE is an architectural platform that defines the Java component model in a multitiered enterprise environment. See "Multitiered Architecture." J2EE can be compared to Microsoft.NET in its purpose and scope. Sun developed the platform in collaboration with IBM, BEA Systems, Oracle Corporation, and a number of other vendors.

J2EE encompasses Sun's Enterprise JavaBeans (EJB), which defines how to build Internet- or intranet-based applications using the Java programming language. Many platforms are supported in this environment, including Sun, Linux, IBM, Apple, and Windows, as well as PDAs, cell phones, and a variety of embedded and specialized systems.

J2EE supports transaction management, life-cycle management, resource pooling, and other features, automatically providing these features to components. The advantage is that developers don't need to code these features themselves, but instead design components to access them. This lets developers concentrate on business logic and user interface design.

Basically, the J2EE platform is defined by components, containers, and connectors. Components are the applications and applets. Containers operate between components and clients to provide services to both. Connections make the J2EE platform portable by providing APIs for existing enterprise vendor offerings.

Figure J-2 illustrates the J2EE model. Note the four tiers of this model. On the left are Web clients or in-house systems running Java applets and applications. These are connected to the middle tier, which, in turn, is connected to the back-end databases and legacy systems via data connectors such as JDBC (Java Database Connectivity) and SQL/Java.

Clients using Web browsers interact via standard HTML with the Web server or run Java applets that have been downloaded from the server. The Java applets may interact with the Web server as well. JSPs (Java Server Pages) dynamically generate Web pages using information

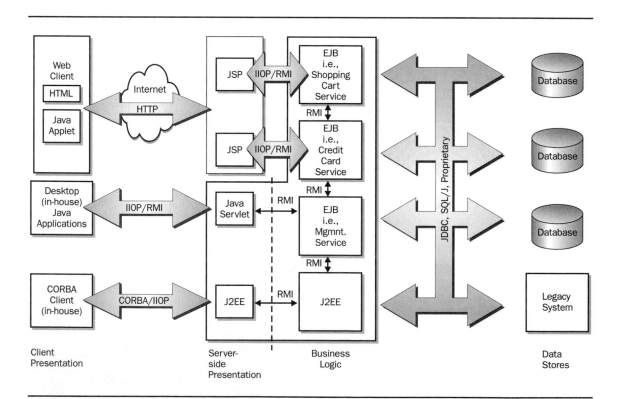

Figure J-2.   *Java 2 Platform, Enterprise Edition (J2EE) model*

obtained from EJBs and back-end databases. Clients running full Java applications connect with Java servlets on the presentation Web servers.

Components communicate via Web standards such as HTTP and HTML, as well as the following:

- **RMI (Remote Method Invocation)** RMI is the basis of distributed object computing in the Java environment. It defines how Java components can interoperate in a multiple Java VM environment. RMI provides the tools that programmers need to create distributed Java applications (objects) that can invoke methods on other Java applications that are running on other Java Virtual Machines, such as remote hosts across the Internet. Invoking a method is like asking another program to do something. A Java object must first obtain a reference to another Java object before it can invoke its methods. It may obtain these references via another Java application, or it may obtain them through a naming service that is built into RMI.

- **JMS (Java Messaging Service)** JMS is a message-oriented communication protocol for the J2EE environment that provides an alternative to RMI. JMS follows both the point-to-point messaging and publish-and-subscribe techniques. Point-to-point is like an e-mail message. The message goes in a queue and is picked up by the recipient. With publish and subscribe, clients make a request to a server to be updated when some specific information changes. That's the subscribe part. When the information changes, the server publishes it and notifies the subscribers. Publish and subscribe is a tremendous advantage for the Internet because it reduces the traffic caused by people and components that must constantly check back with a server to see if information has changed.

- **IIOP (Internet Inter-ORB Protocol)** IIOP is an OMG (Object Management Group) specification for the CORBA environment. It carries GIOP (General Inter-ORB Protocol) over TCP/IP (GIOP specifies the format for message exchange between ORBs). The OMG modified IIOP so that it could also serve as a transport for RMI, thus making Java and CORBA interoperability possible. With IIOP, Java components can interact with programs in the CORBA environment that were written with non-Java languages such as C++ and COBAL. RMI works in Java-only environments, while IIOP provides interoperability among heterogeneous environments.

- **XML (Extensible Markup Language)** XML is a meta-markup language for defining structured data that provides advanced methods for viewing and manipulating data. XML is portable data. In distributed computing environments, XML has become a key part of transporting data across networks. Sun's JAXP (Java Application Programming Interface for XML Parsing) is a development tool that helps Java developers build Java applications that support XML. XML is especially useful in e-commerce and Web publishing applications.

The business logic layer contains Enterprise JavaBeans components, which provide various types of business services. These components may be commercially available or built in-house. They are used to assemble general business applications. For example, an e-commerce site could be built by combining components that provide "shopping cart" services, customer service features, credit card transaction services, and other special user interfaces.

Related Entries   ActiveX; API (Application Programming Interface); Client/Server Computing; COM (Component Object Model); CORBA (Common Object Request Broker Architecture); DBMS (Database Management System); Distributed Applications; Distributed Computer Networks; Distributed Object Computing; Embedded Systems; Microsoft.NET; Middleware and Messaging; Mobile Computing; MOM (Message-Oriented Middleware); Multitiered Architectures; Network Appliances; Object Technologies; ORB (Object Request Broker); RPC (Remote Procedure Call); SOAP (Simple Object Access Protocol); Sun Microsystems; Thin Clients; Web Technologies and Concepts; *and* XML (Extensible Markup Language)

Note   *A complete set of links is available at the Linktionary Web site.*

Linktionary!—Tom Sheldon's Encyclopedia of Networking updates	http://www.linktionary.com/j/java.html
Sun Microsystem's Java Web site (contains complete documentation, developer info, and support)	http://java.sun.com/
Another Sun Java site	http://www.sun.com/java/
Sun's JavaBeans page	http://splash.javasoft.com/beans/
Sun's Java 2 Platform, Enterprise Edition	http://java.sun.com/j2ee/
JavaWorld Online Magazine	http://www.javaworld.com/
Java Boutique	http://javaboutique.internet.com/
Webmonkey Java topics	http://hotwired.lycos.com/webmonkey/programming/java/
Cetus links for objects and components	http://cetus-links.org/
Network World Fusion Java information	http://www.nwfusion.com/netresources/java.html

Jigsaw

Jigsaw is a full-blown HTTP server, written entirely in Java. It is designed to be portable (run on any machine running Java), extensible (extended by writing new resource objects), and efficient (minimizes file system accesses with caching). Information is available at the World Wide Web Consortium.

Jigsaw—The W3C's Web Server	http://www.w3.org/pub/WWW/Jigsaw/.

Jitter

See Delay, Latency, and Jitter.

Jukebox Optical Storage Devices

A *jukebox* is an optical disk device that can automatically load and unload optical disks and provide as much as 500 gigabytes of near-line information. The devices are often called *optical disk libraries*, *robotic drives*, or *autochangers*. Jukebox devices may have up to 50 slots for disks, and either a picking device traverses the slots, or the slots move to align with the picking device. The arrangement of the slots and picking devices affects performance, depending on the space between a disk and the picking device. Seek times are around 85 milliseconds and transfer rates are in the 700-Kbit/sec range.

Jukeboxes are used in high-capacity storage environments such as imaging, archiving, and HSM (hierarchical storage management). HSM is a strategy that moves little-used or unused files from fast magnetic storage to optical jukebox devices in a process called *migration.* If the files are needed, they are demigrated back to magnetic disk. After a certain period of time or nonuse, the files on optical disk might be moved to magnetic tape archives.

Related Entries   Backup and Data Archiving; Data Center Design; Data Protection; Disaster Planning and Recovery; Fault Tolerance and High Availability; Mirroring; Optical Libraries; Storage Management Systems; *and* Storage Systems

Luminex	http://www.luminex.com/
Maxoptix	http://www.maxoptix.com/
Rising Edge Technologies	http://www.risingedge.com

Jumbo Frames

A proprietary technique used by Alteon Networks to expand the size of Ethernet frames from 1,500 bytes to 9,000 bytes. Jumbo frames can improve throughput on Gigabit Ethernet networks. The idea is to reduce the frame header overhead. Since Gigabit Ethernet processes many frames per second, reducing the number of headers to process and increasing the frame size gives users the benefits of higher data throughput and lower server CPU utilization, regardless of their network infrastructure.

Note that if jumbo frames cross a non-supporting router, the router will break the frames down into 1,500-byte frames.

More information is available at http://www.alteonwebsystems.com.

Kerberos Authentication Protocol

Kerberos is a symmetric-key authentication scheme developed at MIT for verifying the identities of users and devices in client/server network environments. Kerberos is called a *trusted third-party authentication protocol*, meaning that it runs on a server that is separate from any client or server. The name comes from the three-headed dog that guarded the entrance to Hades.

The Kerberos server is called the *AS (authentication server)*. When a client needs to access some server, the clients access the Kerberos server to obtain a ticket. Possession of the ticket defines access. This assumes that both the client and the server trust the "third-party" Kerberos authentication server.

The IETF manages the Kerberos specification, although Microsoft has taken some liberties in changing the protocol to fit its needs in Windows 2000. Kerberos version 5 is outlined in RFC 1510 (The Kerberos Network Authentication Service, September 1993).

Kerberos was created by MIT's Project Athena, a test project for enterprise-wide computing that took place in the late 1980s. Kerberos is available for public use and the source code is available free on the Web sites listed later.

Kerberos provides security for remote logons and can provide a single logon solution so users do not need to log on every time they access a new server. The AS stores passwords for all users in a central database. It issues credentials that clients use to access servers within the *realm* of the AS. A realm includes all the users and servers that the AS server tracks, as explained in a moment. The AS server is physically secured and managed by a single administrative staff. Since it authenticates users, application servers are relieved of this task. They "trust" the credentials issued by an AS for a particular client.

In any communication that requires encryption, there is always a security risk in getting the encryption key to the parties involved. The key might be compromised in transit. An important Kerberos feature is that the AS provides a way to safely distribute an encryption key to a client and a server that need to engage in secure transactions. This shared key is called a *session key*.

An AS operates within a *realm*, a security domain in which a specific security policy is set. Realms can trust other realms, meaning that if a user is authenticated by an AS in one realm, the trusting realm will not require that the user be reauthenticated to access a server in its realm. In other words, it trusts that another AS has properly identified and validated a user.

Here are some important Kerberos features:

- For this discussion, a client is software that acts on behalf of a user.

- Before a client can access a server, it must obtain credentials from the AS.

- The credentials that a client needs to access a server include a *server ticket*. A server ticket has specific time parameters and only allows a specific user at a specific client computer to access a specific server. A user may hold numerous tickets at the same time to access multiple servers.

- The initial objective is to get a *TGT (ticket-granting ticket)* from the AS to the client. A TGT (not to be confused with a server ticket) is analogous to a permit or a license. With a TGT, a client has the authority to obtain server tickets from a *TGS (ticket-granting server)*. A TGS may be running on the AS computer.

■ The purpose of a TGT is to eliminate the need for users to type a password every time they want to access a new server. When a TGS receives a request for a ticket that includes the TGT, it uses the information in the TGT to validate the user and does not require the user to reenter a password.

■ The TGT includes the user's ID and network address, as well as the ID of the TGS. It also includes a timestamp that provides some protections from hackers. In addition, it includes the all-important session key (which is eventually distributed to the client and the target server that the user wants to access). The TGT is encrypted with a key known only to the AS and TGS. Therefore, only the TGS can decrypt the TGT after it is sent from the AS.

■ The AS does not send the TGT directly to the target server. It is sent to the client, where it is saved for use in all future ticket requests. When the user attempts to access a server, the TGT is sent to the TGS. The TGS decrypts the TGT and compares its contents with information provided by the user to determine authenticity, then returns a ticket to the user for the target server.

The authentication and authorization scheme is pictured in Figure K-1 and outlined here:

1. The first step is for the client to get a TGT. This step also validates the user. A simple request for a TGT is sent to the AS. The AS, which has a copy of the client's password, encrypts the TGT with a key derived from the user's password.

2. When the client receives this response, the user is prompted for a password that can decrypt the response. Only the authentic user should be able to enter a password that can decrypt the response, so the scheme effectively validates the user.

3. Once the response is decrypted, the client has a copy of the TGT. To access a server, the client sends a request to the TGS that contains the ID of the target server, the user's ID, and the TGT to prove the authenticity of the user.

4. The TGS decrypts the TGT and views its contents. If everything checks out, the TGS builds a server ticket for the target server and encrypts it with a key shared in common with the target server. The server ticket is encrypted again by the TGS with a key derived from the user's password and returned to the client.

5. The client decrypts the response to extract the server ticket and the session key. The ticket is then forwarded to the target server along with the user ID. Note that the ticket also contains an encrypted form of the user ID.

6. The target server decrypts the ticket and compares the user ID sent with the ticket to the user ID that was encrypted in the ticket. If they match, the user is granted access to the server.

The ticket contains the session key, which was also sent to the client. Now, both client and server have a session key they can use to encrypt and decrypt messages sent across the network, thus providing private communications.

K

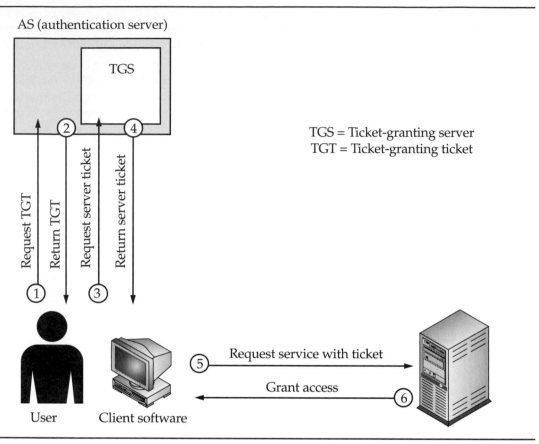

Figure K-1.   *Kerberos authentication scheme*

An enhancement to the authentication process is available by requiring that users enter a token ID, which is an ID obtained from a credit card–like device that generates tokens. Users carry the token card with them. It displays values that are synchronized with the server, and the user enters these values when logging in.

While the Kerberos scheme implements symmetric (single-key or secret-key)–encryption techniques, some vendors are supporting public-key authentication schemes for the initial user authentication. Microsoft is providing this feature in its Kerberos implementation and has submitted a proposal to the IETF that recommends the technique.

For more information on Kerberos, refer to the Web sites listed at the end of this topic. Also refer to RFC 1964 (The Kerberos Version 5 GSS-API Mechanism, June 1996), and RFC 2712 (Addition of Kerberos Cipher Suites to Transport Layer Security, October 1999).

Related Entries   Authentication and Authorization; Certificates and Certification Servers; Digital Signatures; Key Distribution and Management; PKI (Public-Key Infrastructure); Public-Key Cryptography; Security; Smart Cards; *and* Token-Based Authentication

Linktionary!—Tom Sheldon's Encyclopedia of Networking updates	http://www.linktionary.com/k/kerberos.html
IETF Working Group: Kerberos (krb-wg)	http://www.ietf.org/html.charters/krb-wg-charter.html
IETF Working Group: Kerberized Internet Negotiation of Keys (kink)	http://www.ietf.org/html.charters/kink-charter.html
Kerberos. IETF Working Group: Common Authentication Technology (cat)	http://www.ietf.org/html.charters/cat-charter.html
Kerberos: The Network Authentication Protocol (MIT Kerberos page)	http://web.mit.edu/kerberos/www/
Kerberos document references	http://nii.isi.edu/info/kerberos
Lenny Miceli's Kerberos information and help page	http://ubvms.cc.buffalo.edu/~tkslen/kerberos.html

Kernel

K

Kernels are the core components of operating systems. They are the central portion that manages memory, files, peripherals, and system resources. The kernel typically runs processes and provides interprocess communication among those processes. Common core functions include scheduling and synchronization of events, communication among processes (message passing), memory management, management of processes, and management of input and output routines.

Related Entries   Linux; Microsoft Windows; Network Operating Systems; Operating Systems; *and* UNIX

Linktionary!—Tom Sheldon's Encyclopedia of Networking updates	http://www.linktionary.com/k/kernel.html
Gemal's Psyched Site (Linux kernels)	http://www.gemal.dk/linux/

Key Distribution and Management

Keys are used as part of encryption and authentication functions to lock and unlock messages. While a particular encryption *algorithm* is often published and well known, the keys used to make each encryption unique must be kept secure and private. But there are logistics problems in exchanging keys. If you send an encrypted message to a friend, your friend will need a key to decrypt the message. The process of getting that key to your friend may be compromised. This section describes methods for exchanging keys in secure ways over open networks like the Internet.

The one thing to avoid in any key exchange is obvious: never send the actual key over the network in the open. If Alice and Bob need to exchange keys, they may be able to do so over the phone (if it's a relatively short alphanumeric string). They could also meet in person or use a public-key scheme as described later. In any case, once they have a "shared secret key," they can use it for authentication and to establish trust.

For example, Bob can make sure he is connected with Alice by having Alice prove that she knows the secret key, without Alice actually sending the secret key across the wire. How is this done? Bob sends Alice some random text, and Alice encrypts it with the secret key and returns it to Bob. Bob also encrypts the ransom text with his secret key, and then compares the results to what Alice returned. If they are the same, Alice must be authentic and trust is established.

An important point is that application data is never encrypted with the shared secret key. Once two parties have established trust by confirming to one another that they know the shared secret, they create mutually agreed upon "session" keys to protect application data. These are one-time keys that are not reused for future sessions. This avoids the possibility that someone who did capture the key could use it in the future (replay attack).

Still, Bob and Alice must have previously exchanged a key. This is not always practical, especially when the parties involved don't know each other, as is common in e-commerce transactions. The public-key cryptography scheme provides another solution. A mutually shared key can be constructed on the spot without any previous exchange of information with a simple technique: Bob combines his private key with Alice's public key, and Alice combines her private key with Bob's public key. This will create a new shared key, but the scheme requires a public-key infrastructure to work.

The Kerberos system, discussed under its own heading in this book relies on a central key server for key distribution, but this system works best within an enterprise, not on the global Internet. Asymmetric public keys solve this problem as discussed in a moment.

Manual Key Exchange

This topic seems obvious. If two people want to communicate securely, they can meet to exchange keys, or send them via courier. To avoid compromise, the keys can be split up with part sent via courier, part exchanged over a phone (hopefully, the phone is not bugged), and part being something that both parties know (assuming that both parties can agree on what that thing must be without compromising it to an eavesdropper).

In the case of two devices that will establish secure sessions across a wide area link, a network administrator may configure the passwords and keys for each box, and then physically deliver the boxes or have them shipped in a secure way. These techniques work well if there are only a small number of sites or users, and if the sites are owned by the same enterprise (or at least within the same administrative domain). They also work for users in the same organization that want to exchange information securely, assuming those users can just meet to exchange keys.

However, manual techniques do not work well over public networks with unknown parties. That is where public-key cryptography, discussed next, comes into play.

Public Keys and Certificates

Public-key cryptography is an asymmetric-key technique in which users have two keys, one public and one private. Material encrypted with one key in the pair can be decrypted with the other, and vice versa. However, in most cases, it is computationally infeasible to encrypt large amounts of data with public/private keys. A symmetric key is much faster. Therefore, public-key cryptography is often used only to authenticate a remote user or server and to exchange a secret key (e.g., the sender encrypts a secret key with the recipient's public key).

Once this secret key is exchanged, all further application data is encrypted with the secret key, not the public/private key pairs.

Certificate authorities (CAs) usually manage public keys by verifying the owner and binding the key with information about the owner into a certificate. The certificate is signed with the CA's private key to provide integrity. Signing a certificate with a private key "locks" its contents. In addition, the CA's public key can be used to prove that the certificate was locked by the CA's private key, thus providing authenticity.

In the public-key scheme, the CA manages key distribution via certificates. If you need someone's public key in order to send them a private message, you obtain their certificate from their CA. Alternatively, you can have the person send you their certificate. But how do you know the certificate is authentic? The certificate authority signed it with its private key; therefore, you can verify it with the CA's public key.

RFC 1422 (Certificate-Based Key Management, February 1993) describes certificates and key management.

Another method for distributing keys is to extend the existing DNS (Domain Name System) so that it has a new record type to hold certificates.

In the IPSec scheme, the root certificate authority can be specified in the IPSec policy. This root CA is trusted by IKE, the Internet Key Exchange algorithm (discussed later). IKE can request that the root CA send certificates to other computers that wish to establish communications. Note that multiple root CAs may be specified, including CAs that are running on an enterprise network.

See "Public, Key Cryptography" for more details.

Diffie-Hellman Key Exchange

Whitfield Diffie and Martin Hellman published the first public-key algorithm in the 1970s. The algorithm is referred to as the Diffie-Hellman key exchange. It enables two parties to agree on a key that can be used to encrypt subsequent messages that are exchanged between the parties.

According to RFC 2631 (Diffie-Hellman Key Agreement Method, June 1999), "Diffie and Hellman describe a means for two parties to agree upon a shared secret in such a way that the secret will be unavailable to eavesdroppers. This secret may then be converted into cryptographic keying material for other (symmetric) algorithms."

The key exchange requires that both parties already have their own public/private key pairs. Each party then combines its private key with the other's public key to create a unique secret number that is the same for both parties, even though nothing of value has been exchanged between the parties that an eavesdropper could detect. The secret number is partially derived from each party's private key, which is never revealed. Next, the secret number is converted into a shared symmetric cryptographic key that can be used to encrypt all subsequent message exchanges between the parties.

IKE (Internet Key Exchange)

The IETF's IKE (Internet Key Exchange) protocol is an automatic security-negotiation and key-management service. IKE is used with the IPSec (IP Security) protocol by computers that need to negotiate *security associations* (SAs) with one another. An SA is a connection between two systems, established for the purpose of securing the packets transmitted across the connection. IPSec defines a variety of security features that can be applied to an SA, such as authentication of packet headers and/or encryption of entire packets (tunneling). IPSec is important for VPN deployment, although other protocols are available. See "IPSec (IP Security)."

IKE is considered a hybrid protocol for negotiating VPNs. It is defined in Internet RFC 2409, (The Internet Key Exchange, November 1998) and was created by combining techniques used in the following previously defined protocols:

■ **ISAKMP (Internet Security Association and Key Management Protocol)**   ISAKMP is defined in RFC 2408 (Internet Security Association and Key Management Protocol, November 1998), which provides a framework for authentication and key exchange without specifically defining such a framework. The protocol is key exchange independent, meaning it supports many different key exchange methods. Also see RFC 2407 (The Internet IP Security Domain of Interpretation for ISAKMP, November 1998).

■ **OAKLEY**   Two previously authenticated parties use this protocol to agree on keying methods such as "perfect forward secrecy for keys," "identity protection," and "authentication." Perfect forward secrecy means that keys used to protect data transmissions must not be used to create additional keys. The basic mechanism is the Diffie-Hellman key-exchange algorithm. OAKLEY is defined in RFC 2412 (The OAKLEY Key Determination Protocol, November 1998). Note that IKE does not implement the entire OAKLEY protocol, nor is it completely dependent on it.

■ **SKEME**   This is an IEEE-defined key-exchange technique that provides anonymity, reputability, and quick key refreshment. IKE does not implement the entire SKEME protocol, only its public-key encryption method—SKEME's concept of fast rekeying using an exchange of nonces (challenges).

Two computers that wish to establish communications use predefined keys, public keys, or symmetric keys to authenticate themselves. Once authenticated, a primary security association is set up and a master key is generated. Following that, sessions and session keys can be established between the systems. See "IPSec (IP Security)" for more on this topic. Note that the full IPSec topic is located at the Linktionary! Web site (http://www.linktionary.com/i/ipsec.html).

A related protocol called GKMP (Group Key Management Protocol) describes the ability to create and distribute keys within arbitrary-sized groups without the intervention of a global/centralized key manager. See RFC 2094 (Group Key Management Protocol Architecture, July 1997).

Key Recovery

Key recovery is usually part of a key-management scheme. If a key is lost, the data encrypted with that key may not be recoverable. Key recovery is an "emergency" method for gaining access to a key or to the data. Several key recovery methods are available. One that the government likes is *key escrow*. With this method, an encryption key is split into several pieces and the pieces are distributed to several trustees. If the key is needed to recover data, the trustees must all agree to combine their keys. A court order may be issued to obtain the key parts in the event of criminal activity.

Another method is session key escrow. A session is an exchange of data between two systems. The session may be encrypted with a one-time session key that is generated on the spot and never used again. To provide key recovery, the session key is encrypted with the public key of an escrow agency and forwarded to the escrow agency. The escrow agency has these keys to decrypt data if necessary.

While key recovery may be a responsible activity for organizations that want to monitor the activities of their employees, government involvement in key recovery concerns many citizen rights groups.

Related Entries   Authentication and Authorization; Certificate Systems; Cryptography; Digital Signatures; DSS (Digital Signature Standard); Hash Functions; IPSec (IP Security); Kerberos Authentication Protocol; One-Time Password Authentication; PKI (Public-Key Infrastructure); Public-Key Cryptography; Secret-Key Cryptography; Security; SKIP (Simple Key management for Internet Protocols); Token-Based Authentication; *and* VPN (Virtual Private Network)

Linktionary!—Tom Sheldon's Encyclopedia of Networking updates	http://www.linktionary.com/k/ key_exchange.html
VPNC (Virtual Private Network Consortium)	http://www.vpnc.org/
ICSA (International Computer Security Association) certifies IPSec products	http://www.icsa.net/
IBM Redbook: A Comprehensive Guide to Virtual Private Networks; Volume III: Cross-Platform Key and Policy Management	http://www.redbooks.ibm.com/abstracts/ sg245309.html
IETF Working Group: IP Security (ipsec)	http://www.ietf.org/html.charters/ ipsec-charter.html
NIST (National Institute of Standards and Technology)	http://csrc.nist.gov/
NIST Key Recovery page	http://csrc.nist.gov/keyrecovery/
Interesting Netscape paper discussing the mechanisms of public-key authentication and encryption	http://developer.netscape.com/tech/security/ ssl/howitworks.html

Key Encryption Methods

Key encryption technologies are used to encrypt and decrypt data. A key is a value that is used with cryptographic algorithms to encrypt some input (called *plaintext*). The output is called *ciphertext*. Given the same input and the same algorithm, a different key will produce different ciphertext. See "Cryptography," "Public-Key Cryptography," and "PKI (Public-Key Infrastructure)."

KeyNote Trust Management System

See Trust Relationships and Trust Management. Also see RFC 2704 (The KeyNote Trust-Management System Version 2, September 1999).

Key Telephone Systems

Often referred to as just KTS, a key telephone system is a premises telephone system that is best known by the phones that have buttons for calling inside an organization and for placing calls outside through the public telephone network. A key telephone system is in the same category as a PBX (private branch exchange), except that key systems rely on the telephone company switching equipment, while PBXs rely on a central control unit located at the customer site. In other words, with a key system, the dial tone is generated at the telephone company central office. A full PBX generates its own dial tones. Key systems also do not require dialing a number to gain an outside line since all lines are already directly connected to the telephone company central office. On a PBX system, lines are connected to the PBX, and the PBX makes connections to the central office when the outside number is dialed.

Related Entries   Centrex (CENTRal Exchange); PBX (Private Branch Exchange); Telecommunications and Telephone Systems; *and* Voice/Data Networking.

L2TP (Layer 2 Tunneling Protocol)

L2TP is a tunneling protocol that delivers PPP (point-to-point protocol) sessions across an ATM network, frame relay network, or the Internet.

L2TP can help reduce the cost of remote dial-up networking for users who normally dial into a corporate network over a long-distance connection. L2TP is often called a "virtual dial-up protocol" because it extends a dial-up PPP session across the Internet. Consider the traditional dial-up session without tunneling: a remote user in Los Angeles who needs to connect with the corporate network in New York dials the home office remote access telephone number. A dedicated circuit is created across the PSTN from L.A. to New York. Obviously, this is not a cost-effective way to access the corporate network. In addition, the long-distance call does not meet the digital requirements for V.90 modems, so the data rate is usually around 33 Kbits/sec or worse, not the 56 Kbits/sec rate that is possible with V.90 modems. See "Modems" for an explanation.

With L2TP, the remote user connects to the Internet via a local ISP or by using one of the national ISPs that have local dial-up numbers throughout the country. As shown in the following illustration, native PPP runs over the dial-up link between the user and the CO. An L2TP access concentrator (LAC) then virtually extends PPP across the Internet to an L2TP network server (LNS), which is located at the corporate network. This is where the PPP session officially terminates.

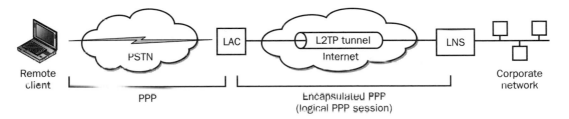

1. The client dials the ISP using an analog phone or ISDN. In this case, the client's computer is configured with PPP, although a client may also run L2TP directly.

2. When the call arrives at the ISP's LAC, the LAC performs a call check by contacting a RADIUS server. The RADIUS server responds with an accept or reject message. If accepted, the replay will also specify that an L2TP tunnel is needed.

3. The LAC creates a tunnel to the LNS at the client's corporate site. This is done by sending a message to UDP port 1701. An authentication procedure takes place between the LAC and the LNS.

4. A tunnel is set up and the client begins communicating with the corporate LCP using PPP. The client first sends PPP authentication information to the LCP, which in turn authenticates the client.

The client's PPP frames are encapsulated into IP packets with an L2TP tunneling header and sent across the Internet connection. The LCP strips off the L2TP header to access the PPP frames. Note that the LAC does not authenticate the client during the set-up phase, but it does check with RADIUS to make sure that the dial-up session is allowed. The client is authenticated by the corporate server, just as if he or she logged on from a node directly attached to that network.

L2TP is used by carriers to provide outsourcing services. The carrier establishes a pool of modems (usually in a RAC—remote access concentrator) and leases the modems to ISPs. Many ISPs want to establish a wider presence by expanding their coverage areas. Rather than building new PoPs in those areas, they can lease modems that exist in the carrier's CO. The carrier then forwards dial-up subscriber traffic to the ISP's PoP over L2TP tunnels. Redback Networks is one such vendor that makes equipment for doing this as shown in the following illustration. When a client dials in, an L2TP tunnel session is set up across a link to the smaller service provider or corporate site. The corporate end of the tunnel may be accessible across a variety of networks, include frame relay, ATM, or the Internet. The following illustrates a situation in which multiple smaller ISPs lease modems in a pool that exist at a carrier CO. L2TP tunnels exist between the carriers RAS server and the smaller service providers LNSs.

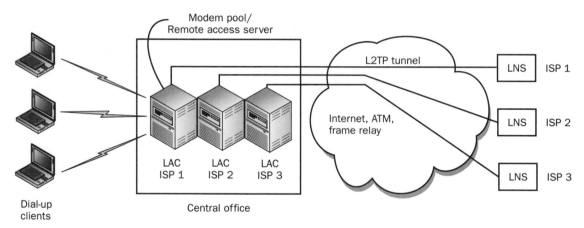

Keep in mind that PPP is a point-to-point protocol, meaning that it normally operates across a circuit with a termination point at both ends. L2TP extends the PPP session "virtually" across an IP network where it terminates at an NAS (network access server). The NAS is usually at the corporate network site to which the remote user wishes to connect. Because the PPP packets traverse the Internet, no long-distance charges are incurred. This allows the remote user to dial in to a local service provider network from any location and connect with the corporate network. The advantage for the corporate network is that PPP terminates at its site, not at the local carrier central office or ISP that the remote user initially dials into. This allows the enterprise to run its own RADIUS server, which provides AAA (authentication, authorization, and accounting).

L2TP is not quite a VPN (virtual private network) technology, although it is close. L2TP in its native form lacks the security of a true VPN. However, RFC 2888, "Secure Remote Access with L2TP" (August 2000), explains how L2TP can be combined with IPSec (IP Security) to create a secure environment.

PPTP (point-to-point tunneling protocol) is a Microsoft-developed protocol that provides virtual dial-up services similar to L2TP. L2TP was derived from PPTP features and features of an earlier Cisco protocol called L2F (Layer 2 Forwarding). L2TP supports TACACS+ and RADIUS authentication. PPTP does not. L2TP also supports more protocols than PPTP, including IPX, SNA, and others. Microsoft continues to support PPTP as a tunneling protocol for its Windows products, but L2TP is preferred over PPTP. IPSec is now the Internet standard for tunneling and secure VPNs. While L2TP is still used, IPSec is preferred when full VPN support is required. As mentioned, RFC 2888 describes how L2TP and IPSec can be used together.

The following RFCs describe L2TP:

- RFC 2661, "Layer Two Tunneling Protocol 'L2TP'" (August 1999)

- RFC 2809, "Implementation of L2TP Compulsory Tunneling via RADIUS" (April 2000)

- RFC 2888, "Secure Remote Access with L2TP" (August 2000)

- RFC 3070, "Layer Two Tunneling Protocol (L2TP) over Frame Relay" (February 2001)

Related Entries   Access Control; Authentication and Authorization; Communication Server; DIAMETER; IPSec (IP Security); Mobile Computing; Modems; MPLS (Multiprotocol Label Switching); NAS (Network Access Server); PPP (Point-to-Point Protocol); PPTP (Point-to-Point Tunneling Protocol); RADIUS (Remote Authentication Dial-In User Service); Remote Access; Roaming; Security; TACACS (Terminal Access Controller Access Control System); Tunnels; *and* VPN (Virtual Private Network)

Linktionary!–Tom Sheldon's Encyclopedia of Networking updates	http://www.linktionary.com/l/l2tp.html
Cisco documention: Access VPDN Dial-In Using L2TP	http://www.cisco.com/univercd/cc/td/doc/cisintwk/intsolns/l2tp/
Cisco paper: "Layer 2 Tunneling Protocol"	http://www.cisco.com/warp/public/cc/pd/iosw/prodlit/l2tun_ds.htm
IETF Working Group: Layer Two Tunneling Protocol Extensions (l2tpext)	http://www.ietf.org/html.charters/l2tpext-charter.html
Redback Networks	http://www.redbacknetworks.com
L2TPD open source implementation of L2TP	http://www.marko.net/l2tp/

Label Switching

Label switching is technique for overcoming the inefficiency of traditional layer 3 hop-by-hop routing. Labels are assigned to packets that allows network devices to forward packets in layer 2 at high speed. The label points to an entry in a forwarding table that specifies where the packet should be forwarded. This label switching technique is much faster than the traditional routing method where each packet is examined before a forwarding decision is made. According to RFC 2475 (An Architecture for Differentiated Services, December 1998):

Examples of the label switching (or virtual circuit) model include Frame Relay, ATM, and MPLS. In this model path forwarding state and traffic management or QoS state is established for traffic streams on each hop along a network path. Traffic aggregates of varying granularity are associated with a label switched path at an ingress node, and packets/cells within each label switched path are marked with a forwarding label that is used to lookup the next-hop node, the per-hop forwarding behavior, and the replacement label at each hop. This model permits finer granularity resource allocation to traffic streams, since label values are not globally significant but are only significant on a single link; therefore resources can be reserved for the aggregate of packets/cells received on a link with a particular label, and the label switching semantics govern the next-hop selection, allowing a traffic stream to follow a specially engineered path through the network.

A related topic is "Multilayer Switching," which discusses silicon-based wire-speed routing devices that examine not only layer 3 packet information, but also layer 4 (transport) and layer 7 (application) information.

Label switching is normally done within a specific network (autonomous system), such as a network service provider backbone. Large enterprise networks may also use the techniques to boost performance and take advantage of traffic engineering. Label switching uses layer 3 routing protocols to gather information about network routes and then build layer 2 forwarding tables from that information. Packets going into the network are given a label that maps them to a label switched path (LSP). An LSP may be engineered to provide traffic control and QoS.

The advantage of label switching for service providers is the ability to do traffic engineering and forward traffic across *explicit routes*. An explicit route is an LSP that has a defined path that provides minimal delay, guaranteed bandwidth, and one-hop routes to a specific destination.

The label switching network consists of *LSRs (label switching routers)*, some of which exist as edge devices. The ingress LSR looks up the packet's destination IP address in a routing table and assigns it an appropriate label. No further packet examination is required in the network since the label specifies a specific LSP. At the other end of the LSP, an egress LSR removes the labels and forwards the packets via traditional routing.

An LSP is a switched path, similar to a virtual circuit in the ATM or frame relay environment. LSPs work in one direction, so two LSPs are required to carry traffic in both directions between two endpoints. Label switching is also a form of tunneling in which a variety of protocol packets may be transmitted across the network.

An ingress LSR has the task of assigning a label to an incoming packet. The LSR assigns a label based on various criteria, such as the port the packet arrives on, its destination address, the type of applications, or the contents of the ToS (Type of Service) field in an IP header (Diff-Serv defines the ToS field).

In a conventional routing environment, routing protocols such as RIP and OSPF discover and distribute information about routes on an internetwork. This information is used to control the forwarding of packets. In a label switching network, LSRs are multilayer switching devices that run routing software and perform switching. The routing software accumulates information about layer 3 routes and uses this information to map those routes to labels. The information is then distributed to other LSRs, which use it to build label switched paths. Of course, administrators can explicitly define LSPs across the networks.

Several label switching techniques are outlined here.

■ **Topology-driven label assignment**   This is the method just discussed in which label assignments are derived from routing protocol information.

■ **Signaling/request/control-driven label assignment**   In this scheme, applications make a request to have a label assigned to a traffic flow. A signaling/control protocol makes the request and the LER responds by adding or changing entries in its forwarding table and assigning labels to those entries. There are two primary signaling models: CF-LDP (Constraint-Based Label Distribution Protocol) and RSVP-LSP (Resource Reservation Protocol-LSP). See "MPLS (Multiprotocol Label Switching)" for more information on these techniques.

■ **Traffic-driven label assignment**   In this scheme, label assignment and distribution is triggered by the arrival of data at an ingress LSR. This approach may be used to minimize the number of label assignments (i.e., there are relatively few flows and they are short-lived); but if the number of traffic flows grows too large, the overhead of assigning labels may overwhelm the network. High-performance packet-classification equipment will be necessary. A problem with this approach is that the network must detect a flow, but a flow may end before it can be detected.

A protocol called GSMP (General Switch Management Protocol) has been developed by the IETF that allows routers to control a label switch. GSMP provides an interface for switch configuration control and reporting, port management, connection control, QoS, and traffic engineering control, and the reporting of statistics and asynchronous events. More information is available at the GSMP Working Group site given later.

Related Entries   ARIS (Aggregate Route-Based IP Switching); ATM (Asynchronous Transfer Mode); Bandwidth Management; Congestion Control Mechanisms; Constraint-Based Routing; CSR (Cell-Switched Router), Toshiba; Cut-Through Routing; Differentiated Services (Diff-Serv); IP Navigator; IP over ATM; IP Switching, Ipsilon, Nokia; MPLS (Multiprotocol Label Switching); Multilayer Switching; Network Access Services; Network Core Technologies; Optical Networks; Prioritization of Network Traffic; QoS (Quality of Service); Switching and Switched Networks; Tag Switching; Traffic Management, Shaping, and Engineering; Tunnels; *and* VPN (Virtual Private Network)

Linktionary!—Tom Sheldon's Encyclopedia of Networking updates	http://www.linktionary.com/l/label_switching.html
IETF MPLS Working Group	http://www.ietf.org/html.charters/mpls-charter.html
Label switch, router control of. IETF Working Group: General Switch Management Protocol (gsmp)	http://www.ietf.org/html.charters/gsmp-charter.html
Multilayer routing page by Noritoshi Demizu	http://www.watersprings.org/links/mlr/
MPLS Forum	http://www.mplsforum.com/
TechFest multilayer switching page	http://www.techfest.com/networking/mlayer.htm

Lambda Circuits

A lambda circuit is an individual wavelength of light for transmitting data on a strand of fiber-optic cable. Using separate lasers, each tuned to a slightly different frequency, multiple lambdas can be projected down a single fiber strand to carry multiple streams of data.

DWDM (dense wavelength division multiplexing) is the technology for projecting multiple lambda circuits on fiber strands. Currently, 200 lambdas per fiber is common, but thousands are possible.

Lambda networking is essentially frequency division multiplexing in the light range with each lambda occupying a part of the light spectrum in the same way that radio and TV stations occupy a part of the radio spectrum. Think of each lambda as being a different color of light, each of which can carry many gigabits of data. Each lambda is separated by a guard band of a certain width. The better the tuning, the more lambdas per fiber.

Related Entries   Fiber-Optic Cable; Optical Networks; *and* WDM (Wavelength Division Multiplexing)

Linktionary!—Tom Sheldon's Encyclopedia of   http://www.linktionary.com/l/lambda.html
Networking updates

LAN (Local Area Network)

A LAN is a shared communication system to which many computers are attached. A LAN, as its name implies, is limited to a local area. This has to do more with the physical characteristics of the medium than the fact that many early LANs were designed for departments, although the latter accurately describes a LAN as well.

When is a network no longer a LAN? If you connect two LANs together via a router, you create an internetwork as shown in Figure L-1, although you still have two LANs. LANs are OSI layer 2 technologies. A router involves OSI layer 3. The LANs on each side of the router are distinct communication systems that contain their own broadcasts and addressing schemes. A router joins LANs and transmits packets between them based on a layer 3 addressing scheme (IP or IPX, for example), not the layer 2 addressing scheme used by individual LANs.

LANs began to appear in the early 1970s. They grew from earlier point-to-point connections where a single wire connected two systems. It made sense to let multiple computers share the same cable, but in doing so, an arbitration mechanism was needed to ensure that only one computer transmitted at once on the cable. Actually, the concept for Ethernet came out of a satellite communication system in which many devices shared the uplink.

Arbitration methods are called *medium access controls*. Some methods have each workstation determine whether the cable is in use. Other methods use a central controller that gives each station access in turn. See "MAC (Medium Access Control)."

LANs have different topologies, the most common being the *linear bus* and the *star configuration*. In the former, a cable snakes through a building from one workstation to another. In the star configuration, each workstation is connected to a central hub with its own cable. Each has its advantages and disadvantages. Interestingly, the most popular network, Ethernet, can be designed with a variety of topologies, although internally it still operates as a shared bus. See "Topology."

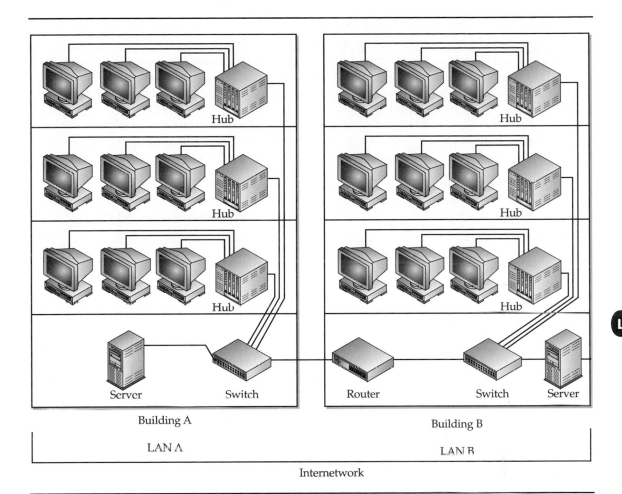

Figure L-1. *Two LANs joined via a router to create an internetwork*

Data is packaged into *frames* for transmission on the LAN. At the hardware level, each frame is transmitted as a bit stream on the wire. A frame is usually addressed for a single computer, although a *multicast address* can be used to transmit to all workstations on the LAN. Higher-layer protocols such as IP and IPX package data into datagrams that are capable of crossing router boundaries into other LANs. See "Network Architecture," "Framing in Data Transmissions," "Datagram and Datagram Services," and "Packets and Packet-Switching Networks" for more details.

LAN Distance and Size Limitations

One of the reasons why LANs are considered "local" is because there are practical limitations to the distance of a shared medium and the number of workstations you can connect to it. For example, if you tried to build a single LAN for an entire organization, there might be so many workstations attempting to access the cable at the same time that no real work would get done.

The electrical characteristics of the cable also dictate LAN limitations. Network designers must find a balance among the type of cable used, the transmission rates, and signal loss over distance. Coaxial cable allows higher transmission rates over longer distances, but twisted-pair wire is cheap and easy to install.

Delay is another factor. On Ethernet networks, workstations on either end of a long cable may not even detect that they are transmitting at the same time, thus causing a collision that results in corrupted data. You can use the following devices to extend a LAN or improve its performance:

- **Repeaters and repeater hubs**   Extends the distance limitations of Ethernet cable by boosting the signal. A repeater hub is a multiport device for building star-configured topologies with twisted-pair cable. See "Repeater" and "Ethernet" for details.

- **Bridges**   Provides repeater functions along with selective filtering of traffic to reduce congestion and contention. See "Bridges and Bridging" for details.

- **Switches**   Basically a multiport bridge that segments a network into many smaller collision domains while maintaining the broadcast characteristics. Greatly improves the performance of LANs. See "Switching and Switched Networks" and "VLAN (Virtual LAN)."

- **Routers**   As mentioned, these devices connect multiple LANs together to create internetworks. See "Internetworking" and "IP (Internet Protocol)" for more details. There are also layer 3 switching routers, as discussed under "Multilayer Switching."

As mentioned, see "Ethernet" for a more detailed discussion of the most popular LAN technology today. Also see "Fast Ethernet," "Gigabit Ethernet," and "Network Design and Construction." Other topics include "Token Ring Network" and "Wireless LANs." See "Network Concepts" for a list of network and LAN tutorial sites on the Web. RFC 2285 (Benchmarking Terminology for LAN Switching Devices, February 1998) outlined the terminology for LAN switching devices.

Related Entries   Access Method, Network; Addresses, Network; Backbone Networks; Bridges and Bridging; Broadcast; Broadcast Domain; Broadcast Networking; Cable and Wiring; Campus Network; Collisions and Collision Domains; Connection-Oriented and Connectionless Services; CSMA/CD (Carrier Sense Multiple Access/Collision Detection); Data Communication Concepts; Datagram and Datagram Services; Data Link Protocols; Ethernet; IEEE 802 Standards; MAC (Media Access Control); Network Architecture; Network Concepts; Network Connection Technologies; Network Design and Construction; Network Layer Protocols; Network Management; Network Operating Systems; NIC (Network Interface Card); OSI (Open Systems Interconnection) Model; Packets and Packet-Switching Networks; Peer-to-Peer Communication; Point-to-Point Communications; Reliable Data Delivery Services; Repeater; Routers; Routing; Servers; Switching and Switched Networks; TCP (Transmission Control Protocol); Thin Clients; TIA/EIA Structured Cabling Standards; Token Ring Network; Topology; Transport Protocols and Services; Virtual Circuit; VLAN (Virtual LAN); WAN (Wide Area Network); Wireless LANs; *and* Wireless PANs (Personal Area Networks)

Linktionary!—Tom Sheldon's Encyclopedia of Networking updates | http://www.linktionary.com/l/lan.html

IEEE 802 LAN/MAN Standards Committee | http://grouper.ieee.org/groups/802/

LAN Construction Set by Web 66 | http://web66.coled.umn.edu/Construction/

Cisco technology information | http://www.cisco.com/univercd/cc/td/doc/cisintwk/index.htm

Cisco Documentation: LAN Technologies Technical Tips | http://www.cisco.com/warp/public/473/

Cisco Documentation: Designing Switched LAN Internetworks | http://www.cisco.com/univercd/cc/td/doc/cisintwk/idg4/nd2012.htm

"LAN Troubleshooting and Baselining" by Wandel & Goltermann | http://download.wg.com/articles/pocketguide.pdf

"Native LAN Services" paper discusses stretching LANs across the WAN | http://www.larscom.com/whatnew/wp_nativeLAN.htm

Novell papers about LAN connectivity | http://developer.novell.com/research/topical/lan_wan_interconnectivity.htm

Links to LAN tutorial by Dwight Baker | http://www.wizard.com/users/baker/public_html/NetTutor.html

TechFest LAN links | http://www.techfest.com/networking/lan.htm

ITPRC.com (see Technologies section) | http://www.itprc.com/

See "Network Concepts" for an extensive set of links

LAN Drivers

A LAN driver is a workstation or server software module that provides an interface between a NIC (network interface card) and the upper-layer protocol software running in the computer. The driver is designed for a specific NIC. Drivers are usually installed during the initial installation of a network-compatible client or server operating system. The setup program asks which type of NIC is installed in the system and installs the appropriate driver. If the setup program does not have a driver, you are usually asked to insert a disk from the NIC manufacturer that contains a driver. The driver is then integrated into the protocol stack (or stacks) of the computer.

Figure L-2 illustrates where in the protocol stack the IEEE LAN drivers are located. The actual drivers are in the MAC (Medium Access Control) sublayer to the data link layer. The upper portion, called the LLC (Logical Link Control), provides a connection point for those drivers into the upper layers and acts as a software bus, delivering packets from upper layers to the appropriate LAN.

Novell and Microsoft have developed special interface support standards that let one or more interface cards work with one or more network protocols, Novell's standard is ODI (Open Data link Interface) and Microsoft's standard is NDIS (Network Device Interface

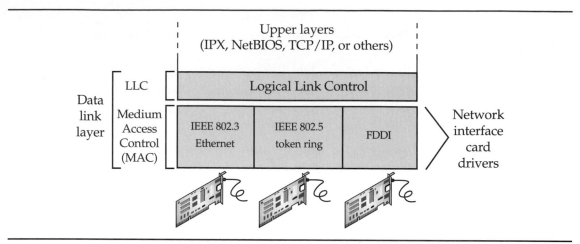

Figure L-2. *LAN drivers in relation to the protocol stack*

Specification). Both support multiple protocols on a single network and multiple network interface cards in a single machine.

Related Entries Access Method, Network; Addresses, Network; Data Link Protocols; LLC (Logical Link Control); MAC (Media Access Control); NDIS (Network Driver Interface Specification); Network Concepts; Network Connection Technologies; Network Operating System; NIC (Network Interface Card); *and* ODI (Open Data-link Interface)

LANE (LAN Emulation)

LANE was defined by the ATM Forum in 1995 as a way to allow legacy networks such as Ethernet, token ring, and FDDI to use an ATM network as backbone connection. In July of 1997, the ATM Forum ratified an enhanced LANE specification called LANE 2.0, which adds support for QoS and other necessary features.

Integrating ATM with legacy LANs is not easy. Keep in mind that ATM is a connection-oriented technology. It requires that virtual circuits exist between source and destination before any data can be sent. Data is transmitted in fixed-length cells. Legacy LANs transmit data in variable-length frames over a shared connectionless network.

What LANE does is automate SVC (switched virtual circuit) setup across ATM networks for LAN clients. Before LANE, administrators had to manually configure PVCs (permanent virtual circuits) between hosts.

Another thing LANE does is map MAC (Media Access Control) addresses to ATM addresses. It also defines a scheme for encapsulating higher-level protocol datagrams into ATM cells and delivering them across the ATM backbone. Since LANE emulates layer 2 protocols (data link layer), it can transport higher-layer protocols such as TCP/IP and SPX/IPX without modification. This allows existing LAN applications to be used without change. They don't need to know that the underlying network is cell based rather than frame based, or that it uses virtual connections rather than a connectionless scheme.

Since LANE operates in layer 2 (the MAC layer), it is limited to creating bridged networks (and not routed networks) over the ATM switching fabric. You can create multiple ELANs, but if you want clients in those ELANs to talk to each other, you'll need to implement external routers. This external router is often called the "one-armed router."

 LANE is covered in more detail at the Linktionary! Web site.

MPOA (Multiprotocol over ATM) is a related technology that provides inter-ELAN routing directly on the ATM network so that separate routers are not needed. MPOA adds a cut-through routing service that allows clients on different ELANs to connect with one another using the routes learned by the MPOA routing service. MPOA is derived from LANE. The problem with LANE is the requirement that traffic go through an external router when the underlying ATM network is fully capable of creating a direct connect between two devices connected to different VLANs. MPOA adds this capability. See "MPOA (Multiprotocol over ATM)."

Related Entries   ATM (Asynchronous Transfer Mode); IP over ATM; MPLS (Multiprotocol Label Switching); MPOA (Multiprotocol over ATM); *and* Multilayer Switching

Linktionary!— Tom Sheldon's Encyclopedia of Networking updates	http://www.linktionary.com/l/lane.html
The ATM Forum	http://www.atmforum.com
ATM Forum MPOA and LAN Emulation specifications and documents listing	http://www.atmforum.com/atmforum/specs/approved.html
3Com White Papers Index	http://www.3com.com/technology/tech_net/white_papers/index.html
LANE Working Group information at Anixter	http://www.anixter.com/techlib/whiteppr/network/d0504p10.htm
Video and Audio Streams Over an IP/ATM Wide Area Network, UBC TEVIA Project, June 1997	http://www.cs.ubc.ca/nest/dsg/tevia_files/techreport/node13.html
TechFest ATM links	http://www.techfest.com/networking/atm.htm

LAN Emulation

LAN emulation is a method of emulating the characteristics of a LAN over a switched ATM (Asynchronous Transfer Mode) network backbone. See "LANE (LAN Emulation)" for a continuation of this topic.

LAN Management

See Network Management.

LAN Manager, Microsoft

See Microsoft LAN Manager.

LAN Server, IBM

See IBM LAN Server; OS/2 Warp Server.

LAP (Link Access Procedure)

The LAP protocols are part of a group of data link layer protocols for framing and transmitting data across point-to-point links. LAP originates from IBM SDLC (Synchronous Data Link Control), which IBM submitted to the ISO for standardization. The ISO developed HDLC (High-level Data Link Control) from the protocol. Later, the CCITT (now referred to as the ITU) modified HDLC for use in its X.25 packet-switching network standard. It called the protocol LAP (Link Access Procedure), but later updated it and called it LAPB (LAP Balanced).

This section discusses LAPB and several derivatives of LAPB. You can also refer to "SDLC (Synchronous Data Link Control)" and "HDLC (High-level Data Link Control)" for additional information.

LAPB transmissions typically take place over physical point-to-point links. It is a full-duplex protocol, meaning that each station can send and receive commands and responses over separate channels to improve throughput. The protocol is bit oriented, meaning that the data is monitored bit by bit. Bit-oriented information in the LAPB frame defines the structure for delivering data and command/response messages between communicating systems. The frame format for LAPB is similar to the frame type for HDLC. Refer to that topic for more details.

As mentioned, LAPB is the data link protocol for X.25. Related LAP protocols for other data communication technologies are outlined next.

MLP (Multilink Procedure)   MLP is an extension of LAPB that allows for multiple physical links, thus providing better throughput. As shown in Figure L-3a, a device that has multiple LAPB links will implement MLP as an upper-layer management protocol to allocate frames to the links. MLP sees the multiple LAPB links as a pool of links for transmitting information from higher-layer protocols as frames. Higher-level software does not need to be aware that multiple links exist. The MLP layer handles distributing frames among the links, and thus gives upper layers full access to the links.

LAPM (Link Access Procedure for Modems)   This is the data link protocol used by V.32 error-correcting modems. When two LAPM modems establish a session, as pictured in Figure L-3b, they transmit data in frames using bit-oriented synchronous techniques. An attached computer still sends data to the LAPM modems as standard asynchronous input, but the modem transmits it as frames.

LAPD (Link Access Procedure D-Channel)   LAPD is the protocol used on ISDN's (Integrated Services Digital Network) D channel. Call setup and other signaling takes place on the D channel. Data transmissions take place on B channels. LAPD is the ITU Q.921 protocol.

LAPF (Link Access Procedure for Frame-Mode Bearer Services)   LAPF is designed for use with frame relay. It is similar to LAPD in its frame format except that there is no Control field in the frame. Thus, LAPF is used for carrying data only and there is no signaling at the data link layer for performing flow control and error control. End systems perform these functions in higher-layer protocols.

Related Entries   Data Communication Concepts; Data Link Protocols; Frame Relay; HDLC (High-level Data Link Control); ISDN (Integrated Services Digital Network); Modems; *and* SDLC (Synchronous Data Link Control)

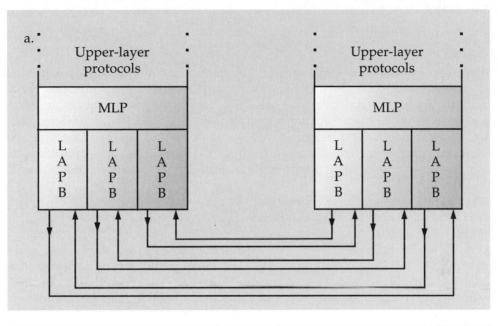

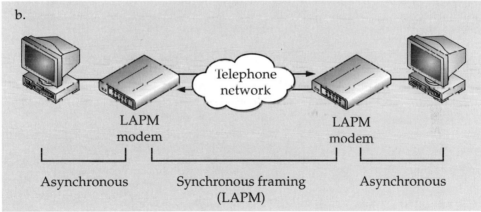

Figure L-3.   *LAP (Link Access Protocol) connection methods*

Linktionary!—Tom Sheldon's Encyclopedia of Networking updates   http://www.linktionary.com/l/lap.html

LAPB tutorial at Sangoma   http://www.sangoma.com/support_learning.cfm

Gory Fairhurst's HDLC protocol tutorial   http://www.erg.abdn.ac.uk/users/gorry/course/dl-pages/hdlc.html

HDLC Tutorial at RAD Data Communications   http://www.rad.com/networks/1994/hdlc/hdlc.htm

Asynchronous HDLC FAQ	http://ftp.uni-erlangen.de/pub/other/Documents/ ISO/async-HDLC

Last Mile Services

"Last mile" is a metaphor that refers to any of the communication links that connect homes and offices to carrier networks and the Internet. A variety of services can provide broadband data connectivity to carrier and service provider networks and the Internet. Broadband generally refers to services above 56 Kbits/sec (typical modem). The communication links may include cable (CATV), local loop twisted-pair cable, wireless systems, and fiber-optic systems. At the end of the last mile are homes, small businesses, apartment buildings, condominium projects, office buildings, and so on. Buildings with multiple occupants are often referred to as MTUs (multi-tenant units).

The "local loop" refers to the copper twisted-pair telephone wire that links the telephone company central office with homes and businesses. Local loop services are a subset of last mile services.

Besides dial-up lines, DSL is the only service that can provide a nonshared link all the way to the subscriber. This is because DSL runs on top of the twisted-pair telephone circuit. The subscriber gets all the bandwidth. DSL can be used as a shared link as well. For example, a DSL link may connect all the users in an apartment building to the central office and Internet.

Related Entries   Cable (CATV) Data Networks; Circuit-Switching Services; CO (Central Office); Communication Services and Providers; DBS (Direct Broadcast Satellite); DSL (Digital Subscriber Line); FTTH (Fiber To The Home); HALO (High Altitude Long Operation); Home Networking; ISDN (Integrated Services Digital Network); ISPs (Internet Service Providers); LMDS (Local Multipoint Distribution Service); Local Loop; Modems; Network Access Services; NPN (New Public Network); PON (Passive Optical Network); Residential Broadband; Satellite Communication Systems; Service Providers and Carriers; Telecommunications and Telephone Systems; Wireless Broadband Access Technologies; Wireless Communications; Wireless LANs; *and* Wireless Local Loop

Linktionary!—Tom Sheldon's Encyclopedia of Networking updates	http://www.linktionary.com/l/last_mile.html
The Last Mile channel at stardust.com	http://www.stardust.com/lastmile/
Cisco article describing last mile services	http://www.cisco.com/warp/public/784/ packet/lastmile.html
FSAN (Full Service Access Network) consortium	http://www.fsanet.net/

LATA (Local Access and Transport Area)

The RBOCs (Regional Bell Operating Companies), which are now more properly referred to as the ILECs (incumbent local exchange carriers), operate within specific geographical areas, which are divided into service areas called LATAs (local access and transport areas). LATAs were defined during the restructuring of AT&T in 1984, and there are close to 200 of them.

The carriers that handle services within a LATA are referred to as *LECs (local exchange carriers)*. ITOs (independent telephone companies) are non-incumbent telephone companies, some of which operate in areas where they compete with the RBOCs. Therefore, they are local exchange carriers that compete with the RBOCs and are called *competitive LECs* or

CLECs. See "Service Providers and Carriers" for a description of LECs, CLECs, and other types of service providers.

Services provided within a LATA are called *intra-LATA* services. Any service provided outside the LATA is an *inter-LATA* service, and these services are provided by *IXCs* *(interexchange carriers),* which include MCI Worldcom, US Sprint, and AT&T. All LECs must provide an access point into the LATA areas to interexchange carriers. This access point is called the *POP (point of presence).*

Note that the Telecommunications Reform Act of 1996 makes it possible for IXCs to offer services in local (intra-LATA) areas, and for the LECs and RBOCs to offer long-distance services. Consequently, a variety of network services are now available that disrupt the incumbent carriers, including cable access, wireless services, and fiber services to the home or office. As interest in VoIP (Voice over IP) has increased, many competing service providers emerged. Refer to "NPN (New Public Network)."

Related Entries   CO (Central Office); Communication Services and Providers; ISPs (Internet Service Providers); IXC (Interexchange Carrier); Local Loop; NPN (New Public Network); PoP (Point of Presence); PSTN (Public-Switched Telephone Network); RBOCs (Regional Bell Operating Companies); Service Providers and Carriers; Telecommunications and Telephone Systems; *and* Wireless Communications

Linktionary!—Tom Sheldon's Encyclopedia of Networking updates	http://www.linktionary.com/l/lata.html
LATA map of the United States at Robotics.net	http://www.robotics.net/clec/LATA_Map.html

Latency

According to RFC 1242 (Benchmarking Terminology for Network Interconnection Devices, July 1991), latency for store-and-forward devices is the time interval starting when the last bit of the input frame reaches the input port, and ending when the first bit of the output frame is seen on the output port. For bit-forwarding devices, latency is the time interval starting when the end of the first bit of the input frame reaches the input port, and ending when the start of the first bit of the output frame is seen on the output port. Variability of latency is called "jitter." See "Delay, Latency, and Jitter."

Layer 2/Layer 3/Layer 4 Switching

See Multilayer Switching; IP over ATM; *and* Label Switching.

Layered Architecture

See Network Architecture.

LDAP (Lightweight Directory Access Protocol)

LDAP is a client/server protocol for accessing information in network directories such as Novell Directory Services (NDS), Microsoft Active Directory, or directories that follow the X.500 standard. However, LDAP has everything you need to make a directory service, including an information model, a naming model, and an API. RFC 2251 (Lightweight Directory Access Protocol version 3, December 1997) defines the most recent version of LDAP.

Several other topics are related to LDAP, including "Directory Services," "Name Services," and "Service Advertising and Discovery."

A directory service is to a network what white pages and yellow pages are to the telephone system. Like the white pages, a directory service can be used to look up a person or object (file service, printer, etc.) by name. Like the yellow pages, a directory service can be used to look up someone or something by the type of service they offer or some description. A directory service is essentially a *lookup* database, although network administrators use it to keep track of and manage network users and network resources.

LDAP Operation

LDAP is based on a client/server model in which clients make queries to one or more LDAP-compatible directory servers. Servers respond to queries with an appropriate answer or with a pointer to another LDAP server that can handle the query. Client queries take the form of *operations* for adding, deleting, and modifying directory entries, or querying the directory database for information based on specific criteria. An LDAP API provides standard function calls that programmers can use to build LDAP applications.

LDAP has its roots in the OSI X.500 directory standard. The "lightweight" portion of its name comes from the fact that LDAP is a scaled-down version of an earlier protocol. LDAP was originally designed to work as a front-end client for X.500 directory services. A protocol called DAP (Directory Access Protocol) provides the interface for accessing these services. However, DAP requires the full OSI protocol stack, as well as lots of memory and processing power. LDAP is a stripped-down version of DAP that runs over the TCP transport protocol, bypassing the session and presentation layer functions required with X.500 DAP.

LDAP Information Model and Schemas

RFC 2251 describes the LDAP data or information model. LDAP assumes there are one or more servers providing access to a DIT (directory information tree). The tree has *entries* with unique distinguished names (DNs) that describe their exact location in the tree. These entries define people and real objects in the world such as computers, printers, mobile devices, and so on. Entries have *attributes* and *values*. Think of an entry like a record in a database. Attributes are the fields of the record (Name, Address, City, and so on), and values are the allowable values that can be entered into the fields. Values can be forced to conform to some syntax.

For example, RFC 2798 (Definition of the inetOrgPerson LDAP Object Class, April 2000) describes an LDAP entry for defining people who are associated with an organization in some way. Some of the defined attributes include display name, employee number, employee type, JPEG photograph, preferred language, vehicle identification, and so on.

While there are general guidelines for designing a directory tree, no two directories are likely to be exactly the same. Think about a business-to-business extranet connection between two companies. The companies want to share their directory information about the people and resources in their respective companies. But each organization has defined its own directory tree scheme (entries and attributes). What is needed is a scheme that defines the entries, attributes, and values of a particular directory and serves as a map to the tree so that clients and applications know how to access the tree. The schema serves as a key to joining different directories.

With LDAP version 3, an LDAP-compliant directory server has a way to exchange its schema information with other LDAP servers or clients. RFC 2252 (LADPv3 Attributes, December 1997) defines a framework for developing schemas. RFC 2256 (A Summary of the

X.500(96) User Schema for use with LDAPv3) provides an overview of the attribute types and object classes defined by the ISO and ITU-T committees for use by directory clients.

LDAP Developments

As mentioned, RFC 2251 describes the latest version of LDAP, LDAP version 3. Earlier descriptions appear in RFC 1777 (Lightweight Directory Access Protocol, March 1995). RFC 1617 (Naming and Structuring Guidelines for X.500 Directory Pilots, May 1994) is slightly dated, but provides guidelines for planning a directory structure. A complete list of related RFCs may be found at the Linktionary! Web site.

The features and services provided in LDAP 3.0 include all the features of LDAP version 2 as defined in RFC 1777 and the following:

- Allows interdirectory server-to-server updates between X.500 and non-X.500 directories.

- Directory servers may refer clients to other directory servers. This allows a server to offload the work, rather than going to the other server itself, getting the information, and then passing it back to the client.

- Supports replication of data from server to server via LDAP Data Interchange Format (LDIF), an import/export facility that represents directory information in a text format.

- Has a more extensive security model that supports new Internet security standards such as TLS (Transport Layer Security).

- A directory's schema information (which defines how directory entries represent real-world objects) may be communicated to clients.

RFC 2589 (Lightweight Directory Access Protocol (v3): Extensions for Dynamic Directory Services, May 1999) describes new techniques that LDAP can use to deal with short-term directory information. There are *static directories* that contain information that "persists" over a long period of time and there are *dynamic directories* that contain short-term information that must be periodically refreshed or removed after a time-out period. For example, when a remote client logs on, information about that client is dynamically entered into the directory. This information is periodically updated until the client logs off, then disappears after a time-out period. RFC 2589 defines how to deal with this information.

An important concept for any directory service is to make the information available to all users on a network. Replication can make information more readily available to remote users and provide fault tolerance. An IETF working group called LDAP Duplication/Replication/Update Protocols (ldup) is standardizing the following replication methods:

- **Multi-master replication**   A replication model that allows changes to any replica without first notifying the other replicas.

- **Master-slave, or single-master replication**   A replication model in which there is one master directory and one or more slaves. The master control writes on the replicated data.

Another IETF working group called LDAP Extension (ldapext) is working on a number of LDAP extensions, including the ability of LDAP servers to create a sorted scrollable list of search results for clients, methods for LDAP clients to discover LDAP servers, the ability to carry LDAP over UDP (rather than TCP), improved language control, and the ability to sign directory information for security reasons.

There are two free LDAP server implementations listed at the end of this topic. One is available from the University of Michigan and the other is available from Critical Angle. These servers are stripped down and do not require the overhead typically required by a full X.500 service.

The Directory Interoperability Forum was formed to advance open directories based on LDAP standards. The forum is a group of open directory providers who plan to work through standards bodies to accelerate the evolution and adoption of directory-based applications.

Eventually, the Internet may have a global directory with a standard schema. Until then, the LDAP-compatible directory systems developed by Novell, Microsoft, and others will continue to serve users.

Related Entries   CIP (Common Indexing Protocol); CNRP (Common Name Resolution Protocol); DEN (Directory Enabled Networks); Directory Services; Handle System; Metadata; Microsoft Active Directory; Name Services; NDS (Novell Directory Services); NIS (Network Information System); Search and Discovery Services; Service Advertising and Discovery; SLP (Service Location Protocol); URI (Uniform Resource Identifier); URN (Uniform Resource Name); WebDAV; *and* X.500 Directory Services

Linktionary!—Tom Sheldon's Encyclopedia of Networking updates	http://www.linktionary.com/l/ldap,html
The Directory Interoperability Forum	http://www.opengroup.org/directory/
Complete list of directory services and LDAP RFCs	http://olymp.wu-wien.ac.at/manuals/rfc-ldap.html
LDAP Duplication/Replication/Update Protocols (ldup)	http://www.ietf.org/html.charters/ldup-charter.html
LDAP Extension (ldapext)	http://www.ietf.org/html.charters/ldapext-charter.html
University of Michigan LDAP pages and sldap server software	http://www.umich.edu/~dirsvcs/ldap/ldap.html
OpenLDAP, community-developed (open source) LDAP software	http://www.openldap.org/
IBM Redbooks, Understanding LDAP	http://www.redbooks.ibm.com/abstracts/sg244986.html
Google Web Directory: LDAP	http://directory.google.com/Top/Computers/Software/Internet/Servers/Directory/LDAP/

See "Directory Services" for additional links.

LDP (Label Distribution Protocol)

LDP (Label Distribution Protocol) is a protocol used in MPLS (Multiprotocol Label Switching) environments by LSR (Label Switching Routers) to inform other LSRs of the label assignment they have made. LDP allows LSRs to agree with one another on the meaning of labels so that one device knows which label to use in order to forward traffic through another device. RFC 3036 (LDP Specification, January 2001) and RFC 3037 (LDP Applicability, January 2001) describe LDP. Refer to "MPLS (Multiprotocol Label Switching)" for more information.

Learning Bridges

A bridge is a device that joins networks to create a much larger network. Both networks retain the same network addressing scheme, and broadcasts on one network will propagate across the bridge if the address of a frame matches the address of a workstation on the other side of the bridge. A learning bridge, also called an *adaptive bridge*, "learns" which network addresses are on one side of the bridge and which are on the other so it knows how to forward packets it receives. See "Bridges and Bridging."

Leased Line

A leased line is a permanent or switched communication circuit between a customer site and a service provider's wide area network, or between two sites owned by a customer (a private line). Leased lines almost always refer to carrier-based TDM circuits, although, in general, any communication link with monthly fee could be called a leased line. This topic discusses carrier TDM circuits.

Local and long-distance carriers provide leased lines to organizations for a fixed monthly fee. The bandwidth on the lines is fixed, and since they typically use time division multiplexing, the latency is bounded, which is good for supporting real-time voice and video. An organization can install leased lines between its remote sites to support intracompany phone calls and data transmissions. Multiplexers are used to carry voice and data over leased lines.

Leased lines are the traditional method for building WANs (wide area networks). Since they provide dedicated always-on service, they are often called *dedicated private lines*. Wide area networks built with leased lines are often called *private WANs*. A leased line is one option for organizations that need to connect distant sites across public areas. Other alternatives include wireless radio and optical point-to-point systems for metropolitan areas, or satellite links for longer distances. See "Communication Services and Providers" for an overview of alternative services.

The most-often-used high-speed digital line service is the *T1 circuit*, which provides transmission rates of 1.544 Mbits/sec. A T1 line can provide 24 channels for voice or data at 64-Kbit/sec bandwidth each. Customers who don't need the full T1 bandwidth can opt for fractional T1, which provides digital services in increments of 64 Kbits/sec. Multiple T1 lines can be aggregated as described under "Inverse Multiplexing" and "Link Aggregation." Another circuit-based service is ISDN (Integrated Services Digital Network), which provides the equivalent of switched leased-line services starting in increments of 64 Kbits/sec. See "ISDN (Integrated Services Digital Network)" for more information.

For a continuation of this topic and a further description of leased lines, see "TDM Networks." A related topic is "WAN (Wide Area Network)."

Related Entries   Bandwidth on Demand; Bandwidth Reservation; Bonding; Circuit; Circuit-Switching Services; Communication Service Providers; CSU/DSU (Channel Service Unit/Data Service Unit); Data Communication Concepts; DDR (Dial-on-Demand Routing); Dial-Up Line; DSL (Digital Subscriber Line); E Carrier; IADs (Integrated Access Devices); IMA (Inverse Multiplexing over ATM); Leased Line; Link Aggregation; Load Balancing; Local Loop; MAN (Metropolitan Area Network); MLPPP (Multilink PPP); Multiplexing and Multiplexers; NADH (North American Digital Hierarchy); Network Access Services; Packets and Packet-Switching Networks; Point-to-Point Communications; Service Providers and Carriers; SONET (Synchronous Optical Network); T Carrier; Telecommunications and Telephone Systems; Voice over IP (VoIP); VPNs (Virtual Private Networks); *and* WAN (Wide Area Network)

Linktionary!—Tom Sheldon's *Encyclopedia of Networking* updates

http://www.linktionary.com/l/leased_line.html

LEC (LAN Emulation Client)

See LANE (LAN Emulation).

LEC (Local Exchange Carrier)

A LEC is a telephone company that operates within a local area called the LATA (local access and transport area). The ILECs (incumbent LECs) are the result of the breakup of AT&T in 1984, which created seven independent RBOCs (Regional Bell Operating Companies) in the U.S. These included Pacific Bell, NYNEX, GTE, and others, but mergers and consolidations have changed the original gang of seven to a few larger companies that are now more appropriately called ILECs, rather than RBOCs. Most ILECs operate across a number of LATAs.

The CAPs (competitive access providers) and CLECs (competitive LECs) compete with the ILECs in the same service areas. Any non-incumbent carrier is called an ITC (independent telephone company), but some ITCs operate in areas where they do not compete with ILECs.

The IXCs (interexchange carriers) provide inter-LATA service (basically, long-distance service). Common IXCs are AT&T and MCI Worldcom. More recently, the CLECs are morphing into what are called *ICPs (integrated communications providers)*, which provide a variety of "new public network" services, including Web hosting and Internet access. Another acronym is BLEC (broadband LEC).

Refer to "Service Providers and Carriers" for a more complete discussion of these service providers.

Linktionary!—Tom Sheldon's Encyclopedia of Networking updates

http://www.linktionary.com/l/lec.html

LECS (LAN Emulation Configuration Server)

See LANE (LAN Emulation).

Legacy Systems

Legacy systems are computer systems that a company already has in place and must maintain even though new computing technologies are available and being installed. There is usually a need to maintain backward compatibility with or connections to legacy systems. Originally, the term "legacy system" was used to refer to existing mainframe systems, but now the term is used more widely. For example, you'll often hear about legacy networks (e.g., coaxial cable Ethernet), legacy databases (i.e., databases that hold historical information), and legacy software. Legacy software must be maintained because it is often the only way to access legacy databases.

LEO (Low Earth Orbit) Satellite

Satellite systems are employed for telephone and data communications. There are geostationary satellites flying in high orbit (22,000 miles) where they can maintain the same position above the earth's surface at all times. The only problem, with such high-flying satellites is that there is a noticeable delay in real-time communications, and the power requirements to communicate with the satellites is too high for portable devices.

LEOs are more practical for mobile communication devices like mobile phones, PDAs, and automobile communication systems. An LEO satellite orbits in a relatively low earth orbit of a few hundred miles. In this orbit, the round-trip time for transmission is minimal, as are the power requirements for earth-bound communication devices. The downside of LEO satellites is that a fleet of them is required. Because of their low orbit, they move faster relative to a point on the surface, so a fleet of LEO satellites is required to maintain communications over a single point. As one LEO moves out of position, the other moves in. Each satellite covers an area that could be compared to a cell in a cellular system, except that the cell moves as the satellite orbits.

See "Satellite Communication Systems" for more information.

 Linktionary!—Tom Sheldon's Encyclopedia of Networking updates   http://www.linktionary.com/s/satellite.html

LES (LAN Emulation Server)

See LANE (LAN Emulation).

Licensing, Electronic

Electronic software licensing provides automatic tracking of software usage to ensure that an organization stays within its software licensing requirements and legal boundaries for software usage.

A typical licensing package holds keys that allow users to access software applications. Each key is a license that has been purchased from the software vendor. The licensing program delivers keys to users who request the use of an application. When all the keys are in use, other users can't access applications until a key becomes available or more keys are added. Licensing programs usually include controls that prevent unauthorized users from accessing programs or prevent users from holding a key for too long.

See "Electronic Software Distribution and Licensing."

Line Conditioning

Line conditioning is a technique to improve the quality of electrical or communication links. Several line-conditioning methods are described below:

- *Electrical power conditioning* equipment is designed to smooth out problems with electrical power that can damage sensitive computer equipment. Power problems that are conditioned include surges, spikes, and transients, as well as hum caused by neutral-to-ground connections. Battery backups can protect against drops in power that cause sags (brownouts). See "Power and Grounding Problems and Solutions."

- *Line conditioning* is also something that the telephone company will do when you lease high-speed services such as T1. The CSU (channel service unit) installed at customer sites also provides its own line conditioning functions in the form of equalization functions and signal regeneration.

■ *Line conditioners* are also available for modem connections. These line conditioners can help improve problems with the local loop, such as ambient line noise that reduces throughput. If the line is free of noise, a modem can operate at its full potential. Line conditioners of this sort provide impedance matching, which can reduce the reflections that are generated by electrical signals as they travel across the local loop. They also balance the electrical current that flows between sites to reduce analog ambient line noise and keep signal frequencies strong to reduce circuit loss and increase line quality.

■ *Repeaters,* such as those used to extend Ethernet networks are a form of line conditioner. They reamplify attenuated signals and perform other functions that condition the signal.

Related Entries   DSL (Digital Subscriber Line); ISDN (Integrated Services Digital Network); Local Loop; Modems; Power and Grounding Problems and Solutions; *and* T Carrier

Linktionary!—Tom Sheldon's Encyclopedia of Networking updates	http://www.linktionary.com/l/line_conditioning.html
"Expecting 56k (V.90/X2/K56)?" (describes phone line problems)	http://www.hal-pc.org/~wdg/56k.html

Link Aggregation

Link aggregation is the bonding together of two or more data channels into a single channel that appears as a single, higher-bandwidth logical link. Aggregated links also provide redundancy and fault tolerance if each of the aggregated links follows a different physical path. Link aggregation may be used to improve access to public networks by aggregating modem links or digital lines. Link aggregation may also be used in the enterprise network to build multigigabit backbone links between Gigabit Ethernet switches.

Link aggregation is sometimes referred to as load balancing since traffic loads are distributed across multiple links. However, this book refers to load balancing as a data center technique in which incoming requests from clients are distributed to two or more servers. See "Load Balancing." This topic is about balancing network traffic loads across multiple communication links.

Aggregation is sometimes called *inverse multiplexing* or *IMUX*. If multiplexing is the aggregation of multiple low-speed channels into a single high-speed link, then inverse multiplexing is the "spreading" of data across multiple links. It allows for the configuration of fractional bandwidth on an incremental scale to meet bandwidth requirements. Link Aggregation is also called *trunking*.

Bandwidth on demand or *bonding* refers to the ability to add lines to increase bandwidth as needed. In this scheme, the line is connected automatically as the bandwidth needs require it. Aggregation is common with ISDN connections. The basic rate interface supports two 64Kbits/ sec links. One may be used for phone calls while the other is simultaneously used for data. The two may be bonded to create a 128-Kbits/sec data link.

Link aggregation for dial-up lines is now relatively simple. Desktop operating systems such as Microsoft Windows support MLPPP (Multi-Link PPP), which is a protocol for bonding together multiple dial-up links running PPP (Point-to-Point Protocol). See "MLPPP (Multilink PPP)."

Multilink router connections over WAN links are possible with protocols such as Cisco's Distributed MLPPP protocol. The protocol provides a way to combine T1/E1 lines on a Cisco 7500 series router into a bundle that has the combined bandwidth of multiple T1/E1 lines. The protocol allows some increment of T1/E1 to be installed. For example, a "bundle" could contain four T1 lines. The protocol is geared toward ISPs.

Multiple links can be configured for backup purposes or to obtain more temporary bandwidth. The alternate links should follow different paths to guard against local disasters. For example, links could come into the building in different locations, across different local loops and even different carriers. However, aggregation may not be possible if the same equipment is being used at all ends.

VRRP (Virtual Router Redundancy Protocol) is a protocol that allows several routers on a multiaccess link to utilize the same virtual IP address. One router will be elected as a master, with the other routers acting as backups in case of the failure of the master router. With VRRP, several routers share a virtual IP and MAC address. VRRP lets routers automatically route around failures, ensuring uninterrupted net operations. See "VRRP (Virtual Router Redundancy Protocol)."

Link aggregation is considered a traffic-engineering technique that can reduce congestion and allocate additional resources when necessary. Efficient traffic engineering reduces packet loss and transit delays and, therefore, improves overall throughput. The link aggregation techniques discussed next involve adding physical network links. Another form of aggregation is to create redundant virtual links through large mesh networks, as is done in ATM and MPLS networks. For example, PNNI (Private Network-to-Network Interface) is a layer 2 routing protocol for ATM networks for adding aggregated links between ATM switches.

Link Aggregation in the Enterprise Network

Enterprise link aggregation techniques allow trunking in Ethernet networks. Administrators will be able to combine multiple Ethernet channels between switches, or between switches and servers. For example, four Fast Ethernet lines could be connected between a switch and a server to provide combined throughput of up to 400 Mbits/sec. All of the links then appear as a single logical link. The links also provide redundancy and protection against failure. Several link aggregation techniques are outlined here.

■ **IEEE 802.3 Link Aggregation Standard**   The IEEE 802.3ad Working Group is developing a link aggregation protocol that will provide a standard aggregation technique that vendors can use to create interoperable aggregation products. The IEEE points out that it prefers to use the term *link aggregation* rather than *trunking*. 802.3ad uses LACP (Link Aggregation Control Protocol) to manage the link configuration and then distribute loads among the links. Management functions include adding new links, removing links, and diverting traffic when a link fails. The standard provides link identification, status monitoring, and synchronization across the links.

■ **ALB (Adaptive Load Balancing)**   Intel developed ALB to meet the throughput requirements in bandwidth-intensive environments. With ALB, four 100-Mbit/sec Ethernet channels can be combined into a single 400-Mbit/sec channel between a switch and a server. The cards are installed in a server and configured to work together as a "team" under ALB. All of the adapters are wired to a single switch. ALB assigns the entire team a single network address. The ALB software drivers include an intelligent, adaptive agent that distributes the data traffic evenly among the links by dynamically analyzing the traffic flow from the server.

- **Cisco Fast EtherChannel**   Fast EtherChannel (FEC) is a trunking technology developed by Cisco that balances links in the network backbone of campus environments. It groups together from two to four full-duplex Fast Ethernet channels to provide fault-tolerant high-speed links among switches, routers, and servers. Bandwidth is scalable in increments of 200 Mbits/sec up to 800 Mbits/sec for Fast Ethernet. With Gigabit Ethernet, Fast EtherChannel will scale up to multigigabit capacity. Fast EtherChannel is similar to Intel's ALB (Adaptive Load Balacing). Fast EtherChannel handles the task of load balancing traffic across the multiple links. Load balancing evenly distributes traffic across redundant parallel paths. If any one link fails, the other links automatically take up the balance of the load without interruption. Fast EtherChannel load balancing is integrated with the Cisco Catalyst 5000 family's LAN switch architectures.

Related Entries   Anycasting; Bandwidth Management; Bandwidth on Demand; Congestion Control Mechanisms; Data Center Design; DDR (Dial-on-Demand Routing); Ethernet; Fast Ethernet; Gigabit Ethernet; Inverse Multiplexing; Load Balancing; MLPPP (Multilink PPP); Network Concepts; Network Connection Technologies; Network Design and Construction; Serial Communication and Interfaces; Switching and Switched Networks; Throughput; Traffic Management, Shaping, and Engineering; *and* WAN (Wide Area Network)

Linktionary!—Tom Sheldon's Encyclopedia of Networking updates	http://www.linktionary.com/l/link_aggregation.html
IEEE P802.3ad Link Aggregation Task Force	http://grouper.ieee.org/groups/802/3/ad/index.html
3Com Link Aggregation and Support for IEEE 802.3ad	http://www.3com.com/technology/tech_net/white_papers/500666.html
Cisco document: Distributed Multilink PPP for Cisco Routers	http://www.cisco.com/univercd/cc/td/doc/product/software/ios120/120newft/120t/120t7/mlppp7.htm
Cisco Fast EtherChannel	http://www.cisco.com/warp/public/cc/techno/media/lan/ether/channel/index.shtml
Bitpipe.com (search for "link aggregation")	http://www.bitpipe.com

Link-State Routing

Routing protocols discover routes on interconnected networks and build routing tables that provide routers with packet-forwarding information. *Dynamic routing protocols* (as opposed to manually configured static routing) automatically discover routes and create routing tables without operator intervention. Since network topologies are subject to change at any time (a link may fail), dynamic protocols are essential for routing around failed links in large internetworks.

Routing protocols may use *distance-vector routing* or *link-state* algorithms (also called *shortest path first* or *SPF* algorithms). Distance-vector routing can best be described as forwarding packets by getting directions along the way. Link-state routing is a better technique for larger networks. Routers use it to build a topological database that describes routes on the entire internetwork.

This information is used to build routing tables with more accurate routing information. Link-state routing also responds faster to changes in the network. Link-state routing is now the preferred routing method for most organizations and Internet service providers.

The most common link-state routing protocol is OSPF (Open Shortest Path First). Other link-state protocols include IS-IS (Intermediate System to Intermediate System), an OSI protocol, and Novell's NLSP (NetWare Link Services Protocol). Distance-vector routing includes RIP (Routing Information Protocol), Cisco's IGRP (Internet Gateway Routing Protocol), and Apple's RTMP (Routing Table Maintenance Protocol).

OSPF is an internal routing protocol used within autonomous systems, such as service provider networks, universities, and private companies. Exterior routing protocols operate between autonomous systems. BGP (Border Gateway Protocol) is an exterior routing protocol.

The most important concept for link-state routing is that routers gather information about routes over the entire network. Link-state routers gather this information from neighbors and pass it on to other neighbors. Eventually, all the routers have information about all the links on the network. Then, each router runs the *Dijkstra shortest path algorithm* to calculate the best path to each network and create routing tables.

As mentioned, link-state routing responds faster to broken links or the addition of links. Routes can be based on the avoidance of congested areas, the speed of a line, the cost of using a line, or various priorities. OSPF (Open Shortest Path First) is the most common routing protocol to use the link-state algorithm. Refer to the OSPF topic for more details about the operation of link-state routing.

Related Entries Distance-Vector Routing; IP (Internet Protocol); IS-IS (Intermediate System-to-Intermediate System) Routing; NLSP (NetWare Link Services Protocol); OSPF (Open Shortest Path First); Routing; Routers; Routing on the Internet; *and* VRRP (Virtual Router Redundancy Protocol)

 Linktionary!—Tom Sheldon's Encyclopedia   http://www.linktionary.com/l/link_state_routing.html of Networking updates

Linux

Linux is a UNIX-like 32-bit operating system that runs on a variety of platforms, including Intel, SPARC, PowerPC, and DEC Alpha processors, as well as multiprocessing systems. The operating system is essentially free and you can download it from the Web. You can buy fully supported commercial versions from Red Hat, Caldera Systems, and other companies.

Linux is a "user-developed" product, meaning that many of its components and drivers have been developed by users around the world who ran the operating system for their own use. The original operating system was developed by Linus Torvalds as a college project. It is now well supported and gaining ground as a respectable operating system despite its homegrown roots. The operating system is used by many Web site developers and is now available as an embedded system, either as a small software kernel or burned into a chip.

Anyone planning to use Linux for production use should first make sure that the applications they need to use run on the operating system, and that appropriate drivers are available to support hardware and software. You can check the Web site given later for more information. Here are some basic Linux facts:

- Linux distribution is governed by the *GNU Public License,* which states that distributors can charge for the operating system so long as the source code is included.
- Linux is a full 32-bit cross-platform operating system. A 64-bit kernel that supports SMP (symmetrical multiprocessing) is also available for advanced processors such as the Compaq/DEC Alpha and the Sun UltraSparc.
- The operating system supports TCP/IP networking and Internet protocols, as well as Java. It is well suited for use as an Internet server and an Internet firewall.
- Linux conforms to standards for UNIX-like operating systems. It combines features of UNIX System Five and Berkeley System Distribution (BSD). See "UNIX" for a further description of features available in Linux.
- Programs intended for the SCO and SVR4 UNIX systems will run unaltered. Literally thousands of programs are ready to run for Linux. With Java support, that number grows even bigger.
- Documentation is provided as HOWTO files, which are written by users and developers and are freely available at some of the Web sites given later.

On the Web, Linux is one of the most well-documented and talked-about products around. You can visit many different sites for more information about the latest releases of Linux and programs written for Linux. Linux International (LI) is a nonprofit association that promotes the growth of Linux. The LI Web site has historical information, Linux resources, links, mailing lists, documentation, FAQs (Frequently Asked Questions), and other information.

Distributors such as Red Hat, Caldera, Walnut Creek, and WorkGroup Solutions bundle the basic Linux kernel with additional utilities and product support. Some of the versions are quite sophisticated and include cross-platform utilities that interoperate with other operating systems. Here is a list of Linux distributors:

Caldera Systems	http://www.caldera.com/
Corel Corp.	http://linux.corel.com/
Debian (based on Linux kernel)	http://www.debian.org/
MandrakeSoft, Inc., Linux Mandrake	http://www.linux-mandrake.com/en/
Red Hat, Inc.	http://www.redhat.com/
The Slackware Linux Project	http://slackware.com/
SuSE, Inc.	http://www.suse.com
WorkGroup Solutions, Inc.	http://www.wgs.com/

Neoware's NeoLinux is an embedded Linux distribution that is specifically designed for network appliances. The embedded operating system is based on Official Red Hat Linux and is meant for use in cash registers, firewalls, routers, interactive Web kiosks, thin clients, security devices, and wireless appliances. Refer to http://www.neoware.com.

Related Entries   CDE (Common Desktop Environment); DCE (Distributed Computing Environment); Embedded Systems; File Server; File Sharing; File Systems; Motif; Multiprocessing; Network Appliances;

Network Operating Systems; NFS (Network File System); Open Group; Open Source Software; Servers; Thin Clients; UNIX; UNIX File System; *and* X Window

Linktionary!—Tom Sheldon's Encyclopedia of Networking updates	http://www.linktionary.com/l/linux.html
Linux Online	http://www.linux.org/
Linux International (LI)	http://li.org/
Linux KernelNotes.org	http://www.kernelnotes.org/
GNU's Not Unix!	http://www.gnu.org/
The Linux Professional Institute (Certification for the Linux Community)	http://www.lpi.org/
Linux Documentation Project	http://www.linuxdoc.org/
LinuxWorld On-line Magazine	http://www.linuxworld.com/
Linux Today	http://linuxtoday.com/
Linux Weekly News	http://www.lwn.net/
Linux Links at Netfusion	http://www.nwfusion.com/netresources/linux.html
VA Linux Systems	http://www.valinux.com/

See "UNIX" for related links.

LISTSERV

LISTSERV is the name of a mailing list product sold by L-Soft International, Inc., that has its roots in the original mailing list server product created by Eric Thomas in 1986. Refer to the heading "Mailing List Programs" for a discussion of this topic.

LLC (Logical Link Control)

The LLC is part of the data link layer in a protocol stack. The data link layer controls access to the network medium and defines how upper-layer data in the form of packets or datagrams is inserted into *frames* for delivery on a particular network. The underlying physical layer then transmits the framed data as a stream of bits on the network medium.

The IEEE 802.2 standard defines LLC, which is positioned in the protocol stack as pictured in Figure L-4. Note that LLC resides on the upper half of the data link layer. The MAC (Medium Access Control) sublayer is where individual shared LAN technologies such as Ethernet are defined. Early on, the data link layer contained only LLC-like protocols; but when shared LANs came along, the IEEE positioned the MAC sublayer into the lower half of the data link layer.

Basically, LLC provides a common interface, and provides reliability and flow-control features. It is a subclass of HDLC (High-level Data Link Control), which is used on wide area links. LLC can provide both connection-oriented and connectionless services.

The LLC acts like a software bus, allowing multiple higher-layer protocols to access one or more lower-layer networks. For example, a server may have multiple network interface cards (and an Ethernet and a token ring card). The LLC will forward packets from upper-layer

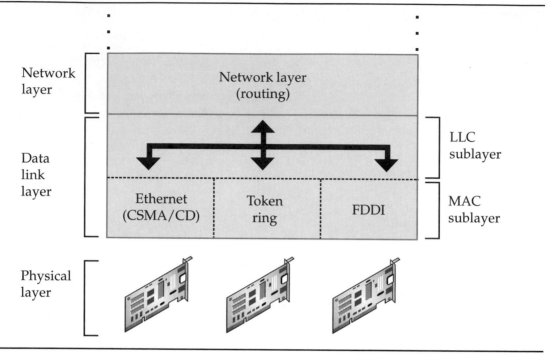

Figure L-4. *How LLC fits into the protocol stack*

protocols to the appropriate network interface. This scheme allows upper-layer protocols to operate without specific knowledge of the lower-layer network in use.

Note that the MAC layer is responsible for appending the actual physical address of the destination computer to the frame. The physical address is the hardwired address on the network interface card for the destination.

Related Entries   Bridges and Bridging; Connection-Oriented and Connectionless Services; Data Link Protocols; Ethernet; Framing in Data Transmissions; HDLC (High-level Data Link Control); IEEE 802 Standards; LAN (Local Area Network); MAC (Media Access Control); Network Concepts; NIC (Network Interface Card); Token Ring Network; *and* Virtual Circuits

Linktionary!—Tom Sheldon's Encyclopedia of Networking updates	http://www.linktionary.com/l/llc.html
Godred Fairhurst's Data Comm Tutorial on LLC	http://www.erg.abdn.ac.uk/users/gorry/course/lan-pages/llc.html
Optimized Engineering Corporation Ethernet Introduction	http://www.optimized.com/COMPENDI/TabOfCon.htm

LMDS (Local Multipoint Distribution Service)

LMDS is a radio system developed by Bellcore as a wireless local loop system that can be used in areas where installing physical cable is prohibitive, such as rural areas. While LMDS will never provide data rates comparable to fiber, it can provide the most economical way to provide high-speed last-mile connections for business in metro areas. Alcatel calls LMDS "wireless IP." The service is categorized as "fixed wireless," which really means that roaming between cells or other LMDS systems is usually not allowed. It also implies that subscribers are normally stationary, although antennas and equipment may be moved but the antenna must be aligned afterward.

LMDS uses a point-to-multipoint radio topology where a base station broadcasts to subscriber antennas. The subscriber to base station link is point to point. Point-to-multipoint and related topologies are illustrated and discussed further under the topic "Wireless Broadband Access Technologies."

Data rates are sufficient to support voice, video, data, and Internet access services. Bandwidth is shared, so actual data rates per subscriber will vary; but a typical system has a shared downstream bandwidth of 1.5 Gbits/sec and an upstream bandwidth of 200 Mbits/sec. Since the bandwidth is shared, a typical subscriber may obtain downstream data rates of 30 Mbits/sec to 150 Mbits/sec.

Figure L-5 illustrates a typical LMDS system (as defined by Alcatel). A wireless base station connects to SONET rings. The base station to subscriber range is 5 to 8 km (3 to 5 mi). The transmitter sits on a tall building or stand. It covers an area of 60 to 90 degrees. Thus, 4 to 6 transmitters are required to cover a full area. Multiple cells can be created to overcome line-of-sight problems. Repeaters and reflectors may also be used to cover areas that are not in the line-of-sight. Note that satellites and HALO (High Altitude Long Operation) systems overcome line-of-sight problems by positioning the transmitters high above the subscriber.

Point-to-point connections may be used to connect outlying systems to the wired network. At customer premises sites, outdoor antennas are connected to indoor multiplexing units that, in turn, are connected to internal networks. Figure L-5 illustrates the use of an Alcatel 9900 LMDS system that is designed for MTUs (multiple tenant units), office buildings, and small to medium–sized enterprises.

The LMDS frequency bands are allocated at various ranges in the electromagnetic spectrum. In the United States, the FCC split 493 markets into two blocks, a 1,150-MHz "A" block and a 150-MHz "B" block, as follows:

- Block A   27.50 to 28.35 GHz
- Block A   29.10 to 29.25 GHz
- Block A   31,07 to 31.22 GHz
- Block B   31.00 to 31.07 GHz
- Block B   31.22 to 31.30 GHz

In addition, Telegent has allocations around 24 GHz and Winstar has allocations around 39 GHz in the United States. With LMDS bandwidth of over 1 GHz in the U.S., LMDS has a

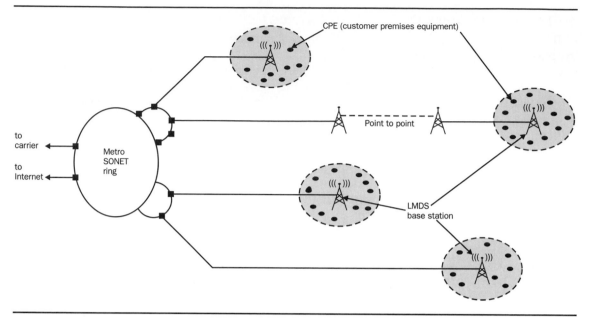

Figure L-5.   *LMDS topology (source: Alcatel)*

huge amount of spectrum. In comparison, the various mobile cellular bands are approximately 30 MHz in width. Here are some additional LMDS features:

- LMDS is a viable access technology and a cost-effective alternative to laying cable in metropolitan areas.

- Due to the high-frequency allocations, LMDS supports high data rates that are ideal for business users.

- The range from base station to receiver is limited to a few miles. The high-frequency waves dissipate over short distances. At the highest frequency (39 MHz), the range is limited to about one mile.

- Rain causes serious attenuation of LMDS signals, more so in the higher frequencies.

- Requires line of sight between antennas, which can create nonservice holes in areas where there are buildings, lots of trees, and other obstructions.

- A typical metro system may have a layout similar to a mobile cellular network with multiple cells and multiple users per cell.

- Base stations connect to wired networks such as the Internet and the PSTN.

LMDS is often compared to another wireless broadband access system called MMDS (Multichannel Multipoint Distribution Services). Both are point-to-multipoint broadcast systems and both provide two-way access services. However, there are some major differences. MMDS operates at 2.5 to 2.7 GHz in the United States and 3.4 to 3.7 GHz in other countries. Its coverage area is typically 32 to 48 km (20 to 30 mi), which means that a small number of antenna sites can cover most metro areas. Typical downstream data rates to the subscriber are from 128 Kbits/sec to 3 Mbits sec, and may go as high as 10 Mbits/sec. MMDS service is ideal for home users because the data rate and the cost of using the system are well matched to a home user's requirements. In contrast to MMDS, LMDS is ideal for business uses because it provides much higher data rates.

LMDS provides more bandwidth than MMDS; but the LMDS frequency range is affected by rain, which causes signal fading over long distances. Most important, LMDS requires line of sight which reduces its coverage area.

Currently, standards groups such as the IEEE are working on developing standard air interfaces. Some vendors have been using FDD (frequency division duplexing), which allocates separate frequency bands for upstream and downstream traffic. A more bandwidth-efficient technique called TDD (time division duplexing) is being used by Ensemble Communications and has been submitted for standardization. TDD toggles upstream and downstream traffic on the same channel, in scheduled time slots. See "Wireless Broadband Access Technologies."

The IEEE wireless initiatives are also referred to as IEEE 802.16 Wireless MAN (Metropolitan Area Network). The mission of Working Group 802.16 is "to develop standards and recommended practices to support the development and deployment of fixed broadband wireless access systems." Initially, the group focused on LMDS bands.

N-WEST (National Wireless Electronic Systems Testbed) is a U.S. Department of Commerce project that promotes broadband wireless technologies, particularly LMDS. N-WEST includes testbed facilities equipped with prototype LMDS systems that will be used to develop operational standards and performance assessment. The N-WEST Web site is at http://nwest.nist.gov/.

For a complete list of LMDS operators, vendors, and related publications, see the WCA (Wireless Communications Association International) Web site listed here.

Related Entries   HALO (High Altitude Long Operation); MAN (Metropolitan Area Network); MMDS (Multichannel Multipoint Distribution Services); Network Access Services; Satellite Communications; Wireless Broadband Access Technologies; Wireless Communications

Linktionary!—Tom Sheldon's Encyclopedia of Networking updates	http://www.linktionary.com/l/lmds.html
"What is LMDS" by Roger Marks	http://nwest.nist.gov/lmds.html
N-WEST (National Wireless Electronic Systems Testbed)	http://nwest.nist.gov/
WCA (Wireless Communications Association International).	http://www.wcai.com
BWA (Broadband Wireless Association)	http://www.broadband-wireless.org/
IEEE 802.16 Working Group on Broadband Wireless Access (IEEE Wireless MAN)	http://grouper.ieee.org/groups/802/16/
U.S. FCC LMDS Auction page	http://www.fcc.gov/wtb/auctions/lmds1.html
Web ProForum Local Multipoint Distribution System (LMDS) Tutorial	http://www.iec.org/tutorials/lmds/
Ensemble Communications	http://www.ensemblecom.com

Load Balancing

Load balancing is the process of distributing some load across multiple links, servers, processors, or other devices in order to improve performance and overcome deficiencies in existing equipment. This topic is primarily about *server load balancing*, which is the process of distributing requests from clients across a group of servers.

Another type of load balancing takes place in *aggregated communication links*, where network traffic is distributed across two or more links that appear as a single link with high bandwidth (and redundancy). See "Link Aggregation."

Still another type of load balancing occurs in *multiprocessor systems*, where processing loads are distributed across multiple processors in the same computer, or across an array of computers that are configured into a multiprocessing cluster. For example, a single complex task may be broken into pieces that can be simultaneously processed on different processors. See "Multiprocessing" for more information.

As mentioned, this topic will focus on server load balancing, a hot topic when you consider that most Web sites are overworked and old server configurations are unlikely to handle the load. Multiple servers are required, some that perform specialized tasks, so the job of a server load balancer is to receive incoming traffic and send that traffic to available servers or servers that are most appropriate for a particular task. These servers are represented by a virtual IP address. Traffic destined for the IP address is intercepted by load balancers and distributed to servers in a server farm or cluster. Also see "InfiniBand" for information about switching technology for servers.

Figure L-6 illustrates a typical load-balancing solution for a Web site. Requests arrive at the load-balancing devices and are distributed to servers in the server array. Besides distributing loads, load balancing provides high availability: if a server fails, the load balancer automatically sends requests to other servers. In addition, a server can be taken down for service without affecting user service since the load balancer distributes requests to the other servers that are still running.

Load balancers may be custom-designed network appliances, switches with advanced programmable functionality, or software-based applications that run on standard server platforms such as Microsoft Windows 2000 or UNIX environments. Microsoft NLB (Network Load Balancing), also called MLBS (Microsoft Load Balancing Server), works in Microsoft Windows 2000 clustering environments to balance incoming IP traffic among the nodes in the cluster. Like other load-balancing services, NLB provides scalability and high availability to enterprise-wide TCP/IP services, such as Web, proxy, VPN, streaming media, and other services.

A typical load-balancing device includes forwarding algorithms such as the following:

■ Forward the most recent request to the least busy server.

■ Forward traffic in a round-robin fashion to each server (this is sometimes called the "card-dealer" approach).

■ Assign weights to servers based on their processing capabilities and forward the most requests to servers with the highest weight.

■ Forward based on layer 4 information such as the source and destination IP address, or port number (type of application).

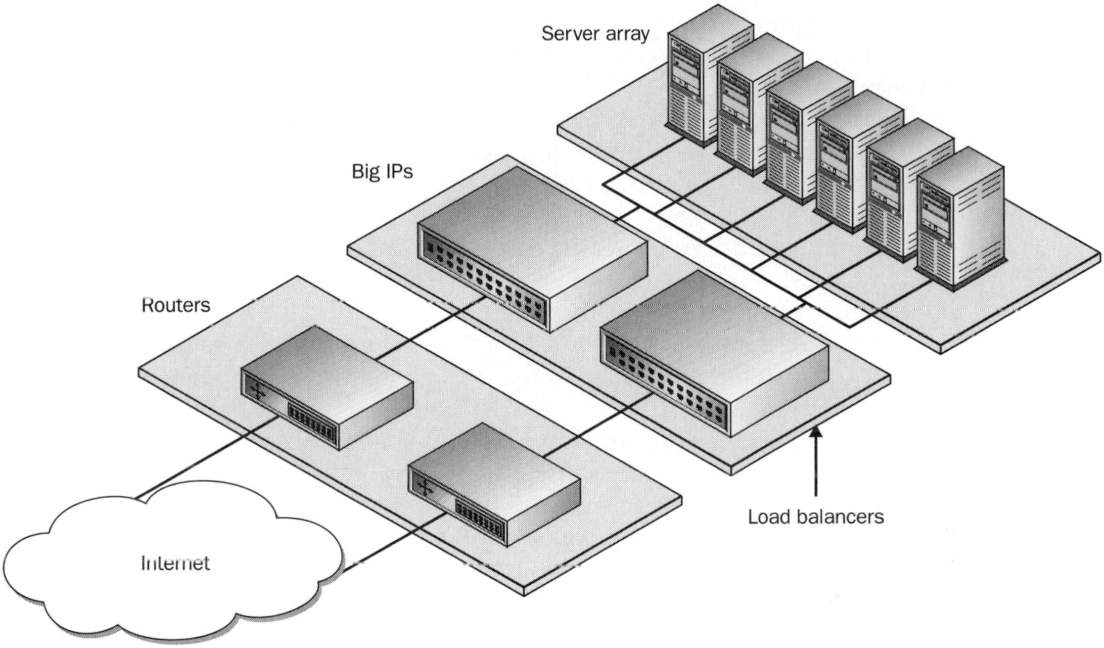

Figure L-6.   *A load-balanced Web site (source: F5 Networks)*

- Forward based on layer 7 information such as the requested URL, which contains directory and file information.
- Forward based on information in cookies
- Forward requests to servers based on the ability to process the request. For example, forward database requests to database servers and Web requests to Web servers.
- Forward requests to servers based on *persistent* sessions, i.e., if a server is already servicing a session, continue to forward related or similar requests to that server.

Note that multiple requests from a single client may be satisfied by multiple servers. This speeds performance. For example, a typical Web page contains many objects, including pictures, text, and sound. One server in a cluster may provide text while another may provide pictures and sound. To the person viewing the Web page, it appears as if they are connected to a single Web server.

Devices that examine the URL and other "application-specific" information for load-balancing purposes are called layer 7 devices. The URL provides information about the requested content, including the directory name and the filename. Cookies are also used as discussed in a moment.

Persistence is important because it ensures that a client continues to work with the same server throughout a transaction that spans a number of TCP connections. For example, at an e-commerce shopping site, the load balancer will make sure a client's requests continue to go to the same server, because that server may be caching shopping cart information for the client. Persistence also optimizes cache performance. For example, information in a URL (directory or filename) can be used to direct requests to a server that has recently cached the requested information.

Cookies are also important in load-balancing environments as a way to identify users. Source IP addresses cannot always be trusted as an accurate user identifier. Users on the other side of proxy environments like America Online may be assigned a different IP address for each connection made across a proxy server. Cookies can provide "user-aware" persistence. When a user first connects with a Web site, the server that handles the request creates or modifies a cookie with session information and returns it to the user. The cookie information is then used to maintain persistence during the session.

Cookies can also provide service-level information. For example, the cookie may indicate that the user is a gold-service customer, so the user's requests go to the highest performance server. However, handling cookies is processor intensive. The load balancer must first establish a TCP connection with the client, and then capture the cookie when it arrives, parse the cookie to find the required information, and determine the appropriate server for the request. The load balancer will need to buffer information from the client until it can determine the nature of the cookie.

High-end layer 7 load balancers are typically, high-performance devices with fast switching fabrics and network processors that can handle instantaneous processing loads of busy Web sites. Alteon Web Systems has designed a series of Web switches that implement advanced network processor technology and a distributed processing architecture. Each port has a network processing ASIC that combines a layer 2 packet engine with two RISC processors onto a single chip. Up to 10 of these network processors are interconnected over an 8-Gbits/sec switch backplane. The packet engine in each network processor switches layer 2 packets in hardware while the network processors support layer 3 through layer 7 switching in software. The switch is basically a parallel processing system in which 20 RISC network processors process traffic simultaneously, regardless of the physical ports through which session traffic traverses. It is a virtual matrix of memory and processor resources that can instantly process traffic from any port. Alteon's Series 700 is built around a 180 Gbits/sec cross-bar switching fabric and includes addition features, such as a QoS managers. It also includes hardware processing assistance for layer 7 content switching, which is necessary to maintain wire speed at the gigabit rates of all ports.

F5 Networks is one of the leaders in load balancing and a variety of other products that can be used to optimize Web site design, including content distribution. Extreme Networks integrates F5 Networks' server load-balancing source code in its own wire-speed switching devices. F5 Networks' load-balancing and high-availability devices provide the following features:

- Prioritizes and controls traffic based on source, destination, and types of traffic.
- Provides central-location control of servers, devices, and content.
- Balances multiple IP protocols and network devices, including firewalls, routers, cache servers, and multimedia servers.
- Manages server and application failures and directs traffic to functioning servers and applications.
- Provides persistence modes to seamlessly process user requests and maintain the link between the site and the customer.

■ Provides cookie-based persistence, source, server, SSL persistence; URL, IP, port, and HTTP header load balancing.

Extreme Networks has designed a series of high-end load-balancing devices that provide all-in-one service and reduce the hardware requirements of load balancing. Figure L-7 illustrates a multidevice hardware configuration and the Extreme solution. In the "before" illustration, multiple layer 2 switches are required to provide distributed connections between routers and load balancers, and between load balancers and servers. In the "after" approach, Extreme Networks' wire-speed switches provide all the switching and load-balancing functions.

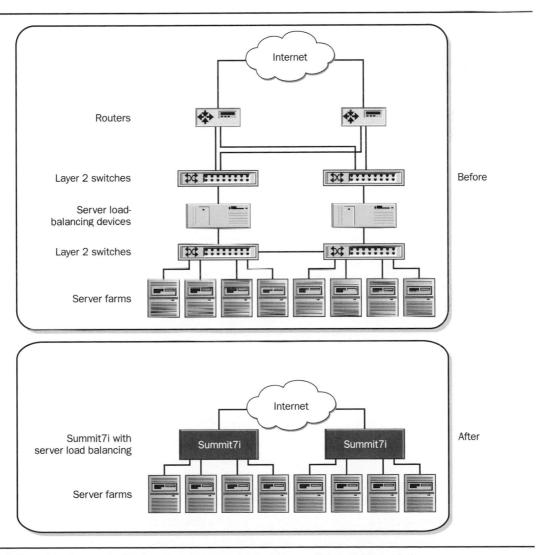

Figure L-7. *A before and after load-balancing scenario (source: Extreme Networks)*

Load balancing is not confined to a single geographic Web site. It may be distributed across the Internet, with multiple sites hosting the same content. For example, a load balancer may forward requests to servers that are geographically closer to the client making the requests. This setup supports disaster recover—if a site fails, the workload is automatically redirected to the backup site. It also supports content distribution.

Early Internet-based load-balancing techniques used DNS for load balancing. The DNS load-balancing technique would select an IP address from a list of IP addresses for the same domain using a round-robin approach. The technique is discussed in RFC 1794 (DNS Support for Load Balancing, April 1995). Basically, the DNS zone transfer program periodically shuffles the order of resource records for server nodes based on a predetermined load-balancing algorithm. However, the timing of this method may not match real-world requirements of today. In addition, all hosts in the server pool are assumed to have equal capability to offer all services, which may not always be the case. Many commercial Internet load balancers implement a more intelligent selection algorithm for choosing Web sites in the DNS list.

RFC 2391 (Load Sharing Using IP Network Address Translation, August 1998) describes LSNAT, which extends NAT (Network Address Translation) to offer load-sharing techniques. RFC 3074 (DHC Load Balancing Algorithm, February 2001) describes a load-balancing algorithm that enables multiple, cooperating servers to decide which one should service a client, without exchanging any information beyond initial configuration.

Related Entries   ASIC (Application-Specific Integrated Circuit); Bandwidth Management; Clustering; Congestion Control Mechanisms; Content Distribution; Cookies; Data Center Design; Distributed Computer Networks; Embedded Systems; Link Aggregation; Multilayer Switching; Multiprocessing; Network Appliances; Network Concepts; Network Design and Construction; Network Processors; Policy-Based Management; Switch Fabrics and Bus Design; Switching and Switched Networks; Traffic Management, Shaping, and Engineering; *and* Web Caching

Linktionary!—Tom Sheldon's Encyclopedia of Networking updates	http://www.linktionary.com/l/load_balancing.html
Google Web Directory: Load Balancing	http://directory.google.com/Top/Computers/Software/Internet/Site_Management/Load_Balancing/
Alteon WebSystems	http://www.alteonwebsystems.com/
Cisco Systems (Local Director)	http://www.cisco.com
Enterasys Networks	http://www.enterasys.com/
Extreme Networks	http://www.extremenetworks.com
F5 Networks	http://www.f5.com
Foundry Networks	http://www.foundry.com
Radware	http://www.radware.com
Red Hill Networks	http://www.redhill-networks.com
Microsoft (search for "load balancing"	http://www.microsoft.com
Acuitive, Inc., white papers	http://www.acuitive.com/rr.html
Bitpipe.com (search for load balancing)	http://www.bitpipe.com

IBM paper on server load balancing	http://www.networking.ibm.com/white/serverload.html
Microsoft paper: "Network Load Balancing Technical Overview"	http://www.microsoft.com/windows2000/library/howitworks/cluster/nlb.asp
Distributed Computing: An Overview	http://www.geocities.com/SiliconValley/Vista/4015/pdcindex.html
Load Balancing links and information by Kang Sung Il	http://rtlab.kaist.ac.kr/~sikang/load/

Local Loop

The local loop is a pair of wires that connect telephone subscribers to the telephone company's CO (central office). The CO is where telephone company switching equipment is located. Some neighborhood buildings are remote switching offices that are connected to a main office via a trunk cable (coaxial or fiber). The two copper wires are individually insulated and twisted around one another to reduce crosstalk.

Usually, two pairs are wired to each home or business to support a second phone. Bundles of wires are connected to apartment and office buildings. The local loop is based on the analog signal technologies that have been used in the phone system for the past 100 years. The cable to each home includes two copper twisted-pair wires. It is estimated that there are over 600 million local loop lines installed throughout the world. This copper infrastructure is the incumbent telephone company's largest asset.

In some areas, a DLC (digital loop carrier) system aggregates the subscriber calls within a neighborhood, office building, or industrial park and multiplexes the calls over a single line (T1/E1 or fiber) back to the telephone company central office.

The local loop is often called the *last mile*, but the local loop refers specifically to the telephone company's twisted-pair copper wire. "Last mile" is a generic term that refers to a variety of access methods, including cable (CATV), wireless local loop, and so on.

The local loop has some limitations that severely restrict its data-carrying capabilities. First, a modem is required to convert computer digital signals to analog signals for transmission across the analog local loop. Second, the signaling on the cable is cut off above 3,100 Hz to reduce line noise. While the range below 3,100 Hz is adequate for voice, the cutoff severely limits data transmissions, as explained next. Third, the further a subscriber is from the telephone company central office, the worse the attenuation and line noise. This can be corrected somewhat with line conditioning, but the maximum distance is about 3.5 miles. See "Modems" for a discussion about 56K modem technology. Also see "MLPPP (Multilink PPP)" for a discussion of modem bonding techniques that can double access rates over analog lines.

DSL (Digital Subscriber Line) is the technology that can remove the limitations of the local loop and provide, potentially, megabits per second of throughput over the local loop. DSL transmissions use a frequency range on the copper local loop cable above the voice band. Basically, the telephone company installs DSL equipment and customers install DSL modems. See "DSL (Digital Subscriber Line)." Another alternative is ISDN (Integrated Services Digital Network), which extends the carrier's digital network across the local loop to the customer. However, DSL is now the preferred choice and, in many cases, provides more bandwidth at a lower prices than ISDN. The Related Entries discuss other access methods and you can also see "Network Access Services."

Related Entries   Cable (CATV) Data Networks; Circuit-Switching Services; CO (Central Office); Communication Services and Providers; DBS (Direct Broadcast Satellite); DSL (Digital Subscriber Line); FTTH (Fiber To The Home); HALO (High Altitude Long Operation); Home Networking; ISDN (Integrated Services Digital Network); Last Mile Services; Line Conditioning; LMDS (Local Multipoint Distribution Service); MMDS (Multichannel Multipoint Distribution Service); Modems; Network Access Services; NPN (New Public Network); PON (Passive Optical Network); Residential Broadband; Satellite Communication Systems; Service Providers and Carriers; Telecommunications and Telephone Systems; Wireless Broadband Access Technologies; *and* Wireless Local Loop

Linktionary!—Tom Sheldon's Encyclopedia of Networking updates	http://www.linktionary.com/l/local_loop.html
"Expecting 56k (V.90/X2/K56)?" (describes phone line problems) by Bill Garfield (aka "bubba")	http://www.hal-pc.org/~wdg/56k.html
CO (central office) locator (to determine how far you are from your CO	http://www.dslreports.com/coinfo
Wireless local loop tutorial at Web ProForums	http://www.iec.org/tutorials/wll/

Local Procedure Calls

See IPC (Interprocess Communication).

LocalTalk

LocalTalk is a LAN (local area network) protocol that defines AppleTalk packet transmission over a 230.4-Kbit/sec cabling system. LocalTalk was originally called AppleTalk, but Apple changed the name in 1989 to LocalTalk. Apple Computer's network architecture is now called AppleTalk, and it includes the protocols that operate over LocalTalk physical networks.

The original LocalTalk system was primarily designed for the attachment of a few Macintosh computers to an Apple LaserWriter printer. Transmission speeds of LocalTalk are very low (230.4 Kbits/sec), but LocalTalk is important because most Macintosh computers have LocalTalk support built in. LocalTalk is a physical bus topology that is wired with twisted-pair telephone wire in a daisy-chain configuration. The total length of the network cannot exceed 1,000 feet, but additional networks can be attached using repeaters, bridges, or routers. Up to 32 nodes can be attached to a network segment, but performance degrades rapidly on busy networks of 20 or more nodes.

Related Entries   AFP (AppleTalk Filing Protocol); Apple Computer; AppleShare; *and* Network Concepts

Apple Tech Info Library (search for LocalTalk)	http://til.info.apple.com/
LocalTalk Characteristics by TEC	http://techedcon.com/refguide/ LocalTalk_Characteristics.htm

Login Scripts

Login scripts are critical for setting up the environments of network users. A *login script* is a series of commands that execute when a user logs on. The commands placed in login scripts can map network drives for users, switch them to specific drives, display menus, and start applications.

In many network operating system environments, there is one login script that runs when a user logs on. In NetWare 4.x, there are up to four login scripts, any of which may execute when a user logs on. A *default login script* runs when a user first logs in and creates a number of environmental settings. However, administrators (and users to some extent) can override the default login script by creating a personal login script. Each user also has a *personal login script* that can contain commands of their choosing.

In NDS (Novell Directory Service), two other login scripts are the *container login script* and the *profile login script*. A container is a branch in the NDS tree that relates to a department, division, or branch of the organization. When a user logs on, the login script for the container they belong to runs. This means that each department or division can have its own login script in addition to the default user login scripts. A profile login script belongs to a group of users who don't necessarily belong to the same container. For example, a profile login script can execute commands for a group of managers.

Related Entries   Access Control; Account, User; Authentication and Authorization; Logons and Logon Accounts; Network Operating Systems; Rights and Permissions; Security; *and* Users and Groups

Logons and Logon Accounts

Logon (or login) is a procedure that a user follows to gain access to a privileged system, such as a network, a file server, a database, a Web server, or some other system. Logon software usually runs when the workstation is turned on or when a user types a command such as **LOGON** or **LOGIN**. The logon procedure asks for an account name and a password. If the user enters either of these incorrectly, the logon procedure usually allows another chance for the user to log on. After a certain number of repeated failures to supply the correct logon information, the system assumes the user is an intruder and locks the account from further logon attempts.

Users typically log onto a user account and are then given access to a system. The user account may be part of a directory service such as NDS (Novell Directory Services). Accounts are created by system administrators and stored on security servers. Users may be required to log on to every system they attempt to access. Pass-through security systems or single sign-on systems allow users to log on once and carry their security credentials to other servers. Those servers trust the original logon and allow users access. These schemes are typically implemented on intranets. See "Authentication and Authorization" for a continuation of this topic.

Access to resources is based on access control lists. See "Access Control" and "ACL (Access Control List)" for more information.

A user account may have various security restrictions applied to it. A supervisor may apply logon restrictions to the user account that do the following:

- Restrict the time the user can log on, thus preventing the user from logging on after hours.
- Specify the workstation where a user logs on, preventing the user from logging on at unsupervised workstations.

- Require unique passwords, thus forcing the user to create a password unlike one the user recently used.

- A logon restriction can define an expiration date for the account, locking out the user after a certain period of time.

Related Entries Access Control; Account, User; Authentication and Authorization; Biometric Access Devices; Certificates and Certification Systems; CHAP (Challenge Handshake Authentication Protocol); Kerberos Authentication Protocol; Login Scripts; One-Time Password Authentication; Rights and Permissions; Security; Smart Cards; Token-Based Authentication; *and* Users and Groups

Linktionary!—Tom Sheldon's   http://www.linktionary.com/l/logon.html
Encyclopedia of Networking updates

Long-Distance Carriers

See Communication Services and Providers; IXC (Interexchange Carrier); and Service Providers and Carriers.

Lotus Domino

Lotus Domino is a server technology that transforms Lotus Notes into an Internet application server that allows Web clients to interactively participate in a Notes environment and access dynamic data and applications on Notes servers. A key feature of Domino is that developers can leverage the Notes application development environment to create Web applications. Versions of Domino are available for Windows NT and Windows 2000 platforms, Solaris/ SPARC, Solaris/Intel Edition, AIX, and OS/2.

Related Entries Collaborative Computing; Electronic Mail; Groupware; Lotus Notes; Microsoft Exchange; *and* Workflow Management

Lotus Domino Web site   http://domino.lotus.com

Lotus Notes

Lotus Notes is an enterprise-wide, client/server-based messaging system that integrates groupware, forms generation, and document flow for large network environments. It also includes full support for the Internet and the Web, and provides a base for development of custom applications that automate business processes.

The latest versions include integration with desktop productivity tools, including Lotus SmartSuite and Microsoft Office, Microsoft Internet Explorer integration, enhanced contact management, and POP3 support for Internet mail.

Notes is an organization-wide messaging system that incorporates enterprise calendaring and scheduling. It supports mobile users with replication techniques that keep remote users in touch and synchronized with the rest of the organization. Notes provides full security to protect the privacy of information stored on servers in databases, documents, and messages.

Related Entries Collaborative Computing; Electronic Mail; Groupware; Lotus Domino; Microsoft Exchange; *and* Workflow Management

Lotus   http://www.lotus.com

LU (Logical Unit) Entities

An LU (logical unit) is a session in an IBM SNA (Systems Network Architecture) environment, usually between a terminal and a mainframe computer. Typically, more than one LU can take place at the same time. See "SNA (Systems Network Architecture)."

LVDS (Low-Voltage Differential Signaling)

LVDS is an industry standard that defines a high-speed, low-power, data-signaling technique that is implemented in a variety of connection technologies. The fastest and longest SCSI disk interfaces implement LVDS. LVDS is also used in new high-speed switching fabrics such as InfiniBand, and in system area networks. LVDS is also used in digital camera interfaces and has even been used to drive LCD displays in laptop computers. LVDS is defined by ANSI/TIA/EIA-644 (EIA-644), which specifies electrical characteristics of the driver output and receiver input. Guidelines for bus configuration, cables, and termination are given, but protocols, connectors, and bus structures are not defined in the standards.

LVDS overcomes some of the limitations of more traditional signaling standards such as RS-422. LVDS cuts down on noise and boosts data rates by using extremely low voltage levels (350 mV compares to 2.4 V), which translates to low radiation and less power consumption. Most important, differential signaling allows the receiver to filter out noise. This is done by sending signals across two wires simultaneously, each with opposing current and voltage swings. The actual data is read as the difference in amplitude between the signals on the two wires. If noise is induced, it will appear on both lines, but the signal information remains unchanged. Since the signal has improved noise immunity, voltage can be reduced and data rate can be increased.

LVDS is ideal for building high-speed multipoint switching fabrics directly onto backplanes. The current trend is to move away from parallel buses like PCI to high-speed switching fabrics that allow simultaneous point-to-point transmissions between multiple components and devices. Normally, the close spacing in such a design would create noise and signal interference. BLVDS (bus LVDS), developed by National Semiconductor, supports low-power, high-speed multipoint switching with low noise and interference. According to Texas Instruments, LVDS drivers and receivers can support speeds up to 400 Mbps, consume 1/8 the power of RS-422, and radiate 1/10 the EMI of the best single-ended input/output (I/O).

Related Entries   InfiniBand; Network Connection Technologies; SCSI (Small Computer System Interface); Serial Communication and Interfaces; *and* Switch Fabrics and Bus Design

 Linktionary!—Tom Sheldon's *Encyclopedia of*   http://www.linktionary.com/l/lvds.html
Networking updates

National Semiconductor's LVDS Interface Web site   http://www.national.com/appinfo/lvds/

MAC (Media Access Control)

In the IEEE 802 protocols for shared multiaccess LANs, the data link layer is divided into two sublayers, as shown next. The upper LLC (Logical Link Control) layer provides a way to address a station on a LAN and exchange information with it. The lower MAC layer provides the interface between the LLC and the particular network medium that is in use (Ethernet, token ring, and so on).

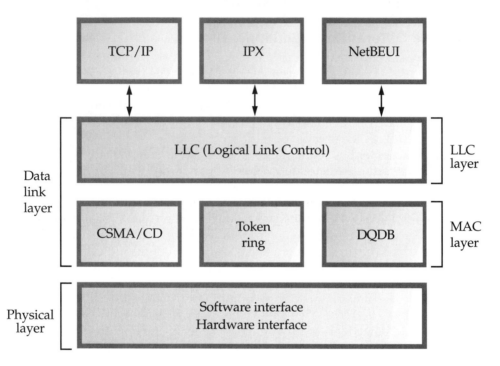

The MAC layer frames data for transmission over the network, and then passes the frame to the physical layer interface where it is transmitted as a stream of bits. Framing packages information into distinct units that are transmitted one at a time on the network. If a frame is corrupted during transmission, only it needs to be resent—not the entire transmission.

Individual LAN addresses are defined in the MAC layer. A network interface card such as an Ethernet adapter has a hardwired address that is assigned at the factory. This address follows an industry standard that ensures that no other adapter has a similar address. Therefore, when you connect workstations to an IEEE network, each workstation will have a unique MAC address. Workstations on the same LAN use the MAC address to forward packets to one another. When LANs are connected in an internetwork, higher-level addressing schemes such as IP (Internet Protocol) identify networks and nodes across the internetwork.

The other job of the MAC layer is to arbitrate access to the medium that is shared by all the computers attached to the LAN. If two stations were to transmit at the same time, the data would be corrupted. The primary access methods are *carrier sensing* (nodes listen for a carrier tone on the cable and may transmit when the line is free) and *token passing* (nodes must have possession of a token before they can transmit). The following topics discuss various LAN access methods:

- ALOHA (has historical reference)
- CSMA/CD (Carrier Sense Multiple Access/Collision Detection)
- Token Bus Network
- Token Ring Network

Other access methods include DQDB (Distributed Queue Dual Bus), used with metropolitan area networks, and CDPD (Cellular Digital Packet Data), used for wireless communications. *Multiplexing* allows multiple devices to transmit on a channel at the same time. The channel is divided into time slots, by frequency, or by other methods. See "Multiplexing and Multiplexers."

Related Entries   ALOHA; Bridges and Bridging; Broadcast Domain; Broadcast Networking; Collisions and Collision Domains; CSMA/CD (Carrier Sense Multiple Access/Collision Detection); Ethernet; FDDI (Fiber Distributed Data Interface); IEEE 802 Standards; LAN (Local Area Network); MAN (Metropolitan Area Network); Multiplexing and Multiplexers; NDIS (Network Driver Interface Specification); Network Concepts; NIC (Network Interface Card); ODI (Open Data link Interface); *and* Token Ring Network

Linktionary!—Tom Sheldon's Encyclopedia of Networking updates	http://www.linktionary.com/m/mac.html
Novatech OSI model page (see Data Link Layer section)	http://www.echelon.ca/handyman/nettech/
Optimized Engineering network tutorials	http://www.optimized.com/COMPENDI/TabOfCon.htm
Gorry Fairhurst's data communications tutorials	http://www.erg.abdn.ac.uk/users/gorry/eg3561/syllabus.html

Mac OS

In 1984, Apple Computer introduced the Macintosh, one of the first widely available personal computers with a graphical user interface operating system based on a familiar metaphor, the desktop. Over the years, the Macintosh operating system evolved to provide more and more features for its users. In 1994, Apple introduced its System 7.5 operating system to provide users with greater efficiency and productivity, including the ability to use both 680 × 0–based Macs and Power Macintosh systems. At that time, the operating system was named *Mac OS*.

In mid-1997, Apple released Mac OS 8, a multithreaded system for executing multiple tasks simultaneously, such as launching applications and copying files. It also enhances the user interface and includes Internet access support in the form of TCP/IP, PPP (Point-to-Point Protocol), Netscape or Microsoft Web browsers, and the PointCast network. In March of 2001, Mac OS 9 was superceded by Mac OS X, which has a UNIX-based foundation called Darwin. Darwin evolved from a joint effort by Apple engineers and programmers in the Open Source software community. Mac OS X also has improved Java support and graphics rendering, as well as support for multiprocessor Power Mac G4 computers.

M

Related Entries   AFP (AppleTalk Filing Protocol); Apple Computer; Apple Open Transport Protocol; AppleShare; AppleTalk; File Sharing; File Systems; LocalTalk; *and* Network Operating Systems

Apple Mac OS Web site   http://www.macos.apple.com

Apple Mac OS X   http://www.apple.com/macosx/

MAE (Metropolitan Area Exchange)

A MAE is a form of *Internet exchange* where Internet backbone operators and/or regional network operators peer with one another. *Peering* is a relationship in which different network authorities agree to exchange route advertisements and traffic. Internet exchanges are also called NAPs (network access points).

The MAEs are a special version of the NAPs that are implemented as metropolitan area networks. Basically, the network reaches out to connect with major providers in the service areas they cover. MAE-West is in California's Silicon Valley and MAE-East is in the Washington, DC, area. MAE is a trademark of MCI Worldcom, which acquired the MAEs in its purchase of MFS (Metropolitan Fiber Systems) Communications.

Refer to "Internet Architecture and Backbone" for more information, or visit the following Web sites:

Worldcom MAE information site   http://www.mae.net/

MFS Communications MAE information   http://www.mfst.com/MAE/doc/mae-info.html

Mailing List Programs

First, the industry now commonly calls mailing list programs "listservers," but this is a name owned by L-Soft International, Inc., which makes the LISTSERV mailing list program, originally created by Eric Thomas in 1986. This section will discuss LISTSERV and Majordomo, a similar mailing list program.

A mailing list program is a program that uses Internet protocols to automate e-mail message distribution to members of a mailing list. Members subscribe to a mailing list, then receive a copy of all e-mail messages sent to the list. Any member can create a new message or respond to a message that was sent by another user. New messages and response messages are automatically forwarded to members of the list. A mailing list is usually set up to disseminate information about a particular topic, such as computers, politics, finance, stocks, or many other topics.

Mailing lists are excellent tools for organizations to use for in-house discussions or to provide open discussions with customers or clients. For example, Microsoft uses mailing lists when beta testing its products. Beta testers receive prerelease copies of a product and participate in mailing list discussions about that product. Many problems and technical details are often hammered out in heated mailing list discussions before the product is released.

A mailing list implements a *mail list exploder*. When a message is sent to the mailing list, it is exploded, meaning that duplicates of the message are sent to everyone on the list. Recipients usually receive a message in a few minutes on the Internet. However, some recipients may choose to have messages sent in digest form, which means messages are bundled in a package and sent once per week (or some other interval).

Generally, subscriptions to a list are open to all. To subscribe, a user sends a request to the mailing list server in an e-mail message. The server then adds the user to the list and returns a set of instructions for using the list. The user can send another message to unsubscribe from the list at any time. However, a list administrator or owner can screen subscribers, drop subscribers that are being rude, or perform other management functions.

As users exchange messages, they create message threads that can be archived and reviewed at any point. One message thread may spawn another message thread. Mailing list programs create logs of messages that are archived and can be reviewed at any time. Users can obtain a log file for a particular time period or use database functions to search for messages related to a specific topic or sent by a person of interest.

The two most popular mailing list programs are outlined here:

- **LISTSERV**   As mentioned, the original mailing list server is LISTSERV, written in 1986 by Eric Thomas and now sold by L-Soft international, Inc. Mr. Thomas still oversees development of the product. It was originally designed for IBM mainframes, but is now available on VM, VMS, Windows NT, Windows 95, Macintosh, and 13 brands of UNIX. Note that LISTSERV is always spelled in uppercase and is a trademark. Other products are often called "listserv" programs, but they are really mailing list programs.

- **Majordomo**   Like LISTSERV, Majordomo is a mailing list program for automating and managing mailing lists. The product is free to download from the Great Circle Web site listed later. Its name comes from the latin "major domus"—"master of the house." Majordomo does not have the commercial aspect of LISTSERV, nor does it have all of LISTSERV's features. Readers should visit the sites listed later to compare the features of the two products. Note that Majordomo runs on UNIX platforms and uses Sendmail, the UNIX mail agent.

Related Entries   Chat; Collaborative Computing; Distributed Applications; Electronic Mail; Groupware; Instant Messaging; IRC (Internet Relay Chat); *and* Sendmail

Linktionary!—Tom Sheldon's Encyclopedia of Networking updates	http://www.linktionary.com/m/mailing_list.html
L-Soft LISTSERV	http://www.lsoft.com
Majordomo list server	http://www.greatcircle.com/majordomo
IFLANET Internet mailing list resource page	http://www.ifla.org/I/training/listserv/lists.htm
Yahoo! Internet mailing lists page	http://dir.yahoo.com/computers_and_internet/internet/mailing_lists/
Google Web Directory	http://directory.google.com/Top/Computers/Internet/Mailing_Lists/Directories/

Mainframe

A mainframe is a central processing computer system that gets its name from the large frame or rack that holds the electronics. Mainframes are based on the central processing model of computing, in which all processing and data storage is done at a central system and users connect to that system via "dumb terminals." The most common mainframes were made by IBM, although major systems were also made by Sperry Rand, Burroughs, NCR, Honeywell, and others.

Mainframes are now considered legacy systems and they are no longer being produced, although supercomputers are an evolution of mainframe systems. In the 1970s, DEC (Digital Equipment Corporation) began producing "minicomputer" systems that provided medium-size businesses and university departments with their own powerful computer system that rivaled the mainframe in many ways. Then, in the 1980s, PCs and LANs started to encroach on the mainframe and minicomputer market, distributing computer power out to desktops.

Many thought that the mainframe would fade away in the 1990s, but mainframes have been reborn into client/server environments and as powerful Web servers. The topics "IBM Host Connectivity," "DLSw (Data Link Switching)," and "TN3270" discuss methods for accessing IBM mainframes across enterprise networks.

Legacy applications and data give mainframes their sticking power. IDC (International Data Corporation) estimates that nearly three-quarters of all data still resides on mainframe systems. Managers have not been anxious to move this information to network servers or other platforms. The cost and risk of failure in making such a move is too high. The current trend is to build data warehouses that extract, summarize, collate, clean up, and present data from back-end production and legacy systems in a way that makes it more accessible to users. See "Data Warehousing" for more on this topic.

A good reason to keep mainframes running is that they were designed from the ground up to run mission-critical transaction processing applications with high-performance, fail-safe operation and reliable security. Keeping mainframe systems, applications, and data alive has kept many technicians, programmers, and database experts employed well past their retirement years. In fact, IBM still sells systems that are part of the old mainframe family. Its G5 and G6 parallel processing servers are part of the System/390 family. In 1996, IBM shipped over 500,000 System/390 systems.

Web technologies are also opening mainframe systems up to the rest of the network, allowing administrators to get rid of incompatible protocols and cumbersome gateways. Software is now available from IBM and other vendors that lets Web clients access mainframe data directly using Web browsers and TCP/IP protocols. While the mainframe lives, traditional mainframe protocols such as IBM SNA (System Network Architecture) are giving way to TCP/IP.

Related Entries   Clustering; Data Warehousing; DB2, IBM; Distributed Computer Networks; Enterprise Network; Fault Tolerance and High-Availability; IBM (International Business Machines); IBM Host Connectivity; Multiprocessing; Servers; SNA (Systems Network Architecture); Supercomputer; *and* TN3270

Linktionary!—Tom Sheldon's Encyclopedia of Networking updates	http://www.linktionary.com/m/mainframe.html
IBM's enterprise servers page	http://www.servers.ibm.com/
IBM's networking hardware page	http://www.networking.ibm.com/
Pictures from the IBM Museum in Endicott	http://www.mindspring.com/~demosthenian/museum.html

Interesting pictures of mainframes	http://www.telnet.hu/hamster/oldiron/e_ibms.html
"Mainframe Server Software Architectures" at Carnegie Mellon	http://www.sei.cmu.edu/str/descriptions/mssa.html
Crossroads mainframe connectivity page	http://www.crossroads.com/products/mainframe/
Bitpipe (search for "mainframe")	http://www.bitpipe.com/
About.com (search for "mainframe")	http://compnetworking.about.com/
Search390.com (S/390-specific search engine)	http://search390.techtarget.com/
Mainframe Service Providers	http://www.mfsp.com/
SimoTime Enterprises (transforming mainframe application for the Internet)	http://www.simotime.com/
Yahoo!'s Mainframes page	http://dir.yahoo.com/Business_and_Economy/ Business_to_Business/Computers/Hardware/ Systems/Mainframes/

Majordomo

See Mailing List Programs.

MAN (Metropolitan Area Network)

Metropolitan area networks connect businesses to businesses, and businesses to WANs and the Internet. A MAN is typically a backbone optical network that spans a metropolitan area, usually in a ring configuration. The telephone companies have provided MAN services in the form of SONET rings for years. These services are based on TDM (time division multiplexing), which is more suitable for voice than data. Customers connect into the ring via ISDN, T1, fractional T1, and even T3 lines. However, even for short distances, these connections are expensive.

A new era of computer networking is emerging with new MAN technologies that extend Ethernet LAN networks across the MAN via fiber-optic links. Most important, these services are being offered by carriers that compete with the incumbent phone companies, and they are cheap. An organization can obtain a 10-Mbit/sec link between its offices in a metropolitan area for under $400 per month. A 100-Mbit/sec link may cost under $1,000 per month. The new networks are also extremely flexible. In some cases, customers can access the provider's Web site and fill out a form to obtain an immediate service upgrade for a special event such as a videoconference.

Gigabit Ethernet MANs are being offered in major metropolitan areas by several companies, including IntelliSpace, Telseon, Yipes Communications, and XO Communications. The Web sites are listed later. Figure M-1 illustrates the traditional telco network and the Yipes IP over fiber network.

Wireless optical networks are emerging from carriers such as Terabeam (http://www.terabeam.com). These systems are sometimes called *free-space optical systems*. Terabeam holds a trademark on "Fiberless Optical." The networks are designed to provide high data rates in metropolitan areas without the need to install cable. Terabeam's systems are installed on top of one or more buildings or towers in a metropolitan area, much like a wireless cellular system. Customers within the range of the hub connect via an infrared transceiver that sits inside a window of their building. The system is based on IP over Ethernet.

M

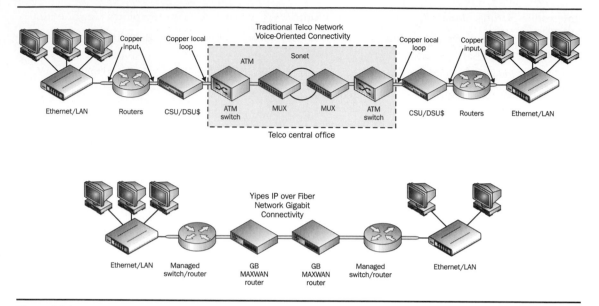

Figure M-1.   *Yipes IP over fiber metropolitan area network*

As mentioned, SONET has been the primary transport for metropolitan area networking. A variety of wireless access technologies are discussed under "Wireless Broadband Access Technologies." Another technology is DPT (Dynamic Packet Transport), a Cisco-developed SONET-like technology that transports packets across fiber-optic rings. See "DPT (Dynamic Packet Transport)."

The IEEE 802.17 Resilient Packet Ring Working Group (RPRWG) is defining a MAN access protocol called Resilient Packet Ring Access Protocol for use in local, metropolitan, and WAN environments. The IETF IP over Resilient Packet Rings (iporpr) Working Group is working with the IEEE on its resilient packet ring technology. Refer to the Web sites listed at the end of the section.

The IEEE 802.16 Working Group on Broadband Wireless Access is creating the IEEE 802.16 family of WirelessMAN standards for wireless metropolitan area networks. IEEE 802.16 specifies the medium access control layer and physical layers of the air interface of interoperable fixed point-to-multipoint broadband wireless access systems. The specification enables transport of data, video, and voice services with a focus on the 5 to 6–GHz range and the unlicensed bands between 2 and 11 GHz. Physical layers are specified for both licensed and unlicensed bands. The working group also includes the WirelessHUMAN (Wireless High-Speed Unlicensed Metropolitan Area Networks) project, which is developing wireless data services in the unlicensed spectrum, primarily 5–6 GHz.

Related Entries   Cable (CATV) Data Networks; DBS (Direct Broadcast Satellite); DPT (Dynamic Packet Transport); DSL (Digital Subscriber Line); Electromagnetic Spectrum; Ethernet; Gigabit Ethernet; HALO (High Altitude Long Operation); HDR (High Data Rate); IEEE 802 Standards; Infrared Technologies; Internet Connections; Last Mile Services; LMDS (Local Multipoint Distribution Service); Local Loop;

MAN (Metropolitan Area Network); Microwave Communications; MMDS (Multichannel Multipoint Distribution Services); Network Access Services; Network Core Technologies; OFDM (Orthogonal Frequency Division Multiplexing); Optical Networks; Packet-Radio Data Networks; Residential Broadband; Resilient Packet Rings; Satellite Communication Systems; Service Providers and Carriers; SONET (Synchronous Optical Network); Telecommunications and Telephone Systems; UWB (Ultra Wideband); WAN (Wide Area Network); Wireless Broadband Access Technologies; Wireless Communications; Wireless LANs; Wireless Local Loop; Wireless Mobile Communication; *and* Wireless PANs (Personal Area Networks)

Linktionary!—Tom Sheldon's Encyclopedia of Networking updates	http://www.linktionary.com/m/man.html
10 Gigabit Ethernet Alliance	http://www.10gea.org/
IntelliSpace	http://www.intellispace.com/
Yipes Communications	http://www.yipes.com/
Telseon	http://www.telseon.com/
XO Communications	http://www.xo.com/
Resilient Packet Ring Alliance Web site	http://www.rpralliance.org/
IEEE Broadband Wireless Access Working Group Web site	http://wirelessman.org/
IEEE Resilient Packet Ring Working Group Web site	http://www.ieee802.org/17/
IETF Working Group: IP over Resilient Packet Rings (iporpr)	http://www.ietf.org/html.charters/iporpr-charter.html

Managed Systems

See ASP (Application Service Provider); Co-Location Services; Outsourcing; *and* MSP (Management Service Provider).

Management

See MSP (Management Service Provider); Network Management.

MAPI (Messaging Application Programming Interface)

MAPI is a Microsoft API that helps ensure system independence for messaging applications. It has become widely supported in the industry. MAPI provides a layer of functionality between applications and underlying messaging systems, helping developers create products that are compatible with a wide range of systems and platforms. MAPI is often called "messaging middleware," and, like other middleware products, it helps to promote the creation of products and speed their release to market.

The MAPI architecture has three layers. At the top are MAPI-compliant applications. In the middle is the MAPI subsystem, which has programming interfaces and a service provider interface. The MAPI service providers are at the bottom. They include store providers, message transfer agents, and address book providers. MAPI clients communicate through the MAPI subsystem to MAPI service providers. The MAPI service provider performs the requested action for the client and passes the action back through the MAPI subsystem to the MAPI client. It is only necessary to make a client application MAPI compliant in order for the application to access the service provider functionality. A specific interface is not required for each provider. This is similar to the way in which applications that use the Microsoft Windows printing subsystem do not require drivers for every available printer.

Related Entries   API (Application Programming Interface); Electronic Mail; *and* Middleware and Messaging

Microsoft	http://www.microsoft.com
Electronic Messaging Association	http://www.ema.org
Netlingo MAPI FAQ	http://www.netlingo.com/more/mapi.html
Eudora MAPI FAQ	http://www.eudora.com/developers/mapi.html

Markup Language

A markup language defines how documents should be formatted. In this sense, it is a metalanguage—a language that describes a formatting and markup language. The term "markup" is historically based on the marks made by copy editors to pages that indicate how they should be formatted and typeset. In the early days of computer typesetting, there were many different typesetting systems, and each used its own proprietary markup language. This language consisted of special control characters to indicate the beginning and end of some formatting. The markups were so obscure that users quickly realized a standard markup language was needed to reduce confusion. That led to SGML (Standard Generalized Markup Language). HTML (Hypertext Markup Language) is a markup language that defines hypertext, a markup language that defines jumps to different parts of a document or, in a hypermedia environment like the Web, to other documents.

Related Entries   Document Management; EDI (Electronic Data Interchange); HTML (Hypertext Markup Language); Hypermedia and Hypertext; Metadata; SGML (Standard Generalized Markup Language); *and* XML (Extensible Markup Language)

Media Access Control Methods

See Access Method, Network; MAC (Media Access Control).

Media Gateway

A media gateway is part of the *softswitch architecture,* an architecture that is used in the convergence of voice and data networks. A service provider or carrier can replace expensive and bulky class 5 voice telephone switches with less expensive softswitches that support the interaction of Internet telephony and PSTN networks. See "Softswitch" and "Voice over IP (VoIP)" for more information.

Megaco

Megaco is a protocol that operates between a media gateway and a media gateway controller, allowing the media gateway controller to control the media gateway. Megaco was developed as part of the convergence movement, which brings voice and data together on the packet-switched Internet. Megaco is an abbreviation of "media gateway controller." It has been defined by the IETF and the ITU (which designates it as H.248).

A media gateway and a media gateway controller are components of *softswitch architecture*. Service providers and carriers can replace class 5 voice switches with softswitches. A class 5 switch is a big and expensive telephone switch normally located in central offices all over the world. It accepts dial-up telephone calls from users and creates circuits across a hierarchy of telephone switches. A softswitch breaks the class 5 switching architecture into the gateway and gateway controller. The media gateway translates between circuit-switched voice traffic and packet-based traffic. The media gateway controller, sometimes called the *call agent* or *softswitch*, controls the switch and other traffic functions.

A softswitch supports the integration of the Internet and the PSTN. Until convergence is complete, both networks will exist and there will be a need for integration. For example, IP telephone users will no doubt want to connect with a PSTN telephone user, and vice versa. This means that Internet protocol devices will need to talk to the SS7-based devices that control PSTN voice calls, and vice versa.

In 1999, the IETF and the ITU formally agreed to work on a single protocol, which is known as Megaco/H.248. The ITU has largely taken over this development as H.248. This is discussed further under "Voice over IP (VoIP)." A related protocol is SIP (Session Initiation Protocol), an IETF-developed application layer control protocol for setting up, maintaining, and terminating voice and videoconferencing sessions. It allows different media gateway controllers to communicate and allows end users to request services from media gateway controllers. See "SIP (Session Initiation Protocol)."

Megaco is described in RFC 3015 (Megaco Protocol Version 1.0, November 2000). Also see RFC 3054 (Megaco IP Phone Media Gateway Application Profile, January 2001). The IETF Media Gateway Control (megaco) Working Group is developing this standard.

Related Entries   Convergence; CTI (Computer-Telephony Integration); H.323 Multimedia Conferencing Standard; MGCP (Media Gateway Control Protocol); Multimedia; NPN (New Public Network); PBX (Private Branch Exchange); PINT (PSTN-Internet Interworking); QoS (Quality of Service); SPIRITS (Service in the PSTN/IN Requesting Internet Service); Softswitch; SS7 (Signaling System 7); Telecommunications and Telephone Systems; Unified Messaging; Videoconferencing; Voice/Data Network, *and* Voice over IP (VoIP)

Linktionary!—Tom Sheldon's Encyclopedia of Networking updates	http://www.linktionary.com/m/megaco.html
IETF Working Group: Media Gateway Control (megaco)	http://www.ietf.org/html.charters/megaco-charter.html
ISC (International Softswitch Consortium)	http://www.softswitch.org
Network Magazine article "Megaco and MGCP" by Doug Allen	http://www.networkmagazine.com/article/NMG20001004S0013
ITPRC Computer Telephony links	http://www.itprc.com/voice.htm
About.com telephony Web page	http://compnetworking.about.com/compute/compnetworking/cs/telephony1/

See "Voice over IP (VoIP)" and "Voice/Data Networking" for more links.

MEMS (Micro-Electromechanical Systems)

A MEMS is a semiconductor device with embedded mechanical components. For example, optical switches are created with MEMs that contain numerous tiny moving mirrors that reflect light along different paths. By applying a specific voltage, the mirrors can be precisely rotated and held in place to direct any input to any output. Switches may typically have thousands of inputs, outputs, and switching mirrors. MEMS may also contain sensors, or tiny valves or gears.

Related Entries   ASIC (Application-Specific Integrated Circuit); Embedded Systems; Network Processors; RISC (Reduced Instruction Set Computer); Switch Fabrics and Bus Design; *and* Switching and Switched Networks

Linktionary!—Tom Sheldon's Encyclopedia of Networking updates	http://www.linktionary.com/m/mems.html
The MEMS Clearinghouse	http://mems.isi.edu/

Message Digest Protocols

There are cryptographic processes that can produce unique "fingerprints" of messages that prove to the receiving party that the messages have not been altered. Some part of the message, such as the header text, is run through a one-way hashing function that produces an output that serves as a unique identification for the message. The output is called a *message digest*. When a person receives such a message, she can run a similar hash function to create a message digest that should exactly match the digest sent with the message. If the digests do not match, the message is considered invalid since any alteration will change the results of the hash and produce a different message digest.

See "Digital Signatures" and "Hash Functions."

Message-Oriented Middleware

See MOM (Message-Oriented Middleware).

Messaging Services, Mobile

Mobile messaging services allow users to enter a short message (maximum 160 characters) from the keyboard of a mobile device and have that message forwarded to a recipient or a group of recipients. The message is sent using e-mail–like store-and-forward techniques, where the message first goes to a messaging system and then on to the recipients.

SMS (Short Messaging Service) was originally designed for GSM mobile phone systems, but is now available for a variety of other phone systems. It is called G-Mail on the GSM networks in Europe, where billions of SMS messages are being sent per month. SMS is evolving into EMS (enhanced messaging service) and MMS (Multimedia Messaging Services). See "SMS (Short Messaging Service)." Also see "Packet Radio Data Networks," "SMR (Specialized Mobile Radio)," and "Wireless Mobile Communications."

Messaging Systems

There are a variety of different types of messaging in the networking environment. People exchange messages in real time or in non-real time via chat, instant messaging, and electronic mail messaging. There are also mobile messaging services, as described in the previous topic.

Messaging is also used by applications to exchange information across network connections in non-real time. In this context, messaging is a programming tool that provides middleware functionality. See "Middleware and Messaging" and "MOM (Message-Oriented Middleware)."

Related Entries   Chat; Collaborative Computing; Electronic Mail; FAX Servers and Network Faxing; Groupware; Instant Messaging; IRC (Internet Relay Chat); MAPI (Messaging Application Programming Interface); Middleware and Messaging; MOM (Message-Oriented Middleware); Peer-to-Peer Communication; SMS (Short Messaging Service); *and* Unified Messaging

Metadata

Meta means "about," so metadata is "about data," or, more specifically, "information about data." There is metadata that describes the fields and formats of databases and data warehouses. There is metadata that describes documents and document elements, such as Web pages, research papers, and so on. And there are metadirectories that describe how information is organized in directories (see "Metadirectories" and "Directory Services").

 A full version of this topic is at the Linktionary! Web site listed later.

An important feature of metadata is that it provides concise information about documents and data that improves searching. For example, compare searching entire sets of documents for keywords as opposed to searching descriptive indexes of those documents. A number of services have been defined for this. See "Search and Discovery Services."

Microsoft categorizes metadata as either technical or business oriented. *Technical metadata* supports developers and works like "glue" to link tools, applications, and systems into a solution. For example, it covers database structure, installed applications, and server systems. *Business metadata* makes the services of the enterprise environment more understandable to end users by describing business objects and processes to ease browsing, navigation, and querying of data.

Metadata for Database Management

Most people who are vaguely familiar with metadata think of database management systems. A database contains fields such as Name, Address, City, and so on. Metadata names these fields, describes the size of the fields, and may put restrictions on what can go in the field (for example, numbers only).

If you were to transfer a database file to someone without also giving them the metadata information, the file would appear to the recipient as a long string of characters. The metadata delineates in terms of the alignment of character blocks how the data should be extracted into fields and records. Therefore, metadata is information about how data is extracted, and how it may be transformed. It is also about indexing and creating pointers into data. Database design is all about defining metadata schemas.

The MDC (Meta Data Coalition) is a coalition of vendors and users with a common interest in defining, implementing, and evolving metadata interchange format standards. MDC manages the OIM (Open Information Model), a set of metadata specifications to facilitate sharing and reuse in the application development and data warehousing domains. The data model is based on industry standards such as UML, XML, and SQL.

Document Metadata

Anyone who uses an advanced word processing program such as Microsoft Word can view and edit document metadata. For example, on the File menu, choose Properties. A dialog box appears that has general information about the document such as creation date, size, and so on. A Summary tab has metadata fields such as Title, Subject, Author, Manager, Company, Category, Keywords, and Comments. This information follows the definition for metadata: it is data about the data in the document and you can search for documents by searching this information.

Metadata takes the form of *named element/value* pairs. For example, the element City may have the value New York. A *schema* defines the vocabulary of a particular set of metadata (that is, element names and formatting rules). The metadata may be included with the document or stored in separate files. A schema is a separate file that is referenced from the document.

Different industries usually choose to define schemas that fit their needs, but several standard global schemas have been developed. An important aspect of metadata is that it be machine readable, meaning that it is in a form that applications can access and use without human intervention. The *Dublin Core* metadata scheme defines a standard set of elements that can be used across a broad set of documents. Library researchers played a big part in defining the Dublin Core, which should give you an idea of how and why it is used. The Dublin Core provides the basis for a standardized electronic card catalog for electronic documents.

One of the best examples of the use of metadata is XML, which defines metadata in DTDs (Document Type Definition) files. XML provides a universal way to exchange business information. Various industries have created their own XML standards to represent information specific to their industry. See "XML (Extensible Markup Language)" for more information. Also see "Electronic Commerce" for a discussion of how XML is used for business transactions.

Metadata Recommendations and Standards

A number of vendors, organizations, consortiums, international standards bodies, and working groups are developing metadata recommendations and standards. Some examples are given here.

- **IFLA (The International Federation of Library Associations and Institutions)** An international body representing the interests of library and information services and their users. See http://www.ifla.org/.

- **IETF (Internet Engineering Task Force)** The IETF has a number of projects underway to define metadata usage on the Internet and Web. See "CIP (Common Indexing Protocol)," "Handle System," and "URN (Uniform Resource Names)."

- **W3C Metadata and Resource Description project groups** The W3C's Metadata Activity Group is developing ways to model and encode metadata. The group has developed RDF (Resource Description Framework) and PICS (Platform for Internet Content Selection). See http://www.w3.org/Metadata/.

■ **Dublin Core**   As mentioned, the Dublin Core is an attempt at standardizing a core set of metadata elements. RFC 2413 (Dublin Core Metadata for Resource Discovery, September 1998) describes the metadata elements. See http://dublincore.org/. The Dublin Core is also covered at the Linktionary! Web site.

■ **Digital Object Identifier (DOI) System**   An identification system for intellectual property in the digital environment developed for the publishing industry. One implementation is the *Handle System*, discussed under its own topic in this book. See http://www.doi.org/.

■ **<indecs> (interoperability of data in e-commerce systems)**   <indecs> is an international collaborative project that seeks to develop a framework of metadata standards to support network commerce in intellectual property. See http://www.indecs.org/.

■ **IEEE Learning Technology Standards Committee (LTSC)**   This committee is developing a metadata model for interactive learning and computer-aided instruction that lets learners or instructors search for and access learning objects. See http://ltsc.ieee.org/.

■ **IMS (Instructional Management System) Learning Resources Metadata Specification**   This specification is a result of a collaborative effort that included the IEEE LTSC, Dublin Core, W3C, and other specifications. See http://www.imsproject.org.

■ **ISO TC46**   An ISO committee that is standardizing metadata for libraries, archiving, and publishing. See http://www.iso.ch/meme/TC46.html.

■ **MARC Standards (Library of Congress)**   The MARC (Machine-Readable Cataloging) formats are standards for the representation and communication of bibliographic and related information in machine-readable form. See http://lcweb.loc.gov/marc/.

■ **Data Document Initiative (DDI)**   DDI is an example of a community-specific metadata. DDI covers datasets in the social and behavioral sciences. See http://www.icpsr.umich.edu/DDI/.

■ **MPEG-7 (Moving Picture Experts Group-7)**   MPEG-7 is a content representation standard for multimedia information such as moving pictures and audio.

The preceding is only a partial list of metadata initiatives and standards. Others are related to specific industries. Some of these models are discussed in more detail at the Linktionary! site given later.

Related Entries   CIP (Common Indexing Protocol); CNRP (Common Name Resolution Protocol); Data Warehousing; Directory Services; Document Management; Name Services; OIM (Open Information Model); Repository; Schema; Search and Discovery Services; Service Advertising and Discovery; SLP (Service Location Protocol); WebDAV; UML (Universal Modeling Language); URN (Universal Resource Name); *and* XML (Extensible Markup Language)

Linktionary!—Tom Sheldon's Encyclopedia of Networking updates	http://www.linktionary.com/m/metadata.html
The Meta Data Coalition	http://www.mdcinfo.com
Object Management Group (see UML topics)	http://www.omg.org
Metadata at W3C	http://www.w3.org/Metadata/
"Metadata Architecture, Documents, Metadata, and Links" by Berners-Lee	http://www.w3.org/DesignIssues/Metadata
Metadata for Digital Libraries: a Research Agenda	http://www.ercim.org/publication/ ws-proceedings/EU-NSF/metadata.html
Metadata, Links at Washington University	http://www.cait.wustl.edu/infosys/infosys.html
Metadata information at OII (see metadata items in index)	http://158.169.50.95:10080/oii/en/alpha.html

Metadirectories

A metadirectory adds interoperability to directory services by serving as a single point of access to multiple directory services. The metadirectory allows different directory services to exchange information, or it provides a form of middleware that allows applications to access different directories using a consolidated view of those directories.

Directories contain elements that describe objects in the real world, such as computers, folders, objects, managed resources, and even people. These elements have names and, like the fields in a database, changing values. For example, one directory might store a person's last name as an element called "lastname." Another might store the same information in an element called "surname." A metadirectory provides a way to either *join* or view these differently named elements as the same thing, using one of these techniques:

- Merge the two directories into a new metadirectory where lastname and surname are merged into a single element.

- View the two directories as they are (without merging them into a new directory), but view the two differently named elements as the same element.

The join aspect of metadirectories goes beyond directories that have similar elements with different names. Consider a user who has multiple identities on a network, such as their logon name and e-mail name. A metadirectory can help to resolve these differences as well.

See "Directory Services" and "Metadata."

Metro Access Network

This is the terminology being used to refer to new Gigabit Ethernet and 10-Gigabit Ethernet metropolitan access networks. See "MAN (Metropolitan Area Network)" and "Network Access Services."

MGCP (Media Gateway Control Protocol)

MGCP is a protocol that operates between a media gateway and a media gateway controller, allowing the media gateway controller to control the media gateway. MGCP was developed as part of the convergence movement, which brings voice and data together on the packet-switched Internet. MGCP is defined in RFC 2705 (Media Gateway Control Protocol Version 1.0, October 1999).

A media gateway and a media gateway controller are components of *softswitch architecture*. Softswitch devices replace class 5 voice switches in converged networks. A class 5 switch is a large telephone switch located in carrier central offices all over the world. It accepts dial-up telephone calls from users and creates circuits across a hierarchy of telephone switches. A softswitch breaks the class 5 switching architecture into the gateway and gateway controller, thus creating a less expensive and more flexible platform. To support convergence, the media gateway translates between circuit-switched voice traffic and packet-based traffic.

A softswitch supports the integration of the Internet and the PSTN (public-switched telephone network). Until convergence is complete, both networks will exist and there will be a need for integration. For example, IP telephone users will no doubt want to connect with a PSTN telephone user, and vice versa. This means that Internet protocol devices will need to talk to the SS7-based devices that control PSTN voice calls, and vice versa.

The media gateway controller is sometimes called the *call agent* or just *softswitch*. MGCP assumes that call control is located in these intelligent devices and that they synchronize with one another across a network to send commands to and control gateways. The call agents are expected to execute whatever commands they receive from other call agents, based on a set of defined behaviors.

The status of MGCP is unknown at this writing. In 1999, the IETF and the ITU formally agreed to work on a single protocol, which is known as Megaco/H.248. The ITU has largely taken over this development as H.248. See "Megaco," "Softswitch," and "Voice over IP (VoIP)" for more information.

Related Entries   Convergence; CTI (Computer-Telephony Integration); H.323 Multimedia Conferencing Standard; Megaco; Multimedia; NPN (New Public Network); PBX (Private Branch Exchange); PINT (PSTN-Internet Interworking); QoS (Quality of Service); Softswitch; SPIRITS (Service in the PSTN/IN Requesting Internet Service); SS7 (Signaling System 7); Telecommunications and Telephone Systems; Unified Messaging; Videoconferencing; Voice/Data Networks; *and* Voice over IP (VoIP)

Linktionary!—Tom Sheldon's Encyclopedia of Networking updates	http://www.linktionary.com/m/mgcp.html
IETF Working Group: Media Gateway Control (megaco)	http://www.ietf.org/html.charters/megaco-charter.html
ISC (International Softswtich Consortium)	http://www.softswitch.org

MIB (Management Information Base)

A MIB is defined in SNMP (Simple Network Management Protocol), a network management protocol used in TCP/IP environments. With an SNMP-compatible network management system, network administrators can monitor and manage computers and other devices (such as routers and printers) connected to the network.

A MIB is a data file that contains a complete collection of all the objects that are managed in a network. "Objects" are variables that hold information about the state of some process running on a device or that include textual information about the device, such as a name and description. This information is strictly defined so that different management systems can access and use the information.

A particular device will have many objects that describe it. An *SNMP agent* runs in each SNMP-managed device and is responsible for updating object variables. The management system then queries the SNMP agent to gain information about a system. In contrast, the agent may also alert the management system about special events on a device.

There are groups of SNMP objects, such as "system," "interface," "IP," and "TCP." A MIB group called "System" contains objects that hold variables such as a device's name, its location, and other descriptive information. The interface group holds information about network adapters and tracks statistics such as bytes sent and received on the interface. The IP group has objects that track packet flow, packet fragmentation, dropped packets, and similar information. The TCP group has objects that keep track of connections.

Related Entries   Network Management; SNMP (Simple Network Management Protocol)

Microsoft

Microsoft Corporation was founded in 1975 by William H. Gates and Paul G. Allen. In 1981, Microsoft and IBM introduced MS-DOS and started the personal computer revolution. Today, Microsoft focuses on producing and marketing a broad range of products for personal computing, including development tools and languages, application software, systems software, hardware peripherals, books, and multimedia applications. Microsoft products of interest to network administrators and users are covered under the Related Entries.

Related Entries   COM (Component Object Model); IntelliMirror; Microsoft.NET; Microsoft Active Directory; Microsoft BackOffice; Microsoft Exchange; Microsoft Windows; Microsoft Windows File System; *and* SOAP (Simple Object Access Protocol)

Microsoft	http://www.microsoft.com/
Microsoft Developer Web site	http://www.msdn.microsoft.com/

Microsoft.NET

Microsoft.NET is a distributed object computing architecture platform that supports component software for enterprises and Web-based applications. In Microsoft's .NET vision, applications are constructed using multiple "Web Services" that work together to provide data and services for applications. A previous version of Microsoft.NET was called Microsoft DNA. The new platform and its evolution from the old architecture are illustrated at the Web site listed later.

All of the Windows .NET 2000 building blocks share a common component model in COM+, which builds on earlier COM services and preserves existing application environments. The family of solutions includes the following.

- Windows 2000 server, which includes Web Services, transaction services, messaging, data access, clustering, and IP load-balancing services

- Visual Studio.NET, a development environment

- BizTalk Server 2000, an XML-based business-to-business commerce solution (supports XML-formatted business documents)

- Commerce Server 2000, a business-to-consumer commerce server

- Exchange Server, a messaging and groupware platform

- SQL Server 2000, a database solution

- Host Integration Server 2000, a server for integrating data on legacy hosts

- Application Center 2000, a solution that supports high-availability server arrays (server farms)

- Mobile Information 2001 Server, a server to support mobile users

The architecture for .NET is a multitiered client/server model. Clients access a middle-tier presentation and business logic server (typically, a Web server). The middle-tier server accesses the back-end databases and legacy systems, retrieves data based on user requests, and then forwards the data to the client as an HTML Web page.

A Web Service is programmable application logic that is accessible using standard Internet protocols. Web Services combine aspects of component-based development and the Web. Like components, Web Services represent black-box functionality that can be reused without worrying about how the service is implemented. Unlike current component technologies, Web Services is not accessed via object-model–specific protocols, such as DCOM, RMI, or IIOP. Instead, Web Services is accessed via HTTP and XML.

In addition, the Web Service interface is defined strictly in terms of the messages the Web Service accepts and generates. Consumers of Web Service can be implemented on any platform in any programming language, as long as they can create and consume the messages defined for the Web Service interface. Five requirements are necessary for service-based development, including standard data representation, common message format, a service description language, a service discovery protocol, and a service provider discovery protocol.

Data is represented with XML and delivered in SOAP (Simple Object Access Protocol) messages via HTTP. A language called WSDL (Web Services Description Language) is used to describe services. An XML-based protocol called Disco is used to discover services at a site, and a mechanism called UDDI (Universal Description, Discovery, and Integration) defines how to advertise services and how Web Service consumers can find services. Similar mechanisms are discussed under "Service Advertising and Discovery."

A platform similar to Microsoft.NET is Sun Microsystem's Java 2 Platform, Enterprise Edition (J2EE), which is discussed under the Java heading. Both .NET and J2EE support distributed object computing and component software technologies for enterprise and Internet environments.

Related Entries COM (Component Object Model); CORBA (Common Object Request Broker Architecture); Distributed Computer Networks; Distributed Object Computing; Java; Microsoft; Microsoft.NET; Microsoft Active Directory; Microsoft BackOffice; Microsoft Exchange; Microsoft Windows; Microsoft Windows File System; Middleware and Messaging; MOM (Message-Oriented

Middleware); Multitiered Architectures; Service Advertising and Discovery; SOAP (Simple Object Access Protocol); UDDI (Universal Description, Discovery, and Integration); Web Technologies and Concepts; *and* XML (Extensible Markup Language)

Microsoft .NET developer center	http://msdn.microsoft.com/net/
Microsoft Web solutions platforms overview	http://microsoft.com/business/products/webplatform/overview.asp
UDDI (Universal Description, Discovery, and Integration) Web site	http://www.UDDI.org/

Microsoft Active Directory

A directory service can provide white page and yellow page services in distributed computing environments. It allows people and applications to look up other people or services in a hierarchical database. See "Directory Services" for a general description.

Microsoft Active Directory combines features of the Internet's DNS (Domain Name System) locator service and X.500 naming. With it, administrators can unify and manage multiple name spaces over heterogeneous systems. The core protocol for the service is LDAP (Lightweight Directory Access Protocol), which allows the service to work across operating system boundaries and integrate multiple name spaces. Because of this cross-platform capability, administrators can manage other vendors' directory services from Active Directory and reduce administrative workload.

The services go beyond simple name lookup. Administrators can locate and manage resources throughout the organization, including user and group accounts, computers, filing systems, peripheral devices, connection devices, database systems, and Internet connections.

Directory services also include the following features:

- Support for multimaster replication, which allows updates to occur at servers that are closest to the operator rather than at a master server
- Support for short life-span services such as Internet telephony, videoconferencing, and chat services
- Interoperable with NetWare environments and backward compatible with Windows NT domain services
- Programmable via a wide range of scripting languages
- Go beyond providing simple white page and yellow page services by providing a wide variety of query, administrative, registration, and resolution needs

Microsoft Active Directory supports Internet and OSI naming formats. For example, Internet e-mail addresses such as *name@company*.com are supported. DNS locator services and X.500 standards are combined. In addition, a Web browser can be used to access directory services via the HTTP protocol using a URL name such as http://server.company.com/service. *LDAP URLs and X.500 names are also supported, which have a form similar to the following:*

LDAP://*server.company.com*/CN=*user*,OU=*department*,OU=*division*,O=*company*,C=*country*

The Active Directory domain tree can be compared to Novell's NDS (Novell Directory Services) tree, except that Microsoft has retained its domain model, which was available in previous versions of Windows NT. Domains are represented by partitions of the directory tree, and domains can be subdivided into OU (organizational unit) containers. Each OU can become an administrative unit that is managed by a person delegated by some higher-level administrator.

The "container" concept allows administrators to build a hierarchical structure of organizations, departments, people, and resources. Administrators and users can "drill down" through the hierarchy to locate people and resources. A global catalog also exists that allows users to easily find an object no matter where it is in the tree.

The hierarchical structure allows for decentralized administration while maintaining security. In previous versions of Windows NT, the domain was the scope of administration and security. With Microsoft Active Directory, security can be administered independently within each domain, within a subtree of OUs that are part of a domain, or within a single OU.

Related Entries   DEN (Directory Enabled Networks); Directory Services; LDAP (Lightweight Directory Access Protocol); Microsoft; Microsoft Windows; Name Services; NDS (Novell Directory Services); NIS (Network Information System); Replication; Search and Discovery Services; Service Advertising and Discovery; *and* X.500 Directory Services

Microsoft Active Directory home page

http://www.microsoft.com/windows2000/ guide/server/features/directory.asp

Refer to "Directory Services" for other links.

Microsoft BackOffice

Microsoft BackOffice is a suite of server-based business and productivity applications that run on Windows NT and Windows 2000 platforms. Microsoft BackOffice Server 2000 is specifically designed to run on Windows 2000 and includes the following components. For additional information, visit Microsoft's BackOffice Web site.

- **SQL Server**   A relational database component for managing and storing data.

- **Host Integration Server**   A host connectivity component that provides Windows, Macintosh, DOS, and OS/2 clients with access to AS/400 and IBM mainframes.

- **SMS (System Management Server)**   A network management component that provides a central place to manage network hardware and software, software distribution, troubleshooting, and application management.

- **Exchange Server**   An electronic mail, messaging, and groupware system. See "Microsoft Exchange Server."

- **ISA (Internet Security and Acceleration) Server**   This server provides security, caching, and Internet connectivity via proxy services.

Related Entries   Microsoft; Microsoft.NET; Microsoft Exchange; *and* Microsoft Windows

Microsoft BackOffice Server Web site

http://www.microsoft.com/backofficeserver/

Microsoft DNA (Digital interNet Application)

DNA is a distributed object computing platform that was the forerunner of Microsoft.NET, Microsoft's latest Web solutions platform. See "Microsoft.NET."

Microsoft Exchange

Microsoft Exchange provides enterprise-wide information exchange by integrating electronic mail, scheduling, electronic forms, and document sharing. It also provides a basis for creating special applications that can take advantage of an enterprise-wide messaging system. With Microsoft Exchange, organizations create an enterprise-wide message system that gives everyone in the organization quick access to information. Exchange also connects with the Internet and other networks outside the organization to provide global messaging.

Exchange is a client/server product that is provided in the form of Exchange Server and Exchange clients. Exchange Server is the "engine" for exchanging information, both throughout the enterprise and outside the enterprise. Exchange clients have a full range of messaging services at their disposal, including electronic mail, address book management, and others, as discussed later.

Microsoft Exchange supports *electronic forms* so that workgroups can exchange "structured information" that can be distributed throughout the enterprise. In addition, *public folders* serve as repositories for shared messages, forms, documents, applications, and databases. These folders can be replicated to other locations, placing information closer to users who need it and reducing network traffic. Exchange synchronizes replicated folders to ensure that users are working with the latest information. Shared *discussion databases,* similar to bulletin board chat sessions, are also supported in Exchange so that people can have a place to field and discuss ideas.

An example of how shared folders and information exchange can benefit an organization is best seen in the example of a customer-support organization. Problems that have been tackled by one support person can be documented in a shared database. Other support people can check this database before working on similar problems. Similarly, ideas can be shared and discussed companywide. Shared discussion databases provide a perfect place to exchange ideas. People can read a history of a conversation and reply at any time. This eliminates the constraints of one-time meetings and phone conversations that are not documented for others to review.

Exchange provides messaging services, information services, directory services, and connectivity services. It also supports remote access, X.400 messaging standards, Internet mail standards, IBM PROFS/OfficeVision, and IBM SNADS (SNA Distributed Services) gateways. Exchange supports MAPI (Messaging Application Programming Interface) so you can create custom message-enabled applications, and ODBC (Open Database Connectivity) so you can access stored information in a variety of data formats.

Related Entries   Collaborative Computing; Electronic Mail; Groupware; Lotus Domino; Lotus Notes; MAPI (Messaging Application Programming Interface); Microsoft; Microsoft.NET; Microsoft Active Directory; Microsoft BackOffice; Microsoft Windows; Microsoft Windows File System; *and* Workflow Management

 Microsoft Exchange Server Web site   http://www.microsoft.com/exchange/

Microsoft Windows

The Microsoft Windows family of products began as a graphical user interface that ran on top of the DOS operating system. The first versions of Windows were important because of their multitasking capabilities, which allowed them to run multiple applications at the same time. Today, the operating system has grown into a full-featured operating system for desktop users and network server applications. The product lineup as of this writing is described here:

- **Windows CE**   A "small footprint" operating system designed for specialized computing devices such as hand-held PCs, telephones, and consumer devices such as television sets.

- **Windows 98**   At the time of this writing, this is the most pervasive desktop operating system. It is fully integrated with Internet/Web technologies and supports new multimedia hardware technologies and entertainment platforms. The user interface and desktop were altered from previous versions by integrating Web-browser–like features into the standard desktop.

- **Windows ME (Millennium Edition)**   This is a follow-on to Windows 98 designed specifically for home users. It includes advanced digital media features, a simplified user interface, home networking, and broad support for consumer hardware and software.

- **Windows XP (Xperience)**   With Windows XP, Microsoft continues its refinement of the user interface and features to support home users. Visual themes improve usability by stepping users through common tasks. A remote access feature lets you access your mom's computer and clean up the desktop. A significant feature is that XP is based on Windows 2000 technology.

- **Windows NT Workstation and Server**   These two operating systems were Microsoft's high-end platforms during the latter half of the 1990s. Windows 2000, described next, is the follow-on operating system.

- **Windows 2000 Professional and Advanced Server**   These are Microsoft's latest high-end desktop workstation and server operating system.

For more information on these systems, refer to the Web site listed here.

Related Entries   Microsoft; Microsoft.NET; Microsoft Active Directory; Microsoft BackOffice; Microsoft Exchange; Microsoft Windows File System; *and* Network Operating Systems

Microsoft's Windows site	http://www.microsoft.com/windows/
Google Web Directory Windows page	http://directory.google.com/Top/Computers/ Software/Operating_Systems/Windows/
Yahoo! Windows directory	http://dir.yahoo.com/Computers_and_Internet/ Software/Operating_Systems/Windows/
J. Helmig's World of Windows Networking	http://www.wown.com/
Google Web Directory Windows page	http://directory.google.com/Top/Computers/ Software/Operating_Systems/Windows/

M

Microsoft Windows File Systems

Microsoft operating systems support the following files systems. The available file system depends on the version of the operating system, as listed in Table M-1. The structure of volumes formatted by each of these file systems, as well as the way each file system organizes data on the disk, are significantly different. Note that the newest operating systems include support for all previous file systems. Operating system versions that support multiple file systems give users a choice of which version to install.

- **FAT (File Allocation Table)**   FAT has been a part of Microsoft operating systems since the original MS-DOS. This file system has limited security features and poorer performance than NTFS.

- **NTFS (NT File System)**   NTFS was introduced with the original release of Windows NT. It includes features such as advanced file system security, recovery from write failures (transaction file system), support for large volumes, long filenames, and improved performance. The remainder of this topic covers NTFS as it is being implemented in all new Microsoft operating systems.

In addition, Windows also supports the following optical disk file systems:

- **CDFS (Compact Disk File System)**   CDFS support enables Windows to read data from CD-ROM devices. The Microsoft implementation of CDFS support adheres to the ISO 9660 specification.

- **UDF (Universal File System)**   UDF is a file system defined by the Optical Storage Technology Association (OSTA). UDF is compliant with ISO-13346 and is the successor to CDFS (ISO-9660). UDF is targeted for DVD, CD-ROM, and data interchange between operating systems. It supports long filenames, Unicode filenames, access control lists (ACLs), read-write (not just mastering), and bootable disk.

Note that Microsoft's *Distributed File System*, or DFS is a network file system, rather than a disk-oriented file system. It presents a logical view of distributed physical storage, allowing

Operating System	File System Format of Volume
Windows 2000	NTFS 5, FAT16, and FAT32
Microsoft Windows NT	NTFS and FAT16
Microsoft Windows 95 (release 2) and Microsoft Windows 98	FAT16 and FAT32
Windows 95 prior to Windows 95 (release 2)	FAT16
Microsoft MS-DOS	FAT16

Table M-1.   *Microsoft File Systems*

file systems that are distributed across a network to be united into a single name space. See "DFS (Distributed File System), Microsoft." Also see "File Systems" for a description of other file systems.

Windows NT and Windows 2000 operating systems provide a choice of FAT16, FAT32, or NTFS. During installation, you can choose to install one of these file systems. FAT versions would only be selected when backward compatibility is required. NTFS provides advanced file permissions that can keep files private. See "Rights and Permissions."

NTFS 5 is the file system for Windows 2000. It has most of the features of NTFS and also provides complete content indexing and built-in hierarchical storage management. A major new feature is dynamic volume management, which allows for live configuration changes without rebooting. There are also advanced backup, restore, and disaster recovery tools. An encrypting file system allows data to be stored in a cipher format on NTFS volumes. A disk quota feature allows administrators to manage the disk space of users. NTFS 5 also includes a remote storage server facility that can migrate files from primary storage to secondary storage (tape or optical disk). See "Storage Management Systems."

NTFS is designed for quick file operations on very large hard drives. It includes a file recovery system and built-in attributes to handle security and access control. When you format a partition on a disk drive with the NTFS file system, the partition is initialized as an NTFS volume. This volume contains the MFT (master file table), which holds information about every file in the volume. The information is stored in 2,048-byte records and operates like a relational database. Files are identified by a number, which depends on the file's position in the MFT and a special sequence number.

The *cluster* is the fundamental unit of disk allocation for NTFS. A default cluster size is selected based on the size of the drive, but a 512 , 1,024-, 2,048-, or 4,096-byte allocation size can be selected. Using a large allocation unit size is better for large files, but storing small files in large allocation units is a waste of disk space. If the drive will hold a lot of small files, the lower allocation size is preferable. However, storing large files on a drive with small allocations can lead to fragmentation, which reduces performance.

Allocation Size	Disk Size
512 bytes	< 512MB
1,024 bytes	512MB to 1GB
2,048 bytes	1GB to 2GB
4,096 bytes	> 2GB

Directories and files on NTFS partitions can be compressed to obtain as much as a 50-percent reduction in the size of a text file or a 40-percent reduction in the size of an executable file. You can select one or more files, directories, or subdirectories, and choose to compress or uncompress them. You also can set the compressed attributes for files. If you choose to compress or uncompress a directory, files currently in the directory are not affected. Only files you add to the directory are affected. Note that compression does not adversely affect performance. Files are compressed incrementally in the background. When a user accesses a compressed file, decompression takes place automatically.

There are two aspects to file system security for computers connected to networks. The first is restricting access to information on a local computer to people who log on to that computer. The second is restricting access to information that is shared over the network. When a directory is shared, users can access it from workstations attached to the network, based on permissions.

To make information on a Windows system available to other users on a network, you share a folder (or an individual file). When you share a folder, all the files and all the subfolders in it are shared as well. You can then change the access permissions on any file or folder in the shared folder if you need to block access.

Related Entries   Access Control; Account, User; ACL (Access Control List); Attributes; Authentication and Authorization; CIFS (Common Internet File System); Compression Techniques; Data Management; Data Protection; DFS (Distributed File System), Microsoft; File Sharing; File Systems; Microsoft; Microsoft Active Directory; Microsoft Windows; NAS (Network Attached Storage); Network Operating Systems; Novell NetWare File System; Replication; Rights and Permissions; Samba; SMB (Server Message Blocks); Storage Management Systems; Storage Systems; Transaction Processing; UNIX File System; Users and Groups; *and* Volume and Partition Management

Linktionary!—Tom Sheldon's Encyclopedia of Networking updates	http://www.linktionary.com/m/microsoft_filesystem.html
Microsoft (search for NTFS)	http://www.microsoft.com/
Microsoft Windows 2000 file system	http://www.microsoft.com/windows2000/

Microwave Communications

Microwaves are short-wavelength, high-frequency signals that occupy the electromagnetic spectrum 1,000 MHz (1 GHz) to 1,000 GHz (1 terahertz). This is just above the radio frequency range and just below the infrared range. The entire range is huge, but much of it is not used for data communications, especially at the high-end due to water absorption. See "Electromagnetic Spectrum."

Here are some microwave facts and figures:

■ Wavelengths under 10 GHz are about ½ meter or less, while wavelengths over 10 GHZ are in the centimeter range. Wavelengths over 100 GHz are in the millimeter range—about the size of a pinhead.

■ Long-wavelength, low-frequency microwaves (5–10 centimeter wavelengths, below 10 GHz) will propagate up to 30 miles and are not affected much by rain. However, they tend to bounce off objects, which creates signal reflections called "multipath" (discussed later).

■ Short-wavelength, high-frequency microwaves (1–5 centimeter wavelength, above 10 GHz) are distance limited to less than 5 miles. These frequencies are absorbed by rain and moisture in the environment. Signal reflection (multipath) is not a problem since the reflections are usually absorbed before they cause problems.

■ A typical microwave oven has an electron tube that generates a 2.45-GHz microwave signal to heat your leftovers.

- Cellular PCS mobile phone systems operate in the 1.9-GHz range.

- A typical cordless phone operates in the unlicensed wireless band at 2.4 GHz. So do wireless LANs, Bluetooth PANs (personal area networks), and a range of other consumer electronic devices. Interference is a problem.

- The IEEE 802.11a wireless LAN standard operates in the 5-GHz range at data rates as high as 54 Mbits/sec.

- Satellite communication systems use microwave frequencies in various ranges starting at 1.6 GHz and going up to 30.5 GHz. The ranges include uplink and downlink channels. See "Satellite Communication Systems."

- MMDS (Multichannel Multipoint Distribution Service), a fixed broadband wireless for long-range local access (48 km/30 mi), operates in the ranges of 2.5–2.7 GHz and 3.4–3.7 GHz.

- LMDS (Local Multipoint Distribution Services), a fixed broadband wireless system for short-range local access (8 km/5 mi), operates in the range of 10 GHz to 43 GHz.

Microwave systems are useful when cable is difficult or impractical to install. Line of sight is required in most cases, although new technologies ease this requirement somewhat. Typical applications include satellite-to-ground links, LAN bridging between buildings in metropolitan areas, and point-to-point links across large open areas such as swamps and lakes.

A point-to-point microwave transmission system consists of two directional antennas as shown here. Generally, the antennas need to be pointed at one another, but exact alignment (line of sight) is only critical as the frequency increases. An antenna mounted on a 300-foot tower can focus on an antenna 50 miles away. This extended distance is possible due to the lack of obstructions and reflections.

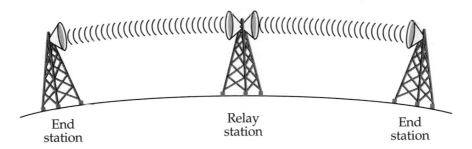

End station   Relay station   End station

Unlike a radio broadcast that sends signals in all directions, microwave antennas are point-to-point communication systems. Relay stations equipped with signal amplifiers can be used to extend transmissions over much longer distances. A relay station consists of two antennas, each focused on a distant antenna in a different direction.

Small, short-distance microwave systems are easy to install and ideal for small business. For example, you can establish a microwave communication link between two buildings by mounting an antenna in a window of each building and focusing the antennas on one another. Such systems provide considerable savings by bypassing the local exchange carrier. In campus environments, microwave systems may be more practical than burying cable.

A typical microwave user is an organization that has offices over five miles apart in metropolitan areas. Universities are common users, as are hospitals and city/county governments. CATV service providers use microwave systems to link their networks. The telephone companies also use microwave extensively along with fiber-optic cable to replace older analog systems. As the cellular communication system expands, service providers use microwave systems to interconnect outlying base stations. Microwave systems are also used as backup lines to provide continuous service in case other transmission systems fail.

The MMDS and LMDS systems are interesting because of their potential to provide network access services in metropolitan areas. MMDS was originally designated for one-way transmission of wireless cable TV signals to rural areas. It has been called "wireless cable." But DBS (Direct Broadcast Satellite) systems proved more popular and, today, MMDS is considered more important as a network access technology. A typical MMDS system consists of a base station antenna and subscribers at fixed locations. One antenna site can cover most metro areas, but a system can be scaled by dividing an area into cells and reusing frequencies, as is done in mobile cellular systems. See "MMDS (Multichannel Multipoint Distribution Service)."

LMDS can provide high-speed last-mile connections for businesses in metro areas. LMDS provides more bandwidth than MMDS, but the LMDS frequency range is affected by rain, which causes signal fading over long distances. Most important, LMDS requires line of sight, which reduces its coverage area. See "LMDS (Local Multipoint Distribution Service)."

However, new metro Ethernet services appearing in most large metropolitan areas may shut out MMDS and LMDS. These services offer inexpensive LAN bridging and Internet access across metropolitan areas at data rates above 10 Gbits/sec, and they offer a practical alternative to carrier leased circuits. See "MAN (Metropolitan Area Networks)."

Microwave systems suffer from signal reflections which occur when signals bounce off nearby objects. The reflected signal combines with the actual signal creating *multipath* problems. The echo signal is received slightly later than the primary signal and can seriously corrupt digital data signals. The frequency bands used by MMDS have long propagation distances and, thus, high amounts of multipath.

The Cisco paper "Overcoming Multipath in Non-Line-of-Sight High-Speed Microwave Communication Links" (see the Web site list) discusses Cisco's use of OFDM (orthogonal frequency division multiplexing) to overcome the problems of multipath. An OFDM receiver synchronizes reflected signals so that they appear to the receiver as if they are arriving in a single stream from a single location. The technique also improves the upstream and downstream data rates. Cisco's version of OFDM is called Vector OFDM or VOFDM. Wi-LAN of Canada claims Cisco's VOFDM infringes on its patented Wideband-OFDM or W-OFDM.

Related Entries   Bluetooth; Communication Services and Providers; DBS (Direct Broadcast Satellite); Electromagnetic Spectrum; HALO (High Altitude Long Operation); HDR (High Data Rate); Infrared Technologies; Last Mile Services; LMDS (Local Multipoint Distribution Service); Local Loop; MAN (Metropolitan Area Network); MMDS (Multichannel Multipoint Distribution Service); Modulation Techniques; Network Access Services; Network Concepts; OFDM (Orthogonal Frequency Division Multiplexing); Optical Networks; Radio Communication and Networks; Residential Broadband; Satellite Communication Systems; Service Providers and Carriers; Spread Spectrum Signaling; Telecommunications and Telephone Systems; UWB (Ultra Wideband); WAN (Wide Area Network); Wireless Broadband Access Technologies; Wireless Communications; Wireless LANs; Wireless Local Loop; *and* Wireless PANs (Personal Area Networks)

Linktionary!—Tom Sheldon's Encyclopedia of Networking updates	http://www.linktionary.com/m/microwave.html
Paul Wade's online microwave antenna book	http://www.qsl.net/n1bwt/contents.htm
Stratex Networks microwave tutorial	http://www.dmcstratexnetworks.com/solutions/this-is-microwave.html
Cisco white paper: "Overcoming Multipath in Non-Line-of-Sight High-Speed Microwave Communication Links"	http://www.cisco.com/warp/public/cc/pd/witc/wt2700/mulpt_wp.htm
U.S. FCC Microwave Services page	http://www.fcc.gov/wtb/microwave/
Microwave Journal	http://www.mwjournal.com/
Broadband Guide	http://www.broadband-guide.com/
Broadband Wireless Association	http://www.broadband-wireless.org/index.html
Bitpipe (search for "microwave")	http://www.bitpipe.com/
Network Magazine tutorials	http://www.networkmagazine.com/static/tutorial/index.html

Middleware and Messaging

Middleware is a layer of software or functionality that sits between one system and another, and provides a way for those systems to exchange information or connect with one another even though they have different interfaces. Messaging is one of the methods that has become integral to the way that middleware is implemented. Middleware and messaging may be employed within an organization to tie together its LAN and legacy systems, its diverse clients and back-end databases, and its local and remote systems. Middleware is also important for Web applications.

Middleware helps applications work together across multiple platforms or operating system environments. Developers write applications that interface with the middleware layer rather than re-creating the functions that the middleware layer can provide. Middleware is used in the enterprise to make client/server applications work across the enterprise network and in Web environments to link clients with applications that reside on servers at multiple locations.

Enterprise application integration or EAI is the process of creating information infrastructures that support the deployment of new applications and processes within organizations. EAI typically describes middleware in terms of topologies:

- A *hub* approach integrates message exchanges, object brokering, data transformations, and so on, at a central location called the *application server*. An application server typically connects Web servers with back-end database servers. It is part of a multitiered architectural approach.

- A *bus* approach implements software in network systems, which provides a sort of *virtual bus* on which messages and objects are exchanged. CORBA's object request broker (ORB) can be considered a bus.

M

■ The *point-to-point* approach uses remote procedure calls or other mechanisms to let applications talk to each other directly over the network. This is the more traditional approach that is still viable in many situations.

The following types of middleware are available for building distributed applications, heterogeneous networks, and Internet-based distributed software systems. The main difference among these systems is whether they offer synchronous (real-time point-to-point connections) or asynchronous operation. Some offer both. Synchronous middleware tends to be more reliable and responsive since systems are actively involved in the exchange of information, but development and maintenance is more difficult than the more relaxed asynchronous methods.

■ **Database middleware**   This is a layer of software that lets clients access database systems from a variety of operating systems or applications. SQL is the earliest two-tier client/server form of middleware. It reduced the need to transfer large amounts of information to clients by efficiently selecting and moving just the records that are needed. It also runs stored procedures directly at the database server, rather than moving the data to the client and requiring the client to run the procedures. This is a form of three-tiered architecture (client, application processing, server), except that the middle tier is running as a stored procedure on the database server. Microsoft's ODBC (Open Database Connectivity) now fills this role in many systems. Microsoft's OLE DB provides similar services. See "DBMS (Database Management System."

■ **RPCs (Remote Procedure Calls)**   RPCs are an early form of middleware in which a client makes a request to a server to run some procedure. RPCs are synchronous in that the requesting application waits for a response from the server. Multiple calls are usually required to get something done, which can affect network bandwidth for complex tasks. RPCs are best used for simple interactions between clients and servers, not complex transactions. This is a problem in today's multitasking environments. See "RPC (Remote Procedure Call)" for more information.

■ **MOM (message-oriented middleware)**   Messaging middleware uses an *asynchronous* approach where the sender does not actively wait for a response. It is like e-mail, where a person picks up messages when they log on. There are two primary types of messaging middleware. *Message queuing* is like an e-mail system in which a server queues up messages for delivery. The server can be configured to force an immediate exchange if possible, and it may examine messages for security reasons or to alter formats. *Publish and subscribe* is a model that has become popular on the Web. You subscribe to a service that publishes information. As new information is published, it is sent to your Web browser. In an enterprise environment, information may be broadcast to everyone. See "MOM (Message-Oriented Middleware)" for more information.

■ **ORBs (object request brokers)**   Sometimes referred to as a "logical bus," an ORB provides an interface that objects can use to communicate with other objects in distributed network environments. However, not all systems are object oriented, especially legacy systems, so ORBs may be limited in some environments. See "ORB (Object Request Broker)" for more information.

■ **TP (transaction processing) monitors**   These provide a high level of monitoring and control for processes occurring between objects to ensure that operations complete successfully. If even one of the operations fails, all operations are rolled back. TPs are naturally synchronous and resource consuming, but they need to be in order to ensure data integrity. See "Transaction Processing" for more information.

■ **XML-based middleware**   XML has become the latest, and possibly most important, middleware component. XML allows developers to create documents for exchanging structured information across the Internet. XML provides a standard way to describe information and, therefore, is a potentially universal data exchange mechanism. *XML application servers* (XAS) combine XML and data access technologies with middleware functionality. The Microsoft.NET platform uses XML to describe application logic and data, SOAP (Simple Object Access Protocol) to package it, and HTTP to deliver it. SOAP defines how to create an HTML header and XML file that can call a program on another computer and pass information to it in a format and layout that the computer will immediately recognize. This is similar to RPCs (remote procedure calls), but Microsoft views SOAP as a move away from the RPC model (which is the basis of COM+) and a move toward a message-passing model.

■ **E-mail middleware**   Yes, e-mail is a form of messaging middleware. In fact, e-mail could be called middleware for people. Many collaborative applications exchange information by sending mail automatically in the background. Many electronic business systems use e-mail to exchange documents such as invoices and purchase orders.

Application servers have become synonymous with middleware. An application server is a "middle server" in a three-tiered architecture, which is an evolution of the two-tiered client/ server model. They may provide any or all of the middleware services described earlier. Application servers interface with databases and information systems on the back end and clients, usually Web server clients, on the front end. The servers may perform relatively simple functions such as building Web pages on-the-fly with data obtained from back-end servers. The servers may also provide more sophisticated functions, such as transaction processing in electronic commerce applications.

Application servers and three-tiered architectures help organizations build sophisticated data centers that distribute incoming client requests among multiple application servers, which, in turn, make requests, to back-end services. See "Multitiered Architecture" for a description and illustrations.

An interesting read related to middleware is RFC 2768 (Network Policy and Services: A Report of a Workshop on Middleware, February 2000). It talks about middleware in terms of network components such as AAA (authentication, authorization, and accounting), policy framework, directories, resource management, networked information discovery and retrieval services, quality of service, security, and operational tools.

Related Entries   ActiveX; API (Application Programming Interface); Application Server; ASP (Application Service Provider); Back-End Systems; Client/Server Computing; Clustering; COM (Component Object Model); Content Distribution; CORBA (Common Object Request Broker Architecture); Data Mart; Data Warehousing; DBMS (Database Management System); Distributed Applications; Distributed Computer Networks; Distributed Object Computing; Electronic Commerce;

IBM Host Connectivity; Java; Load Balancing; Metadata; Microsoft.NET; MOM (Message-Oriented Middleware); Multiprocessing; Multitiered Architectures; Named Pipes; Network Design and Construction; Object Technologies; ODBC (Open Database Connectivity); ORB (Object Request Broker); Pipes; RPCs (Remote Procedure Calls); SOAP (Simple Object Access Protocol); Sockets API; SQL (Structured Query Language); Transaction Processing; *and* XML (Extensible Markup Language)

Linktionary!—Tom Sheldon's Encyclopedia of Networking updates	http://www.linktionary.com/m/middleware.html
OMG (Object Management Group)	http://www.omg.org/
Open Applications Group middleware API specification	http://www.openapplications.org/oamas/loadform.htm
Carnegie Mellon message-oriented middleware page	http://www.sei.cmu.edu/str/descriptions/momt.html
Carnegie Mellon middleware page	http://www.sei.cmu.edu/str/descriptions/middleware.html
Internet2 Middleware page (middleware for advanced network applications)	http://www.internet2.org/html/middleware.html
CAIT Web links page	http://www.cait.wustl.edu/infosys/infosys.html
Bitpipe (search for "middleware")	http://www.bitpipe.com/
Google Web Directory middleware page	http://directory.google.com/Top/Computers/Software/Networking/Middleware/
"Massively Distributed Systems" by Dan Nessett (3Com)	http://www.3com.com/technology/tech_net/white_papers/503056.html
EAI (enterprise application integration) paper at Xpragma	http://www.xpragma.com/eai_wp.htm
Standish Group middleware paper	http://www.standishgroup.com/buscrit.html
Intranet Design Magazine's intranet development page	http://idm.internet.com/webdev/index.html
ServerWatch application servers page	http://serverwatch.internet.com/appservers.html
Application server zone	http://www.appserver-zone.com

MIME (Multipurpose Internet Mail Extension)

MIME is an IETF (Internet Engineering Task Force) standard originally defined in 1992 for sending a variety of different types of information (data types) via Internet electronic mail. Basically, MIME is what lets you attach just about any type of file to an Internet mail message. Previously, electronic mail messages could only handle text. What MIME does is provide standard ways to encode data types for transmission in electronic mail. MIME supports binary files, non-US-ASCII character sets, images, sound, video, and documents that are stored in special formats (such as compressed files). MIME also supports special fonts in the message itself.

A typical e-mail message consists of a header that includes the fields Data, To, From, and Subject, followed by the text of the message. RFC 1049 (A Content-Type Header Field for

Internet Messages, March 1988) added a header that could describe a particular format for the message content, although the entire content had to be the same.

MIME's contributions are multipart attachments for messages and a way for users to choose the type of encoding they want to use. Each part of the message can hold a different data type. One way to understand MIME messages is to envision two or more separate e-mail messages, each with different data types, that are bundled together into a single message and going to the same destination. Each part of the message is called a *body part* and can contain text, graphics, audio, or video.

MIME adds information to the header of an e-mail message, such as the following:

- **MIME-Version**   This indicates that the message conforms to MIME. This field is required.

- **Content-Type**   This header indicates the type of data. Each body part in the message can be preceded by a Content-Type. There are seven major content types and a number of subtypes.

- **Content-Transfer-Encoding**   This indicates the encoding method used on the body part.

- **Content-ID**   This is an optional field that uniquely identifies a body part for reference elsewhere.

- **Content-Description**   This is another option field that can be used to describe a body part.

A more complete description of MIME parts is at the Linktionary! Web site. Here is a listing of the primary RFCs that describe MIME. Many others exist, and they are listed at the Linktionary! Web site.

- RFC 2045 (MIME, Part One: Format of Internet Message Bodies, November 1996)

- RFC 2046 (MIME, Part Two: Media Types, November 1996)

- RFC 2047 (MIME, Part Three: Message Header Extensions for Non-ASCII Text, November 1996)

- RFC 2048 (MIME, Part Four: Registration Procedures, November 1996)

- RFC 2049 (MIME, Part Five: Conformance Criteria and Examples, November 1996)

- RFC 2854 (The 'text/html' Media Type, June 2000)

Related Entries   Electronic Mail; S/MIME (Secure Multipurpose Internet Mail Extension)

Linktionary!—Tom Sheldon's Encyclopedia of Networking updates	http://www.linktionary.com/m/mime.html
IETF Working Group: S/MIME Mail Security (smime)	http://www.ietf.org/html.charters/smime-charter.html
OII's Web page for electronic mail and newsgroup protocols	http://158.169.50.95:10080/oii/en/E-mail.html

RAD Data Communications MIME tutorial	http://www.rad.com/networks/tutorial.htm
The MIME Information page	http://www.hunnysoft.com/mime/
Mail/MIME FAQ	http://www.faqs.org/faqs/mail/mime-faq/
Internet Mail Consortium (see S/MIME link)	http://www.imc.org/
EMA (Electronic Messaging Association)	http://www.ema.org/

Mirroring

Mirroring is the process that exactly duplicates information in one location to another. It can be done locally—say, between disk drives in the same system—or globally, such as when information on a server is duplicated to a server in other parts of the world. Many Web sites mirror their content to other servers, bringing information closer to users, and reducing the distance and number of router hops that data must travel to get to a user. Content distribution is all about getting Web-based information closer to users.

Most network operating systems and many desktop operating systems support disk mirroring. In this type of mirroring, stored data on a primary drive is continuously copied to a second storage device in real time so that both devices hold the same information. Mirroring is a form of fault tolerance that protects data from equipment failure. There are several different types of mirroring, as described here and pictured in Figure M-2.

- **Mirroring**   Data is copied from on-disk controller (channel) to two disk drivers. If one drive fails, the other is still operational.

- **Duplexing**   Data is duplicated over two disk channels and stored on two drives. This method extends fault tolerance to the controller.

- **Server duplexing**   This method provides fault tolerance by duplicating the entire file server. If one server fails, the other provides continuous service to users. For example, Novell's *System Fault Tolerance* provides server duplexing.

- **Replication**   A strategy of duplicating critical files and directories from a server at one location to a server at another location to make that information more accessible to users at the remote location and also to provide redundancy and backup. See "Redundancy" and "Replication."

- **Clustering**   A cluster is a group of servers that share access to the same resources and service clients equally. Should one of the servers go down, the others take up the processing load. Clustered servers may access the same disk systems, which may be mirrored or in a RAID configuration. See "Clustering."

- **Mirror site**   A mirror site is a duplicate data center, located at another site, that contains duplicate systems and data. The duplicate data center should go into operation as the primary site if the master data center site fails for any reason. Companies running mission-critical applications will often create mirrored sites. See "Data Center Design."

Many organizations today outsource in order to obtain the benefits and features of the mirror techniques described earlier. They may also choose to co-locate duplicate equipment at

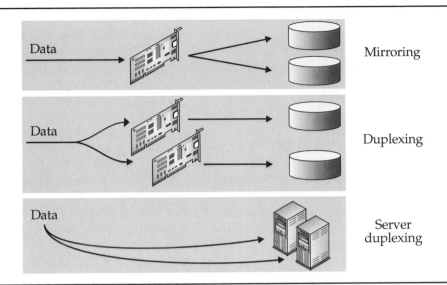

Figure M-2. *Disk and server mirroring*

public Internet data centers. Outsourcing and/or co-location allows organizations to gain all the management and security benefits of Internet data centers. See "Outsourcing."

Content distribution is an advanced, highly managed form of mirroring. It improves performance of Web sites by placing copies of content at caching servers close to users. These servers are placed at ISP sites and Internet data centers by companies such as Akamai. One can imagine a ring of content distribution devices surrounding the Internet. When users access Web sites, the content they are looking for is likely to be cached in a content distribution server near them. See "Content Distribution." Also see "Web Caching."

Related Entries   Backup and Data Archiving; Clustering; Content Delivery; Data Center Design; Data Migration; Data Protection; DBMS (Database Management System); Directory Services; Disaster Planning and Recovery; Fault Management; Fault Tolerance and High Availability; Load Balancing; Microsoft Active Directory; NDS (Novell Directory Services); Proxy Caching; Proxy Servers; Redundancy; Replication; SAN (Storage Area Network); Servers; Storage Management Systems; Storage Systems; Transaction Processing; Two-Phase Commit; Web Caching; *and* Web Technologies and Concepts

Linktionary!—Tom Sheldon's Encyclopedia of Networking updates	http://www.linktionary.com/m/mirroring.html
Bitpipe (search for "mirror")	http://www.bitpipe.com/
Google Web Directory mirroring information	http://directory.google.com/Top/Computers/ Software/Internet/Site_Management/Mirroring//
Amdahl paper: "Remote Data Mirroring for Disaster Recovery"	http://www.amdahl.com/doc/products/ess/ plat400/mm002873/contents.html

MLPPP (Multilink PPP)

PPP Multilink is a bandwidth-on-demand protocol that can connect multiple links between two systems as needed to provide bandwidth on demand. The technique is often called *bonding* or *link aggregation*. For example, the two 64-Kbit/sec B channels of ISDN can be combined to form a single 128-Kbit/sec data channel. Another example would be to bind one or more dial-up asynchronous channels with a leased synchronous line to provide more bandwidth at peak hours of the day.

MLPPP is defined in RFC 1990, "PPP Multilink Protocol" (August 1996). It is an extension to the PPP (Point-to-Point Protocol). See "PPP (Point-to-Point Protocol)" for information about the basic protocol. Microsoft Windows, Linux, and other operating systems support multilink. Many routers also support Multilink PPP and the ability to connect remote LANs with multiple dial-up or ISDN lines.

PPP Multilink provides the protocols and negotiation features that allow systems to indicate that they are capable of combining multiple physical links into a "bundle." When two systems perform initial session negotiations, they also indicate their ability to establish multilink connections. The protocol will fragment packets to ensure equal distribution across the links so that the lines are used efficiently and to ensure that packets arrive across multiple channels at approximately the same time for efficient reordering.

Links that form the bundle may be different physical links (dial-up or dedicated circuits) or different virtual links (such as multiplexed circuits over ISDN, X.25, or frame relay). The links in the bundle may also be different, such as dial-up asynchronous lines and leased synchronous lines.

MLPPP is defined in RFC 1990 as a method for splitting, recombining, and sequencing datagrams across multiple logical data links. The simple approach is to alternate packets among channels. Packet 1 goes to line 1, packet 2 goes to line 2, and so on, in a round-robin approach. But this can cause packet reordering problems. MLPPP adds a 4-byte sequencing header and simple synchronization rules, which allows packets to be split among parallel channels and kept in proper order.

MLPPP Multilink started out as a way to bond two or more ISDN channels, but is now capable of bonding many different types of connections. It can be used to bundle multiple T1 lines. BACP (Bandwidth Allocation Control Protocol) works in conjunction with MLPPP to provide dynamic channel aggregation. Two peer systems negotiate with one another to change MLPPP bandwidth as needed.

Multilink setup is easy in Microsoft Windows. You install two modems and connect them to two separate phone lines. Then you create a dial-up networking connection and specify one of the modems as the modem to dial when connecting. In the Properties box for the new dial-up networking connection, click the Multilink tab and add the second modem. In actual operation, after the first line dials out, makes a connection, and completes authorization, the second line is dialed and bonded to the first. Your ISP must support this feature and you may need to purchase an additional dial-up account.

Related Entries   BACP (Bandwidth Allocation Control Protocol); Bandwidth Management; Bandwidth on Demand; Bandwidth Reservation; Bonding; Circuit-Switching Services; DDR (Dial-on-Demand Routing); IMA (Inverse Multiplexing over ATM); Inverse Multiplexing; ISDN (Integrated Services Digital Network); Link Aggregation; Load Balancing; Modems; PPP (Point-to-Point Protocol); *and* Trunking

Linktionary!—Tom Sheldon's Encyclopedia of Networking updates	http://www.linktionary.com/m/mlppp.html
IETF Working Group: PPP extensions	http://www.ietf.org/html.charters/pppext-charter.html
Google Web Directory	http://directory.google.com/Top/Computers/
3Com paper: "Using Multilink PPP and Dynamic Bandwidth Allocation"	http://infodeli.3com.com/infodeli/tools/isdn/mlppp/mlppp.htm
Modem Central page about bonding	http://www.56k.com/reports/bonding.shtml
Cisco Documentation: Troubleshooting Async Multilink PPP Operations	http://www.cisco.com/univercd/cc/td/doc/cisintwk/intsolns/asynmppp/index.htm

MMDS (Multichannel Multipoint Distribution Service)

MMDS is a microwave technology that was originally designated for one-way transmission of wireless cable TV signals to rural areas. It has been called "wireless cable." The market for MMDS was seriously affected by the emergence of DBS (Direct Broadcast Satellite). In 1998, the FCC allowed two-way transmissions in the MMDS spectrum, which opened up the service for use as a network access technology, particularly for Internet access. MMDS service is ideal for home users because the data rate and the cost of using the system are well matched to a home user's requirements.

MMDS operates at 2.5–2.7 GHz in the United States and 3.4–3.7 GHz in other countries. Typical downstream data rates to the subscriber are from 128 Kbits/sec to 3 Mbits/sec and may burst as high as 10 Mbits/sec. Major MMDS license holders are Sprint and Worldcom.

A typical MMDS system consists of a base station antenna and subscribers at fixed locations. The range from base to subscriber is about 32–48 km (20–30 mi), which means that one antenna site can cover most metro areas. MMDS systems can be scaled by dividing an area into cells and reusing frequencies, as is done in mobile cellular systems. This also helps to overcome minor problems with obstructions. MMDS does not require strict line of sight, so antenna placement is easier and the system is cheaper to install.

Microwave systems suffer from signal reflections in which the primary signal is received with the addition of echo signals that have bounced off nearby objects. This combination of primary and echo signals is called *multipath*. The echo signal is received slightly later than the primary signal and can seriously corrupt digital data signals. The frequency bands used by MMDS have long propagation distances and, thus, high amounts of multipath.

The Cisco paper "Overcoming Multipath in Non-Line-of-Sight High-Speed Microwave Communication Links" (see the Web link) discusses Cisco's use of OFDM (orthogonal frequency division multiplexing) to overcome the problems of multipath. An OFDM receiver synchronizes reflected signals so that they appear to the receiver as if they are arriving in a single stream from a single location. The technique also improves the upstream and downstream data rates. See "OFDM (Orthogonal Frequency Division Multiplexing)."

MMDS is often compared to LMDS (Local Multipoint Distribution Services). Both are point-to-multipoint wireless broadcast systems and both provide two-way access services.

M

However, there are some major differences. LMDS operates above 24 GHz where antennas require line of sight and the range is much less. However, LMDS offers more bandwidth, and thus higher data rates. While MMDS is ideal for home users and small businesses, LMDS is best for larger businesses.

The IEEE wireless initiatives are also referred to as IEEE 802.16 Wireless MAN (Metropolitan Area Network). The mission of Working Group 802.16 is "to develop standards and recommended practices to support the development and deployment of fixed broadband wireless access systems." Initially, the group focused on LMDS bands.

For a complete list of MMDS operators, vendors, and related publications, see the WCA (Wireless Communications Association International) Web site listed shortly.

Related Entries   Communication Services and Providers; DBS (Direct Broadcast Satellite); Electromagnetic Spectrum; HALO (High Altitude Long Operation); HDR (High Data Rate); Infrared Technologies; Last Mile Services; LMDS (Local Multipoint Distribution Service); Local Loop; MAN (Metropolitan Area Network); Network Access Services; Network Concepts; OFDM (Orthogonal Frequency Division Multiplexing); Radio Communication and Networks; Residential Broadband; Satellite Communication Systems; Service Providers and Carriers; (Ultra Wideband); Wireless Broadband Access Technologies; Wireless Communications; Wireless LANs; Wireless Local Loop; *and* Wireless PANs (Personal Area Networks)

Linktionary!—Tom Sheldon's Encyclopedia of Networking updates	http://www.linktionary.com/m/mmds.html
WCA (Wireless Communications Association International)	http://www.wcai.com
BWA (Broadband Wireless Association)	http://www.broadband-wireless.org/
IEEE 802.16 Working Group on Broadband Wireless Access (IEEE Wireless MAN)	http://grouper.ieee.org/groups/802/16/
Cisco paper: "Overcoming Multipath in Non-Line-of-Sight High-Speed Microwave Communication Links"	http://www.cisco.com/warp/public/cc/pd/witc/wt2700/mulpt_wp.htm
Hybrid Networks "An Introduction to Fixed Broadband Wireless Technology"	http://www.hybrid.com/info/primer.htm
Wi-LAN, Inc.	http://www.wi-lan.com

Mobile Computing

Most computer users are connected to networks, and have access to data and devices on those networks. They connect to the Internet and communicate with other users via electronic mail. They work in collaborative groups in which they share schedules and other information. However, when users hit the road, they can lose contact with the people and resources they are accustomed to working with. Fortunately, there is plenty of support for mobile users:

- Operating systems like Microsoft Windows support mobile users with a host of features, including dial-up networking, docking station support, data synchronization with desktop systems and network servers, deferred printing and faxing, and wireless support such as infrared connections. See "Microsoft Windows."

■ IntelliMirror is a set of management technologies built into Microsoft Windows 2000 that provides desktop change and configuration management. With IntelliMirror, users' data, personal computer settings, and computing environment follow them to other locations. See "IntelliMirror."

■ Electronic mail is one of the best support tools for mobile users, who can travel and receive messages when they arrive at their destination. File exchanges are also made easy by attaching files to e-mail. See "Electronic Mail" and "Instant Messaging."

■ Collaborative applications help people work in groups and exchange information from anywhere. See "Collaborative Computing" and "Groupware."

■ High-speed wireless office LANs let people stay connected to the corporate network from anywhere in the office, not just from the cable attachment at their desktop. See "Wireless LANs."

■ Wireless PAN (personal area network) technologies such as Bluetooth allow groups of nearby users (for example, people in meetings) to form spontaneous wireless network connections and exchange information. See "Bluetooth" and "Wireless PANs (Personal Area Networks)."

■ Wireless messaging services help people stay in touch. See "SMR (Specialized Mobile Radio)," "SMS (Short Messaging Service)," and "WAP (Wireless Application Protocol)."

■ New metropolitan cellular networks are providing higher data rates, which means that mobile users can travel away from their normal wired connections and still obtain fast connect speeds. See "Wireless Mobile Communications."

■ Wireless data protocols let mobile users take advantage of cellular phone systems for data transfers. See "Wireless Mobile Communications."

■ WAP (Wireless Application Protocol) is a protocol for delivering Web content to mobile users. See "WAP (Wireless Application Protocol)."

■ Mobile IP lets mobile computing devices change their point of attachment to the Internet without changing their IP address. It supports "nomadic roaming." See "Mobile IP."

■ Roaming lets mobile Internet users access Internet service providers at their remote location while maintaining a relationship with a home ISP. The home ISP handles all access billing, authentication, and so on. This assumes that ISPs have joined into "confederations." See "Roaming" and VPN (Virtual Private Network).

■ Virtual dial-up protocols like L2TP and VPNs (virtual private networks) let users establish secure connections across the Internet to their home office from a local dial-up number, thus avoiding long-distance charges. See "L2TP (Layer 2 Tunneling Protocol)" and "VPN (Virtual Private Network)."

■ Remote access services allow users to dial into their corporate networks and operate on the network as if they were locally attached. Many remote access services take advantage of VPN technology. See "Remote Access."

M

The Web provides an incredible amount of support for mobile users. Users can access familiar resources (Web sites and search engines) anywhere they can connect. Some other examples include

- Web-based e-mail systems let people view their e-mail from any computer equipped with a Web browser. People on vacation can use hotel computers to check their mail. Web-based e-mail systems keep user mail on the server until the user returns to his or her home mail client and downloads the messages for archiving on desktop systems.

- Web-based storage allows users to store files on Internet servers and access those files after traveling to a new location. This is an incredible resource for users with small handheld devices that may not have their own storage. See "SSP (Storage Service Provider)" and "File Sharing" for information about Internet file-sharing services.

Related Entries   Accounting on the Internet; Authentication and Authorization; Bandwidth Management; Distributed Computer Networks; Embedded Systems; ISPs (Internet Service Providers); L2TP (Layer 2 Tunneling Protocol); Modems; Network Applicances; Peer-to-Peer Communication; RADIUS (Remote Authentication Dial-In User Service); Thin Clients; *and* VPN (Virtual Private Network)

Linktionary!—Tom Sheldon's Encyclopedia of Networking updates	http://www.linktionary.com/m/mobile_computing.html
Mobile IP Web resources by Charles Perkins	http://www.computer.org/internet/v2n1/mobile.htm
Mobile Computing online	http://www.mobilecomputing.com/
Google Web Directory: Mobile Computing	http://directory.google.com/Top/Computers/Mobile_Computing/
Network Computing (see Mobile and Wireless heading)	http://www.nwc.com/
MobileInfo.com	http://www.mobileinfo.com/
Bitpipe (search for "mobile computing")	http://www.bitpipe.com

Mobile IP

Traditionally, IP has assumed that a host on the Internet always connects to the same point of attachment. Any person or system that wants to send datagrams to that host addresses the datagrams to an IP address that identifies the subnetwork where the host is normally located. If the host moves, it will not receive those datagrams.

Today, a growing number of Internet users move their systems from place to place. If you normally connect to an ISP (Internet service provider) to establish an Internet connection and receive Internet mail, you'll need to dial long distance into that ISP if you travel to another state or country. The alternative is to dial in via a VPN connection or to have a different IP address at your destination location, but this does not help if people are used to contacting you at another IP address.

Mobile IP, as defined in IETF RFC 2002 (IP Mobility Support, October 1996), provides a mechanism that accommodates mobility on the Internet. It defines how nodes can change their point of attachment to the Internet without changing their IP address.

Mobile IP assumes that a node's IP address remains the same as it is moved from one network location to another. It also allows a user to change from one media type to another (for example, from Ethernet to a wireless LAN). This is not to be confused with "roaming," which allows users to roam among groups of Internet service providers while maintaining a user account with just one of those providers. Roaming is concerned with the movement of users, not hosts or subnets. See "Roaming."

Mobile IP consists of the entities described in the following list. A mobile user has a "home network" where his or her computer is normally attached. The home IP address is the address assigned to the user's computer on that network. When the computer moves to another network, datagrams will still arrive for the user at the home network. The home network will know that the mobile user is at a different location, called the "foreign network," and will forward the datagrams to the mobile user at that location. Datagrams are encapsulated and delivered across a tunnel from the home network to the foreign network.

- **Mobile node**   This is the mobile host computer or router that changes its point of attachment from one network or subnetwork to another without changing its home IP address. When the mobile node moves, it continues to communicate with other Internet nodes via its home IP address.

- **Home agent**   This is a router on the home network that can tunnel datagrams to a mobile node when it is away from its home network. The router maintains current location information for the mobile node.

- **Foreign agent**   When a mobile user visits another site and connects to that network, the visited network is known as the foreign network. The foreign agent resides in a router on the foreign network and is the endpoint of the tunnel established with the home network. The foreign agent "detunnels" and delivers datagrams to the mobile node.

Tunneling is a process of encapsulating datagrams into other datagrams for delivery across a network. Encapsulation is required because the datagrams are addressed to the network from which they are being shipped! By encapsulating the datagrams, the outer datagram can be addressed to the foreign network where the mobile user now resides. Note that the mobile node uses its home address as the source address of all IP datagrams that it sends, even when it is connected to a foreign network.

The important point is that the mobile node retains its IP address whether it is connected to the home network or some foreign network. When the mobile system is away from its home network, the home agent on the home network maintains a "care of" address that is the IP address of the foreign agent where the mobile node is located.

When a mobile node is attached to its home network, it operates without mobility services. If the mobile node is returning from a foreign network, it goes through a process that reregisters it as being attached to the home network rather than the foreign network. The details of this procedure are outlined in RFC 2002 (IP Mobility Support, October 1996).

When a node moves to a foreign network, it obtains a "care of" address on the foreign network. The mobile node operating away from home then registers its new "care of" address with its home agent through the exchange of registration information. When datagrams arrive for the mobile node at the home network, the home agent on that network intercepts the

M

datagrams and tunnels them to the mobile node's "care of" address, which, as mentioned, is usually the foreign agent router. This router then unencapsulates the datagrams and forwards them to the mobile host.

Related Entries   Accounting on the Internet; Authentication and Authorization; Bandwidth Management; IntelliMirror; ISPs (Internet Service Providers); Mobile Computing; Policy-Based Management; RADIUS (Remote Authentication Dial-In User Service); Remote Access; Roaming; Voice over IP (VoIP); *and* VPN (Virtual Private Network)

Linktionary!—Tom Sheldon's Encyclopedia of Networking updates	http://www.linktionary.com/m/mobile_ip.html
GRIC (Global Reach Internet Connection)	http://www.gric.net/
IETF Working Group: Roaming Operations (roamops)	http://www.ietf.org/html.charters/roamops-charter.html
IETF Working Group: IP Routing for Wireless/Mobile Hosts (mobileip)	http://www.ietf.org/html.charters/mobileip-charter.html
"Mobile Networking Through Mobile IP" by Charles E. Perkins	http://www.computer.org/internet/v2n1/perkins.htm
Mobile IP Web resources by Charles E. Perkins	http://www.computer.org/internet/v2n1/mobile.htm

Modems

Modems (*mo*dulators/*dem*odulators) are data communication devices that convert digital signals to analog signals, and vice versa. Modems allow digital transmissions over analog telephone lines. They allow people to connect their computers with other computers, corporate office LANs, and the Internet. Modems are used to establish connections of the telephone company's *local loop,* which is the analog copper cable that runs between homes and businesses to the telephone company central office (CO). The phone company then switches the call like any other voice call to create a point-to-point link to the destination.

Before the Internet, the usual connection was for one user to dial another user, or for a user to dial into a modem at a bulletin board, place of business, or a school (rather than connect through the Internet, as discussed next). In these cases, the connection is modem to modem across the PSTN, as shown at the top in Figure M-3. Note that in the figure, the computer's outgoing digital signal is converted to an analog signal for transmission across the copper local loop to the CO. At the CO, the analog signal is converted back to digital for transmission across its digital backbones. At the destination CO, the signal is once again converted from digital to analog and transmitted to the end user's modem, where it is converted back to digital. Remember all those conversions. Later in this topic, the problems they cause will be discussed.

Today, most users dial into the Internet, where they connect with other users via e-mail, collaborative applications, instant messaging, and so on. Users also connect with their home networks over the Internet by using secure VPN technology. This allows users to dial into a local number and connect to the corporate office across the Internet. The bottom half of Figure M-3 illustrates how most modem connections are made in today's Internet-connected environment. The important point of this configuration is that the ISP is connected to the telephone company's

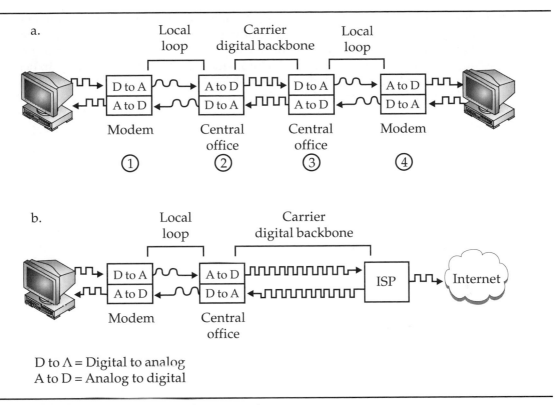

Figure M-3. *Traditional and 56K modem connections*

CO with a digital connection. This configuration makes high-speed 56-Kbit/sec modem technology possible, as explained later in this topic under "V.90 56-Kbit/sec Modems."

There are two types of modems:

- **Consumer voice-grade modems** Most off-the-shelf modems are designed to allow PC users to communicate over the voice phone system. The modems employ compatible communication techniques that comply with several standards, most notably the ITU V series standards (previously called the CCITT standards).

- **Broadband modems** These are modems for nontelephone system connections. A company may set up its own dedicated lines or microwave towers and use broadband modems to achieve very high data rates between those sites.

A modem puts an AC (alternating current) *carrier* signal on the line (in the 1,000–2,000-Hz range) and adds digital information to this signal. A modem at the receiving end then extracts the digital information from the carrier signal. Modulation and demodulation are covered more fully under "Modulation Techniques." Two other related topics are "Error Detection and Correction" and "Signals."

There are some restrictions in the local loop. Long ago, the telephone company established the frequency range of 300–3,300 Hz as the range for voice. The telephone switching system filters out higher frequencies to eliminate noise. Unfortunately, this filtering equipment prevents taking advantage of higher frequencies and wider bandwidth that could help boost data transmission rates. Therefore, a number of techniques, including encoding and compression, have been developed to squeeze as much digital data into the 300–3,300-Hz range as possible. As a side note, the digital subscriber services discussed under "DSL (Digital Subscriber Line)" allow higher frequencies (and higher data rates) on the local loop because they bypass the telephone company's traditional voice switching equipment (class 5 switches).

A voice-grade modem may be either an external box or an internally mounted circuit board. The PC Card format is also available for portable computers. The external modem connects to a computer serial port via an RS-232 serial cable. Serial connection methods are discussed under "Serial Communication and Interfaces."

Carriers and service providers often have racks of modems that users dial into. These are connected to remote access servers that manage the modems and authenticate users. Modems are usually integrated into RAC (remote access concentrator) devices. See "NAS (Network Access Server)," "RADIUS (Remote Authentication Dial-In User Service)," "Remote Access," and "Roaming."

Modems are asynchronous, synchronous, or both. An asynchronous transmission can be compared to the sporadic flow of cars on a highway, while a synchronous transmission can be compared to a steady stream of boxcars on a train track. In asynchronous mode, data is framed and each frame is sent independently. The receiver must be able to detect when a frame starts and ends. In asynchronous mode, a clock signal separates the beginning and end of each frame of data. Synchronous modems are generally more efficient and are typically used for dedicated links between two sites. Most consumer modems are asynchronous. See "Asynchronous Communications" and "Synchronous Communications."

When one modem "calls" another, the destination modem answers and a signal exchange takes place that establishes the parameters for a communication session. The negotiation process determines the maximum signaling rate available between the two modems, as well as the use of compression. Negotiation and signaling are established by the modem standards discussed later.

A full-duplex modem will send signals in both directions at the same time and at the same rate. Newer high-speed (56-Kbit/sec) voice-grade modems such as the V.90 series are asymmetrical, meaning that the download channel has a higher rate than the upload channel.

Modem Standards

The following table lists some of the ITU-T modem standards. The modulation techniques described in the table are FSK (frequency-shift keying), PSK (phase-shift keying), QAM (quadrature amplitude modulation), and TCM (trellis-coded modulation). See "Modulation Techniques."

V.22	1,200 bits/sec, full-duplex, PSK encoding
V.22bis	2,400 bits/sec, full-duplex, QAM encoding
V.32	Asynchronous/synchronous, 4,800/9,600 bits/sec, QAM encoding

V.32bis	Asynchronous/synchronous, 14,400 bits/sec, TCM encoding
V.35	Defines high data rates over combined circuits
V.42	Defines error checking standards
V.42bis	Defines modem compression using the Lempel Ziv method
V.44	The newest data compression standard, announced with V.92 in 2000
V.34	A standard for 28 Kbits/sec using TCM encoding
V.34+	Boosts V.34 to 33.6 Kbits/sec
V.90	56 Kbits/sec download speed, assuming only one digital-to analog conversion
V.92	Improves the upload speed of the V.90 standard from 33.6 Kbits/sec to 47 Kbits/sec

V.90 56-Kbit/sec Modems

Two competing modem standards emerged in the late 1990s to take advantage of higher throughput rates that were made possible by the configuration shown earlier in the bottom of Figure M-3. Note that the ISP is connected to the CO with a digital connection. This allows for a cleaner modem signal and faster rates, as explained in a moment. The two competing standards were U.S. Robotics X2 and Lucent/Rockwell Semiconductor Systems K56flex. Both companies rushed to release 56K products, creating two standards and a lot of consumer confusion. 56K technology requires that ISPs also install compatible modems, so the technology advanced slowly at first because ISPs could not decide on which standard to use.

In 1998, the ITU created the V.90 standard, which is designed for connections that are digital at one end and have only one digital-to analog conversion. V.90 harmonized the two competing X2 and K56flex proposals and has become a worldwide standard.

V.90 specifies up to 56 Kbits/sec in the downstream mode and 31.2 Kbits/sec in the upstream mode. However, it is very unlikely that anyone can reach those speeds

The lastest modem standard is V.92, which is V.90 (56 Kbits/sec) technology with a few refinements and some new features. "V.PCM upstream" allows for upstream communication at up to 48 Kbits/sec (V.90 supported on 31.2 Kbits/sec upstream). The hit rate should be high since most people always dial the same number for Internet access. "Modem on hold" allows a modem to suspend a data call and take an incoming voice call. When the data call resumes, a transmission continues where it left off. This feature benefits homes with only one line, and is a useful feature if you've ever tried to call someone that has been online for hours. "Quick connect" shortens connect times by up to 50%. The modem uses stored settings from previous calls (if they can be used) rather than renegotiating during the connect phase. This feature is also useful in conjunction with "modem on hold" since it speeds up the resumption of the call.

Be aware of so-called "soft modems" (also called "Winmodems" or "controllerless modems"). These modems use your computer's processors instead of an on-board processor. They are cheap because they have fewer chips, but it's a good idea to pay a little more for a full-function modem. Some soft modems run modulation/demodulation in hardware, but run other functions such as compression, error control, and V.90 protocols in software. HSP (host signal processing) modems run everything in software and are really nothing more than plug-in telephone jacks. You're paying for software. Usually, low price is the only indicator that a modem is a soft-modem. Look at the box carefully. If it indicates that the modem only runs under Windows, it's a softmodem.

56K Technology

While the V.9x standards define a rate of 56 Kbits/sec, this is never met due to rate restrictions, line noise, and cable distance. Estimates are that less than 30 percent of the lines in the U.S. are clean enough to let these modems operate near top speed. The shorter the distance of the local loop, the better. The Web site "Expecting 56k (V.90/X2/K56)?" listed later explains some of the problems for V.90 modems and how distance from the CO makes a difference.

Look again at Figure M-3. At the top, there are multiple analog-to-digital (ADC) and digital-to-analog (DAC) conversions. In the bottom part of the figure, the ISP is connected to the CO via a digital line. This eliminates the analog connection between the CO and the ISP, and thus eliminates excess ADC and DAC conversions. But the link between the end user and the CO is still over the analog local loop, and this requires signal conversions.

With 56K modem technology, the upstream rate is lower than the downstream rate. This is due to the fact that the upstream channel requires an analog-to-digital conversion at the CO. Analog-to-digital conversion is not exact. The analog signal is sampled at regular intervals and the samples are rounded off to come up with a digital representation of the analog wave. The rounding off introduces quantization errors that affect signal quality. The solution is to use a lower data transfer rate.

In contrast, digital-to-analog conversion can produce a near-perfect analog representation of a signal so that no information is lost. The CO sends this clean signal on the downstream line to the end user, where it arrives in a well-defined state. When the end user's modem receives this signal, it must do an analog-to-digital conversion; but it is working with a clean signal, so the conversion is fairly accurate. However, this conversion does limit a line that could potentially deliver 64 Kbits/sec to a line that can handle about 56 Kbits/sec.

The newer V.92 standard improves the upload speed, but the asymmetry is still there, it's just not as bad. Practically speaking, the lower upload speed is not a problem with most people because more information is usually downloaded (e.g., one mouse click downloads an entire Web page).

Related Entries   Asynchronous Communications; Bell Modem Standards; Bonding; Capacity; Data Communication Concepts; Dial-Up Line; DSL (Digital Subscriber Line); Error Detection and Correction; Flow-Control Mechanisms; Home Networking; Inverse Multiplexing; ISDN (Integrated Services Digital Network); Line Conditioning; Link Aggregation: Local Loop; MLPPP (Multilink PPP); Modulation Techniques; Remote Access; Serial Communication and Interfaces; Signals; Synchronous Communications; Telecommunications and Telephone Systems; Telephony; Virtual Dial-Up Services; *and* WAN (Wide Area Network)

Linktionary!—Tom Sheldon's Encyclopedia of Networking updates	http://www.linktionary.com/m/modems.html
"Curt's High Speed Modem Page"	http://www.teleport.com/~curt/modems.html
ModemHelp.org	http://www.modemhelp.org/
About.com (see RAS and Modems subject)	http://compnetworking.about.com/

Intel 56K modem technology page	http://www.intel.com/network/technologies/56k.htm
"Why you won't get 56K"	http://www.yes-web.net/no56.htm
Expecting 56k (V.90/X2/K56)?	http://www.hal-pc.org/~wdg/56k.html
3Com article: "Analog Multi-link Bonding"	http://www.3com.com/news/4p_multilink.html
TechFest Modems page (extensive links)	http://www.techfest.com/hardware/modem.htm
Christopher Ostmo's modem site (has extensive resource list)	http://modems.rosenet.net/

Modulation Techniques

Modulation is a technique used to transmit some information (digital or analog) by encoding the information onto an analog carrier signal. Modulation is used by modems to transmit digital data signals over analog transmission lines such as the public telephone network. Modems at each end of the communication link perform the digital-to-analog and analog-to-digital conversion.

The information signal is modulated onto an analog signal at a specific frequency called the *carrier*. The receiving modem demodulates the signal and extracts the digital information from it. Since the carrier wave is at a specific frequency, the receiver simply tunes to that frequency, then receives and extracts the signal. Radio receivers are also called radio tuners because you tune into the carrier frequency of the radio station you want to listen to.

There are three traditional modulation techniques, as described next and pictured in Figure M-4. The original digital signal is shown at the top. Below that are the modulation techniques applied by the following methods.

■ **AM (amplitude modulation)**   In AM, the height or amplitude of the wave is changed between two levels to match the digital data input. This technique was used in some of the early modems, but has too many limitations for high-speed data transmissions.

■ **FM (Frequency modulation)**   In FM, the frequency of a signal changes depending on the binary input. When FM is used to transmit digital signals, it is called *FSK (frequency-shift keying)* because only two frequencies are transmitted.

■ **PM (phase modulation)**   In this method, the period of the wave is shifted by one-fourth, one-half, or three-fourths of its period. The shift in the waves can represent some binary value to the receiver. Note that the shift occurs in relation to the preceding wave period. Since there are four different wave types, as shown in the following illustration, it is possible to represent four different bit values (00, 01, 10, 11) per pulse.

No shift
bit value = 00

1/4 shift
bit value = 01

1/2 shift
bit value = 10

3/4 shift
bit value = 11

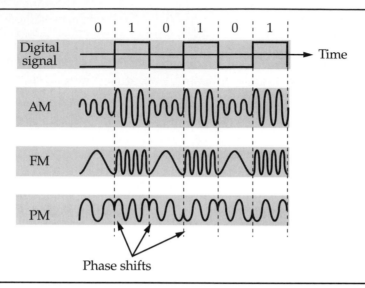

Figure M-4.   *Modulation techniques*

Note that a baud is a pulse signal in the carrier, while bits per second is the rate of information transmitted on the line. The earliest modems transmitted one bit per baud, meaning that a 300-baud modem actually did transmit 300 bits/sec. Modern modems use an encoding technique in which each baud can represent multiple bits of information. For example, in two-way communications, the baud limit is 1,200 pulses per second, but by encoding up to eight bits per baud, a data rate of 9,600 bits/sec can be achieved.

The technique of encoding multiple bits into a baud is called *QAM (quadrature amplitude modulation)*. This scheme extends the concept of phase modulation by using two different amplitude levels and by shifting the wave by one-fourth, by one-half, or by three-fourths of its period. Thus, eight bit values can be represented as listed here:

Bit Value	Phase Shift	Amplitude
000	None	1
001	None	2
010	¼	1
011	¼	2
100	½	1
101	½	2
110	¾	1
111	¾	2

By shifting the wave in even smaller increments, it is possible to represent even more bit values. With 16 values (4 bits in width), it is possible to transmit at 9,600 bits/sec over a 2,400-baud line. Further expansion achieves data rates of 28,800 bits/sec. Even higher rates are achieved by using compression and other techniques. See "Modems."

Spread spectrum signaling is a unique approach to sending information. Instead of transmitting on a single carrier frequency, signals are spread out over a very wide frequency range, often over 200 times the bandwidth of the original signal. Imagine trying to signal to someone in the dark. One technique would be to use a flashlight to signal with Morse code. This requires that the other person be looking directly at you. Another technique is to flash a light bulb. The former is similar to the carrier techniques discussed here since the signal occupies a very narrow range. The latter is more like spread spectrum. You don't even need to be looking directly at the light. The bulb spreads the signal out and you can receive it by just watching the sky light up. Spread spectrum broadcasts in bands where noise is prominent, but does not rise above the noise, so the signal is relatively secure.

OFDM (orthogonal frequency division multiplexing) is another interesting technique for transmitting information. It has become popular lately due to the development of fast signal processors (DSPs). Data signals are divided over a large number of separate carrier waves. The receiving system reconstructs the message from the separate carriers. OFDM is also called a DMT (discrete multitone) system or MCM (multicarrier modulation). OFDM is important in broadband wireless systems as it helps to overcome signal reflection problems, called *multipath*. See "OFDM (Orthogonal Frequency Division Multiplexing)."

M

Related Entries   ADC (Analog-to-Digital Conversion); Analog Transmission Systems; Asynchronous Communications; Bandwidth; Bell Modem Standards; Cable and Wiring; Capacity; Channel; Circuit; Compression Techniques; Data Communication Concepts; Error Detection and Correction; Modems; Multiplexing and Multiplexers; OFDM (Orthogonal Frequency Division Multiplexing); Radio Communication and Networks; Signals; Signaling; Spread Spectrum; Throughput; Virtual Circuit; *and* Wireless Communications

Linktionary!—Tom Sheldon's Encyclopedia of Networking updates	http://www.linktionary.com/m/modulation.html
Cisco paper: "Overcoming Multipath in Non-Line-of-Sight High-Speed Microwave Communication Links"	http://www.cisco.com/warp/public/cc/pd/witc/wt2700/mulpt_wp.htm
Andrew Bateman radio design course: Transmitter & Receiver Architectures	http://www.avren.com/Courses/TX_RX_Architectures_plain.htm
Asynchronous Serial Transmission	http://www-scm.tees.ac.uk/users/a.clements/Async/async.htm

MOM (Message-Oriented Middleware)

MOM is a middleware communication mechanism that provides applications with a way to establish a communication dialog using non-real-time (asynchronous) connectionless techniques. A communication dialog may consist of multiple messages going back and forth between applications, in much the same way that two people might exchange a series of e-mail messages. Messages use the store-and-forward model in which they are sent to queues and held for the recipient to pick up at a later time. For example, a user might send an order request to an e-commerce server. The request may be processed immediately or sit in a queue where it awaits processing. Some requests may be processed during off-hours.

MOM can be contrasted with RPCs (remote procedure calls). RPCs provide connection-oriented links between applications in client/server environments, while MOM is generally connectionless. RPCs require tight integration between applications and the network. In contrast, MOM uses the store-and-forward model. Both RPCs and MOM have advantages and are used for different application requirements. MOM's queued message technique is appropriate when delays are acceptable. It is popular in Web environments where RPCs are difficult to implement.

With message-oriented middleware, applications can continue processing after sending messages and do not need to wait for a connection and a reply from the recipient. Applications may be running at different times to communicate. If systems in the message path are temporarily offline, message delivery continues when those systems resume operation. In addition, messages can be prioritized to ensure faster delivery and delivery can be guaranteed to provide assurance that a message will make it to the destination. Once a system receives a message, it can return an acknowledgment at the request of the sender.

Two messaging techniques are common. *Point to point* is like an e-mail message. The message goes in a queue and is picked up by the recipient. It may travel across many queues. With *publish and subscribe*, clients make a request to a server to be updated when some specific information changes. That's the subscribe part. When the information changes, the server publishes it and notifies the subscribers. Publish and subscribe is a tremendous advantage for the Internet because it reduces the traffic caused by people and components that must constantly check back with a server to see if information has changed.

Several common message-oriented middleware systems are outlined here:

- **MSMQ (Microsoft Message Queuing)**   MSMQ implements the point-to-point messaging model, but a publish-and-subscribe model is available in Microsoft's COM+. MSMQ provides guaranteed message delivery, efficient routing, security, and priority-based messaging.

- **IBM MQSeries**   MQSeries is supported on IBM platforms and operating systems, DEC VMS, Tandem Guardian and Himalaya, HP UX, Sun Solaris, SCO UNIX, and Microsoft Windows. MQSeries links with Lotus Notes to give Notes users access to transactions and data on other systems.

- **JMS (Java Message Service)**   The J2EE (Java 2 Enterprise Edition) environment includes JMS, which provides both point-to-point and publish-and-subscribe models. See "Java."

- **XML and SOAP**   The Microsoft.NET platform uses XML to describe application logic and data, SOAP (Simple Object Access Protocol) to package it, and HTTP to deliver it. SOAP defines how to create an HTML header and XML file that can call a program on another computer and pass information to it in a format and layout that the computer will immediately recognize. This is similar to RPCs (remote procedure calls), but Microsoft views SOAP as a move away from the RPC model that is the basis of COM+, and a move toward a message-passing model. See "Microsoft.NET."

MOM is becoming more important with the growth of the Web. Direct real-time connections between systems is not always possible. MOM can provide virtual connections that may support existing applications, or it can be seen as a new model for building client/server applications that work over the Internet. MOM works in cooperation with other types of middleware products to provide a dynamic distributed network environment. It provides more than data access by supporting interoperability among applications.

Related Entries   Application Server; Client/Server Computing; CORBA (Common Object Request Broker Architecture); Data Mart; Data Warehousing; DBMS (Database Management System); Distributed Applications; Distributed Computer Networks; Distributed Object Computing; Java; Metadata; Microsoft.NET; Middleware and Messaging; Multitiered Architectures; Named Pipes; Object Technologies; ORB (Object Request Broker); Pipes; RPCs (Remote Procedure Calls); SOAP (Simple Object Access Protocol); Transaction Processing; *and* XML (Extensible Markup Language)

Linktionary!—Tom Sheldon's Encyclopedia of Networking updates	http://www.linktionary.com/m/mom.html
OMG (Object Management Group)	http://www.omg.org/
Carnegie Mellon message-oriented middleware page	http://www.sei.cmu.edu/str/descriptions/momt.html
Carnegie Mellon middleware page	http://www.sei.cmu.edu/str/descriptions/middleware.html
CAIT Web links page	http://www.cait.wustl.edu/infosys/infosys.html

MOSPF (Multicast OSPF)

See Multicasting.

MOSS (MIME Object Security Services)

See PEM (Privacy-Enhanced Mail).

Motif

Motif is the industry-standard graphical user interface promoted by The Open Group. It is defined by the IEEE 1295 specification and is used on more than 200 hardware and software platforms. Motif provides application developers, end users, and system vendors with an environment for building applications with a standardized presentation on a wide range of platforms. Motif is the leading user interface for the UNIX-based operating system.

Motif provides application portability across a variety of platforms, allowing application developers to leverage their development work and customers to make valuable software investments. Motif is also the base graphical user interface toolkit for the CDE (Common Desktop Environment).

Related Entries   CDE (Common Desktop Environment); DCE (Distributed Computing Environment); Linux; Motif; Open Group; UNIX; *and* X Window

MW3 Web site (X and Motif information)	http://www.cen.com/mw3
The Open Group's Motif Web page	http://www.opengroup.org/motif/
Motif FAQ	http://www.faqs.org/faqs/motif-faq/
Jennifer Myers's Web page (see X-Window System section for links)	http://www.geek-girl.com/unix.html
Operating System Tutorials (see X-Windows & Motif section)	http://www.wizard.com/users/baker/public_html/OSTutor.html

MP3

MP3 is a compression technology that has become popular recently due to the massive exchange of music on the Internet via peer-to-peer applications such as Napster. MP3 stands for (MPEG Layer 3). MPEG (Moving Pictures Experts Group) is a joint committee of the ISO (International Standards Organization) and the EC (Electrotechnical Commission). Most MPEG standards deal with compression of video. MP3 supports a range of compression ratios, including 4:1 (4 to 1), 6:1, 10:1, and 12:1. Compressed music files are greatly reduced down to a size that can be transferred in a few minutes over a 56-Kbit/sec dial-up line.

MP3 software and hardware are now widely available. An MP3 player is a small pocket device that stores MP3 files in memory or on removable memory cards. A typical player can hold hours of music. Some use recordable CD-ROMs that store hundreds of MP3 files, which are small in size due to the compression.

For more information, visit the MP3 Web site at http://www.mp3.com. Also see "File Sharing," "Multimedia," and "Peer-to-Peer Communication."

MPLS (Multiprotocol Label Switching)

MPLS is an IETF-defined protocol that overcomes some of the shortcomings of IP-based networks. MPLS is meant for service provider core networks or large enterprise networks. It brings traffic engineering, bandwidth management, and quality of service to IP networks. A form of MPLS is used to set up and manage wavelength optical circuits (lambdas) on the core optical networks of the Internet.

 This topic is covered in more detail at the Linktionary! Web site.

MPLS's key feature is the ability to build virtual circuits across IP networks. These VCs are called *label switched paths (LSPs)*. LSPs are similar to virtual circuits in ATM and frame relay networks. Labels are attached to packets, which help MPLS nodes forward the packet across an LSP. The labels are like tracking slips on express delivery packages. They contain an index into a forwarding table, which specifies the next hop for the packet. Nodes in the core MPLS network do not need to examine packets and perform next-hop routing tasks. The label carries the information that determines which path a packet should take.

MPLS supports traffic engineering to provide traffic prioritization and QoS. For example, a path can be created that provides high bandwidth and low delay for "premium" customers who are willing to pay for it. In another example, multiple paths can be defined between two endpoints to provide load balancing and backup service in the event of a line failure. This is similar to using metrics in IP routing to force traffic in one direction or another, but it is much more powerful.

Paths can be engineered using manual or automatic techniques. MPLS supports *explicit routing*, in which network engineers define specific paths across a network for specific types of traffic. MPLS also supports *constraint-based routing*, in which the path is selected on-the-fly as a packet traverses the network, based on parameters that constrain the forwarding direction. Constraint-based routing involves programming traffic-engineering parameters into the network.

An MPLS network is typically a large group of core switches that span a large geographic area, usually an entire country. AT&T, Global Crossing, and other providers have MPLS networks. MPLS may also be used in metropolitan area networks. Terabeam uses MPLS in its "Fiberless Optical" network. Periphery networks are attached to the edges of the MPLS network via LERs (label edge routers), as shown in Figure M-5. The core contains LSRs (label switching routers). The periphery networks may be operated by regional ISPs, local network operators, or even private companies.

MPLS is an IETF specification based on label switching approaches developed by several vendors, including Cisco (Tag Switching), IBM (ARIS or Aggregate Route-Based IP Switching), and Lucent/Ascend (IP Navigator, originally developed by Cascade). MPLS integrates layer 2 switching and layer 3 routing as pictured in Figure M-6. For ATM switches, MPLS adds routing functionality, creating a hybrid switching router. Layer 3 components are IP routing controls (OSPF and BGP), which replaces standard ATM Forum routing and control protocols.

M

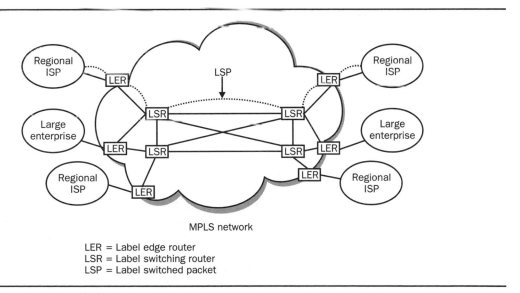

MPLS network

LER = Label edge router
LSR = Label switching router
LSP = Label switched packet

Figure M-5.   *An MPLS network can be viewed as a cloud that is one hop across.*

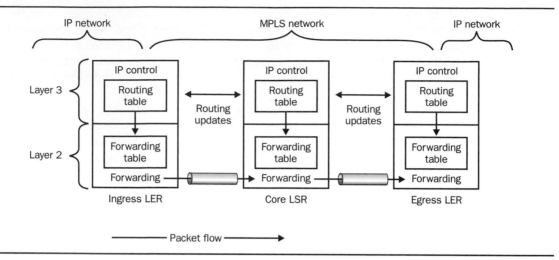

Figure M-6.   *MPLS separates control functions from switching functions.*

Prior to these approaches, several techniques were developed to overlay IP on top of ATM. The ATM Forum's MPOA (Multiprotocol over ATM) is an example. The overlay models provide shortcut routing of IP packets across an ATM backbone, but the underlying ATM network protocols are used unchanged. However, these earlier techniques were not as scalable as MPLS.

MPLS Basic Operation

As shown in Figure M-5, LSRs are core devices that switch packets, and LERs are edge devices that connect with external networks, determine routes, and add or remove labels. An LSP is a concatenation of switch hops that form an end-to-end forwarding path. An LSP starts at an *ingress* LER, crosses one or more LSRs, and ends at an *egress* LER.

When a packet arrives at an MPLS network, the ingress LER does most of the work of handling the packet. It looks at the packet's IP address, determines a route, assigns an LSP, and attaches a label. The packet is then forwarded into the LSP, where it is switched across a series of LSRs until it reaches the egress LER. The label is removed and the packet is forwarded on its way via standard IP routing.

The default MPLS label assignment and label-forwarding process starts with each label switching device learning about the network to which it is directly attached. Routing protocols such as OSPF and BGP are used to build routing tables. MPLS devices then build label-forwarding tables from the routing information and distribute the label information to neighbor as shown in Figure M-7. The tables provide information about how labels should be applied. A label is like shorthand notation that indexes the forwarding decision made by routers.

Figure M-7 may look complicated, but the process is quite simple. Looking at LER 2 on the upper right, note that a label table has been built for the two network prefixes. Label 9 is assigned to 172.16 and label 10 is assigned to 129.10. LER 2 distributes these label assignments

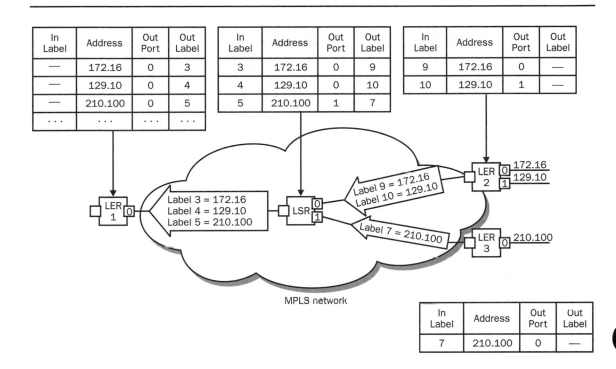

Figure M-7. *MPLS label assignments*

to the LSR in the middle of the MPLS network. In this exchange, LER 2 is saying, "If you send me a packet for network 172,16, attach label 9 to that packet. If you send me a packet for network 129.10, attach label 10 to that packet."

The LSR in the middle of the network receives label assignments from both LER 2 and LER 3, and then builds its own label table. Note that it creates a table entry for each network it knows about on its out ports. It then assigns a label to each one of these entries and forwards the label assignment to LER 1. The LSR is basically saying to use label 3, 4, or 5 for networks 172.16, 129.10, or 210.100, respectively.

Figure M-8 illustrates the label-forwarding process, using the label assignments just described. The steps are outlined here:

1. A packet arrives at the ingress edge router LER 1, which examines the packet's IP address to determine which LSP to use. LER 1's label table indicates that destination address prefix 172.16 should be assigned label 3 and should be sent out port 0.

2. Having been sent out LER 1's port 0, the packet now arrives at the middle LSR. The LSR looks up label 3 in its forwarding table and discovers that label 9 should be attached to the packet and that it should be forwarded out port 0. *It swaps label 3 with label 9 before forwarding the packet.*

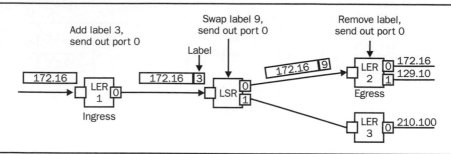

Figure M-8. *MPLS label forwarding*

3. Now the packet arrives at the next hop, LER 2, which looks at the label and determines from its routing table that label 9 indicates port 0. Since LER 2 is the egress LER, there is no further need for a label. The existing label is discarded and the packet is forwarded onto IP network 172.16.

Label swapping as described in step 3 takes place at core LSRs, not ingress and egress LERs. The swap operation consists of looking up the incoming label to determine the outgoing label and the output port.

As mentioned, this topic is covered in more detail at the Linktionary! Web site. Refer to the following RFCs for additional information. The IETF Working Group for MPLS listed later provides additional information.

- RFC 2702, "Requirements for Traffic Engineering Over MPLS" (September 1999)
- RFC 3031, "Multiprotocol Label Switching Architecture" (January 2001)
- RFC 3033, "Signaling for the Internet Protocol" (January 2001)
- RFC 3036, "LDP Specification, RFC 3036" (January 2001)

Related Entries   ATM (Asynchronous Transfer Mode); Bandwidth Management; Congestion Control Mechanisms; Constraint-Based Routing; Differentiated Services (Diff-Serv); IP over ATM; IPSec (IP Security); Label Switching; Multilayer Switching; Network Access Services; Network Core Technologies; Optical Networks; Prioritization of Network Traffic; QoS (Quality of Service); Routers; Routing; Switch Fabrics and Bus Design; Switching and Switched Networks; Traffic Management, Shaping, and Engineering; Tunnels; VPN (Virtual Private Network); *and* WAN (Wide Area Network)

Linktionary!—Tom Sheldon's Encyclopedia of   http://www.linktionary.com/m/mpls.html
Networking updates

IETF MPLS Working Group   http://www.ietf.org/html.charters/mpls-charter.html

MPLS Forum   http://www.mplsforum.com/

MPLS Resource Center   http://www.mplsrc.com/

Noritoshi Demizu Multilayer Switching Page   http://infonet.aist-nara.ac.jp/member/nori-d/mlr/

Nortel Networks MPLS Web page   http://www.nortelnetworks.com/mpls

Juniper Networks MPLS white papers   http://www.juniper.net/techcenter/techpapers/

Bitpipe (search for "MPLS")   http://www.bitpipe.com/

MPλS (Multiprotocol Lambda Switching)

In this scheme, MPLS is used in a control plane above an optical network to set up and manage wavelength paths, which are essential optical virtual circuits, across an all-optical network. See "MPLS (Multiprotocol Label Switching)" and "Optical Networks."

MPOA (Multiprotocol over ATM)

MPOA is an ATM Forum specification for overlaying layer 3 network routing protocols like IP over an ATM switched network environment. It allows organizations to take advantage of the bandwidth and scalability of ATM while retaining legacy LANs, the ability to create VLANs (virtual LANs), and the ability to route between those VLANs.

 Note   *This topic is covered at the Linktionary! Web site. Refer to http://www.linktionary.com/m/ mpoa.html.*

MPP (Massively Parallel Processor) Systems

See Multiprocessing.

MSP (Management Service Provider)

An MSP is a service provider that offers system and network management tools and expertise. An MSP typically has its own data center that runs advanced network management software such as HP OpenView or Tivoli. It uses these tools to actively monitor and provide reports on aspects of its customer's networks, including communication links, network bandwidth, servers, and so on. The MSP may host the customer's Web servers and application servers at its own site. The services provided by MSPs have been called "Web telemetry" services. The MSP Association defines MSPs as follows:

> Management Service Providers deliver information technology (IT) infrastructure management services to multiple customers over a network on a subscription basis. Like Application Service Providers (ASPs), Management Service Providers deliver services via networks that are billed to their clients on a recurring fee basis. Unlike ASPs, which deliver business applications to end users, MSPs deliver system management services to IT departments and other customers who manage their own technology assets.

TriActive is an example of an MSP. It provides management and monitoring of PCs, servers, networks, and Web sites from its own NOC (network operations center), which is hosted by Exodus Communications. Exodus ensures that the NOC has fully redundant power, network connectivity, routing, and switching to ensure maximum reliability and integrity. A "microagent" interacts with customer systems to provide system management. The agent is lightweight and designed for use over the Internet. It acts as a universal agent invoking and managing other agents and programs as required for specific actions

The service is delivered via the Web through a secure Internet portal that lets customers view management information, based on their role in the organization. For example, CIOs can view overall management information while help desk technicians can check call queues, escalations, and open ticket status. Systems analysts can conduct asset inventories and view virus reporting.

Objective Systems Integrators is another management service provider that provides software solutions for unified network, service application, and process management. OSI was recently acquired by Agilent Technologies. A list of other MSPs may be found at the MSP Association Web site.

Related Entries   ASP (Application Service Provider); Data Center Design; Fault Tolerance and High Availability; ISPs (Internet Service Providers); Network Management; Outsourcing; Service Providers and Carriers; SSP (Storage Service Provider); *and* Web Technologies and Concepts

Linktionary!—Tom Sheldon's Encyclopedia of Networking updates	http://www.linktionary.com/m/msp.html
MSP Association	http://www.mspassociation.org/
TriActive	http://www.triactive.com.
Objective Systems Integrators (now Agilent)	http://www.osi.com
AUTOMATOS, Inc.	http://www.automatos.com/
searchSystemsManagement.com	http://searchsystemsmanagement.techtarget.com/

MTA (Message Transfer Agent)

In the X.400 Message Handling System developed by the CCITT (now the ITU), an MTA is like a post office through which messages are exchanged between systems. The MTA provides store-and-forward services. See "X.400 Message Handling System."

MTU (Maximum Transmission Unit)

An MTU is a parameter that specifies how much data a frame for a particular network can carry. This parameter becomes an issue when networks are interconnected and the networks have different MTU sizes. When a datagram arrives at a router that must be forwarded onto a network with a smaller MTU size, the router fragments the packet into pieces that will fit into the frames of the next-hop network.

Refer to "Fragmentation and Reassembly" for more information about this topic.

Multicasting

Multicasting is a way of efficiently transmitting text, audio, and video on the Internet or an internal network to a select group of people, much like a conference call includes a select group of people. Instead of sending information in individual packets to each recipient, a single message is sent to a multicast group, which includes all the people that want to participate in the multicast session. While multicasting is possible on a variety of networks, this topic concentrates on Internet multicasting.

Note *Full coverage of this topic is available at the Linktionary! Web site.*

Multicasting is a one-to-many transmission. In contrast, the traditional method of sending messages on the Internet, called *unicasting*, is a one-to-one transmission. If multicasting is comparable to a conference call, then unicasting is like a private call between two people. Broadcasting is a one-to-all technique in which messages are sent to everybody. Routers block broadcasts from propagating everywhere.

Multicasting provides a way for one host to send packets to a selective group of hosts. The key word is "selective." Users choose to be part of a specific multicast. Multicast packets then travel to the user from the multicast source. An important point is that multicast packets only travel across routes where there is an end user that has requested to be part of the multicast. This keeps multicast packets from crossing parts of the network that do not have multicast participants. Still, on the Internet, a multicast group is potentially huge, with members located around the world.

The trick to multicasting is that users indicate to their local router that they want to be part of a particular multicast group. That router then indicates to the next router closest to the source of the multicast that it wants to receive the multicast. This process continues until a path is established between the multicast source and the person who wants to join the multicast. The result is that only routers that need multicast packets for end systems actually receive those packets. Nonparticipating routers do not receive the packets, making the process more efficient.

As shown in Figure M-9, you can imagine a tree of routers that branch from the multicast source and connect to end systems that want to receive the multicast. If a router has no hosts that want to receive the multicast, it excludes itself from the tree.

Most multicasts are multimedia related, although a multicast host may simply broadcast a message or an occasional news item to participants. This sounds similar to electronic mailing lists, but IP Multicast uses special addressing and special protocols to achieve high-performance and efficiency. See "Webcasting" for an example of how multicasting is used.

RTP (Real-Time Transport Protocol) is a protocol that works in conjunction with multicasting to transport real-time audio, video, simulation data, and other information over multicast networks. While IP Multicast defines how to set up multicast groups, RTP defines how to transport real-time information to the members of the groups and monitor the quality of the information that is delivered. Refer to "RTP (Real-time Transport Protocol)" for more information.

M

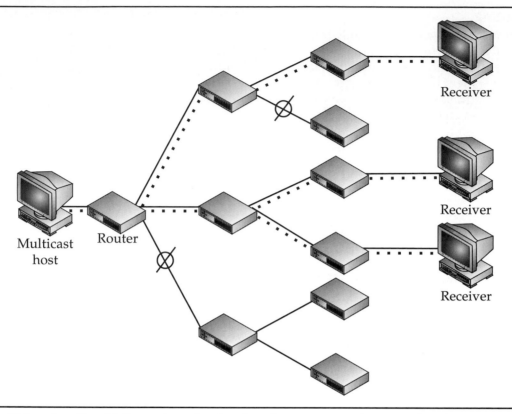

Figure M-9. *A multicast follows a tree of routers from the source to end systems that choose to receive the multicast.*

IP Multicast Protocols

IP Multicast is an open IETF (Internet Engineering Task Force) standard for distributing data to multiple recipients. The multicast recipient group can change dynamically. A host may decide to join or leave a group at any time, and a host may be a member of more than one multicast group. In addition, any host can be a multicast source by simply sending packets addressed to a particular multicast group.

Routers in this scheme must be "multicast enabled." When a multicast source transmits a multicast datagram, the local router forwards the packet to other routers with attached networks that include members of the multicast group.

IP Multicast uses class D addressing, which is a special form of the IP address designed for multicasting. The class scheme for IP addresses is discussed under "IP (Internet Protocol)." The first four bits of a class D address identify it as a class D address. The remaining 28 bits identify a particular multicast group. A class D address can be compared to the channel number of a TV station. When you tune in to a particular class D address, you receive packets that are being multicast by other systems that multicast on the address.

Several protocols are related to IP multicast. These are outlined here and discussed further at the Linktionary! Web site:

- **IGMP (Internet Group Management Protocol)**   Multicast receivers must indicate their desire to be included in a multicast session. This is done with IGMP, a protocol that runs between hosts and their immediately neighboring multicast routers. In addition, a multicast router can use IGMP to occasionally broadcast a query on a network to determine if any hosts still want to receive broadcasts from the multicast transmitters from which it is accepting packets.

- **DVMRP (Distance Vector Multicast Routing Protocol)**   DVMRP is a distance vector routing protocol for multicast. DVMRP is used when a router receives a multicast packet and it wants to find out if other multicast routers it has connections to need to receive the packet (that is, they have attached hosts that are members of the group). DVMRP sends the packet to all attached routers and waits for a reply. Routers with no group members return a "prune" message, which essentially prevents further multicast messages for that group from reaching the router.

- **MOSPF (Multicast Open Shortest Path First)**   As the name implies, MOSPF is an Open Shortest Path First routing protocol. MOSPF routers build maps of the network topology, including the location of islands and tunnels, and then determine the best path through the network to a particular multicast router. Note that MOSPF is designed for use within autonomous systems.

- **PIM (Protocol-Independent Multicast)**   PIM is a new concept for multicast routing and is an alternative to DVMRP and MOSPF. It uses two modes: PIM-dense and PIM-sparse. Dense mode operates like DVMRP. It floods the network with traffic— a bad thing unless the group has enough participants to warrant such an action. PIM-sparse avoids flooding (and wasted bandwidth) in cases where a group is small. Instead, a *rendezvous point* is established and all members send packets to it.

- **MTP (Multicast Transport Protocol)**   MTP defines a flow-controlled multicasting transport protocol that operates on top of any network protocol as long as the data link layer includes multicast. MTP ensures that all messages are delivered reliably, in order, and at the same time. MTP can retransmit packets to a specific branch of a multicast group, thus reducing excess traffic in branches that don't need the retransmission.

For more information, refer to the IETF Working Groups page listed later. A number of working groups are defining various aspects of multicasting, and their Web sites provide links to drafts and related RFCs. See "Webcasting" for related information.

An industry consortium called the IPMI (IP Multicast Initiative) is dedicated to advancing IP Multicasting and making information about it available.

Related Entries   Anycasting; Broadcast; Broadcasting on the Internet; Collaborative Computing; Content Distribution; Distributed Computer Networks; Internet Radio; IP (Internet Protocol); MP3; Multimedia; Newsfeed Services; NNTP (Network News Transport Protocol); Peer-to-Peer Communication; Routing; RSVP (Resource Reservation Protocol); RTP (Real-Time Transport Protocol); Transport Protocols and Services; Videoconferencing; *and* Webcasting

Linktionary!—Tom Sheldon's Encyclopedia of Networking updates	http://www.linktionary.com/m/multicast.html
IETF Working Groups	http://www.ietf.org/
IPMI (IP Multicast Initiative)	http://www.ipmulticast.com
Bitpipe (search for "multicasting")	http://www.bitpipe.com/
Google Web Directory (search for "multicast")	http://directory.google.com/Top/Computers/
3Com Paper: "Introduction to IP Multicast Routing" by Chuck Semeria and Tom Maufer	http://www.3com.com/nsc/501303.html
Cisco Paper: "Internet Protocol (IP) Multicast"	http://www.cisco.com/univercd/cc/td/doc/ cisintwk/ito_doc/ipmulti.htm

Multihoming

The basic description of a multihomed host is a computer that has multiple network connections. On the Internet, a multihomed system is one that is connected to two upstream service providers. Several Internet RFCs discuss this:

- RFC 1787, "Routing in a Multi-provider Internet" (April 1995)
- RFC 2260, "Scalable Support for Multi-homed Multi-provider Connectivity" (January 1998)
- RFC 2270, "Using a Dedicated AS for Sites Homed to a Single Provider" (January 1998)
- RFC 2901, "Guide to Administrative Procedures of the Internet Infrastructure" (August 2000)
- RFC 1998, "An Application of the BGP Community Attribute in Multi-home Routing" (August 1996)

Still another description is as a Web server that supports multiple domains in the same system. When Web clients connect to one of the domains, they cannot tell they are accessing a system that is supporting other domains. UNIX systems, Windows 2000 Server, and other operating systems currently support multihomed features. Microsoft calls a multihomed Web server a *virtual server*.

A multihomed server is one that has two or more network interface cards installed. Alternatively, single NICs can have multiple IP addresses with some operating systems.

Related Entries   Clustering; Internet Connections; Load Balancing; Routers; Routing; Routing on the Internet; Servers; *and* Web Technologies and Concepts

Linktionary!—Tom Sheldon's Encyclopedia of Networking updates	http://www.linktionary.com/m/multihoming.html
Avi Freedman's multihoming paper	http://www.netaxs.com/~freedman/bgp/bgp.html
Frequently Asked Questions on Multihoming and BGP	http://info.connect.com.au/docs/routing/general/ multi-faq.shtml#q1

Multilayer Switching

Multilayer switching is an evolution of LAN and internetworking technologies. Multilayer devices combine aspects of OSI layer 2 (the data link layer) and OSI layer 3 (the network layer) into hybrid switches that can route packets at wire speed. A basic switch is a multiport bridge. These switches were developed to allow microsegmentation of LANs into large broadcast domains with small collision domains. See "Switching and Switched Networks" for an overview of the evolution of switches.

As the technology developed, hardware-based routing functions were also added, then higher-level functions such as the ability to look deep inside packets for information that could aid in the packet-forwarding process. Thus, multilayer switches are devices that examine layer 2 through layer 7 information. These layers are described here. See "OSI (Open Systems Interconnection) Model" for a complete description.

- **Layer 1**   The physical layer, where hardware connections and electrical or optical signaling is defined.

- **Layer 2**   The data link layer, where access to media is defined. Ethernet, ATM, and other networking technologies are defined here. So are bridges and switches.

- **Layer 3**   The routing layer, where internetworking is defined. Routing is defined here. Multilayer switches use information from this layer.

- **Layer 4**   The transport layer sets up connection-oriented sessions. Multilayer switches obtain information from this layer about the application in use—specifically, the port ID—and use it to make switching and routing decisions.

- **Layers 5 through 7**   In the Internet Protocol suite, these layers are informally grouped together and called the "application layer." Information in the layer includes actual application instructions and data. However, so-called layer 7 multilayer switches examine information in the URL—such as the directory or filename—or look at information inside cookies, rather than examining application instructions or data in the packet.

A significant feature of multilayer switches is that they have hardware-based processing power to look deep inside packets for information that can be used to make routing and traffic management decisions. This is handled by ASICs and/or network processors. See "ASIC (Application-Specific Integrated Circuit)" and "Network Processors."

Multilayer switches are referred to by many names: *layer 2 routers, layer 3 switches, routing switches,* and *switching routers.* You will also hear about *wire-speed router,* which refers to the multilayer switche's ability to handle the incoming traffic of all its ports without causing congestion. In other words, it operates at the combined speed of all the wires coming into it.

A layer 3 switch is a hardware-based multiport router. Older routers were software based and had limited ports and processing speeds. A typical software router forwards 500,000 packets per second. A layer 3 switch with built-in high-speed routing at each port can forward up to 50 million packets per second. The devices are also relatively inexpensive, so network managers gain great flexibility in designing networks.

With the availability of inexpensive routing, the question then is where to route. In the past, this decision was constrained by the slow performance of routers. For example, a design consideration with software-based routers was to limit the number of these interconnection devices. If a packet were traveling across multiple networks, each router would add some amount of packet-processing delay. In addition, these routers were susceptible to congestion caused by traffic bursts, so each router was a potential place where packets could be dropped.

Today's high-speed layer 3 switches completely change the way routers may be deployed. Instead of seeing routers as devices that can create bottlenecks, they are valued for their ability to subdivide networks into autonomous networks, control internetwork traffic, and provide security. Since layer 3 switches are inexpensive, they can be deployed throughout the network wherever a network architect feels that routing instead of switching is needed.

Multilayer switches provide traditional routing at high speeds, which should not be confused with the following packet-forwarding techniques that are normally implemented over a backbone network of switches:

- **Cut-through routing**   This method is often called "route once, switch many." It is a packet-forwarding technology. Packets are examined to determine if they constitute a flow (many packets going to the same destination). If so, all subsequent packets in the flow are delivered across a fast switched path (ATM virtual circuit). See "IP over ATM" and "Cut-Through Routing."

- **Label switching**   This method tags packets before they enter a network and the tags are used to switch packets along a fast switched path. See "Label Switching" and "MPLS (Multiprotocol Label Switching)."

Multilayer switches may include support for these functions, but multilayer switches may also be relatively simple and inexpensive devices designed for LANs.

Silicon-Based Routing

Multilayer switches were developed to overcome the bottleneck of software-based routers. By integrating routing functions in hardware, performance was improved. Multilayer switches use ASICs (application-specific integrated circuits) and network processors, which are low-cost, high-speed circuits that implement routing directly in hardware, eliminating some or all software routing techniques. These devices handle real-time switching on their own, rather than relying on a central processor and routing software.

Eventually, routing performance moved from 50,000 packets per second to millions of packets per second. Terabit routers designed for use on the Internet have internal switching rates in the multiterabits/sec range. For example, Juniper Network's M40 systems have a routing capacity of over 800 Gbits/sec.

Functions integrated into hardware include parsing and validating the header, performing a table lookup, determining the next hop, updating the header, and forwarding it to an output queue. Functions that may be done with software include handling errors, fragmenting packets if necessary, processing IP multicast packets, handling non-IP routing (IPX, DECnet, and so on), and other functions that are rarely used. Also, routing protocols such as RIP, OSPF, and BGP, as well as network management functions, are executed in the background by separate processors.

Switch manufacturers design their products to perform at speeds that are an aggregate of all the ports on the device. For example, if a switch has ten Gigabit Ethernet ports, the switching fabric should operate at 10 Gbits/sec.

High-speed routing and forwarding is not the complete story of multilayer switches. As the capabilities of these hardware-based systems improved, designers began adding unique enhancements. Special *network processors* were added to perform *deep-packet classification* and to make unique forwarding decisions. Network processors are used in the following devices:

- **Server load balancers**   These devices distribute incoming service requests to a group of servers. The simplest method is to forward packets to the least busy server, but advanced techniques include forwarding packets based on type of application or whether a server has recently cached information that can be used to satisfy the request.

- **Bandwidth managers**   These devices use multilayer information to allocate network bandwidth and provide QoS for specific types of traffic. For example, voice may be routed to a voice-specific, high-bandwidth pipe.

As the cost of building multilayer switches decreases, vendors have integrated new features into their switches. The most important are QoS features that support VoIP (Voice over IP) and other multimedia applications. For example, Extreme Networks' switches include fully integrated policy-based QoS features. The company's high-end Internet Data Center switch includes VLAN aggregation, wire-speed layer 1–4 access lists, wire-speed server load balancing, Web cache redirection, and policy-based QoS. Other enhancements include fault-tolerant features such as hot-swappable modules, load-sharing power supplies, and link aggregation (connecting multiple switches with two or more links).

QoS support in Ethernet multilayer switches is supported via the IEEE 802.1p and 802.1q protocols (now officially part of IEEE 802.1D-1998). These are layer 2 protocols that prioritize traffic. Prioritization is really a queuing technique in which the highest-priority traffic goes into high-priority queues at switches that are serviced ahead of other queues. Several techniques are used to identify and tag traffic, including the layer 3 port number, which identifies the application, the IP address, and information inserted by Diff-Serv–compatible devices. See "Differentiated Services (Diff-Serv)."

Once the application information is read, the packet may be handled with a predefined level of priority or routed along a specific path. This is defined in policies, usually located in a policy server or directory service. Multilayer switching devices refer to these servers to obtain policy information (rather than being individually programmed by administrators). See "Policy-Based Management" and "DEN (Directory Enabled Networks)."

Packets may be directed based on *class of service*. If a packet is found to be part of a real-time multimedia application, it can be given a higher level of priority than packets that are not time critical, such as e-mail.

A switch may perform traffic shaping, which is a technique of managing and prioritizing traffic in order to avoid or smooth out congestion. Some stations may burst traffic into the network. Traffic shaping helps to smooth out these bursts by forcing the sender to transmit over a longer period of time. This allows other traffic to get through and prevents sudden glitches that can affect real-time traffic.

Related Entries   ASIC (Application-Specific Integrated Circuit); ATM (Asynchronous Transfer Mode); Backbone Networks; Bandwidth Management; Bridges and Bridging; Broadcast Domain; Collisions and Collision Domains; Congestion Control Mechanisms; CoS (Class of Service);

Cut-Through Routing; Data Center Design; Edge Devices; Ethernet; Fast Ethernet; Gigabit Ethernet; Internetworking; IP over ATM; Label Switching; LAN (Local Area Network); Load Balancing; MPLS (Multiprotocol Label Switching); Network Connection Technologies; Network Design and Construction; Network Processors; Optical Networks; Policy-Based Management; Prioritization of Network Traffic; QoS (Quality of Service); Queuing; Routers; Switch Fabrics and Bus Design; Switching and Switched Networks; Tag Switching; Throughput; Traffic Management, Shaping, and Engineering; VLAN (Virtual LAN); *and* Voice/Data Networks

Linktionary!—Tom Sheldon's Encyclopedia of Networking updates	http://www.linktionary.com/m/ multilayer_switching.html
The ATM Forum	http://www.atmforum.com
MultilayerSwitch.com (the definitive site for multilayer switching)	http://www.multilayerswitch.com/
Switching Links at Netfusion	http://www.nwfusion.com/netresources/ switching.html
Extreme Networks (see Technology page)	http://www.extremenetworks.com/technology/
Alcatel Wire-Speed Routing Guide	http://www.ind.alcatel.com/library/whitepapers/ pe_wirespeed_toc.html
Anritsu Multilayer Switching reference guide (a "must have")	http://www.global.anritsu.com/products/ networking/
Alcatel Wire-Speed Routing Guide	http://www2.ind.alcatel.com/library/ whitepapers/pe_wirespeed_toc.cfm
TechFest Multilayer Switching page	http://www.techfest.com/networking/mlayer.htm
Bitpipe.com (search for "multilayer switching")	http://www.bitpipe.com/
Noritoshi Demizu's Multi Layer Routing Web page	http://www.watersprings.org/links/mlr/
3Com Multilayer Switching Home page (numerous papers)	http://www.3com.com/technology/mls/
3Com's Layer 3 Switching site	http://www.3com.com/solutions/key_net/ layer3_switching/
3Com paper: "Layer 3 Switching, An Introduction," by Robert Ciampa	http://www.3com.com/technology/tech_net/ white_papers/500660.html
Entersys switching white papers	http://www.enterasys.com/products/ whitepapers/
Foundry Networks Gigabit Info Center	http://www.foundrynet.com/whitepapers.html
Network World Fusion Switching Web page	http://www.nwfusion.com/netresources/ switching.html
Hewlett-Packard Switches and Hubs	http://www.hp.com/rnd/index.htm
Nortel Networks (high-end switches)	http://www.nortelnetworks.com/products/ switching/
Cisco paper: "Layer 3 Switching—Looking Beyond Performance," by Stuart Hamilton	http://www.cisco.com/warp/public/784/packet/ july98/12.html

Multilink Point-to-Point Protocol

See MLPPP (Multilink PPP).

Multimedia

Multimedia is a term that describes multiple forms of information, including audio, video, graphics, animation, text, and a variety of virtual reality types. The interest in multimedia is surging. At one point, Microsoft and Real Networks reported over 100,000 downloads per day from their respective streaming media players. *Webcasting*, a multicast technology that broadcasts multimedia from a single server to many users, is expected to grow to represent over 70 percent of Internet traffic.

| Note | *This is a synopsis of the full topic. Refer to the Linktionary! Web site given later.* |

The major themes of multimedia networking include the following:

- Voice, video, and data are converging on a single network in both the enterprise and the Internet. The so-called NPN (new public network) is a convergent network that can deliver voice and video with the same quality as the PSTN.

- Traffic prioritization, QoS-enabling features, and bandwidth management are critical for delivering real-time traffic over packet networks (in contrast to the circuit-based PSTN).

- Multicast provides a transport for Webcasting streaming audio and video from one source to large groups of users. No licenses are required for Webcasting, and just about anyone can set up an Internet radio or TV station. Examples of streaming multimedia include live Web cameras, live sporting events, live concerts, and distance learning.

- Voice has a relatively constant low bit rate and can be compressed to a 16-Kbit/sec stream and still maintain reasonable quality. Small numbers of dropped packets are acceptable and there is no reason for the source to retransmit since they would arrive out of sync at the destination.

- Video is composed of a continuous stream of data; but because of the way compression algorithms work, the stream may vary in bandwidth. When scenes change, a burst of new image data is added to the data stream. Some packet loss is acceptable.

- Some streaming data is sensitive to delay and cannot tolerate dropped packets, such as a sensor that supplies continuous data. A QoS channel may be required.

There are two aspects of multimedia content delivery that you need to consider: *real-time delivery* and *stored playback* (also called *on-demand*). In the real-time delivery model, quality of service is essential. Packets must be delivered with minimal delay. For live voice conversations, latency greater than 200 ms is noticeable by humans. Stored playback transmits multimedia in a more relaxed fashion and in one direction. An example is watching a recorded video.

Delivering multimedia from end to end over networks requires adequate bandwidth, compatible protocols, and quality of service. Enterprise networks can be overprovisioned to handle streaming multimedia, but bursts can still disrupt live flows, so prioritization and traffic management may be required. Bandwidth can be reserved for scheduled events such as videoconferences by using resource reservation protocols. Traffic can also be classified and marked with priority codes using differentiated services techniques. Refer to the following topics in this book for more information:

- Congestion Control Mechanisms
- Differentiated Services (Diff-Serv)
- Integrated Services (Int-Serv)
- QoS (Quality of Service)
- RSVP (Resource Reservation Protocol)
- Traffic Management, Shaping, and Engineering

Streaming Media Protocols

Streaming is a method of delivering real-time or stored information such as audio and video across networks with a reasonable amount of QoS. In the case of RealNetworks' streaming media, a song or video starts to play before the entire content arrives. In other words, data continues to download in the background while the song or video plays. No space is used on a hard drive to store the content. The IETF and the World Wide Web Consortium (W3C) have created the following streaming media protocols:

- **RTP (Real-time Transport Protocol)**   RTP is a protocol that is optimized in various ways for the delivery of real-time data such as live and/or interactive audio and video over IP packet-switched networks. RTP runs over UDP and uses its multiplexing and error-checking features. Other similar transports are supported. RTP is described in more detail at the Linktionary! Web site and the other sites listed next.

Linktionary!—Tom Sheldon's Encyclopedia of Networking updates	http://www.linktionary.com/r/rtp.html
IETF Audio/Video Transport Working Group	http://www.ietf.org/html.charters/avt-charter.html
RTP (Real-time Transport Protocol) Overview	http://www.cs.columbia.edu/~hgs/rtp
IPMI (IP Multicast Initiative)	http://www.ipmulticast.com/

- **RTSP (Real-time Streaming Protocol)**   RTSP is a multimedia control protocol. According to the RFC 2326, "Real time Streaming Protocol" (April 1998), RTSP acts as a "network remote control" for multimedia servers. The protocol was designed to serve up multimedia from a cluster of hosts (virtual hosts). It is an application-level protocol that establishes and controls one or more time-synchronized streams of continuous media. No files are stored at the receiver. RealNetworks' RealPlayer is an example of an RTSP application. It provides play, fast forward, pause, and other controls. Real-Networks developed the protocol in conjunction with Netscape and submitted it to the IETF for standardization. Refer to the following sites for more information.

Linktionary!—Tom Sheldon's Encyclopedia of Networking updates	http://www.linktionary.com/r/rtsp.html
IETF MMUSIC Working Group	http://www.ietf.org/html.charters/mmusic-charter.html
RealNetworks RTSP information	http://www.realnetworks.com/devzone/library/rtsp/index.html
RTSP Information page by Henning Schulzrinne	http://www.cs.columbia.edu/~hgs/rtsp/

■ **SMIL (Synchronized Multimedia Integration Language)**   SMIL (pronounced "smile") is an easy-to-learn XML-based markup language for authoring TV-like multimedia presentations with timelines, layout areas, and so on. SMIL helps producers create synchronized presentations that include streaming audio, streaming video, images, text, or any other media type. For example, an opening logo can rotate for five seconds, followed by an audio and video stream, interspersed with periodic displays of text or pictures. Producers can use SMIL to create training courses, product presentations, or multimedia events for the Web. SMIL require RTSP applications such as RealPlayer for presentation. Microsoft has a similar technology called TIME (Times Interactive Multimedia Extensions) that applies SMIL concepts to HTML documents. Microsoft calls it "HTML+TIME." The following sites provide more information:

SMIL Information at W3C	http://www.w3.org/AudioVideo/
Web Developer's SMIL page	http://www.stars.com/Authoring/Languages/XML/SMIL/
Webopedia SMIL links	http://webopedia.internet.com/TERM/S/SMIL.html

ITU Multimedia Conferencing Recommendations

The ITU H.32x is a series of conferencing and communications standards that cover, among other things, conferencing over ISDN, PSTN, and packet-switched networks. They include H.320 (desktop conferencing over ISDN lines), H.323 (conferencing over IP-based networks), and H.324 (conferencing over the public-switched telephone network). H.323 allows IP telephony hardware and software from different vendors to interoperate over IP networks. It defines all the components necessary for a videoconferencing network, including terminals (conference-enabled desktop systems); gateways (translators between different networks); gatekeepers (management and control); and MCUs (multipoint control units), which support multipoint conferencing.

See "H Series ITU Recommendations," "H.323 Multimedia Conferencing Standard," and "Voice over IP (VoIP)" for more information.

Internet Multimedia Protocols

The Internet was not designed with real-time traffic in mind. Therefore, many strategies, recommendations, and protocols have been developed to provide these features. While

M

delivering real-time data over packet-switched networks is inefficient when compared to circuit-based models, the trade-off in convenience and cost makes it worthwhile. The Internet is pervasive and supports a true distributed computing model. Long-distance Internet telephone calls are essentially free.

The IETF MMUSIC (Multiparty Multimedia Session Control) Working Group is developing protocols to support Internet multimedia sessions, with an emphasis on videoconferencing. The group has developed a document called "The Internet Multimedia Conferencing Architecture" that defines an architecture for multimedia conferencing on the Internet. This section outlines the basic architecture. You can refer to the MMUSIC Web site listed later to read the entire document.

The conferencing architecture developed for the Internet is far more general than the ITU standards discussed previously. In particular, the Internet is more scalable to large groups, and allows new media and applications to be added. The architecture has been adapted for IP telephony (Voice over IP or VoIP). Some other important features of the architecture are listed here:

- The architecture takes advantage of efficient multicasting to distribute information to multiple parties.

- It relies on new service models that provide QoS by reserving capacity and prioritizing traffic.

- It corrects delay problems by using transport protocols such as RTP that send timing information so the recipient can synchronize and properly play back the multimedia streams.

- It supports applications such as whiteboards and shared editors.

- It defines conference policy methods (who can listen, who can speak), how participants find each other, and how they communicate.

- It defines security measures to enforce conference policies.

The Internet multimedia conferencing protocol stack is pictured in Figure M-10.

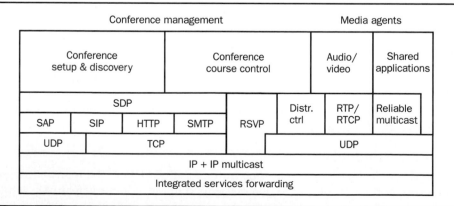

Figure M-10. *Internet multimedia conferencing protocol stack*

The most important of the Internet protocols related to teleconferencing and Internet multimedia sessions are described here. Each of these is described under its own topic heading in this book. A general overview of the Internet Multimedia Conferencing Architecture is provided later.

- **SIP (Session Initiation Protocol)**   A protocol for initiating sessions and inviting users to participate in multimedia sessions. See RFC 2543, "SIP: Session Initiation Protocol" (March 1999). The IETF Session Initiation Protocol (sip) Working Group is continuing development on SIP. See http://www.ietf.org/html.charters/sip-charter.html. Also see "SIP (Session Initiation Protocol)."

- **SAP (Session Announcement Protocol)**   SAP is a protocol to announce Internet multicast conferencing sessions. A conference is announced by periodically multicasting a UDP announcement packet to a multicast address and port. Because SAP is designed for multicast, it is suitable for setting up conference calls, not one-on-one calls. The IETF MMUSIC Working Group developed SAP. It is defined in RFC 2974, "Session Announcement Protocol" (October 2000).

- **SDP (Session Description Protocol)**   SDP is a protocol that describes a format for conveying descriptive information about multimedia sessions. This information includes session name and purpose, session time, type of media (voice or video), media format (MPEG, for example), transport protocol and port number, bandwidth requirements, and contact information. SDP is not a transport protocol, but relies instead on SIP or SAP to deliver the session information to destinations. For example, a caller can send SDP descriptive information in a SIP INVITE message. The callee then responds with acknowledgments regarding the descriptions that it can accept. See RFC 2327, "SDP: Session Description Protocol" (April 1998). The IETF MMUSIC Working Group is continuing development on SDP.

SIP is considered a better choice for telephony on the Internet than the ITU H.323 standard. It is a very simple protocol compared to the complex H.323 family of protocols. SIP was originally designed as a protocol to inform people about multiparty conferences. It would then set up and tear down the calls.

An important SIP feature is that it works across a variety of applications and media. SIP gets the most attention as an IP telephony call setup protocol, but it can also be used to set up just about any kind of multimedia session. An important SIP concept is that it consists of a set of simple text commands. These are composed using basic HTTP syntax. That puts SIP call controls on the same level as using a Web browser or even sending an e-mail message. The commands are easy to understand across the Web, and provide a simple and radical departure from the complex call setup schemes of H.323.

The following IETF Working Groups are developing recommendations and specifications for multimedia over the Internet. The sites list important drafts and RFCs.

- Multiparty Multimedia Session Control (mmusic) is developing protocols to support Internet teleconferencing sessions. The group's focus is on supporting the loosely controlled conferences that are pervasive on the Mbone (multicast backbone) today. The group is working on protocols for distributing session descriptions, securing session announcements, and controlling on-demand delivery of real-time data. Refer to http://www.ietf.org/html.charters/mmusic-charter.html.

■ Audio/Video Transport Working Group (avt) is working on protocols for real-time transmission of audio and video over UDP and IP multicast. In particular, the group is focused on RTP (Real-time Transport Protocol). Refer to http://www.ietf.org/html.charters/avt-charter.html.

■ Session Initiation Protocol (sip) Working Group is developing SIP, a text-based protocol similar to HTTP or SMTP, for initiating interactive communication sessions between users. These sessions include voice, video, chat, interactive games, and virtual reality. See "SIP (Session Initiation Protocol)." Refer to http://www.ietf.org/html.charters/sip-charter.html.

Related Entries   Collaborative Computing; Compression Techniques; CTI (Computer-Telephony Integration); Groupware; G Series ITU Recommendations; H Series ITU Recommendations; H.323 Multimedia Conferencing Standard; Internet Radio; Multicasting; Prioritization of Network Traffic; QoS (Quality of Service); RTP (Real-time Transport Protocol); T Series ITU Recommendations; Videoconferencing; Voice/Data Networks; Voice over IP (VoIP); Webcasting; *and* Web Technologies and Concepts

Linktionary!—Tom Sheldon's Encyclopedia of Networking updates	http://www.linktionary.com/m/multimedia.html
H.323 tutorial at Web ProForums	http://www.iec.org/tutorials/h323/
OII (Open Information Interchange) Electronic Conferencing Standards	http://158.169.50.95:10080/oii/en/confer.html
IMTC (International Multimedia Teleconferencing Consortium)	http://www.imtc.org
Interactive Multimedia & Collaborative Communications Alliance	http://www.imcca.org/
"Conferencing Software for the Web" by David R. Woolley (probably one of the best link pages available on this topic)	http://thinkofit.com/webconf/
"Multimedia Over IP: RSVP, RTP, RTCP, RTSP" by Chunlei Liu	http://www.cis.ohio-state.edu/~jain/cis788-97/ip_multimedia/index.htm

Multiplexing and Multiplexers

Multiplexing is a technique of combining multiple channels of information over a single circuit or transmission path. Multiplexing may also take place in software, where multiple threads of information are delivered to a device or process at the same time.

TCP/IP allows a single computer to multiplex two or more connections across a single network link at the same time. This occurs when you run two different programs to access the Internet, such as a Web browser and an e-mail program. Both programs use the same link to access different sites. Each application is assigned a specific port number in your computer by the TCP (or UDP) protocol. The combination of port number and IP address is called a *socket*.

When multiple sockets are in place on a single system, that system is multiplexing. See "TCP (Transmission Control Protocol)" and "Connection Establishment."

Packet and cell multiplexing techniques interleave the transmissions of multiple users across a packet-switched or cell-switching network. See "Packets and Packet-Switching Networks" and "Cells and Cell Relay."

The remainder of this topic covers channel multiplexing. There are two primary multiplexing techniques, as pictured in Figure M-11. FDM (frequency division multiplexing) divides the frequency spectrum of a circuit into bands and transmits each channel on a specific band, as shown in Figure M-11a. TDM (time division multiplexing) divides a circuit into time slots and assigns a channel to a repeating set of slots, as shown in Figure M-11b. FDM and TDM are discussed in the following sections.

A third technique, called "inverse multiplexing," is shown in Figure M-11c. Instead of putting multiple channels on a single line, it multiplexes one or more channels across two or more physical circuits. The extra lines may be permanent or temporary (to handle traffic bursts). See "Inverse Multiplexing" and "Link Aggregation" for more information.

FDM (Frequency Division Multiplexing)

FDM is a broadband analog transmission technique in which multiple signals are transmitted over a single cable simultaneously, as shown in Figure M-11a. FDM was used in the early telephone system. Each data or voice signal is modulated onto a carrier at a different frequency. An analogy can be found in radio broadcasting. Multiple stations transmit at the same time. To listen to a particular station, you tune your radio to the frequency that the radio station broadcasts on. The frequency range of a circuit is subdivided into narrow bands, and each band then carries a different transmission signal. Guard bands separate the subdivided transmission bands to minimize interference.

In North America, AT&T once used a hierarchical FDM scheme for transmitting signals on systems that have different capacities. A basic group in the hierarchy is 12 channels. The bandwidth of this group is 48 kHz and occupies the frequency range of 60–108 kHz. The first channel occupies the 60–64-kHz range, the second channel occupies the 64–68-kHz range, and so on up to the 12th channel, which occupies the 104–108-kHz range. The next level in the hierarchy consists of five groups combined to carry 60 channels (called a supergroup) in the frequency range of 312–552 kHz. The hierarchy extends up into higher frequencies, with groups that contain 300, 600, 900, and so on, up to 10,800 voice channels.

A voice conversion requires a 3,000-Hz channel, but 4,000 Hz is allocated per channel so there is adequate separation between the channels to avoid crosstalk, as shown here.

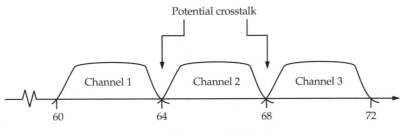

Frequency (kHz)

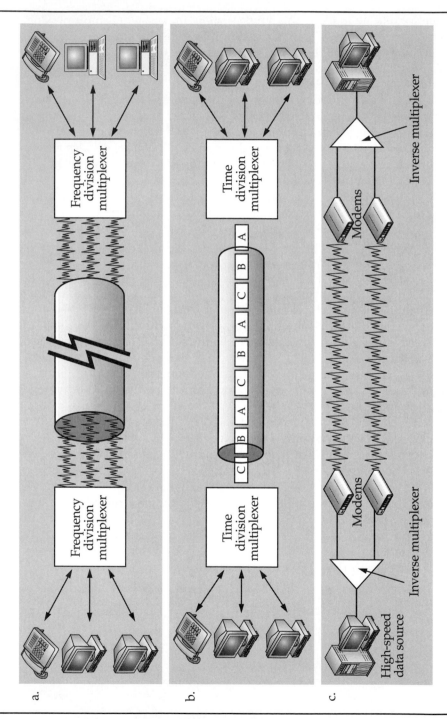

Figure M-11. *Multiplexing techniques*

WDM (wavelength division multiplexing) is a variation of FDM that is used on fiber-optic cables. Two or more wavelengths in the infrared range are transmitted through a single fiber-optic cable. Think of infrared beams occupying slightly different frequency ranges. The original WDM systems could transmit signals on two or four different wavelengths. These wavelengths are often called "lambdas," and they are essentially optical circuits, each of which can transmit an entirely different signal at OC-48 rates (2.4 Gbits/sec). Current DWDM (dense WDM) systems can transmit up to 100 wavelengths per fiber, and future systems will transmit up to 1,000 or more wavelengths per fiber. See "WDM (Wavelength Division Multiplexing)" and "Optical Networks."

OFDM (orthogonal frequency division multiplexing) is another multiplexing technique t hat has become popular lately due to the development of fast digital signal processors (DSPs). Data signals are divided over a large number of separate carrier waves. The receiving system reconstructs the message from the separate carriers. OFDM is also called a DMT (discrete multitone system) or MCM (Multicarrier Modulation). OFDM is important in broadband wireless systems, as it helps to overcome signal reflection problems called "multipath. " See "OFDM (Orthogonal Frequency Division Multiplexing)."

TDM (Time Division Multiplexing)

TDM is a baseband technology in which individual channels of data or voice are interleaved into a single stream of framed bits across a communication channel, as shown in Figure M-12. Analog inputs (voice) are digitized using PCM (pulse code modulation) or other compression techniques.

Each input channel gets a repeating interleaved time segment so that all channels equally share the medium that is used for transmission. If a channel has nothing to send, the slot is still dedicated to the channel and remains empty. While this is inefficient, it guarantees that each channel has the time slots its needs for its own data.

Multiplexing schemes such as T1 can handle 24 voice channels (4 kHz wide). Backbone trunks carry even more channels. A T3 trunk can carry 28 T1 lines. These trunks are used

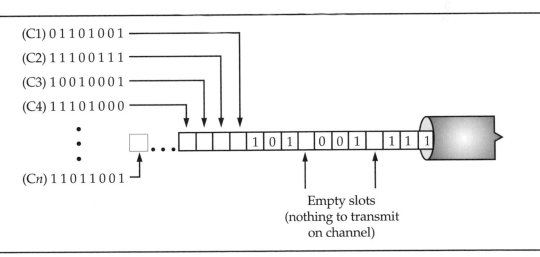

Figure M-12.   *TDM multiplexing*

between carrier COs (central offices), although fiber-optic cable trunks using OC (optical carrier) technology are now more common. See "OC (Optical Carrier" and "SONET (Synchronous Optical Network)."

The T1 carrier is the most common time division multiplexed line. As shown in Figure M-13, there are 24 repeating time slots of 8 bits each. Voice signals are digitized by codecs (*coder-dec*oders) and 7 bits from each channel are placed in one of the slots. The 8th bit in each slot is used for signaling. An entire frame consists of 24 8-bit slots with one extra bit used by the frame itself for synchronization. The entire frame is 193 bits in length. Each of the 24 channels has a data rate of 64 Kbits/sec, yielding a 1.544-Mbit/sec T1 line.

T1 lines are part of the North American Digital Hierarchy (NADH). It was originally created by AT&T and is now used in North America and Japan. A similar but slightly different hierarchy exists in Europe. In NADH terms, a T1 line is a DS-1 and it consists of 24 DS-0 (64-Kbit/sec) channels. A T3 line, which is called a DS-3, consists of 28 T1 lines or 672 DS-0 channels. See "T Carriers." The NADH hierarchy fits into the OC (optical carrier) hierarchy of SONET, which is described under "OC (Optical Carrier)" and "SONET (Synchronous Optical Network)."

Two related technologies used in the wireless environment are CDMA (Code Division Multiple Access) and TDMA (Time Division Multiple Access). These are covered under their own headings.

STDM (Statistical Time Division Multiplexing)

As mentioned, time division multiplexing allocates time slots to channels even if there is nothing to transmit on the channel. This is an inefficient use of bandwidth. One channel may be overtaxed while another is underused.

Statistical multiplexers solve this problem by dynamically allocating time slots and using the line more efficiently. Statistical multiplexers use processors and buffering techniques to allocate slots. Because buffering can add delays, the processors must be fast enough to keep up with the incoming data while allocating it efficiently to time slots. There are, of course, various

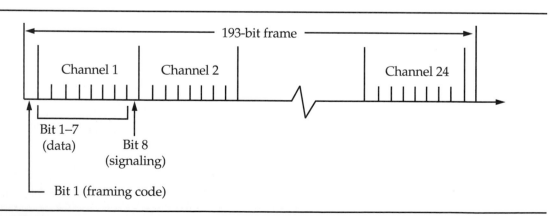

Figure M-13.   *The T1 carrier frame format*

other techniques to improve multiplexer performance, including compression, which is practical to do on-the fly with high-performance equipment.

Multiplexer Configurations

Multiplexers (or MUXs as they are often called), are devices that combine signals from various sources—such as a PBX (private branch exchange), asynchronous terminals, or a bridge connected to a WAN—and transmit those signals as a single data stream over a digital line. Figure M-14 illustrates how a multiplexer connects internal equipment to a T1 leased telephone line. Note that a CSU/DSU (channel service unit/data service unit) connects the multiplexer to the T1 line.

Refer to "TDM Networks" for more information about building network connections with T1 lines and multiplexers. Note that new and inexpensive network access technologies are now available that reduce the need for expensive carrier-based TDM lines. These include metropolitan Ethernet networks and metropolitan wireless systems. Refer to "MAN (Metropolitan Area Network)" and "Network Access Services."

Related Entries Analog Transmission Systems; Asynchronous Communications; Bandwidth; Cable and Wiring; Capacity; CDMA (Code Division Multiple Access); Channel; Circuit; Compression Techniques; Concentrator Devices; Data Communication Concepts; Dedicated Circuits; E-Carrier; Electromagnetic Spectrum; IADs (Integrated Access Devices); IMA (Inverse Multiplexing over ATM); Inverse Multiplexing; MLPPP (Multilink PPP); Modems; Modulation Techniques; Network Connection Technologies; OFDM (Orthogonal Frequency Division Multiplexing); Parallel Interface; Point-to-Point Communications; Private Network; Radio Communication and Networks; Serial Communication and Interfaces; Signals; SONET (Synchronous Optical Network); Spread Spectrum Signaling; T Carriers; TDMA (Time Division Multiple Access); TDM Networks; Telecommunications and Telephone Systems; Throughput; Virtual Circuit; WAN (Wide Area Network); WDM (Wavelength Division Multiplexing); *and* Wireless Communications

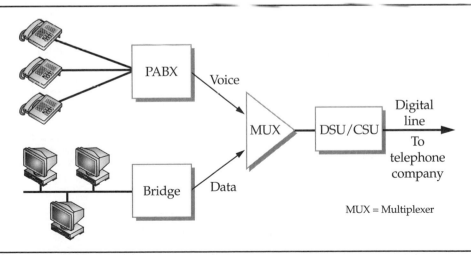

Figure M-14. *Multiplexing voice and data traffic*

Linktionary!—Tom Sheldon's Encyclopedia of Networking updates	http://www.linktionary.com/m/multiplexers.html
TechFest WAN links	http://www.techfest.com/networking/wan.htm
Muliplexing, TCP, and UDP	http://www.aciri.org/floyd/tcp_mux.html
"Netheads versus Bellheads," by T.M. Denton Consultants	http://www.tmdenton.com/netheads.htm
Bitpipe (search for "multiplexing")	http://www.bitpipe.com/
Network Magazine tutorials	http://www.networkmagazine.com/static/tutorial/index.html

Multiprocessing

A multiprocessor system is a computer that uses more than one processor to process the workload. Off-the-shelf multiprocessor systems are now common. A motherboard that supports Intel processors can be purchased for a few hundred dollars. Most network operating systems now support multiprocessing. Superservers may include an array of processors, along with a custom high-performance bus, tens of megabytes of error-correcting memory, RAID (redundant array of inexpensive disks) systems, and redundant features such as multiple power supplies. Figure M-15 illustrates multiprocessing system configurations. On the left, four processors share the same bus. On the right, six multiprocessor systems are interconnected via a high-speed switching fabric.

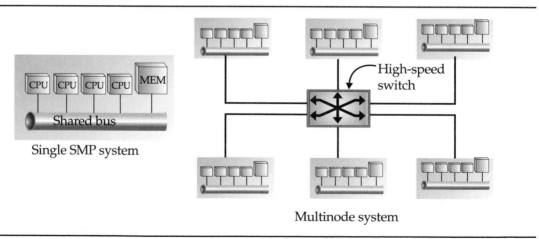

Figure M-15.   *Single-node and multinode multiprocessing configurations*

There are two ways to utilize the processors in a multiprocessing system, asymmetrically and symmetrically:

- **Asymmetrical multiprocessing system** Processors equally share all resources in the system, but work on dedicated tasks. For example, one processor may handle system I/O (input/output) while another handles application processing. Asymmetrical multiprocessing systems do not balance workloads. A processor handling one task can be overworked while another processor sits idle.

- **Symmetrical multiprocessing system** In this design, the operating system distributes the workload evenly among processors so that no processor sits idle while another is overworked. Processors share system resources such as memory and disk I/O. The performance of symmetrical multiprocessing systems increases for all tasks as processors are added. Operating systems that take advantage of symmetrical multiprocessing systems are more complex, but most network operating systems support symmetrical multiprocessing.

The Beowulf HOWTO (see Web site listed later) uses an interesting supermarket analogy to explain multiprocessing. A single-tasking operating system is like a supermarket with one cash register. All the customers must go through the same checkout line. A multitasking operating system is like a supermarket with multiple checkout lines. When the store is busy, more cashiers are needed. However, each cashier still handles one customer at a time, so the amount of time that a customer has to wait to get checked out is still the same. To reduce each customer's wait time, the items they are buying could be split up and given to multiple cashiers. If four cashiers handled the task, then each customer's checkout time should be reduced to one quarter of what it was. However, the items must be distributed to the different cashiers, and then gathered back together.

Note that multiprocessing does not guarantee performance. Consider the supermarket analogy. If we're going to ring up a single customer's items across several registers, there must be enough items to make this worthwhile. With just a few items, it is more efficient to ring the items up at a single register rather than distribute them to multiple registers.

SMP and Parallel Architectures

There is a range of multiprocessing systems. The difference is in how resources are shared among the processors and computers, whether systems are designed for basic load balancing, or whether processing tasks are divided and processed in parallel across the processors (or both). Two basic models exist:

- **Loosely coupled, shared-nothing model** Each processor has its own private memory space and disk space. A variation of this is that each processor accesses private memory and shared disks.

- **Tightly coupled model** In this model, all processors share memory and disk space. This model may also be implemented across systems in a cluster.

Multithreading is the process of splitting a single task into pieces (threads) and processing those pieces at the same time across multiple processors. Multithreading is also called *parallel processing*. Parallel processing may be done across servers in a cluster or by very large system. With this in mind, we have the following system categories:

- **SMP computer**   This is a single-box system with multiple processors that run an SMP-capable operating system that divides the workload among the processors. Off-the-shelf SMP systems are basically load-balancing systems designed for multiuser environments. Requests from multiple users or applications are distributed evenly across the processors. Some applications take advantage of multithreading. An SMP system is under the control of a single SMP-capable operating system, so all the processors share the same memory and disk space (tightly coupled). SMP systems have scalability problems. The shared bus can become saturated with traffic as more processors are added, and if one of the processors fails, the entire system may shut down. New switching fabric designs are more scalable, as discussed under "Switch Fabrics and Bus Design."

- **Basic clusters**   A cluster is a group of computers that provides high-availability, fault tolerance, and load balancing. Optionally, clusters may support SMP, as discussed next. Basic clusters are ideal for Web sites. A separate load-balancing device is installed to distribute requests among the servers. Clusters may perform a rudimentary type of parallel processing. For example, multiple servers may perform the same search across multiple databases. All the servers usually share access to the same storage devices. " If one server goes down, the others take over its workload (high availability). If fault tolerance is used, each server is duplicated so that if the primary server fails, its backup takes over. In the fault-tolerant configuration, server pairs must run in parallel at all times, duplicating one another's memory, cache, and disk states. See "Clustering" and "Load Balancing" for more information.

- **SMP clusters**   Special operating systems or OS extensions are required to support SMP/parallel processing across clusters. One such system is Beowulf, which has been around since the early 1990s. Beowulf is described as "a multi computer architecture which can be used for parallel computations." Another architecture is NUMA (discussed later). Coordinating parallel activities across multiple computers is not an easy task. There are synchronization and latency issues—interconnects must be fast enough to make it worthwhile to distribute processing among multiple systems rather than just running them on a single SMP computer.

- **MPP (massively parallel processing) systems**   This is really a supercomputer-class system that is usually dedicated to processing a single task across multiple processors to a fast completion. MPP systems are often custom built and use custom operating systems. See "Supercomputer" for more information.

In the Beowulf systems, a server control node manages the cluster of servers and hands tasks off to slave nodes. A Beowulf cluster acts like a single machine and new slave nodes can be plugged in at any time to scale the system. Beowulf systems are built with commodity hardware running the Linux operating system and interconnected with Ethernet switches.

An important concept is how machines communicate. In a single SMP computer, processors communicate via shared memory. Shared memory is fast and efficient. If one processor needs to pass some information to another, it puts it in memory and the other picks it up. Multicomputer clusters require distributed memory communications, meaning that some message-passing scheme is required to pass memory contents from one node to another. Common message-passing APIs for parallel systems include *PVM (parallel virtual machine)* and *MPI (message passing interface)*. PVM permits UNIX and/or Windows NT/Windows 2000 computers hooked together by a network to be used as a single large parallel computer. PVM and MPI Web sites are listed later.

The message-passing scheme is inefficient, so a high-performance SMP cluster will need a shared memory system. NUMA (Non-Uniform Memory-Access) architecture implements a distributed memory model in which shared memory appears as a single *coherent* block of memory to all processors in a cluster. It defines a standard memory-management method that allows systems to coordinate memory access. Basically, all the available memory across the group system is available for use by any system. If one node needs to access memory on another system, NUMA manages the exchange.

In clustered environments, the VI Architecture has contributed greatly to improvements in throughput and response time. VI helps overcome problems of traditional networks that introduce excessive loads on the CPU and create latencies. With VI, server applications running in clusters can bypass the operating systems and protocol stacks and communicate directly with applications running in other servers. According to Giganet, Inc., this produces a 40-percent reduction in system overhead, higher throughput, faster response time, and greater user scalability. Giganet has extensive papers on VIA, as well as clustered and multiprocessing systems. See "VI Architecture."

According to Thomas Sterling, writing in *Electronic Engineering Times* (July 10, 2000, p. 85), the fastest computers in the world deliver on the order of a teraflop of performance, or one trillion floating-point operations per second. Today, the largest Beowulf system operates at 200 Gflops, while some of the fastest microprocessors run at 1 Gflop. Sterling estimates that parallel systems built with these microprocessors will achieve 10 Gflops within a few years. He estimates that by 2010, petaflop-scale systems will be available. See also "Supercomputer."

The U.S. government and a number of research institutes are researching HPC (high-performance computing). The research is focusing on hardware and software issues related to massive parallel systems and supercomputers. You can refer to the sites listed later for more information. Massive parallel processing requires a complex management system to handle tasks that may be spread across hundreds or even thousands of computers and processors. The topic "Distributed Computer Networks" discusses a variety of parallel processing systems and projects, including some that are run on computers attached to the Internet.

Note that parallel processing is also used in the world of Web content switching and load balancing. Alteon Web Systems (http://www.alteonwebsystems.com) has designed a series of Web switches that implement up to 20 RISC network processors to process traffic simultaneously.

Reliable server pools can be used for providing highly available services by using a set of servers in a pool. The IETF Reliable Server Pooling (rserpool) Working Group is developing an architecture and protocols for the management and operation of server pools supporting highly reliable applications, and for client access mechanisms to a server pool. The group is specifically addressing network fault tolerance, highly available services, resistance against malicious attacks, and scalability. The working group is located at http://www.ietf.org/html.charters/rserpool-charter.html.

Related Entries Clustering; Data Center Design; Data Warehousing; Distributed Computer Networks; Embedded Systems; Fault Tolerance and High-Availability; High-Speed/High-Performance Networking; Load Balancing; SAN (Storage Area Network); SAN (System Area Network); Servers; Supercomputer; Switch Fabrics and Bus Design; *and* VI Architecture

Linktionary!—Tom Sheldon's Encyclopedia of Networking updates	http://www.linktionary.com/m/multiprocessing.html
Google Web Directory: Parallel Computing	http://directory.google.com/Top/Computers/Parallel_Computing/
IEEE Parascope (a listing of parallel computing aites)	http://computer.org/parascope/
NUMA information at Sequent Computer Systems (now IBM)	http://www.sequent.com/
Data General SMP and ccNUMA information	http://www.dg.com//about/html/beyond_application_bottleneck.html
Giganet, Inc. (information about clusters and VI Architecture)	http://www.giganet.com/
MIT's Alewife large-scale multiprocessing project	http://cag-www.lcs.mit.edu/alewife/
Nan's Parallel Computing Page	http://www.cs.rit.edu/~ncs/parallel.html
"Internet Computing and the Emerging Grid" by Ian Foster at Nature.com (also see links at end)	http://www.nature.com/nature/webmatters/grid/grid.html
NPAC (Northeast Parallel Architecture Center)	http://www.npac.syr.edu/
Center for Research on Parallel Computation	http://www.crpc.rice.edu/CRPC/
PVM (Parallel Virtual Machine) Web site	http://www.csm.ornl.gov/pvm/
The Message Passing Interface (MPI) Standard Web site	http://www-unix.mcs.anl.gov/mpi/index.html
Distributed Computing: An Overview	http://www.geocities.com/SiliconValley/Vista/4015/pdcindex.html

Multitiered Architectures

Multitiered architectures are software models (and hardware models, as discussed later) that extend the basic two-tiered client/server model to three tiers. In the basic two-tiered client/server model, the client requests services and the server provides services. There are software interfaces on the client and the server side that connect with one another to handle these interactions.

However, the two-tiered model has some drawbacks. Both clients and servers run a portion of the application logic, with the servers handling the loads of back-end data management. This requires that client software be installed, managed, and updated on a potentially large number of systems. The two-tier model tends to move large numbers of records across the network to clients that may not always be optimized to handle them. The model is not efficient in distributed wide area network environments like the Internet. For example, a Web client may be a hand-held system with limited memory and processing power. It cannot be relied on to handle front-end processing tasks.

SQL became popular as a form of client/server middleware because it was efficient at selecting and moving just the records that were needed. In addition, it could run stored procedures directly at the database server, rather than moving data to the client and then running procedures on the client. The *three-tiered model* extends this approach by moving application logic (the equivalent of SQL stored procedures) to a middle server called the *application server.* This server performs processing for the client and other tasks as necessary.

The following describes how Microsoft views the functions of the three-tiered model. Figure M-16 illustrates the concepts and shows the supporting hardware. Also refer to Figure J-2 under the topic "Java" for a detailed illustration of software components in a multitiered Java environment.

M

- **Presentation services tier**   Responsible for *gathering* information from the user, *sending* the user information to the business services for processing, *receiving* the results of the business services processing, and *presenting* those results to the user.

- **Business services tier**   Responsible for *receiving* input from the presentation tier, *interacting* with the data services to perform the business operations that the application was designed to automate (for example, income tax preparation, order processing, and so on), and *sending* the processed results to the presentation tier.

- **Data services tier**   Responsible for *storage, retrieval, maintenance,* and *integrity* of data.

By splitting applications into smaller pieces, workloads can be controlled and software development and upgrade are easier. The model has architectural benefits that match network design strategies for distributed systems and data centers. The workload and communication load are divided into pieces that can be handled by specialized devices, such as clustered servers and load balancers. For example, by putting business logic in objects, those objects can be distributed among an array of application servers that handle multiple requests simultaneously. Incoming requests are distributed to application servers via load balancers, as shown on the right in Figure M-16.

The Web is a good example of where to apply the three-tier model. Application developers know little about the potential clients except that they have a near-universal interface: the Web browser. The middle tier accepts requests from clients, retrieves information from the back-end

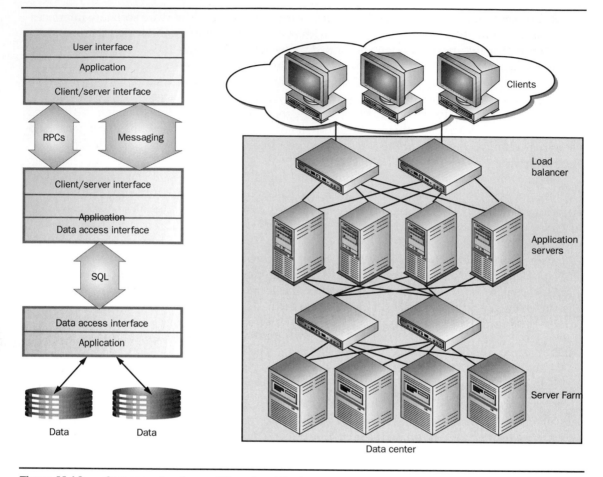

Figure M-16.   *Components of a multitiered architecture*

systems, processes the data, and forwards the results to the client. The client is relieved of a lot of work. Thin clients are a good fit in this model.

The middle tier may provide the following services:

- The code for the middle tier can exist on multiple application servers, all accepting requests from multiple users (via load-balancing switches) and all connecting with the back-end systems.

- Message queuing allows clients to interact asynchronously with the back-end servers. In other words, transactions don't need to follow a precisely timed flow. The client may need to wait for a message from the server.

■ The middle-tier server can provide transaction monitoring, which tracks the order and events of an online exchange to ensure that everything is complete and handled correctly. If not, the transaction is backed out.

■ Distributed object computing services in which application logic and/or data resides in objects that are made available through an ORB (object request broker). An ORB provides a sort of software bus through which objects on one system can make requests of objects on another system. See "Distributed Object Computing."

Java 2 Platform, Enterprise Edition (J2EE) is an architectural platform that defines the Java component model in a multitiered enterprise environment. Basically, the J2EE platform is defined by components, containers, and connectors. Components are the applications and applets. Containers operate between components and clients to provide services to both. Connections make the J2EE platform portable by providing APIs for existing enterprise vendor offerings. See "Java" for more information and a detailed illustration. Also see "Microsoft.NET."

IBM WebSphere Application Server is an e-business application deployment environment that supports Java servlets, Java server pages, and XML to transform static Web sites into dynamic Web sites. The system provides an EJB (Enterprise Java Beans) server for implementing EJB and CORBA components that incorporate business logic, allowing developers to build high-transaction, high-volume e-business applications.

So far, the discussion is related to software architectures and middleware that reside on application servers. Multitiered architectures also apply to network designs with data centers. A typical multitiered architecture within an Internet-connected data center or POP (point of presence) includes powerful routers connecting to Internet service providers or Internet exchanges, a middle layer that includes load-balancing switches (Cisco calls this the distribution layer), the applications servers, and the back-end systems. Traffic arriving at the data center comes in through the routers and is forwarded to the load balancers. The load balancers then distribute the requests to the most appropriate application server (or distribute requests evenly across the servers). See "Load Balancing."

The thin client model represents another aspect of multitier architectures. A thin client is a Web browser device that relies on an external server to run its applications and store its data. It displays information and accepts keyboard inputs. Some systems have small drives to cache objects from Web sites. A typical thin client is the inexpensive Internet appliance you've seen pictured on kitchen counters with TV-like knobs for accessing the interface. Users store data on a server located at a service provider or an online service. Electronic mail is accessed through a Web browser interface on a remote e-mail server. In this model, the service provider is the middle tier. In fact, giant Internet data centers are emerging to support this model. In some cases, the data center caches so much information via content distribution techniques that users are likely to find what they need at the data center rather than out on the bigger Internet. The Internet data center could be referred to as "Internet in a building."

Related Entries   API (Application Programming Interface); Application Server; ASP (Application Service Provider); Browsers, Web; Client/Server Computing; Clustering; COM (Component Object Model); Content Distribution; CORBA (Common Object Request Broker Architecture); Data Center

Design; Data Mart; Data Warehousing; DBMS (Database Management System); Distributed Applications; Distributed Computer Networks; Distributed Object Computing; Electronic Commerce; Enterprise Network; IBM Host Connectivity; Java; Load Balancing; Microsoft.NET; Middleware and Messaging; Network Design and Construction; Object Technologies; ORB (Object Request Broker); Remote Access; RPC (Remote Procedure Call); SAN (Storage Area Network); SQL (Structured Query Language); Thin Clients; *and* Transaction Processing

Linktionary!—Tom Sheldon's Encyclopedia of Networking updates	http://www.linktionary.com/m/multitiered.html
"Three Tier Software Architectures" at Carnegie Mellon	http://www.sei.cmu.edu/str/descriptions/threetier.html
Application server information at Serversatch.Internet.com	http://serverwatch.internet.com/appservers.html
Application Server Zone	http://www.appserver-zone.com/
IBM WebSphere Application Server	http://www-4.ibm.com/software/webservers/appserv/

NADH (North American Digital Hierarchy)

The telephone system has evolved from an analog system to a digital system, at least in the core. Early core transmission facilities used frequency division multiplexing, but in the 1960s this system was largely replaced with the PDH (plesiochronous digital hierarchy), which is a system of multiplexing numerous individual channels into higher-level channels. The system is not synchronous like SONET, but works well with it, as discussed later. The North American version of PDH is called NADH (North American Digital Hierarchy).

The hierarchy uses TDM (time division multiplexing). In this scheme, a circuit is divided into a continuous stream of time slots and multiple channels are multiplexed into the circuit. Traditionally, each channel was a digitized voice call, but video information and data may also occupy a channel. The basic channel is 64 Kbits/sec, which is the amount of bandwidth required to transmit a voice call that has been converted from analog to digital using a sampling rate of 8,000 times per second with the sample represented as an 8-bit value ($8 \times 8,000 =$ 64 Kbits/sec). See "T Carrier" for more on this.

The following table outlines levels in the hierarchy. Levels not shown are used internally by the carriers. The basic channel is a DS-0. A total of 24 DS-0s can be multiplexed into a DS-1, and up to 672 can be multiplexed into a DS-3. Note the last entry is an OC (optical carrier), which is listed to illustrate the next step up in the hierarchy.

Type	Channels	Data Rate
DS-0	1	64 Kbits/sec
DS-1	24	1.533 Mbits/sec
DS-3	672	44.736 Mbits/sec
OC-1*	1 DS-3	51.84 Mbits/sec

*SONET/SDH optical circuit

A T1 circuit is a DS-1 link over two twisted-pair copper cables. It consists of 24 DS-0 channels for a total throughput of 1.544 Mbits/sec, including overhead. A T3 line consists of 24 T1 lines. The phone companies used T carrier lines between its switching offices until the 1980s, when they began deploying fiber-optic cable. T1s, fractional T1s, and T3s are now sold to companies and service providers as access links into carrier networks or as private lines between company sites. They even carry ATM and frame relay traffic. See "E-Carrier," "T-Carrier," and "TDM Networks." See "Network Core Technologies" for an historical perspective on the TDM hierarchy.

SONET (Synchronous Optical Network) and the SDH (Synchronous Digital Hierarchy) define synchronous network hierarchies for transmitting information over optical fiber ring networks. SONET/SDH accommodates the NADH hierarchy. For example, a SONET ADM (add/drop multiplexer) will merge a 45-Mbit/sec DS-3 channel into a 52-Mbit/sec OC-1 channel. See "SONET (Synchronous Optical Network)" and "SDH (Synchronous Digital Hierarchy)."

Related Entries   B-ISDN (Broadband ISDN); Circuit; Circuit-Switching Services; Communication Services and Providers; CSU/DSU (Channel Service Unit/Data Service Unit); Data Communication Concepts; E Carrier; Last Mile Services; Leased Line; Local Loop; MAN (Metropolitan Area Network);

Multiplexing and Multiplexers; Network Access Services; Network Core Technologies; OC (Optical Carrier); Optical Networks; Point-to-Point Communications; Service Providers and Carriers; SONET (Synchronous Optical Network); T Carriers; TDM Networks; Telecommunications and Telephone Systems; *and* WAN (Wide Area Network)

Linktionary!—Tom Sheldon's Encyclopedia of Networking updates	http://www.linktionary.com/n/nadh.html
Committee T1	http://www.t1.org/
"The North American Digital Hierarchy" by Jerry Pople	http://www.it-pub.com/Archives/december/digital.htm
ADSL Forum paper: "General Introduction to Copper Access Technologies"	http://www.adsl.com/general_tutorial.html

NAK (Negative Acknowledgment)

An ACK (acknowledgment) is a confirmation of receipt. When data is transmitted between two systems, the recipient can acknowledge that it received the data. If a station receives packets that are corrupted, it can return a NAK (negative acknowledgment) to the sender. A checksum error may indicate a corrupted packet. A NAK is different than a normal acknowledgment in that it indicates that a packet was received in a corrupted state rather than not received at all.

An alternative to sending a NAK is for the receiving station to not acknowledge that it has received packets. By not receiving an ACK, the sender may assume that the receiver is overflowing or the network is congested and slow down its transmission. Keep in mind that TCP receivers use ACK to inform a sending host that packets have arrived. If the ACK is not sent, the sender assumes packets have been lost. NAK is used to indicate that a packet has been corrupted and to resend it, but there is no need to change the transmission rate.

Related Entries   Acknowledgments; Congestion Control Mechanisms; Connection Establishment; Data Communication Concepts; Error Detection and Correction; Flow-Control Mechanisms; Reliable Data Delivery Services; TCP (Transmission Control Protocol); *and* Transport Protocols and Services

Name Services

A name service, or *resolver service,* allows people to use user-friendly names when working on network-attached computers and accessing network resources. A name is easy to remember. In the background, most networks use numeric addressing schemes or other schemes to identify hosts and resources. Naming services translate a name in one form to an identification in another form. The following describes a variety of naming/resolver services. Some offer basic name/address translation while others offer services to help people find documents and other resources on networks.

■ **DNS (Domain Name System)**   DNS is the most common naming service. It resolves names into IP addresses and is used throughout the Internet. When you access a Web site such as http://www.linktionary.com, the name is first sent to a DNS server, usually at your ISP, that resolves the name into the IP address for the site. The IP address is then used for all further requests. See "DNS (Domain Name Service) and Internet Domains."

- **NetBIOS Naming**   NetBIOS is a networking protocol originally developed by Microsoft and IBM for local area networks. Computers and other resources are assigned names, and all the computers on the network work together to keep track of the names on the local network. This LAN scheme can't be used on router-connected internetworks, not only because it is not designed to cross routers, but also because you don't want every computer on a large internetwork to keep track of every other computer. See "NetBIOS/NetBEUI."

- **The CCSO Nameserver (Ph)**   The Ph Nameserver from the Computing and Communications Services Office (CCSO), University of Illinois at Urbana-Champaign provides a white pages directory service for locating people. RFC 2258 (The Internet Nomenclator Project, January 1998), RFC 2259 (Simple Nomenclator Query Protocol, January 1998), and RFC 2378 (The CCSO Nameserver Architecture, September 1998) provide additional information.

- **WHOIS**   A search and retrieval service for locating users on a network. The protocol was originally used to access a central NICNAME database maintained by the Network Information Center (NIC). This database allowed online lookup of individuals, network organizations, host machines, and other information. See "WHOIS ("Who Is")" for more information.

- **NIS (Network Information Service)**   This is a distributed database that provides a repository for storing information about hosts, users, and mailboxes in the UNIX environment so that users can easily locate those objects and resources. It was originally developed by Sun Microsystems and called YP (Yellow Pages). See "NIS (Network Information Service)."

- **Handle System**   The *Handle System* is a global naming service for documents. It provides *document persistence,* meaning that documents can be found by name, even if their original location is moved. The strategy uniquely identifies documents and stores the information in a name server along with the current location of the document. If the document is moved, the location information is updated. When users need a document, they obtain the current location in a Handle server. See "Handle System" for more details.

- **URN (Uniform Resource Names)**   Like the Handle System, this IETF development assigns names to objects that are independent of their location. For example, the handle urn:isbn:0078823331 identifies a book. When a user want to access information about the book, a request is made to a resolution server, which looks in the namespace called "isbn" to find a book called 0078823331. The server then returns the current URLs. If the URL changes, the name servers are automatically updated so that users can always find the book. See "URN (Uniform Resource Names)."

- **CNRP (Common Name Resolution Protocol)**   An Internet protocol that relieves people from having to remember long and complicated Internet URL (Universal Resource Locators). Instead, you type in "common names" to access resources. CNRP provides a "resolution service" that converts the common name into an Internet address. See "CNRP (Common Name Resolution Protocol)."

N

Note that directory services such as NDS (Novell Directory Service) and Microsoft Active Directory offer many of the features described in these services. See "Directory Services" and "LDAP (Lightweight Directory Access Protocol)" for more information.

RFC 2151 (A Primer On Internet and TCP/IP Tools and Utilities, June 1997) provides a discussion of Internet tools related to naming, searching, indexing, and so on.

Advertising services are related to naming services. They offer a different approach to finding resources and services on a network. The basic idea is that devices with services to offer either broadcast messages that advertise the services they offer (which is inefficient) or listen for messages from clients that are requesting services. See "Service Advertising and Discovery" for more information.

Related Entries   Bots; CIP (Common Indexing Protocol); CNRP (Common Name Resolution Protocol); Directory Services; DNS (Domain Name Service) and Internet Domains; Document Management; Gopher; Handle System; Instant Messaging; Internet; LDAP (Lightweight Directory Access Protocol); Metadata; Name Services; NetBIOS/NetBEUI; NIS (Network Information System); Repository; Resolver Services; Schema; Search and Discovery Services; Service Advertising and Discovery; SLP (Service Location Protocol); URI (Uniform Resource Identifiers); URL (Uniform Resource Locator); URN (Universal Resource Name); WebDAV; Web Technologies and Concepts; WHOIS ("Who is"); WINS (Windows Internet Naming Service); X.500 Directory Services; *and* XML (Extensible Markup Language)

Linktionary!—Tom Sheldon's Encyclopedia   http://www.linktionary.com/n/name_services.html
of Networking updates

Named Pipes

Named pipes is a high-level interface for passing data between processes that are running on separate computers connected by a network. Named pipes is the network version of IPC (interprocess communication) facilities. An IPC provides an interface between processes running in a single, multitasking system. Named pipes is network oriented. Two systems establish a logical connection so they can transfer information. Named pipes enable client/server applications in distributed computing environments.

Related Entries   API (Application Programming Interface); Client/Server Computing; Distributed Applications; Distributed Computer Networks; Distributed Object Computing; IPC (Interprocess Communication); Middleware and Messaging; MOM (Message-Oriented Middleware); Object Technologies; Pipes; RPC (Remote Procedure Call); *and* Sockets API

Linktionary!—Tom Sheldon's Encyclopedia   http://www.linktionary.com/n/named_pipes.html
of Networking updates

Tom Christiansen's interprocess   http://www.perl.com/CPAN-local/doc/
communications page   FMTEYEWTK/IPC/perlipc.html

UNIX named pipes (FIFOs)   http://www.uga.edu/ucns/tti/Computer_Review/
                                                  Winter95/UNIX.html

NAP (Network Access Point)

A NAP is a traffic exchange point in the routing hierarchy of the Internet. It is often called an IX (Internet exchange). There are four original NAPs, which were funded by the NSF (National Science Foundation) and built by major providers during the reorganization of the Internet backbone in the late 1980s. At that time, the NSFNET became the major Internet backbone, but others were available or being built or soon after. When the NSF decided to commercialize the Internet, it proposed the development of Internet exchanges where traffic could be exchanged among backbones. More recently, other Internet exchanges have been built all over the world to handle the massive traffic loads of the Internet.

A NAP consists of switching equipment to which carriers and service providers (national or regional) connect their equipment. No routing is actually done by the NAP equipment. Instead, network service providers co-locate routers at the NAP and connect those routers into the switching equipment. The switching equipment provides any-to-any connectivity to potentially all the other routers at the NAP. The service provider's routers perform all the routing, but use the switching equipment to move packets among the different provider networks access points that are located at the NAP. When service providers agree to exchange traffic at a NAP, they are *peering* with one another. *Peering agreements* define the parameters of traffic exchange.

Most NAPs are designed for use by major network service providers. Other NAPs are available for public use and are meant for local and regional service providers. A MAE (metropolitan area exchange) is a NAP operated by MCI Worldcom that consists of metropolitan fiber-optic rings to which service providers connect, as opposed to service providers running a connection to a centralized facility. MAE-like NAPs are operated by other companies as well.

The public NAPs are often overburdened. Some service providers choose to directly interconnect with one another in an arrangement called *private peering*. One method for doing this is to directly connect their respective routers at the NAP with a dedicated cable, thus bypassing the NAP's switch. Another method is to directly connect their facilities by using leased lines or trenching their own cable. This is usually done when the service providers are geographically closer to one another than they are to the NAP.

At the time the NSF funded the NAPs, it also funded the creation of the *routing arbiter* service, which provided routing coordination in the form of a route server and a routing arbiter database (RADB). Route servers would handle routing tasks at NAPs while the RADB generated the route server configuration files. RADB was part of a distributed set of databases known as the Internet Routing Registry, a public repository of announced routes and routing policy in a common format. ISPs used the information stored in any and all registries to configure their backbone routers, analyze routing policy, and build tools to help in these efforts.

See "Internet Architecture and Backbone," "Peering," and "Routing Registries" for more information on these topics.

Related Entries   Autonomous System; BGP (Border Gateway Protocol); Internet; Internet2; Internet Architecture and Backbone; Internet Connections; Internet Organizations and Committees; ISPs (Internet Service Providers); Network Access Services; Network Core Technologies; NPN (New Public Network);

Peering; PoP (Point of Presence); Registries on the Internet; Routers; Routing; Routing on the Internet; Routing Registries; RPSL (Routing Policy Specification Language); Service Providers and Carriers; *and* STAR TAP

Linktionary!—Tom Sheldon's Encyclopedia of Networking updates	http://www.linktionary.com/n/nap.html
David's Net.Presence Web site (descriptions and lists of network service providers, exchanges, and ISPs)	http://david.remote.net/connectivity/
Worldcom MAE information site	http://www.mae.net/
MFS Communications MAE information	http://www.mfst.com/MAE/doc/mae-info.html
The Ameritech Chicago NAP home page	http://nap.aads.net/main.html
PAIX.net, a neutral Internet exchange	http://www.paix.net/
Equinix IBX (Internet business exchange)	http://www.equinix.com/
Above.net ISX (Internet service exchange)	http://www.above.net/

NAS (Network Access Server)

A NAS is an access gateway. Sometimes it is referred to as a RAS (remote access server) or a media gateway. At any rate, it is a gateway between an external communications network and an internal network. The usual configuration is a server that controls a bank of modems. Users dial into a modem and connect with the access server, which authenticates the users and authorizes access to an internal network. The user typically uses TCP/IP over a PPP connection to access internal resources. This same configuration is used when users dial into Internet service providers, except that the user is given access to the Internet after being authorized by the access server.

The IETF Working Group called Network Access Server Requirements (nasreq) has defined new requirements for modern network access servers with respect to AAA (authentication, authorization, accounting). It considered services such as VPNs, smart authentication methods, and roaming concerns. It developed two Internet RFCs, which provide complete descriptions of network access servers.

- RFC 2881 (Network Access Server Requirements Next Generation NAS Model, July 2000)

- RFC 2882 (Network Access Servers Requirements: Extended RADIUS Practices, July 2000)

Related Entries　　Access Control; Accounting on the Internet; Authentication and Authorization; CHAP (Challenge Handshake Authentication Protocol); Communication Server; Dial-up Line; DIAMETER; EAP (Extensible Authentication Protocol); Internet Connections; ISPs (Internet Service Providers); L2TP (Layer 2 Tunneling Protocol); Mobile Computing; Modems; NAS (Network Access Server); Network Access Services; PoP (Point of Presence); OPSEC (Open Platform for Security); RADIUS (Remote Authentication Dial-In User Service); RAS (Remote Access Server); Remote Access; Roaming;

Security: Servers; TACACS (Terminal Access Controller Access Control System); Terminal Services; Thin Clients; Token-Based Authentication; VPN (Virtual Private Network); *and* WAN (Wide Area Network)

Linktionary!—Tom Sheldon's Encyclopedia of Networking updates	http://www.linktionary.com/n/nas.html
Bitpipe (search for "remote access")	http://www.bitpipe.com/
IETF Working Group: Network Access Server Requirements (nasreq)	http://www.ietf.org/html.charters/nasreq-charter.html
IETF Working Group: Authentication, Authorization and Accounting (aaa)	http://www.ietf.org/html.charters/aaa-charter.html
IETF Working Group: Roaming Operations (roamops)	http://www.ietf.org/html.charters/roamops-charter.html
IETF Working Group: IP Routing for Wireless/Mobile Hosts (mobileip)	http://www.ietf.org/html.charters/mobileip-charter.html

NAS (Network Attached Storage)

NAS is a category of storage devices that attaches directly to a network, allowing clients to access the storage as if it were directly attached to their system. The technique bypasses traditional server attached storage. Storage becomes accessible to users directly across the network and much of the overhead imposed by server and operating system intervention is removed to improve performance.

As an analogy, assume you run a parts warehouse. Salespeople occupy the front of the building and the parts are stored in the back. This is like the traditional server with directly attached storage. Orders go through the sales people and the front office accounting system. As demand grows, you experience a shortage of sales people and physical space. To complete the analogy, you build a customer-oriented warehouse and allow customers to shop directly at the warehouse.

NAS separates storage from servers as do SANs (storage area networks), but a NAS is best defined as a *network appliance* that attaches directly to the enterprise network, while a SAN is a large and complex data center storage system created as a subnetwork of the enterprise network. NAS devices are relatively inexpensive storage peripherals (compared to SAN solutions) that are dedicated to storage and file management. There is no SAN versus NAS decision since both have a place on the enterprise networks. Many organizations that run SANs in their data centers may deploy NAS devices closer to users at the department or workgroup level. This reduces bottlenecks at data centers. A NAS is sometimes used as a local staging system for data obtained from a SAN.

A NAS is usually considered when file servers have reached the limit of their expandability. NAS devices are usually called *filers*, not to be confused with file servers. Servers are often overburdened by trying to be all-purpose machines that provide file services, application services, electronic mail services, and so on. A NAS has a stripped down "thin" operating system that is optimized for file operations. All non-essential operating systems functions are removed, and what remains is usually embedded in hardware. An Ethernet adapter is also installed. Network appliances are like coffee pots and toasters in that they are designed to do one thing really well. In fact, by optimizing response to user requests, filers can provide better response to user requests over a network than the response those users may get from a locally attached hard disk.

A NAS is platform independent, meaning that it works with any client and can store a variety of different file types. While TCP/IP provides a transport service, file access services are usually provided by CIFS (Common Internet File System) and NFS (Network File System).

NASs are sold as preconfigured devices that are ready to run. Setup is about as easy as plugging them into the network. Most are available online as soon as they power up. The administrator then uses a remote management utility to configure access for users. In a directory services environment, this is as simple as adding an object that represents the NAS to a branch of the directory tree. The NAS then obtains all the security rights and permissions assigned to that part of the directory tree.

Technologist George Gilder (http://www.gildertech.com) has a way with words when describing technology. He says that NAS frees storage from the "enslavement of specific server operating systems with specialized file formats and expensive proprietary features."

Gilder points out that cheap and dumb storage devices with thin operating systems and Ethernet controllers are essential for the Internet. In this model, the server operating system "no longer makes the rules and dictates the architectures." According to Gilder, "The rapidly collapsing price of storage dictates architectures that waste storage and economize on processing and customer time. As in bandwidth so in storewidth, abundance trumps intelligence nearly every time." That is why the NAS market has expanded over the last few years.

In fact, increasing bandwidth made the NAS essential. Bandwidth increased to meet demand, even in the access networks, where metro-Ethernets are undoing the leased-line TDM model of the incumbent carriers. As music, video, photos, and other media become easier to capture, manipulate and store, the files are being copied everywhere on the Internet. Users are posting photos and music on Web servers to share with others. The Internet has become a massive storage system. The peer-to-peer trend started by Napster illustrates how file sharing bypasses the controlled storage devices like those in corporate data centers. Users are exchanging information at the edge of networks, not through central storage devices. See "Peer-to-Peer Communication." While enterprise networks will still need secure and centralized storage for corporate data, the rest of the world just needs fast, cheap, and easily accessible storage.

Consider thin clients, those kitchen-top diskless Internet access devices. They rely on storage devices located at ISPs (or more likely some huge regional Internet data center with terabits or storage). If you've ever accessed your e-mail from a Web browser at an airport terminal, you already know the benefits of thin clients and Internet-based storage. You can access your data from anywhere and with any device.

Network Appliance was the pioneer in the NAS field. It developed many of the concepts and created WAFL (Write Anywhere File Layout) to store files in a multiprotocol format. Files in this format can be shared via NFS, CIFS, or HTTP. With WAFL, users can access files, no matter which operating system they use or how the files are stored. WAFL has a number of NAS-specific features. It provides very high performance and supports RAID and quick restart, even after an unclean shutdown.

Microsoft now includes NAS support in its Windows 2000 operating systems. Microsoft uses the brand name "Powered by Windows" to refer to appliances from vendors that run a locked-down, appliance optimized, preinstalled version of the Windows 2000 operating system. Microsoft's NAS supports HTTP, NFS, CIFS, NetWare, Apple Talk, FTP, Kerberos, Fibre Channel, and SCSI.

Note the NAS differs from *IP storage* solutions such as iSCSI and VI Architecture/DAFS (Direct Access File System) solutions, which are meant for data center environments. NAS devices use higher-layer file-sharing protocols such as NFS and CIFS. In contrast, IP storage solutions and the VI Architecture/DAFS encapsulate SCSI and Fibre Channel *block-level storage and access protocols* directly into TCP/IP transports, thus improving disk performance over networks.

The VI Architecture and DAFS provide optimized data transfers in the data center environment. VI adapters allow direct memory-to-memory block-mode data transfers, which is considerably faster than the file-sharing approaches used by NFS and CIFS. DAFS is a file protocol like NFS and CIFS that integrates with VI Architecture devices to allow applications to bypass the normal operating system functions and directly access storage blocks across the network. With DAFS, a client can gain direct access to a disk and transfer data from it directly into local memory without the need to copy data to or from intermediate buffers or to interrupt the operating system. VI Architecture and DAFS are initially confined to data centers because VI requires special interface cards for both clients and servers. DAFS will eventually replace the slower file-level access protocols in NAS devices and boost storage access performance considerably on the enterprise network. See "IP Storage" "DAFS (Direct Access File System)" and "VI Architecture" for more details.

Related Entries   CIFS (Common Internet File System) Protocol; Client/Server Computing; Clustering; DAFS (Direct Access File System); Data Center Design; Data Management; Data Mart; Data Protection; Data Warehousing; Directory Services; Distributed Applications; Distributed Computer Networks; Embedded Systems; Fault Tolerance and High Availability; File Sharing; File Systems; File Transfer Protocols; IP Storage; Load Balancing; Mirroring; Multitiered Architectures; Network Operating Systems; NFS (Network File System); Replication; Rights and Permissions; SAN (Storage Area Network); SCSI (Small Computer System Interface); Search and Discovery Services; Servers; Stateless and Call-Back Filing Systems; Storage Management Systems; Storage Systems; Switching and Switched Networks; *and* VI Architecture

Linktionary!—Tom Sheldon's Encyclopedia of Networking updates	http://www.linktionary.com/n/nas.html
SNIA (Storage Networking Industry Association)	http://www.snia.org/
Storage Management.org	http://www.stormgt.org/
Sun network storage solutions white paper	http://www.sun.com/storage/white-papers/nas.html
STORAGEsearch.com NAS page	http://www.storagesearch.com/nas.html
TechTarget searchStorage.com	http://searchstorage.techtarget.com/
Brian A. Berg's Storage Cornucopia (great links!)	http://www.bswd.com/cornucop.htm
Bitpipe (search for "NAS")	http://www.bitpipe.com/

InfoStor Magazine (search for "NAS")	http://is.pennnet.com/
Microsoft NAS appliance page	http://www.microsoft.com/windows/serverappliance/nas/
Network Appliance	http://www.networkappliance.com/
Nishan Systems SoIP solutions	http://www.nishansystems.com/
Procom Technology	http://www.procom.com
Giganet. Inc. (VI Architecture and NAS solutions)	http://www.giganet.com
EMC Corporation	http://www.emc.com/
Network Storage Solutions	http;//www.nssolutions.com
Excel/Meridian Data	http://www.excelcdrom.com
Adaptec EtherStorage solutions	http://www.adaptec.com/products/solutions/etherstorage.html

NAT (Network Address Translation)

Network address translation is a scheme that allows two connected networks to use different and incompatible IP addressing schemes. Address translation allows hosts on a private internal network to transparently communicate with destinations on an external network or vice versa. NAT also refers to the name of a device that performs these functions.

NATs perform *transparent routing*, which refers to the translation of and routing of datagrams between different address realms. An *address realm* is typically an inside network that uses its own addressing as compared to the external Internet. Traditional routers route packets within a single address realm.

NAT was introduced with RFC 1631 (The IP Network Address Translator, May 1994) and was developed as a follow-up to *supernetting*—that is, CIDR (Classless Inter-Domain Routing). Supernetting was first discussed in RFC 1338 (Supernetting: an Address Assignment and Aggregation Strategy, June 1992), which was later replaced with RFC 1519 (Classless Inter-Domain Routing: an Address Assignment and Aggregation Strategy, September 1993). It was developed as a short-term fix to solve the potential problem of IP address depletion and scaling in routing. The long-term fix was intended to be a new Internet protocol with a larger address space, namely IPv6. However, IPv6 deployment is progressing very slowly, so NATs still provide a valuable service. In addition, they have also been recruited into the firewall brigade because of their talents at hiding internal addresses.

Supernetting changed the way that IP addresses were allocated. The old class-based scheme was thrown out in a favor of a classless scheme in which providers would receive contiguous blocks of addresses and allocate those addresses to lower-level providers. See "CIDR (Classless Inter-Domain Routing)." The important point for this discussion is that service providers were expected to return their former class-based address blocks to the global IP address pool and be allocated new contiguous address blocks. The return of the class-based addresses was critical, because it allowed contiguous address blocks to be reformed and then reassigned to providers. Unfortunately, many organizations refused to give up their address blocks, so the global address space is far from contiguous.

At any rate, renumbering would be required for many networks. If an internal network is directly connected to an external network and the external network changes its addresses, the internal network must also change its addresses. NAT was developed so that organizations could avoid or delay renumbering. If NAT is used, it hides the internal addresses by centralizing them to a single router. NAT allows multiple nodes on the inside network to simultaneously access remote networks using the single IP address.

Today, NAT is used for reasons beyond the original intentions of supernetting schemes. For example, a company may change service providers or reorganize its own internal address plan. In addition, service providers may merge or split, which requires attached networks to renumber or use NAT. Private addressing is also important when an organization has a lot of internal devices that require IP addresses, but those devices will never connect to the global Internet. Some examples are network-connected bank teller machines or cash registers in a retail establishment.

Most important, NAT is used as a security mechanism to hide internal addresses and/or to allow administrators to use any type of addressing they prefer without regard to the global Internet addressing scheme. By allowing networks to use internal addressing schemes, NAT has minimized the address space problem on the Internet.

RFC 1918 (Address Allocation for Private Internets, February 1996) describes private IP network addressing schemes. In this scheme, the private network, called the "internal realm," uses unregistered IP addresses. The RFC recommends three address blocks (1 class A network, 16 contiguous class B networks, and 256 contiguous class C networks). These address blocks are "safe" for security reasons because they are never routed on the global Internet. This can help keep hackers out of the internal network. Because of this feature, organizations are encouraged to use the RFC 1918–specified addresses for internal private networking.

NAT identifies specific traffic flows as *sessions*, in which the traffic belongs to a specific IP address and port and can be identified for address translation. NAT devices modify an end node's address and maintains state about the session traffic so that packets that have had their IP addresses changed can be identified. NATs are similar to firewalls, but you'll still need a full-featured firewall to scan incoming data for viruses and Trojan horses. Note that network address translation is one of the tasks that HTTP proxy servers perform.

A NAT router goes through three phases to translate and address as described here.

- **Address binding**   In this phase, the local node IP address is associated with an external address or vice versa. Once the bindings are in place, they are used for all session-based packet translation. When a new session starts, state is created to keep track of translations for the session. There can be many simultaneous sessions originating from the same host, based on a single address binding.

- **Address lookup and translation**   Once the bindings are made and the state is established for a session, all packets belonging to the session are subjected to an address lookup and translation at the NAT.

- **Address unbinding**   When the private address is no longer needed, the NAT unbinds the address.

The IP address in the headers of packets is replaced with the translated address. In addition, if PAT (port address translation) is being used, the port number in the TCP/UDP header is replaced with a new number. Note that the packet checksum and/or TCP header checksum must be recalculated once new information is inserted into the packet.

An address binding may be fixed using static address assignments or it may be assigned dynamically. With dynamic binding, a pool of IP addresses is available and the NAT draws from the pool when translating to global IP addresses. The address pool should provide enough addresses to match the number of addresses that are needed for global address translation. If not, access will be restricted until NAT unbinds addresses. Static addresses can be used in combination with dynamic addresses to guarantee access to the outside for specific local addresses.

One of the big concerns with NAT is the loss of *transparency*, which is the Internet concept of a single universal logical addressing scheme and the mechanisms by which packets may flow from source to destination essentially unaltered. This is discussed in RFC 2775 (Internet Transparency, February 2000). Other problems are outlined in the RFCs listed later. In particular, RFC 3027 (Protocol Complications with the IP Network Address Translator, January 2001) identifies protocols that do not work well with NAT.

An Internet protocol called RSIP (Realm-Specific Internet Protocol) solves some of the address problems of IPv4 and provides better support for multimedia. The IETF has stated that RSIP is a replacement for NAT (network address translation) and a potential alternative to IPv6. At the same time, RSIP provides a transition path to IPv6 for organizations that implement it.

Two IETF Working Groups are working on NAT:

■ **Network Address Translators (nat)**   This group is working to define NAT operations, limitations of NAT, and the impact of NAT operation on Internet protocols and applications. RSIP is being developed by this group. The group is located at http://www.ietf.org/html.charters/nat-charter.html.

■ **Middlebox Communication (midcom)**   This IETF group uses the term "middlebox" to refer to devices that enforce transport policy, such as firewalls and NATs. These devices need to identify the applications related to datagrams. This requires application-level intelligence. The midcom group is specifying an architecture and framework in which this intelligence is moved to a "midcom agent" which assists the middlebox in its task. By decoupling the application intelligence from the middlebox, complexity is removed and updates are easier. See http://www.ietf.org/html.charters/midcom-charter.html.

The following RFCs provide information about NAT:

■ RFC 1631 (The IP Network Address Translator, May 1994)

■ RFC 2401 (Security Architecture for the Internet Protocol, November 1998)

■ RFC 2663 (IP Network Address Translator Terminology and Considerations, August 1999)

■ RFC 2694 (DNS extensions to Network Address Translators, September 1999)

■ RFC 2709 (Security Model with Tunnel-mode IPsec for NAT Domains, October 1999)

■ RFC 2766 (Network Address Translation - Protocol Translation, February 2000)

- RFC 2775 (Internet Transparency, February 2000)
- RFC 2993 (Architectural Implications of NAT, November 2000)
- RFC 3022 (Traditional IP Network Address Translator, January 2001)
- RFC 3027 (Protocol Complications with the IP Network Address Translator, January 2001)

Related Entries   Access Control; Application-Level Gateway; Attacks and Attackers; Authentication and Authorization; CIDR (Classless Inter-Domain Routing); Filtering; Firewall; Forwarding; Gateway; Hacking and Hackers; Internet; IP (Internet Protocol); IPSec (IP Security); Policy-Based Management; Proxy Servers; Routers; RSIP (Realm-Specific IP); S/WAN (Secure WAN); Security Auditing; Security; SOCKS; Trust Relationships and Trust Management; Tunnels; *and* VPN (Virtual Private Network)

Linktionary!—Tom Sheldon's Encyclopedia of Networking updates	http://www.linktionary.com/n/nat.html
Network Magazine tutorials	http://www.networkmagazine.com/static/tutorial/index.html
Daryl's TCP/IP Primer NAT section	http://www.tcpipprimer.com/nat.cfm
Linus Router Project (free NAT software)	http://linuxrouter.org/
Enterasys NAT paper	http://www.enterasys.com/products/whitepapers/ssr/network-trans/
Network Address Translation Technical Discussion	http://safety.net/nattech.html
Cisco NAT Web site	http://www.cisco.com/warp/public/732/nat/
ICOMSOFT KnowledgeShare NAT page	http://www.vicomsoft.com/knowledge/reference/nat.html

N

NBMA (Nonbroadcast Multiple Access)

An NBMA network is the opposite of a broadcast network. On a broadcast network, multiple computers and devices are attached to a shared network cable or other medium. When one computer transmits frames, all nodes on the network "listen" to the frames, but only the node to which the frames are addressed actually receives the frames. Thus, the frames are broadcast.

A nonbroadcast multiple access network is a network to which multiple computers and devices are attached, but data is transmitted directly from one computer to another over a virtual circuit or across a switching fabric. The most common examples of nonbroadcast network media include ATM (Asynchronous Transfer Mode), frame relay, and X.25.

NHRP (Next Hop Resolution Protocol) is used to determine the NBMA subnetwork addresses of the "NBMA next hop" toward a public internetworking layer address.

Related Entries   ATM (Asynchronous Transfer Mode); CIP (Classical IP over ATM); Frame Relay; IP over ATM; IP Switching, Ipsilon (Nokia); LANE (LAN Emulation); MPLS (Multiprotocol Label Switching); MPOA (Multiprotocol over ATM); Multilayer Switching; NHRP (Next Hop Resolution Protocol); *and* PNNI (Private Network-to-Network Interface)

NC (Network Computer)

A network computer device or "NC" is a stripped down, inexpensive computer that is designed to rely on back-end servers for some or all of its processing requirements. The NC connects to networks via TCP/IP protocols and supports terminal emulation, X Window, Java, and Web browser software. These devices are also called "thin clients," "network appliances," "information appliances," and "Internet appliances."

The NC (Network Computer) concept and name was originally developed by Sun Microsystems, Netscape, and Oracle. NCs were meant to compete with Microsoft's monopoly over the desktop with its Windows operating system. Microsoft soon followed with NetPC, a similar thin client concept that supported Windows. Both the NC and NetPC have faded into obscurity, but thin clients are still important. Today, many include an embedded version of the Linux operating system or Windows CE. See "Thin Clients."

Related Entries   Bootstrapping or Booting; Diskless Workstations; Embedded Systems; Java; Mobile Computing; Network Appliances; Thin Clients; Terminal Services; *and* X Window

Linktionary!—Tom Sheldon's Encyclopedia of Networking updates	http://www.linktionary.com/n/nc.html

NCP (NetWare Core Protocol)

NCP is the principal protocol for transmitting information between a NetWare server and its clients. NCP handles login requests and many other types of requests to the file system and the printing system. IPX (Internetwork Packet Exchange) is the underlying protocol that carries NCP messages. NCP is a client/server LAN protocol. Workstations create NCP requests and use IPX to send them over the network. At the server, NCP requests are received, unpacked, and interpreted.

NCP services include file access, file locking, security, tracking of resource allocation, event notification, synchronization with other servers, connection and communication, print services and queue management, and network management.

Related Entries   Novell NetWare; IPX/SPX (Internetwork Packet Exchange/Sequenced Packet Exchange)

Linktionary!—Tom Sheldon's Encyclopedia of Networking updates	http://www.linktionary.com/n/ncp.html
Novell	http://www.novell.com/
Cisco document: NetWare Protocols	http://www.cisco.com/univercd/cc/td/doc/cisintwk/ito_doc/netwarep.htm
Network Sorcery, NCP formats	http://www.networksorcery.com/enp/protocol/ncp.htm

NDIS (Network Driver Interface Specification)

NDIS is a Microsoft specification that was designed to make it easier for network interface card (NIC) vendors to develop and support products. Before NDIS, NIC vendors had to create drivers that were configured for each possible configuration into which the NIC might be installed. Novell developed a similar interface called ODI (Open Data-Link Interface). This topic is covered in more detail at the Linktionary! Web site.

Related Entries   Microsoft; Microsoft Windows; Network Operating Systems; NIC (Network Interface Card); *and* ODI (Open Data-Link Interface)

Linktionary!—Tom Sheldon's Encyclopedia of Networking updates	http://www.linktionary.com/n/ndis.html
Introduction to NDSI 5.0	http://www.asia.microsoft.com/hwdev/devdes/ndis5.htm
Microsoft HOWTO: Writing WDM/ NDIS Miniports for Windows	http://support.microsoft.com/support/kb/articles/Q224/7/ 84.ASP
NDIS driver interface specification	http://www.dtix.com/product/ndisdrv.html

NDMP (Network Data Management Protocol)

Network Data Management Protocol (NDMP) is an open protocol for managing data stored on network-attached storage devices (specifically, tape devices, although other devices will be supported). The protocol was codeveloped by storage leader Network Appliance and Intelliguard (now part of Legato), NDMP is being actively enhanced and adopted by the storage industry. In April 2000, a new work group for NDMP was created as part of the SNIA (Storage Networking Industry Association) to take responsibility for the development of the protocol standard, interoperability testing, and educational programs on NDMP.

The objective of NDMP is to provide enterprise wide control of backup in heterogeneous environments. It also provides a standardized protocol that vendors can write to and conform with to reduce cross-platform hardware and software development efforts. With NDMP, vendors can concentrate on features and performance rather than writing code for many different platforms and environments. They only need to be concerned with maintaining compatibility with one, well-defined protocol.

This topic is covered in more detail at the Linktionary! Web site and at the NDMP Web site given later.

Related Entries   Backup and Data Archiving; Clustering; Data Management; Data Protection; Disaster Planning and Recovery; Fault Tolerance and High-Availability; IP Storage; Mirroring; NAS (Network Attached Storage); Replication; SAN (Storage Area Network); Storage Management Systems; *and* Storage Systems

Linktionary!—Tom Sheldon's Encyclopedia of Networking updates	http://www.linktionary.com/n/ndmp.html
Network Data Management Protocol Web site	http://www.ndmp.org/
SNIA (Storage Networking Industry Association)	http://www.snia.org/

N

NDS (Novell Directory Services)

Novell NDS eDirectory is a platform-independent directory service with roots in the original NDS (Novell Directory Service) that was introduced with Novell NetWare 4.0. The latest version runs on NetWare, Windows 2000, Solaris, Linux, and Compaq Tru64 UNIX systems. NDS serves as a platform for directory-enabled services such as automated business-relationship management, supply-chain management, and electronic storefronts. Other services include automated provisioning, enhanced security, customer profiling, electronic wallets, automated notification systems, customized Web interfaces, and virtual private networks (VPNs).

> **Note** *The Linktionary! Web site has extended coverage of NDS. Also see "Directory Services" for general information about directory services.*

NDS is designed not only for enterprise networks, but also for ASP (application service providers), ISPs (Internet service providers), and other organizations that need to maintain in-depth, hierarchically linked information about people and a range of "objects," including devices, applications, resources, and services. NDS has an extensible schema and hierarchical tree structure that makes it easy to manage nearly any type of object. LDAP (Lightweight Directory Access Protocol) is the native protocol used for interaction with other directory services.

NDS eDirectory helps unify Internet, intranet, and extranet resources by helping to extend the reach of existing infrastructure to customers and supply-chain partners in a secure way. DNS Federation is a feature that lets business partners manage objects in one another's directory trees. For example, you could assign a user in a supplier's company access rights to a database in your own company. No new object is required in your company database. Instead, you go to the user object in the supplier's directory and grant the rights.

DirXML provides a way to synchronize information in legacy directories. DirXML uses LDAP to connect with other directories and XML as a standard format for information exchange. It can be used to ensure consistent information among internal and external directories.

Due to the directory-oriented nature of NDS, managing security, certificates, cryptography, authentication, and other security technologies is easy. Users authenticate to the directory when they log on. Authentication is handled with passwords encrypted over SSL (Secure Sockets Layer) to X.509v3 certificates and smart cards. The login authentication service is based on the public-key/private-key encryption technology developed by RSA Data Security, Inc., which relies on a private key and a digital signature to verify the user's identity. Once authenticated, all further authentications are handled in the background.

NDS has always supported directory replication. The directory can be partitioned into replicas, and those replicas can be distributed to distant servers to improve initial logon for distant users and provide directory information that is physically closer to users, which is useful if the link to the central database goes down. Any part of the partition, including objects and their attributes, can be selectively copied and distributed.

Related Entries   DEN (Directory Enabled Networks); Directory Services; Discovery Services; LDAP (Lightweight Directory Access Protocol); Metadata; Microsoft Active Directory; Name Services; NIS (Network Information System); Search and Discovery Services; Service Advertising and Discovery; SLP (Service Location Protocol); URI (Uniform Resource Identifier); URN (Uniform Resource Name); Web Technologies and Concepts; WHOIS ("Who is"); *and* X.500 Directory Services

Linktionary!—Tom Sheldon's Encyclopedia of   http://www.linktionary.com/n/nds.html
Networking updates

Novell   http://www.novell.com

NetBIOS/NetBEUI

The NetBIOS (Network Basic Input Output System) was designed by IBM and Sytek to support client/server computing in LAN environments. NetBEUI (NetBIOS Extended User Interface) is a NetBIOS support protocol. According to the paper at the dtool Web site listed later, NetBEUI formalized the transport layer frame that was never standardized in NetBIOS. It specifies how NetBIOS applications send and receive messages over the NetBIOS frame protocol. NetBEUI talks directly to NDIS in the MAC layer, bypassing any internetworking functions, and so is not a routable protocol. IBM used NetBEUI in its LAN Manager Server and Microsoft later adopted it as a LAN networking protocol.

Both NetBIOS and NetBEUI were widely implemented in various versions of Microsoft Windows, although Microsoft now pushes TCP/IP as the network protocol of choice. NetBIOS and NetBEUI are still included in Windows products and some network administrators may find them useful in the small LAN environment. Since you cannot build internetworks with NetBEUI, most organizations have moved to NetBIOS and Windows Sockets over TCP/IP.

Figure N-1 illustrates the protocol structure of a NetBIOS environment. Windows Sockets is another application interface that is shown for comparison and the IPX/SPX protocol is thrown in to show the network layer relationship. Windows Sockets is a Windows implementation of the widely used UC Berkeley Sockets API for TCP/IP environments. Both NetBIOS and Windows Sockets are used in the Windows environment to build distributed network applications.

One advantage of NetBIOS is that it has a simple and easy-to-manage naming service. When you open the Network Neighborhood on a network-connected Windows computer, you may see names of other computers on the network. Each computer has a NetBIOS name, and you can access the computer (or printer) by double-clicking its icon. NetBIOS works in the background on Windows systems to gather and keep a list of the names of other computers (along with their network address). All of the Windows computers are involved in this process.

When Microsoft began supporting TCP/IP in its Windows environment, it added WINS, which resolves NetBIOS names into TCP/IP addresses. See "WINS (Windows Internet Naming Service)." Microsoft also created NetBT (NetBIOS over TCP/IP), which is an interface for connecting NetBIOS applications to the TCP/IP protocols. WINS requires a Windows NT or Windows 2000 computer to operate. An alternative is to run DNS and use Internet-style naming techniques.

More About NetBIOS

NetBIOS provides both a namespace and an application interface. The namespace is flat (not hierarchical) and uses 16 alphanumeric characters. When a computer is connected to a NetBIOS network, it is assigned a name such as "JohnsPC." Names are assigned during the installation of the operating system, but may be changed later.

The first time the computer interacts with the network, it "bids" for use of the name. If the name is not already in use, no conflicts occur and the computer gets to use the name. Other

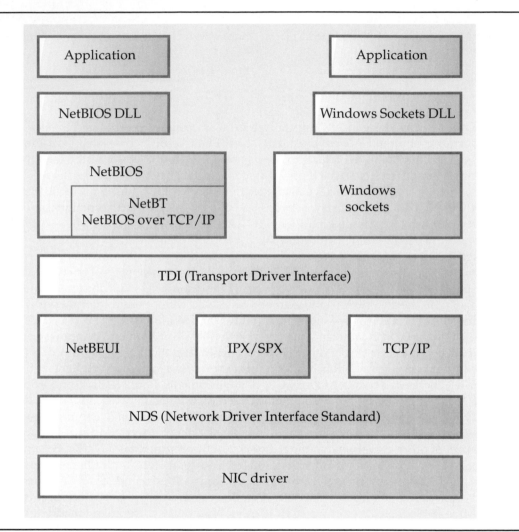

Figure N-1. *NetBIOS and associated protocols*

computers on the network learn about the new computer and its name through a broadcasting scheme (or through a WINS server) and cache the name for future reference.

NetBIOS is an application interface that allows applications to access network services provided by network transports such as NetBEUI, SPX/IPX, and TCP/IP. NetBT (NetBIOS over TCP/IP) is a Microsoft interface for connecting NetBIOS-compatible applications to TCP/IP. Programmers traditionally used NetBIOS to create LAN applications for the IBM LAN Server, Microsoft LAN Manager, and OS/2 environments.

Network applications that run on NetBIOS-compliant networks use NetBIOS to locate other resources and establish connections with those resources. NetBIOS establishes logical links or *sessions* between computers and then use those sessions to exchange data reliably between systems. Computers can exchange data in the form of NetBIOS requests or in the form of an SMB (Server Message Block).

NetBIOS broadcasts information about the location of servers and the names of those servers. If a workstation responds to the messages, the server no longer sends it messages. If a workstation doesn't respond because it is turned off or has a defective network interface card, the server sends messages every few minutes in an attempt to get a response. This traffic can burden a network, but it can be controlled with various mechanisms.

NetBIOS is well established and still supported in many environments, even though newer protocols are available. NetBIOS is also well understood, and there are many applications that use it. It will be around for some time.

Several Internet RFCs provide information about NetBIOS over TCP/IP networks:

- RFC 1001 (Protocol standard for a NetBIOS service on a TCP/UDP transport: Concepts and methods, March 1987)

- RFC 1002 (Protocol standard for a NetBIOS service on a TCP/UDP transport: Detailed specifications, March 1987)

- RFC 1088 (Standard for the transmission of IP datagrams over NetBIOS networks, February 1989)

- RFC 2097 (The PPP NetBIOS Frames Control Protocol, January 1997)

Related Entries   ActiveX; API (Application Programming Interface); Client/Server Computing; COM (Component Object Model); Distributed Applications; Distributed Computer Networks; Distributed Object Computing; IPC (Interprocess Communication); Java; Microsoft.NET; Middleware and Messaging; MOM (Message-Oriented Middleware); Multitiered Architectures; Named Pipes; Object Technologies; Pipes; Resolver Services; RPC (Remote Procedure Call); Service Advertising and Discovery; SMB (Server Message Blocks); SOAP (Simple Object Access Protocol); Sockets API; *and* WinSock

Linktionary!—Tom Sheldon's Encyclopedia of Networking updates	http://www.linktionary.com/n/netbios.html
dtool (Digital Tool) Web site NetBIOS/NetBEUI page	http://www.dtool.com/netbios.html
Microsoft (search for "NetBIOS")	http://www.microsoft.com
Google Web Directory (search for "NetBIOS")	http://directory.google.com/Top/Computers/
NetBIOS over TCP/IP (illustrates name resolution methods)	http://www.ftq.com/tcpip/netbios.htm
Gavin Winston's NetBIOS specification page	http://members.tripod.com/~Gavin_Winston/NETBIOS.HTM
Tim Evans NetBIOS/NetBEUI NBF Networking page	http://ourworld.compuserve.com/homepages/TimothyDEvans/contents.htm
What is SMB, NetBIOS etc.?	http://huizen.dds.nl/~jacco2/samba/smb.html
Cisco NetBIOS browsing and routing information	http://www.cisco.com/warp/public/108/Netbios.html

Netcasting

Netcasting (or "Webcasting") is an alternative to Web browsing. With Web browsing, users go out on the Web and look for information. With Netcasting, information is automatically delivered to users' desktops. Netcasting is often referred to as "push" technology because content is pushed from a Web server and delivered to users who have requested receipt of the content. Content may include the latest news, weather, stock quotes, or software updates. See "Webcasting."

NetPC

The NetPC is a form of thin client, which is a stripped-down computer that relies on computing resources in central servers for most of its functions. The NetPC conforms to a design specification developed by Microsoft and Intel. The concept was to create a very inexpensive sealed computer that was easy for network administrators to set up and manage. However, the NetPC concept has failed to catch on and is no longer important. In its place, Microsoft has developed Windows 2000 Terminal Services and the Windows-based terminal (WBT). See "Thin Clients" and "Terminal Services" for more information.

Netscape

Netscape Communications was started in 1994 by Jim Clark, an investor who was involved with Silicon Graphics, Inc., and Marc Andreessen, one of the coauthors of the Mosaic Web browser. The company's first product was a spin-off of Mosaic called Netscape Navigator. It became an instant success, and when Netscape went public in August of 1994, its stock made one of the biggest one-day jumps in history. Netscape is now owned by AOL-Time Warner.

NetWare, Novell

See Novell NetWare.

Network Access Methods

See "Access Method, Network;" *and* MAC (Medium Access Control).

Network Access Services

Network access services provide businesses with communication links to carrier and service provider wide area networks. A telephone is connected via twisted-pair copper wire (the local loop) to the public telephone network where switches connect calls. Internet users can connect to the Internet over the same local loop or use a variety of other services, including cable TV connections, wireless connections, and fiber-optic connections. This topic surveys traditional and emerging network access methods.

The traditional access method is the public-switched telephone network. The earliest IBM mainframe systems communicated over standard phone lines using protocols such as BSC (Binary Synchronous Communication) and later SDLC (Synchronous Data Link Control). The early Internet (then called ARPANET) was connected with a mesh of AT&T long-distance telephone lines that provided 50-Kbit/sec throughput.

The PSTN and its TDM (time division multiplexing) architecture have defined network access for years. Only recently has this changed as cable TV companies and CLECs (competitive local exchange carriers) provide alternative services that are not restricted to the time slotting of the TDM system and the restrictions of a backbone transport network designed and built by the world's telephone companies. Alternative services include metropolitan optical networks running Ethernet and broadband wireless systems (radio, microwave, or infrared). A central theme with new network access services is convergence of voice and data networks into an all-packet-switched network that interconnects with the older PSTN for backward compatibility. This is the so-called NPN (new public network). The concept is to improve the quality of service on the Internet to support voice and other real-time traffic with the same reliability as the circuit-switched PSTN.

As mentioned, the telephone network was designed to carry multiple digitized voice phone calls over a single trunk. In the case of the North American T1 trunk, an analog voice call is digitized into a 64-Kbit/sec stream and inserted into a continuous series of interleaved time slots on the trunk. TDM is good for voice because it supports the real-time streaming nature of voice, but it is not so good for data, which is usually transmitted in bursts. Allocating burst data to repeating time slots is inefficient.

The incumbent telephone carriers still hold a monopoly on access services in many areas, and they are not about to give up a service that is profitable to them in order to build a new costly network. One telephone company executive said that telephone carriers would continue to push TDM circuits until telephone switching equipment is fully depreciated (2010 in some cases), even though more efficient data services could be established.

New Service Providers and Networks

Common service providers are the ILECs (incumbent local exchange carriers), CLECs (competitive local exchange carriers), and ICPs (integrated communications providers). The ILECs are the phone companies that formerly had a monopoly in most service areas. They used to be called the RBOCs (regional Bell operating companies), but due to mergers and acquisitions, this title no longer applies. The Telecom Act unbundled the local loop, allowing hundreds of new service providers to compete in the access market. Under the Act, ILECs must offer network interconnections, co-location of equipment at central offices (on a lease basis and space permitting), access to unbundled elements, and resale of bandwidth at wholesale prices.

The CLECs appeared in the latter half of the 1990s, after the Telecom Act of 1996 opened up the local market to competition. The original CLECs modeled themselves after the ILECs, wholesaling some ILEC services and providing bandwidth and services of their own. The original CLECs had to deploy costly and complex class 5 switches to provide voice services in order to compete with the ILECs. Later, the CLECs went into the high-bandwidth access business by offering DSL services to home users and fiber-optic access to buildings and business parks. One of the defining features of current CLECs is that they have installed integrated access switches from vendors like Santera, Redback Networks, and others. These switches integrate class 5 voice switch functionality with support for any type of data service, including dial-up, DSL, frame relay, ATM, wireless, and others.

ICPs are basically CLECs and other competitive providers that offer a full range of high-speed access services to support the requirements of home and business users. Most have installed the integrated access switches.

An MSPP (multiservice provisioning platform) is a complex and expensive device that sits between customers and the core network. It consolidates diverse traffic streams coming from customers and forwards those streams to the appropriate backbones. Some traffic will go to the PSTN, some will go to the Internet, and some will go to DWDM optical networks that make up the backbone of the carrier or service providers' networks. Traffic with high priority or a need for QoS may go into DWDM optical circuits (lambdas) that are provisioned to provide a high quality of service and a direct path to a specific destination. See "Network Core Technologies."

Data arriving from customer premises equipment does so in a variety of formats such as TDM, DSL, ATM, frame relay, IP, Ethernet, and wireless. The MSPP must process these protocols to ensure that traffic is routed to the appropriate destinations.

The Tachion Networks Fusion 5000 Broadband Services Switch is essentially a "collapsed central office" that integrates class 5 business voice features, packet-based voice and data, and other key ingredients of a traditional central office, such as SS7. It merges transport, switching, routing, and signaling into one highly compact system. A single Fusion 5000 can replace more than a half dozen disparate systems in a traditional central office.

This topic continues at the Linktionary! Web site. Also refer to the related entries for more information about network access services.

Related Entries   ATM (Asynchronous Transfer Mode); Broadband Communications and Networking; Cable (CATV) Data Networks; Circuit-Switching Services; CO (Central Office); DBS (Direct Broadcast Satellite); DPT (Dynamic Packet Transport); DSL (Digital Subscriber Line); DTM (Dynamic Synchronous Transfer Mode); Edge Devices; Frame Relay; FTTH (Fiber To The Home); Gigabit Ethernet; HALO (High Altitude Long Operation); IMA (Inverse Multiplexing over ATM); Infrared Technologies; IInternet Architecture and Backbone; SDN (Integrated Services Digital Network); Last Mile Services; LMDS (Local Multipoint Distribution Service); Local Loop; MAN (Metropolitan Area Network); Microwave Communications; MMDS (Multichannel Multipoint Distribution Services); Multiplexing and Multiplexers; Optical Networks; PON (Passive Optical Network); PoP (Point of Presence); PoS (Packet over SONET); Residential Broadband; Satellite Communication Systems; SONET (Synchronous Optical Network); T Carriers; TDM Networks; Telecommunications and Telephone Systems; Telecommunications Regulation; Voice/Data Networks; Voice over IP (VoIP); WDM (Wavelength Division Multiplexing); Wireless Broadband Access Technologies; *and* Wireless Local Loop

Linktionary!—Tom Sheldon's Encyclopedia of Networking updates	http://www.linktionary.com/n/network_access.html
Redback Networks	http://www.redback.com
Tachion Networks	http://www.tachion.com/
Cisco integrated access page	http://www.cisco.com/warp/public/779/servpro/solutions/integrated/
Web ProForums (see various access topics)	http://www.iec.org/tutorials/
Bell Labs T1 Carrier Tutorial	http://www.bell-labs.com/technology/access/
Telco Exchange Telecom Pricing Tools	http://www.telcoexchange.com/
The Last Mile channel at stardust.com	http://www.stardust.com/lastmile/
Web ProForums communications technology tutorials	http://www.iec.org/tutorials/

Network Addressing Schemes

See Addresses, Electronic Mail; Addresses, Network; *and* MAC (Medium Access Control).

Network Analyzers

Network analyzers are devices for testing network cable for compliance to specified standards, troubleshooting cable problems, analyzing problems, and monitoring network health. In general, network analyzers are infrastructure testing and troubleshooting tools. There are *network testers* for testing copper and fiber cable, and there are *sniffers* and *protocol analyzers* to monitor network traffic. Often, these devices are combined in the same unit.

Another type of tool used by administrators is a network monitoring system, which often runs as part of a complete software-based network management system. It uses protocols such as SNMP (Simple Network Management Protocol) and RMON (Remote Monitoring) to monitor the status of equipment on the network. Information is obtained from management agents running in those systems. See "Network Management."

This topic covers testing equipment, sniffers, and protocol analyzers. These are usually portable devices carried by technicians. The general theme with cable test equipment is to certify a cable installation. This provides assurance that an existing or just-installed cable plant will support the high-frequency requirements of particular networking technology, such as Gigabit Ethernet or ATM. Different categories of copper cable (Category 5, Category 5e, Category 6) must pass various tests in order to be certified. Many things can go wrong during installation, including excessive bending of cable or improper connector installations that cause crosstalk on a cable. See "Cable and Wiring" for a general discussion of cable and cable characteristics that can be tested.

The TIA/EIA structured cabling standards define how to design, build, manage and test a cable system. Most network test equipment tests for the specifications outlined in this cable standard. See "TIA/EIA Structured Cabling Standards."

Cable testing is performed to look for problems like noise (induced by motors, heaters, and lights), power problems caused by bad AC power, bad cables and connectors, cables that are too long, and grounding problems. Other problems may include faulty NICs, loose connections, and improper network topologies. The following tests are common, and most devices will perform most if not all of them:

- Signal tracers that generate tones into a wire that can be traced by a separate signal receiver. This device helps locate specific wires at the other end of a cable bundle.

- Integrity tests help find the location where wires are broken or damaged.

- Wiremap tests check for correct pairing, reversed pairs, split pairs, and transposed pairs.

- Signal tests measure attenuation (signal loss), near-end crosstalk (NEXT), far-end crosstalk (FEXT), signal-to-noise ration, and return loss (reflections caused by impedance mismatches).

- Cable parameter tests include noise, resistance, capacitance (helps locate link or installation faults), and characteristic impedance (helps locate signal reflections).

- TDRs (time domain reflectometers) perform a test that can determine the length of a link and the distance to a fault in the link. Cable lengths cannot exceed specifications.

- Traffic simulators inject signals into networks connections that simulate network or telephone signals for testing purposes.

Fiber-optic testers are used to evaluate fiber-optic cable installations. Different types of fiber-optic cable (single mode, multimode, inside plant, outside plant, and so on) are tested at common wavelengths (850 nm, 1,300 nm, 1,310 nm, 1,550 nm) for attenuation. Loss in connectors and splices is also evaluated.

Protocol Analyzers

A protocol analyzer is attached to a network to capture network traffic. The captured frames are displayed in raw or filtered form for network technicians to evaluate.

Network analyzers operate in what is called *promiscuous mode*. They listen to all traffic on a network, not just traffic that has been addressed to them. The technician can choose to capture frames transmitted by a particular network computer or frames that carry information for a particular application or service. The captured information is then monitored to evaluate network performance, locate bottlenecks, or even track security breaches. Traffic filters are essential because of the amount of information passing through the analyzer.

There are low-end and high-end network analyzers. Some of the high-end network analyzers may cost tens of thousands of dollars. At the other end of the spectrum are software-based network analyzers that are available as freeware. In fact, many network analyzers are distributed on the Internet by the hacker community for the express purpose of capturing sensitive information on networks, such as passwords.

Low-end analyzers are designed for traditional Ethernet or token ring LANs. High-end analyzers are designed to handle the traffic loads of high-speed networks such as ATM and Gigabit Ethernet. Devices that analyze gigabit-speed traffic are expensive. These devices must have huge buffers (1 GB or better) and/or processors that can analyze traffic at wire speed. Some common tests and features are outlined here:

- Identify excessive packet collisions and alert you when such conditions are occurring.

- Identify framing problems such as illegal frames (too short or too long), frame check sequence errors, and alignment errors.

- Filter traffic on any part of a packet and save specific packets to disk for later analysis.

- Accumulate statistical information, such as the number of packets per second or the number of packets transmitted by a particular system. Provide reports, preferably in graphical format.

- Monitor and analyze bandwidth usage for the purpose of optimizing networks or WAN links.

- Ability to analyze fiber-optic cable as well as copper cable.

Many protocol analyzers may generate their own test packets under your control, which lets you test the carrying capacity of a network or test the operations of devices on the network. Most analyzers can only capture packets on the network segment to which they are attached. You may need to take the analyzer to other physical locations to monitor traffic. More advanced analyzers can tap other network segments, but this may generate excess traffic across network boundaries during analysis.

Many network management software packages include RMON (Remote Monitoring) tools that can perform many of the functions described here. For example, a remote monitoring utility may collect statistics about a network segment and deliver it to the primary management station on a scheduled basis. Capturing actual traffic for later delivery is usually impractical. In fact, many network analyzers are incapable of monitoring switched networks, leaving RMON as the only way to capture and/or analyze traffic between switches and desktop systems.

Many vendors rent their network testing devices. Be sure to check the Web sites listed later. Some low-end models only support one type of network. Also consider the hardware platform and operating system required by the software or device; whether the device can be used remotely; the types of statistics it provides; the layer of the protocol stack (that is, data link, network, and application layers) where it operates; the type of capturing and decoding provided (that is, does it decode packets and provide precapture and postcapture filtering); and whether the device can generate its own traffic for modeling. Also, does the device support switched networks and VLANs (Virtual LANs)?

Related Entries   Cable and Wiring; CIM (Common Information Model); CMIP (Common Management Information Protocol); DMI (Distributed Management Interface); DMTF (Distributed Management Task Force); MIB (Management Information Base); Network Management; Performance Measurement and Optimization; RMON (Remote Monitoring); SNMP (Simple Network Management Protocol); Testing, Diagnostics, and Troubleshooting; TIA/EIA Structured Cabling Standards; *and* WBEM (Web-Based Enterprise Management)

Linktionary!—Tom Sheldon's Encyclopedia of Networking updates	http://www.linktionary.com/n/network_analyzer.html
Google Web Directory protocol analyzers page	http://directory.google.com/Top/Computers/Software/Networking/Network_Performance/Protocol_Analyzers/
Etherreal free network protocol analyzers for UNIX and Windows	http://www.ethereal.com/
Digitech-LeCroy	http://www.digitechinc.com/
Network Instruments	http://www.networkinstruments.com/
Sniffer Technologies	http://www.sniffer.com/
Acterna, LLC	http://www.acterna.com/
Spirent SmartBits performance analyzers	http://www.netcomsystems.com/
Fluke Corporation	http://www.fluke.com/

RAD Com	http://www.radcom-inc.com/
Robert Graham's Sniffing FAQ	http://www.robertgraham.com/pubs/sniffing-faq.html
Charles Spurgeon's Ethernet Analyzers page	http://www.ots.utexas.edu/thernet/enet-analyzers.html
Wandel & Goltermann "LAN Troubleshooting and Baselining" guide	http://download.wg.com/articles/pocketguide.pdf

See "Cable and Wiring" for more links.

Network Appliances

The idea of a "network appliance" conjures up images of network-attached coffee pots, toasters, and pop machines. See "(CPCP) Coffee Pot Control Protocol" for some amusement. In reality, network appliances are devices that are designed to serve up information to end users with the speed of a short-order cook. They are designed to minimize the overhead imposed by server operating systems by being optimized to handle a specific task. Network Appliance, a company, specializes in NAS (network attached storage) devices, which are off-the-shelf, preconfigured *filers* (not to be confused with file servers) that connect directly to networks without the need for a front-end server. The devices are plug-and-play, meaning that they can be plugged into a network and offer services immediately with minimal configuration. See "NAS (Network Attached Storage)."

The general description of a network appliance is a single-purpose device in which all nonessential functions are stripped away. What remains is an inexpensive device with a simplified embedded operating system and an Ethernet network interface.

Perhaps the best example of a network appliance that has been around for years, but never really called a network appliance, is the printer—specifically, a *network-attached* printer. It does one thing really well—it attaches to the network with ease—and it is ready to use immediately. It also does not need to be connected to a server, which is often overburdened with excess tasks.

Network appliances are usually associated with storage devices, but the plug-and-play concept also applies to a whole range of other network devices, including Web servers, e-mail servers, caching devices, load balancers, and more.

Thin clients are a form of network appliance, but instead of being servers of information, they are access devices. A thin client is a terminal-like device, usually diskless, that relies on back-end servers for processing and storage. On the Web, this device is called a *Web terminal*, and is often a diskless kitchen-counter device that relies on Internet-based servers for storage. A small disk may be present to maintain a cache for storing Web page information.

A *Web appliance* is a specialized Web terminal that relies on the Web for some of its operations, or just benefits from Web-based operations. Consider a digital camera with a built-in Web interface. After taking pictures, users can quickly upload the pictures to a Web server for storage and make them available to other users. Since the camera sports a Web browser interface, users can access photo-editing programs at a photo Web sites and edit stored pictures on the spot. In this model, the user is relying on the processing power of Web-based servers. The camera is only providing the interface that allows users to run photo software on the servers.

Another example is a TV set-top box that automatically updates program schedule information from a Web server. Other examples are a Web phone and a Web PBX. They are specialized devices that provide plug-and-play capabilities and Web interfaces.

In general, a big feature of appliances is ease of use. For example, some kitchen-top Web browsers replace the traditional mouse-based interface with one that could be used by a person that has been hiding in the backwoods for the last 30 years.

A new class of services is evolving to support network appliances. Service advertising and discovery protocols define standard methods for users and devices to find out the capabilities of other devices and for devices to advertise their capabilities. See "Service Advertising and Discovery."

This discussion continues under the following topics:

- **Distributed Computer Networks**   Discusses the explosion of small devices all over the Web.

- **Embedded Systems**   Discusses the push to Web-enable small devices, including embedded operating system for appliances.

- **Peer-to-Peer Communication**   Discusses community-oriented information-sharing techniques.

- **Thin Clients**   Discusses a range of Web appliances and network terminal devices. Also see "Terminal Services."

- **Wireless PANs (Personal Area Networks)**   Describes wireless networks that allow users of portable devices to join in spontaneous networks and share information.

Related Entries   Bluetooth; Directory Services; GPS (Global Positioning System); Home Networking; Internet; Java; Mobile Computing; NAS (Network Attached Storage); Network Processors; RTOS (Real-Time Operating System); Servers; *and* Web Technologies and Concepts

Linktionary!—Tom Sheldon's Encyclopedia of Networking updates	http://www.linktionary.com/n/network_appliance.html
The Appliance Culture: Simpler is Better	http://www.netapp.com/tech_library/app_culture.html
Network Appliance	http://www.networkappliance.com/
Net Integration Technologies	http://www.net-itech.com/
National Semiconductor information appliances info	http://www.national.com/appinfo/solutions/
Transmeta network appliance processors	http://www.transmeta.com/
Filanet	http://www.filanet.com/
F5 Networks	http://www.f5.com/
Bitpipe (search for "appliance")	http://www.bitpipe.com/

Network Applications

See Distributed Applications.

Network Architecture

Network architectures define the standards and techniques for designing and building communication systems for computers and other devices. In the past, vendors developed their own architectures and required that other vendors conform to this architecture if they wanted to develop compatible hardware and software. There are proprietary network architectures such as IBM's SNA (Systems Network Architecture) and there are open architectures like the OSI (Open Systems Interconnection) model defined by the International Organization for Standardization.

If an architecture is open, no one vendor controls it and many vendors are free to design software and hardware that works with the architecture. The Internet is successful because it uses an open architecture that caught on as a worldwide network standard. Anyone is free to contribute recommendations that may eventually become standards and protocols within the architecture. In the meantime, the OSI model has not caught on, although it is still used as a reference to compare different architectures. Even the Internet protocols are commonly discussed in terms of their relationship to the OSI standard.

Common network architectures include the OSI protocol model, the Internet protocols, Apple Computer's AppleTalk, IBM's SNA (Systems Network Architecture), and Novell's SPX/IPX. Some of these are compared in Figure N-2.

An architecture is a blueprint that might be compared with an organizational chart. It has multiple layers and each underlying layer provides *services* to the layer above it, just like the office staff in a company provides support services for managers and other staff.

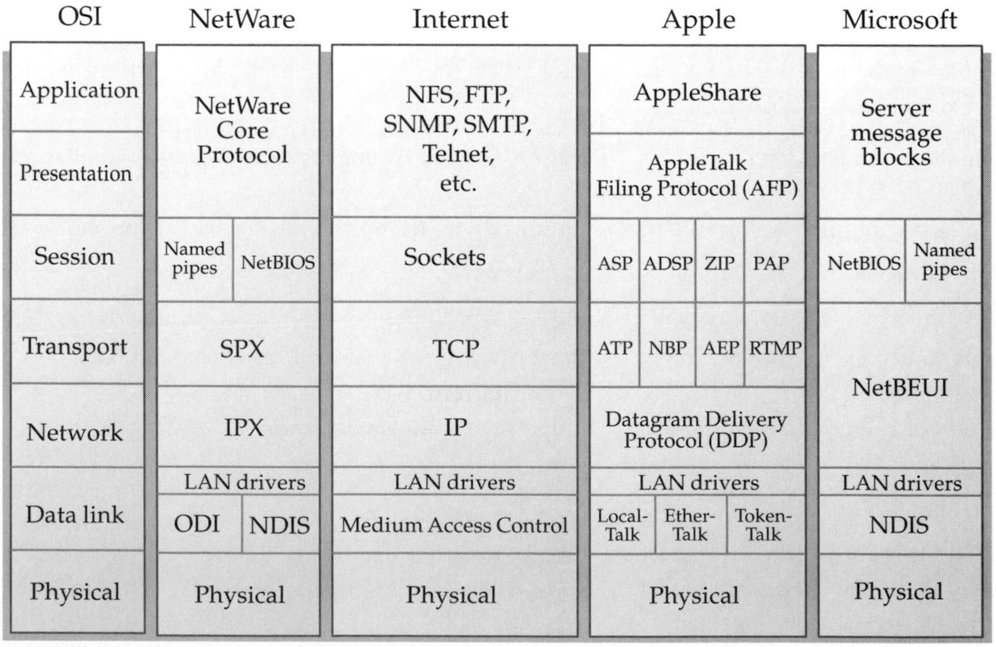

OSI	NetWare		Internet	Apple				Microsoft	
Application	NetWare Core Protocol		NFS, FTP, SNMP, SMTP, Telnet, etc.	AppleShare				Server message blocks	
Presentation				AppleTalk Filing Protocol (AFP)					
Session	Named pipes	NetBIOS	Sockets	ASP	ADSP	ZIP	PAP	NetBIOS	Named pipes
Transport	SPX		TCP	ATP	NBP	AEP	RTMP	NetBEUI	
Network	IPX		IP	Datagram Delivery Protocol (DDP)					
Data link	LAN drivers		LAN drivers	LAN drivers				LAN drivers	
	ODI	NDIS	Medium Access Control	Local-Talk	Ether-Talk	Token-Talk		NDIS	
Physical	Physical		Physical	Physical				Physical	

Figure N-2.   *Common network architecture models*

One of the most important reasons for layering network architectures is to simplify software and hardware development. To create a product such as a network switch, a developer only needs to make sure that product is compatible with the protocols that work in layer 2 of the protocol stack. This allows products from different vendors to connect to the same network and work together. Layered models divide network operations into less complex components.

Take a look at the OSI model on the left in Figure N-2. As mentioned, the OSI model is a standard that is used to compare other network models. At the bottom is the *physical* layer that defines cabling and connectors. Above that, the *data link* layer defines how bits are framed and transmitted across the physical link. Above that, the *network* layer defines how to interconnect different networks. The *transport* layer provides reliability services to ensure that packets are transmitted properly between sender and receiver. Higher layers provide application support services. *See* "OSI (Open Systems Interconnection) Model."

Protocol Concepts

A layered architecture is referred to as a *protocol stack* because each layer has one or more *protocols* that provide specific network and communication services.

Look again at the Internet model in Figure N-2. The IP is at the OSI network layer. It provides basic packet networking services over interconnected networks. The TCP protocol is in the transport layer where it provides a reliable data exchange service. Note that the Internet does not define any particular lower-layer services at the data link and physical layer. That is because Internet services run on just about any network hardware and network service!

Figure N-3 illustrates the basic communication model, using a simple three-layer network architecture for clarity. Note that the three layers define the basic set of communication services. At the top layer, a user application has information to send to the application in the other system. It passes this information down to the data exchange services, which know how to exchange information across networks and hide the details from the application. At the bottom layer, bits are transmitted between systems.

Throughout this process, information is passed down the protocol stack on one computer, transmitted to the other computer, and then passed up through the protocol stack.

Layers in protocol stacks have a *peer relationship* with one another across networks. As an analogy, imagine the creation of a formal agreement between two embassies. At the top, formal negotiations take place between ambassadors, but in the background diplomats and officers work on documents, define procedures, and perform other activities. Diplomats have rank, and each rank performs some service for higher-ranking diplomats. The ambassador at the highest level passes orders down to a lower-level diplomat. That diplomat communicates with a diplomat of equal rank at the other embassy. Diplomats at different levels follow established diplomatic procedures based on the rank they occupy. For example, an officer at a particular level may provide language translation services or technical documentation. This officer communicates with a peer at the other embassy regarding translation and documentation procedures.

In the diplomatic world, a diplomat at one embassy simply picks up the phone and calls his or her peer at the other embassy. In the world of network communication, software protocol processes at each layer exchange information across a *virtual connection* as shown in Figure N-4. The messages they exchange must be packages in a packet that is crossing the network and then unpackaged by the peer process at the receiver. The process of packaging (encapsulating) upper layer information is illustrated in Figure N-5.

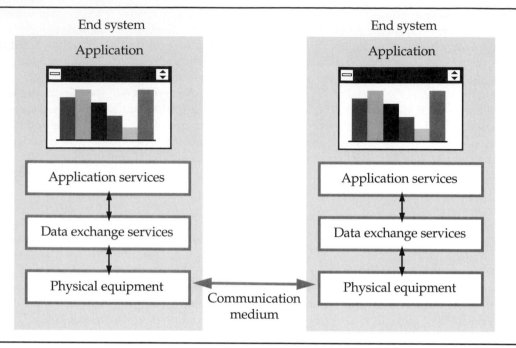

Figure N-3. *Network architecture*

As information passes down through the protocol layers, it forms a packet called the *PDU (protocol data unit),* using OSI terminology. Processes in each layer add *PCI (protocol control information)* to the PDU in the form of messages that are destined for peer entities in the other

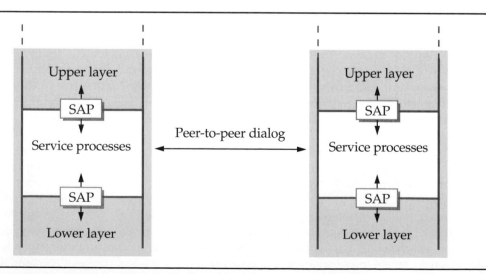

Figure N-4. *Communication process between two separate protocol stacks*

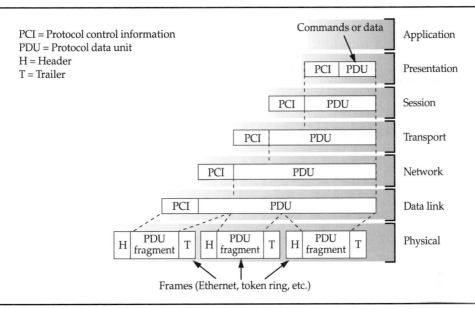

PCI = Protocol control information
PDU = Protocol data unit
H = Header
T = Trailer

Figure N-5. *How data and/or messages are packaged for transport to another computer*

system. Although entities communicate with their peers, they must utilize the services of lower layers to get those messages across. *SAPs (service access points)* are the connection points that entities in adjacent layers use to communicate messages; they are like addresses that entities in other layers or other systems can use when sending messages to a system.

Note that in the Internet protocol suite, the information formed at the application layer (data, commands, instructions) is called a *message*. A message is sent to the transport layer where it is bundled into what is called a *segment* in TCP parlance. Segments are sent to the network layer, where they are packaged into *datagrams*. Finally, datagrams are sent to the physical layer, where they are framed for transmission across the network.

The peer-to-peer conversations that take place between communicating systems are best seen in the transport layer. Transport layer protocols such as TCP are responsible for reliable data delivery. They use various techniques to ensure that packets are delivered in the right order and that they are retransmitted if lost. They also provide *flow control* to prevent the recipient from receiving more packets than it can handle and *congestion controls* to handle network traffic problems. All of these services are handled by message exchanges between transport layer protocols. See "Transport Protocols and Services."

Related Entries   Access Method, Network; Best-Effort Delivery; Bridges and Bridging; Connection Establishment; Connection-Oriented and Connectionless Services; Data Communication Concepts; Data Link Protocols; Datagrams and Datagram Services; Encapsulation; Error Detection and Correction; Flow-Control Mechanisms; Fragmentation and Reassembly; Framing in Data Transmissions; Internetworking; IP (Internet Protocol); LAN (Local Area Network); MAC (Media Access Control); Network Concepts; Network Layer Protocols; OSI (Open Systems Interconnection) Model; Packets and Packet-Switching Networks; Point-to-Point Communications; Reliable Data Delivery Services; Routing; Sequencing of Packets; TCP (Transmission Control Protocol); *and* Transport Protocols and Services

Linktionary!—Tom Sheldon's Encyclopedia of Networking updates	http://www.linktionary.com/n/network_architecture.html
Noritoshi Demizu's Internetworking technical resources page	http://www.watersprings.org/links/inet/
Cisco internetworking technology overviews	http://www.cisco.com/univercd/cc/td/doc/cisintwk/ito_doc/
"The World of Protocols" at Protocols.com	http://www.protocols.com/
Novell's protocol links page	http://developer.novell.com/research/topical/netware_servers.htm
Google Web Directory protocols page	http://directory.google.com/Top/Computers/Internet/Protocols/
About.com protocols page (click "Protocol" in subject list)	http://compnetworking.miningco.com/

See "Network Concepts" for more links, including tutorial sites.

Network Computer Devices

See NC (Network Computer) Devices; Thin Client; *and* Terminal Services.

Network Concepts

A network is a communication system that allows users to access resources on other computers and exchange messages with one another. It allows users to share resources on their own system or access shared resources on other systems. Obviously, it is the topic of this entire book, so this section will guide you to the appropriate sections that discuss networking technology. See "Data Communication Concepts" for a similar outline of basic communication concepts.

Before networks, there were centrally controlled mainframe computers built by IBM and other vendors. See "Mainframe" and "SNA (Systems Network Architecture)."

In the late 1960s and early 1970s, a community of researchers started developing the concept of connecting computers together and using packets and packet switches to exchange information. They were creating the early Internet by connecting large mainframes and minicomputers. See "Internet."

In the late 1970s, microcomputer systems began to appear. They soon dominated small offices and workgroups everywhere. It made sense to connect them together so users could communicate with one another and share network resources like printers and disks. The LAN concept took hold in corporations. See "LAN (Local Area Network)." Also refer to the related entries in the LAN section.

Actually, the LAN concept was developed by Robert Metcalfe, who was working with the Internet engineers. He developed the idea after running across a paper describing a satellite communication system called ALOHA at a friend's house. Metcalfe applied the concept to a cabled system and called it Ethernet. Internet engineers loved UNIX and soon connected their systems with Ethernet. In turn, these networks were connected to the Internet via routers.

Meanwhile, LANs (primarily PC and Macintosh LANs) were being installed everywhere. While Ethernet is the dominant LAN technology today, ARCNET had its day and IBM made token ring popular, although it didn't catch on like Ethernet. In the mid-1980s, most LANs were still confined to workgroups and departments. Some organizations connected these LANs to their mainframes and allowed users to exchange e-mail using mainframe e-mail systems. But soon it just made sense to interconnect the entire organization. For a while, this was attempted by joining LANs with bridges, but bridged networks have scalability and security problems. See "Bridges and Bridging."

Fortunately, the Internet engineers had already developed an internetworking device called the router. Routers were developed as gateways devices for the Internet. They interconnect different types of networks while providing a secure barrier between them. This is critical on the Internet, where interconnected networks are autonomous systems operated by different authorities. See "Routers," "Routing," and "Routing on the Internet."

An important feature of routers is that they support an internetwork addressing scheme that assigns a unique address to each individual network that is connected to the internetwork. Routers keep track of these addresses, thus allowing packets to be forwarded from any network to any other network across a mesh of router-connected networks. See "Packets and Packet-Switching Networks."

The TCP/IP protocol suite provides the internetwork addressing scheme and transport scheme for router-connected networks. IP provides the "overlay" addressing scheme and internetwork routing. See "Internetworking," "Internet Protocol Suite," "IP (Internet Protocol)," and "TCP (Transmission Control Protocol)."

Routers were soon appearing in corporate networks to join department and workgroup LANs into enterprise-wide networks. This meant a conversion to TCP/IP protocols. At first there was some resistance, but when the World Wide Web exploded on the scene in the 1990s, no one doubted the advantage of the Internet protocol suite. Web technologies solved an incredible number of hardware and software interoperablitity problems. In fact, the term "interoperability" is rarely heard today because Web technologies minimized the problem.

LAN technologies improved over the years. Ethernet went from 10 Mbits/sec to 100 Mbits/sec (Fast Ethernet) to 1,000 Mbits/sec (Gigabit Ethernet). In addition, switching technologies improved not only performance but the way that networks were designed. See "Network Design and Construction," "Ethernet," "Fast Ethernet," and "Gigabit Ethernet." Switching technologies are discussed under "Switching and Switched Networks."

Another improvement was the multilayer switch, which combined switching and routing into a high-performance hardware-based device that allowed network designers to put routing wherever needed at a relatively inexpensive price in order to segregate networks, provide security, or control traffic. See "Multilayer Switching."

Application development in LAN and internetwork environments was dominated by client/server computing for years, but more recently distributed object computing technologies have prevailed, partly as a result of the Web. The traditional two-tiered client/server model grew into the three-tiered distributed object model. Middleware and messaging technologies simplify the process of connecting applications and processes across global networks. See "Client/Server Computing," "Middleware and Messaging," "DBMS (Database Management System),"

N

"Distributed Applications," "Distributed Object Computing," "Multitiered Architectures," and "Object Technologies."

As mentioned, Web technologies played an important part in redefining access to data, the sharing of data, and the design of network applications. An *intranet* is an internal network built with Web technologies while an *extranet* is a business-to-business network with links across the Internet. See "Web Technologies and Concepts" and "Intranets and Extranets."

Recently, core Internet networks have improved with optical switching and the overprovisioning of bandwidth. The last bottleneck is the local access network, which not surprisingly is still controlled to a large extent by the incumbent telephone companies. They require packet-switched network users to adjust to their TDM (time division multiplexing) hierarchy in order to take advantage of metropolitan and wide area network links. These T1, T3, and fractional T1 lines are expensive and inefficient. Fortunately, the access market is changing. In the last few years, competitors have installed fiber-optic cable throughout metropolitan areas and are offering flexible bandwidth options using native protocols (Ethernet) at less than half what the carriers were charging. See "MAN (Metropolitan Area Network)," "Network Access Services," "Network Core Technologies," "TDM Networks," and "WAN (Wide Area Network)."

The final part of this story (at least for this edition) is that the Internet is becoming *the* network. With fast connections, enterprises are starting to outsource much of their data services to service providers that run Internet data centers. See "ASP (Application Service Providers)," "MSP (Management Service Provider)," and "SSP (Storage Service Provider)." Also see "Outsourcing," These service providers have data centers that are staffed by professionals 24/7 and that provide all the security and high availability that enterprise data managers can only dream of. See "Data Center Design" and "Fault Tolerance and High Availability."

Outsourcing makes sense because the Internet provides global connections and Internet data centers with direct connections to fast backbones. The cost of equipment and management is shared by all the customers of the service providers. Secure connections can be made across virtual private networks. See "VPN (Virtual Private Network)."

Even users are taking advantage of this scheme. Many are using Web appliances, which are Web-based terminals that rely on Internet applications servers, storage servers, and e-mail servers. All information is stored on the Web. The Internet is essentially becoming a giant storage network. See "Distributed Computer Networks," "NAS (Network Attached Storage)," "Network Appliances," and "Thin Clients."

P2P (peer-to-peer), made famous by Napster community-based file sharing, disrupts the traditional centrally managed storage model. End users host personal collections of music, electronic books, videos, photographs, technical information, software drivers, and so forth on their own computers. P2P software then helps the community of users locate and access files on other user's computers. In this model, end-systems become informal Web storage devices, or what some have called "media collection devices." P2P bypasses the central control that administrators have over information stored on file servers and promotes user-to-user data exchange on the Internet. P2P software features have expanded to support instant messaging, advanced searching, and mailing list support. See "Peer-to-Peer Communication."

A number of other topics are "QoS (Quality of Service)," "Voice/Data Networks," "Mobile Computing," "Security," "Wireless Communications," and "Wireless LANs."

Networking Tutorials on the Web

The following Web sites provide useful and interesting tutorials about networks and networking concepts. Some of the sites present course material, while others present vendor-oriented material.

Cisco Documentation (see links in "Technology Information" section)	http://www.cisco.com/univercd/home/home.htm
3Com technology tutorials (see white papers section)	http://www.3com.com/technology/
Web ProForums	http://www.iec.org/tutorials/
Techguide.com (white papers for technology professionals)	http://www.techguide.com/
Daryl's TCP/IP Primer	http://ipprimer.windsorcs.com/section.cfm
Gorry Fairhurst's WWW course	http://www.erg.abdn.ac.uk/users/ink/course/syllabus.html
Network Magazine networking tutorials	http://www.networkmagazine.com/static/tutorial/index.html
"Data Communications" by Brian Brown	http://www.cit.ac.nz/smac/dc100www/dc_000.htm
Smart Computing (search for topics of interest)	http://www.smartcomputing.com/
IBM Redbooks (See "networking" portal)	http://www.redbooks.ibm.com/
Dwight's network tutorials links list	http://www.wizard.com/users/baker/public_html/NetTutor.html
Lucent Internetworking systems (see Library)	http://www.lucent.com/ins/library/
Internetworking topics at the University of Wolverhampton	http://www.scit.wlv.ac.uk/~jphb/comms/
InterOperability Lab tutorials	http://www.iol.unh.edu/training/
IRT (Internet-Related Technologies) links to technology tutorials	http://www.irt.org/
Light Reading optical networking technologies	http://www.lightreading.com/
Optimized Engineering Corporation Tutorials	http://www.optimized.com/COMPENDI/TabOfCon.htm
RAD Data Communications tutorials	http://www.rad.com/networks/tutorial.htm
3Com Solutions and Technologies page	http://www.3com.com/technology/

N

Links to Networking Topics

The following links provide additional links to networking topics on the Internet or white papers about vendor-specific products:

Linktionary!—Tom Sheldon's Encyclopedia of Networking updates	http://www.linktionary.com/n/network_concepts.html

Noritoshi Demizu's Internetworking technical resources page	http://www.watersprings.org/links/inet/
IEEE links page	http://www.computer.org/internet/links.htm
Microsoft's Networking and RAS Web page	http://www.microsoft.com/technet/network/
Communications and Networking page at Yahoo!	http://dir.yahoo.com/Computers_and_Internet/Communications_and_Networking/
About.com computer networking topics	http://compnetworking.about.com/
ITPRC (Information Technology Professional's Resource Center)	http://www.itprc.com/
Lucent's internetworking systems resource library (also see white papers section)	http://www.lucent.com/ins/library/
Links at Washington University School of Engineering	http://www.cait.wustl.edu/infosys/infosys.html
Bitpipe (search for any topic)	http://www.bitpipe.com/
Google Web Directory	http://directory.google.com/Top/Computers/
OII index of standard for open information exchange	http://158.169.50.95:10080/oii/en/alpha.html
John Scouries' telecommunication sites page	http://ccnga.uwaterloo.ca/~jscouria/telsites.html
Telecoms Virtual Library	http://www.analysys.com/vlib/

Network Connection Technologies

Network connection technologies are used to connect peripherals to computers, computers to computers, computers to network devices, network devices to network devices, and so on. The following sections list each of the topics in which these technologies are discussed.

Peripheral Interconnects   Asynchronous Communications; Cable and Wiring; Fiber-Optic Cable; Fibre Channel; FireWire; HIPPI (High-Performance Parallel Interface); HSSI (High-Speed Serial Interface); InfiniBand; Infrared Technologies; IP Storage; Parallel Interface; SCSI (Small Computer System Interface); Serial Communication and Interfaces; SSA (Serial Storage Architecture); Switch Fabrics and Bus Design; Synchronous Communications; USB (Universal Serial Bus); *and* VI Architecture

LAN/Enterprise Network   ATM (Asynchronous Transfer Mode); Cable and Wiring; Ethernet; Fast Ethernet; FDDI (Fiber Distributed Data Interface); Fiber-Optic Cable; Gigabit Ethernet; Infrared Technologies; LAN (Local Area Network); LocalTalk; Microwave Communications; Token Ring Network; Wireless LANs; *and* Wireless PANs (Personal Area Networks)

Broadband/Metro/Wide Area Networking   ATM (Asynchronous Transfer Mode); Cable (CATV) Data Networks; DBS (Direct Broadcast Satellite); DSL (Digital Subscriber Line); Fiberless Optical Networking; Fiber-Optic Cable; Fibre Channel; Frame Relay; FTTH (Fiber to the Home); Gigabit Ethernet; HALO (High Altitude Long Operation); Infrared Technologies; ISDN (Integrated Services Digital Network); LMDS (Local Multipoint Distribution Service); Microwave Communications; MMDS (Multichannel Multipoint Distribution Service); Optical Networks; PON (Passive Optical Network); Residential Broadband; Satellite Communication Systems; SONET (Synchronous Optical Networks); T Carriers; WDM (Wavelength Division Multiplexing); Wireless Broadband Access Technologies; *and* Wireless Local Loop

Connection Devices and Switching/Routing Techniques   Bridges and Bridging; Concentrator Devices; Multilayer Switching; Multiplexing and Multiplexers; Repeaters; Routers; Switch Fabrics and Bus Design; Switching and Switched Networks; *and* VI Architecture

General Technology Overviews   Communication Services and Providers; Data Communication Concepts; Data Link Protocols; High-Speed/High-Performance Networking; Home Networking; Internet Connections; Internetworking; LAN (Local Area Network); Last Mile Services; Local Loop, Modulation Techniques; Multiplexing and Multiplexers; Network Access Services; Network Concepts; Network Core Technologies; Optical Networks; Point-to-Point Communications; Residential Broadband; Routing; Serial Communication and Interfaces; Service Providers and Carriers; Signals; Storage Systems; Telecommunications and Telephone Systems; WAN (Wide Area Network); Wireless Communications; *and* Wireless Local Loop

Linktionary!—Tom Sheldon's Encyclopedia of Networking updates	http://www.linktionary.com/n/network_connections.html
Cisco documents about internetworking technology	http://www.cisco.com/univercd/cc/td/doc/cisintwk/ito_doc/index.htm

Network Core Technologies

A core network is a central network into which other networks feed. It must have the bandwidth to support the aggregate bandwidth of all the networks feeding into it. Traditionally, the core network has been the circuit-oriented telephone system. More recently, alternative optical networks bypass the traditional core and implement packet-oriented technologies. Figure N-6 provides a timeline of the development of core networks, starting with the early telephone system.

In the beginning, there were copper-based analog phone systems that connected people in local communities. Telephones connected to central switching offices where operators—and later, electronic switching equipment—joined telephone lines to create end-to-end circuits between callers. Multiple conversations were delivered over a single wire between switching offices and over long-distance lines using frequency division multiplexing, which retains the analog nature of the calls. This analog system existed until the 1960s when digital technologies began to appear.

The first digital system was installed by AT&T in 1962. It was a T1 trunk that could carry 24 voice calls over two pairs of copper telephone wire. The calls were digitized using PCM (pulse code modulation) and multiplexed on the line using TDM (time division multiplexing). Note that the "T" stands for terrestrial (as opposed to satellite transmissions) and the "1" is an abbreviation for the 1.544-Mbit/sec signal rate. Digital systems are superior to analog systems in many ways, including the ability to transport more calls on the same line at higher quality over longer distances. Digital switching equipment began appearing in the 1970s.

T1 lines are part of the North American Digital Hierarchy. The NADH was originally created by AT&T and is now used in North America and Japan. A similar hierarchy in Europe multiplexes 30 voice calls into a 2-Mbit/sec circuit. In NADH terms, a T1 line is a DS-1 and it consists of 24 DS-0 (64-Kbit/sec) channels. A T3 line, which is called a DS-3, consists of 28 T1 lines or 672 DS-0 channels. The important point is that individual voice calls are multiplexed into lines that carry 24 calls (T1) for delivery between switching offices, and T1s are multiplexed into T3 for delivery over the long haul.

N

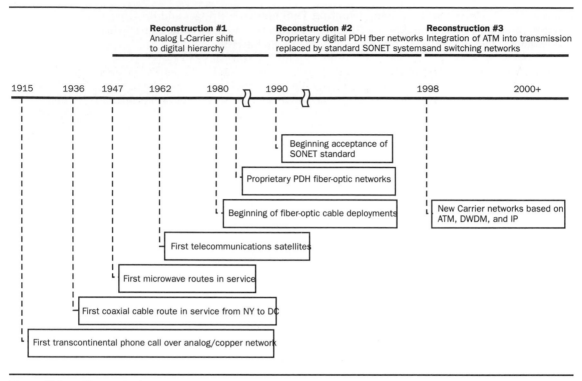

Figure N-6.   *Transmission evolution timeline (Source: Ascend, now Lucent)*

When fiber-optic technology appeared, it became possible to multiplex even more calls into trunks that could extend over much longer distances. The digital hierarchy was eventually extended up into an optical carrier (OC) hierarchy. The SONET/SDH standards are built on this hierarchy, as described next. The first optical networks were designed for digitized voice calls. The new networks are based on packet data, including the transport of voice in packets.

SONET/SDH Optical Networks

SONET was first proposed in the 1980s, and the first optical networks began appearing shortly thereafter. The ITU adapted SONET to create SDH, which became a worldwide standard for building optical telecommunications networks. SONET is now considered a subset of SDH, but the terminology "SONET/SDH" is common in North America. With SONET/SDH, the copper-oriented digital hierarchy was extended into the optical realm, although the hierarchy is based on OC (Optical Carrier).

A SONET/SDH network is pictured in Figure N-7. Small access rings connect to larger regional or backbone rings, which in turn attach to regional and national rings. Transition from smaller rings to larger rings involves a transition to higher OC levels. Access loops typically operate at OC-3 (155 Mbits/sec). These feed into OC-12 (622 Mbits/sec) or OC-48 (2.4 Gbits/sec) regional rings, which in turn may feed into backbone rings operating at OC-96 (4.9 Gbits/sec) or OC-192 (10 Gbits/sec).

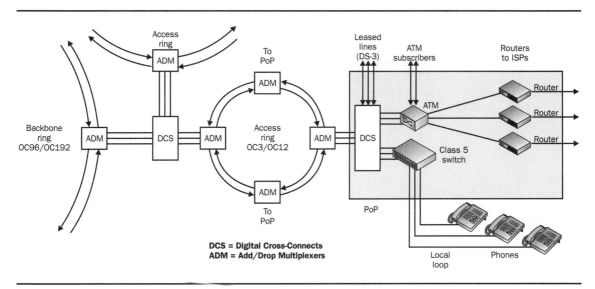

Figure N-7. *SONET optical network rings and carrier PoP (Point of Presence) facility*

Rings are interconnected via ADMs (add/drop multiplexers) and DCSs (digital cross-connects) as shown. In addition, PoP facilities interconnect with access rings via add/drop multiplexers. Optical-to-electrical and electrical-to-optical conversions take place at the connection point. Digital cross connects within the PoP provide a connection point for voice and data traffic.

An ADM does not terminate and demultiplex the entire range of signals on a fiber-optic cable, but instead adds or drops subrate signals. If a signal needs to be switched to another ring, it is dropped from one ring and added to another. For SONET, this means performing an optical-to-electrical-to-optical conversion.

ATM and IP over SONET

SONET was designed with constant bit rate voice in mind. In contrast, cell-oriented (ATM) and packet-oriented (IP) traffic are bursty in nature, not constant. ATM was defined by the telecommunications industry, and so it works well with SONET. ATM works above the SONET layer and provides the mechanisms for encapsulating data in cells and delivering it across the SONET network via permanent or switched virtual circuits. As an analogy, SONET can be compared to the freeway system, while ATM can be compared to the vehicles (ATM cells) and the paths (ATM virtual circuits) that those vehicles take.

ATM over SONET is used by the majority of carriers. It was implemented in the mid-1990s because it was one of the few networking technologies that could deliver the performance levels that were being demanded by the growing voice and data networks. RFC 1483 (Multiprotocol Encapsulation over ATM Adaptation Layer 5, July 1993) defines how to deliver IP packets over ATM networks. The technique is not ideal. IP packets must be segmented to fit into ATM cells. Cells carry the so-called *cell tax* (almost 10 percent of a cell is allocated to header information), which "steals" bandwidth that could be used to carry data. In addition, virtual circuits must be established between all the points that packets might travel.

In the early-1990s, many large ISPs were using T1 and T3 trunks to interconnect their various PoPs (within regional area or national areas), but as Internet traffic increased, these trunks were insufficient. ATM provided a solution with its interfaces running at OC-3 (155 Mbits/sec) and higher. Figure N-8 illustrates an ISP with five PoPs. Each PoP has a core ATM switch surrounded by a collection of IP routers. The PoPs are interconnected over wide-area SONET networks. The ATM switches in the PoPs provide a layer 2 switching fabric over which any layer 3 router can obtain connections to any other router. This IP over ATM network is often configured with statically defined virtual circuits, which become more difficult to configure and manage as the network grows. Various schemes to automate the process are discussed under "IP over ATM."

The original reasons why ATM was selected for the core of ISP networks were speed, virtual circuit capabilities, predictable performance, and the ability to engineer traffic if necessary. Today, gigabit and terabit routers made by Pluris, Juniper and others provide many of these same features with advanced routing technologies. The ATM layer is no longer needed. A single terabit router supports thousands of interconnections within a single system, and router-to-router interconnections are done across an optical switching fabric. Juniper has been

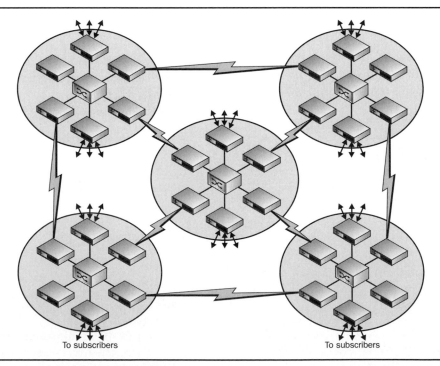

To subscribers   To subscribers

Figure N-8.   *IP over ATM backbone network*

actively pursuing router-based traffic engineering solutions with its support for MPLS (Multiprotocol Label Switching).

PoS (Packet over SONET) is a technique that eliminates the ATM layer and delivers packets directly over SONET links. See "PoS (Packet over SONET)" for more information. The technique is described in RFC 2615 (PPP over SONET/SDH, June 1999).

The next stage in core development is to remove both ATM and SONET and run IP directly over DWDM wavelength circuits. In this scheme, MPLS is used in the control plane to set up wavelength circuits across the optical core in much the same way that it sets up LSPs (label switched paths) across switched networks.

This discussion continues under the topic "Optical Networks." Also see "Network Access Services."

Related Entries   6Bone and IPv6; Abilene; ATM (Asynchronous Transfer Mode); B-ISDN (Broadband ISDN); Broadband Communications and Networking; E Carrier; Edge Devices; End Systems and End-to-End Connectivity; Fiber-Optic Cable; Internet; Internet Architecture and Backbone; IP over ATM; Lambda Circuits; MAN (Metropolitan Area Network); Microwave Communications; MPLS (Multiprotocol Label Switching); PoP (Point of Presence); PoS (Packet over SONET); SONET (Synchronous Optical Network); T Carriers; TDM Networks; Telecommunications and Telephone Systems; Virtual Circuit; WAN (Wide Area Network); WDM (Wavelength Division Multiplexing); *and* Wireless Broadband Access Technologies

Linktionary! Tom Sheldon's *Encyclopedia of Networking* updates	http://www.linktionary.com/n/network_core.html
Juniper Networks Tech Center	http://www.juniper.net/techcenter/
Pluris Terabit Info Center	http://www.pluris.com/terabitsInfopapers.cfm
Web ProForum (see optical networking topics in list)	http://www.iec.org/tutorials/
Noritoshi Demizu multilayer routing Web page (see optical and MPLS links)	http://www.watersprings.org/links/mlr/

Network Design and Construction

Anyone who is tasked with designing or upgrading a network is faced with a job similar to making pigs fly. As mentioned in RFC 1925 (Fundamental Truths of Networking, April 1996), it can be done with enough thrust. When it comes to network design, just replace "thrust" with "bandwidth." If you're up late designing networks, refer to RFC 1925 for some entertainment.

This topic provides an overview of enterprise networking technology. It references related topics in this book and provides pointers for designing networks. The three main areas to be concerned with in designing a network are as follows:

- ■ **Infrastructure**   The cabling system, network devices, and architecture design (topology) of the network

- ■ **Routing and route management**   Standard routing, cut-through routing, label switching, MPLS, and so forth

- ■ **Control and management**   Prioritization, QoS, and management

Note that WAN access networks and public network core technologies are discussed under "Network Access Services," "Network Core Technologies," "NPN (New Public Network)," and "Optical Networks."

From Backbones to Multilayer Switched Networks

The traditional enterprise network was a collection of departmental LANs that were installed independently of one another and then interconnected using a *distributed backbone* networking technology such as FDDI. As shown here, FDDI uses a redundant dual-ring topology that can be "snaked" through buildings or campus environments to interconnect LANs. The 100-Mbit/sec data rate of FDDI was an ideal fit for early 10-Mbit/sec Ethernet LANs. It had enough bandwidth to handle the relatively small amount of internetwork traffic.

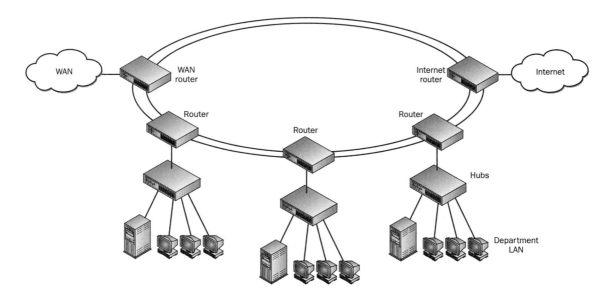

This backbone model assumed that 80 percent of the network traffic stayed within the local LAN. This assumption was based on the fact that servers were located within departments and internetwork traffic was limited to e-mail, occasional queries to servers in other departments, or WAN access across the backbone. Today, this model has changed. Servers are now located in consolidated data centers and almost all users access external connections—primarily the Internet. Today, 80 percent of the traffic is outside of local LANs.

Many departmental LAN have been subsumed into the enterprise network, where servers are managed in data centers that provide security, fault tolerance, and maintenance. In a switched network environment, the physical department LAN has been replaced by VLANs (virtual LANs) that consist of workgroups of users who may be located anywhere on the internetwork. The next few sections describe the progression from early distributed backbone networks to collapsed backbones to fully switched networks with layer 3 switching devices.

Hierarchical Wiring and Collapsed Backbones

Cabling is the essential element of any network design. It has its own architecture, independent of the switching and routing architectures that may be used. See "TIA/EIA Structured Cabling Standards" for a description of hierarchical wiring standards that provide an intelligent and logical solution for wiring a network that supports future growth and bandwidth requirements.

Hierarchical networking supports a *collapsed backbone* rather than the distributed backbone described earlier. A collapsed backbone is a backbone that has been reduced down to silicon on the backplane of an enterprise wiring hub or switch. The network is configured in a star topology where each major network segment connects via its own cable to the hub or switch, as shown here.

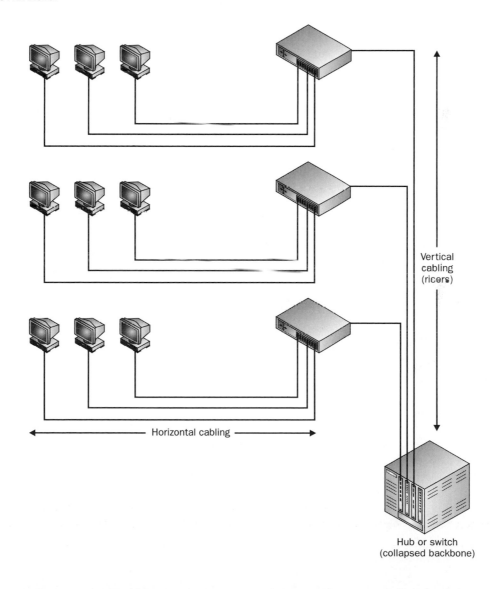

Vertical
cabling
(ricers)

Horizontal cabling

Hub or switch
(collapsed backbone)

Hierarchical cabling and network designs provide better troubleshooting and fault isolation. They also help administrators design networks with better traffic flow that can help avoid congestion. Users in the same group can communicate with one another through the same hub or switch without sending traffic all the way to the backbone hub or switch, but the backbone still provides a connection point to every other point in the network.

Switching Environments

A layer 2 switch is basically a multiport bridge that can be used to create a multisegment broadcast network. Switches may be directly connected with other switches to expand the network into a larger broadcast network. Each port on a switch is a separate network segment. A computer connected to a port does not share its segment with other computers, so there is no contention on that port and collisions are minimized. See "Switching and Switched Networks" for a complete discussion.

Figure N-9 illustrates a typical switched environment built with layer 2 switches. The basic design is flat and hierarchical:

- **Flat any-to-any connection topology**   All the nodes are part of the same broadcast domain, and any node can potentially connect with any other node.

- **Hierarchical structure**   The switching capacity of the network nodes increases as you move up the hierarchy. At the bottom, 10-Mbit/sec hubs or switches connect to Fast Ethernet switches (100 Mbits/sec), and these in turn connect to a Gigabit Ethernet (1 Gbit/sec) core switch.

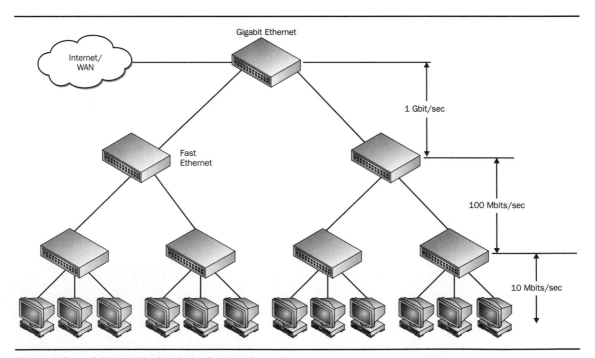

Figure N-9.   *A hierarchical switched network topology*

Figure N-10 illustrates a variation of this topology that is scaled for improved performance. The 10-Mbit/sec Ethernet users on the lower right have been upgraded to 100-Mbit/sec Fast Ethernet. A switch is installed that allows link aggregation between this level in the network and the next level, where a Gigabit Ethernet hub exists. Also note that two back-end Gigabit Ethernet hubs are interconnected with two aggregated links that provide 200 Gbits/sec of throughput.

The IEEE 802.3ad working group has developed trunking and link aggregation standards. Link aggregation provides improved bandwidth through load balancing and fault tolerance (if one link fails, the other is still usable). See "Link Aggregation."

Layer 3 Switching and Network Design

The networks discussed here are built with layer 2 switches, which promotes a flat network topology. This may not be practical for security and management reasons, especially as the network grows. Some areas of the network such as data centers or Web sites require the type of traffic control that can only be achieved with VLANs and routers.

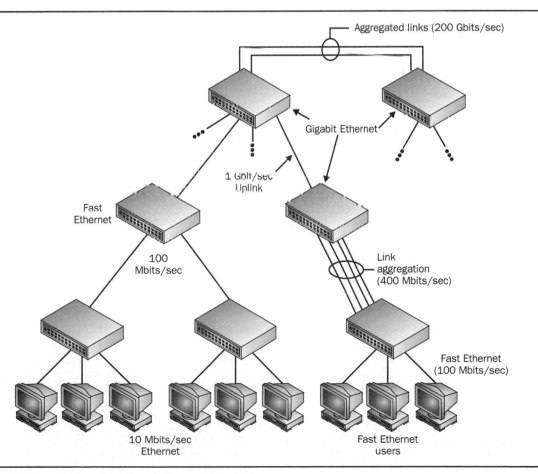

Figure N-10.   *Link aggregation to improve bandwidth*

A VLAN divides a flat network into two or more logical subnetworks. Members of VLANs can be anywhere on the network, forming workgroups that broadcast to one another but maintain autonomy from the rest of the network. Routers are introduced into the network to join VLANs. Packets going between VLANs cross the router. See "VLAN (Virtual LAN)" for more information.

Routers may be used in strategic locations. In Figure N-10, a router could be inserted at the top of the network hierarchy to join the two Gigabit Ethernet switches into an internetwork.

The *layer 3 switch* is the most practical device for creating switched networks. A layer 3 switch is a hardware-based multiport router. It provides high-speed layer 2 switching and the benefits of routing at very high speeds. Older routers were software-based and limited in functionality and speed. A typical software router forwards 500,000 packets per second. A layer 3 switch can forward up to 50 million packets per second or more. They are relatively inexpensive and give the network architect added design flexibility.

With the availability of inexpensive routing, the question then is where to route. In the past, this decision was constrained by the slow performance of routers. For example, a design consideration with software-based routers was to limit the number of these interconnection devices. If a packet were traveling across multiple networks, each router would add some amount of packet processing delay. In addition, routers were susceptible to congestion caused by traffic bursts, so each router was a potential place where packets could be dropped.

Today's high-speed layer 3 switches completely change the way that routers may be deployed. Instead of seeing routers as devices that create autonomous networks and forward packets between networks, routers are valued for their ability to build internetworks, handle layer 3 information, and provide prioritization and QoS based on that information.

Since layer 3 switches are inexpensive, they can be deployed throughout the network wherever a network architect feels that routing instead of switching is needed. Since they operate at wire speed, there is no performance penalty, so network architects can use routing and layer 3 information as useful features in network design.

Figure N-11 illustrates a fully redundant switched network built with a mixture of layer 2 switches and layer 3 Gigabit Ethernet switches. Here, layer 3 switches allow for extreme scalability of the network and the use of redundant links.

Multilayer Switching, Prioritization, and QoS

Traffic prioritization and QoS may be accomplished in two ways on IP networks. One method is for applications or policy servers to signal the level of QoS that a particular flow of packets needs. So far, this method has been difficult and impractical.

An alternative is to use switches that contain powerful *network processors* in multilayer switches that can classify traffic based on policies and rules. This is the method used by Extreme Networks and other vendors of multilayer switches. Extreme's switches are equipped with packet classification engines that compare information in packets against policies. The switches then put packets into queues that service packets based on their classification. The switches may read IEEE 802.1D-1998 (formerly 802.1p prioritization) tags, or examine information deep within the packet such as application type to determine packet priority.

Multilayer switches are sometimes called layer 4 switches or even layer 7 switches. A layer 4 switch evaluates traffic based on port number, TCP session information, or tags. Layer 7

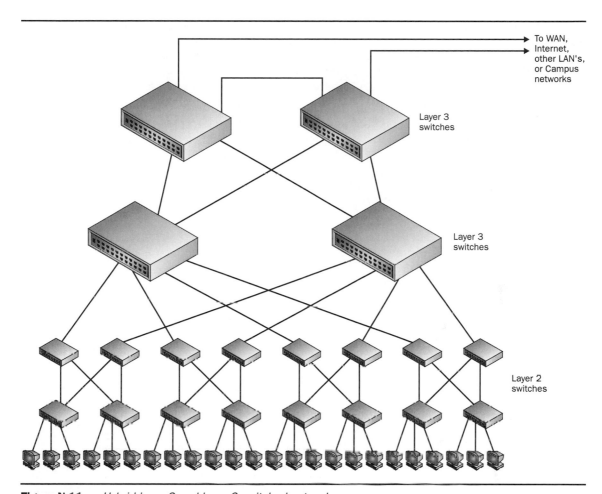

To WAN,
Internet,
other LAN's,
or Campus
networks

Layer 3
switches

Layer 3
switches

Layer 2
switches

Figure N-11. *Hybrid layer 2 and layer 3 switched network*

switches can evaluate URLs to obtain target server directory and file information, and many will evaluate the contents of cookies for forwarding information. These switches may be used to balance loads across servers in a server farm (called server load balancing) or to manage prioritization and QoS. See "Multilayer Switching," QoS (Quality of Service)," and "Prioritization of Network Traffic."

Server Farms, SANs, and NAS

Hierarchical network designs are especially important when it comes to locating network services. Centralizing these services is important in some environments. A hierarchical network, with its increasing levels of bandwidth, dictates that services be placed at the top of the hierarchy if they are to be accessed by all users. Of course, some services may be placed closer to users and layer 3 switches may be used to control access to those areas of the network.

The following topics are related to network services and how they may be designed into the network:

- **Data Center Design**   This topic provides an overview of data centers where servers, storage, and other network services are centralized for efficient access and management.

- **Clustering**   A cluster is a collection of servers that are interconnected via their own high-speed network or a switching fabric. The servers operate as if they are a single server. If one server goes down, the others can take over its load.

- **SAN (Storage Area Network)**   Refer to the topic for information about networks designed specifically for storage devices.

- **NAS (Network Attached Storage)**   A NAS is a storage device that does not require a front-end server. It attaches directly to networks.

- **Load Balancing**   This topic covers multilayer switches that distribute requests to servers in server farms and clusters.

Related Entries   ATM (Asynchronous Transfer Mode); Backbone Networks; Bandwidth Management; Cable and Wiring; DEN (Directory-Enabled Networking); Enterprise Network; Ethernet; Fiber-Optic Cable; Gigabit Ethernet; Intranets and Extranets; IP (Internet Protocol); LAN (Local Area Network); Link Aggregation; Load Balancing; Multilayer Switching; Multitiered Architectures; Network Concepts; Policy-Based Management; Power and Grounding Problems and Solutions; QoS (Quality of Service); Routers; Routing; Structured Cabling Standards; Switching or Switched Networks; Throughput; TIA/EIA Structured Cabling Standards; Topology; Traffic Management, Shaping, and Engineering; VLAN (Virtual LAN); VPN (Virtual Private Network); *and* WAN (Wide Area Network)

Linktionary!—Tom Sheldon's Encyclopedia of Networking updates	http://www.linktionary.com/n/network_design.html
About.com Network Design page (links to articles)	http://compnetworking.about.com/compute/compnetworking/cs/design/
Network design manual at Network Computing	http://www.networkcomputing.com/netdesign/series.htm
Technology guides at Network Computing	http://www.networkcomputing.com/
Cisco Documentation: Internetworking Design Guide	http://www.cisco.com/univercd/cc/td/doc/cisintwk/idg4/index.htm
Cisco Documentation: Internetworking Technology Overview	http://www.cisco.com/univercd/cc/td/doc/cisintwk/ito_doc/index.htm
Cisco Documentation: Designing Large-Scale IP Internetworks	http://www.cisco.com/univercd/cc/td/doc/cisintwk/idg4/nd2003.htm
Anixter Technical Library	http://www.anixter.com/techlib/
3Com Technical Library	http://www.3com.com/technology/tech_net/white_papers/
Enterasys Whitepapers	http://www.enterasys.com/products/whitepapers/

Intel Paper: Scalable Technologies, Essential strategies for rapidly changing network environmen	http://www.intel.com/network/white_papers/scalable_tech.htm
Intel Paper: Extending Virtual LANs to the Server	http://www.intel.com/network/white_papers/extending_lans.htm
Extreme Networks (see Technology page)	http://www.extremenetworks.com/
The Information Technology Professional's Resource Center	http://www.itprc.com/
"Examples of Network Equipment," by Gory Fairhurst	http://www.erg.abdn.ac.uk/users/gorry/course/equip-pages/lan-example-equip.html

Network Interface Card

See NIC (Network Interface Card).

Network Layer Protocols

The OSI (Open Systems Interconnection) model is a standard defined by the International Organization for Standardization. It is a layered architecture in which each layer defines a specific type of communication. The bottom layer, called the physical layer, is responsible for transmitting these messages as bit streams across a physical medium. The layers immediately above the physical layer define how data is packaged for transport over the physical network. Further up the protocol stack are layers that define how sessions between computers are established and managed. The uppermost layers define how applications interface with the network. The OSI model helps developers create products that work over a large variety of platforms and operating systems.

The network layer is the third layer of the protocol stack, just above the physical and data link layers. It is the routing layer and the layer that is responsible for network addressing. In the Internet protocol suite, IP resides in the network layer. Note the following:

- The network layer is also called the *internetwork* layer because it provides the functionality that allows different types of networks to be joined and share a common addressing scheme. See "Internetworking."

- IP (Internet Protocol) is the most common network layer protocol. Others include Novell's IPX and IBM's APPN (Advanced Peer-to-Peer Networking). See "IP (Internet Protocol)."

- Network layer protocols offer best-effort services, as opposed to transport layer services, which provide reliable data delivery services. See "Best-Effort Services" and "Reliable Data Delivery Services."

- Network layer protocols such as IP are connectionless, as opposed to transport layer services, which are connection-oriented. See "Connection-Oriented and Connectionless Services."

A common way to think of the network layer is as a service provider to the transport layer. In the TCP/IP protocol suite, IP provides connectionless (unreliable) packet delivery services, while TCP provides transport layer, connection-oriented services. See "TCP (Transmission Control Protocol)" and "Transport Protocols and Services" for more information about the transport layer.

RFC 2956 (Overview of 1999 IAB Network Layer Workshop, October 2000) describes the "state of the network layer and its impact on continued growth and usage of the Internet." In particular, it discusses NAT (network address translation), firewalls, IPv6, addressing, and various routing issues.

Related Entries   Best-Effort Delivery; Connection-Oriented and Connectionless Services; Data Communication Concepts; Datagram and Datagram Services; Data Link Protocols; IP (Internet Protocol); IPX/SPX (Internetwork Packet Exchange/Sequenced Packet Exchange); Internetworking; Network Architecture; OSI (Open Systems Interconnection) Model; Packets and Packet-Switching Networks; Router; Routing; TCP (Transmission Control Protocol); *and* Transport Protocols and Services

Linktionary!—Tom Sheldon's Encyclopedia of Networking updates	http://www.linktionary.com/n/network_layer.html
Cisco document: OSI: The Network Layer	http://www.cisco.com/warp/public/535/2.html
Network Magazine (see network layer section)	http://www.networkmagazine.com/static/tutorial/index.html

Network Management

Network management involves active and passive monitoring of network resources for the purpose of troubleshooting, detecting potential problems, improving performance, documentation, and reporting. This section discusses management applications and protocols, but of course, there are many other management tasks such as backing up data, providing security, training users, setting policies, and so on.

The ISO developed a network management model that maps out the major functions of network management systems. The model defines these five areas, which are explained in more detail in the Cisco paper listed later.

- **Performance management**   Measure and track network variables such as throughput, user response time, and line utilization.

- **Configuration management**   Monitor network and system configuration information to track the affects of software and hardware elements.

- **Accounting management**   Measure network-utilization so that individual or group use of network resources can be tracked and regulated.

- **Fault management**   Detect, log, notify users of, and, if possible, automatically fix network problems to keep the network running effectively.

- **Security management**   Control access to network resources.

A diversity of management applications and protocols are available. Full-blown management packages use *agents* to collect information from devices all over an enterprise network and send that information back to a central *management station*. The network administrator, working at a management console, produces reports and graphs about the state of the network from this information. Agents may also provide alerts that warn of problems or performance degradations. Most management applications of this type are built around the Internet's SNMP (Simple Network Management Protocol). A newer extension to this protocol is RMON (Remote Monitoring). Both are discussed under separate sections in this book.

Management applications are also available to provide remote desktop and configuration management, software installation and licensing management, network asset management, help desk management, performance and protocol analysis, resource and bandwidth management, capacity planning and simulation.

Many enterprises choose to outsource their management tasks to service providers that offer so-called "managed services." Service providers may take responsibility for a variety of functions, including communication services, applications, disk management, electronic commerce services, and any of the other ISO-defined services listed earlier. See "MSP (Management Service Provider)" and "Outsourcing."

This book discusses a wide variety of management topics as listed here. New Web-based management techniques are discussed under the WBEM (Web-Based Enterprise Management) topic. The DEN (Directory-Enabled Networks) and CIM (Common Information Model) topics cover systems for managing network information. Topics such Bandwidth Management describe the various techniques for managing capacity. Additional information is available at the Linktionary! Web site.

Related Entries   Administrator Account; Agent, Network Management; ASP (Application Service Provider); Auditing; Bandwidth Management: Cable and Wiring; Capacity Planning; CIM (Common Information Model); CMIP (Common Management Information Protocol); Configuration Management; Data Protection; DEN (Directory-Enabled Networks); Directory Services; DME (Distributed Management Environment); DMI (Distributed Management Interface); DMTF (Distributed Management Task Force); Electronic Software Distribution and Licensing; Fault Management; Fault Tolerance and High Availability; IntelliMirror; IPMI (Intelligent Platform Management Interface); MIB (Management Information Base); MSP (Management Service Provider); NDMP (Network Data Management Protocol); Network Analyzers; Network Management; OpenView Management System; Performance Measurement and Optimization; Ping (Packet Internet Groper); Policy-Based Management; Prioritization of Network Traffic; QoS (Quality of Service); Redundancy; RMON (Remote Monitoring); Security Auditing; SNMP (Simple Network Management Protocol); SSP (Storage Service Provider); SystemView, IBM; Testing, Diagnostics, and Troubleshooting; TIA/EIA Structured Cabling Standards; TMN (Telecommunications Management Network); Traffic Management, Shaping, and Engineering; WBEM (Web-Based Enterprise Management); Webmaster; Wired for Management; *and* Zero Administration for Windows Initiative

Linktionary!—Tom Sheldon's Encyclopedia of Networking updates	http://www.linktionary.com/n/network_management.html
The Simple Web (network management information and links)	http://snmp.cs.utwente.nl/
Network management links	http://netman.cit.buffalo.edu/
David Blight's network management links	http://www.ee.umanitoba.ca/~blight/telecommunications/nm.html

Google Web Directory network management page	http://directory.google.com/Top/Computers/Software/Internet/Network_Management/
Bitpipe (search for "network management")	http://www.bitpipe.com/
About.com network management and QoS page	http://compnetworking.about.com/compute/compnetworking/cs/netmanagement/
Network Management links at ITPRC.com	http://www.itprc.com/nms.htm
Cisco documentation: "Network Management Basics"	http://www.cisco.com/univercd/cc/td/doc/cisintwk/ito_doc/nmbasics.htm
IETF (see "Network Management"area)	http://www.ietf.org/html.charters/wg-dis.html
Network World Fusion network management page	http://www.nwfusion.com/netresources/manage.html
MSP Association	http://www.mspassociation.org/
searchSystemsManagement.com	http://searchsystemsmanagement.techtarget.com/

Network Operating Systems

Network operating systems are the gatekeepers to applications and data on LAN and enterprise networks. They are built on the client/server model and are designed to serve clients. Authentication and access control are a network operating system's most important features. A list of clients is maintained in the form of user accounts, and those users are authenticated and authorized to access various server resources. An accounting system may keep track of user activities. A NOS generally provides a shared file system and a set of security features and controls to control user access to network resources.

The most important network operating systems on the market today are listed in the following table, along with the Web site address where you can obtain more information. Each of these operating systems is described elsewhere in this book.

Novell NetWare	http://www.novell.com
Windows 2000 Server	http://www.microsoft.com/windows/
IBM OS/2 Warp Server	http://www-4.ibm.com/software/os/warp/warp-server/
Sun Microsystems Solaris	http://www.sun.com/solaris/
UNIX and Linux (multiple vendors)	(See "UNIX" and "Linux" in this book for links list)

Some desktop operating systems provide peer-to-peer file- and printer-sharing services that are similar to the services offered by full-featured NOSs. However, peer-to-peer environments usually lack the security and access controls that are necessary in corporate environments. Most high-end NOSs run as dedicated servers and are strictly controlled by an administrator who manages the system, sets security policies, and controls who can access the system. Client computers run redirector software that sends requests for network service to a designated network server.

Only a few years ago, each network operating system seemed to have its own niche and provided a set of features or functions that set it apart from other network operating systems. Today, most network operating systems have similar features, use the TCP/IP protocol for internetworking, and include Web server and intranet support.

The best place to find comparative information about operating systems is at magazine sites that feature articles that evaluate NOSs. Several Web sites are listed later. Use the following as a checklist for evaluating networking operating systems. Note that the systems mentioned above generally have these features, although it is still worthwhile to compare the levels of these features among operating systems:

- OS features such as support for SMP (symmetrical multiprocessing), processor support, protocol support, and automatic hardware detection.

- Strong security features such as authentication, authorization, logon restrictions, and access controls, with support for X.509v3 certificates, smart cards, and other advanced security systems.

- Support for name and directory services. Microsoft has Active Directory. Novell has NDS (Novell Directory Services). LDAP compatibility is another requirement.

- File, print, and Web services facilities, including RAID support levels, backup services, and replication capabilities.

- Management, administration, and auditing tools that use graphical interfaces and that operate from remote consoles.

- Internetworking, routing, and WAN support.

- Client operating system support and support for remote dial-up users.

- Services such as virus checking, software distribution, software and hardware inventory, and server-to-server replication.

- Ability to run mission-critical applications with support for fault tolerance and high-availability systems.

- Clustering capabilities.

As mentioned, this is just a partial list of comparative features that should be included in advanced network operating systems. Refer to the following related entries for more information about specific features.

Related Entries   Access Control; Access Rights; Account, User; Accounting Services; ACL (Access Control List); Administrator Account; Attributes; Auditing; Authentication and Authorization; Cache and Caching Techniques; Client/Server Computing; Clustering; Data Management; Data Protection; Directory Attributes and Management; Directory Services; Distributed Applications; Distributed Computer Networks; Embedded Systems; Fault Tolerance and High Availability; File Server; File Sharing; File Systems; File Transfer Protocols; Linux; Logons and Logon Accounts; Login Scripts; Microsoft Active Directory; Microsoft Windows; Microsoft Windows File Systems; Mirroring; Multiprocessing; NAS (Network Attached Storage); NDS (Novell Directory Services); Network Appliances; Novell NetWare; Novell NetWare File System; OS/2 Warp; Replication; Rights and Permissions; RTOS

(Real-Time Operating System); SAN (Storage Area Network); Servers; Storage Systems; Sun Microsystems Solaris; Thin Clients; UNIX; UNIX File System; *and* Users and Groups

Linktionary!—Tom Sheldon's Encyclopedia of Networking updates	http://www.linktionary.com/n/nos.html
Information Systems Meta-List at Washington University (see operating systems section)	http://www.cait.wustl.edu/infosys/infosys.html
Google Web Directory operating system page	http://directory.google.com/Top/Computers/Software/Operating_Systems/
Bitpipe (search for "network operating system")	http://www.bitpipe.com/
About.com network operating system page	http://compnetworking.about.com/compute/compnetworking/cs/networknos/
Network Magazine tutorials	http://www.networkmagazine.com/static/tutorial/index.html
Network World Fusion network operating system page	http://www.nwfusion.com/netresources/nos.html
TechWeb Planet IT (search for "network operating system")	http://www.planetit.com/
Review of Operating Systems	http://tunes.org/Review/OSes.html

Network Operations Center

See NOC (Network Operations Center); Data Center Design.

Network Processors

Network processors are integrated circuit devices that combine the speed of ASIC (application-specific integrated circuits) with a CPU to provide high-performance networking solutions. ASIC technology is widely used to classify, filter, and forward IP traffic. However, The problem with ASICs is that they are hardwired with a specific feature set. If the feature set is changed or upgraded, the ASIC must be replaced. When new standards come along (MPLS and Diff-Serv are examples a recent standards developments), ASICs must be replaced, while network processors can be reprogrammed.

Network processors solve this problem and provide increased performance. A network processors is a high performance programmable I/O device. The programmability is what sets network processors apart from ASICs. Network processors reduce time to market for vendors who build network devices by enabling them to write code for a communications processor, as opposed to creating one-shot ASICs. This strategy also extends the lifetime of devices by allowing vendors to add new features to devices.

The network processor can be programmed to support custom algorithms. The processors are optimized to perform a variety of functions in network devices, including frame classification, filtering, forwarding, marking, policing, traffic shaping, and Diff-Serv routing. These features are associated with switches that provide QoS, traffic prioritization, and traffic management. Policies that control the flow of traffic are implemented in software, so these policies are easily upgraded.

Network processors are used in the same way as ASICs. They are placed in the data path of network switching devices and connected directly to the physical interface. The processors may also perform framing, segmentation and reassembly, and other functions.

EZchip's TOPcore network processor technology integrates many small and fast processors, each optimized to perform specific tasks and able to deliver tenfold improvement in performance over other network processor architectures based on generic RISC processors. The four TOPs (task-optimized processors) are TOPparse (packet parse and classify), TOPsearch (search and lookup), TOPresolve (forwarding and QoS decisions), and TOPmodify (packet modification). A system can perform complex packet manipulation and seven-layer packet processing at 10-Gigabit/OC-192 rates, scalable to 40-Gigabit/OC-768.

Related Entries   ASIC (Application-Specific Integrated Circuit); CISC (Complex Instruction Set Computer); Cut-Through Architecture; Embedded Systems; Network Appliances; RISC (Reduced Instruction Set Computer); Routers; RTOS (Real-Time Operating System); Switch Fabrics and Bus Design; *and* Switching and Switched Networks

Linktionary!—Tom Sheldon's Encyclopedia of Networking updates	http://www.linktionary.com/n/network_processor.html
Intel network processor family page	http://developer.intel.com/design/network/products/npfamily/
EZchip TOPcore network processor	http://www.ezchip.com/
Alcatel	http://www.alcatel.com/
PMC-Sierra	http://www.pmcsierra.com/
Conexant Systems	http://www.conexant.com/
Communications Components: The Evolving Value Chain	http://connected.jpmhq.com/issue42/4.html
Linley Group Network Processor Central	http://www.linleygroup.com/npu/

Network, Public

See NPN (New Public Network); Telecommunications and Telephone System.

Network Service Providers

Specifically, a network service provider, or NSP, provides network services to other network organizations such as regional ISPs. In the Internet hierarchy, there are local ISPs, regional ISPs, and NSPs, which provide backbone networks and support transit traffic across those networks. See "NSP (Network Service Provider)" and "Internet Architecture and Backbone."

Other types of network service providers and the services they offer are discussed under "Communication Services and Providers," "ISPs (Internet Service Providers)," "Network Access Services," and "Service Providers and Carriers."

Newsfeed Services

See Webcasting.

Newsgroups

See NNTP (Network News Transport Protocol).

NFS (Network File System)

NFS is a client/server distributed file service that provides transparent file-sharing network environments. NFS was originally designed by a small team at Sun Microsystems in the 1980s, but it is now an open Internet protocol. It was defined by RFC 1094 (version 2) and updated with RFC 1813 (version 3) in 1995. NFS is now a set of X/Open specifications (defined as X/Open90 and X/Open91). The AFS (Andrew File System) is a version of NFS.

NFS runs on a full range of systems, from PCs to mainframes, in local and global environments. Multiple types of clients can access shared NFS file systems. While NFS is available in the public domain and from many vendors, Sun Microsystems also sells and supports the service. It includes the NIS+ enterprise naming service with its version of NFS and offers an Internet version of NFS called WebNFS, as discussed later in this section. NFS is comparable to CIFS, a Microsoft development that extends SMB (Server Message Blocks) over the Internet. NFS could also be compared to DAFS (Direct Access File System), except that DAFS is a block-level access protocol that is designed to work with VI Architecture in data center environments.

An important distinction between NFS and Internet FTP (File Transfer Protocol) is that NFS does not need to transfer a file fully to a client's system. Instead, only the blocks of the file that the client needs are transferred across the network link, thus reducing network traffic. NFS servers broadcast or advertise the directories that they share. A shared directory is often called a *published* or *exported* directory. Information about shared directories and who can access them is stored in a file that is read by the operating system when it boots.

The process of accessing files in a publish directory is called "file mounting." An automounter process is available that automatically mounts files on demand when a user attempts to access a file. Prior knowledge of a file's location is not necessary.

NFS version 3 provides integrity features for files that may be opened by multiple users simultaneously. If several people were accessing the same file and some of those people were writing changes to the file, then other people must know about the changes that have been made. NFS solves this problem by implementing a lock manager to lock the sections of a file that are currently being accessed by different people. A status monitor works with the lock manager to ensure that people accessing and making changes to a file do not "collide."

NFS version 3 also implements a global namespace that lets users move to different network locations but still access files with the same naming scheme used at their "home site." This feature also benefits applications that are configured to access files based on specific location names.

Security features in NFS include an authentication and authorization service to check user IDs and access rights before allowing them to access a file. NFS can also be configured to use other security services such as Kerberos. Encryption services such as DES (Data Encryption Standard) can also be implemented. NFS also implements ACLs (access control lists) that hold authorization information to define exactly how an authenticated user can access a file. See "Rights and Permissions" for information about NFS ACLs.

Sun has extended NFS to operate on the Internet with WebNFS. WebNFS basically makes information on NFS servers available to users of Web browsers and Java applets over the Internet. It also allows users to access NFS servers through corporate firewalls. WebNFS is a complete file system for the Web, unlike FTP and HTTP. It supports in-place editing of files so users don't need to download and edit a file, then send it back in separate operations.

Files on the Internet appear as local files to users and are accessed using the NFS URL (Uniform Resource Locator) format such as nfs://*server*/*directory*/*filename*. WebNFS builds on NFS technology to bring file access and distribution to the Web. Web NFS has been designed to be much more efficient at bandwidth utilization over the Internet than NFS. This improves performance when downloading software from Web sites. Automatic error and crash recovery is also provided.

The following RFCs describe NFS. Also refer to the IETF Network File System Version 4 (nfsv4) Working Group, which is advancing the NFS technology.

- RFC 1094 (NFS: Network File System Protocol Specification. Sun Microsystems, March 1989)
- RFC 1813 (NFS Version 3 Protocol Specification, June 1995)
- RFC 2054 (WebNFS Client Specification, October 1996)
- RFC 2055 (WebNFS Server Specification, October 1996)
- RFC 2224 (NFS URL Scheme, October 1997)
- RFC 2623 (NFS Version 2 and Version 3 Security Issues, June 1999)
- RFC 2624 (NFS Version 4 Design Considerations, June 1999)
- RFC 2755 (Security Negotiation for WebNFS, January 2000)
- RFC 3010 (NFS Version 4 Protocol, December 2000)

Related Entries   ACL (Access Control List); AFS (Andrew File System); CIFS (Common Internet File System); Client/Server Computing; DAFS (Direct Access File System); Data Management; Directory Services; Distributed Applications; Distributed Computer Networks; File Sharing; File Systems; File Transfer Protocols; NAS (Network Attached Storage); Network Operating Systems; Rights and Permissions; Servers; Stateless and Call-Back Filing Systems; Storage Systems; UNIX; *and* UNIX File System

Linktionary!—Tom Sheldon's Encyclopedia of Networking updates	http://www.linktionary.com/n/nfs.html
Sun Microsystems WebNFS site	http://www.sun.com/software/webnfs/
IETF Working Group: Network File System Version 4 (nfsv4)	http://www.ietf.org/html.charters/nfsv4-charter.html
The PC-Mac TCP/IP & NFS FAQ list	http://www.rtd.com/pcnfsfaq/faq.html
Network Appliance (search for "NFS" in Tech Library)	http://www.netapp.com/tech_library/

NGN (Next Generation Network)

This is another name for the "new public network" or NPN. NPN, while not yet a reality, is an evolution of the existing incumbent carrier telephony networks to a single converged network. The old circuit-switched model gives way to a packet-oriented multiservice (voice, video, data) network that supports QoS (quality of service) and unique hybrid services such as Internet call waiting. See "NPN (New Public Network)."

NHRP (Next Hop Resolution Protocol)

There is a whole range of protocols and schemes that attempt to integrate IP and ATM networks. Classical IP over ATM, or CIP, is one such method. CIP uses an ATM network as its underlying data link network. CIP implements the concept of a *LIS (logical IP subnet)*, which is a closed logical IP subnetwork consisting of a group of hosts.

In CIP, an ATM attached host communicates with an ATMARP server to resolve IP-to-ATM address mappings. All communications within a LIS can take place over ATM PVCs or SVCs. All communication between different LISs requires an IP router to forward the packets. What NHRP does is provide a way for inter-LIS traffic to use ATM SVCs (shortcut paths) rather than go through the router. This improves performance as traffic flows across a direct switched virtual circuit. NHRP makes the ATM network appear as a *single-hop* between source and destination.

Shortcut routing works as follows. If a long flow of packets is being transmitted, NHRP makes a decision about whether the flow is going to be long enough to warrant setting up a virtual connection. The decision is based on a default number of packets, usually ten. If a flow exists, NHRP goes to work to obtain the destination ATM address so a virtual circuit can be set up. An NHRP query goes out over the routed hop-by-hop path (which consists of individual ATM circuits between routers) to the destination and the answer is returned along this path to the source. The source then establishes a virtual circuit across the ATM network directly to the destination, bypassing the hop-by-hop routers and improving performance.

Note that NHRP is an *address resolution* protocol that queries other routers across logical IP networks on top of ATM networks. NHRP resolves the given IP address of a destination, no matter what LIS, into its corresponding ATM address. Once the ATM address is known, a virtual circuit can be set up between LISs.

This topic is covered in more detail at the Linktionary! Web site. Three important RFCs are listed here. Others are listed at the Web site.

- RFC 1932 (IP over ATM: A Framework Document, April 1996)
- RFC 2332 (NBMA Next Hop Resolution Protocol, April 1998)
- RFC 2333 (NHRP Protocol Applicability Statement, April 1998)

The ATM Forum integrated LANE and NHRP to provide a generic bridging and routing environment called MPOA (Multiprotocol over ATM).

Related Entries   ATM (Asynchronous Transfer Mode); IP over ATM; IP Switching, Ipsilon (Nokia); LANE (LAN Emulation); MPOA (Multiprotocol over ATM); NHRP (Next Hop Resolution Protocol); *and* PNNI (Private Network-to-Network Interface)

Linktionary!—Tom Sheldon's Encyclopedia of   http://www.linktionary.com/n/nhrp.html
Networking updates

NIC (Network Interface Card)

NICs are adapters installed in a computer that provide the connection point to a network. Each NIC is designed for a specific type of network, such as Ethernet, token ring, FDDI, ARCNET, and others. A NIC provides an attachment point for a specific type of cable, such as coaxial cable, twisted-pair cable, or fiber-optic cable. NICs for wireless LANs typically have an antenna for communication with a base station.

NICs are defined by physical and data link layer specifications. These physical specifications define mechanical and electrical interface specifications. The mechanical specifications define the physical connection methods for cable. The electrical specifications define the framing methods used to transmit bit streams across the cable. They also define the control signals that provide the timing of data transfers across the network. The data link layer specifications define the medium access method (Ethernet CSMA/CD, token ring, and so forth) in accordance with the IEEE 802.x standards (or possibly other standards). See "MAC (Media Access Control)" for more information.

Network interface cards are available in two categories: those that follow standard specifications, and those that follow the specifications but add enhancements to boost performance. Some of these special features are discussed later. Keep in mind that differences in hardware design among interface cards on a network can slow performance. For example, a network card with a 32-bit interface typically sends data to a 16-bit card faster than the 16-bit card can process it. To solve this bottleneck, *memory buffers* are implemented to capture and hold incoming data, preventing data overflows and allowing the 32-bit card to complete its transmission, even while the 16-bit card continues to process the information it has collected in its buffer.

Another type of bottleneck occurs between the network interface card and the memory of the computer. There are four methods for moving information from the network interface card into the computer once it has been received. With *DMA (direct memory access)*, a controller takes charge of the system bus and transfers data from the NIC to a memory location, thus reducing CPU load. With the *shared memory* option, NICs have their own memory that the system processor can access directly, or both the CPU and NIC share a block of system memory that both can directly access. With the *bus mastering* technique, a network adapter can transfer information directly to system memory without interrupting the system processor.

Global addressing ensures that every network interface card has a unique identifying node address. Token ring and Ethernet card addresses are hardwired on the card. The IEEE (Institute of Electrical and Electronic Engineers) is in charge of assigning addresses to token ring and Ethernet cards. Each manufacturer is given a unique code and a block of addresses. When installing a card, it is a good idea to determine the card address and write it down for future reference. You can also use a diagnostics utility supplied with the card to determine its address after you've installed the card in a system. You might also find the address on a label attached to the card.

N

Most network cards come with a socket for remote-boot PROM (programmable read-only memory). You use remote-boot PROMs on diskless workstations that can't boot on their own but instead boot from the network server. A diskless workstation is less expensive than a system with floppy disk and hard disk drives. It is also more secure because users can't download valuable data to floppy disk or upload viruses and unauthorized software.

Related Entries   Access Method, Network; Collisions and Collision Domains; CSMA/CD (Carrier Sense Multiple Access/Collision Detection); Data Communication Concepts; Data Link Protocols; Ethernet; LAN (Local Area Network); MAC (Media Access Control); NDIS (Network Driver Interface Specification); Network Architecture; Network Concepts; ODI (Open Data-Link Interface); Servers; *and* Token Ring Network

Linktionary!—Tom Sheldon's Encyclopedia of Networking updates	http://www.linktionary.com/n/nic.html
KMJ Communications NIC information page	http://www.kmj.com/nic.html
ATM Network Interface Card Evaluation	http://www.anl.gov/ECT/network/racarlson/evaluation.html
Techguide.com: "Server NICS in the Contemporary LAN Architecture"	http://www.techguide.com/
Jato Technologies: Optimizing Network Interface Cards for operation in a Standard High Volume Server	http://www.level1.com/pressrel/optimizingcards.pdf
Gorry Fairhurst network interface card page	http://www.erg.abdn.ac.uk/users/gorry/course/lan-pages/nic.html
3Com white papers page	http://www.3com.com/technology/tech_net/white_papers/index.html
PC Magazine article: "Server NICs with Tricks"	http://www.zdnet.com/adverts/eprints/intel/pcmg/80831lf.html

NII (National Information Infrastructure)

The NII is the so-called "data superhighway" that is designed to make information available to the public in many forms, including video programming, scientific or business databases, images, sound recordings, library archives, and other media. Public databases are available at locations throughout the country, such as libraries, museums, government agencies, and research facilities. The U.S. government has vast quantities of information in the Library of Congress, the Smithsonian, and elsewhere that it will make available.

NII is promoted by NIST (National Institute of Standards) in the U.S. The High-Performance and High-Speed Networking Act of 1993 calls for federal organizations to coordinate their efforts in defining and building the NII.

Related Entries   6Bone and IPv6; Abilene; Active Networks; GII (Global Information Infrastructure); Internet; Internet2; Internet Architecture and Backbone; Internet Organizations and Committees; Internet Standards; NIST (National Institute of Standards and Technology); NREN (National Research and Education Network); Qbone; Standards Groups, Associations, and Organizations; STAR TAP; *and* vBNS (Very high speed Backbone Network Service)

Linktionary!—Tom Sheldon's Encyclopedia of   http://www.linktionary.com/n/nii.html
Networking updates

NII white papers   http://bob.nap.edu/html/wpni3/

United States National Information   http://nii.nist.gov/
Infrastructure Virtual Library

NIS (Network Information System)

NIS is a distributed database that provides a repository for storing information about hosts, users, and mailboxes in the UNIX environment. It was originally developed by Sun Microsystems and called YP (Yellow Pages). NIS is used to identify and locate objects and resources that are accessible on a network.

NIS has been upgraded to NIS+, which includes better administrative support for large organizations, stronger security, and improved distribution of updates to other NIS+ databases. In particular, NIS+ supports data encryption and authentication over secure RPC.

A typical network will consist of at least one NIS server, but other NIS servers may exist to service different NIS domains. A master-slave configuration is also possible, where a master NIS server distributes the NIS database to one or more slave NIS servers. When changes take place, the master NIS server automatically updates the slaves. This arrangement allows clients to access "nearby" servers with the assurance that they are working with the must recent information.

The NIS+ implementation in Solaris 2.0 consists of 16 information tables that store network information. The most common tables are described below:

- **Hosts**   Information about hosts on the network, such as their network address and hostname
- **Ethers**   Ethernet addresses for hosts
- **Networks**   Information about networks in the domain
- **Services**   Available IP services and their port numbers
- **Password**   Information about passwords and pointers to the shadow file
- **Cred**   Access credentials for users
- **Group**   Information about groups in a domain
- **Auto_Home**   Home directories for users
- **Bootparams**   Information used by diskless workstations

Information is accessed using NIS+ commands or by using management program. The usually procedure is to first select the table to search and specify the search criteria. More recently, directory services such as Sun's Directory Services have become popular. Refer to "Directory Services" and "LDAP (Lightweight Directory Access Protocol)" for more information.

Related Entries   CIP (Common Indexing Protocol); CNRP (Common Name Resolution Protocol); Directory Services; DNS (Domain Name Service); Document Management; Handle System; Internet; LDAP (Lightweight Directory Access Protocol); Metadata; Name Services; NetBIOS/NetBEUI; Search and

Discovery Services; Service Advertising and Discovery; URI (Uniform Resource Identifier); URL (Uniform Resource Locator); URN (Universal Resource Name); *and* WHOIS ("Who is")

Linktionary!—Tom Sheldon's Encyclopedia of Networking updates	http://www.linktionary.com/n/nis.html
SunWorld's NIS+ page	http://www.sunworld.com/sunworldonline/swol-09-1996/swol-09-security.html
NIS FAQ	http://beta.ece.ucsb.edu/~wesc/nis+faq.html
The Linux NIS(YP)/NYS/NIS+ HOWTO by Thorsten Kukuk	http://www.linux.org.tw/CLDP/HOWTO/NIS-HOWTO.html
Linux NIS(YP) Server and Tools	http://www.suse.de/~kukuk/nis/

NIST (National Institute of Standards and Technology)

NIST is a U.S. government agency that was established to assist industry in the development of technology. It is an agency of the U.S. Department of Commerce's Technology Administration. NIST has consolidated the activities of the CSL (Computer Systems Laboratory) and the CAML (Computing and Applied Mathematics Laboratory) into a new information technology laboratory. The NIST Web site is at http://www.nist.gov.

NLSP (NetWare Link Services Protocol)

NLSP is a NetWare routing protocol that was developed by Novell for IPX (Internetwork Packet Exchange) internetworks and as a replacement for RIP (Routing Information Protocol). It is derived from IS-IS (Intermediate System-to-Intermediate System), the link-state routing protocol developed by the ISO (International Organization for Standardization). Routers running NLSP exchange information about network links, the cost of paths, IPX network numbers, and media types. They use this information to build routing tables.

Related Entries   LAN (Local Area Network); Network Architecture; Network Concepts; Network Layer Protocols; Novell; Novell NetWare; RIP (Routing Information Protocol); Routers; *and* Routing

Linktionary!—Tom Sheldon's Encyclopedia of Networking updates	http://www.linktionary.com/n/nlsp.html
Linktionary! — Tom Sheldon's Encyclopedia of Networking updates	http://www.linktionary.com/i/ipx.html
Novell	http://www.novell.com

NNI (Network Node Interface), ATM

NNI in ATM means Network Node Interface. It is the standard interface between ATM switches. The term is also used with frame relay. See "ATM (Asynchronous Transfer Mode)."

NNTP (Network News Transport Protocol)

The NNTP protocol is the delivery mechanism for the USENET newsgroup service. USENET runs on the Internet and other TCP/IP-based networks and provides a way to exchange messages, articles, and bulletins throughout the Internet. Articles are put in central databases throughout the Internet and users access the database to get the articles they need. This reduces network traffic and eliminates the need to store a copy of each article on every subscriber's system.

There are thousands of different newsgroups related to computers, social issues, science, the humanities, recreation, and other topics. See "USENET" for more information on USENET itself. This topic discusses the operation of the NNTP protocol.

USENET servers use NNTP to exchange news articles among themselves. NNTP is also used by clients who need to read news articles on USENET servers. The server-to-server and user-to-server connections are described here:

- **Server-to-server exchanges** In the server-to-server exchange, one server either requests the latest articles from another server (*pull*) or allows the other server to *push* new articles to it. In either case, both servers engage in a conversation in which specific newsgroup information is requested and then delivered. A primary goal is to prevent the sending system from sending articles that the receiver already has. Select newsgroups and articles can be blocked.

- **User-to-server connections** Users run news readers, which are now included with most Web browsers. The user first connects with a newsgroup server (usually located at an ISP (Internet service provider), then downloads a list of available newsgroups. The user can then subscribe to a newsgroup and begin reading articles available in that group or post new articles.

Before NNCP, USENET servers used UUCP (UNIX-to-UNIX Copy Program) to exchange information. UUCP is a "flood broadcast" mechanism. Hosts send new news articles they receive to other hosts, which in turn forward the news on to other hosts that they feed. Usually, a host receives duplicates of articles and must discard those duplicates—a time-consuming process and waste of bandwidth.

NNTP uses an interactive command and response mechanism that lets hosts determine which articles are to be transmitted. A host acting as a client contacts a "server" host using NNTP, and then inquires if any new newsgroups have been created on any of the serving host systems. An administrator can choose to create similar newsgroups on the host he or she manages.

During the same NNTP session, the client requests information about new articles that have arrived in all or some of the newsgroups. The server then sends the client a list of new articles and the client can request transmission of some or all of those articles. The client can refuse to accept articles that it already has.

Readers interested in the details of NNTP commands and responses should read RFC 977 (A Proposed Standard for the Stream-Based Transmission of News, February 1986).

Some organizations may prefer to set up their own USENET systems on their TCP/IP-based intranet rather than deploy groupware and collaborative applications. If you plan on setting up your own news server, refer to "USENET."

Related Entries   Broadcasting on the Internet; Chat; Collaborative Computing; Instant Messaging; Internet Radio; IRC (Internet Relay Chat); Mailing List Programs; Multicasting; Multimedia; Peer-to-Peer Communication; VBI (Vertical Blanking Interval); *and* Webcasting

Linktionary!—Tom Sheldon's Encyclopedia of Networking updates	http://www.linktionary.com/n/nntp.html
IETF Working Group: NNTP Extensions (nntpext)	http://www.ietf.org/html.charters/nntpext-charter.html
Google Web Directory: public news servers	http://directory.google.com/Top/Computers/Usenet/Public_News_Servers/

NOC (Network Operations Center)

A NOC is like a data center, but it may house only network switching equipment and management systems. In contrast, a data center houses storage devices and possibly SANs (storage area networks). Both a NOC and an Internet data center may provide collocation services, which is the rental of space for other providers' equipment.

Related Entries   ASP (Application Service Provider); Collocation; Data Center Design; Fault Tolerance and High-Availability Systems; Internet Architecture and Backbone; Internet Connections; ISP (Internet Service Provider); NSP (Network Service Provider); Outsourcing; POP (Point-of-Presence); Service Providers and Carriers; *and* Web Technologies and Concepts

Linktionary!—Tom Sheldon's Encyclopedia of Networking updates	http://www.linktionary.com/n/noc.html
Exodus Internet data center (take the visual tour)	http://www.exodus.net/idc/

Node

A node is a network-connected device such as a workstation, a server, or a printer. Network connection devices such as bridges and routers are not usually referred to as nodes on a network, even though they have network addresses.

In the IP addressing scheme, network nodes such as computers are called "hosts," while routers are sometimes called "gateways," an older term that is rarely used today because gateways refer to application layer devices that join systems or networks and provide translation services between them.

Related Entries   Data Communication Concepts; Edge Devices; End Systems and End-to-End Connectivity; Front-End System; Network Concepts; *and* Point-to-Point Communications

NOS (Network Operating Systems)

See "Network Operating Systems."

Novell

Novell has been a major influence in the growth of the microcomputer industry. It developed Z-80-based microcomputers in the 1970s and created its first networking products in the early 1980s. In 1983, when IBM announced the IBM Personal Computer XT, which had a hard disk, Novell quickly responded with a product that converted the hard disk system into a file-sharing system. Workstations attached to the server with a star-configured cabling system known as S-Net.

During the 1980s, Novell expanded its product line with the popular NetWare network operating system. In 1993, Novell announced NetWare version 4. Its most important feature was NDS (NetWare Directory Services), which enabled network administrators to organize users and network resources such as servers and printers the way people naturally access them. NDS is discussed further under "NDS (Novell Directory Services)."

Today, Novell markets NDS for use on a number of non-Novell operating systems. In addition, its NetWare operating system now fully supports the TCP/IP protocol suite and Web technologies. The Linktionary! Web site provides a more detailed history of the NetWare product line.

Related Entries   IPX/SPX (Internetwork Packet Exchange/Sequenced Packet Exchange); LAN (Local Area Network); NCP (NetWare Core Protocol); NDS (Novell Directory Service); Network Operating Systems; *and* Novell NetWare

Linktionary!—Tom Sheldon's Encyclopedia of Networking updates	http://www.linktionary.com/ /.html
Novell	http://www.novell.com/

Novell Directory Services

See NDS (Novell Directory Services).

Novell NetWare

Novell calls NetWare a NSE (network services engine), It provides a wide range of built-in services, including directory services, security, routing, messaging, management, file and print services, TCP/IP support, and SMP (symmetric multiprocessing). It also provides a platform for expanded services such as telephony, multimedia services, Internet and intranet browsing and publishing, and more. NetWare version 6 was released in early 2001.

Through NDS (Novell Directory Services), NetWare provides a single view of the network. NDS is a distributed database that holds information about network users and network resources everywhere on the network, even global networks. Users log in once to access resources anywhere, as opposed to having to log in every time they attempt to access a resource. See "NDS (Novell Directory Services)" for more information.

Accounting features let administrators track user access to resources and charge users for use of those resources. The services can be used to collect real charges from users (such as students in an educational environment) or to simply collect usage information. A licensing service lets administrators monitor the use of licensed applications.

NetWare uses a highly secure logon sequence that implements public-/private-key authentication schemes, and an auditing feature that monitors and records networkwide events. The security features are handled through the NDS directory services tree.

NetWare performs automatic file-by-file compression to increase storage capacity. Compression is performed as a background process that has minimal effect on server performance. NetWare also supports automated data migration to transfer infrequently accessed files from expensive online storage to nearline or offline storage devices such as optical disk and tape. See "Storage Management Systems" for more details.

The latest version supports up to 32 systems in a cluster to provide a highly available system. The SMP feature supports up to 32 processors. Novell Storage Services (NSS) handles any storage requirements by supporting billions of volumes and directories, with each volume capable of holding billions of files, each one up to 8 terabytes in size. It also takes advantage of all the processors available in the server.

There are many additional features of NetWare, too numerous to mention here. You can get additional information by visiting Novell's Web site at the address given at the end of this section or by referring to the additional Novell entries in this book.

Related Entries   Client/Server Computing; Directory Services; Distributed Computer Networks; File Systems; IPX/SPX (Internetwork Packet Exchange/Sequenced Packet Exchange); Multiprocessing; NCP (NetWare Core Protocol); NDS (Novell Directory Services); Network Concepts; Network Operating Systems; Novell; *and* Novell NetWare File System

Linktionary!—Tom Sheldon's Encyclopedia of Networking updates	http://www.linktionary.com/n/netware.html
Novell	http://www.novell.com/
Novell Users International	http://www.novell.com/nui/
Novell Resource List at Network Professionals Resource Center	http://www.inetassist.com/url15.htm
Yahoo! NetWare page	http://dir.yahoo.com/computers_and_internet/ communications_and_networking/netware/
About.com Novell NetWare networking page	http://compnetworking.miningco.com/compute/ hardware/compnetworking/msubnovell.htm
Google Web Directory for NetWare	http://directory.google.com/Top/Computers/ Software/Operating_Systems/Network/NetWare/
Novell NetWare links at Inter-Corporate Computer & Network Services	http://www.inter-corporate.com/kb/library/

Novell NetWare File System

The NetWare filing system consists of servers with storage systems that have one or more volumes of information. The first volume on a server is called SYS. Additional volumes can be assigned a name of choice, such as VOL1, VOL2, and so on. Each volume has its own directory structure.

The way you reference a server, its volumes, and the directories of a volume is illustrated next. For example, the following refers to a file called BUDGET.XLS in the BUDGDOCS directory on the APPS volume of the ACCTG server:

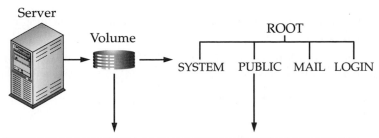

SERVERNAME/VOLNAME:DIRECTORY/SUBDIRECTORY

A NetWare volume is the highest level of storage in the NetWare filing system. It is a physical amount of hard disk storage space. You can expand a volume at any time by adding more physical disk space and making it a part of any existing volume. Volumes appear as objects in the NDS (Novell Directory Services) directory tree, so they are easy to locate by administrators and users from anywhere on the network. A NetWare 4.11 server supports up to 64 volumes.

The NetWare UFS (Universal File System) provides many performance-enhancing features as described here:

- **Elevator seeking**   Prioritizes incoming read requests according to how they can best be accessed by the read head in relation to its current location

- **File caching**   Minimizes the number of times the disk is accessed by holding commonly accessed information in memory

- **Background writes**   Handles disk writes separately from disk reads so that data is written to disk when disk requests from users have minimized

- **Overlapped seeks**   Improves read performance if two or more hard disks are connected to their own controller (disk channel) by allowing NetWare to access each controller simultaneously

- **Turbo FAT**   Indexes the file allocation tables of files over 2MB so that the locations of their segments are immediately available

- **File compression**   Increases disk space by up to 63 percent by compressing files as a background process

- **Block suballocation**   Maximizes disk space by allocating partial disk blocks to small files

NetWare also includes several important features that ensure the survivability and quick recovery of data on servers, as described here:

- **Read-after-write verification**   Verifies writes by reading every write after it is written.

- **Duplicate directories**   Provides a backup of the directory structure by duplicating it on disk.

- **Duplicate FAT**   Provides a backup of the file allocation table by duplicating it on disk.

- **Hot Fix**   Detects and corrects disk defects by automatically marking potentially bad sectors as unwritable.

- **TTS (Transaction Tracking System)**   Protects files from incomplete writes. If a record in a database is being altered and the server goes down, incomplete writes are backed out.

- **SFT (System Fault Tolerance)**   Provides redundancy in hardware by allowing administrators to duplicate disk controllers and mirror hard drives.

Related Entries   File Systems; NCP (NetWare Core Protocol); NDS (Novell Directory Services); Network Concepts; Network Operating Systems; Novell; Novell NetWare; *and* Rights and Permissions

Linktionary!—Tom Sheldon's Encyclopedia   http://www.linktionary.com/n/netware_fs.html
of Networking updates

Novell   http://www.novell.com/

NPN (New Public Network)

The "new public network" or "next generation network" as it is sometimes called, is the convergence of the PSTN (public switched telephone network) and the Internet (or at least Internet-based technologies) into a new network that is a packet-oriented, multiservice (voice, video, data) network. Its most defining feature is that it should provide the same level of guaranteed service for voice on a packet network that the PSTN provides on a circuit-switched network. The NPN is essentially the Internet with full support for voice and video and backward compatibility with the PSTN.

   This topic is covered in more detail at the Linktionary! Web site.

The development of this new network is being driven by a need to move beyond the centralized control of communication services that the carriers now hold. Deregulation is pushing the telecommunications industry to move to a model that is based on open market competition. In addition, customers are demanding new services, and competitive carriers are supplying them. Packet-switched networks are based on the concept of intelligent end devices that run any application the user chooses. This is counter to the PSTN model, in which the end devices (telephones) are dumb and the network is smart. Packet networks will eventually disrupt the 100-year-old phone system. In the meantime, the old and the new must coexist. One thing the telephone network has going for it is high availability. It is available 99.999 percent of the time, which translates to 5 minutes of downtime per year.

The NPN is a merging of the best features of the PSTN and Internet. It has the following characteristics:

- It is a converged public network made up of many providers using the distributed model of the Internet, but many of its features come from both the Internet and PSTN.

- The network is built on open standards and nonproprietary equipment that easily interconnects.

■ The new network is *distributed*, meaning that intelligence is not centralized in the network but moves out to smart edge devices (PCs, smart phones, PDAs, and so forth). New services are easy to create in the NPN because they are created at the edge (by simply installing an application) rather than in the network.

■ All forms of communication, including voice, video, data, and telecommunications are supported.

■ The circuit-oriented, TDM-based hierarchy built on the 64-Kbit/sec digitized voice call will eventually be replaced.

■ While the PSTN was optimized for constant bit rate, narrowband, connection-oriented traffic, the new network is built for variable bit rate, connectionless traffic.

■ Bandwidth is abundant, but the network contains enough intelligence to allocate bandwidth and provide guaranteed service. While the traditional Internet is a best-effort delivery service, the new network will provide guaranteed QoS via virtual circuits and traffic engineering.

■ The NPN provides fault tolerance and high-availability features of the circuit-oriented PSTN, features that are sorely lacking in the Internet. When was the last time your phone didn't work or your 911 call didn't go through?

■ The NPN will require intelligence that supports customer service demands, such as bandwidth on demand. This calls for network services such as policy management (to determine who can get the services), accounting, billing, and security.

The ability to create new services at end devices is perhaps the most important feature of the NPN. The telephone companies offer a relatively limited set of services, such as caller ID and call waiting. These services are configured within the carrier network itself. If you want a service, you request it from the network by pressing buttons on the keypad. For example, you press *69 to have the carrier redial the last person that called you. Think about it. With the PSTN, the 12-digit keypad is your user interface. On the Internet, a Web browser is your interface. Which would you rather have?

Related Entries   AT&T; Bandwidth Management; Call Center Operations; Circuit; Circuit-Switching Services; Communication Services and Providers; Data Communication Concepts; Distributed Computer Networks; DSL (Digital Subscriber Line); ISDN (Integrated Services Digital Network); Leased Line; Local Loop; MAN (Metropolitan Area Network); Multimedia; Network Access Services; Network Core Technologies; Optical Networks; Packets and Packet-Switching Networks; PINT (PSTN-Internet Interworking); QoS (Quality of Service); Service Providers and Carriers; Softswitch; SONET (Synchronous Optical Network); SPIRITS (Service in the PSTN/IN Requesting InTernet Service); SS7 (Signaling System 7); Telecommunications and Telephone Systems; Telecommunications Regulation; Voice/Data Networks; Voice over IP (VoIP); *and* WAN (Wide Area Network)

Linktionary!—Tom Sheldon's Encyclopedia of Networking updates	http://www.linktionary.com/n/npn.html
ITC (Internet & Telecoms Convergence Consortium)	http://itel.mit.edu/
The Softswitch Consortium	http://www.softswitch.org

Intelligent Network Forum	http://www.inf.org/
"Netheads versus Bellheads" by T. M. Denton Consultants (With François Ménard and David Isenberg)	http://www.tmdenton.com/netheads.htm
David Isenberg's Web site	http://www.isen.com
Converge Network Digest (a resource for what's new in network convergence).	http://www.convergedigest.com/
Hambrecht & Quist Connected article: "When Worlds Collide" (discusses next-generation networks)	http://connected.hamquist.com/worldsCollide.html
Web ProForum (see numerous papers on convergence, multiservice networks, and next-generation networks)	http://www.iec.org/tutorials/
Jeff Pulver's Pulver.com Web site (IP telephony, instant messaging, presence information, etc.)	http://www.pulver.com/
Jeff Pulver's Gateways (an online guide to PSTN/IP gateway resources and next-generation telcos)	http://www.pulver.com/gateway/
Lucent's Resource Library (many Telecom- and NPN-related papers).	http://www.lucent.com/ins/library/whitepap.html
IP Telephony Resources Page	http://www.computer.org/internet/telephony/index.htm

NREN (National Research and Education Network)

The NREN is the backbone data network of the Internet, administered by the NSF (National Science Foundation). It succeeded the NSFnet (National Science Foundation network) as the major Internet network for research and education in the United States as of the signing of the "High-Performance Computing Act of 1991," a bill sponsored by then Senator Al Gore. It calls for a high-capacity (gigabits per second) network and the coordination of networking efforts among federal organizations.

Related Entries   6Bone and IPv6; Abilene; Active Networks; GII (Global Information Infrastructure); Internet; Internet2; Internet Architecture and Backbone; Internet Organizations and Committees; Internet Standards; NIST (National Institute of Standards and Technology); NREN (National Research and Education Network); NSF (National Science Foundation) and NSFnet; Qbone; Standards Groups, Associations, and Organizations; STAR TAP; *and* vBNS (Very high speed Backbone Network Service)

Linktionary!—Tom Sheldon's Encyclopedia of Networking updates	http://www.linktionary.com/n/nren.html

NSA (National Security Agency)

The National Security Agency/Central Security Service is responsible for protecting U.S. communications, as well, as for producing foreign intelligence information. It a separately organized agency within the Department of Defense. Within NSA is INFOSEC, which provides security information about information systems. The NSA site is at http://www.nsa.gov.

NSF (National Science Foundation) and NSFnet

The NSF is a U.S. government agency that promotes and funds science research, scientific projects, and the infrastructure required for scientific research. In the mid-1980s, it became interested in the technology of the ARPANET and started funding the development of a backbone network that would link academic and research sites. Initially, these sites were its supercomputer centers. By the late 1980, it began building the NSFNET.

NSFNET was a testbed that led to the development of high-speed networking technologies. Later, NSF turned the NSFNET over to commercial use and the Internet expanded using the technology developed by the NSF project. This project is discussed under "Internet Architecture and Backbone."

Later, NSF funded the vBNS (very high speed Backbone Network Service), which was an experiment in much higher backbone speeds and improved router. Today, NSF supports the work of Internet2, a collaborative project sponsored by UCAID (University Corporation for Advanced Internet Development), a consortium of over 180 U.S. universities. Internet2 is testing even more advanced Internet technologies.

The following RFCs provide more information about the NSF's role in the early Internet. Also see "Routing on the Internet" for historical information about the development of routing techniques in the NSFNET.

- RFC 1074 (NSFNET backbone SPF-Based Interior Gateway Protocol, October 1988)
- RFC 1092 (EGP and Policy Based Routing in the new NSFNET Backbone, February 1989)
- RFC 1093 (NSFNET Routing Architecture, February 1989)
- RFC 1133 (Routing between the NSFNET and the DDN, 1989)
- RFC 1136 (Administrative Domains and Routing Domains: A Model for Routing in the Internet, December 1989)
- RFC 1222 (Advancing the NSFNET Routing Architecture, May 1991)
- RFC 1482 (Aggregation Support in the NSFNET Policy-Based Routing Database, June 1993)
- RFC 1930 (Guidelines for creation, selection, and registration of an Autonomous System, March 1996)

Related Entries   6Bone and IPv6; Abilene; Active Networks; GII (Global Information Infrastructure); Internet; Internet2; Internet Architecture and Backbone; Internet Organizations and Committees; Internet Standards; NIST (National Institute of Standards and Technology); NREN (National Research and Education Network); Qbone; Routing on the Internet; Standards Groups, Associations, and Organizations; STAR TAP; *and* vBNS (Very high speed Backbone Network Service)

Linktionary!—Tom Sheldon's Encyclopedia of Networking updates	http://www.linktionary.com/n/nfs.html
National Science Foundation	http://www.nsf.gov
The NSFNET Backbone Project	http://www.merit.edu/nsfnet/

See "Internet Architecture and Backbone" for more links.

NSP (Network Service Provider)

A network service provider is a carrier or other provider that provides services, primarily bandwidth and Internet exchange services, to local and regional ISPs (Internet service providers). See "Internet Architecture and Backbone" for more information.

NTFS (New Technology File System)

See Microsoft Windows File System.

NTP (Network Time Protocol)

NTP is an Internet protocol that devices can use to obtain the most accurate time possible via radio or atomic clocks at various locations on the Internet. The protocol can synchronize the time of a computer client or server to another server or reference time source. Time provided by NTP servers is typically accurate within milliseconds.

SNTP (Simple Network Time Protocol) is an adaptation of the Network Time Protocol (NTP), which is used to synchronize computer clocks in the Internet. SNTP can be used when the ultimate performance of the full NTP implementation described in RFC-1305 (Network Time Protocol Version 3, March 1992) is not needed or justified.

Refer to the following RFCs for more information:

- RFC 1128 (Measured Performance of the Network Time Protocol in the Internet system, October 1989)

- RFC 1129 (Internet Time Synchronization: The Network Time Protocol, October 1989)

- RFC 1165 (Network Time Protocol over the OSI Remote Operations Service, June 1990)

- RFC 1305 (Network Time Protocol Specification, Implementation, March 1992)

- RFC 2030 (Simple Network Time Protocol Version 4 for IPv4, IPv6 and OSI, October 1996)

Linktionary!—Tom Sheldon's Encyclopedia of Networking updates	http://www.linktionary.com/n/ntp.html
Time Synchronization Server	http://www.eecis.udel.edu/~ntp/

NUMA (Non-Uniform Memory Access)

See Multiprocessing.

OAG (Open Applications Group)

The Open Applications Group is a nonprofit consortium that promotes business software integration, especially in the area of ERP (enterprise resource planning) applications and XML integration. The Open Applications Group was originally comprised of eight ERP vendors, including American Software, CODA Financials, Dun&Bradstreet Software, Marcam, Oracle, PeopleSoft, SAP, and Software 2000. OAG consists of over 37 members including customer organizations, systems integrators, and middleware vendors, and as well as application software vendors.

In the mid-1990s, the OAG developed a model for business software component interoperability called OAGIS (Open Application Group Integration Specification). The model consists of an application architecture, business software component definitions, component integration scenario diagrams, detail definitions of the APIs necessary to integrate business software components, and a full data dictionary describing the individual elements of the APIs. Along with this model is a repeatable process that enables companies to design integrated business software components.

The OAG is dedicated to developing XML for electronic commerce and business applications. It publishes XML-based business information and has developed methods that help businesses quickly integrate XML into their business processes and supply chain functions. In particular, the OAG's work has made XML the standard for data description in ERP applications, which, in turn, has promoted standard definitions for business processes and better integration of supply chain applications and processes.

The OAG Web site is at http://www.openapplications.org/.

Related Entries   EDI (Electronic Data Interchange); Electronic Commerce; ERP (Enterprise Resource Planning); Metadata; Web Technologies and Concepts; Workflow Management, *and* XML (Extensible Markup Language)

OBI (Open Buying on the Internet)

OBI is a freely available design/framework for business-to-business commerce transactions on the Web. It was designed by American Express and SupplyWorks, Inc. OBI is designed to help implementers reduce the cost of doing purchase transactions on the Web and to stimulate Internet commerce. The goal is to reduce costs, improve the overall buy-pay process, and increase service levels to end users using Internet technology. Microsoft, Netscape, Oracle, Open Market, and a number of other companies back the specification. CommerceNet also plays a role in the OBI by managing the specifications.

OBI is meant to complement and not replace existing EDI infrastructures. According to the OBI Consortium, "OBI was created for the purchase of non-strategic, indirect materials by large, distributed requisitioner populations." The OBI Consortium sees EDI as technology and standards for simplifying the purchasing of direct, or "production," materials through tight integration with MRP (materials resource planning) systems.

Related Entries   Certificates and Certification Systems; EDI (Electronic Data Interchange); Electronic Commerce; IOTP (Internet Open Trading Protocol); *and* SET (Secure Electronic Transaction)

Linktionary!—Tom Sheldon's Encyclopedia of Networking updates	http://www.linktionary.com/o/obi.html
Open Buying on the Internet Consortium	http://www.openbuy.org
CommerceNet	http://www.commerce.net

Object Management Architecture

See OMA (Object Management Architecture).

Object Technologies

Object-oriented technology takes software development beyond procedural programming into a world of reusable programming that simplifies development of applications. Operating systems and applications are created as multiple modules that are linked together to create a functional program. Any module can be replaced or updated at any time without a need to update the entire operating system or program. Modules may also be located in different locations, thus supporting distributed computing and the Internet.

Object-oriented programming methods and the concept of reusable objects help ease the job of building applications. Component technology is about applying object technologies to building business applications. The same concept of reusability applies, but it applies to modular components that can be distributed across enterprise networks and the Internet. See "Distributed Object Computing" for information.

A Web browser can be thought of as a container into which users can add objects that provide additional functionality. For example, a user might connect with a Web server and download an object in the form of a Java applet or an ActiveX component that improves the feature set of the Web browser itself or provides some utility that runs inside the Web browser, such as a mortgage calculation program from a real estate Web site.

Dan Nessett of 3Com points out some interesting concepts related to object technologies in his excellent paper "Massively Distributed Systems" (see the link listed later). According to Nessett, two prevalent ways of organizing computations on distributed systems are as follows:

- Move processing logic to the data as is done with active networking and Java applets (i.e., objects move within the distributed system and carry both code and data).

- Move data to a system that will process the data as is done with NFS (Network File System), World Wide Web, FTP, and Gopher.

Nessett continues the discussion with the following: "If the object consists primarily of data, it will closely approximate moving data to the processing. If it consists primarily of code, it will closely approximate moving processing to the data."

Objects are like boxes with internal code or data that performs some action when the external interface is manipulated. Consider a list of files that appears within a scrollable window (in Microsoft Windows, for example). The window is actually an object with external controls. It contains a list of files, and you can click the button at the top of any column to sort the data on that column. The same "window" object is used throughout the operating system to display files and let users manipulate the display of files. Programmers can access the same "window" object to use in their own programs. There is no need to create new "window" objects as new programs are developed.

In terms of program development and object-oriented databases, an object is a self-contained package of data and/or procedures with external functions. In a database environment, an object may hold data such as names and addresses. In a programming environment, an object is more appropriately called a *module*, and it may hold processing logic (methods), rules, and procedures.

An analogy is an ATM (automated teller machine). You don't care about the internal workings of the machine. You use the external interface to request cash, account balances, and other features. An object's external interface can be compared to the buttons on the automated tellers. You can request a service from an object and it will provide that service; but, as a user, you never manipulate the object in any way that might change the way it provides services. In fact, objects only work with other objects by manipulating their external interfaces. They never access data inside another object directly.

A recent encounter with my electric toothbrush and shaver inspires another analogy. The little internal electric motors can be seen as objects. Externally, their high-speed back-and-forth motion is translated into a rotating brush or slicing blades, depending on the device. You don't care about the inside of the motor, only what it does. And the same motor can be used over again in different products.

Objects are like building blocks. They are reusable and may be combined to create complete programs. If a program needs updating, only the objects that need updating are replaced. Objects interact with one another by exchanging messages. An object acting as a client makes requests of an object that acts as a server. The objects may switch those roles at any time.

Objects are categorized into hierarchical *classes* that define different types of objects. Parent classes have characteristics that are passed down to subclasses of the object. This is called *class inheritance*. In a database, the class "people" has the subclasses of "male" and "female" (and hermaphrodite in some places). Each subclass has *generalized* features inherited from its parents, along with *specialized* features of its own. In a network environment, objects may be located on many different computers, and they talk to each other using network protocols.

An ORB (object request broker) is a message-passing middleware interface that helps objects locate one another and establish communications. For applications on different computers that need to work together, distributed object technologies provide a way to decouple applications from the underlying networks and systems.

An important concept with objects is that they more accurately represent the procedures and functions of a business. Object technology is also critical on the Web. It is the basis of component software, which makes wide-area distributed application deployment a reality. You may continue this topic by referring to "Distributed Object Computing," which discusses the importance of object-oriented technology in the network and Internet environment. Also see "Java," "COM (Component Object Model)," and "Microsoft.NET."

The World Wide Web is a massively distributed system full of objects. There are Web sites with documents that contain both objects and referrals to other objects. Dan Nessett, in the previously mentioned paper, talks about how the presentation of massively distributed objects to technically naïve users will require new interfaces. One example is to represent objects as virtual spaces. In this scheme, "a first-level object might be represented as a virtual world, its constituent objects as countries, then cities, streets, houses, rooms, and so on." Another way to think of this is a file system in which users navigate on the screen through a virtual university or library to get to the documents and objects they want.

Related Entries   ActiveX; API (Application Programming Interface); Application Server; Client/Server Computing; COM (Component Object Model); Compound Documents; CORBA (Common Object Request Broker Architecture); DBMS (Database Management System); Distributed Applications; Distributed Computer Networks; Distributed Object Computing; Interoperability; IPC (Interprocess Communication); Java; Metadata; Microsoft.NET; Middleware and Messaging; MOM (Message-Oriented Middleware); Multitiered Architectures; Named Pipes; OLE DB; OMA (Object Management Architecture); ORB (Object Request Broker); Pipes; RPC (Remote Procedure Call); SOAP (Simple Object Access Protocol); Sockets API; Transaction Processing; *and* Web Technologies and Concepts

Linktionary!—Tom Sheldon's Encyclopedia of Networking updates	http://www.linktionary.com/o/object.html
Terry Montlick's *interesting* object technology introduction	http://catalog.com/softinfo/objects.html
Bob Hathaway's object-orientation FAQ	http://www.cyberdyne-object-sys.com/oofaq2/
Ricardo Devis's object-oriented page	http://www.arrakis.es/~devis/oo.html
OMG (Object Management Group)	http://www.omg.org
SIGS Publications Online	http://www.sigs.com/
Object-oriented information sources	http://www.sente.ch/cetus/software.html
Jeff Sutherland's Object Technology Web site	http://jeffsutherland.com/
Object computing links at Washington University	http://www.cait.wustl.edu/infosys/infosys.html
White Paper: CORBA, COM, and Other Object Standards and Their Relevance to Development of Interoperable Systems	http://www2.dcnicn.com/cals/cals_97f/task07/html/Non-CDRL/whitepaper.html
Object Technology page by Kang Sung-IL	http://rtlab.kaist.ac.kr/~sikang/oo/index.html
"Massively Distributed Systems" by Dan Nessett of 3Com	http://www.3com.com/technology/tech_net/white_papers/503056.html

More links are under "Distributed Object Computing."

OC (Optical Carrier)

The existing method for carrying digitized voice signals over twisted copper wire is known as the NADH (North American Digital Hierarchy). This hierarchy defines levels of digital streams, starting with DS-0, which defines a single channel for carrying a digitized voice signal. DS-0 has a bit rate of 64 Kbits/sec. The next level up, DS-1, has a rate of 1.544 Mbits/sec and carries 24 DS-0 channels with some overhead. DS-3 consists of 28 DS-1 channels. See "NADH (North American Digital Hierarchy)."

STS (Synchronous Transport Signal) is a standard for defining high-capacity digital circuits. However, STS circuits are usually discussed as OC (optical carrier) circuits because the high data rates usually require fiber-optic cable. Table O-1 lists the STS hierarchy using the OC terminology. Keep in mind, however, that STS includes electric signals over copper cables, while the OC rates refer to optical signals over fiber-optic cable.

OCs are the digital hierarchies of the SONET standard, which defines a complete fiber-optic ring network built on the OC levels described next. SONET is a physical layer specification that defines dual-ring optical networks for metropolitan and long distance applications.

Note   *The letter "c" attached to the OC level indicates that the OC is not channelized (divided into multiplexed circuits), but that the entire bandwidth is used as a single channel. For example, OC-48c is a single 2.4-Gbit/sec channel.*

OC-768 at 40Gbits/sec is on the horizon for SONET systems. Transmitters that can handle the rate are just emerging, as well as new types of fiber (see "Fiber-Optic Cable"). The transmission rates will limit the distance of the systems, and they will initially be deployed in metropolitan area networks. However, some vendors have said that OC-192 is the end of the road for SONET due to emerging optical networks that employ multi-wavelength DWDM (dense wave division multiplexing). See "Network Core Technologies," "Optical Networks," and "WDM (Wavelength Division Multiplexing)."

STS/OC Level	Data Rate (Mbits/sec)	Number of DS0s	Number of DS1s	Number of DS3s
OC-1	51.84	672	28	1
OC-3	155.52	2,016	84	3
OC-6	311.04	4,032	168	6
OC-9	466.56	6,048	252	9
OC-12	622.08	8,064	336	12
OC-18	933.12	12,096	504	18
OC-24	1,244.16	16,128	672	24
OC-36	1,866.24	24,192	1,008	36
OC-48	2,488.32	32,256	1,344	48
OC-96	4,976.00	64,512	2,688	96
OC-192	9,952.00	129,024	5,376	192

Table O-1.   *OC (Optical Carrier) Levels*

Related Entries Cable and Wiring; Fiber-Optic Cable; Lambda Circuits; Multiplexing and Multiplexers; NADH (North American Digital Hierarchy); Network Core Technologies; Optical Networks; PON (Passive Optical Network); SONET (Synchronous Optical Network); Carriers; WAN (Wide Area Network); *and* WDM (Wavelength Division Multiplexing)

 Linktionary!—Tom Sheldon's Encyclopedia of   http://www.linktionary.com/o/oc.html
Networking updates

ODBC (Open Database Connectivity)

ODBC is a database connectivity architecture that provides a way for clients to access a variety of heterogeneous databases. The latest version, ODBC 3.0, is based on the CLI (Call-Level Interface) specifications from X/Open and ISO/IEC for database APIs. ODBC uses a single programming interface that is open and not tied to any vendor's database. Microsoft developed ODBC and has continued to develop it as a standard. See "OLE DB" for related information.

ODBC has the following features:

- It uses SQL (Structured Query Language) for operations that access a database.

- It contains a library of function calls for accessing DBMS (database management system) data. The function calls can be used to execute SQL statements.

- Clients do not need to know the location of a database, the type of database, or the communication method used to access it.

- ODBC applications have universal access to any database that has an ODBC driver written for it. These databases are called *data sources*.

- Data sources include everything from Oracle relational databases to Microsoft Excel spreadsheet data files.

- Because different DBMSs have widely different functions, the ODBC API was designed in a way that lets an application know what functions are available from a particular database's ODBC driver.

The ODBC environment is pictured in Figure O-1. It consists of applications that conform to ODBC and databases that have ODBC driver modules written for them.

The *application* provides an interface through which users can connect to a data source, make requests for data, and update data. The *driver manager* is the communication link between the application and the *drivers*. ODBC applications only communicate with the driver manager and not directly with drivers. The ODBC driver converts the call to a format that the *data source* can use. Once the data source processes the call, it returns the results to the ODBC driver and the ODBC driver forwards the results to the driver manager.

In the multitiered client/server model, the middle-tier server connects with back-end databases. The middle-tier server is responsible for running the different ODBC drivers that connect with back-end databases. The client only needs to run front-end applications, such as a Web browser, to connect with the back-end services. This is the Web model. See "Middleware and Messaging" for more information.

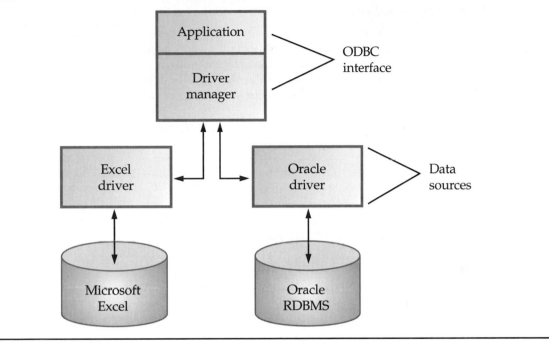

Figure O-1. *The ODBC client/server environment*

Related Entries   Client/Server Computing; COM (Component Object Model); Data Warehousing; DBMS (Database Management System); Distributed Applications; Distributed Computer Networks; Distributed Object Computing; DRDA (Distributed Relational Database Architecture); IBM Host Connectivity; Interoperability; Middleware and Messaging; Multitiered Architectures; Object Technologies; OLE DB; SQL (Structured Query Language); *and* Transaction Processing

Linktionary!—Tom Sheldon's Encyclopedia of Networking updates	http://www.linktionary.com/o/odbc.html
Microsoft universal data access Web site	http://www.microsoft.com/data/
Microsoft ODBC Web site	http://www.microsoft.com/data/odbc/
Roth Consulting's Official Win32::ODBC home page	http://www.roth.net/perl/odbc/
OpenLink Software	http://www.openlinksw.com/
OpenAccess	http://www.atinet.com/
Simba Technologies	http://www.simba.com

ODI (Open Data-Link Interface)

NetWare uses a protocol-independent structure known as ODI to provide simultaneous support for different protocols on the network and the ability to install and support multiple NICs (network interface cards) in the same computer. The ODI interface resides in the data link layer (relative to the OSI protocol stack). ODI standardizes the development of network interface card drivers so that vendors don't need to write separate drivers to work with each of the different network protocols.

ODI may be implemented on servers or workstations. It allows computers to connect to the network with different communication protocols such as TCP/IP, IPX, AppleTalk, or others.

Related Entries   LAN (Local Area Network); MAC (Media Access Control); NDIS (Network Driver Interface Specification; Network Concepts; Network Operating System; NIC (Network Interface Card); *and* Novell NetWare

ODMA (Open Document Management API)

See Document Management.

OFDM (Orthogonal Frequency Division Multiplexing)

OFDM is a multicarrier transmission technique that has been around for years, but only recently became popular due to the development of digital signal processors (DSPs) that can handle its heavy digital processing requirements. OFDM is being implemented in broadband wireless access systems as a way to overcome wireless transmission problems and to improve bandwidth. OFDM is also used in wireless LANs as specified by the IEEE 802.11a and the ETSI HiperLAN/ 2 standards. It is also used for wireless digital radio and TV transmissions, particularly in Europe.

With OFDM, a high-speed digital message is divided into a large number of separate carrier waves. The receiving system reconstructs the message from the separate carriers. The technique is a coding or transport scheme, rather than a modulation scheme. It could be compared to the way that CDMA (code division multiple access) is a coding scheme. OFDM is a multicarrier modulation (MCM) scheme in which many parallel data streams are transmitted at the same time over a channel, with each transmitting only a small part of the total data rate. DMT (discrete multitone) is a similar system used in copper-based DSL (Digital Subscriber Line) systems to overcome transmission problems.

OFDM could be compared to sending a message across a parallel data cable with the message split across the multiple transmit wires in the cable. A single carrier system is like sending the message across a serial cable that has one transmit wire. However, OFDM is usually done in a wireless environment in which individual carriers (frequency bands) carry the individual parallel data streams. According to Wi-LAN, OFDM was "reborn" with the introduction of processors that were capable of generating the different individual carriers.

OFDM is important in broadband wireless systems such as MMDS (Multichannel Multipoint Distribution Services). Signals in these systems are prone to multipath, which occurs when radio signals are reflected off of objects such as buildings and trees. The reflections arrive slightly later than the original signal, corrupting it. Equalizers have been used to cancel out reflected signals, but they are often inadequate.

OFDM avoids multipath problems by sending message bits with a slight pause between each transmission. Imagine yelling "hello!" into a canyon. If you immediately yell a second time, the echo from the first hello mixes with the second hello. If this were data, the receiver might have trouble reading an accurate signal. However, if you wait for the first echo to dissipate, you can yell "hello" again with little echo mixing. Think of an OFDM transmitter pausing momentarily to allow reflections to dissipate before sending the next set of bits. According to Wi-LAN, the data rate must be slowed down just enough so that any reflected (and delayed) bits are late by less than one bit time. Obviously, pausing a transmission reduces data rates, but OFDM is transmitting across multiple channels, so it actually improves the data rate. One can imagine a multilane bridge where cars travel slowly but in parallel across multiple lanes.

An important concept is that the individual carriers are placed very close to one another, unlike FDM (frequency division multiplexing), which inserts guard bands to separate channels. By allowing overlap, carriers can be squeezed closer together, and thus bandwidth is used more efficiently. At the same time, the modulated signals are kept *orthogonal* so they do not interfere with one another. Any digital modulation technique can be applied to the carriers. Just before transmission, all the modulated carriers are added together and then sent across the available spectrum. At the receiver, the individual carriers are first separated, and then demodulated.

Wi-LAN holds patents on W-OFDM (Wideband OFDM), which sets spacing between carriers so that any frequency errors between transmitter and receiver are minimized. Wi-LAN heads up the OFDM Forum. Cisco has developed a similar scheme called VOFDM (Vector OFDM), which it pushes in its Broadband Wireless Internet Forum (BWIF).

OFDM is competing with CDMA. While it has more robust transmission capabilities, it is currently more expensive to implement. Other techniques, such as UWB (Ultra WideBand) and free space optical networking (i.e., Terabeam's trademark Fiberless Optical), are also available.

Related Entries   CDMA (Code Division Multiple Access); DSL (Digital Subscriber Line); Electromagnetic Spectrum; Home Networking; IEEE 802 Standards; LMDS (Local Multipoint Distribution Service); MAN (Metropolitan Area Network); Microwave Communications; MMDS (Multichannel Multipoint Distribution Services); Modulation Techniques; Multiplexing and Multiplexers; Residential Broadband; Spread Spectrum Signaling; UWB (Ultra Wideband); Wireless Broadband Access Technologies; Wireless Communications; Wireless LANs; Wireless Local Loop; *and* Wireless Mobile Communications

Linktionary!—Tom Sheldon's Encyclopedia of Networking updates	http://www.linktionary.com/o/ofdm.html
Wi-LAN (see white papers about OFDM)	http://www.wi-lan.com/
OFDM Forum	http://www.ofdm-forum.com
BWIF (Broadband Wireless Internet Forum).	http://www.bwif.org/
Cisco Fixed Wireless Web page	http://www.cisco.com/warp/public/779/servpro/solutions/wireless/
Cisco paper: "Overcoming Multipath in Non-Line-of-Sight High-Speed Microwave Communication Links"	http://www.cisco.com/warp/public/cc/pd/witc/wt2700/mulpt_wp.htm

Paper on multicarrier modulation by Jean-Paul Linnartz	http://diva.eecs.berkeley.edu/~linnartz/issue.html
OFDM Modulation tutorial (interactive!!)	http://www.ee.ed.ac.uk/~acmc/OFDMTut.html
OFDM by László Házy	http://www.sce.carleton.ca/~hazyl/OFDM/
OFDM Receivers for Broadband-Transmission by Michael Speth	http://www.ert.rwth-aachen.de/Projekte/Theo/OFDM/www_ofdm.html

OIM (Open Information Model)

According to the Meta Data Coalition, the OIM is a set of metadata specifications to facilitate sharing and reuse in the application development and data warehousing domains. OIM is described in UML (Unified Modeling Language) and is organized in easy-to-use and easy-to-extend subject areas. The data model is based on industry standards such as UML, XML, and SQL.

UML is a language for modeling information systems and software artifacts. The UML can be used to visualize, specify, construct, and document knowledge about software-intensive systems and their purpose at an abstract level. The goals of the UML are to unify the most prominent modeling methodologies into a ready-to-use expressive modeling language that is simple and extensible.

Refer to the following Web sites for more information.

Related Entries   Metadata; UML (Unified Modeling Language); and Repository; XML (Extensible Markup Language)

Linktionary!—Tom Sheldon's Encyclopedia of Networking updates	http://www.linktionary.com/o/oim.html
Microsoft Repository and OIM (Open Information Model) information	http://msdn.microsoft.com/repository/default.asp
Meta Data Coalition	http://www.mdcinfo.com/
Object Management Group (see UML information)	http://www.omg.org/

OLAP (Online Analytical Processing)

OLAP defines a class of software that analyzes data (usually historical data) to find patterns and trends. A data analyst uses OLAP software to view data in a multidimensional format, rather than the two-dimensional row and column format. In the multidimensional format, the intersection of relevant data becomes much more apparent, so data is easier to group and summarize. The analyst then creates reports that are used for critical business decisions. OLAP is sometimes referred to as *data mining*.

Data comes from data warehouses and OLTP (online transaction processing) database systems. A data warehouse may contain legacy data, while an OLTP system is the actual day-to-day business system that collects and processes business data. In contrast, OLAP systems are used to read the data warehouse information and make sense of it. The data analyst may spend long periods sifting through data, or may work with summarizations of that data that are more likely to reveal trends and hidden information.

Related Entries   Data Mart; Data Warehousing; DB2, IBM; DBMS (Database Management System); Electronic Commerce; ERP (Enterprise Resource Planning); IBM Host Connectivity; Metadata; OLE DB; Portal; Repository; SQL (Structured Query Language); *and* Transaction Processing

Linktionary!—Tom Sheldon's Encyclopedia of Networking updates	http://www.linktionary.com/o/olap.html
OLAP Council (white papers and links)	http://www.olapcouncil.org
The Data Warehousing Institute	http://www.dw-institute.com
The International Data Warehousing Association	http://www.idwa.org
OLAP links	http://www.pvv.ntnu.no/~akselh/olap.html l
Online bibliography by Joachim Hammer	http://www.cise.ufl.edu/~jhammer/online-bib.htm
"On-Line Analytical Processing" by Kevin Rasmussen and Yesim Tabanoglu	http://misdb.bpa.arizona.edu/~mis696g/Reports/olap/olappape.htm
Executive Information Systems (numerous white papers on OLAP and related topics)	http://www.dkms.com/

OLE (Object Linking and Embedding)

OLE is a Microsoft Windows feature that provides a way to integrate objects from diverse applications. An *object* is a block of information from a spreadsheet, a graphic from a drawing program, or an audio clip from a sound program. It may also be an executable program.

This topic is covered at http://www.linktionary.com/o/ole.html.

OLE DB

OLE DB is a set of Microsoft data access interfaces that provides universal data integration over an enterprise's network regardless of the data type. OLE DB is designed for nonrelational as well as relational information sources on disparate platforms. These include electronic mail and file system stores, text data, graphical data, and custom business objects.

OLE DB allows data sources to share their data through common interfaces without having to implement database functionality that is not native to the data store. OLE DB is a freely published specification designed with industry-wide participation. It is part of Microsoft's UDA (Universal Data Access) strategy, which consists of three core technologies: OLE DB, ActiveX Data Objects (ADO), and Open Database Connectivity (ODBC).

While Microsoft's ODBC (Open Database Connectivity) will continue to provide a unified way to access relational data, OLE DB is meant for database products that are assembled with component technology. OLE DB provides data access to and manipulation of both SQL (Structured Query Language) and non-SQL data sources. OLE DB Provider for ODBC uses existing ODBC drivers to access relational data. This provides consistency and interoperability in an enterprise's network, from the mainframe to the desktop. It also works over the Internet.

OLE DB is the fundamental COM (Component Object Model) building block for storing and retrieving records, and unifies Microsoft's strategy for database connectivity. It is used throughout Microsoft's line of applications and data stores. For example, Microsoft recently released an OLE DB for Data Mining specification, which includes support for a markup language called PMML (Predictive Model Markup Language). PMML is a standard defined by the Data Mining Group.

OLE DB is based on the concept of *data consumers* and *data providers*. A client such as a user with a Web browser is the typical consumer. According to Microsoft, "a provider is a set of COM components that contain a series of interfaces. Because these are standard interfaces, any OLE DB consumer can access data from any provider. Since providers are COM objects, consumers can access them in any language (C++, Basic, Java, etc)."

Related Entries   Client/Server Computing; COM (Component Object Model); Data Mining; Data Warehousing; DBMS (Database Management System); Distributed Applications; Distributed Computer Networks; Distributed Object Computing; DRDA (Distributed Relational Database Architecture); IBM Host Connectivity; Interoperability; Microsoft.NET; Microsoft Windows; Middleware and Messaging; Multitiered Architectures; Object Technologies; ODBC (Open Database Connectivity); OLAP (Online Analytical Processing); OLE (Object Linking and Embedding); SOAP (Simple Object Access Protocol); SQL (Structured Query Language); *and* Transaction Processing

Linktionary!—Tom Sheldon's Encyclopedia of Networking updates	http://www.linktionary.com/o/oledb.html
Microsoft OLE DB Web site	http://www.microsoft.com/data/oledb/
Microsoft universal data access Web site	http://www.microsoft.com/data/
OLE DB Resource Center	http://www.oledb.com/
OLE DB Web links	http://www.oledb.com/new/links.html
The Data Mining Group	http://www.dmg.org/

OLTP (Online Transaction Processing)

See Transaction Processing.

OMA (Object Management Architecture)

OMA is an architecture developed by the OMG (Object Management Group) that provides an industry standard for developing object-oriented applications to run on distributed networks. The goal of the OMG is to provide a common architectural framework for object-oriented applications based on widely available interface specifications. See "OMG (Object Management Group)."

The OMA reference model identifies and characterizes components, interfaces, and protocols that comprise the OMA. It consists of components that are grouped into application-oriented interfaces, industry-specific vertical applications, object services, and ORBs (object request brokers). The ORB defined by the OMG is known more commonly as CORBA (Common Object Request Broker Architecture).

Refer to "CORBA (Common Object Request Broker Architecture)" for more information.

OMG (Object Management Group)

OMG is an organization that represents over 700 software vendors, software developers, and end users. OMG describes its mission as developing "The Architecture for a Connected World." It was established in 1989 to promote object technologies on distributed computing systems. To this end, it has developed a common architectural framework for object-oriented applications based on an open and widely available interface specification called OMA (Object Management Architecture).

Refer to "CORBA (Common Object Request Broker Architecture)" for more information.

 OMG (Object Management Group)   http://www.omg.org

One-Time Password Authentication

A basic authentication scheme is for a server to request a password from the client. The client types the password and sends it over the wire to the server. This technique is vulnerable to eavesdroppers who may be monitoring the line with sniffers and network analyzers. Captured information can be used by a hacker in what is called a "replay attack" to illegally log on to a system. Even an encrypted password can be used in this manner.

A challenge/response is a security mechanism for verifying the identity of a user or system without the need to send the actual password across the wire. The server sends a challenge, which is a string of alpha or numeric characters, to a client. This client then combines the string with its password and, from this, a new password is generated. The new password is sent to the server. If the server can generate the same password from the challenge it sent the client and the client's password, then the client must be authentic. See "CHAP (Challenge Handshake Authentication Protocol)."

An OTP (one-time password) system generates a series of passwords that are used to log on to a specific system. Once one of the passwords is used, it cannot be used again. The logon system will always expect a new one-time password at the next logon. This is done by decrementing a sequence number. Therefore, the possibility of replay attacks is eliminated.

The series of passwords is created by the client, which combines a *seed* value with a secret password that only the client knows. This combination is then run through either the MD4 or MD5 hash functions repeatedly to generate the sequence of passwords.

Smart cards and token-based authentication methods use one time passwords. The IETF has developed an OTP that is based on the earlier Bellcore S/KEY one-time password system. A number of Internet RFCs discuss one-time passwords. These include RFC 1760 (The S/KEY One-Time Password System, February 1995), RFC 2243 (OTP Extended Responses, November 1997), RFC 2289 (A One-Time Password System, February 1998), and RFC 2444 (The One-Time-Password SASL Mechanism, October 1998). Also see RFC 1511 (Common Authentication Technology Overview, September 1993), RFC 1704 (On Internet Authentication, October 1994), and RFC 2401 (Security Architecture for the Internet Protocol, November 1998).

Related Entries   Access Control; Authentication and Authorization; Biometric Access Devices; CHAP (Challenge Handshake Authentication Protocol); Cryptography; Digital Signatures; DSS (Digital Signature Standard); EAP (Extensible Authentication Protocol); FORTEZZA; Hash Functions; Kerberos

O

Authentication Protocol; Logons and Logon Accounts; Passwords; Public-Key Cryptography; Secret-Key Cryptography; Security; Smart Cards; *and* Token-Based Authentication

Linktionary!—Tom Sheldon's Encyclopedia of Networking updates	http://www.linktionary.com/o/one_time_password.html
IETF Working Group: One Time Password Authentication (otp)	http://www.ietf.org/html.charters/otp-charter.html
The Java OTP Calculator by Harry Mantakos	http://www.cs.umd.edu/~harry/jotp/
S/KEY information and programs	http://math.lanl.gov/~aric/Skey/

One-Way Hash Functions

There are cryptographic processes that can produce unique "fingerprints" of messages that prove to the receiving party that the messages have not been altered. Some part of the message, such as the header text, is run through a one-way hashing function that produces an output that serves as a unique identification for the message. The output is called a *message digest*. When a person receives such a message, they can run a similar hash function to create a message digest that should exactly match the digest sent with the message. If the digests do not match, the message should be considered invalid since any alteration will change the results of the hash and produce a different message digest.

This topic is discussed further under "Hash Functions."

Related Entries   Cryptography; Digital Signatures; DSS (Digital Signature Standard); Hash Functions; One-Time Password Authentication; Security; *and* Token-Based Authentication

OpenDoc

OpenDoc was a compound document standard similar to Microsoft's OLE (Object Linking and Embedding). It was developed by Apple, Borland, IBM, and other companies. Apple was the main supporter of the standard. In 1997, Component Integration Labs, a developer of OpenDoc standards, announced that it was closing its site and that it accepted the strength of the component ideas within JavaBeans. At the same time, a number of other companies, such as IBM, decided to use JavaBeans instead of OpenDoc as well. See "Java."

Open Group

The Open Group is an international consortium of vendors, government agencies, and educational institutions that develops standards for open systems. It was formed in 1996 as the holding company for OSF (Open Software Foundation) and X/Open Company, Ltd. Under the Open Group umbrella, the two organizations work together to deliver technology innovations and widespread adoption of open systems specifications.

The Open Group is involved in testing and certification of products to assure that they conform to specification. Conforming products receive the Open Brand mark to signify that they fulfill all the criteria of open computing.

TOGAF (The Open Group Architectural Framework) is an architectural framework that provides a tool for developing a broad range of different IT architectures. TOGAF enables IT staff to design, evaluate, and build the right architecture for an organization. TOGAF includes a foundation architecture of generic services and functions, and a development model that provides a road map for developing a custom architecture. TOGAF is built around the SIB (standards information base), which is a collection of National and International Standards, certain proprietary standards, and Open Group technical standards that have been scrutinized by and adopted by the Open Group. A listing is located at http://www.opengroup.org/sib.htm.

Related Entries   CDE (Common Desktop Environment); DCE (Distributed Computing Environment); Interoperability; ISO (International Organization for Standardization); Motif; Open Systems; OSI (Open Systems Interconnection) Model; UNIX; *and* X Window

 The Open Group   http://www.opengroup.org

Open Source Software

UNIX and Linux are the best examples of open source software, with Linux being the most successful in terms of community involvement. Linux is an operating system in which the source code is freely available and where development is done for the community of users. See "Linux."

According to "The Open Source Definition" at Opensource.org, open source software may be freely distributed and must comply with the following criteria:

- The license should not prevent some party from selling the software as part of a bundle of software from different sources. No royalties need be paid.

- Source code must be included.

- License must allow modifications and derived works.

- An author's original code can be protected by allowing patch files that modify the program at build time.

- The license must not discriminate against any person or group of persons.

- The rights attached to the program must apply to all to whom the program is redistributed without the need for additional licenses.

- The rights attached to the program must not depend on the program's being part of a particular software distribution.

- The license must not place restrictions on other software that is distributed along with the licensed software.

 Linktionary!—Tom Sheldon's Encyclopedia of   http://www.linktionary.com/o/opensource.html
Networking updates

"Open Source Business Model" by Selena Sol   http://www.wdvl.com/Software/Open/Source/
business_model.html

Open source information at Web Developer's   http://www.stars.com/Software/Open/
Virtual Library

Opensource.org	http://www.opensource.org/
Brainfood.com free software solutions	http://www.brainfood.com/
Free Software Foundation	http://www.fsf.org/fsf/

See "Linux" for additional links related to free software.

Open Systems

"Open systems" loosely defines computer architectures, computer systems, computer software, and communication systems in which the specifications are published and available to everyone. An open system encourages the development of compatible vendor products. Customers benefit from open systems because they can choose from a wide variety of products that work with the system and, most important, are easily interconnected with other vendors' products. An open environment provides standard communication facilities and protocols, or provides a way to use a variety of protocols.

Open systems are defined by vendors, consortiums of vendors, government bodies, and worldwide standards organizations. Typically, the sponsoring vendor, consortium, or standards organization controls the specifications, but works with other vendors and users at public meetings to define the specifications. Recent trends have moved away from striving for complete openness and more toward acceptance of in-place standards. For example, TCP/IP has proved more popular than the OSI protocols due to the popularity of the Internet and other factors.

A number of organizations are involved in the development of open standards, including the IEEE (Institute of Electrical and Electronic Engineers), the International Standards Organization, The Open Group, the OMG (Object Management Group), and a number of Internet organizations described under "Internet Organizations and Committees."

The OSI protocols have served as the model for open systems design for the last decade, although TCP/IP and Internet protocols now dominate. Interoperability has been achieved through Web technologies, middleware, ORBs (object request brokers), and other technologies. Refer to "Interoperability" for more information.

Related Entries   CDE (Common Desktop Environment); DCE (Distributed Computing Environment); Interoperability; ISO (International Organization for Standardization); Java; Middleware and Messaging; Motif; Open Group; Open Systems; OSI (Open Systems Interconnection) Model; and Web Technology and Concepts

Open Transport Protocol

See Apple Open Transport Protocol.

OpenView Management System

OpenView is a family of network management products designed by Hewlett-Packard. Both OpenView and Sun Microsystems' SunNet Manager use a platform architecture approach in which a platform is designed that handles all the core functions required for a network management system. These functions include communication protocol interfaces, data definitions, and other management features. Other products designed by the platform vendor or other vendors then plug into or interface with the platform and gain all its built-in functions, such as access to a multiprotocol network, multivendor systems, and data management schemes.

Related Entry   Network Management

Linktionary!—Tom Sheldon's Encyclopedia of Networking updates	http://www.linktionary.com/n/network_management.html
Hewlett-Packard OpenView page	http://www.hp.com/openview/
OpenView Forum	http://www.ovforum.org/

OpenVMS

OpenVMS is a DEC (now Compaq) multiuser operating system that supports Digital's VAX and Alpha series computers. It is an open software environment that supports open standards such as OSF/Motif, POSIX, XPG3, and the OSF DCE (Distributed Computing Environment). It also includes networking support, distributed computing support, and multiprocessing.

Compaq's OpenVMS Web page   http://www.openvms.compaq.com/

Operating Systems

See Network Operating Systems.

OPSEC (Open Platform for Security)

OPSEC is a security integration platform that lets network administrators manage all aspects of security in an open extensible environment. OPSEC was originally created by Check Point Software, but has since become an industry-wide standard security framework. Over 150 partners offer OPSEC-compliant products.

OPSEC offers a complete set of interoperable security components to meet enterprise security requirements. A software development kit from Check Point is used to integrate security components with Check Point's FireWall-1/VPN-1. Any product that adheres to the OPSEC specification may be integrated.

The following security products and standards are integral parts of the OPSEC framework:

- **RADIUS (Remote Authentication Dial-In User Service)**   Dial-up authentication services. FireWall-1 and other access control devices can check with RADIUS servers before allowing access to a network or system.

- **VPN (Virtual Private Network)**   Check Point's VPN module supports tunnels over the Internet or intranets. IP packets are encrypted with a variety of algorithms. IPSec (IP Security) is also supported.

- **X.509 Certificates**   OPSEC supports the X.509 standard, which defines certificate format and management. X.509 certificates hold public keys and provide authentication for those keys by way of being signed by a certificate authority.

- **SNMP (Simple Network Management Protocol)**   OPSEC interoperates with SNMP, allowing security components to exchange messages with SNMP-compliant management systems such as HP OpenView, Sun Solstice; and IBM TME.

- **LDAP (Lightweight Directory Access Protocol)**   LDAP is a directory service that provides a global place to store and retrieve data such as user records and X.509 certificates.

The OPSEC Alliance is dedicated to guaranteeing interoperability at the policy level among security applications. The alliance certifies products and OPSEC compliance so customers can be assured of product integration.

Related Entries   CDSA (Common Data Security Architecture); Cryptography; Digital Signatures; Firewall; Hacking and Hackers; IPSec (IP Security); LDAP (Lightweight Directory Access Protocol); RADIUS (Remote Authentication Dial-In User Service); S/WAN (Secure WAN); Security; Security Auditing; SNMP (Simple Network Management Protocol); Trust Relationships and Trust Management; Tunnels; VPN (Virtual Private Network); X.509 Certificates

Linktionary!—Tom Sheldon's Encyclopedia of Networking updates	http://www.linktionary.com/o/opsec.html
OPSEC.com	http://www.opsec.com/
OPSEC Alliance	http://www.checkpoint.com/opsec
Check Point Software Technologies	http://www.checkpoint.com/

Optical Carrier Standards

See OC (Optical Carrier).

Optical Libraries

Optical disk library systems are designed to bring data normally stored on microfiche or paper to an online device where it is quickly accessible by network users. An optical disk library can also supplement magnetic tape backup systems or serve as an intermediate storage device for data that is "migrating" to magnetic tape in an *HMS (hierarchical management system)*.

In an HMS system, little-used files or files that have been marked for migration are moved from magnetic disk to optical disk, where they remain available to users. In this scheme, the optical disk is called *near-line storage*, as shown in Figure O-2. Eventually, they are moved to magnetic tape for archiving purposes. While magnetic tape offers a convenient, removable, and economical storage media, its sequential access method makes it unsuitable for online data retrieval.

Hierarchical systems will move files on optical disk to magnetic disk when requested by a user. Users are often unaware that the files are from an optical disk, except for a slight delay in accessing the files while they are moved from near-line to online storage. A hierarchical management system keeps a copy of the directory for near-line files available online to users.

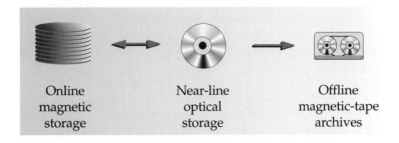

Figure O-2.   *Optical disk libraries*

This topic is covered further under "Storage Management Systems."

Linktionary!—Tom Sheldon's   http://www.linktionary.com/s/storage_management.html
Encyclopedia of Networking updates

Brian A. Berg's Storage Cornucopia page   http://www.bswd.com/cornucop.htm

Optical Networks

An optical network is a network in which the physical layer technology is fiber-optic cable. Cable trunks are interconnected with *optical cross-connects (OXCs)*, and signals are added and dropped at *optical add/drop multiplexers (OADMs)*. The holy grail is an *all-optical network*. In this scheme, an optical wavelength (which acts like a data circuit) stays in the optical realm from end to end.

In contrast, most optical networks have implemented OEO (optical-electrical-optical) switches, which convert optical signals to electrical signals for processing, and then back again to optical signals for the next leg of the trip. The optical-to-electrical conversion adds delay and introduces possible errors as the signals are converted, moved up the protocol stack, and processed by software or firmware. The all-optical network avoids this process. At this writing, components that make the all-optical network a reality are emerging. These are discussed next.

Early optical networks transmitted one signal over a fiber strand. With WDM (wavelength division multiplexing), multiple infrared wavelength signals (called *lambdas*) may be transmitted over a single fiber strand. Today, precision lasers and optical amplifiers allow hundreds and potentially thousands of signals to be transmitted across a single fiber over distances that span continents. These systems are called DWDM (dense wavelength division multiplexing) systems.

The telephone carriers were the first to take advantage of optical networking gear. They built fiber-optic trunks in the 1980s, but by the 1990s, the SONET/SDH optical networking standards were in place and allowed the telephone companies to build global optical networks that supported the existing time division multiplexing methods used by the telephone system. SONET/SDH networks are long spans of fiber constructed as resilient rings in metropolitan, regional, and national networks. As WDM technologies developed, SONET capacity was increased by upgrading to equipment that allows multiple wavelengths per fiber. In addition, WDM systems were used to build high-capacity, long-haul, point-to-point trunks to interconnect SONET networks. These networks had to expand to accommodate not only voice traffic but also the boom in data traffic. See "Network Core Technologies" and "SONET (Synchronous Optical Network)" for more information.

The basic architecture of the Internet is a mesh topology that supports packet switching. The carrier's SONET networks are TDM networks designed for circuit-oriented voice calls. While SONET easily carries Internet traffic, these networks cannot scale to match the Internet's exploding bandwidth requirements. Today, the Internet runs over many high-speed optical backbones designed specifically for Internet traffic. Many of the backbones are built with DWDM trunks.

The traditional carrier networks are built with four layers of support, as shown on the left in the following illustration. In this model, IP rides on top of ATM, which provides QoS, and SONET, which provides multiplexing and fault tolerance. DWDM may be used at the physical layer, which provides large capacity. The evolution of the carrier networks to an IP over optical network is illustrated on the right. First, ATM is replaced with MPLS-enabled routers, which set up optical paths across existing SONET networks. These networks already exist. Finally, SONET is eliminated and IP is delivered directly across optical wavelength circuits that are controlled by a version of MPLS that supports point-and-click provisioning of lambdas across the core optical transport network.

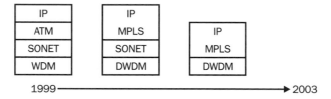

A typical all-optical network is pictured in Figure O-3. Besides the fiber cable and lasers, the main components of an optical network are the OXCs and the OADMs. An OXC is a photonic switch that has a large number of full-duplex ports, each of which can connect to any other port. The OADM extracts wavelength signals from a cable and reinserts new signals on available wavelengths. Note that each fiber link transports multiple lambda circuits, which follow what is called an "optical channel trail," "lightpath," or "wavelength circuit." Some of these circuits "drop out" at OXCs and continue on other fibers. Others drop out at OADMs, where an optical-to-electrical conversion takes place and packets (or cells or TDM) are then forwarded in the electrical domain via routers or switches. In the figure, two separate circuits in different parts of the network are both using lambda 3. This illustrates how the same wavelengths may be reused on different parts of the network.

An important point is that all-optical devices cannot examine packets and make routing decisions. Packets must first be converted to the electrical domain so the header bits can be processed by semiconductor devices. Once a routing decision is made, the packets can be forwarded again in the optical domain. This is the way that current IP/optical networks work; but the goal is to eventually perform optical packet switching, although that is probably a few years away. A temporary solution is *burst multiplexing*. It brings together multiple IP packets, assembled at an edge device, and transfers them as a burst through a core optical transport

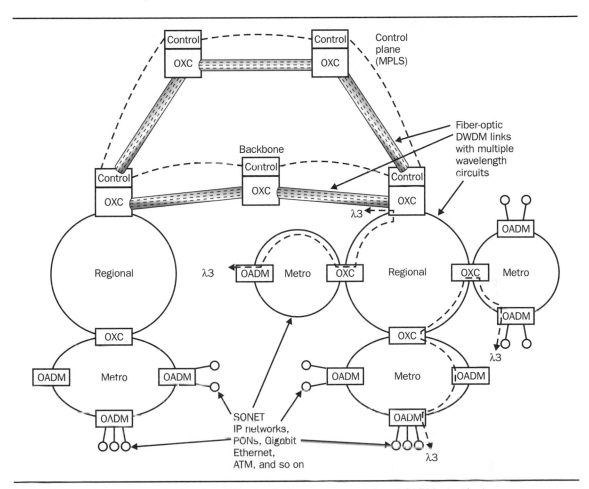

Figure O-3.   *Optical network showing OXCs (optical cross-connects) and OADMs (optical add/drop multiplexers)*

network on an express basis. The header information is carried in a separate wavelength that guides the packet bursts through the network. Only the header information must be processed in the electrical domain while the data burst travels in the optical domain. This reduces the processing loads in the electrical domain.

Most optical networks are long-haul carrier and service provider networks, but many IP-oriented networks are being built in the metropolitan areas. The optical network edge keeps moving closer to end users. The edge consists of gigabit and terabit routers made by Juniper, Sycamore, Cisco, and others. They switch packets in the electrical domain and aggregate large amounts of traffic for delivery across optical wavelength circuits. These routers are located at Internet exchanges and Internet data centers. Feeding the data centers are a variety of regional, metropolitan, campus, and business networks. These feeder networks are SONET, cable networks, PONs (passive optical networks), and wireless networks.

Optical Network Components

The basic components of a WDM trunk are pictured in the following illustration. An electrical- to-optical converter converts electrical signals to optical signals, and a laser injects those signals into the multiplexer. The multiplexer directs multiple light signals into a single fiber. A demultiplexer at the opposite end separates each wavelength and sends it to an optical-to-electric converter. The precision of the multiplexer determines how many wavelengths can be injected into the fiber. The Avanex PowerMux is capable of processing any number of optical signals at any channel spacing and at any bit rate. By cascading multiple PowerMuxes in a tree topology, the company has put up to 800 channels on a single fiber.

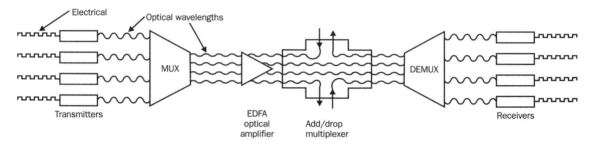

For long-haul trunks, amplifiers are required at intervals of 40 km to 80 km, depending on the cable and amplifier type. Amplifiers are typically EDFAs, which amplify optical signals in the optical domain (i.e., there is no need to convert to electrical to regenerate the signals, as was the case in older systems). EDFAs may be combined with Raman amplifiers to extend distance. See "Fiber Optic Cable" for more information.

One of the advantages of DWDM systems is the ability to easily tap any of the individual wavelengths without disturbing the others. A typical optical network will have multiple add-drop points along the span. An OADM adds and drops whole wavelengths at a time. When a wavelength is dropped, all the information it carries is forwarded to routers or switches at the drop location. The wavelength can then be reused for traffic going to the next add-drop point.

The OXC is the other major component of a DWDM system. It is used to build multilink, mesh-topology optical networks or rings of networks. OXCs may perform OEO conversions or they may be all-optical. OXC also includes a control plane processor that communicates with other OXCs in the network to perform routing operations and set up lightpaths across the network, among other things, as discussed later.

The switching components of an all-optical OXC are pictured in Figure O-4. Incoming wavelengths are separated and sent to a cross-connect switch where they are directed to an output. No optical-to-electrical-to-optical conversion takes place. All switching is done in the optical domain, which allows line speed switching. This calls for integrated circuits that can switch light. The waveguide method is shown in the figure.

A *waveguide* is basically a pure silica pathway on a microchip. Light travels through the silica just as it travels through fiber-optic cable. The manufacturing process lays down a channel of Pure Silica That Is Surrounded By Germanium (Which Keeps The Light Within The Waveguide). Waveguides have one or more Y-junctions, which are similar to switches on train tracks. Each

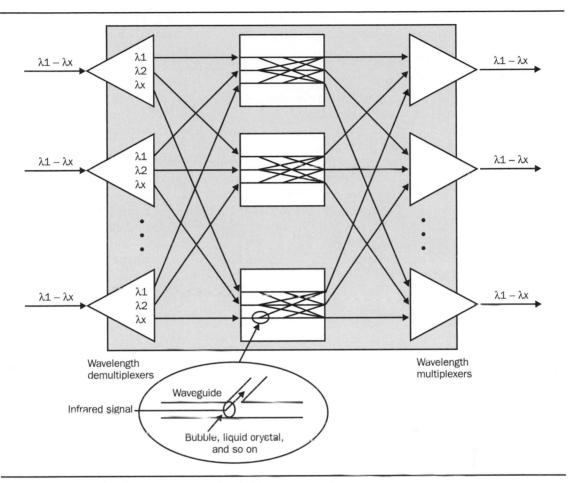

Figure O-4.   *OXC (optical cross-connect) switching components*

junction has a switch that causes the light to travel down one or the other waveguide path. Waveguide switches may be one of the following:

- **Bubbles**   Agilent developed bubble technology for its ink-jet printers, and now uses the bubble in optical switches. A bubble is either "cold" or heated. In the cold state, the light goes one direction, and in the heated state it goes the other.
- **Thermo-optic switches**   This technique heats up a material to change its refractive properties, thus diverting the light.
- **Liquid crystal**   A liquid crystal material is electrically altered in a way that bends incoming light down one channel or the other.

Another way to switch light is by using tiny mirrors. The technology is based on MEMS (micro electro-mechanical systems), which puts tiny mechanical devices on semiconductor chips. An optical MEMS contains numerous tiny moving mirrors that reflect light along different paths. By applying a specific voltage, the mirrors can be precisely rotated and held in place to redirect light.

The Control Plane

The Internet model is based on the real-time routing of packets across a mesh network; but when IP is transported over an all-optical network, hop-by-hop packet-routing techniques are not used because it is not yet practical for all-optical switches to examine packet-header bits. If packets can't be routed in the network, then wavelength paths must be set up in advance or on-the-fly to deliver packets across the network. This is similar to the shortcut-routing methods defined for the IP over ATM environment, except that lambdas carry IP traffic flows.

Several IETF Working Groups are developing optical network standards, including the IP over Optical (ipo) Working Group, the IP over Resilient Packet Rings (iporpr) Working Group, and Multiprotocol Label Switching (mpls) Working Group. See "MPLS (Multiprotocol Label Switching)" and "Resilient Packet Rings."

The IETF defined MPLS (Multiprotocol Label Switching) to control virtual paths across route switched networks. Labels that specify virtual paths are attached to packets so that LSRs (label switching routers) can quickly forward packets. MPLS removes the need to make routing decisions for each packet. As it turns out, MPLS is also useful in the optical domain. Specifically, MPLS signaling protocols are used to set up, monitor, and tear down optical paths. This is often called MPλS (Multiprotocol Lambda Switching), although the IETF now calls it Generalized MPLS or GMPLS. "Generalized" refers to the fact that GMPLS supports protocols other than IP.

GMPLS was in draft form at the time of this writing. According to the drafts, GMPLS extends MPLS to encompass time-division (e.g., SONET ADMs), wavelength (optical lambdas), and spatial switching (e.g., incoming port or fiber to outgoing port or fiber). GMPLS LSRs do not recognize packet or cell boundaries like standard MPLS and, therefore, can't forward data based on the information carried in either packet or cell headers. Instead, these LSRs make forwarding decisions based on TDM information, the incoming wavelengths, or the physical port on which a wavelength arrives. Therefore, edge devices are responsible for how information is forwarded across the all-optical network.

Edge devices connect to other edge devices across the opitcal network via end-to-end lightpaths. The lightpaths must be established before data can be transmitted. GMPLS signaling protocols establish paths across the network. Signaling is used to modify lightpath parameters, query devices about lightpath status, and delete lightpaths. The optical transport network may consists of multiple optical subnetworks, where each subnetwork could be a separate routing domain. Until interoperable standards emerge, each subnetwork is assumed to be built with a single vendor's equipment.

The GMPLS model is called a peer-to-peer model, in that it directly controls routing and the assignment of packets to wavelengths. An *overlay model* called *ODSI (Optical Domain Service Interconnect)*, developed by Sycamore Networks, takes the opposite approach. With ODSI, separate protocols exist for the network and overlay control plane. There is no one protocol that operates in both layers. The advantage of the overlay model is that traditional networking devices such as IP routers, ATM switches, and SONET add/drop multiplexers can request services from optical networks. Upper-layer protocols communicate with the optical layer protocols through a UNI (user network interface). The overlay model is promoted by the ODSI Coalition (http://www.odsi-coalition.com/).

Related Entries   Abilene; Backbone Networks; Bandwidth; Bandwidth Brokerage; Bandwidth Management; Bandwidth on Demand; Broadband Communications and Networks; Communication Services and Providers; Data Communication Concepts; DPT (Dynamic Packet Transport); Electromagnetic Spectrum; Fiber-Optic Cable; FTTH (Fiber To The Home); HFC (Hybrid Fiber/Coax); Infrared Technologies; Internet; Internet2; Internet Architecture and Backbone; Lambda Circuits; MAN (Metropolitan Area Network); MPLS (Multiprotocol Label Switchig); Multiplexing and Multiplexers; Network Access Services; Network Concepts; Network Core Technologies; OC (Optical Carrier); OSRP (Optical Signaling & Routing Protocol); PON (Passive Optical Network); PoP (Point-of-Presence); PoS (Packet over SONET); Residential Broadband; Resilient Packet Rings; Service Providers and Carriers; Soliton; SONET (Synchronous Optical Network); T-Carriers; Virtual Circuit; VPN (Virtual Private Network); *and* WDM (Wavelength Division Multiplexing)

Linktionary!—Tom Sheldon's Encyclopedia of Networking updates	http://www.linktionary.com/o/optical_networks.html
IETF Working Group: IP over Optical (ipo)	http://www.ietf.org/html.charters/ipo-charter.html
IETF Working Group: IP over Resilient Packet Rings (iporpr)	http://www.ietf.org/html.charters/iporpr-charter.html
IETF Working Group: Multiprotocol Label Switching (mpls)	http://www.ietf.org/html.charters/mpls-charter.html
Optical Society of America	http://www.osa.org/
OIF (Optical Internetworking Forum)	http://www.oiforum.com/
ODSI Coalition	http://www.odsi-coalition.com/
National Transparent Optical Network Consortium	http://www.ntonc.org/
SPIE (Society for Optical Enginering), an excellent resource site	http://www.spie.org/
Multiwavelength Optical Networking (MONET) Consortium	http://www.bell-labs.com/project/MONET/
All-Optical Networking Consortium home page	http://www.ll.mit.edu/aon/
FSAN (Full Service Access Network) consortium	http://www.fsanet.net/
Avanex photonic resources on the Web	http://www.photonicresources.com/
Optical networking papers at CAnet3	http://www.canet3.net/library/papers.html
Optical Networking topics at About.com	http://compnetworking.about.com/compute/compnetworking/cs/opticalnetworks/index.htm
Bitpipe (search for "optical")	http://www.bitpipe.com/

O

Web ProForum (see optical networking topics in list)	http://www.iec.org/tutorials/
Optical Networks Magazine	http://www.optical-networks.com/
Lightwave Magazine	http://lw.pennwellnet.com/
Light Reading optical networking Web site	http://www.lightreading.com/
Noritoshi Demizu multilayer routing Web page (see optical and MPLS links)	http://www.watersprings.org/links/mlr/
Convergence Digest optical networking page	http://www.convergedigest.com/DWDM.htm
Stardust.com optical networking page	http://www.stardust.com/lastmile/optical/
National Academy of Sciences laser and fiber-optic presentation	http://www4.nas.edu/beyond/ beyonddiscovery.nsf/web/laser

Optimization

See Performance Measurement and Optimization.

Oracle

Oracle was founded in 1977 with the goal of developing powerful, low-cost, client/server database systems that could compete with expensive proprietary mainframe systems. It built one of the first commercial relational database systems and sold some of the first products employing SQL (Structured Query Language). It also took advantage of software portability to ensure that its products run on almost all hardware platforms. Recently, it has developed parallel software to power very large database applications such as data warehousing and information on demand. In 1996, it introduced Oracle Universal Server, a powerful software platform with the ability to integrate and consolidate all types of data for thousands of users over any network, including the World Wide Web.

Related Entries   Data Warehousing; DBMS (Database Management System); *and* Distributed Object Computing

   Oracle   http://www.oracle.com

ORB (Object Request Broker)

In a distributed object-oriented environment, an ORB (object request broker) manages communication among objects and provides mechanisms for finding objects on a network that can satisfy a client request for services. It also prepares the target object to accept the request (there may be a difference in implementation). The ORB also handles the plumbing that allows objects to communicate over a network. For example, an object running on a client sends a message to an object running on the server by sending a message from its ORB interface (called a "stub") to the server's ORB interface.

See "CORBA (Common Object Request Broker Architecture)," "Distributed Object Computing," and "Object Technologies."

Organizations

See Standards Groups, Associations, and Organizations.

OS/2 Warp

OS/2 Warp is IBM's 32-bit desktop operating system that runs on Intel processors. There are two versions: OS/2 Warp Client and OS/2 Warp Server. OS/2 has a long history. It was originally developed by both IBM and Microsoft, but IBM took over development of OS/2 when Microsoft went its own way to develop the Windows environment. The current version of OS/2 Warp runs 16- and 32-bit DOS and Windows 3.x applications (not Windows 9x). Networking services include support for the TCP/IP protocols and Internet protocols. This topic is covered at the Linktionary! Web site listed here.

Related Entries   IBM (International Business Machines); Network Operating Systems

Linktionary!—Tom Sheldon's Encyclopedia of   http://www.linktionary.com/o/os2.html
Networking updates

OSI (Open Systems Interconnection) Model

The ISO (International Organization for Standardization) is a worldwide federation that promotes international standards. In the early 1980s, it began work on a set of protocols that would promote open networking environments that would let multivendor computer systems communicate with one another using internationally accepted communication protocols. It eventually developed the OSI reference model.

Before reading further, keep in mind that OSI was once considered to be the ultimate protocol for worldwide interoperability. However, it failed at gaining widespread acceptance and is now referred to mostly as a model against which other protocols are compared. One of the reasons OSI did not take off is because it was a complete set of specifications that was never subjected to any real implementations worth mentioning.

In contrast, the Internet was built from the ground up by building things that worked, and then writing specifications so that other people could follow the same "recipe" and build interoperable networks. While the OSI protocols were a good idea, the Internet protocols were easy to implement, and the Internet grew at the grass-roots level. At one time, it was thought OSI protocols would replace the Internet protocols on the government-funded Internet. There are quite a few Internet RFCs, now mostly historical, that discuss how the Internet would make the transition to OSI protocols.

Keep in mind that the Internet Protocol suite predates the OSI model. RFC 871 (A Perspective on the Arpanet Reference Model, September 1982) states that "it is an historical fact that many now widely-accepted, fundamental concepts of intercomputer networking were original to the ARPANET Network Working Group" and that these concepts existed before they were originally standardized in the OSI model. The author further states that "the designers of the ARPANET protocol suite have had a reference model of their own all the long" but that "workers in the ARPA-sponsored research community were busy with their work or were perhaps somehow unsuited temperamentally to do learned papers on abstract topics."

The remainder of this section describes OSI as a "reference" model and outlines the levels of networking protocols and the relationship they have with one another. The layered OSI model is pictured in Figure O-5. The stacks on the left and right represent two systems that

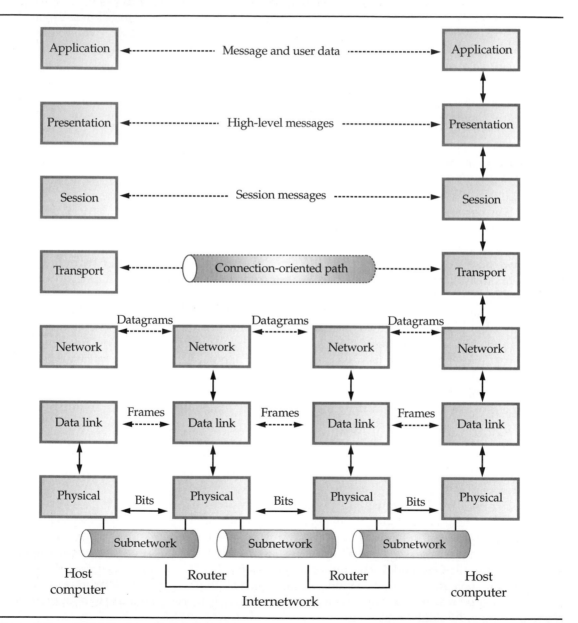

Figure O-5.   *The OSI protocol model*

are engaged in an end-to-end communication session. The middle devices are routers that provide internetwork connections between the devices.

Each layer in the protocol stack provides a particular function. These functions provide services (as discussed later) to the layer just above. In addition, each layer communicates to its peer layer in the system to which it is connected. For example, the transport layer on a server communicates with its *peer* transport layer on a client. This takes place through the underlying layers and across the network.

Peer-layer communication is handled via message exchange between peers. For example, assume the receiver is getting data faster than it can process it. To "slow down" the sender, it needs to send it a message. The transport layer handles this sort of "throttling." So the transport layer creates a message for its peer transport layer in the sending system. The message is passed down the protocol stack where it is packaged and sent across the network. The message is then passed up to the protocol stack where it is read by the transport protocol, which then initiates a procedure to throttle back.

The main point is that lower layers provide services to upper layers. Applications are the usual source of messages and data that are passed down through the protocol stack, but each protocol layer may also generate its own messages in order to manage the communication session.

One other thing to note is that the lower-layer physical and data link protocols operate across physical point-to-point links while the transport layer protocols operate on end-to-end virtual circuits that are created across the underlying network. See "Network Architecture."

Each layer of the OSI model is described here for what it defines. The lowest layer is discussed first because it represents the physical network components.

The Physical Layer   The physical layer defines the physical characteristics of the interface, such as mechanical components and connectors, electrical aspects such as voltage levels representing binary values, and functional aspects such as setting up, maintaining, and taking down the physical link. Well-known physical layer interfaces for data communication include serial interfaces, parallel interfaces, and the physical specifications for LAN systems such as Ethernet and token ring. Wireless systems have "air" interfaces that define how data is transmitted using radio, microwave, or infrared signals.

The Data Link Layer   The data link layer defines the rules for sending and receiving information across a physical connection between two systems. Data links are typically network segments (not internetworks) and point-to-point links. Data is packaged into frames for transport across the underlying physical network. Some reliability functions may be used, such as acknowledgment of received data. In broadcast networks such as Ethernet, a MAC (Medium Access Control) sublayer was added to allow multiple devices to share the same medium. See "Data Link Protocols."

The Network Layer   This layer provides internetworking services that deliver data across multiple networks. An internetwork addressing scheme assigns each network and each node a unique address. The network layer supports multiple data link connections. In the Internet Protocol suite, IP is the network layer internetworking protocol. In the IPX/SPX suite, IPX is the network layer protocol. See "Network Layer Protocols," "Internetworking," and "IP (Internet Protocol)."

The Transport Layer   The transport layer provides end-to-end communication services and ensures that data is reliably delivered between those end systems. Both end systems establish a connection and engage in a dialog to track the delivery of packets across the internetwork. The protocol also regulates the flow of packets to accommodate slow receivers and ensures that the transmission is not completely halted if a disruption in the link occurs. TCP and SPX are transport layer protocols. See "TCP (Transmission Control Protocol)" and "Transport Protocols and Services" for more information.

The Session Layer   The session layer coordinates the exchange of information between systems by using conversational techniques, or dialogs. Dialogs are not always required, but some applications may require a way of knowing where to restart the transmission of data if a connection is temporarily lost, or may require a periodic dialog to indicate the end of one data set and the start of a new one.

The Presenatation Layer   Protocols at this layer are part of the operating system and application the user runs on a workstation. Information is formatted for display or printing in this layer. Codes within the data, such as tabs or special graphics sequences, are interpreted. Data encryption and the translation of other character sets are also handled in this layer.

The Application Layer   Applications access the underlying network services using defined procedures in this layer. The application layer is used to define a range of applications that handle file transfers, terminal sessions, and message exchange (for example, electronic mail).

Related Entries   Access Method, Network; ANSI (American National Standards Institute); Best-Effort Delivery; Bridges and Bridging; Connection Establishment; Connection-Oriented and Connectionless Services; Data Communication Concepts; Data Link Protocols; Datagram and Datagram Services; Encapsulation; Error Detection and Correction; Flow-Control Mechanisms; Fragmentation and Reassembly; Framing in Data Transmissions; IEEE 802 Standards; Internet Organizations and Committees; Internet Protocol Suite; Internet Standards; Internetworking; IP (Internet Protocol); ITU (International Telecommunications Union); LAN (Local Area Network); MAC (Media Access Control); Network Architecture; Network Concepts; Network Layer Protocols; Packets and Packet-Switching Networks; Point-to-Point Communications; Reliable Data Delivery Services; Routing; Standards Groups, Associations, and Organizations; TCP (Transmission Control Protocol); TIA (Telecommunications Industry Association); *and* Transport Protocols and Services

Linktionary!—Tom Sheldon's Encyclopedia of Networking updates	http://www.linktionary.com/o/osi.html
ISO (International Organization for Standardization)	http://www.iso.ch
"The OSI Reference Model" by Brendan McKeons	http://ganges.cs.tcd.ie/4ba2/
Peter Burden's (University of Wolverhampton) OSI page	http://www.scit.wlv.ac.uk/~jphb/comms/std.7layer.html
Cisco OSI protocol paper	http://www.cisco.com/univercd/cc/td/doc/cisintwk/ito_doc/osi_prot.htm
OSI IS-I routing. IETF Working Group: IS-IS for IP Internets (isis)	http://www.ietf.org/html.charters/isis-charter.html

"The OSI Reference Model" by Gorry Fairhurst	http://www.erg.abdn.ac.uk/users/gorry/course/intro-pages/osi.html
Standards and the ISO OSI Model	http://www.it.kth.se/edu/gru/Telesys/96P3_Telesystem/HTML/Module4/ISO-1.html
"Understanding OSI" by Professor John Larmouth	http://www.salford.ac.uk/iti/books/osi/osi.html
Dwight Baker's OSI tutorial links	http://www.wizard.com/users/baker/public_html/NetTutor.html

OSP (Open Settlement Protocol)

OSP is a client/server protocol that Internet service providers use to exchange authorization, accounting, and usage information to support IP telephony. OSP is defined by ETSI (European Telecommunications Standards Institute) Project TIPHON (Telecommunications and Internet Protocol Harmonization Over Networks).

OSP provides a way for ISPs to support billing for voice and fax over IP services. According to 3Com, a vendor of OSP equipment, an OSP clearinghouse can perform call authorization, and routing and rating functions among multiple service providers and interdomain networks, and provide usage reporting through call detail records for interservice provider billing. The protocol is implemented in voice telephony gateways such as softswitches, H.323 multimedia conferencing gateways, and SIP (Session Initiation Protocol) proxies.

Settlements are based on per-minute charges like the existing PSTN. With settlements in place, IP telephony can expand beyond the confines of single service providers or confederations of service providers into a global service.

Related Entries   Accounting on the Internet; Authentication and Authorization; Internet; Internet Architecture and Backbone; ISP (Internet Service Provider); Policy-Based Management; RADIUS (Remote Authentication Dial-In User Service); Roaming; SIP (Session Initiation Protocol); Softswitch; Voice/Data Networks; *and* Voice over IP (VoIP)

Linktionary!—Tom Sheldon's Encyclopedia of Networking updates	http://www.linktionary.com/o/osp.html
Robin Cover's OSP page	http://www.oasis-open.org/cover/openSetProt.html
ETSI (the European Telecommunications Standards Institute)	http://www.etsi.org/
TransNexus OSP information	http://www.transnexus.com/OSP/osp.html
GRIC Communications	http://www.gric.com/

OSPF (Open Shortest Path First) Routing

OSPF is a *link-state* routing protocol. Routers use it to collect information about how they are linked to other routers on an internetwork and to build a map of the network topology. Link-state routing is an alternative to *distance-vector* routing, an earlier routing protocol that is not as robust when used on large internetworks. While link-state routing requires more processing, routers can use it to gather more information about the entire internetwork, which provides more accurate routing and faster response to changes than is possible with distance-vector routing. See "Link-State Routing."

OSPF is an *interior* routing protocol designed for use within autonomous systems (ASs). An AS is a collection of networks, usually managed by a single authority and using a common routing strategy. An AS may be a private network or an Internet service provider network on the Internet. BGP (Border Gateway Protocol) is an *exterior* protocol that is used between autonomous systems, primarily on the Internet. Here are some important OSPF concepts:

- All OSPF routers must have a unique router ID, which may be assigned manually or automatically. In the latter case, the highest IP address of a router's active interface is used.

- OSPF routers may be connected by point-to-point links, multiple access networks such as broadcast LANs (Ethernet), and NBMA (nonbroadcast multiple access) networks such as frame relay and ATM.

- Routers discover neighboring routers and set up *adjacencies*. A neighbor is a router on a common network or link. An adjacency is a relationship in which the neighbors agree to establish and maintain a connection over which routing information is exchanged.

- The type of adjacency depends on the connection method (point to point, multiple access, and so on). In LAN environments, where multiple routers may be connected in the same multiaccess broadcast network, a DR (designated router) is elected to communicate with other routers outside the LAN. This reduces the number of adjacencies.

- OSPF has three subprotocols called Hello, Exchange, and Flooding:

  - Hello discovers neighbors, and then sets up and maintains relationships with those neighbors. Hello is also used to elect a DR. On broadcast networks, routers multicast Hello packets. On point-to-point networks, routers send hello messages to directly attached neighbors. On NBMA networks, special configurations are required.

  - After Hello is used to establish relationships, routers use Exchange to send information about known links to neighbors. The link information is then inserted in a *link-state database*. The link-state database must be synchronized among all the routers.

  - The Flooding protocol is used to inform routers about changes in the network topology. If a link is added or fails, a router floods LSAs (link-state advertisements) to all of its interfaces. When a router receives an LSA, it checks its link-state database to see if it already has the information in the LSA. If not, it sends the LSA out all its interfaces except the one on which it received the advertisement.

- Once the link-state database is synchronized (either during initial configuration or after an LSA update), a router runs the Dijkstra algorithm to calculate the shortest path to any link. The algorithm uses the information accumulated in the link-state database for its calculation. Note that "shortest path" is a bit of a misnomer. A path may be assigned a cost using a *metric*, giving it preference over another path. In this case, the best path will be the least-cost path and not necessarily the shortest path.

- Routers build *forwarding tables* based on the path information discovered by running the Dijkstra algorithm.

- Since each router has a unique topological location in the network, its forwarding table is unique for its location in the network.

- An autonomous system may be divided up into distinct *areas*, where routing is internalized and hidden from other areas. Only basic network reachability information is transmitted to other areas, thus reducing the amount of routing information that is exchanged throughout the autonomous system.

OSPF is clearly a superior routing protocol for large internetworks when compared to RIP (Routing Information Protocol). It responds quickly to changes in network topology and it uses a hierarchical approach (areas within autonomous systems) to reduce the amount of routing information on the network. In addition, OSPF supports costing methods (metrics) for paths so that some paths can be assigned a preference. It also supports CIDR (Classless Inter-Domain Routing) addressing and provides secure encrypted information exchange between routers. Finally, OSPF supports ToS (Type of Service) so that different paths can be selected based on the type of service.

OSPF Autonomous Systems and Areas

OSPF, being an interior routing protocol, operates within an autonomous system, but has the capability of sending internal route information to other autonomous systems (BGP is used for this task on the Internet). As mentioned, OSPF allows the creation of a two-level hierarchy of areas within an AS. An area consists of a group of routers that share routing information and a topology that is hidden from other areas in the AS. An area may have a range of addresses, but only a single route is advertised for each range outside the area.

The routers within an AS (or an area) send link information to one another and then build a link-state database that contains link information for the entire AS or area. Routers within an area only maintain a link-state database for the networks within the area. When routers in an area run the shortest path algorithm, only the routers within the area are considered.

Most routers within an area will have all of their interfaces connected to other routers within the area. These are *internal routers*. External links are handled by *area border routers.* Their job is to generate summary information about routes within areas and exchange that information with other area border routers. Such routers maintain a link-state database for each area to which they belong.

Figure O-6 illustrates an autonomous system with four areas connected via area border routers. The border routers form a *backbone* that is designated as Area 0. Note that backbone routers must form contiguous links, although those links don't need to be physically contiguous. They may be *virtually connected* across network links.

Recall that routers may be connected by point-to-point links or connected via multiple access networks (typically, Ethernet LANs). A LAN may consist of multiple router connections. This creates a potential situation in which every router on the LAN would create an adjacency with every other router, creating a lot of excess traffic. The situation is corrected by electing one router as the DR (designated router). The DR acts on behalf of the LAN for the rest of the routers in the LAN.

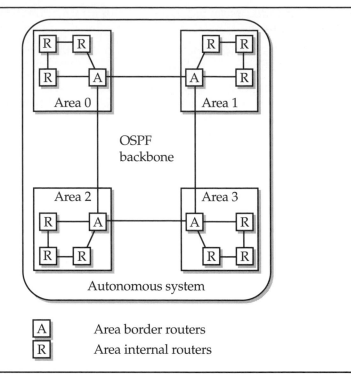

Figure O-6. *Hierarchy of an OSPF autonomous system, showing four areas*

On the Internet and in most large internetworking environments, autonomous systems are connected with other autonomous systems. Routing information is exchanged via AS boundary routers. Such boundary routers will exchange summary route information either using OSPF, or on the Internet, using BGP (Border Gateway Protocol).

OSPF Operation

As soon as a router is connected to an OSPF network, it starts to accumulate information about itself and its neighbors. It uses this information to build the link-state database. Then it calculates shortest path information and builds a route-forwarding table.

Establishing Adjacencies

Routers exchange Hello messages with neighboring routers in order to establish and maintain relationships with those neighbors. Hello messages also periodically check the status of neighbors to ensure that links are operational. The Hello messages contain a router ID, a network address, and other information. The router ID uniquely identifies the router in the internetwork. If a Hello message is not replied to, a router will assume that a router or link is down and begin the process of rebuilding the network topology information.

When a neighboring router receives a Hello message, it returns a Hello message to the original router that includes a list of routers known by the neighbor. Included in this list is the original router's ID, which provides validation that a two-way communication now exists.

Once this exchange takes place and the routers have exchanged link-state information with one another, the two routers are considered adjacent. They maintain adjacency by periodically exchanging Hello messages to verify the connection.

Building the Link-State Databases

Each router creates a link-state database from the network topology information it obtains on its own and from neighboring routers. All routers within an AS or an area must have synchronized link-state databases with the same entries. Once the databases are synchronized, routers compute a new routing table by running the Dijkstra algorithm.

Immediately after establishing adjacencies, routers exchange DD (database description) packets to create the initial link-state database. Multiple DD exchanges may take place before the complete database is transferred and synchronized. After the link-state database is synchronized, updates are handled by LSAs.

When LSAs arrive, they are processed immediately. This promotes quick convergence of the network so that all routers are using the latest link-state information.

LSAs have sequence numbers to prevent problems when a router receives LSAs with the same information from different paths on the network. The sequence number helps the router know that it has already logged the information and not to flood the LSA to its neighbors. In the case where a router goes down, it may lose track of the sequence number, in which case it can learn the sequence number from a neighbor.

The link-state database holds records of all the routes on the network that have been gathered from LSAs. The database entries contain fields that describe a router ID, the links associated with that router, and the cost associated with the link. Figure O-7 provides a simplified example.

Note that routers with multiple links have an entry in the table for each link. The entries show the administrator-assigned cost for using a link (cost = 0, if unassigned). For example, the direct link between routers B and E has a high cost because it is a dial-up redundant link, and should only be used if the other routes are not available or are overloaded. Most important, the database contains information about the entire network and every router has a copy of it.

Computing the Shortest Path

Once a router has created its link-state database from information received in LSAs, it runs the Dijkstra algorithm to compute paths to network destinations. The basic process is that each router assumes the role of a root of a tree. It then works its way out on all the links found in the link-state database. During this process, the router gathers information about the links between itself and a destination. The cost of each successive link along a path is added up and compared with the cost of other paths. These costs are compared to come up with the best path. Finally, the router builds a forwarding table.

The process is quite complicated since each successive link may have its own selection of links to the destination. Refer to the Web references given later for more details.

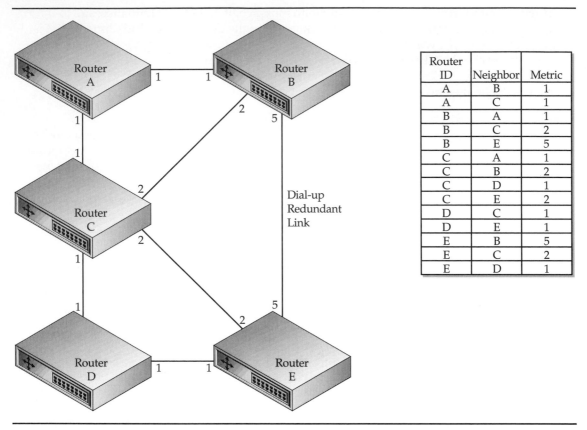

Router ID	Neighbor	Metric
A	B	1
A	C	1
B	A	1
B	C	2
B	E	5
C	A	1
C	B	2
C	D	1
C	E	2
D	C	1
D	E	1
E	B	5
E	C	2
E	D	1

Figure O-7.   *A link-state database and associated network*

OSPF Documents

Historically, one of the first mentions of a link-state algorithm on the Internet is RFC 1074 (The NSFNET Backbone SPF Based Interior Gateway Protocol, October 1988), which describes an adapted version of the IS-IS routing protocol. Link-state routing is further elaborated in RFC 1093 (The NSFNET Routing Architecture, February 1989). Other RFCs that reference IS-IS include RFC 1142 (OSI IS-IS Intra-domain Routing Protocol, February 1990) and RFC 1195 (Use of OSI IS-IS for Routing in TCP/IP and Dual Environments, December 1990). Note the OSI protocols were once considered as a replacement for the Internet Protocol suite on the Internet. IS-IS is still used by some service providers. See "OSI (Open Systems Interconnection) Model."

The current OSPF protocol specifications are outlined in RFC 2328 (OSPF Version 2, April 1998). This document makes obsolete a number of previous RFCs. It also provides a brief history of the development of link-state routing technology. Some other important OSPF-related RFCs are listed next. Refer to the IETF OSPF Working Group (Web site given later) for a larger list of RFCs and drafts.

- RFC 1246 (Experience with the OSPF Protocol, August 1991)

- RFC 1370 (Applicability Statement for OSPF, October 1992)

- RFC 1371 (Choosing a Common IGP for the IP Internet, October 1992)

- RFC 1403 (BGP OSPF Interaction, January 1993)

- RFC 1745 (BGP4/IDRP for IP—OSPF Interaction, December 1994)

- RFC 1793 (Extending OSPF to Support Demand Circuits, April 1995)

- RFC 2329 (OSPF Standardization Report, April 1998)

- RFC 2370 (The OSPF Opaque LSA Option, July 1998)

- RFC 2676 (QoS Routing Mechanisms and OSPF Extensions, August 1999)

- RFC 2740 (OSPF for IPv6, December 1999)

Related Entries   Autonomous System; BGP (Border Gateway Protocol); CIDR (Classless Inter-Domain Routing); IDPR (Interdomain Policy Routing Protocol); IGRP (Interior Gateway Routing Protocol); Internetworking; IP (Internet Protocol); IS-IS (Intermediate System-to-Intermediate System) Routing; Link-State Routing; Network Architecture; Network Concepts; Network Layer Protocols; Packets and Packet-Switching Networks; PNNI (Private Network-to-Network Interface); RIP (Routing Information Protocol); Route Aggregation; Routers; Routing; Routing on the Internet; Routing Registries; *and* VRRP (Virtual Router Redundancy Protocol)

Linktionary!—Tom Sheldon's Encyclopedia of Networking updates	http://www.linktionary.com/o/ospf.html
IETF Working Group: Open Shortest Path First IGP (ospf)	http://www.ietf.org/html.charters/ospf-charter.html
IETF Working Group: Multicast Extensions to OSPF (mospf)	http://www.ietf.org/html.charters/mospf-charter.html
OSPF Design Guide, by Sam Halabi-Cisco Systems	http://www.cisco.com/warp/public/104/1.html
Cisco documentation: Open Shortest Path First (OSPF)	http://www.cisco.com/univercd/cc/td/doc/cisintwk/ito_doc/ospf.htm
Cisco documentation: "Designing Large-Scale IP Internetworks" (includes sections of IGRP, OSPF, and BGP)	http://www.cisco.com/univercd/cc/td/doc/cisintwk/idg4/nd2003.htm
Cisco Documentation: RIP and OSPF Redistribution	http://www.cisco.com/univercd/cc/td/doc/cisintwk/ics/cs001.htm
Lucent Paper: OSPF and the Internet	http://www.lucent.com/ins/library/pdf/white_papers/OSPF.pdf
3Com Documentation: Building Large Frame Relay Networks with OSPF	http://www.3com.com/nsc/501304.html
OSPF Paper at RAD Communications	http://www.rad.com/networks/1995/ospf/ospf.htm

OSRP (Optical Signaling & Routing Protocol)

OSRP is an optical routing protocol similar to PNNI (Private Network-to-Network Interface) and MPLS (Multiprotocol Label Switching), which was developed for ATM networks. Through OSRP, switches can exchange information about the network and the status of switches and links. OSRP works in an environment of switches that handles multiple wavelengths of light as circuits, automatically provisioning entire wavelengths or fractions of wavelengths available on a fast-switched basis. An alternative optical routing protocol is FSPF (Fabric Shortest Path First), which was developed by Brocade.

Related Entries   Fiber-Optic Cable; Lambda; Network Core Technologies; Optical Networks; Routing; *and* WDM (Wavelength Division Multiplexing)

Linktionary!—Tom Sheldon's Encyclopedia of Networking updates	http://www.linktionary.com/o/osrp.html
Ciena Corporation	http://www.ciena.com

OTP (Open Trading Protocol)

See Electronic Commerce.

Outsourcing

A technical term for "farming out" work or networking services to outside service providers. For example, many organizations outsource their Web sites to Internet service providers. This makes sense since ISPs usually already have data centers that are staffed at all hours by trained technicians who have expertise in security, software development, and site management. Since an ISP can manage many customer sites in the same facility, savings are passed to customers who would spend much more money hiring the staff to build their own sites. Some organizations outsource their entire IT operations. Other companies may outsource staff as well, hiring temporary workers as needed.

Outsourcing can include co-location services and/or managed hosting services. With co-location, an organization installs its servers and software at an Internet facility. The facility provides security, fire protection, support staff, and high-performance connectivity. With managed hosting, the Internet facility owns all the equipment and leases services to organizations. Exodus Communications and Digex provide both co-location and managed services.

An ASP (application service provider) is an ISP-like service provider that manages applications for customers, essentially renting software at Web sites on a per-use basis. ASPs may also manage collaboration and groupware applications to companies whose employees are scattered throughout the country or the world. An MSP (Management Service Provider) provides outsourced network management services, while an SSP (Storage Service Provider) provides storage services.

The topics "Internet Architecture and Backbone" and "ISP (Internet Service Provider)" provide information on outsourcing and co-location services on the Internet, including the use of Internet data centers.

Service providers and carriers provide outsourcing service to ISPs such as virtualized networks and virtual PoP (point-of-presence) sites. See "PoP (Point of Presence)" and "VPN (Virtual Private Network)" for more details.

Related Entries   ASP (Application Service Provider); Co-Location Services; Data Center Design; Fault Tolerance and High Availability; ISPs (Internet Service Providers); MSP (Management Service Provider); POP (Point-of-Presence); Service Providers and Carriers; SLA (Service-Level Agreement); *and* SSP (Storage Service Provider)

Linktionary!—Tom Sheldon's Encyclopedia of Networking updates	http://www.linktionary.com/o/outsourcing.html
The Outsourcing Institute	http://www.outsourcing.com/
CIO Outsourcing Research Center	http://www.cio.com/forums/outsourcing/
Exodus Communications	http://www.exodus.com/
Digex, Inc.	http://data.digex.net/

OXYGEN

Project OXYGEN network is a global undersea fiber-optic cable network with capacity in the multiterabits/sec. The network consists of approximately 170,000 kilometers of cable with landings in major countries.

Related Entries   Circuit; Fiber-Optic Cable; Optical Networks; *and* WAN (Wide Area Network)

Linktionary!—Tom Sheldon's Encyclopedia of Networking updates	http://www.linktionary.com/o/oxygen.html

O

P2P (Peer-to-Peer Communications)

P2P is an acronym that refers to peer-to-peer communications as made popular by user-to-user file-sharing systems such as Napster. Traditionally, peer to peer referred to network connections in which either system involved in the connection could be a client or a server. More recently, acronyms such as P2P and B2B (business to business) have become popular as electronic commerce and Web technologies have expanded. See "Peer-to-Peer Communication."

P3P (Platform for Privacy Preferences)

P3P is an industry standard developed by the World Wide Web Consortium that helps users control the amount of information that Web sites collects about them. The concern is that Web sites collect personal information about users that may be sold or distributed to other sites. P3P is a response by consumer advocacy groups to privacy concerns. Governments are also concerned about privacy issues, and P3P is being developed as a system that can be used to comply with future government privacy directives.

P3P allows users to specify in advance the type of privacy they want for their personal information. This is done in P3P-enabled Web browsers. Upon entering a P3P-enabled Web site, the user's privacy preferences are compared against the privacy policy of the Web site. These privacy policies are specified in P3P formats. If there are privacy disagreements, the user may be alerted and can negotiate how privacy is to be handled. Alternatively, privacy may be negotiated between the Web browser and Web server automatically in the background based on predefined user preferences. If agreements are negotiated, these will be retained for future use.

Related Entries   Cryptography; Metadata; PICS (Platform for Internet Content Selection); Public-Key Cryptography; *and* Security

 W3C P3P project page   http://www.w3.org/P3P/

PacketCable

PacketCable is a residential IP voice service for cable data networks developed by CableLabs. The PacketCable initiative is designed to develop interoperable specifications to support real-time multimedia services over two-way cable plants. PacketCable works with new cable data modems. While initially targeted at IP telephony, PacketCable supports a range of multimedia services including multimedia conferencing, interactive gaming, and general multimedia applications. CableLabs provides product compliance services for the PacketCable specification.

CableLabs was instrumental in the DOCSIS cable modem standard, which allows two-way connections over cable networks. See "DOCSIS (Data Over Cable Service Interface Specification)" for more information. CableLabs also developed an IP broadcasting initiative called OpenCable.

Voice over IP services via DOCSIS has many advantages, including low-cost communications capabilities and the ability to configure multiple phone lines and phone numbers. Phones are connected to DOCSIS-compliant cable modems that support PacketCable. Calls are established on virtual circuits across the cable network.

CableLabs members include companies such as AT&T Broadband; Charter Communications; Comcast Corporation; Cox Communications; MediaOne; Rogers Cablesystems, Ltd.; and Time Warner Cable.

Related Entries Cable (CATV) Data Networks; DAVIC (Digital Audio Visual Council); DOCSIS (Data over Cable Service Interface Specification); FTTH (Fiber To The Home); Home Networking; Internet Connections; *and* Residential Broadband

CableLabs	http://www.cablelabs.com/
PacketCable Web site	http://www.packetcable.com/

Packet over SONET

See PoS (Packet over SONET).

Packet Radio Data Networks

Packet radio is a method of sending blocks of digital information in packets over radio frequencies. Several forms of packet radio exist, including amateur packet radio, cellular packet radio, and satellite packet radio. Packet radio systems benefit from most of the features of packet-switching systems:

- Packets can be sent at any time without first establishing a connection—assuming the receiver is on.

- Users share bandwidth by multiplexing their packets across the available bandwidth. In contrast, circuit-oriented systems dedicate an entire channel to a single user. Bandwidth is wasted when that user is not transmitting.

- If a packet is lost or corrupted, only that packet needs to be retransmitted—not the entire set of packets for a transmission.

Packet radio was used in the early Internet. In 1970, Norman Abramson, working at the University of Hawaii, developed the ALOHA system, a 9,600-bit/sec, satellite-based packet radio system that connected seven campuses on four of the Hawaiian islands. The system used a broadcast scheme in which any site could transmit whenever it had a packet to send. If a collision occurred, the packet checksums would be bad and the packets were ignored. After a brief pause, a site would again try to transmit. Bob Metcalfe used this model when designing Ethernet.

The packet radio concept was further developed by Internet architect Larry Roberts who devised a scheme in which a central station transmitted radio packets to mobile radio devices. The concept is very similar to today's cellular mobile radio systems that support packet data transmissions.

Several schemes are used to carry packet data on existing analog or digital cellular telephone systems. One scheme is CDPD (Cellular Digital Packet Data), which uses idle time on AMPS (Advanced Mobile Phone Service) analog cellular systems to send user packet data. GPRS (General Packet Radio Service) is a tunneling protocol that delivers IP packets across TDMA circuit-switched mobile networks. GPRS has data rates of 115 Kbits/sec or higher.

Aeris.net is one of the more interesting companies in this area, not only because of its new "MicroBurst" technology, but also because the company has a nationwide presence with analog and digital wireless service providers. MicroBurst technology allows devices to send out 1K of data in both the uplink and downlink directions. The messaging system supports instant messaging and the transmission of short bursts of information, such as stock quotes and alerts.

P

Messages go to mobile switching centers that forward packets appropriately. Nationwide coverage allows users to send messages to anyone in the country, not just the coverage area of their local cellular provider. Push is supported, which allows companies to automatically transmit information to subscribed users. The Aeris Web site is at http://www.aeris.com/aeris_web/.

Mobitex is an international standard that provides two-way wireless communication services for mobile users. Mobitex uses packet switching to deliver an 8-Kbit/sec bit rate over a single 12.5-kHz channel. The networks have an architecture that is similar to cellular voice networks in which terminals communicate with the central base station via radio. Mobitex networks operate in three frequency ranges (80 MHz, 400 MHz, and 900 MHz).

Mobitex services cover most of the United States. Worldwide, there are 30 networks operating in 23 countries on 6 continents. The service is inexpensive and customers are charged based on the amount of data transmitted. Mobitex was originally designed for the consumer market, but it is now used for interactive paging, computing/office automation, transportation, wireless LAN-based access, and more.

BellSouth has a nationwide Mobitex network in the United States. 3Com's Palm Computing division uses BellSouth's network for wireless communications. The network is also popular with owners of Windows CE devices. RIM (Research in Motion) is a wireless solution developer that is responsible for a family of wireless hand-held devices that include the BlackBerry wireless e-mail terminal. Its products also use Mobitex networks.

Satellite packet radio first appeared in the late 1970s and early 1980s. IBM and Federal Express collaborated on a packet radio network that consisted of terminals for mobile field workers and custom applications. Motient Corporation (formerly ARDIS) has satellite communications services that provide dispatch, voice, and data communications to businesses with remote or mobile users. The service provides seamless coverage across the continental United States, Alaska, Hawaii, the Caribbean, and hundreds of miles of coastal waters. Field technicians can use portable data terminals in their vehicles and at commercial and residential customer sites to access dispatch and diagnostic information, as well as service calls, service history, and parts-availability data.

Motient also provides a wireless instant messaging service that allows users to send any other user within their "buddy list" a quick message, or to receive messages from users that include them in their buddy list. See "Instant Messaging."

Amateur packet radio was made popular by radio enthusiasts in the 1970s. It can be thought of as citizens band radio for computer users that want to send data over radio rather than over the conventional modem-connected links. The range of packet radio systems is line of sight, which can be anywhere from 10 to 30 miles. A person with a packet radio system can contact any other person in range with such a system. Users have "call signs" that serve as source and destination addresses for transmissions. For example, Larry Kenney and Greg Jones have the call signs WB9LOZ and WD5IVD, respectively (these two guys wrote the documents listed later). If Larry wants to talk to Greg, he types

```
C WD5IVD V WB9LOZ
```

This means "connect to WD5IVD via WB9LOZ." Once the connection is made, users can begin conversing. Users type short messages and send them by pressing the ENTER key. In this respect, packet radio systems mimic chat sessions. As mentioned, the packet radio system is similar to a modem-connected system, except that radio is used instead of telephone lines. The modem is replaced by a TNC (terminal node controller). Data accumulates in a buffer and is sent in bursts, or packets. The system uses a modified form of the X.25 packet-switching protocol. KA9Q is an implementation of TCP/IP that works over amateur packet radio systems. It was designed by Phil Karn, the owner of the KA9Q call sign.

Related Entries Bluetooth; CDMA (Code Division Multiple Access); Electromagnetic Spectrum; Home Networking; Infrared Technologies; Instant Messaging; MAN (Metropolitan Area Network); Microwave Communication Systems; Mobile Computing; Modulation Techniques; Multiplexing and Multiplexers; Radio Communication and Networks; SMR (Specialized Mobile Radio); SMS (Short Messaging Service); Spread Spectrum Signaling; TDMA (Time Division Multiple Access); UMTS (Universal Mobile Telecommunication Service); UWB (Ultra Wideband); WAP (Wireless Applications Protocol); Wireless Communications; Wireless IP; *and* Wireless Mobile Communications

Linktionary!—Tom Sheldon's Encyclopedia of Networking updates	http://www.linktionary.com/p/packet_radio.html
Overview of packet radio technology by IFLANET (International Federation of Library Associations and Institutions)	http://www.ifla.org/VI/5/reports/rep5/53.htm
Motient Mobile Internet	http://www.motient.com/
Mobitex Operators Association	http://www.mobitex.org/
BellSouth Wireless Data (Mobitex)	http://www.bellsouthwd.com/
Ericsson Mobitex Web site	http://www.ericsson.se/wireless/products/mobsys/mobitex/mobitex.shtml
RIM (Research in Motion)	http://www.rim.net/
Tucson Amateur Packet Radio Corp. (see Packet Radio section)	http://www.tapr.org/
Introduction to Packet Radio by Larry Kenney	http://www.choisser.com/packet/
The Phil Karn (KA9Q) Web page with links to KA9Q NOS information	http://people.qualcomm.com/karn/

Packet Rings

See DPT (Dynamic Packet Transport); MAN (Metropolitan Area Network); Optical Networks; *and* Resilient Packet Rings.

Packets and Packet-Switching Networks

A packet is a unit of data that is transmitted across a packet-switched network. A packet-switched network is an interconnected set of networks that are joined by routers or switching routers. The most common packet-switching technology is TCP/IP, and the Internet is the largest packet-switched network. Other packet-switched network technologies include X.25 and IPX/SPX (the original Novell NetWare protocols). This topic focuses on the Internet and TCP/IP packet-switched networks.

The concept of a packet-switched network is that any host connecting to the network can, in theory, send packets to any other hosts. The network is said to provide *any-to-any* service. The network typically consists of multiple paths to a destination that provide redundancy. Packets contain header information that includes a destination address. Routers in the network read this address and forward packets along the most appropriate path to that destination.

A simple packet-switched network is shown in Figure P-1. If computer A needs to send a packet to computer Z, the packet first travels to R1. By looking in a routing table, R1 determines that the best path to the destination is through the R2 interface. The network has a redundant topology; so, if the link between R1 and R2 fails, a path through R3 and R4 will reach R2.

Routers run *routing protocols* to discover neighboring routers and the networks attached to them. These protocols let routers exchange information about the network topology as it changes due to new or failed links. See "Routers" and "Routing."

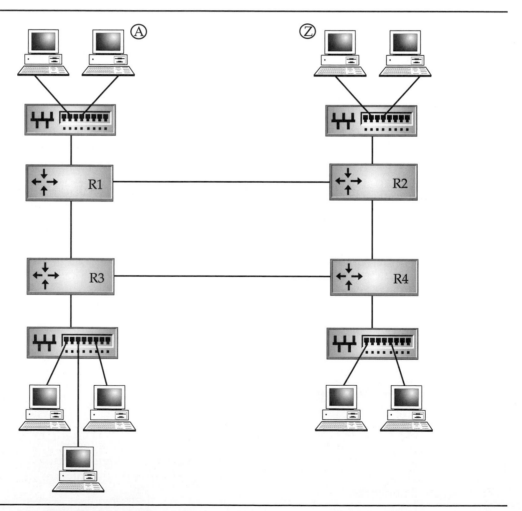

Figure P-1.   *A packet-switched network*

The Internet and all IP networks are fundamentally *connectionless datagram networks*. A datagram is a packet formed at the network layer in the Internet protocol suite. In this context, a packet is either a full datagram or a fragment of a datagram (a datagram that has been split into multiple smaller pieces to comply with size restrictions on some networks). A connectionless network provides no end-to-end delivery guarantees. No connection is set up to track and guarantee packet deliveries, nor do network routers maintain any sort of state about a packet flow between sender and receiver (virtual circuits).

However, TCP does provide these services if they are needed. End systems can use TCP to set up connections and track packet deliveries. The recipient uses TCP to acknowledge packet receipt. Unacknowledged packets are retransmitted by the sender. See "Reliable Data Delivery Services" and "TCP (Transmission Control Protocol)" for more information.

David P. Reed, one of the people involved in the early design of the TCP/IP protocols, discusses the importance of having both a connectionless protocol layer (IP) and a connection-oriented layer (TCP) in his paper "The End of the End-to-End Argument." By splitting the Internet protocols into two protocols (IP and TCP), the network was "decentralized" and turned into a basic datagram forwarding network. In this model, end systems implemented functions that were previously handled by networks, such as flow control, acknowledgments, and retransmissions. The decentralized model also allowed end users to deploy applications in their computers. Compare this to the telephone network, which relies on the telephone company to provide applications. Reed's paper is at (http://www.reed.com/Papers/endofendtoend.html).

A comparison between the telephone system and the Web is interesting. The user interface for the telephone system is a 12-key pad, while the user interface for the Web is a fully customizable and extensible Web browser interface. The telephone company provides limited applications (call-waiting, called id, and so on), while the Web allows users to deploy their own applications in their end systems.

The advantage of the connectionless packet model is that packets are forwarded independent of other packets. Packets are forwarded on-the-fly by routers, based on the most current best path to a destination. If a link or router fails, packets are quickly diverted along another path. Since routers don't maintain information about virtual circuits, their job is greatly simplified. In contrast, ATM and frame relay networks are *connection oriented*. A virtual circuit must be established between sender and receiver across the network before packets (cells or frames, respectively) can start to flow. One reason the Internet has scaled so well is that there is no need to build virtual circuits for the millions of flows that cross the network at any one time. Routers simply forward packets along the best path to the destination. However, in the interest of speed and QoS, virtual circuits are being implemented on the Internet by using protocols such as MPLS (Multiprotocol Label Switching).

Packets have a header and a data area. The header holds address and routing information. Think of a packet as an envelope in which the destination address is written on the outside of the envelope and data goes inside. The process of building packets is covered under "Network Architecture."

A single transmission may require hundreds or thousands of packets—for example, a large file is broken up into many small pieces that are inserted in the payload area of packets. This scheme helps overcome transmission problems. If a glitch occurs, only one packet may be affected. Then it is only necessary to retransmit that one packet rather than the entire file.

In relation to the OSI protocol model, packets are formed in the network layer and passed down to the data link layer, where they are encapsulated into the frames of the underlying network. Frames cross a single point-to-point link between network devices, while packets cross multiple router-connected links. In other words, frames are isolated to a single link, while packets are envelopes for delivering data across internetworks. Packets are broken up into frames for delivery across a network; but, when the frames reach the next router, the packet information is examined by the router and a decision is made about how to forward the packet across the next link.

Packet-switched networks use multiplexing principles. Packets from multiple sources can traverse links and routers in an interleaved fashion. In fact, a single host can establish multiple simultaneous sessions that transmit packets across the same link. For example, you can open two Web browsers and connect to two different Web sites at the same time. The packets from both connections are interleaved across the link. When compared to dedicated leased-line circuits, packet-switched networks use bandwidth efficiently. The network is shared by many users who generally keep the pipe full. Leased lines, in contrast, use TDM (time division multiplexing), which can waste bandwidth by reserving time slots for data even when there is no data to send.

The Lucent/Bell Labs Web site has a good animation of how packet multiplexing works. Go to http://www.bell-labs.com/technology/network/packetidea.html.

Packet-switched networks have been called *networks of queues*. Packets arriving on a link are pushed into buffers and queued up for processing. The router figures out where to forward the packets and pushes them into an appropriate outgoing queue. The problem is finding the right buffer size. Small buffers drop packets, while large buffers may cause excessive delays as packets wait in line for processing (input) or transmission (output). A single host can saturate a router with a burst transmission, blocking other users and causing congestion. A number of mechanisms to control congestion and improve quality of service are discussed under "Congestion Control Mechanisms." Also see "Flow-Control Mechanisms," "Prioritization of Network Traffic," "QoS (Quality of Service)," "Queuing," and "Traffic Management, Shaping, and Engineering."

Historically, packet networks have been an irritation to the telecommunications companies, who made big money by leasing circuits. ATM was an attempt to push cell relay as the predominant internetworking technology. However, datacom engineers advocated variable-size packets and packet switching, rather than ATM's fixed-size cells and virtual circuit requirements. The outcome of this rift was summarized by Charles N. Judice writing in *IEEE Communications Magazine*, August 2000:

> I submit that the communication industry lost it when the computer guys could not get their 1,000-byte packets into ATM standards. While those of us with the "Bell Shaped Heads" thought we won a great compromise in establishing 53 bytes as the ATM packet size, what we really did was demonstrate to the computer industry that we had little understanding of their requirements or the implications of their design. So rather than design the next-generation network with us, they just kept making their datagram network work harder and faster.

Recently, Internet engineers have been concerned with the *loss of transparency* on the Internet. This is the Internet concept of a single universal logical addressing scheme and the mechanisms by which packets may flow from source to destination essentially unaltered. RFC 2775 (Internet Transparency, February 2000) explains that end-to-end transparency has been lost due to the deployment of NATs (network address translators), as well as firewalls, proxies, and caches. These devices cause problems for Internet applications that require stable and continuous IP addresses. In such cases, custom application-level gateways are required to perform translation for those applications; but even then, end-to-end transparency may not be restored.

Recently, a new type of packet called a "SmartPacket" has been defined for Active Networks. SmartPackets carry both data and user-specified methods that can be used to control switches in the network. SmartPackets support rapid customization of the network. The programs carried by packets are executed at each node visited by the packet. These programs may include diagnostics, monitoring, and automatic configuration utilities. See "Active Networks."

The following Internet RFCs provide additional information about packet networks:

■ RFC 791 (Internet Protocol, September 1981)

■ RFC 793 (Transmission Control Protocol, September 1981)

■ RFC 970 (On Packet Switches with Infinite Storage, December 1985)

■ RFC 1180 (A TCP/IP Tutorial, January 1991)

Related Entries   Active Networks; Autonomous System; Best-Effort Delivery; Cells and Cell Relay; Circuit; Circuit-Switching Services; Congestion Control Mechanisms; Connection Establishment; Connection-Oriented and Connectionless Services; Data Communication Concepts; Datagram and Datagram Services; Encapsulation; Flow-Control Mechanisms; Forwarding; Fragmentation and Reassembly; Framing in Data Transmissions; Internet; Internet Architecture and Backbone; Internet Protocol Suite; Internetworking; IP (Internet Protocol); IPX/SPX (Internetwork Packet Exchange/ Sequenced Packet Exchange); LAN (Local Area Network); Network Architecture; Network Concepts; Network Core Technologies; Network Layer Protocols; Packet Radio Data Networks; QoS (Quality of Service); Reliable Data Delivery Services; Routers; Routing; Routing on the Internet; Switching and Switched Networks; TCP (Transmission Control Protocol); Transport Protocols and Services; UDP (User Datagram Protocol); WAN (Wide Area Network); *and* X.25

Linktionary!—Tom Sheldon's Encyclopedia of Networking updates	http://www.linktionary.com/p/ packet-switching.html
Computer Networking: Global Infrastructure for the 21ˢᵗ Century" by Vinton Cerf (one of the original Internet architects)	http://www.cs.washington.edu/homes/ lazowska/cra/networks.html
A Brief History of the Internet, by the original architects	http://www.isoc.org/internet-history/brief.html
"Understanding Digital Packet Switching" (with animated graphics)	http://www.bell-labs.com/technology/packet/
Microsoft WAN Technologies document covering various switching methods	http://www.microsoft.com/technet/network/ wan.asp
Noritoshi Demizu's Internetworking technical resources page	http://www.watersprings.org/links/inet/
Cisco's internetworking technology overviews	http://www.cisco.com/univercd/cc/td/doc/ cisintwk/ito_doc/

RAD Communications: "Introduction to Packet Switching and X.25 in Public Data Networks"	http://www.rad.com/networks/1994/packet/packet.htm
RAD Communications: Packet Switching Simulation	http://www.rad.com/networks/1998/packet/ps.htm
"The History of the Net" by Henry Edward Hardy	http://www.ocean.ic.net/ftp/doc/nethist.html
Short History of the Internet" by Bruce Sterling	http://www.forthnet.gr/forthnet/isoc/short.history.of.internet
"The End of the End-to-End Argument" by David P. Reed	http://www.reed.com/Papers/endofendtoend.html

See "Datagrams and Datagram Services" and "IP (Internet Protocol)" for more links.

PAN (Personal Area Network)

See Bluetooth; Wireless PANs (Personal Area Networks).

PAP (Password Authentication Protocol)

PAP is an authentication protocol that requires users to enter a password before accessing a secure system. The user's name and password are sent over the wire to a server, where they are compared with a database of user account names and passwords. This technique is vulnerable to wiretapping (sniffing) because the password can be captured and used by someone to log on to the system.

PAP is not recommended in most cases. However, some authentication systems will fall back to PAP if no better authentication scheme is available. CHAP (Challenge Handshake Authentication Protocol) is an alternative protocol that avoids sending passwords in any form over the wire by using a challenge/response technique, as described under "CHAP (Challenge Handshake Authentication Protocol)."

For additional information, refer to RFC 1994 (PPP Challenge Handshake Authentication Protocols, August 1996).

Related Entries   Authentication and Authorization; CHAP (Challenge Handshake Authentication Protocol); Cryptography; One-Time Password Authentication; Passwords; PPP (Point-to-Point Protocol); Public-Key Cryptography; Secret-Key Cryptography; Security; Smart Cards; *and* Token-Based Authentication

Linktionary!—Tom Sheldon's Encyclopedia of Networking updates	http://www.linktionary.com/p/pap.html
Linus HOWTO document about PAP	http://www.linuxdoc.org/HOWTO/PPP-HOWTO/pap.html

Parallel Interface

A parallel interface provides a multiline data channel in which bits are sent across multiple conductors simultaneously. The bits must stay in synchronization as they cross the wires, so the parallel interfaces are limited in distance. Parallel interfaces are usually associated with printer connections, but several technologies implement parallel interfaces, including

- **HIPPI (High-Performance Parallel Interface)**   HIPPI is a high-performance parallel interface that is used in data centers and supercomputer applications.
- **SCSI (Small Computer System Interface)**   SCSI is a parallel interface for disk storage devices that is characterized by 50-pin or 68-pin connectors.
- **OFDM (Orthogonal Frequency Division Multiplexing)**   OFDM is a multicarrier modulation (MCM) scheme in which many parallel data streams are transmitted at the same time over a channel with each transmitting only a small part of the total data rate.
- **PCI bus**   The PCI bus is the peripheral interface bus inside most desktop PCs and servers. Most systems implement the 32-bit PCI bus, but 64-bit PCI bus systems should be selected when high I/O speeds are required. PCI-X is a high-bandwidth version of the PCI bus that operates at 133 MHz with data rates over 1 GB/sec in 64-bit mode. See "Servers" and "Switch Fabrics and Bus Design" for more information.

Typically, printers are connected via parallel ports and communication devices are connected via serial ports. Traditional IBM PC parallel printer cables have a 25-pin D connector on the PC side and a Centronics connector on the printer side. This interface is called *SPP (standard parallel port)*.

Today, parallel ports follow the IEEE 1284 standards defined in the early 1990s. It specifies the traditional 25-pin D connector and Centronics connector, as well as a new 36-conductor connector that is smaller than the Centronics connector. The connector has better electrical and physical properties.

The parallel interface has been expanded with *EPP (enhanced parallel port)* and *ECP (extended capabilities port)* while retaining backward compatibility with the original SPP:

- EPP has a bidirection mode that allows both devices to communicate. Intelligent printers, for example, use this mode to report status information back to the PC. EPP is also ten times faster than the original Centronics interface.
- ECP has all the features of EPP and also provides data compression via RLE (run length encoding). Repetitive scanner and printer data benefits from this compression. Under Windows, ECP uses DMA channels and buffers to move data.

EPP and ECP modes must be enabled in the BIOS setup of computers. Most printers today support these modes. The best choice in most cases is the one called "EPP/ECP." If a device does not support these modes, the older SPP mode is used.

Related Entries   Asynchronous Communications; EIA (Electronic Industries Alliance); FireWire; HIPPI (High-Performance Parallel Interface); HSSI (High-Speed Serial Interface); Infrared Technologies; LVDS (Low-Voltage Differential Signaling); Modems; Network Connection Technologies; OFDM (Orthogonal Frequency Division Multiplexing); SCSI (Small Computer System Interface); Signals; SSA (Serial Storage Architecture); Switch Fabrics and Bus Design; Synchronous Communications; *and* USB (Universal Serial Bus)

Linktionary!—Tom Sheldon's Encyclopedia of Networking updates	http://www.linktionary.com/p/parallel_interface.html
Craig Peacock's Beyond Logic site (see Parallel Port Interfacing section)	http://www.beyondlogic.org/
Warp Nine Engineering (see 1284 info section)	http://www.fapo.com/
Parallel Port Central by Jan Axelson	http://www.lvr.com/parport.htm
IBM Parallel Port FAQ/Tutorial (dated, but useful information on the original interface)	http://home.rmi.net/~hisys/parport.html
PCGuide: See Troubleshooting and Repair section	http://www.pcguide.com/

Parallel Processing

See Clustering; Multiprocessing; Servers; Supercomputer; *and* Switch Fabrics and Bus Design.

Partitions and Partition Management

See Replication; Volume and Partition Management.

Passwords

A password is a secret code required to log on or access a secure system. A password is used in conjunction with an account name. Normally, a password is assigned to a user account in advance by a network administrator or automatically by a security system. The user may be allowed to change this password the first time they log on.

User accounts, account names, and passwords are part of AAA (authentication, authorization, and accounting) schemes. *Authorization* is the act of verifying the identity of a user attempting to log on. Once authenticated, users are allowed to access network resources based on previously assigned *authorizations*. *Accounting* is the act of collecting information about resource usage for auditing and billing purposes.

Microsoft Windows desktop systems provide an opportunity for users to enter a logon name and password. Many people bypass this feature, but it is important if you log on to secure systems on local or remote networks. What the logon account does is securely store passwords that are used to access other systems. The option "remember this password" is available when logging on to servers and sites. If the user does not enter a logon name and password when starting Windows, this feature is disabled since Windows doesn't know who is using the system.

Obviously, passwords must be kept secure. They should never be written down. Real words should always be avoided, as they are susceptible to dictionary attacks. A dictionary attack occurs when a hacker uses an automated program to try every word in the dictionary, plus other slang words, abbreviations, and so on.

While passwords like "Qp&yTxT8e3" are secure, they are also extremely difficult to remember. A more effective method is to create a phrase and use the first letter of each word as the password. For example, the password "Mbiot4oJ" is derived from "My birthday is on the 4th of July." A mix of uppercase and lowercase letters and numbers strengthens the password.

So-called "Trojan horse" programs are programs that some unscrupulous person installs on a computer to capture passwords as they are typed in by unsuspecting users. The program is often installed when people leave their computers unattended. Users should beware of executable programs sent via e-mail from unknown sources. Unsuspecting users who run these executables may see some funny or interesting program on their screen, but in the background the program may be installing a monitoring utility that sends captured passwords or other information via e-mail to a hacker!

Clear-text passwords should never be sent across communication channels that can be tapped. This includes all networks and the Internet. Anyone with a monitoring tool (packet sniffer) can watch for packets that contain passwords and capture the passwords for later use. Encryption is a good idea, but even better are techniques such as CHAP that never send passwords across the line. CHAP uses a scheme that only requires that users prove they know the password without actually sending the password. See "CHAP (Challenge Handshake Authentication Protocol)."

So far, the assumption has been that passwords are reusable—the same password is used over and over again. But such a password can be discovered or monitored, and reused by an unauthorized person at a later time. See "One-Time Password Authentication" and "Token-Based Authentication" for alternative authentication techniques.

RFC 1439 (The Uniqueness of Unique Identifiers, March 1993) provides useful information about identifying unique user names and passwords. RFC 2196 (Site Security Handbook, September 1997) provides information on passwords and authentication techniques.

Related Entries   Access Control; Account, User; Anonymous (Guest) Access; Authentication and Authorization; Biometric Access Devices; CHAP (Challenge Handshake Authentication Protocol); Cryptography; Digital Signatures; EAP (Extensible Authentication Protocol); Hash Functions; Kerberos Authentication Protocol; One-Time Password Authentication; PAP (Password Authentication Protocol); Public-Key Cryptography; Rights and Permissions; Secret-Key Cryptography; Security; Token-Based Authentication, *and* Users and Groups

Linktionary!—Tom Sheldon's Encyclopedia of Networking updates | http://www.linktionary.com/p/password.html

"Passwords—Strengths and Weaknesses" by Gary C. Kessler | http://www.hill.com/library/archives/password.shtml

A guide to UNIX account passwords and password security | http://www.acs.calpoly.edu/policies/passwords.html

Path MTU Discovery

See Fragmentation and Reassembly.

PBX (Private Branch Exchange)

A PBX is a telephone switch located on the premises of a company. It allows telephone users to set up circuit-switched voice calls among other users in the same company or to set up calls across the public-switched telephone network. People calling into the company dial a single number. The PBX routes the call to the appropriate extension. Internal users have a number of outgoing lines for making calls over the public network. By connecting internal users with other internal users, the PBX avoids the need for an internal call to be set up across the telephone company's switch.

The telephone company CO (central office) is the location of the switches that connect telephones for an entire town or metropolitan area and provide trunks to the much larger regional, national, and global telephone system. The PBX moves part of this switching system to the customer premises. As shown in Figure P-2, telephones (called extensions) connect to the PBX. The PBX is then connected to the telephone company's central office via a dedicated line, such as a digital T1 line that supports 24 voice or data channels.

Calls coming into the organization are automatically directed to an appropriate extension. The caller may dial this extension directly (called *DID* or *direct inward dialing*), select it in response to an automated message, or have an attendant connect the call to an extension. A PBX will also connect any internal extension with any other internal extension (station-to-station calling), or provide DOD (direct outward dialing).

Centrex is a telephone company service offering that locates PBX-like switching equipment at the carrier site, not the customer premises. Basically, the carrier creates a PBX for a customer in its switching equipment. This outsources PBX service to the telephone company, which is more capable of managing the services. In addition, Centrex makes it easy to keep up with the latest telephone technologies. Carriers can easily offer you new Centrex phone services. In contrast, a PBX may require an expensive upgrade to support those same services. In a decision about whether to use Centrex or PBX, Centrex is usually the preferred solution for small- to medium-size companies. Larger companies usually benefit from purchasing their own on-site PBX equipment.

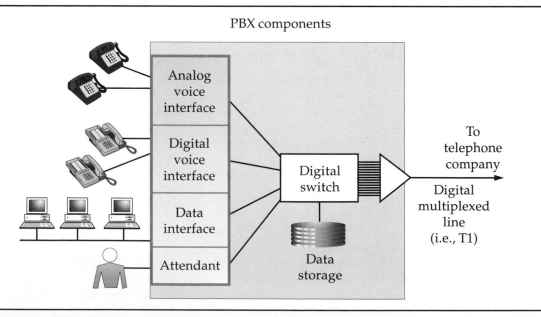

Figure P-2.   *PBX (private branch exchange)*

Traditional PBX vendors include companies like Lucent, Nortel, and Siemens. Modern PBXs use digital switching and controls, and support both analog and digital devices. The PBX vendor may support analog voice phones, but more likely will require that its own digital phones be used with the system. Digital phones may be single-line or multiline phones. Many PBXs also provide digital interfaces for data terminals and PCs. The latest generation of PBXs also support LAN connections. A wireless in-building telephone system is another PBX feature that supports cordless phones for people who need to walk around the building.

Single-board PBXs exist that may be installed in a network server to provide a relatively inexpensive PBX solution for small businesses. A typical board includes a T1 interface that supports 24 voice lines with optional expansion boards, if necessary. The systems support desktop CTI (computer-telephony integration). Administrators can manage the devices via PC-based management software. Users can dial a call, transfer calls, set up conference calls, or manage voice mail from their desktops.

The latest trend is to direct calls over the Internet. Voice must be digitized and packetized. Internet calls may take place directly between end users who have telephone-equipped PCs, or traditional telephone calls may be directed to an "IP-PBX" that handles routing calls over the Internet to other Internet users, or to switches that connect into the PSTN. See "Voice/Data Networks" and "Voice over IP (VoIP)."

Related Entries   Call Center Operations; Centrex (CENTRal Exchange); Circuit; Circuit-Switching Services; Convergence; CTI (Computer-Telephony Integration); Fax Servers and Network Faxing; H.323 Multimedia Conferencing Standard; Leased Line; Local Loop; MAN (Metropolitan Area Network); Megaco; MGCP (Media Gateway Control Protocol); Multiplexing and Multiplexers; NPN (New Public Network); PINT (PSTN and Internet Interworking); QoS (Quality of Service); Service Providers and Carriers; Softswitch; SPIRITS (Service in the PSTN/IN Requesting InTernet Service); SS7 (Signaling System 7); TAPI (Telephony API); Telecommunications and Telephone Systems; Unified Messaging; Videoconferencing; Voice/Data Networks; *and* Voice over IP (VoIP)

Linktionary!—Tom Sheldon's Encyclopedia of Networking updates	http://www.linktionary.com/p/pbx.html
The PhoneZone (one of the best sources for PBX information)	http://www.phonezone.com
Bitpipe (search for PBX)	http://www.bitpipe.com
AltiGen Communications, Inc.	http://www.altigen.com
Diallogic Corporation	http://www.dialogic.com
Lucent Technologies	http://www.lucent.com
NexPath	http://www.nexpath.com
Nortel (Northern Telecom)	http://www.nortel.com
Siemens Nixdorf Information Systems, Inc.	http://www.sni-usa.com
VocalTec Communications Ltd. (Internet telephony products)	http://www.vocaltec.com

P

PCI (Peripheral Component Interface)

See Switch Fabrics and Bus Design.

PDH (Pleiochronous Digital Hierarchy)

See NADH (North American Digital Hierarchy); E Carrier; *and* T Carrier

Peer-to-Peer Communication

This topic discusses various forms of peer-to-peer communications, including peer communications in the OSI protocol stack, traditional peer-to-peer networking (as compared to client/server networking), and community-based P2P (peer-to-peer) networking techniques made famous by Napster.

In the world of political negotiations, "peer to peer" refers to communications between diplomats of the same rank. In the networking environment, "peer to peer" refers to communications between similar processes running in different computers, or communication between devices that are equal with regard to how they exchange information and control communications.

The OSI protocol stack provides a commonly accepted layering of communications processes. The bottom layer defines physical connections, while the top layer defines applications processes. In between are connectionless and connection-oriented communication processes that establish connections between two points (data link layer) or across internetworks. A conversation takes place between peer protocol layers in each system. For example, transport protocols in one system exchange information with transport protocols in the other system. See "Network Architecture" for more information.

"Peer to peer" also refers to network communications that bypass servers and allow hosts to directly communicate. This is significant in enterprise networks where most exchanges take place through servers (i.e., the client/server model). Windows 9x includes peer-to-peer networking support that allows any host to establish a communication session with an equal relationship with another host. There is no need to go through a server. In the client/server architecture, clients must contact a server that usually controls access and message exchange.

P2P, Napster, and Edge Networking

P2P refers to peer-to-peer "community-oriented" information exchange tools that were popularized when Napster hit the scene. While the Napster trend started as a way to exchange MP3 music files, it has since turned into a sophisticated networking technology that helps users locate information on other user's computers and access it directly.

The P2P concept is that information is stored on user's computers. With software like Napster and Gnutella, users search for a song and the software displays a list of peers who have the song stored on their computers. The locations are displayed and the user selects the closest site or the site with the best download speed or music quality. Flycode (started by early Napster founders) describes its peer-to-peer software as software that connects members' hard drives to create a global, virtual library of noninfringing content. When a member requests a specific piece of digital content, Flycode sends him or her directly to another member's hard drive within a matter of seconds to retrieve the file.

P2P promotes a network storage model different from the traditional Web server storage model. End users host personal collections of music, electronic books, videos, photographs, technical information, software drivers, and so forth, on their own computers. Information is widely distributed, rather than stored on a relatively few servers. User computers become servers, or what some have called "media collection devices." This distributed file sharing concept is not new. It has been around for some time in collaborative software and Microsoft Windows' peer-to-peer networks. What Napster did was introduce software that simplified peer-to-peer content distribution among users without any controls imposed by network administrators (or the owners of copyrighted material, but that is another story). Software features quickly expanded to support instant messaging, advanced searching, and mailing list support.

In the enterprise (and on the Internet), peer-to-peer networking bypasses the central control that administrators have over information that is stored on file servers. Consequently, P2P has been called "server bypass" technology. While administrators normally prefer that all information access be handled by servers for security and control reasons, some administrators like the P2P concept because it reduces the traffic load on busy centralized servers. That in itself makes P2P a viable networking concept. However, it also opens users up to hacker attacks since connections and exchanges are not protected by traditional server-based security mechanisms. Still, P2P is not going away soon.

Users in departments or workgroups often need to share similar information. If they are connected to the same LAN segment, traffic stays local if they are sharing it off their own storage devices. In a wireless environment, users may be able to directly connect with one another and exchange files, thus keeping traffic completely off local networks or the Internet. In a hybrid approach, P2P software helps users locate the files they need on a nearby computer that is accessible via wireless connections. In some cases, a Web server may instantly move that information to a nearby server so the end user can access it using a short-distance Bluetooth wireless connection. Thus, P2P promotes networking at the edge. This concept is further explored at the Linktionary! Web site.

Developers are using the P2P concept as the basis for new collaboration software and automatic software distribution. P2P is also finding its way into online user-to-user swap meets, product exchanges, and auctions.

See the section "Internet Distributed File Sharing" under the topic "File Sharing" for more information, and a list of P2P software and information sites. Also see the topic "Distributed Computer Networks."

Related Entries   Collaborative Computing; Content Distribution; CU-SeeME; Distributed Computer Networks; File Sharing; File Transfer Protocols; Groupware; ICQ (I-Seek-You); Instant Messaging; Internet Radio; IRC (Internet Relay Chat); MP3; Multicasting; Multimedia; Unified Messaging; Videoconferencing; *and* Webcasting

Linktionary!—Tom Sheldon's Encyclopedia of Networking updates	http://www.linktionary.com/p/peer2peer.html
Peer-to-Peer (P2P) page at About.com	http://compnetworking.about.com/compute/compnetworking/cs/peertopeer/

ECompany WebGuide (search for "P2P")	http://www.ecompany.com/
Google Web Directory: File Sharing	http://directory.google.com/Top/Computers/Software/Internet/Clients/File_Sharing/
Napster	http://www.napster.com
Flycode.com	http://www.flycode.com/

Peering

The Internet is made up of independently managed but interconnected networks called *autonomous systems* or *ASs*. Lower-level service providers need to use the routes across higher-level service providers. Many national service providers also need to exchange routes with one another. Peering refers to a relationship between two service providers that agree to exchange traffic and routing policies, usually across a direct link that the two service providers establish. An analogy is the way that states allow the free exchange of traffic across their highway systems.

Peering agreements may take place between local ISPs or ISPs that provide the major backbone networks of the Internet. For example, consider two ISPs that service the same area. If those two ISPs develop a peering agreement, users in the same area can exchange packets across the shortest path (between the two local ISPs) rather than going through an intermediate exchange that both ISPs are connected to (and have peering agreements with).

Large ISPs that cover specific regions of the country will peer with one another to allow packets to flow smoothly and along the best paths between source and destination. Not all peering is equal. While big ISPs may peer with one another at no charge, smaller ISPs may need to pay to peer with the larger ISP, or go through alternative peering sites (which are usually overworked). Alternative peering sites are called *Internet exchange* or *NAPs (network access points)*, and these provide public peering so that any ISP can move traffic on the Internet. In the early and mid-1990s, the U.S. government built an experimental backbone network called the NSFNET that provided transit services among regional networks. The backbone concept was successful, but a single backbone was inadequate. Today's Internet consists of many interconnected backbones, as well as regional networks that peer with one another. See "Internet Architecture and Backbone" for more details on this structure.

Note that direct links between ISPs is usually accomplished by running a cable between routers that are co-located at an Internet exchange such as one of the NAPs.

Peering also involves the exchange of routing information among networks. Each autonomous system has its own routing policies and interior routing methods. Thus, an AS is often called a *routing domain*. The BGP exterior routing protocol is used to exchange routing information among ASs. Two BGP peers exchange information about the routes they can reach. The information is in aggregated form and describes only the prefixes (see "Route Aggregation").

While interior routing is usually based on metrics derived from topology, link speed, and load, exterior routing decisions are based on policy-based rules. BGP can understand policy rules, but a mechanism to publish or communicate the policies is still required. A *routing registry* provides this functionality by giving ASs a way to publicize their routing policies. RPSL (Routing Policy Specification Language) is used to specify routing policies. The IRR (Internet Routing

Registry) is the primary means of coordinating routing policy on an Internet-wide basis. It contains announced routes and routing policy in a common format that ISPs access to configure their backbone routers. These issues are discussed further under "Routing Registries."

A related document is RFC 2650 (Using RPSL in Practice, August 1999), which discusses the RPSL language and peering policies. See Section 2.1 on common peering policies for information. Other RFCs of interest are RFC 1786 (Representation of IP Routing Policies in a Routing Registry, March 1995), RFC 1787 (Routing in a Multi-provider Internet, April 1995), and RFC 2260 (Scalable Support for Multi-homed Multi-provider Connectivity, January 1998).

A form of peering also takes place between ISPs and the carriers. An ISP will peer with a CLEC—for example, to gain access to its SS7 network connections and, therefore, access to the public-switched network. This allows the ISP to route VoIP (Voice over IP) calls to and from the traditional telephone network.

Related Entries   Autonomous System; BGP (Border Gateway Protocol); Communication Services and Providers; Exterior Routing; IDPR (Interdomain Policy Routing Protocol); Internet; Internet Architecture and Backbone; Internet Connections; Internet Organizations and Committees; Internetworking; ISPs (Internet Service Providers); MAN (Metropolitan Area Network); Network Access Services; Network Core Technologies; NPN (New Public Network); Outsourcing; POP (Point of Presence); Registries on the Internet; Route Aggregation; Routing; Routing on the Internet; Routing Registries; Service Providers and Carriers; Telecommunications and Telephone Systems; Voice over IP (VoIP); *and* WAN (Wide Area Network)

Linktionary!—Tom Sheldon's Encyclopedia of Networking updates	http://www.linktionary.com/p/peering.html
Internet Operators.org (see Documents section)	http://www.iops.org/
The Commercial Internet eXchange Association	http://www.cix.org/
Merit Web route servers, peering, and statistics	http://www.rsng.net/routeservers.html
RIPE document: "Representation of IP Routing Policies in a Routing Registry"	http://www.ripe.net/ripe/docs/ripe-181.html
Geoff Huston's "Interconnection, Peering, and Settlements" document (excellent!)	http://www.isoc.org/inct99/1e/1e_1.htm
"Internet Service Provider Peering" by Geoff Huston	http://www.users.on.net/tomk/docs/settleme.htm
Network Worlds MAEs and peering page	http://www.nwfusion.com/edge/research/maes.html
TidBITS article: "Border Wars on the Net" by Glenn Fleishman	http://www.tidbits.com/tb-issues/TidBITS-383.html#lnk4
"Settlement Systems for the Internet" by Maria Farnon and Scott Huddle	http://ksgwww.harvard.edu/iip/cai/farnon.html
"Internet Exchanges: Policy Driven Evolution" by Bilal Chinoy and Tim Salo	http://ksgwww.harvard.edu/iip/cai/chinsal.html
"Scaleable Internet Interconnection Agreements and Integrated Services," by Joseph Bailey and Lee McKnight	http://ksgwww.harvard.edu/iip/cai/mcknight.html

PEM (Privacy-Enhanced Mail)

To provide privacy of electronic mail, mechanisms are needed to assure both sender and receiver that messages are confidential, that messages are from an authentic source, that messages have not been altered or corrupted, and that the sender cannot repudiate (disown) the message.

PEM was one of the first standards for securing the text of e-mail messages. PEM was defined by the IETF as a way to encrypt 7-bit text messages. It also defined a hierarchical structure for distributing and verifying digital signatures. PEM specifies a public-key infrastructure for key exchange over large networks like the Internet. However, the specification was deficient and newer standards have been developed, as discussed under "PKI (Public-Key Infrastructure)."

When MIME (Multipurpose Internet Mail Extension) was introduced as a way to add binary attachments to e-mail, PEM became less important because of its support for only 7-bit text messages. PEM was then extended with MOSS (MIME Object Security Standard), a protocol with PEM compatibility and support for MIME attachments. However, MOSS is difficult to implement and use. S/MIME is a de facto standard for securing mail messages that can replace PGP (Pretty Good Privacy) and PEM (Privacy-Enhanced Mail). See "MIME (Multipurpose Internet Mail Extension)" for more information.

Related Entries   Electronic Mail; MIME (Multipurpose Internet Mail Extension); Name Services; PGP (Pretty Good Privacy); *and* PKI (Public-Key Infrastructure)

 Linktionary!—Tom Sheldon's Encyclopedia of Networking updates   http://www.linktionary.com/p/pem.html

Performance Measurement and Optimization

This material is posted at the Linktionary! Web site. Also see "Capacity Planning," "Configuration Management," "Network Management," *and* "Testing, Diagnostics, and Troubleshooting."

 Linktionary!—Tom Sheldon's Encyclopedia of Networking updates   http://www.linktionary.com/p/performance.html

Perl

Perl stands for "Practical Extraction and Report Language." It is a programming language that processes text. In this respect, it is a scripting and report tool. Recently, programmers have been using Perl to build CGI (Common Gateway Interface) scripts for Web servers. More information about Perl is available at the Web sites listed here.

Related Entries   CGI (Common Gateway Interface); HTML (Hypertext Markup Language); HTTP (Hypertext Transfer Protocol); Hypermedia and Hypertext; Java; Metadata; SGML (Standard Generalized Markup Language); WebDAV; Web Technologies and Concepts; *and* XML (Extensible Markup Language)

Perl language home page   http://www.perl.com

The Perl Institute   http://www.perl.org

Yahoo!'s Perl page	http://www.yahoo.com/Computers_and_Internet/Programming_Languages/Perl
Perl authoring: a page about Perl with extensive links	http://www.stars.com/Authoring/Languages/Perl/
Tom Christiansen's "Acquiring Perl Software" Web page	http://language.perl.com/info/software.html
IRT (Internet Related Technologies) Web page (see Perl section)	http://www.irt.org/

Permissions in Windows NT/Windows 2000

See Rights and Permissions.

Personal Area Network

See Wireless PANs (Personal Area Networks).

PGP (Pretty Good Privacy)

PGP is an encryption and digital signature utility for adding privacy to electronic mail and stored data. Phil Zimmermann designed PGP in the early 1990s on the principle that e-mail, like conversations, should be private. In addition, both sender and receiver need assurances that messages are from an authentic source, that messages have not been altered or corrupted, and that the sender cannot repudiate (disown) the message. PGP can assure privacy and nonrepudiation. It also provides a tool to encrypt information on disk.

PGP was expanded over the years by an all-volunteer collaborative effort guided by Zimmermann. It is discussed in RFC 1991 (PGP Message Exchange Formats, August 1996). RFC 2015 (MIME Security with Pretty Good Privacy, October 1996) also discusses PGP.

PGP is designed to integrate into popular e-mail programs and operate on major operating systems such as Windows and Macintosh. It uses a graphical user interface to simplify the encryption process. The package uses public-key encryption techniques in which the user generates two keys—one for distributing to the public and the other to hold privately. These keys can then be used to encrypt and digitally sign messages, as discussed under "Public-Key Cryptography" and "Digital Signatures."

PGP supports *key servers*, so users can place their public keys in a place where other people can access the keys. The PGP certificate model differs from the traditional public-key model. The traditional model relies on a hierarchy of CAs (certificate authorities) to validate certificates and the keys within them. The PGP model relies on individuals to attest to the validity of certificates by signing a name/key association. According to RFC 2693 (SPKI Certificate Theory, September 1999), "the theory was that with enough such signatures, that association could be trusted because not all of these signers would be corrupt. This was known as the "web of trust" model. It differed from X.509 in the method of assuring trust in the <name,key> binding, but it still intended to bind a globally unique name to a key. With PEM and PGP, the intention was for a keyholder to be known to anyone in the world by this certified global name."

PGP is an alternative to RSA's S/MIME (Secure MIME). S/MIME uses RSA (Rivest, Shamir, Adleman) public-key algorithms, while PGP uses Diffie-Hellman public-key management algorithms. The results are generally the same. An older and less robust privacy protocol is PEM (Privacy-Enhanced Mail), which never gained widespread acceptance and has fallen into disuse.

In late 1997, the IETF began evaluating S/MIME as an Internet standard for e-mail privacy, but dropped it due to RSA licensing and some security issues. In September of 1997, the 20-year patents on Diffie-Hellman public-key management expired, so the IETF began evaluating Phil Zimmermann's Open PGP. Open PGP uses both strong public-key and symmetric cryptography to provide confidentiality, key management, authentication, and digital signature services. More recently, both S/MIME (version 3) and Open PGP are back in favor with the IETF, which has a working group for both, as listed later. Open PGP is also discussed in RFC 2440 (Open PGP Message Format, November 1998).

Related Entries   Certificates and Certification Systems; Cryptography; Digital Signatures; Electronic Mail; MIME (Multipurpose Internet Mail Extension); PEM (Privacy Enhanced Mail); PKI (Public-Key Infrastructure); Public-Key Cryptography; S/MIME (Secure Multipurpose Internet Mail Extension); Secret-Key Cryptography; Security; *and* X.509 Certificates

Linktionary!—Tom Sheldon's Encyclopedia of Networking updates	http://www.linktionary.com/p/pgp.html
Network Associates PGP Web site (formerly Phil Zimmermann's Web site)	http://www.pgp.com
PGP information and link sites	http://thegate.gamers.org/~tony/pgp.html
Internet Mail Consortium (see Open PGP link)	http://www.imc.org
Electronic Messaging Association	http://www.ema.org
Peter Gutmann's Security and Encryption-related Resources and Links	http://www.cs.auckland.ac.nz/~pgut001/links.html
PGP paper by Steven Shepard at Hill Associates	http://www.hill.com/library/archives/pgp.shtml
PGP. IETF Working Group: An Open Specification for Pretty Good Privacy (openpgp)	http://www.ietf.org/html.charters/openpgp-charter.html

Physical Layer, OSI Model

OSI (Open Systems Interconnection) is a layered model for defining and building communication systems. It is defined by the ISO (International Organization for Standardization). The lower layers define physical components and transmission schemes, the middle layers define communication management routines, and the upper layers define how applications connect into the model.

The physical layer is the lowest layer of the OSI model. It defines mechanical aspects like connectors, latches, and circuit-to-circuit assignments. It also defines electrical aspects like voltage levels representing binary values and resistance, functional aspects like grounding, and procedural aspects like transmitting bits across the medium in use.

Well-known physical layer interfaces for data communication include EIA RS-232 and RS-449. Well-known local area network systems are Ethernet, token ring, and FDDI (Fiber Distributed Data Interface), which have physical layer specifications such as the type of cable and connectors to use.

Related Entries   Cable and Wiring; Data Communication Concepts; Ethernet; Fast Ethernet; Fiber-Optic Cable; Gigabit Ethernet; Network Architecture; Network Concepts; Network Connection Technologies; OSI (Open Systems Interconnection) Model; Power and Grounding Problems and Solutions; Signals; *and* Testing, Diagnostics, and Troubleshooting

PICS (Platform for Internet Content Selection)

PICS is a W3C specification for describing the content of resources with a metadata label. PICS was originally designed as a way for parents and teachers to gain control over the Web sites and pages that children could access on the Internet. The PICS standards facilitate the following:

- **Self-rating**   Content providers voluntarily label the content they create and distribute.

- **Third-party rating**   Independent labeling services associate labels with content created by others. These services may devise their own labeling, and multiple services may label a particular provider's content.

- **User control**   Allows parents and teachers to use ratings and labels from a variety of sources to filter the content that children can see.

Related Entries   Cryptography; Metadata; P3P (Platform for Privacy Preferences); Public-Key Cryptography; *and* Security

    World Wide Web Consortium PICS site   http://www.w3.org/PICS/

PIM (Protocol Independent Multicast)

See Multicasting.

Ping (Packet Internet Groper)

Ping is a utility associated with UNIX, the Internet, and TCP/IP networks. Since most network operating systems now support TCP/IP, they also include a Ping utility. Ping is the equivalent to yelling in a canyon and listening for the echo. You "ping" another host on a network to see if that host is reachable from your host. The command takes the form ping *ipaddress*, where *ipaddress* is the numeric IP address of the host you want to contact.

Ping uses ICMP (Internet Control Message Protocol) for its operation. Specifically, it sends an ICMP echo request message to the designated host. If the device is reachable before a time-out period, your host will receive an ICMP echo reply message. Ping can be used as a troubleshooting tool when communication problems occur. The first thing to do is ping the address of the machine you are working with. This tells you that the network interface card is working. Next, ping the destination system. If no response is heard, try pinging another system just to see if the network is reachable. If another system responds, the network is probably OK and the destination network or host may have a problem. If possible, go to the destination and ping that machine to see if its network connection is working. If not, check the configuration settings, the connection, or the network interface card itself.

Related Entries   Cable and Wiring; ICMP (Internet Control Message Protocol); Internet Protocol Suite; IP (Internet Protocol); Network Analyzers; Network Management; Performance Measurement and

Optimization; Ping (Packet Internet Groper); RMON (Remote Monitoring); SNMP (Simple Network Management Protocol); *and* Testing, Diagnostics, and Troubleshooting

Daryl's TCP/IP Primer (see Troubleshooting section)	http://www.tcpipprimer.com/section.cfm
Ping information at NetworkingNews.org	http://www.networkingnews.org/networking/ping.html
Webmonkey article: "Examine Your Network with Ping and Traceroute"	http://hotwired.lycos.com/webmonkey/geektalk/97/42/index3a.html?collection=backend
Microsoft document: "Troubleshooting IP Configuration"	http://msdn.microsoft.com/library/winresource/dnwinnt/S7723.HTM
Gorry Fairhurst ICMP Web page	http://www.erg.abdn.ac.uk/users/gorry/course/inet-pages/icmp.html

PINT (PSTN and Internet Interworking)

The traditional circuit-based PSTN (public-switched telephone network) is giving way to the packet-switched model of the Internet. In a few years, people will make voice calls over the Internet with ease and with a high quality of service. In the meantime, both the Internet and the PSTN will exist. There are many instances when Internet users need to access the PSTN and PSTN users need to access Internet telephony services. In the former, an Internet telephony user needs to call a telephone on the PSTN. In the latter, a PSTN telephone user needs to connect with an IP-based telephony system.

The IETF PINT Working Group has addressed the arrangement through which Internet applications can request PSTN services. The IETF SPIRITS (Service in the PSTN/IN Requesting InTernet Service) Working Group has addressed the opposite arrangement in which PSTN users request services that require an interaction between the PSTN and the Internet. Some examples covered by SPIRITS include Internet call waiting, Internet caller-ID delivery, and Internet call forwarding. See "SPIRITS (Service in the PSTN/IN Requesting InTernet Service)" for more information.

PINT-defined services handles situations where Internet users request a telephone call to a PSTN terminal such as a telephone or fax machine. Services that PINT addresses often appear on Web pages, such as click-to-dial, click-to-fax, click-to-fax-back, and voice callback services. For example, a user visiting a Web shopping site may need more information about a product they want to buy. A click-to-fax-back button initiates a sequence that sends information to the user's fax machine through the PSTN.

The original motivation for PINT-defined services was the desire to invoke the following three telephone network services from within an IP network:

- **Request to call**   An IP host makes a phone call to the PSTN.
- **Request to fax content**   An IP host causes a fax to be sent to a PSTN fax.
- **Request to speak/send/play content**   Causes content to be spoken out. For example, a Web page has a button that, when pressed, causes a PINT request to be passed to the PSTN, resulting in the content of the page (or other details) being spoken to the person.

The typical scenario involves an Internet-to-PSTN gateway. An IP host sends a request to a PSTN gateway, which in turn relays the request into a telephone network, upon which the telephone network performs the requested call service. PINT Services uses both SIP (Session Initiation Protocol) and SDP (Session Description Protocol). SIP is used to invite a remote server into a session. The invitation contains an SDP description of the media session that the user would like to take place.

See RFC 2458 (Toward the PSTN/Internet Inter-Networking—Pre-PINT Implementations, November 1998) and RFC 2848 (The PINT Service Protocol: Extensions to SIP and SDP for IP Access to Telephone Call Services, June 2000).

Related Entries   Call Center Operations; Convergence; CTI (Computer-Telephony Integration); H.323 Multimedia Conferencing Standard; IN (Intelligent Network); Megaco; MGCP (Media Gateway Control Protocol); NPN (New Public Network); OSP (Open Settlement Protocol); PBX (Private Branch Exchange); QoS (Quality of Service); SAP (Session Announcement Protocol); SDP (Session Description Protocol); SIP (Session Initiation Protocol); Softswitch; SPIRITS (Service in the PSTN/IN Requesting InTernet Service); SS7 (Signaling System 7); Telecommunications and Telephone Systems; Videoconferencing; Voice/Data Networks; *and* Voice over IP (VoIP)

Linktionary!—Tom Sheldon's Encyclopedia of Networking updates	http://www.linktionary.com/p/pint.html
IETF Working Group: PSTN and Internet Internetworking (pint)	http://www.ietf.org/html.charters/pint-charter.html
Bell Labs PINT Working Group home page	http://www.bell-labs.com/mailing-lists/pint/

Pipes

Pipes are IPC (interprocess communication) features of the UNIX, Windows, and OS/2 operating systems. Pipes are like queues in which one process running in the multitasking operating system can store information it wants to pass to itself, to another process running on the computer, or to multiple processes running on the computer. The information is stored on a first-in, first-out basis and flows as a stream of bits that is not altered during transmission. A pipe is opened like a file and read from or written to in the manner of a file. Pipes are unidirectional in that one pipe is used to read and another is used to write information.

Named pipes are logical structures in a server that other systems access when they need to use the resources of the server. Named pipes are a networking extension of the IPC mechanism. A named pipe is a communication channel used to transfer information among programs, processes, and devices over the network. It is the basis for the communication mechanism between the client and advanced client/server applications such as SQL (Structured Query Language) servers and communication servers.

Pipes are normally used by programs and network processes, but users can take advantage of pipes at the UNIX or DOS command line to redirect the output of one command into another command or redirect the output of a command into a file. For example, the DOS command `DIR > FILELIST.TXT` sends the directory listing into a file called filelist.txt. The command `DIR | SORT` sorts a directory listing.

Related Entries   API (Application Programming Interface); Client/Server Computing; COM (Component Object Model); Connection Establishment; Distributed Applications; Distributed Computer Networks; Distributed Object Computing; IPC (Interprocess Communication); Java; Middleware and Messaging; Multitiered Architectures; Named Pipes; NetBIOS/NetBEUI; Object Technologies; RPC (Remote Procedure Call); Sockets API; Transaction Processing; *and* WinSock

PKCS (Public-Key Cryptography Specification)

See Public-Key Cryptography; PKI (Public-Key Infrastructure).

PKI (Public-Key Infrastructure)

A public-key infrastructure (PKI) is a full system for creating and managing public keys used for encrypting data and exchanging those keys among users. A PKI may be installed on an enterprise network, or it may be available in the public environment. A PKI is a complete system for managing keys that includes policies and working procedures.

PKI is about distributing keys in a secure way. Whitfield Diffie and Martin Hellman developed the concept of asymmetric public-key cryptography in 1976, but it was RSA (Rivest, Shamir, Adleman) Data Systems that turned it into a workable and commercial system. Today, RSA is the most popular public-key scheme.

A little history is useful in understanding the need for PKI and how it relates to public keys. RFC 2693, (SPKI Certificate Theory, September 1999) discusses the early problems of distributing keys between parties who were sharing encrypted information. Prior to the invention of public-key cryptography, it was necessary for two parties to exchange keys using potentially unreliable methods. Picture a secret agent carrying a key in a briefcase that is handcuffed to his wrist. Diffie and Hellman's public-key cryptography scheme simplified key exchange. Two related topics are "Key Distribution and Management" and "Public-Key Cryptography."

Here are the important points of the scheme, according to RFC 2693:

- A user generates a pair of inverse transformations, E and D.

- D is kept secret by the user. It is never communicated to anyone across any channel.

- E is the public "enciphering key." It can be given to other people, even placed in public directories where anyone (people you don't even know) can access it.

The advantage of this scheme is that the public key is placed in a public location where it can be accessed by anyone to encrypt messages to be sent to the owner of that key. When the owner receives the message, the private key is used to decrypt it. In fact, the private key is the only key that can decrypt it.

With the public keys now freely available in public places, the need for couriers was eliminated. But if you obtain a key from a public place, of course you'll want some assurance that it is the actual key for the party you wish to communicate with in a secure way. This requires that you trust the party holding the public keys—thus, the concept of a trusted third party (certificate authorities, as described in a moment).

Diffie and Hellman originally thought that the keys should be stored in a large public file, referenced by the name of the keyholder. This file was essentially a white pages directory, with name and key, similar to a phone book's list of names and phone numbers. But this file could potentially become quite large and would need to be stored at a place where it could be managed. According to RFC 2693, Loren Kohnfelder came up with the idea of breaking each name/key combination out of the large file and into separate records. These individual records could be digitally "signed" by encrypting or hashing them with the public key of the trusted third party. Kohnfelder called this signed record a *certificate*, and the trusted third parties that managed and signed the certificates became known as *certificate authorities (CAs)*. *Signing* is analogous to a tamper-proof seal on a bottle—if the seal has been tampered with, you don't trust the contents. For a discussion of how certificates are used, see "SSL (Secure Socket Layer)."

Building Trust

The *public-key cryptography* scheme is an essential part of doing business on the Internet. It makes it possible for people who don't know each other to interact in secure ways. The scheme is also useful for internal networks as a way to authenticate users and provide secure communications.

Trust is an important aspect of this scheme. In an untrusted environment such as the Internet, two parties must rely on a trusted third party. The third party vouches for the authenticity of other parties so that they may safely communicate. This third party is called a *certificate authority* due to the electronic and cryptographic mechanisms it uses to provide trust.

A certificate authority (CA) is a national or international entity that is government regulated, much like a bank. It issues certificates that contain information about people and businesses that it has verified are authentic. A matching public key is inserted in the certificate and the whole packet is signed with the CA's private key. The signing creates a unique fingerprint that locks the contents of the certificate so that alterations can be detected. The authenticity of the certificate can be verified with the CA's public key.

CAs make public keys widely available to Internet users who need to exchange information and do business with unknown users. By signing certificates, a CA guarantees the binding between public key and user, which prevents masquerading.

The binding of public keys and user information in a certificate allows for a variety of unique features and applications, such as these:

- **Authentication**   If Bob has access to Alice's certificate, he also has her public key. Alice can send messages to Bob that she has encrypted with her private key. If Bob can open the messages with Alice's public key, the messages must be authentic.

- **Digital signing**   In the preceding scheme, a public key is used to encrypt an entire message. This can be computationally intensive. An alternative scheme is to run the message through a hash function and encrypt the resulting message digest, which is a relatively small block of data. The message digest can be verified by the recipient.

- **Nonrepudiation**   If a sender signs a document with his or her private key, the public key can provide proof that it was signed, thus preventing someone from later denying that they sent a message.

All of this relies on the fact that public keys can be trusted. The certificate provides this trust from a certificate authority. But this brings up the question "can you trust the certificate authority?"

PKI Structure and Services

A PKI is a system that provides protocols and services for managing public keys in an intranet environment or throughout the Internet. A global PKI is a potential goal, but whether that is possible or even desirable is questionable. Interoperability among existing systems and services is being developed through protocols and standards. For example, the X.509 standard defines a standard certificate format and layout. See "X.509 Certificates."

PKI structure is being defined by the Internet standards groups, as well as by government agencies such as the U.S. National Institute of Standards (NIST). A PKI structure is *rooted*, meaning that it has a hierarchy in which one CA vouches for another. For example, you obtain a certificate from a CA that can be validated with that CA's public key. But how can you be sure the certificate and the public key are authentic? The solution is that lower-level CAs are certified by higher-level CAs, and those CAs are certified by yet higher-level CAs. You can trace a *chain of trust* up through the hierarchy until you get to the root CA. Currently, there is no global root and that may never happen. Instead, there are many root CAs throughout the world, some of which are managed by government agencies.

An immediate goal is to make the use of security functions easy. Fortunately, desktop and server operating systems, Web browsers, and other applications are making this happen. While encryption and signing are often defined in what appear to be manual steps, these processes are often handled automatically and transparently for the user.

A certificate authority will typically provide the following as part of its public-key infrastructure services:

- **Client evaluation and registration services**   A set of procedures to check the credentials of clients, possibly based on government regulation.

- **Certificate creation**   The registered identities of clients are stored in certificates along with their public keys, and the certificates are signed by the CA.

- **Certificate repository and distribution**   A place to store certificates where they will be available to users and applications on demand. LDAP (Lightweight Directory Access Protocol) now appears to be the preferred method for storing certificates, although proprietary directory services (i.e., Microsoft Windows Active Directory) are also used.

- **Certificate revocation**   If a private key is compromised or the person owning that key no longer matches the identification within a certificate (say, they were fired from their job), a certificate must be revoked. Because any certificate may be revoked, all applications should check with certifying authorities before using the keys or information in certificates. Alternatively, revocation lists can be created and distributed among the CAs in a public infrastructure.

- **Chain of trust**   Certificate authorities should trust relationships with one another so that certificates and keys issued by different authorities can be verified.

- **Update services**   Certificates will require periodic updating with new information or replacement keys.

- **Security and backup**   A service that keeps information about clients must ensure that the information is protected from attack and disasters.

■ **Key recovery**   An optional feature is to provide a way to recover data should a private key required to decrypt that data become lost.

The last service, key recovery, is controversial. Governments want to do it for law enforcement purposes, but privacy groups want to keep private keys private no matter what.

X.509 and the IETF PKIX (Public-Key Infrastructure X.509)

As mentioned, a standard certificate format has been developed called X.509. It was defined in 1988 as part of the work done to develop the ITU X.500 directory services standard. The latest version of X.509 (3.0) was released in 1996. X.509 defines a certificate format for binding public keys to X.500 distinguished path names. X.509 supports both secret-key (single-key) cryptography and public-key cryptography. The original intention was to define the keyholder that could modify a particular X.500 directory node, and the original X.509 data record was originally designed to hold a password instead of a public key. X.509 has since become an important part of the public-key infrastructure.

The IETF PKIX (Public-Key Infrastructure X.509) Working Group is developing X.509-based PKI standards. In particular, the group is defining the life cycle of an X.509 certificate. It is also trying to promote interoperability among X.509 implementations. The Web site given later provides a complete list of drafts and RFCs related to this project.

The papers at the IETF Web sites listed later are interesting and enlightening (and amusing). Anyone interested in how certificates can and will be used should visit this site. Carl Ellison's "Generalized Certificates" paper is very humorous and informative. See "X.509 Certificates" in this book for more information and illustrations about these standard certificates.

SPKI (Simple PKI)

The IETF SPKI Working Group has developed digital certificate standards that are more concerned with authorization than authentication. This is different from the original goal of certificates as stated earlier, which was to bind names and keys. SPKI certificates are meant to authorize some action, give permission, and grant a capability to or for a keyholder.

SPKI certificates are usually not meant to be published, as are public keys. Instead, keyholders distribute the keys directly to a verifier. The certificates may be stored in a global repository such as LDAP, a global PGP key server, or the DNS database. The SPKI Working Group explicitly states that these decisions should be decided by the keyholder, not some defined standard.

The working group also states that SPKI certificates should carry the minimum information necessary to accomplish the task of authorization or whatever else is being done. Requiring any additional information would be considered "a dossier and therefore a privacy violation." A minimum of information is required to prove permission levels. In fact, one use envisioned is for secret balloting where the certificate is anonymous.

SPKI certificates were also meant to be used in constrained environments such as smart cards, or small embedded systems where code and memory requirements are small. Simplicity is important. The fields are limited to just what is necessary to "get the job done," with few if any optional fields.

Basically, SPKI is meant to provide security for a range of Internet applications. Some interesting uses are presented in RFC 2692, including applications in banking (i.e., a certificate to give permission to write electronic checks), personal use (i.e., a certificate testifying to a friend's reputation), software validation (i.e., a certificate that indicates some software is authentic), and so on. The list is both interesting and entertaining (I wondered whether I was being spoofed).

PKCS (Public-Key Cryptography Standards)

PKCS is a series of specifications developed by RSA Laboratories to advance the use of public-key cryptography. The specifications were first developed in 1991. There are up to 15 separate documents that define everything from RSA cryptography standards to certificate standards to token interface standards. The complete set of documents is available at RSA's Web site give later. Also see RFC 2898 (listed shortly).

IETF RFCs

The two IETF working groups mentioned earlier (PKIX and SPKI) are developing public-key infrastructure standards. The Web sites (listed later) provide a complete list of related drafts and RFCs. Some of the more important RFCs related to PKI are listed here. A complete list is available at the Linktionary! Web site.

- RFC 2401 (Security Architecture for the Internet Protocol, November 1998)
- RFC 2437 (PKCS #1: RSA Cryptography Specifications Version 2.0, October 1998)
- RFC 2527 (Internet X.509 Public-Key Infrastructure Certificate Policy and Certification Practices Framework, March 1999)
- RFC 2692 (SPKI Requirements, September 1999)
- RFC 2693 (SPKI Certificate Theory, September 1999)
- RFC 2898 (PKCS #5: Password-Based Cryptography Specification, Version 2.0, September 2000)

Related Entries   Authentication and Authorization; Certificates and Certification Systems; Cryptography; Digital Signatures; DSS (Digital Signature Standard); EAP (Extensible Authentication Protocol); Electronic Commerce; FORTEZZA; Hacking and Hackers; Hash Functions; IPSec (IP Security); Kerberos Authentication Protocol; Key Distribution and Management; One-Time Password Authentication; OPSEC (Open Platform for Security); PGP (Pretty Good Privacy); Public-Key Cryptography; Quantum Cryptography; Secret-Key Cryptography; Security; SKIP (Simple Key Management for Internet Protocols); SSL (Secure Sockets Layer); TLS (Transport Layer Security); Token-Based Authentication; Trust Relationships and Trust Management; *and* X.509 Certificates

Linktionary!—Tom Sheldon's Encyclopedia of Networking updates	http://www.linktionary.com/p/pki.html
PKI Forum	http://www.pkiforum.org/
IETF Public-Key Infrastructure (X.509) (pkix) charter	http://www.ietf.org/html.charters/pkix-charter.html
IETF Simple Public-Key Infrastructure (spki) charter	http://www.ietf.org/html.charters/spki-charter.html

RSA's PKCS (Public-Key Cryptography Standards) page	http://www.rsasecurity.com/rsalabs/pkcs/
NIST's PKI page	http://csrc.ncsl.nist.gov/pki
The Open Group's PKI page	http://www.opengroup.org/public/tech/security/pki/
PKI Law Web site	http://www.pkilaw.com/
"Ten Risks of PKI: What You're Not Being Told About Public Key Infrastructure" by C. Ellison and B. Schneier	http://www.counterpane.com/pki-risks.html
Baltimore learning center PKI page	http://www.baltimore.ie/library/pki/pki-components.html

PKIX (Public-Key Infrastructure X.509)

See PKI (Public-Key Infrastructure); X.509 Certificates

PNNI (Private Network-to-Network Interface)

PNNI is a link-state routing protocol for ATM networks that automatically finds paths in the network using neighbor discovery techniques and then assists in setting up SVCs (switched virtual circuits) between end systems. In this respect, PNNI is both a signaling and routing protocol. A signaling plane assists in setting up virtual circuits while routing functions provide a mechanism to route ATM cells between switches or autonomous ATM networks.

PNNI is an ATM Forum protocol that was designed using concepts borrowed from the Internet's OSPF link-state routing protocol. One of its primary features is the ability to support the integration of multivendor ATM switches. PNNI provides a standard signaling protocol so that multivendor ATM equipment can exchange topology information.

Note that PNNI is an abbreviation for "Private Network-to-Node Interface" or "Private Network-to-Network Interface." *Node* refers to an ATM switch. The two different names reflect the fact that PNNI works between two ATM switches in the same network or between separate, autonomous ATM networks.

PNNI is a dynamic routing protocol. Before PNNI, ATM network administrators used manual techniques or interim protocols to configure PVCs (permanent virtual circuits) across networks. As a network grows, setting up such static routes can be labor intensive. A PVC is a specific path through the network defined by multiple links. Each link must be defined for each path. As the number of PVCs grows, it is virtually impossible for administrators to keep up with the configuration task. PNNI helps administrators set up and manage paths by dynamically configuring SVCs.

PNNI is a source-routing protocol as compared to the Internet's hop-by-hop routing scheme. In the hop-by-hop scheme, packet-forwarding decisions are made individually by each router based on previously exchanged route topology information. When a router receives a packet, it looks up the packet's destination address in a routing table and forwards the packet appropriately. As for ATM networks, virtual circuits across the network must be established before cells start to flow. Paths are selected based on QoS requirements or other factors. There is no decision making at each switch about which path a cell should be forwarded on. Previously exchanged PNNI information is used to determine the best path through the network.

PNNI is an important reason why ATM is a great choice for enterprise backbones and carrier core networks. With PNNI, ATM switches can be connected with multiple links in a mesh configuration. All the links between points can provide load sharing, and links can be added or removed without disrupting the network.

Each ATM switch is called a node, and multiple nodes can be organized into what are called *peer groups*. The link that joins nodes in the same peer group is called a "horizontal link." Nodes in the peer group exchange information with one another, such as reachability, QoS, and topology information. Nodes within peer groups exchange "hello" messages that contain the identity of their immediate neighbors. The information is synchronized to create a topology database that provides nodes with the most current view of the peer group's topology, as well as link metrics, bandwidth, and other information.

A typical PNNI network consists of multiple peer groups that may be configured in a flat or hierarchical configuration. As shown in Figure P-3, peer groups connect with one another via *border nodes* and *border links*. A *peer group leader* is elected in each group to exchange reachability and topology information across borders to other peer groups.

In a hierarchical configuration, topology information that is exchanged between peer groups is aggregated, which helps cut down on the amount of information exchanged between groups. This structure is best for large networks. Aggregation is a hierarchical routing technique that represents a large block of addresses with a single identifier (summarization). The postal ZIP code provides an analogy. For example, all mail with ZIP codes 9*xxxx* is directed to the West

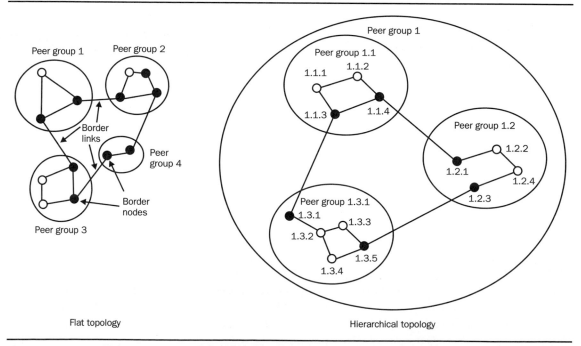

Figure P-3.   *The PNNI hierarchy and address aggregation simplifies the exchange of topology information.*

Coast where the remaining digits are used to further route the mail. Note the hierarchical numbering scheme on the right in Figure P-3 (simplified for clarity). The entire group is called peer group 1. Each individual group has an address in the form 1.x and each individual node has an address in the form 1.x.y. Nodes in peer group 1.1 do not need to know the addresses of nodes in peer group 1.2. They only need to be concerned with its peer group address (1.2).

While hierarchical structures and aggregation reduce the amount of information that must be exchanged across the network, they also reduce the amount of network information that is available to nodes. A flat topology in which topology information is not aggregated can produce better route selections since nodes have more topology information to work with.

PNNI architecture and addressing is covered further in a paper about PNNI by Michael Patterson at the Enterasys Networks Web site given later.

PAR (PNNI Augmented Routing)

PAR is an extension to PNNI routing that distributes information about non-ATM services. In this way, it can be thought of as an advertising service. The information can be distributed (flooded) in an ATM network as part of the PNNI topology. Currently, PAR can flood IPv4-related protocol information such as OSPF or BGP. A PAR-capable device is able to provide access to non-ATM services located on or behind itself and then flood that information using PNNI routing. Other nodes can examine this information to find desired services that are reachable through the ATM network.

Overlay routing provides a good example of how PAR is used. PAR-capable routers can advertise the routing protocol supported on their interface along with their IP address and subnet, and other protocol-specific details. PAR-capable routers can also learn about other routers on the network that support the same routing protocols. Basically, PAR allows an overlay network to be established automatically on an ATM backbone in a dynamic way that does not require manual configuration. An additional set of protocols, called Proxy PAR, allows clients that are not PAR capable to interact with PAR-capable devices.

PAR also supports filtering in a way that allows the implementation of VPNs (virtual private networks). In a service provider network, each customer can be assigned a unique VPN ID. PAR information is tagged with the VPN ID making the information unique to a particular customer. Information that can be filtered includes VPN ID, and IP address (including a subnet mask), as well as protocol flags. The VPN ID is part of all Proxy PAR registrations and queries, allowing services of a given customer to be available only to clients in that customer's network.

Related Entries   ATM (Asynchronous Transfer Mode); IP over ATM; Link-State Routing; OSPF (Open Shortest Path First) Routing; QoS (Quality of Service); *and* Routing

Linktionary!—Tom Sheldon's Encyclopedia of Networking updates	http://www.linktionary.com/p/pnni.html
ATM Forum	http://www.atmforum.com
ATM Forum PNNI and PAR information	http://www.atmforum.com/atmforum/specs/approved.html
Enterasys (formerly Cabletron Systems) PNNI paper by Michael Patterson	http://www.enterasys.com/products/whitepapers/pnni-1/

PNNI Paper by Mika Loukola	http://www.tml.hut.fi/Opinnot/Tik-110.551/1997/pnni/
PNNI paper at IBM	http://www.networking.ibm.com/pnni/pnniwp.html
Cisco documentation: Designing ATM Internetworks	http://www.cisco.com/univercd/cc/td/doc/cisintwk/idg4/nd2008.htm

Point-to-Point Communications

A point-to-point connection is a dedicated communication link between two systems or processes. Think of a wire that directly connects two systems. The systems use that wire exclusively to communicate. The opposite of point-to-point communications is broadcasting, where one system transmits to many.

A telephone call is a circuit-oriented, point-to-point link between two phones. However, calls are usually multiplexed across telephone company trunks; so, while the circuit itself may be virtual, the users are engaging in a point-to-point communication session.

An end-to-end connection refers to a connection between two systems across a switched network. For example, the Internet is made up of a mesh of routers. Packets follow a hop-by-hop path from one router to the next to reach their destinations. Each hop consists of a physical point-to-point link between routers. Therefore, a routed path consists of *multiple* point-to-point links. In the ATM and frame relay environment, the end-to-end path is called a *virtual circuit* that crosses a predefined set of point-to-point links.

A shared LAN such as Ethernet provides a form of point-to-point communications. Keep in mind that on shared LANs, all nodes listen to signals on the cable, so broadcasting is supported. However, when one node addresses frames to another node and only that node receives the frames, one could say that the two nodes are engaged in point-to-point communications across a shared medium.

Point-to-multipoint connections are possible over multidrop links. A mainframe and its terminals is an example. The device that provides the multipoint connection is usually an intelligent controller that manages the flow of information from the multiple devices attached to it.

Point-to-point communications is defined in the physical and data link layers of the OSI protocol stack.

Related Entries   Asynchronous Communications; Circuit; Circuit-Switching Services; Connection-Oriented and Connectionless Services; Data Communication Concepts; Data Link Protocols; Dial-Up Line; E-Carrier; End Systems and End-to-End Connectivity; HDLC (High-level Data Link Control); Internetworking; LAN (Local Area Network); LAP (Link Access Procedure); LLC (Logical Link Control); Network Concepts; OSI (Open Systems Interconnection) Model; PPP (Point-to-Point Protocol); SDLC (Synchronous Data Link Control); Serial Communication and Interfaces; Synchronous Communications; T-Carriers; TDM Networks; *and* Virtual Circuit

Policy-Based Management

Policy-based management provides a way to allocate network resources, primarily network bandwidth, QoS, and security (firewalls), according to defined business policies. As the requirement for QoS increases with the use of Voice over IP (VoIP) and other real-time applications, the requirement for bandwidth allocation based on policy increases. Policy definitions are a response to questions such as these:

- Who and what can access which resources on the network?
- What is the highest priority traffic, what is the lowest priority traffic, and what levels of traffic are in between?
- What traffic must have guaranteed delivery?
- How is bandwidth allocated to ensure guaranteed delivery?
- What traffic is eligible for discard when the network becomes busy and congested?

A policy-based management system allows administrators to define rules based on these types of questions and manage them in the policy system. These rules take the form "If *condition*, then *action*." A condition may be a user or group, the time of day, the application type, or the network address. Policy rules are then distributed to network resources. Policy-based management systems are best for large networks where large numbers of devices are easier to manage from a central location. Public networks will also use a form of policy management to allocate resources, but resource allocation is based on SLAs (services level agreements) established with customers.

Resources include devices that manage network bandwidth, security, IP addresses, storage, processors, and agents, as well as systems that manage services such as billing, accounting, and service mapping (i.e., mapping an RSVP request to an ATM SVC). Locator services are also required to help resource managers find one another. See "SLP (Service Location Protocol)" and "Service Advertising and Discovery."

In the last few years, network elements such as layer 3 switches and multilayer switches have gained the intelligence and processing speed to provide QoS and policy-based decision making. These devices have the ability to monitor and evaluate traffic without delay and make QoS and policy-related decisions. See "Multilayer Switching."

The IETF Policy Framework (POLICY) Working Group has developed a policy management architecture that is considered the best approach for policy management on the Internet. It includes the following components, as pictured in Figure P-4:

- **Policy management service**   A graphical user interface for specifying, editing, and administering policy.
- **Dedicated policy repository**   A place to store and retrieve policy information, such as an LDAP server or a DEN (Directory Enabled Network) device.
- **PDP (policy decision point)**   A resource manager or policy server that is responsible for handling events and making decisions based on those events (i.e., at time x do y), and updating the PEP configuration appropriately.
- **PEP (policy enforcement point)**   PEP exists in network nodes such as routers, firewalls, and hosts. It enforces the policies based on the "if condition then action" rule sets it has received from the PDP.

■ **LPDP (local policy decision point)**   This is a scaled-down PDP that exists within a network node and is used in cases when a policy server is not available. Basic policy decisions can be programmed into this component.

A variety of protocols may be used to communicate policy information between the PDP and the PEP. COPS (Common Open Policy Service) is the usual protocol, although DIAMETER or even SNMP may be used. COPS is a client/server protocol that provides transport services for moving policy information among IP network nodes. It also provides the transport for policy queries and responses. By moving policy information to different subnets, users can log on at other locations and receive the same service they receive from their home network.

COPS was developed by the IETF RSVP Admission Policy (RAP) Working Group, which is developing a scalable policy control model for RSVP. The group is working with the IETF POLICY Working Group to ensure that COPS supports policy information exchange between PDPs and PEPs. A complete set of related drafts and RFCs is located at the RAP site given later. Directories have become a crucial part of policy-based management. They are used to store and retrieve policy information. The IETF is working with the DMTF (Desktop Management Task Force) to define how policies are implemented in its DEN (Directory Enabled Network) specification. DEN defines a standard directory services architecture and schema that can be used to store network policy and configuration information. It also defines a distributed database that can be replicated to other locations; a consistent data model (structure of the data—that is, how real-world objects are defined in the directory); and LDAP (Lightweight Directory Access Protocol), a protocol that applications use to access the directory. With DEN, network administrators can integrate network information and policies in a single database that is consistent across the enterprise.

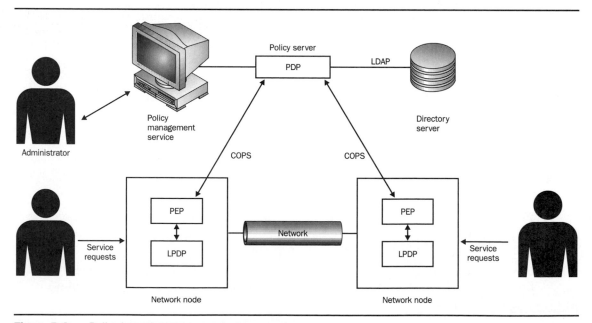

Figure P-4.   *Policy-based management components*

A typical policy transaction starts with a resource request to some device by a user or another network device. For example, a user may request access to a router interface that leads to the Internet. The router forwards the request to the PDP in the policy server using the COPS protocol. The policy server then queries one or more directory servers (via LDAP) to determine the user's authorization. The information is then used to build a "policy lease" that is sent back to the router. The router then implements and enforces the policy via its policy enforcement point.

Cisco QoS Policy Manager (QPM) enables end-to-end quality of service for enterprise networks. Network administrators use QPM as a complete system for application- and user-based centralized policy control, and automated reliable policy deployment. The QPM Web site is listed later.

SOCKS v5 is an IETF standard that can support policy management and border control (firewalls) for IP networks. SOCKS is interoperable with new security models such as IPSec.

The following Internet RFCs provide more information on policy management. Additional information is available at the Linktionary! Web site.

- RFC 2216 (Network Element Service Specification Template, September 1997)
- RFC 2748 (The COPS (Common Open Policy Service) Protocol, January 2000)
- RFC 2749 (COPS Usage for RSVP, January 2000)
- RFC 2750 (RSVP Extensions for Policy Control, January 2000)
- RFC 2751 (Signaled Preemption Priority Policy Element, January 2000)
- RFC 2752 (Identity Representation for RSVP, January 2000)
- RFC 2753 (A Framework for Policy-Based Admission Control, January 2000)
- RFC 2768 (A Report of a Workshop on Middleware, February 2000)
- RFC 2990 (Next Steps for the IP QoS Architecture, November 2000)
- RFC 3052 (Service Management Architectures Issues and Review, January 2001)
- RFC 3060 (Policy Core Information Model—Version 1 Specification, February 2001)
- RFC 3084 (COPS Usage for Policy Provisioning or COPS-PR, March 2001)

Related Entries   Accounting on the Internet; Admission Control; Bandwidth on Demand; BGP (Border Gateway Protocol); CoS (Class of Service); DEN (Directory Enabled Networks); DIAMETER; Differentiated Services (Diff-Serv); Directory Services; Integrated Services (Int-Serv); IntelliMirror; Multilayer Switching; Network Management; Prioritization of Network Traffic; QoS (Quality of Service); Queuing; Repository; RSVP (Resource Reservation Protocol); SOCKS; SBM (Subnet Bandwidth Manager); Switching and Switched Networks; Traffic Management, Shaping, and Engineering; *and* VoIP (Voice over IP)

Linktionary!—Tom Sheldon's Encyclopedia of Networking updates	http://www.linktionary.com/p/policy.html
IETF Working Group: Policy Framework (policy)	http://www.ietf.org/html.charters/policy-charter.html
IETF Working Group: Resource Allocation Protocol (rap)	http://www.ietf.org/html.charters/rap-charter.html

DMTF (Desktop Management Task Force)	http://www.dmtf.org/
Bitpipe (search for "policy-based management")	http://www.bitpipe.com/
SearchNetworking.com (search for "policy-based management")	http://searchnetworking.techtarget.com/
About.com Computer Networking subject and search page	http://compnetworking.about.com/
The Policy channel at stardust.com	http://www.stardust.com/policy
Policy-Based Network links page (slightly dated, but useful)	http://www.ee.umanitoba.ca/~blight/networks/PBN.html
"Building a Policy-Driven Infrastructure" by John McConnell	http://www.lucent.com/ins/library/pdf/white_papers/realnetwp.pdf
Lucent document: Policy-Based Networking	http://www.lucent.com/ins/library/pdf/white_papers/policy.pdf
Cisco QoS Policy Manager Web page	http://www.cisco.com/warp/public/cc/pd/wr2k/qoppmn/
Extreme Networks	http://www.extremenetworks.com/
Allot Communications (QoS and policy solutions for service providers and enterprises)	http://www.allot.com/
F5 Networks (see white papers section)	http://www.f5.com/
Novell ZENworks directory-enabled network management	http://www.novell.com/products/zenworks/

Policy-Based Routing on the Internet

See Peering; Routing on the Internet; *and* Routing Registries.

Polling

Polling is a technique in which one device continually monitors multiple other devices or makes requests from those devices, usually one after the other. Polling may also be done randomly or according to a predefined schedule. Polling is used by management applications to check the state of devices. It may read status information, then add that information to a log file or database for future reference. Many multiport network devices use polling techniques to check the status of ports or to service nodes attached to those ports. Each port may be serviced one after the other in a fair way, or some ports may be given priority service. Queue managers use polling techniques to service queues. See "Queuing."

PON (Passive Optical Network)

PON is one solution to the lack of bandwidth in the so-called "last mile." Home users have limited choices for gaining fast access to the Internet (telephone or cable systems). Likewise, enterprises have been limited to carrier T1 and T3 offerings, although wireless, optical, and satellite services are now more viable. PON provides another solution in metropolitan areas. It is being used in FTTH (Fiber To The Home). A hybrid PON system extends fiber cable to carrier remote terminals and then takes advantage of DSL services over the copper wire into homes.

Passive optical networking is a "resurrected" fiber-optic cable technology that was originally designed for cable TV networks. More recently, it has gained interest as an architecture that can provide high-speed access in metropolitan areas. PON is now an ITU specification.

With PON, a single fiber extends from a service provider's facility to a location near a group of homes or businesses. "Passive" implies that the system does not require power or active electronic components between the service provider and customer. It consists only of the optical fiber, splitters, splice points, and connectors. A single fiber provides service to multiple customers as compared to older systems that required a separate fiber to each customer. PONs can be used over great distances and are ideal for rural areas.

The basic PON architecture is pictured in Figure P-5. The concept is to run a fiber cable trunk from the service provider's head end toward the subscribers. The system has the following components:

- **OLT (optical line termination)**   The termination of the PON fiber cable at the service provider facility.

- **ONT (optical network terminal)**   The termination at the subscriber location.

- **OAS (optical access switch)**   A switch at the service provider that aggregates cells/packets from all the subscribers and provides a connection to the Internet and the PSTN.

- **POS (passive optical splitter) or "splitters"**   Splits the trunk and light signal at any point along the path into a multipoint tree topology.

- **ONUs (optical network units)**   Provides fan-out connections to subscribers. Up to 32 splits and up to 64 ONUs are supported per PON trunk. The subscriber connections from the ONU may be coaxial cable, twisted-pair copper, fiber-optic cable, or even wireless.

- **IOT (intelligent optical terminal)**   This is basically an ONU that is designed for business connections. It provides enterprises with a variety of voice and data services, much like an integrated access device.

The bandwidth of the PON trunk ranges from 155 Mbits/sec to 622 Mbits/sec. Each split reduces this bandwidth, so the bandwidth available to a subscriber depends on the number of splits between the subscriber and the head end. For example, a 622-Mbit/sec trunk that has been split to support 32 ONUs will provide the subscribers attached to the ONU with up to 19.5 Mbits/sec. This bandwidth is shared among the subscribers. Numerous techniques may be employed to organize the traffic on the cable, including ATM, Ethernet, FDM (frequency division multiplexing), and WDM (wavelength division multiplexing).

The FSAN (Full Service Access Network) consortium decided on ATM PON (APON), which became the ITU G.983 standard. G.983 is outlined at the FSAN Web site listed later. APON uses well-known technologies and provides guaranteed QoS due to the fixed size of ATM cells and ATM-specific QoS protocol features. Terawave Communication supports APON and has descriptive information at its Web site.

A group of companies led by Cisco and Corning are promoting the use of Ethernet PONs. The group claims that Ethernet is a more logical choice for PONs than ATM because most

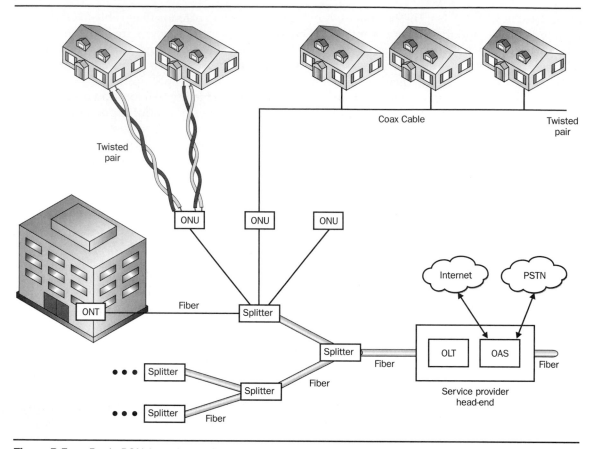

Figure P-5. *Basic PON (passive optical network) configuration*

enterprises are already wired with Ethernet. The IEEE formed the "Ethernet in the First Mile Study Group" to evaluate Ethernet PONs and other access technologies.

Related Entries   Cable (CATV) Data Networks; Communication Services and Providers; Internet Connections; Fiber-Optic Cable; FTTH (Fiber to the Home); HFC (Hybrid Fiber/Coax); Home Networking; Last Mile Services; Local Loop; Network Access Services; Optical Networks; Residential Broadband; *and* Service Providers and Carriers

Linktionary!—Tom Sheldon's Encyclopedia of Networking updates	http://www.linktionary.com/p/pon.html
SearchNetworking.com (search for "PON")	http://searchnetworking.techtarget.com/
Converge Network Digest optical networking directory	http://www.convergedigest.com/ DirectoryOptical.htm

FSAN (Full Service Access Network) consortium	http://www.fsanet.net/
IEEE Ethernet Web page (see "Ethernet in the First Mile Study Group")	http://grouper.ieee.org/groups/802/3/
Terawave Communications	http://www.terawave.com/
Optical Solutions	http://www.opticalsolutions.com/
Lightwave Magazine Online	http://www.light-wave.com
Light Reading ("the global site for optical networking")	http://www.lightreading.com/
Convergence Digest passive optical networking page	http://www.convergedigest.com/DWDM/pons.htm

PoP (Point of Presence)

A PoP is a place where communications services are available to subscribers. Internet service providers have one or more PoPs within their service area that local users dial into. This may be co-located at a carrier's central office. Most ISPs have multiple PoPs in different geographic locations so subscribers can dial into a number that is local to them. If you were to visit a PoP facility, you would see racks of modems, routers, servers, and communications gear. Some PoPs provide co-location services, since much of the equipment is owned by different service providers.

For the telephone system, the closest point of presence for subscribers is the neighborhood CO. A PoP is also defined as a place where long-distance telephone service providers (interexchange carriers, or IXCs) connect into regional and local telephone systems. In the U.S., FCC rules specify that local exchange carriers (LECs) must make space available in their facilities so that a long-distance carrier can connect with the local telephone system. PoPs in the telephone system are the result of the 1984 breakup of AT&T into a long-distance company and a number of LECs. Part of the judgment stipulated that the new LECs were to open their facilities to long-distance carriers for competitive reasons and to give customers a choice of long-distance carriers.

Virtual PoP

More recently, local exchange carriers, have gotten into the business of providing outsourcing "virtual PoP" services to ISPs. The concept is that the LEC/CLEC has all the facilities to manage the infrastructure for an ISP, including dial-up access ports, Internet backbone connections, VPNs, Voice over IP, QoS services, and network management. The ISP leases services from the LEC/CLEC and, in so doing, becomes a reseller of services in local areas, including customer help desk and management services. See "ISP (Internet Service Provider)" for more information.

A paper called "The CLEC Business Opportunity in Managed Port Services" at the Lucent Web site given later describes the virtual PoP concept further. The paper outlines the evolution of ISP networks as follows:

■ The early ISPs employed banks of analog modems at their sites. Remote access servers (RASs) were installed to handle dial-up users.

- Analog modem banks gave way to RACs (remote access concentrators), which integrate hundreds of modems in a single device.

- The next logical step was to co-locate the RACs at the central office or CLEC site, thus forming what is called a *megaPoP*. The RAC terminates the analog portion of a 56K call and transports it digitally to an ISP over a T1 or similar trunk. This is required to fully support V.90 modem technology. See "Modems" for an explanation. In addition, it allowed the carrier to separate data calls and voice calls, thus relieving the voice network from data calls that are usually connected for long periods of time.

- The next step is the creation of the virtual PoP. It evolves from a desire of the ISP to manage subscribers but not networks. Basically, the LEC takes ownership of all RACs, the PSTN interface, and high-speed Internet connections, and sells all services to ISPs.

This configuration lets ISPs expand their presence by leasing modems in any number of PoPs, thus providing local dial-up service for their subscribers. See "L2TP (Layer 2 Tunneling Protocol)" for an example of how this works. Also see "Internet Architecture and Backbone," which contains a subsection called "PoPs and Internet Data Center" that describes and illustrates various service provider facilities. In particular, refer to Figure I-6.

Another type of PoP is the Internet exchange, which is a location where many Internet network service providers meet to exchange traffic and peer with one another. The facility usually includes a central switch and racks where service providers install their routers. The routers connect into the switch and exchange traffic across its switching fabric. Internet exchanges were originally funded by the government. See "Internet Architecture and Backbone."

Another category of PoP is the GigaPoP, which has been defined by the Internet2 consortium. Internet2 is a group of universities that is developing and deploying advanced network applications and technology for tomorrow's Internet. New technologies developed by Internet2 are being deployed onto the existing Internet. The Internet2 consortium defines a GigaPoP as a regional network interconnect point that provides access to the inter-GigaPoP network. A GigaPoP is designed to support very high-speed access and aggregation of traffic.

Physically, a GigaPoP is a secure and environmentally conditioned location that houses communications equipment. It provides a termination point for circuits from Internet2 member networks and from wide-area data-transport networks. These inter-GigaPoP network links only carry traffic among Internet2 sites.

Related Entries   Access Provider; CO (Central Office); Co-Location Services; Content Distribution; Data Center Design; Internet; Internet2; Internet Architecture and Backbone; Internet Connections; ISPs (Internet Service Providers); L2TP (Layer 2 Tunneling Protocol); LATA (Local Access and Transport Area); Local Loop; Mobile Computing; NAP (Network Access Point); NAS (Network Access Server); Network Access Services; Network Core Technologies; NPN (New Public Network); Outsourcing; Peering; Remote Access; Roaming; Service Providers and Carriers; SS7 (Signaling System 7); Telecommunications and Telephone Systems; VPN (Virtual Private Network); WAN (Wide Area Network); *and* Web Caching

Linktionary!—Tom Sheldon's Encyclopedia of Networking updates

http://www.linktionary.com/p/pop.html

Bitpipe (search for "pop")

http://www.bitpipe.com/

SearchNetworking.com (search for "pop")   http://searchnetworking.techtarget.com/

Nortel iPoP (Internet Point of Presence) Web page   http://www.nortelnetworks.com/products/01/ipop/

Internet2 Gigapop information   http://www.internet2.edu/html/gigapops.html

POP (Post Office Protocol)

POP is an Internet mail server protocol that provides an incoming message storage system. It works in conjunction with the SMTP (Simple Mail Transfer Protocol), which provides the message transport services required to move mail from one system to another. The current version is called POP3, as defined in RFC 1939 (Post Office Protocol—Version 3, May 1996). Other related RFCs are listed later.

One goal of POP3 developers was to keep the protocol simple. If more sophisticated operations are needed, IMAP4 (Internet Message Access Protocol) should be considered. IMAP is covered elsewhere.

In-house networks may consist of a single POP server that holds all users' mailboxes. Large corporations may have individual POP servers for each department or division. The Internet has the biggest network of POP servers in the world. Schools, companies, and ISPs (Internet service providers) maintain Internet-connected POP servers that allow people all over the world to exchange mail. An ISP's POP server, for example, holds mailboxes for the customers of that ISP.

POP is dependent on SMTP (Simple Mail Transfer Protocol). A mail server must run both protocols if it is to receive and forward messages with other mail systems. The job of exchanging messages is handled by the SMTP protocol. Messages are routed from one mail server to another until they reach their destinations. The SMTP then hands the messages to the POP server, which puts them into a mailbox. If the destination POP server is offline, the most recent POP server to receive the message will hold it until it can be forwarded to the destination POP server. The destination POP server then puts the mail in the recipient's mailbox for retrieval.

POPs centralized mailbox scheme ensures that recipients get their mail even if their computer is not on, because the mail is held by the next-to-last POP server until it can be picked up. The POP server screens users to make sure that only the intended recipient accesses mail in a mailbox. A user's e-mail address and password are enough to prove their identity, although more secure systems using certificates are available.

Users run an SMTP-compatible mail client to connect with a POP server and download mail from their mailbox. As soon as the user connects, the mail is downloaded. One thing that POP does not do is let users keep some of their mail at the POP server for later retrieval. Mobile users need this feature. If you are working at someone else's computer or on a small hand-held, you may wish to only retrieve some of your mail. Some people like to keep incoming mail in an archive, which means that all mail must be downloaded to the computer where that archive is located. Downloading mail from a remote location defeats that scheme. One solution is to use Web e-mail while on the road, which lets users read their mail on a Web page while keeping the mail on the server for later download. The IMAP protocol is a successor to POP that allows users to read selective messages and keep unread messages on the mail server for later download.

Several other RFCs are related to POP. RFC 2449 (POP3 Extension Mechanism, November 1998) describes POP3 extensions. RFC 2595 (Using TLS with IMAP, POP3 and ACAP, June 1999) describes security options for POP. RFC 1734 (POP3 AUTHentication command, December 1994) describes the optional AUTH command for indicating an authentication mechanism to the server, performing an authentication protocol exchange, and optionally negotiating a protection mechanism for subsequent protocol interactions.

Related Entries Collaborative Computing; Directory Services; Electronic Mail; Groupware; IMAP (Internet Message Access Protocol); Instant Messaging; Intranets and Extranets; Mailing List Programs; Sendmail; *and* SMTP (Simple Mail Transfer Protocol)

Linktionary!—Tom Sheldon's Encyclopedia of Networking updates	http://www.linktionary.com/p/pop3.html
About.com Computer Networking subject and search page (search for "pop3")	http://compnetworking.about.com/
Electronic Messaging Association	http://www.ema.org
Internet Mail Consortium	http://www.imc.org
Mini FAQ on Client-Server Mail Protocols	http://www.rdlab.carnet.hr/NetLab/faq/client.html
RAD Communications POP tutorial	http://www.rad.com/networks/tutorial.htm
Google Web Directory: E-mail	http://directory.google.com/Top/Computers/Internet/E-mail/

Portal

If you've accessed the Web, you've no doubt been to a portal, so it seems odd to define it here. The simplest definition of a portal is a Web site with a lot of hyperlinks to other places. But portals may also host their own content such as news, sports, and weather, as do portal sites such as AltaVista, America Online, MSN (Microsoft Network), Yahoo!, or MSNBC. A portal is a place to hang out on the Web and jump off to other locations. Portals have been called "on-ramps" to the rest of the Web. One of the best examples of a portal front page is at http://www.yahoo.com. It's simple and to the point, and helps people get to where they want to go in a hurry. This interface has remained nearly unchanged for years.

The term "hub" has been used to describe an advanced type of portal that goes beyond the "on-ramp" concept. A hub is supposed to be harder to build than a portal, as it contains more than just links to other sites. Hubs target communities of people with the same interests, such as investing, hobbies, politics, movies, and so on. They are built by experts in the fields of interest being presented by the hub. These sites typically provide chat rooms, discussion groups, online conferences, papers, and other information related to the community interest. Space.com is a hub for people interested in outer space and astronomy. MP3.com is a hub for people interested in digital music. It's usually not hard to find these sites. Just type **www.*name*.com**, where *name* is the topic of interest. For example, try replacing *name* with "movies" or "garden."

Organizations may create their own "intranet portals" or "intranet hubs." These portals and hubs provide jumping off points for employees to other sites within the company, or to sources of information such as medical and retirement benefits information. They may also lead to sources of legacy information owned by the company, such as research data, patent information, customer information, and so on. This gets into the realm of EIPs (enterprise information portals), as discussed next.

EIP (Enterprise Information Portal)

In November 1998, the term "enterprise information portal" was coined by Christopher Shilakes and Julie Tylman of Merrill Lynch as a new type of application that "enables companies to unlock internally and externally stored information, and provides users a single gateway to personalized information needed to make informed business decisions." Joseph M. Firestone of Executive Information Systems (see links later) summarizes the definition of EIPs as presented by Shilakes and Tylman:

- EIPs use both "push" and "pull" technologies to transmit information to users through a standardized Web-based interface.

- EIPs provide "interactivity"—the "ability to 'question' and share information on" user desktops.

- EIPs integrate disparate applications, including content management, business intelligence, data warehouse/data mart, data management, and other data external to these applications into a single system that can "share, manage, and maintain information from one central user interface." An EIP is able to access both external and internal sources of data and information. It is able to support a bidirectional exchange of information with these sources. And it is able to use the data and information it acquires for further processing and analysis.

- EIPs exhibit the trend toward "verticalization" in application software. That is, they are often "packaged applications" providing "targeted content to specific industries or corporate functions."

Firestone notes that EIPs can be confused with data warehouses, and he notes that while data warehouses are associated with legacy data and OLTP (online transaction processing), he notes that EIPs "integrate and amalgamate data and information from such diverse sources as Web documents, research reports, contracts, government licenses, brochures, purchase orders, data warehouses, data marts, legacy systems, enterprise application servers, and any document with content relevant for some corporate interest."

Gerry Murray of International Data Corporation relates portals to commuting and predicts that corporations will make their entire infrastructure available as a portal for employees to access anywhere. He has outlined the following types of portals:

- **Enterprise information portals**   Makes information assets available to people.

- **Enterprise collaborative portals**   Gives people the tools they need to collaborate, including e-mail, chat, instant messaging, groupware, conferencing, and workflow software.

P

■ **Enterprise expertise portals**   Helps people connect with other people who have specific interests or expertise. Also provides people with expert tools to access and analyze data, or perform other tasks.

■ **Enterprise knowledge portals**   A combination of the preceding three types of portals.

Related Entries   ASP (Application Service Provider); Content Distribution; Data Warehousing; Metadata; Middleware and Messaging; Multitiered Architectures; OLAP (Online Analytical Processing); Repository; SAN (Storage Area Network); *and* XML (Extensible Markup Language)

Linktionary!—Tom Sheldon's Encyclopedia of Networking updates	http://www.linktionary.com/p/portal.html
Bitpipe (search for "portal")	http://www.bitpipe.com/
About.com Computer Networking (choose "Portals" under Subject)	http://compnetworking.about.com/
Executive Information Systems has numerous white papers on enterprise information portals	http://www.dkms.com/
destinationCRM.com (search for "portal")	http://www.destinationcrm.com/
"Enterprise Information Portals And Enterprise Knowledge Portals" by Joseph M. Firestone	http://www.dkms.com/EKPandEIP.html
"Defining the Enterprise Information Portal" by Joseph M. Firestone	http://www.dkms.com/EIPDEF.html
"Building Corporate Portals using XML," an excerpt from a book describing metadata and XML by Clive Finkelstein and Peter Aiken	http://www.isy.vcu.edu/~paiken/publications/bcp/indexbcp.htm
2Bridge, leading provider of enterprise portal solutions	http://www.2bridge.com/
Brio Technology (see Library)	http://www.brio.com/
Plumtree (maker of corporate portal software)	http://www.plumtree.com/

Ports, TCP/IP

Computers have a variety of physical hardware ports over which data is transmitted between input/output devices and external peripherals. A typical computer has parallel printer ports, serial ports, USB ports, a keyboard connector, and a mouse connector. Likewise, software processes running in computers need "software ports" to connect with other software processes. Interprocess communication (IPC) takes place between these ports.

In the Internet Protocol suite, the TCP and UDP protocols use ports to support interprocess communications between different networked devices. A single host may have multiple processes running at the same time, connected to one or more computers. Each of these processes is *multiplexed* through the same network interface and local network link. In other words, packets from each of these processes are interleaved and sent through the network interface. A port can be thought of as a *message queue* through which these packets pass.

Each process must be distinguished from other processes, and this is done with port numbers. Ports are numbered from 0 to 65536. The most popular applications and protocols, such as FTP, SMTP and SNMP, are preassigned to "well-known" ports. RFC 1700 (Assigned Numbers, October 1994) outlines these ports, although the list is slightly outdated. The Web sites listed later have additional information.

An application that provides a network service opens its assigned port and waits for messages to arrive on that port. For example, a Web server opens port 80. When a Web browser contacts a Web server, it directs its messages to port 80, the "well-known HTTP services port." Likewise, SNMP opens port 161. All SNMP management applications know to use this port. Some applications use multiple ports. If you use FTP (File Transfer Protocol) to request a file from an FTP server, the request is sent over one channel and the file is transmitted back over another channel. FTP uses ports 20 and 21.

Keep in mind that a port only identifies one process running in one computer. The port is combined with the IP address of the host to create a *socket*. This is like combining a name with an address on an envelope to identify a mail recipient at a postal address.

A socket identifies a process running in a specific computer, so it is one end of a *logical connection* across a packet-switched network. The other end of a connection is identified by another socket. Therefore, a pair of sockets forms a connection and the connection is uniquely identified by the "local socket/foreign socket" address pair. Once a connection is made, the connected systems can begin to exchange data. See "Connection Establishment," "Flow-Control Mechanisms," and "TCP (Transmission Control Protocol)" for more information.

Note that ports and sockets are associated with "long-term connections," something that is specific to TCP and UDP. Both are *connection-oriented* transport layer protocols. IP is a network layer connectionless protocol. Source port and destination port numbers are inserted into fields in the TCP and UDP packet headers. IP headers have source and destination IP address fields. The combination of the port numbers in the TCP or UDP header and the IP addresses in the IP header identifies sockets.

Portscanning is a technique that is used to discover the services being offered by a host. An external host attempts to connect to each known port to see whether the target host offers a response. This technique is used by hackers to find vulnerabilities in Internet-connected systems.

Refer to RFC 793 (Transmission Control Protocol, September 1981) and RFC 1180 (A TCP/IP Tutorial, January 1991) for more information about ports.

Related Entries   Channel; Connection Establishment; Flow-Control Mechanisms; Internet Protocol Suite; Pipes; Reliable Data Delivery Services; RPC (Remote Procedure Call); Sockets; TCP (Transmission Control Protocol); *and* Transport Protocols and Services

Linktionary!—Tom Sheldon's Encyclopedia of Networking updates	http://www.linktionary.com/p/port.html
Port Numbers and Services Database	http://www.sockets.com/services.htm
Web ProForums paper: "IP Internetworking Transport Tutorial"	http://www.iec.org/tutorials/ip_int/

PoS (Packet over SONET)

A major goal of service providers is to transport IP packets over underlying physical networks with as little overhead as possible. In the Ethernet LAN environment, IP packets go into

Ethernet frames, a relatively straightforward and efficient mechanism. In the WAN environment, a typical scenario is to put IP packets in ATM packets and then into SONET frames, as shown on the left in Figure P-6.

PoS removes the ATM data link layer, as shown in Figure P-6, to improve performance where ATM cells and switching techniques are not necessary. This is called "IP over SONET" or "packets over SONET," or just "PoS." In Europe, where SDH is used, it is called "packet over SDH." Actually, all these names are misleading because the technology is really "IP-over-PPP-over-SONET/SDH)."

As shown on the right in Figure P-6, the long-term trend is to bypass even SONET and run IP directly over DWDM. This will occur as SONET networks give way to new, more efficient, all-optical networks, as discussed under "Optical Networking."

There are benefits to eliminating the ATM layer. One is reducing the overhead imposed by the so-called ATM "cell tax." This refers to the amount of bandwidth that is used by the ATM header (5 bytes out of every 53-byte cell—nearly 10 percent). The Trillium paper mentioned at the end of this topic notes that IP takes advantage of only 79.6 percent of the line rate when ATM is used, but uses over 95 percent with IP-over-PPP-over-SONET.

IP over ATM is best used with mesh-connected networks that support any-to-any connections and virtual circuits across those connections. ATM is also used in environments where a rich set of QoS parameters is required (i.e., bandwidth management) and where multiple types of services (data, voice, video) must be aggregated over a common transmission infrastructure.

PoS can be viewed as three layers, and each layer is defined by the following Internet RFCs:

- **Top layer: IP encapsulation into PPP** See RFC 1661 (The Point-to-Point Protocol, July 1994)

- **Mid layer: Framing of PPP with HDLC** See RFC 1662 (PPP in HDLC-like Framing, July 1994)

- **Bottom layer: Mapping into SONET** See RFC 2615 (PPP over SONET/SDH, June 1999)

PPP provides a standard method for transporting multiprotocol datagrams over point-to-point links. It includes LCP (Link Control Protocol) for establishing, configuring, and

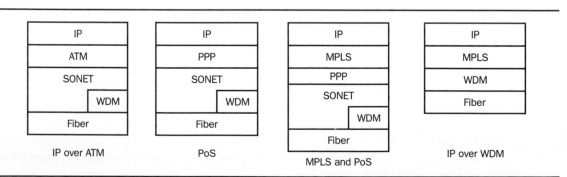

Figure P-6. *PoS (Packet over SONET) removes the ATM layer in the SONET environment.*

testing the data link connection. Refer to RFC 1661 and "PPP (Point-to-Point Protocol)" for more information. RFC 2615 is the primary document that describes the use of PPP over SONET and SDH circuits. All the physical layer requirements, framing, and configuration details are outlined in the RFC.

MPLS extends the functionality of PoS by supporting ATM-like virtual circuits and QoS capabilities in a PoS environment. The layout is shown as "MPLS and PoS" in Figure P-6. With MPLS, routers and switches can build paths through a network for end-to-end packet streams. Packets are then marked with labels that direct them down these paths. Routing decisions are eliminated since labeled packets can be switched at high speeds. The scheme takes full advantage of high-speed optical networks. See "MPLS (Multiprotocol Label Switching)."

RFC 2823 (PPP over Simple Data Link [SDL] Using SONET/SDH with ATM-like framing, May 2000) extends these standards to include a new encapsulation for PPP called SDL (Simple Data Link). SDL provides a very-low-overhead alternative to HDLC-like encapsulation, and can also be used on SONET/SDH links. The IETF Point-to-Point Protocol Extensions (pppext) Working Group has a full list of PPP drafts and RFCs.

Related Entries   ATM (Asynchronous Transfer Mode); DPT (Dynamic Packet Transport); Fiber-Optic Cable; MAN (Metropolitan Area Network); MPLS (Multiprotocol Label Switching); Network Access Services; Network Core Technologies; NPN (New Public Network); Optical Networks; PPP (Point-to-Point Protocol); SONET (Synchronous Optical Network); WAN (Wide Area Network); *and* WDM (Wavelength Division Multiplexing)

Linktionary!—Tom Sheldon's Encyclopedia of Networking updates	http://www.linktionary.com/p/pos.html
IETF Working Group: Point-to-Point Protocol Extensions (pppext)	http://www.ietf.org/html.charters/pppext-charter.html
IP/PPP over SONET/SDH: References	http://www.cis.ohio-state.edu/~jain/refs/snt_refs.htm
Trillium (an Intel company) IP-over-SONET papers	http://www.trillium.com/whats-new/rn_009.html
"Internet Protocol choice: Sonet or ATM?" by Rajeev Gupta (*EETimes* article)	http://www.techweb.com/se/directlink.cgi?EET19971201S0151

POTS (Plain Old Telephone Service)

POTS is the analog telephone service that runs over copper twisted-pair wires and is based on the original Bell telephone system. Twisted-pair wires connect homes and businesses to a neighborhood central office. This is called the *local loop*. The central office is connected to other central offices and long-distance facilities. See "Telecommunications and Telephone Systems" and the other related links next.

Related Entries   Circuit-Switching Services; CO (Central Office); Communication Services and Providers; DSL (Digital Subscriber Line); FTTH (Fiber to the Home); Home Networking; ISDN (Integrated Services Digital Network); Last Mile Services; Line Conditioning; Local Loop; Modems; NPN (New Public Network); PON (Passive Optical Network); Service Providers and Carriers; Telecommunications and Telephone Systems; *and* Wireless Local Loop

P

Power and Grounding Problems and Solutions

Electrical power is rarely supplied as a smooth wave of steady energy. You can see this when lights flicker or when the TV goes haywire while running a blender. Electrical connections are polluted with surges and spikes (collectively called *noise*). You can think of these surges and spikes as shotgun blasts of energy to delicate electrical components. Here's how computer equipment may handle transient energy:

- **Data corruption**   Electrical disturbances may corrupt memory or data transmissions. A program in memory may fail or cause errors that are thought to be program bugs.

- **Equipment failure**   High-energy transients can permanently damage equipment. Small microprocessor circuitry is especially susceptible. Surge suppressors should be used at primary power supply feeds or at individual stations.

- **Slow death**   Equipment that is repeatedly subjected to low-energy surges will fail over time. The delicate circuits in a chip break down, and the equipment eventually fails for no apparent reason.

Improper grounding is also often a source of problems. In fact, surge suppressors are often a cause of grounding problems because many devices route surges to ground. The surges then find their way back into the electrical system, where they cause problems elsewhere.

Electrical environments are *noisy*. Air conditioners, elevators, refrigerators, and even laser printers cause transients when they are switched on and off. The electric company causes transients when it switches grids to balance the system. In fact, any device that uses electricity in a nonlinear way can cause transients that affect other devices. Some common electrical line problems are described here:

- **Noise**   Often referred to as surges, spikes, or transients. Noise problems cause slow or immediate damage to sensitive electronic equipment.

- **Sag**   When circuits become overloaded, the power drops may be below the required level, causing a sag or dropout. A sag might continue for a period of time if the building is incorrectly wired or the utility company is having a problem. A long sag can cause damage to power supplies.

- **Swell**   A swell is the opposite of a sag and can also cause damage to power supplies.

- **Hum**   Hum is high-order harmonics caused by neutral-to-ground connection problems. Such problems indicate a defect in one of the electrical wires to ground. Hum can cause transmission errors in data communication lines. Network performance can suffer if systems must constantly resend corrupted packets.

Grounding Problems

Buildings are wired so that ground connections can drain electrical charges into the earth and protect people from electric shock. Without proper grounding, a charge will pass through a person to the earth. A problem in many buildings and with many computer and network installations is that sensitive electronic equipment and computers are often in the path of the shortest lead to ground. Thus, noise on the ac circuit can infiltrate sensitive electronics through the grounding circuit as well as the hot leads.

Grounding problems are especially prevalent in a network environment because the cabling system can provide a path for *ground loops.* For example, departmental LANs may normally be connected to different sources of power, which are individually grounded. When these department LANs are interconnected, the network cable can form a bridge between the two grounded systems that causes transient energy to seek equilibrium by flowing from ground to ground. In doing so, it flows through the computer systems attached to the cable and causes noise problems. To prevent these problems, equipment connected to different power sources must be electrically isolated.

On a large network, the creation of a single-point ground is usually impossible to achieve. Interconnected networks form links between close or distant points, any one of which can produce electrical problems due to poor wiring. These separate power sources might be in separate buildings, or in a multistory office building that has separate power transformers on every floor or every other floor. Each transformer has its own electrical characteristics and should not be connected to equipment connected to other transformers.

One solution is to connect the entire network to one central power source and ground, as shown in Figure P-7. A power conditioner and an uninterruptible power supply are used at the server. The power conditioner provides dedicated transformer isolation, a clean source of power, and a solid reference ground. Similar devices should be attached to workstations, if possible. A surge suppressor is placed at the feed to the electrical panel. If the surge

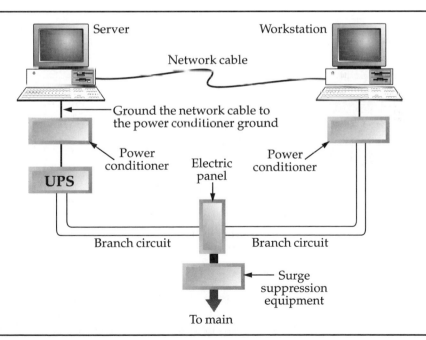

Figure P-7.   *Solving ground problems with a single power source*

suppressors are placed on the branch circuits, they will divert surges to ground and back into the circuits of other systems through the ground connection.

Ensure that a single LAN segment is connected to circuits that branch from a single power source and that no point in the segment shares a ground with other power sources. An electrical contractor can perform this service.

While a single power source is beneficial, it is usually impractical on large networks. One trick is to use nonconductive fiber-optic cable to interconnect networks that are using different power supplies. Figure P-8 illustrates how electrical isolation is maintained between two LAN segments, allowing better control over ground and noise problems.

It is a good idea to buy uninterruptible power supplies and surge suppressors to protect your network equipment. An *uninterruptible power supply* is a battery backup device, generator, or other device that provides a computer with power during an outage. A *surge suppressor* is a device that protects a system against spikes in the electrical power. Most power supplies in desktop systems can handle surges of up to 800 volts. A surge suppressor is required to protect against surges above these levels.

Related Entries   Cable and Wiring; Data Center Design; Data Protection; Disaster Planning and Recovery; Fault Management; Fault Tolerance and High Availability; Fiber-Optic Cable; Line Conditioning; Network Concepts; Network Design and Construction; Redundancy; Testing, Diagnostics, and Troubleshooting; TIA/EIA Structured Cabling Standards; *and* UPS (Uninterruptible Power Supply)

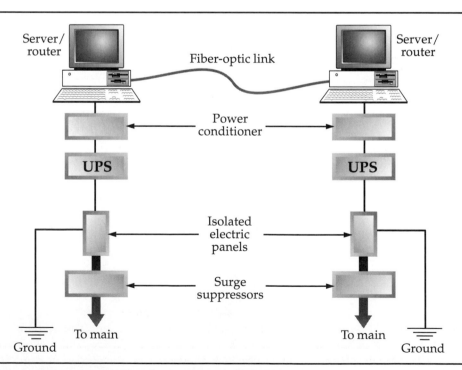

Figure P-8.   *Isolating internetwork subnets with nonconducting cable*

Linktionary!—Tom Sheldon's Encyclopedia of Networking updates   http://www.linktionary.com/p/power_protection.html

Bitpipe (search for "power protection")   http://www.bitpipe.com/

About.com power protection page   http://www.peripherals.about.com/compute/peripherals/cs/powerprotection/

Liebert Solutions   http://www.liebert.com/

Sutton Designs   http://suttondesigns.com

IndustryClick Electrical: power quality assurance page   http://industryclick.com/

APC (American Power Conversion) Corporation   http://www.apcc.com

The Disaster Center   http://www.disastercenter.com/

Disaster Survival Planning Network   http://www.disaster-survival.com/

Binomial International Disaster Recovery Planning   http://www.disasterrecovery.com

Power Line Access Services

Power line access is a technique to deliver data over electrical cables. It is yet another technique to provide high-speed Internet access to home and business users, but the concept has mostly been abandoned. The idea was to run fiber cable close to users, and then use the existing power line cables to connect with user's homes and offices. The systems were supposed to deliver data at multimegabit/sec rates. United Utilities and Nortel Networks were involved in this scheme, but "pulled the plug" in 1999. Other broadband technologies such as DSL and cable modems are considered more practical.

PPP (Point-to-Point Protocol)

Two schemes have been adopted by the Internet community to encapsulate and transmit IP (Internet Protocol) datagrams over serial point-to-point links: SLIP (Serial Line Interface Protocol) and PPP (Point-to-Point Protocol). SLIP is an earlier protocol that has fallen into disuse. PPP predominates because it works with other protocols such as IPX and was designed to overcome problems with the earlier protocol.

PPP is defined in RFC 1661 (The Point-to-Point Protocol, July 1994). RFC 1547 (Requirements for an Internet Standard Point-to-Point Protocol, December 1993) provides historical information about the need for PPP and its development. A series of related RFCs have been written to define how a variety of network control protocols—including TCP/IP, DECnet, AppleTalk, IPX, and others—work with PPP. A complete list of RFCs is available at the Linktionary! Web site.

PPP provides router-to-router, host-to-router, and host-to-host connections. PPP is the protocol used to establish dial-up Internet connections between users and an Internet POP (point of presence). A POP is a facility with banks of remote access equipment (modem banks and access servers) that is located at an ISP or co-located at a service provider facility. When the user dials in, a connection is established and a PPP session is set up between the user's system and the access server. Authentication and IP address assignment is part of the setup. Once complete, the user's computer is an extension of the Internet and the user's serial port and modem have the same functionality as a network interface card connected to the service provider's network.

PPP provides full-duplex bidirectional links that deliver packets in order. This is an important point. The PPP link is point to point as the name implies. It is a circuit dedicated to the user over which packets flow from the user's computer to the service provider's router. PPP provides a flow of frames into which datagrams are encapsulated and sent across the link. One can think of boxcars crossing the PPP link. PPP also supports multiplexing of different network layers protocols, such as TCP/IP, NetBEUI, and IPX, on the same link.

Most PPP implementations use framing derived from HDLC (High-level Data Link Protocol) as described in RFC 1662 (PPP in HDLC-like Framing, July 1994). This framing method is used over asynchronous and synchronous lines using serial communication protocols such as EIA-232-E, EIA-422, and EIA-423, as well as CCITT V.24 and V.35. But other framing mechanisms are supported, as described in the following RFCs. These framing methods are typically used to support router-to-router links in enterprise and Internet backbone networks:

- RFC 2363 (PPP over FUNI, July 1998) describes how PPP can use ATM FUNI (Frame User Network Interface) on point-to-point ATM connections.

- RFC 2516 (A Method for Transmitting PPP Over Ethernet, February 1999) describes how to build PPP sessions and encapsulate PPP packets over Ethernet.

- RFC 2615 (PPP over SONET/SDH, June 1999) describes "IP-over-PPP-over-SONET/SDH," a technique that is used to send IP packets directly over optical networks without using ATM. See "PoS (Packet over SONET)" for more information.

As mentioned, PPP's standard framing method is derived from HDLC, which itself is derived from IBM's SDLC (Synchronous Data Link Protocol). The frame format is pictured in Figure P-9 and described here:

- **Delimiters**   Mark the beginning and ending of the frame
- **Address**   Holds the destination address
- **Control**   Holds the sequence number to ensure proper handling
- **Protocol**   Identifies the protocol contained in the frame (IP, IPX, AppleTalk, and so on)
- **Data**   Contains the data, which can vary in length
- **Frame Check Sequence**   Calculates a check sum used for error checking

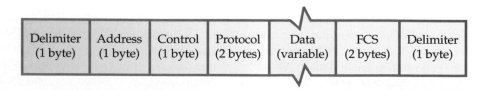

Figure P-9.   *The Point-to-Point Protocol frame format*

The PPP standard also defines an extensible protocol called LCP (Link Control Protocol) that is used during the "link establishment" phase of setting up a connection. LCP establishes encapsulation format options and packet sizes, and also detects looped-back links and determines whether a link is functioning properly or has failed. Once a link is established, LCP negotiates methods for authentication, encryption, and compression.

The original authentication methods were PAP and CHAP, but other authentication methods are possible. RFC 2284 (PPP Extensible Authentication Protocol, March 1998) defines how PPP supports multiple authentication mechanisms. Authentication is a phase that follows the "link establishment" phase, thus allowing the authenticator to request more information before deciding on an authentication mechanism. Supported mechanisms include MD5-challenge, one-time passwords, token cards, and others. RFC 2715 (PPP EAP TLS Authentication Protocol, October 1999) describes how TLS (transport-level security) mechanisms are supported in EAP.

RFC 1968 (The PPP Encryption Control Protocol, June 1996) defines a method for negotiating data encryption over PPP links. RFC 1962 (The PPP Compression Control Protocol, June 1996) defines a method for negotiating data compression over PPP links.

An interesting PPP extension is MLPPP (Multilink PPP), which defines how multiple links can be aggregated into a single bonded link. For example, two PPP links can be established over two modems and two phones lines to a service provider that supports MLPPP. Once the connections are made, the data rate is typically double that of a single line. Performance depends on the modem type and the quality of the connection. See "MLPPP (Multilink PPP)."

L2TP (Layer 2 Tunneling Protocol) is a tunneling protocol that delivers a PPP (Point-to-Point Protocol) session across an ATM network, frame relay network, or the Internet. It provides dial-up VPN (virtual private network) services. See "L2TP (Layer 2 Tunneling Protocol)."

Related Entries   Asynchronous Communications; Authentication and Authorization; Circuit; Compression Techniques; Cryptography; Data Communication Concepts; Data Link Protocols; Dial-Up Line; EAP (Extensible Authentication Protocol); EIA (Electronic Industries Alliance); Framing in Data Transmissions; HDLC (High-level Data Link Control); Internet Connections; L2TP (Layer 2 Tunneling Protocol); LAP (Link Access Procedure); LLC (Logical Link Control); MLPPP (Multilink PPP); Modems; Network Concepts; Network Connection Technologies; Point-to-Point Communications; PoS (Packet over SONET); Routers; Secret-Key Cryptography; Security; Serial Communication and Interfaces; SLIP (Serial Line Internet Protocol); *and* Synchronous Communications

Linktionary!—Tom Sheldon's Encyclopedia of Networking updates	http://www.linktionary.com/p/ppp.html
IETF Point-to-Point Protocol Extensions (pppext) charter	http://www.ietf.org/html.charters/pppext-charter.html
Cisco documentation: Point-to-Point Protocol	http://www.cisco.com/univercd/cc/td/doc/cisintwk/ito_doc/ppp.htm
Ericsson PPP document	http://www.ericsson.com/datacom/emedia/point_to_point.pdf
RAD Data Communications (see PPP tutorial)	http://www.rad.com/networks/tutorial.htm
SLIP/PPP home page by Lai Zit Seng	http://sunsite.nus.edu.sg/pub/slip-ppp/

InComA PPP FAQ	http://www.incoma.ru/protocols/ppp.html
Protocol.com PPP suite Web page	http://www.protocols.com/pbook/ppp.htm
Albert P. Belle WinSock Tuning FAQ	http://www.cerberus-sys.com/~belleisl/ mtu_mss_rwin.html

PPP Multilink

See MLPPP (Multilink Point-to-Point Protocol).

PPS (Packets per Second)

Packets per second (pps) is a measure of throughput for network devices such as bridges, routers, and switches. It's a reliable measurement only if all packet sizes are the same. Vendors will often rate their equipment based on pps, but make sure comparisons are made using the same packet sizes. These rates are discussed under "Throughput."

PPTP (Point-to-Point Tunneling Protocol)

See L2TP (Layer 2 Tunneling Protocol); Modems; *and* VPN (Virtual Private Network).

Premises Distribution System

A premises distribution system, or PDS, is a preplanned network of cabling within a building or campus environment, designed for the transmission of voice and data. The PDS provides a connection point for external communication and links to the public telephone network. A PDS is typically a *structured wiring system* that is designed to implement future services and growth, and accommodate future moves and reconfigurations.

Early premises systems were proprietary, but today most cabling systems follow the TIA/EIA 568 Commercial Building Wiring Standard. This standard provides a uniform wiring system and supports multivendor products and environments. The scope of the specification covers telecommunication wiring for both horizontal wiring (telephone and computer wall outlets to the wiring equipment rooms in a building) and backbone wiring (equipment room to equipment and among buildings in a campus environment). See "TIA/EIA Structured Cabling Standards."

Related Entries   Backbone Networks; Cable and Wiring; Data Communication Concepts; Ethernet; Fast Ethernet; Fiber-Optic Cable; Gigabit Ethernet; ISO/IEC-11801 Cabling Standards; Network Analyzers; Network Concepts; Network Design and Construction; Network Management; Power and Grounding Problems and Solutions; Switching and Switched Networks; *and* TIA/EIA Structured Cabling Standards

Presence Monitoring

See Instant Messaging.

Presentation Layer, OSI Model

OSI (Open Systems Interconnection) is a layered model for defining and building communication systems. It is defined by the ISO (International Organization for Standardization). The lower layers define physical components and transmission schemes, the middle layers define communication management routines, and the upper layers define how applications connect into the model.

The presentation layer is layer 6 in the protocol stack, just below the top-level application layer and above the session layer. The presentation layer provides translation of data, defines data formatting, and provides syntax. The presentation layer prepares incoming data for the application layer, where the user views the data. For outgoing data, the presentation layer translates data from the application layer into a form that is suitable for transfer over the network. There are various encoding rules built into the presentation layer protocols that handle all the data translations.

Related Entries   Data Communication Concepts; Network Architecture; *and* OSI (Open Systems Interconnection) Model

Printing

See IPP (Internet Printing Protocol).

Prioritization of Network Traffic

Prioritization of network traffic is simple in concept: give important network traffic precedence over unimportant network traffic. That leads to some interesting questions. What traffic should be prioritized? Who defines priorities? Do people pay for priority or do they get it based on traffic type (e.g., delay-sensitive traffic such as real-time voice)? For Internet traffic, where are priorities set (at the ingress based on customer preassigned tags in packets, or by service provider policies that are defined by service-level agreements)?

Prioritization is also called CoS (class of service) since traffic is classed into categories such as high, medium, and low (gold, silver, and bronze), and the lower the priority, the more "drop eligible" is a packet. E-mail and Web traffic is often placed in the lowest categories. When the network gets busy, packets from the lowest categories are dropped first.

Prioritization/CoS should not be confused with QoS. It is a subset of QoS. A package-delivery service provides an analogy. You can request priority delivery for a package. The delivery service has different levels of priority (next day, two-day, and so on). However, prioritization does not guarantee the package will get there on time. It may only mean that the delivery service handles that package before handling others. To provide guaranteed delivery, various procedures, schedules, and delivery mechanisms must be in place. For example, Federal Express has its own fleet of planes and trucks, as well as a computerized package tracking system.

Network QoS covers an entire range of bandwidth allocation and service provisioning techniques that deliver packets at guaranteed levels of service. Only ATM (Asynchronous Transfer Mode) networks are designed from the ground up to support QoS. RSVP (Resource Reservation Protocol) is an IETF-defined QoS strategy for TCP/IP networks. It is more than a prioritization and CoS strategy. RSVP supports bandwidth allocation and reservation for specific traffic flows. RSVP was found to be too difficult to implement on the Internet, but many enterprises have found it useful. See "RSVP (Resource Reservation Protocol)." MPLS (Multiprotocol Label Switching) is another QoS strategy that is designed to work across service provider networks on the Internet.

The problem with network priority schemes is that lower-priority traffic may be held up indefinitely when traffic is heavy unless there is sufficient bandwidth to handle the highest load levels. Even high-priority traffic may be held up under extreme traffic loads. One solution is to *overprovision* the network, which is a reasonable option given the relatively low cost of networking gear today.

As traffic loads increase, router buffers begin to fill, which adds to delay. If the buffers overflow, packets are dropped. When buffers start to fill, prioritization schemes can help by forwarding high-priority and delay-sensitive traffic before other traffic. This requires that traffic be classed (CoS) and moved into queues with the appropriate service level. One can imagine an input port that classifies traffic or reads existing tags in packets to determine class, and then moves packets into a stack of queues with the top stack having the highest priority. As traffic loads increase, packets in the topmost stacks are serviced first. See "Queuing."

Prioritization has been used in multiprotocol routers to give some protocols higher priority than other protocols. For example, SNA (Systems Network Architecture) traffic will time-out if it is not delivered promptly, causing retransmissions that degrade network performance. Such protocols should be given high priority. A number of other prioritization/CoS schemes are outlined here:

- **MAC layer prioritization**   In a shared LAN environment such as Ethernet, multiple stations may contend for access to the network. Access is based on first-come, first-serve. Sometimes, two stations attempt simultaneous access, in which case, both stations back off and wait through a time-out period before making another attempt. This is minimized for switched Ethernet where only one station is connected to a switch port. A number of vendor-specific Ethernet priority schemes have been developed. Token ring networks have a priority mechanism in which a reservation bit is set in tokens to indicate priority.

- **VLAN tagging and 802.1p**   The IEEE 802.1Q frame-tagging scheme defines a method for inserting a tag into an IEEE MAC-layer frame that defines membership in a virtual LAN. Three bits within the tag define eight different priority levels. The bit settings serve as a label that provides a signal to network devices as to the class of service that the frame should receive. See "QoS (Quality of Service)," and check under the section "MAC-Layer Prioritization."

- **Network layer prioritization**   The IP packet header has a field called ToS (Type of Service). This field has recently been redefined to work with the IETF's Differentiated Services (Diff-Serv) strategy. Diff-Serv classifies and marks packets so that they receive a specific per-hop forwarding at network devices along a route. The ToS bit is set once, based on policy information, and then read by network devices. Because IP is an internetworking protocol, Diff-Serv works across networks, including carrier and service provider networks that support the service. Therefore, Diff-Serv will support CoS on the Internet, extranets, and intranets. See "Differentiated Services (Diff-Serv)."

Priority settings may be made in several places. The most logical place is the application running in the end user's system. But applications may not support the various schemes that are available, so edge switches may need to infer priority levels for frames or packets by examining the contents of the packets. This is now easily done with so-called "multilayer switches" based on policies that are defined in policy-based management systems. See "Multilayer Switching" and "Policy-Based Management."

RFC 3052 (Service Management Architectures Issues and Review, January 2001) discusses prioritization in the context of service management networks and policy-based management. Another document worth reading is RFC 2990 (Next Steps for the IP QoS Architecture, November 2000).

Related Entries   Admission Control; ATM (Asynchronous Transfer Mode); Bandwidth; Bandwidth Management; Bandwidth on Demand; Capacity; Congestion Control Mechanisms; CoS (Class of Service); Data Communication Concepts; Delay, Latency, and Jitter; Differentiated Services (Diff-Serv); Flow-Control Mechanisms; Integrated Services (Int-Serv); Load Balancing; MPLS (Multiprotocol Label Switching); Multilayer Switching; Multimedia; Policy-Based Management; QoS (Quality of Service); Queuing; Resource Management; Routers; RSVP (Resource Reservation Protocol); RTP (Real-time Transport Protocol); RTSP (Real-Time Streaming Protocol); SBM (Service Bandwidth Manager); SLA (Service-Level Agreement); Tag Switching; TCP (Transmission Control Protocol); Throughput; Traffic Management, Shaping, and Engineering; Transport Protocols and Services; VLAN (Virtual LAN); Voice over IP (VoIP); *and* VPN (Virtual Private Network)

Linktionary!—Tom Sheldon's Encyclopedia of Networking updates	http://www.linktionary.com/p/prioritization.html
Intel paper: "Class of Service and Differentiated Services"	http://www.intel.com/network/white_papers/diff_serv/diffserv.htm
Intel paper: "Layer 2 Traffic Prioritization"	http://www.intel.com/network/white_papers/priority_packet.htm
Hoov's Musings: "Class of Marketing" by Mark Hoover	http://www.acuitive.com/musings/hmv1-3.htm
Lucent white paper. QoS in the LAN	http://www.lucent.com/ins/library/pdf/white_papers/qos_in_lan.pdf
Sally Floyd's Web page. See CBQ (Class-Based Queuing)	http://www.aciri.org/floyd/

Privacy

See Cryptography; P3P (Platform for Privacy Preferences); PICS (Platform for Internet Content Selection); Public-Key Cryptography; *and* Security.

Private-Key Cryptography

Secret-key encryption uses one key, the secret key, that is used to both encrypt and decrypt messages. This is also called symmetric encryption. The term "private key" is often used inappropriately to refer to the secret key. Refer to "Secret-Key Cryptography."

With public-key encryption, a user has two keys, one that is made public and one that is held privately. This is asymmetric encryption. Refer to "Public-Key Cryptography."

P

Private Network

Private network is a term used to describe a wide area network that crosses public properties but that is controlled by an organization. Private networks are created with dial-up or dedicated lines that are leased from local and long-distance carriers. The lines are dedicated to the customer, and so are private. At one time, private networks meant private telephone networks that connected an organization's sites. More recently, the term describes voice and data networks. The topic "TDM Networks" covers private networks.

An alternative to the private network is the VPN (virtual private network), which is built on packet- or cell-switching networks. The carrier preprograms a path through the network, called a *virtual circuit*, and provides a contracted amount of bandwidth (called the *CIR* or *committed information rate*). The advantage of packet switching as compared to leased lines is that you only pay for the bandwidth you need.

Related Entries   Bandwidth on Demand; Circuit-Switching Services; Communication Services and Providers; DSL (Digital Subscriber Line); E-Carrier; IMA (Inverse Multiplexing over ATM); Leased Line; Link Aggregation; Load Balancing; Local Loop; MAN (Metropolitan Area Network); MLPPP (Multilink PPP); Multiplexing and Multiplexers; Network Access Services; NPN (New Public Network); Service Providers and Carriers; T-Carriers; TDM Networks; Telecommunications and Telephone Systems; Virtual Circuits; VPN (Virtual Private Network); *and* WAN (Wide Area Network)

Promiscuous Mode

A network-connected device operating in promiscuous mode captures all frames on a network, not just frames that are addressed directly to it. A network analyzer operates in this mode to capture network traffic for evaluation and to measure traffic for statistical analysis. A hacker may also use a promiscuous mode device to capture network traffic for unscrupulous activities. Network traffic can be encrypted to protect against such eavesdropping. Refer to "Network Analyzers" for a discussion of how promiscuous mode is applied.

Propagation Delay

See Delay, Latency, and Jitter.

Protocol Analyzers

See Network Analyzers.

Protocols and Protocol Stacks

Network architectures are blueprints for building communication systems. The architectures are multilayered and each layer defines a specific type of communication. Bottom layers define how to transmit bits across physical links. Upper layers define how to build network applications that can use networks. Intermediate layers define connectionless and connection-oriented network services. See "Network Architecture" for more information.

Within each layer, specific types of protocols are available to accomplish a specific task. For example, the lower layers define different link protocols such as Ethernet, token ring, ATM, frame relay, and so on. There are perhaps hundreds of protocols that occupy the different layers of the various network architectures. The best place to view a complete list and get additional information on almost all the network protocols available is at the Protocol.com link listed here.

Related Entries   Best-Effort Delivery; Connection Establishment; Connection-Oriented and Connectionless Services; Data Communication Concepts; Datagram and Datagram Services; Data Link Protocols; Encapsulation; Error Detection and Correction; Flow-Control Mechanisms; Fragmentation and Reassembly; Framing in Data Transmissions; Internetworking; IP (Internet Protocol); LAN (Local Area Network); Network Architecture; Network Concepts; Network Layer Protocols; OSI (Open Systems Interconnection) Model; Packets and Packet-Switching Networks; Reliable Data Delivery Services; Routing; TCP (Transmission Control Protocol); and Transport Protocols and Services

Linktionary!—Tom Sheldon's Encyclopedia of Networking updates	http://www.linktionary.com/p/protocols.html
Bitpipe (search for "protocol")	http://www.bitpipe.com/
Google Web Directory protocols page	http://directory.google.com/Top/Computers/Internet/Protocols/
About.com (search for "protocol")	http://compnetworking.about.com/
"The World of Protocols" at Protocols.com	http://www.protocols.com/
Novell's protocol links page	http://developer.novell.com/research/topical/netware_servers.htm
Cazfry's Links to information about protocols. See the Network section.	http://www.hojmark.org/networking/protocols.html

Proxy Caching

See Web Caching.

Proxy Servers

The proxy server can be viewed as a gateway between two networks, usually a private internal network and the Internet. It is sometimes called an *application-level gateway*. The proxy server hides the internal network from the external network. It keeps hackers from accessing or even knowing about internal IP addresses.

A proxy server runs as software on a computer and acts on behalf of a client to make requests outside the client's network. For example, when an internal user attempts to access the Internet, the proxy server intercepts the request and makes the request itself. The internal user never makes a direct request to an outside system. Likewise, when the Internet server returns a response, it is intercepted by the proxy server and transferred to the user. The proxy server can filter all incoming packets and discard any that are not related to an internal request. This prevents hackers from attacking internal systems.

Proxy servers are both firewall and caching systems. Since they provide a centralized location where internal users access the Internet, the proxy server can cache frequently accessed documents from sites on the Internet and make them quickly available for other internal users that need the documents.

This topic is covered in more detail under "Firewall" at the Linktionary! Web site.

Related Entries   Access Control; Apache; Application-Level Gateway; Cache and Caching Techniques; Content Distribution; Firewall; Gateway; Internet; IPSec (IP Security); Multihoming; NAT (Network Address Translation); RSIP (Realm-Specific IP); Security; SOCKS; *and* Web Caching

 Linktionary!—Tom Sheldon's Encyclopedia of   http://www.linktionary.com/f/firewall.html
Networking updates

PSTN (Public-Switched Telephone Network)

See Telecommunications and Telephone Systems.

Public-Key Cryptography

Public-key cryptography provides a way for users to securely exchange information. It also enables a host with other useful security techniques, including authentication (remote connections without the need to exchange sensitive information), digital signing (to provide document integrity), and nonrepudiation (someone cannot deny having sent a message).

Assume Bob and Alice want to exchange private encrypted messages over an unsecure system (like the Internet). They choose an encryption method that will make the messages unreadable to any person who happens to capture the transmissions. Bob encrypts the message using an encryption key. Alice must have this key to decrypt the message. Now, the basic problem: how does Bob get the key to Alice so she can decrypt the message? Bob could call Alice on the phone, but what if the phone line is tapped? Bob could send it via courier, but the key could be compromised. While this seems paranoid, consider that military communications are under constant scrutiny by attackers or foreign defense agencies. The same threat extends into the competitive corporate world and the financial world.

Traditionally, both the sender and receiver have already agreed on a key. Before leaving port, a submarine captain is handed a decoder book that will unscramble encrypted radio messages from home port. This is *symmetric cryptography* (both parties know the same secret key), and it is often referred to as *secret-key cryptography*. DES (Data Encryption Standard) is a common secret-key encryption. These single-key methods are described under "Cryptography" in this book.

But it is not always the case that parties who need to exchange messages know and/or trust each other or have previously exchanged keys. In 1976, Whitfield Diffie and Martin Hellman developed the concept of *asymmetric public-key cryptography*. In this scheme, a person uses a program to generate two keys. The keys are mathematically related through a special function that is very difficult to reverse. One key is kept private and the other is put in a public place, much like phone numbers are listed in a phone book. To send someone a private message, you look up their public key, encrypt the message, and send it to the owner of the key. The owner decrypts the message with their private key. Only the private key can decrypt messages encrypted with the public key. Therefore, the private key must be kept safe and secure.

While Diffie and Hellman developed the concept of asymmetric public-key cryptography in 1976, it was RSA (Rivest, Shamir, Adleman) Data Systems that turned it into a workable and commercial system. Diffie and Hellman originally thought that the keys should be stored in a large public file, referenced by the name of the keyholder. This file was essentially a white pages directory, with name and key, similar to a phone book. But this file could potentially become quite large and would need to be stored at a place where it could be managed. According to RFC 2693, Loren Kohnfelder came up with the idea of breaking each name/key combination out of the large file and into separate records. These individual records could be digitally "signed" by encrypting or hashing them with the public key of a trusted third party. Kohnfelder called this signed record a *certificate*, and the trusted third parties that managed and signed the certificates became known as *certificate authorities (CAs)*.

Figure P-10 illustrates public-key cryptography in action. Bob and Alice want to exchange secure messages. Both Bob and Alice are on the same company network and so have easy access to a corporate certificate server that manages public keys (on public networks, a certificate authority manages keys).

1. Alice and Bob generate a set of keys using software commonly found in Web browsers or e-mail applications.

2. The public key is sent to the public-key server (certificate server) that bundles the key with information about the person into a certificate and signs it with the trusted key assigned to the certificate server.

3. When Bob wants to send a secure message to Alice, he obtains Alice's certificate from the public-key server. This certificate contains Alice's public key, which Bob uses to encrypt the message. He then forwards the message to Alice.

4. Alice receives the message and decrypts it with her private key.

The public-key scheme solves the problem of passing keys to other parties who need to decrypt your messages. In fact, it allows any person to encrypt a message and send it to another person without any prior key exchange. It is not even necessary that the parties know each other, be part of the same organization, or be connected to the same network.

A public-key infrastructure (PKI) is an entire system of managing public keys. It may be implemented within an enterprise network, but usually refers to the hierarchy of CAs in the public environment. It also defines how CAs register users, create and manage certificates, and run their business. The IETF PKIX (Public-Key Infrastructure X.509) Working Group has defined PKI for the Internet. X.509 is an international standard that defines certificate formats and distribution.

This topic is covered in more detail at the Linktionary! Web site. Also see "PKI (Public-Key Infrastructure)."

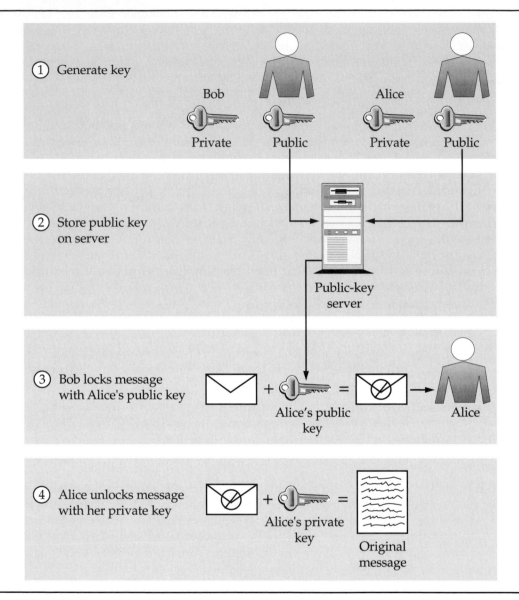

Figure P-10. *Public-key cryptography*

Related Entries   Authentication and Authorization; Certificates and Certification Systems; Cryptography; Digital Signatures; DSS (Digital Signature Standard); EAP (Extensible Authentication Protocol); Electronic Commerce; Hash Functions; IPSec (IP Security); Kerberos Authentication Protocol; Key Distribution and Management; One-Time Password Authentication; Passwords; PGP (Pretty Good Privacy); PKI (Public-Key Infrastructure); Quantum Cryptography; Secret-Key Cryptography; Security; SKIP (Simple Key Management for Internet Protocols); SSL (Secure Sockets Layer); Token-Based Authentication; Trust Relationships and Trust Management; VPN (Virtual Private Network); *and* X.509 Certificates

Linktionary!—Tom Sheldon's Encyclopedia of Networking updates	http://www.linktionary.com/p/public_key.html
IETF Working Group: Common Authentication Technology (cat)	http://www.ietf.org/html.charters/cat-charter.html
RSA Data Security, Inc.	http://www.rsa.com
IEEE Public-Key Cryptography site	http://grouper.ieee.org/groups/1363/
Ron Rivest's Links (possibly the most complete set of links on the Web)	http://theory.lcs.mit.edu/~rivest/crypto-security.html
Entrust Technologies (see white papers)	http://www.entrust.com/
Certicom (specializes in elliptic curve cryptography)	http://www.certicom.com/
OII (Open Information Interchange) information security standards page	http://158.169.50.95:10080/oii/en/secure.html

Additional Web links may be found under the "Security" topic.

Public-Key Infrastructure

See PKI (Public-Key Infrastructure); Public-Key Cryptography.

Public Networks

See NPN (New Public Network).

Push and Pull

See Webcasting.

PVC (Permanent Virtual Circuit)

A virtual circuit is a pathway through a switched, mesh-type network that appears to be a dedicated, physically connected circuit. The virtual circuit is predefined and maintained by the end systems and nodes along the circuit, but the actual pathway through the packet-switched network may change due to routing around downed or busy connections. The important point is that packets are transferred in order over a specific path and arrive at the destination in order.

A PVC is a fixed circuit that is defined in advance by a public network carrier (or a network manager on an internal network). The permanence of the line removes the setup overhead and improves performance. A PVC is used on a circuit that includes routers that must maintain a constant connection in order to transfer routing information in a dynamic network environment. Carriers assign PVCs to customers to reduce overhead and improve performance on their networks.

In contrast, an SVC (switched virtual circuit) establishes a temporary virtual circuit between individual workstations, with sessions lasting only as long as needed. Once a communication session is complete, the virtual circuit is disabled. See "Virtual Circuit" for more information.

QAM (Quadrature Amplitude Modulation)

See Modulation Techniques.

Qbone

Qbone is an Internet2 initiative that is testing quality-of-service capabilities across the Abilene backbone. The tests are meant to demonstrate a network that can provide guaranteed low packet loss, low delay, and low jitter. The Qbone implements edge routers that provide priority tagging via Diff-Serv protocols.

Related Entries   Abilene; Differentiated Services (Diff-Serv); GII (Global Information Infrastructure); Internet; Internet2; Internet Architecture and Backbone; Internet Organizations and Committees; NII (National Information Infrastructure); NIST (National Institute of Standards and Technology); NREN (National Research and Education Network); QoS (Quality of Service); Routing on the Internet; *and* vBNS (Very high speed Backbone Network Service)

The Internet2 page	http://www.ucaid.edu
Merit's Internet2 initiative	http://www.merit.edu/i2/
vBNS QBONE information	http://www.vbns.net/presentations/qbone-plan.html

QoS (Quality of Service)

A network with quality of service has the ability to deliver data traffic with a minimum amount of delay in an environment in which many users share the same network. QoS should not be confused with CoS (class of service). CoS classifies traffic into categories such as high, medium, and low (gold, silver, and bronze). Low-priority traffic is "drop eligible," while high-priority traffic gets the best service. However, if the network does not have enough bandwidth, even high-priority traffic may not get through. Traffic engineering, which enables QoS, is about making sure that the network can deliver the expected traffic loads.

A package-delivery service provides an analogy. You can request priority delivery for a package. The delivery service has different levels of priority (next day, two-day, and so on). However, prioritization does not guarantee the package will get there on time. It may only mean that the delivery service handles that package before handling others. To provide guaranteed delivery, various procedures, schedules, and delivery mechanisms must be in place. For example, Federal Express has its own fleet of planes and trucks, as well as a computerized package tracking system. Traffic engineers work out flight plans and schedule delivery trucks to make sure that packages are delivered as promised.

The highest quality of service is on a nonshared communication link such as a cable that directly connects two computers. No other users contend for access to the network. A switched Ethernet network in which one computer is attached to each switch port can deliver a high level of QoS. The only contention for the cable is between the computers that are exchanging data with one another. If the link is full duplex, there is no contention. Situations that cause QoS to degrade are listed here:

■ Shared network links, in which two or more users or devices must contend for the same communication channel.

- Delays caused by networking equipment (e.g., inability to process large loads).

- Delays caused by distance (satellite links) or excessive hops (cross-country or global routed networks).

- Network congestion, caused by overflowing queues and retransmission of dropped packets.

- Poorly managed network capacity or insufficient capacity. If a link has fixed bandwidth, the only option to improve performance is to manage QoS.

The starting point for providing QoS in any network is to control and avoid congestion. See "Congestion Control Mechanisms" for more information.

Note *This topic is covered in more detail at the Linktionary! Web site.*

What can be done to improve QoS? The obvious solution is to overprovision network capacity and upgrade to the most efficient networking equipment. This is often a practical solution in the private network environment, but not for private WAN links. Another solution is to classify traffic into various priorities and place the highest priority traffic in queues that get better service. This is how bandwidth is divided up in packet-switched networks. Higher-level queues get to send more packets, and so get a higher percentage of the bandwidth. New optical networks in the Internet core provide QoS with excess bandwidth. A single fiber strand can support hundreds or even thousands of wavelength circuits (lambdas). Lambdas can provide single-hop optical pathways between two points with gigabit bandwidth. A single circuit can be dedicated to traffic that needs a specific service level. See "Optical Networks."

Service providers have been reluctant to implement QoS across their networks because of the management and logistics problems. Also, high-speed multilayer switches are needed to classify and forward traffic at line speed, so equipment costs are a consideration. QoS features must also be set up from one end of a network to another, and that is often difficult to accomplish. QoS levels must be negotiated with every switch and router along a path. Still, QoS is getting easier to manage, and, in some cases, it is the only way to optimize network bandwidth.

Leading-edge service providers now offer a range of QoS service levels for Internet traffic. Subscribers specify QoS requirements in SLAs (service-level agreements). Some of the SLA specifications required for QoS are described here:

- **Throughput** An SLA can specify a guaranteed data transfer rate. This is easy on virtual circuit networks such as ATM. It is more difficult on IP networks.

- **Packet loss** When a shared network gets busy, queues in routers and other network devices can fill and start dropping packets. A vendor may guarantee a minimum packet loss.

- **Latency** This is the delay in the time it takes a packet to cross a network. Packets may be held up in queues, on slow links, or because of congestion. The more networking devices a packet crosses, the bigger the delay. Delays of over 100 ms are disruptive to voice.

- **Jitter** Delay that is variable and difficult to interpret.

Of course, the range, location, and ownership of the network will make a big difference in how QoS is applied. An enterprise may wish to install QoS on its own intranet to support voice and video. QoS may also be applied to the LAN/WAN gateway to ensure that private WAN links or VPNs are appropriately loaded and provide quality service for intercompany voice calls, videoconferences, and so on. Most of the focus for QoS technologies is centered on the Internet because it lacks features that can provide QoS.

Service Levels: IP Versus ATM

The Internet is a connectionless packet-switching network, meaning that without any special QoS provisions, all services are best effort. In contrast, leased lines and ATM naturally support QoS because they deliver data in a predictable way. Leased lines such as T1 circuit use TDM (time division multiplexing), which provides fixed-size repeating slots for data. ATM uses fixed-size cells and has built-in traffic engineering parameters to ensure QoS.

Obtaining QoS in IP networks is not so easy, primarily for the following reasons:

- The architecture is routed, meaning that packets may take different paths, which produces unpredictable delays.

- IP is connectionless—that is, it does not have virtual circuit capabilities that could be used to allocate and guarantee bandwidth.

- IP uses variable-size packets, which makes traffic patterns unpredictable.

- Packets from many sources traverse shared links and may burst into routers, causing congestion; packet drops; retransmission; more congestion; and, ultimately, excessive delay that is unsuitable for real-time traffic.

Consider a typical LAN/WAN interface. It is an aggregation point where traffic from many sources inside the network comes together for transmission over the WAN link. If the WAN link has insufficient bandwidth, congestion will occur.

In the preceding scenario, all packets are equal. Packets for mission-critical applications may be dropped, while packets carrying the latest Dilbert cartoon get through. Classification is essential. Fortunately, packet classification is now easy with multilayer routing solutions from vendors such as Extreme Networks. See "Multilayer Switching." Still, the service these devices offer is more CoS oriented. Keep in mind that true QoS requires bandwidth management and traffic engineering across the networks that packets will travel.

ATM networks provide a number of native features to support QoS natively:

- Fixed-size cells (as opposed to IP's variable-length packets) provide predictable throughput. As an analogy, if all boxcars on a train are the same size, you can predict how many will pass a certain point if you know the speed of the train.

- Predictable behavior allows for bandwidth management and the creation of guaranteed service-level agreements.

- ATM is also connection oriented and delivers data over *virtual circuits* that deliver cells in order, an important requirement for real-time audio and video.

- ATM supports admittance control and policing, which monitor traffic and only allow a new flow if the network will support it without affecting the bandwidth requirements of other users.

■ ATM networks "police" traffic to prevent senders from exceeding their bandwidth allocations. If traffic exceeds a certain level, the network may drop packets in that circuit. Packets are classified, with some being more "drop eligible" than other.

As a point of comparison, the Internet has no admittance controls, which is probably good, but it also means that long file transfers can consume bandwidth and prevent other packets from getting through. This is especially disruptive to real-time traffic.

See "ATM (Asynchronous Transfer Mode)," "Admission Control," and "Traffic Management, Shaping, and Engineering."

The following sections describe the various techniques that may be used to provide QoS on the Internet and in enterprise networks. Note that some of these solutions provide only partial QoS, but are required to provide higher levels of service. The various solutions may be categorized as follows:

■ **Congestion management**   Schemes that help reduce congestion when it occurs or that actively work to prevent congestion from occurring.

■ **Classification and queuing techniques**   Traffic is classified according to service levels. Queues exist for each service level, and the highest priority queues are serviced first.

■ **Bandwidth reservation techniques**   Bandwidth is reserved in the network to ensure packet delivery.

■ **Packet tagging and label switching**   Packets are tagged with identifiers that specify a delivery path across a network of switches. The paths can be engineered to provide QoS.

Congestion Management Techniques

Managing network congestion is a critical part of any QoS scheme. TCP has some rudimentary congestion controls. The technique relies on dropped packets. When a packet is dropped, the receiver fails to acknowledge receipt to the sender. The sender assumes that the receiver or the network must be congested and scales back its transmission rates. This reduces the congestion problem temporarily. The sender will eventually start to scale up its transmissions and the process may repeat.

Packets are dropped because a router queue is full or because a network device is using a congestion avoidance scheme, such as RED (random early detection). RED monitors queues to determine when they are getting full enough that they *might* overflow. It then drops packets in advance to signal senders that they should slow down. Fewer packets are dropped in this scheme.

The problem with RED is that it relies on dropping packets to signal congestion. ECN (explicit congestion control) is an end-to-end congestion avoidance mechanism in which a router that is experiencing congestion sets a notification bit in a packet and forwards the packet to the destination. The destination node then sends a "slow down" message back to the sender.

Traffic shaping is a technique that "smoothes out" the flow of packets coming from upstream sources so that downstream nodes are not overwhelmed by bursts of traffic. An upstream node may be a host, or it may be a network device that has a higher data rate than the downstream network. At the same time, some hosts with priority requirements may be allowed to burst traffic under certain conditions, such as when the network is not busy. A traffic shaper is basically a regulated queue that takes uneven and/or bursty flows of packets and outputs them in a steady predictable stream so that the network is not overwhelmed with traffic.

Refer to "Congestion Control Mechanisms" and "Queuing" for more information.

Classification, Admission, and Tagging

Any QoS scheme involves guaranteeing service levels to traffic flows. In a world of infinite bandwidth, all flows could be handled equally. But networks are still bandwidth limited and congestion problems occur due to improper network design. Therefore, traffic must be classified—and, in some cases, tagged—so that downstream devices know what to do with it. Basic classification techniques are outlined here:

- Inspect and classify (differentiate) incoming traffic using various techniques, such as "sniffing" the MAC address, the physical port on which the packet arrived, IEEE 802.1Q VLAN information, IEEE 802.1D-1998 (formerly IEEE 802.1p) information, source and destination IP address, well-known TCP/UDP port numbers, application information at layer 7, such as cookies and other information. Note that some encryption and tunneling schemes make packet sniffing impossible. Some applications never use the same port, and a variety of different applications go to port 80—the Web services port, which makes differentiating on port number difficult.

- If a flow is requesting a particular service, use admission controls to either accept or reject the flow. Admission controls help enforce administrative policies, as well as provide accounting and administrative reporting.

- Schedule the packets into appropriate queues and manage the queues in a way that ensures that each queue gets an appropriate level of service for its class.

Extreme Networks has a line of switches with built-in traffic classification features. Figure Q-1 shows an example of bandwidth allocation for various types of traffic.

Classification requires administrative decisions about how traffic should be classified and where it should be tagged. Administrators might classify traffic based on whether it is best

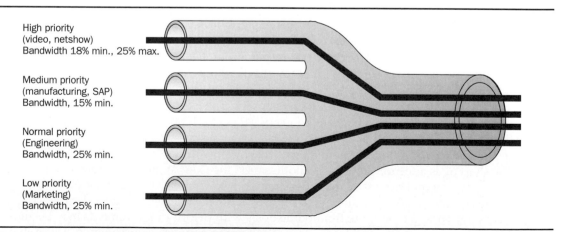

High priority
(video, netshow)
Bandwidth 18% min., 25% max.

Medium priority
(manufacturing, SAP)
Bandwidth, 15% min.

Normal priority
(Engineering)
Bandwidth, 25% min.

Low priority
(Marketing)
Bandwidth, 25% min.

Figure Q-1.   *Bandwidth classification and scheduling (source: Extreme Networks)*

effort and suitable for discard, real-time voice and video, network controls (e.g., OSPF messages), or mission critical.

The following classification schemes identify traffic near its source and mark packets before they enter the network. Network nodes only need to read the markings and forward packets appropriately.

- **IEEE frame tagging** This scheme defines a tag, inserted into an Ethernet frame, which contains three bits that can be used to identify class of service. See the next section for more information.

- **IETF Differentiated Services (Diff-Serv)** Diff-Serv is an IETF specification that works at the network layer. It alters bits in the IP ToS field to signal a particular class of service. Diff-Serv works across networks, including carrier and service provider networks that support the service; and, therefore, it has become an important scheme for specifying QoS across the Internet. Diff-Serv is covered briefly later in this topic and under its own topic.

The first scheme works over LANs, while Diff-Serv works over internetworks. The tag information in MAC-layer frames will be lost if the frame crosses a router. However, some method may be used to capture the information and use it to set Diff-Serv markings.

MAC-Layer Prioritization

As mentioned, the IEEE defined a method for inserting a tag into an IEEE MAC-layer frame that contains bits to define class of service. During development, this was known as Project 802.1p, and you will see it referred to that way in much of the literature. It is now officially part of IEEE 802.1D-1998. The tag defines the following eight "user priority" levels that provide signals to network devices as to the class of service that the frame should receive:

- **Priority 7** Network control traffic such as router configuration messages
- **Priority 6** Voice traffic, such as NetMeeting, that is especially sensitive to jitter
- **Priority 5** Video, which is high bandwidth and sensitive to jitter
- **Priority 4** Controlled load, latency-sensitive traffic such as SNA transactions
- **Priority 3** Better than best effort, which would include important business traffic that can tolerate some delay
- **Priority 2** Best-effort traffic
- **Priority 1** The default mode if none is specified
- **Priority 0** Noncritical traffic such as backups, noncritical replications, some electronic mail, and so on

A method for reordering and moving delay-sensitive real-time traffic to the front of a queue is also defined. A component of this scheme is GARP (Group Address Registration Protocol), which is used by LAN switches and network-attached devices to exchange information about current VLAN configurations. Note that 802.1D-1998 provides at the LAN level what Diff-Serv provides in layer 3 across internetworks. MAC-layer tags may be used to signal a class of service to Diff-Serv.

Two Web sites provide additional information:

Intel paper: "Layer 2 Traffic Prioritization"	http://www.intel.com/network/white_papers/ priority_packet.htm
IEEE 802.1 Working Group Web page	http://grouper.ieee.org/groups/802/1/index.html

IP ToS

The role of the IP ToS field has changed with the development of Diff-Serv. The original meaning of the ToS field was defined in RFC 791 (Internet Protocol, September 1981); however, it was never used in a consistent way. Most routers are aware of the field, but it has little meaning across public networks. Many enterprises have used it internally to designate various classes of service or to prioritize traffic across private WAN links.

The ToS field is divided into two sections: the *Precedence field* (three bits), and a field that is customarily called "Type-of-Service" or "TOS" (five bits). Interestingly, The Precedence field was intended for Department of Defense applications to signal a priority message in times of crisis or when a five-star general wanted to get a good tee time.

Diff-Serv redefined the field as the DS Field (Diff-Serv Field). RFC 2474 (Definition of the Differentiated Services Field in the IPv4 and IPv6 Headers, December 1998) describes this further. See "Differentiated Services (Diff-Serv)."

IETF QoS Solutions

The IETF has been working to define Internet QoS models for many years. The task has not been easy since packets must cross many networks, and providers must agree not only how QoS will be managed, but also how it is paid for. The primary QoS techniques developed by the IETF are Int-Serv (Integrated Services), Diff-Serv (Differentiated Services), and MPLS (Multiprotocol Label Switching), as described next. Each of these is discussed under its own heading elsewhere.

- **Int-Serv (Integrated Services)**   This is a model for providing QoS on the Internet and intranets. The intention of Int-Serv designers was to set aside some portion of network bandwidth for traffic such as real-time voice and video that required low delay, low jitter (variable delay), and guaranteed bandwidth. The Int-Serv Working Group developed RSVP (Resource Reservation Protocol), a signaling mechanism to specify QoS requirements across a network. Int-Serv has scalability problems and it was too difficult to deploy on the Internet. However, RSVP is used in enterprise networks, and its control mechanism for setting up bandwidth across a network is being used in new ways with MPLS.

- **Diff-Serv (Differentiated Services)**   Diff-Serv classifies and marks packets so that they receive a specific per-hop forwarding at network devices along a route. The important part is that Diff-Serv does the work at the edge so that network devices only need to get involved in properly queuing and forwarding packets. Diff-Serv works at the IP level to provide QoS based on IP ToS settings. Diff-Serv is perhaps the best choice for signaling QoS levels available today.

- **MPLS (Multiprotocol Label Switching)**   MPLS is a protocol, designed primarily for Internet core networks, that is meant to provide bandwidth management and quality of service for IP and other protocols. Control of core network resources is accomplished by building *LSPs (label switched paths)* across networks and rapidly forwarding IP packets across the network through these paths. By labeling packets with an indicator of the LSP they are to traverse, it is possible to eliminate the overhead of inspecting packets at every network device along the way. LSPs are similar to virtual circuits in ATM and frame relay networks, and traffic engineering approaches can be used to create LSP that delivers a required level of service.

Policies and Policy Protocols

The final pieces of the QoS picture are policies, policy services, and policy signaling protocols. Most of the QoS systems just described use policy systems to keep track of how network users and network devices can access network resources. A defining feature of a policy system is that it works across a large network and provides policy information to appropriate devices with that network.

A policy architecture consists of the following components, which primarily manage the *rules* that govern how network resources may be used by specific users, applications, or systems. When rules are specified and programmed into policy systems, they are known as *policies*.

- **Policy clients**   Network devices that process network traffic such as switches and routers running various queuing algorithms. Policy clients query policy servers to obtain rules about how traffic should be handled.

- **Policy servers**   This is the central authority that interprets network policies and distributes them to policy clients.

- **Policy information system**   The information about who or what can use network resources is stored in some type of database, usually a directory services database.

This architecture allows network administrators to specify policies for individuals, applications, and systems in a single place—the policy information system. The policy server then uses protocols such as LDAP (Lightweight Directory Access Protocol) or SQL to obtain this information and form policies that can be distributed to policy clients. Policy clients talk to policy servers via network protocols such as COPS (Common Open Policy Service) and SNMP (Simple Network Management Protocol). COPS is an intradomain mechanism for allocating bandwidth resources and it is being adapted for use in establishing policy associated with a Diff-Serv–capable networks.

This topic is covered in more detail under "Policy-Based Management." In addition, RFC 2768 (Network Policy and Services: A Report of a Workshop on Middleware, February 2000) provides useful information about policy.

Additional QoS Information

The following IETF working groups are developing QoS recommendations and standards. Refer to the working group pages for a list of related RFCs and other documents.

Audio/Video Transport (avt)	http://www.ietf.org/html.charters/avt-charter.html
Differentiated Services (Diff-Serv)	http://www.ietf.org/html.charters/Diff-Serv-charter.html
Endpoint Congestion Management (ecm)	http://www.ietf.org/html.charters/ecm-charter.html
Integrated Services (Int-Serv)	http://www.ietf.org/html.charters/Int-Serv-charter.html
Integrated Services over Specific Link Layers (issll)	http://www.ietf.org/html.charters/issll-charter.html
Internet Traffic Engineering (tewg)	http://www.ietf.org/html.charters/tewg-charter.html
Policy Framework (policy)	http://www.ietf.org/html.charters/policy-charter.html
Resource Allocation Protocol (rap)	http://www.ietf.org/html.charters/rap-charter.html
Resource Reservation Setup Protocol (rsvp)	http://www.ietf.org/html.charters/rsvp-charter.html

The following RFCs provide more information about QoS. More specific RFCs are listed under the headings just mentioned.

- RFC 1633 (Integrated Services in the Internet Architecture: An Overview, June 1994)
- RFC 2386 (A Framework for QoS-based Routing on the Internet, August 1998)
- RFC 2430 (A Provider Architecture for Differentiated Services and Traffic Engineering, October 1998)
- RFC 2475 (An Architecture for Differentiated Services, December 1998)
- RFC 2581 (TCP Congestion Control, April 1999)
- RFC 2702 (Requirements for Traffic Engineering over MPLS, September 1999).
- RFC 2915 (Congestion Control Principles, September 2000)
- RFC 2990 (Next Steps for the IP QoS Architecture, November 2000)

Related Entries   Bandwidth on Demand; Bandwidth Management; Bandwidth; Capacity; Congestion Control Mechanisms; CoS (Class of Service); Data Communication Concepts; Delay, Latency, and Jitter; DEN (Directory Enabled Networks); Differentiated Services (Diff-Serv); Directory Services; Flow-Control Mechanisms; Integrated Services (Int-Serv); Load Balancing; MPLS (Multiprotocol Label Switching); Multimedia; Policy-Based Management; Queuing; Routers; RSVP (Resource Reservation Protocol); RTP (Real-time Transport Protocol); RTSP (Real-Time Streaming Protocol); SLA (Service-Level Agreement); TCP (Transmission Control Protocol); Throughput; Traffic Management, Shaping, and Engineering; Transport Protocols and Services; Voice over IP; VLAN (Virtual LAN); *and* VPN (Virtual Private Network)

Linktionary!—Tom Sheldon's Encyclopedia of Networking updates	http://www.linktionary.com/q/qos.html
QoS Alliance	http://www.qosalliance.org/
QoS Forums	http://www.qosforum.com/
Cisco paper: "Quality of Service (QoS) Networking"	http://www.cisco.com/univercd/cc/td/doc/cisintwk/ito_doc/qos.htm

Cisco paper: Advanced QoS Services for the Intelligent Internet	http://www.cisco.com/warp/public/cc/pd/iosw/ioft/ioqo/tech/qos_wp.htm
Internet2 QoS Working Group	http://www.internet2.edu/qos/wg/
QoS links by Paul Ferguson and Geoff Huston, authors of "Quality of Service," a Wiley book.	http://www.wiley.com/compbooks/ferguson/
Ganymede links page (see QoS and other topics)	http://www.ganymede.com/netlinks.phtml
Sally Floyd's References	http://www.aciri.org/floyd/
Extreme Networks	http://www.extremenetworks.com
Microsoft QoS paper	http://www.microsoft.com/windows2000/library/howitworks/communications/trafficmgmt/qosmech.asp
Noritoshi Demizu's multilayer routing page (extensive links)	http://www.watersprings.org/links/mlr/
ITPRC.com Quality of Service page	http://www.itprc.com/qos.htm

See the Related Entries for more links.

Quantum Cryptography

A cryptographic system scrambles and secures information, encrypting it with a key so that others can only get at the information by decrypting the information with the key. However, poorly encrypted information may be cracked by wiley hackers. The most common technique is an attack in which every possible key combination is tried until the information is decrypted. Hundreds of thousands of computers may be put to work in the cracking process. Organized groups on the Internet have been successful at cracking encryptions that supposedly would take years to break. Distributed net is such a project.

Quantum cryptography provides potentially unbreakable encryption. It is used to transmit information by taking advantage of the polarization properties of photons to store the ones and zeros of digital data. Photons have electric fields that vibrate in different directions. The direction indicates the binary value. Typically, standard encryption is used for bulk encryption of data, while quantum cryptography is used to transmit the secret key for that encryption. The technique has been used in fiber cables up to 48 kilometers.

Related Entries   Authentication and Authorization; Certificates and Certification Systems; Cryptography; Digital Signatures; Hash Functions; PKI (Public-Key Infrastructure); Public-Key Cryptography; *and* Security

Linktionary!—Tom Sheldon's Encyclopedia of Networking updates	http://www.linktionary.com/q/quantum_crypto.html
"A Bibliography of Quantum Cryptography" by Gilles Brassard	http://www.cs.mcgill.ca/~crepeau/CRYPTO/Biblio-QC.html
Quantum cryptography tutorial	http://www.cs.dartmouth.edu/~jford/crypto.html

"Quantum Cryptography" by Toby Howard   http://www.cs.man.ac.uk/aig/staff/toby/writing/
PCW/qcrypt.htm

Cryptoanalysis intro by Artur Ekert   http://www.qubit.org/intros/cryptana.html

Queuing

You are familiar with queues as lines of people waiting to buy tickets or to talk to a service representative on the phone. A queue is also a collection of objects waiting to be processed, one at a time. In the networking environment, packets are queued up into the memory buffers of network devices like routers and switches. Packets in a queue are usually arranged in first-in, first-out order, but various techniques may be used to prioritize packets or ensure that all packets are handled fairly, rather than allowing one source to grab more than its share of resources.

Note that a buffer is a physical block of memory, while a queue is a collection of packets waiting in buffers for processing. Queuing algorithms determine how queues are processed. A different type of queuing is message queuing. See "Middleware and Messaging."

Packets may arrive at queues in bursts from multiple devices, and a device may temporarily receive more packets than it can process. Buffers hold packets until a device can catch up. If the device cannot catch up, buffers fill up and new incoming packets are dropped. This is called "tail drop."

Queue management schemes alleviate congestion. One technique drops packets when necessary or appropriate. So-called "stale" packets (voice or video packets that will arrive too late to be used) may also be dropped to free up space in a queue with the assumption that the receiver will drop them anyway. *Scheduling algorithms* determine which packet to send next in order to manage and prioritize the allocation of bandwidth among the flows.

Queue management is a part of packet classification and QoS schemes, in which flows are identified and classified, and then placed in queues that provide appropriate service levels. RFC 1633 (Integrated Services in the Internet Architecture: An Overview, June 1994) describes the router functions that provide "traffic control" functions. The most important for this discussion is the *packet scheduler*, which uses queues to forward different packet streams. Other components include the *classifier*, which identifies and maps packets into queues. Packets of the same class are put into the same queues, where they receive the same treatment by the packet scheduler.

Multiple access networks such as intranets and the Internet are referred to as "networks of queues." In a point-to-point link, the receiver monitors its own queues and signals the sender when it is sending too fast. In packet-switched networks with many senders transmitting at any time, it is impossible to predict traffic levels. Some parts of the network may become more congested than others. The solution is to place queues throughout the network to absorb bursts from one or more senders.

Queuing Methods

This section explains basic queuing techniques. The following questions could be asked about queues when trying to understand how a particular system works:

- How are incoming packets placed into queues?
- What is the order and/or method in which the networking device services its queues?
- What are the strategies for dealing with bursts of traffic and queues that overflow?

There are several queuing methods, including FIFO (first-in, first out), priority queuing, and fair queuing. FIFO is common in all the queuing schemes, as it describes the basic method in which packets flow through queues. You can imagine queues as supermarket checkout lanes. Each lane uses FIFO queuing, but cashiers may change the order to reduce congestion (e.g., pull shoppers from busy lanes into less busy lanes). Shoppers with membership cards, cash, or a small number of items may be pulled into an express lane (prioritization).

- **FIFO queuing**   This is the basic first-in, first-out queuing technique in which the first packet in the queue is the first packet that is processed. When queues become full, congestion occurs and incoming packets are dropped. FIFO relies on end systems to control congestion via congestion control mechanisms.

- **Priority queuing**   This technique uses multiple queues, but queues are serviced with different levels of priority, with the highest priority queues being serviced first. Figure Q-2 illustrates Cisco's priority queuing scheme. When congestion occurs, packets are dropped from lower-priority queues. The only problem with this method is that lower-priority queues may not get serviced at all if high-priority traffic

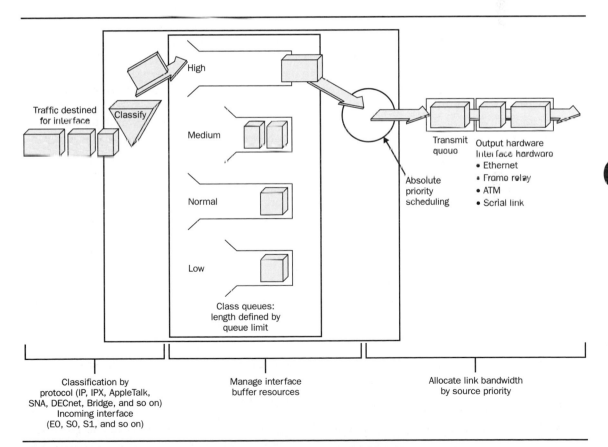

Figure Q-2.   *Cisco's four-level priority queuing scheme (source: Cisco)*

is excessive. Packets are classified and placed into queues according to information in the packets. For example, Cisco routers can be programmed to prioritize traffic for a particular port into high-, medium-, or low-priority queues. Priority schemes may be abused by users or applications that mark packets with priorities that are not allowed. Admission control functions can monitor this. See "Admission Conrol."

■ **Fair queuing**   This method helps solve the problem where some queues may not get serviced because high-priority queues are being serviced. A round-robin approach is used to service all queues in a fair way. This prevents any one source from overusing its share of network capacity. Problems can occur when packets are variable in length and each queue is allowed to release one packet at a time. Some queues will take more time. A byte-oriented scheme may be used to equalize the queues. In addition, some queues may be more full than others and naturally need more service, but a strict, fair queuing scheme will service each queue equally.

■ **WFQ (weighted fair queuing)**   This can be seen as a combination of priority queuing and fair queuing. All queues are serviced so that none are starved, but some queues are serviced more than others. A weight is applied to queues to give some queues higher priority. For example, one queue may get half the available bandwidth and other queues will get an allocation of the remaining bandwidth. Traffic may be prioritized according to packet markings, source and destination IP address fields, port numbers, and information in the ToS field. WFQ weights traffic so that low-bandwidth traffic gets a fair level of priority. If high-priority queues are not in use, lower-priority traffic uses its queues. This prevents high-bandwidth traffic from grabbing an unfair share of resources. WFQ is Cisco's "premier queuing technique" according to the Cisco QoS paper listed later. A unique feature is that it moves real-time interactive traffic to the front of queues and fairly shares the remaining bandwidth among other flows.

■ **CBQ (class-based queuing)**   CBQ is a class-based algorithm that schedules packets in queues and guarantees a certain transmission rate. If a queue is not in use, the bandwidth is made available to other queues. A CBQ-compliant device looks deep in packets to classify packets according to addresses, application type, protocol, URL, or other information. CBQ is more than a queuing scheme. It is also a QoS scheme that identifies different types of traffic and queues the traffic according to predefined parameters.

Queue Behavior

A good document on queue management is RFC 2309 (Recommendations on Queue Management and Congestion Avoidance in the Internet, April 1998). It describes methods for improving and preserving Internet performance, including queue management. Important points are outlined here:

■ Buffering is meant to absorb data bursts and transmit them during the slow period that follows (assuming that occurs).

■ Queue "lockout" occurs when a sender is allowed to monopolize queue space and prevents other connections from getting room in the queue. The sender may be bursting, or sending large packets.

■ The variable length of packets in IP networks (up to 1,500 bytes) makes queue management difficult, and thus QoS is difficult. It is impossible to accurately estimate delay with variable packet sizes.

■ Congestion avoidance mechanisms that operate in TCP hosts can reduce network congestion. These work at the edge of the network. Routers use active queue management techniques to avoid congestion problems. Packets are dropped in anticipation of full queues so that senders slow down. This is appropriate, but maintaining queues in a nonfull state is also not efficient, and "translates to a recommendation that low end-to-end delay is more important than high throughput."

■ Temporary bursts should be allowed. Acting to reduce temporary bursts by dropping packets may be an unnecessary waste of bandwidth.

■ The bigger the queue, the less likely that packets will be dropped off the end of the queue (tail drop). However, large queues can lead to delay problems (a packet may be held when it should be dropped to indicate congestion). Queues should reflect the size of bursts that need to be absorbed. Applications that are affected by delay and jitter, such as voice, need small queues. Non-real-time traffic such as electronic mail, file transfers, and backups benefit from large queues.

■ Two queue disciplines can be used in place of tail drop. "Random drop on full" drops randomly selected packets. "Drop front on full" drops packets at the front of queues. Dropping on the front is used to more quickly notify a sender of congestion. Consider a case where a sender has filled a queue and tail drop occurs. The receiver will continue to receive packets and not know that congestion is occurring until it notices the dropped packet. Dropping at the front tells the receiver right away to signal congestion (by failing to acknowledge).

■ *Active queue management* is the process of dropping packets before buffers overflow. A mechanism called RED (random early detection) detects when a queue is about to overflow by monitoring several threshold levels. When a level is exceeded, packets are dropped "probabilistically" in an attempt to scale back a sender. RED and some variations of RED are discussed under "Congestion Control Mechanisms."

■ Packet bursts are unavoidable. Dropping packets from temporary bursts is not helpful since it will cause the sender to slow down when it may not need to. Keeping average queue size small helps active queue management provide greater capacity to absorb naturally occurring bursts without dropping packets.

■ Small queues reduce delay, which is essential for real-time traffic.

■ Without active queue management, the number of dropped packets increases. TCP hosts steadily increase their transmission rates. If a host reaches a high rate just as the buffer fills, many packets will be dropped. It is best to slow a host down if this situation occurs.

■ Since basic queue management does not provide per-flow state (tracking flows of packets with the same IP source/destination address and port), scheduling methods such as fair queuing, CBQ, and other packet-scheduling methods are needed to fairly allocate bandwidth among flows. Scheduling algorithms and queue management should be seen as complementary, not as replacements for each other.

Traffic-shaping algorithms control queues in a way that smoothes out the flow of packets into networks by hosts or at routers. For example, a host may use what is called a *leaky bucket* at the network interface. The bucket is basically a regulated queue. An application may produce an uneven flow of packets that burst or trickle into the bucket, but the bucket has an imaginary hole in the bottom through which only a certain number of packets can exit in a steady stream. A *token bucket* takes this concept further by allowing a queue to save up permission to send bursts of packets at a later time. A typical algorithm is that for every second of time, a token is saved. If a packet is sent, one of these tokens is destroyed. If no packets are being sent, tokens start to accumulate, which can be used later to burst packets.

UDP may be used by applications that do not need TCP's guaranteed services. UDP does not acknowledge receipt of packets to the sender; therefore, it does not support congestion controls based on dropping packets. When queues fill, UDP will keep sending. Rate controllers can help, as discussed under "Congestion Control Mechanisms."

As mentioned, TCP congestion control mechanisms and active queue management schemes such as RED are discussed under "Congestion Control Mechanisms." Going beyond congestion control mechanisms, there are QoS techniques such as Int-Serv (Integrated Services) and RSVP (Resource Reservation Protocol). See "QoS (Quality of Service)" for an overview and references to related sections. Related RFCs are listed at the Linktionary! Web site.

Related Entries   Acknowledgments; Bandwidth; Bandwidth Management; Capacity; Congestion Control Mechanisms; CoS (Class of Service); Data Communication Concepts; Delay, Latency, and Jitter; Differentiated Services (Diff-Serv); Flow-Control Mechanisms; Integrated Services (Int-Serv); Load Balancing; MPLS (Multiprotocol Label Switching); Policy-Based Management; Prioritization of Network Traffic; QoS (Quality of Service); Routers; RSVP (Resource Reservation Protocol); SLA (Service-Level Agreement); TCP (Transmission Control Protocol); Throughput; ToS (Type of Service); Traffic Management, Shaping, and Engineering; Transport Protocols and Services; Voice over IP; *and* VPN (Virtual Private Network)

Linktionary!—Tom Sheldon's Encyclopedia of Networking updates	http://www.linktionary.com/q/queuing.html
Sally Floyd's References	http://www.aciri.org/floyd/
Cisco paper: "Quality of Service (QoS) Networking"	http://www.cisco.com/univercd/cc/td/doc/cisintwk/ito_doc/qos.htm
UCSC CE/CS high-speed networks Lab (see Projects section)	http://www.cse.ucsc.edu/research/hsnlab/
Noritoshi Demizu's multilayer routing page (extensive links)	http://www.watersprings.org/links/mlr/

Additional links may be found under "Congestion Control Mechanisms" and "QoS (Quality of Service)."

Radio Communication and Networks

Radio communication is usually associated with wireless communication systems like taxicab radios and marine radio, as well as broadcast systems such AM/FM radio and television. Other wireless radio technologies include cordless phones, cellular phones, pagers, garage door openers, walkie-talkies, satellite messaging systems, amateur packet radio, and citizens band radio. Many copper-cable network technologies also operate in the frequency bands allocated to radio. The topic "Electromagnetic Spectrum" has a table that illustrates the most common uses of the radio spectrum.

Radio makes an ideal communication system in areas where cable installation is difficult or not cost effective, and where users are mobile (i.e., the cellular phone system). But, there are bandwidth limitations in the radio spectrum. The microwave range and the infrared range offer higher rates for data communications.

Radio systems may be circuit oriented or packet oriented. In a circuit-oriented system, the available bandwidth is divided into smaller bands that emulate circuits. A single user gets a dedicated transmit and receive channel. This method wastes available bandwidth if nothing is being transmitted. A better approach is to use packets. Packets from multiple users may be multiplexed over one or more channels or over the entire frequency range allocated to the radio system. Bandwidth is used efficiently since it is shared by all users. See "Packet Radio Data Networks."

A typical wireless system consists of a base station transmitter/receiver that operates within a circular radio field. In a cellular phone system, these fields are called *cells*. The radio field may be small, as in the case of small office wireless LANs, or large, as in the case of a metropolitan cellular phone system. A transmitter produces radio waves that are emitted from an antenna. Antennas may be low-frequency aerials or high-frequency masts.

Radio waves have the following characteristics, which impact the design of the radio communication system. Refer to "Electromagnetic Spectrum" for a spectrum chart.

- The higher the frequency, the higher the data rate.

- At lower frequencies, radio waves are omni-directional, meaning that they radiate energy in all directions. If visible, you would see a flood light pattern (as opposed to a beam like a laser).

- At higher frequencies, radio waves are more beam-like.

- Radio waves may propagate as either *ground waves* that follow the earth's surface or *sky waves* that reflect off the ionosphere.

- Radio waves below 3 MHz tend to follow the ground. The lower-frequency waves travel the farthest because they are defracted (bent) as they travel. Note that this frequency range does not support high data rates. It is used for public radio stations and maritime systems. The systems use tall mast antennas and high-power transmitters so that receiving devices can be low powered and inexpensive.

- Radio waves above 3 MHz tend to be absorbed by the ground, but the sky wave portion of the signals propagates well over long distances. The signals are refracted by the ionosphere and bent back to the surface. However, variations in the ionosphere can disrupt signals.

R

■ Radio waves in the 30-MHz to 3-GHz VHF and UHF range (low microwave range) are line of sight. Distance is determined by obstructions and the curvature of the earth. A raised antenna can direct transmissions slightly over the horizon. Devices operating in this range include cellular telephone systems and pagers.

■ The microwave range above 1 GHz is ideal for point-to-point communication links. Microwave frequencies are highly focused line-of-sight waves that can be directed to a single site. The high-frequency range also allows high data rates. See "Microwave Communications."

A typical wireless LAN for use in an office building may have multiple base stations to cover all the different areas of the building. The base stations are then interconnected with copper cable or fiber backbones to a central switch. The backbone design is not much different than a wired network. Workstations benefit from the wireless design. No wires need to be installed to each node and the nodes can usually be moved with few problems.

Related Entries   CDMA (Code Division Multiple Access); Electromagnetic Spectrum; Microwave Communications; Modulation Techniques; Multiplexing and Multiplexers; Packet Radio Data Networks; Satellite Communications Systems; TDMA (Time Division Multiple Access); Telecommunications and Telephone Systems; Wireless Broadband Access Technologies; Wireless Communications; Wireless LAN; *and* Wireless Mobile Communications

Linktionary!—Tom Sheldon's Encyclopedia of Networking updates	http://www.linktionary.com/r/radio_communications.html
"History of Wire and Broadcast Communication" at FCC	http://www.fcc.gov/cib/evol.html
Rune's Land Mobile Radio links	http://rune.tapper.com/lmr/
Radio transmitter and receiver architectures by Andrew Bateman	http://www.avren.com/Courses/ TX_RX_Architectures_plain.htm

See additional links under "Electromagnetic Spectrum."

Radio LANs

See Wireless LANs.

Radio on the Internet

See Internet Radio.

RADIUS (Remote Authentication Dial-In User Service)

RADIUS is a security service for authenticating and authorizing dial-up users. A typical enterprise network may have an access server attached to a modem pool, along with a RADIUS server to provide authentication services. Remote users dial into the access server, and the access server sends authentication requests to the RADIUS server. The RADIUS server authenticates users and authorizes access to internal network resources. Remote users are clients to the access server and the access server is a client to the RADIUS server.

RADIUS was originally developed by Livingston Enterprises for their PortMaster series of network access servers. Lucent Technologies bought Livingston in October 1997, and now claims the software was "invented by the Remote Access Business Unit of Lucent Technologies in 1992." The remainder of this topic draws on RADIUS descriptions provided by Lucent.

Note that RADIUS is an open protocol and is distributed as source code. It is defined in the following Internet RFCs. See "NAS (Network Access Server)" for related RFCs.

- RFC 2139 (RADIUS Accounting, April 1997)
- RFC 2865 (Remote Authentication Dial In User Service (RADIUS), June 2000)

Because RADIUS is open, it can be adapted to work with third-party security products or proprietary security systems. Any access server that supports the RADIUS client protocol can communicate with a RADIUS server.

RADIUS is often referred to as RADIUS AAA, referring to its authentication, authorization, and accounting functions. "Accounting" refers to the ability of RADIUS to gather information about user sessions that can be processed for billing and network analysis. The basic RADIUS authentication system uses its own user database, but other sources of user information include UNIX password files, Sun's NIS (Network Information Service), and directories that can be accessed via LDAP (Lightweight Directory Access Protocol).

The most important feature of RADIUS is its distributed security model. Basically, the communication server (access server or NAS) is separate from the authentication server. This approach is more scalable and secure. The user account information is stored on a central RADIUS server that can be accessed by any number of access servers. This distributed approach is essential for large ISPs that handle hundreds or thousands of dial-up accounts from multiple access servers. An example is pictured in Figure R-1.

Note how the access server is separated from the RADIUS server in a distributed configuration. Access servers typically support dial-up asynchronous or ISDN connections. The access servers talk to the RADIUS servers via the RADIUS protocol, which is outlined in the previously mentioned RFCs.

The RADIUS authentication mechanism works as follows:

1. Users dial in and establish a PPP connection with a network access server.

2. The user and the access server then negotiate an authentication mechanism, usually CHAP (Challenge Handshake Authentication Protocol) or EAP (Extensible Authentication Protocol).

3. The user and the access server exchange authentication information.

4. The access server then packages the access information into an "authentication request packet," along with information about the access server itself and the port being used. The password is encrypted as a precaution against eavesdroppers, using a secret key shared with the RADIUS server.

R

5. The packet is sent to the RADIUS server over whatever connection is in use (LAN, WAN, switch, and so on).

6. When the RADIUS server receives the authentication request packet, it attempts to validate the user against the account information to which it has access. The RADIUS server then returns either an "Authentication Acknowledgment" or an "Authentication Reject" message to the access server.

If a user is validated and an acknowledgment is sent, additional information about the user may be sent as well, such as link requirements and/or policy information that defines service levels for the user. Filters may also be included to restrict access to parts of the network.

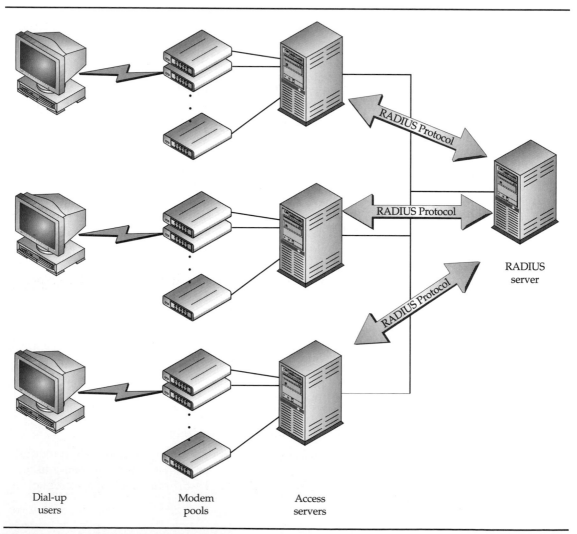

| Dial-up | Modem | Access |
| users | pools | servers |

Figure R-1.   *RADIUS architecture*

Lucent's PortAuthority family of RADIUS servers extends RADIUS with extensible, plug-in modules that enable specific policies. PortAuthority implements policies with what is called the PolicyFlow architecture. The plug-ins can be chained together in a building-block approach. PolicyFlow then defines and manages policy administration across the modules. The modules are Java class files. For example, an ISP implementing PortAuthority can easily switch over from a UNIX password file to a system that stores user data in an LDAP-accessible directory without having to make an immediate migration.

The IETF is evolving RADIUS with its new DIAMETER protocol, which expands on RADIUS with new features, such as the ability to ask for additional logon information beyond the basic authentication, support for roaming users, and the ability to exchange user accounting information among different ISPs. See "DIAMETER" and "Roaming." Also see "Accounting on the Internet." Several topics describe environments in which RADIUS is used. See "Internet Architecture and Backbone" and refer to the section "PoPs and Internet Data Center." Also see "POP (Point of Presence)" and "L2TP (Layer 2 Tunneling Protocol)."

Related Entries   Access Control; Accounting on the Internet; Authentication and Authorization; CHAP (Challenge Handshake Authentication Protocol); Communication Server; Dial-Up Line; DIAMETER; EAP (Extensible Authentication Protocol); Firewall; ISP (Internet Service Provider); L2TP (Layer 2 Tunneling Protocol); Mobile Computing; Modems; NAS (Network Access Server); POP (Point of Presence); Remote Access; Roaming; Security: TACACS (Terminal Access Controller Access Control System); Token-Based Authentication; *and* VPN (Virtual Private Network)

Linktionary!—Tom Sheldon's Encyclopedia of Networking updates	http://www.linktionary.com/r/radius.html
IETF Working Group: Network Access Server Requirements (nasreq)	http://www.ietf.org/html.charters/nasreq-charter.html
IETF Working Group: Authentication, Authorization and Accounting (aaa)	http://www.ietf.org/html.charters/aaa-charter.html
Livingston Enterprises' RADIUS white papers and FAQs	http://www.livingston.com/marketing/products/radius.html
Lucent RADIUS white paper	http://www.lucent.com/ins/library/pdf/white_papers/portawp.pdf
Funk Software's RADIUS page	http://www.funk.com/sbrframe.html
RADIUS Overview at Ericsson	http://www.ericsson.com/datacom/emedia/radius1_overview.pdf
Shiva (now Intel) paper: RADIUS Technology Today and Tomorrow	http://www.shiva.com/remote/samwhitepaperz.html

RAID (Redundant Arrays of Inexpensive Disks)

RAID defines techniques for combining disk drives into arrays. Data is written across all drives, which improves performance and protects data. The alternative is to use one large drive, which does not have the performance benefits of an array and is a single point of failure.

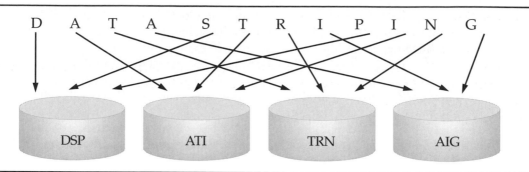

Figure R-2.   *Example of data striping in a RAID system*

A RAID appears as a single drive. Data is written evenly across the drives by using a technique called *striping*. Striping divides data over two or more drives, as shown by the crude example in Figure R-2. The figure shows characters for clarity, but data is usually written in blocks or sectors on each drive. A data file that might take 4 seconds to write on a single drive can be striped to four separate drives in 1 second. Likewise, disk reads are improved because there is a speed advantage in simultaneously reading data from four separate drives.

One form of RAID (level 3, as discussed in the following list) provides redundancy that protects against the failure of one disk in the array. Parity information is generated from the data written to each of the RAID drives, and that parity information is written to a backup drive. If one drive in the array fails, the parity information can be used to rebuild the information that is not available due to the failed drive. However, this parity technique does not provide protection if multiple drives fail. Therefore, some vendors have come up with their own redundancy schemes. Some examples can be found at the Advanced Computer & Network Corp. Web site given later.

Most RAID systems allow *hot replacement* of disks, which means that disks can be replaced while the system is running. When a disk is replaced, the parity information is used to rebuild the data on the disk. Rebuilding occurs while the operating system continues handling other operations, so there is some loss of performance during the rebuilding operation.

RAID levels are outlined in the following list. As mentioned, other levels of RAID have been developed, but some are proprietary. Additional information can be found at the Web sites given later. Note that RAID levels 1, 3, and 5 are most common, while RAID levels 2, 4, and 6 are rarely implemented in commercial products.

- **RAID level 0**   Data is striped over several drives, but there is no redundant drive, so this is not a true fault-tolerant configuration.

- **RAID level 1**   This is a mirroring solution. Data is written in blocks to two separate drives simultaneously.

- **RAID level 2**   This level provides data striping at the bit level over all drives in the array. Additional drives are used to store Hamming codes. Error-correction algorithm reconstructs data from the codes, so mirrored drives are not necessary.

- **RAID level 3**   Data is striped to multiple disks in blocks, and parity information is generated and written to a single parity disk. The information on the parity disk can be used to reconstruct data.

- **RAID level 4**   This level is similar to RAID level 3, except that data is striped in disk sector units rather than as bits or bytes. Parity information is also generated.

- **RAID level 5**   Data is written in disk sector units to all drives in the drive array. Error-correction codes are also written to all drives. This level provides quicker writes because the parity information is spread over all the drives, rather than being written to a single parity drive.

- **RAID level 6**   Similar to RAID level 5, but with added fault tolerance. A second set of parity information is written across all the drives. This is equivalent to double mirroring. This level may be more fault tolerant than necessary and has poor performance.

- **RAID level 10**   This is basically RAID level 1+0, where striping is applied across multiple RAID 1 pairs.

- **RAID level 15**   This is RAID level 1+5, where two complete RAID 5 systems are mirrored for added fault tolerance.

In the event of a failed disk, the most basic systems will require that the entire array go offline until the data on the replacement disk is rebuilt. As mentioned, some systems support hot replacement so that a disk can be replaced while the system continues to run. Data is dynamically reconstructed while the system remains online.

The Adaptec Array Guide provides everything you need to know to understand and build storage array systems. The Web site is listed shortly.

Related Entries   Backup and Data Archiving; Clustering; Data Center Design; Data Migration; Data Protection; Disaster Planning and Recovery; Fault Management; Fault Tolerance and High Availability; File Systems; IP Storage; Mirroring; NAS (Network Attached Storage); Redundancy; Replication; SAN (Storage Area Networks); SCSI (Small Computer System Interface); Servers; Storage Management Systems; *and* Storage Systems

R

Linktionary!—Tom Sheldon's Encyclopedia of Networking updates	http://www.linktionary.com/r/raid.html
The Adaptec Array Guide	http://www.adaptec.com/products/guide/arrayguide01.html
Advanced Computer & Network Corp.'s RAID technology overview	http://www.acnc.com/raid.html
RAID Advisory Board	http://www.raid-advisory.com/
Storage Review.com	http://www.storagereview.com/
RAID vendor links (see RAID heading)	http://www.el.utwente.nl/smi/views/alison/
High-availability white paper by John Mehaffey (discusses mirroring, RAID, and other failover techniques)	http://www.mvista.com/white/highavailability.html

IBM RAID technology paper	http://www.pc.ibm.com/us/infobrf/raidfin.html
"RAID 101" by Lynn Slater	http://members.home.com/slater/raid/index.htm
Brian A. Berg's Storage Cornucopia page	http://www.bswd.com/cornucop.htm

RAP (Resource Allocation Protocol)

RAP is not a protocol itself, but the name of an IETF working group that is attempting to develop standards for providing QoS (Quality of Service) for the Internet. Specifically, the Resource Allocation Protocol Working Group is creating a scalable policy control model for RSVP. The working group also developed COPS (Common Open Policy Service) protocol, which is used in policy-based management.

Related Entries   Integrated Services (Int-Serv); Policy-Based Network Management; QoS (Quality of Service); *and* RSVP (Resource Reservation Protocol)

| Linktionary!—Tom Sheldon's Encyclopedia of Networking updates | http://www.linktionary.com/r/rap.html |
| IETF Working Group: Resource Allocation Protocol (rap) | http://www.ietf.org/html.charters/rap-charter.html |

RARP (Reverse Address Resolution Protocol)

RARP is an Internet protocol that performs the opposite task of ARP (Address Resolution Protocol). It translates a MAC (Medium Access Control) address, which is the address hard-wired into network interface cards, into the IP address that has been assigned to the system with the MAC address. The protocol was originally used to obtain an IP address for Ethernet-connected diskless workstations. Since there is no disk on which to store an IP address, a diskless workstation must obtain the IP address from another source and store it in memory while it is running.

To obtain an IP address, a computer transmits a MAC layer broadcast address (all 1s). A server that supports RARP listens for RARP broadcasts. It reads the source MAC address in the message, and then matches that address in a table with an associated IP address. The server then sends the IP address to the computer.

RARP is outlined in RFC 903 (Reverse Address Resolution Protocol, June 1984). Extensions are covered in RFC 1931 (Dynamic RARP Extensions for Automatic Network Address Acquisition, April 1996).

BOOTP was created at a later time to enhance what RARP provides. BOOTP obtains an IP address, a gateway address, and a name server address from the server running the BOOTP protocol. See BOOTP (BOOTstrap Protocol).

Related Entries   ARP (Address Resolution Protocol); BOOTP; Bootstrapping or Booting; DHCP (Dynamic Host Configuration Protocol); Diskless Workstations; *and* IP (Internet Protocol)

| Linktionary!—Tom Sheldon's Encyclopedia of Networking updates | http://www.linktionary.com/r/rarp.html |

RAS (Remote Access Server)

See Remote Access.

Rate Control

See Congestion Control Mechanisms; QoS (Quality of Service); Queuing; *and* Traffic Management, Shaping, and Engineering.

RBOCs (Regional Bell Operating Companies)

The RBOCs were formed as a result of the breakup of AT&T and are based on a restructuring agreement that took effect in 1984. The final restructuring agreement was the United States District Court's Modification of Final Judgment (MFJ). MFJ ended the Justice Department's suit against AT&T. The RBOCs were organized into seven regional Bell holding companies called Ameritech, Bell Atlantic, Bell South, Nynex, Pacific Telesis, Southwestern Bell, and US West. Each RBOC was assigned a specific geographical area, and each geographical area was divided into service areas called LATAs (local access and transport areas).

The RBOCs are also called the ILECs (incumbent local exchange carriers). In contrast, CAPs (Competitive Access Providers) and CLECs (competitive local exchange carriers) are companies that compete against the RBOCs in the local service areas. IXCs (interexchange carriers) are long-distance service providers such as AT&T, MCI, and Sprint.

The Telecommunications Reform Act of 1996 changed the telecommunications landscape yet again. RBOCs were allowed to merge and the following mergers or acquisitions took place in the following years:

- SBC Communications merged with PacBell (Pacific Telesis) in April 1996.
- Bell Atlantic merged with Nynex in April 1996.
- Qwest Communications bought US West in July 1999.
- SBC Communications merged with Ameritech in October 1999.
- Bell Atlantic merged with GTE in June 2000 and renamed itself Verizon.

So, at this point, it is better to refer to RBOCs as ILECs. They include SBC Communications, Bell Atlantic (now called Verizon), Qwest Communications, and BellSouth.

The Act also attempted to increase competition by opening local markets. RBOCs were required to open their facilities to competitive providers and, if they complied according to the rules, were allowed to expand into long-distance markets. This is discussed further under "Telecommunications Regulation." Also see "Service Providers and Carriers."

Related Entries   AT&T; Communication Services and Providers; ISPs (Internet Service Providers); NPN (New Public Network); PSTN (Public-Switched Telephone Network); Service Providers and Carriers; Telecommunications and Telephone Systems; Telecommunications Regulation; *and* WAN (Wide Area Network)

Linktionary!—Tom Sheldon's Encyclopedia of   http://www.linktionary.com/r/rboc.html
Networking updates

RDF (Resource Description Framework)

See Metadata.

Real-Time Network Services

Real-time network services are designed to deliver real-time information with a high quality of service. Real-time information is live voice and video. Real-time services are designed to deliver real-time information in a timely manner.

The primary property of real-time information is that it must be delivered with a minimum amount of delay and with few dropped packets. However, if packets are lost, it does little good to recover them since the information is live streaming data. This is the opposite of mission-critical data, where every packet must get through without errors.

Because the data from a live source is continuous, it is often called "streaming media." Compression at the source and decompression at the destination is usually required in order to provide timely delivery.

Usually, some amount of packet loss is acceptable, but delay is not. For example, if a few packets are lost, the listener or viewer might not even notice. In a video transmission, missing data appears as a very brief glitch. The receiver may compensate for lost data by filling in information or freezing a frame. In videoconferences, you will often see an image stay still for a moment. Software can compensate for lost data as well.

This topic continues under "Multimedia."

Real-Time Operating System

See RTOS (Real-Time Operating System).

Redirector

A *redirector* is a program running in a network-attached workstation that intercepts network-related requests and redirects them over the network to file servers or peer workstations. For example, if a workstation user makes a request for local files, the redirector forwards the request to the local operating system. If the request is for files on a network server, the redirector forwards the request out over the network to the appropriate server. The request is placed in a packet with the address of the server. Redirector software is individually installed at each workstation along with the driver software for the network interface adapter installed in the computer.

Redundancy

In the world of computer networking, redundant methods are used to protect systems from failure, to protect data from loss and corruption, and to ensure that communication systems stay online and provide a required amount of performance. Some examples are given here:

- Backup and archiving is the most obvious form of redundancy. You create copies of files on alternate disks or backups. The backups are only used when the primary files are lost.

- CRC (cyclic redundancy check) is a method for detecting errors in transmitted data. See "Error Detection and Correction."

- Servers and networking equipment often contain redundant components, such as power supplies, processors, interface cards, and even switching fabrics. If one component goes bad, the redundant component can keep the system up and running. In clustered systems, entire servers and disk systems are duplicated. See "Fault Tolerance and High Availability."

- Redundant power supplies such as battery backup systems or power generators are another form of redundancy. See "Power and Grounding Problems and Solutions."

- RAID data storage systems are based on arrays of redundant disk drives in which data is stored on multiple drives simultaneously, thus providing fault tolerance. See "RAID (Redundant Arrays of Inexpensive Disks)."

- Real-time multimedia transmissions can suffer from excessive packet loss. Since the data is being displayed in real time, recovering a lost packet is usually not feasible. An alternative solution is to create and transmit redundant data streams. Then, if a packet is lost, the missing information may be reconstructed at the receiver from the redundant data that arrives in the following packet(s). See "Multimedia."

- Communication links may be duplicated to provide "on-demand" bandwidth or failover in the event that a primary communication link fails. Link aggregation is a technique in which multiple links are bound together to appear as a single link with a bandwidth of all the links combined. See "Bandwidth on Demand" and "Link Aggregation."

- Load balancing puts redundant equipment such as switches, servers, and storage devices in Web sites and data centers to improve performance and to provide failover options.

Related Entries   Backup and Data Archiving; Clustering; Data Center Design; Data Migration; Data Protection; Disaster Planning and Recovery; Fault Management; Fault Tolerance and High Availability; Load Balancing; Mirroring; Network Management; Power and Grounding Problems and Solutions; Replication; Security; Storage Management Systems; *and* UPS (Uninterruptible Power Supply)

 Linktionary!—Tom Sheldon's Encyclopedia of Networking updates   http://www.linktionary.com/r/redundancy.html

Registries on the Internet

IP addresses on the Internet are distributed in a hierarchical way. At the top of the hierarchy is ICANN (Internet Corporation for Assigned Names and Numbers). ICANN is a nonprofit, international corporation that was formed in 1998 to take over global responsibility for Internet Protocol (IP) address space allocation, protocol parameter assignment, Domain Name System (DNS) management, and root server system management functions. These services were previously performed under U.S. Government contract by the IANA (Internet Assigned Numbers Authority) and other entities. IANA is now a part of ICANN.

ICANN allocates blocks of IP addresses to regional Internet registries. The regional registries then further allocate blocks of IP addresses to local Internet registries within their geographic region. Finally, the local Internet registries assign addresses to end users.

There are currently three regional Internet registries that cover the Americas, Europe, and Asia. The Web sites are given later. These nonprofit organizations provide the following:

- **Registration services**   Approves organizations to receive allocations of IP address space.
- **Routing registry**   A registration service where network operators submit and retrieve router configuration information. The registry serves as a repository for routing policy system information and provides information about IP numbers database.

Refer to Internet RFC 2050 (Internet Registry IP Allocation Guidelines, November 1996) for a more complete description of the Internet registries. Also see RFC 2832 (NSI Registry Registrar Protocol, May 2000) and RFC 2870 (Root Name Server Operational Requirements, June 2000).

RFC 2901 (Guide to Administrative Procedures of the Internet Infrastructure, August 2000) describes the administrative procedures for networks seeking to connect to the global Internet. This includes the steps and operations necessary for address space allocation and registration, routing database registration, and domain name registration.

The IETF Provisioning Registry Protocol (provreg) Working Group is developing protocols related to Internet registries. The provreg Web site is http://www.ietf.org/html.charters/provreg-charter.html.

Related Entries   Autonomous System; BGP (Border Gateway Protocol); CIDR (Classless Inter-Domain Routing); DNS (Domain Name Service) and Internet Domains; Internet; Internet Connections; Internet Organizations and Committees; Internet Standards; ISPs (Internet Service Providers); Route Aggregation; Routing; Routing on the Internet; Routing Registries; Service Providers and Carriers; *and* Standards Groups, Associations, and Organizations

Linktionary!—Tom Sheldon's Encyclopedia of Networking updates	http://www.linktionary.com/r/registries.html
ICANN (Internet Corporation for Assigned Names and Numbers)	http://www.icann.org/
ARIN (American Registry for Internet Numbers)	http://www.arin.net
RIPE NCC (Réseaux IP Européens Network Coordination Centre)	http://www.ripe.net/
APNIC (Asia Pacific Network Information Centre)	http://www.apnic.net/

Relational Database

See DBMS (Database Management System).

Reliable Data Delivery Services

Reliable data delivery services are designed to provide guaranteed and accurate delivery of data over unreliable or best-effort networks. This is done by implementing additional protocols that track packet deliveries and retransmit lost packets. Other services include monitoring the network for congestion and throttling back senders that are contributing to congestion.

IP networks are *best-effort* networks, meaning that the network will deliver packets but provides no guarantees. Packets may be dropped due to congestion. They may also take alternate routers that cause them to arrive after the sender has already sent a replacement packet, causing duplicates at the receiver.

The main point is that the IP network itself does not provide any services to recover from these problems. However, end systems do provide these services. This is a major design feature of the Internet.

David P. Read, one of the people involved in the design of the TCP/IP protocols, writes in "The End of the End-to-End Argument" (http://www.reed.com/Papers/endofendtoend.html) that by splitting the Internet protocols into two protocols (TCP and IP), the network was "decentralized" and turned into a basic datagram forwarding network. In this model, end systems handle functions that were previously handled by networks, such as flow control, acknowledgments, and retransmissions.

One of the reasons for splitting the protocol was that some applications (in particular, live voice), don't need reliability services at all (i.e., for live streaming data, it doesn't make sense to retransmit a lost packet). By separating TCP and IP, applications that need reliability service can go through TCP. Those that don't can access IP through UDP, as described in the upcoming section "Partial Reliable Services."

The following lists the reliable services that TCP implements in end systems. Also see "TCP (Transmission Control Protocol)" for more details.

- **Connection setup and multiplexing**   Reliable data exchange requires the establishment of *connections*. See "Connection Establishment."

- **Positive acknowledgments and flow control**   Examples are *stop-and-wait* and *sliding window*. Both of these schemes provide a form of flow control that keeps the sender from overflowing the receiver with packets (thus preventing excess dropped packets), and an acknowledgment scheme that indicates packet receipt. See "Flow-Control Mechanisms." Also see "TCP (Transmission Control Protocol)."

- **Sequencing of packets**   Sequencing is often called "ordered delivery." Packets are numbered so the receiver can tell if something is missing and can put packets back in the correct order if they arrive at different times (by following different paths).

- **Congestion control mechanisms**   Here, network systems cooperate to alleviate network congestion (a condition in which there is more traffic on the network than can be handled by the network or network devices). The buffers in routers or switches may overflow and start dropping packets. A mechanism is needed in the network itself to alert senders that congestion is occurring and to slow down their transmissions. Refer to "Congestion Control Mechanisms."

- **Error checking to detect corrupted packets**   The sender calculates an FCS (frame check sequence) from the contents of a packet that the receiver can check to make sure the packet is not corrupted. See "Error Detection and Correction" for more details.

Partial Reliable Services

A *partial reliable service* is one that trades off reliability features for performance. TCP's reliability features add considerable overhead. Doing away with one or more of these services when they are not needed improves performance.

UDP (User Datagram Protocol) is an extreme example. UDP is a transport layer service that is stripped down to two basic services: a basic checksum service and a multiplexing service that provides a port-based interface between applications and the IP protocol. Network monitoring programs and multimedia delivery applications use UDP because they do not need the reliability services of TCP. UDP provides these applications with an interface to the network and the sockets they need to form connections with applications on other network systems.

However, there are network applications that need some, but not all, of the reliability features provided by TCP, but more than what is provided by UDP. Some applications don't require ordered delivery, while others can tolerate some loss of data. For example, the results of a database query may not require ordered delivery, while a video stream requires ordered delivery but can tolerate some packet loss. Partial ordered services are services that provide some, but not all, of the services provided by TCP. Internet RFC 1693 (An Extension to TCP: Partial Order Service, November 1994) describes the need for these services and outlines the following four categories:

- **Reliable-ordered services**   Packet delivery is guaranteed (using positive acknowledgments and retransmissions) and packets are numbered so they can be ordered at the destination (sequencing). A file transfer is an example application requiring this service.

- **Reliable-unordered services**   Packet delivery is guaranteed, but sequencing is not critical. A transaction-processing application (e.g., credit card verification) is an example.

- **Unreliable-ordered services**   Some packet loss is acceptable, but sequencing is required. A voice or video application is an example.

- **Unreliable-unordered services**   This service is for applications that do not require guaranteed delivery or sequencing. An example is junk e-mail.

RTP (Real-time Transport Protocol) is an end-to-end delivery service for real-time data such as interactive audio and video. RTP runs on top of UDP, using its multiplexing and checksum features. It does not provide mechanisms for guaranteed and timely delivery, nor does it actively prevent out-of-order delivery. However, RTP does provide a "partial ordered service" in that it sequentially numbers packets and adds timing information for services that might need to reconstruct the original packet sequence. See "Multimedia."

Another interesting protocol in this category is SCTP (Stream Control Transmission Protocol). It is a TCP replacement in voice over IP (VoIP) environments in which a stripped-down transport protocol is needed to carry PSTN signaling messages over IP networks. SCTP is a connection-oriented protocol like TCP that provides many of the reliability features of TCP such as acknowledgments, fragmentation, and sequencing. But SCTP eliminates much of the overhead inherent in TCP that can cause delays. It also provides additional features that optimize it for signal transport. The protocol designers state that SCTP is capable of broader applications including transport of broadcast and streaming data without the need for TCP. See "SCTP (Stream Control Transmission Protocol)."

Related Entries   Acknowledgments; Anycasting; Best-Effort Delivery; Congestion Control Mechanisms; Connection Establishment; Connection-Oriented and Connectionless Services; Error

Detection and Correction; Flow-Control Mechanisms; Fragmentation and Reassembly; Multimedia; Packets and Packet-Switching Networks; QoS (Quality of Service); Queuing; TCP (Transmission Control Protocol); Transport Protocols and Services; *and* UDP (User Datagram Protocol)

Linktionary!—Tom Sheldon's Encyclopedia of Networking updates	http://www.linktionary.com/r/reliable_services.html
Godred Fairhurst's Data Communications Course: Reliability	http://www.erg.abdn.ac.uk/users/gorry/course/arq-pages/reliability.html
"Reliable Messages and Connection Establishment" by Butler W. Lampson	http://research.microsoft.com/lampson/47-ReliableMessages/WebPage.html
"The Transport Layer—An Introduction" by The Transport Group	http://ganges.cs.tcd.ie/4ba2/transport/5.intro1.html
Charles L. Hedrick's TCP/IP tutorial	http://oac3.hsc.uth.tmc.edu/staff/snewton/tcp-tutorial/
The Transport Group Introduction to the Transport Layer	http://ntrg.cs.tcd.ie/4ba2/transport/5.intro.html

Remote Access

Remote access covers a range of techniques that let home users, mobile users, and remote office users access resources on a corporate network, or the Internet in the case of an ISP. Remote access methods should let remote users access a network as if they are directly attached to it and using the same protocols. Note that this topic discusses access to corporate networks, but there are many similarities to connecting with ISPs to access the Internet.

There are two types of remote operations:

■ **Remote control**   In this mode, the dial-up user remotely controls a computer that is connected to the corporate network. Only keyboard commands and screen updates cross the dial-up connection.

■ **Remote node**   In this mode, the user's remote computer becomes another node on the network. All requests and responses cross the dial-up connection, usually via PPP links that encapsulate TCP/IP protocols.

The remote control method can provide better performance for the user, but a dedicated computer must be set up on the corporate LAN that the remote user controls. Access servers that emulate a number of PCs in the same box are available. Remotely controlling a computer at the corporate site cuts down on bandwidth requirements.

The remote node connection allows users to connect to the network using native protocols, such as TCP/IP or IPX. This is the method that most people use to access the Internet by dialing and connecting through an ISP. See "Modems" and "PPP (Point-to-Point Protocol)".

Typical remote access scenarios include home users who access corporate resources via dialup or another access method. The users may dial directly into the corporate network. Another scenario is users who access the corporate network from a business partner's location across an extranet connection or a permanent leased line. Users may access the corporate network from

R

their own computer, or via computer owned by the business partner or a kiosk system at an airport or Internet café.

NAS (Network Access Server)

Remote users typically connect with an NAS (network access server), which terminates calls and provides an end point for a PPP session. A RADIUS server then handles AAA (authentication, authorization, and accounting) functions. See "RADIUS (Remote Authentication Dial-In User Service)."

An NAS is a gateway into another network. It controls a pool of external modems or it is a modular platform that contains many hundreds of modems. The former is usually implemented at a corporate site where only a few remote users need to dial in. The latter is often implemented by organizations with a large mobile work force. ISPs (Internet service providers) also use access servers to provide dial-up access to the Internet for whole communities.

A typical access server answers a dial-in call from a remote user and performs a logon/authentication to verify the user. The access server may hang up the connection and call the user back at a predefined number for security reasons and to reverse the charges on long-distance calls. As mentioned, authentication on many access servers is performed by RADIUS. A newer protocol called DIAMETER is emerging. Microsoft RAS (Remote Access Service) authenticates users who have accounts in Windows NT/Windows 2000 user databases.

If users are geographically remote, an Internet tunnel such as L2TP (Layer 2 Tunneling Protocol) can save long-distances charges by letting users dial local ISPs and connect with the corporate network across the Internet. While L2TP works well, it sends data unencrypted over the public Internet. IPSec (IP Security) is a tunneling and VPN protocol that provides high levels of security for remote access users. See "L2TP (Layer 2 Tunneling Protocol)" and "VPN (Virtual Private Network)." Also see "Mobile Computing" for other information related to remote users.

An IETF working group called Network Access Server Requirements (nasreq) is drafting a functional specification for a NAS (network access server) and the requirements of protocols that will provide that functionality. See "NAS (Network Access Server)."

Today, large service providers and carriers wholesale dial-up and access services to smaller ISPs and other organizations that need to support a large number of remote users at distant locations. The service provider locates racks of modems, authentication servers, and other access equipment at its PoPs. Smaller ISPs then outsource with the service provider by leasing some of the modems. This allows smaller ISPs to establish presence at remote PoPs. Remote users make a call into the local PoP and establish an L2TP or IPSec session across the Internet to the corporate site.

The actual equipment that houses the NAS and modems has become quite sophisticated. Many hundreds or even thousands of modems are concentrated in rack units and are software programmable from a central device to support fast upgrades. Texas Instruments has a paper at the Web ProForum Web site called "The Evolution of the Remote Access Server (RAS) to a Universal Port-Enabled Platform" that describes this further. TI's GoldenPort solution can automatically sense and accommodate any call type on any available port, and it transports voice, fax, and modem calls from traditional POTS interfaces over multiple-packet networks, including IP, frame relay, and ATM.

Related Entries   Access Control; Accounting on the Internet; Authentication and Authorization; Co-Location Services; Communication Server; DIAMETER; Firewall; Gateway; Internet Connections; IPSec (IP Security); ISPs (Internet Service Providers); Mobile Computing; Modems; Network Access Services; Outsourcing; POP (Point of Presence); RADIUS (Remote Access Dial-In User Service); Roaming; *and* VPN (Virtual Private Network)

Linktionary!—Tom Sheldon's Encyclopedia of Networking updates	http://www.linktionary.com/r/ras.html
IETF Working Group: Network Access Server Requirements (nasreq)	http://www.ietf.org/html.charters/nasreq-charter.html
IETF Working Group: IP Security Remote Access (ipsra)	http://www.ietf.org/html.charters/ipsra-charter.html
Nortel paper: "Remote Access Market and Product Evolution."	http://www.firstvpn.com/papers/nortel/remote.pdf
Microsoft remote access Web page	http://www.microsoft.com/windows2000/library/howitworks/communications/remoteaccess/default.asp
Microsoft Networking and RAS page	http://www.microsoft.com/technet/network/
Web ProForum paper: "The Evolution of the Remote Access Server (RAS) to a Universal Port-Enabled Platform"	http://www.iec.org/tutorials/index.html

Repeater

A repeater is a simple physical layer add-on device for extending an electrical, wireless, or optical transmission system over a greater distance. It amplifies signals and transmits the boosted signal on the next cable or wireless segment. Repeaters are necessary because signal strength diminishes over distance, a condition known as *attenuation*. Repeaters are also known as *line conditioners*.

Repeaters on analog transmission lines amplify the incoming signal as is. If the signal is distorted in some way, the distortion is boosted with the rest of the signal. A digital repeater will convert the incoming analog to digital and then forward it as a clean digital signal, although this technique is prone to error if the incoming signal is distorted. Reducing cable distance between repeaters can reduce signal problems. An analog signal can be transmitted about 18,000 meters before a repeater is necessary. A digital signal can be transmitted about 6,000 meters before a repeater is necessary.

Repeaters are used to extend a network segment to reach distant nodes. Expanding the network (as opposed to physically extending it) is something that should be done with repeaters or routers. Think of repeaters as connections to distant workstations rather than as a way to add more workstations.

Optical amplifiers boost signals through the magic of light physics. Photons are injected into the existing signal. This has the effect of boosting the signal. See "Fiber-Optic Cable" and "Optical Networks" for more information.

R

Related Entries   Bridges and Bridging; Ethernet; Line Conditioning; Network Concepts; Routers; *and* Switching and Switched Networks

Linktionary!—Tom Sheldon's Encyclopedia of Networking updates	http://www.linktionary.com/r/repeater.html
Brian Brown's Repeaters and Bridges Web page	http://www.cit.ac.nz/smac/winnt/pt1_7.htm
Gorry Fairhurst "Examples of Network Equipment"	http://www.erg.abdn.ac.uk/users/gorry/course/equip-pages/lan-example-equip.html
Gorry Fairhurst "Repeaters" page	http://www.erg.abdn.ac.uk/users/gorry/course/phy-pages/repeater.html

Replication

Replication is a strategy for automatically copying data to other systems for backup reasons or to make that data more accessible to people at other locations. Replication can also distribute data to multiple servers that can make that information available to multiple simultaneous users. A load-balancing scheme distributes incoming requests to an appropriate server. This is the concept of a clustered system and is often used for busy Web sites.

Mirroring and some forms of RAID (redundant arrays of inexpensive disks) automatically replicate data to other drives to provide fault tolerance. Databases are usually replicated, but replication strategies may also be applied to groups of files or an entire server. Database partitioning and automatic synchronization are some of the requirements. Synchronization involves detecting and resolving file discrepancies, especially in cases when equipment has failed and files may be corrupted or lost. This is especially difficult in real-time replication schemes, where changes must be made at all the replications sites simultaneously or backed off completely.

Organizations with branch offices often use a replication strategy in which entire databases or parts of databases are replicated to the remote offices. This puts the information closer to the users in that office and may eliminate the need for users to access the main database in the corporate office over WAN links. The idea is to provide a consistent view of data for all users, no matter where they are.

Another replication strategy is used for security reasons. Assume a Web server is on the public side of a firewall. That Web server is vulnerable to attack. The Web administrator can maintain a duplicate server inside the firewall where all updates and changes are made. Changes made to this "master" Web server are automatically replicated across the firewall to the public Web server. If the public Web server is attacked, it can be quickly restored from the master. The connection between the servers can be made with non-TCP/IP links such as IPX (Internetwork Packet Exchange), thus preventing Web-based attackers from accessing the master server across the replication link.

The following sections describe file, directory, and database replication schemes.

Web Replications

Replication is common on the World Wide Web. For example, information on a Web server in New York might be replicated to a *mirror site* in Los Angeles. California users can then access the Los Angeles site, thus avoiding extensive router hops to reach the New York site. A proxy caching service performs a replication-like service by copying frequently requested pages into its memory and making sure that the latest versions of those pages are available. This is a "pull" technique.

Another strategy is for Web sites to "push" their most requested pages to proxy servers and cache sites, usually right after changes are made. Pages are usually pushed to "content distribution" sites, which are globally placed Web sites that are specifically designed to put Web content closer to users. See "Content Distribution" and "Web Caching" for more details. Also see the topic "Proxy Servers."

The IETF Web Replication and Caching (wrec) Working Group is developing replication strategies for the Web. Also see RFC 3040 (Internet Web Replication & Caching Taxonomy, January 2001).

File and Directory Replication

Microsoft Windows 2000, Novell NetWare, and other server operating systems use an import/export replication scheme in which a master server is designated an export server and other servers are designated as import servers. The export server replicates data to one or more import servers. Directories on export servers are designated as replication directories. Any files stored in the directories or any files that change are automatically replicated to import servers. Replication takes place automatically on a periodic basis as files are added to the master directory or as information changes. Import servers may be located on the same LAN or across WAN links.

Directory services are common with network operating systems such as Novell NetWare and Microsoft Windows 2000. Directory services are a special kind of database that holds user account information and information about resources on the network. Administrators use the database to manage user accounts and devices. Users access the database to find resources such as printers and storage devices. A directory also holds policy information that describes to network devices the type of service users should be getting.

LDAP is a common directory access protocol that is used by a variety of directory services to provide applications with open access to the directory. An IETF working group called LDAP Duplication/Replication/Update Protocols (ldup) is standardizing the following replication schemes:

- **Multi-master replication** A replication model that allows changes to any replica without first notifying the other replicas.

- **Master-slave, or single-master replication** A replication model in which there is one master directory and one or more slaves. The master control writes on the replicated data.

NDS (Novell Directory Services) is tree structured, as pictured in Figure R-3, and it can be split into two or more *partitions*. A partition can be replicated to another location. In the example, the entire database may be managed by an administrator in New York; but the WestDiv portion of the database is partitioned and replicated to the Los Angeles office, so users at that site have more direct access to the information in that portion of the database. Refer to "NDS (Novell Directory Services)" for more information.

In NDS, there are *master replicas*, *read/write replicas*, and *read-only replicas*. The structure of the database can only be changed on the master replica. Read/write replica information may

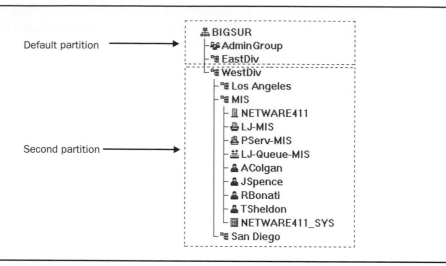

Figure R-3. *NetWare Directory Services can be partitioned and replicated*

be changed, but not the structure. Read-only replicas can only be read and not changed. This hierarchy ensures that changes are properly synchronized across replicated databases. As changes are made, all replicas are automatically updated. These updates are made as soon as possible, but not immediately since constant synchronization would consume network bandwidth. In most cases, small replication delays of directory information do not cause problems.

Microsoft Windows 2000 Active Directory uses a multimaster replication topology in which any domain controller can manipulate the domain database and replicate changes to its replication partners. Domain controllers use USNs (update sequence numbers) to see whether replication partners are up to date. Active Directory includes what is called a "replication topology generator." An administrator determines cost factors for sending data to different locations. This information is then used to build an intersite replication topology.

Active Directory is divided into sites, which are partitions of the database based on IP subnetworks. Sites are important to the topology generator, which generates a topology oriented more within sites than between sites. Intrasite messages are not compressed (which saves CPU cycles). In addition, intrasite replication is immediate and based on changes, while intersite replication is scheduled so as not to affect WAN bandwidth.

Database Replication

Databases such as Oracle, Microsoft SQL, Informix, and others require a high level of synchronized database replication. In many cases, real-time replication is required to maintain synchronization across business transaction databases. In addition, cross-platform support is an important feature in which replication can take place across multiple platforms—for example, between Microsoft SQL Server and Oracle Enterprise Server.

PeerDirect, Inc., specializes in real-time replication architectures. A number of white papers at its Web site outline critical features that are important for corporate database replication. The company advocates a *connection-based replication* scheme as opposed to a *message-based* scheme:

- **Message-based scheme**   This scheme is also called *message queuing* or *store-and-forward* replication. Changes are captured and stored in history queues for later transmission. Queued message packets are delivered through e-mail, FTP, message queuing products, or related methods.

- **Connection-based replication**   This scheme performs point-to-point session-based replication in real time over network connections in which two databases actively participate in the replication session, and simultaneously send and receive changes. There are no change logs or change queues. PeerDirect's real-time replication products read the latest data directly from database and dynamically determine which data has been changed by referencing fixed-size control tables. The method is less complex than other methods and supposedly more efficient.

Microsoft SLQ Server version 7.0 uses a replication model that provides a wide range of features. It builds on previous "publish-and-subscribe" models and includes a number of agents that manage the replication process. These are described shortly. The basic components of Microsoft's SQL Server replication model are outlined here:

- **Publisher**   Makes data available for replication to subscribers and detects data that has changed.

- **Subscribers**   Servers that store replicas and receive updates.

- **Publication**   Information to publish, including tables, specific rows or columns in a table, or stored procedures.

- **Distributor**   A server that contains the distribution database.

- **Pull subscription**   A subscriber that asks for periodic updates of all changes at a publisher. Best for autonomous mobile users.

- **Push subscription**   A publisher propagates changes as they occur to subscribers without a specific request from the subscriber.

- **Snapshot agent**   Creates a picture of the database at a moment in time that can be replicated to other sites. A product catalog with current prices is an example.

- **Distribution agent**   Moves the transactions and snapshot jobs held in distribution database tables to subscribers.

- **Merge agent**   A merge agent moves and reconciles incremental data changes that occurred after the initial snapshot was created.

Microsoft SQL Server supports a range of replication solutions since businesses have different replication requirements. At one end of the spectrum is a need for transactional consistency in which all sites are guaranteed to have the same data values at the same time. An example would be an accounts receivable application in which all sites must have the same invoice updates. At the other end of the spectrum, some amount of site autonomy is allowed.

R

For example, a mobile sales force takes orders on laptop computers and the orders are not put into the system until the salespeople connect to the central office.

SQL Server provides three types of replication, as described here.

Snapshot Replication   A "snapshot" of the data in the database to be replicated is taken at one moment in time and sent to subscribers. An example would be to take a snapshot of the latest product prices and replicate it to the sales staff.

Transactional Replication   Changes to data are monitored and the changes are sent continuously or at scheduled intervals to one or more subscribers. Changes are propagated in near real time with a latency of seconds. For true real-time propagation, a direct network connection between publisher and subscriber is required. To ensure transactional consistency, all changes should be made at the publishing site and only fully committed transactions are sent to subscribers. Subscribers may be allowed to modify replicated data.

Merge Replication   Merge replication provides a high level of autonomy between publisher and subscriber, allowing both to operate independently for periods of time. When the publisher and subscriber reconnect, their changes are merged and conflicts between changes in the data are resolved automatically. The *snapshot agent* and *merge agent* perform merge replications. The *snapshot agent* prepares snapshot files containing schema and data of published tables, stores the files on the *distributor,* and records synchronization jobs in the publication database. The *merge agent* applies to the *subscriber* the initial snapshot jobs held in the distribution database tables. It also merges incremental data changes that occurred after the initial snapshot was created, and reconciles conflicts according to rules you configure or using a custom resolver you create.

For more information about Microsoft SQL Server replication strategies, refer to the Microsoft site given later. Also see "DBMS (Database Management System)" for a list of other database providers and their Web sites.

Related Entries   Backup and Data Archiving; Clustering; Data Center Design; Data Migration; Data Protection; DBMS (Database Management System); DEN (Directory Enabled Networks); Directory Services; Disaster Planning and Recovery; Fault Management; Fault Tolerance and High Availability; File Systems; Jukebox Optical Storage Devices; Microsoft Active Directory; Microsoft Windows File System; Mirroring; Multiprocessing: NAS (Network Attached Storage); NDMP (Network Data Management Protocol); NDS (Novell Directory Services); Optical Libraries; Proxy Servers; Redundancy; SAN (Storage Area Network); SCSP (Server Cache Synchronization Protocol); Storage Management Systems; Storage Systems; Transaction Processing; Web Caching; *and* Web Technologies and Concepts

Linktionary!—Tom Sheldon's Encyclopedia of Networking updates

http://www.linktionary.com/r/replication.html

IETF Working Group: Web Replication and Caching (wrec)

http://www.ietf.org/html.charters/wrec-charter.html

IETF LDAP Duplication/Replication/Update Protocols (ldup)

http://www.ietf.org/html.charters/ldup-charter.html

Caching and Replication in the World Wide Web	http://www.tcd.research.ec.org/cabernet/ workshops/3rd-plenary-papers/13-baentsch.html
Microsoft Windows 2000 Web site	http://www.microsoft.com/windows2000/
Microsoft SQL Server Web page	http://www.microsoft.com/sql/
PeerDirect, Inc. (real-time replication products)	http://www.peerdirect.com
LinkPro Technologies	http://www.linkpro.com/

Repository

A repository in its most basic form is a storehouse for documents, applications, and objects—information in general. A typical company collects a variety of information in database form over time. Some of the information may be about people and some may be about products, marketing, sales, and so on. Each database has different structures, elements, attributes, metadata (information about the data), and so on. At some point, the company may want to share these information assets so that users throughout the company can access, understand, and exploit the information. A repository can provide an "integration environment" for doing just that.

A repository is a central place to share metadata. Metadata is a description of data with a structure that is based on a *common information model*. For example, there are information models that describe business data, geographic data, or medical data. Microsoft developed the OIM (Open Information Model) as an industry standard to describe metadata objects for developing applications and building data warehouses. Standard models can provide a consistent view of data so that developers can create applications that access the data.

Since the repository is a central place for information about corporate data, it is a place where common business rules and data definitions can be enforced. All updates and changes to the way data is described are also made in the repository.

In the data warehousing model, the repository is where data is "extracted," "cleansed," and "integrated" in some way to make it more consumable to users. New models are emerging. Oracle's iFS (Internet File System) is designed to be a repository for a variety of information, including Web pages, media, messages, and so on. The system integrates the relational database and file system worlds and enables integration through XML and Java-based tools.

Microsoft describes its "Microsoft Repository" as follows:

> Repository technology is the integration platform for metadata, acting as the hub for data and component definitions, development and deployment models, reusable software components, and data warehouse descriptions. Integrated metadata management provides a global and consolidated view of the structure and meaning of applications and data—information that usually is scattered throughout the enterprise and buried in individual files, catalogs, or databases.

Microsoft Repository provides a place to integrate metadata for application development and data warehousing. It implements COM and SQL interfaces and ships in Visual Studio and SQL Server. It also includes the OIM, as just described; a repository engine that provides object management; a software development kit and modeling environment; and an XML interchange format that provides a standard way of interchanging instances of OIM.

This topic is covered further under "Metadata," "Data Warehousing," and "OIM (Open Information Model)."

As a side note, there has recently been talk of creating a central repository to store information that is in government databases and auctioning off rights to "mine" that data. Think about the diversity of data, how it is formatted, and how it is stored. Now consider what it will take to give people easy access to those databases.

Related Entries   Client/Server Computing; Data Management; Data Mart; Data Mining; Data Warehousing; DBMS (Database Management System); Directory Services; Distributed Object Computing; Metadata; Middleware and Messaging; Multitiered Architectures; Object Technologies; OIM (Open Information Model); OLAP (Online Analytical Processing); SQL (Structured Query Language); Transaction Processing; UML (Unified Modeling Language); and XML (Extensible Markup Language)

Linktionary!—Tom Sheldon's Encyclopedia of Networking updates	http://www.linktionary.com/r/repository.html
Oracle Internet File System	http://www.oracle.com/database/options/ifs/

Requester Software

Requester software resides in a network-attached workstation. It provides a way for applications running in the workstation to make service requests to devices on the network, such as network servers or bandwidth managers. The requester software serves as a traffic director within the system, diverting commands for local services to the local operating system and diverting commands for network services to the network layer protocols. The network protocols then package information for delivery over the network and send it to the appropriate destination.

Reservation of Bandwidth

See Bandwidth Management; Prioritization of Network Traffic; QoS (Quality of Service); Real-Time Network Services; RSVP (Resource Reservation Protocol); *and* SBM (Subnet Bandwidth Manager).

Residential Broadband

Residential broadband refers to consumer access services rather than business data services. Note that the topic "Home Networking" discusses networking schemes for inside the home. Residential broadband is about access technologies between the home and service providers—specifically, Internet access.

One of the defining features of RBB (residential broadband) networks has been the need to support video services and, more recently, home entertainment services such as virtual reality gaming, downloadable music and video, and multimedia presentations. Other services that benefit from broadband include VoIP (Voice over IP), home schooling, SOHO (small office, home office), and more. There are more than 100 million potential residential customers.

The Cisco document "Residential Broadband Market Drivers" (the Web site is listed at the end of this topic) presents the story of analog and digital TV evolution, as well as new ways to deliver content to the home. It makes some interesting points about how the analog TV spectrum is wasteful and could be better used for other purposes. By 2006, the spectrum may be returned to the government for auction. The Cisco information is by George Abe, author of *Residential Broadband*, a Cisco Press publication.

The Cisco paper mentions that analog TV occupies 6 MHz of bandwidth, while the equivalent signals in digital form (SDTV or standard definition television) can occupy as little as 1.5 MHz due to compression. This allows a broadcaster to have three to five programs where they previously had only one. This new capacity supports unique broadcasting services as well as Internet access services. Some examples are listed here:

- Multiple broadcast from a sporting event, showing different camera angles, with users making the selection of which angle to see.

- TV programs with chat capabilities, in which viewers are using Internet connections to chat with the TV program.

- Virtual channels, in which a broadcaster transmits commands that are executed on viewers' computer-controlled televisions. Images and sounds are not transmitted, but extracted from a local database or created in real time.

The convergence of digital TV and the Internet is taking shape. Electronic program guides were an early example. Users download the guides from Internet sites and use them to select programs or to program their hard-disk–based digital VCRs to record the programs for later viewing.

RFC 2728 (The Transmission of IP Over the Vertical Blinking Interval of a Television Signal, November 1999) discusses how webcasting can be done over television channels. Many PBS channels support this feature. Webcasting is a push technology in which users choose to tune into a variety of broadcasts that are being "pushed" out by a service provider. Push is useful in letting users get just the information they want. For example, a user could choose to view sports news related to a particular team. As broadband capacity increases, the information pushed to users will be full multimedia audio and video clips, not just Web pages. See "Webcasting."

VoD (Video on Demand) is an Internet model that lets users obtain programs and movies on demand, not when the broadcaster chooses to transmit. Users select programs or videos that are transmitted as private data flows to the user. Video compression and high-bandwidth networks make this possible.

An alternative scheme is NVoD (Near Video on Demand). NVoD might be used for popular events like the Olympics or a boxing match. It is similar to pay-per-view, except that the broadcaster staggers the event at, say, 15-minute intervals. Users choose to begin viewing the event at a time that is best for them.

Many new applications are emerging that require broadband, including VoIP (Voice over IP), and audio or video versions of chat rooms. Chat rooms are a form of multipoint-to-multipoint communications in which users establish real-time or near-real-time conference calls with multiple people. This concept can easily be expanded with multimedia. Instead of a list of messages to be read, you click video clips created by other participants.

The various access technologies that provide residential broadband are listed in the Related Entries. Also see "Network Access Services."

Related Entries   Broadband Communications and Networking; Cable (CATV) Data Networks; Communication Services and Providers; DBS (Direct Broadcast Satellite); DSL (Digital Subscriber Line); FTTH (Fiber to the Home); HALO (High Altitude Long Operation); Home Networking; ISDN (Integrated Services Digital Network); Last Mile Services; LMDS (Local Multipoint Distribution Service); Local Loop; MMDS (Multichannel Multipoint Distribution Service); Multicasting; Network Access Services; PON (Passive Optical Network); Satellite Communication Systems; Service Providers and Carriers; Wireless Broadband Access Technologies; Wireless Communications; *and* Wireless Local Loop

Linktionary!—Tom Sheldon's Encyclopedia of Networking updates	http://www.linktionary.com/r/residential_broadband.html
FSAN (Full Service Access Network) consortium	http://www.fsanet.net
Bitpipe (search for "broadband")	http://www.bitpipe.com/
The Last Mile channel at stardust.com	http://www.stardust.com/lastmile/
Cisco document: "Residential Broadband Market Drivers"	http://cio.cisco.com/cpress/cc/td/cpress/design/rbb/ch01.htm
Cisco document: "Technical Foundation of Residential Broadband"	http://cio.cisco.com/cpress/cc/td/cpress/design/rbb/ch02.htm
"Security Considerations for Residential Broadband Access Services" by Brent Chapman	http://www.inetdevgrp.org/19980721/index.htm
NII (National Information Infrastructure) white papers on residential services	http://bob.nap.edu/html/wpni3/

Resilient Packet Rings

A resilient packet ring is a fiber-optic packet network that provides protection against faults. The concept is being implemented in new metropolitan optical networks that coexist with or replace carrier SONET networks. SONET was built from the ground up to support fault tolerance. It implements a dual-ring topology in which one cable waits in standby mode to handle traffic in the event of a fault. If the cable is cut, the ring is reformed over the redundant fiber and data keeps flowing.

As the interest in optical packet-based networks increased, it became obvious that these new networks would need the same fault protection provided by SONET. The IEEE LAN/MAN Standards Committee created the 802.17 standards development project to work on the problem. RPR (resilient packet rings is a new MAC layer standard that defines a resilient packet ring access protocol for use in local, metropolitan, and wide area networks. RPR transfers data packets at rates scalable to many gigabits per second. The new standard uses existing physical layer specifications and new specifications where necessary. According to the IEEE 802.17 group, current metropolitan and WAN fiber-optic rings are using protocols that are neither optimized nor scalable to the demands of packet networks, including speed of deployment, bandwidth allocation and throughput, resiliency to faults, and reduced equipment and operational costs.

Related Entries DPT (Dynamic Packet Transport); Fault Tolerance and High Availability; Link Aggregation; MAN (Metropolitan Area Network); Optical Networks; Redundancy

Linktionary!—Tom Sheldon's Encyclopedia of Networking updates	http://www.linktionary.com/r/ resilient_rings.html
IEEE 802.17 Resilient Packet Ring Working Group	http://www.ieee802.org/rprsg/
Resilient Packet Ring Working Group Web site	http://www.ieee802.org/17/

Resolver Services

Resolver services are generally designed to resolve a name into an address. For example, DNS (Domain Name Service) translates a Web site name such as www.whitehouse.gov into an IP address. When you enter this address into a Web browser's Address field, the Web browser first contacts a DNS server to resolve the name. DNS returns the IP address to your Web browser, which then sends packets to the IP address it was given. Part of this process is locating a suitable DNS server that can resolve the address. Web browsers have a Setup field where the IP address of a primary and secondary DNS server can be found.

There are many other resolver services. In the Windows environment, NetBIOS naming was used for many years as the LAN protocol of choice.

Some interesting new resolver services have emerged to help users find documents on the Internet, independent of their location. The idea is not to rely on a specific Web site address, since Web site locations or the files stored at those locations may change at any time, causing hyperlinks to fail to reference documents at those sites. The resolver service keeps track of documents and provides users with the latest Web address. Web site developers keep the resolver service posted of any changes in with their Web site addresses. A *resolver discovery service* is a service that finds a resolver service.

The important part of this scheme is that documents can contain hyperlinked references to documents that do not rely on physical addresses that might change. See "URN (Universal Resource Name)" and "Handle System."

Other types of resolver services are discussed under "Search and Discovery Services" and "Service Advertising and Discovery."

Related Entries CNRP (Common Name Resolution Protocol); Directory Services; DNS (Domain Name Service) and Internet Domains; Handle System; Metadata; Name Services; NetBIOS/NetBEUI; NIS (Network Information System); Search and Discovery Services; Service Advertising and Discovery; SLP (Service Location Protocol); URN (Universal Resource Naming); WebDAV; *and* WHOIS ("Who is")

Linktionary!—Tom Sheldon's Encyclopedia of Networking updates	http://www.linktionary.com/r/resolver.html

Resource Discovery Services

Resources on enterprise networks and the Internet provide services to users, such as file storage, information searching, printing, electronic messaging, and so on. Almost every device on a network can provide some service. Resource discovery services help users locate the services they need for a specific task. A directory service is one example. It provides a complete database of resources in which a user can search for a service based on service keywords such as "color printer."

Advertising techniques may also be used, in which a device sends out periodic announcements that describe the services it offers. Descriptions of those services should be in a standard format that any device can read and understand. The idea is that mobile users with portable devices who temporarily join networks or move into the realm of ad hoc wireless networks (see "Bluetooth") will need to know about the services offered on those networks.

These topics are further explored under "CNRP (Common Name Resolution Protocol)," "Directory Services," "Search and Discovery Services," and "Service Advertising and Discovery."

Resource Management

Resources on enterprise networks and the Internet consist of information, storage devices, peripherals, applications, networking devices, IP addresses, processing power, and bandwidth. The topic "Network Management" describes user and device management on enterprise networks. More recently, resource management has been associated with bandwidth management.

In a bandwidth-managed network where QoS (Quality of Service) is being provided, a mechanism is required that can estimate the level of QoS that a new user session will need and whether there is enough bandwidth available to service that session. If bandwidth is available, the session is *admitted*. Think about getting a seat on an airplane. The reservation agent provides admission by issuing a ticket if there are seats available.

Bandwidth management is about monitoring, controlling, and enforcing the use of network resources and services. This can be done with a policy-based management system that identifies users and applications, or identifies traffic based on how, when, and where it enters the network. A policy-based management system provides information to networking devices about the type of service users and applications are allowed to consume. Policy information is often stored in directories such as NDS (Novell Directory Service).

Bandwidth allocation may take place on demand, but there is also a need to reserve bandwidth in advance—say, for a teleconference or special event. RSVP (Resource Reservation Protocol) is a protocol for doing this on intranets. It was originally thought that RSVP might work across the Internet, but the protocol had scalability problems and was never widely deployed. In the mean time, MPLS (Multiprotocol Label Switching) was developed and provides a better approach to providing QoS and traffic engineering across the Internet.

Resource management on public networks is difficult because there are many different administrative domains. The IETF and other organizations are developing standard resource and policy management protocols. For example, COPS (Common Open Policy Service) was developed to help resource managers interact with one another and exchange information.

Related Entries   Accounting on the Internet; Admission Control; Bandwidth Brokerage; Bandwidth Management; Bandwidth on Demand; CoS (Class of Service); DEN (Directory Enabled Networks); DIAMETER; Differentiated Services (Diff-Serv); Directory Services; Integrated Services (Int-Serv); IntelliMirror; LDAP (Lightweight Directory Access Protocol); MPLS (Multiprotocol Label Switching) Multilayer Switching; Network Management; Policy-Based Management; Prioritization of Network Traffic; QoS (Quality of Service); Queuing; RSVP (Resource Reservation Protocol); SOCKS; Switching and Switched Networks; Traffic Management, Shaping, and Engineering; *and* VoIP (Voice over IP)

Linktionary!—Tom Sheldon's Encyclopedia of Networking updates

http://www.linktionary.com/r/ resource_management.html

Retransmission

See Acknowledgments; Best-Effort Delivery; Congestion Control Mechanisms; Connection-Oriented and Connectionless Services; Error Detection and Correction; Flow-Control Mechanisms; Queuing; Reliable Data Delivery Service; Transport Protocols and Services; *and* UDP (User Datagram Protocol).

RFC (Request for Comment)

See Internet Standards.

Ricochet

Ricochet is a packet data network operated by Metricom in a few select metropolitan areas. See "Packet Radio Data Networks" for more information.

Rights and Permissions

Network operating systems have access rights (called *permissions* in the Windows NT/Windows 2000 environment) that are assigned by network administrators to grant users access to file systems and directory services (such as Novell Directory Service or Microsoft Active Directory).

 This topic is covered in more detail at the Linktionary! Web site.

Rights/permissions are granted by network administrators, supervisors, or department managers, depending on the management structure. Rights and permissions in file systems are granted to individual users or groups of users and include the ability to read a file but not change it, or the ability to read and change files. These rights/permissions may control the following:

- The time the user can log on or the specific computers the user can operate
- The resources the user can access, such as printers, fax machines, and communication services
- The level of control that administrators or subadministrators have in defining the rights/permissions of the users and/or resources they manage
- The ability to access file systems, as defined at folders in the file system
- The ability to access network resources, as defined in each level of a *directory tree*, such as Microsoft Active Directory or NDS (Novell Directory Services).

Typical rights and permissions include no access, list (view a directory listing), read, add & read (drop a file in a box, but not be able to change it), change, execute a program, change permissions, and take ownership (obtain rights to a directory or file).

R

Typically, a user is granted rights to access files in a particular folder, and rights may be restricted to just that folder. Users who have rights to access files, directories, or objects are usually called *trustees* of those files, directories, or objects.

Inheritance may also be applied, which means that rights *flow down* from the parent folder to subfolders. Inherited rights make administration easy because a user or a group of users can be given access to a whole directory tree in one step. However, administrators/supervisors can block inherited rights to prevent users from accessing specific directories in a tree or set custom rights as appropriate. The fact that rights carry down through the directory tree is of great importance in the planning of directory structures. You should create directory structures that take advantage of the way that rights are set at specific branches of the tree.

The Linkitionary! Web site provides more detail on the individual rights and permissions in Novell NetWare, Microsoft Windows 2000, and UNIX systems.

Related Entries   Access Control; Account, User; Administrator Account; Attributes; Authentication and Authorization; Data Management; Data Protection; Directory Services; File Sharing; File Systems; Logons and Logon Accounts; Microsoft Windows; Microsoft Windows File System; Network Operating Systems; Novell NetWare; Novell NetWare File System; Security; UNIX; UNIX File System; *and* Users and Groups

Linktionary!—Tom Sheldon's Encyclopedia of Networking updates	http://www.linktionary.com/r/rights_permissions.html
Network Appliance Tech Library (click "File Service" and choose a document)	http://www.netapp.com/tech_library/
Microsoft File and Print Services Web page	http://www.microsoft.com/ntserver/fileprint/
Novell directory and file information (see "File Services" under appropriate Operating System heading)	http://www.novell.com/documentation/
Novell Research Network Services Topics (see "File Services")	http://developer.novell.com/research/topical/network_services.htm
AFS directory and file permissions paper at Pittsburgh Supercomputing Center	http://www.psc.edu/general/filesys/afs/setpermissions.html
UNIX file permissions page	http://www.cs.umass.edu/rcfbbl/bbl_security_050395_files.html
UNIX access controls: "Controlling Access to Your Files and Directories"	http://www.mcsr.olemiss.edu/unixhelp/tasks/access_permissions.html

Ring Network Topology

Ring network topology is a closed-loop topology that does not require terminators. The token ring topology forms a logical ring but has the cable layout of a star topology with a central hub. The ring is actually maintained in the hub. When a workstation attaches to the hub, the ring extends out to the workstation through the cable and back again to the hub. If another hub is attached, the ring is maintained by running cables from the ring-out connector on the first hub to the ring-in connector on the second hub, and from the ring-out connector on the second hub to the ring-in connector on the first hub. See "Token Ring Network" and "Topology" for more information.

RIP (Routing Information Protocol)

RIP is a dynamic internetwork routing protocol primary used in *interior* routing environments. A dynamic routing protocol, as opposed to a static routing protocol, automatically discovers routes and builds routing tables. Interior environments are typically private networks (autonomous systems). In contrast, exterior routing protocols such as BGP are used to exchange route summaries between autonomous systems. BGP is used among autonomous systems on the Internet.

RIP uses the distance-vector algorithm developed by Bellman and Ford (Bellman-Ford algorithm). Refer to "Distance-Vector Routing" for more information.

RIP was traditionally used in many TCP/IP and NetWare IPX/SPX internetworks. However, RIP has some drawbacks when used on large networks, especially where traffic is heavy since RIP's routing information exchange generates a lot of traffic of its own. OSPF is an alternative routing protocol now used by most Internet service providers and large organizations.

While OSPF is now the recommended interior routing protocol for large internetworks, RIP is still prevalent. It is simple to use, and, in some cases, you can install and run it without any further configuration. Administrators may want to adjust the cost (metrics) to add preference to some routes.

There are two versions of RIP. RIP version 1 is considered historic, but is still widely used. The latest version is RIP version 2, which is commonly referred to as RIP-2 or RIPv2. If an implementation is called just "RIP," it is probably version 1, not RIPv2.

Historical Information and Internet Documents

RIP has its roots in the early Internet. RFC 823 (The DARPA Internet Gateway, September 1982) mentions distance-vector routing, which is the basis of RIP. But RIP itself has roots in a Xerox protocol called GWINFO, which later became ROUTED (pronounced "route-d") and shipped in BSD UNIX. GWINFO evolved with Xerox Network System (XNS) protocol suite and became XNS Routing Information Protocol. XNS RIP then started showing up in network operating systems' protocol suites, such as Novell IPX/SPX. It is also part of the Microsoft Windows TCP/IP implementation for servers.

The Internet community originally defined RIP in RFC 1058 (Routing Information Protocol, June 1988). The RFC was superseded by RFC 1388, RFC 1723, and eventually RFC 2453 (RIP Version 2, November 1998). RIP version 2 was updated to support variable-length subnet masks and classless routing environments, as discussed under "IP (Internet Protocol)." Reasons for the update are outlined in RFC 1923 (RIPv1 Applicability Statement for Historic Status, March 1996). This RFC essentially places RIPv1 into historical status, even though the protocol is still used.

The IETF working group called Routing Information Protocol (rip) has the latest information about RIP, including the latest RFCs and drafts. Its Web site is listed later. The Linktionary! Web site lists a full set of RIP-related RFCs.

R

RIP Operation

When a RIP router starts up on an IP network, it broadcasts a RIP *request message* on the network in a UDP packet. When the message reaches other RIP routers, they respond by sending their existing routing tables in a *response message* to the new router. After startup, routers automatically send out their routing tables every 30 seconds to make sure that the network routes are up to date (this turns out to be a problem on busy networks).

RIP routing tables contain entries for each of the networks that a router can reach. These entries include information about directly attached routers and routers that it has learned about from the routing tables it received from other routers.

As mentioned, RIP routers transmit their entire routing tables every 30 seconds. Even though most of the information in each update is probably the same as the previous update, the entire table is always sent. This is a major disadvantage of RIP that causes excess traffic on the network. One of the reasons OSPF is preferred is because it sends updates with changes only—not entire routing tables.

When the topology of the network changes, the RIP router that knows about the change is triggered into action and sends routing table updates out on the network. A *triggered update* contains information about the change in the network. As other routers receive updated information, they propagate it on to neighboring routers. A triggered update allows the network to update its routing tables as soon as possible, instead of waiting for the 30-second periodic update.

As each router receives an update, it adds 1 to the hop count of each entry, and then adds the entry to its own database. Each router that receives an update is one more hop away from where the update came from. The hop count ticks up as the update propagates out on the network. One of the drawbacks of RIP is that the maximum hop count is 15, meaning that RIP networks are limited to 16 networks.

Distance-vector routing is based on finding the best route to a destination. A distance-vector table is built by each router. The table contains two primary entries: a vector (destination) and a distance (cost). Distance is based on the hop counts obtained from the routing tables sent by other routers. When first booted, a router sets a cost of 0 for itself, 1 for directly attached neighbors, and infinity for all other destinations. As distance-vector information is received from other routers, a router will integrate the information and build a new routing table for itself. For each destination, it adds the cost found in a neighbor's distance-vector table to the cost of the link to that neighbor. Refer to "Distance-Vector Routing" for more information.

When a router inserts an entry for a destination in its routing table, it also adds an expiration time of 180 seconds. If the route is mentioned in the next routing update, the time is reset to 180 seconds. If the route is not mentioned, the timer expires and the router then starts advertising the route as unreachable for another 120 seconds. If this timer expires, the route is removed from the routing table and this change is propagated throughout the network.

RIP version 1 is a classful routing protocol that follows the "class A, class B, class C" networking scheme. RIP does not support variable-length subnetting and supernetting in the form of CIDR. A classless network addressing scheme is now used on the Internet. OSPF supports classless addressing.

RIP version 2 (RFC 2453) updates the original RIP by providing support for classless addressing (variable-length subnet masking and CIDR). It is also backward compatible with RIP version 1. Version 2 also allows routers to share important additional information used for authentication and multicasting. The IETF Routing Information Protocol (rip) Working Group (Web site given later) developed the version, even though newer link-state protocols were gaining in popularity. The group felt that RIP was still useful on small networks. It is easier to set up and manage than the newer protocols.

RIPng is the newest version of RIP and is designed for compatibility with IPv6-based networks. RIPng is documented in RFC 2080 (RIPng for IPv6, January 1997) and RFC 2081 (RIPng Protocol Applicability Statement, January 1997).

Related Entries　　Autonomous System; Distance-Vector Routing; IGPs (Interior Gateway Protocols); IGRP (Interior Gateway Routing Protocol); Internetworking; IP (Internet Protocol); Network Architecture; IPX/SPX (Internetwork Packet Exchange/Sequenced Packet Exchange); Network Concepts; Network Layer Protocols; OSPF (Open Shortest Path First) Routing; Packets and Packet-Switching Networks; Routers; Routing; Routing on the Internet; *and* VRRP (Virtual Router Redundancy Protocol)

Linktionary!—Tom Sheldon's Encyclopedia of Networking updates	http://www.linktionary.com/r/rip.html
IETF Working Group: Routing Information Protocol (rip)	http://www.ietf.org/html.charters/rip-charter.html
Cisco documentation: "Routing Basics"	http://www.cisco.com/univercd/cc/td/doc/cisintwk/ito_doc/routing.htm
Cisco documentation: "Routing Information Protocol (RIP)"	http://www.cisco.com/univercd/cc/td/doc/cisintwk/ito_doc/rip.htm
Cisco documentation: "RIP and OSPF Redistribution"	http://www.cisco.com/univercd/cc/td/doc/cisintwk/ics/cs001.htm
RIP paper at RAD Communications	http://www.rad.com/networks/1995/rip/content.htm

R

RIPE (Réseaux IP Européens)

RIPE is a nonprofit organization established to administer and register Internet Protocol (IP) numbers in Europe. It allocates blocks of IP addresses that it has received from IANA (Internet Assigned Number Authority). Two similar organizations exist: ARIN (American Registry for Internet Numbers) and APNIC (Asia Pacific Network Information Centre).

Refer to "Registries on the Internet." The RIPE Web site is at http://www.ripe.net.

Related Entries　　Internet; Internet Architecture and Backbone; Internet Organizations and Committees; IP (Internet Protocol); ISPs (Internet Service Providers); Registries on the Internet; Routing; Routing on the Internet; *and* Routing Registries

RISC (Reduced Instruction Set Computer)

Microprocessors have instruction sets called *microcode* that programmers use to create low-level computer programs. The instruction sets perform various tasks, such as moving values into registers or executing instructions to add the values in registers. Microcode can be either simple or complex, depending on the microprocessor manufacturer's preference and the intended use of the chip.

RISC designs, as the name implies, have a reduced set of instructions that improve the efficiency of the processor, but require more complex external programming. RISC designs are based on work performed at IBM by John Cocke. He found that about 20 percent of a computer's instructions did about 80 percent of the work. His 80/20 rule spawned the development of RISC architecture, which reduces the number of instructions to only those that are used most. The other instructions must be implemented in external software.

RISC processors have been used in network switches and routers to handle packet processing. Another processor design is the ASIC (application-specific integrated circuit) architecture. While switches with RISC processors use software-based algorithms, ASICs are hardware-based devices with switching matrixes and processing functions put directly in hardware. This improves performance and lowers cost, but ASICs cannot be upgraded like software-based systems.

Related Entries   ASIC (Application-Specific Integrated Circuit); CISC (Complex Instruction Set Computer); Cut-Through Architecture; MEMS (Micro-Electromechanical Systems); Multilayer Switching; Network Processors; Routers; Switch Fabrics and Bus Design; *and* Switching and Switched Networks

Rlogin

According to RFC 1282 (BSD Rlogin, December 1991), "the rlogin facility provides a remote-echoed, locally flow-controlled virtual terminal with proper flushing of output. It is widely used between UNIX hosts because it provides transport of more of the UNIX terminal environment semantics than does the Telnet protocol, and because on many UNIX hosts it can be configured not to require user entry of passwords when connections originate from trusted hosts. The rlogin protocol requires the use of the TCP. The contact port is 513." Refer to RFC 1282 for more information.

Related Entries   Client/Server Computing; Logons and Logon Accounts; Remote Access; TCP/IP (Transmission Control Protocol/Internet Protocol); *and* Telnet

RMI (Remote Method Invocation)

RMI is the basis of distributed object computing in the Java environment. It defines how Java components can interoperate in a multiple Java VM environment. RMI provides the tools that programmers need to create distributed Java applications (objects) that can invoke methods on other Java applications that are running on other Java virtual machines, such as remote hosts across the Internet. Invoking a method is like asking another program to do something. A Java object must first obtain a reference to another Java object before it can invoke its methods. It may obtain these references via another Java application or it may obtain them through a naming service that is built into RMI.

Related Entries   ActiveX; Client/Server Computing; COM (Component Object Model); Compound Documents; CORBA (Common Object Request Broker Architecture); Distributed Applications; Distributed Computer Networks; Distributed Object Computing; Java; Middleware and Messaging; MOM

(Message-Oriented Middleware); Multitiered Architectures; Object Technologies; ORB (Object Request Broker); RPCs (Remote Procedure Calls); SOAP (Simple Object Access Protocol); *and* Web Technologies and Concepts

RMOA (Real Time Multimedia Over ATM)

RMOA is an ATM Forum specification that defines how ATM's VBR (variable bit rate) may be integrated with H.323. H.323 is an ITU-T recommendation that defines how to support multimedia traffic on best-effort packet-based networks. Refer to http://www.atmforum.com.

RMON (Remote Monitoring)

RMON is an IETF network monitoring and analysis standard similar to SNMP (Simple Network Management Protocol) that was developed to overcome some of the limitations of SNMP. RMON is not a replacement for SNMP. It fits into the SNMP framework as an enhanced data collection system on managed devices. The SNMP protocol may still be used to transfer information from RMON-managed devices to SNMP management stations.

To put these protocols in perspective, assume you are a city planner and you need to monitor traffic at various intersections throughout the city. One way to do this is to have people (called *agents*) stationed at important intersections to gather traffic information. Data entry clerks at a central office call the agents on a regular basis to obtain information about traffic conditions and enter it into a computer for analysis.

The only problem with this technique is the overhead of making all those phone calls. A more efficient method would be to give the agents their own personal computers and have them enter the traffic data as it occurs, and then transfer that data to the central office on a regular basis or upon the request of a manager who needs it. This is what RMON does for SNMP.

Both SNMP and RMON employ *agents*, more commonly called *probes* in RMON, which are software processes running on network devices to collect information about network traffic and store it in a local MIB (management information base). With SNMP, a network management console must continually *poll* the SNMP agents to obtain MIB information, but the constant polling adds to network traffic.

With RMON, probes located in network devices such as hubs, routers, and switches collect and maintain historical information. The network management console does not need to constantly poll probes to get the information. Probes act as servers and the management console is the client in a client/server relationship. SNMP provides the communication layer for transmitting information between RMON probes and management consoles.

The IETF modeled RMON on the capabilities of traditional LAN analyzers. It supports packet capturing and filtering on specific LAN segments and allows network managers to remotely analyze traffic at all seven layers of the protocol stack. RMON can provide useful information about traffic flows that can be used to monitor and manage sessions. It collects statistics that can reveal short-term and long-term trends in traffic. It can also reveal users and systems that use the most bandwidth, and it can sound alarms when certain thresholds are exceeded. If abnormal conditions are detected, the manager can take steps to analyze traffic in more detail with the help of RMON probes.

RMON has the following groups that enable managers to obtain more detailed information about specific activities:

- **Statistics**   Collects and accumulates LAN traffic statistics and errors
- **History**   Collects statistics at defined intervals for use in historical analysis
- **Alarms**   Provides alerts when predefined thresholds are exceeded
- **Host**   Collects information and provides statistics based on MAC (Medium Access Control) addresses
- **HostTopN**   Collects information about which hosts are transmitting the most traffic
- **Matrix**   Collects information about which devices are communicating with one another
- **Events**   Provides a way to trigger actions based on alarms
- **Packet Capture**   Provides a way to select the type of packets to collect
- **Filter**   Provides a way to view only selected packets when analyzing information

RMON 2 expands on the features of the original RMON by providing support all the way up to the application layer. In particular, it lets managers monitor the amount of traffic that is produced by individual applications running in workstations and servers. This feature is useful in client/server network environments and provides information about the actual usage of the network, not just traffic flows. RMON 2 can also provide information about end-to-end traffic flows. The following RFC provides more information:

- RFC 2819 (Remote Network Monitoring Management Information Base, May 2000)

Related Entries   CIM (Common Information Model); CMIP (Common Management Information Protocol); Configuration Management; DMI (Distributed Management Interface); DMTF (Distributed Management Task Force); MIB (Management Information Base); Network Analyzers; Network Management; Performance Measurement and Optimization; SNMP (Simple Network Management Protocol); Testing and Diagnostic Equipment and Techniques; *and* WBEM (Web-Based Network Management)

Linktionary!—Tom Sheldon's Encyclopedia of Networking updates	http://www.linktionary.com/r/rmon.html
IETF Working Group: Remote Network Monitoring (rmonmib)	http://www.ietf.org/html.charters/rmonmib-charter.html
Google Web Directory (search for "RMON")	http://directory.google.com/Top/Computers/
Cisco documentation: "Remote Monitoring (RMON)"	http://www.cisco.com/univercd/cc/td/doc/cisintwk/ito_doc/rmon.htm
Network World Fusion network management page	http://www.nwfusion.com/netresources/manage.html

See "Network Management" for more links.

Roaming

Roaming has several meanings in the telecommunications and networking environment. The cellular phone industry refers to roaming as the ability of a subscriber to move among different service providers. Roaming also applies to wireless LANs. A company that installs wireless LANs throughout its offices may need to set up radio hubs at various points throughout the building. Roaming allows a user with a mobile device to move out of the range of one hub and into the range of another while maintaining a connection with the network. See "Wireless LANs."

Roaming is supported in network operating systems like Microsoft Windows 2000 with its IntelliMirror feature. IntelliMirror is a set of management technologies that provide desktop change and configuration management. User's data, personal computer settings, and the computing environment follows them to other locations as they travel with portable computers. See "IntelliMirror" and "Mobile Computing."

Another form of wireless networking is much broader in scope. The IETF Roaming Operations (roamops) Working Group is developing procedures, mechanisms, and protocols to support users roaming among groups of ISPs. This is different from, but related to, the work of the IP Routing for Wireless/Mobile Hosts Working Group (mobileip) in that the roamops group is not concerned with the movement of hosts or subnets, but of users.

Internet roaming services are offered by confederations of ISPs within a particular region that want to offer better service to their customers. National ISPs in different countries may also offer roaming services. GRIC (Global Reach Internet Connection) is the best example, as discussed later.

Internet RFC 2477 (Criteria for Evaluating Roaming Protocols, January 1999) defines Internet roaming as "the ability to use multiple Internet service providers while maintaining a formal, customer-vendor relationship with only one." RFC 2194 (Review of Roaming Implementations, September 1997) also provides details. The roaming architecture consists of three major subsystems:

- **Phone book subsystem**   The phone book subsystem provides the user with phone numbers that can be dialed from different locations in order to connect into the roaming-enabled network.

- **Authentication subsystem**   This system forwards user authentication information to the user's home ISP for verification.

- **Accounting subsystem**   This system keeps track of the services provided to users so that service providers can be compensated for the services they provide.

RFC 2486 (The Network Access Identifier, January 1999) discusses methods for identifying a roaming user's home authentication server. This is accomplished via the NAI (network access identifier), which is the user identification submitted by a client to a network access server during PPP authentication. RFC 2607 (Proxy Chaining and Policy Implementation in Roaming, June 1999) describes proxy chaining, which is the method that a network access server uses to consult the user's home server and have that home server authenticate the roaming user via the NAI information.

In 1996, ten ISPs in various countries formed the GRIC (Global Reach Internet Connection) with the goal of implementing a global roaming service, and to coordinate billing and settlement among the members. Today, GRIC is composed of over 300 service providers that form one seamless global network called the GRIC Alliance Network.

GRIC offers a variety of roaming services, including a platform that enables service providers to deploy and manage multiple Internet services such as worldwide authentication, authorization, routing, settlement, and provisioning in a way that ensures service providers will be reimbursed for the services they provide. It also offers users logons throughout the world, as well as VPN and VoIP services. See the GRIC Web site listed shortly.

A somewhat related topic is OSP (Open Settlement Protocol), which is a client/server protocol that Internet service providers use to exchange authorization, accounting, and usage information to support IP telephony.

Related Entries   Accounting on the Internet; Authentication and Authorization; Bandwidth Management; DIAMETER; IntelliMirror; ISPs (Internet Service Providers); Mobile Computing; Mobile IP; OSP (Open Settlement Protocol); Policy-Based Management; RADIUS (Remote Authentication Dial-In User Service); Remote Access; Voice over IP (VoIP); *and* VPN (Virtual Private Network)

Linktionary!—Tom Sheldon's Encyclopedia of Networking updates	http://www.linktionary.com/r/roaming.html
GRIC (Global Reach Internet Connection)	http://www.gric.net/
IETF Working Group: Roaming Operations (roamops)	http://www.ietf.org/html.charters/roamops-charter.html
IETF Working Group: IP Routing for Wireless/Mobile Hosts (mobileip)	http://www.ietf.org/html.charters/mobileip-charter.html

Route Aggregation

Route aggregation is a technique of organizing network layer IP addresses in a hierarchical way so that addresses are "topologically significant." Route aggregation in the form of CIDR (Classless Inter-Domain Routing) helped to solve IP address depletion problem in the early 1990s. In addition, route aggregation summarizes routes so there are fewer routes to advertise across the Internet. A service provider is allocated a contiguous block of IP addresses, which it then subnets (divides into smaller allocated blocks) and leases to its downstream subscribers (which may be smaller ISPs). Because these addresses are contiguous, the ISP can advertise one route on the global Internet.

The postal ZIP code system provides an analogy. All mail with ZIP codes 9*xxxx* is directed to the West coast. A mail sorter on the East coast only needs to know that all mail with ZIP codes starting with 9 goes west. On the West Coast, regional and local post offices sort the mail by looking further into the ZIP code. For example, 98*xxx* letters are sent to Washington while 97*xxx* letters are sent to Oregon.

Route aggregation on the Internet is similar. CIDR does away with the old class-based IP address scheme in favor of a classless scheme that supports hierarchical addressing. As mentioned, an ISP is allocated a large block of addresses that it divides up and allocates to downstream ISPs. Allocation is handled by Internet registries, with IANA (Internet Assigned Numbers Authority) at the top. IANA allocates blocks to regional Internet registries, which include ARIN (American Registry for Internet Numbers), RIPE NCC (Réseaux IP Européens

Network Coordination Centre), and APNIC (Asia Pacific Network Information Centre). These regional registries then further allocate blocks of IP addresses to local Internet registries within their geographic region. Finally, the local Internet registries assign addresses to end users. RFC 2050 (Internet Registry IP Allocation Guidelines, November 1996) discusses this hierarchy.

The important concept is that addresses are assigned in contiguous blocks on CIDR bit boundaries defined by a bit mask. For example, the class B address 180.50.0.0 (with the implied subnet mask of 255.255.0.0) is now simply referred to as 180.50.0.0/16. The /16 indicates that the first 16 bits are the network number. An ISP with this address allocation advertises 180.50.0.0/16 on the rest of the Internet. Internet routers outside the ISP's network only need to know this single address. Inside the ISPs network, routers forward incoming packets to the network of sub-ISPs and organizations to which the ISP has allocated addresses.

Note that this scheme is often referred to as "provider-based address allocation" because providers are given a block of addresses that they allocate on their own. Customers get addresses from ISPs, not IANA or other agencies. In addition, addresses are usually leased, which means that they are returned to the ISP's address block if the customer moves out of its area.

Before CIDR, the number of routers to advertise on the Internet was exceeding the capabilities of most hardware. In 1995, there were close to 65,000 routes. As CIDR aggregation has been implemented, the number of routes in the global routing table has reduced to approximately 35,000 routes.

Related Entries   Autonomous System; BGP (Border Gateway Protocol); CIDR (Classless Inter-Domain Routing); Internet Organizations and Committees; Internetworking; IP (Internet Protocol); OSPF (Open Shortest Path First) Routing; Peering; Registries on the Internet; Routing on the Internet; *and* Routing Registries

Linktionary!—Tom Sheldon's Encyclopedia of Networking updates	http://www.linktionary.com/r/route_aggregation.html
ICANN (Internet Corporation for Assigned Names and Numbers)	http://www.icann.org/
ARIN (American Registry for Internet Numbers)	http://www.arin.net
RIPE NCC (Réseaux IP Européens Network Coordination Centre)	http://www.ripe.net/
APNIC (Asia Pacific Network Information Centre)	http://www.apnic.net/
Pacific Bell's Classless Inter-Domain Routing (CIDR) Overview	http://public.pacbell.net/dedicated/cidr.html
Thomas Baumann's CIDR Web pages	http://www.heh.uni-hannover.de/books/os2-peer/peerfaq2/n019.html

Routers

Routers are internetworking devices that connect similar and heterogeneous network segments into *internetworks*. Routers are layer 3 networking devices. In contrast, repeaters operate at the physical layer while bridges (and switches) operate at the data link layer (layer 2). See "Routing," "Internetworking," and "IP (Internet Protocol)" for an overview of the routing process.

The traditional view of a router is a box with two or more interfaces. The interfaces provide connections for networks and/or point-to-point links. There is usually a serial interface for connecting a management console. This interface allows managers to securely configure a router by avoiding sending management information over the network controlled by the router.

The original requirements for routers as defined by the early designers of the Internet was for a switch with the following characteristics:

- Transmit packets across different types of data link layer networks (IP was designed from the start for heterogeneous networking).

- Since different networks have different frame sizes, routers must be able to fragment packets so they fit in the frame size of the underlying network. See "Fragmentation and Reassembly."

- Store a packet temporarily to read its routing information and then forward it. Store and forwarding causes some delay, but newer switching and multilayer switching techniques improve performance.

- Allow routers to drop packets in an overflow situation, but rely on TCP running in end systems to determine that packets have been dropped (or lost).

- Routers do not maintain state information, which is information that can be used to track packet delivery between end systems and detect errors, or reserve bandwidth for flows as is done with RSVP.

Routers also discover, collect, and assemble information about routes on the network that can be used to perform route selection when forwarding packets. This is handled by routing protocols that run in the router, such as RIP, OSPF, or BGP.

A router may perform "firewall-like" functions such as packet filtering and discard. For example, packets may be dropped if they do not match a range of IP addresses or if they are for applications other than those allowed.

The following RFCs provide information about early router design and the router requirements. Refer to "Routing on the Internet" for more information about the early design of the Internet. RFC 875 is a somewhat tongue in cheek, but informative document about internetworks, gateways, and routers

- RFC 823 (DARPA Internet Gateway, September 1982)
- RFC 875 (Gateways, Architecutures, and Heffalumps, September 1982)
- RFC 1812 (Requirements for IP Version 4 Routers, June 1995)

Routers store and forward datagrams and process network layer information. Routers also run routing protocols that discover and gather information about the network topology, calculate routes to other networks, and build routing tables. Some management functions are also required. This requires one or more processors and memory to store routing tables and other information. The topic "Throughput" describes router performance characteristics.

Figure R-4 illustrates the architecture of a traditional router with four interfaces (newer designs are covered later). The device may be a stand-alone dedicated router from a vendor

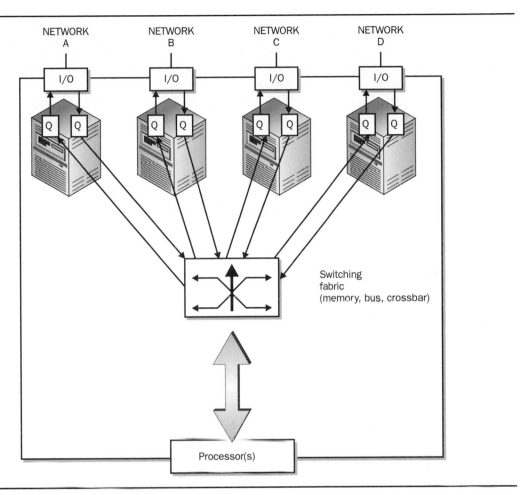

Figure R-4.   *Traditional/legacy router internal architecture*

such as Cisco Systems, or a computer with network interface cards (Ethernet, token ring, and so on) running a network operating system like Novell NetWare, Sun Microsystem's Solaris, or Microsoft Windows 2000.

Buffers are blocks of memory that temporarily hold packets until they can be processed. Note that each interface has input and output buffers. The switching fabric may also have its own buffers. Buffers are a key part of a router. The size of the buffers is critical. Network traffic may burst into the router faster than the router can process the traffic. Buffers temporarily hold packets until they can be processed. If there are too few buffers, the buffers will fill quickly and incoming packets will be dropped. Dropped packets require retransmission, which affects network performance. Too many buffers can cause excessive delay. See "Queuing" for more information on how buffers and queues are handled in routers.

The switching fabric connects all the ports and provides any-to-any connections among those ports. There are several types of switching fabrics. Standard memory may be used to switch packets, but this scheme lacks performance. A shared bus is another method. The most common is a crossbar switch design in which a link exists between every input port and every output port. See "Switch Fabrics and Bus Design" for more information.

When a packet arrives at a router port, it is placed in an input buffer to await processing. An incoming packet may be addressed to the router, but most packets will require forwarding, as described here:

1. Strip off the frame information and retrieve the datagram. Check for errors and forward the datagram to the appropriate protocol forwarding process in the router (for multiprotocol routers).

2. Get the IP network address (the host portion is irrelevant until the datagram reaches the destination network).

3. Look up the address in the routing table to determine how to forward the packet. Find the best match in the table by finding the longest match, meaning that the network address with the most number of bits that match the destination address is used. If no match is found, generate an ICMP error response and send it to the source.

4. Update the IP datagram Time-To-Live field (TTL). If the TTL decrements to zero, discard the datagram (assumes it is in a loop).

5. Make sure the datagram will fit in the MTU (maximum transmission unit) of the next hop network. MTU is the size of the data area for the frame. Datagrams may be fragmented to fit the MTU.

6. Send the packet to the output queue of the appropriate interface. If the queue is full, drop the packet and send an ICMP message to the sender that indicates congestion.

A *layer 3 switch* is a hardware-based multiport router that uses ASICs (application-specific integrated circuits) and/or network processors to greatly improve routing performance. Many of the steps outlined in the preceding are performed directly in hardware as opposed to relying on software and separate CPUs. A typical software router forwards 500,000 packets per second. A layer 3 switch with built-in high-speed routing at each port can forward up to 50 million packets per second. Most devices of this type are now called *multilayer switches* because they can examine information above layer 3. Most can examine application layer data in order to prioritize packets and provide QoS. See "Multilayer Switching."

Multilayer switches are relatively inexpensive, so network managers gain great flexibility in designing routed networks as discussed under "Network Design and Construction."

Note   *This topic continues at the Linktionary! Web site with a discussion of router categories, hybrid routers, and gigabit/terabit routers for the core of the Internet.*

Internet routers and routers for large enterprises support MPLS, which eliminates the traditional hop-by-hop routing technique and replaces it with a label-switching approach that creates fast switched paths through the network. The technique is similar to ATM virtual circuits and brings QoS to the Internet. See "MPLS (Multiprotocol Label Switching)," "Network Core Technologies," and "Optical Networks,"

Related Entries   Active Networks; ASIC (Application-Specific Integrated Circuit); Backbone Networks; Bandwidth Management; Best-Effort Delivery; Congestion Control Mechanisms; Data Communication Concepts; Datagram and Datagram Services; Fragmentation and Reassembly; HSRP (Hot Standby Router Protocol); Internet Architecture and Backbone; Internetworking; IP (Internet Protocol); Label Switching; MPLS (Multiprotocol Label Switching); Multilayer Switching; Network Architecture; Network Concepts; Network Design and Construction; Network Layer Protocols; Network Processors; Packets and Packet-Switching Networks; QoS (Quality of Service); Queuing; RISC (Reduced Instruction Set Computer); Routing; Routing on the Internet; Switch Fabrics and Bus Design; Switching and Switched Networks; Throughput; VLAN (Virtual LAN); VRRP (Virtual Router Redundancy Protocol); *and* WAN (Wide Area Network)

Linktionary!—Tom Sheldon's Encyclopedia of Networking updates	http://www.linktionary.com/r/routers.html
Google Web Directory: Routers and Routing	http://directory.google.com/Top/Computers/Internet/Routers_and_Routing/
Bitpipe (search for "router")	
Cisco documentation: Router Configuration Tutorial	http://www.cisco.com/univercd/cc/td/doc/product/rtrmgmt/netsys/netsysug/routconf.htm
Routing links at Cisco	http://www.cisco.com/warp/public/732/Tech/routing.shtml
Alcatel Wire-Speed Routing Guide	http://www.ind.alcatel.com/library/whitepapers/pe_wirespeed_toc.html
Alcatel White Paper: "Advanced Internetworking—Layer-Three Switching."	http://www.ind.alcatel.com/library/product_catalog/pdfs/f03.pdf
Godred Fairhurst's data communications course: Routers	http://www.erg.abdn.ac.uk/users/gorry/course/inet-pages/router.html
Godred Fairhurst's data communications course: Operation of Routers	http://www.erg.abdn.ac.uk/users/gorry/course/inet-pages/router-opn.html
Juniper Networks technology notes and white papers	http://www.juniper.net/techcenter/
Terabit router information at Pluris	http://www.pluris.com/

Route Servers and Routing Arbiter

See Routing Registries.

Route Switching

See Multilayer Switching.

Routing

This topic discusses routing protocols and algorithms. See "Routers" for a discussion of hardware routing devices and "Multilayer Switching" for a discussion of layer 3 switches (routing switches). A historical perspective on the development of routing on the Internet is referenced under "Routing on the Internet." Also note that this topic covers IP routing, although other routable protocols such as IPX (Internetwork Packet Exchange) exist.

Routing is a packet-forwarding process that takes place on internetworks (i.e., separate networks that are joined by routers), as shown in the following illustration. When a host sends a packet, it is either for a local host on the same network or a host on a remote network. If the packet does not have a local IP network address, the host sends the packet to the default router, which forwards the packet to other networks.

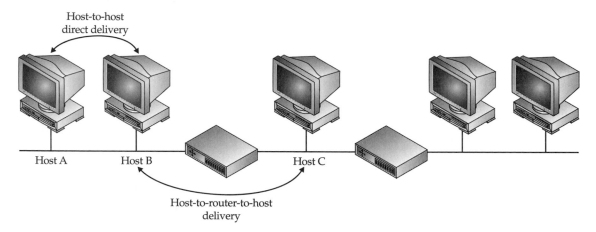

The network in the following illustration is more complex. It consists of a mesh of interconnected networks that provide multiple routing paths. While each router may have its own attached networks and hosts, only two hosts are shown for simplicity. Host A wants to send a packet to host B. Multiple paths exist. Host A sends the packet to its locally attached router and lets the router handle the forwarding.

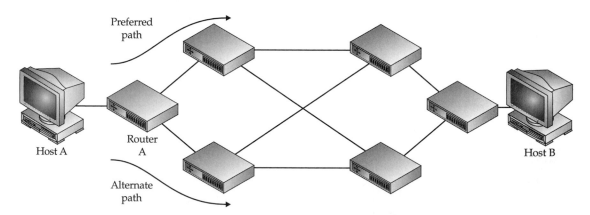

How does the router choose a path? It looks in a routing table that has been created with the help of a *routing protocol*. By looking in its routing table, router A will find two paths. One is preferred, while the other is available should the preferred path go down. An administrator may designate a preferred path by setting metrics.

Routers are responsible for determining the next hop that will get a packet to its destination, not the complete path to the destination. Basic IP routing is called *hop-by-hop* or *destination-based* routing. The technique is like getting directions—a person may point you in the right direction at an intersection. At the next intersection, another person points you in the right direction. Eventually, you get to where you want to go—not by knowing the exact path from the start, but by being pointed along the way as you go. Someone might point you in a direction that avoids construction or dead ends. On a large meshed network with many possible paths, routers may choose paths that avoid congested or temporarily disabled links.

Router-based internetworking is essential for building scalable networks. It promotes a hierarchical network structure and network addressing scheme. Data link layer LANs are limited by size and number of hosts. Routing helps networks grow beyond these limitations. Network designers can use routing to join multiple LANs into internetworks. On the Internet, routers allow independently managed autonomous systems (ASs) to interconnect and exchange traffic while maintaining the autonomy of each network.

Routing Procedures

The original requirement for routers (originally called "gateways") on the early Internet was for a device that could inspect an incoming packet and read its destination address, look this address up in a table, and then forward the packet appropriately. A router may need to fragment packets to fit the frame size of the underlying network. Routers may drop packets in an overflow situation. TCP is responsible for detecting and recovering dropped packets. One of the most comprehensive documents on routing is RFC 1812 (Requirements for IP Version 4 Routers, June 1995).

Originally, the lookup tables were manually configured by network administrators, a process known as *static routing*. Static routing is appropriate for small networks and some dedicated links, but with large networks, *dynamic routing* is a requirement. Network topologies may change at any time when links fail or link metrics are reconfigured. A dynamic routing protocol must discover these changes and update routing tables. Several routing protocols and algorithms have been devised to handle this task, as discussed later.

The internetwork routing process is pictured in Figure R-5 and outlined here. For simplicity, the numeric IP addresses of networks, hosts, and routers are replaced with abbreviations.

1. At the source (A1), a datagram is created with the IP address of the destination host (C1).

2. Since the destination network address is not the same as the current network address, host A1 forwards the datagram directly to the default gateway, router A/B. Note that the datagram is put into one or more frames that have the MAC address of router A/B.

3. The frame arrives at router A/B on port A. The datagram is extracted and the IP address is inspected. The router determines that the destination can be reached through router B/C, so it puts the datagram in a frame type to match network B and attaches the MAC address of router B/C.

4. At router B/C, the frame arrives on port B. The datagram is extracted and the IP address is inspected. The router determines that the host is attached to subnet C, so

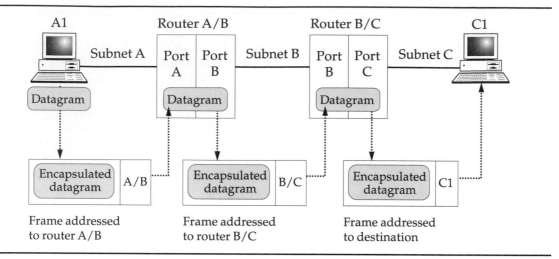

Figure R-5.   *IP packets across mixed networks*

router then puts the datagram in a frame, attaches the MAC address of destination C1, and transmits the frame on the network.

Host C1 sees the frame on the network as being addressed to it, and receives the frame.

To transmit large files, the file is broken into pieces that are put inside numerous packets. Then, if one of the packets is lost, only that packet must be retransmitted and not the entire file. This reliability feature is handled by TCP in the background.

Routing Environments

A basic routing concept is the *autonomous system,* as shown in Figure R-6. The Internet is a collection of autonomous systems in the form of individual service providers and carrier networks that are interconnected by routers, routing protocols, and routing policies. Each autonomous system is managed by its own authority and implements its own internal routing. An autonomous system is essentially a *routing domain*. The same *interior routing protocols* and algorithms are used within a domain. OSPF is the most popular interior routing protocol. Routing among autonomous systems is called *exterior routing*. BGP is the exterior routing protocol for the Internet. Interior routing is sometimes called "intradomain routing" and exterior routing is sometimes called "interdomain routing."

External connections are made via a *border router*, which provides a gateway to the outside world. A border router provides "reachability" information for all of its internal routes to border routers belonging to other ASs. This information is quite succinct and often consists of a single routing table entry (for external routers) that represents all of the internal networks on the other side of the border router. A range of contiguous network addresses may be

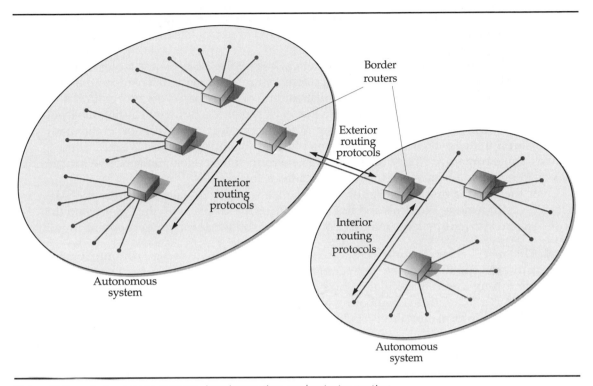

Figure R-6.   *Autonomous system, interior routing, and exterior routing*

represented by a single (larger) network address. This scheme greatly reduces the amount of routing information that must be stored and transmitted on the Internet.

The Internet is made up of many autonomous systems consisting of local, regional, and backbone service providers. See "Internet Architecture and Backbone" for information about the architecture of the Internet.

Routing Protocols and Algorithms

Dynamic routing protocols automatically discover routes on the network and build routing tables. Routers refer to the tables when forwarding packets. As mentioned, there are interior and exterior routing protocols.

The primary interior routing protocols in use today are RIP (Routing Information Protocol) and OSPF (Open Shortest Path First). OSPF is now the most important on large networks and Internet service provider networks, but RIP is still popular for small private networks. The primary exterior routing protocol for exchanging routing information between autonomous systems is BGP (Border Gateway Protocol).

A dynamic routing protocol adjusts to changing network topologies, which are indicated in update messages that are exchanged between routers. If a link attached to a router goes down or becomes congested, the routing protocol running in the router makes sure that other routers know about the change. It then runs a routing algorithm to recalculate the routes on the network and update the routing tables.

Routers store the information about the network in *routing tables*. These tables contain an entry for each known network along with a reference to the interface that leads to that network. The next router in the path will make a similar routing decision based on information it finds in the routing table that it has created. Note that each router has different routing table entries because the reachability of each network is different depending on its location in the mesh.

"Route flapping" is the frequent changing of the availability of routes. When a route changes, some routers are likely not to get the new route information and continue forwarding packets into the old erroneous route (usually called a "black hole").

Over the years, a number of routing protocols have been developed. These include distance-vector routing protocols and link-state routing protocols, with the latter being the most preferred on today's large internetworks. See the following topics for more information:

- **Distance-Vector Routing**   Distance-vector routing protocols base routing decisions on a distance (in terms of the number of hops) and a vector (a direction). The Bellman-Ford algorithm is used to calculate routes once each router has received information about available routes from neighboring routers. See "Distance-Vector Routing" and "RIP (Routing Information Protocol)."

- **Link-State Routing**   Link-state routing provides a way to build a topological database that describes more accurate internetwork routes. The protocols are more suitable for large networks and are now the preferred routing method for most organizations and Internet service providers. The *Dijkstra algorithm* is used to calculate routes. See "Link-State Routing" and "OSPF (Open Shortest Path First)."

You can also refer to "VRRP (Virtual Router Redundancy Protocol)." This protocol provides uninterrupted rerouting in the event of a router failure. It relies on statically configured redundant routers.

Alternative routing techniques are handled in IP over ATM environments, where ATM networks provide the data link layer for IP networks. In this environment, methods are needed to discover routes across the ATM network among routers at the edge of the ATM network. *Cut-through routing* (sometimes called "shortcut routing") is an approach in which a cut-through route is created between end systems as a virtual circuit across an ATM switching fabric. The first few packets are initially routed, but if a long flow is detected, the ATM address of the destination is obtained by the source, which then sets up a virtual connection across the ATM fabric directly to the destination, switching all subsequent packets and bypassing the routers. See "IP over ATM" for more information.

MPLS (Multiprotocol Label Switching) is the latest solution for delivering QoS and traffic engineering across IP networks. It provides explicit routing and constraint-based routing. An explicit route has the characteristics of a virtual circuit in a switched environment. Another alternative to traditional hop-by-hop routing is *explicit routing*. A path is created across a network between two points in advance of sending packets. Packets are tagged with the label of the path and switched across the network.

Constraint-based routing takes this concept further by defining how intelligent routing software can gather information about network loads, bandwidth characteristics, and jitter/delay characteristics. Paths are then selected based on various constraints. An administrator may simply want to balance the load across the network, ensuring that one link is not underused while another is overused. A path may also be selected because it provides enough bandwidth to carry a particular stream. This goes beyond the concept of using metrics to engineer routes. Instead, advanced routing software dynamically selects routes based on the current network environment. See "Traffic Management, Shaping, and Engineering."

Additional Information

The IETF has a number of working groups that are working on routing and routing-related issues. The following IETF Web site has a list of routing-related working groups listed under the topic "Routing Area."

 IETF Working Groups Web page   http://www.ietf.org/html.charters/wg-dir.html

The following RFCs provide information about routing and routing protocols. A more complete list is available at the Linktionary! Web site given later.

- RFC 0791 (Internet Protocol, September 1981)
- RFC 1380 (IESG Deliberations on Routing and Addressing, November 1992)
- RFC 1787 (Routing in a Multi-provider Internet, April 1995)
- RFC 1812 (Requirements for IP Version 4 Routers, June 1995)
- RFC 2791 (Scalable Routing Design Principles, July 2000)
- RFC 2956 (Overview of 1999 IAB Network Layer Workshop, October 2000)
- RFC 2992 (Analysis of an Equal-Cost Multi-Path Algorithm, November 2000)

Related Entries   Active Networks; Autonomous System; Best-Effort Delivery; BGP (Border Gateway Protocol); CLNP (Connectionless Network Protocol); CoS (Class of Service); Datagram and Datagram Services; DNS (Domain Name Service) and Internet Domains; ES-IS (End System-to-Intermediate System) Routing; Fragmentation and Reassembly; Framing in Data Transmissions; HPR (High-Performance Routing); HSRP (Hot Standby Router Protocol); IDPR (Interdomain Policy Routing Protocol); Internet; Internet Architecture and Backbone; Internetworking; IP (Internet Protocol); IP over ATM; IS-IS (Intermediate System-to-Intermediate System) Routing; Label Switching; MPLS (Multiprotocol Label Switching); Multilayer Switching; Network Architecture; Network Concepts; Network Layer Protocols; OSI (Open Systems Interconnection) Model; OSPF (Open Shortest Path First) Routing; Packets and Packet-Switching Networks; Policy-Based Management; QoS (Quality of Service); Registries on the Internet; RIP (Routing Information Protocol); Routers; Routing on the Internet; Routing Registries; RSVP (Resource Reservation Protocol); Traffic Management, Shaping, and Engineering; *and* VRRP (Virtual Router Redundancy Protocol)

Linktionary!—Tom Sheldon's Encyclopedia of Networking updates	http://www.linktionary.com/r/routing.html
Google Web Directory: Routers and Routing	http://directory.google.com/Top/Computers/ Internet/Routers_and_Routing/
Cisco routing protocols page	http://www.cisco.com/public/technotes/ tech_protocol.shtml
Cisco documentation: "Designing Large-Scale IP Internetworks" (includes sections of IGRP, OSPF, and BGP)	http://www.cisco.com/univercd/cc/td/doc/ cisintwk/idg4/nd2003.htm
Cisco documentation: "Routing Basics"	http://www.cisco.com/univercd/cc/td/doc/ cisintwk/ito_doc/routing.htm
Routing links at Cisco	http://www.cisco.com/warp/public/732/Tech/ routing.shtml
Routing links at ITPRC	http://www.itprc.com/routing.htm
Multilayer routing information and links by Noritoshi Demizu	http://www.watersprings.org/links/mlr/

Routing, Multilayer

See Multilayer Switching.

Routing on the Internet

The Internet is a massive internetwork of router-connected networks, consisting of thousands of autonomous systems that are each managed by different authorities. These networks share traffic and exchange routing information. This topic is available at the Linktionary! Web site. It outlines the following topics:

■ Historical development of the Internet, including the first packet switches and routers

■ The building of the early ARPANET from a routing perspective

■ Early routing structures and the development of autonomous system routing

■ The development of the NSFNET and the backbone routing model

■ The emergence of BGP and the scalable Internet

■ Current and future routed networks

The topic at the Linktionary! Web site also includes a complete list of RFCs that describe the historical development of routing on the Internet

Related Entries   Active Networks; Autonomous System; BGP (Border Gateway Protocol); Datagram and Datagram Services; DNS (Domain Name Service) and Internet Domains; GII (Global Information Infrastructure); Internet; Internet2; Internet Architecture and Backbone; Internet Organizations and

Committees; Internet Protocol Suite; Internetworking; Label Switching; Network Concepts; NII (National Information Infrastructure); OSPF (Open Shortest Path First) Routing; Packets and Packet-Switching Networks; Peering; Registries on the Internet; Routing; Routing Registries; Traffic Management, Shaping, and Engineering; *and* vBNS (Very high speed Backbone Network Service)

Linktionary!—Tom Sheldon's Encyclopedia of   http://www.linktionary.com/r/routing_internet.html
Networking updates

Noritoshi Demizu's internetworking technical   http://www.watersprings.org/links/inet/
resources page

Routing Registries

A routing registry is a repository of routing policy information and provides a place where network operators can submit, maintain, and retrieve router configuration information. A registry maintains *route servers* (not to be confused with routers) that coordinate routes among service provider networks, as discussed shortly. Routing servers were introduced to the Internet in 1994 by the Routing Arbiter project, which was part of the NSFNET project and managed by Merit Networks. Routing Arbiter and NAP operations were made into commercial operations in 1996 and NSF launched RSng (Route Server next generation) in 1997.

An AS (autonomous system) is a group of IP networks with its own routing policy and its own interior routing protocols. Thus, an AS is a *routing domain*. An AS uses BGP, an exterior gateway protocol to exchange routing information with other ASs. While interior routing is usually based on metrics derived from topology, link speed, and load, exterior routing decisions are based on policy-based rules. BGP can understand policy rules, but a mechanism to publish or communicate the policies is still required. A routing registry provides this functionality by giving ASs a way to publicize their routing policies. In addition, a relatively new language called RPSL (Routing Policy Specification Language) was developed to specify routing policies.

 Routing Registries and RPSL are discussed further at the Linktionary! Web site.

The IRR (Internet Routing Registry) is now the primary means of coordinating routing policy on an Internet-wide basis. It contains announced routes and routing policy in a common format that network service providers access to configure their backbone routers.

The IRR consists of national and international routing registries, including the RIPE Network Coordination Centre (NCC) in Europe, ANS (Advanced Network Solutions, Inc.), internetMCI, Bell Canada (formerly CA*net), and the RADB (Routing Arbiter Database). The RADB is a component of the IRR and provides unique services: it handles registration for all customers not covered by the other registries and coordinates the routing policies of all the other registries. The Internet also consists of regional registries, which register with one of the above national or international registries.

RPSL is a language for describing routing policy constraints and registering them in the IRR. RPSL replaces a previous language called RIPE-181 that was used through most of the

1990s. RFC 2622 (Routing Policy Specification Language, June 1999) and RFC 2650 (Using RPSL in Practice, August 1999) describe RPSL in detail.

Route Servers

Route servers are an integral part of the Internet. They provide interdomain routing services among service provider routers deployed at Internet interconnection points (NAPs and MAEs), where traffic is exchanged among the different service providers on the Internet. For a discussion of this structure, see "Internet Architecture and Backbone." Also see "Peering."

Route servers gather routing information from ISP routers, process the information according to an ISP's routing policy requirements, and forward the processed routing information to the other ISP routers at the exchange point via BGP-4. Note that route servers are not involved in traffic exchange. ISP routers at the NAPs exchange traffic directly with one another. The route servers only coordinate and provide routing information.

The advantage of placing route servers at NAPs is that ISPs can exchange routes with other ISPs by peering with the route server, rather than full-mesh BGP peering among all the ISPs on the same NAP. This arrangement helps reduce the number of peering sessions each ISP router needs to process. Each ISP may specify a routing policy and the route server processes routing information based on these policies. Policies may include filtering ISPs, specifying particular paths, and specifying which ISPs may exchange routes.

Related Entries   BGP (Border Gateway Protocol); CIDR (Classless Inter-Domain Routing); CIX (Commercial Internet Exchange) Association; DNS (Domain Name Service) and Internet Domains; Internet; Internet Architecture and Backbone; Internet Connections; ISPs (Internet Service Providers); NAP (Network Access Point); NSF (National Science Foundation) and NSFnet; Peering; Registries on the Internet; Route Aggregation; Routers; Routing; *and* Routing on the Internet

Linktionary!—Tom Sheldon's Encyclopedia of Networking updates	http://www.linktionary.com/r/routing_registries.html
Merit global routing and operations page	http://www.merit.edu/internet/
RADB Database Services	http://www.radb.net/
IRR (Internet Routing Registry)	http://www.irr.net/
Route Server next generation project	http://www.rsng.net/
Network Startup Resource Center	http://nsrc.org/

RPC (Remote Procedure Call)

A procedure is a software routine that runs in a computer. A procedure call is a request by one procedure to another procedure for some service. This is relatively easy when both procedures are running in the same computer. A remote procedure call is a request made by a process in one computer to another computer across a network. RPCs are a form of middleware. Other forms of middleware are discussed under "Middleware and Messaging."

Client/server applications use RPCs as shown in the following illustration. If you think of a client/server application as a program that has been split, a server can run the data access portion because it is closest to the data, and the client can run the portion that presents the data to the user and interacts with the user. In this arrangement, the RPC can be viewed as the component that reintegrates the split portions of the program over the network. RPCs are sometimes called *coupling* mechanisms. See "Client/Server Computing"

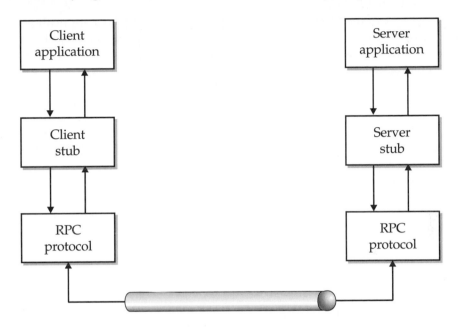

The stub portion of the program allows the procedure call to operate remotely. It translates a call into a remote request and sends it over the network. It also receives remote responses and makes them appear to applications as if they were local responses.

RPCs tend to operate in real time because the calling program usually waits until it receives a response from the called program. In this respect, RPCs are synchronous. RPCs are required in applications in which a procedure should not continue until it receives the information it needs from the remote system. In contrast, MOM (message-oriented middleware) is an asynchronous interprocess communication scheme that uses store-and-forward messaging concepts.

Historically, RPC techniques were investigated as early as 1976 by B. J. Nelson at XEROX PARC. Sun Microsystems popularized the technique with its SunSoft's ONC (Open Network Computing) remote procedure calls (SunRPCs). Millions of systems running NFS (Network File System) use the ONC RPC libraries. The IETF documented the technique in 1988 with the publication of RFC 1057 (RFC 1831, listed next, is more recent). Following is a list of relevant RFCs. Others are listed at the Linktionary! Web site.

- RFC 1831 (RPC: Remote Procedure Call Protocol Specification Version 2, August 1995)
- RFC 1833 (Binding Protocols for ONC RPC Version 2, August 1995)
- RFC 2695 (Authentication Mechanisms for ONC RPC, September 1999)

Alternatives to RPCs are discussed under "Middleware and Messaging" and "Distributed Object Computing." For example, CORBA (Common Object Request Broker Architecture) operates over an ORB (object request broker) architecture that provides better support for a variety of applications, programming languages, and computing platforms. CORBA and other technologies also support messaging, which operates in a more "relaxed" mode than the request-and-wait mode of RPC.

Java is an example of distributed object computing technology. Java applications are capable of running in any Java-enabled device, no matter what platform. RMI (Remote Method Invocation) allows Java applications to invoke methods on Java applications running on other computers. Invoking a method is like asking another program to do something.

XML (Extensible Markup Language) has become a standard for exchanging data across any platform. XML-RPC is a new specification that allows remote procedure calls using HTTP as the transport and XML as the encoding. The mechanism itself is designed for simplicity, but XML allows for the coding of very complex procedures and data structures. The UserLand Software Web site listed later has useful information on XML-RPC. Microsoft's SOAP (Simple Object Access Protocol) implements remote procedures via HTTP, with information in XML format.

RFC 2188 (AT&T/Neda's Efficient Short Remote Operations [ESRO], September 1997) describes an RPC service that is designed specifically for wireless networks. The ESRO protocol provides reliable connectionless remote operation services on top of UDP with minimum overhead.

Related Entries   ActiveX; API (Application Programming Interface); Client/Server Computing; COM (Component Object Model); CORBA (Common Object Request Broker Architecture); Distributed Applications; Distributed Computer Networks; Distributed Object Computing; IPC (Interprocess Communication); Java; Middleware and Messaging; MOM (Message-Oriented Middleware); Multitiered Architectures; Named Pipes; NetBIOS/NetBEUI; Object Technologies; ORB (Object Request Broker); Pipes; Ports; TCP/IP; SOAP (Simple Object Access Protocol); Sockets API; Transaction Processing; Web Technologies and Concepts; *and* XML (Extensible Markup Language)

Linktionary!—Tom Sheldon's Encyclopedia of Networking updates	http://www.linktionary.com/r/rpc.html
IETF Working Group: ONC Remote Procedure Call (oncrpc)	http://www.ietf.org/html.charters/oncrpc-charter.html
Cisco document: Introduction to RPC	http://www.cisco.com/univercd/cc/td/doc/product/software/ioss390/ios390rp/rpintro.htm
"Moving To Distributed Processing Standards . . . Remote Procedure Call"	http://www.ja.net/documents/NetworkNews/Issue44/RPC.html
Ricardo Devis's object-oriented page	http://www.arrakis.es/~devis/oo.html
Netbula (RPC rapid development tools)	http://www.netbula.com/
UserLand Software XML-RPC Web site	http://www.xmlrpc.com/
Software Technology Review RPC Web page	http://www.sei.cmu.edu/str/descriptions/rpc.html#637485

RPSL (Routing Policy Specification Language)

See Routing Registries.

RSA

RSA refers to a data security company and a popular public-key cryptography scheme developed by the founders of the company.

RSA Security was founded in 1982 by the inventors of the RSA public-key cryptosystem, Rivest, Shamir, and Adleman. Today, millions of copies of RSA encryption and authentication technologies are installed worldwide. The RSA scheme is discussed under "Public-Key Cryptosystems." Related topics include "PKI (Public-Key Infrastructure)" and "Certificates and Certification Systems."

RSA technologies are part of existing and proposed standards for the Internet and World Wide Web, ITU (International Telecommunications Union), ISO (International Organization for Standardization), ANSI (American National Standards Institute), and IEEE (Institute of Electrical and Electronic Engineers), as well as business, financial, and electronic commerce networks around the globe. The company develops and markets platform-independent developers' kits and end-user products, and also provides comprehensive cryptographic consulting services.

The company was acquired by Security Dynamics in 1996, but the name RSA Security was retained.

Related Entries   Authentication and Authorization; Certificates and Certification Systems; Cryptography; Digital Signatures; PKI (Public-Key Infrastructure); Public-Key Cryptography; *and* Security

RSA Data Security, Inc.	http://www.rsa.com/
RSA Laboratories	http://www.rsa.com/rsalabs/

RSIP (Realm-Specific IP)

RSIP is an attempt to correct some of the problems with using NAT (network address translation) servers. The major problem with NAT is that it disrupts the end-to-end transparency of the Internet. In a fully transparent environment, a host has an Internet-authorized and -registered IP address that is recognized throughout the global Internet.

In a NAT environment, internal addresses are hidden. A NAT server separates the address space of an internal network from the Internet. The internal network uses private IP addressing schemes. There is a specific set of private IP addresses that Internet routers do not forward for security reasons. These addresses are outlined under "NAT (Network Address Translation)." A NAT server translates between internal and external addressing schemes. It changes the network layer and sometimes the transport layer header of each packet that crosses the NAT router.

The advantage of NAT is that it provides a type of firewall protection and eases the address shortage problem of the Internet. The disadvantage is that NAT prevents some applications from running, such as applications that require IP addresses and ports to remain unmodified between source and destination. In addition, tunneling, and VPN protocols such as IPSec that require end-to-end encryption, do not work well in NAT environments because NAT cannot translate encrypted packet header information.

RSIP restores some of the end-to-end transparency that NAT removes. It replaces the NAT router with an RSIP gateway while maintaining the ability to provide NAT functions for internal hosts that are not RSIP enabled. RSIP also grants a host from one addressing realm (e.g., an intranet) a presence in another addressing realm (an outside network such as the

Internet) so that it may establish end-to-end connectivity with external hosts. RSIP was also created to ease the transition to IPv6 addressing.

In an RSIP environment, an RSIP gateway connects the private and public IP address spaces. The RSIP gateway maintains a pool of public addresses that it "leases" to internal RSIP hosts. When host A needs to establish an end-to-end connection with Internet host B, it negotiates with the RSIP gateway. The RSIP gateway maps public addressing information and parameters to host A's internal address.

When host A connects to Internet host B, it first tunnels packets across the internal network to the RSIP gateway. The RSIP gateway then removes the header and forwards the packets over the Internet. When host B returns packets to the RSIP gateway, the gateway matches information in the packets to previously mapped information and tunnels the packets across the internal network to host A.

RSIP was still under development at the time of this writing. Additional information, including a list of Internet drafts and RFCs, is available at the Web site listed later. It is being developed by the IETF Network Address Translators (nat) Working Group.

RFC 2956 (Overview of 1999 IAB Network Layer Workshop, October 2000) describes the "state of the network layer and its impact on continued growth and usage of the Internet. In particular, it discusses RSIP, NAT (Network Address Translation), firewalls, IPv6, addressing, and various routing issues. RFC 2775 (Internet Transparency, February 2000) discusses transparency issues on the Internet.

Related Entries   Access Control; Authentication and Authorization; CIDR (Classless Inter-Domain Routing); Firewall; Gateway; IPSec (IP Security); NAT (Network Address Translation); Proxy Servers; Security; Tunnels; *and* VPN (Virtual Private Network)

Linktionary!—Tom Sheldon's Encyclopedia of Networking updates	http://www.linktionary.com/r/rsip.html
IETF Network Address Translators (nat) Working Group	http://www.ietf.org/html.charters/nat-charter.html

RSVP (Resource Reservation Protocol)

RSVP is an Internet signaling protocol that is used to set up a type of circuit across an IP network, primarily as a means of providing QoS, for real-time traffic such as voice and video. Guaranteed on-time delivery is essential for delay-sensitive information associated with videoconferencing, voice conversations, and virtual reality. This is not easy on TCP/IP networks. As originally designed, the Internet supports only best-effort delivery of data packets. There is little support for QoS, and IP traffic is especially susceptible to variable queuing delays and congestion losses.

IETF's Integrated Services (int-serv) Working Group developed RSVP as part of its effort to define bandwidth *reservation* techniques for the Internet. By reserving bandwidth, it is possible to provide reasonable levels of QoS. The idea is to identify traffic *flows*, which are streams of packets (voice, video, file transfers, and so on) going to the same destination IP address and port number. Reservations are negotiated with each network device along a route to a destination. If each device has resources to support the flow, a reserved path is set up.

RSVP (Resource Reservation Protocol) works as a signaling protocol. Before any data packets are sent, it sends messages in the forward direction to the destination to request bandwidth reservations. The destination then uses RSVP to send messages back across the same path to set up the reservations. Bandwidth is only reserved if all devices in the path agree to do so. End users or applications make requests for preferential treatment and these requests are evaluated by an *admission control mechanism*, usually in a policy server.

A technical description of RSVP is that it sets up *distributed state* in routers and hosts. This means that routers along a path "remember" flows. However, the original design for routers does not require that they remember flows. Implementing RSVP requires that all routers be upgraded to support it, a daunting task. There were scalability problems and routers had to store potentially huge tables to keep track of all the flows. Thus, there are no significant deployments of RSVP on the Internet although many intranets use it.

More recently, RSVP has been resurrected for use in MPLS networks. RSVP's signaling turns out to be an ideal mechanism for setting up LSPs (label switched paths) across the MPLS networks. The Juniper Network's paper listed later describes the RSVP/MPLS strategy. The IETF Differentiated Services (Diff-Serv) model is considered a more practical way to provide priority service levels in networks. It is more concerned with CoS (class of service) than QoS. Packets are classified and tagged, and then serviced according to their priority level. See "Differentiated Services (Diff-Serv)."

The Reservation Process

The process of setting up a resource reservation starts at the data source with a PATH command that travels through routers along a path to one or more destinations, as shown in the following illustration. Note that RSVP was designed for multicast transmissions, so multiple systems may receive data across the reserved path. The PATH command contains a flow ID that identifies the RSVP session that is being set up. The PATH command also provides information about the type of flow and its bandwidth requirements.

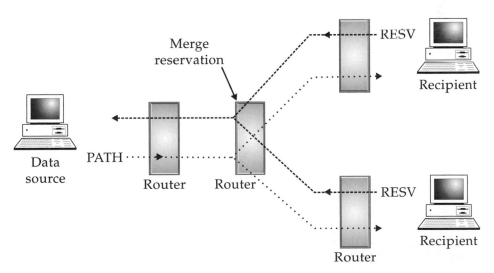

R

The PATH command travels through the potential route, and each router along the way logs the information contained in the PATH command for future reference. It does not reserve the bandwidth just yet. When the recipient systems receive the PATH command, they indicate their willingness to participate in the session by returning an RESV command back across the same route. As each router receives the RESV command, it will reserve the required bandwidth. In a multicast session, some routers may receive multiple RESV commands for the same flow ID. The router simply combines the requests instead of setting up separate resource reservations.

An issue is how routers handle priorities. In a case in which multiple sessions require bandwidth reservations, one of those sessions will no doubt have higher priority than another. One method is to create multiple queues in routers and rank those queues from low to high priority. As packets arrive at a router, they are put in a queue based on a tag in the packet that gives its priority value. The router then forwards packets in the highest level queue first. A *weighted fair queuing algorithm* is used to ensure that at least some of the packets in the lower-level queues also get through.

The following RFCs provide more information on RSVP. Also see RFC listings under "Integrated Services (Int-Serv)" and "QoS (Quality of Service)." Visit the IETF sites listed later for drafts and other related RFCs. The IETF RAP (Resource Allocation Protocol) (rap) Working Group has established policy control extensions for RSVP.

- RFC 1633 Integrated Services in the Internet Architecture: An Overview, June 1994)
- RFC 2205 (Resource ReSerVation Protocol—Version 1 Functional Specification, September 1997)
- RFC 2208 (Resource ReSerVation Protocol—Version 1 Applicability Statement, Some Guidelines on Deployment, September 1997)
- RFC 2209 (Resource Reservation Protocol—Version 1 Message Processing Rules, September 1997)
- RFC 2210 (The Use of RSVP with IETF Integrated Services, September 1997)
- RFC 2212 (Specification of Guaranteed Quality of Service, September 1997)
- RFC 2750 (RSVP Extensions for Policy Control, January 2000)
- RFC 2814 (Subnet Bandwidth Manager, May 2000)

Related Entries   Admission Control; Bandwidth; Bandwidth Management; Capacity; Congestion Control Mechanisms; CoS (Class of Service); Data Communication Concepts; Differentiated Services (Diff-Serv); Integrated Services (Int-Serv); MPLS (Multiprotocol Label Switching); Multicasting; Multimedia; Policy-Based Management; Prioritization of Network Traffic; QoS (Quality of Service); Queuing; SBM (Subnet Bandwith Manager); Traffic Management, Shaping, and Engineering; *and* Virtual Circuits

Linktionary!—Tom Sheldon's Encyclopedia   http://www.linktionary.com/r/rsvp.html
of Networking updates

IETF Working Group: Resource Reservation   http://www.ietf.org/html.charters/rsvp-charter.html
Setup Protocol (rsvp)

IETF Working Group: Integrated Services over Specific Link Layers (issll)	http://www.ietf.org/html.charters/issll-charter.html
IETF Working Group: Integrated Services (intserv)	http://www.ietf.org/html.charters/intserv-charter.html
IETF Working Group: Resource Allocation Protocol (rap)	http://www.ietf.org/html.charters/rap-charter.html
Stardust.com QoS Forum	http://www.qosforum.com/
Cisco document: "Resource Reservation Protocol (RSVP)"	http://www.cisco.com/univercd/cc/td/doc/cisintwk/ito_doc/rsvp.htm
Steven Berson's RSVP page	http://www.isi.edu/div7/rsvp/rsvp.html
Noritoshi Demizu's RSVP links	http://www.watersprings.org/links/mlr/
Juniper paper: "RSVP Signaling Extensions for MPLS Traffic Engineering"	http://www.juniper.net/techcenter/techpapers/200006.html

RTCP (Real-Time Control Protocol)

RTCP is the control protocol for RTP (Real-time Transport Protocol). It is used to periodically transmit control packets to participants in a streaming multimedia session. RTCP's primary function is to provide feedback on the quality of service being provided. This feedback may be used to scale back the sender for flow-control reasons or to keep from congesting the network. The sender may also use the information to change the current compression ratio. RTCP is outlined in 1889 (RTP: A Transport Protocol for Real-Time Applications, January 1996). See "Multimedia" for a discussion of RTP and RTCP.

RTFM (Real-Time Traffic Flow Measurement)

RTFM is a development of the IETF RTFM Working Group, which was tasked with developing a system for measuring and reporting information about traffic flows on the Internet. RTFM can be used to measure traffic in three broad areas, including clients and servers, network segments, and mesh networks (to determine the most used path). See "Performance Measurement and Optimization" for more information.

RTOS (Real-Time Operating System)

An RTOS (real-time operating system) is an operating system that supports a timely response to external events. Robots that move around in real time require real-time operating systems. RTOSs must respond to events as they occur and will return an error if a response is not made in an appropriate time period. A system may also terminate to avoid problems or because it cannot continue due to a failure to operate in real time.

The Real Time Encyclopedia Web site describes a real-time system as a system that responds in a (timely) predictable way to unpredictable external stimuli arrivals. It operates under extreme conditions to provide timeliness and meet deadlines, provide simultaneous processing to support multiple events, react to events in a predictable way, and provide dependability.

Devices that employ embedded systems often use real-time operating systems. See "Embedded Systems."

Related Entries   Embedded Systems; Java; Network Appliances; Network Operating Systems; Network Processors; Real-Time Network Services; Servers; *and* Thin Clients

Linktionary!—Tom Sheldon's Encyclopedia of Networking updates	http://www.linktionary.com/r/rtos.html
Real Time Encyclopedia	http://www.realtime-info.be/
List of real-time operating systems	http://www.realtime-info.be/encyc/techno/publi/faq/rtos_faq_table.htm
Real Time Systems Web page at EG3	http://www.eg3.com/navi/real.htm
Embedded Power Corporation	http://www.embeddedpower.com/
IEEE Real Time Technical Committee	http://cs-www.bu.edu/pub/ieee-rts/Home.html

RTP (Real-time Transport Protocol)

RTP is a protocol that is optimized in various ways for the delivery of real-time data such as live and/or interactive audio and video over IP packet-switched networks. RTP runs over UDP and uses its multiplexing and error-checking features. Other similar transports are supported. RTP is described in more detail at the Linktionary! Web site listed here. Also see "Multimedia" for more information.

Related Entries   Integrated Services (Int-Serv); Multicasting; Multimedia; Prioritization of Network Traffic; QoS (Quality of Service); Real-Time Network Services; Reliable Data Delivery Services; RTSP (Real-Time Streaming Protocol); *and* Transport Protocols and Services

Linktionary!—Tom Sheldon's Encyclopedia of Networking updates	http://www.linktionary.com/r/rtp.html
IETF Audio/Video Transport Working Group	http://www.ietf.org/html.charters/avt-charter.html
RTP (Real-Time Transport Protocol) Overview	http://www.cs.columbia.edu/~hgs/rtp
IPMI (IP Multicast Initiative)	http://www.ipmulticast.com/

RTSP (Real-Time Streaming Protocol)

RTSP is a multimedia control protocol. According to the RFC 2326 (Real Time Streaming Protocol, April 1998), RTSP acts as a "network remote control" for multimedia servers. The protocol was designed to serve up multimedia from a cluster of hosts (virtual hosts). It is an application-level protocol that establishes and controls one or more time-synchronized streams of continuous media. No files are stored at the receiver. RealNetworks' RealPlayer is an example of an RTSP application. It provides play, fast forward, pause, and other controls. RealNetworks developed the protocol in conjunction with Netscape and submitted it to the IETF for standardization. Refer to the following sites for more information.

Related Entries   Integrated Services (Int-Serv); Multimedia; Prioritization of Network Traffic; QoS (Quality of Service); Real-Time Network Services; *and* RTP (Real-time Transport Protocol)

Linktionary!—Tom Sheldon's Encyclopedia of Networking updates	http://www.linktionary.com/r/rtsp.html
IETF MMUSIC Working Group	http://www.ietf.org/html.charters/mmusic-charter.html
RealNetworks RTSP information	http://www.realnetworks.com/devzone/library/rtsp/index.html
RTSP Information page by Henning Schulzrinne	http://www.cs.columbia.edu/~hgs/rtsp/

R

SAA (Systems Application Architecture)

SAA is a set of application, communication, and user-interface specifications for IBM mainframe operating systems such as VM (Virtual Memory) and MVS (Multiple Virtual Memory), midrange operating systems like OS/400 (for IBM AS/400 series), and OS/2 for desktop systems. SAA defined *common applications,* which are applications that can run on any SAA platform. Thus, applications written to SAA can run on a wider range of systems. SAA was an attempt by IBM in the 1980s to provide compatibility among its mainframe and minicomputers, which had previously been developed by different IBM divisions.

Samba

Samba is a suite of programs that provides the same resource-sharing services as Microsoft's SMB (Server Message Blocks). SMB was originally developed for Microsoft operating system environments and is used in Windows 95, Windows 98, Windows NT, and OS/2. Samba provides compatible SMB services for UNIX, NetWare, OS/2, and VMS environments. The primary UNIX platforms are SunOS and Linux, but many other UNIX versions are supported. Samba was originally created by Andrew Tridgell, but it was expanded as a community effort by its users.

Although SMB was primarily designed to work in Microsoft Windows environments, Samba has features that let users of other operating systems use it in modes they are accustomed to. For example, UNIX users can use an FTP-like interface to access shared SMB resources on other servers. Samba includes a NetBIOS name server, which provides the naming service required to browse for shared resources with user-friendly names.

Related Entries   CIFS (Common Internet File System); File Systems; Microsoft Windows; NetBIOS/NetBEUI; Network Operating Systems; *and* SMB (Server Message Blocks)

Linktionary!—Tom Sheldon's Encyclopedia of Networking updates	http://www.linktionary.com/s/samba.html
Andrew Tridgell's Samba page	http://samba.anu.edu.au/samba/
Network Appliance Resource Library (see CIFS-related documents)	http://www.netapp.com/tech_library/

SANs (Storage Area Networks)

SANs are dedicated networks that access to an array of storage devices such as RAID arrays, optical disks, and tape backups. One way to think of a SAN is as a high-speed network within a data center. In contrast, LANs extend outward from the data center. A typical SAN consists of a Fibre Channel subnetwork connected to the enterprise network, as illustrated in Figure S-1. SANs are a radical shift from the traditional server-attached storage because storage is offloaded from servers, freeing up server resources to handle data processing and other tasks.

The SAN concept is to make any storage device available to any user or device on the enterprise network. Any server attached to the SAN can access any disk, which means that any user on the

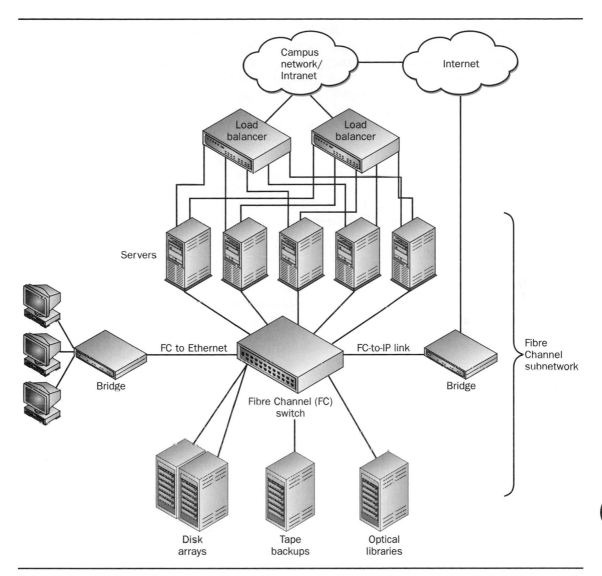

Figure S-1.   *A SAN resides behind the server to provide fast access to an array of storage devices.*

network has access to any disk. This is because the SAN subnetwork provides any-to-any connections between servers and disk. SANs are meant to remove bottlenecks at data centers and to provide scalable storage. Both server elements and disk storage can be expanded at any time. In addition, backups can take place directly over the SAN subnetwork, which removes backup traffic from the enterprise network. High availability and fault tolerance is also easier to support.

A typical enterprise will need to consider SAN technology when its storage requirements approach the terabyte level. Almost any company with large storage requirements should evaluate the technology. Server farms are appropriate up to a point, but SANs can provide better performance and management. A SAN provides any-to-any connectivity among any server and any storage device, and the ability to share storage resources among a variety of servers.

Clustered servers may be part of the SAN environment. A cluster is a group of servers that operate as a single unit but provide load balancing, high availability, and fault tolerance. A cluster is able to handle the load of requests coming from the busiest networks or Web sites.

Note that the SAN subnetwork is often called a *system area network*, although a system area network is not limited to use in a SAN environment. A system area network (I'm being careful not to call it a SAN) may also connect clusters of servers and parallel processing systems. The Fibre Channel component of a SAN is the system area network. The main characteristic is that the devices are generally close to one another (within a data center) and the topology is high-speed switched fabric in most cases.

Another type of storage technology is the NAS (network attached storage). Like SAN, NAS separates storage from servers; but a NAS is better defined as a *network appliance* that attaches directly to the enterprise network, while a SAN is a large and complex data center storage system built around a subnetwork. NAS devices are usually inexpensive storage devices designed for department use or as basic information device. See "NAS (Network Attached Storage)."

SAN Solutions

The storage industry has taken to Fibre Channel and adopted it as the interface of choice for SANs. Fibre Channel provides bandwidth in the range of 266 Mbits/sec to over 4 Gbits/sec over a variety of cable types, including multimode fiber, coaxial cable, and shielded twisted-pair wire. Fibre Channel also supports distances up to 10 km. Fibre Channel Arbitrated Loop (FC-AL), developed with storage connectivity in mind, is a recent enhancement to the standard that supports copper media and loops containing up to 126 devices, or nodes. Devices can be hot-swapped without disrupting the network and the system is fault tolerant.

Fibre Channel supports point-to-point links, scalable bandwidth switched circuits, and arbitrated loops (shared bandwidth loop circuits). Fibre Channel storage interfaces have reached bandwidths of nearly 100 MB/sec when transferring large files. See "Fibre Channel" for more information on alternative implementations of the interface for use in the SAN environment.

While Fibre Channel is the interconnect of choice for the SAN, a typical data center will also contain clusters of servers interconnected with some high-speed switching technology. An example is cLAN (cluster LAN) from Giganet, Inc. An important feature of cLAN is its implementation of the VI (Virtual Interface) Architecture (see the next section), which supports high-speed messaging among applications running in servers by eliminating the overhead of the operating system and network stack.

InfiniBand is a new communication interconnect technology that implements a switched-fabric architecture with a packet-switching communication protocol. It can be used as an interconnect for SANs, as well as system area networks, storage area networks, high-performance clustered systems, and parallel processing systems. See "InfiniBand."

Crossroad Systems specializes in InfiniBand for SANs. It implements a *storage router,* which consolidates storage connections in a single device with a single connection to the switched fabric. Server connections are embedded into the storage router. The storage router can serve as the central point for managing SANs.

Other SAN-Enabling Technologies

The following technologies support SANs, either directly or indirectly. Some of the technologies are emerging, while others have been used in other forms for years in related technologies.

- **VI Architecture**   VIA is designed to reduce the amount of system I/O that CPUs must handle. By reducing I/O-related interrupts, CPUs can dedicate their time to more important tasks. VIA virtualizes a network interface and allows direct links between software processes and network hardware. For example, data transfers can take place directly in memory between applications on different servers in a cluster. Supporters (Microsoft, Compaq, Intel, and others) claim VIA, when used as the messaging interface for applications in SAN nodes, minimizes message-processing delays and allows for more efficient communication within SANs with a reduction in overhead of up to 40 percent.

- **DAFS (Direct Access File System)**   DAFS is a file transfer protocol that improves performance over other file system protocols by allowing file transfers to take place directly between clients and storage systems. DAFS takes advantage of VIA. In a SAN, DAFS allows data to be sent directly from server to server. See "DAFS (Direct Access File System)."

- **IP storage technologies**   The IETF IP Storage (ips) Working Group is developing protocols for encapsulating SCSI and Fibre Channel in an IP-based transport or transports. See "IP Storage."

- **SANs over IP**   Fibre Channel interconnects are fine for data centers, but there is also a need to interconnect geographically distant SANs. Computer Network Technology Corp. (http://www.cnt.com) SAN over IP technology supports storage applications over IP and allows remote SANs to appear as local storage. The technology supports wide area clustering, disaster recovery, and high availability. See "IP Storage."

- **SoIP (Storage over IP)**   This is another IP storage solution developed by Nishan Systems (http://www.nishansystems.com). It translates Fibre Channel data into IP data and allows block-based storage data to traverse IP networks. See "IP Storage."

- **FSPF (Fabric Shortest Path First)**   FSPF solves problems with switch interoperability in the Fibre Channel/SAN environment. It is a new interswitch routing protocol for Fibre Channel switches that allows vendors to create interoperable SAN switching equipment. FSPF is based on OSPF.

- **SRM (Storage Resource Management)**   SRM provides a management view of storage resources from a central management location. With SRM tools, administrators can monitor and configure SAN and other storage devices, but not the data itself. HighGround Systems, Inc., is a provider of SRM products.

S

Associations, Initiatives, Forums, and Coalitions

The following organizations promote SANs, storage products, and interconnect technologies. Getting all the pieces of SANs to work together in an interoperable way is the goal of these groups:

- **SNIA (Storage Networking Industry Association)**   SNIA promotes storage network systems (a SAN by another name). The association is a central point of contact for the SAN industry and is involved in the development of SAN standards. See http://www.snia.org.

- **Fibre Channel Industry Association**   This organization promotes Fibre Channel. Its Web site has a technology section that fully defines how Fibre Channel is used in the SAN environment. See http://www.fibrechannel.org/.

- **FibreAlliance**   The FibreAlliance was formed by a group of storage companies, including EMC Corporation, with the goal of ensuring Fibre Channel SAN management standards, enabling heterogeneous interoperability, and developing methods for managing large-scale enterprise Fibre Channel SANs. See http://www.fiberalliance.com/.

- **Jiro**   Jiro is a Sun Microsystems technology that provides a set of Java and Jini application development interfaces for creating intelligent management services that deploy across network devices, software applications, systems, and storage. Jiro technology provides a set of base management services and the architecture required to manage a SAN. Jiro was formerly called Project StoreX.

Related Entries   Clustering; DAFS (Direct Access File System); Data Center Design; Data Management; Data Protection; Data Warehousing; DBMS (Database Management System); Disaster Planning and Recovery; Distributed Computer Networks; Fault Management; Fault Tolerance and High Availability System; Fibre Channel; File Systems; IP Storage; Load Balancing; Mirroring; Multiprocessing; Multitiered Architectures; NAS (Network Attached Storage); NDMP (Network Data Management Protocol); Replication; Servers; Storage Management Systems; Storage Systems; Switch Fabrics and Bus Design; Switching and Switched Networks; *and* VI Architecture

Linktionary!—Tom Sheldon's Encyclopedia of Networking updates	http://www.linktionary.com/s/san.html
SNIA (Storage Networking Industry Association)	http://www.snia.org/
National Storage Industry Consortium	http://www.nsic.org/
Bitpipe (search for "SAN")	http://www.bitpipe.com
Storage Area Networks.com	http://www.storage-area-networks.com/
SearchStorage.com by techtarget.com	http://www.searchstorage.com/
SAN Links at Netfusion	http://www.nwfusion.com/netresources/sans.html
Brian A. Berg's Storage Cornucopia (great links!)	http://www.bswd.com/cornucop.htm

Giganet, Inc. (now Emulex)	http://www.emulex.com/
Legato Systems SAN Academy	http://www.sanacademy.com/
CNT (Computer Network Technology) storage over IP solutions	http://www.cnt.com/
ADVA storage networking technologies	http://www.san.com/
IBM Enterprise SAN Solutions	http://www.storage.ibm.com/ibmsan/
StorageTek	http://www.storagetek.com/products/
Brocade (see the SAN Solution Center)	http://www.brocade.com/
EMC Corporation	http://www.emc.com/
Gadzoox Networks (see the SAN Library)	http://www.gadzoox.com/
McDATA, Corp. (see SAN Education section)	http://www.mcdata.com/

SAN (System Area Network)

A SAN (system area network) is a relatively local network designed for high-speed interconnection in cluster environments (server to server), multiprocessing systems (processor to processor), and SANs (storage area networks). The architecture is now almost exclusively switched fabric. Fibre Channel is an example of a SAN technology. It provides a high-speed switched environment in which any device on the network can connect with any other device and communicate over a dedicated high-speed link. InfiniBand is another. See "Clustering," "Switch Fabrics and Bus Design," and "SAN (Storage Area Network)."

SAP (Service Advertising Protocol)

See IPX/SPX (Internetwork Packet Exchange/Sequenced Packet Exchange).

SAP (Session Announcement Protocol)

SAP is a protocol to announce Internet multicast conferencing sessions. A conference is announced by periodically multicasting a UDP announcement packet to a multicast address and port. Because SAP is designed for multicast, it is suitable for setting up conference calls, not one-on-one IP telephone calls. The IETF MMUSIC Working Group has developed SAP, which is defined in RFC 2974 (Session Announcement Protocol, October 2000). Also see "SDP (Session Description Protocol)" and "SIP (Session Initiation Protocol)." See "Multimedia" for a general description of multimedia conferencing. Also see "Voice over IP (VoIP)" for related information.

Related Entries   Convergence; CTI (Computer-Telephony Integration); Megaco; MGCP (Media Gateway Control Protocol); Multicasting; Multimedia; NPN (New Public Network); OSP (Open Settlement Protocol); PINT (PSTN-Internet Interworking); QoS (Quality of Service); SDP (Session Description Protocol); SIP (Session Initiation Protocol); Softswitch; SPIRITS (Service in the PSTN/IN Requesting InTernet Service); SS7 (Signaling System 7); TAPI (Telephony API); Telecommunications and Telephone Systems; TRIP (Telephony Routing over IP); Unified Messaging; Videoconferencing; Voice/Data Networking; *and* Voice over IP (VoIP)

Linktionary!—Tom Sheldon's Encyclopedia of Networking updates	http://www.linktionary.com/s/sap.html
IETF Working Group: Multiparty Multimedia Session Control (mmusic)	http://www.ietf.org/html.charters/mmusic-charter.html

SATAN (Security Administrator's Tool for Analyzing Networks)

See Security Auditing.

Satellite Communication Systems

Satellite communication systems consist of Earth-orbiting communications platforms that receive and retransmit signals from earth-based stations. A typical television satellite receives a signal from a base station and broadcasts it to a large number of terrestrial receivers. Signals to satellites are called "uplinks," and signals from satellites are called "downlinks." Uplinks have also been called "shooting the bird." The downlink covers an area called the "footprint," which may be very large or cover a focused area. Satellites use microwave frequencies. Since they are overhead, the transmissions are line of sight to the receiver.

The most common frequency bands for satellites are listed here. See "Electromagnetic Spectrum" and "Wireless Broadband Access Technologies" for more perspective on these bands.

Band	Uplink	Downlink
L/S	1.610 to 1.625 GHz	2.483 to 2.50 GHz
C	3.7 to 4.2 GHz	5.924 to 6.425 GHz
Ku	11.7 to 12.2 GHz	14.0 to 14.5 GHz
Ka	17.7 to 21.7 GHz	27.5 to 30.5 GHz

As pictured in Figure S-2, there are "high-orbit" GEO (geosynchronous satellites), "low-orbit" LEO (low earth orbit) satellites, and satellites in a variety of mid-orbits and elliptical orbits (some spy satellites use these orbits so they can drop in for a close look).

Geosynchronous satellites are placed in high stationary orbits 22,300 miles (42,162 kilometers) above the earth. The satellites are typically used for video transmissions. The speed and height of these satellites allow them to stay synchronized above a specific location on the earth at all times. One problem with high-orbit geosynchronous satellites is that a typical back-and-forth transmission has a delay of about a half second, which causes problems in time-critical computer data transmissions, as discussed in a moment. Satellites in LEO orbit are low enough to minimize this problem.

LEOs are close to the earth, usually within a few hundred kilometers, and inclined to the equatorial plane. Since the satellites are near the earth, earth-based devices don't require as much power to communicate with the satellites. Thus, they are ideal for phones and hand-held devices. However, LEOs are in fast orbits and do not stay stationary above a point on the earth. Therefore, a country-wide or global communication system requires a constellation of satellites

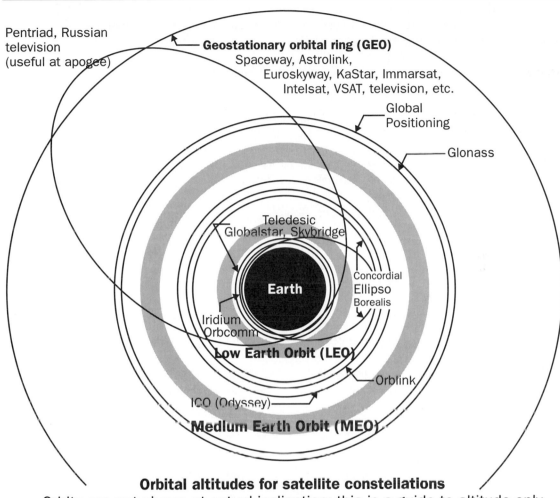

Pentriad, Russian
television
(useful at apogee)

Geostationary orbital ring (GEO)
Spaceway, Astrolink,
Euroskyway, KaStar, Immarsat,
Intelsat, VSAT, television, etc.

Global
Positioning

Glonass

Teledesic
Globalstar, Skybridge

Earth

Concordial
Ellipso
Borealis

Iridium
Orbcomm

Low Earth Orbit (LEO)

Orblink

ICO (Odyssey)

Medium Earth Orbit (MEO)

Orbital altitudes for satellite constellations
Orbits are not shown at actual inclination; this is a guide to altitude only
from Lloyd's satellite constellations.

http://www.ee.surrey.ac.uk/Personal/L.Wood/constellations/

Figure S-2.   *Satellite orbit chart by Lloyd Wood (source: http://www.ee.surrey.ac.uk/Personal/*
L.Wood/constellations/)

that basically project moving footprints above the earth. As one satellite moves out of position,
another takes over coverage. Calls and other transmissions are handed off from one satellite to
another in this process. This is just the opposite of cellular phone systems where people move
in and out of cells.

There is debate about which system is better for data communications: GEO or LEO. While LEOs are ideal for mobile wireless devices, the current trend is to enable GEOs with more bandwidth. Still, the delay of GEOs is a problem for time-critical applications.

 This topic continues at the Linktionary Web site with discussions of satellite applications and specific issues related to using satellites for Internet transmissions.

Related Entries   DBS (Direct Broadcast Satellite); Electromagnetic Spectrum; HALO (High Altitude Long Operation); Microwave Communications; Network Access Services; Network Concepts; Packet Radio Data Networks; Residential Broadband; Service Providers and Carriers; SMR (Specialized Mobile Radio); SMS (Short Messaging Service); Telecommunications and Telephone Systems; WAN (Wide Area Network); Wireless Broadband Access Technologies; *and* Wireless Communications

Linktionary!—Tom Sheldon's Encyclopedia of Networking updates	http://www.linktionary.com/s/satellite.html
IETF TCP over Satellite Working Group archival page	http://tcpsat.lerc.nasa.gov/tcpsat/
IETF Working Group: UniDirectional Link Routing (udlr)	http://www.ietf.org/html.charters/udlr-charter.html
Lloyd's Satellite Constellations (great site, great graphics)	http://www.ee.surrey.ac.uk/Personal/L.Wood/constellations/
Satellite Communications in the Global Internet: Issues, Pitfalls, and Potential	http://www.iif.hu/rendezvenyek/inet97/F5/F5_1.HTM
Satellite Data Networks by Rizwan Mustafa Mir (operational and protocol descriptions)	http://www.cis.ohio-state.edu/~jain/cis788-97/satellite_data/
NASA Satellite Networks & Architectures Branch	http://ctd.lerc.nasa.gov/5610/5610.html
Center for Satellite and Hybrid Communication Networks	http://www.isr.umd.edu/CSHCN/
Tachyon.net fast global TCP/IP Satellite service	http://www.tachyon.net/
Teledesic "Internet-in-the-Sky" constellation	http://www.teledesic.com/
Bitpipe (search for "satellite")	http://www.bitpipe.com/

SBM (Subnet Bandwidth Manager)

SBM is a signaling scheme that provides a method for mapping an Internet-level setup protocol such as RSVP onto IEEE 802–style networks. In particular, it describes the operation of RSVP-enabled hosts/routers and link layer devices (switches and bridges) to support reservation of LAN resources for RSVP-enabled data flows. For example, it can signal 802.1p priorities between network switches or class of service information between RSVP clients and RSVP networks. SBM is described in RFC 2814 (SBM—Subnet Bandwidth Manager: A Protocol for RSVP-Based Admission Control over IEEE 802–Style Networks, May 2000).

For example, SBM is implemented in Microsoft Windows 2000 through ACS (Admission Control Service), which is a QoS component that regulates subnet usage for QoS-enabled applications. The ACS exerts its authority over QOS-aware applications or clients by intercepting RSVP messages and passing the messages' policy information to LPMs (Local Policy Modules) for authentication.

See "QoS (Quality of Service)," "RSVP (Resource Reservation Protocol)," and "Policy-Based Management."

Schema

Information has various properties and descriptions called *metadata*. For example, a mailing address has a name, address, city, state, and ZIP code. The metadata schema is this description of the mailing address. A schema is usually defined by some authority to describe data in a standard way so that it may be accessed by other users or applications.

A *schema* defines the vocabulary of a particular set of metadata (i.e., element names and formatting rules). It is a structural model that defines how objects in the real world, such as people and computers, are represented in the directory database. The schema may define the structure of the database, the names of the objects in it, and the attributes of those objects. An attribute holds values that may need to conform to a particular syntax or range of values.

An analogy is a form that you fill out. It has labeled fields that you write information in. Some fields must be filled out, while others are optional. Some fields have specific rules, such as the date must be formatted. The person creating the form might also create a schema that defines the form.

The W3C (World Wide Web Consortium) defined RDF (Resource Description Framework), which provides a framework for sharing schemas. The descriptions of these vocabulary sets are called RDF schemas. A schema defines the meaning, characteristics, and relationships of a set of properties, and this may include constraints on potential values and the inheritance of properties from other schemas. The RDF language allows each document containing metadata to clarify which vocabulary is being used by assigning each vocabulary a Web address. The schema specification language is a declarative representation language influenced by ideas from knowledge representation (e.g., semantic nets, frames, and predicate logic), as well as database schema specification languages and graph data models.

RFC 2251 (LDAPv3, December 1997) provides a good description of schema. Also see "Metadata" and "Repository."

SCSI (Small Computer System Interface)

SCSI (pronounced "scuzzy") is a family of disk interface systems that provide access services for peripheral I/O devices such as disk drives, CD-ROM discs, optical disks, tape drives, scanners, and other devices. Theoretically, you can plug any vendor's SCSI device into any SCSI controller. Each I/O device is called an LU (logical unit) and each LU is assigned an LUN (logical unit number).

SCSI is normally implemented in host adapters, which provides a shared bus to which peripheral devices attach. Applications make service requests to SCSI, and SCSI issues commands to the logical units that execute the commands. All commands and data cross the SCSI shared bus, which is a parallel interface. Some of the features of the SCSI interface are described here:

- The original SCSI standard supports up to 7 devices on a single host adapter, but new standards support high-speed operation with up to 16 devices and bus lengths of up to 12 meters.

- SCSI devices are "smart" devices with their own control circuitry. They can "disconnect" themselves from the host adapter to process tasks on their own, thus freeing up the bus for other transmissions.

- The bus can handle simultaneous reads and writes.

SCSI has gone through several upgrades, as outlined in Table S-1. New generations are being defined through the joint efforts of the ANSI (American National Standards Institute) X3T10 (SCSI) Committee and the SCSI Trade Association.

The original SCSI was standardized in the late 1980s. It is characterized by a 50-pin connector. By the 1990s, enhancements were made, such as changing the physical connector to a 68-pin connector. New bus widths (more data lines) were devised. These enhancements are called *Wide SCSI*. They include bus widths of 16 bits (2 bytes) or 32 bits (4 bytes), allowing higher data transfer rates and addressing of up to 16 devices instead of the original 8. In addition, fast transfer rates are achieved by using synchronous data transfers instead of asynchronous data transfers.

Ultra SCSI (also called *Fast 20*) was the next advancement. It uses new SCSI chip sets with internal clock speeds that are doubled, thus doubling the megabyte-per-second transfer rates. Basically, Ultra SCSI doubles the transfer rate independent of the bus width. Thus, the original 8-bit SCSI-1 is boosted to 10 MB/sec by applying the Fast enhancements.

Ultra2 SCSI (also called *Fast 40*) was one of the most significant advancements. It uses LVDS (low-voltage differential signaling), which improves the signal-to-noise ratio and allows cable lengths up to 12 meters. Up to this point, SCSI implementations used the *single-ended bus*, which is a signaling scheme that has limited cable lengths. These lengths must be strictly adhered to since the Fast and Ultra SCSI enhancements were achieved by doubling the clock rate, and thus the fundamental frequency at which data is transferred. Doing so required halving the cable lengths to prevent signal degradation.

The *LVDS signaling* scheme used with Ultra2 SCSI improves performance, but the differential bus pushes down the number of devices supported on the bus. LVDS uses extremely low voltage levels, which translates to low radiation and less power consumption. Noise is reduced by sending signals across two wires with opposing voltage levels. The receiver reads the difference in voltage levels and rejects the noise. LVDS is an important signaling technology used in other interconnection schemes such as InfiniBand. See "LVDS (Low-Voltage Differential Signaling)" and "Switch Fabrics and Bus Design."

The current generation, Ultra3 SCSI, was defined in the late 1990s. It defines several new generations of SCSI, including Ultra160 SCSI (160 MB/sec), Ultra320 SCSI (320 MB/sec), and Ultra640 SCSI (640 MB/sec). Ultra 160 SCSI products started shipping in 1999 and Ultra320 SCSI products were appearing in 2001. Adaptec and QLogic are popular sources of SCSI products. Ultra3 SCSI adds features such as the ability to choose the highest possible data transfer rate;

SCSI Trade Association Terms	Maximum Bus Speed (MB/Sec)	Bus Width (Bits)	Maximum Bus Length (Meters)			Maximum Device Support
			Single Ended	LVD	HVD	
				LVD: (low-voltage differential) signaling		
				HVD: (high-voltage differential) signaling		
SCSI-1[2]	5	8	6	[3]	25	8
Fast SCSI[2]	10	8	3	[3]	25	8
Fast/Wide SCSI	20	16	3	[3]	25	16
Ultra SCSI[2]	20	8	1.5	[3]	25	8
Ultra SCSI[2]	20	8	3			4
Wide Ultra SCSI	40	16		[3]	25	16
Wide Ultra SCSI	40	16	1.5			8
Wide Ultra SCSI	40	16	3			4
Ultra2 SCSI[2, 4]	40	8	[4]	12	25	8
Wide Ultra2 SCSI[4]	80	16	[4]	12	25	16
Ultra2 SCSI or Ultra160[6]	160	16	[4]	12	[5]	16
Ultra320	320	16	[4]	12	[5]	16

[1] The listed maximum bus lengths may be exceeded in Point-to-Point and engineered applications.

[2] Use of the word "Narrow" preceding SCSI, Ultra SCSI, or Ultra2 SCSI is optional.

[3] LVD was not defined in the original SCSI standards for this speed. If all devices on the bus support LVD, then 12-meter operation is possible at this speed. However, if any device on the bus is single-ended only, then the entire bus switches to single-ended mode and the distances in the single-ended column apply.

[4] Single ended is not defined for speeds beyond Ultra.

[5] HVD (Differential) is not defined for speeds beyond Ultra2.

Table S-1. *SCSI Trade Association–Endorsed Terminology for SCSI Parallel Interface Technology (source: SCSI Trade Association)*

packetization (transfer multiple commands and messages at once); and QAS (quick arbitrate and select), which provides faster arbitration to reduce connect/disconnect on the bus.

Other recent SCSI developments include VHDCI (Very High Density Cable Interconnect), LUN bridging, and SCSI switching. VHDCI provides high-speed interconnections where space is limited. With LUN bridges, 960 devices can be connected, while expanders allow SCSI cables to extend up to 75 meters. SCSI switching provides the same benefits as other switching technologies.

New SCSI drives that rotate at 15,000 rpms have the potential to deliver a sustained data rate of over 40 MB/sec. A typical server will have four drives, and those drives can produce a combined data rate of 160 MB/sec or more. Clearly, the new Ultra3 SCSI standards are needed. But these new systems must be installed in 64-bit PCI systems since the older 32-bit, 33-MHz PCI bus has a maximum data rate of 133 MB/sec.

Similar technologies include USB (Universal Serial Bus), FireWire (IEEE 1394), Fibre Channel, and InfiniBand. USB is considered a bus for printers, mice, and keyboards. Firewire is competitive with SCSI, but its market has not developed. Fibre Channel is considered a SAN interconnect. In the SAN environment, SCSI is still used for in-the-box drive connections.

S

InfiniBand is a potential PCI replacement, as well as a cluster and SAN interconnection technology.

SCSI-FCP (Small Computer System Interface–Fibre Channel Protocol) is an implementation of Fibre Channel that transports SCSI protocols. SCSI is a disk interface technology that normally runs over a parallel connection. SCSI-FCP is a serial SCSI that allows SCSI-based applications to use an underlying Fibre Channel connection. SCSI-FCP is widely used to connect high-performance servers to storage subsystems, especially in the SAN environment. It provides higher performance (100 Mbits/sec), supports cable lengths up to 10km, and can address up to 16 million devices. Data is transferred in frames rather than blocks.

A new specification called iSCSI (Internet SCSI) is a mapping of SCSI into the TCP/IP protocol. This scheme allows clients to directly connect with a SCSI device across a network and perform block transfer (as opposed to file-level transfers) directly over a network. The communication between an initiator and target occurs over one or more TCP connections. This technology and a similar technology for Fibre Channel are being developed by the IETF IP Storage (ips) Working Group. See "IP Storage" for more information.

Related Entries   Clustering; DAFS (Direct Access File System); Fibre Channel; FireWire; LVDS (Low-Voltage Differential Signaling); NAS (Network Attached Storage); Network Connection Technologies; Parallel Interface; SAN (Storage Area Network); Serial Communication and Interfaces; Servers; SSA (Serial Storage Architecture); Storage Systems; Switch Fabrics and Bus Design; USB (Universal Serial Bus); and VI Architecture

Linktionary!—Tom Sheldon's Encyclopedia of Networking updates	http://www.linktionary.com/s/scsi.html
SCSI Trade Association (hosts a wealth of SCSI information)	http://www.scsita.org
National Storage Industry Consortium	http://www.nsic.org/
SNIA (Storage Networking Industry Association)	http://www.snia.org/
T10 Technical Committee ("the place to find information about I/O interfaces)	http://www.t10.org/
Dan Kegel's Fast Hard Drives Page	http://www.kegel.com/drives
Lacie storage products (see encyclopedia in support area)	http://www.lacie.com/
Toms Hardware Guide	http://www.tomshardware.com/
Gary Field's SCSI Info Central	http://www.scsifaq.org/
Brian A. Berg's Storage Cornucopia Web page	http://www.bswd.com/cornucop.htm
Bitpipe (search for "SCSI")	http://www.bitpipe.com
SearchStorage.com by techtarget.com	http://www.searchstorage.com/
Yahoo!'s SCSI links page	http://www.yahoo.com/Computers_and_Internet/Hardware/Peripherals/SCSI

SCSP (Server Cache Synchronization Protocol)

SCSP is described in RFC 2334 (Server Cache Synchronization Protocol—SCSP, April 1998) as a protocol that attempts to solve the cache synchronization/cache-replication problem, which occurs when a group of servers wish to synchronize information in their caches about the state of clients being served. SCSP algorithms are described as being similar to the routing algorithms used in OSPF (Open Shortest Path First).

Refer to RFC 2334 for additional information. RFC 2335 (A Distributed NHRP Service Using SCSP, April 1998) describes how SCSP is used to synchronize the client information databases held by NHRP (Next Hop Resolution Protocol) servers within a LIS (logical IP subnet). This topic is covered at the Linktionary! Web site.

Related Entries   Cache and Caching Techniques; Clustering; Content Distribution; NHRP (Next Hop Resolution Protocol); Proxy Servers; Replication; Servers; Stateless and Call-Back Filing Systems; *and* Web Caching

Linktionary!—Tom Sheldon's Encyclopedia of   http://www.linktionary.com/s/scsp.html
Networking updates

SCTP (Stream Control Transmission Protocol)

SCTP is a protocol for transporting PSTN signaling messages over IP networks. In addition, the protocol designers state that SCTP is capable of broader applications, including transport of broadcast and streaming data, without the need for TCP. SCTP is a connection-oriented protocol like TCP that provides many of the reliability features of TCP such as acknowledgments, fragmentation, and sequencing. But SCTP eliminates much of the overhead inherent in TCP that can cause delays. It also provides additional features that optimize it for signal transport.

PSTN signaling is important in IP environments when IP telephony clients wish to establish call connections with PSTN telephone users. SCTP provides SS7 (Signaling System 7) functionality over IP networks and, therefore, supports voice call setup over the Internet. In the PSTN, SS7 is an out-of-band signaling system used to set up voice calls. SCTP is used to transport SS7 messages across IP networks and the Internet in situations in which an IP telephony user wants to call a traditional PSTN telephone (or vice versa). These calls are actually set up across signaling and media gateways that translate between SS7 and Internet signaling.

SCTP's special feature is the ability to deliver SS7 messages with little loss and delay. This is critical in order to interface with SS7 since SS7 does not tolerate high delays. In particular, SCTP attempts to reduce delays caused by "head-of-line blocking," which is a queuing problem that can cause delays while some messages wait for other messages to be serviced. TCP causes this problem because it enforces a strict order of delivery. SCTP overcomes the problem by assuming that low delay is more important than order of delivery.

SCTP is described in RFC 2960 (Stream Control Transmission Protocol, October 2000). It was developed by the IETF Signaling Transport (sigtran) Working Group, which is working on related protocols.

Related Entries   Convergence; IN (Intelligent Network); Megaco; MGCP (Media Gateway Control Protocol); Multimedia; NPN (New Public Network); PINT (PSTN-Internet Interworking); SAP (Session Announcement Protocol); SDP (Session Description Protocol); SIP (Session Initiation Protocol); Softswitch; SPIRITS (Service in the PSTN/IN Requesting InTernet Service); SS7 (Signaling System 7); Telecommunications and Telephone Systems; Telecommunications Regulation; TRIP (Telephony Routing over IP); Voice/Data Networks; *and* Voice over IP (VoIP)

Linktionary!—Tom Sheldon's Encyclopedia of Networking updates	http://www.linktionary.com/s/sctp.html
IETF Working Group: Signaling Transport (sigtran)	http://www.ietf.org/html.charters/ sigtran-charter.html
ISC (International Softswitch Consortium)	http://www.softswitch.org

SDH (Synchronous Digital Hierarchy)

SDH is the ITU standard for a synchronous optical network that supports multiple gigabit-per-second transmission speeds over fiber-optic cable. Long-distance and regional telecommunication companies outside of North America implement SDH on their fiber-optic trunk lines. SONET, which is basically a subset of SDH, is used in the United States. Refer to "SONET (Synchronous Optical Network)" for more information.

SDLC (Synchronous Data Link Control)

SDLC is an IBM-defined Data Link Control protocol developed in the 1970s for communication over wide area links to IBM host systems in SNA (Systems Network Architecture) environments. SDLC is based on synchronous, bit-oriented operations as compared to byte-oriented protocols such as BISYNC (Binary Synchronous Communications). This topic is covered at the Linktionary! Web site.

Linktionary!—Tom Sheldon's Encyclopedia of Networking updates	http://www.linktionary.com/s/sdlc.html

SDP (Session Description Protocol)

SDP is a protocol that describes a format for conveying descriptive information about multimedia sessions. When a user wants to join a conference, he or she needs a way to know the multicast group address and the UDP port address for the conference.

SDP was designed as a session directory tool that could be used to advertise multimedia conferences, and communicate the conference addresses and conference tool–specific information necessary for participation. At the same time, SDP was designed for general-purpose use so that it could be used for a wide range of network applications.

This information includes session name and purpose, session time, type of media (voice or video), media format (MPEG, for example), transport protocol and port number, bandwidth requirements, and contact information. SDP is not a transport protocol, but relies instead on SIP (Session Initiation Protocol) or SAP (Session Announcement Protocol) to deliver the session information to destinations. For example, a caller can send SDP descriptive information in a SIP

INVITE message. The callee then responds with acknowledgments regarding the descriptions that it can accept.

See "Multimedia" for more information about multimedia conferencing. Also see RFC 2327 (SDP: Session Description Protocol, April 1998).

Related Entries   Convergence; Megaco; MGCP (Media Gateway Control Protocol); Multimedia; NPN (New Public Network); PINT (PSTN-Internet Interworking); SAP (Session Announcement Protocol); SIP (Session Initiation Protocol); Softswitch; SPIRITS (Service in the PSTN/IN Requesting InTernet Service); SS7 (Signaling System 7); Telecommunications and Telephone Systems; TRIP (Telephony Routing over IP); Voice/Data Networks; *and* Voice over IP (VoIP)

Linktionary!—Tom Sheldon's Encyclopedia of Networking updates	http://www.linktionary.com/s/sdp.html
IETF Working Group: Multiparty Multimedia Session Control (mmusic)	http://www.ietf.org/html.charters/mmusic-charter.html

SDSL (Symmetric Digital Subscriber Line)

See DSL (Digital Subscriber Line).

Search and Discovery Services

One way to view the Web is as a massive storehouse of information—the largest library in the world. Unfortunately, this library is not indexed and cataloged like traditional libraries. One solution is the Web search engine. Search engine Web sites have become some of the most popular sites on the Web. Most portals now include search engines and topical references, which are lists of topics that you "drill down" into to find specific information. This is a good way to find Web pages and documents on the Internet.

One way a search engine works is to go out and scan documents on the Internet and compile lists of keywords in those documents, and then create index files from those lists that users can search. While this technique takes advantage of computer technology (scan and index documents at high speed), the method is not superior to the techniques that have been used for years to catalog books in libraries. What the Web needs is a way to create information about documents using standard formats that any application can access and search. This is metadata—information about data. Searching metadata files is discussed here and in the separate topic "Metadata."

White pages directory services are another category of search service that can help people find other people on the Internet by name or by related information (e-mail address, telephone number, and so on).

There are a number of related topics you may also want to refer to, including

- **Service Advertising and Discovery**   Describes methods for advertising services and for users to find those services. Most of the methods are designed for enterprise networks.

- **Name Services**   Describes name services that resolve resource names into network addresses, allowing people to access services using familiar names.

■ **Directory Services** Describes hierarchical directory systems for storing white pages and yellow pages information about people and resources on networks and the Internet.

Traditional Internet Information Services

Some of the more traditional indexing and searching tools for Internet documents are mentioned next. They are largely text based, as opposed to the graphical user interfaces of Web services. These tools have largely been replaced by Web technologies, but are listed for historical purposes. You can refer to RFC 2151 (A Primer On Internet and TCP/IP Tools and Utilities, June 1997) for more information.

■ **Archie** Creates metadata about documents stored on FTP servers. The metadata is stored in a separate searchable file. Other Archie files can be combined to create a larger database.

■ **Gopher** Gopher is a distributed document search-and-retrieval protocol. It gets its name from the animal that burrows in the ground because it allows users to "drill down" (burrow) into a hierarchy of servers, folders, and documents on a TCP/IP network until a target document is located. Users run a Gopher client that accesses Gopher servers throughout the Internet. See RFC 1436 (The Internet Gopher Protocol, March 1993).

■ **Veronica (Very Easy Rodent-Oriented Netwide Index to Computerized Archives)** An Archie equivalent for Gopher that maintains a Gopher title index and allows users to search across Gopher sites.

■ **Finger** This protocol may be used to find out who is logged on to a host computer or to list information about a specific user. Don't be offended if someone fingers you with this command! See RFC 1288 (The Finger User Information Protocol, December 1992).

■ **WAIS (Aide Area Information Server)** A shareware product used to find information on the Internet by using a single interface to query many databases.

■ **WHOIS (and NICNAME)** WHOIS is used to search databases to find the name of network and system administrators, RFC authors, system and network points of contact and other individuals who are registered in appropriate databases. The usefulness of WHOIS has led to the development of other distributed directory information servers and information retrieval tools. See "WHOIS ("Who is")."

Web-Based Information Services

Web search engines perform a variety of searches on Web documents (HTML, XML, and so on). They may extract keywords from the documents or index metatags, which are the descriptive information tags placed in the source code of Web pages. A search engine implements a program called a *spider* or *Web crawler* that goes out on the Web and retrieves information about Web documents. This information is then cataloged and searched. This description does not do justice to the enormous task of indexing the Web. Millions of documents exist, and each document has many keywords that may be useful in a search.

When users request a search, the keyword list is searched and a list of hits is presented in the user's Web browser. While this technique works well, the results list is often too broad, including many items not directly related to the user's request. This is due to an inability to distinguish among the different meanings of words. The next section discusses methods for improving document and resource searching and discovery.

The OII (Open Information Interchange) search information Web page (http://158.169.50.95:10080/oii/en/search.html) provides a list of search engines and divides them into four categories. The first category includes full-text search engines that analyze documents and Web sites and produce searchable information that is weighted with the most keywords first. Catalog-based search engines categorize information and let users "drill down" into information. Multisearch engines are also called meta-search engines. A good example is "One Look Dictionaries" (http://www.onelook.com/), which searches for a word over multidisciplinary Web dictionary sites and lists definitions by discipline. Finally, Specialist search engines specialize in certain areas, such as medicine, entertainment, computers, and other topics.

The most popular search sites are given here (my personal favorite is Google):

AltaVista Search	http://www.altavista.com
All the Web	http://www.alltheweb.com/
BrightPlanet (performs deep searches into databases)	http://www.brightplanet.com
BullsEye by Intelliseek (multisearch with categorized highlighted search results)	http://www.intelliseek.com
Copernic (multisearch with categorized highlighted search results)	http://www.copernic.com
Dogpile (multisearch)	http://www.dogpile.com/
Excite	http://www.excite.com
Go2Net (multisearch)	http://go2net.com
Google	http://www.google.com
HotBot	http://www.hotbot.com
Go.com	http://www.go.com/
Lycos	http://www.lycos.com
Magellan	http://www.mckinley.com
ProFusion (multisearch)	http://www.profusion.com/
SavvySearch (multisearch)	http://www.savvysearch.com/
WebCrawler	http://www.webcrawler.com
Yahoo!	http://www.yahoo.com

Labeling, Indexing, and Metadata

Imagine a library without a card indexing system. Fortunately, an index exists in the form of card catalogs to help you find books. A similar indexing system is needed for information on the Internet. Ideally, the system should provide a standard way to describe documents so that any application can access the descriptive information. For example, the "Dublin Core" metadata schema defines standard elements for describing documents such as "title," "creator," "subject," "description," "publisher," "date," "type," "format," "rights," and so on. This so-called *schema* can be used to create "data about data," or *metadata*. The metadata can be stored with documents, as is done by including "meta" statements in HTML documents, or it can be stored in catalogs that reference and provide links to documents. Metadata attachments to documents are often called "labels."

Search engines can search through the metadata of individual documents or search the catalogs. Some rating and filtering systems have been developed. A rating system assigns values to content in much the same way movies are rated. The rating is stored in the metadata. Filters can then be used to exclude certain documents based on their rating. The PICS (Platform for Internet Content Selection) is a common labeling and ratings scheme. It is used to add rating to Web pages and is designed primarily as a way to help parents block certain Web sites. See "Metadata" for more information.

XML (Extensible Markup Language) is revolutionizing the way documents are created and the way they can be searched and located. XML provides a way to externally define elements within documents. These elements can then be searched, greatly narrowing the search results. For example, the medical industry can create a standard set of elements related to medical terminology. Since elements have values much like fields in a database, documents can be searched not only to locate specific elements but specific values within those elements.

The *Handle System* is a global naming service for documents. It provides persistence for documents that might move to different locations, so that users can always locate those documents—even after they have been moved. The strategy relies on uniquely identifying each document. This identity is stored in a name server along with the current location of the document. If the document is moved, the location information in the name server must be updated. When users need a document, they find it by going through the name server. The Handle System provides a name resolution system for documents that is analogous to the way that DNS (Domain Name System) resolves Internet names into IP addresses. See "Handle System" for more details.

A related technology is CIP (Common Indexing Protocol). CIP provides a way for information servers to exchange index information about the documents they hold. A server can then answer queries from its own index or look in the indexes received from other servers and make referrals to those servers. See "CIP (Common Indexing Protocol)."

White Pages/Yellow Pages Services

A white pages service can be used to find information on a person or company in various directory databases. You can find an e-mail address, telephone number, and other information based on a name, or, alternatively, you can use it to find a user's name by searching for other known information such as e-mail address, telephone number, and so on. Today, a number of Web sites offer people searching, including the following:

Yahoo! People Search   http://people.yahoo.com/

Internet @ddress.finder   http://www.iaf.net/

| WhoWhere by Lycos | http://www.whowhere.lycos.com/ |
| The X.500 Global Directory Service (search the X.500 global directory for individuals) | http://ganges.cs.tcd.ie/ntrg/x500.html |

At one time, the Internet community and the IETF attempted to standardize the searching techniques. These services were given the name Internet White Pages Services (IWPS). They are discussed in RFC 1684 (Introduction to White Pages Services Based on X.500, August 1994) and in later RFCs.

In particular, RFC 2148 (Deployment of the Internet White Pages Service, September 1997) advocated that "An organization SHOULD publish public E-mail addresses and other public address information about Internet users within their site." That seems ridiculous now with the proliferation of spamming and invasion of privacy issues. However, the white pages effort provided useful information to the Internet community about how to build directory services on the Internet.

RFC 2148 further describes how X.500, an OSI directory services specification, should be used as a model for the data structure and naming scheme without recommending X.500 itself. It points to future directory services implementations that are based on the X.500 model. The RFC recommends LDAP (Lightweight Directory Access Protocol) as the protocol to access data. RFC 2218 (A Common Schema for the Internet White Pages Service, October 1997) defines a common schema.

The Internet Nomenclator Project discussed in RFC 2258 (Internet Nomenclator Project, January 1998) is integrating the hundreds of Ph Nameservers that are publicly available for managing databases about people. Ph is discussed in RFC 2378 (The CCSO Nameserver (Ph) Architecture, September 1998).

The need for an Internet Directory was discussed in RFC 2517 (Building Directories from DNS: Experiences from WWWSeeker, February 1999). It discusses WWWSeeker, an application that finds a Web site given information about the name and location of an organization. The information WWWSeeker searches was obtained from domain registries via WHOIS and other protocols.

CNRP (Common Name Resolution Protocol) is an Internet protocol that relieves people of having to remember long and complicated Internet URLs (Universal Resource Locators). Instead, you type in "common names" to access resources. CNRP provides a "resolution service" that converts the common name into an Internet address. See "CNRP (Common Name Resolution Protocol)."

With the explosion in online business transactions and B2B (business-to-business) transactions, companies doing business on the Web need an easy way to discover one another and publish information that can be used to set up transactions. UDDI (Universal Description, Discovery, and Integration) is a standard that defines a common way for organizations to publish information about business services and provide other organization with information that can be used to integrate business processes. UDDI is more than a directory. The UDDI Business Registry is an implementation of the UDDI specification in which organizations publicly list descriptions of services and methods of engagement. The UDDI specifications take advantage of Internet standards developed by the W3C and the IETF, including HTTP, DNS,

XML, and SOAP. SOAP is a messaging specification originally developed by Microsoft but now promoted by the W3C. The UDDI Web site is http://www.UDDI.org/.

Other related topics are *presence detection* and *instant messaging*. AOL made instant messaging popular. When you log on, your presence is indicated to other people, who may then send you an instant message. The IETF is working on an Internet-scale end-user presence awareness, notification, and instant messaging system. See "Instant Messaging" for more information.

Related Entries   Agent, Internet; CIP (Common Indexing Protocol); CNRP (Common Name Resolution Protocol); Directory Services; DNS (Domain Name Service); Document Management; Handle System; Instant Messaging; LDAP (Lightweight Directory Access Protocol) and Internet Domains; Metadata; Name Services; NIS (Network Information System); Schema; Service Advertising and Discovery; SLP (Service Location Protocol); URI (Uniform Resource Identifier); URL (Uniform Resource Locator); URN (Universal Resource Name); Web Technologies and Concepts; WebDAV; White Pages Directory Services; WHOIS ("Who is"); *and* XML (Extensible Markup Language)

Linktionary!—Tom Sheldon's Encyclopedia of Networking updates	http://www.linktionary.com/s/search.html
The Spire Project (see The Information Research FAQ!)	http://spireproject.com/
OII (Open Information Interchange) Guides (see Internet Searching)	http://158.169.50.95:10080/oii/en/guides.html
Searchtools.com	http://www.searchtools.com/info/
Search Engine Watch	http://www.searchenginewatch.com/
The American Society of Indexers	http://www.asindexing.org/
Terena Reis Pilot Project: "Recent Developments in Indexing, Searching and Information Retrieval Technologies"	http://www.terena.nl/projects/reis/isir/reisnews9908sendex.html

Secret-Key Cryptography

Secret-key encryption uses one key, the secret key, to both encrypt and decrypt messages. This is also called *symmetric encryption*. The term "private key" is often used inappropriately to refer to the secret key. A private key is one of the keys in the public/private key pair for asymmetric cryptography. In this scheme, a user has two keys, one that is made public and one that is held privately. Refer to "Public-Key Cryptography."

In secret-key cryptography schemes, a single key is used to encrypt data. A secret key may be held by one person or exchanged between the sender and the receiver of a message. For example, if you encrypt data for storage on a hard drive, you remember the key and usually don't give it to someone else. But if you want to send secure messages to a business partner using symmetric cryptography, you need to make sure your partner knows the key that will decrypt the messages.

If secret-key cryptography is used to send secret messages between two parties, both the sender and receiver must have a copy of the secret key. However, the key may be compromised during transit. If you know the party you are exchanging messages with, you can give them the

vance. However, if you need to send an encrypted message to someone you have
...et, you'll need to figure out a way to exchange keys in a secure way. One method is to
... via another secure channel or even via overnight express, but this may be risky in some
... See "Key Distribution and Management" for more information.

As mentioned, private-key cryptography is often used to encrypt data on hard drives. The
...son encrypting the data holds the key privately and there is no problem with key distribution.
...cret-key cryptography is also used for communication devices like bridges that encrypt all data
...hat cross the link. A network administrator programs two devices with the same key, and then
personally transports them to their physical locations.

Related Entries   Authentication and Authorization; Biometric Access Devices; CHAP (Challenge
Handshake Authentication Protocol); Cryptography; Digital Signatures; FORTEZZA; Hash Functions;
Key Distribution and Management; One-Time Password Authentication; PAP (Password Authentication
Protocol); Public-Key Cryptography; Security; Smart Cards; *and* Token-Based Authentication

Linktionary!—Tom Sheldon's Encyclopedia of   http://www.linktionary.com/s/secret_key.html
Networking updates

Security

Data and communications security is critical on today's networks. Hackers, Internet intruders,
eavesdroppers, forgers, and other attackers are everywhere. Few people have not heard of
some sort of computer and network attack. Many are victims.

An entire volume could be written on security issues. This section outlines general topics
and points you to resources where you can further your research. Some security topics are
covered elsewhere in this book. You may want to open RFC 2828 (Internet Security Glossary,
May 2000). It provides a useful glossary of security terms.

    The version of this topic at the Linktionary! Web site is extended with more information.

Security Threats and Vulnerabilities

Network security threats are everywhere. Your internal users may be stealing data or inadvertently
revealing sensitive passwords or other material to people who are attempting to infiltrate your
organization. Attackers from the outside may be gaining access through dial-up Internet
connections or external server-to-server connections.

I refer to attackers as *hackers*. This is common in the security community. The opposite of
hackers is a "good citizen." Refer to "Hacking and Hackers" for more details.

An attack is an attempt to take control of a system (a computer, network server, Web site,
and so on) using a variety of methods with the intent to take over the system, or simply to shut
it down or prevent other people from accessing it (a denial-of-service attack). Attacks may also
take place on cryptographic systems information that has been encrypted, such as password
files, secure data files, and so on. There are two primary types of attacks:

- **Passive attack**   Monitoring and collecting information about a system to be used in a
  later attack, or to attack another related system.

■ **Active attack**   An active attack is one in which the atta'
access to a system through unauthorized or illegal m‹

Hackers may monitor the sessions of other users (passive atta‹
the session (active attack). In a *replay attack*, the attacker uses previou‹
to gain access to a system by "replaying" it to the system, which thinks ‹
valid session.

The version of this topic at the Linktionary! Web site has a description of c‹
including impersonation and spoofing, password cracking, eavesdropping and w‹
replay attacks, denial-of-service attacks, and virus/Trojan horse attacks.

An interesting paper related to this topic is "Simulating Cyber Attacks, Defenses, an‹
Consequences," by Fred Cohen. It is available at http://all.net/journal/ntb/simulate/
simulate.html. Also see "Security Auditing" for information about tracking and handling
security incidents.

Security Concepts and Mechanisms

"Security" is an all-encompassing term that describes all the concepts, techniques, and
technologies to protect information from unauthorized access. There are several requirements
for information security:

■ **Confidentiality**   Hiding data, usually with encryption, to prevent unauthorized
viewing and access.

■ **Authenticity**   The ability to know that the person or system you are communicating
with is who or what you think it is.

■ **Access control**   Once a person or system has been authenticated, their ability to access
data and use systems is determined by access controls.

■ **Data Integrity**   Providing assurance that an information system or data is genuine.

■ **Availability**   Making sure that information is available to users in a secure way.

Trust is an important aspect of security. There are many different forms and levels of trust
between people and computer systems. Many exchanges and transactions on the Internet take
place between people who have never met. A third party can provide this trust by verifying
the authenticity of parties in an exchange. Traditionally, banks and escrow companies have
provided this trust. On the Internet, it is provided by CAs (certificate authorities).

Trust management systems provide security services for users and free up applications
from having to provide their own mechanisms for interpreting credentials, authentication,
and policy. A trust management system can be queried by an application with questions about
how trust should be handled. The KeyNote Trust Management System is discussed under the
topic "Trust Relationships and Trust Management."

Security *policies* are an essential part of an organization's general operations. The often-
quoted rule of "denying what is not specifically permitted" provides a good basis for defining
any security policy. While this rule usually applies to firewalls, it also provides a good approach
to overall security.

Physical Security Management

While security is usually associated with some form of cryptography, physical systems must be protected from theft, damage, and corruption. Data must be backed up. In addition, the availablity of data is important. Systems must be kept online, even in the event of fires, floods, and earthquakes. Therefore, some means of replicating systems to other sites is often necessary. Refer to "Backup and Data Archiving," "Data Protection," "Disaster Planning and Recovery," "Fault Management," "Fault Tolerance and High Availability," "Power and Grounding Problems and Solutions," and "Replication."

Cryptography, Keys, and Certificates

There are a number of security mechanisms, most of which are based on some form of cryptography. These mechanisms allow secure data exchange over corporate networks and the Internet. They can be used to hide data, ensure the integrity of messages, and authenticate users or systems.

Cryptography provides the basis for securing data. An encryption algorithm is a mathematical routine that scrambles data, based on a user key, in a way that can be recovered with the same key or key pair. There are two types of encryption algorithms. There are symmetric secret-key algorithms and asymmetric public-key algorithms. These are discussed under "Cryptography" and "Public-Key Cryptography."

The advantage of the public-key scheme is that it eliminates the problems of key exchange. A trusted third party holds the public key and makes it available to other people in the form of a certificate. Certificate authorities bind a person's public key with validated information about that person, thus creating a digital certificate. The structure of the certificate itself (layout and format) is defined by an international standard called X.509. See "Certificates and Certification Systems" and "X.509 Certificates."

Certificates (and their keys) can be used to digitally sign messages. A signed message provides proof that a message is authentic, that it has not been tampered with, and that it has no errors. See "Digital Signatures" and "Hash Function" for more information.

The public-key cryptography scheme is an essential part of doing business on the Internet. By putting public keys in certificates, it is possible for parties who don't know each other to establish secure trusted connections. If both parties trust the certificates issued by a particular CA, then they trust the contents of those certificates. The public keys can then be used for authentication and to establish encrypted communication sessions. A PKI (public-key infrastructure) is an organized hierarchical structure (potentially global) for creating, managing, and distributing certificates. See "PKI (Public-Key Infrastructure)" and "Key Distribution and Management."

AAA (authentication, authorization, and accounting) schemes are required to verify the authenticity of users, and control and track how they access secure systems. There are basic authentication schemes such as shared secret authentication methods, as described under "CHAP (Challenge Handshake Authentication Protocol)." The public-key scheme provides asymmetric (two-key) authentication. Symmetric (secret key) authentication is accomplished with systems such as Kerberos. See "Kerberos Authentication Protocol."

See RFC 2903 (Generic AAA Architecture, August 2000) for information about the AAA architectures. Also refer to "Access Control," "Authentication and Authorization," "Biometric Access Devices," "One-Time Password Authentication," "PAP (Password Authentication Protocol)," "Smart Cards," and "Token-Based Authentication."

S

Securing Connections

A number of protocols exist to secure the connection between systems. Some of these protocols also provide authentication features. For example, PPP (Point-to-Point Protocol) includes the ECP (Encryption Control Protocol), which provides a method to negotiate an encryption method between the two points. See "PPP (Point-to-Point Protocol)" for more information. Secure connections across the Internet can be implemented with VPN technology. IPSec (IP Security) has emerged as the most important protocol for establishing secure connections. See "VPN (Virtual Private Network)" and "IPSec (IP Security)" for more information.

Additional protocols that provide secure links, secure transactions, or tunneling/VPN (virtual private networking) capabilities include "S-HTTP (Secure Hypertext Transfer Protocol)," "SSH (Secure Shell)," "SSL (Secure Sockets Layer)," "TLS (Transport Layer Security)," "L2TP (Layer 2 Tunneling Protocol),""S/WAN (Secure WAN)," and "SET (Secure Electronic Transaction)."

Other Security Topics

There are a number of other security-related topics in this book that are essential to protecting enterprise data. These include "Firewall," "Proxy Servers NAT (Network Address Translation)," "RADIUS (Remote Authentication Dial-In User Service)," "Virus and Antivirus Issues," "Security Auditing," "OPSEC (Open Platform for Security)," and "CDSA (Common Data Security Architecture)."

Security-Related Organizations

There are a variety of security specifications and initiatives, some developed by vendors and some developed by consortiums. Governments also define security specifications. Refer to the following sites.

NIST (National Institute of Standards and Technology)	http://www.nist.gov/
NSA (National Security Agency)	http://www.nsa.gov/
CERT (Computer Emergency Response Team)	http://www.cert.org/
CIAC (Computer Incident Advisory Capability)	http://ciac.llnl.gov/
FIRST (Forum of Incident Response and Security Teams)	http://www.first.org/
EFF (Electronic Frontiers Foundation)	http://www.eff.org/
NetSec Int'l (Network Security International Association)	http://www.netsec-intl.com/

IETF Working Groups and Important RFCs

There are a number of IETF working groups developing security specifications and protocols. Refer to the IETF Web site at http://www.ietf.org/html.charters/wg-dir.html and jump to the Security section. Following are some of the more general security RFCs available on the included CD-ROM. Refer to the individual security topics mentioned earlier for more specific RFCs.

■ RFC 1704 (On Internet Authentication, October 1994)

- RFC 1984 (IAB and IESG Statement on Cryptographic Technology and the Internet, August 1996)
- RFC 2084 (Considerations for Web Transaction Security, January 1997)
- RFC 2196 (Site Security Handbook, September 1997)
- RFC 2316 (Report of the IAB Security Architecture Workshop, April 1998)
- RFC 2350 (Expectations for Computer Security Incident Response, June 1998)
- RFC 2504 (Users' Security Handbook, February 1999)
- RFC 2828 (Internet Security Glossary, May 2000)
- RFC 3013 (Recommended Internet Service Provider Security Services and Procedures, November 2000)

Related Entries   DSS (Digital Signature Standard); EAP (Extensible Authentication Protocol); FORTEZZA; PGP (Pretty Good Privacy); Rights and Permissions; RSIP (Realm-Specific IP); S-HTTP (Secure Hypertext Transfer Protocol); *and* SKIP (Simple Key Management for Internet Protocols)

Linktionary!—Tom Sheldon's Encyclopedia of Networking updates	http://www.linktionary.com/s/security.html
IETF Security Working Groups (see Security Area)	http://www.ietf.org/html.charters/wg-dir.html
InfoSysSec (the most thorough and complete security site on the Web)	http://www.infosyssec.net
RSA's Crypto FAQ (highly recommended!)	http://www.rsa.com/rsalabs/faq/
Ron Rivest's Links—possibly the most complete set of links on the Web	http://theory.lcs.mit.edu/~rivest/crypto-security.html
Bruce Schneier's Counterpane Web site (sign up for the newsletter!)	http://www.counterpane.com/
Google Web Directory Security page	http://directory.google.com/Top/Computers/Security/
Microsoft's Security Web page	http://www.microsoft.com/technet/security/
Peter Gutmann's Security and Encryption-Related Resources and Links	http://www.cs.auckland.ac.nz/~pgut001/links.html
Terry Ritter's "Ciphers by Ritter" Web page	http://www.io.com/~ritter/
GILC (Global Internet Liberty Campaign) Cryptography page with news, government policy, and other resources	http://www.gilc.org/crypto/
Security Links at Telecom Information Resources on the Internet	http://china.si.umich.edu/telecom/net-security.html
Computer and Network Security Reference Index	http://www.vtcif.telstra.com.au/info/security.html

S

Security Auditing

Security auditing is the practice of evaluating the security of networks and systems. It may be done by professional security consulting and auditing services, or it can be done in-house. Auditing may involve evaluating the security of buildings and equipment locations, running background checks on people, evaluating work processes, monitoring systems, scanning computers for security weaknesses, and running intrusion detection systems that can signal possible break-ins.

The advantage of security consulting and auditing services is the third-party perspective of looking at security throughout an organization without preference to individuals, groups, or departments. The consulting agency also specializes in the task and can bring more experience to the project. The downside is that you are bringing unknown people into the organization. It is possible that so-called "reformed hackers" may be working for the company to gather information. Keep in mind that many hackers obtain jobs as janitors in order to gain information that can be used for computer break-ins.

A hierarchy can be established in which the network staff (including administrators) is audited by internal security auditors. These auditors are selected, managed, and audited by an external auditing firm or trusted third party. The external auditing firm may itself be audited by a well-respected national auditing/accounting firm. Some governments operate with a level of distrust where people believe they are being watched. This same strategy can be used to maintain security.

The remainder of this topic covers hardware and software security auditing, but keep in mind that security auditing also involves evaluating the physical site. An interesting paper on "social engineering" is available at the CSI Web site given later. A social engineer is someone who acts like someone else in order to gain information about or access to a system.

Scanners and Intrusion Detection Systems

Security auditing tools and techniques are designed to diagnose the vulnerability of a system, the possible threats it is vulnerable to, and the potential risks if the system is attacked. A vulnerability test is done with a scanner, which evaluates a computer system or network to find known security holes and weaknesses. For example, a scanner might detect that a service is being used that is vulnerable to attack and recommend that the service be disabled. It may also determine that a particular operating system upgrade is needed to fix a security hole.

An IDS (intrusion detection system) is an active monitoring system that detects possible attacks and tracks the attack if possible. An IDS automates the task of monitoring computers, routers, firewalls, links, and other possible attack areas. According to a Carnegie Mellon paper listed later:

> Intrusion detection systems (IDSs) are predicated on the assumption that an intruder can be detected through an examination of various parameters such as network traffic, CPU utilization, I/O utilization, user location, and various file activities. System monitors or daemons convert observed parameters into chronologically sorted records of system activities. Called "audit trails," these records are analyzed by IDSs for unusual or suspect behavior. IDS approaches include rule-based and statistical-based intrusion detection.

Rule-based systems automatically analyze the large amounts of audit trail data collected by intrusion detection systems using expert systems technology. This method assumes that patterns of activity can be detected by examining the audit data. The rule-based method will only detect intrusions that are defined by the rules. The statistical-based systems work on the assumption that an intruder's activity will deviate from normal activity and stand out in the audit data.

Systems like SATAN (Security Administrator's Tool for Analyzing Networks) are available free online to help administrators evaluate their network security. However, while systems like SATAN help administrators, they may also be infected with a utility that lets hackers into your system in the worst way—with a tool that evaluates your security system! Always use tools from respected companies.

The IETF has formed a working group called Intrusion Detection Exchange Format (idwg) that is defining data formats and exchange procedures for sharing information of interest to intrusion detection and response systems, and to management systems that may need to interact with them. Another IETF group called Guidelines and Recommendations for Security Incident Processing (grip) is developing information to assist in handling security incidents in the Internet community. The idwg and grip Web sites are listed later.

Related IETF security and auditing information is in the following RFCs:

- RFC 1948 (Defending Against Sequence Number Attacks. May 1996)
- RFC 2196 (Site Security Handbook, September 1997). This RFC provides extensive information on security incident handling. See Section 5.
- RFC 2350 (Expectations for Computer Security Incident Response, June 1998)
- RFC 2827 (Network Ingress Filtering: Defeating Denial of Service Attacks Which Employ IP Source Address Spoofing, May 2000)
- RFC 2828 (Internet Security Glossary, May 2000)
- RFC 3013 (Recommended Internet Service Provider Security Services and Procedures, November 2000)
- RFC 3067 (TERENA's Incident Object Description and Exchange Format Requirements, February 2001)

Standards for Evaluating Security

If you're going to install security systems and products, it's good to know that the products have been tested and even carry some type of certification that indicates the level of security they provide. The following quote comes by way of security expert Bruce Schneier (http://www.counterpane.com):

> A lot of you are making security products that are an attractive nuisance.... Shame on you. I want you to grow up. I want functions and assurances in security devices. We do not beta test on customers. If my product fails, someone might die.
> —Brian Snow, INFOSEC Technical Director at the National Security Agency, speaking to commercial security product vendors and users at the 2000 Black Hat Briefings security conference.

Schneier goes on to say in his October 15, 2000 CRYPTO-GRAM, "Outside the NSA, assurance is worth very little. The market rewards better capabilities, new features, and faster performance. The market does not reward reliability, bug fixes, or regression testing. The market has its attention firmly fixed on the next big idea, not on making the last big idea more reliable."

The U.S. government has several security evaluation programs that certify security-related products such as operating systems and cryptographic systems. Normally, government agencies can only buy products that are certified by these programs. One such program is FIPS (Federal Information Processing Standards), which was developed by the U.S. National Institute of Standards and Technology (NIST). FIPS certification is required for all products that are sold to U.S. (and Canadian) government agencies.

The so-called "Orange Book" was a set of evaluation criteria developed in the mid-1980s that set the standard for defining security criteria. The book had an orange cover, but its actual title was TCSEC (Trusted Computer System Evaluation Criteria). TCSEC was developed by the U.S. Department of Defense and published by the NCSC (National Computer Security Center), an arm of the NSA. Today, the Orange Book is somewhat dated, but it is still used by many vendors to classify the security level of their systems.

The current standard for evaluating security is spelled out in the ISO's *Common Criteria* standard. Common Criteria is accepted in many countries and provides a way for vendors to sell their products in other countries by labeling their security worthiness. Common Criteria is officially known as ISO/IEC 15408. It is recognized in Australia, Canada, France, Germany, New Zealand, the United Kingdom, and the United States. It provides a common and concise language for specifying security requirements and describing them for products. In the U.S., NIST and the NSA recognize Common Criteria. Private sector laboratories perform testing, and the labs are accredited by the governments of the countries where the labs are located. Countries that support Common Criteria recognize the evaluations done by accredited labs. The following Web sites provide more information:

Common Criteria official Web site	http://www.commoncriteria.org/
ISO Common Criteria Information	http://csrc.nist.gov/cc/

Related Entries   Access Control; Authentication and Authorization; Firewall; Hacking and Hackers; Key Distribution and Management; OPSEC (Open Platform for Security); PKI (Public-Key Infrastructure); Security; *and* Trust Relationships and Trust Management

Linktionary!—Tom Sheldon's Encyclopedia of Networking updates	http://www.linktionary.com/s/security_auditing.html
IETF Working Group: Intrusion Detection Exchange Format (idwg)	http://www.ietf.org/html.charters/idwg-charter.html
IETF G & R for Security Incident Processing (grip)	http://www.ietf.org/html.charters/grip-charter.html
CERT (Computer Emergency Response Team) Web site	http://www.cert.org

ISS (Internet Security Systems) risk management assessment services	http://www.iss.net/
Network Associates	http://www.nai.com/
ISAG (Internet Security Advisors Group)	http://www.isag.com/
Intrusion Detection Paper at Carnegie Mellon Software Engineering Institute	http://www.sei.cmu.edu/str/descriptions/intrusion.html
Intrusion detection paper at Silk Road (interesting and advanced information)	http://www.silkroad.com/papers/published.html
"Intrusion Detection Systems & Multisensor Data Fusion: Creating Cyberspace Situational Awareness" by Tim Bass	http://www.silkroad.com/papers/html/ids/
Intrusion Detection Planning Guide	http://www.cisco.com/univercd/cc/td/doc/product/iaabu/idpg/index.htm
Intrusion detection resources at CSI (Computer Security Institute)	http://www.gocsi.com/
"An Introduction to Intrusion Detection" by Aurobindo Sundaram	http://info.acm.org/crossroads/xrds2-4/intrus.html
Security Administrator's Tool for Analyzing Networks (SATAN)	http://www.fish.com/satan/
CSI "Social Engineering" paper by John Ceraolo	http://www.gocsi.com/devil.htm

See additional security-related links are under "Security."

Segment, Network

A network segment is a data link layer and physical network that is shared by one or more attached nodes. Ethernet and token ring are shared data link layer networks. One segment may be attached to another segment with a bridge to form an extended broadcast domain; but the bridge filters traffic and, in the case of Ethernet, keeps collisions contained within each segment.

Put another way, a very large network may be divided (segmented) with a bridge in order to improve performance and cut down on collisions. If the network is divided equally, only half of the computers are contending for access to the shared network on each segment, but can still send messages across the bridge to other nodes. See "Collisions and Collision Domains."

Further subdivision with bridges is possible, but multiport switches are now the preferred method for segmenting a network. A multiport switch is actually a bridge with multiple ports. Microsegmentation refers to the process of segmenting a network down to the point where one computer is attached to each port and there is no contention or collisions. The switch automatically connects any port with any other port.

Related Entries   Addresses, Network; Broadcast Address; Broadcast Domain; Broadcast Networking; Bridges and Bridging; Collisions and Collision Domains; CSMA/CD (Carrier Sense Multiple Access/Collision Detection); Ethernet; MAC (Media Access Control); *and* Switching and Switched Networks

Segment, TCP

A segment is the unit of end-to-end transmission in the TCP protocol. In general discussion about transmitting information from one node to another, the term "packet" is used loosely to refer to a piece of data. However, the specific packet of data formed by TCP in the transport layer is called a "segment."

When an application needs to send information to another network-attached computer, it forms a message. The message is passed to TCP (assuming a reliable protocol is needed; otherwise, it is sent to UDP), where it is encapsulated into a segment. The segment is sent to IP where it is encapsulated into a datagram. The datagram is sent to the data link layer where it is encapsulated into frames. See "Network Architecture" for more information about this process. Also see "TCP (Transport Control Protocol)."

Sendmail

Sendmail is an SMTP-compatible mail server that has been used for over 20 years in the UNIX and Internet environments. It is an *MTA (message transfer agent)* that transfers messages from user agents and delivers them to mail servers. Like other MTAs, it attempts to deliver mail to the recipient immediately; but if the recipient's mailbox is not available, it queues the message for later delivery.

Historically, Sendmail has been hard to administer and has had a number of security problems. But many of Sendmail's problems have been worked out. Sendmail, Inc., has a commercial version of the package with many enhancements. You can also obtain Sendmail source code from Sendmail.ORG.

Related Entries   Electronic Mail; IMAP (Internet Message Access Protocol); MIME (Multipurpose Internet Mail Extension); POP (Post Office Protocol); *and* SMTP (Simple Mail Transfer Protocol)

Sendmail.ORG	http://www.sendmail.org/
Sendmail, Inc.	http://www.sendmail.com/

Sequencing of Packets

See Reliable Data Delivery Services.

Serial Communication and Interfaces

Serial communication equipment and interfaces transmit signals across point-to-point data links. Bits are sent one after another in a serial stream. Serial connections are commonly used to connect computers to modems. The bit stream traverses the serial link and enters the modem, where it is modulated onto an analog signal for transmission across telephone lines.

Serial lines are normally bidirectional and use one wire for transmit and another for receive. This is a full-duplex link. A half-duplex link uses one wire, and only one end can transmit at a time. The most common Internet protocol to use serial links is PPP, which encapsulated IP datagrams and sends them across a full-duplex link.

A parallel link such as the parallel printer port on the back of a PC sends data across multiple lines at the same time. Imagine bits traveling across eight or more wires simultaneously. Parallel connections have some throughput advantages, but distances are restricted to avoid bit-synchronization problems.

Binary data for serial links is represented in two states on the wire, a positive voltage (usually +5v) for a binary 1 and a negative voltage (–5v) for a binary 0. In order to read the bits correctly, some synchronization and clocking scheme must be used. In asynchronous communications, a transmission starts with a signal drop, which the receiver uses to start its clock. It then reads a start bit, 8 data bits, and a stop bit. The start-stop mode of transmission means that transmission starts over again for each new character, which eliminates any timing discrepancies that may have occurred during the previous transmission.

While asynchronous techniques are simple to implement, the start and stop bits are overhead that waste bandwidth. Synchronous communication techniques send data as large data blocks, say 1,500 to 4,096 bytes. Both sender and receiver stay synchronized during the transmission due to an embedded clock signal in the data stream. Ethernet uses the Manchester signal encoding scheme, which sends a clock pulse along with the data. See "Signals."

Serial and parallel concepts are also used for the data buses and backplanes of computers and networking devices. The common PCI bus in most computers is a parallel bus. But this bus is starting to show its age and is not able to keep up with new faster processors. Increasing its bandwidth causes synchronization and interference problems and requires reducing the length and number of devices that can attach to the bus. Switched fabric buses are starting to replace the serial bus. They consist of multiple switched serial channels that allow any-to-any connections among components and peripherals. Serial links reduce the number of wires and the pin count, which improves cabling distance. InfiniBand is an example. See "Infiniband" and "Switch Fabrics and Bus Designs."

The standards for serial interfacing are the EIA/TIA-232 (DB-25) and the EIA/TIA-574 (DB-9). The former was commonly called the RS-232-C serial interface, but the EIA changed the name in 1987. RS-232 is used for asynchronous and synchronous communications. Synchronous protocols include SDLC, HDLC, Frame Relay, and X.25. See "EIA (Electronic Industries Alliance)" for a description of the serial standards.

Other serial technologies include USB (Universal Serial Bus), Firewire (IEEE 1394), SSA (Serial Storage Architecture), and HSSI (High-Speed Serial Interface), which are discussed under separate headings in this book. Due to their high data transfer rates, these technologies are used to connect disks or build small local networks.

Related Entries Asynchronous Communications; Circuit; Data Communication Concepts; Data Link Protocols; EIA (Electronic Industries Alliance); FireWire; HDLC (High-level Data Link Control); HSSI (High-Speed Serial Interface); Infrared Technologies; LAP (Link Access Procedure); LLC (Logical Link Control); LVDS (Low-Voltage Differential Signaling); Modems; Network Architecture; Network Connection Technologies; Parallel Interface; Point-to-Point Communications; PPP (Point-to-Point Protocol); SDLC (Synchronous Data Link Control); Signals; SSA (Serial Storage Architecture); Switch Fabrics and Bus Design; Synchronous Communications; *and* USB (Universal Serial Bus)

Linktionary!—Tom Sheldon's Encyclopedia of Networking updates	http://www.linktionary.com/s/serial_communications.html
TAL Technologies "Introduction to Serial Communication"	http://www.taltech.com/introserial.htm
Sangoma.com (see TechDesk)	http://www.sangoma.com/
RAD Data Communications RS-232 tutorial	http://www.rad.com/networks/tutorial.htm
Optimized Engineering RS-232 tutorial	http://www.optimized.com/COMPENDI/TabOfCon.htm
Cisco Documentation: Troubleshooting Serial Line Problems	http://www.cisco.com/univercd/cc/td/doc/cisintwk/itg_v1/tr1915.htm
TechFest information about protocols that use serial communications	http://www.techfest.com/networking/wan.htm
DCB (Data Comm for Business) papers about serial connectivity	http://www.dcbnet.com/apnotes.html
Craig Peacock's Beyond Logic site (see Serial/RS-232 Interfacing section)	http://www.beyondlogic.org/
PCGuide (see troubleshooting and repair section)	http://www.pcguide.com/

Servers

A server is either a hardware-based processing device or a software-based process that provides services to network users. This topic describes the former: servers, processors, server components, racks, and related components.

A server is a network-connected computer system that provides services to network users or Web services to Internet users. Servers may be located anywhere on the network, but for large companies, they are usually located in secure centrally managed data centers. Collections of servers are often called "server farms." Servers may be configured in clusters, which are interconnected sets of servers that provide fault tolerance and load balancing (sending user requests to the available or appropriate server). Clustered servers may also provide parallel processing, in which a task is split and processed on several computers simultaneously (see "Clustering" and "Multiprocessing").

A typical server farm consists of Web servers (Internet or intranet), file servers, FTP servers, mail servers, application servers, and database servers. Some form of load balancing is used to distribute requests among the servers. Data centers may be located in multiple locations to provide redundancy and protection from local disasters. Replication techniques are used to keep data synchronized among systems.

Over the last few years, a typical server was an Intel processor–based system with a PCI (Peripheral Component Interconnect) bus and SCSI disks. That formula is changing. The PCI bus is inadequate for today's high-speed processors. Custom systems exist, such as those with multiple PCI buses, but new bus designs are required to build high-performance systems that match today's processors and multiprocessor systems. Some are discussed later.

In addition, servers are being built in highly scalable rack-mount configurations that support fast interconnects, redundancy, fault tolerance, clustering, and parallel processing. Only a few years ago, such systems were called "superservers." Today, you can order them over the phone without much thought about configuration. This topic will focus on new server configurations.

Some of the things to consider when buying a server are outlined here:

- Will the applications running on the server require high-speed processing or will it require fast and efficient disk I/O? Perhaps it will require both?

- Are multiple servers required for load balancing and high availability (a busy Web site) or for parallel processing (e.g., data analysis and simulations)?

- If multiple processors are to be used, an SMP (symmetrical multiprocessing)–capable operating system is required, such as Microsoft Windows 2000.

- Off-the-shelf systems now support up to eight processors. Some systems support up to 32 Intel Itanium processors. Further scaling can be achieved through clustering.

- Is there a physical space limitation or co-location requirement that will require rack-mount systems?

- New SCSI disk interfaces are rated as high 320 MB/sec and 640 MB/sec. Alternative interfaces include Fibre Channel and FireWire.

- Does the server support new high-performance peripheral interfaces such as InfiniBand?

Intel's Xeon server systems feature Intel's Profusion chipset, which supports up to eight Intel Xeon processors. The systems are designed for rack-mount form factors. The Profusion chipset is a buffered cross-bar switch managing five interconnected 100-MHz buses. Two buses support four processors each, two support memory, and the fifth bus supports the I/O subsystem. This multiple bus design allows processors, memory, and I/O to have direct paths to each other, keeping traffic on each bus down to a minimum. See the Intel Web site listed later.

Intel's Itanium processors are design for high-end servers. The Itanium has a 64-bit architecture and implements a VLM (very large memory) architecture that supports up to 10 GB of RAM. The chip can be configured in 4-, 8-, and 32-processor systems.

Sun Microsystems makes servers that are popular as Internet servers and Web servers. IBM makes a line of systems that excel at transaction processing, fault tolerance, and high availability. Some IBM systems are backward compatible with IBM legacy operating systems and software.

Server Architectures

As mentioned, the primary server architecture for microprocessor-based systems has been PCI, a shared parallel peripheral bus. PCI supports multiple processors; but because the bus is shared, there is a limit to the number of peripherals that can be added before the bus is overloaded. Most systems implement the 32-bit PCI bus, but 64-bit PCI bus systems should be selected where high I/O speeds are required. PCI-X is a high-bandwidth version of the PCI bus that operates at 133 MHz with data rates over 1 GB/sec in 64-bit mode.

The problem with I/O is that it interrupts the CPU, reducing the ability of a server to handle real processing tasks. I_2O is a specification that defines techniques for offloading I/O from the CPU to an "intelligent processor." Performance improves as the host is relieved of interrupt-intensive I/O tasks. Version 2.0 of the I$_2$O specification, adopted in April 1999, supports 64-bit addressing, as well as switched fabric I/O architectures.

CompactPCI is a "ruggedized" PCI implementation that supports screw-down components. CompactPCI is designed for mobile systems or mission-critical systems. The pin and socket connectors are more reliable than standard PCI connectors, and the bus supports hot swapping of peripherals, which is required in high-availability systems.

While PCI-X offers the highest performance yet in the PCI bus standard, its parallel bus design effectively limits its useful life. Parallel bus designs are subject to electrical problems that restrict bandwidth and bus length. In addition, the bus is shared, which creates contention problems that grow worse as a system is expanded.

InfiniBand is a likely successor to PCI. It resolves all the problems of PCI and adds many features that will be essential for scaling server systems into high-performance multiprocessor systems. InfiniBand is a point-to-point switching fabric that sets up high-speed switched links between devices. PCI will coexist in some InfiniBand systems, but a major InfiniBand feature is that it off-loads I/O from the motherboard and processor, freeing the processor from interrupts.

Multiprocessing and Clustering

Most network operating systems are able to efficiently run applications across multiple processors via SMP (symmetrical multiprocessing) support. Thus, a four-processor system could theoretically complete a task four times faster than a single-processor system. An SMP system is able to distribute tasks evenly across processors. The basic form of SMP is really load balancing. Each processor is kept busy by the operating system, which distributes loads evenly.

Multiprocessor servers have become commodity items, and major network operating systems such as Windows 2000, Novell NetWare, UNIX, and Linux support SMP out-of-the-box. Keep in mind that basic services such as file services, print services, electronic mail, and database access are more disk intensive than processor intensive, so fast I/O may be more important than multiprocessing. Also, clusters of servers may be built to provide load balancing, high availability, and fault tolerance, rather than parallel processing. Clustering allows a set of servers to share the same resources (storage area network) or to provide load balancing and high availability (Web sites and server farms). Microsoft Windows 2000 DataCenter supports a four-node cluster with expanded support planned for the future. See "Clustering," "Multiprocessing," and "Load Balancing."

Supercomputer systems support a special form of parallel processing where a single highly complex task (simulations, real-time analysis, sequencing the human genome, and so on) is split up and processed in parallel on multiple processors or multiple computers. Distributed.net is a project that employs the idle processing time on thousands of Internet computers to solve complex tasks. See "Distributed Computer Networks" and "Supercomputer."

Reliable server pools can be used for providing highly available services by using a set of servers in a pool. The IETF Reliable Server Pooling (rserpool) Working Group is developing an architecture and protocols for the management and operation of server pools supporting highly reliable applications, and for client access mechanisms to a server pool. The group is specifically addressing network fault tolerance, highly available services, resistance against malicious attacks, and scalability. The Web site is listed later.

Boxes and Racks

The traditional server resides in its own box with its own fans, power supplies, local bus, storage devices, and so on. Many data centers have hundreds of these devices on shelving units. However, the trend is moving toward modular, rack-mount systems. Racks are critical where space is limited, such as the rented space at a service provider or carrier. In fact, rack mounts are usually required since service providers are running out of space.

Many rack-mount modular devices are the equivalent of *network appliances*. They are preconfigured, ready-to-install devices that provide a specific task such as Web services. The systems may be sealed, although they support OS and application upgrades. Most important, modules from the same vendors may be preconfigured to cooperate with other modules in a managed environment. A software management tool allows administrators to access and manage any of the modules in a standard way.

Rack modules are often referred to in terms of their "U," which is a measure of height. A 1U unit is 1.75 inches in height. That measure is used to determine how much vertical space the unit will require in the rack itself. A 2U module is 3.5 inches high. There are also 2.5U units (4.3 inches), 5U units (8.75 inches), and even 8U units (14 inches). Check the Telenet System Solutions, Sag Electronic, or General Technics Web pages for information and illustrations about rack-mount products. Some things to look for in boxes and rack-mount systems are outlined here:

- The ability to install redundant parts such as fans and power supplies.
- Cable management systems that guide and support cables.
- Hot-swap components (i.e., the ability to change out components without shutting down the system).
- Number of drive bays: up to 3 for 1U, 5 for 2U, and 13 for an 8U.
- PCI slots may be limited to 1 in 1U units, but 8U units may have over 6 slots.
- Include space for a UPS (uninterruptible power supply).

InfiniBand optimizes rack-mount design by removing the bus from the server and moving it out to switches that provide interconnects for peripheral devices.

The SSI initiative (Server System Infrastructure) is an effort to standardize the specifications of common server system elements. The initiative covers two primary server elements: power supplies and electronic bays. The initiative is similar to such desktop PC efforts as ATX and NLX, which define common packaging elements for the server market. SSI extends the longevity of server packaging chassis into future system generations. It also eases development costs, promotes better component integration, and broadens the supply base for server system elements.

Related Entries   Cache and Caching Techniques; CISC (Complex Instruction Set Computer); Clustering; Data Center Design; Data Management; Data Protection; Data Warehousing; Disaster Planning and Recovery; Distributed Computer Networks; Embedded Systems; Fault Tolerance and High-Availability; File Systems; InfiniBand; Load Balancing; Mainframe; Mirroring; Multiprocessing; NAS (Network Attached Storage); NC (Network Computer); Network Appliances; Network Processors; NIC (Network Interface Card);

Performance Measurement and Optimization; RAID (Redundant Arrays of Inexpensive Disks); Redundancy; Replication; RISC (Reduced Instruction Set Computer); SAN (Storage Area Network); SAN (System Area Network); SCSI (Small Computer System Interface); Supercomputer; Switch Fabrics and Bus Design; Testing, Diagnostics, and Troubleshooting; UPS (Uninterruptible Power Supply); *and* Web Caching

Linktionary!—Tom Sheldon's Encyclopedia of Networking updates	http://www.linktionary.com/s/servers.html
IETF Working Group: Reliable Server Pooling (rserpool)	http://www.ietf.org/html.charters/rserpool-charter.html
PCI Special Interest Group	http://www.pcisig.com
I₂O Special Interest Group	http://www.intelligent-io.com/
SSI (Server System Infrastructure) Initiative	http://www.ssiforum.org/
IBTA (InfiniBand Trade Association)	http://www.infinibandta.org/
TechWeb (latest information about servers and networking)	http://www.techweb.com/
Network World Fusion (latest information about servers and networking)	http://nwfusion.com/
WebServer Compare (the definitive guide to Web server specs)	http://serverwatch.internet.com/articles/
ServerWatch.com	http://serverwatch.internet.com/
ZDNet eWeek (see Servers Resource Center)	http://www.zdnet.com/eweek/
Tom's Hardware Guide (excellent information on processors and motherboards!)	http://www.tomshardware.com/
Intel server products page	http://developer.intel.com/design/servers/
Hitex Chip Directory	http://www.embeddedlinks.com/chipdir/
IXtreme rack servers	http://hardware.bsdi.com/
Sag Electronics	http://www.sagelectronics.com/
General Technics	http://www.gtweb.net/
"The Processor-Memory Bottleneck: Problems and Solutions" by Nihar R. Mahapatra and Balakrishna Venkatrao	http://info.acm.org/crossroads/xrds5-3/pmgap.html
VitalSigns Papers (see Server Performance section)	http://www.vitalsigns.com/insights/performance.html
Intel white paper: "Planning and Building a Data Center"	http://www.intel.com/network/white_papers/
"How to Build Your Own 1U Rack Mount Server and Save a Bundle" by Tom Adelstein	http://linuxtoday.com/stories/15158.html

Service Advertising and Discovery

Services on networks can be advertised so that users can discover them. A number of protocols and schemes are available to support service advertising and discovery. For example, service advertising and discovery is important as mobile devices and mobile wireless devices proliferate on networks. These devices may connect to networks at varying locations. A service discovery and advertising protocol is an important tool to help these devices find services on the network wherever they connect, and to let other network users know about the services they are offering.

Keep in mind that as networks evolve, a variety of services will be offered. For example, network services such as file, print, and applications services can be advertised to "foreign" mobile users who temporarily connect to a network. But other possibilities exist, especially in the wireless realm. For example, an airport could have numerous small wireless networks that are limited in range to about 10 or 20 feet. As you walk into the range of one of these networks, various service advertisements appear on your portable device. These may be advertisements for peripherals like printers that you can use, but they could also be commercial advertisements.

If you are familiar with instant messaging, you are familiar with service advertising protocols. When a person in your "buddy list" signs on to the network, you receive an alert and you can start chatting with them over the network via special chat software, Internet phone, or videoconferencing software. In the case of the airport wireless networks mentioned previously, advertising protocols can alert you to friends who are located in the general vicinity. Their wireless device is advertising their personal ID and your wireless device listens for IDs and looks them up in your personal address book. If a friend is nearby, your device gets excited and starts beeping.

Two earlier advertising services that were developed for LAN environments include SAP (Service Advertising Protocol) and NetBIOS (Network Basic Input/Output System). These are discussed under their own heading.

A number of new approaches have been developed to provide enhanced service advertising and discovery in dynamic network environments such as the wireless and mobile computing networks, where devices frequently connect and disconnect from the network. When a device comes online, it advertises its services or listens for advertisements of available services.

One technique a device may use to locate a service on the network is to send out a multicast packet that contains a service request. Network devices that are providing services listen for multicast packets and then determine whether they can satisfy the request for services being made by the client. If so, the service will respond to the client with a positive message.

Here are some architectures and schemes related to service discovery, advertising, and acquisition:

■ **Salutation**   The Salutation architecture is a royalty-free service discovery and service management product from the Salutation Consortium, a nonprofit corporation. Salutation is an open standard, independent of operating system, communications protocol, hardware platform, or vendor-imposed limitations. It was created to provide service discovery for a broad range of network appliances and equipment in a platform-, OS-, and network-independent environment. Devices can use it to advertise and describe their capabilities and discover the capabilities of other devices by using search features.

■ **SLP (Service Location Protocol)**   SLP is an IETF standard designed to make it easy for network clients to discover the available services on a network and learn information about the configuration of those services. Many vendors support SLP in their operating systems, including Apple, IBM, Novell, and Sun Microsystems. The IETF Service Location Working Group is developing SLP and similar services. See "SLP (Service Location Protocol)."

■ **Microsoft.NET**   The Microsoft.NET platform for Web Services is a development environment based on building applications with "Web Services." The technique is similar to building distributed objects, but is based on HTTP and XML. Data is represented with XML and delivered in SOAP (Simple Object Access Protocol) messages via HTTP. A language called WSDL (Web Services Description Language) is used to describe services. An XML-based protocol called Disco is used to discover services at a site and a mechanism called UDDI (Universal Description, Discovery, and Integration) defines how to advertise services and how Web Service consumers can find services. See Microsoft.NET.

■ **SSDP (Simple Service Discovery Protocol)**   SSDP is a Microsoft service location protocol that is part of Microsoft's Universal Plug and Play (UpnP) initiative. It is oriented toward home networks. Like SLP, it enables devices to request information about services on a network and to advertise their presence and the services they offer.

■ **Bluetooth**   This is a wireless connectivity specification that enables electronic devices to talk spontaneously and allows instant wireless connectivity between computers, mobile phones, and portable devices. Bluetooth includes its own service discovery protocol that locates services offered by devices within the vicinity of a user's Bluetooth device. Currently, Bluetooth's service discovery protocol is being mapped to the Salutation architecture. See "Bluetooth."

■ **Jini**   This is a Java-based technology defined by Sun Microsystems. When Jini-enabled devices connect to networks, they establish impromptu Java-oriented networks that let users immediately access network resources and services. The technology is designed to support any device that "passes digital information in or out" according to Sun. Devices register with the network when they connect, which makes them available to other devices. For example, when a printer is attached and gets registered, it makes its driver available on the network and this driver gets downloaded to clients when they need to use the printer.

■ **JetSend (Hewlett-Packard)**   JetSend is code that is embedded in devices to allow them to directly exchange information. Devices become either senders or receivers. JetSend gives devices the intelligence to know their own capabilities and negotiate the best way to exchange information with other devices. No external operating systems need to get involved. No special drivers are needed to connect with other devices. All JetSend devices can immediately communicate. JetSend is a transport-independent protocol that works across any bidirectional transport, including TCP/IP, IR, IEEE 1394, and others. It is ideal for PDAs, digital cameras, copiers, network-attached printers and scanners, fax machines, and other devices.

- ■ **Inferno by Lucent Technologies**   A real-time network operating system that provides a software infrastructure for creating distributed network applications. Inferno is more like a file system that operates over a variety of transport protocols. It is designed to provide connectivity over the Internet, public telephone networks, cable television, and satellite broadcast networks. Inferno includes network and security protocols. It has a very small memory footprint and can be used as a stand-alone OS on information appliances.

A lot of the work being done in this area is for home networking and network appliance configuration. In particular, Jini and Microsoft's UPnP are designed to help devices connect and cooperate.

The IETF Resource Capabilities Discovery (rescap) Working Group is developing services that distribute information about resources or services to the global Internet. The IETF Service Location Protocol (svrloc) Working Group has developed procedures for discovering services.

Related Entries   Bluetooth; Directory Services; Embedded Systems; Home Networking; Instant Messaging; Java; Microsoft.NET; Mobile Computing; Network Appliances; Search and Discovery Services; *and* SLP (Service Location Protocol)

Linktionary!—Tom Sheldon's Encyclopedia of Networking updates	http://www.linktionary.com/s/service_advertising.html
Salutation Consortium	http://www.salutation.org
IETF Working Group: Service Location Protocol (svrloc)	http://www.ietf.org/html.charters/svrloc-charter.html
IETF Working Group: Resource Capabilities Discovery (rescap)	http://www.ietf.org/html.charters/rescap-charter.html
Microsoft (search for SSDP)	http://www.microsoft.com/
Sun Microsystems JINI network technology	http://www.sun.com/jini/
The Official Bluetooth Web site	http://www.bluetooth.com/
Jetsend home page	http://www.jetsend.com

Service Providers and Carriers

Anyone with an Internet access account and a telephone is familiar with service providers and carriers. You pay them money every month. However, "service providers" and "carriers" are broad categories. This section describes the different types of service providers and carriers and the service they offer.

In the beginning, at least in the United States, there was one phone company: AT&T. The *ILECs (incumbent local exchange carriers)* are the result of the breakup of AT&T in 1984. That breakup created seven independent RBOCs (Regional Bell Operating Companies). These included Pacific Bell, NYNEX, GTE, and others, but mergers and consolidations have changed the original gang of seven. An LEC is a telephone company that operates within a local area called the LATA (Local Access and Transport Area). Most ILECs operate across a number of LATAs.

The IXCs (interexchange carriers) provide services between LATAs. ILECs are required to create a point of presence that IXCs can connect to and provide long-distance services to local users.

A nonincumbent telephone company is called an ITC (Independent Telephone Company). However, some ITCs operate in noncompetitive areas, i.e., rural areas that are not covered by the RBOCs or any other phone companies.

CAPs (competitive access providers) are carriers that built their own metropolitan SONET rings and offered private metropolitan or wide area networking services to businesses that could bypass the incumbent carriers. The first CAP was Merrill Lynch, which installed a transmission facility in New York to bypass the New York Telephone Company and directly connect to the interexchange carrier. The Merill Lynch enterprise became Teleport Communications Company. Other CAPs followed, such as Metropolitan Fiber Systems.

The Telecom Act of 1996 permitted CLECs (competitive local exchange carriers) to set up operations in the same areas as the ILECs and offer competitive phone service. The Telecom Act of 1996 stipulates that ILECs must offer services to CLECs at wholesale prices, and allow CLECs to plug into the existing phone system and gain access to SS7 signaling. Technically, CLECs get access to UNEs (unbundled network elements), which basically gives CLECs access to the local loop and subscribers at the end of those wires.

The latest provider is generally called an ICP (integrated communications provider), which may own a variety of assets including local loop, SONET, cable TV, and wireless systems. ICPs may offer a full range of services including voice and data services, Internet access, Web hosting and co-location services, and infrastructure outsourcing (leasing dial-up access equipment to other ISPs). They also provide IP telephony services and Internet/PSTN integration.

For more information about the formation of these service providers and carriers, see "Telecommunications Regulation." That topic describes some of the problems that the ILECs and CLECs are having with current regulation. Also see "Telecommunications and Telephone System," "LATA (Local Access and Transport Area)," and "RBOC (Regional Bell Operating Company."

The carriers described in the preceding section have their roots in the telecommunications system. But a range of other service providers grew out of the development of the Internet. Originally, the Internet was a collection of links between universities and research facilities that were involved in U.S. Government research. In the late 1980s, the NSF (National Science Foundation) built the NSFNET, a backbone network with a hierarchical structure. The hierarchy of the network is what is important here. Regional networks connected to the backbone and local networks connected to the regional networks. When NSF turned the Internet over to commercial use, the regional networks turned into commercial NSPs (network service providers) and the local networks turned into ISPs (Internet service providers). NSPs provide backbone services or connections to the backbone and sell bandwidth to downstream service providers. ISPs sell Internet access services to subscribers. Note that NSPs may also provide ISP-like services and some ISPs are big enough to build their own networks. There is no solid definition of what is an NSP and what is an ISP, except that an ISP generally manages end-users' subscriptions and accounting services. See "Internet Architecture and Backbone" and "ISP (Internet Service Providers."

Also part of the mix are cable TV service providers, wireless services providers, and satellite services. See "Cable (CATV) Data Networks," "Wireless Broadband Access Technologies," "Satellite Communication Systems," and "DBS (Direct Broadcast Satellite)."

There are also service providers that build *Internet exchanges,* which are the facilities where many service providers come together and exchange traffic. NAPs (Network Access Points) are Internet exchanges. See the topic "Internet Architecture and Backbone," which contains a section called "PoPs and Internet Data Center." Also see "NAP (Network Access Point)," "Peering," and "PoP (Point of Presence)."

Not all service providers sell access and bandwidth. The following service providers offer so-called "managed services:"

- **ASP (application service provider)**   These are providers that rent software applications and provide all the necessary support to manage those applications. See "ASP (Application Service Provider)."

- **MSP (Management service provider)**   An MSP provides system management services, actively monitoring and reporting on a customer's networks, communication links, bandwidth, servers, and so on. See "MSP (Management Service Provider)."

- **SSP (storage service providers)**   An SSP is a service provider that makes disk space available, either to individuals or to large companies. The space may be used for backups or to service mobile users. Data is protected because the SSP provides redundant, secure, and managed facilities. See "SSP (Storage Service Provider)." Internet file sharing services are covered under the topic "File Sharing."

An important service provider model has emerged over the last few years. This is the "wholesale service provider." These are providers who have constructed large networks of fiber cable in metropolitan areas and across wide areas, and who have built large PoPs to provide equipment co-location and wholesale services. Wholesale IP services allow other ISPs to lease equipment and services without building their own infrastructure. This allows the wholesaler to concentrate on hardware and service, including frequent upgrades, and allows ISPs to concentrate on selling services to and supporting end users. This model allows ISPs to grow without investing in infrastructure equipment and reinvesting in new technology. By leasing modems and other access equipment from wholesaler, ISPs can establish presence at CO and PoPs in much wider areas and offer local dial-up to their subscribers.

Some claim that this model will eventually threaten the ISP, but others claim that it allows ISP to expand and grow. If an ISP builds its own facilities, it may soon become a victim of obsolescence. If it leases, the burden of keeping up with new technologies is on the wholesaler. See "PoP (Point of Presence)" for more information.

Related Entries   ASP (Application Service Provider); AT&T (American Telephone and Telegraph); Cable (CATV) Networks; CO (Central Office); Fault Tolerance and High Availability; FTTH (Fiber To The Home); HALO (High Altitude Long Operation); Internet; Internet Architecture and Backbone; Internet Connections; Internet Organizations and Committees; ISPs (Internet Service Providers); Last Mile Services; LATA (Local Access and Transport Area); LMDS (Local Multipoint Distribution Service); Local Loop; MAN (Metropolitan Area Network); MMDS (Multichannel Multipoint Distribution Service); Network Access Services; Network Core Technologies; NPN (New Public Network); Outsourcing;

Peering; PON (Passive Optical Network); PoP (Point of Presence); PSTN (Public-Switched Telephone Network); RBOCs (Regional Bell Operating Companies); Remote Access; Residential Broadband; Satellite Communication Systems; SSP (Storage Service Provider); Standards Groups, Associations, and Organizations; Telecommunications and Telephone Systems; Telecommunications Regulation; Voice/Data Networking; Voice over IP (VoIP); WAN (Wide Area Network); Wireless Broadband Access Services; Wireless Communications; *and* Wireless Local Loop

Linktionary!—Tom Sheldon's Encyclopedia of Networking updates	http://www.linktionary.com/s/service_providers.html
Bitpipe (search for "service provider")	http://www.bitpipe.com/
Telcotimes and CLEC News Magazine	http://www.telcotimes.com/
CLEC.com	http://www.clec.com/
Telcoexchange	http://www.telcoexchange.com/
Telephony World.com	http://www.telephonyworld.com/
Jeff Pulver's Gateways (an online guide to PSTN/IP gateway resources and next-generation telcos)	http://www.pulver.com/gateway/

See "ISP (Internet Service Provider)" for a list of ISP-related sites.

Session Layer, OSI Model

The OSI (Open Systems Interconnection) model is a standard defined by the International Organization for Standardization that defines a layered protocol architecture for data communication. A layer of functionality in one computer communicates with its peer layer in other computers. This is discussed under "Network Architecture."

   The session layer provides protocols that applications use to establish sessions with one another across a network or other communication system. The session layer is not used much in modern network communications because it was primarily designed to specify how sessions are set up between remote time-sharing systems. Authentication routines are defined in this layer.

SET (Secure Electronic Transaction)

Secure transactions are critical for electronic commerce on the Internet. In order for merchants to automatically and safely collect and process payments from Internet clients, a secure protocol is required that is supported by major credit card companies, vendors, consumers, and software developers. The SET protocol was developed by Microsoft, IBM, Netscape, GTE, Visa, and MasterCard for this purpose. The SET specification is currently managed by SET Secure Electronic Transaction LLC, which promotes and supports the use of SET on the Internet.

   This topic is covered at the Linktionary! Web site listed later.

Related Entries   Certificates and Certification Systems; Digital Signatures; EDI (Electronic Data Interchange); Electronic Commerce; IOTP (Internet Open Trading Protocol); *and* OBI (Open Buying on the Internet)

Linktionary!—Tom Sheldon's Encyclopedia of Networking updates	http://www.linktionary.com/s/set.html
SET Secure Electronic Transaction LLC	http://www.setco.org/
Globeset (SET products and services)	http://www.globeset.com/
MasterCard SET site	http://www.mastercard.com/shoponline/set/
Visa SET site	http://www.visa.com/nt/ecomm/set/

SFT (System Fault Tolerance)

SFT is the fault-tolerant system built into NetWare operating systems. *Fault tolerance* is the more general term for SFT. Fault tolerance allows you to provide redundancy for hardware in a system. With SFT, you can install two disks and then mirror the contents of the main disk to the secondary disk (see "Mirroring"). If the main disk fails, the secondary disk takes over. The disk controller can also be duplicated, or duplexed, to further protect from hardware failure. Novell SFT Level III takes redundancy a step further by duplexing entire servers. If the primary server goes down, the secondary server takes over without an interruption.

Related Entries   Clustering; Data Center Design; Data Migration; Data Protection; Disaster Recovery; Fault Management; Fault Tolerance and High Availability; Mirroring; *and* Replication

SGML (Standard Generalized Markup Language)

SGML is an open standard markup language that specifies how documents should be formatted. In this sense, it is a metalanguage—a language that describes a formatting and markup language. The term *markup* is historically based on the marks made by copy editors to pages that indicate how they should be formatted and typeset. In the early days of computer typesetting, there were many different typesetting systems and each used its own proprietary markup language. This language consisted of special control characters to indicate the beginning and end of some formatting. The markups were so obscure that users quickly realized a standard markup language was needed to reduce confusion.

Two organizations, the Graphics Communications Association and ANSI, went to work on the problem in 1980. They eventually combined their work, and in 1986, the ISO introduced it as SGML (Standard Generalized Markup Language). The most important part of SGML is that files contain standard ASCII text, which means they are portable from one system to another. SGML goes beyond simple document formatting by defining document structures and relationships. Document parts are defined in a hierarchical tree, and formatting is applied based on that hierarchy. Information in documents is translated to perform actions or formatting on other systems.

An SGML document consists of the actual text file (called the *document instance*) and a separate DTD (Document Type Definition) file. The DTD specifies the rules for tagging the document and defines all the ways that the document instance can be laid out and formatted. Since the DTD defines how the associated document will look, the DTD can be changed at any time to alter the document's appearance. In addition, DTDs can be created by various industries and organizations to define specific types of document layouts.

S

HTML, the markup language used for Web pages, is related to SGML. More recently, XML (Extensible Markup Language) was introduced as a way to define the elements in documents with tags so they can be extracted into databases, spreadsheets, and by programs.

Related Entries   Document Management; HTML (Hypertext Markup Language); Hypermedia and Hypertext; *and* XML (Extensible Markup Language)

Linktionary!—Tom Sheldon's Encyclopedia of Networking updates	http://www.linktionary.com/s/sgml.html
World Wide Web Consortium's SGML site	http://www.w3.org/pub/WWW/MarkUp/SGML
OASIS (Organization for Structured Information Standards)	http://www.oasis-open.org/
Robin Cover's SGML Web page	http://www.oasis-open.org/cover/sgml-xml.html

S-HTTP (Secure Hypertext Transfer Protocol)

The native protocol that World Wide Web clients and servers use to communicate is HTTP (Hypertext Transfer Protocol). HTTP is ideal for open communications, but it does not provide authentication and encryption features. S-HTTP was developed to work in conjunction with HTTP to enable clients and servers to engage in private and secure transactions. S-HTTP is especially useful for encrypting forms-based information as it passes between clients and servers.

However, S-HTTP was never fully accepted by Web browser vendors such as Microsoft and Netscape. Instead, a similar protocol called SSL (Secure Sockets Layer) became more popular. SSL provides the same authentication and encryption functionality, but SSL has the added feature of being able to encrypt all data being passed between client and server, including data at the IP level. S-HTTP only encrypts HTTP-level messages.

Still, S-HTTP is supported by a number of products. It supports a variety of cryptographic algorithms and modes of operation. Messages may be protected by using digital signatures, authentication, and encryption. Upon first contact, the sender and receiver establish preferences for encrypting and handling secure messages.

A number of encryption algorithms and security techniques can be used, including DES and RC2 encryption, or RSA public-key signing. In addition, users can choose to use a particular type of certificate, or no certificate at all. In cases in which public-key certificates are not available, it is possible for a sender and receiver to use a session key that they have exchanged in advance. A challenge/response mechanism is also available (see "Challenge/Response Protocol").

The IETF (Internet Engineering Task Force) Web Transaction Security (wts) Working Group is in charge of developing S-HTTP. The Web site is listed later. Relevant RFCs are listed here:

- RFC 2084 (Consideration for Web Transaction Security, January 1997)
- RFC 2616 (HyperText Transfer Protocol—HTTP/1.1, June 1999)
- RFC 2659 (Security Extensions For HTML, August 1999)
- RFC 2660 (The Secure HyperText Transfer Protocol, August 1999)
- RFC 2617 (HTTP Authentication: Basic and Digest Access Authentication, June 1999)

Related Entries   Authentication and Authorization; Cryptography; Digital Signatures; DSS (Digital Signature Standard); HTTP (Hypertext Transfer Protocol); Public-Key Cryptography; RSA; Security; SSL (Secure Sockets Layer); TLS (Transport Layer Security); *and* Web Technologies and Concepts

Linktionary!—Tom Sheldon's Encyclopedia of Networking updates	http://www.linktionary.com/s/shttp.html
IETF Web Transaction Security (wts) Working Group	http://www.ietf.org/html.charters/ wts-charter.html

Signaling for Call Control

Signaling is used in the PSTN (public-switched telephone network) and in various Internet protocols to set up and terminate circuits, virtual circuits, sessions, and so on. Signals may be included in packets that travel the same network as data, or in a separate network. Some example signaling protocols are listed here:

- **SS7 (Signaling System 7)**   The signaling protocol for the PSTN.

- **Q.933**   Frame Relay signaling protocol.

- **PNNI (Private Network-to-Network Interface)**   A signaling protocol for ATM networks used to signal routing topology information and SVC setup.

- **RSVP (Resource Reservation Protocol)**   An Internet protocol that network devices use to request a particular level of QoS across a network of routers.

- **SCTP (Stream Control Transmission Protocol)**   SCTP is designed to transport PSTN signaling messages over IP networks and is used to support VoIP (Voice over IP).

- **SIP (Session Initiation Protocol)**   A simple application layer protocol used to set up, maintain, and terminate multimedia sessions such as voice calls and videoconferences.

MPLS has several signaling protocols that were still being developed at the time of this writing. The protocols set up label switched paths across a network of switches. See "MPLS (Multiprotocol Label Switching)."

Technologies such as voice/data networks, IP telephony, and VoIP (Voice over IP) involve the use of signaling protocols that allow Internet users to send call setup signals into the PSTN, or vice versa. These are outlined under "Voice over IP (VoIP)" and in some of the related entries listed later.

An interesting Internet document is RFC 2719 (Framework Architecture for Signaling Transport, October 1999), which defines an architecture framework for transport of message-based signaling protocols over IP networks. The scope of this work includes definition of encapsulation methods, end-to-end protocol mechanisms, and use of existing IP capabilities to support the functional and performance requirements for signaling transport. RFC 2960 (Stream Control Transmission Protocol, October 2000) defines the actual signaling protocol.

The IETF Signaling Transport (sigtran) Working Group developed RFC 2719 and is working on other aspects of signaling. The working group has additional documents that describe SS7 signaling and the Internet. Also refer to the PINT and SPIRITS related entries listed next.

S

Related Entries   Convergence; H.323 Multimedia Conferencing Standard; IN (Intelligent Network); Megaco; MGCP (Media Gateway Control Protocol); Multimedia; NPN (New Public Network); PINT (PSTN-Internet Interworking); QoS (Quality of Service); RSVP (Resource Reservation Protocol); SAP (Session Announcement Protocol); SCTP (Stream Control Transmission Protocol); SDP (Session Description Protocol); SIP (Session Initiation Protocol); SPIRITS (Service in the PSTN/IN Requesting InTernet Service); SS7 (Signaling System 7); Telecommunications and Telephone Systems; TRIP (Telephony Routing over IP); Voice/Data Networks; *and* Voice over IP (VoIP)

Linktionary!—Tom Sheldon's
Encyclopedia of Networking updates

http://www.linktionary.com/s/signaling.html

IETF Working Group: Signaling
Transport (sigtran)

http://www.ietf.org/html.charters/sigtran-charter.html

Signals

An *analog signal* is a form of propagated energy, such as a sound wave, that vibrates the medium it travels through. Sound waves are measured by their frequency in cycles per second, or *hertz (Hz)*. *Digital signals* are transmitted over media by representing the binary digits as electrical pulses in which each pulse is a signal element. The voltage of the line is varied between a high state and a low state. For example, a binary 1 may be transmitted by applying a high voltage and binary 0 may be transmitted by applying a low voltage. *Bandwidth* is a term that refers to the number of bits per second that can be transmitted over a link.

Figure S-3 depicts both analog and digital signals, with the digital signal shown on top and equivalent analog signal shown below.

Signaling is done at the physical layer across copper cables; fiber-optic cables; and wireless technologies including microwaves, visible light, infrared, and the cellular phone spectrums.

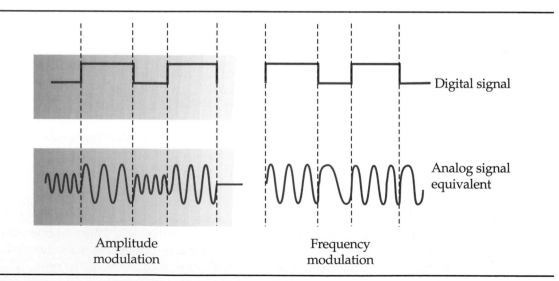

Figure S-3.   *AM and FM representation of digital signals*

As for most LANs, digital data is transmitted as digital signals. For modem connections, data is modulated onto analog signals and demodulated by the receiving modem. In wireless environments, data may be sent in analog or digital form, depending on the technology. See ADC (Analog to Digital Conversion).

As signals travel long distances, the signal is degraded due to attenuation, noise, and interference from other wires (in bundles). These problems are covered under "Cable and Wiring." Analog signals are periodically amplified; but if the signal is corrupted with noise, the noise is amplified. In contrast, digital signals are more reliable over long distances because the digital signal can be easily extracted from the noise and retransmitted.

Signal Encoding Schemes

This section covers digital data transmissions. See "Modulation Techniques" for a discussion of how digital data is transmitted over analog signals.

As mentioned, digital data is transmitted via electrical pulses. A one-to-one correspondence uses a single pulse to represent a bit. This is highly inefficient, so a variety of *encoding schemes* have been developed to more efficiently transmit digital data. The result is that throughput is greatly improved.

Think of sending messages by using flags. Say "flag up" means 1 and "flag down" means 0. A more efficient encoding scheme is to either raise or lower the flag only when there is a binary 1. For example, if the flag is already up, it is lowered. The movement of the flag is the indicator, not whether it is up or down. This will also require some kind of clocking (e.g., signal a bit every second). Assume you want to signal "1001." So, in the first second, the flag is raised (assuming it was down) to indicate the 1. The flag is then held up for two more seconds (the 0 bits), then dropped in the fourth second to indicate the change to a 1 bit.

For digital devices, a receiver must have some way of knowing the beginning and end of bytes in the data stream. In asynchronous communications, byte boundaries are indicated by start and stop bits. In synchronous communications, a clocking mechanism helps the sender and receiver stay synchronized on bit boundaries. The clocking signal may be on a separate wire, but is more often integrated directly into the signal (as discussed later).

Several signaling and encoding schemes are described next and pictured in Figure S-4. The figure illustrates the bit sequence of 0100110001. The goal is to transmit as many bits as possible, to use low voltage levels to reduce the effects of attenuation over large distances, and to provide a synchronization mechanism directly in the signal. The first few examples represent basic signaling, but are rarely used in practice.

- **Unipolar**   In this scheme, 1s are represented by voltage and 0 by no voltage. There is no special encoding.

- **Bipolar**   In this scheme, 1s are represented by positive voltage and 0s by negative voltage. This scheme reduces power requirements and reduces the attenuation of high voltage levels.

- **RZ (return to zero)**   In this scheme, the voltage state returns to zero after a signal state.

- **NRZI (nonreturn to zero, invert on ones)**   In this scheme, the voltage level, whether high or low, does not represent either a binary 1 or a 0. Instead, a change in voltage indicates a binary 1. The next bit is a a 0 if there is no voltage change, or a 1 if there is a voltage change. NRZI is used in slower RS-232 serial communications and for storing data on hard drives. A problem arises on synchronous links with long runs of consecutive bits (potentially thousands of 0s). The receiver may lose synchronization and fail to detect the proper number of 0 bits in the consecutive run. Another problem is that long runs of 0s appear as direct current, which cannot pass through some electrical components. Manchester encoding (discussed next) and other schemes solve these problems by adding clock signals.

- **Manchester**   In this scheme, a signal change always occurs in the middle of a bit, which provides the receiver with a clocking signal that it can synchronize with. A transition to high represents binary 1 and a transition to low represents binary 0. This scheme is used on LANs.

Of course, there are many other encoding schemes. The Web sites listed later provide more information. A system designer chooses a scheme based on the physical restrictions and communication requirements of a system.

Related Entries   ADC (Analog-to-Digital Conversion); Analog Transmission Systems; Bandwidth; Cable and Wiring; Capacity; Channel; Data Communication Concepts; Delay, Latency, and Jitter; Electromagnetic Spectrum; Modulation Techniques; *and* Throughput

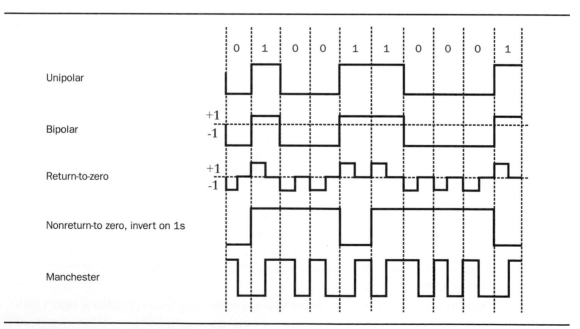

Figure S-4.   *Digital signal encoding schemes*

Linktionary!—Tom Sheldon's Encyclopedia   http://www.linktionary.com/s/signals.html
of Networking updates

Optimized Engineering Corporation (see   http://www.optimized.com/COMPENDI/
several signal encoding sections)   TabOfCon.htm

Gorry Fairhurst's data communications course   http://www.erg.abdn.ac.uk/users/gorry/course/
(see Physical Layer section)   syllabus.html

RAD Data Communications (see Digital   http://www.rad.com/networks/tutorial.htm
Encoding topic)

SIP (Session Initiation Protocol)

SIP is an Internet protocol that provides simple application layer signaling for setting up, maintaining, and terminating multimedia sessions such as voice calls, videoconferences, and even instant messaging sessions. SIP performs many of the functions of the ITU H.323 multimedia conferencing standard, which was largely specified by the telecoms. SIP provides a more-scalable, higher-performance, and more-efficient calling model. Because it is designed on the Internet model, it is inherently distributed and supports the development of telephony applications on Internet systems.

SIP is described in RFC 2543 (SIP: Session Initiation Protocol, March 1999). A related document is RFC 2327 (SDP: Session Description Protocol, April 1998). SDP is a protocol for describing multimedia session for the purposes of session announcement, session invitation, and other forms of multimedia session initiation.

SIP normally runs over UDP or TCP, but it can run over other protocols such as IP, ATM, or X.25. It requires only a datagram service and is independent of the packet layer. It can provide "out-of-band" call setup services in which the SIP exchanges take place over UDP or TCP, but actual data transmission takes place over the public telephone network.

SIP addresses are expressed as URLs. For example, a SIP URL might be sip:+12125551212@ foo.example.com, where foo.example.com is the host serving as a gateway into the PSTN.

The protocol uses a textual syntax similar to HTTP. It consists of requests and responses. In a typical SIP call, the caller sends an INVITE request to the callee. The callee accepts the call by returning a response code to the caller. Either side can terminate the call by sending a BYE request. Authentication and encryption is supported for security reasons. Requests consist of the following components:

- **Methods**   INVITE (identify and locate users and establish a connection), ACK (acknowledge an invitation), BYE (terminate a call), and REGISTER (conveys information about a user's location).

- **Parameters**   The origin and destination of the call and a unique call identifier. May indicate the caller's organization, the call's subject, and the call's priority.

- **Request body**   A description of the call or conference. SDP is one protocol used to describe conferences.

Responses indicate whether a request is still being processed, was successful, can possibly be satisfied by another node, or failed. When a call is redirected, the response indicates the name of the node to be tried. Unsuccessful calls may also return a better time to try again. The possible responses use the same syntax as HTTP and display messages such as "Progress," "Successful Request," "Redirection,' "Incorrect Request," "Server Failure," and "Global Failure."

There are three entities in the SIP environment. The *user agent* receives and initiates calls and may forward the call. A *proxy server* is an intermediary program that acts as both a server and a client for the purpose of making requests on behalf of other clients. A proxy server may, for example, locate a user and then attempt one or more possible network addresses. A *redirect server* accepts a SIP request, maps the address into zero or more new addresses, and returns these addresses to the client.

As mentioned, SIP is similar to HTTP and Web services in its operation. Consider that users make telephone calls in the same way they connect with Web servers. However, so far, SIP is lacking in authentication services and the ability to track calls for billing and accounting purposes. RADIUS and RSVP are considered candidates for this role.

A SIP extension called SIP+ is designed to address the issue of connecting Internet callers with devices connected to the PSTN. SIP+ encapsulates the binary signals required to control PSTN devices into MIME attachments to the SIP message.

A related SIP document is RFC 3050 (Common Gateway Interface for SIP, January 2001), which describes how CGI can be used for service creation in a SIP environment.

RFC 2848 (The PINT Service Protocol: Extensions to SIP and SDP for IP Access to Telephone Call Services, June 2000) provides a description of a protocol for invoking certain telephone services from an IP network. These services include placing basic calls, sending and receiving faxes, and receiving content over the telephone. The protocol is specified as a set of enhancements and additions to the SIP 2.0 and SDP protocols.

SIP is also described in RFC 2458 (Toward the PSTN/Internet Inter-Networking—Pre-PINT Implementations, November 1998). This document is interesting because it describes the arrangements through which Internet applications can request and enrich PSTN telecommunications services. RFC 2458 points out that SIP provides the necessary mechanisms to support services such as call forwarding (no answer, busy, unconditional), callee and calling "numbers" delivery (the numbers can be of any naming scheme), personal mobility (i.e., the ability to reach a called party under a single, location-independent address) even when the user changes terminals, choice of how to reach a party (Internet telephony, mobile, phone, or an answering service), caller and callee authentication, invitation to multicast conferences, and more.

SCTP (Stream Control Transmission Protocol) is a protocol for transporting PSTN signaling messages over IP networks. SCTP is a connection-oriented protocol like TCP that provides many of the reliability features of TCP, such as acknowledgments, fragmentation, and sequencing. But SCTP eliminates much of the overhead inherent in TCP that can cause delays. It also provides additional features that optimize it for signal transport. SCTP's special feature is the ability to deliver SS7 messages with little loss and delay.

See "Multimedia" and "Voice over IP (VoIP)" for more information about how SIP relates to multimedia conferencing and related protocols.

Related Entries   Convergence; H.323 Multimedia Conferencing Standard; IN (Intelligent Network); Megaco; MGCP (Media Gateway Control Protocol); Multicasting; Multimedia; NPN (New Public

Network); PINT (PSTN-Internet Interworking); QoS (Quality of Service); RSVP (Resource Reservation Protocol), SAP (Session Announcement Protocol); SCTP (Stream Control Transmission Protocol); SDP (Session Description Protocol); Search and Discovery Services; Service Advertising and Discovery; Signaling for Call Control; SPIRITS (Service in the PSTN/IN Requesting InTernet Service); SS7 (Signaling System 7); TAPI (Telephony API); Telecommunications and Telephone Systems; TRIP (Telephony Routing over IP); Unified Messaging; Videoconferencing; Voice/Data Networks; *and* Voice over IP (VoIP)

Linktionary!—Tom Sheldon's Encyclopedia of Networking updates	http://www.linktionary.com/s/sip.html
IETF Session Initiation Protocol (sip) Working Group	http://www.ietf.org/html.charters/ sip-charter.html
IETF Multiparty Multimedia Session Control (mmusic) Working Group	http://www.ietf.org/html.charters/ mmusic-charter.html
IETF Working Group: PSTN and Internet Internetworking (pint)	http://www.ietf.org/html.charters/ pint-charter.html
IETF Working Group: Service in the PSTN/IN Requesting InTernet Service (spirits)	http://www.ietf.org/html.charters/ spirits-charter.html
Softswitch Consortium (see Technical Library, Protocols)	http://www.softswitch.org/
The SIP Center	http://www.sipcenter.com/
IP Telephony Signaling by Bjarne Munch, Ericsson	http://www.ericsson.com/iptelephony
SIP Tutorial at *Network Magazine*	http://www.networkmagazine.com/ article/NMG20000727S0028
Henning Schulzrinne's SIP page	http://www.cs.columbia.edu/sip/
Pulver.com (a great site for IP telephony)	http://www.pulver.com/

A complete list of voice over IP and voice/data-related links can be found under "Voice/Data Networks."

SKIP (Simple Key Management for Internet Protocols)

SKIP is a protocol developed by Sun Microsystems to handle key management across IP networks and VPNs. This topic is dicussed at the Linktionary! Web site listed shortly.

Related Entries   Authentication and Authorization; Certificates and Certification Systems; Cryptography; IPSec (IP Security); Key Distribution and Management; Public-Key Cryptography; Security; *and* VPN (Virtual Private Network)

Linktionary!—Tom Sheldon's Encyclopedia of Networking updates	http://www.linktionary.com/s/skip.html
SKIP—Simple Key management for Internet Protocols, IP-Level Cryptography	http://www.skip.org/
SKIP	http://www.sun.com/security/skip/
Simple Key Management for Internet Protocols (SKIP) by Ashar Aziz (also provides general information about key management)	http://www.skip-vpn.org/spec/SKIP.html

S

SLA (Service-Level Agreement)

An SLA is a contract between a service provider and a customer. The service provider may be a telecommunications carrier, an Internet service provider, or any company that provides outsourcing services. The services provided may include dedicated leased lines, shared packet-oriented services, Web hosting services, off-site application management (i.e., ASPs), and off-site network management (i.e., MSPs). The SLA specifies the terms of the agreement and how much the customer will pay for those services. For example, an SLA between a telecom carrier and its customers may specify the following:

- The minimum bandwidth that will be provided

- The amount of burst bandwidth that the customer can use over the minimum and the charge that will be applied to that bandwidth

- The amount of time the service provider guarantees the service will be up and running, usually a percentage such as 99.95 percent of the time (which translates to approximately 5 minutes per day off-time)

- Penalties for not meeting service requirements (e.g., an extra amount of free service in the next month), or nullification of the contract if the provider continues to fail to meet its requirements

- If the service is packet oriented over shared links, the level of QoS that will be provided for specific types of services (e.g., prioritization for real-time traffic such as voice)

- Equipment setup, on-site service assistance, and help desk support

The terms of these contracts are often worded with phrases such as *outage duration* (the amount of time a service is down), *mean time between failures* (the amount of time between service failures), *time to restore* (the amount of time to bring a service back up), *trouble rate* (the number of on-site service calls or phone calls allowed), and *quality of service*. Quality of service has its own set of terms, such as CIR (committed information rate) and CIBR (committed burst information rate), which specify, respectively, the specified data rate and the ability to burst over the specified data rate.

Web ProForums hosts a tutorial called "Carrier Service-Level Agreements (SLAs)." The Web site is listed later. Among other things, the tutorial discusses where performance measurements and troubleshooting should take place: in an end-to-end (from the customer premise location) configuration or within the cloud (carrier switch to carrier switch). It also provides the formulas for various SLA service-level components (measured over a month), including network availability, PVC (permanent virtual circuit) availability, average round-trip network delay, average round-trip PVC delay, effective PVC throughput (frame delivery ratio), mean time to respond, and mean time to repair or restore.

In the telecom world, customers now typically specify the requirements for their service contracts. This change from the past is due to the availability of competing services. Customers can now write up contracts in the form of requests for proposals and submit those to the various providers in their area, and then choose the best. Another reason control over contracts has shifted to the customer is because customers have much better tools for monitoring and logging service levels. In the past, it was difficult to track when service levels were not being met, except when the service was completely down.

While customers may have the upper hand these days, requests for services should be reasonable. A provider may be more than willing to sign a contract for services it cannot meet in the hopes that the customer might be overstating its needs. Customers are often faced with contracting for services when the required service levels are not even known. It may be beneficial to sign short-term agreements, paying a little more than usual just so service requirements can be measured over the particular service being offered.

The Web sites listed shortly offer useful information on formulating service contracts and the things to watch out for. Several magazine sites are listed that provide extensive information about SLAs.

Related Entries   ASP (Application Service Provider); Co-Location Services; Fault Tolerance and High Availability; ISPs (Internet Service Providers); Outsourcing; QoS (Quality of Service); *and* Service Providers and Carriers

Linktionary!—Tom Sheldon's Encyclopedia of Networking updates	http://www.linktionary.com/s/sla.html
Network World Fusion SLA page	http://www.nwfusion.com/netresources/sla.html
Network Computing Magazine (search for SLA)	http://www.networkcomputing.com/
Network Magazine (search for SLA)	http://www.networkmagazine.com/
About.com (search for "service level agreements")	http://www.about.com/
Bitpipe.com (search for SLA)	http://www.bitpipe.com/
Web ProForum Tutorial: "Carrier Service-Level Agreements (SLAs)"	http://www.iec.org/tutorials/carrier_sla/

Sliding-Window Flow Control

See Flow-Control Mechanisms.

SLIP (Serial Line Internet Protocol)

When one TCP/IP system connects with another TCP/IP system over a serial point-to-point communication line (e.g., a dial-up modem), some way is needed to transport IP packets (a network layer activity) across the serial link (a data link layer activity). Basically, IP packets must be encapsulated into data link layer frames to make the trip across the serial link.

Two schemes have been adopted by the Internet community to provide these links: SLIP and PPP (Point-to-Point Protocol). Both protocols transport IP packets, but PPP has replaced

SLIP in nearly all installations. PPP transports other protocols such as DECnet, IPX, and AppleTalk, and supports synchronous transfers, frame error detection, and controls to automatically configure addresses and links. SLIP is described in RFC 1055 (A Nonstandard for Transmission of IP Datagrams Over Serial Lines: Slip, June 1988).

Related Entries   Asynchronous Communications; Dial-Up Line; IP (Internet Protocol); Mobile Computing; Modems; Point-to-Point Communications; PPP (Point-to-Point Protocol); Serial Communication and Interfaces; *and* Synchronous Communications

Slow Start

When a host in a TCP/IP network first starts to transmit onto a shared network, it can be either well mannered or "grabby" about its use of bandwidth. A well-mannered host will start by sending only a few packets and wait for an ACK (acknowledgment). If an ACK is received, it increases the number of packets it sends and keeps increasing in this way until it reaches a transmission rate that does not congest the network. This is called "slow start." Most hosts now use slow start. Those that don't may flood a link with packets that overfill a buffer, causing packets from other hosts to be dropped. Dropped packets require retransmissions that further affect network performance. Various congestion control mechanisms are available that work in the network to prevent unmannered hosts from flooding the network. See "Congestion Control Mechanisms."

SLP (Service Location Protocol)

SLP is an Internet protocol that is designed to make it easy for network clients to discover the available services on a network and learn information about the configuration of those services. Users don't need to know the name of a host that provides a service. Instead, they can query for a particular type of service and SLP will locate that service and return a network address. The protocol allows users to find network devices that perform specific functions, such as a printer that provides double-sided color printing.

SLP has become important for VoIP (Voice over IP), where SLP can be used by SIP (Session Initiation Protocol) clients to query for available services. SIP is an Internet signaling protocol used for setting up, maintaining, and terminating multimedia sessions such as voice calls and videoconferences. With SLP, clients query to find services based on the characteristics of those services. Similar services are described under "Service Advertising and Discovery."

The IETF's Service Location (srvloc) Working Group is developing SLP. SLP is defined in RFC 2165 (Service Location Protocol, June 1997) and updated in RFC 2608 (Service Location Protocol, Version 2, June 1999). A related document is RFC 2609 (Service Templates and Service Schemes, June 1999), which describes "service URLs." Service URLs include attributes that define services. Also see RFC 2614 (An API for Service Location, June 1999), RFC 3059 (Attribute List Extension for the Service Location Protocol, February 2001), and RFC 3082 (Notification and Subscription for SLP, March 2001).

SLP is meant for enterprise networks with shared services, but not for large enterprise WANs with thousands of services or the global Internet. SLP's designers envisioned that the protocol would be used in every device connected to the network. A number of Java-based embedded networking devices are using SLP to announce themselves on the network.

An SLP network consists of the following components:

- **User agent**   A process that runs on the user's system to acquire service information from service agents and directory agents.

- **Service agent**   A basic service advertising process that works on behalf of multiple services to provide information about those services.

- **Directory agent**   A process used on larger networks to provide a single repository for information when multiple service agents exist. It collects information from multiple service agents and stores it in a repository.

Small networks can be configured so that services register themselves with service agents, and the service agents make the information available to other devices. Services on networks can be advertised so that users can discover them. On larger networks, directory agents can be used to keep track of available services for clients. This technique is especially useful in network environments that consist of mobile devices that constantly connect and disconnect from the network. The directory agents dynamically track when and where devices are attached, automatically managing changes on the network.

SLP consists of service types, which define a "service scheme" that includes attributes, values, and protocol behavior. Attributes describe the characteristics of a service. Service types are cataloged by a default naming authority, which is currently ICANN (Internet Corporation for Assigned Names and Numbers).

Note that larger networks will benefit from full-blown directory services such as NDS (Novell Directory Services) or Microsoft Active Directory, although these services don't necessarily have the ability to dynamically manage change on the network. See "Directory Services" for more information.

Many vendors support SLP in their operating systems, including Apple, IBM, Novell, and Sun Microsystems. The Salutation Consortium is working on SLP extensions. See the Web address later.

Microsoft has its own protocol called SSDP (Simple Service Discovery Protocol). SSDP is part of Microsoft Universal Plug and Play initiative, and it is oriented toward home networks. Like SLP, it enables devices to request information about services on a network and to advertise their presence and the services they offer.

Related Entries   Bluetooth; Directory Services; Embedded Systems and Architectures; Home Networking; Instant Messaging; Java; Metadata; Mobile Computing; NPN (New Public Network); PINT (PSTN-Internet Interworking); SAP (Session Announcement Protocol); SDP (Session Description Protocol); Search and Discovery Services; *and* Service Advertising and Discovery

 Linktionary!—Tom Sheldon's Encyclopedia   http://www.linktionary.com/s/slp.html
of Networking updates

| IETF Working Group: Service Location Protocol (svrloc) | http://www.ietf.org/html.charters/svrloc-charter.html |
| Salutation Consortium | http://www.salutation.org |

Smart Cards

A smart card is a card about the size of a credit card that can store information and, in most cases, contains a microprocessor that can perform some activities as programmed by the card's issuer. A phone card is an example of a simple smart card. It allocates a specific amount of time for phone calls and keeps track of usage. Smart cards may also track digital cash. A more "intelligent" smart card may run a relatively sophisticated program.

Unlike *stripe cards,* which have magnetic strips on the outside of the card, smart cards hold information internally and so are much more secure. They are also tamper resistant. Smart cards are often used as token authentication devices that generate access codes for secure systems.

In this role, the card generates a value every few minutes that the user enters (along with a user name and password) when logging on to a secure system. The value generated by the card is synchronized in time with a security system on the network that the user is trying to gain access to.

Smart cards have gained rapid industry acceptance in all sorts of applications. Microsoft and a number of other vendors are using the devices to authenticate mobile and remote users. Several industry organizations have been formed to standardize and promote smart card usage (see Web sites later).

Smart cards provide unique security by storing user's credentials (private keys) in a tamper-resistant package. Users must enter a unique password to use the credentials on the smart card. Smart card deployment can provide higher levels of security than traditional logon methods in which the user password is the basis for the authentication. With smart cards, the user password and the private keys on the smart card provide a two-way authentication scheme—that is, something the user knows and something the user has (the smart card).

Deploying smart cards throughout an organization is not an easy task, but the benefits are clear. However, there are some things to consider when evaluating the deployment of smart cards. For best results, deploy smart cards to everyone in the organization, since security is compromised if some people can log on without strong authentication. You could also separate networks with firewalls into high-security and low-security segments. Smart card deployment will require that someone manage the smart cards, issuing new cards, tracking the cards, and revoking cards.

The Java Card specifications enable Java technology to run on smart cards and other devices with limited memory. The Java Card API allows applications written for one smart card platform enabled with Java Card technology to run on any other such platform.

Related Entries   Access Control; Authentication and Authorization; Biometric Access Devices; Certificates and Certification Systems; CHAP (Challenge Handshake Authentication Protocol);

Cryptography; Digital Signatures; EAP (Extensible Authentication Protocol); FORTEZZA; Hash Functions; Kerberos Authentication Protocol; Key Distribution and Management; One-Time Password Authentication; Secret-Key Cryptography; Security; *and* Token-Based Authentication

Linktionary!—Tom Sheldon's Encyclopedia of Networking updates	http://www.linktionary.com/s/smart-card.html
SCIA (Smart Card Industry Association)	http://www.scia.org/
Smart Card Forum	http://www.smartcardforum.org/
AMERKORE's Smart Card Resource Center	http://www.smart-card.com
Global Chipcard Alliance	http://www.chipcard.org
Smart Card Case Study. IBM Redbooks	http://www.redbooks.ibm.com/abstracts/sg245239.html
Microsoft Smart Cards information	http://www.microsoft.com/security/tech/smartcards/default.asp
Gemplus, a smart card solutions provider	http://www.gemplus.com/
Sun's Java Card Technology Web site	http://java.sun.com/products/javacard/

SMB (Server Message Blocks)

SMB is a high-level file-sharing protocol for exchanging information in the Microsoft Windows network environment. It is the native file-sharing protocol for Windows 95, Windows 98, Windows NT, and OS/2 operating system environments. It is also used in pre-Windows 95 versions of the Windows operating system for file sharing across networks. The new CIFS (Common Internet File System), which allows file sharing across the Internet or intranet, is based on SMB. SMB is also widely available in the UNIX and VMS environments in the form of Samba. See "Samba" for more information.

SMB provides redirector services that allow a client to locate files on other network computers running SMB and open, read, write to, and delete those files. NetBIOS is used to establish logical connections, or sessions, between networked computers. NetBIOS also uses a unique logical name to identify workstations on the network. Once a session is established, a two-way conversation takes place in which the following types of SMB messages are exchanged:

- **Session control**   Commands that start and end a redirector connection to shared resources at a server
- **File**   Messages to gain access to files at a server
- **Printer**   Messages to send print jobs to shared printers or get information about print queues
- **Message**   Provides a way to send messages to or receive messages from other network-attached workstations

S

Related Entries   CIFS (Common Internet File System); DFS (Distributed File System), Microsoft; File Systems; Microsoft Windows File Systems; NetBIOS/NetBEUI; Network Operating Systems; Rights and Permissions; *and* Samba

Linktionary!—Tom Sheldon's Encyclopedia of Networking updates	http://www.linktionary.com/s/smb.html
Microsoft (search for SMB)	http://www.microsoft.com/
Samba site at Australian National University	http://samba.anu.edu.au
Network Appliance Tech Library (search for SMB)	http://www.netapp.com/tech_library/
Network Computing Magazine (search for SMB to see a variety of SMB articles)	http://www.networkcomputing.com/
Syntax Enterprise Services supplies SMB servers	http://www.syntax.com/

SMDS (Switched Multimegabit Data Service)

SMDS is a LEC (local exchange carrier) service that allows customers to extend their LANs across metropolitan and wide area networks. SMDS was developed by Bellcore and is based on the IEEE 802.6 MAN service. It is offered as a service by LECs in some metropolitan areas. This topic is covered in more detail at the Linktionary! Web site:

Linktionary!—Tom Sheldon's Encyclopedia of Networking updates	http://www.linktionary.com/s/smds.html

SMIL (Synchronized Multimedia Integration Language)

See Multimedia

S/MIME (Secure Multipurpose Internet Mail Extension)

S/MIME is an extension of the popular MIME (Multipurpose Internet Mail Extension) electronic mail standard that adds security to protect against interception and e-mail forgery. Because S/MIME is an extension of MIME, it easily integrates with existing electronic messaging products. The demand for e-mail security is growing, along with a demand to validate the authenticity of messages. It is too easy for someone to post a message in a public forum that appears to be from someone else. E-mail security lets users electronically sign messages to prove their origin. Basically, S/MIME is designed to secure messages from prying eyes.

RSA Data Systems promotes S/MIME and VeriSign has set up a certificate hierarchy that supports S/MIME. The Web sites for these companies are listed later.

Securing electronic mail has been problematic. Ease of use is one of the problems. Too many security schemes is another. There were two early attempts to standardize secure e-mail that have failed. These were PEM (Privacy Enhanced Mail) and MOSS (MIME Object Security Services). In the mean time, PGP (Pretty Good Privacy) has become a de facto standard and is now being developed as a standard by the IETF.

S/MIME version 2 is defined in RFC 2311 (S/MIME Version 2 Message Specification, March 1998) and RFC 2312 (S/MIME Version 2 Certificate Handling, March 1998). S/MIME v2 was considered as an IETF standard, but was rejected because the IETF felt that it was encumbered by patents held by RSA Data Security. In addition, S/MIME v2 used weak 40-bit key cryptography.

The IETF standardized S/MIME version 3 in 1999. This version is defined in RFC 2632 (S/MIME Version 3 Certificate Handling, June 1999), RFC 2633 (S/MIME Version 3 Message Specification, June 1999), and RFC 2634 (Enhanced Security Services for S/MIME, June 1999).

S/MIME v3 provides authentication, message integrity and nonrepudiation of origin (via digital signatures), and privacy and data security (via encryption). S/MIME is normally used to secure outgoing mail and interpret incoming secure mail. It may also be used to secure data across HTTP links. S/MIME v3 cryptographically enhances MIME body parts according to CMS (cryptographic message syntax), which is described in RFC 2630 (Cryptographic Message Syntax, June 1999). The Cryptographic Message Syntax describes an encapsulation syntax for data protection. Refer to the RFC for more information. Also see "Cryptography," "Public-Key Cryptography" and "X.509 Certificates."

An alternative encryption scheme is PGP, or Pretty Good Privacy, which has been used as a digital encryption and digital signature utility since 1991. The IETF working group called An Open Specification for Pretty Good Privacy (openpgp) is working to define Open-PGP standards. Open-PGP software uses a combination of strong public-key and symmetric cryptography to provide security services for electronic communications and data storage. These services include confidentiality, key management, authentication, and digital signatures.

Related Entries   Certificates and Certification Systems; Cryptography; Digital Signatures; Electronic Mail; MIME (Multipurpose Internet Mail Extension); PGP (Pretty Good Privacy); Public-Key Cryptography; Secret-Key Cryptography; Security; *and* X.509 Certificates

Linktionary!—Tom Sheldon's Encyclopedia of Networking updates	http://www.linktionary.com/s/smime.html
IETF Working Group: S/MIME Mail Security (smime)	http://www.ietf.org/html.charters/smime-charter.html
RSA's S/MIME Central page	http://www.rsasecurity.com/standards/smime/
VeriSign, Inc.	http://www.verisign.com
Internet Mail Consortium (see S/MIME link)	http://www.imc.org/

SMP (Symmetric Multiprocessing)

See Multiprocessing.

SMR (Specialized Mobile Radio)

SMR is a land-based radio service that provides one-to-many and many-to-one communications. SMR has also been called trunked radio or public access mobile radio. In terms of application,

SMR systems are designed to help roaming field personnel stay in touch with the home office and are often called "dispatch services."

SMR services were established in the late 1970s in the United States when the FCC allocated spectrum for land-based commercial mobile communications. In other words, some commercial operator sets up the system and provides services to subscribers for a fee.

An SMR system consists of base station transmitters and end-user radio equipment. The system uses trunking, which means that several radio channels are pooled so that users within an area have access to any free channel within the pool.

SMR end users may operate in either an "interconnected" mode or a "dispatch" mode. In interconnected mode, the SMR unit can act as a mobile telephone because it is connected through the base station to the public-switched telephone network. In dispatch mode, over-the-air communications can take place between two or more mobile units, or between mobile units and fixed units (and end user's office and a truck).

Companies using the service include construction companies, delivery services, and transportation services that have dispatch operations in a central office. More recently, SMR systems have been expanded to support fax services and data services. The service has traditionally been analog, but the bandwidth is now being used for more-efficient digital operations. Digital services include two-way acknowledgment paging and inventory tracking, credit card authorization, automatic vehicle location, fleet management, inventory tracking, remote database access, and voice mail.

SMR operates in the 800 MHz and 900 MHz frequency ranges with a total spectrum of approximately 19 MHz (14 MHz in the 800-MHz band and 5 MHz in the 900-MHz band). The 800-MHz SMR systems operate on two 25-kHz channel pairs, while the 900-MHz systems operate on two 12.5-kHz channel pairs. Additional information about SMR and its frequency spectrum allocations may be found at the FCC Web site given later. In September 2000, the FCC auctioned 700-MHz "guard band" frequencies consisting of 2-MHz and 4-MHz bands that can be used for the services described here, but not for cellular or PCS services due to possible interference.

Nextel Communications (http://www.Nextel.com) and Southern Communications (http://www.southernco.com) are major holders of SMR spectrum.

Related Entries   Mobile Computing; Packet Radio Data Networks; SMS (Short Messaging Service); Wireless Communications; *and* Wireless Mobile Communications

Linktionary!—Tom Sheldon's Encyclopedia of Networking updates	http://www.linktionary.com/s/smr.html
FCC Specialized Mobile Radio Service Web page	http://www.fcc.gov/wtb/smrs/
Nielson Communications (SMR products)	http://www.nielsoncom.com/
Rune's Land Mobile Radio links	http://rune.tapper.com/lmr/

SMS (Short Messaging Service)

SMS is a unique messaging service that allows users to enter a short message (maximum 160 characters) from the keyboard of a mobile device and have that message forwarded to a recipient or a group of recipients. The message is sent using e-mail-like store-and-forward techniques, where the message first goes to a messaging system and then on to the recipients. SMS is sometimes called a "wireless instant messaging service."

SMS was originally designed for GSM mobile phone systems, but is now available for a variety of other phone systems. It is called G-Mail on the GSM networks in Europe, where billions of SMS messages are being sent per month. The systems are evolving into EMS (Enhanced Messaging Service) and MMS (Multimedia Messaging Services) according to Mobilesms.com. Packet radio services offer an alternative to circuit-oriented SMS. See "Packet Radio Data Networks."

SMS uses bandwidth in the signal path of the mobile phone system. This signal path is where call setup, ring signals, caller ID, and voice mail notification take place. The signal path is different than the phone path, so a voice call can be taking place at the same time that a message is being sent or received. Messages may be directed to Internet addresses or fax machines. In addition, a confirmations receipt may be requested so the sender knows the recipient has received the message.

To use SMS, you need an SMS-capable mobile phone and a subscription to a mobile phone service that supports SMS. You also need a messaging account so messages can be directed to you through the SMS store-and-forward system.

Messages may not be limited to 160 characters for long. Compression techniques and the ability to string several SMS messages together open the system to more functionality.

One of the drawbacks is the difficulty of creating a message on a mobile phone keypad. Some of the newer devices have enhanced keyboards, but they are not as compact as phones. SMS usage is scattered in the United States due to the use of different network standards. It may only be possible to send a message to someone within the same local calling area, and not across carrier boundaries. However, national SMS roaming is being developed by the GSM Alliance.

The definitive source for SMS information is Mobilesms.com. The site hosts an incredible amount of information about mobile services.

Related Entries   Instant Messaging; Mobile Computing; Packet Radio Data Networks; SMR (Specialized Mobile Radio); SMS (Short Messaging Service); WAP (Wireless Application Protocol); Wireless Communications; *and* Wireless Mobile Communications

Linktionary!—Tom Sheldon's Encyclopedia of Networking updates	http://www.linktionary.com/s/sms.html
Mobilesms.com	http://www.mobilesms.com/
GSM Alliance	http://www.gsm-pcs.org

S

SMTP (Simple Mail Transfer Protocol)

SMTP is a simple protocol that controls the exchange of e-mail messages between two mail servers. The protocol is used in the Internet and is defined by the IETF. Using SMTP, a process can transfer mail to another process on the same network or to some other network via a relay or gateway process accessible to both networks. A mail message may pass through a number of intermediate relay or gateway hosts on its path from sender to ultimate recipient. The basic SMTP model is pictured in the following illustration.

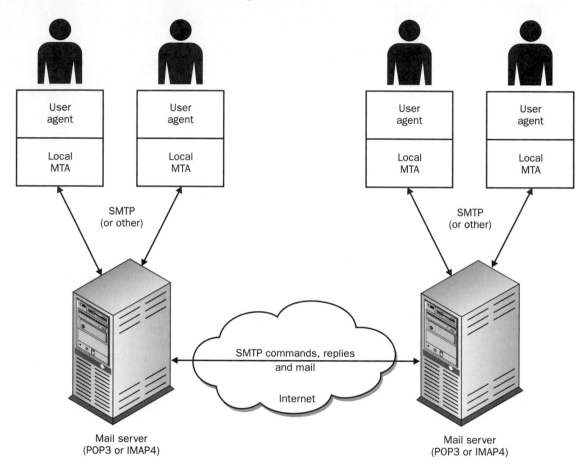

The model consists of user agents, which are applications that provide e-mail services (create and view messages). The MTA (message transfer agent) is the component that uses the SMTP protocol to forward messages to other MTAs. In the illustration, a user creates a message and chooses Send. The message is queued locally with other Outbox messages for delivery at a designated time. The local MTA forwards the messages to the relay MTA, which may be a corporate e-mail server located at the LAN/Internet connection, or a mail server at an ISP that home users connect with across their dial-up connection.

SMTP uses a client/server relationship. The client is the system with mail to send. It establishes a two-way transmission channel to an SMTP server over a TCP connection.

When sender and receiver are connected via the same transport service (on the same network), mail transmissions occur directly between the sender and receiver. When they are not connected to the same transport service, transmission occurs via one or more relay SMTP servers. Large organizations will set up their own relay servers to manage incoming and outgoing mail. These servers typically stay online all the time and may provide various security features. Mail servers run message-handling protocols such as POP3 (Post Office Protocol, version 3) and IMAP4 (Internet Mail Access Protocol, version 4). Both offer mail-drop and mail-forwarding services, and both use SMTP to exchange mail. SMTP is like the mail carrier while POP and IMAP4 are like the post offices. IMAP4 is a new and more flexible protocol that is a replacement for POP3.

When users connect to the mail server, the server authenticates the users and gives them access to their mailboxes. Messages are then downloaded to their computers. IMAP4 improves this model by allowing users to keep mail in their mailboxes on the mail server, rather than have it automatically download to their computers. This is useful for remote mobile users.

SMTP messages may be transferred in a series of hops to the ultimate destination. In this case, a series of connections is established between relay servers. There is a handoff of responsibility from one server to the next, and each server must either deliver a message or report back to the sender that delivery failed.

SMTP uses a basic request and response mechanism to transfer mail. A few simple commands make this exchange possible. The commands are formed with ASCII (text). The simple command structure makes it easy to build mail servers and clients for any platform. A client initiates a mail transaction by sending a series of commands that specify the originator and destination of the mail and transmission of the message content. The server responds to each command. The commands normally progress one at a time, but a pipelining feature is outlined in RFC 2920 (SMTP Service Extension for Command Pipelining, September 2000) that allows multiple commands to be sent to a server in a single TCP send operation.

Internet mail was originally defined in RFC 821 (Simple Mail Transfer Protocol, August 1982). Note that the IETF Detailed Revision/Update of Message Standards (drums) Working Group was updating RFC 821 and other relevant RFCs at the time of this writing. The group is also reviewing future directions in messaging on the Internet. Refer to the DRUMS Web site for the latest SMTP documents.

The IETF Message Tracking Protocol (msgtrk) Working Group is designing a diagnostic protocol that a sender can use to request information about the submission, transport, and delivery of a message regardless of its delivery status.

RFC 2852 (Deliver by SMTP Service Extension, June 2000) defines extensions to define message delivery time, not in terms of priorities but to specify that the message should be dropped if it is not delivered within a specified time period. The extensions could also be used to specify that a "delayed" message be returned to the sender if a message is delayed.

Other RFCs are described under "Electronic Mail," and a complete list of mail-related RFCs is located at the Internet Mail Consortium Web site (http://www.imc.org/rfcs.html).

Related Entries   Collaborative Computing; Electronic Mail; Groupware; Intranets and Extranets; Middleware and Messaging; POP (Post Office Protocol); Sendmail; *and* Workflow Management

Linktionary!—Tom Sheldon's Encyclopedia of Networking updates	http://www.linktionary.com/s/smtp.html
IETF Working Group: Detailed Revision/ Update of Message Standards (drums)	http://www.ietf.org/html.charters/drums-charter.html

IETF Working Group: Message Tracking Protocol (msgtrk)	http://www.ietf.org/html.charters/msgtrk-charter.html
SMTP Tutorial at RAD Data Communications	http://www.rad.com/networks/1998/smtp/smtp.htm
The IMAP Connection	http://www.imap.org
IMAP Information Center	http://www.washington.edu/imap
Internet Mail Consortium	http://www.imc.org
Open Information Interchange (OII) electronic mail page	http://158.169.50.95:10080/oii/en/E-mail.html

SNA (Systems Network Architecture)

SNA is an IBM architecture that defines a suite of communication protocols for IBM systems and networks. SNA is an architecture like the OSI model. There is a protocol stack and various architectural definitions about how communication takes place at the various levels of the protocol stack.

Note   *This topic is covered in more detail at the Linktionary! Web site.*

SNA was originally designed for IBM mainframe systems. One could refer to this original SNA as "legacy SNA." The "new SNA" is APPN (Advanced Peer-to-Peer Networking). Legacy SNA is based on the older concept of centralized processing, where the mainframe was the central computing node. Dumb terminals attached to the central processor and did two things: accepted keyboard input from users, and displayed calculated results or query replies from the mainframe.

As desktop computers and LANs started to appear in the 1980s, it became obvious that personal computing (i.e., running programs on a local computer rather than a central computer) was the wave of the future. This was not so obvious to IBM engineers. There were attempts to maintain the legacy SNA architecture by integrating these new systems as dumb terminals, even though they had their own processing power.

Eventually, IBM saw the benefits of allowing these "smart terminals" to handle some of the processing load. It created APPN to support client/server computing and it began to recognize PC-based applications as being important for the enterprise. APPN is very similar to TCP/IP, and, for a while, many people thought that APPN would eventually supersede TCP/IP. In other words, TCP/IP was the experimental model and APPN would be the working model. Today, APPN is considered a legacy architecture.

By the 1990s, IBM's mainframe systems changed roles from being central processing systems to being just another server on the network—but a very fast server. IBM's high-powered systems can provide the kind of processing power, high availability, and fault tolerance that is needed to keep up with growing traffic at Web sites and corporate data centers. Most important, a vast amount of legacy data is still available on IBM systems. SNA and APPN are still critical in these environments.

Related Entries   APPN (Advanced Peer-to-Peer Networking); IBM (International Business Machines); *and* Mainframe

 Linktionary!—Tom Sheldon's Encyclopedia of   http://www.linktionary.com/s/sna.html
Networking updates

Sniffer

A sniffer is another name for a network analyzer. See "Network Analyzers" for more information.

SNMP (Simple Network Management Protocol)

SNMP is a popular management environment and network protocol. It was defined by the Internet community for TCP/IP networks. The IETF refers to SNMP as the "Internet-standard Management Framework" or, simply, the "Framework." The term "framework" is important because, as mentioned, SNMP defines both a protocol and an architecture for managing networks. The framework is also used when building network management applications or management devices.

SNMPv1 was originally defined in RFC 1067 (A Simple Network Management Protocol, August 1988) although it was based on an earlier protocol defined in RFC 1028 (A Simple Gateway Monitoring Protocol, November 1987). Note that SNMPv1 is now defined in the updated RFC 1157 (A Simple Network Management Protocol, May 1990). Work was started on SNMPv2 in the early 1990s. A primary goal was to improve security, add new management features, and make information retrieval more efficient. But SNMPv2 development fell into chaos and the IETF disbanded it, only to have it resurface as SNMPv3. SNMPv3 includes many of the original goals of SNMPv2.

 The SNMP environment and its management information base are discussed in more detail at the Linktionary! Web site.

One of the best documents for SNMP is RFC 2570 (Introduction to Version 3 of the Internet-Standard Network Management Framework, April 1999). It provides an introduction to the latest version, as well as a list of relevant RFCs for each SNMP version.

An alternative management model is WBEM (Web-Based Enterprise Management), which takes advantage of Web technologies. WBEM is designed to complement existing management standards such as SNMP and DMI (Distributed Management Interface). It uses CIM (Common Information Model) as its inventory model and XML to package information for transfer from one place to another. XML has many advantages in the management environment. See "WBEM (Web-Based Enterprise Management)."

Related Entries   Agent, Network Management; CIM (Common Information Model); CMIP (Common Management Information Protocol); Configuration Management; DMI (Distributed Management Interface); DMTF (Distributed Management Task Force); Fault Management; Fault Tolerance and High Availability; IPMI (Intelligent Platform Management Interface); MIB (Management Information Base); MSP (Management Service Provider); NDMP (Network Data Management Protocol); Network Analyzers; Network Management;

OpenView Management System; Performance Measurement and Optimization; RMON (Remote Monitoring); SystemView, IBM; Testing, Diagnostics, and Troubleshooting; *and* WBEM (Web-Based Enterprise Management)

Linktionary!—Tom Sheldon's Encyclopedia of Networking updates	http://www.linktionary.com/s/snmp.html
IETF Working Group: SNMP Version 3 (snmpv3)	http://www.ietf.org/html.charters/snmpv3-charter.html
IETF Working Group: Configuration Management with SNMP (snmpconf)	http://www.ietf.org/html.charters/snmpconf-charter.html
IETF Working Group: Distributed Management Working Group (disman)	http://www.ietf.org/html.charters/disman-charter.html
IETF Working Group: SNMP Agent Extensibility (agentx)	http://www.ietf.org/html.charters/agentx-charter.html
Network World Fusion Network Management Web page	http://www.nwfusion.com/netresources/manage.html
Bitpipe (search for "SNMP")	http://www.bitpipe.com/
Cisco Documentation on SNMP	http://www.cisco.com/univercd/cc/td/doc/cisintwk/ito_doc/snmp.htm
SNMP Research International	http://www.snmp.com/
TechFest SNMP links list	http://www.techfest.com/networking/netmgmt.htm
David C. Blight's telecom links (see Network Management section)	http://www.ee.umanitoba.ca/~blight/telecom.html

SOAP (Simple Object Access Protocol)

SOAP is a Microsoft/Lotus/IBM-developed protocol for exchanging information in distributed environments. It provides a common message-passing protocol that uses HTTP to carry messages that are formatted in XML (Extensible Markup Language). One of the key objectives of SOAP is to provide a way for business applications running on the Internet or in other distributed environments to talk to each other using XML as the basis for information exchange. Programs on different computers can connect without regard to operating system or platform. Microsoft sees SOAP as a way for Web sites to provide application services via SOAP-based interfaces. SOAP is now a W3C specification.

SOAP defines how to create an HTML header and an XML file that can call a program on another computer and pass information to it in a format and layout that the computer will immediately recognize. This is similar to RPCs (remote procedure calls), but Microsoft views SOAP as a move away from the RPC model, which is the basis of COM+, and a move toward a message-passing model.

From a competitive point of view, Microsoft is embracing XML due to its ability to provide interoperability over the Internet. XML is a framework for representing and exchanging information among many different systems. The major advantage of XML files is that they are self-descriptive and the recipients can easily extract information from them.

SOAP consists of three parts:

- The SOAP envelope (wrapper) construct defines an overall framework for expressing what is in a message, who/what should deal with it, and whether it is optional or mandatory.
- The SOAP encoding rules define a serialization mechanism that can be used to exchange instances of application-defined data types.
- The SOAP RPC representation defines a convention that can be used to represent remote procedure calls and responses.

Microsoft touts SOAP's ability to pass messages through firewalls. Since SOAP uses HTTP as a transport mechanism, SOAP messages can pass through firewalls without the usual security checks. This has the potential of being a major security problem since potentially dangerous commands can hide inside SOAP messages.

Similar schemes already exist for other platforms. IIOP (Internet Inter-ORB Protocol) allows CORBA-based object interaction over TCP/IP networks. In particular, Java applets can use IIOP to communicate with objects on remote servers. Sun Microsystem's RMI (Remote Method Invocation) allows objects in the Java environment to interact with one another. But Microsoft sees SOAP as far superior to these methods. XML and SOAP are the major components of Microsoft.NET, Microsoft's distributed object computing development platform. See "Microsoft.NET."

Related Entries   ActiveX; Client/Server Computing; COM (Component Object Model); CORBA (Common Object Request Broker Architecture); Distributed Applications; Distributed Computer Networks; Distributed Object Computing; Java; Microsoft.NET; Middleware and Messaging; MOM (Message-Oriented Middleware); Multitiered Architectures; Object Technologies; ORB (Object Request Broker); RPC (Remote Procedure Call); Web Technologies and Concepts; *and* XML (Extensible Markup Language)

Linktionary!—Tom Sheldon's Encyclopedia of Networking updates	http://www.linktionary.com/s/soap.html
Microsoft SOAP Web site	http://msdn.microsoft.com/xml/general/
W3C SOAP documentation	http://www.w3.org/TR/SOAP/
UserLand Soap.Weblogs.Com	http://soap.weblogs.com/

Socket

A socket is the endpoint of a connection over a TCP/IP network, much like a phone is the endpoint of a connection in the telephone network. A socket is the combination of a TCP port and an IP address. Ports are logical interfaces for applications, and they are assigned numbers. For example, The Web's HTTP protocol is located at port 80. Using the telephone analogy, the TCP port is then like a telephone number and the IP address is the location of the phone. A socket is like a phone that has been assigned a phone number. However, a typical host can have many sockets active at the same time (multiplexing).

A socket is created during a connection setup between two systems when a process makes a request to a remote machine to open a connection at a specific port. Once the connection is set up, data transfers can begin.

Sockets are the main abstraction of the socket interface, which was originally developed in the Berkeley implementation of UNIX. The socket interface is an API, and a socket is the place where an application process makes a connection to some other process over a network. See "Sockets API,."

RFC 675 (Specification of Internet Transmission Control Program, December 1974) provides a clear description of TCP, ports, and sockets. See section 2.2 ("Sockets and Addressing").

Related Entries   Connection Establishment; Ports, TCP/IP; Reliable Data Delivery Services; TCP (Transmission Control Protocol); *and* Transport Protocols and Services

Sockets API

The socket interface is a de facto (nonstandardized) API (application programming interface) that was originally developed in the Berkeley implementation of UNIX. A socket interface is used to access TCP/IP networking services and create connections to processes running on other hosts.

Socket APIs are what allow applications to bind with ports and IP addresses on hosts. If an application needs the services of TCP, it uses a *stream socket,* which provides connection-oriented, bidirectional, reliable data flows between systems. A *datagram socket* is used by applications that do not need TCP's reliable services. Datagram sockets go through UDP.

In the Windows environment, sockets is known as "Windows Sockets" or "WinSocks." An API similar to sockets is Microsoft's NetBT (NetBIOS over TCP/IP).

An expanded version of this topic is at the Linktionary! Web site:

Linktionary!—Tom Sheldon's Encyclopedia of Networking updates	http://www.linktionary.com/s/sockptsapi
WinSock Development Information	http://www.sockets.com/

SOCKS

SOCKS is a *circuit-level proxy gateway* that provides security based on sessions (i.e., at the TCP layer). It provides a secure channel between two TCP/IP hosts—a SOCKS-enabled client on the internal network and an outside Web server. SOCKS provides firewall services, as well as auditing, management, fault tolerance, and other features. With SOCKS in place, an internal corporate network can be connected to the Internet in a way that allows internal users to access servers on the Internet while providing firewall protection against outside intruders. NEC Corporation has promoted SOCKS.

When a client needs to contact a Web server on the Internet, the request is intercepted by the SOCKS server. The SOCKS server relays this request to the target Web server. It may first evaluate whether the request is allowed based on predefined policies. When the response arrives from the Web server, the SOCKS server evaluates the packet before relaying it to the internal client. Thus, the SOCKS server can collect, audit, screen, filter, and control data flowing and application-level calling features like caller ID and call waiting. This model has made it very difficult for the telephone company to add new features. The convergence proponents replace the Class 5 switch with a "softswitch architecture" that has these components:

- **Media gateway** The media gateway is just the switch portion of the Class 5 switch. Switching technology has advanced tremendously over the past few years, and vendors can easily produce inexpensive media gateways that can handle many more calls in a smaller size than Class 5 switches.

- **Media gateway controller** This component runs the call control and application-level calling features in a server that supports easy software upgrades and expansion of features. The media gateway translates between circuit-switched voice traffic and packet-based traffic. It is also called the "call agent" and it controls the media gateway.

The media gateway is a relatively inexpensive "dumb box" that translates packets into circuits and circuits into packets. As such, the media gateway has become a commodity item and is appearing in rack-mounted systems at carrier POPs that support co-location. In contrast, the media gateway controller holds all the intelligence. It supports the integration of SS7 and Internet protocols, and maintains information about traffic flows that can be used for billing purposes.

Since the media gateway and the media gateway controller are separated, a protocol is needed that allows the media gateway controller to control the media gateway. In 1999, the IETF and the ITU formally agreed to work on a single protocol, which is known as Megaco/ H.248. The ITU has largely taken over this development as H.248. This is discussed further under "Voice over IP (VoIP)." A related protocol is SIP (Session Initiation Protocol), an application layer control protocol for setting up, maintaining, and terminating voice and videoconferencing sessions. It allows different media gateway controllers to communicate and allows end users to request services from media gateway controllers. See "SIP (Session Initiation Protocol)."

An example softswitch is the Alcatel 1000, which is designed to support the gradual migration from voice-centric to data-centric environments. It provides the brains for a converged voice and data network, handles call setup and establishes control paths, controls the trunking gateways that convert TDM signals (PSTN voice calls) to voice over IP, and supports all services in the existing PSTN IN (Intelligent Network).

The Softswitch Consortium Web site has a list of product vendors. This topic continues under "Voice over IP (VoIP)." A full set of Web links is also located under that topic. Also see "Voice/Data Networks."

The IETF PINT Working Group has addressed the arrangement through which Internet applications can request PSTN services. The IETF SPIRITS (Service in the PSTN/IN Requesting InTernet Service) Working Group has addressed the opposite arrangement in which PSTN users request services that require an interaction between the PSTN and the Internet. Some examples covered by SPIRITS include Internet call waiting, Internet caller-ID delivery, and Internet call forwarding. See "SPIRITS (Service in the PSTN/IN Requesting InTernet Service)" and "PINT (PSTN-Internet Internetworking)" for more information.

in and out of the network. SOCKS also provides the foundation for other critical networking services such as security, management, auditing, and accounting.

SOCKS 5 was created by a committee of industry supporters and submitted to the IETF for standardization. It extends SOCKS to include UDP, extends the framework to include provisions for generalized strong authentication schemes, extends the addressing scheme to encompass domain-name and IPv6 addresses. The primary focus was to provide strong authentication for inbound connections. This strengthens the security and gives network administrators better control of access to internal systems by public network users. A variety of negotiable authentication schemes can be used. SOCKS 5 also provides a secure way to run streaming audio and video across firewalls. More recently, SOCKS has emerged as a protocol for implementing policy-based networking at network borders.

SOCKS 5 is outlined in RFC 1928 (SOCKS Protocol Version 5, March 1996), RFC 1929 (Username/Password Authentication for SOCKS V5, April 1996), and RFC 1961 (GSS-API Authentication Method for SOCKS Version 5, June 1996).

Related Entries   Firewall; IPSec (IP Security); NAT (Network Address Translation); Policy-Based Management; Proxy Servers; Security; VPN (Virtual Private Network); *and* Web Caching

Linktionary!—Tom Sheldon's Encyclopedia of Networking updates	http://www.linktionary.com/s/socks.html
SOCKS home page, hosted by NEC	http://www.socks.nec.com/
SOCKS technical resources at stardust.com	http://www.stardust.com/policy/socks.htm
Aventail Corp.	http://www.aventail.com

Softswitch

Softswitch refers to an architecture for a device that supports the integration of IP telephony and the PSTN. In the NPN, the traditional circuit-switched voice network will slowly give way to a packet-oriented voice and data network based on Internet technology. See "NPN (New Public Network)."

Softswitches are an alternative form of Class 5 switch. A Class 5 switch is a big expensive telephony switch, located in central offices all over the world. It accepts dial-up telephone calls from users and creates circuits across a hierarchy of telephone switches, some local, and some regional, national, or international. Call setup and management is handled by SS7 (Signaling System 7), which runs as an out-of-band signaling protocol to control PSTN switching equipment. See "Telecommunications and Telephone Systems" for more details about this system.

Proponents of the convergence of voice and data on an all-packet network point out the superiority of the packet model. Bandwidth and QoS to support voice are quickly becoming a reality in the Internet. However, the PSTN and the Internet will coexist for some time and there will be a need for integration. For example, until convergence is complete, IP telephone users will no doubt want to connect with a PSTN telephone user, and vice versa. This means that Internet protocol devices will need to talk to SS7 devices, and vice versa. That calls for a gateway.

Proponents of convergence also point out the inflexibility of the traditional telephone switch. Wrapped up in one big device are switching, call setup and management features,

Related Entries   Call Center Operations; Circuit-Switching Services; CO (Central Office); Convergence; CTI (Computer-Telephony Integration); H.323 Multimedia Conferencing Standard; IN (Intelligent Network); Local Loop; Megaco; MGCP (Media Gateway Control Protocol); Multicasting; Multimedia; Network Access Services; NPN (New Public Network); OSP (Open Settlement Protocol); PBX (Private Branch Exchange); PINT (PSTN-Internet Interworking); QoS (Quality of Service); SAP (Session Announcement Protocol); SCTP (Stream Control Transmission Protocol); SDP (Session Description Protocol); SIP (Session Initiation Protocol); SPIRITS (Service in the PSTN/IN Requesting InTernet Service); SS7 (Signaling System 7); TAPI (Telephony API); Telecommunications and Telephone Systems; Telecommunications Regulation; TRIP (Telephony Routing over IP); Unified Messaging; Videoconferencing; Voice/Data Networking; *and* Voice over IP (VoIP)

Linktionary!—Tom Sheldon's Encyclopedia of Networking updates	http://www.linktionary.com/s/softswitch.html
ISC (International Softswitch Consortium)	http://www.softswitch.org/
Alcatel	http://www.alcatel.com/
The Parlay Group	http://www.parlay.org
Multiservice Switching Forum	http://www.msforum.org/
IETF Working Group: Media Gateway Control (megaco)	http://www.ietf.org/html.charters/megaco-charter.html
Marconi softswitch Web page	http://www.marconi.com/html/solutions/ intelligentpacketnetworkssoftswitch.htm

Software Distribution

See Electronic Software Distribution and Licensing.

Solaris, SunSoft

See Sun Microsystems Solaris.

Soliton

Solitons are waves that propagate with little energy loss and keep their shape, even after colliding with other waves. The phenomenon was first observed in water, but solitons in the form of light pulses are being employed in fiber-optic transmission systems to enhance distance and performance. The soliton serves as the method for encoding digital signals onto the cable. Soliton-based equipment emits a short pulse of laser light that propagates through fiber-optic cable with no chromatic dispersion. See the Linktionary! Web site for more information.

Related Entries   Fiber-Optic Cable; Optical Networks; *and* WDM (Wavelength Division Multiplexing)

Linktionary!—Tom Sheldon's Encyclopedia of Networking updates	http://www.linktionary.com/s/soliton.html

S

SONET (Synchronous Optical Network)

SONET is a standard that defines telecommunication transmissions over fiber-optic cables. It defines the access methods, framing, and other parameters for transporting digital information over an optical communication system. SONET was first proposed by Bellcore (now Telcordia) in the mid-1980s, and then standardized by the ANSI (American National Standards Institute). The ITU adapted SONET to create SDH (Synchronous Digital Hierarchy), a worldwide telecommunication standard. SONET is a subset of SDH that is used in North America. SONET technology issues are managed by NSIF (Network and Services Integration Forum).

SONET was designed as a means to deploy a global telecommunication system, and so SONET/SDH is widely deployed by the world carriers. It uses standardized rates to ensure that telecommunication companies around the globe can interconnect their systems with little trouble. SONET removes the boundaries between the telephone companies of the world. But SONET is not limited to carrier networks. SONET may run directly to large enterprises in metropolitan areas or be used to build campus networks.

SONET Features

SONET defines the way that the telephone companies transmit digital voice and data over optical networks. It also uses an OC (optical carrier) a hierarchy where many lower-speed links can be multiplexed into high-speed links. SONET allows the construction of large multi-ring networks in which all the rings are synchronized. In the older PDH (plesiochronous digital hierarchy), an example of which is described under "NADH (North American Digital Hierarchy)," the clock speeds of individual transmission lines is identical to all other lines, but they are not locked synchronously. This can cause bits to "slip" out of synchronization over time, and various compensators must be used to avoid the problem.

One of SONET's most important features is its self-healing fiber-optic ring configuration. This is called APS (automatic protection switching), and it helps SONET survive breaks, earthquakes, backhoe accidents, or similar problems that might disrupt service. SONET rings contain two fibers, one that transmits signals in one direction and the other that waits in standby protection mode. If the fiber is cut, transmissions are looped back onto the secondary fiber on both sides of the break to form a new ring around the break.

Four-fiber rings are common to provide a fully redundant SONET network. A Sprint SONET ring using this design is pictured in Figure S-5. In the event of a fiber cut or component failure, calls are rerouted around failure points in milliseconds. The system is a four-fiber, bidirectional, line-switched SONET ring (4 BLSR), as two fibers carry traffic while another two are on standby, or in "protect" mode, ready to take over in the event of a service disruption.

A large-scale interconnected SONET network consists of many rings of varying sizes and speeds, as shown in Figure S-6. A metropolitan area contains a set of interconnected rings, with smaller-capacity rings connected to larger-capacity rings. The metropolitan ring is connected to regional rings, which connect with other cities. The *ADM (add/drop multiplexer)* adds and extracts streams at the junction of SONET networks or at a PoP (point of presence). An ADM does not

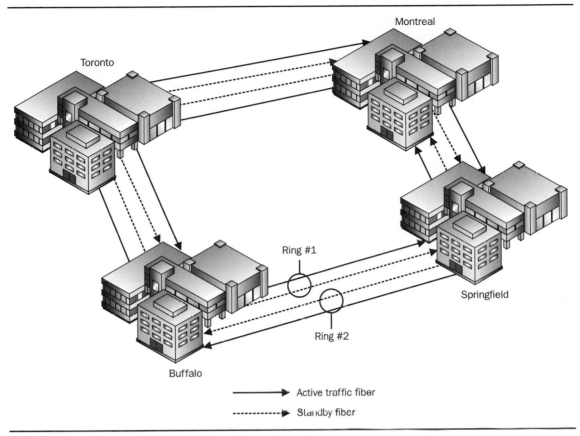

Figure S-5. *Sprints bidirectional, four-fiber SONET ring*

terminate and demultiplex the entire range of signals on a fiber-optic cable, but instead pulls out (or inserts) only subrate signals. If a signal needs to be switched to another ring, the ADM extracts it and then adds it into the other ring. For SONET, this means performing an optical-to-electrical-to-optical conversion. Note that a DCS (digital cross-connect) is usually located at the point where rings connect via ADMs. Its purpose is to allow multiple lower-speed rings to connect into a higher-speed ring.

SONET networks may also be built with linear trunks or a combination of linear and ring topologies. The linear trunks are used to extend SONET to buildings and campuses. The long-haul network may be SONET, but may also be high-capacity DWDM trunks as described under "Optical Networks."

The SONET digital hierarchy complies with the OC (optical carrier) standards described under "OC (Optical Carrier)."

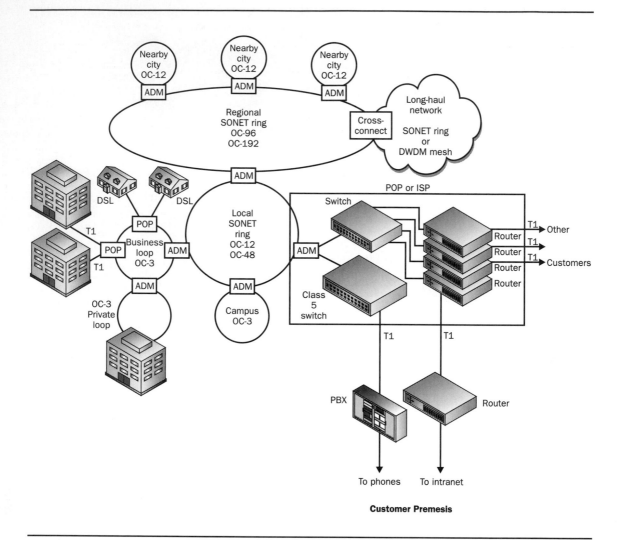

Figure S-6.   *Interconnected SONET ring*

Individual SONET channels are merged into a higher-level channel using time division multiplexing. In this scheme, each channel gets a specific time slot in the transmission. SONET multiplexes a variety of data streams, called *tributaries*, into higher and higher OC levels. This is pictured in Figure S-7.

SONET carries data and control information in 810-byte frames that travel across the fiber in a synchronous stream. Control information is embedded in the frame and is referred to as

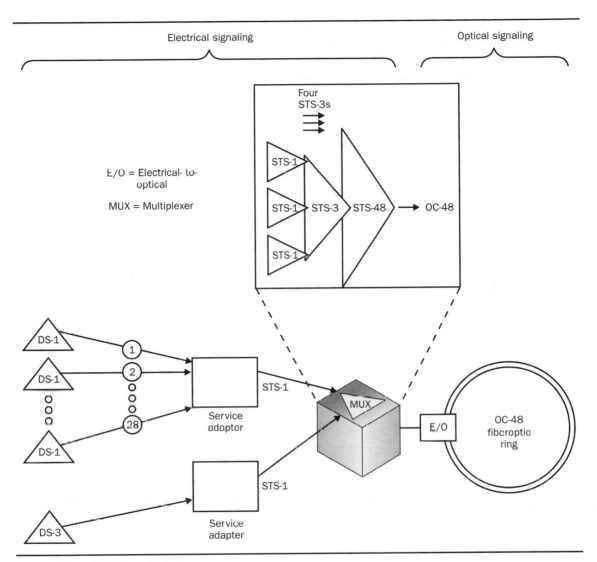

Figure S-7.　*SONET multiplexing*

the *overhead.* SONET's layered architecture is pictured in Figure S-8. The path, line, and section layers are described next, and each includes some information in the overhead section of the SONET frame. A *photonic sublayer* is the lowest layer that specifies properties of the fiber and the light.

- **Path sublayer**　This sublayer is involved with end-to-end connections across repeaters and multiplexers. It provides control signaling and error monitoring between the endpoints (path termination equipment) on the network. Path information is added into the DS-1 signals when they are multiplexed into the tributaries. The information includes a signal label, a path status, and path trace.

- **Line sublayer** This sublayer multiplexes path layer connections into the optical links. This layer also performs performance monitoring and protection switching.

- **Section sublayer** This sublayer handles a single point-to-point link, such as between the original source and a repeater. Frame generation and error monitoring is also handled in this sublayer.

ATM runs on top of SONET and provides a variety of services, including virtual circuits and QoS (Quality of Service) features. *PoS (Packet over SONET)* is a protocol that puts IP packets directly into SONET frames, eliminating the overhead needed to run IP-over-ATM-over-SONET. Vendors such as Cisco have developed PoS products to support the fast-growing Internet/intranet infrastructure. PoS allows service providers to install well-understood SONET networks, but use it more efficiently by eliminating ATM overhead. In addition, PoS can help reduce the need for intermediate SONET ADMs (add/drop multiplexers).

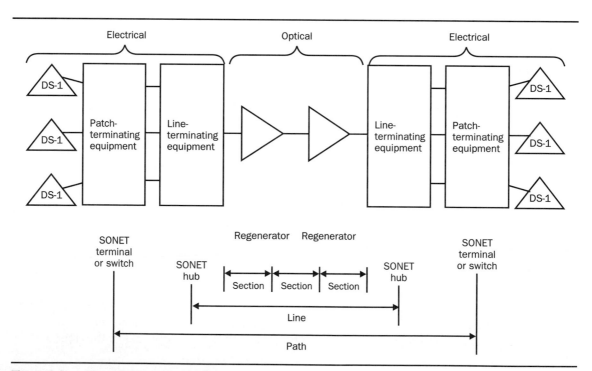

Figure S-8. *The SONET physical layers*

SONET Versus Optical Mesh Networks

SONET networks are scalable and their fault-tolerant features provide fast restoration when links fail. They also provide guaranteed service levels for voice traffic. But SONET is showing its limitations when carrying data traffic. SONET was designed for multiplexed voice streams, not bursty data networks.

New optical core networks employ DWDM technology based on wavelength circuits. A single fiber cable can carry hundreds and potentially thousands of wavelength circuits. In fact, a single wavelength can support the entire traffic load of a SONET fiber. In the new network, IP is transported directly across the DWDM optical network, bypassing ATM and SONET. See "Network Core Technologies" and "Optical Networks" for a continuation of this topic. Also see "NPN (New Public Network)."

Related Entries   ATM (Asynchronous Transfer Mode); B-ISDN (Broadband ISDN); Broadband Communications and Networking; Cable and Wiring; DPT (Dynamic Packet Transport); Fiber-Optic Cable; Internet Architecture and Backbone; MAN (Metropolitan Area Network); Multiplexing and Multiplexers; NADH (North American Digital Hierarchy); Network Access Services; Network Core Technologies; NPN (New Public Network); Optical Networks; PoS (Packet over SONET); T Carriers; TDM Networks: Telecommunications and Telephone Systems; WAN (Wide Area Network); *and* WDM (Wavelength Division Multiplexing)

Linktionary!—Tom Sheldon's Encyclopedia of Networking updates	http://www.linktionary.com/s/sonnet.html
ATIS (Alliance for Telecommunications Industry Solutions)	https://www.atis.org/
Optical Internetworking Forum	http://www.oiforum.com/
Network and Services Integration Forum (NSIF)	http://www.atis.org/atis/sif/sithom.htm
SONET Tutorials at Web ProForum	http://www.iec.org/tutorials/index.html
Nortel SONET white paper (extensive illustrations of a range of SONET networks)	http://www.nortelnetworks.com/products/01/sonet/collateral/sonet_101.pdf
Lucent's Optical Networking page (extensive links)	http://www.lucent-optical.com/resources/
KMI Corporation (fiber-optic market research)	http://www.kmicorp.com/
SONET Pocket Guide by Wandel & Goltermann	http://download.wg.com/brochures/sonet.pdf
Cisco's Packet over SONET/SDH White paper	http://www.cisco.com/warp/public/cc/pd/rt/12000/tech/posdh_wp.htm
SONET/SDH Links at TechFest	http://www.techfest.com/networking/wan.htm
LightRiver Technologies	http://www.sonet.com/
About.com (search for "SONET")	http://compnetworking.about.com/compute/compnetworking/
Bitpipe.com (search for "SONET")	http://www.bitpipe.com/

S

Source Routing

Source routing is a way of moving a packet through a network in which the path is predetermined by the source or some device that tells the source about the path. The path information is placed in the packet. When the packet arrives at a switching device, no forwarding decision is necessary. The device looks at the path information in the packet to determine the port on which it should forward the packet. This is the opposite of hop-by-hop IP routing, where packets contain only the destination address and routers at each junction in the network determine how best to forward the packet.

With source routing, the end systems are smart and the network does simple layer 2 switching. With network routing, the intelligence is in the network and the end systems do not get involved in the routing process. Both have merit. The Internet has become a success because routers take care of learning the network topology and making forwarding decisions. This simplifies host connections. On the other hand, performance can be improved by setting up routes in advance and doing "fast switching" in the network.

Source routing assumes that the source knows about the topology of the network, and can therefore specify a path. However, it is not always possible to expect end-user's systems to learn a network's topology. This gets more difficult as the network grows, and is nearly impossible on the Internet where different provider networks are joined together. From a security point of view, it is unwise to allow the sender to control the path of packets through the network.

Explicit routing is similar to source routing, except that the source gets a predefined path from a third-party device that has determined routes or had them configured by an administrator. MPLS (Multiprotocol Label Switching) supports explicit routing.

IBM Token Ring networks use a *source-routing* scheme that can provide network devices with information about where packets should go and how to get there. In source routing, the packets themselves hold the forwarding information. While this sounds like routing, the source-routing bridge is simply a forwarding device that knows the addresses of other bridges.

Related Entries   Cut-Through Routing; MPLS (Multiprotocol Label Switching); Multilayer Switching; Routing; Switching and Switched Networks; Token Ring Network; Traffic Management, Shaping, and Engineering; *and* VPN (Virtual Private Network)

Linktionary!—Tom Sheldon's Encyclopedia of Networking updates	http://www.linktionary.com/s/source_routing.html
Cisco Documentation: Designing SRB Internetworks	http://www.cisco.com/univercd/cc/td/doc/cisintwk/idg4/nd2004.htm#xtocid263530

Spanning Tree Algorithm

Spanning tree algorithms are executed between bridges in layer 2 networks to find redundant paths in the network and block the paths. See "Bridges and Bridging".

SPIRITS (Service in the PSTN/IN Requesting InTernet Service)

The IETF called "Working Group" Service in the PSTN/IN Requesting InTernet Service (spirits) Working Group is addressing how services supported by IP network entities can be started from

IN (Intelligent Network) requests, as well as the protocol arrangements through which PSTN (Public-Switched Telephone Network) can request actions to be carried out in the IP network—in other words, how PSTN can execute telephony services on IP networks.

Some examples covered by SPIRITS include Internet call waiting, Internet caller-ID delivery, and Internet call forwarding. RFC 2995 (Pre-SPIRITS Implementations of PSTN-Initiated Services, November 2000) describes an Internet call-waiting service that allows subscribers to use their telephone lines for Internet access and also be notified of incoming voice calls.

Related Entries   Convergence; IN (Intelligent Network); Megaco; MGCP (Media Gateway Control Protocol); Multimedia; NPN (New Public Network); PINT (PSTN-Internet Interworking); SAP (Session Announcement Protocol); SCTP (Stream Control Transmission Protocol); SDP (Session Description Protocol); Signaling for Call Control; SS7 (Signaling System 7); Telecommunications and Telephone Systems; TRIP (Telephony Routing over IP); Unified Messaging; Videoconferencing; Voice/Data Networks; *and* Voice over IP (VoIP)

Linktionary!—Tom Sheldon's Encyclopedia of Networking updates	http://www.linktionary.com/s/spirits.html
IETF Working Group: PSTN and Internet Internetworking (pint)	http://www.ietf.org/html.charters/spirits-charter.html

Spread Spectrum Signaling

Wireless mobile communications and wireless LANs can use a variety of schemes to transmit analog or digital information between base stations and users. One method is to transmit at a specific frequency, much like a radio station transmits at a frequency that you dial on your radio. For example, the AMPS mobile cellular telephone system operates in the 824-MHz to 894-MHz frequency range. This range is divided into a pool of 832 full-duplex channel pairs (one sends, one receives). Calls are made over the channels.

The only problem with this scheme is that anyone with an appropriate radio receiver can listen in on a target frequency. The other problem is that the frequency occupies a narrow band that is susceptible to interference, either accidental or malicious. Spread spectrum is a technique of spreading a signal out over a very wide bandwidth, often over 200 times the bandwidth of the original signal.

Spread spectrum technology was first used in World War II as a way to provide jamproof radio communication for guided torpedoes. A spread spectrum transmitter spreads the signals out over a wide frequency range using one of the following techniques:

- **Direct sequence spread spectrum**   In this scheme, the data to transmit is altered by a bit stream that is generated by the sender. The bit stream represents every bit in the original data with multiple bits in the generated stream, thus spreading the signal across a wider frequency band. If 100 bits are used to represent each bit of data, the signal is spread out to 100 times its original bandwidth. The source generates a pseudorandom bit stream to modulate the original data and the destination generates the same bit stream to demodulate what it receives. Spread spectrum broadcasts in bands where noise is prominent, but does not rise above the noise. Its radio signals are too weak to interfere with conventional radios and have fewer FCC (Federal Communications Commission) restrictions.

- **Frequency hopping spread spectrum**   In this technique, the original data signal is not spread out, but is instead transmitted over a wide range of frequencies that change at split-second intervals. Both the transmitter and the receiver jump frequencies in synchronization during the transmission so a jammer would have difficulty targeting the exact frequency on which the devices are communicating. The frequencies are derived from a table that both the sender and receiver follow.

CDMA (Code Division Multiple Access) is a digital cellular standard that uses wideband spread spectrum techniques for signal transmission. CDMA is employed in cellular phone systems and has become the top choice for new high-bandwidth 3G (third-generation) phones because of its spectral efficiency. CDMA is also used in wired systems such as shared cable access networks so that the shared spectrum is used more efficiently.

Related Entries   CDMA (Code Division Multiple Access); Electromagnetic Spectrum; Wireless Broadband Access Technologies; Wireless Communications; Wireless LANs; *and* Wireless Mobile Communications

Linktionary!—Tom Sheldon's Encyclopedia of Networking updates	http://www.linktionary.com/s/spread_spectrum.html
Spread Spectrum Scene Online	http://sss-mag.com
Wireless Nets Consulting Services	http://www.wireless-nets.com/whitepaper_spread.htm
Amateur Radio Spread Spectrum	http://www.tapr.org/tapr/html/ssf.html

SPX (Sequenced Packet Exchange)

See IPX/SPX (Internetwork Packet Exchange/Sequenced Packet Exchange).

SQL (Structured Query Language)

SQL, pronounced "see-quel," was originally developed by IBM in the mid-1970s as a database query language to operate on the VM/370 and MVS/370 operating systems. It was later commercialized by Oracle Corporation, after which many other companies jumped on the bandwagon. Today, SQL is viewed as an interface to access data on many different types of database systems, including mainframes, midrange systems, UNIX systems, and network servers.

In the 1980s, the process of standardizing the language was initiated by ISO (International Organization for Standardization), the ANSI (American National Standards Institute), and X/Open (now part of The Open Group). Standardization is an ongoing process, and the latest implementation, called SQL3, was being standardized at the time of this writing. SQL3 includes object-oriented technology. For historical reference, SQL2 was standardized in 1992 and is commonly referred to as SQL-92. More information about ongoing standardization can be found at the SQL Standards home page listed at the end of this topic.

In the client/server environment, the user's front-end application interfaces to a DBMS (database management system) engine running on a back-end server. The interface between the front end and the back end is a specific API (application programming interface). While SQL provided a standard for accessing databases, there were differences in the way each system was implemented. Database systems have traditionally been tied to a specific front-end interface that did not work with just any client-side application. One of the following programming interfaces is usually implemented:

- **Embedded SQL** In this approach, SQL statements are embedded into the source code of programs that are written in a host language such as C. A typical embedded SQL program contains a number of SQL statements, but these statements cannot be directly compiled into C, so they are precompiled to make them compatible with the host language and the program is then compiled for execution. The program can then operate directly with the database because the SQL statements are embedded in it.

- **CLI (Call-Level Interface)** With this approach, programs must call a set of external functions in an API library in order to work with the database. CLI is normally used when the client and server are on two different systems and the API is located on the client system. The client application makes a call to the API, and the API communicates with the DBMS.

More recently, so-called "middleware" products have emerged that operate between the client and server to allow users to access any back-end server using a variety of front-end applications. They hide the differences between access languages and database APIs.

Refer to "DBMS (Database Management System)" for a more complete discussion of database technologies, and associated connectivity and middleware technologies.

Related Entries Client/Server Computing; Data Management; Data Mart; Data Migration; Data Mining; Data Protection; Data Warehousing; DB2; IBM; DBMS (Database Management System); Distributed Computer Networks; DRDA (Distributed Relational Database Architecture); Metadata; Middleware and Messaging; Multitiered Architectures; ODBC (Open Database Connectivity); OLAP (Online Analytical Processing); OLE DB; Replication; Repository; SAN (Storage Area Network); Transaction Processing; *and* Z39.50

Linktionary!—Tom Sheldon's Encyclopedia of Networking updates	http://www.linktionary.com/s/sql.html
SQL Standards home page	http://www.jcc.com/SQLPages/jccs_sql.htm
SQL Access Group	http://www.opengroup.org
Washington University Information Systems Meta-List	http://www.cait.wustl.edu/infosys/infosys.html
"SQL for Web Nerds" by Philip Greenspun	http://www.arsdigita.com/books/sql/

SS7 (Signaling System 7)

SS7 is an out-of-band signaling system used by the carriers to set up telephone calls. It is a protocol standard defined by the ITU. Network elements in the public-switched telephone network use SS7 to exchange information used not only to set up calls but to control the network. Part of SS7's call setup process is to create a circuit for the call through the telephone network and then place the call on the circuit.

SS7 is a message-based system that operates on a network that is separate from the digital lines that carry calls. This differs from early telephone signaling systems in which signals were transmitted as multifrequency tones in the same channels as calls. In addition, SS7 enables advanced services that were not possible in the older system, such as toll-free numbers, caller ID, call forwarding, call waiting, and local number portability.

SS7 messages sent between telephony switches set up and terminate calls and indicate the status of terminals involved in calls. These signals are carried over a *separate data network* known as CCS (Common Channel Signaling). The protocol used by CCS is SS7 (Signaling System 7). The entire system is called the IN (Intelligent Network). See "Telecommunications and Telephone System" for a more detailed explanation.

The PSTN was designed for one thing: voice communications. It consists of interconnected networks of voice switches located at COs (central offices) and telephone exchanges. Terminals (phones and faxes) are attached to these points via access connections (the local loop). Networks owned by different carriers are interconnected to form the global telephone network.

The network consists of a transport plane that contains telephone switching nodes called SSPs (service switching points). Above this is the SS7 signaling plane. SS7 can be described as an "overlay network," meaning that its service logic is decoupled from the switching nodes. SS7 messages are transmitted in the upper-layer signaling plane, but the messages are directed at telecom equipment in the lower SSP plane. Another part of this system is the SCP (service control point), which is a database server where service control information is hosted. Telecom equipment uses SS7 to query SCPs about how to handle calls.

A typical service of the "intelligent" network is SRF (special resource function), which plays recorded messages and prompts users to respond with inputs from the telephone keypad. Captured digits can be passed on to the SCP, which may use them in its query of the service database. Calling card services use this feature.

SS7 has been getting a lot of attention as interest in VoIP (Voice over IP) grows. One thing that is needed in the VoIP environment is a way to transport SS7 messages over IP networks or to transfer call-setup requests from IP users into the PSTN. See "Voice over IP (VoIP)."

Related Entries   Circuit-Switching Services; Convergence; IN (Intelligent Network); Local Loop; Megaco; MGCP (Media Gateway Control Protocol); Multimedia; NPN (New Public Network); PINT (PSTN-Internet Interworking); PSTN (Public Switched Telephone Network); SAP (Session Announcement Protocol); SCTP (Stream Control Transmission Protocol); SDP (Session Description Protocol); Signaling for Call Control; Telecommunications and Telephone Systems; Voice/Data Networks; *and* Voice over IP (VoIP)

Linktionary!—Tom Sheldon's Encyclopedia of Networking updates	http://www.linktionary.com/s/ss7.html
IETF Working Group: Signaling Transport (sigtran)	http://www.ietf.org/html.charters/sigtran-charter.html
Web ProForums (see several SS7 topics)	http://www.iec.org/tutorials/index.html
Performance Technologies SS7 Tutorial (see Learning Center)	http://www.microlegend.com/

Protocols.com Web page about the SS7 Suite	http://www.protocols.com/protoc.shtml
SS7 Overview at TechFest	http://www.techfest.com/networking/
Lucent white paper: SS7 Solutions for Internet Access	http://www.livingston.com/marketing/whitepapers/
RAD Data Communications SS7 tutorial	http://www.rad.com/networks/tutorial.htm

SSA (Serial Storage Architecture)

SSA is a high-performance serial interface that is commonly used to connect peripheral devices like disk drives, optical disks, printers, and scanners to computer workstations and servers. It can handle up to two 20-MB/sec transmissions at the same time (in opposite directions) on a single port. A typical interface has two ports, so an SSA system has a total bandwidth of 80 MB/sec.

SSA was originally developed by IBM, but it was further developed by the ANSI (American National Standards Institute) subcommittee called X3T10.1. SSA is also specified as a physical layer serial interface in the SCSI-3 standard. Although SCSI designers have achieved high data rates with parallel SCSI, serial designs such as SSA are considered critical for high-data-rate performance and to boost cabling distances to devices.

An SSA connection consists of a shielded four-wire cable (two pairs). The distance between the host and a peripheral can be up to 25 meters (82 feet). At this writing, the longest SCSI cable distance was 25 meters (with 32 meters planned in the future). Devices can be configured in daisy-chain fashion or connected to switch boxes in a star configuration. A loop configuration is also available to provide a fault-tolerant cabling path that has no single point of failure.

Related Entries   Fibre Channel; Firewire; Network Connection Technologies; SCSI (Small Computer System Interface); Serial Communication and Interfaces; *and* Storage Systems

SSH (Secure Shell)

SSH is a "secure shell," which means it provides encrypted "virtual" terminal (Telnet) and file transfer sessions. It also supports authenticated remote logon. It is designed to replace UNIX commands such as **rlogin**, **rsh**, and **rcp**, which have been found to be vulnerable to attacks. SSH provides the mechanisms that allow clients and servers to negotiate secure connections. SSH can create secure remote X sessions for X Window System users.

The protocol was originally developed by Tatu Ylönen, who went on to start SSH Communications Security, now the primary supporter of SSH products. Other vendors, such as F-Secure and Van Dyke Corporation, implement SSH in their security products. SSH is available for Microsoft Windows, UNIX platforms, and other platforms.

SSH provides confidentiality through the support of encryption techniques such as DES, Triple-DES, IDEA, BlowFish, TwoFish, and CAST. Authentication and integrity is provided by passwords or public keys (DSA and RSA), or via Kerberos. Smart cards and token-based authentication are also supported.

Multiple SSH connections can be cascaded so an authenticated user can make secure connections to multiple hosts on a network through the same tunnel. Thus, a remote user can connect to a corporate network and access e-mail, file servers, and other services.

Two versions exist: SSH1 and SSH2. According to SSH Communication Security, SSH1 should be replaced with SSH2 to achieve improved flexibility, better scalability to organizations with

S

thousands of users, and better security. Information about SSH2 is available at the company's Web site given later.

The IETF's secsh (Secure Shell) Working Group was working on SSH and SSH2, but the drafts that were developed are no longer up on the Web site and no RFCs have come out of this group.

Related Entries   Authentication and Authorization; Cryptography; Digital Signatures; DSS (Digital Signature Standard); Kerberos Authentication Protocol; Public-Key Cryptography; RSA; Security; S-HTTP (Secure Hypertext Transfer Protocol); SSL (Secure Sockets Layer); *and* TLS (Transport Layer Security)

IETF Working Group: Secure Shell (secsh)	http://www.ietf.org/html.charters/secsh-charter.html
SSH Communications Security	http://www.ssh.org/
F-Secure Corporation SSH products	http://www.europe.f-secure.com/
Van Dyke Corporation SSH1/SSH2 software	http://www.vandyke.com/

SSL (Secure Sockets Layer)

SSL is a Web protocol for establishing authenticated and encrypted sessions between Web servers and Web clients. SSL starts with a handshake routine that first establishes a TCP/IP connection. Next, the server is authenticated to the client by verifying its public key. Once authenticated, the server selects the strongest cryptographic algorithm supported by both the client and server and within the restrictions enforced by a particular country. Next, a shared secret key is generated that is used to encrypt all data flowing between the client and server. Finally, an encrypted SSL connection is established.

As mentioned, all the information that is sent between client and server is encrypted, including all HTTP requests and responses, as well as the URL being requested by clients. This level of encryption ensures the protection of sensitive information such as credit card numbers, access authorization information (user names), and sensitive data returned by the server.

Because encryption is computationally intensive, SSL sessions are usually only employed when transmitting sensitive information. A typical session goes like this:

1. A user decides to buy something online and clicks a hyperlink called "Buy online through our secure server."

2. The hyperlink establishes an SSL connection. An SSL connection is indicated in the Browser Address field with a URL that starts with "https" instead of "http."

3. Once the transaction is complete, the user clicks another hyperlink to return to the normal HTTP mode and the encrypted SSL session is terminated.

This jumping in and out of secure mode is required to prevent unnecessary encryption of data that reduces performance. However, a user can choose to connect with any SSL-compliant site and obtain full SSL security by typing **https** in the Address field when entering the URL for the site. The "s" in the URL tells the client and server to initiate SSL and connect with an SSL port.

SSL is used by a variety of applications to establish secure connections. For example, the IETF's directory services standard, LDAP (Lightweight Directory Access Protocol), uses SSL to establish secure connections between clients. Other applications may use SSL as well. A typical Web site is configured with SSL ports and non-SSL ports. SSL uses port 443 by default, although other ports can be configured. Other SSL ports include port 465 (SSL SMTP mail send), port 995 (SSL POP3 mail retrieve), 563 (SSL USENET), and 636 (SSL LDAP).

SSL History and Versions

SSL was originally developed by Netscape, then submitted to the IETF (Internet Engineering Task Force) for standardization. There are several versions of SSL, and two look-alike protocols. Microsoft considered the original SSL protocol to be lacking in some security features, so it created PCT (Private Communication Technology). Later, Netscape and others created SSL 3.0 to include the features Microsoft added. Now SSL 3.0 is the most common protocol, although Microsoft still supports PCT. A related protocol that is not as popular as SSL is S-HTTP (Secure HTTP), which is discussed elsewhere.

The IETF sought to standardize SSL, but did not like its use of the RSA Security's proprietary cryptographic technology; so it began work on TLS (Transport Layer Security), which uses Diffie-Hellman public-key cryptography. TLS is basically SSL 3.0, but only the transport layer is secured. Higher-layer protocols can run on top of TLS, but do not benefit from its security. TLS is outlined in RFC 2246 and discussed elsewhere. See "TLS (Transport Layer Security)."

Netscape produced a reference version of SSL called SSLRef that is available free. SSLeay is a free implementation of SSL that implements SSL versions 2 and 3, as well as TLS version 1. SSLeay was developed by Tim J. Hudson. The latest incarnation of his work is OpenSSL. Information about all of these implementations is available at the OpenSSL Web site given later.

The U.S. government now allows 128-bit encryption for use in browsers, allowing a high level of security for banking and financial transactions. Products like Microsoft's SGC (Server Gated Cryptography), an extension of SSL, support this higher level of encryption. Other transaction security protocols exist, such as SET (Secure Electronic Transaction), that provide higher levels of security for business transactions.

When Netscape originally designed SSL, it was meant to secure credit card transactions over the Internet, but the protocol became popular for securing Web connections in general. Still, SSL has some limitations, and other protocols are more practical for building corporate connections and extranets. Tunneling protocols such as PPTP and L2TP are more practical for building dial-up connections for remote users or site-to-site connections. The IETF's new IPSec protocol is especially useful for building secure tunnels across the Internet or intranets, particularly since it can encrypt and encapsulate entire packets, thus hiding all information from eavesdroppers. See "IPSec (IP Security)" for more information.

A typical configuration might consist of Web clients accessing Web servers using SSL and the Web servers accessing back-end databases and application servers using IPSec.

SSL Features and Benefits

SSL benefits electronic commerce and other Web communications by protecting data in transit from eavesdroppers and tampering. With SSL, browsers and servers can *authenticate* one another, then *encrypt* data transmitted during a session.

SSL (and PCT) provide the following services:

■ **Authentication** Clients can verify that a server is authentic (and not a fake) by checking the server's certificate and verifying it with the public key of the certifying

S

authority that issued the certificate. The server can authenticate the client in the same way if the client has a certificate (this is optional in SSL).

- **Confidentiality** A session key is created that both client and server use to encrypt exchanged data.

- **Integrity** Messages may be individually signed (using hash routines) to ensure that they are authentic and have not been altered during transit. The hash creates a unique message digest that is sent with transmitted data and verified by the receiver. Signing also prevents the sender from repudiating the message (denying having sent it).

SSL and Certificates

SSL relies on *digital certificates,* which combine a public key with the credentials of the person, company, or server to which that key belongs. *Certification authorities (CAs)* issue certificates, signing them with their own private keys so that certificates may be authenticated. Refer to "Certificates and Certification Systems," "Digital Signatures," and "Public-Key Cryptography" for more details.

SSL requires that Web servers have certificates. When a user connects to the Web server, the server sends the user its certificate. The user can verify that the certificate is authentic (this is usually handled automatically in the background). Once verified, the public key in the certificate is used to encrypt messages that only the server can decrypt with its private key.

Note that a certificate is "bound" to a Web site. In other words, the certificate says that it works only at a particular IP address (or range of addresses). The idea is that the client must know they are connected to an authentic Web site and not a spoof of that site. The certificate binds a public key with a named entity. This same certificate can be bound to a particular Web site, so if someone steals the certificate and tries to set up a new Web site, that Web site must have an IP address that is already assigned to the real site—and an error would occur if the hacker attempted to do so.

Microsoft Windows 2000 supports SSL public-key certificate authentication. Certificates may be conveniently stored in Microsoft's Active Directory by mapping certificates to existing accounts. After a user has been identified via their certificate and public key, the server still needs to determine the client's access rights on the system. This can come from the Active Directory, but may also be defined in the client's certificate as a mapping that determines authorization to resources.

SSL Cryptographic Support

When the client and the server first connect, they negotiate which type and level of cryptographic technology to use. Because the strength of cryptography is restricted in some countries, the server will choose the highest level of cryptography that is supported by both client and server.

SSL separates encryption, authentication, and data integrity algorithms so that different algorithms may be used for different applications and in different environments. For example, long keys may be used for authentication while short keys are used for encryption (longer keys require more processing). In addition, use of long keys is regulated in some countries.

SSL supports the DES (Data Encryption Standard), Triple-DES, DSA (Digital Signature Algorithm), RSA Security RC2 and RC4, MD5 (Message Digest 5), SHA-1 (Secure Hash Algorithm-1), and SKIPJACK. These are discussed further under "Crytography."

SSL 3.0 Handshake and Connection Routine

There are two subprotocols in the SSL suite. These are the *handshake protocol* (SSL Handshake Protocol or SSLHP) and the *record protocol* (SSL Record Protocol or SSLRP). SSLRP defines the message formats for exchanging data and performs the job of packaging data and applying a MAC (message authentication code). SSLHP defines the dynamic exchange of messages between client and server. During the handshake, the server is authenticated to the client, a cryptographic algorithm is selected, the client is optionally authenticated to the server, shared session keys are generated, and an encrypted SSL connection is established.

The handshake starts when a client connects with a server, as shown in Figure S-9. The server's certificate and public key are used for the initial authentication. After authentication, a symmetric one-time session key is created that both client and server will use to encrypt all subsequent data. Symmetric algorithms are used because their encryption/decryption performance is much faster than public/private-key encryption.

Note   *These steps assume only the client needs to authenticate the server. If the server also needs to authenticate the client, the client must have a certificate and send it to the server in step 5.*

1. Client: "Hello server. I want to use SSL. Here's my SSL version number, some randomly generated data, my cipher settings, and some other useful information."

2. Server: "Hello client. Here's my certificate, SSL version number, some randomly generated data, my cipher settings, and some other useful information. By the way, do you have a certificate?"

3. The client authenticates the server by validating the certificate. The steps to validating a certificate are outlined under the topic "Certificates and Certification Systems." See the section "Validating a Certificate."

4. The client and server are ready to establish a secret session key. The client generates what is called a "premaster secret," then encrypts it with the server's public key and sends it to the server.

5. The server uses its private key to decrypt the premaster secret it received from the client. Now, both the client and the server follow the same steps to create a master secret from the premaster.

6. Both the client and server send a "finished" message to one another to indicate that the negotiation is complete. To create the message, the master key is combined with all the previously sent messages and hashed. If both parties can verify the "finished" messages received from the other, then an SSL connection is established and all subsequent data is securely transmitted using session keys derived from the master key.

S

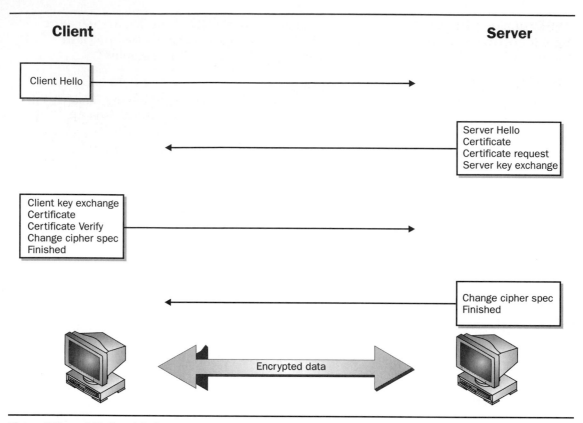

Figure S-9. *SSL Handshake*

Related Entries   Certificates and Certification Systems; Cryptography; Digital Signatures; Electronic Commerce; Hash Functions; PKI (Public-Key Infrastructure); Public-Key Cryptography; Security; SET (Secure Electronic Transaction); S-HTTP (Secure Hypertext Transfer Protocol); TLS (Transport Layer Security); VPN (Virtual Private Network); Web Technologies and Concepts; *and* X.509 Certificates

Linktionary!—Tom Sheldon's Encyclopedia of Networking updates	http://www.linktionary.com/s/ssl.html
IETF Transport Layer Security (tls) Working Group	http://www.ietf.org/html.charters/tls-charter.html
IETF Web Transaction Security (wts) Working Group (information about S-HTTP)	http://www.ietf.org/html.charters/wts-charter.html
OpenSSL Project	http://www.openssl.org/
Peter Gutman's security links (search for many SSL links)	http://www.cs.auckland.ac.nz/~pgut001/links.html
Analysis of the SSL 3.0 Protocol by Wagner and Schneier	http://www.counterpane.com/ssl.html

SSO (Single Sign-On)

See Authentication and Authorization.

SSP (Storage Service Provider)

An SSP offers managed storage services, which means it provides disk storage space that it leases to companies. The SSP manages terabytes of storage and provides all backup, fault tolerance, high availability, security, fire protection, and 24-hour service for organizations that do not want to manage these services on their own. SSP should not be confused with free Internet storage sites that tailor their services to end users. The managed storage model is the same, but SSPs orient their services to companies that require mission-critical services. See "File Sharing" for more information about user-oriented file sharing services and a list of Web sites that provide those services.

Companies faced with building their own fault-tolerant and highly available network or even SAN (storage area network) may want to contract with an SSP. An SSP can build and manage these systems at the customer site or provide access to their own facilities. If customers choose to lease storage at the SSP point of presence, adequate bandwidth between sites will be essential. This is getting to be less of a problem in metropolitan areas where metro-Ethernet, wireless, and optical networks provide low-cost, high-bandwidth services.

Exodus Communications provides a variety of storage, Web hosting, communications, and other Internet-related services. It manages giant Internet data centers. You can take a virtual tour by going to the Exodus site listed later. StorageNetworks is another SSP that has over 50 points of presence. The more PoPs, the better. If a company has offices in various cities, it can contract with an SSP that has PoPs in those same cities. The SSP can then handle mirroring and data replication of the customer's data to get that data closer to end users. Even if an organizaton manages its own storage, it may choose an SSP to manage storage in remote locations or to manage data that is needed at the "front line" where Web clients access data.

Xdrive Technologies provides storage solutions for individuals, enterprises, and service providers. In particular, it promotes the concept of Web storage to support collaborative applications and groups of remote or mobile users. It provides a private-label Web-based interface that service providers can offer to customers.

Related Entries   ASP (Application Service Provider); Backup and Data Archiving; Co-Location; Data Protection; Data Warehousing; Disaster Planning and Recovery; Fault Tolerance and High Availability; File Sharing; File Systems; ISPs (Internet Service Providers); Mirroring; MSP (Management Service Provider); Network Management; Outsourcing; Peer-to-Peer Communication; Redundancy; Replication; Storage Management System; *and* Storage Systems

Linktionary!—Tom Sheldon's Encyclopedia of Networking updates	http://www.linktionary.com/s/ssp.html
StorageNetworks	http://www.storagenetworks.com/
Managed Storage International	http://www.managedstorage.com/
Centripetal Internet storage utility company	http://www.centripetal.com/
Exodus Communications	http://www.exodus.com/

Xdrive Technologies	http://www.xdrive.com/
Bitpipe (search for "SSP" "and "managed storage")	http://www.bitpipe.com/
searchStorage.com (search for "managed storage")	http://searchstorage.techtarget.com/
Google Web Directory: storage and storage services page	http://directory.google.com/Top/Computers/Hardware/Storage/

Standards Groups, Associations, and Organizations

The primary groups, standards, and organizations related to networking and the Internet are listed in the following table. Refer to the related headings in this book for more information. A complete list of standards organizations, associations, consortiums, and other groups would fill a whole book. Therefore, this section provides links to sites on the Web that have links to standards groups, organizations, and associations. Also refer to "Internet," "Internet Standards," and "Internet Organizations and Committees" for information about Internet-related organizations and standards.

ACM (Association of Computing Machinery), a great information site	http://www.acm.org/
ANSI (American National Standards Institute)	http://www.ansi.org
Committee T1	http://www.t1.org/
EIA (Electronic Industries Association)	http://www.eia.org
ETSI (European Telecommunications Standards Institute)	http://www.etsi.org/
FCC (Federal Communications Commission), a great site for radio and wireless information	http://www.fcc.gov/
IAB (Internet Architecture Board)	http://www.iab.org/iab/
IANA (Internet Assigned Numbers Authority)	http://www.iana.org/
ICANN (Internet Corporation for Assigned Names and Numbers)	http://www.icann.org/
IEC (International Electrotechnical Commission)	http://www.iec.ch/
IEEE (Institute of Electrical and Electronic Engineers), Inc.	http://www.ieee.org/
IETF (The Internet Engineering Task Force)	http://www.ietf.org/
Information Technology Association of America	http://www.itaa.org/
Internet Society	http://www.isoc.org/
IRTF (Internet Research Task Force)	http://www.irtf.org/
ISO (International Organization for Standardization)	http://www.iso.ch
ITU (International Telecommunications Union)	http://www.itu.ch
NSF (National Science Foundation)	http://www.nsf.gov/
The Open Group	http://www.opengroup.org/
TIA (Telecommunications Industry Association)	http://www.tiaonline.org/
W3C (World Wide Web Consortium)	http://www.w3c.org

Related Entries   ANSI (American National Standards Institute); IEEE 802 Standards; Internet Organizations and Committees; Internet Protocol Suite; Internet Standards; ISO (International Organization for Standardization); ITU (International Telecommunications Union); OSI (Open Systems Interconnection) Model; Telecommunications and Telephone Systems; *and* TIA (Telecommunications Industry Association)

Linktionary!—Tom Sheldon's Encyclopedia of Networking updates	http://www.linktionary.com/s/standards.html
Linktionary!—Tom Sheldon's Encyclopedia of Networking updates	http://www.linktionary.com/i/internet_standards.html
Open Information Interchange standards bodies list	http://158.169.50.95:10080/oii/en/fora.html
Google Web Directory: Standards page	http://directory.google.com/Top/Computers/Hardware/Standards/
Telecoms Virtual Library (complete subject list with subpages of links)	http://www.analysys.com/vlib/
Prof. Jeffrey MacKie-Mason's links (see various categories for associations, standards bodies, and telecom policies)	http://china.si.umich.edu/telecom/telecom-info.html
C&C Standards page	http://www.cmpcmm.com/cc/standards.html
RAD Data Communications (see Standards)	http://www.rad.com/networks/tutorial.htm
Protocol.com list of standards organizations and forums	http://www.protocols.com/hot.htm
ACM (Association of Computing Machinery) special interest groups	http://www.acm.org/sigs/
Networking Standards list at TechFest	http://www.techfest.com/networking/standard.htm

STAR TAP

STAR TAP (Science, Technology, and Research Transit Access Point) is an advanced networking infrastructure and test bed funded by the NSF Advanced Networking Infrastructure and Research division. It facilitates interconnection and interoperability of advanced international networking in support of applications, performance measuring, and technology evaluations. The STAR TAP anchors the international vBNS connections program. It is a peering location for international research organizations and networks, including vBNS, Abilene (Internet2); Esnet (U.S. Department of Energy), DREN (U.S. Department of Defense), NREN (NASA), and CERN. A number of international networks are also connected to STAR TAP.

Physically, STAR TAP connects with the Ameritech network access point (NAP) in Chicago, as does the vBNS and other high-speed research networks. It enables traffic to flow to international collaborators from over 100 U.S. leading-edge research universities and supercomputer centers that are now, or will be, attached to the vBNS or other high-performance U.S. research networks.

STAR TAP's connectivity supports international collaboration among researchers around the globe. The network is used to test emerging network applications such as real-time

S

applications, streaming video, simulations, broadband services, remote device control, and large distributed processing applications.

Related Entries   Abilene; Active Networks; GII (Global Information Infrastructure); Internet; Internet2; Internet Architecture and Backbone; Internet Organizations and Committees; NAP (Network Access Point); NII (National Information Infrastructure); NIST (National Institute of Standards and Technology); NPN (New Public Network); NREN (National Research and Education Network); Peering; POP (Point of Presence); Registries on the Internet; Routing; Routing on the Internet; Routing Registries; Supercomputer; *and* vBNS (Very high speed Backbone Network Service)

   STAR TAP Web site   http://www.startap.net/

Stateful Inspection Technology

Stateful inspection is a firewall technology developed by Check Point Software and implemented in its FireWall-1 product. Stateful inspection actively tracks all TCP and UDP connections during their life. When a packet arrives from outside the firewall, it must belong to a TCP or UDP connection that is being tracked. If not, the packet is dropped. See "Firewall."

Stateful and Stateless Connections

Keeping *state* or being *stateful* means that some device is keeping track of another device or a connection, either temporarily or over a long period of time. When I put someone's name in my address book and note their birthday and phone number, one could say that I am maintaining state for that person. On the Web, a cookie is a stateful mechanism that allows Web servers to keep track of information about people, as described in a moment.

A *stateful connection* is one in which some information about a connection between two systems is retained for future use. In some cases, the connection is kept open even though the two systems might not be transmitting information (i.e., the connection itself retains state).

In contrast, a *stateless connection* is one in which no information is retained by either sender or receiver. The sender transmits a packet to the receiver and does not expect an acknowledgment of receipt. The recipient receives the packet without any prior connection setup.

A TCP connection-oriented session is a stateful connection because both systems maintain information about the session itself during its life. For example, the receiving computer keeps track of packets received and their sequence, and the sender. It periodically sends an acknowledgment to the sender that it has received a group of packets. IP is a stateless connection protocol. Network routers do not keep track of packet flows in a way that might improve packet delivery, although new protocols are making this possible.

In the case of a Web server, a client connects with the server and downloads some pages. The client and server then disconnect and the server does not maintain any information in its cache about the client that could be used for the next connection, which comes if the client clicks a hyperlink on the page. A new connection must be set up to handle that action.

Stateless systems are efficient if users tend to make few and infrequent requests from servers. However, stateless systems are inefficient if the client needs to make a large number of requests from the same server. Each request requires a setup phase that requires time and the exchange of packets that add traffic to the network. Sophisticated client/server applications require connection-oriented sessions in which the server caches information about the client during the session. This is especially true in transaction-processing systems where information on both the client and server system must be written in synchronization and verified.

RFC 2616 (HTTP/1.1, June 1999) describes the latest version of HTTP. One of its most important features is the ability to maintain persistent connections. In the older HTTP, each object on the page (graphic images, for example) required its own connection setup for transfer to the host. With HTTP/1.1, the client and server maintain a connection to exchange all of the objects on a page and then the connection is closed. However, HTTP/1.1 is still considered stateless, meaning that the server does not store any information about the client during the connection.

HTTP state management is discussed in RFC 2964 (Use of HTTP State Management, October 2000) and RFC 2965 (HTTP State Management Mechanism, October 2000) discusses specify ways to create a stateful session with "cookies." A cookie is a small file, stored on a client system by a server that contains data to be used during future sessions with the server. See "Cookies."

RFC 2140 (TCP Control Block Interdependence, April 1997) discusses sharing TCP state among similar concurrent connections or across similar connection instances.

Related Entries   Client/Server Computing; Cookies; DBMS (Database Management System); File Systems; HTTP (Hypertext Transfer Protocol); IP (Internet Protocol); *and* Web Technologies and Concepts

Linktionary!—Tom Sheldon's Encyclopedia of Networking updates	http://www.linktionary.com/s/state.html
Cookie Central	http://www.cookiecentral.com/

Stateless and Call-Back Filing Systems

Shared file systems must deal with multiple versions of files. For example, if two people request a file and make changes to it at the same time, three versions of the file exist—one per user and the original at the server. One solution is to lock a file so that only one person can edit it at a time. There are two synchronization methods that can also be used:

- **Stateless systems**   The server doesn't track files sent to clients. Clients must keep track of changes made to the original on the server. NFS is a stateless system.

- **Call back systems**   In this method, the server maintains state information about files by tracking who has the files and the changes made. The server uses a *call back promise* technique to inform clients when another client has changed a file.

AFS (Andrew File System) and CIFS (Common Internet File System) are call back systems. As clients change files, other clients holding copies of the files are called back and notified of changes. See "File Systems."

Static Routing

An internetwork is a collection of networks joined by routers. Paths through the network must be found and made available to the router so it knows the best path on which to forward a packet to its destination. *Static routing* is the process a network administrator does to manually configure network routes. The alternative is dynamic routing. If the internetwork is small, static routing may be the best approach; but if it is large, dynamic routing is preferred. Note that in a dynamic routing environment, some paths may be manually configured to control the routing environment.

Dynamic routing requires routing algorithms. Dynamic routing protocols assist in the automatic creation of routing tables. Network topologies are subject to change at any time. A link may fail unexpectedly, or a new link may be added. A dynamic routing protocol must discover these changes, automatically adjust its routing tables, and inform other routers of the changes.

Most routers support both static and dynamic routing.

Related Entries   Routers; Routing; *and* VRRP (Virtual Router Redundancy Protocol)

Storage Management Systems

Storage management systems consist of data storage devices and storage management software that provide online and near-line access to data, as well as archival storage of data. A typical system consists of online hard disk storage, writable optical disks, and tape backup systems. As data on hard drives becomes old or falls into disuse, it is transferred to near-line optical disk storage where it is still readily available if necessary. After a certain time, near-line data that is no longer used may be transferred to tape backup systems and archived. Because data is moved to a hierarchy of devices, these systems are usually called HSM (hierarchical storage management) systems.

Note that HSM systems that send data to slower tape and optical systems have fallen out of favor due to price declines in magnetic storage. It now makes sense to build large storage systems, including RAID systems, and keep everything online. In addition, many enterprise, are taking advantage of managed storage services offered by SSPs (storage service providers). See "SSP (Storage Service Provider)" and "Outsourcing."

An extended version of this topic is at the Linktionary! Web site.

Related Entries   Clustering; Data Center Design; Data Migration; Data Protection; Disaster Planning and Recovery; Fault Management; Fault Tolerance and High Availability; Jukebox Optical Storage Devices; Redundancy; Replication; SSP (Storage Service Provider); *and* Storage Systems

Linktionary!—Tom Sheldon's Encyclopedia of Networking updates	http://www.linktionary.com/s/sms.html
Microsoft Enterprise Class Storage paper	http://www.microsoft.com/windows2000/library/howitworks/fileandprint/storage.asp
IEEE Storage System Standards Working Group	http://www.ssswg.org/
Storage search.com	http://www.storagesearch.com/

Storage over IP (SoIP)

Storage over IP or SoIP is a technology for accessing storage devices over TCP/IP networks. Storage becomes accessible to users directly across the network, and much of the overhead imposed by server and operating system intervention is removed to improve performance. This terminology is a trademark to Nishan Systems. Since the IETF is working to standardize similar storage access technologies, it chose to use the name "IP Storage" for its Working Group and related technology. Refer to "IP Storage" for more information.

Storage Service Provider

See SSP (Storage Service Provider).

Storage Systems

Storage system technologies encompass the full range of data storage techniques, including magnetic disk, tape, and optical storage systems. This topic is discussed at the Linktionary! Web site. There, you will find a description of hard disk technologies and interface techniques, tape technologies and formats, and optical disk technologies. Also refer to the other Web sites listed here.

Related Entries   Backup and Data Archiving; Cache and Caching Techniques; Clustering; DAFS (Direct Access File System); Data Center Design; Data Management; Data Protection; Disaster Planning and Recovery; Fibre Channel; File Systems; IP Storage; Mirroring; NAS (Network Attached Storage); Optical Libraries; RAID (Redundant Arrays of Inexpensive Disks); SAN (Storage Area Network); SCSI (Small Computer System Interface); Servers; SSA (Serial Storage Architecture); *and* Storage Management Systems

Linktionary!—Tom Sheldon's Encyclopedia of Networking updates	http://www.linktionary.com/s/storage.html
Bitpipe (search for "storage")	http://www.bitpipe.com/
Google Web Directory: storage page	http://directory.google.com/Top/Computers/Hardware/Storage/
LaCie hard drive encyclopedia	http://www.lacie.com/scripts/support/encyclopedia1.cfm
Brian A. Berg's Storage Cornucopia	http://www.bswd.com/cornucop.htm
Storage Networking Industry Association	http://www.snia.org/
searchStorage.com	http://searchstorage.techtarget.com/

Store-and-Forward Networking

"Store and forward" is a phrase used in many networking technologies. Packets are stored and forwarded through routers, as discussed under "Routers" and "Routing Protocols and Algorithms." Network applications use store-and-forward messaging when real-time connections are not essential, as discussed under "MOM (Message-Oriented Middleware)." Finally, electronic mail systems use store-and-forward techniques to move e-mail from one user to another across messaging servers, as discussed under "Electronic Mail."

Streaming Transmission

See Multimedia

Striping

See RAID (Redundant Arrays of Inexpensive Disks).

Structured Cabling Standards

Structured wiring or cabling is a preplanned cabling system that is designed with growth and reconfiguration in mind. Structured wiring forms an infrastructure that is usually hierarchical in design with high-speed backbones or interconnects. The backbone or interconnects must be high speed because periphery networks connect to it. Enterprise hubs and switches are at the top of the hierarchy. Departmental or workgroup hubs and switches connect to these. Then entire systems may connect to a data center.

The EIA and the TIA developed a wiring standard for commercial buildings called the *TIA/ EIA 568 Commercial Building Wiring Standard*. This standard provides a uniform wiring system and supports multivendor products and environments. It defines cables, communication connectors, jacks, plugs, adapters, baluns, patch panel systems, and electronic components. It also defines cable distance limitation, topologies, and physical specifications. Thus, a building can be wired without any prior knowledge of the data communication equipment that will use it. The cable plant is easy to manage and faults are easy to isolate.

Related Entries   Backbone Networks; Cable and Wiring; Data Communication Concepts; Network Concepts; Network Design and Construction; Switching and Switched Networks; *and* TIA/EIA Structured Cabling Standards

Web ProForums Structured Cabling System (SCS) Tutorial	http://www.iec.org/tutorials/scs/index.html

Subnetting

See IP (Internet Protocol).

Sun Microsystems

Sun Microsystems, located in Mountain View, California, was founded in 1982 on the premise that "the network is the computer." By the mid-1990s, the company's revenues were in the $6 billion range and it provided a full range of software and hardware products, including operating systems, high-performance workstations, and network equipment. Sun Microsystem's philosophy is based on open, nonproprietary systems. Its technologies are designed to be freely adopted by any manufacturer.

Related Entries   Java; Sun Microsystems Solaris

Sun Microsystems, Inc.	http://www.sun.com
Sun's Java Source page	http://java.sun.com
Sun Microsystems Laboratories	http://www.sunlabs.com/

Sun Microsystems Solaris

The Solaris operating environment is based on industry-standard UNIX System V Release 4. It has been optimized for distributed network environments, and performance enhanced for running database and Web applications. It is designed for multiprocessing (up to 128 CPUs on a single system) and 64-bit computing; and with built-in Solaris Network Cache Accelerator, it optimizes Web server performance. Solaris is Java enabled and includes support for the Java VM (Virtual Machine). The HotJava browser is also included. Centralized administration features allow administrators to control the operating system remotely.

The latest release includes CDE (Common Desktop Environment) as the default desktop. CDE is based on the X Window System Motif desktop and provides a consistent look and feel across UNIX platforms.

The operating system is designed for Web networking (intranets) and enterprise networking. It includes WebNFS, a version of the popular Network File System that is designed for use on the Web and intranets. Network computing features in Solaris include ONC (Open Network Computing) technology—a TCP/IP-based set of services, facilities, and APIs that include file and printer sharing, data exchange, RPC (remote procedure call), and distributed naming services. NIS+ Global Directory Services provides a secure, high-performance, distributed data repository for network and system management information. The operating system also includes DCE (Distributed Computing Environment).

Sun Cluster software increases the availability and capacity of the Solaris Operating Environment by enabling core services, such as devices, file systems, and networks, to operate seamlessly across a cluster.

Solaris runs on SPARC, Intel, and PowerPC platforms. Multiprocessor systems are supported, and Solaris uses symmetrical multiprocessing techniques to take full advantage of these systems. Multithreading is supported, which allows applications to be broken into segments that execute simultaneously on each processor.

Related Entries   Java; Network Operating Systems; Sun Microsystems; *and* WebNFS (Network File System)

 Sun Microsystems' Solaris Web site   http://www.sun.com/solaris/

S

Supercomputer

Supercomputers are the fastest and most expensive computer systems.

Actually, supercomputer specifications keep expanding as processing power increases. In addition, many "off-the-shelf" multiprocessor and parallel-processing systems sold today perform at yesterday's supercomputer speeds. Supercomputers are generally designed for special applications (e.g., predicting weather or modeling of nuclear weapons explosions). They are usually owned by governments, academic institutions, research groups, and companies with special analytical requirements such as Celera Genomics, which mapped the human genome.

An article at ElectronicNews Online (http://www.electronicnews.com/) titled "High-Tech Runs into an Export Control Wall," by Tam Harbert (March 1999) quotes Dan Hoydysh, director of Unisys Corp.'s Washington office, as saying that the U.S. government needs to change how it defines supercomputers and lift its restrictions on current systems. The government now classifies a supercomputer as a system that provides 2,000 MTOP (millions of theoretical operations per second). Hoydysh notes that single Intel Pentium III chips are close to this level. A computer with two Pentium chips exceeds the government classification and is subject to export restrictions.

The Pittsburgh Supercomputing Center is building the most powerful computer in the world with funding from the National Science Foundation. The "terascale" system is being built with Compaq computers. Terascale refers to computational power beyond a teraflop (trillion calculations per second). The system consists of 682 Compaq AlphaServers, each of which contains four Alpha microprocessors built with Compaq computers and is designed for public use. Some applications include analyzing the structure and dynamics of proteins useful in drug design, storm-scale weather forecasting, earthquake modeling, and modeling of global climate change.

According to Cray, Inc., "computational simulation is accepted today as the third element of science, complementing theory and experimentation." Cray was one of the original supercomputer manufacturers. In the early 1990s, Digital Equipment (now owned by Compaq) managed to put the Cray supercomputer design onto a single Alpha processor. Recently, a new Cray has emerged to develop supercomputing systems for science and new product development. Cray systems have powered major breakthroughs in computational physics, chemistry, engineering, environmental science, and medicine.

Related Entries   Clustering; Distributed Computer Networks; High-Speed/High-Performance Networking; Internet2; Multiprocessing; SAN (Storage Area Network); Servers; STAR TAP; *and* Switch Fabrics and Bus Design

Linktionary!—Tom Sheldon's Encyclopedia of Networking updates	http://www.linktionary.com/s/supercomputer.html
Pittsburgh Supercomputer Center	http://www.psc.edu/

The Linktionary! Web site contains the full set of links for "supercomputer."

Supernetting

See CIDR (Classless Inter-Domain Routing).

SVC (Switched Virtual Circuit)

A virtual circuit is a predefined path through a packet-switched network. Defining a virtual circuit defines the path that packets will take through the network and relieves routers of the need to make routing decisions for each packet. Virtual circuits improve performance for long transmissions but are not necessary for short transmissions. An SVC is a temporary virtual circuit that is set up on-the-fly, as opposed to a PVC (permanent virtual circuit), which is programmed into a network for continuous use. See "Virtual Circuit" for more information.

S/WAN (Secure WAN)

S/WAN was originally an initiative of RSA Security, in conjunction with leading firewall and TCP/IP stack vendors. S/WAN's goal is to help companies build secure firewall-to-firewall connections over the Internet between their company sites or between business partners. Basically, S/WAN creates secure VPNs (virtual private networks). All data that is transmitted between sites is encrypted to hide it from wiretappers. Connections mimic a private leased line over the Internet.

S/WAN uses the IETF's *IPSec* specification as the basis for implementing interoperability among different firewall and TCP/IP products. S/WAN devices sit at the edge of a network where it connects with the Internet. An encrypted tunnel is established across the Internet with another S/WAN device. All outgoing packets are encrypted, then encapsulated into a new packet with a new header. The new header is used to route the encrypted packet through the network because the header of the encrypted packet cannot be read by routers.

An open-source version of S/WAN called FreeS/WAN provides VPN services in the Linux environment. The software allows Linux-based systems to provide secure gateway services and VPN connections. FreeS/WAN was envisioned by John Gilmore, cofounder of the EFF (Electronic Frontier Foundation), a group that works on Internet privacy issues. FreeS/WAN encrypts data packets with 168-bit Triple-DES, which is currently considered to be very secure.

Related Entries   Cryptography; IPSec (IP Security); L2TP (Layer 2 Tunneling Protocol); Security; Tunnels; VPN (Virtual Private Network); *and* WAN (Wide Area Network)

Linktionary!—Tom Sheldon's Encyclopedia of Networking updates	http://www.linktionary.com/s/swan.html
RSA Security	http://www.rsasecurity.com/
FreeS/WAN.org	http://www.freeswan.org/
IETF IPSec charter	http://www.ietf.org/html.charters/ipsec-charter.html

Switch Fabrics and Bus Design

Switch fabrics and buses are pathways on computing and network devices that provide chip-to-chip, adapter-to-adapter, or device-to-device pathways for transferring information within computing and network devices.

In servers, the PCI bus is the most popular server bus, but it is showing its age as new super-fast processors emerge. Alternative technologies, including switching fabrics, have been developed to support data transfers that can keep up with today's high-speed processors. Switching fabrics are also used in network and telephony switches. Some of the new motherboard and backplane switch and hub architectures extend out of the box so that multiple peripheral devices may be interconnected to the same high-speed bus.

In a multiprocessor system, multiple processors are interconnected in the same chassis via a bus or a switch with an internal switching fabric. Multiprocessor switching fabrics are discussed here. Also see "Multiprocessing."

Optical cross-connects are used in all-optical networks to direct DWDM wavelength circuits across optical networks without the need to convert to electrical signals for switching and then back to light. These switches uses mirror arrays, bubbles, holograms, and a variety of other technologies. See "Optical Networks."

Bus and Switch Designs

The PCI (Peripheral Component Interconnect) is the most common bus today, but as mentioned, its limited bandwidth is no match for today's high-speed processors. A number of improvements were made to boost PCI's performance, but these improvements provided only a temporary fix. Parallel buses are restricted by crosstalk and synchronization problems that only get worse when the bandwidth or distance is increased.

To overcome these problems, point-to-point switching architectures are being employed in high-performance systems. External connections are typically serial links with four-wire cable or fiber-optic cable, rather than complex multi-pin parallel connections. The contention of bus designs is eliminated; and both send and receive can occur simultaneously between two endpoints, thus providing double the normal throughput. A serial interconnect can stretch much greater distances than parallel interconnects.

A network switch has one primary goal: to move packets from some input port to some output port as quickly as possible. Ideally, a switch is *nonblocking*, meaning that there is adequate bandwidth to handle all incoming ports without dropping packets. Packets may be queued momentarily, but not dropped. A *wire-speed* device forwards packets at the same speed as the attached links. A nonblocking wire-speed device is not a simple thing to build if you consider that traffic from all the input may be momentarily directed to a single output port!

The next few sections outline the major interconnect architectures: shared memory, shared bus, and switching (crossbar) fabrics. These are illustrated in Figure S-10.

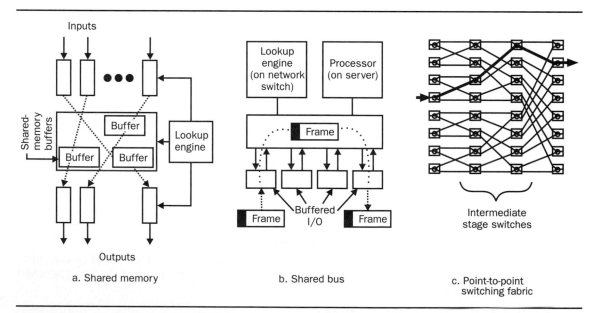

a. Shared memory   b. Shared bus   c. Point-to-point
                                                     switching fabric

Figure S-10.   *Buses and switch fabrics*

Shared Memory Design

The shared memory design illustrated in S-10a is the least complex. When data arrives on an input port, it is stored in memory at the port where it is temporarily buffered and possibly classified. The data is then moved into shared memory where it is assigned a buffer. A lookup engine maps the buffer to some output port. The data is then moved to the output queue. A single lookup engine may manage all ports, or each port may have its own lookup engine.

High-end shared memory systems such as those built by Juniper Networks avoid copying frames from input buffers to output buffers. Frames are placed directly in shared memory as they arrive at the port, and then are immediately moved to an output port to reduce latency. The Juniper design is nonblocking and operates at wire speed.

Shared memory devices can be built with off-the-shelf memory chips, although excessive movement of data to and from memory creates delays. But since memory is shared, it is readily available to any ports that are experiencing excessive traffic.

Shared Bus Architecture

The shared bus design illustrated in Figure S-10b provides a common bus over which the various I/O ports can exchange information. The design is often called a multidrop bus architecture since additional I/O ports may be plugged into the bus. The design is used extensively in desktop PCs, servers, hubs, switches, and many other devices. It is a well-known design and easily expandable, although attaching too many devices to a shared bus will eventually overload it. Therefore, bus designs have fallen out of favor as processor and network data rates have increased.

Note that each port has its own buffer area for temporarily holding incoming and outgoing data, if necessary. The bus is used for data exchange only. A separate shared buffer area could be used, but the design would be inefficient since data would have to move across the bus to the shared memory area, and then back on the bus to the output port. Contention is a problem with shared buses. The situation is similar to a shared Ethernet network, where only one node can transmit on the bus at a time. Other nodes must wait. If waits are excessive, I/O buffers may overflow, causing dropped frames.

Contention problems can be alleviated by implementing multiple buses so that any I/O port can use one of the buses to connect with any other I/O port. The more buses the better, but this design really leads to the switching fabric design, as discussed next. A TDM (time division multiplexing) design may also be used in which each port has an allocated number of time slots on the bus for transmitting information. A slot changer arranges the slots as necessary so that output from one port goes to the appropriate input on another port.

Point-to-Point Switching Fabrics

The switching fabric design illustrated in Figure S-10c has multiple input ports and multiple output ports connected by a matrix of switching points that provide any-to-any, point-to-point links among ports. Links are set up on-the-fly for the duration of the data exchange and multiple links can be active at once. The point-to-point design is often referred to as a *channel-oriented switched fabric*, *crosspoint matrix,* or a *crossbar*. The illustration shows a generic fabric with eight inputs and eight outputs, but hundreds of ports are possible and individual switching units may be interconnected to create an extensive switching fabric, as described later.

Point-to-point switching fabrics are essential for high-performance switches, multiprocessor systems, and system area networks. The architecture is engraved onto chips and the chips are mounted in multiport network devices. The multipoint architecture extends outside the box from ports to devices. A major advantage of switching fabrics is their scalability. As new connections are required, switching elements can be added that automatically integrate into the fabric.

Two-dimensional fabrics provide two choices at each hop through the fabric. Multidimensional switching fabric improves on this by providing multiple path choices per hop. This results in any two points being fewer hops away than in a two-dimensional design. According to Pluris, which makes multistage fabrics called "hypercubes," the more dimensions a fabric has, the fewer the hops needed between input and output ports and, therefore, the lower the latency and jitter for traffic passing through the router. Pluris' hypercube enables a great diversity of routes between input and output nodes. Having multiple equivalent paths through the fabric provides the added advantages of load balancing and redundant links.

Switched Fabric Example: RACE

RACE is a low-cost switching fabric developed by Mercury Computer Systems. It is an example of a chip-level point-to-point circuit switching fabric that can be used to build multiprocessor systems for medical image processing, military signal processing, and other applications. The architecture is ideal for embedded systems in which an application is dedicated to a specific task. This differs from multitask time-sharing systems that require complex operating systems and expensive hardware.

A RACE parallel multiprocessor system consists of multiple Intel i860 microprocessors interconnected with RACEway chips as shown in Figure S-11. The figure illustrates the RACEway chip and a "fat-tree" network interconnect topology built with the chips. Note

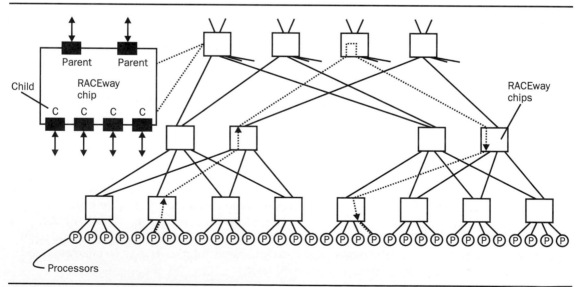

Figure S-11.   *The RACEway chip and RACE network interconnect topology (source: Mercury Computer Systems)*

that each chip has six bidirectional channels, two of which connect to "parents" and four that connect to "children." In the network topology, each chip has two parents and four children. Processors are located at the bottom, and a path between two processors is indicated by the dotted line.

A typical system consists of 32 processors, but large systems with as many as 700 processors have been built. RACEway chips support point-to-point bidirectional communications, one direction at a time, with bandwidth of 160 MB/sec. Latency is approximately 1 microsecond. Each chip has a 32-bit data path.

The chip-level network has many of the characteristics of much larger networks. Source-path routing is used to define paths through the network. Outgoing messages are then assigned the path and appropriately forwarded at each node in the network fabric. An adaptive routing option is also supported in which the network can choose between several different paths to prevent message blocking. A one-to-many broadcast is also possible where at any hop along a path, the path specifier can say "all children." The message is then sent to all the children of that particular chip.

RACE is typically installed as a secondary bus in VME bus systems (described later). A system can then run both buses simultaneously to handle multiprocessing, I/O, and other tasks. The network approach is highly scalable. Additional RACEway chips can be added at any time to support additional processors.

Bus Standards

A number of bus and backplane standards exist, and new standards are being developed to handle high-performance network and server requirements. In addition, new bus designs have emerged that directly connect the internal bus of server systems with other servers to allow cross-system communications and the sharing of external disk systems and peripherals.

PCI (Peripheral Component Interconnect)

The PCI bus was first developed in the early 1990s by Intel and introduced in 1992. It rapidly developed as an industry standard and is now widely used in a variety of Intel- and non-Intel-based devices. The PCI bus is a parallel, 32-bit shared-bus architecture. The first version ran at 33 MHz with 32-bit or 64-bit bus widths. The 33-MHz, 64-bit bus can move data at 264 MB/sec. A 66-MHz version was introduced in 1995 that raised the transfer rate to 528 MB/sec on the 64-bit version of the bus.

PCI-X extended PCI in late 1999 with a faster clock rate and other enhancement designed to improve bandwidth. It operates at 133 MHz with data rates over 1 GB/sec for the 64-bit bus. PCI-X is targeted toward high-end servers and workstations. PCI-X boards also support the ability to remove and replace boards in a running system (hot-plugability). PCI-X is compatible with PCI at the bus level so that older PCI boards can be plugged into the bus. The bus runs at the level of the lowest speed device attached to it. PCI-X also implements an enhanced protocol that increases the efficiency of data transfers and helps the bus achieve higher clock frequencies.

The most important features that PCI introduced in the PC world were interrupt sharing (which helped reduce interrupt conflicts common on ISA systems), automatic configuration, and, of course, a big boost in throughput. Initially, PCI was well suited to the 100-MHz processors of the day. Today, PCI cannot provide the type of I/O that can satisfy new high-speed processors and the throughput requirements of Gigabit Ethernet network connections. For example, a full-duplex Gigabit Ethernet connection can put as much as 200 MB/sec of data on the PCI bus. The 32-bit, 33-MHz PCI bus can handle 133 MB/sec. New SCSI drives that rotate at 15,000 rpms have the potential to deliver a sustained data rate of over 40 MB/sec. A typical server with four drives has a combined data rate of 160 MB/sec or more.

Clearly, the older PCI architecture is a bottleneck. The new specifications improve on it, but the PCI bus has an upper speed limit because it is a shared parallel interconnect. There are technical limitations to boosting the bandwidth and the bus is shared, which means there will always be contention. An alternative strategy is to keep the PCI bus for legacy I/O cards and add a mezzanine/daughterboard that provides an alternative high-speed bus directly to the processor, as discussed later.

The CompactPCI standard (discussed shortly) is a physical enhancement of PCI. The pins and sockets are ruggedized and the cards are designed for front-loading into rack-mount units.

Switching fabrics can be used to scale PCI systems. The concept, often called "virtual PCI," is to allow communication between PCI segments across a switching fabric such as RACE or RapidIO (discussed later). Mercury Computer Systems is currently working with Cypress Semiconductor to develop a transparent PCI switching fabric using the existing RACEway switching fabric. With the addition of a RACEway–to–PCI bridge chip, RACE crossbars will act as a transparent PXP (PCI-to-switching-fabric-to-PCI bridge) fabric.

Intel's Xeon server systems feature Intel's Profusion chipset, which supports up to eight Intel Xeon processors. The systems are designed for rack-mount form factors. The Profusion chipset is a buffered cross-bar switch managing five interconnected 100-MHz buses. Two buses support four processors each, two support memory, and the fifth bus supports the I/O subsystem. This multiple bus design allows processors, memory, and I/O to have direct paths to each other, keeping traffic on each bus down to a minimum.

The PCI Special Interest Group is an association that now monitors the PCI architecture specification and promotes PCI development in various ways. Visit these Web sites for more information:

PCI Special Interest Group	http://www.pcisig.com/
PCI-X information at Compaq	http://www.compaq.com/newsroom/pr/1998/pr090998d.html
PICMG (PCI Industrial Computer Manufacturers Group)	http://www.picmg.org/

CPCI (CompactPCI)

CompactPCI is an industrial version of the standards PCI bus, implemented with rugged Eurocard packaging. The socket connectors are designed to be front-loaded into rack-mount systems. The computer telephony industry, under the direction of PICMG, has extended the CompactPCI system architecture to support analog and digital telephone connectors.

CompactPCI is widely used in industrial applications such as real-time machine control and data acquisition. It is also used in military systems due to its ruggedness. Its high bandwidth makes it ideal for data communications and it is widely used in telecom and telephony products.

Unique features include support for eight PCI slots (as opposed to four in the standard PCI bus). Cards are designed for rugged use and include connectors, card guides, and screw-down face plates that firmly hold cards in their cages. The pin and socket connectors are more reliable than standard PCI connectors. The bus supports hot swapping of peripherals, which makes it useful when fault tolerance is required. The following Web sites provide more information:

CompactPCI information at ZiaTech	http://www.ziatech.com/cpcimain.htm
PCI Source.com (PCI and CompactPCI info)	http://www.pcisource.com/

VMEbus (Versa Module Eurocard bus)

VMEbus is a computer architecture defined in the early 1980s by a group including Motorola, Mostek, and Signetics. VMEbus is derived from the VERSAbus, which was defined by Motorola in 1979 for its 68000 processor. The upgrade to the VMEbus introduced a 32-bit data path and a wider addressing range. In addition, the Eurocard mechanical standard was selected due to its rugged connector design. Therefore, VMEbus is a combination of Motorola's VersaBus electrical specifications and the Eurocard mechanical specifications. Many subsequent revisions have been made, and the architecture has been publicly defined by ANSI, VITA, IEC, and the IEEE.

The VMEbus implements a master-slave architecture in which master modules transfer data to and from slave modules. Many masters can exist on the bus, so it is called a multiprocessing bus. A bus arbiter is used to manage which master module gets access to the bus. There are five sub-buses called the *data transfer bus,* the *data transfer arbitration bus,* the *priority interrupt bus,* the *utility bus,* and the *serial bus.* The bus is nonclocked (asynchrononous), so a handshaking signal is used for data transfers. The data rate is 40 MB/sec.

The most recent version of VMEbus, called VME64, was introduced in 1995. It has enhancements such as higher bandwidths, larger address spaces, and easier-to-use cards. Bandwidth is increased to 80 MB/sec. A superset of VME64 was introduced in 1997 called VME64 Extension (VME64x). It includes a new 160-pin connector family, user-defined I/O pins, hot-swap capability, and bandwidth up to 160 MB/sec among other features. A company called Arizona Digital released a proprietary VME bus called VME320 in 1997. It has a data rate of 320 MB/sec with a peak rate of 500 MB/sec.

VMEbus modules may be single height (3U boards) or double height (6U boards). The "U" indicates a measure of 1.75 inches. 3U modules use 24-bit addressing and 16-bit data paths. 6U modules use 32-bit addressing and 32-bit data paths. 9U boards are also available from some vendors. Smaller cards are used in system designs with limited space.

Several so-called "secondary buses" boost the performance of VME data transfers. FPDP (Front-Panel Data Port) is an ANSI standard that provides a 32-bit parallel I/O bus between two or more VMEbus boards. It supports data rates up to 160 MB/sec with a new version supporting 400 MB/sec. FPDP is also used to acquire data from external sources. RACE may also be used to implement a switched fabric on VME boards. Still another secondary VME bus is SKYchannel, an ANSI standard architecture that implements a nonblocking *packet-switched* architecture operating at 320 MB/sec. Data is collected in variable-sized packets with a header that contains an absolute destination memory address. That address may be across an interconnected VME chassis.

Like the CompactPCI bus, VMEbus is used for rugged industrial-use applications such as machine control, data acquisition, engine control systems, and military applications. The bus is designed for harsh environments where there are extremes in temperature, high shock, and vibrations. VMEbus supports a variety of operating system, many of which are real-time operating systems created by VMEbus vendors.

VMEbus is managed by VITA (VMEbus International Trade Association). Visit http://www.vita.com. A VMEbus primer is at http://www.matrix.com/news/primer.htm.

Mezzanines (Daughterboards)

A mezzanine card is designed to overcome the limited real estate on VME, CompactPCI, and other computer boards. With a mezzanine card, manufacturers can add new I/O functions on standard backplanes to increase the functionality and performance of systems beyond the original design. The IEEE has defined a parent mezzanine standard called CMC (Common Mezzanine Card), which specifies the mechanical specifications of a mezzanine card and the host's mechanical interface. Many mezzanine cards provide a direct high-speed data path to the processor or other motherboard component that bypasses the backplane bus. This overcomes the mismatch between existing low-speed bus standards and high-speed processors.

A variety of CMC "children" standards take advantage of the CMC mechanical specifications. One of the most common is PMC (PCI Mezzanine Card), which provides a way to add PCI bus functionality to VME, CompactPCI, and Multibus II computers. PMC was pioneered by Intel. It uses PCI electrical, logical, and software layer specifications and the CMC physical and mechanical specifications. A typical PMC board has four surface mount connectors (P1–P4) for attaching PCI I/O. P1 and P2 support 32-bit PCI, P3 supports 64-bit PCI, and P4 is used to route signals from the mezzanine to rear panel backplane connectors.

Several common standards are listed next. Additional information is available from GroupIPC, a group of companies that promotes mezzanine solutions, and the VITA Web site. Web sites for both are listed later.

- **IP (IndustryPack) Modules**   In the late 1980s, IP became an industry standard for adding I/O functionality. Current IP modules provide point-to-point multiplexed secondary bus expansions. See the CERN Web page at http://wwwinfo.cern.ch/ce/ms/mezzanines/ip-top.html provides more information.

- **M-Modules**   This is a mezzanine standard developed in Europe that has become an ANSI specification. It provides a point-to-point nonclocked secondary bus with theoretically no speed limits.

- **PMC (PCI Mezzanine Card)**   As described in the preceding text, PMC is a PCI-based add-on.

- **VIM (Velocity Interface Mezzanine)**   This standard was designed for ultra-high-speedprocessors. It provides direct 400 MB/sec data channels to each of four processors on VMEbus and CPCI boards.

Switching Architectures

Switching architectures can be used to support chip-to-chip, board-to-board, and box-to-box (or rack-to-rack) interconnects. The first two categories imply server motherboards, multiprocessor systems, embedded systems, network devices, and other boxed systems. The latter category supports multibox systems, clusters, and system area networks.

The following high-speed architectures are made possible by using LVDS (low-voltage differential signaling), which cuts down on noise and boosts data rates. LVDS uses extremely low voltage levels, which translates to low radiation and less power consumption. Most important, differential signaling allows the receiver to filter out noise. LVDS is ideal for building high-speed multipoint switching fabrics directly onto backplanes. See "LVDS (Low-Voltage Differential Signaling)" for more information.

RapidIO

RapidIO is a switched-fabric interconnect architecture for chip-to-chip– and board-to-board– level system designs. It defines a high-performance interconnect architecture designed for passing data and control information between microprocessors, DSPs, communications and network processors, system memory, and peripheral devices within a system. RapidIO is initially targeted at high-performance embedded applications such as networking, storage, multimedia, and signal processing. It was designed to replace current processor and peripheral bus technologies such as PCI and proprietary processor buses. Note that InfiniBand (discussed later) is a switched fabric architecture targeted at box-to-box and rack-to-rack links.

The initial RapidIO specification defines physical layer technology suitable for interconnects across standard printed circuit board technology. The use of LVDS allows high data transfer rates exceeding 10 Gbits/sec. RapidIO implements a packet-switched interconnect architecture conceptually similar to Internet Protocol (IP).

RapidIO is the result of collaboration between Mercury Computer Systems and Motorola. The technology has been turned over to the RapidIO Trade Association. Visit http:// www.rapidio.org. Mercury Computer Systems (http://www.mc.com/) is a specialist in RapidIO and RACE.

Fibre Channel

Fibre Channel is an interconnection standard for storage devices, servers, and SANs (storage area networks). It consists of a switched architecture that supports both optical and copper connections at speeds from 266 Mbits/sec to 4Gbits/sec. See "Fibre Channel."

Fibre Channel is common in the SAN environment. Qlogic's SANbox switches can be connected as shown in Figure S-12 to interlink Fibre Channel storage and processor devices. The connection options described here support different levels of resiliency, scalability, and performance.

- **Cascading**   An inexpensive network in which devices are daisy-chained. This option is appropriate for only a few devices and where interswitch traffic is low. Scaling the system reduces performance if interswitch traffic is high.

- **Mesh**   In this configuration, every switch is directly connected to every other switch, which reduces hops, even as the fabric scales. However, the number of interswitch connections grows dramatically as new switches are added.

- **Multistage cross-connect**   QLogic recommends this architecture for fabrics above 8 to 10 switches or for fabrics that require a high degree of redundancy. Note that two switches are dedicated to providing cross-connects among the other switches.

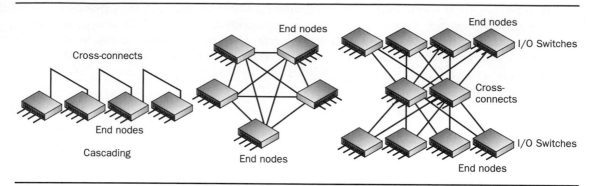

Figure S-12. *QLogic SANbox configurations*

The multistage cross-connect fabric can be expanded in several ways. First, additional cross-connect links can be added at any time (e.g., two each between each cross-connect and switch). This increases the fabric capacity and nonblocking percentage. Second, additional I/O switches can be added to increase the number of end ports. Third, additional cross-connects can be added to improve overall system performance, especially after adding additional I/O switches and end ports.

InfiniBand

InfiniBand is a new communication interconnect technology that implements a switched-fabric architecture with a packet-switching communication protocol. It can be used as a replacement for standard backplane buses such as PCI, and as an interconnect for system area networks (clusters) and storage area networks (disk access). It can also be used as a high-speed interconnection for parallel processing systems.

InfiniBand replaces familiar server bus architectures such as PCI with a switched fabric. In servers, InfiniBand allows system I/O to be removed from the motherboard and extended out via an InfiniBand link to external devices. I/O control is moved from the central processor to the switch fabric. This frees the CPU from I/O tasks and overcomes the bandwidth and slot restrictions of bus architectures. Servers become CPU modules in rack systems, along with disks and other components, all interconnected via InfiniBand. See "InfiniBand."

Other Bus and Switching Standards

The following standards are related to the bus and switching technologies previously discussed:

- **I₂O**   The problem with I/O is that it interrupts the CPU, reducing the ability of a server to handle real processing tasks. I₂O is a specification that defines techniques for offloading I/O from the CPU to an "intelligent processor." The I₂O architecture relieves the host of interrupt-intensive I/O tasks, greatly improving I/O performance in high-bandwidth applications such as networked video, groupware, and client/server processing. Version 2.0 of the I₂O specification, adopted in April 1999, supports 64-bit addressing, as well as switched-fabric I/O architectures. See http://www.intelligent-io.com/.

- **VI Architecture**   The VI (Virtual Interface) Architecture standardizes the interface for high-performance clustering. The interface specifies logical and physical components, as well as connection setup and data transfer operations. It was announced in 1997 by Intel, Microsoft, and Compaq. The VIA Web site is http://www.viarch.org.

- **CSIX (Common Switch Interface)**   CSIX is an interface between switching fabric and switch processing logic. It defines the interface between core interconnect fabric silicon and upper-layer switch-processing silicon. CSIX is being promoted by the CSIX Consortium.

Related Entries   ASIC (Application-Specific Integrated Circuit); ATM (Asynchronous Transfer Mode); Cells and Cell Relays; Relay; Clustering; Cut-Through Architecture; Data Center Design; Distributed Computer Networks; Embedded Systems; LVDS (Low-Voltage Differential Signaling); Multilayer Switching; Multiprocessing; Network Concepts; Network Connection Technologies; Network Processors; RISC (Reduced Instruction Set Computer); SAN (Storage Area Network); SCSI (Small Computer System Interface); Serial Communication and Interfaces; Servers; Switching and Switched Networks; USB (Universal Serial Bus); *and* VI Architecture

Linktionary!—Tom Sheldon's Encyclopedia of Networking updates	http://www.linktionary.com/s/switch_fabrics.html
Google Web Directory: Buses page	http://directory.google.com/Top/Computers/ Hardware/Buses/
eg3.com (resources for embedded systems)	http://www.eg3.com/
CSIX (Common Switch Interface) Consortium	http://www.csix.org/
Enterasys Networks PowerCast switching fabric paper	http://www.enterasys.com/products/whitepapers/ powercast/

Switching, Multilayer

See Multilayer Switching.

Switching and Switched Networks

Network switches are multipoint connection devices that provide a point of attachment for a single computer or another device (hub or switch) that has multiple computers attached to it. The most important feature is that any device attached to one port can directly communicate with a device on another port over what is essentially a private link.

The significance of this technology can be seen when compared to older Ethernet shared LAN technologies. The traditional coaxial cable Ethernet LAN implements a linear cable topology that is shared by all the computers attached to it. Only one device can transmit at a time, so some computers will need to wait while another is transmitting. Computers "listen" for signals on the cable to see if it is being used.

Network switching reduces or removes the sharing of the network and the problems that result from sharing, such as contention (when computers wait to use the cable), collisions (when two systems attempt to use the cable at the same time), and delays caused by contention and collisions. See "Collisions and Collision Domains" and "CSMA/CD (Carrier Sense Multiple Access/Collision Detection)."

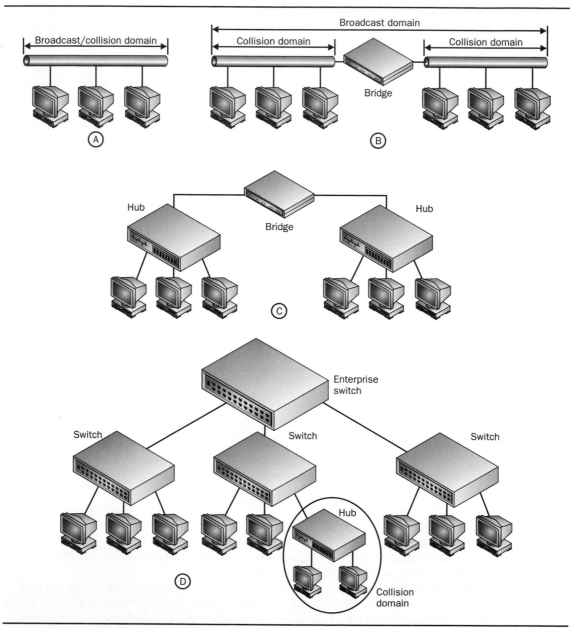

Figure S-13. *A bridge divides a network into two collision domains, but maintains a single broadcast domain.*

Figure S-13 illustrates the evolution of switching. In (A), all the workstations are attached to a single shared segment and must deal with the problems described previously. Many of these problems are solved via *segmentation*, as shown in (B), where the network is divided and rejoined with a bridge. This create two "collision domains" but retains a single broadcast domain. A collision domain is a group of network nodes that are contending for the same shared communication medium. Contention occurs in collision domains when two or more stations attempt to use the medium at the same time. By splitting the network, contention and collisions are reduced because there are fewer nodes per segment.

In (C), the linear network is replaced with a hub to create a *star topology*. This is basically the same network as (B), but the network topology is a star configuration. In (D), the switch provides multiport bridging. Each port provides dedicated bandwidth to the device attached to it. Any port can be bridged to any other port so that an end-to-end private link can be established between any two devices. Note that when two end stations are connected together, they contend with one another for access to the channel. A *full-duplex link* solves this by providing a dedicated wire pair for sending and receiving.

Notice that hubs can be attached to a single port, which means that all the stations attached to the hub share the same switch port. The assumption is that the users attached to the hub don't generate much network traffic, except possibly between other users on the same hub.

This model in (D) may be used on a small department level or as the topology for entire enterprise networks. It is extremely scalable. Switched networks do not lose performance as new switches are added, assuming higher-level switches provide adequate bandwidth. See "Network Design and Construction" for information about building hierarchical networks with switches.

You'll hear a lot about multilayer switches, layer 3 switches, layer 4 switches, and so on. These are "enhanced switches" with added functionality such as routing (thus, it's a multiport router) and packet inspection functionality that can provide prioritization and QoS. A switch with routing functionality is sometimes called a "layer 3 switch" or a "router switch." They are described under the topic "Multilayer Switching."

Since basic switches are layer 2 devices, networks built with them are flat, meaning that they are not subnetted into separate routing domains. Multilayer switches support routing. However, networks that are constructed with basic switches can be virtually separated into separate routing domains by using VLAN technology. See "VLAN (Virtual LAN)."

Many switches are now optimized for load balancing. They inspect and distribute traffic across multiple channels and to multiple devices (servers and storage). Packets are forwarded based on layer 4 and layer 7 information, including information at the application layer, such as the requested URL, cookies, or even processing requirements. For example, a database request is forwarded to a database server and Web requests to Web servers. Forwarding may also be based on *persistent* sessions in a case in which a server is already servicing a session and packets related to the same session should go to the same server. See "Load Balancing."

This topic continues in "Network Design and Construction," which describes how to design and build enterprise networks with switches.

Related Entries   ASIC (Application-Specific Integrated Circuit); ATM (Asynchronous Transfer Mode); Backbone Networks; Bridges and Bridging; Broadcast Domain; Broadcast Networking; Cells and Cell Relay; Collisions and Collision Domains; CSMA/CD (Carrier Sense Multiple Access/Collision Detection); Cut-Through Architecture; Data Center Design; Ethernet; Gigabit Ethernet; Internetworking; IP over

ATM; MPLS (Multiprotocol Label Switching); Multilayer Switching; Multitiered Architectures; Network Connection Technologies; Network Design and Construction; Network Processors; Routers; Switch Fabrics and Bus Design; *and* VLAN (Virtual LAN)

Linktionary!—Tom Sheldon's Encyclopedia of Networking updates	http://www.linktionary.com/s/switching.html
CSIX (Common Switch Interface Consortium)	http://www.csix.org
Entersys switching white papers	http://www.enterasys.com/products/whitepapers/
Foundry Networks Gigabit Info Center	http://www.foundrynet.com/whitepapers.html
Network World Fusion Switching Web page	http://www.nwfusion.com/netresources/switching.html
TechFest Multilayer Switching page	http://www.techfest.com/networking/mlayer.htm
Cisco documentation: Internetworking Design Basics	http://www.cisco.com/univercd/cc/td/doc/cisintwk/idg4/nd2002.htm
Cisco documentation: Designing Switched LAN Internetworks	http://www.cisco.com/univercd/cc/td/doc/cisintwk/idg4/nd2012.htm
Cisco documentation: How LAN Switches Work	http://www.cisco.com/warp/public/473/lan-switch-cisco.shtml

More switching links are available at the Linktionary! Web site.

Symmetrical Multiprocessing

See Multiprocessing.

Synchronous Communications

When devices exchange data, there is a flow or stream of information between the two. In any data transmission, the sender and receiver must have a way to extract individual characters or blocks (frames) of information. Imagine standing at the end of a data pipe. Characters arrive in a continuous stream of bits, so you need a way to separate one block of bits from another. In asynchronous communications, each character is separated by the equivalent of a flag so you know exactly where characters are located. In synchronous communications, both the sender and receiver are synchronized with a clock or a signal encoded into the data stream.

In synchronous communications, the sender and receiver must synchronize with one another before data is sent. To maintain clock synchronization over long periods, a special bit-transition pattern is embedded in the digital signal that assists in maintaining the timing between sender and receiver. One method of embedding timing information is called *bipolar encoding,* as pictured in Figure S-14. In this method, the bit stream pictured at the top is meshed with the clock pulse pictured in the middle to produce the transmission signal shown at the bottom.

Synchronous communications are either character oriented or bit oriented. Character-oriented transmissions are used to send blocks of characters such as those found in ASCII (American Standard Code for Information Interchange) files. Each block must have a starting flag similar to asynchronous communications so the receiving system can initially synchronize with the bit

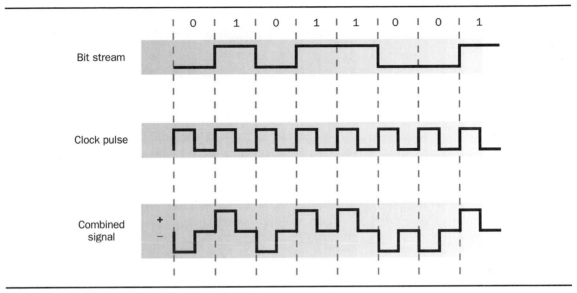

Figure S-14. *Bipolar encoding for synchronous communications*

stream and locate the beginning of the characters. Two or more control characters, known as SYN (synchronous idle) characters, are inserted at the beginning of the bit stream by the sender. These characters are used to synchronize a block of information. Once correct synchronization has been established between sender and receiver, the receiver places the block it receives as characters in a memory buffer.

Bit-oriented synchronous communication is used primarily for the transmission of binary data. It is not tied to any particular character set, and the frame contents don't need to include multiples of eight bits. A unique 8-bit pattern (01111110) is used as a flag to start the frame.

An entirely different form of synchronous communications can be seen in the form of chat and instant messaging. Like a voice telephone call, a chat or instant messaging session is live and each user responds to the other in real time. In contrast, discussion forums and electronic mail are *asynchronous communications*. Some amount of time may pass before a person responds to a message. In a discussion forum, a message sits in a message queue for other people to read and respond to at any time, or until the message falls out of the queue. These two forms of communication, which are accessible to any Internet user from just about any Web-attached system, may be the most profound aspect of the Internet. They promote a new form of instant global communication and collaboration. In the case of discussion forums and e-mail, delayed communication gives respondents time to think about their response and gather information from other sources before responding.

Related Entries Asynchronous Communications; Data Communication Concepts; Data Link Protocols; HDLC (High-level Data Link Control); *and* SDLC (Synchronous Data Link Control)

Optimized Engineering Corp.
Async & Sync page

http://www.optimized.com/COMPENDI/RS-AsSy.htm

Cisco documentation: Synchronous Data
Link Control and Derivatives

http://www.cisco.com/univercd/cc/td/doc/cisintwk/
ito_doc/sdlcetc.htm

SystemView, IBM

SystemView is an enterprise-wide network management system that recognizes and manages systems in heterogeneous environments. It was one of IBM's first products to recognize industry-standard protocols such as TCP/IP, and not just IBM's own SNA (Systems Network Architecture) protocols. In 1996, IBM acquired Tivoli Systems, Inc., and in this process the Tivoli division took over development of IBM's SystemView products. It also linked SystemView with its own environment, TME (Tivoli Management Environment).

Related Entries   IBM (International Business Machines); Network Management

Tivoli Systems, Inc.

http://www.tivoli.com

T Carriers

The T carrier services use TDM (time-division multiplexing) techniques to transmit multiple voice or data over digital trunk lines. An example is to connect a multi-line enterprise PBX to the phone company over a single line. The most common T carriers are T1 (1.544 Mbits/sec) and T3 (45 Mbits/sec). Note that the "T" stands for terrestrial (as opposed to satellite transmissions), and the 1 is an abbreviation for the 1.544-Mbit/sec signal rate.

A T1 or T3 is a digital circuit that is based on the PDH (plesiochronous digital hierarchy), which is a system of multiplexing numerous individual channels into higher-level channels. In North America, this hierarchy is called NADH (North American Digital Hierarchy). The base channel rate is called DS-0 and it holds one digitalzed voice call at a data rate of 64 Kbits/sec. The higher rates are DS-1, which carries 24 channels, and DS-3, which carries 672 channels.

Voice phone calls are digitized using PCM (pulse-code modulation). PCM is a sampling technique in which the voltage level of an analog signal is read 8,000 times per second. This 8,000-Hz sampling rate is two times the highest frequency of the range used to carry voice (300 to 4,000 Hz) and produces a relatively good digital representation. Each voltage level sample is converted to an 8-bit value. A single digitized voice call requires 64,000 bits/sec of bandwidth (8,000 samples/sec × 8 bits/sample).

The TDM circuit is created by repeating a T1 frame that contains twenty-four 8-bit time slots, as shown in the following illustration. Each slot holds a single voltage level sample from each voice channel.

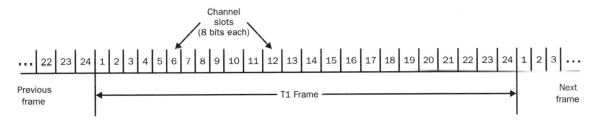

One frame follows another, and each slot in a frame is reserved for a channel, even if there is nothing to send. Each frame contains a total of 193 bits (24 slots × 8 bits + 1 bit to synchronize the frame). Since the sample rate is 8,000 Hz, there must be 8,000 frames per second (with each frame holding one sample from each channel). Therefore, the T1 line rate is 1,544 Mbits/sec (8,000 frames/sec × 193 bits/frame).

There is also a fractional T1, which is an offering that lets customers lease T1 service in single channel increments. A full T1 line is installed, but customers only pay for the incremental service required. This keeps costs low but allows for scaling the service.

Both T1s and T3s were originally used in the carrier networks to connect switching offices. Later, optical cables (and an optical carrier hierarchy) were used in the carrier core network, but T1s and T3s are still used as feeder lines. They are also sold as leased lines to organizations and Internet service providers that need high capacity voice and data access trunks.

The most common T1 configuration is between an organization's PBX and the telephone switching office. Since a T1 carries 24 voice phone calls, up to 24 calls can be made through the PBX and across the T1 circuit. Without this digital multiplexing technology, 24 individual twisted pairs of wire would be needed to connect the calls.

The following illustration shows how multiple T1s may be used to build wide area data networks. On the left, six T1 lines are used to interconnect four sites. While these lines provide private dedicated connections, the cost of leasing six lines—especially for long-distance links—can be excessive. An alternative is to connect into a carrier's packet-switched network as shown on the right. In this configuration, short T1 lines connect into the carrier's local point of presence and the packet network provides any-to-any links among the sites at a cheaper rate over long distances. See "TDM Networks" for more information about building local and wide area networks with T1/T3 circuits.

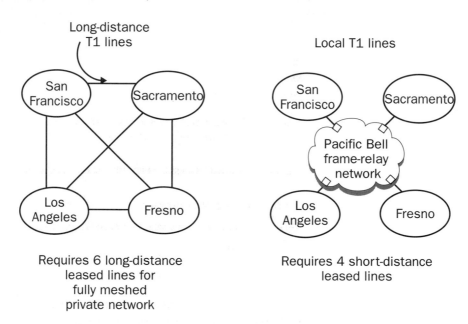

T1 lines are usually dedicated point-to-point connections that are leased from a carrier. They are not easily changed to accommodate moves or temporary office locations, and the line rate is inflexible. You pay for the full bandwidth, even if its not being used. If you need more bandwidth temporarily, you'll need to supplement the line with a bandwidth-on-demand line. If you plan to build a long-distance WAN, dedicated T carriers are prohibitively expensive. ATM, frame relay, and Internet VPNs provide a better solution.

The carriers have dominated the local access market for years with their expensive T1 and T3 access offerings. Recently, competitors have installed fiber optic cable to the doorsteps of businesses in metropolitan areas and are now offering cheaper and faster services. See "MAN (Metropolitan Area Network)."

Related Entries   Bandwidth on Demand; Circuit; Circuit-Switching Services; Communication Services Providers; CSU/DSU (Channel Service Unit/Data Service Unit); DSL (Digital Subscriber Line); Leased Line; Local Loop; MAN (Metropolitan Area Network); Multiplexing and Multiplexers; NADH (North American Digital Hierarchy); Network Access Services; Packets and Packet-Switching Networks; Point-to-Point Communications; Service Providers and Carriers; SONET (Synchronous Optical Network); TDM Networks; Telecommunications and Telephone Systems; Voice over IP (VoIP); VPNs (Virtual Private Network); *and* WAN (Wide Area Network)

Linktionary!—Tom Sheldon's Encyclopedia of Networking updates	http://www.linktionary.com/t/t-carrier.html
Marconi WAN tutorial	http://www.marconi.com/html/education/wanmenu.htm
Larus Corporation "T1 Repeatered Line Transmission Engineering"	http://www.laruscorp.com/t1tut.htm
Bell Labs T1 Carrier tutorial	http://www.bell-labs.com/technology/common/ t1carrier.html
Quabbin Wire & Cable Co. "T1 and T3 Circuits Provide LAN to WAN Interconnection"	http://www.quabbin.com/tech_briefs/tech2.html
"All You Wanted to Know About T1 But Were Afraid to Ask" by Bob Wachtel	http://www.dcbnet.com/notes/9611t1.html
Everything T1 Web page	http://www.everythingt1.com/
Telco Exchange Telecom Pricing Tools	http://www.telcoexchange.com/
Bitpipe.com (search for "T1")	http://www.bitpipe.com/
TechFest T1 Overview	http://www.techfest.com/networking/wan/t1.htm
Paradyne's DSL Sourcebook (provides good overview of telecom technologies)	http://www.paradyne.com/sourcebook_offer/sb_pdf.html

TACACS (Terminal Access Controller Access Control System)

TACACS is an authentication scheme that can be used to validate users who are attempting to gain access to information servers, networks, and remote access servers. TACACS was originally developed by the U.S. Department of Defense and BBN Planet Corp. and then further developed by Cisco. There are three versions of the protocol: the original TACACS as just mentioned, XTACACS (Extended TACACS), and TACACS+. The first two versions are discussed in RFC 1492 (An Access Control Protocol, Sometimes Called TACACS, July 1993). TACACS+ is the latest version and should be used whenever TACACS is called for. TACACS is also discussed in RFC 2975 (Introduction to Accounting Management, October 2000). Note that TACACS, in general, is no longer being maintained.

TACACS runs as a distinct third-party authentication server that provides verification services. Basically, it off-loads user authentication to another server. When a user attempts to gain access to a secure system, the secure system first prompts the user for a name and password. The system then passes this information to the TACACS server and requests authentication services. The original TACACS was quite simple, and Cisco extended it to create TACACS+, which is modular in design and supports plug-in authentication, authorization, and accounting schemes. The system supports physical card key devices or token cards, and supports Kerberos secret-key authentication. An alternative to TACACS+ is RADIUS, which is an Internet standard. Refer to "RADIUS (Remote Authentication Dial-In User Service)" for more information.

T

Related Entries Accounting on the Internet; Authentication and Authorization; Communication Server; Mobile Computing; NAS (Network Access Server); RADIUS (Remote Authentication Dial-In User Service); Remote Access; Security; *and* Token-Based Authentication

Cisco Document: The TACACS Authentication Protocols	http://www.cisco.com/warp/public/480/4.html
Robert Kiessling's TACACS FAQ	http://www.de.easynet.net/tacacs-faq/tacacs-faq.html

Tag Switching

Tag Switching is a Cisco proprietary technology designed to merge the intelligence of routing with the performance of layer 2 (data link) switching networks. It was designed for routed IP networks or switched ATM and Ethernet networks. The architecture is discussed in RFC 2105 (Cisco Systems' Tag Switching Architecture Overview, February 1997). Cisco calls Tag Switching a prestandard implementation of the IETF's MPLS (Multiprotocol Label Switching). Cisco has worked with the IETF to incorporate the features and benefits of Tag Switching into MPLS. See "Label Switching" and "MPLS (Multiprotocol Label Switching)."

Related Entries ATM (Asynchronous Transfer Mode); Differentiated Services (Diff-Serv); IP over ATM; Label Switching; MPLS (Multiprotocol Label Switching); *and* Multilayer Switching

Linktionary!—Tom Sheldon's Encyclopedia of Networking updates	http://www.linktionary.com/t/tag_switching.html
Multilayer Routing page by Noritoshi Demizu	http://www.watersprings.org/links/mlr/

TAPI (Telephony API)

TAPI is a Microsoft for developing CTI (computer-telephony integration) applications. TAPI abstracts the hardware layer so that developers can create products that are network and device independent. TAPI applications be designed for intranet phone systems, PBXs, the public- switched telephone network, and IP networks. TAPI is based on the Microsoft Windows platform and is complemented by other Microsoft APIs, such as Win32, MAPI, SAPI (Speech API), and media control interfaces.

TAPI consists of two interfaces Vendors who develop CTI applications write to the API on the top side. The lower part of TAPI is called the SPI (service provider interface). It provides an interface for devices like PBXs, key telephones, ISDN, the analog phone system, cellular systems, Centrex, and other types of telephone devices.

Related Entries CTI (Computer-Telephony Integration); Voice/Data Networks; *and* Voice over IP (VoIP)

Linktionary!—Tom Sheldon's Encyclopedia of Networking updates	http://www.linktionary.com/t/tapi.html
IP Telephony with TAPI	http://www.microsoft.com/windows2000/library/howitworks/communications/telephony/iptelephony.asp

Tariff

A tariff is a record that is posted with regulatory commissions such as the FCC (Federal Communications Commission) or state regulatory commission describing the prices, terms, and conditions of a telecommunications service offering. An example of a tariff service is basic telephone service. Regulated utilities are required to post tariffs that are approved by an appropriate regulatory agency.

Related Entries   Network Access Services; Service Providers and Carriers; Telecommunications and Telephone System; Telecommunications Regulation; *and* WAN (Wide Area Network)

Linktionary!—Tom Sheldon's Encyclopedia of Networking updates	http://www.linktionary.com/t/tariff.html
TariffNet.com tariff library (see "telecom tariffs")	http://www.intelesource.com/
Tariffonline	http://www.tollusa.com/
Telecom Tariffs Finally Die in 2001	http://www.metagroup.com/metaview/mv0356/mv0356.html

TCP (Transmission Control Protocol)

TCP is a subset of the *Internet protocol suite*, which is often called TCP/IP, although the acronym TCP/IP refers to only two of the many protocols in the Internet protocol suite. Still, most people refer to the Internet protocols as TCP/IP and that style is retained here. For a description of the entire suite, refer to "Internet Protocol Suite."

   This topic is covered in more detail at the Linktionary! Web site.

The Internet Protocol suite consists of a set of protocols that provide a variety of networking services as shown in Figure T-1. TCP and UDP (User Datagram Protocol) are transport layer components that provide the connection point through which applications access network services. TCP and UDP use IP, which is a lower-layer best effort delivery service. IP encapsulates TCP and UDP information in *datagrams* and delivers the information across router-connected internetworks. See "IP (Internet Protocol)" and "UDP (User Datagram Protocol)."

TCP is a connection-oriented protocol that provides the flow controls and reliable data delivery services listed next. These services run in the host computers at either end of a connection, not in the network itself. Therefore, TCP is a protocol for managing end-to-end connections, as shown in Figure T-2. Since end-to-end connections may exist across a series of point-to-point connections, they are often called *virtual circuits*.

- **Connections**   Two computers set up a connection to exchange data. The systems synchronize with one another to manage packet flows and adapt to congestion in the network.

- **Full-duplex operation**   A TCP connection is a pair of virtual circuits (one in each direction). Only the two end systems can use the connection.

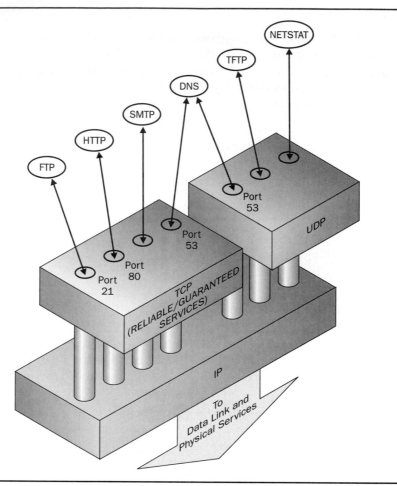

Figure T-1.   *TCP in relation to UDP, IP, and applications*

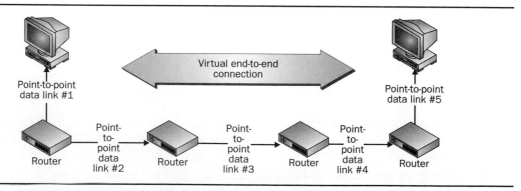

Figure T-2.   *TCP establishes end-to-end connections over router-connected networks*

- **Error checking**   A checksum technique is used to verify that packets are not corrupted.

- **Sequencing**   Packets are numbered so that the destination can reorder packets and determine if a packet is missing.

- **Acknowledgements**   Upon receipt of one or more packets, the receiver returns an acknowledgement (called an "ACK") to the sender indicating that it received the packets. If packets are not ACKed, the sender may retransmit the packets (or terminate the connection if it thinks the receiver has crashed).

- **Flow control**   If the sender is overflowing the receiver by transmitting too quickly, the receiver drops packets. Failed ACKs alert the sender to slow down or stop sending.

- **Packet recovery services**   The receiver can request retransmission of a packet. Also, if packet receipt is not ACKed, the sender will resend the packets.

Reliable data delivery services are critical for applications such as file transfers, database services, transaction processing, and other mission-critical applications in which every packet must be delivered—guaranteed. See "Reliable Data Delivery Services" for a general overview of reliable services.

While TCP provides these reliable services, it depends on IP to delivery packets. IP is often referred to as an *unreliable* or *best effort* service. While it seems odd to build a network that is unreliable, the original Internet architects wanted to remove as many services from the network itself to support fast packet delivery rather than reliability. Routers do not keep track of packets or do anything to ensure delivery. They just forward packets.

The assumption was that end systems would be relatively smart devices with memory and processors. The end devices could handle all the reliability functions rather than the network. This was actually a radical approach at the time, but the implications have been profound. It meant that end systems would become the focus of application development for the Internet, not the network.

In contrast, the telephone network implements an architecture in which end devices (phones) are dumb and the network is supposedly "smart." The only problem with this model is that you can't run applications on your phone that take advantage of the network. In fact, you are totally dependent on the phone company to deploy new applications (call waiting and caller ID are examples). Compared to the Internet, the phone system is a dinosaur. Consider that the user interface for the Web is a full-color graphical browser, while the interface for the telephone network is a 12-key pad!

While end-systems provide TCP's reliability functions, not all applications need them. For example, there is no need to recover lost packets in a live video stream. By the time they are recovered, the viewer has will have already seen the barely visible glitch caused by the missing packet. These applications just need speed. So UDP was created to provide an application interface to the network for real-time applications that don't need TCP's extra services. UDP provides a very simple port connection between applications and IP.

The topic "Reliable Data Delivery Services" has a subsection called "Partial Reliable Services" that describes several Internet protocols that provide some but not all of TCP's reliable services but more than what UDP provides. An example is RTP (Real-time Transport Protocol), a multimedia delivery protocol that provides what is called a "partial ordered service." RTP sequentially numbers packets and adds timing information for services that might need to reconstruct the original packet sequence.

See "Internet" for more information about the structure of the Internet and a history of its development. TCP is described in RFC 793 (Transmission Control Protocol, September 1981). Related documents with revisions and updates are listed later. Also see RFC 1180 (A TCP/IP Tutorial, January 1991).

TCP Features

An end-to-end connection actually extends up through the TCP layer to the application that is using the network services. Note the ports in Figure T-1. The most common applications such as HTTP (Web services) and FTP (File Transfer Protocol) use ports that are "well known," so clients can connect to them to access a particular service without having to query on what port that service is running. For example, Web browsers automatically connect with port 80, FTP uses port 21, and Gopher use port 70.

A typical session involves sending packets from a source IP address and port to a destination IP address and port. The combination port and IP address is called a *socket*. You can think of a socket as the end of a connection. If a connection is like a circuit or wire, then the socket is the end of that wire, much like a telephone exists at the end of a voice circuit. Packets flow across networks between sockets. These packet flows can be identified by an IP address/port number combination.

TCP Segment Properties

A TCP segment is the packet of information that TCP uses to exchange data with its peers (TCP running on other hosts). The segment is what gets encapsulated into an IP datagram and transmitted across the network. See "Network Architecture" for a description of how information is exchanged between protocol layers.

Segments have a 20-byte header and a variable-length Data field. The fields of the TCP segment are described here and pictured in Figure T-3. Keep in mind that either station may send a segment that contains just header information and no data to provide the other system with session control information, such as an acknowledgment that a segment was received.

- ■ **Source and Destination Ports**   Contains the port numbers of the sockets at the source and destination sides of the connection.

- ■ **Sequence Number**   This field contains a sequential number for the receiver, which is a sequential number that identifies the data in the segment and where it belongs in the stream of data that has already been sent. The receiver can use the sequence number to reorder packets that have arrived out of order or to determine that a segment is missing. This field is used by the sliding-window algorithm.

- ■ **Acknowledgment Number**   This field is used by the receiver to indicate to the sender in a return message that it has received a previously sent packet. The number in this field is actually the sequence number for the next segment that the receiver expects. That number is calculated by incrementing the value in the Sequence Number field. This field is used by the sliding-window algorithm. Refer to "Flow-Control Mechanism" for a description.

- **TCP Header Length**   Specifies the length of the header.
- **Codes**   This field is reserved.
- **URG (*urgent*)**   This bit is set to 1 if there is information in the Urgent Pointer field of the header.
- **ACK (*acknowledgment*)**   If ACK is set to 1, it indicates that the segment is part of an ongoing conversation and the number in the Acknowledgment Number field is valid. If this flag is set to 0 and SYN is set to 1, the segment is a request to establish a connection.
- **PSH (*push*)**   A bit set by the sender to request that the receiver send data directly to the application and not buffer it.
- **RST (*reset*)**   When set, the connection is invalid for a number of reasons and must be reset.
- **SYN (*synchronize*)**   Used in conjunction with ACK to request a connection or accept a connection. SYN=1 and ACK=0 indicates a connection request. SYN=1 and ACK=1 indicates a connection accepted. SYN=0 and ACK=1 is an acknowledgment of the acknowledgment.
- **FIN (*finish*)**   When set, this bit indicates that the connection should be terminated.

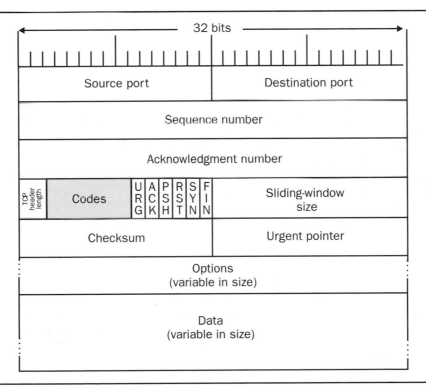

Figure T-3.   *The TCP segment layout*

■ **Sliding Window Size**   Indicates how much space is available in the receiver's buffers. The field is used by the receiver to inform the sender that it needs to speed up or slow down its transmissions. If the receiver wants the sender to stop transmitting altogether, it can return a segment with 0 in this field.

■ **Checksum**   Provides an error-checking value to ensure the integrity of the segment.

■ **Urgent Pointer**   This field can be used by the sender to indicate a location in the data where some urgent data is located.

■ **Options**   A variable set aside for special options.

■ **Data**   A variable-length field that holds the messages or data from applications.

These many different fields are used to set up and control connections, as well as to provide the reliability services that guarantee data delivery. The next section provides some insight into how these features are used.

A Typical TCP Session

Assume a client needs to connect with a server. First, the client must contact the server and request a connection. After the connection is established, various control parameters for the connection are negotiated. After data transmission begins, a sliding window flow-control scheme is used to manage data transfer.

A connection is established via a *three-way handshake*, as described next. This handshake helps define the start of a new TCP connection, and prevents a host from being confused by duplicate packets generated by a previous connection that arrives late.

1. Host A (the sender) sends a TCP segment to host B with the SYN flag set to 1 and the ACK flag set to 0.

2. Host B returns a segment to host A in which both the SYN and ACK flags are set to 1.

3. Host A can now acknowledge to host B that it received its ACK. It sends a segment in which ACK=1 and SYN=0.

Included these steps is a negotiation of an initial sequence number for the client and for the server (each uses its own sequence number scheme). Host A sends its starting number to host B and host B acknowledges that number by incrementing it and returning the number to host A. The same process is used to negotiate host B's starting sequence number.

After data is transmitted, the session is terminated. Host A sends a FIN=1 to host B. Host B then responds with ACK=1 and FIN=1 and host A responds to that with ACK=1.

TCP uses a *keep-alive* feature to keep connections open and manage connections. Keep-alive verifies that the computer at the other end of a connection is still available.

A single host can set up multiple connections over the TCP/IP network at any time. This is called *multiplexing*. If multiple applications or network processes are running, each may set up a connection to a different computer. For example, you can simultaneously open multiple Web browsers and connect with multiple sites.

TCP uses flow controls, sliding windows, and various other mechanisms to manage sessions. These are discussed further under the following headings:

- "Connection Establishment"
- "Flow-Control Mechanisms"
- "Congestion Control Mechanism"

The topic congestion control discusses techniques that TCP uses to control congestion. Specifically, TCP relies on dropped packets as a signal that the receiver or network is overloaded! Much work has gone into improving this technique.

The Linktionary! Web site continues this discussion by outlining TCP performance issues and techniques that have been put into place to improve TCP performance.

There are an incredible number of RFCs related to TCP, too many to list here. Refer to the Linktionary! Web site for the complete list. A number of IETF Working Groups are developing extensions to TCP or working on updates. Refer to the IETF Web site given later and see the Transport Area section.

Related Entries   Acknowledgment; Bandwidth Management; Best-Effort Delivery; Congestion Control Mechanisms; Connection Establishment; Connection-Oriented and Connectionless Services; Constraint-Based Routing; Data Communication Concepts; Data Link Protocols; Delay, Latency, and Jitter; Differentiated Services (Diff-Serv); End Systems and End-to-End Connectivity; Flow-Control Mechanisms; Integrated Services (Int-Serv); Internet; Internet Protocol Suite; Load Balancing; MPLS (Multiprotocol Label Switching); Multimedia; Network Architecture; Packets and Packet-Switching Networks; Policy-Based Management; Ports, TCP/IP; Prioritization of Network Traffic; QoS (Quality of Service); Reliable Data Delivery Services; RSVP (Resource Reservation Protocol); Socket; TCP (Transmission Control Protocol); Throughput; Traffic Management, Shaping, and Engineering; *and* UDP (User Datagram Protocol)

Linktionary!—Tom Sheldon's Encyclopedia of Networking updates	http://www.linktionary.com/t/tcp.html
IETF Transport Area Working Groups	http://www.ietf.org/html.charters/wg-dir.html#Transport_Area
Daryl's TCP/IP Primer	http://ipprimer.2ndlevel.net/
Google Web Directory: Internet protocols page	http://directory.google.com/Top/Computers/Internet/Protocols/
IBM's TC/IP Tutorial and Technical Overview (#GG24-3376-05)	http://www.redbooks.ibm.com/abstracts/gg243376.html/
Noritoshi Demizu's Internetworking technical resources page	http://www.watersprings.org/links/inet/
Uri's TCP/IP Resources List (FAQs, tutorials, guides, Web pages & sites, and books about TCP/IP)	http://www.faqs.org/faqs/internet/tcp-ip/resource-list/

T

Internet Protocols paper at Cisco

http://www.cisco.com/univercd/cc/td/doc/cisintwk/
ito_doc/ip.htm

Information Technology Professional's
Resource Center (see various TCP/IP
topics, including FAQs)

http://www.itprc.com/tcp_ip.htm

The Linktionary! Web site has additional links related to TCP.

TCP/IP (Transmission Control Protocol/Internet Protocol)

The Internet Protocol suite is a set of internetworking protocols that is more commonly referred
to as "TCP/IP." However, TCP/IP refers to only two of the protocols in the Internet Protocol
suite: TCP (Transmission Control Protocol) and IP (Internet Protocol). Many other protocols
are part of TCP/IP, including UDP (User Datagram Protocol), RTP (Real-time Transport
Protocol), and application-level protocols such as FTP and HTTP. See the related entries
here for more information.

Related Entries   Best-Effort Delivery; Connection-Oriented and Connectionless Services; Internet
Protocol Suite; IP (Internet Protocol); Network Architecture; Packets and Packet-Switching Networks;
Reliable Data Delivery Services; TCP (Transmission Control Protocol); UDP (User Datagram Protocol)

TDD (Time Division Duplexing)

See "Wireless Broadband Access Technologies" and "TDMA (Time Division Multiple Access)"

TDM (Time Division Multiplexing)

See Multiplexing and Multiplexers.

TDMA (Time Division Multiple Access)

TDMA is a wireless digital communication scheme for cellular phone systems that allocates
time slots to multiple users within a single channel. It works over existing AMPS (Advanced
Mobile Phone Service) frequencies, providing digital service instead of analog service for up
to three calls per channel. This topic is covered in more detail at the Linktionary! Web site.
Also see "Wireless Mobile Communications" in this book.

Related Entries   CDMA (Code Division Multiple Access); Packet-Radio Data Networks; Satellite
Communication Systems; Wireless Broadband Access Technologies; Wireless Communications; *and*
Wireless Mobile Communications

Linktionary!—Tom Sheldon's
Encyclopedia of Networking updates

http://www.linktionary.com/t/tdma.html

Web ProForums TDMA tutorial

http://www.iec.org/tutorials/tdma/

Universal Wireless Communications
Consortium (TDMA-EDGE information)

http://www.uwcc.org/

See "Wireless Communications" for a more complete list of wireless-related links.

TDM Networks

TDM is a multiplexing technique that divides a circuit into multiple channels based on time. The technique is associated with telephone company voice services. T1 and T3 circuits are divided into multiple channels using time division multiplexing. The most common TDM circuit for business users is the T1 line (1.544 Mbits/sec). It consists of 24 multiplexed 64-Kbit/sec voice channels. Each channel may carry a single phone call, or the entire circuit may be dedicated to data.

Time division multiplexing was designed to delivery a steady stream of data, i.e., digitized voice. The data rate for each channel is exactly what is need to carry a digitized voice—64Kbits/sec. The techniques used to arrive at this figure are discussed under "NADH (North American Digital Hierarchy)."

While companies have long used TDM circuits for both voice and data, TDM circuits are not ideal for data because data tends to be bursty. The repeating time slots do a good job at delivering the streaming bits of digitized voice, but data bursts fill up the slots unevenly. When there is no data to send, bandwidth goes unused. When data bursts, there is usually not enough bandwidth.

A TDM network is a *private network* because the TDM links are dedicated for the traffic of the customer that leases the lines. No other users share the links. For real-time data services, bandwidth and latency are predictable. The customer usually maintains all the endpoint equipment and gets full use of the line to deliver any type of information they want to send (data/voice/video).

Since TDM circuits are point-to-point links, multipoint metropolitan and wide area network that require full interconnection must be built with multiple circuits, as shown in the following illustration.

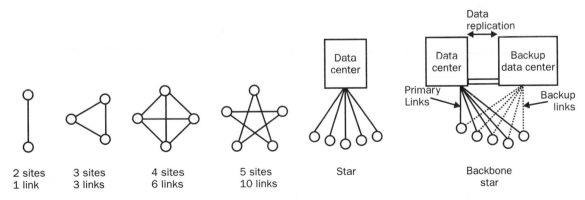

Note that as the number of sites grows, the number of links required for a fully meshed network increases proportionally to the number of sites. This is truly a problem for large companies with many sites or service providers trying to build large interconnected networks. One solution is to consider a *star* or *backbone star* topology, as shown on the right. In this configuration, every site is connected to a central site, which manages all message exchanges and provides a central data center. The backbone star provides redundancy. If the central data center fails, the other takes over. If a primary link to a remote site fails, a dial-up or switched high-speed link can be established to the backup data center.

A traditional T1 line is a local loop twisted-pair copper wire that is *conditioned*, meaning that the signal is regenerated at regular intervals (every 6,000 feet except for the first and last, which are 3,000 feet from the endpoints) to maintain a high signal quality. Two pairs of wire are required. Some common T1 connection scenarios are pictured in Figure T-4, and the equipment for these connections is described here:

- **CSU/DSU (channel service unit/data service unit)**   The CSU/DSU is the actual connection point for the T1 wires. It provides line diagnosis and keep-alive functions for the line. The T1 line connects to the unit via an RJ connector and the bridge/router connects via a V.35 interface. The CSU/DSU provides signal conversion and clocking between the two communication channels.

- **Multiplexer**   A multiplexer (also called a *channel bank*) directs multiple voice and/or data channels onto a T1 line. Many multiplexers have built-in CSU/DSU for direct connection to T1 lines.

- **Bridge or router**   The bridge or router provides the interface that allows internal servers and networks to use the T1 link as a network extension or interconnection.

In Figure T-4a, the entire T1 line is used for data. In T-4b, a multiplexer fills the time slots in the T1 channel with voice and data. Some of the channels are reserved for voice, and the remaining bandwidth is allocated to data. In Figure T- 4c, a T1 inverse multiplexer is used to combine multiple T1 lines into a single high-bandwidth channel between two network sites.

While private TDM networks have the advantage of dedicated nonshared bandwidth and privacy, the cost can be high. The lease rate increases with distance. The data rate is fixed as well. You pay the lease rate whether you fully utilize the line or not. If more bandwidth is needed, you may need one or more supplemental lines or bandwidth-on-demand links. These lines can be multilinked, as discussed under "Inverse Multiplexing" and "MLPPP (Multilink PPP)."

Many organizations need to change their wide area network connections as markets change, as workgroups form and disband, or as mergers take place. In this case, fast packet-switching services such as frame relay provide a more flexible solution than TDM WANs, especially for long-distance connections. Packet services offer bandwidth on demand and the ability to switch connections. In addition, they can mimic dedicated circuits through "virtual circuit" capabilities. These "cloud" type networks provide any-to-any links at a low cost because many users share the services.

Frame relay is a suitable alternative to long-distance TDM circuits simply because the cost is much less and it is easier to build connections to many different offices (you don't need a dedicated fixed-bandwidth circuit). A TDM circuit such as T1 and T3 is the traditional method of connecting an office into the frame relay network. The TDM circuit spans the short hop between the customer and the carrier's point of presence. However, many customers are looking for alternatives to this traditional T1 or T3 access link. One solution is frame over DSL, which uses cheaper DSL connections to send data into frame relay clouds. Many see DSL and

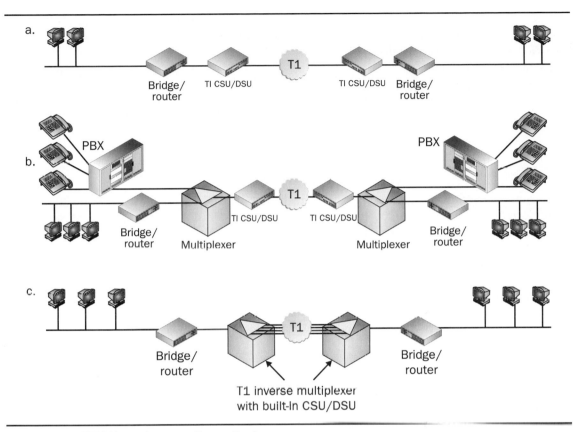

Figure T-4. *TDM Network connection methods*

services such as frame over DSL as a threat to the LEC's TDM circuit business. Rhythms NetConnections (http://www.rhythms.com/) is providing frame over DSL in its service areas.

Another method for building wide area networks is building VPNs (virtual private networks) over the Internet. See "VPN (Virtual Private Network)" for more details. Many other services for building wide area networks are discussed under "Network Access Services" and "WAN (Wide Area Network)."

Related Entries   Bandwidth on Demand; Bandwidth Reservation; Bonding; Circuit; Circuit-Switching Services; Communication Services and Providers; CSU/DSU (Channel Service Unit/Data Service Unit); Data Communication Concepts; DDR (Dial-on-Demand Routing); Dial-up Line; DSL (Digital Subscriber Line); E Carrier; IADs (Integrated Access Devices); IMA (Inverse Multiplexing over ATM); Leased Line; Link Aggregation; Load Balancing; Local Loop; MAN (Metropolitan Area Network); MLPPP (Multilink PPP); Multiplexing and Multiplexers; NADH (North American Digital Hierarchy); Network Access Services; Packets and Packet-Switching Networks; Point-to-Point Communications; Service Providers and Carriers; SONET (Synchronous Optical Network); T Carrier; Telecommunications and Telephone Systems; Voice over IP (VoIP); VPNs (Virtual Private Network); *and* WAN (Wide Area Network)

Linktionary!—Tom Sheldon's Encyclopedia of Networking updates	http://www.linktionary.com/t/tdm_newtork.html
"All You Wanted to Know About T1 But Were Afraid to Ask" by Bob Wachtel	http://www.marconi.com/html/education/wanmenu.htm
	http://www.dcbnet.com/notes/9611t1.html
Everything T1 Web page	http://www.everythingt1.com/
Bitpipe.com (search for "TDM")	http://www.bitpipe.com/

Telecommunications and Telephone Systems

"Telecommunications" is derived from the Greek "tele" (distant) and "communicate" (sharing). In modern terms, telecommunication is the electronic transmission of sound, data, facsimiles, pictures, voice, video, and other information between systems using either analog or digital signaling techniques. Transmissions may take place over guided media (copper cables and fiber-optic cables) or unguided media (wireless radio, microwave, and infrared).

The voice telephone systems are generally referred to as the PSTN (public-switched telephone network). You will also hear the phone system referred to as POTS (plain old telephone system). The system was designed from the ground up for voice. It is a circuit-switching system that sets up voice circuits across a hierarchy of digital switching systems connected by copper and optical cables.

Most of the telecommunication systems around the world are regulated by governments and international organizations. In the United States, the interstate telecommunication industry is regulated by the FCC. Regulation is a controversial topic, and one that affects nearly all aspects of metropolitan and wide area voice and data networking.

The telecommunication environment is now populated with a number of carriers and service providers, include the ILECs, IXCs (interexchange carriers), CAPs (competitive access providers), CLECS (competitive LECs), ISPs (internet service providers), and ICPs (integrated communications providers). These are discussed under "Service Providers and Carriers." The changes in the regulatory environment that spawned their creation are discussed under "Telecommunications Regulation."

As mentioned, the FCC regulates telecommunications in the United States. On a global scale, several organizations recommend telecommunication standards and develop policies that encourage cooperation. The primary standards organizations are the ITU (International Telecommunication Union), ISO (International Standards Organization), and the IEC (International Electrotechnical Commission). These organization are discussed under their own headings in this book.

Structure of the Telephone Network

The public-switched telephone network (PSTN) consists of transmission components, switching components, and facilities for maintenance equipment, billing systems, and other internal components. *Transmission components (links)* define the cable or wireless infrastructure for transmitting signals. *Switching components (nodes)* include transmitters and receivers for setting up voice circuits.

The existing telecommunication systems in the Unites States consist largely of copper twisted-pair wiring in the local loop (the wiring from the phone company to homes and offices) and fiber-optic cable or microwave systems for backbone trunks and long-distance lines. The local loop still uses analog transmission methods for voice calls.

Figure T-5 illustrates service areas and facilities. LECs (local exchange carriers) operate within specific franchised service areas (basically service monopolies) called LATAs (local access and transport areas). LATAs were defined during the split-up of AT&T. The border of a LATA defines where local service ends and long-distance service begins. A LATA is associated with one or more telephone area code. LECs may be one of the incumbent carriers and a competitive access provider. The local carrier typically has several switching offices (called central offices, or COs) within the same LATA.

An *IXC (interexchange carrier)* is any long-distance provider, such as AT&T, MCI, or US Sprint, that provides services between the LECs. The LECs are required to provide a point of presence (an interface) for the IXCs. Communication facilities employed by the IXCs include fiber-optic cable, ground-based microwave towers, and satellite-based microwave systems.

Switching Hierarchy

The telephone system was originally designed as a hierarchy of switches that set up calls across COs, across LATAs, or across long-distance connections. This hierarchy is pictured in Figure T-6.

The hierarchy can be traced back to the first phone systems. In the late 1800s, when telephones were first introduced, people would buy a pair of phones and run a wire between the phones. Soon, cities were enmeshed in telephone cables running in all directions. Savvy entrepreneurs like Alexander Graham Bell built telephone companies so customers could run their wires to a single location and let operators connect them with other phones via a manually operated switching system. At first, customers could only connect with other customers at the switch, but soon, trunk lines were established between phone companies and everybody could call everybody else in the same local area. This grew into the hierarchy of switches that eventually extended to outlying areas and other cities. See "Network Core Technologies" for a description of how this system developed into an optical system.

Note in Figure T-6 that calls within the same CO do not need to be switched any further up the hierarchy than the local CO. A call attached to another CO within the same LATA may go directly to that CO if a line exists, or go through a tandem or long-distance carrier. InterLATA calls are handled by IXCs such as AT&T or MCI. The calls circuits are set up to the IXC's point of presence within the LATA, then out across the long-distance lines and into a point of presence at the other end. The point of presence may be within the local carriers CO or a separate building that may be just next door.

While this system can be explained as a hierarchical structure, today, almost all switching offices are now interconnected to avoid congestion. In addition, a nonhierarchical dynamic routing system is used, as explained later. In Figure T-6, the dotted lines indicate the addition of these trunks. Still, hierarchical terminology is used to describe switching equipment.

The original switches were manually configured by operators. Later, mechanical switches were developed, such as the rotary wiper switches that moved through contacts were arranged in a circle. ESS (electronic switching systems) started to appear in the 1960s. At first, the switches were electromechanical, with the electronic components being added to reduce the number of mechanical parts. Eventually, all-electric switches were developed using solid-state

T

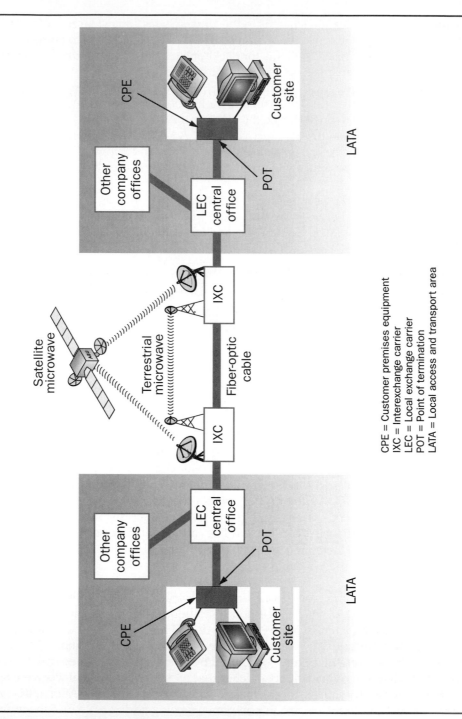

Figure T-5. *Telephone network service areas and facilities*

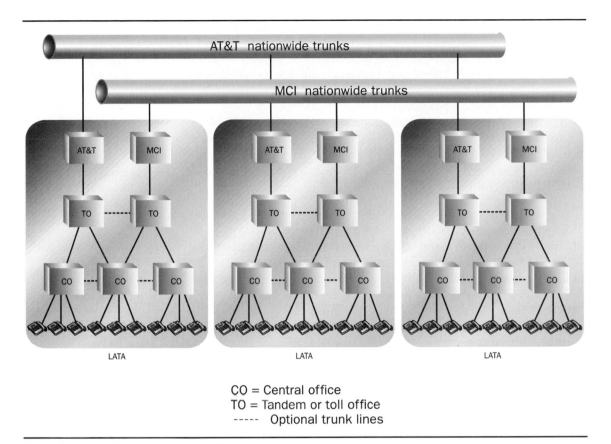

CO = Central office
TO = Tandem or toll office
----- Optional trunk lines

Figure T-6.   *Switching hierarchy of the telephone system*

components and no mechanical parts. Today, switches are programmable digital systems that support unique services such as call forwarding and caller ID, as described later under "IN (Intelligent Network)."

A Class 5 switch is an end office switch that is located at a CO. Customers are attached to these switches. They provide POTS (plain old telephone service), local numbering, emergency services, and other services. COs connect to tandem office, and the Class 5 switches interconnect with Class 4 switches in the tandem office. Tandem switches provide connections among COs and connections into higher-level switches. There is little differentiation among Class 1 through Class 3 switches. They are often called regional, sectional, or intercity switched, respectively.

In the 1980s, AT&T replaced the static hierarchical network scheme with a dynamic routing scheme called DNHR (Dynamic Non-Hierarchical Routing). DNHR is similar to IP routing. A paper by Greg Trangmoe listed later describes DNHR.

The telephone system now uses digital signaling except in the local loop. When an analog voice signal reaches a central office, it is digitized and multiplexed into a digital trunk line that connects to another CO or a tandem office.

Analog voice is digitized using PCM (pulse-code modulation), a sampling technique in which the voltage level of an analog signal is read 8,000 times per second. This 8,000-Hz sampling rate is two times the highest frequency of the range used to carry voice (300 to 4,000 Hz) and produces a relatively good digital representation. Each voltage level sample is converted to an 8-bit value that is transmitted across the line. A single digitized voice call requires 64,000 bits/sec of bandwidth (8,000 samples/sec × 8 bits/sample).

The carriers use TDM (time division multiplexing) to transmit multiple voice calls over a single line. A single call has a data rate of 64 Kbits/sec as just described. This is called a DS-0 in NADH (North American Digital Hierarchy). A total of 24 DS-0s are multiplexed into a T1 circuit. A T3 line, which is called a DS-3, consists of 28 T1 lines or 672 DS-0 channels. At higher levels, DS signal are multiplexed into SONET neworks, which use the OC (optical carrier) scheme. See "NADH (North American Digital Hierarchy)" and "OC (Optical Carrier)."

DLC (Digital Loop Carrier)

DLC is a system that lets the telephone companies extend telephone services to outlying areas. Picture a small town with a single telephone company central office. All the copper wires for all the phones extend back to this central office. Now, suppose a subdivision is built outside town. To provide service, the telephone company installs a digital loop carrier system near the subdivision. All the subscribers in the subdivision connect to the DLC system, which itself is connected back to the central office via a trunk line (T1/E1) or fiber-optic connection.

With DLC, it is not necessary to run copper cable for every subscriber back to the central office. A DLC basically terminates the copper loop in local neighborhoods. The outlying DLC systems may be either remote offices that house DLC equipment to support entire neighborhoods or they may be small *remote terminals*, which are typically installed in office buildings and support approximately 100 subscribers.

DLC poses problems for CLECs that want to reach remote customers and offer DSL services. The CLEC must run a cable out to the remote terminal in order to access the copper loops. They may have trouble establishing a presence at the site and ILECs have not been accommodating to their needs.

PBX Systems and Multichannel Lines

The bottom of the hierarchy in Figure T-6 seems to indicate that all lines from COs terminate at a single phone. In fact, the phone company extends multichannel digital lines (T1 and T3 lines) into businesses that have multiple phones. The business sets up a PBX (private branch exchange) that essentially provides an extension of the telephone company's switching system into the local business. The telephone company can then route all calls for phones within a business to the PBX and rely on the PBX to distribute those calls. Centrex is a PBX that the carrier maintains at its own facility. Subscribers lease Centrex services rather than buy their own PBX. In either case, a digital trunk extends from the carrier to the customer site. See "PBX (Private Branch Exchange)" and "Centrex (CENTRal Exchange)" in this book.

IN (Intelligent Network)

IN is the intelligent portion of the public telephone network that contains the logic for routing calls, establishing connections, and providing advanced features such as unique customer services and custom programming of the network. You will hear about the *AIN (Advanced*

Intelligent Network). It was supposed to provide a way for customers to deploy services, but was never fully developed. For more information, see "Intelligent Network (IN)," a paper written by Telecordia and available at the Web ProForum site listed later.

Before the IN, the telephone network consisted of hardwired switching systems. These hardwired systems were difficult to upgrade. As new features and services were requested from customers, new switches had to be designed, manufactured, and installed. That process could take years. In addition, different carriers used switches from different vendors, so services were difficult to implement across carrier service areas.

In the mid-1960s, SPC (stored program control) switches were developed that allowed the carrier to program new services directly into the switch. In the 1970s, the networks were further enhanced with the introduction of CCS (Common Channel Signaling) networks and SS7 (Signaling System 7) protocol. CCS networks have a signaling path that is separate from the actual voice call circuit. Call setup information is handled by SS7 and the information is transferred via packets across an overlay packet-switching network. The components of the network are pictures in Figure T-7.

The network consists of a transport plane that provides circuit-switched telephone connections. Calls are multiplexed onto trunk lines via time division multiplexing. These nodes are connected to the SS7 signaling plane via SSPs (service switching points). The signaling plane is a packet-switched network that carries SS7 messages. The STPs (service transfer points) are the switching nodes of this network and the SCPs (service control points) are database servers where service control information is hosted.

The system goes to work when a caller lifts the handset on a telephone. The telephone is connected to a switch at a CO. This switch detects that the phone is "off-hook" and responds with a dial tone. It then listens for the dialed digital tones that represent the destination telephone. The digits are passed up to the SS7 network and the SCPs, which determine the route to the destination CO. A circuit is then set up in the transport layer When the called party answers, the circuit is completed. Analog speech is then digitized and delivered across the circuit.

The Intelligent Network provides unique services. For example, a service called SRF (special resource function) plays recorded messages and prompts users to respond with inputs from the telephone keypad. The SSPs capture the digits and pass them up to the service layer, where they are routed via SS7 messages to appropriate SCPs. The SCP may use the information to query the service database and provide a suitable response. Calling card services user this feature.

The primary advantage of a separate signaling system is that the phone network becomes more flexible and allows for the introduction of new services, such as the range of three-digit services (800, 888, 900, etc.). For example, with caller ID, the caller's telephone number is transferred across the SS7 signaling path.

The Intelligent Networking Forum was formed in 1995 to further the use of the IN and stimulate global market growth for distributed network intelligence products and services across public telephony, data, and enterprise networks. The Web address is given later.

While the Intelligent Network is a good idea (anybody that uses caller ID will agree) for a voice communication system, David Isenberg argues in his classic essay "Rise of the Stupid Network" that the Intelligent Network is based on assumptions that are detrimental to the deployment of new data-oriented network services. These assumptions include a belief that the infrastructure is limited and bandwidth is scarce, that human voice generates the most traffic,

T

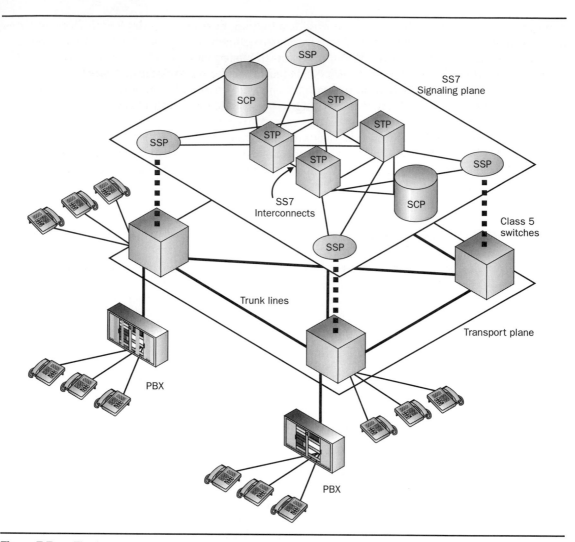

Figure T-7.   *The legacy PSTN network architecture*

that circuit switching is all that matters, and that the telephone company should control the network. Isenberg notes that the telephone companies developed the Intelligent Network to counter threats to its infrastructure, but that this response is much like the way sailing merchants responded to the threat of steam by inventing faster sailing ships in the mid-1800s!

In contrast, the Internet is built on the assumption that the network should be dumb and fast, and that end systems are smart. The original Internet architects removed as many services from the network as possible to reduce complexity and provide fast packet-switching services. Routers do not keep track of packets or do anything to ensure delivery. They just forward packets.

The assumption was that end systems would have processors and memory and be able to provide reliability services such as detecting errors and recovering lost packets. This design has been profound. It meant that end systems would become the focus of application development for the Internet, not the network provider. The telephone network may be "smart," but telephones are dumb. You can't run applications on your phone like you can on a PC. In fact, you are totally dependent on the phone company to deploy new applications (call waiting and caller ID are examples). Compared to the Internet, the phone system is a dinosaur. Consider that the user interface for the Web is a full-color graphical browser while the interface for the telephone network is a 12-key pad!

The NPN (new public network) is an emerging communication system that converges the PSTN (public-switched telephone network) and the Internet. It is a packet-switched network that will deliver voice with the same reliability now provided by the PSTN. See "NPN (New Public Network)."

Carrier and Service Provider Resources

The following Web sites provide links to telecommunications companies. Due to mergers and acquisitions, some of the links at these sites may redirect you to other sites or fail. Still, these sites are the best source for links. See "Service Providers and Carriers" for additional information.

Telecom's Virtual Library	http://www.analysys.com/vlib/
Jeffrey K. MacKie-Mason's Telecom Information Resources	http://china.si.umich.edu/telecom/
NextGen Telcos and ITSPs	http://www.pulver.com/nextgen/
Telecommunication Companies list by David C. Blight	http://www.ee.umanitoba.ca/~blight/ telecommunications/telco.html
Service Providers list by David C. Blight	http://www.ee.umanitoba.ca/~blight/ telecommunications/telecom28.html
Telco Exchange (gateway for telecom services)	http://www.telcoexchange.com/
Lucio Goelzer's Telecommunication Resources list	http://www.goelzer.net/telecom/index.shtml

Related Entries   AIN (Advanced Intelligent Network); AT&T; B-ISDN (Broadband ISDN); Call Center Operations; Centrex (CENTRal EXchange); Circuit; Circuit-Switching Services; CO (Central Office); Communication Services and Providers; CTI (Computer-Telephony Integration); Data Communication Concepts; DSL (Digital Subscriber Line); ISDN (Integrated Services Digital Network); Leased Line; Local Loop; NADH (North American Digital Hierarchy); Network Access Services; Network Core Technologies; NPN (New Public Network); Optical Networks; Service Providers and Carriers; Softswitch; SONET (Synchronous Optical Network); SS7 (Signaling System 7); T Carriers; Telecommunications Regulation; Voice/Data Networks; Voice over IP (VoIP); *and* WAN (Wide Area Network)

Linktionary!—Tom Sheldon's Encyclopedia of Networking updates	http://www.linktionary.com/t/ telecommunications.html
Intelligent Network Forum	http://www.inf.org/
Committee T1 (creates telecom standards in the U.S.)	http://www.t1.org/

ETSI (European Telecommunications Standards Institute)	http://www.etsi.org/
ITU (International Telecommunication Union)	http://www.itu.int/
United States FCC (Federal Communications Commission) consumer information	http://www.fcc.gov/cib/
Bell Labs Innovations (see Technology section)	http://www.bell-labs.com/
Telecordia Technologies (formerly Bellcore)	http://www.telecordia.com/
IEC (International Engineering Consortium)	http://www.iec.org/
Web ProForum Tutorial: "Fundamentals of Telecommunications"	http://www.iec.org/tutorials/fund_telecom/
Web ProForum Tutorial: "Signaling System 7 (SS7)"	http://www.iec.org/tutorials/ss7/
Web ProForum Tutorial: "Intelligent Network (IN)"	http://www.iec.org/tutorials/in/
Paradyne's DSL Sourcebook (provides good overview of telecom technologies)	http://www.paradyne.com/sourcebook_offer/sb_pdf.html
David Isenberg and his paper "Rise of the Stupid Network"	http://www.isen.com/
A Comparative Study of Dynamic Routing in Circuit-Switched Networks by Greg Trangmoe	http://www.ece.arizona.edu/~trangmoe/dyroute/dyroute.html
"Netheads versus Bellheads" by T. M. Denton Consultants (With François Ménard and David Isenberg)	http://www.tmdenton.com/netheads.htm
"Technology in the Local Network," a GTE Laboratories paper	http://bob.nap.edu/html/wpni3/ch-53.html
Yahoo! Telecommunications page	http://dir.yahoo.com/science/engineering/electrical_engineering/telecommunications/
ePanorama — Telephone technology page (good technology overview)	http://www.us-epanorama.net/telephone.html
Telecommunications Magazine	http://www.telecoms-mag.com/
Telephony World.com	http://www.telephonyworld.com/
CLEC.com	http://www.clec.com/

Telecommunications Regulation

Traditionally, the telecommunication industry around the world has been regulated by governments and international organizations. More recently, telecom regulations are being liberalized and even removed to promote healthy competition. In the deregulated environment, many new competitive carriers have appeared. Many new and unique services are being offered, and bandwidth is exploding as new service providers scramble to install fiber or wireless access systems in metro areas.

Customers no longer need to lease private line TDM-based circuits to build metropolitan and wide area networks. Many new options are available, including metro-Ethernet access networks. In addition, a new packet-oriented public network is emerging that converges the best features of the PSTN and the Internet. See "NPN (New Public Network)."

With all these benefits, why was the industry regulated in the first place? In the United States, regulation began in 1866 with the signing of the Post Roads Act, which gave the U.S. Postmaster General control over the telegraph industry. Today, in the United States, the interstate telecommunication industry is regulated by the FCC (Federal Communications Commission), which was formed with the Communications Act of 1934. Individual state PUCs (public utility commissions) regulate communications within their jurisdictions. The FCC also regulates the use of wireless radio frequencies through a system of spectrum allocation and licensing.

AT&T (American Telephone and Telegraph) played an important part in the formation of the U.S. telecommunication system. It became so large that the government brought a number of antitrust suits against it over the years. In 1913, AT&T was forced to divest itself from Western Union and allow independent carriers to use its long-distance networks. With the 1921 Graham Act, Congress created exceptions to antitrust laws for telecommunications companies that would allow them to build what were essentially monopolistic infrastructures within their service areas. To provide balance, the companies were required to provide *universal service*, which dictated that all customers be treated equally.

Eventually, AT&T assumed dominant control of this structure, and by 1984 AT&T was forced by the Justice Department to break up into seven regional holding companies called the RBOCs (regional Bell operating companies), in addition to the research division called Bellcore (now Lucent). This "divestiture" opened up the long-distance telephone business to competition. Competitors such as Sprint and MCI (Microwave Communications Inc.) quickly began building microwave and fiber-optic long-distance infrastructure. In the local area, the RBOCs were required to provide a PoP (point of presence) within their switching offices for long-distance providers.

The RBOCs provide their services within specific geographic areas called LATAs (local access and transport areas). A LATA basically separates local and long-distance telephone markets. A LEC (local exchange carrier) has a franchise within a LATA (intraLATA) to provide services. The RBOCs and the independent LECs were limited to providing local phone service, producing yellow pages, and selling equipment, but were restricted from providing long-distance service, information services, and cable TV services.

InterLATA telecommunication refers to services provided between LATAs by IXCs (interexchange carriers) such as AT&T, MCI, US Sprint, and others. RBOCs must provide all interexchange carriers with equal access to their LATA facilities. Users can therefore choose which interexchange carrier (AT&T, MCI, US Sprint, and others) they want to use.

Up until early 1996, the RBOCs and AT&T services were regulated and prices were fixed for services. For example, *tariffs* that controlled interLATA service rates could not be changed without approval from the federal government. IntraLATA tariffs were controlled at the state level. The *Telecommunications Reform Act of 1996* changed that. It was designed to open local and long-distance markets to alternative providers (cable, cellular, broadcast companies) that were allowed to provide services in both local and long-distance areas. This allowed for *end-to-end packaging* of services, so customers could purchase services across both local and wide areas from a single provider.

A driving concept was that no one company could control the head end of the local loop, which directly connects to homes and businesses. The Act required that the incumbent carriers further open their facilities to CLECs, provide space (if available) in central offices for co-location of competitor's equipment, provide access to the unbundled network elements, and provide services at wholesale prices.

The Telecom Act of 1996 stipulates that ILECs must offer services to CLECs at wholesale prices and allow CLECs to plug into the existing phone system and gain access to SS7 signaling. Technically, CLECs get access to UNEs (unbundled network elements), which basically gives CLECs access to the local loop and subscribers at the end of those wires.

The FCC dissolved the 62-year-old tariff system for long-distance carriers and opened the pricing system up to negotiable contracts. It also dissolved the pricing rules that controlled what incumbent carriers could charge competitors for access to their networks. However, in 1999, the U.S. Supreme Court ruled that the FCC should once again impose national pricing guidelines. Conformance to those guidelines is used as a qualifier in determining an incumbent carrier's ability to expand into long-distance services.

The ILECs are not required to go out of their way to help CLECs deploy advanced services. The CLECs want to co-locate advanced equipment in the ILEC COs that would support a variety of extended services such as DSL, fiber, and wireless, but the ILECs are resisting and claim that the current Act does not require them to open up their facilities in this way.

There is some question whether the Telecommunications Act can be used to regulate networks as they evolve. In other words, does the Act only apply to the way the network was structured in 1996, or should its wording evolve as the network evolves? For example, the ILECs appear to be altering the infrastructure in ways that sidestep the Act in order to lock out CLECs. In some areas, the ILECs are removing copper loops and installing fiber. Do they have the right to remove copper loops that CLECs depend on for their own business?

In another example, ILECs are improving DSL service by building remote central offices that are closer to users. This reduces the length of the copper loop and the remote office is trunked back to ILEC facilities via fiber cable. The problem for CLECs is that without ILEC cooperation, they will need to run their own cable out to the remote offices, build a facility, and hope that they can connect advanced services. The ILECs argue that the Act does not require them to assist the CLECs in deploying advanced services in this environment.

An industry group including Microsoft, Intel, Compaq, and a number of carriers issued a petition to the FCC calling for even less regulation. The petition called "Ten Principles for the Promotion of Widespread Deployment of Advanced Services" may be found at the Progress and Freedom Foundation Web site given later, with commentary by Jeffrey A. Eisenach. The petition offers some interesting points, but it does tend to favor the incumbent carrier's point of view regarding regulation.

As mentioned, the FCC regulates telecommunications in the United States. Committee T1 is a U.S. organization concerned with public network standards in the Unites States. It is supported by both ANSI (American National Standards Institute) and the FCC. In Europe, the ETSI (European Telecommunications Standards Institute) is concerned with telecommunication standards for Eastern and Western Europe. On a global scale, the primary standards organizations are the

ITU (International Telecommunication Union), ISO (International Standards Organization), and the IEC (International Electrotechnical Commission). Their Web site addresses are given here. The ITU and ISO are described elsewhere in this book.

Related Entries   AT&T; CO (Central Office); Communication Services and Providers; Local Loop; Network Access Services; Network Core Technologies; NPN (New Public Network); Service Providers and Carriers; Telecommunications and Telephone Systems; Voice/Data Network; Voice over IP (VoIP); *and* WAN (Wide Area Network)

Linktionary!—Tom Sheldon's Encyclopedia of Networking updates	http://www.linktionary.com/t/telco_regulation.html
United States FCC (Federal Communications Commission) consumer information	http://www.fcc.gov/cib/
Committee T1 (creates telecom standards in the U.S.)	http://www.t1.org/
ETSI (European Telecommunications Standards Institute)	http://www.etsi.org/
ITU (International Telecommunication Union)	http://www.itu.int/
Telecommunications Act of 1996	http://www.fcc.gov/telecom.html
Journalism Resources by Karla Tonella (numerous papers about regulation and telecom/Internet law)	http://bailiwick.lib.uiowa.edu/journalism/mediaLaw/index.html
Lucio Goelzer's Telecommunication Resources list (see Regulation section)	http://www.goelzer.net/telecom/index.shtml
Prof. Jeffrey MacKie-Mason's Telecom Policy and Regulation links page	http://china.si.umich.edu/telecom/policy.html
"Ten Principles for the Promotion of Widespread Deployment of Advanced Services" paper at Progress and Freedom Foundation	http://www.pff.org/popdec98.html

Telecommuting

See Mobile Computing.

Teledesic

Teledesic is an "Internet in the sky" company that is establishing a constellation of satellites to support a global packet network. It was recently allocated two 500-MHz spectrum bands in the spectrum in the 28.6–29.1-GHz and 18.8–19.3-GHz ranges. Teledesic will offer speeds matching fiber optics and services such as Internet access, videoconferencing, and interactive multimedia. The company is backed by Microsoft's Bill Gates, Craig McCaw (of cable and cellular network fame), and Saudi princes.

Related Entries   Broadband Communications and Networking; Communication Services and Providers; DBS (Direct Broadcast Satellite); HALO (High Altitude Long Operation); Home Networking; Internet Connections; Last Mile Services; Microwave Communications; Network Access Services; Residential Broadband; Satellite Communication Systems; *and* Wireless Communications

ICO Teledesic home page   http://www.teledesic.com

Lloyd's satellite constellations Teledesic page   http://www.ee.surrey.ac.uk/Personal/L.Wood/ constellations/teledesic.html

Telematics

Telematics is the combination of telecommunications and data processing. It refers to the transmission of data across distances. The best example is the use of advanced computer and communications equipment and information services to bring mobile computing to the automobile. GM's OnStar is an example of a system that has been in use for some time.

Ford started equipping telematic wireless Web access and navigation systems to its cars in 2001. The systems are called Wingcast and are based on Qualcomm's CDMA wireless technology.

Clarion's AutoPC will likely be the first general-purpose car computer. It uses speech recognition to allow drivers to control the radio and other car features with voice commands.

Telephony

Telephony is all about converting sounds such as voice for delivery over a medium, such as copper wire or radio waves. Telephony is different from telegraphy (Morse code) and teletype (later facsimile).

See "Telecommunications and Telephone Systems."

Telnet

Telnet is the login and terminal emulation protocol common on the Internet and in UNIX environments. It operates over TCP/IP networks. It allows users to log into remote host systems and provides basic communication functions between hosts. Originally, Telnet was a simple terminal program that sent all user input to the remote host for processing. Newer versions perform more processing locally, thus providing better response and reducing the amount of information transferred over the link to the remote host. Administrators often use Telnet to control remote servers.

Telnet was developed in the early days of the Internet when the network interconnected mainframe systems built by IBM, DEC, Honeywell, and Xerox. According to *Where Wizards Stay Up Late* (Katie Hafner and Matthew Lyon, 1996, Touchstone), "Telnet was conceived in order to overcome simple differences, such as establishing a connection and determining what kind of character set to use." Thus, Telnet helped pave the way for rapid expansion of the Internet.

Telnet is a client/server process in which the user invokes the Telnet application on the local system and sets up a link to a Telnet process running on a remote host. The user issues requests at the keyboard that are passed to the Telnet client running in his or her system. Telnet then transmits the requests to the Telnet server on the remote host. Through this process, users can initiate programs on the remote host and run those programs from their own systems as if they were attached directly to the remote host. Most processes run on the remote host. It receives requests from the user's system and processes them in its workspace, thus reducing traffic over the link.

Telnet was originally defined in RFC 854 (Telnet Protocol Specification, May 1983). A number of other RFCs were written to enhance this RFC. These are outlined in the References section of RFC 2877 (5250 Telnet Enhancements, July 2000). In 2000, RFCs 2941–2944 and RFCs 2946–2953 were written to define Telnet authentication and encryption options.

Related Entries   Internet; Internet Protocol Suite; *and* Remote Access

Linktionary!—Tom Sheldon's Encyclopedia of Networking updates	http://www.linktionary.com/t/telnet.html
IETF Working Group: Telnet TN3270 Enhancements (tn3270e)	http://www.ietf.org/html.charters/tn3270e-charter.html
Telnet protocol information	http://www.scit.wlv.ac.uk/~jphb/comms/telnet.html
RAD Communication Telnet Tutorial	http://www.rad.com/networks/1997/telnet/index.htm

Terabit Routers

See Routers.

Terminal Servers

Terminal servers (not to be confused with "terminal services," discussed under the next heading) can connect large numbers of terminals to mainframe or minicomputer systems over a LAN (local area network). The terminals are attached to the terminal server via RS-232 serial interfaces, and the terminal server is connected to an Ethernet or token ring network. The network then serves as the link between the host system and the terminals. A terminal server is basically an asynchronous multiplexer that connects not only terminals but computers, modems, printers, and other peripherals to the host system. The terminal server has a number of serial ports and the appropriate network interface.

Terminal servers are not gateways because the attached terminal devices are using a communication protocol that is compatible with the host. When a personal computer is attached to a host through a terminal server, it runs a terminal emulation program that lets it mimic the communication protocols of a terminal. Note, however, that the terminal server does encapsulate data from terminals for transport over the network to the host system.

T

Terminal Services

Terminal services work in conjunction with thin clients to provide a network-based client/server computing environment in which much of the processing load is shifted from the client to the server. The thin client and the terminal server operate in what is called a thin-client computing environment. Terminal services refer to the software that resides on back-end servers that host multiple, simultaneous thin clients. Servers in this environment must manage the sessions and applications of multiple users. However, there is reduced network traffic, reduced client cost, and ease of management. Thin clients are ideal for users that perform just a few tasks, such as order processing and retail sales, or in call center and kiosk environments.

In terms of functionality, thin clients fall between dumb terminals and smart full-function desktop PCs. While terminals servers perform the bulk of processing, thin clients provide high-resolution GUI displays and keyboard functionality. They also include embedded operating systems such as Windows CE or Linux. See "Thin Clients" for a more complete description.

One category of thin clients is specifically designed to be a Web terminal. They are capable of accessing any Web site and running the Java applets or other code at those sites. Some include hard drives to cache Web objects (the drives are not meant for permanent storage).

There are three primary terminal services vendors: Microsoft, Citrix, and Sun Microsystems (although Sun does not refer to its product as "terminal services" as described later). Microsoft has two separate products: Windows NT 4 Terminal Server Edition and Windows 2000 with Terminal Services. Citrix sold its original product to Microsoft and now sells advanced terminal services products.

Citrix developed its concept of thin-client computing in 1990 with multiuser products that ran on IBM OS/2. Later, it started developing for the Windows NT and introduced a multiuser environment called WinFrame. WinFrame allows the Windows NT server to host multiple, simultaneous client sessions. Users still see the familiar Windows desktop and interface, but the server does most of the processing. Citrix is also responsible for developing the WBT (Windows-Based Terminal) architecture.

Winframe is based on Citrix's *ICA (Independent Computing Architecture)*, a general-purpose presentation services protocol for Microsoft Windows. It is similar to X Window in the UNIX environment and allows applications to execute on a WinFrame multiuser Windows application server. Only the user interface, keystrokes, and mouse movements are transferred between the server and the client device over any network or communications protocol, minimizing the resources used by the client. ICA runs over TCP/IP, NetBEUI, IPX/SPX, and PPP, as well as remote communication protocols such as ISDN, frame relay, and ATM.

By distributing the Windows architecture, Windows applications can perform at very high speeds over low-bandwidth connections. Most important, inexpensive thin clients were developed to take advantage of the server-centric processing model.

Citrix initially tried to obtain a source code license for Windows NT 4.0, but Microsoft had been working up its own thin-client computing concept. Eventually, Microsoft decided that it was interested enough in WinFrame to license Citrix's software and integrate it with Windows NT 4.0 to create Windows TSE (Terminal Server Edition). It also integrated WinFrame into Windows 2000. Both versions are designed to run the Windows desktop and Windows-based applications on a variety of platforms, including those that normally would not be able to run Windows such as Macintosh and UNIX. In the meantime, Citrix continued to evolve WinFrame and eventually developed an enhancement product called MetaFrame, as discussed later.

One thing that Microsoft did not do was license Citrix's ICA protocol as the communication protocol between terminal services and thin clients. It instead developed its own protocol called *RDP (Remote Desktop Protocol)*. RDP and ICA are very similar in functionality, but ICA operates over very "thin" links (as low as 20 Kbits/sec) and supports Macintosh, UNIX, and Java clients, while RDP supports only 32-bit Windows applications. Recently, Microsoft enhanced RDP with encryption, printer support, clipboard redirection, and a variety of other features listed at the Microsoft Web site given later.

Once WinFrame was integrated into Windows, Citrix began work on MetaFrame, which works with Windows Terminal Server Edition and Windows 2000 to provide more features and administrative control. Citrix MetaFrame uses ICA to gain performance over RDP. An important feature is load balancing, which Microsoft recently added to its own products. Load balancing allows a terminal server to route requests to appropriate servers within a cluster of servers. MetaFrame gives administrators additional control over how applications are displayed on thin clients (e.g., resolution and number of colors). Refer to the Citrix Web site for more information.

Sun Microsystems has developed its own thin-client strategy, but Sun prefers to use "information appliance" terminology when describing its products. Its *Sun Ray Appliances* and *Hot Desk Architecture* products perform all computing on one or more centralized, shared machines. Sun Ray appliances support Solaris, Java, Microsoft NT 4.0 TSE (via Citrix MetaFrame), other UNIX platforms, and 3270/5250 platforms. Sun Ray server software runs on SPARC servers under the control of the Solaris operating system. This software provides system management and administration, including authentication of users, server group management, and redirection of input and output to the Sun Ray appliances. Administrative functions such as managing authentication policies are also included in the Sun Ray server software. All Sun Ray server software resides on the servers—nothing is stored on or downloaded to the Sun Ray appliances.

Related Entries   BOOTP (BOOTstrap Protocol); Bootstrapping or Booting; Diskless Workstations; Embedded Systems; Java; Microsoft Windows; Mobile Computing; NC (Network Computer) Devices; Network Appliances; Remote Access; Thin Clients; *and* X Window

Linktionary!—Tom Sheldon's Encyclopedia of Networking updates	http://www.linktionary.com/t/term_serv.html
Citrix Systems	http://www.citrix.com
Microsoft Terminal Services Web page	http://www.microsoft.com/WINDOWS2000/library/technologies/terminal/
Sun Microsystems Information Appliances page	http://www.sun.com/sunray/
Sun Microsystems Sun Ray Server Software	http://www.sun.com/products/sunray/software/

Testing, Diagnostics, and Troubleshooting

Testing, diagnostics, and troubleshooting covers a wide range of topics, including testing and certifying cable, network protocol analysis, benchmarking, performance analysis, and so on. Network technicians carry a variety of tools to troubleshoot network problems and test for compliance. See "Network Analyzers" for more information.

Network testing and diagnostics should be proactive—that is, it is extremely useful to have equipment that can monitor the condition of the network and warn you of impending problems. That is where network management systems based on SNMP (Simple Network Management Protocol) and RMON (Remote Monitoring) come in handy. These systems gather up and display useful information about the condition of networks and provide statistical information that can help you justify your management techniques and requirements for new equipment. See "Network Management" for more information.

This topic could fill an entire book. The Web sites listed next, including the Linktionary! Web site, provide a more information related to network troubleshooting and diagnostics.

Related Entries   Cable and Wiring; CIM (Common Information Model); CMIP (Common Management Information Protocol); DMI (Distributed Management Interface); DMTF (Distributed Management Task Force); Error Detection and Correction; MIB (Management Information Base); Network Analyzers; Network Management; Performance Measurement and Optimization; Ping (Packet Internet Groper); Power and Grounding Problems and Solutions; RMON (Remote Monitoring); SNMP (Simple Network Management Protocol); TIA/EIA Structured Cabling Standards; *and* WBEM (Web-Based Enterprise Management)

Linktionary!—Tom Sheldon's Encyclopedia of Networking updates	http://www.linktionary.com/t/testing.html
AnalogX (a great site for public domain testing tools)	http://www.analogx.com/
Interactive Ethernet Network Troubleshooting	http://www.networkcomputing.com/netdesign/troubleintro.html
Cisco Internetwork Troubleshooting Guides (extensive)	http://www.cisco.com/univercd/cc/td/doc/cisintwk/itg_v1/index.htm
Benchmark FAQ	http://hpwww.epfl.ch/bench/bench.FAQ.html
Daryl's TCP/IP Primer on Troubleshooting	http://ipprimer.windsorcs.com/section.cfm
Enterasys Networks Technical Documentation (see troubleshooting)	http://www.cabletron.com/support/manuals/overview.html
Bob Cerelli's Windows page	http://www.onecomputerguy.com/
Bitpipe.com (search for "troubleshooting")	http://www.bitpipe.com
About.com network troubleshooting links page	http://compnetworking.about.com/compute/compnetworking/cs/troubleshooting/
Novell Research Network Administrator Information & Tools Topics	http://developer.novell.com/research/topical/network_admin_info_tools.htm
Microsoft document: Troubleshooting IP Configuration	http://msdn.microsoft.com/library/winresource/dnwinnt/S7723.HTM
IETF Working Group: Benchmarking Methodology (bmwg)	http://www.ietf.org/html.charters/bmwg-charter.html

TFTP (Trivial File Transfer Protocol)

TFTP is an Internet file transfer protocol similar to FTP (File Transfer Protocol), but it is scaled back in functionality so that it requires fewer resources to run. TFTP uses the UDP (User Datagram Protocol) rather than TCP (Transmission Control Protocol), which allows TFTP to be used when the reliability features of TCP are not required and may add excessive overhead. TFTP also differs from FTP in that it only supports file transfers and does not have the user interface features that FTP has. The command set is minimized so the users cannot get directory listings. There is also no login procedure. TFTP is defined in RFC 1350 (The TFTP Protocol, July 1992).

Related Entries   File Systems; File Transfer Protocols; *and* FTP (File Transfer Protocol)

Thin Clients

The definition of a thin client has changed over the last few years as the market has changed. One overriding definition is that a thin client is a computer at the lowest price possible. That means removing some features such as disk drives and relying on network-attached servers for storage needs. Some devices have disk drives, but they are used more for caching than for permanent data storage.

Thin clients inhabit the feature space somewhere between dumb terminals and smart, full-featured desktop computers. They have features of X-terminals and diskless workstations. Devices that fall into the thin-client category include desktop (and kitchen top) Internet terminals, handheld devices, wireless PDAs, and even smart phones. A common characteristic is that thin clients are in sealed cases with no expansion slots, no hard drives, and limited upgrade capabilities. This helps cut costs. Thin clients can be categorized as follows:

- **Web/e-mail appliances**   These devices are oriented to consumers who need a simple device to view Web pages and check e-mail. They are often pictured on kitchen counter-tops and are specifically designed for Web access. Built-in processors are meant to run Java applets or other code downloaded from Web pages. Web browsers are part of the firmware. A disk drive may exist for caching, but users can also store files at Web-based storage sites.

- **Network terminals**   These devices are designed for enterprise environments where users perform limited tasks such as data entry or transactions (e.g., at the order counter or in a call center). Most of the processing is performed by *terminal servers*, which run applications for users and provide a network-based desktop that is accessible from any thin client anywhere on the network. A special protocol is used to exchange screen and keyboard information between the thin client and the back-end server.

The most common network terminal is the WBT (Windows-Based Terminal), which is designed to operate with Microsoft's Terminal Server products. Citrix developed the concept of the thin client in the Windows environment with its WinFrame terminal services software. It outlined the WBT specification and created a thin-client communications protocol called *ICA (Independent Computing Architecture)* that allows applications to execute on a multiuser Windows application server. Only the user interface, keystrokes, and mouse movements are transferred between the server and the client device. See "Terminal Services" for more information.

The Network Computer or NC was another early thin-client/network terminal concept defined by Sun Microsystems, Netscape, and Oracle. NCs support terminal emulation, X Window, Java, and Web browser software. They use non-Intel processors and were originally meant to compete with Microsoft's monopoly over the desktop with its Windows operating system. The NC never took hold, but the concept served as a model for future designs. Note that Microsoft and Intel developed a similar concept called the NetPC, but it has fallen into obscurity. As described under "Terminal Services," Microsoft joined forces with Citrix and now promotes the WBT design.

Following is a list of the most common characteristics for thin clients. Products may differ, depending on the design philosophy. Note that the product descriptions below describe enterprise network appliances that work with back-end terminal services:

■ Thin clients include high-resolution color displays and graphics systems to support complex GUIs such as Windows.

■ Operating systems may be embedded. Many devices included embedded Windows CE or Linux.

■ Some products remove *everything* from the desktop except the resources needed for the human interface (screen, keyboard, etc.). All computing, including running Java applets, is performed by back-end servers.

■ Stateless desktops are supported, meaning that the desktop does not reside in the local machine but on back-end servers. Users can log in from any thin client on the network to access their desktop, much like bank ATMs allow customer to access their accounts from any location.

■ Typically, there are no expansion slots or user-configurable features, which helps to reduce costs.

■ Floppy drives are eliminated, which provides security (users can't upload viruses or download critical data).

■ Hard disks may exist, but only as caches. Data is stored on network servers, which removes the worry of protecting and securing data at every desktop.

■ Software updates are easier with most of the software located on central servers, Administrators don't need to worry about updating every client system individually.

■ The devices work well over low-bandwidth dial-up links because only screen and keyboard information is being transferred.

The case against thin clients goes like this: A thin client is dependent on enterprise servers or Web servers. If those devices are not available, the device is not usable. In addition, the price of full-featured desktop PCs has dropped dramatically, so these systems make more sense for home users and some enterprise users. Still, the security of a diskless terminal for users who perform special tasks such as order entry is compelling in terms of network administration.

The Linktionary! Web site provides a list of thin-client systems and features.

Related Entries   ASP (Application Service Provider); BOOTP (BOOTstrap Protocol); Bootstrapping or Booting; Diskless Workstations; Embedded Systems; Java; Mobile Computing; Multitiered Architectures; Network Appliances; Remote Access; Terminal Services; *and* X Window

 Linktionary!—Tom Sheldon's Encyclopedia of   http://www.linktionary.com/t/thin_client.html
Networking updates

Thin Planet (a Web site for thin client and ASP experts)	http://www.thinplanet.com/
Boundless Technologies	http://www.boundless.com/
Citrix Systems (terminal services software)	http://www.citrix.com
Compaq Computers	http://www5.compaq.com/products/thinclients/
IBM NetVista Thin Clients	http://www.pc.ibm.com/us/netvista/thinclient.html
Insignia Solutions (Accelerated Java solutions for Internet appliances)	http://www.insignia.com/
Maxspeed Corporation (Windows and Linux thin clients)	http://www.maxspeed.com/
Neoware (thin clients and NewLinux software)	http://www.neoware.com/
Netpliance	http://www.netpliance.com/
Network Computing Devices ("The Thin Client Company")	http://www.ncd.com/
Network World thin-client computing section	http://www.nwfusion.com/netresources/thin.html
Sun Microsystems Sun Ray Appliances and Hot Desk Architecture	http://www.sun.com/sunray/
The New Internet Computer Company (an Oracle spin-off)	http://www.thinknic.com/
Wyse Technology (Winterm thin clients)	http://www.wyse.com/

Three-Tier Client-Server Model

See Multitiered Architectures.

Throttling

Throttling is a term used to describe methods used by transport layer protocols to slow down a sender. The receive host may use the techniques or network devices may use throttling to avoid network congestion. See "Flow-Control Mechanisms," "Congestion Control Mechanisms," "Queuing," and "Traffic Management, Shaping, and Engineering"

Throughput

Throughput is the number of bits transmitted per second through a communication medium or system. It is also referred to as *data rate* or *wire speed*. Throughput is measured after data transmissions because a system will add delay caused by processor limitations, network congestion, buffering inefficiencies, transmission errors, traffic loads, congestion, or inadequate hardware designs. Throughput varies over time with traffic and congestion. In addition, data is packaged in frames and packets that contain header information, so if you are trying to measure actual data throughput, you need to subtract the bits used for overhead. The topic "Delay, Latency, and Jitter" describes some of the things that affect throughput.

Fast Ethernet is rated at 100 Mbits/sec, but after delays and protocol inefficiencies, the actual user data transfer rate is much less, possibly less than 50 percent of Fast Ethernet's specified data rate. The perceived speed of a shared Ethernet LAN will be worse as more users access the system. Collisions occur, which cause stations to back off, wait, then try to retransmit.

As mentioned, the header information of frames and packets significantly reduces the throughput of actual data. Headers contain source and destination address, handshaking information, error checking codes, and so on. For example, an ATM cell can hold 53 bytes of information, but five bytes of that is reserved for header information, so only 48 bytes of actual user data gets transported in the cell. The more header information, the less data sent. Only about 90 percent of the capacity of an ATM circuit is available for transmitting actual data. In addition, some protocols require that individual frames and packets or groups of frames and packets be acknowledged by the receiver. This creates excess traffic that is not sending real data.

Network devices like routers have store and forwarding delays that reduce throughput. So-called wire-speed devices are nonblocking, meaning that they don't hold up packets, even when fully loaded. A wire-speed device must have an internal capacity to move all the data coming in from all ports without delay, even when all ports are at maximum capacity.

Congestion and queuing problems cause dropped packets that exacerbate the delay problem. See "Congestion Control Mechanisms" for more information.

The following tables describe the packet-forwarding capabilities of various devices. The first table outlines the packet's-per-second rating of the three Ethernet technologies.

Ethernet (10 Mbits/sec)	14,880 pps
Fast Ethernet	148,800 pps
Gigabit Ethernet	1.4 million pps

The packet-per-second rates of various router and switch designs are listed here:

Traditional and legacy routers	From 5,000 to 500,000 pps
Traditional router designs with enhanced architectures	1 million pps
Routing switches	1 to 10 million pps
Gigabit routers	20 million pps
Core routers designed for Internet backbone networks	100 million pps or more

Throughput Considerations for TCP

Throughput is a big issue in the Internet and several RFCs discuss the problem. RFC 1323 (TCP Extensions for High Performance, May 1992) describes TCP extensions to improve performance over high-bandwidth long-delay networks such as cross-country fiber-optic links. The RFC refers to these links as "long, fat pipes." Another interesting document is RFC 2488 (Enhancing TCP Over Satellite Channels, January 1999).

Throughput is determined by the speed (data rate in bits/sec) of link and the propagation delay, which is relatively long on cross-country fiber links and satellite links. Congestion and errors add to delay. A pipe's capacity is determined by obtaining its *bandwidth-delay products*—that is, multiplying the bandwidth by the round-trip delay time. The idea is to match the capacity of the pipe with the TCP window size so that the pipe is always full. When congestion or errors occur, TCP hosts slow down their transmissions, which means that pipes may not be fully used until the transmitting hosts reestablish the window size that matches the network capacity. See "Flow-Control Mechanisms."

Related Entries Bandwidth; Bandwidth Management; Bandwidth on Demand; Cable and Wiring; Channel; Circuit; Data Communication Concepts; Delay, Latency, and Jitter; Electromagnetic Spectrum; *and* Signals

 Linktionary!—Tom Sheldon's Encyclopedia of   http://www.linktionary.com/t/throughput.html
Networking updates

TIA (Telecommunications Industry Association)

The TIA serves as the voice of the communications and information technology industry. Its members include vendors, service providers, and organizations that get involved in all aspects of modern communications networks. The TIA gets involved in legislative efforts, international marketing opportunities, tradeshow sponsorship, and standards development. The TIA works in association with the EIA (Electronic Industries Association), and recently affiliated with the MultiMedia Telecommunications Association to work jointly on the convergence of computing technologies and communications. The TIA's Web site provides educational material related to network design and cabling.

Related Entries IEEE 802 Standards; Internet Organizations and Committees; ISO (International Organization for Standardization); ITU (International Telecommunications Union); *and* Standards Groups, Associations, and Organizations

 TIA site   http://www.tiaonline.org

EIA (Electronic Industries Association)   http://www.eia.org/

MMTA (MultiMedia Telecommunications   http://www.mmta.org/
Association)

TIA/EIA Structured Cabling Standards

In the mid-1980s, the TIA (Telecommunications Industry Association) and the EIA (Electronic Industries Association) began developing methods for cabling buildings, with the intent of developing a uniform wiring system that would support multivendor products and environments. In 1991, the TIA/EIA released the TIA/EIA 568 Commercial Building Telecommunication Cabling standard. Note that the ISO/IEC-11801 Generic Customer Premises Cabling standard is an international cabling standard that is based on the ANSI/TIA/EIA-568 cabling standard.

The TIA/EIA structured cabling standards define how to design, build, and manage a cabling system that is structured, meaning that the system is designed in blocks that have very specific performance characteristics. The blocks are integrated in a hierarchical manner to create a unified communication system. For example, workgroup LANs represent a block with lower-performance requirements than the backbone network block, which requires high-performance fiber-optic cable in most cases. The standard defines the use of fiber-optic cable (single and multimode), STP (shielded twisted pair) cable, and UTP (unshielded twisted pair) cable.

The initial TIA/EIA 568 document was followed by several updates and addendums as outlined below. A major standard update was released in 2000 that incorporates previous changes.

- **TIA/EIA-568-A-1995 (Commercial Building Telecommunications Wiring Standards)** Defines a standard for building cable system for commercial buildings that support data networks, voice, and video. It also defines the technical and performance criteria for cabling.

- **TIA/EIA-568-A updates (1998-1999)**   The TIA/EIA-568 was updated several times through this time period. Update A1 outlined propagation delay and delay skew parameters. Update A2 specified miscellaneous changes. Update A3 specified requirements for bundled and hybrid cables. Update A4 defined NEXT and return loss requirements for patch cables. Finally, update A5 defined performance requirements for Enhanced Category 5 (Category 5E).

- **TIA 568-B.1-2000 (Commercial Building Telecommunications Wiring Standard)**   The year 2000 update packages all the previous addendums and service updates into a new release and, most important, specifies that Category 5E cable is the preferred cable type that can provide minimum acceptable performance levels. Several addendums were also released that specify technical information for 100-ohm twisted-pair cable, shielded twisted-pair cable, and optical fiber cable.

- **TIA/EIA-569-A-1995 (Commercial Building Standard for Telecommunications Pathways and Spaces)**   This standard defines how to build the pathways and spaces for telecommunication media.

- **TIA 570-A-1998 (Residential and Light Commercial Telecommunications Wiring Standard)**   This standard specifies residential cabling.

- **TIA/EIA-606-1994 (Building Infrastructure Administration Standard)**   This standard defines the design guidelines for managing a telecommunications infrastructure.

- **TIA/EIA-607-1995 (Grounding and Bonding Requirements)**   This standard defines grounding and bonding requirements for telecommunications cabling and equipment.

The current trend is to evolve the standards to support high-speed networking such as Gigabit Ethernet and define advanced cable types and connectors such as four-pair Category 6 and Category 7 cable. Category 6 is rated for channel performance up to 200 MHz, while Category 7 is rated up to 600 MHz. See "Cable and Wiring" for more information about cable types.

The remainder of this section discusses the TIA/EIA-568 standard in general, rather than any specific release. According to TIA/EIA 568 documents, the wiring standard is designed to provide the following features and functions:

- A generic telecommunication wiring system for commercial buildings
- Defined media, topology, termination and connection points, and administration
- Support for multiproduct, multivendor environments
- Direction for future design of telecommunication products for commercial enterprises
- The ability to plan and install the telecommunication wiring for a commercial building without any prior knowledge of the products that will use the wiring

The layout of a TIA/EIA 568-A structured cable system is illustrated in Figure T-8. The hierarchical structure is apparent in the multifloor office building. A vertical backbone cable runs from the central hub/switch in the main equipment room to a hub/switch in the telecommunication closet on each floor. Work areas are then individually cabled to the equipment in the telecommunication closet. The logical hierarchy is illustrated in Figure T-9.

The TIA standard defines the parameters for each part of the cabling system, which includes work area wiring, horizontal wiring, telecommunication closets, equipment rooms and cross-connects, backbone (vertical) wiring, and entrance facilities. Each of these is described next. Additional details, specifications, and illustrations are available at the Siemon's Web site listed later.

Work Area The work area wiring subsystem consists of the communication outlets (wallboxes and faceplates), wiring, and connectors needed to connect the work area equipment (computers, printers, and so on) via the horizontal wiring subsystem to the telecommunication closet. The standard requires that two outlets be provided at each wall plate—one for voice and one for data.

Horizontal Wiring The horizontal wiring system runs from each workstation outlet to the *telecommunication closet*. The maximum horizontal distance from the telecommunication closet to the communication outlets is 90 meters (295 feet) independent of media type. An additional 6 meters (20 feet) is allowed for patch cables at the telecommunication closet and at the workstation, but the combined length cannot exceed 10 meters (33 feet). As mentioned earlier, the work area must provide two outlets. The horizontal cable should be four-pair 100-ohm UTP cable (the latest standards specify Category 5E), two-fiber 62.5/125-mm fiber-optic cable, or multimode 50/125-mm multimode fiber-optic cable. Coaxial cable is no longer recommended.

Telecommunication Closet The telecommunication closet contains the connection equipment for workstations in the immediate area and a cross-connection to an equipment room. The telecommunication closet is a general facility that can provide horizontal wiring connections, as well as entrance facility connections. There is no limit on the number of telecommunication closets allowed. Some floors in multistory office buildings may have multiple telecommunication closets, depending on the floor plan. These may be connected to an equipment room on the same floor.

Equiptment Rooms and Main Cross-Connects An equipment room provides a termination point for backbone cabling that is connected to one or more telecommunication closets. It may also be the main cross-connection point for the entire facility. In a campus environment, each building may have its own equipment room, to which telecommunication closet equipment is

T

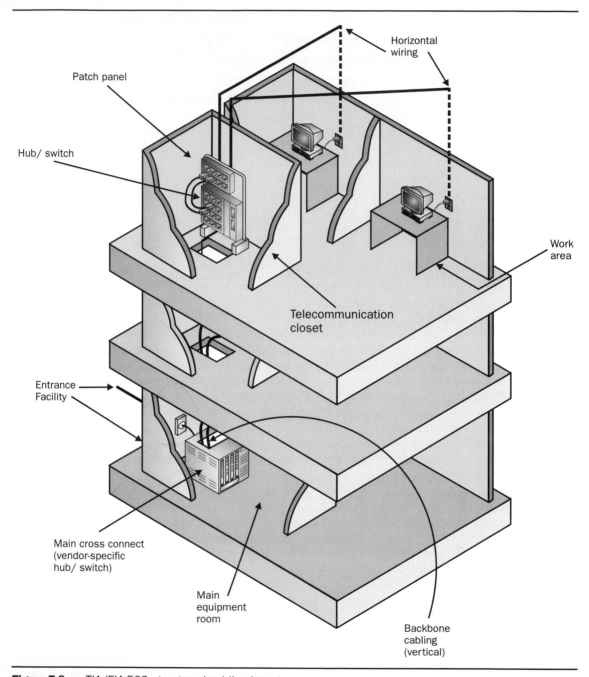

Figure T-8. *TIA/EIA-568 structured cabling layout*

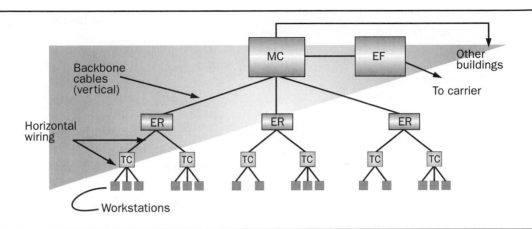

Figure T-9.   *Logical hierarchy of a TIA/EIA-568-A structured cabling system*

connected, and the equipment in this room may then be connected to a central campus facility that provides the main cross-connect for the entire campus.

Backbone Wiring   The backbone wiring runs up through the floors of the building (risers) or across a campus and provides the interconnection for equipment rooms and telecommunication closets. The distance limitations of this cabling depend on the type of cable and facilities it connects. Refer to Figure T-11 and the following table. Note that UTP is limited to 90 meters.

Cable Type	MC to ER
Multimode fiber	2,000m (6,560 ft)
Single-mode fiber	3,000m (9,840 ft)
UTP (<5MHz)	800m (2,624 ft)

Entrance Facilities   The entrance facility contains the telecommunication service entrance to the building. This facility may also contain campus-wide backbone connections. It also contains the *network demarcation point,* which is the interconnection to the local exchange carrier's telecommunication facilities. The demarcation point is typically 12 inches from where the carrier's facilities enter the building, but the carrier may designate otherwise.

Related Entries   Backbone Networks; Cable and Wiring; Data Communication Concepts; Ethernet; Fast Ethernet; Fiber-Optic Cable; Gigabit Ethernet; ISO/IEC-11801 Cabling Standards; Network Analyzers; Network Concepts; Network Design and Construction; Network Management; Performance

T

Measurement and Optimization; Power and Grounding Problems and Solutions; Switching and Switched Networks; *and* Testing, Diagnostics, and Troubleshooting

Linktionary!—Tom Sheldon's Encyclopedia of Networking updates	http://www.linktionary.com/t/tia_cabling.html
TIA online Web site	http://www.tiaonline.org
EIA (Electronic Industries Association)	http://www.eia.org/
ISO (International Standards Organization)	http://www.iso.ch/
MMTA (MultiMedia Telecommunications Association)	http://www.mmta.org/
Siemon Cabling Systems standards overview (excellent illustrations!)	http://www.siemon.com/standards/overview_ind.asp
Cabletesting.com cabling standards documents (describes latest updates!)	http://www.cabletesting.com/ Cabling_Standards_Documents_Overview.html
Anixter technical library with documents about structured cabling	http://www.anixter.com/techlib/
Hubbell Premise Wiring Company	http://www.hubbell-premise.com/
Fluke Corporation	http://www.fluke.com
Wirescope, an Agilent company (see Standards sections)	http://www.wirescope.com
Web ProForums paper: "Structured Cabling System (SCS)" by Lucent	http://www.iec.org/tutorials/scs/
Structured Cabling article at Voice & Data Magazine	http://www.voicendata.com/aug99/s-cabling.html

Time Synchronization Services

Distributed network systems require time synchronization to ensure accurate timestamping and event executions. Time synchronization helps establish and maintain the order of events. A time service keeps track of time in networks and determines the accuracy associated with each clock used to synchronize time. The service provides fault-tolerant clock synchronization for systems in both local and wide area networks. The NTP (Network Time Protocol) may be used to obtain time values from outside sources. The Tymserve 2000 Network Time Server from Datum, Inc. provides NTP time-service functions.

NDS (Novell Directory Services) provides an example of how time-synchronization services help to keep the activities of servers synchronized. NDS holds information about user accounts and network resources. Changes must be copied (replicated) to all servers where the NDS database is stored. Time synchronization helps to ensure that everything is kept synchronized.

There are two time-synchronization schemes. The first uses a *single-reference time server* for relatively small, geographically close networks. The time server is the sole source of time on the network. Any time changes are set on this server, and then others synchronize with it. The other method is used for geographically distant networks and includes the following time servers:

■ **Primary server**   A primary server synchronizes time with other primary time servers or a reference time server, and provides the correct time to secondary time servers.

■ **Reference server**   A reference server gets its time from an external source (such as a radio clock) and is a contact to what the outside world says the time should be.

All other servers on the network can be *secondary time servers*, which get their time from single reference, primary, or reference time servers and do not participate in the establishment of a common time over the network. Note that the master time signal is obtained from public time servers.

Related Entries   NDS (Novell Directory Services); NTP (Network Time Protocol)

Linktionary!—Tom Sheldon's Encyclopedia of Networking updates	http://www.linktionary.com/t/time_synchronization.html
TimeSync site	http://www.eecis.udel.edu/~ntp
Public time servers list	http://www.eecis.udel.edu/~mills/ntp/servers.html
Datum, Inc.	http://www.datum.com
Mark McCutcheon's Internet links page (see Time section)	http://www.cs.ubc.ca/spider/mjmccut/internet.html

TLS (Transport Layer Security)

TLS is the IETF's version of SSL (Secure Socket Layer) version 3.0. The IETF sought to standardize SSL, but did not like its use of the RSA Security's proprietary cryptographic technology, so it began work on TLS (Transport Layer Security), which uses Diffie-Hellman public-key cryptography. TLS also uses HMAC TLS as outlined in RFC 2246 (The TLS Protocol, Version 1.0, January 1999). See "SSL (Secure Socket Layer)" as well.

HMAC (Hashed Message Authentication Code) is a core protocol that is considered essential for security on the Internet along with IPSec, according to RFC 2316 (Report of the IAB, April 1998). It is not a hash function, but a mechanism for message authentication that uses either MD5 or SHA-1 hash functions in combination with a shared secret key (as opposed to a public/private-key pair). Basically, a message is combined with a key and run through the hash function. The result is then combined with the key and run through the hash function again. This 128-bit result is truncated to 96 bits and becomes the MAC.

RFC 2104 (HMAC: Keyed-Hashing for Message Authentication, February 1997) describes how HMAC should be used in preference to older techniques, notably keyed hash functions. Keyed hashes based on MD5 are especially to be avoided, given the hints of weakness in MD5. HMAC is the preferred shared-secret authentication technique and it should be used with SHA-1. It can be used to authenticate any arbitrary message and is suitable for logins.

The following RFCs provide more information about TLS:

■ RFC 2246 (The TLS Protocol, Version 1.0, January 1999) defines the initial version of the TLS protocol.

T

■ RFC 2712 (Addition of Kerberos Cipher Suites to Transport Layer Security, October 1999) proposes enhancing TLS to support Kerberos.

■ RFC 2817 (Upgrading to TLS Within HTTP/1.1, May 2000) describes how to use the upgrade mechanism in HTTP/1.1 to initiate TLS over an existing TCP connection.

■ RFC 2818 (HTTP over TLS, May 2000) describes how to use TLS (Transport Layer Security) to secure HTTP connections over the Internet.

Related Entries   Certificates and Certification Systems; Cryptography; Digital Signatures; Hash Functions; Kerberos Authentication Protocol; PKI (Public-Key Infrastructure); Public-Key Cryptography; Security; SET (Secure Electronic Transaction); S-HTTP (Secure Hypertext Transfer Protocol); *and* SSL (Secure Sockets Layer)

Linktionary!—Tom Sheldon's Encyclopedia of Networking updates	http://www.linktionary.com/t/tls.html
IETF Transport Layer Security (tls) Working Group	http://www.ietf.org/html.charters/tls-charter.html
Security Links at Telecom Information Resources on the Internet	http://china.si.umich.edu/telecom/net-security.html

Additional security-related links are under the "Security" heading.

TMN (Telecommunications Management Network)

TMN is a management architecture defined by the ITU for managing equipment and services in telecommunications networks. As telecommunications networks became more distributed and less centralized in the 1990s, the carriers and the ITU began work on a management system that could be used administer multivendor telecommunications equipment. The Web sites listed next provide descriptive information and commentary about these systems.

Related Entries   Network Management; Telecommunications and Telephone Systems

Linktionary!—Tom Sheldon's Encyclopedia of Networking updates	http://www.linktionary.com/t/tmn.html
Web ProForums paper: Telecommunications Management Network (TMN)	http://www.iec.org/tutorials/tmn/
Telecommunications network management white paper at Ericsson	http://www.ericsson.com/datacom/ emedia/network_management.pdf
Managing Networks in Transition, by Christophe De-Maindreville, Telecommunications Magazine online	http://www.telecoms-mag.com/issues/ 200010/tci/managing_networks.html

TN3270

TN3270 is a special version of the Internet's Telnet protocol that allows users with non-3270-compatible systems to access IBM hosts. It transfers 3270 display terminal data by emulating a subset of the Telnet protocol. TN3270 provides terminal-to-host connections for TCP/IP users over intranets or the Internet. The TN3270 hosts connect to Telnet servers that are in turn connected to the host via SNA or non-SNA methods.

Note that 3270 display terminal data differs from traditional display terminal data in that it is block mode and uses EBCDIC instead of ASCII character representation. Therefore, Telnet must be modified to support 3270 emulation.

When LANs were first being implemented in enterprise environments, so-called terminal networks existed to connect IBM 3270 display terminals with IBM hosts. Rather than have two networks—one for the LAN and one for the terminal-to-host connections—companies wanted to use the LAN for terminal-to-host connections.

SNA (Systems Network Architecture) gateways such as Microsoft SNA Server support TN3270 clients by allowing TN3270 users on a TCP/IP LAN to access a host mainframe through an add-on server package that runs on SNA Server. OpenConnect Systems makes a line of TN3270-compatible software that runs on SNA Server. The company also has products that let Web clients access mainframe data.

RFC 1576 (TN3270 Current Practices, January 1994) provides a good overview of TN3270. RFC 1205 (5250 Telnet Interface, February 1991) describes a similar emulation technique.

RFC 2355 (TN3270 Enhancements, June 1998) describes a protocol that more fully supports 3270 devices than do traditional TN3270 practices. It defines a method of emulating both the terminal and printer members of the 3270 family of devices via Telnet and it provides for the ability of a Telnet client to request that it be assigned a specific device name (also referred to as "LU name" or "network name"). It also defines support for a variety of functions such as the ATTN key, the SYSREQ key, and SNA response handling.

RFC 3029 (TN3270E Service Location and Session Balancing, January 2001) describes the implementation of SLP (Service Location Protocol) and session balancing with TN3270 emulator.

The IETF Telnet TN3270 Enhancements (tn3270e) Working Group is working to update and extend the standards specified in the previously mentioned RFCs.

Related Entries   APPN (Advanced Peer-to-Peer Networking); DLSw (Data Link Switching); IBM (International Business Machines); IBM Host Connectivity; *and* SNA (Systems Network Architecture)

Linktionary!—Tom Sheldon's Encyclopedia of Networking updates	http://www.linktionary.com/t/tn3270.html
IETF Telnet TN3270 Enhancements (tn3270e) Working Group	http://www.ietf.org/html.charters/tn3270e-charter.html
Cisco documentation: TN3270 Design and Implementation	http://www.cisco.com/univercd/cc/td/doc/cisintwk/dsgngde/tn3270/
OpenConnect Systems, Inc.	http://www.oc.com
IntelliTerm by Distinct Corp.	http://www.distinct.com/intelliterm/intelliterm.htm

Token and Token-Passing Access Methods

A token is a special control frame on token ring, token bus, and FDDI (Fiber Distributed Data Interface) networks that determines which stations can transmit data on a shared network. The node that has the token can transmit. Unlike contention-based networks, such as Ethernet, workstations on token-based networks do not compete for access to the network. Only the station that obtains the token can transmit. Other stations wait for the token rather than trying to access the network on their own. On Ethernet networks, "collisions" occur when two or more workstations attempt to access the network at the same time. They must back off and try again later, which reduces performance—especially as the number of workstations attached to a network segment increases.

In token ring networks, a station takes possession of a token and changes one bit, converting the token to a SFS (start-of-frame sequence). A field exists in the token in which workstations can indicate the type of priority required for the transmission. The priority setting is basically a request to other stations for future use of the token. The other stations compare a workstation's request for priority with their own priority levels. If the workstation's priority is higher, the other stations will grant the workstation access to the token for an extended period.

Related Entries   FDDI (Fiber Distributed Data Interface); MAC (Media Access Control); Network Concepts; Token Bus Network; *and* Token Ring Network

Token-Based Authentication

Token-based authentication is a security technique that authenticates users who are attempting to log in to a server, a network, or some other secure system. These devices strengthen the logon sequence. Today, most remote authentication schemes do not send passwords over the wire, either in the clear or encrypted. Remote users who need to access corporate servers are assigned a user account and given a secret password that is known to the user and the server. A successful authentication takes place if a user can prove to a server that he or she knows the shared secret without actually transmitting that secret across the wire.

CHAP (Challenge Handshake Authentication Protocol) provides the best example of this technique. Basically, the server sends a random message to the user. The user then appends the shared secret password to the message and runs it through a hash function, producing a message digest. This is returned to the server, which has also produced a message digest from the same information. The server compares the two message digests and, if they compare, the remote user is considered authentic.

But what if the user's password is compromised? Token-based authentication provides a way to strengthen this scheme by requiring the client to enter yet another piece of information. This is called *two-factor authentication*. Users provide something that they know (their password), and something they have (a one-time value generated by the token device). Organizations often assign tokens to remote and mobile users who need to access internal systems from outside locations.

A token device is about the size of a credit card with a built-in computer that generates information for the user to enter during logon. SecurID, a "token authenticator" from RSA Security, uses a time-based technique in which the device displays a number that changes every minute in synchronization with a security server at the corporate site. When users log in, they are prompted for the value on the SecurID card. The value changes constantly and is called a *one-time password*, It cannot be reused at a later date by someone who manages to capture the password.

Software-based token devices are also available that provide much the same functionality as hardware tokens. They consist of software programs that run in portable computers.

However, some feel that this approach is less secure than hardware tokens because the software system could be more easily compromised.

ActivCard, a manufacturer of token-based authentication devices, employs several modes of operation in its token devices:

■ In the "challenge/response" mode, a user attempting to access a secure site is issued a *challenge* by the host authentication server. This alphanumeric value appears on the user's screen and the user enters it into the token device. The token device then computes a *response* (using its special algorithm) based on the random challenge and a secret key. The response appears on the token device's display and the user types it in the computer and sends it to the authentication server. The authentication server has also generated an appropriate response that it compares to the one generated by the user's token. If they are the same, the user is granted access. If the login fails, the server issues a new challenge with each new logon attempt.

■ In ActivCard's time-plus-event challenge/response mode, the token and the authentication software calculate unique passwords based on an event counter and an internal clock. Time/event synchronous authentication uses the number of passwords already processed by both the token and the authentication server for a particular service on a sequential basis to calculate passwords. The result is an even stronger level of security when it comes to user authentication.

Kerberos, which is discussed elsewhere in this book, is a security server system that provides a software-based token and one-time password authentication scheme. Security server systems that can take advantage of token authentication include RADIUS (Remote Authentication Dial-In User Service) and TACACS (Terminal Access Controller Access Control System).

The following Internet RFCs provide additional information about this security technology:

■ RFC 1510 (The Kerberos Network Authentication Service version 5, September 1993)

■ RFC 1511 (Common Authentication Technology Overview, September 1993)

■ RFC 1704 (On Internet Authentication, October 1994)

■ RFC 1994 (Challenge Handshake Authentication Protocol, August 1996)

■ RFC 2289 (A One-Time-Password System, February 1998)

■ RFC 2401 (Security Architecture for the Internet Protocol, November 1998)

■ RFC 2808 (The SecureID SASL Mechanism, April 2000) defines authentication mechanisms for RSA Security SecurID token card products.

Related Entries   Access Control; Authentication and Authorization; Biometric Access Devices; Certificates and Certification Systems; CHAP (Challenge Handshake Authentication Protocol); Cryptography; Digital Signatures; EAP (Extensible Authentication Protocol); FORTEZZA; Hash Functions; Kerberos Authentication Protocol; Key Distribution and Management; One-Time Password Authentication; Secret-Key Cryptography; Security; *and* Token-Based Authentication

 Linktionary!—Tom Sheldon's Encyclopedia   http://www.linktionary.com/t/token_security.html
of Networking updates

ActivCard site	http://www.activcard.com
RSA Security SecurID Authenticators	http://www.rsasecurity.com/products/securid/authenticators.html
Amerkore's The Smart Card Resource Center	http://www.chipcard.org
Global Chipcard Alliance	http://www.smart-card.com
Network Computing Magazine article on Token Authentication	http://www.networkcomputing.com/1018/1018f1.html

Token Bus Network

A token bus network is similar to a token ring network in that a station must have possession of a token before it can transmit on the network (see "Token and Token-Passing Access Methods"). However, the topology and token-passing method are different. The IEEE 802.4 Committee has defined token bus standards as broadband networks, as opposed to Ethernet's baseband transmission technique. The Manufacturing Automation Protocol (MAP) developed by General Motors for manufacturing floor networks uses IEEE 802.4. ARCNET (Attached Resource Computing Network) is a token bus network, although it does not conform to the IEEE 802.4 standards.

The topology of the network can include groups of workstations connected by long trunk cables. These workstations branch from hubs in a star configuration, so the network has both a bus and star topology. Token bus topology is well suited to groups of users that are separated by some distance. IEEE 802.4 token bus networks are constructed with 75-ohm coaxial cable using a bus topology. The broadband characteristics of the 802.4 standard support transmission over several different channels simultaneously.

The token and frames of data are passed from one station to another following the numeric sequence of the station addresses. Thus, the token follows a logical ring rather than a physical ring. The last station in numeric order passes the token back to the first station. The token does not follow the physical ordering of workstation attachment to the cable. Station 1 might be at one end of the cable and station 2 might be at the other, with station 3 in the middle.

While token bus is used in some manufacturing environments, Ethernet and token ring standards have become more prominent in the office environment.

Related Entries   ARCNET; IEEE 802 Standards; Token and Token-Passing Access Methods; Token Ring Network; *and* Topology

   IEEE 802.4 Token Bus Web page   http://grouper.ieee.org/groups/802/4/

Token Ring Network

Token ring is the IEEE 802.5 standard for a token-passing ring network with a star-configured physical topology. Internally, signals travel around the network from one station to the next in a ring. Physically, each station connects to a central hub called a MAU (multistation access unit). The MAU contains a "collapsed ring," but the physical configuration is a star topology.

When a station is attached, the ring is extended out to the station and then back to the MAU as shown. If a station goes offline, the ring is reestablished with a bypass at the station connector.

Token ring was popular for an extended period in the late 1980s and 1990s, especially in IBM legacy system environments. IBM developed the technology and provided extensive support for connections to SNA systems. More recently, Ethernet, Fast Ethernet, and Gigabit Ethernet technologies have pushed token ring and other LAN technologies to the sidelines. You can refer to the Linktionary! Web site listed below for the full version of this topic.

Related Entries   LAN (Local Area Network); Network Concepts; Network Design and Construction; Token and Token-Passing Access Methods; *and* Token Bus Network

Linktionary!—Tom Sheldon's Encyclopedia of Networking updates	http://www.linktionary.com/t/token_ring.html
IEEE 802.5 Web Site	http://www.8025.org/
HSTRA (High Speed Token Ring Alliance).	http://www.hstra.com/
TechFest token ring technical summary	http://www.techfest.com/networking/lan/token.htm
TechFest token ring links	http://www.techfest.com/networking/lan.htm
Madge Networks (a major token ring vendor)	http://www.madge.com/
Token Ring Links at Network World Fusion	http://www.nwfusion.com/netresources/token.html
Cisco Documentation: Token Ring/IEEE 802.5	http://www.cisco.com/univercd/cc/td/doc/cisintwk/ito_doc/tokenrng.htm
Cisco Documentation: Troubleshooting Token Ring	http://www.cisco.com/univercd/cc/td/doc/cisintwk/itg_v1/tr1906.htm
RAD Communications token ring tutorial	http://www.rad.com/networks/1996/toknring/toknring.htm
Token Ring FAQ (frequently asked questions)	http://www.faqs.org/faqs/LANs/token-ring-faq/

Topology

A network topology is the physical layout of a network. There are local network topologies and enterprise network or WAN (wide area network) topologies. LAN topologies consist of the designs described below and pictured in the following illustration.

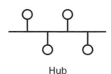

Hub

Star

Star-
Configured
Ring

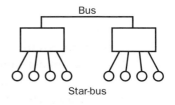

Bus

Star-bus

- **Bus** A single trunk cable connects each workstation in a daisy-chain topology. Signals are broadcast to all stations, but packets are received only by the station to which they are addressed. Ethernet implements this topology. A break in the cable affects the entire network. Traditional Ethernet uses this topology

- **Star** Workstations attach to hubs and signals are broadcast to all stations or passed from station to station. A break in the cable only affects the attached workstation.

- **Star-configured ring** A ring network in which signals are passed from one station to another in a circle. The physical topology is a star in which workstations branch from concentrators or hubs, but the logical topology is a hub. Token ring is an example of this topology.

- **Star/bus configuration** A network that has groups of star-configured workstations connected with long linear bus trunks. Ethernet 10Base-T and Fast Ethernet use this topology.

Enterprise networks and wide area networks expand on these topologies as pictured in this illustration:

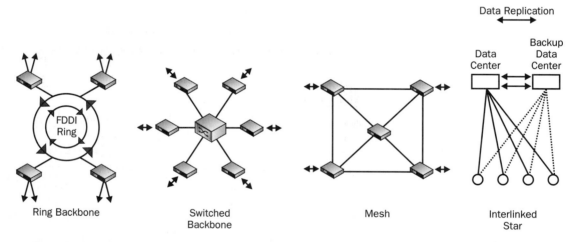

Ring Backbone   Switched Backbone   Mesh   Interlinked Star

- **Ring backbone network** A high-speed network that interconnects many lower-speed networks, delivering frames or packets among them. The backbone may be linear, ring, or mesh. An organization may build a backbone network that snakes through a building, or install a hub that has a high-speed "collapsed backbone" inside a box.

- **Switched core backbone** The switched core is usually an ATM switch or mesh of ATM switches that provide virtual circuits among all the interconnected networks. Service providers and Internet exchanges have used this configuration to interconnect the different networks that make up the Internet.

- **Mesh network** A network consisting of interconnected routers and/or switches with multiple paths and the ability to route around failed links. The Internet is a mesh network.

■ **Interlinked star**   This is a hierarchical topology that provides redundant links and high-availability for private WANs and service provider networks. Each data center has links to the remote sites, but the backup data links may be in standby mode only (i.e., dial-on-demand). The data centers are interconnected and data is replicated across the link.

Related Entries   Backbone Networks; Bridges and Bridging; Campus Network; Ethernet; Gigabit Ethernet; Network Concepts; Network Design and Construction; Switched Fabrics and Bus Design; Switching and Switched Networks; Token Ring Network; WAN (Wide Area Network); *and* Wireless Broadband Access Technologies

Linktionary!—Tom Sheldon's Encyclopedia of   http://www.linktionary.com/t/topology.html
Networking updates

ToS (Type of Service)

The IP datagram header contains an 8-bit field called ToS (Type of Service). The field has been part of the IP header since the beginning, but it was rarely used until the recent introduction of Differentiated Services (Diff-Serv).

ToS was outlined in RFC 791 (Internet Protocol, September 1981). It was then clarified in RFC 1349 (Type of Service in the Internet Protocol Suite, July 1992). In the early days, some attempts were made to specify how it could be used to compute separate routes through networks depending on type of service specifications. The field was defined with two parts, a precedence value and the ToS bits. The precedence value occupies the leftmost 3 bits and was meant to privide a form of priority queuing. The ToS bits specified how the network should make trade-offs between throughput, delay, reliability, and cost.

The IETF Differentiated Services Working Group redefined the ToS field and renamed it the Differentiated Services field. Six bits of the DS field are used as a codepoints to select the PHB (per-hop behavior), which defines how packets are queued at network nodes. This discussion continues under the topic "Differentiated Services (Diff-Serv)."

Traffic Management, Shaping, and Engineering

Traffic management is concerned with controlling and allocating network bandwidth, reducing delay, and minimizing congestion on networks. It encompasses the management of network capacity, measuring and modeling traffic, and analyzing performance. The basic idea is to manage network resources efficiently and give client/subscribers the bandwidth and service levels they need. For the carrier networks, these levels are negotiated in SLAs (service level agreements). At the same time, clients and subscribers traffic must be managed to ensure that it does not use bandwidth that would affect the service levels of other users. This requires admittance controls (only admit traffic that is allowed and no excess that would affect other service levels) and policing (monitor traffic on an ongoing basis).

Related to traffic management is *capacity planning*, which involves measuring and modeling network traffic in order to schedule and provision network bandwidth for current and future requirements. See "Capacity Planning."

Traffic management is relatively easy in ATM networks since ATM was designed with controls to manage traffic. The opposite is true with the Internet protocols, which contains no built-in traffic management features except for the manipulation of routing metrics. For example, Figure T-10a illustrates an IP-based wide area network with four sites connected by T1 leased lines. Site A is connected to site B and site C via separate T1 lines. Site B and C are then connected to site D with leased lines. The topology is basically a loop. A can get to D by going through either B or C. A preference for the route through C rather than B can be established by assigning a higher metric value to the A-B link or the B-D link. In the figure, the B-D link metric is increased to 2, thus increasing the A-B-D metric to a total of 3 while the A-C-D metric remains at 2.

The manipulation of IP metrics may be appropriate for corporate networks, but it totally inadequate for ISP networks. It is very difficult to distribute traffic across multiple links in an efficient way to prevent overloading of some links and underloading of others. The more links, the more difficult the problem. Consequently, in the mid-1990s, many service providers installed ATM core networks to take advantage of ATM's QoS, virtual circuit capabilities, and built-in traffic engineering. As shown in Figure T-10b, the ATM core is surrounded by routers and a mesh of ATM virtual circuits is established in the core to provide any-to-any connectivity among all the

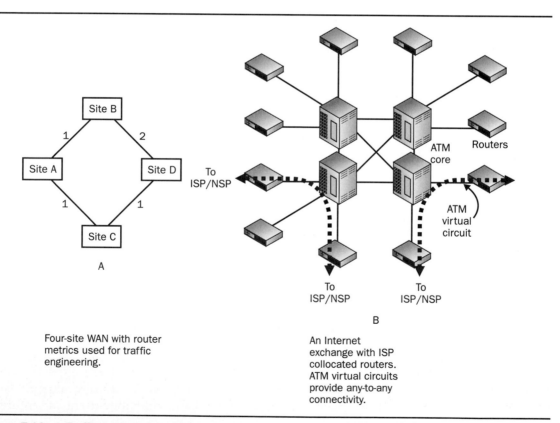

Four-site WAN with router metrics used for traffic engineering.

An Internet exchange with ISP collocated routers. ATM virtual circuits provide any-to-any connectivity.

Figure T-10.   *Traffic engineering with simple IP metrics or ATM virtual circuits.*

routers. This architecture is used at Internet exchanges where many ISPs and network service providers come together and exchange traffic. See "Internet Architecture and Backbone."

Some extensions were developed to help TCP/IP manage congestion, but these do not provide the QoS levels of ATM. More recently, QoS and traffic management techniques have been developed for the Internet in the form of MPLS (Multiprotocol Label Switching). Adding to MPLS are advanced high-performance routing and switching hardware plus an improvement in network capacity that supports over-provisioning of network bandwidth.

ATM traffic management is discussed first, following by traffic management schemes for the Internet. Also see "Load Balancing" and "Link Aggregation" for related information. For more information about QoS and prioritization, see "QoS (Quality of Service)" and "Prioritization of Network Traffic."

ATM Traffic Engineering

ATM was built from the ground up with QoS in mind. It's fixed cell size and built-in traffic management parameters help network administrators properly provision and manage ATM networks to provide QoS. The important point is that everything that is needed to provide QoS is built into ATM, unlike the Internet protocols, which have been hacked and extended in various way to provide various service levels, but not achieving the level of QoS that ATM has.

The primary means for delivery QoS in ATM networks are sophisticated traffic management functions and the ability to differentiate traffic into different service classes. The ATM Forum has defined the following *service categories* to ensure that the service requirements of applications are met. For a more complete description, see "ATM (Asynchronous Transfer Mode)" and see the subsection called "ATM Traffic Management, Quality of Service, and Service Contracts."

- **CBR (constant bit rate)**   Provides a fixed amount of bandwidth that is always available.
- **rt-VBR (real time-variable bit rate)**   This is similar to CBR in that a peak cell rate is specified, but network bandwidth is only used when data is sent.
- **nrt-VBR (non-real time-variable bit rate)**   This service is meant for bursty traffic of the type that is common on LANs.
- **UBR (unspecified bit rate)**   This service does not guarantee bandwidth and allows cells to be dropped if there is not enough bandwidth.
- **ABR (available bit rate)**   This parameter takes advantage of unused bandwidth. A customer gets a specific bandwidth, but can use more if it is available.
- **GFR (guaranteed frame rate)**   GFR offers various quality of service commitments, specifically for IP traffic. GFR is an alternative to UBR services.

Along with these service levels are a number of parameters that measure traffic and network performance and provide information that can be used to control traffic and level of QoS. These are described under the subheading "ATM QoS Parameters" in the ATM topic. The following traffic management functions are used to monitor and manage network traffic and network congestion:

- **CAC (connection admission control)**   When an ATM switch sets up a virtual circuit, it uses CAC to ensure that they can meet the requested QoS without affecting the QoS of existing connections.

- **Policing, or UPC (usage parameter control)**   This is used to check for valid virtual circuits and virtual paths and determine the conformity of traffic-to-traffic descriptors. Invalid cells may be discarded completely or tagged with a CLP (cell loss priority) of 1, indicating that they may be dropped if necessary to meet bandwidth requirements.

- **Traffic shaping**   What traffic shaping does is change the spacing of cells on a connection, thus increasing the delay of those cells. Shaping is performed to better utilize network resources and meet traffic constraints (avoid dropping cells).

The following Web sites provide more information on ATM QoS and traffic management. Also see RFC 2761 (Terminology for ATM Bendmarking, February 2000).

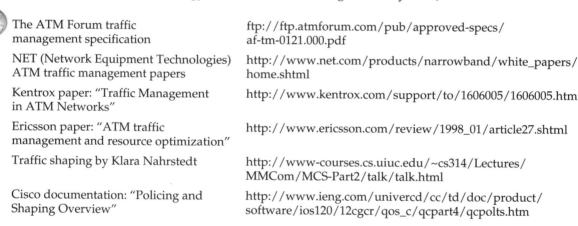

The ATM Forum traffic management specification	ftp://ftp.atmforum.com/pub/approved-specs/af-tm-0121.000.pdf
NET (Network Equipment Technologies) ATM traffic management papers	http://www.net.com/products/narrowband/white_papers/home.shtml
Kentrox paper: "Traffic Management in ATM Networks"	http://www.kentrox.com/support/to/1606005/1606005.htm
Ericsson paper: "ATM traffic management and resource optimization"	http://www.ericsson.com/review/1998_01/article27.shtml
Traffic shaping by Klara Nahrstedt	http://www-courses.cs.uiuc.edu/~cs314/Lectures/MMCom/MCS-Part2/talk/talk.html
Cisco documentation: "Policing and Shaping Overview"	http://www.ieng.com/univercd/cc/td/doc/product/software/ios120/12cgcr/qos_c/qcpart4/qcpolts.htm

Internet Traffic Engineering

Unlike ATM, the Internet was designed from the ground up for best-effort service rather than QoS. Routing protocols and TCP's transport layer services are showing their inefficiencies in the face of massive amounts of real-time traffic. At one point, RSVP (Resource Reservation Protocol) was developed to provide bandwidth management in the Internet, but it required too much in the way of support from routers, which had to be upgraded in most cases. RSVP is now used on enterprise networks, but not throughout the Internet.

The IETF Traffic Engineering Working Group (TEWG) is developing, specifying, and recommending principles, techniques, and mechanisms for traffic engineering in the Internet. According to the group, Internet traffic engineering is concerned with optimizing network performance and efficiently using network resources by measuring, modeling, characterizing, and controlling Internet traffic. The concept is to maintain network performance even when loads shift or routes fail. Traffic engineering is also concerned with planning of network capacity to ensure that the network is designed and provisioned to handle the anticipated traffic loads.

The traffic engineering environment consists of links that connect two nodes, and paths which are sequences of links between an origin and destination node. A route is a set of different paths between the source and destination. A call is a connection across the network to support a particular data flow, which could be a voice call established using the PSTN SS7 signaling protocol or a Web-based HTTP session.

According to TEWG, traffic management functions include call routing (translating number/name to routing address), connection or bearer-path routing methods, QoS resource management, routing table management, and dynamic transport routing. These functions may be *decentralized* and distributed to the network nodes, *centralized* and allocated to a centralized controller such as a bandwidth broker, or performed by a hybrid combination of these approaches. Network administrators can use network measurements and modeling techniques for capacity management. The information can be used to adjust routing tables as needed to balance traffic loads and correct problems in the network.

Refer to the TEWG for more information. A number of drafts and RFCs are posted on the Web site listed later. Also refer to the MPLS Working Group for more information. The most recent solution and one that is proving useful is MPLS, which is described next.

See "QoS (Quality of Service)" for a discussion of the various techniques that have been employed in LANs and IP networks to provide prioritization and rudimentary traffic control. Also see "Differentiated Services (Diff-Serv)," "Integrated Services (Int-Serv)," "Policy-Based Networking," and "Prioritization of Network Traffic." The Diff-Serv topic describes a number of traffic control features such as traffic classifiers, markers, policy systems, bandwidth brokers, and traffic conditioners. A traffic conditioner meters and polices traffic, then drops or shapes traffic as needed.

A number of techniques have been developed to avoid congestion in TCP networks, including RED (random early discard), ECN (explicit congestion notification), and TCP rate control. See "Congestion Control Mechanisms." Queuing methods such as FIFO queuing, priority queuing, fair queuing, WFQ (weighted fair queuing), and CBQ (class-based queuing) help manage traffic within routers and other network devices. See "Queuing." The topic also discusses algorithms that control queues such as leaky buckets and token buckets.

Also see the RFCs listed later. In particular, RFC 2990 (Next Steps for the IP QoS Architecture, November 2000) provides useful information related to emerging techniques.

Currently, MPLS is considered the best approach for providing QoS on the Internet as described next. However, several attempts were made to add QoS to the Internet protocols. See "Integrated Services (Int.Serv)."

MPLS Traffic Engineering

MPLS switches traffic across LSRs (label-switched routers) in the MPLS network. A path is set up across a network of LSRs using manual or automatic techniques. This path extends from an ingress LER (label edge router) to an egress LER. Packets traversing the MPLS network are assigned *labels* that specify which path they are to follow across the network. Therefore, the path is called a "label switched path" or LSP. LSPs are generally set up for traffic flows, which consists of a series of datagrams that are traveling between the same source and destination (an IP phone call, for example).

MPLS traffic engineering approaches are integrated into layer 3 networking functions so that routing of IP traffic can be optimized. LSPs are defined with a "constraint-based" routing approach, in which the LSP is defined as the shortest path that can be established that meets the resource requirements of the traffic and the resources that the network can offer. The resource requirements of the traffic include bandwidth requirements, media requirements, and priority over other flows. If links or nodes fail, new constraints may be adopted and new LSPs may be formed to comply with those constraints.

MPLS uses two different approaches to traffic engineering. One is to build routes on a hop-by-hop basis using LDP (label distribution protocol). The other is to engineer the routes using explicit routing techniques such as TE-RSVP (traffic engineering-resource reservation protocol) and CR-LDP (constraint-based label distribution protocol). In the explicit routing approach, class of service and quality of service parameters are predefined. MPLS and LDP are discussed under "MPLS (Multiprotocol Label Switching)." See "RSVP (Resource Reservation Protocol)" for information about RSVP.

The TE-RSVP approach uses previously defined RSVP techniques to set up a path across the network. Basically, a message is sent across the network from the ingress LER to the egress LER. As the message crosses the network, intermediate LSRs along the path reads the message and prepare to allocate bandwidth for the path. Once the message reaches the egress LER, that LER sends a reservation message back across the same path to the ingress LER. When the LSRs along the path receive this message, they commit to the bandwidth reservation. When the ingress LER receives the message, it sends a confirmation message back across the path to all the LSRs and the egress LER. This path setup scheme also provides a way to specify traffic engineering services, such as QoS and traffic parameters, LSP failure notification, the ability to replace an existing LSP with a higher-priority LSP, and LSP management.

The CR-LDP extends the existing LDP protocol defined in the MPLS specification, but extends it with constraint-based explicit routing parameters. CR-LDP is considered more versatile than the TE-RSVP approach and it uses the existing LDP protocol. The path set up is similar to TE-RSVP, where a set up request travels from the ingress to the egress, and then a mapping message is returned in the backward direction. However, CR-LDP can specify a variety of parameters to define explicit routes through the network. These can specify particular data rates, bandwidth requirements, and weights. Priorities can also be set to prevent one LSP from preempting another and paths may be reconfigured on the fly to provide better optimization.

The following references provide more information about MPLS traffic engineering. Also refer to the tewg and mpls Working Groups listed next for a complete list of RFCs and drafts related to traffic engineering.

 Web ProForum paper: "A Comparison of MPLS Traffic-Engineering Inititatives"   http://www.iec.org/tutorials/

MPLS Resource Center   http://www.mplsrc.com/

Juniper paper: "Traffic Engineering for the New Public Network" by Chuck Semeria   http://www.juniper.net/techcenter/

Cisco document: "MPLS Traffic Engineering"   http://www.cisco.com/univercd/cc/td/doc/product/software/ios120/120newft/120t/120t7/te120_7t.htm

The following Internet RFCs provide additional information on MPLS and the other traffic engineering techniques described above.

- RFC 2309 (Recommendations on Queue Management and Congestion Avoidance in the Internet, April 1998)
- RFC 2386 (A Framework for QoS-based Routing in the Internet, August 1998)
- RFC 2430 (A Provider Architecture for Differentiated Services and Traffic Engineering, October 1998)
- RFC 2475 (An Architecture for Differentiated Services, December 1998)
- RFC 2581 (TCP Congestion Control, April 1999)
- RFC 2702 (Requirements for Traffic Engineering over MPLS, September 1999)
- RFC 2915 (Congestion Control Principles, September 2000)
- RFC 2963 (A Rate Adaptive Shaper for Differentiated Services, October 2000)
- RFC 2990 (Next Steps for the IP QoS Architecture, November 2000)

Related Entries   Bandwidth; Bandwidth Management; Bandwidth on Demand; Capacity; Congestion Control Mechanisms; CoS (Class of Service); Data Communication Concepts; Delay, Latency, and Jitter; Differentiated Services (Diff-Serv); Flow-Control Mechanisms; Integrated Services (Int-Serv); Internet Architecture and Backbone; Load Balancing; MPLS (Multiprotocol Label Switching); Multimedia; Network Access Services; Network Core Technologies; NPN (New Public Network); Policy-Based Management; QoS (Quality of Service); Queuing; Routers; RSVP (Resource Reservation Protocol); RTP (Real-time Transport Protocol); RTSP (Real-Time Streaming Protocol); SLA (Service Level Agreement); TCP (Transmission Control Protocol); Throughput; Transport Protocols and Services; Voice over IP (VoIP); VLAN (Virtual LAN); *and* VPN (Virtual Private Networks)

Linktionary!—Tom Sheldon's Encyclopedia of Networking updates	http://www.linktionary.com/t/traffic_engineering.html
IETF Working Group: Internet Traffic Engineering (tewg)	http://www.ietf.org/html.charters/tewg-charter.html
IETF Working Group: Multiprotocol Label Switching (mpls)	http://www.ietf.org/html.charters/tewg-charter.html
Sally Floyd's information page with information about queuing, rate control, and congestion management	http://www.aciri.org/floyd/
Bitpipe (search for "traffic engineering")	http://www.bitpipe.com/
Noritoshi Demizu's multi layer routing page	http://www.watersprings.org/links/mlr/
Cisco documentation: "Quality of Service (QoS) Networking"	http://www.cisco.com/univercd/cc/td/doc/cisintwk/ito_doc/qos.htm

Transaction Processing

A transaction is a discrete unit of work that is typically part of a business transaction. An OLTP (online transaction processing) system operates in real time to collect and process transaction-related data and post changes to shared databases and other files. In online transaction processing, transactions are executed immediately, as opposed to batch processing, in which a batch of transactions is stored over a period of time and then executed later. Due to the speed of today's systems, batch processing is no longer necessary in most environments. The results of an OLTP are immediately available in the database, assuming that transactions complete. The most common examples of OLTPs are airline reservation systems and banking transactions systems.

Database management systems execute transactions using SQL (Structured Query Language) statements. IBM defined the following types of transactions early on in its transaction systems:

- One statement at a time executed against one database
- A *unit of work,* which includes multiple statements executed on one database
- A *distributed unit of work* that involves multiple statements executed on multiple databases with one statement per database at a time
- A *distributed request* that involves multiple statements executed on multiple databases, with multiple statements per database at a time

Obviously, as transactions are distributed to multiple databases, safety mechanisms must be used to ensure data integrity. A feature of transaction processing is the ability to *roll back* a transaction that cannot be completed (for example, because of insufficient funds, lack of credit, a power loss, or a failed link). A transaction must be either fully completed or rolled back so the database returns to its pretransaction state. A *transaction monitor* is the program that monitors this process. As a user steps through a transaction, changes are made to a database. If the user needs to abort the transaction, the transaction monitor makes sure that all affected databases revert to their pretransaction states.

There are four requirements, collectively called "ACID," for transaction processing in distributed environments:

- **Atomicity**   Defines individual units of work. If a transaction is distributed, all the subtransactions that affect data at separate sites must execute together as a single transaction, either to completion or rolled back if incomplete. To keep data at multiple sites consistent, a *two-phase commit* procedure is used, as described next.
- **Consistency**   Consistency is basically a requirement that databases move from one state to another in coordination. The transaction monitor must verify that all affected data is consistent.
- **Isolation**   Transactions must execute in isolation until completed, without influence from other transactions. Also, the results of a transaction are not available until the transaction is final and complete.
- **Durability**   This property has to do with the final commitment of a transaction. Once a transaction is verified to be accurate on all affected systems, it is committed and from then on cannot be rolled back.

Two-Phase Commit

Transaction processing changes data on multiple systems that may be connected via unreliable communication systems. The opportunity to fail in completing a transaction on one or more systems or during any part of the transaction is great. Therefore, a rollback mechanism is essential in order to protect data. As mentioned, a transaction must be either fully completed or rolled back so the database returns to its pretransaction state. A *transaction monitor* is the program that monitors this process. As a user steps through a transaction, changes are made to a database. If the user needs to abort the transaction, the transaction monitor makes sure that all affected databases revert to their pretransaction states.

Two-phase commit separates the writing of data into two phases, each ending with a verification of completeness. In the following steps, assume that no faults occur during the transaction:

1. The database systems involved in the transaction hold the data to commit to the database in memory.

2. The transaction monitor sends a "precommit" command to the database systems.

3. The database systems reply that they are ready to commit.

4. On hearing back from every database system, the transaction monitor sends a "commit" command.

5. The database systems reply that they successfully committed the data.

6. The transaction monitor completes the transaction when it receives a response from all database systems that data was successfully committed.

If the transaction monitor fails to hear a response from every database system in steps 3 and 5, the transaction monitor alerts the systems to roll back their transactions.

Transaction Processing Environments

IBM's CICS (Customer Information Control System) is one of the most well-known and established transaction-processing environments. CICS was originally developed to monitor transactions on IBM mainframes. It provides a programming environment for developers and manages transactions between users and applications. IBM makes CICS available for mainframe systems, UNIX systems, and PC platforms.

On the Internet, millions of computers are connected and participating in electronic commerce that involves transaction processing across multiple remote systems. Coordinating these transactions is even more critical because of the unpredictable nature of the Internet. Many systems simply hand off transactions to back-end mainframe servers running CICS.

The Internet presents an environment for transaction processing that is quite different from the mainframe and database-oriented models such as CICS, where the environment is relatively homogeneous and centrally located. The Internet model consists of distributed applications running on clients and servers with a variety of operating systems and platforms. Software is built with object-oriented programming techniques and component technology. The concept of *OTMs (object transaction monitors)* has been developed to handle transactions in this environment.

IONA Technologies is a leading provider of OTMs. Its Orbix OTM uses CORBA object request broker technology to manage and secure transactions. The company's entire product line is designed to help developers create enterprise applications and Web e-business solutions

T

using object and component technologies. Its iPortal Application Server provides application logic and supports Sun's Enterprise JavaBeans and Java 2 Platform Enterprise Edition specification (J2EE). J2EE handles transactions automatically, allowing developers to build transactional applications without worrying about the transaction details.

In a Java environment, developers can develop transaction controls with the Java Transaction API (JTA). JTA specifies standard Java interfaces between a transaction manager and the parties involved in a distributed transaction system, including the resource manager, the application server, and the transactional applications. The JTA specification was developed by Sun Microsystems in cooperation with leading industry partners in the transaction-processing and database system arena.

Some of the traditional transaction-processing monitor vendors such as IBM, BEA, GemStone Systems, and Oracle have altered their strategies to support Java-based transactions. These vendors enhance OTM with products that provide reliable transaction-processing support over distributed environments. For example, GemStone's Object Transaction Monitor (OTM) manages transactions performed across multiple, heterogeneous databases using CORBA services. The OTM supplies a standard infrastructure for building J2EE applications that can initiate or participate in two-phase, fully recoverable transactions that are controlled at the object level. The product provides J2EE component supports that synchronize with CORBA services.

Microsoft Transaction Server

Microsoft supports transactions in its Windows environment through Microsoft Transaction Server (MTS). MTS is based on COM+, a technology for building enterprise-level components and electronic commerce applications that use Web interfaces. MTS manages communications between components via DCOM (Distributed COM), and so provides TP monitoring and an object request brokering in one package. A feature called MSDTC (Microsoft Distributed Transaction Coordinator) handles two-phase commit across multiple data sources.

MTS provides "middleware" functionality in that it hides the complexities of transaction processing from the program developers, allowing developers to concentrate on the functionality of their applications. It aids in the development of multitier applications, which consist of client applications, application servers, and back-end database systems that store and provide access to information. The application servers reside in the middle tier and provide application logic. Clients communicate with the application server using a variety of protocols including SOAP (Simple Object Access Protocol). SOAP is a Microsoft/Lotus/IBM-developed protocol for exchanging information in distributed environments. It provides a common message-passing protocol that uses HTTP to carry messages that are formatted in XML (Extensible Markup Language).

MSDTC is the entity that monitors and manages transactions between components. When a transaction begins, a *transaction object* is created by the TM (transaction manager) to represent the transaction. The application that initiated the transaction makes calls to RMs (resource managers), which are participants in the transaction. RMs are typically tied to relational databases. The TM tracks the activities of the RMs during the transaction. If a problem occurs, the TM will abort the transaction. If the application that called the transaction completes its work, the DTC can commit the transaction changes to the databases.

Internet Transaction-Processing Support

Internet designers have realized for years that the TCP and UDP protocols are not ideal for distributed applications, which require a transaction-oriented style of communications. These applications must have a way to guarantee that work being done happens atomically, where each node reaches the same conclusion and terminates its work properly. TCP favors a virtual circuit style of communications but has no TP functions, while UDP does not provide enough services. Several solutions and protocols have been proposed over the years to develop a protocol between TCP and UDP that supports transaction-oriented communications. The following RFCs shed some light on early TP developments in the Internet:

- RFC 955 (Towards a Transport Service for Transaction Processing Applications, September 1985)
- RFC 962 (TCP-4 Prime, November 1985)
- RFC 1379 (Extending TCP for Transactions – Concepts, November 1992)
- RFC 1644 (T/TCP – TCP Extensions for Transactions Functional Specification, July 1994)

In 1998, Microsoft and Compaq started promoting TIP (Transaction Internet Protocol) to support transactions that span multiple Web servers and electronic transactions on the Internet. The TIP designers felt that traditional transaction protocols were too tied to vendors and that there was a need to provide transaction functionality that works across heterogeneous systems and platforms.

TIP is "lightweight" in terms of overhead. It provides two-phase commit functionality and operates by setting up a second communication channel over which transaction monitoring and commitments take place. TIP simply informs end systems that a transaction either was successful or failed. The end system is then responsible for taking further action.

TIP is defined in RFC 2371 (Transaction Internet Protocol, July 1998). RFC 2372 (TIP Requirements and Supplemental Information, July 1998) describes the purpose (usage scenarios), and requirements for TIP. The TIP technical brief listed next provides additional TIP perspective.

Related Entries   ActiveX; COM (Component Object Model); CORBA (Common Object Request Broker Architecture); DBMS (Database Management System); Distributed Applications; Distributed Computer Networks; Distributed Object Computing; Electronic Commerce; Fault Tolerance and High Availability; Java; Middleware and Messaging; Multitiered Architectures; Object Technologies; ORB (Object Request Broker); *and* Web Technologies and Concepts

Linktionary!—Tom Sheldon's Encyclopedia of Networking updates	http://www.linktionary.com/t/transaction_processing.html
"Transaction Processing Monitor Technology" at Carnegie Mellon	http://www.sei.cmu.edu/str/descriptions/tpmt.html
"Database Two Phase Commit" page at Carnegie Mellon	http://www.sei.cmu.edu/str/descriptions/dtpc.html

"A Detailed Comparison of Enterprise JavaBeans (EJB) & The Microsoft Transaction Server (MTS) Models" by Gopalan Suresh Raj	http://members.tripod.com/gsraj/misc/ejbmts/ejbmtscomp.html
Transaction Internet Protocol Technical Brief	http://himalaya.compaq.com/view.asp?IOID=442
Transaction Processing Performance Council (defined benchmarks)	http://www.tpc.org/
Transaction Internet Protocol Technical Brief	http://himalaya.compaq.com/view.asp?IOID=442
Java Transaction API (JTA) Web page	http://java.sun.com/products/jta/
Bitpipe (search for "transaction processing")	http://www.bitpipe.com
IBM Transaction Systems Web page (including CICS link)	http://www-4.ibm.com/software/ts/
IONA Technologies	http://www.iona.com
BEA Systems	http://www.beasys.com
Transarc (Encina)	http://www.transarc.com

Transfer Rates

See Delay, Latency, and Jitter.

Transport Layer, OSI Model

The transport layer is layer 4 in the OSI protocol stack. It resides above the physical, data link, and network layers and just below the session layer. It provides a messaging service for the session layer and hides the underlying network from the upper layers. Transport services in general are discussed in the next section, "Transport Protocols and Services."

Related Entries   Connection-Oriented and Connectionless Services; Data Communication Concepts; OSI (Open Systems Interconnection) Model; Protocol Concepts; TCP (Transmission Control Protocol); *and* Transport Protocols and Services

Transport Layer Security (TLS)

See TLS (Transport Layer Security).

Transport Protocols and Services

Transport protocols occupy layer 4 of the OSI protocol model. The protocols at this level provide connection-oriented sessions and reliable data delivery services. The transport layer sits on top of layer 3 networking services. In the Internet Protocol suite, TCP provides transport services, while IP provides network services. In Novell's SPX/IPX protocol suite, SPX (Sequenced Packet Exchange) provides transport services, while IPX (Internetwork Packet Exchange) provides network services. NetBIOS is also a transport layer protocol.

Network layer protocols like IP provide *best effort* services—that is, they deliver packets but don't guarantee that the packets will actually be delivered. Think about the postal service. It delivers letters, but you don't know that it was received unless you arrange to have a delivery confirmation returned to you. Some applications, such as real-time voice and video, do not need TCP's services. In a real-time stream, it does not make sense to recover a lost packet. Speed of delivery is more important, so UDP (a limited services transport protocol) is used.

Transport layer protocols provide delivery guarantees that are essential for file transfers and mission-critical applications. TCP uses IP, but adds the reliability services at the cost of more overhead and slightly reduced performance. These services operate over a "virtual connection" that is established between sender and receiver. When a session begins, the sender uses a handshaking technique to establish a connection with the receiver. During the session, sender and receiver engage in a dialog that manages the flow of data to prevent from overflowing the receiver and confirms the receipt of TCP segments. A communication session goes like this:

1. Establish a connection (virtual circuit).

2. Negotiate session parameters.

3. Manage data transfers and ensure that data is reliably delivered.

4. Terminate the connection.

The services provided by transport protocols are listed here with references to appropriate sections in this book that provide more detailed descriptions. You should also refer to "TCP (Transmission Control Protocol)" for detailed information on the Internet's transport protocol. A related section is "UDP (User Datagram Protocol)."

■ **Connection setup and multiplexing** The sender must contact the receiver before its starts sending data packets. They engage in a three-way handshake operation to establish the connection, then start transmitting data. A single computer can establish multiple connections with multiple computers at the same time, a feature called multiplexing (since the packets for these different connections are transmitted over the same network connection). See "Connection Establishment" for details.

■ **Flow control mechanisms** While slow start and congestion control are used to avoid network congestion, flow controls help prevent the sender from overflowing the receiver with too much data. These controls are essential because the receiver drops packets when it is overloaded and those packets must be retransmitted, potentially increasing network congestion and reducing system performance. See "Flow-Control Mechanisms."

■ **Slow start and congestion control** Once a connection has been made, the sender starts sending packets, slowly at first so it does not overwhelm the network. If congestion is not bad, it picks up the pace. This is called "slow start." Later, congestion controls help the sender scale back if the network gets busy. See "Congestion Control Mechanisms" for more details.

■ **Reliability services** These services are used to retransmit corrupt, lost, and dropped packets. *Positive acknowledgements* confirm to the sender that the recipient actually received a packet (failure to transmit this acknowledgement means "resend the packet"). Sequencing is used to number packets so that packets can be put back in order and lost packets can be detected. Error checking detects corrupted packets. Refer to "Reliable Data Delivery Services" and "TCP (Transmission Control Protocol)" for more information.

Related Entries   Acknowledgments; Best-Effort Delivery Services; Connection Establishment; Congestion Control Mechanisms; Connection Establishment; Connection-Oriented and Connectionless Services; Data Communication Concepts; Error Detection and Correction; Flow-Control Mechanisms; Network Architecture; Packets and Packet-Switching Networks; QoS (Quality of Service); Reliable Data Delivery Services; RTP (Real-time Transport Protocol); TCP (Transmission Control Protocol); Transport Protocols and Services; UDP (User Datagram Protocol); *and* Virtual Circuit

Linktionary!—Tom Sheldon's Encyclopedia of Networking updates	http://www.linktionary.com/t/transport.html
The Transport Layer- An Introduction, by The Transport Group	http://ganges.cs.tcd.ie/4ba2/transport/5.intro1.html
Transport Layer Protocols tutorial by Xiannong Meng	http://www.cs.panam.edu/~meng/Course/CS6345/Notes/chpt-6/node1.html
IETF Working Groups (see Transport Area)	http://www.ietf.org/html.charters/wg-dir.html
The Transport Layer: Tutorial and Survey. University of Delaware	http://www.cis.udel.edu/~amer/PEL/survey/
Links to papers about multiplexing in the transport layer	http://www.aciri.org/floyd/tcp_mux.html

TRIP (Telephony Routing over IP)

TRIP is an Internet protocol that supports the discovery and exchange of IP telephony gateway routing tables between providers. TRIP is discussed in RFC 2871 (A Framework for Telephony Routing over IP, June 2000).

   An IP telephony gateway is a device that provides a link between the tradition circuit-oriented PSTN and an IP packet-switched network. It allows users on IP networks to originate calls that are forwarded to the PSTN and allows PSTN callers to make calls to Internet phone users.

   See "Voice over IP (VoIP)."

Troubleshooting

See Testing, Diagnostics, and Troubleshooting.

Trunking

See Link Aggregation; Load Balancing.

Trust Relationships and Trust Management

Trust is essential among people who engage in business transactions, but on the Internet people are often required to trust someone they have never met. Likewise, business transactions often require that computers communicate with one another and exchange sensitive information. Trust must be established. The usual technique is to involve a third party that is trusted by both parties. A certificate authority is an example of a third party that issues digital certificates. Trust relationships are also important in the enterprise, where interdivision or interdepartment trust is required.

Trust relationships are established between systems so those systems can exchange information without the need for an administrator or other person to actively monitor and authorize those exchanges. Trust relationships also benefit users. Systems in trust relationships may trust the authentication performed by partner systems. Clients can log in once and access other trusted systems without the need to continually log in.

The Windows NT domain model illustrates the bidirectional nature of some trust relationships (note that the NT domain model is used for example only as Windows 2000 now uses a directory services model). A Windows NT domain is a collection of network resources controlled by a central authority. A typical enterprise may have separate domains for each of its divisions or departments. Trust relationships among these domains may be *one-way* or *two-way* (bidirectional).

An example of a one-way trust would be established by accounting or auditing departments that need to access another department's servers for auditing purposes. There is no need to set up trust in the other direction from the departments into the accounting or auditing department.

A two-way trust relationship allows two domains to trust one another. If a user is properly authenticated in one domain, the other domain trusts the credentials of that user and allows the user to access appropriate systems. Domain administrators still control access to system resources. The trust relationship merely means that the list of users that can be granted access is expanded with the addition of users from the other domain. The trust relationship also consists of a secure channel between the servers in each domain that control user accounts.

The trust relationships are set up by administrators in a cooperative way. The administrator in the first domain designates the second domain as a trusting domain. The administrator in second domain then completes the trust arrangement by designating the first domain as a trusted domain.

A similar trust model applies to the Internet, which is a collection of autonomous systems in the form of individual service provider and carrier networks that are interconnected by routers, routing protocols, and routing policies. Each autonomous system is managed by its own authority and implements its own internal routing. The authority for one AS will allow traffic from another AS to cross its networks. The trust relationship allows the exchange of routing information and other management information.

Similarly, organizations that build extranets and engage in B2B (business-to-business) relationships require trust, since users in one organization will more than likely need to access systems in the other organization. In fact, trust relationships are pervasive in the global information system. Banks and credit organizations exchange information with businesses, while insurance companies exchange information with hospitals and medical offices. Knowing how much information is exchange, you start to wonder about privacy and the strength of the security involved in these trust relationships.

One problem is that malicious users can potentially exploit trust relationships to gain access to other systems. For example, a hacker might be unsuccessful in an attack against some system, but then attack a system that is in a trust relationship with the original target. The second system may be easier to attack, or the hacker may already have an account on that system (possibly

T

obtained by hacking still another system). Through the trust relations, the hacker can follow a path into other systems. This is called a "backdoor" attack.

Trusted Third Parties or TTPs

As mentioned, trusted third parties act as intermediaries between parties for a variety of trust requirements, including authentication services and electronic commerce. A trusted third party may be a security server within an enterprise, as is the case with the Kerberos authentication system. In the business world, TTPs are certificate authorities, accounting firms, banks, government agencies, and so on.

Certificate Authorities

A certificate authority is a third party that can guarantee the authenticity of keys in the public-key scheme as described under "Public-Key Cryptography." A certificate authority guarantees that a public key is authentic. On the Internet, certificate authorities (CAs) like VeriSign, Commerce Net, and even the U.S. Postal Service provide key management. What a CA does is obtain the public key and registration information from clients, verify the information, then bind the key with the user information into a certificate.

A certificate authority creates certificates, which are electronic packages that bind a user's name and other information with the user's public key. The certificate is then signed by a CA. Signing is a cryptographic technique that "locks down" the contents of the certificate so that tampering can be detected. You can compare it to putting a protective seal on a medicine bottle. One must trust that the public key used to verify a certificate is itself authentic. The trust comes from the fact that a CA's public key is in a certificate that has been signed by a higher-level authority and this trust extends up a hierarchy of trust to authorities such as government agencies or international organizations. This hierarchy of trust is part of a public key infrastructure. See "PKI (Public Key Infrastructure)" and "Certificates and Certification Systems."

TTP Service Providers

On the Internet, new electronic trading systems have emerged that call for trust in a variety of forms. *TTP service providers* have emerged to provide a full range of trust services. For example, if you are engaging in electronic transactions with other businesses that you know nothing about, a TTP can provide the assurances that you need for safe electronic commerce. For example, is a business site real or is it spoofed? Is the content authentic or has it been altered? Can other people easily pose as you and gain access to your online accounts? Is your personal information kept confidential and secure? Is information exchanged securely? TTP service providers can also provide accounting, auditing, and tracking services for online transactions.

The OII (Open Information Interchange) Web site presents a good discussion of trust services and what users of trust services should expect in the way of service offerings and the way that TTPs conduct their business. It discusses the need to closely evaluate TTPs, specify required services, write security policies, and establish contracts. A TTP should be evaluated in a number of ways. Check to see if it is accredited by national or international groups and whether its operations can be verified. Check its service levels—that is, the type of services and when they are available. Check its contract, liabilities, and policy statements. Also check to see how confidentiality is maintained.

The OII site also discusses service requirements, including secure archiving of information, timestamping transactions, ensuring evidence of transmission or origination, ensuring the authenticity of entities involved, notarizing activities, auditing, and payment/billing services.

KeyNote Trust Management Systems

KeyNote is a trust management system that has been evolving since 1997. It is now specified in RFC 2704 (The KeyNote Trust-Management System Version 2, September 1999). KeyNote supports a wide variety of applications, including IPSec policy control and electronic payment systems. KeyNote provides a language for describing and implementing security policies, trust relationships, and digitally signed credentials. Developers can create security policies and credentials that grant people or processes the ability to perform specific trusted actions. When an entity makes a request for some action, the KeyNote application submits a description of the action along with a copy of its local security policy to the KeyNote interpreter. KeyNote then "approves" or "rejects" the action according to the rules given in the application's security policy.

RFC 2704 is an interesting read for anyone interested in learning more about trust management systems. It describes the components of such a system, such as languages for describing actions, mechanisms for identifying people or processes, a policy specification language, a language for specifying "credentials" that allows principals to delegate authorization to other principals, and a compliance checker, which determines how actions should be handled given a policy and a set of credentials. RFC 2792 (DSA and RSA Key and Signature Encoding for the KeyNote Trust Management System, March 2000) specifies RSA and DSA key and signature encodings, and binary key encodings for use in KeyNote.

"Web of Trust" Alternatives

Wave Systems, maker of the EMBASSY E-Commerce System (EMBedded Application Security SYstem), takes a different approach to trust. It believes that the current "web-of-trust" system has limitations and has developed a chip that moves trust to the end user's system. The chip is designed to be installed on motherboards. As a hardware device, it is more resistant to hacker attacks than software-only approaches.

EMBASSY moves the point of "trust" to the place where the transaction takes place. The concept is that if the client devices are trusted and secured, the need to secure other network components is minimized. EMBASSY provides a secure repository for storing private and sensitive information and establishes a programmable environment for executing applications and cryptographic algorithms. EMBASSY was developed in conjunction with Hewlett-Packard, RSA Data Security, Sun Microsystems, VeriSign, and Aladdin Knowledge Systems.

Related Entries   Authentication and Authorization; Certificates and Certification Systems; Cryptography; Digital Signatures; Domains, Windows NT; EDI (Electronic Data Interchange); Electronic Commerce; Extranet; IPSec (IP Security); Kerberos Authentication Protocol; Key Distribution and Management; Metadata; PKI (Public-Key Infrastructure); Public-Key Cryptography; Security; SET (Secure Electronic Transaction); SSL (Secure Sockets Layer); TLS (Transport Layer Security); VPN (Virtual Private Network); *and* X.509 Certificates

 Linktionary!—Tom Sheldon's Encyclopedia of Networking updates   http://www.linktionary.com/t/trust.html

OII (Open Information Interchange) Guide to Trust Services	http://158.169.50.95:10080/oii/en/trust.html
Wave Systems	http://www.wavesys.com/
Matt Blaze's Crypto.com page (see Trust Management section)	http://www.crypto.com/

T Series ITU Recommendations

The T series recommendations are ITU standards that define multimedia data networks, particularly videoconferencing. A synopsis is given here. Refer to the ITU Web site listed later for a complete list and a description of each recommendation.

- **T.0–T.107**   Telematic services, facsimile standards, and videotex services, including coding, compression, and imaging

- **T.120–T.140**   Multipoint data communication service for use in multimedia conferencing environments

- **T.170–T.176**   Protocols for interactive audiovisual services, including coded representation of multimedia and hypermedia objects

- **T.190–T192**   Cooperative document handling

- **T.411–T.441**   ODA (Open Document Architecture) and interchange format, DTAM (Document Transfer And Manipulation).

Related Entries   Compression Technique; FAX Servers and Network Faxing; G Series ITU Recommendations; H.323 Multimedia Conferencing Standard; H Series ITU Recommendations; ITU (International Telecommunications Union); Multimedia; Videoconferencing; *and* X Series ITU Recommendations

| ITU T series recommendations | http://www.itu.int//itudoc/itu-t/rec/t/ |

Tunnels

Tunnels are virtual paths across networks that either deliver encrypted packets or packets that are of a different protocol type than the network itself. When a tunnel is used to delivery foreign packets, it can be compared to a ferry that carries cars across a river or channel. An example of a tunnel is pictured in Figure T-11. The tunneling process involves *encapsulating* a packet from the source network into a packet of the intermediate network. When the packet arrives at the destination network, it is removed from the packet and forwarded on the network.

An organization that has two IPX networks that are separated by a large TCP/IP network can join the two IPX networks by encapsulating IPX packets into IP packets for delivery across the TCP/IP network. Tunneling is also often used to deliver nonroutable protocols such as SNA (Systems Network Architecture) or NetBEUI (NetBIOS Extended User Interface) across a routed network. Encapsulation is used to transport Ethernet frames across an FDDI backbone network. The Ethernet frame is placed inside an FDDI frame and sent across the FDDI backbone. When

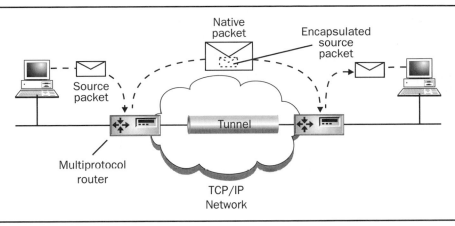

Figure T-11.   *A tunnel delivers packets across an intermediate network*

the packet reaches the Ethernet/FDDI attached to the destination network, it is unencapsulated and sent to the destination.

Tunneling has become popular in building private secure network links—that is, VPNs (virtual private networks) across public networks such as the Internet. To build a VPN, a company installs encrypting routers at either end of the virtual link. All data traffic sent between the sites, no matter what protocol is used, can be placed in IP packets that are routed to the other site. The data in the packets is encrypted to keep it private. When packets are encrypted (i.e., a virtual private network), they are essentially foreign packets that must be encapsulated because the intermediate networks cannot read the header information. The header is usually encrypted for security reasons; however, the IETF IPSec (IP Security) protocol provides an option for encrypting just the data and not the header.

Tunneling may also provide a form of source routing or constraint-based routing, in which an encrypted path is set up in advance to deliver packets from source to destination in a very efficient manner. This is the approach of MPLS (Multiprotocol Label Switching) in combination with IPSec. Normal routing decisions are bypassed and replaced with fast switching options.

Two other popular tunneling protocols are PPTP (Point-to-Point Tunneling Protocol) and L2TP (Layer 2 Tunneling Protocol). PPTP is used to encrypt and encapsulate IP, IPX, or NetBEUI traffic in an IP packet. L2TP extends this concept across X.25, frame relay, or ATM networks. One advantage that PPTP and L2TP have over IPSec tunneling is the ability to easily support dial-up remote access users. The reason is because the protocols support PPP user authentication. This is the same authentication that most ISPs use for dial-up Internet access accounts.

Several Internet RFCs provide more information about encapsulation and encrypted tunnels. Also see "L2TP (Layer 2 Tunneling Protocol)," IPSec (IP Security)," and "VPN (Virtual Private Network)" for more information about tunnels and related RFCs.

- RFC 1234 (Tunneling IPX traffic through IP networks, June 1991)
- RFC 1853 (IP in IP Tunneling, October 1995)

- RFC 2003 (IP Encapsulation within IP, October 1996)
- RFC 2004 (Minimal Encapsulation within IP, October 1996)
- RFC 2983 (Differentiated Services and Tunnels, October 2000)
- RFC 3053 (IPv6 Tunnel Broker, January 2001)
- RFC 3077 (A Link-Layer Tunneling Mechanism for Unidirectional Links, March 2001)

Related Entries　ATM (Asynchronous Transfer Mode); Congestion and Congestion Control; Differentiated Services (Diff-Serv); IP over ATM; IPSec (IP Security); L2TP (Layer 2 Tunneling Protocol); Label Switching; MPLS (Multiprotocol Label Switching); Multilayer Switching; QoS (Quality of Service); Traffic Management, Shaping, and Engineering, VPN (Virtual Private Network)

Linktionary!—Tom Sheldon's Encyclopedia of　　　　http://www.linktionary.com/t/tunnels.html
Networking updates

See "VPN (Virtual Private Networks)" for related links.

Two-Factor Authentication

See Token-Based Authentication.

Two-Phase Commit

See Transaction Processing.

Two-Tier Client/Server Model

See Multitiered Architecture.

UDA (Universal Data Access)

UDA (Universal Data Access) is Microsoft's strategy for providing access to information across the enterprise. UDA provides access to a variety of information sources, including relational and nonrelational, and an easy-to-use programming interface that is tool and language independent. Microsoft's UDA Web site is http://www.microsoft.com/data/.

UDDI (Universal Description, Discovery, and Integration)

With the explosion in online business transactions and B2B (business-to-business) transactions, companies doing business on the Web need an easy way to discover one another and publish information that can be used to set up transactions. UDDI (Universal Description, Discovery, and Integration) is a standard that defines a common way for organizations to publish information about business services and provide other organizations with information that can be used to integrate business processes. UDDI is more than a directory. The UDDI Business Registry is an implementation of the UDDI specification in which organizations publicly list descriptions of services and methods of engagement. The UDDI specifications take advantage of Internet standards developed by the W3C and the IETF, including HTTP, DNS, XML, and SOAP. SOAP is a messaging specification originally developed by Microsoft but now promoted by the W3C.

Related Entries   Electronic Commerce; Microsoft.NET; Search and Discovery Services; SOAP (Simple Object Access Protocol); *and* XML (Extensible Markup Language)

UDDI (Universal Description, Discovery, and Integration) Web site

http://www.UDDI.org/

UDP (User Datagram Protocol)

The TCP/IP protocol stack pictured in Figure U-1 consists of a *best-effort* network layer protocol (IP) and a *reliable* transport layer protocol (TCP). Reliable services can ensure that packets are delivered to a host in the correct order (e.g., if a packet is dropped, TCP can arrange to resend it, as opposed to relying on IP and the network layer to resend it). TCP also supports flow and congestion controls. Best-effort services simply deliver packets. UDP sits next to TCP in the transport layer of the protocol stack, but provides fewer services than TCP. Both TCP and UDP use IP for packet delivery.

When applications developers create programs for TCP/UDP/IP networks, they can choose TCP or UDP at the transport layer. The main difference is that TCP provides reliability and congestion control services, while UDP trades off those services to improve performance. A comparative list of TCP/UDP functions is provided later. Most applications use TCP because reliability is crucial. For example, FTP uses TCP to ensure that an exact copy of a file is delivered to the recipient. Multimedia applications use UDP because they can tolerate some loss, as discussed later. Actually, multimedia applications typically run RTP (Real-time Transport Protocol) on top of UDP. RTP is a service for controlling the transmission rate of real-time multimedia.

The most important thing that TCP and UDP share in common is the ability to establish a host-to-host communication channel for delivering packets between processes running in two different computers. In other words, these protocols provide a way for two applications to communicate. Therefore, they are *end-to-end protocols*.

U

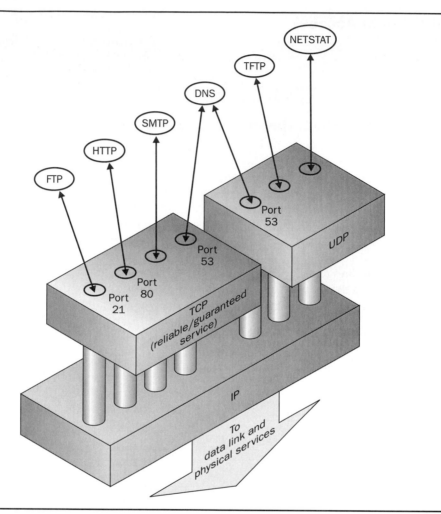

Figure U-1.   *UDP bypasses TCP's services for applications that don't need them.*

When a user accesses a Web site, one or more temporary sessions are established between client and server applications in order to exchange packets. One session might be opening a Web page while another downloads a file. When more than one session is established, packets from those sessions are "multiplexed" across the same link. Some method is needed to differentiate the packets of one session from the packets of another.

Both TCP and UDP use ports and port numbers to identify application protocols. For example, Web services (HTTP) use port 80, FTP uses port 21, and Gopher uses port 70. A typical session involves sending packets from a source IP address and port to a destination IP address and port. TCP and UDP packet headers contain source and destination port address information. These packets flow between the applications at either end of the connection. Therefore, they are often called "flows." Many QoS techniques identify these flows (by looking at port addresses in packets) and give flows a particular quality of service.

The UDP header, pictured next, illustrates how port addressing is the primary function of UDP. The header is mostly port-addressing fields. Compare this to the TCP header in Figure T-3. A checksum is used to detect corrupted packets. If an application requires more reliable service than this, TCP or supplemental protocols must be used.

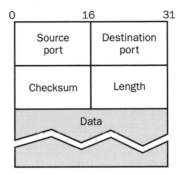

The endpoint of a connection is called a *socket*. It consists of a host's IP address and a port number. Therefore, a socket identifies a specific application running on a specific computer and is the endpoint of a connection. How does a client know which port to use when initially forming packets to send to a server? The usual method is to connect with well-known ports. These are published in RFC 1700 (Assigned Numbers, July 1992). While ports are predefined, sockets do not exist until a connection is established. Multiple connections may use the same port number, but each connection is differentiated by the local and remote addresses associated with that connection.

Here is a comparison of the most important services offered by TCP and UDP:

Service	TCP	UDP
Connection setup	Takes time, but TCP does this to ensure reliability.	No connection required.
Guaranteed message delivery	Returns ACKs (acknowledgments).	Since UDP does not return ACKs, the receiver cannot signal that packets have been successfully delivered. Lost packets are not retransmitted.
Packet sequencing (provide information about the correct order of packets)	Sequentially numbers packets.	UDP does not insert sequence numbers. The packets are expected to arrive as a continuous stream or they are dropped.
Flow controls	The receiver can signal the sender to slow down.	ACKs, which are used in TCP to control packet flow, are not returned.
Congestion controls	Network devices can take advantage of TCP ACKs to control the behavior of senders.	Without ACKs, the network cannot signal congestion to the sender.

U

As mentioned, UDP minimizes delays for real-time traffic. The primary objective is to deliver packets on time. At the same time, some amount of packet drop is acceptable. For example, a single dropped packet in a video stream may not be detectable to a viewer, but attempting to recover the packet may cause delays that are detectable. About 5 percent of the packets in a voice stream can be dropped without detection. With multimedia traffic, speed is more important than reliability, and that is why application developers choose UDP.

Applications using UDP must provide some form of flow control on their own. For example, if a videoconferencing application notices that packets are being dropped, it may dynamically increase the compression ratio (and thus reduce quality) or drop packets on its own in a controlled way to match available bandwidth on the network, while still providing quality that it considers reasonable. It does not rely on UDP for this, and using TCP for flow and congestion control would be inefficient.

In fact, most real-time applications have their own special flow-control requirements that the generic control provided by TCP cannot provide. Basically, UDP-based real-time applications must be "self-regulating." RTP can rely on RTCP (Real-time Control Protocol) to control transmission rates when packets are dropped. RTCP is a feedback mechanism that helps real-time applications work within the available bandwidth of the network.

Keep in mind that real-time applications that use UDP will still attempt to grab network bandwidth, possibly causing congestion in the network. While real-time applications may be able to control the flow between end systems, they do nothing to prevent flows from congesting the network. That is a traffic management issue, as discussed under "Traffic Management, Shaping, and Engineering." Refer to RFC 768 (User Datagram Protocol, August 1980) and RFC 1180 (A TCP/IP Tutorial, January 1991) for more information about UDP.

David P. Read, one of the people involved in the design of the TCP/IP protocols, writes in "The End of the End-to-End Argument" that by splitting the Internet protocols into two protocols (TCP and IP), the network was "decentralized" and turned into a basic datagram-forwarding network. In this model, end systems handle functions that were previously handled by networks, such as flow control, acknowledgments, and retransmissions. By splitting the protocols, it was necessary to create UDP for applications that needed to bypass TCP's services.

Related Entries   Congestion Control Mechanisms; End Systems and End-to-End Connectivity; Internet; Internet Protocol Suite; IP (Internet Protocol); Multimedia; Network Concepts; Reliable Data Delivery Protocols; RTP (Real-time Transport Protocol); RTCP (Real-Time Transport Control Protocol); TCP (Transmission Control Protocol); TCP/IP (Transmission Control Protocol/Internet Protocol); Traffic Management, Shaping, and Engineering; *and* Transport Protocols and Services

Linktionary!—Tom Sheldon's Encyclopedia of Networking updates	http://www.linktionary.com/u/udp.html
Gorry Fairhurst on UDP (see "Transport Protocols and Applications" section)	http://www.erg.abdn.ac.uk/users/gorry/course/syllabus.html
Winsock: UDP Tutorial (how to make a UDP application)	http://durrow.com/borland_udp_main.html

ULSNET (Ultra Low-Speed Networking)

ULSNET is a low-speed, low-efficiency networking system proposed by Vincent Cerf in 1991. According to RFC 1217 (Memo from the Consortium for Slow Commotion Research, April 1991), the military places a high premium on ultrarobust systems capable of supporting communication in extremely hostile environments. A major contributing factor in the survivability of systems is a high degree of redundancy. The network defined in this RFC 1217 is an amusing spoof. See "Internet Entertainment" for more spoofs.

UML (Unified Modeling Language)

According to the Meta Data Coalition, UML is a language for modeling information systems and software artifacts. The UML can be used to visualize, specify, construct, and document knowledge about software-intensive systems and their purpose at an abstract level. The goals of the UML are to unify the most prominent modeling methodologies into a ready-to-use expressive modeling language that is simple and extensible. The modeling language was developed by Rational Software Corporation and partners and was adopted by the OMG in November 1997. The UML continues to evolve though this standards body.

The Unified Modeling Language (UML) is the modeling standard for specifying and representing metadata in the MDC OIM. Based on the formal representation of the metadata specification in the UML, it is possible to generate automatically all the necessary deliverables to deploy implementations of the specifications in tools or repositories.

Refer to the Web sites listed here for more information.

Related Entries   Data Warehousing; Metadata; OIM (Open Information Model); Repository; *and* XML (Extensible Markup Language)

Linktionary!—Tom Sheldon's Encyclopedia of Networking updates	http://www.linktionary.com/u/uml.html
Meta Data Coalition	http://www.mdcinfo.com/
Object Management Group (see UML information)	http://www.omg.org/

UMTS (Universal Mobile Telecommunication Services)

UMTS is an ETSI standard for third-generation GSM (Global System for Mobile Communications). According to the Mobile Lifestreams Web site given later, "UMTS is Europe's vision for 3G and a very powerful one too for mobile multimedia." UMTS can be viewed as a mobile Internet scheme.

The radio access technology is called UTRA (UMTS Terrestrial Radio Access), and is based on W-CDMA. UTRA has two different modes: FDD (frequency duplex division) and TDD (time duplex division). These modes allow the system to work well in wide areas, tight urban areas, or indoors. Transmission rates can go as high as 2 Mbits/sec for stationary users in small cells.

UMTS is designed to meet the requirements of IMT-2000, which is basically a target standard for providing data rates as high as 2Mbits/sec. IMT-2000 was outlined by the ITU and the mobile communications industry. The name refers to the data rate, not the year.

U

The ITU's intentions are to make IMT-2000 a global framework for wireless communications across satellite and terrestrial systems for mobile and stationary users. Users will be able to move across geographic areas and service provider systems with any IMT-2000 device.

See "Wireless Mobile Communications" for a continuation of this topic and related wireless mobile topics.

Related Entries   CDMA (Code Division Multiple Access); Electromagnetic Spectrum; Mobile Computing; Packet Radio Data Networks; Spread Spectrum Signaling; WAP (Wireless Applications Protocol); Wireless Broadband Access Technologies; Wireless Communications; Wireless IP; Wireless LANs; *and* Wireless Mobile Communications

Linktionary!—Tom Sheldon's Encyclopedia of Networking updates	http://www.linktionary.com/u/umts.html
Mobile Data Evolution Web site	http://www.mobileumts.com/
ITU IMT-2000 information	http://www.itu.int/imt/
UMTS Forum	http://www.umts-forum.org
ETSI (European Telecommunications Standards Institute) (UMTS technical body located here)	http://www.etsi.org/
Wireless Data Forum	http://www.wirelessdata.org/

UNI (User Network Interface)

UNI defines physical and protocol interfacing specifications for devices that are connected at the edges of ATM networks. This includes user systems that are connected to a private ATM switch or the connection between a private ATM switch and an ATM switch owned by a public carrier. The other important ATM interface is NNI (Network-to-Network Interface), which defines interfaces between ATM switches in a core or backbone network. NNI automatically constructs full-mesh PVC connections across the backbone, while UNI allows end systems to establish SVCs across switches in the ATM mesh network.

Related Entry   ATM (Asynchronous Transfer Mode)

ATM Forum UNI information	http://www.atmforum.com/atmforum/specs/approved.html

Unified Messaging

Unified messaging is about unifying all types of messages into a single box. For example, e-mail, voice-mail, faxes, and phone messages are accessible from the same box. Alternatively, people use many different devices to communicate. Unified messaging helps people that use different communication devices, media, and technologies to communicate at any time and under their own control.

Refer to the Web sites listed at the end of this topic for more information.

Related Entries   Addresses, Electronic Mail; Collaborative Computing; Directory Services; Electronic Mail; Fax Servers and Network Faxing; Groupware; IMAP (Internet Message Access Protocol); Instant Messaging; Mailing List Programs; Microsoft Exchange; MIME (Multipurpose Internet Mail Extension); Name Services; POP (Post Office Protocol); Search and Discovery Services; SMTP (Simple Mail Transfer Protocol); *and* Workflow Management

Linktionary!—Tom Sheldon's Encyclopedia of Networking updates	http://www.linktionary.com/u/unified_messaging.html
Unified Messaging.com	http://www.unified-messaging.com/
Messagepoint	http://www.messagepoint.com/
Intranet Design Magazine article: "Towards a Universal Inbox"	http://idm.internet.com/foundation/g5-1.shtml
5GM	http://www.5gm.com/

Universal Service

The Telecommunications Act of 1996 specified that telephone services should have "just and reasonable rates accomplished through allocation of a reasonable share of common costs." The idea was to ensure that special at-risk groups were ensured continuous service. Three programs are available, including Lifeline, Link-Up America, and the Universal Service Fund program. USF is of the most interest here. It funds LECs in rural areas and subsidizes a small fraction of the telecommunications-related costs associated with connecting schools, libraries, and nonprofit rural health care providers to the Internet.

As telephone service moves to the Internet where it is potentially unregulated, there is a question about where the funds for universal service will come from.

Related Entry   Telecommunications and Telephone Systems

The Benton Foundation's Universal Service and Universal Access Virtual Library	http://benton.org/Policy/Uniserv/uniserv.html

UNIX

The UNIX operating system was developed at AT&T Bell Laboratories by Ken Thompson and Dennis Ritchie in 1969 and the early 1970s. The original versions were designed to run on DEC PDP-11 16-bit computers and VAX 32-bit computers. The name "UNIX" comes from UNICS (Uniplexed Information and Computing System), a tongue-in-cheek play on words derived from Multics. Multics was an early time-sharing (allows many tasks to be automatically interspersed) operating system created as a test platform in 1964 by General Electric, Massachusetts Institute of Technology, and AT&T, although AT&T eventually dropped out of the collaborative effort. Multics is historically recognized as the first operating system to implement most of the multitasking features now common in most operating systems.

In 1973, Bell Labs completely rewrote UNIX in the C programming language. This made UNIX highly portable, and it now contains system components written in a common, well-known programming language that is easily recompiled to work on a variety of systems. About the same time, *pipes* were introduced into the operating system, which provided a way to combine data from different programs.

Around 1975, AT&T made the operating system available on an open basis to universities and colleges for use in research projects and computer science programs. This was a major step in the popularization of UNIX, and from this, many variants were created (the releases originating from AT&T's original work are now called the System V release, or SVR). The University of California at Berkeley produced some of the most important work on UNIX outside Bell Labs. The versions it created became known as the *Berkeley Software Distributions*, or *BSDs*. U.C. Berkeley added TCP/IP networking and ported UNIX to the DEC VAX.

Peter H. Salus notes in his book *Casting the Net* (Addison-Wesley, 1995, page 128) that Steve Holmgren played an important part in putting the Net on UNIX (as opposed to putting UNIX on the Net) by writing RFC 681 (Network UNIX, May 1975). This RFC describes Holmgren's experience with connecting the operating system to the Net.

AT&T eventually merged its UNIX development under a single unit called UNIX System Laboratories, or USL. In 1991, Novell and AT&T joined forces to create Univell, a company with the goal of developing UnixWare, a desktop UNIX system with built-in Novell NetWare support. Then, in 1993, Novell purchased USL and formed the USG (UNIX Systems Group) to manage UnixWare.

With the purchase of USL, Novell gained control of UNIX SVR4, to the dismay of other UNIX vendors. In an attempt to consolidate the industry on a common UNIX operating system, Novell gave the UNIX trademark to the X/Open organization (described shortly). But the UNIX and NetWare engineers could not build an operating system that leveraged the best features of both UNIX and NetWare. Novell began to see UNIX as a threat to its long-standing NetWare product and sold UNIX off to the Santa Cruz Operation in December of 1995.

The X/Open group was founded in 1984 by Bull, Nixdorf, Philips, Siemens, and other companies to promote open UNIX standards by testing for conformity among products. X/Open now grants the UNIX trademark to UNIX implementations that are compatible with a set of specifications that promote the portability of applications between operating systems. In 1996, The Open Group was created with the merger of X/Open and the OSF (Open Software Foundation). The Open Group manages UNIX standards such as the CDE (Common Desktop Environment) graphical user interface and Motif graphical user interface toolkit. The Open Group can be found under the topic "Open Group."

Another effort to promote portability of applications across UNIX environments was the creation of POSIX (Portable Operating System Interface for UNIX) by the IEEE community in the early 1980s. However, POSIX is not just a standard for UNIX. It has been implemented on other operating system platforms, such as DEC VMS.

All of this standardization has caused vendors to explain their products in wording that resembles the following (this taken from DEC's Web site): "Digital UNIX Operating System is a 64-bit advanced kernel architecture based on Carnegie-Mellon University's Mach V2.5 kernel design with components from BSD (Berkeley Software Distribution) 4.3 and 4.4, UNIX System V, and other sources. Digital UNIX is Digital Equipment Corporation's implementation of the OSF's OSF/1 R1.0, R1.1, and R1.2 technology, and the Motif graphical user interface and programming environment."

Before the release of freely available Linux, Sun Microsystems' Solaris was perhaps the most popular UNIX system. It is a BSD UNIX with many of the features of the SVR releases. Refer to "Sun Microsystems Solaris" for more information. Still another interesting variant is FreeBSD, a version of UNIX that is based on the Berkeley BSD releases and that runs on Intel processors. The FreeBSD operating system is free and can be obtained at the Web site given later.

Linux is another free UNIX-like operating system that runs on a variety of platforms, including Intel, SPARC, PowerPC, and DEC Alpha processors, as well as multiprocessing systems. Linux is a "user-developed" product, meaning that many of its components and drivers have been developed by users around the world who run the operating system for their own use. See "Linux" for more information.

General Features of UNIX

UNIX is a multiuser system that supports networking and distributed file systems such as Sun Microsystems' NFS (Network File System) or the Open Software Foundation's implementation of the AFS (Andrew File System). The traditional operating system consists of a small kernel that runs processes such as user applications and services. The UNIX kernel is a solid core that changes little from system to system, while processes are added at the user's discretion. This design approach makes it easy for the user to add new services or remove unnecessary services. It also makes upgrades easier since the entire operating system does not need to be recompiled.

Users interact with the operating system through a *shell*, which is also a process that accepts user input and performs various tasks. Because the shell is a replaceable process, there are many variations, such as the Bourne shell, the C shell, and the Korn shell. Graphical user interfaces such as Motif have been developed as replacements for text-based shells.

The file system is hierarchical. There is a root directory and branching subdirectories, and each subdirectory can have its own set of subdirectories. Devices such as displays and printers have device names that are handled in the same way as files. For example, a user could direct the output of a process or file listing to the display or a printer by using the display or printer name in a command. The piping feature provides a way to direct the output of one command, such as a sort, into another command.

UNIX and the TCP/IP protocols are closely linked. Every UNIX implementation now includes TCP/IP and support for Ethernet. In addition, Sun Microsystems' NFS is the common distributed file-sharing system included with UNIX, although the AFS is also used. Thus, UNIX provides in one package the ability to install a powerful operating system on a computer that lets users share files and run programs on other users' computers through one of the most common and powerful networking protocols in the industry.

UNIX is the predominant operating system used by the Internet community, with the Linux version now getting a lot of attention from system administrators. Microsoft Windows 2000 is a contender, but many doubt that it is as reliable and scalable as the UNIX variants. UNIX has been around for years and is well tested.

Related Entries   CDE (Common Desktop Environment); DCE (Distributed Computing Environment); Linux; Motif; Multiprocessing; Network Operating Systems; NFS (Network File System); Open Group; Rights and Permissions; Sun Microsystems Solaris; UNIX File System; *and* X Window

Linktionary!—Tom Sheldon's Encyclopedia of Networking updates	http://www.linktionary.com/u/unix.html
The Open Group	http://www.opengroup.org
Bell Labs Paper: "How UNIX was Created"	http://www.bell-labs.com/history/unix/
Compaq's Tru64 UNIX Website	http://www.tru64unix.compaq.com/
SCO (Santa Cruz Operation)	http://www.sco.com
FreeBSD Web Site (see handbook!)	http://www.freebsd.org
UNIX help for Users	http://www.mcsr.olemiss.edu/unixhelp/
Network Startup Resource Center UNIX networking tools	http://www.nsrc.org/lowcost.html
Jennifer Myers's UNIX Reference Desk	http://www.geek-girl.com/unix.html
Network Appliance's database of UNIX papers (very extensive)	http://www.netapp.com/tech_library/
Indiana University's Unix System Administration Independent Learning	http://www.uwsg.indiana.edu/usail
UNIX FAQs	http://www.cis.ohio-state.edu/hypertext/faq/ usenet/unix-faq/faq/top.html
Hans Kuhn's UNIX System Administration Tools	http://darkwing.uoregon.edu/~hak/unix.html
Unix Review.com	http://www.unixreview.com/
History and Timeline of UNIX at The Open Group	http://www.unix-systems.org/what_is_unix/ history_timeline.html
The UNIX Guru Universe	http://www.ugu.com/
ITPRC UNIX and Linux links	http://www.itprc.com/nos.htm
CAIT Information Systems Meta-List (see "Operating Systems" topic)	http://www.cait.wustl.edu/infosys/infosys.html

UNIX File System

The UNIX file system is a hierarchical, tree-structured namespace that is designed to help users organize and access files. The namespace consists of directories that hold files. UNIX file systems consist of the following:

- *Disk-based file systems* store files on magnetic media, CD-ROMs, and other media. Sun Microsystems Solaris uses three formats, including ufs (UNIX file system), which is based on the BSD file allocation table file system; hsfs (High Sierra and ISO 9660 file system), a CD-ROM file system; and pcfs (PC file system), which provides access to data on DOS-formatted disks.

■ *Network file systems* provide network-wide file sharing and file access. NFS (Network File System) and rfs (remote file sharing) file systems are commonly used.

■ *Pseudo file systems* are virtual file systems that exist in temporary memory and provide a place to store files or directory entries for fast access.

File systems can be mounted and unmounted at any time. A mounted file system is available for use. If it is a network file system, it is available for remote users on the network to access.

As mentioned, the UNIX file system is hierarchical in structure and starts with a root directory (called /) from which all other directories branch. The root directory and subdirectories hold other files and other subdirectories. UNIX includes some unique subdirectories where system files are stored, including **/bin**, **/etc**, and **/dev**. A typical UNIX directory structure is pictured in the following illustration.

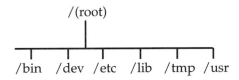

UNIX has three access file permissions—read, write, and execute—and these are issued to three categories of users: owner, group, and others. Each of these is described here:

■ **read (r)**   Allows the user to read a file or list the contents of a directory

■ **write (w)**   Allows the user to write to (change) a file or do a number of things in a directory, including create, rename, and delete a file

■ **execute (x)**   Allows the user to run a program or search a directory

The three categories of users are described here:

■ **owner (u)**   The owner of a file

■ **group (g)**   A group of users to which the owner of a file belongs

■ **others (o)**   All other users

Information on viewing and setting permissions is available at the UNIX file permissions page listed at the end of this topic.

Commands in the UNIX environment such as **ls** (list), **cat** (catalog), and the FTP (File Transfer Protocol) utility display file permissions in a format similar to the following:

-rw-r--r--	1	Tom	Research	1009	Nov 11 1996		stars.gif
drwxrwxr-x	2	DC	Research	512	Sep 16 02:03		stats

U

The first column of the file listing displays the permissions, and the remaining columns define the following in order: number of links, owner, group, file size, date, and filename. The permissions are listed as shown here:

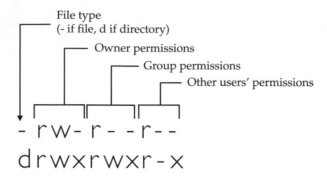

The UNIX system also defines special types of files that represent physical devices such as printers, terminals, and tape drives. Because devices are defined in this way, it is possible to direct the output of some command to the devices as if you were storing information in a file. If the device is a printer, it will print the output. Special device files are stored in the **/dev** directory. UNIX *pipes* are temporary files that store information that is being directed from one place to another.

Related Entries   Access Control; ACL (Access Control List); AFS (Andrew File System); Attributes; Data Management; Data Protection; File Sharing; File Systems; File Transfer Protocols; Linux; Network Operating Systems; NFS (Network File System); Rights and Permissions; Sun Microsystems Solaris; *and* UNIX

Linktionary!—Tom Sheldon's Encyclopedia of Networking updates	http://www.linktionary.com/u/unix_file_system.html
AFS Directory and File Permissions paper at Pittsburgh Supercomputing Center	http://www.psc.edu/general/filesys/afs/setpermissions.html
UNIX file system information	http://www.sao.nrc.ca/imsb/rcsg/documents/basic/node22.html
UNIX file permissions page	http://www.cs.umass.edu/rcfbbl/bbl_security_050395_files.html
UNIX directory information	http://www.mcsr.olemiss.edu/unixhelp/tasks/index.html
Jennifer Myers's UNIX Reference Desk	http://www.geek-girl.com/unix.html
The UNIX Guru Universe	http://www.ugu.com/

UPS (Uninterruptible Power Supply)

A UPS provides electrical power to computers or other devices during a power outage and can be one of the following:

- A battery system

- A rotary UPS that uses the inertia of a large flywheel to carry the computer system through brief outages
- Internal combustion motors that run AC generators

UPS devices come in two forms: online and standby. A *standby* device kicks in only when the power goes down. It must, therefore, contain special circuitry that can switch to backup power in less than five milliseconds. An *online* device constantly provides the source of power to the computer. Because of this, it doesn't need to kick in. If the outside source of power dies, the batteries within the unit continue to supply the computer with power. Although online units are the best choice, they are more expensive than standby units. But because online units supply all the power to a computer, that power is always clean and smooth.

When purchasing a battery backup system, you need to know the following about the devices:

- The amount of time the UPS battery supplies power
- Whether the UPS provides a warning system to the server when the UPS is operating on standby power
- Whether the UPS includes power-conditioning features that can clip incoming transient noise
- The life span of the battery and how it degrades over time
- Whether the device warns you when the batteries can no longer provide backup power
- When the batteries need to be replaced

You also need to know the power requirements of the devices you'll hook to the UPS. For a server installation, this might include the CPU (and any added devices), the monitor, external routers, concentrator units, and wiring centers. You can find out the power requirements of these devices by looking at the backs of the equipment. Labels on the equipment list the power drawn by the units. UPSs have a VA (volt-ampere) rating, which is the line voltage multiplied by the current (amperes). You'll need to add up the power requirements of the equipment you plan to attach to the UPS, and then purchase a UPS that can handle the load. Start by obtaining the amp rating on the back of each device you plan to hook up, and multiply that rating by the voltage (usually 120 volts); then add the values obtained for each device and select a UPS that can handle at least 20 percent over that load.

A UPS attached to a file server usually requires an additional cable that alerts the file server when the UPS is running on standby power. The server will then proceed with shutdown procedures. Check with the UPS vendor to make sure this feature is available for the operating systems you have in mind.

Some vendors have developed advanced features for their power protection equipment. American Power Conversion's Smart-UPS series provides network managers with diagnostic information via a software control program called PowerChute. The software is installed on the server and communicates with the UPS over a cable. Managers can then track power quality, UPS operating temperature, line frequency, UPS output voltage, maximum and minimum line power, battery strength, line voltage, and UPS load.

Related Entries   Data Center Design; Data Protection; Disaster Planning and Recovery; Fault Management; Fault Tolerance and High Availability; *and* Power and Grounding Problems and Solutions

Linktionary!—Tom Sheldon's Encyclopedia of Networking updates	http://www.linktionary.com/u/ups.html
The UPS Warehouse, Power Control Group	http://www.the-ups-warehouse.co.uk/
American Power Conversion Corp.	http://www.apcc.com
JT Packard & Associates' power supplies	http://www.jtpackard.com
Battery Wholesale Distributors' battery FAQ	http://www.mywebplace.com/batterywholesale/batinfo.html

URI (Uniform Resource Identifier)

A URI provides a way to identify abstract or physical resources on the World Wide Web. It is a syntax for encoding the names and addresses of objects. The URI is a general form for creating some kind of address. A URL (Uniform Resource Locator) is a specific address used with some protocol such as HTTP or FTP that follows the general URI format.

Note   *An expanded version of this topic is at the Linktionary! site listed shortly.*

Tim Berners-Lee outlined the concept of URI in RFC 1630 (Universal Resource Identifiers in WWW: A Unifying Syntax for the Expression of Names and Addresses of Objects on the Network as Used in the World-Wide Web, June 1994).

According to Berners-Lee, the URI concept is based on the fact that network resources can be mapped into a concept of "objects" that have some kind of name, address, or identifier. There are many types of objects on many types of systems. Thus, it is important to define the concept of a universal set of all objects, and a universal set of names and addresses for those objects. Names in different namespaces can then be treated in a common way, even though they may have different characteristics.

Related Entries   CIP (Common Indexing Protocol); CNRP (Common Name Resolution Protocol); Directory Services; DNS (Domain Name Service) and Internet Domains; Document Management; Handle System; Internet; LDAP (Lightweight Directory Access Protocol); Metadata; Name Services; NIS (Network Information System); Search and Discovery Services; Service Advertising and Discovery; SLP (Service Location Protocol); URL (Uniform Resource Locator); URN (Universal Resource Name); WebDAV; *and* Web Technologies and Concepts

Linktionary!—Tom Sheldon's Encyclopedia of Networking updates	http://www.linktionary.com/u/uri.html
Guide to URLs	http://www.netspace.org/users/dwb/url-guide.html
W3C's URL guide	http://www.w3.org/Addressing/Addressing.html
IETF Working Group: Uniform Resource Names (urn)	http://www.ietf.org/html.charters/urn-charter.html

URL (Uniform Resource Locator)

Most people are familiar with URLs. They are the addresses you type in a Web browser Address field that start with http://, followed by the name of a Web site. URLs also refer to addresses used with other Internet protocols, such FTP, Gopher, NNTP (Network News Transport Protocol), Telnet, and WAIS (Wide Area Information Servers), among others. URLs are instances of a broader class of identifiers known as Uniform Resource Identifiers (URIs). See "URI (Uniform Resource Identifiers)" for more information.

A resource is an object on the Internet or an intranet that resides on a host system. Objects include directories and an assortment of file types. A URL is the address of an object, a pointer to its location on a server/directory in a particular domain. According to RFC 1738 (Uniform Resource Locators, December 1994), the syntax for a URL is as follows:

> *<scheme>:<scheme-dependent-information>*

The *scheme* portion identifies a particular protocol such as HTTP, FTP, and so on. The *scheme-dependent-information* identifies a domain, a server and/or directory, and a particular file. For example, the following address identifies the document *security.html* in the *papers* directory at the NTResearch Web site:

> http://www.ntresearch.com/papers/security.html

One of the downsides of URLs is that they specifically identify a particular path to a file on a particular host. If you embed such a URL in a document and the location of the file changes, then you need to update the URL in the document. This is impractical for some documents, such as those that include bibliographic references and are stored for years. Uniform Resource Names (URNs) provide a way to overcome this problem by providing persistent, location-independent identifiers for Internet resources. See "URN (Uniform Resource Name)" for more information.

Related Entries   DNS (Domain Name Service) and Internet Domains; Internet; Name Services; Search and Discovery Services; Service Advertising and Discovery; SLP (Service Location Protocol); URI (Uniform Resource Identifier); URN (Universal Resource Name); *and* Web Technologies and Concepts

Linktionary!—Tom Sheldon's Encyclopedia of Networking updates	http://www.linktionary.com/u/url.html
Guide to URLs	http://www.netspace.org/users/dwb/url-guide.html
W3C's URL guide	http://www.w3.org/Addressing/Addressing.html

URL Parsing

URL parsing is a function of traffic management and load-balancing products that scan URLs to determine how to forward traffic across different links or into different servers. A URL includes a protocol identifier (http, for Web traffic) and a resource name, such as www.microsoft.com. The first component could be used to direct traffic to Web servers (as opposed to FTP or other servers). The resource is the added dimension that gives URL parsing an advantage over products that evaluate only layer 4 information (IP address and port). This topic is covered further under "Load Balancing."

Related Entries Congestion Control Mechanisms; Load Balancing; *and* URL (Uniform Resource Locator)

URN (Uniform Resource Name)

A URN, like a URL (Uniform Resource Locator), provides a reference to some resource on the Internet or an intranet, but a URN goes further by providing *persistence*, which is a way to identify a resource independent of its location. If the location changes, the resource can still be found. The scheme was initially outlined in RFC 1737 (Requirements for Uniform Resource Names, December 1994). URNs provide stable names for resources whose location may change over time. The URN remains globally unique for the life of the document, which could be forever. The same URN is never assigned to two different resources. A URL, on the other hand, refers to a specific location. If that location changes, the URL becomes "broken."

 This topic is covered at the Linktionary! Web site listed later.

Related Entries CIP (Common Indexing Protocol); CNRP (Common Name Resolution Protocol); Directory Services; DNS (Domain Name Service) and Internet Domains; Document Management; Handle System; Internet; LDAP (Lightweight Directory Access Protocol); Metadata; Name Services; NIS (Network Information System); Search and Discovery Services; Service Advertising and Discovery; SLP (Service Location Protocol); URI (Uniform Resource Identifier); URL (Uniform Resource Locator); WebDAV; Web Technologies and Concepts; White Pages Directory Services; *and* WHOIS ("Who is")

Linktionary!—Tom Sheldon's Encyclopedia of Networking updates	http://www.linktionary.com/u/urn.html
IETF Working Group Uniform Resource Names (urn)	http://www.ietf.org/html.charters/urn-charter.html
Uniform Resource Names, A Progress Report	http://www.dlib.org/dlib/february96/02arms.html
URN Interoperability Project (TURNIP)	http://www.dlib.org/dlib/march96/briefings/03turnip.html
Guide to URLs	http://www.netspace.org/users/dwb/url-guide.html
W3C's URL guide	http://www.w3.org/Addressing/Addressing.html
Recent Developments in Indexing, Searching, and Information Retrieval Technologies (REIS)	http://www.terena.nl/projects/reis/isir/reisnews9908sendex.html
The Best of Distributed Objects: Naming and Directories	http://www.bodo.org/July98.html
Lessons Learned from the Early Adoption of URNs in an Intranet Environment	http://www.isoc.org/inet99/4m/4m_2.htm

USB (Universal Serial Bus)

USB is a data communication standard for a peripheral bus that was developed by Intel and Microsoft. It is a replacement for the plethora of connectors and ports on the back of desktop PCs and provides an interface for computer-telephony devices. Instead of having separate connections for keyboard, mouse, printer, modem, joystick, audio devices, CD-ROMs, digital cameras, and other devices, USB provides a single port for connecting all of the devices. USB eliminates many of the problems associated with the PC, such as the need to open the computer to install adapter cards, change dip switches, and configure IRQs (interrupt requests).

USB defines the ports and the bus topology with data transfer rates up to 12 Mbits/sec. A single cable up to 5 meters in length is used to daisy-chain devices to a single port. Up to 63 devices can be added to the port at any time without rebooting the system. The topology is a tiered star, which allows peripherals to be connected to repeater hubs that provide multiple port connectors. In some cases, hubs may need power. USB also supplies power to some devices so they will not need power cords or batteries. USB even allows devices to communicate their power requirement needs with the USB host controller.

Related Entries   Asynchronous Communications; EIA (Electronic Industries Association); FireWire; HSSI (High-Speed Serial Interface); LVDS (Low-Voltage Differential Signaling); Modems; Network Connection Technologies; Parallel Interface; Serial Communication and Interfaces; Signals; SSA (Serial Storage Architecture); Switch Fabrics and Bus Design; *and* Synchronous Communications

Linktionary!—Tom Sheldon's Encyclopedia of Networking updates	http://www.linktionary.com/u/usb.html
Universal Serial Bus Implementers Forum home page	http://www.usb.org
Microsoft Corporation (search for USB)	http://www.microsoft.com
New Bus Architectures: How CardBus Fits with IEEE 1394, USB, PCI and Others	http://www.pc-card.com/papers/new_bus.htm
Craig Peacock's Beyond Logic site (see USB section)	http://www.beyondlogic.org/

USENET

USENET is a newsgroup service for implementing discussion groups on the Internet and other TCP/IP-based networks. Originally, USENET relied on a message exchange system called UUCP (UNIX-to-UNIX Copy Program). Today, message delivery is primarily handled by an Internet protocol called NNTP (Network News Transport Protocol). USENET is described in detail at the Linktionary! Web site listed shortly.

Related Entries   Chat; Collaborative Computing; Instant Messaging; IRC (Internet Relay Chat); Mailing List Programs; Multicasting; Multimedia; NNTP (Network News Transport Protocol); Unified Messaging; Videoconferencing; *and* Webcasting

Linktionary!—Tom Sheldon's Encyclopedia of Networking updates	http://www.linktionary.com/u/usenet.html
IETF Working Group: Usenet Article Standard Update (usefor)	http://www.ietf.org/html.charters/usefor-charter.html

U

| IETF Working Group: NNTP Extensions (nntpext) | http://www.ietf.org/html.charters/nntpext-charter.html |
| Internet Software Consortium INN (InterNetNews package) | http://www.isc.org/products/INN/ |

Users and Groups

Network operating systems provide security by requiring that all users log on by typing their user account name and a password. Once a user is verified or authenticated, the user can access the network based on the rights they have been granted throughout the network. Some network operating systems require users to log on every time they access a resource at a different location on the network. The usual technique is to incorporate user authentication features that verify the authenticity of a user one time for all resources on a network. Trust relationships are established so that one server "trusts" that another server has properly authenticated a user.

User accounts hold information about the user, including any restrictions they have on a network. For example, a user might be restricted to logging on at a specific workstation or during a specific time. Groups are collections of users that network administrators create to simplify user management. It is far easier to include users in a group, and then assign network access rights to the group, than it is to assign those rights individually to each user. Groups also simplify messaging. For example, it's easier to send an electronic mail message to a group called "Managers" than to each person in that group individually. Managers should create groups for users, projects, and management purposes when planning and setting up the network, and then add user accounts to groups as users are added to the network.

A user account is granted certain rights and permissions to network resources. These accounts may have the following restrictions (from NetWare):

- **Account balance restrictions**   You can restrict a user's access to the system and its resources by specifying a credit limit. A credit limit is a balance in an account that depletes as time and resources are used. Once depleted, the user can't log on to the system until given more credit.

- **Expiration restrictions**   You can set an expiration date and time for a user account. The account is closed at the time specified. You might use this restriction for temporary employees.

- **Password restrictions**   The administrator or a supervisor can specify the length and uniqueness of logon passwords. You can force users to change their passwords at regular intervals and to use passwords that they haven't used recently.

- **Disk space restrictions**   Disk space restrictions help administrators control how much disk space users can use.

- **Connection restrictions**   Connection restrictions can limit the number of stations a user can log on to simultaneously.

- **Time restrictions**   Time restrictions specify the times, in half-hour blocks, when users can log on to the system.

■ **Station restrictions**   Station restrictions prevent a user from logging on at any station other than the specified workstation. This prevents users from logging on at unsupervised workstations where their activities cannot be monitored. In NetWare, these restrictions can be assigned individually to each account or assigned as default settings that are applied when new accounts are created.

Groups

Groups are collections of users or user accounts. You create groups to simplify the task of managing and defining rights for large numbers of users. It's also easier to send messages to groups than it is to send messages to each individual user within a group. Groups have names and can include users who work on similar projects, belong to the same department, or even belong to a club within the company. A user can belong to more than one group. For example, a user might belong to the *manager* or *administrator's* group, the *advisory* group, and the *golf* group.

You assign directory and file access rights (permissions in Windows NT) to groups in the same way you can assign those rights to users. However, it is much easier to assign the rights to groups, and then add users to the group. The user then gets all the rights and privileges of that group. Groups should be defined when planning a network and created before adding any users. Then, as you create new user accounts, you can add a user to a group. A user can be a member of more than one group.

Here are some examples of ways you could use groups:

■ A word processing group with rights to run a word processing program and store files in its data directories.

■ Electronic mail groups to simplify message addressing. For example, create a group called Managers, Employees, or Temporaries.

■ A management group that has rights to create new user accounts.

■ A backup group that has special access rights to back up directories.

Another interesting aspect of groups is that they provide a convenient way to change or remove the rights of a large number of users at the same time. You can delete an entire group, or you can remove users from a group. When users are removed from a group, they still retain an account on the system, but any rights they had with the group are no longer valid.

Related Entries   Account, User; Access Rights; Attributes; Authentication and Authorization; Data Management; Data Protection; Directory Services; File Sharing; File Systems; Logons and Logon Accounts; Microsoft Windows; Microsoft Windows File System; Network Operating Systems; Novell NetWare; Novell NetWare File System; Operating Systems; Rights and Permissions; UNIX; UNIX File System; *and* Users and Groups

UTP (Unshielded Twisted-Pair) Cable

See Cable and Wiring.

UUCP (UNIX to UNIX Copy Program)

UUCP is a UNIX file transfer command that may be used to copy files to another location on the same system or from a local system to a remote system. When copying files between systems, the source and destination filenames and the source and destination computer names are specified. In the following example, the first entry following the command is the source and the second is the destination. The exclamation point separates the host name from the filename.

```
uucp mycomputer!sourcefilename yourcomputer!destinationfilename
```

Refer to the following Web address for complete description and syntax: http://www.unet.univie.ac.at/aix/cmds/aixcmds5/uucp.htm.

UWB (Ultra Wideband)

UWB is based on a discovery by Larry Fullerton (Time Domain's founder) that single radio frequency (RF) monocycles could be transmitted through an antenna; and by precisely positioning these monocycles in time, a matched receiver could recover the transmissions, thus opening up a whole new wireless medium. The technique does not rely on sine waves, does not require an assigned frequency, and transmits data on random low-powered signals that are indistinguishable from noise. Time Domain compares it to sending Morse Code at 40 million dots and dashes per second. The technology can potentially transmit at 1 Gbit/sec. UWB can interfere with other radio signals, so low power is used; but doing so limits the range.

Related Entries   Radio Communications and Networks; Wireless Communications

Linktionary!—Tom Sheldon's Encyclopedia of Networking updates	http://www.linktionary.com/u/uwb.html
Time Domain	http://www.timedomain.com/

VBI (Vertical Blanking Interval)

Television signals include a nonviewable portion of signal that carries no visual information. It is called VBI (vertical blanking interval) and can be used to carry other information, usually close-captioned signals for the hearing impaired. Internet designers are now using it to transmit unidirectional digital information from Web sites to Web clients.

The model for sending information over VBI is often called "data broadcasting." The technique is a one-way transmission from the station to users, just like television. Stations broadcast popular information such as stock quotes, sports news, and so on. Users cannot interact with the Web server, but the technique is useful for delivering specific content and reduces the load on the actual Internet. Instead of sending this bulk news information to each subscriber individually over the Internet, the information is broadcast at periodic intervals to a special browser, which shows the latest updates. Anyone can choose to tune into the broadcast and select just the news items they want to view.

A company called WavePhore transmits data over PBS stations nationwide. All you need is a TV card in your computer to receive the transmissions, which appear in a special browser on your desktop. Since the service relies on over-the-air television signals, it is always on and a user's browser is constantly updated with the latest news.

RFC 2728 (The Transmission of IP Over the Vertical Blanking Interval of a Television Signal, November 1999) describes a method for broadcasting IP data using the VBI. It includes a description for compressing IP headers on unidirectional networks, a framing protocol identical to SLIP, a forward error-correction scheme, and the NABTS (North American Basic Teletext Standard) byte structures.

Related Entries   Broadcasting on the Internet; Multicasting; Newsfeed Services; NNTP (Network News Transport Protocol); *and* Webcasting

Linktionary!—Tom Sheldon's Encyclopedia of Networking updates	http://www.linktionary.com/v/vbi.html
WavePhore Web site	http://www.wavo.com/

vBNS (Very high speed Backbone Network Service)

The NSF (National Science Foundation) has played an important role in the development of the Internet. It played an early role that was critical in defining the structure of the Internet. In the mid-1980s, it funded the NSFnet, and in 1990, the NSFnet took over the role of ARPANET (Advanced Research Projects Agency Network). The NSFnet connected five supercomputer centers in the United States. NSF is also involved in the NREN (National Research and Education Network) and the NII (National Information Infrastructure) programs.

In 1995, the NSFnet was shut down and NSF commercialized the Internet, but NFS continued to fund research into high-speed networking with the vBNS project. The vBNS was implemented as an IP-over-ATM network, with IP packets encapsulated into ATM cells for transport over a SONET OC-12 (622 Mbits/sec) infrastructure. In early 1999, Abilene, the newest addition to the Internet backbone, was brought online as a follow-up to the successful vBNS. See "Abilene" and "Internet."

V

Related Entries Abilene; Active Networks; GII (Global Information Infrastructure); Internet; Internet2; Internet Architecture and Backbone; Internet Organizations and Committees; NII (National Information Infrastructure); NIST (National Institute of Standards and Technology); NREN (National Research and Education Network); Peering; Registries on the Internet; Routing; Routing on the Internet; Routing Registries; STAR TAP; and Supercomputer

Linktionary!—Tom Sheldon's Encyclopedia of Networking updates	http://www.linktionary.com/v/vbns.html
MCI's vBNS site	http://www.vbns.net/
NLANR (National Laboratory for Applied Network Research) vBNS site	http://www.nlanr.net/VBNS/vBNS.html
NLANR ES Frequently Asked Questions	http://www.ncne.org/faq/
The Internet2 Initiative Web site	http://www.internet2.edu/
A Brief History of the Internet, by the original architects	http://www.isoc.org/internet-history/brief.html

VI Architecture

The Virtual Interface (VI) Architecture specification defines a high-bandwidth, low-latency networking architecture that was designed for creating clusters of servers and SANs (Storage Area Networks). *Clustering* is a technique of linking systems together in a way that makes them appear as a single system. In the past, clustering was achieved through proprietary solutions. The VI Architecture is an attempt to standardize the interface for high-performance clustering. The interface specifies logical and physical components, as well as connection setup and data transfer operations.

The VI Architecture was announced in 1997 by Intel, Microsoft, and Compaq, and it is the result of contributions from over 100 industry operations.

The goal of the architecture is to improve the performance of distributed applications by reducing the latency associated with critical message-passing operations. This is done by reducing the system software processing required to exchange messages. The network interface is moved much closer to the application, increasing its functionality, and better matching its features to application requirements. The result is a substantial reduction in processing overhead along the communication paths that are critical to performance.

VI Architecture bypasses the traditional interrupt-driven designs in place of a polling design. The traditional network operating system virtualizes network hardware into a logical set of connection points. Clients attach to these points and send requests for services as calls into the server operating system. The operating system must handle these interrupts, which can be processor intensive. VI Architecture alters this scheme in order to eliminate the operating system overhead. It provides consumers (clients such as other servers or thin clients) with a direct *virtual interface* into the server hardware.

VI Architecture is a transport, independent, memory-to-memory network transfer technology. It supports bulk data transfers and allows applications to directly access VI Architecture hardware without operating system intervention. In other words, consumers have direct access to remote disks and can transfer data directly from those disks into their own memory. There is no need to copy data to or from intermediate buffers as is the case traditional network transport systems.

DAFS (Direct Access File System) uses VI Architecture as its underlying transport mechanism. DAFS is a file transfer protocol that provides a consistent view of files to a heterogeneous environment of servers that may be running different operating systems. See "DAFS (Direct Access File System)."

Related Entries   Clustering; DAFS (Direct Access File System); Data Center Design; Distributed Computer Networks; InfiniBand; IP Storage; Multiprocessing; Network Connection Technologies; SAN (System Area Network); Servers; Storage Management Systems; Switch Fabrics and Bus Design; *and* Switching and Switched Networks

Linktionary!—Tom Sheldon's Encyclopedia of Networking updates	http://www.linktionary.com/v/vi_architecture.html
VI Architecture Specification	http://www.viarch.org
Intel's VI Architecture home page	http://developer.intel.com/design/servers/vi/
DAFS Collaborative Web site	http://www.dafscollaborative.org/

Videoconferencing

Network videoconferencing is a tool for communicating via audio, video, and data in real time. Until recently it was a pricey tool, but low-priced components (such as cameras), multimedia PCs, and an increasing demand for collaboration over the Internet and intranets have pushed the development of the technology.

The appeal of network videoconferencing derives from the breadth of interaction it offers; the user can see as well as hear the individual or members of the group at the other end. Even low-end videoconferencing systems offer interesting features such as document/application sharing and whiteboard tools that work across electronic conferencing links. These tools and applications make collaboration easy and reduce travel expenses.

Other factors contributing to the growing interest in videoconferencing include better compression techniques, maturing standards that encourage interoperability, high-speed LANs and WANs that support the data requirements of video, and high-performance multimedia computers. In addition, operating systems are multimedia enabled. Microsoft Windows includes a videoconferencing package called NetMeeting.

New uses for videoconferencing are also helping to drive development. In work environments, it is being used for tech support, distance learning, telemedicine, job recruiting interviews, direct sales, legal work, telecommuting, and manufacturing. It can also cut travel costs.

When it comes to choosing videoconferencing systems, buyers should have a clear idea of how the system will be used because there are many trade-offs between price and functionality. Common features include zoom, panning, voice detection (so the camera can follow the voice), noise cancellation, and collaboration features such as whiteboarding software. Most video-conferencing software is designed to dynamically increase compression ratios and drop back frame rates when congestion occurs on the network. Even under these conditions, most systems will maintain an acceptable voice quality, even while the video quality drops.

V

Videoconferencing systems can be categorized in several ways. There are high-end professional systems, and there are low-end "talking-head" systems designed for the home and small office. Another differentiator is the communication technology and protocols used:

- **ITU H.320 systems**   These systems tend to be professional-quality videoconferencing systems that operate over point-to-point circuits such as ISDN and T1 links (switched or dedicated, depending on your needs).

- **ITU H.323 systems**   These systems are designed to work over packet-switched networks such as the Internet where service quality cannot be guaranteed. They are basically "video over IP" systems that tend to have poor quality over the Internet but work well in the LAN environment. However, as bandwidth and quality of service improve on the Internet, these systems will provide better service.

- **IETF protocol–based systems**   The IETF's SIP (Session Initiation Protocol) and related protocols (RTP, RTCP, and SDP) are oriented toward more versatile Internet multimedia. These protocols are discussed later.

- **Proprietary systems**   Many vendors have their own nonstandard video delivery systems that work over circuits, frame relay networks, or ATM networks.

Without sufficient bandwidth, packets are lost or dropped and the video appears jerky. Television operates at about 30 fps (frames per second), and the image shows no jerkiness or blurring. The fastest room systems operate at 24 to 30 fps. Anything below 10 fps appears as a series of still pictures that periodically update. An acceptable rate for low-bandwidth networks is 15 fps, but the video still has an unnatural appearance. To achieve frame rates of 20 to 22 fps, 384 to 512 Kbits/sec of bandwidth are needed. However, unless you are doing one-way presentations, you'll need double that bandwidth to support audio and video streams in both directions.

Obviously, systems designed to work directly over the Internet are more economical and easily support multipoint sessions (connections to multiple locations). Because these systems run on desktop computers and over packet-switched networks, they support applications such as collaboration and whiteboarding tools.

Many home and small business users may be satisfied with Internet-based video-conferencing systems such as CuSeeMe and Microsoft NetMeeting, which are designed to operate at low data rates over packet-switched networks. Some support the aggregation of multiple phone connections to boost performance. The systems operate at 3 to 10 fps, making fast movements undetectable. These systems are best used for talking-head meetings where people point to things in pictures or parts of objects that are being discussed. In fact, audio is often the major consideration in videoconferencing. If the audio is good, users will tolerate video that's not up to television standards.

CUSeeMe by CUSeeMe Networks has established a large user base. It uses a unique protocol developed specifically for TCP/IP networks and the Internet to manage, receive, and rebroadcast video and audio data. Special software-only algorithms reduce the amount of data to transmit over the wire and allow the system to work quite well over dial-up lines.

Microsoft NetShow is a multimedia platform for delivering interactive content, including audio and illustrated audio (images and sound). It is based on Internet standards, including IP multicast and RTP, and includes both client and server components to add the power of traditional broadcasting systems (audio and video) to HTTP. It supports multicast so multiple users can "tune into" a single broadcast. NetShow supports many popular formats, including illustrated audio (images synchronized with an audio track). Files in WAV, AVI, QuickTime, PowerPoint, JPEG, GIF, PNG, and URL formats can all be used to generate illustrated audio.

Videoconferencing Standards

New videoconferencing standards have moved manufacturers away from proprietary systems and in the direction of interoperability. The ITU has developed a number of standards for audio and video conferencing. The H series recommendations are ITU standards that define audiovisual and multimedia systems. See "H Series ITU Recommendations." The ITU G.700 series recommendations are related to digital transmission systems, in particular, coding of analog signals into digital signals. See "G Series ITU Recommendations."

In particular, H.320 standard (1990) is an umbrella standard that supports interoperability among different vendors' videoconferencing equipment over switched digital phone lines (specifically, ISDN). H.320 was designed for circuits, not for the packet-switched Internet. The newer H.323 standard (1996) supports LANs and packet-switched networks. H.323 is a videoconferencing standard that builds on the H.320 standard. On LANs, H.323 allows managers tighter control over how videoconferencing uses network resources. See "H.323 Multimedia Conferencing Standard."

Products like Microsoft NetMeeting and CUSeeME are built upon H.323 standards. H.323 supports a variety of performance levels and an H.323/H.320 gateway will link H.320 ISDN and H.323 videoconferencing systems. Yet another new standard promises to improve dial-up videoconferencing. The H.324 standard allows H.324-compliant devices to connect over standard telephone lines.

The T.120 series of standards for "audiographic teleconferencing" were ratified by the ITU in late 1996. These standards define protocols for transporting, controlling, and displaying multimedia conferencing information. See "T Series ITU Recommendations."

Internet protocols related to teleconferencing and Internet multimedia sessions in general are listed next. A general overview of the Internet multimedia conferencing architecture is described under "Multimedia."

- **SDP (Session Description Protocol)**   A protocol to distribute and describe Internet teleconferencing sessions. See "SDP (Session Description Protocol)."

- **SAP (Session Announcement Protocol)**   A protocol to announce Internet teleconferencing sessions. See "SAP (Session Announcement Protocol)."

- **SIP (Session Initiation Protocol)**   A protocol for initiating sessions and inviting users. See "SIP (Session Initiation Protocol)."

- **RTP (Real-time Transport Protocol)**   A protocol for real-time transmission of audio and video over UDP and IP multicast. See "RTP (Real-time Transport Protocol)."

- **RTSP (Real-Time Streaming Protocol)**   A protocol to control on-demand delivery of real-time data. See "RTSP (Real-Time Streaming Protocol)."

- **SCCP (Simple Conference Control Protocol)**   A protocol for managing tightly controlled sessions.

V

Multimedia standards in general, including videoconferencing, voice over IP, and others, are covered under "Multimedia." The topic "Compression Techniques" discusses methods for compressing video. In particular, the MPEG (Moving Picture Experts Group) has developed a set of standards for compressing video that is used throughout the industry. Another related topic of interest is "QoS (Quality of Service)." It discusses methods for providing enough bandwidth to deliver high-quality multimedia data.

Internet Working Groups and RFCs

The following IETF Working Groups are developing recommendations and specifications for delivering multimedia over the Internet:

- Multiparty MUltimedia SessIon Control (mmusic) is developing protocols to support Internet teleconferencing sessions. The group's focus is on supporting the loosely controlled conferences that were pervasive on the MBone (multicast backbone). The group is working on protocols for distributing session descriptions, securing session announcements, and controlling on-demand delivery of real-time data.

- The Audio/Video Transport Working Group (avt) is working on protocols for real-time transmission of audio and video over IDP and IP multicast. In particular, the group is focused on RTP (Real-time Transport Protocol).

- The Session Initiation Protocol (SIP) Working Group is developing SIP, a text-based protocol, similar to HTTP or SMTP, for initiating interactive communication sessions between users. These sessions include voice, video, chat, interactive games, and virtual reality. See "SIP (Session Initiation Protocol)."

The following Internet RFCs provide additional information. Note that there are many RFCs related to this topic. The following are the most useful. Other RFCs are listed at the working group sites mentioned previously or at the Linktionary! Web site.

- RFC 1193 (Client Requirements for Real-Time Communication Services, November 1990)
- RFC 1324 (A Discussion on Computer Network Conferencing, May 1992)
- RFC 1453 (A Comment on Packet Video Remote Conferencing and the Transport/ Network Layers, April 1993)
- RFC 1819 (Internet Stream Protocol Version 2 Protocol Specification, August 1995)
- RFC 1889 (RTP: A Transport Protocol for Real-Time Applications, January 1996)
- RFC 2326 (Real-Time Streaming Protocol, April 1998)
- RFC 2327 (SDP: Session Description Protocol, April 1998)
- RFC 2543 (SIP: Session Initiation Protocol, March 1999)

Related Entries   Collaborative Computing; Compression Techniques; CTI (Computer-Telephony Integration); Groupware; G Series ITU Recommendations; H.323 Multimedia Conferencing Standard; H Series ITU Recommendations; Multicasting; Multimedia; Prioritization of Network Traffic; QoS (Quality of Service); Signaling for Call Control; SIP (Session Initiation Protocol); Telecommunications and Telephone Systems; T Series ITU Recommendations; Voice/Data Networks; *and* Voice over IP (VoIP)

Linktionary!—Tom Sheldon's Encyclopedia of Networking updates	http://www.linktionary.com/v/videoconferencing.html
IETF Working Group: Multiparty Multimedia Session Control (mmusic)	http://www.ietf.org/html.charters/mmusic-charter.html
IETF Working Group: Audio/Video Transport (avt)	http://www.ietf.org/html.charters/avt-charter.html
IETF Working Group: Session Initiation Protocol (sip)	http://www.ietf.org/html.charters/sip-charter.html
OII (Open Information Interchange) Electronic Conferencing Standards	http://158.169.50.95:10080/oii/en/confer.html
IMTC (International Multimedia Teleconferencing Consortium)	http://www.imtc.org
Interactive Multimedia & Collaborative Communications Alliance	http://www.imcca.org/
Conferencing Software for the Web by David R. Woolley (probably one of the best link pages available on this topic)	http://thinkofit.com/webconf/
CUSeeMe Networks (merged with First Virtual Communications)	http://www.cuseeme.com/ or http://www.fvc.com/
H.323 Tutorial at Web ProForums	http://www.iec.org/tutorials/h323/
Internet Conferencing page at About.com	http://netconference.about.com/internet/netconference/
Digital Horizon's Desktop Video Conferencing Guide	http://www.broadband-guide.com/news/dhnewssept96/dh1.html
Adriana Fourcher's VideoConference.com site	http://www.videoconference.com/
GVC Net Multimedia Communications (see Conferencing section)	http://www.gvcnet.com/

VINES, Banyan

See Banyan Vines.

Virtual Circuit

A virtual circuit is a point-to-point communication link between two end stations on a switched network (ATM, frame relay, IP, or Internet). A virtual circuit is designed to emulate the characteristics of a physical circuit on a switched network. An example of a physical circuit is the analog telephone line between your home and the telephone company central office. It is physical wire that is dedicated to single call. No one else uses it. The bandwidth is not shared.

A switched network consists of many links interconnected by switches. Emulating a circuit means defining a temporary or permanent path across the links, perhaps with specific bandwidth characteristics and minimal delay characteristics. An engineer may set up a virtual circuit to follow a specific path that avoids congestion or uses lines that have higher bandwidth. Alternatively, a path may be set up on-the-fly based on the demands of an application. For example, a virtual circuit can be configured in advance that provides the specific bandwidth requirements and minimal delay characteristics that are necessary for a videoconference. The path is "remembered" by links in the form of tables that describe the forwarding behavior for specific packets. Packets may be marked, or their destinations may be determined by examining address and port information. Switches compare this to table entries and make "fast" forwarding decision based on it.

The technique of defining paths through a network in advance of sending packets is often called *explicit routing*. In particular, explicit routing involves traffic engineering in order to obtain various levels of QoS (quality of service). MPLS provides this on the Internet.

As mentioned, a virtual circuit may be created on-the-fly or set up for more permanent use. The former is called an *SVC (switched virtual circuit)* while the latter is called a *PVC (permanent virtual circuit)*. PVCs are usually set up by technicians who use engineering techniques to find the optimal path across a network. A variety of techniques may be used to set up SVCs. In one technique, called "cut-through routing," network devices look for packet flows that are going to the same destination. When a flow is detected, a PVC is set up to rapidly switch the packets.

The Related Entries provide more information about virtual circuits. An expanded version of this topic is at the Linktionary! Web site.

Related Entries   ATM (Asynchronous Transfer Mode); Bandwidth Reservation; Cells and Cell Relay; Circuit; Cut-Through Routing; Dedicated Circuit; End Systems and End-to-End Connectivity; Frame Relay; IP over ATM; Label Switching; Lambda Circuits; Leased Line; MPLS (Multiprotocol Label Switching); Private Network; QoS (Quality of Service); RSVP (Resource Reservation Protocol); Traffic Management, Shaping, and Engineering; *and* VPN (Virtual Private Network)

 Linktionary!—Tom Sheldon's Encyclopedia   http://www.linktionary.com/v/virtualcircuit.html
of Networking updates

Virtual Dial-Up Services

See L2TP (Layer 2 Tunneling Protocol); Modems; *and* VPN (Virtual Private Network).

Virtual Machine, Java

See Java.

Virtual Reality

See Web3D.

Virus and Antivirus Issues

A *virus* is a computer program that infects other programs with copies of itself. It clones itself from disk to disk or from one system to another over computer networks. A virus executes and does its damage when the program it has infected executes. Besides viruses, your systems are also vulnerable to other types of destructive programs that are not classified as viruses. These include *worms, Trojan horses,* and *logic bombs*.

Note *This topic continues at the Linktionary! Web site with more details and descriptions of viruses, Trojan horses, and various protection strategies.*

The damage caused by viruses may be harmless, such as displaying a happy birthday message for the creator on the appropriate day. Alternatively, the virus may do considerable damage by destroying boot records, file tables, and valuable data on disk. To maintain a protective stance against virus threats, you must back up constantly and stay in contact with the organizations and vendors listed at the end of this section. Most of the Web sites have extensive information on viruses, including databases, recent activities, and even virus hoaxes.

Some interesting (and historical) Internet documents related to security and viruses are listed here:

- RFC 1135 (The Helminthiasis of the Internet, December 1989)
- RFC 2196 (Site Security Handbook, September 1997)
- RFC 2504 (Users' Security Handbook, February 1999)
- RFC 2828 (Internet Security Glossary, May 2000)

Related Entries   Access Control; Authentication and Authorization; Backup and Data Archiving; Biometric Access Devices; Data Protection; Disaster Planning and Recovery; Hacking and Hackers; Replication; Rights and Permissions; Security; *and* Security Auditing

Linktionary!—Tom Sheldon's Encyclopedia of Networking updates	http://www.linktionary.com/v/virus.html
CSI (Computer Security Institute)	http://www.gocsi.com
Data Rescue data recovery services	http://www.datarescue.com/
Trend Micro antivirus software	http://www.antivirus.com
Network Associates (McAfee)	http://www.nai.com/
Symantec Corporation	http://www.symantec.com
F-Secure Corporation (formerly Data Fellows)	http://www.f-secure.com/
Central Command AVP (AntiViral Toolkit Pro) Virus Encyclopedia	http://www.avpve.com/
IBM's antivirus research Web site	http://www.research.ibm.com/antivirus/
Bruce Schneier on the new breeds of viruses, worms, and other malware	http://www.counterpane.com/crypto-gram-9906.html
NetSec Int'l (Network Security International Association), an organization that provides information about the antivirus industry	http://www.netsec-intl.com/
Deploying Enterprise-wide Virus Protection	http://www.techguide.com/
Vmyths.com (truths about computer virus myths & hoaxes)	http://www.vmyths.com/

V

VLAN (Virtual LAN)

Most enterprises have moved toward the switched network paradigm, in which computers are connected to dedicated ports on Ethernet switches, Gigabit Ethernet switches, ATM switches, or other types of switches. Switching devices support network designs in which the entire network is one big flat network as opposed to many subnetworks interconnected by routers. In a flat network, all workstations are in the same broadcast domain. Any computer can directly communicate with any other computer. This has advantages and disadvantages that will be discussed here.

A flat network easily interconnects all systems into a single broadcast domain, but a single broadcast domain has drawbacks related to security, network traffic problems, and a loss of local management. Some administrators prefer traditional subnetwork designs, which can be introduced into flat switched network designs with VLANs. The IEEE 802.1Q VLAN standard was rolled out to provide important VLAN techniques required to build large switched networks. The IEEE standard is discussed later.

A basic VLAN is pictured in Figure V-1. All the computers are connected to the same network. Two logical subnets in the form of VLANs overlay the physical network. In older physical LAN models, all the computers in Sales were connected to the same physical network within the same physical area. In the VLAN model, a computer at any location on the physical network can participate in a VLANs. For example, users in different buildings on the same campus can be part of the same VLAN group, broadcasting messages to one another and sharing the same group servers, printers, and other resources.

Keep in mind that the underlying physical network for VLANs is a flat switched network. VLANs overlay this topology. Routers are still needed to forward packets between VLANs, as shown on the left in Figure V-2. They provide a way for each VLAN to maintain its autonomy and broadcast nature while forwarding packets between VLANs when necessary. Routing allows administrators to put security policies in place as well, such as packet-filtering techniques, as discussed under "Firewall." An optimally designed network will have VLANs configured to reduce as much inter-VLAN routing as possible.

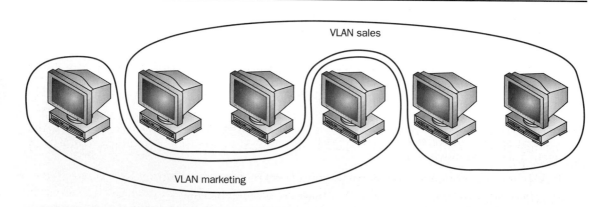

Figure V-1.   *VLAN's logical subdivisions of a single flat network*

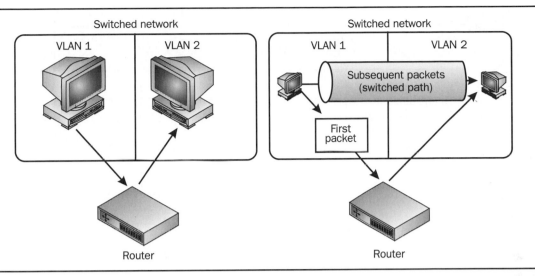

Figure V-2.   *Inter-VLAN transfers can take advantage of switching routers.*

While routing adds the advantages of subnetworking back into the flat switched network topology, routing packets is slower than switching them (unless layer 3 routing is used, which reduces the need for VLANs, as discussed later). Even though a network may be subdivided into VLANs, the underlying network is still capable of switching packets to any computer at high speed. So the "route first, then switch" (or "cut-through" routing) technique is applied to boost performance. A router is initially used to establish a route between two systems in different VLANs and to provide security aspects of verifying that the two systems can set up a connection. Once the route is established and security is checked, packets are switched using the layer 2 switching fabric. This basically avoids moving all but the first few packets through the slow router once it has done its job. In some environments, a route server calculates routes, but all packets are switched. See "IP over ATM."

Figure V-3 illustrates how VLANs are configured. The bottom of the illustration shows the structure of the physical LAN. Backbone switches and local area switches provide VLAN configuration functions.

The network administrator includes a computer (or user) in a VLAN based on a switch port address, a computer hardware address (the MAC, or Medium Access Control address of a network interface card), an IP address, or some other method. In Figure V-3, when computer B transmits, it sends a message that is broadcast to all the computers in the Marketing VLAN, which includes computers E, G, H, and J. If computer B needs to send a message to a user in the Research VLAN, the message must be routed. This is handled by a routing function in the backbone switch or by a separate router.

VLANs are essential in organizations in which users move from one group to another, or the structure of the organization is such that members of the same workgroup are located in different physical locations. VLANs let scattered group members share common resources, such as storage devices, and be part of the same broadcast domain. In other words, traffic generated by users in a

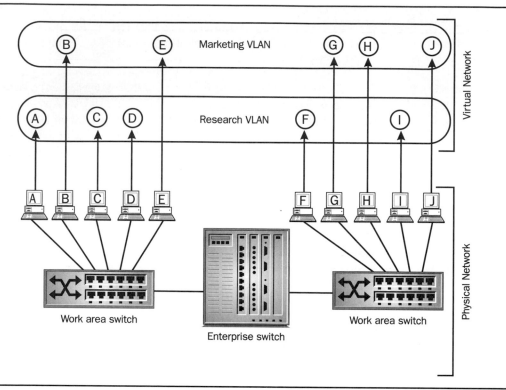

Figure V-3.   *VLANs overlay the physical network topology*

group should stay confined to their group. If users are highly mobile and move from one office to another as part of their job, the network administrator can use VLAN techniques to keep the user within a broadcast group no matter where they plug into the network.

With the advent of routing switches, as described under "Multilayer Switching," VLAN usage has fallen off. Routing switches perform routing in hardware, which removes the performance problem of traditional software-based routers. These switches are said to route at wire speed. Thus, high-performance, inexpensive, well-understood routing via routing switches has supplanted VLANs. Still, many of these routing switches support VLAN technologies, so VLANs can be configured if necessary.

VLANs have always been difficult to configure, while routed subneting is well understood. In addition, the network design supported by VLANs is not as practical in enterprise networks where traffic heads straight for enterprise data centers and the Internet, rather than servers and other devices within "local" groups.

VLAN Configuration Methods

Switching architectures are ideal for the creation of VLANs. The first VLANs were configured manually. Then, as the technology became better understood and more popular, more advanced techniques were employed. The following sections describe the various techniques that can be used to build VLANs. Many vendors are implementing some or all of these techniques. For example, the more advanced methods rely on IP protocols, but networks that use both IP and nonroutable protocols such, as NetBIOS, may need to use the MAC-based method described next in addition to the IP methods.

Port Configuration Methods   The port configuration method is really a way to configure separate LANs within the same box. The resulting LANs are technically not VLANs because they are configured as distinct wiring configurations. The network administrator ties together specific ports on hub or switching devices to create individual LANs. For example, ports 2, 4, 5, and 8 are grouped as LAN #1, and ports 1, 3, 6, 7, 9, and 10 are grouped into LAN #2. Two backplane designs are used in hub or switch devices to allow LAN configuration: *multibus backplanes* or *TDM (time division multiplexing)* backplanes. With the multibus design, each bus represents a LAN and ports are linked to a specific bus. In the TDM design, specific time slots on a single bus are owned by a specific LAN. Because LANs are configured within the hub or switch itself, it is not possible with some hubs or switches to bridge a LAN configured in one device with a LAN configured in another device.

MAC-Based VLANs   The MAC address is the hardwired address built into network interface cards. The network administrator essentially creates a table that defines which MAC addresses belong with what VLAN. Compared to port configuration methods, this method provides true VLAN capabilities because membership in a VLAN is not directly tied to a specific hardware port. Configuration is done in software and a computer can usually belong to two or more VLANs. In addition, if a computer is moved to another location, it still belongs to the same VLAN because its MAC address moves with it.

Layer 3 VLANs   This type of VLAN uses layer 3 information to build VLANs based on internetwork protocol addresses. For example, in Figure V-3, all the computers in the Marketing VLAN might have IP address 100.200.1.x (where x is a specific number for each workstation), while computers in the Research VLAN have the IP address 100.200.2.x. A layer 3 switch is capable of looking at the network address in a frame and forwarding the frame based on information in a table the matches the network address with membership in a particular VLAN. Like the MAC-based VLANs, moves are easy because the port of the workstation does not determine VLAN membership. However, looking at the layer 3 address can cause performance problems. The layer 3 approach can be extended to include more routing functionality right in the switch, and that is what many vendors have done with their high-end switches. You can refer to "Multilayer Switching" to learn about the architectural details of these switches.

IP Multicast VLANs   In this approach, a VLAN is defined by membership in an IP *multicast group*. IP multicasting is a way for one workstation to transmit to some but not all workstations on a network. The workstations that receive the transmissions are known as the multicast group. Multicasting is basically one-to-many communication supported by Internet standards. Multicasting is set up by using IP class D addresses. Routers must be multicast enabled to use this feature. Multicasting is a two-way process. Routers set up multicasting among themselves, but a router only does multicasting if some host on its attached network has requested to be a member of a multicast group. Routers without any need to be part of a particular multicast do

V

not get involved, in order to avoid unnecessary traffic. Multicasting is dynamic in that workstations can join and drop out of a multicast group at any time. Using this feature to create VLANs is useful and flexible. Multicasting also allows the VLAN to span WAN-based routers.

Rules-Based VLANs   Some vendors have implemented "rules-based" VLAN configuration techniques, which allows administrators to create VLANs based on information contained in packets that switches look at and evaluate. This method involves creating rules in software that are followed to determine VLAN membership. While this technique adds a lot of flexibility, setup and maintenance can be complex. For example, a VLAN might be described with these rules:

> All stations with subnet address 200.100.10.x
> > excluding these IP addresses: 200.100.10.5, 200.100.10.6
> > excluding these MAC addresses: 06-1A-0A-05-3C-02-04

IEEE 802.1Q Frame Tag

The IEEE 802.1Q frame tag defines a method for inserting a tag into an IEEE MAC-layer frame that defines membership in a virtual LAN. During the standardization process, engineers sneaked in an extra few bits to define class of service. During development, this was known as Project 802.1p, but officially, the scheme is called IEEE 802.1D-1998. Prioritization is discussed under "QoS (Quality of Service)" and "Prioritization of Network Traffic."

802.1Q is designed to simplify VLAN configuration and management. It specifies a way to define and set up VLANs in frame-based networks such as Ethernet and token ring. IEEE 802.1Q promotes interoperability among vendor VLAN equipment. It is a tagging scheme in which a VLAN ID is inserted into the layer 2 frame header. The VLAN ID associates a frame with a specific VLAN and provides the information that switches need to create VLANs across the network.

Three bits of the 802.1Q tag define priority, while 12 bits define the VLAN ID. The standard defines the forwarding of frames based on tag information, explicit sharing of VLAN information and exchange of topology information, and VLAN management and configuration.

A VLAN protocol called GARP (Generic Attribute Registration Protocol) propagates topology information to network switches and end stations via tags. Also, a registration protocol called GVRP (GARP VLAN Registration Protocol) controls various aspects of the VLAN join/drop process. Network management systems and policy servers also use GVRP to provide administrative control.

Related Entries   ATM (Asynchronous Transfer Mode); Bridges and Bridging; Broadcast Address; Broadcast Domain; Broadcast Networking; Emulated LAN; Ethernet; Gigabit Ethernet; Internetworking; IP over ATM; LAN (Local Area Network); LANE (LAN Emulation); MAC (Media Access Control); Network Design and Construction; QoS (Quality of Service); Routing; Switching and Switched Networks; *and* Virtual Circuits

Linktionary!—Tom Sheldon's Encyclopedia of Networking updates	http://www.linktionary.com/v/vlan.html
IEEE 802.1 Working Group	http://grouper.ieee.org/groups/802/1/

Gigabit Ethernet Alliance	http://www.gigabit-ethernet.org
The ATM Forum's MPOA, VLANS and Distributed ROUTER paper	http://www.atmforum.com/atmforum/library/53bytes/backissues/v4-3/article-04.html
Alcatel Wire-Speed Routing Guide	http://www.ind.alcatel.com/library/whitepapers/pe_wirespeed_toc.html
Intel paper: "Extending Virtual LANs to the Server"	http://www.intel.com/network/white_papers/extending_lans.htm
Cisco VLAN Roadmap	http://www.cisco.com/warp/public/538/7.html
Cisco paper: "LAN Switching"	http://www.cisco.com/univercd/cc/td/doc/cisintwk/ics/cs010.htm
Cisco Paper: "Designing Switched LAN Internetworks"	http://cisco.com/univercd/cc/td/doc/cisintwk/idg4/nd2012.htm
Cabletron 802.1Q VLAN Users Guide	http://www.cabletron.com/support/manuals/overview.html
Foundry Networks paper: "Implementing Virtual LANs in High Speed Packet Networks"	http://www.foundrynet.com/wpvol5.html
VLAN information and links at Netfusion	http://www.nwfusion.com/netresources/vlan.html

VLSM (Variable Length Subnet Masking)

See CIDR (Classless Inter-Domain Routing); Route Aggregation.

VMS (Virtual Memory System)

See OpenVMS.

VoATM (Voice over ATM)

See Voice/Data Networks.

VoFR (Voice over Frame Relay)

See Voice/Data Networks.

Voice/Data Networks

Voice and data networking is about the trends and technologies for merging voice and data communication on a single network. It is part of a broader "multiservice networking" concept that combines all types of communication onto a single network. Practically speaking, the single network is a packet-based IP intranet, the Internet, or special service provider networks that provide Internet-like services. Some other methods for combining voice and data are mentioned here, but the general trend is toward IP-based voice and data networking.

Ironically, even though the trend is toward IP-based multiservice networks, IP is the least capable technology to support real-time multimedia. IP is a best-effort service with no QoS (quality of service). Other technologies such as ATM are better suited to real-time traffic, and they are discussed here. Still, IP networks and the Internet are pervasive, widely distributed, relatively inexpensive to operate, and extremely flexible when it comes to adding new applications, protocols, and services. Most of its QoS problems (primarily delay and lack of resiliency) are being resolved by classifying real-time traffic like voice and giving it priority over other traffic.

Several other topics cover other details about carrying voice, video, and other traffic over data networks. See "Compression Techniques," "Multimedia," "QoS (Quality of Service)," and "Voice over IP (VoIP)."

Some of the goals of integrating voice and data, either within the enterprise or over the wide area, include the following:

- Create end-to-end voice-over-data connections to enable VoIP (voice over IP). VoIP operates above the underlying network layers and supports distributed applications.

- In the wide area, reduce the costs of interoffice and long-distance telephone calls by moving those calls to more-efficient and less-expensive packet-switched networks (frame relay, ATM, or the Internet). This is called "toll bypass," and it makes especially good sense when connecting international locations.

- Consolidate enterprise voice and data networks into a single network that is easier to maintain.

- Enable new and interesting CTI (computer-telephony integration) applications. CTI is about putting telephones and telephony applications into PCs and hand-helds. Some examples include interactive voice response, network-based fax services (including fax on demand and fax back), unified messaging, caller information, and so on. Keep in mind that traditional telephony services have been constrained by the carrier's voice-only network (and the 12-key button arrangement of the phone!).

One of the best reasons to support packet telephony can be seen in the service limitations of the traditional telephone system. The switches are mostly proprietary with embedded call control functions and service logic. That makes it difficult to add new services. In contrast, new services are easy to add in the IP telephony world because users simply add new telephony applications on their computers and communicate with other users who are running the same telephony applications. There is no need for the network to support the services—all the network should do is just transport the packets.

The traditional circuit-switched network is based on 64-Kbit/sec circuits over multiplexed TDM circuits. These are inefficient because a time slot is reserved even if the line is silent, thus wasting bandwidth. Also, the channels lack the bandwidth to handle video and advanced data services. Packet-switched networks are much more efficient. Packets from many sources are statistically multiplexed so there is no wasted bandwidth (empty slots as in TDM). Bandwidth is shared and costs are reduced. Many different communication methods can be combined on the same network, including voice, video, e-mail, voice mail, call center services, Web access, and so on. Packet networks, especially the Internet, are widely distributed. Many devices are accessible, including computers, hand-held devices, information appliances, wireless portable devices, and phones.

Voice and Data Models

There are two broad areas of discussion for voice and data networking. The first is about private voice networks. Organizations want to put voice on the data networks that interconnect their offices, thus reducing the cost of voice—especially for remote offices. The technologies for doing this are described in the following sections.

The following trend can be identified as voice and data converge:

- Organizations build private WANs to carry voice calls between remote offices. Internally, voice and data are handled by separate networks.

- IP telephony is introduced into the enterprise, carrying some voice calls and conferences among internal users and across the private WAN.

- As the new public packet networks ramp up for voice and new protocols come online, more and more voice calls are handled across the Internet or special public networks that are optimized to carry packet-based voice.

- IP telephony applications can be enhanced well beyond the limited range of simple services that were offered by the old PSTN.

VoIP operates at layer 3 of the protocol stack and is media independent. In other words, by implementing VoIP, you are free to use any underlying layer 2 LAN or WAN technology, including ATM and frame relay. This topic covers voice networking in general. See "Voice over IP (VoIP)" for additional information.

Another way to look at the advantages of VoIP is that it enables end-to-end telephony services. ATM and frame relay are WAN technologies that end at the WAN connection. VoIP operates in the next level up, encompassing all the underlying network technologies from end to end.

PBX (Private Branch Exchange) and Integrated Access Devices

The traditional PBX is a box that routes telephone calls internally among employees and routes external calls to the PSTN. A user typically dials 9 to dial an outside line. Internal telephones connect to traditional PBXs via circuit-switched analog lines and the PBX connects to the PSTN via channelized trunks (T1, T3, and so on). A T1 has 24 TDM-based channels, meaning it can support 24 simultaneous calls (one channel is used for signaling). DIDs (direct inward dial numbers) are actual phone numbers assigned to each of the internal phones. PBXs may include a variety of telephony services, including voice mail, queues to put calls on hold (and play music), and IVR (interactive voice response), which can provide Touch-Tone menus of selections for dial-in users.

New PBX and IAD (integrated access device) designs that support voice over data may be configured in one of two ways, as described next. Note that in both cases, the PBX/IAD may be connected to the PSTN and to external sites via T1 trunks or over packet-switched networks (Internet, frame relay, or ATM). Figure V-4 illustrates the available configurations, including internal phones connected via circuit-switched analog lines to the PBX, and Internet phones connected to the PBX via packetized voice over the enterprise data network.

Voice over ATM (VoATM)

ATM is a cell-switching technology that naturally supports the multiplexing of many calls and data transmissions at the same time. ATM provides circuit emulation, either permanent or switched. An ATM permanent virtual circuit may be set up between remote sites to emulate a leased line. ATM switched virtual circuits may be used for temporary connections, as is usually the case with voice phone calls.

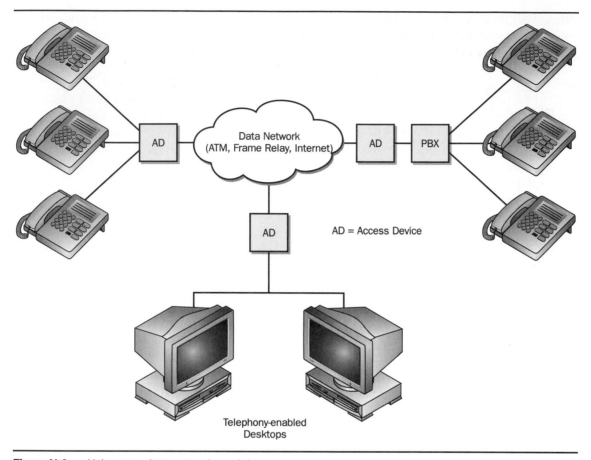

Figure V-4.   *Voice over data network model*

Technologies for carrying voice over ATM are called VoATM or VToA (voice telephony over ATM). The latter is actually the name of an ATM Forum working group. The specification defines ADPCM voice compression and silence suppression and the packetizing of voice over ATM. The most common method for transporting voice over ATM is at ATM Adaptation Layer 1 (AAL1), which supports CBR (constant bit rate) services. A CBR service produces a stream of bits. Up to 248 voice calls can be multiplexed over a 1-Mbit/sec ATM virtual circuit. Several Web sites with additional information are listed here:

ATM Forum VToA specifications (see   http://www.atmforum.com/atmforum/specs/approved.html
Voice & Telephony over ATM section)

Web ProForums VToA paper   http://www.iec.org/tutorials/vtoa/index.html)

Cisco Document: "Multiservice   http://www.cisco.com/univercd/cc/td/doc/cisintwk/
Access Technologies"   ito_doc/multiacc.htm

Voice over Frame Relay (VoFR)

Voice over frame relay is another technology that is considered useful for "toll bypass" and the cost savings inherent in avoiding calls over the PSTN. Frame relay provides any-to-any switched or permanent virtual circuits so organizations can build private WANs among their remote offices. Access to the frame relay network for voice is handled by VFRADs (voice frame relay access devices). The Frame Relay Forum has developed a Voice over Frame Relay standard called FRF.11 that defines how to transport compressed voice data over a frame relay network. The standard assumes that voice has been subjected to extensive compression and uses less than 8 Kbits/sec of bandwidth (compared to 64 Kbits/sec for uncompressed digitized voice). FRF.11 allows interoperability among different vendors' equipment. Several Web sites with additional information are listed here:

Frame Relay Forum	http://www.frforum.com
Motorola's Frame Relay resource center	http://www.mot.com/networking/frame-relay/
Cisco Document: "Multiservice Access Technologies"	http://www.cisco.com/univercd/cc/td/doc/cisintwk/ito_doc/multiacc.htm

Voice over DSL (Digital Subscriber Line)

Many small- to medium-size businesses are using DSL for their business access needs. It is possible to mix voice and data over DSL lines using VoDSL techniques, which code voice and multiplex it over the line using a protocol such as ATM or IP. VoDSL provides a way to combine voice and Internet access over the local loop. Up to 16 voice lines may be possible. A VoDSL configuration consists of an access device that codes speech and transmits it to a DSLAM (DSL access multiplexer) in the carrier central office. Voice and data are encapsulated in ATM cells and transferred across the network where they are split off, with the voice being sent to telephony switches and the data being routed to the Internet. Additional information is available at the following sites:

DSL Forum	http://www.dslforum.org
Jetstream Communications	http://www.jetstream.com/
VoDSL Tutorial at Web ProForum	http://www.iec.org/tutorials/voice_dsl/

Voice over Cable

Like VoDSL, voice over cable networks (the legacy CATV networks) are interested in providing voice service over access links to home and small business users. In the past, the cable network was one way, delivering television broadcasts to subscribers. More recently, cable providers have upgraded their networks to support two-way transmission—primarily to give subscribers Internet access. This also allows voice—in particular, IP telephony—since the cable networks support IP.

Refer to "Cable (CATV) Data Networks" and the following Web site for more information.

Voice over Cable (VoCable) Tutorial at Web ProForum	http://www.iec.org/tutorials/vocable/

Related Entries   Call Center Operations; Circuit-Switching Services; Compression Techniques; Convergence; CTI (Computer-Telephony Integration); H.323 Multimedia Conferencing Standard; Megaco;

MGCP (Media Gateway Control Protocol); Multicasting; Multimedia; Network Access Services; NPN (New Public Network); OSP (Open Settlement Protocol); PBX (Private Branch Exchange); PINT (PSTN-Internet Interworking); QoS (Quality of Service); SAP (Session Announcement Protocol); SCTP (Stream Control Transmission Protocol); SDP (Session Description Protocol); Signaling for Call Control; SIP (Session Initiation Protocol); Softswitch; SPIRITS (Service in the PSTN/IN Requesting InTernet Service); SS7 (Signaling System 7); Telecommunications and Telephone Systems; TRIP (Telephony Routing over IP); Videoconferencing; *and* Voice over IP (VoIP)

Linktionary!—Tom Sheldon's Encyclopedia of Networking updates

http://www.linktionary.com/v/voice-data.html

A complete set of links is available at the Linktionary! Web site.

Voice Mail

See Unified Messaging.

Voice over IP (VoIP)

In just a few years, the old circuit-switched voice-centric communications network will give way to a data-centric, packet-oriented network that seamlessly supports data, voice, and video with a high quality of service. The switching equipment, protocols, and links are already being put into place. A transition network is currently in place that joins the packet data world with the circuit-switched world. Integrated access solutions are being installed that support integrated data, voice, and other media into the Internet or the PSTN.

Despite a number of technological issues, real-time multimedia transmission (voice and video) over IP networks and the Internet has largely been worked out. Advanced compression techniques have reduced voice data transfer rates from 64 Kbits/sec to as little as 6 Kbits/sec. *Voice over IP* or *VoIP* can potentially allow users to call worldwide at no charge (except for the fee paid to service providers for Internet access). A user's IP address basically becomes a phone number. Additionally, computer-based phone systems can be linked to servers that run a variety of interesting telephony applications, including PBX services and voice messaging.

Internet telephony is breaking down the distinctions between telecommunications services and the Internet, sparking reevaluations of the entire industry from technical, economic, and regulatory points of view. The government is taking a hands-off attitude regarding growth of the Internet telephony industry. A few years ago, a Federal Communications attorney said the FCC wants to encourage growth of Internet telephony and had no plans to regulate it soon.

One of the best reasons to support packet telephony can be seen in the service limitations of the traditional telephone system. The switches are mostly proprietary with embedded call control functions and service logic. That makes it difficult to add new services. In addition, the end devices—telephones—are limited in functionality to a 12-key pad! In contrast, new services are easy to add in the IP telephony world because users simply add new telephony applications on their computers and communicate with other users who are running the same telephony applications. There is no need to put additional support in the network itself for these services—all the network has to do is transport packets with good quality of service.

The new model reverses the thinking of the old model. The old model was "dumb endpoints driven by an intelligent network." The new model is intelligent endpoints communicating over a relatively dumb packet-based best-effort network.

While phone calls on the Internet rarely achieve the level of quality of circuit-switched calls, the quality is improving; the connection is often as good as or better than cellular, which is prone to packet errors and distortion due to its wireless nature. The market has found that many customers will tolerate a small decrease in the quality of the call for the significantly reduced cost of an IP telephone call. Savings on fax calls may be even greater. In fact, transmitting fax over the Internet is very practical because real-time delivery is not required. Many service providers are building special networks designed to provide a high quality of service for customer multimedia applications.

Quality of IP telephony is affected by latency, which is basically the amount of time between when someone speaks and when the listener hears. People who talk across satellite links know about this gap and are often able to adjust to it. *Jitter* is the real problem. Jitter is variations in delay. People can get used to talking across satellite links because the delay is constant. You get used to the slight pause. But if the amount of delay changes as the call proceeds, the effect is annoying. When voice is transmitted over packet networks, jitter occurs when packets get held up in queues during unpredictable and momentary bursts of traffic. RTP (Real-time Transport Protocol) is specifically designed to smooth out jitter by synchronizing packets based on timestamps. Virtually all IP telephony applications use RTP.

The remainder of this topic covers new and emerging telephony protocols and models. Specific concepts such as voice compression, codecs, silence suppression, echo cancellation, jitter, and QoS are not covered here. You can refer to "Compression Techniques," "Multimedia," "QoS (Quality of Service)," and "Voice/Data Networks" for additional information.

The PSTN Legacy Architecture

It's important to understand the architecture of the legacy public-switched telephone network to understand the equipment, software, and protocols involved in VoIP integration. The situation for the next few years will be that the existing PSTN will slowly give way to a new public packet network. In the meantime, the existing PSTN must be leveraged because millions of users and non-IP devices are connected to it. In addition, it supports a variety of voice services such as 800 and 900 numbers. An Internet telephony device wanting to connect with one of these devices must use PSTN signaling. Here are the possible Internet/PSTN interconnection scenarios:

- Internet user/device to PSTN user/device (packet to circuit)
- PSTN user/device to Internet user/device (circuit to packet)
- PSTN user/device to PSTN user/device across the Internet (circuit to packet to circuit).
- Internet user/device to Internet user/device across the PSTN (packet to circuit to packet)

In each of these cases, some translation is required to convert from one signaling method to another. In the PSTN, signals are messages sent between telephony switches to set up and terminate calls and indicate the status of terminals involved in calls. These signals are carried

V

over a *separate data network* known as CCS (Common Channel Signaling). The protocol used by CCS is SS7 (Signaling System 7). The entire system is called the IN (Intelligent Network). Refer to "Telecommunications and Telephone System" for a description of this network.

VoIP can be seen as part of the *overlay network,* but built with media gateways and media gateway controllers (also called "softswitches"). A softswitch could be called a "soft" SSP (service switching point). It transmits IP-based voice signals into the SS7 network and translates them so that the SCP (service control point) can act in the same way it responds to signals from SS7-compatible devices. In either case, the SCP sends appropriate signals to control the SSP.

VoIP Standards

When talking about standards, the first thing to mention is that the term "VoIP" was actually coined by the VoIP Forum to describe Voice over IP using ITU H.323 standards. However, "VoIP" has become a generic term for referring to the range of standards that support voice over IP. Those include the ITU standards, IETF standards, and others.

ITU H.323 has dominated the market in terms of the number of devices installed. H.323 is a multimedia conferencing standard that is quite complex. While it works well for videoconferencing, most vendors feel that it is too complex for IP telephony, which is possible by using much simpler protocols. Still, H.323 is considered a pioneering protocol for packet voice and video. The IETF's SIP (Session Initiation Protocol) is now seen as being more important for VoIP.

H.323 Multimedia Conferencing Standard

H.323 is part of a family of the ITU-T Recommendations that specify multimedia communications services such as real-time audio, video, and data over a variety of communication services, including multipoint links where multiple users participate in the same exchange (such as a videoconference). The ITU calls H.323 a recommendation for a "visual telephone system" that works over LANs. It does not provide quality of service controls, because it is packet-based, but QoS can be obtained by relying on other means as discussed under "QoS (Quality of Service)." The IETF's RTP is the transport protocol for this scheme.

An H.323 environment consists of H.323 terminals (phones, and telephony-enabled PCs), gateways to the public telephone network, gatekeepers (management functions), and multipoint control units. It also includes a set of additional protocols for encoding and decoding audio and video data, as well as protocols that define how it is packetized. There are also protocols the define call signaling and control.

H.323 gateways connect different systems and devices (e.g., IP-based H.323 terminals to the PSTN). Gateways perform the appropriate mapping of call signals and control protocols between systems. *H.323 gatekeepers* are systems that manage a group of H.323 terminals and gateways within a "zone." A zone can be thought of as a management area consisting of a group of related terminals, gateways, and multiuser conferencing devices. Gatekeepers provide address translation functions between H.323 addresses and IP addresses. They also provide supervisory functions (admitting or rejecting users), bandwidth allocation, and call signaling functions.

See "H.323 Multimedia Conferencing Standard" for more information.

ETSI TIPHON

ETSI (European Telecommunications Standards Institute) has established the TIPHON (Telecommunications and Internet Protocol Harmonization Over Networks) Working Group to ensure that users connected to IP-based networks can communicate with users in switched-circuit networks such as the PSTN, ISDN, and GSM, and vice versa. While ETSI is a European body, it cooperates with the ITU and IETF. ETSI developed the GSM standard.

TIPHON includes working groups that are identifying various aspects of implementing VoIP, including interoperability, charging/billing, security, call control procedures, information flows, protocols, and QoS. See "OSP (Open Settlement Protocol)," for example.

TIPHON relies on H.323 gatekeeper, gateway, and terminal specifications. The gateway is subdivided into a signaling gateway (mediates signals between IP and the switched circuit networks), a media gateway (connects two different networks and performs translations), and the media gateway controller (translates and maps signaling information among the different networks).

The media gateway controller controls the media gateway by creating, modifying, and deleting connections, as well as specifying media formats and inserting information into media streams. The media gatekeeper provides functions such as authentication, admission policy, call signaling, and accounting.

There are many issues related to end-user addressing, as pointed out in Bjarne Munch's "IP Telephony Signalling" paper (see the Ericsson Web site at the end of this topic). These issues relate "user friendliness, routing mechanisms, number mobility, and service mobility." In the switched circuit network, users are identified by ITU-T E.164 telephone numbers. In the packet network, IP addresses (and various aliases) are used.

The ETSI TIPHON Web site is at http://www.etsi.org/tiphon/.

IETF IP Telephony Standards

The IETF model for VoIP centers around SIP (Session Initiation Protocol). SIP is a control protocol operating in the application layer for setting up, maintaining, and terminating voice and videoconferencing sessions. SIP uses text-based messages and operates in much the same way as the client/server protocol of the Web (i.e., HTTP). SIP provides an overall messaging system for all types of multimedia applications and works just as well for electronic commerce and collaborative computing applications.

In fact, your phone number in an IP-based phone system uses the same URL format as a Web site address or e-mail address. Transferring phone calls to other locations is similar to clicking a hyperlink to switch to a different Web page. In addition, instant messaging and presence protocols can help users create phone call buddy lists and assist in call connections. For example, presence protocols can help locate a person to call, no matter where they are connected to the Net. Presence protocols will be critical in locating and calling mobile Internet phone users.

SIP has gained favor throughout the packet voice community. It is highly adaptable and supports multivendor interoperability among devices. Tests have shown that SIP works well and provides much faster call setup times than H.323.

SIP's distinguishing factor is that it uses the "intelligence at the edge" model. SIP relies on endpoint devices to control packet-based telephony services. In other words, two endpoint SIP devices can set up their own call across the Internet without any devices in the network getting involved, although in practice other devices will be involved if QoS is required or the call must go through the PSTN.

Since the SIP model is based on intelligent edge devices, developers are free to create telephony services and applications that are not restricted by the old service models of the traditional telephone network. In fact, designing telephony applications is very similar to creating Web client/server applications. Developers familiar with HTTP, XML, and other Web development tools instantly recognize SIP. Other protocols that are implemented in Internet multimedia devices include RTP (Real-time Transport Protocol), SAP (Session Announcement Protocol), and SDP (Session Description Protocol). See "Multimedia" for more information.

Media Gateways and Controllers

A telephony gateway is a network element that provides conversion between the audio signals carried on telephone circuits and data packets carried over the Internet or over other packet networks. A media gateway essentially replicates the behavior of the PSTN on the Internet. The purpose of these gateways and their associated protocols is to interconnect the Internet packet world with the switched circuit telephony world of the PSTN.

Gateways have three functional elements as pictured in Figure V-5 and described, next. These elements may be combined into a single box or physically separated into multiple boxes. By separating the functions, a distributed model can be built in which a single media control

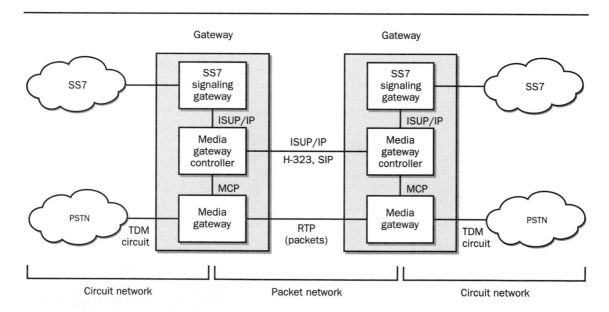

Figure V-5.   *Functional elements of a media gateway (Source: Bjarne Munch, Ericsson)*

device can control many *distributed* media gateways. This separation is referred to as the softswitch architecture. See "Softswitch."

■ **SS7 signaling gateway**   Provides an SS7 STP (signal transfer point) function involving the switched circuit network and a protocol conversion between the SS7 network and IP transport protocols. A signaling gateway basically repackages SS7 signals for IP or IP signals for SS7.

■ **MGC (media gateway controller)**   The MGC handles registration, management, and control functionality of resources in the media gateway. It performs protocol conversion between PSTN signaling protocols and IP telephony. It gathers information about IP and circuit flows and provides that information to billing and management systems.

■ **MG (media gateway)**   A basic device that terminates PSTN switched circuits (trunks and local loops) and converts from pulse code modulated information to packetized information, and vice versa. Also handles RTP media streams across the IP network.

As mentioned, a distributed model for media gateways separates the call-control and signaling planes from the transport layer media gateways, as pictured in Figure V-6. Separating these functions improves scalability. New features can be added to a few controller devices rather than to many media gateways. This model also promotes commodity devices that will bring down the cost of VoIP.

RFC 2705 (Media Gateway Control Protocol, October 1999) provides a general description of the media gateway/media gateway controller model. It describes an architecture in which the call control "intelligence" is outside the media gateways and handled by media gateway controllers (also called "call agents"). These elements synchronize with one another to send coherent commands to the media gateways under their control. A control protocol is used to control VoIP gateways from the external call agents. The MGCP model consists of endpoints and connections:

■ *Endpoints* are sources or "sinks" of data and could be physical or virtual. Examples are interfaces on a gateway that terminates a trunk connected to a PSTN switch (e.g., class 5,

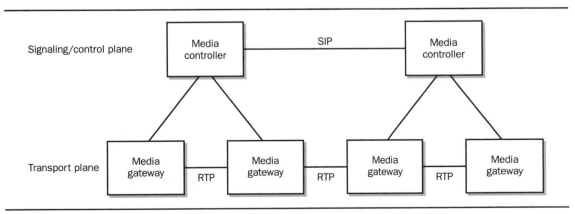

Figure V-6.   *Distributed media gateways and softswitches*

class 4, and so on), or that terminate an analog POTS connection to a phone, key system, or PBX. A gateway that terminates residential POTS lines (to phones) is called a *residential gateway*. Note that there are physical endpoints (hardware) and virtual endpoints (created in software).

■ A *connection* is an association between endpoints over which data is transmitted. Point-to-point and multipoint connections are possible. Connections may exist over IP networks, ATM networks, or internal connections such as TDM backplanes or gateway backplanes. For point-to-point connections, the endpoints of a connection could be in separate gateways or in the same gateway.

Media Control Protocols

Starting in 1998, engineers at Telcordia (formerly BellCore) developed SGCP (Simple Gateway Control Protocol), a master-slave protocol that replicated the functions of a class 5 PSTN switch. Then, Level 3 Communications developed IPDC (Internet Protocol Device Control) as an enhancement to SGCP. The IETF took the best features of SGCP and IPDC and created MGCP. MGCP supports both video and telephony and uses control messages based on simple ASCII encoding. It provides call control features for low-cost, nonintelligent endpoint telephony devices (e.g., dumb phones and gateways). Later, Lucent stepped in with MDCP (Media Device Control Protocol) and the ITU merged the best features of MGCP and MDCP into H.GCP.

The reason for all this development is that network architects are trying to iron out protocols for a future all-IP, next-generation, packet-switched network while maintaining compatibility with the older PSTN. Naturally, there are many opinions on how this should be done.

Media control protocols suport separate control components. Note that SIP is still used in this model as a communication protocol between media controllers. In fact, SIP could be used in place of media control protocols. SIP assumed intelligent end devices, and it may turn out to be the best protocol for maintaining the intelligent edge device model throughout the Internet.

A media control protocol is implemented as a set of transactions composed of commands. The call agent may send commands to gateways that create, modify, and delete connections, or that create notification requests and auditing commands. Gateways may send notification and restart commands to the call agent. All commands include text-based header information following by (optionally) text-based session description information.

Refer to RFC 2705 for additional information. RFC 2805 (Media Gateway Control Protocol Architecture and Requirements, April 2000) provides additional information about media gateways, media controllers, and control protocols.

In late 1998, the IETF developed Megaco based on the previous work and the intention to overcome some of the problems in MGCP. Megaco drafts and documents are available at the IETF Media Gateway Control (megaco) Web site at http://www.ietf.org/html.charters/megaco-charter.html. Also refer to H.248 documents at the ITU (http://www.itu.org).

Megaco assumes that end devices are not intelligent devices (in contrast, SIP assumes that the network consists of distributed intelligent devices). It replaces the gatekeeper functions of the H.323 protocol; supports TDM, ATM, and connectionless IP; and works in a range of gateways, from residential gateways to carrier-size gateways.

In 1999, the IETF and the ITU formally agreed to work on a single protocol. This led to Megaco/H.248. The ITU has largely taken over this development as H.248. However, don't count on H.248 as the final development in this saga. Some feel that the ITU is making it more complex than it needs to be for IP telephony. See RFC 3015 (Megaco Protocol Version 1.0, November 2000) for more information.

Other IP Telephony Protocols

This section describes some of the related protocols and initiatives underway to support IP telephony. Most of the work is being done by the IETF.

IP-PBX (IP-Private Branch Exchange)

A traditional PBX is basically a telephone switch designed for small to large companies. Internet telephones are wired into the box, which then connects inside calls (internal phone to internal phone) or connects calls to/from the PSTN. Phones connect to the traditional PBX over analog phone lines. IP-PBXs use the data network for voice. The IP-PBX connects to the data network and network-connected IP telephones access the IP-PBX.

IP telephony devices are not restricted by the limitations of the old phone system, so end devices and IP-PBXs can provide enhanced functionality and services. These new services are immediately available inside the enterprise that upgrades to IP-PBXs. As packet telephony grows throughout the Internet, users will be able to connect with IP telephony users outside the corporate network and take advantages of new services. See "PBX (Private Branch Exchange)."

CPL (Call Processing Language)

CPL is a processing language that provides a simple and standardized way for users of Internet telephony devices to specify how they want incoming calls handled. CPL is described in RFC 2824 (Call Processing Language Framework and Requirements, May 2000). The IP Telephony (iptel) Working Group (http://www.ietf.org/html.charters/iptel-charter.html) is developing CPL and related protocols.

The traditional phone system does not provide much control in this area, but a simple example would be a telephone that can be programmed by the user to forward calls to another location during a specific time period, or else just record a message. CPL is a simple language that provides a standardized way to describe these behaviors in telephony devices.

Signaling Transport and SCTP (Stream Control Transmission Protocol)

RFC 2719 (Framework Architecture for Signaling Transport, October 1999) defines an architectural framework for transport of message-based signaling protocols over IP networks. It encapsulates methods, end-to-end protocol mechanisms, and use of existing IP capabilities to support the functional and performance requirements for signaling transport.

SCTP is defined in RFC 2960 (Stream Control Transmission Protocol, October 2000). It is meant to be the "signal carrier" in place of TCP. SCTP is a reliable transport protocol operating on top of a connectionless packet network such as IP. The services it offers to users include many of the same services as TCP, but sequencing is removed to reduce delays. SCTP was developed by the IETF Signaling Transport (sigtran) Working Group, which is working on related technologies. See "SCTP (Stream Control Transmission Protocol)."

TRIP (Telephony Routing over IP)

TRIP defines a policy-driven interadministrative domain framework for advertising the reachability of telephony destinations between location servers, and for advertising attributes of the routes to those destinations. TRIP can serve as the telephony routing framework for any signaling protocol. TRIP is similar to BGP-4 in the way that it distributes routing information (telephony information in TRIP's case) between administrative domains. RFC 2871 (A Framework for Telephony Routing over IP, June 2000) defines the framework for TRIP. The work on TRIP is being done by the IP Telephony (iptel) Working Group.

OSP (Open Settlement Protocol)

The purpose of the Open Settlement Protocol is to handle settlements for IP telephony calls among the different carriers that route calls, giving IP telephony the push it needs to expand on a global scale. The protocol supports call authentication, authorization, and accounting techniques, and provides per-minute settlements for VoIP calling. OSP is defined in the ETSI TIPHON project. See "OSP (Open Settlement Protocol)."

JAIN (Java Advanced Intelligent Network)

JAIN is a set of Java technology–based APIs that enable the rapid development of new telecom products and services on the Java platform. JAIN is a Sun Microsystem's initiative that can be used to define and build advanced telecom services that blend IN (Intelligent Network) and Internet technologies. The Java language serves as the basis for creating middleware components and tools for SS7 applications. JAIN allows different IN services to run across a variety of switching platforms from many different vendors. Information is available at http://java.sun.com/products/jain/. The Parlay Group is also involved with JAIN. Its Web site is http://www.parlay.org/.

IETF Working Groups and RFCs

The following IETF working groups are developing IP telephony protocols or are working on related technologies. Additional working groups that are developing QoS are listed under the topic "QoS (Quality of Service)."

The Audio/Video Transport (avt)	http://www.ietf.org/html.charters/avt-charter.html.
IP Telephony (iptel)	http://www.ietf.org/html.charters/iptel-charter.html.
Media Gateway Control (megaco)	http://www.ietf.org/html.charters/megaco-charter.html.
Multiparty Multimedia Session Control (mmusic)	http://www.ietf.org/html.charters/mmusic-charter.html.
PSTN and Internet Internetworking (pint)	http://www.ietf.org/html.charters/pint-charter.html.
Service in the PSTN/IN Requesting InTernet Service (spirits)	http://www.ietf.org/html.charters/spirits-charter.html.
Signaling Transport (sigtran)	http://www.ietf.org/html.charters/sigtran-charter.html.
Telephone Number Mapping (enum)	http://www.ietf.org/html.charters/enum-charter.html.

Internet Fax (fax)	http://www.ietf.org/html.charters/fax-charter.html.
Instant Messaging and Presence Protocol (impp)	http://www.ietf.org/html.charters/impp-charter.html.

The following Internet RFCs provide more information about voice over IP or related multimedia protocols. Also refer the "Multimedia" for other RFCs.

- RFC 2458 (Toward the PSTN/Internet Inter-Networking—Pre-PINT Implementations, November 1998)

- RFC 2705 (Media Gateway Control Protocol, October 1999)

- RFC 2719 (Framework Architecture for Signaling Transport, October 1999

- RFC 2805 (Media Gateway Control Protocol Architecture and Requirements, April 2000)

- RFC 2806 (URLs for Telephone Calls, April 2000)

- RFC 2824 (Call Processing Language Framework and Requirements, May 2000)

- RFC 2833 (RTP Payload for DTMF Digits, Telephony Tones and Telephony Signals, May 2000)

- RFC 2848 (The PINT Service Protocol: Extensions to SIP and SDP for IP Access to Telephone Call Services, June 2000)

- RFC 2871 (A Framework for Telephony Routing over IP, June 2000)

- RFC 2885 (Megaco Protocol, August 2000)

- RFC 2886 (Megaco Errata, August 2000)

- RFC 2897 (Proposal for an MGCP Advanced Audio Package, August 2000)

- RFC 2974 (Session Announcement Protocol, October 2000)

- RFC 2960 (Stream Control Transmission Protocol, October 2000)

Related Entries   Call Center Operations; Circuit-Switching Services; Compression Techniques; Convergence; CTI (Computer-Telephony Integration); H.323 Multimedia Conferencing Standard; Megaco; MGCP (Media Gateway Control Protocol); Multicasting; Multimedia; Network Access Services; NPN (New Public Network); OSP (Open Settlement Protocol); PBX (Private Branch Exchange); PINT (PSTN-Internet Interworking); QoS (Quality of Service); SAP (Session Announcement Protocol); SCTP (Stream Control Transmission Protocol); SDP (Session Description Protocol); Signaling for Call Control; SIP (Session Initiation Protocol); Softswitch; SPIRITS (Service in the PSTN/IN Requesting InTernet Service); SS7 (Signaling System 7); Telecommunications and Telephone Systems; TRIP (Telephony Routing over IP); Videoconferencing; *and* Voice/Data Networks

Linktionary!—Tom Sheldon's Encyclopedia of Networking updates	http://www.linktionary.com/v/voip.html
IP Telephony Signalling by Bjarne Munch, Ericsson	http://www.ericsson.com/iptelephony

iBasis, the world's largest international network for Internet telephony	http://www.ibasis.net/
Henning Schulzrinne's SIP page	http://www.cs.columbia.edu/sip/
Jeff Pulver's Pulver.com Web site (IP telephony, instant messaging, presence information, and so on)	http://www.pulver.com/
Softswitch Consortium	http://www.softswitch.org
Santera	http://www.santera.com
AccessLAN	http://www.accesslan.com

VoIP (Voice over IP)

See Voice over IP (VoIP); Voice/Data Networks.

Volume and Partition Management

Volumes are collections of directories, subdirectories, and files. The term "volumes" as used here applies to the way disk storage is handled in the NetWare environment. Refer to the Linktionary! Web site at http://www.linktionary.com/v/vol_management.html for this topic.

VPN (Virtual Private Network)

Private networks have traditionally been built with dedicated leased lines, dial-up lines, or other links such as satellite or microwave. Links are established among remote sites. The links are "private" because no other traffic except the traffic of the company leasing the links crosses the links.

A *virtual* private network is the creation of private links across public networks such as the Internet. The idea is to create what appears to be a dedicated private link on a shared network using encryption and tunneling techniques. Anybody can create a private connection by encrypting the contents of the traffic being sent across a network, but truly secure VPNs are better built with the cooperation of service providers that can create dedicated paths with guaranteed service levels across their networks.

VPNs are relatively easy in ATM and frame relay networks because the network provider creates virtual circuits across the network that provide dedicated bandwidth and path control for the customer. Traffic is then encrypted by the sender and sent across the virtual circuit. In some cases, the customer outsources all VPN control to the service provider. A short-haul physical link is established to the provider's point of presence and the provider handles all aspects of encryption and path control.

The open environment of the Internet allows anyone to establish a private link by encrypting packets that cross the network. However, the virtual network part of the VPN (as opposed to the private part) requires the cooperation of service providers that can establish virtual circuits using traffic engineering techniques that set up paths with reserved bandwidth. This is possible with MPLS (Multiprotocol Label Switching), which provides traffic engineering for the Internet. As for making the traffic private, IPSec is a good choice.

VPNs across public networks may require the cooperation of a number of providers. For example, if you need a cross-country VPN on a virtual circuit between LA and New York, you may need to enlist the services of several service providers that can cooperatively establish an MPLS path across the Internet.

Before MPLS and IPSec, basic tunneling and encryption schemes were used to build Internet VPNs. L2TP (Layer 2 Tunneling Protocol) is an example of a protocol that encapsulates IP packets in "tunneling" packets that hide the underlying Internet routing structure. L2TP allows users to create what appears to be a local dial-up session into a corporate network across the Internet, thus saving long-distance charges.

This topic continues at the Linktionary! Web site, where you will also find a full set of Web links. Also see the L2TP, MPLS, and IPSec topics.

Related Entries   Access Control; Authentication and Authorization; Communication Server; DIAMETER; IPSec (IP Security); Mobile Computing; Modems; MPLS (Multiprotocol Label Switching); NAS (Network Access Server); PPP (Point-to-Point Protocol); PPTP (Point-to-Point Tunneling Protocol); RADIUS (Remote Authentication Dial-In User Service); Remote Access; Roaming; Security; TACACS (Terminal Access Controller Access Control System); Tunnels; *and* VPN (Virtual Private Network)

 Linktionary!—Tom Sheldon's Encyclopedia of   http://www.linktionary.com/v/vpn.html
Networking updates

VRML (Virtual Reality Modeling Language)

See Web3D.

VRRP (Virtual Router Redundancy Protocol)

In some internetwork environments, networks are connected to other networks via a single router. But that single router is a potential point of failure that can disconnect an entire network from the rest of the internetwork.

VRRP eliminates single points of failure by providing a protocol that supports redundant router connections. An added feature is the ability to do load sharing in which each redundant link carries traffic.

The protocol is designed to help reduce downtime and delays normally associated with lost links and dynamic route configuration. Redundant routers are installed and one is "elected" as the master router. If a router fails, one of the redundant "backup" routers takes over as the master router. The master router sends a special VRRP advertisement packet to the backup routers, usually every second. If advertisements stop, the backups assume the master is down and initiate backup mode, in which the next-in-line router is elected.

An important point is that VRRP provides fast, efficient recovery from failures. Dynamic routing protocols such as RIP and OSPF are time-consuming and inefficient. They must discover failed routes, alert other routers, run routing algorithms to calculate alternate routers, and then build routing tables.

Recovery is so fast in the event of a failure that most end systems may not even notice that the switching over has occurred. In addition, routers in the configuration share a *virtual* IP and MAC address, so that end systems see the routers as having the same address.

V

The following RFCs provide complete details about VRRP. You can also check the EITF VRRP Working Group Web page listed shortly for additional information.

- RFC 2238 (Virtual Router Redundancy Protocol, April 1998)
- RFC 2787 (Definitions of Managed Objects for the Virtual Router Redundancy Protocol, March 2000)

Related Entries   Fault Tolerance and High Availability; HSRP (Hot Standby Router Protocol); IP (Internet Protocol); Routers; Routing; *and* Routing on the Internet

Linktionary!—Tom Sheldon's Encyclopedia   http://www.linktionary.com/v/vrrp.html
of Networking updates

IETF Working Group: Virtual Router   http://www.ietf.org/html.charters/vrrp-charter.html
Redundancy Protocol (vrrp)

VSAT (Very Small Aperture Terminal)

See Satellite Communication Systems.

VTAM (Virtual Telecommunications Access Method

An IBM SNA legacy system includes a mainframe and the software running on that mainframe. The software at the heart of this SNA system is VTAM. IBM mainframes are host-centric processing systems, meaning that the mainframe controls all software and resources. Terminals are attached to the mainframe. In the SNA hierarchy, the mainframe running VTAM is called the Physical Unit type 5, or PU5.

Related Entries   IBM (International Business Machines); SNA (Systems Network Architecture)

W3C (World Wide Web Consortium)

The W3C is an international industry consortium that was founded in 1994 to develop common protocols for the evolution of the World Wide Web. The W3C works with the global community to produce specifications and references that are vendor neutral and freely available throughout the world. Initially, the W3C was established in collaboration with CERN, where the Web originated, with support from DARPA (Defense Advanced Research Projects Agency) and the European Commission. The W3C Web site has a wealth of information about the Internet and emerging protocols and standards. It currently manages a number of Internet standards.

Related Entries   Internet Organizations and Committees; Internet Standards; Standards Groups, Associations, and Organizations; *and* Web Technologies and Concepts

 W3C Web site   http://www.w3.org

WAN (Wide Area Network)

A WAN is generally an extension of an internal network into the wide area using private circuits such as T1 lines or virtual circuits in cell and packet switched networks such as ATM and frame relay. WANs links geographically dispersed offices in other cities or around the globe. Because WANs have been built with private leased lines, bandwidth has traditionally been low and costs have been high, which required careful monitoring and filtering of traffic between sites. WANs can also be constructed across the Internet by implementing VPN (virtual private network) technology. With VPNs private circuits are emulated in the form of encrypted tunnels from one site to another.

Dedicated leased lines (circuit-oriented) such as T1 lines are still common, although expensive. The advantage of leased lines is that they are private—no one else shares the line. An alternative is available with packet-switched networks such as frame relay, ATM, and the Internet. Many users share the networks, which helps lower costs.

Dial-up lines can provide an economical WAN connection in a number of scenarios. For example, a dial-on-demand line can be used to provide additional bandwidth when an existing dedicated leased-line WAN link becomes overburdened. These lines can be multilinked as discussed under "Inverse Multiplexing" and "MLPPP (Multilink PPP)."

Broadband communications is usually considered to be any link with transmission rates above dial-up lines. Broadband transmission systems typically provide channels for data transmissions in different directions and by many different users. Typical broadband communication systems are outlined here and discussed under their own headings in this book.

- **ISDN (Integrated Services Digital Network)**   A circuit oriented service operating at 64-Kbit/sec or 128-Kbit/sec data channel. Primary rate ISDN provides additional bandwidth in increments of 64 Kbits/sec.

- **X.25**   An early packet-switching protocol still used for many low-bandwidth requirements (credit card authorization).

- **ATM (Asynchronous Transfer Mode)**   A cell-switched any-to-any virtual circuit service.

- **Frame relay**   A frame-based any-to-any virtual circuit service.

W

- **Leased lines T1, T3**   A dedicated leased line TDM (time division multiplexing) service. See "TDM Networks."

- **DSL (Digital Subscriber Line)**   A high-speed circuit-oriented service that runs over the local loop.

- **Broadband wireless**   A variety of wireless broadband services are now available or under development. See "Wireless Broadband Access Technologies."

One of the first things to do when designing a WAN is to map out the topology and design what type of connections to use. Should the WAN be circuit oriented (ISDN, T1, and so on) or should it be built across public packet-switched networks (frame relay, ATM, Internet). A private WAN is more expensive to build than a packet-switched WAN, but provides full privacy and dedicated bandwidth. In some cases, dedicated leased lines are the only way to obtain dedicated service and bandwidth requirements.

The following illustration shows various WAN topologies. Note that the star, ring, and fully meshed network are built with circuits, while the packet switched network is built by leasing short-haul lined into a local carrier's PoP (point of presence).

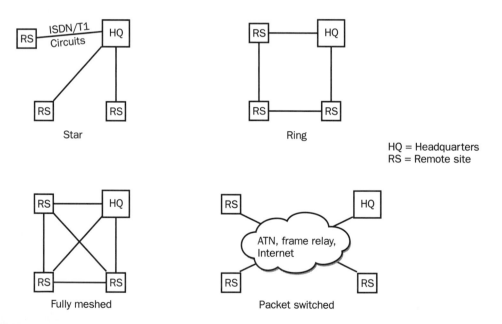

Building a WAN with circuits is a trade-off between cost and fault tolerance. In all cases, servers are located at a central site or headquarters (HQ). The *star configuration* provides a connection for all remote sites to the HQ, but should any link fail, the site connected with that link loses its connectivity. The ring configuration adds fault tolerance. If one link fails, data traffic can be routed through the other link back to the HQ. However, if two links fail, at least one office will be cut off. The fully meshed configuration is very tolerant to faults, but also very expensive since six leased lines are required. The packet-switched network is the least expensive and easiest to configure.

New metro-Ethernet technologies and backbone DWDM optical networks are making WAN deployment easier and cheaper. Customers are no longer restricted to the TDM circuits of the telephone companies. Metro-Ethernet options offer multiple megabits of throughput at a fraction of the cost of leased lines. See "MAN (Metropolitan Area Network)." Other new technologies are outlined under "Network Access Services" and "Network Core Technologies."

The any-to-any connection model of the Internet has proven to be the best way to build global networks. The private WAN may have been replaced by the Internet for some organizations. In its place are firewalls, VPNs (virtual private networks), and tighter security, but at a lower cost with more freedom for users. And when virtual circuits and QoS are required on the Internet, MPLS (Multiprotocol Label Switching) can provide it. The NPN (new public network) refers to public packet-switched data networks that support voice and data with the same reliability and quality of service as the old voice telephone system (at least that is the goal).

Related Entries   ATM (Asynchronous Transfer Mode); Bandwidth Management; Bandwidth on Demand; Capacity; Circuit; Circuit-Switching Services; Communication Services and Providers; Data Communication Concepts; DSL (Digital Subscriber Line); Frame Relay; IMA (Inverse Multiplexing over ATM); Internetworking; ISDN (Integrated Services Digital Network); LMDS (Local Multipoint Distribution Service); Load Balancing; Local Loop; MAN (Metropolitan Area Network); Microwave Communications; Multiplexing and Multiplexers; Network Access Services; Network Design and Construction; NPN (New Public Network); Optical Networks; PON (Passive Optical Network); Private Network; Remote Access; Routers; Satellite Communication Systems; Service Providers and Carriers; SLA (Services Level Agreement); T Carrier; TDM Networks; Telecommunications and Telephone Systems; Topology; Virtual Circuit; Voice/Data Networks; VPN (Virtual Private Network); Wireless Broadband Access Services; Wireless Communications; *and* Wireless Local Loop

Linktionary!—Tom Sheldon's Encyclopedia of Networking updates	http://www.linktionary.com/w/wan.html
Marconi WAN theory tutorial	http://www.marconi.com/html/education/wanmenu.htm
Intel paper: "Wide Area Networking, a User's Guide"	http://www.intel.com/network/white_papers/wide_area.htm
3Com Technology Center (a variety of papers related to WANs)	http://www.3com.com/technology/tech_net/white_papers/index.html
Lucent Internetworking Systems Resource Library (very extensive set of white papers including papers on voice, VPNs, regulation)	http://www.lucent.com/ins/library/whitepap.html
Business Communications Review Networking Topics (an extensive list of excellent articles)	http://www.bcr.com/searchbytopic.htm
ADC Kentrox (see Library)	http://www.kentrox.com/
Cisco Internetworking Technology overview documents	http://www.cisco.com/univercd/cc/td/doc/cisintwk/ito_doc/index.htm

W

Cisco Internetworking Design Guides	http://www.cisco.com/univercd/cc/td/doc/cisintwk/idg4/index.htm
Cisco Internetworking Solutions Guides	http://www.cisco.com/univercd/cc/td/doc/cisintwk/intsolns/index.htm
Cisco Internetwork Troubleshooting Guides	http://www.cisco.com/univercd/cc/td/doc/cisintwk/itg_v1/index.htm
Novell LAN/WAN Interconnectivity white papers	http://developer.novell.com/research/topical/lan_wan_interconnectivity.htm
Mark McCutcheon's Links (very extensive)	http://www.cs.ubc.ca/spider/mjmccut/
Links at ITPRC	http://www.itprc.com/physical.htm
Technology guides at techguide.com	http://www.techguide.com/

WAP (Wireless Application Protocol)

WAP is a worldwide standard for providing Internet communications and advanced telephony services on digital mobile phones, pagers, personal digital assistants and other "smart" wireless terminals. The WAP Forum developed the protocol as a means of transferring information to mobile wireless devices using a standard interface and display format. A complete set of WAP specifications is available at the WAP Forum Web site given later. An extended description of WAP is available at the Linktionary! Web site listed here.

Related Entries   Bluetooth; Electromagnetic Spectrum; HDML (Handheld Device Markup Language); HTML (Hypertext Markup Language); Mobile Computing; Mobile IP; Packet Radio Data Networks; Remote Access; SMS (Short Messaging System); Wireless Broadband Access Technologies; Wireless Communications; Wireless IP; Wireless LANs; *and* Wireless Mobile Communications

Linktionary!—Tom Sheldon's Encyclopedia of Networking updates	http://www.linktionary.com/w/wap.html
WAP Forum	http://www.wapforum.org/
WAP.com, an independent site offering wireless information	http://www.wap.com/
Openwave Systems Internet phone and WAP information	http://www.openwave.com/
"Mobile CT: The Call of the Wireless Web" by Robert Richardson, *Computer Telephony Magazine*	http://www.computertelephony.com/article/CTM20000608S0012

Wavelength Division Multiplexing

See Optical Networks; *and* WDM (Wavelength Division Multiplexing).

Wavelength Routing

See Optical Networks.

WBEM (Web-Based Enterprise Management)

WBEM is a Web-based management architecture originally developed by Microsoft, Compaq, and Cisco, but in 1998 WBEM was turned over to the DMTF (Distributed Management Task Force) for standardization. WBEM uses Web browsers and other technologies to manage enterprise networks. The inventory model used by WBEM is CIM (Common Information Model), which is an object-oriented specification for collecting and sharing enterprise-wide management information. XML (Extensible Markup Language) is used to transfer management data between systems (replacing the Hypermedia Management Protocol defined in an earlier WBEM specification).

Basically, CIM does for management data what SQL does for data in the relational database world. Data is in a (relatively) standard format for easy access by management systems. XML is used to transfer the information around the intranet or the Internet. The data is extracted and placed in XML pages, then transferred to management systems or other entities. XML has many advantages in this environment, and the DMTF has created an XML coding specification for CIM data to simplify data exchange with Web technologies.

The advantage of WBEM is that it provides a common standard that vendors can follow to make their products compatible with a wide variety of management systems. WBEM is designed to complement existing management standards such as SNMP and DMI (Distributed Management Interface) while helping to "consolidate and unify the data provided by existing management technologies." WBEM allows data from a variety of sources to be "described, instantiated, and accessed, regardless of the source." While SNMP can still provide polling and alerts, WBEM and CIM will eventually push it into a legacy protocol status.

Many vendors are supporting WBEM, including Microsoft, which supports WBEM in its Windows 2000 products. Hardware vendors such as Cisco, Compaq, Dell, Hewlett Packard, and others support WBEM in their products. Tivoli and Hewlett Packard support WBEM in their management platforms. Microsoft Windows 2000 includes a CIM object manager called WMI (Windows Management Instrumentation).

WBEM and CIM are closely aligned with the DMTF's DEN (Directory Enabled Networks) specification, which defines a repository for storing information about all sorts of network entities, including user accounts, applications, network devices, and more. The idea is to store management information in a central database that is accessible throughout the network and can be used to associate users with applications and system resource usage for the purpose of policy-based management.

CIM (Common Information Model)

CIM specifies how management information about logical and physical objects on a managed network is stored in management information databases. CIM attempts to provide a consistent and unified view of information so that it can be retrieved by any CIM-compliant network management systems.

CIM consists of a *specification* and a *schema*. The DMTF describes the specification as the language, naming, meta schema, and mapping techniques to other management models such as SNMP MIBs and DMTF MIFs.

The schema is a formal definition of the model. It defines the terms used to express the model and their usage and semantics. Object-oriented constructs are used to describe managed

W

objects. The elements of the schema are classes, properties, and methods. The schema supplies a set of classes with properties and associations that provide a well-understood conceptual framework within which it is possible to organize the available information about the managed environment. There are three levels of object classes:

- **Core schema** Describes classes of managed objects that are applicable to all areas of management.

- **Common schema** An extension of the core model that describes specific classes of managed objects that are common to particular management areas but independent of a particular technology or implementation. The common areas are systems, applications, databases, networks, and devices.

- **Extension schemas** An extension of the common schema that applies to *general environments* such as operating systems or *specific environments* such as Microsoft Windows 2000 operating systems. The general schemas are approved, registered, and released by the DMTF. The specific schemas are merely registered with the DMTF by the vendors or groups that develop them.

CIM will be implemented in two major areas. The first is called "agent to manager flow," in which management information flows from desktops and server. The second is called "manager to manager," which describes management information between elements of a truly distributed management system.

Related Entries CIM (Common Information Model); DEN (Directory Enabled Networks); DMI (Distributed Management Interface); DMTF (Distributed Management Task Force); Network Management; Policy-Based Management; RMON (Remote Monitoring); SNMP (Simple Network Management Protocol); Web Technologies and Concepts; *and* XML (Extensible Markup Language)

Linktionary!—Tom Sheldon's Encyclopedia of Networking updates	http://www.linktionary.com/w/wbem.html
DMTF (Distributed Management Task Force)	http://www.dmtf.org
DMTF's WBEM FAQ	http://www.dmtf.org/pres/rele/faq.html
DMTF's CIM FAQ	http://www.dmtf.org/spec/cimfaq.html
Joe Lindsay's Web Based Management page (very extensive)	http://joe.lindsay.net/webbased.html
Web-Based Management page at POSTECH	http://amazon.postech.ac.kr/wbm/
Network Management links at ITPRC.com	http://www.itprc.com/nms.htm

WCCP (Web Cache Communication Protocol)

WCCP is a Web-caching protocol developed by Cisco. The protocol specifies interactions between one or more routers and one or more Web caches. The purpose of the interaction is to establish and maintain the transparent redirection of selected types of traffic flowing through a group of routers. The selected traffic is redirected to a group of Web caches with the aim of optimizing resource usage and lowering response times. See "Web Caching."

WCS (Wireless Communications Service)

Wireless Communications Service is defined by the Federal Communications Commission as radio communications that may provide fixed, mobile, radio location, or satellite communication services to individuals and businesses within their assigned spectrum block and geographical area. The WCS is capable of providing more advanced wireless phone services that would be able to pinpoint a subscriber in any given locale. The WCS will most likely be used to provide a variety of mobile services, including an entire family of new communication devices utilizing very small, lightweight, multifunction portable phones and advanced devices with two-way data capabilities. WCS systems will be able to communicate with other telephone networks as well as with personal digital assistants, allowing subscribers to send and receive data and/or video messages without connection to a wire.

The WCS is in the 2.3-GHz band of the electromagnetic spectrum from 2,305 to 2,320 MHz and 2,345 to 2,360 MHz. The FCC's auction of WCS licenses help kick off an entirely new industry. Competition in the WCS industry will benefit consumers and businesses. The FCC's licensing plan for this spectrum provides for several new full-service providers of wireless service in each market. Consumers will be able to choose from multiple providers and will receive lower prices and better service as a result.

Related Entries   Electromagnetic Spectrum; Microwave Communications; Mobile Computing; Satellite Communication Systems; WAP (Wireless Application Protocol); Wireless Broadband Access Technologies; Wireless Communications; *and* Wireless Mobile Communications

 FCC WCS Web Site   http://www.fcc.gov/wtb/wcs/wcsfctsh.html

WDM (Wavelength Division Multiplexing)

WDM is an FDM (frequency division multiplexing) technique for fiber-optic cable in which multiple optical signal channels are carried across a single strand of fiber at different wavelengths of light. These channels are also called *lambda circuits*. Think of each wavelength as a different color of light in the infrared range that can carry data.

A fiber-optic cable guides light from end to end. A signal is injected in one end by an LED (light-emitting diode) or by semiconductor lasers. Lasers for silica-based fiber-optic cables produce light in a range called a "window." These windows occupy the near infrared range at wavelengths of 850 nm (nanometer or billionths of a meter), 1,320 nm, 1,400 nm, 1,550 nm, and 1,620 nm. For example, you may see a system described as a 1,550-nm system. Optical multiplexers divide the window into many individual lambdas. Figure W-1 illustrates the output of a 16-channel WDM system operating in the 1,530- to 1,565-nm range. Each lambda circuit is capable of transmitting 2.5 Gbits/sec for a total of 40 Gbits/sec.

As mentioned, optical systems are discussed in terms of their wavelengths (in nanometers). For comparison, red blood corpuscles are about the same size as the wavelengths in the infrared range. A wavelength of 1,550 nm has a frequency of 194,000 GHz (194,000 billion cycles/sec). The frequency increases as the wavelength is shortened. A decrease of only 1 nm increases the frequency by 133 GHz. This is used to advantage by Avanex in its PowerMux optical multiplexer. The PowerMux can put over 800 channels on a single fiber. It separates

W

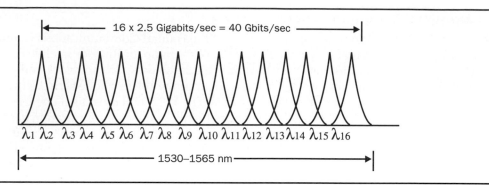

Figure W-1. *16-channel DWDM system*

channels by 12.5 GHz or 0.1 nm. The Avanex Web site (http://www.avanex.com) provides some interesting information about optical systems.

WDM is employed by carriers such as MCI to boost the data rates of their networks dramatically. MCI incorporated Quad WDM (four-wavelength WDM) in its backbone several years ago, instantly quadrupling its network capacity. The backbone operated at 2.5 Gbits/sec before Quad-WDM and at 10 Gbits/sec after installing Quad-WDM multiplexer devices. Since then, MCI has been upgrading to higher-capacity systems.

There are three categories of wavelength division multiplexing:

- **WDM (wavelength division multiplexing)** Two to four wavelengths per fiber. The original WDM systems were dual-channel 1310/1550 nm systems.

- **CWDM (coarse wavelength division multiplexing)** From four to 8 wavelengths per fiber, sometimes more. Designed for short to medium-haul networks (regional and metropolitan area).

- **DWDM (dense wavelength division multiplexing)** A typical DWDM system supports eight or more wavelengths. Emerging systems support hundreds of wavelengths.

The spacing between wavelengths in CWDM is about 10 to 20 nm, while the spacing in DWDM is about 1 to 2 nm. Due to the tight spacing and number of lasers, DWDM systems require elaborate cooling systems. Also, precision light sources and complex optical multiplexers are required to ensure that channels do not interfere with one another. In contrast, CWDM systems are simple and easy to manufacture, and cost much less than DWDM systems. They are also smaller. A CWDM device can be held in your hand, while a DWDM device is a large box that requires rack mounting.

The development of EDFAs (erbium-doped fiber amplifiers) provided a boost in cable distance and capacity for fiber-optic networks. EDFAs can amplify optical signals directly by injecting light into the cable via a light pump. Weak signals enter the amplifier and stimulate excited erbium atoms in the erbium-doped fiber to emit more light, thus preserving the original signal and boosting its output signal. Best of all, EDFAs can simultaneously boost the signals of multiple wavelengths in the same cable. EDFAs work in the 1,500- to 1,600-nm range, so a typical DWDM system has a range of lambda circuits operating in this range.

Prior to the development of EDFAs, *optoelectronic amplifiers* were used to boost optical signals. The process is often called "3R" regeneration, referring to reamplify, regenerate, and retime. Weak incoming light is converted to a voltage signal, amplified, and then converted back to light. This is impractical in high-speed core networks.

With the potential of hundreds of lambdas per fiber, it is practical for carriers to lease entire optical circuits to businesses. For example, a television network could lease lambda circuits to transmit video signals among media centers and stations. Recently, MPLS (Multiprotocol Label Switching) has been considered an ideal protocol for controlling optical switches in DWDM networks. It already controls LSPs (label switched paths) across routed networks and can also be used to control optical paths. This topic continues under "Optical Networks."

Related Entries   Backbone Networks; Cable and Wireless; Circuit; Electromagnetic Spectrum; Fiber-Optic Cable; Infrared Technologies; Lambda Circuits; MPLS (Multiprotocol Label Switching); Multiplexing and Multiplexers; Network Concepts; Network Design and Construction; OC (Optical Carrier); Optical Networks; *and* SONET (Synchronous Optical Network)

Linktionary!—Tom Sheldon's Encyclopedia of Networking updates	http://www.linktionary.com/w/wdm.html
OIF (Optical Internetworking Forum)	http://www.oiforum.com/
Optics.org, photonic resources for scientists and engineers	http://www.optics.org/
OSA (Optical Society of America)	http://www.osa.org/
SPIE (International Society of Optical Engineers)	http://www.spie.org/
AON (All-Optical Networking Consortium)	http://www.ll.mit.edu/aon/
NTONC (National Transparent Optical Network Consortium)	http://www.ntonc.org/
MONET (Multiwavelength Optical Networking Consortium)	http://www.bell-labs.com/project/MONET/
Avanex Web site	http://www.avanex.com/
Photonic Resources on the Web (sponsored by Avanex)	http://www.photonicresources.com/
Light Reading (an excellent site!)	http://www.lightreading.com/
Lightwave Magazine online	http://lw.pennnet.com/
Photonics Online	http://www.photonicsonline.com
Fiber-optic Product News Online	http://www.fpnmag.com/
Web ProForum's DWDM Tutorial	http://www.iec.org/tutorials/dwdm/
WDM Technology (also look for WDM link in this tutorial)	http://www.telcite.fr/nwdmen.htm
Converge! Network Digest Optical Networking article archive	http://www.convergedigest.com/DWDM.htm

W

Web

The *World Wide Web* is often referred to as simply "the Web." Refer to "Web Technologies and Concepts" for more information. Note that the Web is an overlay hyperlinking technology that runs on top of the Internet. Also see "Internet."

Web3D

Web3D is often called virtual reality modeling. It provides a way to deliver interactive 3D objects and artificial worlds across the Internet. An example would be a virtual tour of a house that is for sale in another city. You use a virtual reality–enabled browser to "walk" through the house, pointing left, right, forward, and so on. The Web3D Consortium describes Web3D as follows:

> Web3D blends the intuitive human sense of space and time with user interface interaction and programming language integration producing a truly new and exciting technology for the Internet. The evolution of the Net from command-line to 2D graphical to emergent 3D interfaces reflects ongoing, fundamental progress toward human-centered interface design—that is, toward a more immersive and responsive computer-mediated experience.

Open languages for programming and delivery Web3D include VRML (Virtual Reality Modeling Language), Java3D, and X3D.

VRML provides an interface that delivers virtual graphical three-dimensional worlds to users of Web browsers without consuming an exorbitant amount of bandwidth. VRML is based on an ASCII file format and three-dimensional modeling environments originally developed at Silicon Graphics. The key to VRML is that the descriptions of objects in the three-dimensional world (not the actual graphics) are transmitted to the user. This reduces the bandwidth requirements and makes virtual reality practical on the Web. Another key feature is scaling, which allows the user to move toward an object and watch that object grow in size. VRML provides information that describes an object, no matter what distance the viewer takes.

Although VRML is a coding language, you won't need to do much coding to create virtual worlds. Instead, you create virtual worlds using tools that are essentially three-dimensional painting and modeling packages. VRML files have the extension .wrl (world) and their own MIME type.

Related Entry   Web Technologies and Concepts

Web 3D Consortium	http://www.web3d.org/
VRML at Web Developer's Virtual Library	http://www.stars.com/Authoring/VRML/
About.com Web3D page	http://3dgraphics.about.com/

Web Appliance

See Embedded Systems; Network Appliances; *and* Thin Clients.

Web-Based Network Management

See WBEM (Web-Based Enterprise Management).

Web Caching

The purpose of caching is to reduce latency and network traffic. Caching has been used for local storage since nearly the dawn of computers. Recently accessed information is stored in a cache buffer in case the user needs to access it again. If so, the data is pulled from the cache rather than the slower hard drive. Thus, latency is reduced.

On the Web, latency and traffic are reduced if previously accessed information can be obtained from a local or nearby cache server rather than from the Web server that originated the requested information (called the "origin" server). The information may be stored on the user's local computer, a special caching server within the enterprise, or a caching server geographically closer to the enterprise, usually at a nearby Internet service provider. The caching hierarchy is outlined below and pictured in Figure W-2.

- **Local Web browser caching** (Figure W-2a)   Web page objects and information are stored on a user's hard drive during a first visit to an origin server. The next time the user requests the Web page, the cached information is used if it is still in the cache. A typical client cache has a limited size and removes the oldest information as new information arrives. RFC 2616 (Hypertext Transfer Protocol — HTTP/1.1, June 1999) provides full details on how caching is implemented on the Web and, in particular, in Web browsers.

- **Proxy server caching** (Figure W-2b)   A proxy server is a device that sits at the edge of an enterprise network, usually as a *firewall*. Inside is a *proxy cache* that stores often-accessed information for users inside the firewall. Proxy caches are shared caches. They are discussed further later in this topic.

- **Reverse proxy cache** (Figure W-2c)   A reverse proxy cache is placed near the origin servers, rather than near clients. They may service one or more servers, caching recently requested information so that it is more readily available to clients. Reverse proxy caches are often called *server accelerators* and provide a form of load balancing. The servers that are serviced by reverse proxies are usually configured as a virtual domain with a single physical site address. A relatively new trend is to distribute the accelerators out to service providers, as discussed next. CacheFlow (http://www.cacheflow.com/) produces server accelerator products.

- **Distributed content servers** (Figure W-2d)   A reverse proxy server does not need to be physically near the servers it caches. They can be located at sites that are physically closer to users, such as Internet service provider data centers throughout the world. This is called *content distribution* and a number of companies, including Akamai, Inktomi, and Digital Island, specialize in content distribution systems and software. Typically, these companies arrange to install special caching servers at service provider sites throughout the world, then contract with Web site operators to cache their content on the caching servers. A major feature is that Web servers keep track of where content is cached and "push" updates out to the cache sites to ensure freshness. See "Content Distribution."

Storing Web page objects on local hard drives provides the best service for users, but is limited in a number of ways. Space is limited, and users may not always open the same page twice. The most important feature is its ability to quickly restore a recently viewed page (such

W

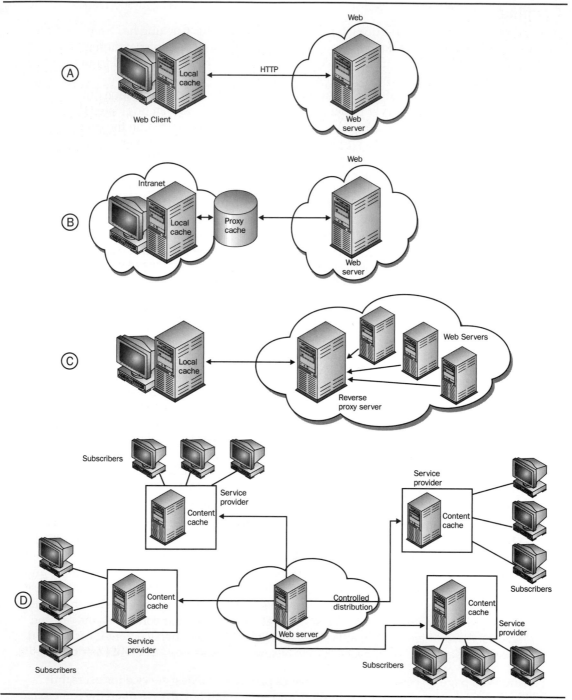

Figure W-2. *Proxy server and proxy caching*

as when a user clicks the Back button in the same general session). A proxy cache is a shared cache that can service many inside users from a centrally managed location. It can also reduce the traffic crossing the Internet access link.

An important goal of any Web-caching scheme is to reduce latency, which improves the quality of service for users. The best way to do this on the Web is to reduce the number of router hops that data must cross to get to the user. Early on, mirror sites were used to store information closer to users. For example, a popular site on the East Coast would be mirrored (replicated) to a server on the West Coast to make it more available to West Coast users. However, users often had to choose a server that was close to them manually. Today, companies like Akamai and Inktomi are providing much better solutions with their content distribution solutions.

Freshness and Staleness

Cache effectiveness is measured in terms of "hit rates," which is the ratio of requests that are satisfied from the cache. The higher the rate the better, but high rates may indicate that some information in the cache is stale. Common hits rates are about 40 percent to 50 percent for Web traffic

A major concern with any type of caching is making sure that data in the cache stays fresh. The caching system can use several techniques to provide freshness:

- Automatically update the cache during nonbusy periods or at timed intervals.

- Monitor expiration dates in Web objects. When the date expires, a device retrieves a new copy from the origin server.

- Request that an object be sent only if it has been modified; otherwise, the current cache object is used.

- Use logs to track objects and monitor their freshness.

- Use heuristic techniques to evaluate header values (such as the last-modified time) and estimate a plausible expiration time.

- Maintain a software relationship with the Web site and allow the Web site to push new and updated objects into the cache.

As mentioned, RFC 2616 provides details on the mechanisms used to manage caches. In particular, see sections 13 and 14 in the RFC. Some objects are never cached, such as secure information and encrypted information. In addition, some objects may be marked in their headers as noncachable by the Web server to ensure that the object is always retrieved from the origin server.

HTTP 1.1 defines several headers for controlling how information is cached. The "Expires" header indicates the date an object expires. The date may be an absolute date or a time based on when the object was last accessed or modified on the server.

Another HTTP 1.1 header is "Cache-Control," which provides instructions to caches on how to handle Web pages. These are discussed in RFC 2616, but Mark Nottingham's caching

W

tutorial provides a more concise list along with useful information on how to control caches. The Web address is listed later.

Proxy Servers and Caches

A proxy server stands between an internal enterprise network and the Internet. It usually provides firewall services. Proxy caches exist inside proxy servers to store Web page information and objects for potentially hundreds or thousands of users on the inside of the proxy server. Any user request may be satisfied by information in the proxy cache.

Internal users never connect directly with external Web servers. Their Web browsers are configured to connect with the proxy server. All requests are sent to the proxy server and the proxy server forwards the requests to the origin servers on behalf of the user. A typical example is a user that requests to see the Dilbert comic of the day. The request is sent to the proxy server, the proxy server forwards the request to the Dilbert server. The comic is returned to the proxy server and placed in the proxy cache, then forwarded to the user. Subsequent user requests are satisfied from the proxy cache for the rest of the day. Next day, the process repeats for the new comic of the day.

Proxy caching has some problems. One is that requests to Web servers are made by the proxy server rather than the end user. This causes some problems when registration or monitoring is required. Another problem is that each Web browser must be configured to use a specific proxy server, although most browsers will attempt to automatically locate a proxy server.

A form of caching known as *transparent caching* does not require that browsers be configured for a specific proxy cache. HTTP requests are automatically intercepted and redirected to caching servers. Layer 4 switches that provide load balancing usually support transparent caching. See "Load Balancing."

Documents at the IETF Web Replication and Caching (wrec) Working Group Web site describe a variety of proxy server types and proxy relationships. There are origin and replica servers, and a master origin server replicates its content to replica servers. Clients may contact master or replica servers. A later section called "Interproxy Communication Protocols" describes the protocols, the proxies, and replicas use, to communicate.

Cache arrays consist of a group of proxy servers that are arranged in a tightly coupled mesh. Client requests are balanced across the mesh. *Network elements* such as layer 4 load-balancing switches can intercept client requests and forward those requests to specific proxies within the array. Protocols for these configurations are discussed under "Network Element Communication Protocols" later in this topic.

Caching proxy meshes are groups of loosely coupled devices that support communication between peer or parent devices. This description is drawn from the previously mentioned IETF Web site and is illustrated in Figure W-3: "An inbound request may be routed to one of a number of intermediate (caching) proxies based on a determination of whether that parent is better suited to resolving the request. For example, Cache Server C and Intermediate Caching Proxy B are peers of the Local Caching Proxy A, and may only be used when the resource requested by A already exists on either B or C. Intermediate Caching Proxies D & E are parents of A, and it is A's choice of which to use to resolve a particular request."

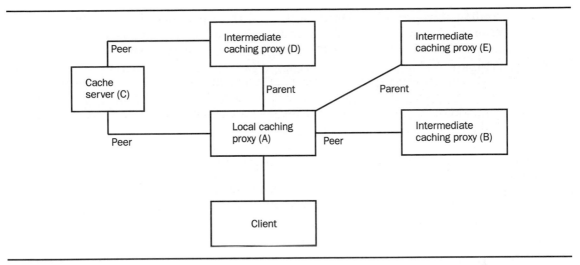

Figure W-3.   *A caching proxy mesh*

Interproxy Communication Protocols

The inter-proxy communication techniques discussed here are used for communication and cooperation between caching proxies. Note that these protocols are being developed by the IETF WREC Working group. Refer to the WREC Web site for update information as some were still under development at the time of this writing.

- **ICP (Internet Cache Protocol)**   ICP permits caches to be queried as to their content, usually by other caches that are hoping to avoid an expensive fetch from a distant origin server. When a proxy server does not have a requested object, it uses ICP to query other proxy servers to find the object. The queried proxy servers return either a HIT or MISS message. If a HIT message is received, the querying proxy server may then send an HTTP request to the responding proxy server. If all the queried proxy servers return a MISS, then the querying proxy server sends a request to the origin server (the server that holds the original content requested by the client). This protocol is discussed fully in RFC 2186 (Internet Cache Protocol version 2, September 1997) and in RFC 2187 (Application of Internet Cache Protocol, September 1997). There is an ICP home page at http://ircache.nlanr.net/Cache/ICP/.

- **HTCP (Hyper Text Caching Protocol)**   HTCP is a protocol for discovering HTTP caching proxies and cached data, managing sets of HTTP caching proxies, and monitoring cache activity. Unlike ICP, HTCP permits full request and response headers to be used in cache management, enabling HTCP replies to describe more accurately the behavior that would occur as a result of a subsequent HTTP request for the same resource. HTCP expands the domain of cache management to include monitoring a remote cache's additions and deletions, requesting immediate deletions,

W

and sending hints about Web objects such as the third-party locations of cachable objects or the measured uncachability or unavailability of Web objects. HTCP is described in RFC 2756 (Hyper Text Caching Protocol, January 2000).

- **Cache digest**   Designed to overcome latency and congestion problems associated with ICP and HTCP. Cache Digests support peering between caching proxies and cache servers without a request-response exchange taking place for each inbound request. Instead, a summary of the contents in cache (the digest) is fetched by other systems that peer with it. With cache digests, it is possible to determine with a relatively high degree of accuracy whether a given resource is cached by a particular system. Cache digests are described further at http://www.squid-cache.org/CacheDigest/.

- **Cache prefilling**   This is a push-caching technique that is well suited to IP-multicast networks because it allows preselected resources to be simultaneously inserted into caches within the targeted multicast group. Different implementations of cache prefilling already exist, especially in satellite contexts.

- **CARP (Cache Array Routing Protocol)**   CARP is a draft protocol that divides URL space among an array of proxies. Requests are intelligently routed to any member of the proxy array that is most likely to be able to handle a request.

A related protocol is SCSP (Server Cache Synchronization Protocol), which is designed to preserve cache information in a redundant server environment. SCSP is described in RFC 2334 (Server Cache Synchronization Protocol-SCSP, April 1998) as a protocol that attempts to solve the cache-synchronization/cache-replication problem, which occurs when a group of servers wishes to synchronize information in their caches about the state of clients being served. SCSP algorithms are described as being similar to those used in OSPF. The protocol works among of a group of servers that work together in synchronization with service clients, such as at a Web site or an enterprise server farm. The servers may also be geographically dispersed, with some being located at remote sites. See "SCSP (Server Cache Synchronization Protocol)"

Network Element Communication Protocols

The following protocols provide cooperation and communication between proxies and network elements such as layer 4 load-balancing switches. These devices generally intercept requests and hand them off to proxies and/or diffuse requests among an array of proxies. As mentioned, these protocols are being developed by the IETF wrec Working Group:

- **WCCP (Web Cache Control Protocol)**   This is currently a Cisco proprietary protocol. WCCP runs between a router functioning as a redirecting network element and proxies that intercept requests. The protocol allows one or more proxies to register with a single router to receive redirected traffic. It also allows one of the proxies, the designated proxy, to dictate to the router how redirected traffic is distributed across the array.

- **NECP (Network Element Control Protocol)**   NECP provides methods for network elements to learn about server capabilities, availability, and hints as to which flows can and cannot be serviced. This allows network elements to perform load balancing across a farm of servers, redirection to interception proxies, and cut-through of flows that cannot be served by the farm. This protocol was still under development at the time of this writing.

- **SOCKS**   SOCKS is a caching proxy to firewall protocol. Firewalls are an integral part of the network infrastructure and SOCKS provides an authenticated tunnel between the caching proxy and the firewall. See "SOCKS" for more information.

Content Distribution

Reverse proxy services have become increasingly important in content distribution schemes. Systems are installed at service provider locations where they are literally "next door" to users, as shown in Figure W-4d. Web pages from sites around the globe may be stored within two router hops of a user. This technique basically automates the mirroring of content from origin servers to distribution servers at service provider sites. The difference between this scheme and previous mirroring schemes is that distribution servers are everywhere on the Internet and special software is used to maintain freshness in the cache.

Distributed caching can relieve a server from sudden bursts of requests that may overwhelm it. By distributing its content to many servers throughout the Internet, a content provider can ensure that it does not become overwhelmed by surges in traffic that may occur following television ads or breaking news.

Delay-sensitive multimedia benefits from distributed caching. A video clip requested from a server that is one or two hops away will not be subject to queuing delays caused by excessive router hops. Storing large files such as video clips in caches near users cuts down on Web traffic.

IETF Working Groups and RFCs

The following IETF working groups are working on Web caching and related protocols. You'll find working drafts and RFCs listed at the Web sites.

Web Replication and Caching (wrec)	http://www.ietf.org/html.charters/wrec-charter.html
HyperText Transfer Protocol (http)	http://www.ietf.org/html.charters/http-charter.html

The previous sections mention RFCs that are relevant to caching. The following RFC provides additional information about caching and replication:

- RFC 2109 (HTTP State Management Mechanism, February 1997) describes HTTP's cookie mechanism. While not a form of caching as described here, Web servers use cookies to cache information about user sessions that can be used during subsequent visits to the site.

- RFC 2227 (Simple Hit-Metering and Usage-Limiting for HTTP, October 1997) describes a "Meter" header, which permits a limited form of demographic information (colloquially called "hit-counts") to be reported by caches to origin servers. It also permits an origin server to control the number of times a cache uses a cached response, and outlines a technique that origin servers can use to capture referral information without "cache-busting."

W

■ RFC 2608 (Service Location Protocol, Version 2, June 1999) describes a protocol that helps network clients to discover the available services on a network and learn information about the configuration of those services. SLP can be used to locate caches. See "SLP (Service Location Protocol)."

■ RFC 3040 (Internet Web Replication and Caching Taxonomy, January 2001) specifies standard terminology and the taxonomy of web replication and caching infrastructure with the goal of establishing a common understanding of the technology.

Related Entries   Cache and Caching Techniques; Clustering; Cookies; Content Distribution; Data Center Design; Gateway; Load Balancing; Mirroring; PoP (Point-of-Presence); Proxy Servers; Replication; SCSP (Server Cache Synchronization Protocol); Servers; SLP (Service Location Protocol); SOCKS; *and* Stateless and Call-Back Filing Systems

Linktionary!—Tom Sheldon's Encyclopedia of Networking updates	http://www.linktionary.com/w/webcaching.html
IETF Working Group: Caching and Replication (wrec)	http://www.ietf.org/html.charters/wrec-charter.html
Brian D. Davison's Web Caching and Content Delivery Resources	http://www.web-caching.com/
Caching.com Internet caching resource center	http://www.caching.com/
NLANR distributed test bed for national information provisioning	http://www.ircache.net/Cache/
NLANR Cache Recommended Reading list	http://ircache.nlanr.net/Cache/reading.html
Squid Web Proxy Cache	http://www.squid-cache.org/
Merit's Internet Web Cache Project	http://www.merit.edu/michnet/cache/
Cisco Document: Network Caching Technologies	http://www.cisco.com/univercd/cc/td/doc/cisintwk/ito_doc/net_cach.htm
Caching Tutorial for Web Authors and Webmasters by Mark Nottingham	http://www.stars.com/Internet/Cache/
The Cache Now! Campaign (good links list and other information)	http://vancouver-webpages.com/CacheNow/
Wojtek Sylwestrzak's W3Cache page with cache related links	http://w3cache.icm.edu.pl/links/
Ingrid Melve's Web Caching Architecture report	http://www.uninett.no/prosjekt/desire/arneberg/
Web Caching—An Introduction by Mark McCutcheon	http://www.cs.ubc.ca/spider/mjmccut/webcache.html
Microsoft Proxy Server	http://www.microsoft.com/proxy/

See "Content Distribution" for related Web links.

Webcasting

What is webcasting? To see a real working example, point your Web browser at eWeek's webcast site (http://www.eweek.com/webcast). You can choose from a list of news items and hear streaming audio and video presentations. A player is required, either RealPlayer from RealNetworks or Microsoft's Windows Media Player. Depending on the bandwidth available, you may see an actual moving image, rather than a series of changing still images. The audio is usually pretty good, though, and certainly beats reading text on the screen, and live interviews give you the emotion of the person speaking.

The technology behind webcasting is streaming audio and video. That means RTP (Real-time Transport Protocol) over UDP (User Datagram Protocol) in most cases. These technologies are outlined under "Multimedia" along with related technologies.

Webcasting is also called "netcasting," "Internet broadcasting," or "data broadcasting," although webcasting is more associated with streaming video and audio. Data broadcasting is more about sending news, stock quotes, and related information to subscribers using "push" techniques. Push is the opposite of "pull," which is what you do when you access Web site. With push, Web sites automatically send you information. E-mail is a push techniques that people use to send other people information, sometimes without the recipient asking for it. Think of push in terms of low-bandwidth data broadcasting (stocks, news, sports headlines). Think of webcasting as full multimedia broadcasting.

The ultimate webcasting technology is multicasting, which is based on special Internet protocols that deliver content along efficient paths from the sender to multiple receivers. The idea is to send packets only along paths that lead to subscribers of the multicast information, thus cutting down on traffic. See "Multicasting."

The webcasting community even has its own organization called the International Webcasting Association. Its Web site is given later. The IWA serves companies that are active in the delivery of multimedia (audio and video) services to consumers or business customers via the Net and other networks. Another association is DiMA (Digital Media Association).

One thing to keep in mind is the U.S. government's Digital Millennium Copyright Act. Special provisions were added for webcasting in 1998 that cover licensing of Internet radio stations, which is essentially audio webcasting. A good source for legal information on this type of webcasting is a set of articles by Sean Flinn at ZDNet Music. The Web site is given below.

Microsoft has done a lot of work to integrate webcasting into its Windows product line. It defines webcasting as a generic term that refers to any automated delivery of personalized and up-to-date information. Webcasting is made possible through the Windows Active Desktop and Active Channels. The Active Desktop provides a common and customizable user interface for organizing webcast sites and information. A typical Active Desktop might contain a weather chart that is updated constantly. Users subscribe to sites that support Active Desktop. Subscription and updates may be handled by CDF (Channel Definition Format), which provides a format that publishers can use to define elements such as media channels, types of information, schedules, and so on. This information helps users subscribe to and manage content.

Webcasting Sites and Services

One of the best examples of webcasting is Yahoo! Broadcast. Yahoo! purchased Broadcast.com to acquire the webcasting technology. The site can be accessed at http://www.broadcast.com/.

It is described as a place where businesses and content providers can deliver corporate communications messages via audio and video streaming. Applications include product launches, press conferences, e-learning, seminars, keynote addresses, annual shareholder meetings, quarterly earnings calls and corporate TV channels. Services include the following:

- Webcasting services such as live and on-demand audio and video broadcasting, pay-per-view broadcasting, secured broadcasting, and multicasting services

- A/V production services, such as live webcast engineering, audio/video production, and satellite connections

- Web and multimedia development, such as synchronized multimedia and front-end interface development (registration, polling, surveying, testing)

NetTalk Live is another webcasting company that combines webcasts with live events on television or radio. It refers to this simultaneous broadcasting as *triplecast*. Viewers watch programs on TV while using their Web browser to interact with the program.

Still another webcasting provider is CNET Networks' TV.com (simply type **tv.com** in your Web browser). The CNET site provides previews and cuts from movie and television shows, as well as its own webcasts.

Content distribution providers such as Akamai, Inktomi and Digital Island provide streaming services that enable Internet content providers and enterprises to host webcasts on their distributed caching networks worldwide. Akamai's network consists of caching servers located at service providers sites around the world. These sites host content "close" to users, which avoids running lengthy multimedia presentations over multiple hops on the Internet.

Microsoft is one of the best sources of information about webcasting technologies. Go to http://www.microsoft.com/windowsmedia/ to view extensive information about media content creation tools, editing tools, and services. Another good source of information is RealNetworks.com. For additional information about streaming multimedia, see "Multimedia."

Related Entries   Broadcasting on the Internet; Collaborative Computing; Content Distribution; Internet Radio; MP3; Multicasting; Multimedia; Newsfeed Services; NNTP (Network News Transport Protocol); Peer-to-Peer Communication; VBI (Vertical Blanking Interval); *and* Videoconferencing

Linktionary!—Tom Sheldon's Encyclopedia of Networking updates	http://www.linktionary.com/w/webcasting.html
International Webcasting Association	http://www.webcasters.org/
DiMA (Digital Media Association)	http://www.digmedia.org/
Interactive Multimedia & Collaborative Communications Alliance	http://www.imcca.org/
RealNetworks.com	http://www.realnetworks.com/
ZDNet Music site (software and tutorials for broadcasters)	http://music.zdnet.com/
Sean Flinn's articles about legal issues related to Webcasting including links to the Digital Millennium Copyright Act documents	http://music.gamespot.com/radiospy/articles/484.html
WavePhore Web site	http://www.wavo.com/

NetTalk Live	http://www.nettalklive.com/
Broadcast.com	http://www.broadcast.com/
Akamai Streaming Services	http://www.akamai.com/
Inktomi Corporation	http://www.inktomi.com/
Digital Island	http://www.digitalisland.net/
Data Channel Corp.	http://www.datachannel.com

WebDAV

The concept behind WebDAV (Web Distributed Authoring and Versioning) is to allow Web clients to remotely perform content authoring on Web content. The original desire was to support efficient and scalable remote editing free of overwriting conflicts by extending HTTP with tools that would allow remote loading, editing, and saving (publishing) of various media types. One goal was to support document management and groupware over the Internet by allowing groups of people to edit and publish documents on Web servers. Keep in mind that remote users do not normally have direct access to the operating systems and storage media functionality at server sites. WebDAV provides the publishing functionality.

In the mid-1990s, a number of extensions for authoring Web documents were independently developed by vendors and groups. In 1998, a group of authors got together to develop a requirements document for Web authoring. This turned into RFC 2291 (Requirements for a Distributed Authoring and Versioning Protocol for the World Wide Web, February 1998). Later, RFC 2518 (HTTP Extensions for Distributed Authoring – WEBDAV, February 1999) defined actual extensions to HTTP such as

- Create, remove, and query Web pages information (authors, creation dates, etc.)
- Create collections of documents and retrieve a listing of the documents (much like creating a folder in a file system)
- Lock documents to prevent more than one person from working on it at the same time
- Instruct servers to copy and move Web resources

The following illustrates the requests that WebDAV clients might execute in order to author a document on a WebDAV server. This diagram courtesy of WebDAV Working Group, UC Irvine.

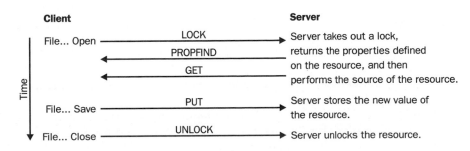

WebDAV information is encoded in either an XML (Extensible Markup Language) request or in an HTTP header. There are many advantages to using XML, not the least of which is the ability to encode characters in ISO 10646 characters sets that provide international support. Another advantage is the ability to add extra XML element to existing structures.

The IETF WWW Distributed Authoring and Versioning (webdav) Working Group has continued to develop WebDAV and has defined a need for other capabilities such as remote management of access permissions on Web resource, the development of a property registry, and other features described at the IETF WebDAV site. The Web address is given below.

The WebDAV Working Group initially had a goal of supporting remote versioning operations, but because of a large scope, a new working group was formed called Web Versioning and Configuration Management (deltav). See the Web address below.

Yet another IETF working group called DAV Searching and Locating (dasl) was formed to define and develop an extensible DAV searching and locating protocol as an application of HTTP. The working group will define protocol elements that enable server-executed queries to locate resources based upon their property values and text content as expressed by the DAV data model.

Related Entries   Collaborative Computing; Document Management; Hypermedia and Hypertext; HTML (HyperText Markup Language); *and* Web Technologies and Concepts

Linktionary!—Tom Sheldon's Encyclopedia of Networking updates	http://www.linktionary.com/w/webdav.html
IETF Working Group: WWW Distributed Authoring and Versioning (webdav)	http://www.ietf.org/html.charters/webdav-charter.html
IETF Working Group: Web Versioning and Configuration Management (deltav)	http://www.ietf.org/html.charters/deltav-charter.html
WebDAV home page	http://www.ics.uci.edu/pub/ietf/webdav/
WebDAV Resources	http://www.webdav.org/

Webmaster

A Webmaster is the administrator/manager of a Web site. Period. However, Webmasters wear many hats. The best description I have seen of a Webmaster was developed by Candis Harrison, Department of Housing and Urban Development, as a description of a webmaster position. The following is a synopsis. See the full description at http://www.itmweb.com/essay532.htm.

"The agency's webmaster manages the content of the agency's entire internet presence. The webmaster determines the management needs and requirements for the internet system. Specific duties include, but are not limited to, the following" (abbreviated list follows):

■ **Planning and management**   This includes promoting the Web site within the organization, developing strategic plans, developing policies for Internet presence, incorporating relevant laws and regulation, identifying opportunities, meeting with contacts to develop plans for the site, setting up meetings and training, and reporting on the status of the Web site to management.

- **Web site development**   Develop and articulate the overall focus and concept of the "home page" and related pages, including research, layout, editing, proofing, and link management. Also monitor chats and webmaster mail, as well as resolve technical problems.

- **Web site maintenance**   Fine-tune site pages based on feedback from users and monthly statistics. Also monitor links and other information for timeliness and accuracy.

- **Marketing/outreach**   Develop and implement marketing plan for home page, demonstrate the Web site to management and staff, provide public relations for the Web site, and represent the Web site at meetings and conferences.

Related Entries   Administrator Account; *and* Network Management

Linktionary!—Tom Sheldon's Encyclopedia of Networking updates	http://www.linktionary.com/w/webmaster.html
IWA (International Webmasters Association)	http://www.iwanet.org/
WOW (World Organization of Webmasters)	http://www.joinwow.org/
IAWMD (International Association of Web Masters and Designers)	http://www.iawmd.com/
AIP (Association of Internet Professionals)	http://www.association.org/
HTML Writers Guild	http://www.hwg.org/
Internet Research Group (see Webmaster Study papers)	http://www.irgintl.com/archive_wp.shtml
CIO Web Professional Research Center	http://www.cio.com/forums/careers/

WebNFS (Network File System)

WebNFS is Sun Microsystem's attempt to bring a file system to the Internet. It is based on the popular NFS (Network File System) that is the primary file system in UNIX and other environments. WebNFS makes file access across the Internet as easy as accessing files on local systems. It is specifically designed to handle the unique problems associated with accessing files across the Internet. It provides enhanced download performance and reliability through automatic error and crash recovery. If a connection is broken in the middle of a file download, the download continues when the connection is restored.

Perhaps the most important feature is that file systems at other locations on the Internet can appear to a user as a file system that is local. WebNFS works through firewalls and implements features such as read-ahead and write-behind to improve data access over the Internet. A file can be referenced with a URL format similar to the following:

    nfs://servername/directory/filename

Another important feature of WebNFS is that it can provide from five to ten times the performance of HTTP (Hypertext Transfer Protocol) when displaying graphics and animation.

W

This is because WebNFS is optimized to use bandwidth efficiently. In addition, files can be edited in place without being downloaded to the user's computer. Because the files are edited in place where other users access them, file integrity is maintained. With other systems, a user may download a file, edit it, and then copy it back—overwriting the original copy of the file, which may have just been changed by another user.

Like NFS, administrators specify which directories or files are to be exported. These are the files that will be available to network users, either on intranets or the Internet. WebNFS handles the task of locating these files, negotiating file access privileges, and locally mounting the files so users at remote locations can access them.

Sun is promoting WebNFS as the best file system for NCs (Network Computers), and for computers that have reduced local file systems and that rely on network-based file systems. Netscape Communications. Oracle, Spyglass, IBM, Apple Computer, and Novell support WebNFS in their product lines. The following Internet RFCs describe WebNFS further:

- RFC 2054 (WebNFS Client Specification, October 1996)
- RFC 2055 (WebNFS Server Specification, October 1996)
- RFC 2623 (NFS Security, RPCSEC_GSS, and Kerberos V5, June 1999)
- RFC 2755 (Security Negotiation for WebNFS, January 2000)

Another file system that has been refined for use on the Internet is Microsoft's CIFS (Common Internet File System), which is an enhanced version of Microsoft's SMB (Server Message Blocks) protocol, the native file sharing protocol for Windows.

Related Entries   CIFS (Common Internet File System); DFS (Distributed File System), Microsoft; Distributed Applications; Distributed Computer Networks; File Sharing; File Systems; File Transfer Protocols; Internet; NAS (Network Attached Storage); Network Operating Systems; NFS (Network File System); Stateless and Call-Back Filing Systems; Storage Systems; *and* Web Technologies and Concepts

Linktionary!—Tom Sheldon's Encyclopedia of Networking updates	http://www.linktionary.com/w/webnfs.html
IETF Working Group; Network File System Version 4 (nfsv4)	http://www.ietf.org/html.charters/nfsv4-charter.html
Sun Microsystems' WebNFS site	http://www.sun.com/webnfs
WebNFS Extensions, The Open Group	http://www.opengroup.org/onlinepubs/009629799/apdxe.htm
Network Appliance Tech Library (search for WebNFS)	http://www.netapp.com/tech_library/

Web Technologies and Concepts

The World Wide Web (or "Web") is a hypertext and hypermedia information system built on top of the Internet. Web clients and Web servers communicate via HTTP and exchange documents and information that is formatted with HTML and XML. The Web browser interface has made a world of information available to everyone. Hypermedia and hypertext is nonlinear information, presented to users in a way that lets them jump from one reference to another with the click of a button. This has created a global library of instantly available information.

On the application development side, distributed object computing technologies and Web-based languages such as Java have changed the way that applications are designed and developed. Wireless technologies are making the Web more available to people wherever they are. Bluetooth and wireless PANs (personal area networks) let people in the same vicinity create spontaneous wireless networks to exchange information. This is "edge-of-the-Internet" networking. Collaborative computing, messaging, groupware systems, unified messaging, instant messaging, videoconferencing and related technologies help people stay in touch and work together over long distances.

Web appliances, Webcasting, embedded systems, and voice telephony, along with improved bandwidth and many other new technologies are making the Web more exciting. Refer to the following topics for more information.

Basic Web Technologies, Web Appliances, Web Devices   Browsers, Web; Client/Server Computing; Collaborative Computing; Content Distribution; Distributed Computer Networks; Embedded Systems; HTML (Hypertext Markup Language); HTTP (Hypertext Transfer Protocol); Java; Microsoft.NET; Network Appliances; Servers; Terminal Services; Thin Clients; *and* Web Caching

Collaboration, Multimedia, Communications   Collaborative Computing; Electronic Mail; Groupware; Instant Messaging; Internet Radio; IRC (Internet Relay Chat); Multicasting; Multimedia; Unified Messaging; Videoconferencing; Voice over IP (VoIP); Web3D; Webcasting; WebDAV; WebTV Networks; Workflow Management; *and* XML (Extensible Markup Language)

File Sharing, Content Distribution, Electronic Commerce   CIFS (Common Internet File System); Electronic Commerce; File Sharing; File Systems; Handle System; Peer-to-Peer Communication; Search and Discovery Services; Service Advertising and Discovery; URI (Uniform Resource Identifier); URN (Uniform Resource Name); *and* WebNFS (Network File System)

Web Security   Certificates and Certification Systems; Cryptography; Digital Signatures; Electronic Commerce; Hash Functions; PKI (Public-Key Infrastructure); Public-Key Cryptography; Security; SET (Secure Electronic Transaction); S-HTTP (Secure Hypertext Transfer Protocol); SSL (Secure Sockets Layer); TLS (Transport Layer Security); VPN (Virtual Private Network); *and* X.509 Certificates

Web Development   ActiveX; COM (Component Object Model); Content Distribution; Distributed Applications; Distributed Computer Networks; Distributed Object Computing; Java; Microsoft.NET; Middleware and Messaging; Multitiered Architecture; Object Technologies; ORB (Object Request Broker); RPCs (Remote Procedure Calls); SOAP (Simple Object Access Protocol), Transaction Processing; Web3D; Web Caching; WebDAV; *and* XML (Extensible Markup Language)

W

Wireless and Mobile Computing   Bluetooth; Home Networking; Infrared Technologies; Mobile Computing; Packet-Radio Data Networks; SMR (Specialized Mobile Radio); SMS (Short Messaging Service); WAP (Wireless Application Protocol); Wireless Communications; Wireless LANs; Wireless Mobile Computing; *and* Wireless PANs (Personal Area Networks)

Related Entries   IEEE 802 Standards; Internet; Internet Architecture and Backbone; Internet Organizations and Committees; Internet Protocol Suite; Internet Standards; IP (Internet Protocol); ISO (International Organization for Standardization); ITU (International Telecommunications Union); OSI (Open Systems Interconnection) Model; Standards Groups, Associations, and Organizations; *and* W3C (World Wide Web Consortium)

Linktionary!—Tom Sheldon's   http://www.linktionary.com/w/web.html
Encyclopedia of Networking updates

WebTV Networks

WebTV is a Microsoft trademark for technology that joins television with the Internet. The term "WebTV" is often used incorrectly to describe any type of TV-based Web services. "WebTV Networks" is the proper use of the name.

According to the WebTV Networks site, WebTV gets you connected to the Web from your TV, allowing you to send e-mail, surf the Web, interact with game shows, participate in polls, chat with other viewers, program your VCR, search for TV listings, and participate in a variety of other interactive TV programming.

WebTV Networks Web   http://www.webtv.net

Ruel.Net Set-Top Page   http://ruel.net/top.box.news/

Yahoo! WebTV links   http://dir.yahoo.com/Computers_and_Internet/
                                  Hardware/Platforms/WebTV/

Whiteboard Applications

A whiteboard in the context of computer networking is part of a collaborative conferencing application that lets multiple users share a common text-based chat board or graphics board. Users can review, create, and update information on the whiteboard. Any changes are visible immediately to other viewers. Microsoft's Netmeeting Whiteboard is object-oriented (versus pixel-oriented), which allows participants to manipulate the contents by clicking and dragging with the mouse. In addition, they can use a remote pointer or highlighting tool to point out specific contents or sections of shared pages.

TeamWave Workplace by TeamWave Software has the usual whiteboard features, such as an interactive surface to draw on and to add text to, and the ability to edit the contents of the whiteboard. It also has the ability to store and retrieve its contents. A unique feature is a set of shared tools that can be placed directly on the whiteboard. Workplace supports an unlimited number of shared whiteboards by storing each whiteboard in its own room. Each room contains a shared whiteboard and its contents. Rooms are kept on a Workplace server and are available anytime from anywhere, and they are available to anyone with access to the server.

The ITU T.120 standards cover voice and still image conferencing facilities.

Related Entries Collaborative Computing; Groupware; Multimedia; T Series ITU Recommendations; *and* Videoconferencing

Linktionary!—Tom Sheldon's Encyclopedia of Networking updates	http://www.linktionary.com/c/collaborate.html
TeamWave Workplace by TeamWave Software	http://www.teamwave.com/
Internet Conferencing page at About.com (search for "whiteboard")	http://netconference.about.com/internet/ netconference/

White Pages Directory Services

See Search and Discovery Services

WHOIS ("Who Is")

WHOIS is an Internet service that returns information from a directory database. It is the earliest and simplest Internet directory service. WHOIS provides search and retrieval services. The protocol was originally used to access a central NICNAME database maintained by the NIC (Network Information Center). This database contained host and network information about the systems connected to the network and the e-mail addresses of system users. RFC 954 (NICNAME/WHOIS October 1985) discusses this early system. It allowed online lookup of individuals, network organizations, host machines, and other information. If you query for a domain name, the service returns an IP address matching that domain name. For more information, refer to the Lintionary! Web site listed here.

Related Entries Directory Services; DNS (Domain Name Service) and Internet Domains; Name Services; NIS (Network Information System); Search and Discovery Services; *and* Service Advertising and Discovery

Linktionary!—Tom Sheldon's Encyclopedia of Networking updates	http://www.linktionary.com/w/whois.html
Allwhois.com, "the most complete whois service on the Internet"	http://www.allwhois.com/
DaveCentral Finger/WHOIS Software Archive	http://www.davecentral.com/finger.html
WHOIS tutorial	http://www.webteacher.org/winnet/finding/ whois.html

W

Windows, Microsoft

All Windows operating system and related topics are listed under "Microsoft Windows" headings.

WINS (Windows Internet Naming Service)

WINS runs on Windows NT Server–based networks. It is a service that keeps a database of computer name-to-IP address mappings so that the NetBIOS computer names used in Windows network environments can be mapped to IP addresses when the underlying network is IP-based. When a user needs to access some computer, the NetBIOS name is referenced, and this name is handed to the nearest WINS server, which then returns an IP address. WINS is almost completely automatic from an administrative point of view. It builds its own database over time and automatically updates itself. WINS does for NetBIOS what DNS does for Internet names.

Related Entries   DHCP (Dynamic Host Configuration Protocol); Directory Services; DNS (Domain Name Service) and Internet Domains; Microsoft Windows; Name Services; NetBIOS/NetBEUI; Search and Discovery Services; *and* Service Advertising and Discovery

Microsoft Document: "Windows NT Server: Dynamic Host Configuration Protocol and Windows Internet Naming Service"	http://msdn.microsoft.com/library/backgrnd/html/msdn_dhcpwins.htm
Microsoft Document: "Windows Internet Naming Service (WINS): Architecture and Capacity Planning"	http://www.microsoft.com/ntserver/nts/techdetails/techspecs/WINSwp98/WINS01-12.asp
Microsoft Document: "Windows 2000 Server Windows Internet Naming Service (WINS) Overview"	http://www.microsoft.com/windows2000/library/howitworks/communications/nameadrmgmt/wins.asp
What is WINS? By CWRUnet Services	http://cnswww.cns.cwru.edu/net/how-to/general/WINS/what-is-WINS.html

WinSock

Sockets is an API (application programming interfaces) that applications use to access TCP/IP networking services. In the Windows environment, sockets is known as "Windows Sockets" or "WinSocks." Refer to "Sockets API" for information about this topic.

Wired for Management

Intel's WfM (Wired for Management) initiative seeks to raise the level of management capabilities for mobile, desktop, and server platforms. It complements Microsoft's ZAWS (Zero Administration for Windows) initiative, which helps administrators manage operating systems and applications. Together, WfM and ZAWS are designed to provide an environment for planning, deploying, and managing distributed computing environments.

According to Intel, WfM defines a baseline set of requirements for managing hardware, including requirements for instrumentation, remote wake-up, power management, and service boot capability. It enables centralized system management, including inventory, fix/repair, configuration, and diagnostics, and provides for off-hours maintenance to minimize downtime. WfM includes support for DMI, as described under "DMI (Distributed Management Interface)." WfM would allow a technician to diagnose and upgrade a remote system while the user of that system continues working on other tasks. It also allows software upgrades in the background or during scheduled hours.

Related Entries   Configuration Management; DMI (Distributed Management Interface); DMTF (Distributed Management Task Force); Network Management; *and* Zero Administration for Windows Initiative

Intel paper: "Building a Managed Computing Environment"	http://www.intel.com/network/white_papers/ managed_environment.htm

Wireless Broadband Access Technologies

Wireless broadband access technologies refers to high-speed wireless access services that businesses can use to build metropolitan area networks or gain Internet access. These wireless services take the place of traditional TDM circuits.

Wireless access systems are usually owned by a service provider that operates within a metropolitan areas. Services include Internet access for businesses, MTUs (multitenant units), and homes, as well as private LAN bridging in metro areas. The topic "Wireless LANs" covers enterprise wireless networking in which an enterprise owns and manages wireless systems used to interconnect its users and systems. Even shorter in range than wireless LANs are wireless PANs (personal area networks) that let nearby users create spontaneous networks. See "Bluetooth" and "Wireless PANs (Personal Area Networks)."

This topic is also about "fixed" wireless systems, as opposed to mobile wireless systems. The cellular telephone system, as covered under "Wireless Mobile Communications," allows users to move about, not only within the range of the local base station but to other cells within the same system and even to other service provider systems. The fixed wireless systems discussed here allow some mobility, but do not typically support the extended roaming features of mobile cellular systems.

Wireless broadband access systems have relatively high data rates and the target subscriber is often an entire enterprise rather than an individual subscriber. Broadband wireless systems can provide bandwidth that exceeds DSL and cable network technologies. Also, the traffic is data, although some of the fixed wireless systems use spectrum that was originally designated for one-way delivery of cable TV.

The IEEE 802.16 specifications are called IEEE 802.16 Wireless MAN, but the working group is called IEEE 802.16 Wireless BWA (Broadband Wireless Access). IEEE 802.16 is covered later. In addition, wireless broadband is called FWBA (fixed wireless broadband access) if the system does not support mobile users, but some systems do allow mobility within a small range of the base station.

The advantage of wireless systems is obvious: there is no need to install cable or rely on existing copper infrastructure that may be inadequate for various reasons. International Data Corporation has estimated that under 10 percent of the office buildings in the United States are reachable by fiber cable. Therefore, wireless access technologies should offer a large market opportunity.

W

Wireless Broadband Topologies

Wireless networks take on three topologies, as illustrated in Figure W-4. The topology used will depend on the applications, the size of the area, the frequency band used (higher frequencies have distance limitations), and the terrain of the area.

- **Point-to-point**   This is wireless direct dedicated connection in which two antennas are directly aligned with one another. A company may use this configuration to link two remote offices. The radio beam may be focused to avoid interference. The configuration usually can provide high bandwidth, especially if lasers, rather than radio waves, are used.

- **Point-to-multipoint**   This is the most common wireless broadband configuration. A base station transceiver transmits and receives radio signals (or optical signals) in all directions. Multiple users share the bandwidth via some form of multiplexing. In large systems, the configuration shown in Figure W-4 may form just one cell in a multicellular coverage area, with each base station linked via a metro fiber-optic cable system. To maximize the available bandwidth, a carrier may divide a coverage area into sectors (like four 90-degree-wide sectors). This allows frequency reuse. Note that in two-way systems, subscriber-to-base-station links are point-to-point.

- **Multipoint-to-multipoint mesh topology**   This is an emerging scheme that provides many benefits. Nokia is an advocate of this technique, and its RoofTop system is outlined later in the topic. The scheme involves placing wireless routers on the exterior of buildings in a topology that mimics the routed topology of the Internet. Client base stations wirelessly connect with one another to form a multipoint interconnected wireless mesh network with potentially multiple data paths. The more clients, the better the reach and coverage. Line-of-site problems inherent in point-to-multipoint systems are eliminated.

In all cases, wireless equipment can be easily moved from one location to another. For example, a company may move from one building to another in the same area. Alternatively, a wireless system might be used to build a temporary network for a conference or one-time event. Wireless systems also make excellent emergency communication systems where installing cables is not realistic in terms of time, cost, and deployment.

Broadband Wireless Frequency Allocations

Broadband wireless occupies the frequency bands from 2 to 42 GHz. The microwave band occupies the spectrum from 2 to 6.7 GHz, and the millimeter-wave band occupies the spectrum from 24 to 40 GHz. Much of this spectrum went unused until around 1993, when advances in digital technologies, including improved modulation techniques and compression algorithms, made it more practical to carry traffic over these short wavelengths.

Currently, some of the bands above 10 GHz are allocated to satellites, point-to-point microwave bridges, radar, and ham radio, but some of these are being reallocated for wireless access solutions.

U-NII (Unlicensed-National Information Infrastructure) specifies unlicensed wireless spectrum at 2.4 GHz and 5 GHz. Licensing is not required to use this spectum. Many products already use the spectrum, including cordless phones, garage door openers, and other devices.

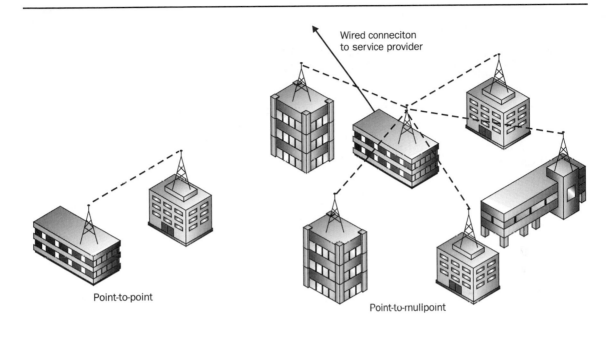

Wired conneciton
to service provider

Point-to-point

Point-to-mulipoint

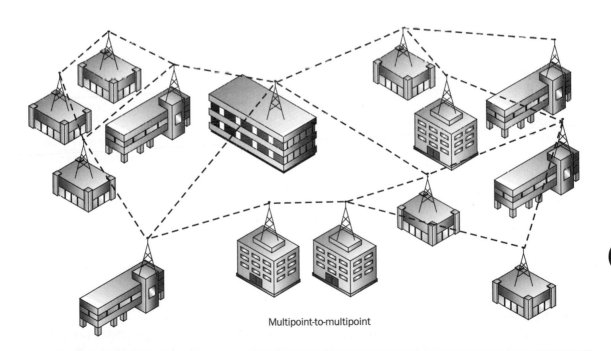

Multipoint-to-multipoint

Figure W-4.   *Wireless topologies (Concept: Nokia)*

In fact, the 2.4-GHz spectrum is so crowded that many companies are focusing on the 5-GHz spectrum and using antennas that are aligned with one another to avoid interference.

Common broadband wireless systems include WLL (wireless local loop) systems operating in the 3.5-GHz range (internationally), MMDS (Multichannel Multipoint Distribution Services) at 2.5–2.7 GHz and 3.4–3.7 GHz, and LMDS (Local Multipoint Distribution Services) at 24 GHz, 28 GHz, 31 GHz, and 38 GHz.

Some of the characteristics of transmitting in the various frequencies are outlined here:

- Higher frequencies support higher data rates, but the waves dissipate more easily over distance. Thus, the higher the frequency, the shorter the distance, so networks using higher frequencies are usually best for urban areas consisting of many smaller cells that reuse frequencies.

- Frequencies above 10 GHz require LOS (line-of-site) between the transmitter and receiver, which means that nonservice "holes" will exist within a service area due to buildings, trees, snow, and other factors. In some areas, only 50 to 60 percent coverage may be achieved. Ways to correct this are discussed later.

- Frequencies below 10 GHz are less restricted by LOS, but the data rates are lower due to lower frequencies.

- Some systems operating in the unlicensed 2.4-GHz band can provide data rates of 10 Mbits/sec, while systems in the 5-GHz band can provide data rates as high as 100 Mbits/sec.

- Rain, snow and fog interfere with signals, so systems in areas that experience these conditions require special engineering. For example, feedback systems can dynamically increase power during heavy rain.

Figure W-5 illustrates how higher frequencies are limited in distance. Note that point-to-point systems tend to have a longer distance than multipoint systems.

Wireless Access Technologies

Following is a list of wireless broadband access technologies. Some of are terrestrial and some are satellite based. Some operate in licensed spectrum, while others use the unlicensed spectrum. All provide fixed services, with some allowing limited mobility.

- **Point-to-point wireless bridges**   Many of the early wireless systems were basic point-to-point bridge systems that companies could use to connect different buildings or service providers could use to build mesh-type wireless metropolitan networks. Microwave and optical (laser) bridges are still popular. An advantage is that they are easy to set up and take down, which makes them useful for one-time events like conferences that take place in multiple buildings in a metro area. Some systems have data rates in Gbits/sec range.

- **Satellite communication systems**   Satellite systems can provide various types of wireless access, although the data rate of some systems barely falls into the category of broadband. LEOS (low earth orbit satellites) are best because there is less latency and

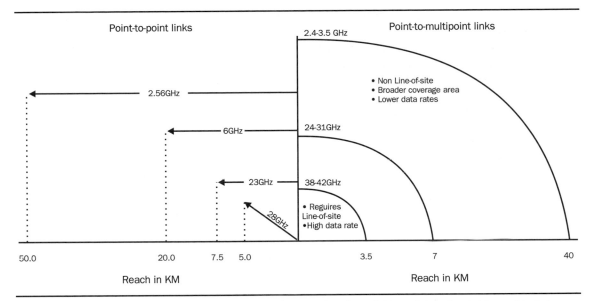

Figure W-5. *Transmission distances at various frequencies for point-to-point and point-to-multipoint systems. (Source: Abbas Masnavi, Cisco Systems)*

lower power requirements. Tachyon (http://www.tachyon.net/) has developed a system that delivers two-way TCP/IP over satellite links with forward channel data rates of 45 Mbits/sec and reverse channel data rates of 256 Kbits/sec. The system is designed for business Internet access, rather than home user.

■ **DBS (Direct Broadcast Satellite)**   DBS is a satellite based digital TV service that has proved to be a successful competitor to terrestrial-based cable TV. In fact, DBS hurt early MMDS operators who planned to develop wireless cable TV systems.

■ **HALOs (High Altitude Long Operation)**   Up in the sky but not quite in outer space is a flying/floating platform called a HALO. HALOs offer network access services by providing communication platforms flying in the stratosphere above cities. The platforms provide uplink and downlink transmissions much like satellites, except that they are closer to earth. The signal propagation times are shorter and the platforms stay over a particular area. HALOs are a good choice for Internet access. They provide data rates as high as 10 Mbits/sec. Two companies are involved in this business. Angel Technologies flies airplanes and uses LMDS 28-GHz spectrum, while the other, Skystation International flies unmanned helium-filled blimps and uses 47-GHz spectrum. See "HALOs (High Altitude Long Operation)."

■ **MMDS (Multichannel Multipoint Distribution Services)**   MMDS is a point-to-multipoint microwave technology that was originally designated for one-way transmission of wireless cable TV signals to rural areas. This market was hurt by DBS. In 1998, the FCC allowed two-way transmissions, which meant that MMDS could be used as a data service and access technology. MMDS bands are centered at 2.1 GHz and

2.6 GHz in the United States and 3.4–3.7 GHz in other countries. The range from the base station is 32 to 48 km (20 to 30 miles), so one or two base stations can cover a metro area. Typical downstream data rates to the subscriber are from 128 Kbits/sec to 3 Mbits/sec and may go as high as 10 Mbits/sec. See "MMDS (Multichannel Multipoint Distribution Services)."

■ **LMDS (Local Multipoint Distribution Services)**   LMDS defines a point-to-multipoint two-way wireless system that occupies various frequency ranges centered around 28 GHz, 29 GHz, and 31 GHz (in the United States). The original concept was developed by Bellcore as a wireless local loop system that could be used instead of laying copper twisted-pair telephone wire to homes in rural areas. In the U.S., it occupies approximately 1.15 GHz of bandwidth with downstream data rates of 1.5 Gbits/sec and upstream rates of 200 Mbits/sec. The range from the base station is about 5 to 8 km (3 to 5 miles), much smaller than MMDS. More antennas are required in metro areas, but the data rate is much higher than MMDS. See "LMDS (Local Multipoint Distribution Services)."

■ **Wireless mesh systems**   Wireless mesh systems are one of the three wireless topologies mentioned earlier. The best example is the Nokia RoofTop system, which is described in the next section.

■ **HDR (High Data Rate)**   HDR is a Qualcomm CDMA-based wireless IP packet data service that provides up to 2.4 Mbits/sec data transfer rate in a 1.25-MHz channel for use by stationary users. Mobile users experience a lower data rate. Qualcomm's CDMA air link technology is designed for data. The peak data rate is 2.4 Mbits/sec on the forward link and 307 Kbits/sec on the reverse link. Qualcomm designed HDR for data only rather than voice and data to avoid compromising the performance of the system. See "HDR (High Data Rate)."

■ **UWB (Ultra Wideband)**   UWB is based on a discovery by Larry Fullerton that single radio frequency (RF) monocycles could be transmitted through an antenna and by precisely positioning these monocycles in time, a matched receiver could recover the transmissions, thus opening up a whole new wireless medium. The technique does not rely on sine waves, does not require an assigned frequency, and transmits data on random low-powered signal that are indistinguishable from noise. Time Domain compares it to sending Morse Code at 40 million dots and dashes per second. The technology can potentially transmit at 1 Gbit/sec. UWB can interfere with other radio signals, so low power is used, but doing so limits the range. The Time Division Web site is at http:// www.timedomain.com/

The next two sections describe unique approaches to wireless metropolitan area networking. Service providers build these system to provide high data rates to customers.

Nokia RoofTop Wireless Mesh System

Nokia's wireless system implements the multipoint-to-multipoint mesh topology pictured in Figure W-4. It is easy to install, relatively cheap, and extremely practical. The system operates in frequency bands that do not require licensing, so installation is relatively painless. Data rates are equivalent to or better than DSL.

Nokia AIR Operating System was designed specifically to handle the unique attributes of outdoor, multihop, wireless networks. The operating system consists of a suite of IP and wireless networking protocols that extend the traditional TCP/IP stack to enable robust IP networking in wireless environments. The physical RF modem is extracted from the operating system layers so that a wide range of RF modems may be used, depending on the topology and local environment. The AIR Operating System consists of a channel access protocol that schedules transmissions to avoid collisions, a neighbor management protocol that monitors the status of neighbor links, a wireless routing protocol, and standard Internet protocols.

Additional protocols handle network security, network management, and automatic software updates across the mesh. The RoofTop wireless routers and bridges use frequency-hopping spread spectrum radios, which prevents eavesdropping. Transmissions in the multihop network are heard only by neighboring routers—not all the routers in the network.

While ISPs may choose to install RoofTop to reach customers, just about anyone with a rooftop, a ladder, and a set of tools can install the system. Each radio needs line-of-site to at least one other node, although multiple links improves the number of routes in the mesh and thus reliability. The network has been called "organic" because it grows from the customer side, not the service provider side. One downside is that each hop adds about 50 ms of latency, which can affect Voice over IP, although Nokia is tuning the system to reduce latency.

Free-Space Optical Networking

A number of companies are developing wireless optical solutions. Products from LightPointe (http://www.lightpointe.com/), for example, enable point-to-point transmissions among buildings up to 2.5 miles apart at data rates up to 622 Mbits/sec using wavelengths in the infrared spectrum. Systems operating in this range do not require licensing.

Even more interesting are point-to-multipoint free-space optical networks. The normal thinking is that light requires line-of-site between sender and receiver or it must be guided (fiber cable). Newer systems rely on the absorption and scattering of light, which in the past has been viewed as a bad thing because it causes signal loss. In such systems, the signal can be pictured as a bright light in fog, where the fog becomes a luminous cloud in the band where the light is absorbed (infrared or ultraviolet).

A wireless optical system designed to operate in this same absorption band will be able to propagate signals between sender and receiver without line-of-site requirements and in environments where there are obstructions such as metro areas with tall buildings. Receiver devices are simply placed in windows.

Two companies produce multipoint free-space optical networking equipment: AirFiber (http://www.airfiber.com/) and TeraBeam (http://www.terabeam.com/). AirFiber's product is actually a mesh network design that is deployed across building rooftops in a metro environment and supports data rates of up to 622 Mbits/sec. TeraBeam has developed a point-to-multipoint system in which users share bandwidth of up to 100 Mbits/sec, with bursting to higher rates possible.

W

Characteristics of Broadband Wireless

LMDS and MMDS advocates point out that broadband wireless can provide better service to more users than DSL. However, higher-frequency services such as LMDS require line-of-site, which reduces coverage area extensively. LOS (line-of-site) is affected by buildings, trees, and even snow. Repeaters and reflecting devices can be used to solve some LOS problems. MMDS provides better coverage than LMDS. While it offers lower data rates, those rates are suited to the home users and small business subscribers in an MMDS coverage area.

Microwave systems suffer from signal reflections in which the primary signal is received with the addition of echo signals that have bounced off nearby objects. This combination of primary and echo signals is called *multipath*. The echo signal is received slightly later than the primary signal and can corrupt digital data.

Multipath problems and solutions are discussed under "Microwave Communications" and "OFDM (Orthogonal Frequency Division Multiplexing)."

Air Interfaces

The air interface for broadband wireless systems has lacked any kind of standards agreement, so a number of proprietary implementations are in use today. However, numerous proposals have been made to the IEEE and other groups. Of these, the following two proposals have gained the most attention. The IEEE Web site listed at the end of this topic provides the most up-to-date information.

DVB Downstream/DOCSIS Upstream

This proposal is based on established television broadcast models. The ETSI DVB (Digital Video Broadcast) is a standard that defines satellite broadcasting in the downstream channel, while DOCSIS (Data Over Cable Service Interface Specification) is a standard used on the upstream channel in cable modems. The idea is to use FDD (frequency division duplexing) in the physical layer and transmit upstream and downstream information on separate frequencies.

DOCSIS and DVB are recommended because the technology already exists and systems could be deployed quickly. However, modifications are necessary to improve latency and interference immunity, as well as to increase the capacity of the referenced standards. These techniques enable the bidirectional delivery of ATM and IP traffic, as well as the distribution of MPEG-2 video from the base station to the subscriber.

TDD (Time Division Duplexing)

The DVB/DOCSIS approach uses FDD, which requires one frequency band for receiving and another for transmitting. TDD uses one channel for both transmitting and receiving. This is accomplished by creating time slots that toggle back and forth between upstream and downstream traffic.

The following illustration shows the difference between FDD and TDD. With FDD, bandwidth is allocated to downstream and upstream traffic in two dedicated frequency bands. Even if data is not being sent, the band is still allocated. In TDD, the downstream and upstream traffic is "toggled" on the same channel. Systems can dynamically allocate more bandwidth to downstream traffic if necessary, making very efficient use of available bandwidth.

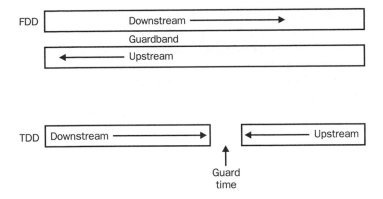

TDD uses bandwidth efficiently because separation of the upstream and downstream channels is done with time spacing, rather than inserting a large guard band between channels. Both the uplink and the downlink use the same frequency, but at different time intervals. Most important, TDD is perfect for carrying data traffic because it can adjust the upstream or downstream bandwidth to match traffic. FDD was designed for voice, which requires symmetric channels. TDD allows asymmetry, which is suited to data. For example, in a burst of data (file transfer) a full upstream channel can be dynamically allocated.

The primary advocate of this model is Ensemble Communications, which points out that its TDD approach, called Adaptix, was developed from the ground up to address point-to-multipoint broadband wireless applications. Ensemble's Adaptix is a proposed standard that is backed by Nokia, Breczecom, 3Com, Siemens, and others.

Ensemble likes to point out that wireless point-to-multipoint networking should not be treated like television broadcasting (as is done with the DVB/DOCSIS model), because such broadcasting treats all customers the same. Adaptix uses several adaptive techniques that can provide individual customers with a service level that meets their needs. For example, the modulation techniques can be dynamically adjusted to accommodate instantaneous changes that affect transmissions, such as changing weather conditions. Another element of Adaptix, Adaptive TDMA, enables the allocation of bandwidth burst by burst to multiple users at multiple locations on demand, all over a single channel.

Wireless Standards and Initiatives

The IEEE wireless initiatives are also referred to as IEEE 802.16 Wireless MAN (metropolitan area network). The mission of Working Group 802.16 is "to develop standards and recommended practices to support the development and deployment of fixed broadband wireless access systems." Initially, the group focused on LMDS bands.

More recently, the group has been looking at MMDS bands and at the U-NII unlicensed bands at 5 GHz. Directional dish antennas are proposed to avoid interference in the band, which is used freely by any number of devices. The group is also working on receivers with

W

multiple antennas and signal-processing components that can help reduce multipath reflections and other interference problems.

A related standard is HiperLAN (Higher-Performance Radio LAN), which is defined by ETSI (European Telecommunications Standards Institute). HiperLAN1 operates at 5.2 GHz, with data rates as high as 24 Mbits/sec. It uses spread spectrum technology. The standard was developed during the 1991–1996 time frame. HiperLAN2 should be complete by the time you read this. It is basically wireless ATM that can provide QoS at greater than 20 Mbits/sec. HiperAccess is an LMDS-like standard. See "Wireless LANs."

The Wireless DSL Consortium is an association of companies including ADC Telecommunications, Nortel Networks, Intel, Conexant Systems, and others that is developing a point-to-multipoint broadband wireless access solution with a physical layer based on TDMA/FDD (time division multiple access/frequency division duplexing). The consortium is developing voice and data services, QoS controls, wireless coverage in non line-of-site areas, and low-cost customer equipment.

N-WEST (National Wireless Electronic Systems Testbed) is a U.S. Department of Commerce project that promotes broadband wireless technologies, particularly LMDS. N-WEST includes test bed facilities equipped with prototype LMDS systems that will be used to develop operational standards and performance assessment. The N-WEST Web site is at http://nwest.nist.gov/.

Related Entries   CDMA (Code Division Multiple Access); Electromagnetic Spectrum; IEEE 802 Standards; Infrared Technologies; Last Mile Services; Local Loop; MAN (Metropolitan Area Network); Microwave Communications; Modulation Techniques; Multiplexing and Multiplexers; Network Access Services; Network Core Technologies; OFDM (Orthogonal Frequency Division Multiplexing); Optical Networks; Packet Radio Data Networks; Residential Broadband; Satellite Communication Systems; Service Providers and Carriers; SMR (Specialized Mobile Radio); Spread Spectrum Signaling; TDMA (Time Division Multiple Access); UWB (Ultra Wideband); WAN (Wide Area Network); Wireless Communications; Wireless LANs; Wireless Local Loop; Wireless Mobile Communications; *and* Wireless PANs (Personal Area Networks)

Linktionary!—Tom Sheldon's Encyclopedia of Networking updates	http://www.linktionary.com/w/ wireless_broadband.html
N-WEST (National Wireless Electronic Systems Testbed)	http://nwest.nist.gov/
WCA (Wireless Communications Association International). See links for a complete list of operators, vendors, publications, and more	http://www.wcai.com
BWA (Broadband Wireless Association)	http://www.broadband-wireless.org/
IEEE 802.16 Working Group on Broadband Wireless Access (IEEE Wireless MAN)	http://grouper.ieee.org/groups/802/16/
U.S. FCC LMDS Auction page	http://www.fcc.gov/wtb/auctions/ lmds1.html
Wireless DSL Consortium	http://www.wdslconsortium.com/
Wi-LAN (see white papers about OFDM)	http://www.wi-lan.com/

OFDM Forum	http://www.ofdm-forum.com
BWIF (Broadband Wireless Internet Forum)	http://www.bwif.org/
WiLAN (with information about OFDM)	http://www.wi-lan.com/
Web ProForums Wireless Broadband Modems Tutorial by Hybrid Networks	http://www.iec.org/tutorials/wire_broad/
Web ProForums LMDS tutorial by Nortel Networks	http://www.iec.org/tutorials/lmds/
Light Reading—The global site for optical networking	http://www.lightreading.com
Cisco Fixed Wireless Web page	http://www.cisco.com/warp/public/779/servpro/solutions/wireless/
Cisco paper: "Overcoming Multipath in Non-Line-of-Sight High-Speed Microwave Communication Links"	http://www.cisco.com/warp/public/cc/pd/witc/wt2700/mulpt_wp.htm
Hybrid Networks "An Introduction to Fixed Broadband Wireless Technology."	http://www.hybrid.com/info/primer.htm
Stardust.com Immobile Wireless Web page (news, links, articles)	http://www.stardust.com/lastmile/immobile/index.htm
Adaptive Broadband	http://www.adaptivebroadband.com/
XO	http://www.xo.com
Ensemble Communications (information about Adaptive TDD)	http://www.ensemblecom.com
Converge Network Digest Broadband Wireless page	http://www.convergedigest.com/BroadbandWireless.htm

Wireless Communications

Wireless communication involves transmitting signals through air and space using radio waves. Wireless spectrum is allocated by governments and international organizations. For example, in the United States, the 800-MHz frequency range is allocated for cellular voice communications. The higher the radio frequency, the greater the bandwidth and data carrying capacity of the wireless system. However, as frequency is increased in a system, its characteristics become more directional (line of site) and the signals are more susceptible to atmospheric conditions such as rain and fog.

Wireless technologies are used to build LANs within building and LANs that bridge buildings. They are also used to provide high-speed access to the Internet or to build metropolitan area networks. Wireless mobile systems with very high data-rates are emerging that allow mobile users to operate as if they are attached to traditional wired networks. A variety of technologies are discussed under various topics in this book, as mentioned later.

The United States FCC Web site provides useful information on wireless spectrum allocation. You can refer to the following Web sites for information on cellular radiotelephone services, general wireless communications services, microwave services, PCS (Personal Communications Service), and others.

W

United States FCC (Federal Communications Commission)	http://www.fcc.gov/
FCC WTB (Wireless Telecommunications Bureau)	http://www.fcc.gov/wtb/
WTB Directory of Wireless Communication Services	http://www.fcc.gov/wtb/services.html
History of Wire and Broadcast Communication	http://www.fcc.gov/cib/evol.html

You'll find addition wireless topics in this book under the following headings:

■ **"Home Networking"**   Discusses methods for networking homes, including wireless systems

■ **"Microwave Communication"**   Discusses wireless systems than operate in different parts of the microwave spectrum, including terrestrial and satellite systems

■ **"Mobile Computing"**   Describes mobile computing technologies

■ **"Packet-Radio Data Networks"**   Describes services offered by nationwide radio data communication services, including short messaing services

■ **"Satellite Communication Systems"**   Discusses the different types of Earth-orbiting communication systems

■ **"Wireless Broadband Access Technologies"**   Discusses technologies that essentially provide wireless local loop services, i.e., wireless access for home and business users to carrier and service provider networks

■ **"Wireless IP"**   Discusses mobile wireless technologies that allow portable IP devices to access the Internet and corporate networks

■ **"Wireless LANs"**   Radio communications for mobile users within a local area and point-to-point connections between buildings and company sites within a campus or metropolitan area

■ **"Wireless Mobile Communications"**   Radio communication over public carrier facilities using packet radio, cellular networks, and satellite stations for users who are "out of the office" and "on the road"

Related Entries   Bluetooth; CDMA (Code Division Multiple Access); DBS (Direct Broadcast Satellite); Electromagnetic Spectrum; HALO (High Altitude Long Operation); HDR (High Data Rate); Home Networking; Infrared Technologies; Microwave Communications; Mobile Computing; Modulation Techniques; Multiplexing and Multiplexers; OFDM (Orthogonal Frequency Division Multiplexing); Packet Radio Data Networks; Residential Broadband; Satellite Communication Systems; SMR (Specialized Mobile Radio); SMS (Short Messaging Service); Spread Spectrum Signaling; TDMA (Time Division Multiple Access); UWB (Ultra Wideband); WAP (Wireless Applications Protocol); Wireless Communications; Wireless Broadband Access Technologies; Wireless LANs; Wireless Mobile Communications; *and* Wireless PAN (Personal Area Networks)

Wireless Organizations

CTIA (Cellular Telecommunications Industry Association)	http://www.wow-com.com
U.S. Wireless Telecommunications Bureau	http://www.fcc.gov/wtb/
Mobile Data Evolution.com	http://www.mobiledataevolution.com/
CDMA One Consortium	http://www.cdg.org/
WirelessReady.org	http://www.sierrawireless.com/alliance/default.asp
ITU IMT-2000 information	http://www.itu.int/imt/
Universal Wireless Communications Consortium (TDMA information)	http://www.uwcc.org/
ETSI (European Telecommunications Standards Institute). UMTS technical body located here	http://www.etsi.org/
UMTS Forum	http://www.umts-forum.org
Wireless Data Forum	http://www.wirelessdata.org/
3GPP (Third Generation Partnership Project)	http://www.3gpp.org
PCIA (Personal Communications Industry Association)	http://www.pcia.com/
WAP Forum	http://www.wapforum.org

Wireless Links

Linktionary!—Tom Sheldon's Encyclopedia of Networking updates	http://www.linktionary.com/w/wireless.html
Wireless Resource List by Prof. Jeff MacKie-Mason	http://china.si.umich.edu/telecom/technical-faqs.html
PaloWireless.com	http://www.palowireless.com/
Telecoms Virtual Library links to wireless vendors	http://www.analysys.co.uk/vlib/mobile.htm
Wireless links by David Blight	http://www.ee.umanitoba.ca/~blight/telecom.html
Wireless links (extensive)	http://china.si.umich.edu/telecom/technical-wireless.html
Yahoo! Wireless links	http://dir.yahoo.com/Science/Engineering/Electrical_Engineering/Telecommunications/Wireless/
Yahoo! Mobile Computing links	http://dir.yahoo.com/computers_and_Internet/Mobile_Computing/
Wireless Telecom links at Lycos	http://www.lycos.com/wguide/wire/wire_144546_47490_3_1.html
Wireless links at ITPRC	http://www.itprc.com/wireless.htm

W

Resources in Wireless Networking, compiled by Prof. Adam Wolisz and Stefan Hauschild	http://www-tkn.ee.tu-berlin.de/bibl/
Wireless Communications Research Center	http://www.cio.com/forums/communications/
Andrew Bateman radio design course: Transmitter & Receiver Architectures	http://www.avren.com/Courses/ TX_RX_Architectures_plain.htm

Wireless IP

Wireless IP obviously refers to using the Internet Protocol over a wireless connection. At one time, the term "wireless IP" referred to CDPD (Cellular Digital Packet Data), a method for transmitting data packets across wireless cellular networks. Today, wireless IP refers to a variety of technologies, including the following:

- **Wireless data protocols**   These protocols typically overlay existing wireless cellular services with a packet-switching scheme that makes efficient use of wireless bandwidth. An entire circuit (or the entire bandwidth of a cellular system) may be used to multiplex data packets from multiple users, or packets may be inserted into the idle time available on any voice channel. See "Wireless Mobile Communications" for more information.

- **Mobile IP**   Mobile IP is about allowing mobile computing devices to change their point of attachment to the Internet without changing their IP address. It is about "nomadic roaming," where a roaming host is connected to the Internet in ways other than its well-known fixed-address domain space. Basically, packets destined to a mobile node are routed first to its home network, where they are intercepted by the mobile node's home agent and then forwarded to the mobile node's most recently reported "care-of" address.

- **MANET (Mobile Ad Hoc Networking)**   MANET is actually the name of an IETF working group that is developing protocols to support routing functionality for nomadic roaming nodes (see above). A system to support roaming requires address management, protocol interoperability enhancements, and the like. MANET is working to extend mobility into the realm of autonomous, mobile, wireless domains, where a set of nodes—which may be combined routers and hosts—themselves form the network routing infrastructure in an ad hoc fashion. Mobile ad hoc networks are envisioned to have dynamic, sometimes rapidly changing random multihop topologies composed of bandwidth-constrained wireless links. Refer to the IETF MANET Working Group Web site listed next.

- **WAP (Wireless Application Protocol)**   WAP is a standard for providing Internet communications and advanced telephony services on digital mobile phones, pagers, personal digital assistants, and other "smart" wireless terminals. WAP is designed to efficiently deliver Web content to mobile users, although that content is limited to the small screen size, memory size, and other constraints of mobile devices. See "WAP (Wireless Application Protocol)."

Note that third-generation (3G) wireless mobile communications fully supports IP. This will provide a standard way to build innovative and interoperable applications for mobile wireless devices. In fact, voice will become just another application that is delivered over IP. This will go well beyond what WAP can deliver (Web pages radically scaled down to display in cell phones). XML (Extensible Markup Language) will play a big role in making Web content available to any type of device, since it provides a means to dynamically adjust content to display in any device. Future phones will be more like wireless PDAs that support a variety of computing applications. They will support Bluetooth for creating ad hoc PANs (personal area networks), allowing users to communicate via IP with people in meetings or sitting next to them on planes.

Related Entries   Bluetooth; Mobile Computing; Mobile IP; Modems; Remote Access; Roaming; Voice over IP (VoIP); VPN (Virtual Private Network); WAP (Wireless Application Protocol); Wireless LANs; *and* Wireless PANs (Personal Area Networks)

IETF Working Group: IP Routing for Wireless/Mobile Hosts (mobileip)   http://www.ietf.org/html.charters/mobileip-charter.html

IETF Working Group: Mobile Ad-hoc Networks (manet)   http://www.ietf.org/html.charters/manet-charter.html

Wireless LANs

Wireless LANs or "WLANs" are the equivalent of wired LANs (usually Ethernet) without the wires. They are meant for office environments and even home use. Other wireless technologies are outlined under "Wireless Communications." Mobile wireless (cellular telephones) is discussed under "Wireless Mobile Communications." Wireless access service (broadband Internet connections) is covered under "Wireless Broadband Access Technologies."

A related wireless technology is the wireless PAN (personal area network), which is a limited-range network for interconnecting mobile devices connecting with peripheral devices. Note that WLANs and PANs are very similar, except that the range of PANs is intentionally limited so that groups of people in the same area (conference room, restaurants, airport terminal) can spontaneously connect. By limiting the range, a typical office can have many different PANs operating at the same time. See "Bluetooth" and "Wireless PANs (Personal Area Networks)."

A typical WLAN consists of a fixed-position wireless transceiver (transmitter/receiver) that broadcasts a signal within an area called a *microcell*. The transceiver is usually called a base station or an access point. Each base station connects to a wired backbone so that users can communicate with users in other microcells or connect with back-end server farms, Internet connections, and other wired network services.

Microcells may cover an office building floor or a workgroup area. Other microcells may exist next to one another or on different floors of an office building. Roaming is possible between WLAN microcells just like roaming is possible with cell phones. As users move out of the range of one microcell and into the range of another, their connection is handed off to the new microcell base station.

Note that *on-demand* networks are also possible. This is where two or more devices communicate directly with one another without going through a base station.

W

WLANs have many advantages:

- They eliminate cable installation, which is especially convenient if the LAN site is a temporary installation or serves a workgroup that might disband in the near future.

- Users can roam the office with small portable devices. In a hospital, doctors and nurses can carry custom patient-monitoring and patient-alert devices.

- Network management is simplified since no physical connections are required.

- Users can bring their portable devices to meetings and remain connected to network services.

- They can provide convenient connections for visiting users.

The last point opens up some interesting scenarios. The range and performance of wireless LANs is so good that several companies are promoting them for wireless remote access in airports, hotels, convention centers, and other places where people might need high-speed access to network resources and the Internet. In airports, wireless LANs may provide users with instant access to information services or Internet connections. In truck stops, wireless networks may provide drivers who have in-truck computers with high-speed Internet access and messaging services.

Wireless Technologies

A wireless network is a radio, microwave, or infrared network. Information is transmitted between the base station and wireless devices on a specific carrier frequency. Information is modulated onto the carrier. Most wireless networks will have multiple microcells and multiple base stations. Neighboring base stations must transmit using different carrier frequencies to prevent interference.

Several wireless technologies may be used:

- **Infrared**   Provide line-of-site connections between devices and supports high-speed connections. Because infrared requires line-of-site, this technique is not as popular as the radiofrequency LANs. Infrared is often used for "conference table networking" or connections to peripherals. Refer to "Infrared Technologies" for more information.

- **Spread spectrum radio**   Spread spectrum is now considered the best technology for wireless LANs. It provides reliability, integrity, and, most important, security. The signal is spread out and appears as background noise to any device that does not know how to tune into the signal. Spread spectrum radio does not interfere with conventional radio because its energy levels are too weak. Two types of spread spectrum exist:

  - **Frequency-hopping spread spectrum**   A narrowband carrier changes frequency in a pattern known to both the transmitter and receiver.

  - **Direct-sequence spread spectrum**   In this scheme, the data to transmit is altered by a bit stream that is generated by the sender. The bit stream represents every bit in the original data with multiple bits in the generated stream, thus spreading the signal across a wider frequency band.

■ **Narrowband (or single-frequency) radio**   This technique is similar to a broadcast from a radio station. Both the transmitter and receiver tune in to a "tight" frequency band. The signal can penetrate walls and is spread over a wide area, so focusing is not required. However, narrowband radio transmissions have problems with radio reflections (ghosting), and certain frequencies are regulated by the FCC.

Wireless LAN Standards

Wireless LANs operate in the so-called unlicensed spectrum at 2.4 GHz and 5 GHz. The spectrum is free to use without a license, just like cordless telephone spectrum opened up 300 MHz of spectrum for unlicensed wireless local area networking. In the United States, Apple Computer was responsible for pushing the FCC (Federal Communications Commission) to unlicense the spectrum so it could be freely used for a variety of wireless needs. Apple has developed products for use in schools where physical rewiring is not affordable. In the United States, the spectrum is called the U-NII (Unlicensed-National Information Infrastructure).

IEEE WLAN Standards

In June of 1997, the IEEE (Institute of Electrical and Electronic Engineers) approved the 802.11 wireless LAN specification, which spelled out interoperability standards for 1-Mbit/sec to 2-Mbit/sec wireless LAN devices. Almost immediately, the technology was outdated, so the IEEE went to work on a 10-Mbit/sec enhancement. The current standard specifies operation in the 2.4-GHz frequency range using spread spectrum and infrared.

The following 802.11 extensions define high-performance wireless Ethernet LAN networks:

■ **IEEE 802.11b**   This extension uses the 2.4-GHz unlicensed band and provides data transfer rates up to 11 Mbits/sec. It specifies direct-sequence spread spectrum radio.

■ **IEEE 802.11a**   This extension uses the 5-GHz unlicensed band and provides data rates from 6 Mbits/sec to 54 Mbits/sec. The radio technology in the IEEE 802.11a is OFDM (orthogonal frequency-division multiplexing). IEEE 802.11a is similar to the HiperLAN/2 standard developed by ETSI, as discussed next.

A Canadian company called Wi-LAN holds patents on OFDM. It is used to improve bandwidth and overcomes a particular type of radio interference called "multipath." The version in IEEE 802.11a (called coded OFDM) was engineered for indoor use. See "OFDM (Orthogonal Frequency Division Multiplexing)."

ETSI HiperLAN

HiperLAN is an ETSI-developed high-speed wireless LAN standard with several configurations that provide LAN data rates as high as 54 Mbits/sec. HiperLAN uses a shared access method similar to CSMA/CD (carrier sense multiple access/collision detection), which is used in Ethernet.

HiperLAN consists of a family of products as outlined in Table W-1. The HiperLAN2 standard will support QoS (Quality of Service) since it is designed upon the ATM standard. HiperAccess is designed to provide fixed access in the "last mile," giving Internet users high-data-rate links to their local ISP. The HiperLink standard is meant to provide high-speed over-the-air point-to-point links, typically between LANs in different buildings of a campus or metropolitan environment.

W

	HiperLAN1	HiperLAN2	HiperAccess	HiperLink
Application	Wireless Ethernet (LAN)	Wireless LAN with a range of up to 200 meters	Wireless local loop with a range of up to 5 kilometers	Wireless point-to-point for connecting HiperLAN and HiperAccess networks
Frequency range	5 GHz	5 GHz	5 GHz	17 GHz
Data rate	19 Mbits/sec	25 to 54 Mbits/sec	25 Mbits/sec	~155 Mbits/sec
Status	Completed and ratified in 1996	Completed in 2000 with compatibility with IEEE 802.11a.	Under development	No current activity

Table W-1.   *Wireless LAN technologies (source: HiperLAN Alliance)*

HiperLAN/2 is of the most interest. It uses OFDM technology like IEEE 802.11a and includes support for prioritization of network traffic. Traffic at higher priorities is allocated bandwidth that cannot be used by traffic at lower priorities. At the same time, high-priority traffic can never take over all the bandwidth.

HiperLAN includes CAC (channel access control), which defines a "listen-before-talking" access mechanism. Devices use CAC to determine if a channel is busy. CAC is an access protocol like Ethernet's CSMA/CD (carrier sense multiple access/collision detection), except that CAC implements a hierarchically independent, nonpreemptive, priority access mechanism.

Related Entries   Bluetooth; CDMA (Code Division Multiple Access); Electromagnetic Spectrum; Ethernet; Home Networking; IEEE 802 Standards; Infrared Technologies; Microwave Communications; Mobile Computing; Modulation Techniques; Multiplexing and Multiplexers; NII (National Information Infrastructure); Packet-Radio Data Networks; OFDM (Orthogonal Frequency Division Multiplexing); PAN (Personal Area Network); Radio Communications and Networks; Residential Broadband; SMR (Specialized Mobile Radio); Spread Spectrum Signaling; UWB (Ultra Wideband); Wireless Communications; Wireless Broadband Access Technologies; Wireless Mobile Communications; *and* Wireless PANs (Personal Area Networks)

Linktionary!—Tom Sheldon's Encyclopedia of Networking updates	http://www.linktionary.com/w/wireless_lan.html
WLANA (Wireless LAN Association)	http://www.wlana.com/
WCA (Wireless Communications Association International)	http://www.wcai.com
IEEE 802.11 WLAN Committee	http://grouper.ieee.org/groups/802/11/
HiperLAN2 Global Forum	http://www.hiperlan2.com/

WECA (Wireless Ethernet Compatibility Alliance)	http://www.wirelessethernet.org/
WirelessLAN.com	http://www.wirelesslan.com/
Palowireless.com IEEE 802.11 Resource Center	http://www.palowireless.com/
Converge Network Digest Wireless LAN page	http://www.convergedigest.com/ WirelessLANs.htm
Stardust.com Wireless Channel	http://www.stardust.com/wireless/
Wi-LAN (see information about OFDM)	http://www.wi-lan.com/
Wireless LAN/MAN Modem Product Directory by Barry McLarnon	http://hydra.carleton.ca/info/wlan.html
David Starobinski's Wireless LANs Page	http://www.rad.com/networks/1994/wireless/ wlan.htm
An IEEE 802.11 WLAN Primer by Bruce Tuch	http://www.csdmag.com/main/feat9709.htm

Wireless Local Loop

Wireless local loop (WLL) refers to a variety of technologies for connecting subscribers to the public-switched telephone network using wireless links, rather than copper wire. In many cases, the bandwidth is much higher than that possible in the copper loop. Wireless local loop is a practical solution for connecting subscribers in countries that do not have the wired infrastructure that is available in the United States. It is also practical in rural areas and new suburban areas as an alternative to laying cable.

An important distinction is that WLL is primarily a fixed wireless service (the subscriber generally stays in one place), while cellular systems offer mobile communication and roaming among different systems. Subscribers install terminals that are linked by radio to the service provider's base stations. Depending on the system, the handset may provide the radio link directly to the base station, which allows the user some mobility. As mentioned, the range of mobility is confined to a specific area and roaming to other areas is usually not possible. Directional antennas may be used to extend range.

WLL services may be deployed in a basic configuration to mimic the local loop or in an advanced configuration that provides advanced services such as video and data access. At the basic level, wireless spectrum allocated to mobile cellular systems may be used for WLL. In some cases (close in urban areas), spectrum allocated to cordless phones may be used. Nokia has developed access nodes that form the link between a GSM radio network and the local exchange. The access node adapts GSM signaling to wireline signaling. The service allows users to have a mobile phone covering an area from one block to a whole town.

Advanced WLL services may be built with LMDS (Local Multipoint Distribution Services), a microwave service that can support multiple two-way voice, video, and data service channels. LMDS operates in the 28-GHz range. In terms of traditional local loop services, LMDS can provide the same quality as the copper local loop. At the same time, it can provide low, medium, and high data rates, depending on user requirements. A system's bandwidth is divided up in a way that allocates some of the bandwidth for voice calls and some for data and video.

See "Wireless Broadband Access Technologies" for information about wireless technologies that may be used in WLL.

W

Related Entries   Broadband Communications and Networking; Last Mile Services; Local Loop; MAN (Metropolitan Area Network); Microwave Communications; Residential Broadband; *and* Wireless Broadband Access Technologies

Linktionary!—Tom Sheldon's Encyclopedia of Networking updates	http://www.linktionary.com/w/wll.html
"Wireless Local Loop (WLL) Tutorial" at Web ProForums	http://www.iec.org/tutorials/wll/
Wireless DSL Consortium	http://www.wdslconsortium.com/

Wireless Messaging

See Instant Messaging; Mobile Computing; Packet Radio Data Networks; SMR (Specialized Mobile Radio); SMS (Short Messaging Service); WAP (Wireless Access Protocol); Wireless Communications; *and* Wireless Mobile Communications

Wireless Mobile Communications

There are a variety of wireless communication systems for transmitting voice, video, and data in local or wide areas. There are point-to-point wireless bridges, wireless local area networks, multidirectional wireless cellular systems, and satellite communication systems.

This topic discusses "mobile" wireless technologies that provide voice and data communication services to mobile users who use cell phones, PDAs, Internet terminals, and related computing devices. Refer to "Wireless Communications" for a list of related wireless topics.

The number of wireless mobile devices is increasing globally. Users equipped with portable computers, PDAs (personal digital assistants), and a variety of small wireless communication devices increasingly need to connect to corporate networks, perform database queries, exchange messages, transfer files, and even participate in collaborative computing. At the same time, wireless systems are achieving higher data rates to support Internet and other data-related applications. The newest mobile communication systems are targeting data rates as high as 2 Mbits/sec.

Cellular Systems and Topology

A cell in a cellular system is a roughly circular area with a central transmitter/receiver base station as shown in Figure W-6 (although the base station may be located off-center to conform to local topology). The station is raised up on a tower or placed on top of a building. Some are located on church steeples. The station has a 360-degree omnidirectional antenna (except when directional transmissions are required) that is tuned to create a cellular area of a specific size. Cells are usually pictured as hexagonal in shape and arranged in a honeycomb pattern. Cell size varies depending on the area. In a city, there are many small cells, while rural area may have very large cells.

Cellular topology provides a way to maintain an adequate number of call channels even though the actual number of channels available to the *entire* service area is small. This is possible through *frequency reuse*. Each cell is assigned a set of channel frequencies, and no *adjoining* cells

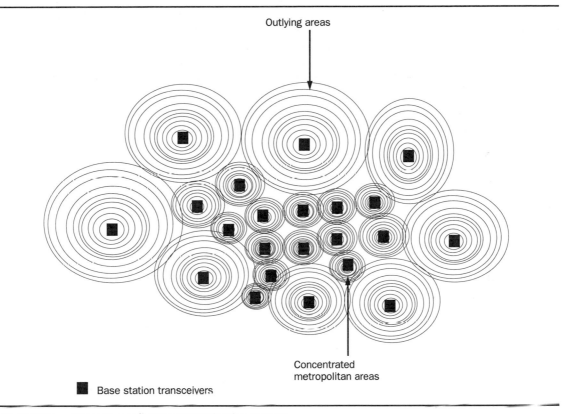

Figure W-6. *Cells in a cellular communication system*

may use those frequencies. However, cells further away may use those frequencies because the distance between cells provides a buffer zone that prevents frequency interference.

The system is scalable, even though it has a finite number of channels. If channel demand increases in a specific area (such as a metro area), the service provider can divide cells into a number of smaller cells. Transmitter power is turned down to fit the new smaller cell size and channel frequencies are allocated so that no adjoining cells use the same channels. However, channel reuse is possible in cells that are at least one cell apart. Thus, frequency reuse and smaller cell size allow the system to scale. Metro areas may have many small cells while rural area may have large cells. The cell size is designed to accommodate the number of people in the area.

When a user turns a phone on, its phone number and serial number are broadcast within the local cell. The base station picks up these signals and informs the switching office that the particular device is located within its area. This information is recorded by the switching office for future reference. An actual call takes place when the user enters a phone number and hits the Send button. The cellular system selects a channel for the user to use during the duration of the call.

As users travel, they may move from one cell to another, necessitating a handoff and the selection of a new channel. While in the vicinity of a cell, mobile phone users are under the control of the transmitter/receiver in that cell. A handoff takes place when the base station in one cell transfers control for a user's call to a base station in another cell. When a base station begins to lose a user's signal, it notifies base stations in all the surrounding cells that the user may be moving into their cells. As the user moves into a new cell, the base station in that cell takes over the call. The frequency of the call is changed to a frequency used in the new cell during the transition. This is because adjoining cells cannot use the same frequencies.

From Analog to Digital Systems

Mobile wireless analog communication systems have been around since the 1950s. The early systems were single channel "over-and-out" systems. Instead of a cellular configuration, a single radio tower serviced a metropolitan area, which severely limited the scalability of the systems. Service quality varied depending on the location of the caller. Later systems added multiple two-way channels but still had limited capacity.

Analog *cellular* services were introduced by AT&T in the 1970s and became widespread in the 1980s. The primary analog service in the United States is called AMPS (Advanced Mobile Phone Service). There are similar systems around the world that go by different names. The equivalent system in England is called TACS (Total Access Communications System).

The AMPS system is a circuit-oriented communication system that operates in the 824-MHz to 894-MHz frequency range. This range is divided into a pool of 832 full-duplex channel pairs (1 send, 1 receive). Any one of these channels may be assigned to a user. A channel is like physical circuit, except that it occupies a specific radiofrequency range and has a bandwidth of 30 kHz. The circuit remains dedicated to a subscriber call until it is disconnected, even if voice or data is not being transmitted.

Cellular systems are described in multiple generations, with third- and fourth-generation (3G and 4G) systems just emerging:

- **1G systems**   These are the *analog* systems such as AMPS that grew rapidly in the 1980s and are still available today. Many metropolitan areas have a mix of 1G and 2G systems, as well as emerging 3G systems. The systems use frequency division multiplexing to divide the bandwidth into specific frequencies that are assigned to individual calls.

- **2G systems**   These second-generation systems are *digital*, and use either TDMA (Time Division Multiple Access) or CDMA (Code Division Multiple Access) access methods. The European GSM (Global System for Mobile communications) is a 2G digital system with its own TDMA access methods. The 2G digital services began appearing in the late 1980s, providing expanded capacity and unique services such as caller ID, call forwarding, and short messaging. A critical feature was seamless roaming, which lets subscribers move across provider boundaries.

- **3G systems**   3G has become an umbrella term to describe cellular data communications with a target data rate of 2 Mbits/sec. The ITU originally attempted to define 3G in its

IMT-2000 (International Mobile Communications-2000) specification, which specified global wireless frequency ranges, data rates, and availability dates. However, a global standard was difficult to implement due to different frequency allocations around the world and conflicting input. So, three operating modes were specified. These are discussed at the Linktionary! Web site. According to Nokia, a 3G device will be a personal, mobile, multimedia communications device that supports speech, color pictures, and video, and various kinds of information content. Nokia's Web site (http://www.Nokia.com) provides interesting information about 3G systems. There is some doubt that 3G systems will ever be able to deliver the bandwidth to support these features because bandwidth is shared. However, 3G systems will certainly support more phone calls per cell.

■ **4G Systems**   On the horizon are 4G systems that may become available even before 3G matures (3G is a confusing mix of standards). While 3G is important in boosting the number of wireless calls, 4G will offer true high-speed data services. 4G data rates will be in the 2-Mbit/sec to 156-Mbit/sec range, and possibly higher. 4G will also fully support IP. High data rates are due to advances in signal processors, new modulation techniques, and smart antennas that can focus signals directly at users. OFDM (orthogonal frequency division multiplexing) is one scheme that can provide very high wireless data rates. OFDM is described under its own heading.

The move to digital technologies opened up the wireless world. It improved capacity, reduced equipment costs, and allowed for the addition of new features. Reduced handset costs meant more people were vying for services and taxing systems. 3G systems add more capacity. In addition, packet technologies were developed that use bandwidth more efficiently. The primary 1G and 2G digital systems are listed here.

■ **Analog cellular**   These are the traditional analog systems such as AMPS and TACS that use frequency division multiplexing. AMPS operates in the 800-MHz range, while TACS operates in the 900-MHz frequency range.

■ **Hybrid analog/digital cellular (usually called digital cellular)**   These systems are analog AMPS systems in which digitized voice and digital data is modulated onto the analog sine wave of the channel being used. They operate in the same 800-MHz range as analog AMPS and even use the same topology and equipment configuration (cells, towers, etc.). The access method may be either TDMA or CDMA, as discussed in the next section.

■ **GSM (Global System for Mobile Communications)**   This is a second-generation mobile system designed from the ground up without trying to be backward compatible with older analog systems. GSM is popular in Europe and Asia, where it provides superior roaming ability among countries. It uses TDMA, but Europe is moving from this system into 3G systems based on a wideband form of CDMA.

W

When digital cellular services were being designed in the early 1980s, the choice was to design a system that was backward compatible with existing analog systems (and used the same frequency allocation) or to design a whole new system. The European community had about seven incompatible analog services, so it created the GSM system from scratch to operate in the 900-MHz range (and later in the 1,800-MHz range).

In the U.S., the digital cellular systems were developed using the AMPS frequency allocation and the TDMA and CDMA access methods. See "CDMA (Code Division Multiple Access)" and "TDMA (Time Division Multiple Access)." In addition, the FCC allocated new bandwidth in the 1,900-MHz frequency range to accommodate what was called PCS (Personal Communication Services). PCS refers to the 1,900-MHz frequency allocation and to mobile systems that provide services beyond voice (such as digital services that support caller ID, messaging, and other features).

As mentioned, these systems are discussed further at the Linktionary! Web site.

Cellular Standards

Keeping track of the analog and digital cellular standards can be difficult. Table W-2 lists the most common standards.

Common Reference Name	Standard	Category	Frequency Band(s)	Comments
Analog cellular	TIA/ EIA-553	FDMA analog cellular	800 MHz	The AMPS standard. Does not support N-AMPS.
Analog cellular (enhanced)	IS-91	FDMA analog cellular	800 MHz	Same as above, but also includes N-AMPS and authentication support.
Narrowband-AMPS (N-AMPS)	IS-88	FDMA analog cellular	800 MHz	Divides one FDMA channel into three smaller channels. Meant for PDA and messaging.
Local AMPS	IS-94	FDMA analog cellular	800 MHz	A low-power cellular system designed for local (in-building) use.
TDMA digital cellular, also called D-AMPS (digital-AMPS)	IS-54	TDMA digital cellular	800 MHz	Same as AMPS, except uses digital TDMA to divide each channel into three time-slotted channels. Does not directly support data.
TDMA digital cellular (enhanced)	IS-136	TDMA digital cellular	800 MHz	An enhancement to above (TIA/ EIA/IS-54) that supports circuit-switched data at 9,600 bits/sec.
CDMA digital cellular	IS-95a	CDMA digital cellular	800 MHz 1,900 MHz	Uses spread spectrum radio and code division multiplexing to put up to 20 conversations on a single band. Data rate is 16 Kbits/sec.

Table W-2.   *Cellular Wireless Standards*

Common Reference Name	Standard	Category	Frequency Band(s)	Comments
CDMA digital cellular (revision b)	IS-95b	CDMA digital cellular	800 MHz 1,900 MHz	A software upgrade to IS-95a that can allocate up to four 16-Kbit/sec channels to a user, allowing up to 64 Kbits/sec for data.
HDR (high data rate)	IS-95c compatible	CDMA		A Qualcomm proprietary IP-based wireless data service.
GSM		TDMA	900 MHz	GSM was designed by the European community as a digital system to replace analog system.
DCS-1800		TDMA	1,800 MHz	This is GSM expanded to the 1,800 MHz range.

Table W-2.   *Cellular Wireless Standards* (continued)

Wireless Data Networking

While early cellular systems were focused on voice, there is now a lot of interest in supporting data transmissions. The older analog and analog/digital hybrid networks were limited in their data rates, but new standards are emerging with a focus on high data rates.

In a circuit-switched wireless network, a dedicated radio channel is allocated to a single transmission. As long as data transmissions are long and continuous (file transfers), a circuit is used efficiently. However, most data transmissions are bursty, and dedicating an entire circuit to them is usually a waste of valuable wireless bandwidth. During idle periods when no data is being sent, bandwidth is still dedicated to the user and not available for others to use.

Packet-switching schemes are best for bursty data traffic. Several packet-switching schemes may be used. In one technique, packets from many users are multiplexed over a single channel. In another technique, packets are inserted into the idle space on any available channel. The busier the network, the less bandwidth that will be available for data. An entire network may be designed just for packet data. Most wireless data systems offer minimal data rates, usually in the 10-Kbit/sec range. That's really only useful for short messaging and occasional Web page lookups. However, new wireless protocols bond multiple channels to increase data rates.

The billing methods help differentiate circuit versus packet switching methods. When you connect over a circuit-switched line, the phone company bills you for the entire duration of the call. With packet-switching systems, you are typically billed by the packet.

Several packet data schemes are outlined here. These are discussed further at the Linktionary! Web site:

■ **CDPD (Cellular Digital Packet Data)**   CDPD provides packet switching on AMPS systems. Data packets are sent when there is idle time on a channel. The system has a limited data rate, usually about 9,600 bits/sec. The CDPD Forum has more information at http://www.cdpd.org.

W

- **Data over GSM networks**   A channel bonding technique called HSCSD (high speed circuit switched data) extends GSM channel capacity to 14.4 Kbits/sec and allows up to four channels to be combined to provide up to 57.6 Kbits/sec throughput.

- **GPRS (General Packet Radio Service)**   Provides packet switching for TDMA circuit-switched networks and data rates of 115 Kbits/sec or higher. GPRS is a tunneling protocol that delivers IP packets across the mobile network to a router that puts them on the Internet.

- **EDGE (Enhanced Data Rates for Global Evolution)**   Improves GSM system data rates with the modified 8PSK (phase shift keying) modulation technique. The combination of GPRS and EDGE boosts the data rate of GSM to 384 Kbits/sec.

This topic continues at the Linktionary! Web site with a discussion of wireless access methods, cellular standards (such as AMPS, GSM, and CDMA systems), wireless data standards, and evolution of the wireless mobile system standards to 3G and IMT-2000.

Related Entries   Bluetooth; CDMA (Code Division Multiple Access); Communication Services and Providers; Electromagnetic Spectrum; HDR (High Data Rate); Home Networking; Infrared Technologies; Last Mile Services; Microwave Communication Systems; Mobile Computing; Network Access Services; Packet Radio Data Networks; Remote Access; Residential Broadband; Satellite Communication Systems; SMR (Specialized Mobile Radio); SMS (Short Messaging Service); Spread Spectrum Signaling; TDMA (Time Division Multiple Access); Telecommunications and Telephone Systems; WAP (Wireless Applications Protocol); Wireless Broadband Access Technologies; Wireless Communications; Wireless IP; *and* Wireless LANs

Linktionary!—Tom Sheldon's Encyclopedia of Networking updates	http://www.linktionary.com/w/wireless_mobile.html
ITU IMT-2000 home page	http://www.itu.int/imt/
3GPP (Third Generation Partnership Project), a group developing GSM, GPRS, and EDGE standards	http://www.3gpp.org/
CDMA Development Group	http://www.cdg.org/
The UMTS Forum	http://www.umts-forum.org/
TDMA-EDGE Web site	http://www.uwcc.org/
Mobile Lifestream's Mobiledataevolution.com Web site	http://www.mobiledataevolution.com/
Mobile Lifestreams	http://www.mobilelifestreams.com/
Nokia's 3G Web site	http://www.nokia.com/3g/
World of Wireless (WOW) Web site	http://www.wow-com.com/
Stardust Wireless page	http://www.stardust.com/wireless/
Andrew Seybold's Wirelessroadmap.com Web site (a great site for information about emerging technologies)	http://www.wirelessroadmap.com/
WINLAB (Wireless Information Network Laboratory), includes technical white papers	http://www.winlab.rutgers.edu/

AT&T's Wireless site	http://www.attws.com
Lucent Wireless Networks page	http://www.lucent.com/wirelessnet/
Nokia (the site to visit for 3G information)	http://www.nokia.com/3g/
Qualcomm Wireless Business Solutions	http://www.qualcomm.com/qwbs/
Ericsson Web site	http://www.ericsson.com/
Wireless news at *Wired Magazine*	http://www.wired.com/news/wireless/
FutureFoneZone (an overview of technologies for future wireless phones)	http://www.mobileipworld.com/wp/ whitepaper.html

Wireless Optical Networking

See Network Access Services; Optical Networks; *and* Wireless Broadband Access Technologies.

Wireless PANs (Personal Area Networks)

A WPAN (Wireless PAN) is a short-distance wireless network specifically designed to support portable and mobile computing devices such as PCs, PDAs, wireless printers and storage devices, cell phones, pagers, set-top boxes, and a variety of consumer electronics equipment. Bluetooth is an example of a wireless PAN that allows devices within close proximity to join together in ad hoc wireless networks in order to exchange information. Many cell phones have two radio interfaces—one for the cellular network and one for PAN connections.

WPANs such as Bluetooth provide the bandwidth and convenience to make data exchange practical for mobile devices such as palm computers. It overcomes many of the complications of other mobile data systems such as cellular packet data systems that require modems and connections through low-bandwidth cellular links. Since WPANs are designed with low power consumption in mind, a range of devices can take advantage of the technology, including digital watches, headsets, heart monitors, and a variety of other devices that can be worn.

The technology was originally designed to replace the cables that allow multiple computers to synchronize their data and exchange files. Since then, the Bluetooth specification has expanded into a communication system that supports smart tetherless devices. In addition, the IEEE has been working on a generic PAN standard, as described later. Service discovery protocols have been developed that helps devices locate and identify the services (printing, projection, sound, etc.) being offered by other devices.

A WPAN can spontaneously form just about anywhere. For example, people in meetings or new friends that have met on a plane can connect to exchange information. Advertising services would allow a users to alert other users of their presence. For example, you might walk into a Bluetooth PAN at an airport and be alerted that someone you know (based on a lookup in your personal address book) is nearby. One can even imagine people advertising information on their systems that is available for download, such as MP3 files or electronic books. This would be practical in a world where publishers compensate people that distribute products via their wireless mobile devices.

Bluetooth networks support Internet gateways so that users with Bluetooth devices can walk into the range of a Bluetooth PAN and gain an Internet connection. Picture "Bluetooth zones" in airports or other public places where users can go to obtain Internet connections.

W

The IEEE 802.15 Working Group for Wireless Personal Area Networks is developing standards for PANs. The Web site address is listed here. The working group is currently working to minimize conflicts between the IEEE WPAN and similar PAN standards such as Bluetooth and WLAN (wireless LAN) standards such as IEEE 802.11, which use the same unlicensed 2.4-GHz frequency range. One goal is to provide interoperability between WPAN devices and 802.11 devices.

The IEEE WPAN group is focused on developing a low power consumption, low complexity, wireless standard that supports devices that are within (or entering) what it calls a POS (Personal Operating Space). A POS typically extends up to 10 meters in all directions from the device, whether it is stationary or in motion. The IEEE WLAN and WPAN design criteria are different in that the former is designed for larger and more permanent networks while the latter is designed for low power consumption devices that can spontaneously form into a network. The low power design supports wearable computing devices.

Related Entries   Bluetooth; Embedded Systems; Home Networking; LAN (Local Area Network); Network Appliances; Microwave Communications; Mobile Computing; Service Advertising and Discovery; SLP (Service Location Protocol); *and* Wireless Communications

IEEE 802.15 Working Group for WPANs	http://ieee802.org/15/
Motorola personal Area networking overview	http://www.motorola.com/bluetooth/pan/

Wiretapping

Wiretapping is the act of tapping into a communication link to listen to a voice conversation or monitor and capture data. Wiretapping is relatively easy on network links. Network analyzers are designed to tap networks and monitor traffic. Anyone with such a device can easily filter out all unwanted traffic to monitor just the packets that they want to monitor, either legally or illegally. End-to-end encryption can secure data from wiretapping threats. Readers should refer to RFC 2804 (IETF Policy on Wiretapping, May 2000).

Related Entries   Cryptography; Hacking and Hackers; IPSec (IP Security); Secret-Key Cryptography; Security; SSL (Secure Sockets Layer); TLS (Transport Layer Security); Tunnels; *and* VPN (Virtual Private Network)

Wiring and Wiring Standards

See Cable and Wiring; *and* TIA/EIA Structured Cabling Standards.

WML (Wireless Markup Language)

WML is a version of HTML that is designed to display Web content on small devices such as cellular phones and handheld devices. WML is being developed as part of WAP (Wireless Application Protocol). See "WAP (Wireless Application Protocol)."

Workflow Management

The purpose of workflow management is to automate and coordinate document procedures in an organization by replacing paper systems with electronic documents. The network provides the routing system that moves documents to and from storage, and among users who need to view and make changes to documents or sign, validate, and authenticate documents. Workflow applications encourage workgroup collaboration by automating processes and eliminating footwork.

The WfMC (Workflow Management Coalition) is an organization that promotes electronic workflow and work management applications. It has helped to establish industry standards that promote interoperability and connectivity among workflow products. The WfMC states that "workflow is concerned with the automation of procedures where documents, information or tasks are passed between participants according to a defined set of rules to achieve, or contribute to, an overall business goal." The WfMC notes that workflow is often associated with business process reengineering, which is concerned with the assessment, analysis, modeling, definition, and subsequent operational implementation of the core business processes of an organization.

Workflow may also occur between organizations across extranet connections using EDI (Electronic Data Interchange) or newer applications based on XML (Extensible Markup Language).

A typical workflow application combines document imaging with electronic messaging and advanced security features such as digital signatures, which can provide proof that documents are from the specified source and that they have been validated by the person indicated in the form.

In accounting environments, documents typically move from clerks to supervisors in various stages of processing and validation. A workflow package can display the forms used by an organization for a clerk to fill out. Some fields in the form are automatically filled out by workflow software, based on the job or the clerk manipulating the form. It's possible to assign predefined routing schemes to forms and eliminate some of the management headaches associated with manual paper flow. Forms are sent directly to the person who is supposed to handle the next step in the procedure. Hang-ups in forms processing can often be handled by automatic features. For example, users can be alerted when a form must be dealt with to prevent overdue charges or other problems caused by late processing.

Publishing is another example of a collaborative environment that can benefit from workflow software. Documents are transferred from writer to editor to production in stages, using the network and its resources to store and eventually print the completed work.

Some of the key features of workflow software are as follows:

- Documents contain routing information that serves to distribute the document to predefined users or devices.
- Documents can have simultaneous access.
- A document is viewed as "under construction" until it exits the workflow process.

W

- The software has a filing system, queue, and workflow manager that keeps the system running.

- Authorized users sign off at various stages, locking parts or all of the document from further editing.

- It delivers work items to the appropriate people and helps them complete a task by issuing alerts, pointing out potential problems and errors, and providing other assistance.

- It provides information in advance for the person processing a form. For example, the workflow software may search out information about a person applying for a loan.

Most workflow software provides some sort of security mechanism, usually in the form of authentication and digital signatures. With this security, a recipient can be sure that the sender and document are valid, and that the document has not been altered during transmission. Likewise, the sender is assured that any alterations to the document by the recipient can be detected.

From a management point of view, workflow software can help an organization track how information is flowing and how to better manage that flow. Workflow software can eliminate many time-consuming and often expensive activities such as meetings, phone calls, and express mail deliveries. But as users take to the new software, bandwidth requirements increase. Workflow software allows users to view large image files, graphics, sound, and even video. This type of traffic can saturate the network.

Workflow and Document Specifications

The WfMC and other organizations have created workflow management and document management specifications that allow products from different vendors to interoperate or that add unique features to existing protocols and standards.

WfMC Workflow Reference Model

The WfMC has developed a workflow reference model based on a generic workflow application structure. The model identifies interfaces that can be standardized in order to allow products to work together. Figure W-7 illustrates the major components and interfaces of the workflow architecture. The three primary components are described below. Refer to the WfMC "Workflow Reference Model" document for details (Web site listed at the end of this section).

- **Workflow enactment service**   A software service that may consist of one or more workflow engines in order to create, manage, and execute workflow instances. Applications may interface to this service via the workflow application programming interface (WAPI).

- **Workflow engine**   A software service or "engine" that provides the runtime execution environment for a workflow instance. A workflow engine can control the execution of a set of processes, or subprocess, instances with a defined scope determined by the range of object types, and their attributes, which it can interpret within the process definition(s).

- **WAPI (Workflow API) and Interchange**   WAPI is a set of API calls and interchange functions supported by a workflow enactment service at its boundary for interaction with other resources and applications. Interchange data formats are also defined.

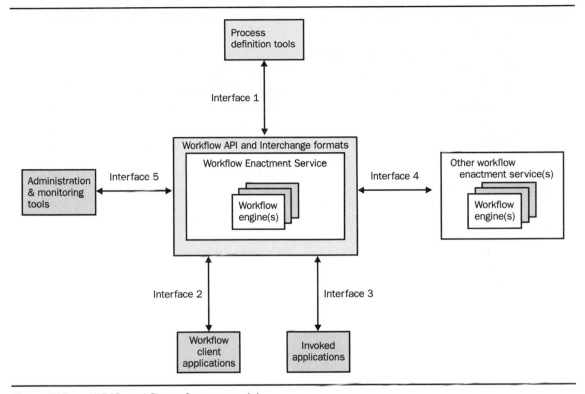

Figure W-7.   *WfMC workflow reference model*

DMA (Document Management Alliance) Specification
The Document Management Alliance (DMA) has created a specification that enables document management systems from different vendors to interoperate. The DMA API provides a client/server programming interface that allows many applications to work together in a uniform way. The DMA model consists of documents in different formats that are stored in a document space. The document space provides a generic place to query and access documents.

DMA can be considered a form of middleware in which there are client interfaces and server interfaces that are designed to run on specific systems. The middleware component allows clients to connect with servers in a transparent way. DMA works well with the WfMC workflow management model. The two together provide both document management and workflow management using standards that support interoperability.

WebDAV (Web Distributed Authoring and Versioning)
WebDAV is an IETF specification that allows remote Web clients to perform content authoring on Web server content. The original desire was to support efficient and scalable remote editing free of overwriting conflicts by extending HTTP with tools that would allow remote loading, editing, and saving (publishing) of various media types. One goal was to support document management and groupware over the Internet by allowing groups of people to edit and publish

W

documents on Web servers. WebDAV provides a way to extend workflow management over the Web. See "WebDAV."

Related Entries   Collaborative Computing; Compound Documents; Distributed Object Computing; Document Management; EDI (Electronic Data Interchange); Electronic Commerce; Electronic Mail; Extranet; Groupware; Handle System; Metadata; OAG (Open Application Group); OLE (Object Linking and Embedding); Transaction Processing; WebDAV; *and* XML (Extensible Markup Language)

Linktionary!—Tom Sheldon's Encyclopedia of Networking updates	http://www.linktionary.com/w/workflow.html
WfMC (Workflow Management Coalition)	http://www.aiim.org
WfMC Workflow Reference Model description	http://www.aiim.org/wfmc/mainframe.htm
Association for Information and Image Management International	http://www.aiim.org
Dragos Manolescu's workflow links	http://dbserver.kaist.ac.kr/~jhson/workflow/wf_collection.html
Workflow tutorial at George Mason University	http://cne.gmu.edu/modules/workflow
Ensemble, from Filenet	http://www.filenet.com
Techguide.com document: Workflow on the Web (see Document Management section)	http://www.techguide.com/

Workgroups

A workgroup is a collection of users attached to a network that share common resources such as server files, printers, and other systems. A few years back, a workgroup was defined by a group of people on the same LAN, which meant that all the users were really within the same area. Now, workgroups can be defined with users from all parts of the network. VLANs provide a way to configure a workgroup by workstation IP address, MAC address, or other criteria. Workgroups may also be defined by mailing lists or membership in webcasting or multicasting groups. The definition is pretty loose.

Related Entries   Collaborative Computing; Electronic Mail; Groupware; Instant Messaging; Multicasting; Unified Messaging; Videoconferencing; VLAN (Virtual LAN); Webcasting; *and* Workflow Management

World Wide Web

See Internet; *and* Web Technologies and Concepts.

World Wide Web Consortium

See W3C (World Wide Web Consortium) or visit the W3C Web site at http://www.w3c.org.

WPAN (Wireless Personal Area Network)

See "Wireless PANs (Personal Area Networks)."

X12 Accredited Standards Committee

X12 is an EDI (Electronic Data Interchange) standard that provides a uniform way for businesses to exchange electronic documents and business transactions. The DISA (Data Interchange Standards Association) was chartered by ANSI (American National Standards Institute) to provide the X12 committee with administrative support. DISA is a not-for-profit organization that supports the development and use of electronic data interchange standards in electronic commerce.

Related Entries   EDI (Electronic Data Interchange); Electronic Commerce; *and* Extranet

Accredited Standards Committee X12 Web page	http://www.x12.org/
X.12, Data Interchange Standards Association, (search for multiple occurrences), C&C Pages	http://www.disa.org/

X.25

The X.25 protocol is an ITU (originally CCITT) recommendation that defines connections of terminals and computers to packet-switching networks. Packet-switching networks route packets of data through a network of switches to destination nodes. In the case of X.25, packets of data up to 128 bytes in size are inserted in HDLC frames, addressed, and forwarded to the intended destination across the X.25 network. Because the service is packet-oriented, many users can share the service simultaneously. It provides any-to-any connections for simultaneous users.

X.25 is a well-established protocol, but is now somewhat dated. Traditionally, X.25 has been used in place of dial-up or leased-line circuits as a way to set up links to remote offices or remote users. In particular, it has been used to connect remote terminals to host systems. For more information, refer to the Linktionary! Web site listed below.

Related Entries   Frame Relay; HDLC (High-level Data Link Control); LAP (Link Access Procedure); NPN (New Public Network); Packets and Packet-Switching Networks; Service Providers and Carriers; Virtual Circuit; *and* WAN (Wide Area Network)

Linktionary!—Tom Sheldon's Encyclopedia of Networking updates	http://www.linktionary.com/x/x25.html
Black Box X.25 information	http://www.blackbox.nl/techweb/protocol/x25.htm
X.25 documentation at Cisco	http://www.cisco.com/univercd/cc/td/doc/cisintwk/ito_doc/x25.htm
Patton Electronics' X.25 Basics	http://www.patton.com/patton/fridayfax/article23.html
X.25 Packet Layer Protocol (PLP) Overview	http://www.techfest.com/networking/wan/x25plp.htm

X.400 Message-Handling System

The ITU (formerly CCITT) defined the X.400 MHS standard, an electronic system for exchanging messages among store-and-forward mail systems. In ISO terminology, X.400 is called MOTIS (Message-Oriented Text Interchange System). The goal of the standard is to provide compatibility among multi-vendor products and interfaces as well as public and private message services.

X.400 was first introduced in 1984 and has been through several enhancements. It outlines the protocols, procedures, components, terminology, and testing methods required to build interoperable e-mail systems. X.400 is based on a distributed client/server model. This topic is covered at the Linktionary! Web site. Internet mail has now become the de-facto mail standard.

Related Entries   Electronic Mail; Groupware; *and* X.500 Directory Services

Linktionary!—Tom Sheldon's Encyclopedia of Networking updates	http://www.linktionary.com/x/x400.html

X.500 Directory Services

X.500 is a CCITT (ITU) recommendation for a "white pages" directory services system that can provide a global "lookup" service for people and objects everywhere. The standard defines a hierarchical tree-structured directory in which countries form the top level of the directory and organizations or organizational units branch from this tree. The original intent was to define an international authority at the root of the tree that would manage the global structure. X.500 can also be installed within an organization as a private directory service and then connected to the global X.500 directory service.

More information on this topic can be found on the Linktionary! Web site.

Related Entries   CIP (Common Indexing Protocol); CNRP (Common Name Resolution Protocol); DEN (Directory Enabled Networks); Directory Services: Handle System; LDAP (Lightweight Directory Access Protocol); Metadata; Microsoft Active Directory; Name Services; NDS (Novell Directory Services); NIS (Network Information System); RDF (Resource Description Framework); Search and Discovery Services; Service Advertising and Discovery; SLP (Service Location Protocol); URI (Uniform Resource Identifier); URN (Uniform Resource Name); WebDAV; White Pages Directory Services; WHOIS ("Who is")

Linktionary!—Tom Sheldon's Encyclopedia of Networking updates	http://www.linktionary.com/x/x500.html
Directory Standards at Open Information Interchange (a great overview with detailed references, including a list of related ITU-T documents)	http://158.169.50.95:10080/oii/en/directory.html
ITU Series X Recommendations	http://www.itu.int/itudoc/itu-t/rec/x/x500up/index.html
"X.500 - The Directory Standard and its Application" by Doug Steedman	http://www.techapps.co.uk/chapx500.html
X.500 directory services information and reports at SURFnet	http://www.surfnet.nl/innovatie/afgesloten/x500/

The X.500 Global Directory Service   http://ganges.cs.tcd.ie/ntrg/x500.html
(search the X.500 global directory for
individuals)

Barbara Shuh's introduction to directories   http://www.nlc-bnc.ca/pubs/netnotes/notes45.htm
and X.500

Colin Robbins's X.500 page at Nexor   http://www.nexor.co.uk/public/directory.html

X.509 Certificates

X.509 is an ITU standard for digital certificates. It is important because it is the basis of the Internet's PKI (public-key infrastructure) standard. The X.509 was first published in 1988 as part of the ITU X.500 directory services standard. The latest version (3.0) was released in 1996. X.500 is a database of named entities (people, computers, printers, and so on) that was meant for global use. Think of a global telephone book. The design was distributed so that organizations could manage the part of the database pertaining to the entities it managed. While X.500 directory services have failed to take hold, X.509 has become the leading framework for certificate services.

 The IETF's PKIX (Public Key Infrastructure X.509) defines the management of X.509 keys. The Web site is given later.

X.509 defines a certificate format for binding public keys to X.500 distinguished path names. X.509 supports both secret-key (single-key) cryptography and public-key cryptography. The original intention was to define the keyholder that could modify a particular X.500 directory node. The original X.509 data record was originally designed to hold a password instead of a public key.

X.509 version 3 defines the field contents of a certificate, which is a record of data that contains 11 major fields as shown in Figure X-1.

The fields in the certificate define the issuing CA, the signing algorithms, how long the certificate is valid, and information about the owner of the certificate. The version 3 extension fields are useful for adding additional information into the certificate. This information can be customized to fit a particular issuer's own requirements. For example, an insurance company could add patient information. A retail chain could add unique customer information. More important, these fields may provide access control information, which authorizes the holder of the certificate to access network or system resources. Thus, version 3 X.509 certificates can play a unique role in managing network security.

An important aspect of certificates that is easy to overlook is their portable nature. When public-key schemes were first created, names and associated keys were listed in the same public file. Later, each name/key pair was broken out into a separate record and then signed by a certificate authority, thus creating "certificates." A certificate may be freely distributed with trust since the content is digitally signed by the issuing certificate authority. This portable nature makes certificates ideal for use in authentication.

As mentioned, X.500 directory services has not achieved its goals, but a slimmer directory services protocol called LDAP (Lightweight Directory Access Protocol) has been derived from

X
Y
Z

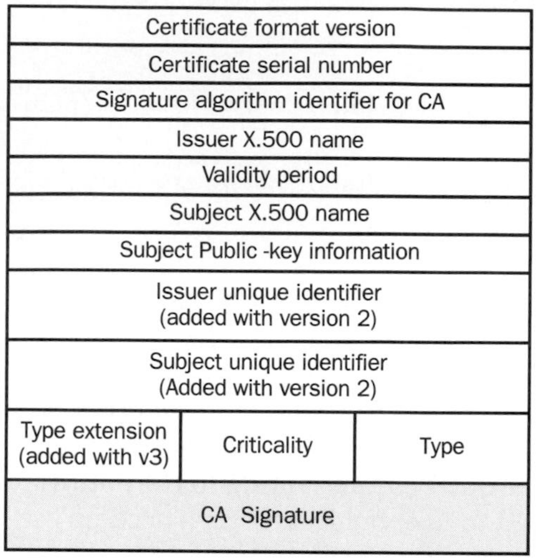

Certificate format version		
Certificate serial number		
Signature algorithm identifier for CA		
Issuer X.500 name		
Validity period		
Subject X.500 name		
Subject Public -key information		
Issuer unique identifier (added with version 2)		
Subject unique identifier (Added with version 2)		
Type extension (added with v3)	Criticality	Type
CA Signature		

Figure X-1.   *X.509 v3 certificate layout (source Entrust)*

parts of X.500. LDAP was defined by the IETF specifically to use on the Internet (or intranets). It is based on some of the features in X.500 and is even interoperable with X.500 (if such installations exist!). Refer to the LDAP heading in the book for more information.

Certificates are typically managed by CAs (certificate authorities), which are public entities, usually regulated, that act as third-party key holders. To create a certificate, the CA combines a user's public key with the user information (as defined by X.509), then signs the information with its private key. Anyone receiving the certificate can verify its authenticity with the CA's public key. The authenticity of the CA's public key can be further verified via the *chain of trust* that exists within the PKI (public-key infrastructure). Certificates, public keys, and PKI are discussed under separate headings in this book.

Related Entries   Access Control; Authentication and Authorization; Certificates and Certification Systems; Cryptography; Digital Signatures; DSS (Digital Signature Standard); EAP (Extensible Authentication Protocol); Hash Functions; IPSec (IP Security); Key Distribution and Management; OPSEC (Open Platform for Security); PKI (Public-Key Infrastructure); Public-Key Cryptography; Secret-Key Cryptography; Security

Linktionary!—Tom Sheldon's Encyclopedia of Networking updates	http://www.linktionary.com/x/x509.html
IETF Simple Public-Key Infrastructure (spki) charter	http://www.ietf.org/html.charters/spki-charter.html
IETF Public-Key Infrastructure (X.509) (pkix) Working Group	http://www.ietf.org/html.charters/pkix-charter.html
NIST's PKI site	http://csrc.ncsl.nist.gov/pki

NIST's PKI Technical Working Group   http://csrc.ncsl.nist.gov/pki/twg/twgindex.html

Security Links at Telecom Information   http://china.si.umich.edu/telecom/net-security.html
Resources on the Internet

xDSL

See DSL (Digital Subscriber Line).

XHTML

See HTML (Hypertext Markup Language).

XML (Extensible Markup Language)

XML is a markup language that is more extensible than HTML and derived from the earlier
SGML (Standard Generalized Markup Language) standard. HTML was also derived from
SGML, but is limited to presenting graphical hyperlinked information on Web pages. XML
allows developers to create more functional documents for exchanging structured information
across the Internet. These documents may be Web pages viewed and manipulated by people
or business documents that are exchanged during automated computer-to-computer business
transactions. XML is a W3C (World Wide Web Consortium) specification. The first release
appeared in February 1998.

XML creates a framework for documents in which data has meaning as defined by tags. In
contrast, data in HTML documents is tagged only with a style. It is formatted, but there is no
description about what a particular block of data is so that some other applications can grab it
and use it in a meaningful way.

As an analogy, compare watching the financial channel on TV to viewing financial Web
pages on the Internet. The TV presents information that you can try to remember. In contrast,
financial Web pages give you information that you can capture and save. If the data is on an
HTML page, that's better than the TV, but not as good as XML. Since HTML does not provide
a description of what information on a page is, you have to highlight the data, copy and paste
it, then edit it to get the data into tabular form. In some cases, it's easier to just retype the data!
XML documents define data inside tagged elements, allowing you to extract the data directly
into spreadsheets or databases.

In traditional data storage, records are defined by lines of text and fields are represented
by the position of the data element in the line (and separated by a character such as a comma).
Now, assume you open the document with a text editor and try to figure out what all the data
is without descriptive information. Not easy. With XML, data is defined by descriptive tags.
For example, the following tag identifies a document author:

      <creator>Tom Sheldon</creator>

Descriptive tags benefit searching, document classification, and so on. Search engines
can easily identify the author as the name between these tags. The industry has worked to
standardize the most common descriptors such as "title," "subject," "publisher," "date," and
so on. Most are defined in the Dublin Core and other metadata standards. See "Metadata." In

addition, entire industries (automotive, medical, construction, and so on) have worked to create their own standard sets of descriptors to define common elements within documents.

By describing data in XML documents with tags, Web pages move from being just "human-readable" to being "computer readable." Documents all over the Web will move from an information presentation paradigm to an information database paradigm. While people will be able to turn XML documents into useful data, the bigger picture is computer-to-computer information exchange and automated business transactions over Internet links.

In a multitiered client/server model, a user accesses a middle-tier presentation and business logic server, which itself accesses back-end databases. The middle-tier server retrieves data from the back-end system based on user requests, then converts the data to XML format and sends it to the client. Since all the data from the back-end server has been identified and tagged by the mid-tier server, the client knows how to identify the data as well. It can reformat the information, use it in other programs, or extract parts of the data as needed.

Markup languages were used as early as the 1960s. Charles Goldfarb at IBM headed a team that created GML (Generalized Markup Language). This later expanded into SGML, which included more automation. In the 1990s, Tim Berners-Lee derived HTML from SGML when he created the technology for the Web. XML is a hybrid of concepts and ideas learned in HTML and SGML, with an emphasis on universal data exchange.

One of the most concise descriptions of XML was made by Simon Phipps, IBM's evangelist for Java and XML, during a chat session (see Web address at the end of the section). He said that XML itself is nothing but the assertion "let's use tags to format data."

Phipps likes to describe the transition to XML as the "last gap" in defining a new world of information sharing. This has been achieved through the following progression of events:

- TCP/IP has become the near-universal communications protocol for connecting information systems.

- Browsers have become the common space into which solutions can be loaded.

- Component technologies such as Java are now established as the standard for platform-neutral computing.

- Data was the last gap. An open data-formatting specification was needed. XML is that specification.

More and more, XML is being selected as a solution for building large software projects. According to the W3C, opting for XML is a bit like choosing SQL for databases: you still have to build your own database and your own programs/procedures that manipulate it, but XML is license-free and there is a growing community of developers with tools and experience.

This topic continues at the Linktionary! Web site with a section describing the basics of XML, along with a list of XML specifications, initiatives, and developments. You'll also find a list of industry-defined schemas.

Related Entries   Distributed Object Computing; Document Management; EDI (Electronic Data Interchange); Electronic Commerce; Handle System; HTML (Hypertext Markup Language); Hypermedia and Hypertext; Metadata; Name Services; OAG (Open Applications Group); OIM (Open Information Model); Portal; Repository; Search and Discovery Services; Service Advertising and Discovery; SGML (Standard Generalized Markup Language); SLP (Service Location Protocol); SOAP (Simple Object Access Protocol); Transaction Processing; WebDAV; *and* Web Technologies and Concepts

Linktionary!—Tom Sheldon's Encyclopedia of Networking updates	http://www.linktionary.com/x/xml.html
W3C's XML page (a must see)	http://www.w3.org/XML/
W3C's other XML pages (see X in alphabetical list)	http://www.w3.org/
XML.com	http://www.xml.com/
XML.org	http://www.xml.org/
OASIS (Organization for Structured Information Standards) promotes SGML, HTML, and XML	http://www.oasis-open.org/
The XML Cover Pages, Robin Cover, Managing Editor	http://www.oasis-open.org/cover/
XML World	http://www.xmlworld.org/
OII Guide to XML and related standards	http://158.169.50.95:10080/oii/en/xmlguide.html
XML Tutorial at GE Global eXchange Services (excellent, worth your time)	http://www.geis.com/
Articles at ACM Crossroads (see "Markup Languages" section)	http://info.acm.org/crossroads/doc/indices/features.html
IBM's XML Zone	http://www.ibm.com/developer/xml/
Simon Phipps comments about XML	http://www.ibm.com/developer/features/feature021599-javaxml.html

X/Open

X/Open Company Ltd. was established to provide standards for the UNIX environment. Its main goal is to promote open systems protocols for UNIX languages, interfaces, networks, and applications. It also promotes portability of applications between the different UNIX environments and supports the IEEE (Institute of Electrical and Electronics Engineers) POSIX (Portable Operating System Interface for UNIX) specifications.

In 1996, The Open Group was formed by merging the OSF (Open Software Foundation) and X/Open Company Ltd. Refer to The Open Group's Web site at http://www.opengroup.org for more information.

XSL (Extensible Style Language)

See XML (Extensible Markup Language).

X
Y
Z

X Series ITU Recommendations

The ITU (International Telecommunications Union) X series of standards is targeted at *data networks* and *open systems communications*. The following provides a general description of the categories. For a complete list of ITU recommendations, refer to the Web site given here.

- **X.1 to X.199**   A variety of data communications and computer networking recommendations
- **X.200**   OSI basic seven-layer reference model descriptions and documents
- **X.300**   Internetworking
- **X.400**   Mail-handling systems
- **X.500**   Directory services
- **X.700**   OSI systems management

Related Entries   G Series ITU Recommendations; H Series ITU Recommendations. ITU (International Telecommunications Union; OSI (Open Systems Interconnection) Model; X.400 Message Handling System; *and* X.500 Directory Services

ITU Recommendations (see X-series   /   http://www.itu.int/itudoc/itu-t/rec/
Recommendations in list)

X Window

The X Window System, or "X" as it is sometimes called, can be thought of as a terminal for UNIX environments with a graphical user interface. X was developed in the early 1990s as a basic client/server system, except that the terminology is reversed from the way people think of client/server today. In a typical X Window arrangement, the user's terminal only displays information and accepts keyboard input. Both the client and server processing is executed at a remote device. Since the remote device (and not the user's terminal) runs the client software, it is called the X client. Since the user's terminal "serves up" the screen information, it is called the X server. X provides an environment for developing graphical client/server applications, and a developer can use a GUI development toolkit such as Motif to create the applications. See "Motif" for more information.

X provides a common windowing system that bridges many platforms. It is the standard graphical engine for UNIX and Linux. X is inherently independent from operating systems and hardware. Many applications are available that integrate X applications to network computers or personal computer environments such as Windows.

X can be used to create and access interactive applications on the Web. The browsers can invoke remote applications, and its integration with HTTP protocols makes access to applications platform independent, allowing "universal access" to any application. Optimization techniques are used to improve performance over WANs and serial lines by using caching, compression, and other techniques.

An interesting aspect of X is that it is the model for "thin clients," small-footprint computers that run Java applications, relying heavily on centralized servers to do much of the work.

The latest version of The X Window System is System 11 Release 6.x (as of this writing, the exact version was release 6.5.1, but further upgrades may occur by the time you read this).

Two Internet RFC provide information about the X Window System:

- RFC 1198 (FYI on the X Window System, January 1991)
- RFC 1013 (X Window System Protocol, Version 11, June 1987)

Related Entries   CDE (Common Desktop Environment); Linux; Motif; Open Group; Terminal Services; Thin Clients; *and* UNIX

Linktionary!— Tom Sheldon's Encyclopedia of Networking updates	http://www.linktionary.com/x/xwindow.html
MW3 Web site (X and Motif information)	http://www.cen.com/mw3
The Open Group's X information	http://www.x.org/
The XFree86 Project	http://www.xfree86.org
Jennifer Myers's Web page (See "X-Window System" section for links)	http://www.geek-girl.com/unix.html
Operating System Tutorials (see "X-Windows & Motif" section)	http://www.wizard.com/users/baker/public_html/OSTutor.html

Z39.50

Z39.50 is a U.S. national standard defining a protocol for computer-to-computer information retrieval. It was developed in 1988 (and revised in 1992) by the National Information Standards Organization (NISO), a standards development body that serves the publishing, library, and information services communities. The protocol is often layered over TCP/IP. Internet RFCs related to Z39.50 include RFC 1729 (Using the Z39.50 Information Retrieval Protocol, December 1994), RFC 1625 (WAIS over Z39.50, June 1994), and RFC 2056 (Uniform Resource Locators for Z39.50, November 1996).

Related Entry   Document Management

Linktionary!—Tom Sheldon's Encyclopedia of Networking updates	http://www.linktionary.com/z/z3950.html
An Overview of the Z39.50 Information Retrieval Standard	http://www.ifla.org/VI/5/op/udtop3/udtop3.htm

Zero Administration for Windows Initiative

The Zero Administration for Windows, or ZAWS, initiative is a Microsoft scheme for managing Windows-based network clients. It automates the task of operating system updates, application installation, desktop configuration, and user access. It allows users to "roam" from location to location while maintaining the same desktop because personal desktop preferences and application information is stored on central servers. The ZAWS initiative is designed to support small-footprint computers such as thin clients as well as other desktop systems.

Key capabilities enabled by the Zero Administration for Windows initiative are as follows:

- Centralized administration and control of desktop computers, with the ability to lock down desktop configurations

- Automatic operating system updates and application installations from a central location

- Stateless desktop computing, with persistent central data storage

- Side-by-side machine replacement in case of desktop hardware failure

- Client-side ability to cache data, thus improving performance, reducing network traffic, and enabling work to continue if the network fails

All of these features allow users to run applications and access data from anywhere without the need to transfer files and applications between computers. ZAWS also helps to reduce help desk and support calls because users operate with a familiar desktop wherever they go and the desktop information is stored in a central location that support staff can both configure and troubleshoot. The desktop configuration can also be locked down to prevent users from changing it in a way that would make the desktop appear confusing the next time they log on.

Microsoft's IntelliMirror is a set of management technologies built into Windows 2000 that provides desktop change and configuration management. With IntelliMirror, user's data, personal computer settings, and computing environment follows them to other locations. Based on policy definitions, IntelliMirror is able to deploy, recover, restore or replace user's data, software, and personal settings in a Windows 2000–based environment. See "IntelliMirror."

Related Entries   Configuration Management; DMI (Distributed Management Interface); DMTF (Distributed Management Task Force); Microsoft Windows; Network Management; Thin Clients; *and* Wired for Management

  Microsoft's Zero Administration for Windows site   http://www.microsoft.com/windows/zak/

Zones and Zone Servers

Zones are subsets of DNS (Domain Name System) namespaces or, in the case of the Internet, *the* DNS namespace. The global DNS namespace includes the names of all sites in an intranet or the Internet, organized hierarchically under the familiar domain "dot com," "dot gov," "dot org," and so on. Within this global DNS namespace are individual *zones of authority*, which are independently managed domains. The administrative authorities are responsible for managing that part of the domain.

For example, under the .com domain are familiar zones such as www.microsoft.com or www.yahoo.com. Zones might be further partitioned into subzones. For example, Microsoft has its own zones for products, support, development tools, and so on.

The defining feature of zones is that they contain *zone servers*, usually two—one primary and one secondary backup system. As for terminology, zone servers = name servers = DNS servers. They are all the same. The primary zone server is where the *zone file* is managed. The secondary zone server gets a read-only copy of this file.

The zone file is a text file that contains a series of *resource records* that bind names to values in the following form:

Name, Value, Type, Class, TTL

Name is the DNS name, while *Value* is an associated IP address. *Type* defines what the DNS record is and thus what kind of information it contains. Some common record types are as follows:

- **Type = A (Address)**   Indicates the record is a name to IP address mapping.

- **Type = NS (Name Server)**   Indicates the record specifies the domain name of servers that provide DNS naming services. A root server in a domain contains an NS record for each second-level server, along with an A record that provides the IP address of the server.

- **Type = CNAME (Canonical Name)**   The record contains a mapping from one domain to another domain. This record defines aliases.

The *Class* field defines a way to specify other entities that might define other type of resource records for the zone file. So far, only the Class IN (Internet) has been used. Finally, the TTL (Time To Live) field specifies how long the record from another server should be allowed to remain cached before it is removed.

Clients query zone servers primarily to obtain IP addresses for a given DNS name. The name is submitted to the server and the server returns an IP address. Often, a server may not have information about a particular name, so the request is forwarded up the hierarchy of name servers until the request can be satisfied.

Related Entries   DNS (Domain Name Service) and Internet Domains; Internet; Routing; Routing on the Internet; *and* TCP/IP (Transmission Control Protocol/Internet Protocol)

 Linktionary!—Tom Sheldon's Encyclopedia of Networking updates

http://www.linktionary.com/z/zones.html

X
Y
Z

Index

A

AAA (authentication, authorization, and accounting), 964, 1117
AAL (ATM Adaptation Layer), 71–72
Abilene, 2–3, 1018
ABONE (Active Backbone), 3
ABR (available bit rate), 77, 1262
Access control entries (ACEs), 5–6
Access control lists (ACLs), 6
Access controls, 3–8
    C2 security rating, 155
    defined, 3–4
    discretionary access control, 5–6
    firewalls, 7
    logon process and, 4–5
    proxy servers, 6–7
    RADIUS, 7
Access providers, 9
Accounting. *See also* Auditing, Security auditing
    Internet, 12–13
    metering and, 12
    passwords and, 964
    roaming and, 12–13
    services, 13
ACD (automatic call distribution), 176
ACEs (access control entries), 5–6

ACID (atomicity, consistency, isolation, durability), 14, 1266–1267
ACK (acknowledgement)
    connection establishment and, 255–256
    flow controls and, 247
    NAK and, 844
    overview of, 14–15
ACL (asynchronous connectionless), 131
ACLs (access control lists), 6
ACR (attenuation to crosstalk ratio), 164
Acrobat, 15–16
ActivCard, 1255
Active Backbone (ABONE), 3
Active Desktop, Microsoft, 1349
Active Directory, Microsoft, 16, 28, 776–777
Active documents, 16
Active Networks (Active Nets), 3, 16–17
Active server pages (ASPs), 17–18
ActiveX, 18–21
    advantages for Web sites, 19–20
    COM and DCOM and, 235–236
    controls, 19–20

    data objects, 330
    defined, 18–19
    features of, 20
    information and support for, 20–21
Adapters, 21
Adaptive bridges, 735
Adaptive Differential Pulse Code Modulation (ADPCM), 31
Adaptive load balancing (ALB), 739–740
ADC (analog-to-digital conversion), 21–23, 31
ADCCP (Advanced Data Communications Control Procedure), 23
Add/drop multiplexer (ADM), 1166–1167. *See also* Multiplexing
Address resolution, 57, 900. *See also* ARP (Address Resolution Protocol)
Addresses, e-mail, 23–24
Addresses, network, 24–27
    ATM addressing, 76
    connection-oriented, 27
    higher-level addressing, 26
    internetwork addressing, 25–26
    MAC addressing, 24–25
    types of, 24

ADM (add/drop multiplexer), 1166–1167. *See also* Multiplexing

Administration, data protection measures, 312

Administrator accounts, 27–30
assigning and protecting, 28
defined, 27–28
lists of tasks, 29
in Windows NT/2000, 11

Admission control, 30–31, 628, 1089

Adobe Acrobat, 15–16

ADOs (ActiveX Data Objects), 20, 330

ADPCM (Adaptive Differential Pulse Code Modulation), 31

ADSL (Asymmetrical Digital Subscriber Line), 31, 406. *See also* DSL (Digital Subscriber Line)

Advanced Data Communications Control Procedure (ADCCP), 23

Advanced Encryption Standard (AES), 279

Advanced Intelligent Network (AIN), 614

Advanced Internet networks, 586

Advanced Mobile Phone Service (AMPS), 1224, 1380–1381. *See also* Wireless mobile communications

Advanced Peer-to-Peer Networking. *See* APPN (Advanced Peer-to-Peer Networking)

Advanced Program-to-Program Communications. *See* APPC (Advanced Program-to-Program Communications)

Advanced Research Projects Agency Network (ARPANET), 58–59, 633, 654–655

Advertising, 31–32. *See also* Service advertising

AES (Advanced Encryption Standard), 279

AES (NIST Advanced Encryption Standard), 279

AFP (AppleTalk Filing Protocol), 32–33

AFS (Andrew File System), 33–35
background of, 33
distributed file systems, 515
features of, 33–34
UNIX and, 1287

AGCN (Arbinet Global Clearing Network), 108

Agents. *See also* Bots
Internet, 35–36
network management, 36, 892
SNMP and RMON, 1067

Aggregate Route-based IP Switching (ARIS), 56

Aggregation, 37. *See also* Link aggregation, Load balancing

AIIM (Association for Information and Image Management International), 397

AIN (Advanced Intelligent Network), 614

ALB (adaptive load balancing), 739–740

Alcatel 1000, 1164

Algorithms
Bellman-Ford, 114–115
block ciphers, 279
Blowfish, 278–279
CAST-128, 278
CAST-256, 278
DES (Data Encryption Standard), 274, 277–278
Diffie-Hellman, 357
digest, 349–350
Dijkstra, 361
distance-vector and link-state, 120, 372–374
DSA (Digital Signature Algorithm), 183
DSS (Digital Signature Standard), 408–409
encryption and, 273, 711
FEAL (Fast Data Encipherment Algorithm), 279
IDEA (International Data Encryption Algorithm), 279
PGP and, 973–974
queuing, 1028
SAFER (Security And Fast Encryption Routine), 279
Skipjack, 279
Triple DES, 277–278
Twofish, 278–279

ALOHA, 38

ALU (average line usage), 110

AM (amplitude modulation), 183–184, 803

America Online (AOL), 9, 202

American National Standards Institute. *See* ANSI (American National Standards Institute)

American Registry for Internet Numbers (ARIN), 56

American Standard Code for Information Interchange (ASCII), 128, 154, 397

American Telephone and Telegraph. *See* AT&T (American Telephone and Telegraph)

American Wire Gauge (AWG), 95

Amplifiers, EDFAs, 936

Amplitude modulation (AM), 183–184, 803

AMPS (Advanced Mobile Phone Service), 1224, 1380–1381. *See also* Wireless mobile communications

Analog-to-digital conversion (ADC), 21–23

Analog transmission, 38–39, 1140
analog lines, 239
cellular services, 1380–1382
compared with digital transmission, 38–39
converting, 39
medium and frequency ranges for, 39
OSI physical layer and, 295–296
waveforms of, 423–424

Andrew File System. *See* AFS (Andrew File System)

Angel Technologies, 576

Anonymous FTP sites, 554

Anonymous (guest) access, 39–40

ANSI (American National Standards Institute), 40–41, 506, 587

Antiviruses, 1306–1307

Any-to-any services, 954

Anycasting, 41–42

AnyNet, 42–43

AOL (America Online), 9, 202

Apache, 43

APIs (application programming interfaces), 43–44

APON (ATM PON), 991

APPC (Advanced Program-to-Program Communications), 44–45. *See also* APPN (Advanced Peer-to-Peer Networking)
conversational APIs, 43
defined, 44
transaction programs of, 44–45

Apple Computer, 45–46
AFP (AppleTalk Filing Protocol), 32–33
Macintosh, 759
Open Transport protocol, 33, 46
overview of, 45

AppleShare, 33, 46–47

AppleTalk, 47–48

AppleTalk Filing Protocol (AFP), 32–33

Application layer, OSI model, 48, 303–304, 943

Application-level gateways, 49, 1013

Application programming interfaces (APIs), 43–44

Application servers, 49–50, 787, 839

Application Service Providers (ASPs), 60–62

Application-Specific Integrated Circuit (ASIC), 59–60, 820, 896

Applications, bandwidth requirements, 106

APPN (Advanced Peer-to-Peer Networking), 50–54
    future developments of, 53
    HPR (High-Performance Routing) as upgrade to, 591
    overview of, 50
    routing environment of, 51–53

APS (automatic protection switching), 1166

Arbinet Global Clearing Network (AGCN), 108

Archives, data. See Backing up and archiving data

ARCNET (Attached Resource Computing Network), 54–55
    configuration of, 55
    token passing in, 8, 54

Area border routers, 947

ARIN (American Registry for Internet Numbers), 56

ARIS (Aggregate Route-based IP Switching), 56

ARP (Address Resolution Protocol), 56–58
    function of, 56–57
    illustration of address resolution process, 57
    RARP and, 57
    RFCs for, 58

ARPA (Advanced Research Projects Agency). See DARPA (Defense Advanced Research Project Agency)

ARPANET (Advanced Research Projects Agency Network), 58–59, 654–655, 654–655

ARQ (automatic repeat request), 457–458

AS (authentication server), Kerberos, 708, 710

AS (autonomous system), 93–95
    BGP and, 118–119
    confederation of, 94
    gateway protocols for, 94
    IGP and, 609
    Internet architecture and, 641–642
    OSPF (Open Shortest Path First) and, 947
    overview of, 93
    peering and, 970
    routing and, 478, 1083

ASCII (American Standard Code for Information Interchange), 128, 154, 397

ASIC (Application-Specific Integrated Circuit), 59–60, 820, 896

ASN (autonomous system number), 647

ASPs (active server pages), 17–18

ASPs (application service providers), 60–62, 952, 1135

Association for Information and Image Management International (AIIM), 397

Asymmetric cryptography, 276, 1014. See also Cryptography

Asymmetrical Digital Subscriber Line (ADSL), 31, 406. See also DSL (Digital Subscriber Line)

Asymmetrical multiprocessing, 62, 835

Asynchronous communications
    discussions forums and, 571, 690
    electronic mail (e-mail) and, 436, 571, 690
    error-correction with, 63–64
    interface standards for, 64
    modems and, 800
    OSI physical layer for, 296–297
    vs. synchronous, 622, 1207

Asynchronous connectionless (ACL), 131

Asynchronous ring mode, FDDI, 497

Asynchronous Transfer Mode. See ATM (Asynchronous Transfer Mode)

AT&T (American Telephone and Telegraph)
    overview of, 82–83, 82–83

role in formation of telecommunication system, 1233

UNIX and, 1285–1286

ATM Adaptation Layer (AAL), 71–72

ATM (Asynchronous Transfer Mode), 65–82. See also CIP (Classical IP over ATM), IP over ATM, IP over SONET
    AAL (ATM Adaptation Layer) and, 71–72
    addressing, 76
    as broadband service, 145
    as cell switching service, 240
    cells and cell relay in, 70–71, 189–190
    CoS and, 271
    CSR (Cell Switched Router) and, 281–282
    edge devices and, 416
    frame relay and, 547
    hybrid networks using, 80–82
    integrating with IP, 900
    interfacing with, 72–74
    inverse multiplexing over, 611–612
    LANE (LAN Emulation) and, 80, 726–727
    MPOA (Multiprotocol over ATM) and, 813
    network design for, 66
    NNI (Network Node Interface) and, 904
    over SONET, 881–883
    overview of, 65–66
    PNNI (Private Network-to-Network Interface) and, 983
    QoS (quality of service) and, 1020–1021
    real-time multimedia over, 1067
    reference model for, 66–70
    service categories of, 77–78
    traffic management, 76–79, 99, 1261–1262
    UNI (User-Network Interface) and, 1284
    virtual circuits and call setup and, 74–76
    vs. Gigabit Ethernet, 565–566
    WANs (wide area networks) and, 1331

ATM PON (APON), 991
Atomicity, consistency, isolation,
    durability (ACID), 14, 1266–1267
Attached Resource Computing
    Network. *See* ARCNET (Attached
    Resource Computing Network)
Attacks/attackers
    biometric access devices
        and, 124
    brute force attacks, 276
    cookies, 264
    overview of, 84
    passive/active, 1115–1116
    replay, 1116
Attenuation, 84, 160–161, 501–502
Attenuation to crosstalk ratio
    (ACR), 164
Attributes, 85, 362
Audio, streaming, 1349
Auditing, 85–87.
    See also Security auditing
        access control and, 5
        data protection measures, 312
        example of system for, 86–87
        network management systems
            for, 86
        resources, 85
        RFCs for, 87
        software metering and
            licensing, 85–86
Authentication and authorization,
    88–93. *See also* Cryptography
        access control and, 4–5
        biometric access devices
            and, 124
        Bluetooth and, 130
        certificates and, 90, 192
        CHAP and, 201
        EAP and, 414
        Kerberos, 90, 708–711
        keys and, 90, 711–712
        one-time passwords, 927–928
        overview of, 88
        PAP and, 962
        passwords and, 964
        PKIs (public key
            infrastructures) and,
            90, 979
        RADIUS and, 1034–1037
        secret key encryption and, 89
        SSL (Secure Sockets Layer)
            and, 1179–1180
        SSO (single sign-on) and,
            90–91

TACACS and, 1212
token-based, 1254–1256
two-factor, 89
working groups and RFCs for,
    91–93
Authentication server (AS), Kerberos,
    708, 710
Authenticode, Microsoft, 93
Authorization. *See* Authentication
    and authorization
Autochangers, 707
Automatic call distribution
    (ACD), 176
Automatic protection switching
    (APS), 1166
Automatic repeat request (ARQ),
    457–458
Autonomous system. *See* AS
    (autonomous system)
Autonomous system number
    (ASN), 647
Availability. *See* Fault tolerance
Available bit rate (ABR), 77, 1262
Average line usage (ALU), 110
AWG (American Wire Gauge), 95

B

B-ISDN (Broadband-Integrated
    Services Digital Network),
    126–127
    ATM and, 66
    ISDN and, 126, 693
    SONET and, 126–127
B2B (business-to-business), 915
Baby Bells, 83, 96.
    See also RBOCs (regional Bell
    operating companies)
Back-end systems, 100
Backbone networks, 96–99
    80/20 and 20/80 rules, 98–99
    collapsed, 885
    core networks, 270
    distributed, 884
    Internet as, 637
    network designs, 884–885
    overview of, 96–98
Backbone star topology, 1222
Backing up and archiving data,
    101–102, 311
BackOffice, 777
Backplane architecture, 100–101

Backup domain controllers (BDCs),
    28, 401
Backward explicit congestion
    notification (BECN), 247, 546
Bandwidth, 102–111. *See also*
    Capacity, Throughput
        admission control and, 30
        brokering, 108
        carriers, 111
        classification, 1021–1022
        data rate and, 158
        defined, 295, 1140
        delays and, 337
        on demand, 110, 112, 693, 738
        DTM and, 411
        effect of protocols on, 102–104
        Gigabit Ethernet and, 565
        managing, 108–110, 586
        overview of, 102–104
        requirements and ratings,
            105–107
        reservation of, 626–627, 1056
        resource management
            and, 1060
        on time of day, 110
Bandwidth Allocation Control
    Protocol (BACP), 112
Bandwidth Allocation Protocol
    (BAP), 112
Banyan VINES, 111–112
Baseband networks, 113
Bastion host, 113
Baud, 113
BDCs (backup domain controllers),
    28, 401
Beans, 114
BECN (backward explicit congestion
    notification), 247, 546
Bell operating companies.
    See RBOCs (regional Bell
    operating companies)
Bell standards, modems, 114
Bellman-Ford distance-vector routing
    algorithm, 114–115
BeOS, 115
Beowulf systems, 836–837
BER (bit error rate), 164
Berkeley Internet Name Domain
    (BIND), 394
Best-effort services, 115–117
    IP and, 65, 116
    overview of, 115–116
    TCP and, 116, 1215, 1271

BGP (Border Gateway Protocol), 117–123
autonomous system domains and, 118–119
CIDR and, 119–120
as exterior routing protocol, 420, 946
iBGP, 119
information exchange on, 121
operation of, 120–122
overview of, 117–118
update message format of, 122
Binary Synchronous Communications (BISYNC), 127–128, 154
BIND (Berkeley Internet Name Domain), 394
Bindery, 123–124
Biometric access devices, 124–125
Bipolar encoding, 1206–1207
BISYNC (Binary Synchronous Communications), 127–128, 154
Bit error rate (BER), 164
Bit errors, 457
Bit-oriented protocols, 128
BizTalk, 432
Block ciphers, 279
Block-level storage access, 851
Block-mode data, 677
Block suballocation, 129
Block transmission, 129
Blowfish, 278–279
Bluetooth, 129–133
embedded systems and, 450
overview of, 129–130
personal area networks and, 131–133
service advertising and, 1132
specifications, 130–131
BNs (border nodes), 52
Bonding, 133, 792
BOOTP (BOOTstrap Protocol), 134
Bootstrapping (booting), 134–135
Border Gateway Protocol (BGP). See BGP (Border Gateway Protocol)
Border nodes (BNs), 52
Bots, 135–136
Bottlenecks, 901
Boundary routers, 117
BRI (basic rate interface), 136, 693

Bridges and bridging, 136–144
defined, 136, 148
Ethernet, 466
functionality of, 139–140
LANs and, 724
learning bridges, 735
load-sharing, 143
MAC sublayer and, 300
networking and, 875, 879
overview of, 136–139
remote techniques for, 143–144
source route bridging, 143
spanning tree algorithm and, 142–143
T1 lines and, 1222
terminology for, 138
transparent bridges, 140–142
types of bridges, 139
Broadband communications, 144–147.
See also Wireless broadband
compared with baseband, 113
defined, 144–145
modems, 799
network connection technologies, 878
residential, 1056–1058
typical systems for, 145–146
WANs and, 1331–1332
Broadband-Integrated Services Digital Network. See B-ISDN (Broadband-Integrated Services Digital Network)
Broadcast addresses, 148, 149
Broadcast domains, 148–149
bridges and, 138
Ethernet and, 234, 461
illustration of, 1204
Broadcast messages, 148
Broadcast networking, 149–150, 855
Broadcast storms, 141–142, 150
Broadcasting, 147, 290, 1299.
See also Webcasting
Brouter (bridge/router), 151
Browsers, Web, 151–152, 1341–1342
Brute force attacks, 276
Bulletin boards, 571
Burst multiplexing, 153, 934
Burst traffic, 152–153
Bus mastering, 901

Bus topology, 153–154. See also Switch fabrics/bus design
backplane architecture and, 100–101
middleware and, 785
network topologies and, 1258
Business metadata, 769
Byte-oriented protocols, 154

C

C2 security rating, 155
Cable and wiring, 155–171
copper cable, ACR (attenuation to crosstalk ratio), 164
copper cable, attenuation, 160–161
copper cable, capacitance, 161
copper cable, FEXT (far-end crosstalk), 163
copper cable, impedance and delay distortion (jitter), 161
copper cable, inductance and NEXT (near-end crosstalk), 162–163
copper cable, noise, 161–162
copper cable, overview, 157–160
high performance, 159
premises distribution system (PDS), 1008
standards, 155, 695–696
structured cabling system, 167–168, 1190
testing, 865
twisted-pair categories, 164–167
types of, 153, 156–157, 462
Cable (CATV). See CATV (cable)
Cable data networks. See CATV (cable) Data Networks
Cable Modem Termination System (CMTS), 170
CableLabs, 959
CAC (connection admission control)
ATM and, 79
QoS and, 30
traffic engineering and, 1262

Cache Array Routing Protocol
(CARP), 1346
Cache arrays, 1344
Cache Digest, 1346
Cache management, 174–176.
See also Web caching
content distribution and,
261–262
gateways as caching
service, 559
HTTP support for, 596
methods, 175–176
overview of, 174
SCSP (Server Cache
Synchronization Protocol)
and, 1107
Caching proxy mesh, 1344–1345
Call agents, 773
Call-back filing systems, 1186
Call centers, 176–178
Call-Level Interface (CLI), 327, 1175
Call Processing Language (CPL),
273, 1325
Campus networks, 178–181
Capacitance, copper cable, 161
Capacity, 181
Capacity planning, 181–182, 1260.
See also Traffic management
CAPs (Competitive Access
Providers), 182–183, 219, 1134
Capstone, 183, 359–360, 408
Capsules, 16
CardBus, 183
CARP (Cache Array Routing
Protocol), 1346
Carrier sense, 300, 758
Carrier sense multiple access/
collision avoidance
(CSMA/CA), 8, 281
Carrier sense multiple access/
collision detection. *See* CSMA/CD
(carrier sense multiple access/
collision detection)
Carrier signal, 183–184
Carriers. *See also* Communication
service providers
E carriers, 413
ILECs, 610–611
LECs, 736
list of, 1133–1134

modulation techniques
and, 803
OC (optical carriers), 880,
918–920
optical networks and, 933–934
overview of, 184
T carriers, 413
telecommunications and,
1231–1233
types of, 736
CAs (certification authorities)
issuing certificates, 192–193
PKIs (public key
infrastructures) and, 979
public keys and, 713
SSL and, 1180
trust relationships and, 1274
X.509 and, 1393–1394
CAST-128, 278
CAST-256, 278
Categories 1-7, twisted-pair cables,
164–167
CATV (cable)
architecture of, 168–170
as broadband service, 146
DSL and, 405
HFC (Hybrid Fiber/Coax)
and, 584–585
PacketCable and, 959
service providers,
238–239, 1135
CATV (cable) data networks, 172–174
operation of, 170–171
overview of, 172
service providers, 172
standards, 173
CBL (Common Business Library), 433
CBQ (class-based queuing), 1030
CBR (constant bit rate), 77
CBR (constraint-based routing),
260, 1081
CCITT (Consultive Committee for
International Telegraphy)
e-mail standards, 23
EIA standards, 420–421
history of, 184–185
ITU and, 699
CCS (Common Channel Signaling),
1176, 1320

CCSO (Computing and
Communications Services
Office), 845
CDDI (Copper Distributed Data
Interface), 185
CDE (Common Desktop
Environment), 185
CDFS (Compact Disk File
System), 780
CDMA (Code Division
Multiple Access)
circuits and, 214
development group for, 187
HFC (Hybrid Fiber/Coax)
and, 585
OFDM (orthogonal frequency
division multiplexing) and,
922–923
overview of, 186–187
S-CDMA, 171
spread spectrum
signaling in, 1174
CDPD (Cellular Digital Packet Data),
188, 960, 1383
CDSA (Common Data Security
Architecture), 188
CEBus (Consumer Electronic
Bus), 189
CEF (Cisco Express Forwarding), 477
Cell Switched Router (CSR), 281–282
Cell switching service, ATM, 240
Cells/cell relay, ATM, 70–71, 189–190
Cellular Digital Packet Data (CDPD),
188, 960, 1383
Cellular systems. *See also* Wireless
mobile communication
analog vs. digital, 1380–1382
CDMA and, 186–187
CDPD and, 188
standards, 1382–1383
topology of, 1378–1380
CENTRal Exchange (Centrex), 190
Central office (CO), 229–230, 753
Centrex (CENTRal Exchange), 190
CERN, 191
CERT (Computer Emergency
Response Team), 191
Certificates, 191–195
authentication/authorization
and, 90

creating, 192–193
overview of, 191–192
PKI and, 193–194, 979
public keys and, 712–713
as security mechanism, 1117
SSL and, 1180
validating, 193
X.509, 931, 1393–1395
Certification authorities. *See* CAs
(certification authorities)
CGI (Common Gateway Interface),
18, 195–196, 972
Challenge Handshake Authentication
Protocol. *See* CHAP
(Challenge Handshake
Authentication Protocol)
Channel aggregation, 666
Channel banks, 1222
Channel multiplexing.
See Multiplexing
Channel-oriented switched fabric,
1195–1196
Channel Service Unit/Data Service
Unit (CSU/DSU), 282–283, 409
Channels, 196–198
bonding, 133
defined, 196
types of, 197
virtual circuits and, 196
CHAP (Challenge Handshake
Authentication Protocol), 198–201
fields of, 200 201
function of, 198
passwords and, 965
process for use of, 199
token-based authentication
and, 1254
vs. PAP, 962
Chat, 201–202
Chat rooms, 571, 690
Check Point Software, 931
CICS (Customer Information Control
System), 202–203, 1268–1269
CIDR (Classless Inter-Domain
Routing), 203–208
ARIN and, 56
BGP and, 117, 119–120
classless addressing, 673
how it works, 205–208
overview of, 203–205
route aggregation with, 37,
1070–1071

supernetting and, 852
support for, 207
CIFS (Common Internet File System),
208–209, 515
CIM (Common Information Model)
directory services and, 342
DMI and, 387–388
overview of, 210
WBEM and, 1335–1336
CIP (Classical IP over ATM), 210–212,
683, 900
CIP (Common Indexing Protocol),
212–213, 579, 1112
Ciphers
block, 279
Blowfish/Twofish, 278–279
CAST-128/CAST-256, 278
DES/Triple Des, 277–278
overview of, 276–277
CIR (committed information rate),
213–214, 247, 544–545
Circuit-level proxy gateways, 1162
Circuit relay firewalls, 216
Circuit switching
DTM and, 411
ISDN and, 239
service providers, 216–218,
238–239
Circuits, 214–216
dedicated vs. switched, 217
illustrations of, 215
types of, 214
CISC (Complex Instruction Set
Computer), 218–219
Cisco Express Forwarding (CEF), 477
Cisco Systems
Fast EtherChannel (FEC), 740
IOS (Internetwork Operating
System), 53
routers, 6
tag switching, 1212
Citrix, 1238–1239
CIX (Commercial Internet
eXchange), 219
Class-based queuing (CBQ), 1030
Class inheritance, 917
Class of Service.
See CoS (Class of Service)
Classes, IP addressing, 673–674
Classical IP over ATM (CIP), 210–212,
683, 900
Classification, bandwidth, 1021–1022

Classless addressing, 673
Classless Inter-Domain Routing.
See CIDR (Classless
Inter-Domain Routing)
CLB (Component Load
Balancing), 227
Clearinghouses, bandwidth, 108
CLECs (competitive local
exchange carriers)
CAPs (Competitive Access
Providers) and, 182
IXC (Interexchange Carrier)
and, 700
LATA (Local Access and
Transport Area) and,
730–731
Network access services
and, 863
overview of, 219–220
service providers, 238, 1134
Telecommunication Reform
Act of 1996 and, 1234–1235
CLI (Call-Level Interface), 327, 1175
Client/server model, 220–224
advantages of, 223
application servers in, 49
back-end systems and, 100
background of, 220
configurations, 221–222
distributed applications
and, 374
enhancements, 223–224
networking and, 875
ODBC and, 921
Clients, 220
CLNP (Connectionless Network
Protocol), 224–225
Cluster controllers, 225
Clustering, 225–228
configurations, 227–228
defined, 225–226
fault tolerance and high
availability and, 489–490
features and benefits, 226
mirroring and, 790
multiprocessing and, 836–837
servers and storage devices
and, 225–226
VI Architecture and, 1300
CMC (Common Mezzanine
Card), 1200

CMIP (Common Management Information Protocol), 228
CMTS (Cable Modem Termination System), 170
CNNs (composite network nodes), 51–52, 51–52
CNRP (Common Name Resolution Protocol), 228
   name services and, 845
CO (central office), 229–230, 753
Co-location services, 232–233
Coaxial cable, 153, 230–231, 465
   defined, 156
   types of, 230
   uses of, 231
   vs. twisted pair, 230
Code Division Multiple Access.
   See CDMA (Code Division Multiple Access)
Codec (coder/decoder)
   converting analog waveforms to digital, 22
   digitizing analog transmissions, 39
Coffee Pot Control Protocol (CPCP), 272
Collaborative computing, 231–232
Collapsed backbones, 96–97
Collision avoidance, 460
Collision detection, 461
Collision domains
   defined, 138
   Ethernet, 461
   illustration of, 1204
   switching and, 1205
   using bridges to isolate, 137–138
Collisions/collision domains, 233–234
   causes of collisions, 233–234
   CSMA/CD and, 233
COM+, 235–236
   Microsoft.NET and, 774
COM (Component Object Model), 234–236, 383
   as basis for ActiveX, 18
   DCOM (Distributed COM) and, 235–236
   MTS (Microsoft Transaction Server) and, 1268
   OLE DB, 926
   overview of, 234–235
   vendor support, 20–21
Commercial Internet eXchange (CIX), 219

Committed information rate (CIR), 213–214, 247, 544–545
Common Business Library (CBL), 433
Common Channel Signaling (CCS), 1176, 1320
Common Data Security Architecture (CDSA), 188
Common Desktop Environment (CDE), 185
Common Gateway Interface (CGI), 18, 195–196, 972
Common Indexing Protocol (CIP), 212–213, 579, 1112
Common information model, 1055
Common Information Model (CIM), 210
Common Internet File System (CIFS), 208–209, 515
Common Management Information Protocol (CMIP), 228
Common Mezzanine Card (CMC), 1200
Common Name Resolution Protocol (CNRP), 228
Common Object Request Broker Architecture. See CORBA (Common Object Request Broker Architecture)
Common Programming Interface for Communications (CPI-C), 45, 50, 272–273
Common Security Services Manager (CSSM), 188
Common Switch Interface (CSIX), 1203
Communication.
   See also Telecommunications
     microwave communications, 782–785
     Peer-to-Peer communication, 968
     synchronous communications, 1206–1208
     transmission rates of, 106–107
Communication controllers, 237
Communication servers, 237–238
Communication service providers, 238–240. See also Carriers
   link providers, 238–239
   local and long distance carriers, 239–240
   types of providers, 238
Compact Disk File System (CDFS), 780
CompactPCI (CPCI), 1198–1199

Competitive Access Providers (CAPs), 182–183, 219, 1134
Competitive Local Exchange Carriers. See CLECs (Competitive Local Exchange Carriers)
Complex Instruction Set Computer (CISC), 218–219
Component Load balancing (CLB), 227
Component Object Model. See COM (Component Object Model)
Component software technology, 241
Component technology, 380–381
Composite network nodes (CNN), 51–52
Compound documents, 18, 241–242
Compression techniques, 103, 242–243
Computer Emergency Response Team (CERT), 191
Computer telephony (CT), 573
Computer-Telephony Integration (CTI), 283–284
Computing and Communications Services Office (CCSO), 845
Concentrator devices, 244
Conferencing, 244
Configuration management, 245, 892
Congestion control, 245–254
   bandwidth and, 109
   delays and, 338
   ECN (Explicit Congestion Notification), 251–252
   FACK and, 14
   fast retransmit/fast recovery, 249–250
   flow control and, 528–529
   frame relay, 247, 545–546
   management resources for, 253
   network architecture, 872
   overview of, 245–246
   QoS (quality of service) and, 1021–1022
   queue management and congestion avoidance, 250
   queuing and, 246
   RED (Random Early Discard), 250–251
   slow start and, 249
   TCP rate control, 247–249, 252
   techniques for managing, 246
   throughput and, 1244
   traffic engineering and, 1263
   transport protocols and, 1272

Connection admission control.
    See CAC (connection
    admission control)
Connection-oriented services
    ATM, 65
    defined, 27
    overview of, 258
    transport layer and, 303
    vs. connectionless, 955–956
Connectionless Network Protocol
    (CLNP), 224–225
Connectionless services, 258–259,
    955–956
Connections, 254–258
    end-to-end, 255
    handshake procedures
        and, 254
    HTTP, 596–597
    Internet types, 645
    process of, 255–257
    stateful/stateless, 1186–1187
Constant bit rate (CBR), 77
Constraint-based routing, 260, 1081
Consultive Committee for
    International Telegraphy.
    See CCITT (Consultive Committee
    for International Telegraphy)
Consumer Electronic Bus
    (CEBus), 189
Containers, 261, 362
Content distribution, 261–263
    caching and, 261–262,
        1341–1342
    mirroring and, 261–262, 791
    multimedia and, 823–824
    providers, 262
    reverse proxy cache and, 1347
Contention, 263
Controlled content distribution
    (CCD). *See* Content distribution
Controllers, embedded, 446–447
Convergence
    CTI (Computer-Telephony
        Integration) and, 283–284
    routing tables, 264
    voice/data, 263
Cookies, 264–266
    cutting, 266
    defined, 264
    load balancing and, 750
    procedure for use of, 265
Copper cable, 157–164
    ACR (attenuation to crosstalk
        ratio), 164
    attenuation, 160–161

capacitance, 161
    FEXT (far-end crosstalk), 163
    impedance and delay
        distortion (jitter), 161
    inductance and NEXT
        (near-end crosstalk),
        162–163
    noise, 161–162
    overview, 157–160
Copper Distributed Data Interface
    (CDDI), 185
CORBA (Common Object Request
    Broker Architecture), 266–270
    architecture of, 267–268
    distributed object computing
        and, 383
    IIOP (Internet Inter-ORB
        Protocol) and, 610
    object interface and operation,
        268–269
    OMA (Object Management
        Architecture) and,
        266–267, 926
    overview of, 266
Core networks, 270
CoS (Class of Service)
    bandwidth management
        and, 109
    Diff-Serv and, 350
    overview of, 270–272
    packets and, 821
    privatization of network traffic
        and, 1009–1011
    vs. QoS, 1018
Coupling mechanisms, 1085
Course wavelength division
    multiplexing (CWDM), 1338
CPCI (CompactPCI), 1198–1199
CPCP (Coffee Pot Control
    Protocol), 272
CPE (Customer Premises
    Equipment), 272
CPI-C (Common Programming
    Interface for Communications),
    45, 50, 272–273
CPL (Call Processing Language),
    273, 1325
Cracking, hackers and, 575
Cray, supercomputers, 1192
Crossbar, 1195–1196
Crosspoint matrix, 1195–1196
Cryptanalysis, 275–276
Cryptography, 273–280
    Advanced Encryption
        Standard (AES) and, 279

Bluetooth and, 130
    Capstone and, 183
    certificates in, 191
    ciphers, block, 279
    ciphers, Blowfish/Twofish,
        278–279
    ciphers,
        CAST-128/CAST-256, 278
    ciphers, DES/Triple Des,
        277–278
    ciphers, overview, 276–277
    cryptanalysis and, 275–276
    digital signatures, 357–360, 408
    e-mail and, 440–441
    encryption process, 274–275
    IPSec and, 686
    Kerberos and, 708
    keys, 89, 711–713
    message digests and, 768
    one-way hash functions, 928
    overview of, 273–274
    PGP (Pretty Good Privacy)
        and, 973–974
    Quantum cryptography, 1027
    S-HTTP (Secure HTTP)
        and, 1138
    as security mechanism, 1117
    Skipjack chip, 183
    SSL (Secure Sockets Layer)
        and, 1180–1181
CSIX (Common Switch
    Interface), 1203
CSMA/CA (carrier sense multiple
    access/collision avoidance), 8, 281
CSMA/CD (carrier sense multiple
    access/collision detection)
    collision sensing with, 233
    contention and, 263
    Ethernet and, 461
    Fast Ethernet and, 480–481
    network access methods, 8
    overview of, 280–281
CSR (Cell Switched Router), 281–282
CSSM (Common Security Services
    Manager), 188
CSU/DSU (Channel Service Unit/
    Data Service Unit), 282–283,
    409, 1222
CT (computer telephony), 573
CTI (Computer-Telephony
    Integration), 283–284
CUSeeMe, 1302
Customer Information Control
    System (CICS), 202–203,
    1268–1269

Customer Premises Equipment (CPE), 272

Cut-through architecture, 284–285, 339, 683

Cut-through routing, 285, 820, 1080

CWDM (course wavelength division multiplexing), 1338

D

DAC (dual attached concentrator), 495

Daemon, 287

DAFS (Direct Access File System)
 fast data access with, 287
 features of, 288
 file systems and, 513–514
 storage solutions and, 678, 851, 1097
 VI architecture and, 287–288
 VI Architecture and, 1301

DARPA (Defense Advanced Research Project Agency), 16–17, 58–59, 289. *See also* Internet Organizations and Committees

DAS (dual-attached station), 495

Data broadcasting, 290, 1299

Data centers, 290–293
 back-end systems and, 100
 design of, 292
 fault tolerance and high availability and, 490
 features of, 290–291
 InfiniBand and, 291–292
 Internet architecture and, 642
 SMCs (service management centers) and, 292–293

Data channels, 133

Data circuit-terminating equipment. *See* DCE (data circuit-terminating equipment)

Data communication, OSI model, 293–304
 application layer, 303–304
 communication protocols, 294
 data link layer, 297–299
 MAC sublayer, 299–301
 network layer, 302
 physical layer, 295–297
 transport layer, 303

Data compression. *See* Compression

Data consumers/data providers, 926

Data encoding. *See* Signaling

Data encryption. *See* Cryptography

Data Encryption Standard. *See* DES (Data Encryption Standard)

Data Exchange Interface (DXI), 73

Data link layer
 bridges, 139–140
 controls, 23, 298–299, 1108
 data communication and, 297–299
 error detection, 298
 Ethernet and, 464
 framing, 298
 LLC (Logical Link Control) and, 299, 743–744
 MAC (Media Access Control) and, 300–301, 758
 NICs (network interface cards) and, 901
 OSI model, 943
 overview of, 305

Data link protocols, 305–308

Data Link Switching (DLSw), 53, 385–386

Data management, 308

Data marts, 309

Data migration, 308, 309–310

Data mining, 135, 310–311, 924–925

Data networks.
 See Voice/data networks

Data over Cable Interface Specification. *See* DOCSIS (Data Over Cable Interface Specification)

Data protection, 308, 311–312

Data rates, 158, 585.
 See also Throughput

Data service unit (DSUs), 282.
 See also CSU/DSU (Channel Service Unit/Data Service Unit)

Data service units (DSUs), 282.
 See also CSU/DSU (Channel Service Unit/Data Service Unit)

Data sources, 920

Data storage, 857

Data striping. *See* RAID (Redundant Arrays of Inexpensive Disks)

Data superhighway, 902

Data switches, 312. *See also* Switching

Data Terminal Equipment (DTE), 297, 410

Data transfer rates, 313, 585

Data transmissions, 313

Data warehousing, 313–318
 architecture of, 315
 client/server model for, 221–222

components of, 314–315
 data management and, 308
 data marts and, 309
 DBMS and, 324
 informational vs. operational systems, 314
 planning and building, 317–318
 summary of information in, 316–317

Database connectivity
 middleware application servers, 328–329
 ODBC, 920–921
 SQL, 327–328
 three-tier model, 328
 tools, 330

Database management system.
 See DBMS (Database Management System)

Database servers, 325

Databases. *See also* DBMS (Database Management System)
 managing, 769–770
 middleware and, 786
 overview of, 318
 replication, 1052

Datacasting, 150

Datagrams, 319–321, 671–672, 872

Datajoiner, 330

Daughterboards (Mezzanines), 1200

DAV (Distributed Authoring and Versioning), 321, 600.
 See also WebDAV

DAVIC (Digital Audio Visual Council), 173, 322–323

DB2, 323

DBMS (database management system), 323–331
 client/server model and, 221, 223
 data management and, 308
 data warehousing and, 324
 database connectivity, middleware application servers, 328–329
 database connectivity, SQL, 327–328
 database connectivity, three-tier model, 328
 database connectivity, tools for, 330
 database servers and, 325
 distributed databases and, 326–327

features of, 323–324
IBM's DB2 and, 323
metadata in, 324
OODBMS, 326
RDBMS, 325–326
DBS (direct broadcast satellite)
microwave and, 784
overview of, 331
wireless broadband and, 1363
DCE (data circuit-terminating
equipment), 297, 333–334
DCE (Distributed Computing
Environment), 33, 334–335
DCOM (Distributed Component
Object Model). See also COM
(Component Object Model)
distributed object computing
architectures, 383
extending COM to
networks, 18
MTS (Microsoft Transaction
Server) and, 1268
overview of, 235–236, 335
vendor support for, 20–21
DDE (Dynamic Data Exchange), 335
DDM (Distributed Data
Management), 44
DDR (Dial-on-Dial Routing), 335–336
DE (discard eligibility), 546
DECnet, 336
Dedicated circuits, 217, 336–337
Dedicated digital services, 239
Dedicated lines, 239, 735
Defense Advanced Research Project
Agency (DARPA), 16–17,
58–59, 289. See also Internet
Organizations and Committees
Delay distortion (jitter), 161
Delay skew, 161
Delays, 337–341
congestion, 338
hardware and processing,
338–339
links and, 339–340
monitoring and
controlling, 340
overview of, 337–338
queuing and, 339
DEN (Directory Enabled Networks),
341–344, 364
Denial-of-service attacks, 40, 84, 344
Dense wavelength division
multiplexing. See DWDM
(dense wavelength
division multiplexing)

Department of Defense, security
standards, 155
DES (Data Encryption Standard).
See also Cryptography
encryption with, 274
NFS (Network File System)
and, 898
overview of, 277–278
security of, 275
as symmetric alogrithm, 276
Destination routing, 1077
Dfs (Distributed File System)
AFS and, 33
benefits of, 345
Dfs volumes, 345–346
features of, 33–34, 516–517
list of distributed file
systems, 515
NFS and, 34
Open Group and, 347
overview of, 344–347
DHCP (Dynamic Host Configuration
Protocol), 135, 347
DIA (Document Interchange
Architecture), 44–45
Diagnostics, 1240
Dial on demand, 112
Dial-on-Demand Routing (DDR),
335–336
Dial-up lines, 348
Dial-up services, 239
DIAMETER, 348–349
DID (direct inward dialing), 966
Diff-Serv (Differentiated Services),
350–357
architecture of, 351–356
bandwidth management
and, 109
CoS and, 271
IETF and, 356
network elements and,
353–356
overview of, 350–351
per-hop behaviors, 352–353
QoS and, 1024
vs. Int-Serv, 627
Diffie-Hellman, 357, 713, 1015
Digest algorithms, 349–350
Digital Audio Visual Council
(DAVIC), 173, 322–323
Digital cellular, 1381
Digital certificates. See Certificates
Digital, converting analog waveforms
to, 21, 31

Digital interNet Application
(DNA), 778
Digital Loop Carrier (DLC), 385,
1228–1229
Digital multimedia libraries, 636
Digital Satellite System (DSS), 331
Digital signal, level 0 (DSO), 22
Digital Signal Processing (DSP),
408, 922
Digital Signal-x (DSx), 409–410
Digital signaling, 295–296, 1140
Digital Signature Algorithm. See DSA
(Digital Signature Algorithm)
Digital Signature Standard (DSS),
359–360, 408–409
Digital signatures, 357–360, 441
PGP (Pretty Good Privacy)
and, 973–974
PKIs (public key
infrastructures) and, 979
Digital Subscriber Line. See DSL
(Digital Subscriber Line)
Digital transmission, 1141
Digital Video Broadcast (DVB), 1366
Digitizing, 39, 360
Dijkstra algorithm, 361
DirecPC system, 331–332
Direct Access File System. See DAFS
(Direct Access File System)
Direct broadcast satellite. See DBS
(direct broadcast satellite)
Direct inward dialing (DID), 966
Direct memory access (DMA), 901
Directories
metadirectories, 772
shared/published, 898
Directory Enabled Networks (DEN),
341–344, 364
Directory services, 361–368
access control and, 5
Active Directory, 16
container objects and, 261
DEN, 341–344
directory enabled networks
and policy management,
365–366
directory structure and
operation, 362–3630
IETF and, 367
LDAP and, 731
list of available services,
366–367
meta-directories, 364–365
name services and, 846
NDS and, 858–859

overview of, 361–362
replication, 366, 733–734, 1051
schema of, 363–364
WHOIS, 1357
Directory Services Markup Language (DSML), 365
DirXML, 858
Disaster planning and recovery, 368–370
Discard eligibility (DE), 546
Discovery. *See also* Search and discovery services, Service advertising
resource discovery services, 1059–1060
services for, 370–371
SLP (Service Location Protocol) and, 1148–1150
source route bridging and, 143
Discretionary access control (DAC), 5–6, 371
Discussion databases, 778
Disk blocks, suballocation, 129
Disk mirroring
backups and, 101
fault tolerance and high availability and, 489
Disk storage systems, 371
Diskless workstations.
See also Thin clients
boot information for, 134
data protection measures, 311
overview of, 371
Dispersion, fiber-optic cable, 502–503
Distance Vector Multicast Routing Protocol (DVMRP), 817
Distance-vector routing
defined, 1080
IGRP and, 609
RIP (Routing Information Protocol) and, 1063–1064
vs. link state routing, 945
Distance-vector routing algorithms, 115, 372–374
Distributed applications, 374–376
Distributed Authoring and Versioning (DAV), 321, 600.
See also WebDAV
Distributed backbones, 96–97
Distributed Component Object Model. *See* DCOM (Distributed Component Object Model)
Distributed computer networks, 376–380

components of, 378
defined, 400
distributed parallel processing, 379
massively distributed systems, 378–379
Distributed computing, 380–384
architectures for, 382–384
component technology and, 380–381
fault tolerance and high availability and, 490
SOAP (Simple Object Access Protocol) and, 1160
Distributed Data Management (DDM), 44
Distributed databases, 326–327
Distributed file sharing, 510–511, 514–517
Distributed File Systems. *See* Dfs (Distributed File System)
Distributed Management Interface (DMI), 387–388
Distributed Management Task Force. *See* DMTF (Distributed Management Task Force)
Distributed mesh design, 632
Distributed Relational Database Architecture (DRDA), 330, 403–404
DLC (Digital Loop Carrier), 385, 1228–1229
DLS (Digital Subscriber Line), 584
DLSw (Data Link Switching), 53, 385–386
DMA (direct memory access), 901
DMA (Document Management Alliance), 1389
DMI (Distributed Management Interface), 387–388
DMTF (Desktop Management Task Force), 1335–1336
DMTF (Distributed Management Task Force), 1335–1336
DEN and, 341
DMI and, 387
electronic software distribution and licensing, 444
initiatives and standards of, 388
DMZ (demilitarized zones), 522
DNA (Digital interNet Application), 778

DNS (Domain Name System), 389–395
e-mail addresses and, 23
hierarchical Internet routing structure and, 389–390
historical and administrative information about, 392–393
name services and, 844
naming hierarchy of, 391–392
operation of, 393–394
resolver services and, 1059
vs. Handle System, 576
DOCSIS (Data Over Cable Interface Specification)
CATV and, 173
overview of, 395–397
vs. DAVIC, 322
wireless broadband interfaces and, 1366
Document Interchange Architecture (DIA), 44–45
Document Management Alliance (DMA), 1389
Document management systems, 397–399
Document Object Model. *See* DOM (Document Object Model)
Document Type Defined (DTD), 1137
Documents
Handle System and, 577–579
metadata for, 770
OpenDoc standard, 928
DOM (Document Object Model), 400
Domain controllers, 401
Domain Name System. *See* DNS (Domain Name System)
Domain registration, 652–653
Domains, Windows NT, 400–402
Downsizing, 402
Downtime, cost of, 487
DPT (Dynamic Packet Transport), 403
DRDA (Distributed Relational Database Architecture), 330, 403–404
DS levels, 409–410
DSA (Digital Signature Algorithm), 183, 359–360, 408–409
DSL (Digital Subscriber Line), 405–408
as broadband service, 146
local loop limitations and, 753
overview of, 405–406
service providers for, 239
versions of, 406–407

vs. CATV, 172
vs. HDSL, 584
WANs and, 1332
DSL Lite (or G.Lite), 407, 569
DSML (Directory Services Markup
    Language), 365
DSO (digital signal, level 0), 22
DSP (Digital Signal Processing),
    408, 922
DSS (Digital Satellite System), 331
DSS (Digital Signature Standard),
    359–360, 408–409
DSUs (data service units), 282. *See
    also* CSU/DSU (Channel Service
    Unit/Data Service Unit)
DSx (Digital Signal-x), 409–410
DTD (Document Type Defined), 1137
DTE (Data Terminal Equipment),
    297, 410
DTM (Dynamic Synchronous
    Transfer Mode), 218, 410–411
Dual attached concentrator
    (DAC), 495
Dual-attached station (DAS), 495
Dual-homed firewalls, 523
Dublin Core metadata
    advertising and, 32
    initiative of, 770
    search and discovery and, 1112
Duplexing
    fault tolerance and high
        availability and, 489
    mirroring and, 412, 790
DVB (Digital Video Broadcast), 1366
DVMRP (Distance Vector Multicast
    Routing Protocol), 817
DWDM (dense wavelength division
    multiplexing), 1338
    ATM and, 66
    lambda circuits and, 722
    optical networks and, 936
DXI (Data Exchange Interface), 73
Dynamic bandwidth allocation, 110
Dynamic Data Exchange, 335
Dynamic DNS, 394
Dynamic Host Configuration
    Protocol (DHCP), 135, 347
Dynamic Packet Transport (DPT), 403
Dynamic routing
    algorithms for, 372
    link-state routing and, 740
    overview of, 412
    protocols for, 1079
    vs. static routing, 1188
Dynamic Synchronous Transfer
    Mode (DTM), 218, 410–411

E

E carriers, 413
E-commerce. *See* Electronic
    commerce (e-commerce)
E-mail. *See* Electronic mail (e-mail)
EAP (Extensible Authentication
    Protocol), 414–415
EAPOE (Extensible Authentication
    Protocol Over Ethernet), 414
EBNs (extended border nodes), 52
ECC (elliptic curbed
    cryptosystem), 408
Echo request message, 603
ECN (Explicit Congestion
    Notification), 251–252
ECP (extended capacities port), 963
ECTF (Enterprise Computer
    Telephony Forum), 573
EDFAs, 501–502, 936
Edge devices, 415–416
EDGE (Enhanced Data Rates for
    Global Evolution), 1384
Edge networking, 968–969
EDI (Electronic Data Interchange),
    416–420
    e-commerce and, 416, 431
    IETF and, 419
    information sharing with, 665
    overview of, 416–418
    standards and initiatives, 418
    X12 and, 1392
    XML and, 418–419
EDMS (Electronic document
    management systems).
    See Document management
EGP (Exterior Gateway Protocol)
    AS (autonomous system)
        and, 94
    overview of, 420
    vs. IGP, 609
EIA (Electronic Industries
    Association), 64, 420–421, 1190,
    1246–1250
EIGRP (Enhanced Interior Gateway
    Routing Protocol), 609
EIP (Enterprise Information Portal),
    997–998
EJB (Enterprise JavaBeans), 383, 703
ELAN (Emulated LAN). *See* LANE
    (LAN Emulation)
Electrical power.
    See Power, grounding
Electromagnetic Interference (EMI),
    451–452. *See* EMI
    (Electromagnetic Interference)

Electromagnetic spectrum, 421–425
    analog, 423–424
    illustration of, 422
    microwave, 424
    wireless, 423
Electronic commerce (e-commerce),
    425–436
    document management
        and, 397
    EDI and, 416
    models for, 431–433
    organizations promoting,
        433–435
    overview of, 425
    payment systems, 428–430
    security, 426–428
    site architecture for, 426
    XML and, 430–431
Electronic Data Interchange. *See* EDI
    (Electronic Data Interchange)
Electronic document
    management systems (EDMS).
    See Document management
Electronic forms, Microsoft
    Exchange, 778
Electronic Industries Association.
    See EIA (Electronic Industries
    Association)
Electronic mail (e-mail), 436–444
    addressing protocols for, 23
    development work, 442–443
    features of, 437–439
    gateways, 559
    how it works, 439–441
    middleware and, 787
    MIME and, 788
    mobile computing and, 795
    overview of, 436–437
    PEM (Privacy-Enhanced Mail)
        and, 972
    S/MIME and, 1152–1153
    security of, 440–441
    SMTP and, 1155–1156
    systems and products, 441–442
Electronic software distribution and
    licensing, 444–445
ELFEXT (equal-level far-end
    crosstalk), 163
Elliptic curbed cryptosystem
    (ECC), 408
EMBASSY, 448, 1275
Embedded SQL, 1175
Embedded systems, 445–451
    communication protocols for,
        449–451
    controllers, 446–447

Java technologies, 449
operating systems, 447–448
overview of, 445–446
Web servers, 448–449
EMI (Electromagnetic Interference), 451–452
Emulated LAN (ELAN).
See LANE (LAN Emulation)
Encapsulation, 452–453
IP over ATM and, 682–683
mobile IP and, 797
tunneling and, 1276
Encoding, 103, 1141–1142.
See also Modulation techniques
Encryption. See Cryptography
End nodes (ENs), 51
End System (ES), 453–454, 591
End System-to-Intermediate System (ES-IS) Routing, 459
End-to-end links, 294, 453–454, 986
End-to-end protocols, 1280
Enhanced Data Rates for Global Evolution (EDGE), 1384
Enhanced Interior Gateway Routing Protocol (EIGRP), 609
Enhanced parallel port (EPP), 963
ENs (end nodes), 51
Enterprise application integration (EAI), 785
Enterprise Computer Telephony Forum (ECTF), 573
Enterprise Information Portal (EIP), 997–998
Enterprise JavaBeans (EJB), 383, 703
Enterprise networks
file sharing for, 508–509
link aggregation in, 739–740
overview of, 454–456
Enterprise Resource Planning.
See ERP (Enterprise Resource Planning)
Enterprise Systems Connection (ESCON), 458
ENUM, 456
Environment Specific Inter-ORB Protocol (ESIOP), 268
EPP (enhanced parallel port), 963
Equal-level far-end crosstalk (ELFEXT), 163
ERP (Enterprise Resource Planning), 456, 915
Error detection/correction
with asynchronous communications, 63–64
data link layer and, 298
data link protocols and, 305

frame relay and, 545
overview of, 457–458
ES (End System), 453–454, 591
ES-IS (End System-to-Intermediate System) Routing, 459
ESCON (Enterprise Systems Connection), 458
ESIOP (Environment Specific Inter-ORB Protocol), 268
EtherLoop, 459–460
Ethernet, 460–476
10Base-2, 470–473
10Base-T, 473–475
adaptations, 462–464
frame formats, 470
frequency ranges of, 103
general features, 461–462
historical information, 460–461
networking devices, 464–469
networking devices, bridges, 466
networking devices, repeaters and hubs, 464–466
networking devices, routers, 468–469
networking devices, switches, 466–468
overview of, 460
Ethernet networks
access methods used by, 8
ALOHA and, 38
ASIC and, 60
bus topology of, 153
collision domains and broadcast domains, 234
LANs and, 875
MANs and, 240
vs. ATM, 80
WANs and, 240
EtherTalk, 476
ETI (Extend the Internet) Alliance, 450–451
ETSI (European Telecommunications Standards Institute),
HiperLAN, 1375–1376
TIPHON, 1321
Exchange, Microsoft, 778
Explicit Congestion Notification (ECN), 251–252
Explicit routing, 477
defined, 1306
label switching and, 720
routing with, 1080
vs. source routing, 1172
Explorer packets, 143
Express Forwarding, 477

Extend the Internet (ETI) Alliance, 450–451
Extended border nodes (EBNs), 52
Extended capacities port (ECP), 963
Extensible Authentication Protocol (EAP), 414–415
Extensible Authentication Protocol Over Ethernet (EAPOE), 414
Exterior Gateway Protocol. See EGP (Exterior Gateway Protocol)
Exterior routing, 478
Exterior routing protocols
AS (autonomous system) and, 641
BGP, 117, 946
IDPR (Interdomain Policy Routing Protocol), 605
vs. interior routing protocols, 420
Extranets, 478–479, 665
Extreme Networks, 750–751

F

F5 Networks, 750–751
Fabric Shortest Path First (FSPF), 1097
Fabric, switched, 480
FACK (forward acknowledgement), 14
Failover, 226, 480
Fair queuing, 1030
Far-end crosstalk (FEXT), 163
Fast CGI, 195
Fast Data Encipherment Algorithm (FEAL), 279
Fast EtherChannel (FEC), 740
Fast Ethernet, 480–485
100Base-FX, 484
100Base-T4, 484
100Base-TX, 482–484
Ethernet versions and, 463
overview of, 480–482
rate of, 102, 103
Fast IP, 485
Fast retransmit/fast recovery (RENO), 249–250
FAT (file allocation table), 512, 780
Fault isolation, 480
Fault management, 486, 892
Fault tolerance, 486–491
clustering and, 225
data management and, 308, 311
high availability and, 488
methods for, 489

overview of, 486–487
SFT (system fault
tolerance), 1137
Fax servers, 492–494
FCC (Federal Communications
Commission), 105
FDDI (Fiber Distributed Data
Interface), 494–497
CDDI and, 185
configuration of, 495–496
operation and access method,
496–497
overview of, 494–495
FDM (frequency division
multiplexing), 170, 214–215,
497, 829–831.
See also WDM (wavelength
division multiplexing)
FEAL (Fast Data Encipherment
Algorithm), 279
FEC (Fast EtherChannel), 740
FEC (forward error correction), 457
FECN (forward explicit congestion
notification), 247, 545–546
Federal Communications
Commission (FCC), 105
FEXT (Far-end crosstalk), 163
Fiber Distributed Data Interface.
See FDDI (Fiber Distributed
Data Interface)
Fiber-optic cable, 497–504.
See also Optical networks, SONET
(Synchronous Optical Network)
attenuation, EDFAs and
Raman amplifiers, 501–502
defined, 156
dispersion, 502–503
ITU specifications for, 500–501
multimode vs. single mode
cable, 499–500
overview of, 497–499
transmission rate of, 103
WDM (wavelength division
multiplexing) and, 1337
Fiber-optic networks, Qwest, 2–3
Fiber-optics
ESCON (Enterprise Systems
Connection) and, 458
infrared technologies and, 620
Fiber To The Home (FTTH),
555–556, 991
Fibre Channel, 504–508
ANSI standards for, 506
connection types used for,
506–507
defined, 504

features of, 504–505
HIPPI (High-Performance
Parallel Interface) and, 588
SANs (Storage Area
Networks) and, 1096
SCSI and, 1105
as switching architecture,
1201–1202
FIFO (first-in, first out), 1029
FIFO (first-in, first-out), 246
File access protocols, 677
File allocation table (FAT), 512, 780
File servers, 508
File sharing, 508–512
distributed, 510–511
enterprise networks and,
508–509
Internet, 509–510
SMB (Server Message Blocks)
and, 1151–1152
Web technologies and, 1355
File systems, 512–518
distributed, 514–517
list of, 512–514
Microsoft Windows, 780–782
NetWare UFS (Universal File
System), 908–910
NFS (Network File System),
898–899
replication, 1051
WebNFS (Network File
System), 1353–1354
File Transfer Access and
Management (FTAM), 519, 553
File Transfer Protocol. *See* FTP
(File Transfer Protocol)
File transfer protocols
FTP (File Transfer
Protocol), 1241
list of, 518–519
TFTP (Trivial File Transfer
Protocol), 1241
UUCP (UNIX-to-UNIX Copy
Program), 1298
Filers, NAS, 849
Filtering, 519–520, 524
Financial Services Technology
Consortium (FSTC), 434
Finger, 520
Firewalls, 520–526
access control with, 7
bastion hosts and, 113
circuit relay firewalls, 216
gateways, 559
overview of, 520–522
passing message through, 1161

RFCs for, 525
stateful inspection technology
for, 1186
terminology for, 522–524
FireWire, 526–527
Firewire (IEEE 1394), 1105
First-in, first out (FIFO), 246, 1029
FIXes (Federal Internet
Exchanges), 638
Flapping, 527
Flat-file databases, 325
Flow control, 528–531
data link layer and, 298–299
data link protocols, 305
network architecture, 872
TCP and, 528–529
types of, 529–531
Flows, 527–528
FM (frequency modulation),
183–184, 803
FORTEZZA, 531–532
Forward acknowledgement
(FACK), 14
Forward error correction (FEC), 457
Forward explicit congestion
notification (FECN), 247, 545–546
Forwarding, 532
Fractional T lines, 145, 533
Fragmentation, 533–537
fragment size and, 534
IP header fields
controlling, 535
overview of, 533–534
path MTU and, 536–537
Frame formats, Ethernet, 470, 707
Frame forwarding, 140
Frame relay, 537–549
ATM internetworking and, 547
bandwidth on demand
and, 111
as broadband service, 145
CIR (committed information
rate) and, 544–545
congestion control, 247,
545–546
as connection-oriented
service, 259
connections setup and
release, 544
error detection and
recovery, 545
features of, 540
frame format for, 542–543
frame switching service, 240
ordering service, 547–548
overview of, 306, 537–539

PVCs, 543
standards for, 539–540
SVCs, 544
voice over, 546–547
WANs and, 1331
Framing, data transmissions, 549–552
data link layer and, 298, 550
data link protocols, 305
Ethernet and, 462
types of, 549
Free space optical systems, 620,
763, 1365
Frequency division multiplexing.
See FDM (frequency
division multiplexing)
Frequency modulation (FM),
183–184, 803
Frequency range
analog transmission, 39
Ethernet, 103
wireless broadband, 1360–1362
Front-end processor (FEP), 244, 553
Front-end system, 553
FSAN (Full Service Access
Network), 991
FSPF (Fabric Shortest Path First), 1097
FSTC (Financial Services Technology
Consortium), 434
FTAM (File Transfer Access and
Management), 519, 553
FTP (File Transfer Protocol)
file transfer protocols and, 518
overview of, 554–555
RFCs for, 555
vs. NFS, 898–899
vs. TFTP, 1241
FTTH (Fiber To The Home),
555–556, 991
Full-duplex transmission
100Base-TX and, 484
defined, 158
Ethernet and, 462
Gigabit Ethernet and, 561
overview of, 556–557
switching and, 1205
vs. simplex, 294
Full Service Access Network
(FSAN), 991

G

G Series, ITU recommendations, 558
Gateway protocols, 94, 118–119
Gateway-to-Gateway Protocol, 560
Gateways, 558–560.
See also Media gateways
application-level gateway, 49
circuit-level proxy, 1162
communication servers
and, 237
IP telephony gateway, 1272
media gateways and
controllers and, 1322–1325
overview of, 558–559
security of, 686
types of, 559–560
GBE (10-Gigabit Ethernet).
See Gigabit Ethernet
General Inter-ORB Protocol (GIOP),
267–268
General Packet Radio Service.
See GPRS (General Packet
Radio Service)
General Switch Management Protocol
(GSMP), 721
Generalized Markup Language
(GML), 599–600, 1396
Generalized MPLS (GMPLS), 938
GEOs (geosynchronous satellites),
1100–1102
GFR (guaranteed frame rate),
77–78, 1262
GID (Group ID), 11
Gigabit Ethernet, 560–568
10 Gigabit Ethernet, 566–568
cabling requirements for, 158
Ethernet versions and, 463
features and specifications,
560–562
MANs and, 772
network configurations,
564–565
over copper (1000Base-T),
563–564
switches for, 564
traffic flow and, 99
vs. ATM, 80–81, 565–566
Gigabyte System Networking (GSN),
572, 587

GigaPOP (Point-of-Presence with
gigabit connections), 233, 994
GII (Global Information
Infrastructure), 568–569
GIOP (General Inter-ORB Protocol),
267–268
G.Lite (or DSL Lite), 407, 569
Global Commerce Initiative
(GCI), 435
Global Information Infrastructure
(GII), 568–569
Global Positioning Satellite
(GPS), 570
Global Reach Internet Connection
(GRIC), 1069–1070
Global System for
Mobile Communications.
See GSM (Global System for
Mobile Communications)
GML (Generalized Markup
Language), 599–600, 1396
GMPLS (Generalized MPLS), 938
Gopher, 569–570
GPRS (General Packet Radio Service),
570, 960, 1384
GPS (Global Positioning
Satellite), 570
Graphical user interfaces (GUIs),
807–808
GRIC (Global Reach Internet
Connection), 1069–1070
Grid environments. See Distributed
computer networks
Grounding problems.
See Power, grounding
Group accounts, 11, 1297
Group ID (GID), 11
Groupware, 570–572
GSM (Global System for Mobile
Communications), 1283. See also
Wireless mobile communications
data over, 1384
digital cellular and, 1381
mobile messaging and, 768
GSMP (General Switch Management
Protocol), 572, 721
GSN (Gigabyte System Networking),
572, 587
Guaranteed frame rate (GFR),
77–78, 1262

Guest (anonymous) access, 39–40
Guest user accounts,
    Windows NT/2000, 11
Guided media, 157, 572

H

H series, ITU recommendations, 573
H.100/H110 computer telephony
    standards, 573
H.323, multimedia conferencing
    standard, 573–575, 1320
Hackers, 84, 575–576, 1115
Half-duplex transmission, 561
HALO (High Altitude
    Long Operation)
        as broadband service, 146
        communication service
            providers, 238
        overview of, 576–577
        wireless broadband and, 1363
Handheld Device Markup Language
    (HDML), 583–584
Handle System
    name services and, 845
    overview of, 577–579
    search and discovery and, 1112
Handover, 480
Handshake, 254
Hash functions, 579–580
    algorithms for, 580
    cryptography and, 274
    digital signatures and, 358
    features of, 579
    one-way hash functions, 928
Hashed message authentication code
    (HMAC), 1252
HCSS (High Capacity Storage
    System), 310
HDLC (High-level Data Link
    Control), 581–583
        ADCCP and, 23
        bit-orientation of, 128
        connection methods with,
            581–582
        data link frames and, 298
        frame structure of, 582
        overview of, 306
        X.25 networks and, 583
HDML (Handheld Device Markup
    Language), 583–584
HDR (High Data Rate), 584, 1364

HDSL (High-Speed Digital
    Subscriber Line), 406, 584
Hewlett-Packard
        JetSend, 1132–1133
        OpenView Management
            System, 930
HFC (Hybrid Fiber/Coax), 584–585
Hierarchical file systems, 101
Hierarchical management system
    (HMS), 932
Hierarchical storage management
    (HSM), 1188. See also Storage
    management systems
Hierarchical wiring, 885–886
High Altitude Long Operation.
    See HALO (High Altitude
    Long Operation)
High availability, 488, 489.
    See also Fault tolerance
High Capacity Storage System
    (HCSS), 310
High Data Rate (HDR), 584, 1364
High-level Data Link Control.
    See HDLC (High-level
    Data Link Control)
High-performance computing
    (HPC), 837
High-Performance File System
    (HPFS), 512
High-Performance Parallel Interface
    (HIPPI), 587–588, 963
High-Performance Routing (HPR),
    IBM, 591
High-Speed Digital Subscriber Line
    (HDSL), 406, 584
High-speed/high-performance
    networking, 585–587
        advanced Internet
            networks, 586
        list of technologies for, 586
        overview of, 585–586
High-Speed Serial Interface
    (HSSI), 592
High-throughput computing
    (HTC), 379
Higher-level addressing, 26
HiperLAN (Higher-Performance
    Radio LAN), 1368
HIPPI (High-Performance Parallel
    Interface), 587–588, 963
Hit rates, Web caching, 1343
HMAC (hashed message
    authentication code), 1252

HMS (hierarchical management
    system), 932
Hop, 590–591
Hop-by-hop routing
    deficiencies of, 719
    destination-based routing
        and, 1077
    vs. source routing, 1172
Host names, IP (Internet Protocol),
    672–674
Hosts
    defined, 591
    internetwork addressing, 25
Hot Standby Router Protocol
    (HSRP), 592
Hot swapping, disks, 1038
HPC (high-performance
    computing), 837
HPFS (High-Performance File
    System), 512
HPR (High-Performance Routing),
    IBM, 591
HSM (hierarchical storage
    management), 1188. See also
    Storage management systems
HSRP (Hot Standby Router
    Protocol), 592
HSSI (High-Speed Serial
    Interface), 592
HTC (high-throughput
    computing), 379
HTCP (Hypertext Caching
    Protocol), 1345
HTML (Hypertext Markup
    Language), 592–595
        CGI and, 195
        hyperlinks with, 599
        markup languages and, 766
        overview of, 592–593
        versions of, 593–594
        vs. HDML, 583
        vs. XML, 1395–1396
        XHTML and, 594
HTTP (Hypertext Transfer Protocol),
    595–599. See also S-HTTP
    (Secure HTTP)
        CIFS and, 209
        connections, 596–597
        developments, 597–598
        file transfer protocols, 519
        overview of, 595–596
        secure connections, 597
        Web browsers and, 151

Hubs
 Ethernet, 464–466
 LANs and, 724
 middleware and, 785
 switching and, 1205
Hybrid Fiber/Coax (HFC), 584–585
Hyperlinks, 151, 599
Hypermedia/hypertext, 599–600
Hypertext Caching Protocol (HTCP),
 1345. *See also* Web caching
Hypertext Markup Language.
 See HTML (Hypertext
 Markup Language)
Hypertext Transfer Protocol.
 See HTTP (Hypertext
 Transfer Protocol)

I

I/O architecture, InfiniBand, 616
I-Seek-You (ICQ), 202, 604–605
I2O (Intelligent I/O), 1202
IAB (Internet Architectural Board),
 601, 650–651
IADs (Integrated Access Devices), 601
IAHC (International Ad Hoc
 Committee), 601
IANA (Internet Assigned Number
 Authority), 392, 602, 652, 1043
iBGP, 119
IBM (International Business
 Machines), 602
 AnyNet, 42
 BISYNC (Binary Synchronous
 Communications), 127
 CICS (Customer Information
 Control System), 202–203
 CPI-C (Common
 Programming Interface for
 Communications), 272–273
 DB2, 323
 DRDA, 403–404
 host connectivity, 602–603
 host gateways, 559
 HPR (High-Performance
 Routing), 591
 SAA (systems application
 architecture), 1094
 SNA (Systems Network
 Architecture), 1158–1159
ICA (Independent Computing
 Architecture), 1238–1239
ICANN (Internet Corporation for
 Assigned Names and Numbers),
 603, 652, 1043

ICI (Intercarrier Interface), 73
ICMP (Internet Control Message
 Protocol), 603–604, 975
ICP (integrated communications
 provider), 238, 1134
ICP (Internet Cache Protocol), 1345
ICQ (I-Seek-You), 202, 604–605
ICSA (International Computer
 Security Association), 605
ICW (Internet Call Waiting), 605
IDEA (International Data Encryption
 Algorithm), 279
IDL (Interface defined Language), 268
IDPR (Interdomain Policy Routing
 Protocol), 605, 694
IDRP (Interdomain Routing
 Protocol), 694
IDS (intrusion detection system), 1120
IEC (International Electrotechnical
 Commission), 605
IEEE 801.2-D (Spanning Tree
 Protocol), 142
IEEE 802.10 Security Working
 Group, 607
IEEE 802.11 Wireless LAN Working
 Group, 607, 1375
IEEE 802.12 Demand Priority
 Working Group, 607
IEEE 802.14 Cable Modem Working
 Group, 173, 608
IEEE 802.15 Wireless Personal Area
 Network (WPAN) Working
 Group, 608
IEEE 802.16 Broadband Wireless
 Access Working Group, 608, 794
IEEE 802.16 Wireless MAN,
 1359, 1367
IEEE 802.17 Resilient Packet Ring
 Working Group, 608, 764
IEEE 802.1 Higher Layer LAN
 Protocols Working Group, 606
IEEE 802.1Q, 1312
IEEE 802.2 Logical Link Control
 Working Group, 606–607
IEEE 802.3 Ethernet Working Group,
 560, 607, 739
IEEE 802.4 Token Bus Working
 Group, 607
IEEE 802.5 Token Ring Working
 Group, 607
IEEE 802.6 Metropolitan Area
 Network Working Group, 607
IEEE 802.7 Broadband TAG, 607
IEEE 802.8 Fiber Optic TAG, 607
IEEE 802.9 Isochronous LAN
 Working Group, 607, 695

IEEE (Institute of Electrical and
 Electronic Engineers)
 802 Standards, 606–608
 ANSI and, 41
 Ethernet specifications,
 463–464
 Ethernet standards, 461
 overview of, 606
IESG (Internet Engineering Steering
 Group), 608, 651
IETF (Internet Engineering
 Task Force)
 Internet standards of, 659–660
 Kerberos specification of, 708
 overview of, 608, 651–652
 security specifications of,
 1118–1119
IGMP (Internet Group Message
 Protocol), 608–609, 817
IGP (Interior Gateway Protocol),
 94, 609
IGRP (Interior Gateway Routing
 Protocol), 609
IIOP (Internet Inter-ORB Protocol)
 CORBA and, 268
 Java and, 705
 overview of, 610
 vs. SOAP, 1161
IISP (Interim Inter-switch Signaling
 Protocol), 610
IKE (Internet Key Exchange), 713–714
ILEC (incumbent local exchange
 carriers). *See also* RBOCs (regional
 Bell operating companies)
 break up of AT&T and, 219
 LATA (Local Access and
 Transport Area) and,
 730–731
 network access services
 and, 863
 overview of, 610–611, 1041
 service providers, 238, 1133
 Telecommunication Reform
 Act of 1996 and, 1234–1235
IM. *See* instant messaging
IMA (Inverse Multiplexing over
 ATM), 611–612, 666
Imaging, 612
IMAP (Internet Message Access
 Protocol), 612–614
 electronic mail (e-mail)
 protocols, 437, 439
 features of, 613
 vs. POP, 612–613
IMP (Interface Message Processor),
 614, 632

Impedance, copper cable, 161
IMPP (Instant Messaging and
    Presence Protocol), 624
IMT-2000 (International Mobile
    Communications-2000). *See*
    Wireless mobile communications
IN (Intelligent Network), 614–615,
    1229–1231
INC (Integrated Network
    Connection), 83
Incident response, security, 616
Incumbent local exchange carriers.
    See ILEC (incumbent local
    exchange carriers)
Independent Computing
    Architecture (ICA), 1238–1239
Independent Telephone Companies
    (ITCs), 1134
Indexing services, 212, 1111–1112
Inductance, copper cable, 162–163
Inferno (Lucent Technologies),
    447, 1133
InfiniBand, 616–618
    components of, 616
    data centers and, 291–292
    I/O architecture and, 616
    network topology, 617
    SANs (Storage Area
        Networks) and, 1096–1097
    as switching architecture, 1202
Information appliances, 618
Information warehouses, 618.
    See also Data warehousing
Information warfare, 618–619
InfoSysSec Web site, 619
Infrared Data Association (IrDA),
    620–621
Infrared technologies, 619–621
    overview of, 619–620
    standards for, 620–621
    use in communications, 620
    Wireless LANs (WLANs)
        and, 1374
Inheritance, rights and
    permissions, 1062
Instant messaging, 622–626
    collaborative computing and,
        231–232
    groupware and, 571
    overview of, 622–624
    protocols for, 624–625
    as synchronous
        communication, 622
Instant Messaging and Presence
    Protocol (IMPP), 624

Institute of Electrical and Electronic
    Engineers. *See* IEEE
    (Institute of Electrical
    and Electronic Engineers)
Integrated Access Devices (IADs), 601
Integrated communications providers
    (ICPs), 238, 1134
Integrated Network Connection
    (INC), 83
Integrated Services Digital Network.
    See ISDN (Integrated Services
    Digital Network)
Integrated Services (Int-Serv),
    626–629
    architecture for, 627–629
    overview of, 626–627
    QoS (quality of service)
        and, 1024
Intelligent I/O (I2O), 1202
Intelligent Network (IN), 614–615,
    1229–1231
Intelligent Platform Management
    Interface (IPMI), 681
IntelliMirror, 629–630, 795
Inter-LATA, 1234
Inter-ORB Protocol (IOP), 268
Interactive Voice Response (IVR), 283
Intercarrier Interface (ICI), 73
Interdomain Policy Routing Protocol
    (IDPR), 605
Interexchange carriers (IXCs).
    See IXCs (interexchange carriers)
Interface defined Language (IDL), 268
Interface Message Processor. *See* IMP
    (Interface Message Processor)
Interfaces. *See* by individual type
Interim Inter-switch Signaling
    Protocol (IISP), 610
Interior Gateway Protocol (IGP),
    94, 609
Interior Gateway Routing Protocol
    (IGRP), 609
Interior routing protocols
    AS (autonomous system)
        and, 641
    compared with exterior, 117
    IS-IS, 694
    OSPF, 946
    vs. exterior routing
        protocol, 420
Interlinked star, network
    topologies, 1259
Intermediate system, 591
Intermediate System-to-Intermediate
    System (IS-IS) Routing, 694
Internal routers, 947

International Ad Hoc Committee
    (IAHC), 601
International Business Machines.
    See IBM (International
    Business Machines)
International Computer Security
    Association (ICSA), 605
International Data Encryption
    Algorithm (IDEA), 279
International Electrotechnical
    Commission (IEC), 605
International Mobile
    Communications-2000
    (IMT-2000). *See* Wireless
    mobile communications
International Organization for
    Standardization. *See* ISO
    (International Organization
    for Standardization)
International Telecommunication
    Union. *See* ITU (International
    Telecommunication Union)
Internet, 630–636
    domains, 391–392
    entertainment, 649–650
    file sharing, 509–510
    history and concepts, 631–634
    mobile computing and, 796
    networking and, 876
    NSF (National Science
        Foundation) and, 913
    overview of, 630–631
    RFCs for, 634
    standards for, 659–661
    traffic engineering, 1262–1263
Internet appliances.
    See Network appliances
Internet Architectural Board (IAB),
    601, 650–651
Internet architecture and backbone,
    637–645
    Internet exchanges and NAPs,
        639–641
    networks and autonomous
        systems, 641–642
    overview of, 637
    PoPs and data centers, 642–644
    topologies, 638
Internet Assigned Number
    Authority. *See* IANA (Internet
    Assigned Number Authority)
Internet Cache Protocol (ICP), 1345
Internet Call Waiting (ICW), 605
Internet connections, 645–649
    ISPs (Internet Service
        Providers), 646–647

routing registries, 647
setting up, 646
Internet Control Message Protocol (ICMP), 603–604, 975
Internet Corporation for Assigned Names and Numbers (ICANN), 393, 603, 652, 1043
Internet Engineering Steering Group (IESG), 608, 651
Internet Engineering Task Force. *See* IETF (Internet Engineering Task Force)
Internet exchanges
FIXes (Federal Internet Exchanges), 638
MAE (Metropolitan Area Exchange), 760
service providers and, 1135
Internet Explorer, 151
Internet fax, 492–493
Internet Group Message Protocol (IGMP), 608–609, 817
Internet Information Server (IIS), 17–18
Internet Inter-ORB Protocol. *See* IIOP (Internet Inter-ORB Protocol)
Internet Key Exchange (IKE), 713–714
Internet Message Access Protocol. *See* IMAP (Internet Message Access Protocol)
Internet multimedia protocols, 825–828
Internet Network Information Center (InterNIC), 652
Internet Open Trading Protocol (IOTP), 432, 668
Internet organizations and committees, 650–653
IP address allocation and domain registration services, 652–653
list of, 650–651
related organizations, 653
Internet Printing Protocol (IPP), 677
Internet Protocol. *See* IP (Internet Protocol)
Internet Protocol Device Control (IPDC), 1324
Internet radio, 658–659
Internet Relay Chat (IRC), 202, 690–691
Internet Research Task Force (IRTF), 289, 651
Internet Routing Registry (IRR), 692, 1083

Internet Security Association and Key Management Protocol (ISAKMP), 714
Internet Server API (ISAPI), 18
Internet service providers. *See* ISPs (Internet service providers)
Internet Society (ISOC), 630, 650
Internet telephony, 661, 1318
Internet2 project, 2, 636–637
Internetwork addressing, 24, 25
Internetwork layer, 891
Internetwork Operating System (IOS), 53, 667–668
Internetwork Packet Exchange/ Sequenced Packet Exchange (IPX/SPX), 661, 688–690
Internetworking
bridges and, 138
network layer and, 302
overview of, 661–662
role of routers in, 1072
InterNIC (Internet Network Information Center), 652
Interoperability, 662–663
Interprocess Communication. *See* IPC (Interprocess Communication)
Intra-LATA services, 731. *See also* LATA (Local Access and Transport Area)
Intranets, 664–665
Intrusion detection system (IDS), 1120. *See also* Security auditing
Inverse multiplexing
bandwidth on demand and, 110
link aggregation and, 738
overview of, 666–667
Inverse Multiplexing over ATM (IMA), 611–612, 666
IONA Technologies, 1268
IOP (Inter-ORB Protocol), 268
IOS (Internetwork Operating System), 53, 667–668
IOTP (Internet Open Trading Protocol), 432, 668
IP addresses
allocation of, 652–653
DHCP and, 347
DNS and, 390
Internet connections and, 646
IP and, 672–674
registries, 1043–1044
using ARP with, 56
using names instead of, 26
IP datagrams, 671–672

IP (Internet Protocol), 669–676
addressing and host names, 672–674
best-effort delivery and, 116
compared with ATM, 65
compared with CLNP, 224
datagrams, 671–672
integrating with ATM, 900
as Internet standard, 654–655
mobile IP, 796–798
as network layer protocol, 891
over SONET, 881–883
overview of, 669–671
wireless, 1372–1373
IP (Internet Protocol) suite. *See* TCP/IP (Transmission Control Protocol/Internet Protocol)
IP (Internet Protocol) version 6. *See* IPv6 (Internet Protocol, version 6)
IP Multicast, 816–817, 1311–1312
IP networks, 1020
IP numbers, 56
IP over ATM, 681–685. *See also* CIP (Classical IP over ATM)
cut-through architecture, 683
encapsulation, 682–683
multilayer switching, 683–684
overview of, 681–685
IP over Cable Data Network (IPCDN), 173
IP over SONET, 999–1001, 1170
IP-PBX (IP-Private Branch Exchange), 1325
IP Performance Metrics (IPPM), 685
IP-Private Branch Exchange (IP-PBX), 1325
IP storage
NAS and, 851
overview of, 677–679
SANs and, 1097
IP Switching, 687–688
IP telephony
cable data networks and, 172
protocols, 1325–1326
standards, 1321–1322
telecommunications and, 661, 688
IPC (Interprocess Communication)
named pipes and, 846
overview of, 679–680
pipes and, 977–978
ports and, 998
IPCDN (IP over Cable Data Network), 173

IPDC (Internet Protocol Device
    Control), 1324
IPMI (Intelligent Platform
    Management Interface), 681
IPP (Internet Printing Protocol), 677
IPPM (IP Performance Metrics), 685
IPSec (IP Security), 685–687, 1193
Ipsilon. *See* Nokia
IPv6 (Internet Protocol, version 6)
    6Bone and, 2
    anycasting, 41–42
    overview of, 674–676
IPX/SPX (Internetwork Packet
    Exchange/Sequenced Packet
    Exchange), 661, 688–690
IRC (Internet Relay Chat), 202,
    690–691
IrDA (Infrared Data Association),
    620–621
IRR (Internet Routing Registry), 692,
    1083
IRTF (Internet Research Task Force),
    289, 651
IS-IS (Intermediate
    System-to-Intermediate System)
    Routing, 694
ISAKMP (Internet Security
    Association and Key Management
    Protocol), 714
ISAPI (Internet Server API), 18
ISDN (Integrated Services Digital
    Network), 692–694
    B-ISDN and, 126–127
    bandwidth on demand
        and, 111
    basic rate, 112
    BRI (basic rate interface)
        for, 136
    as broadband service, 145
    circuit switching, 239
    implementations of, 692
    local loop limitations and, 753
    services and connections, 693
    WANs and, 1331
ISO/IEC-11801 cabling standards,
    695–696
ISO (International Organization for
    Standardization)
    ANSI and, 40
    communication protocols, 294
    overview of, 694–695
    presentation layer, 1008–1009
ISOC (Internet Society), 630, 650
Isochronous services, 695
IsoEthernet, 695

ISPs (Internet service providers)
    as access provider, 9
    as communication service
        providers, 238, 1134
    connecting to Internet with,
        646–647
    Internet architecture and,
        642–643
    overview of, 696–699
ITCs (Independent Telephone
    Companies), 1134
ITU (International
    Telecommunication Union)
    ANSI and, 40
    CCITT and, 184
    fiber-optic cable specifications,
        500–501
    G series recommendations, 558
    H series
        recommendations, 573
    multimedia conferencing
        standard (H.323),
        573–575, 825
    overview of, 699–700
    X series
        recommendations, 1398
ITU-T (International
    Telecommunication
    Union-Telecommunications)
    e-mail standards, 23
    X.500 and, 362
IVR (Interactive Voice Response), 283
IXCs (interexchange carriers)
    communication service
        providers and, 238
    overview of, 700
    PoPs (points of presence)
        and, 993

J

J2EE (Java 2 Platform, Enterprise
    Edition), 703–705, 775, 841
JAIN (Java Advanced Intelligent
    Network), 701, 1326
Java, 701–706
    communication standards, 705
    comparing applets with
        ActiveX controls, 19
    embedded systems, 449
    J2EE, 703–705
    JavaBeans, 702–703
    JVM, 702
    overview of, 701–702

RMI (Remote Method
    Invocation) and, 1066
transaction processing
    and, 1268
Java 2 Platform, Enterprise Edition
    (J2EE), 703–705, 775, 841
Java Advanced Intelligent Network
    (JAIN), 701, 1326
Java Card specification, 1150
Java Database Connectivity
    (JDBC), 330
Java Messaging Service (JMS),
    705, 806
Java Virtual Machine (JVM), 702
JavaBeans, 114, 383, 702–703
JDBC (Java Database
    Connectivity), 330
JetSend, 450, 1132–1133
Jigsaw, 706
Jini, 450, 1132
Jitter (delay distortion), 161.
    See also Delays
JMS (Java Messaging Service),
    705, 806
Jukebox optical storage devices, 707
Jumbo frames, 707
JVM (Java Virtual Machine), 702

K

Kerberos Authentication Protocol,
    708–711
    authentication and
        authorization, 90,
        709–710, 1255
    features of, 708–709
    overview of, 708
    as secret-key cryptographic
        system, 277
Kernels, 711
Key Telephone Systems, 716
Keyed MD5, 580
KeyNote Trust Management System,
    715, 1275
Keys. *See also* PKIs
    (public key infrastructures)
    encryption and authentication
        and, 711–712, 715
    IKE (Internet Key Exchange)
        and, 713–714
    Kerberos, 708–709
    manual exchange, 712
    PGP (Pretty Good Privacy)
        and, 973–974

private, 1114
protocols for management
of, 1145
public, 712–713
recovering, 714–715

L2TP (Layer 2 Tunneling Protocol)
mobile computing and, 795
overview of, 717–719
PPP (Point-to-Point Protocol)
and, 1007
Label Distribution Protocol (LDP),
734, 1264
Label edge routers (LER), 1264
Label switched paths. *See* LSPs
(label switched paths)
Label switching, 719–721, 819
Label switching routers. *See* LSRs
(label switching routers)
Labeling, search and discovery
services, 1111–1112
Lambda circuits, 722, 1337
LAN drivers, 725–726
LANE (LAN Emulation). *See also*
MPOA (Multiprotocol over ATM)
ATM and, 80
CIP (Classical IP over ATM)
and, 210
overview of, 683, 726–727
LANs (local area networks), 722–725
access methods, 8, 759
acknowledgments, 14
addressing for, 27
ATM and, 65
concentrator devices and, 244
as connectionless system, 259
distance and size limitations
of, 723–724
gateways, 559
illustration of, 723
MLPPP (Multilink PPP)
and, 111
mobile computing and, 795
network connection
technologies for, 878
networking and, 874–875
overview of, 722–723
wireless, 1373–1377
LAP Balanced (LAPB), 728
LAP (Link Access Procedure), 306,
728–730
LAPB (LAP Balanced), 728

LAPD (Link Access Procedure
D-Channel), 728
LAPF (Link Access Procedure for
Frame-Mode Bearer Services), 728
LAPM (Link Access Procedure for
Modems), 728
Laser systems, 620
Last mile services, 730, 753
LATA (Local Access and Transport
Area), 730–731, 1234
Latency, 731. *See also* Delays
Layer 2/Layer 3/Layer 4 switching,
887–888.
See also Multilayer switching
Layer 2 Tunneling Protocol. *See* L2TP
(Layer 2 Tunneling Protocol)
Layer 3, VLANs, 1311
LCP (Link Control Protocol), 1007
LDAP (Lightweight Directory Access
Protocol), 731–734
developments of, 733–734
directory access with, 363
electronic mail (e-mail)
protocols, 439
information model and
schemas, 732–733
operation of, 732–733
OPSEC (Open Platform for
Security) and, 932
overview of, 731–732
use of X.500 standard in, 23
LDP (Label Distribution Protocol),
734, 1264
Leaf objects (containers), 362
Leaky bucket, 1032
Learning bridges, 735
Learningware, 636
Leased lines, 336–337, 735
LECs (local exchange carriers)
break up of AT&T and, 219
CAPs (Competitive Access
Providers) and, 182
ILEC (Incumbent Local
Exchange Carriers) and,
610–611
IXC and, 700
LATA (Local Access and
Transport Area) and, 730
overview of, 736
SMDS (Switched Multimegabit
Data Service) and, 1152
Legacy applications, 602, 736, 762
LENs (low-entry nodes), 52
LEOs (low earth orbit), 736–737,
1100–1102

LER (label edge routers), 1264
Licensing, electronic, 737
Lightweight Directory Access
Protocol. *See* LDAP (Lightweight
Directory Access Protocol)
Line conditioners, 737–738, 1049
Link Access Procedure D-Channel
(LAPD), 728
Link Access Procedure for
Frame-Mode Bearer Services
(LAPF), 728
Link Access Procedure for Modems
(LAPM), 728
Link Access Procedure (LAP), 306,
728–730
Link aggregation, 738–740
bandwidth on demand
and, 110
in enterprise networks,
739–740
MLPPP (Multilink PPP)
and, 792
overview of, 738–739
Link Control Protocol (LCP),
414, 1007
Link-state routing, 740–741, 1080
Link-state routing protocols
IS-IS (Intermediate
System-to-Intermediate
System) Routing, 694
list of, 741
OSPF (Open Shortest Path
First), 945
Links, 339–340, 628
Linux
Apache servers for, 43
open source software and, 929
overview of, 741–743
LIS (logical IP subnet), 210–211
LISTSERV, 743, 761
LLC (Logical Link Control), 743–744
bridges and, 139–140
data link layer and, 299, 758
Ethernet and, 464
OSI protocol stack and, 24, 744
overview of, 306
LMDS (Local Multipoint
Distribution Service)
overview of, 745–747
vs. MMDS, 783–784, 793–794
wireless broadband and,
1364, 1366
Load balancing, 748–753.
See also Link aggregation

bandwidth management and, 109
bandwidth on demand and, 110
clustering and, 226
cookies and, 750
distribution of, 752
F5 Networks and, 750–751
fault tolerance and high availability and, 490
forwarding algorithms in, 748–749
link aggregation and, 738
multitiered architecture and, 841
persistence and, 749–750
types of, 748
virtual clusters and, 228
Load-sharing
bridges and, 143
compared with STA, 142
Local Access and Transport Area (LATA), 730–731, 1234
Local area networks. See LANs (local area networks)
Local bridges, 139
Local exchange carriers. See LECs (local exchange carriers)
Local exchange carriers (LECs), 182
Local loop
CO (central office) and, 230
last mile services and, 730
modems and, 798
overview of, 750–754
POTS (Plain Old Telephone Service) and, 1001
wireless, 1377–1378
Local Multipoint Distribution Service. See LMDS (Local Multipoint Distribution Service)
Local procedure calls (LPCs), 679
LocalTalk, 754
Logging, firewalls and, 524
Logic bombs, 1306
Logical connections, 999
Logical IP subnet (LIS), 210–211
Logical Link Control. See LLC (Logical Link Control)
Logical units (LUs), 53, 757
Login scripts, 755
Logon process
access controls and, 4–5
biometric access devices and, 124
overview of, 755–756
telnet and, 1237

Long distance carriers. See Communication service providers
Longitudinal redundancy checking (LRC), 64
Loop resolution, 140
Loops, avoiding, 122
Lossless compression, 243
Lossy compression, 243
Lotus Domino, 756
Lotus Notes, 756
Low earth orbit (LEOs), 736–737, 1100–1102
Low-entry nodes (LENs), 52
Low-voltage differential signaling (LVDS), 757, 1104
LPCs (local procedure calls), 679
LRC (longitudinal redundancy checking), 64
LSAs, link-state databases and, 949
LSPs (label switched paths), 720, 808, 1264
LSRs (label switching routers), 720, 734, 1264
LU 6.2. See APPC (Advanced Program-to-Program Communications)
Lucent Technologies (Inferno), 447, 1133
LUs (logical units), 53, 757
LVDS (low-voltage differential signaling), 757, 1104

M

MAC-based VLANs, 1311
MAC-layer prioritization, 1023–1024
MAC (Media Access Control), 464
addressing, 24–25, 462, 758–759
bridges and, 139–140, 300
LANE (LAN Emulation) and, 726–727
RARP (Reverse Address Resolution Protocol) and, 1040
switching, 300–301
using ARP with, 56–57
Mac OS
AppleShare and, 33
AppleTalk and, 47
overview of, 759–761
MAC sublayer, OSI model, 299–301
Macintosh, Apple Computer, 759
MACs (Message authentication codes), 580

MAE (Metropolitan Area Exchange), 760
Mailing list programs, 760–761
Mainframe computers, 602, 761–763
Majordomo, 761
Management information bases (MIBs), 36, 773–774
Management interface (MI), 387, 681
Management Service Providers (MSPs), 813–814, 1135
Management stations, 892
MANET (Mobile Ad Hoc Networking), 1372
MANs (metropolitan area networks)
Ethernet networks, 240
network connection technologies, 878
networking and, 876
overview of, 763–765
MAPI (Messaging Application Programming Interface), 439, 765–766
Markup languages
development of, 1396
GML (Generalized Markup Language), 600
HDML (Handheld Device Markup Language), 583–584
HTML (Hypertext Markup Language), 592–595
overview of, 766
SGML (Standard Generalized Markup Language), 600, 1137–1138
WML (Wireless Markup Language), 1386
XML (Extensible Markup Language), 1395–1397
Massively distributed systems, 378–379
Massively parallel processing (MPP), 836–837
Maximum Transmission Unit (MTU), 814
MCM (Multicarrier modulation), 922
MD-5, 580
MDC (Meta Data Coalition), 770, 1283
MDCP (Media Device Control Protocol), 1324
Media Access Control. See MAC (Media Access Control)
Media control protocols, 1324–1325
Media Device Control Protocol (MDCP), 1324

Media Gateway Control Protocol (MGCP), 773, 1323–1324
Media gateway controller (MGC), 1323
Media gateways (MGs)
  functions of, 1322–1325
  Megaco and, 766–768
  MGCP (Media Gateway Control Protocol) and, 773
  NAS and, 848
  overview of, 766
  softswitch and, 1164
  types of gateways and, 559
Media, guided, 572
Megaco, 766–768
Memory buffers, 901
MEMS (Micro-Electromagnetic Systems), 768
Merge replication, 1054
Mesh networks, 1259
Message authentication codes (MACs), 580
Message digest, 349–350
  digital signatures and, 358
  hash functions and, 579
  one-way hash functions and, 928
  protocols, 768
Message-oriented middleware. See MOM (message-oriented middleware)
Message transfer agent. See MTA (message transfer agent)
Messaging Application Programming Interface (MAPI), 43, 439, 765–766
Messaging services. See also MOM (message-oriented middleware)
  Microsoft Exchange and, 778
  mobile, 768
  unified messaging, 1284–1285
  wireless, 1378
Messaging systems, 769
Meta Data Coalition (MDC), 770, 1283
Meta-directories, 364–365
Metadata, 769–772
  database management and, 324, 769–770
  defined, 32
  for documents, 770
  recommendations and standards, 770–772
  repositories for, 1055
  schemas and, 1103
  search and discovery services and, 1111–1112

Metadirectories, 772
Metering, Internet accounting, 12
Metro Access Networks, 772
Metropolitan Area Exchange (MAE), 760
Metropolitan area networks. See MANs (metropolitan area networks)
Mezzanines (daughterboards), 1200
MFR (Multilink Frame Relay), 666
MGC (media gateway controller), 1323
MGCP (Media Gateway Control Protocol), 773, 1323–1324
MGs. See Media gateways (MGs)
MI (management interface), 387, 681
MIBs (management information bases), 36, 773–774
Micro-Electromagnetic Systems (MEMS), 768
Microprocessors, RISC (Reduced Instruction Set Computer) and, 1065–1066
Microsoft Active Directory, 16, 28, 776–777
Microsoft Authenticode, 93
Microsoft BackOffice, 777
Microsoft Chat, 691
Microsoft Cluster Service (MSCS), 227
Microsoft Corporation
  NDIS (Network Driver Interface Specification), 856–857
  NetMeeting, 232
  NetShow, 232
  NLB (Network Load Balancing), 748
  overview of, 774
  terminal services and, 1238–1239
  UDA (Universal Data Access) strategy, 925
  webcasting and, 1349–1350
  Zero Administration for Windows (ZAWs), 629, 1358–1359, 1399–1400
Microsoft Dfs (Distributed file systems). See Dfs (Distributed File System)
Microsoft Distributed Transaction Coordinator (MSDTC), 1268–1269
Microsoft DNA (Digital interNet Application), 778
Microsoft Exchange, 778
Microsoft Internet Explorer, 151

Microsoft Internet Information Server, 17–18
Microsoft Load Balancing Server (MLBS), 748
Microsoft Message Queue Server (MSMQ), 43–44, 806
Microsoft Transaction Server (MTS), 19, 1268–1269
Microsoft Windows
  for Express Networks, 447
  files systems of, 780–782
  versions of, 779
Microsoft Windows 98, 779
Microsoft Windows CE, 447–448, 779
Microsoft Windows ME (Millennium Edition), 779
Microsoft Windows NT/2000
  administrator accounts in, 28
  auditing system of, 86–87
  clustering and, 227
  overview of, 779
  security descriptors in, 5–6
  symmetric multiprocessing in, 62
  user accounts in, 11
Microsoft Windows XP ('xperience), 779
Microsoft.NET, 774–776, 1132
Microwave, 424, 782–785, 793–794
Middleware and messaging, 785–788
  client/server model and, 221–222
  EAI topologies, 785–786
  multitiered architecture and, 839–840
  types of, 786–787
Middleware application servers, 328–329
Millennium Edition (Microsoft Windows ME), 779
MIME (Multipurpose Internet Mail Extensions). See also S/MIME (Secure Multipurpose Internet Mail Extension)
  electronic mail (e-mail) protocols, 439
  overview of, 788–790
  PEM (Privacy-Enhanced Mail) and, 972
Mirroring, 790–791
  content distribution and, 261–262, 791
  duplexed systems, 412
  fault tolerance and high availability and, 489

replication and, 1050
types of, 790
MLBS (Microsoft Load Balancing Server), 748
MLP (Multilink Procedure), 728
MLPPP (Multilink PPP)
    BACP and, 112
    dial-up lines and, 348
    handling LAN traffic with, 111
    inverse multiplexing and, 666–667
    overview of, 792–793
    PPP (Point-to-Point Protocol) and, 1007
MMDS (Multichannel Multipoint Distribution Service)
    OFDM (orthogonal frequency division multiplexing) and, 922
    overview of, 793–794
    vs. LMDS, 746–747, 783–784
    wireless broadband and, 1363–1364, 1366
Mobile Ad Hoc Networking (MANET), 1372
Mobile communications. *See* Wireless mobile communications
Mobile computing, 794–796
Mobile IP, 796–798, 1372
Mobile messaging, 768
Mobile users, 7
Mobitex, 960
Modeling language, 1283
Modems (*modulators/demodulators*), 798–803
    56K technology, 802
    baud measurements and, 113
    defined, 295
    overview of, 798–799
    standards, 114, 800–801
    types of, 799
    V.90, 801–802
Modulation techniques, 803–805
MOM (message-oriented middleware), 805–807
    distributed applications and, 375
    middleware and, 786
    types of, 806–807
    vs. RPCs, 806
MOSPF (Multicast OSPF), 817
Motif, 807–808
MP3, 808
MPEG (Moving Pictures Experts Group), 808

MPLS (Multiprotocol Label Switching), 808–813
    comparing ARIS to, 56
    constraint-based routing, 260
    core networks and, 270
    explicit routing, 477
    LDP (Label Distribution Protocol), 734
    operation of, 810–812
    optical networks and, 938
    overview of, 808–810
    QoS (quality of service) and, 1025
    routing with, 1080–1081
    signaling in, 1139
    traffic engineering and, 1264
MPOA (Multiprotocol over ATM), 210, 683, 813
MPP (massively parallel processing), 836–837
MPTN (Multiprotocol Transport Networking), 42
MQSeries, 806
MSCS (Microsoft Cluster Service), 227
MSDTC (Microsoft Distributed Transaction Coordinator), 1268–1269
MSMQ (Microsoft Message Queue Server), 43–44, 806
MSPs (Management Service Providers), 813–814, 1135
MTA (message transfer agent), 437, 814, 1124
MTP (Multicast Transport Protocol), 817
MTS (Microsoft Transaction Server), 19, 1268–1269
MTU (Maximum Transmission Unit), 814
Multicarrier modulation (MCM), 922
Multicast OSPF (MOSPF), 817
Multicast Transport Protocol (MTP), 817
Multicasting, 815–818
    broadcasting and, 149
    collaborative computing and, 231
    defined, 147
    IP Multicast, 816–817
    overview of, 815
    Webcasting and, 150
Multichannel Multipoint Distribution Service. *See* MMDS (Multichannel Multipoint Distribution Service)
Multihomed sites, 647
Multihoming, 818

Multilayer switching, 819–822
    Ethernet, 469
    layers of, 819
    network design and, 887–889
    networking and, 875
    overview of, 683–684
    routers and, 1074–1075
    silicon-based routing, 820–821
    traffic-driven vs. control-driven, 684
Multilink Frame Relay (MFR), 666
Multilink PPP. *See* MLPPP (Multilink PPP)
Multilink Procedure (MLP), 728
Multimedia, 823–828
    content delivery systems for, 823–824
    Internet protocols for, 825–828
    ITU conferencing recommendations, 824–825
    key themes, 823
    SDP (Session Description Protocol) and, 1108–1109
    SIP (Session Initiation Protocol) and, 1143–1145
    standards, 1211
    streaming media, 824–825
    videoconferencing and, 1303–1304
    Web technologies and, 1355
Multimedia conferencing standard, 573–575
Multimedia control protocols, 1101
Multimode cable, 499–500
Multipath, 793
Multiplexing, 828–834
    concentrator devices and, 244
    defined, 295, 1219
    FDM (Frequency Division Multiplexing), 829–831
    inverse multiplexing, 666–667
    multiplexer configurations, 833
    overview of, 828–829
    SONET and, 1169
    STDM (statistical time division multiplexing), 832–833
    T1 lines and, 1222
    TDM (time division multiplexing), 831–832
Multiport bridges, 138, 466
Multiprocessing, 834–838
    asymmetrical vs. symmetrical, 62, 835
    load balancing and, 748
    overview of, 834–835

servers and, 1128
SMP and parallel architectures
for, 835–838
switching fabric and, 1193
Multiprotocol Label Switching.
See MPLS (Multiprotocol
Label Switching)
Multiprotocol over ATM. *See* MPOA
(Multiprotocol over ATM)
Multiprotocol Transport Networking
(MPTN), 42
Multipurpose Internet Mail
Extensions. *See* MIME
(Multipurpose Internet
Mail Extensions)
Multithreading.
See Parallel processing
Multitiered architectures, 838–842
client/server model and,
223–224
clustering and, 227
middle tier applications,
840–841
networks and data centers
and, 841
three-tiered models, 839
two-tiered models, 838–839
Music, MP3, 808
MUXs. *See* Multiplexing

N

NADH (North American Digital
Hierarchy), 843–844, 879
NAK (negative knowledge), 844
Name resolution. *See* DNS (Domain
Name System)
Name services, 844–846
Named pipes, 846, 977
Namespaces, NetBIOS, 859
NAPs (Network Access Points)
Internet exchanges and,
639–641
MAE (Metropolitan Area
Exchange) and, 760
overview of, 847–848
Napster, 876, 968–969
Narrowband radio, 1374–1375
NAS (Network Access Server),
848–849, 1048
NAS (Network Attached Storage)
DAFS and, 287–289
gateways, 560

network appliances and, 868
overview of, 226, 849–852
SANs and, 1096
NAT (network address translation),
852–855
firewalls and, 523
gateways and, 559
overview of, 852–855
RSIP (Realm-Specific Internet
Protocol) and, 1087
National Information Infrastructure
(NII), 902
National Institute of Standards and
Technology (NIST), 904
National Research and Education
Network (NREN), 912
National Science Foundation. *See* NSF
(National Science Foundation)
National Security Agency (NSA),
531, 912
NBMA (Nonbroadcast Multiple
Access) networks, 149, 855
NC (Network Computer), 856, 1242
NCP (NetWare Core Protocol)
distributed file systems, 515
handling service requests
with, 689
overview of, 856
NDIS (Network Driver Interface
Specification), 856–857
NDMP (Network Data Management
Protocol), 857
NDS (Novell Directory Services),
858–859
administrator accounts in, 28
bindery support in, 123
container objects, 261
login scripts, 755
Novell NetWare and, 907
SAP and, 32
user accounts in, 10
Near-end crosstalk (NEXT), 162–163
Near Video on Demand
(NVoD), 1057
NECP (Network Element Control
Protocol), 1346–1347
Negative knowledge (NAK), 844
NeoLinux (Neoware Systems), 447
NetBEUI (NetBIOS Extended User
Interface), 859–861
NetBIOS (Network Basic Input
Output System), 845, 859–861
Netcasting, 862
NetMeeting, Microsoft, 232

NetPC, 862
Netscape, 862
Netscape Navigator, 151
NetShow, Microsoft, 232
NetTalk Live, 1350
NetWare. *See* NDS (Novell Directory
Services), Novell NetWare
NetWare Core Protocol. *See* NCP
(NetWare Core Protocol)
NetWare File System (NWFS), 513
NetWare Link Services Protocol
(NLSP), 904
NetWare UFS (Universal File
System), 513, 908–910
Network Access Points. *See* NAPs
(Network Access Points)
Network Access Server (NAS),
848–849, 1048
Network access services, 862–864
Network address translation.
See NAT (network
address translation)
Network analyzers, 865–868
protocol analyzers and,
866–867
tests performed with, 865–866
types of, 865
Network appliances, 618, 631,
868–869, 1129
Network architecture, 870–874
Network Attached Storage. *See* NAS
(Network Attached Storage)
Network Attached Storage
(NAS), 226
Network Basic Input Output System
(NETBIOS), 845, 859–861
Network Computer (NC), 856, 1242
Network connection technologies,
878–879
Network core technologies, 879–883
ATM and IP over SONET,
881–883
overview of, 879–880
SONET/SDH optical
networks, 880–881
Network Data Management Protocol
(NDMP), 857
Network design, 883–891
backbone model, 884–885
Gigabit Ethernet and, 564
hierarchical wiring for,
885–886
layer 3 switching, 887–888
main areas of, 883

multilayer switching, 888–889
server farms, 889–890
switching environments, 886–887
Network Driver Interface Specification (NDIS), 856–857
Network Element Control Protocol (NECP), 1346–1347
Network elements, 353–356, 1346–1347
Network File System. *See* NFS (Network File System)
Network flow controls, 531
Network Information Service (NIS), 845, 903–904
Network interface cards. *See* NICs (network interface cards)
Network layer, OSI model, 302, 943
Network layer protocols, 891–892
Network Load Balancing (NLB), 227
Network management, 312, 892–894
Network management stations (NMS), 36
Network News Transport Protocol (NNTP), 904–906
Network Node Interface (NNI), 70, 73–74, 904, 904
Network nodes (NNs), 51
Network Operating Systems (NOS), 894–896
Network operations center (NOC), 290, 906
Network processors, 821, 888, 896–897
Network service engines (NSEs), 907
Network terminals, 1242
Network termination (NT), 693
Network testers, 865
Network Time Protocol (NTP), 914, 1251
Network traffic, 866, 1009–1011
Networking, 874–878
concepts, 874–877
high-speed/high-performance, 585–587
at home, 589–590
store-and-forward networking, 1189
topical links, 877–878
tutorials, 877
Networking devices, Ethernet, 464–469
bridges, 466
repeaters and hubs, 464–466
routers, 468–469
switches, 466–468

Networks
access methods used by, 8
bus topology for, 153–154
CMIP (Common Management Information Protocol), 228
interoperability and, 663
segments, 1123–1124
switched, 1203–1206
testing, diagnostics, and troubleshooting, 1240
voice/data networks, 1313–1318
New public network. *See* NPN (new public network)
New Technology File System (NTFS), 512–513, 780–781
Newsfeed services. *See* Webcasting
Newsgroups, 1295.
See also NNTP (Network News Transport Protocol)
Next Generation Network (NGN), 900
Next Hop Resolution Protocol (NHRP). *See* NHRP (Next Hop Resolution Protocol)
NEXT (Near-end crosstalk), 162–163
NFS (Network File System), 898–899.
See also WebNFS (Network File System)
compared with AFS, 33
compared with DFS, 34
distributed file systems, 515
vs. FTP, 898
NGN (Next Generation Network), 900
NHRP (Next Hop Resolution Protocol)
Classical IP over ATM (CIP) and, 211
NBMA and, 855
overview of, 900
NICs (network interface cards)
adapters and, 21
NDIS (Network Driver Interface Specification) and, 856–857
overview of, 901–902
NII (National Information Infrastructure), 902
NIS (Network Information Service), 845
NIS (Network Information System), 903–904
NIST Advanced Encryption Standard (AES), 279

NIST (National Institute of Standards and Technology), 904
NLB (Network Load Balancing), 227
NLSP (NetWare Link Services Protocol), 904
NMS (network management stations), 36
NNI (Network Node Interface), 70, 73–74, 904
NNs (network nodes), 51
NNTP (Network News Transport Protocol), 904–906
NOC (network operations center), 290, 906
Nodes, 906
Noise, 161–162, 1002
Nokia, 687–688, 1364–1365
Non-real time-variable bit rate (nrt-VBR), 77, 1261
Non-Uniform Memory Access (NUMA). *See* Multiprocessing
Nonbroadcast Multiple Access (NBMA) networks, 149, 855
North American Digital Hierarchy (NADH), 843–844, 879
NOS (Network Operating Systems), 894–896
Novell Corporation, 906–907
Novell Directory Services. *See* NDS (Novell Directory Services)
Novell NetWare
advertising in, 31
attributes, 85
bindery in, 123–124
implementation of ACLs in, 6
IPX/SPX, 688–690
NLSP (NetWare Link Services Protocol), 904
overview of, 129, 907–908
Novell Storage Services (NSS), 513
NPN (new public network), 910–912
features of, 910–911
IN (Intelligent Network) and, 615
NGN (Next Generation Network), 900
NREN (National Research and Education Network), 912
Nrt-VBR (non-real time-variable bit rate), 77, 1261
NSA (National Security Agency), 531, 912
NSEs (network service engines), 907
NSF (National Science Foundation)
domain name registration, 392

NREN (National Research and Education Network), 912
overview of, 913
role in development of Internet, 913, 1299
NSFNET, 638, 697, 913, 1299
NSPs (network service providers)
Internet architecture and, 642–643
overview of, 897, 914
service providers and, 1134
vs. ISPs, 696
NSS (Novell Storage Services), 513
NT (network termination), 693
NTFS (New Technology File System), 512–513, 780–781
NTP (Network Time Protocol), 914, 1251
NUMA (Non-Uniform Memory Access). *See* Multiprocessing
NVoD (Near Video on Demand), 1057
NWFS (NetWare File System), 513

O

OADMs (Optical add/drop multiplexers), 933
OAG (Open Applications Group), 915
OAKLEY, 714
OASIS ebXML, 432–433
OASIS (Organization for the Advancement of Structured Information Standards), 384
OBI (Open Buying on the Internet), 431–432, 915
Object Linking and Embedding. *See* OLE (Object Linking and Embedding)
Object Management Architecture (OMA), 266–267, 926
Object Management Group (OMG), 266–267, 927
Object-oriented database management system (OODBMS), 326
Object-oriented technologies, 916–918
class hierarchies and, 917
programming and, 916–917
Object request broker. *See* ORB (object request broker)
Object transaction monitors (OTMs), 1268
OC (optical carriers), 918–920
levels, 919

NADH (North American Digital Hierarchy) and, 918
SONET and, 919
STS (Synchronous Transport Signal) and, 919
types of carriers, 880
ODBC (Open Database Connectivity), 330, 920–921
ODI (Open Data-Link Interface), 922
ODMA (Open Document Management API), 398
ODSI (Optical Domain Service Interconnect), 938
OFDM (orthogonal frequency division multiplexing), 922–924
information transmission with, 805
multipath problems and, 793
multiplexing techniques, 831
overview of, 922–924
parallel interfaces and, 963
OIM (Open Information Model), 770, 924, 1055
OLAP (Online Analytical Processing), 924–925
OLE DB, 925–926
OLE (Object Linking and Embedding)
as basis for COM, 18
COM (Component Object Model) and, 235
database connectivity tools, 330
overview of, 925
OLTP (Online Transaction Processing). *See* Transaction processing
OMA (Object Management Architecture), 266–267, 926
OMG (Object Management Group), 266–267, 927
On demand, multimedia, 823
One-time password authentication, 927–928, 1255
One-way hash functions, 928
Online Analytical Processing (OLAP), 924–925
Online service providers (OSPs), 9
Online storage device, 101
Online Transaction Processing (OLTP). *See* Transaction processing
OODBMS (object-oriented database management system), 326
Open Applications Group (OAG), 915

Open Buying on the Internet (OBI), 431–432, 915
Open Data-Link Interface (ODI), 922
Open Database Connectivity. *See* ODBC (Open Database Connectivity)
Open Document Management API (ODMA), 398. *See also* Document management
Open Group
ActiveX development, 20
CDE and, 185
DCE and, 334
Dfs and, 347
overview of, 928–929
Open Information Model. *See* OIM (Open Information Model)
Open Platform for Security (OPSEC), 931–932
Open Settlement Protocol (OSP), 945, 1326
Open Shortest Path First. *See* OSPF (Open Shortest Path First)
Open Software Foundation (OSF), 334, 928
Open source software, 929–930
Open systems, 930
Open Systems Interconnection. *See* OSI (Open Systems Interconnection) model
Open Transport protocol, Apple Computer, 33, 46
OpenDoc, 928
OpenView Management System, 930–931
Operating systems (OS)
embedded, 447–448
kernel and, 711
networks and, 894–896
OPSEC (Open Platform for Security), 931–932
Optical add/drop multiplexers (OADMs), 933
Optical carriers. *See* OC (optical carriers)
Optical cross-connects (OXCs), 933, 937
Optical disk libraries, 707
Optical Domain Service Interconnect (ODSI), 938
Optical libraries, 932–933
Optical networks, 933–940. *See also* Free space optical systems, SONET (Synchronous Optical Network)
components of, 936–938

control plane of, 938–939

network core technologies, 880–883

overview of, 933–935

PON (Passive Optical Network), 990–993

resilient packet rings and, 1058

SDH (synchronous digital hierarchy) and, 1108

Optical Signaling & Routing Protocol (OSRP), 952

Optoelectronic amplifiers, 1339

Oracle, 940

ORB (object request broker)

CORBA and, 266

distributed applications and, 376

middleware and, 786

object-oriented technologies, 917

overview of, 940

Organization for Economic Corporation and Development (OECD), 435

Organization for the Advancement of Structured Information Standards (OASIS), 384

Orthogonal frequency division multiplexing. *See* OFDM (orthogonal frequency division multiplexing)

OS/2 Warp, 941

OSF (Open Software Foundation), 304, 928

OSI (Open Systems Interconnection) model, 293–304, 941–945

application layer, 48, 303–304

asynchronous communications and, 64

communication protocols, 294

comparing with APPN, 50

comparing with ATM reference model, 69–70

data link layer, 24, 297–299

illustration of, 942

layers of, 943–944

MAC sublayer, 299–301

maintenance of, 694

network architecture and, 870–871

network layer, 302

network layer protocols and, 891

overview of, 941–943

physical layer, 295–297, 974–975

presentation layer, 1008–1009

session layer, 1136

transport layer, 303, 1270

vs. IPX/SPX, 689

OSP (Open Settlement Protocol), 945, 1326

OSPF (Open Shortest Path First), 945–951

autonomous systems and areas, 947–948

building link-state databases, 949

computing shortest path, 949

concepts, 946

distance-vector routing algorithms and, 115

documentation, 950–951

establishing adjacencies, 948–949

as interior routing protocol, 117

IS-IS (Intermediate System-to-Intermediate System) Routing and, 694

link state routing with, 741

vs. IGRP, 609

OSPs (Online service providers), 9

OSRP (Optical Signaling & Routing Protocol), 952

OTMs (object transaction monitors), 1268

Outsourcing

ASPs and, 61

co-location services and, 232–233

network management, 893

networking and, 876

overview of, 952–953

OXCs (Optical cross-connects), 933, 937

OXYGEN, 953

P

P Security (IPSec), 685–687, 1193

P2P (peer-to-peer). *See also* Peer-to-Peer communication

community oriented information exchanges, 968–969

content distribution, 262

Napster and, 876

overview of, 954

P3P (Platform for Privacy Preferences), 954

PACE (Priority Access Control Enabled), 234

Packet errors, 457

Packet filtering, 524

Packet Internet Groper (Ping), 975–976

Packet over SONET (PoS), 999–1001, 1170

Packet overhead, 105

Packet radio, 959–962

amateur, 961

packet switching features of, 959

providers of, 960–961

Packet rings, 962

Packet scheduler, 628

Packet switching

communication service providers, 239

cut-through architecture, 284–285

store-and-forward architecture, 285

vs. circuit switching, 216–217

X.25, 239

Packet switching networks, 954–959

connectionless vs. connection oriented, 955–956

illustration of, 955

multiplexing, 957

overview of, 954

queuing in, 957

PacketCable, 959

Packets. *See also* Packet switching networks

acknowledgments, 14

Active Nets and, 16–17

class of service, 821

defined, 954

header and data area of, 956

multiplexing and, 829

networking and, 875

PoS (Packet over SONET) and, 999–1001

routers and, 1074

Packets per second (Pps), 1008

PANs (personal area networks), 1373

Bluetooth and, 131–133

mobile computing and, 795

wireless, 1385–1386

PAP (Password Authentication Protocol), 962

PAR (PNNI Augmented Routing), 985

Parallel connections, 1125

Parallel interface, 962–964

Parallel processing. *See also*
Clustering, Multiprocessing
defined, 836
distributed, 379
Parity checks, 458
Partial reliable services, 1045–1046
Partition management, 1328
Partitioning. *See also* Replication
databases, 327
directory services, 366
Passive Optical Network (PON),
990–993
Password Authentication Protocol
(PAP), 962
Passwords, 964–965
AAA and, 964
access control and, 4
administrator accounts and, 28
maintaining security of,
964–965
one-time password
authentication,
927–928, 1255
Path MTU Discovery, 536–537
PBX (private branch exchange), 716
Centrex (CENTRal
Exchange), 190
overview of, 965–968
PSTN (public switched
telephone network), 1229
voice/data networks, 1315
PC Cards, 183
PCI bus, 963
PCI (Peripheral
Component Interconnect)
limitations of, 1194
popularity of, 1193
standards, 1197–1198
PCI (protocol control
information), 872
PCM (pulse code modulation),
31, 1209
PCMCIA (Personal Computer
Memory Card International
Association), 183
PDAs (personal digital
assistants), 1378
PDCs (primary domain
controllers), 401
Windows NT, 28
PDF (Portable Document Format), 15
PDH (plesiochronous digital
hierarchy), 843
PDS (Premises distribution
system), 1008
PDU (protocol data unit), 872

Peer relationships, 871
Peer-to-peer. *See* P2P (peer-to-peer)
Peer-to-Peer communication,
968–970. *See also* P2P
overview of, 968
P2P, Napster, and Edge
networking, 968–969
Peering, 970–971
Peering agreements, 847
PEM (Privacy-Enhanced Mail), 972
Per-hop behavior (PHB), 352–353
Performance management, 972
network management, 892
Peripheral Component Interconnect.
See PCI (Peripheral
Component Interconnect)
Peripheral interconnects, 878
Perl (Practical Extraction and Report
Language), 195, 972–973
Permanent virtual circuits. *See* PVCs
(permanent virtual circuits)
Permissions. *See* Rights
and Permissions
Persistence
HTTP (Hypertext Transfer
Protocol) and, 595
load balancing and, 749–750
URNs and, 1294
Personal Applications browser, 151
Personal area networks. *See* PANs
(personal area networks)
Personal Computer Memory Card
International Association
(PCMCIA), 183
Personal digital assistants
(PDAs), 1378
PGP (Pretty Good Privacy), 441,
973–974
Phase modulation (PM), 803
PHB (per-hop behavior), 352–353
Phreaking, 575
Physical circuits, 214–215
Physical layer
flow controls, 529
MAC (Media Access Control)
and, 758
NICs (network interface cards)
and, 901
OSI model, 295–297, 943
Physical layer, OSI model
analog and digital signaling,
295–296
overview of, 974–975
serial interfaces, 297

synchronous and
asynchronous
transmissions, 296–297
transmission media, 297
Physical security, 1117
Piconet, 131–132
PICS (Platform for Internet Content
Selection), 975
PIM (Protocol-Independent
Multicast), 817
Ping (Packet Internet Groper), 603,
975–976
PINT (PSTN-Internet Interworking),
976–977
PIP (Presence Information
Protocol), 32
Pipes, 977–978
UNIX, 680
PKCS (Public-Key Cryptography
Standards), 982
PKIs (public key infrastructures),
978–983
authentication and
authorization, 90
building trust, 979
certificates and, 194
overview of, 978–979
PKCS (Public-Key
Cryptography
Standards), 982
RFCs, 982
SPKI (Simple PKI) and,
981–982
structure and services, 980–981
X.509 and, 981, 1393
PKIX (Public-Key Infrastructure
X.509), 981
Plain Old Telephone Service
(POTS), 1001
Platform for Internet Content
Selection (PICS), 975
Platform for Privacy Preferences
(P3P), 954
Plesiochronous digital hierarchy
(PDH), 843
Plug and Play, 450
PM. *See* Presence monitoring
PM (phase modulation), 803
PNNI Augmented Routing
(PAR), 985
PNNI (Private Network-to-Network
Interface), 983–986
ATM interfacing and, 74
signaling in, 1139
Point-to-point architecture, 786
Point-to-point bus design, 1195–1196

Point-to-point communications, 986
Point-to-point links
    broadcast networking and, 149
    transmission media and, 294
Point-to-Point Protocol. *See* PPP
    (Point-to-Point Protocol)
Point-to-point tunneling protocol
    (PPTP), 719
Point-to-point wireless bridges, 1362
Points of presence. *See* PoPs
    (points of presence)
Policies
    firewalls and, 523
    QoS (quality of service)
        and, 1025
    security, 1116
Policy-based management, 986–990
    admission control and, 30
    architecture of, 987–988
    bandwidth management
        and, 109
    policy decisions, 987
    RFCs, 988
Polling, 990. *See also* Queuing
PON (Passive Optical Network),
    990–993
POP (Post Office Protocol), 437, 438
    overview of, 995–996
    vs. IMAP, 612–613
PoPs (points of presence), 993–995
    Internet architecture and, 642
    ISPs and, 697–698
    IXC (Interexchange Carrier)
        and, 700
    overview of, 993
    virtual PoP, 993–994
Portable Document Format (PDF), 15
Portals, 996–998
    defined, 996
    EIP (Enterprise Information
        Portal), 997–998
Ports
    addressing and, 26
    sockets and, 1161
    TCP/IP, 998–999
Portscanning, 999
PoS (Packet over SONET),
    999–1001, 1170
Post Office Protocol.
    See POP (Post Office Protocol)
POTS (Plain Old Telephone
    Service), 1001
Power, grounding, 1002–1005
Power line access services, 1005
Power line networks, 589

PPP (Point-to-Point Protocol),
    1005–1008
    EAP and, 414
    encapsulation and
        authentication, 1007
    frame format for, 1006
    MLPPP (Multilink PPP) and,
        792–793
    overview of, 306, 1005–1006
    serial links, 1147–1148
pps (packets per second), 1008
PPTP (point-to-point tunneling
    protocol), 719
Practical Extraction and Report
    Language (Perl), 972–973
Premises distribution system
    (PDS), 1008
Presence Information Protocol
    (PIP), 32
Presence monitoring, 622–623,
    624–625
Presentation layer, OSI model, 943,
    1008–1009
Pretty Good Privacy (PGP), 441,
    973–974
PRI (Primary Rate ISDN), 693
Primary domain controllers (PDCs),
    28, 401
Primary Rate ISDN (PRI), 693
Printing, 677. *See also* IPP (Internet
    Printing Protocol)
Priority Access Control Enabled
    (PACE), 234
Priority queuing, 1029–1030
Priority settings, 30
Privacy. *See* Public-Key
    Cryptography, Security
Privacy-Enhanced Mail (PEM), 972
Private branch exchange. *See* PBX
    (private branch exchange)
Private-Key Cryptography.
    See Secret-Key Cryptography
Private keys, 1114
Private Network-to-Network
    Interface. *See* PNNI (Private
    Network-to-Network Interface)
Private networks, 1012
Privatization of network traffic,
    1009–1011
Probes, RMON, 1067
Programming, object-oriented,
    916–917
Promiscuous mode, 866, 1012
Propagation delays, 337
Properties, 85
Protocol analyzers, 866–867

Protocol control information
    (PCI), 872
Protocol data unit (PDU), 872
Protocol-Independent Multicast
    (PIM), 817
Protocol stacks, 871, 1012–1013
Protocols
    communication, 294
    for embedded systems,
        449–451
    stack architecture of,
        1012–1013
Proxies, 523
Proxy caching. *See* Web caching
Proxy servers, 1013–1014
    access control with, 6–7
    application-level gateway, 49
    circuit relay firewalls and, 216
    gateways, 559
    interproxy communication
        protocols, 1345–1346
    SIP (Session Initiation
        Protocol) and, 1144
    Web caching and, 1341–1347
PSTN-Internet Interworking (PINT),
    976–977
PSTN (public switched
    telephone network)
    DLC (Digital Loop Carrier),
        1228–1229
    IN (Intelligent Network)
        and, 615
    Network access services and,
        862–864
    NPN (new public network)
        and, 910
    PBX (private branch
        exchange), 1229. *See also*
        Telecommunications
    PINT (PSTN-Internet
        Interworking) and, 976–977
    SCTP (Stream Control
        Transmission Protocol)
        and, 1107–1108
    signaling in, 1139
    softswitch architecture
        and, 773
    SPIRITS (Service in the PSTN/
        IN Requesting InTernet
        Service), 1172–1173
    switching hierarchy,
        1225–1228
    voice communication
        with, 1224
Public-key cryptography, 273–274,
    1014–1017. *See also* Cryptography

Public-Key Cryptography Standards (PKCS), 982
Public key infrastructure. *See* PKIs (public key infrastructures)
Public-Key Infrastructure X.509 (PKIX), 981
Public keys. *See also* Cryptography, PKIs (public key infrastructures)
  authentication and authorization, 90
  cryptography and, 712–713
  overview of, 191
Public networks, 900
Public switched telephone network. *See* PSTN (public switched telephone network)
Pulse code modulation (PCM), 31, 1209
Push and pull. *See* Webcasting
PVCs (permanent virtual circuits)
  ATM and, 75
  defined, 217, 1306
  frame relay and, 543
  overview of, 1017

Q

Q.933, signaling, 1139
QAM (quadrature amplitude modulation), 804
Qbone, 1018
QoS (quality of service), 1018–1027
  admission control and, 30
  ATM parameters, 79
  bandwidth management and, 104, 109
  classification, admission, and tagging, 1022–1024
  compared with CoS, 271
  congestion management techniques, 1021–1022
  degradation of, 1018–1019
  IETF solutions, 1024–1025
  improving, 1019
  Int-Serv and, 626–627
  IP vs. ATM, 1020–1021
  multilayer switching and, 821, 888
  policies and policy protocols, 1025
  RAP (Resource Allocation Protocol), 1040
  RFCs and working groups, 1025–1026
  routing techniques, 260

RSVP (Resource Preservation Protocol) and, 1088
  SLA specification for, 1019
  vs. CoS, 1009
Quadrature amplitude modulation (QAM), 804
Qualcomm, 186–187, 584
Quality of service. *See* QoS (quality of service)
Quantum cryptography, 1027
Queries. *See* SQL (Structured Query Language)
Queuing, 1028–1032
  ActiveX and, 19
  congestion control and, 246
  CoS and, 270–272
  delays and, 339
  methods for, 1028–1030
  overview of, 1028
  packet switching networks and, 957
  queue behavior, 1030–1032
  queue management and congestion avoidance, 250
Qwest networks, 2–3

R

RAC (remote access concentrators), 800, 994
RACE, 1196–1197
Rack-mounted devices, 1129
RADB (routing arbiter database), 847
Radio communication, 1033–1034
  Internet radio, 658–659
  LMDS (Local Multipoint Distribution Service), 745–747
  overview of, 1033
  SMR (specialized mobile radio), 1153–1154
  UTRA (UMTS Terrestrial Radio Access), 1283
  UWB (Ultra Wideband), 1298
  wave frequencies for, 1033–1034
  WCS (Wireless Communications Service), 1337
  Wireless LANs (WLANs) and, 1374–1375
RADIUS (Remote Authentication Dial-In User Service), 1034–1037
  access control with, 7
  architecture of, 1036

authentication mechanisms, 1035–1036
  DIAMETER and, 348
  extensibility, 1037
  firewalls and, 524
  OPSEC (Open Platform for Security) and, 931
  roaming standard and, 13
RADSL (Rate-Adaptive Digital Subscriber Line), 407
RAID (redundant arrays of inexpensive disks), 1037–1040
  data striping, 1038
  fault tolerance and high availability and, 487, 489
  levels, 1038–1039
  replication and, 1050
Raman amplifiers, 501–502
Random Early Detection (RED), 250–251, 1031
RAP (Resource Allocation Protocol), 1040
RapidIO, 1201
RARP (Reverse Address Resolution Protocol)
  address resolution and, 57
  booting and, 135
  BOOTP as enhancement to, 134
  overview of, 1040
RAS (remote access servers), 848
Rate-Adaptive Digital Subscriber Line (RADSL), 407
RBB (Residential broadband), 1056–1058
RBOCs (regional Bell operating companies). *See also* ILEC (incumbent local exchange carriers)
  AT&T and, 83
  Centrex (CENTRal Exchange), 190
  IXC (Interexchange Carrier) and, 700
  LATA (Local Access and Transport Area) and, 730–731
  Network access services and, 863
  overview of, 96, 1041
RDBMS (relational database management system), 325–326
RDF (Resource Description Framework). *See* Metadata
RDP (Remote Desktop Protocol), 1239

Real-time control protocol
(RTCP), 1091
Real-time delivery, multimedia, 823
Real time multimedia over ATM
(RMOA), 1067
Real-time network services, 1042
Real-time operating system.
See RTOS (real-time
operating system)
Real-time Streaming Protocol.
See RTSP (Real-time
Streaming Protocol)
Real-time traffic flow measurement
(RTFM), 1091
Real-Time Transport Protocol.
See RTP (Real-Time
Transport Protocol)
Real-time-variable bit rate (rt-VBR),
77, 1261
Realm-Specific Internet Protocol
(RSIP). *See* RSIP (Realm-Specific
Internet Protocol)
Realtime fax over IP, 493
Reassembly, 533–537
Receivers, 147
Recovery
data protection and, 311
disaster planning and, 368–370
frame relay, 545
RED (Random Early Detection),
250–251, 1031
Redirect servers, 1144
Redirector, 1042
Reduced Instruction Set Computer.
See RISC (Reduced Instruction
Set Computer)
Redundancy
data management and, 308
fault tolerance and high
availability and, 489, 490
overview of, 1042–1043
Redundant arrays of inexpensive
disks. *See* RAID (redundant arrays
of inexpensive disks)
Redundant bits, 457
Regional Bell operating companies.
See RBOCs (regional Bell
operating companies)
Regional Internet registries
(RIRs), 653
Registries
Internet, 1043–1044
regional, 646
routing registries, 1082–1083
Regulations, telecommunications,
1233–1236

Relational database management
system (RDBMS), 325–326.
See also DBMS (database
management system)
Reliable delivery mechanisms,
1044–1047
flow control and, 528
partial reliable services,
1045–1046
TCP, 1045, 1215
transport protocols and, 1272
Reliable server pools, 838
Remote access, 1047–1049
mobile computing and, 795
NAS (Network Access Server)
and, 1048
types of, 1047
remote access concentrators (RAC),
800, 994
Remote access server (RAS), 848
Remote Authentication Dial-In User
Service (RADIUS). *See* RADIUS
(Remote Authentication Dial-In
User Service)
Remote Desktop Protocol (RDP), 1239
Remote link bridges, 139, 143–144
Remote Method Invocation. *See* RMI
(Remote Method Invocation)
Remote Monitoring (RMON). *See*
RMON (Remote Monitoring)
remote procedure calls (RPCs). *See*
RPCs (remote procedure calls)
Remote vaulting, 101
RENO (fast retransmit/fast
recovery), 249–250
Repeaters
100Base-TX and, 483
defined, 148
Ethernet, 464–466
LANs and, 724
line conditioning and, 738
overview of, 1049
Replay attacks, 84, 1116
Replication, 1050–1055
backups and, 101
data management and, 308
databases, 327, 1052–1054
directory services, 366,
733–734
file and directory, 1051–1052
mirroring and, 790
NDS (Novell Directory
Services) and, 858
overview of, 1050
Web, 1050–1051
Repository, 1055–1056

Request message, RIP, 1064
Requester software, 1056
Réseaux IP Européens (RIPE), 1065
Reservation-based access, 300
Residential broadband (RBB),
1056–1058
Resilient packet rings, 1058–1059
Resolver services, 844–846, 1059
Resource Allocation Protocol
(RAP), 1040
Resource Description Framework
(RDF). *See* Metadata
Resource discovery services,
1059–1060
Resource management, 1060–1061
Resource Preservation Protocol.
See RSVP (Resource
Preservation Protocol)
Resource records, DNS, 393
Resource reservation, 628
Response message, RIP, 1064
Reverse Address Resolution Protocol
(RARP). *See* RARP (Reverse
Address Resolution Protocol)
Reverse proxy cache, 1341–1342, 1347
RFCs
acknowledgments, 14
admission control, 30
advertising, 32
anonymous access, 40
anycasting, 41–42
APPN, 53
ARCNET, 55
ARP (Address Resolution
Protocol), 58
asynchronous
communications, 64
attacks/attackers, 84
auditing, 87
authentication and
authorization, 92
AS (autonomous system)
and, 94
bandwidth utilization, 105
BAP/BACP, 112
BOOTP (BOOTstrap
Protocol), 134
broadcasting, 147, 150
CIP (Classical IP over
ATM), 210
congestion control, 248, 253
cookies, 265–266
CSR (Cell Switched
Router), 282
discretionary access controls
and, 5

DNS and, 392
ECN (Explicit Congestion
  Notification), 251
firewalls, 525
FTP (File Transfer Protocol),
  555
Internet, 634
Internet accounting, 12
IP over ATM, 211
PKIs (public key
  infrastructures), 194, 982
policy-based management, 988
QoS (quality of service),
  1025–1026
queue management, 250
RADIUS accounting, 13
roaming and, 12–13
routing, 1082
security, 1118–1119
TACACS and RADIUS, 7
Ricochet, 1061
Rights and permissions
  assigning in
    Windows NT/2000, 11
  functions of, 1061
  granting and inheriting, 1062
  user accounts, 1296–1297
Ring network topology,
  1062–1063, 1259
RIP (Routing Information Protocol),
  1063–1065
  historical information and
    Internet documents, 1063
  NLSP (NetWare Link Services
    Protocol) and, 904
  operation of, 1064
  overview of, 1063
RIPE (Réseaux IP Européens), 1065
RIRs (Regional Internet
  registries), 653
RISC (Reduced Instruction
  Set Computer)
  ASIC and, 60
  embedded controllers and, 446
  overview of, 1065–1066
  vs. CISC (Complex Instruction
    Set Computer), 219
Rivest, Shamir, Adelman. See RSA
  (Rivest, Shamir, Adelman)
Rlogin, 1066
RMI (Remote Method Invocation),
  705, 1066
RMOA (real time multimedia over
  ATM), 1067
RMON (Remote Monitoring), 867,
  893, 1067–1068

Roaming
  DIAMETER and, 348
  Internet accounting and, 12–13
  mobile computing and, 795
  overview of, 1069–1070
ROAMOPS (Roaming Operations),
  348–349
Robotic drivers, 707
Rollback, 480
Root user accounts, 27. See also
  Administrator accounts
RosettaNet, 433
Route aggregation, 120, 205,
  1070–1071
Route flapping, 205
Route servers, 647, 1083–1084
Route switching.
  See Multilayer switching
Routers, 1072–1075
  area border routers, 947
  broadcast domains and, 149
  Ethernet, 468–469
  filtering with, 519
  internal routers, 947
  LANs and, 724
  legacy architecture of, 1073
  multilayer switching and,
    1074–1075
  packet handling and,
    1073–1074
  redundancy and, 1329–1330
  requirements for, 1072
  T1 lines and, 1222
Routing, 1075–1082.
  See also Multilayer switching
  Active Nets and, 16
  ARIS (Aggregate Route-based
    IP Switching) and, 56
  AS (autonomous system) and,
    93–95
  CSR (Cell Switched Router)
    and, 281–282
  cut-through routing, 285
  DDR (Dial-on-Dial Routing),
    335–336
  distance-vector routing,
    372–374
  dynamic routing, 264,
    412, 1188
  environments, 1078–1079
  ES-IS routing, 459
  explicit routing, 477
  Internet, 1082–1083
  network connection
    technologies and, 879
  network layer and, 302

overview of, 1075–1077
packet switching networks
  and, 955
procedures, 1077–1078
protocols and algorithms,
  1079–1081
RFCs and working
  groups, 1082
static routing, 264, 1187–1188
Routing arbiter database (RADB), 847
Routing Information Protocol. See RIP
  (Routing Information Protocol)
Routing protocols, 1079–1081.
  See also CIDR (Classless
  Inter-Domain Routing)
  ARIS (Aggregate Route-based
    IP Switching) and, 56
  distance-vector and
    link-state, 1080
  dynamic, 1079
  interior vs. exterior, 117–118
  PNNI (Private
    Network-to-Network
    Interface) and, 983
  use of, 1076
Routing registries, 1082–1083
  function of, 970–971
  Internet connections and, 647
  IRR (Internet Routing
    Registry), 692
Routing switches.
  See Multilayer switching
Routing tables, 264, 1080
RPCs (remote procedure calls),
  1084–1086
  conversational APIs, 43
  distributed applications
    and, 375
  IPC (Interprocess
    Communication) and, 679
  middleware and, 786
  vs. MOM, 806
RS-232, 556–557
RSA (Rivest, Shamir, Adelman),
  408–409, 1015, 1087
RSIP (Realm-Specific Internet
  Protocol), 673, 854, 1087–1088
RSVP (Resource Preservation
  Protocol), 1088–1091
  Int-Serv and, 627–628
  overview of, 1088–1089
  reservation process, 1089–1110
  signaling in, 1139
Rt-VBR (real-time-variable bit rate),
  77, 1261

RTCP (real-time control protocol), 1091
RTFM (real-time traffic flow measurement), 1091
RTOS (real-time operating system), 448, 1091–1092
RTP (Real-Time Transport Protocol), 1092, 1303
  multimedia and, 824
  reliable delivery mechanisms and, 1046
  webcasting and, 1349–1350
RTSP (Real-time Streaming Protocol), 824, 1092–1093, 1303
Rubber bandwidth, 110
Rules-based VLANs, 1311–1312

S

S-CDMA (Synchronous Code Division Multiplexing), 171, 585
S-HTTP (Secure HTTP), 597, 1138–1139
S/MIME (Secure Multipurpose Internet Mail Extension), 439, 441, 1152–1153
S/WAN (Secure WAN), 1193
SAA (systems application architecture), 1094
SAFER (Security And Fast Encryption Routine), 279
Salutation architecture, 1131–1132
Samba, 1094
SANs over IP, 1097
SANs (Storage Area Networks), 1094–1099
  associations, initiations, forums, and coalitions, 1098
  Fibre Channel and, 504, 1096
  illustration of, 1095
  InfiniBand and, 1096–1097
  IP storage and, 678
  NAS and, 849
  overview of, 226, 1094–1096
  technologies supporting, 1097
  VI architecture and, 287–288
SAP (Service Advertising Protocol), 31–32, 689
SAP (Session Announcement Protocol), 827, 1099, 1303
SAPs (service access points), 872
SAs (Security associations), 713
SAS (single attached station), 495

SATAN (Security Administrator's Tool for Analyzing Networks), 1121
Satellite communication systems
  communication service providers, 238
  LEOs (low earth orbit) and, 736–737
  microwave and, 783
  overview of, 1100–1102
  packet radio via, 960
  Teledesic, 1236
  wireless broadband and, 1362–1363
SBM (Subnet Bandwidth Manager), 1102–1103
Scalability, 226
Scanners, 22–23
Scatternet, 131–132
SCCP (Simple Conference Control Protocol), 1303
Schemas, 1103
  directory services and, 342, 363–364
  document metadata and, 770
  LDAP and, 732
Science, Technology, and Research Transit Access Point (STAR TAP), 1185–1186
SCO (synchronous connection oriented), 131
Screening routers, 519
SCSI-FCP, 1106
SCSI (Small Computer System Interface), 1103–1106
  compared with similar technologies, 1105–1106
  features of, 1104
  Fibre Channel and, 507
  FireWire and, 526
  parallel interfaces and, 963
  upgrades and versions of, 1104–1105
SCSP (Server Cache Synchronization Protocol), 1107
SCTP (Stream Control Transmission Protocol), 1107–1108
  IP telephony protocols, 1325
  reliable delivery mechanisms, 1046
  signaling in, 1139
  SIP (Session Initiation Protocol) and, 1144
SDH (synchronous digital hierarchy), 880–881, 1108

SDLC (Synchronous Data Link Control), 1108
  ADCCP and, 23
  bit-orientation of, 128
  overview of, 306
  replacing BISYNC (Binary Synchronous Communications), 127
SDP (Session Description Protocol), 827, 1108–1109, 1303
SDSL (Symmetric Digital Subscriber Line), 406. See also DSL (Digital Subscriber Line)
Search and discovery services, 1109–1114
  labeling, indexing, and metadata, 1111–1112
  overview of, 1109–1110
  traditional Internet information services, 1110
  Web-based information services, 1110–1111
  white pages/yellow pages, 1112–1114
Search engines, 35, 1110
Secondary time servers, 1251
Secret-key cryptography, 89, 273, 1014, 1114–1115
Secure connections, 597, 1118
Secure Electronic Transaction (SET), 192, 1136
Secure Hash Standard-1 (SHA-1), 183, 408, 580
Secure HTTP. See S-HTTP (Secure HTTP)
Secure Multipurpose Internet Mail Extension. See S/MIME (Secure Multipurpose Internet Mail Extension)
Secure shell (SSH), 1177–1178
Secure Sockets Layer. See SSL (Secure Sockets Layer)
Secure WAN (S/WAN), 1193
Security, 1115–1120. See also Cryptography
  ASPs and, 61
  CDSA as security middleware, 188
  data management and, 308, 312
  electronic mail (e-mail), 440–441
  gateways, 686
  IPSec (IP Security), 685–687
  network management and, 892

NFS (Network File
System), 898
NSA (National Security
Agency), 912
OPSEC (Open Platform for
Security), 931–932
organizations, 1118
physical security, 1117
RFCs and working groups,
1118–1119
RSA (Rivest, Shamir,
Adelman), 1087
S/WAN (Secure WAN)
and, 1193
secure connections, 1118
theft protection, 311
threats and vulnerabilities,
1115–1116
TLS (Transport Layer
Security), 1251–1252
Web technologies and, 1355
Security Administrator's Tool
for Analyzing Networks
(SATAN), 1121
Security And Fast Encryption
Routine (SAFER), 279
Security associations (SAs), 524, 713
Security auditing, 1120–1123.
See also Auditing
access control and, 5
overview of, 1120
scanners and intrusion
detection, 1120–1121
standards for, 1121–1122
tools for, 85
Security descriptors,
Windows NT/2000, 5–6
Security ID (SID), 5–6
Segments
bridges, 138
network, 1123–1124
TCP, 320–321, 1123, 1217–1218
Sendmail, 1124
Sequenced Packet Exchange
(SPX), 688
Serial communication and interfaces
OSI physical layer and, 297
overview of, 1124–1126
SLIP (Serial Line Interface
Protocol) and, 1147–1148
SSA (Serial Storage
Architecture) and, 1177
Serial Line Interface Protocol.
See SLIP (Serial Line
Interface Protocol)

Serial Storage Architecture
(SSA), 1177
Server Cache Synchronization
Protocol (SCSP), 1107
Server farms, 100, 889–890
Server Message Blocks. *See* SMB
(Server Message Blocks)
Server scripting, ActiveX, 20
Server System Infrastructure
(SSI), 1129
Servers, 1126–1130.
See also Client/server model
architectures for, 1127–1130
boxes and racks, 1129
communication servers,
237–238
LAN-based configurations, 225
multiprocessing and clustering
and, 1128
overview of, 1126–1127
Service access points, 872
Service advertising, 1131–1133
Service Advertising Protocol (SAP),
31–32, 689
Service in the PSTN/IN Requesting
InTernet Service (SPIRITS), 605,
1172–1173
Service level agreements (SLA), 1019,
1146–1147
Service Location Protocol. *See* SLP
(Service Location Protocol)
Service management centers (SMCs),
292–293
Service providers, 1133–1136,
1231–1233
Session Announcement Protocol
(SAP), 827, 1099, 1303
Session Description Protocol. *See* SDP
(Session Description Protocol)
Session Initiation Protocol. *See* SIP
(Session Initiation Protocol)
Session layer, OSI model, 943, 1136
SET (Secure Electronic Transaction),
192, 1136
SFT (system fault tolerance), 1137
SGCP (Simple Gateway Control
Protocol), 1324
SGML (Standard Generalized
Markup Language)
as basis of XML, 1395
markup languages and,
600, 766
overview of, 1137–1138
SHA-1 (Secure Hash Standard-1), 183,
408, 580

Shared bus architecture, 1195
Shared media, 461
Shared memory, 901, 1195
Shared systems, 294
Shielded twisted pair (STP), 482
ShockWave, 151
Short Messaging Service (SMS), 768,
1154–1155
Shortcut routing, 285
SID (Security ID), 5–6
Signaling, 757, 1139–1140
Signaling System 7. *See* SS7 (Signaling
System 7)
Signaling transport, 1325
Signals, 1140–1143
Signing technologies, 93
Silicon-based routing, 820–821
Simple Conference Control Protocol
(SCCP), 1303
Simple Gateway Control Protocol
(SGCP), 1324
Simple Key Management for Internet
Protocols (SKIP), 1145
Simple Mail Transfer Protocol.
See SMTP (Simple Mail
Transfer Protocol)
Simple Network Management
Protocol. *See* SNMP (Simple
Network Management Protocol)
Simple Network Time Protocol
(SNTP), 914
Simple Object Access Protocol.
See SOAP (Simple Object
Access Protocol)
Simple PKI (SPKI), 981–982
Simple Service Discovery Protocol
(SSDP), 1132
Simplex links, vs. full-duplex, 294
Single attached station (SAS), 495
Single-key ciphers. *See* Symmetric
(single-key) ciphers
Single mode cable, fiber-optic,
499–500
Single-reference time server, 1251
Single sign-on (SSO), 90–91.
See also Authentication
SIP (Session Initiation Protocol)
multimedia protocols, 827
overview of, 1143–1145
signaling in, 1139
videoconferencing and, 1303
SKEME, 714
SKIP (Simple Key Management for
Internet Protocols), 1145
Skipjack, 183, 279, 408

Skystation International, 576
SLA (service level agreements), 1019, 1146–1147
Sliding windows, 105, 530–531
SLIP (Serial Line Interface Protocol), 306, 1005, 1147–1148
Slow start, 249, 1148
SLP (Service Location Protocol), 32, 1132, 1148–1150
Small Computer System Interface. *See* SCSI (Small Computer System Interface)
Smart cards
    access control and, 4
    one-time password authentication and, 927
    overview of, 1150–1151
Smart packets, 16
SMB (Server Message Blocks)
    distributed file systems, 515
    overview of, 1151–1152
    Samba and, 1094
SMCs (service management centers), 292–293
SMDS (Switched Multimegabit Data Service), 1152
SMIL (Synchronized Multimedia Integration Language), 825
SMP (symmetric multiprocessing), 62, 225, 836.
    See also Multiprocessing
SMR (specialized mobile radio), 1153–1154
SMS (Short Messaging Service), 768, 1154–1155
SMTP (Simple Mail Transfer Protocol), 1155–1158
    electronic mail (e-mail) protocols, 437–438
    function of, 1156–1157
    illustration of, 1156
    IMAP and, 613
    POP (Post Office Protocol) and, 995
SNA (Systems Network Architecture)
    integrating APPN into, 50
    overview of, 1158–1159
    transitioning to TCP/IP network, 43
Snapshot replication, 1054
Sniffers
    defined, 1159
    hackers and, 575
    network analyzers and, 865

SNMP (Simple Network Management Protocol), 448
    MIBs (management information bases) and, 773–774
    network agents in, 36
    network management with, 893
    OPSEC (Open Platform for Security) and, 932
    overview of, 1159–1160
    RMON (Remote Monitoring) and, 1067
SNTP (Simple Network Time Protocol), 914
SOAP (Simple Object Access Protocol)
    DCOM and, 236
    MOM (message-oriented middleware) and, 806
    overview of, 1160–1161
Socket API, 1162
Sockets
    defined, 26
    overview of, 1161–1162
    UNIX, 680
SOCKS
    caching protocols and, 1347
    firewalls and, 524
    overview of, 1162–1164
Softswitch, 767, 773, 1163–1165
Software, 85, 444–445, 737
SoIP (Storage over IP), 1097
Solaris, Sun Microsystems, 1191
Solitons, 1165
SONET (Synchronous Optical Network), 1166–1171
    as backbone of B-ISDN, 126–127
    DPT and, 403
    features of, 1166–1170
    illustrations of, 1167–1170
    MANs and, 764
    NADH and, 843
    network core technologies, 880–881
    OC (optical carriers) and, 919
    optical mesh networks and, 1171
    PoS (Packet over SONET) and, 999–1001
Source-quench messaging, 530
Source routing, 143, 1172
Spanning tree algorithms (STAs), 142–143, 1172

Spanning Tree Protocol (801.2-D), 142
Specialized mobile radio (SMR), 1153–1154
SPF algorithms, 740
Spiders, 1110
SPIRITS (Service in the PSTN/IN Requesting InTernet Service), 605, 1172–1173
SPKI (Simple PKI), 981–982
Spread spectrum signaling, 805, 1173–1174, 1374
SPX (Sequenced Packet Exchange), 688
SQL (Structured Query Language)
    client/server model and, 221, 223
    database access with, 327–328
    ODBC (Open Database Connectivity) and, 920
    Oracle and, 940
    overview of, 1174–1175
    replication and, 1053–1054
SS7 (Signaling System 7)
    cache management and, 1107
    media gateways and, 1323
    overview of, 1175–1177
    signaling in, 1139
SSA (Serial Storage Architecture), 1177
SSDP (Simple Service Discovery Protocol), 1132
SSH (secure shell), 1177–1178
SSI (Server System Infrastructure), 1129
SSL Handshake Protocol (SSLHP), 1181
SSL Record Protocol (SSLRP), 1181
SSL (Secure Sockets Layer), 597, 1178–1182
    certificates and, 1180
    cryptography and, 1180–1181
    features of, 1179–1180
    handshake and connection routine, 1181–1182
    history and versions, 1179
    overview of, 1178–1179
    use of certificates by, 193
    vs. S-HTTP, 1138
SSLHP (SSL Handshake Protocol), 1181
SSLRP (SSL Record Protocol), 1181
SSO (single sign-on), 90–91.
    See also Authentication
SSP (storage service provider), 1135, 1183–1184

STA (spanning tree algorithm), 142–143

Standard Generalized Markup Language. *See* SGML (Standard Generalized Markup Language)

Standards. *See also* IEEE (Institute of Electrical and Electronic Engineers), RFCs
   asynchronous communications, 64
   cabling, 155, 695–696
   CATV (cable) data networks, 173
   cellular systems, 1382–1383
   CPCI, 1198–1199
   CSIX, 1203
   EDI (Electronic Data Interchange), 418
   EIA telecommunication standards, 420–421
   electronic mail (e-mail), 23
   Fibre Channel, 506
   Frame relay, 539–540
   groups, associations and organizations for, 1184–1185
   I2O, 1202
   infrared technologies, 620–621
   Internet, 659–661
   IP telephony, 1321–1322
   Java, 705
   metadata, 770–772
   mezzanines (daughterboards), 1200
   modems, 114, 800–801
   multimedia, 1211
   PCI (Peripheral Component Interconnect), 1197–1198
   security auditing, 1121–1122
   structured cabling, 696, 1190, 1246–1250
   Switch fabrics/bus design, 1197–1200, 1202–1203
   VI Architecture, 1203
   videoconferencing, 1303–1304
   VMEbus (Versa Module Eurocard bus), 1199–1200
   Voice over IP (VoIP), 1320–1322
   wireless broadband, 1367–1368
   Wireless LANs (WLANs), 1375–1376
   wireless mobile communications, 1382–1383
   Z39.50, 1399

STAR TAP (Science, Technology, and Research Transit Access Point), 1185–1186

Star topology, 1205, 1222, 1258

STAs (spanning tree algorithms), 142–143, 1172

Stateful inspection technology, 1186

Stateful/stateless connections, 1186–1187

Stateless filing systems, 1186

Static routing, 610, 1187–1188

STDM (statistical time division multiplexing), 832–833

Stop-and-wait flow control, 529–530

Storage Area Networks. *See* SANs (Storage Area Networks)

Storage management systems
   disk storage systems, 371
   IP storage, 677–679
   jukebox optical storage devices, 707
   NDMP (Network Data Management Protocol), 857
   networking and, 876
   Novell NetWare and, 908
   overview of, 1188
   SSP (storage service provider), 1135, 1183–1184

Storage over IP (SoIP), 1097, 1188–1189

Storage service provider. *See* SSP (storage service provider)

Storage systems, 1189

Store-and-forward architecture, 338
   fax transmission, 492–493
   forwarding and, 532
   vs. cut-through architecture, 285

Store-and-forward networking, 1189

Stored playback, multimedia, 823

STP (shielded twisted pair), 482

Straight cable, 156

Stream Control Transmission Protocol. *See* SCTP (Stream Control Transmission Protocol)

Streaming media
   Internet radio and, 659
   multimedia and, 824–825
   webcasting and, 1349

Stripe cards, 1150

Striping. *See* RAID (redundant arrays of inexpensive disks)

Structured cabling standards, 696, 1190, 1246–1250

Structured Query Language. *See* SQL (Structured Query Language)

STS (Synchronous Transport Signal), 919

Subnet Bandwidth Manager (SBM), 1102–1103

Subnetting, 205

Sun Microsystems
   overview of, 1190–1191
   terminal services and, 1238–1239
   UNIX support, 1287
   WebNFS (Network File System), 1353–1354

Supercomputers, 837, 1191–1192

Supernetting, 205, 852. *See also* CIDR (Classless Inter-Domain Routing)

Superuser accounts, 27. *See also* Administrator accounts

Surge suppressors, 1004

SVCs (switched virtual circuits)
   ATM and, 75
   defined, 217, 1192, 1306
   frame relay and, 544
   vs. PVCs, 1017

Switch fabric, 480

Switch fabrics/bus design, 1193–1203
   PCI (Peripheral Component Interconnect) and, 1194
   point-to-point designs, 1195–1196
   RACE and, 1196–1197
   shared bus architecture, 1195
   shared memory designs, 1195
   standards, CPCI, 1198–1199
   standards, CSIX, 1203
   standards, I2O, 1202
   standards, mezzanines (daughterboards), 1200
   standards, PCI, 1197–1198
   standards, VI Architecture, 1203
   standards, VMEbus, 1199–1200
   switching architectures, Fibre Channel, 1201–1202
   switching architectures, InfiniBand, 1202
   switching architectures, RapidIO, 1201

Switched core, 1259

Switched Multimegabit Data Service (SMDS), 1152

Switched virtual circuits. *See* SVCs (switched virtual circuits)

Switches
   Ethernet, 466–468
   Gigabit Ethernet, 564
   LANs (local area networks) and, 724

Switching
   ARIS (Aggregate Route-based IP Switching), 56
   environments, 886–887
   MAC sublayer, 300–301
   multilayer switching, 819–822
   network connection technologies, 879
   network design and, 886–887
   networks, 1203–1206
   tag switching, 1212
Switching hierarchy, PSTN (public switched telephone network), 1225–1228
Switching hubs, 484
Symbian, 129
Symmetric cryptography, 1014, 1114
Symmetric Digital Subscriber Line. See SDSL (Symmetric Digital Subscriber Line)
Symmetric multiprocessing, 62, 225, 836. See also Multiprocessing
Symmetric (single-key) ciphers, 276, 277
SYN (synchronized) bits, 255–256
Synchronized Multimedia Integration Language (SMIL), 825
Synchronous Code Division Multiplexing (S-CDMA), 171, 585
Synchronous communications
   chat and instant messaging, 571
   electronic mail (e-mail) and, 436
   instant messaging as, 622
   IRC (Internet Relay Chat) and, 690–691
   modems and, 800
   overview of, 1206–1208
Synchronous connection oriented (SCO), 131
Synchronous Data Link Control. See SDLC (Synchronous Data Link Control)
Synchronous digital hierarchy. See SDH (synchronous digital hierarchy)
Synchronous Optical Network. See SONET (Synchronous Optical Network)
Synchronous token-passing ring mode, 497
Synchronous transmissions, 296–297
Synchronous Transport Signal (STS), 919
System area networks, 1096

System fault tolerance (SFT), 1137
Systems application architecture (SAA), 1094
Systems Network Architecture. See SNA (Systems Network Architecture)

T

T carriers
   bridging across, 145
   as broadband service, 145
   carrier types and, 413
   fractional T1/T3, 533
   leased lines and, 735
   multiplexing and, 832
   NADH (North American Digital Hierarchy) and, 843, 879
   overview of, 1209–1211
   TDM networks and, 1221–1222
   WANs and, 1332
T series, ITU recommendations, 1211
TACACS (Terminal Access Controller Access Control System), 7, 1212
Tag switching, 1212
Tape backups, 101
TAPI (Telephony API), 284, 1213
Tariffs, 1213
TCA (traffic conditioning agreement), 354
TCP/IP (Transmission Control Protocol/Internet Protocol)
   AnyNet and, 43
   comparing APPN to, 50
   DARPA and, 59
   datagrams and, 319
   as Internet standard, 654–655
   internetworking and, 661
   networking and, 875
   overview of, 1220
   ports, 998–999
   vs. UNIX, 1287
TCP SACK (TCP selective acknowledgement), 14
TCP (Transmission Control Protocol), 1213–1220
   acknowledgments, 14
   best-effort delivery and, 116
   congestion control and, 247–249
   as connection-oriented protocol, 259
   development of, 633

   efficiency of packet transmission with, 105
   end-to-end links and, 1215
   features of, 1216–1217
   as Internet standard, 654–655
   rate control, 252
   reliable services and, 1045, 1215–1216
   segment properties, 1217–1218
   segments, 320–321, 1123, 1217–1218
   sessions, 1218–1219
   as transport protocol, 1271
   vs. UDP, 1279–1282
TDD (Time Division Duplexing), 1366–1367
TDM (time division multiplexing)
   circuit types and, 214–215
   dedicated digital services, 239
   defined, 217
   DTM (Dynamic Synchronous Transfer Mode) and, 410
   multiplexing techniques, 831–832
   Network access services and, 862–864
   T carriers and, 1209
   TDM networks, 1221–1224
TDMA (Time Division Multiple Access), 1224
TeamWave Workplace, 1356
Technical metadata, 769
Tele-immersion, 636
Telecommunication Reform Act of 1996, 1234–1235
Telecommunications, 1224–1236
   carrier and service provider resources, 1231–1233
   EIA standards, 420–421
   IN (Intelligent Network), 1229–1231
   Internet telephony, 661
   IP telephony, 688
   Key Telephone Systems, 716
   OSP (Open Settlement Protocol), 945
   PBX (private branch exchange), 965–968
   POTS (Plain Old Telephone Service), 1001
   regulations, 1233–1236
   structure of telephone networks, 1225–1229
   TAPI (Telephony API), 1213
   tariffs, 1213

TMN (telecommunications management network), 1252–1253
UMTS (Universal Mobile Telecommunications Services), 1283–1284
VTAM (Virtual Telecommunications Access Method), 1330
Telecommunications and Internet Protocol Harmonization Over Networks (TIPHON), 1321
Telecommunications Industry Association. See TIA (Telecommunications Industry Association)
Telecommunications management network (TMN), 1252–1253
Telecommuting. See Mobile computing
Teledesic, 1236
Telematics, 1236
Telephone line networks, 589
Telephony, 1236, 1334
Telephony API (TAPI), 284, 1213
Telephony Routing over IP (TRIP), 1272, 1326
Telephony Services API (TSAPI), 284
Television, 1299
Telnet, 1237, 1253–1254
Terminal Access Control Access Control System (TACACS), 7
Terminal Access Controller Access Control System (TACACS), 1212
Terminal servers, 1237–1238, 1242
Terminal services, 1238–1240
Testing, 1240
TFTP (Trivial File Transfer Protocol), 519, 1241
The Open Group Architectural Framework (TOGAF), 928–929
Thicknet (10Base-5), 462
Thin clients, 1241–1243
    characteristics of, 1242–1243
    defined, 1241
    Internet access with, 631
    limitations of, 1243
    multitiered architecture and, 841
    NetPC as, 862

terminal services and, 1238
types of, 1241–1242
Thinnet (10Base-2), 462, 470–473
Three-tiered models, 328–329. See also Multitiered architectures
Three-way handshake, 1219
Throttling, 1244
Throughput, 1244–1245. See also Capacity, Data rates
    Committed Information Rate (CIR), 214
    defined, 102, 295
    delays and, 337
    relationship to bandwidth, 158
    routers and, 1073
    TCP and, 1245
TIA/EIA-568-A cabling standard, 695–696
TIA (Telecommunications Industry Association)
    function of, 1245–1246
    structured cabling standards, 696, 1190, 1246–1250
    telecommunication standards and, 421
Time
    NTP (Network Time Protocol), 914
    synchronization services, 1251
Time Division Duplexing (TDD), 1366–1367
Time Division Multiple Access (TDMA), 1224
Time division multiplexing. See TDM (time division multiplexing)
TIPHON (Telecommunications and Internet Protocol Harmonization Over Networks), 1321
TLS (Transport Layer Security), 1251–1252
TMN (telecommunications management network), 1252–1253
TN3270, 1253–1254
TOGAF (The Open Group Architectural Framework), 928–929
Token-based authentication, 1254–1256
Token bucket, 1032
Token bus networks, 1256–1257

Token passing
    access methods, 1254
    ARCNET and, 54
    FDDI and, 496
    MAC (Media Access Control) and, 300, 758
    network access methods, 8
Token ring networks
    access methods used by, 8
    function of tokens in, 1254
    overview of, 1257
Topologies
    cellular systems, 1378–1380
    overview of, 1258–1259
    WANs, 1332
    wireless broadband, 1360–1361
ToS (Type of Service), 1259
TP. See Transaction processing (TP)
Traceroute utility, 604
Tracking. See Auditing
Traffic conditioners, 354
Traffic conditioning agreement (TCA), 354
Traffic flow. See also Bandwidth
    analyzing network traffic, 866
    backbone networks and, 99
    Int-Serv and, 627
    Internet accounting and, 12
Traffic management, 1259–1265. See also Network traffic
    ATM and, 79, 1261–1262
    bandwidth management and, 109
    firewalls and, 524
    Internet traffic engineering, 1262–1263
    MPLS traffic engineering, 1264–1265
    overview of, 1259–1261
Traffic prioritization, 888
Traffic shaping, 79, 1262
Training, data protection, 312
Transaction monitor, 480, 489
Transaction processing (TP), 1266–1270
    ACID criteria for, 14, 1266–1267
    APPC and, 44–45
    environments, 1267–1268
    Internet support, 1269

middleware and, 787
MTS (Microsoft Transaction
Server) and, 19, 1268–1269
two-phase commit, 1267
types of transactions, 1266
Transactional replication, 1054
Translation bridges, 139
Transmission Control Protocol/
Internet Protocol. *See* TCP/IP
(Transmission Control Protocol/
Internet Protocol)
Transmission media, 297.
See also Cable and wiring
Transmission rates, 103, 106–107, 144
Transmitters, 147
Transparency, 854, 957
Transparent bridges, 140–142
Transparent caching, 1344
Transparent routing, 852
Transport layer, OSI model, 303, 943,
1214, 1270
Transport Layer Security (TLS),
1251–1252
Transport protocols, 1271–1272
Tri-homed firewalls, 523
TRIP (Telephony Routing over IP),
1272, 1326
Triple-DES, 276–278
Trivial File Transfer Protocol (TFTP),
519, 1241
Trojan horses, 965, 1306
Troubleshooting, 1240
Trunking. *See also* Link aggregation,
Load balancing
bandwidth on demand
and, 110
combining links into single
data channels, 133
Ethernet networks, 464
Trust relationships, 1273–1276
KeyNote Trust Management
System, 1275
one-way vs. two-way, 1273
overview of, 1273–1274
PKIs (public key
infrastructures) and,
979–980
security and, 1116

trusted third-parties,
1274–1275
"Web of Trust", 1275
Trusted third-party protocols, 708
TSAPI (Telephony Services API), 284
Tunneling
defined, 686
encapsulation and, 452
functions of, 1276–1277
mobile IP and, 797
Tunneling protocols
IPSec (IP Security), 686
L2TP (Layer 2 Tunneling
Protocol), 717–719
list of, 1277
PPTP (point-to-point tunneling
protocol), 719
Tutorials, networking, 877
Twisted-pair cable
categories, 164–167
defined, 156
Ethernet networks and, 465
shielded and unshielded, 482
types of cable and, 153
vs. coaxial cable, 230
Two-factor authentication, 89
Two-phase commit, 1267
Twofish, 278–279
Type of Service (ToS), 1259

U

UA (user agent), 437
UBR (unspecified bit rate), 77, 1261
UDA (Universal Data Access), 330,
925, 1279
UDDI (Universal Description,
Discovery, and Integration), 1279
UDP (User Datagram Protocol),
1279–1282
congestion control and, 249
as connectionless protocol, 259
header, 1281
as Internet standard, 654–655
reliable delivery mechanisms
and, 1046
transport layer and, 1214

as transport protocol, 1271
vs. TCP, 1279–1282
UFS (Universal File System), 513, 780.
See also NetWare UFS
(Universal File System)
UID (Unique user identification), 10
ULSNET (Ultra Low-Speed
Networking), 1283
Ultra Low-Speed Networking
(ULSNET), 1283
Ultra SCSI, 1104–1105
Ultra Wideband (UWB), 1298, 1364
UML (Unified Modeling Language),
924, 1283
UMTS (Universal Mobile
Telecommunications Services),
1283–1284
Unguided media, 157
UNI (User-Network Interface), 70, 72,
74, 1284
Unified messaging, 1284–1285
Unified Modeling Language (UML),
924, 1283
Uniform Resource Identifier (URI),
1292, 1293
Uniform Resource Locators. *See* URLs
(Uniform Resource Locators)
Uniform Resource Names. *See* URNs
(Uniform Resource Names)
Uninterruptible power supply.
See UPS (uninterruptible
power supply)
Unique user identification (UID), 10
Universal Data Access. *See* UDA
(Universal Data Access)
Universal Description, Discovery,
and Integration (UDDI), 1279
Universal File System (UFS), 513, 780.
See also NetWare UFS
(Universal File System)
Universal in-box, 283
Universal Mobile
Telecommunications Services
(UMTS), 1283–1284
Universal Serial Bus (USB), 1105, 1295
Universal service, 1285
University Corporation for Advanced
Internet Development (UCAID), 2

UNIX, 1285–1288
Apache servers for, 43
CDE and, 185
daemons, 287
features of, 1287–1288
implementation of ACLs in, 6
interprocess communication
mechanisms of, 680
NIS (Network Information
System) and, 903
open source software and, 929
overview of, 1285–1287
user accounts in, 10–11
vs. TCP/IP, 1287
X Window System and, 1391
UNIX file system, 513, 1288–1290
UNIX-to-UNIX Copy Program, 519,
905, 1298
Unreliable (best) effort services, 1215
Unshielded twisted pair (UTP), 482
Unspecified bit rate (UBR), 77, 1261
UPC (usage parameter control),
79, 1262
UPS (uninterruptible power supply)
fault tolerance and high
availability and, 489
overview of, 1290–1292
power outage protection, 1004
URI (Uniform Resource Identifier),
1292, 1293
URL parsing, 1293–1294
URLs (Uniform Resource Locators)
CNRP (Common Name
Resolution Protocol)
and, 228
NFS (Network File System)
and, 899
overview of, 1293
vs. URIs, 1292
URNs (Uniform Resource Names)
CO (central office) and, 229
Handle System and, 579
name services and, 845
overview of, 1294
Usage parameter control (UPC),
79, 1262
USB (Universal Serial Bus), 1105, 1295
USENET, 904–906, 1295

User accounts, 9–11
defined, 9–10
rights and permissions,
1296–1297
in UNIX, 10–11
in Windows NT/2000, 11
User agent (UA), 437
User Datagram Protocol. *See* UDP
(User Datagram Protocol)
User Manager program,
Windows NT/2000, 11
User-Network Interface. *See* UNI
(User-Network Interface)
UTP (unshielded twisted pair), 482
UTRA (UMTS Terrestrial Radio
Access), 1283
UUCP (UNIX-to-UNIX Copy
Program), 519, 905, 1298
UWB (Ultra Wideband), 1298, 1364

V

V.90 modems, 801–802
VBI (Vertical Blanking Interval), 1299
VBNS (very high speed Backbone
Network Service), 913, 1299–1300
VCI (virtual channel identifier), 75
VCs (virtual circuits).
See Virtual circuits (VCs)
VDSL (Very High-Data-Rate Digital
Subscriber Line), 407
Verisign, 194
Versa Module Eurocard bus
(VMEbus), 1199–1200
Vertical Blanking Interval (VBI), 1299
Vertical redundancy checking
(VRC), 64
Very High-Data-Rate Digital
Subscriber Line (VDSL), 407
Very high speed Backbone Network
Service. *See* VBNS (very high
speed Backbone Network Service)
VHDCI (Very High Density Table
Interconnect), 1105
VI (Virtual Interface) Architecture
clustering and, 227
DAFS and, 287–289

overview of, 1300–1301
SANs (Storage Area
Networks) and, 1097
standards, 1203
storage solutions and, 851
VICS (Voluntary Interindustry
Commerce Standards), 434–435
Video on Demand (VoD), 1057
Video, streaming media, 1349
Videoconferencing, 1301–1305
collaborative computing
and, 231
groupware and, 571
protocols used for, 1302
standards, 1303–1304
uses for, 1301
working groups and
RFCs, 1304
VINES, 111
Virtual bus, 785
Virtual channel identifier (VCI), 75
Virtual circuits (VCs)
ATM and, 74–75
channels and, 196
circuit types and, 214–215
connection-oriented networks
and, 27
defined, 217, 986
IP over ATM and, 681
label switched paths (LSPs)
and, 808
overview of, 1305–1306
PVCs and SVCs, 1017, 1192
TCP and, 1215
Virtual clusters, 228
Virtual connections, 871
Virtual Interfaces (VIs), 227, 287–288
Virtual laboratories, 636
Virtual LANs.
See VLANs (virtual LANs)
Virtual path identifier (VPI), 75
Virtual paths (VPs), 74–75
Virtual PoP, 993–994
Virtual private networks. *See* VPNs
(virtual private networks)
Virtual Reality Modeling Language
(VRML), 1340

Virtual Router Redundancy Protocol (VRRP), 739, 1329–1330
Virtual Telecommunications Access Method (VTAM), 1330
Viruses, 1306–1307
VIs (Virtual Interfaces), 227, 287–288
VLANs (virtual LANs), 1308–1313
    configuration of, 1310–1312
    IEEE 802.1Q frame tag and, 1312
    network design and, 888
    overview of, 1308–1310
    switching and, 300
VMEbus (Versa Module Eurocard bus), 1199–1200
VoATM (Voice over ATM), 1315–1316
VoD (Video on Demand), 1057
VoDSL (Voice over DSL), 1317
VoFR (Voice over Frame Relay), 546–547, 1317
Voice data, 263
Voice/data networks, 1313–1318
    goals of integrating voice and data, 1314
    models for, 1314–1317
    PBX (private branch exchange), 1315
    Voice over ATM (VoATM), 1315–1316
    voice over cable, 1317
    Voice over DSL (VoDSL), 1317
    Voice over Frame Relay (VoFR), 1317
    wireless mobile communications and, 1383–1384
Voice gateways, 559
Voice over ATM (VoATM), 1315–1316
Voice over DSL (VoDSL), 1317
Voice over Frame Relay (VoFR), 546–547, 1317
Voice over IP (VoIP), 1318–1328
    media gateways and controllers and, 1322–1325
    overview of, 1318–1319
    PSTN legacy and, 1319–1320
    related protocols, 1325–1326

SLP (Service Location Protocol) and, 1148
SS7 (Signaling System 7) and, 1176
standards, 1320–1322
working groups and RFCs, 1326–1328
Voice telephone systems. *See* PSTN (public switched telephone network)
Voice transmission, 22
VoIP (Voice over IP). *See* Voice over IP (VoIP)
Volume management, 1328
Voluntary Interindustry Commerce Standards (VICS), 434–435
VPI (virtual path identifier), 75
VPNs (virtual private networks)
    AT&T support for, 83
    bandwidth management and, 109
    connecting geographically dispersed users with, 99
    IKE (Internet Key Exchange) and, 714
    mobile computing and, 795
    OPSEC (Open Platform for Security) and, 931
    overview of, 1328–1329
    vs. private networks, 1012
VRC (vertical redundancy checking), 64
VRML (Virtual Reality Modeling Language), 1340
VRRP (Virtual Router Redundancy Protocol), 739, 1329–1330
VTAM (Virtual Telecommunications Access Method), 1330

W

W3C (World Wide Web Coalition), 433, 1331
WAFL (Write Anywhere File Layout), 513–514, 850
WANs (wide area networks), 1331–1334
    acknowledgments, 14

ATM and, 65
backbone networks and, 98
broadband and, 1331–1332
as connection-oriented service, 259
Ethernet networks and, 240
leased lines and, 735
network connection technologies for, 878
networking and, 876
S/WAN (Secure WAN) and, 1193
topologies of, 1332–1333
virtual circuits and, 214
vs. MANs, 763
WAP (Wireless Applications Protocol)
    Bluetooth and, 129
    mobile computing and, 795
    overview of, 1334
    wireless IP and, 1372
Wave Systems, 1275
Wavelength division multiplexing. *See* WDM (wavelength division multiplexing)
Wavelength routing. *See* Optical networks
WBEM (Web-based enterprise management), 210, 1335–1336
WCCP (Web Cache Communication Protocol), 1336, 1346
WCS (Wireless Communications Service), 1337
WDM (wavelength division multiplexing). *See also* Optical networks
    circuits and, 214
    multiplexing techniques and, 831
    overview of, 1337–1339
Web, 1340. *See also* Internet
Web appliances, 868, 1355
Web-based enterprise management (WBEM), 210, 1335–1336
Web Cache Communication Protocol (WCCP), 1336, 1346
Web caching, 1341–1348
    cache management methods, 176

content distribution and, 1347
freshness and staleness and,
1343–1344
illustration of, 1342
overview of, 1341–1343
proxy servers and proxy cache
and, 1344–1347
WCCP (Web Cache
Communication
Protocol), 1336
working groups and RFCs,
1347–1348
Web crawlers, 1110
Web Distributed Authoring and
Versioning. *See* WebDAV (Web
Distributed Authoring
and Versioning)
"Web of Trust", 1275
Web pages, 241
Web servers, embedded, 448–449
Web sites, ActiveX controls on, 19
Web technologies, 1354–1356
Web terminals, 618, 631, 868
Web3D, 1340
Webcasting, 1349–1351
as alternative to Web
browsing, 862
multicasting and, 150
multimedia and, 823
NNTP (Network News
Transport Protocol),
904–906
overview of, 600, 1349
sites and services for,
1349–1350
WebDAV (Web Distributed
Authoring and Versioning), 321,
1351–1352, 1389–1390
Webmaster, 1352–1353
WebNFS (Network File System), 515,
899, 1353–1354
WebTV, 1356

Weighted fair queuing (WFQ),
1030, 1090
Weighted RED (WRED), 251
WEN (Microsoft Windows for
Express Networks), 447
WfM (Wired for Management),
1358–1359
WfMC (Workflow Management
Coalition), 1387, 1388
WFQ (weighted fair queuing),
1030, 1090
White pages, 23, 1112–1114
Whiteboard applications, 1356–1357
WHOIS, 845, 1357
Whois++, 212
Wholesale service providers, 1135
Wide area networks. *See* WANs
(wide area networks)
Wide SCSI, 1104–1105
Windows. *See* Microsoft Windows
WinFrame, 1238–1239
WINS (Windows Internet Naming
Service), 1358
DNS and, 394
WinSocks, 1162, 1358
Wire speed, 1244.
See also Throughput
Wire-speed routers, 819
Wired for Management (WfM),
1358–1359
Wireless Applications Protocol.
See WAP (Wireless
Applications Protocol)
Wireless broadband, 1359–1369
access methods, 1362–1365
air interfaces for, 1366–1367
as broadband service, 146
characteristics of, 1366
Ethernet networks and, 240
frequency ranges, 1360–1362
overview of, 1359

standards and initiatives for,
1367–1368
topologies, 1360–1361
WANs and, 1332
Wireless communications, 1369–1372
HDR (High Data Rate)
and, 584
overview of, 1369
resources for, 1370–1372
roaming and, 1069–1070
SMS (Short Messaging Service)
and, 1154–1155
Web technologies and, 1356
Wireless Communications Service
(WCS), 1337
Wireless home networks, 589–590
Wireless IP, 1372–1373
Wireless LANs (WLANs), 1373–1377
advantages of, 1374
overview of, 1373
radio networks and, 1374–1375
standards, 1375–1376
Wireless local loop (WLL), 1377–1378
Wireless Markup Language
(WML), 1386
Wireless mesh systems, 1364–1365
Wireless messaging, 1378
Wireless mobile communications,
1378–1385
from analog to digital,
1380–1382
CDMA and, 186–187
cellular topology, 1378–1380
data networks, 1383–1384
Ethernet networks and, 240
overview of, 1378
standards, 1382–1383
Wireless PANs, 1385–1386
Wireless service providers
(WSPs), 238
Wireless waveforms, 423
Wiretapping, 1386

Wiring. *See* Cable and wiring
WLANs (Wireless LANs). *See*
    Wireless LANs (WLANs)
WLL (Wireless local loop), 1377–1378
WML (Wireless Markup
    Language), 1386
Workflow management, 1387–1390
    collaborative computing
        and, 232
    document specifications and,
        1388–1390
    groupware and, 571
    overview of, 1387–1388
Workflow Management Coalition
    (WfMC), 1387, 1388
Workgroups, 1390
Workstations, 371
World Wide Web Coalition (W3C),
    433, 1331
World Wide Web (WWW).
    See Internet, Web
Worms, 1306
WRED (weighted RED), 251
Write Anywhere File Layout
    (WAFL), 513–514, 850
WSPs (wireless service
    providers), 238
WWW (World Wide Web).
    See Internet, Web

X/Open Company Ltd., 1397
X series ITU recommendations, 1398
X.25
    overview of, 1391
    packet switching services and,
        239, 583
    WANs and, 1331
X.400 Messaging Handling System,
    23, 1392
X.500 Directory Services, 23, 361–362,
    1392–1393
X.509
    certificates, 192, 1393–1395
    OPSEC (Open Platform for
        Security) and, 931
    PKIs (public key
        infrastructures) and, 981
X12 Accredited Standards
    Committee, 1391
Xdrive Technologies, 1183
XHTML, 594
XML (Extensible Markup Language)
    database connectivity and, 330
    EDI and, 418–419
    embedded systems and, 449
    HTML (Hypertext Markup
        Language) and, 600

    information sharing with, 663
    Java and, 705
    middleware and, 787
    MOM (message-oriented
        middleware) and, 806
    overview of, 1395–1397
    search and discovery and, 1112
    SOAP (Simple Object Access
        Protocol) and, 1160
    use of metadata in, 770
    XHTML and, 594

Yahoo! Broadcast, 1349–1350
Yellow pages, 1112–1114. *See also* NIS
    (Network Information System)

Z39.50, 1399
ZAWs (Zero Administration for
    Windows), 629, 1358–1359,
    1399–1400
Zones, DNS, 393, 1400–1401

INTERNATIONAL CONTACT INFORMATION

AUSTRALIA
McGraw-Hill Book Company Australia Pty. Ltd.
TEL +61-2-9417-9899
FAX +61-2-9417-5687
http://www.mcgraw-hill.com.au
books-it_sydney@mcgraw-hill.com

CANADA
McGraw-Hill Ryerson Ltd.
TEL +905-430-5000
FAX +905-430-5020
http://www.mcgrawhill.ca

**GREECE, MIDDLE EAST,
NORTHERN AFRICA**
McGraw-Hill Hellas
TEL +30-1-656-0990-3-4
FAX +30-1-654-5525

MEXICO (Also serving Latin America)
McGraw-Hill Interamericana Editores S.A. de C.V.
TEL +525-117-1583
FAX +525-117-1589
http://www.mcgraw-hill.com.mx
fernando_castellanos@mcgraw-hill.com

SINGAPORE (Serving Asia)
McGraw-Hill Book Company
TEL +65-863-1580
FAX +65-862-3354
http://www.mcgraw-hill.com.sg
mghasia@mcgraw-hill.com

SOUTH AFRICA
McGraw-Hill South Africa
TEL +27-11-622-7512
FAX +27-11-622-9045
robyn_swanepoel@mcgraw-hill.com

**UNITED KINGDOM & EUROPE
(Excluding Southern Europe)**
McGraw-Hill Education Europe
TEL +44-1-628-502500
FAX +44-1-628-770224
http://www.mcgraw-hill.co.uk
computing_neurope@mcgraw-hill.com

ALL OTHER INQUIRIES Contact:
Osborne/McGraw-Hill
TEL +1-510-549-6600
FAX +1-510-883-7600
http://www.osborne.com
omg_international@mcgraw-hill.com

LICENSE AGREEMENT

THIS PRODUCT (THE "PRODUCT") CONTAINS PROPRIETARY SOFTWARE, DATA AND INFORMATION (INCLUDING DOCUMENTATION) OWNED BY THE McGRAW-HILL COMPANIES, INC. ("McGRAW-HILL") AND ITS LICENSORS. YOUR RIGHT TO USE THE PRODUCT IS GOVERNED BY THE TERMS AND CONDITIONS OF THIS AGREEMENT.

LICENSE

Throughout this License Agreement, "you" shall mean either the individual or the entity whose agent opens this package. You are granted a non-exclusive and non-transferable license to use the Product subject to the following terms:

(i) If you have licensed a single user version of the Product, the Product may only be used on a single computer (i.e., a single CPU). If you licensed and paid the fee applicable to a local area network or wide area network version of the Product, you are subject to the terms of the following subparagraph (ii).

(ii) If you have licensed a local area network version, you may use the Product on unlimited workstations located in one single building selected by you that is served by such local area network. If you have licensed a wide area network version, you may use the Product on unlimited workstations located in multiple buildings on the same site selected by you that is served by such wide area network; provided, however, that any building will not be considered located in the same site if it is more than five (5) miles away from any building included in such site. In addition, you may only use a local area or wide area network version of the Product on one single server. If you wish to use the Product on more than one server, you must obtain written authorization from McGraw-Hill and pay additional fees.

(iii) You may make one copy of the Product for back-up purposes only and you must maintain an accurate record as to the location of the back-up at all times.

COPYRIGHT; RESTRICTIONS ON USE AND TRANSFER

All rights (including copyright) in and to the Product are owned by McGraw-Hill and its licensors. You are the owner of the enclosed disc on which the Product is recorded. You may not use, copy, decompile, disassemble, reverse engineer, modify, reproduce, create derivative works, transmit, distribute, sublicense, store in a database or retrieval system of any kind, rent or transfer the Product, or any portion thereof, in any form or by any means (including electronically or otherwise) except as expressly provided for in this License Agreement. You must reproduce the copyright notices, trademark notices, legends and logos of McGraw-Hill and its licensors that appear on the Product on the back-up copy of the Product which you are permitted to make hereunder. All rights in the Product not expressly granted herein are reserved by McGraw-Hill and its licensors.

TERM

This License Agreement is effective until terminated. It will terminate if you fail to comply with any term or condition of this License Agreement. Upon termination, you are obligated to return to McGraw-Hill the Product together with all copies thereof and to purge all copies of the Product included in any and all servers and computer facilities.

DISCLAIMER OF WARRANTY

THE PRODUCT AND THE BACK-UP COPY ARE LICENSED "AS IS." McGRAW-HILL, ITS LICENSORS AND THE AUTHORS MAKE NO WARRANTIES, EXPRESS OR IMPLIED, AS TO THE RESULTS TO BE

OBTAINED BY ANY PERSON OR ENTITY FROM USE OF THE PRODUCT, ANY INFORMATION OR DATA INCLUDED THEREIN AND/OR ANY TECHNICAL SUPPORT SERVICES PROVIDED HEREUNDER, IF ANY ("TECHNICAL SUPPORT SERVICES"). McGRAW-HILL, ITS LICENSORS AND THE AUTHORS MAKE NO EXPRESS OR IMPLIED WARRANTIES OF MERCHANTABILITY OR FITNESS FOR A PARTICULAR PURPOSE OR USE WITH RESPECT TO THE PRODUCT. NEITHER McGRAW-HILL, ANY OF ITS LICENSORS NOR THE AUTHORS WARRANT THAT THE FUNCTIONS CONTAINED IN THE PRODUCT WILL MEET YOUR REQUIREMENTS OR THAT THE OPERATION OF THE PRODUCT WILL BE UNINTERRUPTED OR ERROR FREE. YOU ASSUME THE ENTIRE RISK WITH RESPECT TO THE QUALITY AND PERFORMANCE OF THE PRODUCT.

LIMITED WARRANTY FOR DISC

To the original licensee only, McGraw-Hill warrants that the enclosed disc on which the Product is recorded is free from defects in materials and workmanship under normal use and service for a period of ninety (90) days from the date of purchase. In the event of a defect in the disc covered by the foregoing warranty, McGraw-Hill will replace the disc.

LIMITATION OF LIABILITY

NEITHER McGRAW-HILL, ITS LICENSORS NOR THE AUTHORS SHALL BE LIABLE FOR ANY INDIRECT, SPECIAL OR CONSEQUENTIAL DAMAGES, SUCH AS BUT NOT LIMITED TO, LOSS OF ANTICIPATED PROFITS OR BENEFITS, RESULTING FROM THE USE OR INABILITY TO USE THE PRODUCT EVEN IF ANY OF THEM HAS BEEN ADVISED OF THE POSSIBILITY OF SUCH DAMAGES. THIS LIMITATION OF LIABILITY SHALL APPLY TO ANY CLAIM OR CAUSE WHATSOEVER WHETHER SUCH CLAIM OR CAUSE ARISES IN CONTRACT, TORT, OR OTHERWISE. Some states do not allow the exclusion or limitation of indirect, special or consequential damages, so the above limitation may not apply to you.

U.S. GOVERNMENT RESTRICTED RIGHTS

Any software included in the Product is provided with restricted rights subject to subparagraphs (c), (1) and (2) of the Commercial Computer Software-Restricted Rights clause at 48 C.F.R. 52.227-19. The terms of this Agreement applicable to the use of the data in the Product are those under which the data are generally made available to the general public by McGraw-Hill. Except as provided herein, no reproduction, use, or disclosure rights are granted with respect to the data included in the Product and no right to modify or create derivative works from any such data is hereby granted.

GENERAL

This License Agreement constitutes the entire agreement between the parties relating to the Product. The terms of any Purchase Order shall have no effect on the terms of this License Agreement. Failure of McGraw-Hill to insist at any time on strict compliance with this License Agreement shall not constitute a waiver of any rights under this License Agreement. This License Agreement shall be construed and governed in accordance with the laws of the State of New York. If any provision of this License Agreement is held to be contrary to law, that provision will be enforced to the maximum extent permissible and the remaining provisions will remain in full force and effect.